BaseBall america®
2012 ALMANAC

BASEBALL AMERICA INC. · DURHAM, N.C.

BaseBall america
2012 ALMANAC

A COMPREHENSIVE REVIEW OF THE 2011 SEASON, FEATURING STATISTICS AND COMMENTARY

Editor
WILL LINGO

Assistant Editors
BEN BADLER, JIM CALLIS, J.J. COOPER, MATT EDDY, CONOR GLASSEY,
AARON FITT, JOSH LEVENTHAL, JOHN MANUEL, NATHAN RODE, JIM SHONERD

Database and Application Development
BRENT LEWIS, TIM COLLINS

Contributing Writer
TOM HAUDRICOURT

Photo Editor
NATHAN RODE

Editorial Assistants
ALEXIS BRUDNICKI, TIM EDNOFF, KYLE DUGAN
MICHAEL KANEN, BRANDON MOREE, BILL WOODWARD

Design & Production
SARA HIATT McDANIEL, LINWOOD WEBB

Cover Photo
JUSTIN VERLANDER BY CLIFF WELCH

BaseBall america

PRESIDENT/PUBLISHER: LEE FOLGER
EDITORS IN CHIEF: WILL LINGO, JOHN MANUEL
EXECUTIVE EDITOR: JIM CALLIS
DESIGN & PRODUCTION DIRECTOR: SARA HIATT McDANIEL
TECHNOLOGY MANAGER: BRENT LEWIS

DISTRIBUTED BY SIMON & SCHUSTER
ISBN-13: 978-1-932391-38-1
STATISTICS PROVIDED BY MAJOR LEAGUE BASEBALL ADVANCED MEDIA
AND COMPILED BY BASEBALL AMERICA

BaseballAmerica.com

EDITOR'S NOTE: Major league statistics are based on final, unofficial 2011 averages. >> The organization statistics, which begin on page 43, include all players who participated in at least one game during the 2011 season. >> Pitchers' batting statistics are not included, nor are the pitching statistics of field players who pitched in less than two games. >> For players who played with more than one team in the same league, the player's cumulative statistics appear on the line immediately after the player's statistics with each team. >> Innings pitched have been rounded off to the nearest full inning.

TABLE OF CONTENTS

ANDREW WOOLLEY

MAJOR LEAGUES

Cards, Rays complete wild comebacks in finale

BY TOM HAUDRICOURT

T he Rays and Red Sox stumbled out of the chute when play began in 2011, and the two teams' fates would intertwine once again on the final day of the season in one of the wildest, craziest finishes ever.

Despite the much-heralded offseason acquisitions of first baseman Adrian Gonzalez and left fielder Carl Crawford, the Red Sox staggered to a 2-10 start, the worst in club history. The Rays also looked unready for prime time, losing eight of their first nine games.

Yet, there they were on the final day of the season, one club trying to hang on and the other attempting a miracle comeback. Boston held a seemingly comfortable nine-game lead on the morning of Sept. 4 in the American League wild card race, but they stumbled to the finish line, allowing Tampa Bay back into the race.

And those teams weren't alone in that agony/ecstasy. Over in the National League, the Braves suffered a similar collapse in the wild card race. Atlanta led by 8½ games on Sept. 5 but started coughing up games in the late going, allowing the Cardinals to come out of nowhere to re-enter the playoff picture.

Baseball fans of all ages considered the season's final day, Sept. 28, perhaps the most glorious and unpredictable in history. Entering play that day, the Red Sox and Rays sat tied for the AL wild card with 90 wins apiece, while the Braves and Cardinals shared the NL edition with 89 victories each. The drama played out in four locations:

■ Atlanta. The Braves hosted the Phillies, who had clinched their fifth straight NL East title on Sept. 17.

■ Baltimore. The Red Sox visited the Orioles, who took to their role of ultimate spoiler.

■ Houston. The Cardinals had the good fortune of playing the Astros, baseball's worst team.

■ St. Petersburg. The Rays hosted the Yankees, who nailed down the AL East on Sept. 22 for their 16th playoff appearance in the last 17 years.

As expected, the Cardinals sailed to the finish line. With ace Chris Carpenter on the mound they rolled past the lowly Astros 8-0, then retreated to the visiting clubhouse at Minute Maid Park to watch on television as the Braves attempted to

Evan Longoria's heroics in Game No. 162 completed the Rays' unlikely comeback

CLIFF WELCH

stave off a complete collapse.

Braves closer Craig Kimbrel, who established a rookie record with 46 saves during the season, failed to hold a 3-2 lead in the ninth by allowing, in succession, a single, a walk, a walk and then the game-tying sacrifice fly. The game lapsed into extra innings, until the Phillies pushed across the go-ahead run in the top of the 13th. Atlanta did not retaliate in the bottom of the inning.

The Braves were done, having lost their last five games—and 18 of their final 26—in a stunning collapse. The Cardinals, who trailed Atlanta by 10½ games on Aug. 25 and by 8½ games at the end of that month, won 23 of their final 32 games to take the wild card by one game.

"We had nothing to lose," Carpenter said. "We were already 'out of it.' People were telling us we were done."

As improbable as the NL finale was, the AL raised the stakes with a wild, late-night finish.

Red Sox closer Jonathan Papelbon whiffed the first two Orioles batters he faced in the bottom of the ninth inning, and he quickly tallied two strikes on third baseman Chris Davis. Boston needed one strike to claim a 3-2 victory, one that would assure it at least a share of the wild card—but Papelbon never recorded that last out. Davis doubled, then right fielder Nolan Reimold followed with another to tie the score. Second baseman Robert Andino then delivered the game-winning single to allow Baltimore to steal a 4-3 victory.

That result flashed on the scoreboard at Tropicana Field, where the Rays incredibly had rallied from a 7-0 deficit in the eighth inning against the Yankees. The Rays tied the score on a two-out, two-strike, ninth-inning home run by pinch-hitter Dan Johnson, who hadn't recorded a hit since April 27 and was batting a meager .109 at the time. The game headed to extra innings.

"I was in the (batting) cage when one of the security guys ran up and said, 'You're hitting,' " Johnson said.

The game remained tied until the bottom of the 12th, when Rays third baseman Evan Longoria sent a line drive down the left-field line that barely cleared the fence in fair territory. Longoria's second homer of the game meant that Tampa Bay had pulled off one of the most remarkable comebacks ever.

"When I hit the ball, I knew it was going to be fair," Longoria said. "We were out there for the better part of five hours, and then everything happened in the final seconds."

Back in Atlanta, the stunned Braves didn't know what to say. "This is tough," catcher Brian McCann said. "This is one of the worst feelings I've ever had coming off a baseball field."

The nine-game lead surrendered by the Red Sox was the largest ever squandered during the month of September. Once in the thick of the battle for the AL East title, Boston finished the final month with a 7-20 record. The Red Sox parted with manager Terry Francona a few days after the collapse, and not long after that, general manager Theo Epstein bolted to the Cubs in a stunning move.

The term "wild card" did not do justice to the events of Sept. 28, 2011, the day the Cardinals and Rays completed their impossible comebacks.

Hot And Not-So-Hot Starts

For all their September and October heroics, fate did not smile on the Cardinals during spring training. Team doctors diagnosed righthander Adam Wainwright with a torn elbow ligament, resulting in Tommy John surgery and a seat on the bench for the entire season. The 29-year-old Wainwright paced all NL pitchers with a 2.53 ERA during the preceding two seasons.

CLIFF WELCH

Manny Ramirez retired rather than sit out 100 games for a second failed drug test

The Brewers' much-heralded offseason acquisition, righthander Zack Greinke, didn't make it out of spring training in one piece, either. Greinke cracked a rib playing a game of pickup basketball at the outset of camp and began the season on the disabled list, missing the first five weeks.

Veteran left fielder/DH Manny Ramirez became a casualty of a different sort. He announced his retirement on April 8, five games into his Rays career, rather than face a 100-game suspension for testing positive for a performance-enhancing drug for the second time in his career. While playing for the Dodgers, Ramirez sat out 50 games beginning in May 2009 after testing positive for human chorionic gonadotropin, a banned female fertility drug often used to help mask steroid use. The New York Times also reported that Ramirez failed an anonymous survey test administered by Major League Baseball in 2003.

Ramirez had signed a one-year free agent deal with the Rays and went 1-for-17 when he walked away from the game at age 38.

The Indians got off to an unexpected hot start in the AL Central, going 18-8 in April and winning 13 consecutive home games at one point. Cleveland faded in the second half, however, to finish at 80-82 and 15 games behind the Tigers.

Elsewhere in the AL Central, the Twins never recovered from a 9-17 start and finished with an AL-worst 63-99 record. The perennial contenders started unraveling amid an avalanche of injuries to key personnel such as catcher Joe Mauer and first baseman Justin Morneau.

Tampa Bay, on the other hand, rebounded from its club-worst 0-6 start to the season. The Rays made it to May with a 15-12 record, becoming the first club to end April with a winning record after losing its first six games.

In a sign of things to come, the pitching-rich Phillies roared through the first month of the season with an 18-8 record, establishing a club mark for victories in April. With free agent import Cliff Lee fortifying a rotation already strong with Roy Halladay, Cole Hamels and Roy Oswalt, the Phillies pitching staff led the NL with a 3.02 ERA, 1.17 WHIP and 3.2-to-1 strikeout-to-walk ratio. Halladay and Lee stood as the most efficient and effective twosome in the NL, each ranking among the top five in ERA, wins, strikeouts, complete games, innings and WHIP.

Angels ace Jered Weaver roared out of the gate, going 6-0, 0.99 during the month of April. He started the All-Star Game for the AL and capped another fine season by going 18-8, 2.41 in 33 turns.

No player started the season hotter than Dodgers right fielder Andre Ethier, who put together a 26-game hitting streak in April. No player in history ever had hit in that many games in a row during the first month.

All was not rosy for the Dodgers, however. The financial troubles of owner Frank McCourt spurred MLB to take over operation of the club in April. Commissioner Bud Selig sent former Rangers executive Tom Schieffer to Los Angeles to oversee the daily business of the team, a move the embattled McCourt challenged legally. The Dodgers reportedly struggled to meet payroll more than once as McCourt's expensive, contentious and protracted divorce from former Dodgers CEO Jamie McCourt played out in public.

"I have taken this action because of my deep concerns regarding the finances and operations of the Dodgers and to protect the best interests of the club," Selig said in announcing the extraordinary move. "The Dodgers have been one of the most prestigious franchises in all of sports, and we owe it to their legion of loyal fans to ensure that this club is being operated properly now and will be guided appropriately in the future."

The Dodgers filed for bankruptcy on June 27, and after more than four months of legal wrangling, McCourt reached a deal with MLB in early November to put the franchise and its media rights up for sale.

CHRIS PROCTOR

Francisco Liriano threw the season's first (and least impressive) no-hitter on May 3

Pitchers Continue To Reign

While the number of regular-season no-hitters decreased from five in 2010 to three in 2011, pitchers continued to enjoy the benefits of a less offensive environment. Scoring declined for the sixth consecutive season in 2011 as offensive output continued to recede from the high-octane 1994-2004 period.

The big league batting average dipped to .255, the lowest figure since 1989. Similarly, the rate per nine innings at which teams scored runs (4.30) and hit home runs (0.94) reached their lowest points since 1992.

Twins lefty Francisco Liriano completed the season's first no-hitter on May 3 in a 1-0 victory against the White Sox. Oddly enough, Liriano's performance just might be the least impressive no-no in major league history—he walked six batters and struck out two, while just 54 percent of his 123 pitches went for strikes. He lowered his ERA from 9.13 to 6.61 with the nine scoreless innings.

Little more than a month later, on June 12, Liriano pitched more effectively in a foiled no-hit bid against the Rangers. He held Texas hitless for seven innings before third baseman Adrian Beltre led off the eighth with a single. In all, Liriano allowed two hits and one run over eight innings. He struck out nine and walked none, and most

CONTINUED ON PAGE 11

Hollywood ending

Matt Kemp fell one home run shy of 40-40

LARRY GOREN

BY JOE HAAKENSON

Matt Kemp was a flirt in 2011.

The Dodgers center fielder flirted with winning the triple crown, and he flirted with becoming the fifth player in baseball history to join the 40-40 club, falling one home run short.

But Kemp also produced in a big way. He batted .324/.399/.586 and led the National League with 39 home runs, 126 RBIs, 115 runs scored and 353 total bases. He made his first all-star team. He stole 40 bases in 51 attempts.

The 27-year-old Kemp performed so well, in fact, that he won the Baseball America Major League Player of the Year award.

Kemp's raw talent and athleticism have led many to believe that he was capable of such a season, but what may have surprised some was how swiftly it came, particularly on the heels of his 2010 campaign.

Kemp hit a career-worst .249 for Los Angeles last year with 28 homers and 19 steals. Some thought he was distracted by a much-publicized relationship with pop star Rihanna.

"Last year there was a lot more attention, but now it's something I've gotten used to," Kemp said. "All that was going on was new to me. Now, the attention is what it is—it's part of the lifestyle. That's what it comes with when you're playing in a city like L.A. Living under the microscope, people are going to assume things and come up with their own opinions. That's what L.A. is"

The relationship with Rihanna reportedly ended last December, and Kemp came to spring training with a new and improved attitude. It also didn't hurt that the Dodgers brought in Davey Lopes as first-base coach and hired the mild-mannered Don Mattingly as the team's manager to replace Joe Torre.

Lopes came over from the Phillies and had an impact on all the Dodgers players, but no one more than Kemp, whose agent Dave Stewart is a former teammate and friend.

"I heard a lot of (negative) statements about him, but what I saw in spring training was totally the opposite," Lopes said. "He did a lot of growing up. I think he recognized he made some mistakes last year and he was going to do everything within his power to correct things. It was not so much that the numbers were bad, but the numbers didn't match up to the abilities Matt has."

Mattingly gave Lopes credit for helping Kemp focus, but emphasized that ultimately it was Kemp who was responsible for getting himself together on and off the field.

"(Lopes) was good for Matt, but honestly, I think Matt was the difference," Mattingly said. "Last year was tough for him and that made him more determined this year. Matt seemed like he was having fun this year.

"He and I had a conversation and I told him, 'Matt, no matter what you do, people are always going to think there's more there.'

"That's the tough part. He can come out next year and be just as focused, do everything exactly the same, give the same effort, play every day and not have the same numbers. That's just the way the game is. But this year, he was the best player in the game."

PREVIOUS 10 WINNERS

2001	Barry Bonds, of, Giants
2002	Alex Rodriguez, ss, Rangers
2003	Barry Bonds, of, Giants
2004	Barry Bonds, of, Giants
2005	Albert Pujols, 1b, Cardinals
2006	Johan Santana, lhp, Twins
2007	Alex Rodriguez, ss, Yankees
2008	C.C. Sabathia, lhp, Indians/Brewers
2009	Joe Mauer, c, Twins
2010	Roy Halladay, rhp, Phillies

Full list: BaseballAmerica.com/awards

everyone agreed he had better stuff that time out.

Three days after Liriano tossed his no-hitter, Cardinals lefty Jaime Garcia took a perfect game into the eighth inning against the Brewers on May 6. In a span of two batters, Garcia lost both the perfecto and no-hitter, first issuing a walk to third baseman Casey McGehee and then allowing a hit to shortstop Yuniesky Betancourt. Garcia settled for a two-hit, eight-strikeout shutout on 102 pitches.

The next night, May 7, Brewers righthander Yovani Gallardo attempted to return the favor, taking a no-hitter into the eighth against the Cardinals. Leading off the St. Louis eighth, third baseman Daniel Descalso singled to break up the bid, but Gallardo and closer John Axford finished with a combined one-hit shutout.

On the same day that Gallardo made his no-hit bid, Tigers ace Justin Verlander navigated the Blue Jays lineup for nine innings without allowing a hit. He previously no-hit the Brewers on June 12, 2007, and he would have had a perfect game but for a one-out walk to catcher J.P. Arencibia in the eighth.

Verlander nearly notched his second no-hitter of the season on June 14 when he held the Indians hitless for 7⅓ innings. Second baseman Orlando Cabrera's one-out single in the eighth denied Verlander his third career no-no—he settled for a two-hit shutout with 12 strikeouts—but it was obvious at that point that he was on his way to a special season. Verlander went 24-5, 2.40 in

34 starts and led the AL in wins, ERA, strikeouts (250) and innings (251).

Angels righty Ervin Santana completed the season's third no-hitter on July 27, though he allowed an unearned run to the Indians in the process. Cleveland scored its lone run in the bottom of the first inning when center fielder Ezequiel Carrera, the leadoff batter, reached on an error by Angels shortstop Erick Aybar, stole second, moved to third on a groundout and then scored on a Santana wild pitch. Santana was flawless otherwise, striking out 10 and walking one.

Even in a year dominated by strong pitching performances, hitters had their say at times. Over a three-week period from mid-May to early June, six players struck three home runs in a game. The Mets' Carlos Beltran accomplished the feat first against the Rockies in Denver on May 12. The other five in chronological order: the Blue Jays' Jose Bautista in Minneapolis (May 15), the Rockies' Jason Giambi in Philadelphia (May 19), the Brewers' Corey Hart at home against the Nationals (May 23), the White Sox's Carlos Quentin in Arlington, Texas, (May 24) and the Giants' Aubrey Huff in St. Louis (June 2).

On May 26 in Philadelphia, the Phillies and Reds locked horns in a 19-inning marathon. Long games are not unusual over the course of a baseball season, but this one had a special twist. Phillies utility infielder Wilson Valdez, who started the game at second base, pitched the 19th inning and plowed through the heart of Cincinnati's order— Joey Votto, Scott Rolen and Jay Bruce—with a

AMERICAN LEAGUE STANDINGS

EAST	W	L	PCT	GB	Manager	General Manager	Attendance	Average	Last Penn.
New York Yankees	97	65	.599	—	Joe Girardi	Brian Cashman	3,653,680	45,107	2009
*Tampa Bay Rays	91	71	.562	6	Joe Maddon	Andrew Friedman	1,529,188	18,879	2008
Boston Red Sox	90	72	.556	7	Terry Francona	Theo Epstein	3,054,001	37,704	2007
Toronto Blue Jays	81	81	.500	16	John Farrell	Alex Anthopoulos	1,818,103	22,446	1993
Baltimore Orioles	69	93	.426	28	Buck Showalter	Andy MacPhail	1,755,461	21,943	1983
CENTRAL	W	L	PCT	GB	Manager	General Manager	Attendance	Average	Last Penn.
Detroit Tigers	95	67	.586	—	Jim Leyland	Dave Dombrowski	2,642,045	32,618	2006
Cleveland Indians	80	82	.494	15	Manny Acta	Chris Antonetti	1,840,835	22,726	1997
Chicago White Sox	79	83	.488	16	Ozzie Guillen/Don Cooper	Ken Williams	2,001,117	24,705	2005
Kansas City Royals	71	91	.438	24	Ned Yost	Dayton Moore	1,724,450	21,290	1985
Minnesota Twins	63	99	.389	32	Ron Gardenhire	Bill Smith	3,168,116	39,113	1991
WEST	W	L	PCT	GB	Manager	General Manager	Attendance	Average	Last Penn.
Texas Rangers	96	66	.593	—	Ron Washington	Jon Daniels	2,946,949	36,382	2011
Los Angeles Angels	86	76	.531	10	Mike Scioscia	Tony Reagins	3,166,321	39,090	2002
Oakland Athletics	74	88	.457	22	Bob Geren/Bob Melvin	Billy Beane	1,476,791	18,460	1990
Seattle Mariners	67	95	.414	29	Eric Wedge	Jack Zduriencik	1,896,321	23,411	Never

*Wild card

PLAYOFFS—Division Series: Tigers defeated Yankees 3-2 and Rangers defeated Rays 3-1 in best-of-five series.
League Championship Series: Rangers defeated Tigers 4-2 in best-of-seven series.

hitless inning. He picked up the win when Raul Ibanez hit a sacrifice fly in the bottom of the 19th to end the 6-hour, 11-minute contest. Valdez threw one pitch to the backstop and hit Rolen with an attempted slider, but he did manage to hit 89 mph with his fastball.

Valdez became the first position player to pick up a victory in the majors since Rockies catcher Brent Mayne on Aug. 22, 2000.

Baseball Suffers 'Killer' Loss

The baseball community suffered a huge loss on May 17 when Hall of Fame slugger Harmon Killebrew died at age 74 from esophageal cancer. Days earlier Killebrew had announced his diagnosis just six months previously.

Killebrew won the 1969 AL MVP award, made the all-star team in 11 seasons and ranked 11th on the all-time home run list with 573. His eight seasons with 40 or more homers tied for second in history to Babe Ruth.

"No individual has ever meant more to the Minnesota Twins organization and millions of fans across Twins territory than Harmon Killebrew," Twins president Dave St. Peter said. "His legacy will be the class, dignity and humility he demonstrated each and every day as a Hall of Fame-quality husband, father, friend, teammate and man."

Many former and current Twins gathered to pay tribute to Killebrew, whose kindness and warmness stood in direct contrast to his brutish power as a player.

"I lost a hero today," said former Twins pitcher Jack Morris, a native of St. Paul, Minn. "To remember the innocence of being a young kid who just looked up to a guy he didn't know because of what he did as a baseball player, something that you hoped that maybe some day you could be like.

"But as a grown man, I look back at him now not as that guy, but as the guy who tried to show me that you don't have to be angry. You don't have to be mad. You can love and share love. We're all going to miss him and we're all going to love him forever."

On May 25, a week after Killebrew's death, came news that former Royals lefthander Paul Splittorff died after a battle with oral cancer and melanoma. He was just 64.

No one who suited up for the Royals was associated longer with the franchise. He traces his roots back to the 25th round of the 1968 draft, the year before Kansas City played its first game. Splittorff went on to pitch 15 years for the club, becoming its all-time leader with 166 wins.

After his retirement in 1984, Splittorff went from the clubhouse to the broadcast booth and was just as popular and respected in that role among fans.

On a less tragic note, but certainly devastating to the chances of the defending World Series champions, Giants catcher Buster Posey missed the bulk of the season after suffering a broken leg in a home-plate collision with the Marlins' Scott Cousins on May 25. Cousins scored from third base on a sacrifice fly to snap a tie in the 12th inning.

NATIONAL LEAGUE STANDINGS

EAST	W	L	PCT	GB	Manager	General Manager	Attendance	Average	Last Penn.
Philadelphia Phillies	102	60	.630	—	Charlie Manuel	Ruben Amaro Jr.	3,680,718	45,441	2009
Atlanta Braves	89	73	.549	13	Fredi Gonzalez	Frank Wren	2,372,940	30,037	1999
Washington Nationals	80	81	.497	21½	J. Riggleman/J. McLaren/ Davey Johnson	Mike Rizzo	1,940,478	24,878	Never
New York Mets	77	85	.475	25	Terry Collins	Sandy Alderson	2,352,596	30,161	2000
Florida Marlins	72	90	.444	30	E. Rodriguez/J. McKeon	Larry Beinfest	1,520,562	19,007	2003
CENTRAL	**W**	**L**	**PCT**	**GB**	**Manager**	**General Manager**	**Attendance**	**Average**	**Last Penn.**
Milwaukee Brewers	96	66	.593	—	Ron Roenicke	Doug Melvin	3,071,373	37,918	^1982
*St. Louis Cardinals	90	72	.556	6	Tony La Russa	John Mozeliak	3,093,954	38,197	2011
Cincinnati Reds	79	83	.488	17	Dusty Baker	Walt Jocketty	2,213,588	27,328	1990
Pittsburgh Pirates	72	90	.444	24	Clint Hurdle	Neal Huntington	1,940,429	24,255	1979
Chicago Cubs	71	91	.438	25	Mike Quade	Jim Hendry	3,017,966	37,259	1945
Houston Astros	56	106	.346	40	Brad Mills	Ed Wade	2,067,016	25,519	2005
WEST	**W**	**L**	**PCT**	**GB**	**Manager**	**General Manager**	**Attendance**	**Average**	**Last Penn.**
Arizona Diamondbacks	94	68	.580	—	Kirk Gibson	Kevin Towers	2,105,432	25,993	2001
San Francisco Giants	86	76	.531	8	Bruce Bochy	Brian Sabean	3,387,303	41,819	2010
Los Angeles Dodgers	82	79	.509	11½	Don Mattingly	Ned Colletti	2,935,139	36,236	1988
Colorado Rockies	73	89	.451	21	Jim Tracy	Dan O'Dowd	2,909,777	35,923	2007
San Diego Padres	71	91	.438	23	Bud Black	Jed Hoyer	2,143,018	26,457	1998

*Wild card ^American League

PLAYOFFS—Division Series: Cardinals defeated Phillies 3-2 and Brewers defeated Diamondbacks 3-2 in best-of-five series.
League Championship Series: Cardinals defeated Brewers 4-2 in best-of-seven series.

A controversy ensued when people questioned the necessity of Cousins' vicious hit on Posey when the catcher was in a vulnerable position. Giants manager Bruce Bochy even suggested a rules change to protect catchers from taking such hits and risking serious injury.

"I think this probably needs to be addressed," Bochy said. "The catcher is so vulnerable."

For his part, Cousins said: "I'm not trying to end anybody's season or anything like that. I was just trying to play hard and score the go-ahead run."

The Giants never recovered from the loss of Posey, the NL rookie of the year in 2010 who helped propel the club to the Fall Classic. San Francisco traded for the Mets' Carlos Beltran in July in an attempt to hang with the Diamondbacks in the NL West race, but the maneuver proved to be fruitless.

Coaches Ride The Carousel

When teams don't meet expectations—realistic or not—people pay with their jobs. A firing spree began in early June when the Athletics dismissed manager Bob Geren on June 9 and replaced him with Bob Melvin, a former big league skipper who had worked as a pro scout for the Mets in 2010.

The A's fell to 27-36 after a nine-game losing streak at the time they fired Geren. "I felt like at this point a change was needed," Oakland GM Billy Beane said. "It got to the point where the emphasis was on the status of the manager on a daily basis instead of the field."

Before the year was through, Melvin signed a three-year extension to remain manager in Oakland.

The ax swung deeper after that when several coaches lost their jobs. The Rangers dismissed hitting coach Thad Bosley on June 8 after several players complained of communication problems. Texas ranked fourth in the AL in runs scored at the time Triple-A coach Scott Coolbaugh took over for Bosley.

The Marlins acted the same day the Rangers did in firing hitting coach John Mallee. Florida replaced Mallee with ESPN analyst Eduardo Perez, whose father Tony serves as a special assistant for the organization. Coincidentally or not, star shortstop Hanley Ramirez's production perked up after the switch from Mallee to Perez. His OPS climbed more than 200 points to .824 following the switch.

Pitching coaches were next. The Orioles' Mark Connor resigned his post on June 14, citing personal reasons, but he later took a job with the Rangers in August as a player-development special

AMERICAN LEAGUE BEST TOOLS

A Baseball America survey of American League managers, conducted at midseason 2011, ranked players with the best tools.

BEST HITTER	BEST CONTROL
1. Adrian Gonzalez, Red Sox	1. Jered Weaver, Angels
2. Miguel Cabrera, Tigers	2. Dan Haren, Angels
3. Jose Bautista, Blue Jays	3. Josh Tomlin, Indians

BEST POWER	BEST PICKOFF MOVE
1. Jose Bautista, Blue Jays	1. Mark Buehrle, White Sox
2 (tie). Miguel Cabrera, Tigers	2. James Shields, Rays
2 (tie). Josh Hamilton, Rangers	3. Justin Verlander, Tigers

BEST BUNTER	BEST RELIEVER
1. Brett Gardner, Yankees	1. Mariano Rivera, Yankees
2. Juan Pierre, White Sox	2. Kyle Farnsworth, Rays
3. Erick Aybar, Angels	3. Daniel Bard, Red Sox

BEST STRIKE-ZONE JUDGMENT	BEST DEFENSIVE C
1. Bobby Abreu, Angels	1. Matt Wieters, Orioles
2. Miguel Cabrera, Tigers	2. Joe Mauer, Twins
3. Kevin Youkilis, Red Sox	3. Alex Avila, Tigers

BEST HIT-AND-RUN ARTIST	BEST DEFENSIVE 1B
1. Derek Jeter, Yankees	1. Mark Teixeira, Yankees
2. Erick Aybar, Angels	2. Adrian Gonzalez, Red Sox
3. Asdrubal Cabrera, Indians	3. Casey Kotchman, Rays

BEST BASERUNNER	BEST DEFENSIVE 2B
1. Jacoby Ellsbury, Red Sox	1. Robinson Cano, Yankees
2. Elvis Andrus, Rangers	2. Dustin Pedroia, Red Sox
3. Brett Gardner, Yankees	3. Ian Kinsler, Rangers

FASTEST BASERUNNER	BEST DEFENSIVE 3B
1. Brett Gardner, Yankees	1. Adrian Beltre, Rangers
2. Jacoby Ellsbury, Red Sox	2. Evan Longoria, Rays
3. Peter Bourjos, Angels	3. Alex Rodriguez, Yankees

MOST EXCITING PLAYER	BEST DEFENSIVE SS
1. Jose Bautista, Blue Jays	1. Elvis Andrus, Rangers
2 (tie). Josh Hamilton, Rangers	2. Asdrubal Cabrera, Indians
2 (tie). Jacoby Ellsbury, Red Sox	3. Erick Aybar, Angels

BEST PITCHER	BEST INFIELD ARM
1. Justin Verlander, Tigers	1. Adrian Beltre, Rangers
2. Jered Weaver, Angels	2. Erick Aybar, Angels
3. C.C. Sabathia, Yankees	3. Jose Bautista, Blue Jays

BEST FASTBALL	BEST DEFENSIVE OF
1. Justin Verlander, Tigers	1. Franklin Gutierrez, Mariners
2. Felix Hernandez, Mariners	2. Adam Jones, Orioles
3. Daniel Bard, Red Sox	3. Shin-Soo Choo, Indians

BEST CURVEBALL	BEST OUTFIELD ARM
1. Justin Verlander, Tigers	1. Shin-Soo Choo, Indians
2. Gio Gonzalez, Athletics	2. Jeff Francoeur, Royals
3. Josh Beckett, Red Sox	3. Ichiro Suzuki, Mariners

BEST SLIDER	BEST MANAGER
1. Felix Hernandez, Mariners	1. Mike Scioscia, Angels
2. C.C. Sabathia, Yankees	2. Ron Gardenhire, Twins
3. Jered Weaver, Angels	3. Joe Maddon, Rays

BEST CHANGEUP	
1. James Shields, Rays	
2. Jered Weaver, Angels	
3. Justin Verlander, Tigers	

consultant. Bullpen coach Mark Adair replaced Connor in Baltimore.

The Astros canned pitching coach Brad Arnsberg

CONTINUED ON PAGE 15

Rays rookie makes good

BY MARC TOPKIN

When 24-year-old Jeremy Hellickson strode up the mound, he gave little indication he was pitching his first full season in the big leagues.

Certainly not the way he handled the pressures of having to face the American League's toughest teams. Not the way he managed his way through constantly tight games.

And, most obviously, not the way he pitched, posting a 13-10, 2.95 record with a .210 opponent average and 20 quality starts that were the best of all major league rookies.

"I know that he is (a rookie), but I don't always process it that way," Rays manager Joe Maddon said.

"Precocious" is the word Rays executive vice president Andrew Friedman uses. "His composure is off the charts," he said. "And that's before you even get to his physical ability."

The Rays kept a close watch on Hellickson, a 2005 fourth-round pick out of Des Moines' Hoover High, even after he won his first three starts in 2010, even more so when a potential move to the bullpen for the stretch run and postseason didn't work out well.

The January 2011 trade of Matt Garza opened a spot in the rotation for Hellickson, but the Rays continued monitoring his innings, giving him an extra day's rest 14 times, and more than that four other times, including a 15-day respite around the all-star break. Including his Game Four start in the AL

ROOKIE OF THE YEAR

Jeremy Hellickson tamed the rugged AL East with a three-pitch repertoire

CLIFF WELCH

Division Series, Hellickson tossed 193 innings.

While the Rays were limiting Hellickson's workload, they also encouraged him to throw more curveballs in concert with a fastball Maddon describes as "sneaky" and a treacherous changeup.

The fastball was Hellickson's primary pitch coming out of high school, but in 2006 Rays minor league pitching guru Dick Bosman showed him the grip for a circle changeup, and Hellickson eventually mastered it.

To get Hellickson to mix in more curveballs, Maddon mentioned it, pitching coach Jim Hickey worked with him on it and teammate James Shields also got involved, showing him a grip that yielded better depth.

The added confidence in his curve gave Hellickson the three-pitch assortment needed for success in the rigorous AL East.

In 10 starts against the Yankees, Red Sox and Blue Jays, Hellickson went 4-2, 3.84 with a 1.31 WHIP, 49 hits, 36 strikeouts and 31 walks in 61 innings. In 19 starts against 12 other teams—including the Tigers (twice), Rangers, Cardinals and Brewers—he went 9-8, 2.53 with a 1.08 WHIP, 97 hits, 81 strikeouts and 41 walks over 128 innings.

"He's an extremely talented pitcher who has the ability to miss bats in the American League," Friedman said. "He fit in really well to our rotation, and we expect him to be a big part of our future success."

PREVIOUS 10 WINNERS

2001	Albert Pujols, of/3b/1b, Cardinals
2002	Eric Hinske, 3b, Blue Jays
2003	Brandon Webb, rhp, Diamondbacks
2004	Khalil Greene, ss, Padres
2005	Huston Street, rhp, Athletics
2006	Justin Verlander, rhp, Tigers
2007	Ryan Braun, 3b, Brewers
2008	Geovany Soto, c, Cubs
2009	Andrew McCutchen, of, Pirates
2010	Jason Heyward, of, Braves

Full list: BaseballAmerica.com/awards

ALL-ROOKIE TEAM 2011

Pos	PLAYER, TEAM	AGE	AB	AVG	OBP	SLG	2B	HR	RBI	SB	RUNDOWN
C	Wilson Ramos, Nationals	23	389	.267	.334	.445	22	15	52	0	Started 106 games, hit for power, thwarted steals
1B	*Eric Hosmer, Royals	21	523	.293	.334	.465	27	19	78	11	Final 317 at-bats: .312/.350/.511 with 14 homers
2B	*Dustin Ackley, Mariners	23	333	.273	.348	.417	16	6	36	6	Ascended quickly to No. 3 hitter in Seattle
3B	Brett Lawrie, Blue Jays	21	150	.293	.373	.580	8	9	25	7	Hit 27 homers between Triple-A and Toronto
SS	*Dee Gordon, Dodgers	23	224	.304	.325	.362	9	0	11	24	Hit .345 with 15 steals after July 31 Furcal deal
CF	Desmond Jennings, Rays	24	247	.259	.356	.449	9	10	25	20	Totaled 22 HR, 37 SB between Triple-A and majors
OF	*Mike Carp, Mariners	25	290	.276	.326	.466	17	12	46	0	Climbed Seattle depth chart at first base, left field
OF	*Lucas Duda, Mets	25	301	.292	.370	.482	21	10	50	1	Led all rookies with .852 OPS (min. 300 PA)
DH	*Freddie Freeman, Braves	21	571	.282	.346	.448	32	21	76	4	Led all rookies in hits (161), on-base percentage

Pos	PITCHER, TEAM	AGE	W	L	SV	ERA	IP	SO	BB	RUNDOWN
SP	Brandon Beachy, Braves	24	7	3	0	3.68	142	169	46	Led all rookies with 10.7 strikeouts per nine innings
SP	Jeremy Hellickson, Rays	24	13	10	0	2.95	189	117	72	Finished second in AL with .210 opponent average
SP	Ivan Nova, Yankees	24	16	4	0	3.70	165	98	57	Went 12-0, 3.25 over final 16 starts; Yankees won 13
SP	Michael Pineda, Mariners	22	9	10	0	3.74	171	173	55	Second among AL starters with 9.1 strikeouts per nine
SP	Vance Worley, Phillies	23	11	3	0	3.01	132	119	46	Went 9-2, 2.83 with 95 SO in 105 IP over final 17 starts
RP	*Chris Sale, White Sox	22	2	2	8	2.79	71	79	27	Hard thrower (95 mph+) stumbled early but not often
RP	Jordan Walden, Angels	23	5	5	32	2.98	60	67	26	Fastball averaged 97.6 mph, second highest in majors
CL	Craig Kimbrel, Braves	23	4	3	46	2.10	77	127	32	Tied for NL lead with 46 saves, set new rookie record

*Bats/throws lefthanded

CONTINUED FROM PAGE 13

on June 14 as they hurtled toward 106 losses, replacing him with special assistant Doug Brocail.

The Indians fired hitting coach Jon Nunnally on June 19, making him the fifth coach to be let go in the month of June. The Indians, who were tied with the Tigers for first place in the AL Central at the time, promoted minor league hitting coordinator Bruce Fields to the big league post.

The Marlins kicked off June by going 1-19 and slipping into last place in the NL East. Manager Edwin Rodriguez resigned on June 19, near the end of an 11-game losing streak. He worked on a one-year deal and did not expect to return in 2012. Florida stunned many by recycling an 80-year-old Jack McKeon as their manager.

Eight years earlier, a 72-year-old McKeon took over the Marlins and led them to the 2003 World Series title.

"You guys got to remember, you all sat in this room and said in 2003 that I was too old," McKeon said at his re-introductory press conference.

Perhaps, but McKeon's return did not turn around the Marlins—they went 40-50—and he announced his retirement (again) following the season. To replace McKeon, Florida acquired manager Ozzie Guillen from the White Sox in a deal that sent prospects Ozzie Martinez and Jhan Marinez to Chicago.

The Marlins had courted Guillen previously, but failed to work out a deal with the White Sox—that is until the outspoken manager forced the issue by demanding either a contract extension

or his release. With two games remaining, Chicago installed pitching coach Don Cooper as the most interim of managers. The White Sox went 1-1.

In a stunning move, Nationals manager Jim Riggleman resigned on June 24. Heightening the absurdity, he walked away after Washington's 1-0 walk-off victory against the Mariners. With the team playing its best baseball of the season, Riggleman asked GM Mike Rizzo to pick up his option for 2012. Rizzo said he wasn't ready to do so and Riggleman decided to leave.

"It's been brewing for a while," he said. "I know I'm not Casey Stengel, but I do feel like I know what I'm doing. It's not a situation where I felt like I should continue on such a short leash."

Rizzo fired back with a statement saying, "I was always taught that one of the cardinal rules of baseball was that no individual can put his interests ahead of those of the team. Jim told me pre-game today that if we wouldn't pick up his team option, then he wouldn't get on the team bus today."

Riggleman's version was a bit different. He said he merely asked for a meeting with Rizzo and was denied. Either way, managers seldom walk away from a club playing well.

The Nationals turned briefly to bench coach John McLaren (three games) before enticing Davey Johnson to return to managing after an 11-year hiatus. Johnson, who had worked as a special assistant to Rizzo, will return as manager in 2012.

The carousel continued as June slipped into July and the first-place Tigers fired pitching coach Rick Knapp and replaced him with bullpen coach Jeff Jones.

All-Time Greats Make History

As the season neared the midway point, Yankees shortstop Derek Jeter approached 3,000 career hits, a plateau never before reached by anyone wearing the famous pinstripes. Not Babe Ruth. Not Lou Gehrig. Not Joe DiMaggio. Not Mickey Mantle.

The question was: Would Jeter be able to reach 3,000 in Yankee Stadium in front of the home fans? A hamstring strain shelved him for 15 days in June, pushing back his timetable and bringing the schedule into play. As the Yankees prepared for a game against Tampa Bay on Saturday, July 9, Jeter stood two hits shy of 3,000. New York had just two games remaining in the homestand before finishing the first half on the road.

Though the Rays threw ace David Price at the Yankees that day, Jeter didn't seem to mind. He went 5-for-5 with a double and a third-inning home run for No. 3,000. He joined Wade Boggs (1999) as the only players ever to reach that milestone with a round-tripper. Amazingly, Jeter had not homered at Yankee Stadium since July 22, 2010, a gap of nearly a year.

Longtime teammates and friends Jorge Posada and Mariano Rivera were the first to greet Jeter after he crossed home plate, though the rest of the Yankees didn't stray far when it came time to mob him.

"You want to hit the ball hard," Jeter said. "I didn't want to hit a slow roller to third base and have it replayed forever. Hitting a home run was the last thing I was thinking about. I was pretty relieved."

But Jeter wasn't done. He knocked in what proved to be the winning run with an eighth-inning single, making the day complete with a 5-4 victory that had the Yankee Stadium crowd of 48,103 roaring.

"I don't think you can script it any better," Yankees manager Joe Girardi said. "This is already movie-ready. To get your 3,000th hit on a home run that ties the game . . . it's just remarkable."

At 37 years and 13 days, Jeter was the fourth-youngest player to accumulate 3,000 career hits. Only Ty Cobb, Hank Aaron and Robin Yount got there at a younger age.

After the game, Jeter stood on the field alone, tipping his cap to the adoring crowd, soaking in a magical day in a Hall of Fame career. He had felt so comfortable and relaxed in the days leading up to the moment that he granted permission to HBO to have a camera crew follow him around and later produce a documentary of the run-up to hit No. 3,000.

NATIONAL LEAGUE BEST TOOLS

A Baseball America survey of National League managers, conducted at midseason 2011, ranked players with the best tools.

BEST HITTER
1. Albert Pujols, Cardinals
2. Joey Votto, Reds
3. Jose Reyes, Mets

BEST POWER
1. Prince Fielder, Brewers
2. Mike Stanton, Marlins
3. Albert Pujols, Cardinals

BEST BUNTER
1. Michael Bourn, Astros/Braves
2. Jose Reyes, Mets
3. Emilio Bonifacio, Marlins

BEST STRIKE-ZONE JUDGMENT
1. Joey Votto, Reds
2. Albert Pujols, Cardinals
3. Prince Fielder, Brewers

BEST HIT-AND-RUN ARTIST
1. Placido Polanco, Phillies
2. Martin Prado, Braves
3. Freddy Sanchez, Giants

BEST BASERUNNER
1. Michael Bourn, Astros
2. Jose Reyes, Mets
3. Andrew McCutchen, Pirates

FASTEST BASERUNNER
1. Michael Bourn, Astros/Braves
2. Jose Reyes, Mets
3. Emilio Bonifacio, Marlins

MOST EXCITING PLAYER
1. Jose Reyes, Mets
2 (tie). Matt Kemp, Dodgers
2 (tie). Albert Pujols, Cardinals

BEST PITCHER
1. Roy Halladay, Phillies
2. Jair Jurrjens, Braves
3. Clayton Kershaw, Dodgers

BEST FASTBALL
1. Aroldis Chapman, Reds
2. Craig Kimbrel, Braves
3. Clayton Kershaw, Dodgers

BEST CURVEBALL
1. Clayton Kershaw, Dodgers
2. Chris Carpenter, Cardinals
3. Tommy Hanson, Braves

BEST SLIDER
1. Carlos Marmol, Cubs
2 (tie). Roy Halladay, Phillies
2 (tie). Sergio Romo, Giants

BEST CHANGEUP
1. Cole Hamels, Phillies
2. Tim Lincecum, Giants
2. Shaun Marcum, Brewers

BEST CONTROL
1. Roy Halladay, Phillies
2. Cliff Lee, Phillies
3. Jeff Karstens, Pirates

BEST PICKOFF MOVE
1. Clayton Richard, Padres
2. Chris Capuano, Brewers
3. Clayton Kershaw, Dodgers

BEST RELIEVER
1. Brian Wilson, Giants
2 (tie). Joel Hanrahan, Pirates
2 (tie). Craig Kimbrel, Braves

BEST DEFENSIVE C
1. Yadier Molina, Cardinals
2. Carlos Ruiz, Phillies
3. Brian McCann, Braves

BEST DEFENSIVE 1B
1. Joey Votto, Reds
2. Albert Pujols, Cardinals
3. Todd Helton, Rockies

BEST DEFENSIVE 2B
1. Brandon Phillips, Reds
2 (tie). Omar Infante, Marlins
2 (tie). Neil Walker, Pirates

BEST DEFENSIVE 3B
1. Ryan Zimmerman, Nationals
2. Placido Polanco, Phillies
3. Scott Rolen, Reds

BEST DEFENSIVE SS
1. Troy Tulowitzki, Rockies
2. Jose Reyes, Mets
3. Alex Gonzalez, Braves

BEST INFIELD ARM
1. Troy Tulowitzki, Rockies
2. Jose Reyes, Mets
3. Rafael Furcal, LAD/Cardinals

BEST DEFENSIVE OF
1. Michael Bourn, Astros/Braves
2. Shane Victorino, Phillies
3. Chris Young, Diamondbacks

BEST OUTFIELD ARM
1. Carlos Gonzalez, Rockies
2. Rick Ankiel, Nationals
3. Jay Bruce, Reds

BEST MANAGER
1. Bruce Bochy, Giants
2. Tony La Russa, Cardinals
3. Clint Hurdle, Pirates

"Just one of those special days," he said. "It's a number that's meant a lot to baseball. To be the only Yankee to do anything is special."

The home run ball from No. 3,000 was corralled by Yankees fan Christian Lopez. Rather than put it up for auction to the highest bidder, he returned it in person to Jeter and was rewarded with bats, balls and jerseys.

"Mr. Jeter deserved it," Lopez said. "It's all his."

More than a month after Jeter collected hit No. 3,000, another of the game's most respected players reached a different, yet still revered, milestone. Twins DH Jim Thome cracked home run Nos. 599 and 600 in an Aug. 15 game in Detroit. He socked a two-run shot in the sixth inning off Tigers righthander Rick Porcello and the milestone blast in the seventh with two aboard against lefty reliever Daniel Schlereth. Both home runs were hit to the opposite field.

"You dream about it but when it finally happens it's kind of surreal," said the 40-year-old Thome, the oldest player to reach 600. "It's a special night, something I'll always cherish. I'll remember the Detroit fans getting on their feet to applaud. That was really cool."

He became the eighth player in history to reach 600 home runs, joining a club that has more than doubled in size in the past decade with the addition of Thome as well as Alex Rodriguez in 2010, Ken Griffey Jr. in '08, Sammy Sosa in '07 and Barry Bonds in '02. Just three sluggers had eclipsed 600 home runs in the first century of major league history: Babe Ruth in 1931, Willie Mays in '69 and Hank Aaron in '71.

"Selfishly, you want to be part of somebody's 600th home run," Twins teammate Michael Cuddyer said. "To have it be a guy like Jim Thome makes it that much cooler because of the type of person he is."

Thome arrived in the majors with a Paul Bunyan physique and maintained it throughout his career. He broke in with the Indians in 1991 and wound up hitting 334 homers for Cleveland in 12 seasons as he helped lead the team to six playoff appearances, including AL pennants in 1995 and '97. Thome moved on to the Phillies, White Sox, Dodgers and Twins before coming full circle to finish the 2011 season with the Indians, courtesy of a late-August trade with Minnesota.

Jeter and Thome weren't alone in the milestone club. Yankees closer Mariano Rivera notched his 602nd career save on Sept. 19, surpassing the all-time mark of 601 established one year earlier by Trevor Hoffman.

The 41-year-old Rivera made his 12th all-star team in 2011 and showed little sign of slowing down. He passed Hoffman with a perfect ninth inning against the Twins in which he locked down a 6-4 victory with his 43rd save of the season.

"It's a blessing," said Rivera, who has eight sea-

ALL-TIME ACHIEVEMENTS

3,000 HITS
Shortstop Derek Jeter collected his 3,000th career hit in Yankee Stadium on July 9, going 5-for-5 in a game started by Rays ace David Price. After slumping through most of the first half, the 37-year-old Jeter hit .327 in the second to pull to within 154 hits of Nap Lajoie and 13th place on the all-time list.

No. Batter	Hits	No. Batter	Hits
1. Pete Rose#	4,256	15. George Brett*	3,154
2. Ty Cobb*	4,189	16. Paul Waner*	3,152
3. Hank Aaron	3,771	17. Robin Yount	3,142
4. Stan Musial*	3,630	18. Tony Gwynn*	3,141
5. Tris Speaker*	3,514	19. Dave Winfield	3,110
6. Cap Anson	3,435	20. Derek Jeter	3,088
7. Honus Wagner	3,420	21. Craig Biggio	3,060
8. Carl Yastrzemski*	3,419	22. Rickey Henderson	3,055
9. Paul Molitor	3,319	23. Rod Carew*	3,053
10. Eddie Collins*	3,315	24. Lou Brock*	3,023
11. Willie Mays	3,283	25. Rafael Palmeiro*	3,020
12. Eddie Murray#	3,255	26. Wade Boggs*	3,010
13. Nap Lajoie	3,242	27. Al Kaline	3,007
14. Cal Ripken	3,184	28. Roberto Clemente	3,000

600 HOME RUNS
Twins DH Jim Thome smacked a pair of opposite-field home runs in an Aug. 15 game in Detroit, giving him 600 for his career. He joined an exclusive club that has welcomed five new members—Bonds, Griffey Jr., Rodriguez, Thome and Sosa—over the course of the past 10 years.

No. Batter	HR	No. Batter	HR
1. Barry Bonds*	762	5. Ken Griffey Jr.*	630
2. Hank Aaron	755	6. Alex Rodriguez	629
3. Babe Ruth*	714	7. Sammy Sosa	609
4. Willie Mays	660	8. Jim Thome*	604

ALL-TIME SAVES LEADERS
Yankees closer Mariano Rivera eclipsed Trevor Hoffman's one-year-old record for career saves, notching No. 602 in a Sept. 19 game at home against the Twins. Rivera, 41, also leads all active pitchers (min. 1,000 innings) with a 2.21 ERA and .210 opponent average. The top 10 for career saves:

No. Pitcher	Saves	No. Pitcher	Saves
1. Mariano Rivera	603	6. Dennis Eckersley	390
2. Trevor Hoffman	601	7. Jeff Reardon	367
3. Lee Smith	478	8. Troy Percival	358
4. John Franco*	424	9. Randy Myers*	347
5. Billy Wagner*	422	10. Rollie Fingers	341

*Bats/throws lefthanded. #Switch-hitter.
Active players in **bold**.

sons of at least 40 saves, one off the record held by Hoffman. "I never thought I'd be doing this for so

CONTINUED ON PAGE 19

Cardinals strike perfect balance

BY DERRICK GOOLD

ST. LOUIS—Back in December 2007, third baseman David Freese had just finished a second season in the Padres system, where he was blocked from above by two prospects at the same position.

In the middle of his meal at a Los Angeles-area Burger King, Freese's cell phone rang. It was an unfamiliar number from a familiar area code, 314, his hometown of St. Louis.

The call changed Freese's career, and it continued the change in John Mozeliak's, too.

Hired as Cardinals general manager less than a month earlier, Mozeliak dialed Freese to welcome him to the organization. His first trade was a memorable one. He dealt team icon Jim Edmonds, in the autumn of his career, to San Diego for Freese, a St. Louis native.

Freese filled a need Mozeliak saw in a future roster, and he also fit a philosophy Mozeliak sought to strengthen.

The dividend of that direction came less than four years later with the 2011 World Series championship. The franchise's 11th title punctuated one of the most unlikely comebacks in history and earned the Cardinals Baseball America Organization of the Year honors.

The season featured league titles for two affiliates, low Class A Quad Cities and Rookie-level Johnson City. A system picked bare by trades and poor drafts earlier in the decade now boasts two of the top pitching prospects in the game: power righthanders Shelby Miller and Carlos Martinez. When the final out of World Series Game Seven settled into left

MIKE JANES

John Mozeliak balanced the Cardinals' roster with stars and supporting players

fielder Allen Craig's glove, he was one of seven homegrown players on the field.

Meanwhile, the return on Mozeliak's first trade proved a whopper. Freese won MVP honors for the World Series.

"When you look at your roster evolution, the way we've put our club together was with star talent and the right complementary players," Mozeliak said.

The Cardinals woke up 10 games out of a playoff spot on Aug. 25, but they renovated their roster through trades and redefined their season. The gutsiest was an eight-player deal with the Blue Jays that cost the Cardinals' Colby Rasmus, long the torchbearer for the new-look system, and brought back Edwin Jackson, Octavio Dotel and Marc Rzepczynski.

Promoted to GM during a caustic period, Mozeliak first unified the front office, and then reorganized it. Jeff Luhnow stopped overseeing both the draft and the system as John Vuch took over as farm director.

Mozeliak's blended roster galvanized in 2011 as first-time regulars like Jon Jay and Craig merged with all-stars Albert Pujols and Lance Berkman to catapult the Cardinals.

PREVIOUS 10 WINNERS	
2001	Houston Astros
2002	Minnesota Twins
2003	Florida Marlins
2004	Minnesota Twins
2005	Atlanta Braves
2006	Los Angeles Dodgers
2007	Colorado Rockies
2008	Tampa Bay Rays
2009	Philadelphia Phillies
2010	San Francisco Giants

Full list: BaseballAmerica.com/awards

CONTINUED FROM PAGE 17

many years and be able to accomplish this record."

After some prodding by teammates Jorge Posada and Alex Rodriguez, Rivera returned to the mound after completing post-game handshakes and hugs. He soaked in the moment with a well-deserved, prolonged ovation from the Yankee Stadium faithful. "I can't describe that feeling because it was priceless," said Rivera, who leads all active pitchers with 1,042 appearances, a 2.21 ERA and a .210 opponent average (min. 1,000 innings).

Hoffman was quick to pay tribute in a prepared statement: "I want to congratulate Mariano Rivera on setting the all-time saves record. It's a great accomplishment and he's still going strong! I have tremendous respect for Mariano, not just for his on-field accomplishments but also for his service to the community."

Moving on to single-season landmarks, White Sox DH Adam Dunn endured a miserable first season in Chicago after signing as four-year, $56 million free agent deal.

After hitting no fewer than 38 home runs in any of the seven previous seasons, Dunn went deep just 11 times in 2011. Worse, he hit an almost inconceivable .159/.292/.277 in 122 games. He fell six plate appearances short of qualifying for the batting title, but considering all position players in history with as many as his 496 PAs, Dunn's .159 average was 20 points lower than any of the other 11,068 members of the sample. Rob Deer held the previous record for hitting .179 over 539 PAs in 1991.

Hall Honors Blyleven, Alomar, Gillick

Though he had to sweat out 14 Hall of Fame elections before gaining entrance, righthander Bert Blyleven earned his plaque in Cooperstown on his next-to-last try. He joined second baseman Roberto Alomar and longtime baseball executive Pat Gillick in being inducted into the game's hallowed halls.

Blyleven first appeared on the 1998 ballot, but he initially received only tepid support by the baseball writers, pulling down just 14.1 percent of votes cast in his second year. He went 287-250 in a 22-year career spent with the Twins, Rangers, Pirates, Indians and Angels. On the strength of a double-plus curveball, Blyleven ranks fifth on the all-time list with 3,701 strikeouts (though he ranked behind only Nolan Ryan and Steve Carlton when he retired) and ninth with 60 shutouts. He helped pitch two teams, the 1979 Pirates and '87 Twins, to World Series championships.

Of the 44 pitchers to debut in 1961 or later—during the game's expansion era—and compile

Derek Jeter homered off David Price for career hit No. 3,000, part of a 5-for-5 day

TOMASSO DeROSA

3,000 innings, Blyleven's 287 wins rank 12th and his 3.31 ERA ranks 14th. However, opponents knocked his candidacy because he fell short of the magical 300-win milestone and because he had few signature seasons on his résumé. He won 20 games in a season only once, he finished as high as third in Cy Young award balloting twice, he made just two all-star teams and he rarely led his league in any category—just strikeouts once, innings twice and shutouts thrice.

But Blyleven finally earned the nod, after years of supporters championing his cause, and it meant no less to him that he had to wait for so long.

"It's been 14 years of praying and waiting," he said. "I'd like to thank the baseball writers of America for, I'd like to say, finally getting it right."

It seemed fitting that Alomar and Gillick entered the Hall of Fame in the same class because of their connection to the glory days of the Blue Jays in the early 1990s, and to a lesser extent the Orioles of the late '90s. Acting as general manager, Gillick engineered the 1990 trade that brought Alomar and Joe Carter from the Padres to Toronto in exchange for Tony Fernandez and Fred McGriff. The move paved the way for consecutive Blue Jays World Series titles in 1992 and '93.

Gillick moved on to Baltimore in '96 and promptly signed Alomar to play second base

CONTINUED ON PAGE 21

MAJOR LEAGUE *ALL-STARS*

ROB CUNI

Jose Bautista went deep 43 times to win his second straight AL home run crown

LARRY GOREN

Clayton Kershaw topped the NL in ERA (2.28), strikeouts (248) and WHIP (0.98)

FIRST TEAM

Pos.	Player, Team	AVG	OBP	SLG	AB	R	H	2B	3B	HR	RBI	BB	SO	SB	CS
C	*Alex Avila, Tigers	.295	.389	.506	464	63	137	33	4	19	82	73	131	3	1
1B	Miguel Cabrera, Tigers	.344	.448	.586	572	111	197	48	0	30	105	108	89	2	1
2B	Dustin Pedroia, Red Sox	.307	.387	.474	635	102	195	37	3	21	91	86	85	26	8
3B	Evan Longoria, Rays	.244	.355	.495	483	78	118	26	1	31	99	80	93	3	2
SS	#Jose Reyes, Mets	.337	.384	.493	537	101	181	31	16	7	44	43	41	39	7
CF	Matt Kemp, Dodgers	.324	.399	.586	602	115	195	33	4	39	126	74	159	40	11
OF	Jose Bautista, Blue Jays	.302	.447	.608	513	105	155	24	2	43	103	132	111	9	5
OF	Ryan Braun, Brewers	.332	.397	.597	563	109	187	38	6	33	111	58	93	33	6
DH	*Prince Fielder, Brewers	.299	.415	.566	569	95	170	36	1	38	120	107	106	1	1

Pos.	Pitcher, Team	W	L	ERA	G	GS	CG	SV	IP	H	R	ER	BB	SO	WHIP
SP	Roy Halladay, Phillies	19	6	2.35	32	32	8	0	234	208	65	61	35	220	1.04
SP	*Clayton Kershaw, Dodgers	21	5	2.28	33	33	5	0	233	174	66	59	54	248	0.98
SP	*C.C. Sabathia, Yankees	19	8	3.00	33	33	3	0	237	230	87	79	61	230	1.23
SP	Justin Verlander, Tigers	24	5	2.40	34	34	4	0	251	174	73	67	57	250	0.92
RP	Mariano Rivera, Yankees	1	2	1.91	64	0	0	44	61	47	13	13	8	60	0.90

SECOND TEAM

Pos.	Player, Team	AVG	OBP	SLG	AB	R	H	2B	3B	HR	RBI	BB	SO	SB	CS
C	Yadier Molina, Cardinals	.305	.349	.465	475	55	145	32	1	14	65	33	44	4	5
1B	*Adrian Gonzalez, Red Sox	.338	.410	.548	630	108	213	45	3	27	117	74	119	1	0
2B	*Robinson Cano, Yankees	.302	.349	.533	623	104	188	46	7	28	118	38	96	8	2
3B	Adrian Beltre, Rangers	.296	.331	.561	487	82	144	33	0	32	105	25	53	1	1
SS	Troy Tulowitzki, Rockies	.302	.372	.544	537	81	162	36	2	30	105	59	79	9	3
CF	*Jacoby Ellsbury, Red Sox	.321	.376	.552	660	119	212	46	5	32	105	52	98	39	15
OF	*Curtis Granderson, Yankees	.262	.364	.552	583	136	153	26	10	41	119	85	169	25	10
OF	Justin Upton, Diamondbacks	.289	.369	.529	592	105	171	39	5	31	88	59	126	21	9
DH	#Lance Berkman, Cardinals	.301	.412	.547	488	90	147	23	2	31	94	92	93	2	6

Pos.	Pitcher, Team	W	L	ERA	G	GS	CG	SV	IP	H	R	ER	BB	SO	WHIP
SP	Josh Beckett, Red Sox	13	7	2.89	30	30	1	0	193	146	65	62	52	175	1.03
SP	*Cliff Lee, Phillies	17	8	2.40	32	32	6	0	233	197	66	62	42	238	1.03
SP	James Shields, Rays	16	12	2.82	33	33	11	0	249	195	83	78	65	225	1.04
SP	Jered Weaver, Angels	18	8	2.41	33	33	4	0	236	182	65	63	56	198	1.01
RP	John Axford, Brewers	2	2	1.95	74	0	0	46	74	59	19	16	25	86	1.14

*Bats/throws lefthanded. #Switch-hitter.

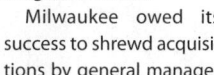

EXECUTIVE OF THE YEAR

Doug Melvin

The Brewers fell just short of the World Series in 2011, but still they won both their first division title and playoff series in 14 years as a National League franchise.

Milwaukee owed its success to shrewd acquisitions by general manager Doug Melvin, who swung offseason trades for Zack Greinke (16-6, 3.83) and Shaun Marcum (13-7, 3.54) that cost the organization top prospects such as Brett Lawrie and Jake Odorizzi.

Melvin also swung a spring-training deal for center fielder Nyjer Morgan and made in-season trades for set-up reliever Francisco Rodriguez and utilityman Jerry Hairston Jr.

PREVIOUS 10 WINNERS

2001: Pat Gillick, Mariners	**2006:** Dave Dombrowski, Tigers
2002: Billy Beane, Athletics	**2007:** Jack Zduriencik, Brewers
2003: Brian Sabean, Giants	**2008:** Theo Epstein, Red Sox
2004: Terry Ryan, Twins	**2009:** Dan O'Dowd, Rockies
2005: Mark Shapiro, Indians	**2010:** Jon Daniels, Rangers

Full list: BaseballAmerica.com/awards

MANAGER OF THE YEAR

Joe Maddon

CLIFF WELCH

The 2011 Rays carried on without Carl Crawford, Matt Garza, Rafael Soriano, Jason Bartlett, Carlos Pena and Joaquin Benoit—all key members of the previous year's American League East division winners. Undaunted, Tampa Bay won 91 games and the AL wild card.

The one constant between the two teams: manager Joe Maddon, who in six years at the helm has taken the low-payroll Rays to the playoffs three times. Though stars such as Evan Longoria and David Price remained, the Rays completely made over their bullpen in 2011 while turning elsewhere to rookies and castoffs.

PREVIOUS 10 WINNERS

2001: Lou Piniella, Mariners	**2006:** Jim Leyland, Tigers
2002: Mike Scioscia, Angels	**2007:** Terry Francona, Red Sox
2003: Jack McKeon, Marlins	**2008:** Ron Gardenhire, Twins
2004: Bobby Cox, Braves	**2009:** Mike Scioscia, Angels
2005: Ozzie Guillen, White Sox	**2010:** Bobby Cox, Braves

Full list: BaseballAmerica.com/awards

CONTINUED FROM PAGE 19

for the Orioles, a club that advanced to the AL Championship Series in both 1996 and '97. Neither the Blue Jays nor Orioles have returned to playoffs since Gillick and Alomar left.

After leaving the Orioles, Gillick also helped build winners in Seattle and Philadelphia. The Mariners advanced to the ALCS in 2000 and '01, winning a single-season record 116 games in the latter season. The Phillies won NL pennants in 2008 and '09, claiming the franchise's second-ever World Series championship in the first year.

Elected in his second year on the ballot, Alomar became the first player to enter the Hall representing the Blue Jays, though he also suited up for the Padres, Orioles, Indians and, as his career wound down, the Mets, White Sox and Diamondbacks. Alomar batted .300/.371/.443 and compiled 2,724 hits, 210 home runs and 474 stolen bases in a 17-year career. He claimed 10 Gold Gloves at second base, a record for the position.

"In the last 25 years, I haven't seen anybody do anything at second base like Robbie Alomar did," Gillick said. "He was a spectacular offensive and defensive player, and I don't think we would have gone to the World Series in '92 without him."

Longtime Philadelphia baseball writer Bill Conlin received the J.G. Taylor Spink Award for distinguished service, while Marlins broadcaster Dave Van Horne was honored with the Ford C. Frick Award for excellence in his field. Famed executive Roland Hemond received the Buck O'Neill lifetime achievement award for his efforts in enhancing the game's impact on society.

Trade Deadline Maneuvering

Pennant races usually begin heating up well after the all-star break, but the Brewers decided not to wait until the July 31 trade deadline to make a move. On the evening of the All-Star Game in Phoenix, July 12, Milwaukee GM Doug Melvin traded for Mets closer Francisco Rodriguez.

The Brewers already had successful closer John Axford in place, but Melvin figured the more the merrier, so K-Rod took over as set-up man. Not surprisingly, the Brewers would not lose a game they led after seven innings for the remainder of the season.

As the deadline approached, the expected flurry of trades materialized. Seeking to boost its failing offense, San Francisco acquired Mets outfielder Carlos Beltran, making the upgrade at the steep cost of top pitching prospect Zack Wheeler. Beltran put up a .920 OPS in 44 games, but the Giants still finished dead last in the league in runs scored and ultimately finished eight games behind the Diamondbacks in the NL West.

The Braves made a move that did work—at least for a while—when they traded four young players to the Astros for speedy center fielder Michael Bourn. The deal did not prevent the Braves from enduring one of the largest late-season collapses in history, however, and Bourn's 42-point drop in on-base percentage following the trade—from .363 down to .321—did little to aid Atlanta's flagging offense.

The Cardinals, refusing to give up on their playoff hopes made over their pitching staff in a three-team deal with the Blue Jays and White Sox. St. Louis received starter Edwin Jackson (5-2, 3.58 in 12 starts after the trade) from Chicago and relievers Octavio Dotel and Marc Rzepczynski from Toronto, while sending Colby Rasmus to the Blue Jays. The 25-year-old Rasmus, a first-round pick in 2005, once was considered the Cardinals' center fielder of the future, but he batted a career-worst .225/.298/.391 in 129 games in 2011.

The Cardinals weren't done dealing. They later traded for veteran Dodgers shortstop Rafael Furcal, who even in a down year provided a superior offensive and defensive alternative to Ryan Theriot.

The Indians went just 12-18 in the 30 games leading up to the trade deadline, but still they refused to cede the AL Central to the Tigers. In a surprising move, Cleveland acquired Rockies ace Ubaldo Jimenez in a deal that cost them their top two pitching prospects, Alex White and Drew Pomeranz, first-round picks in 2009 and 2010.

Jimenez made 11 starts for the Indians but went just 4-4, 5.10, and Detroit ultimately took the Central by 15 games, owing a good deal of its success to the acquisition of Doug Fister from the Mariners. Fister went 8-1, 1.79 in 10 starts for the Tigers and added two effective starts in three tries during Detroit's playoff run.

Even the powerful Phillies felt the need to add a bat to their veteran lineup. Philadelphia acquired right fielder Hunter Pence from the Astros, parting with a four-prospect package that included first baseman Jonathan Singleton, righthander Jarred

ANDREW WOOLLEY

Trade acquisition Hunter Pence balanced the Phillies' lineup and hit .324/.394/.560

Cosart and toolsy right fielder Domingo Santana. Pence helped balance the Phillies' lefty-heavy lineup and batted .324/.394/.560 with 11 homers in 54 games following the trade.

The defending AL champion Rangers completed two July trades for righthanded relievers, first acquiring Koji Uehara from the Orioles and then Mike Adams from the Padres. The duo pitched well for Texas in August and September, but neither pitched all that effectively in the postseason. Uehara allowed five runs (and three home runs) in 1⅓ innings and did not make the World Series roster, while Adams allowed 17 baserunners (two homers) in 8⅓ innings.

Even the Pirates, with a record 18 consecutive losing seasons on their ledger, traded for veteran talent after they found themselves in the NL Central race after the break. The Bucs brought in first baseman Derrek Lee from the Orioles and outfielder Ryan Ludwick from the Padres, but to no avail. Pittsburgh finished 72-90 and wrapped up its 19th straight losing season, despite the fact that Lee batted .337/.398/.584 with seven homers in 28 games.

The Pirates seemed to fall apart after a devastating 19-inning loss to the Braves in Atlanta on July 26. In that game, home-plate umpire Jerry Meals controversially called Julio Lugo safe in a play at the

CONTINUED ON PAGE 24

NL doubles its ASG pleasure

ALL-STAR GAME

Prince Fielder's three-run homer in the fourth propelled the NL to victory

PHOENIX From the first moment he stepped on to the diamond at Chase Field, Diamondbacks fans booed Prince Fielder.

The home fans were angry at Brewers first baseman Prince Fielder because he didn't pick Diamondbacks right fielder Justin Upton, the local favorite, to participate in the home run derby. As captain of the National League contingent, Fielder chose the Dodgers' Matt Kemp, the Cardinals' Matt Holliday and Brewers teammate Rickie Weeks.

Before all was said and done, however, Fielder turned those boos to cheers. His three-run home run off Rangers lefty C.J. Wilson in the fourth inning propelled the NL to a 5-1 victory against the American League.

The win gave the NL its second consecutive All-Star Game triumph after going 13 years with nary a victory. The Brewers very nearly capitalized on the World Series home-field advantage that Fielder won for the NL. Milwaukee came within two wins of advancing to the Series.

Fielder became the first Brewer to be named MVP of the game, and he forgave the booing Arizona fans.

"That's cool," he said. "I get it. Justin Upton is their guy. I didn't take it personal at all."

The 2011 game was notable almost more for those who weren't there. Because they started on the Sunday before the game, the Tigers' Justin Verlander, the Mariners' Felix Hernandez, the Angels' Dan Haren and the Yankees' C.C. Sabathia were unavailable for the AL.

Yankees shortstop Derek Jeter opted not to come, citing aches and pains and general weariness from his push to 3,000 hits. Teammate Alex Rodriguez had an ailing hip and also pulled out of the game.

The original list of 68 players selected to the All-Star Game grew to a whopping 84, an all-time record, as players backed out of the exhibition.

The Yankees' Robinson Cano won the home run derby while his father Jose, who received a cup of coffee with the 1989 Astros, served as his personal pitcher for the event.

JULY 12, 2011

National League 5, American League 1

AMERICAN	AB	R	H	BI	NATIONAL	AB	R	H	BI
Granderson, cf	2	0	0	0	Weeks, 2b	3	1	0	0
Ellsbury, cf	2	0	0	0	Phillips, B, 2b	1	0	0	0
Cabrera, A, ss	2	0	0	0	Beltran, dh	2	1	1	0
Peralta, Jh, ss	2	0	0	0	a-Ethier, ph-dh	1	0	1	1
Gonzalez, Ad, 1b	2	1	1	1	b-Sanchez, G, ph-dh	1	0	0	0
Cabrera, Mi, 1b	0	0	0	0	Kemp, cf	2	1	1	0
Young, M, 3b	1	0	0	0	McCutchen, A, cf	1	0	0	0
Bautista, rf	2	0	1	0	Fielder, 1b	2	1	1	3
Quentin, rf	2	0	0	0	Votto, 1b	2	0	0	0
Hamilton, lf	2	0	1	0	McCann, c	2	0	0	0
Joyce, lf	2	0	1	0	Molina, Y, c	1	0	1	0
Beltre, A, 3b	2	0	1	0	c-Bruce, ph-rf	1	0	0	0
Youkilis, 3b	1	0	1	0	Berkman, rf	1	0	1	0
Cuddyer, 1b	1	0	0	0	Upton, J, rf	2	0	0	0
Ortiz, dh	2	0	0	0	Montero, c	0	0	0	0
a-Konerko, ph	1	0	0	0	Holliday, lf	1	0	0	0
Cano, 2b	2	0	0	0	Pence, lf	2	1	1	0
Kendrick, H, 2b	1	0	0	0	Tulowitzki, ss	2	0	1	0
Avila, c	2	0	0	0	1-Castro, S, pr-ss	1	0	0	0
Wieters, c	1	0	0	0	Rolen, 3b	2	0	0	0
					Sandoval, P, 3b	1	0	1	1
TOTAL	**33**	**1**	**6**	**1**		**31**	**5**	**9**	**5**

American	000	100	000—1
National	000	310	10x—5

LOB—American 6, National 3. **2B**—Molina (1), Sandoval (1). **HR**—Gonzalez (1), Fielder (1). **SB**—Weeks, Castro 2. **PB**—Wieters. **E**—Castro, Bruce. **A**—Bautista, Pence.

AMERICAN	IP	H	R	ER	BB	SO	NATIONAL	IP	H	R	ER	BB	SO
Weaver	1	0	0	0	1	1	Halladay	2	0	0	0	0	1
Robertson	1	1	0	0	0	1	Lee, Cl	1.2	3	1	1	0	0
Pineda	1	0	0	0	0	2	Clippard (W)	0.1	1	0	0	0	0
Wilson, C (L)	1	3	3	3	0	1	Kershaw	1	0	0	0	0	1
Walden	1	2	1	1	0	1	Jurrjens	1.2	1	0	0	0	1
Perez, C	1	1	0	0	0	1	Kimbrel	0.1	0	0	0	1	0
League	1	2	1	1	0	1	Venters	0.2	0	0	0	0	1
Ogando	0.2	0	0	0	0	0	Bell, H	0.1	0	0	0	0	0
Gonzalez, G	0.1	0	0	0	0	1	Hanrahan	0.1	1	0	0	0	1
							Wilson, Br (S)	0.2	0	0	0	0	0

Umpires: HP: Dale Scott. **1B:** Jerry Layne. **2B:** Hunter Wendelstedt. **3B:** Dan Iassogna. **LF:** Ed Hickox. **RF:** Chris Guccione.
T—2:50. **A**—47,994.

CONTINUED FROM PAGE 22

plate that settled matters in favor of the Braves. The throw home clearly arrived before Lugo, and Pirates catcher Mike McKenry appeared to apply the tag in time—and even Lugo's body language suggested that he thought he was out—but Meals motioned safe and the Braves won the six-hour affair.

Pittsburgh lost to Atlanta in extra innings the next night, too, and proceeded to drop 11 of 12 games after the disputed call. The Pirates went 19-43 from July 26 to the end of the season, after beginning the year at 53-47.

Cubs Go In Different Direction

Another disappointing season for the Cubs hit rock bottom on Aug. 12 when mercurial right-hander Carlos Zambrano packed his things and left the team after a tempestuous loss in Atlanta. He surrendered five home runs over 4⅓ innings and was ejected for throwing at Chipper Jones.

Zambrano was only one of many underachieving Chicago players, and longtime GM Jim Hendry finally paid with his job for those failures. On Aug. 19, the Cubs announced that Hendry had been dismissed, a decision he had been informed of weeks before but agreed to postpone until the club's draft picks were signed.

Cubs third baseman Aramis Ramirez, who batted .342/.436/.496 in 33 games following Hendry's dismissal, said the players were at fault, not the GM. "We didn't play the way we should have played," said Ramirez, who invoked his no-trade rights in July to stay with Chicago. "The bottom line is the players have to get it done between the lines, and we didn't do that."

No one could accuse Ricketts of thinking small in finding a replacement for Hendry. Shortly after the regular season ended, the Cubs hired away GM Theo Epstein from the Red Sox. Epstein helped end an 86-year World Series drought in Boston, and he faces a similar challenge in Chicago, where the Cubs haven't won a pennant since 1945 or a World Series since 1908.

Down The Stretch They Come

Dodgers center fielder Matt Kemp hit 39 homers and drove in 126 runs to win two legs of the NL triple crown, but he had to settle for third place with a .324 average. He won BA Major League Player of the Year honors in an otherwise forgettable season in Chavez Ravine.

Beginning on July 26, the Brewers won 27 of 32 games to take control of the NL Central. Milwaukee claimed its first division crown since

ACTIVE LEADERS

Career leaders among players who played in a game in 2011. Batters require 3,000 plate appearances and pitchers 1,000 innings to qualify for percentage titles.

BATTERS			PITCHERS		
AVG	Albert Pujols	.328	ERA	Mariano Rivera	2.21
OBP	Todd Helton	.421	SO/9	Kerry Wood	10.34
SLG	Albert Pujols	.617	BB/9	Roy Halladay	1.85
OPS	Albert Pujols	1.037	HR/9	Mariano Rivera	0.48
R	Alex Rodriguez	1,824	W	Tim Wakefield	200
H	Derek Jeter	3,088	L	Tim Wakefield	180
2B	Ivan Rodriguez	572	SV	Mariano Rivera	603
3B	Carl Crawford	112	IP	Tim Wakefield	3,226.1
HR	Alex Rodriguez	629	SO	Javier Vazquez	2,536
RBI	Alex Rodriguez	1,893	BB	Tim Wakefield	1,205
BB	Jim Thome	1,725	AVG	Mariano Rivera	.210
SO	Jim Thome	2,487	G	Mariano Rivera	1,042
XBH	Alex Rodriguez	1,153	GS	Livan Hernandez	474
SB	Juan Pierre	554	HR	Tim Wakefield	418

1982, when they won the AL East title on the final day of the season.

The Phillies and their "Fearsome Foursome" rotation featuring Roy Halladay, Cliff Lee, Cole Hamels and Roy Oswalt seized control of the NL East as expected and didn't let go. Despite an eight-game losing streak after clinching the NL East, Philadelphia went on to win 102 games, tops in the majors.

The Diamondbacks proved to be the surprise team in the NL by pulling off an improbable worst-to-first charge under fiery skipper Kirk Gibson. Arizona lost 97 times in 2010 but reversed course to win 94 games in 2011, and they held off the defending-champion Giants by eight games.

The Tigers caught fire in September, winning 20 of their final 25 games, and pulled away from the Indians and White Sox in what had been a tense three-team battle in the AL Central for much of the season.

The Angels challenged the Rangers in the AL West for much of the season, but they lost six of their last seven games to end their long-shot pursuit with a whimper. Texas won the West by 10 games after sweeping three games from Los Angeles at home in Arlington.

The Yankees again rose to the top of the AL East, winning 97 games and fending off a season-long challenge by the Red Sox.

But it was those truly wild wild-card races that captured the imagination of baseball fans across the country in the final weeks of the season. Boston and Atlanta appeared to be in total control as the season moved past Labor Day, but once those clubs opened the door, the Rays and Cardinals rushed in to join the playoff party.

ARIZONA DIAMONDBACKS

Joe Paterson	April 2
Josh Collmenter	April 17
Bryan Shaw	June 10
Ryan Cook	July 20
Collin Cowgill	July 26
Paul Goldschmidt	Aug. 1
Wade Miley	Aug. 20
Jarrod Parker	Sept. 27

ATLANTA BRAVES

Matt Young	April 3
Cory Gearrin	April 25
Julio Teheran	May 7
Randall Delgado	June 17
Jose Constanza	July 29
Arodys Vizcaino	Aug. 10
Antoan Richardson	Sept. 4

BALTIMORE ORIOLES

Zach Britton	April 3
Ryan Adams	May 20
Blake Davis	June 22
Matt Angle	July 17
Zach Phillips	Aug. 31
Kyle Hudson	Sept. 4
Pedro Florimon	Sept. 10

BOSTON RED SOX

Jose Iglesias	May 8
Tommy Hottovy	June 3
Kyle Weiland	July 10
Ryan Lavarnway	Aug. 18
Nate Spears	Sept. 6

CHICAGO CUBS

Tony Campana	May 17
D.J. LeMahieu	May 30
Chris Carpenter	June 14
John Gaub	Sept. 12
Steve Clevenger	Sept. 26
Rafael Dolis	Sept. 26

CHICAGO WHITE SOX

Hector Santiago	July 6
Eduardo Escobar	Sept. 2
Shane Lindsay	Sept. 2
Addison Reed	Sept. 4
Dylan Axelrod	Sept. 7

CINCINNATI REDS

Todd Frazier	May 23
Jeremy Horst	May 28
Zack Cozart	July 7
Dave Sappelt	Aug. 7
Devin Mesoraco	Sept. 3

CLEVELAND INDIANS

Alex White	April 30
Ezequiel Carrera	May 20
Josh Judy	May 22
Cord Phelps	June 8
Lonnie Chisenhall	June 27
Zach McAllister	July 7
Jason Kipnis	July 22
Jerad Head	Aug. 28
Nick Hagadone	Sept. 1
Corey Kluber	Sept. 1
Zach Putnam	Sept. 13

COLORADO ROCKIES

Alan Johnson	April 17
Bruce Billings	May 27
Juan Nicasio	May 28
Rex Brothers	June 6
Charlie Blackmon	June 7
Cole Garner	July 4
Jordan Pacheco	Sept. 6
Wilin Rosario	Sept. 6
Tommy Field	Sept. 11
Drew Pomeranz	Sept. 11
Hector Gomez	Sept. 16

DETROIT TIGERS

Brayan Villarreal	April 2
Al Alburquerque	April 15
Andy Dirks	May 16
Charlie Furbush	May 23
Adam Wilk	May 26
Lester Oliveros	July 1
Duane Below	July 20
Chance Ruffin	July 25
Jacob Turner	July 30
Luis Marte	Sept. 1

FLORIDA MARLINS

Brad Hand	June 7
Elih Villanueva	June 15
Matt Dominguez	Sept. 6

HOUSTON ASTROS

Aneury Rodriguez	April 2
Jose Valdez	April 17
Jordan Lyles	May 31
David Carpenter	June 30
Jose Altuve	July 20
J.D. Martinez	July 30
Jimmy Paredes	Aug. 1
J.B. Shuck	Aug. 5
Henry Sosa	Aug. 10
Juan Abreu	Aug. 29
Xavier Cedeno	Sept. 16

KANSAS CITY ROYALS

Nathan Adcock	March 31
Tim Collins	March 31
Aaron Crow	March 31
Louis Coleman	April 21
Eric Hosmer	May 6
Everett Teaford	May 17
Danny Duffy	May 18
Mike Moustakas	June 10
Manny Pina	Aug. 3
Johnny Giavotella	Aug. 5
Salvador Perez	Aug. 10
Kelvin Herrera	Sept. 21

LOS ANGELES ANGELS

Tyler Chatwood	April 11
Alexi Amarista	April 26
Mike Trout	July 8
Garrett Richards	Aug. 10
Jeremy Moore	Sept. 2
Efren Navarro	Sept. 2

LOS ANGELES DODGERS

Ivan De Jesus Jr.	April 1
Jerry Sands	April 18
Javy Guerra	May 15
Rubby de la Rosa	May 24
Josh Lindblom	June 1
Dee Gordon	June 6
Nate Eovaldi	Aug. 6
Justin Sellers	Aug. 12
Tim Federowicz	Sept. 11

MILWAUKEE BREWERS

Eric Farris	July 28
Taylor Green	Aug. 31
Logan Schafer	Sept. 2
Martin Maldonado	Sept. 3
Mike Fiers	Sept. 14

MINNESOTA TWINS

Tsuyoshi Nishioka	April 1
Rene Tosoni	April 28
Brian Dinkelman	June 4
Scott Diamond	July 18
Kyle Waldrop	Sept. 5
Joe Benson	Sept. 6
Liam Hendriks	Sept. 6
Chris Parmelee	Sept. 6

NEW YORK METS

Pedro Beato	April 1
Brad Emaus	April 1
Josh Stinson	Sept. 2
Josh Satin	Sept. 4
Chris Schwinden	Sept. 8

NEW YORK YANKEES

Lance Pendleton	April 15
Amauri Sanit	May 12
Hector Noesi	May 18
Kevin Whelan	June 10
Brandon Laird	July 22
Steve Garrison	July 25
Jesus Montero	Sept. 1
George Kontos	Sept. 10
Austin Romine	Sept. 11
Dellin Betances	Sept. 22
Andrew Brackman	Sept. 22

OAKLAND ATHLETICS

Trystan Magnuson	May 17
Fautino de los Santos	June 4
Jemile Weeks	June 7
Graham Godfrey	June 10
Anthony Recker	Aug. 25
Neil Wagner	Aug. 30
Andrew Carignan	Sept. 2
Michael Taylor	Sept. 2

PHILADELPHIA PHILLIES

Michael Martinez	April 3
Mike Stutes	April 25
Michael Schwimer	Aug. 21
Justin De Fratus	Sept. 18
Joe Savery	Sept. 20

PITTSBURGH PIRATES

Mike Crotta	April 3
Josh Rodriguez	April 5
Daniel Moskos	April 30
Josh Harrison	May 31
Tony Watson	June 8
Chase d'Arnaud	June 24
Eric Fryer	June 26
Aaron Thompson	Aug. 24
Jared Hughes	Sept. 7
Jeff Locke	Sept. 10

SAN DIEGO PADRES

Cedric Hunter	March 31
Evan Scribner	April 26
Logan Forsythe	May 4
Blake Tekotte	May 25
Anthony Rizzo	June 9
Anthony Bass	June 13
Josh Spence	June 24
Luis Martinez	July 15
Erik Hamren	Aug. 1
James Darnell	Aug. 9
Andy Parrino	Aug. 26
Brad Brach	Aug. 31

SAN FRANCISCO GIANTS

Brandon Belt	March 31
Brandon Crawford	May 27
Hector Sanchez	July 15
Steve Edlefsen	Aug. 21
Eric Surkamp	Aug. 27

[SEATTLE MARINERS column]

Brett Pill	Sept. 6

SEATTLE MARINERS

Josh Lueke	April 3
Tom Wilhelmsen	April 3
Michael Pineda	April 5
Carlos Peguero	April 19
Mike Wilson	May 10
Dustin Ackley	June 17
Blake Beavan	July 3
Kyle Seager	July 7
Trayvon Robinson	Aug. 5
Anthony Vasquez	Aug. 23
Alex Liddi	Sept. 7
Steve Delabar	Sept. 11

ST. LOUIS CARDINALS

Eduardo Sanchez	April 13
Pete Kozma	May 18
Tony Cruz	May 24
Maikel Cleto	June 2
Lance Lynn	June 2
Matt Carpenter	June 4
Andrew Brown	June 12
Brandon Dickson	July 2
Adron Chambers	Sept. 6

TAMPA BAY RAYS

Alex Cobb	May 1
Brandon Gomes	May 3
Brandon Guyer	May 6
Robinson Chirinos	July 18
Alexander Torres	July 18
Dane de la Rosa	July 20
Matt Moore	Sept. 14
Russ Canzler	Sept. 15

TEXAS RANGERS

Mason Tobin	April 2
Cody Eppley	April 23
Yoshinori Tateyama	May 24
Mark Hamburger	Aug. 31
Leonys Martin	Sept. 2

TORONTO BLUE JAYS

Luis Perez	April 16
David Cooper	April 29
Eric Thames	May 18
Zach Stewart	June 16
Brett Lawrie	Aug. 5
Henderson Alvarez	Aug. 10
Joel Carreno	Aug. 23
Darin Mastroianni	Aug. 24
Chad Beck	Sept. 13
Danny Farquhar	Sept. 13

WASHINGTON NATIONALS

Brian Broderick	April 3
Cole Kimball	May 14
Ryan Mattheus	June 14
Chris Marrero	Aug. 27
Tom Milone	Sept. 3
Corey Brown	Sept. 6
Steve Lombardozzi	Sept. 6
Brad Peacock	Sept. 6
Atahualpa Severino	Sept. 6

Eric Hosmer and Mike Moustakas

BILL MITCHELL

CLUB BATTING

	AVG	G	AB	R	H	2B	3B	HR	RBI	BB	SO	SB	CS	OBP	SLG
Texas	.283	162	5659	855	1599	310	32	210	807	475	930	143	45	.340	.460
Boston	.280	162	5710	875	1600	352	35	203	842	578	1108	102	42	.349	.461
Detroit	.277	162	5563	787	1540	297	34	169	750	521	1143	49	20	.340	.434
Kansas City	.275	162	5672	730	1560	325	41	129	705	442	1006	153	58	.329	.415
New York	.263	162	5518	867	1452	267	33	222	836	627	1138	147	46	.343	.444
Baltimore	.257	162	5585	708	1434	273	13	191	684	452	1120	81	25	.316	.413
Los Angeles	.253	162	5513	667	1394	289	34	155	629	442	1086	135	52	.313	.402
Chicago	.252	162	5502	654	1387	252	16	154	625	475	989	81	53	.319	.388
Cleveland	.250	162	5509	704	1380	290	26	154	671	494	1269	89	42	.317	.396
Toronto	.249	162	5559	743	1384	285	34	186	704	525	1184	131	52	.317	.413
Minnesota	.247	162	5487	619	1357	259	25	103	572	440	1048	92	39	.306	.360
Oakland	.244	162	5452	645	1330	280	29	114	612	509	1094	117	43	.311	.369
Tampa Bay	.244	162	5436	707	1324	273	37	172	674	571	1193	155	62	.322	.402
Seattle	.233	162	5421	556	1263	253	22	109	534	435	1280	125	40	.292	.348

CLUB PITCHING

	ERA	G	CG	SHO	SV	IP	H	R	ER	HR	BB	SO	AVG
Los Angeles	3.57	162	12	11	39	1465	1388	633	581	142	476	1058	.251
Tampa Bay	3.58	162	15	13	32	1449	1263	614	577	161	504	1143	.234
Oakland	3.71	162	6	12	39	1448	1380	679	597	136	519	1160	.250
New York	3.73	162	5	8	47	1458	1423	657	605	152	507	1222	.256
Texas	3.79	162	10	19	38	1441	1327	677	607	170	461	1179	.244
Seattle	3.90	162	12	10	39	1433	1369	675	621	145	436	1088	.251
Detroit	4.04	162	4	14	52	1440	1406	711	647	149	492	1115	.257
Chicago	4.10	162	6	14	42	1460	1463	706	665	147	439	1220	.261
Boston	4.20	162	2	13	36	1457	1366	737	680	156	540	1213	.247
Cleveland	4.23	162	2	4	38	1453	1482	760	683	153	463	1024	.263
Toronto	4.32	162	7	10	33	1459	1433	761	700	179	540	1169	.256
Kansas City	4.44	162	2	6	37	1451	1487	762	716	163	557	1080	.267
Minnesota	4.58	162	7	8	32	1422	1564	804	724	161	480	940	.281
Baltimore	4.89	162	3	7	32	1447	1568	860	786	210	535	1044	.277

CLUB FIELDING

	PCT	PO	A	E	DP		PCT	PO	A	E	DP
Tampa Bay	.988	4347	1519	73	138	Baltimore	.982	4340	1655	110	159
Chicago	.987	4380	1667	79	129	Cleveland	.982	4360	1689	110	130
Boston	.985	4372	1526	92	120	Seattle	.982	4299	1623	108	152
Kansas City	.985	4354	1700	95	149	Toronto	.982	4376	1703	110	148
Los Angeles	.985	4395	1723	93	157	Texas	.981	4324	1552	114	164
Detroit	.983	4320	1639	103	148	Minnesota	.980	4265	1621	119	153
New York	.983	4375	1569	102	141	Oakland	.979	4343	1529	124	145

INDIVIDUAL BATTING LEADERS *(MINIMUM 2.7 PA/TEAM GAME)*

	AVG	G	AB	R	H	2B	3B	HR	RBI	BB	SO	SB
Miguel Cabrera, Detroit	.344	161	572	111	197	48	0	30	105	108	89	2
Adrian Gonzalez, Boston	.338	159	630	108	213	45	3	27	117	74	119	1
Michael Young, Texas	.338	159	631	88	213	41	6	11	106	47	78	6
Victor Martinez, Detroit	.330	145	540	76	178	40	0	12	103	46	51	1
Jacoby Ellsbury, Boston	.321	158	660	119	212	46	5	32	105	52	98	39
David Ortiz, Boston	.309	146	525	84	162	40	1	29	96	78	83	1
Dustin Pedroia, Boston	.307	159	635	102	195	37	3	21	91	86	85	26
Casey Kotchman, Tampa Bay	.306	146	500	44	153	24	2	10	48	48	66	2
Melky Cabrera, Kansas City	.305	155	658	102	201	44	5	18	87	35	94	20
Alex Gordon, Kansas City	.303	151	611	101	185	45	4	23	87	67	139	17

INDIVIDUAL PITCHING LEADERS *(MINIMUM 0.8 IP/TEAM GAME)*

	W	L	ERA	G	GS	CG	SHO	SV	IP	H	R	ER	BB	SO
Justin Verlander, Detroit	24	5	2.40	34	34	4	2	0	251	174	73	67	57	250
Jered Weaver, Los Angeles	18	8	2.41	33	33	4	2	0	236	182	65	63	56	198
James Shield, Tampa Bay	16	12	2.82	33	33	11	4	0	249	195	83	78	65	225
Doug Fister, Seattle/Detroit	11	13	2.83	32	31	3	0	0	216	193	76	68	37	146
Josh Beckett, Boston	13	7	2.89	30	30	1	1	0	193	146	65	62	52	175
Ricky Romero, Toronto	15	11	2.92	32	32	4	2	0	225	176	85	73	80	178
C.J. Wilson, Texas	16	7	2.94	34	34	3	1	0	223	191	89	73	74	206
Jeremy Hellickson, Tampa	13	10	2.95	29	29	2	1	0	189	146	64	62	72	117
C.C. Sabathia, New York	19	8	3.00	33	33	3	1	0	237	230	87	79	61	230
Gio Gonzalez, Oakland	16	12	3.12	32	32	0	0	0	202	175	81	70	91	197

AWARD WINNERS

Selected by Baseball Writers Association of America

MOST VALUABLE PLAYER

Player	1st	2nd	3rd	Total
Justin Verlander, Detroit	13	3	3	280
Jacoby Ellsbury, Boston	4	13	4	242
Jose Bautista, Toronto	5	7	4	231
Curtis Granderson, New York	3	4	4	215
Miguel Cabrera, Detroit	2	—	9	193
Robinson Cano, New York	—	—	2	112
Adrian Gonzalez, Boston	—	—	1	105
Michael Young, Texas	1	1	1	96
Dustin Pedroia, Boston	—	—	—	48
Evan Longoria, Tampa Bay	—	—	—	27
Ian Kinsler, Texas	—	—	—	25
Alex Avila, Detroit	—	—	—	13
Paul Konerko, Chicago	—	—	—	11
C.C. Sabathia, New York	—	—	—	10
Adrian Beltre, Texas	—	—	—	9
Ben Zobrist, Tampa Bay	—	—	—	7
Victor Martinez, Detroit	—	—	—	7
James Shields, Tampa Bay	—	—	—	7
Mark Teixeira, New York	—	—	—	5
Asdrubal Cabrera, Cleveland	—	—	—	4
Alex Gordon, Kansas City	—	—	—	3
Josh Hamilton, Texas	—	—	—	1
David Robertson, New York	—	—	—	1

CY YOUNG AWARD

Pitcher	1st	2nd	3rd	Total
Justin Verlander, Detroit	28	—	—	196
Jered Weaver, Los Angeles	—	17	8	97
James Shields, Tampa Bay	—	5	9	66
C.C. Sabathia, New York	—	5	7	63
Jose Valverde, Detroit	—	1	3	28
C.J. Wilson, Texas	—	—	—	9
Dan Haren, Los Angeles	—	—	1	7
Mariano Rivera, New York	—	—	—	4
Josh Beckett, Boston	—	—	—	3
Ricky Romero, Toronto	—	—	—	2
David Robertson, New York	—	—	—	1

ROOKIE OF THE YEAR

Player	1st	2nd	3rd	Total
Jeremy Hellickson, Tampa Bay	17	5	2	102
Mark Trumbo, Los Angeles	5	11	5	63
Eric Hosmer, Kansas City	4	4	6	38
Ivan Nova, New York	1	5	10	30
Michael Pineda, Seattle	—	3	2	11
Dustin Ackley, Seattle	—	1	1	6
Desmond Jennings, Tampa Bay	—	1	1	1
Jordan Walden, Los Angeles	—	1	1	1

MANAGER OF THE YEAR

Player	1st	2nd	3rd	Total
Joe Maddon, Tampa Bay	26	1	—	133
Jim Leyland, Detroit	1	13	10	54
Ron Washington, Texas	1	7	5	31
Manny Acta, Cleveland	—	3	7	16
Joe Girardi, New York	—	3	5	14
Mike Scioscia, Los Angeles	—	1	1	4

GOLD GLOVE WINNERS

Selected by AL managers
C—Matt Wieters, Baltimore. 1B—Adrian Gonzalez, Boston. 2B—Dustin Pedroia, Boston. 3B—Adrian Belte, Texas. SS—Erick Aybar, Los Angeles. LF—Alex Gordon, Kansas City. CF—Jacoby Ellsbury, Boston. RF—Nick Markakis, Baltimore. P—Mark Buehrle, Chicago.

SILVER SLUGGER AWARDS

Selected by AL managers, coaches
C—Alex Avila, Detroit. 1B—Adrian Gonzalez, Boston. 2B—Robinson Cano, New York. 3B—Adrian Belte, Texas. SS—Asdrubal Cabrera, Cleveland. OF—Jose Bautista, Toronto; Jacoby Ellsbury, Boston; Curtis Granderson, New York. DH—David Ortiz, Boston.

DEPARTMENT LEADERS

BATTING

GAMES
Miguel Cabrera, Detroit	161
Ichiro Suzuki, Seattle	161
Nick Markakis, Baltimore	160
6 tied at	159

AT-BATS
Ichiro Suzuki, Seattle	677
Jacoby Ellsbury, Boston	660
Melky Cabrera, Kansas City	658
Nick Markakis, Baltimore	641
Juan Pierre, Chicago	639

PLATE APPEARANCES
Jacoby Ellsbury, Boston	732
Dustin Pedroia, Boston	731
Ian Kinsler, Texas	723
Ichiro Suzuki, Seattle	721
Nick Markakis, Baltimore	716

RUNS
Curtis Granderson, New York	136
Ian Kinsler, Texas	121
Jacoby Ellsbury, Boston	119
Miguel Cabrera, Detroit	111
Adrian Gonzalez, Boston	108

HITS
Adrian Gonzalez, Boston	213
Michael Young, Texas	213
Jacoby Ellsbury, Boston	212
Melky Cabrera, Kansas City	201
Miguel Cabrera, Detroit	197

TOTAL BASES
Jacoby Ellsbury, Boston	364
Adrian Gonzalez, Boston	345
Miguel Cabrera, Detroit	335
Robinson Cano, New York	332
Curtis Granderson, New York	322

DOUBLES
Miguel Cabrera, Detroit	48
Jeff Francoeur, Kansas City	47
Robinson Cano, New York	46
Jacoby Ellsbury, Boston	46
Ben Zobrist, Tampa Bay	46

TRIPLES
Peter Bourjos, Los Angeles	11
Austin Jackson, Detroit	11
Curtis Granderson, New York	10
4 tied at	8

EXTRA-BASE HITS
Jacoby Ellsbury, Boston	83
Robinson Cano, New York	81
Miguel Cabrera, Detroit	78
Curtis Granderson, New York	77
Adrian Gonzalez, Boston	75

HOME RUNS
Jose Bautista, Toronto	43
Curtis Granderson, New York	41
Mark Teixeira, New York	39
Mark Reynolds, Baltimore	37
Adrian Beltre, Texas	32
Jacoby Ellsbury, Boston	32
Ian Kinsler, Texas	32

RUNS BATTED IN
Curtis Granderson, New York	119
Robinson Cano, New York	118
Adrian Gonzalez, Boston	117
Mark Teixeira, New York	111
Michael Young, Texas	106

Jacoby Ellsbury

SACRIFICES
Juan Pierre, Chicago	19
Alcides Escobar, Kansas City	18
Elvis Andrus, Texas	16
3 tied at	14

SACRIFICE FLIES
Adam Jones, Baltimore	12
Paul Konerko, Chicago	11
Jeff Francoeur, Kansas City	10
Josh Hamilton, Texas	10
3 tied at	9

HIT BY PITCH
Carlos Quentin, Chicago	23
Sean Rodriguez, Tampa Bay	18
Kevin Youkilis, Boston	14

Gordon Beckham, Chicago	13
3 tied at	12

WALKS
Jose Bautista, Toronto	132
Miguel Cabrera, Detroit	108
Carlos Santana, Cleveland	97
Nick Swisher, New York	95
Ian Kinsler, Texas	89

STOLEN BASES
Coco Crisp, Oakland	49
Brett Gardner, New York	49
Ichiro Suzuki, Seattle	40
Jacoby Ellsbury, Boston	39
Elvis Andrus, Texas	37

Miguel Cabrera

CAUGHT STEALING
Juan Pierre, Chicago	17
Jacoby Ellsbury, Boston	15
Brett Gardner, New York	13
Elvis Andrus, Texas	12
B.J. Upton, Tampa Bay	12

STOLEN BASE PERCENTAGE
Ian Kinsler, Texas	88.2%
Ichiro Suzuki, Seattle	85.1%
Coco Crisp, Oakland	84.5%
Erick Aybar, Los Angeles	83.3%
Austin Jackson, Detroit	81.5%

STRIKEOUTS
Mark Reynolds, Baltimore	196
Austin Jackson, Detroit	181
Adam Dunn, Chicago	177
Curtis Granderson, New York	169
B.J. Upton, Tampa Bay	161

**TOUGHEST TO STRIKE OUT
(AT-BAT PER STRIKEOUT)**
Juan Pierre, Chicago	15.59
Victor Martinez, Detroit	10.59
Vladimir Guerrero, Balt	10.04
Alberto Callaspo, L.A.	9.90
Ichiro Suzuki, Seattle	9.81

GROUNDED INTO DOUBLE PLAYS
Adrian Gonzalez, Boston	28
Miguel Cabrera, Detroit	24
Torii Hunter, Los Angeles	24
David Ortiz, Boston	24
Vladimir Guerrero, Baltimore	23

MULTI-HIT GAMES
Adrian Gonzalez, Boston	66
Melky Cabrera, Kansas City	61
Miguel Cabrera, Detroit	61
Michael Young, Texas	61
2 tied at	59

ON-BASE PERCENTAGE
Miguel Cabrera, Detroit	.448
Jose Bautista, Toronto	.447
Adrian Gonzalez, Boston	.410
David Ortiz, Boston	.398
Alex Avila, Detroit	.389

SLUGGING
Jose Bautista, Toronto	.608
Miguel Cabrera, Detroit	.586
Adrian Beltre, Texas	.561
David Ortiz, Boston	.554
Curtis Granderson, New York	.552

ON-BASE-PLUS-SLUGGING
Jose Bautista, Toronto	1.056
Miguel Cabrera, Detroit	1.033
Adrian Gonzalez, Boston	.957
David Ortiz, Boston	.953
Jacoby Ellsbury, Boston	.928

AVERAGE (LOWEST)
Vernon Wells, Los Angeles	.218
Mark Reynolds, Baltimore	.221
Miguel Olivo, Seattle	.224
Alex Rios, Chicago	.227
Gordon Beckham, Chicago	.230

PITCHING

WINS
Justin Verlander, Detroit	24
C.C. Sabathia, New York	19
Jered Weaver, Los Angeles	18
6 tied at	16

Justin Verlander

TOM DiPACE

LOSSES
Jeremy Guthrie, Baltimore	17
Jeff Francis, Kansas City	16
Fausto Carmona, Cleveland	15
Trevor Cahill, Oaklad	14
Brian Duensing, Minnesota	14
Felix Hernandez, Seattle	14

GAMES
Jose Valverde, Detroit	75
Joel Peralta, Tampa Bay	71
Rafael Perez, Cleveland	71
Joe Smith, Cleveland	71
Daniel Bard, Boston	70
David Robertson, New York	70

GAMES STARTED
Trevor Cahill, Oakland	34
Dan Haren, Los Angeles	34
David Price, Tampa Bay	34
Justin Verlander, Detroit	34
C.J. Wilson, Texas	34

GAMES FINISHED
Jose Valverde, Detroit	70
Brandon League, Seattle	60
Chris Perez, Cleveland	57
Neftali Feliz, Texas	56
Mariano Rivera, New York	54
Jonathan Papelbon, Boston	54

COMPLETE GAMES
James Shields, Tampa Bay	11
Felix Hernandez, Seattle	5
Brandon McCarthy, Oakland	5
7 tied at	4

SHUTOUTS
Derek Holland, Texas	4
James Shields, Tampa Bay	4
Dan Haren, Los Angeles	3
Jason Vargas, Seattle	3
3 tied at	2

SAVES
Jose Valverde, Detroit	49
Mariano Rivera, New York	44
Brandon League, Seattle	37
Chris Perez, Cleveland	36
Jordan Walden, Los Angeles	32
Neftali Feliz, Texas	32

INNINGS PITCHED
Justin Verlander, Detroit	251
James Shields, Tampa Bay	249.1
Dan Haren, Los Angeles	238.1
C.C. Sabathia, New York	237.1
Jered Weaver, Los Angeles	235.2

HITS ALLOWED
Carl Pavano, Minnesota	262
C.C. Sabathia, New York	230
Jeff Francis, Kansas City	224
Brad Penny, Detroit	222
Mark Buehrle, Chicago	221

RUNS ALLOWED
Fausto Carmona, Cleveland	125
Carl Pavano, Minnesota	123
John Lackey, Boston	119
Brad Penny, Detroit	117
A.J. Burnett, New York	115

HOME RUNS ALLOWED
Colby Lewis, Texas	35
A.J. Burnett, New York	31
Max Scherzer, Detroit	29
4 tied at	26

WALKS
Gio Gonzalez, Oakland	91
A.J. Burnett, New York	83
Trevor Cahill, Oakland	82
Ricky Romero, Toronto	80
Francisco Liriano, Minnesota	75
Jon Lester, Boston	75

WALKS PER NINE INNINGS
Josh Tomlin, Cleveland	1.14
Dan Haren, Los Angeles	1.25
Brandon McCarthy, Oakland	1.32
Doug Fister, Sea/Det	1.54
Carl Pavano, Minnesota	1.62

HIT BATTERS
John Lackey, Boston	19
Alfredo Aceves, Boston	15
Fausto Carmona, Cleveland	14
Ricky Romero, Toronto	14
Doug Fister, Sea/Det	12
Brandon Morrow, Toronto	12

STRIKEOUTS
Justin Verlander, Detroit	250
C.C. Sabathia, New York	230
James Shields, Tampa Bay	225
Felix Hernandez, Seattle	222
David Price, Tampa Bay	218

STRIKEOUTS PER NINE INNINGS
Brandon Morrow, Toronto	10.19
Michael Pineda, Seattle	9.11
Justin Verlander, Detroit	8.96
Gio Gonzalez, Oakland	8.78
David Price, Tampa Bay	8.75

STRIKEOUTS PER NINE INNINGS (RELIEVERS)
David Robertson, New York	13.5
Sergio Santos, Chicago	13.1
Vinnie Pestano, Cleveland	12.2
Jonathan Papelbon, Boston	12.2
Koji Uehara, Balt/Tex	11.8

DOUBLE PLAYS
C.J. Wilson, Texas	31
Matt Harrison, Texas	30
Ricky Romero, Toronto	28
Tyler Chatwood, Los Angeles	26
3 tied at	25

PICKOFFS
James Shields, Tampa Bay	12
John Danks, Chicago	7
3 tied at	6

WILD PITCHES
A.J. Burnett, New York	25
Trevor Cahill, Oakland	15
Tim Wakefield, Boston	15
5 tied at	12

WALKS-PLUS-HITS PER INNING
Justin Verlander, Detroit	0.92
Jered Weaver, Los Angeles	1.01
Dan Haren, Los Angeles	1.02
Josh Beckett, Boston	1.03
James Shields, Tampa Bay	1.04

OPPONENT AVERAGE
Justin Verlander, Detroit	.192
Jeremy Hellickson, T.B.	.210
Josh Beckett, Boston	.211
Michael Pineda, Seattle	.211
Jered Weaver, Los Angeles	.212

ERA (WORST)
Brad Penny, Detroit	5.30
Fausto Carmona, Cleveland	5.25
A.J. Burnett, New York	5.15
Jeff Francis, Kansas City	4.82
Rick Porcello, Detroit	4.75

FIELDING

PITCHER
PCT	several tied at	1.000
PO	Felix Hernandez, Seattle	27
A	Ricky Romero, Toronto	41
E	A.J. Burnett, New York	5
	Ervin Santana, Los Angeles	5
	Justin Verlander, Detroit	5
DP	Gavin Floyd, Chicago	6

CATCHER
PCT	A.J. Pierzynski, Chicago	.995
PO	Alex Avila, Detroit	940
A	Russell Martin, New York	96
E	Miguel Olivo, Seattle	11
DP	Alex Avila, Detroit	14
	Matt Wieters, Baltimore	14
PB	Jarrod Saltalamacchia, Boston	26

FIRST BASE
PCT	Casey Kotchman, Tampa Bay	.998
PO	Mark Trumbo, Los Angeles	1281
A	Adrian Gonzalez, Boston	125
E	Miguel Cabrera, Detroit	13
DP	Miguel Cabrera, Detroit	117
	Mark Trumbo, Los Angeles	117

SECOND BASE
PCT	Howard Kendrick, Los Angeles	.992
PO	Robinson Cano, New York	323
A	Robinson Cano, New York	444
E	Jemile Weeks, Oakland	13
DP	Ian Kinsler, Texas	103

THIRD BASE
PCT	Kevin Youkilis, Boston	.967
PO	Evan Longoria, Tampa Bay	124
A	Danny Valencia, Minnesota	260
E	Mark Reynolds, Baltimore	26
DP	Evan Longoria, Tampa Bay	35

SHORTSTOP
PCT	J.J. Hardy, Baltimore	.990
PO	Alcides Escobar, Kansas City	271
A	Alcides Escobar, Kansas City	459
E	Elvis Andrus, Texas	25
DP	Elvis Andrus, Texas	102
	Erick Aybar, Los Angeles	102

OUTFIELD
PCT	Jacoby Ellsbury, Boston	1.000
	Nick Markakis, Baltimore	1.000
PO	Jacoby Ellsbury, Boston	388
A	Alex Gordon, Kansas City	20
E	Adam Jones, Baltimore	8
DP	Melky Cabrera, Kansas City	7

CLUB BATTING

	AVG	G	AB	R	H	2B	3B	HR	RBI	BB	SO	SB	CS	OBP	SLG
St. Louis	.273	162	5532	762	1513	308	22	162	726	542	978	57	39	.341	.425
New York	.264	162	5600	718	1477	309	39	108	676	571	1085	130	35	.335	.391
Milwaukee	.261	162	5447	721	1422	276	31	185	693	481	1083	94	31	.325	.425
Colorado	.258	162	5544	735	1429	274	40	163	697	555	1201	118	42	.329	.410
Houston	.258	162	5598	615	1442	309	28	95	579	401	1164	118	33	.311	.374
Los Angeles	.257	161	5436	644	1395	237	28	117	613	498	1087	126	40	.322	.375
Chicago	.256	162	5549	654	1423	285	36	148	610	425	1202	69	23	.314	.401
Cincinnati	.256	162	5612	735	1438	264	19	183	697	535	1250	97	50	.326	.408
Philadelphia	.253	162	5579	713	1409	258	38	153	693	539	1024	96	24	.323	.395
Arizona	.250	162	5421	731	1357	293	37	172	702	531	1249	133	55	.322	.413
Florida	.247	162	5508	625	1358	274	30	149	596	542	1244	95	41	.318	.388
Pittsburgh	.244	162	5421	610	1325	277	35	107	580	489	1308	108	52	.309	.368
Atlanta	.243	162	5528	641	1345	244	16	173	606	504	1260	77	44	.308	.387
San Francisco	.242	162	5486	570	1327	282	24	121	534	448	1122	85	51	.303	.368
Washington	.242	161	5441	624	1319	257	22	154	594	470	1323	106	38	.309	.383
San Diego	.237	162	5417	593	1284	247	42	91	563	501	1320	170	44	.305	.349

CLUB PITCHING

	ERA	G	CG	SHO	SV	IP	H	R	ER	HR	BB	SO	AVG
Philadelphia	3.02	162	18	21	47	1477	1320	529	495	120	404	1299	.240
San Francisco	3.20	162	3	12	52	1468	1260	578	522	96	559	1316	.232
San Diego	3.42	162	0	10	44	1449	1324	611	551	125	521	1139	.245
Atlanta	3.48	162	3	16	52	1480	1332	605	572	115	521	1332	.240
Los Angeles	3.54	161	7	17	40	1432	1287	612	563	132	507	1265	.241
Washington	3.58	161	3	10	49	1449	1403	643	577	129	477	1049	.256
Milwaukee	3.63	162	1	13	47	1442	1348	638	582	147	440	1257	.246
St. Louis	3.74	162	7	9	47	1462	1461	692	608	136	448	1098	.261
Arizona	3.80	162	5	12	58	1443	1414	662	609	159	442	1058	.257
Florida	3.95	162	7	11	40	1460	1403	702	640	149	500	1218	.253
Pittsburgh	4.04	162	5	11	43	1449	1513	712	650	152	535	1031	.270
Cincinnati	4.16	162	4	5	39	1468	1414	720	678	185	539	1112	.255
New York	4.19	162	6	9	43	1448	1482	742	674	147	514	1126	.265
Chicago	4.33	162	4	5	40	1434	1439	756	690	162	580	1224	.262
Colorado	4.43	162	5	7	41	1448	1471	774	713	176	522	1118	.265
Houston	4.51	162	2	6	25	1435	1477	796	719	188	560	1191	.266

CLUB FIELDING

	PCT	PO	A	E	DP		PCT	PO	A	E	DP
Philadelphia	.988	4431	1620	74	135	San Francisco	.983	4404	1657	104	127
Atlanta	.987	4439	1675	83	131	Washington	.983	4348	1691	104	145
Los Angeles	.986	4296	1511	85	121	Milwaukee	.982	4325	1587	111	130
Arizona	.985	4330	1604	90	131	Pittsburgh	.982	4348	1771	112	154
Cincinnati	.985	4403	1759	91	146	St. Louis	.982	4386	1815	116	167
Florida	.985	4379	1553	93	126	Houston	.981	4305	1632	116	140
San Diego	.985	4348	1694	94	139	New York	.981	4344	1697	116	126
Colorado	.984	4343	1758	98	156	Chicago	.978	4303	1559	134	128

INDIVIDUAL BATTING LEADERS (MINIMUM 2.7 PA/TEAM GAME)

	AVG	G	AB	R	H	2B	3B	HR	RBI	BB	SO	SB
Jose Reyes, New York	.337	126	537	101	181	31	16	7	44	43	41	39
Ryan Braun, Milwaukee	.332	150	563	109	187	38	6	33	111	58	93	33
Matt Kemp, Los Angeles	.324	161	602	115	195	33	4	39	126	74	159	40
Hunter Pence, Houston/Phil.	.314	154	606	84	190	38	5	22	97	56	124	8
Joey Votto, Cincinnati	.309	161	599	101	185	40	3	29	103	110	129	8
Starlin Castro, Chicago	.307	158	674	91	207	36	9	10	66	35	96	22
Aramis Ramirez, Chicago	.306	149	565	80	173	35	1	26	93	43	69	1
Yadier Molina, St. Louis	.305	139	475	55	145	32	1	14	65	33	44	4
Michael Morse, Washington	.303	146	522	73	158	36	0	31	95	36	126	2
Troy Tulowitzki, Colorado	.302	143	537	81	162	36	2	30	105	59	79	9

INDIVIDUAL PITCHING LEADERS (MINIMUM 0.8 IP/TEAM GAME)

	W	L	ERA	G	GS	CG	SHO	SV	IP	H	R	ER	BB	SO
Clayton Kershaw, L.A.	21	5	2.28	33	33	5	2	0	233	174	66	59	54	248
Roy Halladay, Philadelphia	19	6	2.35	32	32	8	1	0	234	208	65	61	35	220
Cliff Lee, Philadelphia	17	8	2.40	32	32	6	6	0	233	197	66	62	42	238
Ryan Vogelsong, S.F.	13	7	2.71	30	28	1	1	0	180	164	62	54	61	139
Tim Lincecum, San Francisco	13	14	2.74	33	33	1	1	0	217	176	74	66	86	220
Cole Hamels, Philadelphia	14	9	2.79	32	31	3	0	0	216	169	68	67	44	194
Ian Kennedy, Arizona	21	4	2.88	33	33	1	0	0	222	186	73	71	55	198
Matt Cain, San Francisco	12	11	2.88	33	33	1	0	0	222	177	82	71	63	179
Hiroki Kuroda, Los Angeles	13	16	3.07	32	32	0	0	0	202	196	77	69	49	161
Madison Bumgarner, S.F.	13	13	3.21	33	33	0	0	0	205	202	82	73	46	191

AWARD WINNERS

Selected by Baseball Writers Association of America

MOST VALUABLE PLAYER

Player	1st	2nd	3rd	Total
Ryan Braun, Milwaukee	20	12	—	388
Matt Kemp, Los Angeles	10	16	6	332
Prince Fielder, Milwaukee	1	4	11	229
Justin Upton, Arizona	1	—	8	214
Albert Pujols, St. Louis	—	—	1	166
Joey Votto, Cincinnati	—	—	4	135
Lance Berkman, St. Louis	—	—	1	118
Troy Tulowitzki, Colorado	—	—	—	69
Roy Halladay, Philadelphia	—	—	1	52
Ryan Howard, Philadelphia	—	—	—	39
Jose Reyes, New York	—	—	—	31
Clayton Kershaw, Los Angeles	—	—	—	29
Shane Victorino, Philadelphia	—	—	—	18
Ian Kennedy, Arizona	—	—	—	16
Cliff Lee, Philadelphia	—	—	—	12
Hunter Pence, Houston/Phil.	—	—	—	10
Pablo Sandoval, San Francisco	—	—	—	7
John Axford, Milwaukee	—	—	—	7
Michael Morse, Washington	—	—	—	5
Carlos Beltran, N.Y./San Fran.	—	—	—	3
Miguel Montero, Arizona	—	—	—	2
Yadier Molina, St. Louis	—	—	—	2
Starlin Castro, Chicago	—	—	—	1
Craig Kimbrel, Atlanta	—	—	—	1
Carlos Ruiz, Philadelphia	—	—	—	1
Mike Stanton, Florida	—	—	—	1

CY YOUNG AWARD

Pitcher	1st	2nd	3rd	Total
Clayton Kershaw, Los Angeles	27	3	2	207
Roy Halladay, Philadelphia	4	21	7	133
Cliff Lee, Philadelphia	—	5	17	90
Ian Kennedy, Arizona	1	3	6	76
Cole Hamels, Philadelphia	—	—	—	17
Tim Lincecum, San Francisco	—	—	—	7
Yovani Gallardo, Milwaukee	—	—	—	5
Matt Cain, San Francisco	—	—	—	3
John Axford, Milwaukee	—	—	—	2
Craig Kimbrel, Atlanta	—	—	—	2
Madison Bumgarner, San Fran.	—	—	—	1
Ryan Vogelsong, San Francisco	—	—	—	1

ROOKIE OF THE YEAR

Player	1st	2nd	3rd	Total
Craig Kimbrel, Atlanta	32	—	—	160
Freddie Freeman, Atlanta	—	21	7	70
Vance Worley, Philadelphia	—	8	16	40
Wilson Ramos, Washington	—	1	3	6
Josh Collmenter, Arizona	—	1	2	5
Danny Espinosa, Washington	—	1	—	3
Darwin Barney, Chicago	—	—	2	2
Kenley Jansen, Los Angeles	—	—	2	2

MANAGER OF THE YEAR

Player	1st	2nd	3rd	Total
Kirk Gibson, Arizona	28	4	—	152
Ron Roenicke, Milwaukee	3	25	2	92
Tony La Russa, St. Louis	1	2	13	24
Charlie Manuel, Philadelphia	—	1	7	10
Fredi Gonzalez, Atlanta	—	—	4	4
Bruce Bochy, San Francisco	—	—	2	2
Clint Hurdle, Pittsburgh	—	—	2	2
Terry Collins, New York	—	—	1	1
Don Mattingly, Los Angeles	—	—	1	1

GOLD GLOVE WINNERS

Selected by NL managers
C—Yadier Molina, St. Louis. 1B—Joey Votto, Cincinnati. 2B—Brandon Phillips, Cincinnati. 3B—Placido Polanco, Philadelphia. SS—Troy Tulowitzki, Colorado. LF—Gerardo Parra, Arizona. CF—Matt Kemp, Los Angeles. RF—Andre Ethier, Los Angeles. P—Clayton Kershaw, Los Angeles.

SILVER SLUGGER AWARDS

Selected by NL managers, coaches
C—Brian McCann, Atlanta. 1B—Prince Fielder, Milwaukee. 2B—Brandon Phillips, Cincinnati. 3B—Aramis Ramirez, Chicago. SS—Troy Tulowitzki, Colorado. OF—Ryan Braun, Milwaukee; Matt Kemp, Los Angeles; Justin Upton, Arizona. P—Daniel Hudson, Arizona.

BATTING

GAMES

Prince Fielder, Milwaukee	162
Matt Kemp, Los Angeles	161
Dan Uggla, Atlanta	161
Joey Votto, Cincinnati	161
4 tied at	159

AT-BATS

Starlin Castro, Chicago	674
Michael Bourn, Hou/Atl	656
Brandon Phillips, Cincinnati	610
Hunter Pence, Hou/Phil	606
Drew Stubbs, Cincinnati	604

PLATE APPEARANCES

Michael Bourn, Hou/Atl	722
Joey Votto, Cincinnati	719
Starlin Castro, Chicago	715
Prince Fielder, Milwaukee	692
Matt Kemp, Los Angeles	689

RUNS

Matt Kemp, Los Angeles	115
Ryan Braun, Milwaukee	109
Albert Pujols, St. Louis	105
Justin Upton, Arizona	105
Joey Votto, Cincinnati	101
Jose Reyes, New York	101

Ryan Braun

HITS

Starlin Castro, Chicago	207
Matt Kemp, Los Angeles	195
Michael Bourn, Hou/Atl	193
Hunter Pence, Hou/Phil	190
Ryan Braun, Milwaukee	187

TOTAL BASES

Matt Kemp, Los Angeles	353
Ryan Braun, Milwaukee	336
Prince Fielder, Milwaukee	322
Joey Votto, Cincinnati	318
Justin Upton, Arizona	313
Albert Pujols, St. Louis	313

DOUBLES

Joey Votto, Cincinnati	40
Carlos Beltran, N.Y./S.F.	39
Justin Upton, Arizona	39
5 tied at	38

TRIPLES

Jose Reyes, New York	16
Shane Victorino, Philadelphia	16
Dexter Fowler, Colorado	15
Michael Bourn, Hou/Atl	10
Starlin Castro, Chicago	9
Seth Smith, Colorado	9

EXTRA-BASE HITS

Ryan Braun, Milwaukee	77
Matt Kemp, Los Angeles	76
Prince Fielder, Milwaukee	75
Justin Upton, Arizona	75
Joey Votto, Cincinnati	72

HOME RUNS

Matt Kemp, Los Angeles	39
Prince Fielder, Milwaukee	38
Albert Pujols, St. Louis	37
Dan Uggla, Atlanta	36
Mike Stanton, Florida	34

RUNS BATTED IN

Matt Kemp, Los Angeles	126
Prince Fielder, Milwaukee	120
Ryan Howard, Philadelphia	116
Ryan Braun, Milwaukee	111

Troy Tulowitzki, Colorado	105

SACRIFICES

Omar Infante, Florida	17
Roy Halladay, Philadelphia	16
Livan Hernandez, Washington	15
Nyjer Morgan, Milwaukee	15
Jason Hammel, Colorado	14

SACRIFICE FLIES

Yuniesky Betancourt, Mil	10
Aubrey Huff, San Francisco	9
6 tied at	8

HIT BY PITCH

Danny Espinosa, Washington	19
Justin Upton, Arizona	19
Nyjer Morgan, Milwaukee	14
Chase Utley, Philadelphia	14
Michael Morse, Washington	13

WALKS

Joey Votto, Cincinnati	110
Prince Fielder, Milwaukee	107
Carlos Pena, Chicago	101
Lance Berkman, St. Louis	92
Andrew McCutchen, Pitt	89

STOLEN BASES

Michael Bourn, Hou/Atl	61
Emilio Bonifacio, Florida	40
Matt Kemp, Los Angeles	40
Cameron Maybin, San Diego	40
Drew Stubbs, Cincinnati	40

CAUGHT STEALING

Michael Bourn, Hou/Atl	14
Emilio Bonifacio, Florida	11
Matt Kemp, Los Angeles	11
6 tied at	10

Joey Votto

STOLEN BASE PERCENTAGE

Tony Campana, Chicago	92.3%
Will Venable, San Diego	89.7%
Eric Young, Colorado	87.1%
3 tied at	86.4%

STRIKEOUTS

Drew Stubbs, Cincinnati	205
Ryan Howard, Philadelphia	172
Danny Espinosa, Washington	166
Mike Stanton, Florida	166
Carlos Pena, Chicago	161

**TOUGHEST TO STRIKE OUT
(AT-BAT PER STRIKEOUTS)**

Jose Reyes, New York	13.10
Yadier Molina, St. Louis	10.80
Placido Polanco, Phil	10.66
Martin Prado, Atlanta	10.60
Albert Pujols, St. Louis	9.98

GROUNDED INTO DOUBLE PLAYS

Albert Pujols, St. Louis	29
Matt Holliday, St. Louis	21
Yadier Molina, St. Louis	21
Starlin Castro, Chicago	20
Joey Votto, Cincinnati	20

MULTI-HIT GAMES

Starlin Castro, Chicago	57
Matt Kemp, Los Angeles	57
Hunter Pence, Philadelphia	57
Jose Reyes, New York	57
2 tied at	55

ON-BASE PERCENTAGE

Joey Votto, Cincinnati	.416
Prince Fielder, Milwaukee	.415
Lance Berkman, St. Louis	.412
Matt Kemp, Los Angeles	.399
Ryan Braun, Milwaukee	.397

SLUGGING PERCENTAGE

Ryan Braun, Milwaukee	.597
Matt Kemp, Los Angeles	.586
Prince Fielder, Milwaukee	.566
Michael Morse, Washington	.550
Lance Berkman, St. Louis	.547

ON-BASE-PLUS-SLUGGING

Ryan Braun, Milwaukee	.994
Matt Kemp, Los Angeles	.986
Prince Fielder, Milwaukee	.981
Lance Berkman, St. Louis	.959
Joey Votto, Cincinnati	.947

AVERAGE (LOWEST)

Casey McGehee, Milwaukee	.223
Carlos Pena, Chicago	.225
John Buck, Florida	.227
Jayson Werth, Washington	.232
Dan Uggla, Atlanta	.233

PITCHING

WINS

Ian Kennedy, Arizona	21
Clayton Kershaw, Los Angeles	21
Roy Halladay, Philadelphia	19
Yovani Gallardo, Milwaukee	17
Cliff Lee, Philadelphia	17

LOSSES

Derek Lowe, Atlanta	17
Hiroki Kuroda, Los Angeles	16
J.A. Happ, Houston	15
7 tied at	14

GAMES

Jonny Venters, Atlanta	85

DEPARTMENT LEADERS

Bill Bray, Cincinnati	79
Craig Kimbrel, Atlanta	79
Jose Veras, Pittsburgh	79
Sean Marshall, Chicago	78
Jason Motte, St. Louis	78
Eric O'Flaherty, Atlanta	78

GAMES STARTED

Chris Carpenter, St. Louis	34
Ryan Dempster, Chicago	34
Derek Lowe, Atlanta	34
17 tied at	33

GAMES FINISHED

Craig Kimbrel, Atlanta	64
John Axford, Milwaukee	63
Francisco Cordero, Cincinnati	63
Carlos Marmol, Chicago	61
Joel Hanrahan, Pittsburgh	59

COMPLETE GAMES

Roy Halladay, Philadelphia	8
Cliff Lee, Philadelphia	6
Clayton Kershaw, Los Angeles	5
Chris Carpenter, St. Louis	4
4 tied at	3

SHUTOUTS

Cliff Lee, Philadelphia	6
Chris Carpenter, St. Louis	2
Jaime Garcia, St. Louis	2
Clayton Kershaw, Los Angeles	2
Anibal Sanchez, Florida	2

SAVES

John Axford, Milwaukee	46
Craig Kimbrel, Atlanta	46
J.J. Putz, Arizona	45
Heath Bell, San Diego	43
Drew Storen, Washington	43

INNINGS PITCHED

Chris Carpenter, St. Louis	237.1
Roy Halladay, Philadelphia	233.2
Clayton Kershaw, L.A.	233.1
Cliff Lee, Philadelphia	232.2
Ian Kennedy, Arizona	222
Daniel Hudson, Arizona	222

HITS ALLOWED

Ricky Nolasco, Florida	244
Chris Carpenter, St. Louis	243
Bronson Arroyo, Cincinnati	227
Brett Myers, Houston	226
Mike Pelfrey, New York	220

Roy Halladay

RUNS ALLOWED

Bronson Arroyo, Cincinnati	119
Ricky Nolasco, Florida	117
Brett Myers, Houston	116
Ryan Dempster, Chicago	111
Mike Pelfrey, New York	111

HOME RUNS ALLOWED

Bronson Arroyo, Cincinnati	46
Brett Myers, Houston	31
Joe Saunders, Arizona	29
Ted Lilly, Los Angeles	28
Chris Capuano, New York	27
Yovani Gallardo, Milwaukee	27

WALKS

Jhoulys Chacin, Colorado	87
Tim Lincecum, San Francisco	86
Chad Billingsley, Los Angeles	84
J.A. Happ, Houston	83
Ryan Dempster, Chicago	82

WALKS PER NINE INNINGS

Roy Halladay, Philadelphia	1.35
Cliff Lee, Philadelphia	1.62
Jeff Karstens, Pittsburgh	1.83
Cole Hamels, Philadelphia	1.83
Ricky Nolasco, Florida	1.92

HIT BATTERS

Tim Hudson, Atlanta	15
Dillon Gee, New York	14
Charlie Morton, Pittsburgh	13
Randy Wolf, Milwaukee	13
Johnny Cueto, Cincinnati	10

STRIKEOUTS

Clayton Kershaw, Los Angeles	248
Cliff Lee, Philadelphia	238
Roy Halladay, Philadelphia	220
Tim Lincecum, San Francisco	220
Yovani Gallardo, Milwaukee	207

STRIKEOUTS PER NINE INNINGS

Zack Greinke, Milwaukee	10.54

Clayton Kershaw, L.A.	9.57
Anibal Sanchez, Florida	9.26
Cliff Lee, Philadelphia	9.21
Tim Lincecum, San Francisco	9.12

STRIKEOUTS PER NINE INNINGS (RELIEVERS)

Craig Kimbrel, Atlanta	14.8
Carlos Marmol, Chicago	12.0
Ernesto Frieri, San Diego	10.9
Tyler Clippard, Washington	10.6
Rafael Betancourt, Colorado	10.5

DOUBLE PLAYS

Joe Saunders, Arizona	28
John Lannan, Washington	26
Jaime Garcia, St. Louis	25
Charlie Morton, Pittsburgh	25
Tim Hudson, Atlanta	24

PICKOFFS

Clayton Kershaw, Los Angeles	9
Chris Narveson, Milwaukee	6
Clayton Richard, San Diego	5
5 tied at	4

WILD PITCHES

Henry Rodriguez, Washington	14
Yovani Gallardo, Milwaukee	12
Jaime Garcia, St. Louis	12
Hiroki Kuroda, Los Angeles	12
Ian Kennedy, Arizona	11
Brandon Beachy, Atlanta	11

WALKS-PLUS-HITS PER INNINGS

Clayton Kershaw, L.A.	0.98
Cole Hamels, Philadelphia	0.99
Cliff Lee, Philadelphia	1.03
Roy Halladay, Philadelphia	1.04
Matt Cain, San Francisco	1.08

OPPONENT AVERAGE

Clayton Kershaw, L.A.	.207
Cole Hamels, Philadelphia	.214
Matt Cain, San Francisco	.217
Tim Lincecum, San Francisco	.222
Ian Kennedy, Arizona	.227

ERA (WORST)

Bronson Arroyo, Cincinnati	5.07
Derek Lowe, Atlanta	5.05
Chris Volstad, Florida	4.89
Ryan Dempster, Chicago	4.80
Jason Hammel, Colorado	4.76

ED WOLFSTEIN

FIELDING

PITCHER

PCT	several tied at	1.000
PO	Brett Myers, Houston	33
A	R.A. Dickey, New York	58
E	Matt Garza, Chicago	7
DP	Livan Hernandez, Washington	7

CATCHER

PCT	Ramon Hernandez, Cincinnati	.998
PO	John Buck, Florida	1008
A	Chris Iannetta, Colorado	82
	Geovany Soto, Chicago	82
E	Geovany Soto, Chicago	13
DP	Brian McCann, Atlanta	14
PB	Josh Thole, New York	16

FIRST BASE

PCT	Todd Helton, Colorado	.997
PO	Joey Votto, Cincinnati	1341
A	Joe Votto, Cincinnati	173
E	Prince Fielder, Milwaukee	15
DP	Albert Pujols, St. Louis	134

SECOND BASE

PCT	Orlando Hudson, San Diego	.993
PO	Neil Walker, Pittsburgh	333
A	Omar Infante, Florida	466
E	Dan Uggla, Atlanta	15
	Rickie Weeks, Milwaukee	15
DP	Neil Walker, Pittsburgh	108

THIRD BASE

PCT	Placido Polanco, Philadelphia	.977
PO	Chase Headley, San Diego	95
A	Placido Polanco, Philadelphia	259
E	Casey McGehee, Milwaukee	20
DP	David Freese, St. Louis	23

SHORTSTOP

PCT	Troy Tulowitzki, Colorado	.991
PO	Starlin Castro, Chicago	267
A	Starlin Castro, Chicago	446
E	Starlin Castro, Chicago	29
DP	Troy Tulowitzki, Colorado	98

OUTFIELD

PCT	Andre Ethier, Los Angeles	1.000
	Shane Victorino, Philadelphia	1.000
PO	Andrew McCutchen, Pittsburgh	414
A	Carlos Gonzalez, Colorado	12
	Gerardo Parra, Arizona	12
E	Justin Upton, Arizona	13
DP	Matt Kemp, Los Angeles	5
	Andrew McCutchen, Pittsburgh	5
	Gerardo Parra, Arizona	5

GEORGE GOJKOVICH

The Cardinals' David Freese, a St. Louis native, established single postseason records for RBIs (21) and total bases (50), winning MVP honors for both the National League finals and World Series

Cards' run culminates in 11th World Series win

BY TOM HAUDRICOURT

Baseball fans agree that there's nothing quite like Game Seven of the World Series. Unless, that is, Game Six offers the high drama that the Cardinals and Rangers staged in 2011.

Twice the Rangers stood one strike away from winning the franchise's first World Series, only to see it slip away both times. The Cardinals made it official the next night with a 6-2 victory in Game Seven that sealed one of the most improbable title runs ever.

The Cardinals knocked out the top-seeded Phillies in the NL Division Series and proceeded to do the same to the No. 2 Brewers in the Championship Series. In the World Series, St. Louis twice snatched victory from the jaws of defeat in Game Six to even things at three games.

In the previous 106 World Series, only one team—the 1986 Mets—had rallied to win it all when one strike away from elimination.

Just 24 hours before the Cardinals claimed the crown, the Rangers seemed poised to win their first championship. Closer Neftali Feliz had two strikes on St. Louis third baseman David Freese with two on and two outs in the bottom of the ninth inning of Game Six. But Freese, who used the postseason as his personal coming-out party, laced a two-run triple over the head of Texas right fielder Nelson Cruz to tie the game at seven apiece.

Despite that bit of heartbreak, the Rangers found themselves in position to win the whole thing again in the top of the 10th when center fielder Josh Hamilton—hobbled by a groin strain—socked his first home run of the World Series, a two-run shot. St. Louis quickly cut the deficit to 9-8 with an RBI groundout in the bottom half of the frame, but Texas once again backed the Cardinals to within one strike of elimination when righthander Scott Feldman worked right fielder Lance Berkman to a 2-2 count.

Again, St. Louis refused to die. Following an intentional walk to Pujols, Berkman laced an RBI single to center that scored Jon Jay from second and knotted the game at nine. Texas failed to score in its half of the 11th, so the Busch Stadium crowd still was buzzing when Freese led off the bottom half of the inning by facing Mark Lowe. Freese promptly connected for a mammoth 428-foot blast to center that won the game 10-9 and set off a wild celebration in St. Louis.

The Cardinals had one more comeback in store for Game Seven, baseball's first in the World Series since 2002. The Rangers tallied two quick runs in the top of the first inning against Cardinals ace Chris Carpenter, who was pitching on short rest. St. Louis answered with two in the bottom of the inning, then they went ahead 3-2 in the third and never looked back. Carpenter and four relievers shut out Texas over the final eight innings to claim the 6-2 victory. St. Louis won its 11th and most improbable championship.

The 28-year-old Freese, who attended high school in suburban St. Louis, won MVP honors of both the World Series and NLCS, becoming the sixth player to do so. He batted a cumulative .397/.465/.794 with five homers in 63 playoff at-bats. Freese set or tied single postseason records with 21 RBIs, eight doubles, 25 hits and 50 total bases.

"You had to be here to believe it," said St. Louis manager Tony La Russa, who a few days after the victory shocked many by announcing his retirement after 16 years at the helm in St. Louis. La Russa left having won two World Series titles with the Cardinals (2006 and '11) and one with the Athletics (1989). He won three other league pennants—1988 and '90 A's, 2004 Cardinals—as well as 2,728 regular-season games, just 35 behind John McGraw for second most all time.

For their part, the Rangers won consecutive American League pennants in 2010-11, but still Texas searched for its first World Series win.

National League Playoffs

The Cardinals' reward for their miracle wild-card finish was a first-round Division Series draw against the 102-win Phillies.

St. Louis and Philadelphia battled to a 2-2 tie after four games, leading to a Game Five clash of aces between the Phillies' Roy Halladay and Carpenter at Citizens Bank Park. The matchup lived up to the hype. St. Louis scored a run in the first inning off Halladay by virtue of a Rafael Furcal leadoff triple followed by a Skip Schumaker double. Carpenter made that run stand up by pitching a three-hit shutout to win 1-0.

Earlier that day, the Brewers pulled out a tense

victory in Game Five of their Division Series against the Diamondbacks—but not before closer John Axford blew his first save since April 18. Arizona tied the score at 2-2 with a run in the ninth, but they did not push across the go-ahead run that inning or in the 10th. Milwaukee center fielder Nyjer Morgan ended the game and the NLDS with an RBI single in the bottom of the 10th to give the Brewers a thrilling 3-2 victory.

The Brewers held home-field advantage for the NLCS, but they could not stop the careening wild-card Cardinals. Milwaukee won Game Four in St. Louis to even the series at two games, but the Cardinals would not lose again in the NLCS. St. Louis won Game Five 7-1 to send the series back to Miller Park, whereupon they jumped on right-hander Shaun Marcum for four first-inning runs and rolled to a 12-6 pennant-clinching victory.

American League Playoffs

Unlike the Cardinals, the Rays were unable to parlay their wild-card charge into postseason success. They shocked the Rangers when rookie lefthander Matt Moore pitched seven shutout innings and catcher Kelly Shoppach socked two homers in a 9-0 romp in Game One in Arlington. But little went right for Tampa Bay after that.

Rays righty James Shields failed to hold a 3-0 lead in Game Two, allowing Texas to avoid falling into a 0-2 hole at home in the series. Tampa Bay had ace lefty David Price lined up for Game Three at home, but Rangers catcher Mike Napoli spoiled the homecoming—his two-run homer in the seventh erased a 1-0 deficit. Texas went on to a 4-2 victory that put them ahead two games to one.

The Rangers claimed victory in the Division Series the next day, winning their third game in a row, 4-3, behind third baseman Adrian Beltre's three home runs.

The other ALDS got off to a fitful start when Game One between the Yankees and Tigers was suspended by rain after two innings, negating the much-anticipated matchup of Yankees ace C.C. Sabathia and Tigers stalwart Justin Verlander.

New York rolled to a 9-3 victory when play resumed the next day, but the Tigers appeared undaunted and took the next two games. Game Three featured a rematch between Sabathia and Verlander, both of whom came back on short rest after their aborted starts in Game One. Verlander pitched eight gritty innings, striking out 11 in a tense 5-4 victory.

Behind beleaguered veteran A.J. Burnett, the Yankees evened the series with a 10-1 romp in Game Four, setting up a decisive Game Five at Yankee Stadium. That contest lived up to expectations, with the Tigers squeezing out a 3-2 victory when closer Jose Valverde struck out Alex Rodriguez to end the game.

"The Yankees are so good that I would by lying if I said it didn't give me a little extra satisfaction to be able to do it (in New York) in the fifth game," Tigers manager Jim Leyland said. "This will be a game I remember for the rest of my life."

The Yankees joined the Phillies as upended No. 1 seeds that failed to advance past the first round, leaving the Tigers and Rangers to square off for the AL pennant. Rain was a factor again, interrupting Game One, but the Rangers eked out a 3-2 win against Verlander and the Tigers.

Weather continued to dominate the headlines when rain postponed Game Two for a day, but nothing could stop Texas slugger Nelson Cruz

AMERICAN LEAGUE CHAMPIONS, 1901–2011

	PENNANT	PCT		PENNANT	PCT		PENNANT	PCT		PENNANT	PCT
1901	Chicago	.610	1918	Boston	.595	1935	Detroit	.616	1952	New York	.617
1902	Philadelphia	.610	1919	Chicago	.629	1936	New York	.667	1953	New York	.656
1903	Boston	.659	1920	Cleveland	.636	1937	New York	.662	1954	Cleveland	.721
1904	Boston	.617	1921	New York	.641	1938	New York	.651	1955	New York	.623
1905	Philadelphia	.622	1922	New York	.610	1939	New York	.702	1956	New York	.630
1906	Chicago	.616	1923	New York	.645	1940	Detroit	.584	1957	New York	.636
1907	Detroit	.613	1924	Washington	.597	1941	New York	.656	1958	New York	.597
1908	Detroit	.588	1925	Washington	.636	1942	New York	.669	1959	Chicago	.610
1909	Detroit	.645	1926	New York	.591	1943	New York	.636	1960	New York	.630
1910	Philadelphia	.680	1927	New York	.714	1944	St. Louis	.578	1961	New York	.673
1911	Philadelphia	.669	1928	New York	.656	1945	Detroit	.575	1962	New York	.593
1912	Boston	.691	1929	Philadelphia	.693	1946	Boston	.675	1963	New York	.646
1913	Philadelphia	.627	1930	Philadelphia	.662	1947	New York	.630	1964	New York	.611
1914	Philadelphia	.651	1931	Philadelphia	.704	1948	Cleveland	.626	1965	Minnesota	.630
1915	Boston	.669	1932	New York	.695	1949	New York	.630	1966	Baltimore	.606
1916	Boston	.591	1933	Washington	.651	1950	New York	.636	1967	Boston	.568
1917	Chicago	.649	1934	Detroit	.656	1951	New York	.636	1968	Detroit	.636

DIVISION ERA (1969-1993)
*Won pennant. ∧ Won first half; defeated Milwaukee 3-2 in playoff. ∧∧ Won first half, defeated Kansas City 3-0.

	EAST	PCT	WEST	PCT	LCS		EAST	PCT	WEST	PCT	LCS
1969	Baltimore*	.673	Minnesota	.599	3-0		Milwaukee	.585	Kansas City	.566	
1970	Baltimore*	.667	Minnesota	.605	3-0	1982	Milwaukee*	.586	California	.574	3-2
1971	Baltimore*	.639	Oakland	.627	3-0	1983	Baltimore*	.605	Chicago	.611	3-1
1972	Detroit	.551	Oakland*	.600	3-2	1984	Detroit*	.642	Kansas City	.519	3-0
1973	Baltimore	.599	Oakland*	.580	3-2	1985	Toronto	.615	Kansas City*	.562	4-3
1974	Baltimore	.562	Oakland*	.556	3-1	1986	Boston*	.590	California	.568	4-3
1975	Boston*	.594	Oakland	.605	3-0	1987	Detroit	.605	Minnesota*	.525	4-1
1976	New York*	.610	Kansas City	.556	3-2	1988	Boston	.549	Oakland*	.642	4-0
1977	New York*	.617	Kansas City	.630	3-2	1989	Toronto	.549	Oakland*	.611	4-1
1978	New York*	.613	Kansas City	.568	3-1	1990	Boston	.543	Oakland*	.636	4-0
1979	Baltimore*	.642	California	.543	3-1	1991	Toronto	.562	Minnesota*	.586	4-1
1980	New York	.636	Kansas City*	.599	3-0	1992	Toronto*	.593	Oakland	.593	4-2
1981	New York*∧	.607	Oakland∧∧	.587	3-0	1993	Toronto*	.586	Chicago	.580	4-2

WILD CARD ERA (1994-PRESENT)
★Won pennant. † Lost ALCS.

	EAST	PCT	CENTRAL	PCT	WEST	PCT	WILD CARD	PCT	LCS
1994	New York	.619	Chicago	.593	Texas	.456	None		
1995	Boston	.597	Cleveland*	.694	Seattle†	.545	New York (E)	.549	4-2
1996	New York*	.568	Cleveland	.615	Texas	.556	Baltimore (E)†	.543	4-1
1997	Baltimore†	.605	Cleveland*	.534	Seattle	.556	New York (E)	.593	4-2
1998	New York*	.704	Cleveland†	.549	Texas	.543	Boston (E)	.568	4-2
1999	New York*	.605	Cleveland	.599	Texas	.586	Boston (E)†	.580	4-1
2000	New York*	.540	Chicago	.586	Oakland	.565	Seattle (W)†	.562	4-2
2001	New York*	.594	Cleveland	.562	Seattle†	.716	Oakland (W)	.630	4-1
2002	New York	.640	Minnesota†	.584	Oakland	.636	Anaheim (W)*	.611	4-1
2003	New York*	.623	Minnesota	.556	Oakland	.593	Boston (E)‡	.586	4-3
2004	New York†	.623	Minnesota	.568	Anaheim	.568	Boston (E)*	.605	4-3
2005	New York	.586	Chicago*	.611	Los Angeles†	.586	Boston (E)	.586	4-1
2006	New York	.599	Minnesota	.593	Oakland†	.574	Detroit (C)*	.586	4-0
2007	Boston*	.593	Cleveland†	.593	Los Angeles	.580	New York (E)	.580	4-3
2008	Tampa Bay*	.599	Chicago	.546	Los Angeles	.617	Boston (E)†	.586	4-3
2009	New York*	.636	Minnesota	.534	Los Angeles†	.599	Boston (E)	.586	4-2
2010	Tampa Bay	.593	Minnesota	.580	Texas*	.556	New York (E)†	.586	4-2
2011	New York	.599	Detroit†	.586	Texas*	.593	Tampa Bay (E)	.562	4-2

when play resumed. The right fielder made post-season history with the first walk-off grand slam—his second homer of the game—to hand Detroit a discouraging 7-3 defeat in 11 innings.

After the Tigers won Game Three at home, Cruz struck again in Game Four—and once again in the 11th inning. His three-run blast handed the Rangers a 3-1 series lead.

The Tigers rallied behind two homers by left fielder Delmon Young to win Game Five, 7-5, and send the series back to Arlington.

That's as far as the Tigers could take it. The Rangers rolled to a 15-5 victory in Game Six to claim their second consecutive AL pennant. Cruz hit yet another home run, giving him six in the series while batting .364/.440/1.273 with two doubles and 13 RBIs in 22 at-bats to claim ALCS MVP honors.

NATIONAL LEAGUE CHAMPIONS , 1901–2011

	PENNANT	PCT		PENNANT	PCT		PENNANT	PCT		PENNANT	PCT
1901	Pittsburgh	.647	1918	Chicago	.651	1935	Chicago	.649	1952	Brooklyn	.627
1902	Pittsburgh	.741	1919	Cincinnati	.686	1936	New York	.597	1953	Brooklyn	.682
1903	Pittsburgh	.650	1920	Brooklyn	.604	1937	New York	.625	1954	New York	.630
1904	New York	.693	1921	New York	.614	1938	Chicago	.586	1955	Brooklyn	.641
1905	New York	.686	1922	New York	.604	1939	Cincinnati	.630	1956	Brooklyn	.604
1906	Chicago	.763	1923	New York	.621	1940	Cincinnati	.654	1957	Milwaukee	.617
1907	Chicago	.704	1924	New York	.608	1941	Brooklyn	.649	1958	Milwaukee	.597
1908	Chicago	.643	1925	Pittsburgh	.621	1942	St. Louis	.688	1959	Los Angeles	.564
1909	Pittsburgh	.724	1926	St. Louis	.578	1943	St. Louis	.682	1960	Pittsburgh	.617
1910	Chicago	.675	1927	Pittsburgh	.610	1944	St. Louis	.682	1961	Cincinnati	.604
1911	New York	.647	1928	St. Louis	.617	1945	Chicago	.636	1962	San Francisco	.624
1912	New York	.682	1929	Chicago	.645	1946	St. Louis	.628	1963	Los Angeles	.611
1913	New York	.664	1930	St. Louis	.597	1947	Brooklyn	.610	1964	St. Louis	.574
1914	Boston	.614	1931	St. Louis	.656	1948	Boston	.595	1965	Los Angeles	.599
1915	Philadelphia	.592	1932	Chicago	.584	1949	Brooklyn	.630	1966	Los Angeles	.586
1916	Brooklyn	.610	1933	New York	.599	1950	Philadelphia	.591	1967	St. Louis	.627
1917	New York	.636	1934	St. Louis	.621	1951	New York	.624	1968	St. Louis	.599

DIVISION ERA (1969-1993)
*Won pennant. ∧ Won first half; defeated Milwaukee 3-2 in playoff. ∧∧ Won first half, defeated Kansas City 3-0.

	EAST	PCT	WEST	PCT	LCS		EAST	PCT	WEST	PCT	LCS
1969	New York*	.617	Atlanta	.574	3-0						
1970	Pittsburgh	.549	Cincinnati*	.630	3-0						
1971	Pittsburgh*	.599	San Francisco	.556	3-1						
1972	Pittsburgh	.619	Cincinnati*	.617	3-2	1982	St. Louis*	.568	Atlanta	.549	3-0
1973	New York*	.509	Cincinnati	.611	3-2	1983	Philadelphia*	.556	Los Angeles	.562	3-1
1974	Pittsburgh	.543	Los Angeles*	.630	3-1	1984	Chicago	.596	San Diego*	.568	3-2
1975	Pittsburgh	.571	Cincinnati*	.667	3-0	1985	St. Louis*	.623	Los Angeles	.586	4-2
1976	Philadelphia	.623	Cincinnati*	.630	3-0	1986	New York*	.667	Houston	.593	4-2
1977	Philadelphia	.623	Los Angeles*	.605	3-1	1987	St. Louis*	.586	San Francisco	.556	4-3
1978	Philadelphia	.556	Los Angeles*	.586	3-1	1988	New York	.625	Los Angeles*	.584	4-3
1979	Pittsburgh*	.605	Cincinnati	.559	3-0	1989	Chicago	.571	San Francisco*	.568	4-1
1980	Philadelphia*	.562	Houston	.571	3-2	1990	Pittsburgh	.586	Cincinnati*	.562	4-2
1981	Montreal∧	.566	Los Angeles*∧∧	.632	3-2	1991	Pittsburgh	.605	Atlanta*	.580	4-3
						1992	Pittsburgh	.593	Atlanta*	.605	4-3
						1993	Philadelphia*	.599	Atlanta	.642	4-2

WILD CARD ERA (1994-PRESENT)
*Won pennant. † Lost ALCS.

	EAST	PCT	CENTRAL	PCT	WEST	PCT	WILD CARD	PCT	LCS
1994	Montreal	.649	Cincinnati	.593	Los Angeles	.509	None		
1995	Atlanta*	.625	Cincinnati†	.590	Los Angeles	.542	Colorado (W)	.535	4-2
1996	Atlanta*	.593	St. Louis†	.543	San Diego	.562	Los Angeles (W)	.556	4-3
1997	Atlanta†	.623	Houston	.519	San Francisco	.556	Florida (E)*	.568	4-2
1998	Atlanta†	.654	Houston	.630	San Diego*	.605	Chicago (C)	.552	4-2
1999	Atlanta*	.636	Houston	.599	Arizona	.617	New York (E)†	.595	4-2
2000	Atlanta	.586	St. Louis†	.586	San Francisco	.599	New York (E)*	.580	4-1
2001	Atlanta†	.543	Houston	.574	Arizona*	.568	St. Louis (C)	.574	4-1
2002	Atlanta	.631	St. Louis†	.599	Arizona	.605	San Francisco (W)*	.590	4-1
2003	Atlanta	.623	Chicago†	.543	San Francisco	.621	Florida (E)*	.562	4-3
2004	Atlanta	.593	St. Louis*	.648	Los Angeles	.574	Houston (C)†	.568	4-3
2005	Atlanta	.556	St. Louis†	.617	San Diego	.506	Houston (C)*	.549	4-2
2006	New York†	.599	St. Louis*	.516	San Diego	.543	Los Angeles (W)	.543	4-3
2007	Philadelphia	.549	Chicago	.525	Arizona†	.556	Colorado (W)*	.552	4-0
2008	Philadelphia*	.568	Chicago	.602	Los Angeles†	.519	Milwaukee (C)	.556	4-1
2009	Philadelphia*	.574	St. Louis	.562	Los Angeles†	.586	Colorado (W)	.568	4-1
2010	Philadelphia†	.599	Cincinnati	.562	San Francisco*	.568	Atlanta (E)	.562	4-2
2011	Philadelphia	.630	Milwaukee†	.593	Arizona	.580	St. Louis (C)*	.556	4-2

THE WORLD SERIES YEAR-BY-YEAR

Year	Winner	Loser	Result
1903	Boston (AL)	Pittsburgh (NL)	5-3
1904	NO SERIES		
1905	New York (NL)	Philadelphia (AL)	4-1
1906	Chicago (AL)	Chicago (NL)	4-2
1907	Chicago (NL)	Detroit (AL)	4-0
1908	Chicago (NL)	Detroit (AL)	4-1
1909	Pittsburgh (NL)	Detroit (AL)	4-3
1910	Philadelphia (AL)	Chicago (NL)	4-1
1911	Philadelphia (AL)	New York (NL)	4-2
1912	Boston (AL)	New York (NL)	4-3-1
1913	Philadelphia (AL)	New York (NL)	4-1
1914	Boston (NL)	Philadelphia (AL)	4-0
1915	Boston (AL)	Philadelphia (NL)	4-1
1916	Boston (AL)	Brooklyn (NL)	4-1
1917	Chicago (AL)	New York (NL)	4-2
1918	Boston (AL)	Chicago (NL)	4-2
1919	Cincinnati (NL)	Chicago (AL)	5-3
1920	Cleveland (AL)	Brooklyn (NL)	5-2
1921	New York (NL)	New York (AL)	5-3
1922	New York (NL)	New York (AL)	4-0
1923	New York (AL)	New York (NL)	4-2
1924	Washington (AL)	New York (NL)	4-3
1925	Pittsburgh (NL)	Washington (AL)	4-3
1926	St. Louis (NL)	New York (AL)	4-3
1927	New York (AL)	Pittsburgh (NL)	4-0
1928	New York (AL)	St. Louis (NL)	4-0
1929	Philadelphia (AL)	Chicago (NL)	4-1
1930	Philadelphia (AL)	St. Louis (NL)	4-2
1931	St. Louis (NL)	Philadelphia (AL)	4-3
1932	New York (AL)	Chicago (NL)	4-0
1933	New York (NL)	Washington (AL)	4-1
1934	St. Louis (NL)	Detroit (AL)	4-3
1935	Detroit (AL)	Chicago (NL)	4-2
1936	New York (AL)	New York (NL)	4-2
1937	New York (AL)	New York (NL)	4-1
1938	New York (AL)	Chicago (NL)	4-0
1939	New York (AL)	Cincinnati (NL)	4-0
1940	Cincinnati (NL)	Detroit (AL)	4-3
1941	New York (AL)	Brooklyn (NL)	4-1
1942	St. Louis (NL)	New York (AL)	4-1
1943	New York (AL)	St. Louis (NL)	4-1
1944	St. Louis (NL)	St. Louis (AL)	4-2
1945	Detroit (AL)	Chicago (NL)	4-3
1946	St. Louis (NL)	Boston (AL)	4-3
1947	New York (AL)	Brooklyn (NL)	4-3
1948	Cleveland (AL)	Boston (NL)	4-2
1949	New York (AL)	Brooklyn (NL)	4-1
1950	New York (AL)	Philadelphia (NL)	4-0
1951	New York (AL)	New York (NL)	4-2
1952	New York (AL)	Brooklyn (NL)	4-3
1953	New York (AL)	Brooklyn (NL)	4-2
1954	New York (NL)	Cleveland (AL)	4-0
1955	Brooklyn (NL)	New York (AL)	4-3
1956	New York (AL)	Brooklyn (NL)	4-3
1957	Milwaukee (NL)	New York (AL)	4-3
1958	New York (AL)	Milwaukee (NL)	4-3
1959	Los Angeles (NL)	Chicago (AL)	4-2
1960	Pittsburgh (NL)	New York (AL)	4-3
1961	New York (AL)	Cincinnati (NL)	4-1
1962	New York (AL)	San Francisco (NL)	4-3
1963	Los Angeles (NL)	New York (AL)	4-0
1964	St. Louis (NL)	New York (AL)	4-3

MORRIS FOSTOFF

Cardinals manager Tony La Russa won his third World Series, his second with St. Louis

Year	Winner	Loser	Result
1965	Los Angeles (NL)	Minnesota (AL)	4-3
1966	Baltimore (AL)	Los Angeles (NL)	4-0
1967	St. Louis (NL)	Boston (AL)	4-3
1968	Detroit (AL)	St. Louis (NL)	4-3
1969	New York (NL)	Baltimore (AL)	4-1
1970	Baltimore (AL)	Cincinnati (NL)	4-1
1971	Pittsburgh (NL)	Baltimore (AL)	4-3
1972	Oakland (AL)	Cincinnati (NL)	4-3
1973	Oakland (AL)	New York (NL)	4-3
1974	Oakland (AL)	Los Angeles (NL)	4-1
1975	Cincinnati (NL)	Boston (AL)	4-3
1976	Cincinnati (NL)	New York (AL)	4-0
1977	New York (AL)	Los Angeles (NL)	4-2
1978	New York (AL)	Los Angeles (NL)	4-2
1979	Pittsburgh (NL)	Baltimore (AL)	4-3
1980	Philadelphia (NL)	Kansas City (AL)	4-2
1981	Los Angeles (NL)	New York (AL)	4-2
1982	St. Louis (NL)	Milwaukee (AL)	4-3
1983	Baltimore (AL)	Philadelphia (NL)	4-1
1984	Detroit (AL)	San Diego (NL)	4-1
1985	Kansas City (AL)	St. Louis (NL)	4-3
1986	New York (NL)	Boston (AL)	4-3
1987	Minnesota (AL)	St. Louis (NL)	4-3
1988	Los Angeles (NL)	Oakland (AL)	4-1
1989	Oakland (AL)	San Francisco (NL)	4-0
1990	Cincinnati (NL)	Oakland (AL)	4-0
1991	Minnesota (AL)	Atlanta (NL)	4-3
1992	Toronto (AL)	Atlanta (NL)	4-2
1993	Toronto (AL)	Philadelphia (NL)	4-2
1994	NO SERIES		
1995	Atlanta (NL)	Cleveland (AL)	4-2
1996	New York (AL)	Atlanta (NL)	4-2
1997	Florida (NL)	Cleveland (AL)	4-3
1998	New York (AL)	San Diego (NL)	4-0
1999	New York (AL)	Atlanta (NL)	4-0
2000	New York (AL)	New York (NL)	4-1
2001	Arizona (NL)	New York (AL)	4-3
2002	Anaheim (AL)	San Francisco (NL)	4-3
2003	Florida (NL)	New York (AL)	4-2
2004	Boston (AL)	St. Louis (NL)	4-0
2005	Chicago (AL)	Houston (NL)	4-0
2006	St. Louis (NL)	Detroit (AL)	4-1
2007	Boston (AL)	Colorado (NL)	4-0
2008	Philadelphia (NL)	Tampa Bay (AL)	4-1
2009	New York (AL)	Philadelphia (NL)	4-2
2010	San Francisco (NL)	Texas (AL)	4-1
2011	St. Louis (NL)	Texas (AL)	4-3

WORLD SERIES BOX SCORES

GAME ONE *October 19*
ST. LOUIS 3, TEXAS 2

TEXAS	AB	R	H	BI	BB	SO	ST. LOUIS	AB	R	H	BI	BB	SO
Kinsler, 2b	4	0	2	0	0	0	Furcal, ss	2	0	0	0	2	1
Andrus, ss	3	0	0	0	0	2	Jay, cf	3	0	0	0	0	0
Hamilton, cf-lf	4	0	0	0	1	1	Pujols, 1b	2	1	0	0	1	0
Young, M, 1b	4	0	0	0	0	0	Holliday, lf	4	1	1	0	0	0
Beltre, A, 3b	4	1	2	0	0	0	Berkman, rf	4	0	2	2	0	0
Cruz, N, rf	3	0	1	0	1	1	Motte, p	0	0	0	0	0	0
Napoli, c	2	1	1	2	1	0	Freese, 3b	2	1	1	0	1	0
Murphy, Dv, lf	2	0	0	0	0	1	Descalso, 3b	0	0	0	0	0	0
a-Gentry, ph-cf	1	0	0	0	0	1	Molina, Y, c	4	0	0	0	0	1
Wilson, C, p	2	0	0	0	0	0	Punto, 2b	2	0	1	0	2	1
Ogando, p	0	0	0	0	0	0	Carpenter, p	2	0	0	0	0	2
b-German, ph	1	0	0	0	0	1	1-Craig, ph	1	0	1	1	0	0
Gonzalez, M, p	0	0	0	0	0	0	Salas, p	0	0	0	0	0	0
Feldman, p	0	0	0	0	0	0	Rzepczynski, p	0	0	0	0	0	0
							Dotel, p	0	0	0	0	0	0
							Rhodes, p	0	0	0	0	0	0
							Schumaker, rf	0	0	0	0	0	0
TOTAL	30	2	6	2	2	7		26	3	6	3	6	5

Texas	000	020	000—2
St. Louis	000	201	00x—3

a-Struck out for Murphy, Dv in the 7th. b-Struck out for Ogando in the 7th. 1-Singled for Carpenter in the 6th.

LOB—Cardinals 8, Rangers 4. 2B—Beltre (1), Holliday (1), Freese (1). HR—Napoli (1). SH—Andrus, Jay, Descalso.

TEXAS	IP	H	R	ER	BB	SO	ST. LOUIS	IP	H	R	ER	BB	SO
Wilson, C (L)	5.2	4	3	3	6	4	Carpenter (W)	6	5	2	2	1	4
Ogando	0.1	1	0	0	0	1	Salas	0.1	1	0	0	1	0
Gonzalez, M	0.1	0	0	0	0	0	Rzepczynski	0.2	0	0	0	0	2
Feldman	1.2	1	0	0	0	1	Dotel	0.2	0	0	0	0	1
							Rhodes	0.1	0	0	0	0	0
							Motte (S)	1	0	0	0	0	0

WP—Wilson. IBB—Punto (by Wilson), Pujols (by Wilson). HBP—Pujols (by Wilson).

T—3:06. A—46,406.

GAME TWO *October 20*
TEXAS 2, ST. LOUIS 1

TEXAS	AB	R	H	BI	BB	SO	ST. LOUIS	AB	R	H	BI	BB	SO
Kinsler, 2b	3	1	2	0	1	0	Furcal, ss	5	0	1	0	0	0
Andrus, ss	4	1	1	0	0	0	Jay, cf	4	0	0	0	0	0
Hamilton, lf	3	0	0	1	0	1	Pujols, 1b	4	0	0	0	0	0
Young, M, 1b	3	0	1	1	0	1	Berkman, rf	4	0	1	0	0	2
Beltre, A, 3b	4	0	1	0	0	2	Motte, p	0	0	0	0	0	0
Cruz, N, rf	3	0	0	0	0	1	Rhodes, p	0	0	0	0	0	0
Napoli, c	3	0	0	0	0	1	Lynn, p	0	0	0	0	0	0
Gentry, cf	2	0	0	0	0	1	Holliday, lf	2	0	0	0	2	1
a-Murphy, Dv, ph	0	0	0	0	0	0	Freese, 3b	3	1	1	0	0	0
b-Torrealba, ph	1	0	0	0	0	1	Descalso, 3b	1	0	0	0	0	0
Chavez, En, cf	0	0	0	0	0	0	Molina, Y, c	3	0	0	0	1	1
Lewis, C, p	2	0	0	0	0	1	Punto, 2b	4	0	2	0	0	1
Ogando, p	0	0	0	0	0	0	Garcia, J, p	1	0	0	0	1	0
c-German, ph	1	0	0	0	0	0	1-Craig, ph	1	0	1	1	0	0
Adams, M, p	0	0	0	0	0	0	Salas, p	0	0	0	0	0	0
Feliz, p	0	0	0	0	0	0	Rzepczynski, p	0	0	0	0	0	0
							Schumaker, rf	1	0	0	0	0	1
TOTAL	29	2	5	2	1	9		33	1	6	1	4	6

Texas	000	000	002—2
St. Louis	000	000	100—1

a-Batted for Gentry in the 8th. b-Struck out for Murphy, Dv in the 8th. c-Grounded out for Ogando in the 8th. 1-Singled for Garcia, J in the 7th. 2-Ran for Molina, Y in the 9th.

LOB— Cardinals 9, Texas 3. 2B—Furcal (1). SF—Hamilton, Young.

SB—Kinsler. E—Kinsler, Pujols.

TEXAS	IP	H	R	ER	BB	SO	ST. LOUIS	IP	H	R	ER	BB	SO
Lewis, C	6.2	4	1	1	2	4	Garcia, J	7	3	0	0	1	7
Ogando	0.1	1	0	0	0	0	Salas	0.1	0	0	0	0	1
Adams, M (W)	1	1	0	0	1	0	Rzepczynski	0.2	0	0	0	0	1
Feliz (S)	1	0	0	0	1	2	Motte (L)	0	2	2	1	0	0
							Rhodes	0.1	0	0	0	0	0
							Lynn	0.2	0	0	0	0	0

Motte pitched to 2 batters in the 9th.

T—3:04. A—47,288.

GAME THREE *October 22*
ST. LOUIS 16, TEXAS 7

ST. LOUIS	AB	R	H	BI	BB	SO	TEXAS	AB	R	H	BI	BB	SO
Furcal, ss	6	1	1	0	0	1	Kinsler, 2b	4	0	0	0	1	1
Craig, rf	5	2	1	1	1	2	Andrus, ss	5	1	2	0	0	2
Pujols, 1b	6	4	5	6	0	0	Hamilton, cf	5	1	1	0	0	0
Holliday, lf	5	3	1	0	1	1	Gentry, cf	0	0	0	0	0	0
Berkman, dh	4	2	2	0	1	1	Young, M, dh	5	2	2	2	0	1
Freese, 3b	4	1	2	2	1	1	Beltre, A, 3b	5	2	4	1	0	0
1-Descalso, pr-3b	0	1	0	0	0	0	Cruz, N, rf	4	1	1	2	1	2
Molina, Y, c	3	1	2	4	1	0	Napoli, 1b	2	0	1	2	0	0
Jay, cf	5	0	0	0	0	1	Murphy, Dv, lf	3	0	0	0	1	0
Theriot, 2b	4	1	1	1	1	0	Torrealba, c	3	0	2	0	1	1
TOTAL	42	16	15	14	6	7		36	7	13	7	4	7

St. Louis	100	434	211—16
Texas	000	330	10x—7

1-Ran for Freese in the 8th.

LOB— Rangers 8, Cardinals 6. 2B—Freese (2), Molina 2 (2), Young (1), Beltre (2). 3B—Pujols 3 (3), Young (1), Cruz (1). SF—Molina, Napoli 2. E—Kinsler, Napoli, Andrus. A—Holliday.

ST. LOUIS	IP	H	R	ER	BB	SO	TEXAS	IP	H	R	ER	BB	SO
Lohse	3	5	3	3	2	3	Harrison (L)	3.2	6	5	3	1	3
Salas	1	4	3	3	0	0	Feldman	1.1	2	3	3	2	0
Lynn (W)	2.1	3	1	1	2	2	Ogando	0.1	3	4	3	2	1
Dotel	1.2	1	0	0	0	1	Gonzalez, M	1.2	1	2	2	1	0
Boggs	1	0	0	0	0	1	Lowe, M	1	2	1	1	0	1
							Oliver	1	1	1	1	0	2

Lohse pitched to 4 batters in the 4th. Salas pitched to 3 batters in the 5th.

IBB—Molina (by Harrison).

T—4:04. A—51,462.

GAME FOUR *October 23*
TEXAS 4, ST. LOUIS 0

ST. LOUIS	AB	R	H	BI	BB	SO	TEXAS	AB	R	H	BI	BB	SO
Furcal, ss	3	0	0	0	1	0	Kinsler, 2b	3	0	1	0	1	1
Craig, rf	3	0	0	0	1	2	Andrus, ss	4	1	2	0	0	0
Pujols, 1b	4	0	0	0	0	0	Hamilton, cf-lf	4	0	1	1	0	1
Holliday, lf	4	0	0	0	0	2	Young, M, dh	3	0	0	0	1	1
Berkman, dh	3	0	2	0	0	1	Beltre, A, 3b	4	0	0	0	0	2
Freese, 3b	3	0	0	0	0	1	Cruz, N, rf	2	1	1	0	2	0
Molina, Y, c	3	0	0	0	0	1	Murphy, Dv, lf	2	1	0	0	2	0
Jay, cf	2	0	0	0	0	0	Gentry, cf	0	0	0	0	0	0
a-Theriot	1	0	0	0	0	1	Napoli, c	2	1	1	3	2	0
Schumaker, cf	0	0	0	0	0	0	Moreland, 1b	4	0	0	0	0	1
Punto, 2b	2	0	0	0	1	0							
TOTAL	28	0	2	0	3	8		28	4	6	4	8	6

St. Louis	000	000	000—0
Texas	100	003	00x—4

a-Struck out for Jay in the 8th.

LOB—Rangers 8, Cardinals 4. 2B—Berkman (1), Hamilton (1), Andrus (1). HR—Napoli (2). PO—Kinsler.

ST. LOUIS	IP	H	R	ER	BB	SO	TEXAS	IP	H	R	ER	BB	SO
Jackson, E (L)	5.1	3	3	3	7	3	Holland, D (W)	8.1	2	0	0	2	7
Boggs	1.2	2	1	1	0	3	Feliz	0.2	0	0	0	1	1
Westbrook	1	1	0	0	1	0							

T—3:07. A—51,539.

GAME FIVE October 24
TEXAS 4, ST. LOUIS 2

ST. LOUIS	AB	R	H	BI	BB	SO	TEXAS	AB	R	H	BI	BB	SO
Furcal, ss	4	0	1	0	0	1	Kinsler, 2b	3	0	0	0	2	0
Craig, rf	2	0	0	0	1	1	Andrus, ss	5	0	1	0	0	2
Pujols, 1b	2	0	0	0	3	1	Hamilton, cf-lf	3	0	1	0	1	0
Holliday, lf	3	1	1	0	2	0	Young, M, dh	4	1	1	0	0	1
Berkman, dh	3	1	0	0	2	3	Beltre, A, 3b	4	1	1	1	0	1
Freese, 3b	4	0	1	0	0	0	Cruz, N, rf	3	1	1	0	1	1
Molina, c	4	0	3	1	0	0	Murphy, Dv, lf	4	0	2	0	0	0
Schumaker, cf	3	0	1	1	0	0	1-Gentry, pr-cf	0	0	0	0	0	0
a-Theriot, ph	0	0	0	0	0	0	Napoli, c	4	0	1	2	0	1
Jay, cf	0	0	0	0	0	0	Moreland, 1b	4	1	1	1	0	1
Punto, 2b	3	0	0	1	2								
TOTAL	**28**	**2**	**7**	**2**	**9**	**8**		**34**	**4**	**9**	**4**	**4**	**7**

St. Louis	020 000 000—2	
Texas	001 001 02x—4	

a-Hit a sacrifice bunt for Schumaker in the 8th. 1-Ran for Murphy, Dv in the 8th.

LOB—Cardinals 12, Rangers 10. 2B—Young (2), Napoli (1). HR—Moreland (1), Beltre (1). E—Carpenter, Murhpy, Wilson.

ST. LOUIS	IP	H	R	ER	BB	SO	TEXAS	IP	H	R	ER	BB	SO
Carpenter	7	6	2	2	2	4	Wilson, C	5.1	4	2	1	5	3
Dotel (L)	0.1	1	2	2	1	1	Feldman	0.2	1	0	0	0	1
Rzepczynski	0.1	2	0	0	0	1	Ogando	1	2	0	0	3	1
Lynn	0	0	0	0	1	0	Oliver (W)	1	0	0	0	0	1
Motte	0.1	0	0	0	0	1	Feliz (S)	1	0	0	0	1	2

Lynn pitched to 1 batter in the 8th. Ogando pitched to 1 batter in the 8th.

WP—Wilson. IBB—Cruz (by Dotel), Kinsler (by Lynn), Pujols (by Wilson), Pujols (by Ogando), Berkman (by Ogando). HPB—Craig (by Feliz).

T—3:31. A—51,459.

GAME SIX October 27
ST. LOUIS 10, TEXAS 9 (11 INNINGS)

TEXAS	AB	R	H	BI	BB	SO	ST. LOUIS	AB	R	H	BI	BB	SO
Kinsler, 2b	5	1	2	2	1	1	Furcal, ss	5	0	0	0	0	0
Andrus, ss	6	1	2	0	0	1	Motte, p	0	0	0	0	0	0
Hamilton, lf-cf	6	2	3	3	0	1	4-Jackson, E, p	0	0	0	0	0	0
Young, M, 1b	4	0	2	1	0	1	5-Lohse, ph	0	0	0	0	0	0
Moreland, 1b	2	0	0	0	0	0	Westbrook, p	0	0	0	0	0	0
Beltre, A, 3b	6	1	1	1	0	1	Schumaker, cf	3	1	1	0	0	0
Cruz, N, rf	6	2	1	1	0	0	Lynn, p	0	0	0	0	0	0
Lowe, M, p	0	0	0	0	0	0	Theriot, 2b	3	0	0	1	0	1
Napoli, c	3	0	2	1	3	1	Pujols, 1b	5	1	1	0	1	1
Gentry, cf	0	1	0	0	1	0	Berkman, rf	5	4	3	3	1	0
a-Murphy, Dv, ph-lf-rh	3	0	1	0	1	0	Holliday, lf	1	0	0	0	2	0
Lewis, C, p	3	0	0	0	0	0	Craig, lf	3	1	1	1	0	1
Ogando, p	0	0	0	0	0	0	Freese, 3b	5	1	2	3	1	1
Holland, D, p	1	1	0	0	0	0	Molina, Y, c	4	0	1	2	1	0
Adams, M, p	0	0	0	0	0	0	Punto, 2b	2	0	0	0	1	2
b-Chavez, En, ph	1	0	0	0	0	0	Dotel, p	0	0	0	0	0	0
Feliz, p	0	0	0	0	0	0	Rzepczynski, p	0	0	0	0	0	0
Oliver, p	0	0	0	0	0	0	2-Laird, ph	0	0	0	0	0	0
Feldman, p	0	0	0	0	0	0	3-Descalso, ph-ss	2	1	2	0	0	0
c-German, ph-lf	1	0	0	0	0	0	Garcia, J, p	1	0	0	0	0	0
							Salas, p	0	0	0	0	0	0
							1-Jay, ph-cf	4	1	2	0	0	0
TOTAL	**49**	**9**	**15**	**9**	**5**	**8**		**43**	**10**	**13**	**10**	**7**	**6**

Texas	110 110 300 20—9	
St. Louis	200 101 012 21—10	

a-Walked for Gentry in the 5th. b-Flied out for Adams, M in the 9th. c-Grounded out for Feldman in the 11th. 1-Grounded out for Salas in the 5th. 2-Batted for Rzepczynski in the 8th. 3-Singled for Laird in the 8th. 4-Batted for Motte in the 10th. 5-Hit a sacrifice bunt for Jackson, E in the 10th.

LOB—Rangers 12, Cardinals 11. 2B—Kinsler (1), Young (3), Pujols (1). 3B—Freese (1). HR—Beltre (2), Cruz (2), Hamilton (1), Berkman (1), Craig (2), Freese (1). SH—Lohse. PO—Holliday. E—Young 2, Holliday, Salas, Freese.

TEXAS	IP	H	R	ER	BB	SO	ST. LOUIS	IP	H	R	ER	BB	SO
Lewis, C	5.1	3	4	2	3	4	Garcia, J	3	5	2	2	2	3
Ogando	0.1	0	0	0	2	0	Salas	2	2	2	0	2	3
Holland, D	2	2	1	1	0	0	Lynn	1.2	4	3	3	0	1
Adams, M	0.1	2	0	0	0	0	Dotel	0.1	1	0	0	0	1
Feliz	1	2	2	2	1	2	Rzepczynski	1	0	0	0	0	0
Oliver	0.1	2	2	2	1	0	Motte	2	2	2	1	1	0
Feldman	0.2	1	0	0	1	0	Westbrook (W)	1	1	0	0	0	0
Lowe, M (L)	0	1	1	1	0	0							

Lowe, M pitched to 1 batter in the 11th.

WP—Ogando, Dotel. IBB—Pujols (by Feldman), Napoli (by Salas).

T—4:33. A—47,325.

GAME SEVEN October 28
ST. LOUIS 6, TEXAS 2

TEXAS	AB	R	H	BI	BB	SO	ST. LOUIS	AB	R	H	BI	BB	SO
Kinsler, 2b	3	0	2	0	1	1	Theriot, 2b	5	0	0	0	0	1
Andrus, ss	2	1	0	0	1	0	Motte, p	0	0	0	0	0	0
Hamilton, cf	4	1	1	0	0	0	Craig, lf	4	2	1	1	1	2
Young, M, 1b	4	0	1	1	0	2	Pujols, 1b	2	2	0	0	1	1
Beltre, A, 3b	3	0	0	0	0	2	Berkman, rf	3	2	1	0	1	0
Cruz, N, rf	4	0	0	0	0	0	Jay, cf	0	0	0	0	0	0
Napoli, c	4	0	1	0	0	1	Freese, 3b	2	0	1	2	2	0
Murphy, Dv, lf	4	0	1	0	0	0	Descalso, 3b	0	0	0	0	0	0
Harrison, p	1	0	0	0	0	1	Molina, Y, c	3	0	2	2	1	0
Feldman, p	0	0	0	0	0	0	Furcal, ss	3	0	2	1	0	0
Wilson, C, p	0	0	0	0	0	0	Schumaker, cf-rf	4	0	0	0	0	2
a-Chavez, En, ph	0	0	0	0	0	0	Carpenter, p	3	0	0	0	0	1
b-Torrealba, ph	1	0	0	0	0	0	Rhodes, p	0	0	0	0	0	0
Adams, M, p	0	0	0	0	0	0	Dotel, p	0	0	0	0	0	0
Gonzalez, M, p	0	0	0	0	0	0	Lynn, p	0	0	0	0	0	0
Ogando, p	0	0	0	0	0	0	1-Punto, ph-2b	1	0	0	0	0	0
TOTAL	**30**	**2**	**6**	**2**	**2**	**7**		**30**	**6**	**7**	**6**	**6**	**7**

Texas	200 000 000—2	
St. Louis	201 020 10x—6	

a-Batted for Wilson, C in the 7th. b-Flied out for Chavez, En in the 7th. 1-Flied out for Lynn in the 8th.

LOB—Cardinals 8, Rangers 6. 2B—Hamilton (2), Young (4), Murphy (1), Freese (3). HR—Craig (3). SH—Harrison, Andrus. PO—Kinsler. E—Pujols.

TEXAS	IP	H	R	ER	BB	SO	ST. LOUIS	IP	H	R	ER	BB	SO
Harrison (L)	4	5	3	3	2	1	Carpenter (W)	6	6	2	2	2	5
Feldman	0.2	0	2	2	3	0	Rhodes	0.1	0	0	0	0	0
Wilson, C	1.1	0	0	0	2	2	Dotel	0.2	0	0	0	0	1
Adams, M	0.2	2	1	1	1	1	Lynn	1	0	0	0	0	1
Gonzalez, M	1	0	0	0	2	0	Motte	1	0	0	0	0	0
Ogando	0.1	0	0	0	0	1							

Carpenter pitched to 1 batter in the 7th.

IBB—Freese (by Feldman). HBP—Pujols (by Feldman), Furcal (by Wilson), Beltre (Carpenter).

T—3:17. A—47,399.

AMERICAN LEAGUE DIVISION SERIES
NEW YORK YANKEES VS· DETROIT TIGERS

DETROIT

PLAYER, POS	AVG	G	AB	R	H	2B	3B	HR	RBI	BB	SO	SB
Alex Avila, c	.063	5	16	0	1	0	0	0	1	2	7	0
Wilson Betemit, 3b	.000	3	8	0	0	0	0	0	0	0	4	0
Miguel Cabrera, 1b	.200	5	15	2	3	0	0	1	3	5	5	1
Brandon Inge, 3b	.429	4	7	3	3	1	0	0	0	0	0	0
Austin Jackson, cf	.125	5	16	3	2	1	0	0	0	4	8	1
Don Kelly, rf	.364	4	11	3	4	0	0	1	2	0	4	0
Victor Martinez, dh	.222	5	18	1	4	0	0	1	3	2	5	0
Magglio Ordonez, rf	.455	4	11	1	5	1	0	0	0	1	2	0
Jhonny Peralta, ss	.222	5	18	0	4	2	0	0	1	1	4	0
Ryan Raburn, lf	.400	3	5	0	2	0	0	0	1	0	3	0
Ramon Santiago, 2b	.143	4	14	0	2	1	0	0	2	0	3	0
Omir Santos, c	—	1	0	0	0	0	0	0	0	0	0	0
Delmon Young, lf	.316	5	19	4	6	0	0	3	3	2	2	0
Totals	**.228**	**5**	**158**	**17**	**36**	**6**	**0**	**6**	**16**	**17**	**47**	**2**

PITCHER	W	L	ERA	G	GS	SV	IP	H	R	ER	BB	SO
Al Alburquerque	0	0	81.00	2	0	0	0.1	2	3	3	1	0
Joaquin Benoit	0	0	2.45	2	0	0	3.2	4	1	1	1	6
Phil Coke	0	0	27.00	1	0	0	1.0	3	3	3	1	1
Doug Fister	1	1	6.52	2	1	0	9.2	12	7	7	4	10
Ryan Perry	0	0	0.00	2	0	0	2.1	3	0	0	0	2
Rick Porcello	0	1	6.00	1	1	0	6.0	5	4	4	1	5
Max Scherzer	1	0	1.23	2	1	0	7.1	4	1	1	4	7
Daniel Schlereth	0	0	10.80	2	0	0	1.2	4	2	2	0	4
Jose Valverde	0	0	6.00	3	0	2	3.0	2	2	2	4	3
Justin Verlander	1	0	5.00	2	2	0	9.0	6	5	5	5	12
Totals	**3**	**2**	**5.73**	**5**	**5**	**2**	**44**	**45**	**28**	**28**	**21**	**50**

NEW YORK

PLAYER, POS	AVG	G	AB	R	H	2B	3B	HR	RBI	BB	SO	SB
Robinson Cano, 2b	.318	5	22	2	7	2	0	2	9	2	4	0
Eric Chavez, ph	.000	1	1	0	0	0	0	0	0	0	1	0
Chris Dickerson, rf	.000	1	1	1	0	0	0	0	0	0	0	0
Brett Gardner, lf	.412	5	17	3	7	1	0	0	5	1	4	0
Curtis Granderson, cf	.250	5	24	4	5	1	1	1	3	4	7	0
Derek Jeter, ss	.250	5	24	6	6	1	0	0	2	1	8	1
Andruw Jones, lf	—	1	0	0	0	0	0	0	1	0	0	0
Russell Martin, c	.176	5	17	3	3	1	0	0	0	2	4	0
Jesus Montero, ph	1.000	1	2	1	2	0	0	0	1	0	0	0
Eduardo Nunez, dh	—	1	0	0	0	0	0	0	0	0	0	1
Jorge Posada, dh	.429	5	14	4	6	0	1	0	0	4	6	0
Alex Rodriguez, 3b	.111	5	18	1	2	0	0	0	3	4	6	0
Nick Swisher, rf	.211	5	19	1	4	0	0	1	1	1	5	0
Mark Teixeira, 1b	.167	5	18	2	3	2	0	0	1	2	5	0
Totals	**.260**	**5**	**173**	**28**	**45**	**8**	**2**	**4**	**26**	**21**	**50**	**2**

PITCHER	W	L	ERA	G	GS	SV	IP	H	R	ER	BB	SO
Luis Ayala	0	0	6.75	2	0	0	1.1	3	1	1	0	0
A.J. Burnett	1	0	1.59	1	1	0	5.2	4	1	1	4	3
Freddy Garcia	0	1	5.06	1	1	0	5.1	6	4	3	0	6
Phil Hughes	0	0	0.00	2	0	0	2.1	2	0	0	4	4
Boone Logan	0	0	0.00	3	0	0	2.1	1	0	0	0	6
Ivan Nova	1	1	4.32	2	1	0	8.1	7	4	4	4	8
Mariano Rivera	0	0	0.00	2	0	0	1.1	0	0	0	0	1
David Robertson	0	0	0.00	2	0	0	2.0	0	0	0	2	0
CC Sabathia	0	0	6.23	3	2	0	8.2	10	6	6	8	11
Rafael Soriano	0	1	1.93	3	0	0	4.2	1	1	1	0	4
Cory Wade	0	0	0.00	1	0	0	2.0	2	0	0	1	2
Totals	**2**	**3**	**3.27**	**5**	**5**	**0**	**44**	**36**	**17**	**16**	**17**	**47**

E—Jeter. **DP**—Detroit 6, New York 3. **LOB**—New York 40, Detroit 32. **SB**—Cabrera, Jackson, Jeter, Nunez. **SH**—Avila, Jackson, Santiago. **SF**—Jones, Rodriguez. **HBP**—Inge (by Ayala), Peralta (by Robertson), Martin 2 (by Scherzer, Verlander), Posada (by Porcello), Teixeira (by Porcello). **IBB**—Cabrera 3 (by Burnett 2 by Sabathia), Cano (by Porcello). **WP**—Schlereth, Verlander, Burnett, Sabathia.

SCORE BY INNINGS

Detroit	502 123 103	—17
New York	302 046 382	—28

Matt Moore pitched seven shutout innings in a surprise ALDS start against Texas

CLIFF WELCH

TEXAS RANGERS VS· TAMPA BAY RAYS

TAMPA BAY RAYS

PLAYER, POS	AVG	G	AB	R	H	2B	3B	HR	RBI	BB	SO	SB
Reid Brignac, ss	.000	3	1	0	0	0	0	0	0	1	0	0
Johnny Damon, dh	.235	4	17	3	4	0	0	1	3	0	4	0
Sam Fuld, rf	.000	3	3	0	0	0	0	0	0	0	1	0
John Jaso, c	.000	2	4	0	0	0	0	0	0	0	1	0
Desmond Jennings, lf	.333	4	15	3	5	1	0	2	2	3	1	0
Elliot Johnson, pr	—	1	0	0	0	0	0	0	0	0	0	0
Matt Joyce, rf	.200	4	15	1	3	1	0	1	4	1	5	0
Casey Kotchman, 1b	.250	4	16	1	4	1	0	0	2	0	1	0
Evan Longoria, 3b	.188	4	16	2	3	0	0	1	3	2	8	0
Sean Rodriguez, ss	.167	4	12	3	2	1	0	0	1	2	0	0
Kelly Shoppach, c	.400	4	10	3	4	0	0	2	6	1	4	0
B.J. Upton, cf	.286	4	14	3	4	3	0	0	0	4	6	1
Ben Zobrist, 2b	.235	4	17	2	4	0	0	0	0	4	4	0
Totals	**.236**	**4**	**140**	**21**	**33**	**7**	**0**	**7**	**21**	**14**	**35**	**1**

PITCHER	W	L	ERA	G	GS	SV	IP	H	R	ER	BB	SO
Juan Cruz	0	0	0.00	2	0	0	2.0	1	0	0	2	2
Wade Davis	0	0	0.00	2	0	0	2.1	1	0	0	1	1
Brandon Gomes	0	0	7.71	3	0	0	2.1	1	2	2	2	3
Jeremy Hellickson	0	1	6.75	1	1	0	4.0	4	3	3	1	1
J.P. Howell	0	0	—	1	0	0	0.0	1	0	0	0	0
Jake McGee	0	0	0.00	1	0	0	0.1	0	0	0	0	0
Matt Moore	1	0	0.90	2	1	0	10.0	3	1	1	3	8
Joel Peralta	0	0	0.00	3	0	0	2.1	1	0	0	2	0
David Price	0	1	4.05	1	1	0	6.2	7	3	3	1	3
James Shields	0	1	12.60	1	1	0	5.0	8	7	7	0	6
Totals	**1**	**3**	**4.11**	**4**	**4**	**0**	**35**	**27**	**16**	**16**	**12**	**24**

TEXAS RANGERS

PLAYER, POS	AVG	G	AB	R	H	2B	3B	HR	RBI	BB	SO	SB
Elvis Andrus, ss	.143	4	14	1	2	0	0	0	0	3	3	0
Adrian Beltre, 3b	.267	4	15	5	4	0	0	3	4	0	1	0
Nelson Cruz, rf	.067	4	15	1	1	0	0	0	0	0	5	0
Craig Gentry, cf	.400	4	5	1	2	0	0	0	0	1	1	2
Josh Hamilton, cf	.267	4	15	1	4	1	0	0	2	1	0	0
Ian Kinsler, 2b	.250	4	16	2	4	2	0	1	3	3	3	1
Mitch Moreland, 1b	.100	3	10	1	1	0	0	1	2	1	1	0
David Murphy, lf	.333	3	6	0	2	0	0	0	1	3	0	0
Mike Napoli, c	.357	4	14	3	5	0	0	1	4	1	5	1
Yorvit Torrealba, dh	.000	1	3	0	0	0	0	0	0	0	0	0
Michael Young, dh	.133	4	15	1	2	0	0	0	0	1	2	0
Totals	**.211**	**4**	**128**	**16**	**27**	**3**	**0**	**6**	**15**	**12**	**24**	**4**

PITCHER	W	L	ERA	G	GS	SV	IP	H	R	ER	BB	SO
Mike Adams	0	0	4.50	3	0	0	2.0	1	1	1	3	1
Scott Feldman	0	0	0.00	1	0	0	3.0	2	0	0	0	4
Neftali Feliz	0	0	2.70	3	0	3	3.1	2	1	1	2	2
Michael Gonzalez	0	0	0.00	2	0	0	0.2	1	0	0	0	2
Matt Harrison	1	0	4.76	2	1	0	5.2	6	3	3	3	9
Derek Holland	1	0	1.42	2	1	0	6.1	7	3	1	2	2
Colby Lewis	1	0	1.50	1	1	0	6.0	1	1	1	2	6
Alexi Ogando	0	0	0.00	3	0	0	2.2	1	0	0	0	2
Darren Oliver	0	0	6.75	2	0	0	1.1	3	1	1	0	1
Koji Uehara	0	0	—	1	0	0	0.0	2	3	3	1	0
C.J. Wilson	0	1	10.80	1	1	0	5.0	7	8	6	1	6
Totals	**3**	**1**	**4.25**	**4**	**4**	**3**	**36.0**	**33**	**21**	**17**	**14**	**35**

E—Beltre, Holland. **DP**—Texas 2, Tampa Bay 1. **LOB**—Tampa Bay 26, Texas 24. **SB**—Upton, Gentry (2), Kinsler, Napoli. **CS**—Gentry, Andrus, Upton (2). **SH**—Gentry. **HPB**—Zobrist (by Wilson), Andrus (by Shields), Beltre (by Shields), Gentry (by Moore), Moreland (by McGee). **IBB**—Hamilton (by Cruz). **WP**—Moore, Price, Shields, Feliz, Harrison, Holland, Lewis.

SCORE BY INNINGS

TAMPA BAY	143	420	412—21
TEXAS	110	602	510—16

AMERICAN LEAGUE CHAMPIONSHIP SERIES
TEXAS RANGERS VS· DETROIT TIGERS

DETROIT TIGERS

PLAYER, POS	AVG	G	AB	R	H	2B	3B	HR	RBI	BB	SO	SB
Alex Avila, c	.080	6	25	1	2	0	0	1	1	0	9	0
Wilson Betemit, ph	.000	1	1	0	0	0	0	0	0	0	1	0
Miguel Cabrera, 1b	.400	6	20	5	8	4	0	3	7	7	6	1
Andy Dirks, rf	.200	2	5	1	1	0	0	0	0	0	1	1
Brandon Inge, 3b	.267	6	15	3	4	0	0	1	1	3	3	0
Austin Jackson, cf	.240	6	25	3	6	1	0	1	4	3	11	0
Don Kelly, rf	.222	5	9	0	2	1	0	0	0	0	0	0
Victor Martinez, dh	.273	6	22	3	6	0	1	1	2	3	1	0
Magglio Ordonez, rf	.000	1	2	0	0	0	0	0	0	1	1	0
Jhonny Peralta, ss	.217	6	23	2	5	1	0	2	2	1	4	0
Ryan Raburn, lf	.261	6	23	4	6	1	0	2	4	4	4	0
Ramon Santiago, 2b	.375	6	24	1	9	1	0	0	0	0	4	0
Danny Worth, pr	—	1	0	0	0	0	0	0	0	0	0	0
Delmon Young, lf	.133	4	15	2	2	0	0	2	3	0	5	0
Totals	**.244**	**6**	**209**	**25**	**51**	**9**	**1**	**13**	**24**	**22**	**50**	**2**

PITCHER	W	L	ERA	G	GS	SV	IP	H	R	ER	BB	SO
Al Alburquerque	0	0	0.00	2	0	0	1.2	0	0	0	2	2
Joaquin Benoit	0	0	0.00	3	0	0	4.0	0	0	0	2	3
Phil Coke	0	0	2.70	4	0	0	3.1	3	1	1	1	2
Doug Fister	1	0	2.45	1	1	0	7.1	7	2	2	0	3
Brad Penny	0	0	27.00	1	0	0	1.2	7	5	5	2	1
Ryan Perry	0	1	9.00	3	0	0	4.0	6	5	4	0	1
Rick Porcello	0	0	4.00	3	1	0	9.0	10	5	4	1	7
Max Scherzer	0	1	9.72	2	2	0	8.1	11	9	9	5	7
Daniel Schlereth	0	0	—	1	0	0	0.0	1	1	1	0	0
Jose Valverde	0	1	8.31	3	0	1	4.1	5	4	4	2	3
Justin Verlander	1	1	5.56	2	2	0	11.1	13	7	7	5	13
Totals	**2**	**4**	**6.05**	**6**	**6**	**2**	**55.0**	**63**	**39**	**37**	**20**	**42**

TEXAS RANGERS

PLAYER, POS	AVG	G	AB	R	H	2B	3B	HR	RBI	BB	SO	SB
Elvis Andrus, ss	.240	6	25	4	6	0	0	0	1	3	2	1
Adrian Beltre, 3b	.222	6	27	4	6	3	0	0	2	2	10	0
Endy Chavez, lf	.000	2	4	0	0	0	0	0	0	0	0	0
Nelson Cruz, rf	.364	6	22	7	8	2	0	6	13	2	4	0
Craig Gentry, cf	.400	3	5	0	2	0	0	0	1	0	0	0
Josh Hamilton, cf	.308	6	26	4	8	4	0	0	5	1	4	0
Ian Kinsler, 2b	.292	6	24	6	7	2	0	0	6	4	2	1
Mitch Moreland, 1b	.111	3	9	0	1	0	0	0	0	1	5	0
David Murphy, lf	.412	5	17	4	7	2	1	0	3	3	2	1
Mike Napoli, c	.292	6	24	6	7	0	0	0	1	3	4	0
Yorvit Torrealba, c	.444	3	9	1	4	1	0	0	0	0	3	0
Michael Young, 1b	.250	6	28	3	7	3	0	1	7	1	6	0
Totals	**.286**	**6**	**220**	**39**	**63**	**17**	**1**	**7**	**39**	**20**	**42**	**3**

PITCHER	W	L	ERA	G	GS	SV	IP	H	R	ER	BB	SO

ANDREW WOOLLEY

The Rangers' Nelson Cruz set a postseason series record with six ALCS home runs

	W	L	ERA	G	GS	SV	IP	H	R	ER	BB	SO
Mike Adams	1	0	2.08	5	0	0	4.1	5	1	1	1	4
Scott Feldman	1	0	0.00	3	0	0	5.2	1	0	0	0	5
Neftali Feliz	0	0	0.00	4	0	1	4.1	1	0	0	2	3
Michael Gonzalez	0	0	0.00	3	0	0	0.2	1	0	0	0	0
Matt Harrison	0	0	3.60	1	1	0	5.0	3	2	2	3	3
Derek Holland	0	0	8.59	2	2	0	7.1	11	7	7	4	5
Colby Lewis	0	1	6.35	1	1	0	5.2	8	4	4	2	6
Alexi Ogando	2	0	1.17	4	0	0	7.2	3	1	1	2	10
Darren Oliver	0	0	0.00	3	0	0	2.2	0	0	0	0	2
Yoshinori Tateyama	0	0	0.00	1	0	0	0.2	1	0	0	0	0
Koji Uehara	0	0	13.50	2	0	0	1.1	3	2	2	1	1
C.J. Wilson	0	1	6.75	2	2	0	10.2	14	8	8	7	11
Totals	**4**	**2**	**4.02**	**6**	**6**	**1**	**56.0**	**51**	**25**	**25**	**22**	**50**

E—Jackson, Porcello, Raburn, Santiago, Young, Andrus, Moreland. **DP**—Detroit 8, Texas 6. **LOB**—Detroit 42, Texas 41. **SB**—Cabrera, Dirks, Andrus, Kinsler, Murphy. **CS**—Jackson, Andrus, Cruz, Kinsler. **SH**—Inge, Peralta, Andrus. **H**—Hamilton (2). **H**—Jackson (by Feldman), Martinez (by Holland), Cruz (by Valverde), Kinsler (by Fister). **IBB**—Cabrera (2, by Adams, Feliz), Ordonez (by Wilson), Beltre (by Valverde), Hamilton (by Porcello), Murphy (by Penny), Napoli (by Valverde). **WP**—Alburquerque, Penny, Verlander, Wilson.

SCORE BY INNINGS

DETROIT	116	256	310	0—25
TEXAS	429	125	431	8—21

NATIONAL LEAGUE DIVISION SERIES
MILWAUKEE BREWERS VS· ARIZONA DIAMONDBACKS

ARIZONA DIAMONDBACKS

PLAYER, POS	AVG	G	AB	R	H	2B	3B	HR	RBI	BB	SO	SB
Henry Blanco, c	.000	1	1	0	0	0	0	0	0	0	0	0
Willie Bloomquist, ss	.318	5	22	3	7	0	0	0	1	1	3	3
Geoff Blum, ph	.000	2	2	0	0	0	0	0	0	0	2	0
Sean Burroughs, 3b	.333	3	3	0	1	0	0	0	0	0	2	0
Josh Collmenter, p	.333	1	3	1	1	0	0	0	0	0	1	0
Collin Cowgill, ph	1.000	2	1	0	1	0	0	0	2	0	0	0
Paul Goldschmidt, 1b	.438	4	16	4	7	0	0	2	6	2	5	1
David Hernandez, p	—	4	0	0	0	0	0	0	0	0	0	0
Aaron Hill, 2b	.278	5	18	3	5	0	0	1	1	5	3	0
Daniel Hudson, p	.000	1	2	0	0	0	0	0	0	0	1	0
Ian Kennedy, p	.250	2	4	0	1	0	0	0	0	0	2	0
John McDonald, ss	.000	2	2	0	0	0	0	0	0	0	0	0
Miguel Montero, c	.300	5	20	3	6	2	0	0	2	2	6	0
Lyle Overbay, 1b	.000	2	4	0	0	0	0	0	0	0	2	0
Micah Owings, p	.000	2	1	0	0	0	0	0	0	0	0	0

PLAYER, POS	AVG	G	AB	R	H	2B	3B	HR	RBI	BB	SO	SB
Jarrod Parker, p	—	1	0	0	0	0	0	0	0	0	0	0
Gerardo Parra, lf	.056	5	18	1	1	1	0	0	0	1	7	0
Joe Paterson, p	—	1	0	0	0	0	0	0	0	0	0	0
J.J. Putz, p	—	3	0	0	0	0	0	0	0	0	0	0
Ryan Roberts, 3b	.350	5	20	2	7	1	0	2	6	0	4	0
Joe Saunders, p	—	1	0	0	0	0	0	0	0	0	1	0
Bryan Shaw, p	—	4	0	0	0	0	0	0	0	0	0	0
Justin Upton, rf	.200	5	20	3	4	0	0	2	3	3	6	0
Chris Young, cf	.389	5	18	5	7	1	0	3	4	2	5	2
Brad Ziegler, p	—	2	0	0	0	0	0	0	0	0	0	0
Totals	**.274**	**5**	**175**	**25**	**48**	**5**	**0**	**10**	**25**	**17**	**49**	**6**

PITCHER	W	L	ERA	G	GS	SV	IP	H	R	ER	BB	SO
Josh Collmenter	1	0	1.29	1	1	0	7.0	2	1	1	2	6
David Hernandez	0	0	3.60	4	0	0	5.0	2	2	2	0	5
Daniel Hudson	0	1	8.44	1	1	0	5.1	9	5	5	0	6
Ian Kennedy	0	1	4.26	2	2	0	12.2	13	6	6	3	8
Micah Owings	1	0	0.00	2	0	0	3.0	2	0	0	0	1
Jarrod Parker	0	0	27.00	1	0	0	0.1	2	1	1	1	0
Joe Paterson	0	0	0.00	1	0	0	0.1	0	0	0	0	1
J.J. Putz	0	1	3.86	3	0	0	2.1	3	1	1	0	0
Joe Saunders	0	0	9.00	1	1	0	3.0	5	3	3	2	1
Bryan Shaw	0	0	0.00	4	0	0	4.0	0	0	0	1	3
Brad Ziegler	0	1	108.00	2	0	0	0.1	4	4	4	2	0
Totals	**2**	**3**	**4.78**	**5**	**5**	**0**	**43.3**	**42**	**23**	**23**	**12**	**31**

MILWAUKEE BREWERS

PLAYER, POS	AVG	G	AB	R	H	2B	3B	HR	RBI	BB	SO	SB
John Axford, p	—	3	0	0	0	0	0	0	0	0	0	0
Yuniesky Betancourt, ss	.278	5	18	5	5	1	0	1	1	0	4	0
Ryan Braun, lf	.500	5	18	5	9	4	0	1	4	3	3	1
Craig Counsell, 2b	.000	2	2	0	0	0	0	0	0	0	0	0
Marco Estrada, p	—	2	0	0	0	0	0	0	0	0	0	0
Prince Fielder, 1b	.278	5	18	2	5	2	0	1	3	2	5	0
Yovani Gallardo, p	.000	2	5	0	0	0	0	0	0	0	1	0
Carlos Gomez, cf	.750	3	4	2	3	0	0	1	2	0	0	2
Taylor Green, ph	.000	1	1	0	0	0	0	0	0	0	0	0
Zack Greinke, p	.500	1	2	0	1	0	0	0	0	0	1	0
Jerry Hairston, 3b	.375	5	16	2	6	2	0	0	3	2	1	0
Corey Hart, rf	.238	5	21	4	5	0	0	1	3	0	3	0
LaTroy Hawkins, p	—	1	0	0	0	0	0	0	0	0	0	0
Mark Kotsay, ph	.000	4	3	1	0	0	0	0	0	0	1	0
George Kottaras, c	.000	1	3	0	0	0	0	0	1	1	1	0
Kameron Loe, p	—	2	0	0	0	0	0	0	0	0	0	0
Jonathan Lucroy, c	.200	4	15	1	3	0	0	0	2	0	5	0
Shaun Marcum, p	.000	1	2	0	0	0	0	0	0	0	1	0
Casey McGehee, ph	.333	3	3	0	1	0	0	0	0	0	1	0
Nyjer Morgan, cf	.188	4	16	1	3	1	0	0	3	1	7	0
Chris Narveson, p	—	2	0	0	0	0	0	0	0	0	0	0
Francisco Rodriguez, p	—	2	0	0	0	0	0	0	0	0	0	0
Takashi Saito, p	—	3	0	0	0	0	0	0	0	0	0	0
Rickie Weeks, 2b	.056	5	18	0	1	0	1	0	1	1	1	0
Randy Wolf, p	.000	1	1	0	0	0	0	0	0	0	0	0
Totals	**.253**	**5**	**166**	**23**	**42**	**10**	**2**	**4**	**23**	**12**	**31**	**3**

PITCHER	W	L	ERA	G	GS	SV	IP	H	R	ER	BB	SO
John Axford	1	0	2.25	3	0	1	4.0	3	1	1	2	5
Marco Estrada	0	0	0.00	2	0	0	3.0	3	0	0	0	5
Yovani Gallardo	1	0	1.29	2	2	0	14.0	10	2	2	3	14
Zack Greinke	0	0	7.20	1	1	0	5.0	8	4	4	0	7
LaTroy Hawkins	0	0	0.00	1	0	0	1.0	0	0	0	2	1
Kameron Loe	0	0	0.00	2	0	0	2.0	3	1	0	0	1
Shaun Marcum	0	1	13.50	1	1	0	4.2	7	7	7	3	3
Chris Narveson	0	0	11.57	2	0	0	2.1	2	3	3	1	5
Francisco Rodriguez	0	0	0.00	2	0	0	2.0	2	0	0	3	4
Takashi Saito	1	0	0.00	3	0	0	3.0	2	0	0	0	2
Randy Wolf	0	1	21.00	1	1	0	3.0	8	7	7	3	2
Totals	**3**	**2**	**4.91**	**5**	**5**	**1**	**44.0**	**48**	**25**	**24**	**17**	**49**

E—Ziegler, Betancourt, Hairston, Weeks. DP—Arizona 3, Milwaukee 2. LOB—Arizona 36, Milwaukee 33. SB—Bloomquist (3), Goldschmidt, Young (2), Braun, Gomez (2). CS—Roberts. SH—Gomez. SF—Hairston (2), Hart. HBP—Goldschmidt (by Saito), Weeks (2, by Kennedy), Morgan (by Kennedy), Fielder (by Collmenter). IBB—Montero (by Marcum), Kotsay (by Ziegler).

SCORE BY INNINGS

ARIZONA	714	171	211	0—25
MILWAUKEE	314	208	220	1—23

PHILADELPHIA PHILLIES VS· ST· LOUIS CARDINALS

ST. LOUIS CARDINALS

PLAYER, POS	AVG	G	AB	R	H	2B	3B	HR	RBI	BB	SO	SB
Lance Berkman, rf	.167	5	18	4	3	1	0	1	4	2	3	1
Mitchell Boggs, p	—	2	0	0	0	0	0	0	0	0	0	0
Chris Carpenter, p	.250	2	4	0	1	0	0	0	0	0	0	0
Adron Chambers, rf	.500	5	2	1	1	0	0	0	1	0	1	0
Allen Craig, rf	.100	3	10	3	1	0	1	0	4	4	4	0
Daniel Descalso, 3b	.000	4	3	0	0	0	0	0	0	0	2	0
Octavio Dotel, p	—	3	0	0	0	0	0	0	0	0	0	0
David Freese, 3b	.278	5	18	1	5	2	0	1	5	0	9	0
Rafael Furcal, ss	.227	5	22	2	5	0	2	0	1	0	3	1
Jaime Garcia, p	.000	1	3	0	0	0	0	0	0	0	0	0
Matt Holliday, lf	.222	4	9	2	2	0	0	0	0	0	3	0
Edwin Jackson, p	.000	1	2	0	0	0	0	0	0	0	1	0
Jon Jay, cf	.167	5	12	0	2	0	0	0	2	3	3	0
Gerald Laird, pr	—	1	0	0	0	0	0	0	0	0	0	0
Kyle Lohse, p	.000	2	2	0	0	0	0	0	0	0	1	0
Yadier Molina, c	.211	5	19	1	4	0	0	0	1	1	5	1
Jason Motte, p	—	3	0	0	0	0	0	0	0	0	0	0
Albert Pujols, 1b	.350	5	20	2	7	3	0	0	1	2	4	1
Nick Punto, 2b	.167	3	6	0	1	0	0	0	0	0	3	0
Arthur Rhodes, p	—	3	0	0	0	0	0	0	0	0	0	0
Marc Rzepczynski, p	—	3	0	0	0	0	0	0	0	0	0	0
Fernando Salas, p	—	3	0	0	0	0	0	0	0	0	0	0
Skip Schumaker, 2b	.600	5	10	1	6	2	0	0	3	0	0	0
Ryan Theriot, 2b	.600	3	10	2	6	2	0	0	1	0	1	1
Totals	**.259**	**5**	**170**	**19**	**44**	**10**	**3**	**2**	**19**	**12**	**45**	**5**

PITCHER	W	L	ERA	G	GS	SV	IP	H	R	ER	BB	SO
Mitchell Boggs	0	0	9.00	2	0	0	2.0	4	2	2	1	1
Chris Carpenter	1	0	3.00	2	2	0	12.0	8	4	4	3	5
Octavio Dotel	1	0	0.00	3	0	0	2.2	0	0	0	0	4
Jaime Garcia	0	1	3.86	1	1	0	7.0	6	3	3	2	3
Edwin Jackson	1	0	3.00	1	1	0	6.0	5	2	2	1	4
Kyle Lohse	0	1	8.44	1	1	0	5.1	7	6	5	1	4
Jason Motte	0	0	0.00	3	0	2	3.1	1	0	0	0	3
Arthur Rhodes	0	0	0.00	3	0	0	1.0	0	0	0	0	2
Marc Rzepczynski	0	0	27.00	3	0	0	1.0	4	3	3	1	0
Fernando Salas	0	0	2.45	3	0	0	3.2	2	1	1	0	2
Totals	**3**	**2**	**4.09**	**5**	**5**	**2**	**44.0**	**37**	**21**	**20**	**8**	**29**

PHILADELPHIA PHILLIES

PLAYER, POS	AVG	G	AB	R	H	2B	3B	HR	RBI	BB	SO	SB
Antonio Bastardo, p	—	2	0	0	0	0	0	0	0	0	0	0
Joe Blanton, p	—	1	0	0	0	0	0	0	0	0	0	0
Ben Francisco, ph	.500	2	2	1	1	0	0	1	3	0	0	0
Ross Gload, ph	.500	3	2	0	1	0	0	0	0	0	1	0
Roy Halladay, p	.167	2	6	0	1	0	0	0	0	0	2	0
Cole Hamels, p	.000	1	2	0	0	0	0	0	0	0	0	0
Ryan Howard, 1b	.105	5	19	1	2	0	0	1	6	1	6	0
Raul Ibanez, lf	.200	4	15	1	3	0	0	1	4	0	5	0
Cliff Lee, p	.000	1	2	0	0	0	0	0	0	0	1	0
Brad Lidge, p	—	3	0	0	0	0	0	0	0	0	0	0
Ryan Madson, p	.000	4	1	0	0	0	0	0	0	0	1	0
Michael Martinez, pr	—	2	0	1	0	0	0	0	0	0	0	0
John Mayberry, lf	.000	2	4	0	0	0	0	0	0	0	2	0
Roy Oswalt, p	.000	1	1	0	0	0	0	0	0	0	0	0
Hunter Pence, rf	.211	5	19	3	4	0	0	0	4	2	2	0
Placido Polanco, 3b	.105	5	19	0	2	0	0	0	0	3	0	0
Jimmy Rollins, ss	.450	5	20	6	9	4	0	0	0	1	1	2
Carlos Ruiz, c	.059	5	17	1	1	0	0	0	0	1	3	0
Michael Stutes, p	—	1	0	0	0	0	0	0	0	0	0	0
Chase Utley, 2b	.438	5	16	5	7	2	1	0	1	3	3	0
Shane Victorino, cf	.316	5	19	2	6	1	0	0	0	2	0	0
Vance Worley, p	—	2	0	0	0	0	0	0	0	0	0	0
Totals	**.226**	**5**	**164**	**21**	**37**	**7**	**1**	**3**	**20**	**8**	**29**	**2**

PITCHER	W	L	ERA	G	GS	SV	IP	H	R	ER	BB	SO
Antonio Bastardo	0	0	0.00	2	0	0	1.0	0	0	0	1	1
Joe Blanton	0	0	0.00	1	0	0	1.0	0	0	0	0	0
Roy Halladay	1	1	2.25	2	2	0	16.0	9	4	4	2	15

	W	L	ERA	G	GS	SV	IP	H	R	ER	BB	SO
Cole Hamels	1	0	0.00	1	1	0	6.0	5	0	0	3	8
Cliff Lee	0	1	7.50	1	1	0	6.0	12	5	5	2	9
Brad Lidge	0	0	0.00	3	0	0	2.0	2	0	0	1	1
Ryan Madson	0	0	2.08	4	0	1	4.1	4	1	1	0	6
Roy Oswalt	0	1	7.50	1	1	0	6.0	6	5	5	1	5
Michael Stutes	0	0	81.00	1	0	0	0.1	3	3	3	1	0
Vance Worley	0	0	6.75	2	0	0	1.1	3	1	1	1	0
Totals	2	3	3.89	5	5	1	44.0	44	19	19	12	45

E—Freese, Molina, Ruiz (2), Victorino. DP—St. Louis 5, Philadelphia 1. LOB—St. Louis 36, Philadelphia 22. SB—Berkman,Furcal, Molina, Pujols, Terriot, Rollins (2). CS—Pujols, Pence, Rollins, Utley. SH—Descalso, Jay, Oswalt. SF—Howard. HBP—Berkman (by Hamels), Holliday (by Oswalt), Utley (by Carpenter), Utley (by Rzepcynski). IBB—Jay (by Hamels), Molina (by Lidge), Pujols (by Halladay), Pence (by Garcia), Ruiz (by Garcia). WP—Garcia, Salas, Halladay. PB—Molina.

SCORE BY INNINGS

PHILADELPHIA	500 503 204	—19
ST. LOUIS	510 105 630	—21

NATIONAL LEAGUE CHAMPIONSHIP SERIES
MILWAUKEE BREWERS VS. ST. LOUIS CARDINALS

ST. LOUIS CARDINALS

PLAYER, POS	AVG	G	AB	R	H	2B	3B	HR	RBI	BB	SO	SB
Lance Berkman, rf	.300	6	20	4	6	0	0	0	2	2	2	1
Mitchell Boggs, p	—	3	0	0	0	0	0	0	0	0	0	0
Chris Carpenter, p	.500	1	2	0	1	0	0	0	0	0	0	0
Adron Chambers, rf	.000	5	3	1	0	0	0	0	1	0	3	0
Allen Craig, lf	.375	5	8	1	3	0	0	1	3	0	1	0
Daniel Descalso, 3b	.333	4	3	1	1	0	0	0	0	0	0	0
Octavio Dotel, p	—	4	0	0	0	0	0	0	0	0	0	0
David Freese, 3b	.545	6	22	7	12	3	0	3	9	2	2	0
Rafael Furcal, ss	.185	6	27	5	5	2	0	1	1	3	0	0
Jaime Garcia, p	.000	2	4	0	0	0	0	0	1	0	2	0
Matt Holliday, lf	.435	6	23	6	10	2	0	1	5	3	7	0
Edwin Jackson, p	.500	2	2	1	1	0	0	0	0	0	0	0
Jon Jay, cf	.240	6	25	7	6	2	0	0	1	3	2	1
Gerald Laird, c	.000	1	1	0	0	0	0	0	0	0	1	0
Kyle Lohse, p	.000	2	3	0	0	0	0	0	0	0	2	0
Lance Lynn, p	.000	5	1	0	0	0	0	0	0	0	1	0
Kyle McClellan, p	—	1	0	0	0	0	0	0	0	0	0	0
Yadier Molina, c	.333	6	24	5	8	3	0	0	2	2	3	0
Jason Motte, p	—	4	0	0	0	0	0	0	0	0	0	0
Albert Pujols, 1b	.478	6	23	5	11	4	0	2	9	4	4	0
Nick Punto, 2b	.133	6	15	0	2	0	0	0	3	2	8	0
Arthur Rhodes, p	—	2	0	0	0	0	0	0	0	0	0	0
Marc Rzepczynski, p	—	5	0	0	0	0	0	0	0	0	0	0
Fernando Salas, p	—	4	0	0	0	0	0	0	0	0	0	0
Ryan Theriot, 2b	.100	4	10	0	1	0	0	0	0	0	1	0
Totals	.310	6	216	43	67	16	0	8	37	19	43	2

PITCHER	W	L	ERA	G	GS	SV	IP	H	R	ER	BB	SO
Mitchell Boggs	0	0	6.00	3	0	0	3.0	4	2	2	1	0
Chris Carpenter	1	0	5.40	1	1	0	5.0	6	3	3	3	3
Octavio Dotel	1	0	2.25	4	0	0	4.0	2	2	1	1	5
Jaime Garcia	0	1	7.27	2	2	0	8.2	13	7	7	3	8
Edwin Jackson	0	0	8.53	2	2	0	6.1	11	6	6	1	5
Kyle Lohse	0	1	6.23	1	1	0	4.1	6	3	3	0	3
Lance Lynn	1	0	0.00	5	0	0	5.1	3	0	0	2	1
Kyle McClellan	0	0	27.00	1	0	0	0.1	2	1	1	0	0
Jason Motte	0	0	0.00	4	0	2	4.2	0	0	0	0	4
Arthur Rhodes	0	0	0.00	2	0	0	0.2	0	0	1	0	1
Marc Rzepczynski	1	0	1.93	5	0	0	4.2	1	1	1	1	4
Fernando Salas	0	0	1.50	4	0	0	6.0	3	1	1	1	6
Totals	4	2	4.25	6	6	2	53.0	51	26	25	14	40

MILWAUKEE BREWERS

PLAYER, POS	AVG	G	AB	R	H	2B	3B	HR	RBI	BB	SO	SB
John Axford, p	—	3	0	0	0	0	0	0	0	0	0	0
Yuniesky Betancourt, ss	.333	6	24	2	8	2	0	1	5	0	3	0
Ryan Braun, lf	.333	6	24	2	8	3	0	1	6	1	6	0
Craig Counsell, 2b	.000	4	2	0	0	0	0	0	0	0	0	0
Marco Estrada, p	—	2	0	0	0	0	0	0	0	0	0	0
Prince Fielder, 1b	.200	6	20	4	4	2	0	2	3	4	4	0
Yovani Gallardo, p	.000	1	1	0	0	0	0	0	1	0	0	0
Carlos Gomez, cf	.200	5	10	1	2	0	0	0	0	0	2	0
Taylor Green, 2b	.000	2	1	0	0	0	0	0	0	0	0	0
Zack Greinke, p	.250	2	4	0	1	0	0	0	0	0	0	0
Jerry Hairston, 3b	.391	6	23	6	9	4	0	0	1	2	3	0
Corey Hart, rf	.250	5	20	2	5	0	0	1	2	2	5	0
LaTroy Hawkins, p	—	3	0	0	0	0	0	0	0	0	0	0
Mark Kotsay, rf	.111	5	9	1	1	0	0	1	1	2	2	0
George Kottaras, c	.000	2	5	0	0	0	0	0	1	0	1	0
Kameron Loe, p	—	3	0	0	0	0	0	0	0	0	0	0
Jonathan Lucroy, c	.294	6	17	2	5	1	0	1	3	0	3	0
Shaun Marcum, p	.000	2	1	0	0	0	0	0	0	0	0	0
Casey McGehee, ph	.000	3	2	0	0	0	0	0	0	1	1	0
Nyjer Morgan, cf	.167	6	12	1	2	1	0	0	0	1	4	0
Chris Narveson, p	.000	4	1	0	0	0	0	0	0	0	1	0
Francisco Rodriguez, p	—	3	0	0	0	0	0	0	0	0	0	0
Takashi Saito, p	—	3	0	0	0	0	0	0	0	0	0	0
Rickie Weeks, 2b	.217	6	23	5	5	1	0	2	3	1	5	0
Randy Wolf, p	.500	1	2	0	1	1	0	0	0	0	0	0
Totals	.254	6	201	26	51	15	0	9	26	14	40	0

PITCHER	W	L	ERA	G	GS	SV	IP	H	R	ER	BB	SO
John Axford	0	0	0.00	3	0	2	3.0	2	0	0	0	4
Marco Estrada	0	0	12.00	2	0	0	3.0	4	4	4	2	4
Yovani Gallardo	0	1	7.20	1	1	0	5.0	8	4	4	5	2
Zack Greinke	1	1	6.17	2	2	0	11.2	15	11	8	4	6
LaTroy Hawkins	0	0	0.00	3	0	0	3.0	2	0	0	2	2
Kameron Loe	0	0	15.43	3	0	0	2.1	10	6	4	1	2
Shaun Marcum	0	2	16.20	2	2	0	5.0	10	9	9	2	2
Chris Narveson	0	0	10.80	4	0	0	5.0	5	6	6	1	8
Francisco Rodriguez	0	0	3.00	3	0	0	3.0	3	1	1	1	4
Takashi Saito	0	0	0.00	3	0	0	4.0	2	0	0	0	3
Randy Wolf	1	0	2.57	1	1	0	7.0	6	2	2	1	6
Totals	2	4	6.58	6	6	2	52.0	67	43	38	19	43

Nyjer Morgan delivered the winning hit of the NLDS but went 2-for-12 in the NLCS

E—Dotel, Theriot, Betancourt, Estrada, Hairston (3), Hart, Weeks (3). DP—St. Louis 7, Milwaukee 6. LOB—St. Louis 44, Milwaukee 38. SB—Berkman, Jay. CS—Holliday, Gomez. SH—Furcal (2), Jackson, Punto, Gomez, Greinke, Wolf. SF—Chambers, Punto, Gallardo. HPB—Berkman (by Saito), Freese (by Greinke), Braun (by Carpenter), Fielder (by Garcia), Gomez (by Dotel), Morgan (by Lohse). IBB—Pujols (2, by Hawkins, Gallardo), Punto (by Gallardo), Fielder (2, by Carpenter, Lynn), Molina (by Narveson). WP—Rzepcynski, Estrada, Gallardo (3).

SCORE BY INNINGS

ST. LOUIS	(11)57 551 531—43
MILWAUKEE	351 591 110—26

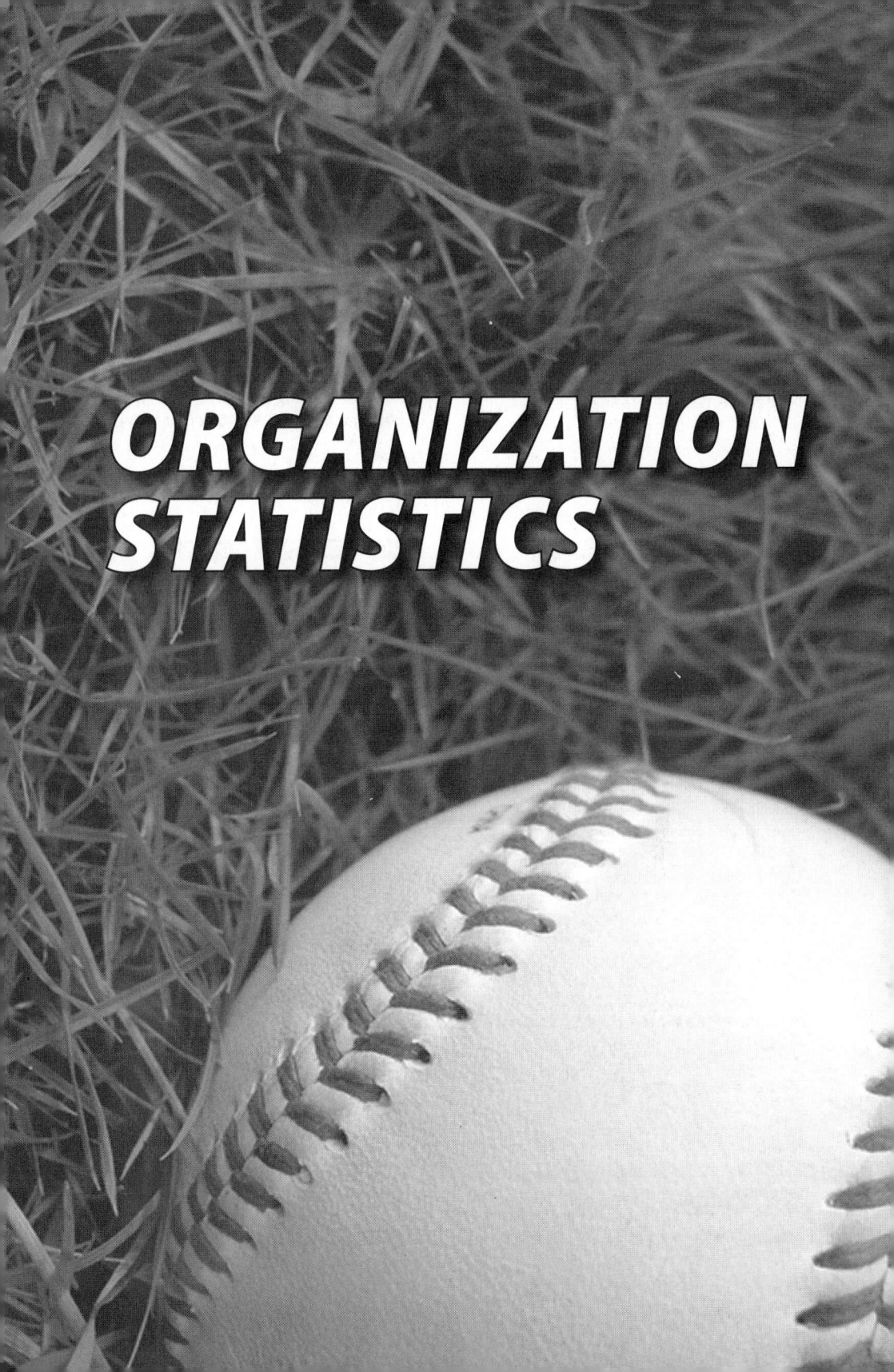

ORGANIZATION STATISTICS

Arizona Diamondbacks

SEASON IN A SENTENCE: Behind a revamped bullpen and front office, the Diamondbacks went from worst to first in capturing the National League West.

HIGH POINT: Following a six-game losing streak that ended on Aug. 22, the Diamondbacks ran off 18 wins in their next 21 games. The streak was spurred by a season high nine-game win streak that finally catapulted Arizona past the defending World Series champion Giants.

LOW POINT: If forced to nitpick in a season that was considered a success on nearly every front, the low point of the came in Game Five of Divisional Series. While the Diamondbacks took it to a winner-take-all game, they fell to the Brewers in extra innings on a walk-off single by outfielder Nyjer Morgan.

NOTABLE ROOKIES: Each side of the ball saw a rookie play a vital role in the team's return to the playoffs. Unconventional righthander Josh Collmenter provided rotation depth and pitched 154 innings with a 3.38 ERA while earning 10 wins. Powerful first baseman Paul Goldschmidt slugged eight home runs in only 177 plate appearances to provide extra punch to the lineup during the final third of the season.

KEY TRANSACTIONS: New general manager Kevin Towers took over for interim GM Jerry Dipoto (who stayed with the organization) and immediately made his imprint. Towers signed closer J.J. Putz as a free agent and traded defensive liability Mark Reynolds to the Orioles for righthander David Hernandez. The moves provided a significant upgrade to the bullpen and upgraded the defense by allowing Ryan Roberts to take over at third. Keeping Kirk Gibson as manager may have been the most important decision, as he brought the same fiery intensity he became known for as a player to the Arizona dugout.

DOWN ON THE FARM: Goldschmidt tied for the Double-A Southern League lead with 30 home runs even though he spent the last part of the season in the big leagues. Lefthander Tyler Skaggs pitched in the Futures Game and placed in the top five for strikeouts in the minor leagues. Righthander Jarrod Parker bounced back from Tommy John surgery and should be ready for a rotation spot as early as 2012. The club held the third and seventh overall picks in the draft and added two premium righthanders in UCLA's Trevor Bauer and Oklahoma prepster Archie Bradley.

OPENING DAY PAYROLL: $53,639,833 (25th)

PLAYERS OF THE YEAR

MAJOR LEAGUE	MINOR LEAGUE
Justin Upton	**Paul Goldschmidt**
of	1b
.289/.369/.529	(Double-A)
31 HR, 39 2B	.306/.435/.626
First Silver Slugger	Southern Lg. MVP

ORGANIZATION LEADERS

BATTING		*Minimum 250 PA
MAJORS		
* AVG	Gerardo Parra	.292
* OPS	Justin Upton	.898
HR	Justin Upton	31
RBI	Justin Upton	88
MINORS		
* AVG	Collin Cowgill, Reno	.354
* OBP	Paul Goldschmidt, Mobile	.435
* SLG	Cody Ransom, Reno	.629
R	A.J. Pollock, Mobile	103
H	David Nick, Visalia	169
	A.J. Pollock, Mobile	169
TB	David Nick, Visalia	253
2B	A.J. Pollock, Mobile	41
3B	Cole Gillespie, Reno	16
HR	Yazy Arbelo, South Bend	31
RBI	Matt Davidson, Visalia	106
BB	Paul Goldschmidt, Mobile	82
SO	Keon Broxton, South Bend/Visalia	172
SB	A.J. Pollock, Mobile	36

PITCHING		#Minimum 75 IP
MAJORS		
W	Ian Kennedy	21
# ERA	Ian Kennedy	2.88
SO	Ian Kennedy	198
SV	J.J. Putz	45
MINORS		
W	David Holmberg, South Bend/Visalia	12
	Tom Layne, Mobile/Reno	12
L	J.R. Bradley, South Bend	16
# ERA	Tyler Skaggs, Visalia/Mobile	2.96
G	Billy Spottiswood, Mobile	51
GS	Eric Smith, Visalia	28
SV	Ryan Cook, Mobile/Reno	19
IP	Wes Roemer, Mobile/Reno	164
BB	Eric Smith, Visalia	85
SO	Tyler Skaggs, Visalia/Mobile	198
# AVG	Tyler Skaggs, Visalia/Mobile	.218

General Manager: Kevin Towers. **Farm Director:** Mike Bell. **Scouting Director:** Ray Montgomery.

Class	Team	League	W	L	PCT	Finish	Manager(s)
Majors	Arizona Diamondbacks	National	94	68	.580	3rd (16)	Kirk Gibson
Triple-A	Reno Aces	Pacific Coast	77	67	.535	5th (16)	Brett Butler
Double-A	Mobile BayBears	Southern	84	54	.609	1st (10)	Turner Ward
High A	Visalia Rawhide	California	63	77	.450	8th (10)	Jason Hardtke
Low A	South Bend Silver Hawks	Midwest	67	72	.482	10th (16)	Mark Haley
Short-season	Yakima Bears	Northwest	33	43	.434	8th (8)	Audo Vicente
Rookie	Missoula Osprey	Pioneer	41	35	.539	t-4th (8)	Hector De La Cruz
Rookie	AZL Diamondbacks	Arizona	20	36	.357	12th (13)	Andy Green
Overall 2011 Minor League Record			385	384	.501	17th (30)	

ORGANIZATION STATISTICS

ARIZONA DIAMONDBACKS
NATIONAL LEAGUE

Batting	B-T	HT	WT	DOB	AVG	vLH	vRH	G	AB	R	H	2B	3B	HR	RBI	BB	HBP	SH	SF	SO	SB	CS	SLG	OBP
Allen, Brandon	L-R	6-2	235	2-12-86	.172	.000	.208	11	29	5	5	0	0	3	7	7	1	0	0	13	1	0	.483	.351
Blanco, Henry	R-R	5-11	225	8-29-71	.250	.266	.222	37	100	12	25	3	1	8	12	12	0	0	0	21	0	1	.540	.330
Bloomquist, Willie	R-R	5-11	185	11-27-77	.266	.303	.249	97	350	44	93	10	2	4	26	23	4	0	2	51	20	10	.340	.317
Blum, Geoff	B-R	6-3	220	4-26-73	.224	.000	.275	23	49	8	11	3	0	2	10	5	1	0	0	9	0	0	.408	.309
Branyan, Russell	L-R	6-4	230	12-19-75	.210	.167	.214	31	62	4	13	5	0	1	2	7	0	0	0	20	0	0	.339	.290
Burroughs, Sean	L-R	6-0	180	9-12-80	.273	.286	.271	78	110	8	30	4	0	1	8	3	0	0	1	15	1	0	.336	.289
Cowgill, Collin	R-L	5-9	185	5-22-86	.239	.275	.212	36	92	8	22	3	0	1	9	8	0	0	0	28	4	2	.304	.300
Drew, Stephen	L-R	6-0	190	3-16-83	.252	.224	.263	86	321	44	81	21	5	5	45	30	1	0	1	74	4	4	.396	.317
Gillespie, Cole	R-R	6-1	200	6-20-84	.333	.000	.500	5	6	2	2	0	0	1	4	1	0	0	0	1	0	0	.833	.429
Goldschmidt, Paul	R-R	6-3	245	9-10-87	.250	.162	.277	48	156	28	39	9	1	8	26	20	0	0	1	53	4	0	.474	.333
Hammock, Robby	R-R	5-10	185	5-13-77	.000	.000	.000	2	2	0	0	0	0	0	0	0	0	0	0	0	0	0	.000	.000
Hill, Aaron	R-R	5-11	200	3-21-82	.315	.281	.326	33	124	23	39	12	2	6	16	12	3	0	1	19	5	4	.492	.386
Johnson, Kelly	L-R	6-1	195	2-22-82	.209	.171	.223	114	430	59	90	23	5	18	49	44	3	0	0	132	13	3	.412	.287
McDonald, John	R-R	5-9	180	9-24-74	.169	.200	.163	19	59	2	10	2	0	0	2	4	0	0	0	9	0	0	.203	.222
Miranda, Juan	L-L	6-0	220	4-25-83	.213	.242	.206	65	174	18	37	8	2	7	23	23	3	0	0	48	0	1	.402	.315
Montero, Miguel	L-R	5-11	215	7-9-83	.282	.195	.308	140	493	65	139	36	1	18	86	47	8	0	4	97	1	1	.469	.351
Mora, Melvin	R-R	5-11	200	2-7-72	.228	.263	.213	42	127	5	29	6	0	0	16	2	2	0	4	24	0	1	.276	.244
Nady, Xavier	R-R	6-2	215	11-14-78	.248	.248	.248	82	206	26	51	11	0	4	35	10	3	0	4	46	2	0	.359	.287
Overbay, Lyle	L-L	6-2	220	1-28-77	.286	.000	.324	18	42	3	12	4	0	1	10	6	1	0	0	11	1	0	.452	.388
2-team total (103 Pittsburgh)					.234			121	394	43	92	21	1	9	47	42	2	0	1	88	2	1	.360	.310
Parra, Gerardo	L-L	5-11	200	5-6-87	.292	.277	.296	141	445	55	130	20	8	8	46	43	3	0	2	82	15	1	.427	.357
Pena, Wily Mo	R-R	6-3	260	1-23-82	.196	.176	.207	17	46	7	9	0	0	5	7	0	0	0	0	19	0	0	.522	.196
Ransom, Cody	R-R	6-2	190	2-17-76	.152	.125	.176	12	33	3	5	2	0	1	4	3	1	0	0	9	1	0	.303	.243
Roberts, Ryan	R-R	5-11	185	9-19-80	.249	.278	.238	143	482	86	120	25	2	19	65	66	2	0	2	98	18	9	.427	.341
Upton, Justin	R-R	6-2	205	8-25-87	.289	.268	.295	159	592	105	171	39	5	31	88	59	19	0	4	126	21	9	.529	.369
Wilson, Josh	R-R	6-0	175	3-26-81	.200	.000	.222	6	10	3	2	1	0	0	1	0	0	0	0	1	0	0	.300	.200
2-team total (54 Milwaukee)					.224			60	85	13	19	5	0	2	5	4	0	0	0	22	1	0	.353	.258
Young, Chris	R-R	6-2	190	9-5-83	.236	.285	.222	156	567	89	134	38	3	20	71	80	4	0	7	139	22	9	.420	.331

Pitching	B-T	HT	WT	DOB	W	L	ERA	G	GS	CG	SV	IP	H	R	ER	HR	BB	SO	AVG	vLH	vRH	K/9	BB/9
Brazoban, Yhency	R-R	6-1	250	11-6-80	0	0	6.00	6	0	0	0	6	8	4	4	1	4	8	.308	.444	.235	12.00	6.00
Castillo, Alberto	L-L	6-3	220	7-5-75	1	0	2.31	17	0	0	0	12	10	3	3	0	7	6	.244	.300	.190	4.63	5.40
Collmenter, Josh	R-R	6-2	235	2-7-86	10	10	3.38	31	24	0	0	154	137	61	58	17	28	100	.237	.250	.225	5.83	1.63
Cook, Ryan	R-R	6-3	200	6-30-87	0	1	7.04	12	0	0	0	8	11	6	6	0	8	7	.333	.313	.353	8.22	9.39
Demel, Sam	R-R	6-0	205	10-23-85	2	2	4.21	34	0	0	0	26	31	13	12	4	13	15	.307	.379	.278	5.26	4.56
Duke, Zach	L-L	6-1	205	4-19-83	3	4	4.93	21	9	1	0	77	101	42	42	6	19	32	.324	.225	.353	3.76	2.23
Enright, Barry	R-R	6-3	220	3-30-86	1	4	7.41	7	7	0	0	38	50	31	31	11	15	21	.325	.309	.337	5.02	3.58
Galarraga, Armando	R-R	6-4	235	1-15-82	3	4	5.91	8	8	0	0	43	47	36	28	13	22	28	.281	.279	.283	5.91	4.64
Gutierrez, Juan	R-R	6-3	260	7-14-83	0	0	5.40	20	0	0	0	18	22	16	11	3	9	23	.275	.351	.209	11.29	4.42
Heilman, Aaron	R-R	6-5	230	11-12-78	4	1	6.88	32	0	0	0	35	48	28	27	8	11	33	.318	.328	.310	8.41	2.80
Hernandez, David	R-R	6-2	250	5-13-85	5	3	3.38	74	0	0	11	69	49	27	26	4	30	77	.193	.171	.212	10.00	3.89
Hudson, Daniel	R-R	6-3	230	3-9-87	16	12	3.49	33	33	3	0	222	217	98	86	17	50	169	.255	.251	.258	6.85	2.03
Kennedy, Ian	R-R	6-0	190	12-19-84	21	4	2.88	33	33	1	0	222	186	73	71	19	55	198	.222	.237	.218	8.03	2.23
Kroenke, Zach	R-L	6-2	205	4-21-84	0	1	9.00	4	0	0	0	4	6	4	4	1	1	3	.333	.000	.429	6.75	2.25
Marquis, Jason	L-R	6-1	210	8-21-78	0	1	9.53	3	3	0	0	11	22	16	12	3	4	5	.386	.542	.273	3.97	3.18
2-team total (20 Washington)					8	6	4.43	23	23	1	0	132	154	74	65	11	43	76	—	—	—	5.18	2.93
Mickolio, Kam	R-R	6-9	255	5-10-84	0	0	6.75	6	0	0	0	7	10	5	5	0	3	7	.357	.500	.300	9.45	4.05
Miley, Wade	L-L	6-1	220	11-13-86	4	2	4.50	8	7	0	0	40	48	20	20	6	18	25	.304	.391	.289	5.63	4.05
Owings, Micah	R-R	6-5	220	9-28-82	8	0	3.57	33	4	0	0	63	56	27	25	8	23	44	.240	.291	.211	6.29	3.29
Parker, Jarrod	R-R	6-1	195	11-24-88	0	0	0.00	1	1	0	0	6	4	0	0	0	1	4	.211	.143	.250	1.59	1.59
Paterson, Joe	R-L	6-1	210	5-19-86	0	3	2.91	62	0	0	1	34	28	11	11	1	15	28	.224	.205	.255	7.41	3.97
Putz, J.J.	R-R	6-5	250	2-22-77	2	2	2.17	60	0	0	45	58	41	15	14	4	12	61	.195	.179	.214	9.47	1.86

Pitching

Pitching	B-T	HT	WT	DOB	W	L	ERA	G	GS	CG	SV	IP	H	R	ER	HR	BB	SO	AVG	vLH	vRH	K/9	BB/9
Saunders, Joe	L-L	6-3	210	6-16-81	12	13	3.69	33	33	1	0	212	210	94	87	29	67	108	.266	.212	.281	4.58	2.84
Shaw, Bryan	B-R	6-1	210	11-8-87	1	0	2.54	33	0	0	0	28	30	9	8	2	8	24	.273	.244	.292	7.62	2.54
Vasquez, Esmerling	R-R	6-1	200	11-7-83	1	1	4.15	31	0	0	0	30	27	16	14	2	13	20	.239	.217	.254	5.93	3.86
Ziegler, Brad	R-R	6-4	205	10-10-79	0	0	1.74	23	0	0	0	21	15	7	4	0	6	15	.208	.316	.170	6.53	2.61

Fielding

Catcher	PCT	G	PO	A	E	DP	PB
Blanco	.995	37	178	13	1	0	1
Montero	.989	134	908	78	11	9	8

First Base	PCT	G	PO	A	E	DP
Allen	1.000	10	77	5	0	9
Branyan	1.000	14	103	6	0	6
Goldschmidt	1.000	43	351	22	0	22
Miranda	.990	46	367	24	4	36
Mora	1.000	1	2	1	0	0
Nady	.993	52	372	32	3	36
Overbay	1.000	11	84	6	0	7

Second Base	PCT	G	PO	A	E	DP
Bloomquist	1.000	1	1	0	0	0
Hill	1.000	33	68	87	0	17

	PCT	G	PO	A	E	DP
Johnson	.988	108	215	263	6	65
Roberts	.968	28	48	73	4	17

Third Base	PCT	G	PO	A	E	DP
Blum	1.000	14	4	24	0	3
Burroughs	.974	20	9	28	1	5
Mora	.965	31	20	63	3	2
Ransom	.905	6	8	11	2	1
Roberts	.964	107	74	197	10	15

Shortstop	PCT	G	PO	A	E	DP
Bloomquist	.979	59	76	155	5	31
Drew	.980	84	119	219	7	48
McDonald	.988	18	28	52	1	8
Ransom	.958	8	4	19	1	2
Roberts	.000	1	0	0	0	0

	PCT	G	PO	A	E	DP
Wilson	1.000	3	4	9	0	1

Outfield	PCT	G	PO	A	E	DP
Bloomquist	1.000	25	41	0	0	0
Cowgill	1.000	25	58	2	0	1
Gillespie	1.000	4	3	0	0	0
Hammock	.000	1	0	0	0	0
Nady	1.000	10	10	1	0	0
Parra	.990	135	288	12	3	5
Pena	.000	1	0	0	0	0
Roberts	1.000	3	4	0	0	0
Upton	.964	159	339	5	13	2
Young	.993	155	394	4	3	2

RENO ACES

TRIPLE-A

PACIFIC COAST LEAGUE

Batting	B-T	HT	WT	DOB	AVG	vLH	vRH	G	AB	R	H	2B	3B	HR	RBI	BB	HBP	SH	SF	SO	SB	CS	SLG	OBP
Abreu, Tony	B-R	5-9	200	11-13-84	.292	.355	.267	120	483	83	141	26	5	10	72	30	6	0	9	84	12	7	.429	.335
Allen, Brandon	L-R	6-2	235	2-12-86	.306	.284	.316	83	304	75	93	21	4	18	66	64	4	0	5	90	7	4	.579	.427
2-team total (10 Sacramento)					.299	—	—	93	344	79	103	23	5	21	72	66	4	0	5	101	7	4	.578	.413
Berroa, Angel	R-R	6-0	195	1-27-77	.320	.333	.314	42	150	22	48	12	2	4	25	7	2	0	2	25	3	1	.507	.354
Blum, Geoff	B-R	6-3	220	4-26-73	.429	.500	.250	4	14	2	6	1	0	0	1	2	0	0	0	0	0	0	.500	.500
Burroughs, Sean	L-R	6-2	180	9-12-80	.412	.485	.377	34	102	19	42	11	2	2	25	7	0	0	0	8	0	2	.618	.450
Castillo, Ramon	R-R	5-11	215	9-6-88	.500	1.000	.000	2	2	0	1	0	0	0	0	0	0	0	0	0	0	0	.500	.500
Cowgill, Collin	R-L	5-9	185	5-22-86	.354	.309	.372	98	395	95	140	24	8	13	70	51	2	0	1	63	30	3	.554	.430
Frey, Evan	L-L	6-0	170	6-7-86	.275	.241	.289	113	389	66	107	14	9	2	38	59	1	0	3	68	22	11	.373	.369
Gillespie, Cole	R-R	6-1	200	6-20-84	.300	.325	.287	137	484	100	145	19	16	12	79	81	10	0	7	91	24	5	.479	.405
Greene, Kyle	L-R	6-1	200	5-26-86	.292	.286	.293	18	48	8	14	4	0	0	8	8	1	0	0	18	0	0	.375	.404
Hallberg, Mark	R-R	5-11	170	12-9-85	.279	.306	.266	114	376	56	105	23	2	6	63	36	3	0	5	22	2	4	.399	.343
Hammock, Robby	R-R	5-10	185	5-13-77	.257	.118	.286	37	101	18	26	7	1	5	21	15	1	0	2	17	0	0	.495	.353
Hester, John	R-R	6-4	228	9-14-83	.263	.154	.320	10	38	4	10	3	0	1	5	4	0	0	1	6	0	1	.421	.326
Langerhans, Ryan	L-L	6-3	220	2-20-80	.308	.405	.261	38	130	23	40	10	2	6	23	39	1	0	1	31	8	1	.554	.468
2-team total (57 Tacoma)					.311	—	—	95	344	69	107	20	2	22	60	76	3	0	3	94	11	7	.573	.437
Manzella, Tommy	R-R	6-2	200	4-16-83	.246	.190	.275	22	61	7	15	0	0	1	3	4	0	0	0	10	1	1	.295	.292
2-team total (109 Oklahoma City)					.232	—	—	131	422	46	98	14	6	8	51	49	4	0	4	126	11	5	.351	.315
May, Lucas	R-R	5-11	195	10-24-84	.270	.231	.288	52	163	31	44	13	0	7	31	23	2	0	2	42	2	2	.479	.363
2-team total (25 Omaha)					.238	—	—	77	248	40	59	15	1	10	44	32	3	0	2	64	2	2	.427	.330
Miranda, Juan	L-L	6-0	220	4-25-83	.229	.176	.254	34	105	17	24	4	1	5	24	20	1	0	0	36	0	1	.429	.357
Owings, Jon Mark	R-R	6-4	195	4-4-85	.333	.000	.667	2	6	2	2	0	0	1	1	0	0	0	0	2	0	0	.833	.333
Pena, Wily Mo	R-R	6-3	260	1-23-82	.363	.413	.345	63	237	52	86	17	3	21	63	25	8	0	1	48	5	2	.726	.439
2-team total (13 Tacoma)					.358	—	—	76	288	63	103	21	3	25	77	34	9	0	1	61	5	2	.712	.440
Ransom, Cody	R-R	6-2	190	2-17-76	.317	.314	.319	101	372	86	118	29	3	27	92	55	2	0	3	94	10	3	.629	.405
Reed, Mark	L-R	5-11	180	4-13-86	.400	.500	.375	4	10	3	4	1	0	0	1	2	0	0	0	3	0	1	.500	.500
Restovich, Michael	R-R	6-6	240	1-3-79	.209	.261	.150	18	43	3	9	1	0	0	2	7	0	0	1	9	0	0	.233	.314
Schmidt, Konrad	R-R	5-10	225	8-2-84	.280	.324	.261	92	346	47	97	24	3	9	45	21	5	0	1	66	1	3	.445	.330
Tracy, Andy	L-R	6-3	230	12-11-73	.288	.194	.322	85	274	55	79	21	2	18	51	55	4	0	3	70	4	0	.577	.411
Wilson, Josh	R-R	6-0	175	3-26-81	.351	.455	.326	16	57	11	20	5	2	1	12	4	2	0	1	7	2	0	.561	.406
Winfree, David	R-R	6-3	230	8-5-85	.321	.375	.298	39	134	27	43	5	1	9	37	15	3	0	5	22	8	1	.575	.389

Pitching	B-T	HT	WT	DOB	W	L	ERA	G	GS	CG	SV	IP	H	R	ER	HR	BB	SO	AVG	vLH	vRH	K/9	BB/9
Bennett, Jeff	R-R	6-3	200	6-10-80	3	0	4.29	24	0	0	0	36	39	19	17	4	19	21	.289	.241	.325	5.30	4.79
Bolsinger, Mike	R-R	6-2	209	1-29-88	0	0	0.00	1	0	0	0	1	1	0	0	0	0	0	.333	.500	.000	0.00	0.00
Brazoban, Yhency	R-R	6-1	250	11-6-80	1	1	2.70	8	0	0	1	10	8	3	3	1	3	11	.216	.176	.250	9.90	2.70
2-team total (15 Round Rock)					4	1	3.22	23	0	0	2	36	31	15	13	6	14	42	—	—	—	10.40	3.47
Castillo, Alberto	L-L	6-3	220	7-5-75	0	0	2.00	8	0	0	0	9	5	2	2	0	5	12	.167	.067	.267	12.00	5.00
Collmenter, Josh	R-R	6-2	235	2-7-86	1	0	1.50	1	1	0	0	6	2	2	1	1	2	7	.105	.143	.000	10.50	3.00
Cook, Ryan	R-R	6-3	200	6-30-87	0	1	2.12	14	0	0	6	17	13	6	4	0	8	12	.224	.150	.263	6.35	4.24
De La Rosa, Eury	L-L	5-9	167	2-24-90	0	0	18.00	1	0	0	0	1	3	2	2	0	1	1	.600	.500	.667	9.00	9.00
DeMark, Mike	R-R	6-0	198	5-20-83	0	0	0.00	2	0	0	0	2	1	0	0	0	0	0	.143	.000	.500	0.00	0.00
Demel, Sam	R-R	6-0	205	10-23-85	0	2	5.06	11	0	0	1	11	11	6	6	1	5	9	.262	.389	.167	7.59	4.22
Duke, Zach	L-L	6-1	205	4-19-83	1	0	8.44	1	1	0	0	5	7	5	5	2	1	2	.304	.500	.200	3.38	1.69
Eitel, Derek	R-R	6-4	200	11-21-87	0	1	5.59	2	1	0	0	10	9	7	6	2	3	6	.237	.300	.214	5.59	2.79
Ellis, Josh	R-R	6-1	200	8-7-84	0	1	13.50	3	0	0	0	3	7	6	5	3	2	2	.389	.429	.364	5.40	5.40
Enright, Barry	R-R	6-3	220	3-30-86	9	5	5.21	21	21	0	0	123	127	71	71	20	42	86	.276	.308	.249	6.31	3.08
Galarraga, Armando	R-R	6-4	235	1-15-82	1	2	9.26	5	5	0	0	23	30	24	24	9	17	16	.300	.383	.175	6.17	6.56
Hamrick, Randy	R-R	6-2	195	8-27-86	0	0	2.25	5	0	0	0	8	10	3	2	0	4	5	.323	.467	.188	5.63	4.50

Pitching	B-T	HT	WT	DOB	W	L	ERA	G	GS	CG	SV	IP	H	R	ER	HR	BB	SO	AVG	vLH	vRH	K/9	BB/9
Hernandez, Gaby	R-R	6-3	215	5-21-86	4	7	5.97	15	15	0	0	86	105	61	57	15	47	53	.301	.264	.332	5.55	4.92
Kroenke, Zach	R-L	6-2	205	4-21-84	10	3	5.89	23	23	0	0	128	173	88	84	14	50	73	.325	.313	.331	5.12	3.51
Layne, Tom	L-L	6-3	185	11-2-84	10	7	6.21	32	15	0	0	122	148	95	84	14	57	56	.303	.272	.318	4.14	4.22
Mahay, Ron	L-L	6-2	190	6-28-71	0	2	9.58	10	0	0	0	10	16	14	11	2	7	8	.340	.368	.321	6.97	6.10
2-team total (12 Memphis)					1	2	5.48	22	0	0	0	21	24	16	13	3	10	16	—	—	—	6.75	4.22
Mickolio, Kam	R-R	6-9	255	5-10-84	3	4	4.97	48	0	0	6	58	58	34	32	4	25	63	.252	.290	.220	9.78	3.88
Miley, Wade	L-L	6-1	220	11-13-86	4	1	3.64	8	8	1	0	54	53	23	22	4	16	56	.255	.218	.268	9.28	2.65
Mulvey, Kevin	R-R	6-1	205	5-26-85	4	9	6.64	19	19	1	0	103	128	83	76	10	44	63	.308	.321	.295	5.50	3.84
Newby, Kyler	R-R	6-4	225	2-22-85	2	3	5.03	13	7	0	0	39	48	23	22	4	19	36	.310	.329	.294	8.24	4.35
Norberto, Jordan	L-L	6-0	195	12-8-86	6	2	4.25	41	0	0	1	49	46	26	23	1	26	54	.249	.253	.245	9.99	4.81
2-team total (6 Sacramento)					6	2	3.79	47	0	0	2	57	52	27	24	2	30	64	—	—	—	10.11	4.74
Owings, Micah	R-R	6-5	220	9-28-82	3	1	4.85	7	7	0	0	39	41	23	21	5	9	27	.266	.350	.176	6.23	2.08
Putz, J.J.	R-R	6-5	250	2-22-77	0	0	0.00	2	0	0	0	2	1	0	0	0	0	3	.143	.000	.200	13.50	0.00
Rodriguez, Rafael	R-R	6-1	195	9-24-84	0	3	9.88	29	1	0	4	37	60	42	41	8	21	18	.364	.344	.387	4.34	5.06
Roemer, Wes	R-R	6-0	205	10-7-86	0	1	3.70	4	4	0	0	24	26	10	10	5	5	18	.271	.291	.244	6.66	1.85
Shaw, Bryan	B-R	6-1	210	11-8-87	1	0	4.58	16	0	0	9	18	14	9	9	4	4	15	.222	.167	.273	7.64	2.04
Stange, Daniel	R-R	6-1	229	12-22-85	3	1	6.14	25	1	0	1	37	41	27	25	6	27	29	.285	.300	.274	7.12	6.63
Stokes, Brian	R-R	6-1	210	9-7-79	1	1	7.02	12	0	0	0	17	23	13	13	1	6	6	.333	.314	.353	3.24	3.24
Torra, Matt	R-R	6-3	225	6-29-84	4	2	6.07	15	15	1	0	86	119	61	58	14	20	41	.331	.297	.365	4.29	2.09
Urquidez, Jason	R-R	6-0	175	9-12-82	4	5	6.29	42	0	0	0	54	68	39	38	7	22	51	.301	.312	.293	8.45	3.64
Vasquez, Esmerling	R-R	6-1	200	11-7-83	2	2	6.18	23	0	0	0	28	26	19	19	3	21	26	.241	.178	.286	8.46	6.83

Fielding

Catcher	PCT	G	PO	A	E	DP	PB
Hammock	.986	13	67	6	1	1	3
Hester	.970	10	59	5	2	1	1
May	.988	42	227	20	3	2	6
Reed	1.000	3	19	2	0	1	2
Schmidt	.990	85	527	40	6	6	6

First Base	PCT	G	PO	A	E	DP
Allen	.994	72	584	41	4	47
Blum	1.000	1	10	1	0	0
Greene	1.000	6	30	4	0	2
Hallberg	1.000	1	11	2	0	0
Hammock	1.000	5	40	1	0	5
Langerhans	1.000	1	12	0	0	0
May	1.000	5	31	1	0	5
Miranda	.996	31	220	17	1	29
Tracy	.989	45	319	27	4	32
Winfree	1.000	1	2	0	0	1

Second Base	PCT	G	PO	A	E	DP
Abreu	.986	86	171	249	6	54
Berroa	.987	16	27	49	1	17
Hallberg	1.000	52	97	147	0	36
Manzella	1.000	1	1	1	0	0
Ransom	1.000	2	3	2	0	1
Wilson	.889	1	2	6	1	1

Third Base	PCT	G	PO	A	E	DP
Abreu	.000	1	0	0	0	0
Blum	1.000	3	0	8	0	0
Burroughs	.966	26	15	41	2	3
Greene	.900	7	3	15	2	3
Hallberg	.976	54	28	92	3	9
Hammock	1.000	11	1	11	0	1
May	1.000	1	0	1	0	0
Ransom	.934	38	18	67	6	5
Tracy	.900	30	13	41	6	4

Shortstop	PCT	G	PO	A	E	DP
Abreu	.955	30	38	88	6	18
Berroa	.979	23	41	51	2	11
Hallberg	1.000	9	7	10	0	1
Manzella	.987	21	24	54	1	12
Ransom	.971	62	93	177	8	29
Wilson	.958	16	23	45	3	16

Outfield	PCT	G	PO	A	E	DP
Allen	1.000	12	23	0	0	0
Berroa	1.000	3	5	0	0	0
Cowgill	.980	98	240	8	5	1
Frey	.973	107	208	9	6	2
Gillespie	.993	134	275	10	2	3
Hammock	1.000	8	12	1	0	1
Langerhans	1.000	37	85	2	0	1
Owings	1.000	2	2	0	0	0
Pena	.972	25	35	0	1	0
Restovich	.900	8	9	0	1	0
Winfree	1.000	32	41	2	0	2

MOBILE BAYBEARS
DOUBLE-A

SOUTHERN LEAGUE

Batting	B-T	HT	WT	DOB	AVG	vLH	vRH	G	AB	R	H	2B	3B	HR	RBI	BB	HBP	SH	SF	SO	SB	CS	SLG	OBP
Comerota, Jimmy	R-R	6-1	175	12-1-86	.188	.125	.250	9	16	0	3	1	0	0	1	2	0	0	0	5	0	0	.250	.278
Easley, Ed	R-R	6-0	200	12-21-85	.273	.357	.239	83	289	37	79	16	0	4	37	32	4	0	2	51	1	2	.370	.352
Eaton, Adam	L-L	5-9	180	12-6-88	.302	.273	.315	56	212	31	64	7	4	4	28	30	9	0	1	35	10	6	.429	.409
Elmore, Jake	R-R	5-10	180	6-15-87	.270	.324	.240	120	381	58	103	19	1	3	41	54	7	0	11	65	15	11	.349	.362
Ford, Josh	R-R	6-1	225	1-17-83	.265	.204	.291	85	306	38	81	18	1	8	36	29	1	0	1	95	0	1	.408	.329
Frey, Evan	L-L	6-0	170	6-7-86	.173	.143	.185	19	75	10	13	2	0	0	5	10	0	0	0	16	2	4	.200	.271
Gallego, Niko	R-R	6-0	150	12-30-85	.208	.143	.231	18	53	4	11	1	0	0	7	3	2	0	0	11	0	1	.226	.276
Goldschmidt, Paul	R-R	6-3	245	9-10-87	.306	.376	.279	103	366	84	112	21	3	30	94	82	5	0	4	92	9	3	.626	.435
Greene, Kyle	L-R	6-1	200	5-26-86	.183	.190	.182	56	109	15	20	6	0	1	11	16	2	0	1	42	0	0	.266	.297
Hallberg, Mark	R-R	5-11	170	12-9-85	.352	.286	.362	15	54	10	19	6	1	0	10	5	0	0	0	3	0	0	.500	.407
Harbin, Taylor	R-R	5-9	175	2-13-86	.270	.262	.274	129	481	68	130	23	1	8	58	40	5	0	7	81	7	7	.372	.328
Kaczrowski, Dan	R-R	5-9	170	6-17-87	.243	.229	.252	80	181	20	44	7	0	1	18	10	1	0	1	18	2	3	.298	.285
Krauss, Marc	L-R	6-2	235	10-5-87	.242	.219	.252	125	433	69	105	25	6	16	65	64	2	0	4	123	3	3	.439	.340
Linton, Ollie	L-L	5-8	160	4-7-86	.284	.297	.280	107	334	53	95	9	4	3	31	41	11	0	6	77	20	8	.362	.375
Marte, Alfredo	R-R	6-0	190	3-31-89	.233	.095	.364	17	43	4	10	1	0	1	6	4	1	0	1	10	1	0	.326	.306
Pollock, A.J.	R-R	6-1	205	12-5-87	.307	.347	.289	133	550	103	169	41	5	8	73	44	4	0	9	86	36	7	.444	.357
Ward, Daryle	L-L	6-2	240	6-27-75	.318	.333	.310	28	85	12	27	7	0	2	18	22	0	0	3	9	1	0	.471	.445
Wheeler, Ryan	L-R	6-4	220	7-10-88	.294	.276	.301	131	480	69	141	30	2	16	89	45	4	0	2	102	3	4	.465	.358

Pitching	B-T	HT	WT	DOB	W	L	ERA	G	GS	CG	SV	IP	H	R	ER	HR	BB	SO	AVG	vLH	vRH	K/9	BB/9
Bauer, Trevor	R-R	6-1	175	1-17-91	1	1	7.56	4	4	0	0	17	20	14	14	2	8	26	.286	.393	.214	14.04	4.32
Brewer, Charles	R-R	6-4	205	4-7-88	5	1	2.58	11	11	2	0	52	48	16	15	2	19	48	.257	.244	.267	8.25	3.27
Cook, Ryan	R-R	6-0	200	6-30-87	1	4	2.25	34	0	0	13	44	28	12	11	2	14	50	.179	.188	.174	10.23	2.86
Corbin, Pat	L-L	6-3	165	7-19-89	9	8	4.21	26	26	1	0	160	172	78	75	15	40	142	.275	.218	.290	7.97	2.25
DeMark, Mike	R-R	6-0	198	5-20-83	3	2	1.85	32	0	0	15	34	26	7	7	2	9	48	.217	.341	.145	12.71	2.38
Ellis, Josh	R-R	6-1	209	8-7-84	2	2	6.00	18	0	0	0	24	26	18	16	1	12	24	.271	.346	.243	9.00	4.50
Henry, Bryan	R-R	6-3	205	2-15-85	7	4	4.65	32	10	0	2	99	115	58	51	15	33	68	.301	.336	.280	6.20	3.01

Pitching

Pitching	B-T	HT	WT	DOB	W	L	ERA	G	GS	CG	SV	IP	H	R	ER	HR	BB	SO	AVG	vLH	vRH	K/9	BB/9
Layne, Tom	L-L	6-3	185	11-2-84	2	0	2.55	3	3	0	0	18	16	5	5	1	6	14	.250	.091	.283	7.13	3.06
Marshall, Evan	R-R	6-2	208	4-18-90	0	0	0.00	1	0	0	0	2	2	0	0	0	0	0	.286	.000	.400	0.00	0.00
Miley, Wade	L-L	6-1	220	11-13-86	4	2	4.78	14	14	0	0	75	74	49	40	6	28	46	.257	.306	.241	5.50	3.35
Munson, Kevin	R-R	6-2	200	1-3-89	0	0	0.00	2	0	0	0	3	3	0	0	0	1	2	.273	.250	.286	6.00	3.00
Newby, Kyler	R-R	6-4	225	2-22-85	8	2	3.87	25	9	0	1	79	72	35	34	9	25	63	.246	.311	.201	7.18	2.85
Ortega, Yonata	R-R	6-1	220	11-11-86	1	0	2.55	14	0	0	1	18	7	8	5	2	11	18	.115	.208	.054	9.17	5.60
Parker, Jarrod	R-R	6-1	195	11-24-88	11	8	3.79	26	26	0	0	131	112	61	55	7	55	112	.236	.274	.209	7.71	3.79
Roemer, Wes	R-R	6-0	205	10-7-86	8	7	4.51	24	23	1	0	140	153	82	70	13	40	97	.285	.265	.304	6.25	2.58
Septimo, Leyson	L-L	6-1	195	7-7-85	2	1	6.37	21	0	0	0	30	20	23	21	1	25	22	.202	.241	.186	6.67	7.58
2-team total (22 Birmingham)					4	2	5.30	43	0	0	0	56	43	39	33	2	41	60	—	—	—	9.64	6.59
Shaw, Bryan	B-R	6-1	210	11-8-87	3	1	0.87	15	0	0	7	21	15	5	2	1	8	15	.200	.195	.206	6.53	3.48
Sinclair, Taylor	L-L	6-3	180	12-23-85	0	0	3.00	5	0	0	0	6	8	3	2	0	5	5	.308	.200	.375	7.50	7.50
Skaggs, Tyler	L-L	6-4	195	7-13-91	4	1	2.50	10	10	0	0	58	45	20	16	4	15	73	.216	.250	.212	11.39	2.34
Spottiswood, Billy	R-R	6-3	210	4-24-85	5	3	2.86	51	0	0	2	72	70	30	23	3	20	61	.252	.273	.238	7.59	2.49
Wilson, Brad	R-R	6-0	184	5-26-87	0	1	13.50	3	2	0	0	9	24	16	14	1	7	5	.500	.600	.429	4.82	6.75
Woodall, Bryan	R-R	6-1	200	10-24-86	4	4	3.43	50	0	0	4	66	68	30	25	5	18	68	.264	.172	.321	9.32	2.47
Zavada, Clay	L-L	6-1	190	6-28-84	3	2	3.43	44	0	0	2	60	67	29	23	4	21	46	.288	.276	.291	6.86	3.13

Fielding

Catcher	PCT	G	PO	A	E	DP	PB
Easley	.998	79	614	43	1	4	7
Ford	.988	63	450	34	6	4	5

First Base	PCT	G	PO	A	E	DP
Goldschmidt	.996	99	877	68	4	87
Greene	1.000	4	22	2	0	2
Ward	.989	25	176	11	2	18
Wheeler	.984	16	111	9	2	16

Second Base	PCT	G	PO	A	E	DP
Comerota	1.000	1	1	3	0	0
Elmore	.981	112	214	315	10	75
Greene	.909	3	4	6	1	1
Hallberg	1.000	8	17	22	0	5
Harbin	.966	7	14	14	1	3

Third Base	PCT	G	PO	A	E	DP
Comerota	1.000	2	1	7	0	1
Elmore	.000	1	0	0	0	0
Greene	.852	10	7	16	4	4
Hallberg	1.000	3	1	9	0	1
Harbin	1.000	4	2	6	0	2
Kaczrowski	.949	19	8	29	2	1
Wheeler	.929	109	65	184	19	12

Shortstop	PCT	G	PO	A	E	DP
Elmore	1.000	3	3	11	0	1
Gallego	.951	15	21	37	3	4
Greene	.000	1	0	0	0	0
Hallberg	1.000	4	5	6	0	1

Catcher	PCT	G	PO	A	E	DP
Kaczrowski	.986	15	27	41	1	14
Harbin	.969	118	161	333	16	80
Kaczrowski	1.000	7	5	15	0	4

Outfield	PCT	G	PO	A	E	DP
Comerota	1.000	1	2	1	0	0
Eaton	.984	54	119	6	2	4
Frey	.966	19	26	2	1	0
Greene	1.000	8	6	0	0	0
Kaczrowski	1.000	4	0	1	0	0
Krauss	.978	106	172	7	4	2
Linton	.976	95	155	10	4	3
Marte	.969	13	31	0	1	0
Pollock	.996	132	275	4	1	1
Septimo	.000	1	0	0	0	0

VISALIA RAWHIDE   HIGH CLASS A

CALIFORNIA LEAGUE

Batting

Batting	B-T	HT	WT	DOB	AVG	vLH	vRH	G	AB	R	H	2B	3B	HR	RBI	BB	HBP	SH	SF	SO	SB	CS	SLG	OBP
Aguila, Roidany	R-R	5-10	175	10-22-90	.250	.000	.500	1	4	0	1	0	0	0	1	0	0	0	0	2	0	0	.250	.250
Blum, Geoff	B-R	6-3	220	4-26-73	.600	.000	.600	2	5	1	3	2	0	1	2	0	0	0	0	0	0	0	1.600	.600
Borchering, Bobby	B-R	6-3	200	10-25-90	.267	.252	.271	135	531	80	142	29	3	24	92	49	5	0	5	162	4	1	.469	.332
Broxton, Keon	R-R	6-3	195	5-7-90	.251	.261	.248	110	406	69	102	14	5	7	44	62	3	0	7	142	27	8	.362	.349
Davidson, Matt	R-R	6-3	225	3-26-91	.277	.286	.274	135	535	93	148	39	1	20	106	52	11	0	8	147	0	1	.465	.348
Eaton, Adam	L-L	5-9	180	12-6-88	.332	.250	.354	65	244	54	81	15	3	6	39	42	14	0	1	41	24	8	.492	.455
Greene, Kyle	L-R	6-1	190	5-26-86	.273	.250	.277	22	77	17	21	6	3	0	10	13	5	0	1	24	0	1	.468	.406
Greer, Brent	R-R	6-0	185	10-16-87	.247	.190	.260	64	223	32	55	13	0	4	27	15	4	0	0	70	4	4	.359	.306
Hilt, Justin	R-R	6-1	205	4-29-88	.189	.250	.179	29	90	11	17	3	0	2	9	14	2	0	1	38	3	1	.289	.308
LaPensee, Ryan	R-R	6-3	190	8-10-88	.244	.246	.243	74	238	19	58	13	0	0	24	16	2	0	2	40	7	4	.298	.295
Marte, Alfredo	R-R	6-0	190	3-31-89	.299	.311	.295	59	234	35	70	15	3	7	33	14	2	0	0	43	5	0	.479	.344
Nick, David	R-R	6-2	180	2-3-90	.300	.350	.286	132	564	99	169	35	5	13	68	30	8	0	3	80	5	5	.449	.342
Owings, Chris	R-R	5-9	175	8-12-91	.246	.279	.237	121	521	67	128	29	6	11	50	15	7	0	4	130	10	4	.388	.274
Owings, Jon Mark	R-R	6-4	195	4-4-85	.282	.172	.307	96	354	52	100	26	2	14	57	34	5	0	2	84	4	2	.486	.352
Perez, Rossmel	B-R	5-9	200	8-26-89	.287	.190	.315	103	349	44	100	12	0	3	41	49	0	0	1	33	6	1	.347	.373
Reed, Mark	L-R	5-11	180	4-13-86	.290	.370	.275	56	179	15	52	8	1	2	4	31	17	0	0	3	36	4	4	.420	.347
Torrez, Raoul	R-R	5-10	180	3-16-88	.231	.250	.225	82	286	43	66	17	2	8	49	29	16	0	5	89	1	0	.388	.330

Pitching

Pitching	B-T	HT	WT	DOB	W	L	ERA	G	GS	CG	SV	IP	H	R	ER	HR	BB	SO	AVG	vLH	vRH	K/9	BB/9
Anderson, Chase	R-R	6-1	175	11-30-87	1	1	5.40	3	3	0	0	13	14	10	8	1	1	20	.259	.120	.379	13.50	0.68
Bauer, Trevor	R-R	6-1	175	1-17-91	0	1	3.00	3	3	0	0	9	7	3	3	1	4	17	.200	.067	.300	17.00	4.00
Belfiore, Mike	R-L	6-2	220	10-3-88	4	4	5.92	35	8	0	0	79	86	58	52	17	57	79	.278	.299	.272	9.00	6.49
Beltre, Cristian	R-R	6-1	195	5-10-85	3	5	6.70	35	0	0	0	44	55	39	33	3	34	42	.301	.246	.331	8.53	6.90
Budrow, Brian	R-R	6-3	215	11-12-86	4	2	4.91	30	1	0	1	51	62	34	28	4	24	36	.305	.372	.256	6.31	4.21
Camacho, Yiomar	R-R	6-1	172	2-24-90	0	1	15.00	1	1	0	0	3	7	5	5	0	1	1	.538	.500	.571	3.00	3.00
Capellan, Victor	R-R	6-2	195	7-24-89	0	1	5.88	23	0	0	0	34	44	24	22	2	20	37	.321	.300	.338	9.89	5.35
Cooper, Blake	R-R	5-11	190	3-30-88	1	0	4.40	10	0	0	1	14	20	8	7	0	5	13	.333	.235	.372	8.16	3.14
De La Rosa, Eury	L-L	5-9	167	2-24-90	0	0	0.00	1	0	0	0	1	1	0	0	0	1	1	.250	.000	.500	9.00	9.00
Duke, Zach	L-L	6-1	205	4-19-83	1	0	1.80	1	1	0	0	5	5	1	1	0	0	4	.263	.250	.273	7.20	0.00
Eitel, Derek	R-R	6-4	200	11-21-87	8	9	6.15	25	22	0	0	123	155	91	84	16	49	105	.313	.329	.300	7.68	3.59
Harden, Trevor	B-R	6-2	215	9-1-87	2	8	6.35	19	18	0	0	101	122	82	71	17	56	77	.303	.333	.279	6.88	5.01
Holmberg, David	R-L	6-4	219	7-19-91	4	6	4.67	13	13	0	0	71	73	44	37	5	35	76	.263	.215	.277	9.59	4.42
Marshall, Evan	R-R	6-2	208	4-18-90	1	1	1.59	15	0	0	4	17	14	6	3	2	5	18	.212	.158	.243	9.53	2.65
Munson, Kevin	R-R	6-2	200	1-3-89	4	3	4.02	42	0	0	0	54	44	27	24	4	41	76	.221	.273	.180	12.75	6.88
Odegaard, Chris	R-R	6-2	220	4-17-87	1	1	9.64	9	1	0	0	14	18	15	15	1	19	17	.316	.296	.333	10.93	12.21
Ortega, Yonata	R-R	6-1	220	11-11-86	3	1	4.81	34	0	0	9	39	37	26	21	3	21	58	.247	.138	.329	13.27	4.81

Pitching	B-T	HT	WT	DOB	W	L	ERA	G	GS	CG	SV	IP	H	R	ER	HR	BB	SO	AVG	vLH	vRH	K/9	BB/9
Rosario, Diogenes	R-R	6-2	179	9-1-88	6	7	5.07	32	18	0	0	119	137	78	67	11	44	88	.291	.304	.284	6.66	3.33
Sinclair, Taylor	L-L	6-3	180	12-23-85	4	2	2.55	45	0	0	4	60	56	19	17	4	22	67	.245	.189	.271	10.05	3.30
Skaggs, Tyler	L-L	6-4	195	7-13-91	5	5	3.22	17	17	0	0	101	81	39	36	6	34	125	.219	.195	.226	11.18	3.04
Smith, Eric	R-R	6-3	220	10-15-88	5	13	6.35	28	28	0	0	150	199	128	106	11	85	103	.325	.361	.300	6.17	5.09
Taylor, Dan	L-L	6-0	205	7-25-87	2	1	4.01	16	2	0	1	34	39	17	15	5	7	35	.300	.250	.316	9.36	1.87
Wilson, Brad	R-R	6-0	184	5-26-87	1	1	4.94	4	4	0	0	24	27	14	13	5	6	19	.300	.286	.303	7.23	2.28
Worthington, Adam	R-R	5-9	190	8-20-87	4	4	4.48	45	0	0	2	62	56	34	31	4	32	69	.238	.253	.230	9.96	4.62

Fielding

Catcher	PCT	G	PO	A	E	DP	PB
Aguila	1.000	1	4	2	0	0	1
Perez	.982	102	823	112	17	9	22
Reed	.995	42	330	37	2	6	6

First Base	PCT	G	PO	A	E	DP
Borchering	.983	68	568	25	10	53
Davidson	.992	66	563	35	5	62
Greene	1.000	3	21	3	0	3
Reed	.962	3	23	2	1	3

Second Base	PCT	G	PO	A	E	DP
Greer	.929	3	7	6	1	4

	PCT	G	PO	A	E	DP
Nick	.976	124	217	314	13	78
Torrez	1.000	15	33	48	0	9

Third Base	PCT	G	PO	A	E	DP
Borchering	.882	57	32	95	17	11
Davidson	.908	56	22	87	11	11
Greer	.900	10	4	14	2	3
Torrez	.933	17	9	33	3	0

Shortstop	PCT	G	PO	A	E	DP
Greer	.928	20	31	46	6	11
Owings	.943	117	174	354	32	83
Torrez	.900	4	3	15	2	2

Outfield	PCT	G	PO	A	E	DP
Broxton	.980	109	234	7	5	2
Eaton	.987	64	148	7	2	1
Greene	1.000	1	16	1	0	0
Greer	.667	1	1	1	1	0
Hilt	.927	28	35	3	3	0
LaPensee	.983	70	110	4	2	0
Marte	.925	56	93	5	8	3
Owings	1.000	1	1	0	0	0
Owings	.975	50	71	8	2	0
Torrez	.980	35	46	3	1	1

SOUTH BEND SILVER HAWKS

LOW CLASS A

MIDWEST LEAGUE

Batting	B-T	HT	WT	DOB	AVG	vLH	vRH	G	AB	R	H	2B	3B	HR	RBI	BB	HBP	SH	SF	SO	SB	CS	SLG	OBP
Arbelo, Yazy	L-R	6-4	229	4-7-88	.247	.193	.271	134	461	68	114	31	0	31	95	73	11	0	4	161	1	0	.516	.361
Bourgeois, Marc	L-R	5-11	205	3-15-89	.224	.188	.242	17	49	3	11	2	1	0	5	5	0	0	0	8	1	1	.306	.296
Broxton, Keon	R-R	6-3	195	5-7-90	.231	.176	.246	20	78	8	18	0	2	0	1	7	0	0	0	30	6	4	.282	.294
Castillo, Ramon	R-R	5-11	215	9-6-88	.196	.169	.208	69	224	21	44	11	2	7	32	11	6	0	1	58	5	2	.357	.252
Freeman, Mike	R-R	6-0	192	8-4-87	.261	.284	.253	70	257	35	67	15	2	0	27	27	2	0	5	39	16	2	.335	.330
Gallego, Niko	R-R	6-0	150	12-29-88	.211	.239	.200	47	161	19	34	6	1	0	13	14	4	0	0	33	5	2	.261	.291
Gomez, Raywilly	B-R	5-11	192	1-25-90	.274	.321	.255	108	390	42	107	15	2	2	50	36	3	0	3	39	2	1	.338	.338
Helm, Matt	R-R	6-1	210	9-1-90	.262	.356	.223	127	451	58	118	27	1	8	60	49	8	0	2	134	16	4	.379	.343
Inciarte, Ender	L-L	5-11	160	10-29-90	.262	.267	.260	116	450	73	118	19	5	1	25	47	2	0	3	59	26	15	.333	.333
Jarrett, Chris	L-L	5-10	170	11-17-88	.198	.213	.193	83	268	34	53	7	5	1	15	21	8	0	2	65	7	2	.272	.274
Montilla, Gerson	R-R	5-10	168	11-13-89	.234	.329	.185	66	244	26	57	20	2	7	30	14	6	0	3	49	7	3	.418	.288
Narodowski, David	R-R	5-9	193	8-3-88	.254	.317	.222	32	122	10	31	8	1	1	7	13	0	0	1	27	3	1	.361	.324
Navarro, Raul	R-R	5-11	167	2-5-92	.205	.222	.200	45	151	18	31	5	1	0	11	14	1	0	0	39	10	2	.252	.277
Ortiz, Roberto	R-R	6-1	195	10-28-88	.210	.198	.217	72	233	24	49	18	2	2	22	18	10	0	3	67	8	3	.330	.292
Pimentel, Jhoan	R-R	5-10	207	7-13-89	.191	.156	.206	51	152	13	29	3	0	1	14	8	0	0	1	26	0	0	.230	.230
Rodriguez, Roberto	L-L	5-11	183	3-22-89	.217	.208	.220	100	332	30	72	14	3	2	21	21	5	0	3	79	6	7	.295	.271
Stone, Bobby	L-L	6-2	220	11-14-89	.193	.278	.169	27	83	7	16	6	0	1	10	12	0	0	2	24	0	0	.301	.289
Walters, Zach	B-R	6-2	195	9-5-89	.302	.278	.313	97	361	69	109	27	6	9	56	42	3	0	3	96	12	10	.485	.377

Pitching	B-T	HT	WT	DOB	W	L	ERA	G	GS	CG	SV	IP	H	R	ER	HR	BB	SO	AVG	vLH	vRH	K/9	BB/9
Bolsinger, Mike	R-R	6-2	209	1-29-88	6	6	2.66	32	13	0	0	102	84	35	30	6	25	91	.228	.195	.256	8.06	2.21
Bradley, J.R.	R-R	6-3	185	6-9-92	6	16	4.98	27	27	1	0	143	169	100	79	16	51	88	.291	.304	.280	5.55	3.22
Budrow, Brian	R-R	6-3	215	11-12-86	2	0	1.59	7	0	0	0	11	6	2	2	0	4	17	.150	.143	.154	13.50	3.18
Burgos, Enrique	R-R	6-4	200	11-23-90	0	2	19.64	2	1	0	0	4	6	8	8	1	5	4	.375	.182	.800	9.82	12.27
Cantwell, Keith	R-R	6-5	215	9-9-87	1	2	5.44	30	0	0	0	45	52	30	27	7	12	49	.286	.310	.263	9.87	2.42
Capellan, Victor	R-R	6-2	195	7-24-89	1	1	4.30	19	0	0	1	23	25	11	11	2	5	21	.278	.300	.260	8.22	1.96
Cooper, Blake	R-R	5-11	190	3-30-88	2	3	3.35	31	0	0	9	40	34	22	15	0	13	38	.221	.246	.204	8.48	2.90
De La Rosa, Eury	L-L	5-9	167	2-24-90	1	0	1.36	39	0	0	10	53	36	11	8	3	13	51	.197	.167	.222	8.66	2.21
Erben, Jeremy	R-R	5-11	195	9-5-88	3	4	2.78	40	0	0	6	55	41	19	17	4	19	65	.204	.173	.217	10.64	3.11
Green, Tyler	R-R	6-1	185	11-24-91	6	8	4.97	25	22	0	1	114	118	70	63	10	49	79	.270	.270	.286	6.24	3.87
Hagens, Bradin	R-R	6-3	210	5-12-89	8	7	4.11	24	24	0	0	125	128	67	57	11	53	79	.265	.268	.263	5.70	3.83
Hamrick, Randy	R-R	6-2	195	8-27-86	0	0	1.93	8	0	0	1	9	9	2	2	0	7	5	.281	.250	.313	4.82	6.75
Hogben, Kable	R-R	6-3	190	7-6-90	0	0	2.84	20	0	0	2	32	26	11	10	0	14	34	.232	.158	.270	9.66	3.98
Holmberg, David	R-L	6-4	219	7-19-91	8	3	2.39	14	14	1	0	83	65	27	22	3	13	81	.212	.268	.187	8.78	1.41
Odegaard, Chris	R-R	6-2	220	4-17-87	4	0	2.20	31	0	0	2	49	37	16	12	1	16	50	.207	.299	.137	9.18	2.94
Robinson, Greg	R-R	6-2	236	7-17-87	0	1	4.15	3	0	0	0	4	4	2	2	0	0	4	.333	.286	.364	8.31	0.00
Schuster, Patrick	R-L	6-1	182	10-30-90	7	4	3.33	27	14	0	0	119	106	52	44	7	41	84	.244	.264	.237	6.35	3.10
Shields, Jeff	R-R	6-3	205	2-22-90	9	13	4.63	27	23	0	0	136	150	82	70	12	31	76	.275	.299	.252	5.03	2.05
Taylor, Dan	L-L	6-0	205	7-25-87	3	2	1.97	21	1	0	2	46	29	13	10	2	7	54	.177	.106	.224	10.64	1.38

Fielding

Catcher	PCT	G	PO	A	E	DP	PB
Castillo	.963	12	71	7	3	0	4
Gomez	.994	88	584	51	4	1	6
Pimentel	.986	48	302	40	5	5	5

First Base	PCT	G	PO	A	E	DP
Arbelo	.986	116	1102	76	17	102
Castillo	.984	25	224	15	4	16

Second Base	PCT	G	PO	A	E	DP
Freeman	.990	61	103	186	3	38
Gallego	.889	6	11	21	4	3
Gomez	1.000	1	2	0	0	0
Montilla	.979	59	112	209	7	46
Narodowski	1.000	2	3	6	0	1
Walters	1.000	11	17	35	0	10

Third Base	PCT	G	PO	A	E	DP
Castillo	1.000	2	2	2	0	0
Gallego	.875	6	2	19	3	2
Helm	.869	96	55	157	32	8
Montilla	1.000	3	0	5	0	1
Narodowski	.900	12	10	26	4	5
Pimentel	1.000	1	1	1	0	0

	PCT	G	PO	A	E	DP
Walters	.930	21	17	49	5	4
Shortstop	**PCT**	**G**	**PO**	**A**	**E**	**DP**
Freeman	.971	9	8	25	1	5
Gallego	.929	31	51	107	12	18
Narodowski	.979	9	13	33	1	8

	PCT	G	PO	A	E	DP
Navarro	.956	43	57	118	8	32
Walters	.946	49	54	155	12	28
Outfield	**PCT**	**G**	**PO**	**A**	**E**	**DP**
Bourgeois	1.000	17	17	1	0	0
Broxton	1.000	20	38	1	0	1

	PCT	G	PO	A	E	DP
Inciarte	.986	116	264	8	4	4
Jarrett	.960	80	96	1	4	0
Ortiz	.966	71	104	8	4	2
Rodriguez	.979	96	133	10	3	2
Stone	.919	25	31	3	3	0

YAKIMA BEARS   SHORT-SEASON
NORTHWEST LEAGUE

Batting	B-T	HT	WT	DOB	AVG	vLH	vRH	G	AB	R	H	2B	3B	HR	RBI	BB	HBP	SH	SF	SO	SB	CS	SLG	OBP
Bell, Carter	R-R	6-1	195	6-12-90	.270	.233	.278	41	163	15	44	8	2	1	17	11	2	0	2	31	1	0	.362	.320
Bourgeois, Marc	L-R	5-11	205	3-15-89	.268	.381	.242	30	112	13	30	8	5	0	11	7	1	0	1	20	2	2	.429	.314
Bream, Tyler	R-R	6-3	210	10-28-89	.235	.224	.238	57	221	24	52	10	1	4	21	11	1	0	0	52	2	0	.344	.275
Comerota, Jimmy	R-R	6-1	175	12-1-86	.322	.404	.300	59	227	31	73	11	3	1	34	26	2	0	3	23	13	2	.410	.391
Hilt, Justin	R-R	6-1	205	4-29-88	.219	.214	.221	59	196	31	43	7	3	11	28	27	3	0	0	83	3	2	.454	.323
Jenkins, Kerry	R-R	6-1	210	5-17-89	.271	.250	.276	48	170	20	46	8	2	1	15	10	5	0	2	37	5	5	.359	.326
Jensen, Matt	R-R	5-10	190	2-20-90	.150	.500	.111	13	40	5	6	1	0	0	2	5	1	0	0	8	2	1	.175	.261
Jones, Zachary	R-R	5-10	170	11-1-88	.279	.316	.274	35	136	14	38	9	1	2	14	13	1	0	0	29	7	1	.404	.347
Kim, Jae Yun	R-R	6-1	185	9-16-90	.232	.438	.193	30	99	9	23	5	0	2	11	5	2	0	0	21	1	0	.343	.283
Moss, Westley	R-R	6-2	165	7-17-88	.269	.184	.286	55	223	29	60	8	2	0	21	22	0	0	3	56	15	8	.323	.331
Narodowski, David	R-R	5-9	193	8-3-88	.217	.200	.222	18	60	10	13	1	0	2	7	9	0	0	0	20	1	1	.333	.319
Navarro, Raul	R-R	5-11	167	2-5-92	.198	.121	.213	56	207	12	41	4	2	0	13	16	1	0	2	49	0	2	.237	.257
Pulfer, Daniel	R-R	5-9	195	2-16-90	.258	.250	.260	59	209	33	54	7	2	2	20	19	5	0	1	19	6	4	.340	.333
Rodriguez, Steven	L-R	6-4	200	1-8-90	.195	.133	.208	27	87	13	17	3	0	0	4	11	6	0	2	16	1	0	.230	.321
Van Winkle, Tyson	R-R	6-1	190	2-2-88	.283	.214	.313	16	46	4	13	2	0	0	6	1	0	0	0	4	0	0	.326	.298
Weber, Garrett	R-R	5-10	165	3-29-89	.292	.269	.298	64	250	32	73	17	1	2	29	19	2	0	1	47	6	1	.392	.346
Zabala, Henry	R-R	6-1	175	10-20-89	.244	.231	.247	55	197	20	48	11	1	3	19	6	3	0	1	30	1	3	.355	.275

Pitching	B-T	HT	WT	DOB	W	L	ERA	G	GS	CG	SV	IP	H	R	ER	HR	BB	SO	AVG	vLH	vRH	K/9	BB/9
Acosta, Victor	R-R	5-11	175	3-10-90	2	0	3.24	9	0	0	1	8	9	5	3	0	7	6	.265	.412	.118	6.48	7.56
Albert, Justin	L-L	6-3	235	5-27-87	5	1	2.17	26	0	0	5	37	36	12	9	0	7	36	.259	.250	.263	8.68	1.69
Blake, Michael	L-L	5-11	190	8-4-90	3	4	5.13	21	0	0	0	26	22	15	15	1	22	47	.227	.379	.162	16.06	7.52
Camacho, Yiomar	R-R	6-1	172	2-24-90	2	2	3.69	7	7	0	0	32	33	18	13	0	12	19	.273	.333	.229	5.40	3.41
Capaul, Alex	R-R	6-2	210	11-2-88	2	3	3.07	15	11	0	0	73	77	36	25	1	10	39	.274	.326	.228	4.79	1.23
De Los Santos, Sammy	R-R	6-1	185	12-9-89	0	2	1.98	20	0	0	3	27	23	9	6	2	8	26	.228	.298	.167	8.56	2.63
Geyer, Cody	R-R	5-11	215	5-4-92	0	0	13.50	3	0	0	0	3	5	5	5	1	4	3	.357	.500	.250	8.10	10.80
Gutierrez, Teofilo	R-R	6-0	180	5-20-90	4	3	4.20	16	12	0	0	81	82	45	38	2	22	56	.264	.262	.265	6.20	2.43
Hamrick, Randy	R-R	6-2	195	8-27-86	0	5	6.42	10	6	2	0	34	44	28	24	3	16	26	.319	.297	.338	6.95	4.28
Hogben, Kable	R-R	6-3	190	7-6-90	1	0	0.53	9	0	0	1	17	6	1	1	0	1	27	.109	.200	.033	14.29	0.53
Kudryk, Adam	L-L	6-6	215	12-31-87	5	4	3.40	15	15	0	0	87	95	44	33	4	34	69	.283	.329	.268	7.11	3.50
Marshall, Evan	R-R	6-2	208	4-18-90	0	0	0.75	11	0	0	2	12	10	4	1	0	2	13	.213	.143	.269	9.75	1.50
Osteen, Adam	R-R	6-3	200	1-24-88	0	0	7.11	5	0	0	0	6	7	6	5	1	2	3	.280	.250	.308	4.26	2.84
Paredes, Willy	R-R	6-3	180	2-2-89	0	1	1.80	7	0	0	0	15	14	3	3	0	4	15	.250	.350	.194	9.00	2.40
Pedrotty, John	L-L	6-4	220	11-28-89	2	4	3.04	15	13	0	0	68	61	29	23	3	29	70	.236	.261	.226	9.26	3.84
Perry, Blake	R-R	6-5	190	2-3-92	1	0	4.09	2	0	0	0	11	7	5	5	0	5	8	.189	.188	.190	6.55	4.09
Reagan, Miles	R-R	6-2	200	11-16-90	0	4	6.23	24	0	0	1	30	26	29	21	0	23	32	.234	.250	.222	9.49	6.82
Robinson, Greg	R-R	6-2	236	7-17-87	2	5	4.66	22	0	0	2	37	37	21	19	2	26	31	.257	.220	.282	7.61	6.38
Wilson, Brad	R-R	6-0	184	5-26-87	3	3	2.84	11	10	0	0	57	59	26	18	2	27	49	.268	.297	.244	7.74	4.26
Zizinia, Drew	R-R	6-2	210	3-14-88	1	2	7.01	19	0	0	0	26	26	22	20	3	14	35	.271	.244	.294	12.27	4.91

Fielding

Catcher	PCT	G	PO	A	E	DP	PB
Jones	.979	10	77	15	2	0	2
Kim	.996	30	230	29	1	2	5
Rodriguez	.991	26	198	24	2	2	4
Van Winkle	.982	16	94	15	2	1	3

First Base	PCT	G	PO	A	E	DP
Bream	.983	25	217	18	4	30
Comerota	.991	52	490	37	5	48
Narodowski	1.000	1	9	1	0	0
Weber	1.000	1	3	0	0	1

Second Base	PCT	G	PO	A	E	DP
Jensen	.931	6	11	16	2	5

	PCT	G	PO	A	E	DP
Jones	1.000	2	4	9	0	0
Narodowski	1.000	1	4	2	0	1
Pulfer	.970	52	111	146	8	37
Weber	.968	18	36	55	3	17

Third Base	PCT	G	PO	A	E	DP
Bell	.904	37	24	79	11	11
Bream	.890	29	13	68	10	3
Jones	.000	1	0	0	0	0
Narodowski	.875	4	1	6	1	0
Weber	.913	8	4	17	2	1

Shortstop	PCT	G	PO	A	E	DP
Narodowski	.966	7	10	18	1	6

	PCT	G	PO	A	E	DP
Navarro	.942	56	82	179	16	43
Weber	.946	19	29	59	5	14

Outfield	PCT	G	PO	A	E	DP
Bourgeois	.962	28	42	8	2	0
Comerota	1.000	7	10	1	0	1
Hilt	.963	56	98	6	4	2
Jenkins	.985	39	64	2	1	0
Jones	1.000	7	9	1	0	0
Moss	.954	55	101	3	5	0
Narodowski	.875	2	7	0	1	0
Zabala	.925	43	58	4	5	0

MISSOULA OSPREY   ROOKIE
PIONEER LEAGUE

Batting	B-T	HT	WT	DOB	AVG	vLH	vRH	G	AB	R	H	2B	3B	HR	RBI	BB	HBP	SH	SF	SO	SB	CS	SLG	OBP
Aguila, Roidany	R-R	5-10	175	10-22-90	.256	.217	.274	53	195	32	50	12	1	12	35	16	3	0	0	46	3	1	.513	.322
Belza, Tom	L-R	6-0	190	7-31-89	.316	.294	.323	63	237	48	75	19	3	7	30	22	0	0	0	51	8	0	.511	.375
Bianco, Justin	L-R	5-11	180	8-24-92	.206	.170	.217	54	199	24	41	8	1	2	20	22	0	0	0	81	5	7	.286	.285
Brown, Breland	R-R	5-9	200	12-12-84	.171	.083	.217	11	35	4	6	2	0	0	3	5	2	0	0	13	1	2	.229	.310
Cardullo, Stephen	R-R	6-0	212	8-31-87	.288	.197	.323	61	219	38	63	14	4	10	38	24	7	0	3	52	3	7	.525	.372
Court, Ryan	R-R	6-2	210	5-28-88	.271	.272	.271	70	273	47	74	14	3	7	33	35	5	0	1	85	5	3	.421	.363

Batting	B-T	HT	WT	DOB	AVG	vLH	vRH	G	AB	R	H	2B	3B	HR	RBI	BB	HBP	SH	SF	SO	SB	CS	SLG	OBP
Ellison, Chris	L-R	6-2	189	12-16-88	.248	.188	.277	60	246	43	61	12	3	6	28	30	2	0	2	68	15	9	.394	.332
Gomez, Jeremia	R-R	6-3	185	2-10-91	.244	.303	.221	35	119	16	29	7	1	4	13	12	1	0	2	37	1	3	.420	.313
Griffin, Jon	R-R	6-7	250	4-29-89	.295	.247	.316	71	278	47	82	12	0	18	59	29	0	0	6	77	4	0	.532	.355
Groff, Eric	R-R	5-11	195	1-25-88	.316	.293	.325	66	269	47	85	23	5	14	48	11	1	0	3	72	10	5	.595	.346
Henry, Bryan	R-R	6-3	220	6-9-89	.220	.200	.231	19	59	8	13	2	1	3	8	1	0	0	1	23	0	1	.441	.230
Jensen, Matt	R-R	5-10	190	2-20-90	.375	.333	.400	3	8	1	3	0	0	0	2	1	0	0	0	3	0	0	.375	.444
Linton, Ty	R-R	6-3	195	1-17-91	.257	.238	.266	39	136	18	35	7	4	3	17	10	3	0	0	53	3	6	.434	.322
Moss, Westley	R-R	6-2	165	7-17-88	.000	.000	.000	3	9	0	0	0	0	0	0	0	0	0	0	6	0	0	.000	.000
Parr, Josh	R-R	5-11	170	9-11-89	.288	.186	.330	34	146	29	42	5	3	3	16	6	6	0	0	21	15	3	.425	.342
Pena, Fidel	R-R	5-10	175	7-19-91	.308	.318	.305	61	240	35	74	10	6	5	34	16	3	0	0	50	12	2	.463	.359

Pitching	B-T	HT	WT	DOB	W	L	ERA	G	GS	CG	SV	IP	H	R	ER	HR	BB	SO	AVG	vLH	vRH	K/9	BB/9
Bradley, Archie	R-R	6-4	225	8-10-92	0	0	0.00	2	1	0	2	1	0	0	0	0	0	4	.143	.000	.200	18.00	0.00
Burgos, Enrique	R-R	6-4	200	11-23-90	4	4	6.56	10	10	0	0	47	57	38	34	4	28	43	.302	.261	.315	8.29	5.40
Capaul, Alex	R-R	6-2	210	11-2-88	0	0	0.00	1	0	0	0	2	1	0	0	0	0	1	.167	.000	.200	5.40	0.00
Darrah, Jesse	L-R	6-2	190	3-28-90	5	2	4.55	14	11	0	0	59	57	36	30	5	25	68	.252	.280	.238	10.31	3.79
Flynn, Conrad	R-R	6-3	190	11-18-88	4	4	6.16	17	6	0	0	61	76	42	42	12	18	59	.309	.270	.331	8.66	2.64
Hernandez, Raymond	R-R	6-1	190	9-1-88	8	3	4.35	14	10	0	0	70	68	38	34	12	18	71	.245	.244	.247	9.09	2.30
Hessler, Keith	L-L	6-4	215	3-15-89	4	0	2.89	23	1	0	0	44	32	17	14	3	20	62	.198	.250	.175	12.78	4.12
Jaime, Johan	L-L	5-11	185	12-7-89	1	3	10.16	21	1	0	0	31	35	37	35	8	24	33	.278	.313	.266	9.58	6.97
Johnson, D.J.	L-R	6-4	235	8-30-89	1	0	2.08	20	0	0	10	26	16	6	6	0	7	32	.176	.200	.164	11.08	2.42
Lara, Victor	R-R	5-10	205	12-3-88	1	3	4.80	22	0	0	1	30	23	18	16	4	21	40	.213	.171	.233	12.00	6.30
Meo, Anthony	R-R	6-2	185	2-19-90	0	0	0.00	1	0	0	0	2	0	0	0	0	0	1	.000	.000	.000	4.50	0.00
Postill, Jason	R-R	6-0	185	6-6-89	1	0	4.61	8	0	0	0	14	9	7	7	1	8	16	.184	.273	.158	10.54	5.27
Price, Dexter	R-R	6-7	220	8-8-90	3	2	4.96	15	11	0	0	65	67	41	36	10	18	47	.263	.266	.260	6.47	2.48
Rowland, Robby	B-R	6-6	205	12-15-91	2	7	8.07	14	14	0	0	68	95	65	61	15	17	52	.335	.324	.341	6.88	2.25
Sample, Matt	R-R	6-5	200	8-16-88	1	0	2.67	24	0	0	3	27	24	9	8	2	10	41	.235	.263	.219	13.67	3.33
Santana, Frank	R-R	6-2	200	2-21-89	1	4	7.24	27	0	0	4	32	37	27	26	3	18	42	.289	.286	.290	11.69	5.01
Siemens, Taylor	L-L	6-5	200	7-1-89	3	1	2.23	14	11	0	0	61	49	28	15	1	25	65	.226	.280	.210	9.64	3.71
Simmons, Seth	R-R	5-9	170	6-14-88	2	2	4.04	26	0	0	1	36	27	20	16	4	20	61	.205	.225	.196	15.39	5.05

Fielding

Catcher	PCT	G	PO	A	E	DP	PB
Aguila	.996	49	452	64	2	5	11
Henry	.950	8	50	7	3	1	5
Pena	1.000	22	189	44	0	3	2

First Base	PCT	G	PO	A	E	DP
Belza	1.000	6	60	4	0	3
Court	1.000	10	79	4	0	7
Griffin	.985	60	537	40	9	45

Second Base	PCT	G	PO	A	E	DP
Belza	.982	11	16	38	1	4
Groff	.948	34	60	86	8	20

	PCT	G	PO	A	E	DP
Jensen	.818	3	4	5	2	1
Pena	.970	30	44	86	4	19

Third Base	PCT	G	PO	A	E	DP
Belza	1.000	1	0	3	0	0
Cardullo	1.000	3	3	6	0	1
Court	.934	55	28	128	11	9
Groff	.968	17	5	25	1	2

Shortstop	PCT	G	PO	A	E	DP
Belza	.917	5	8	3	1	1
Cardullo	.914	35	67	92	15	21
Parr	.951	34	51	104	8	21

	PCT	G	PO	A	E	DP
Pena	1.000	5	8	13	0	3

Outfield	PCT	G	PO	A	E	DP
Belza	.974	26	37	1	1	1
Bianco	.989	54	86	2	1	0
Brown	.833	9	5	0	1	0
Cardullo	1.000	9	19	1	0	0
Ellison	.981	60	100	6	2	1
Gomez	.957	34	42	2	2	0
Linton	.939	39	45	1	3	0
Moss	1.000	3	2	1	0	0

AZL DIAMONDBACKS   ROOKIE

ARIZONA LEAGUE

Batting	B-T	HT	WT	DOB	AVG	vLH	vRH	G	AB	R	H	2B	3B	HR	RBI	BB	HBP	SH	SF	SO	SB	CS	SLG	OBP
Abreu, Jesus	R-R	5-10	155	4-14-92	.262	.200	.281	31	84	21	22	6	3	1	12	29	2	0	1	18	3	0	.440	.457
Alegria, Jose	R-R	6-1	200	11-5-90	.230	.263	.214	23	61	11	14	5	0	2	9	7	1	0	1	16	0	0	.410	.314
Blum, Geoff	B-R	6-3	220	4-26-73	.333	.250	.364	5	15	1	5	0	0	0	1	1	0	0	0	1	0	0	.333	.375
Brito, Socrates	L-L	6-2	197	9-6-92	.275	.218	.293	55	236	29	65	3	7	1	29	13	2	1	3	50	18	10	.360	.315
Castillo, William	R-R	5-10	158	7-11-92	.153	.125	.161	33	72	5	11	0	0	0	8	4	1	2	0	15	1	2	.153	.208
Delgado, Elvin	R-R	5-11	177	8-17-90	.161	.000	.209	21	56	7	9	0	0	0	5	9	0	1		15	2	0	.161	.284
Donahue, Patrick	L-R	5-10	195	7-2-89	.303	.250	.317	47	155	23	47	8	1	1	26	26	3	0	1	13	4	1	.387	.411
Leonard, John	R-R	6-0	159	6-25-92	.229	.283	.211	53	214	25	49	7	0	0	16	25	2	3	1	58	5	3	.262	.314
Mateo, Wagner	L-L	6-2	190	3-30-93	.228	.189	.242	54	206	30	47	9	2	6	25	23	1	0	0	88	4	3	.379	.309
Perez, Michael	L-R	5-11	180	8-7-92	.217	.000	.238	7	23	5	5	2	0	2	3	2	0	0	0	10	1	0	.565	.280
Rogers, Ed	R-R	6-0	190	8-29-78	.213	.100	.243	13	47	4	10	6	0	1	11	5	1	0	0	8	0	0	.404	.302
Ruiz, Pedro	R-R	5-11	165	8-30-91	.291	.391	.270	38	134	28	39	2	2	0	15	22	1	6	0	32	10	5	.396	.395
Soriano, Domingo	R-R	6-1	165	10-29-89	.269	.147	.306	50	145	28	39	8	2	2	16	6	2	1	2	44	10	0	.393	.303
Van Winkle, Tyson	R-R	6-1	190	2-2-88	.226	.125	.261	11	31	10	7	3	0	0	7	1	1	1	3	13	1	0	.323	.375
Weik, Joe	R-R	6-2	215	4-21-88	.266	.263	.267	47	158	26	42	14	3	2	18	14	4	0	3	21	2	3	.430	.335
Williams, Jake	B-L	6-1	190	1-27-91	.241	.333	.213	25	79	9	19	2	1	0	8	11	0	2	0	19	1	1	.291	.333
Williams, Tyler	R-R	6-2	205	1-5-91	.083	.250	.050	10	24	1	2	0	0	0	1	2	0	0	0	20	1	0	.083	.154
Winfree, David	R-R	6-3	230	8-5-85	.250	.200	.286	4	12	1	3	0	0	1	2	4	1	0	0	4	0	0	.500	.471

Pitching	B-T	HT	WT	DOB	W	L	ERA	G	GS	CG	SV	IP	H	R	ER	HR	BB	SO	AVG	vLH	vRH	K/9	BB/9
Acosta, Victor	R-R	5-11	175	3-10-90	1	2	1.69	15	0	0	0	21	12	8	4	0	8	19	.152	.227	.123	8.02	3.38
Brewer, Charles	R-R	6-4	205	4-7-88	0	0	0.00	1	1	0	0	3	3	0	0	0		4	.250	1.000	.182	12.00	0.00
Camacho, Yiomar	R-R	6-1	172	2-24-90	2	3	1.38	6	6	0	0	33	22	9	5	1	4	36	.190	.242	.169	9.92	1.10
Chafin, Andrew	R-L	6-2	205	6-17-90	0	0	0.00	1	1	0	0	1	1	0	0	0	0	2	.250	.000	.500	18.00	0.00
Cruz, Berling	R-R	6-1	183	6-3-91	1	3	5.54	18	0	0	0	26	33	20	16	2	22	26	.303	.263	.324	9.00	7.62
De Jesus, Cesse	R-R	5-11	155	5-16-90	0	2	5.40	4	4	0	0	15	22	11	9	1	5	12	.355	.480	.270	7.20	3.00

Pitching	B-T	HT	WT	DOB	W	L	ERA	G	GS	CG	SV	IP	H	R	ER	HR	BB	SO	AVG	vLH	vRH	K/9	BB/9
Escanio, Bryan	R-R	6-1	185	12-17-91	3	3	5.40	12	9	0	0	55	68	37	33	5	23	55	.305	.410	.248	9.00	3.76
Falcon, Juan	R-R	6-3	200	3-7-92	0	2	13.08	18	3	0	0	21	30	32	31	5	32	18	.333	.323	.339	7.59	13.50
Gerdeman, Ross	R-R	6-3	210	11-7-89	4	2	3.64	14	7	0	0	59	57	25	24	2	13	32	.258	.230	.272	4.85	1.97
Geyer, Cody	R-R	5-11	215	5-4-92	3	2	6.17	20	0	0	1	23	26	18	16	1	12	15	.289	.276	.295	5.79	4.63
Hernandez, Ray	R-R	6-1	190	9-1-88	0	0	0.00	1	0	0	0	1	1	0	0	0	0	2	.250	.000	.333	18.00	0.00
Johnson, Sean	R-R	6-1	205	9-14-89	1	1	6.98	14	0	0	0	19	29	16	15	0	7	21	.345	.333	.352	9.78	3.26
Lebo, Mike	R-R	6-7	225	11-22-88	0	4	4.91	15	3	0	2	44	45	27	24	3	13	26	.259	.268	.254	5.32	2.66
Meo, Anthony	R-R	6-2	185	2-19-90	0	0	0.00	1	1	0	0	1	0	0	0	0	0	2	.000	.000	.000	18.00	0.00
Mulvey, Kevin	R-R	6-1	205	5-26-85	0	1	5.87	2	2	0	0	8	14	5	5	1	0	3	.412	.500	.375	3.52	0.00
Paredes, Willy	R-R	6-3	180	2-2-89	0	0	2.08	2	0	0	0	4	7	1	1	0	0	3	.389	.444	.333	6.23	0.00
Perry, Blake	R-R	6-5	190	2-3-92	1	5	5.00	12	11	0	0	63	65	48	35	3	19	49	.260	.267	.256	7.00	2.71
Platt, Austin	R-R	6-3	190	3-5-92	0	0	9.75	13	0	0	0	12	27	21	13	0	11	11	.458	.500	.429	8.25	8.25
Postill, Jason	R-R	6-0	185	6-6-89	1	2	6.23	6	5	0	0	26	32	19	18	0	7	20	.320	.385	.279	6.92	2.42
Putz, J.J.	R-R	6-5	250	2-22-77	0	0	0.00	2	2	0	0	2	1	0	0	0	0	0	.143	.000	.333	0.00	0.00
Santana, Diony	L-L	6-0	150	1-15-91	0	1	6.49	15	1	0	0	26	30	23	19	1	23	24	.283	.261	.289	8.20	7.86
Urbina, Elroy	L-L	6-1	180	7-22-89	3	3	5.76	22	0	0	1	25	34	26	16	2	10	25	.318	.207	.359	9.00	3.60

Fielding

Catcher	PCT	G	PO	A	E	DP	PB
Alegria	.985	23	117	15	2	2	4
Delgado	.994	20	138	19	1	4	5
Donahue	.967	12	54	5	2	1	4
Perez	.975	5	34	5	1	2	2
Van Winkle	.965	10	68	14	3	1	2

First Base	PCT	G	PO	A	E	DP
Donahue	1.000	2	15	0	0	1
Luciano	1.000	5	32	2	0	5
Mateo	.977	23	192	17	5	15
Weik	.975	21	146	8	4	10
Williams	.991	13	101	6	1	11

Second Base	PCT	G	PO	A	E	DP
Abreu	.914	12	23	30	5	9

	PCT	G	PO	A	E	DP
Castillo	.939	8	11	20	2	4
Donahue	1.000	2	2	4	0	1
Leonard	.955	20	39	45	4	6
Rogers	1.000	1	3	3	0	2
Ruiz	.947	18	42	48	5	10

Third Base	PCT	G	PO	A	E	DP
Abreu	.913	9	4	17	2	3
Blum	.917	4	2	9	1	2
Castillo	1.000	4	0	14	0	0
Donahue	.945	17	16	36	3	7
Luciano	.951	24	14	44	3	3
Ruiz	.955	7	5	16	1	2
Williams	1.000	2	1	0	0	0

Shortstop	PCT	G	PO	A	E	DP
Castillo	1.000	4	6	3	0	2
Leonard	.927	34	39	100	11	14
Rogers	1.000	9	11	24	0	3
Ruiz	.962	14	18	32	2	3

Outfield	PCT	G	PO	A	E	DP
Abreu	1.000	8	13	1	0	1
Brito	.955	55	118	8	6	1
Castillo	1.000	10	16	2	0	0
Luciano	.938	17	28	2	2	0
Mateo	.950	28	38	0	2	0
Soriano	.975	46	72	6	2	1
Weik	1.000	16	25	0	0	0
Williams	.000	1	0	0	0	0
Winfree	.000	2	0	0	0	0

DSL DIAMONDBACKS   ROOKIE

DOMINICAN SUMMER LEAGUE

Batting	B-T	HT	WT	DOB	AVG	vLH	vRH	G	AB	R	H	2B	3B	HR	RBI	BB	HBP	SH	SF	SO	SB	CS	SLG	OBP
Betemit, Felipe	B-R	5-11	182	7-6-91	.146	.167	.135	32	82	12	12	2	1	0	10	19	4	0	0	20	1	3	.195	.333
Bolivar, Anderson	B-R	5-11	165	9-9-92	.241	.184	.263	38	133	18	32	7	0	0	10	16	5	0	1	16	2	1	.293	.342
Garcia, Yorman	R-R	6-1	175	3-17-94	.231	.244	.227	56	182	23	42	8	2	1	19	35	12	0	0	42	2	5	.313	.389
Gonzalez, Michael	R-R	5-11	170	3-12-92	.184	.115	.213	38	87	12	16	3	1	0	12	29	1	0	4	20	0	3	.241	.380
Gutierrez, Yosbel	R-R	5-10	170	1-20-93	.238	.250	.234	27	84	12	20	3	1	0	7	9	8	0	2	24	1	0	.298	.359
Heredia, Juan	R-R	5-11	145	7-4-92	.248	.261	.244	42	105	24	26	5	0	0	4	25	2	0	1	20	2	6	.295	.398
Liriano, Jesse	R-R	6-0	175	10-9-91	.212	.200	.217	47	156	18	33	9	7	1	20	24	8	0	0	66	5	4	.378	.346
Mejias, Ronny	B-R	6-0	170	5-9-94	.179	.097	.196	55	179	27	32	5	1	1	14	35	1	0	0	42	2	3	.235	.316
Perez, Jonathan	R-R	6-0	205	9-14-90	.125	.154	.114	30	48	10	6	2	0	1	5	9	2	0	1	17	1	0	.229	.283
Ramirez, Franyer	L-R	6-0	210	11-27-91	.135	.333	.097	14	37	2	5	2	0	0	2	7	0	0	0	16	0	1	.189	.273
Ramirez, Freddy	R-R	6-0	170	6-27-92	.242	.200	.258	34	91	13	22	3	0	1	9	20	7	0	1	34	1	1	.308	.412
Ramirez, Yefrey	R-R	6-2	165	11-28-93	.169	.162	.172	44	136	18	23	6	0	0	4	22	4	0	1	37	2	0	.213	.301
Ruiz, Pedro	B-R	5-11	165	8-30-91	.257	.214	.274	29	101	18	26	3	2	0	13	35	2	0	2	22	5	4	.327	.450
Santana, Wilmer	L-L	6-0	170	2-19-92	.206	.243	.195	51	170	19	35	2	1	2	14	20	3	0	1	50	3	2	.265	.299
Santiago, Alan	L-R	6-1	170	7-24-90	.253	.229	.262	60	178	20	45	8	0	0	36	38	2	0	3	43	2	5	.298	.385
Silvestre, Valentino	R-R	5-11	177	10-15-93	.223	.200	.237	25	94	10	21	3	0	0	15	10	3	0	0	28	3	1	.255	.318
Valdez, Samuel	R-R	6-2	206	4-2-91	.245	.157	.287	50	159	19	39	10	1	1	18	28	10	0	1	44	0	3	.340	.389
Vargas, Ranfy	R-R	6-2	210	11-16-92	.182	.067	.225	19	55	6	10	3	0	1	3	17	3	0	0	27	0	0	.291	.400

Pitching	B-T	HT	WT	DOB	W	L	ERA	G	GS	CG	SV	IP	H	R	ER	HR	BB	SO	AVG	vLH	vRH	K/9	BB/9
Arauz, Amilcar	R-R	5-10	150	4-17-93	1	0	1.42	10	0	0	1	13	9	3	2	0	4	9	.200	.217	.182	6.39	2.84
Cardenas, David	R-R	5-11	160	1-17-92	0	3	3.72	17	0	0	5	19	20	9	8	2	7	19	.274	.300	.256	8.84	3.26
Cuevas, Enyel	L-L	5-11	140	12-8-92	1	3	5.40	12	0	0	0	22	17	15	13	0	20	19	.218	.333	.203	7.89	8.31
Escanio, Bryan	R-R	6-1	185	12-17-91	0	1	2.61	4	3	0	1	21	19	7	6	0	7	22	.247	.290	.217	9.58	3.05
Gonzalez, Gabriel	R-R	6-2	170	1-23-89	3	1	3.91	17	4	0	0	53	52	25	23	2	19	41	.265	.185	.305	6.96	3.23
Gonzalez, Jose	R-R	6-2	195	12-17-92	3	3	4.18	17	0	0	0	28	33	17	13	2	12	11	.300	.333	.282	3.54	3.86
Guzman, Jean	R-R	5-10	170	11-7-92	0	1	6.59	13	0	0	1	14	10	11	10	0	14	10	.200	.118	.242	6.59	9.22
Hernandez, Luis	R-R	6-2	187	6-22-92	2	6	4.27	13	13	1	0	53	50	34	25	3	38	29	.255	.258	.254	4.96	6.49
Jose, Jose	L-L	6-2	175	7-21-90	2	3	2.41	16	0	0	0	37	30	20	10	0	18	48	.214	.167	.221	11.57	4.34
Matos, Joel	R-R	6-5	200	9-17-92	0	1	9.00	6	2	0	0	10	9	10	10	1	10	6	.243	.211	.278	5.40	9.00
Paredes, Willy	R-R	6-3	180	2-2-89	0	2	4.32	15	0	0	4	25	22	13	12	1	14	30	.232	.125	.286	10.80	5.04
Parra, Geordy	R-R	6-2	165	9-6-93	0	0	1.13	6	2	0	0	8	7	2	1	0	6	18	.218	.200	.229	10.13	3.38
Perez, Jean	L-L	5-11	165	3-1-90	2	2	4.55	16	0	0	0	30	28	20	15	0	17	24	.252	.400	.238	7.28	5.16
Solis, Jency	R-R	6-1	180	2-22-93	1	3	3.90	10	6	0	0	30	38	21	13	2	12	13	.306	.295	.313	3.90	3.60
Soto, Mauricio	R-R	6-1	180	1-16-89	3	5	3.42	13	13	1	0	71	62	39	27	1	21	77	.235	.238	.232	9.76	2.66
Triana, Karl	R-R	6-0	180	10-7-92	3	5	3.06	12	11	1	0	68	56	32	23	1	14	45	.223	.143	.250	5.99	1.86

Pitching	B-T	HT	WT	DOB	W	L	ERA	G	GS	CG	SV	IP	H	R	ER	HR	BB	SO	AVG	vLH	vRH	K/9	BB/9
Valdez, Juan	R-R	6-1	160	3-23-92	3	6	4.70	13	13	0	0	61	64	37	32	2	22	66	.261	.287	.247	9.68	3.23

Fielding

Catcher	PCT	G	PO	A	E	DP	PB
Bolivar	.966	23	146	22	6	1	4
Gutierrez	.977	26	184	29	5	3	6
Perez	1.000	1	1	0	0	0	
Ramirez	1.000	2	4	2	0	0	
Ramirez	.962	21	156	19	7	2	2

First Base	PCT	G	PO	A	E	DP
Betemit	.857	1	4	2	1	0
Perez	.980	15	95	1	2	5
Ramirez	1.000	1	10	0	0	0
Ramirez	.941	3	15	1	1	0
Ramirez	.981	6	48	4	1	6
Valdez	.990	45	386	18	4	37
Vargas	1.000	7	42	7	0	1

Second Base	PCT	G	PO	A	E	DP
Betemit	.929	5	6	7	1	1
Heredia	.727	2	5	3	3	0
Liriano	.959	23	40	53	4	13
Mejias	.967	22	39	49	3	4
Ruiz	1.000	5	16	5	0	2
Silvestre	.958	16	29	40	3	10

Third Base	PCT	G	PO	A	E	DP
Heredia	1.000	1	0	1	0	0
Mejias	.882	15	14	31	6	3
Perez	1.000	6	2	3	0	2
Ramirez	.500	1	0	1	1	0
Ramirez	.888	35	25	70	12	2
Silvestre	.957	6	7	15	1	1

Vargas	.895	12	12	22	4	3

Shortstop	PCT	G	PO	A	E	DP
Heredia	.901	34	50	78	14	17
Mejias	.928	17	23	41	5	9
Ramirez	.875	3	6	8	2	2
Ruiz	.888	22	29	74	13	11
Silvestre	1.000	1	2	3	0	0

Outfield	PCT	G	PO	A	E	DP
Betemit	.935	23	28	1	2	1
Garcia	.976	55	78	4	2	0
Gonzalez	.980	37	46	4	1	1
Santana	.912	49	57	5	6	1
Santiago	.985	57	61	3	1	1
Silvestre	.667	1	2	0	1	0

Atlanta Braves

SEASON IN A SENTENCE: An epic late-season collapse left the Braves out of the playoffs and overshadowed one of the league's best pitching staffs.

HIGH POINT: Following the trade deadline acquisition of center fielder Michael Bourn, the Braves reeled off 17 wins in August, including winning streaks of five and six games. By the end of the month, they stood at 25 games above .500 and held a commanding 8½-game lead in the wild card race over the Cardinals.

LOW POINT: Despite an awful September, Atlanta still just had to win its final game to get into the playoffs. A 4-3 loss in 13 innings to the division rival Phillies came on the heels of a Cardinals win over the Astros, sending St. Louis to the playoffs and eventually the World Series title. Fatigue and injuries struck the pitching staff, but the real culprit was an offense that struggled to score runs. It was one of the worst collapses in baseball history, overshadowed only by the Red Sox' collapse in the American League.

NOTABLE ROOKIES: Craig Kimbrel emerged as one of the game's dominant relievers with a 2.10 ERA, 14.8 strikeouts per nine innings and a rookie-record 46 saves. Brandon Beachy seized a rotation spot and led the NL in strikeout rate (among those with at least 140 IP) while posting a 3.68 ERA. First baseman Freddie Freeman hit in the middle of the order and led the team with 161 hits, as well as hitting 21 home runs. Outfielder Jose Constanza provided a midseason spark, while lefthander Mike Minor and righthanders Randall Delgado and Julio Teheran pitched well in limited duty and should assume bigger roles going forward.

KEY TRANSACTIONS: Fredi Gonzalez took over for longtime manager Bobby Cox, who had been at the helm since 1989. In an effort to find stability in center field, the Braves grabbed Bourn from the Astros at the trade deadline. He hit .278 and stole 22 bases during his 53 games with the Braves.

DOWN ON THE FARM: Teheran earned International League pitcher of the year honors after leading the league in ERA (2.55) and wins (15). Strong seasons by Minor, Delgado and shortstop Tyler Pastornicky put them in line as legitimate options for the 2012 big league roster. The Braves selected lefthander Sean Gilmartin from Florida State with the 28th overall pick in the draft.

OPENING DAY PAYROLL: $87,002,692 (15th)

PLAYERS OF THE YEAR

MAJOR LEAGUE	MINOR LEAGUE
Tim Hudson rhp	**Julio Teheran** rhp
16-10, 3.22	(Triple-A)
158 SO/56 BB	15-3, 2.55
7th in NL in WHIP	IL Pitcher of the Year

ORGANIZATION LEADERS

BATTING		*Minimum 250 PA
MAJORS		
* AVG	Freddie Freeman	.282
* OPS	Brian McCann	.817
HR	Dan Uggla	36
RBI	Dan Uggla	82
MINORS		
* AVG	Tyler Pastornicky, Mississippi/Gwinnett	.314
* OBP	Chris Garcia, Rome	.405
* SLG	Ernesto Mejia, Mississippi	.531
R	Edward Salcedo, Rome	83
H	Andrelton Simmons, Lynchburg	161
TB	Ernesto Mejia, Mississippi	265
2B	Joe Terdoslavich, Lynchburg	52
3B	David Rohm, Rome	8
HR	Ernesto Mejia, Mississippi	26
RBI	Ernesto Mejia, Mississippi	99
BB	Antoan Richardson, Gwinnett/Mississippi	61
SO	Ernesto Mejia, Mississippi	156
SB	Matt Lipka, Rome	28
PITCHING		#Minimum 75 IP
MAJORS		
W	Tim Hudson	16
# ERA	Jonny Venters	1.84
SO	Brandon Beachy	169
SV	Craig Kimbrel	46
MINORS		
W	Julio Teheran, Gwinnett	15
L	Three tied at	11
# ERA	Julio Teheran, Gwinnett	2.55
G	Jaye Chapman, Mississippi/Gwinnett	52
	Benino Pruneda, Mississippi	52
GS	Three tied at	27
SV	Jairo Asencio, Gwinnett	26
IP	Zeke Spruill, Lynchburg/Mississippi	174.2
BB	Caleb Brewer, Rome/Lynchburg	89
SO	Todd Redmond, Gwinnett	142
# AVG	Caleb Brewer, Rome/Lynchburg	.231

2011 PERFORMANCE

General Manager: Frank Wren. **Farm Director:** Kurt Kemp. **Scouting Director:** Tony DeMacio.

Class	Team	League	W	L	PCT	Finish	Manager(s)
Majors	Atlanta Braves	National	89	73	.549	5th (16)	Fredi Gonzalez
Triple-A	Gwinnett Braves	International	78	65	.545	5th (14)	Dave Brundage
Double-A	Mississippi Braves	Southern	61	79	.436	9th (10)	Rocket Wheeler
High A	Lynchburg Hillcats	Carolina	60	78	.435	8th (8)	Rick Albert/Luis Salazar
Low A	Rome Braves	South Atlantic	60	80	.429	11th (14)	Matt Walbeck/Rick Albert
Rookie	Danville Braves	Appalachian	39	29	.574	t-4th (10)	Randy Ingle
Rookie	GCL Braves	Gulf Coast	24	34	.414	12th (15)	Jonathan Schuerholz
Overall 2011 Minor League Record			322	365	.469	27th (30)	

ORGANIZATION STATISTICS

ATLANTA BRAVES
NATIONAL LEAGUE

Batting	B-T	HT	WT	DOB	AVG	vLH	vRH	G	AB	R	H	2B	3B	HR	RBI	BB	HBP	SH	SF	SO	SB	CS	SLG	OBP
Boscan, J.C.	R-R	6-2	215	12-26-79	.333	1.000	.333	4	9	0	3	0	0	0	0	0	0	0	0	5	0	0	.333	.333
Bourn, Michael	L-R	5-11	180	12-27-82	.278	.210	.315	53	227	30	63	8	3	1	18	15	1	0	3	50	22	7	.352	.321
2-team total (105 Houston)					.294	—	—	158	656	94	193	34	10	2	50	53	4	0	4	140	61	14	.386	.349
Conrad, Brooks	B-R	5-11	190	1-16-80	.223	.292	.203	92	103	11	23	5	0	4	13	15	1	0	1	41	2	0	.388	.325
Constanza, Jose	B-L	5-9	150	9-1-83	.303	.385	.257	42	109	21	33	1	1	2	10	6	0	0	0	14	7	4	.385	.339
Diaz, Matt	R-R	6-0	215	3-3-78	.286	.296	.250	16	35	2	10	1	0	0	1	1	0	0	1	8	1	0	.314	.297
2-team total (100 Pittsburgh)					.263	—	—	116	251	16	66	13	1	0	20	12	3	0	2	52	5	2	.323	.302
Freeman, Freddie	L-R	6-5	225	9-12-89	.282	.247	.299	157	571	67	161	32	0	21	76	53	6	0	5	142	4	4	.448	.346
Gonzalez, Alex	R-R	5-11	215	2-15-77	.241	.267	.232	149	564	59	136	27	1	15	56	22	1	0	2	126	2	0	.372	.270
Hernandez, Diory	R-R	6-0	185	4-8-84	.212	.091	.273	22	33	4	7	1	0	1	4	0	0	0	0	5	0	0	.333	.212
Heyward, Jason	L-L	6-5	240	8-9-89	.227	.192	.240	128	396	50	90	18	2	14	42	51	4	0	3	93	9	2	.389	.319
Hicks, Brandon	R-R	6-2	200	9-14-85	.048	.111	.000	17	21	1	1	0	0	0	1	1	0	0	0	9	0	0	.048	.091
Hinske, Eric	L-R	6-2	235	8-5-77	.233	.118	.252	117	236	24	55	10	0	10	28	26	1	0	1	71	0	1	.403	.311
Jones, Chipper	B-R	6-4	210	4-24-72	.275	.268	.278	126	455	56	125	33	1	18	70	51	0	0	6	80	2	2	.470	.344
Lugo, Julio	R-R	6-1	175	11-16-75	.136	.115	.167	22	44	3	6	0	0	0	3	4	0	0	0	11	0	0	.136	.208
Mather, Joe	R-R	6-4	215	7-23-82	.213	.250	.196	36	75	4	16	4	0	1	9	6	0	0	0	23	0	1	.307	.272
McCann, Brian	L-R	6-3	230	2-20-84	.270	.265	.273	128	466	51	126	19	0	24	71	57	2	0	2	89	3	2	.466	.351
McLouth, Nate	L-R	5-11	180	10-28-81	.228	.179	.251	81	267	35	61	12	2	4	16	44	3	0	0	52	4	2	.333	.344
Prado, Martin	R-R	6-1	190	10-27-83	.260	.245	.265	129	551	66	143	26	2	13	57	34	1	0	3	52	4	8	.385	.302
Ramirez, Wilkin	R-R	6-2	190	10-25-85	.231	.222	.250	20	26	5	6	2	0	0	2	4	0	0	0	11	0	2	.308	.333
Richardson, Antoan	B-R	5-8	165	10-8-83	.500	.500	.000	9	4	2	2	0	0	0	0	0	0	0	0	1	0	0	.500	.500
Ross, David	R-R	6-2	205	3-19-77	.263	.240	.275	52	152	14	40	7	0	6	23	16	0	0	0	51	0	1	.428	.333
Schafer, Jordan	L-L	6-1	200	9-4-86	.240	.190	.261	52	196	32	47	6	3	1	7	18	1	0	0	42	15	4	.316	.307
2-team total (30 Houston)					.242	—	—	82	302	46	73	10	3	2	13	28	2	0	1	70	22	4	.315	.309
Uggla, Dan	R-R	5-11	205	3-11-80	.233	.201	.245	161	600	88	140	22	1	36	82	62	7	0	3	156	1	3	.453	.311
Wilson, Jack	R-R	6-0	190	12-29-77	.220	.267	.192	17	41	3	9	1	0	0	1	0	0	0	0	12	0	0	.244	.238
Young, Matt	L-R	5-8	175	10-3-82	.208	.125	.225	20	48	4	10	1	0	0	1	4	0	0	0	6	0	1	.229	.269

Pitching	B-T	HT	WT	DOB	W	L	ERA	G	GS	CG	SV	IP	H	R	ER	HR	BB	SO	AVG	vLH	vRH	K/9	BB/9
Asencio, Jairo	R-R	6-2	180	5-5-84	0	0	6.97	6	0	0	0	16	11	8	1	5	8	.340	.250	.387	6.97	4.35
Beachy, Brandon	R-R	6-3	215	9-3-86	7	3	3.68	25	25	0	0	142	125	62	58	16	46	169	.236	.236	.237	10.74	2.92
Delgado, Randall	R-R	6-3	200	2-9-90	1	1	2.83	7	7	0	0	35	29	12	11	5	14	18	.220	.196	.237	4.63	3.60
Gearrin, Cory	R-R	6-3	200	4-14-86	1	1	7.85	18	0	0	0	18	17	16	16	0	12	25	.243	.393	.143	12.27	5.89
Hanson, Tommy	R-R	6-6	220	8-28-86	11	7	3.60	22	22	0	0	130	106	55	52	17	46	142	.219	.244	.198	9.83	3.18
Hudson, Tim	R-R	6-1	175	7-14-75	16	10	3.22	33	33	1	0	215	189	86	77	14	56	158	.236	.249	.226	6.61	2.34
Jurrjens, Jair	R-R	6-1	200	1-29-86	13	6	2.96	23	23	2	0	152	142	52	50	14	44	90	.249	.270	.233	5.33	2.61
Kimbrel, Craig	R-R	5-11	205	5-28-88	4	3	2.10	79	0	0	46	77	48	19	18	3	32	127	.178	.157	.196	14.84	3.74
Linebrink, Scott	R-R	6-3	220	8-4-76	4	4	3.64	64	0	0	1	54	58	22	22	6	21	42	.282	.304	.268	6.96	3.48
Lowe, Derek	R-R	6-6	230	6-1-73	9	17	5.05	34	34	0	0	187	212	110	105	14	70	137	.285	.285	.286	6.59	3.37
Martinez, Cristhian	R-R	6-1	185	3-6-82	1	3	3.36	46	0	0	0	78	56	30	29	8	19	58	.197	.222	.177	6.72	2.20
Medlen, Kris	B-R	5-10	190	10-7-85	0	0	0.00	2	0	0	0	2	1	0	0	0	2	1	.125	.000	.250	7.71	0.00
Minor, Mike	R-L	6-4	205	12-26-87	5	3	4.14	15	15	0	0	83	93	39	38	7	30	77	.285	.316	.279	8.38	3.27
Moylan, Peter	R-R	6-2	225	12-2-78	2	1	3.24	13	0	0	0	8	12	3	3	0	3	10	.343	.571	.286	10.80	3.24
O'Flaherty, Eric	L-L	6-2	220	2-5-85	2	4	0.98	78	0	0	0	74	59	9	8	2	21	67	.221	.195	.233	8.19	2.57
Proctor, Scott	R-R	6-1	195	1-2-77	2	3	6.44	31	0	0	0	29	31	21	21	5	19	18	.279	.268	.286	5.52	5.83
Sherrill, George	L-L	6-0	230	4-19-77	3	1	3.00	51	0	0	0	36	33	12	12	3	12	38	.248	.256	.236	9.50	3.00
Teheran, Julio	R-R	6-2	175	1-27-91	1	1	5.03	5	3	0	0	20	21	11	11	4	8	10	.276	.340	.172	4.58	3.66
Varvaro, Anthony	R-R	6-0	195	10-31-84	0	2	2.63	18	0	0	0	24	15	7	7	3	11	23	.183	.189	.178	8.63	4.13
Venters, Jonny	L-L	6-3	195	3-20-85	6	2	1.84	85	0	0	5	88	53	19	18	2	43	96	.176	.127	.194	9.82	4.40
Vizcaino, Arodys	R-R	6-0	190	11-13-90	1	1	4.67	17	0	0	0	17	16	9	9	1	9	17	.239	.286	.205	8.83	4.67

Fielding

Catcher	PCT	G	PO	A	E	DP	PB									First Base	PCT	G	PO	A	E	DP
Boscan	1.000	3	18	1	0	0	0	McCann	.995	126	978	78	5	14	7	Conrad	1.000	1	3	0	0	0
								Ross	.992	49	337	32	3	2	2							

Freeman	.996	156	1317	92	6	106
Hernandez	1.000	1	1	0	0	0
Hinske	1.000	13	81	8	0	6
Mather	1.000	1	11	0	0	2
Prado	1.000	2	13	0	0	1

Second Base	PCT	G	PO	A	E	DP
Conrad	1.000	10	8	13	0	4
Lugo	.000	2	0	0	0	0
Uggla	.980	159	294	440	15	86

Third Base	PCT	G	PO	A	E	DP
Conrad	.950	8	6	13	1	0
Hernandez	.714	6	0	5	2	0

Hicks	.667	6	0	2	1	0
Jones	.976	116	65	177	6	19
Lugo	1.000	8	4	13	0	0
Mather	1.000	1	0	1	0	0
Prado	.950	41	12	84	5	6
Wilson	1.000	3	0	3	0	1

Shortstop	PCT	G	PO	A	E	DP
Gonzalez	.981	149	187	434	12	79
Hernandez	1.000	3	1	4	0	1
Hicks	.909	3	3	7	1	2
Lugo	1.000	5	6	6	0	1
Wilson	.977	13	14	28	1	7

Outfield	PCT	G	PO	A	E	DP
Bourn	.991	53	111	3	1	2
Constanza	.985	33	67	0	1	0
Diaz	1.000	12	16	0	0	0
Heyward	.974	122	218	4	6	0
Hinske	1.000	46	65	2	0	0
Mather	.970	25	32	0	1	0
McLouth	.988	79	169	0	2	0
Prado	.983	100	171	6	3	1
Ramirez	.875	7	7	0	1	0
Schafer	.984	51	125	1	2	1
Young	1.000	14	18	0	0	0

GWINNETT BRAVES
TRIPLE-A

INTERNATIONAL LEAGUE

Batting	B-T	HT	WT	DOB	AVG	vLH	vRH	G	AB	R	H	2B	3B	HR	RBI	BB	HBP	SH	SF	SO	SB	CS	SLG	OBP
Boscan, J.C.	R-R	6-2	215	12-26-79	.182	.179	.184	61	203	12	37	8	0	0	8	12	2	0	0	41	0	2	.222	.235
Bowman, Shawn	R-R	6-3	225	12-9-84	.278	.302	.268	52	180	22	50	7	1	8	17	9	2	0	0	52	2	1	.461	.319
Cabrera, Willie	R-R	5-11	185	8-3-86	.125	.250	.100	7	24	2	3	1	0	0	1	2	0	0	1	7	0	0	.167	.185
Carter, Chris	L-L	6-0	230	9-16-82	.338	.222	.380	23	68	10	23	4	0	4	17	7	0	0	0	9	0	0	.574	.400
2-team total (54 Durham)					.286	—	—	77	283	35	81	15	0	14	63	19	2	0	4	37	1	0	.488	.331
Castillo, Wilkin	B-R	6-0	200	6-1-84	.262	.238	.271	80	279	19	73	12	1	5	37	8	1	0	0	47	5	3	.366	.285
Constanza, Jose	B-L	5-9	150	9-1-83	.312	.300	.318	86	333	47	104	2	4	1	25	25	1	0	1	41	23	8	.351	.361
Fiorentino, Jeff	L-R	6-1	185	4-14-83	.260	.222	.270	80	208	30	54	13	0	5	20	28	2	0	3	40	3	1	.394	.349
Gartrell, Stefan	R-R	6-3	230	1-14-84	.260	.271	.255	116	431	67	112	28	0	25	91	42	8	0	2	112	4	2	.499	.335
2-team total (7 Charlotte)					.262	—	—	123	454	70	119	32	0	26	94	44	9	0	2	118	4	2	.504	.338
Gomez, Mauro	R-R	6-2	230	9-7-84	.304	.309	.303	135	506	76	154	34	2	24	90	38	6	0	6	131	6	2	.522	.356
Gotay, Ruben	B-R	5-11	175	12-25-82	.253	.256	.251	72	245	28	62	4	2	3	25	28	0	0	4	36	6	3	.322	.325
Helms, Wes	R-R	6-4	230	5-12-76	.176	.000	.222	9	34	2	6	0	0	0	3	3	2	0	1	9	0	0	.176	.275
Hernandez, Diory	R-R	6-0	185	4-8-84	.201	.207	.199	79	273	19	55	12	1	5	26	7	3	0	1	46	2	2	.308	.229
Heyward, Jason	L-L	6-5	240	8-9-89	.167	.000	.500	2	6	1	1	1	0	0	1	0	0	0	0	1	0	0	.333	.286
Hicks, Brandon	R-R	6-2	200	9-14-85	.252	.293	.233	104	361	52	91	14	1	18	50	41	3	0	0	137	8	3	.446	.333
Kennelly, Matt	R-R	6-1	180	3-21-89	.286	.000	.286	2	7	1	2	1	0	0	1	1	0	0	0	2	0	0	.429	.375
Lucas, Ed	R-R	6-3	205	5-21-82	.218	.213	.220	81	262	25	57	14	1	3	29	28	1	0	2	74	4	0	.313	.294
Lugo, Julio	R-R	6-1	175	11-16-75	.231	.200	.259	13	52	9	12	4	0	1	7	4	0	0	0	8	1	0	.365	.286
Mather, Joe	R-R	6-4	215	7-23-82	.258	.154	.286	18	62	13	16	5	0	1	4	8	0	0	0	14	2	1	.387	.343
McCann, Brian	L-R	6-3	230	2-20-84	.333	.000	.333	2	6	1	2	0	0	0	1	0	0	0	0	1	0	0	.833	.333
McGill, Shawn	R-R	6-4	195	2-29-84	.250	.143	.333	6	16	2	4	1	0	0	0	2	0	0	0	3	0	0	.313	.333
McLouth, Nate	L-R	5-11	180	10-28-81	.500	.000	.500	3	6	2	3	0	0	0	1	2	1	0	0	2	0	0	.500	.667
Nelson, Dan	B-R	5-11	180	2-12-84	.231	.214	.236	40	117	17	27	4	0	4	20	12	0	0	3	21	0	1	.368	.295
Nieves, Wil	R-R	6-0	190	9-25-77	.282	.100	.353	21	71	8	20	2	0	1	6	6	0	0	1	11	1	0	.352	.333
Pastornicky, Tyler	R-R	5-11	170	12-13-89	.365	.387	.356	27	104	15	38	2	0	1	9	8	0	0	1	11	7	3	.413	.407
Prado, Martin	R-R	6-1	190	10-27-83	.176	.333	.143	6	17	2	3	0	0	0	1	3	0	0	0	5	0	0	.176	.300
Ramirez, Wilkin	R-R	6-2	190	10-25-85	.267	.326	.241	81	288	40	77	16	3	11	36	17	1	0	3	70	19	6	.458	.307
Richardson, Antoan	B-R	5-8	165	10-8-83	.333	.000	.500	2	3	1	1	0	0	0	1	0	0	0	0	0	0	0	.333	.500
Schafer, Jordan	L-L	6-1	200	9-4-86	.256	.235	.265	42	164	21	42	8	0	1	21	14	0	0	3	28	6	3	.323	.309
Young, Matt	L-R	5-8	175	10-3-82	.273	.296	.265	99	366	64	100	16	4	1	24	57	2	0	2	59	17	7	.347	.372

Pitching	B-T	HT	WT	DOB	W	L	ERA	G	GS	CG	SV	IP	H	R	ER	HR	BB	SO	AVG	vLH	vRH	K/9	BB/9
Abreu, Juan	R-R	6-0	180	4-8-85	4	2	2.25	41	0	0	1	48	34	18	12	5	27	68	.193	.230	.167	12.75	5.06
Asencio, Jairo	R-R	6-2	180	5-5-84	3	2	1.81	47	0	0	26	55	39	14	11	3	22	70	.196	.255	.143	11.52	3.62
Beachy, Brandon	R-R	6-3	215	9-3-86	1	0	1.80	1	1	0	0	5	4	1	1	2	8	.211	.286	.167	14.40	3.60
Bullock, Billy	R-R	6-6	225	2-27-88	1	0	0.00	1	0	0	0	1	2	0	0	0	0	1	.400	1.000	.250	9.00	0.00
Chapman, Jaye	R-R	6-0	180	5-22-87	2	3	2.98	43	1	0	2	54	40	20	18	5	26	61	.206	.195	.215	10.10	4.31
Cordier, Erik	R-R	6-4	230	2-25-86	5	8	5.13	19	19	0	0	86	88	55	49	9	51	61	.267	.242	.291	6.38	5.34
Delgado, Randall	R-R	6-3	200	2-9-90	2	2	4.15	4	4	0	0	22	19	10	10	4	11	25	.238	.263	.214	10.38	4.57
Flande, Yohan	L-L	6-2	180	1-27-86	8	8	4.01	33	19	0	1	137	155	70	61	9	38	104	.287	.318	.271	6.83	2.50
Gearrin, Cory	R-R	6-3	200	4-14-86	4	1	1.80	35	0	0	4	50	42	11	10	0	20	60	.226	.276	.191	10.80	3.60
Hardy, Rowdy	L-L	6-4	170	10-26-82	0	1	0.00	4	0	0	0	8	6	4	0	0	3	8	.200	.231	.176	9.39	3.52
Hoover, J.J.	R-R	6-3	215	8-13-87	1	1	3.38	12	2	0	1	19	12	8	7	0	12	31	.174	.214	.146	14.95	5.79
Jurrjens, Jair	R-R	6-1	200	1-29-86	1	0	3.00	1	1	0	0	6	4	2	2	1	2	3	.190	.400	.125	4.50	3.00
Lopez, Rodrigo	R-R	6-1	185	12-14-75	6	1	2.59	9	9	0	0	59	59	19	17	2	14	44	.260	.268	.252	6.71	2.14
Lugo, Jose	L-L	6-1	180	4-10-84	1	0	3.00	19	1	0	0	36	34	17	12	3	23	30	.248	.208	.270	7.50	5.75
Marek, Stephen	L-R	6-2	240	9-3-83	0	1	3.38	10	0	0	2	11	8	5	4	0	4	16	.200	.250	.179	13.50	3.38
Martinez, Cristhian	R-R	6-1	185	3-6-82	2	1	2.86	4	4	0	0	22	26	9	7	2	6	18	.291	.321	.277	7.36	0.82
Minor, Mike	R-L	6-4	205	12-26-87	4	5	3.13	16	16	0	0	101	93	43	35	12	27	99	.246	.283	.230	8.85	2.41
Moylan, Peter	R-R	6-2	225	12-2-78	0	1	0.00	6	1	0	0	6	5	1	0	0	4	10	.200	.222	.188	15.00	6.00
Proctor, Scott	R-R	6-1	195	1-2-77	0	1	1.06	14	0	0	3	17	10	3	2	1	5	24	.164	.158	.167	12.71	2.65
2-team total (6 Scranton/W-B)					1	0	1.50	20	0	0	3	24	18	5	4	1	7	32	—	—	—	12.00	2.63
Redmond, Todd	R-R	6-3	215	5-17-85	10	8	2.92	28	27	2	0	170	152	58	55	18	47	142	.241	.268	.218	7.53	2.49
Richardson, Dustin	L-L	6-6	220	1-9-84	1	0	6.00	23	0	0	0	30	30	21	20	4	22	29	.254	.250	.256	8.70	6.60
Shell, Steven	R-R	6-4	215	3-10-83	2	5	4.35	28	7	0	0	60	58	33	29	12	23	54	.251	.316	.203	8.10	3.45
Swaggerty, Ben	L-L	6-1	185	8-8-82	0	0	6.75	15	0	0	0	25	32	20	19	4	18	33	.314	.161	.380	11.72	6.39

Pitching	B-T	HT	WT	DOB	W	L	ERA	G	GS	CG	SV	IP	H	R	ER	HR	BB	SO	AVG	vLH	vRH	K/9	BB/9
Teheran, Julio	R-R	6-2	175	1-27-91	15	3	2.55	25	24	0	0	145	123	46	41	5	48	122	.232	.276	.199	7.59	2.99
Thompson, Jacob	R-R	6-6	235	11-19-86	1	4	8.78	7	7	0	0	27	41	27	26	2	19	25	.363	.415	.333	8.44	6.41
Varvaro, Anthony	R-R	6-0	195	10-31-84	2	8	2.90	38	0	0	1	59	37	23	19	3	35	69	.185	.135	.225	10.53	5.34
Vizcaino, Arodys	R-R	6-0	190	11-13-90	1	0	1.29	6	0	0	0	7	7	3	1	1	0	8	.259	.417	.133	10.29	0.00

Fielding

Catcher	PCT	G	PO	A	E	DP	PB
Boscan	.988	59	528	31	7	3	5
Castillo	.992	58	453	44	4	9	8
Kennelly	1.000	2	13	1	0	0	0
McCann	1.000	1	5	0	0	0	0
McGill	.975	5	38	1	1	1	0
Nieves	.995	21	197	6	1	0	3

First Base	PCT	G	PO	A	E	DP
Bowman	.986	7	63	9	1	6
Carter	.933	3	13	1	1	3
Castillo	1.000	2	11	1	0	1
Gomez	.989	115	840	50	10	78
Helms	.941	2	14	2	1	0
Hicks	1.000	3	12	4	0	0
Lucas	.980	7	43	5	1	2
Mather	1.000	9	59	6	0	6

Second Base	PCT	G	PO	A	E	DP
Castillo	.800	1	1	3	1	0
Gotay	.971	61	108	127	7	32
Hernandez	.958	15	24	45	3	11

	PCT	G	PO	A	E	DP	PB
Hicks	1.000	7	11	26	0	5	
Lucas	.992	33	37	80	1	15	
Nelson	.883	14	21	32	7	7	
Young	.984	25	34	28	1	5	

Third Base	PCT	G	PO	A	E	DP
Bowman	.946	40	32	73	6	5
Castillo	.913	9	7	14	2	0
Gotay	.917	7	5	6	1	0
Helms	.714	2	0	5	2	2
Hernandez	.897	40	10	51	7	3
Hicks	.945	20	14	38	3	5
Lucas	.960	16	7	17	1	0
Lugo	1.000	1	0	3	0	0
Mather	1.000	4	2	4	0	1
Nelson	.938	15	11	19	2	3
Prado	1.000	3	3	4	0	0

Shortstop	PCT	G	PO	A	E	DP
Hernandez	.945	19	22	47	4	13
Hicks	.964	74	104	161	10	32
Lucas	.951	15	19	39	3	10

Lugo	.905	12	17	21	4	6
Pastornicky	.938	27	37	69	7	13

Outfield	PCT	G	PO	A	E	DP
Cabrera	.909	5	7	3	1	0
Carter	1.000	2	5	0	0	0
Castillo	.917	7	10	1	1	0
Constanza	.980	78	141	4	3	0
Fiorentino	.993	69	137	3	1	0
Gartrell	.990	93	190	12	2	2
Hernandez	.000	1	0	0	0	0
Heyward	1.000	2	2	0	0	0
Lucas	.964	14	27	0	1	0
Mather	1.000	5	11	0	0	0
McLouth	1.000	3	2	0	0	0
Prado	.000	1	0	0	0	0
Ramirez	.984	67	119	7	2	1
Richardson	.000	1	0	0	0	0
Schafer	1.000	39	107	1	0	0
Young	.994	76	159	6	1	2

MISSISSIPPI BRAVES

DOUBLE-A

SOUTHERN LEAGUE

Batting	B-T	HT	WT	DOB	AVG	vLH	vRH	G	AB	R	H	2B	3B	HR	RBI	BB	HBP	SH	SF	SO	SB	CS	SLG	OBP
Bowman, Shawn	R-R	6-3	225	12-9-84	.150	.000	.250	6	20	0	3	0	0	0	2	1	0	0	0	7	0	0	.150	.190
Cabrera, Willie	R-R	5-11	185	8-3-86	.264	.285	.254	95	371	46	98	12	5	5	49	25	1	0	2	31	3	4	.364	.311
Dickey, Gavin	R-R	5-11	200	9-29-83	.200	.000	.231	6	15	1	3	1	0	0	0	0	0	0	0	5	0	0	.267	.200
Fiorentino, Jeff	L-R	6-1	185	4-14-83	.238	.167	.250	13	42	8	10	4	0	1	4	6	1	0	0	7	0	0	.405	.347
Harrilchak, Cory	L-L	5-10	175	10-27-87	.266	.238	.275	122	429	44	114	26	5	7	56	42	7	0	4	72	10	7	.399	.338
Henry, Sean	R-R	5-10	180	8-18-85	.277	.326	.255	54	141	20	39	7	0	1	12	12	3	0	2	28	1	2	.348	.342
Jones, Mycal	R-R	5-10	170	5-30-87	.252	.192	.281	100	373	63	94	25	1	7	36	56	7	0	1	90	17	6	.381	.359
Kennelly, Matt	R-R	6-1	180	3-21-89	.262	.243	.269	74	256	29	67	11	0	2	28	30	4	0	1	64	0	1	.328	.347
Kreke, Jordan	R-R	6-1	205	5-21-87	.218	.264	.198	111	354	33	77	12	2	3	33	18	4	0	2	76	2	4	.288	.262
Lemon, Marcus	L-R	5-11	173	6-3-88	.247	.192	.257	56	162	13	40	5	2	0	11	6	1	0	0	30	2	1	.302	.278
Linares, Donell	R-R	6-1	210	10-28-83	.279	.235	.296	114	412	48	115	17	2	7	62	36	9	0	5	43	0	6	.381	.346
Lucas, Ed	R-R	6-3	205	5-21-82	.270	.341	.243	42	159	32	43	6	0	7	26	15	4	0	2	38	0	0	.440	.344
Mejia, Ernesto	R-R	6-5	245	12-2-85	.297	.316	.289	137	499	82	148	37	1	26	99	58	9	0	7	156	4	3	.531	.375
Nelson, Dan	B-R	5-11	180	2-12-84	.314	.309	.315	61	204	39	64	12	1	1	23	23	2	0	1	31	2	1	.397	.387
Pastornicky, Tyler	R-R	5-11	170	12-13-89	.299	.281	.305	90	355	50	106	13	5	6	36	24	2	0	2	34	20	8	.414	.345
Prado, Martin	R-R	6-1	190	10-27-83	.222	.000	.333	2	9	2	2	0	0	0	2	1	0	0	0	1	0	0	.222	.300
Query, Ryan	R-R	5-11	190	8-24-87	.583	.500	.750	5	12	4	7	2	0	1	1	1	1	0	0	3	0	0	1.000	.643
Retherford, C.J.	R-R	5-10	195	8-14-85	.207	.259	.190	41	111	6	23	7	0	1	19	9	4	0	1	18	0	0	.297	.288
Richardson, Antoan	B-R	5-8	165	10-8-83	.283	.346	.244	91	272	64	77	9	0	1	21	60	11	0	1	66	17	5	.327	.430
Rodriguez, Geraldo	R-R	6-1	190	10-25-87	.224	.095	.283	23	67	11	15	6	0	3	5	3	4	0	1	23	0	1	.448	.293
Schlehuber, Braeden	R-R	6-2	205	1-7-88	.233	.273	.219	26	86	7	20	5	0	1	11	9	2	0	1	28	0	0	.326	.316
Sucre, Jesus	R-R	6-0	200	4-30-88	.219	.310	.179	40	137	13	30	5	0	0	10	6	1	0	1	12	0	1	.255	.255
2-team total (32 Jackson)					.217	—	—	72	221	17	48	8	0	1	19	11	1	0	1	19	0	2	.267	.256

Pitching	B-T	HT	WT	DOB	W	L	ERA	G	GS	CG	SV	IP	H	R	ER	HR	BB	SO	AVG	vLH	vRH	K/9	BB/9
Avilan, Luis	L-L	6-2	165	7-19-89	4	8	4.57	36	13	0	1	106	113	66	54	10	36	78	.268	.287	.259	6.60	3.05
Broadway, Mike	R-R	6-5	215	3-30-87	1	0	1.80	4	0	0	0	5	3	1	1	0	2	6	.176	.286	.100	10.80	3.60
Bullock, Billy	R-R	6-6	225	2-27-88	3	1	4.53	50	0	0	11	50	35	27	25	2	34	65	.193	.171	.212	11.78	6.16
Butts, Brett	R-R	6-1	205	4-24-86	0	4	12.00	7	2	0	0	18	20	19	3	16	4	.321	.292	.344	2.57	10.29
Cardenas, Eliecer	R-R	6-2	218	1-30-88	0	0	27.00	5	0	0	0	3	15	14	9	2	6	1	.625	.833	.556	3.00	18.00
Castro, Yeliar	R-R	6-3	180	12-3-87	2	0	3.25	19	0	0	0	28	22	14	10	1	15	29	.212	.211	.212	9.43	4.88
Chapman, Jaye	R-R	6-0	180	5-22-87	1	0	0.64	9	0	0	2	14	5	1	1	5	16	.109	.048	.160	10.29	3.21
Clemens, Paul	R-R	6-4	180	2-14-88	6	5	3.73	20	20	0	0	109	103	57	45	8	44	93	.249	.213	.284	7.70	3.64
Cody, Chris	L-L	6-0	190	1-7-84	3	1	3.46	6	6	1	0	39	42	17	15	4	8	20	.268	.263	.270	4.62	1.85
Cordier, Erik	R-R	6-4	230	2-25-86	0	1	5.40	1	1	0	0	5	6	3	3	1	0	4	.286	.364	.200	7.20	0.00
Crim, Matt	L-L	6-0	195	8-24-87	0	2	5.56	3	3	0	0	11	20	8	7	1	4	10	.377	.417	.366	7.94	3.18
Delgado, Randall	R-R	6-3	200	2-9-90	5	5	3.84	21	21	2	0	117	116	58	50	11	46	110	.258	.224	.290	8.44	3.53
Gustafson, Tim	R-R	6-3	185	12-29-84	1	3	7.28	6	6	0	0	30	37	25	24	5	14	22	.308	.313	.306	6.67	4.25
2-team total (25 Carolina)					4	7	4.84	31	14	0	3	97	97	57	52	11	46	60	—	—	—	5.59	4.20
Hardy, Rowdy	L-L	6-0	170	10-26-82	3	4	3.14	36	0	0	1	49	60	22	17	2	19	40	.303	.238	.347	7.40	3.51
Hoover, J.J.	R-R	6-3	215	8-13-87	2	5	2.48	31	12	0	1	87	65	30	24	5	28	86	.206	.255	.160	8.90	2.90
Kawakami, Kenshin	R-R	5-11	200	6-22-75	2	4	8.41	16	6	0	0	41	56	38	38	9	16	32	.337	.367	.310	7.08	3.54
Lugo, Jose	L-L	6-1	180	4-10-84	3	4	2.73	14	8	0	0	69	60	28	21	2	28	47	.235	.238	.234	6.10	3.63

Pitching

Pitching	B-T	HT	WT	DOB	W	L	ERA	G	GS	CG	SV	IP	H	R	ER	HR	BB	SO	AVG	vLH	vRH	K/9	BB/9
Masters, Chris	L-L	6-0	225	10-1-87	1	0	0.00	1	1	0	0	7	5	0	0	0	1	4	.200	.333	.158	5.14	1.29
Morlan, Eddie	R-R	6-2	220	3-1-86	0	0	6.35	7	0	0	0	6	8	6	4	0	6	5	.333	.286	.353	7.94	9.53
Oberholtzer, Brett	L-L	6-2	230	7-1-89	9	9	3.74	21	21	1	0	128	119	65	53	6	42	93	.249	.214	.263	6.56	2.96
Pruneda, Benino	R-R	5-9	170	8-8-88	2	7	3.50	52	0	0	11	64	55	30	25	3	40	71	.236	.272	.213	9.93	5.60
Shafer, Aaron	L-R	6-5	185	12-2-86	3	2	4.67	7	7	0	0	44	52	25	23	2	14	37	.289	.238	.330	7.51	2.84
Spruill, Zeke	R-R	6-4	184	9-11-89	3	2	3.20	7	7	1	0	45	45	18	16	3	17	16	.266	.228	.300	3.20	3.40
Sullivan, Richard	L-L	6-3	235	4-14-87	4	5	4.19	44	0	0	1	67	74	49	31	4	26	52	.281	.257	.296	7.02	3.51
Swaggerty, Ben	L-L	6-1	185	8-8-82	1	4	4.26	16	0	0	0	19	19	12	9	0	11	32	.247	.121	.341	15.16	5.21
Vizcaino, Arodys	R-R	6-0	190	11-13-90	2	3	3.81	11	8	0	0	50	44	21	21	3	18	55	.234	.207	.257	9.97	3.26
Wilson, Andrew	R-R	6-2	180	7-30-87	0	0	2.13	6	0	0	1	13	12	4	3	0	2	7	.261	.263	.259	4.97	1.42

Fielding

Catcher	PCT	G	PO	A	E	DP	PB
Kennelly	.981	73	578	30	12	5	4
Query	1.000	4	28	3	0	0	2
Schlehuber	1.000	26	160	10	0	2	0
Sucre	.988	38	284	38	4	1	3

First Base	PCT	G	PO	A	E	DP
Bowman	.962	3	22	3	1	4
Linares	.973	7	35	1	1	3
Lucas	1.000	2	12	1	0	0
Mejia	.989	132	956	74	11	74
Retherford	.974	7	32	5	1	2
Rodriguez	1.000	1	10	0	0	1
Sucre	.000	1	0	0	0	0

Second Base	PCT	G	PO	A	E	DP
Cabrera	.876	30	36	49	12	12
Kreke	.977	84	162	184	8	42
Lemon	.977	25	39	47	2	7
Nelson	.955	19	24	39	3	6
Retherford	1.000	9	11	17	0	4

Third Base	PCT	G	PO	A	E	DP
Bowman	1.000	2	0	2	0	0
Kreke	.857	9	3	9	2	1
Linares	.932	95	55	166	16	14
Nelson	.908	26	17	42	6	4
Prado	.750	2	1	2	1	0
Retherford	.968	18	7	23	1	1

Shortstop	PCT	G	PO	A	E	DP
Kreke	.967	18	15	43	2	7

	PCT	G	PO	A	E	DP
Lucas	.929	40	65	105	13	19
Pastornicky	.943	90	111	204	19	36
Outfield	**PCT**	**G**	**PO**	**A**	**E**	**DP**
Cabrera	.972	61	96	8	3	1
Dickey	1.000	4	5	1	0	1
Fiorentino	.929	7	12	1	1	0
Harrilchak	.980	116	235	9	5	2
Henry	1.000	38	69	3	0	0
Jones	.985	97	253	11	4	2
Kreke	1.000	2	2	0	0	0
Lemon	.947	27	35	1	2	0
Nelson	.909	14	17	3	2	0
Richardson	.989	83	176	3	2	0
Rodriguez	.966	16	28	0	1	0

LYNCHBURG HILLCATS

HIGH CLASS A

CAROLINA LEAGUE

Batting	B-T	HT	WT	DOB	AVG	vLH	vRH	G	AB	R	H	2B	3B	HR	RBI	BB	HBP	SH	SF	SO	SB	CS	SLG	OBP
Bethancourt, Christian	R-R	6-2	190	9-2-91	.271	.288	.263	45	166	11	45	6	0	1	20	3	0	0	4	35	3	2	.325	.277
Brownsten, Cory	R-R	6-0	210	6-3-88	.190	.000	.333	6	21	3	4	2	0	0	1	0	0	0	0	3	0	0	.286	.227
Cunningham, Todd	B-R	6-0	200	3-20-89	.257	.220	.280	87	334	59	86	12	4	4	20	33	14	0	1	47	14	6	.353	.348
Davis, Kyle	R-R	5-11	160	1-8-87	.273	.000	.300	5	11	3	3	0	0	1	2	0	0	0	6	2	0	.545	.385
2-team total (15 Winston-Salem)					.127	—	—	20	63	3	8	2	0	1	3	2	1	0	0	27	2	0	.206	.167
Delgado, Ryan	R-R	5-11	215	1-11-88	.357	.429	.286	4	14	0	5	2	0	0	2	0	0	0	0	1	0	0	.500	.357
Gosselin, Phil	R-R	6-1	190	10-3-88	.264	.248	.272	115	424	60	112	24	6	6	63	37	5	0	9	76	6	2	.392	.324
Hefflinger, Robby	R-R	6-4	220	1-3-90	.114	.111	.115	12	44	2	5	2	0	0	3	3	0	0	0	19	0	0	.159	.170
Kleinknecht, Barrett	R-R	6-0	200	7-30-88	.209	.248	.185	83	282	25	59	13	0	7	28	17	6	0	5	56	7	2	.330	.265
Lemon, Marcus	L-R	5-11	173	6-3-88	.260	.236	.270	52	177	21	46	10	1	2	10	17	0	0	0	23	6	3	.362	.325
Leonard, Joe	R-R	6-5	215	8-26-88	.247	.272	.232	110	405	43	100	27	1	8	63	39	1	0	5	88	1	2	.378	.311
McGill, Shawn	R-R	6-4	195	2-29-84	.289	.324	.269	60	201	25	58	11	1	5	18	17	4	0	0	31	3	3	.428	.356
Milligan, Adam	L-R	6-3	210	3-14-88	.291	.276	.298	64	237	35	69	19	4	12	40	16	4	0	1	76	1	0	.557	.345
Query, Ryan	R-R	5-11	190	8-24-87	.211	.333	.100	7	19	4	4	1	1	0	6	4	1	0	1	2	0	0	.368	.360
Rodriguez, Geraldo	R-R	6-1	195	10-25-87	.219	.198	.232	77	260	22	57	17	0	10	46	19	8	0	0	94	3	2	.400	.293
Schlehuber, Braeden	R-R	6-2	205	1-7-88	.248	.170	.297	36	121	18	30	10	0	4	14	9	0	0	1	17	2	1	.430	.298
Simmons, Andrelton	R-R	6-2	170	9-4-89	.311	.316	.309	131	517	69	161	35	6	1	52	29	6	0	6	43	26	18	.408	.351
Spanjer-Furstenburg, Riaan	R-R	6-2	235	2-8-88	.188	.136	.214	17	64	3	12	5	0	0	1	2	0	0	0	15	1	1	.266	.212
Terdoslavich, Joey	B-R	6-2	210	9-9-88	.286	.276	.291	131	483	72	138	52	2	20	82	41	4	0	8	107	2	0	.526	.341
Walker, Kirk	R-R	6-1	170	12-23-88	.000	.000	.000	1	4	0	0	0	0	0	0	0	0	0	0	1	0	0	.000	.000
Ware, L.V.	R-R	5-10	185	3-18-87	.251	.191	.288	115	367	40	92	19	6	7	33	21	15	0	3	98	14	10	.392	.315
Weaver, Matt	R-R	6-0	175	1-27-90	.179	.150	.211	12	39	5	7	0	1	1	4	3	0	0	0	12	0	0	.308	.238
Whitmer, Jace	R-R	6-4	225	12-18-87	.107	.000	.158	8	28	0	3	2	0	0	1	0	0	0	0	7	0	0	.179	.107
Wiley, Keenan	L-L	6-0	175	4-27-87	.285	.272	.291	102	358	59	102	11	5	1	24	22	8	0	2	66	19	5	.352	.338

Pitching	B-T	HT	WT	DOB	W	L	ERA	G	GS	CG	SV	IP	H	R	ER	HR	BB	SO	AVG	vLH	vRH	K/9	BB/9
Brewer, Caleb	R-R	6-3	205	2-2-89	1	2	5.14	4	4	0	0	21	19	13	12	2	20	13	.244	.321	.200	5.57	8.57
Buchter, Ryan	L-L	6-3	185	2-13-87	2	5	3.59	34	0	0	15	43	36	18	17	3	22	49	.237	.222	.241	10.34	4.64
Butts, Brett	R-R	6-1	205	4-24-86	0	0	0.00	1	0	0	0	1	0	0	0	1	1	.000	.000	.000	9.00	9.00
Cardenas, Eliecer	R-R	6-2	218	1-30-88	4	3	0.79	40	0	0	7	57	31	12	5	1	29	75	.159	.186	.144	11.91	4.61
Castro, Yeliar	R-R	6-3	180	12-3-87	0	0	10.38	4	0	0	0	4	4	6	5	0	6	6	.000	.000	.333	16.62	12.46
Crim, Matt	L-L	6-2	180	8-14-87	2	8	5.88	29	8	0	0	72	108	55	47	7	22	47	.353	.278	.379	5.88	2.75
Delgado, Dimasther	L-L	6-2	180	3-3-89	9	6	3.94	23	17	0	0	96	86	50	42	8	48	77	.243	.204	.257	7.22	4.50
Frevert, Matt	R-R	6-1	190	11-16-86	1	3	8.25	10	0	0	1	12	11	11	11	4	5	11	.277	.286	.273	8.25	3.75
Hale, David	R-R	6-2	200	9-27-87	4	6	4.10	28	13	1	0	101	106	52	46	9	30	86	.275	.217	.316	7.66	2.67
Haynes, Jeremy	R-R	6-2	180	5-28-86	2	1	6.14	26	0	0	0	37	38	30	25	5	33	33	.270	.315	.241	8.10	8.10
Jurik, Dan	R-R	6-3	200	6-18-87	0	0	3.45	7	2	0	0	16	15	6	6	3	9	13	.263	.357	.233	7.47	5.17
Kempf, Willie	R-R	6-0	195	9-30-86	3	5	6.75	13	7	0	0	47	57	37	35	10	22	35	.303	.321	.288	6.75	4.24
Lamm, Mark	R-R	6-4	215	3-8-88	1	2	3.16	15	0	0	1	26	17	9	9	2	12	19	.183	.162	.196	6.66	4.21
Lowey, Jason	R-R	5-11	180	12-26-84	0	0	2.25	8	0	0	3	8	6	2	2	2	5	11	.200	.375	.136	12.38	5.63
Masters, Chris	L-L	6-0	225	10-1-87	9	5	3.34	28	23	0	0	148	128	59	55	10	65	122	.237	.183	.256	7.40	3.94
Moran, Gary	R-R	6-8	255	5-21-85	2	1	2.63	5	5	0	0	27	21	10	8	0	7	24	.208	.300	.169	7.90	2.30

Pitching

Pitching	B-T	HT	WT	DOB	W	L	ERA	G	GS	CG	SV	IP	H	R	ER	HR	BB	SO	AVG	vLH	vRH	K/9	BB/9
Rasmus, Cory	R-R	6-1	220	11-6-87	1	5	7.09	7	7	0	0	27	28	28	21	5	12	40	.264	.311	.230	13.50	4.05
Rodgers, Chad	L-L	6-3	185	11-23-87	0	0	0.00	1	0	0	0	1	0	0	0	0	0	1	.000	.000	.000	13.50	0.00
Roth, Robert	R-R	6-1	195	8-5-88	0	0	4.40	9	0	0	0	14	12	8	7	2	8	10	.235	.250	.251	6.28	5.02
Russell, Andrew	R-R	6-0	202	4-27-84	2	2	4.67	33	0	0	0	54	52	33	28	5	16	43	.261	.306	.241	7.17	2.67
Shafer, Aaron	L-R	6-5	185	12-2-86	3	3	3.05	11	10	0	0	65	61	26	22	3	24	40	.250	.289	.227	5.54	3.32
Sims, Blaine	L-L	6-0	185	3-10-89	3	6	3.66	24	12	0	0	84	87	42	34	3	30	52	.275	.301	.266	5.59	3.23
Spruill, Zeke	B-R	6-4	184	9-11-89	7	9	3.19	20	20	0	0	130	108	56	46	7	23	92	.227	.262	.204	6.39	1.60
Talley, Matt	L-L	6-6	225	8-8-89	0	0	5.06	1	1	0	0	5	7	3	3	0	1	0	.350	.333	.364	0.00	1.69
Vizcaino, Arodys	R-R	6-0	190	11-13-90	2	2	2.45	9	9	0	0	40	31	14	11	3	10	37	.207	.182	.226	8.26	2.23
Weber, Ryan	R-R	6-0	170	8-12-90	0	0	3.00	2	0	0	0	6	6	2	2	0	3	3	.261	.125	.333	4.50	4.50
Wilson, Andrew	R-R	6-2	180	7-30-87	2	4	2.70	36	0	0	5	50	44	19	15	5	14	56	.230	.224	.233	10.08	2.52

Fielding

Catcher	PCT	G	PO	A	E	DP	PB
Bethancourt	.968	35	215	26	8	4	4
Brownsten	.978	6	40	4	1	0	1
Delgado	1.000	4	21	5	0	0	0
McGill	.989	56	397	44	5	2	6
Query	1.000	5	36	3	0	0	2
Schlehuber	.989	34	244	38	3	1	1
Whitmer	.974	6	36	2	1	0	0

First Base	PCT	G	PO	A	E	DP
Kleinknecht	.990	13	94	7	1	11
Rodriguez	.987	15	138	10	2	11
Spanjer-Furstenburg	1.000	6	46	4	0	1
Terdoslavich	.989	106	863	72	10	89

Second Base	PCT	G	PO	A	E	DP
Davis	.929	4	4	9	1	3
Gosselin	.964	102	201	251	17	52
Kleinknecht	.970	25	55	76	4	19
Lemon	1.000	3	10	7	0	5
Walker	1.000	1	0	3	0	1
Weaver	.917	5	8	14	2	1

Third Base	PCT	G	PO	A	E	DP
Kleinknecht	.971	32	27	72	3	6
Leonard	.932	100	67	166	17	11
Terdoslavich	1.000	3	5	4	0	0
Weaver	1.000	4	0	3	0	0

Shortstop	PCT	G	PO	A	E	DP
Kleinknecht	1.000	8	17	20	0	5
Leonard	1.000	1	0	3	0	0
Simmons	.958	129	218	417	28	89
Weaver	.800	1	1	3	1	0

Outfield	PCT	G	PO	A	E	DP
Cunningham	.988	81	154	5	2	2
Hefflinger	1.000	10	9	0	0	0
Lemon	.978	49	86	3	2	2
Milligan	.976	47	79	3	2	0
Rodriguez	.977	24	40	3	1	1
Ware	.982	114	207	16	4	0
Weaver	.000	2	0	0	1	0
Wiley	.976	101	192	13	5	1

ROME BRAVES
LOW CLASS A
SOUTH ATLANTIC LEAGUE

Batting	B-T	HT	WT	DOB	AVG	vLH	vRH	G	AB	R	H	2B	3B	HR	RBI	BB	HBP	SH	SF	SO	SB	CS	SLG	OBP
Ahearn, Chris	R-R	5-11	175	5-8-86	.238	.000	.294	7	21	1	5	0	0	0	2	1	1	0	0	4	0	0	.238	.304
Bethancourt, Christian	R-R	6-2	190	9-2-91	.303	.119	.346	54	221	25	67	10	3	4	33	8	1	0	5	27	6	3	.430	.323
Brownsten, Cory	R-R	6-0	210	6-3-88	.136	.000	.188	7	22	1	3	0	0	0	3	0	0	0	3	1	0	0	.136	.240
Dalfonso, Jakob	L-R	6-3	200	1-25-90	.277	.246	.285	72	271	37	75	8	2	9	32	16	5	0	2	47	8	1	.421	.327
Davis, Kyle	R-R	5-11	160	1-8-87	.156	.375	.083	11	32	5	5	1	0	0	2	2	0	0	0	9	1	0	.188	.206
De Los Santos, Fernando	R-R	6-1	180	1-18-90	.250	.500	.000	1	4	0	1	1	0	0	0	0	0	0	0	0	0	0	.500	.250
Delgado, Ryan	R-R	5-11	215	1-11-88	.257	.423	.167	21	74	9	19	4	2	2	13	3	0	0	2	14	0	0	.446	.278
Flores, Juan	R-R	6-2	190	10-2-86	.162	.250	.138	11	37	4	6	1	0	1	3	0	1	0	1	9	0	0	.270	.179
Frierson, Jarred	B-R	5-11	185	3-23-87	.000	.000	.000	2	8	0	0	0	0	0	0	0	0	0	0	1	0	1	.000	.000
Garcia, Chris	L-R	6-2	225	11-25-87	.305	.260	.317	97	348	51	106	24	0	16	67	59	2	0	3	70	1	1	.511	.405
Gattis, Evan	R-R	6-4	230	8-18-86	.322	.430	.290	88	338	58	109	24	2	22	71	25	11	0	2	53	2	4	.601	.386
Hefflinger, Robby	R-R	6-4	220	1-3-90	.256	.276	.251	112	425	55	109	34	3	8	56	24	3	0	8	123	1	1	.407	.296
Jones, Chipper	B-R	6-4	210	4-24-72	.333	1.000	.000	2	3	0	1	0	0	0	1	2	0	0	1	1	0	0	.333	.500
Kleinknecht, Barrett	R-R	6-0	200	7-30-88	.254	.400	.213	30	114	9	29	6	1	4	15	4	2	0	0	16	1	2	.430	.292
Lipka, Matt	R-R	6-1	188	4-15-92	.247	.265	.242	127	530	78	131	21	3	1	37	42	4	0	5	83	28	14	.304	.305
Mueller, Tony	R-R	6-0	190	2-22-90	.217	.220	.217	48	184	23	40	5	1	0	9	5	1	0	0	35	4	3	.255	.242
Query, Ryan	R-R	5-11	190	8-24-87	.161	.250	.130	9	31	2	5	4	0	1	6	4	0	0	0	11	0	0	.387	.257
Rauh, Bobby	R-R	6-0	172	11-25-87	.147	.250	.133	14	34	5	5	0	0	0	3	2	0	0	0	13	1	0	.147	.194
Reyes, Elmer	R-R	5-11	150	11-26-90	.177	.193	.172	64	237	24	42	13	0	1	16	9	7	0	1	35	5	1	.245	.228
Richardson, Hilton	L-L	6-3	200	1-10-89	.218	.186	.230	53	165	17	36	4	2	1	11	17	1	0	0	53	2	3	.303	.295
Rohm, David	R-R	6-3	215	1-22-90	.289	.270	.295	128	481	64	139	32	8	7	58	28	5	0	7	74	3	7	.432	.330
Rose, Kyle	R-R	6-0	165	5-24-89	.206	.267	.182	67	214	24	44	4	1	0	13	20	5	0	0	51	12	6	.234	.289
Salcedo, Edward	R-R	6-3	195	7-30-91	.248	.282	.240	132	508	83	126	27	6	12	68	41	10	0	3	105	23	10	.396	.315
Snitker, Troy	R-R	6-2	210	12-5-88	.222	.000	.286	3	9	0	2	1	0	0	0	0	0	0	0	3	0	0	.333	.222
Weaver, Matt	R-R	6-0	175	1-20-90	.286	.295	.283	52	189	20	54	16	2	2	19	13	1	0	1	34	1	2	.433	.333
Whitmer, Jace	R-R	6-4	225	12-18-87	.273	.308	.250	10	33	4	9	2	0	0	2	4	0	0	0	10	1	0	.333	.385
Wiley, Keenan	L-L	6-0	175	4-27-87	.293	.500	.257	14	41	8	12	1	2	0	5	8	2	0	0	5	3	1	.415	.431

Pitching	B-T	HT	WT	DOB	W	L	ERA	G	GS	CG	SV	IP	H	R	ER	HR	BB	SO	AVG	vLH	vRH	K/9	BB/9
Alsup, Wes	R-R	6-2	205	11-25-86	1	2	8.79	9	0	0	0	14	21	15	14	1	5	14	.344	.286	.375	8.79	3.14
Alvarez, Danilo	R-R	6-0	210	1-14-90	6	5	4.73	33	1	0	0	72	77	49	38	6	29	58	.266	.327	.236	7.22	3.61
Berryhill, Thomas	R-R	5-10	185	12-9-87	0	0	6.91	9	0	0	0	14	21	13	11	1	4	16	.333	.261	.375	10.05	2.51
Brewer, Caleb	R-R	6-3	205	2-2-89	5	9	5.32	23	23	0	0	130	114	95	77	9	69	104	.228	.241	.221	7.18	4.76
Chaffee, Matt	L-L	6-0	185	12-19-88	1	0	2.39	16	0	0	3	26	22	10	7	1	5	27	.220	.250	.211	9.23	1.71
Filak, Dave	R-R	6-4	220	11-24-88	2	5	7.54	11	11	0	0	45	56	46	38	6	33	32	.311	.319	.306	6.35	6.55
Gilmartin, Sean	L-L	6-2	195	5-8-90	2	1	2.53	5	5	0	0	21	18	6	6	3	2	30	.217	.182	.230	12.66	0.84
Hess, Tyler	R-R	6-5	240	8-29-88	1	3	4.53	27	1	0	7	48	43	30	24	2	23	42	.243	.324	.193	7.93	4.34
Jurik, Dan	R-R	6-3	200	6-18-87	1	2	4.20	14	4	0	2	45	47	23	21	3	16	35	.267	.243	.283	7.00	3.20
Kempf, Willie	R-R	6-0	195	9-30-87	5	3	3.84	16	14	0	0	87	98	53	37	4	23	67	.276	.302	.255	6.96	2.39
Kent, Steve	L-L	6-0	200	5-8-89	1	4	7.77	12	8	0	0	49	74	44	42	5	9	37	.347	.228	.391	6.84	1.66
LaPoint, Lucas	R-R	6-3	215	3-30-91	0	0	0.00	1	0	0	0	2	0	0	0	0	1	5	.000	.000	.000	22.50	0.00
Martin, Cody	R-R	6-2	210	9-4-89	1	0	1.48	14	0	0	6	24	18	7	4	2	4	35	.212	.171	.240	12.95	1.48

Pitching

Pitching	B-T	HT	WT	DOB	W	L	ERA	G	GS	CG	SV	IP	H	R	ER	HR	BB	SO	AVG	vLH	vRH	K/9	BB/9
Mertins, Kyle	R-R	6-2	220	2-4-88	1	3	2.25	22	0	0	6	28	29	13	7	0	9	20	.264	.250	.271	6.43	2.89
Miller, Jarrett	R-R	6-1	195	9-28-89	0	1	4.30	8	0	0	0	15	15	11	7	1	8	18	.259	.320	.212	11.05	4.91
Moran, Gary	R-R	6-8	255	5-21-85	4	1	3.50	9	6	0	0	44	48	20	17	1	9	36	.281	.262	.291	7.42	1.85
Northcraft, Aaron	R-R	6-4	225	5-28-90	7	8	3.34	23	19	0	0	113	108	53	42	8	41	88	.254	.291	.230	6.99	3.26
Pacheco, Ronan	L-L	6-6	170	7-29-88	5	9	5.00	21	18	0	0	95	101	61	53	5	40	59	.270	.206	.292	5.57	3.78
Perez, Carlos	L-L	6-2	195	11-20-91	4	10	4.82	28	23	0	1	125	138	89	67	7	66	109	.278	.218	.295	7.85	4.75
Roth, Robert	R-R	6-1	195	8-5-88	0	1	1.32	7	0	0	0	14	8	2	2	0	9	19	.167	.227	.115	12.51	5.93
Schlosser, Gus	R-R	6-4	220	10-20-88	2	0	1.82	19	0	0	8	30	22	6	6	0	4	34	.206	.267	.161	10.31	1.21
Shreve, Chase	L-L	6-3	180	7-12-90	5	6	3.86	34	0	0	4	70	77	33	30	3	26	68	.282	.288	.280	8.74	3.34
Sims, Blaine	L-L	6-0	185	3-10-89	0	2	7.11	4	0	0	0	6	11	6	5	1	4	4	.367	.200	.450	5.68	5.68
Stovall, Tyler	L-L	6-1	180	12-27-89	1	6	5.91	36	1	0	1	53	52	43	35	7	56	47	.255	.185	.280	7.93	9.45
Suschak, Matt	R-R	6-4	205	12-27-88	2	0	6.75	12	0	0	0	20	24	16	15	4	15	16	.304	.375	.255	7.20	6.75
Weber, Ryan	R-R	6-0	170	8-12-90	2	0	2.68	13	6	0	2	44	36	15	13	2	8	32	.222	.241	.212	6.60	1.65

Fielding

Catcher

Catcher	PCT	G	PO	A	E	DP	PB
Bethancourt	.973	50	346	55	11	4	8
Brownsten	.981	7	44	8	1	0	0
Delgado	.978	16	120	13	3	1	3
Gattis	.976	52	358	46	10	6	15
Query	.950	7	69	7	4	1	2
Snitker	1.000	3	24	2	0	0	0
Whitmer	.984	7	57	5	1	0	3

First Base

First Base	PCT	G	PO	A	E	DP
Dalfonso	.992	37	340	14	3	39
Garcia	.987	72	633	34	9	44
Gattis	.943	7	47	3	3	3
Hefflinger	.000	1	0	0	0	0
Kleinknecht	.996	23	221	13	1	18
Weaver	.919	6	32	2	3	2
Whitmer	1.000	1	7	0	0	0

Second Base

Second Base	PCT	G	PO	A	E	DP
Ahearn	.909	5	8	12	2	3
Davis	.969	8	16	15	1	0
Frierson	1.000	1	1	3	0	0
La Stella	.957	60	94	148	11	32
Lipka	1.000	33	62	98	0	27
Reyes	.994	29	58	96	1	15
Weaver	.940	11	16	31	3	4

Third Base

Third Base	PCT	G	PO	A	E	DP
Dalfonso	1.000	7	6	12	0	0
Jones	1.000	1	0	1	0	0
Kleinknecht	.957	7	1	21	1	1
Reyes	.941	18	5	27	2	1
Salcedo	.872	100	67	206	40	14
Weaver	.970	15	10	22	1	1

Shortstop

Shortstop	PCT	G	PO	A	E	DP
Ahearn	1.000	2	2	6	0	0

	PCT	G	PO	A	E	DP
Davis	1.000	2	2	4	0	2
De Los Santos	.833	1	2	3	1	1
Frierson	.667	1	1	3	2	0
Lipka	.964	94	130	271	15	45
Reyes	.963	20	21	57	3	9
Salcedo	.938	19	35	70	7	13
Weaver	.960	7	9	15	1	5

Outfield

Outfield	PCT	G	PO	A	E	DP
Dalfonso	.950	12	19	0	1	0
Flores	.917	10	21	1	2	0
Hefflinger	.991	77	108	6	1	0
Mueller	.983	48	114	2	2	0
Rauh	1.000	13	22	0	0	0
Richardson	.971	52	98	1	3	1
Rohm	.982	127	256	10	5	1
Rose	.973	65	139	4	4	1
Weaver	.955	17	21	0	1	0
Wiley	1.000	14	25	1	0	1

DANVILLE BRAVES

ROOKIE

APPALACHIAN LEAGUE

Batting

Batting	B-T	HT	WT	DOB	AVG	vLH	vRH	G	AB	R	H	2B	3B	HR	RBI	BB	HBP	SH	SF	SO	SB	CS	SLG	OBP
Ahmed, Nick	R-R	6-3	205	3-15-90	.262	.228	.272	59	248	46	65	13	2	4	24	30	3	0	2	46	18	6	.379	.346
Beckwith, William	R-L	6-2	220	8-19-90	.282	.364	.259	58	206	41	58	13	3	11	45	28	12	0	2	46	8	2	.534	.395
Comer, Chad	R-R	6-2	220	8-29-88	.179	.211	.167	24	67	6	12	4	0	0	5	8	3	0	0	13	2	0	.239	.295
De Los Santos, Fernando	R-R	6-1	180	1-18-90	.321	.500	.276	43	131	26	42	14	1	2	14	11	2	0	1	37	2	1	.489	.379
Delgado, Ryan	R-R	5-11	215	1-11-88	.182	.125	.214	7	22	0	4	0	0	0	2	1	0	0	0	2	0	0	.182	.217
DeSantiago, Nick	L-R	5-11	215	4-17-91	.214	.276	.200	46	159	17	34	6	0	0	13	26	0	0	1	42	1	2	.252	.323
Drury, Brandon	R-R	6-2	190	8-21-92	.347	.446	.315	63	265	40	92	23	0	8	54	6	4	0	3	35	3	0	.525	.367
Fleming, Kenny	L-L	6-1	185	9-14-89	.211	.133	.223	47	109	10	23	4	0	1	6	10	2	0	0	24	7	2	.275	.289
Fleming, Kurt	B-R	5-11	193	8-30-91	.243	.140	.273	62	222	29	54	10	5	1	22	12	4	0	3	54	7	4	.347	.290
Kubitza, Kyle	L-R	6-3	190	7-15-90	.321	.154	.353	44	162	36	52	16	3	1	34	24	1	0	2	38	9	3	.475	.407
Larsson, Chase	L-L	6-2	230	11-10-88	.250	.231	.256	61	208	41	52	15	0	8	27	31	7	0	3	36	5	1	.438	.361
Mueller, Tony	R-R	6-0	190	2-22-90	.225	.222	.226	9	40	5	9	2	1	0	5	2	0	0	0	6	3	1	.325	.262
Munson, Sam	R-R	6-1	185	4-9-90	.250	.231	.258	47	172	17	43	9	3	4	36	9	5	0	2	60	3	0	.407	.303
Query, Ryan	R-R	5-11	190	8-24-87	.300	.500	.227	11	30	3	9	2	0	0	5	4	2	0	0	8	0	0	.367	.417
Reyes, Elmer	R-R	5-11	150	11-26-90	.262	.222	.275	52	187	29	49	15	2	1	15	8	7	0	1	29	3	2	.380	.315
Sanchez, Edison	R-R	6-4	195	11-1-90	.256	.243	.260	43	133	15	34	8	1	2	15	25	3	0	3	39	2	0	.376	.378
Skinner, William	R-R	6-0	210	6-9-89	.667	.333	.667	1	6	2	4	2	0	1	3	0	0	0	0	1	0	0	1.500	.667
Stamps, Brian	B-R	5-10	165	12-10-88	.000	.000	.000	3	7	0	0	0	0	0	0	0	0	0	0	3	0	0	.000	.000
Tsai, Meng	R-R	6-0	190	5-13-90	.273	.500	.222	11	11	3	3	2	0	0	2	1	0	0	0	5	0	0	.455	.333
Walker, Kirk	R-R	6-1	170	12-23-88	.133	.125	.136	16	30	6	4	0	0	0	2	2	2	0	0	4	1	0	.133	.235

Pitching

Pitching	B-T	HT	WT	DOB	W	L	ERA	G	GS	CG	SV	IP	H	R	ER	HR	BB	SO	AVG	vLH	vRH	K/9	BB/9
Alvarez, Danilo	R-R	6-0	210	1-14-90	0	1	3.00	2	0	0	0	3	4	1	1	0	0	2	.364	.000	.500	6.00	0.00
Briceno, Rafael	R-R	6-2	175	10-29-90	1	0	2.84	4	3	0	0	19	20	8	6	0	8	15	.274	.269	.277	7.11	3.79
Burns, Jonathan	R-R	6-1	190	6-9-88	0	0	3.38	4	0	0	0	8	6	3	3	1	2	9	.207	.133	.286	10.13	2.25
Chaffee, Matt	L-L	6-0	185	12-19-88	1	0	3.00	4	0	0	0	6	3	2	2	0	1	11	.150	.250	.125	16.50	1.50
Cornely, John	R-R	6-1	195	5-17-89	3	1	2.18	15	0	0	1	33	19	13	8	3	19	50	.165	.220	.135	13.64	5.18
Filak, Dave	R-R	6-4	220	11-24-89	1	6	5.06	13	13	0	0	59	72	48	33	2	19	47	.299	.301	.297	7.21	2.91
Foster, Stephen	L-L	6-0	170	3-4-87	0	0	7.71	1	0	0	0	2	5	2	2	0	1	4	.417	1.000	.364	15.43	3.86
Geronimo, Ignacio	R-R	6-1	170	6-1-91	0	1	8.22	4	0	0	0	8	12	8	7	0	4	6	.343	.417	.304	7.04	4.70
Graham, J.R.	R-R	6-0	185	1-14-90	5	2	1.72	13	8	0	0	58	52	15	11	0	13	52	.245	.270	.232	8.12	2.03
Harper, Ryne	R-R	6-3	155	3-27-89	2	0	0.83	11	0	0	1	22	12	2	2	1	4	26	.164	.138	.182	10.80	1.66
Holland, Adam	R-R	6-5	225	12-15-89	1	0	5.08	9	3	0	0	28	24	16	16	2	10	38	.226	.233	.224	12.07	3.18
Jurik, Dan	R-R	6-3	200	6-18-87	0	2	2.60	9	1	0	0	17	18	7	5	0	3	14	.265	.296	.244	7.27	1.56
Lamm, Mark	R-R	6-4	215	3-8-88	0	0	0.00	2	0	0	0	2	0	0	0	0	0	4	.000	.000	.000	18.00	0.00
LaPoint, Lucas	R-R	6-3	215	3-30-91	4	3	2.19	11	9	1	0	53	57	19	13	4	7	41	.279	.301	.264	6.92	1.18

Pitching

Pitching	B-T	HT	WT	DOB	W	L	ERA	G	GS	CG	SV	IP	H	R	ER	HR	BB	SO	AVG	vLH	vRH	K/9	BB/9
Lopez, Daniel	R-R	6-1	170	5-16-87	0	0	2.45	10	0	0	3	15	16	9	4	0	7	22	.281	.364	.229	13.50	4.30
Lucas, Joe	R-R	6-5	190	4-23-89	0	2	2.10	21	0	0	7	26	16	8	6	1	7	20	.172	.161	.177	7.01	2.45
Martin, Cody	R-R	6-2	210	9-4-89	0	0	0.00	8	0	0	3	9	2	0	0	0	1	14	.069	.167	.000	14.00	1.00
Miller, Jarrett	R-R	6-1	195	9-28-89	3	0	2.21	11	0	0	0	20	11	8	5	0	13	36	.149	.138	.156	15.93	5.75
Perez, Williams	R-R	6-0	185	5-21-91	2	0	3.33	7	4	0	0	24	24	10	9	1	14	27	.261	.387	.197	9.99	5.18
Rivera, Wilson	R-R	6-0	195	10-30-89	2	0	0.90	17	0	0	0	30	16	10	3	0	24	44	.157	.121	.174	13.20	7.20
Ross, Greg	R-R	6-3	200	9-6-89	7	4	3.94	13	11	0	0	62	60	33	27	3	27	46	.259	.323	.213	6.71	3.94
Schlosser, Gus	R-R	6-4	220	10-20-88	0	0	0.00	2	0	0	0	5	1	0	0	0	1	8	.063	.000	.091	14.40	1.80
Silva, Ernesto	R-R	6-4	180	2-5-92	5	5	5.49	14	11	0	0	57	69	44	35	4	17	40	.289	.311	.275	6.28	2.67
Suschak, Matt	R-R	6-0	225	12-27-88	0	0	6.48	6	0	0	0	8	8	6	6	1	7	9	.258	.143	.292	9.72	7.56
Talley, Matt	L-L	6-6	225	8-8-89	0	0	18.00	1	0	0	0	1	2	2	2	0	2	1	.400	.500	.333	9.00	18.00
Winnie, Dan	R-R	6-4	225	3-28-90	3	1	2.13	15	5	0	0	42	30	12	10	2	28	37	.194	.190	.196	7.87	5.95

Fielding

Catcher	PCT	G	PO	A	E	DP	PB
Comer	.994	22	155	18	1	1	2
Delgado	.952	4	32	8	2	0	3
DeSantiago	.988	42	309	27	4	3	11
Query	.988	10	78	3	1	0	2
Tsai	1.000	10	31	2	0	0	2

First Base	PCT	G	PO	A	E	DP
Beckwith	.989	39	337	16	4	30
De Los Santos	.000	1	0	0	0	0
Delgado	1.000	1	8	2	0	0
Sanchez	.990	36	284	8	3	30

Second Base	PCT	G	PO	A	E	DP
De Los Santos	.931	25	44	50	7	9
Drury	1.000	8	12	23	0	6
Reyes	.960	42	60	133	8	24
Walker	1.000	3	6	8	0	1

Third Base	PCT	G	PO	A	E	DP
De Los Santos	.667	4	1	1	1	1
Drury	.916	40	21	66	8	10
Kubitza	.887	28	11	52	8	4
Walker	.889	7	5	11	2	1

Shortstop	PCT	G	PO	A	E	DP
Ahmed	.971	58	88	179	8	40
De Los Santos	1.000	4	3	10	0	1
Reyes	.939	8	11	20	2	5
Walker	1.000	5	4	5	0	1

Outfield	PCT	G	PO	A	E	DP
De Los Santos	1.000	9	8	2	0	1
Fleming	.944	42	48	3	3	0
Fleming	.934	59	81	4	6	0
Kubitza	.000	1	0	0	0	0
Larsson	.978	60	84	7	2	1
Mueller	1.000	9	17	0	0	0
Munson	.956	44	79	7	4	3
Reyes	1.000	1	1	0	0	0
Skinner	1.000	1	5	0	0	0
Stamps	.750	3	3	0	1	0

GCL BRAVES   ROOKIE

GULF COAST LEAGUE

Batting	B-T	HT	WT	DOB	AVG	vLH	vRH	G	AB	R	H	2B	3B	HR	RBI	BB	HBP	SH	SF	SO	SB	CS	SLG	OBP
Alcantara, Aris	R-R	6-2	170	5-5-90	.258	.314	.245	49	178	27	46	9	1	4	23	18	3	0	3	25	9	1	.388	.332
Bowman, Shawn	R-R	6-3	225	12-9-84	.200	.250	.188	7	20	0	4	0	0	0	2	2	0	0	0	5	0	0	.200	.273
Bullard, Christopher	L-R	6-0	215	8-26-89	.248	.321	.229	42	133	14	33	4	2	2	19	12	6	0	4	51	7	4	.353	.329
Comer, Chad	R-R	6-2	220	8-29-88	.000	.000	.000	4	8	0	0	0	0	0	1	0	1	0	1	2	0	0	.000	.100
Cunningham, Todd	B-R	6-0	200	3-20-89	.182	.333	.125	4	11	2	2	0	1	0	4	1	0	0	1	5	1	0	.364	.286
Franco, Carlos	R-R	6-2	170	12-20-91	.239	.258	.234	44	155	22	37	9	1	1	21	15	0	0	0	38	10	0	.329	.306
Garcia, Hector	B-R	6-2	170	6-9-92	.200	.241	.188	42	125	13	25	7	1	0	5	13	4	0	1	36	11	2	.272	.294
Gomez, Victor	R-R	6-1	215	1-10-89	.143	.333	.000	4	7	1	1	0	0	0	0	1	0	0	0	1	0	0	.143	.250
Luna, Ronald	R-R	6-0	145	8-18-92	.270	.222	.281	36	141	18	38	4	1	0	17	5	1	0	3	20	9	3	.312	.293
Marte, Felix	R-R	6-1	180	11-14-90	.269	.342	.246	46	160	23	43	9	1	5	21	20	1	0	0	58	7	1	.431	.354
Moranda, Seth	R-R	6-2	180	9-26-92	.200	.133	.215	25	80	13	16	3	0	0	6	15	5	0	0	20	2	3	.238	.360
Nunez, Anthony	R-R	6-3	205	2-2-90	.232	.077	.304	27	82	8	19	2	0	0	6	1	0	1	14	1	2	.256	.289
Popescu, Nick	B-R	5-10	185	4-23-89	.200	.222	.190	25	60	6	12	1	1	0	4	5	1	0	0	7	4	0	.250	.273
Raffle, Nathan	R-R	5-9	185	7-25-88	.000	.000	.000	5	8	0	0	0	0	0	0	0	0	0	0	3	0	0	.000	.000
Reyes, Gerardo	R-R	5-10	170	2-7-91	.269	.310	.259	41	145	28	39	7	0	0	14	16	7	0	2	10	17	3	.317	.365
Robbins, Logan	R-R	6-0	190	8-4-89	.209	.188	.216	36	129	26	27	5	2	6	16	14	5	0	0	48	12	1	.419	.311
Sanchez, Alejandro	R-R	6-0	183	6-15-92	.200	.333	.158	11	25	4	5	0	0	0	1	2	0	0	0	7	2	0	.200	.259
Skinner, William	R-R	6-0	210	6-9-89	.300	.333	.292	24	80	14	24	6	0	4	18	3	1	0	1	18	2	1	.525	.329
Snitker, Troy	R-R	6-2	210	12-5-88	.200	.182	.205	36	110	9	22	7	0	3	14	8	5	0	1	25	0	1	.345	.282
Stamps, Brian	B-R	5-10	165	12-10-88	.206	.083	.247	43	97	15	20	1	0	2	8	5	3	0	0	40	6	2	.278	.267
Tsai, Meng	R-R	6-0	190	5-13-90	.273	.000	.429	4	11	1	3	1	0	0	1	1	2	0	0	3	0	1	.364	.429
Walker, Kirk	R-R	6-1	170	12-3-88	.290	.353	.269	25	69	13	20	2	2	0	6	6	0	0	0	10	3	1	.377	.347
Weaver, Matt	R-R	6-0	175	1-27-90	.222	.500	.143	3	9	3	2	0	0	1	2	0	0	0	0	3	1	0	.556	.222

Pitching	B-T	HT	WT	DOB	W	L	ERA	G	GS	CG	SV	IP	H	R	ER	HR	BB	SO	AVG	vLH	vRH	K/9	BB/9
Adams, Gardner	R-R	5-9	170	8-23-88	1	1	11.45	12	0	0	0	11	15	14	14	0	11	8	.326	.385	.303	6.55	9.00
Briceno, Rafael	R-R	6-2	175	10-29-90	1	4	4.54	9	9	0	0	42	40	22	21	5	11	40	.241	.080	.310	8.64	2.38
Burns, Jonathan	R-R	6-1	190	6-9-88	0	0	0.00	1	0	0	1	3	2	0	0	0	0	4	.182	.000	.400	12.00	0.00
Butts, Brett	R-R	6-1	205	4-24-86	0	0	5.40	6	1	0	0	7	5	4	4	2	1	4	.227	.429	.133	5.40	1.35
Castillo, Eduardo	R-R	6-2	170	7-27-90	3	3	5.17	11	10	0	0	54	61	36	31	9	13	36	.286	.329	.260	6.00	2.17
Castro, Yeliar	R-R	6-3	180	12-3-87	0	0	3.86	5	1	0	0	7	8	4	3	1	1	7	.267	.083	.389	9.00	1.29
Danieli, Evan	R-R	6-8	225	8-2-89	1	1	37.13	5	0	0	0	3	5	11	11	0	9	2	.417	.333	.444	6.75	30.38
De Luna, Luis	R-R	6-4	200	6-18-90	0	0	6.00	4	0	0	0	3	1	2	2	0	4	2	.100	.000	.167	6.00	12.00
Foster, Stephen	L-L	6-0	170	3-4-87	1	0	1.93	2	0	0	0	5	4	3	1	1	1	0	.200	.333	.143	0.00	1.93
Garcia, Bryam	R-R	5-10	190	11-16-88	1	4	6.08	13	0	0	4	13	20	14	9	0	7	17	.328	.333	.325	11.48	4.73
Geronimo, Ignacio	R-R	6-1	170	6-1-91	0	2	2.45	10	1	0	1	22	16	8	6	1	5	21	.200	.154	.222	8.59	2.05
Gil, Jean Carlos	R-R	6-2	160	10-12-90	2	3	2.91	13	10	0	0	65	65	28	21	6	12	63	.270	.270	.270	8.72	1.66
Gilmartin, Sean	L-L	6-2	195	5-8-90	1	0	9.00	1	1	0	0	2	3	2	2	0	0	1	.333	.000	.375	4.50	0.00
Harper, Ryne	R-R	6-3	215	3-27-89	1	0	0.00	6	0	0	2	9	3	0	0	0	2	11	.107	.100	.111	11.42	2.08
Hashem, Michael	L-L	6-1	220	10-13-88	0	2	5.30	14	0	0	1	19	17	13	11	0	9	12	.239	.143	.263	5.79	4.34
Holland, Adam	R-R	6-5	225	12-15-89	0	0	0.00	2	0	0	0	2	1	0	0	0	0	2	.143	.000	.167	9.00	0.00
Huang, Wei	R-R	6-0	180	3-6-90	1	1	3.54	9	1	0	0	20	18	9	8	0	5	12	.237	.115	.300	5.31	2.21

Pitching	B-T	HT	WT	DOB	W	L	ERA	G	GS	CG	SV	IP	H	R	ER	HR	BB	SO	AVG	vLH	vRH	K/9	BB/9
Jadofsky, Zach	R-R	6-3	210	6-17-90	1	0	10.26	15	0	0	1	17	24	19	19	0	5	14	.338	.333	.340	7.56	2.70
Kawakami, Kenshin	R-R	5-11	200	6-22-75	0	0	15.00	2	1	0	0	3	7	5	5	0	1	3	.467	.000	.583	9.00	3.00
LaFreniere, Frank	R-R	6-5	185	6-2-90	6	3	3.51	12	9	0	0	67	68	34	26	5	6	43	.266	.309	.239	5.81	0.81
Lewis, Matt	R-R	6-3	220	9-25-88	0	1	9.00	3	0	0	0	3	4	3	3	1	4	1	.364	.250	.429	3.00	12.00
Lopez, Daniel	R-R	6-1	170	5-16-87	0	0	0.96	5	2	0	0	9	5	1	1	0	1	9	.156	.286	.056	8.68	0.96
Mendez, Henry	R-R	6-3	195	4-12-89	0	1	6.75	2	0	0	0	1	3	2	1	0	2	0	.500	1.000	.250	0.00	13.50
Otero, Andy	L-L	5-9	160	6-3-92	0	1	8.18	4	3	0	0	11	14	10	10	4	1	14	.304	.344	11.45	0.82
Perez, Williams	R-R	6-0	185	5-21-91	2	0	1.80	6	2	0	0	15	16	8	3	1	3	11	.254	.192	.297	6.60	1.80
Pinto, Alexis	L-L	6-0	170	1-21-90	0	0	3.97	8	0	0	0	11	12	5	5	1	3	13	.261	.308	.242	10.32	2.38
Rasmus, Cory	R-R	6-1	220	11-6-87	0	0	27.00	1	0	0	0	1	2	2	2	0	1	2	.500	.500	.500	27.00	13.50
Robertson, Charlie	L-R	6-5	190	4-30-90	2	3	2.78	16	0	0	1	23	20	8	7	0	8	13	.250	.172	.294	5.16	3.18
Rohrbough, Cole	L-L	6-3	205	5-23-87	0	0	0.00	1	0	0	0	1	1	0	0	0	0	2	.250	.000	.500	18.00	0.00
Talley, Matt	L-L	6-6	225	8-8-89	1	3	2.95	12	6	0	0	43	40	17	14	2	10	31	.250	.283	.237	6.54	2.11
Wright, Clint	R-R	6-6	239	4-29-90	0	0	0.00	8	0	0	0	9	3	0	0	0	3	3	.111	.125	.105	3.12	3.12

Fielding

Catcher	PCT	G	PO	A	E	DP	PB
Comer	1.000	4	25	3	0	1	2
Gomez	1.000	2	6	0	0	0	0
Nunez	.994	27	151	25	1	1	4
Raffle	.667	2	2	0	1	0	0
Snitker	.973	33	195	20	6	4	8
Tsai	1.000	4	20	2	0	0	0

First Base	PCT	G	PO	A	E	DP
Alcantara	.998	44	368	45	1	22
Bowman	1.000	1	5	0	0	0
Franco	.000	1	0	0	0	0
Lobanov	.974	19	145	5	4	12
Walker		2	3	0	0	1

Second Base	PCT	G	PO	A	E	DP
Moranda	1.000	2	2	8	0	1

	PCT	G	PO	A	E	DP
Popescu	.951	14	14	25	2	4
Reyes	.948	38	71	93	9	16
Robbins	.943	8	13	20	2	3
Sanchez	1.000	3	2	5	0	1
Weaver	1.000	1	0	1	0	0

Third Base	PCT	G	PO	A	E	DP
Bowman	1.000	6	2	14	0	1
Franco	.901	33	13	78	10	6
Moranda	.875	3	1	6	1	0
Popescu	.938	8	1	14	1	1
Sanchez	1.000	2	1	1	0	0
Walker	.936	17	9	35	3	0

Shortstop	PCT	G	PO	A	E	DP
Luna	.924	34	48	85	11	15
Moranda	.837	12	14	27	8	3

	PCT	G	PO	A	E	DP
Popescu	1.000	1	0	2	0	0
Robbins	.963	15	20	32	2	5
Sanchez	1.000	3	1	3	0	0
Walker	1.000	2	3	3	0	1

Outfield	PCT	G	PO	A	E	DP
Alcantara	1.000	6	6	1	0	0
Bullard	.983	38	58	0	1	0
Cunningham	1.000	4	3	0	0	0
Garcia	.956	41	83	4	4	0
Marte	.987	44	71	3	1	0
Skinner	1.000	21	34	3	0	1
Stamps	1.000	40	60	4	0	2
Weaver	1.000	2	4	1	0	0

DSL BRAVES   ROOKIE

DOMINICAN SUMMER LEAGUE

Batting	B-T	HT	WT	DOB	AVG	vLH	vRH	G	AB	R	H	2B	3B	HR	RBI	BB	HBP	SH	SF	SO	SB	CS	SLG	OBP
Almanza, Adolfo	R-R	6-1	160	11-11-90	.148	.000	.160	15	27	2	4	0	0	0	1	6	0	0	0	10	0	0	.148	.303
Arno, Robinson	R-R	6-4	216	3-13-93	.241	.216	.246	62	216	26	52	12	0	2	25	16	5	0	3	73	6	1	.324	.304
Caballero, Luis	R-R	6-2	165	7-8-92	.195	.111	.209	46	133	17	26	2	0	0	8	12	10	0	0	25	13	4	.211	.310
Castro, Daniel	R-R	5-11	170	11-14-92	.195	.195	.195	55	195	29	38	7	1	0	18	22	4	0	2	25	10	9	.241	.287
Chevez, Pastor	R-R	6-1	180	7-13-94	.000	.000	.000	3	4	0	0	0	0	0	1	0	0	0	0	3	0	0	.000	.200
Daniel, Emmanuel	R-R	6-1	165	12-25-91	.270	.289	.265	54	174	18	47	11	0	1	21	13	14	0	4	35	5	3	.351	.361
Gomez, Gustavo	R-R	6-1	170	7-19-91	.198	.273	.177	35	101	10	20	1	0	0	6	17	1	0	0	29	3	1	.208	.319
Madrid, Luis	R-R	6-0	165	3-11-93	.257	.182	.275	33	113	14	29	3	1	0	18	8	9	0	0	10	1	1	.301	.354
Maldonado, Erick	R-R	6-1	170	6-17-93	.148	.100	.159	22	54	5	8	2	1	0	2	1	5	0	1	26	0	0	.222	.230
McKenzie, Ibrahim	R-R	6-2	185	2-8-94	.188	.075	.219	60	191	27	36	6	5	2	25	24	20	0	3	62	4	4	.304	.336
Meneses, Joey	R-R	6-3	190	5-6-92	.206	.286	.184	19	63	5	13	0	0	0	4	7	0	0	0	14	0	0	.206	.286
Morel, Jose	B-R	6-1	170	8-2-93	.199	.160	.207	46	136	20	27	1	1	0	9	27	2	0	0	38	6	7	.221	.339
Palacios, Cristian	B-R	6-0	155	1-25-94	.120	.400	.050	12	25	3	3	0	1	0	1	1	1	0	0	12	1	1	.200	.185
Payaro, Camilo	R-R	6-3	206	11-13-90	.000	.000	.000	7	6	0	0	0	0	0	0	0	0	0	0	3	0	0	.000	.000
Peraza, Jose	R-R	5-11	167	4-30-94	.281	.294	.277	66	235	29	66	5	3	1	22	15	10	0	3	27	28	7	.340	.346
Rijkhof, Ruben	R-R	6-1	215	4-25-92	.161	.087	.178	45	124	10	20	3	0	0	8	24	6	0	1	45	1	0	.185	.323
Rivero, Miguel	B-R	6-1	175	6-14-94	.182	.000	.250	15	44	3	8	2	0	0	1	4	1	0	0	9	0	1	.227	.265
Romero, Johan	R-R	5-11	170	9-28-93	.074	.250	.043	18	27	1	2	0	0	0	2	3	1	0	0	8	0	0	.074	.194
Salmeron, Elieser	R-R	5-11	150	7-12-91	.242	.375	.235	27	62	8	15	8	1	1	0	0	9	1	0	0	11	1	4	.286	.404
Sanchez, Carlos	R-R	6-0	178	11-5-93	.205	.367	.152	44	122	13	25	5	0	0	12	21	7	0	0	30	3	1	.246	.353
Velazquez, Victor	R-R	5-11	165	8-26-92	.154	.250	.143	36	78	8	12	2	0	0	5	14	2	0	0	22	0	1	.179	.298

Pitching	B-T	HT	WT	DOB	W	L	ERA	G	GS	CG	SV	IP	H	R	ER	HR	BB	SO	AVG	vLH	vRH	K/9	BB/9
Avendano, Magdiel	R-R	6-1	155	9-11-93	2	1	4.35	23	1	0	6	31	34	17	15	1	6	18	.288	.231	.304	5.23	1.74
Cabrera, Mauricio	R-R	6-2	180	9-22-93	1	5	4.30	19	9	0	0	52	51	38	25	3	24	36	.251	.172	.283	6.19	4.13
Caicedo, Oriel	R-R	6-1	185	3-25-91	1	1	3.52	14	1	0	0	15	12	8	6	1	11	11	.214	.250	.200	6.46	6.46
Caicedo, Oriel L	L-L	5-11	188	1-14-94	3	2	2.10	16	9	0	0	60	43	17	14	1	15	46	.205	.231	.203	6.90	2.25
Cambuston, Jesus	R-R	5-11	187	6-3-94	1	1	5.60	17	1	0	2	27	38	19	17	1	8	21	.339	.267	.366	6.91	2.63
Espinosa, Abraham	R-R	6-1	175	6-3-93	2	4	2.15	14	8	0	0	59	52	23	14	0	10	45	.240	.157	.265	6.90	1.53
Estrella, Roberto	R-R	6-2	175	8-14-92	4	7	3.94	16	9	0	0	48	46	27	21	1	25	29	.253	.306	.225	5.44	4.69
Ferrer, Gerald	R-R	6-2	160	4-20-92	1	1	5.59	15	1	0	0	19	16	16	12	0	23	17	.232	.214	.236	7.91	10.71
Flores, Michael	L-L	6-0	180	8-8-92	0	2	3.63	9	8	0	1	35	35	17	14	1	12	41	.271	.600	.258	10.64	3.12
Garcia, Elvin	L-L	5-11	175	5-14-90	6	3	2.37	14	8	0	1	65	56	20	17	1	3	44	.234	.190	.239	6.12	0.42
Jabalera, Domingo	R-R	6-1	170	11-23-89	1	0	2.45	7	0	0	0	7	5	3	2	0	8	5	.200	.250	.190	6.14	9.82
Medina, Enrique	R-R	5-11	180	3-5-92	1	3	2.63	10	2	0	1	24	19	10	7	0	6	19	.209	.167	.212	7.13	2.25
Montenegro, Jorge	R-R	6-1	170	1-24-91	0	0	0.87	12	1	0	1	21	16	6	2	0	12	22	.213	.227	.208	9.58	5.23
Rosario, Jose	R-R	6-1	160	2-22-94	3	0	4.76	14	0	0	2	17	14	11	9	0	6	10	.226	.118	.267	5.29	3.18

Pitching

Pitching	B-T	HT	WT	DOB	W	L	ERA	G	GS	CG	SV	IP	H	R	ER	HR	BB	SO	AVG	vLH	vRH	K/9	BB/9
Ruiz, Reymi	R-R	6-0	175	1-27-91	2	3	3.91	14	1	0	1	25	22	11	11	0	2	11	.247	.269	.238	3.91	0.71
Ubiera, Andry	R-R	6-0	170	5-22-93	4	1	2.66	14	9	0	1	51	41	20	15	3	23	52	.229	.241	.224	9.24	4.09
Valdez, Elias	L-L	6-3	165	9-4-92	0	0	18.00	3	0	0	0	3	6	6	6	1	2	4	.400	.000	.462	12.00	6.00
Verrier, Ernesto	R-R	6-4	220	8-6-84	2	1	2.77	13	1	0	0	26	26	11	8	0	7	17	.268	.200	.299	5.88	2.42

Fielding

Catcher	PCT	G	PO	A	E	DP	PB
Chevez	.875	3	6	1	1	0	1
Sanchez	.969	44	260	54	10	2	10
Velazquez	.965	36	183	36	8	1	10
Peraza	1.000	2	4	2	0		1

First Base	PCT	G	PO	A	E	DP
Almanza	.944	5	31	3	2	3
Arno	.981	7	50	2	1	4
McKenzie	.985	60	567	34	9	45

Second Base	PCT	G	PO	A	E	DP
Caballero	.917	6	14	8	2	2
Castro	.973	55	137	150	8	29
Gomez	1.000	14	21	27	0	9

Third Base	PCT	G	PO	A	E	DP
Almanza	.857	7	3	9	2	1
Arno	.836	17	15	36	10	5
Caballero	.867	24	12	40	8	4
Gomez	.872	17	15	19	5	1
Madrid	.941	13	8	24	2	1
Peraza	.000	1	0	0	0	0

Shortstop	PCT	G	PO	A	E	DP
Caballero	.943	16	15	35	3	6
Peraza	.944	58	87	181	16	24

Outfield	PCT	G	PO	A	E	DP
Arno	.893	29	24	1	3	0
Daniel	.904	43	63	3	7	0
Gomez	.000	1	0	0	0	0
Maldonado	.880	18	19	3	3	0
Meneses	1.000	18	25	1	0	0
Morel	.936	43	71	2	5	0
Palacios	.769	6	10	0	3	0
Payaro	1.000	6	2	0	0	0
Rijkhof	.892	33	29	4	4	0
Rivero	.952	12	19	1	1	0
Romero	1.000	12	4	1	0	0
Salmeron	1.000	26	25	0	0	0

ATLANTA BRAVES

Baltimore Orioles

SEASON IN A SENTENCE: A season that began with optimism ended in another last-place finish, another season below .500, and another change in the general manager's chair, with Dan Duquette replacing Andy MacPhail.

HIGH POINT: After the Orioles completed a sweep of the Royals on May 26, they sat at 24-24 and just three games out of first place in the American League East, albeit in fourth place. They would not see .500 again. From an excitement standpoint, the high point came on the last day of the season, as the Orioles scrapped their way to a comeback win over the Red Sox that knocked them out of the playoffs.

LOW POINT: There were plenty, but none lower than three inexplicable September starts given to lefthander Brian Matusz. After his season got off to a promising start, Matusz lost his ability to get major league hitters out. He returned to the minors, even getting a start in high Class A, and was effective there, so the Orioles brought him back up in August. He continued to struggle in three rough starts, but the team kept running him out there, and in two of his three September starts he failed to get out of the second inning. He finished with a 10.69 ERA, the worst ever for a pitcher who made at least 10 starts.

NOTABLE ROOKIES: Zach Britton looked like he was going to be the young ace the Orioles have long searched for, but he wore down as the season went on and finished at 11-11, 4.61. Still, when he was at his best he looked like a legitimate frontline major league pitcher. A few other players, such as infielder Ryan Adams, made their major league debuts, but none made significant contributions.

KEY TRANSACTIONS: Bringing in J.J. Hardy before the season solidified the Orioles at shortstop. They sent relievers Koji Uehara and Mike Gonzalez to the Rangers and first baseman Derrek Lee to the Pirates in midseason deals, bringing back four younger players in return, the most notable of whom is righthander Tommy Hunter.

DOWN ON THE FARM: High Class A Frederick was the organization's lone bright spot, finishing with the best record in the Carolina League and winning the league title in the playoffs. The Keys' lineup also featured the system's best prospects in middle infielders Manny Machado and Jonathon Schoop. Double-A Bowie and the Rookie-level Gulf Coast League team were the only others with winning records.

OPENING DAY PAYROLL: $85,304,038 (18th)

ORGANIZATION LEADERS

BATTING
*Minimum 250 PA

MAJORS

* AVG	Vladimir Guerrero	.290
* OPS	Mark Reynolds	.806
HR	Mark Reynolds	37
RBI	Mark Reynolds	86

MINORS

* AVG	Buck Britton, Frederick/Bowie	.297
* OBP	Kyle Hudson, Frederick/Bowie/Norfolk	.375
* SLG	Rhyne Hughes, Norfolk	.465
R	Jonathan Schoop, Delmarva/Frederick	82
H	Jonathan Schoop, Delmarva/Frederick	148
TB	Jonathan Schoop, Delmarva/Frederick	221
2B	Kipp Schutz, Delmarva/Frederick	33
3B	Junior Boni, DSL Orioles	8
HR	Brandon Waring, Bowie	21
RBI	Kipp Schutz, Delmarva/Frederick	72
BB	Brenden Webb, Delmarva	75
SO	Xavier Avery, Bowie	156
SB	Greg Miclat, Bowie	50

PITCHING
#Minimum 75 IP

MAJORS

W	Zach Britton	11
# ERA	Jim Johnson	2.67
SO	Jeremy Guthrie	130
SV	Kevin Gregg	22

MINORS

W	Bobby Bundy, Frederick/Bowie	12
	Jacob Pettit, Delmarva/Frederick	12
L	Rick VandenHurk, Norfolk	13
# ERA	Timothy Bascom, Frederick/Bowie	2.97
G	Sean Gleason, Frederick/Norfolk	59
GS	Steve Johnson, Bowie/Norfolk	27
SV	Sean Gleason, Frederick/Norfolk	32
IP	Oliver Drake, Norfolk/Frederick/Bowie	162.2
BB	Chorye Spoone, Norfolk/Bowie	67
SO	Mike Ballard, Norfolk/Bowie	150
# AVG	Tim Bascom, Frederick/Bowie	.229

2011 PERFORMANCE

General Manager: Andy MacPhail. **Farm Director:** John Stockstill. **Scouting Director:** Joe Jordan.

Class	Team	League	W	L	PCT	Finish	Manager(s)
Majors	Baltimore Orioles	American	69	93	.426	12th (14)	Buck Showalter
Triple-A	Norfolk Tides	International	56	87	.392	13th (14)	Gary Allenson
Double-A	Bowie Baysox	Eastern	75	66	.532	4th (12)	Gary Kendall
High A	Frederick Keys	Carolina	80	59	.576	1st (8)	Orlando Gomez
Low A	Delmarva Shorebirds	South Atlantic	55	85	.393	t-13th (14)	Ryan Minor
Short-season	Aberdeen Ironbirds	New York-Penn	24	51	.320	14th (14)	Leo Gomez
Rookie	GCL Orioles	Gulf Coast	38	22	.633	2nd (15)	Ramon Sambo
Overall 2011 Minor League Record			328	370	.470	26th (30)	

ORGANIZATION STATISTICS

BALTIMORE ORIOLES

AMERICAN LEAGUE

Batting	B-T	HT	WT	DOB	AVG	vLH	vRH	G	AB	R	H	2B	3B	HR	RBI	BB	HBP	SH	SF	SO	SB	CS	SLG	OBP
Adams, Ryan	R-R	5-11	185	4-21-87	.281	.370	.242	29	89	9	25	4	0	0	7	6	1	0	0	25	0	0	.326	.333
Andino, Robert	R-R	6-0	195	4-25-84	.263	.306	.243	139	457	63	120	22	0	5	36	41	3	0	1	83	13	3	.344	.327
Angle, Matt	L-R	5-10	175	9-10-85	.177	.167	.178	31	79	12	14	4	0	1	7	12	1	0	0	13	11	1	.266	.293
Bell, Josh	B-R	6-3	220	11-13-86	.164	.188	.156	26	61	6	10	0	0	0	6	4	0	0	0	25	0	0	.164	.215
Davis, Blake	L-R	5-11	170	12-22-83	.254	.222	.260	25	59	6	15	3	1	1	6	6	0	0	0	13	1	1	.390	.323
Davis, Chris	L-R	6-3	230	3-17-86	.276	.391	.250	31	123	16	34	9	0	2	13	6	0	0	0	39	1	0	.398	.310
2-team total (28 Texas)					.266	—	—	59	199	25	53	12	0	5	19	11	0	0	0	63	1	0	.402	.305
Florimon, Pedro	B-R	6-2	180	12-10-86	.125	.000	.125	4	8	1	1	0	0	0	2	1	0	0	0	6	0	0	.250	.222
Fox, Jake	R-R	6-0	220	7-20-82	.246	.156	.345	27	61	8	15	4	1	2	6	4	2	0	0	8	0	0	.443	.313
Guerrero, Vladimir	R-R	6-3	235	2-9-75	.290	.288	.291	145	562	60	163	30	1	13	63	17	7	0	4	56	2	2	.416	.317
Hardy, J.J.	R-R	6-1	200	8-19-82	.269	.268	.270	129	527	76	142	27	0	30	80	31	2	0	5	92	0	0	.491	.310
Hudson, Kyle	L-L	5-11	175	1-7-87	.143	.000	.167	14	28	3	4	0	0	0	2	0	0	0	0	6	2	0	.143	.143
Izturis, Cesar	B-R	5-9	180	2-10-80	.200	.333	.143	18	30	4	6	0	0	0	1	2	0	0	0	10	0	0	.200	.250
Jones, Adam	R-R	6-3	220	8-1-85	.280	.242	.295	151	567	68	159	26	2	25	83	29	9	0	12	113	12	4	.466	.319
Lee, Derrek	R-R	6-5	240	9-6-75	.246	.275	.236	85	334	39	82	15	1	12	41	25	3	0	2	83	2	1	.404	.302
Markakis, Nick	L-L	6-1	200	11-17-83	.284	.261	.294	160	641	72	182	31	1	15	73	62	7	0	6	75	12	3	.406	.351
Pie, Felix	L-L	6-2	185	2-8-85	.220	.063	.236	85	164	15	36	8	1	0	7	10	0	0	0	32	3	2	.280	.264
Reimold, Nolan	R-R	6-4	215	10-12-83	.247	.225	.258	87	267	40	66	10	3	13	45	28	6	0	4	57	7	2	.453	.328
Reynolds, Mark	R-R	6-2	220	8-3-83	.221	.208	.225	155	534	84	118	27	1	37	86	75	7	0	4	196	6	4	.483	.323
Roberts, Brian	B-R	5-9	175	10-9-77	.221	.188	.235	39	163	18	36	7	1	3	19	12	0	0	1	21	6	1	.331	.273
Scott, Luke	L-R	6-0	205	6-25-78	.220	.167	.231	64	209	24	46	11	0	9	22	24	1	0	2	54	1	1	.402	.301
Snyder, Brandon	R-R	6-2	215	11-23-86	.231	.300	.000	6	13	2	3	1	0	0	1	3	1	0	0	4	0	0	.308	.412
Tatum, Craig	R-R	6-1	225	3-18-83	.195	.278	.174	31	87	7	17	3	0	0	7	6	0	0	1	21	1	0	.230	.245
Wieters, Matt	B-R	6-5	225	5-21-86	.262	.339	.237	139	500	72	131	28	0	22	68	48	2	0	1	84	1	0	.450	.328

Pitching	B-T	HT	WT	DOB	W	L	ERA	G	GS	CG	SV	IP	H	R	ER	HR	BB	SO	AVG	vLH	vRH	K/9	BB/9
Accardo, Jeremy	R-R	6-1	200	12-8-81	3	3	5.73	31	0	0	0	38	43	24	24	5	18	23	.295	.257	.329	5.50	4.30
Arrieta, Jake	R-R	6-4	225	3-6-86	10	8	5.05	22	22	0	0	119	115	70	67	21	59	93	.253	.253	.252	7.01	4.45
Atkins, Mitch	R-R	6-3	230	10-1-85	0	0	8.44	3	3	0	0	11	21	10	10	5	3	7	.412	.440	.385	5.91	2.53
Bergesen, Brad	L-R	6-2	210	9-25-85	2	7	5.70	34	12	1	0	101	119	73	64	16	32	61	.288	.310	.264	5.44	2.85
Berken, Jason	R-R	6-0	205	11-27-83	1	2	5.36	40	0	0	0	47	63	29	28	10	21	41	.318	.391	.261	7.85	4.02
Britton, Zach	L-L	6-3	195	12-22-87	11	11	4.61	28	28	0	0	154	162	93	79	12	62	97	.276	.260	.281	5.66	3.62
Eyre, Willie	R-R	6-0	225	7-21-78	2	2	3.44	19	0	0	0	18	12	7	7	2	5	10	.188	.120	.231	4.91	2.45
Gonzalez, Mike	R-L	6-2	215	5-23-78	2	2	4.27	49	0	0	1	46	46	26	22	7	18	46	.256	.211	.300	8.94	3.50
2-team total (7 Texas)					2	2	4.39	56	0	0	1	53	51	30	26	7	21	51	—	—	—	8.61	3.54
Gregg, Kevin	R-R	6-6	230	6-20-78	0	3	4.37	63	0	0	22	60	58	35	29	7	40	53	.254	.259	.250	7.99	6.03
Guthrie, Jeremy	R-R	6-1	205	4-8-79	9	17	4.33	34	32	2	0	208	213	113	100	26	66	130	.267	.270	.263	5.63	2.86
Hendrickson, Mark	L-L	6-9	240	6-23-74	1	0	5.73	8	0	0	0	11	15	7	7	1	6	5	.349	.240	.500	4.09	4.91
Hunter, Tommy	R-R	6-3	280	7-3-86	3	3	5.06	12	11	0	0	68	88	44	39	11	10	35	.304	.303	.306	4.54	1.30
2-team total (8 Texas)					4	4	4.68	20	11	0	0	85	100	50	44	12	15	45	—	—	—	4.78	1.59
Jakubauskas, Chris	R-R	6-2	215	12-22-78	2	2	5.72	33	6	0	0	72	93	46	46	11	29	52	.316	.348	.290	6.47	3.61
Johnson, Jim	R-R	6-5	230	6-27-83	6	5	2.67	69	0	0	9	91	80	30	27	5	21	58	.238	.220	.258	5.74	2.08
Matusz, Brian	L-L	6-4	190	2-11-87	1	9	10.69	12	12	0	0	50	81	60	59	18	24	38	.372	.327	.387	6.89	4.35
Patton, Troy	B-L	6-1	185	9-3-85	2	1	3.00	20	0	0	0	30	25	10	10	2	5	22	.223	.264	.186	6.60	1.50
Phillips, Zach	L-L	6-1	200	9-21-86	0	0	1.13	10	0	0	0	8	6	1	1	1	2	8	.194	.100	.364	9.00	2.25
Rapada, Clay	L-L	6-5	200	1-9-81	2	0	6.06	32	0	0	0	16	14	11	11	3	7	16	.230	.104	.692	9.92	3.86
Reyes, Jo-Jo	L-L	6-2	230	11-20-84	2	3	6.16	9	5	0	0	31	36	21	21	7	13	23	.293	.216	.326	6.75	3.82
2-team total (20 Toronto)					7	11	5.57	29	25	1	0	141	176	99	87	21	48	87	—	—	—	5.57	3.07
Rupe, Josh	R-R	6-3	210	8-18-82	0	0	5.65	9	0	0	0	14	16	9	9	5	6	7	.276	.259	.290	4.40	3.77
Simon, Alfredo	R-R	6-6	230	5-8-81	4	9	4.90	23	16	0	0	116	128	66	63	15	40	83	.284	.282	.287	6.46	3.11
Strop, Pedro	R-R	6-0	175	6-13-85	2	0	0.73	12	0	0	0	12	8	1	1	0	3	12	.190	.105	.261	8.76	2.19
2-team total (11 Texas)					2	1	2.05	23	0	0	0	22	15	5	5	0	10	21	—	—	—	8.59	4.09
Tillman, Chris	R-R	6-5	210	4-15-88	3	5	5.52	13	13	0	0	62	77	41	38	5	25	46	.301	.300	.302	6.68	3.63
Uehara, Koji	R-R	6-1	190	4-3-75	1	1	1.72	43	0	0	0	47	25	9	9	6	8	62	.152	.136	.171	11.87	1.53

BALTIMORE ORIOLES

Pitching

Pitching	B-T	HT	WT	DOB	W	L	ERA	G	GS	CG	SV	IP	H	R	ER	HR	BB	SO	AVG	vLH	vRH	K/9	BB/9
2-team total (22 Texas)					2	3	2.35	65	0	0	0	65	38	17	17	11	9	85	—	—	—	11.77	1.25
VandenHurk, Rick	R-R	6-5	215	5-22-85	0	0	8.00	4	2	0	0	9	12	9	8	4	8	7	.324	.286	.375	7.00	8.00
Viola, Pedro	L-L	6-1	185	6-29-83	0	0	9.82	4	0	0	0	4	6	4	4	3	2	4	.353	.222	.500	9.82	4.91
Worrell, Mark	R-R	6-1	215	3-8-83	0	0	36.00	4	0	0	0	2	6	8	8	2	2	3	.500	.500	.500	13.50	9.00

Fielding

Catcher	PCT	G	PO	A	E	DP	PB
Fox	1.000	10	38	1	0	0	2
Tatum	.987	30	207	16	3	2	1
Wieters	.995	132	855	70	5	14	1

First Base	PCT	G	PO	A	E	DP
Davis	1.000	16	144	8	0	14
Fox	1.000	6	25	1	0	3
Lee	.991	85	713	52	7	67
Markakis	1.000	3	15	1	0	2
Reynolds	.987	44	370	17	5	45
Scott	1.000	12	84	6	0	8
Snyder	.978	5	42	2	1	3
Tatum	1.000	1	1	0	0	1
Wieters	1.000	1	4	0	0	2

Second Base	PCT	G	PO	A	E	DP
Adams	.982	26	47	62	2	16
Andino	.990	94	159	239	4	63
Davis	.968	18	24	36	2	7
Izturis	.909	3	3	7	1	0
Roberts	.984	39	65	123	3	24

Third Base	PCT	G	PO	A	E	DP
Andino	.983	22	15	42	1	6
Bell	.930	21	17	23	3	1
Davis	.333	1	0	1	2	1
Davis	.848	17	10	18	5	3
Izturis	.000	1	0	0	0	0
Reynolds	.897	114	58	169	26	19

Shortstop	PCT	G	PO	A	E	DP
Andino	.962	30	31	97	5	17

	PCT	G	PO	A	E	DP
Davis	1.000	2	2	2	0	1
Florimon	.900	4	3	6	1	1
Hardy	.990	129	211	403	6	79
Izturis	1.000	12	17	32	0	11

Outfield	PCT	G	PO	A	E	DP
Andino	1.000	3	2	0	0	0
Angle	.969	29	62	0	2	0
Bell	.000	2	0	0	0	0
Fox	1.000	5	5	0	0	0
Hudson	.929	10	13	0	1	0
Jones	.980	148	379	16	8	5
Markakis	1.000	157	311	14	0	3
Pie	1.000	73	100	1	0	0
Reimold	.981	76	150	5	3	0
Scott	.988	45	82	0	1	0

NORFOLK TIDES   TRIPLE-A

INTERNATIONAL LEAGUE

Batting	B-T	HT	WT	DOB	AVG	vLH	vRH	G	AB	R	H	2B	3B	HR	RBI	BB	HBP	SH	SF	SO	SB	CS	SLG	OBP
Abreu, Miguel	R-R	5-10	190	11-14-84	.063	.167	.000	5	16	1	1	0	0	0	0	0	0	0	0	3	1	0	.063	.063
Adams, Ryan	R-R	5-11	185	4-21-87	.284	.337	.265	94	377	46	107	28	3	10	37	30	4	0	3	103	5	2	.454	.341
Angle, Matt	L-R	5-10	175	9-10-85	.271	.213	.296	108	424	67	115	13	3	4	33	47	5	0	5	88	27	3	.344	.347
Bell, Josh	B-R	6-3	220	11-13-86	.253	.216	.269	101	395	62	100	12	2	19	57	40	0	0	3	118	4	0	.438	.320
Booker, Zach	R-R	6-0	220	4-24-85	.000	.000	.000	1	1	0	0	0	0	0	0	0	0	0	0	0	0	0	.000	.000
Davis, Blake	L-R	5-11	170	12-22-83	.280	.250	.291	62	232	28	65	3	3	5	27	15	1	0	3	46	6	5	.384	.323
Donachie, Adam	R-R	6-1	215	3-3-84	.171	.154	.182	14	35	5	6	1	0	3	4	12	0	0	0	12	0	1	.457	.383
Fox, Jake	R-R	6-0	220	7-20-82	.275	.299	.268	68	265	38	73	19	1	12	58	22	10	0	2	52	0	0	.491	.351
Green, Nick	R-R	5-11	185	9-10-78	.208	.213	.205	87	308	31	64	16	0	10	46	25	6	0	5	67	3	1	.357	.276
Hardy, J.J.	R-R	6-1	200	8-19-82	.222	.333	.167	3	9	2	2	0	0	0	3	0	0	0	1	0	0	0	.222	.417
Harris, Brendan	R-R	6-1	200	8-26-80	.225	.231	.222	136	516	50	116	21	2	10	50	37	5	0	3	87	2	2	.331	.282
Henson, Tyler	R-R	6-1	205	12-15-87	.247	.227	.256	123	449	55	111	18	3	3	36	41	3	0	2	98	9	5	.321	.313
Hernandez, Michel	R-R	6-0	215	8-12-78	.167	.125	.174	17	54	4	9	3	0	1	3	3	0	0	0	7	0	0	.222	.250
2-team total (7 Columbus)					.208	—	—	24	77	8	16	5	0	1	5	6	3	0	0	8	0	0	.312	.291
Hester, John	R-R	6-4	228	9-14-83	.251	.265	.245	82	279	22	70	10	0	5	25	27	3	0	0	74	0	3	.341	.324
Hudson, Kyle	L-L	5-11	175	1-7-87	.297	.232	.322	68	246	39	73	7	1	0	11	33	1	0	0	55	26	8	.333	.382
Hughes, Rhyne	L-L	6-2	215	9-9-83	.249	.287	.235	92	342	54	85	25	2	15	59	36	2	0	3	111	3	3	.465	.321
Julius, Jacob	L-L	6-5	210	3-13-86	.222	1.000	.125	3	9	0	2	0	0	0	2	2	0	0	1	4	0	0	.222	.333
Pie, Felix	L-L	6-2	185	2-8-85	.250	.000	.375	7	24	6	6	2	1	0	1	3	0	0	0	4	3	0	.417	.333
Reimold, Nolan	R-R	6-4	215	10-12-83	.237	.238	.237	39	139	16	33	6	0	6	22	18	2	0	2	43	2	1	.410	.329
Rojas, Carlos	R-R	6-1	186	1-11-84	.198	.229	.185	54	172	11	34	3	0	0	6	17	0	0	1	35	2	1	.215	.268
Snyder, Brandon	R-R	6-2	215	11-23-86	.261	.326	.235	114	448	55	117	21	1	14	71	32	5	0	9	91	1	2	.406	.312
Tatum, Craig	R-R	6-1	225	3-18-83	.200	.263	.174	21	65	4	13	3	0	0	7	9	0	0	2	13	0	1	.246	.289
Widlansky, Robbie	L-R	6-2	210	11-6-84	.283	.370	.260	35	127	5	36	5	0	3	12	12	0	0	0	26	0	0	.394	.345

Pitching	B-T	HT	WT	DOB	W	L	ERA	G	GS	CG	SV	IP	H	R	ER	HR	BB	SO	AVG	vLH	vRH	K/9	BB/9
Accardo, Jeremy	R-R	6-1	200	12-8-81	1	1	2.16	26	0	0	2	33	26	9	8	1	11	27	.222	.217	.228	7.29	2.97
Atkins, Mitch	R-R	6-3	230	10-1-85	3	7	5.44	17	17	0	0	94	95	63	57	10	37	74	.264	.222	.298	7.06	3.53
Ballard, Michael	R-L	6-2	180	2-6-84	2	4	4.91	10	9	1	0	51	66	31	28	7	17	38	.319	.340	.312	6.66	2.98
Bergesen, Brad	R-R	6-2	210	9-25-85	2	1	1.64	3	3	1	0	22	14	4	4	1	8	18	.177	.032	.271	7.36	3.27
Berken, Jason	R-R	6-0	205	11-27-83	0	1	3.50	5	4	0	0	18	20	7	7	1	7	16	.299	.294	.303	8.00	3.50
Bierbrodt, Nick	L-L	6-5	215	5-16-78	0	1	6.17	18	0	0	0	23	21	17	16	2	19	12	.239	.261	.231	4.63	7.33
Britton, Zach	L-L	6-3	195	12-22-87	0	1	1.80	1	1	0	0	5	3	1	1	0	1	3	.176	.333	.143	5.40	1.80
Castillo, Alberto	L-L	6-3	220	7-5-75	2	4	1.89	20	0	0	1	33	24	8	7	1	8	26	.216	.286	.174	7.02	2.16
Diaz, Jose	R-R	6-4	300	2-27-84	0	1	5.68	14	0	0	1	13	21	10	8	1	8	10	.368	.455	.314	7.11	5.68
Drake, Oliver	R-R	6-4	210	1-13-87	0	0	0.00	1	0	0	0	2	1	0	0	0	1	2	.143	.000	.250	9.00	4.50
Drese, Ryan	R-R	6-3	245	4-5-76	2	3	6.55	9	6	0	0	44	64	35	32	3	14	11	.360	.343	.370	2.25	2.86
Egan, Pat	R-R	6-7	230	10-25-84	1	2	5.12	21	0	0	0	39	56	29	22	3	16	22	.337	.379	.310	5.12	3.72
Eyre, Willie	R-R	6-0	225	7-21-78	1	0	0.00	3	0	0	0	3	1	0	0	0	1	1	.100	.250	.000	2.70	2.70
Gabino, Armando	R-R	6-3	210	8-31-83	1	2	3.48	17	0	0	0	31	24	15	12	2	20	22	.212	.289	.162	6.39	5.81
George, Chris	L-L	6-2	200	9-16-79	7	5	4.27	27	19	0	0	131	144	67	62	13	56	73	.289	.283	.290	5.03	3.86
Gleason, Sean	L-R	6-0	190	8-21-85	0	1	4.22	9	0	0	0	11	15	6	5	2	0	5	.333	.412	.286	4.22	0.00
Hendrickson, Mark	L-L	6-9	240	6-23-74	2	4	2.87	24	0	0	0	60	52	22	19	9	16	29	.231	.250	.222	4.37	2.41
Jakubauskas, Chris	R-R	6-2	215	12-22-78	0	1	4.05	5	5	0	0	20	23	9	9	3	5	14	.295	.256	.343	6.30	3.15
Johnson, Steve	R-R	6-1	180	8-31-87	2	7	5.56	17	17	0	0	87	101	56	54	7	47	63	.294	.262	.329	6.49	4.84
Matusz, Brian	L-L	6-4	190	2-11-87	2	3	3.46	9	9	1	0	55	51	23	21	4	19	41	.256	.239	.266	6.75	3.13
McCurry, Cole	L-L	6-2	180	9-25-85	5	3	4.15	21	0	0	0	39	40	18	18	4	17	27	.268	.213	.294	6.23	3.92
Patton, Troy	B-L	6-1	185	9-3-85	4	1	1.83	17	2	0	0	44	44	9	9	0	12	30	.257	.283	.248	6.09	2.44

Pitching

Pitching	B-T	HT	WT	DOB	W	L	ERA	G	GS	CG	SV	IP	H	R	ER	HR	BB	SO	AVG	vLH	vRH	K/9	BB/9
Pelzer, Wynn	R-R	6-1	205	6-23-86	0	1	3.09	8	0	0	0	12	9	4	4	0	9	7	.220	.188	.240	5.40	6.94
Phillips, Zach	L-L	6-1	200	9-21-86	1	1	2.63	14	0	0	1	14	12	5	4	0	7	7	.245	.222	.258	4.61	4.61
Rapada, Clay	R-L	6-5	200	3-9-81	0	1	3.92	26	0	0	1	21	24	10	9	1	4	20	.296	.237	.349	8.71	1.74
Rupe, Josh	R-R	6-3	210	8-18-82	2	5	7.07	30	0	0	0	42	50	37	33	5	21	29	.303	.359	.253	6.21	4.50
Spoone, Chorye	R-R	6-1	215	9-16-85	2	1	5.50	8	8	0	0	34	41	26	21	1	26	16	.293	.377	.241	4.19	6.82
Startup, Will	L-L	6-0	195	8-4-84	0	0	10.13	2	0	0	0	3	3	3	3	1	2	1	.273	.400	.167	3.38	6.75
Tanaka, Ryohei	R-R	6-0	169	11-18-82	1	0	3.60	2	2	0	0	10	12	4	4	3	1	4	.308	.400	.250	3.60	0.90
Tillman, Chris	R-R	6-5	210	4-15-88	3	6	5.19	15	15	0	0	76	77	50	44	17	38	54	.258	.257	.259	6.37	4.48
VandenHurk, Rick	R-R	6-5	215	5-22-85	9	13	4.43	26	26	0	0	154	141	83	76	23	40	108	.239	.231	.245	6.30	2.33
Worrell, Mark	R-R	6-1	215	3-8-83	1	6	3.42	52	0	0	21	53	44	25	20	4	22	36	.233	.244	.225	6.15	3.76

Fielding

Catcher	PCT	G	PO	A	E	DP	PB
Booker	1.000	1	1	0	0	0	0
Donachie	.986	13	66	6	1	1	1
Fox	1.000	21	116	12	0	3	1
Hernandez	.990	17	88	8	1	2	1
Hester	.989	78	486	35	6	7	7
Snyder	1.000	1	1	0	0	0	0
Tatum	.984	21	107	14	2	0	1

First Base	PCT	G	PO	A	E	DP
Donachie	1.000	1	9	1	0	0
Fox	.991	28	207	14	2	23
Hester	1.000	2	4	1	0	0
Hughes	.993	33	276	23	2	25
Snyder	.992	86	702	53	6	77
Widlansky	1.000	2	8	1	0	0

Second Base	PCT	G	PO	A	E	DP
Adams	.971	79	144	191	10	44
Davis	1.000	3	11	6	0	2
Green	.973	20	41	67	3	18
Harris	.978	45	82	96	4	32

Third Base	PCT	G	PO	A	E	DP
Bell	.938	91	76	181	17	16
Davis	.875	5	2	12	2	0
Green	.909	3	1	9	1	3
Harris	.989	36	21	67	1	7
Snyder	.900	16	11	25	4	2

Shortstop	PCT	G	PO	A	E	DP
Davis	.917	8	14	19	3	6
Green	.954	36	46	100	7	18
Hardy	1.000	2	1	5	0	2
Harris	.966	51	85	139	8	34

	PCT	G	PO	A	E	DP
Rojas	.979	54	92	141	5	44
Outfield	**PCT**	**G**	**PO**	**A**	**E**	**DP**
Abreu	1.000	5	10	1	0	0
Angle	.988	108	311	10	4	2
Davis	.978	42	87	2	2	1
Fox	.875	4	6	1	1	0
Green	1.000	22	37	2	0	0
Harris	1.000	2	6	0	0	0
Henson	.993	120	286	6	2	1
Hudson	.994	67	160	6	1	1
Hughes	.962	12	24	1	1	1
Julius	1.000	3	6	0	0	0
Pie	1.000	7	11	0	0	0
Reimold	.976	36	79	2	2	0
Snyder	.000	1	0	0	0	0
Widlansky	1.000	19	33	1	0	0

BOWIE BAYSOX   DOUBLE-A
EASTERN LEAGUE

Batting	B-T	HT	WT	DOB	AVG	vLH	vRH	G	AB	R	H	2B	3B	HR	RBI	BB	HBP	SH	SF	SO	SB	CS	SLG	OBP
Abreu, Miguel	R-R	5-10	190	11-14-84	.167	.167	.167	7	18	2	3	0	0	0	1	4	0	0	0	4	3	1	.167	.318
Avery, Xavier	L-L	5-11	180	1-1-90	.259	.229	.272	138	557	72	144	31	2	4	26	49	5	0	1	156	36	14	.343	.324
Baker, Aaron	L-R	6-2	220	9-10-87	.196	.188	.200	15	46	2	9	2	0	0	3	0	0	0	2	19	0	0	.239	.188
Britton, Buck	L-R	6-1	163	5-16-86	.282	.286	.281	82	262	40	74	19	3	3	33	19	5	0	4	40	5	2	.412	.338
Davis, Chris	L-R	6-3	230	3-17-86	.500	.333	.667	2	6	2	3	1	0	0	1	1	0	0	0	2	0	0	.667	.625
Donachie, Adam	R-R	6-1	215	3-3-84	.154	.083	.214	7	26	2	4	1	0	0	3	1	0	0	0	9	0	0	.192	.185
Fiorentino, Jeff	L-R	6-1	185	4-14-83	.250	.158	.297	20	56	6	14	1	1	2	13	10	0	1	0	14	3	0	.446	.358
Florimon, Pedro	B-R	6-2	180	12-10-86	.267	.267	.266	133	454	53	121	27	4	8	60	51	5	0	4	114	15	12	.396	.344
Guerrero, Vladimir	R-R	6-3	235	2-9-75	.250	.250	.000	1	4	1	1	0	0	0	0	0	0	0	0	0	0	0	.250	.250
Hoes, L.J.	R-R	6-1	181	3-5-90	.305	.269	.322	95	344	47	105	17	1	6	54	43	0	0	3	56	16	7	.413	.379
Hudson, Kyle	L-L	5-11	175	1-7-87	.308	.182	.379	28	91	9	28	3	1	0	10	10	0	0	0	24	7	2	.363	.376
Izturis, Cesar	B-R	5-9	180	2-10-80	.240	.167	.263	7	25	3	6	1	0	0	3	2	0	0	1	5	0	1	.280	.286
Joseph, Caleb	R-R	6-3	180	6-18-86	.257	.212	.283	107	374	42	96	15	1	7	41	40	6	0	5	60	5	2	.358	.334
Lee, Derrek	R-R	6-5	240	9-6-75	.667	.000	.667	1	3	0	2	0	0	0	1	0	0	0	0	0	0	0	.667	.750
Lerud, Steve	L-R	6-1	215	10-13-84	.193	.118	.215	73	228	25	44	8	1	5	30	20	5	0	4	86	0	1	.303	.268
Mahoney, Joe	L-L	6-6	240	2-1-87	.289	.274	.295	85	315	43	91	24	5	11	67	25	6	0	9	84	7	2	.502	.344
Miclat, Greg	B-R	5-9	180	7-23-87	.280	.317	.262	120	421	78	118	16	3	2	24	54	8	0	2	94	50	3	.347	.371
Polanco, Joel	R-R	6-2	190	9-27-85	.500	1.000	.000	2	2	0	1	0	0	0	1	0	0	0	0	0	0	0	.500	.500
Rojas, Carlos	R-R	6-1	186	1-11-84	.213	.211	.214	53	141	17	30	5	0	0	9	15	3	0	0	32	0	2	.248	.302
Rooney, Michael	R-R	5-11	172	8-7-88	.000	.000	.000	1	2	0	0	0	0	0	0	0	0	0	0	2	0	0	.000	.000
Rowell, Billy	L-R	6-5	205	9-10-88	.227	.182	.240	41	119	9	27	2	0	0	11	13	1	0	2	41	2	0	.244	.304
Scott, Luke	L-R	6-0	205	6-25-78	.500	1.000	.375	3	10	5	5	1	0	3	7	2	0	0	0	2	0	0	1.500	.583
Stevens, Bobby	R-R	6-0	190	3-30-87	.105	.167	.077	10	19	2	2	1	0	0	0	1	0	0	0	2	0	0	.158	.150
Waring, Brandon	R-R	6-4	195	1-2-86	.222	.234	.216	115	406	60	90	21	3	21	59	33	6	0	3	127	0	0	.443	.288
Welty, Ronnie	R-R	6-2	180	1-19-88	.228	.239	.223	122	391	47	89	20	3	13	45	51	5	0	3	125	11	3	.394	.322
Widlansky, Robbie	L-R	6-2	210	11-6-84	.255	.273	.248	85	310	30	79	21	0	7	45	13	7	0	5	45	1	3	.390	.296

Pitching	B-T	HT	WT	DOB	W	L	ERA	G	GS	CG	SV	IP	H	R	ER	HR	BB	SO	AVG	vLH	vRH	K/9	BB/9
Atkins, Mitch	R-R	6-3	230	10-1-85	1	2	3.38	4	4	0	0	27	21	13	10	2	11	19	.223	.267	.184	6.41	3.71
Ballard, Michael	R-L	6-2	180	2-6-84	8	3	3.33	17	16	1	0	108	89	46	40	12	13	112	.223	.350	.170	9.33	1.08
Bascom, Tim	R-R	6-1	205	1-4-85	9	4	3.11	29	17	0	1	130	113	52	45	8	34	110	.230	.227	.232	7.60	2.35
Bierbrodt, Nick	L-L	6-5	215	5-16-78	1	0	0.78	13	0	0	0	23	20	3	2	1	4	10	.230	.174	.250	3.91	1.57
Britton, Zach	L-L	6-3	195	12-22-87	0	2	5.40	3	3	0	0	12	14	11	7	3	2	15	.286	.250	.297	11.57	1.54
Bundy, Bobby	R-R	6-2	215	1-13-90	1	3	9.60	5	4	0	0	15	25	15	16	3	11	13	.357	.370	.349	7.80	6.60
Clark, Zach	R-R	6-0	195	7-11-83	10	9	5.00	24	23	0	0	139	161	79	77	11	42	81	.300	.335	.272	5.26	2.73
Cooney, Brandon	R-R	6-6	240	8-2-85	2	4	4.18	28	0	0	9	28	25	20	13	1	23	25	.231	.233	.231	8.04	7.39
Diaz, Jose	R-R	6-4	300	2-27-84	0	2	1.41	34	0	0	22	32	21	9	5	2	13	38	.186	.235	.145	10.69	3.66
Drake, Oliver	R-R	6-4	210	1-13-87	3	5	5.20	12	12	2	0	64	77	39	37	8	24	47	.292	.271	.306	6.61	3.38
Egan, Pat	R-R	6-7	230	10-25-84	0	2	2.84	19	0	0	1	25	21	9	8	0	11	22	.221	.158	.263	7.82	3.91
Gabino, Armando	R-R	6-3	210	8-31-83	5	3	3.83	25	1	0	3	47	41	23	20	2	18	52	.238	.274	.212	9.96	3.45

BALTIMORE ORIOLES

Pitching	B-T	HT	WT	DOB	W	L	ERA	G	GS	CG	SV	IP	H	R	ER	HR	BB	SO	AVG	vLH	vRH	K/9	BB/9
Gamboa, Eddie	R-R	6-2	195	12-21-84	2	6	3.05	21	9	0	4	74	60	30	25	7	12	50	.223	.232	.215	6.11	1.47
Johnson, Steve	R-R	6-1	200	8-31-87	5	1	2.16	10	10	0	0	58	40	14	14	7	15	59	.194	.220	.174	9.10	2.31
Klein, Dan	R-R	6-2	190	7-27-88	3	0	1.08	9	0	0	0	17	14	3	2	0	3	16	.230	.286	.200	8.64	1.62
Matusz, Brian	L-L	6-4	190	2-11-87	0	0	0.00	1	1	0	0	6	3	0	0	0	1	1	.143	.000	.176	1.50	1.50
McCurry, Cole	L-L	6-2	180	9-25-85	4	0	0.80	15	0	0	0	34	18	4	3	0	14	44	.155	.057	.198	11.76	3.74
Pelzer, Wynn	R-R	6-1	205	6-23-86	5	7	4.14	29	10	0	1	76	76	41	35	6	45	65	.265	.293	.244	7.70	5.33
Rivero, Raul	R-R	6-0	220	5-6-86	4	2	4.11	40	0	0	2	61	58	30	28	4	14	43	.245	.271	.227	6.31	2.05
Simon, Alfredo	R-R	6-6	230	5-8-81	1	0	3.00	4	4	0	0	18	15	7	6	1	6	20	.221	.200	.242	10.00	3.00
Spoone, Chorye	R-R	6-1	215	9-16-85	5	5	4.11	23	11	1	1	88	83	46	40	5	41	64	.250	.247	.253	6.57	4.21
Tanaka, Ryohei	R-R	6-0	169	11-18-82	0	0	3.09	6	0	0	0	12	11	5	4	1	3	11	.229	.158	.276	8.49	2.31
Viola, Pedro	L-L	6-1	185	6-29-83	3	2	2.04	40	0	0	4	40	26	10	9	2	13	40	.193	.167	.213	9.08	2.95
Zagone, Rick	L-L	6-4	215	9-30-86	4	6	4.84	19	16	1	0	97	113	64	52	15	33	57	.294	.330	.283	5.31	3.07

Fielding

Catcher	PCT	G	PO	A	E	DP	PB
Donachie	.975	4	35	4	1	0	0
Joseph	.997	84	642	73	2	9	6
Lerud	.994	53	326	34	2	1	13
Polanco	1.000	1	2	0	0	0	1

First Base	PCT	G	PO	A	E	DP
Baker	1.000	6	32	1	0	4
Britton	1.000	1	3	0	0	0
Davis	1.000	1	8	0	0	0
Joseph	.846	1	10	1	2	0
Mahoney	.985	71	619	41	10	67
Rowell	.980	27	225	16	5	19
Waring	.979	25	177	11	4	11
Widlansky	.983	21	161	13	3	13

Second Base	PCT	G	PO	A	E	DP
Britton	1.000	16	26	35	0	8

Catcher (cont.)	PCT	G	PO	A	E	DP
Florimon	1.000	1	2	3	0	1
Hoes	.913	6	5	16	2	5
Izturis	.750	2	1	2	1	0
Miclat	.967	114	238	296	18	67
Rojas	1.000	10	10	23	0	6

Third Base	PCT	G	PO	A	E	DP
Britton	.901	31	13	78	10	5
Davis	1.000	1	0	1	0	0
Hoes	.889	9	1	15	2	2
Izturis	.000	1	0	0	0	0
Rojas	.978	37	18	70	2	8
Rooney	1.000	1	0	1	0	0
Rowell	1.000	5	1	5	0	0
Waring	.909	74	38	151	19	10

Shortstop	PCT	G	PO	A	E	DP
Florimon	.959	129	219	383	26	83

(Shortstop cont.)	PCT	G	PO	A	E	DP
Izturis	.800	2	2	2	1	1
Miclat	1.000	3	8	7	0	2
Rojas	1.000	9	13	32	0	5
Stevens	1.000	1	1	2	0	1

Outfield	PCT	G	PO	A	E	DP
Abreu	.900	6	9	0	1	0
Avery	.979	137	274	3	6	1
Britton	.976	23	38	2	1	1
Fiorentino	1.000	17	14	1	0	0
Florimon	1.000	1	2	0	0	0
Hoes	.970	78	124	5	4	1
Hudson	1.000	27	59	2	0	0
Mahoney	1.000	4	5	0	0	0
Stevens	1.000	3	4	0	0	0
Welty	.986	122	215	2	3	0
Widlansky	.951	21	38	1	2	0

FREDERICK KEYS   HIGH CLASS A
CAROLINA LEAGUE

Batting	B-T	HT	WT	DOB	AVG	vLH	vRH	G	AB	R	H	2B	3B	HR	RBI	BB	HBP	SH	SF	SO	SB	CS	SLG	OBP
Abreu, Miguel	R-R	5-10	190	11-14-84	.255	.262	.251	96	361	32	92	18	3	5	43	14	3	0	3	39	31	7	.363	.286
Baker, Aaron	L-R	6-2	220	9-10-87	.386	.524	.261	12	44	8	17	3	0	2	9	6	2	0	1	9	0	0	.591	.472
Bernardo, Luis	R-R	6-0	185	1-16-88	.152	.125	.176	11	33	1	5	0	0	0	6	4	0	0	1	4	0	0	.152	.237
Britton, Buck	L-R	6-1	163	5-16-86	.341	.345	.339	25	91	9	31	9	0	3	30	8	1	0	0	7	1	1	.538	.400
Bumbry, Steve	L-L	5-11	185	4-4-88	.245	.181	.273	109	372	67	91	26	3	11	37	67	5	0	4	124	11	9	.419	.364
Conley, Brian	L-R	6-2	195	5-7-86	.133	.000	.222	7	15	1	2	1	0	0	2	2	2	0	0	3	2	0	.200	.316
Dalles, Justin	R-R	6-2	205	12-30-88	.223	.300	.181	36	112	9	25	4	0	1	8	8	2	0	0	30	0	0	.286	.287
Davis, Glynn	R-R	6-3	170	12-7-91	.250	.250	.500	1	4	0	1	0	0	0	0	0	0	0	0	1	0	0	.250	.250
Donachie, Adam	R-R	6-1	215	3-3-84	.221	.261	.200	22	68	8	15	3	0	3	10	8	0	0	1	20	0	0	.397	.299
Flacco, Mike	R-R	6-5	220	1-17-87	.250	.299	.218	50	168	21	42	10	2	5	22	19	7	0	0	42	3	2	.423	.351
Hoes, L.J.	R-R	6-1	181	3-5-90	.241	.303	.196	41	158	20	38	7	0	3	17	10	3	0	1	25	4	2	.342	.297
Hudson, Kyle	L-L	5-11	175	1-7-87	.279	.258	.291	23	86	12	24	3	0	0	2	10	0	0	0	16	8	6	.314	.354
Julius, Jacob	L-L	6-5	210	3-13-86	.170	.113	.186	77	241	22	41	7	0	8	30	16	3	0	5	88	3	5	.299	.226
Kolodny, Tyler	R-R	6-3	206	3-9-88	.249	.267	.240	67	229	28	57	13	0	4	21	23	16	0	1	48	7	6	.358	.357
Machado, Manny	R-R	6-3	185	7-6-92	.245	.241	.247	63	237	24	58	12	3	5	26	22	0	0	1	48	8	5	.384	.308
Mahoney, Joe	L-L	6-6	240	2-1-87	.500	1.000	.200	3	8	0	4	2	0	0	2	4	0	0	0	1	0	0	.750	.667
Mollenhauer, Dale	L-R	5-10	170	6-26-86	.237	.209	.251	125	409	51	97	18	1	7	33	57	0	0	5	100	30	9	.337	.327
Moore, Kyle	R-R	6-0	190	3-4-86	.000	.000	.000	10	5	0	0	0	0	0	0	0	1	0	0	7	0	0	.000	.063
Mummey, Trent	L-L	5-10	185	1-5-89	.293	.381	.243	15	58	13	17	2	2	1	10	6	1	0	0	8	7	1	.448	.369
Oliveira, Joe	R-R	6-0	195	9-30-87	.308	.300	.313	9	26	3	8	1	1	1	2	2	0	0	0	3	1	0	.538	.357
Rooney, Michael	R-R	5-11	172	8-7-88	.192	.152	.226	40	99	11	19	4	0	0	3	7	3	0	1	20	3	3	.232	.264
Rosa, Garabez	R-R	6-2	166	10-12-89	.212	.237	.200	53	179	15	38	7	1	2	16	3	0	0	0	47	3	0	.296	.225
Schoop, Jon	R-R	6-1	187	10-16-91	.271	.288	.262	79	299	37	81	12	2	5	37	22	4	0	0	44	6	3	.375	.329
Schutz, Kipp	L-L	6-4	205	3-21-88	.212	.135	.244	87	306	39	65	20	0	7	36	22	1	0	2	74	6	9	.346	.266
Starr, Sammie	R-R	5-8	165	5-31-88	.111	.000	.200	3	9	1	1	0	0	0	2	0	0	0	1	0	0	.111	.273
Stevens, Bobby	R-R	6-0	190	3-30-87	.234	.245	.227	79	252	48	59	8	2	8	27	31	9	0	5	57	6	3	.377	.339
Townsend, Tyler	L-R	6-3	215	5-14-88	.317	.280	.340	67	252	43	80	24	2	13	50	11	6	0	2	64	2	2	.583	.358
Ward, Brian	R-R	5-11	200	10-17-85	.254	.274	.243	104	335	43	85	22	0	7	32	42	3	0	4	54	9	2	.382	.339

Pitching	B-T	HT	WT	DOB	W	L	ERA	G	GS	CG	SV	IP	H	R	ER	HR	BB	SO	AVG	vLH	vRH	K/9	BB/9
Atkins, Mitch	R-R	6-3	230	10-1-85	1	1	3.00	2	2	0	0	9	7	3	3	1	0	14	.206	.133	.263	14.00	0.00
Bascom, Tim	R-R	6-1	205	1-4-85	1	0	0.00	1	1	0	0	6	4	0	0	2	7	.200	.000	.267	10.50	3.00
Berry, Ryan	R-R	6-1	195	8-3-88	0	0	0.00	1	1	0	0	4	3	0	0	0	4	.200	.000	.250	9.00	0.00
Bundy, Bobby	R-R	6-2	215	1-13-90	11	5	2.75	20	20	1	0	121	102	43	37	8	31	100	.230	.198	.250	7.44	2.31
Copeland, Scott	R-R	6-3	200	12-15-87	3	2	2.14	6	6	0	0	34	25	8	8	0	15	22	.216	.200	.221	5.88	4.01
Dowdy, Josh	R-R	6-0	200	1-18-87	0	1	10.13	2	0	0	0	3	3	3	3	0	3	2	.300	.333	.286	10.13	10.13
Drake, Oliver	R-R	6-4	210	1-13-87	8	3	2.14	14	13	2	0	97	78	27	23	1	18	80	.224	.217	.229	7.45	1.68
Ferguson, D.J.	R-R	6-1	190	11-27-87	0	1	10.13	1	1	0	0	3	3	3	0	4	1	.273	.000	.375	3.38	13.50
Gleason, Sean	L-R	6-0	190	8-21-85	1	3	4.53	50	0	0	32	48	38	24	24	5	19	58	.212	.298	.172	10.95	3.59

Pitching	B-T	HT	WT	DOB	W	L	ERA	G	GS	CG	SV	IP	H	R	ER	HR	BB	SO	AVG	vLH	vRH	K/9	BB/9
Gurka, Jason	L-L	6-0	170	1-10-88	1	1	3.18	20	0	0	1	28	19	10	10	2	9	34	.192	.250	.169	10.80	2.86
Haughian, Nick	L-L	6-0	205	1-1-87	8	7	3.67	27	21	1	0	135	134	62	55	9	40	102	.267	.260	.269	6.80	2.67
Henry, Randy	R-R	6-3	190	5-10-90	0	3	3.60	9	0	0	1	15	17	6	6	1	2	11	.298	.444	.231	6.60	1.20
Klein, Dan	R-R	6-2	190	7-27-88	0	1	1.15	7	0	0	0	16	9	2	2	3	21	.161	.115	.200	12.06	1.72
Matusz, Brian	L-L	6-4	190	2-11-87	0	0	2.25	1	1	0	0	4	2	1	1	0	2	2	.143	.000	.154	4.50	4.50
McCurry, Cole	L-L	6-2	180	9-25-85	0	0	0.00	1	0	0	0	1	0	0	0	0	0	1	.000	.000	.000	9.00	0.00
Moore, Justin	R-R	6-3	190	7-26-89	3	0	3.40	33	0	0	1	56	41	22	21	4	27	43	.203	.214	.199	6.95	4.37
Moreau, Nathan	L-L	6-4	222	9-15-86	11	12	4.40	27	26	0	0	141	133	80	69	13	60	106	.246	.183	.261	6.77	3.83
Moreland, Kenny	R-R	5-11	200	4-2-86	2	0	3.41	36	0	0	1	61	53	23	23	7	13	41	.240	.215	.254	6.08	1.93
O'Shea, Ryan	L-R	6-1	200	5-29-86	3	6	3.09	25	8	0	2	76	66	28	26	8	23	54	.237	.263	.223	6.42	2.74
Petrini, Chris	R-L	6-0	205	2-11-87	2	2	2.08	30	0	0	3	48	35	15	11	3	21	53	.206	.125	.238	10.01	3.97
Pettit, Jacob	L-L	6-1	185	10-28-86	7	0	1.62	10	10	0	0	56	42	12	10	4	15	41	.213	.231	.211	6.63	2.43
Rasner, Jake	R-R	6-4	210	12-4-86	1	2	10.45	7	4	0	0	21	35	29	24	3	9	11	.376	.316	.418	4.79	3.92
Schrader, Clay	L-R	6-0	200	4-28-90	1	1	1.13	15	0	0	3	24	8	3	3	1	19	35	.101	.143	.078	13.13	7.13
Startup, Will	L-L	6-0	195	8-4-84	3	0	3.14	25	0	0	1	49	38	18	17	6	14	38	.213	.197	.222	7.03	2.59
Tanaka, Ryohei	R-R	6-0	169	11-18-82	9	5	3.33	23	18	0	1	114	118	47	42	9	18	84	.269	.296	.253	6.65	1.43
Tolliver, Ashur	L-L	6-0	170	1-24-88	1	1	3.00	5	0	0	1	9	8	3	3	2	0	8	.229	.000	.267	8.00	0.00
Zagone, Rick	L-L	6-4	215	9-30-86	4	2	2.97	7	7	0	0	36	31	16	12	3	14	27	.231	.227	.232	6.69	3.47

Fielding

Catcher	PCT	G	PO	A	E	DP	PB
Bernardo	.989	11	80	11	1	1	2
Dalles	.984	18	105	19	2	2	2
Donachie	1.000	9	55	3	0	0	1
Moore	1.000	2	3	0	0	0	0
Oliveira	1.000	2	5	0	0	0	1
Ward	.991	101	749	100	8	6	3

First Base	PCT	G	PO	A	E	DP
Baker	1.000	10	94	5	0	8
Dalles	.000	1	0	0	0	0
Donachie	1.000	1	1	0	0	0
Flacco	.995	39	350	22	2	23
Julius	1.000	7	57	2	0	4
Kolodny	.985	25	185	16	3	23
Mahoney	1.000	2	22	1	0	0
Townsend	.998	58	476	28	1	43

Second Base	PCT	G	PO	A	E	DP
Abreu	1.000	2	3	7	0	1
Britton	.957	8	8	14	1	5

Hoes	.971	25	53	47	3	8
Mollenhauer	1.000	1	0	1	0	0
Rooney	1.000	13	22	26	0	8
Rosa	1.000	1	1	5	0	0
Schoop	.975	63	116	159	7	34
Starr	1.000	3	4	4	0	2
Stevens	.973	35	68	74	4	24

Third Base	PCT	G	PO	A	E	DP
Abreu	1.000	1	0	3	0	0
Britton	.824	11	2	12	3	0
Kolodny	1.000	2	1	1	0	0
Mollenhauer	.950	123	83	261	18	21
Rooney	.900	3	1	8	1	1
Schoop	1.000	3	2	8	0	1
Stevens	.000	1	0	0	0	0

Shortstop	PCT	G	PO	A	E	DP
Britton	.000	1	0	0	0	0
Machado	.956	61	88	170	12	30
Rooney	.977	19	29	57	2	12

Rosa	.933	52	91	144	17	38
Schoop	.923	12	12	36	4	3
Stevens	1.000	2	0	3	0	0

Outfield	PCT	G	PO	A	E	DP
Abreu	.983	94	218	7	4	1
Bumbry	.978	107	216	7	5	2
Conley	.900	7	9	0	1	0
Dalles	.000	1	0	0	0	0
Davis	1.000	1	2	0	0	0
Flacco	1.000	5	7	0	0	0
Hoes	.955	17	19	2	1	0
Hudson	1.000	23	40	2	0	1
Julius	.989	48	88	3	1	0
Kolodny	1.000	9	18	0	0	0
Moore	1.000	3	8	0	0	0
Mummey	.964	15	26	1	1	0
Rooney	1.000	1	1	0	0	0
Schutz	.964	76	104	4	4	1
Stevens	1.000	31	52	2	0	0

DELMARVA SHOREBIRDS   LOW CLASS A

SOUTH ATLANTIC LEAGUE

Batting	B-T	HT	WT	DOB	AVG	vLH	vRH	G	AB	R	H	2B	3B	HR	RBI	BB	HBP	SH	SF	SO	SB	CS	SLG	OBP
Bumbry, Steve	L-L	5-11	185	4-4-88	.297	.500	.241	9	37	9	11	3	0	1	5	4	2	0	0	6	1	1	.459	.395
Clinton, Chris	R-R	6-0	186	7-24-89	.000	.000	.000	1	3	0	0	0	0	0	0	0	0	0	0	1	0	0	.000	.000
Conley, Brian	L-R	6-2	195	5-7-86	.250	.000	.250	4	8	1	2	1	0	0	2	6	0	0	0	1	1	1	.375	.571
Dalles, Justin	R-R	6-2	205	12-30-88	.202	.217	.198	27	104	12	21	4	0	4	16	3	3	0	1	25	0	0	.356	.243
Flacco, Mike	R-R	6-5	220	1-17-87	.273	.301	.262	72	264	45	72	20	2	5	41	34	9	0	4	58	5	0	.420	.370
Gaylord, Adam	R-R	6-3	210	5-12-88	.209	.154	.225	83	301	26	63	10	0	1	25	19	5	0	5	66	0	3	.252	.264
Givens, Mychal	R-R	6-1	190	5-13-90	.195	.222	.188	57	210	21	41	7	0	0	15	11	8	0	2	35	6	6	.229	.260
Hornback, Riley	R-R	6-0	185	10-21-89	.212	.259	.186	50	156	24	33	7	0	2	9	26	6	0	1	37	6	1	.295	.344
Julius, Jacob	L-L	6-5	210	3-13-86	.235	.147	.289	29	98	9	23	6	1	1	8	12	1	0	0	23	1	1	.347	.324
Kelly, Ty	L-R	6-0	185	7-20-88	.274	.230	.290	120	457	63	125	13	0	4	46	67	4	0	3	63	11	4	.328	.369
Leonora, Dudley	R-R	6-1	154	12-15-91	.151	.174	.140	22	73	2	11	1	0	0	10	3	1	0	0	13	0	2	.164	.195
Machado, Manny	R-R	6-3	185	7-6-92	.276	.258	.281	38	145	24	40	8	2	6	24	23	1	0	1	25	3	1	.483	.376
Mooney, Mike	B-R	5-8	160	6-12-88	.205	.203	.205	60	210	30	43	5	0	1	16	29	7	0	0	44	3	3	.243	.321
Moore, Kyle	R-R	6-0	190	3-4-86	.000	.000	.000	1	1	0	0	0	0	0	0	0	0	0	0	1	0	0	.000	.000
Mummey, Trent	L-L	5-10	185	1-5-89	.291	.429	.271	14	55	9	16	2	2	2	12	10	0	0	4	11	12	2	.509	.377
Nowak, Jeremy	B-R	6-0	205	3-17-88	.234	.243	.230	62	222	24	52	16	1	3	24	21	3	0	2	51	10	2	.356	.328
Ohlman, Michael	R-R	6-4	205	12-14-90	.224	.202	.234	105	375	38	84	15	2	4	51	48	6	0	2	96	1	2	.307	.320
Oliveira, Joe	R-R	6-0	195	9-30-87	.252	.318	.220	39	135	17	34	7	0	2	20	14	3	0	3	20	3	0	.348	.329
Planeta, Mike	R-R	6-3	195	10-17-89	.220	.222	.219	102	382	40	84	13	3	2	23	14	3	0	4	99	12	6	.285	.251
Pope, Kieron	R-L	6-1	195	10-3-88	.201	.171	.211	41	164	20	33	6	0	3	20	11	3	0	0	53	0	1	.305	.264
Rooney, Michael	R-R	5-11	172	8-7-88	.253	.289	.238	42	150	18	38	11	0	0	9	16	7	0	1	33	5	3	.327	.351
Rosa, Garabez	R-R	6-2	166	10-12-89	.262	.312	.240	66	244	20	64	15	1	3	32	6	0	0	2	57	3	0	.369	.278
Ruettiger, John	L-L	6-1	195	9-21-89	.273	.286	.262	19	77	9	21	6	0	1	8	6	0	0	1	13	1	3	.351	.321
Schoop, Jon	R-R	6-1	187	10-16-91	.316	.375	.299	51	212	45	67	12	3	8	34	20	2	0	3	32	6	4	.514	.376
Schutz, Kipp	L-L	6-4	205	3-21-88	.381	.233	.416	38	155	32	59	13	2	4	36	13	1	0	1	29	2	1	.568	.429
Starr, Sammie	R-R	5-8	165	5-31-88	.194	.400	.095	9	31	2	6	0	0	0	1	3	0	0	0	7	0	2	.194	.286
Webb, Brenden	L-R	6-3	190	2-24-90	.218	.191	.225	121	440	47	96	14	1	4	29	75	3	0	1	152	14	8	.288	.344

Pitching	B-T	HT	WT	DOB	W	L	ERA	G	GS	CG	SV	IP	H	R	ER	HR	BB	SO	AVG	vLH	vRH	K/9	BB/9
Adleman, Tim	R-R	6-5	200	11-13-87	5	7	6.01	28	9	0	0	88	123	70	59	10	24	72	.325	.344	.311	7.34	2.45

Pitching

Pitching	B-T	HT	WT	DOB	W	L	ERA	G	GS	CG	SV	IP	H	R	ER	HR	BB	SO	AVG	vLH	vRH	K/9	BB/9
Baker, David	R-R	6-4	195	4-17-91	3	4	2.82	9	9	0	0	54	40	21	17	5	19	48	.211	.221	.204	7.95	3.15
Berry, Tim	L-L	6-3	180	3-18-91	3	7	5.17	26	26	0	0	117	107	70	67	11	61	96	.251	.286	.242	7.41	4.71
Bridwell, Parker	R-R	6-4	190	8-2-91	0	3	7.06	5	5	0	0	22	23	18	17	0	13	13	.271	.256	.286	5.40	5.40
Bywater, Matt	L-L	6-2	190	6-15-89	0	4	3.77	9	9	0	0	45	38	22	19	3	32	51	.229	.063	.269	10.13	6.35
Copeland, Scott	R-R	6-3	200	12-15-87	5	9	6.58	20	20	0	0	108	136	88	79	10	46	55	.308	.313	.303	4.58	3.83
Cowan, Jake	L-R	6-3	165	6-30-88	0	3	4.46	6	6	0	0	34	36	19	17	0	18	30	.273	.229	.298	7.86	4.72
Dowdy, Josh	R-R	6-0	200	1-18-87	0	0	4.70	7	0	0	0	8	13	4	4	0	4	11	.371	.222	.529	12.91	4.70
Ferguson, D.J.	R-R	6-1	190	11-27-87	1	2	4.69	30	0	0	2	56	66	35	29	5	16	29	.297	.343	.256	4.69	2.59
Gurka, Jason	L-L	6-0	170	1-10-88	2	0	2.52	13	0	0	0	25	28	11	7	4	2	33	.277	.250	.290	11.88	0.72
Henry, Randy	R-R	6-3	190	5-10-90	4	0	1.67	20	0	0	1	38	31	10	7	3	6	29	.223	.193	.244	6.93	1.43
Holloway, Brandon	L-L	6-3	245	4-26-86	0	1	7.50	4	0	0	0	6	7	5	5	2	2	3	.318	.600	.235	4.50	3.00
Martin, Jarret	L-L	6-3	200	8-14-89	5	12	4.96	31	18	0	1	111	107	81	61	8	65	97	.252	.211	.263	7.89	5.29
Noel, Luis	R-R	6-1	175	9-29-87	8	10	4.86	29	18	0	0	120	129	81	65	12	54	92	.271	.273	.270	6.88	4.04
Palsha, Ryan	R-R	6-1	180	5-17-90	2	2	4.25	25	0	0	0	49	51	27	23	3	28	38	.270	.253	.281	7.03	5.18
Petrini, Chris	R-L	6-0	205	2-11-87	1	1	5.40	3	0	0	0	5	5	3	3	1	1	5	.294	.250	.333	9.00	1.80
Pettit, Jacob	L-L	6-1	185	10-28-86	5	4	4.42	16	15	0	0	94	108	52	46	8	30	65	.298	.323	.288	6.25	2.88
Roth, Cameron	L-L	6-1	200	4-5-89	3	2	5.05	32	4	0	1	82	91	48	46	4	33	57	.286	.284	.287	6.26	3.62
Schrader, Clay	L-R	6-0	200	4-28-90	1	1	2.05	12	0	0	2	22	11	7	5	1	13	38	.145	.219	.091	15.55	5.32
Simon, Kyle	R-R	6-5	225	8-18-90	0	2	4.15	8	0	0	0	9	6	4	4	1	2	7	.194	.214	.176	7.27	2.08
Startup, Will	L-L	6-0	195	8-4-84	2	0	1.29	4	0	0	0	7	5	1	1	0	1	8	.192	.000	.294	10.29	1.29
Strong, Travis	R-R	6-3	201	8-13-88	0	2	8.31	7	0	0	0	9	12	10	8	1	8	12	.333	.350	.313	12.46	8.31
Swenson, Aaron	R-R	5-11	200	3-25-87	2	0	5.23	13	0	0	1	21	27	16	12	3	6	11	.300	.265	.321	4.79	2.61
Tolliver, Ashur	L-L	6-0	170	1-24-88	1	2	2.27	24	0	0	0	40	35	10	10	3	16	41	.250	.222	.260	9.30	3.63
Walters, David	R-R	6-3	190	8-13-87	1	6	3.93	48	0	0	30	50	62	31	22	5	12	35	.294	.314	.284	6.26	2.15
Wright, Mike	R-R	6-5	195	1-3-90	1	1	10.54	4	1	0	0	14	21	16	16	3	4	12	.356	.350	.359	7.90	2.63

Fielding

Catcher	PCT	G	PO	A	E	DP	PB
Dalles	.990	23	170	19	2	1	6
Hornback	.990	12	89	11	1	0	5
Ohlman	.970	71	459	54	16	5	18
Oliveira	.976	35	251	35	7	0	7

First Base	PCT	G	PO	A	E	DP
Flacco	.986	68	646	67	10	68
Gaylord	.990	37	363	21	4	26
Hornback	.985	6	64	3	1	5
Julius	.996	29	249	14	1	13
Kelly	.917	1	9	2	1	0

Second Base	PCT	G	PO	A	E	DP
Givens	.954	52	83	168	12	45
Hornback	1.000	2	0	1	0	0
Kelly	1.000	4	8	9	0	3
Leonora	.973	8	17	19	1	5
Mooney	.990	49	81	125	2	23
Rooney	.931	22	45	63	8	12

Rosa	.833	1	3	2	1	1
Schoop	1.000	1	2	1	0	0
Starr	1.000	4	3	11	0	2

Third Base	PCT	G	PO	A	E	DP
Gaylord	.958	36	20	72	4	8
Kelly	.952	65	39	140	9	15
Leonora	.900	7	5	13	2	2
Rooney	.889	2	3	5	1	0
Rosa	.938	10	9	21	2	2
Schoop	.889	20	16	48	8	2
Starr	1.000	2	0	4	0	2

Shortstop	PCT	G	PO	A	E	DP
Gaylord	.000	1	0	0	0	0
Givens	1.000	4	9	9	0	2
Kelly	1.000	1	0	1	0	0
Machado	.961	33	51	120	7	23
Mooney	.667	1	0	2	1	0
Rooney	.918	17	23	55	7	13

Rosa	.935	55	73	159	16	14
Schoop	.949	31	52	114	9	25
Starr	.875	1	0	7	1	1

Outfield	PCT	G	PO	A	E	DP
Bumbry	.923	9	24	0	2	0
Clinton	1.000	1	2	0	0	0
Conley	.900	4	7	2	1	1
Hornback	.938	24	28	2	2	0
Kelly	1.000	42	73	5	0	0
Leonora	1.000	4	4	0	0	0
Mummey	1.000	13	32	0	0	0
Nowak	.976	45	77	5	2	2
Planeta	.978	102	211	12	5	3
Pope	.692	10	9	0	4	0
Ruettiger	1.000	19	46	0	0	1
Schutz	.985	34	63	2	1	0
Webb	.968	121	199	16	7	2

ABERDEEN IRONBIRDS   SHORT-SEASON

NEW YORK-PENN LEAGUE

Batting	B-T	HT	WT	DOB	AVG	vLH	vRH	G	AB	R	H	2B	3B	HR	RBI	BB	HBP	SH	SF	SO	SB	CS	SLG	OBP
Clinton, Chris	R-R	6-0	186	7-24-89	.169	.167	.171	19	65	9	11	1	1	1	5	2	5	0	0	16	3	1	.262	.250
Davis, Adam	R-R	6-0	205	12-15-89	.203	.214	.200	20	59	7	12	3	0	1	3	4	7	0	0	8	0	0	.305	.329
Davis, Glynn	R-R	6-3	170	12-7-91	.271	.320	.250	62	255	34	69	14	0	1	14	25	1	0	1	53	23	9	.337	.337
Givens, Mychal	R-R	6-1	190	5-13-90	.279	.333	.253	74	276	30	77	9	2	1	30	30	7	0	3	40	14	5	.337	.361
Goolsby, Austin	R-R	6-2	185	4-28-88	.183	.214	.167	25	82	8	15	5	0	2	6	8	3	0	1	35	0	1	.317	.277
Hoppy, Kyle	L-L	6-0	195	5-8-91	.216	.231	.209	46	125	13	27	2	1	0	6	17	2	0	1	28	5	2	.248	.317
Hornback, Riley	R-R	6-0	185	10-21-89	.215	.158	.239	19	65	3	14	1	0	0	2	3	0	0	1	14	2	1	.231	.246
Knight, Austin	B-R	5-11	195	2-13-90	.213	.171	.234	63	230	19	49	3	1	0	19	20	1	0	2	47	8	5	.235	.277
Leonora, Dudley	R-R	6-1	154	12-15-91	.242	.211	.256	67	240	19	58	7	0	0	20	7	3	0	2	22	6	2	.271	.270
Moore, Kyle	R-R	6-0	190	3-4-86	—	.000	.000	1	0	0	0	0	0	0	0	0	0	0	0	0	0	0	—	—
Narron, Connor	B-R	6-3	195	11-12-91	.211	.260	.187	71	228	18	48	10	0	0	16	49	4	0	0	47	2	0	.254	.359
Nowak, Jeremy	B-R	6-0	205	3-17-88	.286	.200	.333	8	28	4	8	1	0	2	6	4	1	0	0	7	2	0	.536	.394
Sawyer, Wynston	R-R	6-1	181	11-14-91	.231	.215	.239	71	255	22	59	11	0	3	27	25	4	0	2	61	0	2	.310	.308
Serrata, Martin	B-R	6-1	170	11-3-88	.221	.196	.230	51	153	17	38	6	1	0	14	7	1	0	0	37	3	5	.267	.256
Starr, Sammie	R-R	5-8	165	5-31-88	.284	.348	.262	23	88	18	25	6	1	2	15	13	2	0	1	9	6	1	.443	.385
Vellegia, Joe	R-R	6-7	246	7-23-88	.257	.293	.243	57	210	26	54	12	2	7	35	26	5	0	1	62	1	1	.433	.351
Winegardner, Tommy	B-R	5-10	189	3-11-90	.200	.125	.286	4	15	2	3	2	0	0	1	0	0	0	0	5	0	1	.333	.200
Young, Cody	R-R	6-2	193	1-5-88	.182	.182	.182	8	22	1	4	1	0	0	0	0	1	0	0	9	0	0	.227	.217
Zrenda, Ryan	R-R	6-2	200	6-17-88	.296	.250	.333	9	27	4	8	5	1	0	3	2	1	0	0	5	0	0	.556	.367

Pitching	B-T	HT	WT	DOB	W	L	ERA	G	GS	CG	SV	IP	H	R	ER	HR	BB	SO	AVG	vLH	vRH	K/9	BB/9
Alfonso, Orlando	R-R	6-5	230	8-15-89	1	1	9.00	10	0	0	0	13	20	13	13	1	6	7	.339	.235	.381	4.85	4.15
Baker, David	R-R	6-4	195	4-17-91	1	2	2.45	5	5	0	0	26	17	7	7	2	8	23	.189	.194	.186	8.06	2.81

Pitching

Pitching	B-T	HT	WT	DOB	W	L	ERA	G	GS	CG	SV	IP	H	R	ER	HR	BB	SO	AVG	vLH	vRH	K/9	BB/9
Berry, Ryan	R-R	6-1	195	8-3-88	1	1	4.84	10	2	0	0	22	27	13	12	2	8	19	.293	.209	.367	7.66	3.22
Brandhorst, James	R-R	6-4	240	8-26-87	0	0	4.15	3	0	0	0	4	2	2	2	0	6	5	.154	.000	.200	10.38	12.46
Bridwell, Parker	R-R	6-4	190	8-2-91	2	5	4.53	12	11	0	0	54	56	32	27	2	22	57	.271	.258	.281	9.56	3.69
Cespedes, Angel	R-R	6-2	170	8-27-89	1	4	5.20	21	3	0	2	45	55	34	26	2	17	29	.291	.342	.255	5.80	3.40
Chalas, Miguel	R-R	6-0	170	6-27-92	0	1	6.75	1	1	0	0	4	7	5	3	0	0	6	.368	.500	.333	13.50	0.00
Cooney, Brandon	R-R	6-6	240	8-2-85	0	0	0.00	3	0	0	0	3	2	0	0	0	0	4	.182	.000	.200	12.00	0.00
Cowan, Jake	L-R	6-3	165	6-30-88	0	4	3.54	9	9	0	0	48	38	23	19	2	21	48	.207	.217	.198	8.94	3.91
Drummond, Matt	L-L	6-1	170	4-5-88	0	3	9.45	10	2	0	0	13	21	17	14	2	9	12	.344	.300	.366	8.10	6.08
Erbe, Brandon	R-R	6-4	190	12-25-87	0	1	9.82	4	2	0	0	4	5	4	4	1	1	3	.333	.286	.375	7.36	2.45
Esquivel, Jaime	R-R	6-2	190	5-25-92	0	1	1.80	1	1	0	0	5	2	1	1	0	4	8	.118	.250	.077	14.40	7.20
Fowler, Zachary	L-L	6-4	205	2-27-89	2	0	1.85	13	0	0	0	24	16	9	5	0	6	16	.184	.081	.260	5.92	2.22
Gamboa, Eddie	R-R	6-2	195	12-21-84	0	0	1.29	2	0	0	0	7	4	1	1	0	0	9	.154	.231	.077	11.57	0.00
Hobgood, Matt	R-R	6-4	245	8-3-90	0	6	10.46	8	7	0	0	27	41	34	31	2	23	13	.360	.370	.350	4.39	7.76
Holloway, Brandon	L-L	6-3	245	4-26-86	0	1	9.00	2	0	0	0	4	7	5	4	0	0	1	.389	.333	.400	2.25	0.00
Howard, Trent	L-L	6-2	200	10-16-89	3	2	3.48	11	9	0	0	41	37	20	16	1	14	45	.237	.147	.262	9.80	3.05
Jimenez, Enrico	L-L	6-3	195	2-7-89	3	1	2.77	21	0	0	2	26	21	10	8	2	22	22	.226	.211	.236	7.62	7.62
Jones, Devin	R-R	6-2	170	7-4-90	2	4	6.08	14	0	0	2	24	29	22	16	2	13	21	.290	.303	.284	7.99	4.94
Lebron, Luis	R-R	6-1	180	3-15-85	0	1	5.59	11	0	0	1	10	6	6	6	0	5	11	.167	.333	.048	10.24	4.66
Mazur, Steven	R-R	6-0	195	1-29-88	0	0	11.25	5	0	0	1	4	8	5	5	2	0	3	.421	.500	.364	6.75	0.00
Mota, Jose	R-R	5-11	180	12-18-89	1	4	5.91	18	5	0	3	43	57	32	28	2	13	32	.313	.298	.327	6.75	2.74
Nivar, Jose	B-R	6-1	170	2-28-89	0	0	20.25	1	0	0	0	1	2	3	3	1	3	3	.333	.250	.500	20.25	20.25
Petersime, Zach	R-R	6-3	175	1-19-89	0	3	6.47	17	0	0	0	32	49	26	23	3	13	17	.345	.327	.356	4.78	3.66
Rivera, Jorge	L-L	6-0	200	10-30-90	1	0	0.00	1	0	0	0	3	0	0	0	0	0	2	.000	.000	.000	6.00	0.00
Rodriguez, Eduardo	L-L	6-2	175	4-7-93	0	0	6.75	1	1	0	0	4	6	3	3	1	1	4	.333	.600	.231	9.00	2.25
Schmarzo, Alex	R-R	6-3	200	2-28-89	0	2	6.69	17	1	0	0	36	39	28	27	4	12	23	.273	.367	.223	5.70	2.97
Simon, Kyle	R-R	6-5	225	8-18-90	1	0	0.00	6	0	0	1	8	3	0	0	0	3	2	.120	.214	.000	2.25	3.38
Strong, Travis	R-R	6-3	201	8-13-88	1	0	2.11	12	0	0	0	21	21	6	5	2	6	11	.259	.200	.294	4.64	2.53
Taveras, Sam	R-R	6-1	190	1-4-88	0	0	0.00	2	0	0	0	2	2	0	0	0	4	1	.250	.500	.167	3.86	15.43
Taylor, Matt	R-R	6-1	185	4-1-91	2	1	6.88	10	0	0	0	17	20	14	13	0	15	14	.303	.304	.302	7.41	7.94
Wilson, Tyler	R-R	6-2	185	9-25-89	0	0	2.10	6	6	0	0	30	19	7	7	4	4	24	.176	.179	.173	7.20	1.20
Wirsch, Aaron	R-L	6-5	214	11-15-90	0	2	2.70	3	3	0	0	10	7	6	3	0	10	13	.200	.250	.194	11.70	9.00
Wright, Mike	R-R	6-5	195	1-3-90	2	1	3.77	7	7	0	0	31	29	15	13	3	6	29	.248	.279	.230	8.42	1.74

Fielding

Catcher	PCT	G	PO	A	E	DP	PB
Davis	.985	19	120	8	2	2	6
Goolsby	.982	17	97	10	2	2	9
Hornback	1.000	2	17	1	0	0	1
Moore	1.000	1	1	0	0	0	0
Sawyer	.994	39	296	23	2	1	15

First Base	PCT	G	PO	A	E	DP
Goolsby	1.000	2	15	0	0	2
Hornback	.983	7	53	5	1	6
Narron	1.000	2	3	0	0	0
Sawyer	.990	19	176	15	2	18
Velleggia	.993	49	428	22	3	43

Second Base	PCT	G	PO	A	E	DP
Knight	.920	9	9	14	2	2
Leonora	.970	64	126	224	11	52
Starr	.889	1	2	6	1	2
Zrenda	.968	5	15	15	1	3

Third Base	PCT	G	PO	A	E	DP
Leonora	.000	3	0	0	0	0
Narron	.890	69	43	110	19	5
Starr	.938	4	4	11	1	1
Winegardner	1.000	1	0	2	0	0
Zrenda	.000	2	0	0	0	0

Shortstop	PCT	G	PO	A	E	DP
Givens	.961	68	108	214	13	54
Starr	.950	5	4	15	1	3
Winegardner	.909	2	2	8	1	1

Outfield	PCT	G	PO	A	E	DP
Clinton	.909	18	30	0	3	0
Davis	.993	62	133	4	1	4
Hoppy	.967	40	57	1	2	0
Knight	.988	53	78	5	1	0
Nowak	1.000	8	5	0	0	0
Serrata	.961	45	69	4	3	0
Young	1.000	8	11	0	0	0

GCL ORIOLES   ROOKIE

GULF COAST LEAGUE

Batting	B-T	HT	WT	DOB	AVG	vLH	vRH	G	AB	R	H	2B	3B	HR	RBI	BB	HBP	SH	SF	SO	SB	CS	SLG	OBP
Bernadina, Roderick	R-R	6-1	162	8-10-92	.239	.206	.247	51	184	30	44	14	3	4	28	22	8	0	3	26	6	2	.413	.341
Bream, Doug	L-L	6-2	205	5-30-89	.268	.217	.285	48	183	24	49	10	1	0	19	9	1	0	0	13	1	1	.333	.306
Ciriaco, Moises	R-R	5-11	185	8-31-88	.183	.115	.205	32	109	9	20	1	0	1	12	6	2	0	0	9	6	2	.220	.239
Cleofa, Rojean	R-R	5-11	176	9-11-90	.153	.059	.182	29	72	5	11	5	0	0	4	6	3	0	1	17	0	1	.222	.244
Davis, Adam	R-R	6-0	205	12-15-89	.000	.000	.000	1	1	0	0	0	0	0	0	1	0	0	0	0	0	0	.000	.500
Davis, Glynn	R-R	6-3	170	12-7-91	.435	.375	.467	6	23	4	10	1	0	1	2	4	0	0	0	3	1	1	.652	.519
Edman, Cameron	R-R	6-3	205	6-17-88	.299	.261	.315	26	77	11	23	7	2	1	13	10	4	0	0	9	0	0	.481	.407
Hernandez, Manuel	R-R	6-1	190	8-19-92	.275	.273	.276	49	171	23	47	11	4	1	24	17	5	0	1	52	1	2	.404	.356
Izturis, Cesar	B-R	5-9	180	2-10-80	.000	.000	.000	1	2	0	0	0	0	0	0	0	0	0	0	1	0	0	.000	.000
Lino, Gabriel	R-R	6-3	195	5-17-93	.282	.370	.235	28	78	10	22	6	1	2	11	8	3	0	0	13	1	0	.462	.371
Lorenzo, Gregory	R-R	6-0	160	5-31-91	.232	.250	.227	48	164	25	38	8	6	0	8	14	2	0	1	46	8	5	.354	.298
Moranci, Gino	L-L	6-4	188	1-27-90	.053	.000	.063	7	19	2	1	0	0	0	4	0	0	0	0	6	0	0	.053	.217
Mosby, Michael	R-R	6-0	195	10-30-89	.230	.205	.238	50	174	24	40	7	1	7	30	23	5	0	1	36	3	0	.402	.335
Murphy, Tanner	L-R	6-1	190	7-4-92	.217	.250	.208	18	60	1	13	4	1	0	7	2	2	0	1	16	1	0	.317	.262
Pena, Jerome	B-R	5-11	185	11-6-88	.266	.306	.255	49	177	36	47	8	3	1	21	26	3	0	3	40	3	5	.362	.364
Perez, Pedro	R-R	5-11	170	5-8-91	.269	.200	.286	18	52	4	14	3	0	0	8	5	0	0	1	10	0	0	.327	.328
Rodriguez, Pedro	B-R	5-11	145	4-20-90	.191	.125	.205	31	94	17	18	0	1	0	4	6	0	0	0	16	7	7	.213	.240
Rowell, Billy	L-R	6-5	205	9-10-88	.273	.308	.264	17	66	9	18	6	1	1	7	3	1	0	1	11	1	0	.439	.310
Ruettiger, John	L-L	6-1	195	9-21-89	.462	.500	.444	3	13	3	6	1	0	0	1	0	0	0	0	2	1	1	.538	.500
Simmons, Jalen	R-R	6-4	205	3-16-93	.169	.154	.173	22	65	4	11	4	0	0	4	3	5	0	2	29	1	1	.231	.253
Townsend, Tyler	L-R	6-3	215	5-14-88	.235	.250	.231	5	17	3	4	2	0	1	8	3	0	0	1	4	0	0	.529	.333
Winegardner, Tommy	B-R	5-10	189	3-11-90	.187	.195	.184	41	155	16	29	3	1	0	11	11	1	0	3	40	4	2	.219	.241

Pitching	B-T	HT	WT	DOB	W	L	ERA	G	GS	CG	SV	IP	H	R	ER	HR	BB	SO	AVG	vLH	vRH	K/9	BB/9
Adrian, Yancorix	L-L	6-5	185	7-7-89	0	2	2.70	13	1	0	1	27	24	9	8	2	5	24	.255	.278	.250	8.10	1.69
Berry, Ryan	R-R	6-1	195	8-3-88	0	0	1.80	5	0	0	0	10	5	3	2	1	7	9	.147	.095	.231	8.10	6.30
Blackmar, Mark	R-R	6-3	215	4-28-92	3	0	0.00	10	0	0	4	18	9	0	0	0	8	15	.153	.107	.194	7.64	4.08
Bywater, Matt	L-L	6-2	190	6-15-89	0	0	0.59	6	4	0	0	15	5	2	1	0	9	17	.100	.000	.122	9.98	5.28
Chalas, Miguel	R-R	6-0	170	6-27-92	5	3	2.93	11	7	0	0	46	46	17	15	1	8	42	.266	.247	.281	8.22	1.57
Coffey, Cameron	L-L	6-5	215	9-20-90	4	3	2.21	10	8	0	0	37	35	11	9	0	8	26	.263	.256	.266	6.38	1.96
Erbe, Brandon	R-R	6-4	190	12-25-87	0	0	0.00	1	1	0	0	1	1	0	0	0	0	1	.250	.500	.000	9.00	0.00
Esquivel, Jaime	R-R	6-2	190	5-25-92	5	1	0.95	11	8	0	0	47	25	6	5	2	15	39	.159	.160	.159	7.42	2.85
Fowler, Zachary	L-L	6-4	205	2-27-89	0	0	0.00	3	0	0	1	3	1	0	0	0	0	4	.111	.000	.125	12.00	0.00
Guzman, Juan	R-R	6-0	160	2-25-91	1	2	1.09	12	1	0	1	33	24	5	4	1	7	33	.202	.194	.212	9.00	1.91
Hernandez, Ivan	R-R	6-2	195	7-28-91	1	1	4.43	13	0	0	1	22	23	11	11	4	3	19	.267	.327	.189	7.66	1.21
Hobgood, Matt	R-R	6-4	245	8-3-90	0	0	4.35	5	5	0	0	10	10	6	5	1	3	9	.250	.217	.294	7.84	2.61
Lamb, Chris	L-L	6-1	175	9-6-90	0	0	0.00	1	0	0	0	2	0	0	0	0	1	1	.000	.000	.000	4.50	4.50
Lebron, Luis	R-R	6-1	180	3-15-85	0	0	0.00	1	0	0	0	1	0	0	0	0	0	2	.000	.000	.000	18.00	9.00
Nivar, Jose	B-R	6-1	170	2-28-89	2	0	1.83	16	0	0	0	20	9	4	4	0	15	19	.138	.111	.158	8.69	6.86
Parry, Bennett	L-L	6-6	225	8-7-91	1	0	0.00	2	0	0	0	3	2	1	0	0	1	3	.200	.000	.222	9.00	3.00
Richardson, David	R-R	5-11	170	1-31-91	2	1	1.69	12	0	0	0	16	7	4	3	0	13	13	.137	.120	.154	7.31	7.31
Rivera, Jorge	L-L	6-0	200	10-30-90	4	0	1.20	11	1	0	2	30	23	12	4	0	16	34	.209	.243	.192	10.20	4.80
Rivera, Jose	R-R	6-1	185	8-4-91	0	0	6.48	7	0	0	0	8	13	8	6	0	2	11	.371	.346	.444	11.88	2.16
Rodriguez, Eduardo	R-R	6-2	175	4-7-93	1	1	1.81	11	10	0	1	45	28	17	9	0	17	46	.177	.115	.189	9.27	3.43
Sosa, Israel	L-L	6-2	180	6-6-89	2	1	1.53	7	1	0	0	18	12	5	3	0	4	16	.188	.214	.180	8.15	2.04
Taylor, Matt	R-R	6-1	185	4-1-91	0	0	0.00	2	0	0	0	2	1	0	0	0	0	3	.167	.500	.000	13.50	0.00
Thomas, Corey	R-R	6-2	200	9-23-88	0	0	0.00	1	0	0	0	1	0	0	0	0	1	1	.000	.000	.000	9.00	9.00
Vader, Sebastian	R-R	6-4	175	6-3-92	2	2	2.45	12	11	0	0	48	38	16	13	1	16	44	.216	.230	.202	8.31	3.02
Ward, Dustin	L-L	6-0	175	2-27-90	1	0	0.95	12	0	0	2	19	15	4	2	0	9	25	.211	.000	.227	11.84	4.26
Wilson, Tyler	R-R	6-2	185	9-25-89	0	0	0.00	2	2	0	0	3	0	0	0	0	1	3	.000	.000	.000	9.00	3.00
Wise, Ken	R-R	6-6	225	4-7-90	1	3	6.10	12	0	0	1	21	24	15	14	1	9	23	.282	.265	.306	10.02	3.92
Wooten, Eric	L-L	6-3	180	3-18-90	0	0	3.52	8	0	0	0	8	6	3	3	1	2	6	.222	.667	.167	7.04	2.35
Wright, Mike	R-R	6-5	195	1-3-90	0	0	0.00	1	0	0	0	1	0	0	0	0	0	1	.000	.000	.000	9.00	0.00

Fielding

Catcher	PCT	G	PO	A	E	DP	PB
Davis	1.000	1	8	1	0	0	0
Edman	.990	16	89	15	1	2	2
Lino	.975	26	165	30	5	2	4
Murphy	.980	12	87	9	2	0	3
Perez	.980	18	132	17	3	2	1

First Base	PCT	G	PO	A	E	DP
Bream	.987	38	358	15	5	27
Edman	.990	10	92	3	1	7
Moranci	.983	6	54	3	1	7
Rowell	.984	6	58	2	1	7

	PCT	G	PO	A	E	DP
Townsend	.950	3	17	2	1	1
Second Base						
Ciriaco	.941	3	4	12	1	2
Izturis	1.000	1	2	2	0	0
Pena	.978	44	91	130	5	33
Rodriguez	.957	15	32	57	4	8
Third Base						
Ciriaco	.944	11	6	28	2	4
Mosby	.943	49	35	113	9	12
Shortstop						
Ciriaco	.944	8	13	21	2	6

	PCT	G	PO	A	E	DP
Rodriguez	.960	11	10	38	2	6
Winegardner	.934	41	65	106	12	22
Outfield						
Bernadina	.988	49	77	4	1	2
Cleofa	1.000	24	36	2	0	1
Davis	1.000	6	8	1	0	0
Hernandez	.976	39	39	2	1	0
Lorenzo	1.000	47	73	7	0	1
Ruettiger	1.000	3	5	0	0	0
Simmons	.957	19	19	3	1	1

DSL ORIOLES — ROOKIE

DOMINICAN SUMMER LEAGUE

Batting	B-T	HT	WT	DOB	AVG	vLH	vRH	G	AB	R	H	2B	3B	HR	RBI	BB	HBP	SH	SF	SO	SB	CS	SLG	OBP
Avila, Eliecer	R-R	6-2	175	1-30-90	.203	.150	.231	30	59	6	12	3	0	0	6	7	0	0	0	15	1	2	.254	.288
Bido, Felix	R-R	6-2	170	8-7-91	.222	.204	.229	48	180	19	40	9	1	1	22	10	7	0	0	29	8	4	.300	.289
Boni, Junior	R-R	6-0	175	2-5-91	.275	.231	.295	62	204	45	56	9	8	1	28	36	4	0	2	28	20	6	.412	.390
Capellan, Byron	R-R	5-11	150	8-9-93	.233	.217	.240	68	236	33	55	9	1	0	29	24	4	0	4	45	17	10	.280	.310
Conde, Jhason	R-R	5-11	165	11-20-90	.189	.333	.120	28	37	9	7	0	0	0	6	11	4	0	0	6	4	1	.189	.423
Dominguez, Dioni	B-R	6-1	175	10-20-90	.219	.176	.239	42	105	28	23	3	3	0	6	23	2	0	1	25	8	5	.305	.366
Familia, Elvis	R-R	6-1	190	5-2-91	.119	.000	.143	22	42	9	5	1	0	0	3	16	3	0	0	15	0	0	.143	.393
Hanley, Cesar	B-R	5-11	170	4-4-91	.170	.233	.141	49	94	26	16	2	1	0	8	12	3	0	0	39	8	3	.213	.284
Javier, Jhonatan	R-R	6-1	200	9-16-87	.339	.188	.400	18	56	12	19	5	1	0	7	9	3	0	0	11	5	0	.464	.456
Lartiguez, Oswill	R-R	6-1	179	8-11-92	.261	.286	.252	64	199	31	52	6	2	1	22	30	7	0	0	40	16	10	.327	.377
Ledesma, Ronarsy	R-R	6-1	170	4-19-93	.176	.000	.231	24	51	8	9	2	0	1	9	7	5	0	0	11	1	2	.275	.333
Martinez, Rockny	B-R	6-2	175	7-14-92	.270	.333	.232	39	89	15	24	3	1	0	13	11	6	0	2	12	4	1	.326	.380
Mercedes, Alexander	R-R	6-0	160	3-20-92	.317	.237	.350	55	199	38	63	8	5	1	22	26	5	0	2	18	17	8	.422	.405
Parra, Gustavo	R-R	5-11	172	8-4-90	.186	.188	.186	24	59	4	11	1	3	0	12	6	3	0	1	26	1	0	.305	.290
Pimentel, Jerfry	R-R	6-0	170	12-4-91	.250	.429	.190	16	56	10	14	5	0	0	3	11	1	0	2	9	4	0	.339	.371
Ramirez, Freidderyx	R-R	6-3	175	4-28-92	.240	.294	.220	43	125	17	30	4	2	0	14	12	4	0	2	26	1	2	.304	.322
Taveras, Junior	R-R	5-10	187	12-28-92	.173	.133	.188	45	110	11	19	1	1	0	12	6	2	0	1	18	1	2	.200	.227
Veloz, Hector	R-R	6-2	192	2-1-94	.225	.246	.216	67	227	34	51	16	0	3	31	37	6	0	3	62	6	6	.322	.344

Pitching	B-T	HT	WT	DOB	W	L	ERA	G	GS	CG	SV	IP	H	R	ER	HR	BB	SO	AVG	vLH	vRH	K/9	BB/9
Alba, Victor	R-R	6-2	165	2-11-92	1	0	5.23	10	4	0	0	10	4	7	6	0	15	14	.118	.000	.200	12.19	13.06
Aquino, Wilmer	L-L	5-9	170	12-5-91	1	0	2.77	12	3	0	0	26	20	8	8	2	21	27	.206	.267	.195	9.35	7.27
Bolivar, Miguel	R-R	6-0	180	1-24-92	0	0	11.12	7	1	0	0	6	5	9	7	0	10	2	.227	.167	.250	3.18	15.88
Figueroa, Jose	R-R	6-1	190	3-23-92	3	1	2.76	23	0	0	12	33	24	11	10	0	9	28	.202	.188	.211	7.71	2.48
Garcia, Miguel	R-R	6-1	180	3-24-93	1	1	4.50	4	0	0	0	4	4	2	2	0	1	3	.286	.400	.222	6.75	2.25
Gomez, Carlos	L-L	6-3	190	2-12-94	0	0	0.00	1	0	0	0	1	0	0	0	0	1	1	.500	.000	.500	27.00	0.00

BaseballAmerica.com

Pitching

Pitching	B-T	HT	WT	DOB	W	L	ERA	G	GS	CG	SV	IP	H	R	ER	HR	BB	SO	AVG	vLH	vRH	K/9	BB/9
Jean, Samuel	L-L	6-1	175	6-22-89	7	4	3.11	17	15	1	0	81	66	45	28	2	38	61	.224	.188	.231	6.78	4.22
Louico, Williams	R-R	6-2	180	4-10-90	6	2	2.10	16	15	0	0	86	65	32	20	2	42	69	.212	.228	.202	7.25	4.41
Medina, Jhondaniel	R-R	5-11	158	2-8-93	5	4	3.02	14	13	1	0	66	56	26	22	1	34	60	.232	.196	.259	8.22	4.66
Mercedes, Daniel	R-R	6-4	180	5-12-92	2	1	4.61	14	0	0	1	27	32	24	14	0	16	31	.305	.326	.290	10.21	5.27
Montas, Lorenzo	R-R	6-1	180	12-28-88	0	0	12.00	12	0	0	0	9	9	12	12	2	16	10	.250	.214	.273	10.00	16.00
Perez, Julio	R-R	6-2	175	1-16-92	2	0	4.50	14	0	0	0	20	13	15	10	1	17	7	.197	.120	.244	3.15	7.65
Pina, Edgar	R-R	6-0	172	3-5-93	0	0	8.10	9	0	0	0	7	8	8	6	0	10	12	.296	.286	.308	16.20	13.50
Pinales, Elias	L-L	6-4	155	11-7-92	0	3	5.23	11	8	0	0	31	23	19	18	0	29	26	.205	.174	.213	7.55	8.42
Reyes, Franklin	R-R	6-0	190	1-24-92	0	0	27.00	1	0	0	0	0	3	1	1	0	0	1	.750	1.000	.667	27.00	0.00
Rojas, Yorky	R-R	6-4	185	5-4-91	0	2	10.38	9	2	0	0	17	27	25	20	1	10	11	.360	.306	.410	5.71	5.19
Salas, Domingo	R-R	6-2	170	5-11-91	6	1	1.99	23	0	0	4	50	36	13	11	0	35	45	.206	.210	.204	8.15	6.34
Severino, Janser	R-R	6-2	140	9-16-91	6	2	1.98	14	12	2	0	77	53	25	17	1	28	77	.192	.216	.178	8.96	3.26
Sosa, Israel	L-L	6-2	180	6-6-89	0	1	2.38	4	1	0	0	11	11	4	3	0	7	8	.262	.143	.286	6.35	5.56
Soto, Luis	R-R	6-0	190	8-22-89	0	0	9.00	3	0	0	0	2	0	2	2	0	5	3	.000	.000	.000	13.50	22.50

Fielding

Catcher	PCT	G	PO	A	E	DP	PB
Avila	.968	30	126	23	5	1	6
Hanley	1.000	1	2	1	0	0	0
Ledesma	1.000	4	28	1	0	0	0
Parra	.991	16	96	17	1	1	3
Taveras	.972	44	262	46	9	0	3

First Base	PCT	G	PO	A	E	DP
Avila	1.000	1	2	0	0	0
Bido	.984	48	406	32	7	31
Javier	.970	13	94	3	3	9
Ledesma	1.000	5	39	1	0	1
Parra	1.000	1	3	0	0	0
Ramirez	.975	8	38	1	1	2

Second Base	PCT	G	PO	A	E	DP
Conde	1.000	5	4	6	0	2
Hanley	.976	18	38	45	2	8
Mercedes	.931	51	114	127	18	26
Pimentel	.933	4	8	6	1	1
Taveras	.000	1	0	0	0	0

Third Base	PCT	G	PO	A	E	DP
Conde	1.000	2	0	1	0	0
Pimentel	1.000	1	2	0	0	0
Ramirez	.811	14	7	23	7	4
Veloz	.863	57	43	89	21	6

Shortstop	PCT	G	PO	A	E	DP
Capellan	.949	68	110	189	16	25

	PCT	G	PO	A	E	DP
Conde	.000	1	0	0	0	0
Pimentel	1.000	2	1	8	0	0
Ramirez	.917	2	6	5	1	2

Outfield	PCT	G	PO	A	E	DP
Boni	.949	58	66	8	4	1
Conde	1.000	10	15	1	0	0
Dominguez	.956	41	59	6	3	0
Familia	1.000	18	10	3	0	1
Hanley	1.000	14	13	2	0	0
Lartiguez	.991	64	110	6	1	3
Ledesma	.000	1	0	0	0	0
Martinez	.946	31	33	2	2	1
Pimentel	1.000	3	5	0	0	0
Santana	.000	1	0	0	0	0

Boston Red Sox

SEASON IN A SENTENCE: After the offseason acquisitions of first baseman Adrian Gonzalez and outfielder Carl Crawford, the Red Sox looked like the best team in the game at midseason, but an historic September collapse left Boston out of the playoffs and led to the departure of manager Terry Francona and general manager Theo Epstein.

HIGH POINT: Jacoby Ellsbury had a monster season, and he hit a home run on the last day of August as the Red Sox beat the Yankees 9-5 to take a 1½-game lead in the American League East.

LOW POINT: The month of September—a dismal 7-20 freefall—was punctuated by the final day of the regular season. The Red Sox gave up two runs in the bottom of the ninth in Baltimore to lose 4-3, and then sat in the clubhouse at Camden Yards and watched as the Rays capped a rally from a 7-0 deficit against the Yankees to win in the 12th and claim the wild card. The Red Sox finale ended when Crawford couldn't come up with a sliding catch on Robert Andino's sinking liner to left field. Crawford had a dismal season, never seeming comfortable in the spotlight that comes with wearing a Red Sox uniform.

NOTABLE ROOKIES: Outfielder Josh Reddick seized the right field job, batting .280 with seven homers, and Ryan Lavarnway gave the lineup a late boost. There was not much meaningful playing time for other rookies, but 21-year-old Cuban shortstop Jose Iglesias made his big league debut and righthander Junichi Tazawa made it back to the big leagues as he continued his comeback from Tommy John surgery.

KEY TRANSACTIONS: After the big moves in the offseason for Crawford and Gonzalez, the Red Sox mostly played a pat hand in 2011. They acquired lefthander Erik Bedard from the Mariners in a three-team trade in late July and he made eight starts for the Red Sox, going 1-2. 4.03.

DOWN ON THE FARM: Lavarnway had a breakout season in Double-A and Triple-A, hitting 32 home runs and putting himself in the picture to be the big league catcher in 2012. Third baseman Will Middlebrooks had an all-star season at Double-A Portland (.302, 18 HRs, 80 RBIs). Shortstop Xander Bogaerts hit 16 homers in a half-season for low Class A Greenville as an 18-year-old. Righthander Anthony Ranaudo, who led Louisiana State to a national championship in 2010, went a combined 9-6, 3.97 in two Class A stops in his first pro season.

OPENING DAY PAYROLL: $161,762,475 (3rd)

PLAYERS OF THE YEAR

MAJOR LEAGUE	MINOR LEAGUE
Jacoby Ellsbury	**Ryan Lavarnway**
of	c
.321/.376/.552	(Double-A/Triple-A)
32 HR/39 SB	.290/.376/.563
Won 1st Gold Glove	BA Minors All-Star

ORGANIZATIONAL LEADERS

BATTING		*Minimum 250 PA
MAJORS		
* AVG	Adrian Gonzalez	.338
* OPS	Adrian Gonzalez	.958
HR	Jacoby Ellsbury	32
RBI	Adrian Gonzalez	117
MINORS		
* AVG	Bryce Brentz, Greenville/Salem	.306
* OBP	Alex Hassan, Portland	.404
* SLG	Bryce Brentz, Greenville/Salem	.574
R	Bryce Brentz, Greenville/Salem	91
H	Miles Head, Greenville/Salem	148
TB	Bryce Brentz, Greenville/Salem	263
2B	Reynaldo Rodriguez, Salem/GCL/Lowell/Portland	39
3B	Sean Coyle, Greenville	7
3B	Heiker Meneses, Greenville/Portland/Salem	7
HR	Ryan Lavarnway, Portland/Pawtucket	32
RBI	Bryce Brentz, Greenville/Salem	94
	Will Middlebrooks, Lowell/Portland/Pawtucket	94
BB	Lars Anderson, Pawtucket	80
SO	Jeremy Hazelbaker, Salem/Portland	139
SB	Felix Sanchez, Greenville	55
PITCHING		#Minimum 75 IP
MAJORS		
W	Jon Lester	15
# ERA	Alfredo Aceves	2.61
SO	Jon Lester	182
SV	Jonathan Papelbon	31
MINORS		
W	Stephen Fife, Portland	11
L	Drake Britton, Salem	13
	Stolmy Pimentel, Portland/Salem	13
# ERA	Alex Wilson, Portland/Pawtucket	3.11
G	Blake Maxwell, Pawtucket/Portland	50
GS	Miguel Celestino, Greenville	27
SV	Michael Bowden, Pawtucket	16
	Blake Maxwell, Pawtucket/Portland	16
IP	Miguel Celestino, Greenville	140.2
BB	Hunter Cervenka, Greenville/Lowell	58
SO	Kyle Weiland, Pawtucket	126
#AVG	Manuel Rivera, Greenville/Salem	.229

2011 PERFORMANCE

General Manager: Theo Epstein. **Farm Director:** Mike Hazen. **Scouting Director:** Amiel Sawdaye.

Class	Team	League	W	L	PCT	Finish	Manager(s)
Majors	Boston Red Sox	American	90	72	.556	5th (14)	Terry Francona
Triple-A	Pawtucket Red Sox	International	81	61	.570	2nd (14)	Arnie Beyeler
Double-A	Portland Sea Dogs	Eastern	59	83	.415	12th (12)	Kevin Boles
High A	Salem Red Sox	Carolina	64	75	.460	7th (8)	Bruce Crabbe
Low A	Greenville Drive	South Atlantic	78	62	.557	4th (14)	Billy McMillon
Short-season	Lowell Spinners	New York-Penn	29	45	.392	13th (14)	Carlos Febles
Rookie	GCL Red Sox	Gulf Coast	27	33	.450	11th (15)	George Lombard
Overall 2011 Minor League Record			338	359	.485	20th (30)	

ORGANIZATION STATISTICS

BOSTON RED SOX

AMERICAN LEAGUE

Batting	B-T	HT	WT	DOB	AVG	vLH	vRH	G	AB	R	H	2B	3B	HR	RBI	BB	HBP	SH	SF	SO	SB	CS	SLG	OBP
Anderson, Lars	L-L	6-4	215	9-25-87	.000	.000	.000	6	5	2	0	0	0	0	0	0	0	0	0	3	0	0	.000	.000
Aviles, Mike	R-R	5-10	205	3-13-81	.317	.333	.310	38	101	17	32	6	0	2	8	4	0	0	1	17	4	2	.436	.340
2-team total (53 Kansas City)					.255	—	—	91	286	31	73	17	3	7	39	13	2	0	4	44	14	4	.409	.289
Cameron, Mike	R-R	6-2	210	1-8-73	.149	.143	.161	33	94	9	14	2	0	3	9	8	0	0	2	25	0	0	.266	.212
Crawford, Carl	L-L	6-2	215	8-5-81	.255	.195	.284	130	506	65	129	29	7	11	56	23	3	0	4	104	18	6	.405	.289
Drew, J.D.	L-R	6-1	200	11-20-75	.222	.167	.235	81	248	23	55	6	1	4	22	33	2	0	3	58	0	1	.302	.315
Ellsbury, Jacoby	L-L	6-1	185	9-11-83	.321	.284	.337	158	660	119	212	46	5	32	105	52	9	0	5	98	39	15	.552	.376
Gathright, Joey	L-R	5-10	175	4-27-81	—	.000	.000	7	0	1	0	0	0	0	0	0	0	1	0	0	1	1	—	1.000
Gonzalez, Adrian	L-L	6-2	225	5-8-82	.338	.321	.347	159	630	108	213	45	3	27	117	74	6	0	5	119	1	0	.548	.410
Iglesias, Jose	R-R	5-11	175	1-5-90	.333	1.000	.200	10	6	3	2	0	0	0	0	0	0	0	0	2	0	0	.333	.333
Jackson, Conor	R-R	6-2	215	5-7-82	.158	.111	.200	12	19	2	3	0	0	1	5	2	0	0	1	3	0	0	.316	.227
2-team total (102 Oakland)					.244	—	—	114	352	32	86	17	1	5	43	32	3	0	3	53	3	1	.341	.310
Lavarnway, Ryan	R-R	6-4	225	8-7-87	.231	.294	.182	17	39	5	9	2	0	2	8	4	0	0	0	10	0	0	.436	.302
Lowrie, Jed	B-R	6-0	180	4-17-84	.252	.330	.210	88	309	40	78	14	4	6	36	23	2	0	6	60	1	1	.382	.303
McDonald, Darnell	R-R	5-11	205	11-17-78	.236	.260	.189	79	157	26	37	6	1	6	24	14	2	0	2	33	2	3	.401	.303
Navarro, Yamaico	R-R	5-11	170	10-31-87	.216	.308	.167	16	37	6	8	2	0	1	3	3	0	0	0	9	0	0	.351	.275
2-team total (6 Kansas City)					.250	—	—	22	60	8	15	3	0	1	9	5	0	0	1	14	0	0	.350	.303
Ortiz, David	L-L	6-4	230	11-18-75	.309	.329	.298	146	525	84	162	40	1	29	96	78	1	0	1	83	1	1	.554	.398
Pedroia, Dustin	R-R	5-9	180	8-17-83	.307	.358	.287	159	635	102	195	37	3	21	91	86	1	0	7	85	26	8	.474	.387
Reddick, Josh	L-R	6-2	180	2-19-87	.280	.275	.280	87	254	41	71	18	3	7	28	19	1	0	4	50	1	2	.457	.327
Saltalamacchia, Jarrod	B-R	6-4	235	5-2-85	.235	.209	.247	103	358	52	84	23	3	16	56	24	3	0	1	119	1	0	.450	.288
Scutaro, Marco	R-R	5-10	185	10-30-75	.299	.303	.297	113	395	59	118	26	1	7	54	38	1	0	4	36	4	2	.423	.358
Spears, Nate	L-R	5-11	175	5-3-85	.000	.429	.000	3	4	0	0	0	0	0	0	0	0	0	0	1	0	0	.000	.000
Sutton, Drew	B-R	6-3	200	6-30-83	.315	.214	.350	31	54	11	17	7	0	0	7	3	1	0	0	13	0	0	.444	.362
Varitek, Jason	B-R	6-2	230	4-11-72	.221	.264	.200	68	222	32	49	10	1	11	36	21	4	0	0	67	0	0	.423	.300
Youkilis, Kevin	R-R	6-1	220	3-15-79	.258	.311	.234	120	431	68	111	32	2	17	80	68	14	0	4	100	3	0	.459	.373

Pitching	B-T	HT	WT	DOB	W	L	ERA	G	GS	CG	SV	IP	H	R	ER	HR	BB	SO	AVG	vLH	vRH	K/9	BB/9
Aceves, Alfredo	R-R	6-3	220	12-8-82	10	2	2.61	55	4	0	2	114	84	37	33	8	42	80	.204	.190	.216	6.32	3.32
Albers, Matt	L-R	6-0	225	1-20-83	4	4	4.73	56	0	0	0	65	62	35	34	7	31	68	.251	.263	.243	9.46	4.31
Atchison, Scott	R-R	6-2	200	3-29-76	1	0	3.26	17	0	0	1	30	31	11	11	0	6	17	.279	.289	.273	5.04	1.78
Bard, Daniel	R-R	6-4	215	6-25-85	2	9	3.33	70	0	0	1	73	46	29	27	5	24	74	.179	.211	.136	9.12	2.96
Beckett, Josh	R-R	6-5	225	5-15-80	13	7	2.89	30	30	1	0	193	146	65	62	21	52	175	.211	.186	.245	8.16	2.42
Bedard, Erik	L-L	6-1	200	3-5-79	1	2	4.03	8	8	0	0	38	41	22	17	3	18	38	.275	.255	.284	9.00	4.26
2-team total (16 Seattle)					5	9	3.62	24	24	0	0	129	118	63	52	14	48	125	—	—	—	8.70	3.34
Bowden, Michael	R-R	6-3	215	9-9-86	0	0	4.05	14	0	0	0	20	19	9	9	3	11	17	.241	.258	.229	7.65	4.95
Buchholz, Clay	L-R	6-3	190	8-14-84	6	3	3.48	14	14	0	0	83	76	34	32	10	31	60	.241	.241	.242	6.53	3.38
Doubront, Felix	L-L	6-2	165	10-23-87	0	0	6.10	11	0	0	1	10	12	7	7	1	8	6	.316	.412	.238	5.23	6.97
Hill, Rich	L-L	6-5	220	3-11-80	0	0	0.00	9	0	0	0	8	3	0	0	0	3	12	.115	.071	.167	13.50	3.38
Hottovy, Tommy	L-L	6-1	195	7-9-81	0	0	6.75	8	0	0	0	4	3	3	3	0	3	2	.267	.286	.250	4.50	6.75
Jenks, Bobby	R-R	6-4	275	3-14-81	2	2	6.32	19	0	0	0	16	22	12	11	1	13	17	.328	.278	.387	9.77	7.47
Lackey, John	R-R	6-6	245	10-23-78	12	12	6.41	28	28	0	0	160	203	119	114	20	56	108	.308	.343	.265	6.08	3.15
Lester, Jon	L-L	6-4	240	1-7-84	15	9	3.47	31	31	0	0	192	166	77	74	20	75	182	.234	.207	.244	8.55	3.52
Matsuzaka, Daisuke	R-R	6-0	185	9-13-80	3	3	5.30	8	7	0	0	37	32	24	22	4	23	26	.224	.259	.172	6.27	5.54
Miller, Andrew	L-L	6-7	210	5-21-85	6	3	5.54	17	12	0	0	65	77	43	40	8	41	50	.302	.312	.298	6.92	5.68
Miller, Trever	R-L	6-3	200	5-29-73	0	0	0.00	3	0	0	0	2	0	0	0	0	0	1	.000	.000	.000	4.50	0.00
2-team total (6 Toronto)					0	0	3.18	9	0	0	0	6	6	2	2	1	2	3	—	—	—	4.76	3.18
Morales, Franklin	L-L	6-0	210	1-24-86	1	1	3.62	36	0	0	0	30	30	15	13	4	11	31	.250	.234	.268	8.63	3.06
Okajima, Hideki	L-L	6-1	195	12-25-75	1	0	4.32	7	0	0	0	8	7	4	4	0	5	6	.233	.364	.158	6.48	5.40
Papelbon, Jonathan	R-R	6-4	225	11-23-80	4	1	2.94	63	0	0	31	64	50	22	21	3	10	87	.207	.156	.261	12.17	1.40
Reyes, Dennys	L-L	6-3	250	4-19-77	0	0	16.20	4	0	0	0	2	2	3	3	0	2	1	.333	.333	.333	5.40	10.80
Tazawa, Junichi	R-R	5-11	180	6-6-86	0	0	6.00	3	0	0	0	3	3	2	2	1	1	4	.250	.500	.125	12.00	3.00
Wakefield, Tim	R-R	6-2	210	8-2-66	7	8	5.12	33	23	1	0	155	163	110	88	25	47	93	.267	.246	.282	5.41	2.73
Weiland, Kyle	L-R	6-4	195	9-12-86	0	3	7.66	7	5	0	0	25	29	22	21	5	12	13	.287	.178	.375	4.74	4.38

Pitching	B-T	HT	WT	DOB	W	L	ERA	G	GS	CG	SV	IP	H	R	ER	HR	BB	SO	AVG	vLH	vRH	K/9	BB/9
Wheeler, Dan	R-R	6-3	220	12-10-77	2	2	4.38	47	0	0	0	49	47	24	24	7	8	39	.246	.278	.227	7.11	1.46
Williams, Randy	L-L	6-3	200	9-18-75	0	1	6.48	7	0	0	0	8	10	6	6	0	5	6	.303	.250	.353	6.48	5.40

Fielding

Catcher	PCT	G	PO	A	E	DP	PB
Lavarnway	1.000	8	22	3	0	0	0
Saltalamacchia	.992	101	678	56	6	3	26
Varitek	.993	68	519	28	4	1	6

First Base	PCT	G	PO	A	E	DP
Anderson	.938	6	12	3	1	1
Gonzalez	.997	156	1222	125	4	106
Jackson	1.000	3	9	0	0	0
Lowrie	1.000	4	12	0	0	0
Ortiz	1.000	2	18	0	0	4
Sutton	1.000	5	13	1	0	0
Youkilis	1.000	6	37	5	0	4

Second Base	PCT	G	PO	A	E	DP
Aviles	1.000	7	5	4	0	1
Lowrie	1.000	1	0	2	0	0
Pedroia	.990	159	290	425	7	81

Third Base	PCT	G	PO	A	E	DP
Scutaro	.900	2	3	6	1	1
Spears	.000	1	0	0	0	0
Sutton	.889	7	3	5	1	1

Third Base	PCT	G	PO	A	E	DP
Aviles	.949	22	7	30	2	1
Jackson	1.000	1	1	0	0	0
Lowrie	.948	33	28	64	5	5
Navarro	.882	11	7	8	2	0
Sutton	1.000	8	2	13	0	1
Youkilis	.967	112	87	177	9	15

Shortstop	PCT	G	PO	A	E	DP
Aviles	1.000	8	3	21	0	1
Iglesias	1.000	8	2	3	0	0
Lowrie	.945	49	59	112	10	22
Navarro	1.000	3	2	3	0	1
Scutaro	.972	109	147	269	12	53

	PCT	G	PO	A	E	DP
Sutton	.923	4	6	6	1	2

Outfield	PCT	G	PO	A	E	DP
Aviles	1.000	5	5	0	0	0
Cameron	.980	29	48	0	1	0
Crawford	.987	127	235	1	3	0
Drew	1.000	76	146	3	0	0
Ellsbury	1.000	154	388	6	0	3
Gathright	1.000	4	2	0	0	0
Gonzalez	.000	2	0	0	0	0
Jackson	1.000	6	4	0	0	0
McDonald	.968	67	90	2	3	0
Navarro	1.000	3	6	0	0	0
Reddick	.968	80	145	5	5	1
Spears	1.000	1	1	0	0	0
Sutton	.857	3	6	0	1	0

PAWTUCKET RED SOX

INTERNATIONAL LEAGUE

TRIPLE-A

Batting	B-T	HT	WT	DOB	AVG	vLH	vRH	G	AB	R	H	2B	3B	HR	RBI	BB	HBP	SH	SF	SO	SB	CS	SLG	OBP
Anderson, Lars	L-L	6-4	215	9-25-87	.265	.242	.273	136	491	65	130	31	2	14	78	80	3	0	3	120	5	0	.422	.369
Bermudez, Ronald	R-R	6-1	165	6-6-88	.261	.291	.248	57	180	20	47	15	1	3	21	9	0	0	1	26	0	1	.406	.295
Butler, Daniel	R-R	5-10	190	10-17-86	.333	.000	.333	1	3	1	1	0	0	1	3	0	0	0	0	2	0	1	.333	.333
Carroll, Brett	R-R	6-0	210	10-3-82	.229	.211	.234	24	83	10	19	6	1	1	12	8	1	0	2	20	2	0	.361	.298
Crawford, Carl	L-L	6-2	215	8-5-81	.200	.500	.000	2	5	1	1	0	0	0	1	1	0	0	0	1	0	0	.200	.333
Dlugach, Brent	R-R	6-4	200	3-3-83	.222	.273	.200	63	216	30	48	8	0	6	25	18	1	0	1	86	4	0	.343	.284
Drew, J.D.	L-R	6-1	200	11-20-75	1.000	.000	1.000	1	3	1	3	0	0	0	0	0	0	0	0	0	0	0	1.000	1.000
Exposito, Luis	R-R	6-3	210	1-20-87	.242	.330	.211	89	330	33	80	17	0	8	36	26	1	0	2	79	0	2	.367	.298
Gathright, Joey	L-R	5-10	175	4-27-81	.375	1.000	.286	4	8	3	3	0	0	0	2	1	0	0	0	1	1	0	.375	.444
Iglesias, Jose	R-R	5-11	175	1-5-90	.235	.299	.212	101	357	35	84	9	0	1	31	21	4	0	0	58	12	4	.269	.285
Kalish, Ryan	L-L	6-0	215	3-28-88	.209	.192	.217	22	86	9	18	6	0	0	9	8	0	0	2	20	4	3	.279	.271
Kang, James	R-R	5-9	175	10-19-87	.250	.500	.167	5	8	2	2	0	0	1	4	2	0	0	1	2	0	0	.625	.364
Khoury, Ryan	R-R	5-10	180	3-19-84	.286	.400	.222	8	28	8	8	1	1	1	5	4	0	0	0	4	1	0	.500	.375
Lavarnway, Ryan	R-R	6-4	225	8-7-87	.295	.377	.270	61	227	40	67	18	0	18	55	32	4	0	1	60	1	1	.612	.390
Lin, Che-Hsuan	R-R	6-0	180	9-21-88	.235	.244	.231	85	328	49	77	11	1	2	25	38	7	0	2	51	16	4	.293	.325
Linares, Juan Carlos	R-R	5-11	190	9-7-84	.233	.267	.222	17	60	8	14	5	1	3	12	4	0	0	0	12	0	1	.500	.281
Lowrie, Jed	B-R	6-0	180	4-17-84	.412	.600	.333	5	17	2	7	4	0	0	5	2	0	0	0	1	0	0	.647	.474
Luna, Hector	R-R	6-1	225	2-1-80	.283	.317	.271	113	421	61	119	22	3	14	58	42	3	0	2	67	6	1	.449	.350
McDonald, Darnell	R-R	5-11	205	11-17-78	.345	.000	.435	9	29	6	10	3	0	2	11	5	1	0	0	6	1	2	.655	.457
McKenry, Mike	R-R	5-10	200	3-4-85	.274	.182	.301	29	95	10	26	5	0	3	12	14	1	0	1	24	1	0	.421	.369
Middlebrooks, Will	R-R	6-4	200	9-9-88	.161	.167	.159	16	56	4	9	0	0	2	3	1	0	0	1	18	1	0	.268	.200
Nava, Daniel	B-L	5-10	200	2-22-83	.268	.283	.262	121	441	69	118	27	2	10	48	70	6	0	4	88	10	3	.406	.372
Navarro, Yamaico	R-R	5-11	170	10-31-87	.258	.293	.241	34	128	25	33	8	2	5	13	17	4	0	0	25	3	2	.469	.362
Pichardo, Wilfred	B-R	5-9	146	10-21-89	.000	.000	.000	1	0	0	0	0	0	0	0	0	0	0	0	1	0	0	.000	.000
Reddick, Josh	L-R	6-2	180	2-19-87	.230	.200	.241	52	191	37	44	9	1	14	36	33	0	0	7	39	4	1	.508	.333
Scutaro, Marco	R-R	5-10	185	10-30-75	.455	.500	.444	3	11	4	5	1	0	0	0	1	0	0	0	0	0	0	.545	.500
Sheely, Matt	R-R	5-9	160	8-30-86	.224	.196	.241	43	125	12	28	2	2	0	7	10	5	0	0	33	6	1	.272	.307
Spears, Nate	L-R	5-11	175	5-3-85	.248	.254	.246	96	315	49	78	19	2	8	45	49	6	0	5	69	13	1	.397	.355
Spring, Matt	R-R	6-2	215	11-7-84	.200	.333	.143	3	10	0	2	1	0	0	0	0	0	0	0	5	0	0	.300	.200
Sutton, Drew	B-R	6-3	200	6-30-83	.295	.298	.294	45	166	24	49	13	1	5	27	21	3	0	1	38	0	2	.476	.382
Thomas, Tony	R-R	5-10	180	7-10-86	.212	.237	.203	80	278	35	59	17	1	8	32	21	4	0	3	74	11	3	.367	.275
Valdez, Alex	B-R	6-1	160	9-2-84	.214	.000	.333	5	14	2	3	2	0	1	1	3	0	0	0	6	0	0	.571	.353
2-team total (27 Syracuse)					.165	—	—	32	91	10	15	4	1	3	7	10	1	0	0	23	2	0	.330	.255
Youkilis, Kevin	R-R	6-1	220	3-15-79	.250	.000	.286	2	8	2	2	0	0	1	1	1	0	0	0	0	0	0	.625	.333

Pitching	B-T	HT	WT	DOB	W	L	ERA	G	GS	CG	SV	IP	H	R	ER	HR	BB	SO	AVG	vLH	vRH	K/9	BB/9
Aceves, Alfredo	R-R	6-3	220	12-8-82	1	0	5.63	2	2	0	0	8	6	5	0	4	6	.240	.308	.167	6.75	4.50
Albers, Matt	L-R	6-0	225	1-20-83	0	0	0.00	3	1	0	0	3	1	0	0	0	2	.100	.000	.167	6.00	0.00
Atchison, Scott	R-R	6-2	200	3-29-76	6	2	2.64	36	1	0	5	61	50	20	18	5	9	72	.221	.236	.212	10.57	1.32
Bowden, Michael	R-R	6-3	215	9-9-86	3	3	2.73	41	0	0	16	53	43	19	16	5	18	61	.218	.384	.121	10.42	3.08
Doubront, Felix	L-L	6-2	165	10-23-87	2	5	4.22	18	16	0	0	70	65	37	33	10	26	61	.241	.309	.212	7.81	3.33
Duckworth, Brandon	R-R	6-2	215	1-23-76	8	6	3.97	22	21	0	0	118	113	53	52	11	42	88	.259	.277	.245	6.71	3.20
Fox, Matt	R-R	6-3	190	12-4-82	10	4	3.96	28	21	1	0	130	107	58	57	22	49	122	.230	.262	.207	8.47	3.40
Gonzalez, Miguel	R-R	6-1	170	5-27-84	0	1	1.80	1	1	0	0	5	2	1	1	1	2	5	.125	.125	.125	9.00	3.60
Hill, Rich	L-L	6-5	230	3-11-80	1	0	1.13	10	0	0	1	16	8	3	2	1	5	18	.143	.100	.167	10.13	2.81
Hottovy, Tommy	L-L	6-1	195	7-9-81	2	0	2.75	24	0	0	1	36	23	13	11	8	9	29	.181	.083	.241	7.25	2.25
Jenks, Bobby	R-R	6-4	275	3-14-81	0	0	4.50	2	2	0	0	2	1	1	1	0	1	2	.250	.333	.200	9.00	4.50
Johnson, Kris	L-L	6-4	170	10-14-84	2	2	12.63	8	3	0	0	21	41	31	29	7	6	12	.410	.306	.469	5.23	2.61

Pitching

Pitching	B-T	HT	WT	DOB	W	L	ERA	G	GS	CG	SV	IP	H	R	ER	HR	BB	SO	AVG	vLH	vRH	K/9	BB/9
Kehrt, Jeremy	R-R	6-2	190	12-21-85	1	0	3.45	7	2	0	0	16	19	9	6	3	5	14	.297	.233	.353	8.04	2.87
Lackey, John	R-R	6-6	245	10-23-78	0	0	1.59	1	1	0	0	6	3	1	1	1	0	4	.158	.250	.091	6.35	0.00
Maxwell, Blake	R-R	6-5	255	8-1-84	1	2	2.50	13	0	0	1	18	17	6	5	1	5	8	.262	.263	.261	4.00	2.50
Miller, Andrew	L-L	6-7	210	5-21-85	3	3	2.47	13	12	0	0	66	42	22	18	2	35	61	.181	.122	.209	8.36	4.80
Miller, Trever	R-L	6-3	200	5-29-73	0	0	2.70	3	0	0	0	3	2	1	1	0	0	2	.167	.000	.250	5.40	0.00
Millwood, Kevin	R-R	6-4	230	12-24-74	5	1	4.28	13	13	0	0	74	79	36	35	7	25	66	.278	.279	.278	8.06	3.05
2-team total (2 Scranton/W-B)					6	2	4.68	15	15	1	0	83	93	44	43	10	27	73	—	—	—	7.95	2.94
Morales, Franklin	L-L	6-0	210	1-24-86	0	0	1.42	6	0	0	0	6	3	3	1	1	3	6	.125	.286	.059	8.53	4.26
Neuman, Dennis	R-R	5-11	185	10-18-89	0	1	4.00	5	0	0	2	9	6	9	4	0	8	5	.182	.143	.192	5.00	8.00
Okajima, Hideki	L-R	6-1	195	12-25-75	8	1	2.29	34	0	0	0	51	39	13	13	3	9	48	.211	.190	.220	8.47	1.59
Pena Jr., Tony	R-R	6-2	180	3-23-81	9	6	3.56	33	14	0	3	116	127	51	46	7	36	65	.282	.340	.240	5.03	2.79
Rice, Jason	R-R	5-10	190	5-13-86	4	5	3.69	44	1	0	4	85	77	37	35	6	42	89	.238	.279	.211	9.39	4.43
Ring, Royce	L-L	6-0	220	12-21-80	1	2	4.09	9	0	0	1	11	12	5	5	1	3	8	.300	.077	.407	6.55	2.45
Santeliz, Clevelan	R-R	6-0	180	9-1-86	2	3	4.60	29	0	0	0	43	40	27	22	3	30	37	.245	.246	.245	7.74	6.28
Smith, Greg	L-L	6-1	190	12-22-83	2	1	3.75	4	4	0	0	24	19	10	10	2	7	15	.213	.292	.185	5.63	2.63
2-team total (13 Scranton/W-B)					5	4	4.52	17	14	0	0	82	87	44	41	11	34	51	—	—	—	5.62	3.75
Tazawa, Junichi	R-R	5-11	180	6-6-86	1	1	2.51	8	0	0	0	14	14	4	4	1	3	19	.264	.182	.323	11.93	1.88
Weiland, Kyle	L-R	6-4	195	9-12-86	8	10	3.58	24	24	0	0	128	108	54	51	10	55	126	.232	.202	.258	8.84	3.86
Wheeler, Dan	R-R	6-3	220	12-10-77	0	0	1.93	5	0	0	0	5	3	1	1	1	2	7	.176	.143	.200	13.50	3.86
Williams, Randy	L-L	6-3	200	9-18-75	1	1	1.41	27	0	0	8	32	23	7	5	2	13	36	.204	.081	.263	10.13	3.66
Wilson, Alex	R-R	6-0	215	11-3-86	1	0	3.43	4	4	0	0	21	19	8	8	2	7	24	.235	.306	.178	10.29	3.00

Fielding

Catcher	PCT	G	PO	A	E	DP	PB
Butler	1.000	1	7	1	0	0	0
Exposito	.994	74	610	53	4	6	11
Lavarnway	.996	36	256	23	1	3	4
McKenry	.996	29	215	10	1	2	6
Spring	1.000	3	23	3	0	0	0

First Base	PCT	G	PO	A	E	DP
Anderson	.992	132	1030	65	9	123
Luna	1.000	11	91	7	0	9
Spears	1.000	1	3	1	0	1

Second Base	PCT	G	PO	A	E	DP
Dlugach	1.000	20	42	49	0	18
Kang	1.000	4	9	9	0	2
Khoury	1.000	5	8	14	0	4
Luna	.963	7	15	11	1	4
Navarro	1.000	5	18	16	0	8
Scutaro	1.000	1	1	1	0	0
Spears	.970	37	67	97	5	28
Sutton	.954	17	32	30	3	8

Thomas	.973	52	71	146	6	37

Third Base	PCT	G	PO	A	E	DP
Dlugach	1.000	15	7	36	0	4
Khoury	1.000	1	2	1	0	0
Luna	.948	81	53	110	9	15
Middlebrooks	.917	14	10	23	3	0
Navarro	.850	9	5	12	3	1
Spears	.971	16	9	25	1	3
Sutton	.958	9	3	20	1	2
Youkilis	1.000	1	0	2	0	0

Shortstop	PCT	G	PO	A	E	DP
Dlugach	.964	22	27	54	3	18
Iglesias	.973	97	145	284	12	68
Kang	.000	1	0	0	0	0
Khoury	.750	1	1	2	1	0
Lowrie	1.000	3	5	8	0	4
Navarro	.964	7	10	17	1	7
Scutaro	1.000	1	0	2	0	0
Spears	1.000	4	4	12	0	1

Sutton	.905	7	2	17	2	3
Valdez	1.000	5	5	13	0	1

Outfield	PCT	G	PO	A	E	DP
Bermudez	1.000	51	84	3	0	0
Carroll	1.000	24	37	2	0	0
Crawford	1.000	2	1	0	0	0
Drew	1.000	1	1	0	0	0
Gathright	1.000	4	2	0	0	0
Kalish	.984	18	62	1	1	0
Lin	.987	84	214	9	3	3
Linares	1.000	17	31	2	0	1
McDonald	1.000	7	12	1	0	1
Nava	.994	96	166	2	1	3
Navarro	1.000	11	27	0	0	0
Pichardo	.000	1	0	0	0	0
Reddick	.991	49	104	3	1	1
Sheely	.989	41	88	5	1	3
Spears	.984	36	61	2	1	0
Sutton	.833	5	5	0	1	0
Thomas	1.000	7	6	0	0	0

PORTLAND SEA DOGS   DOUBLE-A

EASTERN LEAGUE

Batting	B-T	HT	WT	DOB	AVG	vLH	vRH	G	AB	R	H	2B	3B	HR	RBI	BB	HBP	SH	SF	SO	SB	CS	SLG	OBP
Bermudez, Ronald	R-R	6-1	165	6-6-88	.292	.273	.300	19	72	6	21	2	1	0	6	2	0	0	0	22	0	1	.347	.311
Butler, Daniel	R-R	5-10	190	10-17-86	.212	.263	.191	21	66	4	14	5	0	0	2	9	1	0	0	11	0	0	.288	.316
Chiang, Chih-Hsien	L-R	6-2	170	2-21-88	.340	.281	.362	88	321	68	109	37	4	18	76	25	10	0	2	61	6	2	.648	.402
Dening, Mitch	L-R	6-1	165	8-17-88	.220	.185	.231	86	264	35	58	11	3	6	36	29	4	0	3	64	3	4	.352	.303
Dent, Ryan	R-R	6-0	190	3-15-89	.206	.286	.180	53	170	20	35	11	0	2	13	17	0	0	2	45	7	3	.306	.275
Dominguez, Drew	R-R	5-11	195	12-27-86	.000	.000	.000	1	4	0	0	0	0	0	1	0	0	0	0	1	0	0	.000	.000
Federowicz, Tim	R-R	5-11	200	8-5-87	.277	.243	.287	90	339	46	94	20	0	8	52	32	3	0	8	63	1	0	.407	.338
Frias, Vladimir	B-R	6-2	170	9-6-86	.250	.317	.211	35	112	10	28	10	0	0	5	3	2	0	1	20	4	1	.339	.280
Gedman, Matt	L-R	6-2	205	9-26-88	.000	.000	.000	1	3	0	0	0	0	0	0	0	0	0	0	0	0	0	.000	.000
Hassan, Alex	R-R	6-3	195	4-1-88	.291	.341	.272	126	454	75	132	34	1	13	64	76	12	0	3	79	8	2	.456	.404
Hazelbaker, Jeremy	L-R	6-3	190	5-26-87	.266	.229	.279	90	354	60	94	18	3	12	41	42	4	0	0	105	35	8	.435	.350
Hedman, Drew	L-L	6-2	200	7-20-86	.000	.000	.000	1	1	0	0	0	0	0	1	0	1	0	1	0	0	0	.000	.333
Hee, Jonathan	B-R	6-0	180	8-11-85	.275	.216	.299	98	331	47	91	26	0	4	40	33	12	0	0	85	3	2	.390	.362
Howell, Jeff	R-R	6-0	205	4-1-83	.316	.714	.226	10	38	6	12	2	1	2	4	1	0	0	0	13	0	0	.579	.333
Khoury, Ryan	R-R	5-10	180	3-19-84	.239	.212	.247	61	234	41	56	12	2	4	26	37	1	0	0	56	5	1	.359	.346
Lavarnway, Ryan	R-R	6-4	225	8-7-87	.284	.318	.268	55	208	35	59	5	0	14	38	25	2	0	4	47	0	0	.510	.360
Lin, Che-Hsuan	R-R	6-0	180	9-21-88	.268	.366	.227	34	138	23	37	5	2	0	11	20	3	0	0	14	12	3	.333	.373
Meneses, Heiker	R-R	5-9	160	7-1-91	.265	.286	.261	24	83	13	22	3	0	0	6	3	3	0	1	25	2	0	.301	.311
Middlebrooks, Will	R-R	6-4	200	9-9-88	.302	.264	.314	96	371	54	112	25	1	18	80	21	4	0	1	95	6	0	.520	.345
Padron, Jorge	L-L	6-1	200	7-20-80	.247	.197	.269	67	243	24	60	7	1	5	28	21	0	0	3	21	1	0	.346	.303
Rodriguez, Reynaldo	R-R	6-0	195	2-7-86	.253	.333	.235	49	186	25	47	15	1	8	32	9	4	0	0	46	0	0	.473	.302
Spring, Matt	R-R	6-2	215	11-2-84	.257	.368	.218	20	74	12	19	9	0	4	13	9	2	0	0	27	0	0	.541	.353
Tejeda, Oscar	R-R	6-1	170	12-26-89	.249	.295	.233	123	457	50	114	24	1	5	41	29	3	0	3	101	13	4	.339	.297
Thomas, Tony	R-R	5-10	180	7-10-86	.300	.000	.353	6	20	3	6	1	0	0	1	1	0	0	0	7	3	0	.350	.333
Valdez, Alex	B-R	6-1	160	9-2-84	.316	.143	.417	6	19	3	6	1	0	0	3	0	0	0	1	2	1	0	.368	.409

BOSTON RED SOX

Batting	B-T	HT	WT	DOB	AVG	vLH	vRH	G	AB	R	H	2B	3B	HR	RBI	BB	HBP	SH	SF	SO	SB	CS	SLG	OBP
2-team total (29 Harrisburg)					.241	—	—	35	108	16	26	7	2	3	15	10	0	0	1	22	3	1	.426	.303
Vazquez, Will	R-R	6-2	190	2-22-85	.111	.273	.040	11	36	3	4	3	0	0	3	3	1	0	0	12	0	0	.194	.200
Wagner, Mark	R-R	6-1	205	6-11-84	.259	.324	.235	36	135	20	35	12	2	6	18	9	1	0	2	28	1	0	.511	.306

Pitching	B-T	HT	WT	DOB	W	L	ERA	G	GS	CG	SV	IP	H	R	ER	HR	BB	SO	AVG	vLH	vRH	K/9	BB/9
Balcom-Miller, Chris	R-R	6-2	210	3-3-89	3	6	4.81	16	16	1	0	82	103	53	44	4	32	75	.310	.345	.275	8.20	3.50
Cabral, Cesar	L-L	6-3	175	2-11-89	2	4	3.52	24	0	0	1	38	41	17	15	3	16	46	.275	.217	.301	10.80	3.76
Clay, Caleb	R-R	6-2	180	2-15-88	1	5	7.47	28	2	0	0	59	72	55	49	9	34	53	.312	.303	.320	8.08	5.19
Doubront, Felix	L-L	6-2	165	10-23-87	1	0	1.80	1	1	0	0	5	4	1	1	0	0	9	.211	.000	.250	16.20	0.00
Fernandes, Kyle	L-L	6-0	190	9-12-85	3	5	3.73	35	0	0	2	63	63	36	26	5	34	57	.256	.217	.276	8.19	4.88
Fields, Josh	R-R	6-0	185	8-19-85	3	0	3.12	9	0	0	1	17	10	6	6	2	10	25	.179	.148	.207	12.98	5.19
Fife, Stephen	R-R	6-3	210	10-4-86	11	4	3.66	19	18	0	0	103	107	47	42	7	37	70	.270	.294	.248	6.10	3.22
Garrison, Seth	B-R	6-5	220	8-13-85	1	2	4.28	20	0	0	0	40	35	19	19	3	18	37	.240	.254	.228	8.33	4.05
Gonzalez, Miguel	R-R	6-1	170	5-27-84	0	5	6.17	15	6	0	0	47	55	41	32	4	19	45	.286	.247	.313	8.68	3.66
Haeger, Charlie	R-R	6-1	210	9-19-83	4	1	3.24	8	8	1	0	50	40	19	18	5	22	49	.226	.193	.255	8.82	3.96
Hottovy, Tommy	L-L	6-1	195	7-9-81	0	0	1.93	8	0	0	1	19	12	4	4	0	4	18	.185	.190	.182	8.68	1.93
Huntzinger, Brock	R-R	6-3	200	7-2-88	5	11	6.17	25	25	0	0	124	159	91	85	23	41	123	.314	.287	.340	8.93	2.98
Jenks, Bobby	R-R	6-4	275	3-14-81	0	0	0.00	1	1	0	0	1	1	0	0	0	0	1	.333	.000	.500	9.00	0.00
Kehrt, Jeremy	R-R	6-2	190	12-21-85	3	2	4.64	22	6	0	1	78	88	48	40	11	23	38	.282	.292	.274	4.40	2.67
Latimer, Will	L-L	6-3	190	12-4-85	0	0	6.14	3	0	0	0	7	9	5	5	0	2	6	.300	.222	.333	7.36	2.45
Lee, Michael	R-R	6-7	220	11-18-86	1	6	5.75	24	17	0	0	88	96	59	56	18	39	67	.282	.278	.284	6.88	4.00
Luis, Santo	R-R	6-4	200	1-27-84	1	1	5.72	16	0	0	0	28	29	18	18	2	16	28	.279	.306	.255	8.89	5.08
Martin, Chris	R-R	6-7	175	6-2-86	0	1	15.88	3	0	0	0	6	12	10	10	2	1	3	.444	.300	.529	4.76	1.59
Maxwell, Blake	R-R	6-5	255	8-1-84	3	4	2.43	37	0	0	15	56	52	22	15	4	16	57	.248	.253	.243	9.22	2.59
Pimentel, Stolmy	R-R	6-3	165	2-1-90	0	9	9.12	15	15	0	0	50	75	57	51	8	23	30	.352	.374	.333	5.36	4.11
Portice, Eammon	R-R	6-2	185	6-18-85	4	8	4.84	37	0	0	0	80	72	51	43	12	33	87	.235	.199	.267	9.79	3.71
Rosario, Charle	R-R	5-10	158	7-23-88	1	0	2.08	4	0	0	0	9	8	5	2	1	1	10	.229	.235	.222	10.38	1.04
Rusch, Matt	R-R	5-11	180	5-20-83	0	3	5.06	4	4	0	0	21	28	14	12	2	4	16	.326	.206	.404	6.75	1.69
Tazawa, Junichi	R-R	5-11	180	6-6-86	3	2	4.70	8	2	0	0	23	20	12	12	3	7	27	.227	.244	.213	10.57	2.74
Wilson, Alex	R-R	6-0	215	11-3-86	9	4	3.05	21	21	0	0	112	103	42	38	8	37	99	.246	.251	.240	7.96	2.97

Fielding

Catcher	PCT	G	PO	A	E	DP	PB
Butler	.985	21	169	23	3	2	5
Federowicz	.982	64	481	65	10	5	1
Howell	1.000	10	80	7	0	5	5
Lavarnway	.995	26	170	26	1	1	3
Spring	1.000	15	123	20	0	3	5
Vazquez	1.000	3	9	1	0	0	1
Wagner	1.000	5	28	4	0	0	0

First Base	PCT	G	PO	A	E	DP
Hedman	1.000	1	6	2	0	0
Hee	.983	32	225	12	4	16
Padron	.990	58	463	44	5	30
Rodriguez	.981	44	325	27	7	35
Spring	1.000	5	32	5	0	2
Vazquez	1.000	3	28	3	0	4
Wagner	1.000	2	22	0	0	2

Second Base	PCT	G	PO	A	E	DP
Frias	.909	3	4	6	1	4
Hee	.958	10	21	25	2	5
Khoury	.974	8	14	24	1	4
Meneses	1.000	3	4	6	0	0
Tejeda	.949	116	169	282	24	52
Valdez	1.000	2	4	1	0	0
Vazquez	1.000	2	2	1	0	0

Third Base	PCT	G	PO	A	E	DP
Dominguez	.000	1	0	0	0	0
Frias	1.000	3	1	3	0	0
Gedman	1.000	1	0	1	0	0
Hee	.960	28	24	48	3	6
Khoury	.946	21	14	39	3	3
Middlebrooks	.936	85	55	136	13	8
Thomas	.909	5	0	10	1	1
Vazquez	.875	3	1	6	1	0

Shortstop	PCT	G	PO	A	E	DP
Dent	.966	44	69	103	6	19
Frias	.953	27	53	68	6	20
Hee	.932	28	45	65	8	14
Khoury	.955	20	35	49	4	9
Meneses	.881	21	28	46	10	9
Valdez	1.000	4	7	11	0	3

Outfield	PCT	G	PO	A	E	DP
Bermudez	1.000	19	44	2	0	1
Chiang	.979	77	131	10	3	1
Dening	.993	81	135	6	1	1
Dent	1.000	7	16	1	0	0
Hassan	.995	119	198	11	1	4
Hazelbaker	.966	85	197	4	7	1
Khoury	1.000	12	19	0	0	0
Lin	.989	34	89	3	1	1

SALEM RED SOX HIGH CLASS A

CAROLINA LEAGUE

Batting	B-T	HT	WT	DOB	AVG	vLH	vRH	G	AB	R	H	2B	3B	HR	RBI	BB	HBP	SH	SF	SO	SB	CS	SLG	OBP
Almanzar, Michael	R-R	6-3	190	12-2-90	.182	.208	.168	61	220	18	40	8	0	2	15	9	3	0	1	55	3	3	.245	.223
Bermudez, Ronald	R-R	6-1	165	6-6-88	.194	.200	.188	9	31	5	6	3	0	0	3	2	1	0	0	4	1	0	.290	.265
Brentz, Bryce	R-R	6-1	180	12-30-88	.274	.296	.263	75	288	48	79	15	1	19	58	26	3	0	4	80	1	1	.531	.336
Butler, Daniel	R-R	5-10	190	10-17-86	.247	.195	.278	91	312	39	77	20	0	11	66	45	7	0	5	56	4	1	.417	.350
Dominguez, Drew	R-R	5-11	195	12-27-86	.200	.333	.000	5	5	1	1	0	0	0	1	1	0	0	0	3	0	0	.200	.429
Escobar, Leonel	R-R	5-10	175	9-4-90	.200	.400	.000	4	10	0	2	0	0	0	1	0	0	0	0	2	0	0	.200	.273
Frias, Vladimir	B-R	6-2	170	9-6-86	.197	.219	.179	24	71	10	14	4	0	3	13	9	3	0	0	16	4	4	.380	.313
Garcia, Joantoni	R-R	5-11	165	9-9-90	.333	.500	.250	2	6	0	2	0	0	0	0	0	0	0	0	2	0	1	.333	.333
Gentile, Zach	L-R	5-8	165	11-1-86	.273	.247	.285	80	253	33	69	10	1	0	20	31	7	0	1	42	3	2	.320	.366
Gibson, Derrik	R-R	6-1	170	12-5-89	.240	.261	.229	128	445	56	107	20	3	1	30	48	6	0	2	86	24	9	.306	.321
Hazelbaker, Jeremy	L-R	6-3	190	8-14-87	.270	.208	.333	34	122	26	34	9	0	5	14	20	2	0	0	34	12	6	.475	.389
Head, Miles	R-R	6-0	215	5-2-91	.254	.287	.234	63	232	27	59	12	1	7	29	20	6	0	1	56	0	2	.405	.328
Hissey, Pete	L-L	6-1	180	1-17-90	.241	.200	.265	97	378	38	91	25	3	2	41	25	7	0	4	93	26	11	.339	.297
Kang, James	R-R	5-9	175	10-19-87	.189	.294	.100	14	37	2	7	1	0	0	2	3	1	0	0	11	1	0	.216	.268
Mailman, David	L-L	6-2	180	10-7-88	.212	.176	.226	79	260	26	55	20	1	6	25	31	1	0	1	70	7	3	.365	.297
Meneses, Heiker	R-R	5-9	160	7-1-91	.356	.406	.333	26	101	23	36	9	5	1	13	8	3	0	1	24	6	1	.574	.416
Padron, Jorge	L-L	6-1	200	7-20-86	.248	.244	.250	60	226	26	56	12	3	2	27	21	3	0	2	25	0	0	.354	.317
Peley, Josue	R-R	6-0	177	12-24-87	.276	.167	.333	36	123	17	34	6	0	0	9	7	0	0	2	27	4	1	.325	.311
Pichardo, Wilfred	B-R	5-9	146	10-21-89	.244	.118	.327	23	86	8	21	4	1	0	6	3	1	0	2	28	2	5	.314	.272
Rodriguez, Reynaldo	R-R	6-0	195	2-7-86	.317	.320	.315	56	202	44	64	24	1	9	43	27	3	0	5	43	7	2	.579	.397

Batting	B-T	HT	WT	DOB	AVG	vLH	vRH	G	AB	R	H	2B	3B	HR	RBI	BB	HBP	SH	SF	SO	SB	CS	SLG	OBP
Spring, Matt	R-R	6-2	215	11-7-84	.250	.156	.304	24	88	13	22	7	0	7	23	6	0	0	0	32	0	1	.568	.298
Valdez, Alex	B-R	6-1	160	9-2-84	.243	.262	.228	39	140	13	34	11	2	1	15	13	0	0	2	40	4	1	.371	.303
Vitek, Kolbrin	R-R	6-2	195	4-1-89	.281	.287	.278	123	473	78	133	22	6	3	43	45	7	0	4	102	10	3	.372	.350
Wagner, Mark	R-R	6-1	205	6-11-84	.264	.297	.240	26	87	14	23	4	0	4	14	14	1	0	2	16	1	0	.448	.365
Wilkerson, Shannon	R-R	6-0	198	7-20-88	.251	.245	.257	102	342	54	86	18	2	10	39	34	4	0	5	70	11	3	.404	.322

Pitching	B-T	HT	WT	DOB	W	L	ERA	G	GS	CG	SV	IP	H	R	ER	HR	BB	SO	AVG	vLH	vRH	K/9	BB/9
Balcom-Miller, Chris	R-R	6-2	210	3-3-89	3	1	2.34	7	7	0	0	35	24	10	9	2	11	37	.205	.190	.213	9.61	2.86
Batista, Anatanaer	R-R	5-10	150	2-2-89	4	3	4.44	27	0	0	2	53	54	31	26	5	26	46	.261	.263	.260	7.86	4.44
Bayer, Jeremiah	R-R	6-2	200	12-26-85	7	4	3.26	36	0	0	4	91	86	35	33	4	32	69	.253	.264	.246	6.82	3.16
Britton, Drake	L-L	6-2	200	5-22-89	1	13	6.91	26	26	0	0	98	111	81	75	12	55	89	.285	.226	.304	8.20	5.07
Cabral, Cesar	L-L	6-3	175	2-11-89	1	0	1.62	12	0	0	8	17	15	5	3	0	5	24	.238	.313	.213	12.96	2.70
Ebert, Tom	R-R	6-6	245	10-31-87	5	6	4.09	31	4	0	1	84	67	40	38	7	37	71	.228	.222	.231	7.64	3.98
Flasher, Jordan	R-R	5-11	165	10-14-87	3	0	2.92	5	0	0	0	12	13	5	4	0	5	5	.302	.357	.276	3.65	3.65
Gleason, Mike	R-R	6-1	195	3-12-88	0	2	6.86	13	0	0	2	20	27	15	15	2	9	16	.333	.433	.275	7.32	4.12
Gonzalez, Miguel	R-R	6-1	170	5-27-84	0	1	1.80	2	2	0	0	5	5	1	1	0	2	4	.263	.273	.250	7.20	3.60
Hernandez, Chris	L-L	6-1	185	12-14-88	10	7	3.18	25	25	1	0	127	112	53	45	8	51	80	.241	.237	.243	5.65	3.60
Herold, Mitch	L-L	6-0	200	6-18-86	1	2	3.35	22	0	0	2	40	31	16	15	1	13	32	.208	.129	.229	7.14	2.90
Hose, T.J.	R-R	5-10	185	4-15-86	1	1	4.22	6	0	0	1	11	11	5	5	2	7	9	.289	.308	.280	7.59	5.91
Latimer, Will	L-L	6-3	190	12-4-85	1	0	2.93	36	0	0	8	77	64	30	25	5	20	61	.226	.203	.233	7.16	2.35
Martin, Chris	R-R	6-7	175	6-2-86	2	1	0.92	13	0	0	4	39	29	4	4	0	6	24	.210	.214	.207	5.49	1.37
Neuman, Dennis	R-R	5-11	185	10-18-89	0	3	5.40	7	0	0	0	12	15	8	7	2	12	8	.313	.200	.364	6.17	9.26
Pimentel, Stolmy	R-R	6-3	165	2-1-90	6	4	4.53	11	10	0	0	52	50	29	26	8	16	35	.259	.296	.238	6.10	2.79
Pressly, Ryan	R-R	6-3	175	12-15-88	6	11	4.50	26	26	0	0	130	125	84	65	9	53	72	.251	.259	.245	4.98	3.67
Ranaudo, Anthony	R-R	6-7	231	9-9-89	5	5	4.33	16	16	0	0	81	80	43	39	6	30	67	.262	.256	.267	7.44	3.33
Rivera, Manuel	L-L	6-0	170	9-1-89	0	2	5.59	5	2	0	2	19	18	12	12	3	10	8	.243	.250	.240	3.72	4.66
Ruiz, Pete	R-R	6-3	205	8-21-87	6	5	5.31	28	15	0	1	115	126	80	68	5	55	94	.282	.300	.270	7.34	4.29
Tazawa, Junichi	R-R	5-11	180	6-6-86	0	1	6.05	6	6	0	0	19	20	13	13	4	6	13	.278	.242	.308	6.05	2.79
Volz, Kendal	R-R	6-5	225	12-2-87	2	3	3.33	31	0	0	2	51	42	19	19	6	12	56	.222	.264	.197	9.82	2.10
2-team total (6 Wilmington)					3	3	3.03	37	0	0	3	62	53	22	21	6	13	63	—	—	—	9.10	1.88

Fielding

Catcher	PCT	G	PO	A	E	DP	PB
Butler	.995	75	504	79	3	3	6
Escobar	1.000	4	20	2	0	1	0
Peley	.990	29	172	32	2	0	9
Spring	1.000	19	111	17	0	1	0
Wagner	.973	13	93	16	3	0	2

First Base	PCT	G	PO	A	E	DP
Almanzar	.989	42	409	22	5	24
Frias	1.000	1	3	1	0	0
Head	.995	59	558	20	3	59
Padron	.978	6	43	1	1	3
Peley	1.000	4	37	1	0	1
Rodriguez	.997	30	319	20	1	24

Second Base	PCT	G	PO	A	E	DP
Frias	.973	14	32	41	2	11

	PCT	G	PO	A	E	DP
Gentile	.990	79	152	241	4	49
Kang	1.000	6	11	18	0	2
Meneses	1.000	16	45	46	0	13
Valdez	1.000	27	63	79	0	16

Third Base	PCT	G	PO	A	E	DP
Almanzar	.926	15	13	50	5	6
Dominguez	1.000	2	0	4	0	0
Garcia	.800	2	2	2	1	1
Kang	1.000	2	0	1	0	0
Meneses	.929	6	3	10	1	0
Valdez	.944	10	8	43	3	3
Vitek	.900	103	40	213	28	13

Shortstop	PCT	G	PO	A	E	DP
Frias	1.000	1	1	4	0	0
Gibson	.966	127	141	402	19	63

	PCT	G	PO	A	E	DP
Kang	.913	5	6	15	2	3
Meneses	.964	5	9	18	1	3
Valdez	1.000	2	4	7	0	2

Outfield	PCT	G	PO	A	E	DP
Bermudez	1.000	8	10	1	0	1
Brentz	.938	70	129	7	9	2
Frias	1.000	7	10	0	0	0
Hazelbaker	.984	34	51	9	1	3
Hissey	.994	97	162	5	1	1
Mailman	.967	74	111	5	4	1
Padron	1.000	17	33	0	0	0
Pichardo	1.000	13	27	0	0	0
Rodriguez	.900	8	8	1	1	0
Wilkerson	.984	97	172	9	3	1

GREENVILLE DRIVE   LOW CLASS A
SOUTH ATLANTIC LEAGUE

Batting	B-T	HT	WT	DOB	AVG	vLH	vRH	G	AB	R	H	2B	3B	HR	RBI	BB	HBP	SH	SF	SO	SB	CS	SLG	OBP
Almanzar, Michael	R-R	6-3	190	12-2-90	.220	.269	.200	50	177	15	39	10	0	2	31	6	6	0	2	38	1	2	.311	.267
Blair, Carson	R-R	6-1	190	10-18-89	.190	.185	.192	33	100	12	19	8	0	3	9	14	0	0	1	40	0	0	.360	.287
Bogaerts, Xander	R-R	6-3	175	10-1-92	.260	.256	.262	72	265	38	69	14	2	16	45	25	2	0	4	71	1	3	.509	.324
Bradley, Jackie	L-R	5-10	180	4-19-90	.333	.000	.385	4	15	2	5	1	0	1	3	0	0	0	0	3	0	0	.600	.333
Brentz, Bryce	R-R	6-1	180	12-30-88	.359	.386	.349	40	170	43	61	10	3	11	36	14	2	0	0	35	2	2	.647	.414
Coyle, Sean	R-R	5-8	175	1-17-92	.247	.262	.242	106	384	77	95	27	7	14	64	60	13	0	7	110	20	6	.464	.362
Dominguez, Drew	R-R	5-11	195	12-27-86	.179	.185	.175	24	84	13	15	0	0	1	6	5	2	0	1	26	3	0	.214	.233
Escobar, Leonel	R-R	5-10	175	9-4-90	.357	.333	.364	4	14	2	5	0	0	0	0	2	0	0	0	4	0	0	.357	.438
Garcia, Jose	R-R	5-11	165	4-23-91	.219	.200	.226	52	215	21	47	6	2	5	28	13	1	0	1	58	14	1	.335	.265
Head, Miles	R-R	6-0	215	5-2-91	.338	.268	.365	66	263	61	89	25	1	15	53	30	3	0	2	53	4	2	.612	.409
Hedman, Drew	L-L	6-2	200	7-20-86	.272	.211	.290	95	324	46	88	21	1	6	45	38	10	0	2	77	9	5	.398	.364
Hernandez, Jayson	R-R	5-10	200	9-2-88	.333	.000	.333	1	3	1	1	0	0	0	0	0	0	0	0	1	0	0	.333	.333
Jacobs, Brandon	R-R	6-1	225	12-8-90	.303	.294	.307	115	442	75	134	32	3	17	80	43	12	0	5	123	30	7	.505	.376
Johnson, Matty	B-R	5-8	165	4-10-88	.289	.250	.306	28	90	17	26	1	1	0	6	13	1	0	0	18	4	4	.322	.385
Kang, James	R-R	5-9	175	10-19-87	.184	.105	.211	25	76	9	14	2	0	0	1	8	2	0	0	36	1	1	.211	.279
LeBlanc, Lucas	R-R	6-3	200	5-7-89	.223	.183	.236	61	238	28	53	8	3	1	31	7	4	0	0	69	10	5	.294	.257
Meneses, Heiker	R-R	5-9	160	7-1-91	.277	.302	.268	51	206	38	57	6	2	2	22	18	8	0	0	56	17	5	.354	.358
Peley, Josue	R-R	6-0	177	12-24-87	.313	.467	.242	13	48	6	15	4	0	0	3	3	2	0	1	5	2	1	.396	.370
Pichardo, Wilfred	B-R	5-9	146	10-21-89	.309	.222	.362	26	94	9	29	7	1	0	5	2	0	0	0	23	6	3	.404	.323
Ramos, Henry	B-B	6-2	187	4-15-92	.262	.272	.258	85	332	40	87	17	4	5	43	17	2	0	3	76	15	6	.383	.299
Renfroe, David	R-R	6-3	200	11-16-90	.240	.216	.250	107	387	43	93	23	3	8	45	28	4	0	4	106	4	3	.377	.296

Batting

Batting	B-T	HT	WT	DOB	AVG	vLH	vRH	G	AB	R	H	2B	3B	HR	RBI	BB	HBP	SH	SF	SO	SB	CS	SLG	OBP
Reyes, Roberto	R-R	6-3	240	8-1-90	.000	.000	.000	1	1	0	0	0	0	0	0	0	0	0	0	1	0	0	.000	.000
Sanchez, Felix	B-R	6-0	165	6-2-90	.233	.202	.244	119	455	81	106	13	4	0	29	43	11	0	1	130	55	10	.279	.314
Shaw, Travis	L-R	6-4	225	4-16-90	.333	.000	.333	2	9	1	3	1	0	0	1	1	0	0	0	0	0	0	.444	.400
Thompson, Jason	B-R	6-1	180	7-30-90	.208	.143	.235	8	24	3	5	1	1	0	1	5	1	0	0	12	0	0	.333	.367
Vazquez, Christian	R-R	5-9	195	8-21-90	.283	.262	.291	105	392	71	111	27	3	18	84	43	5	0	4	84	1	1	.505	.358

Pitching

Pitching	B-T	HT	WT	DOB	W	L	ERA	G	GS	CG	SV	IP	H	R	ER	HR	BB	SO	AVG	vLH	vRH	K/9	BB/9
Celestino, Miguel	R-R	6-6	205	10-10-89	10	6	3.84	27	27	0	0	141	146	74	60	8	33	106	.262	.269	.257	6.78	2.11
Cervenka, Hunter	L-L	6-1	215	1-3-90	0	2	10.80	7	0	0	0	20	22	24	24	2	18	18	.286	.280	.288	8.10	8.10
Couch, Keith	L-R	6-2	210	11-5-89	7	5	3.54	28	18	0	3	137	145	66	54	11	19	123	.267	.329	.227	8.06	1.25
Erasmus, Justin	R-R	6-0	175	1-22-90	4	1	1.11	24	0	0	1	41	37	9	5	2	11	36	.239	.236	.240	7.97	2.43
Flasher, Jordan	R-R	5-11	165	10-14-87	2	2	4.96	18	0	0	1	33	28	21	18	3	18	38	.228	.256	.214	10.47	4.96
Gleason, Mike	R-R	6-1	195	3-12-88	1	0	2.88	14	0	0	5	25	18	8	8	2	10	24	.200	.290	.153	8.64	3.60
Jones, Andrew	R-R	6-3	185	5-1-89	1	1	1.50	8	0	0	2	18	11	3	3	0	2	15	.172	.222	.135	7.50	1.00
Lockwood, Tyler	R-R	6-0	180	12-9-87	5	8	6.00	39	0	0	3	69	106	52	46	8	9	62	.355	.419	.309	8.09	1.17
Martin, Chris	R-R	6-7	175	6-2-86	4	0	2.17	7	1	0	0	29	16	7	7	1	6	28	.163	.167	.162	8.69	1.86
Neuman, Dennis	R-R	5-11	185	10-18-89	2	1	5.94	24	0	0	5	33	28	25	22	9	16	33	.226	.234	.221	8.91	4.32
Olmsted, Michael	R-R	6-6	245	5-2-87	1	0	1.59	18	0	0	4	28	17	7	5	0	9	44	.177	.125	.203	13.98	2.86
Price, Mathew	R-R	6-3	165	7-8-89	0	0	6.75	1	0	0	0	1	3	1	1	0	1	1	.500	.750	.000	6.75	6.75
Ranaudo, Anthony	R-R	6-7	231	9-9-89	4	1	3.33	10	10	0	0	46	35	20	17	4	16	50	.211	.188	.227	9.78	3.13
Rau, Garrett	R-R	6-0	185	12-22-88	3	4	6.14	27	0	0	2	48	53	40	33	4	26	44	.280	.304	.267	8.19	4.84
Rivera, Manuel	L-L	6-0	170	9-1-89	5	4	3.58	20	20	0	0	98	84	43	39	16	23	98	.226	.286	.208	9.00	2.11
Rodriguez, Juan	R-R	6-5	195	12-12-88	2	4	5.19	32	0	0	0	59	57	38	34	3	32	88	.249	.177	.287	13.42	4.88
Rosario, Charle	R-R	5-10	158	7-23-88	6	1	4.66	31	1	0	4	58	71	33	30	4	22	53	.300	.269	.319	8.22	3.41
Stroup, Kyle	R-R	6-6	235	3-13-90	6	6	3.67	21	21	1	0	96	101	44	39	6	26	75	.269	.264	.273	7.06	2.45
Swinson, Scott	R-R	6-2	190	3-11-88	5	5	3.27	25	10	0	0	85	84	37	31	7	17	61	.263	.256	.268	6.43	1.79
Wilson, Tyler	R-R	6-5	192	12-24-89	4	3	3.03	9	6	0	2	39	36	14	13	6	16	19	.245	.222	.258	4.42	3.72
Workman, Brandon	R-R	6-4	195	8-13-88	6	7	3.71	26	26	0	0	131	128	67	54	10	33	115	.260	.249	.265	7.90	2.27

Fielding

Catcher	PCT	G	PO	A	E	DP	PB
Blair	.996	31	214	11	1	2	4
Escobar	1.000	4	31	3	0	0	0
Hernandez	1.000	1	4	0	0	0	0
Peley	1.000	11	83	9	0	0	1
Vazquez	.991	97	788	108	8	2	15

First Base	PCT	G	PO	A	E	DP
Almanzar	.990	36	272	16	3	21
Head	.992	57	469	36	4	41
Hedman	.993	53	423	29	3	37
Shaw	1.000	1	2	0	0	0

Second Base	PCT	G	PO	A	E	DP
Coyle	.959	101	189	274	20	56
Dominguez	1.000	14	21	36	0	10

	PCT	G	PO	A	E	DP
Garcia	1.000	2	3	4	0	1
Kang	.957	6	7	15	1	3
Meneses	.988	18	36	43	1	9
Thompson	.857	2	2	4	1	0

Third Base	PCT	G	PO	A	E	DP
Almanzar	.962	11	8	17	1	2
Dominguez	1.000	4	4	3	0	1
Kang	.846	6	2	9	2	1
Meneses	.951	18	12	46	3	5
Renfroe	.927	100	55	161	17	11
Thompson	.889	6	2	14	2	0

Shortstop	PCT	G	PO	A	E	DP
Bogaerts	.924	71	108	209	26	43
Garcia	.901	45	82	101	20	10

	PCT	G	PO	A	E	DP
Kang	.960	10	20	28	2	8
Meneses	1.000	14	17	31	0	9

Outfield	PCT	G	PO	A	E	DP
Bradley	1.000	4	15	1	0	0
Brentz	.897	38	67	3	8	1
Dominguez	.000	1	0	0	0	0
Hedman	.909	9	10	0	1	0
Jacobs	.977	107	164	8	4	2
Johnson	1.000	23	55	3	0	1
Kang	1.000	1	1	0	0	0
LeBlanc	.981	52	91	11	2	1
Pichardo	.970	14	30	2	1	0
Ramos	.954	80	140	6	7	1
Sanchez	.961	98	214	10	9	0

LOWELL SPINNERS   SHORT-SEASON

NEW YORK-PENN LEAGUE

Batting	B-T	HT	WT	DOB	AVG	vLH	vRH	G	AB	R	H	2B	3B	HR	RBI	BB	HBP	SH	SF	SO	SB	CS	SLG	OBP
Blair, Carson	R-R	6-1	190	10-18-89	.231	.333	.200	3	13	1	3	1	0	0	0	0	0	0	0	6	0	0	.308	.231
Bradley, Jackie	L-R	5-10	180	4-19-90	.190	.286	.143	6	21	5	4	0	0	0	0	4	0	0	0	5	0	2	.190	.320
Cecchini, Garin	L-R	6-2	200	4-20-91	.298	.367	.274	32	114	21	34	12	1	3	23	17	2	0	0	19	12	2	.500	.398
Daeges, Zach	L-R	6-4	225	11-16-83	.000	.000	.000	2	6	0	0	0	0	0	3	0	0	1	0	1	0	0	.000	.333
De La Cruz, Keury	L-L	5-11	170	11-28-91	.263	.246	.268	71	300	31	79	14	6	4	24	10	2	0	6	56	15	11	.390	.292
Dent, Ryan	R-R	6-0	190	3-15-89	.200	.000	.500	1	5	0	1	1	0	0	2	0	0	0	0	2	0	0	.400	.200
Drew, J.D.	L-R	6-1	200	11-20-75	.000			1	2	1	0	0	0	0	0	1	1	0	0	1	0	0	.000	.500
Escobar, Leonel	R-R	5-10	175	9-4-90	.200	.429	.130	10	30	2	6	1	0	0	2	4	2	0	0	5	0	0	.233	.333
Garcia, Joantoni	R-R	5-11	165	9-9-91	.165	.200	.154	52	158	14	26	6	0	3	9	10	0	0	0	48	1	1	.259	.214
Garcia, Jose	R-R	5-11	165	4-23-91	.250	.212	.263	55	212	38	53	11	4	6	24	18	3	0	2	62	22	6	.425	.315
Gedman, Matt	L-R	6-2	205	9-26-88	.169	.188	.164	23	77	4	13	0	0	1	2	3	0	0	0	8	0	0	.208	.200
Hernandez, Jayson	R-R	5-10	200	9-2-88	.252	.292	.242	34	115	12	29	6	1	1	18	9	7	0	3	20	2	0	.348	.336
Ibarra, Adalberto	L-R	5-10	205	4-3-87	.245	.231	.250	16	53	5	13	2	0	0	1	13	1	0	0	9	2	1	.283	.403
Johnson, Matty	B-R	5-8	165	4-10-88	.321	.310	.325	32	109	21	35	6	1	0	8	16	2	0	0	17	15	1	.394	.417
Kalish, Ryan	L-L	6-0	215	3-28-88	.500	.000	.500	2	6	2	3	0	0	0	2	1	0	0	0	1	0	0	.500	.571
LeBlanc, Lucas	R-R	6-3	200	5-7-89	.000	.000	.000	1	3	0	0	0	0	0	0	0	0	0	0	3	0	0	.000	.000
Marquis, Matt	R-R	6-0	200	2-22-90	.337	.476	.290	25	83	12	28	4	0	3	13	10	4	0	1	21	0	2	.494	.429
Middlebrooks, Will	R-R	6-4	200	9-9-88	.333	.000	.400	4	12	4	4	1	0	3	6	2	0	0	1	1	0	1	.167	.400
Moanaroa, Boss	L-R	6-1	200	7-12-91	.241	.275	.230	58	203	23	49	11	3	5	31	29	1	0	0	73	0	0	.399	.339
Moanaroa, Moko	L-L	6-0	215	12-22-89	.260	.214	.279	31	96	9	25	4	0	3	16	11	0	0	0	16	1	1	.427	.336
Natoli, Nick	R-R	6-1	195	1-17-88	.276	.333	.269	11	29	3	8	2	0	0	3	0	0	0	1	0	0	0	.345	.344
Perez, Oscar	R-R	6-1	185	11-9-91	.135	.154	.125	11	37	1	5	0	0	0	1	0	0	0	0	6	0	0	.135	.135
Ramos, Roberto	B-R	5-10	160	9-4-88	.214	.100	.250	21	42	6	9	0	0	0	4	3	0	0	0	14	6	1	.214	.267
Roberson, Tim	R-R	5-10	190	7-19-89	.299	.333	.279	22	67	6	20	2	0	3	9	3	0	0	1	10	0	0	.463	.324

Batting	B-T	HT	WT	DOB	AVG	vLH	vRH	G	AB	R	H	2B	3B	HR	RBI	BB	HBP	SH	SF	SO	SB	CS	SLG	OBP
Robinson, Nick	L-R	6-1	195	3-5-88	.263	.333	.231	9	19	4	5	1	0	0	3	3	0	0	0	3	0	0	.316	.364
Rodriguez, Reynaldo	R-R	6-0	195	2-7-86	.333	.000	.333	4	15	4	5	0	0	1	2	3	0	0	0	5	1	0	.533	.444
Schwindenhammer, Seth	L-R	6-2	205	7-1-91	.213	.296	.183	57	207	26	44	10	1	9	29	17	0	0	1	106	0	2	.401	.271
Shaw, Travis	L-R	6-4	225	4-16-90	.262	.264	.262	57	202	33	53	13	0	8	36	34	2	0	2	47	3	0	.446	.371
Thompson, Jason	B-R	6-1	180	7-30-90	.241	.241	.241	25	87	16	21	3	0	1	5	8	2	0	0	25	2	1	.310	.320
Turocy, Andrew	L-L	6-3	190	12-26-88	.228	.227	.229	49	162	16	37	3	1	1	17	9	1	1	0	36	3	0	.278	.269

Pitching	B-T	HT	WT	DOB	W	L	ERA	G	GS	CG	SV	IP	H	R	ER	HR	BB	SO	AVG	vLH	vRH	K/9	BB/9
Alcantara, Raul	R-R	6-3	180	12-4-92	0	3	6.23	4	4	0	0	17	25	14	12	0	6	14	.333	.273	.381	7.27	3.12
Bastardo, Luis	R-R	6-1	165	5-14-90	3	2	3.45	14	0	0	1	44	30	20	17	3	27	64	.189	.288	.130	12.99	5.48
Brahney, Kevin	L-L	6-5	220	8-8-88	2	0	6.67	17	0	0	0	27	36	23	20	0	17	25	.316	.265	.338	8.33	5.67
Cervenka, Hunter	L-L	6-1	215	1-3-90	2	8	6.84	15	5	0	1	53	51	46	40	5	40	51	.256	.228	.268	8.72	6.84
Diaz, Luis	R-R	6-3	210	4-9-92	4	4	2.53	14	14	0	0	75	57	25	21	3	15	41	.208	.218	.200	4.94	1.81
Doubront, Felix	L-L	6-2	165	10-23-87	0	0	0.00	1	1	0	0	2	0	0	0	0	0	4	.000	.000	.000	18.00	0.00
Garcia, Jason	R-R	6-0	185	11-21-92	3	3	3.88	13	13	0	0	56	52	38	24	1	36	40	.243	.272	.221	6.47	5.82
Herold, Mitch	L-L	6-0	200	6-18-86	0	0	0.00	1	0	0	0	1	0	0	0	0	0	0	.000	.000	.000	0.00	0.00
Holtmeyer, Joe	R-R	6-3	225	11-24-89	0	1	9.90	6	1	0	0	10	13	11	11	4	5	12	.295	.222	.346	10.80	4.50
Huijer, Swen	R-R	6-9	205	11-7-90	2	2	2.43	14	0	0	0	41	32	15	11	3	17	34	.218	.208	.223	7.52	3.76
Huseby, Chris	R-R	6-7	220	1-11-88	0	0	3.00	6	0	0	0	6	6	2	2	0	3	9	.261	.273	.250	13.50	4.50
Jones, Andrew	R-R	6-3	185	5-1-89	1	0	0.87	9	0	0	1	10	8	1	1	0	4	4	.216	.250	.176	3.48	0.00
Lee, Michael	R-R	6-7	220	11-18-86	0	1	2.35	2	2	0	0	8	5	3	2	0	4	8	.179	.118	.273	9.39	4.70
McCarthy, Mike	R-R	6-3	185	11-18-87	1	1	4.64	17	0	0	4	21	16	12	11	2	10	27	.203	.194	.208	11.39	4.22
Ogando, Nefi	R-R	6-2	185	6-3-89	1	5	2.83	15	2	0	0	57	53	26	18	2	31	38	.238	.229	.244	5.97	4.87
Ott, Matty	R-R	6-1	190	4-20-90	2	0	3.75	14	0	0	0	24	20	11	10	1	9	20	.230	.324	.170	7.50	3.38
Pena, Miguel	L-L	6-2	175	10-24-90	1	0	2.35	5	2	0	0	15	10	4	4	0	3	22	.185	.333	.156	12.91	1.76
Scott, Robby	B-L	6-3	220	8-29-89	1	1	1.59	2	0	0	0	6	2	2	1	1	1	5	.111	.182	.000	7.94	1.59
Vellette, Raynel	R-R	6-2	165	6-10-91	2	4	6.50	14	12	0	0	54	59	46	39	9	36	36	.274	.291	.257	6.00	6.00
Vogt, Corey	R-R	6-0	180	8-5-89	0	1	21.00	3	0	0	0	3	4	7	7	0	5	2	.333	.333	.333	6.00	15.00
Wilson, Tyler	R-R	6-5	192	12-24-89	2	3	3.99	7	3	0	0	29	30	18	13	3	7	19	.273	.308	.241	5.83	2.15
Younginer, Madison	R-R	6-4	195	11-3-90	1	6	5.28	14	14	0	0	61	64	42	36	4	31	48	.270	.281	.262	7.04	4.55

Fielding

Catcher	PCT	G	PO	A	E	DP	PB
Blair	1.000	3	20	1	0	0	0
Escobar	.987	10	75	2	1	0	2
Hernandez	.977	34	259	35	7	5	4
Ibarra	1.000	5	33	1	0	0	3
Perez	.978	11	76	14	2	0	5
Roberson	.979	14	80	13	2	0	8

First Base	PCT	G	PO	A	E	DP
Moanaroa	.981	51	382	36	8	40
Moanaroa	.977	10	76	8	2	4
Robinson	1.000	3	18	0	0	2
Rodriguez	1.000	2	16	0	0	0
Shaw	.968	10	79	11	3	5

Second Base	PCT	G	PO	A	E	DP
Garcia	.978	36	59	76	3	17
Gedman	1.000	9	19	25	0	7
Natoli	.857	2	3	3	1	2
Ramos	.933	15	11	31	3	1
Thompson	.968	25	45	46	3	6

Third Base	PCT	G	PO	A	E	DP
Cecchini	.844	26	16	38	10	4
Garcia	1.000	4	2	3	0	0
Gedman	.848	12	12	16	5	2
Natoli	.000	1	0	0	0	0
Robinson	.833	4	1	4	1	1
Shaw	.936	34	26	62	6	7

Shortstop	PCT	G	PO	A	E	DP
Dent	1.000	1	0	4	0	0
Garcia	.915	16	19	24	4	6
Garcia	.932	55	89	143	17	19
Natoli	.900	9	12	15	3	4

Outfield	PCT	G	PO	A	E	DP
Bradley	1.000	5	6	1	0	0
De La Cruz	.964	69	158	3	6	2
Johnson	.987	29	71	3	1	1
Kalish	1.000	1	2	0	0	0
LeBlanc	1.000	1	2	0	0	0
Marquis	1.000	22	40	1	0	1
Moanaroa	1.000	12	10	0	0	0
Schwindenhammer	.975	49	77	2	2	1
Turocy	.974	46	71	5	2	3

GCL RED SOX

ROOKIE

GULF COAST LEAGUE

Batting	B-T	HT	WT	DOB	AVG	vLH	vRH	G	AB	R	H	2B	3B	HR	RBI	BB	HBP	SH	SF	SO	SB	CS	SLG	OBP
Betts, Mookie	R-R	5-9	156	10-7-92	.500	.000	.667	1	4	0	2	0	0	0	2	0	0	0	0	1	0	.500	.500
Chester, David	R-R	6-5	270	3-31-89	.243	.283	.228	46	169	19	41	8	0	9	23	9	7	0	2	42	0	0	.450	.305
Colorado, Jose	L-R	6-1	170	8-26-90	.259	.216	.273	41	147	17	38	10	6	1	17	15	1	0	0	44	3	5	.429	.331
Coste, Carlos	B-R	6-2	186	5-11-93	.158	.000	.250	16	19	0	3	0	0	0	0	2	0	0	0	9	0	0	.158	.158
Dent, Ryan	R-R	6-0	190	3-15-89	.100	.333	.000	4	10	0	1	0	0	0	1	1	0	0	0	2	0	0	.100	.182
Gedman, Matt	L-R	6-2	205	9-26-88	.282	.333	.253	31	117	14	33	5	1	2	15	12	2	0	0	17	1	0	.393	.359
Guerrero, Dreily	B-R	5-11	162	10-12-90	.173	.161	.179	35	98	12	17	4	3	0	8	7	0	0	1	34	3	1	.276	.226
Ibarra, Adalberto	L-R	5-10	205	4-3-87	.423	.000	.500	9	26	2	11	1	0	0	3	4	1	0	0	4	0	0	.462	.516
Jerez, Williams	L-L	6-4	190	5-16-92	.248	.118	.295	32	129	12	32	2	3	0	12	6	1	0	1	33	5	3	.310	.285
Johns, Bryan	R-R	5-9	180	11-18-88	.151	.211	.118	19	53	6	8	1	0	0	3	2	1	0	1	14	1	1	.170	.193
Kapstein, Zach	R-R	6-2	195	5-28-92	.400	.440	.371	22	60	4	24	4	0	1	6	5	2	0	0	13	0	1	.517	.463
Koback, Cody	R-R	6-1	185	4-20-90	.291	.294	.289	19	55	11	16	3	0	1	8	6	7	0	0	14	0	1	.400	.426
LeBlanc, Lucas	R-R	6-3	200	5-7-89	.364	.400	.333	5	11	0	4	1	0	0	0	1	1	0	0	1	0	0	.455	.462
Loya, Jesus	L-R	6-0	170	6-26-90	.267	.203	.295	48	191	25	51	9	0	2	8	12	5	0	1	34	13	3	.346	.325
Marquis, Matt	R-R	6-0	200	2-22-90	.000	.000	.000	1	1	0	0	0	0	0	0	0	1	0	0	0	0	0	.000	.667
Moore, Nick	B-R	6-2	200	12-9-92	.184	.000	.225	15	49	8	9	1	1	1	6	11	1	0	0	17	0	2	.306	.344
Natoli, Nick	R-R	6-1	195	11-9-91	.263	.143	.333	8	19	1	5	2	0	0	6	1	0	0	3	0	0	.368	.462
Perez, Oscar	R-R	6-1	185	11-9-91	.194	.152	.213	36	108	8	21	3	1	1	9	8	0	0	2	24	2	1	.269	.246
Perkins, Kendrick	L-R	6-2	225	9-12-91	.257	.240	.264	49	171	24	44	11	1	3	19	27	1	0	0	62	1	2	.386	.362
Pineda, Jeremias	B-R	5-11	175	11-16-90	.140	.091	.156	16	43	5	6	0	0	0	2	5	2	0	0	16	2	1	.140	.260
Reyes, Roberto	R-R	6-3	240	8-1-90	.216	.172	.233	31	102	11	22	2	0	6	13	3	1	0	0	33	1	0	.412	.245
Robinson, Nick	L-R	6-1	195	3-5-88	.211	.150	.232	25	76	5	16	2	0	0	6	8	0	0	2	20	2	2	.237	.279

Batting

Batting	B-T	HT	WT	DOB	AVG	vLH	vRH	G	AB	R	H	2B	3B	HR	RBI	BB	HBP	SH	SF	SO	SB	CS	SLG	OBP
Rodriguez, Reynaldo	R-R	6-0	195	2-7-86	.000	.000	.000	1	2	0	0	0	0	0	0	0	0	0	0	1	0	0	.000	.000
Swihart, Blake	B-R	6-1	175	4-3-92	.000	.000	.000	2	6	0	0	0	0	0	0	0	0	0	0	2	0	0	.000	.000
Tavarez, Aneury	L-R	5-9	175	4-14-92	.220	.207	.225	33	100	10	22	1	2	3	8	8	4	0	1	40	3	3	.360	.301
Vinicio, Jose	B-R	5-11	150	7-10-93	.291	.351	.262	50	179	22	52	7	5	2	18	7	6	0	1	33	19	10	.419	.337
Weems, Jordan	L-R	6-3	175	11-7-92	.182	.167	.188	14	44	4	8	2	0	0	8	7	1	0	0	16	0	0	.227	.308

Pitching

Pitching	B-T	HT	WT	DOB	W	L	ERA	G	GS	CG	SV	IP	H	R	ER	HR	BB	SO	AVG	vLH	vRH	K/9	BB/9
Alcantara, Mario	R-R	6-2	170	12-27-92	2	6	4.18	11	11	0	0	52	44	31	24	2	20	24	.238	.304	.172	4.18	3.48
Alcantara, Raul	R-R	6-3	180	12-4-92	1	1	0.75	9	9	0	0	48	23	5	4	0	6	36	.147	.153	.144	6.75	1.13
Batista, Anatanaer	R-R	5-10	150	2-2-89	0	0	4.50	2	0	0	0	2	3	1	1	0	1	0	.333	.667	.167	0.00	4.50
Cuevas, William	R-R	6-0	160	10-14-90	2	1	2.79	11	2	0	1	39	32	16	12	2	9	25	.218	.283	.172	5.82	2.09
Dahlstrand, Jacob	R-R	6-5	205	3-26-92	0	3	7.13	8	3	0	0	18	28	22	14	0	6	12	.346	.281	.388	6.11	3.06
Flasher, Jordan	R-R	5-11	165	10-14-87	0	0	4.05	4	0	0	0	7	4	3	3	0	1	4	.160	.100	.200	5.40	1.35
Gomez, Sergio	R-R	6-3	155	8-24-93	1	3	2.68	12	11	0	0	50	38	18	15	4	16	37	.213	.222	.209	6.62	2.86
Good, Zach	L-L	6-3	185	6-8-92	0	1	1.88	9	8	0	0	24	24	11	5	1	6	20	.255	.125	.267	7.50	2.25
Hudson, Jennell	R-R	6-4	185	1-20-90	2	3	9.28	15	0	0	0	21	25	30	22	1	27	11	.309	.302	.316	4.64	11.39
Jones, Andrew	R-R	6-3	185	5-1-89	1	0	2.45	2	0	0	0	4	2	1	1	1	0	2	.167	.250	.125	4.91	0.00
Killen, John	L-L	6-7	185	8-20-90	1	3	8.05	13	0	0	0	19	13	19	17	0	23	16	.191	.188	.192	7.58	10.89
Mateo, Alexander	R-R	5-11	165	4-10-91	0	0	6.89	13	0	0	1	33	54	33	25	5	12	12	.375	.362	.384	3.31	3.31
Melendez, Oscar	R-R	6-1	150	10-13-93	0	1	2.25	2	0	0	0	8	6	2	2	0	1	4	.231	.333	.143	4.50	1.13
Olmsted, Michael	R-R	6-6	245	5-2-87	1	0	0.00	3	0	0	2	4	1	0	0	0	1	4	.083	.000	.167	9.00	2.25
Ortega, Yunior	R-R	5-11	170	8-10-91	5	3	3.43	20	0	0	4	39	32	17	15	5	8	33	.219	.241	.207	7.55	1.83
Parthemore, Renny	R-R	6-5	190	4-7-91	4	1	3.30	14	0	0	0	30	18	15	11	0	20	27	.182	.135	.210	8.10	6.00
Price, Mathew	R-R	6-3	165	7-8-89	0	0	4.50	2	2	0	0	2	2	1	1	0	1	3	.250	.000	1.000	13.50	4.50
Reyes, Dennys	R-L	6-3	250	4-19-77	0	1	9.00	2	2	0	0	2	3	2	2	0	1	1	.375	.000	.375	4.50	4.50
Ring, Royce	L-L	6-0	220	12-21-80	0	0	0.00	1	0	0	1	0	0	0	0	0	0	0	.000	.000	.000	0.00	0.00
Schmeltzer, Jadd	R-R	6-4	240	12-27-88	0	2	2.92	15	0	0	4	25	21	12	8	0	9	12	.233	.265	.214	4.38	3.28
Scott, Robby	B-L	6-3	220	8-29-89	0	0	1.23	4	0	0	2	7	4	1	1	1	1	11	.154	.250	.136	13.50	1.23
Shepard, Brenden	R-R	6-0	190	10-7-87	1	1	4.84	10	0	0	1	22	24	16	12	1	5	16	.276	.242	.296	6.45	2.01
Taveras, Francisco	L-L	6-0	180	5-23-90	5	3	3.62	12	11	0	0	55	60	32	22	0	16	42	.276	.357	.265	6.91	2.63
Vogt, Corey	R-R	6-0	180	8-5-89	0	0	0.00	3	0	0	1	5	0	0	0	0	2	3	.000	.000	.000	5.40	3.60

Fielding

Catcher	PCT	G	PO	A	E	DP	PB
Coste	1.000	12	34	2	0	0	1
Ibarra	.955	5	19	2	1	0	1
Perez	.984	34	146	43	3	2	1
Reyes	1.000	19	85	12	0	0	11
Weems	.954	11	75	8	4	1	5

First Base	PCT	G	PO	A	E	DP
Chester	.990	39	363	17	4	24
Colorado	.977	5	41	2	1	2
Guerrero	1.000	1	2	0	0	0
Kapstein	1.000	7	54	0	0	3
Robinson	1.000	14	126	7	0	8

Second Base	PCT	G	PO	A	E	DP
Gedman	1.000	1	4	3	0	0
Guerrero	.939	13	18	44	4	7

		G	PO	A	E	DP
Johns	1.000	6	19	21	0	6
Natoli	1.000	4	10	9	0	3
Robinson	1.000	10	11	20	0	3
Tavarez	.917	30	55	78	12	14

Third Base	PCT	G	PO	A	E	DP
Gedman	.907	28	17	61	8	8
Guerrero	.932	12	4	37	3	4
Johns	.941	7	5	11	1	1
Moore	.906	15	7	22	3	0
Robinson	.333	1	0	1	2	0

Shortstop	PCT	G	PO	A	E	DP
Betts	.500	1	1	2	3	0
Dent	1.000	2	2	4	0	1
Gedman	.000	1	0	0	0	0
Guerrero	.905	5	7	12	2	1

		G	PO	A	E	DP
Johns	.926	5	10	15	2	2
Natoli	1.000	2	3	5	0	2
Vinicio	.902	50	107	161	29	25

Outfield	PCT	G	PO	A	E	DP
Colorado	1.000	30	57	3	0	1
Guerrero	.667	4	2	0	1	0
Jerez	1.000	32	78	2	0	1
Johns	1.000	1	3	0	0	0
Kapstein	1.000	5	6	2	0	1
Koback	.955	14	19	2	1	0
LeBlanc	1.000	4	2	2	0	0
Loya	.958	46	88	3	4	1
Marquis	1.000	1	2	1	0	0
Perkins	.970	46	61	3	2	0
Pineda	.963	14	25	1	1	0

DSL RED SOX

ROOKIE

DOMINICAN SUMMER LEAGUE

Batting	B-T	HT	WT	DOB	AVG	vLH	vRH	G	AB	R	H	2B	3B	HR	RBI	BB	HBP	SH	SF	SO	SB	CS	SLG	OBP
Aguero, Ynoel	B-R	5-10	170	12-7-90	.303	.238	.326	67	238	39	72	11	2	1	31	46	2	0	1	44	27	3	.378	.418
Amaya, Anthony	L-L	5-10	160	5-1-94	.182	.171	.188	47	137	26	25	8	1	0	13	19	6	0	1	34	2	2	.255	.307
Bogaerts, Jair	R-R	6-2	230	10-7-92	.288	.257	.298	47	156	17	45	8	2	2	27	19	8	0	3	43	0	0	.404	.387
Del Rosario, Robert	R-R	5-11	185	7-25-92	.236	.300	.216	34	127	21	30	6	0	0	21	23	3	0	1	29	9	2	.283	.364
Duncan, Roberto	R-R	6-3	175	2-18-93	.205	.185	.216	38	78	8	16	3	0	0	11	17	10	0	1	24	3	2	.244	.406
Garcia, Andres	R-R	5-9	155	3-12-94	.250	.349	.218	69	256	43	64	5	1	0	17	68	6	0	1	42	11	16	.277	.417
Gonzalez, Aly	R-R	6-1	185	2-9-91	.310	.320	.308	36	116	11	36	5	0	1	21	12	1	0	2	23	0	0	.379	.374
Lopez, Deiner	B-R	6-0	165	5-30-94	.250	.286	.236	61	220	43	55	9	4	1	34	40	12	0	0	48	17	6	.341	.393
Peralta, Aneudis	R-R	5-11	195	8-21-93	.191	.151	.203	64	230	38	44	8	0	1	28	51	7	0	3	43	6	1	.239	.351
Pineda, Jeremias	B-R	5-11	175	11-16-90	.224	.214	.227	18	58	5	13	2	2	1	10	8	1	0	0	25	4	1	.379	.328
Rondon, Cleuluis	R-R	6-0	155	4-13-94	.171	.226	.151	62	205	39	35	6	1	2	27	43	14	0	2	50	14	1	.239	.348
Sopilka, David	R-R	6-0	170	8-30-93	.260	.348	.233	53	192	25	50	10	1	1	30	20	3	0	7	29	1	2	.339	.329
Suarez, Alixon	R-R	6-0	180	7-25-94	.224	.278	.205	62	210	35	47	7	0	2	25	39	11	0	3	45	0	1	.286	.369
Ugas, Juan	R-R	6-0	160	3-21-80	.164	.118	.182	18	61	5	10	2	1	0	5	9	2	0	0	17	0	0	.230	.292
Urena, Lewis	R-R	5-8	145	5-6-91	.500	.000	1.000	2	2	2	1	0	0	0	0	0	0	0	0	0	0	0	.500	.500
2-team total (29 Royals)					.281	—	—	31	96	19	27	2	1	0	13	18	1	0	1	12	9	3	.323	.397

Pitching	B-T	HT	WT	DOB	W	L	ERA	G	GS	CG	SV	IP	H	R	ER	HR	BB	SO	AVG	vLH	vRH	K/9	BB/9
Abreu, William	R-R	6-0	200	1-2-92	1	0	5.06	3	1	0	1	11	8	8	6	0	11	9	.205	.444	.133	7.59	9.28
Aro, Jonathan	R-R	6-0	172	10-10-90	2	2	3.06	9	6	0	0	47	41	22	16	1	4	38	.233	.227	.235	7.28	0.77
Betancourt, Ricardo	L-L	6-2	175	9-9-92	7	1	2.22	12	1	0	0	45	37	14	11	2	12	26	.233	.200	.235	5.24	2.42

Pitching	B-T	HT	WT	DOB	W	L	ERA	G	GS	CG	SV	IP	H	R	ER	HR	BB	SO	AVG	vLH	vRH	K/9	BB/9
Bonnelly, Sully	R-R	6-2	215	10-14-92	3	4	4.26	14	13	0	0	61	50	35	29	5	36	39	.231	.308	.215	5.72	5.28
Cabral, Cesar	R-R	6-1	190	1-2-91	0	0	11.57	2	0	0	0	2	1	3	3	0	2	2	.143	.000	.200	7.71	7.71
Cuevas, William	R-R	6-0	160	10-14-90	1	0	0.00	3	0	0	0	11	8	3	0	0	1	12	.195	.250	.182	10.13	0.84
Espitia, Jose	R-R	6-2	180	9-16-93	0	3	4.45	13	0	0	1	30	23	22	15	3	30	23	.209	.188	.213	6.82	8.90
Fernandez, Jeffry	R-R	6-3	180	3-25-93	0	2	4.20	12	12	0	0	41	34	20	19	1	25	20	.231	.152	.254	4.43	5.53
Garcia, Edwar	R-R	6-4	175	11-19-93	2	4	2.68	13	13	0	0	47	39	20	14	0	29	41	.238	.313	.220	7.85	5.55
Januario, Iago	R-R	6-6	205	1-20-93	1	2	8.10	3	0	0	0	3	4	4	3	0	8	1	.333	.500	.300	2.70	21.60
Jimenez, Ellis	R-R	6-2	175	6-26-92	3	1	2.02	21	0	0	6	49	36	12	11	3	6	39	.208	.206	.209	7.16	1.10
Melendez, Oscar	R-R	6-1	150	10-13-93	4	2	2.58	13	2	0	2	52	63	22	15	2	12	19	.306	.378	.290	3.27	2.06
Montas, Francellis	R-R	6-2	185	3-21-93	0	1	4.26	5	5	0	0	13	7	7	6	0	12	12	.159	.200	.154	8.53	8.53
Osorio, Edwin	R-R	6-2	175	10-20-93	2	3	5.18	14	3	0	0	40	40	28	23	2	25	30	.256	.200	.273	6.75	5.63
Pinales, Carlos	R-R	6-1	180	4-5-92	4	3	2.06	18	0	0	4	39	35	11	9	1	7	46	.230	.265	.220	10.53	1.60
Reyes, Pedro	L-L	6-0	155	5-28-93	5	2	2.88	14	14	0	0	69	56	31	22	2	13	55	.222	.333	.220	7.21	1.70
Taveras, German	R-R	6-2	180	2-15-93	0	1	2.08	5	0	0	1	13	9	3	3	0	9	5	.209	.125	.229	3.46	6.23
Vasquez, Leonel	R-R	6-0	150	2-10-91	2	2	4.42	19	1	0	2	37	41	25	18	1	23	38	.281	.211	.306	9.33	5.65

Fielding

Catcher	PCT	G	PO	A	E	DP	PB
Gonzalez	.971	5	30	4	1	0	0
Sopilka	.981	28	179	32	4	1	5
Suarez	.987	40	261	48	4	2	10

First Base	PCT	G	PO	A	E	DP
Bogaerts	.993	35	280	15	2	20
Duncan	.966	13	50	7	2	3
Gonzalez	.986	18	132	9	2	10
Ugas	.985	14	129	5	2	13

Second Base	PCT	G	PO	A	E	DP
Garcia	.958	45	96	86	8	22

Lopez	.965	26	74	62	5	17

Third Base	PCT	G	PO	A	E	DP
Duncan	.750	5	7	5	4	0
Lopez	.857	3	2	10	2	1
Peralta	.882	64	52	127	24	10

Shortstop	PCT	G	PO	A	E	DP
Lopez	.963	10	15	37	2	5
Rondon	.920	61	101	176	24	24

Outfield	PCT	G	PO	A	E	DP
Aguero	.991	66	108	7	1	3
Amaya	.969	45	87	6	3	1

Del Rosario	1.000	33	71	1	0	0
Duncan	.944	14	15	2	1	0
Garcia	.947	22	36	0	2	0
Gonzalez	1.000	11	10	1	0	0
Lopez	.900	13	25	2	3	1
Pineda	.972	18	35	0	1	0
Sopilka	1.000	1	1	0	0	0
Suarez	.000	1	0	0	0	0
Ugas	1.000	1	1	0	0	0
Urena	1.000	2	2	0	0	0

Chicago Cubs

SEASON IN A SENTENCE: The Cubs were never in contention but had plenty of contentious moments in a frustrating season that ended with a 71-91 record, yet fans saw reason for optimism when general manager Jim Hendry was fired and replaced after the season by Theo Epstein.

HIGH POINT: Shortstop Starlin Castro emerged as a rising star in his first full season in the major leagues and made the cover of Sports Illustrated in an otherwise unmemorable season. Castro, 21, hit .307 and led the National League with 207 hits, the youngest player ever to lead the league in hits and the youngest in franchise history to reach 200 hits. He made 29 errors, but he has outstanding shortstop skills and his defense should improve with experience.

LOW POINT: Pitcher Carlos Zambrano went on one of his trademark tirades and walked out on the team after being ejected from a game in Atlanta on Aug. 12. Zambrano left in the middle of the game, saying he was retiring. He was placed on the disqualified list and did not pitch the rest of the season. Epstein must decide whether to bring the temperamental pitcher back for the final year of a contract that will pay him $18 million.

NOTABLE ROOKIES: Unheralded second baseman Darwin Barney led major league rookies with 47 multi-hit games, hitting .276 with 43 RBIs. Outfielder Tony Campana hit .259 and led the team with 24 stolen bases. First baseman Bryan LaHair hit .288 in 20 games after a standout season at Triple-A Iowa, and fans hope he'll get more of a big league opportunity in 2012.

KEY TRANSACTIONS: The Cubs brought in Matt Garza in January from the Rays in a multi-player trade and he was a workhorse, going 10-10 with a team-best 3.32 ERA and 197 strikeouts in 198 innings. Kerry Wood also returned to the team as a free agent. Though they were out of contention, the Cubs did not unload any of their veterans at the trade deadline.

DOWN ON THE FARM: LaHair tore up the Pacific Coast League, hitting .331 and leading the league with 38 homers and a .664 slugging percentage. Outfielder Brett Jackson established himself as the organization's top prospect, hitting 20 homers and 58 RBIs between Double-A Tennessee and Iowa. The organization spent a team-record $12 million on the draft, with Hendry staying on board until all the key players were signed, led by first-round pick Javier Baez.

OPENING DAY PAYROLL: $125,047,329 (6th)

PLAYERS OF THE YEAR

MAJOR LEAGUE	MINOR LEAGUE
Aramis Ramirez	**Bryan LaHair**
3b	of
.306/.361/.510	(Triple-A)
26 HR/35 2B	.331/.405/.664
Won Silver Slugger	Pacific Coast Lg MVP

ORGANIZATION LEADERS

BATTING		*Minimum 250 PA
MAJORS		
* AVG	Reed Johnson	.309
* OPS	Aramis Ramirez	.871
HR	Carlos Pena	28
RBI	Aramis Ramirez	93
MINORS		
* AVG	Bryan LaHair, Iowa	.331
* OBP	Bryan LaHair, Iowa	.405
* SLG	Bryan LaHair, Iowa	.664
R	Bryan LaHair, Iowa	91
H	Bryan LaHair, Iowa	151
TB	Bryan LaHair, Iowa	303
2B	Bryan LaHair, Iowa	38
3B	Logan Watkins, Daytona	12
HR	Bryan LaHair, Iowa	38
RBI	Bryan LaHair, Iowa	109
BB	Brett Jackson, Tennessee/Iowa	73
SO	Brett Jackson, Tennessee/Iowa	138
SB	Junior Lake, Daytona/Tennessee	38
PITCHING		#Minimum 75 IP
MAJORS		
W	Ryan Dempster	10
	Matt Garza	10
# ERA	Sean Marshall	2.26
SO	Matt Garza	197
SV	Carlos Marmol	34
MINORS		
W	Eric Jokisch, Peoria/Tennessee	10
L	Jay Jackson, Iowa	14
# ERA	Ryan Searle, Daytona/Tennessee	3.03
G	Jeff Beliveau, Daytona/Tennessee	53
	Blake Parker, Tennessee/Iowa	53
GS	Austin Kirk, Peoria	28
SV	Frank Batista, Daytona	26
IP	Austin Kirk, Peoria	151
BB	Cameron Greathouse, Peoria/Boise/AZL Cubs	87
SO	Austin Kirk, Peoria	122
#AVG	Ryan Searle, Daytona/Tennessee	.239

2011 PERFORMANCE

General Manager: Jim Hendry/Randy Bush. **Farm Director:** Oneri Fleita. **Scouting Director:** Tim Wilken.

Class	Team	League	W	L	PCT	Finish	Manager(s)
Majors	Chicago Cubs	National	71	91	.438	t-14th (16)	Mike Quade
Triple-A	Iowa Cubs	Pacific Coast	66	77	.462	12th (16)	Bill Dancy
Double-A	Tennessee Smokies	Southern	83	57	.593	2nd (10)	Brian Harper
High A	Daytona Cubs	Florida State	76	61	.555	2nd (12)	Buddy Bailey
Low A	Peoria Chiefs	Midwest	60	79	.432	15th (16)	Casey Kopitzke
Short-season	Boise Hawks	Northwest	36	40	.474	5th (8)	Mark Johnson
Rookie	AZL Cubs	Arizona	28	28	.500	t-6th (13)	Juan Cabreja
Overall 2011 Minor League Record			349	342	.505	14th (30)	

ORGANIZATION STATISTICS

CHICAGO CUBS

NATIONAL LEAGUE

Batting	B-T	HT	WT	DOB	AVG	vLH	vRH	G	AB	R	H	2B	3B	HR	RBI	BB	HBP	SH	SF	SO	SB	CS	SLG	OBP
Baker, Jeff	R-R	6-2	210	6-21-81	.269	.314	.200	81	201	20	54	12	1	3	23	10	0	0	1	46	0	0	.383	.302
Barney, Darwin	R-R	5-10	180	11-8-85	.276	.290	.273	143	529	66	146	23	6	2	43	22	8	0	4	67	9	2	.353	.313
Byrd, Marlon	R-R	6-0	245	8-30-77	.276	.219	.293	119	446	51	123	22	2	9	35	25	8	0	2	78	3	2	.395	.324
Campana, Tony	L-L	5-8	165	5-3-86	.259	.231	.265	95	143	24	37	3	0	1	6	8	1	0	0	30	24	2	.301	.303
Castillo, Welington	R-R	5-10	210	4-24-87	.154	.000	.200	4	13	0	2	0	0	0	0	0	0	0	0	4	0	0	.154	.154
Castro, Starlin	R-R	6-0	190	3-24-90	.307	.342	.297	158	674	91	207	36	9	10	66	35	2	0	4	96	22	9	.432	.341
Clevenger, Steve	L-R	6-0	195	4-5-86	.250	1.000	.000	2	4	1	1	1	0	0	0	0	1	0	0	0	0	0	.500	.400
Colvin, Tyler	L-L	6-3	210	9-5-85	.150	.057	.170	80	206	17	31	8	3	6	20	14	0	0	1	58	0	0	.306	.204
DeWitt, Blake	L-R	5-11	195	8-20-85	.265	.406	.242	121	230	21	61	11	4	5	26	12	1	0	0	31	1	0	.413	.305
Fukudome, Kosuke	L-R	6-0	200	4-26-77	.273	.273	.273	87	293	33	80	15	2	3	13	46	1	0	0	57	2	2	.369	.374
Hill, Koyie	B-R	6-1	210	3-9-79	.194	.091	.214	46	134	15	26	3	1	2	9	14	0	0	1	40	1	0	.276	.268
Johnson, Reed	R-R	5-10	180	12-8-76	.309	.305	.312	111	246	33	76	22	1	5	28	5	11	0	2	63	2	1	.467	.348
LaHair, Bryan	L-R	6-5	240	11-5-82	.288	.250	.298	20	59	9	17	5	1	2	6	9	0	0	1	18	0	0	.508	.377
Lemahieu, D.J.	R-R	6-4	205	7-13-88	.250	.292	.222	37	60	3	15	2	0	0	4	1	0	0	0	12	0	0	.283	.262
Montanez, Lou	R-R	6-1	195	12-15-81	.222	.250	.143	36	54	6	12	4	0	1	9	2	1	0	0	9	0	1	.352	.263
Pena, Carlos	L-L	6-2	225	5-17-78	.225	.133	.255	153	493	72	111	27	3	28	80	101	4	0	7	161	2	2	.462	.357
Ramirez, Aramis	R-R	6-1	215	6-25-78	.306	.305	.307	149	565	80	173	35	1	26	93	43	10	0	8	69	1	1	.510	.361
Snyder, Brad	L-L	6-3	220	5-25-82	.111	.000	.111	8	9	1	1	0	0	0	0	0	0	0	0	6	0	0	.111	.111
Soriano, Alfonso	R-R	6-1	195	1-7-76	.244	.271	.235	137	475	50	116	27	1	26	88	27	4	0	2	113	2	1	.469	.289
Soto, Geovany	R-R	6-1	220	1-20-83	.228	.296	.207	125	421	46	96	26	0	17	54	45	6	0	2	124	0	0	.411	.310

Pitching	B-T	HT	WT	DOB	W	L	ERA	G	GS	CG	SV	IP	H	R	ER	HR	BB	SO	AVG	vLH	vRH	K/9	BB/9
Berg, Justin	R-R	6-3	225	6-7-84	0	0	3.75	8	0	0	0	12	11	5	5	1	6	6	.250	.294	.222	4.50	4.50
Carpenter, Chris	R-R	6-4	220	12-26-85	0	0	2.79	10	0	0	0	10	12	3	3	1	7	8	.316	.143	.417	7.45	6.52
Cashner, Andrew	R-R	6-6	200	9-11-86	0	0	1.69	7	1	0	0	11	3	2	2	1	4	8	.086	.083	.087	6.75	3.38
Coleman, Casey	L-R	6-0	185	7-3-87	3	9	6.40	19	17	0	0	84	102	62	60	10	46	75	.300	.336	.274	8.00	4.91
Davis, Doug	R-L	6-4	215	9-21-75	1	7	6.50	9	9	0	0	46	59	38	33	2	26	36	.314	.326	.310	7.09	5.12
Dempster, Ryan	R-R	6-2	215	5-3-77	10	14	4.80	34	34	0	0	202	211	111	108	23	82	191	.271	.303	.245	8.50	3.65
Dolis, Rafael	R-R	6-4	215	1-10-88	0	0	0.00	1	0	0	0	1	0	0	0	0	1	1	.000	.000	.000	6.75	6.75
Garza, Matt	R-R	6-4	215	11-26-83	10	10	3.32	31	31	2	0	198	186	90	73	14	63	197	.245	.247	.243	8.95	2.86
Gaub, John	R-L	6-2	210	4-28-85	0	0	6.75	4	0	0	0	3	2	2	2	0	2	3	.200	.000	.500	10.13	6.75
Grabow, John	L-L	6-2	205	11-4-78	3	1	4.76	58	0	0	0	62	67	39	33	9	28	38	.271	.244	.287	5.49	4.04
Lopez, Rodrigo	R-R	6-1	185	12-14-75	6	6	4.42	26	16	0	0	98	116	56	48	18	29	54	.299	.295	.302	4.98	2.67
Maine, Scott	L-L	6-3	215	2-2-85	0	0	10.29	7	0	0	0	7	11	8	8	4	5	5	.344	.125	.417	6.43	6.43
Marmol, Carlos	R-R	6-2	215	10-14-82	2	6	4.01	75	0	0	34	74	54	33	33	5	48	99	.205	.192	.215	12.04	5.84
Marshall, Sean	L-L	6-7	220	8-30-82	6	6	2.26	78	0	0	5	76	66	21	19	1	17	79	.234	.206	.249	9.40	2.02
Mateo, Marcos	R-R	6-1	220	4-18-84	1	2	4.30	23	0	0	0	23	24	11	11	2	10	25	.276	.353	.226	9.78	3.91
Ortiz, Ramon	R-R	6-0	175	5-23-73	1	2	4.86	22	2	0	0	33	31	20	18	6	11	25	.244	.296	.205	6.75	2.97
Russell, James	L-L	6-4	200	1-8-86	1	6	4.12	64	5	0	0	68	76	37	31	12	14	43	.286	.250	.312	5.72	1.86
Samardzija, Jeff	R-R	6-5	225	1-23-85	8	4	2.97	75	0	0	0	88	64	35	29	5	50	87	.200	.208	.195	8.90	5.11
Stevens, Jeff	R-R	6-2	205	9-5-83	0	0	5.14	4	0	0	0	7	4	4	4	1	7	4	.190	.000	.235	5.14	9.00
Wells, Randy	R-R	6-5	230	8-28-82	7	6	4.99	23	23	2	0	135	141	76	75	23	47	82	.269	.263	.273	5.45	3.13
Wood, Kerry	R-R	6-5	210	6-16-77	3	5	3.35	55	0	0	1	51	45	23	19	5	21	57	.236	.227	.240	10.06	3.71
Zambrano, Carlos	B-R	6-5	270	6-1-81	9	7	4.82	24	24	0	0	146	154	80	78	19	56	101	.277	.289	.268	6.24	3.46

Fielding

Catcher	PCT	G	PO	A	E	DP	PB
Castillo	.900	4	16	2	2	0	0
Clevenger	1.000	2	13	0	0	0	0
Hill	.982	45	319	15	6	5	2
Soto	.987	122	899	82	13	7	5

First Base	PCT	G	PO	A	E	DP
Baker	1.000	19	114	7	0	4
Colvin	1.000	4	21	2	0	1
LaHair	1.000	4	15	0	0	3
Lemahieu	1.000	1	8	0	0	1
Pena	.993	153	1116	88	8	104

Second Base	PCT	G	PO	A	E	DP
Baker	.984	18	26	37	1	9
Barney	.981	135	258	349	12	65
DeWitt	.975	18	38	40	2	9
Lemahieu	1.000	15	16	22	0	5

Third Base	PCT	G	PO	A	E	DP
Baker	1.000	11	4	6	0	0
DeWitt	.848	14	6	22	5	3
Lemahieu	.818	11	6	12	4	5
Ramirez	.953	145	68	216	14	18

Shortstop	PCT	G	PO	A	E	DP
Barney	1.000	5	5	10	0	2
Castro	.961	158	267	446	29	82

CHICAGO CUBS

Outfield	PCT	G	PO	A	E	DP
Baker	1.000	11	11	0	0	0
Byrd	.989	118	273	8	3	3
Campana	.989	66	85	1	1	0
Colvin	.991	58	105	2	1	1
DeWitt	1.000	23	33	1	0	0
Fukudome	.987	82	151	5	2	0
Johnson	.976	84	116	5	3	2
LaHair	.958	14	23	0	1	0
Montanez	1.000	25	25	1	0	0
Snyder	.000	1	0	0	0	0
Soriano	.965	128	187	8	7	2

IOWA CUBS — TRIPLE-A
PACIFIC COAST LEAGUE

Batting	B-T	HT	WT	DOB	AVG	vLH	vRH	G	AB	R	H	2B	3B	HR	RBI	BB	HBP	SH	SF	SO	SB	CS	SLG	OBP
Baker, Jeff	R-R	6-2	210	6-21-81	.300	.000	.300	3	10	1	3	1	1	0	1	0	0	0	0	1	0	0	.600	.300
Barney, Darwin	R-R	5-10	180	11-8-85	.357	.333	.375	4	14	3	5	1	0	1	3	0	1	0	0	2	1	0	.643	.400
Byrd, Marlon	R-R	6-0	245	8-30-77	.267	.500	.231	4	15	4	4	1	0	1	3	2	2	0	0	2	1	0	.533	.421
Camp, Matt	L-R	6-0	200	5-29-84	.209	.143	.228	58	187	24	39	10	0	0	20	13	0	0	1	26	2	1	.262	.259
Campana, Tony	L-L	5-8	165	5-30-86	.342	.296	.355	30	120	27	41	8	2	0	9	6	2	0	0	23	8	1	.442	.383
Castillo, Welington	R-R	5-10	210	4-24-87	.286	.313	.275	61	227	38	65	9	0	15	35	20	3	0	1	57	0	0	.524	.351
Clevenger, Steve	L-R	6-0	195	4-5-86	.407	.333	.426	25	86	9	35	3	1	3	15	9	0	0	2	7	1	0	.570	.454
Colvin, Tyler	L-L	6-3	210	9-5-85	.256	.300	.233	50	203	32	52	12	6	7	32	5	0	0	3	55	1	1	.478	.270
Flaherty, Ryan	L-R	6-3	220	7-27-86	.237	.294	.213	49	173	22	41	11	1	5	22	10	0	0	1	44	1	0	.399	.277
Gonzalez, Marwin	B-R	6-1	186	3-14-89	.274	.324	.248	60	197	24	54	12	1	2	19	16	1	0	4	21	3	1	.376	.326
Jackson, Brett	L-R	6-2	210	8-2-88	.297	.279	.306	48	185	39	55	13	2	10	26	28	0	0	1	64	6	1	.551	.388
Johnson, Reed	R-R	5-10	180	12-8-76	.000	.000	.000	3	6	0	0	0	0	0	0	1	2	0	0	3	0	0	.000	.333
LaHair, Bryan	L-L	6-5	240	11-5-82	.331	.284	.352	129	456	91	151	38	0	38	109	60	1	0	6	111	2	0	.664	.405
Lemahieu, D.J.	R-R	6-4	205	7-13-88	.286	.310	.276	58	227	23	65	7	1	3	23	14	2	0	4	27	5	5	.366	.328
Mercedes, Mario	R-R	5-11	195	11-22-86	.500	.500	.500	3	10	0	5	1	1	0	1	1	0	0	0	1	0	0	.800	.545
Montanez, Lou	R-R	6-1	195	12-15-81	.321	.400	.285	92	333	52	107	22	7	7	69	38	5	0	3	47	4	6	.492	.396
Moore, Scott	L-R	6-2	195	11-17-83	.295	.215	.322	123	363	60	107	19	4	9	53	48	6	0	7	79	3	1	.444	.380
Mota, Jonathan	R-R	6-0	180	6-1-87	.289	.268	.301	77	204	24	59	15	1	5	30	9	2	0	3	32	1	1	.446	.321
Ojeda, Augie	B-R	5-9	175	12-20-74	.200	.111	.220	18	50	7	10	1	0	0	3	6	0	0	1	3	0	0	.220	.281
Perez, Fernando	R-B	6-1	195	4-23-83	.238	.200	.257	76	252	43	60	12	2	3	20	27	0	0	0	70	17	2	.337	.312
Ramirez, Max	R-R	5-11	175	10-11-84	.235	.182	.261	11	34	7	8	1	0	1	5	4	0	0	2	7	0	0	.353	.300
3-team total (48 Fresno, 24 Oklahoma City)					.278	—	—	83	266	38	74	15	1	13	48	21	4	0	5	58	0	0	.489	.334
Robinson, Chris	R-R	6-0	220	5-12-84	.316	.343	.304	66	225	26	71	15	0	1	29	6	5	0	2	33	1	1	.396	.345
Scales, Bobby	B-R	6-0	185	10-4-77	.304	.255	.320	68	230	48	70	22	2	9	43	47	3	0	3	58	5	6	.535	.424
Smith, Marquez	R-R	5-10	205	3-20-85	.278	.260	.285	78	259	45	72	18	2	7	36	23	5	0	4	61	0	1	.444	.344
Snyder, Brad	L-L	6-3	220	5-25-82	.290	.267	.300	102	376	48	109	27	3	11	57	27	0	0	2	109	6	1	.465	.336
Soriano, Alfonso	R-R	6-1	195	1-7-76	.077	.000	.250	3	13	3	1	0	0	0	0	0	0	0	0	4	0	0	.077	.077
Spencer, Matt	L-L	6-4	230	1-27-86	.188	.158	.200	27	69	9	13	1	0	1	7	7	0	0	1	17	2	0	.246	.260
Wright, Ty	R-R	6-0	200	2-26-85	.314	.302	.320	46	153	19	48	6	2	1	20	5	0	0	2	22	1	1	.399	.331

Pitching	B-T	HT	WT	DOB	W	L	ERA	G	GS	CG	SV	IP	H	R	ER	HR	BB	SO	AVG	vLH	vRH	K/9	BB/9
Berg, Justin	R-R	6-3	225	6-7-84	4	1	5.16	27	0	0	3	30	29	18	17	4	17	17	.269	.385	.203	5.16	5.16
Berlind, Dan	R-R	6-7	215	12-3-87	0	0	3.00	3	0	0	0	3	5	1	1	0	1	2	.385	.429	.333	6.00	3.00
Bibens-Dirkx, Austin	R-R	6-2	190	4-29-85	4	5	6.07	24	17	0	0	105	125	75	71	18	31	75	.298	.325	.271	6.41	2.65
Bush, Dave	R-R	6-2	205	11-9-79	1	2	6.14	5	5	0	0	22	28	15	15	3	9	12	.318	.281	.339	4.91	3.68
Cabrera, Alberto	R-R	6-4	210	10-25-88	3	6	6.60	19	17	0	0	89	118	67	65	11	53	67	.330	.363	.303	6.80	5.38
Caridad, Esmailin	R-R	5-10	195	10-28-83	2	3	8.27	26	0	0	4	37	51	38	34	5	27	30	.325	.319	.330	7.30	6.57
Carpenter, Chris	R-R	6-4	220	12-26-85	2	3	6.53	22	0	0	1	30	32	25	22	3	23	28	.286	.273	.294	8.31	6.82
Carrillo, Marco	R-R	5-11	215	2-1-87	2	1	6.10	11	2	0	0	31	38	23	21	6	6	25	.306	.360	.270	7.26	1.74
Cashner, Andrew	R-R	6-6	200	9-11-86	0	0	0.00	2	0	0	0	2	0	0	0	0	0	2	.000	.000	.000	9.00	0.00
Chen, Hung-Wen	R-R	5-11	210	2-3-86	1	0	3.00	5	0	0	0	6	7	2	2	1	3	7	.304	.357	.222	10.50	4.50
Coello, Robert	R-R	6-5	250	11-23-84	6	6	4.45	30	11	0	1	95	85	48	47	11	41	94	.240	.264	.223	8.91	3.88
Coleman, Casey	L-R	6-0	185	7-3-87	5	2	3.65	12	12	0	0	74	69	32	30	11	22	54	.254	.296	.223	6.57	2.68
Davis, Doug	R-L	6-4	215	9-21-75	0	0	4.91	1	1	0	0	4	4	2	2	0	0	5	.267	.000	.267	12.27	0.00
Diamond, Thomas	R-R	6-3	250	4-6-83	1	3	8.66	14	5	0	0	45	58	49	43	7	32	46	.314	.326	.301	9.27	6.45
Gaub, John	R-L	6-2	210	4-28-85	4	4	3.42	50	0	0	7	55	42	24	21	6	40	75	.209	.200	.216	12.20	6.51
Harris, Ty'Relle	R-R	6-4	235	12-12-86	0	0	3.00	1	0	0	0	3	3	1	1	1	1	1	.250	.000	.429	3.00	3.00
Jackson, Jay	R-R	6-1	195	10-27-87	8	14	5.34	26	26	0	0	147	180	90	87	10	46	97	.305	.325	.285	5.95	2.82
Maine, Scott	L-L	6-3	215	2-2-85	3	4	3.68	38	0	0	12	51	38	22	21	3	25	72	.203	.214	.197	12.62	4.38
Mateo, Marcos	R-R	6-1	220	4-18-84	1	3	6.87	16	0	0	2	18	20	14	14	3	10	18	.282	.250	.302	8.84	4.91
Mathes, J.R.	L-L	6-3	210	11-9-81	2	4	9.07	9	9	1	0	41	62	44	41	11	16	21	.350	.313	.364	4.65	3.54
Muyco, Jake	R-R	6-0	190	9-16-84	0	0	18.00	2	0	0	0	5	12	10	10	4	0	2	.444	.455	.438	3.60	0.00
Ortiz, Ramon	R-R	6-0	175	5-23-73	6	3	4.26	16	16	0	0	99	115	53	47	12	20	81	.292	.292	.291	7.34	1.81
Parker, Blake	R-R	6-3	225	6-19-85	3	2	2.81	37	0	0	4	51	37	16	16	5	27	60	.201	.154	.236	10.52	4.73
Rusin, Chris	L-L	6-2	185	10-22-86	5	2	4.02	11	9	0	0	63	70	29	28	8	14	46	.293	.270	.303	6.61	2.01
Smit, Kyle	R-R	6-3	170	10-14-87	0	0	10.13	6	0	0	0	5	14	9	6	1	4	3	.467	.571	.375	5.06	6.75
Smith, Carlton	L-R	6-2	205	1-23-86	0	2	10.80	12	0	0	0	15	27	21	18	2	9	9	.386	.480	.333	5.40	5.40
Stevens, Jeff	R-R	6-2	205	9-5-83	0	0	10.03	11	0	0	0	23	40	26	26	5	12	15	.377	.333	.406	5.79	4.63
Struck, Nick	R-R	5-11	185	10-7-89	2	4	5.20	12	11	0	0	62	76	40	36	2	22	38	.311	.405	.233	5.49	3.18
Trinidad, Polin	L-L	6-3	195	11-19-84	0	1	5.06	8	0	0	1	16	22	12	9	0	7	14	.310	.393	.256	7.88	3.94
Wellemeyer, Todd	R-R	6-2	215	8-30-78	0	1	9.82	1	1	0	0	4	8	4	4	0	2	2	.421	.333	.462	4.91	4.91
Wells, Randy	R-R	6-5	230	8-28-82	0	1	13.50	1	1	0	0	4	6	7	6	1	3	3	.333	.375	.300	6.75	6.75

Fielding

Catcher	PCT	G	PO	A	E	DP	PB
Castillo	.989	54	333	35	4	3	8
Clevenger	.994	23	166	12	1	0	2
Mercedes	1.000	3	18	1	0	0	0
Ramirez	1.000	8	64	9	0	0	2
Robinson	.998	60	443	48	1	4	3

First Base	PCT	G	PO	A	E	DP
Baker	1.000	1	8	1	0	2
Colvin	1.000	3	27	4	0	4
LaHair	.992	109	803	50	7	66
Moore	.984	36	286	22	5	25
Robinson	1.000	1	6	3	0	1
Spencer	.968	5	25	5	1	2

Second Base	PCT	G	PO	A	E	DP
Baker	1.000	1	0	2	0	0
Barney	1.000	4	8	4	0	0
Flaherty	1.000	26	53	65	0	20
Gonzalez	1.000	2	3	1	0	1
Lemahieu	.991	21	51	63	1	22
Moore	.956	24	33	53	4	10
Mota	1.000	10	16	16	0	4
Scales	.980	61	83	158	5	23

Smith	1.000	9	15	20	0	8

Third Base	PCT	G	PO	A	E	DP
Flaherty	.882	16	13	32	6	3
Lemahieu	1.000	31	20	62	0	4
Moore	.920	42	20	49	6	6
Mota	.929	8	4	9	1	2
Scales	.818	4	2	7	2	0
Smith	.969	59	35	90	4	7

Shortstop	PCT	G	PO	A	E	DP
Camp	.976	37	44	79	3	16
Gonzalez	.983	54	83	152	4	36
Lemahieu	1.000	5	5	13	0	2
Mota	.968	47	66	114	6	19
Ojeda	.983	17	22	36	1	4

Outfield	PCT	G	PO	A	E	DP
Baker	1.000	1	1	0	0	0

	PCT	G	PO	A	E	DP
Byrd	1.000	4	9	1	0	0
Camp	.936	19	43	1	3	0
Campana	1.000	29	65	1	0	0
Colvin	.966	43	82	4	3	0
Flaherty	1.000	7	11	1	0	0
Jackson	.984	45	118	8	2	1
Johnson	1.000	2	4	0	0	0
LaHair	.955	12	19	2	1	0
Montanez	.994	86	163	8	1	1
Moore	.000	1	0	0	0	0
Perez	.981	69	156	3	3	0
Snyder	.981	89	140	11	3	3
Soriano	1.000	3	3	0	0	0
Spencer	.958	16	22	1	1	0
Wright	.951	34	56	2	3	0

TENNESSEE SMOKIES

DOUBLE-A

SOUTHERN LEAGUE

Batting	B-T	HT	WT	DOB	AVG	vLH	vRH	G	AB	R	H	2B	3B	HR	RBI	BB	HBP	SH	SF	SO	SB	CS	SLG	OBP
Adduci, Jim	L-L	6-2	210	5-15-85	.308	.410	.273	71	237	44	73	13	2	4	20	26	1	0	0	33	21	4	.430	.379
Camp, Matt	L-R	6-0	200	5-29-84	.169	.176	.167	20	65	5	11	3	1	0	2	11	0	0	0	7	1	0	.246	.289
Clevenger, Steve	L-R	6-0	195	4-5-86	.295	.290	.297	95	312	42	92	27	3	5	39	35	0	0	3	39	1	0	.449	.363
Flaherty, Ryan	L-R	6-3	220	7-27-86	.305	.253	.327	83	302	52	92	20	2	14	66	40	0	0	2	55	4	6	.523	.384
Flores, Luis	R-R	5-10	195	11-2-86	.275	.275	.275	40	102	22	28	8	1	7	20	14	3	0	2	16	0	0	.578	.372
Gonzalez, Marwin	B-R	6-1	186	3-14-89	.301	.325	.288	64	216	29	65	18	1	2	20	17	3	0	1	27	4	2	.421	.359
Ha, Jae-Hoon	R-R	6-1	185	10-31-90	.283	.278	.286	61	226	32	64	16	1	3	25	11	3	0	4	28	6	9	.403	.320
Jackson, Brett	L-R	6-2	210	8-2-88	.256	.243	.262	67	246	45	63	10	3	10	32	45	2	0	2	74	15	6	.443	.373
Lake, Junior	R-R	6-3	215	3-27-90	.248	.276	.235	67	242	41	60	10	2	6	17	13	5	0	0	60	19	2	.380	.300
Lalli, Blake	L-R	6-1	205	5-12-83	.287	.288	.286	108	349	40	100	22	1	9	52	39	2	0	3	59	0	0	.433	.359
Lemahieu, D.J.	R-R	6-4	205	7-13-88	.358	.459	.310	50	187	32	67	15	2	2	27	11	0	0	4	22	4	3	.492	.386
Macias, David	B-R	5-9	175	3-7-86	.207	.143	.237	40	87	11	18	3	0	0	6	10	0	0	2	12	0	0	.241	.286
Mercedes, Mario	R-R	5-11	195	11-22-86	.000	.000	.000	1	2	0	0	0	0	0	0	0	0	0	0	0	0	0	.000	.000
Mota, Jonathan	R-R	6-0	180	11-7-86	.221	.233	.213	21	77	5	17	4	0	2	8	2	1	0	0	14	0	1	.351	.250
Na, Kyung-Min	L-L	5-10	170	12-12-91	.000	.000	.000	2	4	0	0	0	0	0	0	0	0	0	0	3	0	0	.000	.000
Perez, Nelson	L-R	6-3	215	11-16-87	.249	.175	.272	88	237	28	59	17	1	8	32	20	3	0	2	87	1	2	.430	.313
Ridling, Rebel	R-R	6-4	230	5-22-86	.309	.361	.280	125	433	79	134	29	0	20	80	43	3	0	5	89	5	2	.515	.372
Samson, Nate	R-R	6-1	190	8-19-87	.236	.244	.228	113	276	45	65	17	3	5	31	22	5	0	2	43	6	5	.373	.302
Soto, Geovany	R-R	6-1	220	1-20-83	.000	.000	.000	2	7	0	0	0	0	0	0	0	0	0	0	1	0	0	.000	.000
Spencer, Matt	L-L	6-4	230	1-27-86	.258	.259	.257	98	322	47	83	21	2	13	63	29	7	0	1	75	4	2	.457	.331
Vitters, Josh	R-R	6-2	200	8-27-89	.283	.299	.275	129	449	56	127	28	2	14	81	22	8	0	8	54	4	10	.448	.322
Wright, Ty	R-R	6-0	200	2-26-85	.333	.279	.366	42	114	21	38	11	0	6	23	23	1	0	3	20	0	1	.588	.440

Pitching	B-T	HT	WT	DOB	W	L	ERA	G	GS	CG	SV	IP	H	R	ER	HR	BB	SO	AVG	vLH	vRH	K/9	BB/9
Beeler, Dallas	R-R	6-5	205	6-12-89	1	5	4.53	9	9	0	0	52	68	31	26	7	7	33	.315	.400	.208	5.75	1.22
Beliveau, Jeff	L-L	6-1	190	1-17-87	6	1	1.89	41	0	0	3	57	37	14	12	7	13	69	.183	.169	.191	10.89	2.05
Berlind, Dan	R-R	6-7	215	12-3-87	1	0	0.00	2	0	0	0	3	2	0	0	0	3	6	.182	.500	.000	18.00	9.00
Bibens-Dirkx, Austin	R-R	6-2	190	4-29-85	2	2	5.40	5	5	0	0	25	26	15	15	3	9	16	.265	.263	.267	5.76	3.24
Buchter, Ryan	L-L	6-3	185	2-13-87	3	0	6.55	10	0	0	0	11	13	11	8	1	11	13	.302	.400	.250	10.64	9.00
Cabrera, Alberto	R-R	6-4	210	10-25-88	6	2	5.36	9	9	0	0	49	60	36	29	4	21	34	.308	.318	.299	6.29	3.88
Cales, David	R-R	5-11	200	7-27-87	0	2	3.86	9	0	0	6	7	4	3	3	1	3	6	.160	.083	.231	3.86	3.86
Caridad, Esmailin	R-R	5-10	195	10-28-83	0	0	7.00	5	0	0	0	9	12	8	7	1	2	10	.316	.357	.292	10.00	2.00
Carpenter, Chris	R-R	6-4	220	12-26-85	1	1	4.38	10	0	0	1	12	10	6	6	2	4	6	.227	.235	.222	4.38	2.92
Carrillo, Marco	R-R	5-11	215	2-1-87	5	4	2.36	29	7	0	3	76	61	26	20	6	32	62	.215	.234	.203	7.31	3.77
Cashner, Andrew	R-R	6-6	200	9-11-86	0	1	6.75	3	3	0	0	3	3	2	2	0	0	6	.273	.200	.333	20.25	0.00
Chen, Hung-Wen	R-R	5-11	210	2-3-86	1	2	4.03	15	4	0	0	29	34	17	13	3	12	22	.298	.325	.284	6.83	3.72
Coello, Robert	R-R	6-5	250	11-23-84	1	2	3.00	4	4	0	0	21	19	7	7	1	7	16	.244	.194	.286	6.86	3.00
Dolis, Rafael	R-R	6-4	215	1-10-88	8	5	3.22	51	4	0	17	73	61	36	26	2	35	48	.227	.222	.231	5.94	4.33
Ebinger, Brent	R-L	6-0	190	6-30-88	0	0	6.75	6	0	0	0	9	13	7	7	2	1	5	.325	.364	.310	4.82	0.96
Garcia, Ramon	R-R	6-2	170	8-2-91	0	1	3.00	1	0	0	0	3	4	1	1	0	0	2	.333	.500	.000	6.00	0.00
Harris, Ty'Relle	R-R	6-4	235	12-12-86	1	0	2.10	17	0	0	0	34	28	9	8	2	27	29	.233	.237	.230	7.60	7.08
Hatley, Marcus	R-R	6-5	220	3-26-88	3	0	4.66	22	0	0	4	29	30	17	15	2	11	20	.278	.347	.220	6.21	3.41
Jokisch, Eric	R-L	6-2	185	7-29-89	1	0	4.11	3	3	0	0	15	16	9	7	0	9	15	.271	.250	.275	8.80	5.28
Loosen, Matt	R-R	6-2	205	4-10-89	0	2	5.73	2	2	0	0	11	6	7	7	2	8	7	.167	.231	.130	5.73	6.55
Martinez, Oswaldo	R-R	6-0	180	5-25-84	4	0	2.34	20	0	0	1	35	29	9	9	1	13	26	.242	.356	.173	6.75	3.38
McNutt, Trey	R-R	6-4	220	8-2-89	5	6	4.55	23	22	0	0	95	120	54	48	5	39	65	.319	.379	.278	6.16	3.69
Parker, Blake	R-R	6-3	225	6-19-85	1	2	4.13	16	0	0	3	24	20	14	11	1	13	20	.227	.139	.288	7.50	4.88
Raley, Brooks	L-L	6-3	185	6-29-88	8	10	4.22	26	25	0	0	136	170	86	64	16	45	80	.307	.288	.313	5.28	2.97
Rhoderick, Kevin	R-R	6-1	190	8-19-88	7	0	3.47	45	0	0	1	57	38	22	22	2	37	58	.189	.205	.180	9.16	5.84
Rusin, Chris	L-L	6-2	185	10-22-86	3	2	3.91	15	15	0	0	76	80	39	33	5	16	49	.268	.174	.297	5.80	1.89
Searle, Ryan	R-R	6-0	190	6-22-89	5	3	3.51	23	11	0	0	85	81	42	33	4	43	66	.258	.336	.204	7.02	4.57
Serrano, Juan Yasser	R-R	5-10	220	3-3-88	0	0	3.00	1	0	0	0	3	2	1	1	0	1	3	.182	.400	.000	9.00	3.00
Smit, Kyle	R-R	6-3	170	10-14-87	2	0	5.40	30	0	0	0	43	54	28	26	3	23	37	.310	.309	.311	7.68	4.78

Pitching	B-T	HT	WT	DOB	W	L	ERA	G	GS	CG	SV	IP	H	R	ER	HR	BB	SO	AVG	vLH	vRH	K/9	BB/9
Sommer, Luke	L-L	6-3	190	6-22-85	0	0	8.10	8	0	0	1	10	18	9	9	4	1	7	.400	.350	.440	6.30	0.90
Stevens, Jeff	R-R	6-2	205	9-5-83	3	0	2.59	25	0	0	2	42	34	12	12	1	16	52	.228	.152	.289	11.23	3.46
Struck, Nick	R-R	5-11	185	10-7-89	1	1	2.31	6	6	1	0	35	42	16	9	0	6	26	.302	.360	.234	6.69	1.54
Suarez, Larry	R-R	6-4	245	12-20-89	0	2	7.31	6	4	0	0	16	22	14	13	2	6	11	.319	.346	.302	6.19	3.38
Whitenack, Robert	R-R	6-5	185	11-20-88	4	0	2.39	7	7	0	0	38	32	10	10	1	13	22	.237	.279	.203	5.26	3.11

Fielding

Catcher	PCT	G	PO	A	E	DP	PB
Clevenger	.996	73	499	55	2	7	6
Flores	.992	32	212	24	2	1	2
Lalli	.985	37	238	18	4	0	1
Macias	1.000	1	3	0	0	0	
Mercedes	.833	1	3	2	1	0	
Soto	1.000	2	6	1	0	0	

First Base	PCT	G	PO	A	E	DP
Clevenger	1.000	9	53	1	0	1
Flaherty	1.000	4	16	1	0	0
Lalli	.991	45	308	21	3	26
Ridling	.993	79	599	63	5	57
Spencer	1.000	3	17	1	0	4
Vitters	.983	32	223	15	4	23

Second Base	PCT	G	PO	A	E	DP
Camp	.978	8	15	29	1	1
Flaherty	.991	37	42	66	1	15
Gonzalez	1.000	15	23	43	0	4

Lemahieu	.969	30	50	74	4	16
Macias	.951	20	44	34	4	16
Mota	.982	13	21	35	1	9
Samson	.981	52	86	122	4	30

Third Base	PCT	G	PO	A	E	DP
Clevenger	1.000	1	1	2	0	0
Flaherty	.939	12	8	23	2	3
Lake	.500	1	0	1	1	0
Lalli	.875	7	5	2	1	0
Lemahieu	1.000	30	13	49	0	4
Macias	1.000	4	1	8	0	2
Mota	1.000	2	1	6	0	2
Samson	.889	12	4	20	3	3
Vitters	.903	100	53	143	21	9

Shortstop	PCT	G	PO	A	E	DP
Camp	.923	8	14	22	3	3
Flaherty	.934	14	15	42	4	10
Gonzalez	.949	45	66	122	10	22

Lake	.934	64	90	181	19	37
Mota	.967	6	13	16	1	8
Samson	.966	16	18	39	2	7

Outfield	PCT	G	PO	A	E	DP
Adduci	.956	68	103	5	5	1
Camp	1.000	3	3	0	0	0
Flaherty	1.000	32	46	3	0	1
Gonzalez	.857	4	6	0	1	0
Ha	1.000	61	136	3	0	0
Jackson	.972	65	135	3	4	0
Lalli	.000	1	0	0	0	0
Macias	1.000	6	6	0	0	0
Na	1.000	2	3	0	0	0
Perez	.962	74	115	10	5	4
Ridling	.985	47	63	1	1	0
Samson	1.000	13	17	1	0	0
Spencer	.964	90	151	10	6	0
Wright	.898	25	43	1	5	1

DAYTONA CUBS   HIGH CLASS A

FLORIDA STATE LEAGUE

Batting	B-T	HT	WT	DOB	AVG	vLH	vRH	G	AB	R	H	2B	3B	HR	RBI	BB	HBP	SH	SF	SO	SB	CS	SLG	OBP
Abreu, Abner	R-R	6-3	187	10-24-89	.244	.250	.242	25	86	8	21	5	1	1	7	5	1	0	0	24	0	0	.360	.293
Bour, Justin	L-R	6-4	250	5-28-88	.277	.182	.311	133	502	65	139	30	1	23	85	46	2	0	8	105	3	2	.478	.335
Brenly, Mike	R-R	6-3	230	10-14-86	.206	.167	.219	96	335	30	69	15	1	0	24	16	4	0	4	53	0	0	.248	.248
Burgess, Michael	L-L	5-11	195	10-20-88	.225	.216	.229	122	426	61	96	24	1	20	68	60	4	0	5	111	1	0	.427	.323
Castillo, Welington	R-R	5-10	210	4-24-87	.238	.333	.212	12	42	6	10	3	0	1	7	6	0	0	1	9	0	0	.381	.327
Cerda, Matt	L-R	5-9	165	6-20-90	.283	.255	.292	109	389	52	110	22	2	1	43	71	3	0	4	71	3	6	.357	.394
Crawford, Evan	R-R	6-2	165	8-5-88	.307	.269	.321	115	446	69	137	24	6	2	50	26	3	0	1	98	32	6	.401	.362
Easterling, Taiwan	R-R	5-11	195	2-24-89	.200	.000	.333	1	5	0	1	0	0	0	0	0	0	0	0	1	0	0	.200	.200
Flores, Luis	R-R	5-10	195	11-2-86	.161	.154	.167	9	31	4	5	0	0	1	3	2	0	0	1	7	0	0	.258	.206
Ha, Jae-Hoon	R-R	6-1	185	10-29-90	.276	.229	.291	71	294	35	81	15	2	8	47	12	4	0	2	39	7	8	.422	.311
Harrington, Dustin	R-R	5-11	180	11-14-88	.221	.286	.183	29	95	11	21	3	0	1	7	2	0	0	0	22	1	1	.284	.237
Lake, Junior	R-R	6-3	215	3-27-90	.315	.327	.311	49	203	39	64	11	4	6	34	6	2	0	3	49	19	4	.498	.336
Macias, David	B-R	5-9	175	3-7-86	.270	.270	.270	37	126	23	34	4	0	2	17	15	2	0	0	22	2	2	.349	.357
Mercedes, Mario	R-R	5-11	195	11-22-86	.182	.200	.172	14	44	3	8	3	0	0	3	2	0	0	1	6	1	1	.250	.213
Noble, Chad	R-R	6-1	210	11-18-87	.234	.195	.250	48	145	15	34	2	0	1	11	12	1	0	0	35	0	1	.269	.297
Opitz, Jake	L-R	6-0	190	7-28-86	.268	.260	.270	85	291	42	78	23	1	8	38	17	1	0	2	60	3	2	.436	.309
Perez, Nelson	L-R	6-3	215	11-16-87	.327	.143	.375	26	101	17	33	4	1	4	17	6	1	0	0	34	1	0	.505	.370
Rohan, Greg	R-R	6-0	205	5-11-86	.345	.429	.308	31	113	16	39	8	1	6	19	9	2	0	0	21	1	0	.593	.403
Silva, Rubi	L-R	5-11	180	6-25-89	.229	.200	.235	29	105	13	24	6	1	2	7	3	0	0	0	22	0	0	.362	.250
Soto, Elliot	R-R	5-9	160	8-21-89	.309	.333	.302	25	81	14	25	2	0	0	5	4	1	0	1	12	1	0	.333	.345
Szczur, Matt	R-R	6-1	195	7-20-89	.260	.255	.262	43	173	20	45	7	2	5	19	5	1	0	1	20	7	0	.410	.283
Valdes, Rafael	R-R	6-2	185	2-21-84	.252	.310	.226	42	135	16	34	9	1	3	18	11	4	0	0	23	0	2	.400	.327
Watkins, Logan	L-R	5-11	170	8-29-89	.281	.228	.297	125	441	70	124	15	12	5	45	44	7	0	5	97	21	5	.404	.352

Pitching	B-T	HT	WT	DOB	W	L	ERA	G	GS	CG	SV	IP	H	R	ER	HR	BB	SO	AVG	vLH	vRH	K/9	BB/9
Antigua, Jeffry	R-L	6-1	170	6-23-90	2	2	2.92	22	8	0	0	83	75	32	27	9	18	81	.240	.208	.255	8.75	1.94
Batista, Frank	R-R	5-10	170	4-26-89	5	3	2.36	51	0	0	26	61	51	18	16	3	20	46	.226	.190	.254	6.79	2.95
Beliveau, Jeff	L-L	6-1	190	1-17-87	0	1	0.52	12	0	0	2	17	13	1	1	0	6	20	.224	.304	.171	10.38	3.12
Buchter, Ryan	L-L	6-3	185	2-13-87	1	0	0.00	6	0	0	1	10	2	0	0	0	3	17	.061	.111	.042	14.81	2.61
Davis, Doug	R-L	6-4	215	9-21-75	1	0	0.00	1	1	0	0	7	2	0	0	0	2	7	.095	.000	.118	9.45	2.70
Del Valle, Frank	L-L	5-11	190	9-16-89	0	2	15.63	2	2	0	0	6	12	11	11	3	6	5	.387	.500	.333	7.11	8.53
Ebinger, Brent	R-L	6-0	190	6-30-88	5	5	7.74	19	3	0	0	43	66	42	37	2	15	30	.355	.328	.367	6.28	3.14
Figueroa, Eduardo	R-R	6-1	185	11-30-88	2	2	2.42	36	0	0	0	71	66	21	19	4	23	56	.250	.237	.260	7.13	2.93
Francescon, Patrick	R-R	5-11	185	1-4-89	0	0	0.00	1	1	0	0	2	2	0	0	0	1	2	.250	.000	.400	9.00	4.50
Guzman, Angel	R-R	6-3	200	12-14-81	0	3	4.26	19	17	0	0	32	41	20	15	3	4	26	.320	.292	.349	7.39	1.14
Harman, Casey	L-L	6-1	210	3-17-89	4	5	4.47	14	9	0	1	58	71	39	29	10	12	48	.300	.255	.313	7.41	1.85
Hatley, Marcus	R-R	6-5	220	3-26-88	0	0	1.76	13	0	0	4	15	10	4	3	0	11	19	.192	.217	.172	11.15	6.46
Kurcz, Aaron	R-R	6-0	175	8-8-90	5	4	3.28	32	12	0	0	82	67	34	30	6	34	91	.222	.194	.247	9.95	3.72
Latham, Jordan	R-R	6-1	180	9-25-86	6	2	4.70	41	0	0	1	61	57	34	32	5	42	57	.248	.302	.202	8.36	6.16
Loosen, Matt	R-R	6-2	205	4-10-89	2	3	4.42	9	6	0	0	37	40	29	18	4	13	39	.274	.288	.263	9.57	3.19
Lorick, Jeff	L-L	6-0	195	12-18-87	8	6	5.38	30	18	0	0	114	133	83	68	10	44	75	.296	.254	.315	5.94	3.48
Martinez, Oswaldo	R-R	6-0	180	9-25-88	1	0	1.50	11	0	0	0	18	11	3	3	1	3	20	.175	.194	.156	10.00	1.50
Negrin, Yoanner	R-R	5-11	190	4-29-84	0	1	10.38	3	0	0	0	4	7	5	5	0	1	5	.368	.571	.250	10.38	2.08

Pitching

Pitching	B-T	HT	WT	DOB	W	L	ERA	G	GS	CG	SV	IP	H	R	ER	HR	BB	SO	AVG	vLH	vRH	K/9	BB/9
Rhee, Dae-Eun	L-R	6-2	190	3-23-89	8	7	4.02	25	17	4	0	128	131	68	57	10	43	117	.265	.258	.272	8.25	3.03
Rhoderick, Kevin	R-R	6-1	190	8-19-88	2	0	1.26	7	0	0	0	14	7	3	2	1	6	19	.143	.179	.095	11.93	3.77
Rosscup, Zach	R-L	6-2	205	6-9-88	4	2	2.54	11	9	0	0	50	43	17	14	4	19	50	.230	.237	.227	9.06	3.44
Searle, Ryan	R-R	6-0	190	6-22-89	1	2	1.59	16	0	0	1	28	18	7	5	2	14	27	.180	.214	.155	8.58	4.45
Serrano, Juan Yasser	R-R	5-10	220	3-3-88	4	1	3.67	28	3	0	0	56	55	28	23	6	20	41	.252	.244	.257	6.55	3.20
Smit, Kyle	R-R	6-3	170	10-14-87	2	2	4.85	9	0	0	2	13	18	11	7	0	8	7	.333	.360	.310	4.85	5.54
Struck, Nick	R-R	5-11	185	10-7-89	6	2	3.42	10	10	0	0	50	55	23	19	2	16	47	.282	.260	.297	8.46	2.88
Suarez, Larry	R-R	6-4	245	12-20-89	1	1	3.00	8	0	0	0	12	13	9	4	3	3	12	.265	.261	.269	9.00	2.25
Wallach, Brett	R-R	6-5	205	12-2-88	3	5	5.74	19	17	0	0	91	106	67	58	6	34	71	.293	.343	.245	7.02	3.36
Whitenack, Robert	R-R	6-5	185	11-20-88	3	0	1.17	4	4	0	0	23	11	5	3	0	1	25	.141	.175	.105	9.78	0.39

Fielding

Catcher	PCT	G	PO	A	E	DP	PB
Brenly	.997	79	620	53	2	6	5
Castillo	.895	3	16	1	2	0	1
Flores	.974	9	68	7	2	1	0
Mercedes	.989	12	74	12	1	0	1
Noble	.987	44	287	27	4	0	3

First Base	PCT	G	PO	A	E	DP
Bour	.987	105	831	52	12	74
Brenly	1.000	6	37	4	0	3
Opitz	.984	22	167	15	3	18
Rohan	1.000	9	63	6	0	2

Second Base	PCT	G	PO	A	E	DP
Cerda	.983	39	81	93	3	21
Macias	.979	21	34	61	2	13

Opitz	.974	11	16	22	1	4
Watkins	.966	72	119	166	10	47

Third Base	PCT	G	PO	A	E	DP
Cerda	.906	63	31	104	14	9
Harrington	.956	27	26	39	3	4
Macias	.950	6	6	13	1	1
Opitz	.941	25	12	36	3	0
Rohan	.818	11	4	14	4	1
Valdes	.958	13	9	14	1	3
Watkins	.000	1	0	0	0	0

Shortstop	PCT	G	PO	A	E	DP
Lake	.940	49	63	156	14	30
Macias	.750	1	1	2	1	0
Soto	.959	24	38	79	5	12

Valdes	.931	25	35	60	7	15
Watkins	.948	45	59	88	8	15

Outfield	PCT	G	PO	A	E	DP
Abreu	1.000	24	45	4	0	0
Burgess	.979	102	174	11	4	2
Crawford	.976	107	196	4	5	2
Easterling	1.000	1	3	1	0	0
Ha	.978	67	167	8	4	3
Macias	1.000	8	5	2	0	0
Opitz	.000	1	0	0	0	0
Perez	.946	23	52	1	3	0
Rohan	1.000	6	13	2	0	1
Silva	.968	26	58	2	2	0
Szczur	.979	40	91	3	2	1
Watkins	1.000	12	13	0	0	0

PEORIA CHIEFS

LOW CLASS A

MIDWEST LEAGUE

Batting	B-T	HT	WT	DOB	AVG	vLH	vRH	G	AB	R	H	2B	3B	HR	RBI	BB	HBP	SH	SF	SO	SB	CS	SLG	OBP
Alcantara, Arismendy	B-R	5-10	160	10-29-91	.271	.278	.269	99	369	45	100	14	5	2	37	16	1	0	0	76	8	8	.352	.303
Andreoli, John	R-R	6-1	215	6-9-90	.111	.000	.136	8	27	3	3	0	0	0	1	3	0	0	0	6	2	0	.111	.200
Borges, Smaily	R-R	6-3	210	1-28-84	.233	.094	.277	36	133	16	31	7	0	3	15	6	3	0	2	32	1	1	.353	.278
Burruel, Sergio	L-R	5-11	210	7-22-91	.203	.143	.219	54	172	11	35	7	0	0	10	27	5	0	2	36	1	1	.244	.325
Cuneo, Ryan	L-R	6-3	190	10-10-88	.263	.226	.276	52	198	25	52	15	1	2	28	15	2	0	4	36	1	0	.379	.315
Easterling, Taiwan	R-R	5-11	195	2-24-89	.277	.231	.291	40	166	18	46	6	1	2	16	8	0	0	3	32	9	4	.361	.305
Fitzgerald, D.J.	R-R	6-0	190	12-20-88	.128	.050	.158	40	141	16	18	4	2	0	9	15	4	0	0	34	4	0	.184	.231
Geiger, Dustin	R-R	6-2	180	12-2-91	.227	.311	.195	43	163	14	37	10	1	1	13	9	2	0	5	38	0	0	.319	.268
Giansanti, Anthony	R-R	5-10	190	9-28-88	.232	.193	.245	125	444	53	103	21	4	11	56	34	7	0	5	80	8	7	.372	.294
Gibbs, Micah	B-R	5-11	223	7-27-88	.245	.224	.252	87	306	32	75	14	1	2	28	49	4	0	2	69	1	2	.317	.355
Jones, Richard	L-R	6-0	215	1-31-88	.309	.234	.332	123	472	62	146	36	0	24	98	32	10	0	5	125	0	3	.538	.362
Klafczynski, Ben	L-R	6-3	195	9-21-88	.243	.162	.270	43	152	8	37	3	0	1	13	14	0	0	0	36	0	0	.283	.307
LePage, Pierre	R-R	5-8	168	2-23-89	.252	.235	.257	65	238	37	60	17	1	2	26	20	3	0	2	20	8	2	.357	.316
Macias, David	B-R	5-9	175	3-7-86	.269	.300	.250	6	26	3	7	1	0	0	1	1	0	0	0	2	0	0	.308	.321
May, Brandon	R-R	6-1	205	1-7-88	.185	.111	.210	32	108	8	20	4	2	0	6	14	1	0	1	40	0	1	.259	.282
Morelli, Jesus	R-R	6-3	180	4-25-90	.244	.190	.261	25	90	9	22	2	0	0	7	2	3	0	1	22	0	0	.267	.281
Na, Kyung-Min	L-L	5-10	170	12-12-91	.258	.276	.250	28	89	10	23	4	0	0	3	9	1	0	0	23	5	1	.303	.333
Noble, Chad	R-R	6-1	210	11-18-87	.167	.000	.500	3	6	0	1	0	0	0	0	1	0	0	0	2	0	0	.167	.286
Rohan, Greg	R-R	6-0	205	5-11-86	.314	.280	.326	76	293	34	92	20	0	5	52	24	4	0	5	50	3	2	.433	.368
Silva, Rubi	L-R	5-11	180	6-25-89	.300	.224	.321	93	390	59	117	16	7	3	37	13	0	0	4	73	6	6	.400	.319
Socorro, Kenny	R-R	5-9	175	6-2-89	.289	.333	.269	10	38	5	11	1	0	0	2	2	0	0	0	1	0	1	.316	.325
Soto, Elliot	R-R	5-9	160	8-21-89	.261	.265	.260	87	318	35	83	11	1	0	24	17	6	0	2	58	4	7	.302	.309
Szczur, Matt	R-R	6-1	195	7-20-89	.314	.385	.292	66	274	55	86	15	1	5	27	21	2	0	1	28	17	5	.431	.366
Valdes, Rafael	R-R	6-2	185	2-21-84	.278	.389	.253	25	97	11	27	5	0	0	11	3	1	0	0	9	1	2	.330	.307

Pitching	B-T	HT	WT	DOB	W	L	ERA	G	GS	CG	SV	IP	H	R	ER	HR	BB	SO	AVG	vLH	vRH	K/9	BB/9
Antigua, Jeffry	R-L	6-1	170	6-23-90	1	2	8.56	10	0	0	1	14	20	18	13	3	6	12	.333	.188	.386	7.90	3.95
Beeler, Dallas	R-R	6-5	205	6-12-89	1	1	1.66	12	11	0	0	43	35	13	8	1	6	35	.222	.206	.232	7.27	1.25
Berlind, Dan	R-R	6-7	215	12-3-87	1	3	4.56	16	0	0	4	26	32	14	13	0	6	14	.308	.442	.213	4.91	2.10
Bristow, Justin	R-R	6-4	220	3-6-87	0	0	4.50	1	0	0	0	2	3	1	1	0	1	2	.333	1.000	.250	9.00	4.50
Del Valle, Frank	L-L	5-11	190	9-16-89	3	2	2.95	9	7	0	0	43	36	17	14	3	11	31	.225	.259	.206	6.54	2.32
Ebinger, Brent	R-L	6-0	190	6-30-88	1	1	0.89	9	0	0	2	20	15	3	2	1	3	10	.205	.267	.163	4.43	1.33
Figueroa, Eduardo	R-R	6-1	185	11-30-88	1	1	4.05	5	0	0	1	7	4	3	3	1	4	6	.190	.300	.091	8.10	5.40
Francescon, Patrick	R-R	5-11	185	1-4-89	1	4	3.89	17	2	0	2	35	36	17	15	3	7	40	.261	.309	.229	10.38	1.82
Garcia, Ramon	R-R	6-2	170	8-2-91	1	3	3.45	7	0	0	0	16	15	7	6	0	3	17	.242	.240	.243	9.77	1.72
Gonzalez, Yohan	R-R	6-4	210	4-15-90	5	6	5.15	40	0	0	3	73	76	46	42	8	29	56	.269	.282	.260	6.87	3.56
Greathouse, Cam	L-L	6-2	230	7-29-90	4	5	4.37	13	12	0	0	58	41	39	28	5	53	49	.200	.253	.167	7.65	8.27
Guzman, Angel	R-R	6-3	200	12-8-81	0	0	2.25	2	2	0	0	4	2	1	1	0	1	2	.154	.222	.000	4.50	2.25
Harman, Casey	L-L	6-1	210	3-17-89	1	1	0.36	16	0	0	0	25	13	3	1	1	4	27	.153	.095	.172	9.59	1.42
Hartman, Ryan	R-R	6-3	180	5-10-92	0	0	19.29	2	0	0	0	2	5	5	5	0	3	1	.500	1.000	.167	3.86	11.57
Hatley, Marcus	R-R	6-5	220	3-26-88	2	1	2.35	13	0	0	3	15	9	5	4	0	8	21	.170	.111	.200	12.33	4.70

Pitching

Pitching	B-T	HT	WT	DOB	W	L	ERA	G	GS	CG	SV	IP	H	R	ER	HR	BB	SO	AVG	vLH	vRH	K/9	BB/9
Hicks, Graham	L-L	6-5	170	2-9-90	1	3	4.01	14	14	0	0	58	55	30	26	7	23	40	.261	.256	.264	6.17	3.55
Jokisch, Eric	R-L	6-2	185	7-29-89	9	3	2.96	25	11	0	1	119	106	41	39	13	32	103	.239	.255	.232	7.81	2.43
Jung, Su-Min	R-R	6-2	190	4-1-90	2	2	5.36	13	3	0	1	44	43	26	26	3	24	19	.276	.293	.265	3.92	4.95
Kirk, Austin	L-L	6-1	200	5-22-90	5	12	4.29	29	28	1	0	151	143	81	72	17	38	122	.250	.240	.254	7.27	2.26
Levitt, Pete	R-R	6-5	235	4-24-89	1	1	4.55	17	0	0	0	28	29	20	14	1	5	21	.266	.232	.302	6.83	1.63
Liria, Luis	B-R	6-2	170	1-15-90	3	3	3.77	10	6	0	2	45	31	24	19	5	20	34	.190	.227	.165	6.75	3.97
Loosen, Matt	R-R	6-2	205	4-10-89	2	1	1.74	6	5	0	0	31	21	6	6	2	6	28	.194	.145	.245	8.13	1.74
Lopez, Robinson	R-R	6-2	190	3-2-91	4	3	5.35	26	4	0	1	69	78	44	41	8	30	35	.294	.299	.291	4.57	3.91
Negrin, Yoanner	R-R	5-11	190	4-29-84	0	0	4.15	2	0	0	1	4	4	2	2	2	1	6	.235	.200	.286	12.46	2.08
Peralta, Starlin	R-R	6-4	180	11-11-90	3	5	5.68	12	12	0	0	57	67	44	36	9	26	40	.290	.308	.276	6.32	4.11
Pichardo, Roderick	R-R	5-10	180	9-24-90	1	1	1.69	12	0	0	2	16	16	4	3	1	7	12	.267	.154	.353	6.75	3.94
Serrano, Juan Yasser	R-R	5-10	220	3-3-88	1	1	2.13	5	0	0	0	13	7	3	3	1	1	4	.159	.167	.154	2.84	0.71
Shafer, Bryce	R-R	6-0	180	11-14-88	0	3	2.79	17	0	0	1	29	27	12	9	1	15	24	.255	.293	.231	7.45	4.66
Simpson, Hayden	R-R	6-0	175	5-20-89	1	6	5.72	16	16	0	0	61	76	51	39	9	27	46	.305	.319	.292	6.75	3.96
Sosa, Alvaro	L-R	6-0	181	6-7-86	4	2	3.42	34	0	0	1	55	52	29	21	2	21	35	.259	.286	.236	5.69	3.42
Suarez, Larry	R-R	6-4	245	12-20-89	0	0	0.00	10	0	0	1	16	13	5	0	1	5	23	.210	.308	.139	12.94	2.81
Thomas, Charles	R-R	6-4	225	7-2-88	0	0	0.00	2	0	0	0	4	3	0	0	0	0	5	.214	.143	.286	12.27	0.00
Wallach, Brett	R-R	6-5	205	12-2-88	1	4	6.49	7	4	0	0	26	29	26	19	0	23	25	.269	.263	.275	8.54	7.86
Wells, Randy	R-R	6-5	230	8-28-82	0	1	2.45	1	1	0	0	4	6	3	1	0	0	1	.333	.357	.250	2.45	0.00
Zambrano, Carlos	R-R	6-5	270	6-1-81	0	0	0.00	1	1	0	0	4	3	1	0	0	3	4	.250	.333	.167	9.00	6.75

Fielding

Catcher

Catcher	PCT	G	PO	A	E	DP	PB
Burruel	.990	54	355	31	4	2	6
Gibbs	.991	84	635	63	6	5	5
Noble	1.000	2	3	1	0	0	0

	PCT	G	PO	A	E	DP	PB
Macias	.962	5	13	12	1	5	
Silva	.936	29	51	81	9	14	
Soto	.989	16	35	53	1	15	
Valdes	1.000	4	8	10	0	3	

	PCT	G	PO	A	E	DP	PB
Socorro	.939	10	15	31	3	7	
Soto	.974	59	91	174	7	44	
Valdes	.929	20	31	61	7	6	

First Base

First Base	PCT	G	PO	A	E	DP
Borges	.000	1	0	0	0	0
Cuneo	.993	33	277	16	2	28
Geiger	1.000	7	50	8	0	5
Giansanti	1.000	1	4	0	0	0
Jones	.986	89	722	44	11	74
Rohan	.992	15	112	8	1	15

Second Base

Second Base	PCT	G	PO	A	E	DP
Alcantara	.918	22	48	53	9	16
Giansanti	1.000	1	3	4	0	0
LePage	.977	63	135	165	7	43

Third Base

Third Base	PCT	G	PO	A	E	DP
Alcantara	.841	23	20	33	10	3
Geiger	.876	35	27	72	14	4
Giansanti	.889	11	8	24	4	3
May	.840	21	15	27	8	4
Rohan	.904	46	29	84	12	10
Soto	1.000	8	5	15	0	2
Valdes	.800	1	2	2	1	0

Shortstop

Shortstop	PCT	G	PO	A	E	DP
Alcantara	.917	52	77	154	21	33
Macias	.667	1	2	0	1	0

Outfield

Outfield	PCT	G	PO	A	E	DP
Andreoli	1.000	6	10	0	0	0
Borges	.977	26	41	1	1	1
Cuneo	1.000	2	1	0	0	0
Easterling	.976	37	77	3	2	0
Fitzgerald	.959	29	45	2	2	0
Giansanti	.976	108	218	24	6	6
Klafczynski	.968	33	57	3	2	1
Morelli	.963	16	26	0	1	0
Na	.932	28	53	2	4	1
Rohan	.929	12	25	1	2	0
Silva	.967	61	138	9	5	2
Szczur	.993	66	141	3	1	1

BOISE HAWKS   SHORT-SEASON

NORTHWEST LEAGUE

Batting	B-T	HT	WT	DOB	AVG	vLH	vRH	G	AB	R	H	2B	3B	HR	RBI	BB	HBP	SH	SF	SO	SB	CS	SLG	OBP
Baez, Javier	R-R	6-0	180	12-1-92	.167	.000	.250	2	6	0	1	0	0	0	1	0	0	0	0	2	0	0	.167	.167
Bieneme, Vismeldy	B-R	5-10	160	3-19-90	.000	.000	.000	1	3	1	0	0	0	0	0	2	0	0	0	2	1	0	.000	.400
Cabeza, Yaniel	R-R	5-11	185	4-19-89	.201	.261	.178	47	164	17	33	7	0	1	17	15	3	0	1	15	2	3	.262	.279
Chen, Pin-Chieh	L-R	6-1	170	7-23-91	.301	.279	.306	60	229	34	69	14	4	2	30	25	0	0	5	44	20	6	.424	.363
Contreras, Willson	R-R	6-1	175	5-13-92	.261	.417	.218	60	222	31	58	5	4	2	27	11	3	0	0	41	3	2	.347	.305
Cuneo, Ryan	L-R	6-3	190	10-10-88	.347	.188	.390	21	75	13	26	10	0	6	29	10	2	0	2	13	0	0	.720	.427
Darvill, Wes	L-R	6-2	175	9-10-91	.256	.255	.256	66	223	29	57	14	0	0	12	29	2	0	0	50	7	4	.318	.346
DeVoss, Zeke	B-R	5-10	171	7-17-90	.311	.313	.310	38	132	28	41	8	1	0	14	32	4	0	0	28	14	4	.386	.458
Fitzgerald, D.J.	R-R	6-0	190	12-20-88	.143	.000	.167	2	7	0	1	0	0	0	0	0	0	0	0	2	0	1	.143	.143
Garcia, Travis	R-R	5-10	190	3-31-89	.280	.000	.368	9	25	4	7	3	1	0	2	2	2	0	1	8	0	0	.480	.367
Golden, Reggie	R-R	5-10	210	10-10-91	.242	.154	.268	64	231	36	56	10	5	7	39	28	4	0	2	68	5	2	.420	.332
Guevara, Jose	R-R	6-1	180	3-17-88	.214	.000	.273	5	14	2	3	0	0	1	2	0	0	0	0	3	0	0	.429	.214
Harrington, Dustin	R-R	5-11	180	11-14-88	.301	.441	.232	29	103	15	31	6	0	0	4	5	1	0	0	23	1	1	.359	.339
Hoilman, Paul	R-R	6-4	240	2-11-89	.252	.278	.245	71	246	46	62	13	0	17	44	49	4	0	1	105	2	0	.512	.383
Klafczynski, Ben	L-R	6-3	195	9-21-88	.221	.214	.222	19	77	6	17	2	1	1	11	6	0	0	1	27	0	0	.312	.274
Lopez, Rafael	L-R	5-9	190	10-2-87	.316	.320	.315	54	196	34	62	8	0	6	37	21	2	0	4	27	1	2	.449	.381
Mercedes, Mario	R-R	5-11	195	11-22-86	.474	.125	.727	5	19	1	9	1	0	0	2	1	0	0	0	1	0	0	.526	.500
Morelli, Jesus	R-R	6-3	180	4-25-90	.273	.231	.300	9	33	3	9	1	0	1	4	2	1	0	0	6	2	0	.394	.333
Na, Kyung-Min	L-L	5-10	170	12-12-91	.171	.235	.153	25	76	10	13	1	0	0	4	9	2	0	0	15	6	3	.184	.276
Noble, Chad	R-R	6-1	210	11-18-87	.257	.667	.219	9	35	6	9	1	0	0	6	3	0	0	1	12	0	0	.286	.308
Romero, Carlos	R-R	6-1	180	5-28-90	.000	.000	.000	1	1	0	0	0	0	0	0	0	0	0	0	0	0	0	.000	.000
Socorro, Kenny	R-R	5-9	175	6-2-89	.200	.190	.204	23	75	5	15	2	0	0	6	5	0	0	1	10	0	0	.227	.247
Springfield, Blair	R-R	5-11	190	2-18-91	.206	.241	.192	32	102	15	21	3	0	2	14	16	0	0	0	25	2	1	.294	.314
Zapata, Oliver	B-R	5-9	180	9-13-92	.224	.235	.221	24	85	15	19	4	2	2	10	8	0	0	1	18	4	3	.388	.287
Zapenas, Brad	R-R	5-11	185	12-4-89	.238	.200	.248	45	151	19	36	7	0	1	18	13	5	0	4	30	0	0	.338	.312

Pitching	B-T	HT	WT	DOB	W	L	ERA	G	GS	CG	SV	IP	H	R	ER	HR	BB	SO	AVG	vLH	vRH	K/9	BB/9
Cruz, Willengton	R-L	6-2	170	8-8-90	1	2	3.71	13	13	0	0	53	50	27	22	5	31	50	.254	.333	.234	8.44	5.23
Fitzgerald, Dustin	R-R	6-4	210	12-6-89	3	1	3.19	20	0	0	2	31	26	18	11	1	23	27	.228	.314	.190	7.84	6.68
Greathouse, Cam	L-L	6-2	230	7-29-90	0	5	7.58	9	0	0	0	19	19	20	16	2	25	25	.257	.238	.264	11.84	11.84
Jensen, Michael	R-R	6-1	185	12-10-90	0	0	0.00	2	0	0	0	2	1	2	0	0	2	2	.143	.000	.200	10.80	10.80

Pitching	B-T	HT	WT	DOB	W	L	ERA	G	GS	CG	SV	IP	H	R	ER	HR	BB	SO	AVG	vLH	vRH	K/9	BB/9
Jung, Su-Min	R-R	6-2	190	4-1-90	0	1	4.15	9	4	0	0	22	15	16	10	2	25	18	.197	.250	.159	7.48	10.38
Kim, Jin-Young	R-R	6-1	190	4-16-92	2	2	7.66	9	2	0	0	25	38	21	21	4	15	16	.376	.289	.429	5.84	5.47
Liria, Luis	B-R	6-2	170	1-15-90	2	1	2.84	5	5	0	0	25	16	10	8	1	7	24	.184	.200	.179	8.53	2.49
Mayora, Hector	R-R	6-1	178	6-22-89	1	3	5.29	11	0	0	0	17	22	13	10	1	9	15	.301	.296	.304	7.94	4.76
McDonald, Sheldon	L-L	5-11	205	11-5-88	0	0	4.91	4	0	0	0	11	14	6	6	2	2	7	.326	.333	.320	5.73	1.64
McKirahan, Andrew	R-L	6-2	195	2-8-90	0	1	2.25	4	0	0	0	4	4	1	1	0	4	6	.250	.429	.111	13.50	9.00
Reed, Austin	R-R	6-3	200	10-31-91	2	7	6.08	15	13	0	0	64	82	51	43	5	25	36	.320	.327	.316	5.09	3.53
Richardson, Colin	R-R	6-1	180	8-13-91	1	0	5.64	15	0	0	1	30	36	20	19	1	12	25	.295	.245	.329	7.42	3.56
Rodriguez, Santo	L-R	6-1	185	9-26-89	0	0	24.00	2	0	0	0	3	7	8	8	1	2	4	.438	.500	.417	12.00	6.00
Rosario, Jose	R-R	6-1	170	8-29-90	6	3	3.53	15	7	0	2	64	67	36	25	1	18	50	.266	.315	.229	7.07	2.54
Sanchez, Yilver	R-R	6-2	198	7-31-90	0	0	4.05	4	0	0	1	7	8	3	3	0	1	4	.308	.286	.333	5.40	1.35
Sandoval, Jean	R-R	6-1	190	7-28-88	2	1	1.13	7	2	0	0	24	15	6	3	1	6	26	.174	.200	.164	9.75	2.25
Shafer, Bryce	R-R	6-0	180	11-14-88	3	2	2.45	23	0	0	12	26	18	7	7	0	11	35	.189	.241	.167	12.27	3.86
Thomas, Charles	R-R	6-4	225	7-2-88	1	2	4.35	17	0	0	0	21	20	14	10	1	21	22	.253	.259	.250	9.58	9.15
Wang, Yao-Lin	R-R	6-0	180	2-5-91	4	4	3.22	14	14	0	0	67	64	25	24	7	20	77	.259	.186	.310	10.34	2.69
Wells, Ben	R-R	6-2	220	9-10-92	4	4	4.66	16	15	0	0	77	83	47	40	4	19	53	.265	.289	.250	6.17	2.21
Zeller, Joe	R-R	5-10	190	10-17-87	2	0	1.95	12	1	0	3	28	26	6	6	0	6	18	.255	.306	.227	5.86	1.95
Zych, Tony	R-R	6-3	190	8-7-90	0	0	0.00	2	0	0	0	2	0	0	0	0	1	2	.000	.000	.000		4.50

Fielding

Catcher	PCT	G	PO	A	E	DP	PB
Cabeza	.995	41	331	32	2	1	6
Guevara	1.000	4	18	0	0	0	0
Lopez	.978	29	193	25	5	1	2
Mercedes	1.000	4	22	5	0	0	1
Noble	1.000	3	18	2	0	0	0
Romero	1.000	1	3	0	0	0	0

First Base	PCT	G	PO	A	E	DP
Contreras	.972	7	66	4	2	9
Cuneo	.973	14	129	14	4	16
Hoilman	.991	54	498	39	5	48
Lopez	1.000	1	8	0	0	0
Noble	1.000	2	14	6	0	1

Second Base	PCT	G	PO	A	E	DP
Bieneme	1.000	1	1	3	0	1
Contreras	.857	2	5	7	2	1

	PCT	G	PO	A	E	DP
Darvill	1.000	9	22	27	0	7
DeVoss	.914	28	57	81	13	22
Garcia	.000	1	0	0	0	0
Harrington	1.000	1	1	3	0	0
Socorro	.955	11	25	39	3	12
Zapenas	.986	27	54	82	2	18

Third Base	PCT	G	PO	A	E	DP
Contreras	.866	46	31	92	19	10
Garcia	1.000	5	2	9	0	1
Harrington	.962	15	16	34	2	8
Socorro	.933	9	7	21	2	1
Zapenas	1.000	6	1	10	0	1

Shortstop	PCT	G	PO	A	E	DP
Baez	.800	2	1	3	1	1
Darvill	.943	57	74	206	17	35
Harrington	.882	6	4	11	2	2

	PCT	G	PO	A	E	DP
Socorro	1.000	1	3	2	0	1
Zapenas	1.000	12	7	39	0	5

Outfield	PCT	G	PO	A	E	DP
Chen	1.000	58	84	3	0	0
Contreras	1.000	6	4	0	0	0
Cuneo	1.000	5	4	0	0	0
DeVoss	1.000	8	5	0	0	0
Fitzgerald	1.000	1	2	0	0	0
Garcia	1.000	2	6	0	0	0
Golden	.950	63	107	6	6	2
Klafczynski	.889	14	14	2	2	0
Morelli	1.000	9	9	0	0	0
Na	.968	22	30	0	1	0
Springfield	.977	26	36	6	1	0
Zapata	.939	24	31	0	2	0

AZL CUBS

ROOKIE

ARIZONA LEAGUE

Batting	B-T	HT	WT	DOB	AVG	vLH	vRH	G	AB	R	H	2B	3B	HR	RBI	BB	HBP	SH	SF	SO	SB	CS	SLG	OBP
Adduci, Jim	L-L	6-2	210	5-15-85	.176	.200	.167	4	17	0	3	0	0	0	0	0	0	0	0	2	2	0	.176	.176
Amaya, Gioskar	R-R	5-11	175	12-13-92	.377	.458	.353	52	204	37	77	11	8	0	36	13	3	0	3	39	13	8	.510	.417
Andreoli, John	R-R	6-1	215	6-9-90	.429	.000	.429	2	7	1	3	0	0	0	0	0	1	0	0	0	1	0	.429	.500
Baez, Javier	R-R	6-0	180	12-1-92	.333	1.000	.273	3	12	2	4	2	0	0	0	0	0	0	0	2	2	0	.500	.333
Bieneme, Vismeldy	B-R	5-10	160	3-19-90	.333	1.000	.250	3	9	2	3	0	0	0	0	0	0	0	0	3	0	1	.333	.333
Cabeza, Yaniel	R-R	5-11	185	4-19-89	.222	.000	.250	3	9	0	2	0	0	0	1	2	0	0	0	2	1	0	.222	.364
Castillo, Welington	R-R	5-10	210	4-24-87	.667	1.000	.600	2	6	2	4	3	0	0	0	3	0	0	0	0	0	0	1.167	.778
Cuneo, Ryan	L-R	6-3	190	10-10-88	.333	.250	.400	2	9	1	3	1	0	0	2	0	0	0	0	1	0	0	.444	.333
Davis, Taylor	R-R	5-11	185	11-28-89	.308	.167	.333	11	39	10	12	1	3	0	10	5	1	0	1	3	0	0	.487	.391
De Jesus, Johan	R-R	5-11	180	8-24-88	.172	.182	.167	9	29	4	5	0	0	0	2	1	1	0	1	10	1	0	.172	.219
DeVoss, Zeke	B-R	5-10	171	7-17-90	.294	.000	.333	4	17	4	5	1	0	0	3	1	1	0	0	4	2	0	.353	.368
Durrence, Ryan	R-R	6-2	230	8-28-88	.247	.286	.234	47	170	24	42	16	1	3	27	12	5	0	1	42	1	3	.406	.314
Easterling, Taiwan	R-R	5-11	195	2-24-89	.500	.625	.450	7	28	10	14	2	2	0	1	1	0	0	0	4	1	2	.714	.517
Garcia, Travis	R-R	5-10	190	3-31-89	.167	.000	.200	5	18	1	3	0	1	0	2	0	0	0	0	3	0	0	.278	.167
Geiger, Dustin	R-R	6-2	180	12-2-91	.342	.368	.333	19	79	14	27	9	2	2	20	3	0	0	0	15	1	3	.582	.366
Gonzalez, Eduardo	L-L	5-10	170	2-9-92	.336	.231	.388	34	119	18	40	2	2	0	13	7	1	0	3	16	5	5	.487	.369
Gonzalez, Gregori	R-R	5-9	170	7-11-89	.330	.357	.322	37	115	30	38	5	6	2	23	4	2	0	3	19	4	4	.530	.355
Guevara, Jose	R-R	6-1	180	3-17-88	.000	.000	.000	1	3	0	0	0	0	0	0	0	0	0	0	1	0	0	.000	.000
Hernandez, Marco	L-R	6-0	170	9-6-92	.333	.241	.365	51	210	39	70	16	5	2	42	16	1	0	5	29	9	7	.486	.375
Inoa, Brain	B-R	5-10	170	2-21-92	.282	.207	.301	40	142	26	40	8	5	0	18	13	0	0	2	36	8	5	.408	.338
Kim, Dong-Yub	R-R	6-4	200	7-24-90	.250	.355	.220	37	140	23	35	9	2	2	13	4	3	0	0	38	12	1	.386	.286
Kwan, Max	R-R	6-2	210	12-30-86	.200	.250	.182	6	15	1	3	0	0	0	2	4	1	0	1	4	0	0	.200	.381
LePage, Pierre	R-R	5-8	168	2-23-89	.667	.000	.667	1	3	0	2	0	0	0	1	0	0	0	0	0	1	0	.667	.667
Lockhart, Daniel	R-R	5-11	165	11-14-92	.219	.000	.241	7	32	1	7	0	0	0	3	2	0	0	0	7	2	1	.219	.265
Lopez, Rafael	L-R	5-9	190	10-2-87	.364	.500	.333	3	11	1	4	1	0	0	2	1	0	0	0	1	0	0	.455	.417
Martin, Darien	R-R	6-2	188	12-11-92	.243	.000	.279	18	70	10	17	0	4	0	8	4	1	0	1	17	3	2	.357	.289
Morelli, Jesus	R-R	6-3	180	4-5-90	.250	.000	.286	2	8	1	2	0	0	0	1	2	1	0	0	0	0	0	.625	.333
Na, Kyung-Min	L-L	5-10	170	12-12-91	.360	.350	.363	28	100	21	36	5	1	0	15	15	2	0	0	15	9	6	.430	.453
Opitz, Jake	L-R	6-0	190	7-28-86	.333	.000	.333	1	3	1	1	0	0	0	1	0	0	0	0	0	0	0	.333	.500
Romero, Carlos	R-R	6-1	180	5-28-90	.246	.357	.209	19	57	6	14	2	0	0	3	3	0	0	0	9	0	0	.281	.283
Rosario, Neftali	R-R	5-11	193	7-22-93	.294	.286	.296	25	102	18	30	5	3	3	17	6	3	0	0	28	1	0	.490	.351
Schlecht, Garrett	L-L	6-2	190	2-15-93	.222	.000	.250	9	27	5	6	0	0	0	3	0	0	0	0	10	0	0	.222	.417

Batting

Batting	B-T	HT	WT	DOB	AVG	vLH	vRH	G	AB	R	H	2B	3B	HR	RBI	BB	HBP	SH	SF	SO	SB	CS	SLG	OBP
Shoulders, Roderick	L-R	6-2	225	9-26-91	.188	.250	.179	8	32	4	6	5	0	0	3	3	0	0	0	10	0	0	.344	.257
Smith, Marquez	R-R	5-10	205	3-20-85	.250	.000	.333	1	4	1	1	0	0	0	0	0	0	0	0	1	1	0	.250	.250
Socorro, Kenny	R-R	5-9	175	6-2-89	.750	.500	1.000	1	4	0	3	2	0	0	3	0	0	0	0	0	0	0	11.250	.750
Springfield, Blair	R-R	5-11	190	2-18-91	.333	.400	.310	11	39	2	13	4	0	1	9	2	1	0	0	9	3	0	.513	.381
Valdez, Jose	B-R	6-1	170	9-5-87	.333	.000	.333	1	3	0	1	0	0	0	1	1	0	0	0	1	0	0	.333	.500
Vogelbach, Daniel	L-R	6-0	250	12-17-92	.292	.667	.238	6	24	4	7	3	0	1	6	2	1	0	0	2	1	0	.542	.370
Zapata, Oliver	B-R	5-9	180	9-13-92	.324	.280	.338	31	102	26	33	4	2	1	12	24	1	0	1	15	12	5	.431	.453

Pitching

Pitching	B-T	HT	WT	DOB	W	L	ERA	G	GS	CG	SV	IP	H	R	ER	HR	BB	SO	AVG	vLH	vRH	K/9	BB/9
Ackerman, Hunter	L-L	6-1	190	10-24-90	0	3	3.68	13	9	0	0	44	46	29	18	3	21	49	.264	.273	.262	10.02	4.30
Del Valle, Frank	L-L	5-11	190	9-16-89	0	0	0.00	3	3	0	0	8	1	0	0	0	3	11	.043	.200	.000	12.38	3.38
Diplan, Rafael	R-R	6-1	190	10-27-91	0	1	7.07	12	0	0	1	14	14	14	11	3	12	8	.264	.238	.281	5.14	7.71
Francescon, Patrick	R-R	5-11	185	1-4-89	0	0	0.00	1	0	0	1	2	1	0	0	0	0	2	.167	.000	.200	9.00	0.00
Garcia, Ramon	R-R	6-2	170	8-2-91	5	0	3.12	9	1	0	0	35	46	14	12	1	7	25	.324	.478	.250	6.49	1.82
Greathouse, Cam	L-L	6-2	230	7-29-90	0	0	4.38	4	0	0	0	12	14	10	6	2	9	13	.280	.500	.250	9.49	6.57
Hartman, Ryan	R-R	6-3	180	5-10-92	3	0	4.39	14	0	0	0	27	27	19	13	3	20	33	.260	.292	.250	11.14	6.75
Hicks, Graham	L-L	6-5	170	2-9-90	0	0	3.38	2	2	0	0	3	3	1	1	0	1	4	.333	.000	.333	13.50	3.38
Jensen, Michael	R-R	6-1	185	12-10-90	0	0	0.00	2	2	0	0	3	1	0	0	0	0	3	.100	.143	.000	9.00	0.00
Jimenez, Alvido	R-R	6-1	160	11-22-91	3	1	2.50	13	0	0	2	36	34	14	10	1	13	22	.262	.286	.250	5.50	3.25
Kim, Jin-Young	R-R	6-1	190	4-16-92	2	0	1.74	6	1	0	0	21	25	10	4	1	3	15	.287	.325	.255	6.53	1.31
Levitt, Pete	R-R	6-5	235	4-24-89	0	0	6.00	3	0	0	1	6	9	4	4	0	2	5	.360	.000	.474	7.50	3.00
Mayora, Hector	R-R	6-1	178	6-22-89	0	0	0.00	2	1	0	0	3	4	3	0	0	2	2	.308	.333	.300	6.75	0.00
McDonald, Sheldon	L-L	5-11	205	11-5-88	0	0	2.25	5	0	0	0	8	8	7	2	0	4	9	.258	.600	.192	10.13	4.50
McKirahan, Andrew	R-L	6-2	195	2-8-90	0	1	1.42	11	0	0	0	13	8	2	2	1	4	18	.178	.200	.171	12.08	2.84
Negrin, Yoanner	R-R	5-11	190	4-29-84	1	0	0.00	3	0	0	0	4	3	0	0	0	3	7	.214	.500	.167	14.54	6.23
Paulino, Amaury	R-R	6-1	175	8-31-91	0	0	0.00	3	2	0	0	3	3	0	0	0	0	1	2	.273	.000	.429	6.00	3.00
Pena, Felix	R-R	6-1	186	2-25-90	3	2	6.92	17	0	0	1	39	48	35	30	8	9	32	.296	.365	.264	7.38	2.08
Peralta, Starlin	R-R	6-4	180	11-11-90	2	1	3.46	3	2	0	0	13	14	5	5	0	2	18	.275	.333	.242	12.46	1.38
Pichardo, Roderick	R-R	5-10	180	9-24-90	1	0	2.08	4	1	0	0	13	10	4	3	1	4	13	.204	.308	.167	9.00	2.77
Pugliese, James	R-R	6-3	195	8-12-92	2	2	4.62	15	9	0	0	39	47	23	20	2	12	32	.296	.323	.277	7.38	2.77
Richardson, Colin	R-R	6-1	180	8-13-91	0	1	12.46	3	0	0	0	4	7	6	6	0	3	3	.350	.222	.455	6.23	6.23
Rodriguez, Santo	L-R	6-1	185	9-26-89	1	3	10.06	16	0	0	0	17	26	25	19	4	10	16	.338	.385	.314	8.47	5.29
Sanchez, Yilver	R-R	6-2	198	7-31-90	1	3	2.39	14	0	0	2	26	36	14	7	0	6	32	.330	.333	.329	10.94	2.05
Sandoval, Jean	R-R	6-1	190	7-28-88	1	1	3.00	8	1	0	0	27	26	15	9	3	7	21	.252	.216	.273	7.00	2.33
Scott, Tayler	R-R	6-3	165	6-1-92	0	0	7.36	2	0	0	0	4	4	3	3	0	1	2	.267	.286	.250	4.91	2.45
Simpson, Hayden	R-R	6-0	170	5-20-89	1	0	8.15	11	9	0	0	18	26	18	16	1	11	11	.356	.346	.362	5.60	5.60
Smith, Brian	L-L	6-0	170	12-14-90	3	4	3.30	14	12	0	0	46	46	22	17	1	23	41	.258	.238	.265	7.96	4.47
Villalba, Luis	L-L	6-2	182	10-28-92	0	1	8.31	4	1	0	0	4	5	5	4	0	4	4	.294	.000	.333	8.31	8.31
Zeller, Joe	R-R	5-10	190	10-17-87	0	0	5.79	2	0	0	1	5	7	6	3	0	1	5	.333	.250	.385	9.64	1.93
Zych, Tony	R-R	6-3	190	8-7-90	0	0	4.50	2	0	0	0	2	2	2	1	0	1	3	.250	.500	.167	13.50	4.50

Fielding

Catcher	PCT	G	PO	A	E	DP	PB
Cabeza	.952	3	19	1	1	0	0
Castillo	1.000	1	5	1	0	0	0
Davis	.956	6	37	6	2	0	1
De Jesus	.977	9	76	9	2	0	3
Guevara	1.000	1	5	1	0	0	0
Inoa	1.000	1	1	0	0	0	0
Lopez	1.000	5	20	2	0	0	0
Romero	.993	18	122	15	1	0	5
Rosario	.974	21	166	20	5	3	8

First Base	PCT	G	PO	A	E	DP
Cuneo	1.000	2	19	5	0	5
Davis	1.000	1	5	1	0	0
Durrence	.979	40	305	15	7	25
Geiger	1.000	7	38	2	0	4
Inoa	.909	3	20	0	2	1
Rosario	1.000	1	6	0	0	0
Shoulders	1.000	5	29	5	0	4
Vogelbach	.962	3	24	1	1	4

Second Base	PCT	G	PO	A	E	DP
Amaya	.950	17	32	44	4	12

	PCT	G	PO	A	E	DP
Bieneme	.875	1	2	5	1	2
DeVoss	.941	3	8	8	1	1
Gonzalez	1.000	1	0	1	0	0
Gonzalez	1.000	3	1	1	0	0
Hernandez	.965	14	27	28	2	3
Inoa	.890	21	34	47	10	8
LePage	.875	1	4	3	1	0
Lockhart	.867	3	7	6	2	3
Smith	1.000	1	2	4	0	2

Third Base	PCT	G	PO	A	E	DP
Amaya	.864	20	19	32	8	2
Bieneme	.000	1	0	0	0	0
Durrence	.750	1	3	0	1	0
Garcia	.889	4	1	7	1	0
Geiger	.938	15	12	33	3	6
Gonzalez	.893	16	5	20	3	2
Hernandez	.900	5	3	6	1	0
Lockhart	1.000	1	3	1	0	0
Opitz	1.000	1	0	2	0	0

Shortstop	PCT	G	PO	A	E	DP
Amaya	.932	18	22	47	5	4

	PCT	G	PO	A	E	DP
Baez	.773	3	4	13	5	5
Hernandez	.953	33	48	94	7	23
Lockhart	.929	3	4	9	1	1
Socorro	1.000	1	1	6	0	1

Outfield	PCT	G	PO	A	E	DP
Adduci	1.000	2	1	0	0	0
Andreoli	1.000	2	2	0	0	0
Durrence	1.000	2	2	0	0	0
Easterling	1.000	7	20	1	0	0
Gonzalez	.906	32	47	1	5	1
Gonzalez	.951	18	31	8	2	2
Inoa	1.000	7	7	2	0	0
Kim	1.000	18	28	1	0	0
Kwan	1.000	3	6	0	0	0
Martin	1.000	18	51	0	0	0
Morelli	1.000	1	1	1	0	1
Na	.984	28	59	2	1	0
Schlecht	1.000	7	12	1	0	0
Springfield	1.000	9	16	2	0	0
Valdez	1.000	1	1	0	0	0
Zapata	.967	30	56	2	2	0

DSL CUBS 1

DOMINICAN SUMMER LEAGUE

ROOKIE

Batting	B-T	HT	WT	DOB	AVG	vLH	vRH	G	AB	R	H	2B	3B	HR	RBI	BB	HBP	SH	SF	SO	SB	CS	SLG	OBP
Baez, Jeffrey	R-R	6-0	180	10-30-93	.300	.154	.340	30	120	27	36	5	1	2	17	12	1	0	0	23	19	3	.408	.368
2-team total (38 Cubs 2)					.282	—	—	68	262	57	74	12	3	5	36	24	5	0	1	55	32	10	.408	.353
Batista, Xavier	R-R	6-3	190	1-18-92	.273	.304	.263	28	99	19	27	6	1	5	17	13	2	0	1	24	4	0	.505	.365
2-team total (39 Cubs 2)					.259	—	—	67	212	36	55	11	2	10	38	36	4	0	4	61	7	4	.472	.371
Cabrera, Frammi	R-R	6-3	170	1-11-90	.253	.211	.264	28	91	15	23	2	0	0	10	14	0	0	0	9	7	5	.275	.352

Batting

Batting	B-T	HT	WT	DOB	AVG	vLH	vRH	G	AB	R	H	2B	3B	HR	RBI	BB	HBP	SH	SF	SO	SB	CS	SLG	OBP
2-team total (41 Cubs 2)					.265	—	—	69	219	34	58	3	0	0	25	29	1	0	2	32	15	10	.279	.351
Calero, Arnaldo	R-R	6-1	175	11-16-93	.204	.091	.237	15	49	3	10	0	0	0	3	3	1	0	0	13	2	1	.204	.264
Casilla, Jose	R-R	6-2	205	1-10-92	.205	.125	.233	42	122	24	25	6	3	2	13	20	4	0	0	46	5	2	.352	.336
Contreras, Edwin	L-L	6-0	190	12-13-93	.162	.167	.160	31	99	8	16	3	2	0	13	11	0	0	2	25	1	2	.232	.241
Cuevas, Varonex	B-R	6-0	165	7-24-92	.165	.294	.124	49	139	18	23	1	2	0	14	27	1	0	3	34	7	6	.201	.300
De La Cruz, Steven	R-R	6-0	183	12-13-93	.086	.143	.071	21	35	2	3	1	0	0	7	8	0	0	1	10	0	0	.114	.250
2-team total (11 Cubs 2)					.164	—	—	32	61	5	10	2	0	0	9	10	9	1	0	1	16	0	0	.197	.278
Encarnacion, Kelvin	B-R	6-0	175	11-23-91	.374	.281	.407	35	123	20	46	1	9	1	17	15	0	0	0	9	25	5	.553	.442
2-team total (31 Cubs 2)					.296	—	—	66	223	38	66	4	11	1	27	35	2	0	0	35	28	8	.426	.396
Figueroa, Darlyn	R-R	6-3	190	12-21-89	.219	.091	.286	10	32	6	7	3	0	0	3	3	1	0	0	9	3	1	.313	.306
2-team total (29 Cubs 2)					.188	—	—	39	112	27	21	6	0	4	14	21	5	0	0	34	6	4	.348	.341
Gonzalez, Antonio	B-R	5-10	170	1-27-94	.196	.087	.232	36	92	11	18	3	1	0	6	20	0	0	0	24	5	5	.250	.339
2-team total (23 Cubs 2)					.214	—	—	59	168	24	36	4	2	0	12	35	0	0	0	47	11	10	.262	.350
Gonzalez, Jasly	R-R	6-3	190	1-28-91	.000	.000	.000	1	1	0	0	0	0	0	0	0	0	0	0	1	0	0	.000	.000
Jimenez, Gabriel	L-L	6-0	188	9-26-93	.150	.107	.165	17	113	17	17	6	1	0	16	25	5	0	0	42	5	3	.221	.329
Mercedes, Enderson	R-R	6-2	180	12-4-92	.140	.083	.156	24	57	6	8	2	0	1	3	3	1	0	0	28	1	2	.228	.197
2-team total (27 Cubs 2)					.188	—	—	51	133	17	25	3	0	1	6	16	2	0	1	52	3	4	.233	.283
Montecino, Jose	B-R	5-11	175	7-31-90	.233	.200	.242	17	43	9	10	1	1	0	2	15	0	0	0	8	4	1	.302	.431
2-team total (32 Cubs 2)					.210	—	—	49	81	19	17	2	1	0	4	25	1	0	1	16	11	4	.259	.398
Montero, Carlos	R-R	6-0	175	7-6-91	.217	.111	.243	15	46	5	10	0	0	0	5	6	1	0	0	5	7	1	.217	.321
Ortega, John	R-R	5-11	152	5-4-94	.227	.313	.200	27	66	20	15	2	0	0	3	22	2	0	0	16	16	5	.258	.433
2-team total (3 Cubs 2)					.260	—	—	30	73	22	19	3	0	0	4	23	0	0	0	17	17	5	.301	.449
Pena, Jhonny	R-R	6-0	190	5-24-92	.204	.259	.186	45	113	10	23	7	0	0	10	15	7	0	0	17	0	0	.265	.333
Pestana, Manuel	R-R	6-0	150	3-9-94	.188	.000	.214	15	32	7	6	1	1	0	7	1	2	0	1	2	2	1	.281	.250
Reyes, Mayke	R-R	6-0	200	4-11-87	.297	.257	.309	55	158	34	47	5	3	3	18	35	11	0	0	25	23	13	.424	.456
Rodriguez, Jesus	B-R	6-0	170	9-5-91	.197	.071	.234	21	61	12	12	0	0	0	11	15	4	0	0	14	6	4	.197	.388
2-team total (36 Cubs 2)					.256	—	—	57	172	35	44	5	3	2	27	24	5	0	1	39	11	8	.355	.361
Sanchez, Francisco	R-R	6-1	170	12-17-93	.191	.245	.174	60	204	26	39	6	2	6	29	25	8	0	4	67	9	6	.328	.299
Suarez, Hector	B-R	6-1	170	5-5-92	.192	.125	.222	25	52	6	10	2	0	0	6	19	3	0	0	19	0	0	.231	.432
2-team total (2 Cubs 2)					.230	—	—	27	61	7	14	3	0	0	8	20	3	0	0	19	0	0	.279	.440
Valerio, Antonio	R-R	6-0	190	3-21-91	.205	.267	.190	21	73	8	15	4	0	1	14	8	0	0	1	15	3	0	.301	.280
2-team total (31 Cubs 2)					.203	—	—	52	148	16	30	5	0	1	20	17	3	0	1	30	4	1	.257	.296

Pitching

Pitching	B-T	HT	WT	DOB	W	L	ERA	G	GS	CG	SV	IP	H	R	ER	HR	BB	SO	AVG	vLH	vRH	K/9	BB/9
Abreu, Gilberto	R-R	6-2	180	8-8-93	1	4	4.84	13	9	0	0	35	29	31	19	1	34	34	.216	.222	.213	8.66	8.66
Cabreja, Enger	R-R	6-2	180	1-28-92	0	3	4.71	14	8	0	1	42	36	30	22	0	38	26	.248	.311	.220	5.57	8.14
Colinas, Augusto	L-L	6-0	178	12-20-92	1	1	2.53	10	0	0	2	21	23	6	6	0	9	19	.288	.375	.278	8.02	3.80
2-team total (10 Cubs 2)					5	2	2.65	20	0	0	2	37	40	12	11	1	12	35	—	—	—	8.44	2.89
De la Cruz, Juancito	R-R	6-3	170	1-21-93	1	4	4.14	15	4	0	0	46	32	28	21	0	28	43	.187	.123	.219	8.47	5.52
Diaz, Alberto	L-L	5-9	157	6-12-91	0	3	3.18	9	0	0	2	11	12	8	4	0	12	6	.316	.667	.286	4.76	9.53
2-team total (2 Cubs 2)					1	3	2.51	11	0	0	2	14	15	8	4	0	14	8	—	—	—	5.02	8.79
Diaz, Jorge	R-R	6-6	190	1-20-92	2	3	9.85	13	6	0	0	25	41	31	27	0	21	17	.383	.455	.351	6.20	7.66
Eusebio, Warner	L-L	5-9	164	9-1-93	2	1	2.19	10	5	0	0	37	26	12	9	1	10	30	.198	.138	.216	7.30	2.43
Frias, Alexander	R-R	6-4	180	5-29-92	0	1	9.00	5	0	0	0	7	9	7	7	0	9	7	.280	.125	.353	9.00	11.57
2-team total (7 Cubs 2)					2	1	5.50	12	0	0	1	18	17	13	11	1	14	12	—	—	—	6.00	7.00
Fuentes, Manuel	L-L	6-1	168	6-6-92	0	4	7.11	14	0	0	1	19	24	18	15	1	16	12	.293	.286	.294	5.68	7.58
Galvez, Carlos	L-L	6-1	170	4-26-90	0	0	1.69	6	0	0	0	11	8	3	2	0	2	6	.205	.250	.200	5.06	1.69
2-team total (15 Cubs 2)					3	1	2.95	21	1	0	0	43	46	19	14	0	12	29	—	—	—	6.12	2.53
Guillen, Luis	R-R	6-1	150	12-16-93	3	1	3.54	7	6	0	0	28	27	13	11	2	8	24	.245	.227	.258	7.71	2.57
2-team total (4 Cubs 2)					3	4	4.24	11	8	0	0	40	39	23	19	3	17	35	—	—	—	7.81	3.79
Leyba, Richard	L-L	6-4	210	10-25-91	0	1	11.93	8	0	0	0	14	26	22	19	0	24	17	.394	.000	.406	10.67	15.07
2-team total (5 Cubs 2)					3	1	6.59	13	0	0	1	29	39	31	21	0	35	27	—	—	—	8.48	10.99
Martinez, Jose	L-L	6-1	160	1-20-94	1	0	2.40	8	0	0	2	15	17	4	4	1	4	13	.279	.333	.265	7.80	2.40
Mejias, Angel	L-L	6-3	180	10-30-93	0	2	2.59	7	6	0	0	24	20	12	7	0	17	15	.227	.083	.250	5.55	6.29
2-team total (1 Cubs 2)					0	2	2.39	8	6	0	0	26	21	13	7	0	19	15	—	—	—	5.13	6.49
Morel, Yomar	R-R	6-1	180	11-18-93	3	3	2.61	9	3	0	0	31	19	14	9	0	17	31	.170	.205	.147	9.00	4.94
Padron, Loiger	R-R	6-0	180	1-31-91	3	1	2.28	10	1	0	0	24	18	8	6	0	12	12	.225	.263	.213	5.70	4.56
2-team total (7 Cubs 2)					6	3	2.44	17	6	0	1	63	40	20	17	0	24	49	—	—	—	7.04	3.45
Pichardo, Roderick	R-R	5-10	180	9-24-90	0	2	2.12	9	0	0	4	17	13	7	4	0	12	28	.206	.185	.222	14.82	6.35
Reyes, Amalio	R-R	6-2	175	5-22-91	0	1	4.50	3	3	0	0	12	10	7	6	1	10	10	.213	.286	.182	7.50	7.50
2-team total (1 Cubs 2)					0	1	4.50	4	3	0	0	14	12	8	7	1	10	12	—	—	—	7.71	6.43
Salazar, Victor	R-R	6-3	178	1-21-93	0	4	6.25	14	7	0	0	36	30	34	25	0	36	19	.224	.218	.228	4.75	9.00
Santana, Alex	R-R	6-1	170	10-23-93	3	0	1.54	7	6	0	0	35	24	12	6	0	6	15	.190	.196	.187	3.86	1.54
2-team total (8 Cubs 2)					4	2	2.67	15	14	0	0	67	59	29	20	3	20	36	—	—	—	4.81	2.67
Severino, Carlos	R-R	6-0	180	8-1-91	0	0	3.65	4	2	0	0	12	13	6	5	0	6	7	.317	.353	.292	5.11	4.38
Telles, Wladimir	R-R	6-1	200	2-5-93	1	1	4.74	13	0	0	0	25	20	14	13	2	15	20	.222	.229	.218	7.30	5.47
2-team total (7 Cubs 2)					2	1	4.50	20	0	0	1	42	40	23	21	3	24	27	—	—	—	5.79	5.14

Fielding

Catcher	PCT	G	PO	A	E	DP	PB
De La Cruz	.979	18	85	10	2	0	1
Pena	.983	34	141	28	3	2	9
Suarez	.938	18	107	14	8	1	6
Valerio	.966	16	98	15	4	1	0

First Base	PCT	G	PO	A	E	DP
Batista	.983	18	115	4	2	6
Cuevas	1.000	2	1	0	0	0
Figueroa	.974	5	33	4	1	1
Jimenez	.987	43	270	31	4	21
Montecino	1.000	1	1	0	0	0

	PCT	G	PO	A	E	DP
Pena	.979	8	42	4	1	3
Pestana	1.000	2	3	0	0	0
Reyes	.967	6	55	4	2	2
Suarez	.900	2	9	0	1	0

Second Base	PCT	G	PO	A	E	DP
Calero	.000	1	0	0	2	0
Cuevas	.980	17	20	30	1	5
Encarnacion	1.000	1	1	0	0	0
Gonzalez	.898	24	15	38	6	0
Montecino	.950	12	21	17	2	5
Ortega	.940	21	37	42	5	7
Reyes	1.000	2	2	3	0	0
Rodriguez	.900	2	4	5	1	1
Sanchez	.900	2	5	4	1	1

Third Base	PCT	G	PO	A	E	DP
Cuevas	.934	25	27	30	4	2
Gonzalez	.875	5	3	4	1	1

	PCT	G	PO	A	E	DP
Montecino	.909	5	3	7	1	1
Montero	.963	13	19	33	2	3
Reyes	.857	3	3	3	1	1
Rodriguez	.924	17	15	46	5	4
Sanchez	.769	3	1	9	3	0
Valerio	.950	5	3	16	1	0

Shortstop	PCT	G	PO	A	E	DP
Cuevas	.757	8	12	16	9	1
Gonzalez	.765	4	3	10	4	1
Ortega	1.000	3	5	9	0	2
Pena	1.000	1	1	0	0	0
Rodriguez	.929	3	7	6	1	1
Sanchez	.886	56	106	120	29	17

Outfield	PCT	G	PO	A	E	DP
Baez	.958	30	64	4	3	1
Batista	1.000	12	13	1	0	0
Cabrera	1.000	28	45	1	0	0
Calero	1.000	10	13	2	0	0
Casilla	.917	31	44	0	4	0
Contreras	.938	30	43	2	3	0
Encarnacion	.978	34	82	5	2	2
Figueroa	.000	1	0	0	0	0
Gonzalez	1.000	2	3	0	0	0
Gonzalez	.000	1	0	0	0	0
Mercedes	.933	19	12	2	1	0
Reyes	.957	28	43	2	2	0

DSL CUBS 2 — ROOKIE

DOMINICAN SUMMER LEAGUE

Batting	B-T	HT	WT	DOB	AVG	vLH	vRH	G	AB	R	H	2B	3B	HR	RBI	BB	HBP	SH	SF	SO	SB	CS	SLG	OBP
Arcila, Delbis	L-L	6-3	190	4-30-93	.258	.173	.283	65	225	42	58	12	4	5	44	36	2	0	0	52	7	4	.413	.365
Baez, Jeffrey	R-R	6-0	180	10-30-93	.268	.190	.300	38	142	30	38	7	2	3	19	12	4	0	1	32	13	7	.408	.340
2-team total (30 Cubs 1)					.282	—	—	68	262	57	74	12	3	5	36	24	5	0	1	55	32	10	.408	.353
Batista, Xavier	R-R	6-3	190	1-18-92	.248	.273	.238	39	113	17	28	5	1	5	21	23	2	0	3	37	3	4	.442	.376
2-team total (28 Cubs 1)					.259	—	—	67	212	36	55	11	2	10	38	36	4	0	4	61	7	4	.472	.371
Bonne, Elieser	R-R	6-2	180	2-17-87	.313	.229	.344	39	128	23	40	9	2	0	13	13	2	0	0	22	17	5	.414	.385
Cabrera, Frammi	R-R	6-3	170	1-11-90	.273	.194	.304	41	128	19	35	1	0	0	15	15	1	0	2	23	8	5	.281	.349
2-team total (28 Cubs 1)					.265	—	—	69	219	34	58	3	0	0	25	29	1	0	2	32	15	10	.279	.351
Candelario, Jeimer	B-R	6-1	180	11-24-93	.337	.280	.362	72	249	50	84	16	2	5	53	50	1	0	5	42	4	4	.478	.443
De La Cruz, Steven	R-R	6-0	183	12-13-93	.269	.333	.235	11	26	3	7	1	0	0	4	1	1	0	0	6	0	0	.308	.321
2-team total (21 Cubs 1)					.164	—	—	32	61	5	10	2	0	0	11	9	1	0	1	16	0	0	.197	.278
Encarnacion, Kelvin	B-R	6-0	175	11-23-91	.200	.100	.225	31	100	18	20	3	2	0	10	20	2	0	0	26	3	3	.270	.344
2-team total (35 Cubs 1)					.296	—	—	66	223	38	66	4	11	1	27	35	2	0	0	35	28	8	.426	.396
Figueroa, Darlyn	R-R	6-3	190	12-21-89	.175	.143	.182	29	80	21	14	3	0	4	14	18	4	0	0	35	6	3	.363	.353
2-team total (10 Cubs 1)					.188	—	—	39	112	27	21	6	0	4	14	21	5	0	0	34	6	4	.348	.341
Gonzalez, Antonio	B-R	5-10	170	1-27-94	.237	.269	.220	23	76	13	18	1	1	0	6	15	0	0	0	23	6	5	.276	.363
2-team total (36 Cubs 1)					.214	—	—	59	168	24	36	4	2	0	12	35	0	0	0	47	11	10	.262	.350
Gonzalez, Gregori	R-R	5-9	170	7-11-89	.000	.000	.000	1	1	0	0	0	0	0	0	0	0	0	0	0	0	0	.000	.000
Mercedes, Enderson	R-R	6-2	180	12-4-92	.224	.211	.228	27	76	11	17	1	0	0	3	13	1	0	1	24	2	2	.237	.341
2-team total (24 Cubs 1)					.188	—	—	51	133	17	25	3	0	1	6	16	2	0	1	52	3	4	.233	.283
Montecino, Jose	B-R	5-11	175	7-31-90	.184	.300	.143	32	38	10	7	1	0	0	2	10	1	0	1	8	7	3	.211	.360
2-team total (17 Cubs 1)					.210	—	—	49	81	19	17	2	1	0	4	25	1	0	1	16	11	4	.259	.398
Ortega, John	B-R	5-11	152	5-4-94	.571	1.000	.500	3	7	2	4	1	0	0	1	1	0	0	0	1	1	0	.714	.625
2-team total (27 Cubs 1)					.260	—	—	30	73	22	19	3	0	0	4	23	2	0	0	17	5	5	.301	.449
Penalver, Carlos	R-R	6-0	170	5-17-94	.272	.286	.266	72	261	51	71	11	2	1	38	35	5	0	4	42	21	8	.341	.364
Perez, Felix	R-R	5-10	170	5-24-92	.250	.333	.200	5	8	2	2	0	0	0	2	0	1	0	0	1	0	0	.250	.333
Petit, Wilfredo	B-R	5-11	165	2-9-93	.196	.077	.220	54	158	17	31	4	0	2	18	14	5	0	1	33	0	3	.259	.281
Puente, Jeffry	L-R	5-10	170	4-21-92	.231	.186	.245	66	182	51	42	7	8	2	33	39	7	0	4	45	11	2	.390	.379
Rodriguez, Jesus	B-R	6-0	170	9-5-91	.288	.259	.298	36	111	23	32	5	3	2	16	9	1	0	1	25	5	4	.441	.344
2-team total (21 Cubs 1)					.256	—	—	57	172	35	44	5	3	2	27	24	5	0	1	39	11	8	.355	.361
Suarez, Hector	B-R	6-1	170	5-5-92	.444	.000	.444	2	9	1	4	1	0	0	2	1	0	0	0	0	0	0	.556	.500
2-team total (25 Cubs 1)					.230	—	—	27	61	7	14	3	0	0	8	20	3	0	0	19	0	0	.279	.440
Valdez, Rander	R-R	6-2	180	9-28-91	.229	.188	.247	45	105	20	24	3	0	1	14	8	6	0	0	27	5	3	.286	.319
Valerio, Antonio	R-R	6-0	190	3-21-91	.200	.167	.222	31	75	8	15	1	0	0	6	9	3	0	0	15	1	1	.213	.310
2-team total (21 Cubs 1)					.203	—	—	52	148	16	30	5	0	1	20	17	3	0	1	30	4	1	.257	.296

Pitching	B-T	HT	WT	DOB	W	L	ERA	G	GS	CG	SV	IP	H	R	ER	HR	BB	SO	AVG	vLH	vRH	K/9	BB/9
Adrian, Daniel	R-R	6-1	175	12-7-90	3	0	3.10	12	0	0	1	29	29	10	10	0	8	24	.266	.375	.221	7.45	2.48
Araujo, Pedro	R-R	6-3	214	7-2-93	4	1	4.45	15	9	0	0	57	52	38	28	2	25	51	.250	.340	.224	8.10	3.97
Arias, Jose	R-R	6-5	220	1-17-91	1	1	2.28	12	10	0	0	43	31	16	11	2	8	50	.197	.240	.178	10.38	1.66
Castro, Javier	R-R	6-0	160	2-10-92	1	2	2.70	5	4	0	0	17	10	10	5	0	9	13	.164	.071	.191	7.02	4.86
Colinas, Augusto	L-L	6-0	178	12-20-92	4	1	2.81	10	0	0	0	16	17	6	5	1	3	16	.270	.143	.286	9.00	1.69
2-team total (10 Cubs 1)					5	2	2.65	20	0	0	2	37	40	12	11	1	12	35	—	—	—	8.44	2.89
Diaz, Alberto	L-L	5-9	157	6-12-91	1	0	0.00	2	0	0	0	3	3	0	0		2	2	.273	.000	.429	6.00	6.00
2-team total (9 Cubs 1)					1	3	2.51	11	0	0	2	14	15	8	4	0	14	8	—	—	—	5.02	8.79
Encarnacion, Antonio	R-R	6-1	170	11-6-91	0	0	4.50	6	0	0	0	6	5	3	3	0	6	4	.227	.500	.200	6.00	9.00
Frias, Alexander	R-R	6-4	180	5-29-92	2	0	3.27	7	0	0	1	11	10	4	4	0	5	5	.238	.200	.250	4.09	4.09
2-team total (5 Cubs 1)					2	1	5.50	12	0	0	1	18	17	13	11	1	14	12	—	—	—	6.00	7.00
Galvez, Carlos	L-L	6-1	170	4-26-90	3	3	3.38	15	1	0	0	32	38	16	12	0	10	23	.325	.400	.318	6.47	2.81
2-team total (6 Cubs 1)					3	3	2.95	21	1	0	0	43	46	19	14	0	12	29	—	—	—	6.12	2.53
Garcia, Victor	L-L	6-2	175	4-1-92	3	3	2.95	14	8	0	0	55	43	26	18	2	27	64	.216	.167	.219	10.47	4.42
Gonzalez, Enyel	R-R	6-2	195	9-4-91	0	1	10.38	2	2	0	0	4	4	8	5	0	3	2	.250	.250	.250	4.15	6.23
Guillen, Luis	R-R	6-1	150	12-16-93	0	3	5.84	2	0	0	0	12	12	10	8	1	9	11	.267	.222	.278	8.03	6.57
2-team total (7 Cubs 1)					3	4	4.24	11	8	0	0	40	39	23	19	3	17	35	—	—	—	7.81	3.79
Leyba, Richard	L-L	6-4	210	10-25-91	3	0	1.26	5	0	0	1	14	13	9	2	0	11	10	.228	.000	.245	6.28	6.91
2-team total (8 Cubs 1)					3	1	6.59	13	0	0	1	29	39	31	21	0	35	27	—	—	—	8.48	10.99

Pitching	B-T	HT	WT	DOB	W	L	ERA	G	GS	CG	SV	IP	H	R	ER	HR	BB	SO	AVG	vLH	vRH	K/9	BB/9
Martinez, Eric	R-R	6-2	185	1-25-90	5	1	1.70	16	3	0	2	42	40	12	8	1	8	22	.253	.244	.256	4.68	1.70
Mejias, Angel	L-L	6-3	180	10-30-93	0	0	0.00	1	0	0	0	2	1	1	0	0	2	0	.250	.000	.250	0.00	9.00
2-team total (7 Cubs 1)					0	2	2.39	8	6	0	0	26	21	13	7	0	19	15	—	—	—	5.13	6.49
Padron, Loiger	R-R	6-0	180	1-31-91	3	2	2.54	7	5	0	0	39	22	12	11	0	12	34	.168	.321	.126	7.85	2.77
2-team total (10 Cubs 1)					6	3	2.44	17	6	0	1	63	40	20	17	0	24	49	—	—	—	7.04	3.45
Pena, Enyelberth	R-R	6-2	175	9-8-90	2	1	5.87	7	0	0	1	15	19	19	10	1	10	15	.288	.333	.271	8.80	5.87
Perez, Hector	R-R	6-1	157	6-25-93	3	0	5.14	10	6	0	0	35	39	21	20	3	16	32	.293	.333	.283	8.23	4.11
Reyes, Amalio	R-R	6-2	175	5-22-91	0	0	4.50	1	0	0	0	2	2	1	1	0	0	2	.250	1.000	.143	9.00	0.00
2-team total (3 Cubs 1)					0	1	4.50	4	3	0	0	14	12	8	7	1	10	12	—	—	—	7.71	6.43
Sanchez, Julio	L-R	6-4	185	12-6-88	2	2	4.13	15	13	0	0	52	56	31	24	2	19	35	.279	.316	.270	6.02	3.27
Santana, Alex	R-R	6-1	170	10-23-93	1	2	3.90	8	8	0	0	32	35	17	14	3	14	21	.292	.200	.322	5.85	3.90
2-team total (7 Cubs 1)					4	2	2.67	15	14	0	0	67	59	29	20	3	20	36	—	—	—	4.81	2.67
Severino, Deuris	R-R	6-1	170	8-26-90	0	0	0.00	1	0	0	0	2	0	0	0	0	2	1	.000	.000	.000	5.40	10.80
Telles, Wladimir	R-R	6-1	200	2-5-93	1	0	4.15	7	0	0	1	17	20	9	8	1	9	7	.290	.211	.320	3.63	4.67
2-team total (13 Cubs 1)					2	1	4.50	20	0	0	1	42	40	23	21	3	24	27	—	—	—	5.79	5.14
Torrez, Daury	R-R	6-3	170	6-11-93	1	2	3.54	16	1	0	1	41	42	19	16	0	5	25	.271	.368	.239	5.53	1.11
Turbi, Francisco	R-R	6-4	210	2-19-88	4	1	3.09	27	0	0	11	32	26	18	11	4	10	29	.218	.150	.232	8.16	2.81

Fielding

Catcher	PCT	G	PO	A	E	DP	PB
De La Cruz	.981	9	49	4	1	0	1
Perez	1.000	2	5	1	0	0	3
Petit	.979	50	265	65	7	2	3
Puente	1.000	1	1	0	0	0	0
Suarez	.857	1	5	1	1	0	2
Valdez	.000	1	0	0	0	0	0
Valerio	.989	31	160	21	2	3	2

First Base	PCT	G	PO	A	E	DP
Arcila	.986	32	266	12	4	28
Batista	.974	12	101	11	3	11
Candelario	1.000	5	22	0	0	1
Figueroa	.949	7	55	1	3	5
Gonzalez	1.000	1	2	0	0	1
Montecino	1.000	13	49	3	0	2
Perez	1.000	1	4	0	0	0
Petit	1.000	3	26	0	0	2

	PCT	G	PO	A	E	DP
Puente	.985	15	128	3	2	9
Rodriguez	1.000	2	5	1	0	0
Suarez	1.000	1	12	0	0	2
Valdez	1.000	2	4	0	0	0

Second Base	PCT	G	PO	A	E	DP
Gonzalez	.842	13	23	25	9	4
Montecino	.974	14	19	19	1	5
Ortega	1.000	3	2	1	0	0
Penalver	1.000	3	7	9	0	1
Petit	1.000	1	0	1	0	0
Puente	.957	35	55	79	6	18
Rodriguez	.967	22	46	41	3	10

Third Base	PCT	G	PO	A	E	DP
Batista	1.000	1	0	1	0	0
Candelario	.913	58	49	129	17	10
Montecino	1.000	3	0	2	0	0
Puente	.824	6	3	11	3	1

	PCT	G	PO	A	E	DP
Rodriguez	.909	12	10	20	3	3
Shortstop	PCT	G	PO	A	E	DP
Gonzalez	.895	4	4	13	2	1
Penalver	.957	67	109	244	16	42
Rodriguez	1.000	4	5	12	0	1

Outfield	PCT	G	PO	A	E	DP
Arcila	.903	35	26	2	3	0
Baez	.970	37	57	7	2	2
Batista	.909	11	10	0	1	0
Bonne	.982	31	51	5	1	1
Cabrera	.964	39	45	9	2	3
Encarnacion	.952	31	56	3	3	2
Figueroa	.950	15	19	0	1	0
Mercedes	.923	16	23	1	2	0
Valdez	.878	31	33	3	5	0

Chicago White Sox

SEASON IN A SENTENCE: The White Sox, boasting the fifth-highest payroll in baseball and bolstered by the offseason signing of Adam Dunn, did not come close to expectations in a tumultuous season that ended with the departure of manager Ozzie Guillen to the Marlins.

HIGH POINT: Paul Konerko reached 2,000 career hits on Aug. 23, on the way to his fifth 30-homer, 100-RBI season in Chicago and arguably his best season. He joined Frank Thomas as the only White Sox to accomplish the feat five times.

LOW POINT: Almost any at-bat for Dunn was a low point for the Chisox, who handed him a $56 million, four-year contract only to see him hit .159 and set a franchise record with 177 strikeouts. A September benching saved Dunn from piling up more strikeouts or having the lowest average among players to qualify for the batting title. The slugger who has averaged 33 home runs a season over his 11-year big league career managed just 11 homers in 2011 and drove in a paltry 42 runs.

NOTABLE ROOKIES: Lefthander Chris Sale had a 2.79 ERA and eight saves while making 58 appearances in his first full professional season. Third baseman Brent Morel hit 10 homers and drove in 41 runs. Righthander Zach Stewart took a perfect game into the eighth inning against the Twins in early September and finished with a one-hit shutout. Righthander Dylan Axelrod went 1-0 in four appearances with a 2.89 ERA.

KEY TRANSACTIONS: The White Sox claimed Philip Humber off waivers from the Athletics before the season, and he became another reclamation success for pitching coach Don Cooper, going 9-9, 3.75. In July, the White Sox traded Edwin Jackson and Mark Teahan to the Blue Jays for righthanders Stewart and Jason Frasor. The biggest move may have come in October, when the Sox named former star Robin Ventura to replace Guillen despite his lack of managerial experience.

DOWN ON THE FARM: Righthander Addison Reed began the season at low Class A Kannapolis and pitched his way to a September callup. The potential closer of the future had a 1.26 ERA with 111 strikeouts and just 14 walks in 78 innings. Axelrod went 9-3, 2.69 between Double-A Birmingham and Triple-A Charlotte. The Sox spent just $2.8 million on the draft and lost their first-round pick for signing Dunn, hurting their efforts to replenish a thin farm system.

OPENING DAY PAYROLL: $127,789,000 (5th)

PLAYERS OF THE YEAR

MAJOR LEAGUE

Paul Konerko
1b
.300/.388/.517
31 HR, 105 RBIs
7th in AL in OPS

MINOR LEAGUE

Addison Reed
rhp
(Lo A/Hi A/AA/AAA)
2-1, 1.26
111 SO, 0.73 WHIP

ORGANIZATION LEADERS

BATTING		*Minimum 250 PA
MAJORS		
* AVG	Paul Konerko	.3
* OPS	Paul Konerko	.905
HR	Paul Konerko	31
RBI	Paul Konerko	105
MINORS		
* AVG	Tyler Kuhn, Charlotte/Birmingham	.333
* OBP	Brady Shoemaker, Kannapolis/Winston-Salem	.391
* SLG	Ian Gac, Winston-Salem	.535
R	Trayce Thompson, Kannapolis	95
H	Tyler Kuhn, Charlotte/Birmingham	168
TB	Ian Gac, Winston-Salem	276
2B	Dan Black, Kannapolis	41
3B	Tyler Kuhn, Charlotte/Birmingham	11
HR	Ian Gac, Winston-Salem	33
RBI	Dan Black, Kannapolis	98
BB	Jim Gallagher, Charlotte	62
SO	Jared Mitchell, Winston-Salem	183
SB	Qualon Millender, Great Falls	28

PITCHING		#Minimum 75 IP
MAJORS		
W	Mark Buehrle	13
# ERA	Mark Buehrle	3.59
SO	Gavin Floyd	151
SV	Sergio Santos	30
MINORS		
W	Cameron Bayne, Charlotte/Birmingham/W-S	14
L	Joseph Serafin, Charlotte/Winston-Salem	11
# ERA	Dylan Axelrod, Birmingham/Charlotte	2.69
G	Shane Lindsay, Birmingham/Charlotte	50
GS	Five tied at	27
SV	Taylor Thompson, Winston-Salem	15
IP	Terry Doyle, Winston-Salem/Birmingham	173
BB	Nevin Griffith, Birmingham	96
SO	Dylan Axelrod, Birmingham/Charlotte	132
# AVG	Dylan Axelrod, Birmingham/Charlotte	.227

General Manager: Ken Williams. **Farm Director:** Buddy Bell. **Scouting Director:** Doug Laumann.

Class	Team	League	W	L	PCT	Finish	Manager(s)
Majors	Chicago White Sox	American	79	83	.488	9th (14)	Ozzie Guillen/Don Cooper
Triple-A	Charlotte Knights	International	69	74	.483	9th (14)	Joe McEwing
Double-A	Birmingham Barons	Southern	71	69	.507	4th (10)	Bobby Magallanes
High A	Winston-Salem Dash	Carolina	69	71	.493	4th (8)	Julio Vinas
Low A	Kannapolis Intimidators	South Atlantic	76	62	.551	5th (14)	Tommy Thompson
Rookie	Great Falls Voyagers	Pioneer	42	34	.553	3rd (8)	Ryan Newman
Rookie	Bristol White Sox	Appalachian	24	44	.353	t-9th (10)	Pete Rose Jr.
Overall 2011 Minor League Record			351	354	.498	18th (30)	

ORGANIZATION STATISTICS

CHICAGO WHITE SOX

AMERICAN LEAGUE

Batting	B-T	HT	WT	DOB	AVG	vLH	vRH	G	AB	R	H	2B	3B	HR	RBI	BB	HBP	SH	SF	SO	SB	CS	SLG	OBP
Beckham, Gordon	R-R	6-0	190	9-16-86	.230	.195	.242	150	499	60	115	23	0	10	44	35	13	0	3	111	5	3	.337	.296
Castro, Ramon	R-R	6-3	240	3-1-76	.235	.289	.130	23	68	6	16	3	0	4	10	7	0	0	0	23	0	0	.456	.307
De Aza, Alejandro	L-L	6-0	190	4-11-84	.329	.263	.338	54	152	29	50	11	3	4	23	17	1	0	0	34	12	5	.520	.400
Dunn, Adam	L-R	6-6	285	11-9-79	.159	.064	.187	122	415	36	66	16	0	11	42	75	4	0	2	177	0	1	.277	.292
Escobar, Eduardo	B-R	5-10	165	1-5-89	.286	.333	.250	9	7	0	2	0	0	0	0	0	0	0	0	1	0	0	.286	.286
Flowers, Tyler	R-R	6-4	245	1-24-86	.209	.135	.247	38	110	13	23	5	1	5	16	14	3	0	2	38	0	1	.409	.310
Konerko, Paul	R-R	6-2	220	3-5-76	.300	.292	.303	149	543	69	163	25	0	31	105	77	8	0	11	89	1	1	.517	.388
Lillibridge, Brent	R-R	5-11	185	9-18-83	.258	.287	.228	97	186	38	48	5	1	13	29	17	7	0	2	62	10	6	.505	.340
Lucy, Donny	R-R	6-2	205	8-8-82	.200	1.000	.111	6	10	1	2	1	0	0	1	1	0	0	0	5	0	0	.300	.273
McPherson, Dallas	L-R	6-4	225	7-23-80	.133	.182	.133	11	15	1	2	0	0	0	0	0	0	0	0	7	0	0	.133	.133
Milledge, Lastings	R-R	5-11	210	4-5-85	.250	.000	1.000	2	4	1	1	1	0	0	0	0	0	0	0	1	0	0	.500	.250
Morel, Brent	R-R	6-2	220	4-21-87	.245	.240	.246	126	413	44	101	18	1	10	41	22	3	0	1	57	5	4	.366	.287
Pierre, Juan	L-L	5-11	175	8-14-77	.279	.329	.264	158	639	80	178	17	4	2	50	43	7	0	3	41	27	17	.327	.329
Pierzynski, A.J.	L-R	6-3	225	12-30-76	.287	.305	.283	129	464	38	133	29	1	8	48	23	5	0	6	33	0	0	.405	.323
Quentin, Carlos	R-R	6-2	235	8-28-82	.254	.297	.241	118	421	53	107	31	0	24	77	34	23	0	5	84	1	1	.499	.340
Ramirez, Alexei	R-R	6-2	175	9-22-81	.269	.268	.269	158	614	81	165	31	2	15	70	51	6	0	5	94	7	5	.399	.328
Rios, Alex	R-R	6-5	210	2-18-81	.227	.287	.204	145	537	64	122	22	2	13	44	27	2	0	4	68	11	6	.348	.265
Teahen, Mark	L-R	6-3	230	9-6-81	.203	.077	.219	51	118	11	24	3	0	3	11	12	0	0	0	28	0	1	.305	.277
2-team total (27 Toronto)					.200	—	—	78	160	14	32	4	0	4	14	16	0	0	0	45	0	1	.300	.273
Viciedo, Dayan	R-R	5-11	230	3-10-89	.255	.406	.186	29	102	11	26	3	0	1	6	9	2	0	0	23	1	0	.314	.327
Vizquel, Omar	B-R	5-9	180	4-24-67	.251	.200	.259	58	167	18	42	7	1	0	8	9	0	0	2	18	1	2	.305	.287

Pitching	B-T	HT	WT	DOB	W	L	ERA	G	GS	CG	SV	IP	H	R	ER	HR	BB	SO	AVG	vLH	vRH	K/9	BB/9
Axelrod, Dylan	R-R	6-0	195	7-30-85	1	0	2.89	4	3	0	0	19	18	6	6	1	9	19	.257	.256	.259	9.16	4.34
Bruney, Brian	R-R	6-3	235	2-17-82	1	0	6.86	23	0	0	0	20	26	15	15	4	12	16	.338	.389	.293	7.32	5.49
Buehrle, Mark	L-L	6-2	230	3-23-79	13	9	3.59	31	31	0	0	205	221	93	82	21	45	109	.277	.251	.288	4.78	1.97
Crain, Jesse	R-R	6-1	215	7-5-81	8	3	2.62	67	0	0	1	65	50	20	19	7	31	70	.215	.184	.233	9.64	4.27
Danks, John	L-L	6-1	215	4-15-85	8	12	4.33	27	27	2	0	170	182	89	82	19	46	135	.274	.270	.275	7.13	2.43
Floyd, Gavin	R-R	6-6	240	1-27-83	12	13	4.37	31	30	1	0	194	180	97	94	22	45	151	.247	.272	.211	7.02	2.09
Frasor, Jason	R-R	5-9	180	8-9-77	1	2	5.09	20	0	0	0	18	20	10	10	3	11	20	.286	.333	.256	10.19	5.60
2-team total (44 Toronto)					3	3	3.60	64	0	0	0	60	58	25	24	7	26	57	—	—	—	8.55	3.90
Gray, Jeff	R-R	6-3	195	11-19-81	0	0	2.70	6	0	0	0	13	13	4	4	1	4	7	.255	.200	.308	4.73	2.70
2-team total (24 Seattle)					0	1	4.28	30	0	0	1	48	52	23	23	4	21	23	—	—	—	4.28	3.91
Harrell, Lucas	B-R	6-2	210	6-3-85	0	0	7.20	3	0	0	0	5	11	4	4	0	1	5	.440	.600	.400	9.00	1.80
Humber, Phil	R-R	6-3	210	12-21-82	9	9	3.75	28	26	0	0	163	151	71	68	14	41	116	.243	.268	.203	6.40	2.26
Jackson, Edwin	R-R	6-3	205	9-9-83	7	7	3.92	19	19	1	0	122	134	55	53	8	39	97	.283	.293	.271	7.18	2.88
Kinney, Josh	R-R	6-1	215	3-31-79	0	0	6.62	13	0	0	0	18	23	13	13	1	7	20	.319	.353	.289	10.19	3.57
Lindsay, Shane	R-R	6-1	205	1-25-85	0	0	12.00	4	0	0	0	6	11	8	8	1	5	6	.379	.385	.375	9.00	7.50
Ohman, Will	L-L	6-2	225	8-13-77	1	3	4.22	59	0	0	0	53	53	26	25	8	17	54	.255	.311	.200	9.11	2.87
Peavy, Jake	R-R	6-1	195	5-31-81	7	7	4.92	19	18	1	0	112	117	61	61	10	24	95	.268	.259	.278	7.66	1.93
Pena, Tony	R-R	6-2	240	1-9-82	1	1	6.20	17	0	0	0	20	25	15	14	2	10	17	.301	.200	.358	7.52	4.43
Reed, Addison	L-R	6-4	215	12-27-88	0	0	3.68	6	0	0	0	7	10	3	3	1	1	12	.313	.313	.313	14.73	1.23
Sale, Chris	L-L	6-6	180	3-30-89	2	2	2.79	58	0	0	8	71	52	22	22	6	27	79	.203	.208	.199	10.01	3.42
Santiago, Hector	R-L	6-0	210	12-16-87	0	0	0.00	2	0	0	0	5	1	0	0	0	1	2	.059	.000	.111	3.38	1.69
Santos, Sergio	R-R	6-2	230	7-4-83	4	5	3.55	63	0	0	30	63	41	25	25	6	29	92	.181	.234	.130	13.07	4.12
Stewart, Zach	R-R	6-2	205	9-28-86	2	5	6.22	10	8	1	0	51	64	35	35	9	13	35	.314	.311	.317	6.22	2.31
2-team total (3 Toronto)					2	6	5.88	13	11	1	0	67	90	44	44	11	18	45	—	—	—	6.01	2.41
Thornton, Matt	L-L	6-6	235	9-15-76	2	5	3.32	62	0	0	3	60	60	34	22	3	21	63	.255	.260	.252	9.50	3.17

Fielding

Catcher	PCT	G	PO	A	E	DP	PB		First Base	PCT	G	PO	A	E	DP					
Castro	.992	21	117	4	1	0	3		Dunn	.986	35	259	24	4	21		McPherson	1.000	6	7	0	0	0
Flowers	.992	31	243	15	2	1	3		Flowers	1.000	3	17	4	0	2		Teahen	1.000	11	40	1	0	1
Lucy	1.000	3	23	1	0	1	0		Konerko	.995	111	975	68	5	89		Viciedo	1.000	4	18	1	0	1
Pierzynski	.995	120	817	65	4	4	4		Lillibridge	.984	22	114	11	2	9		Vizquel	1.000	1	1	1	0	0

CHICAGO WHITE SOX

Second Base	PCT	G	PO	A	E	DP
Beckham	.989	149	272	443	8	84
Escobar	1.000	2	2	1	0	1
Lillibridge	1.000	6	5	4	0	2
Vizquel	.984	16	23	37	1	7

Third Base	PCT	G	PO	A	E	DP
McPherson	1.000	5	2	9	0	0
Morel	.953	125	72	211	14	13

	PCT	G	PO	A	E	DP
Teahen	1.000	28	17	38	0	1
Vizquel	1.000	29	13	31	0	2
Shortstop	PCT	G	PO	A	E	DP
Escobar	1.000	3	0	4	0	0
Ramirez	.977	155	217	457	16	99
Vizquel	1.000	9	8	18	0	3
Outfield	PCT	G	PO	A	E	DP
De Aza	.991	48	104	2	1	0

	PCT	G	PO	A	E	DP
Dunn	1.000	2	1	0	0	0
Lillibridge	1.000	59	87	0	0	0
Milledge	1.000	2	7	0	0	0
Pierre	.976	155	278	5	7	1
Quentin	.994	102	177	2	1	0
Rios	.992	143	349	5	3	3
Teahen	.667	9	2	0	1	0
Viciedo	1.000	21	26	2	0	1

CHARLOTTE KNIGHTS   TRIPLE-A

INTERNATIONAL LEAGUE

Batting	B-T	HT	WT	DOB	AVG	vLH	vRH	G	AB	R	H	2B	3B	HR	RBI	BB	HBP	SH	SF	SO	SB	CS	SLG	OBP
Chavez, Ozzie	B-R	6-1	175	7-13-83	.250	.091	.303	13	44	8	11	1	0	1	5	3	0	0	1	10	2	0	.341	.292
Danks, Jordan	L-R	6-4	210	8-7-86	.257	.256	.257	133	463	65	119	24	6	14	65	57	5	0	1	155	18	4	.425	.344
Dawkins, Gookie	R-R	6-1	180	5-12-79	.233	.192	.251	99	330	31	77	22	0	12	48	32	3	0	2	105	9	4	.409	.305
De Aza, Alejandro	L-L	6-0	190	4-11-84	.322	.306	.330	99	385	64	124	29	5	9	37	33	4	0	4	72	22	11	.494	.378
Escobar, Eduardo	B-R	5-10	165	1-5-89	.266	.248	.273	137	489	55	130	23	4	4	49	27	1	0	4	104	13	8	.354	.303
Flowers, Tyler	R-R	6-4	245	1-24-86	.261	.203	.282	65	222	36	58	8	0	15	32	39	8	0	0	84	2	0	.500	.390
Gallagher, Jimmy	L-L	6-1	195	9-3-85	.246	.261	.239	126	472	72	116	39	2	7	54	62	3	0	3	82	7	2	.381	.335
Garcia, Drew	B-R	6-1	175	4-22-84	.202	.198	.204	104	366	35	74	24	2	8	43	27	2	0	4	116	2	2	.344	.258
Gartrell, Stefan	R-R	6-3	230	1-14-84	.304	.333	.294	7	23	3	7	4	0	1	3	2	1	0	0	6	0	0	.609	.385
2-team total (116 Gwinnett)					.262	—	—	123	454	70	119	32	0	26	94	44	9	0	2	118	4	2	.504	.338
Greene, Justin	R-R	6-0	185	10-10-85	.256	.188	.271	22	86	14	22	4	1	3	11	7	1	0	1	28	2	2	.430	.316
Kuhn, Tyler	L-R	5-10	185	9-9-86	.297	.265	.316	23	91	9	27	4	1	0	4	5	0	0	2	13	0	2	.363	.327
Lucy, Donny	R-R	6-2	205	8-8-82	.158	.147	.162	40	133	11	21	1	0	4	9	10	3	0	0	35	0	0	.256	.233
McPherson, Dallas	L-R	6-4	225	7-23-80	.283	.233	.305	101	392	54	111	27	0	20	69	31	0	0	2	126	1	2	.505	.334
Milledge, Lastings	R-R	5-11	210	4-5-85	.295	.393	.260	123	444	61	131	23	3	12	47	43	6	0	2	63	27	6	.441	.364
Phegley, Josh	R-R	5-10	215	2-12-88	.241	.250	.235	22	79	9	19	4	0	2	6	8	2	0	0	18	0	0	.367	.326
Pierzynski, A.J.	L-R	6-3	225	12-30-76	.200	.000	.200	3	10	2	2	0	0	1	0	1	0	0	0	2	0	0	.200	.273
Price, Jared	R-R	6-2	230	3-18-82	.220	.250	.211	16	50	8	11	3	0	1	7	7	0	0	0	20	0	0	.340	.316
Restovich, Michael	R-R	6-6	240	1-3-79	.220	.308	.200	26	96	11	22	4	0	3	8	7	0	0	0	37	0	0	.365	.282
Ricks, Adam	B-R	5-10	190	9-24-82	.182	.333	.125	4	11	1	2	0	0	0	2	4	1	0	0	3	0	0	.182	.438
Shelton, Kyle	R-R	6-0	184	5-15-86	.159	.111	.171	14	44	4	7	3	0	0	3	4	0	0	0	17	1	0	.227	.229
Teahen, Mark	L-R	6-3	230	9-6-81	.194	.250	.174	8	31	1	6	1	0	0	3	7	0	0	0	9	0	0	.226	.342
Viciedo, Dayan	R-R	5-11	230	3-10-89	.296	.270	.305	119	452	60	134	28	0	20	78	45	5	0	3	83	2	1	.491	.364

Pitching	B-T	HT	WT	DOB	W	L	ERA	G	GS	CG	SV	IP	H	R	ER	HR	BB	SO	AVG	vLH	vRH	K/9	BB/9
Axelrod, Dylan	R-R	6-0	195	7-30-85	6	1	2.27	15	15	0	0	91	74	27	23	2	21	75	.220	.250	.199	7.39	2.07
Ballinger, J.R.	R-R	6-1	190	4-2-88	0	0	0.00	1	0	0	0	3	2	0	0	0	1	2	.200	.000	.286	5.40	2.70
Bayne, Cameron	R-R	6-2	195	2-14-88	0	1	13.50	1	1	0	0	4	13	6	6	0	1	2	.542	.722	.000	4.50	2.25
Bisenius, Joe	R-R	6-4	210	9-18-82	5	1	3.09	13	13	0	0	67	53	29	23	5	39	53	.214	.250	.186	7.12	5.24
Bruney, Brian	R-R	6-3	235	2-17-82	1	0	1.31	19	0	0	7	21	12	3	3	0	9	30	.162	.150	.176	13.06	3.92
Carter, Anthony	L-R	6-3	210	4-4-86	0	2	7.23	35	0	0	3	47	60	39	38	6	26	48	.314	.305	.321	9.13	4.94
Casey, J.C.	R-R	6-3	174	12-13-88	0	0	0.00	1	0	0	0	3	3	0	0	0	1	2	.273	.167	.400	6.00	3.00
Cassel, Justin	R-R	6-2	215	9-25-84	1	0	4.32	2	2	0	0	8	7	4	4	1	2	4	.219	.250	.200	4.32	2.16
Cofield, Kyle	R-R	6-5	220	1-23-87	0	0	9.00	2	0	0	0	2	2	2	2	0	0	2	.333	.500	.250	9.00	0.00
Corley, Tyson	R-R	6-2	200	1-26-86	4	2	4.34	16	0	0	0	29	31	14	14	2	14	14	.277	.306	.254	4.34	4.34
Danks, John	L-L	6-1	215	4-15-85	1	0	2.00	2	2	0	0	9	9	2	2	2	2	6	.265	.125	.308	6.00	2.00
Davis, Doug	R-L	6-4	215	9-21-75	2	5	2.60	9	9	0	0	52	51	20	15	2	12	46	.259	.389	.230	7.96	2.08
Dolsi, Freddy	R-R	6-0	160	1-9-83	3	7	6.87	15	14	0	0	77	96	63	59	13	23	59	.299	.301	.297	6.87	2.68
Harrell, Lucas	B-R	6-2	210	6-3-85	7	3	3.27	13	12	0	0	74	67	28	27	6	26	56	.244	.191	.281	6.78	3.15
Heath, Deunte	R-R	6-4	215	8-8-85	4	7	4.73	30	16	0	1	103	98	62	54	12	62	117	.249	.259	.241	10.26	5.44
Hernandez, Gaby	R-R	6-3	215	5-21-86	4	6	7.69	11	11	0	0	55	76	49	47	12	27	40	.322	.290	.357	6.55	4.42
Humber, Phil	R-R	6-3	210	12-21-82	0	0	7.20	1	1	0	0	5	7	4	4	1	1	5	.318	.545	.091	9.00	1.80
Hynick, Brandon	R-R	6-3	205	3-7-85	1	4	7.85	7	7	0	0	37	51	32	32	10	11	26	.338	.388	.298	6.38	2.70
2-team total (9 Louisville)					1	7	6.75	16	10	0	0	63	73	47	47	12	21	48	—	—	—	6.89	3.02
Infante, Gregori	R-R	6-2	215	7-10-87	1	4	3.35	34	0	0	4	48	50	20	18	5	21	40	.263	.324	.227	7.45	3.91
Kinney, Josh	R-R	6-1	215	3-31-79	6	3	2.77	49	0	0	14	62	49	22	19	2	17	66	.221	.300	.167	9.63	2.48
Kloess, Brandon	R-R	6-2	195	12-9-84	1	0	0.00	4	0	0	0	6	2	0	0	0	0	8	.100	.083	.125	11.37	0.00
Lindsay, Shane	R-R	6-1	205	1-25-85	2	2	1.98	45	0	0	0	64	28	15	14	2	51	78	.132	.109	.153	11.03	7.21
Linza, Keegan	R-R	6-6	230	11-10-88	0	1	21.60	1	0	0	0	2	3	4	4	0	3	0	.500	.500	.500	0.00	16.20
Marquez, Jeff	R-R	6-2	190	8-10-84	3	4	3.97	9	9	1	0	48	53	27	21	5	15	36	.285	.238	.321	6.80	2.83
Nunez, Jhonny	L-R	6-3	215	11-26-85	4	4	4.75	29	5	0	0	47	43	25	25	7	18	50	.246	.294	.215	9.51	3.42
Omogrosso, Brian	R-R	6-4	230	4-26-84	1	1	4.03	11	1	0	0	22	24	11	10	1	8	19	.282	.233	.309	7.66	3.22
Peavy, Jake	R-R	6-1	195	5-31-81	1	1	3.65	4	4	0	0	25	21	10	10	3	1	26	.231	.210	.249	9.49	0.36
Pena, Tony	R-R	6-2	240	1-9-82	0	0	1.69	5	0	0	0	5	3	1	1		2	6	.167	.000	.300	10.13	3.38
Reed, Addison	L-R	6-4	215	12-27-88	0	0	1.27	11	0	0	2	21	8	3	3	2	3	28	.114	.152	.081	11.81	1.27
Remenowsky, Dan	R-R	6-5	245	4-5-84	2	2	4.40	18	0	0	0	29	28	14	14	3	12	25	.252	.256	.250	7.85	3.77
Serafin, Joe	L-L	5-10	185	2-27-86	0	0	3.60	1	1	0	0	5	7	2	2	0	3	4	.318	.364	.273	7.20	5.40
Socolovich, Miguel	R-R	6-1	175	7-24-86	3	2	3.94	29	2	0	1	48	46	24	21	2	25	63	.246	.306	.196	11.81	4.69
Stewart, Zach	R-R	6-2	205	9-28-86	1	1	4.26	1	1	0	0	6	10	3	3	0	0	5	.357	.368	.333	7.11	0.00
Whisler, Wes	L-L	6-5	240	4-7-83	3	2	7.32	13	1	0	0	20	21	18	16	3	22	14	.284	.238	.302	6.41	10.07
Zaleski, Matt	R-R	6-1	190	12-2-81	4	7	4.90	17	16	1	0	90	88	51	49	10	38	66	.261	.261	.261	6.60	3.80

CHICAGO WHITE SOX

Fielding

Catcher

Catcher	PCT	G	PO	A	E	DP	PB
Flowers	.995	65	536	23	3	3	7
Lucy	.997	39	273	17	1	6	0
Phegley	1.000	21	176	6	0	2	4
Pierzynski	1.000	2	8	2	0	0	0
Price	1.000	16	125	6	0	0	5
Ricks	1.000	4	34	0	0	0	0

First Base

First Base	PCT	G	PO	A	E	DP
Dawkins	1.000	2	7	1	0	1
Gallagher	.997	114	942	60	3	79
McPherson	.992	16	122	7	1	10
Shelton	1.000	5	35	4	0	4
Teahen	1.000	2	11	1	0	1
Viciedo	.987	11	70	4	1	2

Second Base

Second Base	PCT	G	PO	A	E	DP
Chavez	.950	8	13	25	2	3
Dawkins	.991	27	41	70	1	15
Escobar	.945	30	60	77	8	23
Garcia	.976	73	121	199	8	44
Kuhn	1.000	3	4	7	0	1
Shelton	1.000	4	8	8	0	2

Third Base

Third Base	PCT	G	PO	A	E	DP
Chavez	1.000	2	1	2	0	0
Dawkins	.959	68	40	125	7	10
Kuhn	1.000	7	4	11	0	1
McPherson	.945	65	43	94	8	9
Shelton	1.000	1	0	1	0	0
Teahen	1.000	4	5	7	0	0

Shortstop

Shortstop	PCT	G	PO	A	E	DP
Chavez	1.000	3	6	7	0	4
Dawkins	1.000	2	4	8	0	1
Escobar	.972	107	109	277	11	51
Garcia	.967	32	36	81	4	11

Outfield

Outfield	PCT	G	PO	A	E	DP
Danks	.997	131	319	9	1	3
De Aza	.964	82	128	5	5	1
Gallagher	.893	13	24	1	3	0
Gartrell	1.000	3	9	0	0	0
Greene	1.000	22	36	0	0	0
Kuhn	1.000	14	22	3	0	0
Lucy	1.000	1	1	0	0	0
Milledge	.993	71	126	10	1	1
Restovich	.000	1	0	0	0	0
Shelton	1.000	2	6	0	0	0
Teahen	1.000	2	1	2	0	0
Viciedo	.974	95	142	8	4	0

BIRMINGHAM BARONS

DOUBLE-A

SOUTHERN LEAGUE

Batting	B-T	HT	WT	DOB	AVG	vLH	vRH	G	AB	R	H	2B	3B	HR	RBI	BB	HBP	SH	SF	SO	SB	CS	SLG	OBP
Bour, Jason	R-R	6-3	215	7-2-86	.278	.314	.255	28	90	13	25	7	0	2	12	0	0	2	23	0	0	.389	.356
Carrithers, Alden	L-R	5-9	165	11-14-84	.276	.277	.275	102	359	49	99	17	5	0	39	51	2	0	5	33	19	3	.351	.365
Colonel, Christian	R-R	6-2	210	12-25-81	.143	.154	.139	15	49	4	7	1	0	0	0	10	2	0	0	16	0	1	.163	.311
Garcia, Drew	B-R	6-1	175	4-22-86	.264	.205	.291	35	125	19	33	9	2	2	20	15	3	0	4	45	1	2	.416	.347
Gilmore, Jon	R-R	6-3	195	8-23-88	.283	.207	.320	50	180	19	51	13	1	3	28	18	3	0	4	32	0	0	.417	.351
Greene, Justin	R-R	6-0	185	10-10-85	.262	.305	.241	95	325	50	85	22	3	8	35	31	7	0	2	122	11	7	.422	.337
Kuhn, Tyler	L-R	5-10	185	9-9-86	.341	.357	.333	107	414	61	141	28	10	1	55	39	6	0	5	64	16	5	.464	.401
Lewis, Ozzie	R-R	6-2	193	3-21-86	.239	.267	.231	20	67	7	16	2	1	2	9	6	0	0	0	24	1	0	.388	.301
Loman, Seth	L-R	6-4	225	12-16-85	.274	.208	.294	122	427	53	117	24	0	19	65	44	24	0	2	122	5	1	.464	.372
Marrero, Christian	L-L	6-1	185	7-30-86	.293	.230	.316	115	420	70	123	25	8	12	59	61	5	0	5	69	10	4	.476	.385
Martinez, Jose	R-R	6-5	170	7-25-88	.295	.222	.328	53	200	19	59	13	1	1	16	15	1	0	2	25	5	2	.385	.344
Oester, Jake	R-R	6-1	190	7-22-86	.216	.273	.188	49	167	11	36	10	0	1	14	15	6	0	1	50	1	0	.293	.302
Paiml, Greg	R-R	6-0	185	8-3-84	.217	.259	.198	108	360	36	78	14	3	2	32	28	7	0	4	110	22	1	.289	.283
Phegley, Josh	R-R	5-10	215	2-12-88	.242	.208	.254	94	364	43	88	21	2	7	50	23	4	0	3	61	1	2	.368	.292
Price, Jared	R-R	6-2	230	3-18-82	.132	.167	.118	31	106	9	14	3	1	1	10	6	2	0	1	42	0	0	.208	.191
Shelton, Kyle	R-R	6-0	184	5-15-86	.248	.298	.214	42	141	20	35	5	0	3	17	17	2	0	2	24	2	3	.348	.333
Short, Brandon	R-R	6-0	190	9-9-88	.262	.240	.271	130	526	75	138	29	5	13	60	36	10	0	6	125	21	9	.411	.318
Sierra, Luis	L-R	5-11	150	7-23-87	.262	.000	.282	11	42	7	11	1	2	1	6	6	0	0	0	5	0	1	.357	.354
Williams Jr., Kenny	B-R	6-0	180	5-22-86	.195	.175	.202	83	318	31	62	11	4	3	26	30	4	0	1	83	4	5	.283	.272
Wilson, Ross	R-R	5-11	185	11-9-88	.229	.286	.214	10	35	5	8	1	0	0	3	6	0	0	0	7	0	0	.257	.341

Pitching	B-T	HT	WT	DOB	W	L	ERA	G	GS	CG	SV	IP	H	R	ER	HR	BB	SO	AVG	vLH	vRH	K/9	BB/9
Axelrod, Dylan	R-R	6-0	195	7-30-85	3	2	3.34	11	9	0	0	59	52	23	22	1	14	57	.237	.264	.219	8.65	2.12
Bayne, Cameron	R-R	6-2	195	2-14-88	2	0	3.50	3	3	0	0	18	15	8	7	2	14	7	.250	.217	.270	3.50	7.00
Bisenius, Joe	R-R	6-4	210	9-18-82	1	0	2.70	6	3	0	1	20	14	6	6	1	16	23	.203	.212	.194	10.35	7.20
Carter, Anthony	L-R	6-3	210	4-4-86	1	0	1.26	12	0	0	5	14	6	3	2	0	5	14	.125	.071	.147	8.79	3.14
Cofield, Kyle	R-R	6-5	220	1-23-87	1	2	2.89	15	0	0	0	28	26	9	9	0	13	23	.257	.250	.263	7.39	4.18
Corley, Tyson	R-R	6-6	200	1-26-86	3	3	5.63	20	0	0	1	32	32	20	20	2	17	17	.269	.333	.225	4.78	4.78
Dolsi, Freddy	R-R	6-0	160	1-9-83	0	0	13.50	2	0	0	0	1	2	2	2	0	1	2	.400	.000	.500	13.50	6.75
Doyle, Terry	R-R	6-4	225	11-2-85	7	5	3.24	15	15	2	0	100	91	38	36	8	22	73	.241	.238	.243	6.57	1.98
Edwards, Justin	L-L	6-0	180	9-7-87	4	8	4.89	28	27	0	0	153	191	103	83	9	52	72	.310	.285	.320	4.24	3.07
Griffith, Nevin	R-R	6-3	210	3-23-89	5	9	6.23	25	22	0	0	108	101	90	75	8	96	85	.250	.219	.276	7.06	7.98
Infante, Gregori	R-R	6-2	215	7-10-87	2	0	0.00	12	0	0	7	15	7	1	0	0	7	14	.132	.190	.094	8.22	4.11
Jones, Nathan	R-R	6-5	185	1-28-86	2	3	3.27	42	0	0	12	63	58	27	23	3	27	67	.243	.280	.219	9.52	3.84
Kloess, Brandon	R-R	6-4	215	12-9-84	2	1	1.31	14	0	0	0	34	21	9	5	2	7	31	.174	.282	.122	8.13	1.83
Leesman, Charlie	L-L	6-4	210	3-10-87	10	7	4.03	27	27	0	0	152	150	79	68	4	83	113	.264	.253	.267	6.69	4.91
Lindsay, Shane	R-R	6-1	205	1-25-85	1	1	4.05	5	0	0	0	7	4	3	3	0	8	12	.182	.333	.077	16.20	10.80
Lowe, Johnnie	R-R	6-5	220	3-21-85	7	4	3.65	30	0	0	0	69	56	32	28	6	35	44	.230	.250	.218	5.74	4.57
Mabee, Henry	R-R	6-4	230	7-10-85	0	1	27.00	3	0	0	0	2	7	8	7	1	3	2	.500	.286	.714	7.71	11.57
Omogrosso, Brian	R-R	6-4	230	4-26-84	0	2	2.51	31	0	0	2	43	36	18	12	2	16	53	.225	.276	.196	11.09	3.35
Peavy, Jake	R-R	6-1	195	5-31-81	0	0	6.23	2	2	0	0	4	9	5	3	0	1	4	.409	.222	.538	8.31	2.08
Reed, Addison	L-R	6-4	215	12-27-88	0	1	0.87	13	0	0	2	21	10	2	2	0	6	33	.143	.156	.132	14.37	2.61
Remenowsky, Dan	R-R	6-5	245	4-7-86	4	2	2.79	26	0	0	7	39	25	13	12	2	10	53	.182	.183	.182	12.34	2.33
Santiago, Hector	R-L	6-0	210	12-16-87	7	5	3.56	15	15	0	0	83	71	34	33	4	39	74	.235	.230	.237	7.99	4.21
Septimo, Leyson	L-L	6-1	195	7-7-85	2	1	4.10	22	0	0	0	26	23	16	12	1	16	38	.230	.200	.243	12.99	5.47
2-team total (21 Mobile)					4	2	5.30	43	0	0	0	56	43	39	33	2	41	60	—	—	—	9.64	6.59
Shirek, Charlie	R-R	6-3	205	10-25-85	4	7	3.87	24	10	0	1	88	94	47	38	6	28	57	.272	.280	.267	5.81	2.85
Socolovich, Miguel	R-R	6-1	175	7-24-86	0	0	0.00	5	0	0	1	7	0	0	0	0	2	7	.000	.000	.000	9.00	2.57
Wickswat, Matt	L-L	6-2	210	8-4-86	0	0	0.00	3	0	0	0	6	7	0	0	0	1	1	.292	.286	.294	1.42	1.42
Zaleski, Matt	R-R	6-1	190	12-2-81	3	3	2.74	8	7	0	0	49	35	17	15	2	14	45	.198	.244	.162	8.21	2.55

CHICAGO WHITE SOX

Fielding

Catcher	PCT	G	PO	A	E	DP	PB
Bour	1.000	25	145	17	0	0	7
Phegley	.993	78	620	51	5	4	16
Price	.986	31	204	14	3	1	5
Sierra	.986	11	65	5	1	1	0

First Base	PCT	G	PO	A	E	DP
Gilmore	.985	20	183	15	3	26
Loman	.986	55	468	30	7	54
Marrero	.997	65	563	36	2	55
Shelton	1.000	8	44	4	0	3

Second Base	PCT	G	PO	A	E	DP
Carrithers	.976	87	151	260	10	70
Garcia	.938	2	5	10	1	2
Kuhn	.994	33	71	107	1	23

	PCT	G	PO	A	E	DP
Paiml	1.000	6	11	15	0	4
Shelton	.955	5	7	14	1	3
Wilson	.960	9	16	32	2	12

Third Base	PCT	G	PO	A	E	DP
Carrithers	1.000	7	3	15	0	2
Colonel	.894	14	11	31	5	2
Gilmore	.893	9	8	17	3	0
Kuhn	.960	31	19	53	3	3
Oester	.890	46	18	103	15	10
Paiml	.932	23	16	39	4	6
Shelton	.914	18	10	43	5	6

Shortstop	PCT	G	PO	A	E	DP
Carrithers	1.000	4	7	16	0	3
Garcia	.932	33	40	84	9	17

	PCT	G	PO	A	E	DP
Kuhn	.972	26	37	66	3	9
Paiml	.971	80	139	262	12	77
Shelton	1.000	1	0	5	0	0

Outfield	PCT	G	PO	A	E	DP
Carrithers	1.000	1	3	0	0	0
Greene	.981	95	204	6	4	1
Kuhn	1.000	20	30	2	0	1
Lewis	.957	10	21	1	1	1
Marrero	.986	41	68	1	1	0
Martinez	.936	51	98	5	7	0
Shelton	1.000	5	12	0	0	0
Short	.992	126	248	10	2	2
Williams Jr.	.970	77	129	2	4	1

WINSTON-SALEM DASH HIGH CLASS A
CAROLINA LEAGUE

Batting	B-T	HT	WT	DOB	AVG	vLH	vRH	G	AB	R	H	2B	3B	HR	RBI	BB	HBP	SH	SF	SO	SB	CS	SLG	OBP
Blanke, Mike	R-R	6-4	220	10-17-88	.236	.250	.227	68	237	25	56	9	0	7	25	22	2	0	3	43	0	0	.363	.303
Bour, Jason	R-R	6-3	215	7-2-86	.183	.155	.210	38	120	9	22	4	0	1	9	8	0	0	1	34	0	0	.242	.233
Ciolli, Nick	L-R	6-2	215	12-6-87	.264	.279	.257	113	375	54	99	17	6	14	62	39	3	0	6	118	7	8	.453	.333
Colligan, Kyle	R-R	6-2	210	4-23-87	.202	.202	.203	90	252	34	51	11	2	8	30	46	2	0	4	69	6	4	.357	.326
Davis, Kyle	R-R	5-11	160	1-8-87	.096	.083	.107	15	52	0	5	2	0	0	2	0	1	0	0	21	0	0	.135	.113
2-team total (5 Lynchburg)					.127			20	63	3	8	2	0	1	3	2	1	0	0	27	2	0	.206	.167
Dubler, Kevin	L-R	6-1	200	2-18-87	.306	.167	.333	12	36	10	11	3	0	3	10	4	1	0	1	4	0	0	.639	.381
Eveland, Kyle	R-R	5-10	175	4-11-87	.091	.000	.200	6	11	1	1	0	0	0	0	1	0	0	0	5	0	1	.091	.167
Gac, Ian	R-R	6-3	245	8-10-85	.279	.309	.263	140	516	91	144	31	1	33	96	58	8	0	5	144	0	1	.535	.358
Martinez, Jose	R-R	6-5	170	7-25-88	.314	.400	.268	80	315	45	99	13	3	5	29	13	2	0	1	44	2	3	.422	.344
Mitchell, Jared	L-L	6-0	205	10-13-88	.222	.229	.219	129	477	74	106	31	8	9	58	52	6	0	4	183	14	6	.377	.304
Oester, Jake	R-R	6-1	190	7-22-86	.252	.291	.221	38	123	10	31	6	1	1	17	7	1	0	1	36	0	2	.341	.295
Saladino, Tyler	R-R	5-11	180	7-20-89	.270	.290	.258	102	397	75	107	26	9	16	55	51	9	0	3	90	7	7	.501	.363
Shelton, Kyle	R-R	6-0	184	5-15-86	.263	.250	.270	17	57	5	15	5	1	0	9	4	1	0	1	11	0	2	.439	.317
Shoemaker, Brady	R-R	6-0	200	5-10-87	.273	.267	.278	19	66	9	18	3	0	0	12	9	0	0	2	16	0	1	.318	.351
Sierra, Luis	L-R	5-11	150	7-23-87	.221	.148	.245	63	213	24	47	12	1	4	27	19	1	0	1	45	1	2	.343	.286
Silverio, Juan	R-R	6-1	175	4-18-91	.276	.250	.294	45	170	28	47	10	3	4	27	10	2	0	1	41	2	1	.441	.322
Spatola, John	L-L	6-0	190	4-2-87	.161	.333	.120	10	31	0	5	2	0	0	1	2	0	0	1	8	0	1	.226	.206
Wagner, Daniel	L-R	6-0	185	7-12-88	.256	.294	.234	132	481	60	123	14	4	1	28	31	1	0	3	64	25	12	.308	.300
Wilkins, Andy	L-R	6-2	225	9-13-88	.278	.230	.301	134	493	72	137	33	0	23	89	56	0	0	4	91	2	2	.485	.349
Yount, Austin	L-R	6-0	185	10-9-86	.214	.093	.250	62	187	18	40	9	2	3	15	23	1	0	2	52	1	0	.332	.300

Pitching	B-T	HT	WT	DOB	W	L	ERA	G	GS	CG	SV	IP	H	R	ER	HR	BB	SO	AVG	vLH	vRH	K/9	BB/9
Ballinger, J.R.	R-R	6-1	190	4-2-88	4	2	5.23	18	0	0	1	41	49	26	24	4	16	33	.288	.265	.298	7.19	3.48
Bassitt, Chris	R-R	6-5	205	2-22-89	0	0	5.40	1	0	0	0	2	2	1	1	0	0	1	.286	.000	.333	5.40	0.00
Bayne, Cameron	R-R	6-2	195	2-14-88	12	8	3.65	23	23	0	0	148	131	69	60	11	51	79	.234	.234	.235	4.80	3.10
Blough, Bryan	R-R	6-1	190	8-29-89	0	0	13.50	1	0	0	0	1	5	2	2	0	0	1	.556	1.000	.333	6.75	0.00
Buch, Ryan	R-R	6-3	205	11-8-87	4	4	4.92	11	11	0	0	57	52	34	31	10	23	48	.246	.300	.214	7.62	3.65
Cassel, Justin	R-R	6-2	215	9-25-84	0	0	0.79	5	1	0	0	11	14	5	1	0	2	4	.298	.357	.273	3.18	1.59
Collop, Justin	R-R	6-1	185	5-30-88	2	3	4.17	15	6	0	0	41	41	21	19	3	13	30	.256	.283	.240	6.59	2.85
Corley, Tyson	R-R	6-6	200	1-26-86	0	1	0.00	3	0	0	2	4	4	5	0	0	1	2	.235	.500	.154	4.50	2.25
Doyle, Terry	R-R	6-4	225	11-2-85	1	5	2.84	11	11	1	0	73	71	27	23	3	11	49	.252	.349	.191	6.04	1.36
Furnish, Brad	B-L	6-1	185	1-19-85	0	2	8.49	4	3	0	0	12	15	12	11	0	7	7	.341	.462	.290	5.40	5.40
Hunt, Leroy	R-R	6-6	240	11-28-87	3	3	4.08	25	0	0	3	46	47	24	21	3	32	28	.280	.333	.258	5.44	6.22
Johnson, Garrett	L-L	6-10	205	9-2-87	0	0	4.32	6	0	0	0	8	7	4	4	0	6	5	.226	.000	.304	5.40	6.48
Kloess, Brandon	R-R	6-2	195	12-9-84	2	2	2.77	21	0	0	6	39	31	17	12	3	13	43	.220	.226	.216	9.92	3.00
Kussmaul, Ryan	R-R	6-4	185	9-19-86	3	1	2.51	41	0	0	6	57	33	19	16	2	21	88	.163	.250	.119	13.81	3.30
Petricka, Jake	R-R	6-5	170	6-5-88	4	7	4.39	13	13	0	0	68	71	39	33	3	26	46	.265	.224	.284	6.12	3.46
Reed, Addison	L-R	6-4	215	12-27-88	2	0	1.59	15	0	0	1	28	21	8	5	1	4	39	.196	.209	.188	12.39	1.27
Rienzo, Andre	R-R	6-3	160	7-5-88	6	5	3.41	25	12	1	0	116	108	50	44	6	66	118	.247	.272	.233	9.16	5.12
Rodriguez, Santos	L-L	6-5	180	1-2-88	2	3	3.77	40	5	0	2	62	70	31	26	4	33	49	.293	.233	.313	7.11	4.79
Santiago, Hector	R-L	6-0	210	12-16-87	2	3	3.68	8	8	0	0	44	38	18	18	7	14	43	.236	.260	.225	8.80	2.86
Santos, Orlando	R-R	6-0	187	12-10-86	3	1	4.47	27	0	0	1	48	47	24	24	3	22	46	.258	.313	.229	8.57	4.10
Sauer, Stephen	R-R	6-2	185	8-13-86	1	0	4.50	5	0	0	0	8	4	4	4	0	4	5	.276	.167	.304	5.63	4.50
Serafin, Joe	L-L	5-10	185	2-27-86	5	11	5.52	25	24	0	0	132	166	86	81	16	49	75	.314	.264	.327	5.11	3.34
Shirek, Charlie	R-R	6-3	205	10-25-85	0	1	7.04	10	0	0	0	15	21	13	12	2	4	11	.328	.348	.317	6.46	2.35
Thompson, Taylor	R-R	6-5	225	6-18-87	7	2	2.52	41	0	0	15	54	42	20	15	1	26	51	.213	.292	.188	8.55	4.36
Van Skike, Jason	R-R	6-4	195	4-10-89	0	0	0.00	1	0	0	1	2	1	1	0	0	0	3	.100	.333	.000	13.50	0.00
Whisler, Wes	L-L	6-5	240	4-7-83	0	1	67.50	3	0	0	0	1	5	5	0	6	1	.500	.500	.000	13.50	81.00
Wickswat, Matt	L-L	6-2	210	8-4-86	6	6	4.03	23	13	0	0	92	93	49	41	11	26	84	.264	.245	.271	8.25	2.55

Fielding

Catcher	PCT	G	PO	A	E	DP	PB
Blanke	.975	67	432	45	12	6	5
Bour	.982	38	252	21	5	1	1
Dubler	.986	11	63	7	1	2	4
Sierra	1.000	31	247	26	0	3	5

CHICAGO WHITE SOX

First Base	PCT	G	PO	A	E	DP
Gac	.981	44	395	21	8	35
Wilkins	.992	96	807	65	7	73
Yount	1.000	1	2	0	0	0

Second Base	PCT	G	PO	A	E	DP
Eveland	1.000	1	3	4	0	1
Oester	.951	8	18	21	2	3
Shelton	1.000	3	11	12	0	3
Sierra	.979	11	22	24	1	6
Silverio	1.000	2	1	4	0	1
Wagner	.968	118	239	303	18	71

Third Base	PCT	G	PO	A	E	DP
Eveland	1.000	2	1	5	0	0
Oester	.932	27	13	55	5	4
Shelton	1.000	6	7	18	0	1
Sierra	.917	13	12	21	3	3
Silverio	.907	42	22	85	11	6
Yount	.932	57	26	111	10	5

Shortstop	PCT	G	PO	A	E	DP
Davis	.953	15	11	50	3	6
Eveland	1.000	1	1	1	0	1
Saladino	.955	102	156	328	23	64
Shelton	.974	8	11	26	1	5

Silverio	1.000	2	4	2	0	2
Wagner	.885	16	24	30	7	7

Outfield	PCT	G	PO	A	E	DP
Ciolli	.979	107	181	8	4	1
Colligan	.968	84	146	5	5	0
Martinez	.959	79	152	10	7	2
Mitchell	.985	127	259	2	4	1
Oester	1.000	2	5	0	0	0
Shoemaker	1.000	17	17	0	0	0
Sierra	1.000	10	7	2	0	0
Silverio	1.000	1	3	1	0	1
Spatola	1.000	10	15	1	0	0

KANNAPOLIS INTIMIDATORS

LOW CLASS A

SOUTH ATLANTIC LEAGUE

Batting	B-T	HT	WT	DOB	AVG	vLH	vRH	G	AB	R	H	2B	3B	HR	RBI	BB	HBP	SH	SF	SO	SB	CS	SLG	OBP
Black, Dan	L-R	6-5	240	7-2-87	.286	.301	.281	135	510	82	146	41	6	18	98	50	7	0	6	109	7	5	.496	.354
Blanke, Mike	R-R	6-4	220	10-17-88	.259	.267	.256	47	170	22	44	13	1	2	18	11	2	0	0	28	0	0	.382	.311
Dubler, Kevin	L-R	6-1	200	2-18-87	.251	.256	.250	52	175	24	44	10	2	3	15	18	2	0	1	34	2	1	.383	.327
Eveland, Kyle	R-R	5-10	175	4-17-87	.228	.184	.243	63	189	29	43	7	0	4	27	24	4	0	2	54	6	1	.328	.324
Gilbert, Kenny	L-L	6-2	185	2-6-89	.257	.250	.260	56	183	25	47	8	2	1	26	12	0	0	3	48	0	2	.339	.298
Gonzalez, Miguel	R-R	5-11	180	12-3-90	.255	.333	.228	55	184	17	47	7	0	2	21	16	3	0	1	34	5	1	.326	.324
Hamme, Ryan	L-R	6-3	210	3-13-87	.218	.000	.250	18	55	10	12	0	1	0	8	6	3	0	1	9	3	1	.255	.323
Harvard, Dusty	L-R	6-3	196	10-28-87	.176	.154	.184	20	51	7	9	0	1	0	5	1	0	0	1	14	0	1	.216	.189
Kuhn, Collin	R-R	6-0	195	11-27-88	.220	.211	.226	35	91	14	20	8	0	3	16	15	3	0	1	32	2	0	.407	.345
Lee, Drew	B-R	5-11	185	3-22-88	.274	.281	.271	94	325	49	89	17	3	5	36	17	3	0	3	79	3	6	.391	.313
Oester, Jake	R-R	6-1	190	7-22-86	.105	.000	.154	6	19	1	2	0	0	0	2	1	0	0	0	6	1	0	.105	.150
Pangilinan, Leighton	L-R	6-3	230	3-6-91	.203	.300	.241	19	64	6	13	3	1	1	9	3	0	0	1	18	0	0	.328	.235
Ramos, Jose	R-R	5-11	190	7-19-87	.167	.250	.000	2	6	0	1	1	0	0	1	0	1	0	0	2	0	0	.333	.286
Ravelo, Rangel	R-R	6-2	210	4-24-92	.317	.300	.327	43	161	11	51	9	0	0	21	12	1	0	0	19	0	1	.373	.368
Sanchez, Carlos	R-R	5-11	175	6-29-92	.288	.373	.254	63	264	44	76	10	1	1	27	15	7	0	1	49	7	8	.345	.341
Semien, Marcus	R-R	6-1	190	9-17-90	.253	.176	.286	60	229	35	58	15	2	3	26	22	2	0	3	53	3	4	.376	.320
Shoemaker, Brady	R-R	6-0	200	5-10-87	.319	.395	.296	99	373	68	119	28	2	11	65	43	9	0	4	78	7	3	.493	.399
Silverio, Juan	R-R	6-1	175	4-18-91	.289	.235	.306	88	329	48	95	29	6	5	58	18	10	0	4	81	4	7	.459	.341
Spatola, John	L-L	6-0	195	4-2-87	.256	.316	.245	42	121	20	31	7	2	4	19	12	3	0	0	28	0	1	.446	.338
Thompson, Trayce	R-R	6-3	195	3-15-91	.241	.306	.216	136	519	95	125	36	2	24	87	60	10	0	4	172	8	4	.457	.329
Vera, Rafael	R-R	6-1	180	11-21-87	.186	.171	.196	57	167	22	31	10	0	0	16	22	7	0	0	43	0	1	.246	.306
Walker, Keenyn	B-R	6-3	195	8-12-90	.228	.273	.206	39	162	25	37	1	2	0	15	14	2	0	1	64	10	4	.259	.296
Wilson, Ross	R-R	5-11	185	11-9-88	.268	.289	.260	79	287	43	77	17	3	2	26	31	10	0	2	55	7	3	.369	.358

Pitching	B-T	HT	WT	DOB	W	L	ERA	G	GS	CG	SV	IP	H	R	ER	HR	BB	SO	AVG	vLH	vRH	K/9	BB/9
Arroyo, Spencer	L-L	6-2	166	8-9-88	10	9	3.70	28	27	0	0	170	188	88	70	18	41	130	.282	.286	.281	6.87	2.17
Bachanov, Jon	R-R	6-4	230	1-30-89	2	4	3.12	14	7	0	1	40	33	18	14	2	14	31	.223	.194	.244	6.92	3.12
Ballinger, J.R.	R-R	6-1	190	4-2-88	2	3	2.18	12	1	0	2	21	26	7	5	0	9	14	.317	.241	.358	6.10	3.92
Bassitt, Chris	R-R	6-5	205	2-22-89	3	1	1.82	16	0	0	1	25	18	6	5	1	6	29	.202	.286	.158	10.58	2.19
Buch, Ryan	R-R	6-3	205	11-8-87	4	3	3.65	8	8	2	0	44	35	23	18	2	17	45	.211	.188	.225	9.14	3.45
Burnside, Paul	R-R	6-4	225	11-20-86	8	4	3.22	19	13	1	1	92	77	41	33	2	31	77	.224	.260	.195	7.51	3.02
Carter, Dexter	R-R	6-6	195	2-5-87	3	5	6.65	14	12	0	0	65	81	50	48	9	30	47	.320	.375	.291	6.51	4.15
Collop, Justin	R-R	6-1	185	5-30-88	1	0	3.55	6	0	0	2	13	11	5	5	0	4	11	.244	.200	.280	7.82	2.84
Cooney, Chase	R-R	6-8	245	12-18-87	2	2	4.10	31	1	0	1	48	44	28	22	6	33	47	.235	.274	.216	8.75	6.14
Furnish, Brad	B-L	6-1	185	1-19-85	0	2	5.10	6	6	0	0	30	35	18	17	3	19	30	.302	.407	.284	5.70	0.90
Heidenreich, Matt	L-R	6-5	185	1-17-91	10	10	4.32	27	27	0	0	154	174	91	74	13	31	101	.277	.284	.272	5.89	1.81
Hunt, Leroy	R-R	6-6	240	11-28-87	1	0	5.79	7	0	0	1	9	6	7	6	0	2	13	.171	.250	.130	12.54	1.93
Johnson, Garrett	L-L	6-10	205	9-2-87	0	0	0.00	1	0	0	0	2	1	0	0	0	2		.143	.000	.167	9.00	0.00
Kelly, Reid	R-R	6-1	182	10-31-86	1	0	3.72	11	0	0	0	19	17	10	8	2	8	22	.239	.231	.244	10.24	3.72
Marin, Terance	R-R	6-1	170	8-21-89	3	1	1.99	26	0	0	1	50	41	16	11	0	11	38	.219	.217	.219	6.89	1.99
McCully, Nick	R-R	5-11	195	9-5-88	5	2	3.17	24	1	0	3	54	39	21	19	0	11	47	.209	.184	.215	7.83	1.83
Moran, Kevin	R-R	6-4	195	7-7-89	1	2	7.33	12	3	0	1	27	29	23	22	0	16	25	.259	.295	.235	8.33	5.33
Negron, Miguel	L-L	6-1	190	8-22-82	1	0	6.23	7	0	0	1	9	11	10	6	1	7	6	.344	.571	.280	6.23	7.27
Negus, Phil	R-R	6-2	205	11-10-87	4	1	3.14	32	12	0	3	92	88	47	32	8	32	82	.246	.263	.233	8.05	3.14
Petricka, Jake	R-R	6-5	170	6-5-88	3	1	2.81	8	8	0	0	42	39	14	13	0	13	48	.255	.241	.263	10.37	2.81
Reed, Addison	L-R	6-4	215	12-27-88	0	0	1.13	4	0	0	0	8	4	1	1	0	1	11	.148	.000	.250	12.38	1.13
Santos, Orlando	R-R	6-0	187	12-10-86	2	0	1.08	12	0	0	1	25	16	3	3	1	6	22	.178	.219	.155	7.92	2.16
Upchurch, Steven	R-R	6-4	180	9-14-89	6	9	4.62	28	12	0	2	90	103	52	46	5	30	70	.292	.331	.263	7.03	3.01
Whisler, Wes	L-L	6-5	240	4-7-83	0	1	2.49	23	0	0	3	25	13	9	7	3	17	24	.159	.034	.226	8.53	6.04
Wilson, Jake	R-R	6-0	195	8-12-87	4	2	1.44	36	0	0	9	50	25	10	8	1	26	63	.147	.176	.134	11.34	4.68

Fielding

Catcher	PCT	G	PO	A	E	DP	PB
Blanke	.982	36	280	40	6	3	2
Dubler	.983	38	272	26	5	1	6
Gonzalez	.973	54	374	55	12	3	12
Ramos	.750	1	6	0	2	0	0
Vera	.942	16	66	15	5	0	4

First Base	PCT	G	PO	A	E	DP
Black	.995	126	1025	111	6	96
Pangilinan	.972	7	66	4	2	6
Spatola	1.000	1	1	0	0	0
Vera	.987	9	71	7	1	6

Second Base	PCT	G	PO	A	E	DP
Lee	.952	42	54	105	8	21
Oester	1.000	1	2	1	0	1
Sanchez	.980	53	89	154	5	38
Semien	.882	4	8	7	2	1
Silverio	1.000	2	4	5	0	1

CHICAGO WHITE SOX

Wilson	.969	39	64	93	5	19

Third Base	PCT	G	PO	A	E	DP
Lee	.917	14	10	23	3	2
Oester	1.000	3	4	2	0	0
Ravelo	.928	41	29	99	10	9
Silverio	.897	82	72	171	28	17
Vera	1.000	3	3	2	0	0

Shortstop	PCT	G	PO	A	E	DP
Eveland	.940	61	89	161	16	35
Sanchez	.949	10	21	16	2	6
Semien	.949	55	87	175	14	31
Silverio	1.000	2	3	3	0	0
Wilson	.906	12	8	21	3	2

Outfield	PCT	G	PO	A	E	DP
Dubler	1.000	1	2	0	0	0
Gilbert	.988	45	76	5	1	0

Hamme	.889	17	15	1	2	1
Harvard	.967	16	27	2	1	0
Kuhn	.985	33	63	3	1	0
Shoemaker	.988	99	162	6	2	1
Spatola	.985	37	62	5	1	0
Thompson	.973	136	307	12	9	2
Vera	.000	1	0	0	0	0
Walker	.978	39	88	3	2	0
Wilson	.889	8	8	0	1	0

BRISTOL SOX   ROOKIE
APPALACHIAN LEAGUE

Batting	B-T	HT	WT	DOB	AVG	vLH	vRH	G	AB	R	H	2B	3B	HR	RBI	BB	HBP	SH	SF	SO	SB	CS	SLG	OBP
Buckner, Grant	R-R	6-2	215	3-21-88	.311	.309	.311	61	235	39	73	20	1	5	36	18	11	0	2	42	2	0	.468	.383
Farris, Cory	L-R	6-0	190	12-29-89	.216	.306	.187	56	204	25	44	8	1	9	27	19	6	0	1	78	0	0	.397	.300
Harvard, Dusty	L-R	6-3	196	10-28-87	.229	.242	.224	26	109	22	25	3	2	1	8	10	1	0	0	30	6	3	.321	.300
Heisler, Adam	L-R	5-10	165	6-7-88	.400	.000	.400	2	5	0	2	0	0	0	0	0	0	0	0	1	0	1	.400	.400
Johnson, Michael	L-R	5-9	175	10-28-88	.276	.220	.290	54	203	37	56	17	3	3	25	18	4	0	2	46	0	2	.433	.344
Keegan, Jordan	R-R	6-0	175	12-23-89	.216	.032	.260	48	162	23	35	4	1	1	4	23	4	0	0	36	0	1	.272	.328
Kuhn, Collin	R-R	6-0	195	11-27-88	.260	.333	.241	31	100	28	26	11	0	4	20	19	8	0	0	19	3	2	.490	.417
Marjama, Mike	R-R	6-2	205	7-20-89	.221	.211	.224	24	86	6	19	2	1	0	7	4	1	0	0	18	0	3	.267	.264
Medina, Martin	R-R	6-0	200	3-24-90	.167	.269	.088	17	60	5	10	5	0	1	6	4	0	0	2	21	0	0	.300	.212
Mercedes, Daurys	R-R	6-1	165	2-26-90	.196	.237	.181	43	143	10	28	7	0	1	12	12	1	0	1	53	3	0	.266	.261
Mosier, Bryce	R-R	6-2	200	5-21-93	.235	.400	.167	10	34	6	8	2	0	0	3	2	2	0	0	5	1	1	.294	.333
O'Connell, Sean	L-R	6-4	181	12-12-91	.167	.083	.190	19	54	4	9	2	0	1	8	5	0	0	0	20	0	0	.259	.237
Puentes, Jerry	R-R	6-1	170	7-18-91	.202	.207	.200	28	89	12	18	5	3	0	5	10	0	0	0	22	0	0	.326	.283
Ramos, Jose	R-R	5-11	190	7-19-87	.320	.750	.238	8	25	0	8	1	0	0	3	0	0	0	0	9	0	1	.360	.320
Ravelo, Rangel	R-R	6-2	210	4-24-92	.384	.526	.333	20	73	10	28	7	1	0	13	2	2	0	1	12	2	0	.507	.410
Robinson, Kyle	R-R	6-3	210	12-2-88	.204	.218	.198	51	186	20	38	15	3	4	21	16	2	0	1	44	1	0	.382	.273
Salgado, Brad	R-R	6-1	185	7-15-91	.187	.238	.171	48	171	15	32	6	1	4	22	16	1	0	4	63	1	1	.304	.255
Sanchez, Carlos	R-R	5-11	175	6-29-92	.250	.000	.333	5	16	4	4	1	0	0	3	5	3	0	0	2	1	2	.313	.500
Schwartz, Mike	L-R	6-0	220	5-4-87	.195	.083	.213	24	87	8	17	3	0	1	13	11	1	0	0	14	0	0	.264	.293
Smith, Kevan	R-R	6-4	240	6-28-88	.396	.500	.365	26	96	24	38	10	1	7	32	14	2	0	0	14	1	2	.740	.482
Tanner, Brent	L-R	6-2	225	10-1-87	.178	.250	.152	14	45	1	8	1	0	0	4	6	1	0	0	17	0	0	.200	.260
Thompson, Drew	L-R	6-1	160	11-7-86	.348	.400	.333	7	23	9	8	3	0	1	7	4	0	0	0	4	0	0	.609	.444
Williams, Tyler	R-R	6-2	205	1-5-91	.263	.273	.259	23	80	7	21	4	1	0	3	7	1	0	0	35	0	0	.338	.330
Wilson, Ross	R-R	5-11	185	11-9-88	.238	.357	.179	11	42	11	10	4	0	0	7	5	0	0	1	10	2	1	.333	.313

Pitching	B-T	HT	WT	DOB	W	L	ERA	G	GS	CG	SV	IP	H	R	ER	HR	BB	SO	AVG	vLH	vRH	K/9	BB/9
Andres, Ricardo	R-R	6-4	205	5-2-91	0	0	6.32	12	0	0	0	16	17	11	11	4	11	8	.293	.316	.282	4.60	6.32
Bassitt, Chris	R-R	6-5	205	2-22-89	0	0	1.08	6	0	0	0	8	9	1	1	0	2	11	.273	.143	.308	11.88	2.16
Blough, Bryan	R-R	6-1	190	8-29-89	1	1	6.38	21	0	0	4	24	36	23	17	4	5	18	.336	.400	.299	6.75	1.88
Bollinger, Ryan	L-L	6-6	185	2-4-91	5	2	4.23	12	12	0	0	62	58	31	29	2	26	65	.247	.239	.249	9.49	3.79
Buch, Ryan	R-R	6-3	205	11-8-87	0	0	0.00	3	3	0	0	8	2	0	0	0	2	13	.077	.250	.000	14.63	2.25
Casey, J.C.	R-R	6-3	174	12-13-88	0	1	7.23	12	0	0	0	19	19	15	15	3	18	.257	.310	.222	8.68	1.45
Cassel, Justin	R-R	6-2	215	9-25-84	0	0	0.00	2	0	0	0	3	2	0	0	0	0	4	.200	.200	.200	0.00	0.00
Cose, Jake	B-R	6-5	195	8-28-90	1	1	8.18	11	0	0	0	11	16	12	10	3	4	9	.327	.273	.370	7.36	3.27
Duque, Jean	R-R	6-3	190	7-17-89	2	9	6.32	14	13	0	0	68	74	58	48	8	32	55	.280	.211	.320	7.24	4.21
Icard, Ethan	R-R	6-2	180	8-28-90	2	7	8.95	13	12	0	0	59	84	61	59	10	35	37	.331	.398	.298	5.61	5.31
Johnson, Garrett	L-L	6-10	205	9-2-87	0	0	4.50	2	0	0	0	2	3	1	1	0	0	3	.333	.000	.333	13.50	0.00
Kibby, Todd	L-L	6-4	240	8-31-91	0	0	3.38	17	5	0	0	37	37	15	14	2	12	36	.264	.156	.296	8.68	2.89
Kiley, Tim	R-R	6-7	225	11-17-88	2	3	5.11	17	0	0	0	25	30	16	14	3	10	28	.291	.351	.258	10.22	3.65
Lane, Matt	R-L	6-6	195	8-11-90	1	2	11.02	17	0	0	1	16	25	23	20	1	7	13	.342	.200	.379	7.16	3.86
Leyer, Euclides	R-R	6-2	172	12-28-92	2	7	6.38	14	14	0	0	66	77	54	47	10	24	53	.287	.262	.303	7.19	3.26
Linza, Keegan	R-R	6-6	230	11-10-88	0	1	3.57	23	0	0	2	23	25	13	9	1	5	22	.278	.258	.288	8.74	1.99
Matos, Darwin	R-R	6-0	170	8-4-90	0	5	4.89	14	8	0	0	50	50	32	27	5	32	49	.267	.297	.252	8.88	5.80
Merkley, Brett	R-R	5-11	165	8-15-87	1	2	6.37	20	0	0	1	30	37	22	21	5	6	28	.308	.353	.291	8.49	1.82
Nunez, Jhonny	L-R	6-3	215	11-26-85	0	0	4.50	3	0	0	0	4	4	3	2	0	2	5	.267	.333	.250	11.25	4.50
Petricka, Jake	R-R	6-5	170	6-5-88	0	0	0.00	2	1	0	0	4	4	0	0	0	0	5	.286	.250	.300	11.25	0.00
Sauer, Stephen	R-R	6-2	185	8-13-86	0	0	0.00	2	0	0	0	3	2	2	0	0	1	2	.154	.200	.125	6.00	3.00
Soptic, Jeff	R-R	6-2	210	4-8-91	0	1	0.00	3	0	0	1	3	2	2	0	0	2	2	.182	.000	.222	6.75	6.75
Van Skike, Jason	R-R	6-4	195	4-10-89	3	1	2.03	19	0	0	0	31	28	10	7	2	7	45	.239	.196	.268	13.06	2.03
Virgili, Andrew	R-R	6-2	205	1-30-90	1	1	4.44	21	0	0	0	24	27	16	12	2	5	21	.273	.242	.288	7.77	1.85

Fielding

Catcher	PCT	G	PO	A	E	DP	PB
Medina	.953	10	71	11	4	0	1
Mosier	.986	10	67	6	1	0	1
O'Connell	.992	19	113	16	1	2	3
Ramos	1.000	4	26	5	0	0	0
Smith	.980	21	176	23	4	3	3
Tanner	.988	11	72	11	1	0	2

First Base	PCT	G	PO	A	E	DP
Buckner	.982	47	415	19	8	34
Medina	1.000	3	29	1	0	6
Robinson	1.000	1	2	0	0	0
Schwartz	.982	18	160	8	3	14
Tanner	.917	1	11	0	1	4

Second Base	PCT	G	PO	A	E	DP
Johnson	.964	35	65	94	6	23

Mercedes	.948	27	41	68	6	16
Puentes	.958	6	7	16	1	5
Sanchez	1.000	1	0	5	0	1
Thompson	1.000	7	6	6	0	1

Third Base	PCT	G	PO	A	E	DP
Buckner	.842	7	3	13	3	1
Johnson	.958	11	2	21	1	0
Marjama	.933	10	5	23	2	3

CHICAGO WHITE SOX

	PCT	G	PO	A	E	DP
Puentes	.864	7	5	14	3	3
Ravelo	.980	18	11	39	1	0
Williams	.886	22	17	45	8	5
Shortstop	PCT	G	PO	A	E	DP
Johnson	.917	8	5	17	2	2
Puentes	.909	10	14	46	6	8

	PCT	G	PO	A	E	DP
Salgado	.939	48	61	139	13	28
Sanchez	1.000	4	9	15	0	6
Outfield	PCT	G	PO	A	E	DP
Farris	.962	45	72	3	3	0
Harvard	.968	26	58	3	2	0
Heisler	1.000	2	2	0	0	0

	PCT	G	PO	A	E	DP
Keegan	.941	46	77	3	5	0
Kuhn	.977	30	41	2	1	1
Mercedes	.927	18	36	2	3	0
Ramos	.000	1	0	0	0	0
Robinson	.974	48	73	3	2	0

GREAT FALLS VOYAGERS
PIONEER LEAGUE

ROOKIE

Batting	B-T	HT	WT	DOB	AVG	vLH	vRH	G	AB	R	H	2B	3B	HR	RBI	BB	HBP	SH	SF	SO	SB	CS	SLG	OBP
De Pinto, Joe	R-R	6-1	180	4-3-89	.285	.368	.262	68	263	49	75	18	3	5	46	34	12	0	3	54	7	2	.433	.388
Douglas, Andrew	R-R	6-0	210	5-27-89	.238	.289	.221	46	151	22	36	8	3	4	16	11	3	0	0	54	17	2	.411	.303
Earley, Michael	R-R	6-0	192	3-15-88	.307	.367	.291	63	228	40	70	17	2	3	34	12	9	0	2	38	5	2	.439	.363
Eveland, Kyle	R-R	5-10	175	4-11-87	.234	.269	.227	40	145	22	34	11	0	3	19	27	1	0	0	43	1	0	.372	.358
Haddow, Mark	R-R	6-2	220	12-2-87	.312	.264	.324	70	269	49	84	16	3	12	51	27	2	0	3	70	4	4	.528	.375
Herbek, David	R-R	6-2	182	4-2-89	.262	.296	.252	70	260	52	68	19	2	5	44	24	14	0	3	61	0	3	.408	.352
Jacquot, Jimmy	R-R	6-1	195	6-15-88	.280	.229	.291	56	207	30	58	12	2	5	35	17	6	0	3	63	0	0	.430	.348
Medina, Martin	R-R	6-0	200	3-24-90	.297	.375	.271	38	128	22	38	9	0	4	29	13	4	0	6	28	0	1	.461	.364
Millender, Qualon	R-R	5-10	170	3-31-87	.270	.235	.280	63	233	41	63	4	0	4	24	39	1	0	2	52	28	11	.330	.375
O'Connell, Sean	L-R	6-4	181	12-12-91	.333	.000	.400	5	12	3	4	0	0	0	0	2	1	0	0	1	3	0	0	.333	.357
Pangilinan, Leighton	L-R	6-3	230	3-6-91	.286	.150	.313	29	119	14	34	4	0	3	19	4	1	0	2	42	0	0	.395	.310
Patino, Jeffer	R-R	5-10	165	10-8-88	.212	.259	.198	33	118	18	25	4	0	3	15	10	1	0	2	27	1	0	.322	.275
Puentes, Jerry	R-R	6-1	170	7-18-91	.158	.000	.207	13	38	5	6	0	0	0	0	4	4	1	0	1	11	0	1	.158	.250
Schwartz, Mike	L-R	6-0	220	5-4-87	.217	.286	.188	9	23	6	5	2	0	1	3	8	1	0	0	2	0	0	.435	.438
Smith, Kevan	R-R	6-4	240	6-28-88	.318	.409	.294	30	107	22	34	12	2	2	16	14	5	0	1	16	1	0	.523	.417
Tanner, Brent	L-R	6-2	225	10-1-87	.111	.125	.105	9	27	2	3	2	0	0	2	3	2	0	0	9	0	0	.185	.250
Thorpe, Randall	R-R	6-1	175	4-2-89	.242	.250	.240	46	157	26	38	9	2	2	15	17	3	0	1	51	14	5	.363	.326
Walker, Keenyn	B-R	6-3	195	8-12-90	.333	.154	.383	15	60	16	20	7	1	0	9	7	4	0	1	17	11	5	.483	.431

Pitching	B-T	HT	WT	DOB	W	L	ERA	G	GS	CG	SV	IP	H	R	ER	HR	BB	SO	AVG	vLH	vRH	K/9	BB/9
Bachanov, Jon	R-R	6-4	230	1-30-89	1	0	2.57	4	0	0	0	7	6	2	2	0	2	9	.231	.375	.167	11.57	2.57
Brase, Stew	R-R	6-3	195	1-20-89	3	2	2.27	19	1	0	1	32	30	18	8	2	12	29	.250	.325	.213	8.24	3.41
Casey, Jarrett	R-L	6-0	185	10-27-87	4	1	4.40	10	0	0	0	47	59	28	23	3	10	45	.317	.377	.293	8.62	1.91
Casey, J.C.	R-R	6-3	174	12-13-88	0	2	7.94	7	0	0	0	11	18	13	10	0	8	8	.391	.611	.250	6.35	6.35
Devenski, Chris	R-R	6-3	195	11-13-90	0	0	2.25	7	0	0	1	8	8	2	2	0	1	9	.258	.143	.292	10.13	1.13
Drake, Blake	R-R	6-5	185	11-12-88	3	2	4.39	17	0	0	0	27	34	18	13	1	11	16	.304	.244	.343	5.40	3.71
Dvorsky, Joe	R-R	6-2	200	9-19-88	4	0	2.93	18	0	0	4	28	20	10	9	3	9	32	.190	.263	.149	10.41	2.93
Evans, Austin	R-R	6-3	220	11-5-87	1	1	5.18	16	0	0	0	24	27	20	14	3	11	34	.281	.211	.328	12.58	4.07
Gehle, Pete	L-L	6-6	240	1-15-88	5	7	4.64	14	14	0	0	69	71	39	36	6	11	65	.255	.190	.274	8.44	1.43
Gulbransen, Jon	L-L	6-0	195	11-16-88	0	1	7.56	17	0	0	0	17	24	14	14	1	11	19	.343	.350	.340	10.26	5.94
Hollis, Jamaal	R-R	6-2	195	12-3-87	1	3	4.94	20	0	0	0	31	36	23	17	6	18	38	.288	.432	.210	11.03	5.23
Johnson, Erik	R-R	6-3	240	12-30-89	0	0	4.50	2	0	0	0	2	4	1	1	0	1	2	.444	.750	.200	9.00	4.50
McCray, Stephen	L-R	6-3	230	10-6-87	3	4	4.85	16	9	0	0	56	68	41	30	10	17	47	.300	.294	.303	7.60	2.75
McMillen, Kyle	L-R	6-2	200	3-14-90	0	1	45.00	2	0	0	0	1	3	7	5	1	3	2	.429	.000	.600	18.00	27.00
Parrent, Brandon	L-L	6-3	215	7-14-90	0	0	3.86	9	5	0	0	28	33	14	12	1	14	21	.311	.476	.271	6.75	4.50
Phippen, Sam	R-R	6-9	210	9-15-87	2	5	5.61	16	11	0	1	59	70	43	37	10	21	66	.293	.278	.303	10.01	3.19
Rath, Kevin	L-L	6-5	220	8-18-89	0	0	6.29	18	0	0	0	24	27	20	17	1	19	22	.287	.226	.317	8.14	7.03
Sanchez, Salvador	R-R	6-6	195	9-13-85	0	0	0.00	2	0	0	0	2	1	0	0	0	0	1	.143	.000	.500	4.50	0.00
Snodgress, Scott	L-L	6-5	210	9-20-89	3	3	3.34	16	12	0	0	59	61	32	22	5	17	68	.262	.242	.269	10.31	2.58
Vance, Kevin	L-R	6-0	208	7-8-90	2	1	4.54	22	1	0	1	36	45	22	18	3	10	58	.294	.349	.273	14.64	2.52
Walters, Blair	L-L	6-0	200	11-8-89	9	4	4.03	14	13	0	0	74	72	36	33	6	17	72	.257	.221	.269	8.80	2.08
Winiarski, Cody	R-R	6-3	190	8-27-89	1	1	1.80	17	0	0	2	20	17	4	4	0	4	29	.224	.136	.259	13.05	1.80

Fielding

Catcher	PCT	G	PO	A	E	DP	PB
Jacquot	.985	35	289	41	5	3	7
Medina	.979	9	87	6	2	1	3
O'Connell	1.000	2	12	3	0	1	1
Smith	.988	25	218	28	3	3	6
Tanner	.985	7	57	7	1	1	5
First Base	PCT	G	PO	A	E	DP	
Jacquot	.989	19	170	10	2	12	
Medina	.967	27	215	20	8	19	
Pangilinan	.971	23	199	4	6	17	
Schwartz	.983	8	48	10	1	3	

Second Base	PCT	G	PO	A	E	DP
De Pinto	.958	63	131	168	13	36
Douglas	.969	6	15	16	1	7
Patino	.970	8	9	23	1	3
Third Base	PCT	G	PO	A	E	DP
Douglas	.826	9	6	13	4	2
Eveland	.932	38	19	77	7	6
Patino	.929	24	15	50	5	4
Puentes	.955	8	3	18	1	1
Shortstop	PCT	G	PO	A	E	DP
Douglas	.000	1	0	0	0	0

	PCT	G	PO	A	E	DP
Eveland	1.000	2	3	4	0	2
Herbek	.962	69	100	204	12	39
Puentes	.923	6	4	8	1	2
Outfield	PCT	G	PO	A	E	DP
Douglas	.917	10	10	1	1	0
Earley	.953	39	36	5	2	0
Haddow	.978	63	127	8	3	2
Millender	.957	62	83	6	4	1
Thorpe	.977	44	82	3	2	1
Walker	1.000	15	16	4	0	0

DSL WHITE SOX
DOMINICAN SUMMER LEAGUE

ROOKIE

Batting	B-T	HT	WT	DOB	AVG	vLH	vRH	G	AB	R	H	2B	3B	HR	RBI	BB	HBP	SH	SF	SO	SB	CS	SLG	OBP
Abreu, Julio	R-R	6-6	210	10-29-91	.211	.294	.186	32	76	6	16	1	0	1	12	16	5	0	3	24	1	1	.263	.370
Alcala, Julio	R-R	6-0	165	12-24-90	.286	.273	.289	58	196	29	56	13	2	0	24	32	4	0	4	31	3	7	.372	.390
Becerra, Ifran	L-R	5-10	155	6-13-91	.242	.170	.265	61	194	40	47	7	2	2	21	37	9	0	2	56	17	6	.330	.384

CHICAGO WHITE SOX

Batting

Batting	B-T	HT	WT	DOB	AVG	vLH	vRH	G	AB	R	H	2B	3B	HR	RBI	BB	HBP	SH	SF	SO	SB	CS	SLG	OBP
Buda, Maurizo	R-R	6-1	175	1-7-92	.262	.250	.265	61	195	25	51	12	0	3	29	23	10	0	2	43	2	2	.369	.365
Del Valle, Jaime	B-R	6-1	170	1-3-90	.230	.167	.242	43	113	14	26	5	4	0	14	18	3	0	1	9	4	3	.345	.348
Fernandez, Andelson	R-R	6-2	170	2-22-91	.187	.241	.171	46	134	11	25	3	1	0	10	13	0	0	3	36	5	6	.224	.253
Garcia, Humberto	B-R	5-10	165	5-20-94	.220	.100	.250	40	100	24	22	3	2	0	5	10	2	0	0	30	10	2	.290	.304
Guerrero, Sandy	R-R	6-1	180	10-14-92	.202	.235	.195	37	104	13	21	6	0	0	5	8	3	0	1	22	1	1	.260	.276
Pascual, Oliver	R-R	5-10	170	11-13-89	.254	.286	.246	27	71	11	18	3	1	2	7	7	0	0	0	9	1	0	.408	.321
Pizzoli, Franco	R-R	5-9	170	2-1-94	.194	.158	.208	28	72	10	14	3	1	1	13	3	3	0	1	12	0	0	.306	.253
Polanco, Luis	R-R	6-3	190	9-30-91	.258	.313	.247	29	93	14	24	3	1	0	10	9	2	0	2	12	0	1	.312	.330
Ramirez, Juan	R-R	6-4	196	8-28-90	.319	.310	.322	44	144	27	46	13	2	3	26	15	5	0	2	28	2	0	.500	.398
Rocha, Jaider	R-R	6-1	185	5-23-93	.150	.143	.151	45	127	11	19	3	1	1	13	30	2	0	0	37	3	5	.213	.321
Rosario, Angel	R-R	5-10	175	12-14-91	.267	.294	.261	52	172	30	46	16	0	0	27	28	4	0	1	22	0	2	.360	.380
Santana, Vladimir	R-R	6-0	165	1-24-91	.236	.291	.218	60	229	40	54	10	5	0	16	37	5	0	2	45	25	11	.323	.352
Santos, Jeffy	B-R	6-2	150	1-4-93	.204	.261	.187	29	98	6	20	3	0	0	6	14	0	0	0	27	5	4	.235	.304

Pitching

Pitching	B-T	HT	WT	DOB	W	L	ERA	G	GS	CG	SV	IP	H	R	ER	HR	BB	SO	AVG	vLH	vRH	K/9	BB/9
Arias, Feny	L-L	6-0	175	5-6-91	3	2	1.95	12	11	1	0	51	41	22	11	0	15	35	.214	.133	.228	6.22	2.66
Bautista, Jose	L-L	6-1	175	3-31-92	0	3	3.14	12	11	0	0	52	45	23	18	2	23	59	.245	.400	.231	10.28	4.01
Brito, Jose	R-R	6-0	175	10-10-90	0	1	8.64	7	2	0	0	8	9	10	8	0	13	4	.300	.267	.333	4.32	14.04
Cabrera, Raldy	R-R	6-0	180	9-25-89	2	0	4.26	19	0	0	1	38	38	25	18	0	20	24	.275	.340	.239	5.68	4.74
Diaz, Evandert	R-R	6-3	190	5-20-92	2	3	3.54	11	6	0	0	41	33	20	16	0	33	32	.243	.227	.257	7.08	7.30
Duque, Jean	R-R	6-3	190	7-17-89	0	0	0.00	1	0	0	0	2	1	0	0	0	1	2	.125	.000	.167	7.71	3.86
Echezuria, Luis	R-R	6-0	179	5-10-91	2	1	4.20	18	0	0	0	30	25	19	14	0	19	22	.227	.271	.194	6.60	5.70
Hernandez, Juandalys	R-R	6-1	165	1-26-91	0	0	36.64	9	1	0	0	5	4	20	19	0	21	3	.267	.167	.333	5.79	40.50
Jaquez, Juan	R-R	6-4	164	12-30-89	0	0	3.71	7	0	0	0	17	17	12	7	1	9	12	.254	.333	.209	6.35	4.76
Jean, Dominque	R-R	6-2	170	11-24-88	3	5	1.95	24	0	0	6	32	17	19	7	2	24	16	.155	.081	.192	4.45	6.68
Magallanes, Yensi	L-L	6-0	185	2-2-93	3	1	1.45	16	0	0	1	31	25	10	5	0	13	38	.217	.250	.211	11.03	3.77
Nieves, Wilce	R-R	6-0	175	5-12-92	5	4	4.82	14	10	1	0	47	40	30	25	3	29	36	.241	.227	.253	6.94	5.59
Olacio, Jefferson	L-L	6-7	230	1-16-94	3	5	5.50	11	11	0	0	38	30	27	23	0	38	42	.227	.353	.209	10.04	9.08
Ortiz, Braulio	R-R	6-5	205	12-20-91	0	1	8.31	6	1	0	0	9	9	11	8	0	11	7	.265	.214	.300	7.27	11.42
Rosario, Carlos	L-L	5-10	160	3-13-88	4	1	2.09	28	0	0	5	47	37	13	11	1	13	36	.219	.208	.221	6.85	2.47
Sanchez, Leopoldo	R-R	6-1	180	6-5-91	5	4	3.22	14	12	1	0	64	53	29	23	1	19	60	.224	.239	.214	8.39	2.66
Valerio, Kelvis	R-R	6-1	160	9-26-91	3	1	1.44	16	2	0	0	50	37	11	8	0	15	26	.214	.222	.209	4.68	2.70
Vargas, Ivan	R-R	6-3	190	8-14-91	0	0	5.14	8	0	0	0	7	6	6	4	0	7	2	.261	.429	.188	2.57	9.00

Fielding

Catcher	PCT	G	PO	A	E	DP	PB
Del Valle	.971	7	28	6	1	0	2
Garcia	1.000	1	1	0	0	0	0
Pascual	.976	7	31	10	1	0	3
Pizzoli	.984	20	106	19	2	1	1
Rosario	.974	47	276	64	9	1	12

First Base	PCT	G	PO	A	E	DP
Abreu	.980	15	93	4	2	10
Alcala	1.000	2	2	0	0	0
Del Valle	.962	9	44	7	2	1
Fernandez	1.000	2	11	0	0	2
Guerrero	.986	32	207	9	3	12
Pascual	1.000	1	1	1	0	0
Pizzoli	1.000	7	56	4	0	8
Polanco	.977	22	158	15	4	11

Second Base	PCT	G	PO	A	E	DP
Becerra	.975	39	71	88	4	18
Garcia	.924	28	45	52	8	9
Santana	.956	15	29	36	3	8

Third Base	PCT	G	PO	A	E	DP
Becerra	1.000	4	2	7	0	1
Fernandez	.850	10	7	10	3	0
Garcia	.000	1	0	0	0	0
Guerrero	.792	10	5	14	5	0
Polanco	.870	11	6	14	3	0
Rosario	1.000	2	1	2	0	0
Santana	.915	47	34	96	12	10

Shortstop	PCT	G	PO	A	E	DP
Fernandez	.933	34	67	87	11	11

	PCT	G	PO	A	E	DP
Garcia	.971	8	14	20	1	3
Guerrero	.000	1	0	0	0	0
Santana	.933	6	8	6	1	1
Santos	.918	28	43	69	10	14

Outfield	PCT	G	PO	A	E	DP
Abreu	.750	5	2	1	1	0
Alcala	.985	52	65	1	1	0
Becerra	.974	25	32	5	1	0
Buda	1.000	60	73	6	0	3
Pascual	1.000	4	2	0	0	0
Ramirez	.979	40	92	1	2	1
Rocha	.968	42	59	1	2	0
Rosario	1.000	1	1	0	0	0

Cincinnati Reds

SEASON IN A SENTENCE: A year after their first playoff appearance and division crown in 15 years, the Reds returned to earth with their 10th losing record in the past 11 seasons, thanks in large part to a pitching staff that couldn't match its 2010 performance.

HIGH POINT: A quarter of the way through the season, the Reds were sitting at 25-17 on the heels of a three-game sweep of the Cardinals. At the time, they were a game and a half up on the rest of the National League Central and looking like a team that could defend its division title. It wouldn't take long for fans to learn otherwise.

LOW POINT: On the heels of a sweep of the Giants, Cincinnati entered August six games back in the division with series coming up against the Astros and Cubs. The Reds could have jumped back into the race with a good week. Instead, Cincinnati went 2-4 against the worst of the division and the season was effectively finished.

NOTABLE ROOKIES: Lefthander Aroldis Chapman proved nearly unhittable (.147 opponent average), but the reliever had trouble aiming his triple-digit fastball, as he walked 41 batters in 50 innings. Zack Cozart claimed the shortstop job in just 11 games, before he was lost for the season to a elbow injury. By the end of the season, catcher Devin Mesoraco, first baseman/outfielder Yonder Alonso, utilityman Todd Frazier and outfielder Dave Sappelt were also seeing major league time.

KEY TRANSACTIONS: With a largely home-grown lineup, the Reds didn't make many tweaks. Outfielder Johnny Gomes was traded away to clear room for prospect Yonder Alonso, but when the Reds faced injuries, they were much more comfortable bringing up replacements from Triple-A. The Reds did sign righthander Bronson Arroyo to a contract extension before the season, only to see him go 9-12, 5.07 while allowing a team-record 46 home runs.

DOWN ON THE FARM: The low Class A Dayton Dragons finished with the best record in the Midwest League (89-43), thanks to a prospect-laden infield of third baseman David Vidal, short-stop Billy Hamilton, second baseman Ronald Torreyes and first baseman Derrick Lutz, and a rotation that included Daniel Corcino, Josh Smith and Daniel Renken. The Reds also had prospects leading the Triple-A Louisville club, although that team was gutted by the promotions of the team's regulars to Cincinnati as the season progressed.

OPENING DAY PAYROLL: $75,947,134 (19th)

PLAYERS OF THE YEAR

MAJOR LEAGUE	MINOR LEAGUE
Joey Votto	**Neftali Soto**
1b	**1b**
.309/.416/.531	Double-A/Triple-A
29 HR, 103 RBIs	.272/.329/.575
Led NL in OBP, BB	31 HR, 80 RBIs

ORGANIZATION LEADERS

BATTING   *Minimum 250 PA

MAJORS

* AVG	Joey Votto	.309
* OPS	Joey Votto	.947
HR	Jay Bruce	32
RBI	Joey Votto	103

MINORS

* AVG	Denis Phipps, Carolina/Louisville	.346
* OBP	Yasmani Grandal, Bake./Carolina/Louisville	.401
* SLG	Neftali Soto, Carolina/Louisville	.576
R	Billy Hamilton, Dayton	99
H	Henry Rodriguez, Bakersfield/Carolina	165
TB	Denis Phipps, Carolina/Louisville	244
2B	Eric Campbell, Bakersfield/Carolina	37
	David Vidal, Dayton	37
3B	Billy Hamilton, Dayton	9
	Kyle Waldrop, Billings	9
HR	Neftali Soto, Carolina/Louisville	31
RBI	David Vidal, Dayton	85
BB	Yasmani Grandal, Bake./Carolina/Louisville	59
SO	Juan Duran, Dayton	152
SB	Billy Hamilton, Dayton	103

PITCHING   #Minimum 75 IP

MAJORS

W	Mike Leake	12
# ERA	Johnny Cueto	2.31
SO	Mike Leake	118
SV	Francisco Cordero	37

MINORS

W	Josh Smith, Dayton	14
L	Curtis Partch, Bakersfield/Carolina	13
# ERA	Josh Smith, Dayton	2.97
G	Donnie Joseph, Carolina	57
GS	Curtis Partch, Bakersfield/Carolina	28
SV	Drew Hayes, Dayton	22
IP	Curtis Partch, Bakersfield/Carolina	160.2
BB	Josh Ravin, Bakersfield/Carolina	82
SO	Josh Smith, Dayton	166
# AVG	Josh Smith, Dayton	.228

General Manager: Walt Jocketty. **Farm Director:** Bill Bavasi. **Scouting Director:** Chris Buckley.

Class	Team	League	W	L	PCT	Finish	Manager(s)
Majors	Cincinnati Reds	National	79	83	.488	9th (16)	Dusty Baker
Triple-A	Louisville Bats	International	73	71	.507	8th (14)	Rick Sweet
Double-A	Carolina Mudcats	Southern	53	86	.381	10th (10)	David Bell
High A	Bakersfield Blaze	California	66	74	.471	7th (10)	Ken Griffey
Low A	Dayton Dragons	Midwest	83	57	.593	1st (16)	Delino DeShields
Rookie	Billings Mustangs	Pioneer	44	32	.579	2nd (8)	Pat Kelly
Rookie	AZL Reds	Arizona	31	25	.554	4th (13)	Jose Nieves
Overall 2011 Minor League Record			350	345	.504	15th (30)	

ORGANIZATION STATISTICS

CINCINNATI REDS
NATIONAL LEAGUE

Batting	B-T	HT	WT	DOB	AVG	vLH	vRH	G	AB	R	H	2B	3B	HR	RBI	BB	HBP	SH	SF	SO	SB	CS	SLG	OBP
Alonso, Yonder	L-R	6-2	240	4-8-87	.330	.154	.360	47	88	9	29	4	0	5	15	10	0	0	0	21	0	0	.545	.398
Bruce, Jay	L-L	6-3	225	4-3-87	.256	.240	.263	157	585	84	150	27	2	32	97	71	5	0	2	158	8	7	.474	.341
Cairo, Miguel	R-R	6-1	220	5-4-74	.265	.319	.253	102	245	33	65	8	2	8	33	18	7	0	3	36	3	4	.412	.330
Cozart, Zack	R-R	6-0	195	8-12-85	.324	.333	.320	11	37	6	12	0	0	2	3	0	0	0	0	6	0	0	.486	.324
Francisco, Juan	L-R	6-2	240	6-24-87	.258	.143	.278	31	93	10	24	7	1	3	15	4	0	0	0	24	1	0	.452	.289
Frazier, Todd	R-R	6-3	220	2-12-86	.232	.360	.195	41	112	17	26	5	0	6	15	7	2	0	0	27	1	0	.438	.289
Gomes, Jonny	R-R	6-1	225	11-22-80	.211	.333	.171	77	218	30	46	8	0	11	31	38	5	0	4	74	5	3	.399	.336
2-team total (43 Washington)					.209	—	—	120	311	41	65	12	1	14	43	48	8	0	5	105	7	3	.389	.325
Hanigan, Ryan	R-R	6-0	200	8-16-80	.267	.275	.265	91	266	27	71	6	0	6	31	35	2	0	0	32	0	0	.357	.356
Heisey, Chris	R-R	6-0	225	12-14-84	.254	.197	.271	120	279	44	71	9	1	18	50	19	5	0	4	78	6	1	.487	.309
Hermida, Jeremy	L-R	6-3	220	1-30-84	.111	1.000	.059	10	18	2	2	0	0	1	3	0	0	0	0	7	0	0	.278	.111
2-team total (20 San Diego)					.190	—	—	30	58	5	11	2	1	2	9	7	1	0	0	26	0	0	.362	.288
Hernandez, Ramon	R-R	6-0	220	5-20-76	.282	.323	.271	91	298	28	84	13	0	12	36	23	5	0	2	41	0	0	.446	.341
Janish, Paul	R-R	6-2	200	10-12-82	.214	.210	.215	114	336	27	72	14	1	0	23	18	4	0	5	46	3	2	.262	.259
Lewis, Fred	L-R	6-2	200	12-9-80	.230	.000	.247	81	183	20	42	7	0	3	19	22	3	0	1	38	2	5	.317	.321
Mesoraco, Devin	R-R	6-1	220	6-19-88	.180	.250	.167	18	50	5	9	3	0	2	6	3	0	0	0	10	0	0	.360	.226
Phillips, Brandon	R-R	6-0	205	6-28-81	.300	.316	.295	150	610	94	183	38	2	18	82	44	9	1	6	85	14	9	.457	.353
Renteria, Edgar	R-R	6-1	200	8-7-75	.251	.304	.239	96	299	34	75	14	0	5	36	24	1	0	3	65	4	2	.348	.306
Rolen, Scott	R-R	6-4	245	4-4-75	.242	.246	.241	65	252	31	61	20	2	5	36	10	4	0	3	36	1	0	.397	.279
Sappelt, Dave	R-R	5-9	195	1-2-87	.243	.267	.234	38	107	14	26	8	0	0	5	7	0	0	0	17	1	1	.318	.289
Stubbs, Drew	R-R	6-4	200	10-4-84	.243	.319	.226	158	604	92	147	22	3	15	44	63	7	0	1	205	40	10	.364	.321
Valaika, Chris	R-R	6-0	210	8-14-85	.280	.800	.150	14	25	3	7	1	1	0	0	2	0	0	0	3	0	0	.400	.333
Votto, Joey	L-R	6-3	220	9-10-83	.309	.333	.299	161	599	101	185	40	3	29	103	110	4	0	6	129	8	6	.531	.416

Pitching	B-T	HT	WT	DOB	W	L	ERA	G	GS	CG	SV	IP	H	R	ER	HR	BB	SO	AVG	vLH	vRH	K/9	BB/9
Arredondo, Jose	R-R	6-0	175	3-12-84	4	4	3.23	53	0	0	0	53	43	21	19	5	31	48	.226	.238	.218	8.15	5.26
Arroyo, Bronson	R-R	6-4	195	2-24-77	9	12	5.07	32	32	1	0	199	227	119	112	46	45	108	.286	.321	.256	4.88	2.04
Bailey, Homer	R-R	6-3	200	5-3-86	9	7	4.43	22	22	0	0	132	136	68	65	18	33	106	.264	.274	.256	7.23	2.25
Bray, Bill	L-L	6-3	225	6-5-83	5	3	2.98	79	0	0	0	48	35	16	16	3	17	44	.202	.182	.232	8.19	3.17
Burton, Jared	R-R	6-5	225	6-2-81	0	0	3.86	6	0	0	0	5	6	2	2	1	3	3	.316	.500	.231	5.79	5.79
Chapman, Aroldis	L-L	6-4	195	2-28-88	4	1	3.60	54	0	0	1	50	24	21	20	2	41	71	.147	.080	.174	12.78	7.38
Cordero, Francisco	R-R	6-3	245	5-11-75	5	3	2.45	68	0	0	37	70	49	20	19	6	22	42	.198	.243	.160	5.43	2.84
Cueto, Johnny	R-R	5-10	220	2-15-86	9	5	2.31	24	24	3	0	156	123	51	40	8	47	104	.220	.209	.229	6.00	2.71
Fisher, Carlos	R-R	6-4	225	2-22-83	0	3	4.50	17	0	0	0	24	25	15	12	3	11	17	.263	.294	.246	6.38	4.13
Horst, Jeremy	L-L	6-3	220	10-1-85	0	0	2.93	12	0	0	0	15	18	6	5	2	6	9	.290	.316	.279	5.28	3.52
Leake, Mike	R-R	6-1	185	11-12-87	12	9	3.86	29	26	0	0	168	159	74	72	23	38	118	.250	.262	.240	6.33	2.04
LeCure, Sam	R-R	6-1	205	5-4-84	2	1	3.71	43	4	0	0	78	57	33	32	10	21	73	.205	.188	.218	8.46	2.43
Maloney, Matt	L-L	6-4	210	1-16-84	0	3	9.16	8	2	0	0	19	36	21	19	7	4	13	.409	.346	.435	6.27	1.93
Masset, Nick	R-R	6-4	240	5-17-82	3	6	3.71	75	0	0	1	70	76	30	29	5	31	62	.273	.287	.270	7.93	3.97
Ondrusek, Logan	R-R	6-8	230	2-13-85	5	5	3.23	66	0	0	0	61	55	25	22	6	28	41	.238	.232	.242	6.02	4.11
Reineke, Chad	R-R	6-6	210	4-9-82	0	1	6.75	2	1	0	0	7	5	6	5	2	6	3	.217	.250	.211	4.05	8.10
Smith, Jordan	R-R	6-4	220	2-4-86	0	0	7.20	17	0	0	0	20	32	16	16	3	8	13	.390	.538	.321	5.85	3.60
Thompson, Daryl	R-R	6-0	205	11-2-85	0	1	15.00	1	0	0	0	3	6	5	5	0	5	0	.429	.364	.667	0.00	15.00
Volquez, Edinson	R-R	6-0	225	7-3-83	5	7	5.71	20	20	0	0	109	106	72	69	19	65	104	.259	.274	.249	8.61	5.38
Willis, Dontrelle	L-L	6-4	225	1-12-82	1	6	5.00	13	13	0	0	76	78	42	42	6	37	57	.271	.127	.305	6.78	4.40
Wood, Travis	R-L	5-11	175	2-6-87	6	6	4.84	22	18	0	0	106	118	57	57	10	40	76	.293	.316	.287	6.45	3.40

Fielding

Catcher	PCT	G	PO	A	E	DP	PB
Hanigan	.993	89	541	29	4	6	2
Hernandez	.998	82	507	41	1	6	3
Mesoraco	.973	16	103	6	3	1	0

First Base	PCT	G	PO	A	E	DP
Alonso	1.000	3	8	3	0	0

	PCT	G	PO	A	E	DP
Cairo	1.000	5	11	0	0	0
Frazier	1.000	1	11	0	0	1
Hernandez	1.000	1	8	0	0	1
Votto	.996	160	1341	173	6	127

Second Base	PCT	G	PO	A	E	DP
Cairo	1.000	13	10	30	0	6

	PCT	G	PO	A	E	DP
Frazier	1.000	2	2	1	0	2
Janish	.955	5	12	9	1	4
Phillips	.992	148	306	409	6	94
Renteria	1.000	4	1	5	0	0
Valaika	1.000	1	3	1	0	0

Third Base	PCT	G	PO	A	E	DP
Alonso	.000	1	0	0	0	0
Cairo	.972	58	31	108	4	13
Francisco	.962	24	14	36	2	1
Frazier	.969	27	19	43	2	1
Janish	.889	8	1	7	1	0
Rolen	.975	63	38	119	4	11
Valaika	1.000	4	4	13	0	2

Shortstop	PCT	G	PO	A	E	DP
Cozart	1.000	11	22	41	0	7
Frazier	1.000	2	2	1	0	0
Janish	.974	103	126	256	10	45
Renteria	.959	86	95	208	13	36
Valaika	1.000	2	1	2	0	1

Outfield	PCT	G	PO	A	E	DP
Alonso	.958	16	22	1	1	0

	PCT	G	PO	A	E	DP
Bruce	.988	155	306	10	4	1
Frazier	1.000	4	3	1	0	0
Gomes	.988	54	81	1	1	0
Heisey	.978	102	134	2	3	0
Hermida	1.000	4	5	0	0	0
Lewis	.988	48	81	3	1	2
Sappelt	1.000	33	51	2	0	1
Stubbs	.992	157	366	8	3	2

LOUISVILLE BATS

TRIPLE-A

INTERNATIONAL LEAGUE

Batting	B-T	HT	WT	DOB	AVG	vLH	vRH	G	AB	R	H	2B	3B	HR	RBI	BB	HBP	SH	SF	SO	SB	CS	SLG	OBP
Alonso, Yonder	L-R	6-2	240	4-8-87	.296	.313	.289	91	358	46	106	24	4	12	56	46	1	0	4	60	6	5	.486	.374
Barton, Brian	R-R	6-3	190	4-25-82	.128	.042	.217	19	47	6	6	1	1	1	7	4	1	0	1	16	2	1	.255	.208
Berry, Quintin	L-L	6-0	175	11-21-84	.056	.000	.111	4	18	2	1	0	0	0	0	0	0	0	0	4	2	0	.056	.056
Castro, Jose	B-R	5-11	172	11-5-86	.267	.273	.263	20	60	7	16	1	1	0	4	3	0	0	3	0	0		.317	.302
Clevlen, Brent	R-R	6-1	205	10-27-83	.247	.182	.269	26	89	9	22	2	1	3	10	7	0	0	0	28	0	1	.393	.302
Cook, David	R-R	5-11	205	7-21-81	.193	.240	.156	24	57	4	11	4	0	0	1	7	3	0	0	17	0	0	.263	.313
Costanzo, Mike	L-R	6-3	215	9-9-83	.216	.171	.232	47	153	15	33	6	0	5	26	14	1	0	5	59	1	1	.353	.277
Cozart, Zack	R-R	6-0	195	8-12-85	.310	.282	.325	77	323	57	100	26	2	7	32	23	2	0	2	51	9	2	.467	.357
Dorn, Danny	L-L	6-2	205	7-20-84	.248	.169	.282	124	448	52	111	30	1	18	74	36	6	0	4	133	2	0	.440	.310
Eymann, Eric	R-R	6-2	195	2-9-84	.186	.150	.217	16	43	4	8	3	0	2	6	1	0	0	1	11	0	0	.395	.200
Francisco, Juan	L-R	6-2	240	6-24-87	.307	.247	.335	74	300	46	92	23	1	15	50	10	3	0	1	65	0	0	.540	.334
Frazier, Todd	R-R	6-3	220	2-12-86	.260	.224	.279	90	315	47	82	18	1	15	46	34	6	0	4	82	17	4	.467	.340
Grandal, Yasmani	B-T	6-2	205	11-8-88	.500	.500	.500	4	12	2	6	2	0	0	2	5	1	0	0	1	0	0	.667	.667
Griffin, Michael	R-R	5-9	200	10-1-83	.195	.256	.143	75	195	17	38	10	1	0	12	7	1	0	1	30	1	1	.256	.225
Heisey, Chris	R-R	6-0	225	12-14-84	.083	.000	.111	4	12	1	1	0	0	1	2	0	0	0	1	5	0	0	.333	.077
Hermida, Jeremy	L-R	6-3	220	1-30-84	.319	.349	.305	105	395	67	126	28	1	17	55	46	8	0	1	97	3	0	.524	.400
Janish, Paul	R-R	6-2	200	10-12-82	.256	.286	.250	13	43	9	11	2	0	1	3	7	2	0	1	4	1	0	.372	.377
Lewis, Fred	R-R	6-2	200	12-9-80	.300	.500	.250	8	20	6	6	1	1	1	3	8	0	0	0	5	1	0	.600	.500
Mesoraco, Devin	R-R	6-1	220	6-19-88	.289	.286	.291	120	436	60	126	36	2	15	71	52	7	0	4	83	1	1	.484	.371
Miller, Corky	R-R	6-1	255	3-18-76	.200	.190	.207	49	145	21	29	6	0	3	11	26	7	0	0	20	1	0	.303	.348
Negron, Kris	R-R	6-0	180	2-1-86	.216	.248	.200	123	417	54	90	16	4	9	45	22	10	0	5	102	11	1	.338	.269
Perez, Felix	L-L	6-2	190	11-14-84	.206	.300	.167	9	34	3	7	1	0	0	1	2	0	0	0	4	1	1	.235	.250
Pfister, Frank	R-R	6-1	205	8-25-86	.333	.000	1.000	3	3	1	1	0	0	0	0	0	0	0	0	1	0	0	.333	.333
Phipps, Denis	R-R	6-2	177	7-22-85	.380	.352	.394	40	158	30	60	12	2	5	26	13	1	0	1	41	4	1	.576	.428
Sappelt, Dave	R-R	5-9	195	1-2-87	.313	.358	.292	74	297	40	93	16	3	7	29	30	2	0	3	39	4	4	.458	.377
Skelton, James	L-R	5-11	165	10-28-85	.000	.000	.000	5	9	0	0	0	0	1	2	0	0	1	2	0	0		.000	.167
Soto, Neftali	R-R	6-2	180	2-28-89	.412	.625	.222	4	17	1	7	0	0	1	4	1	0	0	0	2	0	0	.588	.444
Valaika, Chris	R-R	6-0	210	8-14-85	.261	.305	.242	109	417	39	109	18	0	7	37	21	6	0	6	65	1	0	.355	.302

Pitching	B-T	HT	WT	DOB	W	L	ERA	G	GS	CG	SV	IP	H	R	ER	HR	BB	SO	AVG	vLH	vRH	K/9	BB/9
Arredondo, Jose	R-R	6-0	175	3-12-84	1	1	2.25	6	0	0	0	8	6	3	2	0	2	10	.188	.400	.091	11.25	2.25
Bailey, Homer	R-R	6-3	200	5-3-86	2	1	3.00	6	6	0	0	30	34	10	10	1	6	22	.279	.289	.273	6.60	1.80
Boxberger, Brad	R-R	6-2	200	5-27-88	1	2	2.93	25	0	0	7	28	16	10	9	2	15	36	.167	.182	.154	11.71	4.88
Burton, Jared	R-R	6-5	225	6-2-81	2	0	4.15	11	0	0	0	13	12	6	6	1	5	11	.250	.400	.143	7.62	3.46
Carroll, Scott	R-R	6-4	215	9-24-84	7	8	5.39	25	25	0	0	145	186	92	87	12	47	85	.312	.339	.288	5.26	2.91
Chapman, Aroldis	L-L	6-4	195	2-28-88	0	1	11.12	4	1	0	0	6	9	7	7	0	2	9	.333	.000	.409	14.29	3.18
Christiani, Nick	R-R	5-10	180	7-17-87	2	3	5.30	33	0	0	7	36	46	23	21	2	15	19	.309	.380	.244	4.79	3.79
Cochran, Tom	L-L	6-2	195	10-16-82	7	4	3.55	27	12	0	0	89	71	37	35	8	42	68	.258	.254	.198	6.90	4.26
Cueto, Johnny	R-R	5-10	220	2-15-86	0	2	6.28	4	4	0	0	14	19	12	10	1	6	13	.311	.429	.212	8.16	3.77
Doyle, Pat	R-R	6-2	205	5-12-88	0	0	9.00	1	0	0	0	2	3	2	2	0	2	3	.333	.400	.250	13.50	9.00
Fisher, Carlos	R-R	6-4	225	2-22-83	4	1	3.35	32	0	0	6	40	31	17	15	4	18	40	.212	.179	.241	8.93	4.02
Gil, Jerry	R-R	6-3	210	10-14-82	5	6	3.59	54	0	0	6	63	53	29	25	2	29	58	.233	.314	.184	8.33	4.16
Herrera, Danny Ray	L-L	5-6	165	10-21-84	0	4	3.86	17	0	0	1	19	20	11	8	1	7	15	.274	.333	.250	7.23	3.38
Horst, Jeremy	L-L	6-3	220	10-1-85	1	4	2.81	36	0	0	0	51	41	18	16	2	14	42	.219	.277	.173	7.36	2.45
Hynick, Brandon	R-R	6-3	205	3-7-85	0	3	5.19	9	3	0	0	26	22	15	15	2	10	22	.234	.333	.143	7.62	3.46
2-team total (7 Charlotte)					1	7	6.75	16	10	0	0	63	73	47	47	12	21	48	—	—		6.89	3.02
Jackson, Steven	R-R	6-5	230	3-15-82	0	0	5.59	10	0	0	1	10	10	6	6	0	2	7	.294	.357	.250	6.52	1.86
2-team total (24 Indianapolis)					4	2	4.30	34	0	0	2	46	45	25	22	4	17	22	—	—		4.30	3.33
Johnson, David	R-R	6-5	205	8-25-82	5	2	4.98	36	2	0	1	56	56	35	31	8	23	44	.260	.240	.279	7.07	3.70
Klinker, Matt	R-R	6-4	215	10-8-84	3	1	6.33	6	4	0	0	27	35	19	19	4	7	17	.307	.351	.263	5.67	2.33
Krebs, Joseph	L-L	6-0	200	9-14-84	1	0	6.75	14	0	0	0	21	26	16	16	2	12	15	.299	.179	.356	6.33	5.06
Leake, Mike	R-R	6-1	185	11-12-87	0	1	9.82	2	1	0	0	7	12	8	8	3	0	5	.343	.375	.316	6.14	0.00
LeCure, Sam	R-R	6-1	205	5-4-84	0	1	1.35	4	0	0	1	7	5	1	1	1	2	6	.217	.300	.154	8.10	2.70
Lehr, Justin	R-R	6-2	205	8-3-77	1	2	5.94	12	0	0	0	17	23	11	11	2	7	13	.343	.281	.400	7.02	3.78
Maloney, Matt	L-L	6-4	210	1-16-84	7	1	2.99	14	13	0	0	81	77	29	27	8	11	51	.254	.266	.249	5.64	1.22
McCulloch, Kyle	R-R	6-3	190	3-20-85	0	1	3.09	8	0	0	0	12	18	5	4	1	2	2	.360	.350	.367	1.54	0.77
Mobley, Chris	R-R	5-11	170	8-16-83	1	0	1.23	8	0	0	1	7	5	1	1	0	5	8	.200	.250	.154	9.82	6.14
Reineke, Chad	R-R	6-6	210	4-9-82	9	7	3.84	25	22	0	1	127	143	65	54	13	39	77	.286	.275	.297	5.47	2.77
Smith, Jordan	R-R	6-4	220	2-4-86	0	4	3.08	24	0	0	7	26	25	9	9	2	9	13	.258	.310	.218	4.44	3.08
Tanner, Clayton	R-L	6-2	205	12-5-87	0	0	0.00	1	0	0	0	3	1	0	0	0	2	4	.091	.000	.100	12.00	6.00
Thompson, Daryl	R-R	6-0	205	11-2-85	3	4	4.17	17	15	0	1	91	103	48	42	11	23	82	.286	.305	.270	8.14	2.28

CINCINNATI REDS

Pitching

Pitching	B-T	HT	WT	DOB	W	L	ERA	G	GS	CG	SV	IP	H	R	ER	HR	BB	SO	AVG	vLH	vRH	K/9	BB/9
Volquez, Edinson	R-R	6-0	225	7-3-83	4	2	2.37	13	13	1	0	87	72	31	23	5	29	83	.223	.254	.200	8.55	2.99
Webb, Travis	L-L	6-4	205	8-2-84	0	0	0.00	1	0	0	0	1	0	0	0	0	0	0	.000	.000	.000	0.00	0.00
Willis, Dontrelle	L-L	6-4	225	1-12-82	5	2	2.63	13	13	0	0	75	71	29	22	5	20	67	.250	.222	.263	8.00	2.39
Wood, Travis	R-L	5-11	175	2-6-87	2	3	5.33	10	10	0	0	52	64	33	31	6	17	47	.305	.329	.293	8.08	2.92

Fielding

Catcher	PCT	G	PO	A	E	DP	PB
Grandal	1.000	4	42	1	0	0	0
Mesoraco	.986	97	670	54	10	8	10
Miller	.997	42	290	26	1	0	2
Skelton	1.000	2	15	0	0	0	2

First Base	PCT	G	PO	A	E	DP
Alonso	.989	21	158	16	2	10
Costanzo	.972	15	96	7	3	10
Dorn	.996	89	736	76	3	62
Eymann	.964	9	50	4	2	9
Frazier	1.000	20	164	13	0	17
Miller	1.000	2	4	0	0	1
Soto	1.000	4	28	2	0	5

Second Base	PCT	G	PO	A	E	DP
Castro	.971	18	28	38	2	9
Frazier	1.000	2	3	3	0	0
Griffin	1.000	15	32	29	0	11

	PCT	G	PO	A	E	DP
Negron	.968	33	63	86	5	21
Skelton	.667	1	1	1	1	1
Valaika	.972	85	163	250	12	52

Third Base	PCT	G	PO	A	E	DP
Costanzo	.963	28	14	64	3	5
Eymann	1.000	2	3	5	0	0
Francisco	.959	64	40	125	7	16
Frazier	.950	35	30	83	6	10
Griffin	.917	9	5	6	1	2
Negron	.000	1	0	0	0	0
Pfister	.000	1	0	0	0	0
Valaika	1.000	12	9	23	0	1

Shortstop	PCT	G	PO	A	E	DP
Cozart	.968	75	120	218	11	39
Janish	.959	12	15	32	2	5
Negron	.949	46	70	118	10	30
Valaika	.983	13	18	41	1	4

Outfield	PCT	G	PO	A	E	DP
Alonso	1.000	62	88	3	0	1
Barton	1.000	12	16	0	0	0
Berry	1.000	4	8	0	0	0
Clevlen	.985	25	64	0	1	0
Cook	.969	20	30	1	1	0
Dorn	1.000	31	44	2	0	0
Francisco	.000	1	0	0	0	0
Frazier	1.000	15	26	0	0	0
Griffin	.972	40	67	3	2	1
Heisey	1.000	3	5	0	0	0
Hermida	.989	96	179	2	2	1
Lewis	.900	6	8	1	1	0
Negron	.977	38	82	3	2	0
Perez	1.000	7	12	0	0	0
Phipps	1.000	37	82	4	0	2
Sappelt	.977	72	168	4	4	1
Skelton	.000	1	0	0	0	0

CAROLINA MUDCATS   DOUBLE-A

SOUTHERN LEAGUE

Batting

Batting	B-T	HT	WT	DOB	AVG	vLH	vRH	G	AB	R	H	2B	3B	HR	RBI	BB	HBP	SH	SF	SO	SB	CS	SLG	OBP
Berry, Quintin	L-L	6-0	175	11-21-84	.297	.341	.281	93	320	64	95	16	1	6	41	52	3	0	1	83	40	7	.409	.399
Campbell, Eric	R-R	6-0	205	8-6-85	.265	.226	.283	81	257	33	68	19	0	11	43	18	6	0	0	45	0	3	.467	.327
Castro, Jose	B-R	5-11	172	11-5-86	.314	.314	.317	78	231	25	73	11	0	0	26	5	10	0	3	15	0	1	.364	.353
Coddington, Kevin	R-R	6-4	205	7-21-87	.202	.271	.158	39	124	12	25	6	0	0	11	11	1	0	3	16	2	0	.250	.266
Cook, David	R-R	5-11	205	7-21-81	.256	.277	.248	98	308	54	79	23	0	8	24	49	4	0	0	90	6	3	.409	.366
Costanzo, Mike	L-R	6-3	215	9-9-83	.271	.300	.262	73	255	43	69	18	5	8	36	33	0	0	3	68	2	3	.475	.351
Day, Kyle	L-R	5-11	200	7-13-86	.182	.333	.148	23	33	3	6	2	0	0	2	8	0	0	1	10	1	0	.242	.333
Eymann, Eric	R-R	6-2	195	2-9-84	.188	.333	.100	7	16	1	3	0	0	0	2	0	0	0	0	4	0	0	.188	.188
Fellhauer, Josh	L-L	5-11	175	3-24-88	.278	.263	.283	28	72	12	20	3	0	0	9	10	0	0	0	18	1	2	.319	.366
Fleury, Mark	R-R	6-0	189	5-4-88	.167	.000	.167	2	6	1	1	0	0	1	2	0	1	0	1	3	0	0	.667	.250
Grandal, Yasmani	B-R	6-2	205	11-8-88	.301	.292	.306	45	156	20	47	15	0	4	26	13	2	0	1	39	0	1	.474	.360
Greene, Brodie	R-R	6-1	195	9-25-87	.278	.125	.400	5	18	3	5	1	0	0	2	1	0	0	0	2	0	0	.333	.316
Gregorius, Didi	L-R	6-1	175	2-18-90	.270	.184	.313	38	148	18	40	6	3	2	16	9	0	0	0	25	3	2	.392	.312
Kahaulelio, Jake	R-R	5-10	182	6-7-85	.217	.215	.219	94	276	35	60	11	3	5	34	26	11	0	2	52	2	2	.333	.308
LaMarre, Ryan	R-L	6-2	205	11-21-88	.267	.200	.300	5	15	3	4	1	0	0	3	1	0	0		3	3	0	.333	.421
Lewis, Fred	L-R	6-2	200	12-9-80	.261	.400	.222	7	23	3	6	3	0	0	1	4	0	0	0	4	1	0	.391	.370
McMurray, Chris	R-R	6-1	195	10-12-86	.179	.100	.213	19	67	8	12	2	0	0	7	4	1	0	0	16	0	0	.209	.236
Mendez, Carlos	R-R	6-0	201	9-15-86	.158	.167	.154	8	19	2	3	0	0	1	3	0	0	0		2	1	0	.158	.273
Perez, Felix	L-L	6-2	190	11-14-84	.257	.318	.236	92	327	41	84	16	3	4	32	14	6	0	2	50	7	2	.361	.298
Phipps, Denis	R-R	6-2	177	7-22-85	.328	.316	.333	82	305	53	100	22	5	7	38	27	2	0	4	83	10	6	.502	.382
Puckett, Cody	R-R	5-10	175	4-3-87	.248	.257	.244	96	339	51	84	29	0	15	68	28	7	0	6	80	10	3	.466	.313
Rhinehart, Bill	L-L	6-0	202	11-22-84	.287	.222	.316	36	115	21	33	5	0	7	29	17	2	0	3	30	1	1	.513	.380
Rodriguez, Henry	B-R	5-10	150	2-9-90	.302	.333	.290	69	278	39	84	19	1	5	37	25	4	0	1	43	18	3	.432	.367
Rojas, Miguel	R-R	5-9	175	2-24-89	.259	.282	.248	68	239	26	62	6	0	0	24	16	0	0	3	39	11	7	.285	.302
Skelton, James	L-R	5-11	165	10-28-85	.236	.250	.232	49	127	14	30	9	1	2	16	30	0	0	3	25	2	3	.370	.375
Soto, Neftali	R-R	6-2	180	2-28-89	.272	.318	.253	102	379	70	103	19	3	30	76	25	8	0	2	96	0	1	.575	.329

Pitching

Pitching	B-T	HT	WT	DOB	W	L	ERA	G	GS	CG	SV	IP	H	R	ER	HR	BB	SO	AVG	vLH	vRH	K/9	BB/9
Adkins, James	L-L	6-6	230	11-26-85	0	1	5.74	31	0	0	0	31	33	20	20	3	22	24	.268	.250	.278	6.89	6.32
Arredondo, Jose	R-R	6-0	205	3-12-84	1	0	2.35	6	0	0	0	8	4	2	2	0	4	11	.160	.000	.222	12.91	4.70
Avery, James	R-R	6-0	209	6-10-84	6	12	4.70	27	26	0	0	140	163	89	73	18	54	76	.298	.254	.337	4.90	3.48
Bowman, Drew	R-L	6-3	190	11-8-85	0	0	0.00	2	0	0	0	2	1	0	0	0	2	3	.143	.000	.143	13.50	9.00
Boxberger, Brad	R-R	6-2	200	5-27-88	1	2	1.31	30	0	0	4	34	16	5	5	2	13	57	.139	.196	.094	14.94	3.41
Braun, Jason	R-R	6-5	190	11-24-86	0	0	10.80	4	0	0	0	3	5	4	4	2	1	2	.357	.400	.333	5.40	2.70
Buck, Dallas	R-R	6-2	195	11-11-84	1	5	8.50	8	8	0	0	36	53	43	34	2	20	21	.346	.325	.368	5.25	5.00
Chapman, Aroldis	L-L	6-4	195	2-28-88	1	1	6.14	5	2	0	0	7	5	5	5	1	6	11	.200	.154	.250	13.50	7.36
Christiansen, Nick	R-R	5-10	180	7-17-87	2	0	1.75	20	0	0	3	26	16	5	5	0	5	22	.180	.214	.149	7.71	1.75
Doyle, Pat	R-R	6-2	205	5-12-88	1	0	19.29	2	0	0	0	2	8	5	5	0	2	1	.571	.667	.500	3.86	7.71
Freeman, Justin	R-R	6-1	170	10-22-86	2	4	5.25	54	0	0	1	60	74	39	35	10	25	56	.305	.301	.308	8.40	3.75
Gustafson, Tim	R-R	6-3	185	12-29-84	3	4	3.76	25	8	0	3	67	60	32	28	6	32	38	.244	.274	.225	5.10	4.30
2-team total (6 Mississippi)					4	7	4.84	31	14	0	3	97	97	57	52	11	46	60	—	—	—	5.59	4.28
Hamulack, Tim	L-L	6-2	215	11-14-76	1	3	4.75	31	0	0	3	30	31	17	16	1	16	33	.261	.231	.275	9.79	4.75
Hotchkiss, Jordan	R-R	6-3	220	4-3-86	1	2	5.84	3	3	0	0	12	20	9	8	1	7	8	.364	.364	.364	5.84	5.11
Hynick, Brandon	R-R	6-3	205	3-7-85	4	3	3.67	15	7	0	0	56	52	26	23	2	20	34	.249	.241	.254	5.43	3.20
Jeffords, Jeff	R-R	6-2	205	11-4-84	1	0	7.53	10	0	0	0	14	25	14	12	1	11	10	.397	.500	.314	6.28	6.91

Pitching	B-T	HT	WT	DOB	W	L	ERA	G	GS	CG	SV	IP	H	R	ER	HR	BB	SO	AVG	vLH	vRH	K/9	BB/9
Joseph, Donnie	L-L	6-3	190	11-1-87	1	3	6.94	57	0	0	8	58	67	45	45	8	30	66	.286	.212	.329	10.18	4.63
Klinker, Matt	R-R	6-4	215	10-8-84	6	7	5.23	15	14	2	0	83	100	54	48	9	25	54	.303	.353	.252	5.88	2.72
Lehr, Justin	R-R	6-2	205	8-3-77	1	2	5.44	12	10	0	0	48	57	30	29	8	24	31	.298	.216	.350	5.81	4.50
McCulloch, Kyle	R-R	6-3	190	3-20-85	6	7	5.51	24	14	0	0	95	113	63	58	8	29	53	.303	.321	.289	5.04	2.76
Medina, Ruben	R-R	5-11	157	7-29-86	1	1	4.00	13	0	0	0	18	17	9	8	3	6	10	.262	.273	.250	5.00	3.00
Mobley, Chris	R-R	5-11	170	8-16-83	2	5	6.55	28	0	0	1	33	35	27	24	6	12	43	.269	.325	.244	11.73	3.27
Partch, Curtis	R-R	6-5	227	2-13-87	2	2	6.92	7	7	0	0	39	55	32	30	3	13	33	.337	.373	.313	7.62	3.00
Ravin, Josh	R-R	6-4	220	1-21-88	0	2	7.07	6	6	0	0	28	30	25	22	2	23	21	.288	.270	.299	6.75	7.39
Shunick, Clayton	R-R	6-1	182	9-10-86	0	1	4.91	9	0	0	0	18	20	10	10	1	6	7	.282	.345	.238	3.44	2.95
Tabor, Lee	L-L	6-2	175	12-17-84	0	4	8.39	21	3	0	0	34	38	33	32	4	26	21	.281	.333	.250	5.50	6.82
Thompson, Daryl	R-R	6-0	205	11-2-85	1	4	4.44	9	9	0	0	47	47	28	23	7	17	41	.264	.229	.295	7.91	3.28
Villarreal, Pedro	R-R	6-1	215	12-9-87	7	4	4.42	17	17	1	0	92	92	52	45	11	20	68	.258	.233	.275	6.68	1.96
Webb, Travis	L-L	6-4	205	8-2-84	1	7	4.41	36	5	0	1	69	66	37	34	6	36	89	.251	.275	.236	11.55	4.67

Fielding

Catcher	PCT	G	PO	A	E	DP	PB
Coddington	.991	39	293	23	3	1	3
Fleury	.955	2	18	3	1	0	0
Grandal	.978	42	273	36	7	3	5
McMurray	.994	19	141	14	1	0	1
Skelton	.993	43	257	21	2	2	2

First Base	PCT	G	PO	A	E	DP
Campbell	.986	8	65	5	1	5
Costanzo	.990	29	192	15	2	13
Day	1.000	1	3	1	0	0
Kahaulelio	.992	16	106	12	1	7
Mendez	1.000	1	12	0	0	1
Rhinehart	1.000	3	13	1	0	1
Soto	.995	93	698	53	4	66

Second Base	PCT	G	PO	A	E	DP
Campbell	.000	1	0	0	0	0
Castro	1.000	17	20	31	0	3
Greene	1.000	5	8	10	0	2

	PCT	G	PO	A	E	DP
Kahaulelio	.986	22	35	37	1	10
Mendez	1.000	1	1	0	0	0
Puckett	.971	56	96	141	7	22
Rodriguez	.972	53	97	112	6	33
Rojas	.967	7	17	12	1	5
Skelton	.000	2	0	0	1	0

Third Base	PCT	G	PO	A	E	DP
Campbell	.945	40	31	72	6	5
Castro	.857	14	2	16	3	3
Costanzo	.936	40	31	72	7	3
Kahaulelio	.955	40	20	65	4	4
Mendez	1.000	5	3	11	0	1
Puckett	.667	3	1	5	3	0
Rodriguez	.850	5	3	14	3	0
Rojas	.944	10	11	23	2	2

Shortstop	PCT	G	PO	A	E	DP
Campbell	1.000	1	0	1	0	0
Castro	.985	39	50	83	2	19

	PCT	G	PO	A	E	DP
Eymann	.950	5	4	15	1	2
Gregorius	.953	35	57	104	8	24
Kahaulelio	.867	8	13	13	4	3
Rodriguez	.966	17	28	28	2	9
Rojas	.977	49	83	126	5	21

Outfield	PCT	G	PO	A	E	DP
Berry	.985	84	195	5	3	2
Campbell	.960	22	20	4	1	1
Cook	.968	87	145	8	5	1
Day	1.000	8	8	1	0	0
Fellhauer	.971	23	33	1	1	0
LaMarre	1.000	4	8	0	0	0
Lewis	1.000	7	12	0	0	0
Perez	.945	82	129	9	8	2
Phipps	.984	75	175	9	3	4
Puckett	1.000	38	58	7	0	0
Rhinehart	.965	29	52	3	2	0

BAKERSFIELD BLAZE

HIGH CLASS A

CALIFORNIA LEAGUE

Batting	B-T	HT	WT	DOB	AVG	vLH	vRH	G	AB	R	H	2B	3B	HR	RBI	BB	HBP	SH	SF	SO	SB	CS	SLG	OBP
Bauer, Phil	R-R	6-0	190	2-11-89	.333	.000	.429	3	9	1	3	0	0	0	1	1	0	0	0	3	0	0	.333	.400
Buchholz, Alex	R-R	6-0	182	9-30-87	.284	.306	.276	92	342	47	97	15	1	8	42	27	2	0	5	35	6	8	.404	.335
Campbell, Eric	R-R	6-0	205	8-6-85	.371	.433	.358	46	167	48	62	18	1	9	40	27	7	0	4	24	4	0	.653	.468
Coddington, Kevin	R-R	6-4	205	7-21-87	.362	.385	.353	27	94	21	34	6	0	3	16	7	0	0	1	5	3	2	.521	.402
Fellhauer, Josh	L-L	5-11	175	3-24-88	.281	.271	.284	99	388	56	109	24	1	5	44	46	3	0	0	68	9	10	.387	.362
Fleury, Mark	L-R	6-0	189	5-4-88	.278	.238	.284	51	169	26	47	8	3	3	24	30	1	0	0	42	5	2	.414	.390
Gonzalez, Yovan	R-R	5-10	186	11-11-89	.111	.000	.125	2	9	0	1	0	0	0	0	0	0	0	0	2	1	0	.111	.111
Grandal, Yasmani	B-R	6-2	205	11-8-88	.296	.283	.301	56	206	47	61	14	0	10	40	41	1	0	3	57	0	0	.510	.410
Greene, Brodie	R-R	6-1	195	9-25-87	.287	.325	.275	126	502	79	144	21	6	14	79	41	4	0	3	75	36	9	.436	.344
Gregorius, Didi	L-R	6-1	175	2-18-90	.303	.237	.320	46	188	30	57	12	1	5	28	10	0	0	3	25	8	8	.457	.333
Gualdron, Jose	R-R	5-11	200	7-18-87	.218	.146	.245	49	147	19	32	10	1	2	16	11	1	0	1	34	0	0	.340	.275
Hunt, Stephen	L-L	6-0	190	1-11-89	.291	.200	.310	104	378	44	110	27	3	8	59	36	1	0	1	96	3	3	.442	.353
Jimenez, Jorge	L-R	6-1	215	9-24-84	.256	.211	.274	34	133	19	34	5	1	3	28	3	0	0	2	14	1	2	.376	.268
Kahaulelio, Jake	R-R	5-10	182	6-7-85	.211	.000	.250	5	19	3	4	1	0	0	1	4	0	0	0	1	0	0	.263	.348
LaMarre, Ryan	R-L	6-2	205	11-21-88	.279	.240	.289	117	445	78	124	17	3	6	47	42	8	0	6	97	52	14	.371	.347
Lohman, Devin	R-R	6-1	185	4-14-89	.331	.398	.306	39	130	25	43	10	2	5	17	13	2	0	0	23	4	2	.554	.400
McMurray, Chris	R-R	6-1	195	10-12-86	.000	.000	.000	1	4	0	0	0	0	0	0	0	0	0	0	1	0	0	.000	.000
Means, Andrew	R-R	6-1	214	9-11-86	.249	.250	.248	111	426	58	106	15	3	5	48	18	13	0	2	89	37	10	.333	.298
Mendez, Carlos	R-R	6-0	201	9-15-86	.270	.309	.254	64	237	26	64	13	1	2	28	18	1	0	0	42	1	0	.359	.324
Morillo, Julio	R-R	5-11	176	12-27-87	.333	1.000	.200	2	6	1	2	0	0	0	0	0	0	0	0	4	0	0	.500	.333
Pfister, Frank	R-R	6-1	205	8-25-86	.364	.286	.500	3	11	1	4	1	0	0	1	0	0	0	0	3	1	0	.455	.364
Ramirez, Welinton	R-R	6-0	198	4-13-87	.233	.273	.219	14	43	9	10	5	0	0	6	4	1	0	0	14	0	3	.349	.313
Read, Dayne	R-R	5-11	190	12-31-88	.250	.179	.284	33	120	20	30	4	1	4	15	8	1	0	0	32	9	4	.400	.302
Richburg, Chris	R-R	6-2	210	12-29-85	.262	.302	.247	93	343	44	90	16	1	12	45	16	15	0	3	88	3	3	.420	.321
Rodriguez, Henry	B-R	5-10	150	2-9-90	.340	.345	.339	58	238	37	81	17	0	8	44	14	1	0	1	35	12	7	.513	.378
Weems, Chase	L-R	6-2	190	1-17-89	.167	.000	.167	4	12	1	2	0	0	1	2	0	0	0	0	7	0	0	.417	.167
Wideman, Jordan	R-R	5-11	200	3-14-89	.179	.185	.176	26	78	7	14	3	0	2	10	8	2	0	1	17	0	0	.295	.270

Pitching	B-T	HT	WT	DOB	W	L	ERA	G	GS	CG	SV	IP	H	R	ER	HR	BB	SO	AVG	vLH	vRH	K/9	BB/9
Bowman, Drew	R-L	6-3	190	11-8-85	4	2	4.64	47	0	0	1	66	61	43	34	2	54	78	.237	.234	.239	10.64	7.36
Braun, Jason	R-R	6-5	190	11-24-86	0	0	14.73	8	0	0	0	7	18	13	12	0	9	6	.474	.538	.440	7.36	11.05
Chiu, Tzu-Kai	L-L	6-0	212	9-14-87	1	2	6.82	22	1	0	0	34	48	36	26	7	9	21	.324	.250	.352	5.50	2.36
Crabbe, Tim	R-R	6-4	195	2-20-88	5	5	3.41	21	15	0	0	111	97	48	42	9	46	123	.235	.229	.249	9.97	3.73
Fairel, Matt	L-L	6-4	203	7-8-87	0	6	12.09	7	7	0	0	22	48	36	30	8	14	12	.440	.409	.448	4.84	5.64
Gaffney, Scott	R-R	6-3	186	3-13-86	3	3	6.42	51	0	0	3	62	66	49	44	8	52	49	.276	.253	.288	7.15	7.59

CINCINNATI REDS

Pitching

Pitching	B-T	HT	WT	DOB	W	L	ERA	G	GS	CG	SV	IP	H	R	ER	HR	BB	SO	AVG	vLH	vRH	K/9	BB/9
Hayes, Tyree	R-R	6-0	175	8-8-88	3	3	5.15	20	0	0	1	37	46	26	21	5	17	31	.305	.254	.341	7.61	4.17
Janke, Lance	R-R	6-1	177	10-8-86	4	5	7.03	15	14	0	0	73	92	61	57	6	34	74	.317	.257	.351	9.12	4.19
Jensen, Daniel	R-R	6-8	225	7-25-89	0	0	1.50	1	1	0	0	6	3	1	1	0	1	3	.158	.273	.000	4.50	1.50
Leonard, Matt	L-L	6-0	190	9-2-88	0	0	4.50	1	0	0	0	2	1	1	1	1	1	1	.167	.000	.500	9.00	4.50
Lutz, Derrik	R-R	6-0	210	4-22-85	1	2	3.93	17	0	0	1	18	13	11	8	3	10	14	.194	.240	.167	6.87	4.91
Manno, Chris	L-L	6-3	170	11-4-88	0	1	0.53	13	0	0	2	17	6	2	1	0	6	31	.107	.000	.136	16.41	3.18
Medina, Ruben	R-R	5-11	157	7-29-86	0	0	37.80	2	0	0	0	2	8	10	7	0	3	1	.667	.000	.667	5.40	16.20
Partch, Curtis	R-R	6-5	227	2-13-87	6	11	5.25	21	21	2	0	122	161	92	71	14	28	93	.317	.301	.326	6.88	2.07
Ravin, Josh	R-R	6-4	220	1-21-88	2	8	4.61	19	19	0	0	96	79	56	49	13	59	93	.223	.250	.207	8.75	5.55
Renken, Daniel	R-R	6-3	190	7-5-89	2	0	4.80	6	6	0	0	30	36	24	16	4	13	24	.300	.254	.351	7.20	3.90
Salinas, Doug	R-R	6-4	195	12-5-88	5	2	4.47	47	0	0	14	50	46	27	25	6	19	55	.243	.301	.207	9.83	3.40
Serrano, Mark	L-R	6-1	185	9-14-85	6	9	4.62	18	18	0	0	109	99	61	56	23	38	100	.240	.248	.234	8.26	3.14
Shunick, Clayton	R-R	6-1	182	9-10-86	3	3	2.51	31	1	0	4	68	57	22	19	7	26	72	.226	.286	.188	9.53	3.44
Smith, Ryan	R-R	6-3	205	11-4-89	2	0	0.00	5	0	0	0	7	2	0	0	0	3	3	.100	.167	.071	3.86	3.86
Sulbaran, Juan Carlos	R-R	6-2	220	11-9-89	9	6	4.60	26	26	0	0	137	140	77	70	10	50	155	.264	.254	.270	10.18	3.28
Thurman, Mace	L-L	6-2	187	4-5-87	5	3	5.51	48	1	0	0	65	69	46	40	8	38	61	.270	.206	.293	8.40	5.23
Villarreal, Pedro	R-R	6-1	215	12-9-87	4	3	4.34	10	10	0	0	58	68	31	28	9	8	41	.294	.267	.308	6.36	1.24
Walczak, Jamie	R-R	6-2	195	5-4-87	1	0	5.13	18	0	0	0	26	23	15	15	3	16	35	.247	.147	.305	11.96	5.47
Ware, Chase	R-R	6-4	210	7-16-87	0	0	16.20	2	0	0	0	3	8	7	6	0	3	1	.471	.400	.500	2.70	8.10

Fielding

Catcher	PCT	G	PO	A	E	DP	PB
Coddington	.992	27	231	24	2	2	2
Fleury	.987	40	268	28	4	1	13
Gonzalez	1.000	2	18	3	0	0	1
Grandal	.986	44	389	35	6	4	14
McMurray	1.000	1	9	2	0	0	0
Morillo	1.000	2	11	1	0	0	0
Weems	.968	4	27	3	1	0	2
Wideman	.996	26	230	22	1	2	2

First Base	PCT	G	PO	A	E	DP
Buchholz	.948	8	51	4	3	3
Gualdron	1.000	1	1	0	0	0
Hunt	.984	21	176	12	3	15
Jimenez	.968	11	84	8	3	7
Mendez	.991	41	317	20	3	37
Richburg	.988	62	467	34	6	41

Second Base	PCT	G	PO	A	E	DP
Bauer	1.000	2	4	4	0	1
Buchholz	.800	1	2	2	1	0
Campbell	1.000	1	2	4	0	1
Greene	.978	73	122	184	7	41
Gualdron	.989	20	46	43	1	9
Rodriguez	.955	48	97	117	10	27

Third Base	PCT	G	PO	A	E	DP
Buchholz	.925	75	42	142	15	9
Campbell	.917	39	21	78	9	11
Greene	1.000	1	2	2	0	0
Gualdron	.923	14	9	27	3	4
Jimenez	1.000	2	2	1	0	0
Kahaulelio	1.000	3	0	7	0	0
Mendez	1.000	4	3	10	0	0
Pfister	.667	1	1	1	1	0
Rodriguez	.933	5	4	10	1	0

Shortstop	PCT	G	PO	A	E	DP
Buchholz	1.000	1	1	0	0	0
Greene	.923	49	62	130	16	22
Gregorius	.943	45	84	132	13	25
Gualdron	.967	9	10	19	1	4
Lohman	.917	39	57	75	12	21
Rodriguez	.875	2	2	5	1	1

Outfield	PCT	G	PO	A	E	DP
Campbell	.000	2	0	0	0	0
Fellhauer	.985	95	128	6	2	1
Greene	1.000	2	1	0	0	0
Hunt	.965	60	106	4	4	0
LaMarre	.979	115	267	19	6	2
Means	.971	109	193	16	6	1
Mendez	1.000	9	8	0	0	0
Ramirez	1.000	13	23	6	0	1
Read	.933	32	54	2	4	1

DAYTON DRAGONS
LOW CLASS A
MIDWEST LEAGUE

Batting

Batting	B-T	HT	WT	DOB	AVG	vLH	vRH	G	AB	R	H	2B	3B	HR	RBI	BB	HBP	SH	SF	SO	SB	CS	SLG	OBP
Barnhart, Tucker	B-R	5-8	175	1-7-91	.273	.209	.298	97	326	47	89	24	2	3	43	37	1	0	5	59	2		.387	.344
Berset, Chris	B-R	6-0	195	1-27-88	.215	.146	.235	58	177	27	38	9	1	2	23	33	8	0	2	36	3		.311	.359
Bowe, Theo	L-R	5-9	160	8-5-90	.244	.308	.229	85	266	45	65	7	5	1	24	31	3	0	2	62	20		.320	.328
D'Anna, Dominic	L-R	6-1	215	12-23-88	.286	.329	.271	91	322	47	92	18	1	8	58	50	6	0	5	62	2		.422	.386
Dailey, Brandon	R-R	5-10	170	2-10-92	.000	.000	.000	3	8	0	0	0	0	0	0	1	0	0	0	2	0		.000	.000
Duran, Juan	R-R	6-7	205	9-2-91	.264	.284	.257	104	367	48	97	21	2	16	71	34	2	0	1	152	1		.463	.329
Garton, Josh	L-R	6-2	215	4-27-88	.154	.167	.150	8	26	3	4	1	0	0	1	2	1	0	0	14	0		.192	.241
Hamilton, Billy	B-R	6-1	160	9-9-90	.278	.259	.286	135	550	99	153	18	9	3	50	52	1	0	3	133	103	20	.360	.340
Lohman, Devin	R-R	6-1	185	4-14-89	.208	.120	.236	62	207	14	43	5	1	1	31	17	1	0	2	47	9		.256	.269
Lutz, Donald	L-R	6-4	230	2-6-89	.301	.246	.324	123	465	85	140	23	3	20	75	34	7	0	0	125	5		.492	.358
Matthews, Jaren	L-L	6-1	210	2-20-89	.217	.114	.236	66	217	26	47	7	5	5	21	17	1	0	1	60	7		.364	.272
May, Brennan	R-R	6-0	190	9-25-90	.154	.000	.167	4	13	3	2	1	0	1	3	0	0	0	0	5	0		.462	.154
Muller, Kurt	R-R	5-10	170	7-7-89	.253	.171	.304	26	91	15	23	5	1	0	7	10	5	0	0	14	8		.330	.358
Pfister, Franz	R-R	6-1	205	8-25-86	.192	.182	.198	48	146	15	28	1	0	2	14	7	2	0	4	26	2		.240	.233
Poulk, Drew	R-R	6-3	195	3-14-88	.274	.250	.289	19	62	6	17	5	0	1	10	5	2	0	0	16	1		.403	.348
Rodriguez, Yorman	R-R	6-2	184	8-15-92	.254	.235	.262	79	280	38	71	10	4	7	40	25	2	0	1	84	20		.393	.318
Sierra, Jefry	R-R	5-10	165	4-16-90	.234	.231	.235	105	381	40	89	14	5	0	29	18	2	0	3	117	30		.297	.270
Torreyes, Ronald	R-R	5-9	140	9-2-92	.356	.349	.359	67	278	53	99	9	5	3	41	14	6	0	1	19	12		.457	.398
Vidal, David	R-R	5-11	185	10-23-89	.280	.297	.272	127	454	85	127	37	1	20	85	44	8	0	6	111	3		.498	.350

Pitching

Pitching	B-T	HT	WT	DOB	W	L	ERA	G	GS	CG	SV	IP	H	R	ER	HR	BB	SO	AVG	vLH	vRH	K/9	BB/9
Braun, Jason	R-R	6-5	190	11-24-86	0	0	3.25	17	0	0	0	28	28	11	10	2	18	19	.277	.359	.226	6.18	5.86
Clarke, Mitch	R-L	6-2	220	8-29-90	3	2	2.81	9	6	0	0	42	36	15	13	1	13	29	.240	.192	.265	6.26	2.81
Corcino, Daniel	R-R	5-11	165	8-26-90	11	7	3.42	26	26	1	0	139	128	61	53	10	34	156	.238	.228	.250	10.08	2.20
Crabbe, Tim	R-R	6-4	195	2-20-88	2	2	3.65	8	2	0	1	25	22	13	10	2	7	25	.229	.302	.170	9.12	2.55
Doyle, Pat	R-R	6-2	205	5-12-88	6	4	3.68	37	1	0	2	81	86	43	33	6	30	96	.268	.282	.258	10.71	3.35
Gerson, Starlin	R-R	6-4	195	8-26-88	6	2	3.41	14	12	0	0	69	74	30	26	9	23	55	.272	.292	.257	7.21	3.01
Hayes, Drew	R-R	6-1	190	9-3-87	2	2	1.35	51	0	0	22	60	29	9	9	2	27	89	.141	.172	.116	13.35	4.05
Howell, Blaine	L-L	5-11	210	10-2-88	3	1	1.91	47	0	0	9	66	50	19	14	1	31	67	.216	.232	.206	9.14	4.23
Infante, Ezequiel	L-L	5-10	185	8-31-88	0	2	5.60	16	0	0	0	18	19	12	11	1	19	9	.279	.318	.261	4.58	9.68
Lotzkar, Kyle	R-R	6-4	200	10-24-89	3	2	4.32	14	14	0	0	67	51	34	32	8	25	72	.213	.237	.190	9.72	3.38

Pitching

Pitching	B-T	HT	WT	DOB	W	L	ERA	G	GS	CG	SV	IP	H	R	ER	HR	BB	SO	AVG	vLH	vRH	K/9	BB/9
Martinez, Porfirio	R-R	5-10	175	11-29-89	0	0	24.75	3	0	0	0	4	11	11	11	2	2	6	.500	.333	.700	13.50	4.50
Panerati, Luca	L-L	6-2	167	12-2-89	1	1	4.15	17	0	0	0	35	31	16	16	4	9	25	.238	.250	.231	6.49	2.34
Pearl, Brian	L-R	6-1	190	5-17-88	0	0	4.84	12	1	0	0	22	26	13	12	2	6	30	.274	.237	.298	12.09	2.42
Renken, Daniel	R-R	6-3	190	7-5-89	6	8	3.18	20	20	0	0	113	99	49	40	10	39	141	.234	.259	.212	11.20	3.10
Robles, Tanner	L-L	6-4	205	2-24-89	7	9	5.40	21	20	1	0	87	83	67	52	8	69	85	.249	.198	.275	8.83	7.17
Rogers, Chad	R-R	5-11	175	8-3-89	6	4	2.99	37	1	0	1	69	57	25	23	3	24	72	.227	.231	.224	9.35	3.12
Smith, Josh	R-R	6-2	220	8-7-87	14	7	2.97	26	26	0	0	142	122	57	47	10	33	166	.228	.270	.186	10.50	2.09
Tuttle, Daniel	R-R	6-1	175	8-21-90	4	3	4.87	11	11	0	0	57	58	35	31	2	21	50	.269	.273	.263	7.85	3.30
Walczak, Jamie	R-R	6-2	195	5-4-87	2	0	1.89	11	0	0	0	19	17	8	4	0	8	24	.230	.200	.250	11.37	3.79
Wolford, Dan	R-R	6-2	210	8-19-88	7	1	1.46	43	0	0	1	68	60	15	11	1	23	76	.235	.234	.236	10.11	3.06

Fielding

Catcher	PCT	G	PO	A	E	DP	PB
Barnhart	.998	92	805	118	2	7	6
Berset	.998	52	434	62	1	5	4
Pfister	1.000	1	2	0	0	0	

First Base	PCT	G	PO	A	E	DP
D'Anna	.986	66	467	43	7	44
Lutz	.984	67	535	33	9	38
Matthews	1.000	1	1	0	0	0
Pfister	.986	9	65	3	1	6

Second Base	PCT	G	PO	A	E	DP
Dailey	.875	3	3	4	1	1
Lohman	.938	56	77	135	14	27

	PCT	G	PO	A	E	DP
Pfister	1.000	2	4	2	0	0
Sierra	.952	16	23	36	3	7
Torreyes	.989	67	91	169	3	42

Third Base	PCT	G	PO	A	E	DP
Pfister	.872	19	12	29	6	6
Sierra	.750	2	0	3	1	0
Torreyes	1.000	1	0	2	0	0
Vidal	.965	124	105	169	10	18

Shortstop	PCT	G	PO	A	E	DP
Hamilton	.932	132	218	317	39	67
Lohman	.933	6	7	7	1	0
Pfister	.889	3	5	3	1	1

	PCT	G	PO	A	E	DP
Torreyes	.000	1	0	0	0	0
Outfield	PCT	G	PO	A	E	DP
Bowe	.969	81	151	3	5	1
Duran	.931	92	128	7	10	1
Lutz	1.000	6	9	0	0	0
Matthews	.903	46	61	4	7	1
May	1.000	4	7	0	0	0
Muller	.946	26	34	1	2	0
Pfister	.000	1	0	0	0	0
Poulk	1.000	18	21	0	0	0
Rodriguez	.962	79	120	6	5	0
Sierra	.980	87	177	15	4	2

BILLINGS MUSTANGS
ROOKIE
PIONEER LEAGUE

Batting	B-T	HT	WT	DOB	AVG	vLH	vRH	G	AB	R	H	2B	3B	HR	RBI	BB	HBP	SH	SF	SO	SB	CS	SLG	OBP
Arias, Junior	R-R	6-2	178	1-9-92	.251	.212	.263	61	219	47	55	14	3	8	30	19	3	0	0	74	7	5	.452	.320
Buckley, Sean	R-R	6-4	220	9-3-89	.289	.240	.303	59	225	38	65	11	3	14	41	23	8	0	2	73	6	4	.551	.372
Diaz, Sammy	B-R	5-11	170	2-28-91	.299	.235	.323	38	127	20	38	3	2	2	15	11	0	0	0	19	1	0	.402	.355
Dickinson, Spencer	R-R	5-10	180	9-3-89	.302	.280	.310	29	96	17	29	7	2	2	15	10	5	0	3	28	1	1	.479	.386
Garton, Josh	L-R	6-2	215	4-27-88	.176	.500	.133	6	17	1	3	1	0	0	3	1	0	0	0	5	0	0	.235	.333
Gonzalez, Yovan	R-R	5-10	186	11-11-89	.262	.357	.239	38	141	19	37	5	1	2	24	11	1	0	0	24	1	0	.355	.320
Lohman, Devin	R-R	6-1	185	4-14-89	.322	.333	.317	29	115	23	37	4	0	4	21	16	5	0	2	22	6	2	.461	.420
Maddox, Robert	L-L	6-2	195	10-18-88	.282	.286	.281	63	262	41	74	19	2	16	51	10	6	0	3	73	4	1	.553	.320
Matthews, Jon	R-R	6-3	205	4-6-91	1.000	.000	1.000	2	1	0	1	0	0	0	0	0	0	0	0	0	0	0	01.000	1.000
Muenster, Adam	B-R	5-10	189	4-23-87	.200	.154	.213	16	60	8	12	4	1	1	6	6	0	0	0	9	2	0	.350	.273
Muller, Kurt	R-R	5-10	170	7-7-89	.242	.172	.258	43	157	39	38	7	3	2	18	22	13	0	0	32	24	7	.363	.380
O'Shea, Nicholas	R-R	6-3	220	1-29-89	.255	.283	.242	41	145	22	37	7	1	7	21	10	1	0	1	45	1	0	.462	.306
Perez, Juan	L-R	6-0	180	11-1-91	.268	.261	.271	19	82	14	22	7	2	2	11	9	1	0	1	20	3	3	.476	.344
Poulk, Drew	R-R	6-2	195	3-14-88	.354	.462	.314	24	96	16	34	6	1	6	19	5	0	0	0	30	1	0	.625	.386
Read, Dayne	R-R	5-11	190	12-31-88	.397	.316	.436	15	58	14	23	4	2	4	18	5	2	0	0	11	4	2	.741	.442
Rodriguez, Cristobal	R-R	5-11	165	11-1-89	.257	.320	.238	34	109	14	28	7	0	2	11	7	0	0	2	38	2	4	.376	.297
Selsky, Steven	R-R	6-1	205	7-20-89	.250	.273	.238	8	32	6	8	2	0	1	2	5	1	0	0	11	0	0	.406	.368
Silva, Juan	L-L	6-0	190	1-8-91	.293	.412	.259	41	150	30	44	2	2	4	21	28	1	0	0	43	4	6	.413	.408
Smith, Bryson	R-R	6-1	195	12-17-88	.362	.318	.383	19	69	16	25	4	1	5	18	9	8	0	1	9	1	1	.667	.483
Vicioso, Danny	R-R	6-0	190	10-27-88	.341	.160	.409	28	91	13	31	7	0	3	19	4	1	0	2	17	0	1	.516	.367
Waldrop, Kyle	L-L	6-3	190	11-26-91	.273	.261	.278	68	278	38	76	22	9	5	29	10	3	0	1	65	4	4	.471	.305
Wright, Ryan	R-R	6-1	195	12-3-89	.298	.295	.299	40	161	28	48	11	2	7	32	9	6	0	5	27	6	1	.522	.348

Pitching	B-T	HT	WT	DOB	W	L	ERA	G	GS	CG	SV	IP	H	R	ER	HR	BB	SO	AVG	vLH	vRH	K/9	BB/9
Allen, James	R-R	6-1	197	11-20-89	2	0	1.26	22	0	0	7	29	21	6	4	0	5	39	.198	.313	.149	12.24	1.57
Braun, Jason	R-R	6-5	190	11-24-86	1	0	2.25	10	0	0	1	16	14	5	4	1	5	11	.255	.250	.256	6.19	2.81
Cingrani, Tony	L-L	6-4	200	7-5-89	3	2	1.75	13	13	0	0	51	35	11	10	1	6	80	.190	.200	.188	14.03	1.05
Clarke, Mitch	L-L	6-2	220	8-29-90	1	1	3.60	5	2	0	0	20	23	8	8	2	6	14	.291	.211	.317	6.30	2.70
Contreras, Carlos	R-R	6-0	165	1-8-91	2	1	5.00	18	0	0	0	36	35	20	20	5	23	38	.259	.176	.310	9.50	5.75
Fleece, Nick	R-R	6-2	200	10-24-88	0	0	9.00	3	0	0	0	3	3	3	3	0	2	0	.273	.500	.143	0.00	6.00
Gerson, Starlin	R-R	6-4	175	8-26-88	2	0	0.75	2	2	0	0	12	7	1	1	0	3	10	.167	.231	.138	7.50	2.25
Gonzalez, Aguido	L-L	5-10	185	9-19-86	0	0	0.00	2	0	0	2	2	1	0	0	0	1	0	.167	.000	.200	0.00	4.50
Gonzalez, Carlos	R-R	6-1	195	6-12-90	0	1	5.40	2	2	0	0	10	7	6	6	1	2	10	.206	.111	.240	9.00	1.80
Green, Cole	R-R	6-0	220	5-4-89	4	1	4.24	10	5	0	0	34	39	20	16	5	6	34	.285	.351	.260	9.00	1.59
Guillon, Ismael	L-L	6-3	185	2-13-92	3	6	6.57	15	15	0	0	63	78	57	46	11	46	61	.305	.333	.298	8.71	6.57
Jensen, Daniel	R-R	6-8	225	7-25-89	1	2	6.39	13	2	0	0	31	42	25	22	6	10	24	.323	.333	.318	6.97	2.90
Joyce, Chris	L-L	6-0	195	12-25-89	1	0	2.45	3	0	0	0	4	3	1	1	1	2	1	.273	.000	.429	2.45	4.91
Kemp, Ryan	R-R	6-4	210	9-26-90	3	1	3.48	16	0	0	0	21	13	10	8	0	14	19	.181	.176	.182	8.27	6.10
Leonard, Matt	L-L	6-0	190	9-2-88	2	1	5.23	23	0	0	0	21	31	14	12	1	5	27	.348	.300	.373	11.76	2.18
Lutz, Derrik	R-R	6-0	210	4-22-85	0	0	7.71	6	0	0	0	7	15	6	6	1	1	11	.455	.556	.417	14.14	1.29
Martinez, Porfirio	R-R	5-10	175	11-29-89	1	0	7.61	17	0	0	0	24	30	27	20	2	19	20	.300	.335	.275	7.61	7.23
McMyne, Kyle	R-R	5-11	120	10-18-89	1	1	8.00	10	10	0	0	27	36	24	24	3	14	20	.336	.412	.301	9.00	4.67
Miller, Erik	R-R	6-3	210	4-9-90	3	0	3.45	22	0	0	0	31	39	17	12	1	1	26	.291	.293	.290	7.47	0.29
Moran, Jim	R-R	6-1	180	6-7-90	0	0	6.75	2	0	0	0	3	3	2	2	0	1	2	.273	1.000	.200	6.75	3.38

Pitching	B-T	HT	WT	DOB	W	L	ERA	G	GS	CG	SV	IP	H	R	ER	HR	BB	SO	AVG	vLH	vRH	K/9	BB/9
Mugarian, Wes	R-R	6-0	185	9-18-91	4	5	5.80	15	15	0	0	71	79	58	46	11	40	61	.285	.273	.292	7.70	5.05
Muhammad, El'Hajj	R-R	6-2	200	7-7-91	2	2	4.70	19	0	0	0	44	46	23	23	1	18	45	.267	.244	.276	9.20	3.68
Pearl, Brian	L-R	6-1	190	5-17-88	1	0	3.00	3	0	0	0	6	6	2	2	0	2	8	.261	.167	.294	12.00	3.00
Pinckard, Brooks	L-R	6-1	190	8-15-88	3	2	3.62	28	0	0	10	32	29	19	13	4	13	27	.242	.313	.216	7.52	3.62
Quezada, Radhames	R-R	6-2	175	7-6-90	2	3	3.83	10	10	0	0	49	50	28	21	2	12	55	.256	.257	.256	10.03	2.19
Quinn, Pat	R-R	6-4	200	3-6-90	2	3	4.80	22	0	0	0	30	37	18	16	3	15	25	.303	.324	.294	7.50	4.50

Fielding

Catcher	PCT	G	PO	A	E	DP	PB
Gonzalez	.986	38	306	55	5	5	5
O'Shea	.963	17	139	16	6	1	4
Vicioso	.978	23	194	33	5	3	3

First Base	PCT	G	PO	A	E	DP
Maddox	.991	59	506	34	5	41
O'Shea	1.000	20	152	15	0	11
Vicioso	1.000	1	3	0	0	0

Second Base	PCT	G	PO	A	E	DP
Diaz	.967	23	37	52	3	10
Muenster	.929	11	17	35	4	5
Rodriguez	.838	8	13	18	6	6
Wright	.993	37	64	88	1	20

Third Base	PCT	G	PO	A	E	DP
Arias	.864	37	24	84	17	4
Buckley	.885	28	20	34	7	1
Diaz	.947	7	7	11	1	4
Muenster	1.000	5	5	7	0	0
Rodriguez	.000	1	0	0	0	0

Shortstop	PCT	G	PO	A	E	DP
Arias	1.000	1	3	2	0	1
Diaz	.813	6	10	16	6	4
Lohman	.940	29	47	62	7	16
Perez	.954	19	26	57	4	10
Rodriguez	.913	24	38	77	11	10

Outfield	PCT	G	PO	A	E	DP
Diaz	.000	2	0	0	0	0
Dickinson	1.000	29	42	1	0	1
Garton	.800	2	4	0	1	0
Matthews	.000	1	0	0	0	0
Muller	1.000	42	89	2	0	0
Poulk	.957	18	20	2	1	0
Read	1.000	15	23	1	0	0
Selsky	.941	8	16	0	1	0
Silva	.912	36	44	8	5	3
Smith	1.000	19	26	1	0	0
Waldrop	.950	68	110	5	6	1

AZL REDS   ROOKIE

ARIZONA LEAGUE

Batting	B-T	HT	WT	DOB	AVG	vLH	vRH	G	AB	R	H	2B	3B	HR	RBI	BB	HBP	SH	SF	SO	SB	CS	SLG	OBP
Bauer, Phil	R-R	6-0	190	2-11-89	.185	.182	.186	20	54	8	10	1	0	1	3	10	3	0	0	12	3	0	.259	.343
Dailey, Brandon	R-R	5-10	170	2-10-92	.298	.245	.322	43	171	37	51	5	5	1	27	23	3	0	2	37	17	2	.404	.387
Denove, Chris	R-R	6-1	215	12-9-82	.375	.333	.400	5	16	5	6	2	0	1	5	2	0	0	0	1	0	0	.688	.444
Dickinson, Spencer	R-R	5-10	180	9-3-88	.263	.400	.227	26	95	22	25	6	1	0	14	22	3	0	2	21	7	2	.347	.410
Estevez, Wilfrel	R-R	6-0	177	8-11-90	.217	.000	.260	17	60	9	13	3	1	0	13	7	1	0	0	20	0	1	.300	.309
Fleury, Mark	L-R	6-0	189	5-4-88	.143	.000	.200	3	7	0	1	0	0	0	0	3	0	0	0	1	1	1	.143	.400
Francisco, Juan	L-R	6-2	240	6-24-87	.500	.455	.571	5	18	3	9	3	0	1	3	1	0	0	0	3	0	0	.833	.526
Gomez, Wagner	B-R	6-1	180	12-2-91	.226	.160	.247	31	106	12	24	5	2	3	15	7	1	0	1	33	0	0	.396	.278
Lentz, Matt	L-R	6-3	220	1-10-89	.154	.100	.172	11	39	4	6	1	1	0	3	4	0	0	0	18	1	0	.231	.233
Lopez, Yimmy	R-R	6-0	216	8-19-92	.205	.273	.179	14	39	3	8	1	1	0	7	4	3	0	1	10	2	0	.282	.319
Matthews, Jon	R-R	6-3	205	4-6-91	.229	.333	.197	43	153	25	35	4	5	0	13	15	6	0	0	36	18	7	.320	.322
May, Brennan	R-R	6-0	190	9-25-90	.274	.268	.276	45	164	30	45	11	5	7	32	17	5	0	2	63	11	5	.530	.356
Morillo, Julio	R-R	5-11	176	12-27-92	.255	.154	.294	29	94	19	24	10	1	0	14	14	1	0	1	15	1	4	.383	.355
Perez, Juan	L-R	6-0	180	11-1-91	.346	.263	.379	33	130	28	46	4	5	2	21	16	2	0	0	18	12	1	.496	.424
Puckett, Cody	R-R	5-10	175	4-3-87	.167	.000	.250	2	6	1	1	0	0	1	2	0	0	0	1	3	0	0	.667	.143
Ramirez, Robert	R-R	6-1	170	7-19-92	.243	.219	.250	38	140	22	34	5	3	1	9	8	0	0	2	32	8	3	.343	.280
Rojas, Miguel	R-R	5-9	175	2-24-89	.471	.375	.556	6	17	6	8	3	0	0	6	6	2	0	0	1	4	1	.647	.640
Rosa, Gabriel	R-R	6-4	185	7-2-93	.245	.250	.243	28	106	17	26	5	3	2	10	8	3	0	1	28	4	3	.406	.314
Sanchez, Carlos	L-L	5-10	175	4-4-91	.263	.280	.256	46	179	24	47	14	3	3	28	13	1	0	4	31	1	2	.425	.310
Selsky, Steven	R-R	6-1	205	7-20-89	.338	.261	.373	20	74	17	25	6	0	6	18	12	1	0	1	13	2	1	.662	.432
Smith, Bryson	R-R	6-1	195	12-17-88	.385	.357	.417	6	26	4	10	0	1	0	2	1	1	0	0	6	2	1	.462	.429
Sosa, Fray	R-R	6-1	205	8-29-89	.375	.667	.333	11	24	7	9	3	0	0	3	1	1	0	0	2	0	0	.500	.423
Terry, Joe	L-R	5-11	185	12-18-89	.216	.125	.241	13	37	7	8	2	0	0	8	6	1	0	1	10	5	0	.270	.333
Valor, Humberto	R-R	6-1	186	9-9-92	.207	.300	.182	40	140	18	29	3	2	0	11	14	8	0	0	33	6	6	.257	.315
Wideman, Jordan	R-R	5-11	200	3-14-89	.250	.333	.200	3	8	2	2	1	0	0	1	4	1	0	0	1	0	0	.375	.538
Wright, Ryan	R-R	6-1	195	12-3-89	.318	.167	.375	5	22	4	7	2	1	1	5	0	2	0	0	5	1	2	.636	.375

Pitching	B-T	HT	WT	DOB	W	L	ERA	G	GS	CG	SV	IP	H	R	ER	HR	BB	SO	AVG	vLH	vRH	K/9	BB/9
Alessio, Eric	R-R	6-2	210	9-28-88	1	0	5.14	10	0	0	0	14	23	11	8	1	3	13	.377	.167	.465	8.36	1.93
Amezcua, Tony	R-R	6-0	175	5-27-91	0	0	6.00	3	1	0	0	3	3	2	2	0	1	1	.250	.429	.000	3.00	3.00
Beard, Eliezer	R-R	6-4	202	4-23-91	3	2	6.70	10	7	0	0	42	54	37	31	2	15	44	.312	.308	.314	9.50	3.24
Bender, Joel	L-L	6-4	205	8-3-91	4	3	3.40	12	8	0	0	53	63	30	20	1	17	45	.294	.361	.281	7.64	2.89
Braun, Jason	R-R	6-5	190	11-24-86	1	0	9.95	4	0	0	0	6	10	7	7	0	2	5	.370	.429	.350	7.11	2.84
Burton, Jared	R-R	6-5	225	6-2-81	0	1	9.00	3	3	0	0	4	7	5	4	1	0	6	.389	.400	.385	13.50	0.00
Caceres, Cesar	R-R	6-3	180	8-28-88	1	1	6.08	11	0	0	0	24	25	17	16	1	11	24	.278	.273	.281	9.13	4.18
Chacin, Alejandro	R-R	6-0	200	6-24-93	2	1	1.23	20	0	0	11	22	12	5	3	0	7	34	.158	.160	.157	13.91	2.86
De Los Santos, Abel	R-R	6-1	155	5-17-92	0	2	7.54	11	2	0	0	23	30	19	19	1	8	23	.316	.364	.290	9.13	3.18
Fairel, Matt	L-L	6-3	203	7-8-87	1	1	3.46	4	3	0	0	13	12	5	5	0	3	10	.240	.182	.256	6.92	2.08
French, Justice	R-R	6-4	215	8-2-89	4	4	3.99	11	10	0	0	59	65	31	26	3	6	55	.277	.256	.289	8.44	0.92
Gonzalez, Aguido	L-L	5-10	185	9-19-86	0	0	0.00	1	0	0	0	1	0	0	0	0	1	1	.000	.000	.000	9.00	9.00
Gonzalez, Carlos	R-R	6-1	195	6-12-90	2	3	4.70	12	6	0	0	44	50	27	23	5	12	44	.286	.289	.285	9.00	2.45
Green, Cole	R-R	6-0	220	5-4-89	0	0	0.00	1	0	0	0	1	0	0	0	0	0	1	.000	.000	.000	9.00	0.00
Hayes, Tyree	R-R	6-0	175	8-8-88	0	0	2.70	6	0	0	0	10	12	4	3	0	2	8	.300	.250	.313	7.20	1.80
Joyce, Chris	L-L	6-0	195	12-25-89	1	0	1.13	11	0	0	0	16	12	7	2	0	5	22	.197	.077	.229	12.38	2.81
Kemp, Ryan	R-R	6-4	210	9-26-90	1	0	0.00	0	0	0	0	3	2	2	0	0	6	4	.182	.200	.167	12.00	0.00
Maloney, Matt	L-L	6-4	210	1-16-84	0	0	0.00	1	1	0	0	2	1	0	0	0	0	2	.286	.000	.286	9.00	0.00
Moran, Jim	R-R	6-1	180	6-7-90	1	1	3.54	19	0	0	0	20	23	12	8	1	11	26	.284	.273	.288	11.51	4.87

Pitching	B-T	HT	WT	DOB	W	L	ERA	G	GS	CG	SV	IP	H	R	ER	HR	BB	SO	AVG	vLH	vRH	K/9	BB/9
O'Rear, Lucas	L-R	6-7	240	11-24-88	0	4	9.00	12	6	0	0	41	62	46	41	4	36	29	.354	.410	.325	6.37	7.90
Panerati, Luca	L-L	6-2	167	12-2-89	0	1	3.00	1	1	0	0	6	8	3	2	0	1	2	.296	.000	.308	3.00	1.50
Ramos, Carlos	R-R	6-0	176	11-4-90	1	0	6.14	16	0	0	0	22	24	22	15	1	7	16	.276	.359	.208	6.55	2.86
Robles, Tanner	L-L	6-4	205	2-24-89	2	0	2.77	3	2	0	0	13	7	4	4	0	6	17	.152	.500	.119	11.77	4.15
Smith, Jordan	R-R	6-4	220	2-4-86	0	0	1.50	4	3	0	0	6	6	2	1	1	0	2	.261	.222	.286	3.00	0.00
Tuttle, Daniel	R-R	6-1	175	8-21-90	3	1	3.91	5	3	0	0	23	19	13	10	0	9	35	.221	.412	.174	13.70	3.52
Walczak, Jamie	R-R	6-2	195	5-4-87	2	0	4.70	5	0	0	0	8	8	6	4	0	2	11	.242	.200	.278	12.91	2.35
Yard, Randall	R-R	6-2	175	4-20-89	1	0	4.95	14	0	0	0	20	18	11	11	1	9	19	.243	.231	.250	8.55	4.05

Fielding

Catcher	PCT	G	PO	A	E	DP	PB
Denove	1.000	4	21	3	0	0	1
Fleury	1.000	2	7	3	0	1	0
Gomez	.956	28	219	43	12	4	19
Morillo	.995	24	178	29	1	1	8
Sosa	1.000	4	18	4	0	0	0
Wideman	1.000	2	23	0	0	0	0

First Base	PCT	G	PO	A	E	DP
Bauer	1.000	1	7	1	0	0
Lopez	.982	7	53	1	1	4
Morillo	1.000	2	17	3	0	2
Perez	1.000	4	16	0	0	2
Sanchez	.995	46	399	22	2	32
Terry	1.000	2	13	1	0	2

Second Base	PCT	G	PO	A	E	DP
Bauer	1.000	1	1	1	0	1
Dailey	.962	39	66	110	7	23
Perez	.981	9	21	30	1	7
Puckett	1.000	2	1	1	0	0
Terry	.867	3	10	3	2	1
Wright	.917	4	6	5	1	2

Third Base	PCT	G	PO	A	E	DP
Francisco	.833	3	1	4	1	1
Perez	.750	2	1	2	1	0
Ramirez	.816	30	19	65	19	8
Rosa	.915	25	24	41	6	3

Shortstop	PCT	G	PO	A	E	DP
Dailey	1.000	1	3	4	0	0

	PCT	G	PO	A	E	DP
Perez	.982	14	21	34	1	7
Rojas	1.000	4	2	12	0	2
Valor	.924	40	52	106	13	20

Outfield	PCT	G	PO	A	E	DP
Bauer	.905	15	19	0	2	0
Dickinson	.919	26	52	5	5	1
Estevez	.905	13	18	1	2	0
Lentz	.800	5	3	1	1	0
Matthews	.929	43	63	2	5	0
May	.988	44	75	4	1	2
Selsky	1.000	20	32	2	0	1
Smith	.923	6	11	1	1	0
Terry	1.000	2	2	0	0	0

DSL REDS

ROOKIE

DOMINICAN SUMMER LEAGUE

Batting	B-T	HT	WT	DOB	AVG	vLH	vRH	G	AB	R	H	2B	3B	HR	RBI	BB	HBP	SH	SF	SO	SB	CS	SLG	OBP
Aquino, Aristides	R-R	6-4	190	4-22-94	.188	.146	.201	60	202	27	38	4	4	3	21	21	7	0	2	63	4	10	.292	.284
Arias, Brayan	R-R	6-2	180	11-27-91	.291	.220	.315	51	196	27	57	7	1	1	23	15	2	0	2	37	12	3	.352	.344
Baez, Ariel	R-R	6-0	183	1-22-91	.252	.295	.235	50	159	20	40	10	1	4	28	16	7	0	3	42	2	2	.403	.341
Bueno, Ronald	B-R	5-10	154	10-4-92	.279	.326	.264	60	190	33	53	5	3	0	15	36	3	0	2	36	13	6	.337	.396
Burgos, Deyvi	L-L	6-2	185	7-16-92	.241	.167	.261	18	58	9	14	2	1	0	9	12	1	0	0	8	3	0	.310	.380
Florentino, Oviel	B-R	6-1	160	2-3-94	.192	.185	.195	36	104	10	20	3	0	0	1	5	0	0	0	31	3	3	.221	.229
Galindez, Ronald	R-R	6-0	170	7-29-90	.233	.233	.233	50	163	18	38	4	2	0	17	19	3	0	1	15	11	5	.282	.323
Mejia, Humberto	R-R	6-1	195	10-13-90	.263	.500	.200	8	19	6	5	1	0	0	3	4	3	0	0	7	1	0	.316	.462
Peralta, Henderson	B-R	6-0	195	6-4-91	.183	.179	.184	39	104	15	19	4	1	1	13	9	7	0	0	24	2	1	.269	.292
Peraza, Juan Carlos	R-R	6-2	197	3-11-91	.135	.107	.145	33	104	10	14	4	0	0	5	12	3	0	2	32	1	2	.173	.240
Perez, Moises	L-R	6-1	189	12-24-92	.217	.216	.217	47	129	13	28	6	1	1	15	17	1	0	2	40	1	1	.302	.309
Ramirez, Robert	L-R	6-1	170	7-19-92	.235	.200	.241	8	34	2	8	2	0	0	5	3	0	0	0	6	3	0	.294	.297
Rivas, Jefry	R-R	6-1	175	9-6-92	.191	.222	.180	46	136	21	26	8	1	0	13	19	4	0	0	27	2	3	.265	.308
Soto, Junior	R-R	5-11	180	9-27-91	.222	.364	.176	17	45	3	10	2	0	0	7	5	2	0	2	10	0	0	.267	.315
Suero, Jonathan	B-R	6-0	170	2-28-93	.219	.190	.228	62	187	27	41	7	4	2	16	18	14	0	2	66	7	5	.332	.330
Valdelamar, Jose	R-R	5-11	186	1-10-90	.202	.167	.212	31	84	18	17	3	3	0	11	22	1	0	0	30	4	0	.310	.374

Pitching	B-T	HT	WT	DOB	W	L	ERA	G	GS	CG	SV	IP	H	R	ER	HR	BB	SO	AVG	vLH	vRH	K/9	BB/9
Aybar, Manuel	R-R	6-3	185	1-6-93	1	1	11.93	12	0	0	0	14	15	22	19	1	19	15	.263	.286	.250	9.42	11.93
Cantalizo, Eury	R-R	6-2	185	9-24-91	1	1	2.89	9	1	0	1	19	16	12	6	0	7	14	.219	.280	.188	6.75	3.38
Damian, Pedro	R-R	6-1	170	11-29-92	1	4	2.19	15	3	0	1	37	23	13	9	0	28	42	.187	.217	.169	10.22	6.81
De Leon, John	R-R	6-4	205	10-13-93	1	1	7.94	12	0	0	0	11	9	11	10	0	18	8	.231	.267	.208	6.35	14.29
Diaz, Pedro	R-R	6-0	180	4-29-93	0	3	2.36	15	0	0	3	34	25	16	9	0	18	29	.203	.196	.209	7.60	4.72
Guzman, Jose	R-R	6-3	175	9-18-91	3	5	3.52	14	13	0	0	61	54	32	24	2	38	52	.247	.325	.201	7.63	5.58
Lora, Luis	R-R	6-4	193	12-28-89	1	6	4.56	12	10	1	0	49	40	31	25	1	28	56	.219	.270	.183	10.22	5.11
Peralta, Wandy	L-L	6-1	205	7-27-91	6	1	2.05	12	12	0	0	61	48	17	14	0	29	55	.221	.333	.203	8.07	4.26
Pineda, Lorgi	R-R	6-1	173	10-31-91	3	0	2.09	18	0	0	4	43	38	17	10	0	20	39	.245	.250	.242	8.16	4.19
Polanco, Miguel	R-R	6-4	195	2-26-91	2	2	5.48	14	0	0	0	21	17	18	13	0	30	13	.215	.286	.159	5.48	12.66
Ramirez, Harold	R-R	6-0	197	9-19-92	1	3	3.89	16	4	0	2	42	46	28	18	1	14	27	.286	.231	.312	5.83	3.02
Rosario, Jose	L-L	6-4	209	3-15-91	6	2	2.10	12	12	0	0	60	42	23	14	1	38	47	.194	.194	.193	7.05	5.70
Suarez, Jose	L-L	6-3	180	5-1-91	0	1	8.78	10	2	0	0	13	15	16	13	0	23	13	.288	.333	.279	8.78	15.53
Taveras, Werleen	R-R	5-11	170	8-19-90	4	4	1.96	13	9	1	1	60	45	17	13	1	19	57	.208	.241	.190	8.60	2.87
Tineo, Carlos	R-R	6-5	195	3-12-91	0	1	7.50	10	0	0	0	12	17	14	10	0	12	8	.333	.235	.382	6.00	9.00
Tolentino, Carlos	R-R	6-0	180	5-14-89	1	1	2.20	13	0	0	5	16	10	5	4	0	9	17	.182	.227	.152	9.37	4.96
Williams, Jose	R-R	6-5	200	2-17-91	1	0	2.25	4	2	0	0	12	5	3	3	0	4	13	.119	.143	.095	9.75	3.00

Fielding

Catcher	PCT	G	PO	A	E	DP	PB
Mejia	.987	8	68	6	1	0	0
Peralta	.975	37	223	45	7	2	5
Peraza	.960	17	123	20	6	0	12
Soto	.992	16	112	14	1	2	5

First Base	PCT	G	PO	A	E	DP
Baez	.944	14	77	7	5	10

	PCT	G	PO	A	E	DP
Peraza	.968	15	112	8	4	7
Perez	.982	47	302	21	6	29
Rivas	1.000	3	17	2	0	2
Soto	1.000	1	5	0	0	0

Second Base	PCT	G	PO	A	E	DP
Bueno	.917	28	53	57	10	11
Florentino	.688	6	6	5	5	2

	PCT	G	PO	A	E	DP
Ramirez	.846	2	5	6	2	2
Reynoso	.000	1	0	0	0	0
Rivas	.926	16	32	31	5	10
Suero	.952	27	53	46	5	11

Third Base	PCT	G	PO	A	E	DP
Baez	.949	31	27	48	4	4
Ramirez	1.000	6	9	16	0	1

Rivas	.868	23	12	34	7 2
Suero	.946	16	5	30	2 4

Shortstop	PCT	G	PO	A	E	DP
Bueno	.901	33	47	71	13	13
Florentino	.876	24	37	48	12	9

Perez	.000	1	0	0	0 0
Rivas	1.000	1	0	1	0 0
Suero	.878	20	33	39	10 9

Outfield	PCT	G	PO	A	E	DP
Aquino	.886	50	61	9	9	2

Arias	.957	29	43	1	2 1
Burgos	1.000	15	17	0	0 0
Galindez	.986	40	68	4	1 0
Reynoso	.957	50	83	6	4 1
Valdelamar	.957	30	40	5	2 2

VSL REDS   ROOKIE

VENEZUELAN SUMMER LEAGUE

Batting	B-T	HT	WT	DOB	AVG	vLH	vRH	G	AB	R	H	2B	3B	HR	RBI	BB	HBP	SH	SF	SO	SB	CS	SLG	OBP
Aldazoro, Argenis	L-L	6-2	160	9-17-92	.248	.313	.236	64	210	29	52	12	3	2	27	33	7	0	2	40	10	6	.362	.365
Ariza, Jorge	L-R	6-0	185	7-20-91	.186	.222	.180	21	59	5	11	1	0	0	2	12	0	0	1	7	1	0	.203	.319
Benedetto, Nick	R-R	6-0	150	2-27-93	.187	.273	.172	63	219	33	41	6	3	1	20	12	1	0	1	61	9	5	.256	.232
Cardona, Juan	R-R	5-9	150	2-12-94	.219	.400	.203	22	64	7	14	2	1	0	9	5	4	0	0	18	5	0	.281	.315
Duarte, Jose	R-R	6-2	190	4-23-93	.281	.500	.239	42	135	12	38	9	0	1	20	10	6	0	1	35	1	1	.370	.355
Duque, Andres	R-R	6-3	176	2-9-92	.198	.143	.208	27	86	8	17	3	0	0	9	6	1	0	2	15	0	0	.233	.253
Farinez, Rusbel	R-R	5-9	150	4-27-92	.308	.361	.299	67	240	45	74	15	2	0	25	31	11	0	2	14	20	10	.388	.408
Flores, Ponceano	R-R	6-1	182	4-6-90	.237	.250	.235	33	93	12	22	1	1	0	11	5	7	0	1	13	9	2	.269	.321
Lopez, Yimmy	R-R	6-0	216	8-19-92	.261	.370	.234	39	138	17	36	8	1	2	27	9	7	0	2	32	1	2	.377	.333
Mendez, Miguel	R-R	5-10	160	4-16-93	.341	.342	.341	62	208	45	71	16	5	2	35	13	14	0	2	12	12	6	.495	.414
Mier y Teran, Jonniel	R-R	6-1	170	3-30-94	.188	.150	.195	43	133	13	25	6	3	0	15	20	1	0	1	51	1	3	.278	.297
Moreno, William	R-R	5-11	170	1-17-92	.284	.190	.297	52	169	28	48	7	4	5	24	21	2	0	1	18	4	1	.462	.368
Raga, Jose	R-R	5-11	190	11-20-93	.231	.000	.273	6	13	3	3	0	0	0	2	3	1	0	2	3	0	1	.231	.368
Rivero, Kleyber	R-R	5-10	215	9-13-92	.222	.200	.226	22	63	6	14	4	0	0	2	8	4	0	0	19	2	1	.286	.347
Santoni, Andres	R-R	5-11	170	6-6-91	.256	.294	.249	63	211	28	54	14	2	1	34	23	13	0	4	51	3	2	.355	.359
Valor, Geraldo	R-R	5-10	155	5-2-94	.244	.212	.250	57	197	35	48	10	1	3	26	14	12	0	1	19	7	2	.350	.330
Velazquez, Nestor	R-R	5-11	170	5-28-93	.157	.000	.178	34	83	15	13	0	0	0	5	10	2	0	0	16	9	5	.157	.263

Pitching	B-T	HT	WT	DOB	W	L	ERA	G	GS	CG	SV	IP	H	R	ER	HR	BB	SO	AVG	vLH	vRH	K/9	BB/9
Bier, Deivis	R-R	6-1	180	5-6-87	3	1	5.12	13	0	0	0	19	22	12	11	1	14	11	.282	.308	.269	5.12	6.52
Cardera, Joher	L-L	5-11	155	8-27-94	0	3	4.66	15	1	0	1	19	12	12	10	1	12	8	.185	.100	.200	3.72	5.59
Castellano, Josue	L-L	6-0	190	1-13-92	4	0	1.03	16	0	0	0	44	32	8	5	2	7	34	.206	.185	.211	7.01	1.44
Chiquiin, Jose	R-R	6-4	164	4-24-90	1	2	4.26	14	0	0	0	25	22	14	12	0	9	13	.242	.143	.304	4.62	3.20
De Sousa, Jose	L-L	6-0	180	5-15-92	0	0	4.38	7	2	0	0	12	10	6	6	0	6	16	.217	.444	.162	11.68	4.38
Gonzalez, Luis	L-L	6-1	170	3-25-93	4	3	3.84	13	13	0	0	61	65	30	26	5	13	23	.279	.273	.280	3.39	1.92
Heredia, Jose	L-L	6-3	200	6-12-92	1	1	9.26	13	2	0	0	12	10	14	12	1	23	6	.244	.400	.222	4.63	17.74
Hernandez, Joyce	R-R	6-2	170	10-28-92	3	0	2.93	15	0	0	0	28	20	11	9	0	13	20	.204	.071	.257	6.51	4.23
Mieres, Oswaldo	R-R	6-3	178	5-14-92	7	4	2.33	14	14	0	0	73	54	23	19	1	19	52	.206	.186	.219	6.38	2.33
Moreno, Robert	R-R	5-11	169	9-20-89	4	3	3.31	27	0	0	14	33	25	15	12	4	11	23	.221	.129	.256	6.34	3.03
Morillo, JR	L-L	5-11	167	10-30-91	2	4	4.91	14	5	0	1	44	53	27	24	5	8	30	.296	.360	.286	6.14	1.64
Munoz, Jose	R-R	6-1	180	4-4-92	0	5	6.35	13	10	0	0	45	56	43	32	4	29	19	.316	.373	.294	3.77	5.76
Parra, Jesus	R-R	5-11	175	4-14-91	0	0	6.00	2	2	0	0	3	4	2	2	0	1	3	.333	.250	.375	9.00	3.00
Patino, Carlos	R-R	6-1	160	4-8-93	2	0	1.56	19	0	0	4	35	20	6	6	1	5	29	.163	.147	.169	7.53	1.30
Romero, Franderlin	R-R	6-1	190	2-21-91	3	2	3.02	13	13	1	0	66	69	31	22	3	9	34	.265	.241	.266	4.66	1.23
Sarrameda, Ramon	R-R	6-3	180	7-8-91	4	2	2.41	19	0	0	1	41	43	15	11	2	7	24	.276	.238	.289	5.27	1.54
Torrealba, Julio	L-L	6-1	190	4-24-90	0	2	5.71	12	9	0	0	41	40	28	26	1	23	19	.261	.214	.272	4.17	5.05
Zapata, John	R-R	5-11	190	8-11-92	0	2	8.75	14	1	0	0	24	30	27	23	3	12	7	.319	.294	.333	2.66	4.56

Fielding

Catcher	PCT	G	PO	A	E	DP	PB
Ariza	.973	19	97	13	3	0	4
Duarte	.966	30	137	35	6	3	3
Flores	.976	32	138	23	4	0	7
Raga	.955	4	17	4	1	0	0

First Base	PCT	G	PO	A	E	DP
Duarte	1.000	4	26	2	0	2
Lopez	.966	30	272	16	10	21
Moreno	1.000	1	3	1	0	0
Santoni	.980	41	359	41	8	34
Valor	.000	1	0	0	0	0

Second Base	PCT	G	PO	A	E	DP
Cardona	.963	20	34	44	3	11
Farinez	.954	51	114	116	11	26
Mendez	.818	3	4	5	2	3
Velazquez	1.000	4	7	4	0	1

Third Base	PCT	G	PO	A	E	DP
Farinez	.944	5	5	12	1	1
Mendez	.969	37	35	90	4	4
Santoni	.925	11	8	29	3	3
Velazquez	.913	25	31	53	8	5

Shortstop	PCT	G	PO	A	E	DP
Mendez	.939	24	41	67	7	14
Valor	.932	54	103	170	20	26

Outfield	PCT	G	PO	A	E	DP
Aldazoro	.952	62	116	3	6	3
Benedetto	.976	59	118	5	3	1
Duque	.875	13	13	1	2	0
Mier y Teran	.943	35	50	0	3	0
Moreno	.989	47	87	1	1	0
Rivero	.923	17	21	3	2	1

CINCINNATI REDS

Cleveland Indians

SEASON IN A SENTENCE: The Indians started 30-15 and were in first place in the American League Central in mid-July, but the season went into a tailspin from there as the club finished under .500 for the third straight season.

HIGH POINT: The Indians ended April tied with the Phillies for the best record (18-8) in baseball, outscoring their opponents 141-95 in the season's first month. Indians pitchers had a combined 3.49 ERA in April and opponents hit just .237/.307/.358 against them. Righthanders Justin Masterson and Josh Tomlin anchored the pitching staff, each finishing April with an ERA under 2.50.

LOW POINT: The Indians' run prevention eroded as the season went on, and they gave up more runs each month as the season progressed, including an average of 6.3 per game during a 12-17 September. With the playoffs already out of sight on Sept. 26, the Indians suffered their worst loss of the season, a 14-0 drubbing at division leader Detroit with trade deadline acquisition Ubaldo Jimenez on the mound.

NOTABLE ROOKIES: Vinnie Pestano worked his way through the minor leagues to little hype as a 20th-round pick in 2006, but the 26-year-old righthander was a vital piece of Cleveland's bullpen. He led all Indians relievers in strikeouts and his rate of 12.2 strikeouts per nine innings was the best on the team. Second baseman Jason Kipnis arrived in July and was one of the Indians' best hitters down the stretch. Lonnie Chisenhall could be the third baseman of the future, but the 22-year-old struggled in his first big league stint.

KEY TRANSACTIONS: Hoping to make a push for the playoffs, the Indians dealt four players, including first-round picks Drew Pomeranz and Alex White, to acquire Jimenez. With Colorado, Jimenez's velocity had dropped from 2010 and his 4.46 ERA was a career high. The results weren't any better upon his arrival in Cleveland, as he racked up a 5.10 ERA in 11 starts.

DOWN ON THE FARM: Between the graduations of Chisenhall and Kipnis, the trades of White and Pomeranz and the struggles of prospects at the lower levels, the Indians system thinned significantly. The Columbus Clippers won their second consecutive Triple-A National Championship with a core of young relievers who could help the big league team in 2012, including Zach Putnam, Nick Hagadone, Chen Lee and Josh Judy.

OPENING DAY PAYROLL: $49,190,566 (26th)

PLAYERS OF THE YEAR

MAJOR LEAGUE	MINOR LEAGUE
Carlos Santana	**Zach McAllister**
c	rhp
.239/.351/.457	(Triple-A)
27 HR, 35 2B	12-3, 3.32
3rd in AL in BB (97)	128 SO/155 IP

ORGANIZATION LEADERS

BATTING		*Minimum 250 PA
MAJORS		
* AVG	Travis Hafner	.280
* OPS	Travis Hafner	.810
HR	Carlos Santana	27
RBI	Asdrubal Cabrera	92
MINORS		
* AVG	Tim Fedroff, Akron/Columbus	.308
* OBP	Tim Fedroff, Akron/Columbus	.385
* SLG	Jerad Head, Columbus	.526
R	Carlos Moncrief, Lake County	73
H	Tim Fedroff, Akron/Columbus	151
TB	Jesus Aguilar, Lake County/Kinston	234
2B	Anthony Gallas, Lake County/Kinston/Akron	34
3B	Jason Kipnis, Columbus	9
HR	Jerad Head, Columbus	24
RBI	Jesus Aguilar, Lake County/Kinston	82
BB	Tyler Holt, Kinston	78
SO	Carlos Moncrief, Lake County	158
SB	Ezequiel Carrera, Columbus	35
PITCHING		#Minimum 75 IP
MAJORS		
W	Justin Masterson	12
	Josh Tomlin	12
# ERA	Justin Masterson	3.21
SO	Justin Masterson	158
SV	Chris Perez	36
MINORS		
W	Zach McAllister, Columbus	12
L	Three tied at	12
# ERA	Jeanmar Gomez, Mahoning Valley/Columbus	2.54
G	Dale Dickerson, Lake County/Akron	55
GS	Michael Goodnight, Lake County/Kinston	28
SV	Cory Burns, Akron	35
	Preston Guilmet, Kinston	35
IP	Matt Packer, Akron	169.1
BB	Corey Kluber, Columbus	70
SO	Corey Kluber, Columbus	143
# AVG	Michael Goodnight, Lake County/Kinston	.217

General Manager: Chris Antonetti. **Farm Director:** Ross Atkins. **Scouting Director:** John Mirabelli.

Class	Team	League	W	L	PCT	Finish	Manager(s)
Majors	Cleveland Indians	American	80	82	.494	8th (14)	Manny Acta
Triple-A	Columbus Clippers	International	88	56	.611	1st (14)	Mike Sarbaugh
Double-A	Akron Aeros	Eastern	73	69	.514	6th (12)	Chris Tremie
High A	Kinston Indians	Carolina	76	62	.551	2nd (8)	Aaron Holbert
Low A	Lake County Captains	Midwest	53	86	.381	16th (16)	Ted Kubiak
Short-season	Mahoning Valley Scrappers	New York-Penn	41	34	.547	5th (14)	David Wallace
Rookie	AZL Indians	Arizona	30	26	.536	5th (13)	Anthony Medrano
Overall 2011 Minor League Record			361	333	.520	9th (30)	

ORGANIZATION STATISTICS

CLEVELAND INDIANS
AMERICAN LEAGUE

Batting	B-T	HT	WT	DOB	AVG	vLH	vRH	G	AB	R	H	2B	3B	HR	RBI	BB	HBP	SH	SF	SO	SB	CS	SLG	OBP
Brantley, Michael	L-L	6-2	200	5-15-87	.266	.214	.289	114	451	63	120	24	4	7	46	34	3	0	5	76	13	5	.384	.318
Buck, Travis	L-R	6-2	230	11-18-83	.228	.067	.246	50	149	18	34	11	0	2	18	8	2	1	0	31	1	1	.342	.275
Cabrera, Asdrubal	B-R	6-0	180	11-13-85	.273	.291	.265	151	604	87	165	32	3	25	92	44	11	0	4	119	17	5	.460	.332
Cabrera, Orlando	R-R	5-10	195	11-2-74	.244	.276	.230	91	324	35	79	13	0	4	38	13	3	0	3	40	6	2	.321	.277
Carrera, Ezequiel	L-L	5-10	185	6-11-87	.243	.191	.269	68	202	27	49	8	3	0	14	16	1	0	0	35	10	5	.312	.301
Chisenhall, Lonnie	L-R	6-1	200	10-4-88	.255	.260	.253	66	212	27	54	13	0	7	22	8	1	0	1	49	1	0	.415	.284
Choo, Shin-Soo	L-L	5-11	205	7-13-82	.259	.269	.254	85	313	37	81	11	3	8	36	36	6	0	3	78	12	5	.390	.344
Crowe, Trevor	B-R	5-10	190	11-17-83	.214	.200	.231	15	28	6	6	1	0	0	2	4	0	0	0	9	3	0	.250	.313
Donald, Jason	R-R	6-1	195	9-4-84	.318	.377	.268	39	132	13	42	6	1	1	8	7	3	0	1	35	3	2	.402	.364
Duncan, Shelley	R-R	6-5	225	9-29-79	.260	.245	.273	76	223	29	58	17	0	11	47	19	3	0	2	56	0	1	.484	.324
Everett, Adam	R-R	6-0	180	2-5-77	.217	.143	.256	34	60	9	13	1	0	0	1	5	0	0	0	14	1	0	.233	.277
Fukudome, Kosuke	L-R	6-0	200	4-26-77	.249	.258	.243	59	237	26	59	12	1	5	22	15	3	0	2	53	2	4	.371	.300
Hafner, Travis	L-R	6-3	240	6-3-77	.280	.233	.302	94	325	41	91	16	0	13	57	36	6	0	1	78	0	0	.449	.361
Hannahan, Jack	L-R	6-2	210	3-4-80	.250	.296	.226	110	320	38	80	16	2	8	40	38	2	0	2	80	2	1	.388	.331
Head, Jerad	R-R	6-0	210	11-15-82	.125	.250	.000	10	24	2	3	1	0	0	1	0	0	1	0	5	1	0	.167	.160
Kearns, Austin	R-R	6-3	240	5-20-80	.200	.235	.171	57	150	18	30	5	1	2	7	18	4	0	0	48	0	4	.287	.302
Kipnis, Jason	L-R	5-11	185	4-3-87	.272	.263	.276	36	136	24	37	9	1	7	19	11	2	0	1	34	5	0	.507	.333
LaPorta, Matt	R-R	6-2	215	1-8-85	.247	.207	.260	107	352	34	87	23	1	11	53	23	5	0	5	87	1	0	.412	.299
Marson, Lou	R-R	6-1	200	6-26-86	.230	.297	.191	79	243	26	56	9	2	1	19	24	1	0	2	68	4	2	.296	.300
Phelps, Cord	B-R	6-2	200	1-23-87	.155	.100	.164	35	71	10	11	2	1	1	6	8	0	0	0	17	1	0	.254	.241
Santana, Carlos	B-R	5-11	190	4-8-86	.239	.318	.201	155	552	84	132	35	2	27	79	97	2	0	7	133	5	3	.457	.351
Sizemore, Grady	L-L	6-2	200	8-2-82	.224	.183	.239	71	268	34	60	21	1	10	32	18	6	0	3	85	0	2	.422	.285
Thome, Jim	L-R	6-3	250	8-27-70	.296	.273	.306	22	71	11	21	4	0	3	10	11	0	0	0	23	0	0	.479	.390
2-team total (71 Minnesota)					.256	—	—	93	277	32	71	16	0	15	50	46	0	0	1	92	0	0	.477	.361
Valbuena, Luis	L-R	5-10	195	11-30-85	.209	.250	.194	17	43	4	9	0	0	1	1	1	0	0	0	9	1	0	.279	.227

Pitching	B-T	HT	WT	DOB	W	L	ERA	G	GS	CG	SV	IP	H	R	ER	HR	BB	SO	AVG	vLH	vRH	K/9	BB/9
Carmona, Fausto	R-R	6-4	230	12-7-83	7	15	5.25	32	32	0	0	189	205	125	110	22	60	109	.276	.296	.252	5.20	2.86
Carrasco, Carlos	R-R	6-3	215	3-21-87	8	9	4.62	21	21	1	0	125	130	68	64	15	40	85	.270	.318	.216	6.14	2.89
Durbin, Chad	R-R	6-2	225	12-3-77	2	2	5.53	56	0	0	0	68	86	45	42	12	26	59	.306	.289	.319	7.77	3.42
Germano, Justin	R-R	6-2	210	8-6-82	0	1	5.68	9	0	0	0	13	15	8	8	1	5	5	.288	.273	.316	3.55	3.55
Gomez, Jeanmar	R-R	6-3	170	2-10-88	5	3	4.47	11	10	0	0	58	73	31	29	6	15	31	.303	.319	.289	4.78	2.31
Hagadone, Nick	L-L	6-5	230	1-1-86	1	0	4.09	9	0	0	0	11	4	6	5	0	6	11	.118	.071	.150	9.00	4.91
Herrmann, Frank	R-R	6-4	220	5-30-84	4	0	5.11	40	0	0	0	56	71	35	32	7	16	34	.302	.386	.223	5.43	2.56
Huff, David	L-L	6-2	215	8-22-84	2	6	4.09	11	10	0	0	51	55	35	23	6	11	36	.266	.268	.265	6.39	3.02
Jimenez, Ubaldo	R-R	6-4	210	1-22-84	4	4	5.10	11	11	0	0	65	68	43	37	7	27	62	.261	.239	.283	8.54	3.72
Judy, Josh	R-R	6-4	200	2-9-86	0	0	7.07	12	0	0	0	14	18	11	11	4	4	10	.321	.318	.324	6.43	2.57
Kluber, Corey	R-R	6-4	215	4-10-86	0	0	8.31	3	0	0	0	4	6	4	4	0	3	5	.300	.400	.000	10.38	6.23
Masterson, Justin	R-R	6-6	250	3-22-85	12	10	3.21	34	33	1	0	216	211	89	77	11	65	158	.257	.291	.210	6.58	2.71
McAllister, Zach	R-R	6-6	240	12-8-87	0	1	6.11	4	4	0	0	18	26	16	12	1	7	14	.338	.421	.256	7.13	3.57
Perez, Chris	R-R	6-4	230	7-1-85	4	7	3.32	64	0	0	36	60	46	24	22	5	26	39	.215	.198	.233	5.88	3.92
Perez, Rafael	L-L	6-3	195	5-15-82	5	2	3.00	71	0	0	0	63	59	27	21	2	19	33	.253	.237	.270	4.71	2.71
Pestano, Vinnie	R-R	6-0	200	2-20-85	1	2	2.32	67	0	0	2	62	41	16	16	5	24	84	.184	.280	.115	12.19	3.48
Putnam, Zach	R-R	6-2	225	7-3-87	1	1	6.14	8	0	0	0	7	10	5	5	1	0	9	.313	.231	.368	11.05	0.00
Sipp, Tony	L-L	6-0	190	7-12-83	6	3	3.03	69	0	0	0	62	45	22	21	10	24	57	.201	.229	.180	8.23	3.47
Smith, Joe	R-R	6-2	205	3-22-84	3	3	2.01	71	0	0	0	67	52	16	15	1	21	45	.217	.152	.248	6.04	2.82
Talbot, Mitch	R-R	6-2	200	10-17-83	2	6	6.64	12	12	0	0	64	90	47	47	10	28	36	.344	.388	.301	5.09	3.96
Tomlin, Josh	R-R	6-1	190	10-19-84	12	7	4.25	26	26	0	0	165	157	80	78	24	21	89	.248	.267	.226	4.84	1.14
White, Alex	R-R	6-3	215	8-29-88	1	0	3.60	3	3	0	0	15	14	7	6	3	9	13	.255	.200	.286	7.80	5.40

Fielding

Catcher	PCT	G	PO	A	E	DP	PB
Marson	.990	78	476	43	5	6	5
Santana	.989	95	580	43	7	4	4

First Base	PCT	G	PO	A	E	DP
Duncan	.980	7	44	6	1	4
Hannahan	1.000	8	30	2	0	1
LaPorta	.992	97	807	41	7	69

	PCT	G	PO	A	E	DP
Santana	.994	66	622	43	4	43
Second Base	PCT	G	PO	A	E	DP
Cabrera	.985	83	128	262	6	44
Donald	.989	19	35	51	1	10

Everett	.893	8	8 17 3 5
Kipnis	.963	36	58 100 6 16
Phelps	.933	20	28 42 5 10
Valbuena	1.000	11	19 24 0 7

Third Base	PCT	G	PO	A	E	DP
Cabrera	1.000	4	2	2	0	0
Chisenhall	.940	58	44	114	10	8
Donald	1.000	4	1	7	0	0
Everett	.968	16	2	28	1	4
Hannahan	.983	104	83	208	5	21

Thome	.000	1	0	0	0	0
Shortstop	**PCT**	**G**	**PO**	**A**	**E**	**DP**
Cabrera	.976	151	216	386	15	78
Cabrera	1.000	3	3	4	0	0
Donald	.940	16	17	30	3	6
Everett	1.000	4	4	0	0	0
Valbuena	.000	1	0	0	0	0
Outfield	**PCT**	**G**	**PO**	**A**	**E**	**DP**
Brantley	.988	111	236	5	3	2
Buck	.988	40	80	0	1	0

Carrera	.970	64	128	2	4	0
Chisenhall	.000	1	0	0	0	0
Choo	.978	85	172	9	4	2
Crowe	1.000	14	15	0	0	0
Duncan	.984	39	59	2	1	0
Fukudome	.986	59	143	2	2	2
Head	.938	9	15	0	1	0
Kearns	.991	54	105	1	1	0
Sizemore	.984	56	123	1	2	0
Valbuena	1.000	2	2	0	0	0

COLUMBUS CLIPPERS   TRIPLE-A
INTERNATIONAL LEAGUE

Batting	B-T	HT	WT	DOB	AVG	vLH	vRH	G	AB	R	H	2B	3B	HR	RBI	BB	HBP	SH	SF	SO	SB	CS	SLG	OBP
Bell, Bubba	L-R	6-0	195	10-9-82	.292	.429	.235	8	24	2	7	2	0	0	2	0	0	0		3	1	0	.375	.346
2-team total (67 Buffalo)					.237	—	—	75	186	17	44	12	0	1	20	14	1	0	1	26	10	1	.317	.292
Brown, Jordan	L-L	6-0	205	12-18-83	.278	.226	.317	20	72	10	20	3	1	3	13	11	0	0	0	15	0	0	.472	.373
Buck, Travis	L-R	6-2	230	11-18-83	.256	.150	.309	36	121	21	31	6	1	4	25	19	3	0	2	26	1	1	.421	.366
Carlin, Luke	B-R	5-10	195	12-20-80	.213	.188	.226	63	188	33	40	8	0	5	27	44	2	0	2	45	0	0	.335	.364
Carrera, Ezequiel	L-L	5-10	185	6-11-87	.287	.268	.296	82	328	63	94	8	3	2	25	39	5	0	0	53	35	4	.348	.371
Childs, Dwight	R-R	6-2	190	7-23-88	.000	.000	.000	1	3	0	0	0	0	0	0	0	0	0	0	1	0	0	.000	.000
Chisenhall, Lonnie	L-R	6-1	200	10-4-88	.267	.200	.294	66	255	45	68	15	3	7	45	28	7	0	2	47	0	1	.431	.353
Copeland, Ben	L-L	6-1	190	12-17-83	.133	.100	.200	5	15	2	2	1	1	0	2	1	0	0	0	4	0	0	.333	.188
Crowe, Trevor	B-R	5-10	190	11-17-83	.100	.091	.111	5	20	1	2	0	0	0	1	0	0	0	0	3	2	0	.100	.143
Donald, Jason	R-R	6-1	195	9-4-84	.310	.357	.288	47	174	32	54	12	0	4	15	19	6	0	0	33	7	3	.448	.397
Duncan, Shelley	R-R	6-5	225	9-29-79	.202	.194	.205	33	109	20	22	3	0	5	19	24	2	0	2	24	1	0	.367	.350
Fedroff, Tim	L-R	5-11	220	2-4-87	.272	.263	.279	62	224	29	61	15	1	1	28	35	1	0	2	35	3	2	.362	.370
Goedert, Jared	R-R	6-1	205	5-25-85	.271	.265	.275	79	284	39	77	18	0	15	39	33	1	0	3	60	0	0	.493	.346
Head, Jerad	R-R	6-0	210	11-15-82	.284	.291	.280	114	422	67	120	28	1	24	70	25	11	0	4	99	3	1	.526	.338
Hernandez, Michel	R-R	6-0	215	8-12-78	.304	.429	.250	7	23	4	7	2	0	1	4	3	0	0	0	1	0	0	.522	.385
2-team total (17 Norfolk)					.208	—	—	24	77	8	16	5	0	1	5	6	3	0	0	8	0	0	.312	.291
Hodges, Wes	R-R	6-2	205	9-14-84	.219	.205	.227	32	114	12	25	6	0	2	16	7	2	0	0	31	0	0	.325	.276
Huffman, Chad	R-R	6-1	215	4-29-85	.246	.204	.269	124	431	66	106	30	2	13	58	67	6	0	6	107	5	1	.415	.351
Johnson, Nick	L-L	6-3	235	9-19-78	.201	.115	.244	53	184	20	37	6	0	6	13	26	5	0	0	52	0	1	.332	.316
Kipnis, Jason	L-R	5-11	185	4-3-87	.280	.313	.264	92	343	65	96	16	9	12	55	44	3	0	5	72	12	1	.484	.362
LaPorta, Matt	R-R	6-2	215	1-8-85	.444	.429	.500	2	9	2	4	0	0	1	3	0	0	0	0	1	0	0	.778	.444
McBride, Matt	R-R	6-2	215	5-23-85	.156	.053	.231	12	45	3	7	2	0	1	3	2	0	0	0	8	0	0	.267	.191
Mills, Beau	L-R	6-3	220	8-15-86	.269	.186	.316	35	119	13	32	6	0	7	18	10	1	0	2	22	0	0	.496	.332
Neal, Thomas	R-R	6-2	225	8-17-87	.250	.333	.190	10	36	5	9	1	0	0	1	1	1	0	0	7	1	0	.278	.289
Phelps, Cord	B-R	6-2	200	1-23-87	.294	.281	.301	97	378	51	111	25	4	14	63	51	1	0	4	89	3	6	.492	.376
Phillips, Paul	R-R	5-11	200	4-15-77	.237	.182	.269	78	266	26	63	9	0	3	24	16	2	0	4	26	0	0	.305	.281
Reyes, Argenis	R-R	5-10	180	9-25-82	.313	.256	.364	25	83	9	26	5	0	2	9	4	0	0	0	10	1	0	.446	.345
Rodriguez, Josh	R-R	6-0	185	12-18-84	.193	.200	.190	18	57	6	11	1	0	2	5	6	0	0	0	22	1	0	.316	.270
2-team total (6 Indianapolis)					.229	—	—	24	70	9	16	3	0	2	11	11	0	0	1	24	1	0	.357	.329
Sizemore, Grady	L-L	6-2	200	8-2-82	.250	.333	.200	2	8	1	2	0	0	1	2	2	0	0	0	3	0	0	.625	.400
Smith, Kyle	R-R	6-1	190	12-25-87	.200	.250	.000	4	5	3	1	0	0	0	0	0	0	0	0	3	0	0	.200	.200
Valbuena, Luis	L-R	5-10	195	11-30-85	.302	.280	.316	113	420	64	127	22	0	17	75	46	2	0	3	96	6	3	.476	.372
Webb, Donnie	B-R	5-11	210	4-30-86	.129	.182	.100	11	31	2	4	0	0	0	1	4	0	0	1	8	0	0	.129	.222

Pitching	B-T	HT	WT	DOB	W	L	ERA	G	GS	CG	SV	IP	H	R	ER	HR	BB	SO	AVG	vLH	vRH	K/9	BB/9
Barnes, Scott	L-L	6-4	185	9-5-87	7	4	3.68	16	15	0	0	88	80	41	36	12	34	90	.240	.259	.230	9.20	3.48
Berger, Eric	L-L	6-2	205	4-22-86	0	1	10.05	11	0	0	0	14	26	24	16	2	14	20	.382	.385	.381	12.56	8.79
Brach, Brett	R-R	6-2	190	3-29-88	1	0	3.86	1	0	0	0	5	6	2	2	1	2	1	.316	.600	.214	1.93	3.86
Espino, Paolo	R-R	5-10	190	1-10-87	2	1	3.43	12	5	0	0	39	35	16	15	3	7	41	.229	.232	.227	9.38	1.60
Germano, Justin	R-R	6-2	210	8-6-82	1	2	4.22	16	6	1	3	49	50	23	23	5	4	39	.272	.320	.239	7.16	0.73
Gomez, Jeanmar	R-R	6-3	170	2-10-88	10	7	2.55	21	21	2	0	138	123	54	39	8	49	107	.242	.294	.207	7.00	3.20
Hagadone, Nick	L-L	6-5	230	1-1-86	4	3	3.35	34	0	0	4	48	42	27	18	5	15	53	.228	.127	.271	9.87	2.79
Herrmann, Frank	L-R	6-4	220	5-30-84	0	0	5.91	9	0	0	0	11	13	7	7	1	4	12	.310	.278	.333	10.13	3.38
Huff, David	L-L	6-2	215	8-22-84	9	3	3.87	18	18	0	0	107	111	52	46	10	30	66	.264	.283	.256	5.55	2.52
Judy, Josh	R-R	6-4	200	2-9-86	6	2	3.12	50	0	0	23	52	44	23	18	5	25	60	.230	.280	.198	10.38	4.33
Kluber, Corey	R-R	6-4	215	4-10-86	7	11	5.56	27	27	0	0	151	153	101	93	19	70	143	.263	.257	.268	8.54	4.18
Langwell, Matt	R-R	6-2	225	10-6-84	1	0	4.00	12	0	0	0	18	19	9	8	1	8	17	.264	.296	.244	8.50	4.00
Lee, Chen	R-R	5-11	175	10-21-86	4	0	2.27	21	0	0	1	32	26	9	8	2	12	43	.228	.277	.194	12.22	3.41
Lewis, Jensen	R-R	6-3	220	5-16-84	3	2	5.14	22	0	0	2	28	40	16	16	4	15	22	.342	.412	.288	7.07	4.82
Martinez, Joe	L-R	6-2	190	2-26-83	8	9	4.04	35	16	0	0	118	136	54	53	11	29	101	.290	.306	.277	7.70	2.21
McAllister, Zach	R-R	6-6	240	12-8-87	12	3	3.32	25	25	3	0	155	155	61	57	11	31	128	.261	.286	.241	7.45	1.80
Popham, Marty	R-R	6-6	235	8-4-87	0	0	5.40	1	0	0	0	2	1	1	1	1	2		.286	.333	.250	10.80	5.40
Putnam, Zach	R-R	6-2	225	7-3-87	6	3	3.65	44	0	0	9	69	61	30	28	6	23	68	.233	.205	.253	8.87	3.00
Reichenbach, J.D.	L-L	6-2	180	8-29-87	0	0	0.00	1	0	0	0	1	1	0	0	0	1	1	.250	.500	.000	9.00	9.00
Smith, Carlton	L-R	6-2	205	1-23-86	2	3	4.50	34	0	0	2	46	45	25	23	4	20	46	.259	.292	.239	9.00	3.91
Sturdevant, Tyler	R-L	6-1	191	12-20-85	0	0	4.91	2	0	0	1	4	6	3	2	0	2	4	.353	.800	.167	9.82	4.91
Talbot, Mitch	R-R	6-2	200	10-17-83	4	2	4.26	13	7	0	0	44	54	24	21	4	10	42	.300	.274	.318	8.53	2.03
Todd, Jess	R-R	5-11	210	4-20-86	0	0	11.00	8	0	0	0	9	18	11	11	2	6	6	.450	.571	.385	6.00	6.00
2-team total (2 Scranton/W-B)					0	1	10.97	10	0	0	0	11	19	13	13	2	8	7	—	—	—	5.91	6.75

CLEVELAND INDIANS

Pitching	B-T	HT	WT	DOB	W	L	ERA	G	GS	CG	SV	IP	H	R	ER	HR	BB	SO	AVG	vLH	vRH	K/9	BB/9
White, Alex	R-R	6-3	215	8-29-88	1	0	1.90	4	4	0	0	24	19	7	5	1	5	28	.211	.200	.217	10.65	1.90
Wright, Steve	R-R	6-1	200	8-30-84	0	0	6.75	1	0	0	0	3	5	2	2	0	0	2	.417	.000	.625	6.75	0.00

Fielding

Catcher	PCT	G	PO	A	E	DP	PB
Carlin	.998	60	444	38	1	3	6
Childs	1.000	1	10	3	0	0	0
Hernandez	1.000	7	50	3	0	1	0
McBride	1.000	4	33	3	0	0	0
Phillips	.993	73	611	52	5	6	4

First Base	PCT	G	PO	A	E	DP
Brown	1.000	8	58	4	0	5
Buck	1.000	5	39	4	0	5
Duncan	1.000	4	28	0	0	0
Goedert	1.000	28	206	20	0	19
Hodges	.988	28	240	14	3	22
Huffman	.977	16	117	9	3	12
Johnson	.988	32	230	25	3	27
LaPorta	1.000	2	19	0	0	0
McBride	1.000	3	27	5	0	3
Mills	.989	20	163	20	2	12
Phillips	1.000	1	1	0	0	1

Second Base	PCT	G	PO	A	E	DP
Head	1.000	1	1	1	0	1
Kipnis	.971	80	134	237	11	53
Phelps	.973	44	79	101	5	22
Reyes	.963	14	20	32	2	7
Valbuena	1.000	8	9	17	0	7

Third Base	PCT	G	PO	A	E	DP
Chisenhall	.949	59	40	110	8	9
Donald	.939	19	15	31	3	3
Goedert	.924	44	26	95	10	8
Phelps	.500	1	0	1	1	0
Reyes	.750	3	1	5	2	0
Rodriguez	.923	5	1	11	1	0
Valbuena	.930	15	10	30	3	6

Shortstop	PCT	G	PO	A	E	DP
Donald	.955	25	30	54	4	11
Phelps	.959	40	59	104	7	24
Reyes	.947	7	4	14	1	1
Valbuena	.978	75	92	173	6	35

Outfield	PCT	G	PO	A	E	DP
Bell	1.000	6	18	1	0	0
Brown	.900	7	9	0	1	0
Buck	1.000	22	37	3	0	1
Carrera	.991	82	216	6	2	2
Copeland	1.000	5	6	0	0	0
Crowe	1.000	4	7	0	0	0
Duncan	.975	15	37	2	1	1
Fedroff	.992	59	119	2	1	1
Head	.970	111	186	8	6	1
Huffman	.987	90	150	6	2	0
McBride	1.000	4	8	1	0	1
Neal	.875	6	7	0	1	0
Reyes	.000	1	0	0	0	0
Rodriguez	1.000	13	20	0	0	0
Sizemore	1.000	2	1	0	0	0
Smith	.000	2	0	0	0	0
Valbuena	1.000	11	21	3	0	0
Webb	1.000	8	20	0	0	0

AKRON AEROS

EASTERN LEAGUE

DOUBLE-A

Batting	B-T	HT	WT	DOB	AVG	vLH	vRH	G	AB	R	H	2B	3B	HR	RBI	BB	HBP	SH	SF	SO	SB	CS	SLG	OBP
Apodaca, Juan	R-R	5-11	180	7-15-86	.184	.318	.138	30	87	8	16	3	0	0	6	10	2	0	0	25	1	0	.218	.283
Arnal, Cristo	R-R	6-0	175	9-17-85	.187	.219	.174	72	225	20	42	5	0	0	15	16	1	0	0	33	5	5	.209	.244
Bellows, Kyle	R-R	6-2	204	8-19-88	.229	.248	.222	123	432	48	99	22	2	3	43	36	5	0	2	68	6	5	.310	.295
Cannon, Tyler	B-R	6-0	205	8-30-87	.278	.167	.333	6	18	3	5	3	0	0	2	4	1	0	0	4	0	0	.444	.435
Chen, Chun	R-R	6-1	200	11-1-88	.262	.253	.265	113	412	58	108	24	3	16	70	43	3	0	8	122	2	1	.451	.330
Copeland, Ben	L-L	6-0	190	12-17-83	.265	.264	.266	55	215	32	57	15	1	6	26	19	1	0	1	42	8	2	.428	.326
Diaz, Juan	R-R	6-4	200	12-12-88	.255	.250	.257	133	522	64	133	24	4	9	60	40	3	0	3	116	9	2	.368	.310
Donald, Jason	R-R	6-1	195	9-4-84	.241	.333	.200	9	29	4	7	0	0	0	2	2	0	0	0	6	1	0	.241	.290
Drennen, John	L-L	5-11	195	8-26-86	.240	.195	.259	85	283	30	68	17	4	6	38	43	5	0	1	58	1	0	.392	.349
Fedroff, Tim	L-R	5-11	220	2-4-87	.338	.417	.316	70	266	42	90	13	5	2	35	27	1	0	2	39	7	5	.447	.399
Fontanez, Kevin	R-R	5-11	170	6-21-90	.250	.333	.200	3	8	0	2	0	0	0	0	1	0	0	0	2	0	0	.250	.333
Gallas, Anthony	R-R	6-2	210	12-14-87	.000	.000	.000	1	4	0	0	0	0	0	0	0	0	0	0	3	0	0	.000	.000
Goedert, Jared	R-R	6-1	205	5-25-85	.276	.400	.211	8	29	7	8	2	0	3	9	6	0	0	1	8	0	0	.655	.389
Hafner, Travis	L-R	6-3	240	6-3-77	.500	.000	.600	2	6	2	3	1	0	0	0	1	0	0	0	1	0	0	.667	.571
Henry, Jordan	L-R	6-3	175	6-13-88	.256	.300	.238	119	454	66	116	7	2	0	33	69	0	0	0	75	33	12	.280	.354
Hernandez, Michel	R-R	6-0	215	8-12-78	.323	.321	.324	32	99	15	32	8	0	1	22	22	2	0	2	13	0	0	.434	.448
Johnson, Nick	L-L	6-3	235	9-19-78	.200	.000	.250	2	5	0	1	0	0	0	3	1	0	0	1	0	0	0	.200	.556
Lawson, Matt	R-R	6-0	195	11-18-85	.267	.381	.232	30	90	9	24	5	1	1	7	8	1	0	2	22	0	2	.378	.327
McBride, Matt	R-R	6-2	215	5-23-85	.297	.361	.277	84	310	50	92	24	4	14	53	30	2	0	3	44	3	0	.535	.359
Mills, Beau	L-R	6-3	220	8-15-86	.300	.339	.287	61	230	37	69	16	1	11	49	22	1	0	4	37	0	0	.522	.358
Padron, Raul	L-R	6-0	195	9-17-84	.225	.182	.246	55	200	24	45	12	1	3	22	16	1	0	1	49	1	2	.340	.284
Sanchez, Karexon	B-R	5-10	197	8-22-87	.220	.247	.210	108	350	41	77	12	2	9	40	39	6	0	2	102	16	3	.343	.307
Sizemore, Grady	L-L	6-2	200	8-2-82	.400	1.000	.368	6	20	1	8	3	0	0	3	2	0	0	2	0	0	0	.550	.455
Webb, Donnie	B-R	5-11	210	4-30-86	.214	.188	.223	85	262	34	56	10	3	2	24	27	2	0	3	62	14	5	.298	.289
Weglarz, Nick	L-L	6-3	240	12-16-87	.179	.179	.179	41	134	25	24	8	0	3	12	36	2	0	0	43	0	1	.306	.360

Pitching	B-T	HT	WT	DOB	W	L	ERA	G	GS	CG	SV	IP	H	R	ER	HR	BB	SO	AVG	vLH	vRH	K/9	BB/9
Adams, Austin	R-R	5-11	185	8-19-86	11	10	3.77	26	26	0	0	136	147	68	57	6	63	131	.280	.276	.285	8.67	4.17
Allen, Cody	R-R	6-1	210	11-20-88	0	0	18.00	1	0	0	0	1	3	2	2	0	2	2	.500	.500	.500	18.00	18.00
Barnes, Scott	L-L	6-4	185	9-5-87	1	0	1.64	2	2	0	0	11	5	2	2	0	2	17	.139	.375	.071	13.91	1.64
Berger, Eric	L-L	6-2	205	4-22-86	2	0	2.53	31	2	0	0	57	44	17	16	4	22	67	.213	.176	.230	10.58	3.47
Brach, Brett	R-R	6-2	190	3-29-88	1	2	4.45	5	5	0	0	28	27	17	14	4	12	15	.267	.250	.281	4.76	3.81
Bryson, Rob	R-R	6-1	200	12-11-87	2	0	2.95	16	0	0	0	21	17	9	7	1	12	23	.221	.229	.214	9.70	5.06
Burns, Cory	R-R	6-1	180	10-9-87	2	5	2.11	54	0	0	35	60	47	15	14	3	15	70	.220	.242	.200	10.56	2.26
Carrasco, Carlos	R-R	6-3	215	3-21-87	0	0	9.82	1	1	0	0	4	4	4	4	1	3	3	.267	.333	.222	7.36	7.36
De La Cruz, Kelvin	L-L	6-5	190	8-1-88	5	6	4.19	23	16	0	2	86	70	42	40	3	57	95	.227	.143	.261	9.94	5.97
Dickerson, Dale	R-R	6-2	210	9-11-86	0	0	4.50	2	0	0	0	2	2	1	1	0	1	1	.250	.333	.200	4.50	4.50
Espino, Paolo	R-R	5-10	190	1-10-87	6	0	2.44	22	5	0	1	81	66	22	22	8	18	78	.224	.269	.188	8.67	2.00
Gardner, Joe	R-R	6-4	220	3-18-88	7	8	4.99	19	19	0	0	97	108	73	54	6	47	60	.287	.319	.257	5.55	4.35
Hagadone, Nick	L-L	6-5	230	1-1-86	2	1	1.59	12	0	0	0	23	14	4	4	0	7	24	.175	.219	.146	9.53	2.78
Landis, Kyle	R-R	6-1	185	5-30-86	1	0	4.38	9	0	0	0	12	19	6	6	1	4	12	.352	.261	.419	8.76	2.92
Langwell, Matt	R-R	6-2	225	5-6-86	4	1	2.66	36	1	0	3	51	43	17	15	4	20	54	.226	.183	.259	9.59	3.55
Lee, Chen	R-R	5-11	175	10-21-86	2	1	2.50	23	0	0	0	40	27	16	11	1	16	56	.196	.190	.200	12.71	2.50
McFarland, T.J.	L-L	6-3	209	6-8-89	9	9	3.87	25	25	2	0	137	140	73	59	9	50	103	.265	.221	.281	6.75	3.28
Miller, Adam	R-R	6-4	200	11-26-84	1	4	6.27	23	0	0	1	33	43	24	23	0	16	25	.331	.377	.299	6.82	4.36
Packer, Matt	L-L	6-0	200	8-28-87	9	12	4.31	27	27	1	0	169	175	91	81	16	33	129	.269	.219	.288	6.86	1.75
Petter, Kyle	L-L	6-0	180	4-5-90	0	0	0.00	2	0	0	0	1	0	0	0	0	3	2	.000	.000	.000	13.50	20.25

CLEVELAND INDIANS

Pitching	B-T	HT	WT	DOB	W	L	ERA	G	GS	CG	SV	IP	H	R	ER	HR	BB	SO	AVG	vLH	vRH	K/9	BB/9
Pino, Yohan	R-R	6-2	190	12-26-83	0	0	0.00	2	0	0	0	1	2	0	0	0	0	2	.400	.000	.400	13.50	0.00
2-team total (36 New Hampshire)					4	8	4.08	38	10	1	0	97	92	47	44	15	14	106	—	—	—	9.84	1.30
Pomeranz, Drew	R-L	6-5	230	11-22-88	0	1	2.57	3	3	0	0	14	10	4	4	1	6	17	.200	.095	.276	10.93	3.86
Popham, Marty	R-R	6-6	235	8-4-87	0	1	7.24	4	2	0	0	14	23	11	11	0	5	9	.377	.348	.395	5.93	3.29
Price, Bryan	R-R	6-4	210	11-13-86	2	3	2.79	28	1	0	0	52	50	20	16	5	15	33	.258	.329	.209	5.75	2.61
Smith, Joe	R-R	6-2	205	3-22-84	0	0	2.45	4	0	0	0	4	1	1	1	0	2	7	.083	.000	.100	17.18	4.91
Stowell, Bryce	R-R	6-2	205	9-23-86	1	0	1.86	13	0	0	0	19	12	6	4	1	10	28	.176	.300	.125	13.03	4.66
Sturdevant, Tyler	R-L	6-1	191	12-20-85	3	1	3.30	19	0	0	2	30	30	12	11	2	9	34	.270	.262	.275	10.20	2.70
Wright, Steve	R-R	6-1	200	8-30-84	2	4	5.98	8	7	0	0	47	47	32	31	8	28	35	.269	.311	.246	6.75	5.40

Fielding

Catcher	PCT	G	PO	A	E	DP	PB
Apodaca	.986	28	202	14	3	0	3
Chen	.993	82	651	66	5	6	18
Hernandez	.994	25	154	26	1	0	3
McBride	1.000	5	27	2	0	0	0
Padron	1.000	12	75	19	0	3	3

First Base	PCT	G	PO	A	E	DP
Arnal	.992	19	121	10	1	14
Fontanez	1.000	1	7	1	0	1
Goedert	.960	5	43	5	2	5
Johnson	.800	1	3	1	1	1
McBride	.980	46	321	28	7	37
Mills	.997	39	338	25	1	24
Padron	.994	38	347	14	2	39

Second Base	PCT	G	PO	A	E	DP
Arnal	.968	34	64	88	5	23
Cannon	1.000	2	6	7	0	3
Fontanez	1.000	1	0	1	0	0
Lawson	.976	21	35	47	2	12
Sanchez	.980	91	204	232	9	76

Third Base	PCT	G	PO	A	E	DP
Arnal	1.000	2	0	2	0	0
Bellows	.962	119	68	259	13	26
Cannon	1.000	4	3	10	0	0
Donald	.909	5	2	8	1	0
Lawson	1.000	4	6	4	0	0
Sanchez	.921	18	10	25	3	2

Shortstop	PCT	G	PO	A	E	DP
Arnal	1.000	16	15	28	0	6

Diaz	.966	127	172	391	20	83
Donald	1.000	1	3	2	0	0
Sanchez	1.000	2	3	6	0	2

Outfield	PCT	G	PO	A	E	DP
Arnal	1.000	4	2	0	0	0
Copeland	1.000	50	79	3	0	1
Drennen	.991	76	109	2	1	1
Fedroff	.991	64	99	7	1	1
Gallas	1.000	1	2	0	0	0
Goedert	.000	1	0	0	0	0
Henry	.988	108	243	6	3	1
McBride	1.000	26	46	1	0	0
Sizemore	1.000	5	7	0	0	0
Webb	.986	78	132	4	2	0
Weglarz	.967	24	28	1	1	0

KINSTON INDIANS

HIGH CLASS A

CAROLINA LEAGUE

Batting	B-T	HT	WT	DOB	AVG	vLH	vRH	G	AB	R	H	2B	3B	HR	RBI	BB	HBP	SH	SF	SO	SB	CS	SLG	OBP
Abraham, Adam	R-R	6-0	228	3-27-87	.252	.278	.238	130	456	63	115	31	0	17	72	70	9	0	4	114	5	2	.432	.360
Abreu, Abner	R-R	6-3	187	10-24-89	.244	.212	.261	91	336	42	82	16	5	12	35	22	3	0	3	102	19	3	.429	.294
Aguilar, Jesus	R-R	6-3	241	6-30-90	.257	.283	.239	31	113	12	29	3	0	4	13	11	0	0	0	28	1	0	.389	.323
Burnette, Chase	L-L	6-2	214	5-20-88	.230	.263	.214	74	248	24	57	10	2	4	32	14	3	0	2	74	3	2	.335	.277
Cannon, Tyler	B-R	6-0	205	8-30-87	.246	.254	.241	92	309	36	76	17	4	6	39	36	1	0	2	81	0	4	.385	.325
Casas, Jordan	L-R	5-11	180	3-17-88	.256	.222	.276	32	121	14	31	3	2	0	12	7	1	0	0	23	1	2	.314	.302
Cid, Delvi	R-R	6-2	170	7-19-89	.197	.183	.206	79	234	31	46	5	1	2	9	28	9	0	0	64	28	8	.252	.306
DeGeorge, Dan	R-R	5-10	180	2-19-87	.226	.278	.154	11	31	2	7	0	1	0	5	1	0	0	1	3	0	0	.290	.242
Folgia, Greg	B-R	5-11	195	3-31-88	.176	.083	.227	11	34	4	6	3	0	0	2	1	0	0	0	16	0	0	.265	.200
Frawley, Casey	R-R	5-11	170	9-17-87	.215	.255	.193	127	465	54	100	20	4	11	59	44	9	0	7	111	7	3	.346	.291
Gallas, Anthony	R-R	6-2	210	12-14-87	.197	.266	.141	39	142	14	28	10	0	2	21	12	7	0	3	34	1	0	.310	.287
Greenwell, Bo	L-L	6-0	185	10-15-88	.260	.208	.285	65	235	27	61	12	2	3	23	20	1	0	2	30	5	6	.366	.318
Holt, Tyler	R-R	5-10	187	3-10-89	.254	.211	.281	123	449	66	114	18	4	2	26	78	2	0	2	106	34	6	.323	.365
Martinez, Argenis	B-R	5-11	160	4-8-90	.227	.316	.160	32	88	9	20	3	0	0	6	12	5	0	0	21	4	1	.261	.352
Perez, Roberto	R-R	6-0	227	12-23-88	.225	.192	.244	94	284	30	64	16	1	2	30	62	1	0	1	79	1	0	.310	.365
Pickens, Doug	R-R	6-0	201	6-19-85	.165	.076	.220	76	242	14	40	5	0	2	16	14	5	0	1	60	0	1	.211	.225
Rivas, Ronald	R-R	6-2	184	1-16-88	.143	.083	.174	10	35	2	5	0	0	0	1	3	0	0	0	12	0	0	.143	.211
Smit, Jason	R-R	6-0	165	10-27-89	.217	.333	.176	8	23	3	5	2	1	0	2	2	0	0	0	6	0	0	.391	.280
Smith, Kyle	R-R	6-1	190	12-25-87	.000	.000	.000	3	9	1	0	0	0	0	0	1	0	0	0	5	0	0	.000	.100
Tice, Jeremie	R-R	6-3	219	9-25-86	.258	.263	.255	77	275	39	71	16	0	11	43	36	7	0	2	73	1	1	.436	.356
Toole, Justin	R-R	6-0	180	9-10-86	.258	.264	.255	99	329	39	85	20	1	0	26	16	9	0	0	51	17	3	.325	.311

Pitching	B-T	HT	WT	DOB	W	L	ERA	G	GS	CG	SV	IP	H	R	ER	HR	BB	SO	AVG	vLH	vRH	K/9	BB/9
Allen, Cody	R-R	6-1	210	11-20-88	0	0	0.00	1	0	0	0	3	1	0	0	0	0	3	.100	.250	.000	9.00	0.00
Brach, Brett	R-R	6-2	190	3-29-88	6	9	3.60	21	19	1	0	115	97	48	46	8	37	72	.229	.214	.241	5.63	2.90
Bryson, Rob	R-R	6-1	200	12-11-87	0	0	0.64	10	0	0	1	14	6	1	1	1	3	20	.128	.100	.148	12.86	1.93
Cook, Clayton	R-R	6-3	175	7-23-90	9	9	4.56	25	25	0	0	122	124	70	62	10	53	106	.263	.243	.280	7.80	3.90
Flores, Jose	R-R	6-3	250	6-4-89	4	5	6.02	42	0	0	2	55	72	46	37	2	19	49	.320	.341	.308	7.97	3.09
Goodnight, Michael	R-R	6-4	215	6-10-89	1	0	1.69	1	1	0	0	5	3	1	1	0	0	6	.176	.000	.375	10.13	0.00
Guilmet, Preston	R-R	6-2	200	7-27-87	1	1	2.16	52	0	0	35	58	43	14	14	4	11	60	.202	.226	.186	9.26	1.70
Haley, Trey	R-R	6-3	180	6-21-90	1	1	3.77	19	0	0	1	29	25	14	12	1	17	27	.240	.195	.270	8.48	5.34
House, T.J.	R-L	6-2	215	9-29-89	6	12	5.19	25	24	1	0	130	133	85	75	12	66	89	.269	.287	.263	6.16	4.57
Jimenez, Francisco	L-L	5-11	164	10-2-88	4	3	3.23	26	7	0	0	70	69	29	25	4	23	75	.266	.271	.265	9.69	2.97
Jones, Chris	L-L	6-2	202	9-19-88	7	1	3.36	43	0	0	0	72	65	31	27	6	30	66	.240	.145	.282	8.21	3.73
Landis, Kyle	R-R	6-1	185	5-30-86	9	2	2.15	32	0	0	3	50	33	12	12	5	9	61	.191	.159	.209	10.91	1.61
Mahalic, Joey	R-R	6-3	205	11-28-88	0	0	11.17	5	0	0	0	10	16	13	12	1	5	4	.364	.500	.286	3.72	4.66
McFarland, T.J.	L-L	6-3	209	6-8-89	0	1	2.25	2	2	0	0	12	9	5	3	2	1	12	.191	.150	.222	9.00	0.75
Miller, Adam	R-R	6-4	200	11-26-84	0	1	4.91	8	0	0	1	11	8	7	6	2	5	14	.195	.118	.250	11.45	4.09
Murata, Toru	L-R	6-0	175	5-20-85	3	2	2.36	22	5	0	2	50	37	14	13	2	10	58	.208	.171	.231	10.51	1.81
Pomeranz, Drew	R-L	6-5	230	11-22-88	3	2	1.87	15	15	0	0	77	56	22	16	5	32	96	.202	.130	.220	11.10	3.74
Popham, Marty	R-R	6-6	235	8-4-87	6	2	4.19	22	16	0	0	97	92	47	45	17	19	95	.247	.270	.231	8.84	1.77
Rayl, Mike	L-L	6-5	180	11-1-88	1	3	4.61	8	8	0	0	41	48	23	21	6	13	37	.293	.394	.267	8.12	2.85
Reichenbach, J.D.	L-L	6-2	180	8-29-87	1	0	0.00	2	1	0	0	6	0	0	0	0	2	3	.000	.000	.000	4.50	3.00
Sarianides, Nick	R-R	6-1	200	8-29-89	2	0	4.05	6	0	0	0	13	15	6	6	0	9	6	.300	.308	.297	4.05	6.08

Pitching	B-T	HT	WT	DOB	W	L	ERA	G	GS	CG	SV	IP	H	R	ER	HR	BB	SO	AVG	vLH	vRH	K/9	BB/9
Soto, Giovanni	L-L	6-3	180	5-18-91	4	4	3.23	15	11	0	0	64	56	29	23	5	21	64	.234	.259	.227	9.00	2.95
Sturdevant, Tyler	R-L	6-1	191	12-20-85	4	2	1.98	21	0	0	1	41	31	10	9	3	8	44	.203	.220	.191	9.66	1.76
Turek, Travis	R-R	6-3	200	9-2-87	3	0	3.57	12	0	0	0	23	22	9	9	1	10	17	.262	.115	.328	6.75	3.97
Wright, Steve	R-R	6-1	200	8-30-84	1	2	4.46	7	4	0	0	38	47	28	19	7	16	27	.305	.382	.244	6.34	3.76

Fielding

Catcher	PCT	G	PO	A	E	DP	PB
Abraham	1.000	3	20	6	0	0	
Perez	.991	94	767	87	8	12	4
Pickens	.988	48	300	27	4	2	10

First Base	PCT	G	PO	A	E	DP
Aguilar	.991	25	196	14	2	16
Burnette	.980	63	516	28	11	44
Cannon	1.000	3	22	3	0	2
Pickens	1.000	8	67	5	0	3
Smit	.941	4	30	2	2	2
Tice	1.000	34	249	14	0	20
Toole	.990	13	91	7	1	3

Second Base	PCT	G	PO	A	E	DP
Cannon	.991	47	87	122	2	29
DeGeorge	.947	4	9	9	1	1

Frawley	.985	14	26	39	1	8	
Martinez	.984	30	53	68	2	14	
Rivas	1.000	8	13	21	0	5	
Smith	1.000	2	1	7	0	1	
Toole	.994	38	73	94	1	20	

Third Base	PCT	G	PO	A	E	DP
Abraham	.945	111	75	232	18	14
Cannon	.941	9	4	12	1	1
DeGeorge	.727	7	1	7	3	2
Martinez	.000	1	0	0	0	0
Tice	.000	1	0	0	0	0
Toole	1.000	19	9	36	0	2

Shortstop	PCT	G	PO	A	E	DP
Cannon	.951	12	18	40	3	11
Frawley	.941	109	116	248	23	54

Martinez	1.000	1	1	2	0	0
Rivas	.900	2	1	8	1	0
Smith	.750	1	1	2	1	0
Toole	.970	16	19	46	2	7

Outfield	PCT	G	PO	A	E	DP
Abreu	.978	87	172	3	4	1
Cannon	1.000	7	4	1	0	0
Casas	1.000	31	50	1	0	0
Cid	.969	73	151	5	5	2
Folgia	1.000	8	13	1	0	0
Gallas	.981	32	51	2	1	0
Greenwell	.990	60	99	1	1	0
Holt	.983	111	221	9	4	3
Pickens	1.000	8	8	0	0	0
Smit	.778	2	6	1	2	0
Toole	.900	13	16	2	2	0

LAKE COUNTY CAPTAINS

MIDWEST LEAGUE

LOW CLASS A

Batting	B-T	HT	WT	DOB	AVG	vLH	vRH	G	AB	R	H	2B	3B	HR	RBI	BB	HBP	SH	SF	SO	SB	CS	SLG	OBP
Aguilar, Jesus	R-R	6-3	241	6-30-90	.292	.317	.282	95	349	58	102	27	2	19	69	35	10	0	3	98	1	0	.544	.370
Bartolone, Nick	R-R	5-10	153	10-22-90	.219	.224	.217	106	356	41	78	12	2	0	26	25	3	0	5	70	11	8	.264	.272
Burnette, Chase	L-L	6-2	214	5-20-88	.203	.116	.253	34	118	8	24	8	0	0	7	12	1	0	0	21	1	0	.271	.282
Cannon, Tyler	B-R	6-0	205	8-30-87	.366	.353	.373	30	93	18	34	10	2	3	17	17	1	0	3	20	2	0	.613	.456
Casas, Jordan	L-R	5-11	180	3-17-88	.281	.390	.235	35	139	20	39	4	1	0	12	9	4	0	3	24	3	0	.324	.335
Childs, Dwight	R-R	6-2	190	7-23-88	.270	.364	.231	11	37	4	10	4	0	1	6	2	0	0	0	11	0	0	.459	.308
Choo, Shin-Soo	L-L	5-11	205	7-13-82	.000	.000	.000	3	8	0	0	0	0	0	0	1	0	0	0	2	0	0	.000	.000
Dunn, Henry	R-R	5-7	185	3-26-89	.125	.000	.190	15	32	2	4	1	0	0	0	1	0	0	0	11	0	2	.156	.152
Fields, Aaron	R-R	6-0	190	6-20-88	.239	.250	.235	30	92	9	22	3	0	1	11	4	4	0	0	23	0	3	.304	.300
Fontanez, Kevin	R-R	5-11	170	6-21-90	.196	.069	.241	33	112	10	22	4	0	1	9	8	2	0	1	22	0	0	.259	.260
Gallas, Anthony	R-R	6-2	210	12-14-87	.314	.292	.324	57	207	35	65	24	0	6	21	23	4	0	0	38	4	4	.517	.393
Heere, Brian	L-R	5-11	170	8-6-87	.245	.286	.230	87	277	26	68	9	1	3	35	39	2	0	3	62	0	0	.318	.340
Lavisky, Alex	R-R	6-1	200	1-13-91	.207	.245	.191	49	184	19	38	10	0	8	24	9	2	0	0	66	0	1	.391	.251
Martinez, Argenis	B-R	5-11	160	4-8-90	.235	.170	.255	60	196	21	46	4	1	0	24	29	0	0	3	53	8	1	.265	.329
Moncrief, Carlos	L-R	6-1	210	11-3-88	.233	.197	.248	122	464	73	108	26	7	16	53	76	6	0	3	158	20	7	.422	.346
Monsalve, Alex	R-R	6-2	225	4-22-92	.264	.344	.232	117	458	55	121	21	3	5	44	31	3	0	4	96	7	6	.356	.313
Montero, Moises	R-R	6-0	210	11-4-89	.193	.250	.159	31	109	10	21	8	0	3	11	5	1	0	1	26	0	0	.349	.233
Rodriguez, Luigi	B-R	5-11	160	11-13-92	.250	.220	.264	34	132	10	33	4	2	0	5	14	0	0	1	36	6	5	.311	.320
Rodriguez, Ronny	R-R	6-0	170	4-17-92	.246	.311	.220	98	370	41	91	28	7	11	42	13	3	0	4	83	10	7	.449	.274
Smit, Jason	R-R	6-0	165	10-27-89	.344	.357	.339	26	90	17	31	5	1	2	11	15	3	0	1	24	1	2	.489	.450
Smith, Kyle	R-R	6-1	190	12-25-87	.182	.091	.227	13	33	4	6	2	0	0	2	2	1	0	0	9	0	0	.242	.250
Urshela, Giovanny	R-R	6-0	197	10-11-91	.238	.214	.247	126	505	57	120	24	2	9	46	14	4	0	4	69	3	0	.347	.262
Washington, LeVon	L-R	5-11	170	7-26-91	.218	.235	.212	79	298	35	65	9	4	2	20	49	2	0	1	89	15	6	.315	.331

Pitching	B-T	HT	WT	DOB	W	L	ERA	G	GS	CG	SV	IP	H	R	ER	HR	BB	SO	AVG	vLH	vRH	K/9	BB/9
Allen, Cody	R-R	6-1	210	11-20-88	2	0	0.00	7	0	0	0	17	10	0	0	0	5	28	.164	.194	.133	14.82	2.65
Blair, Kyle	R-R	6-2	236	9-27-88	3	5	5.02	23	14	0	0	81	78	47	45	7	40	70	.255	.297	.209	7.81	4.46
Bryson, Rob	R-R	6-1	200	12-11-87	0	1	4.50	4	0	0	0	4	5	2	2	1	1	5	.294	.333	.200	11.25	2.25
Colon, Joseph	R-R	6-0	167	2-10-90	0	0	3.00	1	1	0	0	6	6	2	2	0	2	4	.261	.429	.000	6.00	3.00
Cook, Cole	R-R	6-6	200	10-18-88	5	11	4.54	20	19	1	0	105	126	66	53	16	35	68	.296	.284	.308	5.83	3.00
Cooper, Jordan	R-R	6-2	190	5-10-89	2	9	4.73	27	16	1	3	105	109	60	55	19	30	68	.267	.262	.271	5.85	2.58
Dew, Owen	R-R	6-2	180	9-26-88	1	4	5.79	8	0	0	0	19	22	15	12	4	6	17	.289	.314	.268	8.20	2.89
Dickerson, Dale	R-R	6-2	210	9-11-86	3	3	2.45	53	0	0	3	70	62	24	19	5	26	48	.243	.295	.195	6.20	3.36
Dischler, Tony	R-R	6-3	190	3-6-89	0	1	22.50	3	1	0	0	6	13	16	15	3	9	7	.433	.467	.400	10.50	13.50
Ehlert, Clayton	R-R	6-1	195	11-2-87	1	2	1.68	38	1	0	16	48	34	11	9	3	7	29	.194	.217	.169	5.40	1.30
Encarnacion, Luis	R-R	6-3	170	10-25-91	2	3	5.00	31	0	0	0	45	31	33	25	1	51	53	.195	.189	.203	10.60	10.20
Goodnight, Michael	R-R	6-4	215	6-10-89	5	12	4.15	27	27	0	0	130	104	72	60	9	66	117	.219	.217	.221	8.10	4.57
Guerrero, Harold	L-L	6-3	215	5-21-90	0	0	1.80	2	0	0	0	5	3	1	1	0	3	5	.167	.143	.182	9.00	5.40
Haley, Trey	R-R	6-3	180	6-21-90	0	0	2.84	8	2	0	1	13	5	4	4	0	8	17	.125	.050	.200	12.08	5.68
Jimenez, Francisco	L-L	5-11	164	10-2-88	2	0	2.37	6	0	0	0	19	10	5	5	0	4	16	.156	.179	.139	7.58	1.89
Landis, Kyle	R-R	6-1	185	5-30-86	0	0	0.00	1	0	0	0	1	0	0	0	0	0	1	.000	.000	.000	9.00	0.00
Mahalic, Joey	R-R	6-2	205	11-28-88	1	5	6.36	23	0	0	0	47	55	45	33	5	35	35	.289	.345	.243	6.75	6.75
Petter, Kyle	L-L	6-0	180	4-5-90	2	5	2.70	22	0	0	2	33	20	12	10	1	17	46	.168	.195	.154	12.42	4.59
Rayl, Mike	L-L	6-5	180	11-1-88	5	5	2.83	17	17	0	0	83	66	28	26	3	13	84	.216	.221	.214	9.15	1.42
Reichenbach, J.D.	L-L	6-2	180	8-29-87	7	2	3.65	30	9	0	0	104	111	56	42	6	26	72	.278	.288	.272	6.25	2.26
Rucinski, Drew	R-R	6-2	180	9-27-88	1	0	0.00	2	0	0	0	3	1	0	0	0	3	7	.091	.000	.250	18.90	8.10
Salazar, Danny	R-R	6-0	180	1-11-90	0	2	3.38	3	3	0	0	8	8	4	3	0	2	7	.258	.188	.333	7.88	2.25
Sarianides, Nick	R-R	6-1	200	8-29-89	5	4	3.86	36	0	0	2	68	70	34	29	7	25	54	.268	.274	.263	7.18	3.33

Pitching	B-T	HT	WT	DOB	W	L	ERA	G	GS	CG	SV	IP	H	R	ER	HR	BB	SO	AVG	vLH	vRH	K/9	BB/9
Sterling, Felix	R-R	6-3	200	3-15-93	2	3	4.14	9	9	0	0	41	31	20	19	4	25	35	.220	.197	.238	7.62	5.44
Stowell, Bryce	R-R	6-2	205	9-23-86	0	1	2.60	10	0	0	0	17	8	5	5	0	10	26	.140	.172	.107	13.50	5.19
Striz, Nate	R-R	6-2	220	10-15-88	0	2	6.88	20	1	0	1	35	36	27	27	3	26	25	.271	.271	.270	6.37	6.62
Wetmore, Kirk	L-L	6-2	205	3-17-89	3	4	5.25	12	11	0	0	58	56	49	34	4	37	34	.252	.241	.259	5.25	5.71
Wright, Steve	R-R	6-1	200	8-30-84	1	2	3.13	9	9	0	0	46	48	30	16	3	24	33	.273	.364	.202	6.46	4.70

Fielding

Catcher	PCT	G	PO	A	E	DP	PB
Childs	1.000	9	77	7	0	0	0
Lavisky	.991	28	204	26	2	2	8
Monsalve	.981	72	498	73	11	4	20
Montero	.992	31	207	27	2	2	5

First Base	PCT	G	PO	A	E	DP
Aguilar	.986	93	814	49	12	85
Burnette	.985	34	316	20	5	29
Cannon	1.000	1	12	0	0	0
Childs	1.000	2	13	2	0	3
Fields	1.000	9	37	4	0	6
Monsalve	1.000	1	7	1	0	0
Smit	1.000	2	18	1	0	2
Smith	.979	5	43	4	1	3

Second Base	PCT	G	PO	A	E	DP
Bartolone	.985	67	123	212	5	50
Cannon	1.000	4	3	12	0	2
Fields	.765	5	4	9	4	1
Fontanez	.975	8	11	28	1	5
Martinez	.970	55	95	165	8	41
Smith	.955	5	4	17	1	4

Third Base	PCT	G	PO	A	E	DP
Cannon	1.000	4	2	5	0	1
Fields	.000	1	0	0	0	0
Fontanez	.882	6	5	10	2	0
Martinez	.700	5	2	5	3	0
Monsalve	.000	1	0	0	0	0
Urshela	.934	126	98	214	22	27

Shortstop	PCT	G	PO	A	E	DP
Bartolone	.913	34	56	101	15	26
Cannon	.966	8	8	20	1	5
Rodriguez	.923	97	168	285	38	62

Outfield	PCT	G	PO	A	E	DP
Bartolone	1.000	5	7	0	0	0
Cannon	1.000	4	2	0	0	0
Casas	.988	34	76	5	1	1
Choo	1.000	2	4	0	0	0
Dunn	1.000	14	17	1	0	0
Gallas	.972	56	101	3	3	2
Heere	.982	61	105	5	2	2
Moncrief	.950	121	206	21	12	1
Rodriguez	.916	34	72	4	7	0
Smit	1.000	23	29	2	0	0
Washington	.961	78	138	11	6	0

MAHONING VALLEY SCRAPPERS   SHORT-SEASON

NEW YORK-PENN LEAGUE

Batting	B-T	HT	WT	DOB	AVG	vLH	vRH	G	AB	R	H	2B	3B	HR	RBI	BB	HBP	SH	SF	SO	SB	CS	SLG	OBP
Barr, John	R-R	6-2	190	6-17-88	.241	.295	.220	47	162	19	39	8	1	0	24	19	6	0	4	24	5	1	.302	.335
Battaglia, Ryan	R-R	6-1	202	6-29-92	.000	.000	.000	6	8	0	0	0	0	0	1	1	0	0	0	5	0	0	.000	.111
Dunn, Henry	R-R	5-7	185	3-26-89	.214	.000	.273	4	14	1	3	0	0	1	6	2	0	0	0	2	0	1	.429	.313
Elliott, Cody	R-R	6-0	170	4-26-90	.224	.232	.222	65	245	40	55	8	4	1	31	22	7	0	4	67	6	2	.302	.302
Fontanez, Kevin	R-R	5-11	170	6-21-90	.211	.308	.160	12	38	5	8	1	0	0	5	3	1	0	1	4	3	0	.237	.279
Frazar, Evan	R-R	6-0	185	3-17-91	.304	.000	.347	19	56	10	17	0	0	1	6	6	5	0	1	14	3	0	.357	.412
Hankins, Todd	R-R	5-11	180	11-18-90	.246	.235	.250	65	240	42	59	10	2	4	43	23	5	0	6	50	14	4	.354	.318
Lavisky, Alex	R-R	6-1	200	1-13-91	.201	.179	.208	68	259	29	52	18	0	5	28	20	7	0	0	71	0	1	.328	.276
Lindor, Francisco	B-R	5-11	175	11-14-93	.316	.200	.357	5	19	4	6	0	0	0	2	1	0	0	0	5	1	0	.316	.350
Lowery, Jake	L-R	5-10	200	7-21-90	.245	.270	.237	69	253	43	62	23	1	6	43	54	1	0	2	56	3	2	.415	.377
MacPhee, Zack	B-R	5-9	175	2-13-90	.143	.000	.182	6	14	1	2	1	0	0	4	0	0	0	0	3	0	1	.214	.333
Montero, Moises	R-R	6-0	210	11-4-89	.000	.000	.000	1	3	0	0	0	0	0	0	0	0	0	0	1	0	0	.000	.000
Myles, Bryson	R-R	5-11	230	9-18-89	.302	.283	.309	50	192	36	58	10	3	1	15	24	5	0	0	32	20	7	.401	.394
Sabourin, Jerrud	L-L	6-2	210	11-2-89	.225	.200	.232	60	209	19	47	13	1	0	27	19	4	0	0	40	0	0	.297	.306
Serna, K.C.	R-R	6-0	185	10-15-89	.265	.436	.204	42	147	20	39	8	1	1	12	12	5	0	1	24	12	5	.354	.339
Siliga, Aaron	L-L	5-10	180	8-24-92	.171	.139	.180	47	158	17	27	7	3	2	15	22	0	0	0	25	8	3	.291	.272
Smith, Jordan	L-R	6-4	205	7-5-90	.300	.254	.318	65	243	36	73	20	1	0	47	35	9	0	3	30	3	1	.391	.403
Wolters, Tony	L-R	5-10	165	6-9-92	.292	.328	.280	69	267	50	78	10	3	1	20	30	11	0	1	49	19	4	.363	.385

Pitching	B-T	HT	WT	DOB	W	L	ERA	G	GS	CG	SV	IP	H	R	ER	HR	BB	SO	AVG	vLH	vRH	K/9	BB/9
Allen, Cody	R-R	6-1	210	11-20-88	3	1	2.14	14	0	0	0	34	21	9	8	1	9	42	.183	.179	.186	11.23	2.41
Anderson, Cody	R-R	6-4	220	9-14-90	0	1	1.80	3	1	0	0	5	4	1	1	0	4	3	.235	.333	.214	5.40	7.20
Araujo, Elvis	L-L	6-6	215	7-15-91	0	0	8.10	2	2	0	0	7	11	6	6	0	7	5	.393	.250	.500	6.75	9.45
Armstrong, Shawn	R-R	6-2	210	9-11-90	0	0	0.00	1	0	0	0	2	1	0	0	0	0	2	.167	.000	.250	9.00	0.00
Cespedes, Ramon	R-R	6-2	174	11-1-90	1	1	4.24	16	0	0	0	23	20	12	11	3	9	27	.225	.263	.196	10.41	3.47
Colon, Joseph	R-R	6-0	167	2-18-90	4	4	3.55	15	14	0	0	71	63	33	28	3	29	57	.237	.223	.248	7.23	3.68
Dischler, Tony	R-R	6-3	190	3-6-89	1	2	4.15	22	0	0	0	39	46	22	18	3	11	24	.291	.304	.281	5.54	2.54
Gomez, Jeanmar	R-R	6-3	170	2-10-88	0	0	2.25	1	1	0	0	4	5	1	1	0	0	3	.294	.364	.167	6.75	0.00
Guerrero, Harold	L-L	6-3	215	5-21-90	2	4	6.14	16	7	0	0	48	49	37	33	2	25	36	.265	.278	.260	6.70	4.66
Jimenez, Danny	L-L	6-2	205	9-23-89	4	3	2.39	17	12	0	0	72	66	30	19	1	24	50	.241	.149	.275	6.28	3.01
Krasne, Will	R-R	6-0	200	11-30-87	3	5	4.01	22	0	0	0	34	25	17	15	3	30	22	.208	.262	.179	5.88	8.02
McKeon, Josh	R-R	6-2	200	10-28-89	0	0	3.00	4	0	0	0	6	5	3	2	0	1	7	.217	.222	.214	10.50	1.50
Nixon, Robert	R-R	6-1	190	11-1-88	7	3	4.82	15	15	0	0	80	99	50	43	8	17	48	.301	.314	.288	5.38	1.90
Petter, Kyle	L-L	6-0	180	4-5-90	2	0	0.00	6	0	0	2	8	2	0	0	0	5	14	.091	.091	.091	16.43	5.87
Radeke, Mason	R-R	6-1	175	6-13-90	2	0	4.53	9	9	0	0	44	44	23	22	6	15	30	.263	.308	.225	6.18	3.09
Roberts, Will	L-R	6-5	195	8-17-90	1	3	3.27	9	8	0	0	41	37	17	15	2	7	29	.247	.297	.209	6.31	1.52
Rondon, Hector	R-R	6-3	180	2-26-88	0	0	3.00	2	2	0	0	3	3	1	1	0	0	2	.250	.400	.143	6.00	0.00
Rucinski, Drew	R-R	6-2	190	12-30-88	2	0	2.84	15	0	0	0	25	27	9	8	3	5	30	.284	.366	.222	10.66	1.78
Sides, Steven	R-R	6-4	215	10-24-90	0	0	4.85	12	0	0	0	13	14	8	7	2	6	13	.259	.235	.270	9.00	4.15
Stowell, Bryce	R-R	6-2	205	9-23-86	0	0	0.00	1	0	0	1	2	1	0	0	0	1	3	.143	.000	.333	13.50	4.50
Striz, Nate	R-R	6-2	220	10-15-88	4	5	3.26	18	1	0	1	47	39	22	17	1	23	49	.238	.225	.247	9.38	4.40
Tejeda, Enosil	R-R	6-0	175	6-21-89	2	2	2.91	28	0	0	12	34	21	14	11	0	15	57	.171	.151	.186	15.09	3.97
Wagoner, Jack	R-R	6-1	205	6-20-89	1	0	1.13	6	0	0	0	8	2	1	1	0	6	6	.077	.083	.071	6.75	6.75
Wetmore, Kirk	L-L	6-2	205	3-17-89	2	1	0.00	3	3	0	0	15	8	3	0	0	3	15	.154	.333	.083	9.00	1.80

Fielding

Catcher	PCT	G	PO	A	E	DP	PB
Battaglia	1.000	5	13	0	0	0	1
Lavisky	.983	48	348	46	7	6	10
Lowery	.978	25	193	26	5	3	6
Montero	1.000	1	7	1	0	0	0

AZL INDIANS

ROOKIE

ARIZONA LEAGUE

Batting	B-T	HT	WT	DOB	AVG	vLH	vRH	G	AB	R	H	2B	3B	HR	RBI	BB	HBP	SH	SF	SO	SB	CS	SLG	OBP
Battaglia, Ryan	R-R	6-1	202	6-29-92	.000	.000	.000	1	3	2	0	0	0	0	0	1	0	0	0	1	0	0	.000	.250
Bradley, Marcus	L-L	5-9	160	8-30-90	.200	.333	.143	8	20	5	4	2	0	0	3	7	0	0	0	8	2	0	.300	.407
Brown, Mark	L-L	5-9	160	9-11-91	.214	.281	.192	43	131	19	28	5	2	0	14	18	1	0	2	36	6	2	.282	.309
Campbell, Andrew	L-R	6-0	155	2-18-92	.265	.290	.254	29	98	13	26	2	1	0	6	13	2	0	0	23	5	2	.306	.363
Castillo, Leonardo	R-R	6-2	190	7-9-93	.303	.250	.322	49	198	25	60	14	1	4	30	6	3	0	0	32	3	0	.444	.333
Cervenka, Martin	R-R	6-1	175	8-3-92	.164	.182	.159	17	55	4	9	1	1	0	1	5	0	0	0	14	0	0	.218	.233
Crowe, Trevor	B-R	5-10	190	11-17-83	.444	1.000	.412	6	18	9	8	3	1	2	8	6	0	0	0	4	2	1	1.056	.583
Dunn, Henry	R-R	5-7	185	3-26-89	.277	.278	.276	15	47	7	13	3	1	0	5	5	0	0	1	8	3	2	.383	.340
Garcia, Robel	B-R	6-0	168	3-28-93	.284	.302	.276	45	169	31	48	10	8	6	24	23	2	0	3	50	7	2	.544	.371
Gonzalez, Erik	R-R	6-1	165	8-31-91	.258	.240	.266	41	159	28	41	2	3	2	14	12	2	0	1	31	5	1	.346	.316
Greenwell, Bo	L-L	6-0	185	10-15-88	.692	1.000	.636	4	13	4	9	4	0	1	6	2	0	0	0	1	1	0	1.231	.733
Haase, Eric	R-R	5-10	180	12-18-92	.300	.333	.286	4	10	2	3	0	0	0	2	1	0	0	0	0	0	0	.300	.364
Jones, Hunter	R-R	6-2	185	8-17-91	.257	.455	.173	23	74	5	19	2	1	0	9	9	0	0	2	9	5	2	.311	.329
Kelly, Jairo	B-R	6-0	170	9-20-92	.278	.188	.316	15	54	6	15	1	2	0	3	7	1	0	1	16	2	1	.370	.365
Lin, Chia-Ching	L-R	6-0	180	1-4-92	.143	.000	.200	18	49	4	7	1	2	0	6	4	0	0	2	20	1	0	.245	.200
Martinez, Jorge	B-R	6-2	170	3-29-93	.256	.255	.256	45	180	25	46	10	2	4	30	16	1	0	4	34	4	3	.400	.313
Nilsson, Mitch	B-R	5-11	165	5-24-91	.358	.467	.327	21	67	9	24	7	0	1	10	7	0	0	0	14	1	0	.507	.419
Ramirez, Jose	B-R	5-9	165	9-17-92	.325	.102	.400	48	194	30	63	13	4	1	20	7	2	0	2	17	12	6	.448	.351
Rodriguez, Luigi	B-R	5-11	160	11-13-92	.379	.394	.371	25	95	18	36	6	2	3	14	5	1	0	2	19	12	5	.579	.408
Romero, Juan	R-R	6-1	175	6-16-93	.225	.175	.245	42	142	19	32	11	2	6	22	13	3	0	3	70	0	1	.458	.298
Tolentino, Patric	R-R	6-4	202	7-18-89	.182	.200	.167	12	22	2	4	1	0	0	5	3	2	0	0	6	0	0	.227	.333
Valerio, Charlie	B-R	6-0	204	11-7-90	.272	.333	.245	40	147	28	40	7	0	5	21	20	1	0	2	30	7	3	.422	.359

Pitching	B-T	HT	WT	DOB	W	L	ERA	G	GS	CG	SV	IP	H	R	ER	HR	BB	SO	AVG	vLH	vRH	K/9	BB/9
Araujo, Elvis	L-L	6-6	215	7-15-91	3	1	2.86	13	11	0	0	63	54	28	20	2	18	58	.228	.151	.262	8.29	2.57
Aviles, Robbie	L-R	6-4	200	12-17-91	0	2	6.52	7	6	0	0	10	13	9	7	0	2	7	.333	.231	.385	6.52	1.86
Blair, Kyle	R-R	6-2	236	9-27-88	0	0	13.50	1	0	0	0	1	3	2	2	0	0	2	.429	.500	.400	13.50	0.00
Carmona, Manuel	R-R	6-0	190	6-21-92	2	1	2.41	20	0	0	4	37	26	17	10	2	15	40	.205	.214	.200	9.64	3.62
Curtis, Matt	R-R	6-3	210	4-3-89	1	2	4.18	17	0	0	4	28	24	14	13	3	9	20	.233	.200	.244	6.43	2.89
De Los Santos, Xavier	R-R	6-0	180	10-13-88	3	1	4.50	16	0	0	0	36	29	18	18	1	20	39	.228	.324	.194	9.75	5.00
DeJesus, Luis	R-R	6-3	173	12-16-91	3	2	3.33	13	9	0	0	46	41	20	17	3	11	45	.238	.225	.242	8.80	2.15
Guerrero, Abel	L-L	6-0	180	12-28-91	0	0	20.25	2	0	0	0	1	3	4	3	0	3	0	.500	.000	.500	0.00	20.25
Haley, Trey	R-R	6-3	180	6-21-90	0	0	0.00	2	1	0	0	3	0	0	0	0	4	0	.000	.000	.000	12.00	0.00
Homblert, Rafael	R-R	6-5	178	9-4-91	2	3	3.80	15	3	0	1	43	44	29	18	3	20	33	.278	.311	.265	6.96	4.22
Lopez, Jose	R-R	6-2	185	3-20-91	1	3	6.42	17	0	0	1	34	40	33	24	1	31	25	.301	.250	.323	6.68	8.29
Lugo, Luis	L-L	6-5	200	3-5-94	0	2	6.14	3	2	0	0	7	10	6	5	1	8	8	.303	.000	.333	9.82	9.82
McKeon, Josh	R-R	6-2	200	10-29-88	1	0	1.00	17	0	0	1	27	15	8	3	0	14	30	.160	.057	.220	10.00	4.67
Merritt, Ryan	L-L	6-0	180	2-21-92	0	0	1.08	4	0	0	1	8	10	3	1	0	2	10	.278	.400	.231	10.80	2.16
Morel, Luis	R-R	6-0	170	11-19-92	0	1	3.60	9	3	0	0	25	23	15	10	2	16	22	.240	.267	.227	7.92	5.76
Morimando, Shawn	L-L	5-11	170	11-20-92	0	0	3.00	3	0	0	0	6	5	3	2	0	2	8	.227	.333	.211	12.00	3.00
Ramirez, Moisses	R-R	5-11	170	3-8-90	3	0	2.70	11	0	0	2	30	24	11	9	2	7	26	.220	.179	.235	7.80	2.10
Reyes, Anthony	R-R	6-2	230	10-16-81	0	1	3.00	3	2	0	0	3	3	1	1	0	2	2	.250	.200	.286	6.00	6.00
Rucinski, Drew	R-R	6-2	190	12-30-88	1	0	4.32	5	0	0	0	8	8	4	4	0	2	10	.250	.364	.190	10.80	2.16
Salazar, Danny	R-R	6-0	180	1-11-90	0	0	2.70	5	5	0	0	7	6	3	2	1	2	11	.231	.286	.211	14.85	2.70
Sisco, Jake	R-R	6-3	185	12-9-91	2	4	5.24	12	8	0	0	34	40	22	20	0	17	31	.303	.290	.307	8.13	4.46
Soto, Giovanni	L-L	6-3	180	5-18-91	0	0	1.80	3	1	0	0	5	4	1	1	0	1	7	.200	.000	.235	12.60	1.80
Sterling, Felix	R-R	6-3	200	3-15-93	2	3	4.10	6	4	0	0	26	26	15	12	3	8	31	.257	.344	.217	10.59	2.73
Valera, Francisco	R-R	6-1	170	10-19-89	0	0	2.25	3	1	0	0	4	2	1	1	0	1	3	.167	.200	.143	6.75	2.25

Fielding

Catcher	PCT	G	PO	A	E	DP	PB
Battaglia	.923	1	9	3	1	1	0
Cervenka	.985	15	117	14	2	0	4
Haase	1.000	4	21	1	0	0	3
Nilsson	1.000	4	28	2	0	0	3
Tolentino	1.000	6	18	3	0	0	0
Valerio	.985	36	278	41	5	2	8

First Base	PCT	G	PO	A	E	DP
Castillo	.981	43	332	24	7	25
Gonzalez	.974	14	107	6	3	7
Tolentino	1.000	1	7	0	0	1
Valerio	.941	2	15	1	1	2

Second Base	PCT	G	PO	A	E	DP
Campbell	1.000	1	1	0	0	0
Garcia	.951	9	19	20	2	3
Ramirez	.959	47	102	131	10	28

Third Base	PCT	G	PO	A	E	DP
Castillo	.933	5	4	10	1	0
Garcia	.893	25	16	51	8	3
Gonzalez	.854	28	20	50	12	5

Shortstop	PCT	G	PO	A	E	DP
Garcia	.946	10	11	24	2	5
Kelly	.905	10	11	27	4	4

Martinez	.890	38	59	95	19	17

Outfield	PCT	G	PO	A	E	DP
Bradley	.000	3	0	0	0	0
Brown	.986	43	66	5	1	1
Campbell	.917	24	20	2	2	0
Crowe	1.000	3	6	0	0	0
Dunn	1.000	13	18	1	0	0
Greenwell	1.000	3	8	0	0	0
Jones	.972	22	35	0	1	0
Lin	.909	17	27	3	3	0
Rodriguez	.961	24	46	3	2	0
Romero	.930	40	52	1	4	0

CLEVELAND INDIANS

DOMINICAN SUMMER LEAGUE

Batting	B-T	HT	WT	DOB	AVG	vLH	vRH	G	AB	R	H	2B	3B	HR	RBI	BB	HBP	SH	SF	SO	SB	CS	SLG	OBP
Acevedo, Carlos	R-R	5-11	180	1-18-93	.205	.200	.206	18	44	2	9	2	0	0	3	1	0	0	0	16	0	0	.250	.222
Aleman, Jose	R-R	5-11	175	8-23-94	.083	.000	.125	10	12	0	1	0	0	0	2	2	0	0	0	4	0	0	.083	.214
Bautista, Claudio	R-R	5-11	170	11-29-93	.225	.310	.195	32	111	12	25	4	0	1	14	10	0	0	2	19	7	3	.288	.285
Boscan, Manuel	B-R	6-0	160	3-10-93	.193	.091	.216	44	119	9	23	4	2	0	10	14	1	0	2	10	2	3	.261	.279
Calderon, Kevin	R-R	5-11	180	4-4-94	.161	.263	.108	28	56	2	9	4	0	0	6	1	0	0	1	13	0	0	.232	.172
Caraballo, Joel	R-R	5-11	140	2-8-94	.215	.160	.235	35	93	16	20	4	1	1	11	13	3	0	0	22	7	0	.312	.330
Castillo, Amauri	R-R	6-2	197	4-4-93	.184	.091	.211	32	98	3	18	3	0	0	8	4	2	0	0	23	1	0	.214	.231
De Jesus, Victor	R-R	6-2	170	1-13-93	.209	.205	.211	65	158	14	33	6	0	1	11	24	3	0	3	48	6	4	.266	.319
De La Cruz, Juan	R-R	6-1	195	8-5-93	.139	.067	.165	44	115	5	16	4	0	0	7	11	3	0	0	21	2	1	.174	.233
De La Cruz, Yunior	R-R	6-0	195	12-23-89	.213	.125	.226	21	61	2	13	2	0	0	5	4	0	0	2	9	0	0	.246	.254
Fledi, Joel	R-R	6-2	180	2-17-93	.182	.250	.143	6	11	1	2	0	0	0	2	1	0	0	0	6	0	0	.182	.357
Galvez, Fermin	L-L	6-3	225	1-25-93	.222	.222	.222	29	81	6	18	5	0	1	8	13	0	0	1	23	0	1	.321	.326
Hernandez, Angel	R-R	6-1	180	9-24-92	.245	.237	.250	41	110	18	27	7	0	0	10	15	6	0	1	25	4	2	.309	.364
Herrera, Juan	R-R	5-11	165	6-28-93	.297	.295	.297	58	192	30	57	11	2	1	20	22	7	0	3	27	7	5	.391	.384
Lora, Felix	R-R	6-3	190	6-18-93	.219	.200	.226	60	196	22	43	16	0	3	23	16	2	0	2	46	3	4	.347	.282
Matos, David	L-L	6-3	180	4-14-93	.145	.167	.139	51	145	12	21	1	1	1	8	27	0	0	1	46	1	0	.186	.286
Mejia, Joel	R-R	5-11	157	4-7-93	.201	.152	.214	55	159	16	32	2	1	0	7	20	4	0	1	22	11	13	.226	.304
Mendoza, Yonathan	B-R	5-11	167	2-10-94	.219	.310	.188	41	114	15	25	4	1	0	14	24	0	0	3	11	2	1	.272	.348
Rincones, Luis	R-R	5-11	165	3-11-94	.242	.182	.255	29	62	12	15	3	1	0	5	8	2	0	0	20	3	1	.323	.347
Soto, Fidias	R-R	6-2	185	1-13-93	.282	.263	.300	32	39	14	11	2	0	1	4	13	3	0	0	12	2	3	.410	.481
Valdez, Ordomar	B-R	5-9	150	4-27-94	.274	.194	.301	47	124	20	34	3	2	0	10	20	2	0	0	20	13	5	.331	.384

Pitching	B-T	HT	WT	DOB	W	L	ERA	G	GS	CG	SV	IP	H	R	ER	HR	BB	SO	AVG	vLH	vRH	K/9	BB/9
Alcantara, Martin	R-R	5-11	180	9-14-91	2	0	2.55	4	3	0	0	18	16	6	5	0	7	12	.239	.400	.192	6.11	3.57
Cabrera, Luis	R-R	6-4	175	7-27-92	0	1	3.50	13	0	0	0	18	14	7	7	2	10	11	.222	.100	.245	5.50	5.00
Cleto, Jeffry	R-R	6-3	190	6-14-91	3	4	1.65	14	13	0	0	65	54	26	12	2	22	37	.208	.208	.233	5.10	3.03
Colon, Frangy	R-R	6-2	170	1-18-93	0	1	3.38	5	0	0	0	8	10	4	3	0	4	5	.294	.500	.250	5.63	4.50
2-team total (5 Astros)					0	2	3.21	10	1	0	1	14	16	6	5	0	8	9	—	—		5.79	5.14
Encarnacion, Estevenson	R-R	6-4	186	6-4-90	7	2	2.70	27	0	0	9	43	26	16	13	0	28	47	.178	.111	.193	9.76	5.82
Encarnacion, Isaias	L-L	6-4	200	7-10-91	0	0	1.80	5	2	0	0	10	5	3	2	0	12	12	.156	.000	.156	10.80	10.80
Estrella, Edward	R-R	6-1	170	1-28-94	1	2	6.35	19	0	0	1	23	28	22	16	0	14	12	.298	.154	.321	4.76	5.56
Garcia, Juan	R-R	6-1	183	12-3-93	0	1	6.50	13	0	0	0	18	15	17	13	0	19	17	.234	.167	.250	8.50	9.50
Lovera, Yeiker	R-R	6-0	175	1-23-93	4	2	2.44	12	11	0	0	59	42	18	16	4	16	33	.198	.261	.181	5.03	2.44
Lugo, Luis	L-L	6-5	200	3-5-94	0	3	3.38	9	7	0	0	29	21	19	11	3	16	36	.194	.200	.194	11.05	4.91
Marte, Juan	R-R	6-4	175	6-24-94	0	0	11.81	6	0	0	0	5	2	7	7	0	14	4	.133	.000	.143	6.75	23.63
Nivar, Juan	R-R	6-1	170	9-24-92	0	1	16.00	10	0	0	0	9	12	18	16	2	14	3	.333	.333	.333	3.00	14.00
Paredes, Alexis	R-R	6-3	175	1-24-92	1	4	4.53	23	4	1	0	52	42	30	26	2	23	37	.226	.323	.206	6.45	4.01
Polanco, Anderson	L-L	6-3	190	9-6-92	3	4	1.77	13	12	0	0	61	38	16	12	2	32	63	.180	.200	.179	9.30	4.72
Puerta, Breily	R-R	5-10	180	6-17-92	2	1	2.57	11	8	0	0	42	33	16	12	0	12	50	.214	.346	.188	10.71	2.57
Ramirez, Moisses	R-R	5-11	170	3-8-90	3	1	1.99	15	0	0	7	23	20	7	5	1	7	21	.247	.308	.235	8.34	2.78
Rivas, Alejandro	R-R	6-1	200	8-21-91	0	0	2.08	3	0	0	0	4	3	2	1	1	2	4	.200	.750	.000	8.31	4.15
Sanchez, Eliezer	R-R	6-4	227	1-11-92	0	4	4.96	10	7	0	1	33	30	21	18	1	21	25	.246	.304	.232	6.89	5.79
Santana, Juan	R-R	6-2	170	7-2-93	4	2	4.14	23	0	0	0	41	39	21	19	0	20	23	.253	.333	.236	5.01	4.35
Villa, Alejandro	R-R	6-2	160	5-29-92	0	0	0.00	1	0	0	0	1	2	0	0	0	1		.500	.000	.500	13.50	0.00
Zapata, Jose	R-R	6-4	200	5-21-93	1	3	3.68	10	1	0	0	22	16	15	9	0	18	20	.200	.143	.205	8.18	7.36

Fielding

Catcher	PCT	G	PO	A	E	DP	PB
Aleman	.977	10	37	5	1	0	4
Calderon	.976	23	72	9	2	0	5
De La Cruz	.975	42	233	38	7	2	5
De La Cruz	.988	20	157	10	2	1	2

First Base	PCT	G	PO	A	E	DP
Acevedo	1.000	1	1	0	0	1
Castillo	.986	10	66	4	1	1
De La Cruz	1.000	1	5	0	0	0
Galvez	.982	24	164	2	3	14
Matos	.990	44	286	10	3	23
Valdez	1.000	1	0	1	0	0

Second Base	PCT	G	PO	A	E	DP
Bautista	.952	5	9	11	1	2

	PCT	G	PO	A	E	DP
Boscan	.988	26	41	40	1	8
Herrera	.952	11	22	18	2	3
Mendoza	.889	3	2	6	1	1
Valdez	.973	38	77	68	4	12

Third Base	PCT	G	PO	A	E	DP
Bautista	.939	23	12	50	4	3
Boscan	.957	7	9	13	1	1
Castillo	.870	22	14	46	9	5
Herrera	.928	25	19	45	5	6
Mendoza	1.000	4	1	6	0	0

Shortstop	PCT	G	PO	A	E	DP
Bautista	.750	3	1	2	1	0
Boscan	.957	6	2	20	1	0
Caraballo	.913	30	45	71	11	13

	PCT	G	PO	A	E	DP
De La Cruz	1.000	1	0	1	0	0
Herrera	.929	7	11	15	2	2
Mendoza	.930	34	41	66	8	9

Outfield	PCT	G	PO	A	E	DP
Acevedo	.895	13	17	0	2	0
De Jesus	.974	62	106	6	3	2
Hernandez	1.000	10	11	0	0	0
Lora	.968	59	84	6	3	2
Mejia	.974	55	110	3	3	0
Rincones	.974	25	36	1	1	1
Soto	.963	25	25	1	1	0

CLEVELAND INDIANS

Colorado Rockies

SEASON IN A SENTENCE: A season that began with high expectations and an 11-2 start ended with the Rockies 21 games out of first place in the National League West, former ace Ubaldo Jimenez traded to the Indians, and general manager Dan O'Dowd summing it up as an "utter disappointment."

HIGH POINT: Troy Tulowitzki turned in another outstanding season, winning a Gold Glove and Silver Slugger award as the top fielder and hitter at shortstop in the NL. He became just the third NL shortstop to win both awards in consecutive seasons, joining Barry Larkin (1995-96) and Edgar Renteria (2002-03). He led NL shortstops in doubles (36), homers (a career-high 30), RBIs (105) and extra-base hits (68).

LOW POINT: Jimenez pitched the Rockies' first no-hitter, won 19 games and posted a 2.88 ERA in 2010, but he was limping along with a 6-9, 4.46 record and diminished velocity in 2011 when the Rockies traded him to the Indians in a deadline deal at the end of July.

NOTABLE ROOKIES: No rookies made a big difference in how 2011 went, but several auditioned for future roles, including two first-round picks who came from the Indians in the Jimenez trade. Righthander Alex White went 2-4, 8.42, largely the result of giving up 12 homers in his seven starts; and lefthander Drew Pomeranz went 2-1, 5.40 in four starts after bouncing back from an emergency appendectomy. Lefthander Rex Brothers made 48 relief appearances, averaging 13.1 strikeouts per nine innings while posting a 2.88 ERA.

KEY TRANSACTIONS: The Jimenez trade was a move toward the future, yielding three of the top pitching prospects in the Indians organization: White, Pomeranz and Joe Gardner.

DOWN ON THE FARM: Outfielder Tim Wheeler, a first-round pick in 2009, hit 33 homers for Double-A Tulsa, establishing himself as one of the organization's best all-around prospects after a mediocre first season. Third baseman Nolan Arenado, a 2009 second-round pick, led the minor leagues with 122 RBIs for Class A Modesto, hitting .298 with 20 homers. Modesto teammate Kent Matthes (.334, 23 HRs, 95 RBIs) was the Cal League MVP, and righthander Chad Bettis (12-5, 3.34) was the league pitcher of the year. Shortstop Trevor Story was rated as the top prospect in the Rookie-level Pioneer League after an impressive first professional season.

OPENING DAY PAYROLL: $88,148,071 (14th)

ORGANIZATION LEADERS

BATTING		*Minimum 250 PA
MAJORS		
* AVG	Troy Tulowitzki	.302
* OPS	Troy Tulowitzki	.916
HR	Troy Tulowitzki	30
RBI	Troy Tulowitzki	105
MINORS		
* AVG	Josh Rutledge, Modesto	.348
* OBP	Josh Rutledge, Modesto	.414
* SLG	Kent Matthes, Modesto	.642
R	Tim Wheeler, Tulsa	105
H	Tim Wheeler, Tulsa	161
TB	Tim Wheeler, Tulsa	300
2B	Kent Matthes, Modesto	39
3B	David Kandilas, Casper	10
HR	Tim Wheeler, Tulsa	33
RBI	Nolan Arenado, Modesto	122
BB	Delta Cleary Jr., Modesto	75
SO	Tim Wheeler, Tulsa	142
SB	Rafael Ortega, Asheville	32

PITCHING		#Minimum 75 IP
MAJORS		
W	Jhoulys Chacin	11
# ERA	Jhoulys Chacin	3.62
SO	Jhoulys Chacin	150
SV	Huston Street	29
MINORS		
W	Chad Bettis, Modesto	12
	Rob Scahill, Tulsa	12
L	Nick Schnaitmann, Modesto/Asheville	13
# ERA	Edwar Cabrera, Asheville/Modesto	3.34
G	Jim Miller, Colorado Springs	65
GS	Chad Bettis, Modesto	27
	Parker Frazier, Modesto	27
SV	Jim Miller, Colorado Springs	24
IP	Chad Bettis, Modesto	169.2
BB	Tyler Matzek, Modesto/Asheville	96
SO	Edwar Cabrera, Asheville/Modesto	217
#AVG	Chad Bettis, Modesto	.225

General Manager: Dan O'Dowd. **Farm Director:** Marc Gustafson. **Scouting Director:** Bill Schmidt.

Class	Team	League	W	L	PCT	Finish	Manager(s)
Majors	Colorado Rockies	National	73	89	.451	11th (16)	Jim Tracy
Triple-A	Colorado Springs Sky Sox	Pacific Coast	64	80	.444	15th (16)	Stu Cole
Double-A	Tulsa Drillers	Texas	68	72	.486	5th (8)	Duane Espy
High A	Modesto Nuts	California	74	66	.529	4th (10)	Jerry Weinstein
Low A	Asheville Tourists	South Atlantic	69	70	.496	9th (14)	Joe Mikulik
Short-season	Tri-City Dust Devils	Northwest	44	32	.579	2nd (8)	Fred Ocasio
Rookie	Casper Ghosts	Pioneer	27	49	.355	8th (8)	Tony Diaz
Overall 2011 Minor League Record			346	369	.484	21st (30)	

ORGANIZATION STATISTICS

COLORADO ROCKIES

NATIONAL LEAGUE

Batting	B-T	HT	WT	DOB	AVG	vLH	vRH	G	AB	R	H	2B	3B	HR	RBI	BB	HBP	SH	SF	SO	SB	CS	SLG	OBP
Alfonzo, Eliezer	R-R	5-11	220	2-7-79	.267	.300	.255	25	75	2	20	1	0	1	9	3	1	0	0	13	0	0	.320	.304
Amezaga, Alfredo	B-R	5-11	165	1-16-78	.242	.200	.278	20	33	5	8	1	0	0	2	3	0	0	1	7	0	0	.273	.297
2-team total (20 Florida)					.182	—	—	40	77	6	14	1	0	0	4	7	0	0	1	14	0	0	.195	.247
Blackmon, Charlie	L-L	6-3	200	7-1-86	.255	.400	.218	27	98	9	25	1	0	1	8	3	0	0	0	8	5	1	.296	.277
Ellis, Mark	R-R	5-10	185	6-6-77	.274	.294	.267	70	263	34	72	13	0	6	25	14	3	0	1	43	7	3	.392	.317
Field, Thomas	R-R	5-9	175	2-22-87	.271	.364	.243	16	48	4	13	0	0	0	3	3	0	0	0	14	0	0	.271	.314
Fowler, Dexter	B-R	6-4	190	3-22-86	.266	.254	.270	125	481	84	128	35	15	5	45	68	6	0	1	130	12	9	.432	.363
Garner, Cole	R-R	6-2	210	12-15-84	.222	.000	.333	4	9	1	2	0	0	0	3	1	0	0	0	6	0	0	.222	.300
Giambi, Jason	L-R	6-3	240	1-8-71	.260	.219	.273	64	131	20	34	6	0	13	32	17	3	0	1	45	0	0	.603	.355
Gomez, Hector	R-R	6-2	180	3-5-88	.333	.000	.667	2	6	1	2	0	0	0	0	1	0	0	0	2	0	0	.333	.429
Gonzalez, Carlos	L-L	6-1	205	10-17-85	.295	.272	.307	127	481	92	142	27	3	26	92	48	7	0	6	105	20	5	.526	.363
Helton, Todd	L-L	6-2	215	8-20-73	.302	.292	.307	124	421	59	127	27	0	14	69	59	3	0	8	71	0	1	.466	.385
Herrera, Jonathan	B-R	5-9	150	11-3-84	.242	.250	.239	104	281	28	68	5	1	3	14	28	1	0	0	40	4	4	.299	.313
Iannetta, Chris	R-R	6-0	230	4-8-83	.238	.241	.237	112	345	51	82	17	1	14	55	70	5	0	4	89	6	3	.414	.370
Kouzmanoff, Kevin	R-R	6-1	210	7-25-81	.255	.281	.242	27	98	11	25	5	0	3	16	4	5	0	1	19	0	0	.398	.315
Lopez, Jose	R-R	6-0	205	11-24-83	.208	.225	.200	38	125	10	26	4	0	2	8	3	1	0	0	15	2	0	.288	.233
2-team total (44 Florida)					.216	—	—	82	231	23	50	12	0	8	21	7	2	0	1	28	2	0	.372	.245
Morales, Jose	B-R	5-11	200	2-20-83	.267	.250	.273	22	60	6	16	3	0	0	7	9	0	0	2	12	0	1	.317	.352
Nelson, Chris	R-R	5-11	175	9-3-85	.250	.245	.252	63	180	20	45	10	1	4	16	7	1	0	1	35	3	1	.383	.280
Pacheco, Jordan	R-R	6-1	190	1-30-86	.286	.385	.241	21	84	5	24	1	0	2	14	3	1	0	0	9	0	0	.369	.318
Pagnozzi, Matt	R-R	6-2	205	11-10-82	.286	.333	.278	7	21	2	6	0	0	0	2	1	1	0	0	8	0	0	.286	.348
2-team total (5 Pittsburgh)					.276	—	—	12	29	2	8	0	0	0	3	1	1	0	0	10	0	0	.276	.323
Rosario, Wilin	R-R	5-11	200	2-23-89	.204	.286	.175	16	54	6	11	3	1	3	8	2	0	0	1	20	0	0	.463	.228
Smith, Seth	L-L	6-3	210	9-30-82	.284	.217	.299	147	476	67	135	32	9	15	59	46	4	0	7	93	10	2	.483	.347
Spilborghs, Ryan	R-R	6-1	200	9-5-79	.210	.207	.212	98	200	22	42	8	1	3	22	19	2	0	2	49	2	2	.305	.283
Stewart, Ian	L-R	6-3	215	4-5-85	.156	.091	.170	48	122	14	19	6	1	0	6	14	0	0	0	37	3	2	.221	.243
Tulowitzki, Troy	R-R	6-3	215	10-10-84	.302	.349	.284	143	537	81	162	36	2	30	105	59	4	0	5	79	9	3	.544	.372
Wigginton, Ty	R-R	6-0	230	10-11-77	.242	.259	.235	130	401	52	97	21	2	15	47	38	5	0	1	84	8	1	.416	.315
Young Jr., Eric	R-R	5-10	180	5-25-85	.247	.234	.256	77	198	34	49	4	3	0	10	26	3	0	1	38	27	4	.298	.342

Pitching	B-T	HT	WT	DOB	W	L	ERA	G	GS	CG	SV	IP	H	R	ER	HR	BB	SO	AVG	vLH	vRH	K/9	BB/9
Belisle, Matt	R-R	6-4	225	6-6-80	10	4	3.25	74	0	0	0	72	77	33	26	5	14	58	.276	.250	.291	7.25	1.75
Betancourt, Rafael	R-R	6-2	215	4-29-75	2	0	2.89	68	0	0	8	62	46	21	20	7	8	73	.203	.220	.189	10.54	1.16
Billings, Bruce	R-R	6-0	200	11-18-85	0	0	4.50	1	0	0	0	2	5	1	1	0	0	0	.556	.600	.500	0.00	0.00
Brothers, Rex	L-L	6-0	205	12-18-87	1	2	2.88	48	0	0	1	41	33	14	13	4	20	59	.217	.193	.232	13.06	4.43
Chacin, Jhoulys	R-R	6-3	215	1-7-88	11	14	3.62	31	31	2	0	194	168	87	78	20	87	150	.231	.232	.230	6.96	4.04
Cook, Aaron	R-R	6-3	215	2-8-79	3	10	6.03	18	17	0	0	97	127	67	65	9	37	48	.326	.349	.303	4.45	3.43
Daley, Matt	R-R	6-2	180	6-23-82	0	0	10.50	7	0	0	0	6	8	7	7	1	2	7	.333	.375	.310	10.50	3.00
De La Rosa, Jorge	L-L	6-1	215	4-5-81	5	2	3.51	10	10	0	0	59	48	25	23	4	22	52	.222	.111	.244	7.93	3.36
Escalona, Edgmer	R-R	6-4	215	10-6-86	0	0	1.75	14	0	0	0	26	17	5	5	3	7	14	.187	.135	.222	4.91	2.45
Gonzalez, Edgar	R-R	6-2	210	2-23-83	0	0	9.00	1	0	0	0	2	5	2	2	0	1	1	.500	.500	.500	4.50	4.50
Hammel, Jason	R-R	6-6	215	9-2-82	7	13	4.76	32	27	0	1	170	175	100	90	21	68	94	.270	.268	.271	4.97	3.59
Jimenez, Ubaldo	R-R	6-4	210	1-22-84	6	9	4.46	21	21	2	0	123	118	68	61	10	51	118	.251	.239	.262	8.63	3.73
Johnson, Alan	R-R	6-1	180	8-24-83	0	0	9.00	1	1	0	0	4	6	5	4	0	3	3	.375	.000	.462	6.75	6.75
Lindstrom, Matt	R-R	6-3	220	2-11-80	2	2	3.00	63	0	0	2	54	52	21	18	3	14	36	.256	.253	.258	6.00	2.33
Miller, Jim	R-R	6-1	200	4-28-82	0	0	2.57	6	0	0	0	7	3	2	2	0	4	5	.130	.167	.118	6.43	5.14
Millwood, Kevin	R-R	6-4	230	12-24-74	4	3	3.98	9	9	0	0	54	58	26	24	9	8	36	.274	.296	.260	5.96	1.33
Morales, Franklin	L-L	6-0	210	1-24-86	0	1	3.86	14	0	0	0	14	10	6	6	2	8	11	.204	.250	.172	7.07	5.14
Mortensen, Clayton	R-R	6-4	185	4-10-85	2	4	3.86	16	6	0	0	58	55	30	25	9	24	30	.257	.281	.240	4.63	3.70
Nicasio, Juan	R-R	6-3	200	8-31-86	4	4	4.14	13	13	0	0	72	73	35	33	8	18	58	.262	.313	.205	7.28	2.26
Paulino, Felipe	R-R	6-2	270	10-5-83	0	4	7.36	18	0	0	0	15	23	12	12	3	7	14	.383	.318	.421	8.59	4.30
Pomeranz, Drew	R-L	6-5	230	11-22-88	2	1	5.40	4	4	0	0	18	19	11	11	0	5	13	.271	.222	.299	6.38	2.45
Reynolds, Greg	R-R	6-7	225	7-3-85	3	0	6.19	13	3	0	0	32	40	22	22	6	10	18	.303	.328	.277	5.06	2.81
Reynolds, Matt	L-L	6-5	240	10-2-84	1	2	4.09	73	0	0	0	51	48	24	23	10	18	50	.255	.292	.217	8.88	3.20

Pitching

Pitching	B-T	HT	WT	DOB	W	L	ERA	G	GS	CG	SV	IP	H	R	ER	HR	BB	SO	AVG	vLH	vRH	K/9	BB/9
Roenicke, Josh	R-R	6-3	200	8-4-82	0	0	3.78	19	0	0	0	17	14	7	7	1	7	12	.233	.158	.268	6.48	3.78
Rogers, Esmil	R-R	6-1	190	8-14-85	6	6	7.05	18	13	0	0	83	110	65	65	14	47	63	.320	.318	.321	6.83	5.10
Romero, J.C.	B-L	5-11	205	6-4-76	1	0	4.32	12	0	0	0	8	12	7	4	1	3	9	.324	.267	.364	9.72	3.24
2-team total (24 Philadelphia)					1	0	4.01	36	0	0	0	25	28	14	11	1	15	19	—	—	—	6.93	5.47
Street, Huston	R-R	6-0	190	8-2-83	1	4	3.86	62	0	0	29	58	62	28	25	10	9	55	.276	.284	.270	8.49	1.39
Stults, Eric	L-L	6-0	225	12-9-79	0	0	6.00	6	0	0	0	12	11	8	8	4	4	7	.229	.158	.276	5.25	3.00
White, Alex	R-R	6-3	215	8-29-88	2	4	8.42	7	7	0	0	36	48	35	34	12	16	24	.324	.365	.294	5.94	3.96

Fielding

Catcher	PCT	G	PO	A	E	DP	PB
Alfonzo	.966	19	128	12	5	2	2
Iannetta	.998	105	733	82	2	7	8
Morales	.962	17	117	8	5	0	3
Pacheco	1.000	2	8	1	0	0	0
Pagnozzi	1.000	7	32	6	0	0	1
Rosario	.990	14	87	16	1	1	3

First Base	PCT	G	PO	A	E	DP
Giambi	.995	23	203	10	1	13
Helton	.997	119	985	104	3	110
Iannetta	1.000	2	4	0	0	0
Pacheco	.991	13	106	2	1	8
Wigginton	1.000	36	181	12	0	10

Second Base	PCT	G	PO	A	E	DP
Amezaga	1.000	5	12	11	0	1
Ellis	.997	64	123	194	1	42
Herrera	.992	62	94	151	2	30

	PCT	G	PO	A	E	DP
Lopez	1.000	11	17	24	0	8
Morales	1.000	2	0	2	0	0
Nelson	.969	29	36	58	3	15
Pacheco	1.000	2	2	2	0	1
Young Jr.	.955	7	10	11	1	5

Third Base	PCT	G	PO	A	E	DP
Amezaga	.000	2	0	0	0	0
Herrera	1.000	9	1	4	0	0
Iannetta	.000	1	0	0	0	0
Kouzmanoff	.938	25	17	44	4	4
Lopez	.934	29	9	48	4	2
Nelson	.917	24	9	35	4	2
Pacheco	.905	7	6	13	2	0
Stewart	.929	42	25	54	6	3
Wigginton	.970	68	33	96	4	15

Shortstop	PCT	G	PO	A	E	DP
Amezaga	.857	2	0	6	1	0

	PCT	G	PO	A	E	DP
Field	.985	15	18	47	1	8
Gomez	.833	2	1	4	1	0
Herrera	.971	21	11	23	1	5
Nelson	.857	2	0	6	1	0
Tulowitzki	.991	140	261	417	6	98

Outfield	PCT	G	PO	A	E	DP
Amezaga	.000	2	0	0	0	0
Blackmon	1.000	27	43	2	0	0
Field	1.000	1	1	0	0	0
Fowler	.975	122	309	6	8	2
Garner	1.000	3	6	0	0	0
Gonzalez	.996	125	219	12	1	2
Smith	.978	129	216	5	5	0
Spilborghs	1.000	64	78	4	0	0
Wigginton	.926	27	24	1	2	0
Young Jr.	.957	43	65	2	3	0

COLORADO SPRINGS SKY SOX

TRIPLE-A

PACIFIC COAST LEAGUE

Batting	B-T	HT	WT	DOB	AVG	vLH	vRH	G	AB	R	H	2B	3B	HR	RBI	BB	HBP	SH	SF	SO	SB	CS	SLG	OBP
Alfonzo, Eliezer	R-R	5-11	220	2-7-79	.319	.368	.286	31	94	21	30	7	0	12	37	2	3	0	2	16	2	1	.777	.347
Amezaga, Alfredo	B-R	5-11	165	1-16-78	.305	.302	.308	67	239	49	73	19	1	4	41	29	4	0	3	36	4	2	.444	.385
Beerer, Scott	R-R	6-1	200	7-4-82	.372	.325	.389	41	148	19	55	12	0	3	28	3	5	0	1	24	1	2	.514	.401
Blackmon, Charlie	L-L	6-3	200	7-1-86	.337	.294	.361	58	243	49	82	19	4	10	49	19	5	0	3	34	12	5	.572	.393
Cantu, Jorge	R-R	6-3	205	1-30-82	.280	.286	.278	30	118	16	33	6	0	5	18	6	1	0	0	16	0	0	.458	.320
Emaus, Brad	R-R	6-0	205	3-28-86	.313	.400	.280	45	163	37	51	10	2	9	28	20	1	0	1	24	3	3	.564	.389
Fields, Josh	R-R	6-1	235	12-14-82	.365	.383	.356	50	178	53	65	20	1	11	45	20	2	0	3	37	7	0	.674	.429
Fowler, Dexter	B-R	6-4	190	3-22-86	.237	.242	.234	24	97	17	23	6	1	2	9	15	1	0	0	24	2	1	.381	.345
Garner, Cole	R-R	6-2	210	12-15-84	.330	.354	.321	46	185	38	61	8	5	8	35	10	3	0	4	47	4	2	.557	.366
Giambi, Jason	L-R	6-3	240	1-8-71	.429	.000	.429	3	7	2	3	0	0	0	3	0	1	0	0	2	0	0	.429	.500
Gonzalez, Carlos	L-L	6-1	205	10-17-85	.300	.333	.286	3	10	1	3	0	0	0	0	0	0	0	0	0	0	0	.300	.300
Jacobs, Mike	L-R	6-3	215	10-30-80	.298	.268	.311	117	429	70	128	30	1	23	97	58	0	0	8	105	3	3	.534	.376
Macri, Matt	R-R	6-2	215	5-29-82	.273	.269	.275	114	374	56	102	24	4	13	65	34	4	0	5	73	1	1	.463	.336
Mather, Joe	R-R	6-4	215	7-23-82	.321	.391	.290	55	209	36	67	14	1	6	31	18	0	0	7	39	3	0	.483	.363
Merchan, Jesus	R-R	5-11	180	3-26-81	.366	.333	.379	26	93	14	34	3	1	0	11	10	0	0	2	9	0	0	.419	.419
2-team total (58 New Orleans)					.301	—	—	84	276	36	83	11	1	2	28	19	3	0	2	27	0	1	.359	.350
Nazario, Radames	R-R	6-0	166	6-14-87	.288	.217	.326	19	66	9	19	7	1	0	9	1	0	0	0	17	0	1	.424	.299
Nelson, Chris	R-R	5-11	175	9-3-85	.329	.337	.325	73	289	52	95	20	5	11	65	17	3	0	5	48	3	3	.547	.366
Pacheco, Jordan	R-R	6-1	190	1-30-86	.278	.316	.265	97	363	57	101	21	3	3	50	30	9	0	6	48	2	2	.377	.343
Pagnozzi, Matt	R-R	6-2	205	11-10-82	.275	.274	.276	54	178	26	49	13	2	3	29	16	1	0	1	40	0	2	.421	.337
Paulk, Mike	L-L	6-2	195	4-23-84	.326	.283	.338	87	288	47	94	19	3	6	33	29	0	0	3	45	1	3	.476	.384
Rohlinger, Ryan	R-R	6-0	195	10-7-83	.284	.262	.292	70	243	49	69	15	5	5	35	37	3	0	2	43	0	2	.449	.382
2-team total (33 Fresno)					.247	—	—	103	364	71	90	19	5	10	51	56	5	0	3	57	2	3	.409	.353
Salazar, Jeff	L-L	6-0	195	11-24-80	.234	.357	.200	30	64	19	15	2	0	3	9	16	1	0	0	14	8	0	.406	.395
Schaeffer, Warren	R-R	6-0	180	1-28-85	.277	.310	.250	26	65	9	18	5	1	0	3	2	0	0	0	13	0	0	.385	.299
Spilborghs, Ryan	R-R	6-0	200	9-5-79	.444	.533	.400	10	45	8	20	3	0	3	10	2	0	0	0	6	0	0	.711	.468
Stewart, Ian	L-R	6-3	215	4-5-85	.275	.267	.279	45	171	29	47	10	1	14	42	22	1	0	1	51	1	0	.591	.359
Taveras, Willy	R-R	6-0	180	12-25-81	.302	.254	.323	97	391	67	118	17	5	10	44	21	1	0	4	51	13	4	.448	.336
Wigginton, Ty	R-R	6-0	230	10-11-77	.286	1.000	.167	2	7	1	2	0	0	0	1	2	0	0	0	1	0	0	.286	.444
Young Jr., Eric	B-R	5-10	180	5-25-85	.363	.320	.385	58	223	61	81	18	9	2	28	39	2	0	5	36	17	1	.552	.454

Pitching	B-T	HT	WT	DOB	W	L	ERA	G	GS	CG	SV	IP	H	R	ER	HR	BB	SO	AVG	vLH	vRH	K/9	BB/9
Billings, Bruce	R-R	6-0	200	11-18-85	6	2	4.47	29	0	0	1	50	58	29	25	4	21	47	.289	.374	.218	8.40	3.75
2-team total (15 Sacramento)					7	2	4.46	44	2	0	1	77	80	44	38	5	34	72	—	—	—	8.45	3.99
Brothers, Rex	L-L	6-2	205	12-18-87	3	2	2.89	25	0	0	0	28	29	10	9	4	15	45	.266	.262	.269	14.46	4.82
Buckner, Billy	R-R	6-2	205	8-27-83	4	8	6.03	23	21	0	0	109	136	91	73	12	52	80	.313	.313	.313	6.61	4.29
Colome, Jesus	R-R	6-2	240	12-23-77	0	2	10.38	10	1	0	0	13	28	16	15	1	4	9	.444	.467	.424	6.23	2.77
Cook, Aaron	R-R	6-3	215	2-8-79	1	0	5.52	2	2	0	0	15	13	9	9	2	2	5	.236	.091	.333	3.07	1.23
Daley, Matt	R-R	6-2	180	6-23-82	1	0	6.28	17	0	0	0	14	20	12	10	2	3	15	.345	.400	.303	9.42	1.88
Escalona, Edgmer	R-R	6-4	215	10-6-86	3	1	3.18	34	0	0	1	40	35	14	14	4	11	40	.241	.221	.260	9.08	2.50
Espineli, Geno	L-L	6-4	195	9-8-82	0	0	30.86	3	0	0	0	2	11	9	8	2	2	5	.611	.333	.667	19.29	7.71
2-team total (31 Fresno)					3	5	6.83	34	4	0	0	57	82	51	43	9	30	34	—	—	—	5.40	4.76
Gonzalez, Edgar	R-R	6-2	210	2-23-83	5	3	5.29	15	14	0	0	80	93	56	47	9	24	53	.291	.323	.256	5.96	2.70

Pitching	B-T	HT	WT	DOB	W	L	ERA	G	GS	CG	SV	IP	H	R	ER	HR	BB	SO	AVG	vLH	vRH	K/9	BB/9
Graham, Andy	R-R	6-4	210	6-29-84	0	2	7.21	31	10	0	0	54	78	49	43	8	33	42	.344	.396	.298	7.04	5.53
Johnson, Blake	R-R	6-5	200	6-14-85	2	1	7.62	20	0	0	0	26	36	28	22	4	8	17	.324	.352	.298	5.88	2.77
2-team total (14 Omaha)					5	2	7.51	34	1	0	1	56	77	53	47	5	25	36	—	—	—	5.75	3.99
Johnson, Alan	R-R	6-1	180	8-24-83	5	11	7.43	26	23	0	0	132	201	118	109	13	60	85	.361	.362	.360	5.80	4.09
Johnston, Andrew	R-R	6-5	205	4-20-84	2	3	8.29	38	0	0	3	42	83	42	39	4	10	26	.423	.476	.384	5.53	2.13
Lindstrom, Matt	R-R	6-3	220	2-11-80	0	0	13.50	2	0	0	0	2	4	3	3	1	0	4	.400	.667	.000	18.00	0.00
Maine, John	R-R	6-4	200	5-8-81	1	3	7.43	11	11	0	0	46	58	48	38	6	37	35	.315	.319	.313	6.85	7.24
Miller, Jim	R-R	6-1	200	4-28-82	8	5	5.25	65	0	0	24	72	93	48	42	7	21	73	.314	.324	.306	9.13	2.63
Molleken, Dustin	L-R	6-4	230	8-21-84	0	0	18.00	1	0	0	0	1	3	2	2	0	1	1	.500	.000	1.000	9.00	9.00
Mortensen, Clayton	R-R	6-4	185	4-10-85	2	8	9.42	15	15	0	0	64	104	71	67	13	29	54	.370	.400	.340	7.59	4.08
Muecke, Josh	L-L	6-3	195	1-9-82	2	4	6.80	10	10	0	0	45	59	42	34	9	25	29	.322	.333	.318	5.80	5.00
Perkins, Dan	R-R	6-4	200	3-5-86	0	1	32.40	1	1	0	0	2	5	6	6	0	5	1	.714	.667	.750	5.40	27.00
Reynolds, Greg	R-R	6-7	225	7-3-85	6	7	6.81	19	19	0	0	110	160	88	83	10	32	65	.343	.360	.328	5.33	2.63
Riordan, Cory	R-R	6-2	225	5-25-86	0	0	3.86	1	1	0	0	7	7	3	3	0	0	4	.259	.333	.200	5.14	0.00
Roenicke, Josh	R-R	6-3	200	8-4-82	0	1	3.52	23	0	0	0	31	30	14	12	3	7	22	.263	.214	.310	6.46	2.05
2-team total (16 Las Vegas)					1	4	4.58	39	0	0	0	53	55	35	27	6	22	42	—	—	—	7.13	3.74
Rogers, Esmil	R-R	6-1	190	8-14-85	1	2	6.26	5	5	0	0	23	36	16	16	3	5	15	.364	.372	.357	5.87	1.96
Romero, J.C.	B-L	5-11	205	6-4-76	0	0	3.38	3	0	0	0	3	2	1	1	0	3	3	.200	.000	.500	10.13	10.13
Street, Huston	R-R	6-0	190	8-2-83	0	0	0.00	2	0	0	0	2	0	0	0	0	0	2	.000	.000	.000	9.00	0.00
Stults, Eric	L-L	6-0	225	12-9-79	4	4	4.63	52	0	0	1	68	76	39	35	11	16	69	.275	.274	.276	9.13	2.12
Torres, Joe	L-L	6-2	195	9-3-82	0	0	0.00	1	0	0	0	1	0	0	0	0	0	0	.000	.000	.000	0.00	0.00
Vargas, Claudio	R-R	6-4	235	6-19-78	2	2	11.08	8	4	0	0	26	50	34	32	6	13	19	.407	.421	.394	6.58	4.50
Weiser, Keith	R-L	6-3	200	9-21-84	1	1	4.11	27	0	0	0	31	39	15	14	4	11	20	.315	.266	.367	5.87	3.23
White, Sean	R-R	6-4	210	4-25-81	4	2	5.68	53	1	0	0	82	103	55	52	6	49	54	.320	.354	.292	5.90	5.36
Williamson, Joey	R-R	6-2	210	1-28-86	2	3	7.12	9	6	0	0	37	53	32	29	5	21	30	.349	.373	.329	7.36	5.15

Fielding

Catcher	PCT	G	PO	A	E	DP	PB
Alfonzo	.981	15	89	13	2	0	0
Pacheco	.991	86	588	51	6	6	8
Pagnozzi	.997	47	322	27	1	3	5

First Base	PCT	G	PO	A	E	DP
Alfonzo	1.000	4	39	0	0	5
Cantu	1.000	15	110	11	0	9
Fields	.959	7	44	3	2	2
Giambi	.923	2	12	0	1	1
Jacobs	.991	104	836	81	8	91
Macri	1.000	2	19	4	0	2
Mather	1.000	1	10	0	0	1
Pagnozzi	1.000	2	9	2	0	1
Paulk	.986	16	121	15	2	19

Second Base	PCT	G	PO	A	E	DP
Amezaga	1.000	11	24	30	0	6
Emaus	.977	39	77	131	5	30
Fields	1.000	1	1	1	0	0
Macri	.970	40	72	89	5	16
Merchan	.962	20	46	54	4	14

Nazario	.975	8	14	25	1	6
Nelson	.970	23	39	58	3	16
Schaeffer	1.000	6	5	19	0	3
Young Jr.	.910	18	32	39	7	9

Third Base	PCT	G	PO	A	E	DP
Cantu	1.000	11	3	11	0	1
Emaus	.750	2	2	1	1	0
Fields	.920	21	12	34	4	1
Macri	.956	55	23	85	5	9
Nelson	.950	12	4	15	1	0
Pacheco	.909	5	2	8	1	0
Rohlinger	.875	3	3	4	1	1
Schaeffer	1.000	11	4	19	0	1
Stewart	.927	40	28	61	7	6
Wigginton	1.000	2	0	5	0	1

Shortstop	PCT	G	PO	A	E	DP
Amezaga	.964	32	43	91	5	23
Macri	1.000	3	3	5	0	2
Merchan	1.000	4	5	15	0	2
Nazario	.948	8	23	32	3	6

Nelson	.955	40	55	114	8	23
Rohlinger	.977	66	133	200	8	44
Schaeffer	1.000	2	5	3	0	0

Outfield	PCT	G	PO	A	E	DP
Amezaga	.982	28	50	6	1	2
Beerer	1.000	34	66	8	0	1
Blackmon	.950	56	102	11	6	4
Fields	1.000	8	11	1	0	0
Fowler	1.000	23	58	2	0	0
Garner	.958	43	65	4	3	0
Gonzalez	1.000	3	6	0	0	0
Macri	1.000	2	1	0	0	0
Mather	.983	49	106	7	2	1
Nazario	1.000	1	1	0	0	0
Paulk	.985	46	64	3	1	1
Salazar	1.000	20	32	0	0	0
Spilborghs	.875	8	7	0	1	0
Taveras	.984	91	174	12	3	0
Young Jr.	.989	45	88	0	1	0

TULSA DRILLERS
DOUBLE-A

TEXAS LEAGUE

Batting	B-T	HT	WT	DOB	AVG	vLH	vRH	G	AB	R	H	2B	3B	HR	RBI	BB	HBP	SH	SF	SO	SB	CS	SLG	OBP
Beerer, Scott	R-R	6-1	200	7-4-82	.290	.248	.308	89	328	52	95	18	0	13	42	16	7	0	1	43	18	5	.463	.335
Cesario, Jimmy	L-R	5-11	200	10-15-85	.317	.364	.305	83	252	30	80	10	2	4	37	19	10	0	3	44	4	1	.421	.384
Daniel, Mike	L-R	6-3	190	8-17-84	.258	.333	.227	26	62	11	16	3	1	1	8	10	1	0	0	12	4	1	.387	.370
Davis, Lars	L-R	6-3	205	11-7-85	.255	.268	.250	48	149	22	38	4	0	6	15	25	5	0	0	37	0	3	.403	.380
Field, Thomas	R-R	5-9	175	2-22-87	.271	.293	.262	134	472	77	128	23	3	17	61	53	12	0	4	108	9	4	.439	.357
Gomez, Hector	R-R	6-2	180	3-5-88	.235	.239	.234	102	425	46	100	23	6	14	50	19	3	0	1	94	16	4	.416	.272
Holcomb, Darin	R-R	5-11	205	12-7-85	.268	.329	.241	74	272	34	73	19	1	4	32	29	3	0	5	46	1	1	.390	.340
McBride, Matt	R-R	6-2	215	5-23-85	.235	1.000	.188	6	17	4	4	0	0	0	2	1	0	0	3	0	0	0	.235	.278
Mitchell, Mike	R-R	6-2	200	8-24-85	.214	.276	.175	81	224	33	48	9	2	3	21	22	4	0	1	52	16	5	.313	.295
Paulsen, Ben	L-R	6-4	205	10-27-87	.241	.188	.267	136	547	69	132	29	4	19	78	40	4	0	4	132	2	3	.413	.296
Rike, Brian	L-L	6-2	200	12-13-85	.252	.232	.258	82	250	30	63	14	0	13	37	23	3	0	3	98	2	5	.464	.319
Rosario, Wilin	R-R	5-11	200	2-23-89	.249	.323	.215	102	405	52	101	15	3	21	48	19	1	0	1	91	1	2	.457	.284
Sardinha, Bronson	L-R	6-1	220	4-6-83	.302	.257	.318	82	275	51	83	16	0	10	31	43	2	0	1	50	7	4	.469	.399
Schaeffer, Warren	R-R	6-0	180	1-28-85	.139	.116	.154	43	108	8	15	5	0	0	10	12	2	0	0	30	1	0	.185	.238
Squier, Jeff	R-R	6-3	190	3-4-87	.235	.143	.300	7	17	0	4	0	0	0	2	0	0	0	0	6	1	2	.235	.316
Wetzel, Erik	R-R	6-1	180	12-25-86	.235	.275	.220	58	183	14	43	6	0	0	20	14	2	0	3	39	5	1	.268	.292
Wheeler, Tim	L-R	6-4	205	1-21-88	.287	.236	.311	138	561	105	161	28	6	33	86	59	12	0	3	142	21	12	.535	.365
Zuanich, Mike	R-L	6-4	225	7-10-86	.261	.308	.224	30	88	16	23	3	0	6	11	9	4	0	1	23	1	1	.500	.353

Pitching	B-T	HT	WT	DOB	W	L	ERA	G	GS	CG	SV	IP	H	R	ER	HR	BB	SO	AVG	vLH	vRH	K/9	BB/9
Cook, Aaron	R-R	6-3	215	2-8-79	0	1	5.79	3	3	0	0	14	16	9	9	1	3	13	.291	.250	.308	8.36	1.93
DeRatt, Alan	R-R	6-5	225	11-6-85	0	1	5.40	3	2	0	0	8	11	5	5	0	2	3	.324	.308	.333	3.24	2.16

COLORADO ROCKIES

Pitching	B-T	HT	WT	DOB	W	L	ERA	G	GS	CG	SV	IP	H	R	ER	HR	BB	SO	AVG	vLH	vRH	K/9	BB/9
Dodson, Stephen	R-R	6-5	200	8-29-85	10	2	3.47	42	0	0	2	62	56	25	24	7	24	48	.242	.235	.247	6.93	3.47
Friedrich, Christian	R-L	6-4	215	7-8-87	6	10	5.00	25	25	0	0	133	156	88	74	20	43	103	.286	.256	.296	6.95	2.90
Froneberger, Isaiah	L-L	5-10	200	6-23-89	0	0	16.88	2	0	0	0	3	5	5	5	1	0	3	.385	.000	.455	10.13	0.00
Gardner, Joe	R-R	6-4	220	3-18-88	3	3	2.48	6	6	0	0	36	31	19	10	1	8	22	.226	.270	.189	5.45	1.98
Houston, Dan	R-R	6-3	205	10-24-86	4	4	4.27	13	13	1	0	78	89	43	37	6	18	51	.288	.270	.298	5.88	2.08
Jarrett, Sean	R-R	6-5	210	4-26-83	1	0	5.86	18	0	0	0	28	35	22	18	6	4	17	.310	.326	.300	5.53	1.30
Jorgenson, Adam	R-R	6-0	185	9-10-85	1	5	5.43	60	0	0	11	70	65	45	42	11	36	64	.257	.240	.268	8.27	4.65
Malone, Chris	R-R	6-4	215	6-28-83	1	0	4.15	4	0	0	0	4	7	3	2	0	2	3	.368	.200	.556	6.23	4.15
Molleken, Dustin	L-R	6-4	230	8-21-84	1	4	4.76	35	0	0	6	45	46	25	24	7	9	41	.264	.309	.236	8.14	1.79
Nicasio, Juan	R-R	6-3	200	8-31-86	5	1	2.22	9	9	1	0	57	48	15	14	3	10	63	.233	.313	.183	10.01	1.59
Pomeranz, Drew	R-L	6-5	230	11-22-88	1	0	0.00	2	2	0	0	10	2	0	0	0	0	7	.063	.125	.042	6.30	0.00
Riordan, Cory	R-R	6-4	200	5-25-86	1	12	5.37	27	22	0	0	142	172	95	85	21	25	100	.301	.298	.303	6.32	1.58
Rogers, Esmil	R-R	6-1	190	8-14-85	0	1	2.25	1	1	0	0	4	5	3	1	1	1	2	.278	.250	.333	4.50	2.25
Scahill, Rob	R-R	6-2	220	2-15-87	12	11	3.92	27	26	1	0	161	164	81	70	12	60	104	.266	.291	.250	5.83	3.36
Sullivan, Josh	R-R	6-4	215	7-5-84	5	9	5.51	25	20	1	0	118	122	82	72	19	54	87	.272	.302	.252	6.65	4.13
Torres, Joe	L-L	6-2	195	9-3-82	3	1	2.28	51	0	0	2	55	45	17	14	5	23	62	.222	.232	.215	10.08	3.74
Turpen, Dan	R-R	6-4	245	8-17-86	2	4	4.83	48	1	0	11	60	63	34	32	5	35	33	.284	.321	.264	4.98	5.28
Weathers, Casey	R-R	6-1	205	6-10-85	2	2	5.32	44	0	0	0	46	32	31	27	3	48	48	.199	.158	.221	9.46	9.46
Weiser, Keith	R-L	6-3	200	9-21-84	1	1	4.84	25	0	0	2	35	36	20	19	4	13	14	.273	.098	.352	3.57	3.31
White, Alex	R-R	6-3	215	8-29-88	1	1	1.65	4	4	0	0	16	10	3	3	1	1	10	.172	.095	.216	5.51	0.55
Williamson, Joey	R-R	6-2	210	1-28-86	3	2	2.42	19	6	0	1	52	45	20	14	5	19	52	.243	.250	.239	9.00	3.29

Fielding

Catcher	PCT	G	PO	A	E	DP	PB
Davis	.994	48	279	34	2	2	8
Rosario	.989	95	652	82	8	8	13

First Base	PCT	G	PO	A	E	DP
Cesario	1.000	3	31	2	0	5
Paulsen	.992	134	1251	61	11	123
Rosario	1.000	1	1	0	0	0
Zuanich	1.000	3	31	1	0	8

Second Base	PCT	G	PO	A	E	DP
Cesario	.961	40	76	122	8	34
Field	.983	96	176	278	8	71
Schaeffer	1.000	1	1	4	0	0

	PCT	G	PO	A	E	DP
Wetzel	.936	11	21	23	3	4
Third Base	PCT	G	PO	A	E	DP
Cesario	.895	9	4	13	2	0
Holcomb	.938	60	33	134	11	12
Paulsen	1.000	1	1	3	0	0
Schaeffer	.975	29	15	62	2	8
Squier	1.000	5	1	6	0	0
Wetzel	.879	45	21	73	13	4

Shortstop	PCT	G	PO	A	E	DP
Field	.968	34	55	95	5	29
Gomez	.963	101	177	324	19	71
Schaeffer	.944	4	4	13	1	3

	PCT	G	PO	A	E	DP
Squier	.833	1	0	5	1	1
Wetzel	.000	1	0	0	1	0
Outfield	PCT	G	PO	A	E	DP
Beerer	.954	73	117	8	6	1
Cesario	1.000	3	1	0	0	0
Daniel	.920	18	21	2	2	0
McBride	1.000	3	4	1	0	0
Mitchell	.960	68	134	9	6	1
Rike	.969	58	90	5	3	1
Sardinha	.974	76	141	8	4	1
Wheeler	.981	137	302	13	6	4
Zuanich	1.000	3	6	0	0	0

MODESTO NUTS   HIGH CLASS A

CALIFORNIA LEAGUE

Batting	B-T	HT	WT	DOB	AVG	vLH	vRH	G	AB	R	H	2B	3B	HR	RBI	BB	HBP	SH	SF	SO	SB	CS	SLG	OBP
Arenado, Nolan	R-R	6-1	205	4-16-91	.298	.333	.288	134	517	82	154	32	3	20	122	47	1	0	14	53	2	1	.487	.349
Christensen, David	R-R	6-1	195	2-11-88	.274	.268	.275	57	179	34	49	11	6	5	21	15	4	0	2	74	3	3	.486	.340
Clark, Jared	R-R	6-4	215	5-9-86	.229	.216	.233	61	214	21	49	11	1	7	33	25	2	0	2	66	0	2	.388	.313
Cleary, Delta	B-R	6-3	180	8-14-89	.235	.234	.235	130	503	96	118	20	4	1	45	75	5	0	4	97	27	16	.296	.337
Gonzalez, Jose	R-R	6-1	165	6-23-87	.210	.204	.213	69	214	27	45	3	0	1	15	24	5	0	2	47	2	2	.238	.302
Gonzalez, Maikol	R-R	5-10	175	3-25-86	.111	.000	.133	9	18	4	2	0	0	0	1	6	0	0	0	7	2	1	.111	.333
Ka'aihue, Kala	R-R	6-2	230	3-29-85	.167	.167	.167	11	36	4	6	0	0	2	5	3	0	0	0	13	0	1	.333	.286
Martinez, Carlos	R-R	5-11	182	9-22-88	.212	.340	.177	78	236	25	50	11	1	6	28	19	6	0	3	63	7	6	.343	.284
Matthes, Kent	R-R	6-2	215	1-8-87	.334	.269	.352	93	371	70	124	39	3	23	95	22	5	0	1	80	7	4	.642	.378
Mesa, Eliezer	R-R	5-11	180	11-24-88	.256	.293	.244	53	164	22	42	7	1	0	13	15	1	0	1	28	1	1	.311	.320
Nina, Angelys	R-R	5-11	165	11-16-88	.294	.310	.290	112	425	63	125	22	5	5	54	29	4	0	5	72	15	10	.405	.341
Robinson, Scott	R-R	6-0	185	7-6-88	.224	.183	.235	89	303	44	68	17	3	2	36	20	3	0	4	86	24	7	.320	.276
Roling, Kiel	R-R	6-3	240	1-23-87	.252	.255	.252	105	412	74	104	24	2	16	58	41	6	0	3	118	3	3	.437	.327
Rutledge, Josh	R-R	6-1	190	4-21-89	.348	.316	.358	113	460	91	160	33	9	9	71	41	12	0	2	91	16	3	.517	.414
Sanders, Joseph	R-R	6-0	195	4-24-88	.211	.333	.191	30	109	14	23	5	0	1	17	3	0	0	0	31	0	0	.284	.232
Sandoval, Orlando	R-R	6-0	185	1-22-86	.233	.255	.224	53	172	27	40	11	3	4	22	11	0	0	0	49	4	2	.401	.316
Seabury, Beau	R-R	6-1	195	6-13-85	.274	.385	.238	31	106	21	29	3	0	2	20	7	2	0	1	26	0	0	.406	.328
Tarleton, Dallas	L-R	5-11	200	8-5-87	.268	.143	.302	56	164	23	44	5	2	0	21	30	2	0	0	44	2	2	.323	.388
Zuanich, Mike	R-L	6-4	225	7-10-86	.366	.260	.397	58	224	59	82	23	2	14	49	30	8	0	2	59	4	3	.674	.455

Pitching	B-T	HT	WT	DOB	W	L	ERA	G	GS	CG	SV	IP	H	R	ER	HR	BB	SO	AVG	vLH	vRH	K/9	BB/9
Bettis, Chad	R-R	6-1	193	4-26-89	12	5	3.34	27	27	0	0	170	142	72	63	10	45	184	.225	.254	.206	9.76	2.39
Cabrera, Edwar	L-L	6-0	160	10-20-87	4	1	3.56	13	13	0	0	81	78	33	32	8	23	107	.252	.315	.238	11.89	2.56
DeRatt, Alan	R-R	6-5	225	11-6-85	6	5	4.87	26	10	0	0	92	107	59	50	7	26	69	.293	.329	.269	6.73	2.53
Frazier, Parker	R-R	6-5	159	11-11-88	11	11	4.50	27	27	0	0	154	171	95	77	15	46	105	.281	.280	.281	6.14	2.69
Gomez, Leuris	R-R	6-0	170	10-20-86	5	3	4.75	38	5	0	0	85	88	52	45	7	35	99	.262	.276	.255	10.44	3.69
Harris, Will	R-R	6-4	225	8-28-84	3	2	5.55	33	0	0	4	47	45	29	29	4	21	55	.254	.279	.241	10.53	4.02
Houston, Dan	R-R	6-3	205	10-24-86	7	1	2.53	13	13	1	0	85	71	35	24	7	22	67	.224	.248	.205	7.07	2.32
Kuo, Sheng-An	R-R	6-2	190	1-1-86	3	3	6.66	48	0	0	10	51	50	40	38	8	19	46	.255	.282	.237	8.06	3.33
Marbry, Michael	R-R	6-3	185	9-3-84	5	3	2.92	50	0	0	16	65	58	27	21	5	20	66	.239	.275	.209	9.19	2.78
Matzek, Tyler	L-L	6-3	210	10-19-90	0	3	9.82	10	10	0	0	33	34	37	36	5	46	37	.266	.346	.245	10.09	12.55
Mead, Kaimi	L-L	5-11	195	8-19-85	0	1	9.39	4	0	0	0	8	9	8	8	2	8	7	.290	.200	.333	8.22	9.39
Perkins, Dan	R-R	6-4	200	3-5-86	4	6	6.22	21	21	0	0	103	116	74	71	7	55	69	.294	.298	.292	6.05	4.82
Rose, Chad	R-R	6-2	200	2-17-88	5	1	4.86	37	0	0	0	54	56	32	29	4	16	47	.265	.275	.260	7.88	2.68

Pitching	B-T	HT	WT	DOB	W	L	ERA	G	GS	CG	SV	IP	H	R	ER	HR	BB	SO	AVG	vLH	vRH	K/9	BB/9
Schnaitmann, Nick	R-R	6-6	190	11-16-89	3	11	10.16	16	14	0	0	67	98	82	76	17	45	44	.346	.266	.413	5.88	6.01
Woods, Coty	R-R	6-2	190	3-14-88	5	4	2.19	49	0	0	1	78	61	20	19	4	33	88	.215	.292	.176	10.15	3.81
Yacko, Kurt	R-R	5-11	180	8-22-87	1	6	1.86	47	0	0	3	73	73	16	15	1	14	64	.267	.309	.239	7.93	1.73

Fielding

Catcher	PCT	G	PO	A	E	DP	PB
Gonzalez	.990	69	522	60	6	4	7
Seabury	.993	31	246	22	2	4	1
Tarleton	.995	50	372	48	2	3	0

First Base	PCT	G	PO	A	E	DP
Clark	.996	32	218	19	1	18
Ka'aihue	.950	5	34	4	2	2
Martinez	1.000	2	6	0	0	2
Roling	.992	73	594	45	5	53
Sanders	1.000	5	36	0	0	4
Zuanich	.993	29	242	24	2	18

Second Base	PCT	G	PO	A	E	DP
Gonzalez	.926	5	12	13	2	3
Martinez	.961	31	46	77	5	14
Nina	.981	105	221	294	10	61
Sanders	.917	5	7	4	1	1

Third Base	PCT	G	PO	A	E	DP
Arenado	.943	131	85	215	18	25
Gonzalez	.000	1	0	0	0	0
Martinez	.833	10	1	9	2	0
Sanders	.867	6	4	9	2	2

Shortstop	PCT	G	PO	A	E	DP
Gonzalez	.750	2	0	3	1	2

	PCT	G	PO	A	E	DP
Martinez	.920	27	30	74	9	12
Nina	1.000	2	4	4	0	0
Rutledge	.943	112	137	263	24	53

Outfield	PCT	G	PO	A	E	DP
Christensen	.968	46	89	2	3	1
Cleary	.987	130	291	10	4	1
Matthes	.948	85	139	6	8	2
Mesa	.932	45	68	1	5	0
Robinson	.980	75	138	6	3	3
Sandoval	.968	49	85	7	3	0
Zuanich	1.000	11	31	1	0	0

ASHEVILLE TOURISTS

LOW CLASS A

SOUTH ATLANTIC LEAGUE

Batting	B-T	HT	WT	DOB	AVG	vLH	vRH	G	AB	R	H	2B	3B	HR	RBI	BB	HBP	SH	SF	SO	SB	CS	SLG	OBP
Adames, Cristhian	B-R	6-0	160	7-26-91	.273	.252	.282	108	399	63	109	17	2	8	44	42	7	0	4	74	2	0	.386	.350
Aguilera, Anthony	R-R	6-0	215	10-30-86	.182	.273	.159	19	55	6	10	4	0	0	5	4	4	0	0	16	0	0	.255	.286
Altobelli, Dom	R-R	6-1	195	3-7-87	.236	.296	.200	24	72	9	17	6	0	2	13	6	1	0	1	27	3	1	.403	.300
Barnes, Avery	R-L	5-11	180	9-17-86	.278	.276	.279	83	327	56	91	24	3	7	39	13	2	0	5	89	19	3	.434	.305
Dickerson, Corey	L-R	6-2	210	5-22-89	.282	.245	.295	106	383	78	108	27	5	32	87	39	8	0	5	99	9	6	.626	.356
Garneau, Dustin	R-R	6-1	215	8-13-87	.255	.258	.254	100	341	71	87	29	4	17	67	58	7	0	5	70	7	3	.513	.370
Laurent, Chandler	R-R	5-10	180	10-17-87	.284	.303	.276	80	303	52	86	21	3	15	50	26	9	0	2	97	17	5	.521	.356
Massanari, Bryce	R-R	6-2	215	4-29-86	.328	.329	.328	69	259	44	85	19	0	14	43	35	7	0	2	64	0	0	.564	.419
Massey, Tyler	L-L	6-0	205	7-21-89	.200	.188	.204	20	65	8	13	5	0	0	10	4	1	0	0	19	3	0	.277	.257
Ortega, Rafael	L-R	5-11	160	5-15-91	.294	.232	.316	113	479	77	141	26	8	9	66	28	3	1	4	90	32	19	.438	.335
Parker, Kyle	R-R	6-0	200	9-30-89	.285	.280	.287	117	445	75	127	23	1	21	95	48	14	0	8	133	2	0	.483	.367
Tanos, Brett	R-R	5-11	175	10-6-88	.285	.302	.279	111	400	76	114	28	3	10	44	71	8	0	2	85	5	4	.445	.401
Tracy, Mark	R-R	6-4	220	1-1-88	.256	.280	.247	79	297	40	76	20	1	9	54	20	2	0	3	120	4	1	.421	.304
Velazquez, Helder	R-R	6-3	165	10-14-88	.270	.310	.255	105	411	61	111	30	1	10	54	23	14	0	2	94	11	2	.421	.329
Wilson, Russell	R-R	6-0	192	11-29-88	.228	.311	.203	61	193	40	44	5	4	3	15	35	7	0	0	82	15	2	.342	.366
Wong, Joey	L-R	5-10	175	4-12-88	.286	.286	.286	101	360	43	103	20	3	6	55	27	11	0	2	61	8	9	.408	.353

Pitching	B-T	HT	WT	DOB	W	L	ERA	G	GS	CG	SV	IP	H	R	ER	HR	BB	SO	AVG	vLH	vRH	K/9	BB/9
Bennigson, Craig	R-L	6-2	230	3-21-87	2	0	8.16	9	0	0	0	14	20	15	13	2	7	18	.323	.231	.347	11.30	4.40
Cabrera, Edwar	L-L	6-0	160	10-20-87	4	2	3.14	13	13	0	0	86	77	33	30	10	18	110	.237	.298	.224	11.51	1.88
Campos, Albert	R-R	6-4	222	2-4-91	6	4	5.19	15	15	0	0	87	111	59	50	5	19	64	.316	.343	.299	6.65	1.97
DeRatt, Alan	R-R	6-5	225	11-6-85	0	2	6.30	2	2	0	0	10	12	7	7	0	3	6	.324	.333	.308	5.40	2.70
Ferrer, Ricardo	R-R	6-2	174	10-11-89	0	3	9.00	6	0	0	0	26	41	26	26	5	16	12	.376	.375	.376	4.15	5.54
Froneberger, Isaiah	L-L	5-10	200	6-23-89	2	1	4.56	22	0	0	0	26	30	13	13	4	15	31	.303	.261	.316	10.87	5.26
Gonzalez, Juan	R-R	6-2	206	4-5-90	3	7	7.90	19	6	0	0	55	78	59	48	7	19	42	.335	.396	.292	6.91	3.13
Head, Stephen	L-L	6-3	220	1-13-84	0	0	9.00	5	0	0	0	9	18	11	9	1	5	6	.429	.438	.423	6.00	5.00
Hungerman, Josh	L-L	6-3	195	9-8-86	2	3	5.92	34	3	0	1	79	97	72	52	9	43	79	.300	.375	.276	9.00	4.90
Kern, Bruce	R-R	6-1	175	4-24-88	6	6	3.74	54	0	0	10	75	79	38	31	5	17	68	.276	.279	.275	8.20	2.05
Matzke, Tyler	L-L	6-3	210	10-19-90	5	4	4.36	12	12	0	0	64	45	35	31	3	50	74	.202	.227	.196	10.41	7.03
McAtee, Brad	R-R	6-5	215	3-15-87	1	5	5.17	22	0	0	0	31	39	28	18	2	13	20	.287	.243	.303	5.74	3.73
Mueller, Josh	R-R	6-4	215	1-18-89	6	7	5.50	27	19	0	1	106	131	72	65	11	48	76	.306	.336	.290	6.43	4.06
Perez, Juan	R-R	6-0	190	5-30-89	4	7	4.87	55	0	0	19	61	73	33	4	22	56	.297	.278	.305	8.26	3.25
Reid, Taylor	R-R	6-3	215	6-8-89	0	2	4.69	38	0	0	2	56	61	33	29	7	28	38	.272	.304	.250	6.14	4.53
Schnaitmann, Nick	R-R	6-6	190	11-16-89	6	2	2.70	9	9	1	0	60	56	22	18	4	15	32	.252	.244	.257	4.80	2.25
Sitton, Kraig	L-L	6-5	190	7-13-88	7	1	4.59	53	0	0	0	69	82	45	35	11	15	53	.307	.180	.345	6.95	1.97
Slaats, Josh	R-R	6-5	225	12-8-88	7	3	4.18	22	22	0	0	125	135	65	58	12	51	103	.274	.263	.280	7.42	3.67
Stavert, Erik	R-R	6-3	185	11-20-87	3	4	7.32	14	13	0	0	63	84	54	51	8	21	51	.321	.338	.314	7.32	3.02
Suarez, Rafael	R-R	6-0	200	5-14-89	2	1	8.38	18	0	0	1	29	38	30	27	7	8	28	.309	.393	.284	8.69	2.48
Tago, Peter	R-R	6-2	170	7-5-92	3	5	7.07	19	19	0	0	90	88	74	71	10	72	58	.267	.314	.233	5.78	7.17

Fielding

Catcher	PCT	G	PO	A	E	DP	PB
Aguilera	1.000	19	138	14	0	2	2
Garneau	.985	97	647	92	11	4	19
Massanari	.996	31	243	22	1	2	1
Tracy	.000	1	0	0	0	0	0

First Base	PCT	G	PO	A	E	DP
Altobelli	.970	10	89	9	3	13
Massanari	.975	13	111	8	3	10
Massey	.987	9	67	7	1	4
Tracy	.982	67	557	34	11	65
Velazquez	.985	50	376	22	6	46

Second Base	PCT	G	PO	A	E	DP
Tanos	.971	43	103	129	7	31
Velazquez	.986	14	35	38	1	15
Wilson	.978	55	112	155	6	46
Wong	.987	29	72	79	2	21

Third Base	PCT	G	PO	A	E	DP
Altobelli	.857	6	1	5	1	0
Tanos	.917	62	37	129	15	13
Velazquez	.845	39	22	71	17	6
Wong	.976	40	32	89	3	11

Shortstop	PCT	G	PO	A	E	DP
Adames	.966	108	161	351	18	79

	PCT	G	PO	A	E	DP
Velazquez	1.000	1	1	3	0	0
Wong	.973	35	41	102	4	20

Outfield	PCT	G	PO	A	E	DP
Barnes	.959	68	111	5	5	1
Dickerson	.970	65	94	3	3	0
Laurent	.961	75	138	8	6	1
Massey	1.000	13	13	0	0	0
Ortega	.980	112	232	18	5	1
Parker	.947	95	171	9	10	2
Velazquez	.000	1	0	0	0	0

TRI-CITY DUST DEVILS

SHORT-SEASON

NORTHWEST LEAGUE

Batting	B-T	HT	WT	DOB	AVG	vLH	vRH	G	AB	R	H	2B	3B	HR	RBI	BB	HBP	SH	SF	SO	SB	CS	SLG	OBP
Aguilera, Anthony	R-R	6-0	215	10-30-86	.308	.000	.400	6	13	4	4	1	0	0	0	3	1	0	0	3	0	0	.385	.471
Altobelli, Dom	R-R	6-1	195	3-7-87	.333	.000	.357	4	15	2	5	1	0	1	5	0	0	0	0	4	0	0	.600	.333
Argyroupolos, Matt	R-R	6-2	195	8-24-88	.136	.091	.152	14	44	2	6	2	0	0	6	2	1	0	0	16	0	1	.182	.191
Ballard, Jordan	R-R	6-3	210	11-9-87	.128	.000	.238	13	39	7	5	0	0	1	7	6	0	0	0	10	0	0	.205	.244
Berggren, Jarod	R-R	6-2	190	10-31-89	.200	.000	.286	3	10	1	2	0	0	0	0	0	0	0	0	3	0	0	.200	.200
Casteel, Ryan	R-R	6-1	205	6-6-91	.273	.333	.258	56	198	31	54	17	2	1	30	24	2	0	2	40	8	5	.394	.354
Crousset, Juan	L-L	5-11	193	4-30-90	.243	.357	.226	32	107	13	26	4	2	3	15	4	1	0	2	32	2	0	.402	.272
Featherston, Taylor	R-R	6-1	185	10-8-89	.231	.152	.250	49	169	19	39	8	3	2	20	17	3	0	0	38	3	1	.349	.312
Hernandez, David	R-R	6-2	165	2-1-88	.256	.250	.258	50	164	20	42	4	0	2	18	13	1	0	1	31	8	6	.317	.313
Humphries, Brian	L-R	6-3	195	3-20-90	.272	.233	.280	63	254	45	69	13	2	2	27	23	3	0	1	39	12	2	.362	.338
Langfels, Jayson	R-R	6-2	205	8-17-88	.233	.122	.267	52	176	27	41	7	5	5	24	19	4	0	1	56	6	2	.415	.320
Massey, Tyler	L-L	6-0	205	7-21-89	.284	.265	.287	68	257	41	73	15	0	7	46	21	4	0	4	51	12	5	.424	.343
McDade, Blake	L-L	6-1	208	7-1-87	.182	.222	.175	29	66	9	12	3	2	0	7	9	2	0	1	15	0	2	.288	.295
Mende, Sam	R-R	6-1	166	1-9-90	.000	1.000	.000	1	4	0	0	0	0	0	0	0	0	0	0	2	0	0	.000	.000
Pirkle, Richard	R-R	6-1	190	8-16-88	.228	.500	.156	19	57	6	13	4	0	1	8	4	3	0	1	19	0	1	.351	.308
Reyes, Leonardo	R-R	6-0	165	8-2-88	.254	.200	.276	50	173	25	44	4	1	2	17	24	1	0	0	32	7	2	.324	.348
Ribera, Jordan	L-R	6-0	225	12-22-88	.242	.222	.246	45	161	17	39	11	0	5	33	19	0	0	1	32	2	1	.404	.320
Shepherd, Jaron	L-R	6-1	175	10-30-88	.272	.250	.275	30	92	15	25	5	1	0	14	14	1	0	0	22	1	2	.348	.374
Simon, Jared	R-R	6-1	210	3-3-89	.243	.189	.258	65	239	32	58	11	1	5	34	30	5	0	1	77	3	3	.360	.338
Smalling, Timothy	R-R	6-3	207	10-14-87	.294	.170	.325	57	238	42	70	19	7	1	21	11	3	0	1	49	4	3	.445	.332
Squier, Jeff	R-R	6-3	190	3-3-87	.156	.133	.163	18	64	5	10	1	1	1	4	3	1	0	0	25	5	1	.250	.206

Pitching	B-T	HT	WT	DOB	W	L	ERA	G	GS	CG	SV	IP	H	R	ER	HR	BB	SO	AVG	vLH	vRH	K/9	BB/9
Alsup, Ben	R-R	6-3	180	9-9-88	3	3	3.23	13	11	0	0	61	56	24	22	4	22	50	.249	.287	.209	7.34	3.23
Ballard, Rhett	R-R	6-5	235	11-13-85	3	2	3.31	20	0	0	1	33	20	17	12	2	24	26	.175	.200	.165	7.16	6.61
Bennigson, Craig	R-L	6-2	230	3-21-87	3	3	2.82	23	0	0	2	45	39	17	14	2	8	45	.234	.196	.248	9.07	1.61
Bergman, Christian	R-R	6-1	180	5-4-88	7	5	2.59	15	15	2	0	97	83	31	28	4	11	68	.226	.216	.232	6.29	1.02
Dennis, Christopher	R-R	6-0	180	3-31-89	1	0	5.04	19	0	0	1	25	27	15	14	0	12	25	.276	.282	.271	9.00	4.32
Ferrer, Ricardo	R-R	6-2	174	10-11-89	2	6	4.39	14	14	0	0	70	82	52	34	9	21	46	.283	.333	.257	5.94	2.71
Froneberger, Isaiah	L-L	5-10	200	6-23-89	0	1	7.71	5	0	0	3	5	10	4	4	0	2	5	.400	.000	.556	9.64	3.86
Gagnon, Tyler	R-R	6-2	175	3-22-89	4	3	2.57	14	14	0	0	74	55	23	21	2	26	64	.205	.226	.190	7.82	3.18
Gonzalez, Nelson	R-R	6-1	168	2-15-90	7	0	1.71	20	4	0	3	58	48	16	11	0	10	49	.223	.214	.229	7.60	1.55
Head, Stephen	L-L	6-3	220	1-13-84	1	0	1.50	3	0	0	0	6	1	1	1	0	4	7	.056	.000	.067	10.50	6.00
Jensen, Chris	R-R	6-2	200	9-30-90	2	1	2.65	8	8	0	0	37	27	15	11	1	10	28	.206	.236	.184	6.75	2.41
Lo, Ching-Lung	R-R	6-6	190	8-20-85	1	2	6.59	9	0	0	0	14	14	10	10	1	10	9	.259	.389	.194	5.93	6.59
Mayo, Vianney	R-R	6-2	200	4-6-90	2	2	2.58	9	9	0	0	45	49	16	13	1	17	36	.283	.268	.294	7.15	3.38
Meaux, Jesse	R-R	6-4	210	8-8-89	0	0	0.00	1	0	0	0	2	0	0	0	0	2	0	.000	.000	.000	9.00	9.00
Padilla, Roberto	L-L	6-3	200	6-29-90	1	0	4.15	2	0	0	0	4	3	2	2	0	7	2	.188	.286	.111	4.15	14.54
Rankin, Will	R-R	6-0	192	5-1-89	1	0	1.00	4	0	0	1	9	3	2	1	0	5	9	.103	.111	.100	9.00	5.00
Roberts, Kenny	R-L	6-1	200	3-9-88	4	2	1.86	27	0	0	10	39	26	10	8	2	7	39	.188	.189	.188	9.08	1.63
Sammy, Jeremiah	L-R	6-2	190	7-13-87	0	0	8.31	4	0	0	0	4	6	4	4	1	5	2	.333	.286	.364	4.15	10.38
Stavert, Erik	R-R	6-3	185	11-20-87	0	1	9.00	1	1	0	0	2	4	3	2	0	2	1	.444	.600	.250	4.50	9.00
Suarez, Rafael	R-R	6-0	200	5-14-89	1	0	2.34	21	0	0	5	42	42	17	11	4	15	30	.253	.239	.263	6.38	3.19
Tilford, Clint	R-R	6-3	195	4-2-88	0	2	22.50	2	0	0	0	2	5	5	5	0	5	0	.333	.000	.333	0.00	22.50

Fielding

Catcher	PCT	G	PO	A	E	DP	PB
Aguilera	1.000	6	30	2	0	0	1
Casteel	.989	54	396	39	5	3	5
Pirkle	.993	19	125	18	1	0	3

First Base	PCT	G	PO	A	E	DP
Argyroupolos	1.000	7	48	4	0	6
Ballard	1.000	5	32	3	0	4
Massey	.975	15	113	3	3	8
McDade	.993	20	134	17	1	11
Ribera	.997	39	335	26	1	33

Second Base	PCT	G	PO	A	E	DP
Altobelli	.875	1	3	4	1	1

	PCT	G	PO	A	E	DP
Hernandez	.972	38	95	111	6	33
Mende	1.000	1	4	4	0	1
Smalling	.969	32	57	99	5	12
Squier	1.000	4	9	17	0	2

Third Base	PCT	G	PO	A	E	DP
Altobelli	.917	3	2	9	1	0
Argyroupolos	1.000	6	4	6	0	1
Ballard	1.000	2	1	4	0	1
Hernandez	.958	8	5	18	1	3
Langfels	.959	52	35	130	7	14
Squier	.850	8	4	13	3	2

Shortstop	PCT	G	PO	A	E	DP
Featherston	.932	49	61	132	14	23
Smalling	.919	23	25	77	9	11
Squier	1.000	4	8	13	0	3

Outfield	PCT	G	PO	A	E	DP
Berggren	1.000	3	6	1	0	0
Crousset	.917	17	22	0	2	0
Humphries	.965	61	131	5	5	1
Massey	.986	44	64	8	1	0
Reyes	1.000	24	50	0	0	0
Shepherd	.951	28	56	2	3	1
Simon	.992	56	125	6	1	1

CASPER GHOSTS

ROOKIE

PIONEER LEAGUE

Batting	B-T	HT	WT	DOB	AVG	vLH	vRH	G	AB	R	H	2B	3B	HR	RBI	BB	HBP	SH	SF	SO	SB	CS	SLG	OBP
Argyroupolos, Matt	R-R	6-2	195	8-24-88	.217	.188	.226	21	69	12	15	1	0	4	8	9	2	0	2	21	0	0	.406	.317
Berggren, Jarod	R-R	6-2	190	10-31-89	.289	.167	.313	15	38	2	11	2	0	0	4	1	5	0	0	16	3	0	.342	.386
Ciriaco, Juan	R-R	5-9	155	7-6-90	.254	.308	.216	28	63	4	16	0	1	0	6	1	0	0	1	17	6	1	.286	.262
De La Cruz, Robert	R-R	5-11	189	10-10-89	.203	.154	.214	40	138	18	28	8	1	3	16	12	1	0	1	35	3	2	.341	.270
De Leon, Miguel	R-R	6-2	195	8-5-91	.317	.125	.364	16	41	7	13	4	0	1	4	5	1	0	0	9	0	0	.488	.404
Herrera, Rosell	B-R	6-3	180	10-16-92	.284	.233	.301	63	243	38	69	6	8	6	34	27	3	0	1	62	5	4	.449	.361
Kandilas, David	R-R	6-2	185	9-14-90	.327	.316	.330	61	248	51	81	17	10	6	35	26	4	0	1	44	15	6	.548	.398
Mende, Sam	R-R	6-1	166	1-9-90	.281	.349	.258	46	171	33	48	11	2	14	39	16	5	0	0	52	7	2	.614	.359

COLORADO ROCKIES

Batting	B-T	HT	WT	DOB	AVG	vLH	vRH	G	AB	R	H	2B	3B	HR	RBI	BB	HBP	SH	SF	SO	SB	CS	SLG	OBP
Ramirez, Michael	R-R	5-10	165	4-27-90	.181	.227	.160	24	72	4	13	3	1	1	14	0	0	0	0	17	0	2	.292	.181
Reyes, Angel	R-R	6-2	195	10-23-90	.181	.160	.188	33	105	21	19	3	1	5	16	5	4	0	1	21	1	0	.371	.243
Riggins, Harold	R-R	6-2	240	3-6-90	.279	.321	.264	67	215	42	60	13	1	8	35	46	6	0	2	85	1	3	.460	.416
Rivera, Jose	R-R	5-10	170	4-18-90	.228	.192	.237	39	123	18	28	5	1	5	17	1	0	0	0	28	2	4	.309	.264
Roja, Yafistel	B-R	5-11	150	10-26-91	.276	.412	.255	36	123	19	34	6	1	1	8	6	1	0	0	24	9	2	.366	.315
Sosa, Francisco	R-R	6-4	180	2-27-90	.254	.275	.246	50	185	21	47	10	3	6	28	13	1	0	1	57	7	4	.438	.305
Story, Trevor	R-R	6-1	175	11-15-92	.268	.216	.289	47	179	37	48	8	2	6	28	26	2	0	2	41	13	1	.436	.364
Swanner, Will	R-R	6-2	185	9-10-91	.264	.351	.238	43	159	33	42	14	1	10	24	20	3	0	0	60	1	2	.553	.357
Thomas, Dillon	L-L	6-1	195	12-10-92	.328	.333	.324	15	58	12	19	2	0	1	7	3	0	0	0	18	2	1	.414	.361
Thomore, Carl	R-R	6-2	212	1-13-93	.192	.111	.217	43	156	25	30	8	3	0	25	18	3	0	0	52	4	1	.301	.288
Yan, Julian	R-R	6-2	180	11-27-91	.249	.255	.247	53	201	22	50	8	2	3	26	11	0	0	2	60	6	1	.353	.285

Pitching	B-T	HT	WT	DOB	W	L	ERA	G	GS	CG	SV	IP	H	R	ER	HR	BB	SO	AVG	vLH	vRH	K/9	BB/9
Barraza, Alejandro	R-R	6-1	205	10-25-90	1	1	6.98	20	0	0	1	39	51	32	30	8	5	34	.315	.317	.313	7.91	1.16
Brewer, Russell	R-R	6-0	200	2-25-88	1	6	4.45	27	0	0	2	30	28	16	15	4	7	33	.243	.333	.155	9.79	2.08
Crocker, Matt	R-L	6-3	190	5-24-89	0	1	5.46	20	0	0	0	28	33	25	17	2	13	19	.289	.341	.260	6.11	4.18
Fernandez, Raul	R-R	6-2	180	6-22-90	4	7	8.20	14	14	0	0	64	91	64	58	11	18	50	.330	.328	.331	7.07	2.54
Gibson, Trevor	R-R	6-3	225	9-6-86	0	0	4.50	2	0	0	0	2	2	2	1	0	0	2	.222	.250	.200	9.00	0.00
Gillingham, Alex	R-R	6-3	200	10-17-89	3	5	5.55	13	12	1	0	62	78	46	38	6	16	50	.299	.330	.275	7.30	2.34
Hart, Brook	L-L	6-5	220	4-10-89	4	1	3.86	17	1	0	1	40	48	21	17	6	12	29	.286	.306	.274	6.58	2.72
Hernandez, Jefri	R-R	6-1	170	4-27-91	2	3	3.99	10	10	0	0	47	54	31	21	5	12	27	.281	.233	.321	5.13	2.28
Hughes, Benjamin	R-R	6-5	215	11-29-89	2	2	6.50	10	5	0	0	36	49	31	26	5	11	38	.320	.282	.354	9.50	2.75
Johnson, Patrick	R-R	5-10	170	8-14-88	0	4	5.35	10	6	0	0	34	37	23	20	2	17	28	.285	.326	.262	7.49	4.54
Mahon, Logan	L-L	6-2	195	9-5-88	0	0	4.50	5	0	0	0	6	6	3	3	0	4	6	.250	.444	.133	9.00	6.00
Mejias, Alving	R-R	6-1	185	12-26-91	0	2	7.49	19	3	0	0	52	82	55	43	8	12	30	.350	.337	.362	5.23	2.09
Parker, Geoff	R-R	6-3	245	3-22-89	3	9	6.89	14	13	0	0	63	81	57	48	6	27	51	.308	.323	.293	7.32	3.88
Rankin, Will	R-R	6-0	192	5-1-89	1	1	6.95	13	0	0	1	22	30	18	17	1	6	20	.330	.281	.356	8.18	2.45
Roliard, Kyle	L-L	6-5	190	2-28-90	1	0	4.76	21	0	0	1	28	27	19	15	2	13	36	.237	.214	.250	11.44	4.13
Sammy, Jeremiah	L-R	6-2	190	7-13-87	1	1	9.13	14	0	0	0	24	48	28	24	7	8	15	.444	.352	.537	5.70	3.04
Winkler, Danny	R-R	6-1	200	2-2-90	4	3	3.92	12	12	0	0	57	64	31	25	6	19	65	.278	.354	.238	10.20	2.98
Wolford, Michael	R-R	6-3	200	5-24-89	0	3	3.86	24	0	0	9	23	21	10	10	2	11	25	.231	.238	.224	9.64	4.24

Fielding

Catcher	PCT	G	PO	A	E	DP	PB
Ramirez	.993	24	119	23	1	2	3
Reyes	.992	29	208	26	2	1	1
Swanner	.984	31	222	21	4	1	9

First Base	PCT	G	PO	A	E	DP
Argyropoulos	.987	8	74	1	1	6
De Leon	.979	9	44	2	1	7
Reyes	1.000	1	9	1	0	0
Riggins	.983	67	563	61	11	49

Second Base	PCT	G	PO	A	E	DP
Ciriaco	.900	10	8	28	4	4
Mende	.929	14	35	43	6	10
Rivera	.961	38	44	102	6	19
Roja	.954	23	30	73	5	14

Third Base	PCT	G	PO	A	E	DP
Argyropoulos	.893	13	6	19	3	0
Ciriaco	1.000	1	1	1	0	0
De Leon	.875	2	2	5	1	0
Herrera	.860	16	15	28	7	1
Mende	.910	31	26	55	8	2
Roja	.750	2	1	2	1	0
Story	.933	15	13	29	3	4

Shortstop	PCT	G	PO	A	E	DP
Ciriaco	.923	8	11	13	2	7
Herrera	.915	41	64	120	17	27
Mende	1.000	2	2	6	0	1
Rivera	1.000	1	2	4	0	1
Story	.915	30	46	83	12	21

Outfield	PCT	G	PO	A	E	DP
Berggren	1.000	15	21	1	0	1
De La Cruz	.929	21	22	4	2	0
Kandilas	.969	61	120	5	4	1
Riggins	1.000	1	3	0	0	0
Sosa	.951	38	38	1	2	0
Thomas	1.000	12	23	1	0	0
Thomore	.938	34	43	2	3	0
Yan	.963	53	100	5	4	2

DSL ROCKIES   ROOKIE

DOMINICAN SUMMER LEAGUE

Batting	B-T	HT	WT	DOB	AVG	vLH	vRH	G	AB	R	H	2B	3B	HR	RBI	BB	HBP	SH	SF	SO	SB	CS	SLG	OBP
Bacilio, Jesus	R-R	6-0	180	4-7-93	.264	.209	.287	46	144	27	38	3	4	2	20	19	9	0	2	21	8	4	.382	.379
Briceno, Jose	R-R	6-0	195	9-19-92	.288	.239	.307	47	160	26	46	10	1	0	18	23	6	0	4	22	12	3	.363	.389
Daza, Yonathan	R-R	6-2	190	2-28-94	.231	.259	.224	49	134	19	31	6	1	0	14	12	6	0	0	16	8	5	.291	.322
De La Cruz, Jose	R-R	6-0	160	6-12-92	.231	.239	.228	63	238	28	55	16	2	1	28	16	5	0	1	41	7	2	.328	.292
Dilone, Miguel	L-R	6-2	175	7-8-93	.268	.261	.270	64	183	25	49	7	1	0	25	46	1	0	4	34	13	15	.317	.410
Galvez, Cesar	B-R	5-9	145	7-24-91	.269	.278	.265	68	234	44	63	7	2	0	26	44	2	0	1	30	47	11	.316	.388
Garcia, Dawin	R-R	6-1	0	8-28-93	.126	.176	.114	30	87	7	11	1	0	1	3	6	0	0	0	35	0	0	.172	.183
Marte, Hamlet	R-R	5-10	180	2-3-94	.181	.368	.113	27	72	5	13	8	0	0	7	8	4	0	2	18	0	1	.292	.291
Morales, Juan	R-R	6-0	180	7-17-92	.192	.000	.217	10	26	3	5	1	0	0	2	2	0	0	1	5	2	0	.231	.241
Morrobel, Eddy	R-R	5-11	185	3-26-93	.183	.250	.157	25	71	7	13	2	0	2	5	7	1	0	0	22	3	2	.296	.266
Pena, Franmy	R-R	5-10	175	8-14-92	.296	.293	.297	35	115	18	34	5	1	5	0	0	0	0	0	3	1	0	.452	.325
Quintin, Cristian	R-R	6-3	165	12-27-93	.185	.167	.192	50	146	24	27	4	3	3	19	17	6	0	1	61	5	0	.315	.294
Roble, Jonathan	B-R	5-11	170	4-25-92	.172	.200	.154	26	64	10	11	3	0	0	3	17	3	0	0	24	4	3	.219	.369
Rosario, Jairo	R-R	5-10	175	1-21-93	.236	.344	.200	37	127	15	30	5	0	0	16	9	2	0	2	22	4	2	.276	.293
Soriano, Wilson	R-R	5-9	140	12-31-91	.258	.333	.235	59	178	32	46	7	1	0	18	17	0	0	0	9	18	8	.309	.323
Tapia, Raimel	L-L	6-2	160	2-4-94	.262	.270	.259	67	248	29	65	6	3	1	35	26	2	0	1	41	15	8	.323	.336

Pitching	B-T	HT	WT	DOB	W	L	ERA	G	GS	CG	SV	IP	H	R	ER	HR	BB	SO	AVG	vLH	vRH	K/9	BB/9
Aquino, Jayson	L-L	6-1	170	11-22-92	8	2	1.30	14	14	3	0	90	55	21	13	1	22	80	.175	.175	.175	8.03	2.21
Estevez, Carlos	R-R	6-4	210	12-28-92	3	2	3.44	8	6	1	0	34	33	14	13	2	14	27	.260	.260	.260	7.15	3.71
Hernandez, Raul	R-R	6-0	175	10-2-92	0	1	0.00	1	1	0	0	5	1	0	0	0	0	5	.167	.111	.222	9.64	3.86
Herrera, Alvin	R-R	6-1	165	3-15-93	0	1	12.66	10	0	0	0	11	14	17	15	1	4	10	.311	.417	.273	8.44	3.38
Jiminian, Johendi	R-R	6-3	165	10-14-92	6	3	3.18	14	14	0	0	68	57	31	24	4	23	47	.230	.261	.213	6.22	3.04

Pitching

Pitching	B-T	HT	WT	DOB	W	L	ERA	G	GS	CG	SV	IP	H	R	ER	HR	BB	SO	AVG	vLH	vRH	K/9	BB/9
Leon, Carlos	R-R	6-2	195	4-10-92	2	0	1.78	21	0	0	2	35	26	10	7	1	9	26	.203	.208	.200	6.62	2.29
Lezama, Angel	R-R	6-0	164	3-1-94	4	4	2.03	13	12	1	0	67	56	27	15	2	5	59	.221	.250	.206	7.97	0.68
Marcano, Angel	L-L	6-1	155	5-4-93	2	0	3.94	14	0	0	0	16	10	10	7	1	11	12	.185	.222	.178	6.75	6.19
Medina, Jose	R-R	6-2	195	9-24-92	1	2	10.13	12	0	0	0	16	24	20	18	2	10	15	.343	.407	.302	8.44	5.63
Medrano, Andres	R-R	6-0	190	4-10-92	5	2	3.00	32	0	0	16	39	32	14	13	3	8	33	.222	.103	.302	7.62	1.85
Montilla, Manuel	R-R	6-4	205	9-7-91	1	3	2.52	23	0	0	1	36	36	17	10	0	11	26	.259	.167	.318	6.56	2.78
Palacios, Javier	R-R	6-1	165	9-29-93	3	2	5.72	15	1	0	0	28	31	21	18	0	6	27	.279	.342	.247	8.58	1.91
Payamps, Joel	R-R	6-2	170	4-7-94	1	3	3.29	10	10	0	0	38	35	17	14	1	18	38	.243	.294	.215	8.92	4.23
Rodriguez, Helmis	L-L	5-11	155	6-10-94	5	2	1.74	11	10	0	1	52	36	16	10	0	17	45	.196	.182	.198	7.84	2.96
Rogers, Randol	R-R	6-3	175	12-31-92	0	0	12.71	5	0	0	0	6	8	9	8	1	2	3	.320	.250	.385	4.76	3.18
Sanchez, Julio	R-R	6-0	160	9-28-91	0	0	3.60	6	0	0	0	5	3	7	2	1	5	3	.167	.143	.182	5.40	9.00
Santana, Jhonriz	R-R	6-1	165	4-22-93	0	0	8.53	7	0	0	0	6	7	8	6	0	9	4	.259	.333	.222	5.68	12.79
Valera, Smit	R-R	6-1	168	7-14-90	0	1	1.80	9	1	0	0	10	7	11	2	0	7	5	.189	.000	.269	4.50	6.30
Valerio, Radhames	L-L	6-2	200	10-17-92	2	0	1.66	13	2	0	0	38	28	10	7	1	9	19	.203	.231	.200	4.50	2.13
Yan, Carlos	R-R	6-5	192	1-28-91	0	0	0.00	1	0	0	1	1	1	0	0	0	0	1	.250	.000	.333	9.00	0.00

Fielding

Catcher	PCT	G	PO	A	E	DP	PB
Bacilio	1.000	1	6	1	0	0	0
Briceno	.974	27	182	39	6	4	4
Marte	1.000	6	37	1	0	0	5
Pena	.963	12	67	10	3	0	1
Rosario	.978	30	193	26	5	0	7
Soriano	1.000	1	3	0	0	0	1

First Base	PCT	G	PO	A	E	DP
Briceno	.985	15	123	10	2	9
Dilone	.914	5	31	1	3	2
Galvez	.981	17	145	12	3	8
Morales	.980	6	47	2	1	1
Morrobel	.992	16	119	9	1	8
Pena	.982	19	160	6	3	8

Second Base	PCT	G	PO	A	E	DP
Dilone	.960	31	49	72	5	14
Galvez	.961	23	52	47	4	8
Garcia	.875	1	2	5	1	1
Morrobel	.833	1	4	1	1	0
Roble	.951	11	13	26	2	1
Soriano	1.000	11	21	25	0	2

Third Base	PCT	G	PO	A	E	DP
De La Cruz	.917	9	2	9	1	2
Dilone	.859	24	19	48	11	2
Galvez	.938	26	24	66	6	3
Morrobel	.571	3	2	6	6	0
Soriano	.867	19	16	36	8	2

Shortstop	PCT	G	PO	A	E	DP
De La Cruz	.938	54	84	143	15	12
Galvez	.929	3	5	8	1	2
Garcia	.860	19	19	30	8	2
Soriano	1.000	4	2	6	0	1

Outfield	PCT	G	PO	A	E	DP
Bacilio	.981	39	48	3	1	0
Daza	.961	49	70	4	3	1
Morales	1.000	3	1	0	0	0
Quintin	.960	47	67	5	3	3
Soriano	.982	29	53	2	1	0
Tapia	.973	66	101	6	3	1

Detroit Tigers

SEASON IN A SENTENCE: The Tigers won the American League Central and beat the Yankees in the Division Series—with another dominant season from Justin Verlander, who threw a no-hitter in May—but they fell short of reaching the World Series in their first trip to the playoffs in five years.

HIGH POINT: With their season on the line in the decisive Game Five of the Division Series in Yankee Stadium, Don Kelly and Delmon Young hit back-to-back home runs in the first inning against the Yankees. Trade deadline acquisition Doug Fister pitched five one-run innings, and the bullpen held on for the 3-2 victory over the team with the AL's best regular-season record.

LOW POINT: The Tigers didn't perform like a playoff team to start the year. By May 2, they were 12-17 and already eight games back in the AL Central after losing seven straight games, including sweeps against Seattle and Cleveland.

NOTABLE ROOKIES: Al Alburquerque became a minor league free agent after the 2010 season before ever reaching the major leagues. He rewarded the Tigers when they took a flyer on him in the offseason, posting the lowest ERA (1.87) of any Tigers reliever and leading the team in strikeouts per nine innings (13.9). Andy Dirks got a callup from Triple-A Toledo in mid-May and split time between all three outfield positions, though he wasn't able to do much damage at the plate.

KEY TRANSACTIONS: Looking to add another reliable starter behind Justin Verlander, the Tigers acquired Fister from the Mariners at the trade deadline for third baseman Francisco Martinez, lefthander Charlie Furbush, outfielder Casper Wells and righthander Chance Ruffin. Fister was brilliant down the stretch and in the postseason, posting a 1.79 ERA with a 57-5 K-BB mark in 70 regular season innings with the Tigers.

DOWN ON THE FARM: Low Class A West Michigan finished 70-69, the only Tigers full-season affiliate to finish over .500. West Michigan third baseman Nick Castellanos got off to a slow start in his first full season but finished well and was the Midwest League's No. 4 prospect. Righthander Jacob Turner pitched well in Double-A Erie and made his major league debut in July. Lefthander Drew Smyly had a 2.07 ERA in 126 innings between high Class A Lakeland and Erie, while 18-year-old righthander Brenny Paulino was the Rookie-level Gulf Coast League's No. 4 prospect.

OPENING DAY PAYROLL: $105,700,231 (10th)

PLAYERS OF THE YEAR

MAJOR LEAGUE	MINOR LEAGUE
Justin Verlander rhp	**Drew Smyly** rhp
24-5, 2.40	(High A/Double-A)
250 SO/251 IP	11-6, 2.07
Won AL triple crown	130 SO/126 IP

ORGANIZATION LEADERS

BATTING   *Minimum 250 PA

MAJORS

* AVG	Miguel Cabrera	.344
* OPS	Miguel Cabrera	1.034
HR	Miguel Cabrera	30
RBI	Miguel Cabrera	105

MINORS

* AVG	Justin Henry, Erie/Toledo	.314
* OBP	Justin Henry, Erie/Toledo	.414
* SLG	Jordan Lennerton, Lakeland	.444
R	Jamie Johnson, Erie	93
H	Nick Castellanos, West Michigan	158
TB	Tony Plagman, Lakeland	229
2B	Nick Castellanos, West Michigan	36
3B	Audy Ciriaco, Erie/Toledo	8
	Ben Guez, Erie/Toledo	8
HR	Ryan Strieby, Toledo	19
RBI	Tony Plagman, Lakeland	97
BB	Jordan Lennerton, Lakeland	92
SO	Ryan Strieby, Toledo	171
SB	Dixon Machado, West Michigan	25

PITCHING   #Minimum 75 IP

MAJORS

W	Justin Verlander	24
# ERA	Justin Verlander	2.40
SO	Justin Verlander	250
SV	Jose Valverde	49

MINORS

W	Jared Wesson, Lakeland	15
L	Trevor Feeney, Lakeland/Toledo/Erie	13
	Luke Putkonen, Erie/Lakeland	13
# ERA	Drew Smyly, Lakeland/Erie	2.07
G	Brendan Wise, Erie/Toledo	53
GS	Trevor Feeney, Lakeland/Toledo/Erie	28
SV	Kenny Faulk, Lakeland	20
IP	Trevor Feeney, Lakeland/Toledo/Erie	160.1
BB	Andrew Oliver, Toledo	80
SO	Andrew Oliver, Toledo	143
# AVG	Drew Smyly, Lakeland/Erie	.227

General Manager: Dave Dombrowski. **Farm Director:** Dan Lunetta. **Scouting Director:** David Chadd.

Class	Team	League	W	L	PCT	Finish	Manager(s)
Majors	Detroit Tigers	American	95	67	.586	3rd (14)	Jim Leyland
Triple-A	Toledo Mud Hens	International	67	77	.465	11th (14)	Phil Nevin
Double-A	Erie SeaWolves	Eastern	67	75	.472	9th (12)	Chris Cron
High A	Lakeland Flying Tigers	Florida State	64	74	.464	8th (12)	Dave Huppert
Low A	West Michigan Whitecaps	Midwest	70	69	.504	7th (16)	Ernie Young
Short-season	Connecticut Tigers	New York-Penn	39	35	.527	t-6th (14)	Andrew Graham
Rookie	GCL Tigers	Gulf Coast	29	31	.483	7th (15)	Basilio Cabrera
Overall 2011 Minor League Record			336	361	.482	23rd (30)	

ORGANIZATION STATISTICS

DETROIT TIGERS
AMERICAN LEAGUE

Batting	B-T	HT	WT	DOB	AVG	vLH	vRH	G	AB	R	H	2B	3B	HR	RBI	BB	HBP	SH	SF	SO	SB	CS	SLG	OBP
Avila, Alex	L-R	5-11	210	1-29-87	.295	.273	.304	141	464	63	137	33	4	19	82	73	3	0	8	131	3	1	.506	.389
Betemit, Wilson	B-R	6-2	220	11-2-81	.292	.250	.307	40	120	11	35	7	3	5	19	11	0	0	2	47	1	0	.525	.346
2-team total (57 Kansas City)					.285	—	—	97	323	40	92	22	4	8	46	31	0	0	5	105	4	1	.452	.343
Boesch, Brennan	L-L	6-4	235	4-12-85	.283	.302	.276	115	428	75	121	25	1	16	54	35	5	0	4	83	5	3	.458	.341
Cabrera, Miguel	R-R	6-4	240	4-18-83	.344	.319	.353	161	572	111	197	48	0	30	105	108	3	0	5	89	2	1	.586	.448
Dirks, Andy	L-L	6-0	195	1-24-86	.251	.323	.239	78	219	34	55	13	0	7	28	11	3	0	0	36	5	2	.406	.296
Guillen, Carlos	B-R	6-1	215	9-30-75	.232	.185	.250	28	95	8	22	2	1	3	13	5	0	0	2	16	1	1	.368	.265
Inge, Brandon	R-R	5-11	190	5-19-77	.197	.245	.170	102	269	29	53	10	2	3	23	24	2	0	3	74	1	1	.283	.265
Jackson, Austin	R-R	6-1	185	2-1-87	.249	.257	.245	153	591	90	147	22	11	10	45	56	4	0	3	181	22	5	.374	.317
Kelly, Don	L-R	6-4	190	2-15-80	.245	.190	.250	112	257	35	63	8	3	7	28	14	3	0	1	32	2	1	.381	.291
Martinez, Victor	B-R	6-2	210	12-23-78	.330	.311	.337	145	540	76	178	40	0	12	103	46	2	0	7	51	1	0	.470	.380
Ordonez, Magglio	R-R	6-0	215	1-28-74	.255	.292	.231	92	329	33	84	10	0	5	32	23	1	0	4	41	2	1	.331	.303
Peralta, Jhonny	R-R	6-2	215	5-28-82	.299	.240	.323	146	525	68	157	25	3	21	86	40	2	0	9	95	0	2	.478	.345
Raburn, Ryan	R-R	6-0	185	4-17-81	.256	.274	.245	121	387	53	99	22	2	14	49	21	3	0	3	114	1	1	.432	.297
Rhymes, Will	L-R	5-9	155	4-1-83	.235	.143	.244	29	85	13	20	3	0	0	2	11	0	1	0	12	1	0	.271	.323
Santiago, Ramon	B-R	5-11	175	8-31-79	.260	.320	.245	101	258	29	67	11	3	5	30	17	4	0	4	38	0	0	.384	.311
Santos, Omir	R-R	6-0	215	4-29-81	.227	.364	.091	11	22	1	5	0	0	0	0	0	0	0	0	4	0	0	.227	.227
Sizemore, Scott	R-R	6-0	185	1-4-85	.222	.381	.143	17	63	8	14	1	0	0	4	10	0	0	0	19	1	1	.238	.329
2-team total (93 Oakland)					.245	—	—	110	368	50	90	22	1	11	56	53	2	0	1	112	5	3	.399	.342
Wells, Casper	R-R	6-2	210	11-23-84	.257	.280	.211	64	113	16	29	10	0	4	12	9	2	0	0	29	1	0	.451	.323
2-team total (31 Seattle)					.237	—	—	95	215	30	51	11	0	11	27	18	7	0	0	71	3	2	.442	.317
Worth, Danny	R-R	6-1	185	9-30-85	.270	.333	.188	30	37	6	10	2	0	0	3	2	0	0	0	9	0	0	.324	.308
Young, Delmon	R-R	6-3	200	9-14-85	.274	.364	.242	40	168	28	46	5	1	8	32	5	2	0	3	30	0	0	.458	.298
2-team total (84 Minnesota)					.268	—	—	124	473	54	127	21	1	12	64	23	2	0	6	85	1	0	.393	.302

Pitching	B-T	HT	WT	DOB	W	L	ERA	G	GS	CG	SV	IP	H	R	ER	HR	BB	SO	AVG	vLH	vRH	K/9	BB/9
Alburquerque, Al	R-R	6-0	195	6-10-86	6	1	1.87	41	0	0	0	43	21	9	9	0	29	67	.142	.176	.113	13.92	6.02
Below, Duane	L-L	6-3	220	11-15-85	0	2	4.34	14	2	0	0	29	28	16	14	2	11	14	.252	.255	.250	4.34	3.41
Benoit, Joaquin	R-R	6-3	220	7-26-77	4	3	2.95	66	0	0	2	61	47	22	20	5	17	63	.218	.248	.184	9.30	2.51
Coke, Phil	L-L	6-1	210	7-19-82	3	9	4.47	48	14	0	1	109	118	64	54	5	40	69	.279	.215	.314	5.71	3.31
Fister, Doug	L-R	6-8	210	2-4-84	8	1	1.79	11	10	0	0	70	54	19	14	4	5	57	.206	.196	.220	7.29	0.64
2-team total (21 Seattle)					11	13	2.83	32	31	3	0	216	193	76	68	11	37	146	—	—	—	6.07	1.54
Furbush, Charlie	L-L	6-5	215	4-11-86	1	3	3.62	17	2	0	0	32	36	18	13	5	16	26	.303	.261	.329	7.24	3.90
2-team total (11 Seattle)					4	10	5.48	28	12	0	0	85	97	59	52	16	30	67	—	—	—	7.07	3.16
Gonzalez, Enrique	R-R	5-10	225	7-14-82	0	0	10.00	8	0	0	0	9	12	10	10	1	7	3	.343	.381	.286	3.00	7.00
Marte, Luis	R-R	5-11	200	8-26-86	1	0	2.45	4	0	0	0	4	6	1	1	0	1	3	.375	.375	.375	7.36	2.45
Oliver, Andy	L-L	6-3	210	12-3-87	0	1	6.52	2	2	0	0	10	11	7	7	3	8	5	.289	.250	.308	4.66	7.45
Oliveros, Lester	R-R	6-0	225	5-28-88	0	0	5.63	9	0	0	0	8	8	5	5	0	4	4	.258	.250	.263	4.50	4.50
2-team total (10 Minnesota)					0	0	4.64	19	0	0	0	21	21	11	11	0	11	13	—	—	—	5.48	4.64
Pauley, David	R-R	6-2	215	6-17-83	0	2	5.95	14	0	0	0	20	26	14	13	4	6	10	.325	.316	.333	4.58	2.75
2-team total (39 Seattle)					5	6	3.16	53	0	0	0	74	64	27	26	6	22	44	—	—	—	5.35	2.68
Penny, Brad	R-R	6-4	230	5-24-78	11	11	5.30	31	31	0	0	182	222	117	107	24	62	74	.306	.264	.345	3.67	3.07
Perry, Ryan	R-R	6-4	200	2-13-87	2	0	5.35	36	0	0	0	37	39	25	22	1	21	24	.277	.292	.263	5.84	5.11
Porcello, Rick	R-R	6-5	200	12-27-88	14	9	4.75	31	31	0	0	182	210	103	96	18	46	104	.292	.321	.248	5.14	2.27
Purcey, David	L-L	6-4	240	4-22-82	1	2	7.23	19	0	0	0	19	21	15	15	1	20	12	.296	.276	.310	5.79	9.64
3-team total (9 Oakland, 5 Toronto)					1	2	5.61	33	0	0	0	34	33	21	21	2	27	22	—	—	—	5.88	7.22
Ruffin, Chance	R-R	6-0	185	9-8-88	0	0	4.91	2	0	0	0	4	5	2	2	2	0	3	.313	.750	.167	7.36	0.00
2-team total (13 Seattle)					1	0	4.08	15	0	0	0	18	18	8	8	4	9	18	—	—	—	9.17	4.58
Scherzer, Max	R-R	6-3	220	7-27-84	15	9	4.43	33	33	0	0	195	207	101	96	29	56	174	.272	.281	.262	8.03	2.58
Schlereth, Daniel	L-L	6-0	206	5-9-86	2	2	3.49	49	0	0	0	49	36	20	19	6	31	44	.209	.174	.244	8.08	5.69
Thomas, Brad	L-L	6-4	235	10-12-77	0	1	9.00	12	0	0	0	11	17	12	11	1	6	7	.386	.400	.375	5.73	4.91
Turner, Jacob	R-R	6-5	210	5-21-91	0	1	8.53	3	3	0	0	13	17	12	12	3	4	8	.315	.400	.241	5.68	2.84
Valverde, Jose	R-R	6-4	255	3-24-78	2	4	2.24	75	0	0	49	72	52	21	18	5	34	69	.198	.230	.158	8.59	4.23
Verlander, Justin	R-R	6-5	225	2-20-83	24	5	2.40	34	34	4	0	251	174	73	67	24	57	250	.192	.174	.215	8.96	2.04

Pitching	B-T	HT	WT	DOB	W	L	ERA	G	GS	CG	SV	IP	H	R	ER	HR	BB	SO	AVG	vLH	vRH	K/9	BB/9
Villareal, Brayan	R-R	6-0	170	5-10-87	1	1	6.75	16	0	0	0	16	21	12	12	3	10	14	.323	.375	.273	7.88	5.63
Weinhardt, Robbie	R-R	6-2	205	12-8-85	0	0	10.80	2	0	0	0	2	4	2	2	0	0	1	.444	.400	.500	5.40	0.00
Wilk, Adam	L-L	6-2	180	12-9-87	0	0	5.40	5	0	0	0	13	14	10	8	3	3	10	.259	.286	.242	6.75	2.03

Fielding

Catcher	PCT	G	PO	A	E	DP	PB
Avila	.995	133	940	73	5	14	7
Kelly	1.000	1	3	0	0	0	1
Martinez	.988	26	141	17	2	3	0
Santos	1.000	10	48	3	0	0	0

First Base	PCT	G	PO	A	E	DP
Cabrera	.991	152	1263	103	13	117
Guillen	1.000	1	2	0	0	0
Kelly	1.000	15	48	7	0	8
Martinez	1.000	6	38	10	0	4
Peralta	1.000	1	1	0	0	0
Raburn	1.000	2	6	0	0	2

Second Base	PCT	G	PO	A	E	DP
Guillen	.983	25	48	69	2	20
Raburn	.950	56	69	122	10	23
Rhymes	.978	24	31	58	2	12
Santiago	.996	75	93	143	1	28
Sizemore	.964	17	22	58	3	12
Worth	1.000	15	9	11	0	2

Third Base	PCT	G	PO	A	E	DP
Avila	.500	1	0	1	1	0
Betemit	.925	40	25	49	6	6
Inge	.964	99	76	163	9	12
Kelly	.961	45	30	64	4	7
Raburn	.909	4	3	7	1	1
Santiago	1.000	5	0	3	0	0

Worth	.944	13	5	12	1	3
Shortstop	**PCT**	**G**	**PO**	**A**	**E**	**DP**
Peralta	.988	145	218	383	7	83
Santiago	.983	27	35	80	2	15

Outfield	PCT	G	PO	A	E	DP
Boesch	.985	101	190	7	3	1
Dirks	.985	71	127	4	2	0
Jackson	.992	152	379	8	3	3
Kelly	.984	58	59	1	1	0
Ordonez	1.000	69	85	7	0	3
Raburn	.948	72	106	4	6	2
Wells	.987	59	73	3	1	2
Young	.973	40	70	3	2	2

DETROIT TIGERS

TOLEDO MUD HENS

TRIPLE-A

INTERNATIONAL LEAGUE

Batting	B-T	HT	WT	DOB	AVG	vLH	vRH	G	AB	R	H	2B	3B	HR	RBI	BB	HBP	SH	SF	SO	SB	CS	SLG	OBP
Ciriaco, Audy	R-R	6-3	195	6-16-87	.093	.118	.081	14	54	2	5	0	0	0	2	2	1	0	1	15	0	1	.093	.138
Diaz, Argenis	R-R	6-0	190	2-12-87	.279	.229	.302	98	340	45	95	17	2	0	25	41	1	0	3	65	3	5	.341	.356
Dirks, Andy	L-L	6-0	195	1-24-86	.325	.260	.355	41	157	30	51	8	1	7	24	12	0	0	2	28	12	2	.522	.368
Guez, Ben	R-R	5-11	180	1-24-87	.278	.296	.271	95	316	41	88	27	3	3	32	21	6	0	2	72	10	9	.411	.333
Guillen, Carlos	B-R	6-1	215	9-30-75	.347	.375	.320	14	49	9	17	6	0	1	9	6	0	0	0	10	1	0	.531	.418
Henry, Justin	L-R	6-3	180	4-30-85	.421	.500	.412	6	19	5	8	2	0	0	1	3	0	0	0	2	1	1	.526	.500
Inge, Brandon	R-R	5-11	190	5-19-77	.287	.395	.229	29	108	18	31	4	0	7	19	17	1	0	0	30	0	0	.519	.389
Iorg, Cale	R-R	6-2	185	9-6-85	.208	.244	.194	88	312	33	65	18	1	5	21	15	5	0	3	79	12	7	.321	.254
Kunkel, Jeff	B-R	5-11	200	3-11-83	.075	.000	.093	19	53	2	4	0	0	1	2	2	1	0	0	13	0	0	.132	.125
Martinez, Victor	B-R	6-2	210	12-23-78	.500	.500	.500	2	6	1	3	1	0	0	2	1	0	0	1	1	0	0	.667	.500
Murrian, John	R-R	6-2	215	6-15-88	.133	.158	.115	14	45	2	6	2	0	0	4	1	0	0	1	12	0	0	.178	.149
Nicolas, Cesar	R-R	6-4	230	4-17-82	.100	.143	.077	7	20	2	2	0	0	0	2	3	2	0	1	9	0	0	.100	.269
Ordonez, Magglio	R-R	6-0	215	1-28-74	.297	.600	.250	9	37	3	11	1	0	2	6	2	0	0	0	9	0	0	.486	.333
Perez, Timo	L-L	5-9	180	4-8-75	.304	.268	.319	122	473	43	144	32	0	6	50	29	2	0	4	41	16	2	.410	.344
Pounds, Bryan	R-R	6-0	195	10-4-85	.287	.258	.300	29	101	8	29	5	0	4	11	8	0	0	1	33	4	1	.455	.336
Rhymes, Will	L-R	5-9	155	4-1-83	.306	.296	.310	104	405	57	124	17	4	3	24	46	2	0	3	46	13	8	.390	.377
Salazar, Jeff	L-L	6-0	195	11-24-80	.226	.246	.216	66	217	39	49	10	1	6	30	38	1	0	1	62	15	4	.364	.342
Santos, Omir	R-R	6-0	215	4-29-81	.245	.286	.233	49	151	12	37	5	0	2	16	3	1	0	3	29	0	0	.338	.259
Scram, Deik	L-R	6-2	180	2-1-84	.267	.417	.212	21	45	4	12	5	0	1	4	13	0	0	0	10	0	0	.444	.431
Sizemore, Scott	R-R	6-0	185	1-4-85	.408	.269	.480	23	76	17	31	7	1	2	15	12	2	0	1	19	3	1	.605	.495
St. Pierre, Max	R-R	6-0	175	4-17-80	.207	.267	.178	77	232	17	48	6	0	4	25	14	3	0	4	40	0	1	.284	.257
Strieby, Ryan	R-R	6-5	235	8-9-85	.255	.248	.257	130	487	66	124	28	0	19	76	60	6	0	4	171	5	2	.429	.341
Thomas, Clete	L-R	5-11	195	11-14-83	.251	.214	.264	113	367	37	92	15	2	12	53	32	3	0	2	130	20	3	.401	.314
Thorman, Scott	L-R	6-3	225	1-6-82	.240	.202	.251	109	388	41	93	11	1	13	58	27	1	0	2	80	9	4	.374	.289
Timpner, Clay	L-L	6-2	195	5-13-83	.111	.000	.176	13	27	3	3	0	0	0	1	4	0	0	0	3	1	0	.111	.226
Wells, Casper	R-R	6-2	210	11-23-84	.370	.375	.368	7	27	4	10	2	2	2	6	3	0	0	0	8	0	0	.815	.433
Worth, Danny	R-R	6-1	185	9-30-85	.256	.255	.256	86	309	45	79	19	4	8	37	36	3	0	1	86	13	2	.421	.338

Pitching	B-T	HT	WT	DOB	W	L	ERA	G	GS	CG	SV	IP	H	R	ER	HR	BB	SO	AVG	vLH	vRH	K/9	BB/9
Alburquerque, Al	R-R	6-0	195	6-10-86	0	0	1.93	4	0	0	0	5	5	1	1	0	2	10	.263	.286	.250	19.29	3.86
Below, Duane	L-L	6-3	220	11-15-85	9	4	3.13	18	18	0	0	115	99	42	40	12	37	83	.232	.168	.254	6.50	2.90
Coke, Phil	L-L	6-1	210	7-19-82	0	0	5.06	1	1	0	0	5	8	3	3	0	2	6	.348	.333	.350	10.13	3.38
Feeney, Trevor	R-R	6-1	185	6-4-86	0	1	27.00	1	0	0	0	3	11	8	8	2	1	3	.611	.625	.600	10.13	3.38
Furbush, Charlie	L-L	6-5	215	4-11-86	5	3	3.17	10	9	2	0	54	35	21	19	7	16	61	.180	.138	.199	10.17	2.67
Gagnier, L.J.	R-R	6-2	210	2-28-85	1	3	7.44	8	5	0	0	33	44	29	27	6	11	22	.319	.407	.253	6.06	3.03
Garcia, Ramon	L-L	6-2	165	10-30-84	1	3	3.92	10	7	0	0	44	48	20	19	5	14	26	.279	.256	.287	5.36	2.89
Gonzalez, Enrique	R-R	5-10	225	7-14-82	4	6	5.48	35	3	0	13	48	52	30	29	7	21	60	.284	.304	.272	11.33	3.97
Hoffman, Matt	L-L	6-2	195	11-18-88	2	5	3.18	49	0	0	0	62	60	26	22	3	23	46	.253	.306	.224	6.64	3.32
Marte, Luis	R-R	5-11	200	8-26-86	1	0	5.40	2	0	0	0	3	3	2	2	0	4	2	.231	.500	.182	5.40	10.80
Ni, Fu-Te	L-L	6-0	170	11-14-82	6	3	3.24	34	12	0	0	111	106	46	40	10	34	93	.245	.260	.239	7.54	2.76
Oliver, Andy	L-L	6-3	210	12-3-87	8	12	4.71	26	26	0	0	147	149	83	77	15	80	143	.272	.327	.250	8.76	4.90
Oliveros, Lester	R-R	6-0	225	5-28-88	1	3	6.43	22	0	0	5	28	30	21	20	7	17	26	.316	.342	.304	8.36	5.46
2-team total (2 Rochester)					1	3	6.10	24	0	0	5	31	39	21	21	8	17	30	—	—	—	8.71	4.94
Ortega, Jose	R-R	5-11	185	10-12-88	1	3	6.30	33	0	0	0	50	61	41	35	7	27	44	.310	.312	.308	7.92	4.86
Oxspring, Chris	L-R	6-1	195	5-13-77	0	1	6.53	8	3	0	0	21	25	16	15	3	9	20	.294	.250	.333	8.71	3.92
Perry, Ryan	R-R	6-4	220	2-13-87	3	0	3.03	20	0	0	7	33	24	12	11	1	9	30	.207	.235	.195	8.27	2.48
Purcey, David	L-L	6-4	240	4-22-82	0	0	2.38	8	0	0	0	11	11	3	3	0	5	7	.262	.278	.250	5.56	3.97
Robowski, Ryan	L-L	5-11	175	2-3-88	0	0	0.00	1	0	0	0	1	1	0	0	0	1	1	.333	.000	.500	9.00	9.00
Ruffin, Chance	R-R	6-0	185	9-8-88	0	1	1.84	15	0	0	9	15	14	4	3	1	6	17	.241	.130	.314	10.43	3.68
Schlereth, Daniel	L-L	6-0	200	5-9-86	1	0	0.77	8	0	0	0	12	6	1	1	0	5	18	.154	.071	.200	13.89	3.86

Pitching	B-T	HT	WT	DOB	W	L	ERA	G	GS	CG	SV	IP	H	R	ER	HR	BB	SO	AVG	vLH	vRH	K/9	BB/9
Simons, Zach	L-R	6-3	200	5-23-85	0	1	5.11	8	0	0	1	12	10	7	7	4	10	10	.213	.250	.185	7.30	7.30
Teufel, Shawn	L-L	6-3	215	7-16-86	1	0	0.00	1	1	0	0	6	3	0	0	0	3	7	.136	.000	.200	10.50	4.50
Thomas, Brad	L-L	6-4	235	10-12-77	0	1	3.48	8	0	0	0	10	10	4	4	1	6	12	.256	.400	.207	10.45	5.23
Turner, Jacob	R-R	6-5	210	5-21-91	0	1	3.12	3	3	0	0	17	15	6	6	1	3	20	.227	.344	.118	10.38	1.56
Villareal, Brayan	R-R	6-0	170	5-10-87	3	5	5.05	17	10	0	0	66	65	40	37	6	29	40	.261	.304	.231	5.45	3.95
Weber, Thad	R-R	6-2	200	9-28-84	5	11	5.65	27	27	1	0	151	176	98	95	28	49	111	.290	.267	.308	6.60	2.91
Weinhardt, Robbie	R-R	6-2	205	12-8-85	1	4	6.49	24	0	0	1	35	36	31	25	3	14	31	.257	.254	.259	8.05	3.63
Wilk, Adam	L-L	6-2	180	12-9-87	8	6	3.24	18	18	0	0	103	105	45	37	15	14	76	.262	.222	.280	6.66	1.23
Wise, Brendan	L-R	6-2	190	1-9-86	5	2	1.90	50	0	0	1	62	57	16	13	3	28	39	.256	.316	.235	5.69	4.09

Fielding

Catcher	PCT	G	PO	A	E	DP	PB
Kunkel	1.000	19	115	9	0	1	0
Murrian	.990	14	96	4	1	0	1
Santos	.992	48	344	15	3	3	4
St. Pierre	.997	77	534	47	2	4	7

First Base	PCT	G	PO	A	E	DP
Nicolas	1.000	1	7	1	0	0
Strieby	.993	111	811	64	6	104
Thorman	.996	33	254	25	1	19

Second Base	PCT	G	PO	A	E	DP
Diaz	.964	17	36	44	3	13
Guillen	.969	11	13	18	1	3
Henry	.867	3	6	7	2	3
Iorg	.900	2	4	5	1	2
Rhymes	.992	89	181	208	3	66

	PCT	G	PO	A	E	DP
Sizemore	.959	22	34	37	3	10
Worth	.957	12	29	37	3	11

Third Base	PCT	G	PO	A	E	DP
Diaz	.958	39	32	81	5	12
Henry	1.000	1	1	1	0	1
Inge	.987	24	18	56	1	5
Iorg	1.000	1	0	1	0	0
Nicolas	1.000	2	1	1	0	0
Pounds	.938	21	16	44	4	3
Worth	.951	60	34	120	8	9

Shortstop	PCT	G	PO	A	E	DP
Ciriaco	.953	14	23	38	3	9
Diaz	.952	42	63	116	9	25
Iorg	.947	82	117	222	19	50
Worth	.947	9	12	24	2	2

Outfield	PCT	G	PO	A	E	DP
Dirks	.982	41	106	1	2	1
Guez	.983	91	164	8	3	3
Henry	1.000	1	2	0	0	0
Iorg	1.000	2	5	0	0	0
Ordonez	.929	6	13	0	1	0
Perez	.983	74	105	9	2	1
Pounds	1.000	5	4	1	0	0
Rhymes	.889	8	8	0	1	0
Salazar	.988	64	163	3	2	0
Scram	1.000	19	40	2	0	1
Thomas	.993	106	263	12	2	2
Thorman	.982	31	49	6	1	0
Timpner	1.000	11	15	2	0	0
Wells	.933	7	14	0	1	0

ERIE SEAWOLVES
EASTERN LEAGUE

DOUBLE-A

Batting	B-T	HT	WT	DOB	AVG	vLH	vRH	G	AB	R	H	2B	3B	HR	RBI	BB	HBP	SH	SF	SO	SB	CS	SLG	OBP
Alvino, Billy	R-R	5-11	200	9-2-87	.000	.000	.000	1	3	0	0	0	0	0	0	0	0	0	0	0	0	0	.000	.000
Bergolla, William	R-R	5-10	195	2-4-83	.174	.250	.158	6	23	3	4	1	0	0	2	1	0	0	1	7	0	0	.217	.200
Bertram, Michael	L-R	6-2	220	2-25-84	.258	.212	.274	82	267	33	69	20	0	5	30	33	6	0	4	75	2	4	.390	.348
Bishop, Rawley	R-R	6-3	205	11-19-85	.266	.314	.245	124	455	58	121	28	0	10	67	52	8	0	6	106	16	4	.393	.347
Calderone, Adam	L-R	6-2	200	3-17-84	.213	.240	.203	28	94	4	20	5	1	1	11	5	0	0	0	19	4	0	.319	.253
2-team total (10 New Hampshire)					.202	—	—	38	129	5	26	7	2	1	19	8	0	1	0	26	5	0	.333	.246
Ciriaco, Audy	R-R	6-3	195	6-16-87	.277	.275	.278	101	390	56	108	23	8	5	55	10	5	0	3	64	5	6	.415	.301
Douglas, Brandon	R-R	6-0	200	8-27-85	.281	.289	.277	124	499	72	140	30	3	3	46	25	5	0	2	57	22	4	.371	.320
Guez, Ben	R-R	5-11	180	1-24-87	.299	.327	.282	38	127	18	38	4	5	4	24	13	3	0	2	22	2	6	.504	.372
Guillen, Carlos	B-R	6-1	215	9-30-75	.250	.000	.250	1	4	0	1	0	0	0	0	0	0	0	0	2	0	0	.250	.250
Henry, Justin	L-R	6-3	180	4-30-85	.309	.326	.300	113	376	52	116	24	6	0	46	62	4	0	2	52	21	8	.404	.410
Holaday, Bryan	R-R	6-0	205	11-19-87	.242	.169	.267	95	330	35	80	18	0	7	42	27	4	0	4	76	6	1	.361	.304
Iorg, Cale	R-R	6-2	185	9-6-85	.167	.179	.161	26	84	8	14	1	0	2	6	4	1	0	0	28	2	1	.250	.213
Johnson, Jamie	L-R	5-9	180	4-26-87	.275	.250	.286	137	534	93	147	33	5	4	51	84	6	0	6	92	14	12	.378	.376
Kunkel, Jeff	B-R	5-11	200	3-11-83	.270	.308	.250	12	37	1	10	0	0	0	8	1	2	0	1	9	0	0	.270	.317
Maggard, Zach	R-R	5-11	181	8-2-88	.000	.000	.000	1	1	0	0	0	0	0	0	0	0	0	0	1	0	0	.000	.000
Martinez, Francisco	R-R	6-1	180	9-1-90	.282	.315	.267	91	348	63	98	14	4	7	46	19	1	0	2	80	7	8	.405	.319
Murrian, John	R-R	6-2	215	6-15-88	.240	.186	.274	42	154	15	37	6	2	5	20	3	2	0	1	42	0	0	.403	.263
Nunez, Gustavo	B-R	5-10	170	2-8-88	.215	.129	.244	34	121	13	26	3	0	2	8	5	1	0	0	27	4	3	.289	.252
Pounds, Bryan	R-R	6-0	195	10-4-85	.273	.261	.279	90	326	48	89	25	1	5	40	41	8	0	4	81	0	4	.402	.364
Retherford, C.J.	R-R	5-10	195	8-14-85	.176	.000	.188	5	17	2	3	1	0	0	2	0	0	0	0	2	0	0	.235	.176
Rockett, Michael	R-R	6-1	180	7-26-87	.261	.214	.274	39	134	17	35	4	1	2	15	4	1	0	2	29	3	1	.351	.284
Roof, Shawn	R-R	5-11	175	8-3-84	.278	.323	.244	61	151	17	42	5	1	0	13	12	3	0	0	19	6	8	.325	.343
Scram, Deik	L-R	6-2	180	2-1-84	.258	.250	.261	67	213	40	55	12	4	7	39	39	3	0	2	68	3	1	.451	.377
Wyatt, Brent	B-R	5-10	185	1-25-85	.162	.000	.190	22	68	7	11	2	0	1	8	9	0	0	0	19	2	1	.235	.260

Pitching	B-T	HT	WT	DOB	W	L	ERA	G	GS	CG	SV	IP	H	R	ER	HR	BB	SO	AVG	vLH	vRH	K/9	BB/9
Brown, Brooks	L-R	6-3	210	6-20-85	3	9	5.67	17	17	0	0	94	111	68	59	10	27	65	.298	.308	.289	6.25	2.59
Crosby, Casey	R-L	6-5	220	9-17-88	9	7	4.10	25	25	0	0	132	122	68	60	11	77	121	.253	.244	.256	8.27	5.26
Feeney, Trevor	R-R	6-1	185	6-4-86	0	1	6.43	3	3	0	0	14	19	10	10	0	5	12	.322	.314	.333	7.71	3.21
Gagnier, L.J.	R-R	6-2	210	2-28-85	4	6	6.04	16	15	1	0	82	86	57	55	13	28	72	.267	.312	.226	7.90	3.07
Garcia, Ramon	L-L	6-2	165	10-30-84	3	3	4.57	23	7	0	0	61	61	32	31	8	16	49	.263	.247	.273	7.23	2.36
Gayhart, Jared	L-R	6-3	195	10-29-86	5	0	3.38	37	2	0	1	67	58	27	25	8	26	58	.244	.226	.260	7.83	3.51
Hamilton, Cory	R-R	6-1	195	4-15-88	1	2	7.80	11	0	0	0	15	19	21	13	1	15	8	.311	.400	.250	4.80	9.00
Hoffman, Matt	L-L	6-2	195	11-18-88	0	0	54.00	1	0	0	0	0	4	2	2	0	2	0	.000	.000	.000	0.00	54.00
Little, Matt	R-R	5-11	180	3-19-88	0	0	3.38	6	0	0	0	8	9	3	3	0	6	4	.321	.167	.438	4.50	6.75
Marte, Luis	R-R	5-11	200	8-26-86	3	0	1.70	23	1	0	3	53	29	10	10	3	18	68	.158	.175	.146	11.55	3.06
Oliveros, Lester	R-R	6-0	225	5-28-88	2	0	0.53	10	0	0	0	17	11	1	1	0	4	28	.193	.179	.207	14.82	2.12
Putkonen, Luke	R-R	6-6	200	5-10-86	1	7	7.57	11	11	0	0	52	68	50	44	8	22	23	.315	.294	.336	3.96	3.78
Robowski, Ryan	L-L	5-11	175	2-3-88	0	1	7.27	6	0	0	0	9	17	8	7	2	3	7	.459	.313	.571	7.27	3.12
Ruffin, Chance	R-R	6-0	185	9-8-88	3	3	2.12	31	0	0	10	34	23	9	8	2	16	43	.190	.255	.149	11.38	4.24
Samuels, Zach	L-R	6-2	180	10-8-86	0	0	3.60	7	0	0	0	10	9	4	4	0	3	6	.243	.200	.273	5.40	2.70
Simons, Zach	L-R	6-3	200	5-23-85	0	1	5.01	15	0	0	1	23	19	13	13	6	13	17	.221	.118	.288	6.56	5.01

Pitching	B-T	HT	WT	DOB	W	L	ERA	G	GS	CG	SV	IP	H	R	ER	HR	BB	SO	AVG	vLH	vRH	K/9	BB/9
Smyly, Drew	L-L	6-3	190	6-13-89	4	3	1.18	8	7	0	0	46	32	10	6	1	15	53	.201	.246	.176	10.45	2.96
Sorensen, Mark	R-R	6-3	205	2-21-86	7	7	6.49	17	17	1	0	97	121	78	70	17	26	56	.308	.308	.307	5.20	2.41
Stohr, Tyler	L-R	6-2	210	9-19-86	0	2	4.21	20	0	0	3	26	22	12	12	3	17	27	.234	.179	.273	9.47	5.96
Turner, Jacob	R-R	6-5	210	5-21-91	3	5	3.48	17	17	0	0	114	102	47	44	9	32	90	.239	.228	.249	7.13	2.53
Voss, Jay	L-L	6-4	195	4-22-87	9	7	3.67	19	19	1	0	115	96	50	47	11	37	101	.228	.224	.230	7.88	2.89
Waite, Rob	R-R	6-3	210	1-9-87	4	4	4.56	40	1	0	2	75	87	43	38	6	29	63	.297	.303	.291	7.56	3.48
Weinhardt, Robbie	R-R	6-2	205	12-8-85	1	1	4.05	16	0	0	1	27	29	12	12	3	11	23	.290	.313	.269	7.76	3.71
Wise, Brendan	L-R	6-2	190	1-9-86	0	1	31.50	3	0	0	0	2	9	7	7	0	2	1	.692	.800	.625	4.50	9.00
Wood, Austin	L-L	6-2	195	11-2-86	5	5	3.16	50	0	0	6	63	57	25	22	5	28	61	.245	.286	.221	8.76	4.02

Fielding

Catcher	PCT	G	PO	A	E	DP	PB
Alvino	1.000	1	6	3	0	0	1
Holaday	.988	92	673	78	9	9	4
Kunkel	1.000	12	75	8	0	1	4
Murrian	.985	40	305	17	5	3	2

First Base	PCT	G	PO	A	E	DP
Bertram	.991	14	104	4	1	7
Bishop	.997	124	1100	69	3	113
Henry	.960	4	22	2	1	2
Pounds	.974	5	34	3	1	1

Second Base	PCT	G	PO	A	E	DP
Douglas	.971	114	194	302	15	72
Henry	1.000	14	28	41	0	16
Iorg	1.000	3	6	3	0	0

Nunez	.957	7	9	13	1	3
Retherford	1.000	3	5	8	0	4
Roof	.963	10	12	14	1	4
Third Base	PCT	G	PO	A	E	DP
Ciriaco	1.000	5	0	3	0	0
Henry	.875	4	1	6	1	2
Iorg	.667	3	1	3	2	1
Martinez	.909	89	81	189	27	18
Pounds	.977	38	20	66	2	6
Roof	.929	6	2	11	1	2
Shortstop	PCT	G	PO	A	E	DP
Bergolla	1.000	6	11	9	0	3
Ciriaco	.964	91	104	275	14	56
Henry	.895	5	8	9	2	2

Iorg	.935	14	13	30	3	3
Nunez	.982	26	39	71	2	21
Roof	.952	6	6	14	1	4
Outfield	PCT	G	PO	A	E	DP
Bertram	1.000	11	14	1	0	0
Calderone	.960	27	48	0	2	0
Guez	.980	36	46	3	1	0
Henry	.969	92	150	6	5	0
Iorg	.857	7	6	0	1	0
Johnson	.990	137	276	12	3	3
Pounds	.938	9	14	1	1	0
Rockett	.985	38	59	6	1	2
Roof	1.000	24	48	1	0	0
Scram	1.000	46	80	4	0	2
Wyatt	1.000	21	37	1	0	0

DETROIT TIGERS

LAKELAND FLYING TIGERS

HIGH CLASS A

FLORIDA STATE LEAGUE

Batting	B-T	HT	WT	DOB	AVG	vLH	vRH	G	AB	R	H	2B	3B	HR	RBI	BB	HBP	SH	SF	SO	SB	CS	SLG	OBP
Bergolla, William	R-R	5-10	195	2-4-83	.274	.333	.251	63	234	31	64	9	0	4	22	19	2	0	2	33	3	2	.363	.331
Brantly, Rob	L-R	6-2	205	7-14-89	.219	.147	.241	39	146	16	32	6	0	3	18	5	0	0	4	17	0	0	.322	.239
Eckerle, Brandon	R-R	5-10	175	11-2-88	.233	.200	.237	13	43	6	10	1	0	0	2	3	0	0	1	8	3	1	.256	.277
Fields, Daniel	L-R	6-1	201	1-23-91	.220	.182	.233	124	432	57	95	14	4	8	46	49	7	0	2	133	4	4	.326	.308
Garcia, Avisail	R-R	6-4	230	6-12-91	.264	.327	.247	129	488	53	129	16	6	11	56	18	6	0	3	132	14	5	.389	.297
Gaynor, Wade	R-R	6-3	225	4-19-88	.213	.198	.218	129	488	58	104	28	3	9	56	38	14	0	4	137	2	2	.338	.287
Guillen, Carlos	B-R	6-1	215	9-30-75	.200	.250	.182	4	15	1	3	2	0	0	2	1	0	0	0	2	0	0	.333	.250
Harrison, Brett	R-R	6-0	185	6-9-92	.500	.500	.500	1	2	0	1	0	0	0	0	0	0	0	0	0	0	0	.500	.500
Jones, Corey	L-R	6-0	190	9-14-87	.259	.255	.261	122	432	45	112	19	0	6	47	33	3	0	7	71	2	1	.345	.312
Kunkel, Jeff	B-R	5-11	200	3-11-83	.222	.200	.235	10	27	5	6	1	1	0	1	2	3	0	0	10	0	0	.333	.344
Lennerton, Jordan	L-L	6-2	217	2-16-86	.285	.205	.311	136	484	75	138	33	1	14	75	92	0	0	3	125	0	0	.444	.397
Loy, Brandon	R-R	6-0	190	5-3-90	.220	.000	.237	12	41	2	9	1	0	0	2	5	0	0	0	8	1	1	.244	.304
Meador, James	R-R	6-0	200	12-9-87	.000	.000	.000	1	2	0	0	0	0	0	0	0	0	0	0	1	0	0	.000	.000
Nunez, Gustavo	B-R	5-10	170	2-8-88	.304	.258	.320	62	260	46	79	10	7	3	18	25	2	0	1	40	14	10	.431	.368
Plagman, Tony	L-L	6-2	211	8-14-87	.257	.219	.270	137	526	62	135	32	4	18	97	50	12	0	8	94	0	1	.435	.331
Rockett, Michael	R-R	6-1	180	7-26-87	.233	.300	.205	52	172	18	40	9	1	0	14	5	0	0	3	44	0	1	.297	.250
Rodriguez, Julio	R-R	6-1	225	8-3-89	.283	.328	.268	66	226	20	64	11	1	1	27	10	6	0	4	28	0	0	.354	.325
Roof, Eric	R-R	6-3	185	11-15-86	.254	.344	.222	40	122	18	31	4	0	1	12	13	3	0	1	35	1	1	.311	.338
Roof, Shawn	R-R	5-10	175	8-3-84	.348	.545	.286	14	46	7	16	2	0	0	7	3	2	0	0	11	4	1	.391	.412
Soares, Ryan	R-R	6-1	195	7-10-87	.263	.417	.222	18	57	8	15	2	0	3	6	1	3	0	0	11	0	0	.456	.311
Wyatt, Brent	B-R	5-10	185	1-25-85	.290	.360	.266	94	334	59	97	19	4	3	30	62	13	0	3	57	9	2	.398	.417

Pitching	B-T	HT	WT	DOB	W	L	ERA	G	GS	CG	SV	IP	H	R	ER	HR	BB	SO	AVG	vLH	vRH	K/9	BB/9
Faulk, Kenny	L-L	6-0	210	5-27-87	2	5	2.56	48	0	0	20	53	50	19	15	3	15	67	.253	.155	.293	11.45	2.56
Feeney, Trevor	R-R	6-1	185	6-4-86	8	11	4.39	24	24	1	0	144	155	73	70	18	30	96	.285	.295	.274	6.01	1.88
Gayhart, Jared	L-R	6-3	195	10-29-86	0	0	0.00	1	0	0	0	1	2	0	0	0	3	.333	.500	.250	20.25	0.00
Gentzler, Dan	R-R	6-0	185	10-9-87	0	3	1.98	10	0	0	2	14	14	7	3	1	1	5	.255	.438	.179	3.29	0.66
Heckaman, Eric	R-R	6-2	215	9-4-86	0	0	3.68	3	0	0	0	7	8	3	3	0	3	8	.286	.308	.267	9.82	3.68
Hess, Kevan	R-R	6-2	190	3-30-88	0	0	3.00	3	0	0	0	6	5	2	2	1	5	4	.250	.000	.385	6.00	7.50
Larez, Victor	R-R	6-3	160	5-28-87	6	4	4.33	21	14	0	0	96	107	57	46	10	18	62	.276	.331	.233	5.83	1.69
Little, Matt	R-R	5-11	180	3-19-88	0	2	4.55	28	0	0	6	30	32	19	15	3	14	23	.262	.333	.200	6.98	4.25
Morrison, Michael	R-R	6-1	210	12-17-87	2	0	2.72	34	1	0	0	46	26	14	14	1	24	50	.160	.185	.144	9.71	4.66
Nelson, Cole	L-L	6-7	235	7-14-89	5	11	4.87	26	17	0	0	105	123	65	57	6	50	87	.299	.314	.294	7.43	4.27
2-team total (5 Fort Myers)					6	12	4.67	31	17	0	0	116	133	70	60	6	56	92	—	—	—	7.16	4.36
Newman, Nate	R-R	6-4	215	12-17-86	1	1	4.63	14	0	0	0	23	30	13	12	3	12	20	.319	.294	.333	7.71	4.63
Paulino, Brenny	R-R	6-4	170	2-21-93	0	2	21.94	2	2	0	0	5	9	9	9	7	.346	.357	.333	11.81	15.19
Pratt, Jordan	R-R	6-3	215	9-25-89	2	0	4.03	13	0	0	0	22	21	13	10	2	3	18	.241	.211	.265	7.25	1.21
Putkonen, Luke	R-R	6-6	200	5-10-86	2	6	5.54	18	8	1	0	65	77	46	40	10	18	52	.297	.342	.259	7.20	2.49
Robowski, Ryan	L-L	5-11	175	2-3-88	2	1	2.35	29	0	0	2	46	43	15	12	2	16	36	.256	.220	.271	5.87	3.13
Samuels, Zach	L-R	6-2	180	10-8-86	1	2	1.79	30	1	0	2	55	43	14	11	1	10	47	.218	.237	.207	7.64	1.63
Sanz, Luis	R-R	6-1	173	11-19-87	0	0	4.50	1	1	0	0	6	6	3	3	1	2	3	.273	.182	.364	4.50	3.00
Smyly, Drew	L-L	6-3	190	6-13-89	7	3	2.58	14	14	0	0	80	71	32	23	1	21	77	.241	.265	.232	8.63	2.35
Sorensen, Mark	R-R	6-3	205	2-21-86	3	4	4.44	9	9	1	0	49	64	37	24	5	9	27	.311	.409	.198	4.99	1.66

Pitching	B-T	HT	WT	DOB	W	L	ERA	G	GS	CG	SV	IP	H	R	ER	HR	BB	SO	AVG	vLH	vRH	K/9	BB/9
Stohr, Tyler	L-R	6-2	210	9-19-86	1	0	3.45	24	0	0	0	31	24	12	12	3	8	23	.214	.259	.167	6.61	2.30
Stroud, Brian	R-R	6-4	215	10-18-88	0	3	8.27	3	3	0	0	16	26	16	15	4	3	13	.361	.467	.286	7.16	1.65
Teufel, Shawn	L-L	6-3	215	7-16-86	4	5	3.78	22	10	1	0	81	74	37	34	10	26	46	.242	.194	.256	5.11	2.89
Voss, Jay	L-L	6-4	195	4-22-87	3	0	3.21	8	6	0	0	34	33	13	12	0	7	30	.256	.256	.256	8.02	1.87
Wesson, Jared	L-L	6-5	190	1-30-86	15	10	4.27	27	27	1	0	148	154	73	70	10	66	96	.273	.205	.298	5.85	4.02
White, Tyler	R-R	6-2	197	8-8-89	0	1	1.05	12	1	0	0	26	16	10	3	0	11	21	.180	.242	.143	7.36	3.86

Fielding

Catcher	PCT	G	PO	A	E	DP	PB
Brantly	.987	29	201	34	3	3	1
Kunkel	1.000	8	53	3	0	0	0
Rodriguez	.972	66	442	45	14	3	7
Roof	.992	37	226	23	2	0	11

First Base	PCT	G	PO	A	E	DP
Lennerton	.994	74	636	41	4	53
Plagman	.988	64	593	39	8	53

Second Base	PCT	G	PO	A	E	DP
Bergolla	1.000	7	12	21	0	4
Guillen	1.000	2	2	4	0	1
Jones	.970	121	197	320	16	74
Nunez	1.000	1	3	8	0	1

Roof	1.000	1	2	2	0	0
Roof	1.000	2	4	7	0	1
Soares	1.000	4	6	13	0	4
Wyatt	1.000	2	1	6	0	0

Third Base	PCT	G	PO	A	E	DP
Bergolla	.900	5	1	8	1	2
Gaynor	.953	128	104	257	18	25
Harrison	.000	1	0	0	0	0
Roof	1.000	3	1	5	0	0
Soares	1.000	3	0	4	0	0

Shortstop	PCT	G	PO	A	E	DP
Bergolla	.956	51	67	150	10	25
Loy	.958	12	16	30	2	8

Nunez	.975	61	102	176	7	34
Roof	1.000	1	1	5	0	1
Roof	.923	5	2	10	1	1
Soares	.955	11	16	26	2	7
Wyatt	.714	1	2	3	2	0

Outfield	PCT	G	PO	A	E	DP
Eckerle	1.000	13	14	0	0	0
Fields	.993	124	276	6	2	1
Garcia	.968	129	232	8	8	1
Meador	1.000	1	3	2	0	0
Plagman	1.000	10	22	1	0	0
Rockett	.991	51	105	6	1	1
Roof	1.000	3	6	0	0	0
Wyatt	.989	91	161	17	2	5

WEST MICHIGAN WHITECAPS

LOW CLASS A

MIDWEST LEAGUE

Batting	B-T	HT	WT	DOB	AVG	vLH	vRH	G	AB	R	H	2B	3B	HR	RBI	BB	HBP	SH	SF	SO	SB	CS	SLG	OBP
Ashenbrenner, Josh	L-R	6-0	190	8-29-87	.295	.400	.275	21	61	10	18	3	0	0	6	7	1	0	0	14	0	0	.344	.377
Azcona, Javier	R-R	6-0	184	9-28-91	.222	.250	.200	3	9	2	2	1	0	1	5	1	0	0	0	3	0	0	.667	.300
Brantly, Rob	L-R	6-2	205	7-14-89	.303	.262	.315	75	284	42	86	16	1	7	44	24	5	0	1	39	2	2	.440	.366
Casali, Curt	R-R	6-2	230	11-9-88	.227	.263	.214	25	75	10	17	7	0	2	14	13	1	0	1	9	0	0	.400	.344
Castellanos, Nick	R-R	6-4	195	3-4-92	.312	.286	.320	135	507	65	158	36	3	7	76	45	3	0	6	130	3	2	.436	.367
Castillo, Luis	R-R	5-11	160	5-15-89	.267	.240	.277	122	468	46	125	26	2	3	38	40	2	0	6	69	5	8	.350	.324
Enos, Ryan	L-L	5-10	185	12-19-87	.204	.250	.196	16	54	5	11	4	0	0	8	5	1	0	1	5	2	1	.278	.279
Gomez, Edwin	B-R	6-3	175	8-26-91	.182	.200	.177	22	77	2	14	3	1	0	5	3	1	0	0	30	0	2	.247	.222
Gulliver, Jimmy	L-R	5-11	175	6-6-86	.157	.000	.167	20	51	5	8	0	0	1	3	3	1	0	0	12	2	1	.216	.218
Hamme, Ryan	L-R	6-3	210	3-13-87	.268	.262	.269	70	254	37	68	15	1	3	24	23	2	0	1	49	2	0	.370	.332
Jones, Clay	R-R	6-1	220	11-11-87	.308	.318	.304	46	156	29	48	11	0	2	21	25	1	0	2	28	0	0	.417	.402
Krizan, Jason	L-R	6-0	180	6-28-89	.239	.237	.240	53	184	13	44	4	1	3	19	13	1	0	0	30	1	1	.321	.293
Machado, Dixon	R-R	6-0	140	2-22-92	.235	.223	.239	124	429	47	101	1	2	0	28	46	4	0	2	77	25	5	.247	.314
McCann, James	R-R	6-2	210	6-13-90	.059	.250	.033	9	34	0	2	1	0	0	1	2	1	0	1	12	0	0	.088	.132
Meador, James	R-R	6-0	200	12-9-87	.000	.000	.000	1	4	0	0	0	0	0	0	0	0	0	0	2	0	0	.000	.000
Moya, Steven	L-R	6-6	220	9-8-91	.204	.193	.208	86	323	38	66	10	1	13	39	12	1	0	1	127	1	1	.362	.234
Nowlin, Billy	R-R	6-1	210	12-16-86	.243	.278	.224	46	152	21	37	4	0	6	17	14	5	0	2	33	0	1	.388	.324
Perez, Hernan	R-R	6-0	160	3-26-91	.258	.254	.260	129	503	69	130	23	3	8	42	38	6	0	8	87	23	6	.364	.314
Polk, P.J.	R-R	5-9	170	12-12-88	.169	.290	.091	40	124	15	21	0	0	0	5	12	2	0	0	28	2	2	.169	.254
Robbins, James	L-L	6-0	225	9-26-90	.251	.250	.251	129	490	55	123	26	1	16	65	16	7	0	2	158	5	0	.406	.283
Rowland, Jeff	L-L	5-10	185	4-1-88	.243	.269	.236	83	255	31	62	11	3	5	19	41	4	0	0	83	7	2	.369	.357
Sanz, Luis	R-R	5-10	165	2-23-91	.294	.425	.228	41	119	6	35	5	0	0	18	8	2	0	1	19	2	1	.336	.346
Soares, Ryan	R-R	6-1	195	7-10-87	.000	.000	.000	2	6	1	0	0	0	0	0	0	0	0	0	0	0	0	.000	.143

Pitching	B-T	HT	WT	DOB	W	L	ERA	G	GS	CG	SV	IP	H	R	ER	HR	BB	SO	AVG	vLH	vRH	K/9	BB/9
Bennett, Daniel	B-R	6-4	220	12-28-88	2	1	0.52	13	0	0	3	17	8	1	1	1	1	17	.140	.120	.156	8.83	0.52
Burgos, Alex	L-L	5-11	192	12-1-90	6	5	2.19	16	16	0	0	95	63	28	23	4	33	89	.189	.152	.207	8.46	3.14
Carreno, Josue	R-R	6-1	170	6-26-91	7	10	4.55	24	23	1	1	125	132	73	63	7	41	115	.270	.273	.269	8.30	2.96
Clark, Tyler	B-R	6-2	185	1-4-89	0	0	2.89	6	0	0	0	9	9	3	3	1	4	6	.250	.313	.200	5.79	3.86
Cooper, Patrick	R-R	6-3	204	8-25-89	5	6	4.00	33	3	0	1	72	58	33	32	3	27	67	.226	.244	.210	8.38	3.38
Crnkovich, Steve	R-R	6-4	192	10-8-87	1	0	6.52	8	0	0	0	10	9	7	7	0	7	7	.250	.333	.208	6.52	6.52
Cruz, Antonio	L-L	5-11	200	10-7-91	2	6	3.11	22	10	0	1	75	68	29	26	5	28	58	.244	.200	.270	6.93	3.35
2-team total (11 Kane County)					3	6	2.73	33	11	0	1	105	91	37	32	7	41	97	—	—	—	8.29	3.50
Eichhorn, Kevin	R-R	6-0	175	2-6-90	11	5	3.61	25	25	2	0	152	148	71	61	10	33	109	.256	.247	.264	6.45	1.95
Ferrell, Jeff	R-R	6-3	185	11-23-90	2	1	3.49	6	6	0	0	28	28	13	11	3	12	24	.267	.271	.263	7.62	3.81
Flynn, Brian	L-L	6-8	239	4-19-90	7	2	3.46	13	13	0	0	68	58	28	26	3	23	57	.235	.259	.223	7.58	3.06
Gentzler, Dan	R-R	6-0	185	10-9-87	1	3	4.32	10	0	0	0	17	24	10	8	1	3	14	.329	.429	.237	7.56	1.62
Hess, Kevan	R-R	6-2	190	3-30-88	1	1	7.85	11	0	0	0	18	19	16	16	0	13	11	.275	.355	.211	5.40	6.38
Hoch, Logan	L-L	6-2	185	5-5-87	0	1	5.13	15	0	0	1	26	27	16	15	3	13	25	.270	.211	.306	8.54	4.44
Larez, Victor	R-R	6-3	160	5-28-87	3	2	5.28	5	5	0	0	29	32	17	17	3	5	15	.276	.322	.228	4.66	1.55
Lebron, Ramon	R-R	6-1	180	2-1-89	3	1	1.83	22	0	0	1	34	18	10	7	1	19	44	.161	.207	.111	11.53	4.98
Mendoza, Clemente	R-R	6-0	170	7-24-90	1	3	7.81	19	0	0	0	28	36	26	24	3	21	23	.327	.306	.338	7.48	6.83
Mercedes, Melvin	R-R	6-3	190	11-2-90	0	0	10.80	2	0	0	0	2	3	2	2	0	1	1	.375	.500	.333	5.40	5.40
Mowry, Tim	R-R	6-5	226	9-28-87	0	0	9.64	3	1	0	0	5	7	6	5	0	2	3	.368	.400	.333	5.79	3.86
Newman, Nate	R-R	6-4	215	12-17-86	1	0	3.24	17	0	0	3	25	25	16	9	2	13	24	.258	.216	.283	8.64	4.68
Rondon, Bruce	R-R	6-2	190	12-9-90	2	2	2.03	41	0	0	19	40	22	11	9	0	34	61	.164	.175	.156	13.73	7.65
Ryan, Kyle	L-L	6-5	180	9-25-91	6	10	3.15	24	24	0	0	137	145	56	48	3	30	99	.283	.242	.296	6.50	1.97

Pitching	B-T	HT	WT	DOB	W	L	ERA	G	GS	CG	SV	IP	H	R	ER	HR	BB	SO	AVG	vLH	vRH	K/9	BB/9
Smith, Brennan	R-R	6-3	200	8-4-89	1	3	4.99	9	7	1	0	40	47	29	22	4	19	27	.294	.312	.277	6.13	4.31
Stroud, Brian	R-R	6-4	215	10-18-88	0	2	4.95	4	4	0	0	20	27	14	11	3	6	10	.318	.341	.293	4.50	2.70
Todd, Jade	R-L	6-2	190	3-22-90	2	1	3.99	17	0	0	2	29	28	14	13	1	8	25	.252	.279	.235	7.67	2.45
Torrealba, Michael	R-R	5-11	150	11-19-89	5	3	2.22	43	1	0	9	81	68	26	20	5	33	89	.230	.244	.218	9.89	3.67
Woolley, Ryan	R-R	6-1	190	2-11-88	1	0	4.44	11	0	0	2	24	24	13	12	5	4	26	.250	.280	.217	9.62	1.48
Zumaya, Richard	R-R	6-0	180	11-10-89	0	1	6.75	5	1	0	0	8	7	6	6	2	9	8	.250	.308	.200	9.00	10.13

Fielding

Catcher	PCT	G	PO	A	E	DP	PB
Brantly	.983	70	507	73	10	8	13
Casali	.995	25	175	18	1	0	3
McCann	.987	9	70	6	1	1	0
Sanz	.993	40	268	35	2	1	2

First Base	PCT	G	PO	A	E	DP
Jones	.980	12	89	8	2	8
Nowlin	1.000	2	15	3	0	2
Robbins	.994	128	1189	63	8	104

Second Base	PCT	G	PO	A	E	DP
Ashenbrenner	.967	14	23	35	2	6

Azcona	.889	2	5	3	1	2
Gulliver	.942	15	20	29	3	7
Perez	.959	112	159	280	19	55

Third Base	PCT	G	PO	A	E	DP
Ashenbrenner	1.000	5	1	10	0	0
Azcona	1.000	1	0	3	0	0
Castellanos	.917	129	63	191	23	18
Gulliver	.900	4	1	8	1	0
Nowlin	1.000	2	0	2	0	0
Soares	1.000	2	0	1	0	0

Shortstop	PCT	G	PO	A	E	DP
Machado	.963	122	197	371	22	75
Perez	.937	17	30	44	5	11

Outfield	PCT	G	PO	A	E	DP
Castillo	.983	119	278	7	5	4
Enos	.926	13	22	3	2	1
Gomez	.949	22	36	1	2	1
Hamme	.938	31	44	1	3	0
Krizan	.978	50	86	4	2	0
Moya	.947	77	141	3	8	1
Polk	.959	36	45	2	2	1
Rowland	.992	77	125	4	1	0

CONNECTICUT TIGERS   SHORT-SEASON

NEW YORK-PENN LEAGUE

Batting	B-T	HT	WT	DOB	AVG	vLH	vRH	G	AB	R	H	2B	3B	HR	RBI	BB	HBP	SH	SF	SO	SB	CS	SLG	OBP
Azcona, Javier	R-R	6-0	184	9-28-91	.232	.286	.212	52	181	20	42	11	2	5	25	8	4	0	1	60	5	3	.398	.278
Casali, Curt	R-R	6-2	230	11-9-88	.278	.385	.217	10	36	7	10	2	0	1	2	6	2	0	0	5	0	0	.417	.409
Collins, Tyler	L-L	5-11	205	6-6-90	.313	.390	.287	42	163	28	51	10	1	8	31	10	3	0	2	17	6	1	.534	.360
Corcino, Edgar	B-R	6-2	190	6-7-92	.278	.750	.143	6	18	1	5	1	0	0	1	1	0	0	0	7	0	0	.333	.316
Gomez, Edwin	B-R	6-3	175	8-26-91	.286	.294	.280	15	42	8	12	1	0	1	1	8	2	0	0	11	3	0	.381	.423
Green, Dean	L-R	6-4	255	6-30-89	.341	.329	.347	65	246	33	84	19	2	7	44	18	5	0	2	35	1	0	.520	.395
Holm, Jeff	L-L	6-2	210	10-17-88	.236	.246	.230	58	208	29	49	8	1	5	25	25	0	0	2	34	11	2	.356	.315
Kaline, Colin	B-R	5-10	150	4-26-89	.222	.182	.247	39	117	10	26	5	0	0	6	19	0	0	1	23	3	2	.265	.328
King, Jason	B-R	6-0	216	6-14-89	.251	.250	.252	53	195	27	49	6	4	6	31	20	8	0	3	39	6	3	.415	.341
Leyland, Patrick	R-R	6-2	200	10-11-91	.220	.214	.224	35	118	9	26	4	0	1	12	8	2	0	1	10	1	0	.280	.279
Maggard, Zach	R-R	5-11	181	8-2-88	.281	.324	.267	36	135	12	38	14	0	2	19	1	3	0	0	42	1	0	.430	.302
McClendon, Bo	R-R	5-10	215	10-4-87	.176	.111	.250	8	17	2	3	0	0	0	2	5	0	0	0	5	0	0	.176	.364
Moreno, Alexander	R-R	6-4	185	4-1-90	.083	.100	.000	6	12	2	1	0	0	0	1	1	0	0	0	7	0	0	.083	.214
Nunez, Alexander	R-R	5-11	172	5-4-90	.000	.000	.000	3	11	0	0	0	0	0	0	0	0	0	0	3	0	0	.000	.000
Ogden, Jonathan	R-R	5-10	175	7-15-88	.091	.000	.125	5	11	1	1	0	0	0	0	2	2	0	0	6	0	0	.091	.333
Perry, Matt	L-R	6-2	190	7-17-87	.260	.250	.264	43	131	16	34	7	0	1	14	14	0	0	0	25	1	1	.336	.331
Polk, P.J.	R-R	5-9	170	12-12-88	.172	.214	.153	32	87	15	15	1	0	1	10	8	2	0	1	21	4	2	.218	.255
Reina, Adolfo	R-R	6-0	210	1-22-90	.000	.000	.000	3	8	1	0	0	0	0	0	1	0	0	0	2	0	0	.000	.111
Rijo, Samir	B-R	6-1	211	6-26-90	.241	.238	.241	25	79	7	19	5	1	0	9	6	0	0	2	18	0	3	.329	.287
Sanz, Luis	R-R	5-10	165	2-23-91	.000	.000	.000	3	10	2	0	0	0	0	0	1	0	0	0	1	0	0	.000	.091
Smith, Les	L-R	6-1	190	12-24-89	.143	.000	.182	25	56	5	8	2	0	1	6	5	0	0	1	16	0	3	.232	.210
Suarez, Eugenio	B-R	5-11	155	7-18-91	.250	.254	.248	58	204	37	51	11	5	5	24	18	4	0	0	43	9	5	.426	.323
Westlake, Aaron	L-R	6-4	235	12-27-88	.264	.290	.253	27	106	14	28	4	1	2	15	10	0	0	0	23	1	0	.377	.328
Wright, Chad	L-R	5-10	190	7-27-89	.261	.283	.254	69	241	37	63	9	0	0	15	41	5	0	1	28	14	7	.299	.378

Pitching	B-T	HT	WT	DOB	W	L	ERA	G	GS	CG	SV	IP	H	R	ER	HR	BB	SO	AVG	vLH	vRH	K/9	BB/9
Avila, Nick	R-R	6-2	220	8-29-88	3	2	4.55	15	0	0	0	28	21	16	14	2	7	18	.210	.231	.197	5.86	2.28
Barfield, Jeff	R-R	6-0	205	2-11-88	2	2	4.11	21	1	0	5	35	35	20	16	1	11	28	.254	.283	.235	7.20	2.83
Barrett, Tyler	R-L	6-2	210	6-23-89	1	1	4.95	6	6	0	0	20	24	16	11	2	10	13	.296	.400	.250	5.85	4.50
Bennett, Daniel	B-R	6-4	220	12-28-88	0	0	1.17	14	0	0	8	15	12	2	2	0	5	22	.226	.235	.222	12.91	2.93
Castillo, Alejandro	L-L	5-10	170	3-2-90	0	0	0.00	1	0	0	0	0	0	0	0	0	3	0	.000	.000	.000	0.00	81.00
Celis, Fernando	R-R	6-1	165	3-27-89	1	4	2.57	18	0	0	0	28	26	9	8	2	9	20	.241	.119	.318	6.43	2.89
Collier, Tommy	R-R	6-2	205	12-3-89	4	1	1.85	7	7	0	0	39	28	8	8	1	10	35	.203	.196	.207	8.08	2.31
Crouse, Matt	L-L	6-4	185	7-1-90	5	1	3.22	13	13	0	0	64	68	25	23	4	13	53	.269	.217	.288	7.41	1.82
Gagnier, Drew	R-R	6-4	225	9-21-88	0	2	9.72	8	0	0	0	8	13	9	9	0	10	4	.371	.471	.278	4.32	10.80
Green, Scott	R-R	6-7	240	8-10-85	1	1	5.79	9	0	0	0	9	11	9	6	0	7	8	.289	.154	.360	6.75	5.79
Guichardo, Rayni	L-L	6-1	165	8-13-91	1	2	5.34	18	1	0	1	29	38	19	17	4	8	21	.317	.372	.286	6.59	2.51
Hess, Kevan	R-R	6-2	190	3-30-88	1	0	0.00	4	0	0	1	6	2	0	0	0	4	4	.105	.000	.222	6.00	6.00
Knudson, Guido	R-R	6-1	185	8-5-89	0	1	8.10	5	0	0	0	3	4	4	3	0	3	1	.250	.333	.200	2.70	8.10
Mendoza, Clemente	R-R	6-0	170	7-24-90	1	1	2.70	7	1	0	0	13	6	6	4	0	7	13	.133	.040	.250	8.78	4.73
Mercedes, Melvin	R-R	6-3	190	11-2-90	3	1	2.67	21	0	0	3	34	32	17	10	0	16	21	.246	.313	.207	5.61	4.28
Palacios, Wilsen	R-R	6-3	180	12-15-89	5	5	3.08	14	14	3	0	79	63	36	27	7	24	48	.216	.234	.202	5.47	2.73
Perez, Pedro	R-R	6-4	170	5-3-88	1	2	4.02	18	2	0	0	31	27	22	14	2	21	32	.229	.241	.219	9.19	6.03
Robertson, Montreal	R-R	6-4	220	6-19-90	0	0	0.00	2	0	0	1	4	3	0	0	0	2	0	.214	.250	.200	0.00	4.91
Sanz, Luis	R-R	6-1	173	11-19-87	6	4	2.81	14	14	3	0	83	67	36	26	4	23	76	.214	.162	.254	8.21	2.48
Smith, Brennan	R-R	6-3	200	8-4-89	4	3	1.53	14	14	2	0	94	76	21	16	3	19	66	.218	.214	.220	6.32	1.82
Woolley, Ryan	R-R	6-1	190	2-11-88	0	2	2.38	11	1	0	0	23	23	10	6	0	5	18	.253	.278	.236	7.15	1.99

Fielding

Catcher

Catcher	PCT	G	PO	A	E	DP	PB
Casali	1.000	8	56	8	0	1	0
Leyland	.967	34	197	11	7	3	12
Maggard	.991	29	202	18	2	1	8
Reina	1.000	3	26	3	0	0	2
Sanz	1.000	3	21	0	0	0	0

First Base

First Base	PCT	G	PO	A	E	DP
Green	.992	29	239	18	2	16
Holm	.988	20	154	16	2	12
Perry	1.000	7	54	4	0	2
Westlake	.981	21	196	14	4	10

Second Base

Second Base	PCT	G	PO	A	E	DP
Azcona	.944	38	56	112	10	16
Kaline	.954	39	47	99	7	11
Nunez	.867	3	8	5	2	1

Third Base

Third Base	PCT	G	PO	A	E	DP
Azcona	.667	2	1	1	1	0
Corcino	.824	6	3	11	3	1
King	.912	44	29	74	10	5
Perry	.939	27	15	47	4	4

Shortstop

Shortstop	PCT	G	PO	A	E	DP
Azcona	.906	15	22	36	6	4

	PCT	G	PO	A	E	DP
Ogden	.875	5	8	6	2	3
Suarez	.927	58	90	150	19	21

Outfield

Outfield	PCT	G	PO	A	E	DP
Collins	.963	40	75	4	3	3
Gomez	1.000	14	21	1	0	0
Holm	.986	40	66	2	1	0
McClendon	1.000	6	7	0	0	0
Moreno	1.000	2	1	0	0	0
Polk	.923	26	46	2	4	2
Rijo	.968	25	29	1	1	1
Smith	.946	21	34	1	2	1
Wright	1.000	69	190	2	0	2

GCL TIGERS   *ROOKIE*

GULF COAST LEAGUE

Batting	B-T	HT	WT	DOB	AVG	vLH	vRH	G	AB	R	H	2B	3B	HR	RBI	BB	HBP	SH	SF	SO	SB	CS	SLG	OBP
Aguasvivas, Juaner	R-R	6-4	248	9-15-89	.315	.310	.316	48	178	26	56	9	3	10	37	12	4	0	4	47	3	0	.567	.364
Collins, Tyler	L-L	5-11	205	6-6-90	.333	.000	.333	1	3	2	1	1	0	0	1	2	0	0	0	0	0	0	.667	.600
Corcino, Edgar	B-R	6-2	190	6-7-92	.201	.273	.177	51	174	23	35	9	0	5	15	20	4	0	1	51	3	2	.339	.296
Cortez, Luis	R-R	6-0	155	1-8-92	.275	.130	.316	28	102	19	28	9	1	1	6	7	3	0	0	21	7	2	.412	.339
De Los Santos, Carlos	B-R	6-0	177	11-1-90	.192	.178	.197	46	167	16	32	6	3	0	11	3	2	0	1	36	4	1	.263	.214
Eckerle, Brandon	R-R	5-10	175	11-2-88	.355	.256	.386	45	166	34	59	5	0	0	12	28	4	0	0	16	18	4	.386	.460
Gibson, Tyler	L-R	6-2	190	6-17-93	.143	.333	.091	4	14	0	2	0	0	0	0	0	0	0	0	9	0	0	.143	.143
Harrison, Brett	R-R	6-0	185	6-9-92	.238	.333	.200	6	21	1	5	0	0	0	1	2	0	0	1	4	0	0	.238	.292
Hudgins, Derrick	R-R	5-11	165	3-10-91	.185	.267	.154	32	108	9	20	1	0	0	8	5	1	0	1	29	5	1	.194	.226
Jones, Clay	R-R	6-1	220	11-11-87	.182	.000	.222	3	11	0	2	0	0	0	1	1	0	0	0	1	0	0	.182	.250
Loy, Brandon	R-R	6-0	190	5-3-90	.333	.000	.333	5	15	3	5	1	0	0	3	4	0	0	0	2	0	0	.400	.474
Matz, Chretien	R-R	6-0	195	9-18-89	.242	.467	.176	22	66	6	16	2	0	0	2	2	2	0	0	18	1	1	.273	.286
Maxfield, Zach	R-R	6-0	200	2-28-88	.272	.059	.328	28	81	11	22	5	0	4	15	13	6	0	0	19	1	2	.481	.410
McCann, James	B-R	6-2	210	6-13-90	.357	.000	.357	5	14	1	5	1	0	1	6	1	1	0	0	1	0	0	.643	.438
Moreno, Alexander	R-R	6-4	185	4-1-90	.214	.375	.150	9	28	4	6	2	1	0	1	3	0	0	0	7	2	0	.357	.290
Purroy, Gabriel	R-R	5-9	160	4-16-92	.266	.357	.246	28	79	12	21	5	0	2	14	9	2	0	1	11	1	0	.405	.352
Reina, Adolfo	R-R	6-0	210	1-22-90	.211	.167	.222	28	90	10	19	4	0	5	13	6	0	0	1	19	1	0	.422	.258
Salgado, Ismael	R-R	6-1	165	1-11-93	.144	.100	.160	38	111	14	16	4	0	0	6	1	2	0	0	20	2	1	.180	.167
Santos, Omir	R-R	6-0	215	4-29-81	.000	.000	.000	2	2	0	0	0	0	0	0	0	0	0	0	1	0	0	.000	.333
Smith, Pat	L-L	6-0	170	10-11-91	.232	.250	.226	54	207	17	48	8	1	6	26	13	1	0	1	47	5	4	.367	.279
Soares, Ryan	R-R	6-1	195	7-10-87	.118	.000	.143	6	17	2	2	1	0	1	2	1	0	0	0	6	0	0	.353	.167
Suarez, Eugenio	B-R	5-11	155	7-18-91	.341	.250	.375	12	44	11	15	7	0	2	9	3	2	0	0	4	2	0	.636	.408
Thigpen, Wes	R-R	6-0	200	6-20-89	.250	.267	.242	31	92	13	23	4	0	2	7	6	1	0	0	7	0	0	.359	.303
Vasquez, Danry	L-R	6-3	169	1-8-94	.272	.275	.271	54	206	25	56	8	1	2	30	7	4	0	2	34	3	2	.350	.306
Westlake, Aaron	L-R	6-4	235	12-27-88	.167	.333	.083	5	18	2	3	1	0	1	4	2	0	0	0	6	0	0	.389	.250

Pitching	B-T	HT	WT	DOB	W	L	ERA	G	GS	CG	SV	IP	H	R	ER	HR	BB	SO	AVG	vLH	vRH	K/9	BB/9
Briceno, Endrys	R-R	6-4	150	2-7-92	2	5	5.34	12	12	0	0	59	72	44	35	2	19	49	.310	.300	.317	7.47	2.90
Castillo, Alejandro	L-L	5-10	170	3-2-90	0	1	2.51	18	0	0	1	29	18	15	8	2	9	31	.168	.080	.195	9.73	2.83
Clark, Tyler	B-R	6-2	185	1-4-89	0	0	3.71	13	0	0	0	17	15	10	7	1	13	25	.238	.200	.256	13.24	6.88
De La Rosa, Edgar	R-R	6-6	215	11-20-90	2	4	3.19	12	12	0	0	68	70	30	24	5	18	50	.277	.379	.246	6.65	2.39
Del Orbe, Emmanuel	R-R	6-3	188	12-20-90	3	0	5.18	15	0	0	0	24	37	20	14	1	10	19	.349	.294	.375	7.03	3.70
Duffey, Jack	L-L	6-2	190	4-18-92	5	3	3.81	11	11	0	0	54	54	26	23	2	17	42	.260	.229	.275	6.96	2.82
Green, Scott	R-R	6-7	240	8-10-85	0	2	4.66	9	0	0	1	10	11	9	5	3	5	6	.268	.105	.409	5.59	4.66
Heckaman, Eric	R-R	6-2	215	5-14-88	1	2	1.14	20	0	0	1	24	16	6	3	0	13	25	.198	.094	.265	9.51	4.94
Kickham, Dan	R-R	6-4	205	12-12-88	2	0	3.68	13	0	0	0	15	8	7	6	1	10	11	.167	.143	.176	6.75	6.14
Knudson, Guido	R-R	6-1	185	8-5-89	1	1	2.74	13	0	0	0	23	18	10	7	0	4	22	.225	.333	.170	8.61	1.57
Lo, Hua-Wei	L-L	5-11	165	12-1-90	0	0	0.00	2	1	0	1	6	4	0	0	0	1	9	.190	.167	.200	13.50	1.50
Matyas, Scott	R-R	6-4	220	1-18-88	0	1	8.44	4	0	0	0	5	5	5	5	1	2	6	.250	.143	.308	10.13	3.38
Paulino, Brenny	R-R	6-4	170	2-21-93	4	3	2.36	11	8	2	0	46	34	19	12	1	18	45	.202	.164	.224	8.87	3.55
Robertson, Montreal	R-R	6-4	220	6-19-90	3	2	2.73	24	0	0	9	26	29	10	8	0	14	22	.290	.325	.267	7.52	4.78
Sabol, Jake	R-R	6-5	220	8-11-88	3	3	3.43	13	10	0	0	66	63	28	25	3	11	39	.251	.250	.251	5.35	1.51
Satterwhite, Cody	R-R	6-4	205	1-27-87	0	0	3.60	8	0	0	1	10	13	7	4	0	2	10	.325	.333	.321	9.00	1.80
Stroud, Brian	R-R	6-4	215	10-18-88	1	4	2.76	6	6	0	0	33	27	16	10	5	6	29	.221	.250	.200	7.99	1.65
Todd, Jade	R-L	6-2	190	3-22-90	2	0	1.08	9	0	0	1	8	5	1	1	0	1	5	.179	.222	.158	5.40	1.08
White, Tyler	R-R	6-2	197	8-8-89	0	0	1.80	4	0	0	0	5	0	2	1	0	2	6	.000	.000	.000	10.80	3.60

Fielding

Catcher

Catcher	PCT	G	PO	A	E	DP	PB
McCann	.967	5	23	6	1	0	0
Purroy	.988	21	144	14	2	2	4
Reina	.989	22	157	18	2	2	5
Salgado	1.000	1	7	0	0	0	0
Santos	1.000	1	2	0	0	0	0
Thigpen	.985	22	122	8	2	0	6

First Base

First Base	PCT	G	PO	A	E	DP
Aguasvivas	.988	46	399	24	5	37
Jones	1.000	2	13	2	0	0
Maxfield	.990	13	91	7	1	5
Westlake	1.000	2	17	3	0	1

Second Base

Second Base	PCT	G	PO	A	E	DP
Corcino	1.000	2	0	3	0	0
Cortez	.000	1	0	0	0	0

	PCT	G	PO	A	E	DP
De Los Santos	.977	27	49	80	3	14
Hudgins	.964	31	47	59	4	15
Maxfield	1.000	1	0	5	0	0
Reina	1.000	1	0	4	0	1
Soares	1.000	6	16	12	0	3

Third Base

Third Base	PCT	G	PO	A	E	DP
Corcino	.899	50	32	92	14	10
Cortez	.600	2	0	3	2	0

	PCT	G	PO	A	E	DP			PCT	G	PO	A	E	DP			PCT	G	PO	A	E	DP
Harrison	.929	5	3	10	1	0		Loy	.895	5	4	13	2	2		Gibson	1.000	4	8	1	0	0
Maxfield	.800	4	0	4	1	0		Suarez	.904	12	19	28	5	6		Matz	1.000	14	17	1	0	0
Reina	.750	2	1	2	1	0		Thigpen	1.000	1	3	4	0	1		Moreno	1.000	4	6	0	0	0
Shortstop	**PCT**	**G**	**PO**	**A**	**E**	**DP**		**Outfield**	**PCT**	**G**	**PO**	**A**	**E**	**DP**		Salgado	.952	28	38	2	2	2
Cortez	.933	25	38	59	7	12		De Los Santos	1.000	1	1	0	0	0		Smith	.977	51	128	2	3	1
De Los Santos	.968	18	35	57	3	10		Eckerle	1.000	39	66	5	0	1		Vasquez	.987	46	72	6	1	2

DSL TIGERS ROOKIE

DOMINICAN SUMMER LEAGUE

Batting	B-T	HT	WT	DOB	AVG	vLH	vRH	G	AB	R	H	2B	3B	HR	RBI	BB	HBP	SH	SF	SO	SB	CS	SLG	OBP
Acevedo, Sandy	L-L	6-0	170	12-25-92	.248	.273	.241	51	149	16	37	3	2	2	17	13	6	0	0	42	11	5	.336	.333
Contreras, Francisco	R-R	6-1	180	12-3-92	.193	.244	.174	54	166	18	32	8	4	1	16	11	6	0	1	34	7	1	.307	.266
Crafort, Samuel	B-R	6-0	147	7-31-93	.212	.164	.231	60	198	21	42	4	5	3	16	26	2	0	1	77	9	10	.328	.308
Delgado, Alwin	R-R	6-3	175	11-3-92	.272	.280	.269	55	184	18	50	12	3	0	13	11	5	0	1	38	7	7	.370	.328
Felipe, Eurys	B-R	5-10	150	3-29-94	.194	.105	.215	34	98	21	19	3	1	0	5	21	2	0	2	16	9	7	.245	.341
Guzman, Raynolds	R-R	6-0	185	3-16-90	.274	.222	.296	62	215	24	59	11	3	1	27	5	6	0	2	14	6	3	.367	.307
Lara, Confesor	R-R	6-2	170	8-7-90	.177	.172	.178	61	215	32	38	3	3	2	12	18	4	0	1	79	12	4	.247	.252
Morillo, Robert	R-R	6-1	188	6-2-91	.180	.130	.222	25	50	6	9	3	0	1	7	6	1	0	0	11	2	1	.300	.281
Ortiz, Samuel	R-R	5-11	155	6-12-91	.255	.241	.262	63	188	30	48	5	5	1	21	27	10	0	5	37	13	10	.351	.370
Oses, Omar	R-R	5-11	159	5-25-93	.203	.192	.208	29	74	7	15	1	0	0	7	3	3	0	3	20	3	0	.216	.253
Pena, Lenny	L-R	6-3	195	3-27-92	.206	.118	.239	48	126	10	26	6	0	3	13	11	3	0	2	41	0	6	.325	.282
Romero, Javier	R-R	6-2	190	2-13-91	.184	.227	.165	55	141	16	26	8	0	0	12	21	5	0	1	42	10	5	.284	.310
Santana, Felix	R-R	5-10	180	8-19-94	.204	.114	.245	49	142	17	29	7	2	3	16	12	7	0	1	43	5	6	.345	.296
Santana, Felix A.	R-R	5-10	180	8-29-91	.087	.143	.063	13	23	2	2	0	0	0	0	1	0	0	0	5	1	0	.087	.125

Pitching	B-T	HT	WT	DOB	W	L	ERA	G	GS	CG	SV	IP	H	R	ER	HR	BB	SO	AVG	vLH	vRH	K/9	BB/9
Abad, Che Yeyne	L-L	5-11	162	6-30-90	0	1	12.60	6	0	0	0	5	6	10	7	0	9	2	.316	.000	.333	3.60	16.20
Acosta, Alvin	R-R	6-2	170	6-12-90	1	1	3.32	10	0	0	0	19	16	11	7	0	13	18	.239	.250	.236	8.53	6.16
Alvarado, Carlos	R-R	6-4	175	10-22-89	2	0	1.64	2	2	0	0	11	9	2	2	1	2	12	.225	.143	.242	9.82	1.64
Aybar, Pedro	R-R	6-2	195	11-21-91	1	1	3.68	10	0	0	0	15	17	8	6	0	13	22	.288	.455	.250	13.50	7.98
Burgos, Cesar	R-R	6-2	185	3-1-93	0	0	0.00	7	0	0	0	7	4	0	0	0	3	10	.154	.100	.188	12.27	3.68
Calderon, Yinio	R-R	6-4	170	11-16-90	0	0	16.20	3	0	0	0	3	3	6	6	0	7	4	.333	.333	.333	10.80	18.90
Ciriaco, Ricardo	R-R	6-0	220	8-18-92	1	6	4.94	29	2	0	1	51	52	34	28	1	29	32	.267	.313	.258	5.65	5.12
Espinal, Yoel	R-R	6-2	200	11-7-92	3	3	2.79	12	12	0	0	48	29	18	15	1	29	51	.177	.194	.173	9.50	5.40
Hidalgo, Luis	R-R	6-1	170	1-18-91	3	4	2.07	14	8	0	0	65	58	28	15	2	15	71	.231	.213	.237	9.78	2.07
Jacobs, Vijandrick	L-L	5-10	185	2-20-94	0	1	7.43	7	3	0	0	13	12	11	11	1	15	13	.267	.000	.279	8.78	10.13
Lachapel, Walter	R-R	6-0	180	8-16-92	1	1	4.70	21	0	0	1	38	45	25	20	1	26	37	.302	.314	.298	8.69	6.10
Lopez, Yorfrank	R-R	6-3	170	12-1-90	2	0	1.98	3	1	0	0	14	14	4	3	1	5	11	.264	.250	.267	7.24	3.29
Manzanillo, Rafael	R-R	6-6	190	10-24-91	2	2	9.78	17	1	0	0	23	15	27	25	0	42	33	.190	.333	.156	12.91	16.43
Montero, Miguel	R-R	6-3	170	12-4-92	0	2	11.93	18	0	0	0	14	11	19	19	0	39	8	.224	.167	.233	5.02	24.49
Morillo, Gregory	R-R	6-2	180	3-4-92	0	3	7.27	18	3	0	0	26	23	32	21	1	28	32	.228	.111	.253	11.08	9.69
Nesbitt, Angel	R-R	6-1	175	12-4-90	1	0	0.00	5	0	0	1	6	4	0	0	0	1	7	.190	.143	.214	10.50	1.50
Paniagua, Adrian	R-R	6-0	195	5-1-91	1	4	6.32	16	9	0	0	37	41	34	26	0	39	45	.297	.357	.282	10.95	9.49
Paulino, David	R-R	6-5	180	2-6-94	0	1	0.00	8	7	0	0	15	8	4	0	0	7	14	.160	.111	.171	8.40	4.20
Perez, Fernando	R-R	6-3	181	12-17-93	0	2	2.10	9	9	0	0	34	23	11	8	1	14	26	.202	.095	.226	6.82	3.67
Rosario, Harold	R-R	5-11	198	10-23-92	3	3	3.22	20	0	0	1	36	26	17	13	0	20	56	.195	.333	.174	13.87	4.95
Solano, Gregory	R-R	6-3	180	7-9-92	3	5	4.75	10	10	0	0	42	33	29	22	0	23	37	.213	.250	.207	7.99	4.97
Valdez, Jose	R-R	6-1	167	3-1-90	1	1	2.29	18	0	0	9	20	13	5	5	0	10	27	.191	.100	.207	12.36	4.58

Fielding

Catcher	PCT	G	PO	A	E	DP	PB
Guzman	.993	46	377	54	3	3	8
Oses	.972	26	185	20	6	1	10
Santana	.952	7	19	1	1	0	3

First Base	PCT	G	PO	A	E	DP
Contreras	1.000	3	10	1	0	0
Guzman	.992	18	117	3	1	18
Morillo	1.000	5	35	1	0	2
Pena	.981	38	241	12	5	22
Romero	.959	20	90	4	4	10

Second Base	PCT	G	PO	A	E	DP
Contreras	1.000	2	0	1	0	0

	PCT	G	PO	A	E	DP
Crafort	.000	1	0	0	0	0
Felipe	.875	8	14	14	4	2
Morillo	.974	19	15	23	1	10
Ortiz	.966	53	111	115	8	32

Third Base	PCT	G	PO	A	E	DP
Contreras	.919	52	45	103	13	7
Delgado	1.000	3	2	1	0	0
Guzman	.000	2	0	0	1	0
Morillo	.571	3	3	1	3	0
Ortiz	.929	9	11	15	2	2
Pena	.852	7	4	19	4	1

Shortstop	PCT	G	PO	A	E	DP
Crafort	.878	9	16	20	5	3
Delgado	.936	55	71	133	14	29
Felipe	.833	5	1	9	2	2
Morillo	.947	5	5	13	1	1

Outfield	PCT	G	PO	A	E	DP
Acevedo	.913	37	40	2	4	0
Crafort	.947	43	47	7	3	1
Lara	.925	59	67	7	6	1
Oses	1.000	2	2	0	0	0
Romero	.975	33	35	4	1	0
Santana	1.000	2	2	0	0	0
Santana	.964	41	48	6	2	1

VSL TIGERS ROOKIE

VENEZUELAN SUMMER LEAGUE

Batting	B-T	HT	WT	DOB	AVG	vLH	vRH	G	AB	R	H	2B	3B	HR	RBI	BB	HBP	SH	SF	SO	SB	CS	SLG	OBP
Alvarado, Jesus	R-R	6-1	160	11-25-91	.301	.235	.324	58	193	29	58	13	1	2	26	18	4	0	1	27	7	8	.409	.370
Carranza, Daniel	R-R	6-1	182	1-25-93	.190	.261	.171	31	105	13	20	6	1	4	13	5	2	0	0	53	0	0	.381	.241
Castro, Harold	L-R	6-0	145	11-30-93	.313	.271	.326	63	252	44	79	10	0	1	32	11	4	0	0	21	24	7	.365	.352
Cortez, Luis	R-R	6-0	155	1-8-92	.229	.143	.261	46	157	18	36	8	0	4	19	10	8	0	3	36	4	1	.357	.303
Gonzalez, David	R-R	5-9	140	12-1-93	.255	.230	.264	68	239	44	61	12	0	1	19	51	3	0	4	33	8	10	.318	.387

DETROIT TIGERS

Batting

Batting	B-T	HT	WT	DOB	AVG	vLH	vRH	G	AB	R	H	2B	3B	HR	RBI	BB	HBP	SH	SF	SO	SB	CS	SLG	OBP
Montero, Jhosua	R-R	5-11	190	1-15-94	.168	.263	.145	30	95	7	16	3	0	2	11	2	2	0	0	26	1	1	.263	.202
Ovalles, Jose	R-R	5-10	190	8-2-93	.226	.147	.253	50	133	25	30	6	0	3	13	31	7	0	2	25	0	0	.338	.393
Perez, Carlos	R-R	6-0	155	2-16-94	.267	.250	.276	49	146	18	39	8	1	0	26	19	3	0	2	28	4	2	.336	.359
Soledad, Jose	R-R	5-11	165	7-22-92	.313	.355	.299	67	249	44	78	17	1	5	39	21	2	0	4	30	15	5	.450	.366
Tenia, Gabriel	R-R	6-0	203	1-18-93	.211	.282	.189	48	161	20	34	5	0	7	25	13	5	0	3	43	0	0	.373	.286
Tovar, Orvin	R-R	5-11	180	8-6-93	.213	.241	.203	67	240	37	51	10	2	2	29	36	3	0	3	34	5	3	.296	.319
Ustariz, Jesus	R-R	6-1	192	4-26-93	.324	.250	.348	50	176	25	57	12	1	3	22	14	5	0	2	21	3	0	.455	.386
Yance, Anderson	L-L	5-11	160	7-25-92	.263	.306	.254	60	209	34	55	11	2	2	16	19	5	0	2	34	11	5	.364	.336

Pitching

Pitching	B-T	HT	WT	DOB	W	L	ERA	G	GS	CG	SV	IP	H	R	ER	HR	BB	SO	AVG	vLH	vRH	K/9	BB/9
Alvarado, Carlos	R-R	6-4	175	10-22-89	3	5	3.57	18	13	0	0	68	69	35	27	3	22	63	.266	.305	.249	8.34	2.91
Belisario, Johan	R-R	5-11	155	8-13-93	0	4	7.50	15	6	0	0	42	61	43	35	10	12	26	.343	.377	.325	5.57	2.57
Camaripano, Junior	L-L	6-2	175	12-21-93	0	2	7.13	15	0	0	1	24	21	22	19	2	24	21	.250	.235	.254	7.88	9.00
Cedeno, Cruz	R-R	6-1	150	10-14-93	3	4	5.58	16	7	0	1	50	57	32	31	8	19	21	.305	.221	.353	3.78	3.42
Hernandez, Daniel	R-R	6-2	160	2-11-92	3	1	3.96	13	11	0	0	52	59	35	23	3	21	34	.284	.263	.295	5.85	3.61
Jacobs, Vijandrick	L-L	5-10	185	2-20-94	2	0	9.00	3	0	0	0	6	3	6	6	0	7	3	.158	.000	.176	4.50	10.50
Lopez, Yorfrank	R-R	6-3	170	12-1-90	2	7	6.94	17	13	0	0	58	81	50	45	3	28	31	.331	.365	.316	4.78	4.32
Mendoza, Jose	R-R	6-1	158	4-1-93	0	2	15.00	10	0	0	0	12	20	20	20	3	6	7	.370	.526	.286	5.25	4.50
Mosquera, Yonny	R-R	5-10	170	1-16-91	2	3	5.91	16	3	0	1	35	42	30	23	6	25	25	.298	.318	.289	6.43	6.43
Nesbitt, Angel	R-R	6-1	175	12-4-90	1	3	4.25	20	7	0	7	53	63	30	25	0	18	32	.303	.268	.316	5.43	3.06
Rodriguez, Jose	R-R	5-11	180	12-30-92	5	0	3.51	19	0	0	0	41	38	19	16	1	25	21	.259	.204	.286	4.61	5.49
Rodriguez, Luis	R-R	6-1	160	5-11-92	1	0	4.50	15	0	0	0	22	17	13	11	2	17	9	.218	.261	.200	3.68	6.95
Rojas, Eduardo	R-R	6-2	175	1-7-94	2	1	4.09	14	6	0	0	44	40	28	20	3	32	16	.247	.167	.270	3.27	6.55
Sanchez, Jairo	R-R	5-11	204	8-11-92	2	0	2.87	21	0	0	3	31	31	13	10	0	21	17	.274	.258	.280	4.88	6.03
Tablante, Jose	L-L	5-10	135	1-18-92	2	6	6.10	18	3	0	3	38	41	30	26	4	17	36	.283	.296	.280	8.45	3.99
Vasquez, Angel	R-R	6-5	190	10-8-93	0	4	8.84	14	2	0	0	19	33	22	19	1	14	8	.384	.348	.397	3.72	6.52
Villaroel, Orlando	R-R	6-1	190	3-18-90	0	1	14.85	6	0	0	0	7	10	13	11	1	16	3	.417	.625	.313	4.05	21.60

Fielding

Catcher	PCT	G	PO	A	E	DP	PB
Montero	.966	11	44	12	2	1	4
Ovalles	.981	43	206	47	5	2	12
Tenia	.981	23	130	26	3	0	5

First Base	PCT	G	PO	A	E	DP
Castro	1.000	1	1	0	0	0
Cortez	.000	1	0	0	0	0
Montero	.958	2	21	2	1	2
Ovalles	1.000	6	45	4	0	4
Soledad	.994	37	334	25	2	30

	PCT	G	PO	A	E	DP
Tenia	.969	16	116	11	4	7
Ustariz	.980	16	135	9	3	12

Second Base	PCT	G	PO	A	E	DP
Castro	.965	57	135	143	10	35
Cortez	.941	4	8	8	1	1
Gonzalez	.966	11	28	29	2	6

Third Base	PCT	G	PO	A	E	DP
Cortez	.926	28	27	60	7	7
Soledad	.917	33	27	72	9	5

	PCT	G	PO	A	E	DP
Ustariz	1.000	15	10	52	0	3

Shortstop	PCT	G	PO	A	E	DP
Castro	.815	6	6	16	5	2
Cortez	.959	13	25	45	3	7
Gonzalez	.954	54	104	184	14	33

Outfield	PCT	G	PO	A	E	DP
Alvarado	.963	57	120	10	5	5
Carranza	.958	11	22	1	1	0
Perez	.948	43	50	5	3	2

Florida Marlins

SEASON IN A SENTENCE: A lack of starting pitching depth, exposed by an injury to star right-hander Josh Johnson, and a down season from shortstop Hanley Ramirez sank the Marlins to a last-place finish in the National League East.

HIGH POINT: Hopes were high in the first third of the season as the Marlins were within two games of the Phillies as late as June 4. The largely homegrown offense looked good as Mike Stanton had already slugged 13 home runs, Logan Morrison had a .922 OPS and Gaby Sanchez held a .321 average.

LOW POINT: It was all downhill from there, as Florida lost 19 of its next 21 games, manager Edwin Rodriguez resigned and the club turned again to Jack McKeon. McKeon was unable to recapture the magic of 2003, when he led the Marlins to a World Series championship after a similar midseason takeover. What will ultimately be the last season of the Florida Marlins—they became the Miami Marlins in November as they move into a new ballpark under Ozzie Guillen in 2012—proved eminently forgettable.

NOTABLE ROOKIES: Righthander Steve Cishek proved to be one of the league's better rookie relievers, with a 2.63 ERA in 55 innings. Lefthander Brad Hand came up from Double-A Jacksonville and had a 4.20 ERA in 12 starts. Outfielder Bryan Peterson helped fill the late-season center-field void and held a .357 on-base percentage while stealing seven bases in 241 plate appearances.

KEY TRANSACTIONS: The Marlins had little to deal at midseason, after making several moves before the season. Signing righthander Javier Vazquez to a free agent deal proved to be a worthy investment; he threw nearly 200 innings while putting up a 3.69 ERA. The most notable move may have been when closer Leo Nunez was placed on the restricted list with a week left in the season, as it turned out his name is actually Juan Carlos Oviedo and he's a year older than previously believed. His status for 2012 remained unresolved.

DOWN ON THE FARM: Low Class A Greensboro captured the South Atlantic League championship, led by outfielders Christian Yelich and Marcell Ozuna and catcher J.T. Realmuto. Yelich, the club's 2010 first-rounder, had a breakout season as he hit .321 with 15 home runs and 32 stolen bases. The Marlins selected a former Cuban defector, righthander Jose Fernandez, with their first-round pick in 2011.

OPENING DAY PAYROLL: $56,944,000 (24th)

PLAYERS OF THE YEAR

MAJOR LEAGUE	MINOR LEAGUE
Mike Stanton	**Christian Yelich**
of	of
.262/356/.537	(Low Class A)
34 HR, 30 2B	.312/.388/.484
2nd in NL in AB/HR	32 2B, 32 SB

ORGANIZATION LEADERS

BATTING		*Minimum 250 PA
MAJORS		
* AVG	Emilio Bonifacio	.296
* OPS	Mike Stanton	.893
HR	Mike Stanton	34
RBI	Mike Stanton	87
MINORS		
* AVG	Christian Yelich, Greensboro	.312
* OBP	Luke Montz, Jacksonville	.391
* SLG	Mark Canha, Greensboro	.529
R	Kevin Mattison, Jacksonville	87
	Marcell Ozuna, Greensboro	87
H	Noah Perio, Greensboro	144
	Christian Yelich, Greensboro	144
TB	Kyle Jensen, Jupiter/Jacksonville	247
2B	Ryan Fisher, Greensboro	36
3B	Kevin Mattison, Jacksonville	16
HR	Kyle Jensen, Jupiter/Jacksonville	27
RBI	Mark Canha, Greensboro	85
BB	Chris Gutierrez, New Orleans/Jacksonville	80
SO	Kyle Skipworth, Jacksonville	143
SB	Kevin Mattison, Jacksonville	38
PITCHING		#Minimum 75 IP
MAJORS		
W	Javier Vazquez	13
# ERA	Edward Mujica	2.96
SO	Anibal Sanchez	202
SV	Leo Nunez	36
MINORS		
W	Tom Koehler, New Orleans	12
	Rob Rasmussen, Jupiter	12
L	Edgar Olmos, Jupiter	17
# ERA	Brad Hand, Jupiter/Jacksonville	3.56
G	Jhan Marinez, Jacksonville	56
GS	Three tied at	28
SV	Sandy Rosario, Jacksonville/New Orleans	27
IP	Elih Villanueva, New Orleans	165
BB	Edgar Olmos, Jupiter	81
SO	Chad James, Jupiter	124
# AVG	Brad Hand, Jupiter/Jacksonville	.233

General Manager: Larry Beinfest. **Farm Director:** Brian Chattin. **Scouting Director:** Stan Meek.

Class	Team	League	W	L	PCT	Finish	Manager(s)
Majors	Florida Marlins	National	72	90	.444	t-12th (16)	E. Rodriguez/B. Hyde/J. McKeon
Triple-A	New Orleans Zephyrs	Pacific Coast	69	74	.483	10th (16)	Greg Norton
Double-A	Jacksonville Suns	Southern	70	70	.500	5th (10)	Andy Barkett
High A	Jupiter Hammerheads	Florida State	60	80	.429	12th (12)	Ron Hassey
Low A	Greensboro Grasshoppers	South Atlantic	79	60	.568	t-2nd (14)	Andy Haines
Short-season	Jamestown Jammers	New York-Penn	35	40	.467	10th (14)	Dave Berg
Rookie	GCL Marlins	Gulf Coast	38	16	.704	1st (15)	Jorge Hernandez
Overall 2011 Minor League Record			351	340	.508	12th (30)	

ORGANIZATION STATISTICS

FLORIDA MARLINS
NATIONAL LEAGUE

Batting	B-T	HT	WT	DOB	AVG	vLH	vRH	G	AB	R	H	2B	3B	HR	RBI	BB	HBP	SH	SF	SO	SB	CS	SLG	OBP
Amezaga, Alfredo	B-R	5-11	165	1-16-78	.136	.077	.161	20	44	1	6	0	0	0	2	4	0	0	0	7	0	0	.136	.208
2-team total (20 Colorado)					.182	—	—	40	77	6	14	1	0	0	4	7	0	0	1	14	0	0	.195	.247
Baker, John	L-R	6-1	220	1-20-81	.154	.500	.154	16	13	0	2	0	0	1	2	0	0	0	0	3	0	0	.154	.267
Bonifacio, Emilio	B-R	5-11	200	4-23-85	.296	.333	.282	152	565	78	167	26	7	5	36	59	1	0	5	129	40	11	.393	.360
Buck, John	R-R	6-3	230	7-7-80	.227	.189	.241	140	466	41	106	15	1	16	57	54	7	0	1	115	0	1	.367	.316
Cameron, Mike	R-R	6-2	210	1-8-73	.238	.214	.243	45	143	18	34	8	0	6	18	20	0	0	0	34	1	0	.420	.331
Coghlan, Chris	L-R	6-0	205	6-18-85	.230	.107	.278	65	269	33	62	20	1	5	22	22	4	0	2	49	7	6	.368	.296
Cousins, Scott	L-L	6-1	195	1-22-85	.135	.000	.159	48	52	5	7	1	0	1	4	6	0	0	0	21	1	1	.212	.224
Dobbs, Greg	L-R	6-1	205	7-2-78	.275	.216	.281	134	411	38	113	23	0	8	49	22	1	0	3	83	0	0	.389	.311
Dominguez, Matt	R-R	6-1	205	8-28-89	.244	.389	.148	17	45	2	11	4	0	0	2	2	1	0	0	8	0	0	.333	.292
Hatcher, Chris	R-R	6-2	205	1-12-85	—	—	—	12	0	0	0	0	0	0	0	0	0	0	0	0	0	0	—	—
Hayes, Brett	R-R	6-1	205	2-13-84	.231	.207	.238	64	130	19	30	9	0	5	16	11	0	0	0	39	0	0	.415	.291
Helms, Wes	R-R	6-4	230	5-16-76	.191	.212	.159	69	110	10	21	5	0	0	6	11	2	0	0	35	0	0	.236	.276
Infante, Omar	R-R	6-0	180	12-26-81	.276	.273	.277	148	579	55	160	24	8	7	49	34	2	0	8	67	4	2	.382	.315
Lopez, Jose	R-R	6-0	205	11-24-83	.226	.176	.250	44	106	13	24	8	0	6	13	4	1	0	1	13	0	0	.472	.259
2-team total (38 Colorado)					.216	—	—	82	231	23	50	12	0	8	21	7	2	0	1	28	2	0	.372	.245
Martinez, Ozzie	R-R	5-10	190	5-7-88	.130	.200	.077	20	23	0	3	0	0	0	1	0	0	0	0	9	0	0	.130	.130
Morrison, Logan	L-L	6-3	235	8-25-87	.247	.241	.249	123	462	54	114	25	4	23	72	54	5	0	4	99	2	1	.468	.330
Murphy, Donnie	R-R	5-10	195	3-10-83	.185	.160	.194	36	92	10	17	4	1	2	9	4	3	0	1	21	0	0	.315	.240
Petersen, Bryan	L-R	6-0	205	4-9-86	.265	.294	.255	74	204	18	54	13	3	2	10	26	5	0	3	49	7	1	.387	.357
Ramirez, Hanley	R-R	6-3	230	12-23-83	.243	.315	.223	92	338	55	82	16	0	10	45	44	2	0	6	66	20	10	.379	.333
Rottino, Vinny	R-R	6-0	215	4-7-80	.167	.400	.000	8	12	1	2	0	0	0	2	0	0	0	0	4	0	0	.167	.286
Sanchez, Gaby	R-R	6-1	225	9-2-83	.266	.295	.257	159	572	72	152	35	0	19	78	74	6	0	7	97	3	1	.427	.352
Stanton, Mike	R-R	6-5	235	11-8-89	.262	.293	.253	150	516	79	135	30	5	34	87	70	9	0	6	166	5	5	.537	.356
Thurston, Joe	L-R	5-11	210	9-29-79	.250	.667	.250	1	4	0	1	0	0	0	0	0	0	0	0	1	0	0	.250	.250
Wise, Dewayne	L-L	5-11	195	2-24-78	.239	.167	.255	49	67	6	16	2	0	0	5	3	1	0	1	21	4	2	.269	.278

Pitching	B-T	HT	WT	DOB	W	L	ERA	G	GS	CG	SV	IP	H	R	ER	HR	BB	SO	AVG	vLH	vRH	K/9	BB/9
Badenhop, Burke	R-R	6-5	220	2-8-83	2	3	4.10	50	0	0	1	64	65	29	29	1	24	51	.265	.264	.266	7.21	3.39
Buente, Jay	R-R	6-2	185	9-28-83	0	1	9.00	1	1	0	0	3	5	4	3	0	3	1	.357	.286	.429	3.00	9.00
Ceda, Jose	R-R	6-4	275	1-28-87	0	1	4.43	17	0	0	0	20	16	11	10	1	12	21	.211	.185	.224	9.30	5.31
Choate, Randy	L-L	6-1	200	9-5-75	1	1	1.82	54	0	0	0	25	13	7	5	3	13	31	.149	.145	.167	11.31	4.74
Cishek, Steve	R-R	6-5	200	6-18-86	2	1	2.63	45	0	0	3	55	45	18	16	1	19	55	.221	.225	.218	9.05	3.13
Dunn, Mike	L-L	6-1	195	5-23-85	5	6	3.43	72	0	0	0	63	51	28	24	9	31	68	.224	.198	.244	9.71	4.43
Hand, Brad	L-L	6-3	200	3-20-90	1	8	4.20	12	12	0	0	60	53	32	28	10	35	38	.241	.300	.224	5.70	5.25
Hensley, Clay	R-R	5-11	190	8-31-79	6	7	5.19	37	9	0	0	68	62	41	39	9	30	46	.238	.171	.305	6.12	3.99
Johnson, Josh	L-R	6-7	250	1-31-84	3	1	1.64	9	9	0	0	60	39	13	11	2	16	56	.185	.209	.156	8.35	2.98
Mujica, Edward	R-R	6-2	215	5-10-84	9	6	2.96	67	0	0	0	76	64	27	25	7	14	63	.233	.220	.245	7.46	1.66
Nolasco, Ricky	R-R	6-2	230	12-13-82	10	12	4.67	33	33	2	0	206	244	117	107	20	44	148	.295	.305	.285	6.47	1.92
Oviedo, Juan	R-R	6-2	190	3-15-82	1	4	4.06	68	0	0	36	64	57	30	29	8	21	55	.235	.270	.203	7.69	2.94
Rosario, Sandy	R-R	6-1	170	8-22-85	0	0	2.45	4	0	0	0	4	5	1	1	0	2	2	.313	.273	.400	4.91	4.91
Sanabia, Alex	R-R	6-2	165	9-8-88	0	0	3.27	3	2	0	0	11	13	4	4	2	3	8	.289	.200	.400	6.55	2.45
Sanches, Brian	R-R	6-0	190	8-8-78	4	1	3.94	39	2	0	0	62	52	32	27	7	36	53	.227	.257	.198	7.74	5.25
Sanchez, Anibal	R-R	6-0	205	2-27-84	8	9	3.67	32	32	3	0	196	187	85	80	14	64	202	.250	.243	.257	9.26	2.93
Vazquez, Javier	R-R	6-2	210	7-25-76	13	11	3.69	32	32	2	0	193	178	91	79	21	50	162	.243	.245	.241	7.57	2.34
Villanueva, Elih	R-R	6-2	235	7-27-86	0	1	24.00	1	1	0	0	3	5	8	8	1	5	2	.357	.400	.250	6.00	15.00
Volstad, Chris	R-R	6-8	230	9-23-86	5	13	4.89	29	29	0	0	166	187	96	90	23	49	117	.289	.305	.273	6.36	2.66
Webb, Ryan	R-R	6-6	215	2-5-86	2	4	3.20	53	0	0	0	51	48	20	18	2	20	31	.255	.276	.238	5.51	3.55

Fielding

Catcher	PCT	G	PO	A	E	DP	PB
Baker	1.000	1	2	0	0	0	0
Buck	.995	135	1008	42	5	5	7
Hayes	1.000	50	254	20	0	2	3

First Base	PCT	G	PO	A	E	DP
Dobbs	1.000	4	21	3	0	2
Hayes	1.000	1	3	0	0	1
Helms	1.000	5	7	0	0	1
Lopez	1.000	8	40	5	0	2
Morrison	1.000	1	6	0	0	0
Sanchez	.996	153	1262	101	5	109

Second Base	PCT	G	PO	A	E	DP
Amezaga	.980	11	21	29	1	6
Bonifacio	1.000	5	5	7	0	1
Helms	1.000	2	1	1	0	0
Infante	.989	146	260	466	8	75
Lopez	1.000	9	9	13	0	2
Murphy	.000	1	0	0	0	0
Thurston	1.000	1	3	4	0	1
Third Base	**PCT**	**G**	**PO**	**A**	**E**	**DP**
Bonifacio	.955	36	17	47	3	8
Dobbs	.943	100	49	132	11	8
Dominguez	.931	16	6	21	2	1

Helms	.938	33	14	31	3	3
Lopez	.941	10	6	10	1	1
Martinez	.000	1	0	0	0	0
Murphy	.963	15	9	17	1	0
Shortstop	**PCT**	**G**	**PO**	**A**	**E**	**DP**
Bonifacio	.966	67	98	154	9	34
Martinez	.750	6	0	3	1	0
Murphy	.986	18	27	46	1	10
Ramirez	.957	86	127	188	14	38
Outfield	**PCT**	**G**	**PO**	**A**	**E**	**DP**
Amezaga	1.000	4	1	0	0	0

Bonifacio	.991	60	105	4	1	0
Cameron	1.000	40	93	3	0	0
Coghlan	1.000	65	157	3	0	1
Cousins	1.000	21	20	3	0	1
Dobbs	1.000	6	12	0	0	0
Hayes	.000	2	0	0	0	0
Morrison	.977	119	207	6	5	0
Petersen	.982	62	106	5	2	2
Rottino	1.000	3	1	1	0	0
Stanton	.980	142	282	10	6	2
Wise	1.000	34	49	0	0	0

NEW ORLEANS ZEPHYRS

TRIPLE-A

PACIFIC COAST LEAGUE

FLORIDA MARLINS

Batting	B-T	HT	WT	DOB	AVG	vLH	vRH	G	AB	R	H	2B	3B	HR	RBI	BB	HBP	SH	SF	SO	SB	CS	SLG	OBP
Aguila, Chris	R-R	5-11	200	2-23-79	.287	.244	.298	117	411	63	118	27	1	22	72	43	5	0	3	123	5	1	.518	.359
Cervenak, Mike	R-R	5-11	195	8-17-76	.298	.322	.288	123	406	66	121	24	1	14	68	36	6	0	2	51	4	3	.466	.362
Coghlan, Chris	L-R	6-0	205	6-18-85	.245	.409	.129	15	53	11	13	4	0	1	7	8	3	0	3	5	3	1	.377	.358
Cousins, Scott	L-L	6-1	195	1-22-85	.222	.000	.286	2	9	1	2	0	0	0	1	1	0	0	0	3	0	0	.222	.300
Davis, Brad	R-R	6-1	190	12-29-82	.267	.297	.261	101	344	40	92	22	1	5	49	27	3	0	3	80	1	0	.381	.324
Dominguez, Matt	R-R	6-1	205	8-28-89	.258	.325	.236	87	325	47	84	18	1	12	55	24	3	0	4	50	0	1	.431	.312
Fermin, Miguel	R-R	5-11	175	2-11-85	.150	.111	.182	11	20	5	3	1	0	0	3	0	0	0	0	9	1	0	.200	.261
Glime, Gregg	B-R	5-11	200	10-29-87	.111	.000	.167	6	9	1	1	0	0	0	0	4	0	0	0	2	0	0	.111	.385
Gotay, Ruben	B-R	5-11	175	12-25-82	.239	.152	.256	62	205	30	49	8	1	6	22	29	3	0	0	45	5	1	.376	.342
Gutierrez, Chris	R-R	5-9	185	3-12-84	.188	.000	.214	6	16	0	3	0	0	0	1	4	0	0	0	2	0	0	.188	.350
Klosterman, Ryan	R-R	5-11	190	5-28-82	.156	.143	.161	29	77	11	12	2	1	3	11	4	2	0	1	16	1	1	.325	.214
Kroeger, Josh	L-L	6-3	230	8-31-82	.284	.255	.291	82	282	48	80	18	0	11	56	36	5	0	2	32	8	5	.465	.372
Lopez, Jose	R-R	6-0	205	11-24-83	.400	.353	.418	32	125	24	50	9	0	9	30	6	2	0	2	12	2	0	.688	.430
Martinez, Ozzie	R-R	5-10	190	5-7-88	.245	.312	.225	88	339	43	83	15	1	3	26	21	5	0	3	57	11	4	.332	.296
Mathews, Aaron	R-R	5-10	215	5-10-82	.162	.176	.158	29	74	5	12	4	2	1	6	3	0	0	1	11	1	0	.311	.192
Merchan, Jesus	R-R	5-11	180	3-26-81	.268	.269	.267	58	183	22	49	8	0	1	17	9	3	0	0	18	0	1	.328	.313
2-team total (26 Colorado Springs)					.301	—	—	84	276	36	83	11	1	1	28	19	3	0	2	27	0	1	.359	.350
Morrison, Logan	L-L	6-3	235	8-25-87	.167	.333	.111	6	24	3	4	2	0	1	5	2	0	0	1	4	0	0	.375	.222
Murphy, Donnie	R-R	5-10	195	3-10-83	.087	.077	.100	6	23	3	2	2	0	0	2	3	0	0	0	4	0	0	.174	.192
Padilla, Jorge	R-R	6-2	205	8-11-79	.337	.447	.293	48	163	30	55	10	1	1	21	19	5	0	4	32	6	2	.429	.414
Pedroza, Sergio	L-R	6-1	180	2-23-84	.222	.000	.250	4	9	2	2	0	0	0	1	3	1	0	0	1	0	1	.556	.300
Petersen, Bryan	L-R	6-0	205	4-9-86	.351	.349	.351	67	248	47	87	21	0	11	36	26	3	1	0	41	6	5	.569	.434
Romero, Alex	L-R	6-0	198	9-9-83	.339	.231	.372	19	56	7	19	4	0	0	5	3	2	0	0	9	0	0	.411	.393
Rottino, Vinny	R-R	6-0	215	4-7-80	.304	.353	.287	119	467	81	142	31	2	10	59	50	3	0	1	62	17	9	.443	.374
Salazar, Oscar	R-R	6-0	195	6-27-78	.221	.206	.225	45	136	12	30	2	1	2	16	6	0	0	1	18	4	1	.294	.252
Sammons, Clint	R-R	6-1	210	5-15-83	.174	.000	.235	9	23	5	4	0	0	3	4	4	1	0	0	11	0	0	.565	.321
Thurston, Joe	L-R	5-11	210	9-29-79	.300	.277	.308	126	453	68	136	34	3	13	59	48	17	0	0	78	12	4	.475	.388
Torres, Andres	B-R	6-2	180	11-12-83	.276	.357	.255	42	134	13	37	8	1	2	19	18	2	0	0	35	8	2	.396	.370
Vazquez, Ramon	L-R	5-11	195	8-21-76	.172	.000	.217	10	29	3	5	1	0	0	1	3	0	0	0	3	0	0	.207	.250
3-team total (20 Las Vegas, 40 Memphis)					.267	—	—	70	240	33	64	8	1	1	32	31	0	0	0	39	2	1	.321	.351
Wise, Dewayne	L-L	5-11	195	2-24-78	.333	.000	.333	2	9	0	3	1	0	0	0	0	0	0	0	4	0	0	.444	.333
2-team total (31 Las Vegas)					.338	—	—	33	142	28	48	11	3	4	19	6	4	0	1	25	8	3	.542	.379

Pitching	B-T	HT	WT	DOB	W	L	ERA	G	GS	CG	SV	IP	H	R	ER	HR	BB	SO	AVG	vLH	vRH	K/9	BB/9
Andrelczyk, Pete	R-R	6-1	185	11-10-85	4	1	1.49	21	1	0	2	36	35	7	6	0	11	27	.259	.250	.266	6.69	2.72
Badenhop, Burke	R-R	6-5	220	2-8-83	1	1	6.75	11	0	0	1	15	20	16	11	1	7	10	.328	.350	.317	6.14	4.30
Buente, Jay	R-R	6-2	185	9-28-83	3	0	1.94	10	5	1	0	42	23	9	9	1	10	44	.163	.151	.176	9.50	2.16
Ceda, Jose	R-R	6-4	275	1-28-87	3	1	1.36	36	0	0	24	40	30	14	6	1	13	53	.201	.150	.236	12.03	2.95
Cishek, Steve	R-R	6-5	200	6-18-86	1	1	2.35	15	0	0	0	23	18	7	6	1	12	19	.217	.313	.157	7.43	4.70
Doolittle, Todd	R-R	5-10	175	11-1-82	3	2	3.08	18	6	1	0	53	52	22	18	6	19	56	.256	.298	.220	9.57	3.25
Downs, Darin	R-L	6-3	210	12-26-84	3	2	4.29	10	5	0	0	36	34	17	17	1	8	39	.250	.356	.198	9.84	2.02
Garate, Victor	L-L	6-1	210	9-25-84	3	3	2.72	43	1	0	2	56	44	23	17	5	34	59	.215	.247	.195	9.43	5.43
Gomez, Mariano	L-L	6-6	240	9-12-82	2	3	8.20	14	3	0	1	26	38	27	24	4	14	18	.339	.250	.389	6.15	4.78
Jennings, Daniel	L-L	6-3	190	4-17-87	1	3	7.04	24	0	0	2	31	34	24	24	3	17	27	.301	.349	.271	7.92	4.99
Koehler, Tom	R-R	6-3	225	6-29-86	12	7	4.97	28	28	0	0	150	144	90	83	18	79	116	.254	.247	.259	6.94	4.73
Madden, Corey	R-R	6-1	195	3-30-84	1	2	4.03	17	0	0	1	22	31	10	10	3	11	30	.330	.432	.263	12.09	4.43
Mata, Frank	R-R	6-1	235	3-11-84	1	6	5.24	35	0	0	2	46	45	29	27	10	21	30	.265	.288	.247	5.83	4.08
McLemore, Mark	L-L	6-2	220	10-9-80	0	2	5.91	4	3	0	0	11	12	8	7	0	14	5	.300	.500	.265	4.22	11.81
Mendez, Adalberto	R-R	6-2	160	2-22-82	1	8	7.33	24	13	0	0	93	97	78	76	13	52	77	.275	.284	.266	7.43	5.01
Parcell, Garrett	R-R	6-5	220	7-12-84	3	2	4.32	36	0	0	1	58	61	37	28	5	25	38	.268	.280	.259	5.86	3.86
Richardson, Dustin	L-L	6-6	220	1-9-84	3	1	3.66	23	0	0	2	32	31	13	13	2	20	35	.256	.341	.208	9.84	5.63
Rosario, Jose	R-R	6-0	170	2-16-86	0	0	3.00	2	0	0	1	6	5	4	2	0	3	5	.217	.222	.214	7.50	4.50
Rosario, Sandy	R-R	6-1	170	8-22-85	0	1	4.05	7	0	0	4	7	5	4	3	0	5	4	.217	.286	.188	5.40	6.75
Sampson, Chris	R-R	6-1	195	5-23-78	9	2	3.71	20	19	1	0	116	139	50	48	15	19	62	.301	.312	.294	4.80	1.47
Sanabia, Alex	R-R	6-2	165	9-8-88	0	3	7.89	4	4	0	0	22	35	21	19	4	3	13	.372	.324	.404	5.40	1.25
Simons, Zach	L-R	6-3	200	5-23-85	0	0	7.27	4	0	0	0	9	10	7	7	2	6	7	.286	.333	.250	7.27	6.23
Trahern, Dallas	R-R	6-3	235	11-29-85	2	2	7.32	7	7	0	0	36	46	35	29	6	22	12	.322	.338	.306	3.03	5.55

Pitching

Pitching	B-T	HT	WT	DOB	W	L	ERA	G	GS	CG	SV	IP	H	R	ER	HR	BB	SO	AVG	vLH	vRH	K/9	BB/9
Valdez, Cesar	R-R	6-2	200	3-17-85	0	1	7.59	8	0	0	0	11	13	9	9	5	3	13	.302	.174	.450	10.97	2.53
Villanueva, Elih	R-R	6-2	235	7-27-86	7	11	5.35	28	28	0	0	165	199	113	98	24	59	105	.305	.306	.305	5.73	3.22
Volstad, Chris	R-R	6-8	230	9-23-86	1	1	4.42	3	3	1	0	18	20	9	9	1	9	14	.290	.275	.310	6.87	4.42
West, Sean	L-L	6-8	260	6-15-86	5	8	5.59	17	17	0	0	87	103	64	54	5	46	56	.299	.279	.308	5.79	4.76

Fielding

Catcher	PCT	G	PO	A	E	DP	PB
Davis	.984	99	674	59	12	5	4
Fermin	1.000	5	11	3	0	0	0
Glime	1.000	4	11	2	0	0	0
Rottino	.997	39	270	33	1	4	5
Sammons	1.000	5	34	5	0	1	0

First Base	PCT	G	PO	A	E	DP
Cervenak	.992	69	490	38	4	49
Gotay	.993	18	136	8	1	11
Kroeger	.992	30	214	22	2	33
Lopez	.979	6	44	3	1	4
Rottino	1.000	11	61	5	0	10
Salazar	.994	21	162	15	1	17
Sammons	1.000	1	10	0	0	0

Second Base	PCT	G	PO	A	E	DP
Gotay	1.000	4	9	14	0	4
Klosterman	1.000	3	3	3	0	1
Lopez	.963	17	33	46	3	14
Martinez	1.000	6	13	12	0	6
Merchan	.963	10	13	13	1	2

Third Base	PCT	G	PO	A	E	DP
Aguila	.000	1	0	0	0	0
Cervenak	.976	18	7	33	1	5
Dominguez	.946	83	61	165	13	21
Gotay	.933	31	16	40	4	3
Klosterman	1.000	1	1	1	0	0
Lopez	.917	6	1	10	1	0
Martinez	1.000	3	2	5	0	1
Merchan	1.000	1	1	2	0	0
Murphy	1.000	1	1	1	0	1
Torres	1.000	2	1	6	0	0
Vazquez	1.000	4	0	3	0	0

Shortstop	PCT	G	PO	A	E	DP
Gutierrez	.957	6	6	16	1	3
Klosterman	.901	16	38	35	8	9
Martinez	.960	80	112	203	13	54

	PCT	G	PO	A	E	DP	PB
Merchan	.961	39	54	94	6	23	
Murphy	.889	3	1	7	1	0	
Thurston	1.000	5	9	15	0	3	
Vazquez	1.000	1	2	2	0	1	

Outfield	PCT	G	PO	A	E	DP
Aguila	.984	104	177	10	3	2
Coghlan	1.000	14	34	3	0	2
Cousins	1.000	2	5	0	0	0
Kroeger	1.000	54	116	5	0	1
Mathews	.977	22	41	2	1	0
Morrison	1.000	5	9	0	0	0
Padilla	.982	48	108	4	2	0
Pedroza	1.000	2	6	0	0	0
Petersen	.986	64	135	9	2	2
Romero	.946	16	35	0	2	0
Rottino	.980	68	137	7	3	2
Salazar	.900	9	9	0	1	0
Thurston	.968	16	29	1	1	1
Torres	1.000	35	83	7	0	2
Wise	1.000	2	9	0	0	0

JACKSONVILLE SUNS

DOUBLE-A

SOUTHERN LEAGUE

Batting

Batting	B-T	HT	WT	DOB	AVG	vLH	vRH	G	AB	R	H	2B	3B	HR	RBI	BB	HBP	SH	SF	SO	SB	CS	SLG	OBP
Baker, John	L-R	6-1	220	1-20-81	.111	.000	.167	3	9	0	1	1	0	0	0	1	0	0	0	5	0	0	.222	.200
Coghlan, Chris	L-R	6-0	205	6-18-85	.211	.286	.167	5	19	3	4	1	0	0	0	4	0	0	0	1	0	0	.263	.348
Curry, Ryan	R-R	5-10	185	4-18-85	.244	.273	.223	112	369	53	90	21	3	8	47	28	8	0	4	58	4	7	.382	.308
Dominguez, Jeff	B-R	6-2	160	7-31-86	.389	.167	.500	6	18	3	7	0	0	1	2	0	0	0	1	4	1	1	.556	.368
Dominguez, Matt	R-R	6-1	205	8-28-89	.133	.286	.000	4	15	1	2	0	0	0	1	3	1	0	0	2	0	0	.133	.316
Dudley, Aaron	L-R	6-3	193	2-17-88	.000	.000	.000	5	4	0	0	0	0	0	0	0	0	0	0	2	0	0	.000	.000
Gran, Paul	R-R	5-11	182	4-7-86	.260	.209	.282	95	292	43	76	23	4	6	42	33	14	0	3	76	9	1	.428	.360
Gutierrez, Chris	R-R	5-9	185	3-12-84	.227	.183	.246	122	392	49	89	17	5	0	47	76	5	0	4	87	4	1	.296	.356
Hatcher, Chris	R-R	6-2	205	1-12-85	.250	—	—	1	4	0	1	0	0	0	0	0	0	0	0	1	1	0	.250	.250
Jensen, Kyle	R-L	6-4	230	5-20-88	.250	.368	.213	21	80	14	20	1	1	5	10	7	0	0	0	23	1	0	.475	.310
Lasater, Ben	R-R	6-3	195	5-25-84	.296	.291	.299	102	348	43	103	25	2	12	60	31	8	0	4	89	0	5	.483	.363
Lis, Erik	L-L	6-1	220	3-8-84	.180	.250	.163	26	61	7	11	3	0	1	7	4	3	0	0	18	0	0	.279	.265
Mattison, Kevin	L-L	6-0	180	9-20-85	.260	.247	.266	130	503	87	131	17	16	8	49	58	17	0	5	127	38	16	.406	.353
Montz, Luke	R-R	6-2	225	7-7-83	.273	.351	.242	118	395	66	108	27	0	22	78	74	7	0	7	95	8	0	.509	.391
Negrych, Jim	L-R	5-10	180	3-2-85	.304	.287	.309	121	398	60	121	22	1	5	46	45	1	0	7	52	11	7	.402	.370
Padilla, Jorge	R-R	6-2	205	8-11-79	.272	.317	.248	53	184	25	50	6	0	4	17	23	0	0	1	27	5	2	.370	.351
Romero, Alex	L-R	6-0	195	9-9-83	.303	.323	.296	104	353	53	107	21	3	7	50	33	11	0	4	38	8	3	.439	.377
Sellers, Neil	R-R	6-0	195	4-3-82	.176	.237	.144	59	170	16	30	10	0	4	16	22	2	0	1	35	0	1	.306	.277
Skipworth, Kyle	L-R	6-4	205	3-1-90	.207	.212	.205	106	396	35	82	12	2	11	49	34	2	0	1	143	0	4	.331	.273
Smolinski, Jake	R-R	5-11	185	2-9-89	.245	.256	.240	116	396	42	97	26	0	7	36	59	1	0	3	57	6	5	.364	.342
Synan, Jeremy	L-R	6-0	193	7-14-86	.338	.333	.339	35	68	17	23	6	3	1	9	13	0	0	0	14	2	1	.559	.444
Torres, Tim	B-R	6-2	180	11-12-83	.239	.323	.193	26	88	6	21	1	0	0	6	9	1	0	0	23	3	1	.250	.316

Pitching

Pitching	B-T	HT	WT	DOB	W	L	ERA	G	GS	CG	SV	IP	H	R	ER	HR	BB	SO	AVG	vLH	vRH	K/9	BB/9
Allison, Jeff	R-R	6-2	195	11-7-84	3	4	6.26	30	4	0	0	65	82	46	45	8	26	29	.313	.407	.247	4.04	3.62
Alvarez, Jose	L-L	5-11	150	5-6-89	2	6	5.35	12	12	0	0	66	80	47	39	9	22	45	.308	.328	.301	6.17	3.02
Andrelczyk, Pete	R-R	6-1	185	11-10-85	5	2	3.06	20	1	0	0	35	30	12	12	4	15	30	.231	.262	.200	7.64	3.82
Benjamin, Ramon	R-L	6-2	180	6-14-87	2	2	4.64	16	0	0	0	21	30	21	11	2	12	16	.337	.414	.300	6.75	5.06
Brady, Mike	R-R	6-0	200	3-21-87	0	0	4.50	1	0	0	0	2	3	1	1	0	1	0	.333	.250	.400	0.00	4.50
Downs, Darin	R-L	6-3	210	12-26-84	2	5	4.83	22	13	0	0	76	87	44	41	7	23	48	.289	.244	.308	5.66	2.71
Evans, Bryan	R-R	6-3	205	2-25-87	3	1	3.38	8	6	0	0	37	38	16	14	1	19	27	.271	.255	.282	6.51	4.58
Hand, Brad	L-L	6-3	200	3-20-90	11	4	3.40	19	18	0	0	109	90	42	41	11	50	71	.231	.234	.230	5.88	4.14
Harvey, Kris	R-R	6-2	200	1-5-84	2	3	6.68	24	0	0	0	32	37	30	24	6	15	23	.289	.226	.333	6.40	4.18
Hensley, Clay	R-R	5-11	190	8-31-79	0	0	2.08	1	1	0	0	4	5	1	1	0	1	7	.278	.250	.286	14.54	2.08
Jennings, Daniel	L-L	6-3	190	4-17-87	4	1	3.16	21	0	0	2	26	26	11	9	1	11	29	.265	.300	.241	10.17	3.86
Kaminska, Kyle	L-R	6-4	180	10-5-88	2	1	3.71	7	0	0	0	17	16	8	7	1	4	12	.242	.115	.325	6.35	2.12
Korpi, Wade	R-L	5-11	185	3-10-86	0	2	2.25	12	0	0	3	16	16	4	4	1	5	11	.267	.231	.294	6.19	2.81
Madden, Corey	R-R	6-1	195	3-30-84	2	1	2.72	25	0	0	0	43	32	15	13	2	18	42	.212	.222	.203	8.79	3.77
Marinez, Jhan	R-R	6-1	165	8-12-88	3	8	3.57	56	0	0	3	58	47	26	23	7	42	74	.223	.188	.246	11.48	6.52
O'Gara, Joey	R-R	6-0	205	4-20-88	7	9	4.55	27	27	0	0	158	181	93	80	11	45	72	.291	.291	.292	4.09	2.56
Parcell, Garrett	R-R	6-5	220	7-12-84	0	0	2.25	3	0	0	0	4	7	1	1	0	1	4	.389	.375	.400	9.00	2.25
Poveda, Omar	R-R	6-4	215	9-28-87	8	6	4.32	27	27	1	0	156	153	83	75	16	54	116	.259	.241	.274	6.68	3.11
Rogers, Jared	R-R	6-7	198	5-9-88	0	1	9.00	1	0	0	0	3	4	3	3	1	0	0	.333	.250	.375	0.00	0.00

Pitching	B-T	HT	WT	DOB	W	L	ERA	G	GS	CG	SV	IP	H	R	ER	HR	BB	SO	AVG	vLH	vRH	K/9	BB/9
Rosario, Jose	R-R	6-0	170	2-16-86	1	0	1.29	4	0	0	0	7	7	1	1	1	3	9	.280	.167	.385	11.57	3.86
Rosario, Sandy	R-R	6-1	170	8-22-85	3	2	4.15	46	0	0	23	48	52	31	22	4	17	46	.274	.236	.297	8.69	3.21
Simons, Zach	L-R	6-3	200	5-23-85	0	2	7.30	8	0	0	0	12	14	11	10	2	6	9	.280	.238	.310	6.57	4.38
Squires, Chris	R-R	6-2	195	3-29-88	0	0	6.14	5	0	0	0	7	9	5	5	0	3	1	.290	.267	.313	1.23	3.68
Taylor, Graham	L-L	6-3	225	5-25-84	3	5	4.09	21	17	0	0	99	125	54	45	15	24	62	.316	.266	.336	5.64	2.18
Trahern, Dallas	R-R	6-3	235	11-29-85	5	4	4.68	24	14	0	1	102	112	61	53	7	39	46	.286	.368	.222	4.06	3.44

Fielding

Catcher	PCT	G	PO	A	E	DP	PB
Baker	1.000	3	9	0	0	0	0
Montz	.979	53	286	42	7	2	5
Skipworth	.985	94	611	44	10	6	12

First Base	PCT	G	PO	A	E	DP
Gran	1.000	2	10	0	0	0
Lasater	.993	81	658	69	5	68
Lis	.989	12	80	7	1	6
Montz	.990	46	366	24	4	37
Sellers	.989	13	90	4	1	5
Torres	1.000	2	21	1	0	4

Second Base	PCT	G	PO	A	E	DP
Curry	.967	90	179	259	15	67
Negrych	.981	56	106	148	5	39

Torres	1.000	5	8	13	0	3

Third Base	PCT	G	PO	A	E	DP
Curry	.933	6	3	11	1	0
Dominguez	1.000	4	5	12	0	1
Gran	.907	61	32	105	14	6
Gutierrez	1.000	1	2	2	0	0
Lasater	.900	5	1	8	1	0
Negrych	.889	39	18	62	10	6
Sellers	.929	33	19	73	7	12
Torres	.000	1	0	0	0	0

Shortstop	PCT	G	PO	A	E	DP
Dominguez	.958	6	6	17	1	0
Gran	.984	16	26	37	1	13
Gutierrez	.948	119	170	339	28	64

Torres	1.000	7	7	14	0	3

Outfield	PCT	G	PO	A	E	DP
Coghlan	1.000	4	5	0	0	0
Curry	1.000	3	7	0	0	1
Jensen	.980	21	48	1	1	0
Mattison	.975	129	374	15	10	4
Montz	.955	10	20	1	1	0
Negrych	1.000	3	3	0	0	0
Padilla	.957	47	87	3	4	0
Romero	.984	88	175	5	3	1
Smolinski	.991	108	206	11	2	1
Synan	.974	20	36	1	1	1
Torres	1.000	12	21	1	0	0

JUPITER HAMMERHEADS   HIGH CLASS A

FLORIDA STATE LEAGUE

Batting	B-T	HT	WT	DOB	AVG	vLH	vRH	G	AB	R	H	2B	3B	HR	RBI	BB	HBP	SH	SF	SO	SB	CS	SLG	OBP
Acosta, Pedro	R-R	6-2	213	7-11-90	.000	.000	.000	1	1	0	0	0	0	0	0	0	0	0	0	0	0	0	.000	.000
Austin, Chase	R-R	6-2	185	12-4-87	.226	.259	.212	105	372	45	84	12	2	10	41	24	9	0	3	60	11	4	.349	.287
Baker, John	L-R	6-1	220	1-20-81	.286	.286	.286	12	28	8	8	2	2	0	1	10	1	0	0	8	0	0	.500	.487
Ceballos, Jose	R-R	6-0	190	12-27-88	.000	.000	.000	4	6	0	0	0	0	0	0	0	0	0	0	3	0	0	.000	.000
Coghlan, Chris	L-R	6-0	205	6-18-85	.343	.250	.370	10	35	4	12	1	0	0	2	5	0	0	1	5	1	1	.371	.415
Cousins, Scott	L-L	6-1	195	1-22-85	.308	.333	.300	5	13	2	4	0	0	0	2	3	0	0	0	4	0	0	.308	.438
Cregar, Chad	L-R	6-4	221	10-30-86	.000	.000	.000	2	7	0	0	0	0	0	0	0	0	0	0	2	0	0	.000	.000
Dominguez, Jeff	B-R	6-2	160	7-31-86	.255	.254	.256	121	470	56	120	20	4	7	59	31	4	0	3	81	25	5	.360	.305
Dominguez, Matt	R-R	6-1	205	8-28-89	.167	.143	.182	4	18	0	3	0	0	0	2	1	1	0	0	3	0	0	.167	.250
Duarte, Jose	R-R	5-10	165	3-7-85	.254	.292	.242	100	374	52	95	22	2	3	34	34	1	0	5	67	19	9	.348	.359
Fermin, Miguel	R-R	5-11	175	2-11-85	.254	.317	.227	43	138	16	35	7	0	4	13	5	1	0	1	31	1	1	.391	.283
Glime, Gregg	B-R	5-11	200	10-29-87	.198	.333	.131	28	91	12	18	4	0	2	9	7	1	0	0	30	0	1	.308	.263
Hord, Dallas	R-R	6-0	175	11-25-87	.226	.250	.217	12	31	2	7	0	0	0	2	3	0	0	0	11	2	0	.226	.294
Infante, Omar	R-R	6-0	180	12-26-81	.600	.000	.600	1	5	0	3	0	0	0	0	0	0	0	0	0	0	0	.600	.600
Jensen, Kyle	R-L	6-4	230	5-20-88	.309	.370	.289	109	391	53	121	20	1	22	66	46	5	0	5	114	0	0	.535	.385
Krick, Taylor	R-R	6-1	200	3-31-88	.246	.270	.232	68	199	21	49	3	0	1	16	27	9	0	1	44	1	3	.276	.360
Lopez, Alfredo	R-R	5-10	160	10-7-89	.337	.269	.339	24	82	7	26	2	1	0	8	2	0	0	15	5	2	.366	.391
Manzanillo, Ernesto	R-R	5-11	165	12-24-88	.243	.253	.240	85	304	21	74	16	1	2	24	12	1	0	3	68	6	3	.322	.272
Morrison, Logan	L-L	6-3	235	8-25-87	.200	.000	.286	3	10	2	2	0	0	1	3	3	0	0	0	4	0	0	.500	.385
Murphy, Donnie	R-R	5-10	195	3-10-83	.130	.333	.059	8	23	4	3	0	1	0	2	5	2	0	0	6	0	0	.217	.333
Ortiz, Jaime	L-L	6-1	220	7-14-88	.255	.290	.244	115	392	38	100	20	2	5	35	31	4	0	6	74	3	1	.355	.312
Othman, Sharif	B-R	6-0	195	3-23-89	.218	.250	.204	24	78	3	17	3	0	1	5	4	1	0	1	20	0	0	.295	.262
Pedroza, Sergio	L-R	6-1	180	2-23-84	.244	.171	.279	39	127	16	31	6	0	4	20	16	2	0	3	21	1	1	.386	.331
Peralta, Rony	L-R	6-0	160	8-19-90	.111	.091	.120	13	36	4	4	0	0	0	2	0	0	0	0	15	0	0	.111	.158
Pertusati, Danny	R-R	6-1	185	4-27-90	.237	.339	.190	119	384	39	91	21	3	6	42	28	3	0	3	85	10	7	.354	.292
Poulk, Dallas	L-R	5-11	175	5-16-88	.261	.281	.257	100	348	40	91	19	2	0	32	41	2	0	0	66	10	7	.328	.343
Ramirez, Hanley	R-R	6-3	230	12-23-83	.476	.333	.500	6	21	6	10	1	1	0	4	1	0	0	0	2	1	0	.619	.500
Smith, Rand	R-R	6-0	190	6-11-87	.306	.250	.333	19	62	7	19	4	0	1	6	7	0	0	0	11	1	2	.419	.377
Synan, Jeremy	L-R	6-0	193	7-14-86	.197	.154	.214	64	238	20	47	9	4	2	19	27	4	0	0	55	1	3	.294	.294
Torres, Jose	R-R	6-0	170	10-22-90	.221	.284	.188	83	253	25	56	11	0	0	16	8	3	0	1	29	7	0	.265	.253
Woods, Nate	R-R	6-6	203	3-28-89	.212	.333	.129	16	52	2	11	2	0	0	4	0	0	0	0	10	0	0	.308	.255

Pitching	B-T	HT	WT	DOB	W	L	ERA	G	GS	CG	SV	IP	H	R	ER	HR	BB	SO	AVG	vLH	vRH	K/9	BB/9
Alvarez, Jose	L-L	5-11	150	5-6-89	6	1	2.96	15	14	0	0	82	79	32	27	2	19	73	.258	.234	.269	8.01	2.09
Battisto, A.J.	R-R	6-0	193	9-30-83	0	0	2.65	10	0	0	0	17	13	5	5	1	5	16	.213	.250	.189	8.47	2.65
Benjamin, Ramon	R-L	6-2	180	6-14-87	5	1	3.29	27	0	0	1	41	36	18	15	1	19	37	.235	.175	.271	8.12	4.17
Buret, Alfredo	R-R	6-1	160	8-22-87	0	0	0.00	2	0	0	0	4	2	0	0	0	3	3	.143	.000	.200	6.23	6.23
Cargill, Collin	R-R	6-2	190	10-6-87	1	1	2.20	11	0	0	1	16	14	5	4	0	8	5	.255	.269	.241	2.76	4.41
Donatello, Sean	R-R	6-2	205	8-24-90	0	0	3.86	1	0	0	0	2	3	1	1	0	0	2	.300	.286	.333	7.71	0.00
Estevez, Albaro	R-R	6-2	180	3-15-89	2	0	0.00	4	0	0	0	5	5	2	0	0	1	3	.263	.167	.308	5.06	1.69
Evans, Bryan	R-R	6-3	205	2-25-87	5	1	1.02	17	5	0	0	53	33	8	6	2	13	43	.178	.159	.196	7.30	2.21
Hand, Brad	L-L	6-3	200	3-20-90	0	1	7.20	1	1	0	0	5	5	5	4	1	5	4	.278	.500	.250	7.20	9.00
Harvey, Kris	R-R	6-2	200	1-5-84	3	2	2.27	21	0	0	0	32	18	9	8	1	12	31	.167	.140	.188	8.81	3.41
Hensley, Clay	R-R	5-11	190	8-31-79	0	1	4.50	1	1	0	0	4	2	2	2	1	2	4	.143	.125	.167	4.50	0.00
James, Chad	L-L	6-3	185	1-23-91	5	15	3.80	27	27	0	0	149	173	77	63	12	51	124	.294	.273	.303	7.47	3.07
Johnson, Graham	R-R	6-6	215	10-13-89	0	4	7.51	33	0	0	1	56	91	58	47	11	34	30	.360	.393	.336	4.79	5.43
Kaminska, Kyle	L-R	6-4	180	10-5-88	3	1	2.33	25	5	0	0	77	69	25	20	5	16	69	.235	.226	.243	8.03	1.86

Pitching

Pitching	B-T	HT	WT	DOB	W	L	ERA	G	GS	CG	SV	IP	H	R	ER	HR	BB	SO	AVG	vLH	vRH	K/9	BB/9
Korpi, Wade	R-L	5-11	185	3-10-86	3	2	2.05	32	0	0	1	53	43	16	12	2	18	48	.228	.210	.236	8.20	3.08
Mincey, Brad	R-R	6-0	190	12-9-88	0	0	0.00	4	0	0	1	6	4	0	0	0	1	7	.190	.250	.111	10.50	1.50
Montgomery, Matt	R-R	6-4	210	7-21-87	3	7	3.39	19	19	1	0	109	120	46	41	6	16	72	.278	.294	.265	5.94	1.32
Neil, Matthew	R-R	6-6	225	9-5-86	2	0	3.48	2	2	0	0	10	11	5	4	1	2	10	.282	.304	.250	8.71	1.74
Nygren, James	R-R	6-0	195	3-8-89	1	0	9.00	1	0	0	0	2	4	2	2	1	1	1	.444	.333	.667	4.50	4.50
Olmos, Edgar	L-L	6-5	180	4-12-90	4	17	6.63	28	28	0	0	128	167	110	94	13	81	101	.318	.278	.332	7.12	5.71
Omahen, John	R-R	6-0	190	3-15-89	1	1	3.72	8	2	0	0	19	17	13	8	1	12	11	.233	.188	.268	5.12	5.59
Peale, Tommy	R-R	6-3	225	11-11-86	0	0	40.50	1	0	0	0	1	1	3	3	0	3	1	.500	1.000	.000	13.50	40.50
Ramos, A.J.	R-R	5-10	210	9-20-86	1	4	1.78	49	0	0	25	51	37	12	10	2	19	71	.200	.274	.152	12.61	3.38
Rasmussen, Rob	R-L	5-10	155	4-2-89	12	10	3.64	28	27	1	0	148	140	75	60	10	71	118	.254	.235	.261	7.16	4.31
Reed, Evan	R-R	6-4	225	12-31-85	0	1	4.02	11	0	0	0	16	9	7	7	0	10	13	.176	.111	.212	7.47	5.74
Rosario, Jose	R-R	6-0	170	2-16-86	3	2	2.31	31	5	0	2	70	62	20	18	2	21	74	.238	.270	.210	9.51	2.70
Sanabia, Alex	R-R	6-2	165	9-8-88	0	2	5.73	2	2	0	0	11	13	8	7	2	0	1	.277	.353	.233	0.82	0.00
Sanches, Brian	R-R	6-0	190	8-8-78	0	1	6.75	1	1	0	0	3	2	2	2	1	0	1	.200	.143	.333	3.38	0.00
Simons, Zach	L-R	6-3	200	5-23-85	0	0	0.00	5	0	0	0	4	4	2	0	0	1	3	.222	.167	.333	6.23	2.08
Solano, Aneurys	R-R	6-1	180	11-18-88	0	0	12.00	5	0	0	0	6	10	9	8	2	6	5	.357	.250	.500	7.50	9.00
Sprague, Holden	R-R	6-2	210	7-24-87	0	0	0.00	1	0	0	0	1	0	0	0	0	1	0	.000	.000	.000	0.00	9.00
Squires, Chris	R-R	6-2	195	3-29-88	0	1	3.65	17	0	0	1	25	26	13	10	0	11	19	.265	.275	.259	6.93	4.01
Toves, Ken	R-L	6-3	180	7-31-89	0	0	7.59	5	0	0	1	11	15	9	9	1	6	9	.341	.455	.303	7.59	5.06
Webb, Ryan	R-R	6-6	215	2-5-86	1	0	2.70	3	1	0	0	3	4	1	1	0	3	3	.333	.400	.286	8.10	8.10

Fielding

Catcher	PCT	G	PO	A	E	DP	PB
Baker	1.000	7	29	2	0	0	1
Ceballos	1.000	3	9	0	0	0	0
Fermin	.997	42	316	19	1	1	3
Glime	.996	26	206	18	1	1	1
Hord	.974	12	67	9	2	1	1
Krick	.991	46	311	32	3	6	8
Othman	.990	15	96	8	1	1	1

First Base	PCT	G	PO	A	E	DP
Austin	.975	5	36	3	1	4
Cregar	1.000	1	7	0	0	1
Krick	.975	9	74	4	2	4
Ortiz	.986	113	868	65	13	96
Pertusati	1.000	6	29	2	0	6
Woods	.956	13	103	5	5	5

Second Base	PCT	G	PO	A	E	DP
Infante	1.000	1	2	7	0	0
Lopez	.982	14	28	28	1	5

	PCT	G	PO	A	E	DP
Manzanillo	.951	10	17	22	2	3
Poulk	.964	93	183	243	16	60
Torres	.971	27	58	78	4	20

Third Base	PCT	G	PO	A	E	DP
Austin	.938	69	57	141	13	19
Dominguez	1.000	4	3	8	0	0
Krick	.875	4	1	6	1	0
Lopez	.950	8	5	14	1	0
Manzanillo	.923	7	7	17	2	3
Murphy	.900	7	1	8	1	0
Peralta	.818	5	2	7	2	0
Pertusati	.871	13	10	17	4	2
Poulk	1.000	1	0	2	0	0
Torres	.916	32	21	55	7	4

Shortstop	PCT	G	PO	A	E	DP
Dominguez	.936	103	166	275	30	56
Manzanillo	.963	7	9	17	1	0
Murphy	1.000	1	0	1	0	0

	PCT	G	PO	A	E	DP
Peralta	.963	8	7	19	1	2
Ramirez	.938	5	8	7	1	1
Torres	.946	25	35	71	6	18

Outfield	PCT	G	PO	A	E	DP
Austin	1.000	24	38	3	0	0
Coghlan	1.000	8	13	0	0	0
Cousins	.923	5	12	0	1	0
Dominguez	1.000	3	1	0	0	0
Duarte	.989	96	247	17	3	2
Jensen	.973	74	104	6	3	2
Krick	1.000	5	2	0	0	0
Manzanillo	.989	50	86	5	1	0
Morrison	1.000	3	8	1	0	1
Pedroza	.982	30	49	5	1	1
Pertusati	.977	98	160	10	4	0
Smith	1.000	18	45	3	0	1
Synan	.975	38	74	4	2	0
Woods	1.000	1	1	0	0	0

GREENSBORO GRASSHOPPERS
LOW CLASS A

SOUTH ATLANTIC LEAGUE

Batting	B-T	HT	WT	DOB	AVG	vLH	vRH	G	AB	R	H	2B	3B	HR	RBI	BB	HBP	SH	SF	SB	CS	SLG	OBP
Black, Danny	L-R	6-2	170	8-19-88	.280	.244	.296	120	415	58	116	18	5	5	51	37	2	0	4	81	32	10	.383	.338
Bonadonna, Joe	R-R	5-8	170	9-6-85	.196	.231	.165	60	163	21	32	6	0	2	9	17	5	0	2	42	13	3	.270	.289
Canha, Mark	R-R	6-2	195	2-15-89	.276	.296	.265	107	384	72	106	22	0	25	85	59	5	0	7	85	7	3	.529	.374
Dudley, Aaron	L-R	6-3	193	2-17-88	.277	.231	.292	64	213	29	59	9	0	5	26	20	4	0	1	54	2	2	.390	.349
Fisher, Ryan	L-R	6-3	195	4-24-88	.258	.212	.279	129	469	74	121	36	4	18	79	38	14	0	3	137	7	3	.467	.330
Galloway, Isaac	R-R	6-2	190	10-10-89	.241	.293	.215	110	431	56	104	26	1	16	54	14	3	0	2	119	17	9	.448	.269
Gimenez, Wilfredo	R-R	6-0	180	12-18-90	.251	.248	.254	72	251	33	63	13	1	3	32	9	4	0	4	44	0	1	.347	.284
Keys, Brent	L-R	6-1	210	7-14-90	.208	.316	.147	17	53	6	11	0	0	0	5	10	2	0	1	14	5	1	.208	.348
McConkey, Brian	L-R	6-2	210	12-17-88	.263	.254	.266	63	213	36	56	13	0	5	26	29	8	0	5	44	1	0	.394	.365
Mendoza, Pedro	R-R	6-0	148	5-11-91	.224	.286	.180	26	85	6	19	4	0	0	9	1	0	0	0	10	2	1	.271	.233
Morales, Jobduan	B-R	5-10	180	6-7-91	.333	.250	.400	3	9	1	3	0	0	0	2	1	0	0	0	3	0	0	.333	.400
Ozuna, Marcell	R-R	6-2	190	11-12-90	.266	.294	.251	131	496	87	132	28	5	23	71	46	2	0	2	121	17	2	.482	.330
Perio, Noah	L-R	6-0	170	11-14-91	.295	.280	.301	119	488	76	144	30	3	6	52	19	3	0	4	64	15	6	.406	.323
Realmuto, J.T.	R-R	6-1	190	3-18-91	.287	.254	.308	96	348	46	100	16	3	12	49	26	6	0	0	78	13	6	.454	.347
Smith, Rand	R-R	6-0	190	6-11-87	.211	.200	.222	8	19	1	4	1	0	0	1	3	0	0	1	8	0	1	.263	.304
Wooster, James	L-L	6-1	200	6-19-89	.242	.118	.270	57	186	33	45	8	1	7	28	12	0	0	2	59	1	0	.409	.285
Yelich, Christian	L-R	6-4	189	12-5-91	.312	.256	.341	122	461	73	144	32	1	15	77	55	3	0	2	102	32	5	.484	.388

Pitching	B-T	HT	WT	DOB	W	L	ERA	G	GS	CG	SV	IP	H	R	ER	HR	BB	SO	AVG	vLH	vRH	K/9	BB/9
Brady, Mike	R-R	6-0	200	3-21-87	7	1	1.91	48	0	0	18	61	40	15	13	4	10	81	.184	.155	.203	11.89	1.47
Buret, Alfredo	R-R	6-1	160	8-22-87	0	0	7.20	3	0	0	0	5	9	5	4	1	0	3	.391	.667	.294	5.40	0.00
Caldera, Alex	L-R	6-3	200	10-1-85	3	1	3.77	6	6	0	0	31	27	16	13	1	13	33	.241	.250	.235	9.58	3.77
Conley, Jordan	R-R	6-1	180	7-19-86	3	2	2.48	41	0	0	3	62	50	19	17	2	14	53	.213	.151	.248	7.74	2.04
Cravey, Kevin	R-R	6-1	180	8-15-87	0	1	6.00	9	0	0	1	15	17	12	10	1	8	12	.288	.444	.220	7.20	4.80
Dayton, Grant	L-L	6-2	200	11-25-87	7	1	2.89	49	0	0	5	72	59	25	23	5	24	99	.223	.183	.237	12.43	3.01
Leverton, James	R-L	6-2	185	5-13-86	3	3	1.61	6	2	0	0	28	22	7	5	0	9	35	.220	.185	.233	11.25	2.89
Manzueta, Jheyson	R-R	6-2	162	12-5-89	2	10	6.56	20	20	0	0	84	84	69	61	12	66	59	.265	.345	.217	6.35	7.10
Mejia, Miguel	R-R	6-2	210	1-19-88	1	2	2.63	9	0	0	0	14	9	5	4	1	2	16	.184	.188	.182	10.54	1.32

Pitching	B-T	HT	WT	DOB	W	L	ERA	G	GS	CG	SV	IP	H	R	ER	HR	BB	SO	AVG	vLH	vRH	K/9	BB/9
Mincey, Brad	R-R	6-0	190	12-9-88	0	0	3.00	1	0	0	0	3	5	4	1	0	3	2	.333	.714	.000	6.00	9.00
Morey, Robert	R-R	6-1	185	11-27-88	7	7	5.14	26	25	1	0	140	163	88	80	14	52	107	.290	.280	.298	6.88	3.34
Nappo, Gregory	L-L	6-0	190	8-25-88	4	1	4.61	9	6	0	0	41	42	23	21	5	9	36	.266	.213	.288	7.90	1.98
Neal, Zach	R-R	6-3	220	11-9-88	7	6	4.16	22	22	0	0	119	124	61	55	12	41	84	.273	.264	.279	6.35	3.10
Oaks, Alan	R-R	6-3	225	4-4-88	1	1	3.15	4	4	0	0	20	20	8	7	1	5	11	.260	.267	.258	4.95	2.25
Ojala, Mike	R-R	6-3	195	8-24-87	4	3	4.42	38	0	0	0	55	47	34	27	7	28	63	.228	.188	.256	10.31	4.58
Peale, Tommy	R-R	6-3	225	11-11-86	0	1	16.20	1	1	0	0	3	7	7	6	0	2	2	.438	.500	.417	5.40	5.40
Rogers, Jared	R-R	6-7	198	5-9-88	5	5	3.16	17	13	0	0	80	87	33	28	6	16	54	.278	.281	.276	6.10	1.81
Shafer, Chris	R-R	6-2	245	5-16-89	4	0	3.60	39	0	0	1	65	61	32	26	5	30	55	.247	.337	.199	7.62	4.15
Sprague, Holden	R-R	6-2	210	7-24-87	0	2	7.94	14	0	0	0	40	52	35	35	7	11	31	.323	.232	.371	7.03	2.50
Squires, Chris	R-R	6-2	195	3-29-88	0	1	11.81	4	0	0	0	5	11	8	7	0	1	4	.440	.500	.412	6.75	1.69
Toves, Ken	R-L	6-3	180	7-31-89	2	0	7.15	7	0	0	0	11	16	9	9	1	3	15	.320	.300	.333	11.91	2.38
Varner, Rett	R-R	6-4	185	2-3-88	8	8	5.29	20	20	0	0	102	125	69	60	15	31	62	.298	.318	.285	5.47	2.74
Veres, Adam	R-R	6-4	230	3-19-88	2	1	4.88	13	0	0	0	24	25	13	13	2	7	18	.275	.355	.233	6.75	2.63
Watson, Sean	R-R	6-2	215	7-24-85	1	1	2.57	12	0	0	9	14	10	4	4	0	13	18	.208	.267	.182	11.57	8.36
Winters, Kyle	R-R	6-4	190	4-22-87	8	3	4.10	19	19	0	0	97	84	51	44	8	27	75	.233	.242	.228	6.98	2.51
Zawacki, Brett	R-R	6-1	190	5-2-89	0	0	2.84	9	1	0	0	19	17	6	6	2	9	10	.246	.286	.229	4.74	4.26

Fielding

Catcher	PCT	G	PO	A	E	DP	PB
Dudley	.992	18	115	6	1	0	5
Gimenez	.992	48	344	44	3	2	10
Morales	1.000	2	18	0	0	0	0
Realmuto	.978	76	535	91	14	9	25

First Base	PCT	G	PO	A	E	DP
Canha	.994	95	771	67	5	71
Dudley	.930	8	52	1	4	8
McConkey	.987	38	302	7	4	30
Morales	1.000	1	4	0	0	1

Second Base	PCT	G	PO	A	E	DP
Black	1.000	9	25	29	0	9

	PCT	G	PO	A	E	DP	PB
Bonadonna	.987	20	33	41	1		12
Mendoza	1.000	1	0	1	0		0
Perio	.953	114	201	291	24		60

Third Base	PCT	G	PO	A	E	DP
Black	1.000	2	1	6	0	2
Bonadonna	1.000	12	16	17	0	5
Dudley	.000	1	0	0	0	0
Fisher	.939	127	72	267	22	18
Mendoza	1.000	2	1	2	0	1

Shortstop	PCT	G	PO	A	E	DP
Black	.960	108	155	251	17	44
Bonadonna	.974	11	19	18	1	6

	PCT	G	PO	A	E	DP
Fisher	1.000	1	1	1	0	1
Mendoza	.971	23	28	71	3	14
Perio	.846	2	5	6	2	3

Outfield	PCT	G	PO	A	E	DP
Bonadonna	.929	9	13	0	1	0
Dudley	.000	1	0	0	0	0
Galloway	.996	108	245	3	1	2
Keys	.968	17	30	0	1	0
McConkey	1.000	1	1	0	0	0
Ozuna	.967	125	278	14	10	5
Smith	.889	7	8	0	1	0
Wooster	1.000	51	94	8	0	1
Yelich	.972	113	207	4	6	1

JAMESTOWN JAMMERS   SHORT-SEASON
NEW YORK-PENN LEAGUE

Batting	B-T	HT	WT	DOB	AVG	vLH	vRH	G	AB	R	H	2B	3B	HR	RBI	BB	HBP	SH	SF	SO	SB	CS	SLG	OBP
Adams, Joshua	R-R	5-11	185	3-7-89	.244	.256	.241	53	205	26	50	13	0	2	29	18	0	0	5	36	1	0	.337	.298
Barnes, Austin	R-R	5-10	190	12-28-89	.288	.250	.299	57	219	33	63	13	0	1	19	25	4	0	1	22	6	1	.361	.369
Behar, Jose	R-R	6-1	200	4-30-89	.000	.000	.000	1	4	0	0	0	0	0	0	0	0	0	0	1	0	0	.000	.000
Castillo, Nestor	B-R	6-2	176	10-24-89	.219	.273	.207	34	114	19	25	1	2	0	9	7	1	0	0	21	7	1	.263	.270
Cooper, Marquise	R-R	5-9	175	10-16-91	.220	.167	.239	60	182	32	40	5	1	4	22	25	7	0	1	54	14	3	.324	.335
Dayleg, Terrence	R-R	6-0	170	9-19-87	.273	.204	.293	62	242	33	66	14	3	4	30	19	8	0	1	46	3	3	.405	.344
Dewitt, Kentrell	L-R	5-11	180	3-20-91	.200	.133	.224	32	115	13	23	2	2	2	13	9	1	0	2	34	4	1	.304	.260
Goetz, Ryan	L-R	5-10	185	5-16-88	.240	.194	.257	61	233	32	56	9	2	2	25	31	2	0	4	51	4	3	.322	.330
Keys, Brent	L-R	6-1	210	7-14-90	.340	.276	.364	26	106	13	36	2	0	1	12	2	0	0	0	9	6	2	.387	.352
Lopez, Alfredo	R-R	5-10	160	10-7-89	.244	.200	.257	14	45	8	11	0	0	0	3	2	0	0	0	10	4	0	.244	.306
McConkey, Brian	L-R	6-2	210	12-17-88	.246	.313	.224	34	130	14	32	3	0	2	14	18	1	0	0	24	1	2	.315	.342
McIntyre, Ryan	L-R	6-1	190	5-26-90	.189	.400	.136	23	74	11	14	1	0	0	5	10	3	0	2	16	3	1	.203	.303
Mendoza, Pedro	R-R	6-0	148	5-11-91	.252	.250	.253	35	131	10	33	4	0	0	9	5	1	0	0	11	1	2	.282	.285
Morales, Jobduan	B-R	5-10	180	6-7-91	.272	.250	.279	52	180	31	49	10	5	4	23	32	1	0	0	38	0	1	.450	.385
Peralta, Rony	L-R	6-0	160	8-19-90	.217	.143	.239	23	92	7	20	1	0	1	9	2	1	0	1	19	1	1	.261	.240
Perez, Yefri	R-R	5-11	162	2-24-91	.198	.278	.176	24	86	6	17	5	1	0	10	2	0	0	2	16	3	0	.279	.213
Rodriguez, Eddie	R-R	6-1	215	7-29-88	.247	.250	.246	28	89	11	22	5	1	0	12	7	3	0	0	14	0	0	.326	.323
Rosa, Viosergy	L-L	6-3	185	6-16-90	.210	.393	.165	41	143	16	30	9	1	1	18	7	3	0	2	54	0	0	.308	.258
Smith, Rand	R-R	6-0	190	6-11-87	.270	.227	.280	30	115	15	31	4	0	3	12	10	2	0	0	19	4	1	.383	.339
Woods, Nate	R-R	6-6	230	3-28-89	.184	.273	.148	10	38	3	7	2	0	1	2	0	0	0	1	8	0	0	.316	.179

Pitching	B-T	HT	WT	DOB	W	L	ERA	G	GS	CG	SV	IP	H	R	ER	HR	BB	SO	AVG	vLH	vRH	K/9	BB/9
Brewer, Blake	R-R	6-5	177	3-2-90	2	1	4.30	21	0	0	1	23	13	11	11	0	30	30	.181	.167	.189	11.74	11.74
Buret, Alfredo	R-R	6-1	160	8-22-87	0	1	4.03	27	0	0	11	29	32	14	13	2	14	28	.281	.364	.203	8.69	4.34
Cargill, Collin	R-R	6-2	190	10-6-87	0	0	6.00	2	0	0	0	3	5	2	2	0	0	1	.357	.667	.273	3.00	0.00
Esch, Jacob	R-R	6-4	190	3-23-91	1	1	4.63	8	0	0	0	12	13	10	6	6	11	.283	.238	.320	8.49	4.63
Estevez, Albaro	R-R	6-2	180	3-15-89	1	1	11.00	7	0	0	0	9	18	11	11	0	7	10	.439	.353	.500	10.00	7.00
Fernandez, Jose	R-R	6-3	215	7-31-92	0	1	19.29	1	1	0	0	2	4	5	5	0	3	4	.400	.429	.333	15.43	11.57
Hodges, Josh	R-R	6-7	235	6-21-91	8	1	3.39	15	15	0	0	88	90	39	33	7	18	50	.272	.284	.263	5.13	1.85
Lowell, Charlie	L-L	6-4	235	10-25-90	0	0	0.00	2	0	0	0	2	1	0	0	0	2	4	.143	.000	.333	18.00	9.00
Lyman, Scott	R-R	6-4	215	3-21-90	0	0	4.50	2	0	0	0	2	4	1	1	0	0	2	.400	.667	.286	9.00	0.00
Manzueta, Jheyson	R-R	6-2	162	12-5-89	0	1	6.61	10	0	0	0	16	15	13	12	0	7	13	.250	.276	.226	7.16	3.86
Mejia, Miguel	R-R	6-2	210	1-19-88	2	1	4.00	6	0	0	1	9	5	4	4	0	1	16	.161	.200	.143	10.00	1.00
Mincey, Brad	R-R	6-0	190	12-9-88	0	1	3.18	12	0	0	0	23	19	8	8	1	6	14	.229	.286	.188	5.56	2.38
Nappo, Gregory	L-L	6-0	190	8-25-88	0	0	0.00	5	2	0	0	14	4	0	0	0	3	22	.087	.091	.086	14.14	1.93
Neil, Matthew	R-R	6-6	225	9-5-86	2	3	3.26	13	13	0	0	66	69	26	24	6	5	61	.262	.232	.290	8.28	0.68
Oliver, Dejai	R-R	6-2	200	8-28-90	1	5	7.27	9	8	0	0	35	48	28	28	3	12	37	.331	.415	.263	9.61	3.12

FLORIDA MARLINS

Pitching	B-T	HT	WT	DOB	W	L	ERA	G	GS	CG	SV	IP	H	R	ER	HR	BB	SO	AVG	vLH	vRH	K/9	BB/9
Peale, Tommy	R-R	6-3	225	11-11-86	3	2	3.17	15	8	0	0	48	41	21	17	2	14	27	.229	.226	.232	5.03	2.61
Petersen, Curtis	R-R	6-3	180	8-28-89	3	3	5.52	23	0	0	0	31	28	23	19	2	24	22	.241	.275	.215	6.39	6.97
Reed, Frankie	L-L	6-1	185	2-12-88	1	1	6.11	12	0	0	0	18	21	12	12	1	5	16	.276	.280	.275	8.15	2.55
Reyes, Helpi	R-R	6-1	175	7-27-92	1	6	5.37	15	12	0	0	60	64	43	36	0	28	32	.279	.291	.268	4.77	4.18
Richards, Stephen	L-L	6-0	180	8-10-88	0	1	10.64	11	0	0	0	11	13	16	13	1	15	13	.283	.294	.276	10.64	12.27
Rodriguez, Jose	R-R	6-1	195	9-24-90	0	1	6.75	1	1	0	0	4	3	4	3	1	3	3	.200	.000	.300	6.75	6.75
Sprague, Holden	R-R	6-2	210	7-24-87	0	1	8.03	7	0	0	0	12	11	12	11	1	13	15	.239	.292	.182	10.95	9.49
Squires, Chris	R-R	6-2	195	3-29-88	1	0	4.66	4	0	0	0	10	10	5	5	3	0	8	.263	.158	.368	7.45	0.00
Topp, Tyler	R-R	6-2	175	11-14-86	1	0	5.23	7	0	0	0	10	9	6	6	1	5	10	.225	.222	.227	8.71	4.35
Toves, Ken	R-L	6-3	180	7-31-89	0	0	0.00	9	0	0	1	12	8	0	0	0	4	13	.190	.077	.241	9.75	3.00
Urena, Jose	R-R	6-3	172	9-12-91	4	7	4.33	15	15	0	0	73	74	38	35	4	29	48	.264	.264	.265	5.94	3.59
Wier, Charles	R-R	6-2	205	7-26-88	4	1	2.64	21	0	0	2	31	28	10	9	1	9	26	.233	.120	.314	7.63	2.64

Fielding

Catcher	PCT	G	PO	A	E	DP	PB
Barnes	.987	31	209	19	3	3	6
Behar	1.000	1	5	1	0	0	0
Morales	.991	27	195	17	2	3	6
Rodriguez	.986	20	129	7	2	1	5
Goetz	.990	19	33	66	1	10	
Lopez	1.000	13	14	34	0	5	
Mendoza	.983	23	40	75	2	23	
Peralta	1.000	2	6	8	0	0	
Perez	1.000	1	0	3	0	0	
Mendoza	.914	10	9	23	3	1	
Peralta	.973	15	30	41	2	11	
Perez	.888	21	35	60	12	11	

First Base	PCT	G	PO	A	E	DP
Dayleg	1.000	15	130	7	0	8
McConkey	.989	21	170	10	2	25
Morales	.986	21	198	10	3	19
Rosa	.960	21	161	7	7	19
Woods	1.000	2	17	1	0	1

Second Base	PCT	G	PO	A	E	DP
Adams	.889	2	1	7	1	0
Barnes	.971	12	22	45	2	12
Dayleg	.962	8	24	26	2	7

Third Base	PCT	G	PO	A	E	DP
Adams	.928	48	32	96	10	14
Dayleg	1.000	2	2	3	0	0
Goetz	.865	15	12	20	5	3
Mendoza	.857	2	1	5	1	0
Peralta	.909	7	1	19	2	1
Perez	1.000	1	2	2	0	0

Shortstop	PCT	G	PO	A	E	DP
Adams	1.000	1	1	3	0	0
Dayleg	.958	30	43	94	6	29

Outfield	PCT	G	PO	A	E	DP
Castillo	.981	33	50	3	1	2
Cooper	.976	56	116	4	3	2
Dayleg	1.000	2	2	0	0	0
Dewitt	.951	28	53	5	3	0
Goetz	.977	25	42	1	1	0
Keys	1.000	26	46	2	0	1
Lopez	1.000	1	3	0	0	0
McConkey	.941	11	16	0	1	0
McIntyre	.943	22	29	4	2	2
Smith	1.000	27	45	3	0	1
Woods	1.000	4	7	0	0	0

GCL MARLINS   ROOKIE

GULF COAST LEAGUE

Batting	B-T	HT	WT	DOB	AVG	vLH	vRH	G	AB	R	H	2B	3B	HR	RBI	BB	HBP	SH	SF	SO	SB	CS	SLG	OBP
Acosta, Pedro	R-R	6-2	213	7-11-90	.238	.333	.200	7	21	1	5	1	0	0	0	1	0	0	0	6	1	0	.286	.273
Behar, Jose	R-R	6-1	200	4-30-89	.196	.000	.265	20	46	11	9	1	0	1	7	8	1	0	1	12	1	0	.283	.321
Burke, Connor	R-R	6-1	195	8-20-92	.145	.100	.153	28	69	5	10	1	0	0	5	10	1	0	0	21	0	0	.159	.263
Caldwell, Tony	R-R	5-10	195	12-2-88	.306	.333	.301	32	98	11	30	3	0	1	10	12	6	0	1	16	2	0	.367	.410
Ceballos, Jose	R-R	6-0	190	12-27-88	.000	.000	.000	3	7	1	0	0	0	0	1	0	0	0	0	1	0	0	.000	.000
Dewitt, Kentrell	L-R	5-11	180	3-20-91	.352	.200	.386	16	54	7	19	2	2	0	4	6	1	0	1	14	2	1	.463	.419
Dice, Brian	R-R	6-1	190	10-8-87	.143	.000	.143	4	7	1	1	0	0	0	0	0	0	0	0	4	0	0	.143	.143
Hernandez, Yeison	B-R	5-10	150	6-29-92	.300	.306	.299	51	180	30	54	6	1	0	17	15	6	0	2	28	13	8	.344	.369
Jackson, Kenny	L-R	6-4	195	7-2-89	.202	.095	.231	37	99	14	20	4	0	0	15	16	0	0	2	22	3	1	.242	.308
Martinez, Juancito	R-R	6-1	170	6-10-89	.275	.313	.269	38	109	22	30	8	2	0	10	2	2	0	1	25	6	3	.385	.298
McIntyre, Ryan	L-R	6-1	190	5-26-90	.385	.250	.444	4	13	2	5	2	0	0	2	1	0	0	0	0	0	0	.538	.429
Muecklisch, Todd	R-R	5-10	175	7-9-88	.000	.000	.000	2	5	0	0	0	0	0	0	1	0	0	0	0	0	0	.000	.167
Munoz, Felix	L-L	6-1	193	4-7-92	.290	.283	.292	50	200	21	58	9	1	1	31	14	0	0	2	26	0	1	.360	.333
Myers, Jonathan	R-R	6-2	210	7-16-87	.256	.143	.281	29	78	9	20	3	1	1	12	12	2	0	3	15	0	0	.359	.358
Ortiz, Luis	B-R	5-10	161	3-14-92	.242	.250	.240	47	149	28	36	4	0	1	9	20	4	0	2	23	11	0	.289	.343
Othman, Sharif	B-R	6-0	195	3-23-89	.000	.000	.000	3	11	0	0	0	0	0	0	1	0	0	7	0	0	0	.000	.083
Pedroza, Sergio	L-R	6-1	192	2-23-84	.455	.333	.500	4	11	3	5	1	0	0	6	4	0	0	0	1	0	1	.545	.600
Perez, Yefri	R-R	5-11	162	2-24-91	.319	.333	.314	14	47	8	15	2	1	0	8	3	0	0	0	8	1	0	.404	.360
Rieger, Ryan	L-L	6-2	205	8-10-90	.600	.500	.625	5	10	3	6	1	0	0	3	4	1	0	0	0	0	0	.700	.733
Sammons, Clint	R-R	6-1	210	5-10-83	.333	1.000	.000	4	6	1	2	0	0	1	2	1	0	0	0	0	0	0	.833	.429
Schultz, John	L-L	5-11	195	5-3-89	.278	.344	.262	46	158	40	44	6	4	0	30	29	3	0	4	33	4	2	.367	.392
Solorzano, Jesus	R-R	6-0	190	8-8-90	.299	.351	.287	51	194	34	58	13	4	3	31	13	5	0	2	30	18	7	.454	.355
Soto, Mayobanez	R-R	6-3	185	5-5-91	.216	.000	.267	15	37	5	8	2	0	1	5	8	1	0	0	2	0	0	.351	.370
Veras, Jhiomar	R-R	6-0	195	6-15-90	.238	.318	.215	32	101	17	24	4	1	3	15	7	3	0	0	24	2	2	.386	.306
Woods, Nate	R-R	6-6	230	3-28-89	.333	.429	.315	24	87	17	29	13	1	2	16	10	8	0	0	12	0	0	.575	.448

Pitching	B-T	HT	WT	DOB	W	L	ERA	G	GS	CG	SV	IP	H	R	ER	HR	BB	SO	AVG	vLH	vRH	K/9	BB/9
Battisto, A.J.	R-R	6-0	193	9-30-83	1	0	0.93	9	3	0	0	10	6	1	1	0	0	11	.176	.182	.174	10.24	0.00
Brice, Austin	R-R	6-4	205	6-19-92	6	0	2.96	11	9	0	0	49	32	20	16	2	33	55	.189	.204	.183	10.17	6.10
Caminero, Arquimedes	R-R	6-4	185	6-16-87	0	0	9.00	1	0	0	0	1	2	1	1	0	1	2	.400	.000	.500	18.00	9.00
Cargill, Collin	R-R	6-2	190	10-6-87	1	0	6.52	6	0	0	1	10	13	8	7	1	4	11	.310	.167	.367	10.24	3.72
Conley, Adam	L-L	6-3	185	5-24-90	0	0	0.00	2	0	0	0	2	1	0	0	0	0	2	.143	.000	.200	9.00	0.00
Del Orbe, Ramon	R-R	5-11	177	2-17-92	4	4	3.67	11	9	0	0	54	39	25	22	4	26	54	.196	.232	.177	9.00	4.33
Donatello, Sean	R-R	6-3	185	8-24-90	3	0	2.97	13	4	0	1	30	20	11	10	0	12	21	.190	.160	.200	6.23	3.56
Esch, Jacob	R-R	6-4	190	3-27-90	2	0	1.29	4	0	0	0	7	4	1	1	0	2	6	.182	.222	.154	7.71	2.57
Fernandez, Jose	R-R	6-3	215	7-31-92	0	0	0.00	1	1	0	0	2	1	1	0	0	1	3	.125	.000	.143	13.50	4.50
Gil, Daniel	R-R	6-5	184	12-15-87	1	1	0.82	18	0	0	6	33	30	7	3	1	9	37	.242	.326	.198	10.09	2.45
Hensley, Clay	R-R	5-11	190	8-31-79	0	0	2.70	1	0	0	0	3	2	1	1	0	0	6	.167	.000	.250	16.20	0.00
Higgins, Tyler	R-R	6-3	230	4-22-91	0	0	27.00	2	0	0	0	1	2	4	4	1	3	1	.286	.500	.166	6.75	20.25

Pitching	B-T	HT	WT	DOB	W	L	ERA	G	GS	CG	SV	IP	H	R	ER	HR	BB	SO	AVG	vLH	vRH	K/9	BB/9
Hope, Mason	R-R	6-3	190	6-27-92	2	0	3.29	7	6	0	0	27	27	11	10	0	7	31	.237	.256	.225	10.21	2.30
Lowell, Charlie	L-L	6-4	235	10-25-90	0	1	40.50	2	0	0	0	1	4	6	6	0	2	2	.571	.000	.571	13.50	13.50
Lyman, Scott	R-R	6-4	215	3-21-90	0	0	0.00	2	0	0	0	2	1	2	0	0	3	1	.143	.000	.167	5.40	16.20
Mincey, Brad	R-R	6-0	190	12-9-88	1	0	0.00	2	0	0	0	4	3	0	0	0	2	6	.188	.000	.214	13.50	4.50
Moore, Walker	R-R	6-4	215	7-4-88	0	1	10.80	1	0	0	0	2	2	2	2	1	0	2	.286	.000	.286	10.80	0.00
Nygren, James	R-R	6-0	195	3-8-89	4	1	1.36	19	0	0	6	33	19	9	5	1	5	34	.162	.163	.162	9.27	1.36
Oliver, Dejai	R-R	6-2	200	8-28-90	0	0	0.00	2	1	0	0	3	1	0	0	0	1	5	.100	.000	.250	15.00	3.00
Omahen, John	R-R	6-0	190	3-15-89	3	0	0.40	10	0	0	0	22	14	7	1	0	5	18	.182	.115	.216	7.25	2.01
Reed, Evan	R-R	6-4	225	12-31-85	0	0	3.12	8	3	0	0	9	15	4	3	0	0	11	.395	.467	.348	11.42	0.00
Reed, Frankie	L-L	6-1	185	2-12-88	1	0	0.00	4	0	0	1	6	3	1	0	0	3	6	.150	.000	.200	9.53	4.76
Rembisz, Scott	R-R	6-1	230	9-26-88	0	0	7.36	4	0	0	0	4	2	3	3	0	2	4	.167	.333	.111	9.82	4.91
Rodriguez, Jose	R-R	6-1	195	9-24-90	4	3	2.04	11	8	0	0	53	35	13	12	1	15	41	.188	.237	.165	6.96	2.55
Rojas, Wilfredo	R-R	6-2	150	8-31-89	0	1	10.13	3	0	0	0	3	4	3	3	1	0	1	.400	.333	.429	3.38	0.00
Sanabia, Alex	R-R	6-2	165	5-8-89	0	0	0.00	3	3	0	0	8	5	1	0	0	0	5	.172	.200	.158	5.63	0.00
Solano, Aneurys	R-R	6-1	180	11-18-88	1	0	2.33	13	0	0	1	19	19	6	5	2	12	14	.264	.294	.255	6.52	5.59
Tamares, Joel	R-R	6-2	155	8-13-90	2	1	2.49	16	0	0	1	25	16	10	7	0	17	24	.178	.154	.188	8.53	6.04
Webb, Ryan	R-R	6-6	215	2-5-86	0	0	0.00	1	1	0	0	2	2	0	0	0	0	2	.286	1.000	.167	9.00	0.00
Weber, Jeremy	R-R	6-5	185	5-21-90	0	1	14.14	3	0	0	0	7	13	11	11	2	3	5	.382	.500	.318	6.43	3.86
Wright, Beau	L-L	6-2	220	1-2-91	2	2	3.98	11	6	0	0	41	44	21	18	0	26	34	.289	.292	.289	7.52	5.75

Fielding

Catcher	PCT	G	PO	A	E	DP	PB
Acosta	.941	6	29	3	2	0	1
Behar	.986	20	125	14	2	0	3
Caldwell	.993	32	241	26	2	2	3
Ceballos	.947	3	14	4	1	0	1
Dice	1.000	3	14	1	0	0	0
Othman	1.000	3	18	2	0	0	0
Sammons	.941	4	14	2	1	0	0

First Base	PCT	G	PO	A	E	DP
Munoz	.982	45	396	33	8	26
Myers	1.000	2	16	0	0	0
Rieger	1.000	2	7	1	0	0
Woods	.984	7	57	3	1	5

Second Base	PCT	G	PO	A	E	DP
Burke	.909	9	7	13	2	3
Hernandez	1.000	3	1	8	0	2
Myers	.947	8	12	6	1	0
Ortiz	.955	46	72	117	9	16
Perez	1.000	1	1	3	0	0

Third Base	PCT	G	PO	A	E	DP
Jackson	.905	36	8	49	6	4
Myers	.444	4	1	3	5	0
Perez	.920	10	9	14	2	0
Soto	.826	7	5	14	4	0
Woods	.929	9	8	18	2	1

Shortstop	PCT	G	PO	A	E	DP
Hernandez	.939	47	73	142	14	20

	PCT	G	PO	A	E	DP
Jackson	1.000	1	2	1	0	0
Myers	.923	4	6	6	1	4
Ortiz	.857	2	3	3	1	0
Perez	.846	3	3	8	2	1

Outfield	PCT	G	PO	A	E	DP
Burke	.000	4	0	0	0	0
Dewitt	1.000	13	13	0	0	0
Martinez	.966	35	54	3	2	1
McIntyre	1.000	3	4	0	0	0
Pedroza	1.000	3	3	1	0	0
Schultz	.977	38	41	2	1	0
Solorzano	.989	51	86	3	1	1
Veras	.907	29	44	5	5	2

DSL MARLINS

ROOKIE

DOMINICAN SUMMER LEAGUE

Batting	B-T	HT	WT	DOB	AVG	vLH	vRH	G	AB	R	H	2B	3B	HR	RBI	BB	HBP	SH	SF	SO	SB	CS	SLG	OBP
Acosta, Pedro	R-R	6-2	213	7-11-90	.253	.222	.269	22	79	14	20	8	0	2	16	8	3	0	1	21	2	1	.430	.341
Astacio, Juan	R-R	6-1	180	9-29-92	.115	.200	.095	8	26	4	3	1	0	0	4	1	0	0	0	9	1	2	.154	.258
Castillo, Felix	R-R	5-11	191	7-16-91	.272	.154	.313	42	151	19	41	9	0	2	12	21	2	0	3	11	1	0	.371	.362
Castro, Victor	R-R	6-1	198	1-10-92	.293	.378	.262	47	167	26	49	14	2	2	30	17	7	0	4	30	4	4	.437	.374
Cordova, Rehiner	B-R	6-0	150	1-11-94	.231	.270	.218	46	147	26	34	2	0	0	7	22	5	0	1	35	1	2	.245	.349
Cuevas, Carlos	R-R	6-1	170	11-26-91	.131	.115	.138	27	84	9	11	1	1	0	3	12	4	0	0	27	3	0	.167	.270
De La Cruz, Dionicio	R-R	6-2	175	1-31-94	.208	.186	.217	62	216	22	45	8	5	1	27	17	3	0	2	62	8	6	.269	.273
De Leon, Miguel	R-R	5-10	160	5-9-93	.168	.105	.194	41	131	12	22	5	2	0	5	15	0	0	1	43	3	5	.237	.252
Del Rosario, Yeison	R-R	6-1	165	2-15-94	.086	.000	.103	14	35	1	3	0	0	0	3	4	2	0	1	26	0	0	.086	.214
Duran, Carlos	L-R	6-1	192	5-24-92	.269	.295	.261	57	197	21	53	11	0	2	24	30	7	0	0	23	2	3	.355	.385
Gonzalez, Randy	L-L	6-3	180	7-18-94	.179	.118	.205	21	56	2	10	3	0	0	2	7	0	0	0	22	0	0	.232	.270
Jimenez, Joel	R-R	5-11	189	4-30-92	.145	.267	.103	45	117	8	17	7	0	2	15	20	4	0	1	38	0	1	.256	.289
Lara, Erick	R-R	6-2	150	3-24-94	.000	.000	.000	5	7	0	0	0	0	0	0	1	0	0	0	6	0	0	.000	.125
Lorenzo, Raffi	R-R	5-10	161	1-1-94	.152	.111	.162	16	46	5	7	3	0	0	1	2	0	0	0	9	2	1	.217	.188
Mota, Juan	R-R	6-1	167	9-17-92	.235	.167	.259	64	230	29	54	7	4	0	25	27	3	0	1	32	4	4	.300	.322
Ramirez, Marc	R-R	6-2	185	7-17-91	.218	.265	.200	51	174	25	38	8	1	1	13	23	8	0	0	51	9	7	.293	.337
Vallejo, Manuel	R-R	6-2	155	9-17-93	.059	.000	.069	17	34	5	2	1	0	0	1	2	0	0	0	20	1	3	.088	.111
Vigil, Rodrigo	R-R	6-0	164	1-3-93	.247	.295	.231	46	174	23	43	8	0	1	13	16	3	0	0	22	2	3	.310	.321

Pitching	B-T	HT	WT	DOB	W	L	ERA	G	GS	CG	SV	IP	H	R	ER	HR	BB	SO	AVG	vLH	vRH	K/9	BB/9
Adames, Jose	R-R	6-2	165	1-17-93	4	2	2.82	13	2	0	1	45	41	22	14	2	18	25	.246	.286	.229	5.04	3.63
Almonte, Jefferies	R-R	6-2	190	5-29-92	2	3	3.60	12	0	0	3	15	9	10	6	1	15	9	.200	.100	.229	5.40	9.00
Batman, Jean	L-L	6-2	190	10-23-92	0	4	3.79	12	8	0	0	38	28	18	16	0	23	34	.214	.333	.205	8.05	5.45
Beltre, Andy	R-R	6-4	195	7-6-93	1	4	4.50	13	8	0	0	50	52	33	25	0	20	52	.259	.226	.270	9.36	3.60
Camilo, Melkis	B-L	6-5	175	5-13-92	0	0	3.38	2	1	0	0	3	3	4	1	0	5	5	.273	.000	.273	16.88	16.88
Castellanos, Gabriel	L-L	6-1	165	12-28-93	0	4	10.20	8	5	0	0	15	17	19	17	2	15	5	.304	.429	.286	3.00	9.00
Cavanerio, Jorgan	R-R	6-1	155	8-18-94	0	3	3.10	12	4	0	1	29	28	18	10	3	6	29	.297	.239	.900	1.86
De La Rosa, Esmerling	R-R	6-2	199	5-15-91	2	5	3.92	12	6	0	1	44	48	30	19	1	13	41	.277	.256	.285	8.45	2.68
Del Pozo, Miguel	L-L	6-1	180	10-14-92	3	3	5.09	12	6	0	0	41	39	27	23	5	25	47	.253	.267	.252	10.40	5.53
Fermin, Yeraldo	R-R	5-11	136	10-2-91	3	3	3.77	12	4	0	0	62	62	31	26	1	13	43	.266	.262	.268	6.24	1.89
Ferreras, Kevin	L-L	6-0	170	7-5-93	0	0	9.31	7	0	0	0	10	9	10	10	1	12	12	.237	.500	.222	11.17	11.17
Garcia, Jarlin	L-L	6-2	170	1-18-93	5	5	3.29	14	8	0	1	52	47	22	19	3	12	46	.241	.400	.228	7.96	2.08
German, Domingo	R-R	6-2	172	8-4-92	2	1	1.82	8	6	0	0	35	38	19	7	0	13	40	.284	.273	.287	10.38	3.38

Pitching	B-T	HT	WT	DOB	W	L	ERA	G	GS	CG	SV	IP	H	R	ER	HR	BB	SO	AVG	vLH	vRH	K/9	BB/9
Jean, Victor	R-R	6-2	185	4-25-94	0	0	9.00	4	0	0	0	6	6	7	6	1	5	8	.250	.333	.222	12.00	7.50
Liriano, German	R-R	6-0	180	6-29-93	0	0	3.48	8	4	0	2	31	27	14	12	3	12	17	.233	.348	.204	4.94	3.48
Mendoza, Yeims	R-R	6-2	155	2-27-93	0	0	4.26	4	0	0	0	6	6	3	3	0	5	5	.250	.200	.263	7.11	7.11
Palin, Nelson	R-R	6-3	182	9-22-92	0	2	40.50	2	0	0	0	1	2	3	3	0	3	1	.500	1.000	.333	13.50	40.50
Ramos, Felix	B-L	6-0	175	12-2-93	1	0	3.33	9	1	0	1	24	19	9	9	1	14	17	.232	.375	.216	6.29	5.18
Rincon, Junior	R-R	6-2	185	12-7-91	0	2	13.50	11	2	0	1	15	30	27	23	1	20	9	.435	.550	.388	5.28	11.74
Santamaria, Rigoberto	R-R	6-2	195	4-27-94	1	2	3.70	12	2	0	2	41	46	18	17	1	6	25	.282	.261	.291	5.44	1.31

Fielding

Catcher	PCT	G	PO	A	E	DP	PB
Acosta	.992	16	106	19	1	1	5
Cariel	1.000	5	32	1	0	0	0
Castillo	.983	23	149	27	3	3	3
Jimenez	.990	30	176	21	2	1	4

First Base	PCT	G	PO	A	E	DP
Acosta	1.000	2	12	0	0	3
Castillo	1.000	5	36	2	0	7
Duran	.980	53	407	33	9	32
Jimenez	.981	6	49	4	1	2
Mota	1.000	6	17	0	0	3

Second Base	PCT	G	PO	A	E	DP
Cordova	1.000	2	2	2	0	1
De Leon	1.000	2	1	2	0	0
Lorenzo	.974	10	11	27	1	5

	PCT	G	PO	A	E	DP
Mota	.970	39	97	96	6	20
Vallejo	1.000	1	1	1	0	1
Vigil	.962	20	58	43	4	10

Third Base	PCT	G	PO	A	E	DP
Castillo	1.000	1	1	1	0	0
Cordova	.957	7	3	19	1	2
Cuevas	.889	11	8	16	3	1
De Leon	.846	33	20	68	16	5
Mota	.841	19	18	35	10	3
Vallejo	1.000	2	1	0	0	0

Shortstop	PCT	G	PO	A	E	DP
Cordova	.938	39	66	101	11	17
De Leon	.789	5	7	8	4	1
Lara	.667	3	2	4	3	2
Vigil	.964	24	47	61	4	8

Outfield	PCT	G	PO	A	E	DP
Astacio	1.000	8	13	0	0	0
Cariel	1.000	4	4	0	0	0
Castro	.934	41	54	3	4	0
Cuevas	.923	10	10	2	1	0
De La Cruz	.975	52	111	4	3	3
De Leon	1.000	2	4	0	0	0
Del Rosario	.929	14	13	0	1	1
Gonzalez	.963	18	24	2	1	0
Lara	1.000	2	1	0	0	0
Lorenzo	1.000	1	1	0	0	0
Ramirez	.950	50	70	6	4	1
Vallejo	.947	11	15	3	1	0

Houston Astros

SEASON IN A SENTENCE: The Astros had the worst season in franchise history, losing 100 games for the first time ever, never posting a winning month and finishing 56-106—easily last place in the National League Central, as well as the worst record in baseball.

HIGH POINT: Houston finished August—its best month at 12-17—with a four-game winning streak, beating the Pirates 2-0 behind seven scoreless innings by J.A. Happ. The Astros did get to play a small role in the pennant race, dropping two of three to the Cardinals in the final series of the season as St. Louis grabbed the wild card on its way to an unlikely World Series title.

LOW POINT: It was a season full of them, as Houston was powerless offensively most of the season, and it was best exemplified by loss No. 102. It was their 11th of 12 shutouts, a 2-0 loss to the Reds and Bronson Arroyo, who led the league in earned runs and home runs allowed but was good enough to shut out Houston.

NOTABLE ROOKIES: Manager Brad Mills tried a lot of new faces, with four Astros jumping all the way from the 2010 instructional league roster to the 2011 major league roster. Corner outfielder J.D. Martinez was the best of the lot, while third baseman Jimmy Paredes, second baseman Jose Altuve and righthander David Carpenter had their moments. No. 1 prospect Jordan Lyles got 94 innings at age 20 but wasn't quite major league-ready, going 2-8, 5.36.

KEY TRANSACTIONS: Needing to rebuild a farm system devastated by a decade of mostly poor drafts, Houston traded outfielders Michael Bourn (to the Braves) and Hunter Pence (to the Phillies) in deadline deals and got back eight players: outfielder Jordan Schafer and seven minor leaguers, led by first baseman/outfielder Jonathan Singleton, righthanders Jarred Cosart and Paul Clemens and lefthander Brett Oberholtzer. Singleton and Cosart instantly became the top hitting and pitching prospects in the organization. The Astros also tried to boost the athleticism in the system through the draft, taking outfielder George Springer with their first-round pick.

DOWN ON THE FARM: For the third time in four seasons, the Astros had the worst winning percentage of any organization. No affiliate posted a winning record, and the system's overall winning percentage was .409. Altuve led the minors in batting at .389 before being promoted to Houston.

OPENING DAY PAYROLL: $70,694,000 (20th)

PLAYERS OF THE YEAR

MAJOR LEAGUE

Carlos Lee
of/1b
.275/.342/.446
18 HR, 94 RBIs
38 2B, 4th in NL

MINOR LEAGUE

Jose Altuve
2b
(High A/Double-A)
.389/.426/.591
10 3B, 10 HR

ORGANIZATION LEADERS

BATTING		*Minimum 250 PA
MAJORS		
* AVG	Hunter Pence	.308
* OPS	Hunter Pence	.827
HR	Carlos Lee	18
RBI	Carlos Lee	94
MINORS		
* AVG	Jose Altuve, Lancaster/Corpus Christi	.389
* OBP	Jose Altuve, Lancaster/Corpus Christi	.426
* SLG	Jose Altuve, Lancaster/Corpus Christi	.591
R	Kody Hinze, Lancaster/Corpus Christi	87
H	Austin Wates, Lancaster	158
TB	Kody Hinze, Lancaster/Corpus Christi	262
2B	Mike Kvasnicka, Lexington	32
3B	Jose Altuve, Lancaster/Corpus Christi	10
HR	Kody Hinze, Lancaster/Corpus Christi	29
RBI	Kody Hinze, Lancaster/Corpus Christi	98
BB	Kody Hinze, Lancaster/Corpus Christi	94
SO	Jonathan Villar, Lanc./Corpus Christi	156
SB	Jonathan Villar, Lanc./Corpus Christi	34

PITCHING		#Minimum 75 IP
MAJORS		
W	Wandy Rodriguez	11
# ERA	Wandy Rodriguez	3.49
SO	Bud Norris	176
SV	Mark Melancon	20
MINORS		
W	Dallas Keuchel, Corpus Christi/Okla. City	10
L	Robert Donovan, Lancaster	14
# ERA	Andy Van Hekken, Okla. City	3.40
G	Ross Wolf, Okla. City	56
GS	Ross Seaton, Corpus Christi	28
SV	Kirk Clark, Lancaster	19
IP	Jake Buchanan, Lanc./Corpus Christi	165.2
BB	Jose Cisnero, Lancaster	75
SO	Jose Cisnero, Lancaster	152
# AVG	Jose Cisnero, Lancaster	.246

General Manager: Ed Wade. **Farm Director:** Fred Nelson. **Scouting Director:** Bobby Heck.

Class	Team	League	W	L	PCT	Finish	Manager(s)
Majors	Houston Astros	National	56	106	.346	16th (16)	Brad Mills
Triple-A	Oklahoma City RedHawks	Pacific Coast	68	75	.476	11th (16)	Tony DeFrancesco
Double-A	Corpus Christi Hooks	Texas	50	90	.357	8th (8)	Tom Lawless
High A	Lancaster JetHawks	California	55	85	.393	10th (10)	Tom Spencer
Low A	Lexington Legends	South Atlantic	59	79	.428	12th (14)	Rodney Linares
Short-season	Tri-City Valley Cats	New York-Penn	33	42	.440	11th (14)	Stubby Clapp
Rookie	Greeneville Astros	Appalachian	25	43	.368	8th (10)	Omar Lopez
Rookie	GCL Astros	Gulf Coast	20	34	.370	15th (15)	Ed Romero
Overall 2011 Minor League Record			310	448	.409	30th (30)	

ORGANIZATION STATISTICS

HOUSTON ASTROS

NATIONAL LEAGUE

Batting	B-T	HT	WT	DOB	AVG	vLH	vRH	G	AB	R	H	2B	3B	HR	RBI	BB	HBP	SH	SF	SO	SB	CS	SLG	OBP
Altuve, Jose	R-R	5-7	170	5-6-90	.276	.321	.262	57	221	26	61	10	1	2	12	5	2	0	1	29	7	3	.357	.297
Barmes, Clint	R-R	6-1	205	3-6-79	.244	.226	.251	123	446	47	109	27	0	12	39	38	7	0	2	88	3	1	.386	.312
Bogusevic, Brian	L-L	6-3	220	2-18-84	.287	.154	.298	87	164	22	47	14	1	4	15	15	1	0	1	40	4	2	.457	.348
Bourgeois, Jason	R-R	5-9	195	1-4-82	.294	.396	.219	93	238	30	70	8	2	1	16	10	0	0	0	24	31	6	.357	.323
Bourn, Michael	L-R	5-11	180	12-27-82	.303	.284	.310	105	429	64	130	26	7	1	32	38	3	0	1	90	39	7	.403	.363
2-team total (53 Atlanta)					.294	—	—	158	656	94	193	34	10	2	50	53	4	0	4	140	61	14	.386	.349
Cancel, Robinson	R-R	6-0	240	5-4-76	.000	.000	.000	2	6	0	0	0	0	0	0	1	0	0	0	4	0	0	.000	.143
Corporan, Carlos	B-R	6-2	220	1-7-84	.188	.243	.171	52	154	9	29	8	1	0	11	10	4	0	2	49	0	0	.253	.253
Downs, Matt	R-R	6-1	185	3-19-84	.276	.340	.257	106	199	29	55	18	0	10	41	17	5	0	1	47	0	0	.518	.347
Durango, Luis	B-R	5-9	155	4-23-86	.167	.000	.167	2	6	0	1	0	0	0	1	1	0	0	0	1	0	0	.167	.286
Hall, Bill	R-R	6-0	210	12-28-79	.224	.308	.194	46	147	18	33	7	2	2	13	8	2	0	1	55	1	1	.340	.272
2-team total (16 San Francisco)					.211	—	—	62	185	24	39	9	2	2	14	11	2	0	1	63	3	2	.314	.261
Inglett, Joe	L-R	5-9	175	6-29-78	.222	1.000	.192	20	27	3	6	1	0	0	1	0	0	0	0	7	0	0	.259	.222
Johnson, Chris	R-R	6-3	220	10-1-84	.251	.260	.248	107	378	32	95	21	3	7	42	16	7	0	4	97	2	2	.378	.291
Keppinger, Jeff	R-R	6-0	185	4-21-80	.307	.421	.272	43	163	22	50	9	0	4	20	4	0	0	2	7	0	1	.436	.320
2-team total (56 San Francisco)					.277	—	—	99	379	39	105	20	0	6	35	12	2	0	4	24	0	1	.377	.300
Lee, Carlos	R-T	6-2	265	6-20-76	.275	.348	.253	155	585	66	161	38	4	18	94	59	3	0	6	60	4	3	.446	.342
Martinez, J.D.	R-R	6-3	200	8-21-87	.274	.360	.247	53	208	29	57	13	0	6	35	13	2	0	3	48	0	1	.423	.319
Michaels, Jason	R-R	6-0	210	5-4-76	.199	.221	.171	89	156	10	31	9	0	2	10	11	1	0	0	31	1	0	.295	.256
Paredes, Jimmy	B-R	6-1	200	11-25-88	.286	.216	.305	46	168	16	48	8	2	2	18	9	0	0	1	47	5	4	.393	.320
Pence, Hunter	R-R	6-4	220	4-13-83	.308	.278	.318	100	399	49	123	26	3	11	62	30	1	0	2	86	7	1	.471	.356
2-team total (54 Philadelphia)					.314	—	—	154	606	84	190	38	5	22	97	56	1	0	5	124	8	2	.502	.370
Quintero, Humberto	R-R	5-9	215	8-2-79	.240	.268	.233	79	262	22	63	12	1	2	25	6	1	0	2	53	1	0	.317	.258
Sanchez, Angel	R-R	6-1	200	9-20-83	.240	.270	.231	110	288	35	69	10	0	1	28	27	1	0	2	44	3	0	.285	.305
Schafer, Jordan	L-L	6-1	200	9-4-86	.245	.294	.236	30	106	14	26	4	0	1	6	10	1	0	1	28	7	0	.311	.314
2-team total (52 Atlanta)					.242	—	—	82	302	46	73	10	3	2	13	28	2	0	1	70	22	4	.315	.309
Shuck, J.B.	L-L	5-11	195	6-18-87	.272	.455	.243	37	81	9	22	2	1	0	3	11	0	0	0	7	2	0	.321	.359
Towles, J.R.	R-R	6-2	190	2-11-84	.184	.149	.200	54	147	11	27	7	0	3	11	13	2	0	2	26	0	0	.293	.256
Wallace, Brett	L-R	6-2	250	8-26-86	.259	.211	.269	115	336	37	87	22	0	5	36	36	3	0	2	91	1	1	.369	.334

Pitching	B-T	HT	WT	DOB	W	L	ERA	G	GS	CG	SV	IP	H	R	ER	HR	BB	SO	AVG	vLH	vRH	K/9	BB/9
Abad, Fernando	L-L	6-2	215	12-17-85	1	4	7.32	29	0	0	0	20	28	18	16	5	9	15	.326	.273	.381	6.86	4.12
Abreu, Juan	R-R	6-0	180	4-8-85	0	0	2.70	7	0	0	0	7	6	2	2	1	3	12	.231	.125	.278	16.20	4.05
Carpenter, David	R-R	6-2	210	7-15-85	1	3	2.93	34	0	0	1	28	28	9	9	3	13	29	.272	.190	.328	9.43	4.23
Cedeno, Xavier	L-L	6-1	165	8-26-86	0	0	27.00	3	0	0	0	2	7	5	5	2	0	0	.636	.500	.714	0.00	0.00
Del Rosario, Enerio	R-R	6-2	180	10-16-85	0	3	4.58	54	0	0	0	53	59	30	27	3	31	31	.280	.311	.263	5.26	5.26
Escalona, Sergio	L-L	6-0	210	8-3-84	2	1	2.93	49	0	0	0	28	24	10	9	3	11	25	.240	.188	.333	8.13	3.58
Figueroa, Nelson	R-R	6-1	185	5-18-74	0	3	8.69	8	5	0	0	29	45	33	28	3	16	17	.352	.278	.380	5.28	4.97
Fulchino, Jeff	R-R	6-5	285	11-26-79	1	4	5.18	36	0	0	0	33	34	19	19	5	18	31	.266	.204	.311	8.45	4.91
2-team total (3 San Diego)					1	4	5.71	39	0	0	0	35	37	22	22	5	22	33	—	—	—	8.57	5.71
Happ, J.A.	L-L	6-6	200	10-19-82	6	15	5.35	28	28	0	0	156	157	103	93	21	83	134	.265	.270	.264	7.71	4.78
Harrell, Lucas	B-R	6-2	210	6-3-85	0	2	3.46	6	2	0	0	13	12	8	5	0	7	10	.240	.357	.194	6.92	4.85
Lopez, Wilton	R-R	6-0	200	7-19-83	2	6	2.79	73	0	0	0	71	72	26	22	6	18	56	.264	.330	.225	7.10	2.28
Lyles, Jordan	R-R	6-4	210	10-19-90	2	8	5.36	20	15	0	0	94	107	61	56	14	26	67	.285	.271	.295	6.41	2.49
Lyon, Brandon	R-R	6-1	200	8-10-79	3	3	11.48	15	0	0	4	13	27	17	17	4	5	6	.409	.632	.259	4.05	3.38
Melancon, Mark	R-R	6-2	215	3-28-85	8	4	2.78	71	0	0	20	74	65	28	23	5	26	66	.234	.243	.228	7.99	3.15
Myers, Brett	R-R	6-4	240	8-17-80	7	14	4.46	34	33	2	0	216	226	116	107	31	57	160	.267	.278	.259	6.67	2.38
Norris, Bud	R-R	6-0	220	3-2-85	6	11	3.77	31	31	0	0	186	177	93	78	24	70	176	.250	.280	.220	8.52	3.39
Pendleton, Lance	L-R	6-3	195	9-10-83	0	0	17.36	4	0	0	0	5	10	9	9	4	1	5	.435	.571	.375	9.64	1.93
Rodriguez, Aneury	R-R	6-4	200	12-13-87	1	6	5.27	43	8	0	0	85	83	57	50	13	32	64	.252	.269	.243	6.75	3.38
Rodriguez, Fernando	R-R	6-3	215	6-18-84	2	3	3.96	47	0	0	0	52	51	24	23	6	30	57	.264	.225	.287	9.80	5.16
Rodriguez, Wandy	R-L	5-11	195	1-18-79	11	11	3.49	30	30	0	0	191	182	81	74	25	69	166	.251	.233	.256	7.82	3.25

Pitching	B-T	HT	WT	DOB	W	L	ERA	G	GS	CG	SV	IP	H	R	ER	HR	BB	SO	AVG	vLH	vRH	K/9	BB/9
Sosa, Henry	R-R	6-1	205	7-28-85	3	5	5.23	10	10	0	0	53	54	31	31	7	23	38	.271	.297	.256	6.41	3.88
Valdez, Jose	R-R	6-4	200	1-22-83	0	0	9.00	12	0	0	0	14	17	14	14	2	7	15	.304	.318	.294	9.64	4.50
Wright, Wesley	R-L	5-11	180	1-28-85	0	0	1.50	21	0	0	0	12	6	2	2	1	5	11	.154	.038	.385	8.25	3.75

Fielding

Catcher	PCT	G	PO	A	E	DP	PB
Cancel	1.000	2	14	0	0	0	1
Corporan	.985	50	371	30	6	5	2
Quintero	.992	77	541	43	5	9	3
Towles	.981	51	284	22	6	3	2

First Base	PCT	G	PO	A	E	DP
Downs	1.000	13	37	4	0	4
Lee	.992	79	578	75	5	59
Wallace	.992	96	659	77	6	32

Second Base	PCT	G	PO	A	E	DP
Altuve	.991	55	80	135	2	25
Bourgeois	1.000	2	1	2	0	1
Downs	.965	27	37	46	3	9
Hall	.976	41	97	67	4	21
Inglett	1.000	3	8	7	0	4
Keppinger	.982	38	57	105	3	19
Sanchez	1.000	19	31	48	0	20

Third Base	PCT	G	PO	A	E	DP
Downs	.920	19	4	19	2	4
Inglett	1.000	2	0	1	0	0
Johnson	.937	101	65	157	15	20
Paredes	.953	46	31	71	5	6
Sanchez	1.000	10	4	16	0	2

Shortstop	PCT	G	PO	A	E	DP
Barmes	.978	122	171	356	12	69
Downs	.800	2	3	1	1	0
Sanchez	.964	46	58	129	7	22

Outfield	PCT	G	PO	A	E	DP
Bogusevic	.978	53	80	9	2	4
Bourgeois	.992	73	116	1	1	0
Bourn	.992	103	256	3	2	0
Downs	1.000	3	4	0	0	0
Durango	1.000	2	3	0	0	0
Lee	.985	80	119	10	2	3
Martinez	.990	52	93	5	1	2
Michaels	1.000	41	59	1	0	0
Pence	.977	100	203	9	5	3
Schafer	1.000	28	66	0	0	0
Shuck	.978	26	44	1	1	0
Wright	.000	1	0	0	0	0

OKLAHOMA CITY REDHAWKS

TRIPLE-A

PACIFIC COAST LEAGUE

Batting	B-T	HT	WT	DOB	AVG	vLH	vRH	G	AB	R	H	2B	3B	HR	RBI	BB	HBP	SH	SF	SO	SB	CS	SLG	OBP
Barmes, Clint	R-R	6-1	205	3-6-79	.333	.500	.250	2	6	2	2	1	0	0	1	1	0	0	0	0	0	0	.500	.429
Barnes, Brandon	R-R	6-2	210	5-15-86	.197	.242	.178	71	229	34	45	13	5	8	27	29	3	0	1	69	5	1	.402	.294
Bogusevic, Brian	L-L	6-3	220	2-18-84	.261	.217	.282	58	218	27	57	11	5	3	35	30	5	0	1	49	20	3	.399	.362
Bourgeois, Jason	R-R	5-9	195	1-4-82	.444	.600	.385	4	18	4	8	3	1	0	1	1	0	0	0	1	0	1	.722	.474
Cancel, Robinson	R-R	6-0	240	5-4-76	.299	.382	.273	94	318	37	95	19	0	4	51	37	2	0	1	59	10	3	.396	.374
Clemens, Koby	R-R	5-11	200	12-4-86	.234	.250	.229	126	384	51	90	21	2	16	55	51	6	0	3	117	4	2	.424	.331
Corporan, Carlos	B-R	6-2	220	1-7-84	.250	.296	.226	22	80	9	20	4	0	3	12	8	2	0	1	16	0	1	.413	.330
DeLome, Collin	L-R	6-2	195	12-18-85	.256	.250	.257	89	262	36	67	16	3	7	29	18	7	0	3	82	9	2	.420	.317
Dopirak, Brian	R-R	6-4	225	12-20-83	.252	.211	.264	57	163	22	41	11	0	6	17	7	1	0	0	40	0	0	.429	.287
Durango, Luis	B-R	5-9	155	4-23-86	.273	.308	.266	47	154	33	42	2	1	0	9	22	0	0	1	23	18	9	.299	.362
2-team total (61 Tucson)					.257	—	—	108	331	69	85	5	4	0	24	41	4	0	2	54	28	14	.296	.344
Esposito, Brian	R-R	6-1	210	2-24-79	.317	.333	.310	16	41	5	13	2	0	1	4	1	0	0	0	5	0	0	.439	.333
Frostad, Emerson	L-R	6-1	210	1-13-83	.143	.000	.143	4	7	0	1	0	0	0	0	2	1	0	0	2	0	0	.143	.400
Goebbert, Jake	L-L	6-0	200	9-24-87	.283	.188	.300	31	106	14	30	8	0	2	15	10	0	0	0	18	0	1	.415	.345
Hernandez, Anderson	B-R	5-9	190	10-30-82	.300	.298	.301	136	510	74	153	25	4	6	52	53	2	0	4	77	21	12	.400	.366
Inglett, Joe	L-S	5-9	175	6-29-78	.071	.000	.087	11	28	1	2	0	0	0	8	0	0	0	9	2	0	.071	.278
Johnson, Chris	R-R	6-3	220	10-1-84	.272	.267	.273	21	81	18	22	7	0	4	15	10	3	0	0	25	1	1	.506	.372
Keppinger, Jeff	R-R	6-0	185	4-21-80	.250	.000	.250	7	28	2	7	0	0	0	0	1	0	0	0	0	0	0	.250	.241
Locke, Drew	R-R	6-1	220	2-28-83	.264	.220	.280	125	375	41	99	26	2	11	58	35	7	0	4	68	9	3	.432	.335
Manzella, Tommy	R-R	6-2	200	4-16-83	.230	.238	.228	109	361	39	83	14	6	7	48	45	4	0	4	116	10	4	.360	.319
2-team total (22 Reno)					.232	—	—	131	422	46	98	14	6	8	51	49	4	0	4	126	11	5	.351	.315
Michaels, Jason	R-R	6-0	210	5-4-76	.300	.400	.200	5	20	0	6	2	0	0	2	2	0	0	0	5	0	0	.400	.364
Navarro, Oswaldo	R-R	6-0	200	10-2-84	.267	.309	.252	107	315	28	84	13	1	2	31	39	3	0	5	45	3	2	.333	.348
Quintero, Humberto	R-R	5-9	215	8-2-79	.286	1.000	.231	4	14	1	4	1	0	0	0	0	1	0	0	5	0	0	.357	.333
Ramirez, Max	R-R	5-11	175	10-11-84	.226	.227	.226	24	84	7	19	3	0	2	14	3	1	0	3	17	0	0	.333	.253
3-team total (48 Fresno, 11 Iowa)					.278	—	—	83	266	38	74	15	1	13	48	21	4	0	5	58	0	0	.489	.334
Schafer, Jordan	L-L	6-1	200	9-4-86	.500	.667	.471	5	20	4	10	2	0	0	3	2	0	0	0	5	3	1	.600	.545
Shuck, J.B.	L-L	5-11	195	6-18-87	.297	.264	.307	108	354	60	105	11	7	0	30	56	4	0	1	30	20	11	.367	.398
Simunic, Andy	R-R	6-0	170	8-7-85	.200	.000	.333	3	5	1	1	0	0	0	0	0	1	0	0	3	0	0	.200	.333
Sutil, Wladimir	R-R	5-10	155	10-31-84	.222	.211	.227	31	63	8	14	2	0	0	3	6	1	0	1	6	2	2	.254	.296
Towles, J.R.	R-R	6-2	190	2-11-84	.276	.304	.268	35	105	19	29	4	0	3	11	18	11	0	1	11	3	0	.400	.430
Vallejo, Jose	R-R	6-0	200	9-11-86	.233	.222	.238	57	146	14	34	3	0	2	12	17	0	0	1	24	2	2	.295	.311
Wallace, Brett	L-R	6-2	250	8-26-86	.356	.091	.427	28	104	16	37	10	0	1	24	15	3	0	4	28	1	0	.481	.437
Wikoff, Brandon	L-R	5-9	170	4-5-88	.154	.000	.182	4	13	0	2	0	0	0	0	1	0	0	0	6	0	1	.154	.214

Pitching	B-T	HT	WT	DOB	W	L	ERA	G	GS	CG	SV	IP	H	R	ER	HR	BB	SO	AVG	vLH	vRH	K/9	BB/9
Abad, Fernando	L-L	6-2	215	12-17-85	2	3	4.80	29	0	0	0	30	32	16	16	4	6	31	.271	.339	.196	9.30	1.80
Abreu, Erick	R-R	6-1	170	8-9-83	0	0	14.54	4	0	0	0	4	7	7	7	1	4	3	.350	.385	.286	6.23	8.31
Abreu, Juan	R-R	6-0	180	4-8-85	1	0	1.86	7	0	0	3	10	8	3	2	0	7	9	.235	.235	.235	8.38	6.52
Arguello, Doug	L-L	6-3	215	11-21-84	5	7	3.67	31	7	0	0	69	52	29	28	4	46	61	.214	.157	.255	8.00	6.03
2-team total (2 Round Rock)					5	7	3.89	33	7	0	0	72	55	32	31	4	49	64		—	—	8.04	6.15
Aristil, Jonnathan	R-R	6-1	160	11-30-86	0	0	0.00	1	0	0	0	1	2	0	0	0	0	1	.400	.667	.000	9.00	0.00
Beltran, Francis	R-R	6-6	255	11-29-79	0	0	19.89	5	0	0	0	6	16	14	14	2	4	5	.471	.500	.455	7.11	5.68
Carpenter, David	R-R	6-2	210	7-15-85	0	0	0.00	19	0	0	9	19	15	0	0	0	6	21	.221	.217	.222	9.95	2.84
Cedeno, Xavier	L-L	6-1	165	8-26-86	2	3	6.23	12	3	0	0	26	32	20	18	2	8	27	.299	.343	.278	9.35	2.77
Chacin, Gustavo	L-L	5-11	205	11-4-80	3	6	5.13	27	9	0	0	67	81	42	38	8	24	37	.303	.357	.279	5.00	3.24
Clemens, Paul	R-R	6-4	180	2-14-88	0	1	15.43	1	1	0	0	5	4	8	8	1	6	6	.250	.286	.222	11.57	11.57
Del Rosario, Enerio	R-R	6-2	180	10-16-85	0	0	0.00	3	0	0	0	3	3	0	0	0	0	0	.300	.500	.000	0.00	0.00
Escalona, Sergio	L-L	6-0	210	8-3-84	1	0	3.18	14	0	0	0	17	15	8	6	0	5	18	.213	.217	.211	9.53	2.65
Fien, Casey	R-R	6-2	195	10-21-83	2	2	4.81	21	0	0	3	24	28	15	13	7	8	24	.289	.364	.226	8.88	2.96
Figueroa, Nelson	R-R	6-1	185	5-18-74	6	7	6.50	16	15	0	0	82	113	63	59	14	30	52	.334	.362	.309	5.73	3.31

Pitching	B-T	HT	WT	DOB	W	L	ERA	G	GS	CG	SV	IP	H	R	ER	HR	BB	SO	AVG	vLH	vRH	K/9	BB/9
Fulchino, Jeff	R-R	6-5	285	11-26-79	1	0	0.56	17	0	0	3	16	11	1	1	0	3	15	.200	.250	.161	8.44	1.69
Gervacio, Sammy	R-R	6-0	175	1-10-85	4	0	4.01	28	0	0	1	34	24	18	15	5	10	26	.197	.160	.222	6.95	2.67
Happ, J.A.	L-L	6-6	200	10-19-82	1	0	1.50	3	3	0	0	18	11	5	3	0	9	16	.177	.280	.108	8.00	4.50
Harrell, Lucas	B-R	6-2	210	6-3-85	5	2	1.72	9	9	0	0	52	42	12	10	0	24	38	.220	.198	.240	6.54	4.13
Hennessey, Brad	R-R	6-2	195	2-7-80	0	3	11.45	7	6	0	0	22	43	31	28	6	5	10	.406	.379	.438	4.09	2.05
Keuchel, Dallas	L-L	6-3	200	1-1-88	1	1	7.50	7	7	0	0	36	52	30	30	5	12	15	.354	.400	.326	3.75	3.00
Leon, Arcenio	R-R	6-1	220	9-22-86	0	0	13.50	1	0	0	0	2	2	3	3	1	1	0	.250	.500	.167	0.00	4.50
Lyles, Jordan	R-R	6-4	210	10-19-90	3	3	3.61	12	10	0	0	62	64	25	25	4	17	42	.277	.269	.285	6.06	2.45
Lyon, Brandon	R-R	6-1	200	8-10-79	0	0	0.00	2	0	0	0	2	2	0	0	0	0	0	.286	.000	.400	0.00	0.00
Meszaros, Danny	R-R	6-0	170	9-6-85	1	1	4.56	18	0	0	0	26	34	17	13	6	14	27	.318	.205	.397	9.47	4.91
Nieve, Fernando	R-R	6-0	220	7-15-82	1	2	7.63	3	3	0	0	15	27	15	13	0	5	17	.380	.308	.422	9.98	2.93
Perez, Sergio	R-R	6-3	230	12-5-84	5	9	4.25	22	21	0	0	110	129	65	52	14	48	71	.296	.321	.271	5.81	3.93
Rodriguez, Fernando	R-R	6-3	215	6-18-84	2	3	1.50	16	0	0	2	24	16	5	4	2	11	33	.190	.088	.260	12.38	4.13
Rowland-Smith, Ryan	L-L	6-3	240	1-26-83	2	10	6.19	22	19	0	1	105	131	77	72	16	41	87	.310	.264	.330	7.48	3.53
Sosa, Henry	R-R	6-1	205	7-28-85	0	0	0.00	1	1	0	0	7	5	0	0	0	3	3	.208	.286	.100	3.86	3.86
2-team total (17 Fresno)					3	1	8.01	18	1	0	0	30	44	30	27	3	20	24	—	—	—	7.12	5.93
Storey, Mickey	R-R	6-2	185	3-16-86	1	0	3.99	23	0	0	2	29	35	13	13	3	12	28	.297	.346	.258	8.59	3.68
Urckfitz, Pat	L-L	6-4	200	7-21-88	0	1	17.47	4	0	0	0	6	16	11	11	1	6	0	.552	.375	.619	0.00	9.53
Valdez, Jose	R-R	6-4	200	1-22-83	1	0	5.66	20	0	0	9	21	23	16	13	4	9	26	.267	.270	.265	11.32	3.92
Van Hekken, Andy	R-L	6-3	185	7-31-79	9	6	3.40	35	19	0	1	130	152	56	49	7	47	111	.295	.331	.277	7.70	3.26
Villar, Henry	R-R	5-11	170	5-24-87	2	1	6.81	10	7	0	0	38	45	31	29	9	25	15	.310	.347	.271	3.52	5.87
Wolf, Ross	R-R	6-0	180	10-18-82	4	3	4.76	56	0	0	3	74	83	46	39	4	27	55	.290	.328	.263	6.72	3.30
Wright, Wesley	R-L	5-11	180	1-28-85	3	1	2.07	39	3	0	2	65	49	17	15	4	23	52	.207	.284	.161	7.16	3.17

Fielding

Catcher	PCT	G	PO	A	E	DP	PB
Cancel	.991	62	403	48	4	4	6
Corporan	.994	20	143	15	1	5	1
Esposito	.986	14	64	5	1	0	0
Frostad	1.000	2	10	0	0	0	0
Quintero	.955	4	20	1	1	0	0
Ramirez	.994	19	156	19	1	4	1
Towles	.996	33	203	23	1	3	0

First Base	PCT	G	PO	A	E	DP
Bogusevic	1.000	8	53	2	0	4
Cancel	.949	16	85	9	5	18
Clemens	.985	89	640	65	11	75
Dopirak	.989	23	164	17	2	18
Navarro	1.000	1	7	2	0	0
Wallace	.996	26	232	21	1	29

Second Base	PCT	G	PO	A	E	DP
Hernandez	.971	63	117	180	9	50
Inglett	1.000	5	12	14	0	5
Keppinger	1.000	6	13	19	0	5
Manzella	1.000	17	30	47	0	15
Navarro	.988	19	30	52	1	12
Sutil	1.000	12	16	23	0	7
Vallejo	.985	51	84	115	3	29
Wikoff	1.000	2	2	4	0	1

Third Base	PCT	G	PO	A	E	DP
Clemens	.730	21	5	22	10	3
Hernandez	.914	41	23	51	7	6
Inglett	1.000	2	2	0	0	0
Johnson	.981	21	21	31	1	4
Manzella	.800	1	1	3	1	0
Navarro	.960	84	39	128	7	20
Simunic	1.000	2	0	3	0	1
Wikoff	1.000	1	1	1	0	0

Shortstop	PCT	G	PO	A	E	DP
Barnes	1.000	2	1	4	0	1
Hernandez	.943	48	67	130	12	34
Manzella	.969	94	144	260	13	77
Sutil	.963	15	22	30	2	10
Vallejo	.000	1	0	0	0	0
Wikoff	1.000	1	2	4	0	0

Outfield	PCT	G	PO	A	E	DP
Barnes	.987	67	145	5	2	3
Bogusevic	.957	52	110	2	5	0
Bourgeois	.857	4	6	0	1	0
Clemens	.800	7	4	0	1	0
DeLome	.968	69	117	4	4	1
Durango	.979	44	93	2	2	2
Goebbert	.955	28	64	0	3	0
Hernandez	.000	1	0	0	0	0
Inglett	1.000	5	6	0	0	0
Locke	.995	102	179	7	1	3
Michaels	1.000	3	5	0	0	0
Schafer	1.000	5	6	0	0	0
Shuck	.971	96	154	11	5	1
Simunic	.000	1	0	0	0	0

CORPUS CHRISTI HOOKS

DOUBLE-A

TEXAS LEAGUE

Batting	B-T	HT	WT	DOB	AVG	vLH	vRH	G	AB	R	H	2B	3B	HR	RBI	BB	HBP	SH	SF	SO	SB	CS	SLG	OBP
Altuve, Jose	R-R	5-7	170	5-6-90	.361	.360	.361	35	144	21	52	9	3	5	25	7	0	0	1	14	5	5	.569	.388
Bailey, Adam	L-L	6-1	195	3-6-88	.323	.250	.368	23	93	11	30	7	0	3	15	2	0	0	1	19	0	1	.495	.333
Barnes, Clint	R-R	6-1	205	3-6-79	.444	.000	.500	2	9	2	4	0	0	0	2	1	0	0	0	1	0	0	.444	.500
Barnes, Brandon	R-R	6-2	210	5-15-86	.286	.364	.238	54	203	25	58	13	0	7	27	14	2	0	2	42	6	3	.453	.335
Bourgeois, Jason	R-R	5-9	195	1-4-82	.200	.286	.000	2	10	1	2	0	0	0	0	0	0	0	0	1	0	0	.200	.200
Esposito, Brian	R-R	6-1	210	2-24-79	.155	.077	.195	38	116	5	18	4	0	0	7	5	0	0	0	29	1	1	.190	.190
Fixler, Jon	R-R	6-1	205	6-13-86	.286	.500	.125	5	14	0	4	0	0	0	0	1	0	0	0	3	0	0	.286	.333
Flores, David	R-R	6-2	220	10-13-86	.203	.216	.196	69	227	27	46	7	0	6	24	19	1	0	3	36	0	0	.313	.264
Frostad, Emerson	L-R	6-1	210	1-13-83	.239	.200	.250	52	159	18	38	5	1	3	11	23	0	0	1	32	1	1	.340	.333
Gaston, Jon	L-R	6-0	215	10-13-86	.236	.230	.238	114	415	39	98	20	5	7	43	27	3	0	1	107	14	1	.359	.287
Goebbert, Jake	L-L	6-0	200	9-24-87	.305	.262	.318	75	272	32	83	18	4	5	34	22	6	0	2	47	2	4	.456	.368
Hernandez, Federico	B-R	6-0	170	2-9-88	.142	.140	.143	49	155	9	22	4	0	3	16	12	0	0	1	31	0	2	.226	.202
Hinze, Kody	R-R	6-0	225	7-29-87	.281	.317	.266	55	199	26	56	7	0	7	28	24	1	0	2	46	0	1	.422	.358
Keppinger, Jeff	R-R	6-0	185	4-21-80	.438	.667	.385	4	16	4	7	1	0	1	2	3	0	0	1	0	0	0	.688	.526
Martinez, J.D.	R-R	6-3	200	8-21-87	.338	.356	.330	88	317	50	107	25	1	13	72	42	4	0	7	55	1	0	.546	.414
Paredes, Jimmy	B-R	6-1	200	11-25-88	.270	.292	.262	93	385	69	104	22	4	10	41	15	2	0	1	84	29	12	.426	.300
Simunic, Andy	R-R	5-10	170	8-7-85	.187	.269	.154	34	91	18	17	3	1	0	4	16	1	0	0	26	3	0	.242	.315
Steele, T.J.	R-R	6-3	205	9-21-86	.214	.298	.179	118	415	55	89	17	4	11	55	16	4	0	3	114	20	6	.354	.249
Sutil, Wladimir	R-R	5-10	155	10-31-84	.284	.391	.234	53	201	28	57	9	0	2	13	19	4	0	2	22	13	3	.358	.357
Thompson, Jose	R-R	6-2	180	5-14-87	.115	.174	.069	18	52	2	6	1	0	0	3	0	0	0	0	18	0	0	.135	.164
Vallejo, Jose	R-R	6-0	200	9-11-86	.146	.125	.160	20	41	2	6	0	0	1	2	6	0	0	5	1	0	0	.146	.167
Van Ostrand, Jimmy	R-R	6-4	210	8-7-84	.306	.313	.304	104	346	41	106	22	2	11	48	43	1	0	3	52	3	3	.477	.382
Villar, Jonathan	B-R	6-1	195	5-2-91	.231	.206	.244	83	324	52	75	16	2	10	26	29	4	0	2	100	14	6	.386	.301
Wallace, Chris	R-R	6-0	205	4-27-88	.244	.267	.231	36	123	17	30	4	0	6	29	12	1	0	0	41	1	0	.423	.316
Wikoff, Brandon	L-R	5-9	170	4-5-88	.308	.286	.317	103	331	40	102	6	0	3	26	47	3	0	1	33	5	3	.353	.398

Pitching

Pitching	B-T	HT	WT	DOB	W	L	ERA	G	GS	CG	SV	IP	H	R	ER	HR	BB	SO	AVG	vLH	vRH	K/9	BB/9
Abreu, Erick	R-R	6-1	170	8-9-83	6	8	4.29	33	18	0	0	124	124	64	59	21	27	111	.259	.297	.230	8.08	1.96
Aristil, Jonnathan	R-R	6-1	160	11-30-86	4	8	6.13	30	21	0	2	120	129	85	82	21	66	117	.269	.262	.275	8.75	4.94
Berner, David	L-L	6-2	205	8-16-87	1	1	9.33	13	0	0	0	18	32	20	19	4	14	12	.390	.400	.386	5.89	6.87
Buchanan, Jake	R-R	6-0	200	9-24-89	0	0	1.29	1	1	0	0	7	6	1	1	0	1	2	.231	.333	.143	2.57	1.29
Carpenter, David	R-R	6-2	210	7-15-85	0	1	4.50	14	0	0	5	14	14	7	7	4	3	17	.259	.304	.226	10.93	1.93
Carrillo, Cesar	R-R	6-3	170	4-29-84	1	1	9.64	5	0	0	0	9	12	10	10	2	7	6	.324	.308	.333	5.79	6.75
Cedeno, Xavier	L-L	6-1	165	8-26-86	5	6	3.95	23	19	0	0	112	98	59	49	8	45	110	.236	.217	.243	8.87	3.63
Clemens, Paul	R-R	6-4	180	2-14-88	2	1	2.35	5	5	0	0	31	23	9	8	3	12	26	.200	.183	.218	7.63	3.52
Cosart, Jarred	R-R	6-3	180	5-25-90	1	2	4.71	7	7	0	0	36	33	20	19	4	13	22	.234	.226	.246	5.45	3.22
Gervacio, Sammy	R-R	6-0	175	1-10-85	1	0	1.38	8	0	0	0	13	11	3	2	0	5	12	.229	.333	.167	8.31	3.46
Greenwalt, Kyle	R-R	6-0	200	9-29-88	4	10	7.86	28	9	0	2	71	96	63	62	16	18	46	.328	.326	.329	5.83	2.28
Hennessey, Brad	R-R	6-2	195	2-7-80	0	1	1.80	4	0	0	0	5	4	1	1	1	0	3	.222	.200	.250	5.40	0.00
Hicks, Chris	R-R	6-4	205	2-17-87	0	0	3.77	13	0	0	0	14	14	9	6	1	7	7	.246	.308	.194	4.40	4.40
James, Brad	R-R	6-2	210	6-19-84	0	2	7.11	4	0	0	0	6	9	5	5	1	8	2	.360	.400	.333	2.84	11.37
Keuchel, Dallas	L-L	6-3	200	1-1-88	9	7	3.17	20	20	1	0	128	116	49	45	9	27	76	.244	.267	.235	5.36	1.90
King, Blake	R-R	6-1	195	4-11-87	0	2	3.76	33	0	0	0	41	25	18	17	3	38	50	.176	.186	.167	11.07	8.41
2-team total (2 Springfield, MO)					0	2	4.07	35	0	0	0	42	32	20	19	4	42	50	—	—	—	10.71	9.00
Leon, Arcenio	R-R	6-1	220	9-22-86	3	4	4.59	47	0	0	0	65	69	44	33	2	48	73	.279	.323	.250	10.16	6.68
Meszaros, Danny	R-R	6-0	170	9-6-85	0	4	5.09	30	0	0	5	35	38	23	20	4	15	44	.273	.250	.293	11.21	3.82
Nevarez, Matt	R-R	6-2	220	2-26-87	0	2	9.00	11	0	0	0	21	22	22	21	0	25	23	.286	.375	.222	9.86	10.71
Oberholtzer, Brett	L-L	6-2	230	7-1-89	2	3	5.27	6	6	0	0	27	28	16	16	3	10	28	.267	.265	.268	9.22	3.29
Perconte, Mike	R-R	6-4	170	3-18-86	0	0	22.85	5	0	0	0	4	15	11	11	3	2	5	.500	.750	.333	10.38	4.15
2-team total (19 Frisco)					3	0	7.71	24	0	0	0	33	42	28	28	6	17	33	—	—	—	9.09	4.68
Robinson, Andrew	R-R	6-1	185	2-13-88	0	1	8.10	2	0	0	0	3	5	3	3	0	2	1	.357	.333	.375	2.70	5.40
Rodriguez, Wandy	R-L	5-11	195	1-18-79	0	0	2.25	1	1	0	0	4	1	1	1	1	1	2	.375	.500	.250	4.50	2.25
Seaton, Ross	L-R	6-4	213	9-18-89	4	9	5.23	28	28	0	0	155	168	103	90	19	47	97	.279	.293	.266	5.63	2.73
Sosa, Henry	R-R	6-1	205	7-28-85	2	0	2.89	3	3	0	0	19	16	7	6	1	4	17	.222	.182	.256	8.20	1.93
Stoffel, Jason	R-R	6-2	225	9-15-88	1	3	5.63	18	0	0	4	16	18	10	10	3	9	19	.265	.265	.265	10.69	5.06
Urckfitz, Pat	L-L	6-4	200	7-21-88	1	5	5.08	31	0	0	1	39	46	29	22	4	26	31	.295	.360	.264	7.15	6.00
Villar, Henry	R-R	5-11	170	5-24-87	2	4	4.06	32	0	0	2	38	42	17	17	3	4	33	.282	.306	.260	7.88	0.96
Wolf, Shane	L-L	6-3	225	9-10-86	1	4	5.98	22	1	0	0	41	52	31	27	4	15	27	.306	.292	.314	5.98	3.32
Zeid, Josh	R-R	6-5	210	3-24-87	0	1	10.13	14	1	0	0	16	23	21	18	5	6	15	.333	.385	.267	8.44	3.38

Fielding

Catcher	PCT	G	PO	A	E	DP	PB
Esposito	.991	29	201	17	2	1	5
Fixler	.938	3	13	2	1	0	
Frostad	.994	42	331	18	2	5	2
Hernandez	.988	48	297	32	4	1	7
Wallace	.986	30	205	7	3	2	1

First Base	PCT	G	PO	A	E	DP
Flores	1.000	6	51	1	0	4
Frostad	1.000	5	35	1	0	4
Goebbert	1.000	4	26	5	0	1
Hinze	.992	46	350	32	3	22
Van Ostrand	.991	87	721	40	7	70

Second Base	PCT	G	PO	A	E	DP
Altuve	.982	25	50	60	2	17
Barnes	1.000	3	5	6	0	0
Keppinger	1.000	2	5	5	0	0
Paredes	.958	46	91	115	9	26

(Catcher cont.)	PCT	G	PO	A	E	DP
Simunic	1.000	2	3	3	0	0
Sutil	1.000	5	9	9	0	3
Thompson	.980	13	22	27	1	4
Vallejo	1.000	5	5	11	0	2
Wikoff	.995	50	68	142	1	27

Third Base	PCT	G	PO	A	E	DP
Altuve	.950	7	5	14	1	0
Flores	.955	57	36	113	7	11
Paredes	.918	43	39	84	11	10
Simunic	.963	11	7	19	1	3
Sutil	.867	4	3	10	2	0
Thompson	.000	3	0	0	0	0
Vallejo	.750	2	1	2	1	0
Van Ostrand	1.000	2	0	2	0	0
Wikoff	.948	24	13	42	3	2

Shortstop	PCT	G	PO	A	E	DP
Barnes	.900	2	1	8	1	1

(Shortstop cont.)	PCT	G	PO	A	E	DP
Sutil	.984	39	56	133	3	25
Villar	.932	83	113	201	23	41
Wikoff	.962	20	26	50	3	8

Outfield	PCT	G	PO	A	E	DP
Bailey	1.000	22	46	1	0	0
Barnes	.982	46	106	2	2	0
Bourgeois	1.000	2	4	0	0	0
Flores	.000	3	0	0	0	0
Gaston	.995	93	187	10	1	2
Goebbert	.972	73	132	8	4	2
Martinez	.983	72	115	4	2	2
Simunic	.968	17	30	0	1	0
Steele	.983	103	221	9	4	3
Sutil	1.000	1	3	0	0	0
Vallejo	1.000	3	2	1	0	0
Van Ostrand	1.000	2	4	0	0	0

LANCASTER JETHAWKS

CALIFORNIA LEAGUE

HIGH CLASS A

Batting	B-T	HT	WT	DOB	AVG	vLH	vRH	G	AB	R	H	2B	3B	HR	RBI	BB	HBP	SH	SF	SO	SB	CS	SLG	OBP
Adamson, Daniel	R-R	5-11	210	9-15-87	.155	.182	.139	18	58	4	9	3	0	1	6	3	1	0	1	28	2	1	.259	.206
Altuve, Jose	R-R	5-7	170	5-6-90	.408	.483	.381	52	213	38	87	13	7	5	34	19	0	0	3	26	19	9	.606	.451
Arrendell, Miguel	L-R	6-0	165	3-26-88	.281	.296	.274	50	178	35	50	11	1	3	19	20	1	0	0	24	1	4	.404	.357
Austin, Jay	L-L	5-11	170	8-10-90	.257	.250	.260	74	315	47	81	17	4	3	37	29	1	0	4	73	17	11	.365	.318
Bailey, Adam	L-L	6-1	195	3-4-86	.289	.244	.313	30	128	15	37	3	0	5	27	5	1	0	2	23	0	0	.430	.316
Castro, Erik	L-R	6-4	200	11-13-87	.259	.234	.269	77	263	32	68	16	0	9	37	35	2	0	0	81	1	3	.422	.350
Comadena, Jordan	R-R	5-10	214	11-16-85	.295	.265	.311	40	95	15	28	8	1	1	16	10	6	0	2	26	1	0	.432	.389
Flores, David	R-R	6-2	220	10-13-86	.311	.300	.316	50	183	28	57	14	0	12	48	17	2	0	3	33	0	2	.585	.371
Garcia, Rene	R-R	6-0	190	3-21-90	.242	.344	.198	86	297	26	72	11	2	1	27	17	3	0	3	41	3	2	.303	.288
Goebbert, Jake	L-L	6-0	200	9-24-87	.260	.259	.260	26	104	16	27	1	0	5	18	10	0	0	2	16	3	0	.413	.319
Heath, Ben	R-R	6-2	220	10-7-88	.262	.222	.280	40	145	19	38	11	0	5	23	15	1	0	1	41	0	1	.441	.333
Hernandez, Federico	B-R	6-0	170	2-9-88	.194	.240	.178	31	98	5	19	4	0	2	9	7	1	0	1	23	0	0	.296	.252
Hinze, Kody	R-R	6-0	225	7-29-87	.323	.394	.299	80	285	61	92	20	0	22	70	70	3	0	2	73	1	0	.625	.458
Hogue, Grant	R-R	6-1	190	6-26-86	.269	.333	.243	109	386	63	104	19	2	1	25	33	11	0	3	67	28	7	.337	.342
Lane, Bryce	R-R	6-0	190	8-24-89	.000	.000	.000	5	14	2	0	0	0	0	0	1	0	0	0	4	0	0	.000	.067
Meyer, Jonathan	R-R	6-1	195	11-1-90	.264	.295	.252	130	484	65	128	23	0	14	72	59	2	0	6	125	1	5	.399	.343
Mier, Jio	R-R	6-2	180	8-26-90	.233	.188	.254	57	206	35	48	7	1	2	23	29	4	0	3	54	5	3	.306	.335

HOUSTON ASTROS

HOUSTON ASTROS

Batting	B-T	HT	WT	DOB	AVG	vLH	vRH	G	AB	R	H	2B	3B	HR	RBI	BB	HBP	SH	SF	SO	SB	CS	SLG	OBP
Rodriguez, Hector	R-R	5-11	150	8-8-89	.111	.000	.118	6	18	2	2	1	0	0	0	1	0	0	0	5	0	0	.167	.158
Simunic, Andy	R-R	6-0	170	8-7-85	.295	.361	.257	67	227	41	67	10	2	5	28	29	0	0	3	59	5	0	.423	.371
Singleton, Jonathan	L-L	6-2	215	9-18-91	.333	.345	.324	35	129	20	43	9	1	4	16	14	3	0	2	40	0	0	.512	.405
Thompson, Jose	R-R	6-2	180	5-14-87	.303	.288	.309	69	267	49	81	14	0	10	46	14	2	0	2	54	2	2	.468	.340
Todd, Alex	R-R	6-2	190	8-15-89	.298	.412	.250	16	57	6	17	4	0	1	2	0	1	0	0	14	0	0	.421	.310
Vallejo, Jose	B-R	6-0	200	9-11-86	.250	.000	.500	2	4	0	1	0	0	0	0	1	0	0	0	3	0	0	.250	.400
Villar, Jonathan	B-R	6-1	195	5-2-91	.259	.333	.235	47	174	26	45	7	4	4	26	25	2	0	3	56	20	6	.414	.353
Wates, Austin	R-R	6-1	179	9-2-88	.300	.292	.304	132	526	85	158	23	9	6	75	47	11	0	6	86	26	7	.413	.366

Pitching	B-T	HT	WT	DOB	W	L	ERA	G	GS	CG	SV	IP	H	R	ER	HR	BB	SO	AVG	vLH	vRH	K/9	BB/9
Alvino, Wander	R-R	5-11	159	2-10-87	3	3	4.19	46	0	0	1	73	67	47	34	7	51	73	.239	.288	.204	9.00	6.29
Berner, David	L-L	6-2	205	8-16-87	1	1	6.21	20	0	0	1	33	45	34	23	8	8	16	.313	.273	.330	4.32	2.16
Buchanan, Jake	R-R	6-0	200	9-24-89	5	10	3.91	25	25	1	0	159	157	92	69	10	35	102	.256	.205	.292	5.79	1.99
Cisnero, Jose	R-R	6-3	185	4-11-89	8	11	6.06	27	27	0	0	123	115	88	83	13	75	152	.246	.286	.216	11.09	5.47
Clark, Kirk	R-R	6-2	202	7-19-88	3	5	7.01	53	0	0	19	53	64	48	41	9	29	50	.296	.295	.297	8.54	4.96
Cruz, Luis	L-L	5-9	170	9-10-90	0	1	14.54	4	4	0	0	13	24	21	21	7	6	10	.407	.286	.444	6.92	4.15
Donovan, Robby	R-R	6-5	230	4-24-88	5	14	6.29	26	26	1	0	137	155	103	96	18	54	94	.291	.323	.262	6.16	3.54
Doran, Bobby	R-R	6-6	235	3-21-89	1	3	9.05	22	13	0	0	67	102	73	67	14	32	41	.355	.369	.344	5.54	4.32
Greenwalt, Kyle	R-R	6-0	200	9-29-88	1	1	1.85	12	0	0	1	24	17	7	5	2	9	18	.202	.111	.246	6.66	3.33
Grimmett, Zach	R-R	6-3	185	2-5-90	6	12	6.81	30	18	0	0	118	151	100	89	22	50	78	.317	.337	.304	5.97	3.82
Hicks, Chris	R-R	6-4	205	2-17-87	2	1	3.28	15	0	0	0	25	19	10	9	3	5	28	.204	.233	.180	10.22	1.82
Meiners, Jeremiah	L-L	6-0	200	8-16-88	0	0	6.23	2	0	0	0	4	7	3	3	1	3	3	.368	.750	.267	6.23	6.23
Musick, Wes	L-L	6-0	190	12-30-86	4	5	4.80	21	5	0	1	54	64	32	29	4	19	51	.306	.269	.318	8.45	3.15
Ness, Michael	R-R	6-4	210	10-20-87	4	6	5.98	42	1	0	0	84	112	68	56	13	24	62	.317	.305	.325	6.62	2.56
Pitkin, Colton	R-L	6-3	210	8-10-89	1	0	6.45	36	0	0	1	52	58	37	37	10	19	37	.287	.255	.298	6.45	3.31
Ramirez, Yordany	R-R	6-1	190	7-31-84	1	1	11.88	19	0	0	0	25	41	33	33	6	21	15	.366	.283	.424	5.40	7.56
Robinson, Andrew	R-R	6-1	185	2-13-88	8	10	6.29	29	21	1	0	127	168	96	89	22	33	91	.318	.383	.271	6.43	2.33
Trinidad, Jose	R-R	5-11	150	7-13-87	1	0	6.75	10	0	0	0	11	15	8	8	3	5	8	.357	.300	.409	6.75	4.22
Urckfitz, Pat	L-L	6-4	200	7-21-88	0	0	2.03	10	0	0	2	13	8	3	3	0	3	17	.163	.200	.147	11.48	2.03
Wolf, Shane	L-L	6-3	225	9-10-86	1	1	6.28	19	0	0	0	29	35	23	20	5	13	25	.302	.241	.322	7.85	4.08

Fielding

Catcher	PCT	G	PO	A	E	DP	PB
Comadena	1.000	16	46	2	0	0	4
Garcia	.984	84	529	69	10	10	9
Heath	.981	28	198	13	4	0	5
Hernandez	.996	29	210	28	1	2	1

First Base	PCT	G	PO	A	E	DP
Castro	.985	15	120	9	2	7
Flores	.996	28	251	20	1	25
Hinze	.994	69	617	47	4	53
Singleton	.981	33	241	22	5	30

Second Base	PCT	G	PO	A	E	DP
Altuve	.979	48	92	137	5	31
Arrendell	.966	13	20	36	2	10
Rodriguez	1.000	3	10	15	0	3
Simunic	.975	30	40	78	3	22
Thompson	.976	42	66	97	4	17

Third Base	PCT	G	PO	A	E	DP
Todd	.969	15	23	39	2	11
Vallejo	1.000	1	2	4	0	0
Arrendell	.833	3	3	2	1	0
Castro	.824	7	7	3	1	
Flores	1.000	8	2	13	0	1
Meyer	.953	118	88	240	16	29
Simunic	.903	9	6	22	3	0
Thompson	.900	4	1	8	1	2

Shortstop	PCT	G	PO	A	E	DP
Arrendell	.927	27	41	60	8	10
Meyer	.857	1	2	4	1	1
Mier	.953	57	80	162	12	36
Rodriguez	.941	3	3	13	1	2
Simunic	.750	1	0	3	1	0
Thompson	.913	13	16	26	4	6

	PCT	G	PO	A	E	DP
Todd	.818	2	3	6	2	1
Vallejo	.000	1	0	0	0	0
Villar	.930	45	62	112	13	24

Outfield	PCT	G	PO	A	E	DP
Adamson	1.000	16	24	1	0	0
Arrendell	.875	4	6	1	1	1
Austin	.973	69	141	1	4	0
Bailey	.964	30	46	7	2	1
Comadena	.957	20	22	0	1	0
Flores	1.000	2	2	0	0	0
Goebbert	.973	24	32	4	1	1
Hogue	.972	106	259	15	8	2
Lane	1.000	4	6	0	0	0
Simunic	.980	31	47	1	1	0
Singleton	.000	1	0	0	0	0
Thompson	1.000	1	2	0	0	0
Wates	.977	124	208	9	5	1

LEXINGTON LEGENDS
SOUTH ATLANTIC LEAGUE
LOW CLASS A

Batting	B-T	HT	WT	DOB	AVG	vLH	vRH	G	AB	R	H	2B	3B	HR	RBI	BB	HBP	SH	SF	SO	SB	CS	SLG	OBP
Adamson, Daniel	R-R	5-11	210	9-15-87	.295	.321	.285	53	183	29	54	11	3	4	29	18	4	0	3	46	2	0	.454	.365
Austin, Jay	L-L	5-11	170	8-10-90	.203	.103	.234	32	123	9	25	7	0	0	16	13	5	0	2	32	6	2	.260	.301
Bailey, Adam	L-L	6-1	195	3-6-88	.282	.260	.289	79	312	45	88	14	2	16	53	19	4	0	2	56	2	2	.494	.329
Burnett, Tyler	L-R	6-0	205	5-9-89	.249	.218	.257	103	366	53	91	16	1	6	32	40	1	0	0	75	21	3	.347	.324
DeShields, Delino	R-R	5-9	188	8-16-92	.220	.237	.213	119	469	73	103	17	2	9	48	52	8	0	5	118	30	11	.322	.305
Heath, Ben	R-R	6-2	220	10-7-88	.245	.270	.232	51	188	19	46	11	0	5	19	11	2	0	2	50	0	0	.383	.291
Hernandez, Enrique	R-R	5-11	170	8-24-91	.247	.291	.231	62	215	30	53	11	0	2	17	31	0	0	0	33	0	2	.326	.341
King, Emilio	R-R	6-1	180	3-19-91	.293	.320	.283	98	362	50	106	24	1	9	42	13	9	0	1	81	3	5	.439	.332
Kvasnicka, Mike	R-R	6-2	200	12-7-88	.260	.283	.251	128	484	59	126	32	4	4	59	46	4	0	2	106	5	5	.368	.328
Lane, Bryce	R-R	6-0	190	8-24-89	.238	.271	.223	67	189	33	45	11	1	4	16	22	4	0	1	45	7	2	.370	.329
McCurdy, Ryan	R-R	5-10	175	12-28-87	.000	.000	.000	1	1	0	0	0	0	0	0	0	0	0	0	0	0	0	.000	.000
Medrano, Jhonny	R-R	6-1	156	9-12-87	.203	.134	.238	60	197	20	40	11	0	5	22	12	2	0	5	53	2	1	.335	.255
Mier, Jio	R-R	6-2	180	8-26-90	.245	.216	.255	57	216	39	53	14	0	5	29	37	1	0	3	58	6	2	.380	.354
Nash, Telvin	R-R	6-1	230	2-20-91	.269	.259	.273	73	268	41	72	16	0	14	37	40	6	0	2	103	2	0	.485	.373
Orloff, Ben	R-R	5-11	170	4-26-87	.284	.314	.277	96	327	51	93	15	4	2	31	27	13	0	3	26	12	6	.373	.359
Pena, Roberto	B-R	6-0	210	6-8-92	.217	.141	.243	82	281	31	61	11	0	5	33	18	2	0	3	50	0	0	.310	.266
Rodriguez, Hector	R-R	5-11	150	8-8-89	.171	.182	.167	12	35	1	6	1	0	0	2	0	1	0	0	12	1	0	.200	.194
Santana, Domingo	R-R	6-5	200	8-5-92	.382	.333	.409	17	68	13	26	4	0	5	21	6	2	0	0	15	1	0	.662	.447
2-team total (96 Lakewood)					.287	—	—	113	418	58	120	33	4	12	53	32	17	0	0	135	5	1	.471	.362
Scott, Jordan	L-R	6-2	180	9-22-91	.277	.000	.317	14	47	6	13	3	0	0	6	3	1	0	1	8	0	1	.340	.327

Batting	B-T	HT	WT	DOB	AVG	vLH	vRH	G	AB	R	H	2B	3B	HR	RBI	BB	HBP	SH	SF	SO	SB	CS	SLG	OBP
Sosa, Ruben	B-R	5-7	170	9-23-90	.206	.143	.250	11	34	6	7	3	0	0	3	4	0	0	0	7	2	0	.294	.289
Wallace, Chris	R-R	6-0	205	4-27-88	.285	.345	.266	66	242	37	69	16	3	14	49	17	12	0	4	52	0	3	.550	.356

Pitching	B-T	HT	WT	DOB	W	L	ERA	G	GS	CG	SV	IP	H	R	ER	HR	BB	SO	AVG	vLH	vRH	K/9	BB/9
Alaniz, R.J.	R-R	6-4	175	6-14-91	7	10	4.44	27	21	0	0	116	111	78	57	11	38	96	.248	.254	.244	7.47	2.96
Bullock, Garrett	L-L	6-3	195	6-9-86	0	0	9.82	3	0	0	0	4	4	4	4	0	3	1	.364	.000	.500	2.45	7.36
Bushue, Tanner	R-R	6-4	180	6-20-91	6	6	4.66	16	16	0	0	77	89	43	40	13	17	51	.284	.282	.286	5.94	1.98
Champion, Adam	L-L	6-7	230	9-22-87	0	0	18.00	1	0	0	0	2	4	4	4	1	1	1	.400	1.000	.333	4.50	4.50
Chowning, Jason	R-R	6-2	178	10-17-87	4	4	2.45	35	0	0	2	59	51	20	16	5	23	60	.233	.276	.210	9.20	3.53
Cruz, Luis	L-L	5-9	170	9-10-90	5	4	4.45	18	14	0	0	91	99	53	45	15	23	92	.276	.298	.269	9.10	2.27
De Leon, Jorge	R-R	6-0	180	8-15-87	6	4	3.42	43	0	0	16	55	48	29	21	5	13	51	.225	.304	.179	8.30	2.11
Dydalewicz, Brad	L-L	6-1	180	3-24-90	0	4	11.03	10	7	0	0	24	34	35	29	4	19	11	.324	.259	.346	4.18	7.23
Foltynewicz, Mike	R-R	6-4	200	10-7-91	5	11	4.97	26	26	0	0	134	149	84	74	10	51	88	.289	.284	.292	5.91	3.43
Garcia, Gabriel	L-L	5-11	140	5-11-89	2	5	3.76	31	0	0	2	69	68	33	29	10	16	68	.252	.185	.273	8.83	2.08
Gouvea, Murillo	R-R	6-2	200	9-15-88	1	3	3.98	30	1	0	1	75	82	43	33	4	29	83	.273	.327	.242	10.00	3.50
Lo, Chia-Jen	R-R	5-11	185	4-7-86	0	0	13.50	2	0	0	0	2	3	3	3	1	2	3	.250	.000	.286	13.50	9.00
Martinez, David	R-R	6-2	180	8-4-87	5	7	4.19	37	5	0	2	67	77	44	31	7	17	44	.282	.308	.269	5.94	2.30
Minaya, Juan	R-R	6-4	185	9-18-90	1	5	6.90	28	9	0	1	77	89	66	59	6	57	76	.299	.294	.301	8.88	6.66
Perez, Juri	R-R	5-11	148	8-8-90	1	0	18.90	2	1	0	0	3	7	7	7	1	2	7	.412	.429	.400	8.90	5.40
Quevedo, Carlos	R-R	6-1	222	9-30-89	8	6	4.53	27	26	0	0	151	193	88	76	22	19	110	.307	.279	.323	6.56	1.13
Ramirez, Yordany	R-R	6-1	190	7-31-84	1	1	5.14	4	0	0	0	7	4	4	4	1	7	5	.160	.000	.211	6.43	9.00
Shirley, Tommy	R-L	6-5	220	11-11-88	0	0	13.50	1	1	0	0	2	1	3	3	0	4	2	.143	.000	.200	9.00	18.00
Sogard, Alex	L-L	6-3	215	7-25-87	3	4	4.14	31	10	0	4	104	112	54	48	12	25	112	.272	.306	.263	9.66	2.16
Streilein, Brian	R-R	6-4	205	11-3-88	5	4	3.99	40	1	0	6	70	71	36	31	8	19	40	.266	.327	.229	5.14	2.44

Fielding

Catcher	PCT	G	PO	A	E	DP	PB
Heath	.995	29	186	22	1	3	5
Pena	.988	82	608	77	8	5	11
Wallace	.995	31	201	15	1	0	4

First Base	PCT	G	PO	A	E	DP
Burnett	.983	79	647	32	12	59
Kvasnicka	1.000	1	4	0	0	0
Medrano	.981	28	240	12	5	17
Nash	.975	33	265	13	7	29
Wallace	1.000	1	2	0	0	1

Second Base	PCT	G	PO	A	E	DP
DeShields	.953	107	196	266	23	65
Hernandez	.929	12	22	30	4	7

	PCT	G	PO	A	E	DP
Orloff	.973	15	32	39	2	12
Rodriguez	1.000	6	6	13	0	3
Sosa	1.000	1	2	1	0	1

Third Base	PCT	G	PO	A	E	DP
Burnett	1.000	1	1	1	0	0
Hernandez	.750	4	3	3	2	0
Kvasnicka	.902	116	70	214	31	22
Medrano	.860	20	8	29	6	1
Rodriguez	.500	2	0	1	1	0

Shortstop	PCT	G	PO	A	E	DP
Hernandez	1.000	3	5	11	0	2
Mier	.962	56	81	175	10	35
Orloff	.962	80	117	236	14	44

	PCT	G	PO	A	E	DP
Rodriguez	.944	4	6	11	1	2

Outfield	PCT	G	PO	A	E	DP
Adamson	.979	53	133	8	3	2
Austin	.953	32	81	0	4	0
Bailey	.977	75	157	13	4	3
Burnett	1.000	7	8	1	0	0
Hernandez	1.000	32	56	4	0	0
King	.981	98	192	14	4	1
Lane	.974	63	104	7	3	0
Medrano	1.000	9	13	0	0	0
Nash	.957	13	20	2	1	1
Santana	.885	16	22	1	3	0
Scott	.895	13	17	0	2	0
Sosa	.941	9	16	0	1	0

TRI-CITY VALLEYCATS   SHORT-SEASON

NEW YORK-PENN LEAGUE

Batting	B-T	HT	WT	DOB	AVG	vLH	vRH	G	AB	R	H	2B	3B	HR	RBI	BB	HBP	SH	SF	SO	SB	CS	SLG	OBP
Arrendell, Miguel	L-R	6-0	165	3-26-88	.219	.176	.234	18	64	5	14	2	0	0	5	7	0	0	0	8	4	0	.250	.296
Davidson, Chase	L-R	6-5	222	1-14-90	.000	.000	.000	1	4	0	0	0	0	0	0	0	0	0	0	2	0	0	.000	.000
Duffy, Matthew	R-R	6-3	215	2-6-89	.298	.293	.299	63	235	36	70	20	1	2	37	15	13	0	2	41	2	2	.417	.370
Epps, Chris	L-R	6-2	172	12-10-88	.212	.385	.154	19	52	16	11	3	0	2	16	8	0	0	0	18	4	2	.385	.414
Gominsky, Justin	R-R	6-4	185	8-26-89	.237	.226	.241	60	232	35	55	9	0	0	18	22	3	0	0	42	12	7	.276	.311
Hamblin, Miles	L-R	6-3	200	10-22-88	.264	.200	.282	59	201	34	53	11	2	4	20	23	3	0	1	44	6	1	.398	.346
Healey, Jacke	R-R	6-2	180	6-26-88	.156	.250	.127	49	154	17	24	7	1	3	19	18	0	0	1	50	8	2	.273	.243
Hinson, John	L-R	6-1	180	9-13-88	.284	.294	.281	43	162	18	46	9	1	2	11	17	0	0	2	26	7	5	.389	.348
Johnson, Neiko	R-R	5-9	165	2-2-88	.235	.163	.263	56	179	29	42	5	0	1	16	39	0	0	2	37	21	4	.279	.393
Johnson, Zachary	R-R	5-11	200	6-16-88	.262	.294	.251	72	271	31	71	12	1	5	40	26	8	0	5	45	1	2	.369	.339
Kiilsgaard, Kellen	L-L	6-2	220	6-16-88	.159	.188	.153	28	88	7	14	2	2	1	12	4	0	0	1	19	2	0	.261	.194
McCurdy, Ryan	R-R	5-10	175	12-28-87	.324	.222	.360	32	102	8	33	6	0	0	17	4	8	0	2	11	2	2	.382	.388
Meredith, Brandon	R-R	6-2	225	12-19-89	.244	.400	.191	35	119	24	29	7	4	1	10	19	5	0	0	29	7	3	.395	.371
Muren, Andrew	R-R	6-0	195	11-22-88	.257	.300	.241	67	222	32	57	7	1	2	21	36	7	0	1	55	8	8	.324	.376
Rodriguez, Hector	R-R	5-11	150	8-8-89	.176	.250	.154	17	51	7	9	0	1	0	3	5	3	0	0	16	2	1	.216	.222
Scott, Jordan	L-R	6-2	180	9-22-91	.235	.167	.273	5	17	4	4	0	1	0	3	6	5	0	0	2	1	1	.353	.409
Springer, George	R-R	6-3	205	9-19-89	.179	.167	.182	8	28	8	5	3	0	1	3	2	3	0	0	2	4	0	.393	.303
Valenzuela, Rafael	L-R	6-1	175	12-20-88	.316	.229	.354	31	114	17	36	10	0	2	18	9	2	0	1	18	2	2	.456	.367
Williams, Bubby	R-R	6-0	190	3-13-89	.206	.216	.202	36	131	16	27	5	1	6	19	3	1	0	4	45	0	2	.397	.223

Pitching	B-T	HT	WT	DOB	W	L	ERA	G	GS	CG	SV	IP	H	R	ER	HR	BB	SO	AVG	vLH	vRH	K/9	BB/9
Belliard, Joan	R-R	6-2	185	3-3-89	1	1	4.82	17	0	0	0	19	19	15	10	2	11	17	.257	.259	.255	8.20	5.30
Blankenship, Travis	L-L	6-1	185	10-16-87	1	2	3.90	21	0	0	0	30	24	20	13	2	8	28	.209	.139	.241	8.40	2.40
Bueno, Kristian	L-L	6-1	175	12-10-88	1	3	6.10	17	0	0	0	21	26	19	14	2	19	18	.283	.154	.333	7.84	8.27
Bullock, Garrett	L-L	6-3	195	6-9-86	0	0	2.51	22	0	0	0	32	25	10	9	1	8	30	.223	.265	.205	8.35	4.18
Champion, Adam	L-L	6-7	230	9-22-87	4	1	3.35	14	5	0	0	46	45	19	17	2	14	31	.259	.313	.227	6.11	2.76
Cole, Ryan	R-R	5-11	205	12-12-87	1	1	2.33	26	0	0	10	27	30	12	7	0	6	25	.280	.229	.322	8.33	2.00
Cotton, Jamaine	R-R	6-2	185	9-27-90	2	1	3.68	5	5	0	0	22	25	10	9	1	5	14	.291	.219	.333	5.73	2.05
Diaz, Dayan	R-R	5-10	156	2-10-89	7	3	1.98	19	1	0	2	50	27	17	11	0	30	70	.158	.159	.157	12.60	5.40

Pitching	B-T	HT	WT	DOB	W	L	ERA	G	GS	CG	SV	IP	H	R	ER	HR	BB	SO	AVG	vLH	vRH	K/9	BB/9
Dufek, Jonas	R-R	6-5	215	6-30-88	3	4	3.71	11	11	1	0	51	55	28	21	2	16	37	.279	.280	.278	6.53	2.82
Gouvea, Murillo	R-R	6-2	200	9-15-88	0	1	10.13	1	1	0	0	3	6	5	3	0	0	3	.400	.400		10.13	0.00
Hallock, Kyle	L-L	6-2	185	8-6-88	3	4	2.63	13	13	0	0	62	58	29	18	3	17	61	.241	.227	.247	8.90	2.48
James, Brad	R-R	6-2	210	6-19-84	1	0	3.18	5	0	0	0	6	4	2	2	0	3	8	.190	.222	.167	12.71	4.76
Lambson, Mitchell	L-L	6-1	198	7-20-90	2	6	4.33	22	0	0	2	35	33	19	17	4	8	39	.248	.286	.226	9.93	2.04
Ordosgoitti, Luis	R-R	6-4	180	9-22-92	0	0	12.00	1	1	0	0	3	7	4	4	0	2	2	.467	.500	.600	6.00	6.00
Perez, Juri	R-R	5-11	148	8-8-90	1	6	5.48	15	15	0	0	67	85	44	41	7	24	67	.313	.312	.313	8.96	3.21
Quezada, Euris	R-R	6-6	210	4-6-89	1	3	6.95	9	9	0	0	34	45	32	26	1	24	24	.317	.250	.378	6.42	6.42
Shirley, Tommy	R-L	6-5	220	11-11-88	0	0	0.00	2	0	0	0	6	3	0	0	0	1	9	.158	.000	.200	13.50	1.50
Smink, Travis	L-L	6-2	200	4-10-87	2	4	4.37	23	0	0	1	45	52	25	22	5	8	33	.294	.275	.302	6.55	1.59
Tropeano, Nicholas	R-R	6-4	205	8-27-90	3	2	2.36	12	12	0	0	53	42	18	14	1	21	63	.212	.176	.243	10.63	3.54
Walter, Andrew	R-R	6-4	215	10-18-90	0	0	3.00	2	2	0	0	6	6	3	2	0	4	8	.261	.333	.235	12.00	6.00

Fielding

Catcher	PCT	G	PO	A	E	DP	PB
Hamblin	.984	39	285	27	5	2	8
McCurdy	.989	29	235	27	3	1	6
Williams	.989	11	89	4	1	0	3

First Base	PCT	G	PO	A	E	DP
Johnson	.979	60	510	44	12	31
Valenzuela	.982	13	103	5	2	7
Williams	1.000	2	21	2	0	2

Second Base	PCT	G	PO	A	E	DP
Arrendell	.968	8	13	17	1	1
Hinson	.952	41	62	116	9	21
Johnson	.927	18	21	30	4	3

	PCT	G	PO	A	E	DP
Johnson	.917	6	9	13	2	1
Rodriguez	.929	3	4	9	1	1

Third Base	PCT	G	PO	A	E	DP
Duffy	.925	59	31	117	12	13
Healey	1.000	1	0	1	0	0
Johnson	1.000	2	1	1	0	0
Johnson	.667	1	0	2	1	0
Rodriguez	.923	6	4	8	1	1
Valenzuela	.875	10	2	12	2	1

Shortstop	PCT	G	PO	A	E	DP
Arrendell	.919	10	12	22	3	0
Healey	.959	45	70	119	8	21

	PCT	G	PO	A	E	DP
Johnson	.875	15	14	42	8	4
Rodriguez	.921	7	12	23	3	4

Outfield	PCT	G	PO	A	E	DP
Epps	.938	17	29	1	2	0
Gominsky	.983	58	113	4	2	0
Johnson	.944	20	33	1	2	0
Kiilsgaard	1.000	19	28	1	0	0
Meredith	.974	32	35	2	1	0
Muren	.972	66	124	14	4	1
Scott	1.000	5	4	0	0	0
Springer	1.000	8	13	0	0	0
Valenzuela	1.000	5	2	0	0	0

GREENEVILLE ASTROS

ROOKIE

APPALACHIAN LEAGUE

Batting	B-T	HT	WT	DOB	AVG	vLH	vRH	G	AB	R	H	2B	3B	HR	RBI	BB	HBP	SH	SF	SO	SB	CS	SLG	OBP
Alvarez, Luis	R-R	5-11	198	2-28-90	.271	.308	.262	38	133	14	36	6	1	2	10	12	5	0	0	19	1	3	.376	.353
Batista, Jean	B-R	6-2	180	11-15-91	.333	.000	.357	12	45	6	15	3	0	2	11	1	0	0	0	13	0	1	.533	.348
Davidson, Chase	L-R	6-5	222	1-14-90	.335	.324	.339	43	161	33	54	13	2	11	44	24	2	0	1	51	8	1	.646	.426
Genoves, Ernesto	R-R	5-11	203	6-4-91	.280	.242	.293	38	125	23	35	9	1	4	21	12	7	0	0	29	0	1	.464	.375
Kiilsgaard, Kellen	L-L	6-2	220	12-16-88	.167	.667	.111	8	30	4	5	1	0	0	1	4	0	0	0	8	0	0	.200	.265
Magee, Josh	R-R	5-10	160	10-1-91	.283	.306	.277	53	184	28	52	9	0	2	19	16	4	0	4	36	16	9	.364	.346
Monzon, Jose	R-R	6-0	170	12-30-91	.200	.222	.194	53	170	27	34	7	1	0	10	25	7	0	0	51	7	1	.253	.327
Moon, Chan	L-R	6-0	160	3-23-91	.207	.152	.224	43	140	19	29	3	3	1	12	16	3	0	0	51	3	1	.293	.302
Moronta, Cristian	R-R	5-10	185	12-5-89	.242	.250	.240	13	33	3	8	2	0	0	0	0	0	0	0	6	0	0	.303	.242
Ovando, Ariel	L-L	6-4	190	9-15-93	.235	.143	.254	44	170	16	40	10	3	2	30	12	0	0	2	51	0	0	.365	.283
Rivera, Darwin	R-R	5-11	180	10-27-91	.224	.178	.238	57	205	23	46	9	0	4	26	13	2	0	2	51	0	2	.327	.275
Sanchez, Ronald	L-R	5-10	180	8-9-91	.167	.111	.185	24	72	7	12	1	0	0	3	9	0	0	0	23	0	0	.181	.259
Scott, Jordan	L-R	6-2	180	9-22-91	.337	.373	.326	60	246	41	83	12	3	1	31	19	2	0	1	37	11	5	.423	.388
Sosa, Ruben	B-R	5-7	170	9-23-90	.248	.214	.264	39	129	25	32	6	1	0	17	22	2	0	1	27	12	3	.310	.364
Todd, Alex	R-R	6-2	190	8-15-89	.159	.240	.134	33	107	13	17	6	0	0	11	12	8	0	2	23	0	1	.215	.287
Vargas, Jose	R-R	6-1	200	4-30-91	.149	.053	.173	27	94	7	14	6	0	1	10	4	3	0	1	26	0	0	.245	.206
Wierzbicki, Jesse	R-R	6-3	200	11-24-88	.265	.333	.250	45	162	35	43	12	1	5	28	22	3	0	3	44	3	0	.444	.358
Wright, Garen	R-R	6-3	230	12-25-90	.253	.357	.203	25	87	14	22	4	1	1	9	5	2	0	0	20	8	2	.356	.309

Pitching	B-T	HT	WT	DOB	W	L	ERA	G	GS	CG	SV	IP	H	R	ER	HR	BB	SO	AVG	vLH	vRH	K/9	BB/9
Batista, Ricardo	L-L	6-1	170	8-19-91	3	4	4.73	12	12	0	0	53	49	31	28	2	34	47	.247	.229	.252	7.93	5.74
Cotton, Jamaine	R-R	6-2	185	9-27-90	4	1	5.45	9	5	0	1	35	46	22	21	2	11	27	.319	.347	.305	7.01	2.86
Dando, Zachary	R-R	6-3	175	1-4-91	1	3	4.91	19	0	0	3	33	23	21	18	3	10	35	.187	.135	.209	9.55	2.73
Del Rio, Danilo	R-R	5-11	179	9-28-90	1	2	5.40	17	2	0	0	42	52	34	25	1	19	17	.302	.288	.308	3.67	4.10
Houser, Adrian	R-R	6-4	205	2-2-93	1	2	4.56	6	6	0	0	26	25	16	13	1	15	19	.258	.184	.333	6.66	5.26
Jones, Mark	R-R	6-7	205	8-29-90	0	0	6.75	16	0	0	0	24	31	22	18	3	14	20	.298	.353	.271	7.50	5.25
Lee, Chris	L-L	6-3	175	8-17-92	1	5	5.18	13	13	0	0	49	53	34	28	4	34	47	.279	.195	.302	8.69	6.29
Meiners, Jeremiah	L-L	6-0	200	8-16-88	2	3	2.90	20	0	0	1	40	34	19	13	1	10	42	.218	.167	.233	9.37	2.23
Mojica, Juan	R-R	6-4	190	2-13-89	0	0	0.00	1	0	0	0	1	0	0	0	0	1	1	.000	.000	.000	9.00	0.00
Ordosgoitti, Luis	R-R	6-4	180	9-22-92	2	4	4.50	9	7	0	0	44	47	29	22	2	7	42	.270	.276	.267	8.59	1.43
Perdomo, Jose	R-R	6-0	180	10-24-91	0	4	9.00	5	5	0	0	18	33	22	18	4	8	21	.379	.357	.390	10.50	4.00
Perez, Tyson	R-R	6-3	215	12-27-89	2	5	5.07	13	13	0	0	55	62	37	31	10	13	49	.281	.314	.252	8.02	2.13
Propst, Brad	R-R	6-1	180	3-18-89	1	3	5.71	17	1	0	1	35	39	28	22	2	10	37	.267	.306	.238	9.61	2.60
Quintero, Rodney	R-R	6-2	215	1-18-90	0	1	5.97	16	0	0	0	29	28	28	19	3	16	32	.246	.220	.260	10.05	5.02
Ramirez, Francis	R-R	6-5	205	1-12-92	1	1	2.89	4	4	0	0	19	12	7	6	1	2	11	.182	.107	.194	5.30	0.96
Shewey, Paris	L-L	5-11	198	2-5-89	1	5	9.82	20	0	0	3	22	35	24	24	6	7	21	.357	.379	.348	8.59	2.86
Smith, Matison	R-R	6-0	185	6-26-88	2	0	2.65	21	0	0	3	34	40	16	10	3	9	45	.286	.294	.281	11.91	2.38
Zuloaga, Scott	R-L	6-4	200	9-20-91	1	0	6.14	24	0	0	0	15	18	11	10	0	7	19	.286	.206	.379	11.66	4.30

Fielding

Catcher	PCT	G	PO	A	E	DP	PB
Alvarez	.974	38	281	53	9	5	12
Genoves	.981	27	184	21	4	3	9

	PCT	G	PO	A	E	DP	PB
Moronta	.965	12	71	11	3	0	7

First Base	PCT	G	PO	A	E	DP
Davidson	1.000	10	103	5	0	9
Genoves	1.000	2	5	0	0	1

Sanchez	.989	24	164	10	2	15
Wierzbicki	.984	37	303	14	5	24

Second Base	PCT	G	PO	A	E	DP
Batista	.909	2	4	6	1	5
Magee	.926	48	94	130	18	25
Moon	.917	3	2	9	1	1
Sosa	.970	20	42	56	3	13
Todd	1.000	1	1	1	0	1

Third Base	PCT	G	PO	A	E	DP
Batista	.667	3	0	2	1	0

Magee	.833	5	7	8	3	0
Moon	.875	5	2	5	1	1
Rivera	.827	57	37	106	30	12
Wierzbicki	.875	3	1	6	1	0

Shortstop	PCT	G	PO	A	E	DP
Batista	.750	3	1	5	2	0
Moon	.954	37	46	98	7	23
Todd	.907	31	38	89	13	18

Outfield	PCT	G	PO	A	E	DP
Davidson	1.000	2	1	0	0	0

Kiilsgaard	1.000	5	5	0	0	0
Monzon	.968	52	116	4	4	0
Ovando	.904	39	60	6	7	1
Scott	.959	60	113	3	5	0
Sosa	1.000	16	24	1	0	1
Vargas	.929	15	23	3	2	1
Wright	.969	22	31	0	1	0

GCL ASTROS

ROOKIE

GULF COAST LEAGUE

Batting	B-T	HT	WT	DOB	AVG	vLH	vRH	G	AB	R	H	2B	3B	HR	RBI	BB	HBP	SH	SF	SO	SB	CS	SLG	OBP
Adamson, Daniel	R-R	5-11	210	9-15-87	.400	.000	.500	2	5	0	2	0	0	0	0	0	1	0	0	1	0	0	.400	.500
Ayarza, Max	B-R	6-0	160	3-11-92	.148	.231	.122	23	54	6	8	1	2	0	3	5	0	0	1	14	1	2	.241	.217
Batista, Jean	B-R	6-2	180	11-15-91	.243	.281	.232	38	144	18	35	7	3	1	18	6	0	0	2	25	6	1	.354	.270
Bourgeois, Jason	R-R	5-9	195	1-4-82	.300	.333	.250	3	10	1	3	0	0	0	4	1	0	0	2	0	0	0	.300	.364
Diaz, Kenny	R-R	5-9	175	5-9-92	.281	.444	.217	13	32	6	9	2	0	1	8	4	1	0	0	8	0	0	.438	.378
Epps, Chris	L-R	6-2	172	12-10-88	.304	.450	.272	35	112	17	34	3	3	4	25	22	2	0	0	36	6	5	.491	.426
Fernandez, Jose	R-R	6-1	170	5-20-93	.245	.214	.252	43	159	21	39	6	3	0	15	14	3	0	0	54	11	3	.321	.318
Gonzalez, Alfredo	R-R	6-1	190	7-13-92	.172	.182	.169	30	93	8	16	3	3	0	9	3	1	0	2	20	3	3	.269	.202
Gonzalez, Kevin	R-R	5-10	190	11-6-87	.250	.250	.250	13	32	2	8	2	0	0	2	4	0	0	0	6	0	0	.313	.333
Gonzalez, Wallace	R-R	6-5	240	2-11-93	.242	.333	.220	18	62	3	15	1	1	0	5	5	1	0	0	16	1	0	.290	.309
Marte, Ydarqui	R-R	6-1	188	10-10-92	.122	.273	.067	17	41	6	5	1	0	0	7	6	0	0	1	10	3	2	.146	.229
Martone, Luca	B-R	5-8	150	10-24-93	.314	.143	.339	29	70	9	22	5	0	0	2	8	0	0	0	17	3	1	.386	.385
McKinney, Jarrod	R-R	5-11	205	10-14-89	.182	.214	.172	35	121	19	22	4	1	0	7	6	3	0	3	42	4	2	.231	.233
Mejia, Yonathan	B-R	6-2	175	9-19-92	.329	.235	.357	40	146	15	48	8	0	0	25	3	4	0	1	29	2	0	.384	.357
Meskin, Jake	R-R	6-2	200	8-6-88	.067	.167	.042	22	30	1	2	0	0	0	4	2	2	0	2	10	0	1	.067	.167
Nash, Telvin	R-R	6-1	230	2-20-91	.385	.400	.375	5	13	5	5	2	0	0	3	0	0	0	0	0	0	0	.538	.500
Redinger, Kyle	R-R	6-3	205	12-19-91	.148	.192	.135	41	122	10	18	6	0	0	8	10	5	0	1	42	0	1	.197	.239
Reynolds, Javaris	L-L	6-1	190	1-24-93	.228	.333	.200	46	158	25	36	3	0	0	4	19	12	0	0	40	15	8	.247	.354
Shults, Justin	L-R	6-3	205	12-2-87	.224	.163	.244	51	174	24	39	10	1	5	29	22	2	0	1	51	2	2	.379	.317
Suniaga, Geber	R-R	5-11	160	6-17-91	.000	.000	.000	7	12	2	0	0	0	0	1	5	0	0	1	8	1	0	.000	.278
Valenzuela, Rafael	L-R	6-1	175	10-20-87	.231	.333	.200	4	13	1	3	1	0	0	2	1	0	0	0	2	0	0	.308	.286
Vizcaino, Kelvin	R-R	6-0	175	9-30-92	.244	.211	.254	29	82	14	20	2	1	2	5	8	1	0	0	23	3	5	.366	.319
Witkowski, Joe	R-R	6-2	215	8-1-88	.220	.375	.190	18	50	2	11	1	1	0	4	3	2	0	0				.280	.291

Pitching	B-T	HT	WT	DOB	W	L	ERA	G	GS	CG	SV	IP	H	R	ER	HR	BB	SO	AVG	vLH	vRH	K/9	BB/9
Abad, Fernando	L-L	6-2	215	12-17-85	0	0	0.00	2	0	0	0	2	1	0	0	0	2		.143	.500	.000	9.00	0.00
Baso, Xavier	R-R	6-0	190	1-12-91	0	0	7.36	3	0	0	0	4	5	3	3	0	2	6	.333	.333	.333	14.73	4.91
Bushue, Tanner	R-R	6-4	180	6-25-91	0	2	7.88	3	3	0	0	8	14	7	7	0	0	7	.368	.333	.412	7.88	0.00
Culbreth, Brandon	R-R	6-4	200	7-27-92	0	2	12.71	5	1	0	0	6	6	9	8	0	7	4	.273	.444	.154	6.35	11.12
Del Rosario, Enerio	R-R	6-2	180	10-16-85	0	0	9.00	1	0	0	0	1	2	1	1	0	0	2	.500	.500	.500	18.00	0.00
Dennison, Steve	L-R	6-7	225	3-5-89	0	1	3.93	14	0	0	0	18	24	14	8	1	5	16	.293	.320	.281	7.85	2.45
Dydalewicz, Brad	L-L	6-1	180	3-24-90	0	1	10.29	8	0	0	0	7	11	8	8	1	7	3	.379	.222	.450	3.86	9.00
Feliz, Michael	R-R	6-4	210	9-28-93	0	3	4.32	12	10	0	0	50	53	35	24	2	21	44	.270	.273	.269	7.92	3.78
Fien, Casey	R-R	6-2	195	10-21-83	1	0	0.00	2	0	0	0	2	1	0	0	0	0	3	.143	.000	.200	13.50	0.00
Ford, Blake	L-R	6-5	215	5-16-88	4	3	1.90	18	0	0	8	24	27	13	5	2	6	20	.276	.273	.276	7.61	2.28
Franco, Enderson	R-R	6-2	170	12-29-92	1	4	2.40	10	10	0	0	47	56	28	23	1	17	26	.303	.255	.321	4.98	3.26
Gill, Justin	R-R	6-3	205	1-1-89	0	0	3.32	20	0	0	1	22	17	12	8	2	10	18	.210	.185	.222	7.48	4.15
Gomez, Pedro	R-R	6-3	204	5-10-91	4	2	4.18	16	0	0	1	28	21	14	13	1	19	17	.226	.200	.233	5.46	6.11
Grills, Evan	R-R	6-4	205	6-13-92	3	1	3.00	13	2	0	0	33	33	13	11	1	7	29	.262	.306	.244	7.91	1.91
Hardoin, Zachary	L-L	5-10	190	7-11-88	0	1	4.70	16	0	0	0	15	12	11	8	0	11	23	.218	.308	.190	13.50	6.46
Holley, Krishawn	R-R	6-0	195	2-8-92	1	2	2.16	13	0	0	0	17	12	6	4	1	8	15	.200	.118	.233	8.10	4.32
Houser, Adrian	R-R	6-4	205	2-2-93	1	2	4.03	6	5	0	0	22	24	12	10	0	10	25	.273	.182	.303	10.07	4.03
Infante, Wilton	R-R	6-1	175	6-14-92	1	0	4.15	6	0	0	0	4	3	4	2	0	3	1	.188	.400	.091	2.08	6.23
Kellogg, Dustin	R-R	6-4	185	2-16-93	1	1	4.26	6	0	0	0	6	7	3	3	1	1	9	.280	.444	.188	12.79	1.42
Mojica, Juan	R-R	6-4	190	2-13-89	0	0	1.42	14	0	0	0	19	18	3	3	0	9	19	.243	.278	.232	9.00	4.26
Musick, Wes	L-L	6-0	190	12-30-86	0	0	6.00	3	0	0	0	6	7	4	4	1	4	6	.292	.400	.263	9.00	6.00
Ordosgoitti, Luis	R-R	6-4	180	9-22-92	0	1	1.50	2	2	0	0	6	8	4	1	0	1	5	.308	.385	.231	7.50	1.50
Pettus, Nate	R-R	6-1	200	10-9-88	0	0	11.25	5	0	0	0	4	3	5	5	0	2	2	.231	.000	.375	4.50	4.50
Ramirez, Francis	R-R	6-5	205	1-12-92	1	2	5.93	8	7	0	0	30	29	23	20	5	20	30	.242	.270	.229	8.90	5.93
Rodriguez, Richard	R-R	6-4	185	3-4-90	0	0	9.82	4	0	0	0	4	4	4	4	1	1	3	.353	.200	.417	7.36	2.45
Rowland-Smith, Ryan	L-L	6-3	240	1-26-83	0	1	1.35	2	2	0	0	7	9	2	1	0	3	7	.310	.000	.375	9.45	4.05
Shirley, Tommy	R-L	6-5	220	11-11-88	0	0	0.00	2	2	0	0	5	2	0	0	0	0	4	.125	.500	.071	7.20	0.00
Tiburcio, Frederick	R-R	6-3	192	11-1-90	3	5	4.47	12	10	0	0	54	54	32	27	0	22	47	.256	.329	.215	7.83	3.64
Valdez, Jose	R-R	6-4	200	1-22-83	0	1	4.50	4	0	0	0	4	3	2	2	0	1	7	.188	.222	.143	15.75	2.25
Walter, Andrew	R-R	6-4	215	10-18-90	0	0	2.45	4	0	0	0	7	6	2	2	0	1	4	.222	.182	.250	4.91	1.23

Fielding

Catcher	PCT	G	PO	A	E	DP	PB
Diaz	.986	11	63	9	1	1	3
Gonzalez	.974	30	225	37	7	3	15

Gonzalez	1.000	12	56	6	0	1	2
Meskin	1.000	18	50	4	0	0	2
Witkowski	1.000	5	22	5	0	0	2

First Base	PCT	G	PO	A	E	DP
Nash	.967	5	29	0	1	3
Redinger	1.000	5	20	2	0	2

Shults	.990	47	360	22	4 28
Valenzuela	1.000	3	22	1	0 0

Second Base	PCT	G	PO	A	E	DP
Ayarza	.947	8	8	10	1	1
Batista	.934	13	24	33	4	4
Martone	.968	27	22	68	3	13
Mejia	.972	15	35	34	2	10

Third Base	PCT	G	PO	A	E	DP
Ayarza	.750	10	4	8	4	1
Batista	.909	12	8	22	3	1

Martone	.000	1	0	0 0 0
Redinger	.904	38	31	63 10 4
Valenzuela	1.000	1	1	0 0 0

Shortstop	PCT	G	PO	A	E	DP
Ayarza	.857	4	6	6	2	0
Batista	.813	9	10	16	6	3
Fernandez	.926	43	63	125	15	20
Mejia	.833	2	2	3	1	1

Outfield	PCT	G	PO	A	E	DP
Adamson	1.000	2	4	0	0	0

Bourgeois	1.000	2	5	0 0 0
Epps	.962	31	48	2 2 1
Gonzalez	.957	15	22	0 1 0
Marte	1.000	13	18	0 0 0
McKinney	.941	30	43	5 3 1
Reynolds	.980	44	97	3 2 0
Shults	1.000	4	7	1 0 1
Suniaga	1.000	6	7	0 0 0
Vizcaino	.962	22	50	1 2 0

DSL ASTROS   ROOKIE

DOMINICAN SUMMER LEAGUE

Batting	B-T	HT	WT	DOB	AVG	vLH	vRH	G	AB	R	H	2B	3B	HR	RBI	BB	HBP	SH	SF	SO	SB	CS	SLG	OBP
Avea, Marlon	R-R	6-1	195	8-31-93	.165	.095	.188	37	85	4	14	0	0	0	9	9	5	0	1	26	2	1	.165	.280
Coa, Pedro	R-R	6-2	190	12-21-92	.186	.182	.188	39	86	5	16	1	0	0	9	7	2	0	0	7	0	0	.198	.263
De La Cruz, Johan	R-R	6-2	190	1-3-93	.237	.243	.234	42	131	17	31	3	0	1	8	13	4	0	0	32	6	2	.282	.324
Gonzalez, Mario	L-R	6-1	195	12-25-91	.273	.162	.302	64	176	29	48	11	1	3	32	50	7	0	4	25	3	2	.398	.443
Hernandez, Teoscar	R-R	6-2	180	10-15-92	.274	.143	.318	65	226	41	62	13	7	7	35	28	4	0	3	42	16	4	.487	.360
Laguna, Mesac	R-R	6-2	185	1-12-92	.267	.289	.260	61	195	17	52	5	1	3	35	10	6	0	3	27	3	4	.349	.318
Medina, Michael	R-R	6-0	190	10-3-93	.113	.071	.126	53	115	18	13	4	0	4	16	36	5	0	0	67	0	2	.252	.346
Murillo, Cristian	L-L	6-1	165	6-1-93	.228	.125	.268	26	57	12	13	6	0	0	4	9	3	0	0	19	2	1	.333	.362
Polanco, Franny	R-R	6-2	185	12-20-91	.292	.289	.294	58	171	15	50	7	0	2	25	9	1	0	3	23	4	4	.368	.326
Rivera, Darwin	R-R	5-11	180	10-27-91	.333	.500	.276	12	39	6	13	5	0	1	4	3	0	0	0	12	0	0	.538	.381
Santana, Juan	R-R	6-1	180	8-16-94	.274	.367	.245	68	248	44	68	11	1	3	28	28	2	0	2	22	9	3	.363	.350
Serrano, Frederick	R-R	6-2	190	8-29-94	.169	.188	.163	24	59	6	10	4	0	0	6	8	3	0	0	29	0	1	.237	.300
Sierra, Andru	B-R	5-9	168	11-13-91	.222	.135	.263	48	117	20	26	4	1	1	4	12	5	0	1	25	5	5	.299	.319
Silfa, Yoel	R-R	5-11	160	7-8-93	.219	.224	.218	68	237	30	52	9	0	2	19	20	4	0	3	28	11	4	.283	.288
Solano, Jose	R-R	6-2	175	3-15-92	.282	.175	.315	65	238	37	67	7	0	2	21	18	7	0	1	45	21	7	.336	.348

Pitching	B-T	HT	WT	DOB	W	L	ERA	G	GS	CG	SV	IP	H	R	ER	HR	BB	SO	AVG	vLH	vRH	K/9	BB/9
Abad, Luis	R-R	6-3	165	4-18-94	0	4	5.29	12	12	0	0	34	22	28	20	0	39	27	.191	.176	.194	7.15	10.32
Arias, Johan	R-R	6-0	170	1-1-92	1	2	7.98	17	0	0	1	29	36	27	26	2	15	20	.305	.389	.290	6.14	4.60
Barrios, Agapito	R-R	6-2	167	11-30-93	3	4	4.60	13	13	0	0	59	55	35	30	3	27	37	.243	.176	.263	5.68	4.14
Colon, Frangy	R-R	6-2	170	1-18-93	0	1	3.00	5	0	0	1	6	6	2	2	0	4	4	.261	.000	.300	6.00	6.00
2-team total (5 Indians)					0	2	3.21	10	1	0	1	14	16	6	5	0	8	9	—	—	—	5.79	5.14
De Leon, Ambiorix	L-L	6-3	185	8-7-91	2	4	4.47	14	10	0	0	56	51	32	28	3	19	44	.239	.100	.246	7.03	3.04
De Los Santos, Samil	R-R	6-4	175	1-8-94	1	3	7.04	9	2	0	0	15	13	19	12	0	20	13	.245	.000	.277	7.63	11.74
Delis, Juan	R-R	6-1	195	5-29-94	1	0	4.44	15	1	0	1	24	23	14	12	0	23	14	.253	.238	.257	5.18	8.51
Feliz, Andres	L-L	6-2	170	10-30-90	1	3	6.15	15	0	0	2	26	25	19	18	2	24	21	.278	.667	.264	7.18	8.20
Ferreira, Edgar	L-L	6-3	180	10-15-92	0	1	11.57	10	2	0	0	14	10	21	18	1	23	18	.204	.000	.204	11.57	14.79
Franzua, Geronimo	L-L	6-1	170	9-25-93	0	6	4.12	11	10	0	0	39	35	32	18	1	29	26	.230	.143	.234	5.95	6.64
Frias, Edison	R-R	6-1	178	12-18-90	1	2	4.24	4	3	0	0	17	18	8	8	2	6	21	.265	.200	.283	11.12	3.18
Guduan, Reymin	L-L	6-4	185	3-16-92	1	3	2.17	13	13	0	0	46	31	19	11	0	42	61	.193	.500	.181	12.02	8.28
Gustave, Jandel	R-R	6-2	160	10-12-92	0	4	12.10	14	1	0	0	19	24	32	26	2	34	19	.320	.250	.324	8.84	15.83
Lozano, Javier	R-R	6-2	190	4-24-93	1	0	1.80	4	0	0	0	5	5	2	1	0	2	1	.263	1.000	.222	1.80	3.60
Martinez, Alexander	R-R	6-2	160	3-11-93	2	2	7.00	16	0	0	0	27	36	27	21	3	14	17	.310	.263	.320	5.67	4.67
Mesa, Victor	R-R	6-2	170	11-26-93	2	0	3.16	11	0	0	0	26	28	16	9	2	10	19	.272	.176	.291	6.66	3.51
Perdomo, Yeudy	L-L	6-1	155	12-19-91	1	1	3.78	7	1	0	0	17	12	8	7	0	8	21	.203	.000	.207	11.34	4.32
Ramirez, Felix	R-R	6-5	150	7-12-90	2	0	1.69	7	0	0	1	16	11	3	3	0	6	13	.204	.250	.190	7.31	3.38
Sanchez, Manuel	R-R	6-3	207	8-3-90	4	0	2.55	15	0	0	1	25	21	13	7	0	12	18	.228	.412	.187	6.57	4.38
Santana, Kelvin	R-R	6-4	190	4-15-90	2	0	0.00	14	0	0	5	20	11	1	0	0	13	31	.159	.000	.180	13.72	5.75
Saucedo, Javier	L-L	5-11	160	9-28-91	1	0	4.84	12	0	0	1	22	32	20	12	2	11	16	.360	.000	.381	6.45	4.43
Yonquelys, Martinez	R-R	6-0	180	4-23-93	1	0	6.48	5	0	0	0	8	9	9	6	2	4	6	.265	.600	.207	6.48	4.32

Fielding

Catcher	PCT	G	PO	A	E	DP	PB
Avea	.988	27	143	16	2	0	5
Coa	.989	24	150	25	2	0	8
Polanco	.962	35	183	46	9	4	7
Serrano	1.000	1	1	0	0	0	0

First Base	PCT	G	PO	A	E	DP
Coa	1.000	5	11	2	0	3
Gonzalez	.984	62	454	26	8	40
Laguna	1.000	5	24	2	0	1
Medina	.956	11	43	0	2	3
Polanco	.895	4	15	2	2	1
Ramirez	1.000	1	1	0	0	0

Second Base	PCT	G	PO	A	E	DP
De La Cruz	.000	1	0	0	0	0

Santana	1.000	2	1	0	0	0
Sierra	.906	9	10	19	3	3
Silfa	.969	58	92	129	7	32
Solano	1.000	10	12	19	0	4

Third Base	PCT	G	PO	A	E	DP
Coa	1.000	5	2	5	0	1
Gonzalez	1.000	2	1	0	0	0
Medina	.732	12	12	18	11	0
Polanco	1.000	1	0	1	0	0
Rivera	.808	7	5	16	5	0
Sierra	.854	13	12	23	6	6
Silfa	.889	8	3	5	1	0
Solano	.869	37	35	71	16	6

Shortstop	PCT	G	PO	A	E	DP
Santana	.915	65	118	183	28	33
Sierra	1.000	1	0	1	0	1
Silfa	.944	7	9	8	1	2

Outfield	PCT	G	PO	A	E	DP
De La Cruz	.983	37	54	4	1	0
Hernandez	.956	59	102	7	5	3
Laguna	.985	56	64	3	1	1
Medina	.920	16	21	2	2	0
Murillo	1.000	10	8	0	0	0
Perdomo	.000	1	0	0	0	0
Polanco	.000	1	0	0	0	0
Serrano	1.000	13	9	0	0	0
Sierra	.947	23	18	0	1	0
Solano	.919	26	33	1	3	0

Kansas City Royals

SEASON IN A SENTENCE: For a team that finished the season 20 games under .500, the 2011 season was an upbeat one for the Royals, as a wave of prospects gave the team a late-season talent boost and hope for brighter days ahead.

HIGH POINT: After Salvador Perez's promotion to be the team's everyday catcher, there were nights where everyone in the Royals lineup was 27 or younger. The youngsters proved to be better than the players they replaced, and Kansas City went 15-10 during September. September baseball is hard to judge, but the Royals took it as a sign the youngsters will be ready to compete in 2012. One holdover, Alex Gordon, turned his career around with a .303/.376/.502 season that included a Gold Glove for his play in left field.

LOW POINT: After an unexpectedly strong start, the Royals fell apart in late May. Kansas City went 6-19 in a stretch that saw it go from three games above .500 to 10 games under. Early in the slide, reliever Vin Mazzaro gave up 14 earned runs in two-plus innings in a 19-1 loss to Cleveland, the most runs a pitcher allowed in that few innings in the modern era of baseball.

NOTABLE ROOKIES: Eric Hosmer hit .293/.334/.465 as the team's everyday first baseman. Third baseman Mike Moustakas had a tougher introduction when he came up at midseason, but after slumping to .182, he ripped off hitting streaks of 15 and 11 games in the final two months to improve to .263. Perez and second baseman Johnny Giavotella arrived sooner than expected, and a solid bullpen included contributions from Aaron Crow, Louis Coleman and Tim Collins. Lefthander Danny Duffy showed flashes after joining the rotation.

KEY TRANSACTIONS: The free-agent signings of outfielders Melky Cabrera and Jeff Francouer provided productive, low-cost additions to an outfield in need of help. Unlike in 2010, the Royals didn't make many trade deadline deals, but they did send away Mike Aviles and Wilson Betemit for some lower-level prospects.

DOWN ON THE FARM: Triple-A Omaha won the Pacific Coast League title and Double-A Northwest Arkansas also made the playoffs, but every other affiliate finished below .500. Several prominent prospects also had down years. Top lefthander John Lamb had to have Tommy John surgery, and Mike Montgomery and Chris Dwyer struggled with command issues.

OPENING DAY PAYROLL: $36,126,000 (30th)

PLAYERS OF THE YEAR

MAJOR LEAGUE	MINOR LEAGUE
Alex Gordon	**Johnny Giavotella**
of	2b
.303/.376/.502	(Triple-A)
23 HR, 45 2B	.338/.390/.481
Won first Gold Glove	9 HR, 34 2B

ORGANIZATION LEADERS

BATTING   *Minimum 250 PA

MAJORS

* AVG	Melky Cabrera	.305
* OPS	Alex Gordon	.878
HR	Alex Gordon	23
RBI	Billy Butler	95

MINORS

* AVG	Johnny Giavotella, Omaha	.338
* OBP	Clint Robinson, Omaha	.399
* SLG	Clint Robinson, Omaha	.533
R	Anthony Seratelli, NW Arkansas	91
H	Clint Robinson, Omaha	164
TB	Clint Robinson, Omaha	268
2B	Clint Robinson, Omaha	35
3B	Paulo Orlando, Omaha/NW Arkansas	12
HR	Clint Robinson, Omaha	23
	Jamie Romak, NW Arkansas	23
RBI	Clint Robinson, Omaha	100
BB	John Whittleman, Wilmington/Omaha	76
SO	Murray Watts, Kane County/Burlington	118
SB	Derrick Robinson, NW Arkansas	55

PITCHING   #Minimum 75 IP

MAJORS

W	Bruce Chen	12
# ERA	Bruce Chen	3.77
SO	Luke Hochevar	128
SV	Joakim Soria	28

MINORS

W	Will Smith, NW Arkansas	13
L	Leondy Perez, Kane County	13
# ERA	Greg Billo, Kane County	1.93
G	Jesse Chavez, Omaha	45
	Kelvin Herrera, Wilm./NW Arkansas/Omaha	45
GS	Six tied at	27
SV	Jesse Chavez, Omaha	16
IP	Jeff Suppan, Omaha	165.2
BB	Chris Dwyer, NW Arkansas	78
SO	Jake Odorizzi, Wilmington/NW Arkansas	157
#AVG	Greg Billo, Kane County	.228

2011 PERFORMANCE

General Manager: Dayton Moore. **Farm Director:** Scott Sharp. **Scouting Director:** Lonnie Goldberg.

Class	Team	League	W	L	PCT	Finish	Manager(s)
Majors	Kansas City Royals	American	71	91	.438	11th (14)	Ned Yost
Triple-A	Omaha Storm Chasers	Pacific Coast	79	63	.556	3rd (16)	Mike Jirschele
Double-A	Northwest Arkansas Naturals	Texas	73	64	.533	3rd (8)	Brian Poldberg
High A	Wilmington Blue Rocks	Carolina	66	72	.478	6th (8)	Brian Rupp
Low A	Kane County Cougars	Midwest	65	74	.468	12th (16)	Vance Wilson
Rookie	Idaho Falls Chukars	Pioneer	33	43	.434	6th (8)	Brian Buchanan
Rookie	Burlington Royals	Appalachian	24	44	.353	t-9th (10)	Nelson Liriano
Rookie	AZL Royals	Arizona	22	34	.393	11th (13)	Darryl Kennedy
Overall 2011 Minor League Record			362	394	.479	24th (30)	

ORGANIZATION STATISTICS

KANSAS CITY ROYALS

AMERICAN LEAGUE

Batting	B-T	HT	WT	DOB	AVG	vLH	vRH	G	AB	R	H	2B	3B	HR	RBI	BB	HBP	SH	SF	SO	SB	CS	SLG	OBP
Aviles, Mike	R-R	5-10	205	3-13-81	.222	.309	.185	53	185	14	41	11	3	5	31	9	2	0	3	27	10	2	.395	.261
2-team total (38 Boston)					.255	—	—	91	286	31	73	17	3	7	39	13	2	0	4	44	14	4	.409	.289
Betemit, Wilson	R-R	6-2	220	11-2-81	.281	.228	.301	57	203	29	57	15	1	3	27	20	0	0	3	58	3	1	.409	.341
2-team total (40 Detroit)					.285	—	—	97	323	40	92	22	4	8	46	31	0	0	5	105	4	1	.452	.343
Butler, Billy	R-R	6-1	240	4-18-86	.291	.306	.287	159	597	74	174	44	0	19	95	66	3	0	7	95	2	1	.461	.361
Cabrera, Melky	B-L	6-0	200	8-11-84	.305	.304	.306	155	658	102	201	44	5	18	87	35	1	0	5	94	20	10	.470	.339
Cain, Lorenzo	R-R	6-2	200	4-13-86	.273	.000	.353	6	22	4	6	1	0	0	1	1	0	0	0	4	0	0	.318	.304
Dyson, Jarrod	L-R	5-9	160	8-15-84	.205	.000	.214	26	44	8	9	1	0	0	3	7	0	0	1	14	11	1	.227	.308
Escobar, Alcides	R-R	6-1	185	12-16-86	.254	.244	.257	158	548	69	139	21	8	4	46	25	4	0	3	73	26	9	.343	.290
Francoeur, Jeff	R-R	6-5	220	1-8-84	.285	.302	.279	153	601	77	171	47	4	20	87	37	8	0	10	123	22	10	.476	.329
Getz, Chris	L-R	6-0	185	8-30-83	.255	.286	.245	118	380	50	97	6	3	0	26	30	3	0	2	45	21	7	.287	.313
Giavotella, Johnny	R-R	5-8	185	7-10-87	.247	.262	.243	46	178	20	44	9	4	2	21	6	1	0	2	32	5	2	.376	.273
Gordon, Alex	L-R	6-2	220	2-10-84	.303	.278	.314	151	611	101	185	45	4	23	87	67	7	0	3	139	17	8	.502	.376
Hosmer, Eric	L-L	6-4	230	10-24-89	.293	.237	.315	128	523	66	153	27	3	19	78	34	1	0	5	82	11	5	.465	.334
Ka'aihue, Kila	L-R	6-4	235	3-29-84	.195	.130	.220	23	82	6	16	4	0	2	6	12	0	0	1	26	0	0	.317	.295
Maier, Mitch	L-R	6-2	210	6-30-82	.232	.229	.233	44	95	19	22	4	3	0	7	16	1	0	1	32	1	0	.337	.345
Moustakas, Mike	L-R	5-11	230	9-11-88	.263	.191	.289	89	338	26	89	18	1	5	30	22	1	0	2	51	2	0	.367	.309
Navarro, Yamaico	R-R	5-11	170	10-31-87	.304	.250	.429	6	23	2	7	1	0	0	6	2	0	0	1	5	0	0	.348	.346
2-team total (16 Boston)					.250	—	—	22	60	8	15	3	0	1	9	5	0	0	1	14	0	0	.350	.303
Pena, Brayan	B-R	5-11	235	1-7-82	.248	.250	.247	72	222	17	55	11	0	3	24	12	2	0	4	24	0	0	.338	.288
Perez, Salvador	R-R	6-3	230	5-10-90	.331	.484	.291	39	148	20	49	8	2	3	21	7	1	0	2	20	0	0	.473	.361
Pina, Manny	R-R	6-0	230	6-5-87	.214	.333	.182	4	14	2	3	2	0	0	1	0	0	0	0	2	0	0	.357	.267
Treanor, Matt	R-R	6-0	205	3-3-76	.226	.195	.234	65	186	24	42	6	0	3	21	33	4	0	2	49	2	2	.306	.351
2-team total (7 Texas)					.214	—	—	72	196	24	42	6	0	3	22	34	4	0	3	53	2	2	.291	.338

Pitching	B-T	HT	WT	DOB	W	L	ERA	G	GS	CG	SV	IP	H	R	ER	HR	BB	SO	AVG	vLH	vRH	K/9	BB/9
Adcock, Nathan	R-R	6-5	220	2-25-88	1	1	4.62	24	3	0	1	60	63	34	31	5	26	36	.272	.260	.281	5.37	3.88
Chavez, Jesse	R-R	6-2	170	8-21-83	0	0	10.57	4	0	0	0	8	12	9	9	3	5	8	.353	.214	.450	9.39	5.87
Chen, Bruce	L-L	6-2	215	6-19-77	12	8	3.77	25	25	1	0	155	152	71	65	18	50	97	.258	.259	.258	5.63	2.90
Coleman, Louis	R-R	6-4	200	4-4-86	1	4	2.87	48	0	0	1	60	44	20	19	9	26	64	.207	.257	.180	9.65	3.92
Collins, Tim	L-L	5-7	170	8-21-89	4	4	3.63	68	0	0	0	67	52	28	27	5	48	60	.216	.210	.221	8.06	6.45
Crow, Aaron	R-R	6-3	190	11-10-86	4	4	2.76	57	0	0	0	62	55	20	19	8	31	65	.237	.311	.175	9.44	4.50
Davies, Kyle	R-R	6-1	210	9-9-83	1	9	6.75	13	13	0	0	61	84	52	46	7	26	50	.332	.338	.325	7.34	3.82
Duffy, Danny	L-L	6-3	200	12-21-88	4	8	5.64	20	20	0	0	105	119	66	66	15	51	87	.287	.266	.295	7.43	4.36
Francis, Jeff	L-L	6-5	220	1-8-81	6	16	4.82	31	31	1	0	183	224	102	98	19	39	91	.301	.277	.309	4.48	1.92
Herrera, Kelvin	R-R	5-10	190	12-31-89	0	1	13.50	2	0	0	0	2	2	3	3	1	0	0	.286	.500	.200	0.00	0.00
Hochevar, Luke	R-R	6-5	210	9-15-83	11	11	4.68	31	31	0	0	198	192	110	103	23	62	128	.252	.269	.231	5.82	2.82
Holland, Greg	R-R	5-10	200	11-20-85	5	1	1.80	46	0	0	4	60	37	13	12	3	19	74	.175	.181	.171	11.10	2.85
Jeffress, Jeremy	R-R	6-0	210	9-21-87	1	1	4.70	14	0	0	1	15	12	8	8	1	11	13	.222	.222	.222	7.63	6.46
Mazzaro, Vin	R-R	6-3	220	9-27-86	1	1	8.26	7	4	0	0	28	39	26	26	4	15	10	.358	.388	.333	3.18	4.76
Mendoza, Luis	R-R	6-3	235	10-31-83	2	0	1.23	2	2	0	0	15	11	3	2	0	5	7	.212	.200	.222	4.30	3.07
O'Sullivan, Sean	R-R	6-2	230	9-1-87	2	6	7.25	12	10	0	0	58	78	52	47	10	26	19	.328	.321	.336	2.93	4.01
Paulino, Felipe	R-R	6-2	270	10-5-83	4	6	4.11	21	20	0	0	125	123	62	57	10	48	119	.265	.265	.265	8.59	3.47
Soria, Joakim	R-R	6-3	200	5-18-84	5	5	4.03	60	0	0	28	60	60	29	27	7	17	60	.259	.242	.277	8.95	2.54
Teaford, Everett	L-L	5-11	155	5-15-84	2	1	3.27	26	3	0	1	44	36	17	16	8	14	28	.281	.197	.253	5.73	2.86
Tejeda, Robinson	R-R	6-2	245	3-24-82	0	1	6.14	9	0	0	0	7	12	5	5	2	3	2	.387	.222	.455	2.45	3.68
Texeira, Kanekoa	R-R	6-2	190	2-6-86	0	0	2.84	6	0	0	0	6	13	2	2	0	3	0	.419	.438	.400	0.00	4.26
Wood, Blake	R-R	6-5	240	8-8-85	5	3	3.75	55	0	0	1	70	66	30	29	5	32	62	.254	.252	.255	8.01	4.13

Fielding

Catcher	PCT	G	PO	A	E	DP	PB
Pena	.995	69	417	25	2	6	4
Perez	.990	39	290	21	3	2	2
Pina	1.000	4	33	1	0	0	0
Treanor	.990	65	389	22	4	5	2

First Base	PCT	G	PO	A	E	DP
Betemit	1.000	3	23	2	0	0
Butler	1.000	11	86	8	0	10

	PCT	G	PO	A	E	DP
Gordon	.964	7	24	3	1	3
Hosmer	.993	127	1096	78	8	101
Ka'aihue	.990	19	181	15	2	14

Second Base	PCT	G	PO	A	E	DP
Aviles	.971	20	45	56	3	16
Betemit	1.000	1	2	2	0	1
Getz	.988	110	189	299	6	69
Giavotella	.972	46	56	117	5	17

Third Base	PCT	G	PO	A	E	DP
Aviles	.910	24	13	48	6	3
Betemit	.961	47	24	99	5	6
Moustakas	.954	89	60	169	11	14
Navarro	1.000	5	2	9	0	1

Shortstop	PCT	G	PO	A	E	DP
Aviles	.933	6	4	10	1	2
Escobar	.980	158	271	459	15	98
Getz	.938	4	5	10	1	2

	PCT	G	PO	A	E	DP
Navarro	1.000	1	1	0	0	0

Outfield	PCT	G	PO	A	E	DP
Cabrera	.991	153	331	13	3	7
Cain	1.000	6	7	0	0	0
Dyson	1.000	17	31	0	0	0
Francoeur	.986	153	327	16	5	4
Gordon	.991	148	312	20	3	2
Maier	1.000	29	64	2	0	0

OMAHA STORM CHASERS   TRIPLE-A
PACIFIC COAST LEAGUE

Batting	B-T	HT	WT	DOB	AVG	vLH	vRH	G	AB	R	H	2B	3B	HR	RBI	BB	HBP	SH	SF	SO	SB	CS	SLG	OBP
Arias, Joaquin	R-R	6-1	170	9-21-84	.232	.263	.217	69	241	37	56	12	4	3	25	14	0	0	2	28	7	1	.353	.272
Aviles, Mike	R-R	5-10	205	3-13-81	.307	.424	.271	35	140	21	43	8	2	9	25	6	0	0	3	17	6	4	.586	.329
Blanco, Gregor	L-L	5-11	170	12-24-83	.196	.250	.175	23	56	13	11	5	0	0	4	17	0	0	0	15	9	1	.286	.384
Cain, Lorenzo	R-R	6-2	200	4-13-86	.312	.289	.322	128	487	84	152	28	7	16	81	40	15	0	3	102	16	6	.497	.380
Clark, Cody	R-R	6-2	195	9-14-81	.233	.205	.242	51	159	18	37	12	0	4	13	12	2	0	1	26	0	0	.384	.293
Dyson, Jarrod	L-R	5-9	160	8-15-84	.279	.329	.263	83	319	69	89	10	3	3	26	35	3	0	0	47	38	2	.357	.356
Eigsti, Ryan	R-R	6-1	205	8-24-85	.000	.000	.000	1	2	0	0	0	0	0	0	0	0	0	0	2	0	0	.000	.000
Falu, Irving	B-R	5-11	180	6-6-83	.301	.339	.285	111	385	50	116	19	9	2	47	35	1	0	4	47	21	11	.390	.358
Giavotella, Johnny	R-R	5-8	185	7-10-87	.338	.333	.339	110	453	67	153	34	2	9	72	40	2	0	5	57	9	5	.481	.390
Hosmer, Eric	L-L	6-4	230	10-24-89	.439	.500	.409	26	98	21	43	5	0	3	15	19	0	0	1	16	3	0	.582	.525
Ka'aihue, Kila	L-R	6-4	235	3-29-84	.272	.348	.242	95	323	43	88	19	0	11	65	57	2	0	6	81	1	1	.433	.379
Lough, David	L-L	5-11	180	1-20-86	.318	.336	.310	114	456	87	145	26	11	9	65	36	4	0	8	49	14	8	.482	.367
May, Lucas	R-R	5-11	195	10-24-84	.176	.115	.203	25	85	9	15	3	1	3	13	9	1	0	0	22	0	0	.329	.263
2-team total (52 Reno)					.238	—	—	77	248	40	59	15	1	10	44	32	3	0	2	64	2	2	.427	.330
Mertins, Kurt	R-R	5-10	188	4-22-86	.274	.250	.294	20	62	7	17	0	1	0	4	2	0	0	1	17	1	0	.306	.292
Moustakas, Mike	L-R	5-11	230	9-15-88	.287	.260	.300	55	223	38	64	15	1	10	44	19	3	0	3	44	1	1	.498	.347
Navarro, Yamaico	R-R	5-11	170	10-31-87	.272	.259	.277	25	92	11	25	3	1	2	9	7	0	0	2	18	3	4	.391	.317
Orlando, Paulo	R-R	6-3	185	11-1-85	.235	.204	.248	58	187	24	44	10	2	1	27	11	0	0	0	30	6	3	.326	.281
Perez, Salvador	R-R	6-3	230	5-10-90	.333	.353	.323	12	48	5	16	5	0	1	10	0	1	0	0	6	0	0	.500	.347
Pina, Manny	R-R	6-0	230	6-5-87	.238	.179	.260	68	210	34	50	13	0	5	25	34	8	0	1	37	0	0	.371	.364
Robinson, Clint	L-L	6-5	235	2-16-85	.326	.318	.330	134	503	86	164	35	0	23	100	58	6	0	4	88	2	1	.533	.399
Whittleman, John	L-R	6-2	195	2-11-87	.500	.000	.500	1	4	0	2	0	0	0	0	0	0	0	0	1	0	0	.500	.500
Zawadzki, Lance	R-R	5-11	195	5-26-85	.233	.179	.252	91	326	44	76	13	6	8	40	25	0	0	0	76	15	3	.383	.288

Pitching	B-T	HT	WT	DOB	W	L	ERA	G	GS	CG	SV	IP	H	R	ER	HR	BB	SO	AVG	vLH	vRH	K/9	BB/9
Castaneda, Federico	R-R	6-3	187	1-26-84	0	0	0.00	2	0	0	0	3	1	0	0	0	0	3	.100	.000	.167	9.00	0.00
Chavez, Jesse	R-R	6-2	170	8-21-83	2	4	3.75	45	0	0	16	58	63	30	24	6	16	54	.281	.255	.300	8.43	2.50
Chen, Bruce	L-L	6-2	215	6-19-77	0	0	6.00	2	2	0	0	9	11	6	6	3	1	8	.297	.250	.320	8.00	1.00
Coleman, Louis	R-R	6-4	200	4-4-86	0	1	3.86	6	0	0	2	7	4	4	3	0	4	16	.167	.200	.143	20.57	5.14
Davies, Kyle	R-R	6-1	210	9-9-83	1	1	0.75	2	1	0	0	12	8	3	1	0	0	14	.182	.158	.200	10.50	0.00
2-team total (6 Las Vegas)					1	1	1.80	8	1	0	0	20	11	6	4	1	3	22	—	—	—	9.90	1.35
Duffy, Danny	L-L	6-3	200	12-21-88	3	1	3.43	8	8	0	0	42	37	17	16	5	10	48	.237	.303	.220	10.29	2.14
Hardy, Blaine	L-L	6-2	220	3-14-87	2	3	7.14	23	0	0	0	29	38	25	23	7	19	23	.304	.319	.295	7.14	5.90
Herrera, Kelvin	R-R	5-10	190	12-31-89	1	0	2.12	14	0	0	6	17	12	5	4	1	7	18	.190	.240	.158	9.53	3.71
Holland, Greg	R-R	5-10	200	11-20-85	2	0	2.08	13	0	0	2	22	13	5	5	1	11	27	.176	.172	.178	11.22	4.57
Jeffress, Jeremy	R-R	6-0	210	9-21-87	2	3	7.13	16	3	0	3	24	27	20	19	5	18	24	.293	.333	.255	9.00	6.75
Johnson, Blake	R-R	6-5	200	6-14-85	3	1	7.42	14	1	0	1	30	41	25	25	1	17	19	.333	.327	.338	5.64	5.04
2-team total (20 Colorado Springs)					5	2	7.51	34	1	0	1	56	77	53	47	5	25	36	—	—	—	5.75	3.99
Lebron, Willy	R-R	6-1	205	3-28-79	1	1	0.55	9	0	0	0	16	12	6	1	1	5	22	.207	.167	.250	12.12	2.76
Mazzaro, Vin	R-R	6-3	220	9-27-86	7	2	4.29	22	22	0	0	124	140	63	59	9	60	107	.286	.284	.287	7.79	4.37
Mendoza, Luis	R-R	6-3	235	10-31-83	12	5	2.18	33	18	1	2	144	126	52	35	5	54	81	.238	.254	.224	5.05	3.37
Miner, Zach	R-R	6-3	200	3-12-82	2	1	1.59	12	0	0	1	23	16	4	4	1	10	20	.193	.207	.185	7.94	3.97
Montgomery, Mike	L-L	6-4	185	7-1-89	5	11	5.32	28	27	0	0	151	157	99	89	15	69	129	.271	.304	.258	7.71	4.12
O'Sullivan, Sean	R-R	6-2	230	9-1-87	8	2	4.22	14	14	0	0	75	85	37	35	6	16	55	.286	.260	.306	6.63	1.93
Pucetas, Kevin	R-R	6-4	225	11-27-84	6	6	4.98	33	12	0	1	107	116	63	59	18	38	67	.273	.279	.268	5.65	3.21
Rollins, Heath	R-R	6-1	185	5-25-85	0	0	16.50	4	0	0	0	6	15	13	11	3	3	2	.455	.583	.381	3.00	4.50
Santiago, Mario	R-R	6-2	210	12-16-84	3	5	5.70	19	4	0	2	47	49	32	30	8	28	33	.271	.266	.275	6.27	5.32
Shell, Steven	R-R	6-4	215	3-10-83	1	2	8.03	8	0	0	0	12	19	12	11	3	4	11	.365	.480	.259	8.03	2.92
Sisk, Brandon	L-L	6-1	210	7-13-85	4	2	1.41	25	0	0	2	32	16	8	5	1	16	30	.148	.194	.125	8.44	4.50
Suppan, Jeff	R-R	6-2	230	1-2-75	11	8	4.78	28	27	2	0	166	186	94	88	23	51	94	.283	.313	.259	5.11	2.77
Teaford, Everett	L-L	5-11	155	5-15-84	3	2	3.34	16	3	0	0	35	23	14	13	5	11	33	.183	.105	.216	8.49	2.83
Tejeda, Robinson	R-R	6-2	245	3-24-82	0	3	3.80	31	0	0	1	45	40	23	19	8	15	43	.241	.304	.196	8.60	3.00
Texeira, Kanekoa	R-R	6-2	190	2-6-86	0	1	5.23	8	0	0	1	10	12	7	6	2	7	4	.286	.238	.333	3.48	6.10
Wood, Blake	R-R	6-5	240	8-8-85	0	0	0.00	5	0	0	0	5	2	0	0	0	0	6	.133	.091		10.80	0.00

Fielding

Catcher	PCT	G	PO	A	E	DP	PB
Clark	.985	48	308	25	5	5	1
Eigsti	1.000	1	3	1	0	0	0
May	.974	25	176	11	5	2	3
Perez	1.000	11	94	10	0	1	0
Pina	.979	66	419	55	10	4	3
Robinson	.988	76	616	43	8	63	

First Base	PCT	G	PO	A	E	DP
Arias	1.000	10	30	7	0	6
Hosmer	.986	23	187	19	3	23
Ka'aihue	.990	43	381	18	4	27

Second Base	PCT	G	PO	A	E	DP
Arias	.905	4	7	12	2	2
Aviles	1.000	1	2	0	0	0
Falu	.988	17	38	44	1	11

Giavotella	.981	105	212	296	10	78
Mertins	.966	8	8	20	1	1
Navarro	.833	4	8	7	3	3
Zawadzki	.889	4	4	12	2	0

Third Base	PCT	G	PO	A	E	DP
Arias	.935	47	29	87	8	9
Falu	.943	25	19	47	4	8
Giavotella	.000	1	0	0	1	0
Mertins	1.000	4	2	5	0	1
Moustakas	.942	51	50	113	10	20

Whittleman	1.000	1	1	0	0	0
Zawadzki	.900	21	20	34	6	2

Shortstop	PCT	G	PO	A	E	DP
Arias	.970	10	6	26	1	3
Aviles	.970	34	42	117	5	26
Falu	.940	28	34	60	6	9
Mertins	1.000	1	1	1	0	0
Navarro	.918	20	39	50	8	9
Zawadzki	.955	53	62	169	11	32

Outfield	PCT	G	PO	A	E	DP
Blanco	1.000	18	28	1	0	1
Cain	.974	127	289	13	8	5
Dyson	.971	79	195	8	6	1
Falu	.985	35	66	1	1	0
Giavotella	1.000	2	2	0	0	0
Lough	.982	114	204	9	4	1
Mertins	.000	1	0	0	0	0
Orlando	.966	52	108	6	4	2
Robinson	1.000	2	2	0	0	0

KANSAS CITY ROYALS

NORTHWEST ARKANSAS NATURALS   DOUBLE-A
TEXAS LEAGUE

Batting	B-T	HT	WT	DOB	AVG	vLH	vRH	G	AB	R	H	2B	3B	HR	RBI	BB	HBP	SH	SF	SO	SB	CS	SLG	OBP
Bianchi, Jeff	R-R	5-10	190	10-5-86	.259	.250	.262	119	444	63	115	23	2	2	48	39	3	0	4	85	20	5	.333	.320
Colon, Christian	R-R	6-1	180	5-14-89	.257	.192	.273	127	491	69	126	14	2	8	61	46	6	0	1	51	17	5	.342	.325
Eigsti, Ryan	R-R	6-1	205	8-24-85	.259	.333	.239	23	58	5	15	6	0	2	10	6	2	0	2	18	1	0	.466	.338
Francis, Nick	R-R	6-3	195	3-5-86	.260	.341	.238	55	192	30	50	8	0	3	25	17	3	0	3	40	12	4	.349	.326
Lisson, Mario	R-R	6-2	220	5-31-84	.293	.346	.272	89	283	58	83	21	0	15	45	31	5	0	1	81	15	2	.527	.372
Mertins, Kurt	R-R	5-10	188	4-22-86	.254	.246	.259	57	173	29	44	12	0	3	29	24	4	0	2	47	4	2	.376	.355
Myers, Wil	R-R	6-3	205	12-10-90	.254	.276	.247	99	354	50	90	23	1	8	49	52	4	0	4	87	9	2	.393	.353
Navarro, Rey	B-R	5-10	175	12-22-89	.271	.304	.261	55	188	26	51	8	0	1	18	14	4	0	2	26	6	3	.330	.332
Orlando, Paulo	R-R	6-3	185	11-1-85	.305	.297	.308	45	167	30	51	5	10	4	24	13	3	0	2	35	8	4	.527	.362
Perez, Salvador	R-R	6-3	230	5-10-90	.283	.338	.262	79	286	35	81	14	0	9	43	16	4	0	1	30	0	1	.427	.329
Pina, Manny	R-R	6-0	230	6-5-87	.250	1.000	.143	3	8	0	2	1	0	0	3	2	0	0	0	3	0	0	.375	.400
Robinson, Derrick	B-L	5-11	170	9-28-87	.251	.322	.224	107	419	56	105	6	2	1	25	46	0	0	3	87	55	15	.282	.323
Romak, Jamie	R-R	6-2	220	9-30-85	.251	.262	.247	123	439	66	110	21	1	23	71	55	8	0	2	88	6	1	.460	.343
Seratelli, Anthony	B-R	6-0	205	2-27-83	.282	.270	.286	129	440	91	124	12	6	9	64	75	5	0	0	92	35	5	.398	.392
Smith, Tim	L-L	6-3	225	6-14-86	.311	.303	.312	69	238	38	74	13	2	10	49	19	3	0	3	37	8	2	.508	.365
Theriot, Ben	L-R	6-1	190	12-8-87	.303	.333	.295	46	122	10	37	9	1	5	22	14	1	0	1	28	0	0	.516	.377
Treanor, Matt	R-R	6-0	205	3-3-76	.263	.000	.333	7	19	2	5	1	0	0	5	4	3	0	0	2	0	0	.316	.462
Van Stratten, Nick	R-R	6-1	185	5-22-85	.236	.279	.218	68	208	30	49	9	3	5	27	17	2	0	1	28	9	2	.380	.298

Pitching	B-T	HT	WT	DOB	W	L	ERA	G	GS	CG	SV	IP	H	R	ER	HR	BB	SO	AVG	vLH	vRH	K/9	BB/9
Baez, Manauris	B-R	5-11	182	8-16-85	1	1	4.46	15	3	0	0	38	41	20	19	5	15	28	.275	.276	.275	6.57	3.52
Barrera, Henry	R-R	6-0	195	11-25-85	0	1	6.00	8	0	0	1	9	10	6	6	2	5	11	.278	.222	.333	11.00	5.00
Basurto, Eric	R-R	6-3	200	4-17-86	2	0	3.38	2	0	0	0	3	4	1	1	0	2	2	.364	.600	.167	6.75	6.75
Baumann, Buddy	L-L	5-10	175	12-9-87	4	3	4.29	25	9	0	2	71	73	38	34	9	28	68	.264	.213	.291	8.58	3.53
Chapman, Kevin	L-L	6-4	210	2-19-88	1	2	4.99	25	0	0	3	40	37	25	22	5	21	50	.255	.226	.277	11.34	4.76
Chen, Bruce	L-L	6-2	215	6-19-77	0	1	18.00	1	1	0	0	2	5	4	4	0	0	2	.500	1.000	.444	9.00	0.00
Davies, Kyle	R-R	6-1	210	9-9-83	0	2	5.63	2	2	0	0	8	10	7	5	0	0	7	.313	.375	.250	7.88	0.00
Dobies, Andrew	L-L	6-1	180	4-20-83	1	1	5.89	12	0	0	1	18	24	15	12	4	6	12	.312	.325	.297	5.89	2.95
Dwyer, Chris	R-L	6-2	210	4-10-88	8	10	5.60	27	27	2	0	141	124	93	88	14	78	126	.238	.253	.231	8.02	4.97
Garcia, Edgar	R-R	6-2	190	9-20-87	2	3	3.47	13	3	0	5	36	29	19	14	6	11	31	.213	.208	.217	7.68	2.72
Hardy, Blaine	L-L	6-2	220	3-14-87	2	1	1.59	19	0	0	8	40	28	11	7	2	16	41	.194	.245	.168	9.30	3.63
Herrera, Kelvin	R-R	5-10	190	12-31-89	4	0	1.75	23	0	0	7	36	22	9	7	4	6	40	.176	.222	.150	10.00	1.50
Jeffress, Jeremy	R-R	6-0	210	9-21-87	1	3	4.26	9	8	0	0	32	32	17	15	2	22	20	.271	.226	.308	5.68	6.25
Johnson, Blake	R-R	6-5	200	6-14-85	1	0	0.43	9	0	0	3	21	14	2	1	1	6	16	.189	.226	.163	6.86	2.57
Keating, Patrick	R-R	6-0	220	6-9-87	3	3	6.16	29	0	0	7	38	42	27	26	9	12	44	.286	.344	.244	10.42	2.84
Lafferty, Brendan	L-L	6-3	180	5-27-86	2	0	4.32	11	0	0	2	25	29	18	12	3	7	20	.287	.294	.280	7.20	2.52
Lamb, John	L-L	6-4	200	7-10-90	1	2	3.09	8	8	0	0	35	33	15	12	3	13	22	.246	.200	.266	5.66	3.34
Lebron, Willy	R-R	6-1	205	3-28-79	3	1	3.83	23	1	0	1	49	43	24	21	2	26	50	.236	.195	.267	9.12	4.74
Miner, Zach	R-R	6-3	200	3-12-82	1	6	7.16	11	11	0	0	44	55	37	35	8	18	24	.302	.298	.306	4.91	3.68
Mozingo, Harold	R-R	6-1	192	3-29-85	1	0	12.75	7	0	0	0	12	22	18	17	2	8	9	.400	.333	.441	6.75	6.00
Odorizzi, Jake	R-R	6-2	175	3-27-90	5	3	4.72	12	12	0	0	69	66	38	36	13	22	54	.254	.276	.222	7.08	2.88
Osuna, Edgar	L-L	6-1	184	11-25-87	6	4	7.89	14	11	0	0	57	78	54	50	13	15	54	.329	.292	.345	8.53	2.37
Paulino, Eduardo	R-R	5-11	176	9-29-85	2	3	5.46	31	0	0	0	58	60	41	35	6	41	41	.275	.235	.301	6.40	6.40
Pimentel, Elisaul	R-R	6-2	170	7-10-88	0	1	6.35	2	2	0	0	6	6	5	4	2	4	6	.261	.111	.357	9.53	6.35
Rollins, Heath	R-R	6-1	185	5-25-85	1	2	4.34	17	5	0	1	48	36	25	23	5	28	27	.207	.190	.216	5.10	5.29
Santiago, Mario	R-R	6-2	210	12-16-84	5	1	2.23	16	7	0	0	65	56	21	16	3	17	44	.228	.184	.265	6.82	2.37
Sisk, Brandon	L-L	6-1	210	7-13-85	3	1	3.77	16	0	0	0	29	23	12	12	2	7	28	.228	.083	.308	8.79	2.20
Smith, Will	R-L	6-5	235	7-10-89	13	9	3.85	27	27	2	0	161	171	78	69	13	45	108	.279	.261	.287	6.02	2.51
Volz, Kendal	R-R	6-5	225	12-2-87	0	0	6.75	3	0	0	1	7	5	5	5	1	4	7	.208	.250	.188	9.45	5.40

Fielding

Catcher	PCT	G	PO	A	E	DP	PB
Eigsti	.993	22	139	13	1	1	0
Perez	.985	77	521	75	9	7	3
Pina	1.000	3	14	0	0	0	0
Theriot	.989	41	258	20	3	4	9
Treanor	.983	7	50	7	1	0	0

First Base	PCT	G	PO	A	E	DP
Lisson	.982	7	49	6	1	6
Romak	.988	68	549	32	7	59
Seratelli	.997	70	577	42	2	66

Second Base	PCT	G	PO	A	E	DP
Bianchi	.993	62	107	171	2	41
Colon	.974	15	27	47	2	13
Mertins	.990	21	37	63	1	22
Navarro	.943	18	36	47	5	11
Seratelli	.991	25	47	64	1	13

Third Base	PCT	G	PO	A	E	DP
Lisson	.919	78	48	133	16	20
Mertins	.942	27	13	52	4	3
Navarro	.932	35	32	64	7	10

Shortstop	PCT	G	PO	A	E	DP
Bianchi	.952	38	54	124	9	27
Colon	.966	99	142	306	16	66
Seratelli	.000	1	0	0	0	0

Outfield	PCT	G	PO	A	E	DP
Francis	.959	52	89	4	4	0
Myers	.965	94	191	4	7	1
Orlando	.980	45	90	7	2	2
Robinson	.978	107	269	4	6	1
Seratelli	.951	31	38	1	2	0
Smith	.955	34	40	2	2	0
Van Stratten	.979	67	128	9	3	3

WILMINGTON BLUE ROCKS HIGH CLASS A

CAROLINA LEAGUE

KANSAS CITY ROYALS

Batting	B-T	HT	WT	DOB	AVG	vLH	vRH	G	AB	R	H	2B	3B	HR	RBI	BB	HBP	SH	SF	SO	SB	CS	SLG	OBP
Batista, Deivy	R-R	5-11	150	5-7-88	.217	.279	.181	97	281	35	61	16	2	2	23	29	3	0	2	88	5	3	.310	.295
Bonilla, Jose	R-R	5-10	188	8-4-88	.210	.179	.224	76	243	21	51	11	0	3	29	30	3	0	3	53	1	1	.292	.301
Caseres, Steven	L-R	6-4	220	3-26-87	.107	.000	.136	8	28	1	3	0	0	0	0	2	0	0	0	12	0	0	.107	.167
Dyer, Jared	R-R	6-2	205	5-29-86	.158	.300	.000	7	19	4	3	1	0	0	0	2	0	0	0	5	0	0	.211	.238
Eigsti, Ryan	R-R	6-1	205	8-24-85	.250	.133	.320	14	40	4	10	1	0	2	5	6	1	0	0	15	0	0	.425	.362
Ferguson, Tim	R-R	6-1	190	10-25-88	.222	.266	.191	111	379	44	84	12	1	6	43	38	2	0	7	90	13	7	.306	.291
Francis, Nick	R-R	6-3	195	3-5-86	.319	.464	.238	51	191	30	61	20	2	7	35	13	0	0	0	40	7	1	.555	.363
Frost, Adam	R-R	5-11	165	10-13-86	.214	.250	.200	5	14	4	3	0	1	0	3	1	0	0	0	2	4	0	.357	.267
Graterol, Juan	R-R	6-1	170	2-14-89	.182	.033	.277	23	77	3	14	2	0	1	5	6	0	0	0	16	0	0	.247	.241
Hall, Gerard	B-R	5-9	170	7-9-88	.255	.200	.268	32	102	9	26	6	1	0	13	6	1	0	0	18	3	2	.333	.303
Jones, Travis	R-R	6-2	200	5-23-89	.231	.300	.188	9	26	4	6	2	0	0	1	3	0	0	1	6	0	0	.308	.300
Lewis, Joey	R-R	6-4	220	10-13-87	.204	.205	.203	77	260	29	53	13	3	7	25	23	2	0	3	79	0	1	.358	.271
Liberto, Michael	R-R	5-7	170	6-21-88	.233	.167	.278	13	30	4	7	2	0	0	5	6	1	0	0	5	2	0	.300	.378
McClure, Alex	B-R	6-0	185	6-16-89	.196	.216	.182	67	240	22	47	4	3	1	13	15	5	0	1	63	14	7	.250	.267
Merrifield, Whit	R-R	6-1	175	1-24-89	.262	.287	.248	126	477	74	125	30	3	5	36	52	4	0	4	89	24	14	.369	.337
Mertins, Kurt	R-R	5-10	188	4-22-86	.264	.250	.275	24	91	15	24	4	0	0	7	6	2	0	0	15	1	2	.308	.323
Morales, Adrian	R-R	5-8	180	11-18-88	.300	.400	.200	3	10	2	3	1	0	0	0	2	0	0	0	2	0	1	.400	.417
Navarro, Rey	B-R	5-10	175	12-22-89	.285	.314	.269	72	277	34	79	17	7	8	41	18	4	0	1	39	5	4	.484	.337
Ortiz, Adrian	L-R	6-0	172	1-14-87	.115	.083	.143	8	26	1	3	3	0	0	1	2	0	0	0	5	0	1	.231	.179
Prades, Yem	R-R	6-2	194	3-8-88	.289	.265	.303	80	305	36	88	16	5	4	24	10	2	0	3	66	11	7	.413	.313
Rodriguez, Julio	R-R	6-1	225	8-3-89	.219	.231	.213	22	73	3	16	5	0	1	8	2	1	0	1	9	0	3	.329	.247
Stovall, Ryan	R-R	5-11	190	12-16-86	.242	.217	.257	58	223	23	54	16	0	2	19	5	3	0	1	53	6	3	.341	.267
Testa, Carlo	L-L	6-3	218	12-16-86	.290	.300	.285	100	366	48	106	27	4	7	43	36	6	0	2	109	18	7	.443	.361
Van Stratten, Nick	R-R	6-1	185	5-22-85	.271	.352	.217	61	229	22	62	14	1	1	27	13	6	0	3	30	10	3	.354	.323
Whittleman, John	L-R	6-2	195	2-11-87	.234	.207	.249	123	415	52	97	24	3	20	68	76	0	0	5	108	2	0	.451	.349

Pitching	B-T	HT	WT	DOB	W	L	ERA	G	GS	CG	SV	IP	H	R	ER	HR	BB	SO	AVG	vLH	vRH	K/9	BB/9
Arguelles, Noel	L-L	6-3	215	1-12-90	4	5	3.20	21	21	0	0	104	93	38	37	6	24	64	.245	.266	.239	5.54	2.08
Baez, Manauris	B-R	5-11	182	8-16-85	1	1	2.33	8	0	0	0	19	20	6	5	1	7	20	.267	.185	.313	9.31	3.26
Barrera, Henry	R-R	6-0	195	11-25-85	0	0	3.00	3	0	0	0	6	6	2	2	0	1	11	.250	.111	.333	16.50	1.50
Caldwell, Allen	L-L	5-11	170	3-29-88	2	0	1.50	9	2	0	1	24	15	5	4	2	4	23	.176	.048	.219	8.63	1.50
Chapman, Kevin	L-L	6-4	210	2-19-88	0	2	4.84	15	0	0	7	22	24	14	12	1	7	40	.264	.200	.295	16.12	2.82
Cuevas, Gary	R-R	6-2	200	5-23-88	0	0	9.00	4	0	0	0	5	6	5	5	0	8	4	.300	.222	.364	7.20	14.40
Dennick, Ryan	L-L	6-0	185	1-10-87	3	7	4.36	35	0	0	4	54	55	30	26	4	14	51	.267	.213	.290	8.55	2.35
Garcia, Edgar	R-R	6-2	190	9-20-87	0	0	2.25	7	0	0	1	12	11	3	3	0	2	11	.239	.353	.172	8.25	1.50
Gibson, Glenn	L-L	6-4	195	9-21-87	0	0	13.06	9	0	0	0	10	25	17	15	3	4	7	.446	.400	.463	6.10	3.48
Herrera, Kelvin	R-R	5-10	190	12-31-89	2	1	0.61	8	0	0	1	15	8	1	1	1	2	12	.160	.150	.167	7.36	1.23
Keck, Jonathon	L-L	6-6	215	6-18-88	0	2	5.56	14	0	0	4	23	26	15	14	0	11	21	.283	.333	.268	8.34	4.37
Lafferty, Brendan	L-L	6-3	180	5-27-86	2	3	4.57	19	0	0	1	43	51	28	22	4	15	33	.287	.250	.300	6.85	3.12
Mariot, Michael	R-R	6-0	190	10-20-88	8	4	3.41	28	28	0	0	100	99	47	38	7	21	80	.248	.260	.241	7.18	1.88
Marks, Justin	L-L	6-3	195	1-12-88	8	8	3.98	28	22	2	0	145	144	66	64	14	49	140	.261	.262	.261	8.71	3.05
Melville, Tim	R-R	6-5	210	10-9-89	11	10	4.32	29	25	0	0	135	152	73	65	7	53	108	.287	.287	.287	7.18	3.52
Odenbach, Dusty	R-R	6-3	225	9-3-87	2	3	3.50	20	0	0	0	46	38	20	18	4	25	36	.233	.212	.247	6.99	4.86
Odorizzi, Jake	R-R	6-2	175	3-27-90	5	4	2.87	15	15	0	0	78	68	30	25	4	22	103	.235	.211	.256	11.83	2.53
Paukovits, Bryan	R-R	6-7	240	6-29-87	2	3	3.46	31	0	0	7	55	52	33	21	1	17	46	.255	.269	.248	7.57	2.80
Pimentel, Elisaul	R-R	6-2	170	7-10-88	6	7	3.59	26	22	1	1	133	129	60	53	10	31	105	.254	.276	.239	7.11	2.10
Rivers, Alex	R-R	5-10	170	8-13-88	0	0	0.00	1	0	0	0	2	0	0	0	0	0	1	.000	.000	.000	4.50	0.00
Sample, Tyler	L-R	6-7	245	6-27-89	7	12	5.25	27	22	0	0	130	146	95	76	11	58	86	.289	.254	.309	5.94	4.01
Stueve, Andrew	R-R	6-0	190	4-7-89	1	0	0.00	2	0	0	0	3	0	0	0	0	0	3	.000	.000	.000	9.00	0.00
Volz, Kendal	R-R	6-5	225	12-2-87	1	0	1.64	6	0	0	1	11	11	3	2	0	1	7	.275	.538	.148	5.73	0.82
2-team total (31 Salem)					3	3	3.03	37	0	0	3	62	53	22	21	6	13	63	—	—		9.10	1.88
White, Cole	R-R	6-2	195	1-22-88	1	0	1.69	2	0	0	1	5	5	1	1	0	2	4	.250	.429	.154	6.75	3.38

Fielding

Catcher	PCT	G	PO	A	E	DP	PB
Bonilla	.987	74	522	69	8	6	9
Dyer	1.000	7	55	4	0	2	2
Eigsti	.989	13	80	14	1	0	1
Graterol	.977	19	147	21	4	2	1
Jones	1.000	9	61	11	0	2	3
Rodriguez	.981	20	134	22	3	5	2

First Base	PCT	G	PO	A	E	DP
Caseres	.975	5	39	0	1	2
Graterol	.906	3	28	1	3	3
Lewis	.998	52	400	38	1	36
Stovall	.985	45	374	18	6	39
Whittleman	.983	35	283	11	5	24

Second Base	PCT	G	PO	A	E	DP
Batista	.947	23	37	52	5	8
Hall	.947	5	9	9	1	4
Liberto	1.000	2	1	5	0	1
Merrifield	.983	40	74	104	3	28
Mertins	.981	14	24	28	1	10
Navarro	.974	55	92	133	6	32

Third Base	PCT	G	PO	A	E	DP
Batista	.927	45	22	79	8	7
Frost	.923	5	4	8	1	1
Liberto	.667	4	2	2	2	1
Morales	1.000	2	1	2	0	0
Navarro	.846	5	0	11	2	1

	PCT	G	PO	A	E	DP
Stovall	.765	5	4	9	4	1
Whittleman	.894	76	51	135	22	14

Shortstop	PCT	G	PO	A	E	DP
Batista	.963	21	27	52	3	15
Hall	.920	27	44	83	11	12
Liberto	.958	7	6	17	1	3
McClure	.969	67	99	185	9	35
Mertins	.927	11	11	27	3	3
Morales	1.000	1	5	4	0	3
Navarro	.952	8	15	25	2	9

Outfield	PCT	G	PO	A	E	DP
Ferguson	.983	87	171	4	3	2
Francis	.953	42	70	11	4	1

Merrifield	.983	85	162	9	3	2	Prades	.988	79	167	2	2	0	Van Stratten	.983	52	112	7	2	3
Ortiz	1.000	6	13	3	0	0	Testa	.987	66	149	3	2	0

KANE COUNTY COUGARS

LOW CLASS A

MIDWEST LEAGUE

Batting

Batting	B-T	HT	WT	DOB	AVG	vLH	vRH	G	AB	R	H	2B	3B	HR	RBI	BB	HBP	SH	SF	SO	SB	CS	SLG	OBP
Adams, Lane	R-R	6-2	198	11-13-89	.230	.286	.214	43	152	22	35	7	2	1	11	14	2	0	2	44	7	2	.322	.300
Aparicio, Julio	R-R	6-2	175	1-4-90	.169	.222	.153	67	231	18	39	10	1	3	14	8	2	0	1	78	1	4	.260	.202
Beltre, Geulin	B-R	6-0	185	10-27-90	.264	.250	.268	122	459	62	121	18	4	3	42	34	3	0	3	92	18	11	.340	.317
Caseres, Steven	L-R	6-4	220	3-26-87	.231	.300	.188	7	26	2	6	1	0	0	2	2	1	0	0	4	0	1	.269	.310
Caxito, Orlando	R-R	5-11	160	2-3-92	.208	.190	.212	81	289	19	60	5	1	3	31	20	0	0	4	70	11	4	.263	.256
Cruz, Fernando	B-R	6-2	205	3-28-90	.227	.059	.333	13	44	2	10	0	0	0	0	1	0	0	0	8	0	2	.227	.244
Cuthbert, Cheslor	R-R	6-1	190	11-16-92	.267	.277	.263	81	300	33	80	13	1	8	51	36	2	0	4	65	2	0	.397	.345
David, Kevin	R-R	6-5	205	4-10-88	.240	.297	.221	42	150	15	36	6	0	1	11	14	3	0	0	28	0	0	.300	.317
Eibner, Brett	R-R	6-3	195	12-2-88	.213	.210	.214	76	272	46	58	13	2	12	31	48	4	0	0	90	2	3	.408	.340
Espinal, Yowill	R-R	6-0	170	4-1-91	.203	.182	.209	91	300	30	61	7	1	3	24	32	0	0	4	97	15	8	.263	.277
Fletcher, Brian	R-R	6-0	190	10-26-88	.328	.383	.312	91	341	54	112	31	3	14	60	24	9	0	2	80	4	4	.560	.386
Franco, Angel	B-R	5-10	155	5-23-90	.249	.211	.260	97	382	49	95	14	6	4	27	36	2	0	1	40	5	6	.348	.316
Graterol, Juan	R-R	6-1	170	2-14-89	.203	.138	.223	35	123	5	25	3	0	0	6	10	0	0	0	12	0	0	.228	.263
Hall, Gerard	B-R	5-9	170	7-9-88	.269	.233	.281	53	171	23	46	15	4	0	16	23	1	0	2	46	4	2	.404	.355
Jenkins, Ryan	R-R	6-2	215	1-26-87	.237	.243	.235	33	118	13	28	7	0	1	14	9	2	0	0	21	0	2	.322	.302
Jones, Travis	R-R	6-2	200	5-23-89	.234	.222	.237	48	154	18	36	6	0	4	16	15	0	0	0	31	2	0	.351	.302
Krebs, Paul	R-R	5-7	175	10-6-86	—	.000	.000	1	0	0	0	0	0	0	0	0	0	0	0	0	0	0	—	—
Kuebler, Jake	R-R	6-0	200	9-3-89	.209	.179	.220	92	339	35	71	17	2	7	30	38	1	0	0	91	5	3	.333	.291
Liberto, Michael	R-R	5-7	170	6-21-88	.190	.333	.083	15	21	2	4	1	0	0	0	8	2	0	0	4	1	1	.238	.452
Llanos, Alex	R-R	6-1	160	9-21-90	.246	.211	.256	85	346	40	85	18	1	5	30	14	1	0	3	83	13	7	.347	.275
Pickett, Jovan	L-L	5-8	160	11-11-87	.267	.227	.277	35	105	16	28	0	2	0	5	10	6	0	0	22	9	4	.305	.364
Stovall, Ryan	R-R	5-11	190	12-16-86	.307	.279	.319	57	205	27	63	15	5	8	31	15	1	0	1	45	5	3	.546	.356
Watts, Murray	L-R	6-7	270	10-9-87	.211	.188	.220	35	114	8	24	3	0	2	13	24	1	0	0	46	0	0	.289	.353

Pitching

Pitching	B-T	HT	WT	DOB	W	L	ERA	G	GS	CG	SV	IP	H	R	ER	HR	BB	SO	AVG	vLH	vRH	K/9	BB/9
Adam, Jason	R-R	6-4	225	8-4-91	6	9	4.23	21	21	0	0	104	94	60	49	9	25	76	.235	.239	.231	6.56	2.16
Billo, Greg	R-R	6-4	220	7-15-90	9	5	1.93	27	18	0	1	135	113	39	29	6	25	119	.228	.218	.237	7.93	1.67
Boruff, Chase	L-R	6-2	195	7-27-88	4	1	2.30	41	0	0	7	67	51	22	17	1	20	63	.207	.217	.198	8.51	2.70
Byrne, Chas	B-R	6-3	185	1-26-89	3	3	3.93	36	0	0	9	55	54	28	24	5	12	53	.251	.269	.234	8.67	1.96
Caldwell, Allen	L-L	5-11	170	3-29-88	4	0	2.39	11	0	0	1	26	20	9	7	2	9	39	.213	.257	.186	13.33	3.08
Carl, Edwin	R-R	6-0	210	8-31-88	0	0	12.00	2	0	0	0	3	7	4	4	0	2	5	.467	.375	.571	15.00	6.00
Cruz, Antonio	L-L	5-11	200	10-7-91	1	0	1.80	11	1	0	0	30	23	8	6	2	13	39	.215	.182	.230	11.70	3.90
2-team total (22 West Michigan)					3	6	2.73	33	11	0	1	105	91	37	32	7	41	97	—	—	—	8.29	3.50
Garrido, Santiago	R-R	6-1	195	10-4-89	2	5	6.34	19	9	0	0	61	75	45	43	6	30	49	.304	.322	.288	7.23	4.43
Giovenco, Mike	R-R	6-6	235	1-4-88	0	2	6.93	13	0	0	0	25	35	23	19	0	19	28	.327	.280	.368	10.22	6.93
Graham, Tyler	R-R	6-4	250	10-5-87	1	0	10.80	6	0	0	0	8	14	11	10	0	4	8	.368	.250	.455	8.64	4.32
Hayenga, Keaton	R-R	6-4	190	7-10-88	1	1	5.85	4	4	0	0	20	21	15	13	0	7	11	.263	.225	.300	4.95	3.15
Hodge, Mitch	R-R	6-2	210	6-15-89	2	1	6.56	26	0	0	1	48	65	38	35	4	24	37	.317	.284	.350	6.94	4.50
Keck, Jonathon	L-L	6-6	215	6-18-88	0	2	3.26	25	0	0	1	39	34	19	14	3	18	35	.233	.261	.220	8.15	4.19
Marimon, Sugar Ray	R-R	6-1	168	9-30-88	3	5	3.68	13	13	0	0	66	55	30	27	6	20	54	.227	.242	.218	7.36	2.73
Mitchell, Jason	R-R	6-2	185	3-13-88	3	1	2.11	10	3	0	1	38	37	11	9	1	5	27	.248	.319	.182	6.34	1.17
Mitchell, Matt	R-R	6-2	205	3-31-89	1	1	6.00	14	0	0	1	24	38	18	16	1	13	13	.384	.413	.358	4.88	4.88
Odenbach, Dusty	R-R	6-3	225	9-3-87	2	1	2.30	14	0	0	0	27	20	10	7	0	11	28	.208	.245	.170	9.22	3.62
Penny, Robbie	L-R	6-3	215	11-8-88	0	3	5.02	3	3	0	0	14	21	12	8	0	5	8	.356	.370	.344	5.02	3.14
Perez, Leondy	R-R	6-1	190	8-19-89	8	13	3.41	27	27	0	0	153	167	77	58	7	29	108	.277	.292	.265	6.35	1.71
Rivers, Alex	R-R	5-10	170	8-13-88	0	1	4.56	10	0	0	1	24	24	14	12	2	3	22	.264	.071	.429	8.37	1.14
Rogers, Nick	R-R	6-2	225	10-2-87	1	1	2.45	20	0	0	9	29	20	8	8	4	12	27	.194	.157	.231	8.28	3.68
Santiago, Leonel	R-R	6-0	180	12-23-89	7	7	3.06	18	18	0	0	109	101	43	37	6	19	92	.245	.280	.212	7.62	1.57
Simmons, Crawford	R-L	6-2	185	6-10-91	0	3	6.93	3	2	0	0	10	13	8	8	0	6	12	.325	.500	.182	10.45	5.23
Ventura, Yordano	R-R	5-11	140	6-3-91	4	6	4.27	19	19	0	0	84	82	43	40	8	24	88	.258	.241	.275	9.39	2.56
White, Cole	R-R	6-2	195	1-22-88	1	0	6.46	13	0	0	0	15	24	11	11	1	9	16	.358	.484	.250	9.39	5.28
Wooley, Nick	R-R	6-2	160	4-18-88	0	3	5.85	8	1	0	0	20	23	16	13	0	8	16	.295	.353	.250	7.20	3.60

Fielding

Catcher	PCT	G	PO	A	E	DP	PB
David	.997	42	279	40	1	1	4
Graterol	.996	23	190	40	1	3	1
Jenkins	.976	33	217	28	6	4	6
Jones	.988	47	368	45	5	4	1

First Base	PCT	G	PO	A	E	DP
Caseres	.977	4	41	1	1	2
Cruz	1.000	8	62	6	0	4
Graterol	.989	9	83	5	1	6
Hall	1.000	1	4	0	0	1
Kuebler	.997	82	719	67	2	51
Liberto	1.000	1	0	0	0	0
Stovall	.990	12	96	2	1	6
Watts	.977	29	250	10	6	23

Second Base	PCT	G	PO	A	E	DP
Espinal	.969	74	110	201	10	42
Franco	.989	62	77	188	3	28
Hall	1.000	1	1	4	0	1
Liberto	.923	7	7	17	2	1

Third Base	PCT	G	PO	A	E	DP
Cruz	1.000	3	0	4	0	0
Cuthbert	.930	78	39	134	13	8
Franco	.908	27	19	40	6	9
Kuebler	.714	2	1	4	2	0
Liberto	.000	2	0	0	0	0
Stovall	.908	34	20	59	8	7

Shortstop	PCT	G	PO	A	E	DP
Caxito	.942	79	128	215	21	40

	PCT	G	PO	A	E	DP
Espinal	.929	16	18	34	4	8
Hall	.960	46	68	126	8	25
Liberto	.938	3	4	11	1	1

Outfield	PCT	G	PO	A	E	DP
Adams	.924	36	58	3	5	2
Aparicio	.982	51	108	0	2	0
Beltre	.953	102	191	10	10	2
Eibner	.994	68	163	2	1	1
Fletcher	.956	84	146	5	7	0
Llanos	.987	71	141	8	2	1
Pickett	.926	14	24	1	2	0
Stovall	1.000	2	4	0	0	0

KANSAS CITY ROYALS

BURLINGTON ROYALS

ROOKIE

APPALACHIAN LEAGUE

Batting	B-T	HT	WT	DOB	AVG	vLH	vRH	G	AB	R	H	2B	3B	HR	RBI	BB	HBP	SH	SF	SO	SB	CS	SLG	OBP
Adams, Lane	R-R	6-2	198	11-13-89	.281	.219	.296	43	167	31	47	9	3	5	20	17	3	0	3	45	9	1	.461	.353
Antonio, Mike	R-R	6-2	190	10-26-91	.262	.238	.268	55	206	30	54	11	0	10	37	17	3	0	4	25	10	5	.461	.322
Bonifacio, Jorge	R-R	6-1	192	6-4-93	.284	.320	.274	62	236	26	67	20	4	7	30	16	3	0	3	58	5	6	.492	.333
Bringas, Adrian	R-R	5-10	185	7-18-89	.227	.262	.217	57	203	23	46	12	0	5	16	15	4	0	1	29	1	1	.360	.291
Brooks, Steven	R-R	6-0	195	1-26-89	.288	.368	.255	21	66	6	19	0	1	0	6	8	2	0	0	17	6	3	.318	.382
Conner, Cameron	L-L	6-2	185	1-16-88	.252	.265	.248	45	159	21	40	6	1	2	11	17	3	0	0	61	17	7	.340	.335
Dyer, Jared	R-R	6-2	205	5-29-86	.254	.091	.288	19	63	3	16	4	0	0	9	5	1	0	0	17	0	1	.317	.319
Figueroa, Yunior	B-R	6-0	170	8-8-90	.206	.429	.148	12	34	3	7	4	0	0	2	6	0	0	0	8	0	1	.324	.325
Hamblen, Derek	R-R	6-0	185	1-6-89	.121	.250	.103	25	66	7	8	1	1	0	3	8	0	0	0	16	3	3	.167	.216
Howard, Anthony	L-L	6-1	180	11-9-90	.151	.091	.160	27	86	15	13	1	1	3	7	9	4	0	0	27	1	0	.291	.263
Pickett, Jovan	L-L	5-8	160	11-11-87	.304	.333	.295	22	79	10	24	3	1	0	4	4	4	0	0	21	6	3	.367	.368
Rodriguez, Jose	B-R	5-8	165	11-25-87	.252	.172	.273	44	139	20	35	5	2	0	14	17	5	0	2	37	17	4	.317	.350
Shin, Jin-Ho	R-R	6-2	200	10-20-91	.219	.054	.268	46	160	17	35	10	0	3	15	16	4	0	1	53	1	1	.338	.304
Smith, Tyler	R-R	6-0	200	7-5-88	.000	.000	.000	1	4	0	0	0	0	0	0	0	0	0	0	1	0	0	.000	.000
Swab, Kenny	R-R	6-2	215	8-20-88	.243	.313	.232	33	111	11	27	3	0	1	15	9	6	0	0	28	0	1	.297	.333
Trapp, Justin	R-R	5-10	165	10-7-90	.259	.300	.249	63	243	45	63	13	4	7	41	29	5	0	4	64	31	7	.432	.345
Watts, Murray	L-R	6-7	270	10-9-87	.222	.204	.227	65	230	32	51	10	0	15	44	41	2	0	2	72	1	1	.461	.342

Pitching	B-T	HT	WT	DOB	W	L	ERA	G	GS	CG	SV	IP	H	R	ER	HR	BB	SO	AVG	vLH	vRH	K/9	BB/9
Baez, Angel	R-R	6-3	196	2-14-91	0	6	7.09	14	14	0	0	47	67	52	37	3	30	41	.321	.378	.289	7.85	5.74
Brown, Rudy	L-L	6-4	225	6-16-88	1	3	4.31	19	2	0	2	40	59	27	19	1	8	47	.335	.304	.350	10.66	1.82
Cantrell, Eric	R-R	6-4	210	7-25-89	0	5	4.53	13	10	0	0	52	52	30	26	0	22	47	.263	.244	.276	8.19	3.83
Culver, Malcom	R-R	6-2	190	2-9-90	2	2	8.03	18	0	0	0	37	46	35	33	8	23	38	.307	.311	.303	9.24	5.59
Ferguson, Andy	R-R	6-1	195	9-30-88	0	3	5.45	20	0	0	1	36	45	28	22	4	15	33	.306	.344	.279	8.17	3.72
Gonzales, Abel	L-L	6-1	195	12-30-87	2	2	4.66	12	0	0	1	29	33	19	15	2	5	25	.277	.317	.256	7.76	1.55
Graffeo, Nick	R-R	6-2	190	12-14-87	4	2	2.04	17	6	0	4	53	37	15	12	4	16	53	.192	.247	.152	9.00	2.72
Graham, Tyler	R-R	6-4	250	10-5-87	2	1	3.09	14	0	0	2	32	24	13	11	3	17	38	.202	.283	.151	10.69	4.78
Hall, Cory	R-R	6-2	232	5-12-88	2	2	5.55	15	0	0	2	36	34	25	22	5	12	31	.246	.222	.262	7.82	3.03
Middendorf, Dave	R-L	6-3	235	1-23-89	1	1	11.42	7	0	0	0	9	21	14	11	2	2	10	.438	.429	.441	10.38	2.08
Mitchell, Jason	R-R	6-2	185	3-13-88	3	1	4.26	6	0	0	0	19	21	14	9	2	8	17	.269	.231	.288	8.05	3.79
Murray, Matt	R-R	6-4	225	12-28-89	2	4	3.40	12	12	1	0	53	43	24	20	5	10	58	.213	.256	.179	9.85	1.70
Pizziconi, Andrea	R-R	6-2	190	10-4-91	1	2	6.81	16	2	0	0	40	42	36	30	6	21	22	.269	.257	.279	4.99	4.76
Ridings, Matt	R-R	6-0	190	10-17-87	3	4	3.92	14	14	0	0	67	65	36	29	5	11	60	.244	.255	.237	8.10	1.49
Rivers, Alex	R-R	5-10	190	8-13-88	1	1	1.02	9	0	0	1	18	14	7	2	0	4	19	.209	.167	.243	9.68	2.04
Rogers, Nick	R-R	6-2	225	10-2-87	0	0	4.91	2	0	0	0	4	4	3	2	0	4	4	.267	.667	.167	9.82	9.82
Yambati, Robinson	R-R	6-3	185	1-15-91	0	5	18.85	8	8	0	0	18	44	44	37	6	11	9	.458	.512	.415	4.58	5.60

Fielding

Catcher	PCT	G	PO	A	E	DP	PB
Dyer	.986	10	68	3	1	0	2
Shin	.986	40	328	28	5	2	9
Smith	1.000	1	3	1	0	0	0
Swab	.967	23	152	24	6	4	4

First Base	PCT	G	PO	A	E	DP
Dyer	.975	4	39	0	1	1
Figueroa	1.000	2	10	1	0	1
Hamblen	1.000	4	25	2	0	1
Watts	.986	61	491	20	7	33

Second Base	PCT	G	PO	A	E	DP
Hamblen	.857	5	11	7	3	1
Rodriguez	.917	23	26	51	7	10
Trapp	.918	45	63	116	16	17

Third Base	PCT	G	PO	A	E	DP
Bringas	.852	56	37	84	21	6
Figueroa	1.000	5	3	4	0	1
Hamblen	.909	11	9	21	3	2

Shortstop	PCT	G	PO	A	E	DP
Antonio	.877	54	55	124	25	20
Hamblen	1.000	2	2	0	0	0

	PCT	G	PO	A	E	DP
Trapp	.900	18	18	36	6	6
Outfield	PCT	G	PO	A	E	DP
Adams	.979	43	93	0	2	0
Bonifacio	.992	60	117	8	1	2
Brooks	1.000	14	23	0	0	0
Conner	.947	39	51	3	3	0
Dyer	1.000	2	1	0	0	0
Hamblen	1.000	3	3	1	0	1
Howard	.911	26	51	0	5	0
Pickett	.965	22	54	1	2	0
Rodriguez	1.000	4	6	0	0	0

IDAHO FALLS CHUKARS

ROOKIE

PIONEER LEAGUE

Batting	B-T	HT	WT	DOB	AVG	vLH	vRH	G	AB	R	H	2B	3B	HR	RBI	BB	HBP	SH	SF	SO	SB	CS	SLG	OBP
Alcantara, Ysmelin	R-R	6-2	180	5-13-90	.256	.000	.323	10	39	4	10	1	0	1	5	2	0	0	1	10	0	0	.359	.286
Antonio, Mike	R-R	6-2	190	10-26-91	.303	.273	.318	8	33	6	10	2	1	1	5	1	0	0	1	6	1	0	.515	.314
Chism, Tyler	R-R	6-0	205	10-6-88	.265	.359	.235	65	260	59	69	11	2	8	36	27	12	0	5	62	7	5	.415	.355
Davis, Runey	R-R	6-0	185	1-2-89	.326	.283	.343	58	193	42	63	18	3	9	42	28	6	0	3	72	7	4	.591	.422
DelGuidice, Nick	R-R	5-11	180	6-1-89	.355	.364	.350	17	62	9	22	7	0	0	10	1	0	0	1	11	1	0	.468	.359
Elder, Chris	L-R	5-11	205	7-5-88	.289	.100	.339	36	142	28	41	9	4	9	27	12	0	0	0	26	1	2	.599	.344
Escobar, Edul	R-R	5-11	185	9-2-90	.287	.298	.282	48	178	21	51	12	0	4	20	7	2	0	1	29	0	0	.421	.319
Espy, Dean	R-R	6-1	210	10-30-89	.318	.365	.300	62	233	43	74	17	1	7	39	20	10	0	3	59	1	1	.489	.391
Fradejas, Justin	R-R	6-0	190	8-21-88	.310	.455	.216	28	84	16	26	4	0	2	10	13	2	0	0	19	1	0	.429	.414
Gallagher, Cam	R-R	6-3	210	12-16-92	.200	.273	.158	8	30	2	6	0	0	1	2	3	0	0	0	4	0	0	.300	.273
Harper, Lance	B-R	6-1	205	7-17-90	.222	.000	.333	6	18	2	4	1	0	0	1	0	0	0	0	3	0	0	.278	.222
Jenkins, Ryan	R-R	6-2	215	1-26-87	.209	.222	.206	13	43	4	9	1	0	1	5	2	0	0	0	10	0	0	.302	.244
Krebs, Paul	R-R	5-7	175	10-6-86	1.000	.000	1.000	2	1	1	1	0	0	0	0	1	0	0	0	0	0	0	1.000	1.000
Liberto, Michael	S-R	5-7	170	6-21-88	.348	.375	.342	26	92	16	32	5	2	0	8	13	2	0	1	12	8	2	.446	.435
Martinez, Adrian	R-R	6-1	158	1-12-91	.222	.256	.212	49	189	19	42	5	1	0	9	9	1	0	0	43	4	0	.259	.261
Mateo, Danny	B-R	6-1	178	8-10-91	.348	.352	.347	56	224	33	78	9	4	4	40	17	0	0	3	43	0	1	.478	.389

KANSAS CITY ROYALS

Batting	B-T	HT	WT	DOB	AVG	vLH	vRH	G	AB	R	H	2B	3B	HR	RBI	BB	HBP	SH	SF	SO	SB	CS	SLG	OBP
Moreno, Henry	R-R	6-2	162	6-6-89	.275	.295	.268	59	240	36	66	19	2	11	41	18	2	0	1	62	0	0	.508	.330
Piterson, Luis	R-R	5-11	155	6-10-90	.298	.333	.285	43	171	25	51	11	2	0	15	14	2	0	2	19	4	3	.386	.354
Sandford, Darian	B-R	5-9	170	4-28-87	.247	.244	.248	46	174	30	43	2	3	0	18	15	1	0	1	44	25	6	.293	.309
Smith, Tyler	R-R	6-0	200	7-5-88	.192	.214	.184	20	52	9	10	1	0	1	5	7	2	0	0	21	0	0	.269	.311
Threlkeld, Mark	R-R	6-3	205	5-2-90	.271	.214	.285	57	221	23	60	16	3	4	31	17	3	0	2	67	3	4	.425	.329

Pitching	B-T	HT	WT	DOB	W	L	ERA	G	GS	CG	SV	IP	H	R	ER	HR	BB	SO	AVG	vLH	vRH	K/9	BB/9
Avinazar, Willian	R-R	6-4	195	2-27-89	0	2	8.58	12	4	0	0	28	38	31	27	3	18	38	.322	.304	.333	12.07	5.72
Brooks, Aaron	R-R	6-4	220	4-27-90	6	2	3.84	15	13	0	0	80	89	42	34	7	8	73	.285	.275	.293	8.25	0.90
Carl, Edwin	R-R	6-0	210	8-31-88	3	1	1.36	21	0	0	5	33	17	6	5	0	3	71	.145	.111	.167	19.36	0.82
Cuevas, Gary	R-R	6-2	200	5-23-88	0	0	4.58	9	0	0	0	18	12	10	9	1	15	23	.179	.172	.184	11.72	7.64
Diaz, Eric	L-L	6-2	184	10-4-88	0	3	10.06	4	4	0	0	17	22	21	19	5	15	16	.324	.259	.366	8.47	7.94
Dooley, Gates	R-R	6-0	205	8-22-88	3	3	6.79	17	7	0	1	61	73	52	46	6	41	57	.304	.274	.328	8.41	6.05
Fassold, Cody	R-R	6-2	230	10-2-88	1	2	4.24	19	0	0	4	23	25	13	11	1	13	27	.263	.200	.300	10.41	5.01
Giovenco, Mike	R-R	6-6	235	1-4-88	1	0	1.64	6	0	0	0	11	11	3	2	0	4	16	.256	.100	.391	13.09	3.27
Johnson, Nathan	R-R	6-3	185	3-31-89	0	1	4.22	14	0	0	2	32	30	17	15	8	9	26	.246	.216	.259	7.31	2.53
Martin, Brennon	L-L	6-3	195	5-5-87	4	6	4.02	15	15	0	0	87	102	50	39	13	9	75	.291	.330	.278	7.73	0.93
Middendorf, Dave	R-L	6-3	235	1-23-89	0	2	6.35	10	0	0	0	17	25	17	12	1	6	15	.316	.219	.383	7.94	3.18
Moen, Kellen	B-R	6-2	185	5-30-88	2	7	7.25	15	13	0	0	58	80	52	47	6	19	51	.325	.373	.281	7.87	2.93
Patton, Spencer	R-R	6-1	185	2-20-88	3	1	3.40	19	2	0	2	40	42	20	15	0	15	56	.261	.338	.208	12.71	3.40
Peacock, Brian	L-L	6-3	190	5-7-90	5	5	4.48	15	14	0	1	74	73	45	37	7	21	89	.259	.238	.268	10.78	2.54
Penny, Robbie	L-R	6-3	215	11-8-88	3	4	9.84	19	4	0	1	47	72	60	51	8	22	50	.350	.462	.257	9.64	4.24
Sanchez, Jose	L-L	5-10	186	4-20-89	2	4	8.17	19	0	0	0	36	46	42	33	3	26	32	.297	.259	.317	7.93	6.44
Wood, Ryan	R-R	6-4	185	5-5-87	0	0	22.50	2	0	0	0	2	7	5	5	1	0	4	.538	.625	.400	18.00	0.00

Fielding

Catcher	PCT	G	PO	A	E	DP	PB
Escobar	.971	48	396	45	13	3	13
Harper	.983	6	51	6	1	0	3
Jenkins	1.000	12	86	13	0	2	1
Krebs	1.000	2	1	0	0	0	0
Smith	.994	20	137	24	1	2	3

First Base	PCT	G	PO	A	E	DP
DelGuidice	1.000	1	11	0	0	1
Espy	.980	48	416	36	9	41
Jenkins	1.000	1	6	0	0	0
Liberto	1.000	1	10	0	0	0
Moreno	.964	28	254	12	10	23

Second Base	PCT	G	PO	A	E	DP
DelGuidice	1.000	3	1	4	0	2
Liberto	.943	13	16	34	3	4
Mateo	.940	23	29	65	6	11
Piterson	.963	41	78	129	8	28

Third Base	PCT	G	PO	A	E	DP
DelGuidice	.900	3	3	6	1	1
Liberto	1.000	2	0	2	0	0
Mateo	.933	17	9	33	3	4
Threlkeld	.912	55	27	107	13	10

Shortstop	PCT	G	PO	A	E	DP
Antonio	.966	8	6	22	1	3
DelGuidice	.947	10	11	25	2	9
Liberto	.946	10	11	24	2	7
Martinez	.947	49	62	151	12	28

Outfield	PCT	G	PO	A	E	DP
Alcantara	.952	9	19	1	1	0
Chism	.959	62	90	3	4	1
Davis	.968	54	87	5	3	2
Elder	.981	35	48	5	1	1
Fradejas	.971	26	33	0	1	0
Sandford	.912	44	51	1	5	0

AZL ROYALS · ROOKIE

ARIZONA LEAGUE

Batting	B-T	HT	WT	DOB	AVG	vLH	vRH	G	AB	R	H	2B	3B	HR	RBI	BB	HBP	SH	SF	SO	SB	CS	SLG	OBP
Adams, Lane	R-R	6-2	198	11-13-89	.357	.333	.364	4	14	5	5	3	0	0	1	3	1	0	0	4	0	1	.571	.500
Allen, Jerrell	R-R	6-2	180	9-6-92	.242	.250	.240	42	149	27	36	5	2	1	12	18	1	0	0	38	5	0	.322	.327
Arteaga, Humberto	R-R	6-1	160	1-23-94	.254	.295	.243	47	213	30	54	11	2	0	28	9	2	0	0	39	8	2	.324	.290
Bello, Rainier	B-R	5-10	165	6-1-92	.284	.286	.284	23	88	15	25	4	0	1	12	5	1	0	1	20	0	0	.364	.326
Blanco, Jerico	R-R	6-1	160	5-25-92	.268	.195	.291	47	168	25	45	9	1	2	23	7	1	0	4	38	3	2	.369	.294
Cuckovich, Nicholas	R-R	6-2	200	10-8-91	.302	.375	.280	37	139	23	42	7	1	0	19	23	6	0	2	39	24	6	.367	.418
David, Kevin	R-R	6-1	205	4-10-88	.185	.333	.167	8	27	5	5	2	1	0	3	2	1	0	1	8	1	0	.333	.258
DelGuidice, Nick	R-R	5-11	180	6-1-89	.408	.286	.433	34	125	32	51	16	2	4	24	10	3	0	2	10	2	2	.664	.457
Gallagher, Cam	R-R	6-3	210	12-6-92	.141	.105	.153	20	78	6	11	0	0	1	7	7	0	0	1	15	0	0	.179	.209
Garcia, Carlos	R-R	6-0	176	3-18-92	.272	.353	.248	40	147	31	40	7	5	0	22	15	1	0	0	27	8	3	.388	.344
Gaylord, Brian	L-R	6-3	210	5-26-89	.200	.220	.194	52	210	29	42	11	2	4	26	15	4	0	1	57	2	1	.329	.265
Gore, Terrance	R-R	5-7	165	6-8-91	.340	.316	.347	35	94	22	32	2	2	0	16	15	4	0	1	21	17	0	.404	.447
Gray, Gabriel	R-R	6-1	190	8-26-93	.219	.000	.250	11	32	5	7	2	1	0	3	0	4	0	1	13	2	0	.344	.297
Howard, Anthony	L-L	6-1	180	11-9-90	.400	.167	.474	8	25	8	10	1	3	3	7	6	0	0	1	8	0	1	1.040	.500
Jenkins, Ryan	R-R	6-2	215	1-26-87	.273	.750	.167	5	22	3	6	1	0	0	3	0	0	0	0	7	0	0	.318	.273
Lane, Travis	R-R	6-2	215	8-10-90	.260	.350	.243	38	131	20	34	6	0	1	22	16	3	0	0	32	3	3	.328	.353
Llanos, Alex	R-R	6-1	160	9-21-90	.190	.250	.176	5	21	1	4	0	1	0	2	0	0	0	0	7	1	1	.286	.190
Marquez, Alexander	R-R	5-11	190	12-10-92	.250	.125	.275	18	48	3	12	2	0	0	7	7	0	0	0	5	0	0	.292	.345
Morales, Adrian	R-R	5-8	180	11-18-88	.323	.286	.337	34	124	22	40	6	0	4	28	22	3	0	0	24	5	3	.468	.436
Smith, Tim	L-L	6-3	225	6-14-86	.091	.000	.125	4	11	0	1	1	0	0	0	2	0	0	0	1	2	1	.182	.231
Toney, D'Andre	R-R	5-10	170	1-24-92	.340	.286	.357	43	150	32	51	12	5	5	29	14	11	0	1	28	7	11	.587	.432

Pitching	B-T	HT	WT	DOB	W	L	ERA	G	GS	CG	SV	IP	H	R	ER	HR	BB	SO	AVG	vLH	vRH	K/9	BB/9
Amador, Ezequiel	R-R	6-1	154	7-26-88	1	0	7.15	5	0	0	0	11	14	10	9	2	6	8	.304	.294	.310	6.35	4.76
Avinazar, Willian	R-R	6-4	195	2-27-89	0	0	7.50	4	1	0	0	6	9	6	5	1	4	4	.360	.125	.471	4.50	6.00
Bangs, Parker	R-R	6-4	210	12-22-87	0	2	6.55	11	0	0	0	22	23	16	16	4	17	28	.274	.316	.262	11.45	6.95
Baumann, Buddy	L-L	5-10	175	12-9-87	0	1	3.86	2	2	0	0	5	3	3	2	0	1	9	.167	.250	.143	17.36	1.93
Blanco, Nicolas	R-R	6-2	190	3-23-87	0	0	3.52	6	0	0	0	8	6	3	3	0	3	5	.276	.250	.294	5.87	3.52
Diaz, Eric	L-L	6-2	184	10-4-88	1	4	5.65	12	9	0	0	51	58	37	32	3	16	42	.294	.452	.265	7.41	2.82
Durden, Andrew	R-R	6-0	200	11-27-88	0	0	9.95	5	0	0	0	6	11	8	7	3	3	4	.379	.308	.438	5.68	4.26

Pitching	B-T	HT	WT	DOB	W	L	ERA	G	GS	CG	SV	IP	H	R	ER	HR	BB	SO	AVG	vLH	vRH	K/9	BB/9
Edelbrock, Casey	R-R	6-3	195	5-20-88	0	2	8.04	8	0	0	0	16	19	16	14	1	5	19	.306	.200	.378	10.91	2.87
Edelen, Brian	R-R	6-2	200	3-7-88	2	1	7.23	15	0	0	0	42	51	39	34	8	18	45	.291	.311	.281	9.57	3.83
Fassold, Cody	R-R	6-2	230	10-2-88	1	0	0.00	1	0	0	0	3	3	0	0	0	2	2	.250	.500	.200	6.00	6.00
Gomez, Omar	L-L	6-2	190	1-26-89	0	0	0.00	2	2	0	0	2	1	1	0	0	1	1	.167	.333	.000	5.40	5.40
Hodgson, Ivor	B-L	6-2	190	4-25-86	0	0	0.00	4	3	0	0	6	4	1	0	0	2	5	.190	.167	.200	7.50	3.00
Johnson, Nathan	R-R	6-2	185	3-31-89	1	0	3.97	7	0	0	3	11	18	7	5	1	1	10	.367	.313	.394	7.94	0.79
Lumpkins, Stephen	R-L	6-8	225	4-16-90	2	1	7.02	10	8	0	0	33	47	31	26	2	22	26	.343	.364	.337	7.02	5.94
Morales, Julio	R-R	6-1	172	11-22-88	3	5	6.64	14	3	0	1	42	50	36	31	1	22	41	.299	.342	.266	8.79	4.71
Ogando, Cesar	R-L	6-3	210	6-6-92	0	4	10.52	12	11	0	0	32	50	40	37	4	24	23	.370	.435	.357	6.54	6.82
Rivers, Alex	R-R	5-10	170	8-13-88	0	0	8.44	2	1	0	0	5	8	6	5	0	2	8	.320	.000	.571	13.50	3.38
Rodriguez, Jonathan	R-R	6-1	165	12-13-88	0	0	4.91	3	1	0	0	4	6	2	2	1	1	2	.429	.571	.286	4.91	2.45
Rosario, Sergio	R-R	5-11	184	8-20-90	1	3	7.71	8	4	0	1	30	29	26	26	3	18	31	.252	.261	.246	9.20	5.34
Runion, Sam	R-R	6-4	220	11-9-88	1	1	1.00	7	2	0	0	9	7	4	1	0	4	10	.200	.176	.222	10.00	4.00
Schulz, Clayton	L-L	6-2	180	6-7-90	2	0	0.00	4	1	0	0	17	9	3	0	0	2	17	.153	.143	.154	9.18	1.08
Simmons, Crawford	R-L	6-2	185	6-10-91	0	0	9.00	1	1	0	0	1	2	1	1	0	0	1	.400	.500	.333	9.00	0.00
Soto, Jorge	R-R	6-3	180	11-1-91	0	0	9.53	4	1	0	0	6	9	6	6	3	6	6	.375	.200	.421	4.76	9.53
Stueve, Andrew	R-R	6-0	190	4-7-89	1	3	2.09	22	1	0	6	43	38	18	10	0	6	40	.233	.218	.241	8.37	1.26
White, Cole	R-R	6-2	195	1-22-88	0	0	12.00	3	0	0	0	3	4	4	4	0	5	3	.333	.200	.429	9.00	15.00
Williams, Ali	R-R	6-2	185	7-8-89	1	1	3.89	13	3	0	0	37	43	28	16	2	10	35	.281	.390	.213	8.51	2.43
Witt, Christian	R-R	6-4	245	10-11-88	3	3	9.11	17	2	0	1	28	42	35	28	4	7	19	.333	.415	.294	6.18	2.28

Fielding

Catcher	PCT	G	PO	A	E	DP	PB
Bello	.974	10	56	20	2	2	12
David	.976	6	35	5	1	1	0
Gallagher	.985	7	58	7	1	0	0
Jenkins	.943	4	29	4	2	1	0
Lane	.984	23	162	23	3	3	9
Marquez	.974	17	91	20	3	0	2

First Base	PCT	G	PO	A	E	DP
Cuckovich	.970	4	29	3	1	0
Gaylord	.983	52	446	28	8	34
Morales	1.000	1	11	0	0	1

Second Base	PCT	G	PO	A	E	DP
Cuckovich	.857	1	1	5	1	1

	PCT	G	PO	A	E	DP
DelGuidice	1.000	12	22	25	0	6
Garcia	.911	39	66	97	16	16
Morales	.926	7	12	13	2	4

Third Base	PCT	G	PO	A	E	DP
Cuckovich	.943	20	18	32	3	2
DelGuidice	.950	14	10	28	2	5
Morales	.899	25	23	48	8	8

Shortstop	PCT	G	PO	A	E	DP
Arteaga	.932	47	68	137	15	17
Cuckovich	.692	3	3	6	4	3
DelGuidice	.800	6	7	13	5	3
Garcia	1.000	2	1	1	0	2

Outfield	PCT	G	PO	A	E	DP
Adams	1.000	4	6	0	0	0
Allen	.951	40	75	3	4	0
Blanco	.988	46	78	3	1	0
Cuckovich	.889	5	8	0	1	0
DelGuidice	1.000	2	1	0	0	0
Gore	.975	30	74	4	2	2
Gray	1.000	11	13	2	0	1
Howard	.778	5	6	1	2	0
Llanos	1.000	4	6	1	0	0
Smith	1.000	4	12	0	0	0
Toney	.955	41	60	4	3	1

DSL ROYALS

ROOKIE

DOMINICAN SUMMER LEAGUE

Batting	B-T	HT	WT	DOB	AVG	vLH	vRH	G	AB	R	H	2B	3B	HR	RBI	BB	HBP	SH	SF	SO	SB	CS	SLG	OBP
Bello, Rainier	B-R	5-10	165	6-1-92	.250	.000	.290	10	36	3	9	2	0	0	3	2	1	0	1	7	0	0	.306	.300
Blanco, Luis	R-R	5-11	155	3-26-93	.257	.091	.299	37	109	19	28	8	0	0	13	14	5	0	1	24	4	6	.330	.364
Flores, Jecksson	R-R	5-11	145	10-28-93	.238	.375	.198	46	143	25	34	3	0	0	15	27	3	0	2	20	10	7	.259	.366
Giron, Jose	R-R	5-11	155	6-27-93	.201	.324	.165	59	149	31	30	6	0	0	17	28	5	0	2	25	11	3	.242	.342
Gomez, Brawlun	R-R	6-2	185	8-5-92	.172	.244	.142	51	151	21	26	7	2	0	24	25	2	0	2	45	12	3	.245	.294
Gonzalez, Cesar	R-R	6-3	185	11-20-93	.240	.262	.231	51	146	16	35	4	0	0	16	18	6	0	2	24	1	4	.267	.343
Gonzalez, Pedro	R-R	6-2	162	1-28-92	.301	.256	.314	52	176	25	53	8	0	1	24	21	11	0	3	22	1	0	.364	.403
Nivar, Pedro	R-R	5-10	170	1-13-92	.186	.250	.170	39	118	16	22	1	1	1	17	16	10	0	1	26	8	2	.237	.331
Patino, Alfredo	R-R	6-0	175	5-18-93	.283	.245	.296	53	191	32	54	4	0	0	21	28	6	0	2	28	18	10	.304	.388
Ramirez, Abraham	R-R	6-2	189	10-17-90	.184	.200	.180	48	125	13	23	5	1	2	14	12	2	0	2	37	0	3	.288	.262
Ramos, Mauricio	R-R	6-1	160	2-2-92	.226	.320	.193	60	190	36	43	8	0	2	26	36	7	0	3	39	3	3	.300	.364
Solano, Jose	R-R	6-1	170	8-17-93	.217	.256	.204	50	152	29	33	8	1	3	15	23	9	0	0	54	13	2	.342	.353
Torres, Ramon	R-R	5-10	155	1-22-93	.260	.229	.269	60	204	35	53	6	3	2	24	26	5	0	4	36	14	5	.309	.351
Urena, Lewis	R-R	5-8	145	5-6-91	.277	.227	.292	29	94	17	26	2	1	0	13	18	1	0	1	12	9	3	.319	.395
2-team total (2 Red Sox)					.281	—	—	31	96	19	27	2	1	0	13	18	1	0	1	12	9	3	.323	.397
Villegas, Luis	R-R	5-10	170	12-2-92	.244	.143	.271	53	164	26	40	8	0	1	23	38	5	0	2	22	6	1	.311	.397

Pitching	B-T	HT	WT	DOB	W	L	ERA	G	GS	CG	SV	IP	H	R	ER	HR	BB	SO	AVG	vLH	vRH	K/9	BB/9
Almonte, Miguel	R-R	6-2	160	4-4-93	0	0	5.40	5	1	0	0	12	7	7	7	0	9	9	.256	.333	.226	6.94	5.40
Brazoban, Jose	R-R	5-9	165	5-28-93	1	0	3.56	9	7	0	0	30	30	18	12	2	12	14	.259	.250	.261	4.15	3.56
Caramo, Yender	R-R	6-0	175	8-25-91	10	3	1.20	13	12	1	0	68	51	11	9	1	8	38	.216	.207	.219	5.05	1.06
Castillo, Darwin	R-R	6-4	180	10-27-92	2	1	6.23	7	2	0	0	17	19	13	12	0	10	15	.275	.125	.295	7.79	5.19
Diaz, Frankelis	R-R	6-0	190	9-25-91	0	3	4.30	7	4	0	1	23	27	17	11	1	4	22	.287	.412	.260	8.61	1.57
Feliz, Igol	R-R	6-3	195	5-31-93	3	0	5.48	10	0	0	0	21	20	13	13	1	11	19	.250	.417	.221	8.02	4.64
Garcia, Dilson	R-R	6-2	184	9-9-91	4	0	1.80	11	3	0	1	35	23	9	7	0	18	29	.190	.156	.202	7.46	4.63
Guevara, Cruz	L-L	6-0	155	5-29-94	1	0	3.86	2	0	0	0	2	1	1	1	0	4	6	.125	.000	.143	23.14	15.43
Machado, Andres	R-R	6-0	175	4-22-93	0	0	4.66	7	1	0	0	10	9	6	5	0	11	7	.250	.250	.250	6.52	10.24
Martinez, Jossiel	L-L	5-10	160	11-9-91	5	0	1.13	16	0	0	5	48	40	10	6	3	9	46	.240	.000	.252	8.69	1.70
Melgar, Luis	R-R	6-3	163	2-5-92	1	1	1.80	12	4	0	0	25	20	6	5	0	8	14	.217	.278	.203	5.04	2.88
Munoz, Jairo	R-R	6-0	180	8-12-91	3	0	2.57	6	0	0	0	7	4	2	2	0	4	7	.174	.000	.222	9.00	5.14
Nina, Aroni	R-R	6-4	160	4-9-90	2	2	3.61	14	9	0	1	47	38	27	19	2	24	53	.221	.167	.235	10.08	4.56
Ortiz, Jesus	R-R	5-10	170	1-6-91	1	5	2.60	15	0	0	4	28	25	16	8	0	14	27	.245	.320	.221	8.78	4.55
Penalo, Victor	R-R	5-10	154	7-12-91	0	0	0.00	1	0	0	0	2	1	0	0	0	1	2	.167	.500	.000	9.00	4.50
Perdomo, Miguel	R-R	6-3	175	4-21-93	2	4	2.70	14	13	0	0	67	54	27	20	1	16	40	.232	.362	.198	5.40	2.43

Pitching	B-T	HT	WT	DOB	W	L	ERA	G	GS	CG	SV	IP	H	R	ER	HR	BB	SO	AVG	vLH	vRH	K/9	BB/9
Polanco, Adelso	R-R	6-3	165	12-20-93	0	1	7.50	6	0	0	0	6	10	8	5	1	4	6	.357	.375	.350	9.00	6.00
Rios, Yamil	L-L	6-0	155	9-24-92	1	1	2.57	7	0	0	0	14	13	10	4	1	10	9	.260	.000	.271	5.79	6.43
Rodriguez, Freddy	R-R	6-3	188	12-1-90	3	0	1.89	14	1	0	2	33	27	9	7	1	12	14	.223	.167	.242	3.78	3.24
Rodriguez, Jose	R-R	6-2	192	9-18-92	2	1	4.04	14	5	0	2	36	32	25	16	0	23	23	.242	.227	.245	5.80	5.80
Rosario, Sergio	R-R	5-11	184	8-20-90	3	0	1.54	8	8	1	0	41	29	7	7	1	10	50	.196	.219	.190	10.98	2.20
Tatis, Yerinson	R-R	6-4	177	1-1-94	2	0	1.88	7	0	0	1	14	10	3	3	0	4	6	.200	.286	.186	3.77	2.51
Velasquez, Angelo	R-R	6-0	160	9-19-91	0	2	12.60	6	0	0	0	10	20	15	14	1	4	8	.426	.556	.395	7.20	3.60

Fielding

Catcher	PCT	G	PO	A	E	DP	PB
Bello	1.000	7	30	8	0	0	1
Gonzalez	.987	14	65	10	1	0	3
Gonzalez	.987	38	237	57	4	0	4
Villegas	.971	22	119	14	4	0	5

First Base	PCT	G	PO	A	E	DP
Gonzalez	.987	35	300	11	4	33
Gonzalez	1.000	11	106	8	0	9
Patino	1.000	1	12	0	0	0
Ramos	1.000	1	6	0	0	0
Villegas	.996	26	243	11	1	21

Second Base	PCT	G	PO	A	E	DP
Blanco	.977	12	23	20	1	10
Flores	.981	26	47	55	2	12
Nina	1.000	1	3	5	0	2
Patino	.964	13	27	26	2	7
Torres	.909	3	3	7	1	1
Urena	.964	23	47	60	4	11

Third Base	PCT	G	PO	A	E	DP
Patino	.847	23	15	46	11	6
Ramos	.911	47	32	132	16	14
Urena	.000	1	0	0	0	0
Villegas	.667	1	0	2	1	0

Shortstop	PCT	G	PO	A	E	DP
Flores	.955	20	31	54	4	7
Torres	.955	52	83	152	11	36

Outfield	PCT	G	PO	A	E	DP
Brazoban	.000	1	0	0	0	0
Giron	.990	57	90	6	1	1
Gomez	.941	51	78	2	5	0
Nivar	.975	34	38	1	1	0
Patino	.000	1	0	0	0	0
Ramirez	.983	46	57	0	1	0
Solano	.970	49	58	7	2	1

Los Angeles Angels

SEASON IN A SENTENCE: With one of the highest payrolls in the game and the starting pitching trio of Jared Weaver, Dan Haren and Ervin Santana, the Angels could never get their offense going enough to keep up with the Rangers in the National League West, costing general manager Tony Reagins his job.

HIGH POINT: On Aug. 21, with the Angels trailing the Rangers by four games, news came from the Angels that they had reached an agreement with Weaver that would keep the Southern California native in Anaheim for the next five years.

LOW POINT: Despite being as close as a game and a half out of first place as late as Sept. 10, the Angels ultimately stumbled at the end as the Rangers cruised to another pennant. Los Angeles finished with a 6-11 stretch that included series losses to the Orioles and Athletics. The season ended on a particularly down note, with a sweep by the Rangers.

NOTABLE ROOKIES: Hard-throwing righthander Jordan Walden took over as closer and registered 32 saves while posting a 2.98 ERA. Slugging first baseman Mark Trumbo replaced the injured Kendry Morales and led all rookies in home runs (29) and RBIs (87). Tyler Chatwood made 25 starts as the fifth starter and held his own with a 4.75 ERA.

KEY TRANSACTIONS: One major transaction played a key role in determining the outcome of the AL West in 2011. Unfortunately, the trade that sent catcher Mike Napoli and outfielder Juan Rivera to the Blue Jays in exchange for outfielder Vernon Wells swayed the division in Texas' favor. Not only did the Angels take on the bulk of Wells' bloated contract, but he went on to put up one of the worst seasons by a position player in 2011. Napoli was traded to Texas and put up the best offensive season of his career, emerging as a star in the postseason. That deal more than any other led to Reagins' dismissal. The Angels hired Diamondbacks assistant GM Jerry Dipoto to replace him.

DOWN ON THE FARM: Going into the season, outfielder Mike Trout was ranked as one of the top prospects in baseball. He validated that acclaim in 2011 as he was named Baseball America's Minor League Player of the Year. As one of the youngest players in Double-A (19), Trout hit .328/.415/.543 with 11 home runs and 33 stolen bases. He also got his feet wet in the big leagues.

OPENING DAY PAYROLL: $138,543,166 (4th)

PLAYERS OF THE YEAR

MAJOR LEAGUE	MINOR LEAGUE
Jered Weaver	**Mike Trout**
rhp	of
18-8, 2.41	(Double-A)
198 SO/236 IP	.326/.414/.544
2nd in AL in ERA, WHIP	BA Minor Lg POY

ORGANIZATION LEADERS

BATTING		*Minimum 250 PA
MAJORS		
* AVG	Alberto Callaspo	.288
* OPS	Howie Kendrick	.802
HR	Mark Trumbo	29
RBI	Mark Trumbo	87
MINORS		
* AVG	Gil Velazquez, Salt Lake	.328
* OBP	Mike Trout, Arkansas	.414
* SLG	Kole Calhoun, Inland Empire	.547
R	Matt Long, Inland Empire/Arkansas	119
H	Kole Calhoun, Inland Empire	166
TB	Kole Calhoun, Inland Empire	280
2B	Paul McAnulty, Salt Lake	41
3B	Jeremy Moore, Salt Lake	18
HR	Kole Calhoun, Inland Empire	22
RBI	Jeff Baisley, Salt Lake	100
BB	Kole Calhoun, Inland Empire	73
	David Harris, Arkansas/Cedar Rapids/I.E.	73
SO	David Harris, Arkansas/Cedar Rapids/I.E.	139
SB	Travis Witherspoon, Cedar Rapids/I.E.	46
PITCHING		#Minimum 75 IP
MAJORS		
W	Jered Weaver	18
# ERA	Jered Weaver	2.41
SO	Jered Weaver	198
SV	Jordan Walden	32
MINORS		
W	Manuel Flores, Salt Lake/Inland Empire	13
L	Eddie McKiernan, Arkansas	12
	Max Russell, Cedar Rapids/Inland Empire	12
# ERA	Matt Shoemaker, Salt Lake/Arkansas	3.15
G	Jeremy Berg, Arkansas/Salt Lake	52
GS	Ariel Pena, Inland Empire/Salt Lake	28
SV	Ryan Brasier, Arkansas/Salt Lake	19
IP	Matt Shoemaker, Salt Lake/Arkansas	177.1
BB	Ariel Pena, Inland Empire/Salt Lake	85
SO	Ariel Pena, Inland Empire/Salt Lake	183
# AVG	Garrett Richards, Arkansas	.233

General Manager: Tony Reagins. **Farm Director:** Abe Flores. **Scouting Director:** Ric Wilson.

Class	Team	League	W	L	PCT	Finish	Manager(s)
Majors	Los Angeles Angels	American	86	76	.531	6th (14)	Mike Scioscia
Triple-A	Salt Lake Bees	Pacific Coast	62	82	.431	16th (16)	Keith Johnson
Double-A	Arkansas Travelers	Texas	68	69	.496	4th (8)	B. Mosiello/T. Takayoshi/B. Mitchell
High A	Inland Empire 66ers	California	69	71	.493	t-5th (10)	Tom Gamboa/Damon Mashore
Low A	Cedar Rapids Kernels	Midwest	61	78	.439	14th (16)	Brent Del Chiaro
Rookie	Orem Owlz	Pioneer	46	30	.605	1st (8)	Tom Kotchman
Rookie	AZL Angels	Arizona	28	28	.500	t-6th (13)	Tyrone Boykin
Overall 2011 Minor League Record			334	358	.483	22nd (30)	

ORGANIZATION STATISTICS

LOS ANGELES ANGELS
AMERICAN LEAGUE

Batting	B-T	HT	WT	DOB	AVG	vLH	vRH	G	AB	R	H	2B	3B	HR	RBI	BB	HBP	SH	SF	SO	SB	CS	SLG	OBP
Abreu, Bobby	L-R	6-0	220	3-11-74	.253	.238	.259	142	502	54	127	30	1	8	60	78	1	0	3	113	21	5	.365	.353
Amarista, Alexi	L-R	5-8	150	4-6-89	.154	.000	.174	23	52	2	8	3	1	0	5	2	0	0	1	8	0	0	.250	.182
Aybar, Erick	B-R	5-10	180	1-14-84	.279	.216	.308	143	556	71	155	33	8	10	59	31	6	0	3	68	30	6	.421	.322
Bourjos, Peter	R-R	6-1	185	3-31-87	.271	.289	.261	147	502	72	136	26	11	12	43	32	10	0	1	124	22	9	.438	.327
Branyan, Russell	L-R	6-4	230	12-19-75	.185	.200	.183	37	65	7	12	2	0	4	12	11	0	0	1	21	2	0	.400	.299
Callaspo, Alberto	B-R	5-9	195	4-19-83	.288	.306	.280	141	475	54	137	23	0	6	46	58	1	0	2	48	8	1	.375	.366
Conger, Hank	B-R	6-1	220	1-29-88	.209	.182	.211	59	177	14	37	8	0	6	19	17	1	0	0	37	0	0	.356	.282
Hunter, Torii	R-R	6-2	225	7-18-75	.262	.287	.252	156	580	80	152	24	2	23	82	62	4	0	3	125	5	7	.429	.336
Izturis, Maicer	B-R	5-8	175	9-12-80	.276	.295	.265	122	449	51	124	35	0	5	38	33	0	4	6	96	8	.334	.334
Kendrick, Howard	R-R	5-10	210	7-12-83	.285	.295	.280	140	537	86	153	30	6	18	63	33	10	1	0	119	14	6	.464	.338
Mathis, Jeff	R-R	6-0	200	3-31-83	.174	.180	.170	93	247	18	43	12	0	3	22	15	2	0	3	75	1	2	.259	.225
Moore, Jeremy	L-R	6-1	190	6-29-87	.125	.250	.000	8	8	3	1	0	0	0	0	0	0	0	0	2	0	0	.125	.125
Navarro, Efren	L-L	6-0	200	5-14-86	.200	.333	.143	8	10	1	2	1	0	0	1	0	0	0	0	1	0	0	.300	.273
Pettit, Chris	R-R	6-0	200	8-15-84	—	.389	.000	1	0	0	0	0	0	0	0	0	0	0	0	0	0	0	—	—
Romine, Andrew	B-R	6-1	190	12-24-85	.125	.000	.182	10	16	2	2	0	0	0	1	0	0	0	6	1	0	.125	.176
Trout, Mike	R-R	6-1	200	8-7-91	.220	.245	.203	40	123	20	27	6	0	5	16	9	2	0	1	30	4	0	.390	.281
Trumbo, Mark	R-R	6-4	220	1-16-86	.254	.264	.249	149	539	65	137	31	1	29	87	25	5	0	4	120	9	4	.477	.291
Velazquez, Gil	R-R	6-2	190	10-17-79	.500	.500	.500	4	6	0	3	0	0	0	1	0	0	0	1	0	0	.500	.429
Wells, Vernon	R-R	6-1	230	12-8-78	.218	.284	.187	131	505	60	110	15	4	25	66	20	1	0	3	86	9	4	.412	.248
Willits, Reggie	B-R	5-11	185	5-30-81	.045	.000	.083	22	22	0	1	1	0	0	1	4	0	0	0	7	0	0	.091	.192
Wilson, Bobby	R-R	6-0	210	4-8-83	.189	.250	.127	57	111	5	21	8	0	1	8	10	0	0	2	16	0	2	.288	.252
Wood, Brandon	R-R	6-3	210	3-2-85	.143	.250	.100	6	14	1	2	1	0	0	0	0	0	0	0	8	0	0	.214	.143

Pitching	B-T	HT	WT	DOB	W	L	ERA	G	GS	CG	SV	IP	H	R	ER	HR	BB	SO	AVG	vLH	vRH	K/9	BB/9
Bell, Trevor	L-R	6-2	200	10-12-86	1	1	3.41	19	0	0	0	34	39	14	13	2	10	17	.291	.281	.300	4.46	2.62
Bulger, Jason	R-R	6-4	210	12-6-78	0	1	0.96	5	0	0	0	9	6	4	1	2	10	7	.182	.250	.118	6.75	9.64
Cassevah, Bobby	R-R	6-3	220	9-11-85	1	1	2.72	30	0	0	0	40	28	12	12	1	19	24	.207	.226	.190	5.45	4.31
Chatwood, Tyler	R-R	6-0	185	12-16-89	6	11	4.75	27	25	0	0	142	166	81	75	14	71	74	.303	.321	.281	4.69	4.50
Downs, Scott	L-L	6-2	210	3-17-76	6	3	1.34	60	0	0	1	54	39	11	8	3	15	35	.199	.160	.222	5.87	2.52
Haren, Dan	R-R	6-5	215	9-17-80	16	10	3.17	35	34	4	0	238	211	91	84	20	33	192	.235	.226	.248	7.25	1.25
Jepsen, Kevin	R-R	6-3	230	7-26-84	1	2	7.62	16	0	0	0	13	21	11	11	2	9	6	.375	.333	.423	4.15	6.23
Kazmir, Scott	L-L	6-0	195	1-24-84	0	0	27.00	1	1	0	0	2	5	5	5	1	2	0	.500	1.000	.286	0.00	10.80
Kohn, Michael	R-R	6-0	200	6-26-86	0	1	7.30	14	0	0	1	12	14	10	10	6	9	9	.280	.286	.276	6.57	6.57
Palmer, Matt	R-R	6-2	235	3-21-79	1	1	5.17	3	3	0	0	16	19	10	9	0	4	7	.306	.286	.317	4.02	2.30
Pineiro, Joel	R-R	6-0	200	9-25-78	7	7	5.13	27	24	0	0	146	182	90	83	16	38	62	.311	.322	.299	3.83	2.35
Ramirez, Horacio	L-L	6-1	220	11-24-79	1	0	6.00	12	0	0	0	9	16	7	6	1	2	4	.432	.318	.600	4.00	2.00
Richards, Garrett	R-R	6-3	215	5-27-88	0	2	5.79	7	3	0	0	14	16	11	9	4	7	9	.291	.367	.200	5.79	4.50
Rodney, Fernando	R-R	5-11	220	3-18-77	3	5	4.50	39	0	0	3	32	26	18	16	1	28	26	.224	.273	.180	7.31	7.88
Rodriguez, Francisco	R-R	6-2	220	2-26-83	0	0	4.61	10	0	0	0	14	13	7	7	2	5	7	.241	.212	.286	4.61	3.29
Santana, Ervin	R-R	6-2	185	12-12-82	11	12	3.38	33	33	4	0	229	207	95	86	26	72	178	.241	.245	.237	7.01	2.83
Takahashi, Hisanori	L-L	5-10	175	4-2-75	4	3	3.57	61	0	0	2	68	58	31	27	7	25	52	.232	.263	.209	6.88	3.31
Thompson, Rich	R-R	6-1	205	7-1-84	1	3	3.00	44	0	0	0	54	46	18	18	5	20	56	.224	.237	.213	9.33	3.33
Walden, Jordan	R-R	6-5	235	11-16-87	5	5	2.98	62	0	0	32	60	49	22	20	3	26	67	.223	.227	.218	9.99	3.88
Weaver, Jered	R-R	6-7	215	10-4-82	18	8	2.41	33	33	4	0	236	182	65	63	20	56	198	.212	.216	.208	7.56	2.14
Williams, Jerome	R-R	6-3	240	12-4-81	4	0	3.68	10	6	0	0	44	45	20	18	6	15	28	.269	.230	.310	5.73	3.07

Fielding

Catcher	PCT	G	PO	A	E	DP	PB
Conger	.983	56	322	27	6	5	1
Mathis	.995	91	512	53	3	4	6
Wilson	.996	47	239	26	1	1	0

First Base	PCT	G	PO	A	E	DP
Branyan	.981	11	47	4	1	11
Kendrick	.992	17	119	10	1	15

Navarro	1.000	8	41	0	0	2
Trumbo	.993	149	1281	93	10	117
Wilson	1.000	6	7	0	0	1
Wood	1.000	1	2	1	0	0

Second Base	PCT	G	PO	A	E	DP
Amarista	.964	14	21	33	2	8
Izturis	.984	49	87	158	4	33

Kendrick	.992	108	161	317	4	63
Velazquez	1.000	2	2	5	0	1

Third Base	PCT	G	PO	A	E	DP
Branyan	1.000	2	0	1	0	0
Callaspo	.959	129	95	255	15	27
Izturis	.964	37	26	55	3	3
Romine	1.000	3	1	2	0	1

Velazquez	1.000	2	0	2	0	0
Wood	1.000	5	7	7	0	4
Kendrick	1.000	23	33	1	0	0
Moore	1.000	5	4	1	0	0

Shortstop	PCT	G	PO	A	E	DP
Amarista	.000	1	0	0	0	0
Aybar	.980	142	240	406	13	102
Izturis	.986	16	25	43	1	8
Romine	.950	7	4	15	1	2

Outfield	PCT	G	PO	A	E	DP
Abreu	.969	28	29	2	1	0
Amarista	1.000	8	9	1	0	0
Bourjos	.989	147	350	7	4	0
Hunter	.989	137	264	15	3	2

Trout	.976	35	80	0	2	0
Trumbo	1.000	11	3	0	0	0
Wells	.990	122	281	4	3	0
Willits	1.000	20	23	0	0	0

SALT LAKE BEES

TRIPLE-A

PACIFIC COAST LEAGUE

Batting	B-T	HT	WT	DOB	AVG	vLH	vRH	G	AB	R	H	2B	3B	HR	RBI	BB	HBP	SH	SF	SO	SB	CS	SLG	OBP
Almanzar, Jean	B-R	5-7	150	2-7-89	.250	.500	.167	3	8	1	2	0	0	0	0	0	0	0	0	0	0	0	.250	.250
Amarista, Alexi	L-R	5-8	150	4-6-89	.292	.290	.293	86	363	49	106	24	5	4	50	22	4	0	3	56	15	8	.419	.337
Armstrong, Cole	L-R	6-3	210	8-24-83	.284	.200	.314	68	190	23	54	14	0	9	30	27	1	0	1	47	2	3	.500	.374
Auer, Tyson	R-R	6-0	188	10-24-85	.280	.296	.273	91	353	51	99	19	4	1	35	15	1	0	1	76	21	12	.365	.311
Aybar, Erick	B-R	5-10	180	1-14-84	.250	.000	.333	1	4	1	1	0	0	0	0	0	0	0	0	1	0	0	.250	.250
Bailey, Dwayne	B-R	6-2	185	8-11-86	.224	.143	.245	24	67	8	15	2	1	0	5	7	0	0	0	22	0	1	.284	.297
Baisley, Jeff	R-R	6-3	220	12-19-82	.303	.241	.332	134	538	85	163	31	3	20	100	38	8	0	5	85	5	1	.483	.355
Bandy, Jett	R-R	6-4	210	3-26-90	.000	.000	.000	1	1	0	0	0	0	0	0	0	0	0	0	0	0	0	.000	.000
Castillo, Angel	R-R	6-3	195	6-7-89	.111	.000	.143	5	18	3	2	1	0	0	1	2	1	0	0	5	1	0	.167	.238
Conger, Hank	B-R	6-1	220	1-29-88	.300	.355	.275	27	100	14	30	4	0	5	26	12	0	0	0	18	0	0	.490	.375
Karcich, Jon	R-R	6-2	195	9-10-87	.250	.250	.250	4	12	2	3	0	0	1	5	1	0	0	0	4	0	0	.500	.308
Kiniry, Rian	L-R	6-0	180	12-12-86	.302	.265	.317	41	116	12	35	6	1	1	14	9	0	0	0	20	7	2	.397	.352
Lopez, Roberto	R-R	6-0	195	10-1-85	.167	.000	.217	10	30	2	5	1	0	0	2	3	1	0	0	2	0	2	.200	.265
McAnulty, Paul	L-R	5-11	225	2-24-81	.311	.273	.329	118	444	67	138	41	0	19	79	42	3	0	5	92	5	3	.532	.370
Melillo, Kevin	L-R	6-0	190	5-14-82	.284	.212	.337	46	155	21	44	9	0	4	19	25	0	0	1	29	5	2	.419	.381
Mercado, Orlando	R-R	5-9	220	3-13-85	.250	.250	.250	5	16	1	4	1	0	0	1	2	0	0	0	2	0	0	.313	.333
Moore, Jeremy	L-R	6-1	190	6-29-87	.298	.252	.315	113	426	76	127	24	18	15	66	21	3	0	6	114	21	10	.545	.331
Navarro, Efren	L-L	6-0	200	5-14-86	.317	.293	.328	133	492	76	156	36	6	12	73	42	2	0	7	78	5	5	.488	.368
Pettit, Chris	R-R	6-0	200	8-11-84	.167	.109	.193	59	209	23	35	8	2	1	14	7	5	0	3	51	3	4	.268	.263
Richardson, Kevin	R-R	6-3	230	9-12-80	.278	.306	.263	73	241	35	67	17	1	10	45	22	5	0	0	90	0	1	.481	.351
Romine, Andrew	B-R	6-1	190	12-24-85	.281	.261	.289	105	381	67	107	9	2	4	35	45	4	0	0	87	23	6	.346	.337
Sandoval, Freddy	B-R	6-1	205	8-16-82	.280	.244	.293	44	157	24	44	7	1	4	20	14	1	0	3	29	5	2	.414	.337
Velazquez, Gil	R-R	6-2	190	10-17-79	.328	.308	.336	123	427	78	140	25	5	8	58	49	4	0	4	60	17	6	.466	.399
Willits, Reggie	B-R	5-11	185	5-30-81	.260	.284	.247	65	227	36	59	5	2	0	15	44	2	0	0	46	5	4	.300	.385

Pitching	B-T	HT	WT	DOB	W	L	ERA	G	GS	CG	SV	IP	H	R	ER	HR	BB	SO	AVG	vLH	vRH	K/9	BB/9
Bay, Bear	R-R	6-3	170	8-7-83	8	11	5.19	28	25	2	0	160	207	98	92	24	40	95	.322	.316	.327	5.35	2.25
Bell, Trevor	L-R	6-2	200	10-12-86	2	5	6.27	11	10	0	0	56	71	41	39	10	13	49	.306	.333	.291	7.88	2.09
Berg, Jeremy	R-R	6-0	180	7-17-86	1	1	4.70	43	0	0	3	61	64	34	32	1	24	47	.281	.347	.233	6.90	3.52
Brasier, Ryan	R-R	6-0	205	8-26-87	2	1	5.00	25	0	0	3	27	26	16	15	2	9	26	.257	.262	.254	8.67	3.00
Browning, Barret	L-L	6-2	205	12-28-84	2	1	4.61	50	2	0	0	66	67	38	34	5	35	47	.280	.228	.319	6.38	4.75
Bulger, Jason	R-R	6-4	210	12-6-78	1	0	4.03	35	0	0	1	38	31	17	17	7	17	49	.230	.182	.263	11.61	4.03
Cassevah, Bobby	R-R	6-3	220	9-11-85	1	3	4.64	18	0	0	0	21	23	13	11	2	10	12	.264	.263	.265	5.06	4.22
Chaffee, Ryan	R-R	6-2	195	5-18-88	1	1	6.52	4	1	0	0	10	13	8	7	3	4	8	.317	.250	.345	7.45	3.72
Chatwood, Tyler	R-R	6-0	185	12-16-89	1	2	5.06	4	4	0	0	16	21	11	9	2	11	11	.323	.409	.279	6.19	6.19
Correa, Manuarys	R-R	6-3	170	1-5-89	0	0	0.00	1	0	0	0	3	2	0	0	0	2	3	.222	.000	.333	10.13	6.75
Diaz, Amalio	R-R	6-2	170	9-10-86	4	2	5.85	34	1	0	0	60	65	50	39	5	37	42	.286	.315	.268	6.30	5.55
Flores, Manuel	L-L	6-2	170	6-1-87	0	0	7.50	1	1	0	0	6	8	5	5	1	0	5	.333	.300	.357	7.50	0.00
Geltz, Steve	R-R	5-10	170	11-1-87	0	0	21.60	2	0	0	0	2	4	4	4	0	2	1	.444	.750	.200	5.40	10.80
Jepsen, Kevin	R-R	6-3	230	7-26-84	1	3	4.45	24	0	0	7	28	32	14	14	4	8	20	.291	.367	.230	6.35	2.54
Junge, Eric	R-R	6-5	220	1-5-77	8	9	5.12	25	25	2	0	160	179	97	91	23	45	102	.288	.296	.283	5.74	2.53
Kazmir, Scott	L-L	6-0	195	1-24-84	0	5	17.02	5	5	0	0	12	22	30	20	0	20	14	.355	.294	.378	8.22	11.74
Ketchner, Ryan	L-L	6-1	190	4-19-82	6	6	6.12	24	18	1	1	107	142	77	73	22	46	50	.326	.317	.330	4.19	3.86
Kohn, Michael	R-R	6-0	200	6-26-86	1	3	4.10	46	0	0	12	48	47	27	22	5	20	64	.253	.308	.213	11.92	3.72
Lawrence, Brian	R-R	6-0	195	5-14-76	2	5	8.07	7	7	0	0	32	48	31	29	5	8	21	.345	.364	.333	5.85	2.23
Meyer, Matt	L-L	6-4	200	1-17-85	1	2	2.30	14	0	0	0	16	15	11	4	1	15	15	.246	.214	.255	8.62	6.32
Ortega, Anthony	R-R	6-0	185	8-24-85	1	3	8.23	20	3	0	0	35	54	35	32	9	15	28	.375	.468	.305	7.20	3.86
Oye, Matt	R-R	6-5	230	2-25-86	0	1	18.90	1	1	0	0	3	8	7	7	0	3	0	.571	.545	.667	0.00	8.10
Palmer, Matt	R-R	6-2	235	3-21-79	9	11	6.44	24	24	0	0	137	170	105	98	14	65	109	.313	.300	.322	7.16	4.27
Pena, Ariel	R-R	6-3	186	5-20-89	0	0	2.25	1	1	0	0	4	4	7	3	1	0	4	.389	1.000	.313	6.75	9.00
Ramirez, Horacio	L-L	6-1	220	11-24-79	3	2	3.96	45	1	0	6	52	52	23	23	8	15	21	.271	.224	.296	3.61	2.58
Rodriguez, Francisco	R-R	6-1	220	2-26-83	0	1	27.00	6	1	0	0	5	12	16	14	1	8	5	.480	.333	.526	9.64	15.43
Shoemaker, Matt	R-R	6-2	225	9-27-86	0	2	8.14	4	4	0	0	21	28	19	19	3	12	12	.326	.321	.333	5.14	5.14
Tullo, Aaron	R-R	6-3	195	3-9-88	0	0	0.00	1	0	0	0	1	0	0	0	0	2	0	.000	.000	.000	0.00	18.00
Williams, Jerome	R-R	6-3	240	12-4-81	7	2	3.91	11	10	1	0	74	78	36	32	10	15	60	.276	.300	.262	7.33	1.83

Fielding

Catcher	PCT	G	PO	A	E	DP	PB
Armstrong	.982	62	338	39	7	5	6
Conger	.983	22	158	14	3	1	1
Mercado	1.000	5	26	8	0	2	1
Richardson	.996	68	407	45	2	4	6

First Base	PCT	G	PO	A	E	DP
Baisley	1.000	3	26	0	0	5

McAnulty	1.000	11	79	4	0	9
Navarro	.998	132	1285	69	3	140
Pettit	1.000	3	11	0	0	4
Richardson	1.000	1	6	1	0	1

Second Base	PCT	G	PO	A	E	DP
Almanzar	.917	2	5	6	1	5
Amarista	.990	53	107	177	3	50

Bailey	.957	14	21	45	3	9
Melillo	.941	6	4	12	1	3
Romine	1.000	25	44	74	0	19
Sandoval	.907	14	14	25	4	9
Velazquez	.995	40	80	123	1	32

Third Base	PCT	G	PO	A	E	DP
Baisley	.973	120	85	270	10	36

LOS ANGELES ANGELS

Melillo	.000	1	0	0	0 0
Romine	.955	8	4	17	1 1
Sandoval	1.000	7	2	14	0 0
Velazquez	.946	12	6	29	2 1

Shortstop	PCT	G	PO	A	E	DP
Amarista	1.000	6	6	23	0	5
Aybar	.800	1	1	3	1	3
Romine	.983	69	114	223	6	55

Velazquez	.968	70	107	229	11	55

Outfield	PCT	G	PO	A	E	DP
Amarista	.947	30	52	2	3	1
Auer	.995	90	192	8	1	3
Bailey	1.000	8	8	0	0	0
Castillo	1.000	5	10	3	0	1
Karcich	1.000	3	6	1	0	0
Kiniry	1.000	38	54	1	0	1

Lopez	1.000	6	9	1	0 0
McAnulty	1.000	20	19	2	0 0
Melillo	1.000	21	21	2	0 0
Moore	.963	107	226	9	9 1
Navarro	1.000	1	2	0	0 0
Pettit	1.000	48	63	4	0 1
Sandoval	1.000	22	28	0	0 0
Velazquez	1.000	1	2	0	0 0
Willits	.975	61	116	1	3 0

ARKANSAS TRAVELERS

DOUBLE-A

TEXAS LEAGUE

Batting	B-T	HT	WT	DOB	AVG	vLH	vRH	G	AB	R	H	2B	3B	HR	RBI	BB	HBP	SH	SF	SO	SB	CS	SLG	OBP
Bailey, Dwayne	B-R	6-2	185	8-11-86	.306	.318	.300	18	62	8	19	5	0	0	7	9	1	0	0	16	2	1	.387	.403
Baird, Dillon	L-R	6-3	190	1-13-88	.196	.065	.227	46	163	14	32	2	1	1	10	12	2	0	1	36	1	1	.239	.258
Bandy, Jett	R-R	6-4	210	3-26-90	.500	.000	.500	1	2	1	1	0	0	1	1	0	0	0	0	0	0	0	2.000	.500
Blackburn, Mitch	L-R	5-8	180	12-21-87	.500	.000	.667	1	4	0	2	0	0	0	0	0	0	0	0	0	0	0	.500	.500
Brossman, Jay	R-R	6-1		1-17-85	.247	.231	.255	22	73	10	18	2	1	2	12	6	0	0	0	17	3	0	.384	.304
Campos, Jesus	R-R	5-10	175	3-6-88	.167	.133	.200	11	30	3	5	2	0	0	5	3	0	0	0	10	0	0	.233	.242
Castillo, Angel	R-R	6-3	195	6-7-89	.216	.158	.245	105	347	44	75	12	1	6	23	23	7	0	3	104	16	5	.308	.276
Cusick, Matt	L-R	5-10	190	5-5-86	.261	.225	.269	63	207	31	54	5	2	4	21	40	0	0	0	28	2	2	.362	.381
Fuller, Clay	B-R	6-2	190	6-17-87	.249	.268	.241	85	277	42	69	10	1	8	34	23	1	0	2	68	10	6	.379	.307
Gailen, Blake	L-L	5-9	180	3-27-85	.208	.227	.203	29	101	12	21	6	2	2	13	17	0	0	0	15	3	2	.366	.322
Giovinazzo, Chris	R-R	6-0	205	11-30-88	.130	.333	.000	8	23	0	3	1	0	0	0	2	0	0	0	3	0	1	.174	.200
Harris, David	B-R	6-0	185	3-10-87	.000	.000	.000	2	2	0	0	0	0	0	0	0	0	0	0	2	0	0	.000	.000
Jacobo, Gabe	R-R	6-3	200	4-14-87	.270	.303	.254	86	341	40	92	13	4	10	49	17	4	0	4	72	2	1	.419	.309
Jimenez, Luis	R-R	6-1	205	1-18-88	.290	.278	.295	125	490	62	142	40	1	18	94	27	11	0	9	72	15	6	.486	.335
Kiniry, Rian	L-R	6-0	180	12-12-86	.111	.000	.120	10	27	2	3	0	0	0	5	0	0	0	0	9	2	2	.111	.250
Long, Matt	L-R	5-11	180	4-30-87	.282	.375	.234	17	71	15	20	5	1	2	11	8	1	0	2	10	8	0	.465	.354
Lopez, Roberto	R-R	6-0	195	10-1-85	.275	.288	.269	92	331	39	91	30	1	12	40	32	9	0	2	59	2	4	.480	.353
Lowrance, Marvin	L-L	6-0	215	7-16-84	.150	.083	.179	12	40	7	6	1	0	0	2	6	0	0	0	12	0	0	.175	.261
Mercado, Orlando	R-R	5-9	220	3-13-85	.266	.283	.259	61	203	15	54	10	0	4	26	18	2	0	3	34	2	3	.374	.327
Mount, Ryan	L-R	6-0	190	8-17-86	.329	.375	.299	47	161	27	53	12	1	5	34	19	3	0	4	39	9	0	.509	.401
Perez, Darwin	B-R	5-10	160	7-27-89	.257	.250	.260	121	424	61	109	15	6	2	51	69	6	0	4	100	23	6	.335	.366
Pettit, Chris	R-R	6-0	200	8-15-84	.195	.192	.197	65	246	40	48	13	1	7	34	29	7	0	4	74	15	2	.341	.294
Ramirez, Carlos	R-R	5-11	210	3-19-88	.222	.000	.333	4	9	1	2	0	0	0	1	0	0	0	0	1	1	0	.222	.222
Rosario, Alberto	R-R	5-10	190	1-10-87	.228	.209	.235	89	290	32	66	6	1	3	26	23	4	0	3	40	5	1	.286	.291
Sumi, Ikko	R-R	5-9	200	10-20-87	.167	.000	.167	2	6	1	0	0	0	0	0	0	0	0	0	0	0	0	.167	.167
Townsend, Jon	R-R	6-0	190	9-24-84	.262	.163	.313	53	145	16	38	7	0	2	17	15	0	0	3	37	1	2	.352	.325
Trout, Mike	R-R	6-1	200	8-7-91	.326	.355	.313	91	353	82	115	18	13	11	38	45	9	0	1	76	33	10	.544	.414
Younger, Adam	R-R	6-2	207	8-25-85	.178	.154	.191	24	73	7	13	3	1	0	2	6	0	0	1	27	1	1	.247	.238

Pitching	B-T	HT	WT	DOB	W	L	ERA	G	GS	CG	SV	IP	H	R	ER	HR	BB	SO	AVG	vLH	vRH	K/9	BB/9
Arenas, Orangel	R-R	6-0	200	3-31-89	9	10	4.48	25	25	0	0	149	176	86	74	12	39	67	.296	.309	.285	4.06	2.36
Berg, Jeremy	R-R	6-0	180	7-17-86	2	1	3.65	9	0	0	0	12	13	5	5	2	3	10	.295	.474	.160	7.30	2.19
Brasier, Ryan	R-R	6-0	205	8-26-87	0	1	0.71	25	0	0	16	25	18	3	2	1	14	26	.198	.135	.241	9.24	4.97
Carpenter, David	R-R	6-3	180	9-1-87	1	0	0.00	19	0	0	5	19	12	0	0	0	5	16	.182	.219	.147	7.71	2.41
Cendejas, Eric	R-R	6-0	175	1-28-88	0	0	0.00	2	0	0	0	2	1	0	0	0	0	1	.125	.200	.000	3.86	0.00
Fish, Robert	L-L	6-2	230	1-19-88	1	0	3.26	24	0	0	2	30	21	11	11	1	18	41	.200	.256	.161	12.16	5.34
Geltz, Steve	R-R	5-10	170	11-1-87	3	3	3.09	32	0	0	0	47	31	16	16	5	14	67	.190	.239	.152	12.92	2.70
Hurst, Kyle	R-R	6-4	230	8-23-85	2	0	4.50	2	2	0	0	10	17	6	5	2	2	6	.370	.286	.440	5.40	1.80
Kiely, Tim	R-R	6-1	190	8-26-85	0	1	9.00	2	0	0	0	3	3	4	3	1	1	2	.250	.250	.250	6.00	3.00
McKiernan, Eddie	R-R	5-11	160	3-21-89	9	12	5.22	27	20	3	1	140	156	91	81	23	31	93	.280	.313	.253	5.99	2.00
Meyer, Matt	L-L	6-4	220	1-17-85	1	2	2.87	15	0	0	2	16	5	6	5	0	13	27	.096	.036	.167	15.51	7.47
Oye, Matt	R-R	6-5	230	2-25-86	0	2	7.36	3	2	0	0	11	16	11	9	2	5	6	.333	.292	.375	4.91	4.09
Perez, Jose	R-R	6-2	180	9-14-87	2	0	3.65	9	0	0	0	12	9	6	5	1	12	16	.200	.267	.167	11.68	8.76
Piazza, Mike	R-R	6-4	205	11-24-86	0	1	3.26	20	0	0	0	30	28	14	11	4	19	25	.243	.246	.241	7.42	5.64
Reckling, Trevor	L-L	6-2	205	5-22-89	4	7	3.73	17	17	2	0	99	104	51	41	11	35	63	.274	.269	.276	5.73	3.18
Richards, Garrett	R-R	6-3	215	5-27-88	12	2	3.15	22	21	3	0	143	123	58	50	10	40	103	.233	.257	.214	6.48	2.52
Sattler, Dan	R-R	6-3	190	11-11-83	1	3	5.40	19	0	0	0	30	24	19	18	1	21	29	.231	.233	.230	8.70	6.30
Scholl, Chris	R-R	5-11	195	10-27-87	4	3	2.32	32	7	0	0	85	61	25	22	7	22	66	.196	.195	.198	6.96	2.32
Shoemaker, Matt	R-R	6-2	225	9-27-86	12	5	2.48	23	23	5	0	156	132	47	43	17	35	129	.228	.258	.201	7.43	2.01
Taylor, Drew	R-L	6-2	195	8-18-86	2	11	5.14	29	19	0	0	112	125	86	64	13	71	73	.287	.308	.277	5.87	5.71
Van Mil, Loek	R-R	7-1	220	9-15-84	3	5	2.04	30	1	0	0	66	53	22	15	4	23	46	.220	.227	.213	6.24	3.12

Fielding

Catcher	PCT	G	PO	A	E	DP	PB
Bandy	1.000	1	4	0	0	0	0
Mercado	.989	50	328	32	4	2	2
Ramirez	1.000	4	16	1	0	0	0
Rosario	.989	89	572	76	7	8	8
Sumi	1.000	2	20	0	0	0	0

First Base	PCT	G	PO	A	E	DP
Baird	.991	25	199	11	2	14

Brossman	.979	17	129	10	3	13
Jacobo	.990	67	538	39	6	42
Lopez	.969	11	90	5	3	6
Mercado	1.000	3	16	3	0	0
Pettit	.988	19	154	17	2	17
Townsend	1.000	1	13	0	0	2
Younger	1.000	1	6	0	0	1

Second Base	PCT	G	PO	A	E	DP
Bailey	.923	14	15	33	4	3
Blackburn	1.000	1	2	3	0	0
Campos	1.000	7	8	16	0	2
Cusick	.987	56	85	136	3	27
Mount	.932	35	57	93	11	25
Perez	1.000	3	5	8	0	2
Townsend	.990	24	40	57	1	11

	PCT	G	PO	A	E	DP
Younger	1.000	8	8	22	0	2
Third Base	**PCT**	**G**	**PO**	**A**	**E**	**DP**
Brossman	.900	5	2	7	1	0
Campos	1.000	2	2	1	0	0
Jacobo	.813	13	8	18	6	4
Jimenez	.940	101	98	186	18	19
Townsend	.941	17	11	37	3	1
Younger	.938	6	3	12	1	0

Shortstop	PCT	G	PO	A	E	DP
Bailey	.947	4	8	10	1	1
Campos	.700	2	5	2	3	0
Perez	.981	117	168	305	9	57
Townsend	.896	12	14	29	5	7
Younger	.929	7	5	8	1	2
Outfield	**PCT**	**G**	**PO**	**A**	**E**	**DP**
Castillo	.995	100	177	7	1	2
Fuller	.990	82	191	5	2	0
Gailen	.984	27	60	3	1	2

	PCT	G	PO	A	E	DP
Giovinazzo	1.000	8	6	1	0	0
Harris	.000	1	0	0	0	0
Jacobo	1.000	2	3	0	0	0
Kiniry	1.000	9	23	0	0	0
Long	1.000	17	64	2	0	1
Lopez	1.000	44	74	6	0	0
Lowrance	1.000	4	3	0	0	0
Mount	1.000	8	10	0	0	0
Pettit	.987	37	76	1	1	0
Trout	.995	89	203	4	1	1

INLAND EMPIRE 66ERS

HIGH CLASS A

LOS ANGELES ANGELS

CALIFORNIA LEAGUE

Batting	B-T	HT	WT	DOB	AVG	vLH	vRH	G	AB	R	H	2B	3B	HR	RBI	BB	HBP	SH	SF	SO	SB	CS	SLG	OBP
Alliman, Terrell	R-R	6-3	185	10-15-88	.071	.182	.000	9	28	2	2	0	0	0	1	3	0	0	0	8	1	0	.071	.161
Bailey, Dwayne	B-R	6-2	185	8-11-86	.275	.278	.274	57	200	34	55	9	3	1	25	23	4	0	1	47	10	2	.365	.360
Baird, Dillon	L-R	6-3	190	1-13-88	.259	.154	.289	50	174	26	45	16	1	5	27	15	0	0	2	48	1	1	.448	.314
Bass, Justin	R-R	5-11	190	4-6-89	.289	.292	.288	53	180	24	52	10	2	1	20	15	4	0	3	22	7	4	.383	.351
Blackburn, Mitch	L-R	5-8	180	12-21-87	.239	.667	.135	17	46	4	11	2	0	0	1	8	0	0	0	12	0	0	.283	.352
Brossman, Jay	R-R	6-1	210	1-17-85	.182	.000	.267	6	22	3	4	1	0	1	6	1	0	0	1	8	1	0	.364	.208
Broussard, Ryan	R-R	5-11	181	9-15-89	.143	.000	.167	6	7	1	1	0	0	0	1	0	0	0	0	3	0	0	.143	.250
Calhoun, Kole	L-L	5-10	200	10-14-87	.324	.303	.332	133	512	94	166	36	6	22	99	73	4	0	4	96	20	10	.547	.410
Campos, Jesus	R-R	5-10	175	3-6-88	.167	.200	.160	13	30	4	5	0	0	0	4	2	0	0	1	8	0	0	.167	.212
Cusick, Matt	L-R	5-10	190	5-5-86	.190	.200	.188	6	21	4	4	2	1	0	2	4	0	0	0	2	0	0	.381	.320
Gomez, Rolando	L-R	5-7	145	6-18-89	.143	.000	.167	2	7	0	1	1	0	0	1	1	0	0	0	2	0	0	.286	.250
Grichuk, Randal	R-R	6-1	195	8-13-91	.283	.100	.326	14	53	13	15	4	2	1	6	3	0	0	1	13	0	0	.491	.316
Haerther, Casey	R-R	6-2	210	10-5-87	.293	.292	.293	117	437	54	128	34	0	8	68	24	2	0	3	73	1	2	.426	.330
Hannick, Chris	R-R	5-10	190	9-26-88	.000	.000	.000	3	8	0	0	0	0	0	0	1	1	0	0	2	0	0	.000	.200
Harris, David	R-R	6-0	185	3-10-87	.309	.275	.323	41	136	22	42	8	3	3	21	23	2	0	3	42	3	1	.478	.409
Hernandez, Brian	R-R	6-1	195	11-25-88	.136	.000	.176	7	22	0	3	1	0	0	1	1	0	0	0	6	0	0	.182	.174
Irvine, Steven	R-R	5-10	185	9-7-87	.248	.235	.252	99	319	41	79	18	4	3	35	27	4	0	5	69	4	4	.357	.310
Jimenez, Jose	L-R	5-10	240	1-2-87	.271	.254	.276	84	291	35	79	17	0	6	35	40	0	0	2	54	1	0	.392	.357
Karcich, Jon	R-R	6-2	195	9-10-87	.208	.232	.200	75	221	27	46	14	1	2	21	20	2	0	1	61	4	3	.308	.279
Kiniry, Rian	L-R	6-0	180	12-12-86	.250	.263	.247	73	276	52	69	7	5	2	20	35	3	0	2	56	14	8	.333	.339
Long, Matt	L-R	5-11	180	4-30-87	.301	.271	.313	121	481	104	145	29	11	16	73	56	10	0	6	86	26	12	.507	.382
Oliver, Eric	R-R	6-1	215	1-29-87	.266	.375	.242	59	222	31	59	13	0	6	39	29	5	0	2	38	2	2	.405	.360
Parks, Jarrod	R-R	6-0	192	5-24-88	.333	.000	.353	7	18	3	6	1	0	0	1	3	0	0	0	4	0	0	.389	.429
Phillips, P.J.	R-R	6-3	170	9-23-86	.244	.292	.226	25	86	9	21	7	0	0	8	10	0	0	1	31	2	2	.326	.320
Ramirez, Carlos	R-R	5-11	210	3-19-88	.348	.309	.365	52	181	28	63	21	0	4	28	16	2	0	2	33	1	0	.530	.403
Rodriguez, Jean	R-R	5-10	205	3-27-89	.143	.000	.167	3	7	1	1	0	0	1	2	0	0	0	0	1	0	0	.571	.143
Segura, Jean	R-R	5-11	160	3-17-90	.281	.217	.302	44	185	26	52	9	4	3	21	15	1	0	1	26	18	6	.422	.337
Sumi, Ikko	R-R	5-9	200	10-20-87	.172	.200	.158	13	29	2	5	1	0	0	4	3	0	0	0	6	0	0	.207	.250
Townsend, Jon	R-R	6-0	190	9-24-84	.349	.357	.345	13	43	7	15	4	0	1	8	4	2	0	0	13	3	2	.512	.429
Wells, Vernon	R-R	6-1	230	12-8-78	.200	.250	.000	2	5	3	1	1	0	0	3	2	0	0	0	1	0	0	.400	.429
Willits, Reggie	B-R	5-11	185	5-30-81	.200	.333	.143	5	20	1	4	1	0	0	3	3	0	0	0	5	0	0	.250	.304
Wing, Michael	R-R	6-1	180	10-25-88	.317	.395	.285	73	293	50	93	17	2	11	54	47	6	0	2	53	1	7	.502	.365
Witherspoon, Travis	R-R	6-2	190	4-16-89	.279	.357	.259	16	68	15	19	4	0	1	10	5	1	0	0	14	2	2	.382	.338
Yakubik, Jerod	L-L	6-2	205	11-30-87	.571	1.000	.500	2	7	1	4	0	0	0	0	0	0	0	0	1	0	0	.571	.571
Younger, Adam	R-R	6-2	207	8-25-85	.234	.175	.257	62	209	25	49	9	3	7	36	20	8	0	4	83	0	1	.407	.320

Pitching	B-T	HT	WT	DOB	W	L	ERA	G	GS	CG	SV	IP	H	R	ER	HR	BB	SO	AVG	vLH	vRH	K/9	BB/9
Boshers, Buddy	L-L	6-3	205	5-9-88	2	5	4.30	43	4	0	1	75	88	43	36	7	41	61	.299	.256	.319	7.29	4.90
Carpenter, David	R-R	6-3	180	9-1-87	0	1	0.93	25	0	0	11	29	23	6	3	1	9	36	.219	.304	.153	11.17	2.79
Cendejas, Eric	R-R	6-0	175	1-28-88	0	0	3.86	7	0	0	0	7	7	4	3	0	1	8	.269	.222	.294	10.29	1.29
Chaffee, Ryan	R-R	6-2	195	5-18-88	2	10	7.26	30	14	0	0	97	114	84	78	11	48	87	.284	.219	.325	8.10	4.47
Correa, Manuarys	R-R	6-3	170	1-5-89	0	0	9.82	5	0	0	0	7	11	10	8	2	4	5	.344	.500	.222	6.14	4.91
DeJiulio, Frank	R-R	6-3	185	8-22-89	0	0	67.50	1	0	0	0	1	3	5	5	0	2	1	.600	1.000	.500	13.50	27.00
Downs, Scott	L-L	6-2	210	3-17-76	1	1	9.00	2	1	0	0	2	5	2	2	0	1	1	.455	.200	.667	4.50	4.50
Evans, Cody	R-R	6-5	190	9-3-83	2	0	3.18	7	3	0	0	28	28	13	10	1	8	11	.255	.200	.231	5.96	0.40
Flores, Manuel	L-L	6-2	170	6-1-87	13	9	5.59	27	26	0	0	158	217	119	98	20	34	119	.321	.286	.331	6.79	1.94
Graham, Caleb	R-R	6-3	220	1-18-87	1	2	3.72	22	0	0	0	36	28	15	15	4	6	36	.214	.244	.200	8.92	1.49
Haynes, Jeremy	R-R	6-2	180	5-28-86	1	2	9.39	4	3	0	0	15	20	16	16	2	17	14	.345	.423	.281	8.22	9.98
Hellweg, Johnny	R-R	6-9	210	10-29-88	6	4	3.73	28	14	0	0	89	75	43	37	2	59	113	.229	.235	.225	11.38	5.94
Hurst, Kyle	R-R	6-4	230	8-23-85	6	5	5.15	18	15	0	0	86	91	56	49	11	34	62	.265	.190	.318	6.51	3.57
Johnson, Kevin	L-R	6-4	240	8-19-88	3	2	3.33	33	0	0	1	51	52	23	19	6	16	42	.260	.213	.281	7.36	2.81
Kelley, Ty	R-R	6-4	196	8-18-88	0	0	4.91	9	0	0	0	8	9	8	6	2	6	8	.333	.438	.295	11.66	3.68
Kenney, Mike	R-R	6-4	212	8-16-86	5	6	5.07	43	0	0	6	71	87	45	40	5	25	56	.301	.363	.267	7.10	3.17
Locke, Stephen	L-L	6-1	188	5-6-86	0	1	10.57	2	2	0	0	8	15	14	9	2	8	1	.441	.333	.452	1.17	9.39
Lopez, Baudilio	R-R	6-0	190	11-20-90	0	0	10.50	5	0	0	0	6	9	7	7	0	5	2	.346	.200	.438	7.50	7.50
Nabors, Kevin	R-R	6-2	220	2-2-88	1	2	6.55	36	0	0	2	44	54	43	32	5	33	42	.286	.304	.278	8.59	6.75
Oye, Matt	R-R	6-5	230	2-25-86	7	4	4.87	32	6	0	4	68	68	40	37	6	25	54	.268	.289	.256	7.11	3.29
Pena, Ariel	R-R	6-3	186	5-20-89	10	6	4.45	27	27	1	0	152	154	88	75	10	81	180	.264	.292	.247	10.68	4.81
Perez, Jose	R-R	6-2	180	9-14-87	2	1	2.33	12	0	0	3	19	16	5	5	0	7	23	.216	.290	.163	10.71	3.26

Pitching	B-T	HT	WT	DOB	W	L	ERA	G	GS	CG	SV	IP	H	R	ER	HR	BB	SO	AVG	vLH	vRH	K/9	BB/9
Piazza, Mike	R-R	6-4	205	11-24-86	0	1	2.78	20	0	0	0	36	24	14	11	0	13	42	.183	.188	.181	10.60	3.28
Pineiro, Joel	R-R	6-0	200	9-25-78	0	0	0.00	1	1	0	0	6	6	3	0	0	2	2	.286	.364	.200	3.18	3.18
Pugliese, Nick	R-R	6-1	205	9-18-85	1	0	7.27	6	0	0	0	9	10	7	7	1	4	6	.270	.294	.250	6.23	4.15
Rodney, Fernando	R-R	5-11	220	3-18-77	0	0	9.00	2	1	0	0	2	2	2	2	0	1	3	.250	.200	.333	13.50	4.50
Russell, Max	L-L	6-2	210	9-21-88	1	2	4.17	7	7	0	0	41	42	21	19	4	8	34	.268	.231	.280	7.46	1.76
Sattler, Dan	R-R	6-3	190	11-11-83	0	0	0.00	2	0	0	0	3	3	0	0	0	0	4	.250	.333	.167	12.00	0.00
Schugel, A.J.	R-R	6-1	190	6-27-89	1	2	5.03	4	4	0	0	20	22	11	11	1	6	15	.278	.357	.235	6.86	2.75
Tillman, Daniel	R-R	6-1	205	3-14-89	1	0	4.50	7	0	0	2	8	7	6	4	1	2	8	.212	.154	.250	9.00	2.25
Wiedenbauer, John	L-L	6-3	185	1-16-88	0	0	1.74	9	1	0	0	10	5	2	2	0	2	6	.139	.154	.130	5.23	1.74
Williams, Harold	L-L	6-4	190	9-23-84	2	5	6.79	15	11	0	0	54	62	41	41	8	29	60	.287	.246	.302	9.94	4.80

Fielding

Catcher	PCT	G	PO	A	E	DP	PB
Hannick	.955	3	16	5	1	0	0
Jimenez	.983	82	619	68	12	7	9
Ramirez	.987	52	405	46	6	2	2
Rodriguez	1.000	3	10	0	0	0	0
Sumi	.967	12	73	15	3	0	2

First Base	PCT	G	PO	A	E	DP
Bailey	1.000	1	10	1	0	0
Baird	.980	5	47	2	1	2
Calhoun	1.000	31	302	14	0	24
Haerther	.984	63	519	35	9	47
Jimenez	1.000	3	14	1	0	1
Karcich	.988	12	81	3	1	5
Oliver	.996	34	259	20	1	22
Yakubik	1.000	1	7	1	0	0

Second Base	PCT	G	PO	A	E	DP
Bailey	.933	9	12	16	2	5
Bass	.833	2	2	3	1	0
Blackburn	.981	13	15	36	1	10
Broussard	1.000	5	7	4	0	2
Campos	1.000	8	14	13	0	4
Cusick	.875	4	4	10	2	3
Irvine	.987	38	62	88	2	17

	PCT	G	PO	A	E	DP
Karcich	.977	33	52	76	3	13
Townsend	.939	9	21	25	3	6
Wing	.958	47	94	111	9	22
Younger	1.000	1	0	2	0	0

Third Base	PCT	G	PO	A	E	DP
Bailey	.950	33	24	72	5	8
Baird	.867	5	2	11	2	0
Blackburn	.667	2	0	2	1	0
Brossman	1.000	5	5	9	0	2
Campos	1.000	1	0	1	0	0
Cusick	.846	2	3	8	2	0
Haerther	1.000	6	3	8	0	0
Hernandez	1.000	6	4	4	0	1
Irvine	.935	60	31	126	11	13
Karcich	.817	22	14	44	13	3
Parks	.857	7	4	2	1	2
Townsend	1.000	5	1	6	0	2
Wing	1.000	6	5	16	0	1
Younger	1.000	3	2	7	0	0

Shortstop	PCT	G	PO	A	E	DP
Bailey	.912	14	22	30	5	7
Blackburn	1.000	3	7	4	0	0
Broussard	.000	1	0	0	0	0

	PCT	G	PO	A	E	DP
Campos	1.000	5	4	7	0	1
Gomez	.833	2	2	3	1	0
Irvine	.950	10	12	26	2	9
Segura	.974	43	63	128	5	20
Wing	.958	17	24	44	3	8
Younger	.948	58	50	168	12	22

Outfield	PCT	G	PO	A	E	DP
Alliman	1.000	5	8	0	0	0
Bailey	.750	5	3	0	1	0
Bass	.968	37	59	2	2	0
Calhoun	.983	94	171	7	3	0
Grichuk	1.000	14	19	1	0	0
Harris	.984	40	61	2	1	1
Irvine	.000	1	0	0	0	0
Karcich	1.000	8	9	0	0	0
Kiniry	.985	70	130	0	2	0
Long	.983	118	218	16	4	7
Oliver	.875	22	21	0	3	0
Wells	1.000	2	3	0	0	0
Willits	.929	4	13	0	1	0
Witherspoon	.972	16	34	1	1	0
Yakubik	1.000	1	1	0	0	0

CEDAR RAPIDS KERNELS

LOW CLASS A

MIDWEST LEAGUE

Batting	B-T	HT	WT	DOB	AVG	vLH	vRH	G	AB	R	H	2B	3B	HR	RBI	BB	HBP	SH	SF	SO	SB	CS	SLG	OBP
Almanzar, Jean	B-R	5-7	150	2-7-89	.226	.185	.242	92	319	34	72	9	2	3	37	15	1	0	3	61	2	3	.295	.260
Alvarez, Ricky	R-R	5-11	217	2-7-89	.257	.271	.252	126	482	54	124	31	1	10	64	13	13	0	6	96	2	2	.388	.292
Bass, Justin	B-R	5-11	190	4-6-89	.274	.229	.291	66	252	24	69	12	3	0	20	16	2	0	3	38	4	8	.345	.319
Blackburn, Mitch	L-R	5-8	180	12-21-87	.200	.125	.250	6	20	5	4	1	0	0	4	0	0	0	0	4	1	0	.250	.333
Campos, Jesus	R-R	5-10	175	3-6-88	.215	.316	.183	55	158	23	34	4	0	0	9	24	6	0	1	38	0	1	.241	.339
Cruz, Jeremy	R-R	6-1	225	4-19-87	.261	.292	.251	119	448	50	117	27	2	9	55	40	3	0	3	89	10	4	.391	.324
Decker, Brandon	L-R	6-3	240	3-22-88	.231	.160	.253	97	338	43	78	15	3	8	34	38	5	0	2	88	2	3	.364	.316
Eichelberger, Dan	R-R	6-0	175	12-30-87	.186	.125	.210	26	86	10	16	4	0	1	11	5	0	0	2	13	3	2	.267	.226
Giovinazzo, Chris	R-R	6-0	205	11-30-88	.167	.130	.186	16	66	6	11	0	0	3	5	1	0	0	3	23	1	1	.167	.236
Gomez, Rolando	L-R	5-7	145	6-18-89	.261	.221	.274	89	345	42	90	16	8	4	37	22	3	0	5	91	15	5	.388	.307
Grichuk, Randal	R-R	6-1	195	8-13-91	.230	.250	.223	32	122	12	28	7	4	2	13	6	1	0	2	29	0	1	.402	.267
Harris, David	B-R	6-0	185	3-10-87	.229	.198	.241	83	280	44	64	13	0	8	35	50	6	0	4	95	12	5	.361	.353
Hatton, Wes	R-R	5-10	165	12-28-90	.200	.167	.213	78	280	27	56	5	7	4	37	23	2	0	1	79	4	3	.311	.265
Heid, Drew	L-R	5-10	175	12-14-87	.270	.172	.299	30	126	15	34	5	0	0	10	9	5	0	1	21	7	2	.310	.340
Hernandez, Brian	R-R	6-1	195	11-25-88	.227	.304	.203	27	97	7	22	4	0	3	17	4	0	0	1	15	1	0	.361	.255
Irvine, Steven	R-R	5-10	185	9-7-87	.176	.000	.300	7	17	3	3	0	0	0	1	6	0	0	0	4	1	0	.176	.391
Jones, Ryan	L-L	6-0	200	5-19-88	.145	.231	.119	18	55	10	8	2	0	0	4	9	4	0	0	19	3	1	.182	.309
Larson, Francis	R-R	6-0	195	5-5-88	.326	.400	.310	23	86	10	28	3	0	2	6	4	1	0	0	21	0	0	.430	.363
Lugo, Carlos	R-R	6-0	190	11-20-89	.208	.300	.143	16	48	4	10	2	0	0	4	3	0	0	0	13	0	0	.250	.356
Martinez, Drew	L-L	5-10	170	4-4-89	.160	.000	.182	9	25	2	4	0	0	0	1	2	0	0	0	8	1	0	.160	.222
Nidiffer, Marcus	R-R	6-2	205	1-13-87	.230	.231	.230	68	204	27	47	11	1	6	24	25	16	0	1	61	2	0	.382	.358
Pardo, Braulio	B-R	5-11	180	10-10-86	.158	.100	.222	7	19	3	3	0	0	0	0	3	0	0	0	6	0	0	.158	.273
Parks, Jarrod	R-R	6-0	192	5-24-88	.169	.133	.179	21	71	5	12	2	0	0	7	8	4	0	0	19	1	0	.197	.289
Ramirez, Carlos	R-R	5-11	210	3-19-88	.259	.143	.287	31	108	20	28	3	0	3	12	15	4	0	1	17	1	2	.370	.367
Witherspoon, Travis	R-R	6-2	190	4-16-89	.245	.252	.243	102	404	60	99	16	4	12	42	36	5	0	3	103	44	9	.394	.313
Workman, Andy	R-R	6-1	200	11-16-88	.171	.000	.240	11	35	3	6	1	0	1	4	5	0	0	0	15	3	0	.286	.275
Yakubik, Jerod	L-L	6-2	205	11-30-87	.227	.222	.229	19	66	4	15	2	0	0	3	0	0	0	1	11	0	1	.258	.257
Young, Kirby	L-R	6-3	195	7-4-88	.100	.000	.100	3	10	1	1	0	0	0	0	0	0	0	0	6	0	0	.100	.100

Pitching	B-T	HT	WT	DOB	W	L	ERA	G	GS	CG	SV	IP	H	R	ER	HR	BB	SO	AVG	vLH	vRH	K/9	BB/9
Baez, Suammy	R-R	6-4	220	9-28-88	1	6	4.72	10	10	0	0	48	50	31	25	1	25	42	.263	.299	.239	7.93	4.72
Correa, Manuarys	R-R	6-3	170	1-5-89	1	1	2.77	32	0	0	3	55	51	20	17	2	14	52	.245	.284	.217	8.46	2.28
Diaz, Jairo	R-R	6-0	195	5-27-91	0	3	8.20	4	4	0	0	19	24	18	17	1	12	10	.320	.360	.300	4.82	5.79
Diemer, Brian	R-R	6-5	240	3-25-88	9	11	4.07	26	25	2	0	133	145	76	60	2	44	75	.277	.296	.260	5.09	2.98

Pitching

Pitching	B-T	HT	WT	DOB	W	L	ERA	G	GS	CG	SV	IP	H	R	ER	HR	BB	SO	AVG	vLH	vRH	K/9	BB/9
Fowler, Seth	R-R	6-3	230	3-3-87	3	5	6.71	20	8	0	1	56	77	44	42	5	25	36	.335	.408	.280	5.75	3.99
George, Bryant	R-R	5-10	178	7-17-88	0	0	1.42	5	0	0	0	6	5	1	1	0	3	5	.217	.300	.154	7.11	4.26
Graham, Caleb	R-R	6-3	220	1-18-87	1	2	3.45	18	0	0	2	31	23	13	12	2	10	35	.209	.243	.192	10.05	2.87
Gregersen, Erik	R-R	6-5	225	9-19-86	1	0	2.25	18	0	0	0	28	20	12	7	1	16	30	.192	.143	.226	9.64	5.14
Jang, Pill Joon	R-R	6-3	190	4-8-88	2	6	5.06	14	14	0	0	75	89	51	42	5	26	45	.301	.326	.276	5.42	3.13
Johnson, Kevin	L-R	6-4	240	8-19-88	1	1	3.38	12	0	0	4	13	9	5	5	1	4	9	.200	.200	.200	6.08	2.70
Kehrer, Tyler	L-L	6-3	210	3-23-88	2	1	4.18	35	0	0	3	47	36	26	22	1	35	55	.214	.172	.240	10.46	6.65
Kelley, Ty	R-R	6-4	196	8-18-88	0	0	3.18	9	0	0	0	17	23	8	6	1	4	9	.324	.344	.308	4.76	2.12
LaTempa, Justin	R-R	6-5	210	11-21-86	5	9	4.31	27	18	0	1	111	112	61	53	10	45	72	.267	.360	.182	5.86	3.66
Lopez, Baudilio	R-R	6-1	190	11-20-90	0	1	15.58	3	3	0	0	9	19	16	15	5	6	8	.442	.533	.393	8.31	6.23
Nichols, Heath	R-R	6-2	180	11-23-88	6	7	3.88	20	20	2	0	114	110	62	49	11	45	77	.255	.289	.226	6.10	3.56
Roach, Donn	R-R	6-1	200	12-14-89	5	5	3.45	45	0	0	2	70	73	33	27	1	20	68	.266	.291	.248	8.70	2.56
Robinson, Dakota	L-L	6-3	190	6-5-88	10	3	2.86	43	0	0	8	72	64	26	23	4	16	65	.246	.279	.221	8.09	1.74
Russell, Max	L-L	6-2	210	9-21-88	5	10	3.79	20	20	0	0	114	101	60	48	14	45	85	.237	.240	.236	6.71	3.55
Schugel, A.J.	R-R	6-1	190	6-27-89	4	3	2.59	25	12	0	1	90	73	34	26	2	39	80	.220	.174	.257	7.97	3.89
Tillman, Daniel	R-R	6-1	205	3-14-89	5	3	2.04	36	5	0	12	66	53	21	15	1	32	70	.218	.187	.243	9.50	4.34

Fielding

Catcher	PCT	G	PO	A	E	DP	PB
Larson	.986	20	124	19	2	3	0
Lugo	.971	16	94	8	3	1	0
Nidiffer	.986	68	443	43	7	6	11
Pardo	1.000	7	45	6	0	0	0
Ramirez	.990	31	262	21	3	1	0

First Base	PCT	G	PO	A	E	DP
Alvarez	.987	63	557	37	8	50
Blackburn	1.000	1	7	0	0	0
Cruz	.957	6	43	2	2	3
Decker	.990	70	649	51	7	61
Yakubik	1.000	2	16	1	0	2

Second Base	PCT	G	PO	A	E	DP
Almanzar	.990	42	63	138	2	30
Campos	.960	9	10	14	1	4

	PCT	G	PO	A	E	DP
Gomez	.920	9	16	30	4	9
Hatton	.941	74	121	227	22	44
Hernandez	1.000	5	10	13	0	4
Irvine	1.000	1	1	2	0	0
Young	.882	3	8	7	2	1

Third Base	PCT	G	PO	A	E	DP
Alvarez	.889	36	29	59	11	7
Blackburn	1.000	1	0	1	0	0
Campos	.934	26	18	39	4	3
Cruz	.912	34	22	61	8	2
Hernandez	.963	22	17	60	3	6
Irvine	1.000	3	1	9	0	1
Parks	.897	21	16	36	6	3

Shortstop	PCT	G	PO	A	E	DP
Almanzar	.960	52	67	172	10	28

	PCT	G	PO	A	E	DP
Campos	.956	22	41	68	5	17
Gomez	.924	70	110	180	24	41

Outfield	PCT	G	PO	A	E	DP
Bass	.988	45	78	3	1	1
Cruz	.969	75	116	7	4	3
Eichelberger	.957	25	45	0	2	0
Giovinazzo	.974	16	35	2	1	0
Gomez	.833	4	5	0	1	0
Grichuk	.986	32	62	6	1	0
Harris	.978	54	85	3	2	0
Heid	.933	30	42	0	3	0
Jones	1.000	17	18	2	0	0
Martinez	1.000	9	20	1	0	0
Witherspoon	.987	101	225	8	3	3
Workman	1.000	10	26	0	0	0
Yakubik	1.000	5	6	0	0	0

LOS ANGELES ANGELS

OREM OWLZ

ROOKIE

PIONEER LEAGUE

Batting	B-T	HT	WT	DOB	AVG	vLH	vRH	G	AB	R	H	2B	3B	HR	RBI	BB	HBP	SH	SF	SO	SB	CS	SLG	OBP
Baker, Abel	L-R	6-1	195	10-26-90	.306	.172	.336	48	157	22	48	10	2	4	33	27	1	0	2	43	1	1	.471	.406
Bandy, Jett	R-R	6-4	210	3-26-90	.333	.000	.400	2	6	2	2	1	0	0	2	0	0	0	0	0	0	0	.500	.333
Brewer, Brandon	L-R	5-9	170	4-2-90	.226	.182	.234	34	133	16	30	6	1	0	18	16	0	0	0	24	2	1	.286	.309
Cowart, Kaleb	B-R	6-3	190	6-2-92	.283	.247	.295	72	283	49	80	12	3	7	40	25	5	0	6	81	11	4	.420	.345
Cron Jr., C.J.	R-R	6-4	235	1-5-90	.308	.317	.304	34	143	30	44	5	1	13	41	10	5	0	1	34	0	0	.629	.371
Giovinazzo, Chris	R-R	6-0	205	11-30-88	.256	.227	.266	28	86	17	22	1	0	2	9	14	1	0	0	29	2	1	.337	.366
Gowens, Brennan	L-R	6-0	195	3-14-90	.182	.375	.120	8	33	3	6	0	0	1	4	2	0	0	0	9	0	1	.273	.229
Hairgrove, Trevor	R-R	6-1	185	9-16-89	.254	.281	.242	55	189	34	48	10	1	3	26	22	6	0	3	31	2	1	.365	.345
Hall, Frazier	L-R	6-4	220	6-3-88	.355	.372	.351	62	228	44	81	19	2	9	46	13	3	0	4	46	1	1	.575	.391
Hatton, Wes	R-R	5-10	165	12-28-90	.311	.368	.269	24	90	11	28	6	1	0	16	8	0	0	0	16	3	2	.467	.367
Jones, Ryan	L-L	6-0	200	5-19-88	.319	.295	.327	67	257	51	82	18	7	12	61	26	3	0	2	48	3	3	.584	.385
Larson, Francis	R-R	6-0	195	5-5-88	.241	.176	.268	15	58	8	14	0	1	2	10	3	1	0	0	10	0	0	.379	.290
Lindsey, Taylor	L-R	6-0	195	12-2-91	.362	.343	.368	63	290	64	105	28	6	9	46	13	3	0	1	46	10	4	.593	.394
Lugo, Carlos	R-R	6-0	190	11-20-89	.000	.000	.000	3	7	0	0	0	0	0	1	2	0	0	0	3	0	0	.000	.222
Mahoney, Kyle	R-R	6-2	220	4-24-89	.200	.222	.167	6	15	5	3	0	0	0	2	2	0	0	0	7	0	0	.200	.368
Martinez, Drew	L-L	5-10	170	4-4-89	.289	.294	.287	39	121	16	35	2	0	0	10	17	2	0	1	27	5	1	.306	.383
Mitchell, Gary	L-R	6-4	235	4-4-89	.300	.257	.310	56	180	42	54	11	3	7	39	29	5	0	2	64	6	2	.511	.407
Pacione, Ricky	B-R	5-9	185	4-25-89	.333	.200	.388	29	69	10	23	0	1	0	8	6	0	0	0	6	2	1	.362	.387
Parks, Jarrod	R-R	6-0	192	5-24-88	.419	.333	.441	12	43	12	18	1	1	3	9	5	4	0	0	12	1	0	.698	.519
Ray, Andrew	R-R	6-1	195	5-1-91	.175	.188	.167	43	126	18	22	4	0	2	13	14	1	0	2	44	3	0	.254	.259
Yakubik, Jerod	L-L	6-2	205	11-30-87	.372	.387	.387	60	215	48	80	17	3	1	34	16	8	0	1	30	2	0	.493	.433

Pitching	B-T	HT	WT	DOB	W	L	ERA	G	GS	CG	SV	IP	H	R	ER	HR	BB	SO	AVG	vLH	vRH	K/9	BB/9
Baez, Suammy	R-R	6-4	220	9-28-88	3	3	6.15	17	1	0	1	26	33	21	18	4	6	36	.303	.320	.298	12.30	2.05
Baker, Garrett	L-L	6-5	215	8-1-89	3	0	8.33	18	0	0	0	31	44	30	29	5	14	26	.336	.364	.330	7.47	4.02
Carlin, Junior	L-L	6-2	165	6-4-88	4	0	1.50	17	0	0	1	30	16	6	5	3	7	35	.162	.160	.162	10.50	2.10
Cendejas, Eric	R-R	6-0	175	1-28-88	1	0	3.16	15	0	0	2	26	20	14	9	1	9	21	.217	.278	.203	7.36	3.16
Clevinger, Mike	R-R	6-4	202	12-21-90	0	0	2.25	3	0	0	0	4	3	1	1	0	2	5	.200	.500	.154	11.25	4.50
Crowley, Ryan	L-L	6-3	190	11-15-90	1	2	5.50	12	11	0	0	38	44	28	23	6	4	31	.297	.212	.322	7.41	0.96
George, Bryant	R-R	5-10	178	7-17-88	0	0	0.00	3	0	0	0	5	3	0	0	0	4	7	.167	.400	.077	6.75	5.06
Gregersen, Erik	R-R	6-5	225	9-19-86	2	0	4.86	10	0	0	0	17	10	9	9	1	7	22	.161	.174	.154	11.88	3.78
Jang, Pill Joon	R-R	6-3	190	4-8-88	1	0	0.00	1	1	0	0	6	1	0	0	0	1	3	.059	.500	.000	4.50	1.50
Johnson, Michael	L-L	6-2	175	2-5-91	1	0	3.21	4	3	0	0	14	16	5	5	2	3	8	.296	.333	.294	5.14	1.93
Kinzer, Taylor	R-R	6-3	213	1-7-88	0	0	5.59	8	0	0	1	9	10	6	6	0	2	5	.342	.333	.345	5.59	3.72
Lopez, Baudilio	R-R	6-1	190	11-20-90	3	6	7.01	13	8	0	0	53	76	47	41	8	18	29	.350	.431	.310	4.96	3.08

LOS ANGELES ANGELS (side tab)

Pitching	B-T	HT	WT	DOB	W	L	ERA	G	GS	CG	SV	IP	H	R	ER	HR	BB	SO	AVG	vLH	vRH	K/9	BB/9
Maronde, Nick	B-L	6-3	205	9-5-89	5	0	2.14	11	11	0	0	46	36	12	11	5	15	50	.217	.200	.220	9.71	2.91
Marshall, Kris	L-L	5-9	165	11-13-87	0	0	7.62	12	0	0	1	13	13	11	11	4	9	16	.260	.214	.278	11.08	6.23
Meade, Aaron	B-L	6-2	185	5-2-88	2	2	5.93	20	6	0	0	44	53	35	29	7	24	48	.296	.171	.326	9.82	4.91
Melioris, Joe	R-R	6-10	240	5-29-90	5	3	8.67	18	9	0	0	54	67	53	52	10	15	40	.313	.303	.318	6.67	2.50
Mutz, Nick	R-R	6-1	190	6-15-90	2	3	2.31	12	0	0	2	23	20	10	6	4	5	25	.230	.208	.238	9.64	1.93
Odom, Logan	L-R	6-6	240	8-2-89	3	2	5.44	15	12	0	0	51	56	33	31	5	32	60	.277	.206	.309	10.52	5.61
Reynolds, Danny	R-R	6-0	170	5-2-91	3	2	4.60	20	0	9	29	33	17	15	1	5	24	.295	.452	.235	7.36	1.53
Riedie, Shane	R-R	6-5	230	1-5-90	0	2	10.38	13	2	0	0	17	30	24	20	4	10	15	.380	.414	.360	7.79	5.19
Sipple, Eddie	L-L	6-1	185	12-27-88	1	0	4.15	15	0	0	1	13	11	7	6	0	7	20	.229	.200	.250	13.85	4.85
Sookee, Aaron	R-R	6-3	172	6-5-91	0	0	13.50	3	0	0	0	5	13	7	7	1	0	6	.500	.200	.571	11.57	0.00
Tullo, Aaron	R-R	6-3	195	3-9-88	1	1	9.00	18	0	0	3	22	27	24	22	2	13	29	.284	.242	.306	11.86	5.32
Vargas-Vila, Daniel	R-R	6-1	205	6-7-89	1	3	3.54	13	12	0	0	56	57	31	22	8	13	56	.264	.203	.296	9.00	2.09
Waller, Shane	R-R	6-0	190	9-22-88	4	0	2.45	13	0	0	1	22	13	6	6	2	9	32	.173	.214	.164	13.09	3.68
Wiedenbauer, John	L-L	6-3	185	1-16-88	0	0	5.79	3	0	0	1	5	4	3	3	0	2	2	.250	.333	.231	3.86	3.86
Wood, Austin	R-R	6-4	225	7-11-90	0	0	20.25	2	0	0	0	1	4	3	3	1	0	1	.500	1.000	.429	6.75	0.00
Yinger, Chad	R-R	6-8	225	7-16-88	0	0	9.00	7	0	0	0	8	16	8	8	2	1	7	.432	.529	.350	7.88	1.13

Fielding

Catcher	PCT	G	PO	A	E	DP	PB
Baker	.992	48	328	65	3	2	9
Larson	.979	15	124	19	3	3	1
Lugo	1.000	3	14	1	0	0	0
Mahoney	.969	5	27	4	1	0	0
Pacione	.971	21	127	7	4	0	6

First Base	PCT	G	PO	A	E	DP
Bandy	1.000	2	12	0	0	1
Cowart	1.000	1	11	1	0	2
Hairgrove	1.000	1	5	0	0	0
Hall	.994	58	470	13	3	41
Yakubik	.985	24	181	10	3	25

Second Base	PCT	G	PO	A	E	DP
Brewer	.960	6	11	13	1	2
Hatton	1.000	10	16	23	0	8
Lindsey	.976	62	114	168	7	44

Third Base	PCT	G	PO	A	E	DP
Cowart	.917	66	48	128	16	17
Hairgrove	.857	2	2	4	1	0
Hatton	1.000	3	0	5	0	1
Parks	.955	5	4	17	1	2
Yakubik	.500	1	0	1	1	0

Shortstop	PCT	G	PO	A	E	DP
Brewer	.931	29	33	75	8	15

	PCT	G	PO	A	E	DP
Hairgrove	.976	51	68	138	5	31
Outfield	PCT	G	PO	A	E	DP
Carlin	.000	1	0	0	0	0
Giovinazzo	.926	28	49	1	4	0
Gowens	.944	8	17	0	1	0
Hatton	.000	1	0	0	0	0
Jones	.972	63	94	9	3	3
Martinez	.985	39	62	2	1	0
Mitchell	.966	44	83	3	3	2
Ray	.933	37	39	3	3	0
Yakubik	.943	40	48	2	3	0

AZL ANGELS

ARIZONA LEAGUE

ROOKIE

Batting	B-T	HT	WT	DOB	AVG	vLH	vRH	G	AB	R	H	2B	3B	HR	RBI	BB	HBP	SH	SF	SO	SB	CS	SLG	OBP
Bandy, Jett	R-R	6-4	210	3-26-90	.307	.382	.289	46	176	32	54	18	0	4	29	10	18	0	4	23	2	0	.477	.394
Bolaski, Michael	R-R	6-3	185	2-5-92	.218	.071	.250	21	78	9	17	3	3	0	10	10	3	0	0	16	2	1	.333	.330
Bolden, Ryan	R-L	6-2	195	9-17-91	.168	.150	.173	29	101	12	17	4	1	0	13	9	3	0	2	48	8	1	.228	.252
Borenstein, Zach	L-R	6-0	205	7-23-90	.274	.318	.264	31	113	21	31	6	4	2	21	17	6	0	0	21	12	1	.451	.397
Clarke, Chevez	B-R	5-11	185	1-9-92	.226	.100	.248	51	195	33	44	5	10	3	27	16	1	0	2	66	5	4	.400	.285
Giovinazzo, Chris	R-R	6-0	205	11-30-88	.308	.500	.273	4	13	3	4	1	0	0	0	2	2	0	0	5	0	0	.385	.471
Gowens, Brennan	L-R	6-0	195	3-14-90	.235	.250	.232	31	98	18	23	2	1	1	14	19	1	0	1	19	6	2	.306	.361
Grichuk, Randal	R-R	6-1	195	8-13-91	.333	.429	.294	7	24	2	8	1	1	0	6	2	0	0	2	4	0	0	.458	.357
Hannick, Chris	R-R	5-10	190	9-26-88	.212	.143	.231	11	33	3	7	2	0	0	6	9	2	0	0	7	0	0	.273	.409
Hernandez, Brian	R-R	6-1	195	11-25-88	.270	.158	.309	20	74	11	20	1	2	0	2	9	1	0	0	10	2	1	.338	.357
Lugo, Carlos	R-R	6-0	190	11-20-89	.182	.500	.111	4	11	3	2	0	0	0	1	4	0	0	1	4	1	0	.182	.375
Mahoney, Kyle	R-R	6-2	220	4-24-89	.302	.250	.323	12	43	5	13	1	0	1	11	5	3	0	2	12	1	0	.395	.396
Moesquit, Kevin	R-R	5-10	180	6-20-91	.265	.323	.253	48	181	32	48	11	3	1	24	33	3	0	2	36	11	5	.376	.384
Nappi, Jason	R-R	6-1	205	4-20-88	.255	.222	.262	43	157	33	40	7	6	3	20	21	5	0	2	53	11	4	.433	.357
Oliver, Eric	R-R	6-1	215	1-29-87	.500	.500	.500	4	12	2	6	1	0	1	2	1	0	0	0	0	0	0	.833	.538
Sandoval, Freddy	B-R	6-1	205	8-16-82	.200	.333	.143	7	20	4	4	0	3	1	5	4	1	0	0	4	0	1	.650	.360
Scioscia, Matt	R-R	6-3	240	9-20-88	.239	.200	.244	12	46	4	11	3	0	0	9	2	0	0	0	10	2	0	.304	.271
Segura, Jean	R-R	5-11	160	3-17-90	.367	.667	.333	8	30	5	11	4	0	1	5	0	0	0	0	3	0	0	.600	.367
Sneed, James	L-L	5-10	170	2-21-92	.000	.000	.000	1	4	0	0	0	0	0	0	0	0	0	0	1	0	1	.000	.000
Soto, Wendell	B-R	5-8	150	5-11-92	.227	.222	.228	35	132	21	30	5	3	2	13	15	0	0	1	38	6	5	.356	.304
Whitley, Jackson	L-L	6-3	220	9-9-92	.260	.286	.254	40	146	16	38	8	4	0	23	23	1	0	0	44	3	1	.370	.365
Workman, Andy	R-R	6-1	200	11-16-88	.291	.300	.289	43	158	31	46	9	3	2	22	22	4	0	0	38	10	5	.424	.391
Young, Kirby	L-R	6-3	195	7-4-88	.455	.250	.531	15	44	15	20	4	1	0	13	7	1	0	2	8	1	2	.591	.519

Pitching	B-T	HT	WT	DOB	W	L	ERA	G	GS	CG	SV	IP	H	R	ER	HR	BB	SO	AVG	vLH	vRH	K/9	BB/9
Alvarado, Josh	R-R	6-0	180	12-20-87	0	0	10.61	11	0	0	0	9	5	11	11	0	17	11	.152	.250	.120	10.61	16.39
Batista, Lay	R-R	6-2	180	8-4-89	3	6	4.04	14	12	0	0	65	65	41	29	4	19	52	.258	.188	.293	7.24	2.64
Burkard, Alex	L-L	6-8	215	1-4-89	5	4	4.97	14	9	0	0	63	70	40	35	2	15	45	.273	.194	.299	6.39	2.13
DeJiulio, Frank	R-R	6-3	185	8-22-89	2	2	7.62	13	5	0	0	26	25	22	22	3	19	26	.248	.156	.290	9.00	6.58
Diaz, Jairo	R-R	6-0	195	5-27-91	4	1	4.08	11	10	0	0	57	59	33	26	3	18	44	.272	.338	.242	6.91	2.83
Efferson, Brandon	R-R	5-11	175	11-25-88	0	4	5.30	19	3	0	4	36	36	24	21	5	10	33	.257	.426	.172	8.33	2.52
Fish, Robert	L-L	6-2	230	1-19-88	0	0	0.00	2	0	0	0	3	3	1	0	0	0	3	.273	.000	.375	9.00	0.00
George, Bryant	R-R	5-10	178	7-17-88	0	0	12.46	6	0	0	0	4	11	8	6	0	3	4	.440	.500	.400	8.31	6.23
Holtman, Johnny	R-R	6-5	225	1-11-88	0	1	3.68	18	0	0	5	22	18	10	9	0	5	23	.231	.208	.241	9.41	2.05
Kelley, Ty	R-R	6-4	196	8-18-88	1	0	7.36	3	0	0	0	4	8	3	3	0	0	2	.333	.000	.615	4.91	0.00
Lodge, Brandon	R-R	6-2	165	8-3-88	0	1	5.48	20	0	0	0	23	28	15	14	3	3	14	.311	.375	.288	5.48	1.17
Marshall, Kris	L-L	5-9	165	11-13-87	1	0	5.79	4	0	0	0	5	6	4	3	0	4	1	.333	.000	.462	1.93	7.71
Martinez, Fabio	R-R	6-3	190	10-29-89	0	0	0.00	2	0	0	0	2	2	0	0	0	1	2	.222	.000	.400	7.71	3.86
McNelis, Brandon	R-R	6-1	215	5-17-88	2	3	3.25	14	9	0	0	53	47	26	19	2	21	49	.239	.250	.233	8.37	3.59

Pitching

Pitching	B-T	HT	WT	DOB	W	L	ERA	G	GS	CG	SV	IP	H	R	ER	HR	BB	SO	AVG	vLH	vRH	K/9	BB/9
Meyer, Matt	L-L	6-4	220	1-17-85	0	0	1.13	6	0	0	0	8	3	1	1	0	1	17	.115	.000	.130	19.13	1.13
Negrete, Jake	R-R	6-3	190	3-8-90	2	0	3.93	16	0	0	2	18	22	8	8	0	4	22	.297	.364	.269	10.80	1.96
Ortega, Anthony	R-R	6-0	185	8-24-85	0	0	1.50	4	1	0	0	6	3	1	1	0	0	5	.143	.125	.154	7.50	0.00
Riedie, Shane	R-R	6-5	230	1-5-90	1	0	4.00	2	2	0	0	9	12	5	4	1	3	6	.343	.333	.344	6.00	3.00
Rodriguez, Francisco	R-R	6-1	220	2-26-83	0	1	8.44	4	2	0	0	5	5	5	5	2	4	5	.263	.250	.286	8.44	6.75
Sattler, Dan	R-R	6-3	190	11-11-83	0	1	1.29	5	0	0	1	7	6	1	1	0	0	7	.231	.125	.278	9.00	0.00
Sookee, Aaron	R-R	6-3	172	6-5-91	3	3	4.63	14	0	0	2	23	23	13	12	1	9	28	.256	.280	.246	10.80	3.47
Tromblee, Stephen	L-L	6-0	205	4-3-89	3	1	2.81	18	0	0	0	26	30	10	8	1	3	27	.294	.400	.276	9.47	1.05
Wiedenbauer, John	L-L	6-3	185	1-16-88	1	0	1.80	7	0	0	0	10	7	2	2	0	0	10	.184	.222	.172	9.00	0.00
Yinger, Chad	R-R	6-8	225	7-16-88	0	0	0.00	4	0	0	2	5	5	0	0	0	2	3	.263	.000	.294	5.40	3.60

Fielding

Catcher	PCT	G	PO	A	E	DP	PB
Bandy	.987	32	261	37	4	2	4
Hannick	1.000	8	52	7	0	0	2
Lugo	1.000	4	32	3	0	0	1
Mahoney	.987	9	69	6	1	1	3
Scioscia	.970	5	28	4	1	0	1

First Base	PCT	G	PO	A	E	DP
Bolaski	.667	1	4	0	2	0
Mahoney	1.000	1	12	0	0	1
Nappi	.987	6	69	5	1	5
Oliver	1.000	3	18	3	0	2
Sandoval	1.000	2	19	1	0	4
Scioscia	1.000	5	45	0	0	5
Whitley	.979	40	354	25	8	33

Second Base	PCT	G	PO	A	E	DP
Bolaski	1.000	1	1	3	0	0
Copa	.966	7	12	16	1	3
Hernandez	1.000	9	9	24	0	2
Moesquit	.975	42	85	113	5	32
Sandoval	1.000	1	1	3	0	0
Young	1.000	1	2	2	0	0

Third Base	PCT	G	PO	A	E	DP
Bolaski	.922	16	21	50	6	4
Borenstein	1.000	4	2	9	0	2
Copa	.750	1	0	3	1	1
Hernandez	.957	11	5	17	1	1
Nappi	.901	25	17	47	7	8
Sandoval	1.000	1	0	1	0	0

Shortstop	PCT	G	PO	A	E	DP
Moesquit	.938	10	15	30	3	5
Segura	.917	5	5	6	1	1
Soto	.919	35	37	88	11	12
Young	.966	14	26	31	2	12

Outfield	PCT	G	PO	A	E	DP
Bolden	.964	28	27	0	1	0
Borenstein	1.000	25	34	1	0	0
Clarke	.969	51	90	5	3	0
Giovinazzo	1.000	3	9	1	0	0
Gowens	.892	24	29	4	4	1
Grichuk	1.000	4	7	0	0	0
Nappi	1.000	1	2	0	0	0
Sandoval	.750	2	2	1	1	0
Sneed	1.000	1	4	0	0	0
Workman	.982	36	52	4	1	0

DSL ANGELS

ROOKIE

DOMINICAN SUMMER LEAGUE

Batting	B-T	HT	WT	DOB	AVG	vLH	vRH	G	AB	R	H	2B	3B	HR	RBI	BB	HBP	SH	SF	SO	SB	CS	SLG	OBP
Alamanzar, Michael	R-R	5-10	185	2-16-91	.215	.071	.255	22	65	9	14	2	4	0	6	9	2	0	1	15	4	1	.369	.325
Aquino, Bladimir	R-R	6-0	190	7-3-93	.091	.000	.100	9	11	3	1	0	0	0	0	8	0	0	0	5	1	0	.091	.474
Beltran, Glenn	R-R	6-2	220	12-23-91	.278	.262	.282	64	223	36	62	11	2	5	33	24	4	0	2	42	12	4	.413	.356
De La Cruz, Ercilio	B-R	5-11	160	10-28-92	.231	.304	.216	47	134	30	31	7	3	0	12	46	3	0	0	46	13	6	.328	.437
Dionicio, Ismael	B-R	5-10	165	7-19-91	.297	.400	.278	47	128	22	38	6	1	0	21	16	1	0	1	30	17	5	.359	.377
Fernandez, Jesus	R-R	6-1	185	3-6-94	.130	.000	.167	9	23	2	3	0	0	0	2	3	1	0	1	8	0	0	.130	.250
Grance, Moises	R-R	5-11	160	12-1-91	.275	.407	.246	45	149	25	41	8	2	3	20	16	1	0	2	35	8	2	.416	.345
Hernandez, Jonattan	B-R	5-11	175	7-11-90	.160	.188	.147	18	50	5	8	4	0	1	10	7	0	0	0	17	0	2	.300	.263
Herrera, Jose	B-R	6-0	155	1-14-93	.132	1.000	.108	17	38	5	5	0	1	0	2	5	3	0	0	12	1	1	.184	.283
Jolly, Luis	R-R	6-2	180	3-21-93	.125	.053	.145	34	88	15	11	2	2	0	11	13	1	0	0	48	4	3	.193	.245
Linares, Raul	B-R	5-11	160	10-4-90	.239	.226	.242	52	159	48	38	12	3	0	22	19	3	0	3	31	27	2	.352	.326
Martinez, Sandy	B-R	5-11	180	7-18-92	.255	.125	.279	37	102	12	26	3	0	0	11	6	1	0	0	7	0	1	.284	.303
Mateo, Steven	R-R	6-2	188	8-19-92	.271	.308	.264	30	85	9	23	3	0	2	22	16	3	0	2	23	0	3	.376	.396
Mendez, Samir	R-R	6-1	215	7-13-92	.288	.250	.295	58	208	32	60	10	0	4	44	11	2	0	5	32	5	2	.394	.323
Montilla, Angel	R-R	6-1	170	4-18-93	.321	.000	.346	8	28	5	9	3	1	0	3	3	2	0	0	7	1	0	.500	.424
Rodriguez, Angel	R-R	5-10	170	4-28-92	.278	.160	.303	44	144	27	40	1	0	0	18	17	6	0	1	35	8	3	.285	.353
Rondon, Jose	R-R	6-1	160	3-3-94	.315	.333	.312	49	165	28	52	1	2	0	21	17	1	0	2	16	9	4	.406	.378
Salcedo, Erick	B-R	5-10	155	6-28-93	.241	.200	.247	38	108	19	26	4	2	0	16	25	4	0	2	14	4	4	.315	.396
Toribio, Pedro	R-R	5-10	158	7-21-90	.316	.268	.329	52	187	50	59	10	10	4	28	13	1	0	4	22	32	4	.540	.354
Villavicencio, Gabriel	R-R	6-0	190	10-3-92	.208	.000	.270	18	48	9	10	1	0	0	4	8	1	0	0	9	2	0	.229	.333
Vivas, Enyelber	R-R	6-1	175	8-26-92	.148	.111	.154	24	61	9	9	1	0	0	7	9	1	0	0	11	2	0	.164	.268

Pitching	B-T	HT	WT	DOB	W	L	ERA	G	GS	CG	SV	IP	H	R	ER	HR	BB	SO	AVG	vLH	vRH	K/9	BB/9
Campos, Alexis	R-R	6-1	160	6-23-92	0	0	0.00	6	0	0	2	8	4	1	0	0	2	9	.148	1.000	.080	10.57	2.35
Cruz, Junior	R-R	6-1	180	4-5-90	6	3	2.13	13	13	1	0	72	59	28	17	1	21	52	.229	.250	.224	6.50	2.63
DeLeon, Ernesto	R-R	6-6	230	11-24-91	0	0	8.44	4	0	0	0	5	6	6	5	1	7	4	.286	.000	.353	6.75	11.81
Garcia, Franklin	R-R	6-3	195	3-23-90	5	2	3.89	15	4	0	0	37	26	20	16	0	14	34	.202	.000	.215	8.27	3.41
Gomez, Jordany	R-R	6-3	180	9-1-90	0	0	11.25	4	0	0	0	4	3	5	5	0	5	1	.214	.000	.273	2.25	11.25
Guerra, Angel	R-R	6-1	180	2-2-93	3	0	2.59	15	0	0	1	31	25	14	9	0	6	26	.214	.150	.227	7.47	1.72
Hurtado, Daniel	R-R	6-1	180	7-25-92	7	3	1.45	14	14	3	0	74	53	23	12	2	20	65	.200	.177	.207	7.87	2.42
Jimenez, Eswarlin	L-L	6-1	187	11-27-91	6	3	1.72	14	12	2	0	68	52	26	13	0	14	72	.215	.188	.217	9.53	1.85
Melo, Ivan	L-L	6-1	165	7-21-94	0	1	2.57	9	0	0	0	14	9	8	4	0	8	17	.184	.333	.163	10.93	5.14
Perez, Gabriel	R-R	6-0	185	6-3-91	10	1	1.47	14	14	1	0	74	41	15	12	2	28	76	.163	.128	.169	9.29	3.42
Ramirez, Orlando	R-R	6-1	170	5-4-92	4	1	1.42	19	0	0	1	38	25	11	6	0	9	39	.188	.269	.168	9.24	2.13
Reyes, Jose	R-R	6-2	160	2-3-93	1	0	1.08	9	0	0	0	17	9	2	2	0	6	13	.164	.000	.180	7.02	3.24
Rodriguez, Jose	R-R	6-4	190	3-10-90	0	0	4.05	5	0	0	0	7	6	4	3	1	7	6	.240	.143	.278	8.10	9.45
Rodriguez, Nataniel	L-L	5-10	185	8-27-90	1	1	4.58	15	0	0	2	20	14	10	10	1	6	23	.203	.000	.237	10.53	2.75
Santana, Francisco	L-L	5-10	155	2-1-93	2	1	2.30	14	1	0	0	27	22	13	7	2	10	22	.216	.333	.204	7.24	3.29
Santiago, Yancarlos	L-L	6-0	180	1-23-91	4	1	1.38	12	12	1	0	65	37	16	10	0	12	82	.164	.125	.167	11.35	1.66
Santos, Edward	R-R	6-2	220	10-22-89	2	0	0.82	17	0	0	4	22	17	2	2	0	6	22	.218	.083	.242	9.00	2.45
Toribio, Roberto	R-R	6-0	180	11-2-89	1	1	1.56	10	0	0	1	17	8	4	3	1	5	12	.140	.154	.136	6.23	2.60

Fielding

Catcher	PCT	G	PO	A	E	DP	PB
Alamanzar	.983	19	101	15	2	2	4
Aquino	1.000	6	23	3	0	0	0
Fernandez	.889	2	6	2	1	0	0
Martinez	.983	35	252	29	5	1	0
Villavicencio	1.000	2	11	3	0	0	0
Vivas	.974	24	172	18	5	1	10

First Base	PCT	G	PO	A	E	DP
Dionicio	1.000	1	4	0	0	1
Grance	1.000	1	11	0	0	0
Hernandez	.983	8	57	2	1	4
Mateo	1.000	2	14	2	0	1
Mendez	.993	44	406	16	3	28
Rodriguez	.959	9	91	2	4	9
Villavicencio	1.000	13	95	2	0	13

Second Base	PCT	G	PO	A	E	DP
Dionicio	.900	8	8	19	3	4
Grance	.981	34	74	82	3	25
Linares	1.000	4	6	5	0	1
Rodriguez	.923	5	6	18	2	5
Salcedo	.786	4	4	7	3	1
Toribio	.967	22	35	54	3	8

Third Base	PCT	G	PO	A	E	DP
Grance	1.000	3	1	8	0	2
Herrera	.881	12	12	25	5	4
Linares	.889	16	8	48	7	8
Mateo	.800	7	3	13	4	2
Rodriguez	.955	10	4	17	1	2
Rondon	.885	30	11	66	10	4

Shortstop	PCT	G	PO	A	E	DP
Dionicio	1.000	1	1	2	0	0
Herrera	1.000	1	0	2	0	1
Rondon	.938	20	26	65	6	8
Salcedo	.950	34	40	94	7	10
Toribio	.937	20	15	59	5	6

Outfield	PCT	G	PO	A	E	DP
Beltran	.976	57	77	5	2	2
De La Cruz	1.000	47	55	2	0	1
Dionicio	.973	30	36	0	1	0
Grance	1.000	2	7	0	0	0
Hernandez	.000	1	0	0	0	0
Jolly	.951	31	39	0	2	0
Linares	.970	25	31	1	1	0
Montilla	1.000	8	10	2	0	1
Rodriguez	.963	20	25	1	1	0

Los Angeles Dodgers

SEASON IN A SENTENCE: The Dodgers enjoyed memorable seasons from Matt Kemp and Clayton Kershaw, yet the team wasn't close to a playoff spot and continued to be overshadowed by negative headlines off the field.

HIGH POINT: Right fielder Andre Ethier went on a 31-game hitting streak in April and May, while Kemp and Kershaw at least gave Dodger fans a distraction from the team's off-field issues. Kershaw defeated Giants rival Tim Lincecum all four times they met, including a pair of 2-1 wins in September that helped sink San Francisco's playoff hopes. Although they were out of the race, the Dodgers did go 41-28 after the all-star break.

LOW POINT: The Dodgers were riddled by injuries and fell out of contention by midseason, even spending a week in the basement of the National League West in early July. Off the field, there were plenty to choose from, from declining attendance to the team filing for bankruptcy as Major League Baseball battled to wrest control of the team from embattled owner Frank McCourt (the two sides agreed to a process for selling the team after the season). But worst of all was when a Giants fan was nearly beaten to death in a Dodger Stadium parking lot after the teams played on Opening Day.

NOTABLE ROOKIES: The Dodgers got plenty of contributions from younger players. Foremost among them was shortstop Dee Gordon, who showed off his athleticism while batting .304/.325/.362. Outfielder Jerry Sands had his moments and hit well in September after strugling during an early season callup. Righthander Rubby de la Rosa posted a 3.71 ERA, but he went down in July and needed Tommy John surgery. With Jonathan Broxton injured for most of the season, righthander Javy Guerra filled the void as closer and went 21-for-23 converting saves.

KEY TRANSACTIONS: The Dodgers brought in four prospects in a pair of deadline deals, although they either have limited upside or are far from the majors. They cleared the way for Gordon by shipping Rafael Furcal to the Cardinals in one of those deals.

DOWN ON THE FARM: The Rookie-level Arizona League squad won its league title and four of Los Angeles' six affiliates qualified for postseason play. One of those was Double-A Chattanooga, which boasted a pitching staff loaded wih arms that could be in the majors soon or have already contributed there, such as de la Rosa.

OPENING DAY PAYROLL: $104.2 million (12th)

PLAYERS OF THE YEAR

MAJOR LEAGUE	MINOR LEAGUE
Matt Kemp	**Scott Van Slyke**
of	of/1b
.324/.399/.586	(Double-A)
39 HR, 40 SB	.348/.427/.595
BA Player of the Year	20 HR, 45 2B

ORGANIZATION LEADERS

BATTING		*Minimum 250 PA
MAJORS		
* AVG	Matt Kemp	.324
* OPS	Matt Kemp	.985
HR	Matt Kemp	39
RBI	Matt Kemp	126
MINORS		
* AVG	Scott Van Slyke, Chattanooga	.348
* OBP	Scott Van Slyke, Chattanooga	.427
* SLG	Scott Van Slyke, Chattanooga	.595
R	Angelo Songco, Rancho Cucamonga	110
H	Angelo Songco, Rancho Cucamonga	167
TB	Angelo Songco, Rancho Cucamonga	310
2B	Angelo Songco, Rancho Cucamonga	48
3B	Alfredo Silverio, Chattanooga	18
HR	Jerry Sands, Albuquerque	29
	Angelo Songco, Rancho Cucamonga	29
RBI	Angelo Songco, Rancho Cucamonga	114
BB	Scott Van Slyke, Chattanooga	65
SO	Kyle Russell, Chattanooga/Albuquerque	154
SB	Elian Herrera, Chattanooga	33
PITCHING		**#Minimum 75 IP**
MAJORS		
W	Clayton Kershaw	21
# ERA	Clayton Kershaw	2.28
SO	Clayton Kershaw	248
SV	Javy Guerra	21
MINORS		
W	Three tied at	12
L	Tim Sexton, Albuquerque/Great Lakes	12
# ERA	Garrett Gould, Great Lakes	2.40
G	Shawn Tolleson, Great Lakes/Rancho/Chatt.	57
GS	Red Patterson, Great Lakes/Rancho	28
	Tim Sexton, Albuquerque/Great Lakes	28
SV	Logan Bawcom, Great Lakes/Rancho	27
IP	Red Patterson, Great Lakes/Rancho	173.1
BB	Chris Withrow, Chattanooga	75
SO	Red Patterson, Great Lakes/Rancho	172
# AVG	Garrett Gould, Great Lakes	.22

General Manager: Ned Colletti. **Farm Director:** De Jon Watson. **Scouting Director:** Logan White.

Class	Team	League	W	L	PCT	Finish	Manager(s)
Majors	Los Angeles Dodgers	National	82	79	.509	7th (16)	Don Mattingly
Triple-A	Albuquerque Isotopes	Pacific Coast	70	74	.486	t-8th (16)	Lorenzo Bundy
Double-A	Chattanooga Lookouts	Southern	77	62	.554	3rd (10)	Carlos Subero
High A	Rancho Cucamonga Quakes	California	80	60	.571	2nd (10)	Juan Bustabad
Low A	Great Lakes Loons	Midwest	72	67	.518	6th (16)	John Shoemaker
Rookie	Ogden Raptors	Pioneer	41	35	.539	t-4th (8)	Damon Berryhill
Rookie	AZL Dodgers	Arizona	34	22	.607	3rd (13)	Jody Reed
Overall 2011 Minor League Record			374	320	.539	3rd (30)	

ORGANIZATION STATISTICS

LOS ANGELES DODGERS

NATIONAL LEAGUE

Batting	B-T	HT	WT	DOB	AVG	vLH	vRH	G	AB	R	H	2B	3B	HR	RBI	BB	HBP	SH	SF	SO	SB	CS	SLG	OBP
Barajas, Rod	R-R	6-2	250	9-5-75	.230	.267	.214	98	305	29	70	13	0	16	47	22	4	0	3	71	0	0	.430	.287
Blake, Casey	R-R	6-2	205	8-23-73	.252	.283	.242	63	202	32	51	10	1	4	26	26	3	0	3	50	1	2	.371	.342
Carroll, Jamey	R-R	5-9	170	2-18-74	.290	.304	.284	146	452	52	131	14	6	0	17	47	2	0	1	58	10	0	.347	.359
Castro, Juan	R-R	5-11	190	6-20-72	.286	.286	.286	7	14	2	4	0	0	0	1	1	0	0	0	4	0	0	.286	.333
De Jesus Jr., Ivan	R-R	5-11	200	5-1-87	.188	.286	.160	17	32	2	6	0	0	0	1	2	0	0	0	11	0	0	.188	.235
Ellis, A.J.	R-R	6-2	225	4-9-81	.271	.360	.233	31	85	8	23	1	1	2	11	14	3	0	0	16	0	1	.376	.392
Ethier, Andre	L-L	6-2	205	4-10-82	.292	.220	.321	135	487	67	142	30	0	11	62	58	3	0	3	103	0	1	.421	.368
Federowicz, Tim	R-R	5-11	200	8-5-87	.154	.200	.125	7	13	0	2	0	0	0	1	2	1	0	0	4	0	0	.154	.313
Furcal, Rafael	B-R	5-8	190	10-24-77	.197	.195	.198	37	137	15	27	4	0	1	12	11	3	0	0	21	5	3	.248	.272
2-team total (50 St. Louis)					.231	—	—	87	333	44	77	15	0	8	28	28	4	0	1	39	9	5	.348	.298
Gibbons, Jay	L-L	6-0	195	3-2-77	.255	.444	.217	24	55	5	14	2	0	1	5	5	1	0	1	14	0	0	.345	.323
Gimenez, Hector	B-R	5-10	225	9-28-82	.143	.333	.000	4	7	0	1	0	0	0	0	0	0	0	0	3	0	0	.143	.143
Gordon, Dee	L-R	5-11	150	4-22-88	.304	.275	.316	56	224	34	68	9	2	0	11	7	0	0	0	27	24	7	.362	.325
Gwynn Jr., Tony	L-R	5-11	195	10-4-82	.256	.200	.273	136	312	37	80	12	6	2	22	23	1	0	2	61	22	6	.353	.308
Hoffmann, Jamie	R-R	6-3	235	8-20-84	.000	.000	.412	2	4	0	0	0	0	0	0	0	0	0	0	1	0	0	.000	.000
Kemp, Matt	R-R	6-3	215	9-23-84	.324	.341	.319	161	602	115	195	33	4	39	126	74	6	0	7	159	40	11	.586	.399
Loney, James	L-L	6-2	205	5-7-84	.288	.213	.312	158	531	56	153	30	1	12	65	42	1	0	5	67	4	0	.416	.339
Miles, Aaron	B-R	5-8	180	12-15-76	.275	.293	.270	136	454	49	125	17	3	3	45	25	3	0	5	49	4	3	.346	.314
Mitchell, Russ	R-R	5-10	210	2-15-85	.157	.115	.200	25	51	5	8	1	0	2	3	7	0	0	0	10	0	0	.294	.259
Navarro, Dioner	B-R	5-9	205	2-9-84	.193	.179	.196	64	176	13	34	6	1	5	17	20	1	0	2	35	0	0	.324	.276
Oeltjen, Trent	L-L	6-1	190	2-28-83	.197	.250	.186	61	71	10	14	1	1	2	6	13	1	0	2	30	6	0	.324	.322
Paul, Xavier	L-R	5-9	205	2-25-85	.273	.000	.300	7	11	0	3	0	0	0	0	0	0	0	0	5	0	0	.273	.273
2-team total (121 Pittsburgh)					.255	—	—	128	243	30	62	6	5	2	20	13	0	0	1	62	16	6	.346	.292
Rivera, Juan	R-R	6-2	230	7-3-78	.274	.254	.281	62	219	24	60	12	1	5	46	21	1	0	5	35	2	1	.406	.333
Sands, Jerry	R-R	6-4	220	9-28-87	.253	.367	.203	61	198	20	50	15	0	4	26	25	1	0	1	51	3	3	.389	.338
Sellers, Justin	R-R	5-10	160	2-1-86	.203	.300	.172	36	123	20	25	9	0	1	13	12	1	2	0	21	1	0	.301	.283
Thames, Marcus	R-R	6-2	220	3-6-77	.197	.167	.233	36	66	4	13	1	1	2	7	4	0	0	0	16	0	0	.333	.243
Uribe, Juan	R-R	5-11	230	3-22-79	.204	.159	.219	77	270	21	55	12	0	4	28	17	6	0	2	60	2	0	.293	.264
Velez, Eugenio	B-R	6-1	170	5-16-82	.000	.000	.000	34	37	5	0	0	0	0	0	1	2	1	0	11	1	0	.000	.075

Pitching	B-T	HT	WT	DOB	W	L	ERA	G	GS	CG	SV	IP	H	R	ER	HR	BB	SO	AVG	vLH	vRH	K/9	BB/9
Billingsley, Chad	R-R	6-1	240	7-29-84	11	11	4.21	32	32	1	0	188	189	98	88	14	84	152	.264	.282	.248	7.28	4.02
Broxton, Jonathan	R-R	6-4	300	6-16-84	1	2	5.68	14	0	0	7	13	15	10	8	2	9	10	.283	.238	.313	7.11	6.39
Cormier, Lance	R-R	6-1	200	8-19-80	0	1	9.88	9	0	0	0	14	22	17	15	4	5	7	.338	.179	.459	4.61	3.29
De La Rosa, Rubby	R-R	6-1	185	3-4-89	4	5	3.71	13	10	0	0	61	54	26	25	6	31	60	.244	.235	.255	8.90	4.60
Elbert, Scott	L-L	6-1	210	8-13-85	0	1	2.43	47	0	0	2	33	27	9	9	1	14	34	.220	.191	.255	9.18	3.78
Ely, John	R-R	6-2	200	5-13-86	0	1	4.26	5	1	0	0	13	12	6	6	2	7	13	.245	.217	.269	9.24	4.97
Eovaldi, Nate	R-R	6-3	195	2-13-90	1	2	3.63	10	6	0	0	35	28	14	14	2	20	23	.230	.275	.197	5.97	5.19
Eveland, Dana	L-L	6-1	235	10-29-83	3	2	3.03	5	5	0	0	30	28	10	10	1	6	16	.257	.278	.253	4.85	1.82
Garland, Jon	R-R	6-6	210	9-27-79	1	5	4.33	9	9	1	0	54	55	26	26	6	20	28	.276	.351	.206	4.67	3.33
Guerra, Javy	R-R	6-0	205	10-31-85	2	2	2.31	47	0	0	21	47	37	12	12	2	18	38	.218	.164	.258	7.33	3.47
Guerrier, Matt	R-R	6-3	195	8-2-78	4	3	4.07	70	0	0	1	66	59	31	30	4	25	50	.233	.204	.253	6.78	3.39
Hawksworth, Blake	R-R	6-3	200	3-1-83	2	5	4.08	49	0	0	0	53	45	29	24	6	17	43	.225	.193	.250	7.30	2.89
Jansen, Kenley	B-R	6-5	255	9-30-87	2	1	2.85	51	0	0	5	54	30	17	17	3	26	96	.159	.163	.156	16.10	4.36
Kershaw, Clayton	L-L	6-3	215	3-19-88	21	5	2.28	33	33	5	0	233	174	66	59	15	54	248	.207	.178	.213	9.57	2.08
Kuo, Hong-Chih	L-L	6-2	240	7-23-81	1	2	9.00	40	0	0	0	27	24	29	27	4	23	36	.242	.289	.204	12.00	7.67
Kuroda, Hiroki	R-R	6-1	190	2-10-75	13	16	3.07	32	32	0	0	202	196	77	69	24	49	161	.254	.264	.244	7.17	2.18
Lilly, Ted	L-L	6-1	195	1-4-76	12	14	3.97	33	33	0	0	193	172	88	85	28	51	158	.238	.210	.246	7.38	2.38
Lindblom, Josh	R-R	6-5	240	6-15-87	1	0	2.73	27	0	0	0	30	21	9	9	0	10	28	.212	.370	.153	8.49	3.03
MacDougal, Mike	B-R	6-4	185	3-5-77	3	1	2.05	69	0	0	1	57	54	16	13	3	29	41	.257	.278	.244	6.47	4.58
Padilla, Vicente	R-R	6-0	230	9-27-77	0	0	4.15	9	0	0	3	9	7	4	4	0	5	9	.226	.462	.056	9.35	5.19
Troncoso, Ramon	R-R	6-1	210	2-16-83	0	0	6.75	18	0	0	0	23	38	18	17	5	4	14	.388	.350	.414	5.56	1.59

Fielding

Catcher	PCT	G	PO	A	E	DP	PB
Barajas	.997	88	651	48	2	4	3
Ellis	1.000	29	167	11	0	2	2
Federowicz	.977	7	37	6	1	0	1
Gimenez	1.000	1	8	0	0	0	0
Navarro	.985	54	421	27	7	5	2

First Base	PCT	G	PO	A	E	DP
Blake	.980	8	45	3	1	2
Loney	.996	150	1129	74	5	90
Mitchell	.969	6	30	1	1	1
Rivera	.982	17	105	4	2	3
Sands	1.000	6	28	0	0	3

Second Base	PCT	G	PO	A	E	DP
Carroll	.980	81	91	160	5	35
Castro	1.000	4	3	11	0	1
De Jesus Jr.	.971	11	12	21	1	2

	PCT	G	PO	A	E	DP
Miles	.992	72	119	139	2	28
Sellers	1.000	12	30	19	0	4
Uribe	1.000	18	31	37	0	11
Velez	1.000	11	10	13	0	2

Third Base	PCT	G	PO	A	E	DP
Blake	.946	45	37	69	6	6
Castro	1.000	1	1	2	0	0
Miles	.928	61	21	82	8	8
Mitchell	1.000	11	7	23	0	0
Sellers	1.000	5	4	11	0	0
Uribe	.978	59	37	96	3	3

Shortstop	PCT	G	PO	A	E	DP
Carroll	.981	66	78	132	4	27
Furcal	.974	36	57	95	4	18
Gordon	.954	54	80	128	10	25
Miles	.000	1	0	0	0	0

	PCT	G	PO	A	E	DP
Sellers	.986	19	25	48	1	16
Uribe	1.000	4	3	5	0	2

Outfield	PCT	G	PO	A	E	DP
Blake	.000	2	0	0	0	0
Ethier	1.000	126	243	8	0	0
Gibbons	1.000	14	16	1	0	0
Gwynn Jr.	.993	121	140	8	1	2
Hoffmann	1.000	1	3	0	0	0
Kemp	.986	159	345	11	5	5
Mitchell	.000	1	0	0	0	0
Oeltjen	.962	23	25	0	1	0
Paul	1.000	5	5	1	0	0
Rivera	1.000	45	70	1	0	0
Sands	1.000	57	89	6	0	1
Thames	.963	17	26	0	1	0
Velez	.800	4	4	0	1	0

ALBUQUERQUE ISOTOPES — TRIPLE-A

PACIFIC COAST LEAGUE

Batting	B-T	HT	WT	DOB	AVG	vLH	vRH	G	AB	R	H	2B	3B	HR	RBI	BB	HBP	SH	SF	SO	SB	CS	SLG	OBP
Becker, Joe	R-R	5-10	184	11-8-85	.310	.281	.325	70	187	24	58	9	3	3	12	14	2	0	0	39	0	0	.439	.365
Blake, Casey	R-R	6-2	205	8-23-73	.143	.200	.111	4	14	1	2	1	0	0	0	2	0	0	0	8	0	0	.214	.250
Castro, Juan	R-R	5-11	190	6-20-72	.400	.400	.200	9	25	6	11	2	1	0	3	2	0	0	0	5	0	0	.600	.481
Closser, J.D.	B-R	5-10	205	1-15-80	.297	.292	.299	69	212	45	63	10	0	10	39	30	0	0	4	33	2	0	.486	.378
Collado, Keyter	R-R	5-9	182	6-8-86	.333	.000	.333	1	3	1	1	0	0	0	0	0	0	0	0	0	0	0	.333	.333
Coon, Brad	L-L	6-0	175	12-11-82	.284	.261	.293	23	81	13	23	3	1	0	7	9	1	0	1	18	1	0	.346	.359
De Jesus Jr., Ivan	R-R	5-11	200	5-1-87	.310	.294	.316	100	387	61	120	19	2	8	59	45	6	0	2	68	4	1	.432	.389
Ellis, A.J.	R-R	6-2	225	4-9-81	.304	.283	.313	59	184	36	56	15	0	2	28	50	7	0	1	23	0	1	.418	.467
Espino, Damaso	R-R	6-1	210	5-8-83	.292	.311	.284	65	202	28	59	4	1	4	32	15	3	0	2	29	2	0	.381	.347
Federowicz, Tim	R-R	5-11	200	8-5-87	.325	.240	.362	25	83	17	27	7	0	6	17	15	2	0	2	20	0	0	.627	.431
Furcal, Rafael	B-R	5-8	190	10-24-77	.385	.250	.444	4	13	2	5	1	0	1	6	3	0	0	0	1	0	0	.692	.500
Gibbons, Jay	L-L	6-0	195	3-2-77	.300	.265	.313	76	263	38	79	12	1	9	46	44	2	0	1	44	1	0	.456	.403
Gordon, Dee	L-R	5-11	150	4-22-88	.333	.311	.339	70	288	51	96	10	6	0	24	18	2	0	3	40	30	4	.410	.373
Hernandez, Bryant	R-R	5-8	170	3-5-88	.333	.167	.444	5	15	4	5	0	1	0	2	0	3	0	0	5	0	0	.467	.444
Hoffmann, Jamie	R-R	6-3	235	8-20-84	.297	.271	.308	133	475	91	141	23	3	22	84	44	5	0	9	102	14	4	.497	.356
Lindsey, John	R-R	6-2	255	1-30-77	.309	.316	.305	75	230	36	71	15	0	13	49	28	10	0	2	59	0	0	.543	.404
Mirabal, Charlie	R-R	5-11	180	4-2-87	.400	.500	.333	2	5	1	2	1	0	0	3	1	0	0	0	1	0	0	.600	.400
Mitchell, Russ	R-R	5-10	210	2-15-85	.283	.294	.278	93	336	66	95	22	2	16	69	46	5	0	5	62	1	1	.503	.372
Ochoa, Ivan	R-R	5-9	160	12-16-82	.257	.217	.277	18	70	7	18	4	0	0	7	7	1	0	1	14	1	0	.314	.329
Oeltjen, Trent	L-L	6-1	190	2-28-83	.339	.370	.328	56	180	33	61	14	3	8	34	25	4	0	1	50	7	4	.583	.429
Ortiz, Wilberto	R-R	5-10	180	1-30-85	.125	.000	.176	11	24	4	3	2	0	0	1	4	1	0	0	5	0	0	.208	.276
Robinson, Trayvon	B-R	5-10	200	9-1-87	.293	.276	.300	100	368	70	108	9	6	26	71	45	3	0	0	122	8	6	.563	.375
2-team total (3 Tacoma)					.289	—	—	103	377	71	109	9	6	26	71	48	3	0	0	126	9	6	.552	.374
Russell, Kyle	L-L	6-5	195	6-27-86	.211	.182	.222	11	38	6	8	2	1	1	3	8	0	0	0	10	1	0	.395	.348
Sands, Jerry	R-R	6-4	220	9-28-87	.278	.248	.291	94	370	78	103	21	3	29	88	38	3	0	7	86	3	1	.586	.344
Sellers, Justin	R-R	5-10	160	2-1-86	.304	.385	.271	89	270	57	82	17	2	14	49	41	5	0	4	57	3	3	.537	.400
Smith, Corey	R-R	6-1	200	4-15-82	.239	.218	.247	66	201	27	48	7	0	7	22	10	0	0	0	50	1	0	.378	.275
Thames, Marcus	R-R	6-2	220	3-6-77	.176	.333	.143	6	17	3	3	1	0	2	4	2	0	0	0	4	0	0	.588	.263
Velez, Eugenio	B-R	6-1	170	5-16-82	.339	.327	.343	55	218	33	74	15	3	2	31	11	1	0	2	36	6	6	.463	.371

Pitching	B-T	HT	WT	DOB	W	L	ERA	G	GS	CG	SV	IP	H	R	ER	HR	BB	SO	AVG	vLH	vRH	K/9	BB/9
Acosta, Ryan	R-R	6-2	170	11-4-88	0	0	6.00	1	0	0	0	3	2	2	2	1	2	1	.182	.000	.333	3.00	6.00
Alvarez, Mario	R-R	6-0	205	3-26-84	1	2	6.43	13	1	0	0	21	29	17	15	3	14	10	.337	.462	.234	4.29	6.00
Bastardo, Alberto	L-L	6-0	160	4-9-84	4	3	5.38	15	15	0	0	72	90	48	43	8	33	65	.308	.313	.306	8.13	4.13
Broxton, Jonathan	R-R	6-4	300	6-16-84	0	0	4.50	2	2	0	0	2	2	1	1	0	1	5	.250	.250	.250	22.50	4.50
Colon, Roman	R-R	6-5	245	8-13-79	2	1	4.85	27	0	0	3	30	33	20	16	5	7	17	.287	.333	.246	5.16	2.12
Corcoran, Roy	R-R	5-10	190	5-11-80	1	2	6.25	19	0	0	1	32	43	22	22	1	16	20	.339	.360	.325	5.68	4.55
De La Rosa, Wilkin	L-L	6-0	185	2-21-85	3	0	2.25	8	0	0	0	8	6	2	2	0	9	6	.214	.250	.167	6.75	10.13
Dedeaux, Adam	L-L	6-0	200	7-1-86	0	0	8.80	10	0	0	0	15	24	15	15	6	11	9	.375	.267	.471	5.28	6.46
Elbert, Scott	L-L	6-1	210	8-13-85	2	0	5.02	13	0	0	3	14	13	9	8	1	9	16	.236	.320	.167	10.05	5.65
Ely, John	R-R	6-2	200	5-13-86	7	8	5.99	25	25	2	0	144	178	109	96	21	44	99	.301	.306	.296	6.17	2.74
Eveland, Dana	L-L	6-1	235	10-29-83	12	8	4.38	25	25	2	0	154	151	83	75	11	61	107	.260	.272	.254	6.25	3.56
Felix, Francisco	R-R	5-11	205	7-28-83	3	2	5.99	26	7	0	0	71	75	47	47	9	37	67	.272	.319	.227	8.53	4.71
Housey, John	L-R	6-3	178	6-4-88	0	0	0.00	1	0	0	0	0	0	0	0	0	0	0	.000	.000	.000	0.00	0.00
Huber, Jon	R-R	6-1	200	7-7-81	0	1	10.24	9	0	0	0	10	17	15	11	2	10	8	.405	.333	.533	7.45	9.31
Jackson, Steven	R-R	6-5	230	3-15-82	0	2	15.88	2	2	0	0	6	11	11	10	2	5	2	.407	.500	.308	3.18	7.94
Keisler, Randy	L-L	6-3	200	2-24-76	7	4	4.67	23	19	0	0	112	118	69	58	10	50	81	.267	.272	.264	6.53	4.03
Kuo, Hong-Chih	L-L	6-2	240	7-23-81	0	0	0.00	2	0	0	0	1	0	0	0	0	1	3	.000	.000	.000	16.20	5.40
Link, Jon	R-R	6-0	205	3-23-84	2	2	4.24	54	1	0	11	68	65	34	32	6	32	63	.260	.347	.175	8.34	4.24
Miller, Justin	R-R	6-2	215	8-27-77	0	1	10.80	3	0	0	1	2	2	2	2	1	4	2	.286	.000	.500	10.80	21.60
3-team total (11 Round Rock, 6 Tacoma)					1	3	5.73	20	0	0	3	22	18	14	14	3	22	19	—	—		7.77	9.00
Monasterios, Carlos	R-R	6-1	205	3-21-86	0	0	9.00	1	1	0	0	4	9	6	4	0	2	4	.450	.375	.750	9.00	9.00

LOS ANGELES DODGERS

Pitching

Pitching	B-T	HT	WT	DOB	W	L	ERA	G	GS	CG	SV	IP	H	R	ER	HR	BB	SO	AVG	vLH	vRH	K/9	BB/9
Newby, Joey	R-R	6-2	205	3-8-82	2	6	6.31	25	5	0	0	51	60	39	36	6	30	42	.291	.272	.304	7.36	5.26
Parisi, Mike	R-R	6-3	215	4-18-83	6	2	5.20	9	9	0	0	55	49	33	32	9	31	36	.241	.245	.237	5.86	5.04
Pfeiffer, David	L-L	6-3	190	8-17-85	1	3	8.00	25	0	0	0	36	52	40	32	11	14	27	.335	.352	.327	6.75	3.50
Redding, Tim	R-R	5-11	230	2-12-78	2	7	6.59	13	13	1	0	70	91	59	51	11	22	48	.319	.329	.307	6.20	2.84
Schlichting, Travis	R-R	6-4	205	10-19-84	5	3	7.10	51	0	0	4	65	78	54	51	11	30	51	.302	.306	.300	7.10	4.18
Sexton, Tim	R-R	6-6	185	6-10-87	3	6	6.86	15	14	0	0	79	121	66	60	13	24	40	.357	.416	.317	4.58	2.75
Snell, Ian	R-R	5-11	200	10-30-81	1	2	11.05	6	5	0	0	22	26	28	27	11	17	18	.295	.302	.289	7.36	6.95
Troncoso, Ramon	R-R	6-1	210	2-16-83	2	4	5.05	35	0	0	0	57	59	36	32	8	26	41	.277	.277	.277	6.47	4.11
Valdez, Merkin	R-R	6-5	230	11-10-81	4	2	3.58	38	0	0	4	50	47	23	20	1	24	43	.251	.280	.223	7.69	4.29
2-team total (12 Round Rock)					5	2	3.29	50	0	0	8	66	61	27	24	2	29	57	—	—	—	7.81	3.97
Villarreal, Oscar	L-R	6-0	215	11-22-81	0	0	6.75	2	0	0	0	3	5	2	2	1	0	3	.385	.333	.500	10.13	0.00

Fielding

Catcher	PCT	G	PO	A	E	DP	PB
Closser	.986	27	194	15	3	3	0
Collado	1.000	1	7	0	0	0	0
Ellis	.991	53	309	23	3	3	6
Espino	.984	46	275	31	5	3	2
Federowicz	1.000	22	162	23	0	3	2

First Base	PCT	G	PO	A	E	DP
Closser	.979	34	253	22	6	28
Ellis	1.000	1	4	2	0	0
Espino	1.000	11	71	5	0	8
Gibbons	1.000	6	41	4	0	3
Lindsey	.995	26	208	8	1	22
Mitchell	.994	23	158	9	1	14
Sands	.990	45	372	28	4	36
Smith	.978	31	215	11	5	27

Second Base	PCT	G	PO	A	E	DP
Becker	.979	25	38	54	2	12
Castro	1.000	2	1	5	0	0
De Jesus Jr.	.989	73	147	205	4	57
Hernandez	1.000	1	0	3	0	0

Mirabal	.833	1	1	4	1	1
Ortiz	1.000	6	9	17	0	2
Sellers	.956	22	39	69	5	14
Velez	.961	31	61	86	6	24

Third Base	PCT	G	PO	A	E	DP
Becker	.985	35	16	48	1	2
Blake	.833	4	0	10	2	2
Castro	1.000	3	1	4	0	0
Closser	1.000	2	0	1	0	0
De Jesus Jr.	.818	10	8	19	6	4
Espino	1.000	1	1	2	0	0
Hernandez	.000	1	0	0	0	0
Mitchell	.965	72	39	127	6	10
Ortiz	1.000	3	0	1	0	1
Sands	1.000	1	0	3	0	0
Sellers	.964	15	12	15	1	3
Smith	.919	29	23	45	6	2
Velez	1.000	2	2	4	0	1

Shortstop	PCT	G	PO	A	E	DP
Castro	1.000	3	3	7	0	1

	PCT	G	PO	A	E	DP
De Jesus Jr.	.900	17	13	32	5	2
Furcal	.905	4	7	12	2	2
Gordon	.940	70	101	197	19	50
Hernandez	.909	2	7	3	1	3
Ochoa	.935	18	26	61	6	11
Sellers	.976	45	80	122	5	37

Outfield	PCT	G	PO	A	E	DP
Closser	.000	1	0	0	0	0
Coon	1.000	20	32	1	0	0
Gibbons	.975	59	75	4	2	2
Hoffmann	1.000	131	222	6	0	0
Link	.000	1	0	0	0	0
Mitchell	1.000	9	11	1	0	1
Oeltjen	.980	52	96	4	2	1
Redding	.000	1	0	0	0	0
Robinson	.995	97	211	2	1	0
Russell	1.000	11	14	1	0	0
Sands	.950	60	90	5	5	2
Sellers	1.000	7	7	0	0	0
Thames	1.000	5	4	0	0	0
Velez	.973	20	34	2	1	0

CHATTANOOGA LOOKOUTS

DOUBLE-A

SOUTHERN LEAGUE

Batting	B-T	HT	WT	DOB	AVG	vLH	vRH	G	AB	R	H	2B	3B	HR	RBI	BB	HBP	SH	SF	SO	SB	CS	SLG	OBP
Baez, Pedro	R-R	6-2	195	3-11-88	.210	.370	.154	32	105	12	22	12	0	2	15	9	1	0	0	28	1	2	.381	.278
Castellanos, Alex	R-R	5-11	180	8-4-86	.322	.324	.321	32	121	30	39	14	4	4	23	15	4	0	3	24	4	1	.603	.406
Cavazos-Galvez, Brian	R-R	6-0	215	5-17-87	.277	.339	.251	116	411	60	114	27	5	14	61	12	10	0	4	63	13	11	.470	.311
Coon, Brad	L-L	6-0	175	12-11-82	.262	.231	.273	80	202	33	53	15	3	0	13	45	3	0	2	38	13	3	.366	.401
Denker, Travis	R-R	5-9	205	8-5-85	.288	.414	.233	66	233	37	67	15	0	10	33	35	2	0	3	45	6	1	.481	.381
Erickson, Gorman	B-R	6-4	220	3-11-88	.275	.216	.308	41	142	18	39	8	0	7	26	11	1	0	1	22	1	0	.479	.329
Garabedian, Alex	R-R	6-2	210	8-26-85	.136	.250	.071	8	22	0	3	1	0	0	1	2	0	0	0	8	0	0	.182	.208
Gimenez, Hector	B-R	5-10	225	9-28-82	.286	.344	.263	66	231	44	66	21	0	11	54	23	1	0	5	46	0	0	.519	.346
Herrera, Elian	B-R	5-11	190	2-1-85	.278	.314	.261	116	378	69	105	17	6	3	35	58	1	0	6	103	33	11	.378	.370
Jackson, Anthony	B-R	5-8	175	6-17-84	.273	.167	.346	20	44	5	12	0	0	1	2	4	0	0	0	10	2	0	.341	.333
Lemmerman, Jake	R-R	6-1	192	5-4-89	.234	.217	.241	21	77	11	18	6	0	2	11	8	2	0	1	22	1	0	.390	.318
Mier, Jessie	R-R	6-1	215	3-5-85	.279	.238	.318	16	43	2	12	1	0	0	6	5	0	0	1	5	0	2	.302	.347
Navarro, Dioner	B-R	5-9	205	2-9-84	.143	.000	.143	5	14	0	2	0	0	0	1	3	0	0	0	1	2	0	.143	.294
Ochoa, Ivan	R-R	5-9	160	12-16-82	.233	.309	.202	84	236	28	55	13	3	1	20	25	2	0	2	39	5	3	.326	.309
Ortiz, Wilberto	R-R	5-10	180	1-30-85	.222	.310	.160	68	171	19	38	12	1	3	21	20	0	3	26	1	0	.357	.306
Pedroza, Jaime	B-R	5-8	167	9-12-86	.250	.159	.278	87	268	28	67	16	3	6	24	40	5	0	0	76	9	6	.399	.358
Ponte, Angelo	R-R	5-11	215	12-16-86	.000	.000	.000	1	1	0	0	0	0	0	0	0	0	0	0	0	0	0	.000	.000
Russell, Kyle	L-L	6-5	195	6-27-86	.259	.174	.282	120	394	61	102	29	4	19	69	45	6	0	2	144	5	1	.497	.342
Silverio, Alfredo	R-R	6-0	205	5-6-87	.306	.306	.306	132	533	90	163	42	18	16	85	30	1	0	6	91	11	12	.542	.340
Smith, Corey	R-R	6-1	200	4-15-82	.283	.303	.273	54	198	33	56	9	2	3	24	17	0	0	3	50	5	0	.394	.335
Van Slyke, Scott	R-R	6-5	195	7-24-86	.348	.370	.339	130	457	81	159	45	4	20	92	65	2	0	5	100	6	5	.595	.427
Wallach, Matt	L-R	6-1	205	2-17-86	.247	.148	.264	76	186	26	46	11	0	3	17	38	11	0	5	30	3	0	.355	.396

Pitching	B-T	HT	WT	DOB	W	L	ERA	G	GS	CG	SV	IP	H	R	ER	HR	BB	SO	AVG	vLH	vRH	K/9	BB/9
Alvarez, Mario	R-R	6-0	205	3-26-84	0	0	5.17	11	1	0	0	16	19	12	9	0	7	13	.306	.250	.367	7.47	4.02
Ames, Steven	R-R	6-1	205	3-15-88	2	2	2.48	28	0	0	5	33	32	10	9	3	11	41	.260	.302	.229	11.30	3.03
Antonini, Mike	R-L	6-2	200	8-6-85	10	9	4.01	27	27	0	0	148	164	85	66	19	42	131	.272	.262	.276	7.97	2.55
Corcoran, Roy	R-R	5-10	190	5-11-80	0	1	9.45	2	1	0	0	7	12	9	7	1	5	2	.400	.467	.333	2.70	6.75
De La Rosa, Rubby	R-R	6-1	185	3-4-89	2	2	2.93	8	8	0	0	40	30	19	13	1	19	52	.199	.194	.203	11.70	4.28
De La Rosa, Wilkin	L-L	6-0	185	2-21-85	1	2	3.15	14	1	0	1	20	23	17	7	0	12	22	.280	.222	.309	9.90	5.40
Eovaldi, Nate	R-R	6-3	195	2-13-90	6	5	2.62	20	19	0	0	103	76	41	30	3	46	99	.203	.188	.215	8.65	4.02
Fife, Stephen	R-R	6-3	210	10-4-86	3	0	4.01	6	6	0	0	34	36	18	15	2	15	25	.271	.292	.250	6.68	4.01
Guerra, Javy	R-R	6-0	205	10-31-85	1	0	1.06	14	0	0	3	17	8	2	2	1	5	15	.145	.222	.108	7.94	2.65
Jackson, Steven	R-R	6-5	230	3-15-82	0	1	7.15	3	3	0	0	11	17	11	9	2	5	9	.378	.542	.190	7.15	3.97
Jansen, Kenley	B-R	6-5	255	9-30-87	0	1	4.50	5	0	0	0	6	2	3	3	1	3	9	.111	.200	.077	13.50	4.50

Pitching	B-T	HT	WT	DOB	W	L	ERA	G	GS	CG	SV	IP	H	R	ER	HR	BB	SO	AVG	vLH	vRH	K/9	BB/9
Lima, Joel	R-R	6-0	165	8-7-89	0	0	0.00	2	0	0	0	3	2	1	0	0	1	4	.182	.250	.143	12.00	3.00
Lindblom, Josh	R-R	6-5	240	6-15-87	1	3	2.13	34	0	0	17	42	30	10	10	3	14	54	.205	.292	.136	11.48	2.98
Martin, Ethan	R-R	6-2	195	6-6-89	5	3	4.02	21	3	0	2	40	31	21	18	3	29	43	.215	.262	.181	9.60	6.47
Miller, Justin	R-R	6-2	190	8-2-87	2	0	7.23	18	0	0	0	24	38	21	19	3	11	14	.369	.409	.339	5.32	4.18
Newby, Joey	R-R	6-2	205	3-8-82	2	1	3.74	7	2	0	0	22	25	9	9	1	7	16	.287	.282	.292	6.65	2.91
Pfeiffer, David	L-L	6-3	190	8-17-85	4	1	3.50	23	3	0	0	46	54	25	18	2	11	31	.286	.338	.254	6.02	2.14
Pomeranz, Stuart	R-R	6-7	220	12-17-84	0	0	27.00	2	0	0	0	1	3	5	4	0	3	2	.375	.600	.000	13.50	20.25
Rice, Scott	L-L	6-6	220	9-21-81	4	4	1.95	34	0	0	1	51	42	17	11	3	17	42	.223	.173	.257	7.46	3.02
Savage, Will	R-R	6-4	215	8-25-84	12	6	3.95	25	23	1	1	141	150	69	62	12	27	87	.273	.311	.241	5.54	1.72
Solano, Javier	R-R	6-0	177	3-31-90	1	0	3.03	19	0	0	1	33	30	14	11	1	16	27	.250	.276	.226	7.44	4.41
St. Clair, Cole	L-L	6-5	225	7-30-86	1	5	3.04	42	0	0	2	50	43	19	17	1	13	46	.242	.278	.212	8.23	2.32
Tolleson, Shawn	R-R	6-2	215	1-19-88	4	2	1.62	38	0	0	12	44	42	14	8	2	11	55	.251	.342	.176	11.17	2.23
Wall, Josh	R-R	6-6	218	1-21-87	4	5	3.93	51	0	0	1	69	72	34	30	6	27	57	.271	.327	.233	7.47	3.54
Walter, Josh	R-R	6-4	250	4-5-85	0	0	1.50	3	0	0	0	6	3	2	1	1	3	3	.143	.300	.000	4.50	4.50
Webster, Allen	R-R	6-3	185	2-10-90	6	3	5.04	18	17	1	0	91	101	53	51	7	36	73	.286	.288	.284	7.22	3.56
Withrow, Chris	R-R	6-3	195	4-1-89	6	6	4.20	25	25	1	0	129	111	68	60	8	75	130	.239	.246	.232	9.09	5.25

Fielding

Catcher	PCT	G	PO	A	E	DP	PB
Erickson	.994	39	300	27	2	3	3
Garabedian	1.000	6	48	4	0	0	0
Gimenez	.994	24	157	11	1	1	1
Mier	.990	16	89	11	1	0	2
Navarro	1.000	3	22	1	0	1	1
Ponte	.000	1	0	0	0	0	0
Wallach	.991	72	513	37	5	4	7

First Base	PCT	G	PO	A	E	DP
Cavazos-Galvez	.977	55	387	34	10	43
Gimenez	.985	31	182	13	3	24
Navarro	.929	2	11	2	1	0
Smith	.988	13	79	4	1	11
Van Slyke	.980	65	399	37	9	37

	PCT	G	PO	A	E	DP
Wallach	1.000	2	5	0	0	1

Second Base	PCT	G	PO	A	E	DP
Denker	.982	24	37	73	2	15
Herrera	.952	52	57	100	8	15
Ortiz	.976	12	17	23	1	8
Pedroza	.977	84	134	203	8	45

Third Base	PCT	G	PO	A	E	DP
Baez	.967	30	13	45	2	6
Denker	.904	45	37	67	11	5
Herrera	.932	24	14	27	3	1
Ortiz	1.000	22	15	24	0	2
Smith	.944	41	25	59	5	6

Shortstop	PCT	G	PO	A	E	DP
Herrera	.932	34	52	71	9	19
Lemmerman	.949	21	40	53	5	15
Ochoa	.953	81	120	206	16	51
Ortiz	.948	25	30	61	5	10

Outfield	PCT	G	PO	A	E	DP
Castellanos	.984	31	60	3	1	0
Cavazos-Galvez	.973	50	68	4	2	0
Coon	.991	65	102	3	1	1
Herrera	1.000	28	35	0	0	0
Jackson	1.000	16	25	2	0	0
Russell	.978	97	168	6	4	3
Silverio	.978	123	254	19	6	4
Van Slyke	.976	73	145	3	3	0

RANCHO CUCAMONGA QUAKES   HIGH CLASS A

CALIFORNIA LEAGUE

Batting	B-T	HT	WT	DOB	AVG	vLH	vRH	G	AB	R	H	2B	3B	HR	RBI	BB	HBP	SH	SF	SO	SB	CS	SLG	OBP
Barajas, Rod	R-R	6-2	250	9-5-75	.389	.250	.429	4	18	4	7	2	0	1	2	1	0	0	0	2	0	0	.667	.421
Becker, Joe	R-R	5-10	184	11-8-85	.400	.667	.000	1	5	0	2	1	0	0	2	0	0	0	0	1	0	0	.600	.400
Blake, Casey	R-R	6-2	205	8-23-73	.375	.333	.500	2	8	2	3	1	0	0	1	0	0	0	0	2	0	0	.500	.375
Buss, Nick	L-R	6-2	195	12-15-86	.328	.366	.313	115	479	86	157	30	8	14	55	27	6	0	3	63	28	10	.511	.369
Cuevas, Noel	R-R	6-2	187	10-2-91	.220	.071	.247	23	91	11	20	4	0	1	11	4	0	0	0	17	2	2	.286	.253
Delmonico, Tony	R-R	6-0	194	4-27-87	.268	.276	.265	111	396	66	106	22	2	12	63	57	23	0	5	99	1	2	.424	.387
Denker, Travis	R-R	5-9	205	8-5-85	.259	.364	.229	55	197	39	51	8	2	15	48	28	2	0	3	38	3	0	.548	.352
Erickson, Gorman	B-R	6-4	220	3-11-88	.305	.297	.309	63	226	37	69	16	4	6	40	41	1	0	4	42	3	2	.491	.408
Furcal, Rafael	B-R	5-8	190	10-24-77	.318	.500	.250	6	22	10	7	0	0	0	1	3	0	0	0	3	1	0	.318	.400
Gallagher, Austin	R-R	6-5	210	11-16-88	.292	.255	.306	111	390	73	114	19	2	13	62	62	1	0	5	70	0	1	.451	.386
Gordon, Dee	L-R	5-11	150	4-22-88	.273	1.000	.200	3	11	4	3	0	0	0	0	1	0	0	0	1	2	1	.273	.333
Guerrero, Pedro	R-R	6-3	185	12-3-88	.274	.250	.281	39	117	16	32	6	3	0	4	10	0	0	1	30	2	3	.376	.328
Jackson, Anthony	R-R	5-8	175	6-17-84	.336	.293	.365	35	143	32	48	5	3	3	30	15	3	0	3	19	10	5	.476	.402
Jean, Ramon	R-R	6-0	160	10-10-87	.247	.284	.233	88	296	42	73	11	1	5	34	10	5	0	2	61	13	7	.341	.281
LaRosa, B.J.	R-R	6-2	200	4-28-88	.182	.200	.176	8	22	1	4	0	0	0	1	0	0	0	0	2	0	1	.182	.217
Lemmerman, Jake	R-R	6-1	192	5-4-89	.293	.265	.304	103	400	71	117	23	2	8	54	47	12	0	5	90	9	3	.420	.379
Mattingly, Preston	R-R	6-2	210	8-28-87	.233	.179	.260	37	116	15	27	3	0	2	11	10	0	0	1	36	7	1	.310	.291
Mier, Jessie	R-R	6-1	215	3-5-85	.156	.091	.182	21	77	7	12	2	0	2	10	4	4	0	0	8	0	0	.260	.235
Ortiz, Wilberto	R-R	5-10	180	1-30-85	.321	.211	.344	30	109	19	35	7	2	1	22	22	2	0	1	17	2	1	.450	.440
Pedroza, B.J.	B-R	5-8	167	7-9-88	.278	.154	.317	30	108	18	30	7	1	4	26	12	5	0	0	22	2	0	.472	.376
Pericht, Mike	R-R	6-5	235	5-23-88	.400	.500	.333	2	10	1	4	0	0	0	1	0	0	0	0	1	0	0	.400	.400
Smith, Blake	L-R	6-2	225	12-9-87	.294	.277	.300	74	293	59	86	24	0	16	63	32	0	0	4	83	3	2	.539	.359
Songco, Angelo	L-R	6-0	195	9-9-88	.313	.255	.337	131	534	110	167	48	4	29	114	42	7	0	5	121	4	3	.581	.367
Thompson, Kevin	R-R	6-3	185	9-16-88	.200	.500	.125	4	10	1	2	0	0	0	0	0	0	0	0	4	0	0	.200	.200
Uribe, Juan	R-R	5-11	230	3-22-79	.500	.500	.500	3	8	2	4	1	0	0	1	0	0	0	0	2	0	0	.625	.556
Wise, J.T.	R-R	6-0	210	6-2-86	.286	.309	.277	97	336	61	96	18	2	17	73	53	3	0	4	90	2	2	.503	.384
Ynoa, Rafael	R-R	6-0	180	8-7-87	.275	.290	.269	126	466	61	128	21	5	3	54	42	2	0	7	69	13	11	.365	.333

Pitching	B-T	HT	WT	DOB	W	L	ERA	G	GS	CG	SV	IP	H	R	ER	HR	BB	SO	AVG	vLH	vRH	K/9	BB/9
Acosta, Ryan	R-R	6-2	170	11-4-88	0	2	10.66	8	0	0	0	13	23	21	15	3	9	12	.377	.545	.282	8.53	6.39
Aguasviva, Geison	L-L	6-2	166	8-3-87	0	1	1.13	6	0	0	0	8	5	2	1	1	2	6	.185	.167	.190	6.75	2.25
Ames, Steven	R-R	6-1	205	3-15-88	0	0	1.17	15	0	0	9	15	10	3	2	1	2	28	.182	.091	.242	16.43	1.17
Bawcom, Logan	R-R	6-2	200	11-9-88	1	2	3.74	21	0	0	13	22	17	10	9	2	12	28	.218	.174	.236	11.63	4.98
Cabrera, Freddie	R-R	6-5	210	1-25-90	1	0	5.91	4	0	0	0	11	12	8	7	1	4	5	.300	.200	.333	4.22	3.38
Carela, Daniel	R-R	6-3	225	9-18-87	0	0	4.35	8	0	0	0	10	13	12	5	0	8	7	.310	.125	.353	6.10	6.97
Frias, Carlos	R-R	6-4	170	11-13-89	1	1	6.19	12	0	0	0	16	17	13	11	3	17	11	.304	.364	.289	6.19	9.56
Garland, Jon	R-R	6-6	210	9-27-79	0	0	5.79	1	1	0	0	5	6	3	3	0	0	3	.300	.308	.286	5.79	0.00

Pitching

Pitching	B-T	HT	WT	DOB	W	L	ERA	G	GS	CG	SV	IP	H	R	ER	HR	BB	SO	AVG	vLH	vRH	K/9	BB/9
Hawksworth, Blake	R-R	6-3	200	3-1-83	0	0	2.25	4	4	0	0	4	2	1	1	0	1	5	.154	.000	.250	11.25	2.25
Housey, John	L-R	6-3	178	6-4-88	0	0	27.00	1	0	0	0	1	3	3	3	1	2	0	.500	.500	.500	0.00	18.00
2-team total (6 High Desert)					1	0	10.03	7	0	0	0	12	19	14	13	4	9	7	—	—	—	5.40	6.94
Jansen, Kenley	B-R	6-5	255	9-30-87	0	0	0.00	2	2	0	0	2	0	0	0	0	0	4	.000	.000	.000	18.00	0.00
Kuo, Hong-Chih	L-L	6-2	240	7-23-81	0	1	6.23	5	1	0	0	4	7	3	3	0	1	7	.350	.250	.375	14.54	2.08
Magill, Matt	R-R	6-3	190	11-10-89	11	5	4.33	26	21	0	0	139	156	78	67	15	52	126	.280	.259	.292	8.14	3.36
Martin, Ethan	R-R	6-2	195	6-6-89	4	4	7.36	16	9	0	0	55	65	48	45	8	37	61	.291	.337	.263	9.98	6.05
Miller, Aaron	L-L	6-3	200	9-18-87	3	2	3.97	10	6	0	0	34	37	19	15	2	18	30	.282	.280	.283	7.94	4.76
Montgomery, Bret	R-R	6-6	250	8-6-85	0	0	3.86	2	0	0	0	5	2	3	2	1	4	7	.111	.167	.083	13.50	7.71
Nestor, Scott	R-R	6-4	225	8-20-84	0	0	10.80	3	0	0	0	3	2	4	4	0	6	4	.154	.143	.167	10.80	16.20
Orenduff, Justin	R-R	6-3	215	5-27-83	0	0	8.74	9	0	0	0	11	11	11	11	1	13	7	.262	.368	.174	5.56	10.32
Ozoria, Arismendy	R-R	6-0	195	8-7-90	7	5	5.40	19	14	0	0	85	94	55	51	16	41	58	.285	.267	.296	6.14	4.34
Padilla, Vicente	R-R	6-0	230	9-27-77	0	0	1.42	4	4	0	0	6	4	1	1	0	1	5	.182	.375	.071	7.11	1.42
Patterson, Red	R-R	6-3	210	5-11-87	7	1	3.91	14	14	1	0	92	78	42	40	10	25	93	.234	.209	.246	9.10	2.45
Redding, JonMichael	R-R	6-1	195	11-16-87	11	7	3.66	25	24	0	0	138	132	64	56	9	52	130	.250	.230	.261	8.50	3.40
Reed, Chris	L-L	6-4	195	5-20-90	0	1	7.71	3	3	0	0	7	9	6	6	1	4	9	.321	.000	.346	11.57	5.14
Roberts, Jordan	L-L	6-2	200	1-5-86	7	4	3.03	36	0	0	0	71	74	29	24	5	19	58	.275	.286	.272	7.32	2.40
Romero, Robert	R-R	5-10	190	3-28-85	0	1	8.56	24	0	0	1	27	31	32	26	2	29	32	.284	.311	.266	10.54	9.55
Santiago, Andres	R-R	6-2	200	10-26-89	8	5	5.03	28	20	0	0	122	150	76	68	10	48	113	.302	.294	.307	8.36	3.55
Smith, Steve	R-R	6-2	210	5-15-86	5	5	3.63	43	0	0	9	69	67	33	28	5	27	59	.251	.203	.289	7.66	3.50
Solano, Javier	R-R	6-0	177	3-31-90	2	3	4.09	26	0	0	3	44	54	24	20	3	9	20	.309	.288	.324	9.20	1.84
Suiter, Andy	L-L	6-3	215	6-10-87	0	2	5.61	25	0	0	0	43	46	30	27	4	31	35	.271	.256	.275	7.27	6.44
Tolleson, Shawn	R-R	6-2	215	1-19-88	2	0	0.93	5	0	0	3	10	2	3	1	1	3	17	.061	.067	.056	15.83	2.79
Vasquez, Luis	R-R	6-4	175	4-3-86	0	2	3.77	13	0	0	0	14	13	8	6	0	21	11	.260	.174	.333	6.91	13.19
Walter, Josh	R-R	6-4	250	4-5-85	3	1	3.74	30	2	0	1	65	63	31	27	6	29	64	.249	.173	.297	8.86	4.02
Webster, Allen	R-R	6-3	185	2-10-90	5	2	2.33	9	9	0	0	54	46	18	14	2	21	62	.228	.176	.265	10.33	3.50
Wilborn, Greg	L-L	6-2	175	6-3-87	2	3	6.85	12	6	0	1	43	48	34	33	3	28	38	.293	.385	.264	7.89	5.82

Fielding

Catcher	PCT	G	PO	A	E	DP	PB
Barajas	1.000	1	4	0	0	0	0
Erickson	.987	53	410	43	6	5	9
LaRosa	.985	8	65	2	1	0	0
Mier	.983	21	162	14	3	1	7
Pericht	1.000	2	15	3	0	0	0
Wise	.990	59	523	68	6	6	9

First Base	PCT	G	PO	A	E	DP
Gallagher	.992	67	488	39	4	54
Mattingly	1.000	1	3	0	0	0
Songco	.988	57	451	32	6	45
Wise	1.000	22	151	17	0	14

Second Base	PCT	G	PO	A	E	DP
Becker	1.000	1	2	4	0	1

	PCT	G	PO	A	E	DP	PB
Denker	.977	9	16	27	1	4	
Guerrero	.982	10	23	33	1	10	
Pedroza	.952	28	44	75	6	22	
Uribe	1.000	2	1	1	0	0	
Ynoa	.969	93	184	258	14	61	

Third Base	PCT	G	PO	A	E	DP
Delmonico	.926	85	42	147	15	13
Denker	.941	40	27	69	6	9
Guerrero	.880	13	4	18	3	1
Ortiz	1.000	6	4	6	0	0

Shortstop	PCT	G	PO	A	E	DP
Furcal	.833	3	5	5	2	1
Gordon	1.000	3	4	7	0	0
Guerrero	.955	12	16	26	2	7

	PCT	G	PO	A	E	DP
Lemmerman	.946	96	125	225	20	44
Ortiz	1.000	1	2	4	0	3
Ynoa	.956	31	49	82	6	21

Outfield	PCT	G	PO	A	E	DP
Buss	.988	113	240	6	3	0
Cuevas	.963	22	52	0	2	0
Jackson	1.000	35	101	1	0	1
Jean	.984	77	120	6	2	2
Mattingly	1.000	28	50	2	0	2
Ortiz	.977	25	41	2	1	0
Smith	.974	72	173	13	5	2
Songco	.952	65	78	2	4	0

GREAT LAKES LOONS

LOW CLASS A

MIDWEST LEAGUE

Batting

Batting	B-T	HT	WT	DOB	AVG	vLH	vRH	G	AB	R	H	2B	3B	HR	RBI	BB	HBP	SH	SF	SO	SB	CS	SLG	OBP
Akins, Nick	R-R	6-1	220	12-25-87	.219	.198	.226	85	302	43	66	11	3	12	45	37	7	0	5	77	0	2	.394	.313
Becker, Joe	R-R	5-10	184	11-8-85	.244	.368	.154	13	45	2	11	0	0	0	5	6	1	0	0	9	0	0	.244	.346
Bosnik, Jesse	L-R	6-2	205	7-23-88	.232	.213	.240	100	336	31	78	20	0	8	42	21	4	0	3	79	2	4	.363	.283
Cilladi, Steve	R-R	5-9	182	3-15-87	.185	.167	.190	12	27	1	5	0	0	1	2	0	0	0	0	5	0	0	.296	.185
Collado, Keyter	R-R	5-9	182	6-8-86	—	.000	.000	1	0	0	0	0	0	0	0	0	0	0	0	0	0	0	—	—
Coyle, Bobby	L-L	6-1	215	3-6-89	.250	.222	.261	98	380	42	95	16	1	9	44	30	1	0	5	68	3	2	.368	.303
Dean, Blake	L-L	6-1	175	2-25-88	.237	.180	.264	96	350	32	83	16	1	9	44	37	2	0	6	47	1	0	.349	.309
Domecus, Steve	R-R	6-3	220	6-29-87	.276	.306	.261	60	210	28	58	11	2	5	23	12	13	0	1	37	2	2	.419	.352
Garcia, Jonathan	R-R	5-11	175	11-11-91	.228	.225	.230	130	464	58	106	28	2	19	63	34	8	0	5	133	2	1	.420	.290
Grider, Casio	R-R	6-1	165	8-17-87	.230	.221	.234	120	417	66	96	22	10	2	25	45	13	0	0	105	31	7	.345	.324
Henderson, Chris	L-R	5-11	190	6-23-88	.220	.216	.221	61	186	17	41	6	1	1	10	19	1	0	2	36	2	2	.280	.293
Hernandez, Bryant	R-R	5-8	170	3-5-88	.185	.288	.138	58	189	22	35	6	2	3	19	14	2	0	2	59	3	1	.286	.246
Iden, David	R-R	5-9	160	3-4-87	.211	.250	.197	31	95	14	20	4	0	0	10	1	0	1	0	20	1	0	.253	.290
Jacobs, Chris	R-R	6-5	257	11-25-88	.288	.224	.318	65	215	31	62	14	0	12	33	34	3	0	0	62	0	0	.521	.393
Landry, Leon	L-R	5-11	185	9-20-89	.250	.250	.250	125	500	59	125	21	11	4	41	37	5	0	2	67	28	12	.360	.307
Lara, Christian	B-R	5-11	185	4-11-85	.261	.286	.252	63	218	35	57	12	2	2	22	35	1	0	6	43	4	4	.362	.358
Mattingly, Preston	R-R	6-2	210	8-28-87	.229	.250	.200	16	48	8	11	2	0	3	8	1	1	0	1	17	1	0	.458	.255
Mirabal, Charlie	R-R	5-11	180	4-2-87	.250	.216	.268	33	108	6	27	4	0	0	7	9	1	0	1	20	1	0	.287	.311
Pederson, Joc	L-L	6-1	185	4-21-92	.160	.267	.114	16	50	4	8	0	0	0	1	7	2	0	0	9	2	0	.160	.282
Pena, Roman	R-R	6-0	190	9-2-86	.226	.267	.213	39	124	19	28	9	2	3	8	22	0	0	1	24	2	0	.403	.340
Pericht, Mike	R-R	6-5	235	5-23-88	.273	.314	.257	92	308	34	84	18	1	11	37	25	13	0	2	92	2	0	.445	.351

Pitching

Pitching	B-T	HT	WT	DOB	W	L	ERA	G	GS	CG	SV	IP	H	R	ER	HR	BB	SO	AVG	vLH	vRH	K/9	BB/9
Acosta, Ryan	R-R	6-2	170	11-4-88	2	2	2.85	18	0	0	2	41	38	16	13	2	13	25	.252	.203	.287	5.49	2.85
Anton, Rick	L-L	6-0	190	6-5-89	1	1	4.00	8	4	0	0	27	31	17	12	0	3	17	.277	.333	.247	5.67	1.00
Bawcom, Logan	R-R	6-2	200	11-2-88	4	1	2.78	31	0	0	14	45	33	18	14	2	16	56	.201	.181	.217	11.12	3.18

Pitching	B-T	HT	WT	DOB	W	L	ERA	G	GS	CG	SV	IP	H	R	ER	HR	BB	SO	AVG	vLH	vRH	K/9	BB/9
Boothe, Robert	R-R	6-2	190	1-30-86	0	0	10.80	3	0	0	0	5	5	6	6	0	8	5	.263	.333	.250	9.00	14.40
Budkevics, Pete	R-R	6-2	165	10-14-87	4	4	3.39	45	0	0	5	85	77	38	32	5	32	71	.246	.212	.271	7.52	3.39
Burgos, Raul	R-R	6-1	210	8-18-87	2	4	4.16	36	0	0	3	67	57	39	31	3	41	42	.234	.280	.190	5.64	5.51
Christenson, Ryan	L-L	6-1	185	1-11-89	7	8	5.05	26	21	0	0	119	146	76	67	6	32	98	.300	.221	.335	7.39	2.41
Cone, Derek	R-R	6-5	210	6-20-90	1	4	5.68	8	4	0	1	25	26	16	16	3	19	20	.260	.293	.237	7.11	6.75
Drowne, Mike	R-L	5-10	175	7-28-88	0	0	9.64	6	0	0	0	9	13	14	10	0	13	7	.310	.385	.276	6.75	12.54
Gomez, Gustavo	R-R	6-1	150	5-24-91	0	2	11.12	5	3	0	0	11	13	14	14	1	9	16	.289	.294	.286	12.71	7.15
Gould, Garrett	R-R	6-4	190	7-19-91	11	6	2.40	27	24	0	0	124	102	47	33	8	37	104	.220	.233	.204	7.57	2.69
Housey, John	L-R	6-3	178	6-4-88	1	2	3.38	14	0	0	1	27	27	12	10	3	12	18	.265	.229	.296	6.08	4.05
Lee, Zach	R-R	6-4	190	9-13-91	9	6	3.47	24	24	0	0	109	101	51	42	9	32	91	.242	.229	.254	7.51	2.64
Matre, Steve	R-R	6-2	185	5-21-88	0	0	0.00	1	0	0	0	2	2	0	0	0	1	1	.286	.500	.200	5.40	5.40
McGough, Scott	R-R	6-0	170	10-31-89	0	4	2.21	20	0	0	8	20	18	6	5	1	6	25	.243	.216	.270	11.07	2.66
Montgomery, Bret	R-R	6-6	250	8-6-85	7	1	2.60	39	1	0	3	90	81	28	26	3	25	79	.233	.231	.251	8.20	1.50
Patterson, Red	R-R	6-3	210	5-11-87	5	4	3.43	14	14	1	0	81	70	33	31	5	20	79	.233	.266	.205	8.74	2.21
Pevsner, Andrew	L-L	6-3	205	10-15-88	1	1	4.25	29	0	0	0	42	43	21	20	4	30	34	.267	.281	.260	7.23	6.38
Rodriguez, Juan	R-R	6-5	195	12-12-88	1	1	1.59	12	0	0	1	17	6	5	3	0	10	20	.105	.136	.086	10.59	5.29
Sanchez, Angel	R-R	6-3	177	11-28-89	8	4	2.82	20	16	0	0	99	72	40	31	5	39	84	.198	.218	.180	7.64	3.55
Sexton, Tim	R-R	6-6	185	6-10-87	3	6	4.18	14	14	1	0	84	86	47	39	7	20	74	.258	.312	.212	7.93	2.14
Stickel, Brant	L-L	6-4	210	1-8-87	0	2	10.80	8	0	0	0	7	14	8	8	0	6	4	.412	.667	.273	5.40	8.10
Tolleson, Shawn	R-R	6-2	215	1-19-88	1	0	0.00	14	0	0	10	15	8	1	0	0	4	33	.154	.120	.185	19.80	2.40
Wilborn, Greg	L-L	6-2	175	6-3-87	4	4	3.74	14	14	0	0	65	60	33	27	4	44	90	.246	.190	.285	12.46	6.09

Fielding

Catcher	PCT	G	PO	A	E	DP	PB
Cilladi	.964	10	74	7	3	0	2
Collado	1.000	1	1	0	0	0	0
Domecus	.977	52	350	32	9	0	6
Pericht	.980	83	678	72	15	4	10

First Base	PCT	G	PO	A	E	DP
Bosnik	1.000	1	1	0	0	0
Dean	.989	80	679	39	8	44
Henderson	.982	24	150	12	3	15
Jacobs	.987	43	345	24	5	25

Second Base	PCT	G	PO	A	E	DP
Grider	.966	94	173	286	16	55
Henderson	1.000	3	3	0	0	0

	PCT	G	PO	A	E	DP	PB
Hernandez	1.000	20	26	48	0	10	
Iden	.973	28	44	64	3	11	

Third Base	PCT	G	PO	A	E	DP
Becker	.929	13	5	21	2	2
Bosnik	.935	98	75	157	16	6
Cilladi	.000	1	0	0	0	0
Henderson	.923	27	14	46	5	2
Iden	.714	3	0	5	2	0
Lara	.923	4	5	7	1	1

Shortstop	PCT	G	PO	A	E	DP
Grider	.851	17	17	40	10	7
Hernandez	.955	35	52	98	7	19
Iden	1.000	2	0	3	0	0

	PCT	G	PO	A	E	DP
Lara	.964	57	87	151	9	27
Mirabal	.978	33	46	88	3	16

Outfield	PCT	G	PO	A	E	DP
Akins	.947	60	105	2	6	1
Coyle	.979	60	89	5	2	0
Domecus	1.000	2	1	1	0	0
Garcia	.975	126	220	12	6	5
Grider	1.000	9	23	2	0	0
Henderson	1.000	1	1	0	0	0
Landry	.984	123	245	5	4	1
Mattingly	1.000	11	18	0	0	0
Pederson	.949	16	34	3	2	0
Pena	.967	24	28	1	1	0

OGDEN RAPTORS

ROOKIE

PIONEER LEAGUE

Batting	B-T	HT	WT	DOB	AVG	vLH	vRH	G	AB	R	H	2B	3B	HR	RBI	BB	HBP	SH	SF	SO	SB	CS	SLG	OBP
Aguilar, Alexis	R-R	5-11	162	6-17-91	.307	.260	.325	45	176	35	54	8	2	4	34	5	6	0	1	26	14	5	.443	.346
Baldwin III, James	L-R	6-3	190	10-10-91	.250	.183	.279	50	196	47	49	9	3	10	39	18	12	0	1	74	22	5	.480	.348
Boudreaux, Justin	R-R	6-1	190	10-3-89	.265	.214	.282	32	113	26	30	7	2	3	21	16	10	0	1	26	16	0	.442	.400
Cuevas, Noel	R-R	6-2	187	10-2-91	.285	.297	.280	60	246	38	70	16	5	8	32	14	3	0	4	55	13	6	.488	.326
Dickson, O'Koyea	R-R	5-11	215	2-9-90	.333	.347	.329	48	189	33	63	10	1	13	38	19	4	0	2	44	1	1	.603	.402
Edge, Andrew	R-R	6-2	230	12-31-87	.253	.327	.220	41	158	31	40	17	2	8	28	8	1	0	0	81	1	0	.538	.293
Hunt, Jeff	L-R	6-2	190	2-13-91	.272	.238	.284	45	151	31	41	9	2	4	17	19	0	0	0	55	2	2	.437	.353
Iden, David	R-R	5-9	160	3-4-87	.476	.545	.400	5	21	6	10	3	0	0	3	2	1	0	0	2	1	0	.619	.542
Kirkland, Matt	R-R	6-2	210	3-13-91	.292	.229	.319	39	161	28	47	7	0	4	30	11	2	0	0	37	0	0	.410	.345
Maynard, Pratt	L-R	6-0	215	11-19-89	.239	.375	.188	25	88	16	21	3	0	2	11	13	2	0	1	24	0	0	.341	.346
Mirabal, Charlie	R-R	5-11	180	4-2-87	.315	.294	.326	34	146	28	46	8	0	3	25	7	2	0	0	26	11	2	.432	.355
Morales, Enlly	R-R	5-11	168	9-13-89	.260	.194	.304	25	77	12	20	4	0	0	7	4	4	0	1	19	1	1	.312	.326
O'Brien, Chris	B-R	6-0	219	7-24-89	.267	.333	.222	4	15	2	4	1	0	0	2	0	0	0	0	2	0	0	.533	.267
Pederson, Joc	L-L	6-1	185	4-21-92	.353	.284	.377	68	266	54	94	20	2	11	64	36	3	0	5	54	24	5	.568	.429
Ponte, Angelo	R-R	5-11	215	12-16-86	.000	.000	.000	2	1	0	0	0	0	0	0	1	0	0	0	1	0	0	.000	.500
Schaus, Jeff	L-R	6-2	205	4-7-89	.273	.333	.250	8	33	5	9	1	1	0	3	3	0	0	0	6	0	0	.364	.333
Schebler, Scott	L-R	6-1	208	10-6-90	.285	.326	.268	70	295	44	84	17	8	13	58	13	5	0	2	97	1	1	.529	.324
Shines, Devin	R-L	5-9	185	5-15-89	.400	1.000	.000	1	5	1	2	1	0	0	2	0	1	0	0	1	0	0	.600	.500
Thompson, Kevin	R-R	6-3	185	9-16-88	.241	.400	.208	11	29	6	7	1	0	0	5	3	1	0	0	6	2	2	.276	.333
Vazquez, Jan	B-R	5-10	165	4-29-91	.253	.167	.295	27	91	10	23	5	0	1	10	9	0	0	0	23	1	1	.341	.333
Wingo, Scott	L-R	5-11	175	3-25-89	.275	.286	.272	32	109	37	30	8	0	4	17	28	12	0	2	30	7	2	.459	.464
Winker, Joey	L-L	6-1	190	8-28-89	.111	.000	.125	4	18	1	2	0	0	1	1	1	0	0	0	5	0	0	.278	.158
Woodward, Scott	L-R	6-2	205	12-3-88	.219	.275	.185	34	105	25	23	8	2	4	12	13	5	0	0	26	4	1	.448	.333

Pitching	B-T	HT	WT	DOB	W	L	ERA	G	GS	CG	SV	IP	H	R	ER	HR	BB	SO	AVG	vLH	vRH	K/9	BB/9
Anton, Rick	L-L	6-0	190	6-5-89	0	1	1.59	6	0	0	0	11	5	3	1	1	13	.238	.200	.241	6.88	0.53	
Cabrera, Freddie	R-R	6-5	210	1-25-90	1	1	8.44	7	2	0	0	21	35	24	20	8	7	17	.376	.467	.333	7.17	2.95
Cone, Derek	R-R	6-5	210	6-20-90	3	3	5.03	10	10	0	0	48	49	28	27	7	23	57	.266	.289	.250	10.61	4.28
De Aza, Carlos	R-R	6-3	178	5-4-90	2	2	7.02	22	0	0	1	33	39	29	26	4	12	25	.287	.300	.281	6.75	3.24
Dedeaux, Adam	R-R	6-0	200	7-1-86	0	0	13.50	5	0	0	0	14	28	18	18	3	7	9	.421	.529	.375	6.75	5.25
Dominguez, Jose	R-R	6-0	160	8-7-90	0	3	18.00	3	3	0	0	10	26	22	20	2	3	9	.464	.348	.545	8.10	2.70
Drowne, Mike	R-L	5-10	175	7-28-88	1	1	4.56	21	0	0	3	24	23	13	12	0	26	31	.253	.208	.269	11.79	9.89

LOS ANGELES DODGERS

Pitching	B-T	HT	WT	DOB	W	L	ERA	G	GS	CG	SV	IP	H	R	ER	HR	BB	SO	AVG	vLH	vRH	K/9	BB/9
Eadington, Eric	R-L	6-2	220	2-9-88	1	0	0.00	9	0	0	0	10	7	0	0	0	2	13	.179	.167	.185	11.32	1.74
Garcia, Yimi	R-R	6-1	175	8-18-90	4	2	3.10	20	1	0	4	52	46	23	18	4	19	71	.236	.261	.228	12.21	3.27
Gomez, Gustavo	R-R	6-1	150	5-24-91	5	1	4.87	13	13	0	0	61	57	40	33	9	36	81	.245	.321	.201	11.95	5.31
Handke, Chris	R-R	6-10	235	3-19-88	0	1	6.66	16	4	0	0	26	22	23	19	3	29	27	.227	.265	.206	9.47	10.17
Lima, Joel	R-R	6-0	165	8-7-89	3	1	5.71	21	0	0	1	35	41	25	22	9	11	34	.287	.362	.250	8.83	2.86
Martinez, Brandon	R-R	6-4	150	11-25-90	6	3	4.07	15	15	0	0	73	66	40	33	6	44	58	.237	.212	.250	7.15	5.42
Matre, Steve	R-R	6-2	185	5-21-88	0	1	5.82	11	0	0	0	17	26	12	11	2	5	22	.342	.333	.346	11.65	2.65
McGough, Scott	R-R	6-0	170	10-31-89	1	1	4.76	6	0	0	2	6	8	4	3	0	0	8	.320	.375	.294	12.71	0.00
Nishijimi, Kazuki	L-L	6-1	190	2-28-89	2	1	5.51	14	1	0	0	33	44	28	20	4	2	27	.303	.282	.311	7.44	0.55
Noriega, Juan	R-R	5-7	145	9-3-90	0	0	0.00	2	0	0	0	2	1	0	0	0	2	0	.154	.000	.167	13.50	0.00
O'Sullivan, Ryan	R-R	6-2	190	9-5-90	0	1	6.48	3	3	0	0	8	7	7	6	1	6	5	.250	.143	.286	5.40	6.48
Purpura, Robert	R-R	6-0	185	2-26-87	1	1	6.75	8	0	0	0	12	16	9	9	5	4	14	.314	.353	.294	10.50	3.00
Rodriguez, Yimy	R-R	6-2	215	9-1-87	3	3	4.06	16	1	0	1	44	44	23	20	3	16	43	.251	.309	.225	8.73	3.25
Sanchez, Raydel	R-R	6-0	205	3-11-90	4	5	4.66	15	15	0	0	75	89	54	39	11	16	77	.283	.372	.220	9.20	1.91
Shelton, Matt	R-R	6-4	205	11-30-88	4	2	2.05	19	0	0	1	26	21	10	6	1	8	30	.214	.278	.177	10.25	2.73
Stickel, Brant	L-L	6-4	210	1-8-87	0	0	10.13	5	0	0	0	5	9	6	6	1	3	7	.391	.333	.412	11.81	5.06
Thomas, Mike	L-L	6-2	185	1-6-89	0	2	7.90	6	2	0	0	14	20	12	12	2	9	14	.364	.526	.278	9.22	5.93
West, Jason	R-R	5-11	185	7-30-88	0	0	0.00	2	0	0	0	2	2	0	0	0	1	1	.286	.500	.200	5.40	5.40

Fielding

Catcher	PCT	G	PO	A	E	DP	PB
Edge	.975	30	274	39	8	1	5
Maynard	.989	19	157	17	2	0	4
O'Brien	.944	3	30	4	2	2	0
Ponte	1.000	2	5	0	0	0	0
Vazquez	.972	26	211	29	7	3	3
Boudreaux	.920	32	37	89	11	18	
Mirabal	.957	34	40	117	7	13	
Thompson	.800	3	1	3	1	1	

First Base	PCT	G	PO	A	E	DP
Dickson	.988	42	373	24	5	24
Kirkland	.975	34	294	15	8	21

Second Base	PCT	G	PO	A	E	DP
Aguilar	.901	22	38	44	9	7
Hunt	1.000	1	2	0	0	0
Iden	.926	5	11	14	2	6
Morales	.957	24	38	74	5	12
Wingo	.982	29	57	104	3	17

Third Base	PCT	G	PO	A	E	DP
Aguilar	.857	12	6	18	4	0
Hunt	.816	42	24	60	19	3
Thompson	1.000	6	3	11	0	0
Woodward	.778	20	11	24	10	1

Shortstop	PCT	G	PO	A	E	DP
Aguilar	.914	9	10	22	3	5

Outfield	PCT	G	PO	A	E	DP
Baldwin III	.950	47	90	5	5	0
Cuevas	.974	53	74	1	2	0
Pederson	.952	62	91	9	5	2
Schaus	1.000	3	1	0	0	0
Schebler	.978	52	86	2	2	0
Shines	.000	1	0	0	0	0
Winker	1.000	4	2	1	0	0
Woodward	1.000	10	7	0	0	0

AZL DODGERS

ROOKIE

ARIZONA LEAGUE

Batting	B-T	HT	WT	DOB	AVG	vLH	vRH	G	AB	R	H	2B	3B	HR	RBI	BB	HBP	SH	SF	SO	SB	CS	SLG	OBP
Akins, Nick	R-R	6-1	220	12-25-87	.360	.000	.429	7	25	4	9	1	0	2	6	4	0	0	0	8	1	0	.640	.448
Boudreaux, Justin	R-R	6-1	190	10-3-89	.216	.333	.194	12	37	7	8	2	1	0	4	4	1	0	0	9	1	0	.324	.310
Brett, Beau	L-L	6-3	185	7-14-89	.160	.100	.175	18	50	8	8	2	0	0	2	8	1	0	1	10	1	0	.200	.283
Capellan, Jose	R-R	6-0	190	10-10-90	.270	.200	.288	25	74	6	20	2	0	1	12	10	0	0	1	14	3	1	.338	.353
Ethel, J.J.	R-R	6-2	180	5-22-89	.303	.000	.333	12	33	6	10	4	0	1	7	3	1	0	0	3	0	0	.515	.378
Ethier, Devon	R-R	6-0	165	6-4-90	.119	.200	.108	27	42	9	5	2	0	0	2	9	0	0	0	17	0	0	.167	.275
Franco, Bladimir	R-R	6-1	172	2-4-91	.211	.043	.244	40	142	21	30	7	1	3	19	9	1	0	1	51	0	2	.338	.261
Gibbons, Jay	L-L	6-0	195	3-2-77	.286	1.000	.167	2	7	1	2	0	0	0	2	0	0	0	0	3	0	0	.286	.250
Hernandez, Bryant	R-R	5-8	170	3-5-88	.359	.222	.382	19	64	18	23	3	1	1	8	8	5	0	0	11	3	2	.484	.468
Holland, Malcolm	R-R	5-11	165	6-18-92	.159	.143	.164	25	69	11	11	1	0	0	3	9	0	0	0	18	5	1	.174	.256
Jackson, Anthony	B-R	5-8	175	6-17-84	.231	.000	.273	3	13	2	3	0	0	0	0	1	0	0	0	3	0	0	.231	.286
Jarrin, Stefan	R-R	5-10	170	8-27-90	.213	.000	.260	23	61	9	13	5	0	0	7	7	2	0	0	18	0	0	.295	.314
Lincoln, Joe	R-R	6-4	210	9-16-88	.667	.000	.667	1	3	1	2	1	0	0	1	0	1	0	0	0	0	0	1.000	.750
Lugo, Ronny	R-R	6-2	170	2-18-90	.230	.167	.246	26	87	13	20	2	2	0	11	6	1	0	0	20	6	2	.299	.287
Morales, Delvis	B-R	6-1	146	8-29-90	.277	.250	.283	38	137	26	38	3	3	0	12	14	1	0	1	25	8	6	.343	.346
Morales, Enlly	R-R	5-11	168	9-13-89	.286	.500	.200	3	14	0	4	1	0	0	3	0	0	0	0	2	0	0	.357	.286
Nam, Tae-Hyeok	R-R	6-0	209	3-13-91	.221	.111	.244	30	104	14	23	5	1	2	19	4	0	4	2	37	1	1	.346	.303
O'Brien, Chris	B-R	6-0	219	7-24-89	.294	.125	.326	42	153	23	45	15	3	3	33	18	2	0	5	30	0	3	.490	.365
Ogle, Tyler	R-R	5-11	193	8-9-90	.167	.000	.214	6	18	4	3	0	0	0	2	0	0	0	0	1	0	0	.167	.167
Oguisten, Faustino	R-R	6-2	165	1-17-91	.300	.000	.316	13	20	5	6	0	0	0	2	3	0	0	0	2	1	0	.300	.391
Ponte, Angelo	R-R	5-11	215	12-16-86	1.000	.000	1.000	1	1	1	1	0	0	0	0	0	0	0	0	0	0	0	2.000	1.000
Rosa, Gianison	L-R	6-0	205	10-15-89	.221	.133	.242	31	77	14	17	5	2	1	11	21	1	0	0	29	1	1	.377	.394
Santana, Alex	R-R	6-4	200	8-21-93	.238	.243	.237	50	189	30	45	10	3	1	19	10	6	0	0	64	8	1	.339	.298
Shines, Devin	R-L	5-9	185	5-15-89	.318	.333	.315	52	211	45	67	14	2	4	31	24	7	0	4	48	13	4	.460	.398
Smith, Blake	L-R	6-2	225	12-9-87	.450	.000	.563	6	20	7	9	2	0	4	10	3	0	0	0	1	0	0	1.150	.522
Taylor, Kevin	L-R	6-0	200	7-13-91	.000	.000	.000	2	5	0	0	0	0	0	0	1	0	0	0	1	0	0	.000	.167
Thompson, Kevin	R-R	6-3	185	9-16-88	.333	.333	.333	9	18	6	6	0	0	0	2	1	0	0	1	2	0	0	.333	.350
Wallach, Matt	L-R	6-1	205	2-17-86	.125	.000	.125	3	8	0	1	1	0	0	2	1	0	0	0	4	0	0	.250	.222
Wingo, Scott	L-R	5-11	175	3-25-89	.450	.500	.444	7	20	1	9	0	1	0	0	5	0	0	0	2	0	2	.550	.560
Winker, Joey	L-L	6-1	190	8-28-91	.374	.400	.368	43	163	35	61	17	6	4	46	20	3	0	4	37	4	0	.626	.442

Pitching	B-T	HT	WT	DOB	W	L	ERA	G	GS	CG	SV	IP	H	R	ER	HR	BB	SO	AVG	vLH	vRH	K/9	BB/9
Barlow, Scott	R-R	6-3	170	12-18-92	0	1	27.00	2	0	0	0	2	5	5	5	1	2	1	.500	1.000	.375	5.40	10.80
Bastardo, Alberto	L-L	6-0	160	4-6-84	0	3	3.24	3	3	0	0	8	7	4	3	0	4	8	.241	.222	.250	8.64	4.32
Bolt, Garrett	R-R	6-4	215	9-23-89	0	2	6.48	9	0	0	0	8	10	8	6	1	7	13	.294	.278	.313	14.04	7.56
Boothe, Robert	R-R	6-2	190	1-30-86	0	0	2.57	8	5	0	0	21	16	11	6	0	14	13	.219	.222	.217	5.57	6.00
Cabrera, Freddie	R-R	6-5	210	1-25-90	0	1	2.40	6	2	0	0	15	14	6	4	0	1	14	.246	.190	.278	8.40	0.60

Pitching	B-T	HT	WT	DOB	W	L	ERA	G	GS	CG	SV	IP	H	R	ER	HR	BB	SO	AVG	vLH	vRH	K/9	BB/9
Carela, Daniel	R-R	6-3	225	9-18-87	1	0	6.11	9	2	0	1	18	15	12	12	1	15	16	.246	.250	.244	8.15	7.64
Chamra, Rob	R-R	6-4	225	3-22-88	3	0	3.92	16	0	0	0	21	22	9	9	3	13	15	.289	.357	.250	6.53	5.66
Cone, Derek	R-R	6-5	210	6-20-90	0	1	4.50	4	4	0	0	18	15	9	9	1	8	19	.234	.194	.273	9.50	4.00
Dedeaux, Adam	L-L	6-0	200	7-1-86	0	0	27.00	1	0	0	0	0	2	2	1	0	1	1	.667	1.000	.500	27.00	27.00
Dominguez, Jose	R-R	6-0	160	8-7-90	4	1	3.50	10	10	0	0	44	38	20	17	3	13	43	.236	.190	.265	8.86	2.68
Downing, Gregg	L-L	5-10	175	11-8-90	2	0	5.48	18	0	0	0	23	26	15	14	4	13	24	.302	.286	.306	9.39	5.09
Eadington, Eric	R-L	6-2	220	2-9-88	1	1	1.59	9	0	0	0	11	10	2	2	0	6	18	.233	.333	.179	14.29	4.76
Fructuoso, Beyker	R-R	6-4	205	4-8-90	0	1	7.94	7	0	0	0	6	7	5	5	0	4	7	.318	.222	.385	11.12	6.35
Jensen, David	L-L	6-6	215	12-29-87	1	0	6.00	3	0	0	0	3	4	2	2	0	1	3	.308	1.000	.250	9.00	3.00
Laney, Matt	L-L	6-4	235	9-2-88	2	0	0.74	12	4	0	0	24	13	5	2	0	9	24	.155	.182	.145	8.88	3.33
Matre, Steve	R-R	6-2	185	5-21-88	0	0	1.35	7	0	0	0	7	6	1	1	0	1	3	.231	.429	.158	4.05	1.35
Medina, Bolivar	L-L	6-2	175	8-11-88	0	1	13.50	7	0	0	0	7	12	12	10	2	5	6	.364	.200	.393	8.10	6.75
Mesa, Luis	R-R	6-4	170	7-13-90	5	3	4.59	14	14	0	0	65	73	37	33	6	21	50	.285	.333	.273	6.96	2.92
Miller, Aaron	L-L	6-3	200	11-8-87	1	0	0.00	1	0	0	0	2	1	0	0	0	1	3	.143	.000	.250	13.50	4.50
Noriega, Juan	R-R	5-7	145	9-3-90	0	0	0.00	6	1	0	0	13	9	0	0	0	2	21	.191	.188	.194	14.54	1.38
Purpura, Robert	R-R	6-0	185	2-26-87	1	0	0.00	8	0	0	2	10	5	0	0	0	1	8	.143	.083	.174	6.97	0.87
Ruiz, Abner	L-L	6-1	180	4-1-89	0	0	10.13	3	0	0	0	3	4	4	3	0	1	3	.364	.000	.364	3.38	10.13
Stem, Craig	R-R	6-5	215	1-5-90	0	1	3.65	11	0	0	0	12	17	8	5	0	4	11	.315	.389	.278	8.03	2.92
Stickel, Brant	L-L	6-4	210	1-8-87	0	2	1.56	12	0	0	1	17	7	4	3	1	5	13	.125	.167	.114	6.75	2.60
Suiter, Andy	L-L	6-3	215	6-10-87	1	0	0.00	8	0	0	0	10	1	1	0	0	2	12	.034	.200	.000	10.80	1.80
Takano, Kazuya	R-R	6-1	170	11-10-92	3	3	6.81	13	5	0	0	38	52	31	29	8	11	33	.329	.329	.330	7.75	2.58
Tamares, Daniel	R-R	6-3	170	12-20-89	0	1	2.11	13	1	0	0	21	13	7	5	0	8	33	.176	.182	.171	13.92	3.38
Thomas, Mike	L-L	6-2	185	1-6-89	2	1	2.49	12	4	0	0	22	21	8	6	2	4	34	.244	.200	.254	14.12	1.66
Villa, Francisco	R-R	6-0	194	4-1-92	1	1	7.80	11	1	0	1	15	23	15	13	2	6	15	.348	.321	.368	9.00	3.60
West, Jason	R-R	5-11	185	7-30-88	2	0	0.52	15	0	0	4	17	13	1	1	0	5	23	.213	.238	.200	11.94	2.60

Fielding

Catcher	PCT	G	PO	A	E	DP	PB
Capellan	.980	25	170	29	4	2	8
Ethel	.989	11	80	7	1	0	3
Lincoln	1.000	1	7	2	0	0	
O'Brien	.987	23	190	32	3	2	6
Ogle	.966	5	25	3	1	0	0
Ponte	1.000	1	5	1	0	0	0
Wallach	1.000	3	16	4	0	0	0

First Base	PCT	G	PO	A	E	DP
Brett	.992	18	119	7	1	7
Nam	.989	29	261	5	3	19
Valdez	.984	16	122	2	2	12

Second Base	PCT	G	PO	A	E	DP
Hernandez	1.000	6	9	18	0	2

Holland	.920	24	43	49	8	10	
Jarrin	.903	19	30	35	7	11	
Morales	.944	3	6	11	1	0	
Oguisten	.750	7	5	4	3	1	
Taylor	1.000	1	1	1	0	0	
Thompson	.909	2	5	5	1	2	
Wingo	1.000	7	9	19	0	2	

Third Base	PCT	G	PO	A	E	DP
Franco	.985	19	13	51	1	2
Santana	.832	38	15	69	17	8
Valdez	.800	3	1	3	1	0

Shortstop	PCT	G	PO	A	E	DP
Boudreaux	.973	9	18	18	1	6
Hernandez	.951	10	13	26	2	2

Jarrin	1.000	1	0	1	0	0
Morales	.927	37	41	98	11	18
Oguisten	.875	4	4	3	1	0
Thompson	1.000	4	6	11	0	0

Outfield	PCT	G	PO	A	E	DP
Akins	1.000	6	10	1	0	1
Ethier	.950	21	19	0	1	0
Franco	.880	16	22	0	3	0
Gibbons	1.000	1	1	0	0	0
Lugo	.949	26	33	4	2	1
Rosa	.909	23	20	0	2	0
Shines	.984	52	118	7	2	2
Smith	1.000	5	10	0	0	0
Winker	1.000	41	47	1	0	0

DSL DODGERS

ROOKIE

DOMINICAN SUMMER LEAGUE

Batting	B-T	HT	WT	DOB	AVG	vLH	vRH	G	AB	R	H	2B	3B	HR	RBI	BB	HBP	SH	SF	SO	SB	CS	SLG	OBP
Coplin, Edwin	R-R	6-5	185	9-4-90	—	.000	.000	2	0	0	0	0	0	0	0	0	0	0	0	0	0	0	—	—
Cordero, Josmar	R-R	5-10	175	9-10-91	.283	.133	.324	42	138	20	39	9	2	2	20	11	6	0	1	20	4	1	.420	.359
De La Cruz, Detriano	R-R	6-3	195	11-27-91	.208	.000	.238	9	24	4	5	1	0	0	1	5	0	0	0	7	1	0	.250	.345
Garcia, Juan	L-L	6-1	180	6-14-93	.182	.190	.179	40	99	11	18	4	2	0	5	9	1	0	1	37	2	6	.263	.255
Heredia, Henry	R-R	5-8	170	8-23-91	.197	.143	.220	24	71	4	14	4	0	0	9	2	4	0	1	22	0	0	.254	.256
Infante, Jorky	B-R	6-0	155	2-24-91	.210	.227	.205	32	105	11	22	4	0	0	6	15	2	0	0	16	6	5	.248	.320
Javier, Jose Luis	R-R	5-10	160	10-31-92	.235	.231	.237	16	51	9	12	2	1	0	5	2	0	0	0	17	5	1	.314	.264
Linares, Jonathan	R-R	6-0	160	4-29-93	.300	.143	.385	7	20	3	6	4	0	0	3	3	0	0	0	2	1	0	.500	.391
Martinez, Vladimir	B-R	6-2	173	6-26-92	.222	.156	.236	54	176	22	39	4	0	0	20	25	6	0	2	25	6	2	.244	.335
Moreno, Jose	R-R	6-0	187	6-30-90	.265	.176	.294	21	68	9	18	4	0	1	8	4	0	0	0	12	2	0	.368	.306
Oguisten, Faustino	R-R	6-2	165	1-17-91	.333	.412	.306	25	66	11	22	3	1	0	7	8	1	0	0	8	9	3	.409	.413
Pena, Gregory	B-R	6-0	175	12-10-91	.303	.262	.315	61	188	37	57	7	5	3	31	23	4	0	1	31	23	6	.441	.389
Perez, Jesus	R-R	6-1	180	7-19-93	.333	.000	.500	2	6	1	2	0	0	0	1	0	0	0	0	1	1	1	.333	.429
Reyes, Jorge	R-R	6-0	160	9-7-90	.182	.250	.167	20	44	9	8	1	0	0	4	5	2	0	0	14	3	0	.205	.294
Rivas, Webster	R-R	6-0	195	8-8-90	.279	.357	.264	55	172	26	48	10	1	2	23	22	2	0	0	24	0	4	.384	.367
Rodriguez, Jean	R-R	6-0	191	12-10-92	.288	.300	.285	53	177	29	51	10	0	4	25	12	4	0	0	38	3	3	.412	.347
Rodriguez, Leo	R-R	5-11	160	12-11-91	.278	.315	.265	63	209	25	58	9	0	1	22	21	4	0	1	23	6	6	.335	.353
Rojas, Jeffry	B-R	6-0	170	8-18-92	.235	.278	.222	51	153	19	36	2	0	1	17	9	8	0	3	21	1	1	.268	.306
Roso, Adrian	R-R	6-0	165	8-18-91	.167	.053	.193	32	102	13	17	4	0	0	7	17	2	0	0	27	8	5	.206	.298
Santana, Melvin	R-R	5-10	160	10-4-91	.245	.268	.238	56	192	31	47	11	4	0	17	25	5	0	2	28	10	3	.344	.344
Soriano, Abinaer	R-R	6-0	175	10-9-91	.216	.154	.230	46	139	24	30	8	2	1	17	10	2	0	1	44	5	4	.324	.276
Sosa, Rutinel	L-L	6-2	170	6-18-91	.167	.000	.222	11	24	3	4	1	0	0	2	0	0	0	0	8	0	2	.208	.231
Tejeda, Claudio	R-R	6-0	170	12-29-92	.167	.500	.100	5	12	4	2	0	0	0	1	2	0	0	0	1	0	0	.167	.333

Pitching	B-T	HT	WT	DOB	W	L	ERA	G	GS	CG	SV	IP	H	R	ER	HR	BB	SO	AVG	vLH	vRH	K/9	BB/9
Alcantara, Geuris	R-R	6-2	185	5-29-92	0	0	12.27	3	0	0	0	4	7	5	5	1	7	3	.438	.500	.429	7.36	17.18
Angeles, Aris	R-R	6-0	179	9-9-89	1	3	2.73	15	0	0	2	30	24	13	9	1	12	25	.222	.281	.197	7.58	3.64

Pitching	B-T	HT	WT	DOB	W	L	ERA	G	GS	CG	SV	IP	H	R	ER	HR	BB	SO	AVG	vLH	vRH	K/9	BB/9
Araujo, Victor	R-R	5-11	171	11-9-89	3	4	1.80	13	11	1	1	60	43	17	12	3	13	61	.196	.260	.178	9.15	1.95
Binns, Simon	R-R	6-3	170	7-1-93	0	0	9.82	7	0	0	0	7	9	10	8	0	10	9	.290	.143	.333	11.05	12.27
Bock, Edinson	R-R	6-2	190	4-15-94	1	0	3.68	6	0	0	0	7	2	5	3	0	9	9	.083	.000	.105	11.05	11.05

Pitching	B-T	HT	WT	DOB	W	L	ERA	G	GS	CG	SV	IP	H	R	ER	HR	BB	SO	AVG	vLH	vRH	K/9	BB/9
Botello, Ariel	R-R	6-2	217	11-15-89	0	0	4.26	4	0	0	0	6	9	3	3	1	0	6	.333	.667	.167	8.53	0.00
Canelo, Willie	L-L	6-2	180	5-27-92	0	0	0.00	1	0	0	0	0	1	0	0	0	1	0	1.000	.000	1.000	0.00	27.00
Chavez, Giordanny	R-R	6-3	185	4-19-91	3	4	3.78	13	10	1	0	48	48	24	20	0	18	29	.270	.200	.284	5.48	3.40
De Dios, Leandro	R-R	5-11	184	6-20-89	0	0	0.00	1	0	0	0	1	1	0	0	0	1	3	.200	.000	.200	27.00	9.00
Diaz, Jose Agusto	R-R	5-11	185	1-15-91	2	0	0.67	19	0	0	2	27	22	6	2	0	11	23	.232	.235	.231	7.67	3.67
Gonzalez, Sawil	R-R	6-3	180	3-24-90	1	2	5.23	14	0	0	2	21	13	13	12	2	15	26	.181	.091	.197	11.32	6.53
Lantigua, Daniel	R-R	6-3	180	5-29-92	0	1	0.00	1	0	0	0	1	3	3	0	1	1	0	.500	.000	.600	0.00	13.50
Martinez, Jonathan	R-R	6-1	170	6-27-94	5	1	1.67	12	2	0	1	32	19	8	6	1	12	31	.168	.316	.138	3.34	3.34
Mateo, Jackson	R-R	6-0	193	8-22-92	5	1	1.62	15	15	0	0	72	49	19	13	2	18	52	.190	.250	.179	6.47	2.24
Mendez, Irvit	R-R	6-6	225	4-11-90	0	0	3.38	2	0	0	0	3	4	1	1	0	1	3	.333	1.000	.273	10.13	3.38
Pena, Ariel	R-R	6-4	208	1-8-92	1	1	5.32	11	3	0	1	24	26	22	14	1	14	14	.271	.222	.282	5.32	5.32
Shellon, Andrew	R-R	6-2	150	1-6-93	2	2	5.40	15	0	0	3	18	11	11	11	2	13	13	.172	.308	.137	6.38	6.38
Silverio, Luis	L-L	6-3	190	6-6-91	1	2	7.04	17	0	0	0	23	32	22	18	1	21	24	.333	.000	.376	9.39	8.22
Sulbaran, Miguel	L-L	5-10	165	3-19-94	6	1	2.81	13	11	0	0	58	37	19	18	2	18	52	.179	.143	.181	8.12	2.81
Tamarez, Moises	R-R	6-3	195	3-6-93	0	0	2.00	8	0	0	1	18	12	7	4	1	6	10	.185	.071	.216	5.00	3.00
Taveras, Samuel	R-R	6-5	175	9-20-89	5	1	2.02	11	7	0	1	49	30	11	11	1	13	29	.175	.182	.174	5.33	2.39
Velasquez, Abdiel	R-R	6-3	184	3-4-93	1	4	4.05	12	9	0	0	47	54	30	21	3	18	38	.287	.417	.257	7.33	3.47

Fielding

Catcher	PCT	G	PO	A	E	DP	PB
Cordero	.991	17	101	11	1	0	1
Linares	1.000	7	33	5	0	0	0
Moreno	1.000	19	110	13	0	0	4
Rivas	.980	41	248	47	6	2	2
Rodriguez	1.000	1	1	0	0	0	0

First Base	PCT	G	PO	A	E	DP
Cordero	.987	17	135	14	2	8
Heredia	.965	21	136	2	5	7
Pena	1.000	1	1	0	0	0
Rivas	.989	11	85	2	1	4
Rodriguez	.984	17	118	8	2	8
Rojas	.970	18	130	1	4	11

Second Base	PCT	G	PO	A	E	DP
Infante	1.000	7	11	12	0	1
Martinez	.972	40	72	69	4	11
Oguisten	1.000	1	1	1	0	0

	PCT	G	PO	A	E	DP
Reyes	1.000	2	2	2	0	1
Rodriguez	.951	10	19	20	2	5
Santana	.906	21	47	40	9	8
Tejeda	1.000	1	0	2	0	0

Third Base	PCT	G	PO	A	E	DP
Infante	.902	27	21	53	8	3
Oguisten	.941	11	8	24	2	2
Perez	1.000	1	0	1	0	0
Reyes	.853	10	9	20	5	0
Rodriguez	.949	11	5	32	2	0
Rojas	.901	25	13	51	7	2
Santana	1.000	1	0	2	0	0

Shortstop	PCT	G	PO	A	E	DP
Infante	1.000	2	1	1	0	0
Javier	.885	13	22	24	6	4
Martinez	.667	1	1	1	1	0
Martinez	.667	2	2	2	2	0

	PCT	G	PO	A	E	DP
Oguisten	.918	13	19	26	4	6
Rodriguez	1.000	1	1	4	0	0
Rodriguez	.942	46	51	127	11	13
Santana	1.000	2	0	2	0	0
Tejeda	.933	5	6	8	1	2

Outfield	PCT	G	PO	A	E	DP
Cordero	.000	1	0	0	0	0
De La Cruz	1.000	9	15	1	0	0
Garcia	.915	36	41	2	4	1
Heredia	1.000	1	1	0	0	0
Infante	.000	1	0	0	0	0
Martinez	1.000	13	18	1	0	1
Pena	.980	59	93	4	2	1
Reyes	.875	5	7	0	1	0
Rodriguez	.946	30	52	1	3	0
Roso	.905	28	37	1	4	1
Soriano	.939	45	76	1	5	1
Sosa	.875	6	7	0	1	0

Milwaukee Brewers

SEASON IN A SENTENCE: In the last season of Prince Fielder's contract the Brewers were in win-now mode, and win they did, as a potent offense and rebuilt pitching staff got the team featured on the cover of Sports Illustrated, and led them to a division title and the National League Championship Series.

HIGH POINT: With one out in the bottom of the 10th inning and the score tied 1-1 in Game Five of the Division Series against the Diamondbacks, outfielder Nyjer Morgan singled up the middle to score speedy outfielder Carlos Gomez. The single gave the Brewers a 2-1 victory over the Diamondbacks and marked the first time since 1982 that the franchise advanced to the LCS.

LOW POINT: The top of Milwaukee's rotation—Yovani Gallardo, Zack Greinke and Shaun Marcum—was a key to its successful season, but the trio combined for 1-4, 8.78 mark in the NLCS against the Cardinals, as the Brewers fell in six games.

NOTABLE ROOKIES: Many of the system's top prospects were dealt in deals to acquire Greinke and Marcum, but 28-year old righthander Marco Estrada was a valuable, versatile contributor to the pitching staff. He was used mostly in relief but also made seven starts, compiling a 4.08 ERA om 93 innings.

KEY TRANSACTIONS: The Greinke and Marcum deals were made in anticipation of Fielder's free agency, as general manager Doug Melvin knew the team needed to shore up its rotation. He gave up a number of the system's best prospects in the deals, but any Brewers fan would thank him for doing so. Acquiring utility infielder Jerry Hairston proved to be an important move, as he took over for struggling third baseman Casey McGehee, and Francisco Rodriguez shored up the bullpen.

DOWN ON THE FARM: As four of the previous year's Top 10 Prospects were traded away, the Brewers experienced a down year in talent throughout their system. Righthander Wily Peralta was one of the bright spots, as he took a giant step forward and was one of the top pitchers in the Double-A Southern League before earning a late-season promotion to Triple-A. After not signing their first-round pick in 2010, the Brewers held two first-round picks in 2011 and used them both on college pitchers, taking Texas righthander Taylor Jungmann 12th overall and Georgia Tech lefthander Jed Bradley with the 15th pick.

OPENING DAY PAYROLL: $85,497,333 (17th)

PLAYERS OF THE YEAR

MAJOR LEAGUE	MINOR LEAGUE
Ryan Braun	**Michael Fiers**
of	rhp
.332/.397/.597	(Double-A/Triple-A)
33 HR, 111 RBIs	13-3, 1.86
Led NL in SLG, XBH	132 SO/126 IP

ORGANIZATION LEADERS

BATTING   *Minimum 250 PA

MAJORS

* AVG	Ryan Braun	.332
* OPS	Ryan Braun	.994
HR	Prince Fielder	38
RBI	Prince Fielder	120

MINORS

* AVG	Taylor Green, Huntsville/Nashville	.336
* OBP	Taylor Green, Huntsville/Nashville	.412
* SLG	Taylor Green, Huntsville/Nashville	.58
R	Mat Gamel, Nashville	90
H	Scooter Gennett, Brevard County	167
TB	Mat Gamel, Nashville	266
2B	Sean Halton, Huntsville	39
3B	Three tied at	8
HR	Mat Gamel, Nashville	28
RBI	Mat Gamel, Nashville	96
BB	Nick Shaw, Wisconsin	82
SO	Brock Kjeldgaard, Brevard Co./Huntsville	141
SB	Reggie Keen, Wisconsin	41

PITCHING   #Minimum 75 IP

MAJORS

W	Yovani Gallardo	17
# ERA	Yovani Gallardo	3.52
SO	Yovani Gallardo	207
SV	John Axford	46

MINORS

W	Michael Fiers, Huntsville/Nashville	13
L	Maverick Lasker, Brevard County/Wisconsin	13
# ERA	Michael Fiers, Huntsville/Nashville	1.86
G	Roque Mercedes, Huntsville/Brevard County	49
GS	Three tied at	28
SV	Greg Holle, Wisconsin	19
IP	Sam Narron, Nashville	160
BB	Amaury Rivas, Nashville	81
SO	Tyler Thornburg, Wisconsin/Brevard County	160
# AVG	Michael Fiers, Huntsville/Nashville	.182

General Manager: Doug Melvin. **Farm Director:** Reid Nichols. **Scouting Director:** Bruce Seid.

Class	Team	League	W	L	PCT	Finish	Manager(s)
Majors	Milwaukee Brewers	National	96	66	.593	2nd (16)	Ron Roenicke
Triple-A	Nashville Sounds	Pacific Coast	71	73	.493	t-6th (16)	Don Money
Double-A	Huntsville Stars	Southern	64	73	.467	8th (10)	Mike Guerrero
High A	Brevard County Manatees	Florida State	62	76	.449	11th (12)	Jeff Isom
Low A	Wisconsin Timber Rattlers	Midwest	67	72	.482	11th (16)	Matt Erickson
Rookie	Helena Brewers	Pioneer	30	46	.395	7th (8)	Joe Ayrault
Rookie	AZL Brewers	Arizona	17	39	.304	13th (13)	Tony Diggs
Overall 2011 Minor League Record			311	379	.451	29th (30)	

ORGANIZATION STATISTICS

MILWAUKEE BREWERS

NATIONAL LEAGUE

Batting	B-T	HT	WT	DOB	AVG	vLH	vRH	G	AB	R	H	2B	3B	HR	RBI	BB	HBP	SH	SF	SO	SB	CS	SLG	OBP
Almonte, Erick	R-R	6-2	245	2-1-78	.103	.158	.000	16	29	1	3	0	0	1	3	0	0	0	0	4	0	0	.207	.103
Betancourt, Yuniesky	R-R	5-11	210	1-31-82	.252	.229	.258	152	556	51	140	27	3	13	68	16	2	0	10	63	4	4	.381	.271
Boggs, Brandon	B-R	5-11	210	1-9-83	.158	.167	.154	16	19	4	3	0	0	2	3	2	3	0	0	8	1	0	.474	.273
Braun, Ryan	R-R	6-1	210	11-17-83	.332	.350	.327	150	563	109	187	38	6	33	111	58	5	0	3	93	33	6	.597	.397
Carroll, Brett	R-R	6-0	210	10-3-82	.000	.000	.500	2	3	0	0	0	0	0	0	0	0	0	0	1	0	0	.000	.000
Counsell, Craig	L-R	6-0	180	8-21-70	.178	.333	.172	107	157	19	28	2	1	1	9	20	3	0	2	21	2	1	.223	.280
Farris, Eric	R-R	5-9	180	3-3-86	.000	.000	.333	.000	1	1	0	0	0	0	0	0	0	0	0	0	0	0	.000	.000
Fielder, Prince	L-R	5-11	275	5-9-84	.299	.282	.306	162	569	95	170	36	1	38	120	107	10	0	6	106	1	1	.566	.415
Gamel, Mat	L-R	6-0	215	7-26-85	.115	.000	.150	10	26	1	3	1	0	0	2	1	0	0	0	4	0	0	.154	.148
Gomez, Carlos	R-R	6-4	215	12-4-85	.225	.278	.191	94	231	37	52	11	3	8	24	15	2	0	2	64	16	2	.403	.276
Green, Taylor	L-R	5-11	200	11-2-86	.270	.500	.270	20	37	2	10	3	0	0	1	0	0	0	0	6	0	0	.351	.270
Hairston Jr., Jerry	R-R	5-10	190	5-29-76	.274	.212	.297	45	124	18	34	10	0	1	7	11	3	0	0	16	1	0	.379	.348
2-team total (75 Washington)					.270	—	—	120	337	43	91	21	1	5	31	33	5	0	0	46	3	2	.383	.344
Hart, Corey	R-R	6-6	235	3-24-82	.285	.333	.272	130	492	80	140	25	4	26	63	51	4	0	1	114	7	6	.510	.356
Kotsay, Mark	L-L	6-0	210	12-2-75	.270	.462	.259	104	233	18	63	13	1	3	31	21	0	0	1	27	3	0	.373	.329
Kottaras, George	L-R	6-0	190	5-10-83	.252	.174	.273	49	111	15	28	6	1	5	17	10	0	0	1	26	0	1	.459	.311
Lopez, Felipe	B-R	6-0	205	5-12-80	.182	.000	.216	16	44	4	8	0	0	0	3	4	0	0	1	7	0	0	.182	.245
Lucroy, Jonathan	R-R	6-0	190	6-13-86	.265	.291	.259	136	430	45	114	16	1	12	59	29	2	0	3	99	2	1	.391	.313
Maldonado, Martin	R-R	6-1	225	8-16-86	.000	.000	.222	3	1	0	0	0	0	0	0	0	0	0	0	1	0	0	.000	.000
McGehee, Casey	R-R	6-1	220	10-12-82	.223	.169	.239	155	546	46	122	24	2	13	67	45	1	0	8	104	0	3	.346	.280
Morgan, Nyjer	L-L	6-0	175	7-2-80	.304	.209	.316	119	378	61	115	20	6	4	37	19	14	0	3	70	13	4	.421	.357
Nieves, Wil	R-R	5-11	190	9-25-77	.140	.118	.152	20	50	2	7	2	0	0	3	0	0	0	0	12	0	0	.180	.189
Reed, Jeremy	L-L	6-0	195	6-15-81	.000	.000	.000	7	7	0	0	0	0	0	0	0	0	0	0	2	0	0	.000	.000
Rivera, Mike	R-R	6-1	235	9-8-76	.333	.600	.333	1	6	0	2	0	0	0	0	0	0	0	0	1	0	0	.333	.333
Schafer, Logan	L-L	6-1	180	9-8-86	.333	.333	.333	8	3	1	1	0	0	0	1	0	0	0	0	1	0	0	.333	.500
Weeks, Rickie	R-R	5-10	215	9-13-82	.269	.261	.271	118	453	77	122	26	2	20	49	50	8	0	3	107	9	2	.468	.350
Wilson, Josh	R-R	6-0	175	3-26-81	.227	.213	.250	54	75	10	17	4	0	2	4	4	0	0	0	21	1	0	.360	.266
2-team total (6 Arizona)					.224	—	—	60	85	13	19	5	0	2	5	4	0	0	2	24	1	0	.353	.258

Pitching	B-T	HT	WT	DOB	W	L	ERA	G	GS	CG	SV	IP	H	R	ER	HR	BB	SO	AVG	vLH	vRH	K/9	BB/9
Axford, John	R-R	6-5	195	4-1-83	2	2	1.95	74	0	0	46	74	59	19	16	4	25	86	.212	.188	.233	10.51	3.05
Braddock, Zach	L-L	6-2	230	8-23-87	0	1	7.27	25	0	0	0	17	16	15	14	2	11	18	.239	.250	.231	9.35	5.71
De La Cruz, Eulo	R-R	5-10	215	3-12-84	0	0	2.77	11	0	0	0	13	10	4	4	0	5	9	.213	.185	.250	6.23	3.46
DiFelice, Mark	R-R	6-2	190	8-23-76	0	0	12.00	3	0	0	0	3	4	4	4	1	2	3	.250	.167	.333	9.00	6.00
Dillard, Tim	R-R	6-4	225	7-19-83	1	1	4.08	24	0	0	0	29	26	13	13	3	4	27	.241	.300	.206	8.48	1.26
Estrada, Marco	R-R	6-0	180	7-5-83	4	8	4.08	43	7	0	0	93	83	45	42	11	29	88	.243	.204	.276	8.55	2.82
Fiers, Mike	R-R	6-3	200	6-15-85	0	0	0.00	2	0	0	0	2	2	0	0	0	1	3	.250	.500	.200	9.00	13.50
Gallardo, Yovani	R-R	6-2	210	2-27-86	17	10	3.52	33	33	1	0	207	193	92	81	27	59	207	.245	.257	.235	8.99	2.56
Green, Sean	R-R	6-6	230	4-20-79	0	1	5.40	14	0	0	0	12	14	8	7	0	6	7	.280	.353	.242	5.40	4.63
Greinke, Zack	R-R	6-2	190	10-21-83	16	6	3.83	28	28	0	0	172	161	82	73	19	45	201	.245	.245	.245	10.54	2.36
Hawkins, LaTroy	R-R	6-5	220	12-21-72	3	1	2.42	52	0	0	0	48	50	15	13	1	10	28	.260	.207	.300	5.21	1.86
Herrera, Danny Ray	L-L	5-6	165	10-21-84	0	0	21.60	2	0	0	0	2	6	5	4	1	1	0	.600	.400	.800	0.00	5.40
2-team total (16 New York)					0	1	4.66	18	0	0	0	10	13	6	5	1	3	5	—	—	—	4.66	2.79
Kintzler, Brandon	R-R	5-10	185	8-1-84	1	1	3.68	9	0	0	0	15	14	9	6	3	3	15	.250	.000	.268	9.20	1.84
Loe, Kameron	R-R	6-8	240	9-10-81	4	7	3.50	72	0	0	1	72	65	30	28	4	16	61	.240	.250	.233	7.63	2.00
Marcum, Shaun	R-R	6-0	195	12-14-81	13	7	3.54	33	33	0	0	201	175	84	79	22	57	158	.232	.271	.195	7.09	2.56
McClendon, Mike	R-R	6-5	225	4-3-85	3	0	2.63	9	0	0	0	14	15	5	4	1	3	10	.273	.208	.323	6.59	1.98
Mitre, Sergio	R-R	6-3	225	2-16-81	0	1	3.27	22	0	0	0	33	30	14	12	3	10	14	.240	.235	.243	3.82	2.73
Narveson, Chris	L-L	6-3	205	12-20-81	11	8	4.45	30	28	0	0	162	160	82	80	17	65	126	.257	.212	.265	7.01	3.62
Rodriguez, Francisco	R-R	6-0	195	1-7-82	4	0	1.86	31	0	0	0	29	23	7	6	1	10	33	.209	.228	.189	10.24	3.10
2-team total (42 New York)					6	2	2.64	73	0	0	23	72	67	22	21	4	26	79	—	—	—	9.92	3.27
Saito, Takashi	L-R	6-2	200	2-14-70	4	2	2.03	30	0	0	0	27	21	6	6	2	9	23	.216	.279	.167	7.76	3.04
Stetter, Mitch	L-L	6-4	220	1-16-81	0	0	5.14	16	0	0	0	7	8	4	4	2	1	7	.296	.211	.500	9.00	1.29
Wolf, Randy	L-L	6-0	205	8-22-76	13	10	3.69	33	33	0	0	212	214	95	87	23	66	134	.266	.246	.270	5.68	2.80

Fielding

Catcher	PCT	G	PO	A	E	DP	PB
Kottaras	1.000	36	171	8	0	0	2
Lucroy	.993	132	976	63	7	6	1
Maldonado	1.000	3	4	0	0	0	
Nieves	.992	17	109	8	1	0	1
Rivera	1.000	1	13	2	0	1	0

First Base	PCT	G	PO	A	E	DP
Almonte	1.000	2	3	0	0	0
Fielder	.990	159	1332	84	15	113
Gamel	1.000	2	18	1	0	1
Kotsay	1.000	11	27	1	0	4
McGehee	1.000	5	6	0	0	1
Wilson	.000	1	0	0	0	0

Second Base	PCT	G	PO	A	E	DP
Counsell	1.000	25	18	37	0	9
Green	1.000	7	6	9	0	0

	PCT	G	PO	A	E	DP
Hairston Jr.	.969	27	33	60	3	11
Lopez	.977	11	19	23	1	5
Weeks	.969	115	175	291	15	65
Wilson	1.000	10	12	21	0	4

Third Base	PCT	G	PO	A	E	DP
Counsell	.960	14	5	19	1	1
Gamel	.833	3	3	2	1	0
Green	1.000	5	2	7	0	2
Hairston Jr.	1.000	5	4	4	0	0
Lopez	.000	1	0	0	0	0
McGehee	.942	147	72	255	20	17
Wilson	.875	13	2	5	1	1

Shortstop	PCT	G	PO	A	E	DP
Betancourt	.965	149	167	418	21	85
Counsell	.980	23	19	30	1	6
Hairston Jr.	1.000	1	1	2	0	1

	PCT	G	PO	A	E	DP
Wilson	.950	8	9	10	1	4

Outfield	PCT	G	PO	A	E	DP
Almonte	1.000	7	2	0	0	0
Boggs	1.000	5	2	0	0	0
Braun	.996	147	259	8	1	2
Carroll	1.000	1	3	0	0	0
Counsell	.000	1	0	0	0	0
Gamel	1.000	1	1	0	0	0
Gomez	1.000	87	183	5	0	1
Hairston Jr.	1.000	12	24	2	0	1
Hart	.992	126	251	3	2	1
Kotsay	.942	54	79	2	5	0
Morgan	.992	111	244	5	2	1
Schafer	.000	2	0	0	0	0
Wilson	1.000	3	2	0	0	0

NASHVILLE SOUNDS
PACIFIC COAST LEAGUE

TRIPLE-A

Batting	B-T	HT	WT	DOB	AVG	vLH	vRH	G	AB	R	H	2B	3B	HR	RBI	BB	HBP	SH	SF	SO	SB	CS	SLG	OBP
Almonte, Erick	R-R	6-2	245	2-1-78	.303	.327	.296	83	244	43	74	15	1	6	42	31	0	0	1	46	2	1	.447	.380
Arlis, Patrick	R-R	6-0	229	12-18-80	.300	.000	.333	5	10	2	3	1	0	0	0	1	0	0	0	2	0	0	.400	.364
Boggs, Brandon	B-R	5-11	210	1-9-83	.241	.148	.280	94	270	45	65	19	1	9	38	53	8	0	0	82	3	5	.419	.381
Brown, Jordan	L-L	6-0	205	12-18-83	.317	.213	.339	100	353	50	112	28	0	8	51	12	3	0	6	32	2	0	.465	.340
Buller, Dayton	R-R	6-0	190	6-22-81	.300	.286	.333	4	10	3	3	2	0	0	0	4	0	0	0	2	0	0	.500	.500
Carroll, Brett	R-R	6-0	210	10-3-82	.281	.291	.277	93	335	66	94	14	2	15	51	34	7	0	3	73	9	3	.469	.356
Farris, Eric	R-R	5-9	180	3-3-86	.271	.267	.273	134	538	70	146	26	5	6	55	32	6	0	4	70	21	7	.372	.317
Figueroa, Luis	B-R	5-9	165	2-16-74	.296	.273	.313	9	27	1	8	2	0	0	3	4	0	0	0	1	0	0	.370	.387
Gamel, Mat	L-R	6-0	215	7-26-85	.310	.213	.347	128	493	90	153	29	0	28	96	46	4	0	2	84	2	0	.540	.372
Gindl, Caleb	L-L	5-9	205	8-31-88	.307	.326	.300	126	472	84	145	23	5	15	60	63	1	0	0	93	6	5	.472	.390
Gonzalez, Andy	R-R	6-3	215	12-15-81	.240	.100	.275	25	50	6	12	1	0	1	6	6	0	0	1	9	0	0	.320	.316
Green, Taylor	L-R	5-11	200	11-2-86	.336	.267	.357	120	420	74	141	36	1	22	88	55	4	0	5	72	1	0	.583	.413
Hart, Corey	R-R	6-6	235	3-24-82	.133	.000	.154	5	15	1	2	2	0	0	1	0	0	0	0	3	0	0	.267	.133
Katin, Brendan	R-R	6-1	223	1-28-83	.239	.205	.257	34	109	22	26	9	0	11	25	11	1	0	0	41	0	0	.624	.314
Kottaras, George	L-R	6-0	190	5-10-83	.343	.379	.329	29	102	19	35	8	1	4	21	16	0	0	0	29	0	1	.559	.432
Lopez, Felipe	B-R	6-0	205	5-12-80	.250	.000	.273	4	12	1	3	0	0	0	1	4	1	0	0	1	0	0	.250	.471
Machado, Anderson	B-R	6-0	189	1-25-81	.156	.100	.175	27	77	7	12	1	0	1	8	11	0	0	1	17	0	1	.208	.258
Maldonado, Martin	R-R	6-1	225	8-16-86	.321	.290	.330	39	134	23	43	5	0	8	25	16	5	0	1	21	0	0	.537	.410
Maysonet, Edwin	R-R	6-1	195	10-17-81	.290	.290	.290	103	383	57	111	24	2	3	39	27	8	0	3	70	2	1	.386	.347
Morgan, Nyjer	L-L	6-0	175	7-2-80	.500	.000	.667	2	4	1	2	0	0	0	0	2	0	0	0	1	1	0	.500	.667
Nieves, Wil	R-R	5-11	190	9-25-77	.170	.292	.125	23	88	3	15	2	0	1	6	4	1	0	1	11	0	0	.227	.213
Nowak, Chris	R-R	6-5	225	2-21-83	.159	.176	.148	19	44	2	7	0	0	1	4	8	0	0	1	11	3	1	.227	.283
Reed, Jeremy	L-L	6-0	195	6-15-81	.233	.214	.240	36	103	7	24	5	2	1	6	11	1	0	1	15	4	1	.350	.310
Rivera, Mike	R-R	6-1	235	9-8-76	.238	.220	.245	61	193	16	46	10	0	7	31	19	3	0	1	55	2	1	.399	.315
Sanchez, Juan	R-R	5-11	170	1-16-87	.000	.000	.000	3	3	0	0	0	0	0	0	0	0	0	0	0	0	0	.000	.000
Schafer, Logan	L-L	6-1	180	9-8-86	.331	.244	.363	40	169	31	56	13	2	5	23	17	4	0	2	18	5	3	.521	.401
Wheeler, Zelous	R-R	5-10	220	1-16-87	.275	.188	.314	17	51	7	14	3	1	1	6	9	0	0	0	8	0	0	.431	.383

Pitching	B-T	HT	WT	DOB	W	L	ERA	G	GS	CG	SV	IP	H	R	ER	HR	BB	SO	AVG	vLH	vRH	K/9	BB/9
Braddock, Zach	L-L	6-2	230	8-23-87	0	0	4.76	6	0	0	1	6	4	3	3	0	7	10	.200	.375		15.88	11.12
Butler, Josh	R-R	6-5	200	12-11-84	9	8	5.15	28	28	0	0	142	171	95	81	24	76	96	.302	.294	.308	6.10	4.83
De La Cruz, Eulo	R-R	5-10	215	3-12-84	7	6	3.88	25	23	0	0	137	130	67	59	14	63	126	.249	.224	.268	8.28	4.14
DiFelice, Mark	R-R	6-2	190	8-23-76	2	1	2.17	17	3	0	6	29	25	7	7	3	6	31	.227	.196	.250	9.62	1.86
Dillard, Tim	R-R	6-4	225	7-19-83	4	2	3.58	17	0	0	1	38	31	19	15	3	13	30	.228	.286	.178	7.17	3.11
Fiers, Mike	R-R	6-3	200	6-15-85	8	1	1.11	12	10	1	0	65	41	18	8	4	22	69	.174	.165	.183	9.60	3.06
Flores, Randy	L-L	6-0	190	7-31-75	1	1	3.27	10	0	0	2	11	13	7	4	2	4	11	.277	.350	.222	9.00	3.27
2-team total (19 Tucson)					2	3	3.03	29	0	0	2	30	30	16	10	3	10	30	—	—		9.10	3.03
Green, Sean	R-R	6-6	230	4-20-79	1	5	3.91	33	0	0	6	46	41	22	20	3	27	40	.252	.271	.237	7.83	5.28
Greinke, Zack	R-R	6-2	190	10-21-83	0	1	4.70	2	2	0	0	8	10	4	4	1	2	9	.333	.263	.455	10.57	2.35
Hand, Donovan	R-R	6-4	210	4-20-86	2	6	3.60	39	0	0	1	55	66	24	22	6	21	32	.308	.275	.333	5.24	3.44
Hawkins, LaTroy	R-R	6-5	220	12-21-72	0	0	0.00	2	0	0	0	1	0	0	0	0	2	1	.000	.500	.000	6.75	13.50
Henderson, Jim	L-R	6-5	190	10-21-82	3	1	5.93	20	0	0	0	30	24	20	20	4	23	30	.220	.232	.208	8.90	6.82
Herrera, Danny Ray	L-L	5-6	165	10-21-84	1	0	1.48	29	0	0	2	43	32	8	7	2	8	39	.203	.173	.217	8.23	1.69
Hinton, Robert	R-R	6-1	205	10-21-84	1	0	7.88	6	0	0	0	8	8	7	7	3	4	9	.250	.417	.150	10.13	4.50
James, Justin	R-R	6-3	215	9-13-81	2	2	4.41	27	0	0	1	35	41	20	17	0	17	23	.293	.309	.282	5.97	4.41
Kintzler, Brandon	R-R	5-10	185	8-1-84	0	0	0.00	1	0	0	0	1	0	0	0	0	0	2	.000	.000	.000	18.00	0.00
Marzec, Eric	R-R	6-0	190	1-13-88	0	0	0.00	2	0	0	0	3	1	0	0	0	1	1	.111	.167	.000	3.00	3.00
McClendon, Mike	R-R	6-5	225	4-3-85	5	6	3.53	38	0	0	8	59	61	28	23	2	19	48	.264	.304	.227	7.36	2.91
Meadows, Dan	L-L	6-6	223	11-3-87	0	2	4.04	20	1	0	1	36	33	16	16	4	13	35	.248	.321	.200	8.83	3.28
Narron, Sam	L-L	6-7	200	7-12-81	6	7	5.12	28	26	1	0	160	190	99	91	22	48	91	.302	.322	.292	5.12	2.70
Parra, Manny	L-L	6-3	205	10-30-82	0	1	6.10	7	1	0	0	10	12	8	7	0	5	8	.293	.538	.179	6.97	4.35
Peralta, Wily	R-R	6-2	240	5-8-89	2	0	2.03	5	5	0	0	31	21	7	7	0	11	40	.193	.179	.208	11.61	3.19

Pitching

Pitching	B-T	HT	WT	DOB	W	L	ERA	G	GS	CG	SV	IP	H	R	ER	HR	BB	SO	AVG	vLH	vRH	K/9	BB/9
Rivas, Amaury	R-R	6-2	217	12-20-85	7	12	4.72	28	28	0	0	151	151	88	79	14	81	108	.260	.251	.269	6.45	4.84
Rogers, Mark	R-R	6-2	226	1-30-86	0	2	13.20	5	5	0	0	15	21	23	22	1	22	12	.333	.433	.242	7.20	13.20
Saito, Takashi	L-R	6-2	200	2-14-70	0	0	0.00	6	0	0	6	3	1	0	0	0	0	7	.158	.222	.100	11.12	0.00
Segovia, Zack	R-R	6-2	245	4-11-83	5	4	3.98	45	0	0	2	63	70	31	28	6	38	50	.280	.295	.271	7.11	5.40
Stetter, Mitch	L-L	6-4	220	1-16-81	0	0	10.80	2	0	0	0	2	2	2	2	1	0	1	.286	.250	.333	5.40	0.00
Wright, Chase	L-L	6-2	205	2-8-83	5	6	6.07	21	12	0	1	76	104	54	51	6	37	44	.340	.280	.366	5.23	4.40

Fielding

Catcher	PCT	G	PO	A	E	DP	PB
Arlis	1.000	2	15	0	0	0	
Buller	.968	4	27	3	1	0	0
Kottaras	.990	28	172	17	2	1	3
Maldonado	.997	38	282	29	1	3	1
Nieves	1.000	22	158	12	0	2	1
Rivera	.997	52	369	29	1	3	0

First Base	PCT	G	PO	A	E	DP
Almonte	.981	33	281	24	6	33
Brown	.975	11	75	2	2	4
Gamel	.988	102	828	78	11	82
Gonzalez	1.000	1	8	0	0	1
Nowak	1.000	1	7	0	0	0
Reed	1.000	1	1	2	0	0
Rivera	1.000	1	10	0	0	0

Second Base	PCT	G	PO	A	E	DP
Farris	.983	107	214	306	9	74

Figueroa	1.000	1	1	3	0	0
Gonzalez	.962	6	9	16	1	4
Green	.990	26	42	56	1	12
Lopez	1.000	2	6	8	0	2
Machado	1.000	1	5	10	0	3
Maysonet	1.000	3	6	7	0	2

Third Base	PCT	G	PO	A	E	DP
Figueroa	1.000	1	1	0	0	0
Gamel	.880	20	13	31	6	4
Gonzalez	.933	7	3	11	1	2
Green	.945	94	47	158	12	16
Lopez	.750	2	0	3	1	0
Nowak	1.000	12	7	17	0	0
Wheeler	.905	16	4	34	4	3

Shortstop	PCT	G	PO	A	E	DP
Farris	.928	25	42	61	8	10
Figueroa	.960	6	6	18	1	4

Machado	.970	19	24	41	2	10
Maysonet	.953	98	166	303	23	66
Sanchez	.000	1	0	0	0	0

Outfield	PCT	G	PO	A	E	DP
Almonte	1.000	5	4	0	0	0
Boggs	.970	76	126	5	4	0
Brown	.978	73	130	3	3	0
Carroll	.986	89	202	17	3	2
Gindl	.973	124	245	9	7	1
Hart	1.000	5	6	0	0	0
Katin	1.000	17	25	1	0	0
Morgan	1.000	2	3	0	0	0
Reed	.971	26	33	1	1	0
Schafer	.990	40	96	6	1	2

HUNTSVILLE STARS

SOUTHERN LEAGUE

DOUBLE-A

Batting

Batting	B-T	HT	WT	DOB	AVG	vLH	vRH	G	AB	R	H	2B	3B	HR	RBI	BB	HBP	SH	SF	SO	SB	CS	SLG	OBP
Buller, Dayton	R-R	6-0	190	6-22-81	.165	.167	.164	27	85	6	14	3	1	0	8	8	0	0	0	32	0	1	.224	.237
Caufield, Chuck	R-R	6-1	218	7-6-83	.265	.270	.262	33	102	15	27	7	0	3	16	2	5	0	0	27	3	3	.422	.312
Cline, Matt	R-R	5-10	188	10-18-85	.237	.244	.234	91	274	45	65	12	2	2	19	36	7	0	2	54	3	1	.318	.339
Davis, Khris	R-R	6-0	195	12-21-87	.210	.182	.225	35	124	10	26	7	1	2	16	10	1	0	1	23	0	0	.331	.272
De La Rosa, Anderson	R-R	6-0	199	8-1-84	.239	.250	.235	61	184	19	44	9	1	5	26	7	3	0	0	41	0	2	.380	.278
Gonzalez, Andy	R-R	6-3	215	12-15-81	.306	.425	.262	44	147	21	45	12	0	3	17	31	1	0	0	30	0	0	.449	.430
Green, Taylor	L-R	5-11	200	11-2-86	.364	.000	.444	3	11	2	4	1	0	0	3	0	1	0	1	3	0	0	.455	.385
Halton, Sean	R-R	6-5	265	6-7-87	.298	.312	.292	116	439	49	131	39	1	7	65	32	4	0	7	83	6	1	.440	.346
Haydel, Lee	L-L	5-11	180	7-15-87	.274	.255	.280	120	449	49	123	16	6	0	26	37	0	0	1	101	17	18	.323	.329
Jones, Brandon	L-L	6-1	215	12-10-83	.229	.254	.233	68	230	35	55	13	2	4	34	31	3	0	1	59	1	0	.365	.336
Kjeldgaard, Brock	R-R	6-5	215	1-22-86	.271	.313	.250	61	203	18	55	9	2	6	27	17	6	0	3	66	2	1	.424	.341
Komatsu, Erik	L-L	5-10	175	10-1-87	.294	.233	.323	93	320	48	94	19	1	6	40	53	2	0	4	44	13	6	.416	.393
Lucroy, Jonathan	R-R	6-0	190	6-13-86	.273	.333	.250	4	11	3	3	1	0	0	4	6	0	0	0	1	1	0	.364	.529
Machado, Anderson	B-R	6-0	189	1-25-81	.000	.000	.000	9	8	1	0	0	0	0	2	2	0	0	0	3	0	0	.000	.200
Maldonado, Martin	R-R	6-1	215	8-16-86	.264	.281	.258	64	208	24	55	13	0	3	34	19	9	0	2	56	2	1	.370	.349
Miranda, Sergio	B-R	5-9	193	3-5-87	.270	.209	.291	109	356	49	96	16	2	0	29	30	5	0	4	41	1	6	.326	.332
Morris, Hunter	L-R	6-2	200	10-7-88	.353	.333	.357	4	17	6	6	1	1	1	2	0	0	0	0	1	0	0	.706	.353
Ortiz, Yancarlos	B-R	5-9	200	9-15-84	.063	.000	.000	9	16	0	1	0	0	0	0	2	0	0	0	4	1	0	.063	.167
Riggans, Shawn	R-R	6-2	200	7-25-80	.167	.000	.200	7	6	0	1	0	0	0	0	1	0	0	0	2	0	0	.167	.286
Sanchez, Juan	R-R	5-11	170	1-16-87	.100	.000	.100	4	10	0	1	1	0	0	0	0	0	0	0	2	0	0	.200	.100
Schafer, Logan	L-L	6-1	180	9-8-86	.302	.263	.318	50	189	31	57	9	4	0	19	17	3	0	0	25	10	5	.392	.368
Statia, Hainley	B-R	5-10	180	1-19-86	.279	.327	.256	95	297	42	83	16	4	2	40	36	1	0	4	38	3	1	.380	.355
Wheeler, Zelous	R-R	5-10	220	1-16-87	.272	.286	.265	65	228	34	62	20	0	8	32	30	9	0	1	49	7	0	.465	.377
Wilson, Steffan	R-R	6-1	220	5-24-86	.236	.236	.237	123	419	48	99	17	1	6	50	36	1	0	4	90	4	2	.325	.296

Pitching

Pitching	B-T	HT	WT	DOB	W	L	ERA	G	GS	CG	SV	IP	H	R	ER	HR	BB	SO	AVG	vLH	vRH	K/9	BB/9
Bowman, Michael	R-R	6-2	203	5-2-87	6	12	5.27	26	26	0	0	135	167	81	79	19	57	61	.316	.367	.270	4.07	3.80
Byrd, Darren	R-R	6-3	200	10-24-86	5	3	2.95	41	0	0	7	64	58	26	21	2	32	50	.243	.188	.283	7.03	4.50
Dunn, Jameson	R-R	6-4	225	1-6-87	1	0	6.00	3	0	0	0	3	3	2	2	0	2	0	.300	.250	.333	0.00	6.00
Fiers, Mike	R-R	6-3	200	6-15-85	5	3	2.64	22	8	0	5	61	42	21	18	7	14	63	.189	.167	.208	9.24	2.05
Frerichs, Corey	R-R	5-11	200	5-7-86	1	0	9.00	7	0	0	0	11	16	15	11	2	7	8	.340	.391	.292	6.55	5.73
Hand, Donovan	R-R	6-4	210	4-20-86	0	0	2.38	9	0	0	1	11	16	3	3	0	1	12	.348	.385	.333	9.53	0.79
Heckathorn, Kyle	R-R	6-6	225	6-17-88	0	4	7.18	7	7	0	0	36	45	34	29	7	17	24	.296	.313	.284	5.94	4.21
Henderson, Jim	L-R	6-5	190	10-21-82	4	1	2.64	22	0	0	5	31	22	9	9	4	8	39	.198	.234	.172	11.45	2.31
Hinton, Robert	R-R	6-1	205	8-13-84	1	3	1.67	37	0	0	2	54	44	13	10	4	19	58	.226	.190	.252	9.67	3.17
James, Justin	R-R	6-3	215	9-13-81	0	0	3.38	3	0	0	0	3	3	1	1	0	1	5	.273	.333	.250	16.88	3.38
Luetge, Lucas	L-L	6-3	200	3-24-87	1	3	3.13	46	1	0	3	69	63	29	24	3	23	69	.247	.175	.296	9.00	3.01
Manzanillo, Santo	R-R	6-0	190	12-20-88	0	1	2.21	20	0	0	7	20	13	5	5	2	12	19	.181	.167	.190	8.41	5.31
Meadows, Dan	L-L	6-6	223	11-3-87	6	2	1.51	21	0	0	1	42	28	9	7	1	10	39	.192	.232	.167	8.42	2.16
Mercedes, Roque	R-R	6-3	185	10-28-86	0	3	6.95	27	0	0	4	34	52	28	26	7	19	35	.356	.364	.350	9.36	5.08
Merklinger, Dan	L-L	6-1	195	11-19-85	9	9	4.10	28	28	1	0	158	156	87	72	18	57	153	.258	.245	.263	7.58	3.25
Peralta, Wily	R-R	6-2	240	5-8-89	9	7	3.46	21	21	1	0	120	106	57	46	9	48	117	.243	.272	.217	8.80	3.61
Sanchez, Jesus	R-R	5-11	202	9-24-87	4	7	4.91	30	14	0	1	99	104	60	54	13	47	66	.271	.254	.285	6.00	4.27

Pitching	B-T	HT	WT	DOB	W	L	ERA	G	GS	CG	SV	IP	H	R	ER	HR	BB	SO	AVG	vLH	vRH	K/9	BB/9
Scarpetta, Cody	R-R	6-3	244	8-25-88	8	5	3.85	23	23	0	0	117	100	61	50	8	61	98	.234	.169	.280	7.54	4.69
Seidel, R.J.	R-R	6-5	200	9-3-87	1	4	5.87	9	4	0	0	31	34	24	20	6	12	26	.279	.273	.282	7.63	3.52
Wooten, Rob	R-R	6-4	190	7-21-85	3	3	3.38	36	0	0	7	43	41	20	16	3	15	41	.252	.231	.271	8.65	3.16
Wright, Chase	L-L	6-2	205	2-8-83	0	3	8.90	7	5	0	0	29	41	31	29	6	19	19	.336	.300	.348	5.83	5.83

Fielding

Catcher	PCT	G	PO	A	E	DP	PB
Buller	1.000	24	198	22	0	1	3
De La Rosa	.983	54	344	52	7	4	9
Lucroy	1.000	4	32	3	0	1	0
Maldonado	.990	61	409	63	5	2	4

First Base	PCT	G	PO	A	E	DP
Gonzalez	1.000	2	9	1	0	1
Halton	.994	115	846	87	6	75
Morris	1.000	4	37	3	0	4
Wilson	.994	24	161	14	1	13

Second Base	PCT	G	PO	A	E	DP
Cline	1.000	38	64	81	0	17
Miranda	.988	85	148	194	4	43

	PCT	G	PO	A	E	DP
Ortiz	1.000	2	0	5	0	1
Statia	1.000	19	32	55	0	7
Wheeler	.885	5	14	9	3	3

Third Base	PCT	G	PO	A	E	DP
Gonzalez	.900	16	13	23	4	2
Green	1.000	3	0	4	0	0
Miranda	1.000	3	2	4	0	0
Wheeler	.976	58	39	123	4	10
Wilson	.914	61	42	96	13	11

Shortstop	PCT	G	PO	A	E	DP
Cline	.935	49	65	92	11	19
Gonzalez	.908	25	37	62	10	11
Miranda	.000	1	0	0	0	0

	PCT	G	PO	A	E	DP
Ortiz	.600	4	1	2	2	0
Sanchez	1.000	4	3	5	0	1
Statia	.963	70	109	175	11	35
Wheeler	1.000	1	0	1	0	0

Outfield	PCT	G	PO	A	E	DP
Caufield	1.000	23	38	1	0	1
Davis	.979	29	47	0	1	0
Haydel	.968	114	205	8	7	0
Jones	.980	57	91	6	2	1
Kjeldgaard	.974	53	111	3	3	0
Komatsu	.990	86	186	3	2	1
Schafer	.992	48	122	4	1	1
Wilson	.972	23	33	2	1	0

MILWAUKEE BREWERS

BREVARD COUNTY MANATEES HIGH CLASS A
FLORIDA STATE LEAGUE

Batting	B-T	HT	WT	DOB	AVG	vLH	vRH	G	AB	R	H	2B	3B	HR	RBI	BB	HBP	SH	SF	SO	SB	CS	SLG	OBP
Brownstein, Mike	R-R	5-10	175	8-9-87	.243	.167	.270	40	136	15	33	5	1	0	9	13	1	0	0	32	5	2	.294	.313
Caufield, Chuck	R-R	6-1	218	7-6-83	.258	.316	.233	39	128	23	33	1	2	1	6	13	5	0	1	27	6	4	.406	.347
Davis, Kentrail	L-R	5-9	195	6-29-88	.245	.224	.253	132	507	76	124	19	8	8	46	37	18	0	2	97	33	8	.361	.317
Davis, Khris	R-R	6-0	195	12-21-87	.309	.329	.303	90	304	50	94	21	1	15	68	51	9	0	7	70	10	5	.533	.415
Dean, Brent	R-R	6-1	210	7-26-86	.224	.214	.227	19	58	9	13	3	1	2	9	4	0	0	2	22	1	1	.414	.266
Dennis, Chris	L-R	6-1	205	9-15-88	.169	.000	.192	27	83	11	14	1	0	2	10	12	0	0	0	39	2	1	.253	.274
Gennett, Scooter	L-R	5-9	164	5-1-90	.300	.282	.307	134	556	74	167	20	6	9	51	27	4	0	6	69	11	10	.406	.334
Kjeldgaard, Brock	R-R	6-5	215	1-22-86	.268	.400	.222	65	231	39	62	9	2	18	49	26	10	0	1	75	13	2	.558	.366
Krieger, Scott	R-R	6-0	215	1-30-87	.270	.329	.249	88	300	45	81	7	3	8	39	20	5	0	5	108	7	4	.427	.321
McCraw, Sean	L-R	6-0	185	3-11-86	.188	.174	.194	49	149	16	28	7	0	3	21	16	1	0	0	35	0	0	.295	.271
Morris, Hunter	L-R	6-2	200	10-7-88	.271	.281	.268	126	501	75	136	28	5	19	67	18	5	0	7	84	7	3	.461	.299
Neda, Rafael	R-R	6-1	215	10-12-88	.222	.000	.250	3	9	0	2	0	0	0	3	0	1	0	0	2	0	0	.222	.300
Prince, Josh	R-R	6-0	180	1-26-88	.281	.339	.265	75	249	41	70	11	0	5	24	17	3	0	2	37	24	8	.386	.332
Richardson, D'Vontrey	R-R	6-1	200	7-30-88	.284	.235	.304	97	359	47	102	13	7	3	41	22	3	0	4	70	9	13	.384	.327
Roberts, Michael	R-R	6-2	185	8-28-87	.264	.385	.225	18	53	3	14	2	0	0	6	4	0	0	0	13	1	0	.302	.316
Sanchez, Juan	R-R	5-11	170	1-16-87	.245	.242	.246	63	204	16	50	11	0	1	19	14	4	0	0	30	5	5	.314	.306
Schafer, Logan	L-L	6-1	190	9-8-86	.306	.278	.333	9	36	4	11	0	0	1	5	0	0	1	5	4	1	1	.306	.390
Vucinich, Shea	R-R	6-1	185	12-1-88	.260	.282	.252	125	427	59	111	22	1	9	51	47	12	0	3	122	13	10	.379	.348
Zarraga, Shawn	R-R	6-0	260	1-21-89	.272	.254	.278	69	235	22	64	9	1	4	35	16	3	0	1	31	9	2	.370	.325

Pitching	B-T	HT	WT	DOB	W	L	ERA	G	GS	CG	SV	IP	H	R	ER	HR	BB	SO	AVG	vLH	vRH	K/9	BB/9
Anundsen, Evan	R-R	6-3	215	5-17-88	5	2	3.86	32	11	1	1	89	101	43	38	8	24	62	.287	.343	.235	6.29	2.44
Blanks, Bradley	R-R	6-4	185	3-17-85	2	0	3.77	22	0	0	5	31	30	14	13	3	11	26	.248	.255	.243	7.55	3.19
Bucci, Nick	R-R	6-2	180	7-16-90	8	11	3.84	26	25	1	0	150	143	73	64	12	51	119	.247	.247	.246	7.14	3.06
Burgos, Hiram	R-R	6-1	210	8-4-87	6	8	4.89	24	22	0	0	120	142	70	65	13	35	80	.302	.314	.290	6.02	2.63
Conner, Mitchell	R-R	6-3	210	7-26-88	2	2	10.61	6	0	0	0	9	12	11	11	0	2	8	.293	.364	.211	7.71	1.93
Crawford, Skyler	R-R	6-1	175	4-20-88	0	0	3.38	12	0	0	0	21	18	9	8	1	10	9	.234	.250	.222	3.80	4.22
Frerichs, Corey	R-R	5-11	200	5-7-86	0	3	6.00	14	0	0	2	18	17	13	12	2	12	19	.254	.226	.278	9.50	6.00
Greinke, Zack	R-R	6-2	190	10-21-83	0	0	0.00	1	1	0	0	3	1	0	0	0	0	4	.100	.000	.500	12.00	0.00
Hawkins, LaTroy	R-R	6-5	220	12-21-72	0	0	4.91	3	0	0	0	4	6	3	2	1	0	5	.375	.400	.333	12.27	0.00
Heckathorn, Kyle	R-R	6-6	225	6-17-88	5	6	3.95	15	15	1	0	80	82	40	35	8	21	65	.267	.294	.236	7.34	2.37
Lasker, Maverick	R-R	6-2	190	2-17-90	3	8	5.74	15	14	0	0	58	68	48	37	5	32	46	.297	.299	.294	7.14	4.97
Manzanillo, Santo	R-R	6-0	190	12-20-88	1	0	1.52	28	0	0	10	41	31	9	7	2	14	43	.200	.190	.211	9.36	3.05
Marzec, Eric	R-R	6-0	190	1-13-88	1	0	1.74	8	1	0	0	21	17	4	4	1	5	9	.230	.257	.205	3.92	2.18
Mercedes, Roque	B-R	6-3	185	10-28-86	2	2	2.25	22	0	0	12	28	22	8	7	1	11	25	.232	.297	.190	8.04	3.54
Nieves, Efrain	L-L	6-0	169	11-15-89	3	0	4.86	41	0	0	0	63	70	38	34	7	27	53	.286	.220	.325	7.53	3.86
Pascual, Rolando	R-R	6-6	245	2-8-89	0	2	11.88	26	0	0	0	25	33	38	33	0	33	15	.333	.298	.365	5.40	11.88
Pokorny, Jon	R-L	6-2	225	4-4-88	5	3	3.77	44	0	0	0	60	57	28	25	5	28	55	.250	.198	.279	8.30	4.22
Rogers, Mark	R-R	6-2	226	1-30-86	0	3	9.37	5	5	0	0	16	22	20	17	4	15	17	.301	.297	.306	9.37	8.27
Rosario, Adrian	R-R	6-4	180	9-30-89	4	5	5.83	16	14	0	0	66	79	48	43	9	33	39	.300	.277	.323	5.29	4.48
2-team total (1 St. Lucie)					4	5	5.80	17	14	0	0	68	84	49	44	9	34	41	—	—	—	5.40	4.48
Ross, Austin	R-R	6-2	200	8-12-88	4	4	7.49	13	13	0	0	64	85	60	53	8	27	44	.318	.331	.304	6.22	3.82
Ruiz, Manuel	L-L	6-5	175	12-12-88	0	0	5.14	2	2	0	0	7	4	5	4	0	8	9	.154	.222	.118	11.57	10.29
Seidel, R.J.	R-R	6-5	200	9-3-87	3	3	3.31	23	3	0	1	49	42	27	18	3	17	28	.237	.198	.279	5.14	3.12
Thornburg, Tyler	R-R	5-11	185	9-29-88	3	6	3.57	12	12	0	0	68	45	30	27	5	33	84	.186	.239	.136	11.12	4.37
Watten, Trey	R-R	6-3	180	12-16-86	1	4	9.17	14	0	0	0	18	31	20	18	0	12	7	.403	.512	.278	3.57	6.11
Willinsky, Mark	R-R	6-4	215	3-14-87	2	4	6.90	29	0	0	6	46	70	35	35	1	14	38	.354	.419	.304	7.49	2.76
Wooten, Rob	R-R	6-4	190	7-21-85	2	0	2.53	12	0	0	1	21	15	6	6	0	3	18	.190	.208	.161	7.59	1.27

Fielding

Catcher	PCT	G	PO	A	E	DP	PB
Dean	.982	16	102	5	2	0	0
McCraw	.994	49	285	36	2	5	4
Neda	.905	3	15	4	2	0	0
Roberts	.976	17	119	5	3	3	5
Zarraga	.991	60	420	34	4	1	3

First Base	PCT	G	PO	A	E	DP
Dennis	.971	3	29	4	1	0
Kjeldgaard	.983	18	160	13	3	13
Krieger	.941	3	15	1	1	4
Morris	.981	115	950	42	19	97

Second Base	PCT	G	PO	A	E	DP
Brownstein	.958	4	6	17	1	3
Gennett	.967	134	251	395	22	89
Sanchez	1.000	1	2	2	0	1

Third Base	PCT	G	PO	A	E	DP
Brownstein	.927	15	9	29	3	6
Morris	.857	6	5	7	2	1
Sanchez	.879	16	4	25	4	1
Vucinich	.938	102	74	196	18	21

Shortstop	PCT	G	PO	A	E	DP
Brownstein	.961	19	23	50	3	6
Prince	.958	72	100	195	13	41

	PCT	G	PO	A	E	DP
Sanchez	.952	34	50	90	7	27
Vucinich	.956	15	23	42	3	13
Outfield	PCT	G	PO	A	E	DP
Brownstein	.000	1	0	0	0	0
Caufield	.949	31	54	2	3	0
Davis	.970	129	252	10	8	1
Davis	.987	82	148	1	2	0
Dennis	1.000	2	4	0	0	0
Kjeldgaard	1.000	28	49	0	0	0
Krieger	.985	33	66	1	1	0
Richardson	.970	94	217	12	7	2
Sanchez	1.000	12	27	2	0	0
Schafer	.909	8	9	1	1	0

WISCONSIN TIMBER RATTLERS

LOW CLASS A

MIDWEST LEAGUE

Batting	B-T	HT	WT	DOB	AVG	vLH	vRH	G	AB	R	H	2B	3B	HR	RBI	BB	HBP	SH	SF	SO	SB	CS	SLG	OBP
Brownstein, Mike	R-R	5-10	175	8-9-87	.277	.245	.293	45	148	20	41	8	0	2	20	24	2	0	2	25	8	3	.372	.381
Dennis, Chris	L-R	6-1	205	9-15-88	.263	.265	.262	51	179	26	47	10	3	8	35	24	1	0	2	51	4	1	.486	.350
Garfield, Cameron	R-R	6-1	195	5-23-91	.118	.333	.071	6	17	3	2	1	0	0	2	1	1	0	0	3	0	1	.176	.211
Garvey, Robbie	L-L	5-8	165	4-26-89	.197	.115	.216	45	137	14	27	2	1	1	9	8	1	0	1	38	5	3	.248	.245
George, Carlos	R-R	6-2	165	2-6-89	.238	.250	.232	26	80	4	19	1	0	0	9	2	2	0	0	16	1	3	.250	.274
Gomez, Carlos	R-R	6-4	215	12-4-85	.333	.000	.333	4	12	3	4	0	0	0	0	1	0	0	0	3	1	.333	.385
Hawn, Cody	L-R	6-1	195	8-11-88	.294	.237	.314	101	377	56	111	24	0	6	50	51	4	0	3	85	3	4	.406	.382
Hopkins, Greg	R-R	6-1	200	11-22-88	.229	.250	.221	114	415	54	95	16	3	7	53	21	4	0	3	88	16	4	.333	.271
Keen, Reggie	R-R	5-10	180	12-2-87	.263	.306	.244	111	411	60	108	16	7	3	30	25	9	0	2	77	41	14	.358	.318
Macias, Brandon	R-R	5-10	185	10-10-88	.264	.308	.254	22	72	11	19	6	0	0	6	3	3	0	0	9	3	1	.347	.321
Mittelstaedt, T.J.	L-R	5-10	185	2-13-88	.293	.237	.311	113	379	72	111	13	4	12	46	76	2	0	4	116	28	7	.443	.410
Neda, Rafael	R-R	6-1	215	10-12-88	.114	.000	.125	10	35	3	4	0	0	0	4	3	0	0	0	3	0	0	.114	.184
Paciorek, Joey	R-R	6-2	225	9-20-88	.257	.320	.221	40	144	17	37	7	1	2	14	12	1	0	0	35	0	3	.361	.318
Pechek, Tony	B-R	6-2	195	10-12-86	.159	.125	.179	48	151	11	24	7	1	0	10	13	1	0	1	41	0	0	.219	.229
Ramirez, Nick	L-L	6-3	225	8-1-89	.197	.241	.185	36	137	11	27	12	0	3	23	9	1	0	2	36	0	0	.350	.248
Rivera, Yadiel	R-R	6-2	175	5-2-92	.194	.143	.207	32	103	6	20	2	1	1	5	4	0	0	0	34	0	0	.262	.224
Roberts, Tyler	R-R	6-2	226	10-25-90	.211	.229	.205	46	152	14	32	9	0	4	27	12	2	0	2	58	1	0	.349	.274
Rogers, Jason	R-R	6-2	250	3-13-88	.275	.329	.248	64	240	29	66	15	2	6	37	22	2	0	4	48	6	1	.429	.336
Romero, Franklin	R-R	5-11	180	6-24-88	.227	.178	.248	93	304	30	69	9	7	2	31	6	4	0	3	92	19	12	.322	.249
Shaw, Nick	R-R	5-11	160	8-25-88	.260	.261	.260	126	465	80	121	16	6	2	40	82	4	0	3	82	8	7	.333	.374
Stang, Chad	R-R	6-2	190	3-26-89	.269	.209	.292	65	238	30	64	10	6	2	14	14	3	0	2	50	12	5	.387	.315
Walker, Mike	L-R	6-3	215	6-12-88	.274	.292	.266	105	369	54	101	20	1	15	72	60	8	0	0	120	7	5	.455	.387

Pitching	B-T	HT	WT	DOB	W	L	ERA	G	GS	CG	SV	IP	H	R	ER	HR	BB	SO	AVG	vLH	vRH	K/9	BB/9
Arnett, Eric	R-R	6-5	230	1-25-88	0	4	5.00	5	5	0	0	27	31	19	15	1	8	25	.284	.373	.207	8.33	2.67
Bashara, Charly	L-L	6-1	190	5-31-87	4	5	5.23	23	9	0	0	72	91	53	42	12	19	41	.304	.267	.321	5.10	2.36
Braddock, Zach	L-L	6-2	180	8-23-87	0	0	0.00	2	2	0	0	5	0	0	0	1	7	.000	.000	.000	13.50	1.93
Britt, Dan	R-R	6-4	180	3-13-88	6	3	3.99	30	4	0	0	70	67	35	31	6	19	56	.259	.255	.261	7.20	2.44
Cravy, Tyler	R-R	6-3	180	7-13-89	3	2	5.75	15	0	0	0	20	27	14	13	0	10	29	.307	.342	.280	12.84	4.43
Crawford, Skyler	R-R	6-1	175	4-20-88	0	0	3.00	4	0	0	0	9	5	3	3	2	4	5	.152	.071	.211	5.00	4.00
Dunn, Jameson	R-R	6-4	225	1-6-87	2	0	3.00	6	5	0	0	27	21	9	9	2	10	20	.221	.222	.220	6.67	3.33
Garman, Brian	L-L	5-10	180	7-19-88	4	3	3.18	41	1	0	3	62	60	28	22	1	34	61	.254	.200	.280	8.81	4.91
Hall, Brooks	R-R	6-5	200	6-26-90	7	5	4.13	19	18	0	0	100	100	51	46	7	25	63	.279	.274	.283	5.65	2.24
Holle, Greg	R-R	6-8	240	11-16-88	1	4	4.57	41	0	0	19	61	52	33	31	1	24	45	.229	.250	.217	6.64	3.54
Howell, Del	L-L	6-3	185	9-6-87	3	9	5.66	19	16	1	0	83	87	59	52	12	52	50	.278	.347	.256	5.44	5.66
Keeling, Thomas	L-L	6-3	185	3-30-88	1	3	5.89	19	0	0	2	18	13	16	12	1	16	22	.194	.042	.279	10.80	7.85
Krestalude, Damon	R-R	6-4	185	6-5-89	0	0	9.26	7	1	0	0	12	17	12	12	3	11	8	.347	.316	.367	6.17	8.49
Lasker, Maverick	R-R	6-2	190	2-17-90	1	5	5.56	11	8	0	1	44	44	30	27	5	11	34	.259	.281	.248	7.01	2.27
Lintz, Seth	R-R	6-1	170	2-7-90	1	0	2.53	8	0	0	0	11	7	3	3	0	5	12	.179	.176	.182	10.13	4.22
Marzec, Eric	R-R	6-0	190	1-13-88	3	2	1.77	32	0	0	4	46	29	14	9	2	27	55	.182	.194	.174	10.84	5.32
Medlen, Casey	R-R	6-0	155	8-4-89	1	1	3.00	16	0	0	0	27	20	10	9	0	5	35	.194	.278	.149	11.67	1.67
Miller, Matt	R-R	6-6	220	1-30-88	6	8	4.38	22	21	2	0	111	102	64	54	4	55	89	.246	.272	.230	7.22	4.46
Nelson, Jimmy	R-R	6-6	245	6-5-89	8	9	4.38	26	25	1	0	146	146	81	71	9	65	120	.266	.276	.257	7.40	4.01
Parra, Manny	L-L	6-3	205	10-30-82	1	0	0.00	1	0	0	0	2	0	0	0	0	0	4	.000	.000	.000	18.00	0.00
Rosario, Adrian	R-R	6-4	180	9-30-89	0	1	1.34	19	0	0	5	34	21	7	5	2	12	42	.183	.178	.186	11.23	3.21
Ross, Austin	R-R	6-2	200	8-12-88	6	3	3.25	13	12	1	0	69	58	30	25	2	23	70	.221	.176	.253	9.09	2.99
Thornburg, Tyler	R-R	5-11	185	9-29-88	7	0	1.57	12	12	2	0	69	49	14	12	5	12	76	.203	.157	.246	9.96	3.28
Wawrzasek, Stosh	R-R	6-0	225	8-30-90	1	1	4.10	36	0	0	1	53	52	27	24	5	27	54	.252	.238	.262	9.23	4.61
Williams, Alan	L-L	6-3	195	3-5-90	1	1	3.38	13	0	0	2	19	12	7	7	1	9	21	.179	.115	.220	10.13	4.34

Fielding

Catcher	PCT	G	PO	A	E	DP	PB
Garfield	1.000	4	21	2	0	0	3
Neda	.975	10	72	7	2	0	0
Paciorek	.975	39	318	36	9	4	12

Pechek	.984	48	338	25	6	2	5
Roberts	.980	46	308	37	7	3	9
First Base	PCT	G	PO	A	E	DP
Dennis	.939	4	29	2	2	6

Hawn	.993	72	620	42	5	60
Ramirez	.993	31	284	14	2	15
Rogers	.979	4	46	0	1	4
Walker	.985	30	257	12	4	19

MILWAUKEE BREWERS

Second Base	PCT	G	PO	A	E	DP
Brownstein	.984	30	45	78	2	15
Hopkins	.959	25	46	70	5	12
Macias	1.000	5	5	18	0	0
Mittelstaedt	.975	27	42	73	3	15
Shaw	.983	59	95	195	5	37

Third Base	PCT	G	PO	A	E	DP
Brownstein	.667	2	0	2	1	0
Hopkins	.950	87	64	183	13	17

	PCT	G	PO	A	E	DP
Macias	.974	12	4	33	1	1
Shaw	.000	1	0	0	0	0
Walker	.881	42	13	61	10	3

Shortstop	PCT	G	PO	A	E	DP
Brownstein	.922	14	15	32	4	5
George	.920	26	51	53	9	15
Macias	.933	4	5	9	1	2
Rivera	.924	32	49	85	11	19
Shaw	.962	69	73	183	10	35

Outfield	PCT	G	PO	A	E	DP
Dennis	1.000	19	24	3	0	0
Garvey	.954	44	59	3	3	1
Gomez	1.000	4	6	1	0	0
Hopkins	1.000	2	1	0	0	0
Keen	.971	109	219	15	7	1
Mittelstaedt	.974	77	109	5	3	0
Rogers	1.000	32	33	1	0	0
Romero	.946	88	166	9	10	2
Stang	.971	65	124	9	4	3

HELENA BREWERS   ROOKIE
PIONEER LEAGUE

Batting	B-T	HT	WT	DOB	AVG	vLH	vRH	G	AB	R	H	2B	3B	HR	RBI	BB	HBP	SH	SF	SO	SB	CS	SLG	OBP
Allison, Kenny	R-R	6-3	185	2-21-90	.255	.288	.235	43	137	18	35	4	3	2	22	16	3	0	0	41	5	4	.372	.346
Berberet, Parker	R-R	6-3	205	10-20-89	.240	.239	.241	68	262	41	63	15	2	7	40	33	3	0	5	71	1	3	.393	.327
Dean, Brent	R-R	6-1	210	7-26-86	.286	.111	.368	8	28	3	8	3	0	1	6	2	0	0	0	11	0	1	.500	.333
Dhanani, Kyle	R-R	6-3	195	9-6-87	.266	.288	.257	59	233	29	62	13	0	2	28	14	5	0	0	54	7	7	.348	.321
Dishon, Johnny	R-R	5-11	193	3-21-89	.257	.200	.279	57	202	32	52	6	3	6	25	29	4	0	2	85	21	6	.406	.359
Elliot, Douglas	R-R	6-2	210	8-31-88	.154	.000	.250	4	13	2	2	1	0	0	0	2	0	0	0	2	0	0	.231	.267
Elmore, Gant	R-R	5-7	175	9-9-88	.171	.056	.203	25	82	9	14	2	0	0	4	10	1	0	0	27	2	1	.195	.269
Felix, Steve	L-R	6-1	215	4-21-88	.231	.077	.269	19	65	12	15	5	0	5	18	6	5	0	1	14	0	1	.538	.338
Garvey, Robbie	L-L	5-8	165	4-26-89	.238	.121	.267	46	168	20	40	11	1	0	17	17	3	0	3	41	9	4	.315	.314
McMahan, Ben	R-R	6-0	201	10-14-89	.315	.420	.268	39	162	26	51	10	1	7	25	3	1	0	1	36	3	0	.519	.329
Nemeth, Michael	L-R	6-1	200	4-4-89	.213	.219	.211	47	155	15	33	5	0	1	16	26	1	0	3	29	1	2	.265	.324
Paciorek, Joey	R-R	6-2	225	9-20-88	.259	.000	.304	7	27	5	7	3	0	2	3	5	0	0	0	8	0	1	.593	.375
Ramirez, Nick	L-L	6-3	225	8-1-89	.369	.472	.313	23	103	23	38	9	0	8	30	2	1	0	1	22	0	1	.689	.383
Rivera, Yadiel	R-R	6-2	175	5-2-92	.248	.213	.263	74	330	47	82	14	7	8	38	14	3	0	0	91	7	3	.406	.285
Roberts, Tyler	R-R	6-0	226	10-25-90	.263	.291	.244	42	133	20	35	11	0	2	14	16	2	0	0	39	0	0	.391	.351
Rogers, Jason	R-R	6-2	250	3-13-88	.296	.375	.263	7	27	3	8	1	0	1	3	2	0	0	0	5	0	1	.444	.345
Sanchez, Ruben	L-L	6-2	180	8-20-91	.227	.200	.235	12	44	3	10	3	0	0	2	3	0	0	0	10	1	2	.295	.277
Walla, Max	L-L	5-11	195	4-12-91	.285	.263	.294	69	253	40	72	16	2	4	29	30	6	0	0	72	5	6	.411	.374
Williams, Adrian	R-R	6-0	175	1-3-91	.238	.250	.233	56	206	31	49	3	1	0	15	14	4	0	0	57	12	8	.262	.299

Pitching	B-T	HT	WT	DOB	W	L	ERA	G	GS	CG	SV	IP	H	R	ER	HR	BB	SO	AVG	vLH	vRH	K/9	BB/9
Albury, Sean	R-R	5-11	180	3-24-89	0	0	0.90	16	0	0	6	20	12	4	2	0	5	27	.169	.222	.136	12.15	2.25
Arnett, Eric	R-R	6-5	230	1-25-88	4	2	5.19	9	9	0	0	52	64	40	30	7	9	49	.296	.180	.331	8.48	1.56
Barnes, Jacob	R-R	6-2	230	4-14-90	2	1	2.12	18	0	0	2	30	25	7	7	3	6	43	.227	.270	.205	13.04	1.82
Cravy, Tyler	R-R	6-3	180	7-13-89	3	4	4.76	14	11	0	0	70	70	45	37	6	19	81	.258	.222	.279	10.41	2.44
Crawford, Skyler	R-R	6-1	175	4-20-88	0	0	3.00	3	0	0	0	6	5	4	2	0	2	9	.227	.167	.250	13.50	3.00
Gagnon, Drew	R-R	6-4	195	6-26-90	0	3	8.05	8	7	0	1	19	25	19	17	1	10	27	.321	.600	.254	12.79	4.74
Goforth, David	R-R	6-0	188	10-11-88	4	0	4.43	19	0	0	2	41	44	25	20	5	10	42	.277	.157	.333	9.30	2.21
Harvey, Seth	L-R	6-2	205	1-20-88	2	1	2.70	16	0	0	1	33	27	12	10	1	17	46	.225	.167	.250	12.42	4.59
Jones, Alex	R-R	6-6	190	3-3-87	1	2	4.10	21	0	0	1	37	40	21	17	0	6	39	.280	.302	.270	9.40	1.45
Keeling, Thomas	L-L	6-3	185	3-30-88	0	1	5.61	20	0	0	1	34	23	22	21	6	18	41	.195	.231	.185	10.96	4.81
Lintz, Seth	R-R	6-1	170	2-7-90	0	1	6.39	6	0	0	0	13	20	11	9	2	8	12	.377	.100	.442	8.53	5.68
Moye, Andy	R-R	6-5	180	9-11-87	7	3	4.48	15	15	0	0	78	87	45	39	15	19	76	.279	.279	.279	8.73	2.18
Pierce, Chad	R-R	6-1	215	11-20-87	2	4	6.64	15	5	0	0	39	50	36	29	4	19	33	.314	.306	.318	7.55	4.35
Shackelford, Kevin	R-R	6-5	215	4-7-89	3	5	4.15	15	8	0	0	65	74	34	30	8	10	31	.285	.351	.247	4.29	1.38
Strong, Mike	L-L	6-0	175	11-17-88	2	7	6.10	15	13	0	0	62	63	53	42	11	30	55	.263	.227	.270	7.98	4.35
Toledo, Tommy	R-R	6-3	185	12-13-88	1	5	4.26	10	5	0	0	38	33	25	18	6	21	35	.246	.292	.221	8.29	4.97
Williams, Alan	L-L	6-3	195	3-5-90	1	1	2.57	9	0	0	4	14	11	4	4	0	5	28	.216	.000	.262	18.00	3.21
Williams, Mark	R-R	6-4	225	8-12-89	1	0	3.38	6	0	0	0	8	8	5	3	0	3	8	.258	.250	.267	9.00	3.38
Williamson, Brandon	R-R	6-2	180	4-22-89	1	2	5.64	8	3	0	0	22	21	14	14	2	3	19	.250	.185	.281	7.66	1.21

Fielding

Catcher	PCT	G	PO	A	E	DP	PB
Berberet	.984	30	279	27	5	2	4
Dean	.985	8	59	5	1	0	4
Elliot	.947	2	16	1	1	0	0
Paciorek	.972	4	29	6	1	0	2
Roberts	.981	40	311	41	7	5	7

First Base	PCT	G	PO	A	E	DP
Berberet	1.000	23	189	14	0	22
Felix	.933	6	41	3	3	5
Nemeth	1.000	29	230	14	0	24
Ramirez	.977	15	124	5	3	9

	PCT	G	PO	A	E	DP
Rogers	.984	7	53	8	1	3

Second Base	PCT	G	PO	A	E	DP
Elmore	.949	25	38	73	6	20
Williams	.969	53	101	147	8	27

Third Base	PCT	G	PO	A	E	DP
Dhanani	.923	58	41	90	11	10
Nemeth	.846	18	8	25	6	5
Williams	1.000	2	0	2	0	0

Shortstop	PCT	G	PO	A	E	DP
Dhanani	1.000	1	0	2	0	0

	PCT	G	PO	A	E	DP
Rivera	.935	74	97	233	23	47
Williams	1.000	1	2	2	0	0

Outfield	PCT	G	PO	A	E	DP
Allison	.972	26	32	3	1	0
Dishon	.951	57	91	7	5	1
Felix	.000	1	0	0	1	0
Garvey	1.000	44	78	4	0	1
McMahan	.931	23	25	2	2	0
Rogers	1.000	1	3	0	0	0
Sanchez	.840	11	21	0	4	0
Walla	.962	69	139	11	6	5

AZL BREWERS   ROOKIE
ARIZONA LEAGUE

Batting	B-T	HT	WT	DOB	AVG	vLH	vRH	G	AB	R	H	2B	3B	HR	RBI	BB	HBP	SH	SF	SO	SB	CS	SLG	OBP
Arias, Hitaniel	R-R	6-6	202	9-20-90	.237	.282	.223	42	169	16	40	7	2	2	28	7	2	0	0	60	3	3	.337	.275

Batting

Batting	B-T	HT	WT	DOB	AVG	vLH	vRH	G	AB	R	H	2B	3B	HR	RBI	BB	HBP	SH	SF	SO	SB	CS	SLG	OBP
Berard, Kevin	R-R	5-10	170	12-3-91	.293	.114	.338	46	174	33	51	8	1	1	13	22	6	0	3	43	14	3	.368	.385
Dowell, Malcolm	R-R	6-0	190	4-21-93	.209	.250	.198	30	110	15	23	1	2	0	10	19	2	0	0	37	5	4	.255	.336
Felix, Steve	L-R	6-1	215	4-21-88	.375	.231	.400	26	88	14	33	5	3	4	23	9	9	0	2	18	8	4	.636	.472
Franco, Matthew	L-L	6-1	200	12-9-92	.160	.167	.159	30	100	8	16	1	0	0	3	19	0	0	0	37	5	3	.170	.294
Garcia, Jose	R-R	6-3	195	3-5-91	.250	.216	.260	43	164	23	41	6	7	0	13	4	3	0	1	43	7	1	.372	.279
Garfield, Cameron	R-R	6-1	195	5-23-91	.361	.667	.333	9	36	7	13	3	1	2	10	2	0	0	0	9	0	0	.667	.395
Harris, Jalen	R-R	6-2	210	7-7-92	.234	.250	.230	44	171	18	40	6	3	1	19	19	0	0	0	54	8	2	.322	.311
Jenkins, Renaldo	R-R	6-0	190	3-1-93	.253	.233	.257	45	166	26	42	6	2	0	23	21	2	0	2	49	15	6	.313	.340
Macias, Brandon	R-R	5-10	185	10-10-88	.239	.200	.247	30	109	15	26	8	1	2	10	12	6	0	1	20	6	4	.385	.344
Martinez, Andres	R-R	6-2	188	1-26-92	.232	.172	.250	40	125	20	29	4	1	5	16	8	4	0	2	50	5	5	.400	.295
Mendoza, Alejandro	R-R	5-11	156	2-12-92	.314	.000	.367	11	35	5	11	1	0	0	2	3	1	0	0	12	0	1	.343	.385
Neda, Rafael	R-R	6-1	215	10-12-88	.278	.250	.286	7	18	6	5	1	0	0	2	6	3	0	0	2	0	1	.444	.519
Ogrinc, Gerard	R-R	6-3	230	2-5-88	.000	.000	.000	3	7	0	0	0	0	0	0	0	0	0	0	4	0	0	.000	.000
Pharr, Jimmie	R-R	6-0	185	5-26-89	.263	.250	.265	29	95	16	25	6	1	3	16	21	2	0	1	28	0	4	.442	.403
Puello, Ronny	R-R	6-6	200	10-23-89	.106	.042	.125	31	104	3	11	2	0	0	7	7	1	0	1	40	0	1	.125	.168
Reed, Michael	R-R	6-0	190	11-18-92	.232	.000	.255	14	56	11	13	4	2	0	5	5	0	0	0	17	1	0	.375	.295
Sanchez, Ruben	R-R	6-2	180	8-20-91	.375	.000	.500	7	32	6	12	2	1	2	5	2	0	0	0	7	2	3	.688	.412
Weisenburger, Adam	R-R	5-10	185	12-13-88	.276	.273	.277	33	116	13	32	6	2	0	7	18	2	0	0	17	1	2	.362	.382

Pitching

Pitching	B-T	HT	WT	DOB	W	L	ERA	G	GS	CG	SV	IP	H	R	ER	HR	BB	SO	AVG	vLH	vRH	K/9	BB/9
Conner, Mitchell	R-R	6-3	210	7-26-89	0	2	4.09	11	0	0	1	11	9	6	5	2	3	17	.225	.333	.105	13.91	2.45
Davis, Greg	R-R	6-4	220	3-13-89	1	3	8.61	13	0	0	0	23	37	22	22	1	8	15	.370	.394	.358	5.87	3.13
Francisco, Michael	R-L	6-4	224	8-4-88	0	0	2.82	14	0	0	1	22	19	9	7	1	11	25	.229	.136	.262	10.07	4.43
Glynn, Elliott	L-L	6-1	160	1-13-89	2	1	4.86	11	0	0	0	17	20	9	9	0	6	14	.294	.389	.260	7.56	3.24
Howell, Del	L-L	6-3	185	9-6-87	0	2	1.06	3	3	0	0	17	11	5	2	1	5	12	.172	.333	.109	6.35	2.65
James, Justin	R-R	6-3	215	9-13-81	0	0	0.00	3	3	0	0	4	5	0	0	0	0	2	.385	.500	.333	4.50	0.00
Keller, Daniel	R-R	6-5	190	6-30-92	2	2	7.06	12	5	0	0	29	40	24	23	0	10	21	.315	.282	.330	6.44	3.07
Lopez, Jorge	R-R	6-4	165	2-10-93	0	0	2.25	4	4	0	0	12	13	3	3	0	3	10	.265	.357	.143	7.50	2.25
Medlen, Casey	R-R	6-0	155	8-4-89	0	1	2.35	6	0	0	0	8	6	5	2	0	6	9	.194	.182	.200	10.57	7.04
Oviedo, Jose	R-R	6-2	165	11-30-88	0	2	5.14	10	2	0	1	14	15	11	8	0	6	16	.254	.143	.289	10.29	3.86
Peterson, Stephen	L-L	6-3	210	11-6-87	1	2	3.00	14	0	0	0	27	23	12	9	2	8	32	.235	.250	.230	10.67	2.67
Pierce, Joel	L-R	6-4	200	12-21-92	0	4	9.00	13	2	0	0	27	42	31	27	4	12	21	.350	.469	.307	7.00	4.00
Rivero, Francisco	R-R	6-2	204	3-11-91	0	0	3.38	6	2	0	0	11	9	6	4	1	3	10	.220	.211	.227	8.44	2.53
Rogers, Mark	R-R	6-2	226	1-30-86	0	0	4.85	5	3	0	0	13	13	9	7	1	5	11	.250	.182	.300	7.62	3.46
Ruiz, Manuel	L-L	6-5	175	12-12-88	4	1	3.56	14	1	0	0	43	30	25	17	2	32	50	.197	.172	.203	10.47	6.70
Saba, Jeffrey	R-R	6-2	152	9-7-91	2	4	5.48	14	7	0	0	48	64	43	29	5	12	28	.317	.303	.325	5.29	2.27
Schaub, Michael	R-R	6-2	180	5-31-92	2	4	2.60	13	4	0	1	45	39	23	13	2	20	35	.231	.286	.204	7.00	4.00
Stetter, Mitch	L-L	6-4	220	1-16-81	0	0	12.27	4	2	0	0	4	10	6	5	0	1	5	.500	.500	.500	12.27	2.45
Thompson, Chad	R-R	6-8	210	2-6-91	1	1	5.82	9	2	0	0	17	19	13	11	0	6	16	.284	.333	.261	8.47	3.18
West, Will	L-L	6-4	170	7-23-92	1	3	3.99	13	5	0	0	38	51	28	17	3	8	42	.307	.206	.333	9.86	1.88
Whalen, Connor	L-L	6-3	195	4-19-88	0	2	5.11	11	0	0	1	12	20	8	7	0	3	16	.345	.250	.370	11.68	2.19
White, Michael	R-R	6-6	190	9-11-89	1	4	6.28	14	6	0	1	43	50	32	30	3	20	41	.281	.313	.261	8.58	4.19
Wright, Brae	L-L	6-4	205	11-1-83	0	1	7.11	5	5	0	0	6	10	8	5	0	3	6	.357	.250	.400	8.53	4.26

Fielding

Catcher	PCT	G	PO	A	E	DP	PB
Felix	.900	1	9	0	1	0	1
Garfield	.983	7	53	4	1	0	1
Neda	1.000	6	49	7	0	0	2
Ogrinc	1.000	2	6	2	0	0	0
Pharr	.972	22	152	23	5	0	11
Weisenburger	.963	25	177	34	8	2	5

First Base	PCT	G	PO	A	E	DP
Arias	.959	36	310	20	14	27
Felix	.979	9	85	8	2	4
Harris	1.000	11	98	1	0	8

Second Base	PCT	G	PO	A	E	DP
Berard	.935	26	37	78	8	17

	PCT	G	PO	A	E	DP
Jenkins	.947	14	28	43	4	6
Macias	.972	7	9	26	1	1
Martinez	.900	2	5	4	1	0
Mendoza	.927	10	12	26	3	7

Third Base	PCT	G	PO	A	E	DP
Harris	.864	26	23	53	12	4
Macias	.800	5	1	7	2	0
Martinez	.909	27	32	58	9	4

Shortstop	PCT	G	PO	A	E	DP
Berard	.939	11	21	41	4	9
Jenkins	.873	29	46	71	17	15
Macias	.885	17	22	47	9	9

Outfield	PCT	G	PO	A	E	DP
Berard	1.000	7	13	0	0	0
Dowell	.844	30	37	1	7	0
Felix	.909	9	10	0	1	0
Franco	.957	29	42	2	2	0
Garcia	.978	42	86	4	2	1
Glynn	1.000	1	5	2	0	0
Macias	1.000	2	2	0	0	0
Martinez	.000	1	0	0	0	0
Puello	.954	29	55	7	3	3
Reed	.955	14	20	1	1	0
Rogers	1.000	1	2	0	0	0
Sanchez	.846	7	11	0	2	0

DSL BREWERS

DOMINICAN SUMMER LEAGUE

ROOKIE

Batting	B-T	HT	WT	DOB	AVG	vLH	vRH	G	AB	R	H	2B	3B	HR	RBI	BB	HBP	SH	SF	SO	SB	CS	SLG	OBP
Abreu, Joan	R-R	5-11	180	7-15-90	.256	.286	.250	21	43	9	11	1	0	0	1	5	2	0	0	7	2	4	.279	.360
Arcia, Orlando	R-R	6-0	165	8-4-94	.294	.353	.283	64	218	47	64	16	1	6	36	30	4	0	2	20	13	4	.459	.386
Castillo, Francisco	B-R	5-11	170	6-4-93	.245	.150	.259	48	155	22	38	5	3	0	15	12	3	0	1	18	12	11	.316	.310
Colatosti, Raphachel	R-R	6-1	0	7-3-93	.247	.474	.177	41	81	11	20	2	0	0	6	11	4	0	0	11	5	3	.272	.365
De La Cruz, Jorge	R-R	6-1	180	9-9-92	.159	.182	.154	28	63	2	10	2	0	0	4	5	2	0	0	23	0	0	.190	.243
De Leon, Juan	R-R	6-4	217	2-27-92	.237	.176	.250	57	186	21	44	6	0	3	12	17	6	0	1	51	0	0	.317	.319
Hernandez, Yonki	B-R	5-10	160	10-5-90	.258	.150	.285	61	198	38	51	3	8	1	17	37	11	0	2	48	21	9	.369	.399
Hinojosa, Dionis	R-R	6-1	180	8-14-90	.282	.286	.282	61	177	28	50	2	3	1	18	29	7	0	0	31	29	9	.345	.404
Matos, Sthervin	R-R	6-1	185	2-13-94	.274	.400	.255	38	113	18	31	5	2	1	16	17	6	0	1	20	13	3	.381	.394
Mejia, Deyvi	R-R	6-0	195	11-3-89	.313	.467	.285	56	195	24	61	14	1	3	37	15	7	0	3	28	1	0	.441	.377

Batting

Batting	B-T	HT	WT	DOB	AVG	vLH	vRH	G	AB	R	H	2B	3B	HR	RBI	BB	HBP	SH	SF	SO	SB	CS	SLG	OBP
Mejia, Natanael	R-R	6-0	175	7-10-92	.151	.000	.180	25	73	3	11	2	0	0	2	5	0	0	0	21	0	2	.178	.205
Mendoza, Alejandro	R-R	5-11	156	2-12-92	.220	.222	.219	26	82	11	18	4	0	1	11	8	1	0	0	17	5	2	.305	.297
Mondesi, Raul	R-R	5-10	182	8-23-92	.267	.389	.238	54	187	24	50	4	1	5	26	16	4	0	2	44	5	8	.380	.335
Otano, Leudi	R-R	5-11	180	2-21-91	.147	.000	.152	15	34	2	5	1	0	0	1	7	1	0	0	13	1	2	.176	.310
Pena, Carlos	R-R	5-11	190	9-28-92	.125	.000	.170	22	64	9	8	1	0	0	1	10	0	0	0	13	1	0	.141	.243
Pena, Jose	R-R	6-2	192	3-3-93	.183	.067	.209	50	169	12	31	9	1	3	26	18	1	0	2	45	0	6	.302	.263
Rubio, Elvis	R-R	6-3	215	7-2-94	.170	.133	.177	36	94	9	16	4	0	1	7	12	8	0	1	18	1	0	.245	.313
Sanchez, Ruben	L-L	6-2	180	8-20-91	.323	.182	.400	11	31	8	10	0	0	1	6	3	2	0	1	1	5	2	.419	.405
Sotelo, Julio	R-R	5-11	182	4-1-91	.105	.000	.111	9	19	1	2	0	0	0	1	3	0	0	0	4	1	0	.105	.227

Pitching

Pitching	B-T	HT	WT	DOB	W	L	ERA	G	GS	CG	SV	IP	H	R	ER	HR	BB	SO	AVG	vLH	vRH	K/9	BB/9
Arias, Doni	R-R	6-3	187	7-26-92	3	2	2.61	15	0	0	2	21	14	7	6	1	9	11	.187	.118	.207	4.79	3.92
Belen, Javier	R-R	6-4	190	10-19-91	1	1	5.48	16	0	0	0	23	22	19	14	3	20	15	.244	.471	.192	5.87	7.83
Dicent, Joel	R-R	6-3	176	8-4-91	4	3	2.70	11	11	1	0	60	44	24	18	3	22	54	.208	.148	.232	8.10	3.30
Francisco, Juan	R-R	6-5	180	12-15-90	5	1	3.24	13	4	1	0	42	28	21	15	3	28	34	.187	.231	.171	7.34	6.05
Gomez, Milton	R-R	6-1	172	4-22-94	3	3	4.61	9	7	0	0	27	31	22	14	1	9	23	.292	.233	.316	7.57	2.96
Lorenzo, Leonard	R-R	6-0	190	7-16-91	3	0	2.13	7	7	0	0	42	30	13	10	1	17	36	.197	.125	.223	7.65	3.61
Mateo, Yheris	R-R	5-9	163	10-19-90	0	1	8.44	4	0	0	1	5	6	5	5	0	5	7	.300	.500	.250	11.81	8.44
Montano, Eliezer	L-L	6-7	170	10-21-91	2	2	4.93	11	8	1	0	49	45	31	27	2	21	33	.247	.375	.235	6.02	3.83
Mora, Elvis	R-R	6-1	170	2-7-92	3	3	6.14	12	2	0	0	22	24	16	15	2	13	14	.293	.294	.292	5.73	5.32
Ortega, Jorge	R-R	6-1	165	6-20-93	4	6	3.16	13	11	2	0	74	69	30	26	5	12	45	.252	.293	.234	5.47	1.46
Padilla, Marcos	L-L	6-2	175	1-1-94	0	0	4.98	11	0	0	0	22	22	18	12	2	17	8	.250	.286	.247	3.32	7.06
Peguero, Pedro	R-R	6-6	215	8-10-93	0	0	9.95	4	0	0	0	6	7	7	7	0	11	2	.280	.333	.263	9.95	15.63
Perez, Osmel	R-R	6-3	196	7-28-93	2	1	4.00	5	3	0	0	18	19	11	8	4	2	13	.284	.286	.283	6.50	1.00
Reyes, Eduard	R-R	6-0	174	8-23-90	1	1	1.56	4	2	0	0	17	17	6	3	0	3	18	.246	.333	.228	9.35	1.56
Rizzo, Gian	R-R	6-1	160	9-5-93	4	1	1.82	13	10	1	1	64	60	14	13	1	14	67	.248	.254	.246	9.37	1.96
Santiago, Juan	L-L	5-11	176	12-23-90	1	0	3.54	13	4	0	1	28	18	15	11	0	25	23	.176	.364	.154	7.39	8.04
Sosa, Carlos	R-R	6-6	236	9-6-91	2	0	1.08	25	0	0	19	25	18	4	3	0	5	32	.194	.375	.156	11.52	1.80
Torrez, Orlando	R-R	6-3	195	4-14-92	4	0	0.96	13	1	0	1	28	18	8	3	1	13	23	.182	.261	.158	7.39	4.18
Ventura, Angel	R-R	6-2	185	4-7-93	2	2	6.00	12	1	0	1	24	25	19	16	3	16	16	.278	.375	.257	6.00	6.00

Fielding

Catcher	PCT	G	PO	A	E	DP	PB
Mejia	.978	20	115	21	3	0	3
Mejia	1.000	23	144	23	0	2	2
Otano	1.000	9	63	8	0	0	0
Pena	.981	21	139	15	3	1	3
Sotelo	1.000	5	22	4	0	0	0

First Base	PCT	G	PO	A	E	DP
Abreu	.000	1	0	0	0	0
De La Cruz	1.000	5	30	1	0	2
De Leon	.983	43	283	9	5	19
Matos	.980	8	45	5	1	4
Mejia	.963	25	196	11	8	21
Mendoza	1.000	3	5	0	0	3
Sotelo	1.000	1	2	0	0	0

Second Base	PCT	G	PO	A	E	DP
Abreu	.929	3	3	10	1	3
Castillo	.913	38	53	62	11	11
Colatosti	.970	17	31	33	2	7
Mendoza	.967	22	46	41	3	8
Otano	.750	1	2	1	1	0

Third Base	PCT	G	PO	A	E	DP
Abreu	.966	12	8	20	1	1
Colatosti	.857	11	6	18	4	4
De La Cruz	.914	19	17	15	3	0
De Leon	.909	12	5	25	3	5
Matos	.885	31	21	64	11	0

Shortstop	PCT	G	PO	A	E	DP
Abreu	.000	1	0	0	1	0
Arcia	.957	62	144	193	15	37
Castillo	.882	6	3	12	2	1
Colatosti	.822	14	12	25	8	1

Outfield	PCT	G	PO	A	E	DP
Castillo	.909	4	9	1	1	0
Colatosti	.000	1	0	0	0	0
Hernandez	.964	53	103	3	4	1
Hinojosa	.990	54	99	5	1	1
Mondesi	.986	45	71	2	1	0
Otano	1.000	1	1	0	0	0
Pena	.968	39	59	2	2	0
Rubio	.935	22	24	5	2	0
Sanchez	1.000	5	9	1	0	0

Minnesota Twins

SEASON IN A SENTENCE: The Metrodome may be gone, but the roof caved in on the Twins in 2011, as they posted the worst record in the American League by losing 99 games—the franchise's worst season since 1982, the Metrodome's first season.

HIGH POINT: The Twins looked like they might bounce back from a slow start at midseason, and a three-run eighth-inning rally on July 20 against the first-place Indians brought them to 46-51, just five games back in the American League Central, though still in fourth place.

LOW POINT: The bounceback never materialized, and in September the Twins fell apart as the weight of injuries, poor pitching, poor defense and no power on offense came together. The Twins lost 11 straight games in a 2-19 stretch, and franchise cornerstone Joe Mauer had his miserable season ended by an upper respiratory infection. It was the latest in a series of injury lows for Mauer, whose bat and defense slid after he went on the disabled list early in the season with bilateral leg weakness. He also required a trip to the Mayo Clinic and had his toughness questioned in the media.

NOTABLE ROOKIES: Minnesota was counting on more from middle infielder Tsuyoshi Nishioka, imported from Japan, but he posted a .527 OPS and was insufficient defensively at shortstop. Outfielder Ben Revere, a 2007 first-round pick, also lacked power but led the team with 34 steals while replacing the injured Denard Span in center field. Australian Luke Hughes provided some power, as did shortstop Trevor Plouffe, a 2004 first-rounder, but neither was effective defensively.

KEY TRANSACTIONS: The team's collapse and what owner Jim Pohlad termed a "difference in philosophy" led to the firing of general manager Bill Smith after four seasons, the first GM firing since the franchise moved to Minnesota. Terry Ryan, his predecessor and a senior adviser during Smith's tenure, took the job back, saying he felt recharged after his time away. Jim Thome hit his 600th home run on Aug. 15, then was traded 11 days later to the Indians.

DOWN ON THE FARM: Triple-A Rochester was awful again, leading to the firing of manager Tom Nieto, but the rest of the system rallied to around .500. Rookie-level Elizabethton shined with outfielder Eddie Rosario (21) and Miguel Sano (20) ranking atop the organization in home runs, despite playing a short-season schedule.

OPENING DAY PAYROLL: $112,737,000 (9th)

ORGANIZATION LEADERS

BATTING		*Minimum 250 PA
MAJORS		
* AVG	Joe Mauer	.287
* OPS	Michael Cuddyer	.805
HR	Michael Cuddyer	20
RBI	Danny Valencia	72
MAJORS		
* AVG	Yangervis Solarte, New Britain	.329
* OBP	Aaron Bates, Rochester	.408
* SLG	Joe Benson, GCL/New Britain	.491
R	Brian Dozier, Fort Myers/New Britain	92
H	Brian Dozier, Fort Myers/New Britain	157
TB	Brian Dozier, Fort Myers/New Britain	241
2B	Yangervis Solarte, New Britain	36
3B	Brian Dozier, Fort Myers/New Britain	12
HR	Eddie Rosario, Elizabethton	21
RBI	Chris Parmelee, New Britain	83
BB	Chris Herrmann, Fort Myers/New Britain	79
SO	Lance Ray, Beloit	132
SB	Brian Dozier, Fort Myers/New Britain	24
	Daniel Santana, Beloit	24
PITCHING		#Minimum 75 IP
MAJORS		
W	Three tied at	9
# ERA	Scott Baker	3.14
SO	Scott Baker	123
SV	Matt Capps	15
MINORS		
W	B.J. Hermsen, Beloit/Fort Myers	13
L	Scott Diamond, Rochester	14
	Eric Hacker, Rochester	14
# ERA	Adrian Salcedo, Beloit	2.93
G	Kyle Waldrop, Rochester	56
GS	Bobby Lanigan, New Britain	27
SV	Bruce Pugh, Fort Myers/New Britain	17
IP	Bobby Lanigan, New Britain	153.2
BB	Blake Martin, Fort Myers/New Britain	77
SO	Manuel Soliman, Beloit	120
# AVG	Steve Hirschfeld, New Britain	.246

2011 PERFORMANCE

General Manager: Bill Smith. **Farm Director:** Jim Rantz. **Scouting Director:** Deron Johnson.

Class	Team	League	W	L	PCT	Finish	Manager(s)
Majors	Minnesota Twins	American	63	99	.389	14th (14)	Ron Gardenhire
Triple-A	Rochester Red Wings	International	53	91	.368	14th (14)	Tom Nieto
Double-A	New Britain Rock Cats	Eastern	72	70	.507	7th (12)	Jeff Smith
High A	Fort Myers Miracle	Florida State	63	76	.453	10th (12)	Jake Mauer
Low A	Beloit Snappers	Midwest	69	69	.500	8th (16)	Nelson Prada
Rookie	Elizabethton Twins	Appalachian	42	26	.618	2nd (10)	Ray Smith
Rookie	GCL Twins	Gulf Coast	31	29	.517	6th (15)	Ramon Borrego
Overall 2011 Minor League Record			330	361	.478	25th (30)	

ORGANIZATION STATISTICS

MINNESOTA TWINS

AMERICAN LEAGUE

Batting	B-T	HT	WT	DOB	AVG	vLH	vRH	G	AB	R	H	2B	3B	HR	RBI	BB	HBP	SH	SF	SO	SB	CS	SLG	OBP
Benson, Joe	R-R	6-1	205	3-5-88	.239	.118	.278	21	71	3	17	6	1	0	2	3	0	0	0	21	2	2	.352	.270
Butera, Drew	R-R	6-1	195	8-9-83	.167	.215	.148	93	234	19	39	9	1	2	23	11	2	0	1	42	0	0	.239	.210
Casilla, Alexi	B-R	5-9	185	7-20-84	.260	.236	.272	97	323	52	84	21	4	2	21	28	3	0	3	45	15	4	.368	.322
Cuddyer, Michael	R-R	6-2	220	3-27-79	.284	.311	.272	139	529	70	150	29	2	20	70	48	4	0	3	95	11	1	.459	.346
Dinkelman, Brian	L-R	5-11	195	11-10-83	.301	.273	.306	23	73	5	22	1	0	0	4	4	1	0	0	14	2	0	.315	.346
Holm, Steve	R-R	6-0	205	10-21-79	.118	.000	.133	6	17	1	2	1	0	0	0	1	0	0	0	4	0	0	.176	.167
Hughes, Luke	R-R	5-11	205	8-2-84	.223	.196	.236	96	287	31	64	12	0	7	30	24	3	0	1	79	3	2	.338	.289
Kubel, Jason	L-R	6-0	220	5-25-82	.273	.254	.283	99	366	37	100	21	1	12	58	32	1	0	2	86	1	1	.434	.332
Mauer, Joe	L-R	6-5	235	4-19-83	.287	.234	.319	82	296	38	85	15	0	3	30	32	3	0	2	38	0	0	.368	.360
Morneau, Justin	L-R	6-4	235	5-15-81	.227	.144	.270	69	264	19	60	16	0	4	30	19	3	0	2	44	0	0	.333	.285
Nishioka, Tsuyoshi	B-R	6-1	175	7-27-84	.226	.203	.239	68	221	14	50	5	0	0	19	15	1	0	0	43	2	4	.249	.278
Parmelee, Chris	L-L	6-1	230	2-24-88	.355	.316	.368	21	76	8	27	6	0	4	14	12	0	0	0	13	0	0	.592	.443
Plouffe, Trevor	R-R	6-2	200	6-15-86	.238	.308	.212	81	286	47	68	18	1	8	31	25	4	0	3	71	3	3	.392	.305
Repko, Jason	R-R	5-11	200	12-27-80	.226	.292	.188	67	133	21	30	2	0	2	11	6	2	0	0	38	7	2	.286	.270
Revere, Ben	L-R	5-9	170	5-3-88	.267	.265	.268	117	450	56	120	9	5	0	30	26	2	0	0	41	34	9	.309	.310
Rivera, Rene	R-R	5-10	230	7-31-83	.144	.179	.132	45	104	9	15	3	0	1	5	8	1	0	1	32	0	0	.202	.211
Span, Denard	L-L	6-0	210	2-27-84	.264	.240	.273	70	284	37	75	11	5	2	16	27	0	0	0	36	6	1	.359	.328
Thome, Jim	L-R	6-3	250	8-27-70	.243	.245	.242	71	206	21	50	12	0	12	40	35	0	0	1	69	0	0	.476	.351
2-team total (22 Cleveland)					.256	—	—	93	277	32	71	16	0	15	50	46	0	0	1	92	0	0	.477	.361
Tolbert, Matt	B-R	6-0	185	5-4-82	.198	.200	.197	87	207	22	41	10	2	0	11	11	4	0	0	31	3	2	.266	.252
Tosoni, Rene	L-R	6-0	195	7-2-86	.203	.286	.188	60	172	20	35	7	1	5	22	14	3	0	0	42	0	2	.343	.275
Valencia, Danny	R-R	6-2	220	9-19-84	.246	.309	.224	154	564	63	139	28	2	15	72	40	0	0	4	102	2	6	.383	.294
Young, Delmon	R-R	6-3	200	9-14-85	.266	.270	.264	84	305	26	81	16	0	4	32	18	0	0	2	55	1	0	.357	.305
2-team total (40 Detroit)					.268	—	—	124	473	54	127	21	1	12	64	23	2	0	5	85	1	0	.393	.302

Pitching	B-T	HT	WT	DOB	W	L	ERA	G	GS	CG	SV	IP	H	R	ER	HR	BB	SO	AVG	vLH	vRH	K/9	BB/9
Baker, Scott	R-R	6-4	215	9-19-81	8	6	3.14	23	21	1	0	135	126	50	47	15	32	123	.248	.267	.215	8.22	2.14
Blackburn, Nick	R-R	6-4	240	2-24-82	7	10	4.49	26	26	1	0	148	183	91	74	19	54	76	.305	.295	.316	4.61	3.28
Burnett, Alex	R-R	6-0	220	7-26-87	2	5	5.51	66	0	0	0	51	50	32	31	4	21	33	.263	.263	.264	5.86	3.73
Capps, Matt	R-R	6-2	245	9-3-83	4	7	4.25	69	0	0	15	66	66	31	31	10	13	34	.262	.264	.260	4.66	1.78
Diamond, Scott	L-L	6-3	215	7-30-86	1	5	5.08	7	7	0	0	39	51	25	22	3	17	19	.317	.323	.315	4.38	3.92
Duensing, Brian	L-L	6-0	205	2-22-83	9	14	5.23	32	28	1	0	162	193	102	94	21	52	115	.299	.217	.330	6.40	2.89
Dumatrait, Phil	R-L	6-2	210	7-12-81	1	3	3.92	45	0	0	1	41	45	22	18	5	25	29	.276	.237	.310	6.31	5.44
Hacker, Eric	B-R	6-1	230	3-26-83	0	0	0.00	2	0	0	0	5	4	1	0	0	4	2	.235	.125	.333	3.38	6.75
Hendriks, Liam	R-R	6-1	200	2-10-89	0	2	6.17	4	4	0	0	23	29	16	16	3	6	16	.312	.333	.282	6.17	2.31
Hoey, Jim	R-R	6-6	210	12-30-82	1	2	5.47	26	0	0	0	25	34	20	15	4	13	14	.330	.326	.333	5.11	4.74
Hughes, Dusty	L-L	5-10	185	6-29-82	1	0	9.95	15	0	0	0	13	19	14	14	4	8	11	.365	.360	.370	7.82	5.68
James, Chuck	L-L	6-0	190	11-9-81	0	0	6.10	8	0	0	0	10	12	7	7	1	4	8	.293	.357	.259	6.97	3.48
Liriano, Francisco	L-L	6-2	215	10-26-83	9	10	5.09	26	24	1	0	134	125	81	76	14	75	112	.244	.235	.253	7.50	5.02
Manship, Jeff	R-R	6-2	210	1-16-85	0	0	8.10	5	0	0	0	3	5	3	3	0	4	2	.385	.500	.286	5.40	10.80
Mijares, Jose	L-L	6-0	230	10-29-84	0	2	4.59	58	0	0	0	49	53	31	25	4	30	30	.275	.253	.292	5.51	5.51
Nathan, Joe	R-R	6-4	225	11-22-74	2	1	4.84	48	0	0	14	45	38	26	24	7	14	43	.222	.198	.247	8.66	2.82
Oliveros, Lester	R-R	6-0	225	5-28-88	0	0	4.05	10	0	0	0	13	13	6	6	0	7	9	.277	.222	.310	6.08	4.73
2-team total (9 Detroit)					0	0	4.64	19	0	0	0	21	21	11	11	0	11	13	—	—	—	5.48	4.64
Pavano, Carl	R-R	6-5	250	1-8-76	9	13	4.30	33	33	3	0	222	262	123	106	23	40	102	.294	.289	.300	4.14	1.62
Perkins, Glen	L-L	6-0	210	3-2-83	4	4	2.48	65	0	0	2	62	55	19	17	2	21	65	.244	.222	.259	9.49	3.06
Slama, Anthony	R-R	6-3	200	1-6-84	0	0	0.00	2	0	0	0	2	0	0	0	2	3	.000	.000	.000	11.57	7.71
Slowey, Kevin	R-R	6-3	205	5-4-84	0	8	6.67	14	8	0	0	59	78	44	44	10	5	34	.321	.345	.300	5.16	0.76
Swarzak, Anthony	R-R	6-4	210	9-10-85	4	7	4.32	27	11	0	0	102	111	53	49	9	26	55	.275	.253	.301	4.85	2.29
Waldrop, Kyle	R-R	6-5	215	10-27-85	1	0	5.73	7	0	0	0	11	10	7	7	1	6	5	.233	.056	.360	4.09	4.91

Fielding

Catcher	PCT	G	PO	A	E	DP	PB		PCT	G	PO	A	E	DP	PB
Butera	.989	93	418	38	5	3	7	Holm	1.000	6	33	1	0	1	0
								Mauer	.987	52	291	18	4	2	4
								Rivera	.988	44	231	16	3	1	1

First Base	PCT	G	PO	A	E	DP
Cuddyer	.995	46	355	23	2	31
Hughes	.997	36	278	13	1	26
Mauer	.994	18	158	11	1	15
Morneau	.998	56	440	44	1	52
Parmelee	.989	20	164	12	2	19
Plouffe	.000	1	0	0	0	0

Second Base	PCT	G	PO	A	E	DP
Casilla	.977	56	85	174	6	38
Cuddyer	.989	17	35	52	1	7
Dinkelman	1.000	11	24	32	0	8
Hughes	.989	37	79	108	2	25
Nishioka	.923	6	10	14	2	8

	PCT	G	PO	A	E	DP
Plouffe	.986	17	32	36	1	10
Tolbert	.979	36	61	78	3	23

Third Base	PCT	G	PO	A	E	DP
Hughes	.949	13	10	27	2	2
Tolbert	1.000	6	2	3	0	1
Valencia	.949	147	73	260	18	20

Shortstop	PCT	G	PO	A	E	DP
Casilla	.969	36	56	101	5	23
Nishioka	.964	60	96	172	10	34
Plouffe	.944	45	73	111	11	33
Tolbert	.973	31	41	66	3	19

Outfield	PCT	G	PO	A	E	DP
Benson	.957	20	44	0	2	0
Cuddyer	.974	77	142	6	4	1
Dinkelman	1.000	10	20	0	0	0
Kubel	.992	58	110	9	1	3
Mauer	1.000	1	3	0	0	0
Plouffe	1.000	13	19	1	0	1
Repko	.988	55	78	2	1	0
Revere	.976	106	285	3	7	0
Span	.995	67	206	1	1	0
Tosoni	.968	42	87	4	3	0
Young	.967	75	144	4	5	1

MINNESOTA TWINS

ROCHESTER RED WINGS — TRIPLE-A
INTERNATIONAL LEAGUE

Batting	B-T	HT	WT	DOB	AVG	vLH	vRH	G	AB	R	H	2B	3B	HR	RBI	BB	HBP	SH	SF	SO	SB	CS	SLG	OBP
Bailey, Jeff	R-R	6-2	200	11-19-78	.252	.281	.240	127	428	65	108	24	6	15	63	61	10	0	3	99	7	2	.442	.357
Bates, Aaron	R-R	6-4	230	3-10-84	.316	.277	.333	106	358	57	113	23	0	7	37	53	5	0	3	90	1	1	.439	.408
Brown, Matt	R-R	6-0	210	8-8-82	.225	.316	.187	34	129	12	29	7	1	3	10	10	1	0	0	41	1	1	.364	.286
Chang, Ray	R-R	6-0	210	8-24-83	.269	.313	.252	42	167	18	45	7	0	2	17	14	0	0	2	26	0	0	.347	.322
Dinkelman, Brian	L-R	5-11	195	11-10-83	.243	.265	.234	127	469	54	114	27	1	3	41	45	7	0	4	93	7	2	.324	.316
Fernandez, Jair	R-R	6-1	220	12-10-86	.250	.235	.258	17	48	6	12	6	0	1	8	5	0	0	0	14	1	0	.438	.321
Gardenhire, Toby	B-R	6-0	190	9-11-82	.247	.239	.251	103	332	30	82	14	0	4	40	18	1	0	1	46	1	1	.325	.287
Hollimon, Michael	R-R	6-1	185	6-14-82	.257	.243	.266	29	101	22	26	8	3	2	10	18	1	0	0	24	1	0	.455	.375
Holm, Steve	R-R	6-0	205	10-21-79	.179	.238	.156	47	151	13	27	6	0	1	13	17	2	0	2	38	0	0	.238	.267
Hughes, Luke	R-R	5-11	205	8-2-84	.231	.171	.256	30	117	16	27	6	1	4	11	10	0	0	2	18	2	0	.402	.287
Kubel, Jason	L-R	6-0	220	5-25-82	.333	.250	.357	5	18	3	6	1	0	1	2	3	0	0	0	4	0	0	.556	.429
Lambin, Chase	B-R	6-2	195	7-7-79	.274	.289	.268	134	471	49	129	24	5	6	46	45	8	0	5	112	1	6	.384	.344
Lehmann, Danny	R-R	5-11	185	9-5-85	.204	.105	.242	43	137	11	28	5	0	2	13	11	4	0	0	21	0	0	.285	.283
Martin, Dustin	L-L	6-2	215	4-4-84	.265	.241	.275	136	490	64	130	26	5	15	69	54	5	0	5	108	9	3	.431	.341
Morneau, Justin	L-R	6-4	235	5-15-81	.367	.308	.412	7	30	8	11	4	0	1	8	1	0	0	0	2	0	0	.600	.387
Nishioka, Tsuyoshi	B-R	6-1	175	7-27-84	.333	.667	.222	3	12	0	4	1	0	0	1	2	0	0	0	1	0	0	.417	.429
Plouffe, Trevor	R-R	6-2	200	6-15-86	.313	.333	.304	51	192	33	60	11	3	15	33	21	3	0	3	39	3	1	.635	.384
Reed, Jeremy	L-L	6-0	195	6-15-81	.000	.000	.000	4	15	0	0	0	0	0	0	1	0	0	0	2	0	0	.000	.063
Repko, Jason	R-R	5-11	200	12-27-80	.216	.286	.174	10	37	4	8	1	0	2	5	6	0	0	1	11	2	0	.405	.318
Revere, Ben	L-R	5-9	170	5-3-88	.303	.263	.319	32	132	15	40	3	1	1	9	6	1	0	0	11	8	2	.364	.338
Rivera, Rene	R-R	5-10	230	7-31-83	.268	.293	.259	43	149	15	40	12	0	5	24	11	2	0	1	27	0	0	.450	.325
Roberts, Brandon	R-R	6-0	185	11-9-84	.267	.307	.250	71	255	28	68	9	2	2	17	14	6	0	1	41	14	8	.341	.319
Romero, Nick	B-R	6-1	200	7-15-87	.000	.000	.000	1	2	1	0	0	0	0	0	1	2	0	0	1	0	0	.000	.500
Singleton, Steve	L-R	6-0	185	9-12-85	.252	.200	.276	41	143	17	36	8	1	3	17	6	3	0	1	25	1	1	.385	.294
Span, Denard	L-L	6-0	210	2-27-84	.205	.091	.250	10	39	4	8	1	0	0	2	0	0	0	0	5	3	0	.231	.205
Tolbert, Matt	B-R	6-0	185	5-4-82	.136	.000	.182	17	59	7	8	1	1	0	3	10	0	0	2	11	5	3	.186	.254
Tosoni, Rene	L-R	6-0	195	7-2-86	.226	.228	.226	73	274	30	62	14	0	6	32	20	2	0	1	68	4	0	.343	.283
Young, Delmon	R-R	6-3	200	9-14-85	.290	.400	.238	9	31	5	9	3	0	2	5	1	0	0	0	5	0	0	.581	.313

Pitching	B-T	HT	WT	DOB	W	L	ERA	G	GS	CG	SV	IP	H	R	ER	HR	BB	SO	AVG	vLH	vRH	K/9	BB/9
Baldwin, Andy	R-R	6-5	215	10-20-82	7	13	5.51	25	24	2	0	144	160	92	88	33	34	107	.279	.280	.278	6.70	2.13
Bazardo, Yorman	R-R	6-2	230	7-11-84	0	1	4.71	9	3	0	0	21	21	11	11	3	8	17	.266	.314	.227	7.29	3.43
Burnett, Alex	R-R	6-0	220	7-26-87	0	0	7.36	4	0	0	1	4	5	3	3	1	1	3	.333	.429	.250	7.36	2.45
DeVries, Cole	R-R	6-2	185	2-12-85	4	2	3.90	30	2	0	0	62	74	30	27	4	18	42	.298	.344	.272	6.06	2.60
Diamond, Scott	L-L	6-3	215	7-30-86	4	14	5.56	23	23	2	0	123	158	85	76	11	36	90	.311	.361	.289	6.59	2.63
Diamond, Thomas	R-R	6-3	250	4-6-83	0	4	8.25	7	5	0	0	24	32	22	22	6	15	27	.320	.273	.357	10.13	5.63
Dumatrait, Phil	R-L	6-2		7-12-81	0	1	1.15	15	0	0	4	16	10	4	2	1	11	12	.179	.063	.225	6.89	6.32
Gibson, Kyle	R-R	6-6	210	10-23-87	3	8	4.81	18	18	0	0	95	109	57	51	11	27	91	.282	.279	.286	8.59	2.55
Gutierrez, Carlos	R-R	6-3	225	9-22-86	2	3	4.62	43	0	0	0	62	60	41	32	2	31	57	.246	.179	.303	8.23	4.48
Hacker, Eric	B-R	6-1	230	3-26-83	7	14	6.10	26	25	0	0	136	161	103	92	18	50	98	.294	.287	.300	6.50	3.32
Hendriks, Liam	R-R	6-1	200	2-10-89	4	4	4.56	9	9	0	0	49	52	26	25	0	3	30	.277	.229	.314	5.47	0.55
Hoey, Jim	R-R	6-6	210	12-30-82	1	3	3.83	33	0	0	9	42	32	20	18	6	21	38	.211	.228	.200	8.08	4.46
Hughes, Dusty	L-L	5-10	185	6-29-82	3	1	4.29	43	2	0	1	57	55	32	27	6	24	68	.231	.211	.270	10.80	3.81
James, Chuck	L-L	6-0	190	11-9-81	3	2	2.30	38	0	0	1	63	49	16	16	4	27	67	.213	.207	.216	9.62	3.88
Manship, Jeff	R-R	6-2	210	1-16-85	1	2	4.32	11	3	0	0	25	24	12	12	4	4	21	.245	.239	.250	7.56	1.44
Mullins, Ryan	L-L	6-6	180	11-13-83	1	4	8.80	7	6	0	0	30	47	30	29	6	10	24	.362	.250	.411	7.28	3.03
Nathan, Joe	R-R	6-4	225	11-22-74	0	0	0.00	3	1	0	0	3	2	1	0	0	1	5	.200	.333	.000	15.00	3.00
Oliveros, Lester	R-R	6-0	225	5-28-88	0	0	3.00	2	0	0	0	3	2	1	1	1	0	4	.182	.250	.143	12.00	0.00
2-team total (22 Toledo)					1	3	6.10	24	0	0	5	31	39	21	21	8	17	30	—	—	—	8.71	4.94
Perkins, Glen	L-L	6-0	200	3-2-83	0	0	0.00	2	1	0	0	3	4	0	0	0	2	3	.333	.250	.375	6.00	0.00
Slama, Anthony	R-R	6-3	200	1-6-84	3	2	2.92	27	0	0	1	37	27	15	12	4	16	42	.201	.308	.134	10.22	3.89
Slowey, Kevin	R-R	6-3	205	5-4-84	1	2	3.55	7	7	0	0	38	44	16	15	3	5	29	.288	.255	.304	6.87	1.18
Stevens, Jake	L-L	6-2	215	3-15-85	1	2	4.70	29	4	0	0	54	68	38	28	6	21	50	.298	.235	.333	8.39	3.52
Stuifbergen, Tom	R-R	6-3	261	9-26-88	1	0	1.80	1	1	0	0	5	4	2	1	1	0	5	.200	.300	.100	9.00	0.00
Suarez, Dennis	R-R	5-11	200	3-13-84	0	1	6.48	5	0	0	0	25	27	18	18	4	10	11	.273	.246	.310	3.96	3.60
Swarzak, Anthony	R-R	6-4	210	9-10-85	2	1	3.90	6	6	1	0	32	35	14	14	3	7	25	.267	.188	.343	6.96	1.95

Pitching	B-T	HT	WT	DOB	W	L	ERA	G	GS	CG	SV	IP	H	R	ER	HR	BB	SO	AVG	vLH	vRH	K/9	BB/9
Tarsi, Mike	R-L	6-8	202	8-11-86	0	0	0.00	2	0	0	0	3	0	0	0	0	3	0	.000	.000	.000	0.00	9.00
Waldrop, Kyle	R-R	6-5	215	10-27-85	5	5	3.87	56	0	0	3	79	84	39	34	7	18	44	.276	.307	.261	5.01	2.05

Fielding

Catcher	PCT	G	PO	A	E	DP	PB
Fernandez	1.000	16	98	9	0	1	3
Gardenhire	1.000	1	2	1	0	1	0
Holm	.993	44	280	22	2	1	0
Lehmann	.992	43	323	28	3	1	0
Rivera	.991	43	304	23	3	3	4

First Base	PCT	G	PO	A	E	DP
Bailey	1.000	92	765	60	0	62
Bates	.992	42	345	34	3	35
Brown	.958	2	20	3	1	1
Morneau	.951	5	35	4	2	6
Plouffe	1.000	7	47	4	0	7

Second Base	PCT	G	PO	A	E	DP
Brown	1.000	1	3	1	0	0
Chang	1.000	2	3	5	0	0
Dinkelman	.969	44	58	98	5	20
Gardenhire	.990	45	80	117	2	35
Hollimon	.973	7	16	20	1	8
Hughes	.960	18	29	43	3	12

Lambin	.800	1	0	4	1	0
Plouffe	.943	9	15	18	2	0
Singleton	.972	28	56	84	4	16
Tolbert	1.000	2	5	3	0	0

Third Base	PCT	G	PO	A	E	DP
Brown	.923	26	12	48	5	2
Gardenhire	.909	6	3	7	1	0
Hughes	.963	13	6	20	1	1
Lambin	.914	101	48	175	21	9
Plouffe	1.000	1	1	5	0	1
Singleton	1.000	1	3	2	0	0

Shortstop	PCT	G	PO	A	E	DP
Chang	.986	38	49	93	2	17
Gardenhire	.943	46	62	120	11	28
Hollimon	1.000	5	7	11	0	5
Lambin	.902	8	14	23	4	3
Nishioka	1.000	3	2	8	0	2
Plouffe	.976	27	34	88	3	19
Singleton	1.000	10	10	21	0	4

Tolbert	.955	13	24	40	3	11

Outfield	PCT	G	PO	A	E	DP
Bailey	.927	26	34	4	3	1
Bates	1.000	6	5	0	0	0
Brown	1.000	3	7	0	0	0
Dinkelman	1.000	75	142	4	0	0
Gardenhire	1.000	5	10	1	0	0
Hollimon	1.000	17	21	1	0	0
Kubel	1.000	3	7	0	0	0
Lambin	1.000	4	4	0	0	0
Martin	.987	121	217	7	3	1
Plouffe	1.000	7	10	1	0	1
Reed	1.000	4	13	0	0	0
Repko	.967	10	27	2	1	1
Revere	.963	31	77	0	3	0
Roberts	1.000	64	129	4	0	0
Span	1.000	10	24	0	0	0
Tosoni	.969	69	119	6	4	1
Young	1.000	4	3	0	0	0

NEW BRITAIN ROCK CATS

DOUBLE-A

EASTERN LEAGUE

Batting	B-T	HT	WT	DOB	AVG	vLH	vRH	G	AB	R	H	2B	3B	HR	RBI	BB	HBP	SH	SF	SO	SB	CS	SLG	OBP
Benson, Joe	R-R	6-1	205	3-5-88	.285	.270	.289	111	400	69	114	28	4	16	67	56	13	0	3	109	13	9	.495	.388
Bigley, Evan	R-R	6-1	200	3-9-87	.253	.261	.250	133	487	59	123	34	3	7	56	35	8	0	3	108	5	6	.378	.311
Cates, Chris	R-R	5-3	145	4-15-85	.205	.216	.201	79	200	25	41	8	0	0	11	14	1	0	2	22	0	2	.245	.258
Chang, Ray	R-R	6-0	210	8-24-83	.270	.250	.274	23	89	10	24	9	0	1	22	5	2	0	1	14	1	1	.404	.320
De San Miguel, Allan	R-R	5-9	200	2-1-88	.190	.000	.216	13	42	5	8	2	0	0	3	0	0	0	0	15	0	0	.238	.244
Dolenc, Mark	R-R	6-3	218	11-8-84	.266	.289	.257	131	418	40	111	15	5	3	47	31	7	0	5	125	17	12	.347	.323
Dozier, Brian	R-R	5-11	190	5-15-87	.318	.385	.296	78	311	60	99	22	7	7	34	28	5	0	0	46	11	7	.502	.384
Fernandez, Jair	R-R	6-1	220	12-10-86	.205	.065	.298	25	78	11	16	3	0	1	11	15	1	0	0	26	0	0	.282	.340
Hanson, Nate	R-R	6-0	195	2-8-87	.238	.235	.238	60	202	21	48	13	1	2	22	16	2	0	8	27	1	0	.342	.289
Herrmann, Chris	L-R	6-0	195	11-24-87	.258	.164	.281	97	337	53	87	14	5	7	46	64	2	0	0	68	9	3	.392	.380
Hollimon, Michael	B-R	6-1	185	6-14-82	.223	.197	.231	97	349	60	78	11	2	16	52	46	0	0	4	94	9	2	.404	.311
Lehmann, Danny	R-R	5-11	185	9-5-85	.309	.286	.317	20	55	11	17	6	0	0	4	7	1	0	1	9	0	1	.418	.391
Parmelee, Chris	L-L	6-1	230	2-24-88	.287	.226	.310	142	530	76	152	30	5	13	83	68	3	0	9	94	0	1	.436	.366
Rohlfing, Dan	R-R	6-0	185	2-12-89	.247	.250	.246	54	166	19	41	7	0	0	21	12	0	0	0	33	1	2	.289	.298
Romero, Deibinson	R-R	6-1	200	9-24-86	.256	.272	.251	121	414	55	106	27	2	11	58	40	7	0	7	93	1	2	.411	.327
Singleton, Steve	L-R	6-0	185	9-12-85	.295	.286	.297	41	166	24	49	17	0	3	13	6	4	0	2	14	2	2	.452	.331
2-team total (27 Reading)					.295	—	—	68	261	37	77	25	0	4	26	10	4	0	2	27	4	3	.437	.329
Solarte, Yangervis	B-R	5-11	176	7-7-87	.329	.339	.326	121	459	64	151	36	3	7	49	24	5	0	2	38	5	4	.466	.367

Pitching	B-T	HT	WT	DOB	W	L	ERA	G	GS	CG	SV	IP	H	R	ER	HR	BB	SO	AVG	vLH	vRH	K/9	BB/9
Albers, Andrew	R-L	6-1	195	10-6-85	4	1	2.91	13	5	0	0	43	44	15	14	0	7	34	.288	.261	7.06	1.45
Arias, Santos	R-R	5-11	162	3-17-87	1	0	9.90	18	2	0	0	30	51	38	33	4	19	15	.375	.361	.387	4.50	5.70
Bromberg, David	L-R	6-5	245	9-14-87	1	3	6.08	8	7	0	0	37	50	25	25	3	15	23	.336	.406	.275	5.59	3.65
Darnell, Logan	L-L	6-2	210	2-2-89	1	1	5.58	5	5	0	0	31	38	26	19	3	4	20	.317	.400	.282	5.87	1.17
Davis, Tony	B-L	5-11	185	1-16-88	2	2	2.57	17	0	0	0	28	23	9	8	1	12	24	.225	.313	.186	7.71	3.86
Dean, Pat	L-L	6-1	180	5-25-89	0	1	4.50	1	1	0	0	6	9	3	3	0	1	3	.346	.286	.417	4.50	1.50
DeVries, Cole	R-R	6-2	185	2-12-85	0	0	2.28	15	0	0	9	28	17	9	7	3	5	33	.170	.119	.207	10.73	1.63
Guerra, Deolis	R-R	6-5	245	4-17-89	8	7	5.59	37	10	0	1	95	102	67	59	11	28	95	.273	.228	.307	9.00	2.65
Hauser, Matt	R-R	6-2	195	3-30-88	0	0	3.38	1	0	0	0	3	3	1	1	0	4	.273	.000	.000	13.50	0.00
Hendriks, Liam	R-R	6-1	200	2-10-89	8	2	2.70	16	15	2	0	90	85	30	27	5	18	81	.248	.223	.269	8.10	1.80
Hirschfeld, Steve	R-R	6-5	226	9-8-85	8	8	3.73	30	21	0	1	128	117	54	53	10	43	90	.246	.253	.241	6.33	3.02
Jacobson, Brett	R-R	6-6	205	11-9-86	5	6	4.56	38	13	1	1	101	86	56	51	9	58	80	.240	.287	.204	7.15	5.19
Lanigan, Bobby	R-R	6-4	220	5-5-87	8	9	4.45	27	27	0	0	154	184	93	76	13	40	101	.299	.302	.297	5.92	2.34
Martin, Blake	L-L	6-2	182	6-19-86	3	6	6.23	22	10	0	0	61	63	48	42	4	58	45	.275	.213	.298	6.68	8.60
Mullins, Ryan	L-L	6-6	180	11-13-83	1	0	0.00	1	0	0	0	3	2	0	0	1	2	.182	.000	.286	6.00	3.00
Osterbrock, Dan	R-L	6-3	190	1-27-87	0	0	18.47	2	2	0	0	6	14	14	13	2	5	2	.438	.167	.500	2.84	7.11
Pugh, Bruce	R-R	6-3	180	7-18-88	0	3	9.33	13	0	0	4	18	20	19	19	4	16	21	.282	.294	.270	10.31	7.85
Robertson, Tyler	L-L	6-5	220	12-23-87	10	3	3.61	55	0	0	16	90	87	42	36	6	29	88	.252	.252	.252	8.83	2.91
Schuld, Matt	R-R	6-3	210	12-7-87	2	2	8.12	17	5	0	1	41	55	39	37	6	21	27	.331	.354	.310	5.93	4.61
Steedley, Spencer	L-L	6-2	194	5-31-85	4	5	4.52	30	7	0	0	64	75	33	32	3	30	50	.302	.294	.319	7.07	4.24
Stevens, Jake	L-L	6-2	215	3-15-85	1	3	6.59	16	0	0	2	27	36	20	20	6	11	20	.321	.286	.333	6.59	3.62
Suarez, Dennis	R-R	5-11	200	3-13-84	1	6	5.48	12	12	0	0	66	70	48	40	7	28	35	.271	.308	.232	4.80	3.84
Tarsi, Mike	R-L	6-8	202	8-11-86	3	0	4.22	26	0	0	1	32	37	24	15	1	19	26	.282	.195	.322	7.31	5.34
Watts, Dakota	R-R	6-5	201	11-16-87	1	2	7.86	23	0	0	2	34	42	34	30	3	19	28	.294	.283	.301	7.34	4.98

Fielding

Catcher	PCT	G	PO	A	E	DP	PB
De San Miguel	.991	13	99	8	1	1	1
Fernandez	.992	18	103	15	1	1	1
Herrmann	.984	60	404	28	7	3	4
Lehmann	.978	20	120	16	3	2	2
Rohlfing	.992	40	246	15	2	3	3

First Base	PCT	G	PO	A	E	DP
Hanson	.996	29	213	18	1	22
Parmelee	.995	110	817	90	5	89
Romero	.973	8	63	9	2	8

Second Base	PCT	G	PO	A	E	DP
Cates	.917	7	3	8	1	0
Chang	1.000	1	4	1	0	1
Dozier	.982	15	21	34	1	6

	PCT	G	PO	A	E	DP
Hollimon	.968	22	39	52	3	11
Singleton	.991	21	50	58	1	18
Solarte	.974	89	145	231	10	59

Third Base	PCT	G	PO	A	E	DP
Cates	.905	14	10	9	2	0
Chang	.946	20	17	36	3	7
Dozier	1.000	1	1	0	0	0
Hanson	1.000	4	2	6	0	0
Hollimon	.900	3	4	5	1	1
Romero	.937	109	77	222	20	13
Singleton	.000	1	0	0	0	0

Shortstop	PCT	G	PO	A	E	DP
Cates	.959	54	84	125	9	39
Dozier	.983	60	84	142	4	34

	PCT	G	PO	A	E	DP
Hollimon	.935	20	28	58	6	9
Singleton	.978	13	17	28	1	9

Outfield	PCT	G	PO	A	E	DP
Benson	.992	100	245	11	2	5
Bigley	.962	127	262	13	11	3
Cates	1.000	2	1	0	0	0
Chang	.000	1	0	0	0	0
Dolenc	.974	127	219	10	6	2
Hanson	1.000	3	4	0	0	0
Herrmann	1.000	23	41	3	0	0
Hollimon	1.000	18	36	0	0	0
Parmelee	.979	21	42	5	1	1
Rohlfing	1.000	10	17	0	0	0
Solarte	.962	16	24	1	1	0

FORT MYERS MIRACLE
FLORIDA STATE LEAGUE

HIGH CLASS A

Batting	B-T	HT	WT	DOB	AVG	vLH	vRH	G	AB	R	H	2B	3B	HR	RBI	BB	HBP	SH	SF	SO	SB	CS	SLG	OBP
Arcia, Oswaldo	L-R	6-0	210	5-9-91	.263	.210	.285	59	213	27	56	14	2	8	32	9	3	0	2	53	1	1	.460	.300
Beresford, James	L-R	6-1	162	1-19-89	.270	.257	.277	131	485	51	131	12	1	0	37	43	2	0	6	63	4	8	.299	.328
Casilla, Alexi	B-R	5-9	185	7-20-84	.000	.000	.000	1	2	0	0	0	0	0	0	0	0	0	0	0	0	0	.000	.000
De Los Santos, Estarlin	B-R	5-10	185	1-20-87	.194	.267	.170	17	62	5	12	3	1	1	4	3	1	0	0	19	1	1	.323	.242
Dozier, Brian	R-R	5-11	190	5-15-87	.322	.386	.293	49	180	32	58	11	5	2	22	27	6	0	2	20	13	4	.472	.423
Goncalves, Jonathan	R-R	5-11	159	5-13-89	.227	.220	.230	94	300	40	68	16	2	0	23	47	4	0	2	66	8	3	.293	.337
Hanson, Nate	R-R	6-0	195	2-8-87	.267	.301	.248	52	206	24	55	12	0	4	29	16	3	0	1	31	0	0	.383	.327
Hawkins, Jamaal	R-R	5-9	180	10-27-88	.232	.254	.219	51	155	15	36	11	0	0	10	10	4	0	0	48	1	2	.303	.296
Herrmann, Chris	L-R	6-0	195	11-24-87	.310	.393	.271	24	87	14	27	5	1	1	16	15	0	0	2	6	1	0	.425	.404
Hicks, Aaron	B-R	6-2	185	10-2-89	.242	.263	.228	122	443	79	107	31	5	5	38	78	1	0	3	110	17	9	.368	.354
Hidalgo, Anderson	R-R	5-9	192	9-5-88	.274	.333	.241	100	347	45	95	22	1	6	44	27	4	0	2	65	0	2	.395	.332
Kelly, Paul	R-R	6-0	185	10-19-86	.125	.000	.250	3	8	1	1	0	0	0	0	2	1	0	0	1	1	0	.125	.364
Kubel, Jason	L-R	6-0	220	5-25-82	.000	.000	.000	2	3	0	0	0	0	0	0	1	3	0	0	0	0	0	.000	.500
Liddle, Steven	L-L	6-1	205	11-24-87	.220	.160	.244	102	328	38	72	16	1	2	28	38	2	0	6	78	0	1	.293	.299
Mauer, Joe	L-R	6-5	235	4-19-83	.261	.182	.333	7	23	3	6	2	0	1	6	3	1	0	0	1	0	0	.478	.370
McCallum, Derek	L-R	5-11	185	3-22-88	.191	.333	.128	22	68	4	13	0	0	2	10	0	0	0	0	17	0	2	.191	.295
Morales, Angel	R-R	6-1	180	11-24-89	.264	.235	.276	33	121	17	32	6	0	3	13	13	0	0	4	36	3	2	.388	.326
Nishioka, Tsuyoshi	B-R	6-1	175	7-27-84	.333	.143	.600	4	12	4	4	1	0	0	1	2	1	0	0	2	1	0	.417	.467
Pinto, Josmil	R-R	5-11	230	3-31-89	.262	.301	.239	64	221	21	58	11	1	5	32	12	2	0	1	36	1	0	.389	.305
Rams, Danny	R-R	6-2	230	12-19-88	.239	.231	.244	87	309	32	74	16	3	8	42	26	6	0	1	100	0	1	.388	.310
Rohlfing, Dan	R-R	6-0	185	2-12-89	.272	.345	.235	49	173	25	47	8	1	2	13	13	1	0	2	37	1	2	.364	.323
Romero, Nick	B-R	6-1	200	7-15-87	.200	.229	.185	114	400	32	80	17	3	2	52	44	6	0	4	84	6	1	.273	.286
Santana, Ramon	R-R	5-9	152	6-20-86	.244	.221	.260	50	164	13	40	13	1	3	22	10	4	0	0	46	0	1	.390	.303
Williams, Reggie	L-R	6-2	180	11-5-88	.234	.259	.223	58	197	21	46	7	1	3	23	18	0	0	3	35	2	2	.325	.294

Pitching	B-T	HT	WT	DOB	W	L	ERA	G	GS	CG	SV	IP	H	R	ER	HR	BB	SO	AVG	vLH	vRH	K/9	BB/9
Albers, Andrew	R-L	6-1	195	10-6-85	4	1	1.55	22	2	0	4	52	48	11	9	2	7	46	.247	.279	.233	7.91	1.20
Bowen, Ricky	R-R	6-3	178	8-6-87	1	2	3.83	20	3	0	1	40	36	22	17	3	16	48	.235	.180	.272	10.80	3.60
Darnell, Logan	L-L	6-2	210	2-2-89	8	3	4.17	15	15	0	0	86	95	43	40	6	25	46	.286	.255	.300	4.80	2.61
Dean, Pat	L-L	6-1	180	5-25-89	3	6	6.67	11	11	0	0	58	83	51	43	8	15	36	.332	.329	.333	5.59	2.33
Dempster, Clint	L-L	6-0	180	8-29-89	2	0	7.89	11	0	0	0	22	40	22	19	5	6	16	.388	.296	.421	6.65	2.49
Garcia, Jhon	R-R	6-1	216	5-19-87	3	5	3.82	33	9	0	2	78	82	40	33	6	30	62	.274	.207	.329	7.18	3.48
Hauser, Matt	R-R	6-2	195	3-30-88	2	6	2.16	24	0	0	7	42	37	12	10	3	16	44	.237	.250	.227	9.50	3.46
Hermsen, B.J.	R-R	6-5	235	12-1-89	2	1	4.39	5	5	0	0	27	34	14	13	1	6	20	.312	.346	.281	6.75	2.03
Holbrooks, Kane	R-R	6-3	230	6-8-87	5	9	4.87	19	16	1	0	94	122	60	51	8	26	47	.318	.308	.324	4.48	2.48
Hunt, Shooter	R-R	6-3	200	8-16-86	2	0	7.38	28	0	0	1	43	40	42	35	3	61	46	.250	.304	.209	9.70	12.87
Ibarra, Edgar	L-L	6-0	189	5-31-89	5	10	5.16	32	16	1	0	106	133	73	61	13	49	77	.306	.248	.336	6.52	4.15
Martin, Blake	L-L	6-2	182	6-19-86	2	0	3.09	13	0	0	1	23	14	8	8	1	19	18	.182	.138	.208	6.94	7.33
Mullins, Ryan	L-L	6-6	180	11-13-83	0	2	8.64	4	2	0	0	8	9	9	8	2	4	5	.273	.222	.292	5.40	4.32
Munoz, Miguel	R-R	6-2	182	8-4-88	1	1	9.00	2	2	0	0	6	7	6	6	1	5	2	.318	.154	.556	3.00	7.50
Nelson, Cole	L-L	6-7	235	7-14-89	1	1	2.61	5	0	0	0	10	10	5	3	0	6	5	.250	.273	.241	4.35	5.23
2-team total (26 Lakeland)					6	12	4.67	31	17	0	0	116	133	70	60	6	56	92	—	—	—	7.16	4.36
Osterbrock, Dan	R-L	6-3	190	1-27-87	2	0	2.95	4	3	0	0	18	19	7	6	1	2	9	.253	.360	.200	4.42	0.98
Pugh, Bruce	R-R	6-3	180	7-18-88	2	4	4.53	30	0	0	13	46	50	29	23	6	16	54	.279	.273	.284	10.64	3.15
Schuld, Matt	R-R	6-3	210	12-7-87	4	1	3.99	15	11	0	0	70	72	35	31	2	19	46	.263	.237	.287	5.91	2.44
Slowey, Kevin	R-R	6-3	205	5-4-84	0	1	3.75	4	4	0	0	12	9	5	5	1	1	9	.205	.118	.259	6.75	0.75
Stillings, Brad	L-R	6-4	208	1-20-88	2	3	6.96	14	8	0	0	43	58	37	33	5	22	29	.331	.309	.351	6.12	4.64
Stuifbergen, Tom	R-R	6-3	261	9-26-88	5	9	4.40	23	22	1	0	117	151	70	57	10	19	75	.319	.332	.306	5.79	1.47
Thielbar, Caleb	L-L	6-0	200	1-31-87	1	0	0.00	3	1	0	0	7	1	0	0	0	5	5	.042	.125	.000	6.14	6.14
Tippett, Brad	R-R	6-2	185	2-11-88	0	1	7.23	9	0	0	0	19	27	16	15	4	4	11	.329	.289	.353	5.30	1.93
Tomshaw, Matthew	L-L	6-2	200	12-17-88	0	0	2.13	7	4	0	0	25	24	7	6	1	4	10	.255	.320	.232	3.55	1.42
Tone, Matt	L-L	6-1	219	2-17-88	2	5	5.37	40	1	0	1	64	65	40	38	4	44	52	.263	.203	.292	7.35	6.22
Watts, Dakota	R-R	6-5	201	11-16-87	2	2	4.60	25	0	0	8	31	32	16	16	1	14	25	.271	.327	.227	7.18	4.02
Wimmers, Alex	L-R	6-2	195	11-1-88	2	3	4.20	11	4	1	1	40	28	22	19	5	22	39	.189	.134	.235	8.63	4.87

Fielding

Catcher	PCT	G	PO	A	E	DP	PB
Herrmann	1.000	6	28	5	0	0	0
Mauer	1.000	6	38	4	0	0	1
Pinto	.996	43	270	13	1	1	6
Rams	.992	55	348	29	3	1	14
Rohlfing	.985	34	230	25	4	3	4

First Base	PCT	G	PO	A	E	DP
Hanson	.996	52	459	38	2	47
Liddle	.988	52	378	29	5	34
Rams	.917	2	11	0	1	0
Rohlfing	1.000	1	7	0	0	0
Romero	.987	36	280	19	4	14

Second Base	PCT	G	PO	A	E	DP
Beresford	.977	37	61	107	4	16
Casilla	1.000	1	2	4	0	1
De Los Santos	.970	15	26	38	2	8

	PCT	G	PO	A	E	DP	
Dozier	.972	13	27	42	2	9	
Hawkins	.982	46	62	101	3	20	
Hidalgo	1.000	1	0	2	0	0	
Romero	.970	10	15	17	1	2	
Santana	.933	4	5	9	1	0	
Williams	.968	23	32	60	3	7	

Third Base	PCT	G	PO	A	E	DP
Dozier	.857	2	3	3	1	0
Hawkins	1.000	2	2	0	0	0
Hidalgo	.937	76	70	108	12	7
Romero	.915	51	34	84	11	3
Williams	.889	14	7	33	5	5

Shortstop	PCT	G	PO	A	E	DP
Beresford	.960	96	136	244	16	49
De Los Santos	1.000	2	3	6	0	2
Dozier	.970	33	54	109	5	23

	PCT	G	PO	A	E	DP
Hawkins	1.000	3	5	5	0	1
Kelly	1.000	3	8	8	0	2
Nishioka	.875	4	4	10	2	1
Romero	1.000	2	3	7	0	0

Outfield	PCT	G	PO	A	E	DP
Arcia	.971	54	97	3	3	0
Goncalves	.990	93	192	9	2	3
Herrmann	.960	15	23	1	1	0
Hicks	.978	121	331	18	8	10
Kubel	1.000	1	2	0	0	0
Liddle	.959	49	88	6	4	1
McCallum	.963	17	24	2	1	0
Morales	.984	32	60	2	1	0
Rohlfing	.941	9	14	2	1	0
Romero	.000	0	0	0	0	0
Santana	.976	26	37	4	1	0
Williams	.947	13	17	1	1	0

BELOIT SNAPPERS

LOW CLASS A

MIDWEST LEAGUE

Batting	B-T	HT	WT	DOB	AVG	vLH	vRH	G	AB	R	H	2B	3B	HR	RBI	BB	HBP	SH	SF	SO	SB	CS	SLG	OBP
Arcia, Oswaldo	L-R	6-0	210	5-9-91	.352	.364	.347	20	71	18	25	8	1	5	18	9	0	0	1	16	2	2	.704	.420
Arias, Jhonatan	R-R	5-10	180	2-18-89	.151	.118	.159	28	86	5	13	1	0	0	5	5	0	0	0	20	1	0	.163	.198
Bryant, Adam	R-R	5-11	170	5-21-89	.245	.154	.276	59	208	25	51	17	4	1	25	21	3	0	3	51	0	3	.380	.319
Choi, Hyeong-rok	L-R	5-11	189	8-23-89	.192	.400	.143	10	26	5	5	1	1	0	2	1	1	0	0	9	0	0	.308	.250
Glad, Gunner	R-R	6-0	190	8-14-86	.175	.194	.167	36	120	10	21	5	0	2	11	12	0	0	1	22	1	4	.267	.248
Goncalves, Jonathan	R-R	5-11	159	5-13-89	.261	.385	.212	13	46	5	12	3	0	0	3	8	0	0	2	9	3	1	.326	.357
Gonzales, Mike	L-R	6-6	270	6-16-88	.289	.284	.290	116	412	66	119	27	1	15	76	53	5	0	7	105	4	0	.468	.371
Grimes, Tyler	R-R	5-10	187	7-3-90	.225	.257	.214	42	138	22	31	5	4	4	17	10	6	0	1	53	5	2	.406	.316
Hawkins, Jamaal	R-R	5-9	180	10-27-88	.226	.147	.256	37	124	23	28	7	0	1	10	14	6	0	1	32	10	1	.306	.331
Knudson, Kyle	R-R	6-3	210	9-12-87	.226	.250	.218	33	115	12	26	3	0	1	17	6	1	0	1	33	0	2	.278	.268
Leer, Andy	R-R	6-2	200	1-3-88	.215	.266	.199	98	335	40	72	14	1	3	35	37	5	0	5	103	4	5	.290	.298
Lin, Wang-Wei	L-R	6-0	191	6-28-88	.276	.200	.296	117	413	58	114	20	1	4	40	55	8	0	0	80	12	10	.358	.372
McCallum, Derek	L-R	5-11	181	3-22-88	.187	.175	.189	75	225	21	42	10	0	2	23	19	5	0	6	65	2	3	.258	.259
Ortiz, Danny	L-L	5-11	166	1-5-90	.239	.256	.233	129	468	58	112	33	4	10	71	37	2	0	6	96	7	5	.391	.294
Parker, Matt	R-R	6-1	210	2-9-88	.176	.000	.176	6	17	0	3	1	0	0	1	1	0	0	0	5	0	0	.235	.222
Perez, Jairo	R-R	5-10	160	6-10-88	.337	.371	.327	74	276	56	93	20	1	15	60	32	5	0	2	48	11	5	.580	.413
Pinto, Josmil	R-R	5-11	230	3-31-89	.250	.417	.150	9	32	4	8	3	0	1	9	2	0	0	2	10	0	0	.438	.278
Ray, Lance	R-L	6-1	194	9-2-89	.253	.214	.265	132	470	76	119	34	1	16	74	55	6	0	6	132	10	6	.432	.335
Roberts, Nate	L-L	6-2	200	2-25-89	.302	.205	.326	68	222	55	67	12	4	4	34	28	29	0	1	48	9	4	.446	.443
Santana, Daniel	B-R	5-11	173	11-7-90	.247	.293	.231	104	365	55	90	15	5	7	41	25	4	0	5	98	24	15	.373	.298
Streich, Tobias	R-R	6-0	218	4-5-88	.212	.263	.194	71	217	31	46	6	1	4	16	21	7	0	1	42	0	2	.304	.301
Williams, Reggie	R-R	6-2	180	11-5-88	.316	.333	.311	23	76	14	24	4	0	3	10	9	1	0	1	10	0	1	.447	.378

Pitching	B-T	HT	WT	DOB	W	L	ERA	G	GS	CG	SV	IP	H	R	ER	HR	BB	SO	AVG	vLH	vRH	K/9	BB/9
Achter, A.J.	R-R	6-5	205	8-27-88	5	8	4.52	19	19	0	0	100	97	59	50	13	35	108	.256	.306	.233	9.75	3.16
Boer, Madison	R-R	6-4	215	11-9-89	0	0	6.75	8	0	0	2	8	12	7	6	0	1	12	.343	.438	.263	13.50	1.13
Carter, Bart	L-L	6-1	208	7-8-87	1	2	3.12	18	0	0	0	26	21	10	9	2	7	30	.216	.364	.173	10.38	2.42
Darnell, Logan	L-L	6-2	210	2-2-89	2	2	3.78	6	6	0	0	33	24	17	14	5	8	24	.192	.147	.209	6.48	2.16
Dean, Pat	L-L	6-1	180	5-25-89	2	0	2.86	8	8	0	0	44	40	15	14	4	9	37	.242	.256	.238	7.57	1.84
Dempster, Clint	L-L	6-0	180	8-29-89	4	2	2.14	31	0	0	6	46	26	13	11	4	13	44	.166	.148	.175	8.55	2.53
Fuentes, Nelvin	L-L	6-0	196	4-7-89	3	3	3.29	29	0	0	0	38	30	18	14	3	11	43	.204	.184	.214	10.10	2.58
Garcia, Martire	L-L	5-11	150	3-1-90	2	1	5.57	14	1	0	0	21	19	16	13	1	25	22	.244	.250	.242	9.43	10.71
Gonzalez, Jose	L-L	5-9	166	2-3-90	5	3	2.47	48	0	0	13	62	49	21	17	2	23	63	.210	.143	.239	9.15	3.34
Guerra, Pedro	R-R	6-0	180	1-9-90	2	1	5.04	6	5	0	0	25	28	15	14	4	11	39	.277	.346	.204	14.04	3.96
Hauser, Matt	R-R	6-2	195	3-30-88	3	0	1.40	17	0	0	5	19	13	3	3	1	13	27	.186	.280	.133	12.57	6.05
Hermsen, B.J.	R-R	6-5	235	12-1-89	11	7	3.10	21	20	1	0	125	131	62	43	10	31	81	.271	.313	.241	5.85	2.24
Lobanov, Andrey	L-L	6-3	171	1-25-90	0	7	6.79	21	7	0	0	53	77	45	40	7	17	42	.330	.386	.313	7.13	2.89
O'Rourke, Ryan	R-L	6-3	217	4-30-88	5	5	3.18	34	17	0	1	110	116	45	39	7	32	107	.272	.250	.281	8.73	2.61
Salcedo, Adrian	R-R	6-4	175	4-24-91	6	6	2.93	29	20	1	0	135	131	56	44	4	27	92	.252	.262	.245	6.13	1.80
Soliman, Manuel	R-R	6-2	185	8-11-89	7	11	3.97	28	25	1	0	136	128	73	60	17	50	120	.250	.260	.243	7.94	3.31
Spangler, Sam	L-L	6-2	195	9-24-89	0	1	3.38	13	1	0	0	24	14	12	9	2	18	22	.171	.172	.170	8.25	6.75
Tonkin, Mike	R-R	6-7	220	11-19-89	4	3	3.87	48	3	0	2	77	82	41	33	3	24	69	.271	.234	.292	8.10	2.82
Tootle, Ben	R-R	6-2	185	1-9-88	1	1	7.71	26	0	0	0	30	30	30	26	2	28	21	.250	.170	.301	6.23	8.31
Weller, Blayne	R-R	6-5	220	1-30-90	6	6	3.99	40	6	0	0	86	91	46	38	5	38	73	.280	.291	.273	7.67	3.99

Fielding

Catcher	PCT	G	PO	A	E	DP	PB
Arias	.996	27	228	26	1	3	4
Knudson	1.000	32	266	27	0	0	2
Parker	1.000	6	33	4	0	2	1
Pinto	.987	9	64	10	1	1	2

	PCT	G	PO	A	E	DP	PB
Streich	.992	70	464	59	4	3	17

First Base	PCT	G	PO	A	E	DP
Gonzales	.986	89	722	45	11	62
Leer	1.000	12	76	6	0	7
Ray	.992	41	350	17	3	26

Second Base	PCT	G	PO	A	E	DP
Arias	1.000	1	1	2	1	0
Bryant	.958	34	61	100	7	16
Choi	.800	2	2	2	1	1
Glad	.970	16	27	38	2	10

Grimes	1.000	10	19	33	0	7
Hawkins	.970	25	44	52	3	8
Leer	1.000	12	22	25	0	5
McCallum	.951	18	33	45	4	8
Perez	1.000	12	34	29	0	8
Santana	.970	9	10	22	1	6
Williams	.952	5	10	10	1	3

Third Base	PCT	G	PO	A	E	DP
Bryant	1.000	3	0	6	0	0
Choi	.950	8	4	15	1	1
Glad	.871	11	8	19	4	1

Gonzales	1.000	1	1	0	0	0
Hawkins	1.000	2	0	4	0	0
Leer	.942	64	42	138	11	9
Perez	.864	49	30	78	17	2
Williams	1.000	6	3	12	0	2

Shortstop	PCT	G	PO	A	E	DP
Bryant	1.000	15	22	45	0	10
Grimes	.949	30	46	65	6	14
Hawkins	.949	9	17	20	2	4
Leer	1.000	11	18	30	0	4
Santana	.924	78	112	216	27	41

Outfield	PCT	G	PO	A	E	DP
Glad	1.000	8	15	1	0	0
Goncalves	.935	13	28	1	2	0
Leer	1.000	1	1	0	0	0
Lin	.979	115	226	11	5	3
McCallum	1.000	42	52	2	0	1
O'Rourke	.000	1	0	0	0	0
Ortiz	.971	109	184	17	6	5
Ray	.964	84	160	3	6	1
Roberts	.948	31	53	2	3	1
Santana	1.000	15	29	1	0	0
Williams	.941	11	16	0	1	0

ELIZABETHTON TWINS — ROOKIE

APPALACHIAN LEAGUE

Batting	B-T	HT	WT	DOB	AVG	vLH	vRH	G	AB	R	H	2B	3B	HR	RBI	BB	HBP	SH	SF	SO	SB	CS	SLG	OBP
Arias, Jhonatan	R-R	5-10	180	2-18-89	.313	.500	.250	5	16	2	5	0	0	1	2	5	0	0	0	5	0	0	.500	.476
Goodrum, Niko	B-R	6-3	170	2-28-92	.275	.261	.278	59	204	39	56	10	3	2	20	21	4	0	1	56	8	1	.382	.352
Hejma, Matej	R-R	6-6	215	5-4-90	.225	.320	.188	27	89	12	20	3	0	1	8	6	4	0	0	30	0	1	.292	.303
Henderson, Brandon	R-R	6-2	180	4-18-89	.153	.238	.125	32	85	8	13	2	1	0	4	5	2	0	0	33	1	0	.200	.217
Kepler, Max	L-L	6-4	180	2-10-93	.262	.351	.240	50	191	29	50	11	3	1	24	23	3	0	2	54	1	1	.366	.347
Koch, Matthew	R-R	6-0	210	11-21-88	.273	.273	.273	12	44	6	12	6	0	2	9	5	0	0	2	13	0	0	.545	.333
Koelling, Tyler	R-R	6-0	195	5-1-89	.228	.267	.217	34	136	19	31	6	0	5	22	12	0	0	0	21	2	2	.382	.291
Larson, Roy	R-R	6-5	205	12-23-87	.202	.185	.209	28	94	8	19	5	0	1	16	6	0	0	4	34	0	1	.287	.240
Lockwood, Nick	R-R	6-1	175	1-7-91	.260	.196	.283	52	208	32	54	13	1	1	22	10	7	0	1	42	3	1	.346	.314
Parker, Matt	R-R	6-1	210	2-9-88	.277	.174	.303	31	112	18	31	6	0	2	10	9	2	0	0	19	0	0	.384	.341
Pettersen, Adam	R-R	5-9	170	11-19-88	.286	.333	.268	17	56	16	16	2	0	1	7	7	3	0	1	9	1	0	.375	.388
Rhodes, Rory	R-R	6-7	200	7-28-91	.261	.333	.240	43	157	21	41	12	1	2	15	22	3	0	0	72	2	3	.389	.363
Rodriguez, Jairo	R-R	5-11	180	8-24-88	.208	.250	.191	26	96	9	20	2	0	1	8	5	2	0	2	20	1	1	.260	.257
Rosario, Eddie	L-R	6-0	170	9-28-91	.337	.308	.349	67	270	71	91	9	9	21	60	27	0	0	0	60	17	6	.670	.397
Sano, Miguel	R-R	6-3	195	5-11-93	.292	.313	.285	66	267	58	78	18	7	20	59	23	2	0	1	77	5	4	.637	.352
Vargas, Kennys	B-R	6-5	215	8-1-90	.322	.349	.313	44	174	27	56	11	0	6	33	15	1	0	1	50	0	0	.489	.377
Williams, J.D.	B-R	5-11	183	11-20-90	.324	.365	.308	50	185	30	60	12	1	4	24	25	1	0	1	58	10	5	.465	.406

Pitching	B-T	HT	WT	DOB	W	L	ERA	G	GS	CG	SV	IP	H	R	ER	HR	BB	SO	AVG	vLH	vRH	K/9	BB/9
Alloway, Nick	R-R	6-4	225	1-6-89	0	0	3.25	19	0	0	0	28	26	17	10	1	18	25	.260	.167	.300	8.13	5.86
Atherton, Tim	R-R	6-2	195	11-7-89	3	0	1.50	6	4	0	0	24	14	4	4	3	5	29	.175	.100	.220	10.88	1.88
Bashore, Matt	L-L	6-2	200	4-6-88	0	0	3.24	12	3	0	0	17	13	8	6	2	8	15	.213	.118	.250	8.10	4.32
Boer, Madison	R-R	6-4	215	11-9-89	2	1	2.60	15	0	0	9	17	13	5	5	1	2	31	.203	.143	.233	16.10	1.04
Carter, Bart	R-R	6-1	208	7-8-87	2	0	1.42	6	0	0	0	13	8	3	2	0	2	24	.174	.063	.233	17.05	1.42
Christensen, Derek	R-R	6-1	180	6-19-89	5	2	2.84	19	6	0	0	57	43	22	18	6	26	61	.207	.136	.252	9.63	4.11
Ciurcina, Cesar	R-R	5-11	192	10-23-90	2	5	9.35	16	4	0	1	35	51	42	36	7	22	29	.342	.310	.363	7.53	5.71
Evans, Steven	L-L	6-4	210	8-9-89	3	1	1.54	21	0	0	0	23	15	6	4	0	11	24	.188	.174	.193	9.26	4.24
Gruver, Steven	L-L	6-2	205	6-30-89	1	0	3.45	23	0	0	1	31	30	13	12	1	10	32	.252	.206	.271	9.19	2.87
Guerra, Pedro	R-R	6-0	180	1-9-90	2	1	3.70	10	6	0	0	41	42	20	17	4	7	41	.266	.270	.264	8.93	1.52
Hurlbut, David	L-L	6-3	180	11-24-89	3	6	4.50	13	12	0	0	66	82	39	33	7	12	51	.300	.250	.316	6.95	1.64
Jewell, Garrett	R-R	6-1	190	6-17-90	0	0	7.36	8	0	0	0	7	11	10	6	2	4	2	.333	.286	.346	2.45	4.91
Johnson, Cole	R-R	6-3	200	10-6-88	1	1	2.14	12	0	0	1	21	19	10	5	1	8	22	.247	.211	.259	9.43	3.43
Jones, Tyler	R-R	6-4	215	9-5-89	0	0	12.86	4	1	0	0	7	16	10	10	2	2	8	.432	.421	.444	10.29	2.57
Kimes, Corey	L-L	6-4	240	5-2-90	0	0	3.38	5	0	0	0	5	5	5	2	0	6	6	.250	.000	.294	10.13	10.13
Limon, Marcus	R-R	6-4	195	4-20-89	3	1	4.26	5	5	0	0	25	24	13	12	5	9	19	.258	.233	.270	6.75	3.20
Parker, Justin	L-L	6-4	195	4-21-90	0	2	6.87	7	4	0	0	18	29	19	14	6	3	10	.358	.348	.362	4.91	1.47
Shibuya, Tim	R-R	6-1	190	9-14-89	8	2	3.30	13	13	0	0	74	70	32	27	7	11	70	.249	.263	.242	8.55	1.34
Spangler, Sam	L-L	6-2	195	9-24-87	0	0	4.50	5	0	0	1	10	10	5	5	1	4	12	.263	.375	.233	10.80	3.60
Summers, Matt	R-R	6-1	205	8-17-89	1	1	0.87	20	0	0	6	21	11	2	2	0	5	36	.153	.000	.234	15.68	2.18
Van Steensel, Todd	R-R	6-1	190	1-14-91	5	2	5.68	13	10	0	0	57	60	40	36	10	17	58	.263	.240	.275	9.16	2.68
Williams, Corey	L-L	6-1	190	7-4-90	1	1	3.86	7	0	0	1	12	12	6	5	0	5	11	.261	.278	.250	8.49	3.86

Fielding

Catcher	PCT	G	PO	A	E	DP	PB
Arias	.984	5	54	7	1	0	1
Koch	1.000	7	68	4	0	0	0
Parker	.993	31	258	26	2	5	2
Rodriguez	.984	26	222	27	4	3	2

First Base	PCT	G	PO	A	E	DP
Kepler	1.000	3	25	1	0	0
Rhodes	.990	34	276	14	3	22
Vargas	.987	34	294	19	4	29

Second Base	PCT	G	PO	A	E	DP
Goodrum	.944	5	9	8	1	0
Lockwood	.991	51	89	126	2	31
Pettersen	.957	16	29	38	3	12

Third Base	PCT	G	PO	A	E	DP
Larson	.943	23	7	43	3	4
Sano	.905	48	35	108	15	9

Shortstop	PCT	G	PO	A	E	DP
Goodrum	.905	54	84	144	24	32

Sano	.836	16	17	39	11	6

Outfield	PCT	G	PO	A	E	DP
Hejma	.952	20	20	0	1	0
Henderson	.967	29	52	6	2	3
Kepler	.951	45	57	1	3	1
Koelling	1.000	20	35	1	0	0
Rosario	.985	65	122	6	2	0
Williams	.962	33	48	2	2	0

MINNESOTA TWINS

GULF COAST LEAGUE

Batting	B-T	HT	WT	DOB	AVG	vLH	vRH	G	AB	R	H	2B	3B	HR	RBI	BB	HBP	SH	SF	SO	SB	CS	SLG	OBP
Arcia, Oswaldo	L-R	6-0	210	5-9-91	.500	.333	.600	2	8	1	4	1	1	0	1	0	0	0	0	1	0	0	.875	.500
Benson, Joe	R-R	6-1	205	3-5-88	.222	.250	.200	3	9	2	2	1	0	0	2	0	0	0	0	2	1	1	.333	.364
Chang, Ray	R-R	6-0	210	8-24-83	.300	1.000	.222	3	10	0	3	1	0	0	0	1	0	0	0	0	0	0	.400	.364
Chapman, Phillip	R-R	5-11	196	3-28-89	.308	.383	.246	33	104	18	32	12	1	0	21	11	6	0	4	21	1	1	.442	.392
Cross, Kelly	B-R	6-3	205	3-21-92	.129	.192	.104	29	93	3	12	2	0	0	2	15	0	0	0	31	0	0	.151	.250
De Los Santos, Estarlin	B-R	5-10	185	1-20-87	.143	.154	.138	11	42	2	6	1	0	0	1	0	0	0	0	6	1	1	.167	.143
Guillen, Wander	R-R	5-11	170	8-24-92	.317	.353	.292	14	41	6	13	0	1	0	5	4	1	0	1	3	1	0	.366	.383
Hendricks, Joshua	R-R	6-3	217	11-9-91	.275	.263	.282	47	160	19	44	8	2	0	18	10	0	0	1	30	2	1	.350	.316
Leachman, Drew	R-R	6-3	200	4-21-89	.237	.250	.231	44	135	15	32	4	1	0	20	19	2	0	2	19	2	2	.304	.335
Mejia, Aderlin	B-R	5-11	170	5-12-92	.210	.229	.202	38	119	14	25	1	0	0	11	14	0	0	1	11	2	6	.218	.291
Morales, Angel	R-R	6-1	180	11-24-89	.214	.500	.167	4	14	2	3	1	0	1	4	0	0	0	1	1	0	0	.500	.200
Ortiz, Kelvin	R-R	5-11	178	10-19-91	.189	.250	.155	45	111	14	21	7	0	3	12	13	2	0	0	37	1	3	.333	.286
Pimentel, Candido	B-R	5-11	160	7-19-90	.250	.191	.281	45	136	16	34	1	1	0	6	21	0	0	0	31	8	5	.272	.350
Pimentel, Javier	R-R	6-2	175	3-13-94	.167	.250	.121	28	102	10	17	5	2	1	10	5	3	0	0	19	1	1	.284	.227
Polanco, Jorge	B-R	5-11	165	7-5-93	.250	.333	.202	51	172	21	43	8	3	1	16	15	3	0	1	24	6	4	.349	.319
Quesada, Michael	R-R	6-0	180	2-1-90	.211	.130	.253	41	133	20	28	7	2	3	15	18	3	0	1	27	4	0	.361	.316
Roberts, Brandon	L-R	6-0	185	11-9-84	.333	.000	.500	3	9	3	3	0	0	0	1	1	0	0	0	1	0	0	.333	.400
Rodriguez, Dereck	R-R	6-1	160	6-5-92	.156	.094	.190	29	90	4	14	4	0	0	5	5	2	0	0	35	2	0	.200	.216
Rodriguez, Jairo	R-R	5-11	180	8-24-88	.300	.333	.286	3	10	1	3	0	0	0	1	1	0	0	1	1	0	.300	.333
Silvania, Kelvin	L-L	6-1	185	10-3-90	.276	.370	.233	27	87	5	24	5	0	1	9	6	3	0	1	18	0	1	.368	.340
Torres, Julio	B-R	5-11	170	10-29-93	.214	.200	.222	31	84	8	18	0	0	0	4	7	3	0	0	17	1	2	.214	.298
Trinidad, Romy	R-R	6-2	170	5-14-91	.321	.300	.333	8	28	3	9	3	0	0	4	2	0	0	0	3	1	0	.429	.367
Wickens, Stephen	R-R	5-10	170	3-5-89	.245	.234	.254	36	106	13	26	8	1	0	10	17	4	0	0	15	1	4	.340	.370
Younis, Jacob	B-R	5-8	187	7-10-93	.219	.270	.191	34	105	15	23	2	0	0	9	11	2	0	2	26	7	3	.238	.300

Pitching	B-T	HT	WT	DOB	W	L	ERA	G	GS	CG	SV	IP	H	R	ER	HR	BB	SO	AVG	vLH	vRH	K/9	BB/9
Arevalo, Ricardo	R-R	6-3	210	2-28-91	0	4	3.60	13	9	0	0	40	39	25	16	1	20	37	.252	.172	.308	8.33	4.50
Atherton, Tim	R-R	6-2	195	11-7-89	0	0	2.25	4	1	0	0	8	1	2	2	0	2	12	.042	.077	.000	13.50	2.25
Bromberg, David	L-R	6-5	245	9-14-87	0	0	9.00	3	1	0	0	5	5	5	5	0	3	5	.263	.222	.300	9.00	5.40
Chen, Hung Yi	R-R	5-10	190	9-25-92	0	4	4.33	12	10	0	1	35	45	21	17	1	5	38	.310	.295	.333	9.68	1.27
Cicio, Nick	L-L	5-9	170	4-9-89	2	0	1.74	13	0	0	2	21	16	5	4	0	2	20	.213	.211	.214	8.71	0.87
Fawbush, Nathan	R-R	6-7	193	7-3-90	2	1	5.61	8	5	0	0	26	30	16	16	2	7	20	.319	.429	.231	7.01	2.45
Herr, Tyler	R-R	6-8	220	10-8-90	5	3	2.65	19	0	0	0	37	39	14	11	1	16	22	.285	.279	.290	5.30	3.86
Johnson, Cole	R-R	6-3	200	10-6-88	1	1	0.00	7	0	0	1	14	7	1	0	0	1	12	.152	.059	.207	7.71	0.64
Krogstad, J.R.	R-R	6-2	199	8-25-88	0	0	0.00	3	0	0	0	4	2	0	0	0	1	3	.143	.222	.000	6.23	2.08
Limon, Marcus	R-R	6-2	195	4-20-89	0	3	2.31	12	0	0	1	23	16	7	6	2	4	21	.195	.250	.143	8.10	1.54
Manship, Jeff	R-R	6-2	210	1-16-85	0	0	1.50	2	2	0	0	6	5	1	1	0	0	5	.227	.333	.100	7.50	0.00
Mata, Angel	R-R	6-2	190	12-3-92	0	1	1.46	12	11	0	0	37	23	8	6	0	19	30	.184	.230	.141	7.30	4.62
Montanez, Josue	L-L	6-2	195	1-15-92	1	0	5.25	8	0	0	0	12	15	8	7	1	4	14	.300	.357	.278	10.50	3.00
Munoz, Miguel	R-R	6-2	182	8-4-88	1	1	6.00	3	0	0	0	6	6	4	4	1	4	0	.261	.300	.231	0.00	6.00
Nunez, Luis	L-L	5-11	160	9-26-93	5	0	1.67	16	0	0	5	32	23	8	6	0	6	37	.200	.316	.177	10.30	1.67
O'Neill, Bobby	R-R	6-3	220	7-15-89	3	3	2.27	11	10	0	0	40	36	14	10	3	7	27	.254	.216	.294	6.13	1.59
Ramirez, Gerardo	R-R	6-2	165	1-17-94	0	0	3.12	10	0	0	0	17	15	8	6	0	6	12	.231	.286	.167	6.23	3.12
Robb, Hein	L-L	6-0	185	5-12-92	0	2	3.82	11	11	0	0	38	39	21	16	0	17	29	.262	.381	.242	6.93	4.06
Sanudo, Gonzalo	L-R	6-3	215	10-1-92	0	1	5.66	12	0	0	1	19	15	13	0	7	22	.244	.281	.217	9.58	3.05
Solbach, Markus	R-R	6-5	195	8-26-91	3	3	1.91	15	0	0	1	28	26	10	6	0	8	17	.252	.245	.260	5.40	2.54
Tomshaw, Matthew	L-L	6-2	200	12-17-88	3	0	2.16	11	0	0	1	17	14	7	4	1	2	17	.209	.294	.180	9.18	1.08
Trau, Mark	R-R	6-5	176	6-27-91	0	1	1.08	12	0	0	0	17	7	2	2	0	16	10	.130	.143	.121	5.40	8.64
Wahl, Kyle	R-R	6-2	180	11-17-88	5	1	2.23	16	0	0	2	32	21	9	8	1	13	35	.186	.182	.188	9.74	3.62
Wimmers, Alex	L-R	6-2	195	11-1-88	0	0	0.00	1	0	0	0	1	0	0	0	0	1	1	.000	.000	.000	9.00	9.00

Fielding

Catcher	PCT	G	PO	A	E	DP	PB
Chapman	.967	21	135	10	5	2	1
Cross	.975	19	132	21	4	2	6
Quesada	.971	19	147	21	5	3	4
Rodriguez	.967	3	23	6	1	0	1
Younis	.857	1	5	1	1	0	1

First Base	PCT	G	PO	A	E	DP
Hendricks	.995	42	350	30	2	39
Pimentel	1.000	4	8	0	0	0
Quesada	1.000	4	32	4	0	5
Silvania	.976	20	151	9	4	16
Wickens	1.000	1	11	0	0	0

Second Base	PCT	G	PO	A	E	DP
Chang	1.000	1	2	1	0	1
De Los Santos	1.000	3	0	9	0	0
Guillen	.933	3	3	11	1	1
Mejia	.926	13	24	39	5	9

	PCT	G	PO	A	E	DP
Polanco	.918	10	22	23	4	5
Torres	.953	20	26	55	4	14
Wickens	.976	19	33	47	2	13
Younis	1.000	2	2	2	0	0

Third Base	PCT	G	PO	A	E	DP
Guillen	.786	10	4	18	6	3
Leachman	.000	1	0	0	0	0
Mejia	1.000	3	2	3	0	0
Pimentel	.897	19	14	38	6	5
Polanco	.957	14	5	17	1	0
Younis	.816	20	6	25	7	1

Shortstop	PCT	G	PO	A	E	DP
Chang	1.000	1	1	2	0	0
De Los Santos	.964	7	7	20	1	3
Mejia	.948	23	38	72	6	17
Pimentel	.950	4	8	11	1	5
Polanco	.908	19	24	55	8	17

	PCT	G	PO	A	E	DP
Wickens	.962	10	18	33	2	9

Outfield	PCT	G	PO	A	E	DP
Arcia	1.000	2	1	0	0	0
Benson	1.000	2	1	0	0	0
Chapman	1.000	3	2	0	0	0
Leachman	.963	40	48	4	2	0
Morales	1.000	3	7	1	0	1
Ortiz	.961	40	72	1	3	1
Pimentel	.959	42	69	2	3	2
Pimentel	1.000	2	1	0	0	0
Polanco	1.000	10	11	0	0	0
Quesada	1.000	10	14	3	0	0
Roberts	1.000	3	3	0	0	0
Rodriguez	.976	29	38	2	1	0
Trinidad	1.000	8	7	0	0	0
Wickens	1.000	4	4	0	0	0
Younis	1.000	1	1	0	0	0

DOMINICAN SUMMER LEAGUE

MINNESOTA TWINS

Batting	B-T	HT	WT	DOB	AVG	vLH	vRH	G	AB	R	H	2B	3B	HR	RBI	BB	HBP	SH	SF	SO	SB	CS	SLG	OBP
Arias, Victor	B-R	5-11	170	3-26-91	.226	.182	.250	45	124	20	28	4	1	0	17	17	3	0	3	30	17	7	.274	.327
Baez, Dubal	R-R	6-0	175	6-14-93	.250	.286	.228	35	92	28	23	2	0	0	13	17	11	0	0	22	14	3	.272	.425
Ciprian, Ernesto	R-R	6-2	175	2-9-91	.221	.113	.273	57	190	28	42	7	6	2	26	23	7	0	1	55	7	3	.353	.326
Concepcion, Eddy	B-R	5-11	185	1-25-93	.195	.250	.175	41	133	13	26	4	0	0	15	16	5	0	1	30	2	3	.226	.303
Estaba, Pedro	B-R	5-10	165	8-4-92	.208	.308	.171	17	48	6	10	4	0	0	5	4	1	0	0	11	2	0	.292	.283
Gallardo, Felix	R-R	6-1	178	6-25-91	.105	.053	.132	22	57	7	6	1	0	0	3	11	2	0	0	17	2	2	.123	.271
Gonzalez, Erick	R-R	6-1	184	5-4-91	.286	.246	.306	59	189	39	54	9	4	1	23	53	2	0	1	28	13	4	.392	.445
Guillen, Wander	R-R	5-11	170	8-24-92	.188	.211	.178	18	64	9	12	5	2	1	11	6	5	0	0	17	1	0	.375	.307
Jimenez, Ronald	R-R	6-1	170	1-22-94	.266	.232	.281	52	177	29	47	7	0	0	22	15	4	0	3	42	14	7	.305	.332
Martinez, Carlos	R-R	5-11	170	4-6-94	.185	.111	.217	40	119	17	22	5	1	0	19	22	8	0	2	41	5	3	.244	.344
Martinez, Felix	R-R	6-2	175	12-6-88	.138	.080	.161	36	87	15	12	2	1	0	14	17	7	0	2	26	0	3	.184	.319
Pacheco, Adonis	L-L	5-11	175	7-14-91	.285	.258	.300	58	186	24	53	7	7	0	22	22	1	0	0	33	16	8	.398	.364
Pimentel, Javier	R-R	6-2	175	3-13-94	.220	.261	.206	25	91	14	20	4	2	2	15	9	0	0	1	31	1	1	.374	.287
Polanco, Joel	R-R	5-11	175	8-15-92	.205	.286	.165	44	127	18	26	8	1	0	13	27	6	0	1	35	3	7	.283	.366
Ramirez, Jose	B-R	5-10	165	9-6-91	.256	.260	.254	52	164	34	42	2	1	0	18	40	4	0	2	32	20	10	.280	.410
Silva, Jhon	B-R	5-11	160	6-5-93	.208	.167	.220	31	77	9	16	3	0	0	6	8	0	0	0	29	4	3	.247	.282
Ynojoso, Jonatan	B-R	5-11	150	10-23-92	.186	.037	.231	44	118	23	22	2	1	0	14	26	2	0	2	30	5	6	.220	.338

Pitching	B-T	HT	WT	DOB	W	L	ERA	G	GS	CG	SV	IP	H	R	ER	HR	BB	SO	AVG	vLH	vRH	K/9	BB/9
Abreu, Jose	R-R	5-11	170	7-13-92	3	1	1.30	11	6	0	0	42	28	9	6	0	12	29	.196	.145	.235	6.26	2.59
Bonilla, Sterling	R-R	6-0	165	2-26-92	1	3	2.73	13	9	1	0	53	52	25	16	0	13	43	.252	.296	.230	7.35	2.22
De La Cruz, Melciades	R-R	6-1	190	5-12-93	1	1	2.29	12	8	0	0	39	30	16	10	1	13	38	.207	.087	.263	8.69	2.97
Florentino, Yeison	R-R	6-3	180	1-16-92	1	2	3.16	20	0	0	3	26	22	16	9	0	15	18	.224	.273	.185	6.31	5.26
Jimenez, Jose	R-R	6-3	215	12-12-91	1	2	2.53	12	6	0	0	32	26	13	9	1	13	29	.232	.317	.183	8.16	3.66
Jorge, Felix	R-R	6-2	170	1-2-94	2	1	2.67	9	5	0	1	27	19	12	8	0	9	26	.192	.174	.208	8.67	3.00
Landa, Yorman	R-R	6-0	175	6-11-94	2	2	3.38	12	6	0	0	32	19	23	12	1	26	31	.170	.216	.147	8.72	7.31
Martinez, Edgar	R-R	6-0	145	9-1-90	2	1	0.32	18	1	0	5	28	20	6	1	0	9	12	.200	.289	.145	3.86	2.89
Nunez, Francisco	R-R	6-3	180	12-28-91	9	1	1.47	20	1	0	5	49	29	12	8	1	8	61	.166	.127	.183	11.20	1.47
Rosario, Randy	L-L	6-0	160	5-18-94	2	4	3.86	13	8	0	0	35	28	22	15	0	19	26	.212	.167	.219	6.69	4.89
Suarez, Carlos	R-R	6-1	182	11-24-92	0	0	9.39	12	0	0	1	15	22	19	16	0	16	8	.328	.360	.310	4.70	9.39
Subero, Junior	R-R	6-0	180	3-14-92	3	4	0.77	12	10	0	0	47	29	8	4	2	16	49	.178	.219	.152	9.45	3.09
Vargas, Javier	R-R	6-1	185	1-28-93	3	1	4.33	11	5	0	0	27	26	20	13	1	17	26	.271	.364	.222	8.67	5.67
Vasquez, Jose	R-R	6-0	170	3-27-91	4	0	6.35	11	0	0	1	17	22	14	12	0	9	16	.328	.130	.432	8.47	4.76
Villasana, Elias	R-R	6-1		3-22-93	4	1	2.48	20	0	0	1	40	27	14	11	1	20	32	.200	.174	.213	7.20	4.50
Zarzuela, Ezequiel	R-R	6-1	170	11-18-90	3	2	2.60	19	0	0	3	35	30	16	10	1	19	40	.227	.208	.238	10.38	4.93
Zoquiel, Reyson	L-L	5-11	175	11-5-93	1	0	5.00	8	3	0	0	18	16	12	10	2	15	11	.235	.250	.234	5.50	7.50

Fielding

Catcher	PCT	G	PO	A	E	DP	PB
Concepcion	.983	16	104	14	2	3	8
Gallardo	1.000	13	91	10	0	0	4
Gonzalez	1.000	1	3	0	0	0	
Martinez	.982	16	99	9	2	0	3
Polanco	.988	32	218	26	3	2	5

First Base	PCT	G	PO	A	E	DP
Arias	.933	5	24	4	2	3
Concepcion	.962	7	48	2	2	3
Gallardo	1.000	2	22	1	0	1
Gonzalez	.993	17	136	14	1	14
Martinez	.981	14	99	2	2	11
Martinez	1.000	1	8	1	0	0
Martinez	.971	19	148	19	5	11
Polanco	1.000	10	86	4	0	8

Second Base	PCT	G	PO	A	E	DP
Arias	1.000	5	2	12	0	3

	PCT	G	PO	A	E	DP	PB
Baez	.968	19	24	36	2	3	
Estaba	1.000	2	2	0	0	0	
Gonzalez	1.000	1	0	2	0	0	
Jimenez	.979	12	17	30	1	9	
Martinez	.897	8	21	14	4	4	
Ramirez	.991	22	47	58	1	15	
Ynojoso	.875	8	14	14	4	3	

Third Base	PCT	G	PO	A	E	DP
Arias	.894	12	17	25	5	3
Estaba	.895	13	3	31	4	2
Guillen	.860	16	11	38	8	4
Jimenez	.750	1	0	3	1	0
Martinez	.824	10	6	22	6	3
Martinez	1.000	1	1	2	0	0
Martinez	.000	1	0	0	0	0
Pimentel	.857	12	3	21	4	4
Ramirez	.885	7	5	18	3	1

Shortstop	PCT	G	PO	A	E	DP
Arias	.667	1	2	0	1	0
Baez	.867	5	4	9	2	3
Jimenez	.888	36	53	105	20	18
Pimentel	.935	8	9	20	2	4
Ramirez	.932	12	17	51	5	4
Ynojoso	.897	9	12	14	3	2

Outfield	PCT	G	PO	A	E	DP
Arias	1.000	21	22	4	0	1
Ciprian	.961	53	65	8	3	1
Gonzalez	.982	42	53	1	1	0
Pacheco	.918	46	74	4	7	2
Ramirez	.929	10	13	0	1	0
Silva	1.000	31	39	4	0	0
Ynojoso	.966	19	26	2	1	1

New York Mets

SEASON IN A SENTENCE: In Game 162, Jose Reyes clinched the first batting title in Mets history, bunting for a single and taking himself out of the game, and summing up the Mets' year in one play: individual brilliance with little else to distinguish a fourth-place team.

HIGH POINT: On July 29, the Mets improved to a season-best four games over .500, beating the Nationals behind the 10th victory by rookie righthander Dillon Gee. July was the team's third straight winning month, but New York was just 22-32 the rest of the way.

LOW POINT: In May, the New Yorker magazine profiled owner Fred Wilpon and how he lost millions of dollars in Bernie Madoff's infamous Ponzi scheme. Wilpon criticized Mets stalwarts such as Reyes and David Wright in the piece, and spent much of the rest of the season chasing new investors and fending off lawsuits.

NOTABLE ROOKIES: Injuries at first base and the July trade of Carlos Beltran to the Giants provided opportunity for Lucas Duda, and the 25-year-old responded with 10 homers in the second half. Gee came back to earth in the second half but still led the team in wins at 13-6, 4.43, while grinder Justin Turner got nearly 500 plate appearances and wound up as the regular second baseman, hitting 30 doubles. Rule 5 pick Pedro Beato had his moments out of the bullpen.

KEY TRANSACTIONS: Beltran led the Mets in home runs, even though he was traded to the Giants at the end of July. In return, the Mets received high Class A righthander Zach Wheeler, a power-armed, high-ceiling prospect. New York got much less for closer Francisco Rodriguez, obtaining A-ball righty Adrian Rosario and 5-foot-7 lefty Danny Ray Herrera from the Brewers in an earlier deadline deal.

DOWN ON THE FARM: Righthander Matt Harvey, a 2010 first-round pick, reached Double-A in his debut and led the organization in wins and strikeouts while going 13-5, 3.32 overall. Righthander Jenrry Mejia had Tommy John surgery, but righty Jeurys Familia took a significant step forward. And 22-year-old left fielder Juan Lagares wound up hitting .349, good for fifth in the minors, while reaching Double-A. Both high Class A St. Lucie and low Class A Savannah lost in their league championship series, while short-season Brooklyn lost a playoff series to rival Staten Island.

OPENING DAY PAYROLL: $118,847,309 (7th)

PLAYERS OF THE YEAR

MARC LEVINE

MAJOR LEAGUE	MINOR LEAGUE
Jose Reyes	**Matt Harvey**
ss	rhp
.337/.384/.493	(High A/Double-A)
Won NL batting title	13-5, 3.32
Led NL with 16 3B	156 SO/136 IP

ORGANIZATION LEADERS

BATTING   *Minimum 250 PA

MAJORS

* AVG	Jose Reyes	.337
* OPS	Carlos Beltran	.904
HR	Carlos Beltran	15
RBI	Carlos Beltran	66

MINORS

* AVG	Juan Lagares, St. Lucie/Binghamton	.349
* OBP	Josh Satin, Binghamton/Buffalo	.411
* SLG	Juan Lagares, St. Lucie/Binghamton	.5
R	Matt Den Dekker, St. Lucie/Binghamton	103
H	Juan Lagares, St. Lucie/Binghamton	164
TB	Matt Den Dekker, St. Lucie/Binghamton	248
2B	Josh Satin, Binghamton/Buffalo	43
3B	Rafael Fernandez, St. Lucie/Savannah	12
HR	Brahiam Maldonado, Binghamton	28
RBI	Valentino Pascucci, Buffalo	91
BB	Valentino Pascucci, Buffalo	76
SO	Matt Den Dekker, St. Lucie/Binghamton	156
SB	Jordany Valdespin, Binghamton/Buffalo	37

PITCHING   #Minimum 75 IP

MAJORS

W	Dillon Gee	13
# ERA	R.A. Dickey	3.28
SO	Chris Capuano	168
SV	Francisco Rodriguez	23

MINORS

W	Matt Harvey, St. Lucie/Binghamton	13
L	Mark Cohoon, Binghamton/Buffalo	14
# ERA	Darin Gorski, St. Lucie	2.08
G	Dale Thayer, Buffalo	54
GS	Mark Cohoon, Binghamton/Buffalo	27
SV	Josh Edgin, Savannah/St. Lucie	27
IP	Chris Schwinden, Binghamton/Buffalo	148.2
BB	Ryan Fraser, Savannah	63
SO	Matt Harvey, St. Lucie/Binghamton	156
# AVG	Taylor Whitenton, Savannah	.193

General Manager: Sandy Alderson. Farm Director: Adam Wogan. Scouting Director: Chad MacDonald.

Class	Team	League	W	L	PCT	Finish	Manager(s)
Majors	New York Mets	National	77	85	.475	10th (16)	Terry Collins
Triple-A	Buffalo Bisons	International	61	82	.427	12th (14)	Tim Teufel
Double-A	Binghamton Mets	Eastern	65	76	.461	10th (12)	Wally Backman
High A	St. Lucie Mets	Florida State	72	68	.514	6th (12)	Pedro Lopez
Low A	Savannah Sand Gnats	South Atlantic	79	60	.568	t-2nd (14)	Ryan Ellis
Short-season	Brooklyn Cyclones	New York-Penn	45	29	.608	2nd (14)	Rich Donnelly
Rookie	Kingsport Mets	Appalachian	39	29	.574	t-4th (10)	Frank Fultz
Rookie	GCL Mets	Gulf Coast	27	29	.482	8th (15)	Luis Rojas
Overall 2011 Minor League Record			388	373	.510	11th (30)	

ORGANIZATION STATISTICS

NEW YORK METS

NATIONAL LEAGUE

Batting	B-T	HT	WT	DOB	AVG	vLH	vRH	G	AB	R	H	2B	3B	HR	RBI	BB	HBP	SH	SF	SO	SB	CS	SLG	OBP
Baxter, Mike	L-R	6-0	190	12-7-84	.235	.000	.250	22	34	6	8	2	1	1	4	5	1	0	0	9	0	0	.441	.350
Bay, Jason	R-R	6-2	210	9-20-78	.245	.300	.228	123	444	59	109	19	1	12	57	56	2	0	6	109	11	1	.374	.329
Beltran, Carlos	B-R	6-1	215	4-24-77	.289	.232	.310	98	353	61	102	30	2	15	66	60	2	0	4	61	3	0	.513	.391
2-team total (44 San Francisco)					.300			142	520	78	156	39	6	22	84	71	3	0	4	88	4	2	.525	.385
Davis, Ike	L-L	6-4	230	3-22-87	.302	.163	.372	36	129	20	39	8	1	7	25	17	1	0	2	31	0	0	.543	.383
Duda, Lucas	L-R	6-4	255	2-3-86	.292	.274	.297	100	301	38	88	21	3	10	50	33	7	0	5	57	1	0	.482	.370
Emaus, Brad	R-R	6-0	205	3-28-86	.162	.250	.138	14	37	2	6	0	0	0	1	4	1	0	0	9	0	0	.162	.262
Evans, Nick	R-R	6-2	220	1-30-86	.256	.236	.264	59	176	26	45	10	2	4	25	15	1	0	2	48	0	1	.403	.314
Hairston, Scott	R-R	6-0	205	5-25-80	.235	.247	.216	79	132	20	31	8	1	7	24	11	2	0	0	34	1	1	.470	.303
Harris, Willie	L-R	5-9	195	6-22-78	.246	.355	.230	126	240	36	59	11	0	2	33	36	4	0	2	62	5	4	.317	.351
Hu, Chin-Lung	R-R	5-11	190	2-2-84	.050	.067	.000	22	20	2	1	0	0	1	0	1	1	0	0	1	11	1	0	.050	.091
Martinez, Fernando	L-R	6-1	205	10-10-88	.227	.250	.222	11	22	3	5	2	0	1	2	1	0	0	0	7	0	0	.455	.261
Murphy, Daniel	L-R	6-2	205	4-1-85	.320	.299	.326	109	391	49	125	28	2	6	49	24	3	0	2	42	5	5	.448	.362
Nickeas, Mike	R-R	6-0	215	2-13-83	.189	.115	.259	21	53	4	10	1	0	1	6	4	0	0	0	11	0	1	.264	.246
Pagan, Angel	B-R	6-2	200	7-2-81	.262	.262	.261	123	478	68	125	24	4	7	56	44	1	0	5	62	32	7	.372	.322
Pascucci, Valentino	R-R	6-6	270	11-17-78	.273	.333	.000	10	11	1	3	0	0	1	2	0	0	0	0	3	0	0	.545	.273
Paulino, Ronny	R-R	6-3	250	4-21-81	.268	.289	.254	78	228	19	61	13	0	2	19	15	1	0	3	38	0	0	.351	.312
Pridie, Jason	L-R	6-1	205	10-9-83	.231	.194	.237	101	208	28	48	11	3	4	20	24	0	0	1	64	7	1	.370	.309
Reyes, Jose	B-R	6-1	200	6-11-83	.337	.325	.341	126	537	101	181	31	16	7	44	43	0	0	4	41	39	7	.493	.384
Satin, Josh	R-R	6-2	200	12-23-84	.200	.300	.133	15	25	3	5	1	0	0	2	1	1	0	0	11	0	0	.240	.259
Tejada, Ruben	R-R	5-11	185	10-27-89	.284	.266	.289	96	328	31	93	15	1	0	36	35	6	0	3	50	5	1	.335	.360
Thole, Josh	L-R	6-1	215	10-28-86	.268	.167	.280	114	340	22	91	17	0	3	40	38	4	0	3	47	0	2	.344	.345
Turner, Justin	R-R	6-0	210	11-23-84	.260	.234	.270	117	435	49	113	30	0	4	51	39	10	0	1	59	7	2	.356	.334
Wright, David	R-R	6-0	210	12-20-82	.254	.256	.254	102	389	60	99	23	1	14	61	52	3	0	3	97	13	2	.427	.345

Pitching	B-T	HT	WT	DOB	W	L	ERA	G	GS	CG	SV	IP	H	R	ER	HR	BB	SO	AVG	vLH	vRH	K/9	BB/9
Acosta, Manny	R-R	6-4	215	5-1-81	4	1	3.45	44	0	0	4	47	50	21	18	6	15	46	.269	.244	.270	8.81	2.87
Batista, Miguel	R-R	6-1	210	2-19-71	2	0	2.64	9	4	1	0	31	22	9	9	0	14	15	.208	.265	.158	4.40	4.11
2-team total (26 St. Louis)					5	2	3.60	35	5	1	0	60	49	29	24	2	33	31	—	—	—	4.65	4.95
Beato, Pedro	R-R	6-4	220	10-27-86	2	1	4.30	60	0	0	0	67	59	41	32	5	27	39	.240	.261	.226	5.24	3.63
Boyer, Blaine	R-R	6-3	245	7-11-81	0	2	10.80	5	0	0	1	7	13	8	8	2	1	1	.433	.286	.563	1.35	1.35
Buchholz, Taylor	R-R	6-3	220	10-13-81	1	1	3.12	23	0	0	0	26	22	10	9	5	7	26	.234	.324	.175	9.00	2.42
Byrdak, Tim	L-L	5-11	190	10-31-73	2	1	3.82	72	0	0	1	38	34	20	16	3	19	47	.239	.224	.279	11.23	4.54
Capuano, Chris	L-L	6-3	220	8-19-78	11	12	4.55	33	31	1	0	186	198	99	94	27	53	168	.270	.220	.286	8.13	2.56
Carrasco, D.J.	R-R	6-4	215	4-12-77	1	3	6.02	42	1	0	0	49	67	35	33	7	16	27	.337	.354	.325	4.93	2.92
Dickey, R.A.	R-R	6-2	220	10-29-74	8	13	3.28	33	32	1	0	209	202	85	76	18	54	134	.256	.263	.251	5.78	2.33
Gee, Dillon	R-R	6-1	210	4-28-86	13	6	4.43	30	27	1	0	161	150	85	79	18	71	114	.248	.224	.265	6.39	3.98
Herrera, Danny Ray	L-L	5-6	165	10-21-84	0	1	1.13	16	0	0	0	8	7	1	1	0	2	5	.250	.200	.250	5.63	2.25
2-team total (2 Milwaukee)					0	1	4.66	18	0	0	0	10	13	6	5	1	3	5	—	—	—	4.66	2.79
Igarashi, Ryota	R-R	5-11	200	5-28-79	4	1	4.66	45	0	0	0	39	43	20	20	2	28	42	.276	.217	.308	9.78	6.52
Isringhausen, Jason	R-R	6-3	235	9-7-72	3	3	4.05	53	0	0	7	47	36	23	21	6	24	44	.211	.257	.178	8.49	4.63
Misch, Pat	R-L	6-2	190	8-18-81	1	0	10.29	6	0	0	0	7	11	8	8	1	4	5	.344	.357	.333	6.43	5.14
Niese, Jon	L-L	6-4	215	10-27-86	11	11	4.40	27	26	0	0	157	178	88	77	14	44	138	.284	.259	.291	7.89	2.52
O'Connor, Mike	L-L	6-3	185	8-17-80	0	1	2.70	9	0	0	0	7	5	2	2	0	3	8	.200	.308	.083	10.80	4.05
Parnell, Bobby	R-R	6-4	200	9-8-84	4	6	3.64	60	0	0	6	59	60	29	24	4	27	64	.258	.231	.271	9.71	4.10
Pelfrey, Mike	R-R	6-7	250	1-14-84	7	13	4.74	34	33	2	0	194	220	111	102	21	65	105	.286	.277	.294	4.88	3.02
Rodriguez, Francisco	R-R	6-0	195	1-7-82	2	2	3.16	42	0	0	23	43	44	15	15	3	16	46	.265	.313	.194	9.70	3.38
2-team total (31 Milwaukee)					6	2	2.64	73	0	0	23	72	67	22	21	4	26	79	—	—	—	9.92	3.27
Schwinden, Chris	R-R	6-3	215	9-22-86	0	2	4.71	4	4	0	0	21	23	13	11	1	6	17	.274	.216	.319	7.29	2.57
Stinson, Josh	R-R	6-4	210	3-14-88	0	2	6.92	14	0	0	1	13	14	10	10	1	7	8	.286	.333	.258	5.54	4.85
Thayer, Dale	R-R	6-0	195	12-17-80	0	3	3.48	11	0	0	0	10	12	4	4	0	0	5	.308	.500	.231	4.35	0.00
Young, Chris	R-R	6-10	260	5-25-79	1	0	1.88	4	4	0	0	24	12	5	5	3	11	22	.146	.104	.206	8.25	4.13

NEW YORK METS

Fielding

Catcher	PCT	G	PO	A	E	DP	PB
Nickeas	1.000	20	118	6	0	0	4
Paulino	.983	68	375	30	7	3	6
Thole	.997	102	657	44	2	4	16

First Base	PCT	G	PO	A	E	DP
Davis	.997	36	287	34	1	22
Duda	.995	43	350	15	2	30
Evans	.992	45	360	35	3	23
Murphy	.991	52	419	36	4	36
Pascucci	.800	1	4	0	1	1
Satin	1.000	8	48	5	0	6

Second Base	PCT	G	PO	A	E	DP
Emaus	1.000	11	16	37	0	5
Hairston	.000	1	0	0	0	0
Harris	1.000	10	10	22	0	2

Hu	.941	10	9	7	1	1
Murphy	.978	24	36	55	2	5
Tejada	.984	55	95	146	4	31
Turner	.978	78	144	206	8	36

Third Base	PCT	G	PO	A	E	DP
Evans	1.000	2	0	1	0	0
Harris	.938	7	4	11	1	0
Murphy	.933	28	13	43	4	4
Satin	.000	1	0	0	0	0
Turner	.949	36	25	50	4	3
Wright	.929	101	68	180	19	9

Shortstop	PCT	G	PO	A	E	DP
Hu	1.000	1	1	0	0	0
Reyes	.968	124	175	361	18	75
Tejada	.956	41	53	120	8	18

Turner	.800	1	2	2	1	0
Wright	1.000	1	1	0	0	0

Outfield	PCT	G	PO	A	E	DP
Baxter	1.000	13	12	1	0	0
Bay	.991	122	220	4	2	1
Beltran	.994	91	150	4	1	2
Duda	.987	46	75	1	1	0
Evans	1.000	9	9	0	0	0
Hairston	.957	35	44	0	2	0
Harris	1.000	44	63	0	0	0
Martinez	.800	3	4	0	1	0
Murphy	1.000	1	1	0	0	0
Pagan	.968	121	302	5	10	1
Pridie	.984	75	120	2	2	0

BUFFALO BISONS   TRIPLE-A

INTERNATIONAL LEAGUE

Batting	B-T	HT	WT	DOB	AVG	vLH	vRH	G	AB	R	H	2B	3B	HR	RBI	BB	HBP	SH	SF	SO	SB	CS	SLG	OBP
Adams, Russ	L-R	6-0	205	8-30-80	.180	.111	.192	23	61	5	11	1	0	1	5	9	1	0	0	9	1	1	.246	.296
Baxter, Mike	L-R	6-0	190	12-7-84	.188	.214	.180	18	64	4	12	0	2	1	7	5	1	0	0	19	1	0	.297	.257
Bell, Bubba	L-R	6-0	195	10-9-82	.228	.231	.228	67	162	15	37	10	0	1	18	12	1	0	1	23	9	1	.309	.284
2-team total (8 Columbus)					.237	—	—	75	186	17	44	12	0	1	20	14	1	0	1	26	10	1	.317	.292
Botts, Jason	B-R	6-5	250	7-26-80	.268	.341	.242	59	168	20	45	10	2	3	19	32	0	0	1	45	1	0	.405	.383
Chavez, Raul	R-R	5-11	245	3-18-73	.199	.169	.210	80	241	12	48	10	0	1	22	6	0	0	5	33	0	0	.253	.214
Duda, Lucas	L-R	6-4	255	2-3-86	.302	.268	.318	38	129	22	39	8	0	10	24	23	3	0	2	27	0	0	.597	.414
Evans, Nick	R-R	6-2	220	1-30-86	.313	.338	.304	64	249	31	78	13	0	8	32	26	0	0	2	50	3	0	.462	.375
Feliciano, Jesus	L-L	5-10	190	6-6-79	.263	.153	.300	121	391	43	103	12	1	4	37	30	9	0	3	32	7	5	.330	.328
Figueroa, Luis	B-R	5-9	165	2-16-74	.294	.333	.280	101	371	54	109	21	2	1	37	32	1	0	4	40	1	5	.369	.348
Fisher, Michael	B-R	6-2	188	3-22-85	.259	.200	.282	66	251	36	65	11	0	4	21	24	2	0	1	46	1	5	.351	.327
Hernandez, Luis	B-R	5-10	190	6-26-84	.240	.245	.238	121	404	43	97	15	2	6	54	22	2	0	4	73	7	3	.332	.280
Hu, Chin-Lung	R-R	5-11	190	2-2-84	.194	.091	.250	13	31	3	6	2	0	0	1	0	1	0	0	11	0	0	.258	.219
Lutz, Zach	R-R	6-1	222	6-8-86	.295	.274	.304	61	220	38	65	12	0	11	31	27	3	0	0	70	0	0	.500	.380
Malo, Jonathan	R-R	6-2	180	9-29-83	.143	.176	.111	27	35	3	5	0	0	0	2	1	0	0	1	7	0	0	.143	.162
Manriquez, Salomon	R-R	6-1	200	9-15-82	.321	.214	.357	27	56	6	18	3	0	1	7	3	0	0	0	5	0	0	.429	.356
Martinez, Fernando	R-R	6-1	205	10-10-88	.260	.185	.291	63	223	29	58	11	0	8	30	18	6	0	2	60	0	4	.417	.329
Nickeas, Mike	R-R	6-0	215	2-13-83	.214	.240	.203	60	168	15	36	9	0	2	15	16	2	0	3	27	0	0	.304	.286
Nieuwenhuis, Kirk	L-R	6-3	215	8-7-87	.298	.254	.320	53	188	33	56	17	2	6	14	32	1	0	0	59	5	2	.505	.403
Pascucci, Valentino	R-R	6-6	270	11-17-78	.264	.238	.274	130	443	58	117	29	1	21	91	76	3	0	1	149	1	2	.476	.375
Paulino, Ronny	R-R	6-3	250	4-21-81	.200	.000	.278	7	25	2	5	1	0	0	2	1	0	0	0	4	0	0	.240	.231
Perez, Fernando	R-R	6-1	195	4-23-83	.188	.209	.174	40	112	18	21	2	1	1	5	18	0	0	1	30	5	3	.250	.298
Pridie, Jason	L-R	6-1	205	10-9-83	.186	.263	.150	14	59	8	11	1	0	3	6	3	0	0	0	12	1	0	.356	.226
Reyes, Raul	L-L	6-0	195	12-30-86	.200	.158	.222	18	55	7	11	5	0	2	8	2	1	0	0	19	0	0	.400	.241
Ryan, Dusty	R-R	6-4	235	9-2-84	.185	.250	.158	8	27	4	5	1	0	0	2	0	0	0	0	13	0	0	.222	.241
Satin, Josh	R-R	6-2	200	12-23-84	.317	.422	.270	38	145	17	46	8	0	1	16	14	1	0	0	33	1	2	.393	.381
Tejada, Ruben	R-R	5-11	185	10-27-89	.246	.231	.252	54	207	26	51	7	3	3	21	19	2	0	1	30	4	2	.353	.314
Turner, Justin	R-R	6-0	210	11-23-84	.300	.273	.310	10	40	6	12	3	2	0	2	2	2	0	0	6	0	0	.475	.364
Valdespin, Jordany	L-R	6-0	190	12-23-87	.280	.263	.290	27	107	7	30	8	0	2	9	4	0	0	1	25	4	4	.411	.304

Pitching	B-T	HT	WT	DOB	W	L	ERA	G	GS	CG	SV	IP	H	R	ER	HR	BB	SO	AVG	vLH	vRH	K/9	BB/9
Acosta, Manny	B-R	6-4	215	5-1-81	1	0	1.77	20	0	0	4	20	13	6	4	0	17	27	.186	.120	.222	11.95	7.52
Alvarez, Manny	R-R	5-11	215	12-18-85	0	2	10.29	7	0	0	0	7	11	8	8	0	3	3	.367	.417	.333	3.86	3.86
Batista, Miguel	R-R	6-1	210	2-19-71	3	0	4.24	10	8	0	0	47	46	25	22	4	25	36	.261	.356	.163	6.94	4.82
Beato, Pedro	R-R	6-4	220	10-27-86	1	0	0.00	1	0	0	0	1	2	0	0	0	1	0	.400	1.000	.000	0.00	6.75
Bonser, Boof	R-R	6-4	265	10-14-81	0	0	2.45	1	1	0	0	4	3	1	1	0	2	4	.231	.000	.500	9.82	4.91
Carrasco, D.J.	R-R	6-1	215	4-12-77	2	3	3.47	9	8	0	0	47	46	23	18	4	17	37	.261	.321	.233	7.14	3.28
Chacin, Gustavo	L-L	5-11	205	11-4-80	0	1	12.00	12	1	0	0	15	33	22	20	4	8	10	.423	.118	.508	6.00	4.80
Cohoon, Mark	L-L	6-2	195	9-15-87	4	11	6.11	18	18	0	0	94	120	68	64	11	38	51	.321	.241	.344	4.87	3.63
De La Torre, Jose	R-R	5-9	175	10-17-85	2	2	0.89	15	0	0	0	20	14	5	2	0	12	17	.194	.208	.188	7.52	5.31
Egbert, Jack	L-R	6-3	220	5-12-83	0	3	4.50	7	4	0	0	22	23	11	11	2	10	11	.271	.316	.234	4.50	4.09
Fossum, Casey	L-L	6-1	160	1-6-78	0	4	6.56	9	6	0	0	36	46	28	26	3	16	24	.322	.260	.355	6.06	4.04
Gee, Dillon	R-R	6-1	205	4-28-86	1	1	4.63	2	2	0	0	12	7	8	6	1	5	8	.171	.050	.286	6.17	3.86
Hampson, Justin	L-L	6-1	205	3-8-80	3	3	3.41	52	0	0	1	58	57	28	22	5	16	56	.253	.216	.281	8.69	2.48
Igarashi, Ryota	R-R	5-11	200	5-28-79	0	1	0.87	21	0	0	5	31	15	7	3	2	9	34	.140	.085	.183	9.87	2.61
Lujan, John	R-R	6-1	230	5-10-84	3	4	2.40	36	1	0	2	49	50	15	13	3	13	41	.270	.176	.333	7.58	2.40
Mejia, Jenrry	R-R	6-0	205	10-11-89	1	2	2.86	5	5	0	0	28	16	10	9	1	14	21	.168	.244	.111	6.67	4.45
Misch, Pat	R-L	6-1	190	8-18-81	8	9	4.00	22	22	1	0	142	142	71	63	18	41	94	.260	.247	.265	5.97	2.60
O'Connor, Mike	L-L	6-3	185	8-17-80	5	5	5.22	39	0	0	0	60	69	36	35	7	19	66	.288	.207	.333	9.85	2.83
Owen, Dylan	R-R	5-11	185	7-12-86	6	7	4.26	25	20	0	0	116	110	62	55	10	44	91	.249	.259	.241	7.04	3.40
Parnell, Bobby	R-R	6-4	200	9-8-84	0	0	3.38	8	0	0	1	8	7	3	3	1	2	11	.233	.100	.300	12.38	2.25
Schwinden, Chris	R-R	6-3	215	9-22-86	8	8	3.95	26	26	0	0	146	138	71	64	14	48	134	.250	.236	.262	8.28	2.97
Stinson, Josh	R-R	6-4	210	3-14-88	3	7	7.44	13	13	0	0	62	77	54	51	7	33	32	.312	.331	.294	4.67	4.82

Pitching	B-T	HT	WT	DOB	W	L	ERA	G	GS	CG	SV	IP	H	R	ER	HR	BB	SO	AVG	vLH	vRH	K/9	BB/9
Sweeney, Brian	R-R	6-2	200	6-13-74	5	5	4.34	32	8	0	1	85	92	46	41	11	22	67	.274	.349	.229	7.09	2.33
Tankersley, Taylor	L-L	6-0	210	3-7-83	1	1	5.79	48	0	0	0	56	67	37	36	7	37	72	.294	.295	.293	11.57	5.95
Thayer, Dale	R-R	6-0	195	12-17-80	4	3	2.66	54	0	0	21	71	54	23	21	8	15	66	.214	.217	.213	8.37	1.90
Turgeon, Erik	R-R	6-0	170	3-25-87	0	0	27.00	1	0	0	1	0	1	1	1	1	0	0	.500	.000	.500	0.00	0.00

Fielding

Catcher	PCT	G	PO	A	E	DP	PB
Chavez	.995	78	527	62	3	8	3
Manriquez	1.000	12	69	6	0	0	1
Nickeas	.995	56	375	28	2	1	5
Paulino	.938	5	27	3	2	0	0
Ryan	.947	8	31	5	2	0	0

First Base	PCT	G	PO	A	E	DP
Baxter	1.000	3	20	1	0	3
Duda	1.000	8	41	9	0	5
Evans	.991	26	194	18	2	22
Lutz	.991	14	107	7	1	6
Manriquez	.889	3	14	2	2	2
Nickeas	1.000	1	0	1	0	0
Pascucci	.986	85	660	42	10	55
Satin	.989	10	80	11	1	13

Second Base	PCT	G	PO	A	E	DP
Adams	1.000	2	1	4	0	1
Figueroa	.987	14	40	38	1	10
Fisher	.925	13	27	22	4	5

	PCT	G	PO	A	E	DP
Hernandez	.980	90	173	223	8	56
Hu	.947	6	7	11	1	4
Malo	1.000	4	8	5	0	2
Satin	.971	7	15	18	1	4
Tejada	1.000	1	1	4	0	1
Turner	.955	8	20	22	2	4
Valdespin	1.000	7	13	20	0	4

Third Base	PCT	G	PO	A	E	DP
Adams	.900	14	11	16	3	1
Evans	1.000	10	4	11	0	0
Figueroa	.971	15	8	26	1	4
Fisher	.965	51	33	78	4	4
Lutz	.957	35	26	64	4	3
Malo	.889	6	2	6	1	0
Satin	.893	22	12	38	6	2
Turner	1.000	2	5	1	0	0

Shortstop	PCT	G	PO	A	E	DP
Figueroa	.951	50	69	125	10	27
Hernandez	.961	21	36	63	4	14

Hu	1.000	2	2	4	0	1
Tejada	.948	53	56	143	11	32
Valdespin	.924	20	22	51	6	11

Outfield	PCT	G	PO	A	E	DP
Baxter	.920	14	20	3	2	2
Bell	.990	59	99	2	1	1
Botts	.932	41	53	2	4	0
Duda	.977	31	41	1	1	1
Evans	.983	31	58	1	1	1
Feliciano	.996	115	271	5	1	1
Figueroa	1.000	8	8	0	0	0
Malo	1.000	6	2	0	0	0
Martinez	.978	48	87	2	2	0
Nieuwenhuis	.992	51	124	4	1	1
Pascucci	1.000	3	4	0	0	0
Perez	.961	37	73	1	3	1
Pridie	.968	14	29	1	1	1
Reyes	1.000	17	31	2	0	0

BINGHAMTON METS

EASTERN LEAGUE

DOUBLE-A

Batting	B-T	HT	WT	DOB	AVG	vLH	vRH	G	AB	R	H	2B	3B	HR	RBI	BB	HBP	SH	SF	SO	SB	CS	SLG	OBP
Bell, Bubba	L-R	6-0	195	10-9-82	.261	.167	.294	6	23	4	6	0	0	1	3	1	0	0	0	7	2	0	.391	.292
Blaquiere, Jean Luc	R-R	6-0	196	2-27-86	.229	.318	.176	47	118	20	27	6	0	2	14	22	4	0	0	27	0	1	.331	.368
Campbell, Eric	R-R	6-3	220	4-9-87	.247	.274	.236	126	405	46	100	23	2	4	46	54	8	0	3	75	6	2	.343	.345
Coronado, Jose	B-R	6-1	190	4-13-86	.190	.200	.186	61	142	18	27	6	0	1	11	15	0	0	2	34	0	0	.254	.264
den Dekker, Matt	L-L	6-1	205	8-10-87	.235	.236	.235	72	272	49	64	13	3	11	32	27	5	0	4	91	12	5	.426	.312
Dykstra, Allan	L-R	6-5	215	5-21-87	.267	.272	.265	121	390	57	104	22	1	19	77	69	12	0	4	131	1	1	.474	.389
Feliciano, Jesus	L-L	5-10	190	6-6-79	.324	.500	.300	8	34	4	11	2	0	0	2	0	0	0	0	3	0	2	.382	.324
Fisher, Michael	B-R	6-2	188	3-22-85	.290	.319	.281	56	200	25	58	14	2	3	24	11	1	0	1	34	4	1	.425	.329
Gronauer, Kai	R-R	6-1	215	11-28-86	.253	.206	.266	52	158	19	40	5	1	4	20	14	4	0	2	33	1	0	.373	.326
Guzman, Carlos	L-R	6-0	195	5-24-86	.228	.174	.240	42	123	13	28	4	0	1	15	10	1	0	2	25	1	0	.285	.287
Havens, Reese	L-R	6-1	195	10-20-86	.289	.254	.307	58	211	37	61	15	1	6	26	27	2	0	2	59	2	0	.455	.372
Lagares, Juan	R-R	6-1	175	3-17-89	.370	.321	.394	38	162	21	60	11	3	2	22	5	1	0	1	29	10	2	.512	.391
Maldonado, Brahiam	R-R	5-11	200	9-18-85	.222	.212	.226	131	477	64	106	16	5	28	74	38	6	0	6	146	9	5	.453	.285
Malo, Jonathan	R-R	6-2	180	9-29-83	.240	.250	.234	67	200	30	48	6	3	3	14	17	4	0	1	45	1	1	.345	.311
Manriquez, Salomon	R-R	6-1	200	9-15-82	.254	.283	.242	60	209	21	53	13	0	5	27	13	3	0	2	36	1	0	.388	.304
Ozga, Travis	B-R	6-2	210	12-7-86	.206	.333	.160	9	34	0	7	0	0	0	3	2	0	0	0	5	0	0	.206	.250
Reyes, Jose	B-R	6-1	200	6-11-83	.333	.000	.333	3	9	3	3	0	0	1	1	1	0	0	0	0	0	0	.667	.400
Reyes, Raul	L-L	6-0	195	12-30-86	.292	.330	.280	106	367	47	107	20	4	12	50	23	4	0	1	93	6	4	.466	.339
Romero, Niuman	B-R	6-1	190	1-24-85	.243	.342	.185	32	103	13	25	2	1	0	12	8	0	0	1	24	2	1	.282	.295
2-team total (34 Reading)					.241	—	—	66	212	23	51	5	1	0	23	19	2	0	4	49	6	3	.274	.304
Ryan, Dusty	R-R	6-4	235	9-2-84	.265	.179	.292	34	117	22	31	10	1	5	19	12	4	0	1	42	0	0	.496	.351
Satin, Josh	R-R	6-2	200	12-23-84	.325	.316	.328	94	338	60	110	35	2	11	60	57	4	0	5	91	2	2	.538	.423
Scott, Lorenzo	L-L	6-3	210	3-1-82	.148	.167	.143	29	88	9	13	3	2	0	4	7	1	0	1	42	2	4	.227	.216
Valdespin, Jordany	L-R	6-0	190	12-23-87	.297	.292	.299	107	404	62	120	24	3	15	51	21	7	0	2	68	33	14	.483	.341

Pitching	B-T	HT	WT	DOB	W	L	ERA	G	GS	CG	SV	IP	H	R	ER	HR	BB	SO	AVG	vLH	vRH	K/9	BB/9
Alvarez, Manny	R-R	5-11	215	12-18-85	0	0	3.00	2	0	0	1	3	4	1	1	1	0	2	.333	.400	.286	6.00	0.00
Brooks, Ricky	R-R	6-3	180	7-18-84	2	8	3.95	53	1	0	1	82	89	39	36	6	21	58	.276	.231	.306	6.37	2.30
Carson, Robert	L-L	6-3	220	1-23-89	4	11	5.05	25	24	0	0	128	154	88	72	14	55	91	.299	.300	.298	6.38	3.86
Cohoon, Mark	L-L	6-2	195	9-15-87	1	3	3.81	9	9	0	0	52	59	31	22	7	17	44	.284	.333	.271	7.62	2.94
Cruz, Rhiner	R-R	6-2	205	11-1-86	3	2	4.14	36	0	0	7	59	43	27	27	4	39	51	.202	.163	.228	7.82	5.98
Egbert, Jack	L-R	6-3	205	5-12-83	1	1	1.88	7	0	0	5	24	17	6	5	2	6	17	.195	.111	.233	6.38	2.25
Familia, Jeurys	R-R	6-3	185	10-10-89	4	4	3.49	17	17	0	0	88	85	43	34	10	35	96	.249	.331	.194	9.86	3.59
Harvey, Matt	R-R	6-4	210	3-27-89	5	3	4.53	12	12	0	0	60	58	32	30	4	23	64	.254	.270	.242	9.65	3.47
Holt, Brad	R-R	6-4	194	10-13-86	8	8	4.71	34	13	0	0	94	75	57	49	7	57	74	.211	.217	.206	7.11	5.48
Kaplan, Jeff	R-R	6-0	190	7-9-85	0	0	4.50	3	0	0	0	4	5	2	2	0	2	4	.333	.125	.571	9.00	4.50
Lujan, John	R-R	6-1	230	5-10-84	0	3	3.48	15	0	0	7	21	19	10	8	3	8	25	.244	.280	.226	10.89	3.48
McHugh, Collin	R-R	6-2	195	6-19-87	8	2	2.89	18	16	1	2	93	78	32	30	2	32	100	.223	.258	.197	9.64	3.09
Merritt, Roy	L-L	6-0	170	9-22-85	1	1	5.26	31	3	0	0	51	71	31	30	2	12	38	.324	.373	.306	6.66	2.10
Moore, Brandon	R-R	6-3	190	1-24-86	10	8	4.47	26	25	0	1	133	156	85	66	12	42	105	.287	.339	.251	7.11	2.84
Niesen, Eric	L-L	6-0	185	9-4-85	0	5	7.94	27	0	0	0	28	31	25	25	4	31	22	.287	.237	.314	6.99	9.85
Owen, Dylan	R-R	5-11	185	7-12-86	1	1	6.75	4	1	0	0	8	13	7	6	0	7	5	.371	.400	.350	5.63	7.88
Powers, Michael	R-R	6-3	180	4-7-86	2	0	3.38	6	0	0	0	13	11	5	5	1	8	8	.229	.286	.150	5.40	5.40

Pitching	B-T	HT	WT	DOB	W	L	ERA	G	GS	CG	SV	IP	H	R	ER	HR	BB	SO	AVG	vLH	vRH	K/9	BB/9
Ramirez, Edgar	R-R	6-4	250	11-30-83	1	2	3.48	17	2	0	0	31	27	17	12	3	10	22	.231	.222	.236	6.39	2.90
Sage, Brandon	L-L	6-2	210	10-3-86	1	1	7.84	16	0	0	1	21	26	18	18	4	13	18	.306	.290	.315	7.84	5.66
Schwinden, Chris	R-R	6-3	215	9-22-86	0	0	0.00	2	0	0	0	3	2	0	0	0	0	5	.200	.000	.500	15.00	0.00
Stinson, Josh	R-R	6-4	210	3-14-88	4	3	3.99	27	2	0	6	47	46	22	21	1	16	39	.257	.273	.245	7.42	3.04
Stoner, Tobi	B-R	6-2	215	12-3-84	4	6	5.76	18	16	0	0	91	111	64	58	17	26	57	.306	.291	.316	5.66	2.58
Turgeon, Erik	R-R	6-0	170	3-25-87	5	4	5.33	51	0	0	7	73	91	51	43	10	21	52	.307	.331	.290	6.44	2.60

Fielding

Catcher	PCT	G	PO	A	E	DP	PB
Bailey	1.000	1	14	0	0	0	0
Blaquiere	.988	38	215	32	3	3	3
Gronauer	.995	51	352	34	2	2	7
Manriquez	1.000	38	242	19	0	4	3
Ryan	.985	27	193	10	3	2	5

First Base	PCT	G	PO	A	E	DP
Campbell	.989	43	256	24	3	22
Dykstra	.983	87	636	43	12	54
Fisher	.978	5	43	2	1	3
Manriquez	.975	12	75	4	2	8
Ozga	1.000	4	19	3	0	3
Satin	.988	10	75	4	1	2
Schwaner	1.000	1	1	0	0	0
Wunderlich	1.000	1	6	2	0	1

Second Base	PCT	G	PO	A	E	DP
Coronado	1.000	5	7	8	0	0
Fisher	.980	11	17	33	1	5

Guevara	1.000	1	1	1	0	0
Havens	.952	51	75	123	10	23
Malo	1.000	20	40	51	0	9
Romero	1.000	1	1	0	0	0
Satin	.965	37	63	73	5	20
Valdespin	.967	25	40	49	3	5

Third Base	PCT	G	PO	A	E	DP
Campbell	.909	56	28	112	14	9
Coronado	.800	13	0	8	2	1
Fisher	.924	27	14	47	5	4
Malo	.922	24	15	32	4	1
Ozga	1.000	7	2	13	0	0
Price	1.000	1	1	2	0	0
Romero	1.000	2	1	4	0	0
Satin	.945	37	29	40	4	5

Shortstop	PCT	G	PO	A	E	DP
Coronado	.950	38	40	74	6	11
Dietrich	.800	1	3	5	2	1

Malo	.944	9	13	21	2	4
Reyes	1.000	3	3	3	0	0
Romero	.946	27	32	73	6	8
Valdespin	.925	78	121	200	26	41

Outfield	PCT	G	PO	A	E	DP
Bell	1.000	6	17	0	0	0
Campbell	.923	25	35	1	3	0
den Dekker	.994	72	164	1	1	0
Feliciano	1.000	8	20	0	0	0
Glaesmann	1.000	1	1	0	0	0
Guzman	.987	35	73	4	1	1
Kiermaier	1.000	1	3	2	0	0
Lagares	.980	38	93	4	2	1
Maldonado	.954	112	213	16	11	2
Malo	.962	16	25	0	1	0
Reyes	.977	104	206	11	5	1
Rogers	1.000	1	5	0	0	0
Scott	.986	28	69	2	1	0
Tinoco	1.000	1	3	0	0	0

ST. LUCIE METS

HIGH CLASS A

FLORIDA STATE LEAGUE

Batting	B-T	HT	WT	DOB	AVG	vLH	vRH	G	AB	R	H	2B	3B	HR	RBI	BB	HBP	SH	SF	SO	SB	CS	SLG	OBP
Baxter, Mike	L-R	6-0	190	12-7-84	.438	.000	.467	4	16	2	7	2	0	0	4	1	0	0	1	2	0	0	.563	.444
Bay, Jason	R-R	6-2	210	9-20-78	.500	.800	.286	4	12	5	6	0	0	2	4	4	0	0	0	0	0	0	1.000	.625
Bouchard, Matt	R-R	6-0	185	12-12-86	.208	.214	.206	15	48	7	10	3	0	0	5	7	0	0	0	10	2	0	.271	.309
Brown, J.B.	L-R	6-1	220	4-30-89	.200	.200	.200	23	80	9	16	1	1	0	7	3	0	0	0	20	1	1	.238	.229
Centeno, Juan	L-R	5-9	172	11-16-89	.318	.333	.314	52	157	22	50	5	1	1	11	12	1	0	1	22	3	1	.382	.368
Coronado, Jose	B-R	6-1	190	4-13-86	.222	.000	.333	15	36	4	8	0	0	0	9	0	0	0	0	8	1	0	.222	.378
den Dekker, Matt	L-L	6-1	205	8-10-87	.296	.325	.283	67	267	54	79	19	8	6	36	24	5	0	2	65	12	5	.494	.362
Doyle, Dock	L-R	6-0	200	3-24-86	.296	.375	.255	24	71	12	21	4	0	2	11	7	0	0	0	14	0	1	.437	.359
Fernandez, Rafael	L-L	6-1	171	8-3-88	.281	.286	.280	10	32	5	9	1	0	0	4	5	0	0	2	8	1	0	.313	.359
Flores, Wilmer	R-R	6-3	175	8-6-91	.269	.293	.258	133	516	52	139	26	2	9	81	27	6	0	8	68	2	2	.380	.309
Gomez, Gilbert	R-R	6-3	190	8-24-86	.307	.160	.380	22	75	9	23	4	1	4	10	9	1	0	0	17	4	0	.547	.388
Havens, Reese	L-R	6-1	195	10-20-86	.273	.500	.143	3	11	1	3	2	0	0	2	2	0	0	0	5	0	0	.455	.385
Lagares, Juan	R-R	6-1	175	3-17-89	.338	.375	.319	82	308	51	104	15	6	7	49	21	1	0	2	47	5	6	.494	.380
Lutz, Zach	R-R	6-1	222	6-3-86	.000	.000	.000	2	8	0	0	0	0	0	1	1	0	0	0	2	0	0	.000	.111
Marte, Jefry	R-R	6-1	187	6-21-91	.248	.253	.246	131	483	56	120	22	2	7	55	41	7	0	6	86	14	2	.346	.313
Ozga, Travis	B-R	6-2	210	12-7-86	.262	.297	.240	56	168	21	44	8	1	0	14	21	0	0	0	39	0	1	.321	.344
Pagan, Angel	B-R	6-2	200	7-2-81	.226	.000	.259	8	31	6	7	1	1	1	2	4	1	0	0	5	0	2	.419	.333
Paulino, Ronny	R-R	6-3	250	4-21-81	.176	.375	.000	5	17	1	3	1	0	0	2	0	0	0	0	4	0	0	.235	.176
Pena, Francisco	R-R	6-2	230	10-12-89	.223	.286	.195	95	319	28	71	13	0	5	37	20	3	0	0	50	3	1	.310	.275
Ponce, Dimas	R-R	5-11	140	1-22-91	.333	.667	.167	4	9	0	3	0	0	0	2	0	0	0	0	4	0	0	.333	.333
Puello, Cesar	R-R	6-2	195	4-1-91	.259	.254	.261	117	441	67	114	21	5	10	50	18	20	0	6	103	19	9	.397	.313
Ryan, Dusty	R-R	6-4	235	9-2-84	1.000	.000	1.000	1	1	0	1	0	0	0	2	3	0	0	0	1	0	0	1.000	1.000
Sandoval, Rylan	R-R	5-10	185	8-10-87	.224	.231	.220	94	313	44	70	14	1	8	35	23	7	0	0	78	2	2	.351	.292
Shields, Robbie	R-R	6-1	195	12-7-87	.269	.263	.271	20	67	14	18	5	0	1	12	8	0	0	2	9	0	0	.388	.338
Vaughn, Cory	R-R	6-3	225	5-15-89	.219	.271	.199	63	210	29	46	8	1	9	29	23	5	0	2	53	2	3	.395	.308
Welch, Stefan	L-R	6-3	175	8-12-88	.271	.216	.296	129	436	55	118	19	3	16	53	57	9	0	7	105	3	1	.438	.361
Wright, David	R-R	6-0	210	12-20-82	.476	.333	.533	6	21	9	10	3	0	0	2	6	0	0	0	3	1	0	.619	.593
Zapata, Pedro	R-R	6-4	185	10-3-87	.292	.327	.275	117	452	62	132	21	7	3	42	23	5	0	1	86	36	6	.389	.333

Pitching	B-T	HT	WT	DOB	W	L	ERA	G	GS	CG	SV	IP	H	R	ER	HR	BB	SO	AVG	vLH	vRH	K/9	BB/9
Allen, Kyle	R-R	6-3	195	2-12-90	6	11	6.28	26	20	1	0	106	131	87	74	9	59	74	.305	.301	.308	6.28	5.01
Beaulac, Eric	R-R	6-5	190	11-13-86	0	1	3.27	13	1	0	0	22	28	10	8	2	7	23	.308	.211	.377	9.41	2.86
Bennett, Hamilton	R-L	6-1	180	6-26-88	0	0	3.00	1	0	0	0	3	4	1	1	0	0	1	.333	.000	.364	3.00	0.00
Carr, Nick	R-R	6-1	195	4-9-87	3	0	2.40	22	0	0	8	30	26	8	8	3	14	34	.236	.267	.215	10.20	4.20
Church, John	R-R	6-3	235	11-4-86	5	2	4.03	35	4	1	0	74	71	39	33	3	31	46	.258	.292	.228	5.62	3.79
Cruz, Rhiner	R-R	6-2	205	11-1-86	2	1	2.77	8	0	0	0	13	9	9	4	1	6	18	.200	.143	.250	12.46	4.15
Edgin, Josh	L-L	6-1	225	12-17-86	2	1	2.06	25	0	0	11	35	30	10	8	2	13	35	.233	.184	.253	9.00	3.34
Egbert, Jack	L-R	6-3	220	5-12-83	0	2	4.37	5	5	0	0	23	33	15	11	0	4	12	.347	.370	.327	4.76	1.59
Familia, Jeurys	R-R	6-3	185	10-10-89	1	1	1.49	6	6	0	0	36	21	7	6	1	8	36	.171	.170	.171	8.92	1.98
Gorski, Darin	L-L	6-4	210	10-6-87	11	3	2.08	27	21	3	1	139	109	40	32	11	29	140	.212	.171	.227	9.09	1.88
Harvey, Matt	R-R	6-4	210	3-27-89	8	2	2.37	14	14	0	0	76	67	24	20	5	24	92	.238	.273	.198	10.89	2.84
Hilliard, Chris	L-L	6-0	175	10-26-87	0	0	27.00	1	0	0	0	1	4	3	3	1	1	2	.571	1.000	.400	18.00	9.00

NEW YORK METS

Pitching	B-T	HT	WT	DOB	W	L	ERA	G	GS	CG	SV	IP	H	R	ER	HR	BB	SO	AVG	vLH	vRH	K/9	BB/9
Kaplan, Jeff	R-R	6-0	190	7-9-85	2	5	3.45	45	0	0	12	57	51	24	22	3	24	44	.238	.202	.276	6.91	3.77
Kolarek, Adam	L-L	6-3	215	1-14-89	0	1	7.36	5	0	0	0	7	13	6	6	0	4	3	.382	.389	.375	3.68	4.91
Mazzoni, Cory	R-R	6-1	190	10-19-89	1	1	2.57	6	0	0	0	7	7	4	2	1	1	8	.250	.300	.222	10.29	1.29
McHugh, Collin	R-R	6-2	195	6-19-87	1	2	6.31	9	6	0	1	36	47	27	25	3	14	39	.318	.289	.347	9.84	3.53
Morel, Estarlin	R-R	6-0	185	10-2-89	2	1	3.78	32	0	0	1	52	45	27	22	7	14	36	.231	.146	.313	6.19	2.41
Morla, Ronny	R-R	6-3	190	5-19-88	0	2	13.89	9	0	0	0	12	27	19	18	1	8	9	.466	.435	.486	6.94	6.17
Moviel, Scott	R-R	6-11	235	5-7-88	5	10	5.10	26	23	1	0	125	177	84	71	3	34	66	.340	.336	.344	4.74	2.44
Niesen, Eric	L-L	6-0	185	9-4-85	3	3	3.00	24	0	0	1	36	30	18	12	2	6	32	.222	.178	.244	8.00	1.50
Parnell, Bobby	R-R	6-4	200	9-8-84	0	0	0.00	1	1	0	0	1	0	0	0	0	0	0	.000	.000	.000	0.00	9.00
Peavey, Greg	R-R	6-2	185	7-11-88	5	4	3.97	13	10	1	0	59	66	31	26	1	15	39	.289	.317	.266	5.95	2.29
Powers, Michael	R-R	6-3	180	4-7-86	6	5	2.90	33	2	0	0	71	67	34	23	3	19	60	.245	.263	.229	7.57	2.40
Rodriguez, Armando	R-R	6-3	250	1-28-88	4	4	3.96	16	16	0	0	75	60	38	33	11	29	74	.218	.230	.206	8.88	3.48
Rosario, Adrian	R-R	6-		9-30-89	0	0	4.50	1	0	0	0	2	5	1	1	0	1	2	.556	.500	.600	9.00	4.50
2-team total (16 Brevard County)					4	5	5.80	17	14	0	0	68	84	49	44	9	34	41	—			5.40	4.48
Sage, Brandon	L-L	6-2	210	10-3-86	2	3	4.63	23	0	0	0	35	40	19	18	6	10	18	.292	.298	.289	4.63	2.57
Santana, Johan	L-L	6-0	210	3-13-79	0	0	1.80	2	2	0	0	5	5	1	1	0	0	5	.263	.250	.267	9.00	0.00
Stoner, Tobi	B-R	6-2	215	12-3-84	1	1	7.80	3	3	0	0	15	21	13	13	3	2	10	.339	.394	.276	6.00	1.20
Weldon, Todd	R-R	6-4	215	7-21-87	0	0	0.00	1	0	0	0	1	2	1	0	0	0	0	.400	.333	.500	0.00	0.00
Wheeler, Zack	R-R	6-4	185	5-30-90	2	2	2.00	6	6	0	0	27	26	6	6	0	5	31	.252	.264	.240	10.33	1.67

Fielding

Catcher	PCT	G	PO	A	E	DP	PB
Centeno	.985	45	235	33	4	3	9
Doyle	1.000	11	52	7	0	1	2
Paulino	1.000	3	9	2	0	0	0
Pena	.989	91	682	57	8	5	6
Ryan	1.000	1	15	0	0	1	1

First Base	PCT	G	PO	A	E	DP
Ozga	.980	20	140	7	3	10
Welch	.998	124	1025	62	2	107

Second Base	PCT	G	PO	A	E	DP
Bouchard	.962	9	25	26	2	4
Brown	.942	23	37	61	6	15
Centeno	.000	1	0	0	0	0
Coronado	1.000	10	17	22	0	6
Havens	1.000	3	3	7	0	0

	PCT	G	PO	A	E	DP
Sandoval	.966	82	108	237	12	53
Shields	.975	17	27	51	2	11

Third Base	PCT	G	PO	A	E	DP
Bouchard	1.000	3	2	8	0	2
Coronado	.750	3	1	2	1	0
Lutz	1.000	1	1	0	0	0
Marte	.902	122	65	193	28	24
Ozga	.667	1	1	1	1	0
Ponce	1.000	4	1	3	0	0
Sandoval	.857	7	4	8	2	1
Wright	1.000	4	1	5	0	0

Shortstop	PCT	G	PO	A	E	DP
Bouchard	1.000	2	3	5	0	1
Coronado	1.000	2	3	7	0	3
Flores	.966	129	195	370	20	79

	PCT	G	PO	A	E	DP
Sandoval	.941	5	4	12	1	2
Shields	1.000	3	2	4	0	0

Outfield	PCT	G	PO	A	E	DP
Baxter	1.000	2	4	0	0	0
Bay	1.000	4	6	0	0	0
den Dekker	.993	65	138	7	1	2
Doyle	.000	1	0	0	0	0
Fernandez	1.000	5	6	0	0	0
Gomez	.946	20	32	3	2	1
Lagares	.982	59	105	2	2	1
Ozga	1.000	11	16	0	0	0
Pagan	1.000	7	16	0	0	0
Puello	.961	116	235	9	10	4
Sandoval	1.000	3	1	0	0	0
Vaughn	.948	57	84	8	5	2
Zapata	.968	82	176	7	6	2

SAVANNAH SAND GNATS   LOW CLASS A
SOUTH ATLANTIC LEAGUE

Batting	B-T	HT	WT	DOB	AVG	vLH	vRH	G	AB	R	H	2B	3B	HR	RBI	BB	HBP	SH	SF	SO	SB	CS	SLG	OBP
Bonfe, Joe	R-R	6-4	220	12-28-87	.254	.286	.243	85	303	37	77	11	1	3	28	26	3	0	1	67	8	0	.327	.318
Brown, J.B.	L-R	6-1	220	4-30-89	.188	.500	.143	4	16	1	3	0	0	0	2	0	0	0	0	4	0	0	.188	.188
Butler, Jet	B-R	6-2	200	10-6-87	.205	.143	.226	26	83	6	17	3	1	1	5	2	1	0	0	17	0	0	.301	.233
Ceciliani, Darrell	L-L	6-1	220	6-22-90	.259	.283	.252	109	421	62	109	23	4	4	40	52	8	0	0	96	25	8	.361	.351
Cordero, Albert	R-R	5-11	175	1-14-90	.286	.287	.285	104	385	38	110	15	2	6	44	15	9	0	5	69	1	1	.382	.324
Farrell, Patrick	R-R	6-3	210	12-29-86	.095	.250	.059	8	21	2	2	1	0	0	1	1	0	0	0	7	0	0	.143	.136
Fernandez, Rafael	L-L	6-1	171	8-3-88	.264	.207	.284	115	428	60	113	23	12	6	63	65	6	0	3	122	20	4	.416	.367
Forsythe, Blake	R-R	6-2	220	7-31-89	.235	.216	.241	105	370	44	87	24	4	9	43	56	2	0	6	123	0	1	.395	.334
Gamboa, Juan Carlos	L-R	5-7	152	4-18-91	.455	.333	.500	4	11	1	5	1	1	0	3	2	0	0	0	0	0	0	.727	.538
Harris, Alonzo	R-R	5-11	165	11-16-89	.270	.250	.278	109	355	56	96	11	4	4	28	28	4	0	2	65	15	6	.358	.329
Honeck, Sam	L-L	6-2	210	6-19-87	.227	.203	.235	75	269	23	61	21	1	3	36	28	3	0	1	61	0	1	.346	.306
Lawley, Dustin	R-R	6-1	195	4-11-89	.273	.500	.143	3	11	2	3	2	0	1	1	0	0	0	0	4	0	0	.727	.273
Maron, Cam	L-R	6-1	175	1-20-91	.250	.250	.000	1	4	0	1	0	0	0	0	0	0	0	0	2	0	0	.250	.250
Nieves, Luis	R-R	6-1	160	12-15-88	.238	.222	.243	87	366	38	87	15	1	3	26	20	2	0	0	45	10	0	.297	.312
Rodriguez, Aderlin	R-R	6-3	210	11-18-91	.221	.202	.227	131	516	59	114	23	2	17	78	29	3	0	3	106	2	1	.372	.265
Rodriguez, Javier	R-R	6-2	165	4-4-90	.209	.227	.203	26	86	10	18	3	1	4	4	9	0	0	0	15	0	1	.407	.284
Shields, Robbie	R-R	6-1	195	12-7-87	.274	.302	.264	60	226	30	62	20	4	2	26	29	1	0	4	36	9	4	.425	.354
Tejada, Miguel	R-R	6-1	175	11-11-90	.125	.000	.125	4	8	1	1	0	0	0	0	0	0	0	0	7	0	0	.125	.125
Torres, Juan	R-R	6-1	180	10-7-88	.169	.100	.193	25	77	5	13	2	0	2	8	2	0	0	0	18	0	0	.273	.190
Tovar, Wilfredo	R-R	5-10	160	8-11-91	.251	.276	.243	131	491	70	123	21	3	2	41	44	8	0	7	53	15	9	.318	.318
Vaughn, Cory	R-R	6-3	225	5-1-89	.286	.368	.261	68	245	33	70	14	2	4	30	36	14	0	1	64	8	5	.408	.405

Pitching	B-T	HT	WT	DOB	W	L	ERA	G	GS	CG	SV	IP	H	R	ER	HR	BB	SO	AVG	vLH	vRH	K/9	BB/9
Almonte, Yohan	R-R	6-1	150	11-9-89	8	8	3.91	24	23	1	0	122	115	62	53	15	27	83	.251	.240	.258	6.12	1.99
Bennett, Hamilton	R-L	6-1	180	6-26-88	2	0	1.83	34	0	0	14	54	30	12	11	1	15	56	.166	.175	.161	9.33	2.50
Cuan, Angel	L-L	5-11	150	5-29-89	10	3	3.56	32	14	0	1	124	125	56	49	10	16	99	.262	.212	.277	7.19	1.16
Edgin, Josh	L-L	6-1	225	12-17-86	1	0	0.87	24	0	0	16	31	14	4	3	0	10	41	.135	.148	.130	11.90	2.90
Fraser, Ryan	R-R	6-3	190	8-27-88	7	9	3.58	28	21	0	1	138	140	64	55	13	63	90	.271	.267	.273	5.86	4.10
Germen, Gonzalez	R-R	6-1	175	9-23-87	7	7	3.93	26	21	0	0	119	126	56	52	9	35	111	.271	.247	.287	8.39	2.65
Goeddel, Erik	R-R	6-3	185	12-20-88	3	5	3.39	15	13	0	0	72	58	29	27	5	24	67	.220	.250	.203	8.41	3.01
Hebert, Mike	R-R	6-3	180	8-11-90	3	2	3.44	10	2	1	1	34	25	16	13	0	11	32	.202	.270	.172	8.47	2.91
Huchingson, Chase	L-L	6-5	197	4-14-89	7	2	1.82	27	8	0	0	84	61	24	17	1	25	91	.203	.203	.203	9.75	2.68

Pitching	B-T	HT	WT	DOB	W	L	ERA	G	GS	CG	SV	IP	H	R	ER	HR	BB	SO	AVG	vLH	vRH	K/9	BB/9
Kolarek, Adam	L-L	6-3	215	1-14-89	7	0	2.22	21	1	0	5	53	41	16	13	1	19	55	.214	.164	.234	9.40	3.25
Leduc, Guillaume	R-R	6-4	192	7-28-87	2	3	5.97	20	0	0	0	32	37	26	21	2	14	17	.285	.283	.286	4.83	3.98
Morla, Ronny	R-R	6-3	190	5-19-88	3	3	2.53	34	0	0	10	46	26	15	13	2	25	50	.160	.175	.151	9.71	4.86
Peavey, Greg	R-R	6-2	185	7-11-88	6	2	3.12	14	14	0	0	78	75	31	27	3	11	69	.256	.204	.289	7.96	1.27
Rojas, Luis	R-R	5-10	185	7-29-89	1	5	4.87	29	0	0	0	44	45	28	24	3	32	26	.269	.281	.262	5.28	6.50
Sage, Brandon	L-L	6-2	210	10-3-86	2	0	2.45	8	0	0	0	15	14	5	4	0	5	5	.264	.200	.279	3.07	3.07
Weldon, Todd	R-R	6-4	215	7-21-87	3	1	3.80	12	0	0	0	21	21	12	9	2	16	11	.263	.303	.234	4.64	6.75
Whitenton, Taylor	R-R	6-3	190	2-20-88	5	5	2.49	26	22	1	1	112	77	39	31	6	48	119	.193	.226	.170	9.56	3.86
Zavala, Gabriel	R-R	6-3	180	5-14-87	2	5	4.70	32	0	0	1	44	39	26	23	3	29	36	.248	.230	.260	7.36	5.93

Fielding

Catcher	PCT	G	PO	A	E	DP	PB
Cordero	.968	64	452	57	17	5	14
Farrell	1.000	7	44	3	0	0	0
Forsythe	.986	67	523	50	8	4	8
Torres	1.000	5	28	2	0	0	1

First Base	PCT	G	PO	A	E	DP
Bonfe	.995	42	359	20	2	36
Butler	1.000	12	86	2	0	5
Farrell	1.000	1	1	0	0	0
Honeck	.991	75	624	55	6	59
Tejada	.000	1	0	0	0	0
Torres	.980	13	93	4	2	9

Second Base	PCT	G	PO	A	E	DP
Brown	.923	3	6	6	1	0
Butler	1.000	5	7	10	0	3
Gamboa	1.000	2	4	0	0	0
Harris	.935	6	11	18	2	5
Nieves	.988	77	128	188	4	48
Shields	1.000	9	17	28	0	7
Tejada	1.000	3	3	4	0	2
Tovar	.982	37	72	94	3	23

Third Base	PCT	G	PO	A	E	DP
Bonfe	.875	10	4	24	4	0
Lawley	1.000	2	1	7	0	0
Rodriguez	.878	127	91	226	44	19

Shortstop	PCT	G	PO	A	E	DP
Gamboa	1.000	1	0	3	0	0
Nieves	.950	7	5	14	1	4
Shields	.935	38	52	107	11	21
Tovar	.959	94	136	257	17	59

Outfield	PCT	G	PO	A	E	DP
Bonfe	.933	28	53	3	4	0
Butler	1.000	7	4	1	0	0
Ceciliani	.983	95	226	4	4	1
Fernandez	.942	113	248	13	16	2
Harris	.978	92	169	12	4	4
Lawley	.000	1	0	0	0	0
Rodriguez	.915	25	38	5	4	1
Vaughn	.983	63	111	5	2	0

BROOKLYN CYCLONES   SHORT-SEASON

NEW YORK-PENN LEAGUE

Batting	B-T	HT	WT	DOB	AVG	vLH	vRH	G	AB	R	H	2B	3B	HR	RBI	BB	HBP	SH	SF	SO	SB	CS	SLG	OBP
Brown, Brandon	R-R	6-1	180	7-28-87	.303	.326	.293	40	142	27	43	5	0	6	17	13	0	0	0	34	5	0	.465	.361
Brown, Dylan	R-R	6-3	210	10-21-87	.147	.077	.190	9	34	2	5	0	0	1	3	1	1	0	0	11	1	0	.235	.194
Brown, J.B.	L-R	6-1	220	4-30-89	.200	.333	.176	5	20	1	4	0	0	0	2	1	0	0	0	5	0	0	.200	.238
Carpenter, Tyler	R-R	5-10	190	7-7-88	.125	.000	.188	9	24	3	3	1	0	0	1	4	0	0	0	11	0	0	.167	.250
Clark, Jonathan	L-R	6-1	180	9-28-90	.143	.000	.156	12	35	2	5	0	0	0	1	4	1	0	0	14	0	0	.143	.250
Evans, Phillip	R-R	5-10	185	9-10-92	.125	1.000	.000	2	8	1	1	0	0	0	0	0	0	0	0	0	0	0	.125	.125
Frenzel, Cole	L-R	6-2	208	3-13-90	.238	.154	.254	43	160	23	38	4	1	1	20	17	4	0	3	35	1	0	.294	.321
Greene, Chase	R-R	5-11	180	4-22-90	.256	.233	.268	29	86	12	22	2	1	1	4	15	1	0	0	15	3	2	.337	.373
Harrison, Brian	R-R	6-2	180	12-15-88	.237	.237	.238	62	219	31	52	7	0	3	30	23	9	0	2	45	2	0	.311	.332
Leyva, Carlos	L-R	5-8	170	4-29-89	.206	.167	.214	10	34	5	7	0	0	0	2	2	3	0	0	3	2	0	.206	.308
Lucas, Richard	R-R	6-1	205	11-2-88	.300	.222	.326	69	250	46	75	19	3	6	41	31	6	0	4	66	2	2	.472	.385
Muno, Danny	B-R	5-11	175	2-9-89	.355	.310	.370	59	220	45	78	23	3	2	24	43	3	0	0	39	9	4	.514	.466
Pugh, Tillman	R-R	6-0	190	2-19-89	.344	.300	.364	13	32	8	11	1	1	1	3	6	0	0	0	12	4	1	.531	.447
Reyes, Jose	B-R	6-2	200	6-11-83	.333	.000	.333	1	3	1	1	1	0	0	0	0	0	0	0	0	0	0	.667	.333
Rivera, T.J.	R-R	6-1	190	10-27-88	.326	.417	.290	15	43	6	14	2	0	0	5	2	0	0	2	7	0	1	.372	.340
Rodriguez, Javier	R-R	6-2	165	4-4-90	.257	.317	.238	67	249	32	64	22	2	4	43	34	4	0	5	62	5	0	.410	.349
Stewart, Luke	L-R	6-4	205	2-29-88	.176	.000	.205	17	51	5	9	3	1	1	5	11	0	0	0	20	0	0	.333	.323
Taijeron, Travis	R-R	6-2	200	1-20-89	.299	.315	.293	56	194	24	58	13	5	9	44	22	7	0	2	64	0	0	.557	.387
Thurber, Charley	L-L	6-4	220	12-28-89	.271	.415	.239	58	221	26	60	14	1	0	26	19	1	0	2	55	1	1	.344	.329
Tijerina, Ismael	R-R	6-0	165	8-19-89	.223	.220	.224	46	157	24	35	7	0	0	9	18	1	0	0	24	3	3	.268	.307
Torres, Juan	R-R	6-1	180	10-7-88	.174	.000	.267	7	23	2	4	0	0	2	3	2	2	0	0	5	0	0	.435	.296
Valdez, Amauris	R-R	5-11	194	8-24-88	.133	.125	.136	22	75	4	10	0	0	1	4	2	1	0	1	16	0	0	.173	.165
Zapata, Nelfi	R-R	6-0	203	12-13-90	.269	.133	.308	20	67	7	18	3	0	2	14	1	0	0	2	9	0	0	.403	.271

Pitching	B-T	HT	WT	DOB	W	L	ERA	G	GS	CG	SV	IP	H	R	ER	HR	BB	SO	AVG	vLH	vRH	K/9	BB/9
Aldama, Eduardo	R-R	6-1	175	12-23-89	3	5	5.37	14	14	0	0	60	61	37	36	5	29	68	.261	.256	.264	10.14	4.33
Beaulac, Eric	R-R	6-5	190	11-13-86	1	0	2.35	5	0	0	0	8	7	5	2	0	4	7	.226	.263	.167	8.22	4.70
Camarena, Marcos	R-R	6-3	202	9-8-90	3	3	3.13	13	13	0	0	63	62	25	22	5	12	51	.251	.266	.235	7.25	1.71
Carnevale, Hunter	R-R	5-11	200	8-27-88	1	1	1.08	12	0	0	2	17	12	3	2	0	5	19	.211	.250	.189	10.26	2.70
Carr, Nick	R-R	6-1	195	4-19-87	0	0	2.35	6	0	0	1	8	7	2	2	0	5	5	.269	.500	.227	5.87	5.87
Chism, T.J.	L-L	5-10	190	8-9-88	3	0	1.14	27	0	0	6	32	21	6	4	0	7	30	.179	.163	.189	8.53	1.99
De La Torre, Jose	R-R	5-9	175	10-17-85	0	0	0.00	3	0	0	0	3	2	0	0	0	1	6	.182	.200	.167	18.00	3.00
Fontanez, Randy	R-R	6-1	205	5-18-89	1	2	2.82	12	7	0	0	38	39	16	12	2	10	26	.279	.279	.278	6.10	2.35
Gould, Jeremy	R-L	6-4	205	6-6-88	1	3	3.26	26	0	0	5	30	30	15	11	2	10	46	.252	.219	.264	13.65	2.97
Hauptman, Casey	R-R	6-4	220	1-1-89	1	2	3.38	18	0	0	0	29	36	16	11	1	8	19	.310	.288	.328	5.83	2.45
Hilliard, Chris	L-L	6-0	175	10-26-87	3	1	3.48	8	8	0	0	31	36	14	12	2	9	18	.288	.304	.283	5.23	2.61
Leathersich, Jack	R-L	5-11	205	7-14-90	0	0	0.71	9	0	0	1	13	6	1	1	0	3	26	.136	.111	.154	18.47	2.13
Leduc, Guillaume	R-R	6-4	192	7-28-87	0	0	5.06	5	0	0	0	5	8	3	3	0	0	4	.333	.500	.214	6.75	0.00
Mazzoni, Cory	R-R	6-1	190	10-19-89	1	0	0.00	6	1	0	0	6	5	0	0	0	2	10	.238	.143	.286	15.00	3.00
Mitchell, Bret	R-R	6-2	190	12-10-88	0	1	1.93	1	1	0	0	5	6	2	1	0	2	2	.316	.444	.200	3.86	3.86
Montero, Rafael	R-R	6-0	170	10-17-90	1	0	3.60	2	0	0	0	5	3	2	2	1	1	5	.176	.143	.200	9.00	1.80
Pill, Tyler	R-R	6-1	185	5-29-90	1	0	3.86	7	1	0	0	7	4	3	3	0	3	9	.174	.100	.231	11.57	3.86
Seng, Tyson	L-R	6-1	180	8-5-93	3	1	0.90	17	0	0	2	30	27	5	3	0	5	32	.252	.163	.313	9.60	1.50
Tapia, Domingo	R-R	6-4	186	12-16-91	1	0	0.00	1	1	0	0	6	5	0	0	0	0	6	.227	.333	.154	9.00	0.00

Pitching	B-T	HT	WT	DOB	W	L	ERA	G	GS	CG	SV	IP	H	R	ER	HR	BB	SO	AVG	vLH	vRH	K/9	BB/9
Tovar, Orlando	L-L	6-3	213	3-26-88	5	1	3.09	21	0	0	1	35	38	15	12	2	12	26	.281	.234	.307	6.69	3.09
Vazquez, Carlos	L-L	5-11	180	9-3-91	4	2	3.61	15	14	0	0	67	72	32	27	4	14	52	.276	.350	.243	6.95	1.87
Walters, Jeff	R-R	6-3	170	11-6-87	4	6	3.32	14	14	0	0	65	62	29	24	3	24	48	.251	.296	.212	6.65	3.32
Weldon, Todd	R-R	6-4	215	7-21-87	4	1	2.56	21	0	0	6	32	22	10	9	1	10	39	.193	.250	.152	11.08	2.84
Winnick, Steve	R-R	6-1	195	9-16-87	4	0	2.97	26	0	0	0	33	24	11	11	1	11	20	.203	.191	.211	5.40	2.97
Yanez, Ernesto	R-R	6-0	162	1-22-90	0	1	5.54	8	0	0	1	13	13	9	8	1	5	8	.255	.143	.297	5.54	3.46

Fielding

Catcher	PCT	G	PO	A	E	DP	PB
Carpenter	.980	9	45	4	1	0	1
Carrillo	.977	27	242	17	6	0	3
Torres	.971	4	32	2	1	0	2
Valdez	.987	22	136	14	2	3	5
Zapata	.979	19	127	12	3	0	4

First Base	PCT	G	PO	A	E	DP
Frenzel	.997	43	355	15	1	34
Harrison	.958	3	23	0	1	4
Lucas	.982	13	101	6	2	5
Stewart	1.000	17	125	6	0	12
Torres	1.000	1	12	0	0	0

Second Base	PCT	G	PO	A	E	DP
Brown	.960	28	53	67	5	15
Brown	1.000	4	10	11	0	3
Leyva	.973	10	17	19	1	7
Rivera	.981	13	23	29	1	8
Tijerina	.967	23	41	76	4	17

Third Base	PCT	G	PO	A	E	DP
Brown	.000	1	0	0	0	0
Harrison	.922	35	21	50	6	4
Lucas	.926	38	25	63	7	3
Muno	1.000	2	1	3	0	0

Shortstop	PCT	G	PO	A	E	DP
Brown	.857	1	2	4	1	1

	PCT	G	PO	A	E	DP
Evans	1.000	2	5	5	0	1
Muno	.952	52	75	141	11	31
Reyes	1.000	1	0	1	0	0
Tijerina	.962	24	30	72	4	14

Outfield	PCT	G	PO	A	E	DP
Brown	1.000	4	3	1	0	0
Brown	.933	8	14	0	1	0
Clark	1.000	6	19	0	0	0
Greene	.930	28	38	2	3	0
Pugh	.962	12	24	1	1	1
Rodriguez	.981	57	96	6	2	1
Taijeron	.978	54	86	4	2	1
Thurber	.992	58	115	3	1	1

KINGSPORT METS
ROOKIE

APPALACHIAN LEAGUE

Batting	B-T	HT	WT	DOB	AVG	vLH	vRH	G	AB	R	H	2B	3B	HR	RBI	BB	HBP	SH	SF	SO	SB	CS	SLG	OBP
Brown, Dylan	R-R	6-3	210	10-21-87	.268	.364	.244	33	56	10	15	5	1	1	5	4	4	0	0	20	0	1	.446	.359
Carpenter, Tyler	R-R	5-10	190	7-7-88	.273	.000	.375	5	11	1	3	0	0	1	1	0	0	0	0	3	0	0	.545	.273
Clark, Jonathan	L-R	6-1	180	9-28-90	.205	.176	.212	30	83	10	17	3	1	0	8	11	2	0	0	29	3	3	.265	.313
Concepcion, Julio	R-R	6-4	194	9-5-89	.299	.360	.283	60	241	32	72	15	3	2	33	6	3	0	3	46	4	1	.411	.320
De La Cruz, Yucarybert	R-R	6-0	160	10-23-90	.251	.222	.260	58	227	39	57	8	4	1	19	12	2	0	1	46	7	5	.335	.293
Evans, Phillip	R-R	5-10	185	9-10-92	.364	.000	.400	3	11	3	4	2	0	0	3	1	0	0	0	2	0	0	.545	.417
Gamboa, Juan Carlos	L-R	5-7	152	4-18-91	.256	.375	.243	19	78	12	20	4	3	0	10	6	0	0	2	15	4	2	.423	.302
Glenn, Jeff	R-R	6-3	185	9-22-91	.255	.290	.246	48	157	17	40	15	0	3	19	15	2	0	1	45	3	1	.408	.326
Lawley, Dustin	R-R	6-1	195	4-11-89	.284	.417	.250	57	232	37	66	17	3	9	43	14	3	0	6	48	5	5	.500	.325
Leyva, Carlos	L-R	5-8	170	4-29-89	.205	.125	.226	16	39	9	8	1	0	0	4	5	0	0	1	3	1	0	.231	.289
Maron, Cam	L-R	6-1	175	1-20-91	.318	.200	.348	58	201	38	64	8	1	3	24	38	3	0	0	34	4	2	.413	.434
Moreno, Nestor	B-R	5-11	195	6-21-88	.260	.304	.247	34	96	14	25	2	0	0	12	10	1	0	1	18	1	1	.281	.333
Nimmo, Brandon	L-R	6-3	185	3-27-93	.111	.000	.125	3	9	1	0	0	0	0	3	0	0	0	5	0	0	.111	.333
Pron, Greg	R-R	6-6	195	1-3-89	.318	.283	.327	58	211	42	67	14	1	7	34	24	2	0	2	53	6	1	.493	.389
Pugh, Tillman	R-R	6-0	190	2-19-89	.252	.212	.267	39	123	14	31	7	1	3	19	13	1	0	0	39	6	2	.398	.328
Rivera, T.J.	R-R	6-1	190	10-27-88	.290	.235	.303	27	93	17	27	6	0	1	14	8	1	0	0	16	3	1	.387	.353
Sanchez, Alexander	R-R	6-3	200	11-28-90	.254	.067	.318	13	59	7	15	3	0	2	10	1	0	0	0	4	1	0	.407	.267
Shepherd, Tant	R-R	6-0	200	8-1-89	.241	.227	.243	40	137	29	33	10	1	3	15	13	5	0	1	29	3	1	.394	.327
Stewart, Luke	L-R	6-4	205	2-29-88	.234	.190	.241	42	137	25	32	6	2	6	28	21	0	0	1	43	2	1	.438	.333
Tejada, Miguel	R-R	5-11		11-90	.160	.091	.179	14	50	8	8	0	0	4	8	1	1	0	0	20	0	0	.400	.192
Zurcher, Chad	R-R	6-1	170	8-25-88	.283	.222	.302	38	113	21	32	6	0	0	11	16	3	0	0	11	5	3	.336	.386

Pitching	B-T	HT	WT	DOB	W	L	ERA	G	GS	CG	SV	IP	H	R	ER	HR	BB	SO	AVG	vLH	vRH	K/9	BB/9
Birdwell, Peter	R-R	6-4	225	2-3-87	0	0	9.95	3	0	0	0	6	9	8	7	0	1	7	.321	.286	.333	9.95	1.42
Bradford, Chase	R-R	6-1	185	8-5-89	0	0	3.51	21	0	0	1	33	35	14	13	2	7	37	.271	.262	.276	9.99	1.89
Diaz, Miller	R-R	6-1	209	6-22-92	1	1	5.35	9	6	0	1	34	39	21	20	1	21	22	.300	.244	.329	5.88	5.61
Emmons, Dustin	R-R	6-1	205	9-26-89	2	0	3.78	17	1	0	0	33	39	20	14	2	10	21	.283	.286	.281	5.67	2.70
Frias, Darwin	R-R	6-0	192	2-18-92	1	2	2.25	20	0	0	2	24	20	9	6	2	12	23	.222	.300	.183	8.63	4.50
Kountis, Jonathan	R-R	6-3	220	3-15-88	0	0	15.19	5	0	0	0	5	10	10	9	1	2	5	.400	.500	.353	8.44	3.38
Lake, Robert	R-R	6-2	185	1-4-89	0	0	7.82	8	0	0	0	13	22	13	11	1	3	11	.379	.400	.368	7.82	2.13
Lugo, Jacob	R-R	6-4	185	11-17-89	5	2	3.66	11	10	0	0	47	42	27	19	5	20	44	.235	.227	.239	8.49	3.86
McDowall, Kenny	R-R	6-3	185	8-14-90	2	1	3.00	8	0	0	0	15	12	5	5	1	6	10	.211	.227	.200	6.00	3.60
Mitchell, Bret	R-R	6-2	190	12-10-88	5	1	2.95	7	7	0	0	40	24	15	13	2	12	38	.175	.211	.150	8.62	2.72
Montero, Rafael	R-R	6-0	170	10-17-90	2	1	4.24	4	4	0	0	17	17	8	8	2	6	9	.258	.333	.214	4.76	3.18
Morris, Akeel	R-R	6-1	170	11-14-92	3	2	3.86	11	11	1	0	51	30	28	22	5	38	61	.166	.169	.164	10.69	6.66
Picca, Mark	L-L	6-2	200	5-31-89	1	1	3.70	18	0	0	1	24	22	16	10	5	5	23	.237	.143	.277	8.51	1.85
Robles, Hansel	R-R	5-11	185	8-13-90	3	1	2.68	15	0	0	1	37	28	13	11	2	16	44	.211	.189	.219	10.22	3.89
Sheppard, Chad	R-R	6-4	210	11-25-88	2	1	5.31	15	0	0	0	20	17	13	12	2	14	29	.221	.333	.179	12.84	6.20
Tapia, Domingo	R-R	6-4	186	12-16-91	5	5	3.78	11	11	0	0	50	50	28	21	3	16	30	.258	.242	.265	5.40	2.88
Urbina, Juan	L-L	6-2	170	5-31-93	4	6	5.95	12	12	0	0	56	68	43	37	9	20	49	.300	.419	.272	7.88	3.21
Valenzuela, Brian	L-L	5-10	155	10-21-89	2	4	5.63	10	6	0	1	40	53	31	25	2	14	29	.314	.200	.361	6.53	3.15
West, Jared	R-R	6-1	180	7-30-88	0	1	1.96	19	0	0	10	23	21	11	5	0	6	21	.239	.267	.224	8.22	2.35
Yanez, Ernesto	R-R	6-0	162	1-22-90	1	0	0.40	11	0	0	2	22	16	2	1	1	4	14	.203	.231	.189	5.64	1.61
Ynoa, Gabriel	R-R	6-2	158	5-26-93	0	0	4.50	2	0	0	1	8	6	4	4	4	0	6	.207	.083	.294	6.75	0.00

Fielding

Catcher	PCT	G	PO	A	E	DP	PB
Carpenter	1.000	4	16	7	0	0	0
Glenn	.980	30	221	24	5	0	3
Maron	.976	30	220	20	6	4	2
Moreno	1.000	11	64	8	0	0	1

First Base	PCT	G	PO	A	E	DP
De La Cruz	.000	1	0	0	0	0
Moreno	.933	15	105	7	8	9
Sanchez	1.000	4	38	1	0	3
Shepherd	1.000	15	127	7	0	8
Stewart	.991	41	327	11	3	36

Second Base	PCT	G	PO	A	E	DP
De La Cruz	.942	27	49	64	7	16
Gamboa	.750	1	1	2	1	0
Leyva	.982	15	21	35	1	8
Rivera	.971	18	26	41	2	7
Zurcher	.988	16	29	53	1	14

Third Base	PCT	G	PO	A	E	DP
De La Cruz	1.000	2	0	1	0	0
Lawley	.904	26	20	65	9	10
Rivera	.900	7	0	9	1	0
Sanchez	.815	9	5	17	5	1
Shepherd	.887	23	10	37	6	1
Tejada	.762	8	5	11	5	0
Zurcher	.667	1	1	1	1	1

Shortstop	PCT	G	PO	A	E	DP
De La Cruz	.975	29	36	79	3	19
Evans	.833	3	3	7	2	1
Gamboa	.947	16	25	46	4	4

	PCT	G	PO	A	E	DP
Rivera	1.000	1	0	4	0	0
Tejada	.852	6	5	18	4	4
Zurcher	.919	14	24	33	5	9

Outfield	PCT	G	PO	A	E	DP
Brown	.963	29	25	1	1	0
Clark	1.000	28	48	1	0	1
Concepcion	.990	59	100	3	1	0
Lawley	.982	24	54	1	1	1
Nimmo	1.000	3	8	0	0	0
Pron	1.000	54	98	5	0	1
Pugh	.986	37	66	3	1	1

GCL METS   ROOKIE

GULF COAST LEAGUE

Batting	B-T	HT	WT	DOB	AVG	vLH	vRH	G	AB	R	H	2B	3B	HR	RBI	BB	HBP	SH	SF	SO	SB	CS	SLG	OBP
Alvarez, Hector	R-R	5-11	170	2-14-91	.229	.316	.203	27	83	6	19	5	0	0	6	12	0	0	0	13	0	0	.289	.326
Batista, Sneider	R-R	5-11	182	9-13-90	.240	.214	.248	47	171	19	41	9	1	0	17	13	2	0	0	19	3	3	.304	.301
Carpenter, Tyler	R-R	5-10	190	7-7-88	.278	.000	.385	6	18	1	5	0	0	0	2	0	0	0	0	3	0	0	.278	.278
De Leon, Jeyckol	R-R	6-2	185	7-25-90	.234	.048	.278	33	111	10	26	5	1	0	17	7	4	0	0	27	0	0	.297	.303
De Wolf, Thomas	L-R	6-3	198	12-22-89	.179	.375	.129	14	39	5	7	1	0	0	2	6	3	0	1	15	1	1	.205	.327
Evans, Phillip	R-R	5-10	185	9-10-92	.333	.333	.333	4	15	3	5	2	0	0	1	2	0	0	0	3	0	1	.467	.412
Gamboa, Juan Carlos	L-R	5-7	152	4-18-91	.340	.357	.333	17	53	10	18	4	0	0	3	9	0	0	0	15	0	0	.415	.435
Gomez, Gilbert	R-R	6-3	190	3-8-92	.248	.133	.279	38	141	16	35	9	0	2	22	13	3	0	1	39	4	2	.355	.323
Gronauer, Kai	R-R	6-1	215	11-28-86	.238	.250	.231	6	21	2	5	3	0	0	6	3	0	0	0	4	0	0	.381	.333
Hu, Chin-Lung	R-R	5-11	190	2-2-84	.184	.286	.167	13	49	8	9	0	0	0	1	8	0	0	0	7	2	1	.184	.298
Hutson, Ryan	R-R	6-2	195	9-19-88	.205	.143	.224	46	151	24	31	10	0	2	18	34	0	0	1	30	1	1	.311	.349
Leyva, Carlos	L-R	5-8	170	4-29-89	.333	.667	.250	4	15	2	5	2	1	0	7	2	0	0	0	3	0	0	.600	.412
Mercedes, Ariel	R-R	6-1	190	10-15-91	.240	.286	.228	30	100	9	24	3	1	0	9	7	2	0	0	26	2	1	.290	.303
Nimmo, Brandon	L-R	6-3	185	3-27-93	.241	.125	.286	7	29	5	7	0	0	2	4	3	0	0	0	9	0	0	.448	.313
Pina, Eudy	R-R	6-3	188	4-12-91	.223	.200	.228	52	202	30	45	7	3	2	16	12	6	0	1	60	4	4	.317	.285
Ponce, Dimas	R-R	5-11	140	1-22-91	.196	.273	.178	35	112	14	22	3	2	1	9	14	2	0	2	30	1	0	.286	.292
Rivero, Jorge	B-R	6-0	183	1-6-89	.232	.278	.221	26	95	9	22	1	1	1	7	13	0	0	0	12	0	6	.295	.324
Rohan, Eddie	R-R	6-0	205	8-15-88	.222	.125	.243	18	45	8	10	2	0	0	4	7	8	0	1	9	0	0	.267	.410
Ryan, Dusty	R-R	6-4	235	9-2-84	.222	.333	.200	6	18	4	4	3	0	0	2	5	0	0	0	8	0	0	.389	.391
Santana, Randoll	R-R	6-0	165	11-12-90	.215	.321	.177	32	107	10	23	5	1	2	11	6	3	0	0	22	3	2	.336	.276
Schafer, Justin	R-R	6-1	190	6-12-88	.226	.286	.208	8	31	2	7	2	0	0	3	2	0	0	1	5	0	1	.290	.265
Soto, Breiner	R-R	6-2	147	2-23-90	.221	.267	.213	26	95	11	21	4	0	0	9	10	0	0	0	16	2	3	.263	.295
Tabb, Brandon	R-R	5-10	185	12-8-90	.244	.333	.222	21	45	4	11	3	0	0	1	1	0	1	1	12	1	0	.311	.271
Tuschak, Joe	L-R	6-0	185	10-17-92	.204	.045	.244	32	108	15	22	2	0	0	12	15	4	0	2	34	2	0	.222	.318

Pitching	B-T	HT	WT	DOB	W	L	ERA	G	GS	CG	SV	IP	H	R	ER	HR	BB	SO	AVG	vLH	vRH	K/9	BB/9
Arias, Martires	R-R	6-7	207	11-10-90	0	1	7.71	11	0	0	0	14	19	14	12	0	13	12	.333	.345	.321	7.71	8.36
Baldonado, Alberto	L-L	6-2	160	2-1-93	2	2	3.71	11	6	0	0	44	41	20	18	2	17	26	.247	.333	.228	5.36	3.50
Bay, Shane	L-L	6-2	225	2-29-92	1	0	3.27	7	0	0	0	11	13	4	4	0	4	8	.289	.200	.314	6.55	3.27
Beaulac, Eric	R-R	6-5	190	11-13-86	0	1	16.88	2	2	0	0	3	2	5	5	0	4	1	.250	1.000	.143	3.38	13.50
Budgell, Matt	R-R	6-2	150	9-30-92	0	1	5.74	7	2	0	0	16	18	11	10	0	5	10	.316	.214	.349	5.74	2.87
Carr, Nick	R-R	6-1	195	4-19-87	0	0	0.00	2	2	0	0	2	2	0	0	0	1	2	.250	.200	.333	9.00	4.50
De La Torre, Jose	R-R	5-9	175	10-17-85	0	0	2.25	5	5	0	0	4	4	3	1	0	3	6	.250	.429	.111	13.50	6.75
Diaz, Miller	R-R	6-1	209	6-22-92	0	0	0.00	2	1	0	0	8	3	0	0	0	2	5	.107	.300	.000	5.63	2.25
Dotson, Zach	L-L	6-1	180	10-30-90	0	0	54.00	2	0	0	0	1	4	6	6	0	5	0	.667	.000	.667	0.00	45.00
Fulmer, Michael	R-R	6-3	200	3-15-93	0	1	10.13	4	3	0	0	5	9	7	6	0	4	10	.346	.625	.222	16.88	6.75
Gant, John	R-R	6-3	175	8-6-92	0	1	6.48	4	1	0	0	8	8	6	6	1	3	5	.286	.500	.227	5.40	3.24
Goeddel, Erik	R-R	6-3	185	12-20-88	0	0	1.50	3	3	0	0	6	5	1	1	0	2	7	.217	.154	.300	3.00	3.00
Gomez, Carlos	R-R	6-1	160	3-30-91	0	1	1.59	8	0	0	1	11	8	2	2	0	2	7	.205	.400	.083	5.56	1.59
Gsellman, Robert	R-R	6-4	200	7-18-93	0	1	4.15	7	1	0	1	13	15	6	6	1	2	8	.288	.211	.333	5.54	1.38
Hebert, Mike	R-R	6-3	180	8-11-90	3	0	2.65	4	1	0	0	17	14	5	5	1	2	15	.230	.158	.262	7.94	1.06
Hilario, Julian	R-R	6-1	190	8-17-90	1	3	2.81	11	5	0	0	42	41	19	13	0	15	34	.258	.259	.257	7.34	3.24
Hodge, Lachlan	L-L	6-2	185	2-3-89	0	0	27.00	1	1	0	0	1	3	3	3	1	2	0	.333	.000	.500	0.00	18.00
Lake, Robert	R-R	6-2	185	1-4-89	0	0	3.46	5	0	0	0	13	10	7	5	1	7	8	.208	.167	.233	5.54	4.85
Lara, Rainy	R-R	6-4	180	3-14-91	1	2	2.22	16	0	0	6	24	23	7	6	0	7	18	.261	.273	.255	6.66	2.59
McDowall, Kenny	R-R	6-3	185	8-14-90	1	0	0.00	4	0	0	0	5	0	0	0	0	3	1	.000	.000	.000	1.80	5.40
Merritt, Roy	L-L	6-0	170	9-22-85	0	0	5.14	7	2	0	0	7	9	8	4	0	2	4	.310	.286	.318	5.14	2.57
Missigman, Craig	R-R	6-4	175	8-5-93	1	1	5.48	9	3	0	1	23	17	16	14	1	6	18	.200	.130	.226	7.04	2.35
Monrroy, Isaac	L-L	5-10	155	10-9-90	3	3	3.86	19	0	0	2	23	20	11	10	0	4	29	.227	.225	.225	11.19	1.54
Montero, Rafael	R-R	6-0	170	10-17-90	1	2	1.45	7	4	0	1	31	28	11	5	0	6	32	.228	.186	.250	9.29	1.74
Pill, Tyler	R-R	6-1	185	5-29-90	0	0	4.50	2	0	0	0	2	3	1	1	0	0	1	.375	.400	.333	4.50	0.00
Ruff, Rich	R-R	6-3	215	12-14-88	0	1	5.54	12	0	0	1	13	12	8	8	1	8	8	.250	.231	.257	5.54	5.54
Sheppard, Chad	R-R	6-3	210	11-25-88	1	0	0.00	2	0	0	0	2	0	0	0	0	2	4	.000	.000	.000	18.00	9.00
Villasmil, Edioglis	R-R	6-2	164	4-10-92	3	2	4.38	10	6	0	0	37	30	18	18	1	22	30	.227	.304	.171	7.30	5.35
West, Jared	R-R	6-1	180	7-30-88	0	0	0.00	3	0	0	0	2	1	0	0	0	0	1	.125	.000	.250	0.00	0.00
Wheeler, Beck	R-R	6-3	215	12-13-88	0	0	0.87	14	0	0	2	21	8	3	2	1	9	20	.121	.154	.100	8.71	3.92
Ynoa, Gabriel	R-R	6-2	158	5-26-93	2	3	3.00	10	7	0	0	48	51	17	16	1	4	21	.277	.348	.235	3.94	0.75

Fielding

Catcher	PCT	G	PO	A	E	DP	PB
Alvarez	.977	21	118	12	3	1	2
Carpenter	1.000	5	42	5	0	0	1
De Leon	.984	17	113	14	2	3	4
Gronauer	1.000	4	20	2	0	0	0
Rohan	1.000	16	71	9	0	0	2
Ryan	.958	4	22	1	1	0	3

First Base	PCT	G	PO	A	E	DP
Alvarez	.900	2	8	1	1	1
De Leon	.990	14	97	6	1	8
Hutson	.983	45	384	24	7	33

Second Base	PCT	G	PO	A	E	DP
Batista	.977	10	21	21	1	5
Hu	.950	4	8	11	1	3
Leyva	1.000	3	6	12	0	1
Rivero	.968	24	54	66	4	16
Santana	.931	6	15	12	2	5
Tabb	.962	16	19	31	2	5

Third Base	PCT	G	PO	A	E	DP
Batista	.900	37	20	61	9	6
Ponce	.976	25	18	62	2	6

Shortstop	PCT	G	PO	A	E	DP
Evans	.923	4	5	19	2	2

	PCT	G	PO	A	E	DP
Gamboa	.919	15	14	20	3	3
Hu	.978	8	12	32	1	9
Ponce	.939	12	15	16	2	3
Santana	.969	26	41	84	4	13

Outfield	PCT	G	PO	A	E	DP
De Wolf	1.000	12	9	0	0	0
Gomez	1.000	36	82	2	0	1
Mercedes	.944	28	31	3	2	1
Nimmo	1.000	6	13	0	0	0
Pina	.982	44	100	8	2	3
Soto	.951	20	38	1	2	0
Tuschak	1.000	25	42	0	0	0

DSL METS 1

ROOKIE

DOMINICAN SUMMER LEAGUE

Batting	B-T	HT	WT	DOB	AVG	vLH	vRH	G	AB	R	H	2B	3B	HR	RBI	BB	HBP	SH	SF	SO	SB	CS	SLG	OBP
Abreu, Adrian	R-R	6-0	185	6-14-91	.203	.194	.207	44	123	18	25	4	2	2	15	23	3	0	1	26	5	5	.317	.340
Canelon, Leon	R-R	5-11	150	9-10-91	.260	.240	.267	37	100	18	26	2	0	0	4	10	1	0	1	22	3	2	.280	.330
2-team total (3 Mets2)					.274	—	—	40	106	19	29	2	0	0	5	11	1	0	1	22	4	2	.292	.345
Chavez, Anthony	R-R	6-2	185	11-8-92	.219	.152	.241	58	187	25	41	14	1	0	25	17	4	0	2	57	9	3	.305	.295
Cruzado, Victor	R-R	5-11	178	6-3-92	.203	.222	.195	18	59	4	12	2	0	1	8	12	0	0	0	21	0	3	.288	.338
2-team total (28 Mets2)					.250	—	—	46	152	19	38	10	1	1	23	28	1	0	5	39	6	5	.349	.360
De La Cruz, Maikis	R-R	5-11	174	9-6-90	.316	.394	.274	28	95	11	30	6	1	0	13	11	1	0	1	12	8	4	.400	.389
2-team total (45 Mets2)					.321	—	—	73	265	40	85	19	1	0	31	27	4	0	2	39	33	12	.400	.389
Decena, Joan	R-R	6-3	195	9-9-91	.264	.298	.252	60	212	26	56	13	1	3	30	12	6	0	0	54	8	4	.377	.322
Figuera, Jose	R-R	6-2	178	6-10-93	.216	.152	.241	41	116	11	25	7	1	0	15	10	4	0	0	36	7	5	.293	.300
Leal, Miguel	R-R	6-0	184	7-4-91	.275	.294	.270	54	149	16	41	4	0	0	18	18	1	0	3	17	2	1	.302	.351
Lupo, Vicente	R-R	6-0	180	11-26-93	.197	.125	.220	49	132	21	26	7	1	5	13	23	2	0	0	59	5	0	.379	.325
Machillanada, Alex	R-R	5-11	177	10-1-91	.206	.111	.240	13	34	1	7	0	0	0	3	5	0	0	1	6	1	1	.206	.300
2-team total (32 Mets2)					.272	—	—	45	92	11	25	4	0	0	5	17	1	0	2	14	6	3	.315	.384
Maracaro, Alvin	R-R	5-9	177	2-10-93	.298	.278	.306	41	121	19	36	4	2	0	13	7	5	0	1	25	10	3	.364	.358
Marmolejos, Merqui	R-R	5-11	184	10-10-93	.245	.179	.270	32	102	16	25	4	1	1	5	11	2	0	0	25	2	2	.333	.330
2-team total (26 Mets2)					.234	—	—	58	188	27	44	10	3	2	24	18	5	0	1	49	5	3	.351	.316
Moscote, Victor	R-R	6-1	155	5-10-94	.143	.167	.125	14	28	3	4	1	0	1	3	0	0	0	0	8	0	0	.286	.226
2-team total (15 Mets2)					.131	—	—	29	61	9	8	1	1	2	3	6	1	0	0	17	0	1	.279	.221
Ortega, Luis	R-R	5-10	187	4-5-93	.429	.333	.500	3	7	1	3	1	0	0	1	0	0	0	0	3	0	0	.571	.429
2-team total (38 Mets2)					.225	—	—	41	80	13	18	6	1	0	3	5	2	0	1	18	0	1	.325	.284
Peguero, Eris	L-R	6-1	175	11-29-89	.308	.299	.312	63	237	37	73	9	4	1	20	19	7	0	0	37	30	9	.392	.376
Perez, Pedro	B-R	6-1	190	8-31-94	.262	.297	.247	61	210	26	55	9	1	2	38	25	5	0	3	47	15	2	.343	.350
Rodriguez, Jean	B-R	6-0	157	9-3-92	.189	.000	.280	19	37	1	7	1	0	0	3	3	0	0	0	7	1	1	.216	.250
2-team total (36 Mets2)					.218	—	—	55	119	12	26	3	1	0	8	12	1	0	0	27	5	1	.261	.295
Ruiz, Yeixon	B-R	6-0	155	3-19-91	.245	.190	.265	65	233	44	57	4	3	0	14	25	8	0	2	29	20	5	.288	.336
Sierra, Johanny	R-R	6-4	180	1-3-92	.111	.100	.118	13	27	4	3	0	1	0	1	2	1	0	0	10	2	0	.185	.200
2-team total (20 Mets2)					.179	—	—	33	78	12	14	2	1	0	4	12	1	0	0	26	6	1	.231	.297
Weijgertse, Kevin	R-R	6-4	176	2-22-91	.218	.381	.118	23	55	5	12	2	0	0	6	11	3	0	1	7	1	1	.255	.371
2-team total (39 Mets2)					.240	—	—	62	146	18	35	2	0	0	17	40	3	0	2	27	2	5	.253	.408

Pitching	B-T	HT	WT	DOB	W	L	ERA	G	GS	CG	SV	IP	H	R	ER	HR	BB	SO	AVG	vLH	vRH	K/9	BB/9
Almonte, Gaby	R-R	6-0	185	8-15-92	1	0	3.38	4	0	0	1	8	4	4	3	0	5	5	.143	.250	.125	5.63	5.63
2-team total (9 Mets2)					1	4	3.00	13	9	1	1	48	42	24	16	0	19	34	—	—	—	6.38	3.56
Baez, Carlos	L-L	6-6	200	5-26-91	0	0	5.40	9	0	0	0	7	7	10	4	0	9	9	.250	.250	.250	12.15	12.15
2-team total (10 Mets2)					0	3	11.77	19	2	0	0	13	14	28	17	0	26	18	—	—	—	12.46	18.00
Bautista, Miguel	R-R	5-11	158	12-11-92	2	3	3.86	12	1	0	1	21	23	16	9	2	9	18	.277	.250	.288	7.71	3.86
2-team total (8 Mets2)					3	3	3.58	20	2	0	1	38	34	23	15	2	19	29	—	—	—	6.93	4.54
Caminero, Franly	L-L	5-11	175	12-3-92	1	2	2.73	13	6	0	0	33	26	17	10	2	23	25	.211	.200	.213	6.82	6.27
Chivilli, Cristian	R-R	6-2	200	2-19-91	1	3	4.42	19	7	0	2	39	32	21	19	1	25	28	.230	.250	.222	6.52	5.82
Estevez, Ramon	R-R	6-0	165	10-27-90	2	2	2.42	15	2	0	1	52	43	27	14	0	17	61	.223	.200	.232	10.56	2.94
Feliz, Gabriel	L-L	5-11	160	11-12-92	6	4	2.57	17	2	0	1	42	32	19	12	1	24	36	.205	.143	.211	7.71	5.14
German, Audry	R-R	5-11	163	8-16-92	0	0	2.59	8	3	0	0	24	14	7	7	0	17	16	.165	.111	.190	5.92	6.29
2-team total (8 Mets2)					2	1	4.79	16	3	0	0	41	31	24	22	0	23	27	—	—	—	5.88	5.01
Gonzalez, Marcos	R-R	6-0	175	10-22-92	1	1	9.45	3	0	0	0	7	13	7	7	2	2	4	.406	.500	.375	5.40	2.70
Martinez, Wimbert	R-R	6-2	175	12-18-93	1	1	3.48	17	1	0	1	31	19	17	12	1	16	26	.181	.139	.203	7.55	4.65
Mateo, Luis	R-R	6-3	185	3-22-90	6	1	2.00	13	13	0	0	63	44	17	14	1	5	80	.194	.157	.210	11.43	0.71
Montero, Rafael	R-R	6-0	170	10-17-90	1	1	1.00	4	4	0	0	18	7	2	2	1	2	20	.119	.143	.105	10.00	0.00
Nuez, Yoryi	R-R	6-1	153	2-13-93	1	3	4.60	6	2	0	1	16	12	10	8	0	13	19	.211	.222	.205	10.91	7.47
2-team total (10 Mets2)					5	6	3.78	16	6	0	1	50	38	33	21	0	40	48	—	—	—	8.64	7.20
Ortega, Flabio	R-R	6-1	170	8-19-90	1	0	1.47	10	0	0	8	18	17	4	3	0	7	27	.236	.045	.320	13.25	3.44
Perez, Andres E.	R-R	6-2	184	2-8-91	1	2	2.10	7	5	0	0	26	24	12	6	1	11	29	.242	.200	.257	10.17	3.86
2-team total (10 Mets2)					4	3	2.04	17	9	0	1	62	46	21	14	1	25	66	—	—	—	9.63	3.65
Ramos, Eduard	R-R	6-2	195	2-22-92	0	0	7.36	7	0	0	0	7	11	9	6	0	5	6	.344	.300	.364	7.36	6.14
2-team total (8 Mets2)					1	1	5.26	15	1	0	0	26	35	21	15	0	17	14	—	—	—	4.91	5.96
Rengel, Luis	R-R	6-2	165	3-19-90	2	3	1.48	15	9	0	0	55	53	21	9	0	11	52	.249	.311	.224	8.56	1.81

Pitching	B-T	HT	WT	DOB	W	L	ERA	G	GS	CG	SV	IP	H	R	ER	HR	BB	SO	AVG	vLH	vRH	K/9	BB/9
Reyes, Persio	R-R	6-2	151	3-17-93	2	1	0.00	5	4	0	0	24	15	3	0	0	3	23	.176	.056	.209	8.63	1.13
2-team total (11 Mets2)					4	2	1.95	16	14	0	0	74	52	21	16	2	21	58	—	—	—	7.05	2.55
Reyes, Ruben	R-R	6-4	178	9-22-90	1	2	7.02	13	3	0	0	17	16	18	13	0	22	16	.258	.235	.267	8.64	11.88
2-team total (9 Mets2)					1	3	6.62	22	6	0	2	34	33	31	25	2	36	43	—	—	—	11.38	9.53
Rodriguez, Miguel	R-R	6-3	186	8-27-91	0	1	4.26	10	0	0	0	19	26	16	9	1	9	7	.313	.333	.304	3.32	4.26
Rodriguez, Waldo	L-L	5-11	176	10-20-90	0	0	5.68	5	0	0	0	6	11	6	4	0	2	3	.423	.333	.435	4.26	2.84
Romero, Johel	R-R	6-3	220	4-16-91	1	2	3.15	13	0	0	2	20	14	10	7	1	12	15	.194	.313	.161	6.75	5.40
Rosario, Lenny	L-L	6-1	162	5-15-91	2	2	4.84	8	3	0	0	22	18	19	12	1	23	22	.217	.000	.234	8.87	9.27
2-team total (9 Mets2)					3	5	4.40	17	9	0	0	43	37	34	21	1	46	43	—	—	—	9.00	9.63
Valdez, Carlos	L-L	6-0	170	9-30-90	1	2	4.12	7	5	0	0	20	21	13	9	1	7	15	.266	.000	.276	6.86	3.20
2-team total (4 Mets2)					1	3	4.26	11	9	0	0	32	35	19	15	1	13	24	—	—	—	6.82	3.69

Fielding

Catcher	PCT	G	PO	A	E	DP	PB
Abreu	.991	40	274	39	3	3	10
Leal	.981	24	178	25	4	0	4
Machillanada	.991	13	93	12	1	0	4
Moscote	1.000	4	9	0	0	0	1
Ortega	1.000	1	5	6	0	0	0
Ruiz	1.000	1	6	1	0		1

First Base	PCT	G	PO	A	E	DP
Abreu	.944	3	16	1	1	1
Leal	.984	25	184	6	3	15
Marmolejos	.931	11	94	1	7	9
Moscote	.957	6	43	1	2	3
Perez	.973	12	105	5	3	11
Weijgertse	.994	23	157	12	1	7

Second Base	PCT	G	PO	A	E	DP
Canelon	1.000	1	1	2	0	0

(Second Base cont.)	.824	6	13	15	6	4
Cruzado	.824	6	13	15	6	4
Maracaro	.946	22	40	47	5	8
Rodriguez	1.000	6	8	6	0	0
Ruiz	.950	41	76	114	10	26

Third Base	PCT	G	PO	A	E	DP
Chavez	.886	20	10	29	5	1
Cruzado	1.000	1	0	3	0	0
Marmolejos	.900	5	0	9	1	0
Perez	.860	38	26	60	14	2
Rodriguez	.929	6	3	10	1	0
Ruiz	.854	15	9	26	6	2

Shortstop	PCT	G	PO	A	E	DP
Canelon	.929	34	54	103	12	20
Chavez	.877	41	42	93	19	14
Rodriguez	.800	3	3	5	2	0

Outfield	PCT	G	PO	A	E	DP
Cruzado	.000	1	0	0	0	0
De La Cruz	.957	27	38	6	2	1
Decena	.970	59	88	8	3	3
Figuera	.930	39	39	1	3	0
Lupo	.976	34	39	1	1	0
Maracaro	1.000	4	3	0	0	0
Marmolejos	.000	1	0	0	0	0
Peguero	.966	63	83	3	3	0
Ruiz	1.000	1	1	0	0	0
Sierra	1.000	7	8	1	0	0

DSL METS 2   ROOKIE

DOMINICAN SUMMER LEAGUE

Batting	B-T	HT	WT	DOB	AVG	vLH	vRH	G	AB	R	H	2B	3B	HR	RBI	BB	HBP	SH	SF	SO	SB	CS	SLG	OBP
Bernal, Michael	R-R	6-1	195	12-27-91	.274	.283	.272	67	215	44	59	7	5	11	36	37	7	0	1	68	17	11	.507	.396
Canelon, Leon	R-R	5-11	150	9-10-91	.500	.000	.500	3	6	1	3	0	0	1	1	0	0	0	0	1	0		.500	.571
2-team total (37 Mets1)					.274	—	—	40	106	19	29	2	0	0	5	11	1	0	1	22	4	2	.292	.345
Caraballo, Oswald	R-R	6-2	180	1-5-93	.225	.182	.234	49	129	15	29	2	1	0	11	18	2	0	1	12	5	5	.256	.327
Cruzado, Victor	B-R	5-11	178	6-3-92	.280	.212	.317	28	93	15	26	8	1	0	15	16	1	0	5	18	6	2	.387	.374
2-team total (18 Mets1)					.250	—	—	46	152	19	38	10	1	1	23	28	1	0	5	39	6	5	.349	.360
De La Cruz, Maikis	R-R	5-11	174	9-6-90	.324	.387	.309	45	170	29	55	13	0	0	18	16	3	0	1	27	25	8	.400	.389
2-team total (28 Mets1)					.321	—	—	73	265	40	85	19	1	0	31	27	4	0	2	39	33	12	.400	.389
Hato, Bjorn	R-R	6-1	160	6-26-91	.200	.278	.177	38	80	18	16	3	0	0	9	21	2	0	0	16	7	6	.238	.379
Hilario, Manuel	R-R	5-10	172	2-10-92	.220	.238	.215	62	177	27	39	10	4	2	28	37	15	0	3	38	22	8	.356	.392
Liriano, Victor	R-R	6-4	193	5-23-93	.189	.231	.175	32	106	14	20	2	0	1	7	7	5	0	0	31	5	3	.236	.271
Machillanada, Alex	R-R	5-11	177	10-1-91	.310	.556	.265	32	58	10	18	4	0	0	2	12	1	0	1	8	5	2	.379	.431
2-team total (13 Mets1)					.272	—	—	45	92	11	25	4	0	0	5	17	1	0	2	14	6	3	.315	.384
Marmolejos, Merqui	R-R	5-11	184	10-10-93	.221	.222	.220	26	86	11	19	6	2	1	19	7	3	0	1	24	3	1	.372	.299
2-team total (32 Mets1)					.234	—	—	58	188	27	44	10	3	2	24	18	5	0	1	49	5	3	.351	.316
Moscote, Victor	R-R	6-1	155	5-10-94	.121	.286	.077	15	33	6	4	0	1	1	2	3	1	0	0	9	0	1	.273	.216
2-team total (14 Mets1)					.131	—	—	29	61	9	8	1	1	2	3	6	1	0	0	17	0	1	.279	.221
Ortega, Luis	R-R	5-10	187	4-5-93	.205	.083	.230	38	73	12	15	5	1	0	2	5	2	0	1	15	0	1	.301	.272
2-team total (3 Mets1)					.225	—	—	41	80	13	18	6	1	0	3	5	2	0	1	18	0	1	.325	.284
Ramos, Natanael	R-R	5-10	170	6-19-93	.148	.267	.109	28	61	10	9	4	0	0	4	7	3	0	0	8	0	1	.213	.268
Reyes, Alfredo	R-R	6-2	160	10-4-93	.191	.200	.190	52	188	25	36	2	1	1	19	26	3	0	2	44	6	6	.229	.297
Reyes, Mauricio	B-R	5-10	160	6-1-92	.130	.200	.111	37	69	11	9	3	0	0	1	10	0	0	1	19	3	4	.174	.238
Rivero, Jorge	B-R	6-0	183	1-6-89	.292	.214	.315	37	120	17	35	8	6	0	17	12	3	0	2	14	10	3	.458	.365
Rodriguez, Jean	B-R	6-0	157	9-3-92	.232	.083	.257	36	82	11	19	2	1	0	5	9	1	0	0	13	6	4	.280	.315
2-team total (19 Mets1)					.218	—	—	55	119	12	26	3	1	0	8	12	1	0	0	20	7	5	.261	.295
Rondon, Pedro	R-R	6-1	180	4-30-92	.235	.394	.174	39	119	16	28	2	0	0	15	22	2	0	2	32	9	4	.252	.359
Sanchez, Elvis	R-R	6-2	190	2-8-94	.157	.167	.154	70	198	26	31	4	0	3	20	62	6	0	4	73	5	3	.222	.367
Sierra, Johanny	R-R	6-4	160	1-3-92	.216	.250	.205	20	51	8	11	2	0	0	3	10	0	0	0	16	4	1	.255	.344
2-team total (13 Mets1)					.179	—	—	33	78	12	14	2	1	0	4	12	1	0	0	26	6	1	.231	.297
Weijgertse, Kevin	R-R	6-4	176	2-22-91	.253	.158	.278	39	91	13	23	0	0	0	11	29	0	0	1	20	1	4	.253	.430
2-team total (23 Mets1)					.240	—	—	62	146	18	35	4	0	0	14	40	3	0	2	27	2	5	.253	.408

Pitching	B-T	HT	WT	DOB	W	L	ERA	G	GS	CG	SV	IP	H	R	ER	HR	BB	SO	AVG	vLH	vRH	K/9	BB/9
Almonte, Gaby	R-R	6-0	185	8-15-92	0	4	2.93	9	9	1	0	40	38	20	13	0	14	29	.244	.216	.252	6.53	3.15
2-team total (4 Mets1)					1	4	3.00	13	9	1	1	48	42	24	16	0	19	34	—	—	—	6.38	3.56
Baez, Carlos	L-L	6-6	200	5-26-91	0	3	18.47	10	2	0	0	6	7	18	13	0	17	9	.280	1.000	.217	12.79	24.16
2-team total (9 Mets1)					0	3	11.77	19	2	0	0	13	14	28	17	0	26	18	—	—	—	12.46	18.00
Bautista, Miguel	R-R	5-11	158	12-11-92	1	0	3.24	8	1	0	0	17	11	7	6	0	10	11	.180	.222	.173	5.94	5.40
2-team total (12 Mets1)					3	3	3.58	20	2	0	1	38	34	23	15	2	19	29	—	—	—	6.93	4.54
Blanco, Rolgenis	R-R	6-0	160	2-7-93	0	0	8.38	8	0	0	0	10	15	11	9	1	9	3	.341	.000	.375	2.79	8.38

Pitching

Pitching	B-T	HT	WT	DOB	W	L	ERA	G	GS	CG	SV	IP	H	R	ER	HR	BB	SO	AVG	vLH	vRH	K/9	BB/9
Brochero, Doxon	R-R	6-2	170	3-7-94	0	0	45.00	3	0	0	0	1	1	5	5	0	6	1	.250	.000	.333	9.00	54.00
Canelon, Kevin	L-L	6-1	175	1-16-94	1	2	7.08	11	1	0	0	20	25	19	16	0	16	24	.309	.400	.303	10.62	7.08
Celas, Jose	R-R	6-1	180	1-12-91	0	0	40.50	1	1	0	0	1	1	3	3	0	2	0	.333	.000	.333	0.00	27.00
Coronado, Carlos	R-R	5-11	176	9-26-91	1	2	2.96	15	0	0	4	24	28	17	8	2	8	16	.283	.208	.307	5.92	2.96
Encarnacion, Jose	R-R	6-4	190	10-11-90	1	1	6.50	8	3	0	0	18	20	17	13	1	22	19	.274	.350	.245	9.50	11.00
Fana, Jose	R-R	6-2	193	10-19-90	3	4	4.36	22	6	0	2	54	58	34	26	1	20	27	.269	.316	.258	4.53	3.35
German, Audry	R-R	5-11	163	8-16-92	2	1	7.94	8	0	0	0	17	17	17	15	0	6	11	.274	.000	.293	5.82	3.18
2-team total (8 Mets1)					2	1	4.79	16	3	0	0	41	31	24	22	0	23	27	—	—	—	5.88	5.01
Lebron, Hector	L-L	6-1	190	4-19-92	1	4	7.71	23	2	0	1	37	38	42	32	1	36	34	.268	.333	.266	8.20	8.68
Nuez, Yoryi	R-R	6-1	153	2-13-93	4	3	3.41	10	4	0	0	34	26	23	13	0	27	29	.210	.219	.207	7.60	7.08
2-team total (6 Mets1)					5	6	3.78	16	6	0	1	50	38	33	21	0	40	48	—	—	—	8.64	7.20
Perez, Andres E.	R-R	6-2	184	2-8-91	3	1	2.00	10	4	0	1	36	22	9	8	0	14	37	.171	.214	.158	9.25	3.50
2-team total (7 Mets1)					4	3	2.04	17	9	0	1	62	46	21	14	1	25	66	—	—	—	9.63	3.65
Ramos, Eduard	R-R	6-2	195	2-22-92	1	1	4.42	8	3	0	0	18	24	14	9	0	12	8	.333	.385	.322	3.93	5.89
2-team total (7 Mets1)					1	1	5.26	15	3	0	0	26	35	23	15	0	17	14	—	—	—	4.91	5.96
Reyes, Persio	R-R	6-2	151	3-17-93	2	1	2.88	11	0	0	0	50	37	18	16	2	18	35	.214	.184	.222	6.30	3.24
2-team total (5 Mets1)					4	2	1.95	16	14	0	0	74	52	21	16	2	21	58	—	—	—	7.05	2.55
Reyes, Ruben	R-R	6-4	178	9-22-90	0	1	6.23	9	3	0	2	17	17	13	12	2	14	27	.258	.333	.235	14.02	7.27
2-team total (13 Mets1)					1	3	6.62	22	6	0	2	34	33	31	25	2	36	43	—	—	—	11.38	9.53
Rodriguez, Edgar	R-R	6-2	155	8-31-94	0	1	29.70	4	0	0	0	3	10	11		0	3	4	.500	.250	.563	10.80	8.10
Rodriguez, Euner	R-R	6-0	170	2-10-94	2	3	7.09	27	1	0	1	33	36	31	26	0	34	21	.281	.226	.299	5.73	9.27
Rosario, Lenny	L-L	6-1	162	5-15-91	1	3	3.92	9	6	0	0	21	19	15	9	0	23	21	.264	.167	.273	9.15	10.02
2-team total (8 Mets1)					3	5	4.40	17	9	0	0	43	37	34	21	1	46	43	—	—	—	9.00	9.63
Santiago, Paul	R-R	5-11	165	1-12-92	0	1	7.03	11	3	0	1	24	32	32	19	1	27	23	.308	.333	.301	8.51	9.99
Solano, Yoseibis	R-R	6-1	190	4-22-93	0	1	9.00	2	0	0	0	1	0	1	1	0	5	0	.000	.000	.000	0.00	45.00
Soriano, Cristian	L-L	6-3	184	9-5-91	3	3	6.81	21	2	0	0	36	37	31	27	1	21	34	.261	.182	.267	8.58	5.30
Valdez, Carlos	L-L	6-0	170	9-30-90	1	0	4.50	4	4	0	0	12	14	6	6	0	6	9	.318	.286	.324	6.75	4.50
2-team total (7 Mets1)					1	3	4.26	11	4	0	0	32	35	19	15	1	13	24	—	—	—	6.82	3.69

Fielding

Catcher	PCT	G	PO	A	E	DP	PB
Hilario	.969	20	138	19	5	1	6
Machillanada	.981	29	129	26	3	0	5
Moscote	.982	10	52	4	1	1	3
Ortega	.988	21	69	15	1	0	3
Ramos	.980	27	122	25	3	1	4

First Base	PCT	G	PO	A	E	DP
Barrera	.333	1	1	0	2	0
Cruzado	1.000	1	2	1	0	0
Hato	.900	5	7	2	1	1
Hilario	.991	15	100	9	1	4
Liriano	1.000	2	3	0	0	1
Machillanada	.875	1	6	1	1	1
Marmolejos	.980	7	48	2	1	4
Moscote	.962	5	24	1	1	0
Ortega	.926	7	24	1	2	1
Ramos	1.000	1	1	0	0	0
Rivero	1.000	1	1	0	0	0
Rodriguez	1.000	1	2	0	0	0
Sanchez	.973	14	72	1	2	2
Weijgertse	.993	39	267	15	2	18

Second Base	PCT	G	PO	A	E	DP
Canelon	1.000	1	5	7	0	1
Cruzado	1.000	4	6	3	0	1
Hato	.933	9	4	10	1	1
Hilario	.857	2	2	4	1	0
Marmolejos	.933	7	5	9	1	1
Moscote	1.000	1	1	1	0	0
Ortega	1.000	2	2	2	0	0
Reyes	.891	19	22	19	5	5
Rivero	.963	22	37	40	3	5
Rodriguez	.951	17	33	25	3	6
Rondon	.919	12	12	22	3	2

Third Base	PCT	G	PO	A	E	DP
Hato	1.000	2	4	2	0	0
Marmolejos	.818	10	3	15	4	0
Ortega	.833	2	2	3	1	0
Reyes	.750	2	0	3	1	0
Rivero	1.000	5	6	4	0	0
Rodriguez	.875	10	4	10	2	0
Sanchez	.860	58	36	75	18	2

Shortstop	PCT	G	PO	A	E	DP
Canelon	1.000	1	0	1	0	0
Hato	.905	20	19	38	6	5
Marmolejos	.000	1	0	0	0	0
Ortega	.000	1	0	0	0	0
Reyes	.901	52	80	138	24	14
Reyes	1.000	5	1	2	0	0
Rivero	.938	7	11	19	2	3
Rondon	1.000	1	3	4	0	2

Outfield	PCT	G	PO	A	E	DP
Bernal	.927	61	96	5	8	1
Caraballo	.944	44	64	3	4	1
Cruzado	.984	24	55	5	1	1
De La Cruz	.978	45	85	6	2	0
Hato	.000	2	0	0	0	0
Hilario	.900	10	15	3	2	1
Liriano	.930	30	39	1	3	0
Ortega	1.000	2	1	0	0	0
Rondon	1.000	8	6	1	0	1
Sierra	1.000	19	26	1	0	0

New York Yankees

SEASON IN A SENTENCE: The Yankees ranked second in the majors in runs and ranked first in walks and home runs, powering their way past the Rays and Red Sox to win the American League East, but their aim is always higher and they fell short in a five-game Division Series loss to the Tigers.

HIGH POINT: After the Red Sox had dominated the season series to that point, the Yankees beat them 4-2 on Sept. 1 at Fenway Park, and won again the next day while the Red Sox lost to take over first place in the division. New York won 12 of its next 19 games, then rallied with a two-run pinch-hit single by catcher/DH Jorge Posada to beat the Rays 4-2 at Yankee Stadium and clinch the division as the Red Sox ultimately slid out of the playoffs. C.C. Sabathia anchored the pitching staff, going 19-8, 3.00, while Curtis Granderson was an MVP candidate.

LOW POINT: For the second straight season, the Yankees' season ended with Alex Rodriguez striking out to end a playoff series. Rodriguez still has six years and more than $140 million left on his contract and played just 99 games in 2011, ending a streak of 13 consecutive seasons of at least 30 home runs and at least 100 RBIs.

NOTABLE ROOKIES: After failing to sign Cliff Lee in the offseason, the Yankees turned to veteran pitchers Bartolo Colon and Freddy Garcia but got more mileage out of 24-year-old Ivan Nova. He went 16-4, 3.70, leading all rookies in pitching wins. Eduardo Nunez proved to be a useful utilityman, and Jesus Montero flashed his potential with a strong September.

KEY TRANSACTIONS: Colon and Garcia were effective, cheap pickups inthe offseason, making 51 starts between them, but Colon wore down and wasn't available in the playoffs. Cory Wade, another low-cost pickup who started the year in the Rays system, wound up winning six games out of the bullpen and pitched 40 effective innings. The Yankees ended up not making any major deadline moves, surprising given the state of their pitching behind Sabathia.

DOWN ON THE FARM: Triple-A Scranton/Wilkes-Barre failed the make the playoffs for the first time as a Yankees affiliate, and Double-A Trenton also didn't reach the playoffs. But short-season Staten Island and the Rookie-level Gulf Coast League club both won league championships.

OPENING DAY PAYROLL: $202,689,028 (1st)

PLAYERS OF THE YEAR

MAJOR LEAGUE	MINOR LEAGUE
Curtis Granderson	**Jesus Montero**
of	c
.262/.364/.552	(Triple-A)
41 HR, 25 SB	.288/.348/.467
Led AL in R, RBIs	18 HR, 19 2B

ORGANIZATION LEADERS

BATTING   *Minimum 250 PA

MAJORS

* AVG	Robinson Cano	.302
* OPS	Curtis Granderson	.916
HR	Curtis Granderson	41
RBI	Curtis Granderson	119

MINORS

* AVG	Walter Ibarra, Tampa	.297
* OBP	Kyle Roller, Charleston/Tampa	.371
* SLG	Jorge Vazquez, Scranton	.516
R	Abraham Almonte, Tampa	92
H	Robert Lyerly, Tampa/Trenton	149
TB	Jorge Vazquez, Scranton	235
2B	Corban Joseph, Trenton	38
3B	Abraham Almonte, Tampa	11
HR	Jorge Vazquez, Scranton	32
RBI	Jorge Vazquez, Scranton	93
BB	Ramon Flores, Charleston	61
SO	Cody Johnson, Trenton/Tampa	194
SB	Raymond Kruml, Trenton/Scranton	40

PITCHING   #Minimum 75 IP

MAJORS

W	C.C. Sabathia	19
# ERA	C.C. Sabathia	3.00
SO	C.C. Sabathia	230
SV	Mariano Rivera	44

MINORS

W	D.J. Mitchell, Scranton	13
L	Shane Greene, Charleston	14
# ERA	David Phelps, GCL/Scranton	2.99
G	Pat Venditte, Trenton	51
GS	Three tied at	27
GS	Shane Greene, Charleston	27
GS	Adam Warren, Scranton	27
SV	Kevin Whelan, Scranton	23
IP	D.J. Mitchell, Scranton	161.1
BB	Andrew Brackman, Scranton	75
SO	Dellin Betances, Trenton/Scranton	142
#AVG	Dellin Betances, Trenton/Scranton	.217

2011 PERFORMANCE

General Manager: Brian Cashman. **Farm Director:** Mark Newman. **Scouting Director:** Damon Oppenheimer.

Class	Team	League	W	L	PCT	Finish	Manager(s)
Majors	New York Yankees	American	97	65	.599	1st (14)	Joe Girardi
Triple-A	Scranton/WB Yankees	International	73	69	.514	7th (14)	Dave Miley
Double-A	Trenton Thunder	Eastern	68	73	.482	8th (12)	Tony Franklin
High A	Tampa Yankees	Florida State	74	64	.536	5th (12)	Luis Sojo
Low A	Charleston RiverDogs	South Atlantic	55	85	.393	t-13th (14)	Aaron Ledesma
Short-season	Staten Island Yankees	New York-Penn	45	28	.616	1st (14)	Tom Slater
Rookie	GCL Yankees	Gulf Coast	37	23	.617	3rd (15)	Carlos Mendoza
Overall 2011 Minor League Record			352	342	.507	13th (30)	

ORGANIZATION STATISTICS

NEW YORK YANKEES

AMERICAN LEAGUE

Batting	B-T	HT	WT	DOB	AVG	vLH	vRH	G	AB	R	H	2B	3B	HR	RBI	BB	HBP	SH	SF	SO	SB	CS	SLG	OBP
Cano, Robinson	L-R	6-0	205	10-22-82	.302	.314	.296	159	623	104	188	46	7	28	118	38	12	0	8	96	8	2	.533	.349
Cervelli, Francisco	R-R	6-1	210	3-6-86	.266	.276	.263	43	124	17	33	4	0	4	22	9	2	0	1	29	4	1	.395	.324
Chavez, Eric	L-R	6-1	210	12-7-77	.263	.304	.255	58	160	16	42	7	1	2	26	14	0	0	1	34	0	0	.356	.320
Dickerson, Chris	L-L	6-3	230	4-10-82	.260	.333	.237	60	50	9	13	2	0	1	7	2	1	0	1	17	4	0	.360	.296
Gardner, Brett	L-L	5-10	185	8-24-83	.259	.233	.265	159	510	87	132	19	8	7	36	60	8	2	2	93	49	13	.369	.345
Golson, Greg	R-R	6-0	190	9-17-85	.182	.167	.200	9	11	1	2	0	0	0	0	1	0	0	0	2	1	0	.182	.250
Granderson, Curtis	L-R	6-1	185	3-16-81	.262	.272	.258	156	583	136	153	26	10	41	119	85	12	0	7	169	25	10	.552	.364
Jeter, Derek	R-R	6-3	195	6-26-74	.297	.349	.277	131	546	84	162	24	4	6	61	46	6	0	5	81	16	6	.388	.355
Jones, Andruw	R-R	6-1	230	4-23-77	.247	.286	.172	77	190	27	47	8	0	13	33	29	3	0	0	62	0	0	.495	.356
Laird, Brandon	R-R	6-1	215	9-11-87	.190	.273	.100	11	21	3	4	0	0	1	3	0	0	0	4	0	0	.190	.292
Martin, Russell	R-R	5-10	230	2-15-83	.237	.211	.248	125	417	57	99	17	0	18	65	50	5	0	3	81	8	2	.408	.324
Molina, Gustavo	R-R	6-1	245	2-24-82	.167	.000	.333	3	6	0	1	1	0	0	0	0	0	0	0	0	0	0	.333	.167
Montero, Jesus	R-R	6-3	235	11-28-89	.328	.500	.216	18	61	9	20	4	0	4	12	7	1	0	0	17	0	0	.590	.406
Nunez, Eduardo	R-R	6-0	155	6-15-87	.265	.277	.259	112	309	38	82	18	2	5	30	22	0	0	1	37	22	6	.385	.313
Pena, Ramiro	B-R	5-11	175	7-18-85	.100	.071	.115	23	40	5	4	0	0	1	4	2	1	0	1	11	0	0	.175	.159
Posada, Jorge	B-R	6-2	215	8-17-71	.235	.092	.269	115	344	34	81	14	0	14	44	39	2	0	2	76	0	2	.398	.315
Rodriguez, Alex	R-R	6-3	230	7-27-75	.276	.277	.276	99	373	67	103	21	0	16	62	47	5	0	3	80	4	1	.461	.362
Romine, Austin	R-R	6-0	220	11-22-88	.158	.000	.188	9	19	2	3	0	0	0	1	0	0	0	0	5	0	0	.158	.200
Swisher, Nick	B-L	5-11	210	11-25-80	.260	.327	.232	150	526	81	137	30	0	23	85	95	5	0	8	125	2	2	.449	.374
Teixeira, Mark	B-R	6-3	220	4-11-80	.248	.302	.223	156	589	90	146	26	1	39	111	76	11	0	8	110	4	1	.494	.341

Pitching	B-T	HT	WT	DOB	W	L	ERA	G	GS	CG	SV	IP	H	R	ER	HR	BB	SO	AVG	vLH	vRH	K/9	BB/9
Ayala, Luis	R-R	6-2	190	1-12-78	2	2	2.09	52	0	0	0	56	51	17	13	5	20	39	.256	.250	.263	6.27	3.21
Betances, Dellin	R-R	6-8	260	3-23-88	0	0	6.75	2	1	0	0	3	1	2	2	0	6	2	.125	.167	.000	6.75	20.25
Brackman, Andrew	R-R	6-10	230	12-4-85	0	0	0.00	3	0	0	0	2	1	0	0	0	3	0	.100	.000	.143	0.00	11.57
Burnett, A.J.	R-R	6-4	230	1-3-77	11	11	5.15	33	32	0	0	190	190	115	109	31	83	173	.260	.256	.264	8.18	3.92
Carlyle, Buddy	L-R	6-3	210	12-21-77	0	1	4.70	8	0	0	0	8	5	4	4	1	7	9	.185	.000	.263	10.57	8.22
Chamberlain, Joba	R-R	6-2	240	9-23-85	2	0	2.83	27	0	0	0	29	23	10	9	3	7	24	.228	.250	.208	7.53	2.20
Colon, Bartolo	R-R	5-11	265	5-24-73	8	10	4.00	29	26	1	0	164	172	85	73	21	40	135	.267	.297	.238	7.39	2.19
Garcia, Freddy	R-R	6-4	250	10-6-76	12	8	3.62	26	25	0	0	147	152	63	59	16	45	96	.268	.284	.255	5.89	2.76
Garrison, Steve	B-L	6-1	195	9-12-86	0	0	0.00	1	0	0	0	1	0	0	0	0	0	0	.000	.000	.000	0.00	0.00
Gordon, Brian	L-R	6-0	190	8-16-78	0	1	5.23	2	2	0	0	10	12	6	6	3	3	4	.300	.231	.333	3.48	2.61
Hughes, Phil	R-R	6-5	240	6-24-86	5	5	5.79	17	14	1	0	75	84	48	48	9	27	47	.283	.312	.234	5.67	3.25
Kontos, George	R-R	6-3	215	6-12-85	0	0	3.00	7	0	0	0	6	4	2	2	1	3	6	.190	.200	.188	9.00	4.50
Laffey, Aaron	L-L	6-0	200	4-15-85	2	1	3.38	11	0	0	0	11	13	4	4	0	5	6	.310	.222	.467	5.06	4.22
2-team total (36 Seattle)					3	2	3.88	47	0	0	0	53	67	24	23	7	21	30	—	—	—	5.06	3.54
Logan, Boone	R-L	6-5	225	8-13-84	5	3	3.46	64	0	0	0	42	43	20	16	4	13	46	.261	.260	.262	9.94	2.81
Marquez, Jeff	R-R	6-2	190	8-10-84	0	0	2.25	3	0	0	0	4	5	1	1	0	0	2	.278	.125	.400	4.50	0.00
Mitre, Sergio	R-R	6-3	225	2-16-81	0	0	11.81	4	0	0	0	5	9	9	7	0	4	2	.375	.556	.267	3.38	6.75
Noesi, Hector	R-R	6-3	200	1-26-87	2	2	4.47	30	2	0	0	56	63	29	28	6	22	45	.286	.302	.272	7.19	3.51
Nova, Ivan	R-R	6-4	225	1-12-87	16	4	3.70	28	27	0	0	165	163	74	68	13	57	98	.258	.240	.275	5.33	3.10
Pendleton, Lance	L-R	6-3	195	9-10-83	0	0	3.21	11	0	0	0	14	10	5	5	2	10	8	.200	.273	.143	5.14	6.43
Proctor, Scott	R-R	6-1	195	1-2-77	0	3	9.00	8	0	0	0	11	19	13	11	6	12	11	.388	.304	.462	9.00	9.82
Rivera, Mariano	R-R	6-2	185	11-29-69	1	2	1.91	64	0	0	44	61	47	13	13	3	8	60	.215	.240	.191	8.80	1.17
Robertson, David	R-R	5-11	195	4-9-85	4	0	1.08	70	0	0	1	67	40	9	8	1	35	100	.170	.156	.186	13.50	4.73
Sabathia, C.C.	L-L	6-7	290	7-21-80	19	8	3.00	33	33	3	0	237	230	87	79	17	61	230	.255	.207	.273	8.72	2.31
Sanit, Amauri	R-R	5-8	205	7-4-79	0	0	12.86	4	0	0	0	7	12	10	10	0	3	4	.353	.500	.188	5.14	3.86
Soriano, Rafael	R-R	6-1	230	12-19-79	2	3	4.12	42	0	0	2	39	33	18	18	4	18	36	.229	.302	.173	8.24	4.12
Valdes, Raul	L-L	5-11	190	11-27-77	0	0	2.70	6	0	0	0	7	8	2	2	1	2	8	.308	.294	.333	10.80	2.70
Wade, Cory	R-R	6-2	190	5-28-83	6	1	2.04	40	0	0	0	40	33	10	9	5	8	30	.221	.246	.202	6.81	1.82
Whelan, Kevin	R-R	6-0	200	1-8-84	0	0	5.40	2	0	0	0	2	0	1	1	0	5	1	.000	.000	.000	5.40	27.00

Fielding

Catcher	PCT	G	PO	A	E	DP	PB								
Cervelli	.980	41	278	18	6	1	3	Martin	.990	125	866	96	10	8	4
								Molina	1.000	3	9	1	0	0	0
								Montero	1.000	3	12	1	0	0	0
								Posada	1.000	1	7	2	0	0	0

Romine	.980	8	46	3	1	0 0

First Base	PCT	G	PO	A	E	DP
Chavez	1.000	3	12	1	0	0
Laird	.955	3	16	5	1	3
Posada	.988	14	74	6	1	8
Swisher	1.000	11	29	2	0	4
Teixeira	.997	147	1229	73	4	114

Second Base	PCT	G	PO	A	E	DP
Cano	.987	157	323	444	10	97
Cervelli	1.000	1	0	1	0	0
Martin	1.000	1	1	0	0	0

Nunez	1.000	16	12	28	0	3
Pena	1.000	7	7	9	0	2
Posada	1.000	1	0	1	0	0

Third Base	PCT	G	PO	A	E	DP
Cervelli	.000	2	0	0	0	0
Chavez	1.000	42	26	60	0	9
Laird	1.000	9	3	7	0	1
Martin	.500	3	0	1	1	0
Nunez	.919	40	22	46	6	7
Pena	.880	13	5	17	3	3
Rodriguez	.973	89	54	165	6	13

Shortstop	PCT	G	PO	A	E	DP
Jeter	.972	122	140	280	12	60
Nunez	.913	50	46	101	14	17
Pena	.867	4	8	5	2	2

Outfield	PCT	G	PO	A	E	DP
Dickerson	.944	52	34	0	2	0
Gardner	.985	156	322	7	5	3
Golson	1.000	9	7	0	0	0
Granderson	.992	155	354	11	3	1
Jones	.989	57	88	1	1	1
Nunez	1.000	4	4	0	0	0
Swisher	.996	141	273	9	1	1

SCRANTON/WILKES-BARRE YANKEES

INTERNATIONAL LEAGUE

TRIPLE-A

Batting	B-T	HT	WT	DOB	AVG	vLH	vRH	G	AB	R	H	2B	3B	HR	RBI	BB	HBP	SH	SF	SO	SB	CS	SLG	OBP
Bernier, Doug	R-R	6-0	185	6-24-80	.237	.224	.243	95	291	32	69	13	4	0	29	37	3	0	1	78	4	1	.309	.328
Brewer, Dan	R-R	5-11	195	7-19-87	.278	.240	.297	46	151	17	42	9	1	0	9	14	2	0	0	47	8	4	.351	.347
Castro, Kelvin	R-R	6-3	164	12-14-87	—	.000	.000	2	0	0	0	0	0	0	0	0	0	0	0	0	0	0	—	—
Cervelli, Francisco	R-R	6-1	210	3-6-86	.154	.000	.154	3	13	2	2	0	0	0	0	1	1	1	0	0	5	0	0	.154	.267
Dickerson, Chris	L-L	6-3	230	4-10-82	.241	.211	.252	57	212	33	51	10	1	2	16	30	3	0	1	63	18	4	.325	.341
Gil, Jose	R-R	6-0	205	9-4-86	.250	.333	.200	6	16	2	4	1	0	0	0	0	0	0	0	4	0	0	.313	.250
Golson, Greg	R-R	6-0	190	9-17-85	.263	.216	.280	105	384	55	101	9	7	8	33	30	9	0	1	105	15	5	.385	.330
Krum, Austin	L-L	5-10	195	1-19-86	.246	.245	.246	64	224	33	55	10	2	0	13	26	3	0	3	51	9	4	.308	.328
Kruml, Ray	L-R	5-11	175	8-5-85	.150	.000	.231	12	40	3	6	1	0	0	3	6	0	0	0	11	3	1	.175	.261
Laird, Brandon	R-R	6-1	215	9-11-87	.260	.271	.255	123	462	51	120	27	0	16	69	17	4	0	6	84	0	0	.422	.288
Lamb, Mike	L-R	6-1	205	8-9-75	.296	.320	.288	53	203	27	60	13	2	6	26	13	4	0	1	29	0	0	.468	.348
Maruszak, Addison	R-R	6-1	195	12-24-86	.125	.000	.143	3	8	1	1	0	0	0	0	0	0	0	0	3	0	0	.125	.125
Maxwell, Justin	R-R	6-5	235	11-6-83	.260	.375	.234	48	177	36	46	8	1	16	35	26	1	0	0	72	11	2	.588	.358
Molina, Gustavo	R-R	6-0	245	2-24-82	.253	.255	.252	47	162	9	41	6	0	4	21	7	1	0	1	37	0	0	.364	.287
Montero, Jesus	R-R	6-3	235	11-28-89	.288	.328	.273	109	420	52	121	19	1	18	67	36	4	0	3	98	0	0	.467	.348
Nunez, Luis	R-R	5-11	160	11-21-86	.234	.322	.189	78	256	25	60	14	0	2	27	13	3	0	4	33	3	0	.313	.275
Parraz, Jordan	R-R	6-3	215	10-8-84	.289	.297	.286	126	443	66	128	28	6	9	52	42	9	0	1	91	5	4	.440	.362
Pena, Ramiro	B-R	5-11	175	7-18-85	.273	.350	.242	55	209	27	57	12	1	4	18	20	1	0	0	35	3	2	.397	.339
Pilittere, P.J.	R-R	6-0	215	11-23-81	.209	.130	.250	22	67	4	14	2	0	0	5	8	0	0	0	11	0	0	.239	.293
Rodriguez, Alex	R-R	6-3	230	7-27-75	.400	.000	.400	2	5	0	2	0	0	0	0	1	2	0	0	0	1	0	0	.400	.571
Romine, Austin	R-R	6-0	220	11-22-88	.133	.333	.000	4	15	1	2	0	0	0	0	1	0	0	0	3	0	0	.133	.133
Russo, Kevin	R-R	5-11	190	7-8-84	.273	.308	.259	113	450	53	123	19	6	4	46	33	5	0	4	103	12	4	.369	.327
Tiffee, Terry	R-R	6-3	215	4-21-79	.345	.258	.380	29	110	16	38	12	0	3	18	6	1	0	0	18	0	0	.536	.348
Vazquez, Jorge	R-R	5-11	225	3-15-82	.262	.271	.258	118	455	67	119	20	0	32	93	30	8	0	7	166	0	0	.516	.314

Pitching	B-T	HT	WT	DOB	W	L	ERA	G	GS	CG	SV	IP	H	R	ER	HR	BB	SO	AVG	vLH	vRH	K/9	BB/9
Arias, Wilkins	L-L	6-1	150	11-4-80	0	0	13.50	1	0	0	0	1	1	1	1	0	0	0	.333	.500	.000	0.00	0.00
Ayala, Luis	R-R	6-2	190	1-12-78	0	0	1.80	3	0	0	0	5	6	1	1	0	0	7	.375	.375	.375	12.60	0.00
Banuelos, Manny	L-L	5-11	155	3-13-91	2	2	4.19	7	7	1	0	34	36	17	16	2	19	31	.277	.217	.310	8.13	4.98
Betances, Dellin	R-R	6-8	260	3-23-88	0	3	5.14	4	4	1	0	21	16	12	12	2	15	27	.208	.162	.250	11.57	6.43
Brackman, Andrew	R-R	6-10	230	12-4-85	3	6	6.00	33	13	0	1	96	82	65	64	10	75	75	.236	.221	.250	7.03	7.03
Carlyle, Buddy	L-R	6-3	210	12-21-77	2	2	3.98	27	2	0	1	43	35	19	19	5	16	31	.223	.308	.163	6.49	3.35
Flores, Randy	L-L	6-0	190	7-31-75	1	3	3.07	29	0	0	4	29	27	10	10	3	5	20	.245	.259	.232	6.14	1.53
Garcia, Freddy	R-R	6-4	250	10-6-76	1	0	4.50	1	0	0	0	4	8	2	2	1	0	0	.444	.571	.364	0.00	2.25
Gordon, Brian	R-R	6-0	190	8-16-78	0	0	0.00	1	1	0	0	5	4	0	0	0	0	2	.222	.300	.125	12.60	0.00
2-team total (12 Lehigh Valley)					5	0	1.04	13	10	0	0	60	43	11	7	4	7	63	—	—		9.40	1.04
Hall, Shaeffer	R-L	6-1	205	10-2-87	1	0	2.84	1	1	0	0	6	5	2	2	1	0	3	.238	.125	.308	4.26	0.00
Hernandez, Fernando	R-R	5-11	210	7-31-84	0	0	9.00	1	0	0	0	2	4	2	2	0	2	5	.400	.500	.333	22.50	9.00
Igawa, Kei	L-L	6-1	210	7-13-79	1	0	2.78	4	4	0	0	23	18	8	7	2	13	12	.222	.200	.230	4.76	5.16
Kensing, Logan	R-R	6-1	190	7-3-82	1	1	4.28	21	0	0	4	27	32	16	13	5	13	32	.291	.326	.269	10.54	4.28
Kontos, George	R-R	6-3	215	6-12-85	4	4	2.62	40	4	0	2	89	72	27	26	12	26	91	.221	.281	.182	9.17	2.62
Laffey, Aaron	L-L	6-0	200	4-15-85	0	1	7.36	2	1	0	0	4	5	5	3	0	2	1	.333	.167	.444	2.45	4.91
Millwood, Kevin	R-R	6-4	230	12-24-74	1	1	8.00	2	2	1	0	9	14	8	8	3	2	7	.359	.350	.368	7.00	2.00
2-team total (13 Pawtucket)					6	2	4.68	15	15	1	0	83	93	44	43	10	27	73	—	—		7.95	2.94
Mitchell, D.J.	R-R	6-0	160	5-13-87	13	9	3.18	28	24	3	0	161	155	60	57	10	63	112	.256	.251	.261	6.25	3.51
Noesi, Hector	R-R	6-3	200	1-26-87	1	1	3.28	6	5	0	0	25	28	11	9	0	9	17	.280	.321	.227	6.20	3.28
Norton, Tim	R-R	6-5	230	5-23-83	1	0	0.00	1	0	0	0	1	0	0	0	0	0	2	.250	.000	.333	18.00	0.00
Nova, Ivan	R-R	6-4	225	1-12-87	1	2	3.38	3	3	0	0	16	16	6	6	3	2	18	.258	.216	.320	10.13	1.13
Pendleton, Lance	L-R	6-3	195	9-10-83	3	4	3.11	18	10	0	1	58	52	23	23	7	24	45	.235	.261	.212	6.08	3.24
Phelps, David	R-R	6-2	185	10-9-86	6	6	3.19	18	18	1	0	107	115	42	38	11	26	90	.278	.271	.286	7.55	2.18
Pope, Ryan	R-R	6-3	210	5-21-86	2	1	8.14	14	0	0	0	21	29	19	19	3	7	20	.330	.359	.306	8.57	3.00
Prior, Mark	R-R	6-5	230	9-7-80	0	0	0.00	1	0	0	0	1	0	0	0	0	0	0	.000	.000	.000	0.00	0.00
Proctor, Scott	R-R	6-1	195	1-2-77	0	0	2.57	6	0	0	0	7	8	2	2	0	2	6	.276	.133	.429	10.29	2.57
2-team total (14 Gwinnett)					1	0	1.50	20	0	0	3	24	18	5	4	1	7	32	—	—		12.00	2.63
Romero, J.C.	B-L	5-11	205	6-4-76	1	0	2.92	11	0	0	0	12	11	5	4	0	5	10	.234	.174	.292	7.30	3.65
2-team total (5 Syracuse)					1	0	2.33	16	0	0	0	19	14	6	5	0	6	15	—	—		6.98	2.79
Sanit, Amauri	R-R	5-8	205	7-4-79	2	1	5.21	10	2	0	0	19	24	11	11	4	7	25	.304	.237	.366	11.84	3.32

Pitching	B-T	HT	WT	DOB	W	L	ERA	G	GS	CG	SV	IP	H	R	ER	HR	BB	SO	AVG	vLH	vRH	K/9	BB/9
Schmidt, Josh	R-R	6-4	175	11-14-82	5	2	2.81	19	0	0	1	32	28	11	10	3	12	29	.241	.268	.217	8.16	3.38
Silva, Carlos	R-R	6-4	280	4-23-79	2	1	3.52	4	4	0	0	23	21	9	9	4	4	13	.241	.234	.250	5.09	1.57
Sisco, Andy	L-L	6-10	270	1-13-83	2	0	1.88	16	0	0	0	14	8	3	3	0	12	15	.167	.227	.115	9.42	7.53
Smith, Greg	L-L	6-1	190	12-22-83	3	3	4.84	13	10	0	0	58	68	34	31	9	27	36	.304	.333	.293	5.62	4.21
2-team total (4 Pawtucket)					5	4	4.52	17	14	0	0	82	87	44	41	11	34	51	—	—	—	5.62	3.75
Soriano, Rafael	R-R	6-1	230	12-19-79	1	0	4.50	2	0	0	0	2	1	1	1	1	0	2	.143	.250	.000	9.00	0.00
Texeira, Kanekoa	R-R	6-2	190	2-6-86	0	1	22.85	5	0	0	0	4	16	13	11	1	3	4	.552	.545	.556	8.31	6.23
Todd, Jess	R-R	5-11	210	4-20-86	0	1	10.80	2	0	0	0	2	1	2	2	0	2	1	.250	.000	.250	5.40	10.80
2-team total (8 Columbus)					0	1	10.97	10	0	0	0	11	19	13	13	2	8	7	—	—	—	5.91	6.75
Valdes, Raul	L-L	5-11	190	11-27-77	1	0	0.00	3	0	0	0	3	5	0	0	0	0	2	.385	.600	.250	6.00	0.00
Wade, Cory	R-R	6-2	190	5-28-83	1	0	0.00	1	0	0	0	2	2	0	0	0	0	1	.400	.000	.500	5.40	0.00
2-team total (21 Durham)					3	1	1.17	22	0	0	0	38	36	5	5	4	6	35	—	—	—	8.22	1.41
Warren, Adam	R-R	6-2	215	8-25-87	6	8	3.60	27	27	1	0	152	145	68	61	13	53	111	.249	.274	.228	6.56	3.13
Whelan, Kevin	R-R	6-0	200	1-8-84	2	3	2.75	45	0	0	23	52	38	16	16	5	14	54	.202	.174	.225	9.29	2.41
Wordekemper, Eric	R-R	6-1	215	8-8-83	3	3	3.60	42	0	0	2	50	52	20	20	2	22	33	.274	.282	.268	5.94	3.96

Fielding

Catcher	PCT	G	PO	A	E	DP	PB
Cervelli	1.000	2	16	0	0	0	1
Gil	1.000	6	44	6	0	0	1
Molina	.989	36	244	21	3	4	2
Montero	.997	88	615	38	2	7	7
Pilittere	1.000	10	62	10	0	1	1
Romine	1.000	4	32	0	0	0	1

First Base	PCT	G	PO	A	E	DP
Laird	.992	15	120	5	1	7
Lamb	.994	21	168	5	1	20
Maruszak	1.000	1	3	0	0	0
Pilittere	1.000	1	3	0	0	0
Tiffee	.990	15	94	7	1	11
Vazquez	.992	94	712	65	6	85

Second Base	PCT	G	PO	A	E	DP
Bernier	.956	10	21	22	2	7
Nunez	1.000	56	108	146	0	40
Pena	1.000	5	11	12	0	3
Russo	.984	76	117	198	5	45

Third Base	PCT	G	PO	A	E	DP
Bernier	1.000	3	0	7	0	0
Laird	.968	104	68	171	8	23
Lamb	1.000	9	3	4	0	0
Maruszak	1.000	1	1	2	0	1
Nunez	1.000	2	0	3	0	0
Pena	1.000	1	0	1	0	1
Rodriguez	.857	2	4	2	1	0
Russo	.923	28	15	33	4	5
Vazquez	1.000	7	4	14	0	1

Shortstop	PCT	G	PO	A	E	DP
Bernier	.987	81	100	200	4	49
Maruszak	1.000	1	2	2	0	0
Nunez	.931	15	23	31	4	6
Pena	.981	48	71	131	4	35

Outfield	PCT	G	PO	A	E	DP
Brewer	1.000	38	84	3	0	1
Dickerson	.967	51	115	2	4	0
Golson	.996	101	251	17	1	2
Krum	1.000	63	138	6	0	0
Kruml	1.000	12	17	1	0	0
Laird	.917	11	11	0	1	0
Maxwell	1.000	45	120	6	0	1
Parraz	.981	107	196	8	4	2
Russo	1.000	14	26	2	0	1

TRENTON THUNDER · DOUBLE-A
EASTERN LEAGUE

Batting	B-T	HT	WT	DOB	AVG	vLH	vRH	G	AB	R	H	2B	3B	HR	RBI	BB	HBP	SH	SF	SO	SB	CS	SLG	OBP
Almonte, Zoilo	B-R	5-11	165	6-10-89	.251	.282	.231	46	175	23	44	11	1	3	23	14	1	0	1	45	4	1	.377	.309
Baker, Ryan	R-R	5-9	205	11-9-84	.125	.000	.129	11	32	4	4	1	0	0	2	2	1	0	1	20	0	0	.156	.194
Brewer, Dan	R-R	5-11	195	7-19-87	.229	.000	.267	10	35	3	8	2	1	0	5	3	0	0	1	11	3	1	.343	.282
Gil, Jose	R-R	6-0	205	9-4-86	.253	.290	.241	73	249	30	63	17	0	6	35	33	3	0	3	40	2	1	.394	.344
Jeter, Derek	R-R	6-3	195	6-26-74	.500	.000	.500	2	4	1	2	0	0	0	2	0	0	0	1	0	0	0	.500	.667
Johnson, Cody	L-R	6-4	240	8-18-88	.226	.200	.231	74	297	37	67	16	1	15	45	20	2	0	2	138	1	0	.438	.277
Joseph, Corban	L-R	6-0	168	10-28-88	.277	.252	.287	131	499	75	138	38	8	5	58	59	1	0	2	104	4	3	.415	.353
Krum, Austin	L-L	5-10	195	1-19-86	.255	.286	.242	70	278	39	71	10	4	2	30	33	4	0	3	51	19	3	.342	.340
Kruml, Ray	L-R	5-11	175	8-5-85	.290	.250	.306	114	452	70	131	13	8	5	35	31	0	0	1	107	37	11	.387	.335
Leslie, Myron	B-R	6-3	220	5-2-82	.333	.667	.167	3	9	1	3	0	0	0	0	1	0	0	0	2	0	0	.333	.400
Lyerly, Rob	L-R	6-2	200	7-23-87	.246	.222	.258	68	272	36	67	16	1	4	34	15	3	0	1	93	2	0	.357	.292
Mack, DeAngelo	R-L	5-10	190	11-19-86	.248	.219	.258	40	121	12	30	5	0	4	17	16	5	0	1	28	3	1	.388	.357
Maruszak, Addison	R-R	6-1	195	12-21-86	.244	.234	.249	108	344	40	84	22	2	7	47	52	4	0	5	69	2	6	.381	.346
Mesa, Melky	R-R	6-1	190	1-31-87	.251	.231	.260	105	386	58	97	24	4	9	46	36	9	0	1	129	18	13	.404	.329
Mujica, Yadil	L-R	6-1	170	1-1-85	.233	.250	.226	54	172	20	40	4	0	1	14	14	1	0	0	22	3	1	.273	.294
Pena, Ramiro	B-R	5-11	175	7-18-85	.429	.000	.429	2	7	1	3	0	0	0	2	0	0	0	0	1	0	0	.429	.429
Pirela, Jose	B-R	5-10	191	11-21-89	.239	.246	.237	128	468	50	112	21	4	8	45	25	13	0	7	88	9	7	.353	.292
Place, Jason	R-R	6-3	205	5-8-88	.148	.300	.114	14	54	6	8	1	1	1	4	0	1	0	0	15	1	1	.259	.164
Romine, Austin	R-R	6-0	220	11-22-88	.286	.319	.273	85	336	43	96	13	0	6	47	32	3	0	2	60	2	2	.378	.351
Rye, Jack	L-L	6-1	200	3-8-86	.167	.333	.111	8	24	2	4	0	1	1	1	3	0	0	6	8	0	0	.375	.259
Sublett, Damon	L-R	6-1	190	9-22-85	.280	.227	.297	54	182	24	51	8	7	2	28	33	0	0	1	55	1	0	.434	.389
Suttle, Bradley	B-R	6-2	205	1-24-86	.215	.123	.238	86	326	41	70	18	6	9	47	40	7	0	3	108	4	1	.390	.311

Pitching	B-T	HT	WT	DOB	W	L	ERA	G	GS	CG	SV	IP	H	R	ER	HR	BB	SO	AVG	vLH	vRH	K/9	BB/9
Anderson, Brian	R-R	6-2	220	3-11-82	1	0	1.17	7	0	0	0	8	7	2	1	0	1	9	.250	.300	.222	10.57	1.17
Arbiso, Cory	R-R	6-3	210	4-21-86	5	5	5.23	40	9	0	0	83	112	54	48	4	27	52	.323	.343	.309	5.66	2.94
Arias, Wilkins	L-L	6-1	150	11-4-80	4	1	2.31	29	0	0	2	35	19	10	9	3	13	39	.153	.235	.126	10.03	3.34
Banuelos, Manny	L-L	5-11	155	3-13-91	4	5	3.59	20	20	0	0	95	94	46	38	7	52	94	.263	.229	.277	8.87	4.91
Betances, Dellin	R-R	6-8	260	3-23-88	4	6	3.42	21	21	0	0	105	86	49	40	7	55	115	.219	.247	.196	9.83	4.70
Duff, Grant	R-R	6-6	210	12-19-82	0	0	6.00	8	0	0	0	9	13	6	6	2	7	5	.342	.400	.304	5.00	7.00
Flannery, Ryan	R-R	6-4	245	1-6-86	0	0	9.00	4	0	0	0	5	10	6	5	1	6	7	.400	.333	.462	12.60	10.80
Garrison, Steve	B-L	6-1	195	9-04-86	2	4	5.95	17	16	0	0	76	102	58	50	12	20	46	.317	.269	.345	5.47	2.38
Hall, Shaeffer	R-L	6-1	205	10-2-87	10	8	4.12	26	24	0	1	151	179	85	69	14	38	97	.294	.282	.298	5.79	2.27
Halsey, Brad	L-L	6-1	185	2-14-81	2	1	4.88	23	0	0	0	31	41	27	17	2	24	24	.301	.286	.310	6.89	6.89
Hernandez, Fernando	R-R	5-11	210	7-31-84	6	4	5.91	33	0	0	7	35	55	24	23	6	15	39	.353	.350	.354	10.03	3.86
Heyer, Craig	R-R	6-3	195	11-15-85	10	9	4.54	28	24	0	0	147	166	88	74	9	38	75	.286	.288	.284	4.60	2.33
Horne, Alan	R-R	6-4	195	1-5-83	0	2	12.79	7	1	0	2	6	8	13	9	0	13	3	.308	.333	.294	4.26	18.47

Pitching	B-T	HT	WT	DOB	W	L	ERA	G	GS	CG	SV	IP	H	R	ER	HR	BB	SO	AVG	vLH	vRH	K/9	BB/9
Hughes, Phil	R-R	6-5	240	6-24-86	1	0	1.86	2	2	0	0	10	6	2	2	0	4	11	.176	.214	.150	10.24	3.72
Igawa, Kei	L-L	6-1	210	7-13-79	2	2	4.31	16	6	0	1	54	52	26	26	8	24	40	.255	.284	.241	6.63	3.98
Madrigal, Warner	R-R	6-1	235	3-21-84	0	0	20.25	2	0	0	0	1	2	3	3	1	2	2	.333	.500	.250	13.50	13.50
Marquez, Jeff	R-R	6-2	190	8-10-84	2	0	2.25	3	3	0	0	20	9	7	5	2	3	11	.138	.147	.129	4.95	1.35
Millwood, Kevin	R-R	6-4	230	12-24-74	1	0	0.00	1	1	1	0	7	1	0	0	0	4	3	.048	.000	.100	3.86	5.14
Norton, Tim	R-R	6-5	230	5-23-83	1	0	1.55	22	0	0	6	29	12	6	5	2	8	44	.124	.111	.131	13.66	2.48
Okamoto, Naoya	L-L	5-10	185	7-28-83	1	0	3.76	21	0	0	2	38	31	19	16	3	21	26	.218	.326	.167	6.10	4.93
Pope, Ryan	R-R	6-3	210	5-21-86	0	2	3.20	22	0	0	6	20	19	11	7	1	5	21	.257	.303	.220	9.61	2.29
Romanski, Josh	L-L	6-0	185	10-18-86	0	1	2.04	13	1	0	0	18	20	5	4	2	6	14	.294	.414	.205	7.13	3.06
Schmidt, Josh	R-R	6-4	175	11-14-82	3	2	1.83	24	0	0	9	34	18	7	7	1	13	48	.155	.125	.139	12.58	3.41
Silva, Carlos	R-R	6-4	280	4-23-79	0	0	0.00	1	1	0	0	6	3	1	0	0	0	6	.136	.250	.000	9.00	0.00
Stoneburner, Graham	R-R	6-1	190	9-29-87	1	5	4.17	11	11	0	0	58	72	36	27	3	20	36	.310	.320	.300	5.55	3.09
Texeira, Kanekoa	R-R	6-2	190	2-6-86	0	1	10.64	11	0	0	2	11	24	18	13	2	3	7	.444	.480	.414	5.73	2.45
Valdes, Raul	L-L	5-11	190	11-27-77	0	0	0.00	2	0	0	0	2	0	0	0	0	0	2	.000	.000	.000	10.80	0.00
Venditte, Pat	R-B	6-1	180	6-30-85	3	7	3.40	51	0	0	0	90	80	37	34	7	31	88	.244	.213	.266	8.80	3.10
Whitley, Chase	R-R	6-4	220	6-14-89	3	4	3.38	19	1	0	1	43	46	21	16	6	19	37	.280	.276	.284	7.80	4.01

Fielding

Catcher	PCT	G	PO	A	E	DP	PB
Baker	.960	11	66	6	3	0	1
Gil	.991	59	430	35	4	6	7
Maruszak	1.000	4	21	1	0	0	0
Romine	.993	71	506	48	4	4	7

First Base	PCT	G	PO	A	E	DP
Gil	.992	13	108	10	1	11
Leslie	1.000	2	17	2	0	2
Lyerly	.979	55	441	28	10	46
Maruszak	.998	58	470	32	1	37
Rye	.983	6	53	4	1	2
Suttle	.986	7	66	3	1	7

Second Base	PCT	G	PO	A	E	DP
Joseph	.962	127	243	344	23	78
Mujica	1.000	1	0	2	0	0
Pirela	.963	13	28	24	2	9

Third Base	PCT	G	PO	A	E	DP
Lyerly	.667	10	6	14	10	2
Maruszak	.955	36	25	80	5	13
Mujica	.957	19	8	37	2	3
Suttle	.930	77	55	171	17	14

Shortstop	PCT	G	PO	A	E	DP
Jeter	.909	2	1	9	1	3
Mujica	.950	30	35	80	6	14
Pena	.800	2	0	4	1	0

	PCT	G	PO	A	E	DP
Pirela	.921	113	154	276	37	62

Outfield	PCT	G	PO	A	E	DP
Almonte	.976	40	78	5	2	1
Brewer	1.000	7	14	0	0	0
Johnson	1.000	3	2	0	0	0
Krum	1.000	66	139	4	0	0
Kruml	.983	108	231	7	4	3
Mack	1.000	38	53	2	0	1
Maruszak	.905	9	19	0	2	0
Mesa	.980	99	241	8	5	2
Mujica	1.000	4	7	0	0	0
Place	.933	13	27	1	2	0
Rye	1.000	1	3	0	0	0
Sublett	.960	38	71	1	3	0

TAMPA YANKEES　　　　　　　　　　　HIGH CLASS A

FLORIDA STATE LEAGUE

Batting	B-T	HT	WT	DOB	AVG	vLH	vRH	G	AB	R	H	2B	3B	HR	RBI	BB	HBP	SH	SF	SO	SB	CS	SLG	OBP
Abeita, Mitch	R-R	6-0	185	4-7-86	.221	.214	.223	61	199	18	44	10	1	2	20	33	3	0	0	49	0	2	.312	.340
Adams, David	R-R	6-2	190	5-15-87	.308	.318	.300	12	52	6	16	3	0	0	4	4	1	0	0	8	0	2	.365	.368
Alcantara, Jorge	R-R	6-1	195	8-9-91	.111	.500	.000	7	9	2	1	0	0	0	0	0	0	0	0	2	0	0	.111	.111
Almonte, Abe	B-R	5-9	205	6-27-89	.268	.319	.251	131	537	92	144	27	11	4	52	52	2	0	4	100	30	11	.382	.333
Almonte, Zoilo	B-R	5-11	165	6-10-89	.293	.338	.277	70	259	38	76	15	3	12	54	31	2	0	4	60	14	4	.514	.368
Angelini, Carmen	R-R	6-2	185	9-22-88	.257	.154	.318	9	35	5	9	1	2	0	4	1	0	0	1	10	0	2	.400	.341
Blaser, Tyson	R-R	6-2	225	12-8-87	.154	.000	.207	15	39	5	6	1	0	0	2	2	5	0	0	14	0	0	.179	.283
Brewer, Dan	R-R	5-11	195	7-19-87	.333	.500	.286	2	9	1	3	0	1	0	0	0	0	0	0	2	0	0	.556	.333
Castro, Kelvin	R-R	6-3	164	12-14-87	.268	.316	.249	95	336	54	90	15	7	5	45	24	2	0	3	82	8	3	.399	.318
Cervelli, Francisco	R-R	6-1	210	3-6-86	.300	.000	.300	3	10	0	3	0	0	0	0	0	0	0	0	2	0	0	.300	.300
Chavez, Eric	L-R	6-1	210	12-7-77	.333	.500	.231	6	21	4	7	2	0	1	3	2	0	0	0	4	0	0	.571	.391
Grote, Taylor	R-R	6-2	195	12-5-88	.185	.110	.214	73	260	27	48	11	0	2	26	35	2	0	1	90	2	1	.250	.285
Heathcott, Slade	L-L	6-1	190	9-28-90	.600	.000	.600	1	5	2	3	0	0	0	0	0	0	0	0	1	0	0	1.200	.600
Higashioka, Kyle	R-R	6-0	205	4-20-90	.238	.111	.300	46	164	21	39	10	0	4	16	14	1	0	1	22	1	0	.372	.300
Hurst, Jon	R-R	5-11	195	10-18-88	.500	.000	.500	1	2	1	1	0	0	0	0	2	0	0	0	0	0	0	.500	.500
Ibarra, Walter	R-R	5-11	180	11-1-87	.297	.283	.302	100	390	59	116	24	3	6	52	19	6	0	8	65	10	7	.421	.333
Johnson, Cody	L-R	6-4	240	8-18-88	.326	.395	.299	39	135	26	44	10	1	6	22	11	3	0	1	56	0	0	.548	.387
Landoni, Emerson	B-R	5-10	146	2-18-89	.254	.224	.266	83	236	27	60	7	2	1	20	11	6	0	1	47	2	2	.314	.300
Lyerly, Rob	L-R	6-2	200	12-2-87	.315	.318	.314	64	260	32	82	16	5	4	46	18	2	0	1	56	4	2	.462	.363
Mack, DeAngelo	R-L	5-10	190	11-19-86	.300	.204	.333	59	207	26	62	14	4	3	30	20	2	0	2	33	2	2	.464	.364
Mahoney, Kevin	L-R	6-1	205	5-11-87	.266	.205	.286	46	158	21	42	9	1	5	20	18	4	0	2	46	1	0	.430	.352
Medchill, Neil	L-R	6-4	220	6-25-87	.225	.160	.248	59	191	38	43	7	0	11	25	32	0	0	1	64	4	1	.435	.335
Mesa, Melky	R-R	6-1	190	1-31-87	.167	.000	.200	4	12	1	2	1	0	0	1	3	2	0	0	4	1	0	.250	.412
Murphy, J.R.	B-R	6-0	190	5-13-91	.259	.222	.269	23	85	8	22	6	0	1	14	2	0	0	2	9	0	0	.365	.270
Murton, Luke	R-R	6-4	222	5-21-86	.274	.288	.268	116	423	44	116	28	1	8	62	40	6	0	4	82	2	5	.402	.342
Mustelier, Ronnier	R-R	5-10	210	8-8-84	.333	.366	.318	31	126	20	42	13	1	3	24	8	1	0	0	15	6	1	.524	.378
Place, Jason	R-R	6-3	205	5-8-88	.213	.250	.194	13	47	3	10	3	1	1	5	3	0	0	0	16	0	1	.383	.260
Rabago, Hector	R-R	5-10	185	8-24-88	.232	.313	.200	23	56	7	13	2	0	1	8	6	1	0	2	14	0	0	.321	.308
Rodriguez, Alex	R-R	6-3	230	7-27-75	.333	.667	.000	2	6	1	2	1	0	1	2	1	0	0	0	0	0	0	1.000	.429
Roller, Kyle	L-R	6-1	250	3-27-88	.265	.239	.273	60	211	27	56	13	0	7	28	12	2	0	1	65	1	0	.427	.365
Segedin, Rob	R-R	6-3	220	11-10-88	.245	.238	.247	52	188	32	46	4	1	2	21	15	3	0	0	40	4	1	.309	.311

Pitching	B-T	HT	WT	DOB	W	L	ERA	G	GS	CG	SV	IP	H	R	ER	HR	BB	SO	AVG	vLH	vRH	K/9	BB/9
Allen, Scottie	R-R	6-1	170	7-3-91	3	4	7.21	16	9	0	0	49	66	42	39	9	21	37	.325	.350	.301	6.84	3.88
Black, Sean	R-R	6-3	185	4-23-88	6	9	7.02	24	22	0	0	110	146	96	86	17	41	67	.321	.322	.319	5.47	3.34
Burawa, Daniel	R-R	6-3	190	12-30-88	2	2	3.66	20	0	0	2	39	41	18	16	0	9	31	.272	.339	.228	7.09	2.06
Casanova, Reinier	R-R	6-0	215	3-3-87	1	1	6.60	11	0	0	1	15	14	11	11	0	11	15	.296	.294		9.00	6.60

NEW YORK YANKEES

Pitching	B-T	HT	WT	DOB	W	L	ERA	G	GS	CG	SV	IP	H	R	ER	HR	BB	SO	AVG	vLH	vRH	K/9	BB/9
Claiborne, Preston	R-R	6-2	215	1-21-88	3	7	3.11	38	0	0	5	81	73	33	28	8	30	75	.243	.274	.213	8.33	3.33
De La Cruz, Joel	R-R	6-1	190	6-9-89	0	1	3.00	1	0	0	0	3	2	1	1	0	1	3	.182	.167	.200	9.00	3.00
Flannery, Ryan	R-R	6-4	245	1-6-86	3	1	1.24	36	0	0	19	44	34	8	6	0	5	35	.209	.200	.217	7.21	1.03
Gil, Daniel	R-R	6-3	190	4-24-89	7	2	4.66	32	7	0	0	77	93	46	40	7	28	48	.294	.336	.260	5.59	3.26
Gipson, Mike	R-R	6-1	195	9-15-88	0	1	2.95	9	0	0	0	18	15	6	6	1	6	11	.227	.171	.290	5.40	2.95
Halsey, Brad	L-L	6-1	185	2-14-81	0	0	0.00	1	0	0	0	1	0	0	0	0	1	0	.000	.000	.000	9.00	0.00
Heredia, Jairo	R-R	6-1	190	10-8-89	8	2	3.29	13	12	0	0	68	60	26	25	8	16	68	.233	.254	.212	8.96	2.11
Hinojosa, Joaquin	R-R	5-11	185	4-18-89	0	1	13.50	1	0	0	0	1	2	2	2	0	2	1	.333	.333	.333	6.75	13.50
Marquez, Jeff	R-R	6-2	190	8-10-84	1	1	6.08	4	4	0	0	13	17	9	9	2	4	7	.333	.318	.345	4.73	2.70
Marshall, Brett	R-R	6-0	195	3-22-90	9	7	3.78	27	26	0	0	140	142	67	59	6	48	114	.271	.259	.283	7.31	3.08
Marte, Ronny	R-R	6-1	175	2-26-86	1	1	3.57	39	0	0	3	68	73	29	27	3	18	53	.268	.268	.269	7.01	2.38
Nuding, Zach	R-R	6-4	250	3-29-90	0	0	0.00	1	1	0	0	3	3	0	0	0	1	1	.273	.167	.400	3.00	3.00
O'Brien, Mikey	R-R	5-11	185	3-3-90	4	3	3.04	10	8	0	0	47	38	16	16	5	22	31	.226	.306	.167	5.89	4.18
Perez, Kelvin	R-R	6-1	140	10-10-85	0	0	6.43	8	0	0	0	14	20	12	10	1	5	15	.328	.351	.292	9.64	3.21
Pope, Ryan	R-R	6-3	210	5-21-86	0	0	0.00	4	0	0	0	5	1	0	0	0	2	4	.059	.000	.143	7.20	3.60
Prior, Mark	R-R	6-5	230	9-7-80	0	0	2.57	2	2	0	0	3	2	2	0	2	2	.154	.167	.143	6.00	6.00
Quintana, Jose	L-L	6-0	170	1-24-89	10	2	2.91	30	12	0	1	102	86	35	33	5	28	88	.236	.223	.243	7.76	2.47
Ramirez, Jose	R-R	6-1	155	1-21-90	0	5	8.14	6	6	0	0	24	35	25	22	3	11	25	.337	.311	.372	9.25	4.07
Romanski, Josh	L-L	6-0	185	10-18-86	7	5	3.16	17	17	0	0	88	96	41	31	7	15	69	.277	.241	.288	7.03	1.53
Silva, Carlos	R-R	6-4	280	4-23-79	0	0	2.57	2	2	0	0	7	8	2	2	1	2	9	.296	.316	.250	11.57	2.57
Sneed, Kramer	L-L	6-3	185	10-7-88	2	3	3.69	16	3	0	0	39	44	18	16	1	15	42	.289	.229	.317	9.69	3.46
Solbach, Michael	R-R	6-3	185	7-31-85	6	4	3.12	28	4	0	1	69	69	28	24	1	23	56	.265	.280	.252	7.27	2.99
Soriano, Rafael	R-R	6-1	230	12-19-79	0	1	11.57	2	2	0	0	2	4	3	3	1	0	1	.444	.400	.500	3.86	0.00
Stoneburner, Graham	R-R	6-1	190	9-29-87	0	0	3.86	3	2	0	0	19	16	8	8	3	5	15	.239	.250	.229	7.23	2.41
Turley, Nik	L-L	6-6	230	9-11-89	0	0	6.14	2	2	0	0	7	11	8	5	1	1	5	.344	.077	.526	6.14	1.23
Whitley, Chase	R-R	6-4	220	6-14-89	0	1	1.68	23	0	0	6	48	41	13	9	2	10	40	.233	.282	.187	7.45	1.86

Fielding

Catcher	PCT	G	PO	A	E	DP	PB
Abeita	.985	59	410	45	7	5	6
Blaser	.977	14	73	12	2	0	3
Cervelli	1.000	2	12	2	0	0	0
Higashioka	.983	44	311	33	6	3	7
Hurst	1.000	1	6	0	0	0	0
Murphy	1.000	17	112	14	0	0	2
Rabago	1.000	11	36	9	0	0	0

First Base	PCT	G	PO	A	E	DP
Abeita	1.000	1	6	0	0	0
Blaser	1.000	1	1	0	0	0
Landoni	1.000	1	3	0	0	0
Lyerly	.982	13	100	8	2	13
Mahoney	1.000	16	129	6	0	13
Murton	.985	79	648	51	11	65
Rabago	.857	1	6	0	1	0
Roller	.991	36	312	15	3	31
Segedin	1.000	3	4	0	0	0
Solbach	1.000	1	3	1	0	0

Second Base	PCT	G	PO	A	E	DP
Adams	1.000	10	17	31	0	10
Alcantara	1.000	2	3	3	0	1
Castro	.966	58	118	190	11	45
Ibarra	1.000	19	38	54	0	12
Landoni	.964	42	67	120	7	21
Mahoney	.952	11	24	35	3	11
Mustelier	.963	6	11	15	1	2
Rabago	1.000	2	2	2	0	1

Third Base	PCT	G	PO	A	E	DP
Alcantara	1.000	1	0	1	0	0
Castro	.952	9	8	12	1	1
Chavez	1.000	3	1	5	0	1
Landoni	.889	12	5	11	2	1
Lyerly	.878	48	17	62	11	6
Mahoney	.977	17	13	29	1	5
Murphy	.909	5	1	9	1	0
Murton	1.000	2	1	0	0	0
Mustelier	.000	2	0	0	0	0
Rabago	.955	7	10	11	1	0
Segedin	.938	43	29	77	7	7

Shortstop	PCT	G	PO	A	E	DP
Angelini	.978	9	20	24	1	6
Castro	.953	30	53	90	7	27
Ibarra	.970	81	93	266	11	48
Landoni	.943	21	23	60	5	11

Outfield	PCT	G	PO	A	E	DP
Alcantara	1.000	1	2	0	0	0
Almonte	.981	126	302	7	6	0
Almonte	.992	66	123	4	1	1
Brewer	1.000	2	1	0	0	0
Grote	.951	70	129	8	7	4
Heathcott	1.000	1	1	0	0	0
Johnson	1.000	23	39	0	0	0
Landoni	1.000	4	3	0	0	0
Mack	.961	42	74	0	3	0
Medchill	.955	47	83	1	4	0
Mesa	1.000	2	7	0	0	0
Murton	1.000	1	1	0	0	0
Mustelier	.961	25	44	5	2	2
Place	1.000	7	7	0	0	0
Segedin	.938	9	15	0	1	0

CHARLESTON RIVERDOGS

LOW CLASS A

SOUTH ATLANTIC LEAGUE

Batting	B-T	HT	WT	DOB	AVG	vLH	vRH	G	AB	R	H	2B	3B	HR	RBI	BB	HBP	SH	SF	SO	SB	CS	SLG	OBP
Arcia, Francisco	B-R	6-0	155	9-14-89	.429	.000	.429	3	7	1	3	1	0	0	2	2	0	0	0	2	0	0	.571	.556
Brown, Shane	R-R	5-11	197	1-11-88	.321	.306	.326	35	131	18	42	8	0	0	15	14	8	0	0	12	1	0	.382	.418
Castro, Kelvin	R-R	6-3	164	12-14-87	.264	.143	.314	18	72	11	19	2	2	3	11	2	0	0	0	17	2	0	.472	.284
De Leon, Kelvin	R-R	6-2	180	10-29-90	.221	.206	.228	118	453	54	100	23	1	14	60	32	7	0	1	147	0	1	.369	.282
Farnham, Jeff	R-R	6-1	190	8-30-87	.232	.333	.190	42	142	16	33	8	0	2	12	14	2	0	0	27	2	1	.331	.310
Felix, Anderson	B-R	6-0	175	5-11-92	.217	.218	.216	116	438	55	95	27	3	6	39	52	5	0	3	129	16	7	.333	.305
Ferraro, Mike	L-L	6-2	200	5-31-88	.254	.429	.202	35	122	18	31	7	0	1	6	3	0	0	1	30	1	1	.336	.300
Flores, Ramon	L-L	5-10	150	3-26-92	.265	.277	.261	125	468	59	124	26	2	11	59	61	3	0	0	93	13	2	.400	.353
Grote, Taylor	L-R	6-2	195	12-5-88	.213	.211	.213	25	94	11	20	7	2	1	8	10	0	0	0	40	2	0	.362	.288
Heathcott, Slade	L-L	6-1	190	9-28-90	.271	.286	.266	52	210	36	57	11	4	4	16	19	4	0	1	57	6	7	.419	.342
Higashioka, Kyle	R-R	6-0	205	4-20-90	.223	.237	.217	36	130	14	29	6	0	4	13	9	2	0	2	19	0	0	.362	.280
Lassiter, Garrison	L-R	6-1	185	12-22-89	.274	.143	.299	64	212	19	58	10	1	1	23	26	2	0	2	64	2	1	.344	.355
Lopez, Daniel	R-R	6-2	175	1-17-92	.429	.500	.400	3	7	3	3	0	0	0	1	4	0	0	1	1	0	0	.429	.667
Mahoney, Kevin	L-R	6-1	190	5-11-87	.261	.275	.256	67	245	39	64	11	3	3	31	26	4	0	4	55	2	0	.367	.337
Mojica, Jose	R-R	6-0	145	12-26-88	.262	.282	.254	108	386	41	101	25	2	0	42	26	3	0	2	66	6	1	.337	.312
Murphy, J.R.	B-R	6-0	190	5-13-91	.297	.403	.255	63	256	31	76	23	0	6	32	19	0	0	2	38	2	0	.457	.343
Roller, Kyle	L-R	6-1	235	3-27-88	.305	.231	.333	50	187	30	57	18	0	9	29	16	7	0	1	46	1	0	.545	.379
Rosario, Jose	R-R	5-11	160	11-29-91	.143	.000	.200	5	21	1	3	1	0	0	2	1	1	0	0	4	2	0	.190	.217
Sanchez, Gary	R-R	6-2	220	12-2-92	.256	.244	.260	82	301	49	77	16	1	17	52	36	2	0	4	93	2	1	.485	.335

Batting	B-T	HT	WT	DOB	AVG	vLH	vRH	G	AB	R	H	2B	3B	HR	RBI	BB	HBP	SH	SF	SO	SB	CS	SLG	OBP
Segedin, Rob	R-R	6-3	220	11-10-88	.323	.317	.325	61	226	33	73	15	3	5	34	23	7	0	4	39	3	2	.482	.396
Sosa, Eduardo	L-L	6-0	180	3-14-91	.255	.221	.266	79	310	35	79	15	3	2	28	20	2	0	1	79	14	2	.342	.303
Toussen, Jose	R-R	6-1	155	11-13-89	.263	.341	.235	84	315	40	83	8	3	0	23	30	4	0	0	43	18	5	.308	.335
Wilson, Wes	R-R	6-0	210	8-18-89	.308	.200	.375	4	13	0	4	0	0	0	3	1	0	0	0	2	0	0	.308	.357

Pitching	B-T	HT	WT	DOB	W	L	ERA	G	GS	CG	SV	IP	H	R	ER	HR	BB	SO	AVG	vLH	vRH	K/9	BB/9
Allen, Scottie	R-R	6-1	170	7-3-91	4	2	7.86	9	8	0	0	45	71	40	39	8	12	29	.368	.366	.369	5.84	2.42
Barreda, Manuel	R-R	5-11	165	10-8-88	4	3	4.50	45	6	0	0	74	67	44	37	4	49	82	.247	.250	.246	9.97	5.96
Burawa, Daniel	R-R	6-3	190	12-30-88	3	2	3.63	19	0	0	3	45	36	21	18	6	15	35	.226	.167	.248	7.05	3.02
Dott, Aaron	R-L	6-4	215	5-17-88	2	1	1.99	18	0	0	2	32	21	7	7	2	8	39	.186	.143	.205	11.08	2.27
Evarts, Steve	L-L	6-3	180	10-13-87	1	5	5.65	7	7	0	0	37	42	27	23	2	21	27	.292	.471	.236	6.63	5.15
Forer, Nathan	R-R	6-1	172	6-6-88	2	8	5.13	31	8	0	3	67	86	56	38	11	22	35	.309	.364	.279	4.73	2.97
Gerritse, Brett	R-R	6-4	220	3-4-91	1	0	2.40	6	1	0	0	15	8	4	4	0	4	12	.295	.154	.400	7.20	2.40
Gipson, Mike	R-R	6-1	195	9-15-88	0	2	6.04	6	4	0	0	22	30	16	15	6	7	19	.313	.297	.322	7.66	2.82
Greene, Shane	R-R	6-4	210	11-17-88	5	14	4.37	27	27	0	0	138	141	88	67	9	68	128	.265	.256	.269	8.35	4.43
Kahnle, Tommy	R-R	6-1	220	8-7-89	3	5	4.22	40	0	0	2	81	69	50	38	1	49	112	.223	.260	.205	12.44	5.44
Lewis, Freddy	L-L	6-2	210	12-16-86	0	0	0.00	2	0	0	0	2	4	7	0	0	7	3	.333	.000	.364	16.20	37.80
Martinez, Richard	R-R	6-1	194	7-19-88	0	2	11.29	11	1	0	0	18	27	26	23	3	15	19	.338	.250	.375	9.33	7.36
Montgomery, Mark	R-R	5-11	205	8-30-90	0	0	1.85	22	0	0	14	24	17	5	5	0	11	41	.183	.152	.200	15.16	4.07
Nuding, Zach	R-R	6-4	250	3-29-90	7	6	4.48	20	20	0	0	98	87	58	49	11	44	82	.232	.252	.222	7.51	4.03
Nuno, Vidal	L-L	5-11	195	7-26-87	2	1	1.80	7	7	0	0	40	37	9	8	4	2	37	.248	.235	.252	8.33	0.45
O'Brien, Mikey	R-R	5-11	185	3-3-90	3	4	3.24	14	14	0	0	72	65	37	26	5	23	68	.241	.295	.206	8.46	2.86
Perez, Kelvin	R-R	6-1	140	10-10-85	0	4	4.66	39	0	0	8	56	50	29	29	4	39	62	.243	.241	.244	9.96	6.27
Ramirez, Jose	R-R	6-1	155	1-21-90	5	7	4.90	15	15	0	0	79	84	51	43	9	32	74	.276	.239	.297	8.43	3.65
Recchia, Mike	R-R	6-1	210	4-2-89	3	1	2.33	22	0	0	0	46	37	15	12	3	10	29	.220	.239	.208	5.63	1.94
Reyes, Yobanny	R-R	6-0	165	11-29-88	1	3	4.78	21	0	0	0	26	27	16	14	1	17	24	.276	.233	.309	8.20	5.81
Rodriguez, Wilton	R-R	6-3	195	11-6-90	0	0	5.94	9	0	0	0	17	20	12	11	2	8	22	.303	.214	.327	11.88	4.32
Rondon, Francisco	L-L	6-1	160	4-10-90	2	3	4.67	19	0	0	0	35	26	22	18	1	21	42	.210	.194	.215	10.90	5.45
Sneed, Kramer	L-L	6-3	185	10-7-88	3	6	4.18	17	7	0	0	65	58	33	30	10	13	68	.232	.234	.232	9.46	1.81
Turley, Nik	L-L	6-6	230	9-11-89	4	6	2.51	15	15	0	0	82	70	32	23	8	21	82	.224	.250	.219	8.96	2.30

Fielding

Catcher	PCT	G	PO	A	E	DP	PB
Arcia	.900	2	8	1	1	0	0
Farnham	1.000	28	237	34	0	7	1
Higashioka	.991	10	91	15	1	1	1
Murphy	.977	38	304	36	8	4	3
Sanchez	.986	60	482	70	8	4	26
Wilson	1.000	4	22	3	0	1	0

First Base	PCT	G	PO	A	E	DP
Brown	1.000	3	21	0	0	4
Castro	1.000	1	7	0	0	0
Farnham	.970	10	56	8	2	7
Flores	.989	23	164	16	2	8
Mahoney	.994	59	489	38	3	43
Roller	.992	47	340	26	3	34

Second Base	PCT	G	PO	A	E	DP
Castro	.933	3	8	6	1	3

	PCT	G	PO	A	E	DP
Felix	.965	115	226	267	18	63
Mahoney	1.000	1	3	2	0	0
Mojica	1.000	4	6	10	0	2
Toussen	.967	19	35	54	3	11

Third Base	PCT	G	PO	A	E	DP
Castro	.800	9	5	19	6	1
Lassiter	.921	53	30	98	11	9
Mahoney	1.000	7	3	5	0	1
Mojica	.875	10	4	17	3	1
Murphy	1.000	8	5	15	0	1
Segedin	.891	43	34	80	14	8
Toussen	.846	12	15	18	6	2

Shortstop	PCT	G	PO	A	E	DP
Castro	.875	5	3	11	2	3
Lassiter	.966	8	13	15	1	3
Mojica	.915	94	119	216	31	48

	PCT	G	PO	A	E	DP
Rosario	.938	5	8	7	1	1
Toussen	.910	32	46	65	11	15

Outfield	PCT	G	PO	A	E	DP
Brown	.947	12	18	0	1	0
De Leon	.953	108	197	4	10	0
Ferraro	.984	32	59	3	1	2
Flores	.985	102	183	9	3	1
Grote	.886	20	28	3	4	0
Heathcott	.974	39	109	4	3	1
Lopez	.800	3	4	0	1	0
Segedin	.947	15	18	0	1	0
Sosa	.975	77	150	8	4	2
Toussen	1.000	19	33	3	0	1

STATEN ISLAND YANKEES   SHORT-SEASON

NEW YORK-PENN LEAGUE

Batting	B-T	HT	WT	DOB	AVG	vLH	vRH	G	AB	R	H	2B	3B	HR	RBI	BB	HBP	SH	SF	SO	SB	CS	SLG	OBP
Austin, Tyler	R-R	6-2	200	9-6-91	.323	.217	.356	27	96	16	31	10	1	3	14	10	4	0	2	23	7	0	.542	.402
Bichette Jr., Dante	R-R	6-1	215	9-26-92	.143	.000	.143	2	7	1	1	0	0	1	1	1	0	0	0	2	0	1	.571	.250
Brown, Shane	R-R	5-11	197	1-11-88	.446	.385	.479	22	74	21	33	6	1	2	5	13	3	0	0	7	0	1	.635	.544
Castillo, Ali	R-R	5-10	165	6-19-89	.224	.302	.193	49	152	24	34	8	1	0	11	9	0	0	2	21	3	2	.289	.264
Culver, Cito	B-R	6-0	185	8-26-92	.250	.324	.224	69	276	40	69	14	2	2	33	30	1	0	3	57	10	0	.337	.323
Gamel, Ben	L-L	5-10	156	5-17-92	.289	.319	.280	55	190	20	55	19	1	2	30	24	3	0	3	50	7	2	.432	.373
Grice, Cody	R-R	6-0	220	1-19-90	.241	.179	.260	46	166	22	40	4	3	1	23	18	3	0	3	41	11	3	.319	.321
Gumbs, Angelo	R-R	6-0	175	10-13-92	.264	.238	.271	51	197	32	52	11	4	3	29	20	1	0	2	57	11	7	.406	.332
Liccien, Jhorge	R-R	6-0	165	10-10-90	.157	.100	.181	34	102	8	16	5	0	0	9	7	3	0	1	36	0	0	.206	.230
McCoy, Nick	R-R	5-10	180	3-2-87	.162	.160	.162	37	99	6	16	3	0	0	8	10	3	0	4	21	0	0	.192	.250
Nunez, Reymond	R-R	6-4	210	9-25-90	.272	.258	.277	69	257	25	70	20	0	3	32	20	2	0	3	80	0	0	.385	.326
Pena, Henry	L-R	6-0	180	10-26-90	.000	.000	.000	3	7	0	0	0	0	0	0	1	0	0	0	7	0	0	.000	.125
Rinard, Bobby	R-R	6-2	180	11-9-88	.208	.194	.214	44	120	22	25	4	0	2	17	11	1	0	1	28	6	0	.292	.278
Stevenson, Casey	L-R	6-3	200	5-18-88	.272	.264	.276	48	158	23	43	9	0	3	27	19	8	0	2	28	1	0	.386	.374
Tejeda, Isaias	R-R	6-0	195	10-28-91	.333	.000	.333	1	3	1	1	0	0	0	0	0	0	0	0	0	0	0	.333	.333
Williams, Mason	L-R	6-0	150	8-21-91	.349	.397	.332	68	269	42	94	11	6	3	31	20	2	0	3	41	28	12	.468	.395
Wilson, Wes	R-R	6-0	210	8-18-89	.244	.467	.133	15	45	8	11	2	0	0	3	0	3	0	3	6	0	1	.289	.275
Wilson, Zach	R-R	6-1	205	8-6-90	.316	.310	.239	65	234	39	60	15	1	10	31	20	13	0	2	40	0	1	.457	.346

Pitching	B-T	HT	WT	DOB	W	L	ERA	G	GS	CG	SV	IP	H	R	ER	HR	BB	SO	AVG	vLH	vRH	K/9	BB/9
Arneson, Zach	R-R	6-2	190	11-17-88	2	1	3.57	15	0	0	1	18	18	8	7	1	8	17	.269	.292	.256	8.66	4.08

Pitching	B-T	HT	WT	DOB	W	L	ERA	G	GS	CG	SV	IP	H	R	ER	HR	BB	SO	AVG	vLH	vRH	K/9	BB/9
Brebbia, John	R-R	6-1	185	5-30-90	0	1	0.00	5	0	0	0	8	5	3	0	1	0	8	.172	.357	.000	9.00	0.00
Cotham, Caleb	R-R	6-3	215	11-6-87	0	1	1.71	12	0	0	0	21	21	7	4	1	9	29	.250	.310	.218	12.43	3.86
DeLuca, Evan	L-L	6-1	195	3-9-91	3	3	4.27	11	11	0	0	46	42	25	22	0	32	43	.247	.250	.246	8.35	6.22
Garrison, Steve	B-L	6-1	195	9-12-86	0	0	0.00	1	1	0	0	5	4	0	0	0	1	4	.235	.000	.235	7.20	1.80
Gerritse, Brett	R-R	6-4	220	3-4-91	3	0	1.25	12	0	0	0	22	14	5	3	1	10	20	.171	.125	.200	8.31	4.15
Hobbs, Dustin	R-R	6-2	200	8-18-89	4	1	6.91	15	0	0	0	27	34	24	21	3	13	22	.306	.325	.296	7.24	4.28
Hughes, Phil	R-R	6-5	240	6-24-86	0	0	2.08	1	1	0	0	4	3	1	1	1	1	7	.188	.333	.154	14.54	2.08
Lewis, Freddy	L-L	6-2	210	12-16-86	5	0	4.03	23	0	0	0	29	29	16	13	1	19	25	.271	.355	.237	7.76	5.90
Maines, Corey	R-R	6-0	195	10-16-88	0	0	16.20	2	0	0	0	2	4	3	3	0	1	2	.500	.333	.600	10.80	5.40
Martinez, Richard	R-R	6-1	194	7-19-88	2	1	5.35	9	8	0	0	35	40	26	21	3	17	26	.292	.280	.299	6.62	4.33
Mitchell, Bryan	L-R	6-2	175	4-19-91	1	3	4.09	14	14	0	0	62	65	34	28	5	31	59	.275	.310	.250	8.61	4.52
Montgomery, Mark	R-R	5-11	205	8-30-90	0	0	2.25	4	0	0	1	4	3	1	1	0	2	10	.200	.000	.250	22.50	4.50
Morton, Taylor	R-R	6-3	194	12-18-91	1	0	5.40	1	1	0	0	5	6	3	3	0	2	3	.300	.222	.364	5.40	3.60
Nuno, Vidal	L-L	5-11	195	7-26-87	5	0	0.72	8	0	0	1	25	14	3	2	0	3	29	.161	.091	.185	10.44	1.08
Oliver, Will	R-R	6-2	185	7-4-87	5	2	3.42	15	14	0	0	68	70	31	26	7	28	57	.275	.220	.310	7.51	3.69
Paullus, Robert	R-R	6-1	190	8-31-89	1	2	3.86	20	0	0	3	30	21	15	13	3	12	41	.186	.119	.225	12.16	3.56
Pinder, Branden	R-R	6-3	210	1-26-89	2	2	1.16	24	0	0	14	31	16	4	4	1	5	38	.152	.263	.090	11.03	1.45
Recchia, Mike	R-R	6-1	210	4-2-89	3	2	3.00	9	0	0	0	15	18	9	5	0	3	19	.300	.227	.342	11.40	1.80
Richardson, Matt	R-R	6-1	175	5-28-90	0	0	3.48	11	0	0	0	10	6	5	4	0	17	8	.176	.273	.130	6.97	14.81
Rodriguez, Wilton	R-R	6-3	195	11-6-90	1	4	4.13	15	14	0	0	65	70	33	30	3	29	49	.279	.298	.265	6.75	3.99
Rondon, Francisco	L-L	6-1	160	4-19-88	1	0	0.00	4	0	0	0	7	3	0	0	0	6	13	.143	.000	.167	16.20	8.10
Tracy, Matt	L-L	6-3	212	11-26-88	1	2	3.04	17	6	0	0	47	41	20	16	1	16	48	.232	.270	.221	9.13	3.04
Varce, Zach	R-R	6-0	195	12-14-88	2	0	5.76	8	3	0	0	25	27	17	16	2	12	27	.270	.250	.288	9.72	4.32
Wetherell, Phil	R-R	6-5	225	10-9-89	4	2	2.40	25	0	0	3	30	23	14	8	2	15	41	.202	.178	.217	12.30	4.50

Fielding

Catcher	PCT	G	PO	A	E	DP	PB
Liccien	.987	34	268	28	4	1	7
McCoy	.990	36	260	41	3	6	4
Tejeda	1.000	1	8	0	0	1	
Wilson	.980	13	93	6	2	0	6

First Base	PCT	G	PO	A	E	DP
Austin	.968	5	28	2	1	2
Nunez	.989	65	570	35	7	53
Stevenson	1.000	3	26	2	0	2
Wilson	1.000	1	6	1	0	0

Second Base	PCT	G	PO	A	E	DP
Castillo	.978	28	33	101	3	20

	PCT	G	PO	A	E	DP
Gumbs	.952	44	68	109	9	21
Stevenson	1.000	3	1	9	0	0

Third Base	PCT	G	PO	A	E	DP
Austin	.904	18	13	34	5	5
Bichette Jr.	1.000	2	2	4	0	0
Castillo	.939	12	9	22	2	0
Stevenson	.932	17	11	30	3	1
Wilson	.903	26	20	45	7	5

Shortstop	PCT	G	PO	A	E	DP
Castillo	1.000	2	2	6	0	2
Culver	.946	67	125	175	17	45
Stevenson	.955	6	2	19	1	3

Outfield	PCT	G	PO	A	E	DP
Brown	1.000	13	15	0	0	0
Castillo	1.000	2	2	0	0	0
Gamel	.978	51	82	5	2	1
Grice	1.000	45	63	3	0	1
Pena	.000	1	0	0	1	0
Rinard	.980	37	49	1	1	0
Stevenson	.958	13	23	0	1	0
Williams	.984	63	119	8	2	1
Wilson	1.000	7	3	0	0	0

GCL YANKEES   ROOKIE
GULF COAST LEAGUE

Batting	B-T	HT	WT	DOB	AVG	vLH	vRH	G	AB	R	H	2B	3B	HR	RBI	BB	HBP	SH	SF	SO	SB	CS	SLG	OBP
Adams, David	R-R	6-2	190	5-15-87	.429	.333	.486	17	56	13	24	9	0	1	11	5	1	0	2	10	2	1	.643	.469
Alcantara, Jorge	R-R	6-1	195	8-9-91	.264	.278	.259	27	72	11	19	7	0	1	6	12	1	0	0	24	6	1	.403	.376
Anderson, Jake	L-R	6-0	170	12-3-91	.215	.292	.188	33	93	12	20	6	2	0	8	9	1	0	0	32	6	0	.323	.291
Austin, Tyler	R-R	6-2	200	9-6-91	.390	.391	.390	20	82	13	32	8	1	3	22	5	2	0	0	16	11	0	.622	.438
Bichette Jr., Dante	R-R	6-1	215	9-26-92	.342	.400	.313	52	196	33	67	17	3	3	47	30	10	0	4	41	3	3	.505	.446
Bird, Greg	L-R	6-3	215	11-9-92	.083	.000	.143	4	12	0	1	0	0	0	0	1	0	0	0	4	0	0	.083	.154
Blaser, Tyson	R-R	6-2	225	12-8-87	.167	.500	.000	9	6	2	1	0	0	0	2	1	1	0	0	1	0	0	.167	.375
Brewer, Dan	R-R	5-11	195	7-19-87	.375	.667	.200	3	8	4	3	1	0	0	4	3	0	0	0	2	2	0	.500	.545
Calderon, Yeicok	L-L	6-2	185	12-23-91	.225	.237	.221	40	151	18	34	11	3	6	25	8	1	0	3	54	5	2	.457	.264
Cave, Jake	L-L	6-0	179	12-7-92	.000	—	—	1	1	0	0	0	0	0	0	1	0	0	0	0	0	0	.000	.500
Custodio, Claudio	R-R	5-10	155	10-30-90	.325	.326	.324	39	157	46	51	9	1	1	19	22	8	0	0	40	26	2	.414	.433
Duran, Matt	R-R	6-1	205	5-1-93	.301	.231	.333	23	83	13	25	6	1	3	17	9	1	0	3	21	0	0	.506	.365
Hurst, Jon	R-R	5-11	195	10-18-88	.667	.667	.667	9	9	3	6	0	0	0	4	2	1	0	0	1	0	0	.667	.750
James, Justin	L-L	6-5	230	11-24-90	.230	.238	.226	25	74	15	17	6	0	0	10	10	4	0	1	19	2	2	.311	.348
Jones, Austin	L-R	6-1	205	8-20-92	.260	.200	.286	15	50	3	13	1	0	0	2	5	0	0	0	17	0	0	.280	.327
Kuo, Fu-Lin	R-R	6-0	185	1-7-91	.250	.350	.191	34	108	20	27	6	1	3	22	18	2	0	2	26	1	3	.407	.362
Lopez, Daniel	R-R	6-2	175	1-17-92	.304	.268	.321	47	168	31	51	11	4	3	16	14	5	0	1	27	22	3	.470	.372
Mustelier, Ronnier	R-R	5-10	210	8-8-84	.500	.500	.500	5	20	3	10	1	0	0	3	1	0	0	0	2	3	1	.550	.524
Pena, Henry	L-R	6-0	180	10-26-90	.245	.278	.229	24	53	10	13	4	1	1	8	10	0	0	1	27	0	0	.415	.359
Rosario, Jose	R-R	5-11	160	11-29-91	.331	.333	.330	43	172	38	57	6	5	6	28	6	5	0	0	28	11	4	.529	.372
Santana, Ravel	R-R	6-2	160	5-1-92	.296	.220	.330	41	162	43	48	11	3	9	29	17	1	0	3	40	10	3	.568	.361
Taveras, Damian	R-R	6-1	205	11-28-89	.305	.278	.313	28	82	9	25	11	0	0	13	13	3	0	1	20	0	0	.439	.414
Tejeda, Isaias	R-R	6-0	195	10-28-91	.331	.347	.323	39	148	34	49	11	3	6	27	11	7	0	0	20	5	3	.568	.404
Valera, Jackson	R-R	6-1	175	4-8-92	.244	.237	.247	35	131	14	32	8	0	2	22	7	6	0	1	13	0	1	.351	.310

Pitching	B-T	HT	WT	DOB	W	L	ERA	G	GS	CG	SV	IP	H	R	ER	HR	BB	SO	AVG	vLH	vRH	K/9	BB/9
Agramonte, Kenedy	R-R	5-10	150	12-4-90	1	0	1.69	9	0	0	0	11	7	7	2	0	12	14	.179	.158	.200	11.81	10.13
Casanova, Reinier	R-R	6-0	215	3-3-87	0	0	0.00	3	0	0	0	4	3	1	0	0	2	5	.188	.200	.182	11.25	4.50
Checo, Mariel	R-R	6-3	190	10-16-89	1	0	2.00	22	0	0	4	27	18	6	6	2	16	41	.184	.220	.158	13.67	5.33
Cotham, Caleb	R-R	6-3	215	11-6-87	0	0	4.50	1	1	0	0	2	2	2	1	0	1	3	.222	.000	.222	13.50	4.50

Pitching	B-T	HT	WT	DOB	W	L	ERA	G	GS	CG	SV	IP	H	R	ER	HR	BB	SO	AVG	vLH	vRH	K/9	BB/9
Cowsert, Cory	L-R	6-0	185	1-19-88	3	2	2.53	21	0	0	3	21	18	6	6	0	9	31	.225	.250	.208	13.08	3.80
Cruz, Dawerd	R-R	6-1	170	12-7-88	4	1	5.97	11	5	0	0	35	41	31	23	3	16	35	.279	.296	.269	9.09	4.15
De La Cruz, Joel	B-R	6-1	190	6-9-89	2	0	5.10	17	0	0	0	30	30	20	17	3	12	19	.256	.268	.250	5.70	3.60
Encinas, Gabe	R-R	6-3	195	12-21-91	3	0	5.08	12	11	0	0	51	57	32	29	3	18	46	.284	.307	.265	8.06	3.16
Feliciano, Pedro	L-L	5-10	190	8-25-76	0	0	0.00	1	1	0	0	1	0	0	0	0	0	1	.000	.000	.000	9.00	0.00
Gipson, Mike	R-R	6-1	195	9-15-88	0	1	1.80	3	1	0	0	5	1	1	1	0	1	4	.063	.111	.000	7.20	1.80
Hinojosa, Joaquin	R-R	5-11	185	4-18-89	0	1	3.24	16	0	0	7	17	20	8	6	2	3	11	.299	.077	.439	5.94	1.62
Isabel, George	R-R	6-6	230	9-9-89	1	0	3.54	16	0	0	0	20	11	11	8	0	14	21	.153	.172	.140	9.30	6.20
Johnson, Trevor	L-L	6-3	190	7-29-88	0	2	17.05	8	0	0	0	6	12	14	12	1	11	4	.400	.364	.421	5.68	15.63
Mahoney, Dan	R-R	6-3	195	2-17-88	0	0	23.14	3	0	0	0	2	3	6	5	1	5	1	.300	.333	.286	3.86	19.29
Maines, Corey	R-R	6-0	195	10-16-88	1	1	3.12	14	0	0	1	17	13	7	6	1	4	18	.210	.333	.159	9.35	2.08
Marquez, Jeff	R-R	6-2	190	8-10-84	0	0	0.00	2	2	0	0	4	1	0	0	0	2	5	.071	.000	.077	11.25	4.50
Marte, Damaso	L-L	6-2	215	2-14-75	0	1	81.00	1	0	0	0	0.2	6	6	6	0	0	0	.750	.000	.857	0.00	0.00
Martinez, Daniel	L-L	6-2	170	6-4-90	1	0	1.02	13	0	0	0	18	15	5	2	0	12	21	.208	.333	.167	10.70	6.11
Morton, Taylor	R-R	6-3	194	12-18-91	3	2	1.98	12	6	0	0	50	49	19	11	1	8	35	.254	.311	.227	6.30	1.44
Nuding, Zach	R-R	6-4	250	3-29-90	0	0	2.57	3	1	0	0	7	6	2	2	0	0	8	.214	.333	.158	10.29	0.00
Phelps, David	R-R	6-2	185	10-9-86	1	1	0.00	2	2	0	0	7	4	2	0	0	1	5	.154	.000	.235	6.43	1.29
Polanco, Reynaldo	R-R	6-2	178	5-20-93	3	6	6.86	11	5	0	0	39	45	35	30	6	15	38	.283	.183	.343	8.69	3.43
Prior, Mark	R-R	6-5	230	9-7-80	0	0	1.13	7	6	0	0	8	3	2	1	0	2	13	.107	.000	.125	14.63	2.25
Rodriguez, Edwin	R-R	6-0	150	5-16-90	4	1	3.20	16	0	0	0	39	32	16	14	2	12	41	.224	.197	.244	9.38	2.75
Rutckyj, Evan	R-L	6-5	213	1-31-92	5	3	4.76	12	8	0	0	45	42	30	24	4	24	37	.240	.189	.254	7.35	4.76
Sharp, Hayden	R-R	6-6	195	10-30-92	0	0	15.75	4	1	0	0	4	12	9	7	0	1	5	.500	.545	.462	11.25	2.25
Smith, Adam	R-R	6-3	200	12-15-89	0	0	81.00	2	0	0	0	0.1	2	6	3	0	5	0	.500	.000	.500	0.00	135.00
Stoneburner, Graham	R-R	6-1	190	9-29-87	0	0	3.77	4	3	0	0	14	12	9	6	0	3	10	.226	.273	.194	6.28	1.88
Texeira, Kanekoa	R-R	6-2	190	2-6-86	0	0	0.00	3	2	0	0	5	3	2	0	0	1	3	.167	.250	.100	5.40	1.80
Triplet, David	R-R	5-11	185	1-28-87	0	0	6.75	2	0	0	0	3	3	3	2	0	5	2	.300	.167	.500	6.75	16.88
Varce, Zach	R-R	6-0	195	12-14-88	1	0	3.94	6	5	0	0	16	18	9	7	0	6	18	.273	.263	.277	10.13	3.38
Vinas, Leonel	R-R	5-10	165	8-27-91	2	1	9.69	14	0	0	2	13	17	15	14	5	9	9	.304	.261	.333	6.23	6.23

Fielding

Catcher	PCT	G	PO	A	E	DP	PB
Blaser	1.000	7	16	1	0	0	0
Hurst	.889	7	16	0	2	0	2
Taveras	1.000	1	5	0	0	0	0
Tejeda	.965	37	295	32	12	1	12
Valera	.984	22	171	18	3	0	1

First Base	PCT	G	PO	A	E	DP
Austin	.989	10	83	3	1	11
Duran	.952	9	59	1	3	2
Jones	.988	10	80	3	1	4
Kuo	.942	16	108	6	7	9
Pena	.727	2	8	0	3	0
Taveras	.989	14	78	8	1	7
Valera	.982	6	48	6	1	4

Second Base	PCT	G	PO	A	E	DP
Adams	1.000	15	15	33	0	8
Alcantara	1.000	3	4	8	0	2
Anderson	.932	30	35	47	6	8
Kuo	.962	7	11	14	1	3
Rosario	.922	19	26	45	6	8

Third Base	PCT	G	PO	A	E	DP
Alcantara	.000	2	0	0	1	0
Austin	.917	6	1	10	1	0
Bichette Jr.	.945	45	30	74	6	10
Duran	.833	6	2	13	3	0
Kuo	1.000	2	4	7	0	0
Rosario	1.000	1	0	3	0	0

Shortstop	PCT	G	PO	A	E	DP
Alcantara	.000	1	0	0	1	0
Anderson	.667	1	1	1	1	0
Custodio	.904	38	67	94	17	21
Rosario	.938	23	46	60	7	10

Outfield	PCT	G	PO	A	E	DP
Alcantara	.941	19	31	1	2	0
Brewer	1.000	2	1	0	0	0
Calderon	.968	37	56	4	2	1
Cave	.000	1	0	0	0	0
James	.886	23	30	1	4	0
Kuo	1.000	7	6	1	0	0
Lopez	.950	44	92	3	5	0
Mustelier	1.000	5	5	1	0	0
Pena	1.000	20	25	0	0	0
Santana	.950	41	92	3	5	0

DSL YANKEES 1   ROOKIE

DOMINICAN SUMMER LEAGUE

Batting	B-T	HT	WT	DOB	AVG	vLH	vRH	G	AB	R	H	2B	3B	HR	RBI	BB	HBP	SH	SF	SO	SB	CS	SLG	OBP
Aquino, Melvin	R-R	5-11	160	7-14-92	.203	.261	.185	53	192	23	39	2	1	2	10	11	7	0	0	52	8	3	.255	.271
Arias, Gian	B-R	5-11	179	10-6-91	.234	.318	.202	54	158	28	37	5	1	3	16	41	4	0	1	35	12	5	.335	.402
Castillo, Ali	R-R	5-10	165	6-19-89	.286	.200	.333	6	14	3	4	1	0	0	1	0	1	0	0	3	3	1	.357	.333
De La Rosa, Elio	R-R	6-0	185	4-18-91	.251	.319	.225	48	167	18	42	4	1	3	25	16	5	0	0	39	1	0	.341	.335
Duran, Francisco	R-R	6-2	185	10-3-91	.206	.095	.255	28	68	10	14	0	1	1	3	8	1	0	0	19	4	1	.279	.299
Figueroa, Jose	L-R	5-10	170	12-9-92	.200	.174	.213	26	70	11	14	5	1	1	9	13	2	0	1	22	1	2	.343	.337
Fulgencio, Edwin	R-R	6-2	190	7-22-91	.267	.000	.308	4	15	2	4	2	0	1	5	1	0	0	0	5	0	0	.600	.313
2-team total (8 Yankees 2)					.244	—		12	41	3	10	3	0	1	7	4	0	0	0	14	0	0	.390	.311
Gonzalez, Maldueno	R-R	5-11	215	3-7-91	.200	.000	.222	6	10	0	2	0	0	0	1	0	0	0	0	6	0	0	.200	.273
Guzman, Miguel	R-R	5-11	157	7-18-90	.160	.143	.167	14	25	4	4	0	0	0	1	5	0	0	0	8	1	1	.160	.300
2-team total (3 Yankees 2)					.154	—		17	26	5	4	0	0	0	1	5	0	0	0	8	1	1	.154	.290
Herrera, Roybell	R-R	5-11	177	12-30-90	.235	.182	.254	26	85	11	20	3	0	3	6	3	2	0	0	26	0	1	.376	.278
Leonora, Ericson	R-R	5-11	174	8-25-92	.252	.250	.253	58	218	32	55	15	1	8	42	17	5	0	0	56	5	4	.440	.321
Lopez, Jerison	R-R	5-11	177	8-24-91	.333	.000	.333	1	3	0	1	0	0	0	1	0	0	0	0	1	0	0	.333	.333
2-team total (44 Yankees 2)					.278	—		45	133	24	37	10	2	1	18	14	1	0	1	27	3	2	.406	.349
Lopez, Jose	R-R	5-10	178	8-13-91	.279	.292	.274	34	86	10	24	4	0	0	8	9	2	0	0	22	1	1	.326	.361
Moronta, Eladio	R-R	5-11	175	12-16-88	.299	.364	.277	47	174	32	52	10	1	5	27	15	9	0	8	40	7	2	.454	.369
Oliberto, Mikeson	R-R	5-10	164	8-23-90	.274	.323	.253	31	106	8	29	3	0	1	7	7	5	0	0	18	11	5	.330	.347
2-team total (31 Yankees 2)					.300	—		62	217	26	65	10	1	3	25	17	5	0	1	45	17	8	.396	.363
Orozco, Jamiel	R-R	5-11	160	1-29-93	.209	.242	.192	54	182	18	38	6	1	2	19	18	3	0	2	32	2	2	.286	.288
Perez, Fernando	B-R	6-2	160	12-9-90	.189	.128	.210	55	185	28	35	5	1	2	15	38	6	0	0	72	5	3	.259	.345
Polanco, Jose	R-R	6-1	190	5-22-91	.204	.222	.197	54	167	26	34	5	2	4	16	24	0	0	2	60	7	2	.329	.301
Polo, Rafael	R-R	6-2	165	4-2-93	.245	.229	.250	55	196	30	48	5	3	0	16	26	4	0	1	41	10	7	.301	.344
Ramos, Abraham	R-R	5-10	150	8-3-92	.294	.278	.300	23	68	8	20	5	0	2	12	3	1	0	1	13	1	2	.456	.329

Pitching	B-T	HT	WT	DOB	W	L	ERA	G	GS	CG	SV	IP	H	R	ER	HR	BB	SO	AVG	vLH	vRH	K/9	BB/9
Bello, Yoely	L-L	6-2	150	12-16-90	3	2	2.68	18	1	0	1	37	27	14	11	1	18	42	.209	.400	.193	10.22	4.38
Beriguete, Victor	R-R	6-1	185	11-6-88	0	2	3.48	12	0	0	0	21	22	12	8	0	12	18	.268	.300	.250	7.84	5.23
Cabrera, Cristofer	R-R	6-0	180	12-25-92	0	3	5.79	9	8	0	0	28	30	29	18	1	19	34	.265	.263	.267	10.93	6.11
Camilo, Gustavo	R-R	5-10	156	1-2-92	0	0	3.15	13	0	0	2	20	20	14	7	0	13	20	.256	.194	.298	9.00	5.85
De La Rosa, Maikel	L-L	6-2	190	11-25-90	0	1	6.38	15	0	0	0	18	22	19	13	0	16	18	.286	.000	.314	8.84	7.85
de la Rosa, Roberto	R-R	6-1	180	3-28-93	0	0	3.00	1	1	0	0	3	3	2	1	0	2	2	.231	.000	.333	6.00	6.00
Gomez, Juan	R-R	6-1	168	12-2-92	0	0	7.45	7	0	0	0	10	9	12	8	1	9	9	.231	.182	.250	8.38	8.38
Heredia, Juan	L-L	6-3	160	1-20-89	4	3	2.38	20	0	0	3	34	30	18	9	0	22	53	.229	.231	.229	14.03	5.82
Mejia, Edison	R-R	6-1	185	7-2-90	2	2	2.91	13	4	0	0	43	39	21	14	3	6	43	.241	.146	.281	8.93	1.25
Mercedes, Melvin	R-R	6-3	170	8-28-89	3	5	2.67	13	10	1	1	57	55	33	17	0	16	52	.239	.293	.221	8.16	2.51
Mojica, Deivi	R-R	6-1	185	3-19-91	4	1	2.82	16	1	0	2	51	55	23	16	1	11	39	.276	.270	.279	6.88	1.94
Pena, Jose	R-R	6-0	190	3-22-91	4	3	3.68	11	4	0	1	37	38	21	15	2	6	42	.260	.288	.245	10.31	1.47
Rincon, Angel	R-R	6-1	180	9-26-92	2	5	2.24	13	12	0	0	60	49	23	15	0	22	60	.214	.231	.207	8.95	3.28
Rivera, Eduardo	R-R	6-5	180	9-24-92	0	1	9.79	14	14	0	0	34	40	43	37	0	42	40	.299	.231	.326	10.59	11.12
Saavedra, Jhon	R-R	6-2	180	2-2-89	3	1	3.19	18	0	0	1	31	30	16	11	0	11	35	.256	.265	.253	10.16	3.19
Soto, Dubeny	R-R	5-11	185	10-30-88	2	0	1.14	15	0	0	4	24	11	4	3	0	5	26	.138	.136	.138	9.89	1.90
Vargas, Cesar	R-R	6-1	160	12-30-91	5	4	2.39	15	15	0	0	72	46	25	19	1	28	85	.184	.182	.185	10.67	3.52

Fielding

Catcher	PCT	G	PO	A	E	DP	PB
Duran	.966	25	152	21	6	1	4
Gonzalez	.957	1	21	1	1	0	0
Herrera	.959	24	194	19	9	1	4
Lopez	.867	1	13	0	2	0	0
Lopez	.970	31	224	31	8	1	7
Vavrusa	1.000	2	12	1	0	0	1

First Base	PCT	G	PO	A	E	DP
Arias	.986	28	197	14	3	13
De La Rosa	.974	43	324	18	9	31
Gonzalez	1.000	2	7	0	0	0
Lopez	1.000	3	21	0	0	1

Second Base	PCT	G	PO	A	E	DP
Arias	.938	3	5	10	1	2

	PCT	G	PO	A	E	DP
Castillo	1.000	4	14	13	0	3
Guzman	.842	8	5	11	3	1
Orozco	.973	43	83	97	5	16
Perez	.938	5	6	9	1	0
Polo	.935	14	29	29	4	8

Third Base	PCT	G	PO	A	E	DP
Aquino	.853	30	26	55	14	6
Arias	.860	21	21	28	8	1
Perez	.714	2	2	3	2	0
Ramos	.846	23	14	41	10	0

Shortstop	PCT	G	PO	A	E	DP
Aquino	.890	21	25	40	8	7
Arias	1.000	1	0	4	0	0
Orozco	.947	10	12	24	2	3

	PCT	G	PO	A	E	DP
Perez	.865	41	45	90	21	18

Outfield	PCT	G	PO	A	E	DP
Arias	1.000	2	2	0	0	0
Duran	1.000	4	3	0	0	0
Figueroa	.966	26	28	0	1	0
Fulgencio	1.000	4	5	1	0	0
Guzman	1.000	3	3	0	0	0
Leonora	.913	55	60	3	6	1
Lopez	1.000	1	1	0	0	0
Moronta	.986	40	64	5	1	3
Oliberto	.941	31	46	2	3	0
Polanco	.923	53	47	1	4	1

DSL YANKEES 2   ROOKIE

DOMINICAN SUMMER LEAGUE

Batting	B-T	HT	WT	DOB	AVG	vLH	vRH	G	AB	R	H	2B	3B	HR	RBI	BB	HBP	SH	SF	SO	SB	CS	SLG	OBP
Brito, Sandy	R-R	6-3	170	6-9-93	.218	.190	.225	62	202	37	44	10	5	3	20	55	5	0	3	81	3	1	.361	.392
Castellon, Alfredo	L-R	6-2	166	6-4-92	.286	.000	.333	8	21	3	6	0	0	0	1	4	0	0	0	5	0	0	.286	.400
Coa, Rainiero	R-R	5-10	170	1-3-93	.308	.188	.339	30	78	11	24	7	0	0	8	10	2	0	1	8	1	1	.397	.396
de Oleo, Eduardo	R-R	5-10	185	1-25-93	.246	.286	.234	44	142	18	35	10	0	1	16	18	1	0	0	36	2	1	.338	.335
Fulgencio, Edwin	R-R	6-2	190	7-22-91	.231	.500	.182	8	26	1	6	1	0	0	2	3	0	0	0	9	0	0	.269	.310
2-team total (4 Yankees 1)					.244	—	—	12	41	3	10	3	0	1	7	4	0	0	0	14	0	0	.390	.311
Gomez, Jhoan	R-R	6-0	175	2-14-93	.241	.220	.247	58	203	31	49	16	0	3	32	20	9	0	4	47	7	4	.365	.331
Guzman, Miguel	R-R	5-11	157	7-18-90	.000	.000	.000	3	1	1	0	0	0	0	0	0	0	0	0	0	0	0	.000	.000
2-team total (14 Yankees 1)					.154	—	—	17	26	5	4	0	0	1	5	0	0	0	8	1	1	.154	.290
Javier, Jose	R-R	5-10	160	9-16-92	.271	.200	.287	46	133	24	36	9	2	2	20	20	4	0	4	25	13	1	.414	.373
Lopez, Daniel	R-R	6-2	175	1-17-92	.424	.600	.393	11	33	14	14	0	3	0	4	3	5	0	1	4	4	0	.606	.524
Lopez, Jerison	R-R	5-11	177	8-24-91	.277	.152	.320	44	130	24	36	10	2	1	18	14	1	0	1	26	3	2	.408	.349
2-team total (1 Yankees 1)					.278	—	—	45	133	24	37	10	2	1	18	14	1	0	1	27	3	2	.406	.349
Marte, Freite	R-R	5-10	174	11-23-89	.203	.067	.241	21	69	10	14	3	2	1	7	5	1	0	0	24	2	2	.348	.267
Martini, Renzo	R-R	6-1	190	8-25-92	.261	.289	.252	46	141	19	42	15	1	3	34	18	6	0	1	15	0	0	.422	.355
Mojica, Miguel	R-R	6-2	180	8-23-92	.259	.214	.270	47	139	18	36	6	2	1	20	19	0	0	1	31	3	5	.353	.346
Noguera, Freddy	R-R	5-9	160	1-10-91	.342	.333	.345	21	38	11	13	3	0	0	10	1	0	0	0	4	2	1	.421	.359
Oliberto, Mikeson	R-R	5-10	164	8-23-90	.324	.310	.329	31	111	18	36	7	1	2	18	10	0	0	1	27	6	3	.459	.377
2-team total (31 Yankees 1)					.300	—	—	62	217	26	65	10	1	3	25	17	5	0	1	45	17	8	.396	.363
Pina, Julio	R-R	5-9	190	6-18-91	.370	.526	.286	22	54	15	20	6	0	2	10	5	0	0	0	11	0	2	.593	.424
Reyes, Allison	R-R	6-0	165	9-16-92	.235	.326	.212	59	230	28	54	11	0	2	20	32	7	0	1	44	15	11	.309	.344
Reynoso, Victor	R-R	6-3	190	12-29-87	.258	.304	.248	44	132	31	34	6	0	3	15	6	3	0	1	26	3	3	.371	.303
Romero, Wilmer	R-R	6-1	185	12-19-93	.226	.212	.231	57	212	24	48	8	3	5	28	18	4	0	0	65	1	4	.363	.299
Tamarez, Christopher	R-R	6-2	170	10-25-93	.197	.245	.182	55	208	30	41	5	0	1	24	19	4	0	8	32	0	3	.236	.268
Valera, Junior	R-R	6-0	180	9-27-92	.167	.143	.182	7	18	2	3	0	0	0	1	2	0	0	0	4	1	1	.167	.250

Pitching	B-T	HT	WT	DOB	W	L	ERA	G	GS	CG	SV	IP	H	R	ER	HR	BB	SO	AVG	vLH	vRH	K/9	BB/9
Aquino, Daury	R-R	6-1	179	4-4-91	3	4	3.27	16	3	0	0	44	47	28	16	1	12	34	.269	.306	.259	6.95	2.45
Batista, Jean	R-R	6-4	175	10-27-91	2	4	4.11	13	11	0	0	61	66	37	28	3	17	55	.281	.265	.285	8.07	2.49
Bautista, Rony	L-L	6-7	200	9-17-91	1	9	4.53	14	14	0	0	58	61	42	29	0	29	57	.275	.111	.282	8.90	4.53
Bello, Hector	L-L	6-1	175	5-19-91	1	3	5.91	20	2	0	1	43	46	41	28	3	34	42	.282	.000	.295	8.86	7.17
Canela, Erick	R-R	6-1	155	10-2-90	1	3	2.61	14	13	0	0	59	51	28	17	1	17	55	.233	.180	.253	8.44	2.61
de Leon, Nestor	R-R	6-2	200	6-22-89	0	1	13.50	4	0	0	0	3	10	5	5	2	0	2	.625	.667	.600	5.40	0.00
De Los Santos, Alexander	R-R	6-2	180	8-16-90	2	1	4.03	15	0	0	1	29	30	22	13	2	14	22	.259	.250	.260	6.83	4.34
Delgado, Johansel	R-R	5-11	155	12-3-90	1	0	2.05	15	0	0	1	22	20	8	5	0	9	14	.256	.200	.270	5.73	3.68
Garcia, Samuel	R-R	6-0	180	3-4-93	1	3	3.92	21	1	0	2	41	46	24	18	2	22	42	.269	.349	.242	9.15	4.79

Pitching	B-T	HT	WT	DOB	W	L	ERA	G	GS	CG	SV	IP	H	R	ER	HR	BB	SO	AVG	vLH	vRH	K/9	BB/9
Gonzalez, Felipe	R-R	6-2	165	8-15-91	3	4	2.35	13	13	1	0	57	59	22	15	1	19	43	.282	.232	.301	6.75	2.98
Joseph, Francis	R-R	5-10	165	10-4-93	1	0	3.32	10	0	0	0	22	18	10	8	0	9	13	.234	.267	.226	5.40	3.74
Mateo, Andres	R-R	5-11	200	4-24-91	2	1	6.62	15	0	0	0	18	13	17	13	0	27	17	.213	.316	.167	8.66	13.75
Matos, Juan	R-R	6-2	190	10-6-93	0	1	4.05	2	2	0	0	7	4	5	3	0	4	3	.167	.400	.105	4.05	5.40
Niebla, Luis Alberto	R-R	6-2	180	1-4-91	6	1	1.72	17	0	0	0	31	20	9	6	0	4	31	.185	.150	.193	8.90	1.15
Nunez, Julian	R-R	6-7	190	7-11-89	0	0	7.36	7	0	0	0	7	7	8	6	1	9	2	.292	.222	.333	2.45	11.05
Perez, Elvin	R-R	6-4	193	8-3-90	2	3	6.99	18	0	0	1	28	31	30	22	2	17	23	.270	.171	.313	7.31	5.40
Peroza, Yunior	R-R	6-2	155	8-9-91	0	2	4.22	12	12	0	0	53	60	34	25	4	20	35	.296	.182	.327	5.91	3.38
Santana, Gabriel	R-R	6-2	170	11-9-89	0	0	0.00	1	0	0	0	1	0	0	0	0	0	0	.000	.000	.000	0.00	0.00
Tolentino, Israel	R-R	6-4	190	1-11-88	0	4	7.91	15	0	0	3	19	20	22	17	0	25	16	.263	.333	.246	7.45	11.64

Fielding

Catcher	PCT	G	PO	A	E	DP	PB
Castellon	1.000	3	17	1	0	0	2
Coa	.988	30	142	25	2	4	11
de Oleo	.976	39	266	60	8	2	14
Pina	.951	14	68	10	4	0	3

First Base	PCT	G	PO	A	E	DP
Lopez	.988	37	300	22	4	23
Martini	.989	26	181	6	2	19
Reynoso	.969	16	111	13	4	9

Second Base	PCT	G	PO	A	E	DP
Javier	.920	26	50	54	9	13
Lopez	1.000	1	1	0	0	0
Noguera	.947	13	17	19	2	6

	PCT	G	PO	A	E	DP
Reyes	.904	35	90	70	17	18
Valera	.909	4	4	6	1	1

Third Base	PCT	G	PO	A	E	DP
Gomez	.866	53	48	113	25	10
Javier	1.000	1	0	2	0	1
Lopez	1.000	4	2	6	0	0
Martini	.964	18	17	37	2	5
Noguera	1.000	2	1	2	0	0

Shortstop	PCT	G	PO	A	E	DP
Guzman	1.000	1	0	2	0	0
Javier	.929	4	4	9	1	2
Noguera	.000	1	0	0	0	0
Reyes	.956	20	29	58	4	17

	PCT	G	PO	A	E	DP
Tamarez	.905	49	60	121	19	18
Valera	.875	2	2	5	1	1

Outfield	PCT	G	PO	A	E	DP
Brito	.911	49	67	5	7	2
Fulgencio	1.000	6	4	1	0	0
Lopez	.913	10	18	3	2	0
Marte	.919	20	33	1	3	1
Mojica	.953	47	98	4	5	1
Oliberto	1.000	29	40	6	0	1
Pina	.500	1	1	0	1	0
Reynoso	.959	30	46	1	2	0
Romero	.984	45	58	4	1	1

NEW YORK YANKEES

Oakland Athletics

SEASON IN A SENTENCE: The Athletics hoped to be a factor in 2011, but injuries to the pitching staff and another season with a punchless offense sent the team to its fourth losing season in five years.

HIGH POINT: The A's routed the Angels 14-0 on May 17, with Gio Gonzalez throwing seven one-hit, shutout innings, to briefly move into a tie for first in the American League West with a 22-20 record. Gonzalez built upon a strong 2010 season by finishing 10th in the AL in ERA and making the all-star team. Rookie second baseman Jemile Weeks provided the A's an offensive spark, hitting .303 with 22 steals after taking over the everyday job in June.

LOW POINT: Oakland's stay atop the division was short, as the team promptly lost six in a row. Things bottomed out a couple of weeks later when the A's lost 10 straight games from May 30-June 9, a stretch that included getting swept by the Orioles in a three-game series, during which they mustered just four runs. The A's fired manager Bob Geren during the streak, replacing him with Bob Melvin.

NOTABLE ROOKIES: For the success Oakland's young pitchers have had, the organization has struggled mightily to produce hitters to go with them. So it was a welcome development to see Weeks, a first-round pick in 2008, seize the second base job and have a stellar offensive rookie season, leading the team in average—no other A's regular batted over .270—and finishing second with 22 steals. Guillermo Moscoso, a 27-year-old rookie righthander, was a revelation in the rotation, posting a 3.38 ERA and .212 opponent average.

KEY TRANSACTIONS: Moscoso was acquired from the Rangers in a minor trade in January. The A's were active on the trade front during the season, though most of their deals involved sending veterans to contending clubs for young players. Mark Ellis, Conor Jackson and Brad Ziegler were among those dealt away. Scott Sizemore, brought over from the Tigers in late May for lefty David Purcey, took over as the regular third baseman.

DOWN ON THE FARM: Triple-A Sacramento finished with the best record in the Pacific Coast League but came up short in the PCL playoffs. Four of Oakland's domestic affiliates reached post-season play. Outfielder Michael Choice, the 2010 first-round pick, belted 30 home runs for high Class A Stockton in his first full season.

OPENING DAY PAYROLL: $66,536,500 (21st)

PLAYERS OF THE YEAR

MAJOR LEAGUE	MINOR LEAGUE
Gio Gonzalez	**Michael Choice**
lhp	of
16-12, 3.12	(High Class A)
197 SO/202 IP	.285/.376/.542
4th in AL in SO/9	30 HR, 28 2B

ORGANIZATION LEADERS

BATTING *Minimum 250 PA

MAJORS

* AVG	Jemile Weeks	.303
* OPS	Josh Willingham	.809
HR	Josh Willingham	29
RBI	Josh Willingham	98

MINORS

* AVG	Wes Timmons, Midland/Sacramento	.341
* OBP	Jermaine Mitchell, Midland/Sacramento	.430
* SLG	Jai Miller, Sacramento	.588
R	Jermaine Mitchell, Midland/Sacramento	115
H	Jermaine Mitchell, Midland/Sacramento	178
TB	Jermaine Mitchell, Midland/Sacramento	284
2B	Matt Carson, Sacramento	34
	Josh Whitaker, Burlington	34
3B	Jermaine Mitchell, Midland/Sacramento	16
HR	Jai Miller, Sacramento	32
RBI	Jai Miller, Sacramento	88
BB	Conner Crumbliss, Stockton	96
SO	Dusty Coleman, Sacramento/Stockton	185
SB	Nino Leyja, Burlington	28

PITCHING #Minimum 75 IP

MAJORS

W	Gio Gonzalez	16
# ERA	Gio Gonzalez	3.12
SO	Gio Gonzalez	197
SV	Andrew Bailey	24

MINORS

W	Graham Godfrey, Midland/Sacramento	14
L	Shawn Haviland, Midland	12
# ERA	Blake Hassebrock, Burlington	2.64
G	Trey Barham, Midland	56
GS	Josh Bowman, Burlington	28
GS	Robert Gilliam, Stockton	28
SV	Jose Guzman, Stockton	20
IP	Robert Gilliam, Stockton	164.1
BB	Gary Daley, Sacramento/Stockton/Midland	67
SO	Robert Gilliam, Stockton	156
	A.J. Griffin, Burlington/Sac./Mid./Stockton	156
# AVG	A.J. Griffin, Burlington/Sac./Mid./Stockton	.238

General Manager: Billy Beane. **Farm Director:** Keith Lieppman. **Scouting Director:** Eric Kubota.

Class	Team	League	W	L	PCT	Finish	Manager(s)
Majors	Oakland Athletics	American	74	88	.457	10th (14)	Bob Geren/Bob Melvin
Triple-A	Sacramento River Cats	Pacific Coast	88	56	.611	1st (16)	Darren Bush
Double-A	Midland RockHounds	Texas	63	77	.450	6th (8)	Steve Scarsone
High A	Stockton Ports	California	75	65	.536	3rd (10)	Webster Garrison
Low A	Burlington Bees	Midwest	76	62	.551	4th (16)	Aaron Nieckula
Short-season	Vermont Lake Monsters	New York-Penn	39	35	.527	t-6th (14)	Rick Magnante
Rookie	AZL Athletics	Arizona	27	29	.482	8th (13)	Marcus Jensen
Overall 2011 Minor League Record			368	324	.532	6th (30)	

ORGANIZATION STATISTICS

OAKLAND ATHLETICS

AMERICAN LEAGUE

Batting	B-T	HT	WT	DOB	AVG	vLH	vRH	G	AB	R	H	2B	3B	HR	RBI	BB	HBP	SH	SF	SO	SB	CS	SLG	OBP
Allen, Brandon	L-R	6-2	235	2-12-86	.205	.167	.224	41	146	18	30	9	2	3	11	11	0	0	1	55	2	0	.356	.259
Barton, Daric	L-R	6-0	205	8-16-85	.212	.253	.193	50	236	27	50	13	0	0	21	39	2	0	3	47	2	1	.267	.325
Carter, Chris	R-R	6-4	245	12-18-86	.136	.050	.208	15	44	2	6	0	0	0	2	6	0	0	0	20	0	0	.136	.174
Crisp, Coco	B-R	5-10	185	11-1-79	.264	.211	.289	136	531	69	140	27	5	8	54	41	1	0	6	65	49	9	.379	.314
DeJesus, David	L-L	5-11	190	12-20-79	.240	.174	.265	131	442	60	106	20	5	10	46	45	11	0	4	86	4	3	.376	.323
Ellis, Mark	R-R	5-10	185	6-6-77	.217	.236	.210	62	217	21	47	11	1	1	16	8	3	0	1	32	7	2	.290	.253
Jackson, Conor	R-R	6-2	215	5-7-82	.249	.254	.246	102	333	30	83	17	1	4	38	30	3	0	2	50	3	1	.342	.315
2-team total (12 Boston)					.244	—	—	114	352	32	86	17	1	5	43	32	3	0	3	53	3	1	.341	.310
Kouzmanoff, Kevin	R-R	6-1	210	7-25-81	.221	.231	.218	46	136	13	30	6	0	4	17	8	1	0	4	27	2	0	.353	.262
LaRoche, Andy	R-R	6-1	195	9-13-83	.247	.286	.231	40	93	10	23	6	1	0	5	8	2	0	0	19	0	0	.333	.320
Matsui, Hideki	L-R	6-2	210	6-12-74	.251	.273	.242	141	517	58	130	28	0	12	72	56	1	0	9	84	1	1	.375	.321
Miller, Jai	R-R	6-3	205	1-17-85	.250	.500	.000	7	12	3	3	0	0	1	2	0	0	0	0	5	0	0	.500	.250
Pennington, Cliff	B-R	5-10	215	6-15-84	.264	.270	.262	148	515	57	136	26	2	8	58	42	1	0	4	104	14	9	.369	.319
Powell, Landon	B-R	6-2	265	3-19-82	.171	.185	.167	36	111	10	19	3	0	1	4	11	0	0	0	32	0	0	.225	.246
Recker, Anthony	R-R	6-2	240	8-29-83	.176	.286	.100	5	17	3	3	1	0	0	4	0	0	0	0	7	0	0	.235	.333
Rosales, Adam	R-R	6-1	195	5-20-83	.098	.114	.077	24	61	5	6	0	0	2	8	4	1	0	1	13	0	0	.197	.162
Sizemore, Scott	R-R	6-0	185	1-4-85	.249	.276	.237	93	305	42	76	21	1	11	52	43	2	0	1	93	4	2	.433	.345
2-team total (17 Detroit)					.245	—	—	110	368	50	90	22	1	11	56	53	2	0	1	112	5	3	.399	.342
Sogard, Eric	L-R	5-10	190	5-22-86	.200	.000	.237	27	70	7	14	3	0	2	4	4	0	0	0	13	0	0	.329	.243
Suzuki, Kurt	R-R	5-11	195	10-4-83	.237	.233	.239	134	460	54	109	26	0	14	44	38	7	0	7	64	2	2	.385	.301
Sweeney, Ryan	L-L	6-4	225	2-20-85	.265	.159	.286	108	264	34	70	11	3	1	25	33	0	0	1	48	1	1	.341	.346
Taylor, Michael	R-R	6-5	255	12-19-85	.200	.211	.182	11	30	4	6	0	0	1	1	5	0	0	0	11	0	0	.300	.314
Weeks, Jemile	B-R	5-9	160	1-26-87	.303	.287	.310	97	406	50	123	26	8	2	36	21	4	0	4	62	22	11	.421	.340
Willingham, Josh	R-R	6-2	215	2-17-79	.246	.208	.264	136	488	69	120	26	0	29	98	56	11	0	8	150	4	1	.477	.332

Pitching	B-T	HT	WT	DOB	W	L	ERA	G	GS	CG	SV	IP	H	R	ER	HR	BB	SO	AVG	vLH	vRH	K/9	BB/9
Anderson, Brett	L-L	6-4	235	2-1-88	3	6	4.00	13	13	1	0	83	86	40	37	8	25	61	.270	.303	.252	6.59	2.70
Bailey, Andrew	R-R	6-3	240	5-31-84	0	4	3.24	42	0	0	24	42	34	18	15	3	12	41	.218	.227	.206	8.86	2.59
Balfour, Grant	R-R	6-2	195	12-30-77	5	2	2.47	62	0	0	2	62	44	17	17	8	20	59	.199	.191	.207	8.56	2.90
Billings, Bruce	R-R	6-0	200	11-18-85	0	0	12.60	3	0	0	0	5	8	9	7	1	6	7	.348	.375	.333	12.60	10.80
Blevins, Jerry	L-L	6-6	175	9-6-83	0	0	2.86	26	0	0	0	28	24	14	9	2	14	26	.235	.256	.220	8.26	4.45
Braden, Dallas	L-L	6-1	185	8-13-83	1	1	3.00	3	3	0	0	18	18	7	6	2	5	15	.265	.333	.250	7.50	2.50
Breslow, Craig	L-L	5-11	190	8-8-80	0	2	3.79	67	0	0	0	59	69	29	25	4	21	44	.296	.352	.261	6.67	3.19
Cahill, Trevor	R-R	6-4	225	3-1-88	12	14	4.16	34	34	0	0	208	214	102	96	19	82	147	.269	.264	.274	6.37	3.55
Carignan, Andrew	R-R	5-11	205	7-23-86	0	0	4.26	6	0	0	0	6	8	4	3	1	2	5	.276	.143	.318	7.11	2.84
Cramer, Bobby	L-L	6-1	205	10-28-79	0	1	1.08	5	0	0	0	8	6	1	1	1	1	6	.200	.000	.273	6.48	1.08
De Los Santos, Fautino	R-R	6-2	225	2-15-86	3	2	4.32	34	0	0	0	33	27	19	16	4	17	43	.220	.173	.254	11.61	4.59
Devine, Joey	R-R	6-0	235	9-19-83	1	1	3.52	26	0	0	0	23	18	9	9	0	11	20	.214	.268	.163	7.83	4.30
Fuentes, Brian	L-L	6-4	230	8-9-75	2	8	3.70	67	0	0	12	58	52	30	24	6	20	48	.237	.265	.221	6.48	3.09
Godfrey, Graham	R-R	6-3	215	8-9-84	1	2	3.96	5	4	0	0	25	32	14	11	3	5	13	.305	.267	.356	4.68	1.80
Gonzalez, Gio	R-L	6-0	205	9-19-85	16	12	3.12	32	32	0	0	202	175	81	70	17	91	197	.230	.253	.224	8.78	4.05
Harden, Rich	L-R	6-1	195	11-30-81	4	4	5.12	15	15	0	0	83	87	48	47	17	31	91	.267	.232	.297	9.91	3.38
Magnuson, Trystan	L-R	6-7	210	6-6-85	0	0	6.14	9	0	0	0	15	15	11	10	3	5	11	.250	.091	.342	6.75	3.07
McCarthy, Brandon	R-R	6-7	200	7-7-83	9	9	3.32	25	25	5	0	171	168	73	63	11	25	123	.258	.256	.260	6.49	1.32
Moscoso, Guillermo	R-R	6-1	200	11-14-83	8	10	3.38	23	21	0	0	128	102	59	48	14	38	74	.212	.225	.197	5.20	2.67
Norberto, Jordan	L-L	6-0	195	12-8-86	0	0	8.10	6	0	0	0	7	8	6	6	0	7	6	.308	.333	.294	5.40	9.45
Outman, Josh	L-L	6-1	185	9-14-84	3	5	3.70	13	9	0	0	58	62	27	24	4	23	35	.277	.217	.299	5.40	3.55
Purcey, David	L-L	6-4	240	4-22-82	0	0	2.13	9	0	0	0	13	9	3	3	1	3	7	.191	.313	.129	4.97	2.13
3-team total (19 Detroit, 5 Toronto)					1	2	5.61	30	0	0	0	34	33	21	21	2	27	22	—	—	—	5.88	7.22
Ross, Tyson	R-R	6-6	230	4-22-87	3	3	2.75	9	6	0	0	36	33	12	11	1	13	24	.252	.250	.254	6.00	3.25
Wagner, Neil	R-R	6-0	195	1-1-84	0	0	7.20	6	0	0	0	5	6	7	4	1	3	4	.300	.429	.231	7.20	5.40
Wuertz, Michael	R-R	6-3	210	12-15-78	0	0	6.68	39	0	0	0	34	37	25	25	5	26	32	.280	.241	.311	8.55	6.95
Ziegler, Brad	R-R	6-4	205	10-10-79	3	2	2.39	43	0	0	1	38	38	14	10	0	13	29	.264	.396	.198	6.93	3.11

Fielding

Catcher	PCT	G	PO	A	E	DP	PB
Powell	.992	33	237	15	2	2	1
Recker	.978	5	44	1	1	0	0
Suzuki	.993	129	914	55	7	7	5

First Base	PCT	G	PO	A	E	DP
Allen	.989	41	334	19	4	24
Barton	.988	65	596	39	8	72
Carter	.986	11	64	4	1	5
Ellis	1.000	2	15	3	0	2
Jackson	.997	50	345	17	1	27
LaRoche	1.000	1	13	2	0	0
Powell	1.000	1	8	2	0	1
Rosales	1.000	5	36	2	0	2

Second Base	PCT	G	PO	A	E	DP
Ellis	.994	59	127	189	2	50

	PCT	G	PO	A	E	DP	PB
LaRoche	1.000	8	7	9	0	2	
Rosales	1.000	3	3	4	0	1	
Sizemore	1.000	1	0	1	0	0	
Sogard	.933	3	5	9	1	2	
Weeks	.969	96	148	261	13	49	

Third Base	PCT	G	PO	A	E	DP
Jackson	1.000	6	3	6	0	0
Kouzmanoff	.922	46	29	78	9	9
LaRoche	.905	27	10	28	4	4
Rosales	.833	6	4	6	2	1
Sizemore	.934	91	54	129	13	10
Sogard	1.000	10	5	13	0	0

Shortstop	PCT	G	PO	A	E	DP
LaRoche	.966	9	3	25	1	3
Pennington	.964	147	216	374	22	90

Rosales	.913	7	9	12	2	3	
Sogard	.974	14	15	22	1	2	

Outfield	PCT	G	PO	A	E	DP
Crisp	.997	133	321	2	1	1
DeJesus	.984	122	240	6	4	1
Jackson	.988	46	79	4	1	2
Matsui	.982	27	53	3	1	2
Miller	1.000	5	2	0	0	0
Rosales	1.000	2	4	0	0	0
Sweeney	1.000	92	150	3	0	0
Taylor	.920	11	23	0	2	0
Willingham	.988	96	159	3	2	1

SACRAMENTO RIVER CATS

PACIFIC COAST LEAGUE

Batting	B-T	HT	WT	DOB	AVG	vLH	vRH	G	AB	R	H	2B	3B	HR	RBI	BB	HBP	SH	SF	SO	SB	CS	SLG	OBP
Allen, Brandon	L-R	6-2	235	2-12-86	.250	.400	.200	10	40	4	10	2	1	3	6	2	0	0	0	11	0	0	.575	.286
2-team total (83 Reno)					.299	—	—	93	344	79	103	23	5	21	72	66	4	0	5	101	7	4	.578	.413
Barton, Daric	L-R	6-0	205	8-16-85	.197	.167	.209	17	61	10	12	2	0	0	4	14	0	0	0	16	0	0	.230	.347
Canham, Mitch	L-R	6-2	205	9-25-84	.280	.250	.286	8	25	2	7	0	0	0	5	0	0	0	7	0	0	.280	.400
Cardenas, Adrian	L-R	6-0	205	10-10-87	.314	.344	.300	127	491	70	154	28	4	5	51	47	2	0	3	56	13	6	.418	.374
Carson, Matt	R-R	6-2	200	7-1-81	.285	.303	.277	90	368	61	105	34	1	19	65	27	3	0	2	88	11	1	.538	.338
Carter, Chris	R-R	6-4	245	12-18-86	.274	.241	.286	75	296	55	81	18	2	18	72	42	3	0	3	85	5	1	.530	.366
Coleman, Dusty	R-R	6-2	185	4-20-87	.333	.182	.400	10	36	5	12	3	0	0	4	1	0	0	0	14	0	2	.417	.351
Donaldson, Josh	R-R	6-0	220	12-8-85	.261	.250	.266	115	444	79	116	28	0	17	70	51	6	0	2	100	13	4	.439	.344
Ellis, Mark	R-R	5-10	185	6-6-77	.200	.000	.222	3	10	0	2	1	0	0	1	1	0	0	0	0	0	0	.300	.273
Galarraga, Joel	R-R	5-11	185	3-20-82	.406	.364	.429	8	32	8	13	2	0	0	3	1	0	0	0	3	0	0	.469	.424
Heether, Adam	R-R	6-0	195	1-14-82	.153	.100	.207	20	59	8	9	0	0	1	8	16	1	0	0	17	1	0	.203	.342
Horton, Josh	L-R	6-2	215	2-19-86	.217	.161	.246	26	92	8	20	3	0	1	14	8	1	0	2	11	2	0	.283	.282
Kouzmanoff, Kevin	R-R	6-1	210	7-25-81	.302	.321	.293	61	262	41	79	24	1	13	58	11	5	0	1	36	1	1	.550	.341
Ladendorf, Tyler	R-R	6-0	210	3-7-88	.211	.250	.200	4	19	2	4	1	0	0	1	0	0	0	0	6	0	0	.263	.250
LaRoche, Andy	R-R	6-1	195	9-13-83	.254	.308	.234	54	197	24	50	12	0	4	29	19	6	0	2	24	3	2	.376	.335
Miller, Jai	R-R	6-3	205	1-17-85	.276	.263	.282	110	410	81	113	24	4	32	88	54	8	0	3	179	16	0	.588	.368
Mitchell, Jermaine	L-L	6-0	205	11-2-84	.302	.231	.329	56	232	48	70	14	3	5	28	39	0	0	1	47	13	5	.453	.401
Parker, Steve	L-R	6-2	200	9-3-87	.320	.250	.333	5	25	4	8	0	0	0	2	2	0	0	6	0	0	.320	.370
Peterson, Shane	L-L	6-0	195	2-11-88	.293	.196	.331	46	167	31	49	7	3	6	32	23	0	0	1	37	2	1	.479	.377
Powell, Landon	B-R	6-3	265	3-19-82	.283	.143	.344	12	46	6	13	0	0	1	5	7	0	0	0	9	0	0	.348	.377
Recker, Anthony	R-R	6-2	240	8-29-83	.287	.327	.271	99	345	61	99	24	1	16	48	56	4	0	5	81	7	5	.501	.388
Rosales, Adam	R-R	6-1	195	5-20-83	.265	.196	.297	40	147	23	39	5	1	3	22	13	1	0	3	32	1	1	.374	.323
Sizemore, Scott	R-R	6-0	185	1-4-85	.267	.222	.286	9	30	11	8	2	0	1	3	12	0	0	1	4	2	1	.433	.465
Sogard, Eric	L-R	5-10	190	5-22-86	.298	.306	.294	79	315	55	94	16	2	5	37	40	4	0	3	34	13	3	.410	.381
Taylor, Michael	R-R	6-5	255	12-19-85	.272	.229	.289	93	349	51	95	16	0	16	64	46	3	0	2	80	14	5	.456	.360
Timmons, Wes	R-R	6-0	185	7-12-79	.321	.250	.348	56	190	34	61	14	0	3	34	30	8	0	1	10	5	3	.442	.432
Tolleson, Steve	R-R	5-11	190	11-1-83	.274	.239	.287	46	175	29	48	6	0	5	19	31	2	0	1	37	8	2	.394	.388
2-team total (77 Tucson)					.275	—	—	123	487	77	134	27	2	9	55	60	5	0	4	93	24	5	.394	.358
Weeks, Jemile	B-R	5-9	160	1-26-87	.321	.298	.331	45	184	30	59	6	4	3	22	29	2	0	1	32	10	4	.446	.417
Willingham, Josh	R-R	6-2	215	2-17-79	.200	.000	.333	2	5	1	1	0	0	1	2	2	0	0	0	2	0	0	.800	.429

Pitching	B-T	HT	WT	DOB	W	L	ERA	G	GS	CG	SV	IP	H	R	ER	HR	BB	SO	AVG	vLH	vRH	K/9	BB/9
Bailey, Andrew	R-R	6-3	240	5-31-84	0	0	0.00	4	0	0	0	4	3	0	0	0	1	3	.200	.200	.200	6.75	2.25
Balfour, Grant	R-R	6-2	195	12-30-77	0	0	9.00	1	0	0	0	1	2	1	1	0	1	0	.400	.333	.500	0.00	9.00
Banwart, Travis	R-R	6-4	205	2-14-86	9	9	4.63	27	25	0	0	150	145	87	77	22	46	120	.250	.296	.215	7.22	2.77
Bateman, Joe	R-R	6-1	185	5-6-80	2	1	5.40	26	0	0	2	43	53	26	26	4	15	35	.299	.361	.257	7.27	3.12
Benacka, Mike	R-R	6-2	210	8-2-82	0	1	6.35	4	0	0	0	6	7	6	4	3	6	4	.333	.444	.250	6.35	9.53
Billings, Bruce	R-R	6-2	200	11-18-85	1	0	4.44	15	2	0	0	26	22	15	13	1	13	25	.232	.200	.255	8.54	4.44
2-team total (29 Colorado Springs)					7	2	4.46	44	2	0	1	77	80	44	38	5	34	72	—	—	—	8.45	3.99
Blevins, Jerry	L-L	6-6	175	9-6-83	2	0	4.85	27	0	0	0	30	25	16	16	3	7	35	.227	.188	.258	10.62	2.12
Cabrera, Fernando	R-R	6-4	225	11-16-81	4	3	2.71	53	0	0	9	63	49	22	19	6	26	73	.216	.247	.196	10.43	3.71
Capra, Anthony	L-L	6-1	200	4-3-87	1	1	1.80	1	1	0	0	5	3	1	1	0	2	4	.188	.333	.154	7.20	5.40
Carignan, Andrew	R-R	5-11	205	7-23-86	0	0	2.16	13	0	0	0	17	11	5	4	1	7	19	.186	.211	.175	10.26	3.78
Chulk, Vinnie	R-R	6-2	200	12-19-78	3	4	3.36	54	0	0	4	70	58	26	26	5	26	55	.227	.257	.206	7.11	3.36
Cramer, Bobby	L-L	6-1	205	10-28-79	1	0	4.03	6	6	0	0	22	22	11	10	3	12	26	.253	.258	.250	10.48	4.84
Daley, Gary	R-R	6-3	200	11-1-85	1	1	8.00	2	2	0	0	9	11	9	8	2	5	1	.314	.143	.429	1.00	5.00
De Los Santos, Fautino	R-R	6-2	225	2-15-86	0	0	1.83	15	0	0	0	20	18	4	4	0	12	21	.247	.172	.295	9.61	5.49
DeHoyos, Gabe	R-R	5-11	260	4-14-80	0	1	6.17	8	0	0	1	12	15	8	8	0	3	10	.313	.217	.400	7.71	2.31
Devine, Joey	R-R	6-0	235	9-19-83	4	0	4.24	23	0	0	3	23	21	15	12	11	2	9	35	.183	.206	.165	13.50	0.77
DiNardo, Lenny	L-L	6-2	220	9-19-79	3	5	6.49	13	9	0	0	61	76	53	44	8	25	41	.302	.352	.282	6.05	3.69
Eyre, Willie	R-R	6-0	225	7-21-78	4	5	3.48	39	2	0	9	62	63	29	24	5	28	45	.269	.198	.328	6.53	4.06
Farquhar, Danny	R-R	5-11	180	2-17-87	0	0	0.00	4	0	0	1	8	7	1	0	0	3	9	.233	.308	.176	10.13	3.38

Pitching

Pitching	B-T	HT	WT	DOB	W	L	ERA	G	GS	CG	SV	IP	H	R	ER	HR	BB	SO	AVG	vLH	vRH	K/9	BB/9
2-team total (50 Las Vegas)					4	5	4.07	54	0	0	15	60	70	33	27	4	21	52	—	—	—	7.84	3.17
Godfrey, Graham	R-R	6-3	215	8-9-84	14	3	2.68	19	18	0	0	107	92	38	32	6	30	89	.227	.223	.230	7.46	2.52
Griffin, A.J.	R-R	6-5	215	1-28-88	0	1	3.00	1	1	0	0	6	6	3	2	1	2	8	.273	.250	.300	12.00	3.00
Harden, Rich	L-R	6-1	195	11-30-81	0	0	3.52	2	2	0	0	8	3	3	3	1	3	12	.115	.083	.143	14.09	3.52
Hernandez, Carlos	L-L	5-11	155	3-4-87	8	7	5.27	19	19	0	0	109	135	70	64	12	32	80	.308	.261	.326	6.59	2.63
Hollingsworth, Ethan	R-R	6-2	200	5-4-87	1	0	5.06	2	2	0	0	11	13	6	6	2	4	7	.310	.375	.294	5.91	3.38
Hornbeck, Ben	R-L	6-5	180	7-22-87	1	0	1.13	6	0	0	0	8	6	2	1	0	4	7	.207	.273	.167	7.88	4.50
Hunter, Brett	R-R	6-4	215	6-27-87	0	0	0.00	2	0	0	0	3	1	0	0	0	1	4	.100	.333	.000	12.00	3.00
Lansford, Jared	R-R	6-0	190	10-22-86	0	0	4.50	2	0	0	1	2	4	1	1	0	1	3	.444	.000	.444	13.50	4.50
Magnuson, Trystan	L-R	6-7	210	6-6-85	4	2	2.98	30	0	0	5	45	34	20	15	4	19	46	.210	.242	.188	9.13	3.77
Marti, Yadel	R-R	5-11	180	7-22-79	5	1	4.92	16	14	0	0	82	100	51	45	11	33	50	.304	.291	.315	5.47	3.61
Mathis, Doug	R-R	6-3	220	6-7-83	0	1	6.33	4	4	0	0	21	27	16	15	1	9	10	.303	.256	.348	4.22	3.80
2-team total (13 Fresno)					0	5	4.27	17	17	0	0	86	92	49	41	6	40	64	—	—	—	6.67	4.17
Moscoso, Guillermo	R-R	6-1	200	11-14-83	3	3	3.88	9	8	0	0	46	41	22	20	3	16	52	.230	.235	.227	10.10	3.11
Mye, Chaz	L-L	6-3	200	4-27-88	0	0	0.00	1	0	0	0	1	0	0	0	0	1	0	.000	.000	.000	0.00	9.00
Norberto, Jordan	L-L	6-0	195	12-8-86	0	0	1.08	6	0	0	1	8	6	1	1	1	4	10	.207	.333	.174	10.80	4.32
2-team total (41 Reno)					6	2	3.79	47	0	0	2	57	52	27	24	2	30	64	—	—	—	10.11	4.74
Outman, Josh	L-L	6-1	185	9-14-84	8	3	3.91	17	17	0	0	78	77	47	34	7	47	72	.256	.231	.269	8.27	5.40
Perlman, Max	R-L	6-7	235	2-2-88	1	0	2.00	2	2	0	0	9	6	2	2	0	2	3	.188	.250	.150	3.00	2.00
Ross, Tyson	R-R	6-6	230	4-22-87	3	2	7.61	9	9	0	0	37	52	34	31	5	22	34	.325	.260	.386	8.35	5.40
Souza, Justin	R-R	6-1	185	10-22-85	3	1	4.85	26	0	0	0	43	43	24	23	8	11	31	.264	.288	.244	6.54	2.32
Wagner, Neil	R-R	6-0	195	1-1-84	2	1	3.10	22	0	0	2	29	27	10	10	2	10	34	.241	.271	.219	10.55	3.10
Wuertz, Michael	R-R	6-3	210	12-15-78	0	0	9.00	3	1	0	0	3	3	3	3	0	2	5	.250	.333	.222	15.00	6.00

Fielding

Catcher

Catcher	PCT	G	PO	A	E	DP	PB
Canham	1.000	1	2	0	0	0	0
Donaldson	.977	71	546	53	14	9	7
Galarraga	.979	6	43	3	1	0	1
Powell	.984	9	58	3	1	1	1
Recker	.994	61	497	34	3	4	6

First Base

First Base	PCT	G	PO	A	E	DP
Allen	1.000	5	32	1	0	3
Barton	.993	17	128	7	1	11
Canham	1.000	3	26	3	0	1
Carter	.995	49	374	15	2	38
Donaldson	1.000	1	1	0	0	1
Galarraga	1.000	1	2	0	0	0
Heether	1.000	3	18	1	0	1
LaRoche	1.000	3	25	2	0	3
Parker	1.000	1	13	0	0	1
Peterson	.986	16	128	8	2	11
Recker	.995	25	174	19	1	17
Timmons	1.000	26	213	11	0	18

Second Base

Second Base	PCT	G	PO	A	E	DP
Cardenas	.978	35	67	68	3	14

(continued)

	PCT	G	PO	A	E	DP
Donaldson	1.000	2	4	7	0	2
Ellis	1.000	2	5	4	0	0
Horton	.947	5	8	10	1	3
LaRoche	.970	33	52	79	4	22
Parker	.000	1	0	0	0	0
Rosales	.952	6	4	14	1	1
Sizemore	1.000	1	2	2	0	0
Timmons	.938	16	33	42	5	9
Tolleson	1.000	12	24	27	0	6
Weeks	.965	43	75	119	7	26

Third Base

Third Base	PCT	G	PO	A	E	DP
Cardenas	.886	13	8	23	4	0
Carter	.800	3	2	2	1	0
Donaldson	.944	27	18	50	4	1
Horton	.970	15	12	20	1	4
Kouzmanoff	.970	56	45	85	4	12
Parker	1.000	4	1	8	0	1
Rosales	1.000	4	2	6	0	0
Sizemore	.923	8	4	8	1	1
Timmons	1.000	11	9	13	0	1
Tolleson	.933	9	4	10	1	0

Shortstop

Shortstop	PCT	G	PO	A	E	DP
Cardenas	1.000	3	3	7	0	1
Coleman	1.000	10	11	33	0	5
Horton	.962	6	11	14	1	4
Ladendorf	1.000	4	7	20	0	7
LaRoche	.967	14	20	38	2	9
Rosales	.984	32	47	78	2	14
Sogard	.976	73	119	167	7	34
Tolleson	.963	7	8	18	1	4

Outfield

Outfield	PCT	G	PO	A	E	DP
Allen	1.000	6	4	0	0	0
Canham	1.000	1	1	0	0	0
Cardenas	.974	44	74	0	2	0
Carson	.971	83	195	9	6	3
Carter	1.000	7	4	0	0	0
Donaldson	.600	2	3	0	2	0
Heether	.931	15	27	0	2	0
Miller	.980	108	240	3	5	2
Mitchell	.973	47	141	2	4	1
Peterson	.982	26	55	1	1	1
Taylor	.972	88	167	7	5	3
Tolleson	.842	11	15	1	3	0

MIDLAND ROCKHOUNDS

DOUBLE-A

TEXAS LEAGUE

Batting	B-T	HT	WT	DOB	AVG	vLH	vRH	G	AB	R	H	2B	3B	HR	RBI	BB	HBP	SH	SF	SO	SB	CS	SLG	OBP
Barfield, Jeremy	R-L	6-5	240	7-12-88	.257	.216	.276	131	495	56	127	24	3	11	72	42	4	0	3	90	1	1	.384	.318
Canham, Mitch	L-R	6-2	205	9-25-84	.226	.297	.203	45	155	22	35	5	2	0	18	15	2	0	2	30	2	0	.284	.299
Carter, Yusuf	R-R	6-2	205	2-6-85	.169	.130	.182	21	89	7	15	5	1	2	7	1	0	0	0	31	2	1	.315	.178
Christian, Jason	L-R	6-3	170	6-16-87	.273	.281	.271	36	128	20	35	6	1	1	10	10	1	0	1	32	5	2	.375	.324
Green, Grant	R-R	6-3	180	9-27-87	.291	.329	.272	127	530	76	154	33	1	9	62	39	6	0	6	119	6	8	.408	.343
Heether, Adam	R-R	6-0	195	1-14-82	.255	.268	.247	101	365	63	93	21	0	13	62	45	22	0	4	72	6	1	.419	.367
Horton, Josh	L-R	6-2	215	2-19-86	.000	.000	.000	1	3	0	0	0	0	0	0	0	0	0	0	1	0	0	.000	.000
Ladendorf, Tyler	R-R	6-0	210	3-7-88	.225	.298	.193	125	432	55	97	17	3	6	35	47	6	0	2	87	6	5	.319	.308
Mitchell, Jermaine	L-L	6-0	205	11-2-84	.355	.333	.368	74	304	67	108	15	13	10	50	54	1	0	1	65	14	13	.589	.453
Nunez, Juan	R-R	6-2	220	8-27-87	.000	.000	.000	1	1	0	0	0	0	0	0	0	0	0	0	1	0	0	.000	.000
Ortiz, Ryan	R-R	6-3	195	9-29-87	.237	.283	.212	47	152	19	36	4	0	2	14	21	8	0	1	40	2	0	.303	.357
Paramore, Petey	B-R	6-2	195	10-30-86	.192	.196	.189	45	151	19	29	2	1	3	16	24	2	0	2	42	0	0	.278	.307
Parker, Steve	L-R	6-2	200	9-3-87	.286	.285	.286	132	504	72	144	30	2	10	74	69	2	0	1	107	1	1	.413	.373
Peterson, Shane	L-L	6-0	195	2-11-88	.260	.119	.310	59	227	33	59	16	1	3	27	30	5	0	1	38	11	1	.379	.357
Rivero, Jose	R-R	6-3	220	1-8-90	.154	.333	.100	4	13	1	2	1	0	0	2	2	0	0	0	3	0	0	.308	.267
Spina, Mike	R-R	6-1	220	12-17-86	.282	.244	.300	129	483	64	136	32	3	10	75	70	10	0	5	110	1	0	.422	.380
Sulentic, Matt	L-R	5-10	170	10-6-87	.272	.255	.278	124	493	64	134	22	1	6	46	46	3	0	4	94	24	7	.357	.335
Timmons, Wes	R-R	6-0	185	7-12-79	.365	.321	.390	39	156	21	57	6	0	5	28	8	3	0	2	11	0	0	.500	.402
Walton, Kent	R-R	6-1	185	12-11-86	.235	.167	.282	37	119	16	28	5	0	1	15	16	2	0	2	39	3	1	.303	.331

Pitching	B-T	HT	WT	DOB	W	L	ERA	G	GS	CG	SV	IP	H	R	ER	HR	BB	SO	AVG	vLH	vRH	K/9	BB/9
Barham, Trey	L-L	6-0	215	11-7-85	6	2	2.95	56	0	0	1	61	58	23	20	5	27	48	.267	.273	.262	7.08	3.98

OAKLAND ATHLETICS

Pitching	B-T	HT	WT	DOB	W	L	ERA	G	GS	CG	SV	IP	H	R	ER	HR	BB	SO	AVG	vLH	vRH	K/9	BB/9
Bateman, Joe	R-R	6-1	185	5-6-80	0	0	3.00	4	0	0	0	9	5	3	3	0	2	7	.161	.083	.211	7.00	2.00
Bergmann, Jason	R-R	6-3	220	9-25-81	1	7	5.65	16	14	0	0	78	84	54	49	8	37	53	.285	.301	.264	6.12	4.27
Capra, Anthony	L-L	6-1	200	4-3-87	1	7	5.36	20	20	0	0	97	106	67	58	8	54	82	.280	.333	.257	7.58	4.99
Carignan, Andrew	R-R	5-11	205	7-23-86	0	0	3.18	11	0	0	3	11	10	4	4	1	3	15	.238	.238	.238	11.91	2.38
Daley, Gary	R-R	6-3	200	11-1-85	6	7	5.18	20	19	0	0	106	121	72	61	5	50	78	.289	.274	.303	6.62	4.25
De Los Santos, Fautino	R-R	6-2	225	2-15-86	0	0	2.89	8	0	0	3	9	8	3	3	1	4	15	.222	.154	.261	14.46	3.86
DiNardo, Lenny	L-L	6-2	220	9-19-79	1	2	3.51	6	4	0	0	26	28	10	10	3	1	20	.275	.231	.302	7.01	0.35
Godfrey, Graham	R-R	6-3	215	8-9-84	0	0	0.00	1	1	0	0	4	3	2	0	0	1	6	.200	.333	.111	13.50	2.25
Gray, Sonny	R-R	5-11	200	11-7-89	1	0	0.45	5	5	0	0	20	15	1	1	0	6	18	.214	.225	.200	8.10	2.70
Griffin, A.J.	R-R	6-5	215	1-28-88	2	3	6.47	6	6	0	0	32	39	24	23	6	11	20	.293	.269	.318	5.63	3.09
Haviland, Shawn	R-R	6-2	200	11-10-85	6	12	7.08	27	27	0	0	144	205	133	113	24	42	110	.330	.339	.323	6.89	2.63
Hernandez, Carlos	L-L	5-11	155	3-4-87	4	1	5.27	8	8	0	0	43	57	28	25	6	10	37	.315	.326	.312	7.80	2.11
Hollingsworth, Ethan	R-R	6-2	200	5-4-87	6	5	3.61	17	16	0	1	95	107	47	38	8	23	66	.287	.321	.260	6.27	2.19
Hornbeck, Ben	R-L	6-5	180	7-22-87	0	0	14.73	4	0	0	0	4	8	6	6	0	2	7	.444	.400	.500	17.18	4.91
Hunter, Brett	R-R	6-4	215	6-27-87	4	2	4.73	23	0	0	0	27	28	18	14	3	16	25	.264	.310	.234	8.44	5.40
Lansford, Jared	R-R	6-0	190	10-22-86	3	5	4.54	48	0	0	9	79	87	45	40	7	27	48	.285	.346	.237	5.45	3.06
Marti, Yadel	R-R	5-11	180	7-22-79	2	0	0.75	2	2	0	0	12	7	1	1	0	2	7	.163	.148	.188	5.25	1.50
Meloan, John	R-R	6-3	225	7-11-84	1	3	4.67	25	0	0	5	27	28	21	14	2	20	25	.269	.298	.246	8.33	6.67
Murray, Justin	R-R	6-4	200	5-11-87	0	5	6.49	7	7	0	0	35	47	29	25	6	15	21	.333	.346	.326	5.45	3.89
Ortiz, Jonathan	R-R	5-10	190	5-11-87	5	2	4.02	42	0	0	1	65	62	30	29	7	24	60	.250	.288	.222	8.31	3.32
Sewell, Lance	L-L	6-3	195	6-17-86	0	0	10.29	6	0	0	0	7	16	14	8	2	7	8	.432	.500	.400	10.29	9.00
Smyth, Paul	R-R	5-11	210	4-1-87	5	3	4.85	40	0	0	1	65	67	39	35	8	29	59	.273	.283	.266	8.17	4.02
Souza, Justin	R-R	6-1	185	10-22-85	1	0	1.33	14	0	0	1	20	9	3	3	2	2	17	.125	.121	.128	7.52	0.89
Storey, Mickey	R-R	6-2	185	3-16-86	3	3	4.03	27	0	0	4	38	41	17	17	3	13	31	.281	.328	.247	7.34	3.08
Thornton, Zack	R-R	6-3	213	5-19-88	0	0	0.00	1	0	0	0	3	1	0	0	0	1	4	.100	.000	.000	12.00	3.00
Trinidad, Polin	L-L	6-3	195	11-19-84	4	4	6.91	18	9	0	0	56	70	47	43	6	19	32	.314	.319	.311	5.14	3.05
Wagner, Neil	R-R	6-0	195	1-1-84	1	3	3.38	28	0	0	4	37	31	18	14	0	13	53	.225	.235	.218	12.78	3.13
Williamson, Fabian	R-L	6-2	175	10-20-88	0	0	6.35	10	2	0	0	23	29	17	16	3	16	17	.315	.250	.338	6.75	6.35

Fielding

Catcher	PCT	G	PO	A	E	DP	PB
Canham	.989	34	261	18	3	3	7
Carter	.969	16	141	14	5	0	4
Nunez	1.000	1	3	0	0	0	0
Ortiz	.973	45	304	22	9	2	12
Paramore	.988	45	297	23	4	0	4

First Base	PCT	G	PO	A	E	DP
Heether	.987	7	69	5	1	10
Parker	.966	9	79	5	3	7
Spina	.994	126	1132	77	7	109
Timmons	1.000	1	11	1	0	0

Second Base	PCT	G	PO	A	E	DP
Christian	.959	21	38	55	4	19

	PCT	G	PO	A	E	DP
Heether	.946	26	39	83	7	19
Horton	1.000	1	1	2	0	0
Ladendorf	.970	64	104	192	9	39
Timmons	.994	34	50	120	1	23

Third Base	PCT	G	PO	A	E	DP
Canham	1.000	4	2	10	0	0
Christian	.962	8	7	18	1	2
Heether	.929	12	7	32	3	3
Parker	.936	118	69	224	20	21

Shortstop	PCT	G	PO	A	E	DP
Christian	1.000	6	4	11	0	2
Green	.942	79	115	225	21	50
Ladendorf	.954	57	87	161	12	40

	PCT	G	PO	A	E	DP
Timmons	1.000	2	2	12	0	2

Outfield	PCT	G	PO	A	E	DP
Barfield	.975	127	251	20	7	4
Green	.970	47	97	1	3	0
Heether	.927	32	48	3	4	0
Ladendorf	1.000	7	19	1	0	0
Mitchell	1.000	65	148	6	0	1
Peterson	1.000	56	102	4	0	0
Rivero	1.000	1	1	0	0	0
Sulentic	.966	67	110	4	4	0
Walton	1.000	24	34	0	0	0

STOCKTON PORTS

HIGH CLASS A

CALIFORNIA LEAGUE

Batting	B-T	HT	WT	DOB	AVG	vLH	vRH	G	AB	R	H	2B	3B	HR	RBI	BB	HBP	SH	SF	SO	SB	CS	SLG	OBP
Aliotti, Anthony	L-L	6-0	204	7-16-87	.276	.198	.295	127	457	73	126	20	1	11	66	80	9	0	3	123	2	1	.396	.392
Carter, Chris	R-R	6-4	245	12-18-86	.333	.500	.300	6	24	3	8	0	0	3	7	4	0	0	0	8	0	0	.708	.429
Choice, Michael	R-R	6-0	215	11-10-89	.285	.320	.276	118	467	79	133	28	1	30	82	61	10	0	4	134	9	5	.542	.376
Christian, Jason	L-R	6-3	170	6-16-87	.259	.259	.259	40	143	19	37	2	2	3	19	11	0	0	2	43	6	1	.364	.308
Coleman, Dusty	R-R	6-2	185	4-20-87	.240	.279	.229	120	462	71	111	27	4	15	66	46	6	0	5	171	21	4	.413	.314
Crumbliss, Conner	L-R	5-8	175	4-19-87	.268	.248	.274	120	426	75	114	18	4	7	52	96	5	0	5	85	24	7	.378	.404
Dixon, Rashun	R-R	6-2	210	8-27-90	.243	.218	.251	125	456	74	111	19	5	11	47	47	3	0	2	135	3	5	.379	.317
Gil, Leonardo	R-R	6-1	160	8-18-87	.256	.299	.239	97	352	47	90	12	3	6	39	25	6	0	3	123	5	4	.358	.313
Gilmartin, Michael	R-R	6-0	180	7-14-87	.264	.193	.287	124	492	71	130	25	9	14	75	51	6	0	5	124	4	6	.437	.338
Johnston, Jonathan	L-R	6-0	195	2-13-84	.318	.000	.438	8	22	7	7	1	0	0	2	1	0	0	0	6	0	0	.364	.423
LeVier, Mitch	L-L	5-11	185	1-12-88	.218	.145	.237	99	367	45	80	14	3	15	48	22	3	0	3	102	2	3	.395	.266
Lipkin, Ryan	R-R	6-1	200	10-8-87	.248	.263	.244	83	314	44	78	20	1	6	47	14	4	0	1	51	3	2	.376	.288
Nunez, Juan	R-R	6-2	200	8-27-87	.268	.250	.269	16	56	8	15	0	0	2	5	0	0	0	0	14	0	0	.268	.328
Ortiz, Ryan	R-R	6-3	195	9-29-87	.340	.364	.333	28	97	17	33	5	0	4	21	21	1	0	2	22	0	0	.515	.455
Paramore, Petey	B-R	6-2	195	10-30-86	.235	.174	.250	31	119	19	28	2	0	7	21	14	2	0	3	25	0	0	.429	.319
Richard, Myrio	R-R	6-1	190	8-27-88	.292	.267	.298	107	432	65	126	29	1	8	57	43	7	0	3	69	27	10	.419	.363
Stafford, Rhett	R-R	6-2	220	3-1-89	.000	.000	.000	2	5	0	0	0	0	0	0	0	0	0	0	1	0	0	.000	.000
Stassi, Max	R-R	5-10	205	3-15-91	.231	.200	.242	31	121	22	28	6	0	2	19	16	2	0	0	22	1	1	.331	.331
Walton, Kent	R-R	6-1	185	12-11-86	.317	.286	.324	11	41	5	13	2	1	1	9	6	0	0	1	8	0	1	.488	.396

Pitching	B-T	HT	WT	DOB	W	L	ERA	G	GS	CG	SV	IP	H	R	ER	HR	BB	SO	AVG	vLH	vRH	K/9	BB/9
Benacka, Mike	R-R	6-2	210	8-2-82	1	0	2.84	22	0	0	1	32	25	11	10	3	15	30	.214	.073	.289	8.53	4.26
Brown, Jake	R-L	6-2	220	12-28-86	5	7	5.55	20	18	0	1	99	123	77	61	16	19	53	.301	.292	.303	4.82	1.73
Carignan, Andrew	R-R	5-11	205	7-23-86	1	0	0.00	9	0	0	5	11	4	1	0	0	2	12	.108	.267	.000	9.82	1.64
Daley, Gary	R-R	6-3	200	11-1-85	3	0	3.21	6	6	0	0	34	28	16	12	4	12	22	.226	.225	.226	5.88	3.21

Pitching

Pitching	B-T	HT	WT	DOB	W	L	ERA	G	GS	CG	SV	IP	H	R	ER	HR	BB	SO	AVG	vLH	vRH	K/9	BB/9
Deal, Scott	R-R	6-3	195	12-11-86	6	3	4.92	41	0	0	1	64	75	41	35	6	26	43	.291	.346	.267	6.05	3.66
Doolittle, Ryan	R-R	6-3	185	3-25-88	3	0	2.21	5	2	0	1	20	17	5	5	1	3	24	.215	.450	.136	10.62	1.33
Duran, Omar	L-L	6-3	209	2-26-90	0	0	1.42	4	0	0	0	6	2	1	1	0	5	3	.100	.000	.111	4.26	7.11
Gilliam, Rob	R-R	6-1	195	11-29-87	12	7	5.04	28	28	0	0	164	165	102	92	24	48	156	.263	.281	.251	8.54	2.63
Griffin, A.J.	R-R	6-5	215	1-28-88	5	3	3.57	12	12	0	0	71	64	31	28	8	14	82	.246	.262	.235	10.44	1.78
Guzman, Jose	R-R	5-11	185	11-5-87	2	5	2.91	48	0	0	20	68	50	23	22	5	28	71	.203	.216	.195	9.40	3.71
Hart, Michael	R-R	6-0	227	2-9-87	1	4	5.26	19	0	0	0	26	34	20	15	7	6	19	.312	.400	.286	6.66	2.10
Hodsdon, Scott	R-R	6-1	185	5-31-85	0	1	18.00	2	0	0	0	3	7	7	6	1	2	4	.467	.333	.556	12.00	6.00
Hoehn, Connor	R-R	6-1	205	7-5-89	2	3	5.21	36	0	0	7	48	39	32	28	11	12	59	.214	.292	.171	10.99	2.23
Hornbeck, Ben	R-L	6-5	180	7-22-87	0	0	0.84	7	0	0	1	11	11	1	1	0	1	16	.268	.167	.310	13.50	0.84
Hunter, Brett	R-R	6-4	215	6-27-87	1	0	1.35	12	0	0	1	20	12	4	3	1	6	17	.171	.156	.184	7.65	2.70
Huttenlocker, A.J.	L-L	6-3	190	8-5-86	4	0	1.83	41	0	0	0	69	62	17	14	3	12	60	.242	.273	.234	7.83	1.57
Lansford, Josh	R-R	6-2	215	7-31-84	3	6	2.78	41	0	0	4	58	42	22	18	4	11	68	.200	.179	.214	10.49	1.70
Leaper, J.J.	R-R	6-1	160	3-3-87	0	0	54.00	1	0	0	0	1	7	7	6	3	2	0	.778	1.000	.600	0.00	18.00
Lyman, Jeff	R-R	6-3	225	1-14-87	0	0	7.94	8	0	0	0	11	15	10	10	1	6	14	.313	.313	.313	11.12	4.76
Marti, Yadel	R-R	5-11	180	7-22-79	0	0	0.00	1	0	0	0	2	0	0	0	0	1	1	.000	.000	.000	4.50	4.50
McCarthy, Brandon	R-R	6-7	200	7-7-83	1	0	0.00	2	2	0	0	10	7	2	0	0	0	8	.200	.235	.167	7.20	0.00
Mederos, Chris	R-R	6-3	175	5-17-87	0	0	5.11	11	0	0	0	12	11	8	7	2	3	14	.229	.280	.174	10.22	2.19
Murphy, Sean	B-R	6-6	215	8-23-88	1	0	1.50	1	1	0	0	6	6	1	1	0	1	5	.261	.250	.273	7.50	1.50
Murray, Justin	R-R	6-4	200	5-11-87	0	0	6.75	2	0	0	0	3	4	2	2	0	0	1	.364	.000	.444	3.38	0.00
Mye, Chaz	L-L	6-3	200	4-27-88	0	0	0.00	1	0	0	0	1	1	0	0	0	1	0	.200	.000	.250	6.75	6.75
Peterson, Max	L-L	6-2	210	6-27-88	1	1	9.00	7	0	0	0	10	12	10	10	2	3	9	.286	.182	.323	8.10	2.70
Ross, Tyson	R-R	6-6	230	4-22-87	0	0	9.00	1	1	0	0	1	2	1	1	0	1	1	.400	1.000	.250	9.00	9.00
Schultz, Bo	R-R	6-3	215	9-25-85	0	0	14.85	7	0	0	1	7	11	14	11	0	5	4	.367	.429	.348	5.40	6.75
Simmons, James	R-R	6-3	220	9-29-86	3	2	5.48	13	8	0	0	43	56	29	26	5	6	36	.313	.294	.320	7.59	1.27
Smith, Murphy	R-R	6-3	210	8-25-87	6	9	3.94	26	24	0	1	137	151	80	60	10	33	100	.282	.312	.260	6.57	2.17
Straily, Dan	R-R	6-2	220	12-1-88	11	9	3.87	28	26	0	0	161	160	78	69	10	40	154	.260	.229	.279	8.63	2.24
Williamson, Fabian	R-L	6-2	175	10-20-88	3	5	7.53	12	10	0	0	49	60	41	41	8	29	40	.314	.267	.323	7.35	5.33
Wuertz, Michael	R-R	6-3	210	12-15-78	0	0	12.00	3	2	0	0	3	6	4	4	1	1	7	.400	.500	.364	21.00	3.00

Fielding

Catcher	PCT	G	PO	A	E	DP	PB
Johnston	.969	8	54	9	2	0	2
Lipkin	.989	78	554	52	7	1	6
Nunez	.975	16	144	15	4	1	1
Ortiz	.977	23	205	12	5	2	5
Paramore	.989	20	176	10	2	3	1

First Base	PCT	G	PO	A	E	DP
Aliotti	.991	123	1071	91	10	90
Carter	.978	5	40	4	1	7
Gil	.993	14	124	9	1	11

Second Base	PCT	G	PO	A	E	DP
Christian	.958	6	10	13	1	3
Crumbliss	.975	94	197	264	12	65
Gilmartin	.968	43	68	114	6	20

Third Base	PCT	G	PO	A	E	DP
Christian	.913	20	6	36	4	4
Crumbliss	1.000	1	2	4	0	1
Gil	.900	82	45	135	20	15
Gilmartin	.921	43	19	74	8	5

Shortstop	PCT	G	PO	A	E	DP
Coleman	.945	118	176	337	30	60
Gilmartin	.958	23	26	65	4	13

Outfield	PCT	G	PO	A	E	DP
Choice	.973	98	206	7	6	1
Crumbliss	.961	22	46	3	2	1
Dixon	.975	121	223	9	6	2
LeVier	.977	79	120	6	3	1
Richard	.966	96	165	8	6	0
Stafford	1.000	2	5	1	0	1
Walton	.938	11	15	0	1	0

BURLINGTON BEES

LOW CLASS A

MIDWEST LEAGUE

Batting

Batting	B-T	HT	WT	DOB	AVG	vLH	vRH	G	AB	R	H	2B	3B	HR	RBI	BB	HBP	SH	SF	SO	SB	CS	SLG	OBP
Cabrera, Yordy	R-R	6-1	205	9-3-90	.231	.156	.259	101	359	59	83	21	5	6	47	31	5	0	6	110	23	6	.368	.297
Consigli, Royce	L-R	6-2	217	9-7-91	.247	.207	.263	127	474	60	117	18	5	7	49	59	5	0	2	83	16	9	.350	.335
Crisotomo, Jose	L-R	6-1	181	4-20-89	.325	.297	.333	46	169	19	55	9	2	3	20	12	1	0	3	22	7	5	.456	.368
House, Tyreace	R-R	5-10	175	3-1-88	.190	.170	.196	108	348	46	66	7	0	0	27	43	4	0	2	81	27	6	.210	.285
Kirby-Jones, A.J.	R-R	5-10	215	10-2-88	.240	.190	.257	94	325	45	78	18	0	13	50	56	5	0	0	101	1	1	.415	.360
Kirkland, Wade	R-R	5-10	197	4-4-89	.217	.208	.221	83	258	38	56	16	1	3	26	20	8	0	3	73	5	3	.322	.291
Landaeta, Douglas	R-R	6-1	199	11-25-88	.250	.220	.262	110	420	51	105	23	2	5	35	23	6	0	3	89	10	4	.364	.296
Leyja, Nino	R-R	5-10	175	10-2-90	.235	.185	.252	113	421	72	99	20	5	6	35	47	6	0	1	118	28	5	.349	.320
Nester, John	R-R	6-1	210	5-28-89	.213	.162	.232	82	249	30	53	17	1	3	23	38	5	0	3	72	4	3	.325	.318
Nunez, Juan	R-R	6-2	220	8-27-88	.105	.154	.080	12	38	3	4	1	0	0	3	4	0	0	0	7	0	0	.132	.190
Petitti, Daniel	R-R	6-1	190	5-12-88	.143	.160	.129	19	56	3	8	0	1	0	3	2	0	0	0	15	0	0	.179	.172
Pineda, Ryan	R-R	5-11	180	4-17-89	.255	.241	.261	84	263	37	67	18	2	3	29	30	3	0	4	63	6	6	.373	.333
Rivero, Jose	R-R	6-3	220	1-8-90	.196	.132	.220	60	194	19	38	7	1	2	22	20	3	0	3	62	5	1	.273	.277
Taylor, Beau	L-R	6-0	200	2-13-90	.293	.172	.322	43	147	16	43	7	0	2	17	18	0	0	1	34	1	3	.367	.367
Thompson, Tony	R-R	6-4	219	12-19-88	.259	.272	.256	108	397	46	103	15	1	14	59	37	7	0	5	57	3	0	.408	.330
Whitaker, Josh	R-R	6-3	235	2-8-89	.326	.347	.316	113	396	67	129	34	3	17	68	44	7	0	1	107	10	2	.556	.402

Pitching

Pitching	B-T	HT	WT	DOB	W	L	ERA	G	GS	CG	SV	IP	H	R	ER	HR	BB	SO	AVG	vLH	vRH	K/9	BB/9
Bowman, Josh	R-R	6-2	195	9-9-88	8	6	3.55	28	28	0	0	155	148	74	61	9	44	98	.253	.291	.216	5.70	2.56
Brown, Jake	R-L	6-2	220	12-28-86	4	0	1.62	8	7	0	0	50	36	14	9	1	6	39	.198	.216	.193	7.02	1.08
Castillo, Jeiler	R-R	6-0	155	10-26-87	0	1	4.32	8	0	0	0	8	8	4	4	1	9	6	.258	.308	.222	6.48	9.72
Frankoff, Seth	R-R	6-5	200	8-27-88	0	1	11.25	5	5	0	0	12	21	16	15	0	9	7	.404	.583	.250	5.25	6.75
Griffin, A.J.	R-R	6-5	215	1-28-88	8	0	1.56	8	8	0	0	52	36	10	9	2	5	46	.187	.225	.159	7.96	0.87
Hart, Michael	R-R	6-0	227	2-9-87	3	2	1.46	20	0	0	2	37	18	9	6	2	16	37	.142	.130	.151	9.00	3.89
Hassebrock, Blake	R-R	6-4	212	7-15-89	7	8	2.64	26	26	0	0	140	133	64	41	9	46	110	.249	.282	.220	7.09	2.96
Joseph, Jonathan	R-R	6-1	180	5-17-88	6	4	5.67	21	14	0	0	81	89	59	51	11	31	73	.280	.299	.255	8.11	3.44
Long, Nathan	R-R	6-2	210	2-9-86	8	8	3.42	26	15	0	3	108	97	49	41	6	42	92	.244	.266	.221	7.67	3.50

Pitching	B-T	HT	WT	DOB	W	L	ERA	G	GS	CG	SV	IP	H	R	ER	HR	BB	SO	AVG	vLH	vRH	K/9	BB/9
Macias, Jose	R-R	6-2	180	7-18-89	8	4	3.46	16	16	0	0	81	81	40	31	3	18	62	.260	.279	.242	6.92	2.01
Mederos, Chris	R-R	6-3	175	5-17-87	2	1	0.93	13	0	0	5	19	9	2	2	0	4	25	.134	.192	.098	11.64	1.86
Murphy, Sean	B-R	6-6	215	8-23-88	1	3	6.33	15	6	0	0	43	57	31	30	5	10	34	.328	.316	.337	7.17	2.11
Peterson, Max	L-L	6-2	210	6-27-88	2	2	4.34	19	0	0	0	37	33	20	18	4	26	43	.241	.186	.282	10.37	6.27
Tenholder, Daniel	R-R	6-1	207	7-6-88	4	3	3.02	40	0	0	11	54	50	21	18	4	18	58	.240	.309	.180	9.73	3.02
Thomson, Matt	R-R	6-4	220	3-22-88	0	0	6.75	2	0	0	0	4	7	3	3	0	3	5	.412	.400	.429	11.25	6.75
Thornton, Zack	R-R	6-3	213	5-19-88	5	4	2.39	40	0	0	5	83	62	27	22	2	22	82	.204	.212	.196	8.89	2.39
Treinen, Blake	R-R	6-4	215	6-30-88	1	1	3.67	18	0	0	2	27	20	13	11	1	7	29	.202	.255	.154	9.67	2.33
Tyson, Drew	R-R	6-5	195	8-11-89	5	4	3.81	33	0	0	0	54	52	28	23	6	19	36	.246	.308	.200	5.96	3.15
Urlaub, Jeff	L-L	6-2	160	4-24-87	1	2	3.93	14	0	0	0	18	18	12	8	3	6	23	.250	.286	.227	11.29	2.95
Vail, Tyler	R-R	6-1	208	11-3-91	1	4	5.68	13	13	0	0	57	68	38	36	6	28	34	.296	.331	.259	5.37	4.42
Vidal, Pedro	R-R	6-3	194	7-31-87	6	3	1.95	36	0	0	5	69	46	24	15	5	23	73	.185	.207	.164	9.48	2.99
Walz, T.J.	R-R	6-0	175	11-21-88	0	1	3.86	10	0	0	0	19	13	9	8	2	7	16	.194	.300	.108	7.71	3.38

Fielding

Catcher	PCT	G	PO	A	E	DP	PB
Nester	.989	79	587	60	7	7	10
Nunez	.933	12	73	11	6	2	0
Petitti	.988	19	143	16	2	2	2
Taylor	.984	31	219	23	4	1	2

First Base	PCT	G	PO	A	E	DP
Kirby-Jones	.991	74	610	50	6	53
Rivero	.909	2	9	1	1	1
Thompson	.956	14	105	3	5	6
Whitaker	.979	55	449	53	11	38

Second Base	PCT	G	PO	A	E	DP
Kirkland	.950	11	18	39	3	7
Leyja	.956	91	126	244	17	40
Pineda	.969	43	76	110	6	26

Third Base	PCT	G	PO	A	E	DP
Kirkland	.910	31	18	53	7	3
Leyja	.786	11	6	16	6	1
Nester	1.000	2	0	1	0	0
Pineda	.950	22	11	27	2	2
Thompson	.949	87	72	132	11	13

Shortstop	PCT	G	PO	A	E	DP
Cabrera	.910	95	149	234	38	46
Kirkland	.923	38	49	95	12	21
Pineda	.892	7	7	26	4	5

Outfield	PCT	G	PO	A	E	DP
Consigli	.987	116	223	10	3	2
Crisotomo	.972	43	70	0	2	0
House	.991	106	221	0	2	0
Landaeta	.995	104	178	14	1	3
Pineda	.750	5	3	0	1	0
Rivero	.965	44	74	9	3	2
Whitaker	.933	11	25	3	2	1

VERMONT LAKE MONSTERS
NEW YORK-PENN LEAGUE

SHORT-SEASON

Batting	B-T	HT	WT	DOB	AVG	vLH	vRH	G	AB	R	H	2B	3B	HR	RBI	BB	HBP	SH	SF	SO	SB	CS	SLG	OBP
Affinito, Chris	R-R	6-3	230	2-10-87	.209	.231	.205	24	86	17	18	6	0	2	8	13	3	0	0	36	2	0	.349	.333
Bercume, Jeff	L-R	5-8	175	6-15-87	.154	.667	.000	4	13	0	2	0	0	0	1	1	1	0	0	3	2	1	.154	.267
Clime, Neudy	R-R	5-11	185	2-1-89	.056	.000	.100	11	18	2	1	1	0	0	1	1	0	0	0	5	1	0	.111	.105
Crocker, Bobby	R-R	6-3	220	5-1-90	.322	.364	.306	32	118	19	38	5	0	3	15	8	1	0	1	22	6	1	.441	.367
Fabiaschi, Michael	R-R	5-11	185	8-17-88	.282	.190	.329	40	124	18	35	8	0	1	20	18	2	0	0	32	4	1	.371	.382
Jamieson, Sean	R-R	6-0	193	3-2-89	.235	.206	.245	69	260	39	61	9	1	3	21	37	9	0	0	53	27	5	.312	.350
Lewis, Chad	R-R	6-3	200	12-10-91	.238	.179	.258	70	265	32	63	11	1	4	40	13	5	0	7	72	4	1	.332	.279
Lopez, Diomedes	R-R	6-2	195	1-30-89	.196	.174	.202	32	107	16	21	3	0	6	15	11	4	0	1	40	1	1	.393	.293
Macklin, Xavier	R-R	6-1	190	9-5-90	.230	.184	.246	43	152	8	35	7	1	0	12	10	2	0	0	47	3	2	.289	.287
Oberacker, Chad	L-L	5-11	195	1-14-89	.293	.207	.313	47	157	24	46	5	2	0	12	20	0	0	1	32	13	2	.350	.371
Pan, Zhi Fang	B-R	6-1	170	11-12-90	.336	.359	.327	37	143	22	48	4	0	1	22	12	1	0	2	27	8	4	.385	.386
Petitti, Daniel	R-R	6-1	190	5-12-88	.286	.500	.250	4	14	1	4	0	0	0	1	0	0	0	0	7	0	1	.286	.286
Rickles, Nick	R-R	6-3	225	2-2-90	.310	.325	.305	41	145	16	45	9	2	2	33	12	2	0	3	24	5	1	.441	.364
Roberts, Sam	L-R	6-1	190	2-23-89	.232	.133	.254	32	82	12	19	1	0	1	7	18	0	0	1	20	1	2	.280	.366
Robinson, Dusty	R-R	6-0	205	9-9-89	.219	.128	.258	36	128	22	28	6	2	7	22	8	1	0	0	34	6	1	.461	.270
Shipman, Aaron	L-L	6-0	175	1-27-92	.254	.222	.263	63	201	34	51	8	1	0	19	42	1	0	0	39	17	3	.303	.385
Tanis, Jacob	R-R	6-1	200	6-30-89	.221	.273	.200	49	154	18	34	6	0	1	11	17	4	0	0	42	6	3	.279	.314
Taylor, Beau	L-R	6-0	200	2-13-90	.111	.000	.125	5	18	1	2	0	0	0	1	0	0	0	0	4	0	0	.111	.111
Tripp, Jordan	R-R	6-4	215	10-27-89	.225	.211	.230	63	218	35	49	11	1	5	24	23	8	0	3	76	11	2	.353	.317
Vollmuth, B.A.	R-R	6-3	215	12-23-89	.500	.429	.571	4	14	8	7	4	1	0	6	2	1	0	0	3	0	1	.929	.588

Pitching	B-T	HT	WT	DOB	W	L	ERA	G	GS	CG	SV	IP	H	R	ER	HR	BB	SO	AVG	vLH	vRH	K/9	BB/9
Bailey, Andrew	R-R	6-5	215	3-30-89	1	0	2.34	26	0	0	0	42	35	17	11	2	22	37	.222	.271	.192	7.87	4.68
Castillo, Jeiler	R-R	6-0	155	10-26-87	1	1	5.75	20	0	0	1	36	39	27	23	3	13	23	.273	.200	.342	5.75	3.25
Chitwood, Logan	R-R	6-1	185	3-28-89	2	0	4.18	19	0	0	0	32	34	17	15	1	10	26	.264	.273	.257	7.24	2.78
Duran, Omar	L-L	6-3	209	2-26-90	0	1	4.00	7	0	0	0	9	8	6	4	0	7	11	.242	.214	.263	11.00	7.00
Frankoff, Seth	R-R	6-5	200	8-27-88	6	3	2.34	14	14	2	0	73	54	25	19	1	27	63	.208	.242	.174	7.77	3.33
Granier, Drew	R-R	6-0	180	11-24-88	1	1	1.91	7	7	0	0	28	21	11	6	0	22	34	.214	.222	.210	10.80	6.99
Hughes, Ryan	L-L	6-7	245	5-20-88	1	0	6.00	19	0	0	0	27	36	18	18	2	11	18	.321	.405	.271	6.00	3.67
Kilcrease, Nathan	R-R	5-6	170	8-17-89	3	4	2.67	20	1	0	1	30	26	12	9	0	5	28	.228	.120	.313	8.31	1.48
Macias, Jose	R-R	6-2	175	7-18-89	2	2	3.27	4	4	0	0	22	20	8	8	2	6	21	.241	.256	.225	8.59	2.45
Menna, J.C.	R-R	6-2	175	12-24-88	2	7	5.70	14	11	0	0	54	60	43	34	7	39	40	.290	.283	.296	6.71	6.54
Mye, Chaz	L-L	6-3	200	4-27-88	0	0	9.00	2	0	0	0	2	4	2	2	1	2	3	.444	.400	.500	13.50	9.00
Paez, Argenis	R-R	6-3	180	10-20-90	0	2	6.14	4	4	0	0	15	16	13	10	1	11	10	.262	.371	.115	6.14	6.75
Peters, Tanner	R-R	6-0	150	8-6-90	1	1	1.35	21	0	0	11	27	12	4	4	1	8	33	.135	.122	.150	11.14	2.70
Potter, Eric	L-L	6-4	215	11-26-89	0	0	3.12	12	0	0	0	17	23	6	6	0	8	19	.329	.444	.256	9.87	4.15
Powers, Brent	L-L	6-1	205	5-25-89	4	2	3.84	14	12	0	0	63	74	32	27	5	15	44	.292	.294	.292	6.25	2.13
Tyson, Drew	R-R	6-5	195	8-11-89	1	0	0.00	2	0	0	1	3	2	0	0	0	0	3	.182	.250	.143	9.00	0.00
Urlaub, Jeff	L-L	6-2	160	4-24-87	3	1	1.67	23	0	0	5	38	27	12	7	1	4	49	.200	.189	.207	11.71	0.96
Vail, Tyler	R-R	6-1	208	11-3-91	1	5	6.05	10	10	0	0	39	35	30	26	4	25	22	.248	.274	.228	5.12	5.82
Walz, T.J.	R-R	6-0	175	11-21-88	4	0	0.41	11	0	0	0	22	14	1	1	0	3	27	.182	.091	.250	11.05	1.23
Wunderlich, Kurt	R-R	6-2	210	8-22-89	2	5	5.33	14	11	0	0	52	61	35	31	8	21	30	.298	.306	.292	5.16	3.61

Fielding

Catcher	PCT	G	PO	A	E	DP	PB
Lopez	.972	31	214	26	7	2	7
Petitti	1.000	4	28	5	0	0	0
Rickles	.981	39	286	30	6	5	2
Taylor	.966	3	23	5	1	0	1

First Base	PCT	G	PO	A	E	DP
Affinito	.989	21	161	13	2	13
Lewis	.974	35	241	25	7	22
Rickles	1.000	1	6	3	0	0
Tanis	.977	21	156	15	4	15

Second Base	PCT	G	PO	A	E	DP
Clime	1.000	7	7	5	0	0

Fielder	PCT	G	PO	A	E	DP
Fabiaschi	.970	24	45	86	4	16
Pan	.978	29	56	78	3	18
Roberts	1.000	23	38	59	0	6
Third Base						
Fabiaschi	.909	15	7	23	3	5
Lewis	.892	38	27	64	11	5
Tanis	.957	22	10	34	2	6
Vollmuth	.900	4	4	5	1	0
Shortstop						
Clime	1.000	1	0	2	0	0
Fabiaschi	.667	1	1	1	1	0
Jamieson	.970	68	122	174	9	28

Fielder	PCT	G	PO	A	E	DP
Pan	.867	3	5	8	2	2
Roberts	1.000	4	6	11	0	1
Outfield						
Bercume	1.000	4	4	0	0	0
Crocker	.981	27	48	4	1	2
Macklin	.972	27	35	0	1	0
Oberacker	.983	27	57	0	1	0
Robinson	.889	25	40	0	5	0
Shipman	.975	59	115	1	3	1
Tripp	.975	57	115	4	3	1

AZL ATHLETICS
ARIZONA LEAGUE
ROOKIE

Batting	B-T	HT	WT	DOB	AVG	vLH	vRH	G	AB	R	H	2B	3B	HR	RBI	BB	HBP	SH	SF	SO	SB	CS	SLG	OBP
Alexander, Dayton	R-R	6-1	195	2-4-91	.243	.174	.256	44	144	13	35	7	1	0	12	14	3	0	2	30	5	2	.306	.319
Baez, Luis	R-R	6-3	165	5-24-91	.230	.250	.222	40	152	19	35	7	3	2	14	7	1	0	1	36	2	2	.355	.267
Booker, Austin	L-R	5-10	170	4-11-88	.250	.250	.250	19	56	7	14	0	0	0	3	3	0	0	0	11	2	0	.250	.288
Boras, Shane	B-R	5-9	160	11-24-89	.224	.200	.231	18	49	3	11	2	0	0	6	3	0	0	0	7	1	0	.265	.269
Bostick, Chris	R-R	5-11	185	3-24-93	.442	.636	.390	14	52	13	23	6	1	1	5	3	1	0	0	12	4	0	.654	.482
Contreras, Franklin	R-R	6-2	165	6-10-90	.169	.133	.180	24	65	6	11	4	0	0	5	5	0	0	1	23	1	0	.231	.225
Crocker, Bobby	R-R	6-3	220	5-1-90	.261	.320	.238	24	88	14	23	4	3	0	4	5	2	0	0	22	2	2	.375	.316
De La Cruz, Jonatan	R-R	6-0	160	5-28-88	.203	.167	.214	24	74	4	15	5	0	1	7	8	0	0	0	13	1	1	.311	.280
Leyland, Josh	L-R	6-1	220	7-6-91	.322	.286	.333	20	59	11	19	6	0	0	9	15	1	0	1	19	0	1	.424	.461
Marte, Miguel	R-R	6-3	230	8-29-89	.299	.303	.298	39	137	20	41	11	0	6	26	9	7	0	2	38	0	1	.511	.368
Mateo, Reynaldo	R-R	5-9	209	7-16-89	.266	.207	.283	39	128	21	34	8	2	6	25	9	8	0	3	38	0	0	.500	.345
Peralta, Jensi	R-R	6-2	180	7-2-91	.301	.290	.304	38	123	20	37	9	4	1	16	14	1	0	0	34	2	1	.463	.377
Petitti, Daniel	R-R	6-1	190	5-12-88	.218	.150	.239	27	87	13	19	7	0	1	14	9	5	0	2	25	2	1	.333	.320
Ramsey, Rashad	L-L	6-0	175	5-10-92	.224	.167	.243	23	49	9	11	1	0	0	2	6	0	0	0	18	3	0	.245	.309
Rickles, Nick	R-R	6-3	225	2-2-90	.304	.333	.300	6	23	5	7	2	2	0	2	3	1	0	0	4	1	0	.565	.407
Robinson, Dusty	R-R	6-0	205	9-9-89	.239	.364	.200	12	46	9	11	1	0	1	5	6	0	0	0	9	0	0	.326	.327
Rojas, Kelvin	R-R	6-2	188	8-7-90	.379	.588	.326	48	169	38	64	11	4	3	35	16	4	0	2	42	3	1	.544	.440
Solano, Wilfredo	R-R	6-2	185	1-15-93	.244	.297	.228	45	164	21	40	7	0	1	20	8	4	0	1	33	5	0	.305	.294
Soto, Michael	R-R	6-0	195	11-17-91	.209	.053	.271	20	67	9	14	5	0	3	11	8	0	0	1	18	1	0	.418	.289
Stafford, Rhett	R-R	6-2	220	3-1-89	.265	.235	.274	41	151	29	40	6	2	5	29	21	2	0	1	43	2	2	.430	.360
Vollmuth, B.A.	R-R	6-3	215	12-23-89	.148	.000	.182	8	27	3	4	0	0	1	2	3	2	0	0	6	0	0	.259	.281
Welch, Dan	R-R	6-2	205	4-24-89	.200	.000	.333	1	5	2	1	0	0	0	1	0	0	0	0	0	0	0	.200	.200

Pitching	B-T	HT	WT	DOB	W	L	ERA	G	GS	CG	SV	IP	H	R	ER	HR	BB	SO	AVG	vLH	vRH	K/9	BB/9
Acevedo, Rony	R-R	6-2	165	9-18-88	3	2	7.43	15	1	0	1	23	29	23	19	2	11	20	.315	.412	.259	7.83	4.30
Avila, Andres	R-R	6-0	185	6-20-90	3	5	5.20	15	13	0	0	62	83	46	36	6	16	71	.310	.308	.311	10.25	2.31
Azor, Jose	R-R	6-2	185	10-12-88	1	4	11.52	17	0	0	0	25	37	42	32	4	27	19	.339	.417	.301	6.84	9.72
Capra, Anthony	L-L	6-1	200	4-3-87	0	0	0.00	1	1	0	0	5	1	0	0	0	3	.067	.000	.077	5.40	0.00	
Doolittle, Ryan	R-R	6-3	185	3-25-88	0	2	13.50	4	1	0	0	5	14	7	7	1	0	7	.500	.583	.438	13.50	0.00
Duran, Omar	L-L	6-3	209	2-26-90	1	0	1.50	8	0	0	1	18	11	6	3	0	5	16	.180	.200	.174	8.00	2.50
Eppley, Nate	R-R	6-6	205	10-28-88	0	0	3.58	18	0	0	2	28	31	16	11	1	9	23	.284	.244	.309	7.48	2.93
Figueroa, Pedro	L-L	6-0	215	11-23-85	0	0	4.50	2	2	0	0	2	3	1	1	0	0	6	.300	.667	.143	27.00	0.00
Gagnier, Drew	R-R	6-4	225	9-21-88	2	0	4.20	7	0	0	1	15	14	9	7	1	9	12	.241	.391	.143	7.20	5.40
Girdwood, Thomas	R-R	6-2	200	3-14-89	0	0	13.50	2	0	0	0	2	4	4	3	0	1	3	.400	.500	.375	13.50	4.50
Granier, Drew	R-R	6-0	180	11-24-88	5	1	1.57	6	3	0	0	23	12	4	4	1	7	35	.152	.238	.121	13.70	2.74
Gray, Sonny	R-R	5-11	200	11-7-89	0	1	4.50	1	1	0	0	2	4	1	1	0	0	2	.444	.600	.250	9.00	0.00
Juma, Alexis	R-R	6-1	180	5-23-88	0	2	14.54	2	1	0	0	4	10	10	7	0	4	5	.417	.333	.467	10.38	8.31
Krol, Ian	L-L	6-1	180	5-9-91	0	0	0.00	3	3	0	0	5	0	0	0	0	0	6	.000	.000	10.80	0.00	
Lamb, Chris	B-L	6-1	185	6-29-90	0	0	0.00	3	0	0	0	5	2	1	0	0	1	4	.118	.000	.167	7.20	1.80
Larsen, Aaron	R-L	6-1	190	3-1-87	3	3	7.09	11	6	0	0	46	60	39	36	4	24	32	.326	.358	.308	6.31	4.73
Leon, Arnold	R-R	6-1	205	9-6-88	0	1	8.53	5	5	0	0	6	6	6	6	0	0	8	.273	.273	.273	11.37	5.68
Mota, David	R-R	6-4	265	2-18-87	0	1	8.83	13	0	0	0	17	25	19	17	1	17	17	.338	.276	.378	8.83	8.83
Mye, Chaz	L-L	6-3	200	4-27-88	2	0	1.01	15	0	0	4	27	25	6	3	1	6	25	.255	.185	.282	8.44	2.03
Paez, Argenis	R-R	6-3	180	10-20-90	4	2	4.17	11	7	0	0	50	47	36	23	3	27	51	.245	.250	.241	9.24	4.89
Paulino, Gregory	R-R	6-3	180	2-4-93	1	1	3.21	8	5	0	0	28	23	16	10	3	8	14	.235	.257	.222	4.50	2.57
Perlman, Max	R-L	6-7	235	2-2-88	2	2	2.76	13	5	0	0	42	29	15	13	2	11	44	.187	.123	.233	9.35	2.34
Potter, Eric	L-L	6-4	215	11-26-89	0	0	1.29	8	0	0	4	14	9	2	2	0	3	22	.188	.176	.194	14.14	1.93
Rodriguez, Kevin	L-L	6-4	190	6-26-91	0	0	9.95	5	0	0	0	6	12	8	7	0	5	6	.387	1.000	.296	8.53	7.11
Simmons, James	R-R	6-3	220	9-29-86	0	0	0.00	2	2	0	0	5	1	0	0	0	0	4	.063	.000	.100	7.20	0.00
Tanner, Cecil	R-R	6-6	240	4-23-90	0	1	7.40	15	0	0	1	21	17	17	17	0	27	26	.215	.108	.310	11.32	11.76
Treinen, Blake	R-R	6-4	215	6-30-88	0	0	0.00	3	0	0	0	3	3	0	0	0	1	7	.250	.400	.143	21.00	3.00

Fielding

Catcher	PCT	G	PO	A	E	DP	PB
Mateo	.974	25	183	38	6	1	8
Petitti	.971	27	205	28	7	4	4
Rickles	1.000	6	60	6	0	2	1
Stafford	1.000	5	21	1	0	0	0
Welch	1.000	1	12	1	0	1	0

First Base	PCT	G	PO	A	E	DP
De La Cruz	1.000	2	1	0	0	0
Leyland	.970	17	142	20	5	12

Marte	.976	36	292	33	8	19
Soto	.977	6	41	1	1	3

Second Base	PCT	G	PO	A	E	DP
Booker	.900	13	27	27	6	6
Boras	.962	15	21	30	2	6
Bostick	.957	5	13	9	1	3
Contreras	.889	22	24	40	8	6
De La Cruz	.969	10	13	18	1	2
Solano	.897	8	10	16	3	3

Third Base	PCT	G	PO	A	E	DP
Baez	.966	15	8	20	1	1

De La Cruz	.933	14	9	19	2	1
Peralta	.900	24	17	28	5	2
Soto	.900	4	4	5	1	1
Vollmuth	.905	5	3	16	2	3

Shortstop	PCT	G	PO	A	E	DP
Baez	.667	1	1	1	1	0
Booker	1.000	2	1	2	0	0
Bostick	.926	8	7	18	2	2
Peralta	.870	13	15	25	6	6
Solano	.919	38	40	96	12	13

Outfield	PCT	G	PO	A	E	DP
Alexander	.970	44	62	2	2	2
Baez	.929	27	25	1	2	0
Booker	1.000	1	2	0	0	0
Contreras	.000	1	0	0	0	0
Crocker	1.000	10	16	0	0	0
Peralta	1.000	1	1	0	0	0
Ramsey	1.000	23	22	1	0	0
Robinson	1.000	10	15	3	0	2
Rojas	.958	46	65	4	3	1
Stafford	.982	35	51	5	1	0

DSL ATHLETICS ROOKIE

DOMINICAN SUMMER LEAGUE

Batting	B-T	HT	WT	DOB	AVG	vLH	vRH	G	AB	R	H	2B	3B	HR	RBI	BB	HBP	SH	SF	SO	SB	CS	SLG	OBP
De La Cruz, Vicmal	L-L	6-0	185	11-20-93	.318	.349	.309	58	192	29	61	13	5	1	28	37	5	0	1	27	10	5	.453	.438
De La Rosa, Anderson	R-R	6-1	180	8-12-91	.239	.056	.286	29	88	10	21	3	0	1	10	15	2	0	0	17	1	4	.307	.362
Ledezma, Diego	R-R	6-5	170	8-14-90	.165	.176	.162	34	91	5	15	2	0	0	7	6	0	0	0	22	0	0	.187	.216
Martinez, Hiram	B-R	6-1	143	9-30-92	.095	.000	.133	8	21	1	2	1	0	0	0	0	0	0	0	2	0	2	.143	.095
Martinez, Wilman	R-R	5-11	204	1-13-93	.225	.185	.233	54	160	14	36	3	0	0	7	22	6	0	2	26	3	2	.244	.337
Mendez, Gregorio	R-R	5-11	182	9-30-92	.125	.000	.167	4	8	1	1	0	0	0	0	1	0	0	0	2	0	0	.125	.222
Nunez, Renato	R-R	6-1	185	4-4-94	.268	.167	.291	53	194	20	52	12	0	5	28	6	4	0	2	42	1	2	.407	.301
Osorio, Luis	B-R	6-1	155	4-5-91	.307	.250	.319	48	166	36	51	9	2	0	15	15	3	0	0	34	8	5	.386	.375
Paz, Andy	R-R	6-0	170	1-5-93	.315	.250	.333	24	73	8	23	3	0	0	7	14	4	0	0	10	3	3	.356	.451
Penalo, Rodolfo	B-R	5-7	130	8-27-92	.250	.278	.242	27	80	11	20	2	1	1	9	11	1	0	2	12	8	7	.338	.340
Raga, Argenis	R-R	6-1	176	7-22-94	.200	.111	.219	47	155	13	31	4	0	0	14	10	2	0	2	15	4	3	.226	.254
Rivas, Jesus	R-R	6-0	180	3-22-94	.179	.219	.169	54	162	15	29	1	1	1	16	12	1	0	4	41	0	0	.216	.235
Rosario, Jose	R-R	6-5	219	9-2-90	.288	.281	.289	52	153	17	44	10	0	2	15	21	3	0	1	25	1	1	.392	.382
Santana, Gabriel	R-R	6-0	165	8-23-92	.244	.278	.237	64	205	26	50	6	1	0	17	21	18	0	1	24	4	9	.283	.363
Sayegh, Jose	R-R	6-2	180	12-7-91	.133	.188	.124	36	105	9	14	2	1	0	7	13	4	0	1	42	0	1	.171	.252
Sosa, Alfredo	R-R	5-10	189	1-18-93	.139	.107	.147	52	137	23	19	6	0	0	5	25	4	0	1	44	4	2	.182	.287
Zarraga, Jonesy	R-R	6-1	170	6-3-92	.206	.167	.213	34	126	15	26	1	2	0	6	12	6	0	0	31	8	6	.246	.306

Pitching	B-T	HT	WT	DOB	W	L	ERA	G	GS	CG	SV	IP	H	R	ER	HR	BB	SO	AVG	vLH	vRH	K/9	BB/9
Acevedo, Rony	R-R	6-2	165	9-18-88	0	0	0.00	3	3	0	0	4	1	0	0	0	1	4	.083	.250	.000	9.00	2.25
Alejo, Yordy	R-R	6-2	186	11-13-93	0	6	6.68	15	0	0	0	31	36	28	23	4	18	10	.305	.304	.305	2.90	5.23
Almonte, Edward	R-R	6-2	176	1-12-90	4	4	3.75	19	0	0	0	60	62	31	25	0	21	33	.276	.436	.242	4.95	3.15
Astacio, Andres	R-R	6-3	180	8-20-90	3	2	3.24	19	1	0	3	42	47	17	15	2	9	29	.281	.311	.270	6.26	1.94
Benzant, Leonel	R-R	6-6	213	12-20-91	0	4	3.71	9	8	0	1	34	34	16	14	2	9	20	.266	.217	.276	5.29	2.38
Castillo, Jose	R-R	6-2	185	2-22-91	0	1	10.80	6	0	0	0	5	6	6	6	2	7	5	.300	.250	.313	9.00	12.60
Cruzado, Fernando	R-R	6-2	210	10-25-89	3	2	3.83	13	9	0	0	47	55	27	20	2	16	35	.293	.286	.295	6.70	3.06
De Los Santos, Robinson	R-R	6-3		7-21-90	0	0	0.00	1	1	0	0	2	3	3	0	0	1	3	.333	.500	.200	16.20	5.40
Gonzalez, Darwin	L-L	6-3	183	11-24-92	3	0	3.98	19	0	0	0	41	38	25	18	2	31	30	.245	.000	.268	6.64	6.86
Jose, Luis	R-R	6-4	195	9-26-87	0	2	3.13	14	0	0	6	23	19	10	8	1	8	14	.224	.217	.226	5.48	3.13
Mata, Anderson	L-L	5-11	165	11-17-93	2	3	4.50	15	8	0	0	36	30	27	18	2	38	30	.236	.000	.254	7.50	9.50
Navas, Carlos	R-R	6-1	170	8-13-92	0	0	13.50	1	1	0	0	1	1	0	0	0	0	0	.000	.000	.000	0.00	0.00
Nolasco, Alex	L-L	6-4	190	9-11-90	1	3	4.46	18	2	0	0	34	25	21	17	1	32	25	.200	.214	.214	6.55	8.39
Paulino, Gregory	R-R	6-3	180	2-4-93	1	3	1.36	8	7	0	0	33	30	12	5	0	9	23	.242	.375	.210	6.27	2.45
Perez, Cristhian	R-R	6-2	180	9-13-91	2	1	3.30	14	11	0	0	57	63	27	21	3	13	32	.278	.241	.289	5.02	2.04
Rosario, Jose	R-R	6-2	170	11-28-90	1	1	3.68	6	0	0	0	7	8	6	3	0	4	4	.267	.400	.240	4.91	4.91
Suniaga, Elihoref	R-R	6-1	170	5-5-92	2	2	3.98	11	7	0	0	20	17	9	9	0	8	16	.224	.063	.267	7.08	3.54
Torres, Jose	L-L	6-2	165	9-24-93	1	5	3.99	14	11	0	0	50	45	27	22	1	24	33	.242	.294	.237	5.98	4.35
Trinidad, Victor	R-R	6-0	173	12-23-90	3	6	2.70	23	0	0	3	40	35	15	12	1	18	42	.241	.158	.271	9.45	4.05
Veliz, Victor	L-L	5-11	170	10-6-93	0	1	3.18	7	2	0	0	17	17	8	6	0	11	11	.262	.286	.259	5.82	5.82

Fielding

Catcher	PCT	G	PO	A	E	DP	PB
Ledezma	.977	29	135	36	4	2	4
Mendez	1.000	4	19	2	0	0	0
Paz	.942	17	82	16	6	2	1
Raga	.963	21	118	11	5	0	4
Ramirez	.963	10	47	5	2	0	1

First Base	PCT	G	PO	A	E	DP
Martinez	.973	31	235	13	7	20
Paz	1.000	2	5	0	0	0
Rivas	1.000	7	45	1	0	4
Rosario	.990	44	359	21	4	29
Trinidad	1.000	2	1	0	1	0

Second Base	PCT	G	PO	A	E	DP
Martinez	.944	5	9	8	1	2
Osorio	.984	30	54	73	2	20
Paz	.500	1	1	0	1	0
Penalo	.935	23	55	46	7	9

Raga	.955	15	29	34	3	8
Santana	.960	4	14	10	1	4

Third Base	PCT	G	PO	A	E	DP
Martinez	.750	2	2	1	1	1
Martinez	.944	14	11	23	2	4
Nunez	.851	53	43	129	30	13
Osorio	.800	3	2	6	2	0
Rivas	1.000	3	3	6	0	0
Santana	1.000	3	2	11	0	0

Shortstop	PCT	G	PO	A	E	DP
Martinez	.821	6	8	15	5	4
Osorio	.950	10	17	40	3	5
Raga	1.000	1	0	2	0	0
Santana	.952	58	110	170	14	32

Outfield	PCT	G	PO	A	E	DP
Almonte	.500	1	1	0	1	0
De La Cruz	.942	43	62	3	4	1

De La Rosa	.971	20	32	2	1	2
Duinkerk	.875	6	5	2	1	0
Osorio	1.000	3	1	0	0	0
Rivas	1.000	44	53	2	0	0
Sayegh	.956	31	39	4	2	1
Sosa	.977	50	78	7	2	3
Zarraga	1.000	33	60	5	0	2

Philadelphia Phillies

SEASON IN A SENTENCE: Riding baseball's best rotation in recent memory, the Phillies won a franchise-best 102 games and had World Series-or-bust aspirations, but they tripped up against the eventual champion Cardinals in the National League Division Series.

HIGH POINT: Philadelphia clinched its fifth consecutive NL East title at home on Sept. 19 when Roy Oswalt tossed seven shutout innings in a 9-2 defeat against none other than the Cardinals. The champagne celebration that ensued was joyous but the only one the Phillies got to take part in.

LOW POINT: Slugger Ryan Howard ruptured his Achilles tendon trying to get out of the batter's box on the final out of the Division Series loss, sending him to the ground in a heap and leaving the Phillies' hopes in the dust of the first-base line.

NOTABLE ROOKIES: Pitchers Vance Worley and Mike Stutes didn't make the 25-man roster out of spring training but were called up shortly thereafter and stuck for the rest of the season, then contributed during the postseason. Worley filled in admirably for injured starters Oswalt and Joe Blanton, going 11-3, 3.01 in 21 starts, while Stutes made 57 appearances out of the bullpen.

KEY TRANSACTIONS: Along with bringing back Cliff Lee to fortify the rotation in a free agent coup in December, Philadelphia traded for Astros outfielder Hunter Pence at midseason, finding a righthanded power-hitting replacement for the departed Jayson Werth. The Phillies gave up top hitting prospect Jonathan Singleton and top pitching prospect Jarred Cosart in the deal. Veteran talent evaluator Chuck LaMar resigned in September and was replaced by Joe Jordan as farm director.

DOWN ON THE FARM: The Phillies have traded 17 prospects in the last four years to acquire Blanton, Lee, Oswalt, Pence and Halladay. Those moves have left the system thin on impact talent, though there's still depth and several players have a chance to contribute in 2012: hard-throwing relievers Phillippe Aumont and Justin De Fratus and slick-fielding shortstop Freddy Galvis. In an effort to replenish the system through the draft, scouting director Marti Wolever focused on projectable, high-ceiling athletes and he made an effort to stockpile lefthanded pitching. Former top prospect Domonic Brown no longer qualifies for rookie consideration, and he split the year between Philadelphia and Triple-A Lehigh Valley after a hand injury during spring training.

OPENING DAY PAYROLL: $172,976,379 (2nd)

PLAYERS OF THE YEAR

MAJOR LEAGUE	MINOR LEAGUE
Roy Halladay rhp	**Julio Rodriguez** rhp
19-6, 2.35	(High Class A)
220 SO/234 IP	16-7, 2.76
1st in CG, 2nd in IP	168 SO/157 IP

ORGANIZATION LEADERS

BATTING   *Minimum 250 PA

MAJORS

* AVG	Carlos Ruiz	.283
* OPS	John Mayberry	.854
HR	Ryan Howard	33
RBI	Ryan Howard	116

MINORS

* AVG	Michael Spidale, Reading	.326
* OBP	Matt Rizzotti, Reading	.392
* SLG	Matt Rizzotti, Reading	.511
R	Rich Thompson, Lehigh Valley	81
H	Michael Spidale, Reading	161
TB	Matt Rizzotti, Reading	255
2B	Darin Ruf, Clearwater	43
3B	Rich Thompson, Lehigh Valley	8
HR	Cody Overbeck, Reading/Lehigh Valley	24
	Matt Rizzotti, Reading	24
RBI	Matt Rizzotti, Reading	84
BB	Matt Rizzotti, Reading	79
SO	Anthony Hewitt, Lakewood	149
SB	Rich Thompson, Lehigh Valley	48

PITCHING   #Minimum 75 IP

MAJORS

W	Roy Halladay	19
# ERA	Roy Halladay	2.35
SO	Cliff Lee	238
SV	Ryan Madson	32

MINORS

W	Julio Rodriguez, Clearwater	16
L	J.C. Ramirez, Reading	13
# ERA	Julio Rodriguez, Clearwater	2.76
G	Justin Friend, Clearwater/Reading	55
GS	Brian Bass, Lehigh Valley	28
	Austin Hyatt, Reading	28
SV	Justin Friend, Clearwater/Reading	28
IP	Jonathan Pettibone, Clearwater	161
BB	Ervis Manzanillo, Lakewood	71
SO	Trevor May, Clearwater	208
# AVG	Julio Rodriguez, Clearwater	.186

2011 PERFORMANCE

General Manager: Ruben Amaro Jr. **Farm Director:** Benny Looper. **Scouting Director:** Marti Wolever.

Class	Team	League	W	L	PCT	Finish	Manager(s)
Majors	Philadelphia Phillies	National	102	60	.630	1st (16)	Charlie Manuel
Triple-A	Lehigh Valley Iron Pigs	International	80	64	.556	4th (14)	Ryne Sandberg
Double-A	Reading Phillies	Eastern	74	68	.521	5th (12)	Mark Parent
High A	Clearwater Threshers	Florida State	75	63	.543	3rd (12)	Dusty Wathan
Low A	Lakewood BlueClaws	South Atlantic	68	69	.496	10th (14)	Chris Truby
Short-season	Williamsport Crosscutters	New York-Penn	43	33	.566	4th (14)	Mickey Morandini
Rookie	GCL Phillies	Gulf Coast	27	32	.458	t-9th (15)	Rolando de Armas
Overall 2011 Minor League Record			367	329	.527	7th (30)	

ORGANIZATION STATISTICS

PHILADELPHIA PHILLIES

NATIONAL LEAGUE

Batting	B-T	HT	WT	DOB	AVG	vLH	vRH	G	AB	R	H	2B	3B	HR	RBI	BB	HBP	SH	SF	SO	SB	CS	SLG	OBP
Bowker, John	L-L	6-1	205	7-8-83	.000	.000	.000	12	13	0	0	0	0	0	0	0	0	0	0	7	0	0	.000	.000
2-team total (19 Pittsburgh)					.133	—	—	31	30	0	4	1	0	0	2	2	0	0	1	11	0	1	.167	.188
Brown, Domonic	L-L	6-5	205	9-3-87	.245	.281	.237	56	184	28	45	10	1	5	19	25	0	0	1	35	3	1	.391	.333
Francisco, Ben	R-R	6-1	190	10-23-81	.244	.245	.243	100	250	24	61	10	1	6	34	33	5	0	3	42	4	4	.364	.340
Gload, Ross	L-L	6-1	190	4-5-76	.257	.000	.266	93	113	3	29	8	0	8	3	0	0	0	0	23	0	0	.327	.276
Howard, Ryan	L-L	6-4	240	11-19-79	.253	.224	.266	152	557	81	141	30	1	33	116	75	7	0	5	172	1	0	.488	.346
Ibanez, Raul	L-R	6-2	220	6-2-72	.245	.211	.256	144	535	65	131	31	1	20	84	33	2	0	5	106	2	0	.419	.289
Kratz, Erik	R-R	6-4	255	6-15-80	.333	.000	1.000	2	6	2	1	0	0	0	0	0	0	0	0	1	0	0	.500	.333
Martinez, Michael	B-R	5-9	145	9-16-82	.196	.176	.203	88	209	25	41	5	2	3	24	18	0	0	2	35	3	0	.282	.258
Mayberry Jr., John	R-R	6-6	230	12-21-83	.273	.306	.250	104	267	37	73	17	1	15	49	26	2	0	1	55	8	3	.513	.341
Moss, Brandon	L-R	6-0	210	9-16-83	.000	.000	.000	5	6	0	0	0	0	0	0	0	0	0	0	2	0	0	.000	.000
Orr, Pete	L-R	6-1	195	6-8-79	.219	.167	.222	46	96	7	21	3	0	4	6	2	0	0	1	19	3	0	.250	.279
Pence, Hunter	R-R	6-4	220	4-13-83	.324	.405	.303	54	207	35	67	12	2	11	35	26	0	0	3	38	1	1	.560	.394
2-team total (100 Houston)					.314	—	—	154	606	84	190	38	5	22	97	56	1	0	5	124	8	2	.502	.370
Polanco, Placido	R-R	5-10	190	10-10-75	.277	.336	.257	122	469	46	130	14	0	5	50	42	3	0	8	44	3	0	.339	.335
Rollins, Jimmy	B-R	5-8	170	11-27-78	.268	.240	.278	142	567	87	152	22	2	16	63	58	3	0	3	59	30	8	.399	.338
Ruiz, Carlos	R-R	5-10	205	1-22-79	.283	.265	.288	132	410	49	116	23	0	6	40	48	10	0	1	48	1	0	.383	.371
Sardinha, Dane	R-R	6-0	215	4-8-79	.219	.333	.174	15	32	8	7	1	0	1	4	1	0	0	0	13	0	0	.250	.419
Schneider, Brian	L-R	6-1	210	11-26-76	.176	.125	.188	41	125	11	22	4	0	2	9	11	1	0	1	35	0	0	.256	.246
Utley, Chase	L-R	6-1	200	12-17-78	.259	.187	.285	103	398	54	103	21	6	11	44	39	14	0	2	47	14	0	.425	.344
Valdez, Wilson	R-R	5-11	170	5-20-78	.249	.250	.249	99	273	39	68	14	4	1	30	18	0	0	2	41	3	3	.341	.294
Victorino, Shane	B-R	5-9	190	11-30-80	.279	.308	.271	132	519	95	145	27	16	17	61	55	6	0	0	63	19	3	.491	.355

Pitching	B-T	HT	WT	DOB	W	L	ERA	G	GS	CG	SV	IP	H	R	ER	HR	BB	SO	AVG	vLH	vRH	K/9	BB/9
Baez, Danys	R-R	6-3	225	9-10-77	2	4	6.25	29	0	0	0	36	43	28	25	5	13	18	.293	.327	.272	4.50	3.25
Bastardo, Antonio	L-L	5-11	195	9-21-85	6	1	2.64	64	0	0	8	58	28	17	17	6	26	70	.144	.145	.143	10.86	4.03
Blanton, Joe	R-R	6-3	245	12-11-80	1	2	5.01	11	8	0	0	41	52	23	23	5	9	35	.319	.299	.333	7.62	1.96
Carpenter, Drew	R-R	6-3	240	5-18-85	0	0	7.71	6	0	0	0	9	13	8	8	2	4	10	.333	.294	.364	9.64	3.86
2-team total (6 San Diego)					0	0	7.98	12	0	0	0	15	19	13	13	3	7	16	—	—	—	9.82	4.30
Contreras, Jose	R-R	6-4	255	12-6-71	0	0	3.86	17	0	0	5	14	11	6	6	0	8	13	.220	.056	.313	8.36	5.14
De Fratus, Justin	B-R	6-4	220	10-21-87	1	0	2.25	5	0	0	0	4	1	2	1	0	3	3	.083	.200	.000	6.75	6.75
Halladay, Roy	R-R	6-6	230	5-14-77	19	6	2.35	32	32	8	0	234	208	65	61	10	35	220	.239	.273	.206	8.47	1.35
Hamels, Cole	L-L	6-3	195	12-27-83	14	9	2.79	32	31	3	0	216	169	68	67	19	44	194	.214	.249	.204	8.08	1.83
Herndon, David	R-R	6-5	230	9-4-85	1	4	3.32	45	0	0	1	57	54	26	21	9	24	39	.258	.354	.200	6.16	3.79
Kendrick, Kyle	R-R	6-3	210	8-26-84	8	6	3.22	34	15	0	0	115	110	50	41	14	30	59	.255	.234	.270	4.63	2.35
Lee, Cliff	L-L	6-3	190	8-30-78	17	8	2.40	32	32	6	0	233	197	66	62	18	42	238	.229	.196	.239	9.21	1.62
Lidge, Brad	R-R	6-5	215	12-23-76	0	2	1.40	25	0	0	1	19	16	3	3	0	13	23	.225	.097	.325	10.71	6.05
Madson, Ryan	L-R	6-6	200	8-28-80	4	2	2.37	62	0	0	32	61	54	16	16	2	16	62	.243	.198	.278	9.20	2.37
Mathieson, Scott	R-R	6-3	230	2-27-84	0	0	0.00	4	0	0	0	5	9	0	0	0	3	5	.409	.615	.111	9.00	5.40
Oswalt, Roy	R-R	6-0	190	8-29-77	9	10	3.69	23	23	0	0	139	153	60	57	10	33	93	.280	.276	.284	6.02	2.14
Perez, Juan	R-L	6-0	175	9-3-78	1	0	3.60	8	0	0	0	5	1	2	2	0	5	8	.063	.000	.143	14.40	9.00
Romero, J.C.	B-L	5-11	205	6-4-76	0	0	3.86	24	0	0	0	16	16	7	7	0	12	10	.262	.208	.297	5.51	6.61
2-team total (12 Colorado)					1	0	4.01	36	0	0	0	25	28	14	11	1	15	19	—	—	—	6.93	5.47
Savery, Joe	L-L	6-3	215	11-4-85	0	0	0.00	4	0	0	0	3	1	0	0	0	2	2	.125	.000	.250	6.75	0.00
Schwimer, Michael	R-R	6-8	240	2-19-86	1	1	5.02	12	0	0	0	14	15	8	8	2	7	16	.278	.400	.172	10.05	4.40
Stutes, Mike	R-R	6-1	185	9-4-86	6	2	3.63	57	0	0	0	62	49	25	25	7	28	58	.218	.212	.222	8.42	4.06
Worley, Vance	R-R	6-2	230	9-25-87	11	3	3.01	25	21	1	0	132	116	47	44	10	46	119	.237	.201	.272	8.13	3.14
Zagurski, Mike	L-L	6-0	225	1-27-83	0	0	5.40	4	0	0	0	3	4	2	2	1	3	4	.286	.167	.375	10.80	8.10

Fielding

Catcher	PCT	G	PO	A	E	DP	PB
Kratz	1.000	1	10	0	0	0	1
Ruiz	.996	128	950	68	4	4	8
Sardinha	1.000	15	86	6	0	3	2

First Base	PCT	G	PO	A	E	DP
Schneider	.997	40	277	9	1	0	(1)
Bowker	1.000	1	1	1	0	0
Gload	.986	10	70	3	1	7

	PCT	G	PO	A	E	DP
Howard	.993	149	1282	70	9	110
Mayberry Jr.	.990	18	89	6	1	9

Second Base	PCT	G	PO	A	E	DP
Martinez	.979	19	21	26	1	6

	PCT	G	PO	A	E	DP
Orr	.982	29	51	61	2	16
Polanco	1.000	1	1	0	0	0
Utley	.990	100	208	275	5	48
Valdez	.989	45	78	95	2	20
Third Base	PCT	G	PO	A	E	DP
Martinez	.968	26	20	41	2	2
Orr	1.000	3	2	5	0	0
Polanco	.977	118	78	259	8	15

	PCT	G	PO	A	E	DP
Ruiz	.000	1	0	0	0	0
Valdez	.939	24	13	33	3	4
Shortstop	PCT	G	PO	A	E	DP
Martinez	.950	13	15	23	2	5
Rollins	.988	138	181	393	7	79
Valdez	.956	25	30	57	4	15
Outfield	PCT	G	PO	A	E	DP
Bowker	1.000	1	4	0	0	0

	PCT	G	PO	A	E	DP
Brown	.951	52	78	0	4	0
Francisco	.973	69	103	4	3	0
Gload	1.000	3	4	1	0	0
Ibanez	.995	134	208	5	1	0
Martinez	.960	14	23	1	1	0
Mayberry Jr.	.981	61	104	2	2	0
Moss	1.000	1	2	0	0	0
Pence	.988	53	81	2	1	0
Victorino	1.000	130	296	0	0	0

LEHIGH VALLEY IRONPIGS — TRIPLE-A

INTERNATIONAL LEAGUE

Batting	B-T	HT	WT	DOB	AVG	vLH	vRH	G	AB	R	H	2B	3B	HR	RBI	BB	HBP	SH	SF	SO	SB	CS	SLG	OBP
Barfield, Josh	R-R	6-0	190	12-17-82	.257	.263	.254	123	452	47	116	23	4	6	55	21	0	0	9	70	12	8	.365	.284
Belliard, Ronnie	R-R	5-9	210	4-7-75	.251	.288	.236	53	199	27	50	8	1	3	23	17	1	0	2	36	3	1	.347	.311
Bocock, Brian	R-R	5-11	185	3-9-85	.224	.222	.225	81	272	22	61	6	1	4	27	26	0	0	2	71	2	4	.298	.290
2-team total (14 Indianapolis)					.226	—	—	95	301	25	68	7	1	4	28	28	0	0	3	78	3	4	.296	.289
Bozied, Tagg	R-R	6-3	225	7-24-79	.238	.276	.221	62	189	31	45	13	2	11	31	35	5	0	0	73	0	4	.503	.371
Brown, Domonic	L-L	6-5	205	9-3-87	.261	.273	.253	41	138	22	36	6	0	3	15	28	4	0	4	33	12	4	.370	.391
Cust, Jack	L-R	6-1	245	1-7-79	.250	.222	.273	6	20	3	5	2	0	1	2	3	0	0	0	3	0	0	.500	.348
Frandsen, Kevin	R-R	6-0	185	5-24-82	.303	.352	.281	77	284	32	86	13	3	4	40	11	16	0	6	31	10	3	.412	.356
Galvis, Freddy	B-R	5-10	170	11-14-89	.298	.216	.333	33	121	15	36	6	1	0	8	3	0	0	0	18	4	2	.364	.315
Hudson, Robbie	R-R	6-0	170	8-31-83	.133	.250	.115	12	30	2	4	1	0	0	1	1	0	0	0	8	1	1	.167	.161
Kratz, Erik	R-R	6-4	255	6-15-80	.288	.291	.286	103	358	56	103	19	0	15	53	38	11	0	2	72	2	0	.466	.372
Larish, Jeff	L-R	6-2	200	10-11-82	.240	.221	.247	75	254	33	61	12	1	13	37	33	1	0	0	85	1	1	.449	.330
Mayberry Jr., John	R-R	6-6	230	12-21-83	.265	.294	.253	28	113	16	30	8	0	4	15	5	0	0	4	23	2	0	.442	.287
Miller, Matt	R-R	6-2	210	12-26-82	.219	.273	.190	15	32	2	7	0	0	0	6	4	1	0	2	10	0	1	.219	.308
Moss, Brandon	L-R	6-0	210	9-16-83	.275	.269	.278	124	436	66	120	31	1	23	80	62	4	0	4	127	4	6	.509	.368
Naughton, Joel	L-R	6-1	210	8-27-86	.231	.333	.143	4	13	1	3	0	0	0	1	0	0	0	0	3	0	0	.231	.231
Orr, Pete	L-R	6-1	195	6-8-79	.267	.259	.270	75	281	40	75	16	2	5	26	17	7	0	1	56	15	5	.391	.324
Overbeck, Cody	R-R	6-1	200	6-5-86	.279	.282	.277	68	226	15	63	11	1	6	26	12	6	0	1	67	0	0	.416	.331
Podsednik, Scott	L-L	6-0	185	3-18-76	.245	.000	.271	14	53	4	13	6	1	0	3	6	0	0	0	15	2	0	.396	.286
Polanco, Placido	R-R	5-10	190	10-10-75	.000	.000	.000	2	6	0	0	0	0	0	0	1	0	0	0	1	0	0	.000	.143
Rivero, Carlos	R-R	6-3	200	5-20-88	.185	.250	.133	7	27	1	5	2	1	1	5	1	1	0	1	6	0	0	.444	.233
Romero, Niuman	B-R	6-1	190	1-24-85	.000	.000	.000	1	1	0	0	0	0	0	0	0	0	0	0	1	0	0	.000	.000
Sardinha, Dane	R-R	6-0	215	4-8-79	.140	.120	.147	29	93	6	13	3	0	1	10	2	0	0	3	32	0	0	.172	.238
Sullivan, Cory	L-L	6-0	200	8-20-79	.210	.192	.216	36	100	15	21	4	0	0	14	20	0	0	2	18	2	0	.250	.336
Suomi, John	L-R	5-11	200	10-5-80	.286	.111	.333	19	42	4	12	2	1	1	5	3	0	0	1	9	0	0	.452	.326
Thompson, Rich	L-R	6-3	185	4-23-79	.276	.242	.289	124	424	81	117	25	8	5	30	37	16	0	3	84	48	4	.408	.354
Young, Delwyn	B-R	5-10	190	6-30-82	.244	.205	.261	146	442	51	108	30	0	11	50	51	3	0	3	109	0	1	.387	.298

Pitching	B-T	HT	WT	DOB	W	L	ERA	G	GS	CG	SV	IP	H	R	ER	HR	BB	SO	AVG	vLH	vRH	K/9	BB/9
Aumont, Phillippe	L-R	6-7	255	1-7-89	0	0	3.18	18	0	0	3	23	21	9	8	0	14	37	.244	.257	.235	14.69	5.56
Bass, Brian	R-R	6-2	215	1-6-82	8	10	3.81	28	28	1	0	158	170	79	67	13	56	105	.278	.290	.269	5.97	3.18
Bonine, Eddie	R-R	6-5	220	6-6-81	3	4	5.16	11	10	0	0	45	58	27	26	3	8	44	.310	.288	.325	8.74	1.59
Brummett, Tyson	R-R	6-0	180	8-15-84	1	4	5.82	7	6	0	0	34	41	22	22	6	11	20	.306	.310	.303	5.29	2.91
Bump, Nate	R-R	6-2	195	7-24-76	5	9	4.97	26	25	1	0	134	172	83	74	11	29	66	.319	.357	.285	4.43	1.95
Bush, Dave	R-R	6-2	205	11-9-79	1	2	3.91	4	4	0	0	23	20	10	10	3	6	16	.233	.242	.226	6.26	2.35
Carpenter, Drew	R-R	6-3	240	5-18-85	5	1	1.79	34	1	0	0	60	48	13	12	2	11	65	.213	.225	.206	9.70	1.64
Chapman, Chance	R-R	6-4	200	2-27-84	2	2	5.29	17	0	0	0	32	37	22	19	5	10	27	.289	.333	.260	7.52	2.78
Contreras, Jose	R-R	6-4	255	12-6-71	0	0	0.00	1	1	0	0	2	2	0	0	0	0	0	.286	.000	.500	0.00	0.00
De Fratus, Justin	B-R	6-4	220	10-21-87	2	3	3.73	28	0	0	7	41	35	19	17	3	11	56	.230	.254	.213	12.29	2.41
Edell, Ryan	L-L	6-1	215	7-6-83	5	5	3.27	17	10	0	0	77	80	31	28	8	11	60	.269	.202	.298	7.60	1.29
Feierabend, Ryan	L-L	6-3	225	8-22-85	10	8	5.39	28	23	0	0	132	146	84	79	20	41	92	.283	.203	.309	6.27	2.80
Gordon, Brian	L-R	6-0	190	8-16-78	5	0	1.14	12	9	0	0	55	39	11	7	4	7	56	.197	.176	.215	9.11	1.14
2-team total (1 Scranton/W-B)					5	0	1.04	13	10	0	0	60	43	11	7	4	7	62	—	—	—	9.40	1.04
Grilli, Jason	R-R	6-5	225	11-11-76	4	1	1.93	28	0	0	3	33	26	8	7	2	12	43	.217	.204	.225	11.85	3.31
Heilman, Aaron	R-R	6-5	230	11-12-78	0	0	8.38	9	0	0	0	10	14	9	9	1	6	8	.350	.375	.333	7.45	5.59
2-team total (7 Indianapolis)					2	0	4.42	16	0	0	1	18	17	9	9	1	9	14	—	—	—	6.87	4.42
Herndon, David	R-R	6-5	230	9-4-85	2	2	2.45	8	0	0	1	15	15	4	4	1	2	14	.263	.259	.267	8.59	1.23
Mathieson, Scott	R-R	6-3	230	2-27-84	2	2	3.28	30	12	0	5	82	71	31	30	9	50	83	.230	.221	.235	9.07	5.47
Oswalt, Roy	R-R	6-0	190	8-29-77	0	0	2.70	2	2	0	0	10	8	3	3	1	4	8	.222	.444	.148	7.20	3.60
Perez, Juan	R-L	6-0	175	9-3-78	0	5	5.70	36	0	0	4	36	37	24	23	5	25	53	.262	.250	.269	13.13	6.19
Redding, Tim	R-R	5-11	230	2-12-78	0	3	5.16	5	4	0	0	23	37	17	13	1	7	14	.308	.424	.556	5.56	2.78
Savery, Joe	L-L	6-3	215	11-4-85	4	0	1.80	18	0	0	2	25	23	6	5	0	6	26	.258	.192	.286	9.36	2.16
Schwimer, Michael	R-R	6-8	240	2-19-86	9	1	1.85	47	0	0	10	68	51	15	14	4	22	86	.203	.307	.133	11.38	2.91
Stutes, Mike	R-R	6-1	185	9-4-86	2	1	1.80	7	0	0	1	10	9	3	2	0	4	14	.250	.308	.208	12.60	3.60
Walrond, Les	L-L	6-3	205	11-7-76	0	1	1.23	12	0	0	0	15	9	2	2	0	9	15	.173	.167	.176	9.20	5.52
Worley, Vance	R-R	6-2	230	9-25-87	5	2	2.31	9	9	1	0	51	41	13	13	5	12	50	.219	.214	.223	8.88	2.13
Zagurski, Mike	L-L	6-0	225	1-27-83	4	0	2.65	46	0	0	11	54	43	18	16	3	27	63	.226	.215	.232	10.44	4.47

Fielding

Catcher	PCT	G	PO	A	E	DP	PB
Kratz	.991	101	807	69	8	9	9
Naughton	1.000	4	27	0	0	0	0
Sardinha	.987	29	215	18	3	1	4
Suomi	.976	10	78	4	2	1	1

PHILADELPHIA PHILLIES

First Base	PCT	G	PO	A	E	DP
Bozied	.990	25	188	10	2	18
Frandsen	.989	10	81	5	1	9
Larish	.996	51	443	25	2	44
Mayberry Jr.	1.000	1	8	0	0	1
Overbeck	.995	60	515	36	3	65

Second Base	PCT	G	PO	A	E	DP
Barfield	.984	108	189	302	8	77
Frandsen	1.000	24	41	53	0	21
Hudson	1.000	3	5	5	0	1
Orr	.982	14	14	42	1	8

Third Base	PCT	G	PO	A	E	DP
Belliard	.951	49	42	94	7	13

Bozied	.917	9	4	18	2	4
Frandsen	.896	21	10	33	5	2
Larish	.927	19	14	37	4	3
Orr	.977	47	25	102	3	10
Overbeck	.000	1	0	0	1	0
Polanco	1.000	1	1	0	0	0
Rivero	.882	7	1	14	2	4

Shortstop	PCT	G	PO	A	E	DP
Bocock	.957	81	104	251	16	63
Frandsen	.947	23	23	67	5	12
Galvis	.977	33	43	87	3	16
Hudson	.963	9	6	20	1	4
Orr	.950	9	5	14	1	4

Outfield	PCT	G	PO	A	E	DP
Barfield	1.000	7	18	1	0	0
Bozied	1.000	8	10	2	0	0
Brown	.939	38	59	3	4	2
Larish	1.000	1	2	0	0	0
Mayberry Jr.	.982	27	53	2	1	0
Miller	.833	6	5	0	1	0
Moss	.976	112	192	15	5	3
Orr	1.000	7	12	0	0	0
Podsednik	.963	14	25	1	1	0
Sullivan	1.000	30	38	2	0	0
Thompson	.992	117	253	6	2	0
Young	.969	84	123	3	4	1

READING PHILLIES

DOUBLE-A

EASTERN LEAGUE

Batting	B-T	HT	WT	DOB	AVG	vLH	vRH	G	AB	R	H	2B	3B	HR	RBI	BB	HBP	SH	SF	SO	SB	CS	SLG	OBP
Chavez, Ozzie	B-R	6-1	175	7-13-83	.262	.353	.244	29	107	10	28	4	0	1	10	9	3	0	0	21	1	7	.327	.336
Clevlen, Brent	R-R	6-1	205	10-27-83	.336	.500	.297	32	113	26	38	12	0	6	20	21	0	0	0	34	5	2	.602	.440
Evans, Terry	R-R	6-4	210	1-19-82	.184	.170	.193	48	141	22	26	9	0	6	17	9	5	0	2	49	1	2	.376	.255
Figueroa, Paco	R-R	5-11	180	2-19-83	.259	.280	.252	68	185	25	48	8	1	0	17	32	3	0	1	29	6	4	.314	.376
Frandsen, Kevin	R-R	6-0	185	5-24-82	.500	.500	.500	1	4	1	2	0	0	1	2	1	0	0	0	1	0	1	1.250	.600
Frey, Chris	L-L	6-1	180	8-11-83	.286	.000	.300	5	21	2	6	2	0	2	5	0	0	0	0	4	0	0	.667	.286
Galvis, Freddy	B-R	5-10	170	11-14-89	.273	.261	.277	104	422	63	115	22	4	8	35	28	6	0	1	68	19	11	.400	.326
Garcia, Harold	B-R	5-11	190	10-25-86	.300	.286	.302	12	50	5	15	3	0	2	4	2	0	0	0	11	2	1	.480	.327
Gosewisch, Tuffy	R-R	5-11	180	8-17-83	.247	.318	.224	109	369	41	91	19	0	13	66	20	8	0	6	61	4	6	.404	.295
Hanzawa, Troy	R-R	5-9	155	9-12-85	.077	.111	.059	8	26	6	2	0	0	0	0	2	1	0	0	3	0	1	.077	.172
Hernandez, Fidel	R-R	5-11	190	1-18-86	.267	.281	.264	59	172	27	46	7	0	2	15	12	0	0	1	16	3	2	.343	.314
Kennelly, Tim	R-R	6-0	180	12-5-86	.215	.159	.234	61	181	18	39	8	3	3	21	11	3	0	0	44	5	2	.343	.272
Lubanski, Chris	L-L	6-3	210	3-24-85	.189	.000	.217	19	53	5	10	0	1	1	5	2	1	0	1	16	3	1	.283	.228
Miller, Matt	R-R	6-2	210	12-26-82	.243	.222	.250	20	74	8	18	3	1	0	1	5	1	0	0	7	2	0	.311	.300
Mitchell, Derrick	R-R	6-3	210	1-5-87	.265	.240	.274	135	476	67	126	24	2	19	79	40	6	0	6	110	20	10	.443	.326
Overbeck, Cody	R-R	6-1	200	6-5-86	.275	.257	.283	62	233	43	64	6	0	18	46	19	2	0	3	58	1	6	.532	.331
Rivero, Carlos	R-R	6-3	200	5-20-88	.275	.326	.257	129	491	70	135	36	0	15	66	38	5	0	4	106	5	3	.440	.331
Rizzotti, Matt	L-L	6-5	265	12-24-85	.295	.336	.278	139	499	73	147	34	1	24	84	79	4	0	5	125	4	1	.511	.392
Romero, Niuman	B-R	6-1	190	1-24-85	.239	.270	.222	34	109	10	26	3	0	0	11	11	2	0	3	25	4	2	.266	.312
2-team total (32 Binghamton)					.241	—	—	66	212	23	51	5	1	0	23	19	2	0	4	49	6	3	.274	.304
Schneider, Brian	L-R	6-1	210	11-26-76	.250	.000	.300	7	24	2	6	1	0	0	1	3	0	0	0	4	0	0	.292	.333
Singleton, Steve	L-R	6-0	185	9-12-85	.295	.111	.314	27	95	13	28	8	0	1	13	4	0	0	0	13	2	1	.411	.323
2-team total (41 New Britain)					.295	—	—	68	261	37	77	25	0	4	26	10	4	0	2	27	4	3	.437	.329
Slayden, Jeremy	L-R	6-0	185	7-28-82	.500	.000	.600	2	6	1	3	1	0	0	2	0	0	0	0	1	0	0	.667	.500
Spidale, Mike	R-R	6-1	190	3-12-82	.326	.297	.336	133	494	65	161	16	3	5	35	28	12	0	2	51	20	10	.401	.375
Suomi, John	L-R	5-11	200	10-5-80	.348	.000	.356	19	46	4	16	3	0	1	3	1	1	0	0	2	2	0	.478	.375
Susdorf, Steve	L-L	6-1	195	3-28-86	.339	.382	.326	78	242	51	82	20	0	6	35	25	3	0	1	48	7	1	.496	.406
Victorino, Shane	B-R	5-9	190	11-30-80	.333	.250	.429	4	15	2	5	1	0	1	3	1	0	1	0	2	1	2	.600	.389

Pitching	B-T	HT	WT	DOB	W	L	ERA	G	GS	CG	SV	IP	H	R	ER	HR	BB	SO	AVG	vLH	vRH	K/9	BB/9
Aumont, Phillippe	L-R	6-7	255	1-7-89	1	5	2.32	25	0	0	4	31	23	16	8	2	11	41	.195	.160	.221	11.90	3.19
Brummett, Tyson	R-R	6-0	180	8-15-84	4	8	4.52	30	11	0	0	92	103	53	46	11	28	72	.282	.259	.300	7.07	2.75
Chapman, Chance	R-R	6-4	200	2-27-84	0	0	0.00	5	0	0	1	7	5	0	0	1	7	.227	.200	.250	9.45	1.35
Cisco, Mike	R-R	5-11	190	5-23-87	8	0	1.59	29	0	0	3	62	39	12	11	6	29	51	.182	.187	.179	7.36	4.19
Cloyd, Tyler	R-R	6-3	190	5-16-87	6	3	2.78	18	17	0	0	107	101	35	33	7	15	99	.250	.294	.214	8.35	1.27
Contreras, Jose	R-R	6-4	255	12-6-71	0	0	0.00	1	0	0	0	1	2	0	0	0	1	1	.400	.250	1.000	9.00	9.00
De Fratus, Justin	B-R	6-4	220	10-21-87	4	2	2.10	23	0	0	8	34	28	11	8	1	14	43	.224	.173	.260	11.27	3.67
Diekman, Jacob	L-L	6-4	190	1-21-87	0	1	3.05	53	0	0	3	65	47	29	22	3	44	83	.199	.099	.262	11.49	6.09
Edell, Ryan	L-L	6-1	215	7-6-83	5	1	3.50	12	12	0	0	72	79	34	28	6	9	50	.279	.270	.282	6.25	1.13
Ellis, Jordan	R-R	6-2	198	9-11-85	1	1	8.65	19	0	0	0	26	34	25	25	5	16	28	.312	.314	.310	9.69	5.54
Esposito, Joe	L-R	5-11	220	5-15-85	5	5	5.48	14	14	0	0	66	75	44	40	8	30	56	.293	.290	.296	7.68	4.11
Friend, Justin	R-R	6-1	200	6-21-86	1	4	3.38	29	0	0	9	29	29	11	11	1	8	31	.254	.208	.288	9.51	2.45
Hyatt, Austin	R-R	6-2	180	5-23-86	12	6	3.85	28	28	0	0	154	136	69	66	20	49	171	.235	.201	.262	9.97	2.86
Kissock, Chris	R-R	6-4	195	5-2-85	3	7	4.82	37	7	0	1	103	107	62	55	9	25	69	.272	.276	.267	6.05	2.19
Lidge, Brad	R-R	6-5	215	12-23-76	0	0	4.91	4	0	0	0	4	3	2	2	0	1	5	.214	.250	.167	12.27	2.45
Loop, Derrick	R-L	6-3	220	12-11-83	1	3	5.29	19	2	0	0	34	34	21	20	6	15	32	.258	.065	.360	8.47	3.97
Ramirez, J.C.	R-R	6-3	225	8-16-88	11	13	4.50	26	26	3	0	144	144	84	72	15	55	69	.262	.242	.270	5.56	3.44
Rosenberg, B.J.	R-R	6-2	215	9-17-85	5	7	4.28	39	14	0	2	109	114	56	52	11	38	103	.275	.266	.285	8.48	3.13
Savery, Joe	L-L	6-3	215	11-4-85	1	0	1.00	6	0	0	0	9	7	1	1	0	0	14	.212	.125	.294	14.00	0.00
Walrond, Les	L-L	6-3	205	11-7-76	4	1	2.08	21	0	0	3	30	25	7	7	1	13	32	.227	.200	.246	9.49	3.86
Zeid, Josh	R-R	6-5	210	3-24-87	2	3	5.65	21	11	0	2	64	63	43	40	9	27	56	.265	.309	.227	7.92	3.82

Fielding

Catcher	PCT	G	PO	A	E	DP	PB
Gosewisch	.994	108	851	69	6	2	6
Kennelly	.980	31	214	25	5	2	4
Schneider	1.000	3	25	1	0	0	0
Suomi	1.000	10	63	6	0	0	0

First Base	PCT	G	PO	A	E	DP
Hernandez	1.000	7	33	2	0	4
Kennelly	1.000	7	36	8	0	3

Overbeck	.997	36	279	29	1	19
Rizzotti	.988	96	690	53	9	64
Susdorf	1.000	5	32	2	0	1

Second Base	PCT	G	PO	A	E	DP
Chavez	.943	6	13	20	2	7
Figueroa	.991	58	96	122	2	24
Frandsen	1.000	1	2	4	0	1
Garcia	1.000	12	22	28	0	5
Hernandez	.962	30	61	67	5	20
Kennelly	1.000	1	0	2	0	0
Romero	.992	30	54	68	1	9
Singleton	1.000	19	47	31	0	10

Third Base	PCT	G	PO	A	E	DP
Figueroa	1.000	2	0	2	0	0

Hernandez	.929	12	12	27	3	4
Kennelly	.667	2	0	2	1	0
Overbeck	.750	1	0	3	1	0
Rivero	.915	126	84	186	25	15

Shortstop	PCT	G	PO	A	E	DP
Chavez	.967	23	32	55	3	15
Galvis	.964	104	144	288	16	44
Hanzawa	.929	7	4	22	2	5
Hernandez	1.000	7	5	12	0	2
Rivero	1.000	1	2	1	0	1
Romero	.750	3	1	2	1	0
Singleton	.960	6	13	11	1	5

Outfield	PCT	G	PO	A	E	DP
Clevlen	.952	31	60	0	3	0

Evans	1.000	39	64	2	0	0
Figueroa	1.000	5	4	0	0	0
Frey	1.000	5	11	0	0	0
Kennelly	.920	18	19	4	2	1
Lubanski	.900	5	9	0	1	0
Miller	.939	20	30	1	2	0
Mitchell	.987	132	295	5	4	0
Overbeck	.929	9	12	1	1	0
Slayden	1.000	2	4	0	0	0
Spidale	.986	127	210	5	3	1
Susdorf	.982	60	104	5	2	2
Victorino	1.000	3	11	1	0	1

CLEARWATER THRESHERS

HIGH CLASS A

FLORIDA STATE LEAGUE

Batting	B-T	HT	WT	DOB	AVG	vLH	vRH	G	AB	R	H	2B	3B	HR	RBI	BB	HBP	SH	SF	SO	SB	CS	SLG	OBP
Barnes, Jeremy	R-R	5-10	190	4-13-87	.267	.298	.253	100	367	36	98	23	0	9	45	33	5	0	1	86	0	1	.403	.335
Bocock, Brian	R-R	5-11	185	3-9-85	.286	.000	.333	2	7	1	2	0	0	0	1	0	0	0	1	1	0	0	.286	.250
Brown, Domonic	L-L	6-5	205	9-3-87	.368	.333	.385	5	19	4	7	1	0	2	4	2	0	0	0	3	0	0	.737	.429
Castro, Leandro	R-R	5-11	175	6-15-89	.277	.231	.295	56	231	38	64	11	3	10	31	5	4	0	0	33	10	2	.481	.304
Chavarin, Angel	L-R	6-0	176	10-22-90	.500	1.000	.000	2	2	0	1	0	0	0	0	0	0	0	0	0	0	0	.500	.500
Dabbs, Mike	L-R	6-0	185	3-29-87	.212	.240	.200	27	85	7	18	2	0	0	4	6	2	0	0	18	1	4	.235	.280
Frandsen, Kevin	R-R	6-0	185	5-24-82	.400	.500	.333	3	10	1	4	2	0	0	1	0	0	0	0	0	0	0	.600	.400
Gillies, Tyson	L-R	6-2	195	10-31-88	.154	.000	.182	3	13	1	2	2	0	0	0	0	0	0	0	1	0	0	.308	.154
Gonzalez, Gustavo	R-R	6-0	0	1-23-91	.600	.000	.600	3	5	1	3	0	0	1	4	0	0	0	0	0	0	0	1.200	.600
Gump, Brian	L-L	6-2	195	6-16-87	.217	.154	.234	86	249	28	54	6	3	5	22	18	3	0	1	81	8	7	.325	.277
Hankerd, Cyle	R-R	6-3	215	1-24-85	.248	.227	.253	31	109	14	27	4	1	6	23	9	2	0	0	15	0	0	.468	.317
Hanzawa, Troy	R-R	5-9	155	9-12-85	.223	.255	.209	112	364	38	81	19	3	3	33	17	9	0	0	75	3	2	.316	.274
Hernandez, Cesar	B-R	5-10	160	5-23-90	.268	.233	.282	119	421	47	113	7	4	4	37	23	1	0	2	80	23	10	.333	.306
Hernandez, Fidel	R-R	5-11	190	1-18-86	.160	.185	.146	22	75	4	12	0	0	0	3	0	0	0	1	11	0	0	.160	.158
James, Jiwan	B-R	6-4	180	4-11-89	.268	.240	.279	130	526	76	141	26	6	4	38	40	7	0	2	120	31	16	.363	.327
Lafrenz, Bronco	R-R	6-1	190	2-6-87	.193	.200	.190	23	83	6	16	3	0	1	5	5	1	0	0	18	0	0	.265	.247
Langley, Torre	R-R	5-9	175	10-9-87	.195	.125	.212	16	41	0	8	0	0	0	5	4	1	0	2	11	0	0	.195	.271
Mattair, Travis	R-R	6-5	210	12-21-88	.207	.265	.195	57	188	19	39	10	0	6	26	16	3	0	1	48	4	0	.356	.279
Myers, D'Arby	R-R	6-3	175	12-9-88	.235	.216	.242	44	136	16	32	2	3	1	9	5	2	0	1	30	5	1	.316	.271
Payton, Matt	L-R	5-9	185	2-3-88	.391	.667	.294	6	23	3	9	0	0	2	1	1	0	0	0	1	0	0	.391	.440
Quaranto, Kevin	L-R	6-3	215	5-13-88	.714	.500	.800	3	7	1	5	1	0	0	1	3	0	0	0	2	0	0	.857	.800
Ruf, Darin	R-R	6-3	220	7-28-86	.308	.358	.291	133	484	72	149	43	1	17	82	56	10	0	4	95	0	1	.506	.388
Ruiz, Carlos	R-R	5-10	205	1-22-79	.333	.000	.333	1	3	1	1	0	0	0	0	0	0	0	0	0	0	0	.333	.333
Schoenberger, Alan	B-R	5-10	160	1-19-89	.180	.160	.187	34	100	12	18	3	1	1	8	8	0	0	1	23	1	1	.260	.239
Singleton, Jonathan	L-L	6-2	215	9-18-91	.284	.189	.324	93	320	48	91	14	0	9	47	56	1	0	5	83	3	3	.413	.387
Stumpo, Bob	B-R	6-4	220	7-17-87	.750	.000	.750	1	4	0	3	0	0	0	0	0	0	0	0	0	0	0	.750	.750
Suomi, John	L-R	5-11	200	10-5-80	.182	.200	.174	11	33	3	6	1	0	2	2	3	0	0	0	7	0	0	.394	.250
Tripp, Brandon	L-R	6-2	200	4-2-85	.322	.194	.355	42	152	22	49	13	0	5	20	8	4	0	1	38	0	0	.507	.370
Utley, Chase	L-R	6-1	200	12-17-78	.281	.200	.353	9	32	4	9	2	0	1	4	3	1	0	0	6	1	0	.438	.361
Valle, Sebastian	R-R	6-1	170	7-24-90	.284	.368	.253	91	348	34	99	19	2	5	40	13	2	0	2	84	0	0	.394	.312

Pitching	B-T	HT	WT	DOB	W	L	ERA	G	GS	CG	SV	IP	H	R	ER	HR	BB	SO	AVG	vLH	vRH	K/9	BB/9
Alaniz, Adrian	R-R	6-2	200	3-12-84	1	0	7.71	9	0	0	0	9	14	10	8	3	5	7	.359	.316	.400	6.75	4.82
Bastidas, Leonel	R-R	6-3	184	6-26-89	0	0	0.00	1	0	0	0	2	2	0	0	0	0	0	.250	.250	.250	0.00	0.00
Buchanan, David	R-R	6-3	190	5-11-89	3	2	3.90	6	6	0	0	32	37	15	14	4	11	24	.289	.339	.246	6.68	3.06
Cameron, Dustin	R-R	6-1	210	11-5-81	0	0	7.71	4	0	0	0	5	7	6	4	0	1	3	.350	.375	.333	5.79	1.93
Chapman, Chance	R-R	6-4	200	2-27-84	1	1	3.68	7	0	0	0	7	8	4	3	1	1	12	.258	.308	.222	14.73	1.23
Cloyd, Tyler	R-R	6-3	190	5-16-87	3	1	2.75	13	5	0	0	39	31	12	12	3	7	39	.212	.143	.276	8.92	1.60
Colvin, Brody	R-R	6-3	195	8-14-90	3	8	4.71	22	21	0	0	117	131	67	61	10	42	78	.289	.273	.302	6.02	3.24
Contreras, Jose	R-R	6-4	255	12-6-71	0	1	40.50	1	1	0	0	1	4	3	3	0	0	0	.667	.500	1.000	0.00	0.00
Cosart, Jarred	R-R	6-3	180	5-25-90	9	8	3.92	20	19	0	0	108	98	55	47	7	43	79	.243	.203	.286	6.58	3.58
Ellis, Jordan	R-R	6-2	198	9-11-85	1	0	0.00	6	0	0	0	9	4	0	0	0	2	14	.138	.125	.154	14.54	2.08
Esposito, Joe	L-R	5-11	220	5-15-85	2	2	3.55	21	2	0	0	46	42	22	18	3	24	38	.258	.256	.259	7.49	4.73
Friend, Justin	R-R	6-1	200	6-21-86	2	3	2.12	26	0	0	19	30	20	8	7	1	8	30	.190	.137	.241	9.10	2.43
Loomis, Andy	L-L	5-10	175	11-25-85	1	2	1.14	28	0	0	3	32	27	6	4	0	10	39	.231	.186	.276	11.08	2.84
Loop, Derrick	R-L	6-3	220	12-3-83	2	1	1.13	24	0	0	3	32	22	6	4	2	16	30	.202	.100	.261	8.44	4.50
Lugo, Ebelin	R-R	6-2	190	4-23-90	2	3	4.45	38	1	0	3	59	64	33	29	8	12	49	.284	.264	.303	7.52	1.84
Madson, Ryan	L-R	6-6	200	8-28-80	0	0	0.00	1	1	0	0	1	0	0	0	0	0	1	.000	.000	.000	9.00	0.00
May, Trevor	R-R	6-5	215	9-23-89	10	8	3.63	27	27	3	0	151	121	65	61	8	67	208	.221	.229	.214	12.37	3.98
McGuire, Mike	R-R	6-7	240	6-29-86	0	0	9.00	14	0	0	0	18	28	19	18	0	8	19	.337	.357	.317	9.50	4.00
Oswalt, Roy	R-R	6-0	190	8-29-77	0	0	5.40	1	1	0	0	5	7	3	3	0	1	5	.318	.333	.316	9.00	1.80
Palica, Tommy	L-L	6-3	215	7-21-87	1	1	7.66	14	0	0	0	25	24	21	21	2	10	18	.255	.258	.254	6.57	3.65
Pettibone, Jon	R-R	6-5	200	7-19-90	10	11	2.96	27	27	0	0	161	149	62	53	5	34	115	.248	.244	.253	6.43	1.90
Pettis, Eric	R-R	6-2	200	6-9-88	2	2	3.27	37	0	0	3	55	50	20	20	5	12	46	.243	.261	.228	7.53	1.96
Rodriguez, Julio	R-R	6-4	195	8-29-90	16	7	2.76	27	27	0	0	157	102	49	48	13	56	168	.186	.213	.159	9.65	3.22

PHILADELPHIA PHILLIES

Pitching

Pitching	B-T	HT	WT	DOB	W	L	ERA	G	GS	CG	SV	IP	H	R	ER	HR	BB	SO	AVG	vLH	vRH	K/9	BB/9
Savery, Joe	L-L	6-3	215	11-4-85	0	0	0.00	1	0	0	0	2	2	0	0	0	0	1	.250	.000	.400	4.50	0.00
Shreve, Colby	R-R	6-5	210	1-5-88	1	1	3.55	7	0	0	0	13	16	6	5	3	3	14	.314	.250	.355	9.95	2.13
Sosa, Juan	R-R	6-2	165	10-11-89	1	0	2.90	17	1	0	1	31	23	14	10	2	9	28	.207	.218	.196	8.13	2.61
Stephens, Jay	R-R	6-5	200	10-10-84	0	0	10.80	4	0	0	0	3	4	5	4	0	4	3	.267	.222	.333	10.80	10.80
Whatcott, Jordan	R-R	6-0	198	6-10-85	4	1	2.57	45	0	0	11	63	61	18	18	3	18	46	.266	.320	.225	6.57	2.57

Fielding

Catcher	PCT	G	PO	A	E	DP	PB
Lafrenz	.995	23	170	18	1	5	4
Langley	1.000	16	86	15	0	0	5
Quaranto	1.000	3	27	2	0	0	1
Ruiz	1.000	1	5	0	0	0	0
Stumpo	1.000	1	9	0	0	0	1
Suomi	1.000	11	78	11	0	1	0
Valle	.998	90	737	68	2	7	11

First Base	PCT	G	PO	A	E	DP
Hankerd	1.000	4	34	2	0	4
Ruf	.992	74	596	49	5	52
Savery	.993	19	137	14	1	18
Singleton	.984	46	337	26	6	27

Second Base	PCT	G	PO	A	E	DP
Frandsen	1.000	1	1	4	0	1
Hernandez	.975	119	202	298	13	67

Hernandez	.938	3	7	8	1	2
Mattair	1.000	2	2	4	0	1
Schoenberger	.889	14	9	31	5	4
Utley	1.000	7	8	10	0	2

Third Base	PCT	G	PO	A	E	DP
Barnes	.945	71	52	104	9	9
Hernandez	.900	8	2	7	1	0
Mattair	.949	55	27	85	6	6
Payton	.857	3	0	6	1	0
Ruf	.857	3	4	2	1	0
Schoenberger	.750	5	0	3	1	0

Shortstop	PCT	G	PO	A	E	DP
Bocock	1.000	2	0	6	0	1
Frandsen	1.000	2	2	6	0	0
Gonzalez	.667	3	2	2	2	0
Hanzawa	.970	112	174	281	14	66

Hernandez	1.000	7	9	19	0	1
Payton	.900	3	2	7	1	2
Schoenberger	.947	19	20	34	3	9

Outfield	PCT	G	PO	A	E	DP
Brown	1.000	5	3	0	0	0
Castro	.975	51	114	3	3	1
Dabbs	.984	27	58	2	1	1
Gillies	1.000	3	11	0	0	0
Gump	.978	75	126	5	3	2
Hankerd	.980	25	45	5	1	1
Hernandez	1.000	4	9	0	0	0
James	.986	130	274	9	4	2
Myers	.987	40	71	3	1	0
Ruf	.857	6	10	2	2	1
Savery	.944	12	17	0	1	0
Singleton	.942	30	46	3	3	0
Tripp	1.000	34	47	4	0	1

LAKEWOOD BLUECLAWS
SOUTH ATLANTIC LEAGUE
LOW CLASS A

Batting

Batting	B-T	HT	WT	DOB	AVG	vLH	vRH	G	AB	R	H	2B	3B	HR	RBI	BB	HBP	SH	SF	SO	SB	CS	SLG	OBP
Alonso, Carlos	R-R	5-11	205	2-15-88	.313	.275	.330	48	160	17	50	10	0	2	21	25	7	0	1	13	2	1	.413	.425
Altherr, Aaron	R-R	6-5	190	1-14-91	.211	.097	.241	41	147	20	31	6	0	1	15	11	2	0	2	47	12	0	.272	.272
Alvarez, Miguel	R-R	6-1	172	8-27-89	.257	.252	.260	90	319	38	82	18	1	1	24	9	3	0	2	78	17	4	.329	.282
Barnes, Jeremy	R-R	5-10	190	4-13-87	.230	.333	.197	22	87	11	20	5	0	1	10	3	2	0	4	10	1	0	.322	.260
Batts, Stephen	R-R	6-0	200	2-14-86	.188	.000	.255	18	64	9	12	4	0	3	9	5	5	0	1	20	1	0	.391	.293
Collier, Zach	L-L	6-2	185	9-8-90	.255	.299	.237	112	416	50	106	24	6	1	36	40	7	0	4	99	35	13	.349	.328
Dabbs, Mike	L-R	6-0	185	3-29-87	.279	.286	.277	25	86	12	24	7	0	3	11	0	3	0	1	11	5	0	.465	.300
Duran, Edgar	R-R	5-11	155	2-10-91	.234	.300	.245	112	401	36	94	8	3	4	42	24	4	0	7	79	15	7	.299	.280
Franco, Maikel	R-R	6-1	180	8-26-92	.123	.217	.071	17	65	6	8	2	0	1	6	1	1	0	0	15	0	0	.200	.149
Hewitt, Anthony	R-R	6-1	190	4-27-89	.240	.273	.227	119	454	62	109	21	6	14	55	17	9	0	0	149	36	5	.405	.281
Hillman, Drew	R-R	6-0	200	5-4-89	.190	.200	.186	15	58	4	11	4	0	1	4	2	2	0	0	9	0	0	.310	.242
Langley, Torre	R-R	5-9	175	10-9-87	.220	.375	.190	17	50	1	11	0	0	1	3	1	0	1	11	1	0	.240	.273
Lanning, Jeff	R-R	6-0	210	1-1-87	.260	.314	.239	43	123	23	32	8	0	5	12	11	3	0	1	30	2	0	.447	.333
Mattair, Travis	R-R	6-5	210	12-21-88	.266	.244	.278	33	124	15	33	8	1	2	18	7	1	0	1	35	0	1	.395	.308
Mendez, Geancarlo	R-R	6-2	170	11-17-89	.244	.205	.261	80	291	38	71	15	3	3	33	29	2	0	1	44	11	3	.347	.316
Miramontes, Kenny	R-R	5-9	180	7-18-88	.100	.200	.000	3	10	1	1	0	0	0	0	1	0	0	0	3	0	0	.100	.182
Murphy, Jim	R-R	6-4	240	9-16-85	.268	.286	.260	129	463	64	124	35	1	22	77	59	11	0	4	123	1	0	.490	.361
Payton, Matt	L-R	5-9	185	2-3-88	.143	.000	.167	3	7	0	1	0	0	0	0	0	0	0	3	0	0	.143	.143
Perdomo, Carlos	R-R	5-10	168	4-25-90	.255	.273	.244	77	263	32	67	8	3	0	27	25	3	0	3	25	15	9	.308	.323
Rice, Bill	L-R	5-11	185	9-7-88	.293	.314	.284	35	123	19	36	3	3	1	8	12	2	0	1	21	8	5	.390	.362
Rupp, Cameron	R-R	6-1	240	9-28-88	.272	.343	.237	99	324	33	88	19	1	4	44	31	8	0	4	96	0	0	.373	.346
Santana, Domingo	R-R	6-5	200	8-5-92	.269	.267	.269	96	350	45	94	29	4	7	32	26	15	0	0	120	4	1	.434	.345
2-team total (17 Lexington)					.287	—	—	113	418	58	120	33	4	12	53	32	17	0	0	135	5	1	.471	.362
Schoenberger, Alan	R-R	5-10	160	1-19-89	.197	.211	.192	36	137	17	27	8	1	1	9	10	2	0	1	41	1	1	.292	.260
Singleton, Steve	L-R	6-0	185	9-12-85	.186	.250	.161	11	43	5	8	2	0	1	1	1	0	0	0	5	1	1	.302	.205
Unda, Luis	L-L	6-1	155	1-28-90	.000	.000	.000	3	8	0	0	0	0	0	0	0	0	0	0	2	0	0	.000	.000
Victorino, Shane	B-R	5-9	190	11-30-80	.167	.000	.167	2	6	1	1	0	0	0	2	1	0	0	0	2	0	0	.167	.286

Pitching

Pitching	B-T	HT	WT	DOB	W	L	ERA	G	GS	CG	SV	IP	H	R	ER	HR	BB	SO	AVG	vLH	vRH	K/9	BB/9
Biddle, Jesse	L-L	6-4	225	10-22-91	7	8	2.98	25	24	0	0	133	104	51	44	5	66	124	.219	.211	.221	8.39	4.47
Blanton, Joe	R-R	6-3	245	12-11-80	0	0	0.00	1	1	0	0	1	0	0	0	0	0	0	.000	.000	.000	0.00	0.00
Bonilla, Lisalberto	R-R	6-1	164	6-6-90	4	5	2.80	26	15	1	4	106	91	38	33	8	29	95	.229	.282	.185	8.07	2.46
Borup, Jake	R-R	6-5	210	5-6-87	1	0	5.91	6	0	0	0	11	16	9	7	3	2	11	.308	.348	.276	9.28	1.69
Buchanan, David	R-R	6-3	190	5-11-89	11	5	3.38	20	20	1	0	125	115	60	47	6	32	86	.246	.240	.250	6.19	2.30
Castillo, Lendy	R-R	6-1	170	4-8-89	4	2	2.54	21	2	0	0	46	37	16	13	1	16	46	.220	.271	.184	9.00	3.13
Claypool, Garett	R-R	6-2	170	8-21-88	5	7	3.47	27	23	0	0	137	111	60	53	12	46	151	.223	.201	.240	9.90	3.01
Davis, Rye	R-R	6-5	250	12-11-88	0	0	6.00	2	0	0	0	3	3	2	2	1	2	3	.250	.429	.000	9.00	6.00
Duke, Ryan	R-R	6-0	180	9-27-88	0	0	1.15	15	0	0	6	16	7	2	2	0	5	18	.132	.107	.160	10.34	2.87
Hollands, Mario	L-L	6-5	205	8-26-88	6	6	4.24	28	15	0	0	98	109	53	46	5	36	73	.283	.269	.289	6.73	3.32
Johnson, Chase	R-R	6-5	245	4-29-88	4	6	4.31	38	0	0	0	71	73	37	34	3	27	64	.268	.309	.241	8.11	3.42
Johnson, Jay	R-L	6-2	210	12-21-89	1	5	2.94	40	0	0	5	49	41	22	16	0	35	49	.228	.208	.236	9.00	6.43
Knigge, Tyler	R-R	6-4	215	10-27-88	4	3	3.32	43	0	0	4	65	58	29	24	4	24	54	.243	.237	.246	7.48	3.32
Lidge, Brad	R-R	6-5	215	12-23-76	0	0	2.25	4	2	0	0	4	5	1	1	0	0	5	.313	.286	.333	11.25	0.00
Lugo, Ebelin	R-R	6-2	190	4-23-90	0	3	7.20	3	0	0	0	5	8	5	4	2	1	2	.400	.222	.545	3.60	1.80
Manzanillo, Ervis	L-L	6-2	160	8-25-91	8	7	5.02	26	25	0	0	118	114	73	66	5	71	105	.257	.200	.277	7.99	5.40

Pitching	B-T	HT	WT	DOB	W	L	ERA	G	GS	CG	SV	IP	H	R	ER	HR	BB	SO	AVG	vLH	vRH	K/9	BB/9
McGuire, Mike	R-R	6-7	240	6-29-86	2	1	7.45	9	0	0	0	10	12	9	8	1	9	11	.308	.333	.292	10.24	8.38
Morgado, Bryan	L-L	6-3	205	12-8-88	0	0	2.08	5	0	0	0	9	8	4	2	0	4	5	.258	.231	.278	5.19	4.15
Neris, Hector	R-R	6-2	175	6-14-89	2	1	3.86	19	0	0	0	35	34	21	15	6	9	43	.245	.161	.312	11.06	2.31
Pettis, Eric	R-R	6-2	200	6-9-88	0	1	1.23	10	0	0	2	15	9	5	2	1	4	9	.180	.150	.200	5.52	2.45
Romero, J.C.	B-L	5-11	205	6-4-76	0	0	0.00	1	0	0	0	1	0	0	0	0	1	1	.000	.000	.000	9.00	9.00
Shreve, Colby	R-R	6-5	210	1-5-88	5	5	2.75	33	3	0	2	72	71	35	22	4	27	65	.259	.262	.257	8.13	3.38
Sosa, Juan	R-R	6-2	165	10-11-89	3	2	4.17	30	0	0	10	41	36	20	19	5	15	33	.243	.276	.222	7.24	3.29
Wright, Austin	L-L	6-4	235	9-26-89	1	2	2.67	7	7	0	0	34	29	12	10	2	9	41	.238	.200	.253	10.96	2.41

Fielding

Catcher	PCT	G	PO	A	E	DP	PB
Langley	1.000	17	116	8	0	0	2
Lanning	.985	34	240	25	4	3	4
Rupp	.982	98	716	96	15	9	13

First Base	PCT	G	PO	A	E	DP
Alonso	.800	1	4	0	1	0
Batts	1.000	2	22	0	0	4
Lanning	1.000	5	35	2	0	1
Mendez	1.000	4	20	1	0	2
Murphy	.991	128	1067	74	10	100

Second Base	PCT	G	PO	A	E	DP
Alonso	.984	42	83	107	3	25
Barnes	.914	15	32	32	6	13
Payton	1.000	2	4	8	0	2
Perdomo	.965	48	95	128	8	32

	PCT	G	PO	A	E	DP
Schoenberger	.960	32	45	75	5	11

Third Base	PCT	G	PO	A	E	DP
Alonso	.909	4	4	6	1	0
Barnes	.905	6	6	13	2	3
Batts	.941	11	13	19	2	3
Franco	1.000	17	10	27	0	3
Hillman	.870	11	5	15	3	1
Mattair	.929	33	13	66	6	5
Mendez	.905	43	31	64	10	9
Perdomo	.500	1	0	2	2	0
Schoenberger	.667	2	1	1	1	0
Singleton	.879	11	8	21	4	2

Shortstop	PCT	G	PO	A	E	DP
Duran	.950	111	136	305	23	61
Miramontes	.846	3	5	6	2	1

	PCT	G	PO	A	E	DP
Perdomo	.938	26	32	59	6	8

Outfield	PCT	G	PO	A	E	DP
Altherr	.979	39	92	3	2	1
Alvarez	.964	74	126	9	5	0
Batts	.846	5	10	1	2	0
Collier	.966	108	222	6	8	0
Dabbs	.935	20	27	2	2	0
Hewitt	.962	80	170	6	7	1
Mendez	.952	10	18	2	1	0
Rice	.962	31	48	3	2	2
Santana	.956	49	81	5	4	1
Schoenberger	1.000	1	3	0	0	0
Victorino	.000	2	0	0	0	0

WILLIAMSPORT CROSSCUTTERS

SHORT-SEASON

NEW YORK-PENN LEAGUE

Batting	B-T	HT	WT	DOB	AVG	vLH	vRH	G	AB	R	H	2B	3B	HR	RBI	BB	HBP	SH	SF	SO	SB	CS	SLG	OBP
Alonso, Carlos	R-R	5-11	205	2-15-88	.429	.400	.444	5	14	4	6	2	0	0	4	3	1	0	0	2	0	0	.571	.556
Altherr, Aaron	R-R	6-5	190	1-14-91	.260	.250	.263	71	269	41	70	12	2	5	31	13	5	0	4	52	25	4	.375	.302
Amaro, Luis	L-L	5-11	175	1-17-89	.182	.000	.200	18	33	6	6	1	0	0	3	3	0	0	1	11	0	0	.212	.243
Asche, Cody	L-R	6-1	180	6-30-90	.192	.119	.208	68	239	14	46	11	0	2	19	24	3	0	1	50	0	3	.264	.273
Black, Taylor	R-R	6-1	180	2-17-89	.212	.222	.209	58	184	14	39	8	2	1	17	14	5	0	2	29	2	2	.293	.283
Clark, Nolan	R-R	6-0	200	7-8-90	.133	.333	.000	8	15	1	2	0	0	0	3	6	1	0	0	8	1	1	.133	.409
Diaz, Francisco	B-R	5-10	158	3-21-90	.211	.185	.220	36	109	17	23	5	0	0	7	16	1	0	1	19	3	1	.257	.315
Dugan, Kelly	B-R	6-3	195	9-18-90	.284	.200	.313	47	176	25	50	4	4	2	21	14	4	0	4	34	6	0	.386	.343
Franco, Maikel	R-R	6-1	180	8-26-92	.287	.239	.301	54	202	19	58	17	1	2	38	25	1	0	1	30	0	0	.411	.367
Hillman, Drew	R-R	6-0	200	5-4-89	.000	.000	.000	1	3	0	0	0	0	0	0	0	1	0	0	1	0	0	.000	.250
Hudson, Kyrell	R-R	6-1	180	12-6-90	.275	.273	.276	68	269	31	74	11	4	1	18	18	1	0	1	63	28	11	.357	.322
Jimenez, Witer	B-R	6-1	180	4-12-89	.152	.091	.171	13	46	2	7	0	0	0	2	1	0	0	0	10	2	2	.152	.204
Lavin, Peter	L-L	5-11	180	12-27-87	.314	.222	.347	32	137	20	43	9	2	2	9	7	0	0	1	20	5	0	.453	.345
Martinez, Harold	R-R	6-3	210	5-3-90	.256	.273	.251	67	234	38	60	13	1	2	31	37	2	0	4	61	3	1	.346	.357
Mendez, Geancarlo	R-R	6-2	170	11-17-89	.200	.278	.148	14	45	6	9	1	2	0	5	3	0	0	1	10	1	0	.311	.245
Miramontes, Kenny	R-R	5-9	180	7-18-88	.226	.120	.271	30	84	10	19	1	0	0	13	12	3	0	2	15	4	1	.238	.337
Murray, Pat	R-R	6-2	220	12-24-86	.244	.273	.234	22	86	10	21	5	0	1	10	5	1	0	0	18	0	0	.337	.293
Payton, Matt	L-R	5-9	185	2-3-88	.222	.000	.250	4	9	0	2	1	0	0	2	1	0	0	0	3	0	1	.333	.300
Stassi, Brock	L-L	6-2	190	8-7-89	.200	.083	.222	50	150	14	30	2	0	1	14	18	2	0	2	15	3	0	.233	.291
Stumpo, Bob	B-R	6-2	220	7-17-87	.267	.281	.263	44	146	25	39	9	1	1	23	16	4	0	3	25	0	0	.363	.349
Unda, Luis	L-L	6-1	155	1-28-90	.207	.000	.218	19	58	8	12	3	0	0	6	0	0	0	0	10	0	0	.259	.207

Pitching	B-T	HT	WT	DOB	W	L	ERA	G	GS	CG	SV	IP	H	R	ER	HR	BB	SO	AVG	vLH	vRH	K/9	BB/9
Arias, Gabirel	R-R	6-2	185	12-6-89	1	2	2.97	24	0	0	7	36	36	12	12	0	12	31	.261	.304	.232	7.68	2.97
Barnes, Casey	R-R	6-0	170	5-19-88	0	0	9.82	2	0	0	0	4	5	5	4	1	2	1	.294	.300	.286	2.45	4.91
Bastidas, Leonel	R-R	6-3	184	6-26-89	1	3	8.15	4	4	0	0	18	28	20	16	2	5	14	.346	.382	.319	7.13	2.55
Birmingham, Jim	L-L	6-5	180	8-2-88	1	0	2.31	8	0	0	1	12	7	3	3	0	5	14	.163	.118	.192	10.80	3.86
Brough, Austin	L-L	6-4	190	12-9-87	2	3	0.47	20	0	0	1	38	35	11	2	2	5	23	.254	.111	.323	5.45	1.18
Campbell, Matt	R-R	6-2	195	9-10-87	3	0	1.59	14	1	0	1	28	25	6	5	0	9	12	.236	.218	.255	3.81	2.86
Cusick, Paul	R-R	6-3	195	9-26-88	0	0	0.00	2	0	0	0	3	5	2	0	0	1	3	.333	.333	.333	8.10	2.70
Duke, Ryan	R-R	6-0	180	9-27-88	0	0	0.00	6	0	0	1	7	3	0	0	0	0	9	.120	.000	.188	11.05	0.00
Fick, Cody	R-R	6-0	195	10-20-87	3	1	3.89	15	2	0	0	37	29	19	16	3	22	28	.213	.140	.256	6.81	5.35
Garner, Perci	R-R	6-3	225	12-13-88	1	1	1.20	8	4	0	1	30	29	7	4	0	9	30	.252	.269	.238	9.00	2.70
Gomez, Juary	R-R	6-2	200	5-23-90	4	1	2.84	24	0	0	10	38	32	13	12	2	10	31	.227	.141	.299	7.34	2.37
Herbst, Gregory	R-R	6-6	235	7-26-89	0	1	36.00	1	1	0	0	1	5	4	4	0	1	0	.625	.600	.667	0.00	9.00
Kleven, Colin	R-R	6-5	200	4-15-91	4	6	4.84	14	14	0	0	67	68	41	36	5	28	42	.261	.295	.235	5.64	3.76
Martinez, Lino	L-L	6-0	160	9-17-92	6	2	2.79	13	13	0	0	68	64	25	21	3	23	46	.258	.318	.225	6.12	3.06
Morgado, Bryan	L-L	6-3	205	12-8-88	2	0	2.36	12	3	0	1	34	28	12	9	2	13	39	.217	.250	.202	10.22	3.41
Morgan, Adam	L-L	6-1	195	2-27-90	3	3	2.01	11	11	0	0	54	42	18	12	2	14	43	.206	.314	.149	7.21	2.35
Murray, Colton	R-R	6-0	195	4-22-90	1	2	3.00	22	0	0	0	30	28	12	10	1	12	23	.241	.255	.231	6.90	3.60
Neris, Hector	R-R	6-2	175	6-14-89	1	1	1.13	15	0	0	0	24	17	3	3	1	8	29	.198	.263	.146	10.88	3.00
Nesseth, Mike	R-R	6-5	225	4-19-88	3	6	3.21	14	14	0	0	62	56	31	22	2	19	34	.240	.282	.198	4.96	2.77
Pirela, Jesus	R-R	6-0	155	3-13-89	3	0	4.34	17	0	0	0	29	27	17	14	0	17	31	.245	.292	.210	9.62	5.28

Pitching	B-T	HT	WT	DOB	W	L	ERA	G	GS	CG	SV	IP	H	R	ER	HR	BB	SO	AVG	vLH	vRH	K/9	BB/9
Stewart, Ethan	L-L	6-5	210	1-19-91	1	0	2.00	2	2	0	0	9	9	3	2	1	6	6	.281	.333	.250	6.00	6.00
Wright, Austin	L-L	6-4	235	9-26-89	3	1	3.38	8	7	1	0	35	30	13	13	1	13	44	.231	.244	.225	11.42	3.38

Fielding

Catcher	PCT	G	PO	A	E	DP	PB
Clark	1.000	5	20	2	0	0	0
Diaz	.976	35	254	33	7	3	2
Stumpo	.979	39	254	26	6	2	8

First Base	PCT	G	PO	A	E	DP
Dugan	1.000	5	53	3	0	4
Mendez	.967	7	50	8	2	4
Murray	.974	21	172	14	5	18
Stassi	.993	49	379	45	3	32

Second Base	PCT	G	PO	A	E	DP
Alonso	1.000	3	9	9	0	4

	PCT	G	PO	A	E	DP
Asche	.954	64	109	201	15	40
Miramontes	.974	7	15	22	1	4
Payton	1.000	2	2	8	0	0

Third Base	PCT	G	PO	A	E	DP
Franco	.947	34	25	65	5	5
Martinez	.928	41	35	81	9	11
Mendez	.714	1	1	4	2	1

Shortstop	PCT	G	PO	A	E	DP
Black	.922	58	92	156	21	31
Miramontes	.956	23	33	54	4	10
Payton	.875	1	3	4	1	2

Outfield	PCT	G	PO	A	E	DP
Altherr	.964	70	125	7	5	1
Amaro	.875	13	7	0	1	0
Dugan	.973	38	67	5	2	2
Hudson	.961	67	118	4	5	1
Jimenez	.950	10	18	1	1	0
Lavin	.972	31	67	3	2	0
Mendez	.000	2	0	0	0	0
Unda	.955	12	21	0	1	0

GCL PHILLIES
GULF COAST LEAGUE

ROOKIE

Batting	B-T	HT	WT	DOB	AVG	vLH	vRH	G	AB	R	H	2B	3B	HR	RBI	BB	HBP	SH	SF	SO	SB	CS	SLG	OBP
Castillo, Jorge	B-R	5-10	170	10-19-90	.194	.292	.165	35	103	10	20	5	0	1	9	3	2	0	4	26	2	1	.272	.223
Chavarin, Angel	L-R	6-0	176	10-22-90	.091	.182	.061	24	44	2	4	3	0	0	4	0	0	0	0	13	0	0	.159	.167
Duffy, Chris	L-R	6-2	200	12-17-87	.293	.282	.298	38	123	21	36	6	0	1	27	21	2	0	2	32	0	0	.504	.399
Ford, Trey	R-R	6-2	200	7-25-90	.242	.217	.247	39	120	14	29	4	1	3	13	17	3	0	0	27	2	4	.367	.350
Gonzalez, Gustavo	R-R	6-2	0	1-23-91	.275	.300	.262	26	91	12	25	1	0	1	5	7	2	0	2	15	2	0	.319	.333
Greene, Tyler	R-R	6-2	175	12-1-92	.276	.214	.295	17	58	9	16	6	0	0	4	11	0	0	1	23	5	1	.379	.386
Hill, John	L-R	6-3	205	2-11-89	.226	.357	.188	33	62	5	14	2	0	0	12	8	1	0	2	16	2	0	.258	.315
Hillman, Drew	R-R	6-0	200	5-4-89	.253	.179	.286	25	91	11	23	5	2	0	6	5	3	0	1	10	1	1	.352	.310
Holland, Matthew	L-L	6-3	215	8-21-87	.236	.333	.209	35	110	19	26	7	0	4	15	9	3	0	1	26	1	0	.409	.309
Jimenez, Witer	B-R	6-1	180	4-12-89	.235	.267	.229	23	85	12	20	5	2	1	5	7	0	0	2	15	6	3	.376	.287
Langley, Torre	R-R	5-9	175	10-9-87	.333	.500	.286	4	9	0	3	2	0	0	5	1	0	0	0	2	0	0	.556	.400
Lavin, Peter	L-L	5-11	180	12-27-87	.299	.216	.330	32	134	22	40	10	2	2	19	6	0	0	2	20	8	1	.448	.324
Marshall, Michael	R-R	6-3	235	8-25-88	.229	.333	.206	23	83	9	19	7	0	1	12	11	1	0	1	15	0	0	.349	.323
Miranda, Jorge	R-R	6-0	164	5-26-91	.096	.182	.073	20	52	5	5	0	0	0	4	5	2	0	0	17	1	2	.096	.203
Moore, Logan	L-R	6-3	190	8-22-90	.225	.182	.245	30	71	6	16	0	0	1	9	2	0	0	1	17	0	0	.268	.243
Myers, D'Arby	R-R	6-3	175	12-9-88	.222	.500	.143	2	9	0	2	0	0	0	0	0	0	0	0	1	0	0	.222	.222
Numata, Chace	B-R	6-0	175	8-14-92	.154	.000	.167	9	13	1	2	0	0	0	1	1	1	0	0	1	0	0	.154	.267
Podsednik, Scott	L-L	6-0	185	3-18-76	.300	.000	.375	3	10	2	3	2	1	0	1	2	0	0	0	1	1	0	.700	.417
Pointer, Brian	L-L	6-0	190	1-28-92	.278	.143	.313	47	169	30	47	12	4	6	25	17	3	0	1	47	8	0	.503	.353
Quaranto, Kevin	L-R	6-3	215	5-13-88	.240	.000	.286	16	25	3	6	3	1	0	1	5	2	0	0	8	0	0	.440	.406
Rice, Bill	L-R	5-11	185	9-7-88	.306	.250	.321	11	36	6	11	2	1	0	5	0	0	0	1	4	2	1	.417	.297
Rios, Nerio	B-R	6-0	150	10-5-91	.600	.000	.600	3	5	1	3	0	0	0	0	0	0	0	0	1	1	0	.600	.600
Solarte, Bernardo	R-R	6-0	161	1-23-92	.188	.296	.149	38	117	15	19	3	0	2	11	10	9	0	1	30	4	3	.277	.314
Valenzuela, Carlos	R-R	5-11	170	9-18-90	.331	.351	.325	43	160	20	53	9	1	2	18	11	2	0	1	31	2	0	.438	.379
Villalobos, Alejandro	R-R	5-11	170	8-20-91	.285	.333	.270	44	165	17	47	4	4	0	14	10	4	0	0	5	7	5	.358	.341

Pitching	B-T	HT	WT	DOB	W	L	ERA	G	GS	CG	SV	IP	H	R	ER	HR	BB	SO	AVG	vLH	vRH	K/9	BB/9
Barnes, Casey	R-R	6-0	170	5-19-88	2	1	5.74	3	3	0	0	16	18	10	10	3	1	8	.295	.438	.244	4.60	0.57
Best, Carlos	R-R	6-2	170	1-13-91	1	1	7.04	4	0	0	0	8	9	6	1	2	6	.310	.333	.294	7.04	2.35
Birmingham, Jim	L-L	6-5	180	8-2-88	2	1	1.37	14	0	0	8	20	9	5	3	0	9	25	.138	.333	.094	11.44	4.12
Campbell, Matt	R-R	6-2	195	9-10-87	0	0	0.00	1	0	0	0	1	1	0	0	0	0	1	.333	.000	.500	9.00	0.00
Chapman, Chance	R-R	6-4	200	2-27-84	0	1	13.50	2	1	0	0	2	5	3	0	1	1	.500	.250	.667	4.50	4.50
Cota, Fabian	L-L	6-1	170	4-13-92	1	0	3.52	15	0	0	0	23	21	10	9	1	12	25	.250	.467	.203	9.78	4.70
Cusick, Paul	R-R	6-3	195	9-26-88	3	2	4.14	16	1	0	0	37	31	19	17	1	15	36	.220	.194	.229	8.76	3.65
Davis, Rye	R-R	6-5	250	12-11-88	1	1	1.88	15	0	0	4	24	15	5	5	1	8	22	.169	.130	.182	8.25	3.00
Durham, Ian	R-R	6-4	200	1-31-89	1	0	3.62	18	0	0	2	32	36	20	13	2	10	24	.293	.158	.353	6.68	2.78
Fritsch, Craig	R-R	6-4	190	12-29-87	0	1	9.58	13	0	0	1	10	7	11	11	2	18	9	.184	.182	.185	7.84	15.68
Giles, Kenny	R-R	6-2	190	9-20-90	1	1	5.79	3	0	0	0	5	6	4	3	1	3	7	.333	.333	.333	13.50	5.79
Gonzalez, Luis	L-L	6-2	170	1-17-92	3	2	5.74	12	7	0	0	42	51	30	27	0	24	40	.298	.259	.306	8.50	5.10
Inch, Steven	R-R	6-4	190	2-1-91	0	1	5.70	8	5	0	0	24	31	17	15	1	9	20	.316	.350	.308	7.61	3.42
Kinder, Andre	L-L	6-1	195	11-26-88	1	1	2.92	13	1	0	2	25	17	9	8	2	12	31	.193	.333	.177	11.31	4.38
McGuire, Mike	R-R	6-7	240	6-29-86	0	0	4.50	1	1	0	0	2	3	1	1	0	0	2	.375	.333	.400	9.00	0.00
Minarek, Marek	R-R	6-5	176	6-28-93	0	0	6.00	2	0	0	0	3	5	2	2	1	4	.385	.600	.250	12.00	3.00
Morales, Luis	R-R	6-4	212	3-16-93	0	0	13.50	2	0	0	0	3	5	4	4	2	1	4	.417	1.000	.364	13.50	3.38
Musser, Jonathan	R-R	6-5	205	12-19-91	1	6	6.44	14	9	0	0	43	52	35	31	2	26	25	.294	.242	.324	5.19	5.40
Oviedo, Ramon	R-R	6-4	160	7-24-90	4	2	3.86	12	10	0	0	56	51	27	24	3	22	46	.248	.153	.286	7.39	3.54
Rios, Yacksel	R-R	6-3	185	6-27-93	0	1	8.74	10	0	0	0	11	14	12	11	0	14	10	.298	.214	.333	7.94	11.12
Serrano, Jorge	R-R	6-2	180	9-21-93	0	0	9.35	7	0	0	0	9	12	12	9	1	11	3	.364	.364	.364	3.12	11.42
Stewart, Ethan	L-L	6-5	210	1-19-91	4	4	3.62	11	11	0	0	55	57	32	22	5	21	54	.274	.237	.282	8.89	3.46
Warner, Josh	R-R	6-3	185	10-10-92	2	6	6.91	12	10	0	0	55	72	48	42	7	12	48	.314	.258	.335	7.90	1.98

Fielding

Catcher	PCT	G	PO	A	E	DP	PB
Chavarin	.968	23	80	12	3	0	7

	PCT	G	PO	A	E	DP	PB
Hill	.984	31	163	17	3	1	3
Langley	1.000	4	11	6	0	1	0

	PCT	G	PO	A	E	DP	PB
Moore	.986	28	120	16	2	1	4
Numata	1.000	8	28	6	0	1	2

	PCT	G	PO	A	E		DP
Quaranto	1.000	12	42	2	0	0	2

First Base	PCT	G	PO	A	E	DP
Duffy	.987	28	222	14	3	11
Holland	.972	14	100	5	3	1
Marshall	1.000	20	163	11	0	9
Quaranto	1.000	1	5	1	0	1

Second Base	PCT	G	PO	A	E	DP
Valenzuela	1.000	28	41	68	0	9
Villalobos	.952	31	53	65	6	10

Third Base	PCT	G	PO	A	E	DP
Ford	.922	34	25	70	8	4

	PCT	G	PO	A	E	DP
Hillman	.935	17	8	35	3	2
Valenzuela	.962	11	2	23	1	0

Shortstop	PCT	G	PO	A	E	DP
Ford	.667	3	4	6	5	0
Gonzalez	.956	25	33	53	4	6
Greene	.948	17	15	40	3	8
Rios	.800	3	0	4	1	0
Rios	.625	1	1	4	3	1
Valenzuela	1.000	1	2	1	0	0
Villalobos	.958	13	17	29	2	4

Outfield	PCT	G	PO	A	E	DP
Castillo	.953	28	40	1	2	0
Holland	.909	7	10	0	1	0
Jimenez	1.000	22	44	2	0	0
Lavin	1.000	30	68	4	0	0
Miranda	1.000	15	17	1	0	0
Myers	1.000	2	1	0	0	0
Podsednik	1.000	3	8	0	0	0
Pointer	.969	41	87	6	3	1
Rice	.967	11	28	1	1	0
Solarte	1.000	34	42	5	0	0

DSL PHILLIES

ROOKIE

DOMINICAN SUMMER LEAGUE

Batting	B-T	HT	WT	DOB	AVG	vLH	vRH	G	AB	R	H	2B	3B	HR	RBI	BB	HBP	SH	SF	SO	SB	CS	SLG	OBP
Almonte, Marlin	R-R	5-11	180	9-28-93	.167	.167	.167	21	48	3	8	1	0	0	4	5	2	0	0	13	2	2	.188	.273
Berroa, Eladio	B-R	5-8	155	2-2-91	.207	.219	.203	68	222	26	46	5	6	1	32	20	6	0	5	50	11	8	.297	.285
Cardozo, Jairo	B-R	5-11	160	1-27-94	.244	.167	.262	56	156	20	38	3	0	0	13	15	4	0	3	34	8	5	.263	.320
Cepeda, Rommel	R-R	5-11	180	11-13-91	.210	.200	.213	56	162	18	34	7	0	2	14	16	7	0	1	38	6	4	.290	.306
Contreras, Roberto	L-R	6-3	170	7-12-94	.127	.133	.125	29	63	10	8	2	1	1	4	10	2	0	0	32	0	0	.238	.267
De La Cruz, Rafael	R-R	6-2	200	7-29-91	.257	.241	.263	45	109	19	28	9	0	2	18	16	5	0	0	29	3	1	.394	.377
Dicen, Francisco	R-R	6-3	180	9-9-90	.227	.250	.214	11	22	0	5	0	0	0	3	1	0	0	0	5	1	0	.227	.261
Esquea, Edwin	R-R	6-0	200	9-11-91	.216	.150	.235	34	88	12	19	3	0	1	7	9	4	0	2	20	4	2	.284	.311
Francisco, Delvi	R-R	6-1	190	8-24-92	.307	.286	.315	44	153	21	47	7	1	0	15	21	2	0	0	23	12	6	.366	.398
Gonzalez, Diego	R-R	5-11	170	3-16-91	.345	.286	.368	47	174	21	60	6	0	0	14	11	4	0	1	20	23	17	.379	.395
Marine, Felix	R-R	6-0	180	5-25-90	.233	.229	.234	56	146	19	34	11	0	2	15	14	5	0	0	31	7	2	.349	.321
Miranda, Pedro	R-R	6-0	180	7-6-92	.272	.250	.276	35	92	14	25	5	1	0	8	14	0	0	0	22	5	9	.304	.368
Mora, Angelo	B-R	5-11	151	2-25-93	.246	.245	.246	54	171	21	42	7	3	0	18	10	2	0	1	29	7	5	.322	.293
Morales, Yeisson	R-R	6-3	195	4-28-92	.196	.200	.195	37	107	15	21	6	1	0	9	15	4	0	0	30	3	3	.271	.317
Olmo, Yan	R-R	6-3	200	12-15-90	.277	.364	.243	58	191	26	53	6	0	3	17	19	11	0	0	31	19	4	.356	.376
Ramirez, Riswish	B-R	5-11	170	11-1-91	.265	.261	.267	44	113	10	30	0	2	0	16	5	2	0	0	15	4	6	.301	.308
Rios, Fernando	R-R	6-0	175	8-22-92	.217	.273	.167	16	23	5	5	2	0	0	1	2	2	0	0	5	0	0	.304	.333
Torres, Robinson	R-R	5-10	160	2-12-92	.220	.154	.243	61	150	25	33	5	1	1	21	18	9	0	5	29	19	4	.287	.330

Pitching	B-T	HT	WT	DOB	W	L	ERA	G	GS	CG	SV	IP	H	R	ER	HR	BB	SO	AVG	vLH	vRH	K/9	BB/9
Alejo, Francibel	L-L	6-3	170	1-21-93	5	4	3.51	15	13	1	1	74	63	42	29	3	27	52	.223	.150	.228	6.30	3.27
Angulo, Rivar	L-L	6-3	185	7-1-91	0	1	7.94	11	0	0	0	11	11	10	10	0	19	10	.194	.000	.200	7.94	15.09
Bautista, Erinzon	R-R	6-4	180	11-26-89	1	0	1.57	11	2	0	4	29	20	5	5	1	6	33	.202	.357	.176	10.36	1.88
Cairo, Welinton	L-L	6-2	180	7-7-89	0	2	4.50	10	0	0	1	12	8	6	6	0	11	19	.182	.200	.179	14.25	8.25
Casimiro, Ranfi	R-R	6-8	200	7-16-92	2	2	3.21	8	6	0	0	28	16	12	10	3	17	26	.157	.229	.119	8.36	5.46
Dela Cruz, Luis	R-R	6-3	180	8-17-90	0	0	8.59	5	0	0	0	7	8	7	7	1	9	3	.267	.333	.222	3.68	11.05
Dottin, Henry	R-R	6-3	170	10-10-92	1	0	18.00	8	0	0	0	7	10	18	14	2	15	8	.313	.143	.360	10.29	19.29
Emelenciano, Pedro	R-R	6-4	175	7-23-93	0	0	10.66	10	0	0	0	13	13	17	15	0	20	6	.283	.200	.323	4.26	14.21
Joaquin, Ulises	R-R	5-11	165	6-11-92	4	4	3.34	15	10	0	2	65	46	27	24	1	21	44	.194	.221	.183	6.12	2.92
Lorenzo, Jorge	R-R	6-2	175	9-29-90	4	3	3.65	20	1	0	4	37	36	26	15	2	19	25	.254	.268	.248	6.08	4.62
Marte, Juan	R-R	6-4	160	5-8-90	1	2	5.21	6	3	0	0	19	18	13	11	0	7	21	.254	.286	.240	9.95	3.32
Morel, Darbin	R-R	6-3	195	7-23-93	0	0	19.64	5	0	0	0	4	7	14	8	1	9	2	.438	.333	.500	4.91	22.09
Oviedo, Ramon	R-R	6-4	160	7-24-90	1	1	3.00	3	3	0	0	12	11	5	4	0	6	9	.262	.240	.294	6.75	4.50
Reyes, Julio	R-R	6-3	200	4-19-91	4	4	3.29	14	8	0	1	55	49	31	20	1	31	47	.230	.284	.205	7.74	5.10
Santos, Felix	R-R	5-11	170	9-10-90	2	0	2.48	18	0	0	5	29	22	11	8	0	7	22	.210	.208	.210	6.83	2.17
Santos, Gregorio	R-R	6-3	190	3-1-93	3	1	4.60	17	4	0	1	43	51	23	22	1	18	25	.305	.280	.316	5.23	3.77
Sierra, Adrian	L-L	5-11	155	1-10-91	0	8	5.79	14	9	0	2	51	69	43	33	1	22	44	.321	.444	.310	7.71	3.86
Solano, San Lazaro	R-R	5-11	170	12-17-90	1	0	0.00	1	0	0	0	2	1	0	0	0	0	3	.143	.000	.200	13.50	0.00
Sosa, Yari	R-R	6-0	180	9-30-90	9	1	1.73	13	12	2	0	83	55	17	16	2	16	59	.190	.136	.205	6.37	1.73
Vasquez, Gerard	R-R	6-2	190	6-3-94	0	0	10.32	10	0	0	0	11	11	14	13	1	8	11	.262	.214	.286	8.74	14.29

Fielding

Catcher	PCT	G	PO	A	E	DP	PB
Cepeda	.972	54	334	41	11	2	4
De La Cruz	.970	17	57	8	2	2	0
Esquea	.942	13	74	7	5	1	2
Marine	1.000	2	2	0	0	0	0
Rios	1.000	1	1	0	0	0	0

First Base	PCT	G	PO	A	E	DP
Cepeda	1.000	1	5	0	0	0
De La Cruz	.993	24	132	8	1	9
Esquea	.983	15	107	7	2	8
Marine	.980	46	363	24	8	32
Rios	1.000	5	20	1	0	1

Second Base	PCT	G	PO	A	E	DP
Berroa	1.000	3	11	7	0	4

	PCT	G	PO	A	E	DP
Cardozo	.951	27	34	43	4	9
Mora	.879	9	14	15	4	3
Ramirez	.942	31	51	47	6	9
Torres	.949	29	44	50	5	9

Third Base	PCT	G	PO	A	E	DP
Berroa	.919	64	47	145	17	8
De La Cruz	.722	6	3	10	5	0
Ramirez	.857	6	0	6	1	0
Torres	1.000	9	3	20	0	1

Shortstop	PCT	G	PO	A	E	DP
Berroa	1.000	3	1	8	0	0
Cardozo	.930	32	38	82	9	11
Mora	.939	47	71	145	14	24
Ramirez	.000	1	0	0	0	0

	PCT	G	PO	A	E	DP
Torres	1.000	1	2	1	0	0

Outfield	PCT	G	PO	A	E	DP
Almonte	1.000	11	8	0	0	0
Cardozo	1.000	1	1	0	0	0
Contreras	1.000	10	12	0	0	0
Dicen	.778	7	6	1	2	0
Francisco	.957	44	62	4	3	0
Gonzalez	.973	47	69	4	2	2
Marine	1.000	8	10	1	0	1
Miranda	1.000	29	36	3	0	2
Olmo	.991	57	101	4	1	3
Torres	1.000	24	28	3	0	1

VENEZUELAN SUMMER LEAGUE

Batting	B-T	HT	WT	DOB	AVG	vLH	vRH	G	AB	R	H	2B	3B	HR	RBI	BB	HBP	SH	SF	SO	SB	CS	SLG	OBP
Astudillo, Willians	R-R	5-9	182	10-14-91	.361	.349	.364	52	194	31	70	8	3	1	25	15	7	0	1	2	11	5	.448	.424
Briceno, Jesus	L-R	6-0	160	4-12-92	.278	.000	.306	31	54	7	15	4	0	0	0	11	0	0	0	6	0	0	.352	.400
Chavez, Albertin	R-R	5-10	172	1-21-92	.284	.250	.293	59	215	31	61	11	0	2	28	20	3	0	1	19	6	8	.363	.351
Fajardo, Rosmel	R-R	6-2	177	7-19-92	.221	.286	.196	53	154	28	34	5	2	2	11	19	3	0	0	24	8	4	.318	.318
Fernandez, Rafael	R-R	5-10	168	5-13-92	.240	.143	.256	18	50	2	12	0	0	0	1	2	1	0	1	5	0	0	.240	.278
Garcia, Alejandro	R-R	6-3	150	7-22-94	.160	.190	.150	40	81	7	13	0	1	0	4	5	2	0	0	23	1	4	.185	.227
Garcia, Wilson	B-R	5-11	160	1-11-94	.264	.318	.248	60	197	20	52	9	0	1	22	17	3	0	1	20	3	0	.325	.330
Herrera, Francisco	R-R	5-11	185	9-15-93	.283	.333	.269	29	99	17	28	7	0	2	11	14	1	0	0	12	4	2	.414	.377
Machado, Gregorio	B-R	6-1	184	10-28-91	.213	.241	.205	53	141	23	30	8	1	2	18	11	8	0	0	25	5	2	.326	.306
Martinez, Gustavo	R-R	5-11	155	9-22-93	.243	.261	.239	38	111	15	27	1	0	0	2	11	0	0	0	11	9	5	.252	.311
Mayorga, Jose	R-R	5-10	175	8-20-92	.260	.206	.273	58	177	22	46	5	0	0	26	19	4	0	0	11	1	3	.288	.345
Morelos, Jair	L-R	5-10	150	2-2-94	.280	.238	.292	58	186	14	52	4	1	0	22	13	3	0	1	11	7	7	.312	.335
Oberto, Wilmer	L-L	5-11	188	11-2-92	.185	.171	.191	47	124	15	23	5	0	3	13	28	2	0	3	35	6	5	.298	.338
Olivera, Deiber	R-R	5-11	155	8-25-92	.250	.125	.286	14	36	4	9	5	0	0	4	2	0	0	0	4	1	0	.389	.289
Oliveros, Jose	R-R	5-10	195	5-24-92	.395	.375	.400	13	43	7	17	5	1	1	4	7	0	0	0	3	1	2	.628	.480
Perdomo, Alexander	B-R	5-9	155	5-24-93	.174	.133	.194	15	46	5	8	1	0	0	5	5	1	0	1	4	1	1	.196	.264
Rivas, Frank	R-R	5-11	180	7-17-92	.195	.389	.136	35	77	2	15	2	0	0	4	4	2	0	1	17	2	0	.221	.250
Rodriguez, Herlis	L-L	6-0	157	6-10-94	.289	.310	.285	45	159	19	46	5	3	2	19	15	2	0	1	20	3	7	.396	.356
Silva, Francisco	R-R	5-11	155	5-12-91	.167	.167	.167	23	54	5	9	0	0	0	2	4	3	0	1	8	1	2	.167	.258
Villegas, Enderson	R-R	5-10	168	1-31-92	.284	.300	.275	39	109	6	31	5	1	0	11	13	3	0	1	16	2	1	.349	.373

Pitching	B-T	HT	WT	DOB	W	L	ERA	G	GS	CG	SV	IP	H	R	ER	HR	BB	SO	AVG	vLH	vRH	K/9	BB/9
Arteaga, Alejandro	R-R	6-2	176	4-30-94	0	0	6.75	3	1	0	0	4	5	3	3	1	2	1	.313	.200	.364	2.25	4.50
Bohorquez, Liberio	R-R	6-0	170	9-23-92	1	2	5.20	14	0	0	0	28	32	19	16	3	14	25	.294	.290	.295	8.13	4.55
Calanche, Jean	R-R	6-1	150	12-31-92	0	4	4.97	9	2	0	0	25	28	15	14	1	14	15	.304	.290	.311	5.33	4.97
Escaray, Atilio	R-R	6-2	153	12-29-89	3	0	7.20	15	0	0	1	30	35	26	24	1	28	25	.299	.371	.268	7.50	8.40
Gonzalez, Jhonnis	R-R	6-1	180	7-3-92	0	0	13.50	4	0	0	0	5	8	7	0	4	2	.364	.429	.333	3.86	7.71
Gonzalez, Jorge	L-L	5-11	175	3-30-90	3	1	1.99	8	4	0	0	32	28	10	7	1	6	14	.235	.176	.245	3.98	1.71
Gonzalez, Severino	R-R	6-1	153	9-28-92	1	1	2.11	17	0	0	1	43	36	13	10	0	3	29	.228	.267	.212	6.12	0.63
Guzman, Jorge	R-R	6-1	201	8-14-91	3	3	2.22	13	6	0	1	45	39	21	11	2	13	42	.228	.208	.236	8.46	2.62
Izurriaga, Ely	L-L	5-11	188	6-29-90	4	3	1.64	23	0	0	12	44	36	9	8	0	17	49	.231	.292	.220	10.02	3.48
Leon, Luis	R-R	6-2	166	11-24-89	0	2	3.91	13	0	0	1	23	26	11	10	0	11	20	.280	.286	.277	7.83	4.30
Martinez, Manaure	R-R	6-1	155	12-31-91	3	1	2.25	14	3	0	2	28	28	8	7	3	10	26	.267	.297	.250	8.36	3.21
Mendez, Ronald	R-R	6-5	211	2-27-93	2	5	4.97	13	13	0	0	58	64	41	32	3	33	27	.286	.292	.283	4.19	5.12
Mora, Audrys	L-L	5-11	170	6-14-93	1	3	3.43	15	1	0	0	39	34	17	15	0	15	28	.243	.273	.237	6.41	3.43
Morales, Luis	R-R	6-4	212	3-16-93	0	3	4.11	5	5	0	0	15	16	11	7	0	6	8	.262	.148	.353	4.70	3.52
Parada, Douglas	L-L	6-1	233	2-27-93	0	2	5.40	5	0	0	0	7	9	10	4	0	4	4	.321	.667	.227	5.40	5.40
Rivas, Manuel	R-R	6-1	169	10-15-90	4	2	3.22	14	11	0	0	73	51	30	26	2	34	57	.204	.217	.198	7.06	4.21
Rojas, Keive	R-R	6-0	170	2-26-93	2	4	3.75	13	13	0	0	62	75	34	26	4	26	44	.302	.298	.305	6.35	3.75
Silva, Yovan	R-R	6-0	209	2-6-90	3	4	3.11	12	11	0	0	64	45	25	22	5	34	42	.205	.226	.198	5.94	4.81

Fielding

Catcher	PCT	G	PO	A	E	DP	PB
Astudillo	.950	3	17	2	1	0	1
Briceno	.967	5	25	4	1	0	2
Fernandez	.969	5	24	7	1	1	1
Garcia	1.000	30	168	37	0	6	3
Mayorga	.993	19	110	34	1	1	2
Oliveros	.974	4	32	5	1	0	1
Rivas	.980	18	85	14	2	2	5
Villegas	1.000	1	3	1	0	0	1

First Base	PCT	G	PO	A	E	DP
Briceno	1.000	2	1	1	0	0
Fajardo	.000	1	0	0	0	0
Fernandez	.985	8	60	5	1	4
Garcia	.995	22	171	15	1	15
Herrera	1.000	1	13	0	0	0
Mayorga	1.000	6	45	5	0	2
Oberto	.986	12	69	3	1	3
Oliveros	1.000	7	54	1	0	3

Rivas	.982	10	49	6	1	5
Villegas	.985	21	180	14	3	14

Second Base	PCT	G	PO	A	E	DP
Astudillo	1.000	4	8	11	0	1
Chavez	.984	43	89	95	3	15
Mayorga	.923	7	14	10	2	2
Olivera	.971	10	16	17	1	3
Perdomo	1.000	13	27	28	0	6

Third Base	PCT	G	PO	A	E	DP
Astudillo	.934	41	45	96	10	8
Chavez	.929	10	8	18	2	2
Herrera	.885	18	11	35	6	3
Mayorga	.833	2	1	4	1	0
Olivera	.500	3	1	2	1	0
Silva	.571	3	0	4	3	0

Shortstop	PCT	G	PO	A	E	DP
Astudillo	.909	5	7	13	2	3

Chavez	.000	1	0	0	0	0
Herrera	1.000	1	1	1	0	0
Morelos	.932	57	88	160	18	26
Perdomo	.000	2	0	0	0	0
Silva	.855	21	28	37	11	6

Outfield	PCT	G	PO	A	E	DP
Astudillo	1.000	1	0	0	0	0
Briceno	1.000	7	1	2	0	0
Chavez	.000	1	0	0	0	0
Fajardo	.923	32	46	2	4	1
Garcia	.939	37	42	4	3	1
Machado	.933	52	81	3	6	2
Martinez	1.000	30	32	3	0	1
Mayorga	.905	18	17	2	2	0
Oberto	.985	36	63	3	1	1
Rodriguez	.991	44	103	8	1	1

Pittsburgh Pirates

SEASON IN A SENTENCE: The Pirates seemed poised to snap the worst losing streak in American professional sports history after climbing to first place in mid-July, but the team's pitching couldn't keep carrying an anemic offense and they collapsed in the second half, finishing with a losing record for the 19th straight season.

HIGH POINT: The Pirates were the talk of baseball when they surged to first place in the National League Central on July 19 with a 51-44 record following James McDonald's 1-0 victory over the Reds. Pitching and defense (and a soft schedule) were key to the Pirates' first-half surge, and even after the midsummer swoon, their unheralded rotation finished with a respectable 4.04 ERA. Journeyman reliever Joel Hanrahan emerged as a legitimate closer, recording 40 saves in 44 attempts. Andrew McCutchen's production dipped with little help around him, but he shone defensively in center field.

LOW POINT: The Pirates were six games above .500 and had won two straight when they dropped a 19-inning affair with the Braves after umpire Jerry Meals' blown call at home. Pittsburgh lost 12 of its next 14 games and never recovered.

NOTABLE ROOKIES: The Pirates got most of their top rookies to the big leagues in 2010. This season's top contributors were catcher Michael McKenry, who replaced injured veterans Ryan Doumit and Chris Snyder; scrappy outfielder Alex Presley, who injected some energy into the lineup; and infielders Josh Harrison and Chase d'Arnaud. Lefty relievers Tony Watson and 2007 first-round pick Danny Moskos also contributed.

KEY TRANSACTIONS: When Lyle Overbay didn't hit at first base, the Pirates traded for veteran Derek Lee, who slugged seven homers but was bothered by injuries. They also added outfielder Ryan Ludwick at the July 31 deadline from the Padres in an effort to find offensive punch.

DOWN ON THE FARM: Outfielder Robbie Grossman led the minors in walks and hit .294/.418/.451 at high Class A Bradenton in his best season as a pro. Outfielder Starling Marte won the Double-A Eastern League batting title, while righthander Kyle McPherson blossomed, reaching the EL and leading the organization in strikeouts. Righty Jameson Taillon, the 2010 No. 2 overall draft pick, threw well while limited to strict pitch counts, but 2009 first-rounder Tony Sanchez had a poor year as Marte's teammate in Altoona.

OPENING DAY PAYROLL: $45,047,000 (28th)

PLAYERS OF THE YEAR

MAJOR LEAGUE	MINOR LEAGUE
Andrew McCutchen	**Starling Marte**
of	of
.259/.364/.456	(Double-A)
23 HR, 23 SB	.332/.370/.500
5th in NL in BB/SB	EL batting champion

ORGANIZATION LEADERS

BATTING		*Minimum 250 PA
MAJORS		
* AVG	Neil Walker	.273
* OPS	Andrew McCutchen	.820
HR	Andrew McCutchen	23
RBI	Andrew McCutchen	89
MINORS		
* AVG	Ramon Cabrera, Bradenton	.343
* OBP	Robbie Grossman, Bradenton	.418
* SLG	Starling Marte, Altoona	.5
R	Robbie Grossman, Bradenton	127
H	Starling Marte, Altoona	178
TB	Starling Marte, Altoona	268
2B	Starling Marte, Altoona	38
3B	Andy Vasquez, West Virginia	13
HR	Jordy Mercer, Altoona/Indianapolis	19
RBI	Elevys Gonzalez, Bradenton	83
BB	Robbie Grossman, Bradenton	104
SO	Quincy Latimore, Altoona	140
SB	Drew Maggi, West Virginia	32

PITCHING		#Minimum 75 IP
MAJORS		
W	Kevin Correia	12
# ERA	Jeff Karstens	3.38
SO	James McDonald	142
SV	Joel Hanrahan	40
MINORS		
W	Phil Irwin, Bradenton/Altoona	13
L	Sean Gallagher, Indianapolis	12
# ERA	Brett Lorin, Bradenton	2.84
G	Justin Thomas, Indianapolis	63
GS	Kyle McPherson, Bradenton/Altoona	28
SV	Noah Krol, Altoona	24
IP	Kyle McPherson, Bradenton/Altoona	161
BB	Justin Wilson, Indianapolis	67
SO	Kyle McPherson, Bradenton/Altoona	142
# AVG	Kyle McPherson, Bradenton/Altoona	.226

General Manager: Neal Huntington. **Farm Director:** Kyle Stark. **Scouting Director:** Greg Smith.

Class	Team	League	W	L	PCT	Finish	Manager(s)
Majors	Pittsburgh Pirates	National	72	90	.444	t-12th (16)	Clint Hurdle
Triple-A	Indianapolis Indians	International	76	68	.528	6th (14)	Dean Treanor/Jeff Branson
Double-A	Altoona Curve	Eastern	64	77	.454	11th (12)	P.J. Forbes
High A	Bradenton Marauders	Florida State	74	63	.540	4th (12)	Carlos Garcia
Low A	West Virginia Power	South Atlantic	69	69	.500	8th (14)	Gary Robinson
Short-season	State College Spikes	New York-Penn	31	44	.413	12th (14)	Kimera Bartee
Rookie	GCL Pirates	Gulf Coast	34	26	.567	4th (15)	Tom Prince
Overall 2011 Minor League Record			348	347	.501	16th (30)	

ORGANIZATION STATISTICS

PITTSBURGH PIRATES

NATIONAL LEAGUE

Batting	B-T	HT	WT	DOB	AVG	vLH	vRH	G	AB	R	H	2B	3B	HR	RBI	BB	HBP	SH	SF	SO	SB	CS	SLG	OBP
Alvarez, Pedro	L-R	6-3	235	2-6-87	.191	.158	.198	74	235	18	45	9	1	4	19	24	2	0	0	80	1	0	.289	.272
Bowker, John	L-L	6-1	205	7-8-83	.235	.200	.235	19	17	0	4	1	0	0	2	2	0	0	0	4	0	1	.294	.316
2-team total (12 Philadelphia)					.133	—	—	31	30	0	4	1	0	0	2	2	0	0	0	11	0	1	.167	.188
Brown, Dusty	R-R	6-0	180	6-19-82	.107	.000	.130	11	28	2	3	0	0	0	0	1	0	0	0	10	1	0	.107	.138
Cedeno, Ronny	R-R	6-0	190	2-2-83	.249	.220	.258	120	413	43	103	25	3	2	32	30	0	0	5	93	2	5	.339	.297
Ciriaco, Pedro	R-R	6-0	170	9-27-85	.303	.222	.333	23	33	4	10	2	1	0	6	1	0	0	0	6	2	1	.424	.324
d'Arnaud, Chase	R-R	6-1	200	1-21-87	.217	.255	.198	48	143	17	31	6	2	0	6	4	1	0	1	36	12	2	.287	.242
Diaz, Matt	R-R	6-0	215	3-3-78	.259	.295	.225	100	216	14	56	12	1	0	19	11	3	0	1	44	4	2	.324	.303
2-team total (16 Atlanta)					.263	—	—	116	251	16	66	13	1	0	20	12	3	0	2	52	5	2	.323	.302
Doumit, Ryan	B-R	6-1	215	4-3-81	.303	.315	.299	77	218	17	66	12	1	8	30	16	1	0	0	35	0	1	.477	.353
Fryer, Eric	R-R	6-2	215	8-26-85	.269	.250	.278	10	26	5	7	0	0	0	3	0	0	0	7	1	1	.269	.345
Harrison, Josh	R-R	5-8	185	7-8-87	.272	.226	.293	65	195	21	53	13	2	1	16	3	0	0	1	24	4	1	.374	.281
Jaramillo, Jason	B-R	6-0	215	10-9-82	.326	.364	.313	23	43	1	14	3	0	0	6	2	0	0	0	12	1	0	.395	.356
Jones, Garrett	L-L	6-4	240	6-21-81	.243	.147	.262	148	423	51	103	30	1	16	58	48	2	0	4	104	6	3	.433	.321
Lee, Derrek	R-R	6-5	240	9-6-75	.337	.333	.338	28	101	16	34	2	1	7	18	8	3	0	1	27	0	0	.584	.398
Ludwick, Ryan	R-L	6-3	215	7-13-78	.232	.267	.220	38	112	14	26	5	0	2	11	19	0	0	1	37	0	0	.330	.341
2-team total (101 San Diego)					.237	—	—	139	490	56	116	23	0	13	75	51	4	0	6	124	1	1	.363	.310
McCutchen, Andrew	R-R	5-10	190	10-10-86	.259	.277	.253	158	572	87	148	34	5	23	89	89	9	6	6	126	23	10	.456	.364
McKenry, Mike	R-R	5-10	200	3-4-85	.222	.167	.239	58	180	17	40	12	0	2	11	14	0	0	2	49	0	1	.322	.276
Overbay, Lyle	L-L	6-2	220	1-28-77	.227	.252	.217	103	352	40	80	17	1	8	37	36	1	0	1	77	1	1	.349	.300
2-team total (18 Arizona)					.234	—	—	121	394	43	92	21	1	9	47	42	2	0	1	88	2	1	.360	.310
Pagnozzi, Matt	R-R	6-2	205	11-10-82	.250	.400	.000	5	8	0	2	0	0	0	1	0	0	0	0	2	0	0	.250	.250
2-team total (7 Colorado)					.276	—	—	12	29	2	8	0	0	0	3	1	1	0	0	10	0	0	.276	.323
Paul, Xavier	L-R	5-9	205	2-25-85	.254	.074	.278	121	232	30	59	6	5	2	20	13	0	0	1	57	16	6	.349	.293
2-team total (7 Los Angeles)					.255	—	—	128	243	30	62	6	5	2	20	13	0	0	1	62	16	6	.346	.292
Pearce, Steve	R-R	5-11	210	4-13-83	.202	.213	.191	50	94	8	19	2	0	1	10	7	1	0	2	21	0	0	.255	.260
Presley, Alex	L-L	5-9	190	7-25-85	.298	.231	.327	52	215	27	64	12	6	4	20	13	1	0	1	40	9	3	.465	.339
Rodriguez, Josh	R-R	6-0	185	12-18-84	.083	.000	.083	7	12	1	1	0	0	0	1	1	1	0	0	8	0	0	.083	.214
Snyder, Chris	R-R	6-4	240	2-12-81	.271	.310	.254	34	96	13	26	3	0	3	17	17	1	0	3	23	0	1	.396	.376
Tabata, Jose	R-R	5-11	220	8-12-88	.266	.297	.258	91	334	53	89	18	1	4	21	40	4	0	3	61	16	7	.362	.349
Toregas, Wyatt	R-R	5-11	210	12-2-82	.000	.000	.000	3	4	0	0	0	0	0	0	0	0	0	0	1	0	0	.000	.000
Walker, Neil	B-R	6-3	215	9-10-85	.273	.269	.275	159	596	76	163	36	4	12	83	54	4	0	8	112	9	6	.408	.334
Wood, Brandon	R-R	6-3	210	3-2-85	.220	.241	.209	99	236	25	52	9	0	7	31	19	0	0	1	65	0	0	.347	.277

Pitching	B-T	HT	WT	DOB	W	L	ERA	G	GS	CG	SV	IP	H	R	ER	HR	BB	SO	AVG	vLH	vRH	K/9	BB/9
Ascanio, Jose	R-R	5-11	195		0	0	7.11	8	0	0	0	6	10	5	5	2	2	5	.345	.294	.417	7.11	2.84
Beimel, Joe	L-L	6-3	215	4-19-77	1	1	5.33	35	0	0	0	25	34	17	15	6	9	17	.321	.302	.333	6.04	3.20
Burres, Brian	L-L	6-2	185	4-8-81	1	0	3.86	5	2	0	0	14	12	6	6	4	4	10	.226	.167	.234	6.43	2.57
Correia, Kevin	R-R	6-3	200	8-24-80	12	11	4.79	27	26	1	0	154	175	90	82	24	39	77	.287	.277	.294	4.50	2.28
Crotta, Mike	R-R	6-6	235	9-25-84	0	1	9.28	15	0	0	0	11	20	11	11	2	5	7	.392	.353	.412	5.91	4.22
Grilli, Jason	R-R	6-5	225	11-11-76	2	1	2.48	28	0	0	1	33	24	10	9	2	15	37	.200	.238	.179	10.19	4.13
Hanrahan, Joel	R-R	6-4	245	10-6-81	1	4	1.83	70	0	0	40	69	56	17	14	1	16	61	.220	.195	.241	8.00	2.10
Hughes, Jared	R-R	6-7	235	7-4-85	0	1	4.09	12	0	0	0	11	9	5	5	1	4	10	.220	.214	.222	8.18	3.27
Karstens, Jeff	R-R	6-3	185	9-24-82	9	9	3.38	30	26	1	0	162	163	69	61	22	33	96	.263	.288	.242	5.32	1.83
Leroux, Chris	L-R	6-6	225	4-14-84	1	1	2.88	23	0	0	0	25	26	9	8	0	7	24	.257	.368	.190	8.64	2.52
Lincoln, Brad	L-R	6-0	210	5-25-85	2	3	4.72	12	8	0	0	48	54	27	25	6	16	29	.286	.349	.236	5.48	3.02
Locke, Jeff	L-L	6-1	215	11-20-87	0	3	6.48	4	4	0	0	17	21	12	12	3	10	5	.323	.300	.327	2.70	5.40
Maholm, Paul	L-L	6-2	220	6-25-82	6	14	3.66	26	26	1	0	162	160	72	66	11	50	97	.262	.265	.261	5.38	2.77
McCutchen, Daniel	R-R	6-2	210	3-26-83	5	3	3.72	73	0	0	0	85	87	38	35	7	33	47	.272	.308	.250	5.00	3.51
McDonald, James	L-R	6-4	200	10-19-84	9	9	4.21	31	31	0	0	171	176	86	80	24	78	142	.268	.302	.246	7.47	4.11
Meek, Evan	R-R	6-0	220	5-12-83	1	1	3.48	24	0	0	0	21	27	11	8	1	12	17	.310	.324	.300	7.40	5.23
Morton, Charlie	R-R	6-5	230	11-12-83	10	10	3.83	29	29	2	0	172	186	82	73	6	77	110	.281	.364	.220	5.77	4.04
Moskos, Daniel	R-L	6-1	210	4-28-86	1	1	2.96	31	0	0	0	24	29	11	8	0	9	11	.302	.364	.250	4.07	3.33
Ohlendorf, Ross	R-R	6-4	240	8-8-82	1	3	8.15	9	9	0	0	39	60	38	35	9	15	27	.364	.352	.369	6.28	3.49

Pitching	B-T	HT	WT	DOB	W	L	ERA	G	GS	CG	SV	IP	H	R	ER	HR	BB	SO	AVG	vLH	vRH	K/9	BB/9
Olson, Garrett	R-L	6-1	210	10-18-83	1	1	2.08	4	0	0	0	4	2	1	1	0	3	4	.125	.286	.000	8.31	6.23
Resop, Chris	R-R	6-3	225	11-4-82	5	4	4.39	76	0	0	1	70	73	34	34	8	30	79	.269	.255	.277	10.21	3.88
Thompson, Aaron	L-L	6-2	190	2-28-87	0	0	7.04	4	1	0	0	8	13	6	6	2	6	1	.382	.500	.333	1.17	7.04
Veras, Jose	R-R	6-6	235	10-20-80	2	4	3.80	79	0	0	1	71	54	32	30	6	34	79	.206	.184	.220	10.01	4.31
Watson, Tony	L-L	6-4	220	5-30-85	2	2	3.95	43	0	0	0	41	34	18	18	6	20	37	.228	.279	.193	8.12	4.39
Wood, Tim	R-R	6-0	180	11-16-82	0	3	5.63	13	0	0	0	8	8	5	5	1	8	2	.286	.286	.286	2.25	9.00

Fielding

Catcher	PCT	G	PO	A	E	DP	PB
Brown	1.000	10	49	3	0	1	3
Doumit	.983	60	321	26	6	1	4
Fryer	.979	8	42	5	1	0	0
Jaramillo	1.000	14	65	2	0	0	0
McKenry	.987	58	359	24	5	2	1
Pagnozzi	1.000	2	12	1	0	0	0
Snyder	1.000	33	201	17	0	1	5
Toregas	1.000	2	5	1	0	0	0

First Base	PCT	G	PO	A	E	DP
Bowker	1.000	1	3	0	0	0
Jones	.989	34	257	17	3	27
Lee	.996	28	226	22	1	16
Overbay	.991	98	836	60	8	90
Pearce	.989	16	81	9	1	9
Wood	1.000	9	42	0	0	2

Second Base	PCT	G	PO	A	E	DP
Cedeno	1.000	1	0	3	0	0
d'Arnaud	1.000	1	1	1	0	0
Harrison	.923	6	8	16	2	5
Rodriguez	1.000	1	1	3	0	0
Walker	.992	159	333	442	6	108
Wood	1.000	3	2	1	0	0

Third Base	PCT	G	PO	A	E	DP
Alvarez	.935	66	55	145	14	15
Ciriaco	1.000	2	1	2	0	1
d'Arnaud	.929	12	11	28	3	4
Harrison	.956	50	31	100	6	7
McKenry	.000	1	0	0	0	0
Pearce	.895	10	6	11	2	1
Wood	.973	61	27	83	3	9

Shortstop	PCT	G	PO	A	E	DP
Cedeno	.978	125	191	397	13	72
Ciriaco	.966	7	9	19	1	2
d'Arnaud	.936	29	27	61	6	14
Rodriguez	1.000	4	5	6	0	2
Wood	.974	19	31	43	2	12

Outfield	PCT	G	PO	A	E	DP
Bowker	.000	1	0	0	0	0
Ciriaco	1.000	2	1	0	0	0
Diaz	.970	57	62	3	2	0
Jones	.994	90	155	2	1	1
Ludwick	.984	35	59	1	1	1
McCutchen	.984	155	414	9	7	5
Paul	.990	96	97	4	1	0
Pearce	.800	5	4	0	1	0
Presley	.988	51	77	2	1	1
Tabata	.988	88	157	4	2	2

INDIANAPOLIS INDIANS   TRIPLE-A
INTERNATIONAL LEAGUE

Batting	B-T	HT	WT	DOB	AVG	vLH	vRH	G	AB	R	H	2B	3B	HR	RBI	BB	HBP	SH	SF	SO	SB	CS	SLG	OBP
Alvarez, Pedro	L-R	6-3	235	2-6-87	.256	.205	.279	35	125	16	32	5	1	5	19	22	0	0	1	42	0	1	.432	.365
Bocock, Brian	R-R	5-11	185	3-9-85	.241	.143	.273	14	29	3	7	1	0	0	1	2	0	0	1	36	0	0	.276	.281
2-team total (81 Lehigh Valley)					.226	—	—	95	301	25	68	7	1	4	28	28	0	0	3	78	3	4	.296	.289
Bowker, John	L-L	6-1	205	7-8-83	.306	.234	.337	106	421	56	129	27	1	15	76	27	1	0	2	73	2	3	.482	.348
Brown, Dusty	R-R	6-0	180	6-19-82	.285	.244	.299	54	172	18	49	17	0	7	28	22	2	0	3	35	0	2	.506	.367
Cedeno, Ronny	R-R	6-0	190	2-2-83	.267	.000	.308	4	15	2	4	1	0	1	1	0	0	0	5	0	0	.467	.313
Ciriaco, Pedro	R-R	6-0	170	9-27-85	.231	.209	.242	71	277	31	64	7	3	2	24	5	0	0	2	49	13	7	.300	.243
Clement, Jeff	L-R	6-1	225	8-21-83	.271	.500	.224	22	59	5	16	5	0	1	5	7	1	0	0	15	0	0	.407	.358
d'Arnaud, Chase	R-R	6-1	200	1-21-87	.264	.344	.226	74	288	43	76	12	6	4	37	23	5	0	1	53	20	4	.389	.328
Doumit, Ryan	R-R	6-1	215	4-3-81	.231	.167	.250	8	26	4	6	1	0	3	4	1	0	0	4	0	0	.346	.355
Durham, Miles	R-R	6-4	205	3-21-83	.233	.182	.261	74	219	24	51	10	4	2	24	11	1	0	4	66	5	3	.342	.268
Ford, Shelby	R-R	6-3	185	12-15-84	.304	.000	.318	8	23	5	7	2	0	2	4	2	0	0	5	0	1	.652	.360
Friday, Brian	R-R	5-11	190	12-16-85	.238	.318	.204	67	223	31	53	14	1	3	22	30	3	0	5	53	6	3	.350	.330
Fryer, Eric	R-R	6-2	215	8-26-85	.203	.265	.179	38	118	16	24	5	1	2	11	21	2	0	0	30	3	0	.314	.333
Hague, Matt	R-R	6-3	225	8-20-85	.309	.308	.310	141	534	70	165	37	3	12	75	47	9	0	4	68	4	3	.457	.372
Harrison, Josh	R-R	5-8	185	7-8-87	.310	.343	.295	62	226	35	70	15	2	5	23	15	6	0	2	28	13	5	.460	.365
Hernandez, Gorkys	R-R	6-0	185	9-7-87	.283	.287	.281	126	424	48	120	25	9	1	40	35	8	0	1	91	21	9	.392	.348
Jaramillo, Jason	B-R	6-0	215	10-9-82	.276	.340	.241	46	134	13	37	7	0	2	23	17	3	0	1	22	1	1	.373	.368
Lambo, Andrew	L-L	6-3	210	8-11-88	.184	.207	.173	60	185	19	34	11	0	3	17	17	2	0	2	48	1	0	.292	.257
Ludwick, Ryan	R-L	6-3	215	7-13-78	.385	1.000	.308	4	13	3	5	1	0	1	5	3	0	0	0	2	0	0	.692	.500
Marte, Andy	R-R	6-1	205	10-21-83	.202	.148	.226	97	287	32	58	15	0	7	37	27	4	0	2	60	2	0	.328	.278
Mercer, Jordy	R-R	6-3	191	8-27-86	.239	.306	.213	60	226	39	54	13	1	6	21	13	8	0	0	43	3	3	.385	.304
Norman, Anthony	R-R	6-0	185	10-20-84	.235	.000	.250	11	34	4	8	3	0	0	3	1	0	0	1	12	1	0	.324	.250
Pearce, Steve	R-R	5-11	210	4-13-83	.267	.000	.320	7	30	5	8	2	0	3	6	0	0	0	0	9	0	0	.633	.267
Perez, Miguel	R-R	6-3	235	9-25-83	.211	.286	.167	8	19	0	4	0	1	0	1	2	0	0	0	7	0	0	.316	.286
Picart, Greg	B-R	5-11	175	9-25-84	.000	.000	.000	2	5	0	0	0	0	0	0	0	0	0	0	0	0	0	.000	.000
Presley, Alex	L-L	5-9	190	7-25-85	.333	.343	.329	87	342	58	114	18	5	8	41	28	4	0	2	54	22	8	.485	.388
Rodriguez, Josh	R-R	6-0	185	12-18-84	.385	.429	.333	6	13	3	5	2	0	0	6	5	0	0	1	2	0	0	.538	.526
2-team total (18 Columbus)					.229	—	—	24	70	9	16	3	0	2	11	11	0	0	1	24	1	0	.357	.329
Tabata, Jose	R-R	5-11	220	8-12-88	.333	.200	.391	9	33	6	11	6	0	0	2	5	0	0	0	4	0	2	.515	.421
Toregas, Wyatt	R-R	5-11	210	12-2-82	.133	.150	.125	22	60	6	8	3	0	0	8	4	1	0	0	15	0	0	.183	.200
Watts, Kris	L-R	6-1	209	7-15-84	.250	.143	.276	12	36	5	9	3	1	0	2	0	3	0	0	5	0	0	.389	.308
Wimberly, Corey	B-R	5-8	170	10-26-83	.238	.182	.265	56	172	17	41	5	3	0	11	8	4	0	0	19	15	6	.302	.288

Pitching	B-T	HT	WT	DOB	W	L	ERA	G	GS	CG	SV	IP	H	R	ER	HR	BB	SO	AVG	vLH	vRH	K/9	BB/9
Ascanio, Jose	R-R	5-11	195	5-2-85	2	3	4.91	30	5	0	1	44	50	25	24	2	15	50	.282	.313	.255	10.23	3.07
Beimel, Joe	L-L	6-3	215	4-19-77	0	0	0.00	2	0	0	0	2	0	0	0	0	0	3	.000	.000	.000	13.50	0.00
Boyer, Blaine	R-R	6-3	245	7-11-81	0	0	13.50	11	0	0	0	8	14	14	12	3	9	8	.359	.333	.375	9.00	10.13
Burres, Brian	L-L	6-2	185	4-8-81	5	9	4.66	25	23	0	0	129	140	71	67	18	45	95	.279	.267	.284	6.61	3.13
Claggett, Anthony	B-R	6-3	195	7-15-84	0	0	1.42	4	0	0	0	6	3	1	1	0	4	5	.158	.167	.154	7.11	5.68
Crotta, Mike	R-R	6-6	235	9-25-84	0	0	5.91	11	0	0	0	11	11	7	7	2	2	5	.256	.286	.241	4.22	1.69
Dubee, Michael	R-R	6-3	185	1-12-86	0	1	9.53	4	0	0	0	6	8	7	6	2	5	3	.348	.364	.333	4.76	7.94
Figueroa, Nelson	R-R	6-1	185	5-18-74	1	1	4.00	3	3	1	0	18	20	8	8	0	4	14	.282	.333	.192	7.00	2.00
Gallagher, Sean	R-R	6-2	220	12-30-85	5	12	5.11	29	23	0	0	132	131	81	75	15	65	98	.263	.319	.212	6.68	4.43

PITTSBURGH PIRATES

Pitching	B-T	HT	WT	DOB	W	L	ERA	G	GS	CG	SV	IP	H	R	ER	HR	BB	SO	AVG	vLH	vRH	K/9	BB/9
Heilman, Aaron	R-R	6-5	230	11-12-78	2	0	0.00	7	0	0	1	9	3	0	0	0	3	6	.107	.100	.111	6.23	3.12
2-team total (9 Lehigh Valley)					2	0	4.42	16	0	0	1	18	17	9	9	1	9	14	—	—	—	6.87	4.42
Hughes, Jared	R-R	6-7	235	7-4-85	3	1	2.11	35	0	0	0	43	35	10	10	1	18	45	.232	.206	.250	9.49	3.80
Jackson, Steven	R-R	6-5	230	3-15-82	4	2	3.96	24	0	0	1	36	35	19	16	4	15	15	.257	.306	.230	3.72	3.72
2-team total (10 Louisville)					4	2	4.30	34	0	0	2	46	45	25	22	4	17	22	—	—	—	4.30	3.33
Leroux, Chris	L-R	6-6	225	4-14-84	6	3	2.80	32	0	0	1	61	48	20	19	1	21	57	.216	.261	.185	8.41	3.10
Lincoln, Brad	L-R	6-0	210	5-25-85	7	8	4.19	19	19	0	0	112	115	55	52	6	21	94	.270	.202	.326	7.58	1.69
Locke, Jeff	L-L	6-1	215	11-20-87	1	2	2.22	5	5	0	0	28	25	8	7	1	9	25	.240	.275	.219	7.94	2.86
Meek, Evan	R-R	6-0	220	5-12-83	0	0	2.25	8	0	0	1	8	6	2	2	1	1	8	.214	.353	.000	9.00	1.13
Meyer, Dan	R-L	6-2	225	7-3-81	0	0	7.45	14	0	0	0	19	17	16	16	3	18	12	.236	.304	.204	5.59	8.38
Moskos, Daniel	R-L	6-1	210	4-28-86	1	1	3.43	30	0	0	3	42	40	17	16	2	11	29	.258	.220	.281	6.21	2.36
Ohlendorf, Ross	R-R	6-4	240	8-8-82	1	1	3.33	4	4	0	0	24	22	10	9	2	8	12	.247	.239	.256	4.44	2.96
Olson, Garrett	R-L	6-1	210	10-18-83	4	3	3.05	24	15	0	0	86	63	35	29	7	47	61	.208	.188	.216	6.41	4.94
Owens, Rudy	L-L	6-3	225	12-18-87	9	7	5.05	21	21	0	0	112	129	65	63	10	32	71	.289	.294	.287	5.69	2.56
Thomas, Justin	L-L	6-3	220	1-18-84	8	2	3.89	63	0	0	3	69	66	32	30	4	24	59	.251	.188	.290	7.66	3.12
Thompson, Aaron	L-L	6-2	190	2-28-87	1	0	2.84	5	4	0	0	19	23	6	6	0	9	10	.295	.226	.340	4.74	4.26
Valdez, Cesar	R-R	6-2	200	3-17-85	1	1	3.86	34	0	0	5	42	36	20	18	2	17	36	.228	.239	.220	7.71	3.64
Veal, Donald	L-L	6-4	240	9-18-84	0	0	5.68	7	0	0	0	6	5	4	4	0	7	7	.217	.300	.154	9.95	9.95
Watson, Tony	L-L	6-4	220	5-30-85	3	3	2.36	26	1	0	0	34	24	10	9	2	11	35	.194	.211	.186	9.17	2.88
Wilson, Justin	L-L	6-2	233	8-18-87	10	8	4.13	30	21	0	3	124	121	68	57	12	67	94	.254	.225	.264	6.80	4.85
Wood, Tim	R-R	6-0	180	11-16-82	2	0	2.84	40	0	0	23	44	32	16	14	1	12	32	.196	.211	.185	6.50	2.44

Fielding

Catcher	PCT	G	PO	A	E	DP	PB
Brown	.994	45	295	24	2	2	6
Doumit	1.000	5	39	1	0	0	1
Fryer	.989	33	240	18	3	2	1
Jaramillo	.992	39	212	27	2	1	0
Perez	.977	7	40	3	1	0	1
Toregas	1.000	17	106	7	0	0	1
Watts	.986	10	66	2	1	1	0

First Base	PCT	G	PO	A	E	DP
Bowker	.988	13	73	8	1	9
Brown	.000	1	0	0	0	0
Clement	1.000	6	55	4	0	3
Durham	.957	4	21	1	1	1
Hague	.987	122	1020	86	15	80
Marte	1.000	4	43	1	0	3
Pearce	.947	2	16	2	1	2

Second Base	PCT	G	PO	A	E	DP
Bocock	.857	1	4	2	1	1
Ciriaco	.944	18	36	31	4	5
d'Arnaud	1.000	22	34	63	0	10
Ford	.958	6	12	11	1	2
Friday	.986	32	52	88	2	16
Harrison	.950	21	38	57	5	13
Mercer	.993	34	59	86	1	17
Rodriguez	1.000	5	10	10	0	2
Wimberly	.972	16	27	43	2	6

Third Base	PCT	G	PO	A	E	DP
Alvarez	.957	31	23	67	4	5
Ciriaco	1.000	1	0	2	0	0
d'Arnaud	1.000	5	9	7	0	1
Friday	.971	13	6	28	1	2
Hague	.959	17	15	32	2	1
Harrison	.897	40	28	68	11	2
Marte	.983	45	24	90	2	10
Pearce	1.000	2	2	2	0	0

Shortstop	PCT	G	PO	A	E	DP
Bocock	1.000	8	8	11	0	2
Cedeno	1.000	3	6	4	0	1
Ciriaco	.951	46	69	106	9	18
d'Arnaud	.980	47	73	124	4	27
Friday	.985	18	14	51	1	6
Harrison	.800	1	3	1	1	0
Mercer	.982	26	39	73	2	12
Pearce	1.000	1	1	1	0	1
Picart	.800	2	2	2	1	1
Rodriguez	1.000	1	1	0	0	0

Outfield	PCT	G	PO	A	E	DP
Bowker	.984	91	176	4	3	0
Ciriaco	1.000	6	6	1	0	0
Durham	.966	64	108	7	4	1
Fryer	1.000	3	6	0	0	0
Hernandez	.987	126	302	11	4	5
Lambo	1.000	45	86	2	0	0
Ludwick	1.000	4	5	1	0	0
Mercer	1.000	1	1	0	0	0
Norman	.909	7	10	0	1	0
Pearce	1.000	2	3	0	0	0
Presley	.979	86	180	7	4	2
Tabata	1.000	7	11	0	0	0
Wimberly	1.000	16	35	3	0	0

ALTOONA CURVE — DOUBLE-A

EASTERN LEAGUE

Batting	B-T	HT	WT	DOB	AVG	vLH	vRH	G	AB	R	H	2B	3B	HR	RBI	BB	HBP	SH	SF	SO	SB	CS	SLG	OBP
Chalk, Brad	L-L	6-1	180	1-20-86	.244	.231	.249	97	266	23	65	7	5	0	36	26	1	0	3	45	4	1	.308	.311
Curry, Matt	L-R	6-1	225	7-27-88	.242	.230	.246	87	302	38	73	16	3	6	39	33	5	0	7	90	1	1	.374	.320
Durham, Miles	R-R	6-4	205	3-21-83	.204	.206	.203	45	157	18	32	10	1	2	19	15	2	0	3	52	4	1	.318	.277
Farrell, Jeremy	R-R	6-3	200	11-11-86	.260	.246	.263	88	312	40	81	18	1	5	38	29	10	0	1	78	4	1	.372	.341
Ford, Shelby	B-R	6-3	185	12-15-84	.194	.174	.205	20	62	5	12	1	0	1	6	1	0	0	1	19	0	1	.258	.203
Fryer, Eric	R-R	6-2	215	8-26-85	.345	.314	.359	37	113	24	39	4	2	5	16	16	1	0	1	21	1	0	.549	.427
Hernandez, Jose	L-R	5-11	195	3-19-86	.165	.182	.149	40	91	6	15	4	1	1	10	5	2	0	2	36	0	1	.264	.220
Holt, Brock	L-R	5-10	165	6-11-88	.288	.185	.320	132	511	62	147	30	9	1	40	50	7	0	5	85	18	10	.387	.356
Lambo, Andrew	L-L	6-3	210	8-11-88	.274	.238	.286	69	252	35	69	17	0	8	41	26	3	0	3	59	4	3	.437	.345
Latimore, Quincy	R-R	5-10	175	2-3-89	.239	.257	.233	128	457	52	109	32	1	15	59	33	8	0	7	140	7	8	.411	.297
Marte, Starling	R-R	6-1	170	10-9-88	.332	.289	.346	129	536	91	178	38	8	12	50	22	11	0	2	100	24	12	.500	.370
Mercer, Jordy	R-R	6-3	191	8-27-86	.268	.318	.251	72	265	40	71	17	1	13	48	23	4	0	6	35	6	3	.487	.329
Norman, Anthony	R-R	6-0	185	10-20-84	.282	.083	.322	29	71	12	20	3	4	0	9	7	0	0	0	16	2	1	.437	.346
Picart, Greg	B-R	5-11	175	9-25-85	.218	.167	.238	56	170	14	37	2	1	1	14	15	2	0	2	35	3	2	.259	.286
Rodriguez, Josh	R-R	6-0	185	12-18-84	.267	.333	.242	57	225	24	60	3	0	5	19	18	1	0	2	41	3	1	.347	.321
Sanchez, Tony	R-R	6-0	215	5-20-88	.241	.261	.235	118	402	46	97	14	1	5	44	47	14	0	2	76	5	5	.318	.340
Sanchez, Yunesky	B-R	6-2	210	5-3-84	.299	.226	.320	42	134	13	40	6	0	2	18	6	2	0	3	18	0	1	.388	.331
Scott, Travis	L-R	6-3	220	4-24-85	.091	.000	.111	10	33	2	3	0	1	0	2	1	0	0	1	5	0	0	.152	.114
Watts, Kris	L-R	6-0	209	7-15-84	.232	.229	.233	71	194	24	45	9	0	3	14	34	2	0	1	37	0	0	.325	.348

Pitching	B-T	HT	WT	DOB	W	L	ERA	G	GS	CG	SV	IP	H	R	ER	HR	BB	SO	AVG	vLH	vRH	K/9	BB/9
Alderson, Tim	R-R	6-6	217	11-3-88	0	4	4.12	42	1	0	0	74	70	39	34	6	27	57	.252	.280	.226	6.90	3.27
Beimel, Joe	L-L	6-3	215	4-19-77	0	0	0.00	4	2	0	0	3	2	0	0	0	1	1	.182	.222	.000	2.70	2.70
Boleska, Tom	R-R	6-0	190	7-30-86	1	1	5.40	12	0	0	0	17	14	10	10	0	12	11	.255	.192	.310	5.94	6.48
Claggett, Anthony	B-R	6-3	215	7-15-84	5	5	3.75	42	0	0	2	62	46	26	26	6	32	36	.213	.253	.179	5.20	4.62
Colla, Mike	R-R	6-2	220	12-23-86	5	11	3.70	29	23	0	0	134	117	58	55	20	39	109	.229	.249	.211	7.34	2.63

Pitching	B-T	HT	WT	DOB	W	L	ERA	G	GS	CG	SV	IP	H	R	ER	HR	BB	SO	AVG	vLH	vRH	K/9	BB/9
Cox, Tyler	R-L	6-3	200	4-19-86	1	0	0.00	1	0	0	0	1	1	0	0	0	0	1	.250	.000	.333	9.00	0.00
Crotta, Mike	R-R	6-6	235	9-25-84	0	0	0.00	1	0	0	0	1	1	0	0	0	0	1	.250	.000	.500	9.00	0.00
Dubee, Michael	R-R	6-3	185	1-12-86	2	6	3.27	43	0	0	6	63	72	26	23	2	16	50	.293	.294	.292	7.11	2.27
Hughes, Jared	R-R	6-7	235	7-4-85	3	4	4.09	13	11	0	0	62	62	31	28	2	18	33	.259	.295	.218	4.82	2.63
Irwin, Phillip	R-R	6-3	220	2-25-87	8	4	3.81	15	14	0	0	87	91	42	37	9	10	69	.264	.267	.261	7.11	1.03
Krol, Noah	B-R	6-2	185	6-6-84	3	5	4.45	54	0	0	24	55	62	30	27	2	19	28	.288	.273	.299	4.61	3.13
Leach, Brian	R-R	6-3	195	4-14-86	0	0	9.00	10	0	0	0	15	14	15	15	0	15	7	.250	.286	.229	4.20	9.00
Leroux, Chris	L-R	6-6	225	4-14-84	1	2	2.57	5	0	0	0	7	9	5	2	2	0	6	.300	.429	.188	7.71	0.00
Locke, Jeff	L-L	6-1	215	11-20-87	7	8	4.03	23	22	0	0	125	118	68	56	9	46	114	.251	.230	.256	8.21	3.31
Loree, Mike	R-R	6-6	226	9-14-86	0	0	1.17	4	0	0	0	8	6	1	1	0	3	11	.207	.188	.231	12.91	3.52
McPherson, Kyle	B-R	6-4	215	11-11-87	8	5	3.02	16	16	0	0	89	75	34	30	7	21	82	.226	.204	.244	8.26	2.12
McSwain, Matt	R-R	6-1	197	8-15-85	2	0	3.76	32	2	0	0	67	60	29	28	11	17	29	.239	.263	.219	3.90	2.28
Moreno, Diego	R-R	6-1	177	7-21-86	0	0	4.91	7	0	0	0	11	10	6	6	1	3	14	.238	.261	.211	11.45	2.45
Morris, Bryan	L-R	6-3	220	3-28-87	3	4	3.35	35	6	0	0	78	72	34	29	2	33	64	.252	.235	.263	7.38	3.81
Ohlendorf, Ross	R-R	6-4	240	8-8-82	0	0	3.86	1	1	0	0	5	5	2	2	1	1	3	.250	.556	.000	5.79	1.93
Pribanic, Aaron	R-R	6-4	200	9-16-86	10	9	3.88	28	27	1	0	153	169	69	66	13	28	71	.282	.263	.301	4.18	1.65
Sinkbeil, Brett	R-R	6-2	210	12-26-84	0	1	4.03	4	4	0	0	22	29	16	10	3	2	23	.302	.297	.305	9.27	0.81
Thompson, Aaron	L-L	6-2	190	2-28-87	4	7	5.16	28	12	0	0	84	100	55	48	6	20	51	.307	.350	.287	5.49	2.15
Veal, Donald	L-L	6-4	240	9-18-84	0	1	7.71	4	0	0	0	5	9	4	4	3	0	3	.391	.400	.389	5.79	0.00
Welker, Duke	L-R	6-7	220	2-10-86	1	0	5.40	8	0	0	0	10	11	7	6	0	1	9	.256	.278	.240	8.10	0.90

Fielding

Catcher	PCT	G	PO	A	E	DP	PB
Fryer	.978	16	82	8	2	1	0
Sanchez	.976	104	665	58	18	5	4
Scott	.971	6	26	8	1	0	1
Watts	.993	22	133	5	1	1	1

First Base	PCT	G	PO	A	E	DP
Curry	.994	87	785	71	5	61
Durham	.991	44	400	30	4	28
Ford	.985	8	60	4	1	11
Sanchez	1.000	6	55	5	0	3

Second Base	PCT	G	PO	A	E	DP
Ford	1.000	2	3	5	0	0
Holt	.980	98	188	293	10	64

Picart	.981	12	21	31	1	2
Rodriguez	.969	32	52	104	5	17

Third Base	PCT	G	PO	A	E	DP
Farrell	.926	86	42	171	17	20
Ford	1.000	5	4	14	0	0
Picart	.939	25	6	40	3	3
Rodriguez	1.000	3	1	6	0	1
Sanchez	.926	28	11	52	5	3

Shortstop	PCT	G	PO	A	E	DP
Ford	.929	3	4	9	1	1
Holt	.973	33	45	97	4	14
Mercer	.976	72	104	228	8	38
Picart	.982	16	19	36	1	6

Rodriguez	.955	22	34	71	5	11

Outfield	PCT	G	PO	A	E	DP
Chalk	.988	77	152	12	2	2
Durham	1.000	2	2	0	0	0
Ford	1.000	1	2	0	0	0
Fryer	1.000	14	15	2	0	0
Hernandez	.962	16	25	0	1	0
Lambo	.924	66	105	5	9	3
Latimore	.970	123	244	12	8	1
Marte	.976	129	308	18	8	4
Norman	.929	12	26	0	2	0
Picart	1.000	1	2	0	0	0

BRADENTON MARAUDERS   HIGH CLASS A

FLORIDA STATE LEAGUE

Batting	B-T	HT	WT	DOB	AVG	vLH	vRH	G	AB	R	H	2B	3B	HR	RBI	BB	HBP	SH	SF	SO	SB	CS	SLG	OBP
Alvarez, Pedro	L-R	6-3	235	2-6-87	.188	.400	.091	6	16	2	3	0	0	1	2	3	2	0	0	5	0	0	.375	.381
Anderson, Calvin	R-R	6-7	240	5-8-87	.271	.265	.274	60	225	31	61	12	1	13	42	20	3	0	3	84	2	1	.507	.335
Baker, Aaron	L-R	6-2	220	9-10-87	.282	.224	.305	103	386	53	109	21	3	15	73	44	1	0	8	92	1	2	.469	.351
Brown, Kelson	R-R	6-3	170	11-7-87	.262	.215	.282	84	260	29	68	10	2	0	27	14	1	0	3	35	4	1	.315	.299
Cabrera, Ramon	B-R	5-7	202	11-5-89	.343	.380	.328	92	327	46	112	25	4	3	53	38	4	0	7	29	5	1	.471	.410
Chambers, Evan	R-R	6-1	210	3-24-89	.234	.189	.252	125	436	57	102	24	2	11	55	70	11	0	6	131	20	12	.374	.350
Cunningham, Jarek	R-R	6-1	195	12-25-89	.258	.221	.272	80	310	53	80	23	6	15	51	17	13	0	4	82	5	2	.516	.320
d'Arnaud, Chase	R-R	6-1	200	1-21-87	.333	.000	.333	4	12	3	4	1	0	1	3	1	0	0	0	2	0		.667	.385
Doumit, Ryan	R-R	6-1	215	4-3-81	.143	.000	.154	5	14	1	2	0	0	0	1	2	0	0	0	3	0	0	.143	.250
Gonzalez, Benji	R-R	5-11	160	1-16-90	.222	.173	.241	120	388	55	86	12	4	1	34	40	4	0	7	88	19	7	.281	.296
Gonzalez, Elevys	B-R	5-11	175	10-23-89	.322	.378	.300	126	454	63	146	36	6	6	83	39	1	0	3	93	7	5	.467	.374
Grossman, Robbie	B-L	6-1	190	9-16-89	.294	.326	.281	134	490	127	144	34	2	13	56	104	6	0	7	111	24	10	.451	.418
Maggi, Drew	R-R	6-0	185	5-16-89	.000	.000	.000	1	1	0	0	0	0	0	0	0	0	0	0	1	0	0	.000	.500
Marquez, Jairo	R-R	6-0	170	4-7-88	.211	.500	.107	14	38	3	8	1	0	0	2	4	0	0	1	3	0	0	.237	.279
Paulino, Carlos	R-R	6-0	170	9-24-89	.299	.304	.297	82	271	44	81	18	4	4	40	18	6	0	4	33	0	2	.439	.351
Pearce, Steve	R-R	5-11	210	4-13-83	.000	.000	.000	3	6	2	0	0	0	0	0	4	0	0	0	2	0	0	.000	.400
Presley, Alex	L-L	5-9	190	7-25-85	.167	.000	.167	2	6	2	1	0	0	0	1	0	0	0	0	0	0	0	.167	.286
Rubinstein, David	R-R	6-2	190	12-15-87	.247	.292	.227	94	300	41	74	13	0	5	42	31	5	0	2	57	8	6	.340	.325
Santos, Adalberto	R-R	5-11	185	9-28-87	.314	.317	.313	105	353	59	111	22	7	7	49	42	5	0	3	55	27	4	.476	.392
Scott, Travis	L-R	6-3	220	4-24-85	.273	.000	.375	3	11	1	3	0	0	0	0	1	0	0	0	1	0	0	.273	.333
Snyder, Chris	R-R	6-4	240	2-12-81	.400	.200	.467	6	20	6	8	2	0	1	8	6	0	0	0	5	0	0	.650	.538
Tabata, Jose	R-R	5-11	220	8-12-88	.125	.500	.000	4	8	1	1	1	0	0	1	3	0	0	0	3	0	0	.250	.364
White, Cole	R-R	6-4	205	4-3-85	.285	.282	.286	45	151	20	43	10	1	3	17	13	3	0	1	39	1	2	.424	.351

Pitching	B-T	HT	WT	DOB	W	L	ERA	G	GS	CG	SV	IP	H	R	ER	HR	BB	SO	AVG	vLH	vRH	K/9	BB/9
Alvarado, Gabriel	R-R	6-2	175	5-19-87	0	1	5.40	5	0	0	0	7	8	4	4	1	7	6	.308	.273	.333	8.10	9.45
Ascanio, Jose	R-R	5-11	195	5-2-85	0	0	9.82	3	2	0	0	4	4	4	4	0	1	6	.286	.333	.250	14.73	2.45
Baker, Nate	L-L	6-3	190	12-27-87	10	8	3.34	29	25	0	0	148	151	80	55	6	51	105	.258	.239	.265	6.37	3.09
Beckman, Ryan	R-R	6-4	185	1-20-89	4	4	3.12	42	0	0	11	52	44	29	18	1	18	46	.226	.190	.252	7.96	3.12
Beimel, Joe	L-L	6-3	215	4-19-77	0	0	0.00	2	2	0	0	2	0	0	0	0	0	2	.000	.000	.000	0.00	0.00
Black, Vic	R-R	6-3	185	5-23-88	1	0	4.05	5	0	0	0	7	8	4	3	1	4	5	.333	.167	.389	6.75	5.40
Cox, Tyler	R-L	6-3	200	4-19-86	2	0	2.60	22	0	0	0	28	18	10	8	1	11	28	.175	.188	.164	9.11	3.58
Cumpton, Brandon	R-R	6-2	198	11-16-88	3	3	3.66	13	12	0	0	66	73	29	27	6	12	42	.280	.232	.315	5.70	1.63
Erickson, Jason	R-R	6-1	200	2-3-87	3	2	4.33	34	3	0	3	71	73	40	34	9	9	51	.262	.268	.258	6.50	2.55

Pitching

Pitching	B-T	HT	WT	DOB	W	L	ERA	G	GS	CG	SV	IP	H	R	ER	HR	BB	SO	AVG	vLH	vRH	K/9	BB/9
Foster, Zach	R-R	6-6	220	5-24-87	3	1	3.11	29	0	0	2	38	25	14	13	2	18	18	.195	.155	.229	4.30	4.30
Inman, Jeff	R-R	6-3	180	11-24-87	2	2	2.18	12	6	1	0	33	28	12	8	2	5	16	.226	.255	.203	4.36	1.36
Irwin, Phillip	R-R	6-3	220	2-25-87	5	0	2.03	10	10	0	0	53	47	15	12	3	12	40	.234	.180	.287	6.75	2.03
Leach, Brian	R-R	6-3	195	4-14-86	3	4	7.62	22	5	0	0	52	62	49	44	7	25	33	.298	.291	.305	5.71	4.33
Lopez, Porfirio	L-L	5-10	160	3-24-90	2	1	5.16	12	0	0	0	23	23	15	13	2	11	18	.277	.296	.268	7.15	4.37
Lorin, Brett	L-R	6-7	245	3-31-87	7	6	2.84	25	17	1	1	117	103	50	37	7	19	99	.230	.185	.266	7.59	1.46
McPherson, Kyle	B-R	6-4	215	11-11-87	4	1	2.89	12	12	1	0	72	62	25	23	4	6	60	.227	.223	.231	7.53	0.75
McSwain, Matt	R-R	6-1	197	8-15-85	3	1	1.89	4	1	0	0	19	15	8	4	1	3	17	.214	.417	.109	8.05	1.42
Meek, Evan	R-R	6-0	220	5-12-83	0	0	0.00	2	1	0	0	2	1	0	0	0	2	.143	.000	.200	9.00	0.00
Miller, Quinton	R-R	6-1	185	11-28-89	5	7	6.56	15	14	0	0	70	93	53	51	3	16	35	.321	.323	.319	4.50	2.06
Moreno, Diego	R-R	6-1	177	7-21-86	2	4	3.21	34	0	0	5	34	26	14	12	2	15	31	.211	.265	.176	8.29	4.01
Navarro, Eliecer	L-L	5-9	177	10-26-87	1	2	6.12	13	1	0	0	32	38	24	22	6	10	31	.292	.283	.298	8.63	2.78
Ohlendorf, Ross	R-R	6-4	240	8-8-82	0	0	4.50	2	2	0	0	8	10	4	4		1	6	.303	.364	.273	6.75	1.13
Ramos, Jhonatan	L-L	5-8	156	8-7-89	4	3	3.72	27	6	0	1	73	83	35	30	7	22	45	.292	.235	.323	5.57	2.72
Sinkbeil, Brett	R-R	6-2	210	12-26-84	2	6	5.11	20	9	0	0	62	65	46	35	6	21	37	.264	.244	.285	5.40	3.06
Veal, Donald	L-L	6-4	240	9-18-84	0	1	2.79	7	4	0	0	19	17	6	6	1	6	18	.236	.269	.217	8.38	2.79
Waldron, Tyler	R-R	6-2	185	5-1-89	4	1	4.25	7	5	0	0	30	35	15	14	3	5	16	.297	.245	.338	4.85	1.52
Welker, Duke	L-R	6-7	220	2-10-86	3	5	2.25	36	0	0	6	52	33	18	13	2	25	41	.186	.163	.209	7.10	4.33

Fielding

Catcher	PCT	G	PO	A	E	DP	PB
Cabrera	.996	78	484	35	2	4	14
Doumit	.857	2	6	0	1	0	0
Marquez	1.000	5	33	0	0	0	1
Paulino	.986	55	312	37	5	1	5
Scott	1.000	3	15	0	0	0	0
Snyder	1.000	4	14	1	0	0	0

First Base	PCT	G	PO	A	E	DP
Baker	.992	99	878	78	8	75
Brown	1.000	5	49	3	0	6
Marquez	1.000	7	36	4	0	2
White	.982	32	245	23	5	21

Second Base	PCT	G	PO	A	E	DP
Brown	.986	42	53	91	2	16
Cunningham	.940	79	136	210	22	49
Maggi	1.000	1	4	0	0	0
Santos	.923	26	38	58	8	13

Third Base	PCT	G	PO	A	E	DP
Alvarez	.889	5	1	15	2	0
Brown	.947	15	15	39	3	4
Gonzalez	.923	124	60	239	25	16
Pearce	1.000	3	0	6	0	0

Shortstop	PCT	G	PO	A	E	DP
Brown	.888	20	27	60	11	9

	PCT	G	PO	A	E	DP
d'Arnaud	1.000	3	6	5	0	0
Gonzalez	.951	120	156	344	26	74

Outfield	PCT	G	PO	A	E	DP
Brown	1.000	4	3	0	0	0
Chambers	.985	124	319	6	5	1
Grossman	.972	133	235	9	7	2
Paulino	1.000	4	5	0	0	0
Presley	1.000	2	1	0	0	0
Rubinstein	.982	89	157	9	3	2
Santos	.983	65	109	6	2	0
Tabata	1.000	2	2	0	0	0
White	.917	7	11	0	1	0

WEST VIRGINIA POWER

LOW CLASS A

SOUTH ATLANTIC LEAGUE

Batting	B-T	HT	WT	DOB	AVG	vLH	vRH	G	AB	R	H	2B	3B	HR	RBI	BB	HBP	SH	SF	SO	SB	CS	SLG	OBP
Avila, Eric	R-R	6-1	165	6-9-90	.216	.260	.201	116	380	44	82	14	1	4	31	27	5	0	2	57	9	7	.289	.275
Bencsko, Justin	L-L	6-1	185	8-13-87	.226	.100	.286	11	31	4	7	3	0	0	2	2	2	0	0	9	0	0	.323	.314
Curry, Matt	L-R	6-1	225	7-27-88	.361	.324	.373	46	155	39	56	15	3	9	34	35	2	0	3	29	6	2	.671	.477
Diaz, Elias	R-R	6-1	175	11-17-90	.221	.257	.210	90	326	38	72	23	3	2	45	23	4	0	2	69	6	1	.328	.279
Emsley-Pai, Kawika	B-R	5-11	195	9-3-88	.250	.356	.204	64	196	30	49	11	2	0	17	46	3	0	1	42	3	5	.327	.398
Freeman, Wes	R-R	6-4	215	1-29-90	.250	.111	.364	5	20	3	5	1	0	0	1	0	0	0	0	8	3	1	.300	.318
Grovatt, Dan	L-L	6-1	195	10-29-88	.284	.276	.287	131	476	70	135	30	5	8	67	61	4	0	8	90	21	9	.418	.364
Howard, Justin	L-L	6-0	205	8-28-87	.262	.246	.268	126	450	64	118	37	2	6	66	78	0	0	3	112	9	7	.393	.369
Lyles, Chase	R-R	6-2	206	1-13-87	.241	.222	.247	70	249	35	60	11	1	4	36	29	5	0	4	44	5	6	.341	.328
Maggi, Drew	R-R	6-0	185	5-16-89	.267	.283	.261	125	484	63	129	27	4	3	45	64	9	0	3	71	32	18	.357	.361
Marquez, Jairo	R-R	6-0	170	4-7-88	.295	.222	.314	16	44	6	13	4	0	0	5	4	0	0	0	7	0	0	.386	.354
Mort, Kevin	R-R	5-9	170	3-10-88	.234	.250	.228	100	321	29	75	10	0	1	36	34	4	0	3	49	5	6	.274	.312
Ngoepe, Gift	B-R	5-10	165	1-18-90	.306	.412	.279	25	85	14	26	5	1	2	5	7	0	0	0	14	3	3	.459	.359
Noris, Rogelio	R-R	6-2	192	3-12-89	.212	.182	.224	91	316	40	67	14	4	9	50	9	4	0	3	91	1	2	.367	.241
Rojas Jr., Mel	B-R	6-3	200	5-24-90	.246	.200	.263	131	508	66	125	16	7	5	46	46	3	0	1	119	23	14	.335	.312
Vasquez, Andy	L-R	6-1	168	10-8-87	.278	.307	.271	113	417	66	116	15	13	5	39	12	4	0	1	78	24	10	.412	.304
White, Cole	R-R	6-4	205	4-3-85	.288	.296	.286	35	132	16	38	9	1	5	23	12	1	0	2	39	3	2	.485	.347

Pitching	B-T	HT	WT	DOB	W	L	ERA	G	GS	CG	SV	IP	H	R	ER	HR	BB	SO	AVG	vLH	vRH	K/9	BB/9
Beckman, Ryan	R-R	6-4	185	1-2-90	0	0	0.00	4	0	0	2	6	5	0	0	0	0	3	.227	.429	.133	4.50	0.00
Black, Vic	R-R	6-3	185	5-23-88	2	1	5.28	22	0	0	1	29	30	21	17	0	16	23	.268	.277	.262	7.14	4.97
Cain, Colton	L-L	6-3	225	2-5-91	8	6	3.64	24	19	0	0	106	92	55	43	6	31	81	.234	.216	.239	6.86	2.62
Castro, Orlando	L-L	5-11	194	3-17-92	1	0	4.11	7	0	0	1	15	17	8	7	4	9	6	.279	.188	.311	3.52	5.28
Cumpton, Brandon	R-R	6-2	198	11-16-88	7	4	4.30	13	12	0	0	67	60	34	32	6	18	48	.240	.258	.229	6.45	2.42
Decker, Kevin	R-R	6-1	185	2-24-88	3	5	3.49	31	0	0	2	59	65	28	23	2	20	55	.272	.276	.270	8.34	3.03
Dodson, Zack	L-L	6-2	190	7-23-90	6	4	2.57	13	13	0	0	67	61	27	19	3	15	46	.246	.246	.246	6.21	2.03
Ennis, Justin	L-L	6-1	210	4-20-88	5	2	4.03	21	0	0	2	45	49	23	20	4	14	29	.282	.250	.297	5.84	2.82
Foster, Zach	R-R	6-6	220	5-24-87	1	1	4.91	11	0	0	0	18	24	10	10	1	5	20	.316	.308	.320	9.82	2.45
Fuesser, Zac	L-L	6-2	190	7-19-90	3	6	3.74	32	11	0	2	108	111	50	45	14	33	95	.274	.278	.273	7.89	2.74
Lopez, Porfirio	L-L	5-10	160	3-24-90	2	4	3.38	19	6	0	2	56	49	23	21	4	21	51	.233	.220	.237	8.20	3.38
Navarro, Eliecer	L-L	5-9	177	10-26-87	5	0	2.83	14	8	0	0	57	50	20	18	7	9	54	.236	.205	.244	8.48	1.41
Payne, Vince	R-R	6-4	175	12-19-90	2	0	5.56	8	0	0	0	11	9	8	7	2	6	3	.231	.167	.259	2.38	4.76
Pounders, Brooks	R-R	6-4	270	9-26-90	5	5	3.68	36	1	0	3	66	61	29	27	9	14	72	.242	.256	.235	9.82	1.91
Ramos, Jhonatan	L-L	5-8	156	8-7-89	0	0	0.00	1	0	0	0	5	3	0	0		1	4	.158	.133	.250	6.75	1.69
Sadler, Casey	R-R	6-4	200	7-13-90	5	5	2.43	35	0	0	4	67	51	20	18	5	17	57	.213	.290	.157	7.70	2.30
Singh, Rinku	L-L	6-2	190	8-8-88	2	1	3.18	12	0	0	0	17	19	6	6	1	7	13	.297	.304	.293	6.88	3.71

Pitching

Pitching	B-T	HT	WT	DOB	W	L	ERA	G	GS	CG	SV	IP	H	R	ER	HR	BB	SO	AVG	vLH	vRH	K/9	BB/9
Stevenson, Trent	L-R	6-6	175	6-1-90	0	3	6.93	22	3	0	3	49	65	40	38	9	13	25	.314	.293	.328	4.56	2.37
Taillon, Jameson	R-R	6-6	225	11-18-91	2	3	3.98	23	23	0	0	93	89	45	41	9	22	97	.249	.205	.278	9.42	2.14
Townsend, Jason	R-R	6-3	190	9-17-88	0	1	2.38	44	0	0	13	53	46	15	14	4	14	46	.238	.262	.227	7.81	2.38
Von Rosenberg, Zack	R-R	6-5	205	9-24-90	5	9	5.73	27	25	0	0	126	143	86	80	19	23	114	.290	.312	.274	8.16	1.65
Waldron, Tyler	R-R	6-2	185	5-1-89	7	6	4.82	19	17	0	0	97	91	53	52	14	26	64	.244	.242	.245	5.94	2.41

Fielding

Catcher	PCT	G	PO	A	E	DP	PB
Diaz	.977	82	613	61	16	4	8
Emsley-Pai	.989	57	390	43	5	5	8
Marquez	1.000	2	13	1	0	0	2

First Base	PCT	G	PO	A	E	DP
Curry	.997	36	302	24	1	21
Howard	.988	63	525	43	7	54
Lyles	.985	34	303	24	5	25
Marquez	.947	2	18	0	1	1
White	.964	6	50	4	2	4

Second Base	PCT	G	PO	A	E	DP
Avila	1.000	1	1	0	0	0

	PCT	G	PO	A	E	DP	PB
Maggi	.813	7	6	7	3	1	
Mort	.994	84	139	207	2	64	
Ngoepe	1.000	12	24	27	0	7	
Vasquez	.954	51	96	132	11	24	

Third Base	PCT	G	PO	A	E	DP
Avila	.927	111	75	269	27	27
Lyles	.941	18	16	32	3	4
Mort	1.000	11	8	15	0	2
Vasquez	.842	6	4	12	3	1

Shortstop	PCT	G	PO	A	E	DP
Maggi	.952	117	148	328	24	65
Mort	1.000	2	3	4	0	1

	PCT	G	PO	A	E	DP
Ngoepe	.976	12	16	24	1	0
Vasquez	.900	10	12	24	4	3

Outfield	PCT	G	PO	A	E	DP
Bencsko	.875	4	5	2	1	0
Freeman	1.000	5	9	0	0	0
Grovatt	.967	127	248	15	9	6
Howard	.946	29	50	3	3	0
Noris	.971	83	127	9	4	0
Rojas Jr.	.984	129	296	4	5	3
Vasquez	.957	51	84	4	4	2
White	1.000	6	8	2	0	0

STATE COLLEGE SPIKES

SHORT-SEASON

NEW YORK-PENN LEAGUE

Batting	B-T	HT	WT	DOB	AVG	vLH	vRH	G	AB	R	H	2B	3B	HR	RBI	BB	HBP	SH	SF	SO	SB	CS	SLG	OBP
Bencsko, Justin	L-L	6-1	185	8-13-87	.271	.185	.310	27	85	13	23	2	1	2	6	11	2	0	0	30	7	3	.388	.367
Bishop, Jorge	R-R	5-10	152	3-12-91	.162	.333	.107	13	37	5	6	0	0	0	2	4	0	0	1	7	2	1	.162	.238
Cayones, Exicardo	L-L	6-0	183	10-9-91	.063	.000	.071	11	32	0	2	0	0	0	0	4	1	0	0	13	1	0	.063	.189
Dickerson, Alex	L-L	6-3	235	5-26-90	.313	.333	.306	41	150	25	47	16	1	3	19	16	5	0	2	28	0	0	.493	.393
Freeman, Wes	R-R	6-4	215	7-9-88	.304	.264	.319	50	191	25	58	14	2	6	25	9	1	0	0	51	11	2	.492	.338
Fuselier, Alex	L-R	6-0	170	9-13-89	.213	.220	.210	52	183	24	39	4	2	0	13	23	4	0	0	36	9	8	.257	.314
Gamache, Daniel	L-R	5-11	190	11-20-90	.231	.143	.255	20	65	6	15	2	1	1	12	5	1	0	1	13	1	1	.338	.292
Garcia, Willy	R-R	6-3	177	9-4-92	.286	.000	.333	3	7	1	2	0	0	0	0	0	0	0	0	0	0	0	.286	.286
Gonzalez, Samuel	R-R	6-0	180	2-24-89	.302	.238	.330	40	139	20	42	5	2	1	15	14	4	0	3	15	3	4	.388	.375
Gourley, Walker	R-R	6-0	185	6-28-91	.180	.270	.143	42	128	11	23	3	0	0	10	7	2	0	2	31	8	0	.203	.230
Hanson, Alen	B-R	5-11	152	10-22-92	.200	.250	.167	3	10	1	2	0	0	0	1	0	0	0	0	2	0	0	.200	.273
Jones, Rodarrick	R-R	6-0	195	7-31-90	.245	.375	.222	17	53	7	13	5	0	0	5	8	3	0	0	11	0	2	.340	.375
Lashmet, Chris	R-R	6-4	230	4-25-89	.231	.234	.230	60	216	15	50	11	0	2	22	21	2	0	1	31	2	2	.310	.304
Lewis, Taylor	L-L	6-0	200	12-18-89	.188	.167	.196	60	186	22	35	1	7	0	17	34	3	0	3	43	16	4	.269	.319
Nowlin, Billy	R-R	6-1	210	12-16-86	.190	.167	.200	5	21	2	4	1	0	0	3	1	0	0	0	2	0	0	.238	.227
Osuna, Jose	R-R	6-2	213	12-12-92	.250	—	—	2	8	2	2	1	0	0	1	1	0	0	0	0	0	0	.375	.333
Polanco, Gregory	L-L	6-4	170	9-14-91	.100	.000	.100	3	10	1	1	0	0	0	1	0	0	0	0	2	0	0	.100	.100
Ponce, Dimas	R-R	5-11	140	1-22-91	.177	.281	.148	45	147	19	26	5	0	0	8	15	7	0	1	18	7	1	.211	.282
Sharp, Brian	R-R	6-0	195	7-30-88	.143	.238	.095	19	63	8	9	2	0	1	5	3	6	0	0	4	0	0	.222	.250
Singer, Kirk	R-R	6-2	170	12-1-89	.236	.220	.241	59	191	23	45	9	5	1	18	17	3	0	2	47	8	5	.351	.305
Skirving, Matt	L-R	6-2	215	12-12-89	.277	.256	.283	48	166	17	46	15	1	3	24	13	4	0	0	38	3	3	.434	.344
Sosa, Junior	L-L	5-10	139	10-3-90	.195	.364	.169	22	82	9	16	2	0	1	9	7	1	0	0	9	3	2	.256	.267
Trent, Derek	L-R	6-1	210	11-6-88	.197	.182	.202	44	142	13	28	9	1	1	10	20	5	0	0	35	1	1	.296	.317
Trinidad, Michaelangel	L-L	5-11	232	8-23-88	.133	.250	.091	4	15	0	2	2	0	0	0	0	0	0	0	4	0	0	.267	.133

Pitching	B-T	HT	WT	DOB	W	L	ERA	G	GS	CG	SV	IP	H	R	ER	HR	BB	SO	AVG	vLH	vRH	K/9	BB/9
Allie, Stetson	R-R	6-2	220	3-13-91	0	2	6.58	15	7	0	0	26	20	20	19	1	29	28	.208	.341	.096	9.69	10.04
Archibald, Cliff	L-R	6-1	190	5-23-90	0	1	4.11	19	0	0	1	31	36	15	14	1	17	22	.288	.207	.358	6.46	4.99
Benedict, Matt	R-R	6-5	220	2-3-89	5	3	3.79	15	15	0	0	71	77	41	30	1	15	39	.271	.233	.303	4.92	1.89
Campos, Fraylin	R-R	5-11	170	1-3-90	1	2	9.00	8	0	0	0	11	13	11	11	0	9	9	.302	.353	.269	7.36	7.36
Castro, Orlando	L-L	5-11	194	3-17-92	2	0	4.76	6	0	0	0	17	20	9	9	0	4	11	.290	.400	.227	5.82	2.12
Cooper, Jordan	R-R	6-3	215	2-16-90	1	4	5.06	13	3	0	0	37	43	27	21	1	14	23	.291	.245	.316	5.54	3.38
De Leon, Emmanuel	B-R	6-1	175	12-25-90	2	2	3.28	21	0	0	5	25	21	10	9	1	8	17	.226	.211	.236	6.20	2.92
Dodson, Zack	L-L	6-2	190	7-23-90	0	1	4.58	4	4	0	0	18	22	12	9	2	4	13	.310	.273	.327	6.62	2.04
Ennis, Justin	L-L	6-1	210	4-20-88	0	0	0.00	2	0	0	0	2	1	0	0	0	1	1	.125	.000	.143	3.86	3.86
Fienemann, Mitchell	R-R	6-4	186	5-28-90	1	2	3.86	13	0	0	5	16	12	9	7	1	8	10	.207	.292	.147	5.51	4.41
Hafner, Ryan	R-R	6-6	205	11-22-91	2	6	3.15	15	14	0	0	66	58	32	23	4	20	31	.229	.261	.204	4.25	2.74
Jefferson, Michael	L-L	6-5	190	7-31-89	2	3	4.33	14	7	0	0	44	37	22	21	4	15	34	.226	.267	.210	7.01	3.09
Kilcrease, Robert	L-L	5-11	175	7-20-90	0	0	2.70	8	0	0	0	10	5	3	3	0	4	11	.139	.083	.167	9.90	3.60
Kingham, Nick	R-R	6-5	220	11-8-91	6	2	2.15	15	15	0	0	71	63	18	17	5	15	47	.238	.234	.240	5.96	1.90
Kleis, Kevin	R-R	6-8	225	8-31-91	1	1	4.26	17	0	0	0	32	36	20	15	0	14	15	.288	.321	.264	4.26	3.98
Lopez, Cesar	R-R	6-3	210	12-3-90	0	0	13.50	1	0	0	0	2	4	3	3	1	0	1	.444	.500	.400	4.50	0.00
Mateo, Diomedes	L-L	6-2	180	10-26-89	0	0	0.00	1	0	0	0	1	0	0	0	0	0	2	.000	.000	.000	18.00	0.00
Montero, Joan	R-R	6-0	186	10-26-88	0	1	8.06	17	0	0	1	26	39	25	23	1	21	21	.345	.366	.333	7.36	7.36
Payne, Vince	R-R	6-4	175	12-19-90	2	1	5.20	15	0	0	1	28	29	17	16	1	11	21	.271	.295	.254	6.83	3.58
Poytress, Josh	R-L	6-2	185	7-20-90	4	3	4.28	17	1	0	2	34	34	19	16	3	10	29	.262	.279	.253	7.75	2.67
Rodriguez, Joely	L-L	6-1	175	11-14-91	0	1	5.40	2	1	0	0	5	12	5	3	0	1	3	.444	.000	.500	5.40	1.80
Singh, Rinku	L-L	6-2	190	8-8-88	0	2	2.16	4	0	0	0	8	10	4	2	0	1	7	.278	.333	.200	7.56	1.08
Stevenson, Trent	L-R	6-6	175	6-1-90	0	4	5.80	7	0	0	0	36	53	23	23	2	3	12	.349	.311	.374	3.03	0.76
Weidman, Bryce	R-R	6-4	210	12-28-90	1	1	8.25	5	1	0	0	12	18	13	11	2	4	5	.340	.227	.433	3.75	3.00

Fielding

Catcher	PCT	G	PO	A	E	DP	PB
Gonzalez	.960	29	168	26	8	2	7
Gourley	1.000	1	5	1	0	0	
Skirving	.986	22	130	15	2	3	0
Trent	.978	25	120	13	3	2	8

First Base	PCT	G	PO	A	E	DP
Dickerson	.982	34	309	17	6	21
Gourley	1.000	3	24	0	0	1
Lashmet	.992	15	114	8	1	11
Nowlin	.872	4	29	5	5	4
Osuna	.909	1	10	0	1	0
Skirving	1.000	18	160	12	0	8
Trinidad	.971	4	30	3	1	2

Second Base	PCT	G	PO	A	E	DP
Bishop	.923	12	20	28	4	5

	PCT	G	PO	A	E	DP
Gamache	.923	9	15	21	3	3
Gourley	.976	20	29	51	2	11
Hanson	1.000	3	3	7	0	1
Ponce	.800	2	3	1	1	0
Sharp	1.000	5	8	13	0	1
Singer	.975	32	66	91	4	20

Third Base	PCT	G	PO	A	E	DP
Bishop	.600	1	0	3	2	0
Freeman	.875	2	2	5	1	1
Gamache	.813	8	2	11	3	0
Gourley	.850	18	12	22	6	1
Lashmet	.927	45	37	77	9	7
Ponce	.800	1	1	3	1	1
Sharp	.875	6	2	12	2	0

Shortstop	PCT	G	PO	A	E	DP
Ponce	.955	42	61	129	9	24
Sharp	.935	7	15	14	2	5
Singer	.923	26	40	68	9	7

Outfield	PCT	G	PO	A	E	DP
Bencsko	1.000	24	40	1	0	0
Cayones	.917	8	11	0	1	0
Freeman	1.000	45	114	5	0	2
Fuselier	1.000	47	98	6	0	3
Garcia	1.000	1	5	0	0	0
Jones	.963	12	26	0	1	0
Lewis	.993	59	140	6	1	4
Mesa	.925	20	32	5	3	1
Nowlin	1.000	1	3	0	0	0
Polanco	.500	2	1	0	1	0
Sosa	.965	22	55	0	2	0

GCL PIRATES

GULF COAST LEAGUE

ROOKIE

Batting	B-T	HT	WT	DOB	AVG	vLH	vRH	G	AB	R	H	2B	3B	HR	RBI	BB	HBP	SH	SF	SO	SB	CS	SLG	OBP
Alvarez, Pedro	L-R	6-3	235	2-6-87	.000	.000	.000	1	1	0	0	0	0	0	0	0	0	0	0	0	0	0	.000	.000
Apomte, Carlos	B-R	5-11	135	2-9-91	.262	.300	.255	28	65	16	17	5	0	0	8	15	3	0	2	11	9	2	.338	.412
Barrios, Jonathan	B-R	5-11	179	12-1-91	.299	.350	.286	25	97	20	29	4	3	1	11	11	2	0	0	24	8	1	.433	.382
Bishop, Jorge	R-R	5-10	152	3-12-91	.186	.071	.208	26	86	12	16	2	0	1	11	9	1	0	1	9	1	3	.244	.268
Carvajal, Jodaneli	R-R	5-9	145	4-20-92	.268	.286	.265	50	194	44	52	8	3	0	12	16	2	0	1	25	15	1	.340	.329
Cayones, Exicardo	L-L	6-0	183	10-9-91	.293	.200	.306	27	82	14	24	5	3	0	12	11	2	0	0	21	2	3	.427	.389
Chi, Ping-Hung	L-R	5-7	145	7-1-91	.200	.500	.000	3	5	3	1	0	0	0	0	4	0	0	0	1	0	0	.200	.556
Child, Dylan	R-R	6-1	181	2-21-91	.234	.231	.235	20	47	5	11	0	0	0	5	2	2	0	1	10	0	1	.234	.288
Clement, Jeff	L-R	6-1	225	8-21-83	.257	.500	.242	9	35	4	9	4	0	0	7	3	0	0	1	7	0	0	.371	.308
Cornelissen, Daan	L-R	6-2	194	7-6-91	.125	.000	.125	6	16	1	2	0	0	0	1	1	0	0	0	7	1	0	.125	.176
Cunningham, Jarek	R-R	6-1	195	12-25-89	.400	.000	.400	2	5	2	2	0	0	0	0	0	2	0	0	0	0	0	.400	.571
Farrell, Jeremy	R-R	6-3	200	11-11-86	.143	.000	.143	4	14	2	2	0	0	0	2	2	1	0	1	5	1	0	.143	.278
Gamache, Daniel	L-R	5-11	190	11-20-90	.350	.000	.389	6	20	6	7	0	0	0	4	3	1	0	1	5	0	0	.350	.440
Garcia, Willy	R-R	6-3	177	9-4-92	.266	.241	.270	47	177	26	47	9	4	5	35	11	6	0	4	49	7	5	.446	.323
Hanson, Alen	B-R	5-11	152	10-22-92	.263	.259	.263	52	198	42	52	13	7	2	35	21	7	0	1	34	24	6	.429	.352
Hornback, Ryan	R-R	6-1	180	7-19-91	.221	.250	.217	25	77	13	17	3	1	0	7	9	0	0	0	8	1	1	.286	.302
Jaramillo, Jason	B-R	6-0	215	10-9-82	.192	.250	.182	7	26	6	5	3	0	0	4	4	1	0	0	8	0	0	.308	.323
Jones, Rodarrick	R-R	6-0	195	7-31-90	.500	1.000	.455	4	12	5	6	0	1	2	6	4	0	0	0	2	0	0	1.167	.625
Lakind, Jared	L-L	6-2	195	3-9-92	.148	.100	.159	34	108	15	16	3	0	4	20	17	1	0	3	43	1	1	.287	.264
Myles, Candon	L-R	5-10	185	10-24-92	.167	.000	.200	2	6	0	1	0	0	0	0	0	0	0	0	1	0	0	.167	.167
Ngoepe, Gift	B-R	5-10	165	1-18-90	.167	.000	.167	2	6	0	1	0	0	0	0	0	1	0	0	1	0	0	.167	.286
Nivar, Gavi	R-R	6-4	185	9-16-89	.247	.067	.280	32	97	12	24	2	1	0	11	7	1	0	1	14	3	5	.289	.302
Osuna, Jose	R-R	6-2	213	12-12-92	.331	—	.389	48	178	28	59	14	3	4	32	18	3	0	1	21	3	2	.511	.400
Pearce, Steve	R-R	5-11	210	4-13-83	.667	.000	.667	1	3	0	2	0	0	0	2	1	0	0	0	1	0	0	.667	.750
Polanco, Gregory	L-L	6-4	170	9-14-91	.237	.278	.226	48	169	34	40	4	4	3	34	24	3	0	5	33	18	0	.361	.333
Ponce, Dimas	R-R	5-11	140	1-22-91	.296	.333	.278	9	27	5	8	0	0	0	3	6	2	0	0	5	0	0	.296	.457
Schoenfeld, Joey	R-R	6-2	187	6-11-91	.190	.000	.235	7	21	1	4	0	0	0	6	2	2	0	1	7	1	0	.190	.308
Schwind, Jonathan	R-R	6-0	185	5-30-90	.347	.444	.330	38	124	31	43	14	2	4	25	13	12	0	0	24	4	1	.589	.456
Sosa, Junior	L-L	5-10	139	10-3-90	.238	.300	.219	15	42	7	10	0	0	1	5	0	0	0	6	5	2	.238	.319
Urena, Luis	R-R	6-5	198	8-21-92	.235	.375	.203	30	85	10	20	5	3	0	10	15	0	0	0	31	4	4	.365	.350

Pitching	B-T	HT	WT	DOB	W	L	ERA	G	GS	CG	SV	IP	H	R	ER	HR	BB	SO	AVG	vLH	vRH	K/9	BB/9
Almonte, Brayan	R-R	6-7	188	10-9-91	0	0	12.46	15	0	0	0	17	23	25	24	3	22	11	.319	.100	.404	5.71	11.42
Burnette, Jake	R-R	6-4	180	8-10-92	0	0	0.00	1	0	0	0	1	1	1	0	0	1	1	.250	.500	.000	9.00	9.00
Campos, Fraylin	R-R	5-11	170	1-9-94	1	1	2.14	12	0	0	3	21	16	5	5	1	7	10	.213	.200	.220	4.29	3.00
Castro, Orlando	L-L	5-11	194	3-17-92	2	0	0.72	5	5	0	0	25	19	3	2	0	2	22	.209	.333	.195	7.92	0.72
Creasy, Jason	R-R	6-4	185	5-13-92	0	0	1.69	3	2	0	0	5	7	3	1	0	3	3	.292	.111	.400	5.06	5.06
Dodson, Zack	L-L	6-2	190	7-23-90	0	1	4.15	3	3	0	0	9	8	5	4	1	3	7	.235	.333	.200	7.27	3.12
Heredia, Luis	R-R	6-6	205	8-10-94	1	2	4.75	12	11	0	0	30	28	16	16	3	19	23	.257	.265	.250	6.82	5.64
Hernandez, Jimy	R-R	6-2	209	5-22-92	3	2	6.16	16	1	0	1	31	38	25	21	3	12	19	.297	.261	.317	5.58	3.52
Herrand, Yhonatan	R-R	6-5	230	9-11-91	0	1	7.94	9	0	0	0	11	9	10	10	0	10	10	.231	.071	.320	7.94	7.94
Inman, Jeff	R-R	6-3	180	11-24-87	0	0	0.00	3	0	0	0	3	0	0	0	0	1	2	.000	.000	.000	6.00	3.00
Jagoditsh, David	B-R	6-7	230	9-4-90	1	0	11.12	6	1	0	0	6	8	8	8	0	7	6	.261	.222	.286	12.71	9.53
Kilcrease, Robert	L-L	5-11	175	3-14-89	1	2	3.75	12	0	0	0	24	24	12	10	0	7	18	.264	.350	.239	6.75	2.63
Lee, Wilson	L-R	6-1	180	12-12-91	1	1	3.89	16	5	0	2	35	36	17	15	7	8	23	.265	.333	.252	5.97	2.08
Lodge, Jackson	L-L	6-1	160	10-12-93	0	2	6.75	16	1	0	0	29	35	24	22	3	3	18	.289	.250	.297	5.52	0.92
Lopez, Cesar	R-R	6-3	210	12-3-90	0	2	5.85	7	7	0	0	20	25	13	13	2	5	14	.300	.222	.319	6.30	2.25
Mateo, Diomedes	L-L	6-2	180	10-26-89	3	2	5.36	15	2	0	0	42	46	28	25	3	16	33	.286	.237	.301	7.07	3.43
Neverauskas, Dovydas	R-R	6-3	175	1-14-93	3	1	3.24	10	2	0	0	25	22	12	9	3	14	18	.237	.286	.215	6.48	5.04
Parsons, Joe	R-R	6-0	201	5-29-89	1	5	5.33	18	0	0	2	25	30	19	15	4	8	19	.294	.314	.284	6.75	2.84
Pevny, Logan	R-R	6-3	190	1-13-92	7	1	4.28	16	3	0	0	40	44	26	19	4	13	23	.270	.283	.264	5.18	2.93
Richardson, Cristopher	L-L	6-0	184	5-8-92	1	0	0.00	3	0	0	0	9	8	1	0	0	4	4	.242	.000	.308	4.15	4.15

Pitching

Pitching	B-T	HT	WT	DOB	W	L	ERA	G	GS	CG	SV	IP	H	R	ER	HR	BB	SO	AVG	vLH	vRH	K/9	BB/9
Sanchez, Isaac	R-R	6-0	170	10-14-92	4	0	4.06	15	1	0	1	31	30	17	14	1	17	20	.254	.316	.225	5.81	4.94
Singh, Rinku	L-L	6-2	190	8-8-88	1	0	0.00	1	0	0	0	4	1	0	0	0	0	5	.077	.000	.091	11.25	0.00
Trepagnier, Bryton	R-R	6-5	180	9-18-91	1	3	6.04	12	3	0	0	28	36	25	19	3	11	14	.308	.298	.314	4.45	3.49
Veal, Donald	L-L	6-4	240	9-18-84	0	0	5.40	1	1	0	0	2	1	1	1	0	2	3	.167	.000	.167	16.20	10.80
Weidman, Bryce	R-R	6-4	210	12-28-90	1	2	3.89	9	9	0	0	37	37	18	16	3	5	25	.266	.189	.294	6.08	1.22

Fielding

Catcher	PCT	G	PO	A	E	DP	PB
Child	.974	16	66	8	2	0	3
Hornback	.994	25	141	17	1	0	6
Jaramillo	.964	4	25	2	1	1	0
Schoenfeld	1.000	6	40	3	0	0	3
Schwind	.951	20	101	16	6	0	7

First Base	PCT	G	PO	A	E	DP
Child	1.000	2	15	3	0	1
Clement	1.000	4	25	1	0	1
Cornelissen	1.000	6	38	3	0	6
Lakind	.978	33	246	15	6	17
Osuna	.989	20	177	11	2	20

Second Base	PCT	G	PO	A	E	DP
Apomte	.974	11	19	19	1	5
Barrios	.971	6	9	25	1	5
Bishop	1.000	4	9	11	0	2
Carvajal	.967	31	68	79	5	15

Third Base	PCT	G	PO	A	E	DP
Cunningham	1.000	1	1	2	0	0
Hanson	.981	13	26	25	1	10
Ponce	1.000	2	2	3	0	2
Schoenfeld	1.000	1	0	1	0	1
Alvarez	.000	1	0	0	0	0
Apomte	.879	16	7	22	4	1
Barrios	.944	17	18	50	4	4
Bishop	.942	20	18	47	4	2
Farrell	1.000	2	1	3	0	1
Gamache	.625	3	5	0	3	0
Pearce	.500	1	1	0	1	0
Ponce	.818	5	4	5	2	0
Schwind	.923	3	4	8	1	2

Shortstop	PCT	G	PO	A	E	DP
Apomte	1.000	1	1	1	0	0
Barrios	1.000	2	3	3	0	2

Outfield	PCT	G	PO	A	E	DP
Bishop	1.000	2	0	3	0	1
Carvajal	.904	17	42	43	9	9
Hanson	.937	39	66	98	11	17
Ngoepe	1.000	1	0	5	0	1
Ponce	.923	4	6	6	1	2
Cayones	1.000	22	25	1	0	0
Chi	1.000	2	1	1	0	1
Garcia	.955	45	97	8	5	2
Jones	1.000	2	1	0	0	0
Myles	1.000	2	3	1	0	0
Nivar	.950	28	36	2	2	1
Osuna	.968	19	28	2	1	0
Polanco	.978	44	123	8	3	4
Sosa	.967	12	28	1	1	0
Urena	.958	26	45	1	2	0

DSL PIRATES

DOMINICAN SUMMER LEAGUE

ROOKIE

Batting	B-T	HT	WT	DOB	AVG	vLH	vRH	G	AB	R	H	2B	3B	HR	RBI	BB	HBP	SH	SF	SO	SB	CS	SLG	OBP
Adames, Yunerky	L-L	6-1	200	8-26-90	.176	.067	.208	24	68	12	12	0	1	0	2	13	3	0	0	14	4	1	.206	.333
Aquiles, Yunior	R-R	6-3	185	11-11-93	.125	.222	.097	27	40	6	5	1	0	0	4	8	1	0	1	18	2	0	.150	.280
Arribas, Danny	R-R	6-0	185	9-30-92	.200	.189	.205	48	125	16	25	5	0	0	12	13	3	0	1	29	1	4	.240	.289
De Aza, Miguel	L-L	6-0	170	11-14-92	.211	.111	.245	29	71	4	15	1	1	0	5	9	4	0	2	19	0	3	.254	.326
Espinal, Edwin	R-R	6-3	210	1-23-94	.269	.409	.233	35	108	8	29	9	0	0	19	20	1	0	2	10	3	2	.352	.382
Fortunato, Raul	R-R	6-2	190	9-5-90	.324	.343	.316	66	244	53	79	10	5	7	32	30	6	0	1	49	34	11	.492	.409
Garcia, Deybi	R-R	5-11	185	2-11-92	.313	.375	.292	15	32	7	10	2	0	0	3	5	3	0	0	4	1	0	.375	.450
Gerald, Yefaine	R-R	6-4	186	6-9-90	.225	.215	.230	62	204	35	46	10	1	4	32	31	5	0	3	54	13	9	.343	.337
Goris, Diego	R-R	6-2	165	12-8-90	.350	.342	.352	68	266	53	93	20	4	5	46	15	3	0	3	28	15	3	.511	.387
Jaquez, Yeffrey	R-R	6-0	180	10-8-92	.115	.500	.045	12	26	2	3	0	0	1	4	5	1	0	0	6	0	0	.231	.281
Jimenez, Jhoanel	B-R	5-11	185	6-19-90	.313	.182	.381	38	64	15	20	5	0	1	10	16	3	0	2	13	3	2	.438	.459
Lopez, Francis	R-R	6-2	200	6-22-92	.000	.000	.000	3	5	0	0	0	0	0	1	0	0	0	0	2	0	0	.000	.000
Ortiz, Jose	R-R	6-0	180	9-15-89	.209	.325	.147	38	115	18	24	6	0	3	25	13	6	0	4	19	0	1	.339	.312
Pena, Ramses	B-R	5-10	152	10-9-92	.174	.108	.198	55	138	26	24	2	0	0	10	24	1	0	2	38	16	5	.188	.297
Polanco, Yomifer	R-R	6-1	187	2-15-93	.225	.071	.263	27	71	7	16	1	0	0	7	8	6	0	0	18	1	2	.239	.353
Polonia, Rodney	L-R	5-10	160	9-19-92	.182	.200	.174	34	66	7	12	3	0	0	7	5	1	0	1	10	0	2	.227	.247
Reyes, Patrick	R-R	6-0	190	9-11-92	.211	.250	.200	10	19	0	4	1	0	0	0	1	0	0	0	6	0	0	.263	.250
Rivera, Maximo	R-R	5-11	182	12-22-92	.215	.235	.208	64	200	40	43	7	2	0	7	29	24	3	0	5	47	16	9	.375	.302
Valdez, Robertson	R-R	6-0	204	10-6-92	.160	.087	.190	29	81	10	13	4	0	0	4	8	3	0	0	20	0	2	.210	.261
Vasquez, Jesus	R-R	6-2	180	12-10-91	.324	.333	.320	66	222	48	72	20	1	11	53	41	7	0	6	58	21	13	.572	.435

Pitching	B-T	HT	WT	DOB	W	L	ERA	G	GS	CG	SV	IP	H	R	ER	HR	BB	SO	AVG	vLH	vRH	K/9	BB/9
Almonte, Brayan	R-R	6-7	188	10-9-91	0	0	7.94	3	2	0	0	6	6	6	5	0	8	5	.261	1.000	.190	7.94	12.71
Baez, Luis	R-R	6-2	185	11-29-89	0	0	5.40	6	0	0	0	8	6	7	5	0	7	5	.188	.000	.207	5.40	7.56
Batis, Raul	L-L	6-1	170	3-5-89	1	2	3.79	12	2	0	0	36	33	19	15	1	16	31	.241	.000	.248	7.82	4.04
Berroa, Javier	R-R	5-11	180	8-5-87	1	1	1.52	15	0	0	2	30	23	9	5	0	14	32	.217	.200	.221	9.71	4.25
Cadet, Martires	L-L	6-2	170	5-9-91	2	2	1.22	12	10	1	0	37	27	10	5	0	23	43	.196	.200	.195	10.46	5.59
De Leon, Christopher	R-R	6-0	158	8-2-92	4	4	2.44	12	9	0	1	48	36	16	13	0	19	38	.205	.235	.192	7.13	3.56
Del Rosario, Mervin	L-L	6-3	190	3-15-92	6	2	3.53	16	9	0	2	51	49	26	20	3	20	19	.253	.222	.254	3.35	3.53
Diaz, Axel	R-R	6-2	170	3-14-91	1	0	18.00	2	0	0	0	1	2	2	2	0	1	1	.000	.000	.000	9.00	9.00
Garcia, Jose	R-R	6-4	180	5-25-88	2	0	4.26	4	0	0	0	6	5	4	3	1	3	9	.208	.000	.250	12.79	4.26
Grullon, Adrian	R-R	6-0	180	9-17-92	0	1	5.40	3	1	0	0	5	6	3	3	2	4	4	.300	.250	.313	7.20	7.20
Henriquez, Cristian	L-L	6-0	175	6-20-92	4	3	4.62	15	1	0	0	37	43	22	19	0	17	26	.293	.200	.296	6.32	4.14
Hernandez, Jimy	R-R	6-2	209	5-22-92	0	1	9.72	3	3	0	0	8	14	11	9	0	5	6	.368	.571	.323	6.48	5.40
Jimenez, Antonio	R-R	6-0	175	3-1-91	0	0	4.91	3	0	0	0	4	1	3	2	0	5	6	.077	.000	.111	14.73	12.27
Lopez, Jovany	L-L	5-10	155	3-11-91	1	1	0.00	2	0	0	0	4	1	2	0	0	1	6	.083	.000	.100	13.50	2.25
Lorenzo, Arquimedes	R-R	6-2	190	5-29-91	0	0	6.00	4	1	0	0	9	15	10	6	3	7	6	.333	.000	.366	6.00	7.00
Mateo, Diomedes	L-L	6-2	180	10-26-89	0	0	4.91	3	0	0	0	4	6	7	4	0	8	6	.222	.000	.231	7.36	9.82
Mendoza, Juan	R-R	6-0	220	1-11-86	2	1	5.12	18	0	0	2	32	30	21	18	1	22	21	.248	.250	.248	5.97	6.25
Merejo, Aneudy	R-R	5-10	155	11-9-90	4	1	1.80	26	0	0	14	35	26	10	7	1	11	37	.205	.200	.206	9.51	2.83
Montero, Yunior	R-R	6-4	175	8-8-93	1	0	0.00	1	1	0	0	5	2	0	0	0	1	6	.118	.200	.000	7.20	1.80
Perez, Clario	R-R	6-1	185	8-30-92	3	2	2.12	14	13	0	0	68	57	21	16	1	15	31	.225	.286	.202	4.10	1.99
Perez, Ricky	R-R	6-3	205	5-31-90	1	0	4.74	6	5	0	0	19	21	11	10	2	7	11	.276	.318	.259	5.21	3.32
Pimentel, Cesilio	L-L	6-2	185	1-5-93	1	1	2.31	7	3	0	0	23	20	11	6	0	7	31	.211	.500	.204	11.96	2.70
Regalado, Jose	R-R	6-3	180	11-19-91	1	2	1.80	4	0	0	0	5	6	3	1	0	2	5	.300	.000	.300	9.00	3.60

Pitching

Pitching	B-T	HT	WT	DOB	W	L	ERA	G	GS	CG	SV	IP	H	R	ER	HR	BB	SO	AVG	vLH	vRH	K/9	BB/9
Richardson, Cristopher	L-L	6-0	184	5-8-92	0	1	3.24	3	0	0	0	8	5	3	3	1	8	6	.172	.000	.179	6.48	8.64
Rodriguez, Ramon	R-R	6-4	196	3-23-93	0	1	4.43	7	4	0	0	22	17	13	11	0	8	22	.195	.158	.206	8.87	3.22
Sanchez, Angel	L-L	6-7	190	3-2-93	0	0	13.50	12	1	0	0	13	22	26	19	3	22	4	.373	.000	.379	2.84	15.63
Sanchez, Isaac	R-R	6-0	170	10-14-92	0	0	16.20	1	0	0	0	2	2	3	3	0	2	1	.286	.000	.286	5.40	10.80
Santamaria, Joaquin	R-R	6-4	175	9-21-89	0	1	27.00	2	0	0	0	0	3	2	1	0	4	1	.750	.500	1.000	27.00	108.00
Santos, Luis	R-R	6-0	182	2-11-91	2	1	2.70	10	0	0	3	23	16	8	7	0	12	23	.205	.182	.209	8.87	4.63
Singh, Rinku	L-L	6-2	190	8-8-88	1	0	2.45	3	0	0	0	11	7	3	3	1	3	7	.194	.000	.212	5.73	2.45
Vilchez, Francisco	R-R	6-0	183	12-28-90	3	2	2.16	7	6	0	0	33	24	10	8	1	8	36	.205	.118	.220	9.72	2.16

Fielding

Catcher	PCT	G	PO	A	E	DP	PB
Arribas	.947	6	18	0	1	0	2
Garcia	.978	14	80	9	2	0	5
Jaquez	1.000	7	42	5	0	0	0
Jimenez	.983	36	142	27	3	0	3
Lopez	1.000	2	3	0	0	0	0
Ortiz	.979	26	160	24	4	4	10
Reyes	.962	10	42	8	2	0	2

First Base	PCT	G	PO	A	E	DP
Adames	.978	22	170	10	4	13
Arribas	1.000	2	7	0	0	1
Espinal	.985	22	183	13	3	18
Goris	.961	11	70	3	3	2
Jaquez	.889	3	16	0	2	1
Ortiz	1.000	1	3	0	0	0

Valdez	.974	19	141	7	4	11

Second Base	PCT	G	PO	A	E	DP
Arribas	.909	5	4	6	1	2
Goris	.989	23	51	42	1	13
Jimenez	1.000	1	1	0	0	0
Pena	.957	15	24	21	2	5
Polonia	.895	29	34	43	9	4
Rivera	.929	17	24	28	4	5
Valdez	1.000	1	1	2	0	0

Third Base	PCT	G	PO	A	E	DP
Arribas	.891	33	34	64	12	7
Espinal	.000	1	0	0	0	0
Goris	.957	12	14	30	2	5
Jaquez	1.000	1	1	2	0	0

Pena	.000	1	0	0	0	0
Rivera	.875	32	18	52	10	3
Valdez	.900	5	2	7	1	3

Shortstop	PCT	G	PO	A	E	DP
Goris	.944	28	38	80	7	10
Pena	.857	38	49	71	20	11
Rivera	.872	13	15	19	5	1

Outfield	PCT	G	PO	A	E	DP
Aquiles	1.000	12	11	1	0	0
De Aza	.875	10	7	0	1	0
Fortunato	.992	65	126	4	1	3
Gerald	.991	60	102	6	1	0
Polanco	1.000	16	28	2	0	2
Vasquez	.952	65	95	5	5	0

VSL PIRATES   ROOKIE
VENEZUELAN SUMMER LEAGUE

Batting	B-T	HT	WT	DOB	AVG	vLH	vRH	G	AB	R	H	2B	3B	HR	RBI	BB	HBP	SH	SF	SO	SB	CS	SLG	OBP
Aponte, Kelly	L-R	6-5	220	6-4-91	.286	.333	.279	61	189	35	54	10	2	6	30	34	4	0	5	42	4	1	.455	.397
Chourio, Bealyn	B-R	6-0	150	3-31-94	.200	.176	.205	32	90	15	18	3	0	0	8	14	1	0	2	16	2	8	.233	.308
Claudio, Anthony	R-R	6-1	180	12-1-92	.164	.154	.167	24	55	6	9	1	0	0	5	5	0	0	0	12	2	3	.182	.233
Elenes, Norman	L-R	6-0	175	7-10-92	.182	.000	.222	4	11	1	2	0	1	0	1	1	0	0	0	5	0	0	.364	.250
Esqueda, Carlos	R-R	5-8	135	12-6-91	.290	.286	.291	18	62	22	18	9	0	1	10	20	7	0	0	8	5	8	.484	.506
Galvez, Jordan	R-R	5-11	157	4-23-92	.308	.294	.310	65	208	34	64	12	1	0	26	20	5	0	5	22	11	12	.375	.374
Gimenez, Carlos	R-R	5-11	190	5-14-90	.247	.158	.276	27	77	9	19	5	0	2	16	5	6	0	2	6	1	4	.390	.333
Herrera, Dilson	R-R	5-10	150	3-3-94	.308	.459	.277	65	214	42	66	19	5	2	27	32	9	0	4	40	16	8	.472	.413
Lugo, Jose	R-R	6-1	200	6-19-90	.051	.000	.061	22	39	5	2	1	1	0	1	9	3	0	0	12	0	1	.128	.275
Marquez, Carlos	L-R	6-2	180	4-29-93	.204	.200	.205	22	54	8	11	1	0	0	11	5	1	0	1	15	2	1	.259	.279
Montilla, Ulises	R-R	5-11	170	5-12-92	.364	.333	.370	70	253	39	92	21	3	3	47	33	4	0	4	17	11	8	.506	.439
Morales, Tomas	R-R	6-0	190	7-30-91	.286	.333	.250	4	7	0	2	0	0	0	1	0	0	0	0	2	2	.286	.286
Moreno, Manuel	R-R	6-0	165	2-18-92	.177	.091	.203	30	96	8	17	2	0	1	8	5	3	0	0	11	0	4	.229	.240
Munoz, Carlos	L-L	5-11	225	6-29-94	.190	.000	.190	9	21	0	4	1	0	0	1	0	1	0	0	2	0	0	.238	.227
Munoz, Edgard	B-R	5-8	150	10-31-91	.360	.308	.370	52	164	42	59	8	1	1	17	23	9	0	0	14	20	15	.439	.464
Rangel, Eduardo	R-R	6-2	188	1-19-93	.244	.200	.254	50	164	19	40	5	0	2	19	14	4	0	0	34	2	5	.311	.319
Roman, Jose	L-L	6-1	200	12-27-90	.317	.175	.345	68	243	39	77	17	0	5	46	34	2	0	1	33	6	3	.449	.404
Salazar, Alexis	R-R	5-11	185	1-26-91	.176	.167	.179	15	34	4	6	2	1	0	3	9	0	0	1	4	0	2	.294	.341
Salazar, Jose	R-R	6-2	174	7-11-94	.222	.250	.216	57	167	38	37	5	0	1	16	17	6	0	3	26	3	4	.269	.311

Pitching	B-T	HT	WT	DOB	W	L	ERA	G	GS	CG	SV	IP	H	R	ER	HR	BB	SO	AVG	vLH	vRH	K/9	BB/9
Barraza, Jesus	R-R	5-10	150	11-3-90	1	1	5.02	22	0	0	7	29	33	20	16	2	9	24	.280	.282	.278	7.53	2.83
Calderin, Oscar	L-L	6-4	175	2-22-91	2	2	4.19	13	4	0	0	34	42	30	16	1	9	14	.282	.174	.302	3.67	2.36
Campos, Luis	R-R	6-0	188	8-28-90	1	3	5.26	17	9	0	1	51	55	33	30	1	30	28	.288	.260	.298	4.91	5.26
Espinoza, Roberto	R-R	6-1	189	5-7-92	4	3	4.37	15	13	0	1	68	67	38	33	3	22	61	.250	.296	.230	8.07	2.91
Gutierrez, Alexander	L-L	6-3	213	3-25-93	1	1	5.17	13	8	0	0	31	31	21	18	2	33	8	.265	.200	.278	2.30	9.48
Lopez, Jovany	L-L	5-10	155	3-11-91	1	3	2.00	13	0	0	0	18	18	5	4	1	6	14	.273	.375	.240	7.00	3.00
Marrujo, Jose	R-R	5-10	189	9-21-92	5	1	1.20	20	0	0	5	45	33	7	6	1	7	40	.208	.302	.172	8.00	1.40
Mendoza, Andres	R-R	6-2	220	6-3-92	1	0	5.08	16	0	0	0	34	33	24	19	1	16	24	.260	.270	.256	6.42	4.28
Mendoza, Jorge	R-R	6-2	160	6-27-94	0	0	9.00	1	0	0	0	1	2	1	1	0	0	1	.500	.000	.667	9.00	0.00
Montilla, Richard	R-R	6-0	143	1-10-91	0	1	31.50	2	0	0	0	2	7	7	7	0	2	2	.643	.571	.714	9.00	9.00
Ortiz, Luis	R-R	6-2	170	12-20-91	6	2	3.56	18	0	0	1	43	31	19	17	4	11	22	.209	.156	.224	4.60	2.30
Otamendi, Andy	L-L	6-0	163	5-15-93	2	1	3.15	11	9	0	0	40	45	20	14	0	12	28	.283	.188	.307	6.30	2.70
Paredes, Jesus	L-L	6-2	162	1-18-93	0	1	7.04	12	0	0	0	15	24	12	12	4	14	4	.375	.375	.375	2.35	8.22
Rico, Luis	L-L	6-1	180	11-29-93	1	1	3.76	9	8	0	0	26	28	12	11	2	11	23	.286	.250	.289	7.86	3.76
Rocha, Oderman	R-R	6-3	165	11-7-92	4	2	3.29	14	13	0	0	55	44	30	20	0	26	52	.217	.222	.215	8.56	4.28
Ruiz, Carlos	R-R	6-2	169	4-13-91	4	3	2.08	18	0	0	1	39	28	17	9	0	18	20	.194	.279	.158	4.62	4.15
Urbina, Dan	R-R	6-3	158	11-27-93	1	1	7.17	9	3	0	0	21	25	19	17	1	13	12	.309	.450	.262	5.06	5.48
Vilchez, Francisco	R-R	6-0	183	12-28-90	5	2	4.78	8	2	0	0	26	34	15	14	0	8	20	.309	.424	.260	6.84	2.73
Vivas, Julio	R-R	6-2	227	10-1-93	1	4	5.55	17	3	0	0	36	41	23	22	0	11	18	.289	.225	.314	4.54	2.78

Fielding

Catcher	PCT	G	PO	A	E	DP	PB
Elenes	.955	4	18	3	1	0	2

Lugo	.988	18	67	14	1	0	3
Marquez	.969	17	87	6	3	0	1

Morales	1.000	4	10	1	0	0	2
Rangel	.986	45	241	34	4	2	17

First Base	PCT	G	PO	A	E	DP
Aponte	.977	33	288	16	7	22
Galvez	.984	11	56	4	1	3
Gimenez	.667	2	2	0	1	0
Lugo	1.000	2	13	0	0	1
Marquez	1.000	1	3	0	0	0
Munoz	1.000	1	1	0	0	0
Rangel	1.000	2	20	1	0	2
Roman	.994	34	333	21	2	24

Second Base	PCT	G	PO	A	E	DP
Chourio	1.000	3	1	5	0	0
Esqueda	.945	9	22	30	3	7
Galvez	.957	28	60	75	6	17
Gimenez	1.000	1	1	0	0	0
Herrera	.000	2	0	0	0	0

	PCT	G	PO	A	E	DP
Montilla	.982	36	75	88	3	17
Salazar	1.000	5	9	12	0	4

Third Base	PCT	G	PO	A	E	DP
Chourio	.000	1	0	0	0	0
Esqueda	.600	1	1	2	2	0
Galvez	.889	8	8	16	3	1
Gimenez	1.000	2	0	1	0	0
Herrera	.882	59	48	146	26	11
Munoz	1.000	1	0	2	0	0
Salazar	1.000	11	4	27	0	4

Shortstop	PCT	G	PO	A	E	DP
Chourio	.938	29	35	87	8	11
Claudio	1.000	1	1	3	0	0
Esqueda	.921	7	10	25	3	1

	PCT	G	PO	A	E	DP
Gimenez	.944	4	6	11	1	2
Munoz	1.000	1	0	2	0	0
Salazar	.938	41	55	112	11	19

Outfield	PCT	G	PO	A	E	DP
Claudio	.966	20	28	0	1	0
Esqueda	1.000	2	3	0	0	0
Galvez	.889	22	22	2	3	0
Gimenez	1.000	20	18	2	0	0
Montilla	.982	33	51	5	1	2
Moreno	.945	30	50	2	3	1
Munoz	.945	47	67	2	4	0
Roman	1.000	4	5	0	0	0
Salazar	.947	15	16	2	1	0
Sucre	.929	55	73	6	6	0

St. Louis Cardinals

SEASON IN A SENTENCE: Left behind in the National League Central by the streaking Brewers, the Cardinals rallied from 10½ games out in the wild-card race, going 18-8 in September, to pass the Braves on the final day of the season, then shocked the Phillies in the Division Series, beat the Brewers in the League Championship Series and overcome the Rangers in seven games for the franchise's 11th World Series championship.

HIGH POINT: It doesn't get more dramatic than Game Six of the 2011 World Series. The Cardinals were down to their last strike twice against the Rangers, in the ninth and 10th innings, but rallied to tie both times. Third baseman David Freese tied the game in the ninth with a two-run, two-out triple off closer Neftali Feliz, and won it in the 11th with a walkoff home run. Chris Carpenter and Freese led the way in Game Seven, a 6-2 victory.

LOW POINT: A 7-0 loss to the Pirates on Aug. 27 left St. Louis 10½ back of the Brewers in the NL Central, and 10 back of the Braves in the wild card.

NOTABLE ROOKIES: When healthy, Allen Craig mashed. He was especially valuable in the postseason, slugging .622 with four home runs, three in the World Series, and he saved a home run with a stellar catch in left field in Game Seven. Daniel Descalso was a valuable infield reserve, even playing some shortstop, while righthander Fernando Salas led the bullpen with 75 innings and 24 saves, though he lost his closer job by playoff time. Lance Lynn, a starter in the minors, pitched well out of the pen in the postseason.

KEY TRANSACTIONS: General manager John Mozielak reshaped his roster on the fly, trading Colby Rasmus to Toronto as part of a three-team deal that netted righties Edwin Jackson and Octavio Dotel and lefty Mark Rzepczynski. He got Rafael Furcal from the Dodgers to take over at shortstop, a sore spot in the season's first 100 games. When it was all over, La Russa announced his retirement, and Mozielak named former catcher Mike Matheny as La Russa's replacement.

DOWN ON THE FARM: St. Louis affiliates posted a .518 winning percentage, and two clubs—low Class A Quad Cities and Rookie-level Johnson City—won championships. Quad Cities outfielder Oscar Taveras won the Midwest League batting title, while righthanders Shelby Miller and Carlos Martinez gave the Cardinals one of the minors' best power-pitching duos.

OPENING DAY PAYROLL: $105,433,572 (11th)

ORGANIZATION LEADERS

BATTING		*Minimum 250 PA
MAJORS		
* AVG	Yadier Molina	.305
* OPS	Lance Berkman	.959
HR	Albert Pujols	37
RBI	Albert Pujols	99
MINORS		
* AVG	Oscar Taveras, Quad Cities	.386
* OBP	Matt Carpenter, Memphis	.417
* SLG	Matt Adams, Springfield	.566
R	Nick Stavinoha, Memphis	84
H	Zack Cox, Palm Beach/Springfield	158
TB	Matt Adams, Springfield	262
2B	Ryan Jackson, Springfield	34
3B	Virgil Hill, Quad Cities/Batavia	7
HR	Matt Adams, Springfield	32
RBI	Nick Stavinoha, Memphis	109
BB	Matt Carpenter, Memphis	84
SO	Xavier Scruggs, Palm Beach	125
SB	Adron Chambers, Memphis	22
	Robelys Reyes, DSL Cardinals	22
PITCHING		#Minimum 75 IP
MAJORS		
W	Kyle Lohse	14
# ERA	Fernando Salas	2.28
SO	Chris Carpenter	191
SV	Fernando Salas	24
MINORS		
W	Michael Blazek, Springfield/Memphis	13
	Anthony Ferrara, Quad Cities	13
L	Eric Fornataro, Palm Beach	13
	Jorge Rondon, Palm Beach/Springfield	13
# ERA	Boone Whiting, Quad Cities	2.41
G	Nick Greenwood, P.B./Memphis/Springfield	62
GS	Nick Additon, Springfield/Memphis	26
	Michael Blazek, Springfield/Memphis	26
SV	Victor Marte, Memphis	31
IP	John Gast, Palm Beach/Springfield	161.1
BB	Michael Blazek, Springfield/Memphis	73
SO	Shelby Miller, Palm Beach/Springfield	170
# AVG	Boone Whiting, Quad Cities	.191

General Manager: John Mozeliak. **Farm Director:** John Vuch. **Scouting Director:** Jeff Luhnow.

Class	Team	League	W	L	PCT	Finish	Manager(s)
Majors	St. Louis Cardinals	National	90	72	.556	4th (16)	Tony La Russa
Triple-A	Memphis Redbirds	Pacific Coast	77	66	.538	4th (16)	Chris Maloney
Double-A	Springfield Cardinals	Texas	62	78	.443	7th (8)	Ron Warner
High A	Palm Beach Cardinals	Florida State	68	70	.493	7th (12)	Luis Aguayo
Low A	Quad Cities River Bandits	Midwest	81	56	.591	2nd (16)	Johnny Rodriguez
Short-season	Batavia Muckdogs	New York-Penn	37	38	.493	8th (14)	Dann Bilardello
Rookie	Johnson City Cardinals	Appalachian	45	23	.662	1st (10)	Mike Shildt
Rookie	GCL Cardinals	Gulf Coast	31	24	.564	5th (15)	Steve Turco
Overall 2011 Minor League Record			401	355	.535	5th (30)	

ORGANIZATION STATISTICS

ST. LOUIS CARDINALS

NATIONAL LEAGUE

Batting	B-T	HT	WT	DOB	AVG	vLH	vRH	G	AB	R	H	2B	3B	HR	RBI	BB	HBP	SH	SF	SO	SB	CS	SLG	OBP
Berkman, Lance	B-L	6-1	220	2-10-76	.301	.277	.307	145	488	90	147	23	2	31	94	92	3	0	4	93	2	6	.547	.412
Brown, Andrew	R-R	6-0	185	9-10-84	.182	.167	.200	11	22	1	4	1	0	0	3	0	0	0	0	8	0	0	.227	.182
Carpenter, Matt	L-R	6-3	200	11-26-85	.067	.000	.071	7	15	0	1	1	0	0	0	4	0	0	0	4	0	0	.133	.263
Chambers, Adron	L-L	5-10	185	10-8-86	.375	.000	.375	18	8	2	3	0	1	0	4	0	0	0	0	1	0	0	.625	.375
Craig, Allen	R-R	6-2	210	7-18-84	.315	.313	.316	75	200	33	63	15	0	11	40	15	1	0	2	40	5	0	.555	.362
Cruz, Tony	R-R	5-11	205	8-18-86	.262	.269	.256	38	65	8	17	5	0	0	6	6	1	0	0	13	0	1	.338	.333
Descalso, Daniel	L-R	5-10	190	10-19-86	.264	.190	.280	148	326	35	86	20	3	1	28	33	3	1	3	65	2	2	.353	.334
Freese, David	R-R	6-2	220	4-28-83	.297	.347	.283	97	333	41	99	16	1	10	55	24	4	0	2	75	1	0	.441	.350
Furcal, Rafael	B-R	5-8	190	10-24-77	.255	.275	.250	50	196	29	50	11	0	7	16	17	1	0	1	18	4	2	.418	.316
2-team total (37 Los Angeles)					.231	—	—	87	333	44	77	15	0	8	28	28	4	0	1	39	9	5	.348	.298
Greene, Tyler	R-R	6-2	190	8-17-83	.212	.209	.213	58	104	22	22	5	0	1	11	13	4	0	0	31	11	0	.288	.322
Hamilton, Mark	L-L	6-4	220	7-29-84	.213	.182	.222	38	47	5	10	3	0	0	4	4	0	0	0	16	0	0	.277	.275
Holliday, Matt	R-R	6-4	235	1-15-80	.296	.256	.306	124	446	83	132	36	0	22	75	60	8	0	2	93	2	1	.525	.388
Jay, Jon	L-L	5-11	200	3-15-85	.297	.287	.299	159	455	56	135	24	2	10	37	28	7	0	4	81	6	7	.424	.344
Kozma, Pete	R-R	6-0	170	4-11-88	.176	.250	.111	16	17	2	3	1	0	0	1	4	0	0	0	4	0	0	.235	.333
Laird, Gerald	R-R	6-1	225	11-13-79	.232	.286	.222	37	95	11	22	7	1	1	12	9	1	0	1	19	1	1	.358	.302
Molina, Yadier	R-R	5-11	230	7-13-82	.305	.284	.311	139	475	55	145	32	1	14	65	33	1	0	4	44	4	5	.465	.349
Patterson, Corey	L-R	5-10	180	8-13-79	.157	.273	.125	44	51	5	8	4	0	0	3	2	0	0	0	12	0	1	.235	.189
Pujols, Albert	R-R	6-3	230	1-16-80	.299	.295	.300	147	579	105	173	29	0	37	99	61	4	0	7	58	9	1	.541	.366
Punto, Nick	B-R	5-9	190	11-8-77	.278	.273	.281	63	133	21	37	8	4	1	20	25	0	0	2	21	1	1	.421	.388
Rasmus, Colby	L-L	6-2	200	8-11-86	.246	.256	.242	94	338	61	83	14	6	11	40	45	0	0	2	77	5	2	.420	.332
Robinson, Shane	R-R	5-9	160	10-30-84	.000	.000	.000	9	7	0	0	0	0	0	0	1	0	0	0	2	0	0	.000	.125
Schumaker, Skip	L-R	5-10	195	2-3-80	.283	.250	.287	117	367	34	104	19	0	2	38	27	2	0	3	50	0	2	.351	.333
Theriot, Ryan	R-R	5-11	180	12-7-79	.271	.310	.256	132	442	46	120	26	1	1	47	29	4	0	2	41	4	6	.342	.321

Pitching	B-T	HT	WT	DOB	W	L	ERA	G	GS	CG	SV	IP	H	R	ER	HR	BB	SO	AVG	vLH	vRH	K/9	BB/9
Augenstein, Bryan	R-R	6-6	230	7-11-86	0	1	9.53	5	0	0	0	6	11	7	6	1	3	6	.407	.600	.294	9.53	4.76
Batista, Miguel	R-R	6-1	210	2-19-71	3	2	4.60	26	1	0	0	29	27	20	15	2	19	16	.241	.294	.218	4.91	5.83
2-team total (9 New York)					5	2	3.60	35	5	1	0	60	49	29	24	2	33	31	—	—	—	4.65	4.95
Boggs, Mitchell	R-R	6-4	215	2-15-84	2	3	3.56	51	0	0	4	61	62	27	24	4	21	48	.266	.247	.276	7.12	3.12
Carpenter, Chris	R-R	6-6	230	4-27-75	11	9	3.45	34	34	4	0	237	243	98	91	16	55	191	.264	.259	.268	7.24	2.09
Cleto, Maikel	R-R	6-3	235	5-1-89	0	0	12.46	3	0	0	0	4	7	6	6	2	4	6	.333	.364	.300	12.46	8.31
Dickson, Brandon	R-R	6-5	190	11-3-84	0	0	3.24	4	1	0	0	8	9	3	3	2	3	7	.290	.182	.350	7.56	3.24
Dotel, Octavio	R-R	6-0	220	11-25-73	3	3	3.28	29	0	0	2	25	16	10	9	1	5	32	.182	.235	.148	11.68	1.82
Franklin, Ryan	R-R	6-3	190	3-5-73	1	4	8.46	21	0	0	1	28	44	27	26	9	7	17	.367	.326	.392	5.53	2.28
Garcia, Jaime	L-L	6-2	215	7-8-86	13	7	3.56	32	32	2	0	195	207	100	77	15	50	156	.273	.308	.264	7.21	2.31
Jackson, Edwin	R-R	6-3	205	9-9-83	5	2	3.58	13	12	0	0	78	91	37	31	8	23	51	.300	.328	.283	5.88	2.65
Lohse, Kyle	R-R	6-2	210	10-4-78	14	8	3.39	30	30	1	0	188	178	80	71	16	42	111	.249	.249	.248	5.30	2.01
Lynn, Lance	R-R	6-5	250	5-12-87	1	1	3.12	18	2	0	1	35	25	12	12	3	11	40	.203	.229	.187	10.38	2.86
McClellan, Kyle	R-R	6-2	215	6-12-84	12	7	4.19	43	17	0	0	142	143	71	66	21	43	76	.260	.206	.297	4.83	2.73
Miller, Trever	R-L	6-3	200	5-29-73	0	1	4.02	39	0	0	1	16	19	7	7	1	10	9	.306	.233	.474	5.17	5.74
Motte, Jason	R-R	6-0	200	6-22-82	5	2	2.25	78	0	0	9	68	49	22	17	2	16	63	.202	.270	.162	8.34	2.12
Rhodes, Arthur	L-L	6-2	220	10-24-69	0	1	4.15	19	0	0	0	9	6	4	4	2	3	6	.207	.313	.077	6.23	3.12
Rzepczynski, Marc	L-L	6-1	205	8-29-85	0	3	3.97	28	0	0	0	23	22	11	10	1	11	28	.259	.171	.320	11.12	4.37
Salas, Fernando	R-R	6-2	200	5-30-85	5	6	2.28	68	0	0	24	75	50	20	19	7	21	75	.186	.214	.164	9.00	2.52
Sanchez, Eduardo	R-R	5-11	170	2-16-89	3	1	1.80	26	0	0	5	30	14	6	6	1	16	35	.144	.158	.136	10.50	4.80
Tallet, Brian	L-L	6-6	220	9-21-77	0	1	8.31	18	0	0	0	13	20	13	12	4	5	9	.339	.261	.389	6.23	3.46
Valdes, Raul	L-L	5-11	190	11-27-77	0	1	3.38	7	0	0	0	5	6	2	2	0	4	7	.273	.300	.250	11.81	6.75
Walters, P.J.	R-R	6-4	200	3-12-85	0	0	9.00	4	0	0	0	4	3	4	4	1	2	3	.188	.143	.222	6.75	4.50
Westbrook, Jake	R-R	6-3	215	9-29-77	12	9	4.66	33	33	0	0	183	208	103	95	16	73	104	.290	.260	.316	5.11	3.58

Fielding

Catcher	PCT	G	PO	A	E	DP	PB
Cruz	1.000	20	90	6	0	1	1
Laird	.985	31	182	12	3	1	3
Molina	.995	137	857	67	5	5	6

First Base	PCT	G	PO	A	E	DP
Berkman	.988	21	154	14	2	18

	PCT	G	PO	A	E	DP
Craig	1.000	2	6	0	0	0
Cruz	1.000	2	8	0	0	4
Freese	1.000	5	8	0	0	2
Hamilton	1.000	8	24	0	0	1
Laird	1.000	1	1	0	0	0
Molina	.750	2	3	0	1	0
Pujols	.992	146	1254	165	11	134

Second Base	PCT	G	PO	A	E	DP
Craig	1.000	8	7	10	0	1
Cruz	.000	1	0	0	0	0
Descalso	1.000	18	24	34	0	6
Greene	.950	25	18	39	3	8
Kozma	1.000	10	7	12	0	5
Punto	.987	45	58	91	2	26
Schumaker	.982	95	139	251	7	47
Theriot	.991	35	41	71	1	23

Third Base	PCT	G	PO	A	E	DP
Carpenter	1.000	5	1	12	0	0
Craig	1.000	2	0	2	0	0
Cruz	1.000	3	0	2	0	0
Descalso	.967	117	51	125	6	18
Freese	.941	88	33	159	12	23
Kozma	.000	1	0	0	0	0
Pujols	.824	7	2	12	3	2
Punto	.923	7	2	10	1	0

Shortstop	PCT	G	PO	A	E	DP
Descalso	.963	13	17	35	2	9
Furcal	.958	49	73	155	10	36
Greene	.965	20	13	42	2	7
Kozma	1.000	3	2	1	0	0
Punto	1.000	8	8	15	0	2
Theriot	.956	91	117	254	17	54

Outfield	PCT	G	PO	A	E	DP
Berkman	.980	126	194	4	4	2
Brown	1.000	7	10	0	0	0
Chambers	.875	11	7	0	1	0
Craig	1.000	48	74	3	0	0
Cruz	1.000	2	1	0	0	0
Greene	1.000	10	6	0	0	0
Hamilton	.000	2	0	0	0	0
Holliday	.985	115	196	4	3	0
Jay	.989	140	273	5	3	4
Patterson	.966	30	27	1	1	1
Rasmus	.987	92	223	4	3	0
Robinson	1.000	9	2	0	0	0
Schumaker	.958	40	22	1	1	0

MEMPHIS REDBIRDS

PACIFIC COAST LEAGUE

TRIPLE-A

Batting	B-T	HT	WT	DOB	AVG	vLH	vRH	G	AB	R	H	2B	3B	HR	RBI	BB	HBP	SH	SF	SO	SB	CS	SLG	OBP
Anderson, Bryan	L-R	6-1	200	12-16-86	.281	.230	.295	98	335	39	94	19	0	8	37	36	5	0	2	76	1	1	.409	.357
Brown, Andrew	R-R	6-0	185	9-10-84	.284	.343	.261	107	359	67	102	12	3	20	73	56	5	0	7	105	4	4	.501	.382
Bynum, Freddie	L-R	6-1	185	3-15-80	.248	.281	.237	75	226	30	56	11	2	3	21	16	1	0	1	49	4	1	.354	.299
Carpenter, Matt	L-R	6-3	200	11-26-85	.300	.336	.286	130	434	61	130	29	3	12	70	84	8	0	6	68	5	4	.463	.417
Chambers, Adron	L-L	5-10	185	10-8-86	.277	.274	.278	128	426	73	118	19	5	10	44	53	10	0	3	90	22	13	.415	.368
Craig, Allen	R-R	6-2	210	7-18-84	.286	.500	.200	10	35	9	10	2	1	1	5	3	1	0	0	3	0	0	.486	.359
Cruz, Tony	R-R	5-11	205	8-18-86	.262	.259	.264	45	149	13	39	5	1	4	25	11	1	0	1	31	0	1	.389	.315
Derba, Nick	R-R	5-10	190	9-9-85	.197	.192	.200	22	61	6	12	2	1	0	10	4	0	0	0	17	0	0	.262	.246
Freese, David	R-R	6-2	220	4-28-83	.231	.000	.231	4	13	1	3	1	0	0	1	1	0	0	0	3	0	0	.308	.286
Garcia, Jose	R-R	5-11	170	2-11-88	.333	.227	.435	18	45	10	15	3	0	0	5	5	0	0	0	7	2	2	.400	.400
Greene, Tyler	R-R	6-2	190	8-17-83	.323	.328	.321	66	254	53	82	19	2	14	43	37	8	0	2	75	19	2	.579	.422
Hamilton, Mark	L-L	6-4	220	7-29-84	.345	.373	.333	69	252	46	87	26	0	2	39	42	4	0	5	44	0	0	.472	.439
Hill, Steve	R-R	5-11	200	3-14-85	.294	.167	.364	6	17	3	5	0	0	3	6	2	0	0	0	5	0	0	.824	.368
Jones, Daryl	L-L	6-0	180	6-25-87	.250	.233	.256	53	120	18	30	7	1	3	15	23	2	0	0	39	2	3	.400	.379
Kozma, Pete	R-R	6-0	170	4-11-88	.214	.252	.196	112	398	48	85	17	2	3	47	36	3	0	6	91	2	2	.289	.280
Laird, Gerald	R-R	6-1	225	11-13-79	.429	.750	.000	2	7	3	3	1	0	0	1	2	0	0	0	1	0	0	.571	.556
Luna, Aaron	R-R	5-11	200	3-28-87	.266	.293	.243	71	203	36	54	7	0	10	33	19	11	0	4	49	5	0	.448	.354
Punto, Nick	B-R	5-9	190	11-8-77	.200	.400	.100	5	15	2	3	0	0	0	0	3	0	0	0	1	0	0	.200	.333
Rapoport, Jim	L-L	5-11	160	6-25-85	.252	.261	.249	76	261	36	66	4	1	3	19	46	2	0	0	31	1	4	.309	.368
Robinson, Shane	R-R	5-9	160	10-30-84	.299	.225	.323	43	167	35	50	8	3	4	23	19	1	0	4	16	9	1	.455	.366
Solano, Donovan	R-R	5-10	185	12-17-87	.284	.329	.260	81	229	22	65	21	1	1	23	19	1	0	4	35	2	0	.397	.336
Stavinoha, Nick	R-R	6-2	240	5-3-82	.270	.247	.280	133	533	84	144	30	1	28	109	44	5	0	4	100	5	1	.488	.329
Vazquez, Ramon	L-R	5-11	195	8-21-76	.275	.371	.240	40	131	21	36	6	0	0	17	18	0	0	0	28	1	1	.321	.362
3-team total (20 Las Vegas, 10 New Orleans)					.267	—	—	70	240	33	64	8	1	1	32	31	0	0	0	39	2	1	.321	.351

Pitching	B-T	HT	WT	DOB	W	L	ERA	G	GS	CG	SV	IP	H	R	ER	HR	BB	SO	AVG	vLH	vRH	K/9	BB/9
Additon, Nick	L-L	6-5	215	12-16-87	4	8	4.56	18	16	0	0	97	94	52	49	14	40	80	.260	.276	.255	7.45	3.72
Augenstein, Bryan	R-R	6-6	230	7-11-86	3	0	4.04	26	1	0	0	36	36	18	16	5	12	35	.250	.311	.205	8.83	3.03
Blazek, Michael	R-R	6-0	180	3-16-89	2	0	3.75	2	2	0	0	12	8	5	5	1	9	6	.205	.208	.200	4.50	6.75
Boggs, Mitchell	R-R	6-4	215	2-15-84	0	2	2.45	4	4	0	0	15	12	5	4	1	5	14	.226	.259	.192	8.59	3.07
Boyer, Blaine	R-R	6-3	245	7-11-81	0	2	13.50	4	4	0	0	16	34	26	24	5	9	5	.466	.486	.447	2.81	5.06
Broderick, Brian	R-R	6-5	205	9-1-86	7	7	5.04	22	15	0	0	91	121	56	51	11	21	45	.324	.316	.330	4.45	2.08
Buursma, Jason	R-R	6-3	200	9-9-85	0	0	3.78	15	0	0	0	17	19	8	7	1	13	5	.292	.483	.139	2.70	7.02
Cleto, Maikel	R-R	6-3	235	5-1-89	5	3	4.29	13	13	0	0	71	57	37	34	6	43	66	.218	.219	.218	8.33	5.43
Dickson, Brandon	R-R	6-5	190	11-3-84	8	9	3.95	26	25	1	0	157	169	75	69	22	32	124	.277	.302	.253	7.09	1.83
Fick, Chuckie	R-R	6-5	187	11-20-85	5	3	2.30	54	0	0	1	70	44	25	18	2	37	61	.180	.172	.186	7.81	4.73
Greenwood, Nick	R-L	6-1	180	9-28-87	0	0	9.00	1	0	0	0	2	4	2	2	0	0	2	.400	.333	.429	9.00	0.00
King, Blake	R-R	6-1	195	4-11-87	2	0	11.08	15	0	0	0	13	9	18	16	2	20	19	.188	.231	.136	13.15	13.85
Kopp, David	R-R	6-3	205	10-22-85	0	0	7.00	8	0	0	0	9	13	9	7	1	5	8	.342	.462	.280	8.00	5.00
Lynn, Lance	R-R	6-5	250	5-12-87	7	3	3.84	12	12	0	0	75	79	33	32	2	25	64	.279	.335	.205	7.68	3.00
Mahay, Ron	L-L	6-2	190	6-28-71	1	0	1.64	12	0	0	0	11	8	2	2	1	3	8	.205	.250	.158	6.55	2.45
2-team total (10 Reno)					1	2	5.48	22	0	0	0	21	24	16	13	3	10	16	—	—	—	6.75	4.22
Marte, Victor	R-R	6-2	255	11-8-80	2	4	1.44	55	0	0	31	62	47	13	10	5	20	52	.210	.216	.205	7.51	2.89
Ottavino, Adam	L-R	6-5	230	11-22-85	7	8	4.85	26	25	0	0	141	154	85	76	14	71	120	.284	.304	.267	7.66	4.53
Parise, Pete	R-R	6-1	180	12-5-84	2	1	3.97	40	0	0	1	57	55	26	25	8	16	32	.253	.247	.257	5.08	2.54
Rauschenberger, Cory	R-R	6-1	185	7-31-84	5	2	2.87	46	2	0	1	75	71	28	24	9	29	32	.256	.267	.246	3.82	3.46
Reifer, Adam	R-R	6-2	195	6-3-86	0	1	1.42	5	0	0	0	6	7	1	1	1	1	1	.318	.250	.357	1.42	1.42
Rundles, Rich	L-L	6-5	210	6-3-81	1	3	1.80	35	0	0	1	30	24	13	6	3	15	29	.224	.176	.268	8.70	4.50
Salas, Fernando	R-R	6-2	200	5-30-85	0	0	0.00	3	0	0	2	3	2	0	0	0	0	4	.222	.000	.400	12.00	0.00
Sanchez, Eduardo	R-R	5-11	170	2-16-89	1	0	0.00	3	0	0	0	3	0	0	0	0	0	3	.000	.000	.000	9.00	0.00
Todd, Jess	R-R	5-11	210	4-20-86	2	4	4.91	41	0	0	0	44	46	25	24	4	14	38	.275	.397	.202	7.77	2.86
Valdes, Raul	L-L	5-11	190	11-27-77	6	2	4.73	27	7	0	0	59	61	32	31	8	11	62	.263	.274	.257	9.46	1.68
Walters, P.J.	R-R	6-4	200	3-12-85	7	4	4.27	17	17	1	0	103	105	51	49	9	42	87	.267	.303	.231	7.58	3.66
2-team total (7 Las Vegas)					8	7	5.17	24	24	1	0	132	149	80	76	13	58	113	—	—	—	7.69	3.94

Fielding

Catcher	PCT	G	PO	A	E	DP	PB
Anderson	.988	92	603	44	8	7	2
Cruz	.990	39	267	21	3	3	2
Derba	.984	17	109	15	2	2	0
Hill	1.000	4	24	2	0	0	0
Laird	1.000	1	5	0	0	0	1

First Base	PCT	G	PO	A	E	DP
Brown	1.000	5	27	0	0	5
Bynum	1.000	6	51	5	0	6
Hamilton	.995	61	551	32	3	78
Laird	1.000	1	7	0	0	1
Stavinoha	.992	75	615	37	5	72

Second Base	PCT	G	PO	A	E	DP
Bynum	.972	48	101	145	7	40
Craig	1.000	1	2	4	0	1
Garcia	.978	9	22	23	1	5

	PCT	G	PO	A	E	DP
Greene	.871	8	11	16	4	4
Kozma	.970	40	70	126	6	40
Luna	1.000	2	1	4	0	1
Punto	.909	4	8	12	2	4
Solano	.960	26	37	58	4	14
Vazquez	.964	28	45	87	5	22

Third Base	PCT	G	PO	A	E	DP
Brown	.000	1	0	0	1	0
Bynum	.000	1	0	0	0	0
Carpenter	.951	122	64	246	16	27
Cruz	1.000	1	0	1	0	1
Freese	1.000	4	3	2	0	0
Kozma	1.000	3	4	1	0	0
Punto	.000	1	0	0	0	0
Solano	.957	16	13	31	2	3
Vazquez	1.000	6	1	7	0	0

Shortstop	PCT	G	PO	A	E	DP
Garcia	1.000	3	7	4	0	3
Greene	.960	56	74	167	10	55
Kozma	.973	66	84	200	8	55
Solano	.978	20	34	55	2	16
Vazquez	.833	4	3	2	1	2

Outfield	PCT	G	PO	A	E	DP
Brown	.966	92	136	8	5	2
Bynum	1.000	8	17	1	0	1
Chambers	.987	124	290	4	4	1
Craig	1.000	6	7	1	0	0
Hamilton	1.000	3	6	0	0	0
Jones	.984	31	62	0	1	0
Luna	.972	55	100	5	3	2
Rapoport	.993	72	144	4	1	1
Robinson	.989	42	89	0	1	0
Stavinoha	.982	40	55	1	1	0

SPRINGFIELD CARDINALS
DOUBLE-A

TEXAS LEAGUE

Batting	B-T	HT	WT	DOB	AVG	vLH	vRH	G	AB	R	H	2B	3B	HR	RBI	BB	HBP	SH	SF	SO	SB	CS	SLG	OBP
Adams, Matt	L-R	6-3	230	8-31-88	.300	.284	.308	115	463	80	139	23	2	32	101	40	4	0	6	90	0	1	.566	.357
Ahmady, Alan	R-R	5-11	200	12-14-87	.117	.045	.158	20	60	5	7	1	0	0	3	9	1	0	1	15	0	0	.133	.239
Bolivar, Domnit	R-R	5-11	165	5-12-89	.298	.300	.296	16	47	5	14	2	1	1	9	3	0	0	1	8	1	0	.447	.333
Castellanos, Alex	R-R	5-11	180	8-4-86	.319	.339	.310	93	354	72	113	21	4	19	62	24	11	0	2	94	10	1	.562	.379
Cox, Zack	L-R	6-0	215	5-9-89	.293	.247	.310	93	352	54	103	19	0	10	48	29	6	0	2	69	0	1	.432	.355
Craig, Allen	R-R	6-2	210	7-18-84	.000	.000	.000	2	6	0	0	0	0	0	1	1	0	0	1	1	0	0	.000	.125
Curtis, Jermaine	R-R	5-11	190	7-10-86	.315	.264	.349	90	276	41	87	12	3	5	32	38	9	0	1	31	0	0	.435	.414
Cutler, Charlie	L-R	6-0	200	7-29-86	.333	.360	.325	62	204	37	68	8	3	5	34	21	3	0	3	28	0	0	.475	.398
Derba, Nick	R-R	5-10	190	9-9-85	.180	.219	.158	30	89	10	16	3	0	2	9	15	0	0	0	27	0	0	.281	.298
Duncan, Eric	L-R	6-3	210	12-7-84	.274	.224	.287	103	351	60	96	21	1	22	62	25	3	0	6	78	3	1	.527	.322
Garcia, Jose	R-R	5-11	170	2-25-88	.318	.351	.300	94	318	49	101	15	0	5	38	24	6	0	2	57	19	7	.412	.374
Henley, Tyler	L-L	5-10	200	6-10-85	.156	.125	.162	15	45	5	7	2	1	1	3	8	1	0	0	11	1	0	.311	.296
Hill, Steve	R-R	5-11	200	3-14-85	.282	.220	.311	31	131	22	37	5	0	11	26	10	0	0	3	35	1	0	.573	.326
Ingram, D'Marcus	R-R	5-9	170	3-10-88	.239	.333	.200	25	92	13	22	5	1	1	9	5	1	0	0	21	2	0	.348	.314
Jackson, Ryan	R-R	6-3	180	5-10-88	.278	.329	.254	135	533	65	148	34	3	11	73	44	4	0	6	91	2	0	.415	.334
Jones, Daryl	L-L	6-0	180	6-25-87	.269	.289	.262	47	145	26	39	5	1	4	20	15	2	0	1	33	1	2	.400	.344
Luna, Aaron	R-R	5-11	200	3-28-87	.250	.429	.184	17	52	13	13	4	0	0	1	12	2	0	0	12	0	1	.327	.409
Perez, Audry	R-R	5-9	180	12-23-88	.261	.270	.255	59	230	28	60	15	0	8	37	5	2	0	3	29	0	0	.430	.279
Pham, Tommy	R-R	6-1	175	3-8-88	.294	.271	.305	40	143	31	42	11	3	5	16	18	1	0	2	40	3	3	.517	.372
Punto, Nick	B-R	5-9	190	11-8-77	.333	.000	.381	7	24	3	8	1	0	0	2	2	0	0	0	3	1	0	.375	.385
Rapoport, Jim	L-L	5-11	160	6-25-85	.221	.270	.204	39	140	24	31	3	0	0	10	19	5	0	1	17	6	2	.243	.333
Robinson, Shane	R-R	5-9	160	10-30-84	.484	.300	.571	7	31	8	15	2	0	3	8	4	2	0	0	1	0	1	.839	.568
Solano, Donovan	R-R	5-10	185	12-17-87	.228	.345	.181	27	101	5	23	7	0	2	10	3	0	0	0	16	0	0	.356	.250
Swauger, Chris	L-L	6-0	195	8-11-86	.296	.317	.287	114	362	52	107	13	2	12	56	24	3	0	2	67	3	4	.442	.343
Tartamella, Travis	R-R	5-11	200	12-17-87	.152	.071	.188	15	46	4	7	1	1	5	3	0	0	0	13	0	0	.217	.204
Vasquez, Niko	R-R	5-11	175	2-26-89	.225	.259	.202	39	138	17	31	10	0	6	20	13	1	0	1	32	0	0	.428	.294

Pitching	B-T	HT	WT	DOB	W	L	ERA	G	GS	CG	SV	IP	H	R	ER	HR	BB	SO	AVG	vLH	vRH	K/9	BB/9
Additon, Nick	L-L	6-5	215	12-16-87	4	1	2.93	10	10	0	0	61	50	23	20	8	15	48	.223	.159	.239	7.04	2.20
Blazek, Michael	R-R	6-0	180	3-16-89	11	6	5.45	24	24	0	0	134	148	90	81	25	64	128	.280	.277	.282	8.62	4.31
Calhoun, Daniel	L-L	6-3	220	9-5-86	0	0	4.66	5	0	0	0	10	16	8	5	2	0	7	.356	.412	.321	6.52	0.00
Castillo, Richard	R-R	5-11	165	10-11-89	1	1	4.30	24	2	0	0	44	61	25	21	4	21	42	.326	.382	.294	8.59	4.30
Cleto, Maikel	R-R	6-3	235	5-1-89	2	2	3.93	7	6	0	0	34	40	19	15	2	12	36	.301	.294	.305	9.44	3.15
Delgado, Ramon	R-R	6-3	195	9-3-86	0	1	9.00	2	0	0	0	3	6	3	3	0	2	2	.462	1.000	.125	6.00	6.00
Freeman, Sam	R-L	5-11	170	6-24-87	2	2	3.03	52	0	0	3	59	53	28	20	5	28	52	.240	.235	.242	7.89	4.25
Frevert, Matt	R-R	6-1	190	11-16-86	1	1	7.50	14	0	0	4	18	20	15	15	4	8	7	.286	.417	.217	3.50	4.00
Gast, John	L-L	6-1	195	2-16-89	4	4	4.08	13	13	1	0	79	80	42	36	9	33	54	.266	.237	.273	6.13	3.74
Greenwood, Nick	R-L	6-1	180	9-28-87	2	4	4.31	59	0	0	2	77	79	42	37	9	21	52	.266	.178	.311	6.05	2.44
Hooker, Deryk	R-R	6-4	185	6-21-89	2	6	4.94	11	11	0	0	58	58	34	32	8	18	39	.266	.309	.234	6.02	2.78
Kelly, Joe	R-R	6-1	165	6-9-88	6	4	5.01	11	11	0	0	59	70	40	33	7	25	51	.306	.337	.282	7.74	3.79
King, Blake	R-R	6-1	195	4-11-87	0	0	13.50	2	0	0	0	1	7	2	2	1	4	0	.875	.667	1.000	0.00	27.00
2-team total (33 Corpus Christi)					0	2	4.07	35	0	0	0	42	32	20	19	4	42	50	—	—	—	10.71	9.00
Kopp, David	R-R	6-3	205	10-22-85	3	5	5.95	23	9	0	4	65	76	50	43	12	25	40	.288	.297	.282	5.54	3.46
Kulik, Ryan	L-L	5-11	205	12-3-85	0	1	8.38	7	0	0	0	15	12	9	1	8	6	15	.357	.412	.320	5.59	7.45
Lyman, Jeff	R-R	6-3	225	1-14-87	0	0	5.23	17	0	0	0	21	18	12	12	4	13	17	.228	.216	.238	7.40	5.66
Miller, Shelby	R-R	6-3	195	10-10-90	9	3	2.70	16	16	0	0	87	72	28	26	2	33	89	.229	.171	.266	9.24	3.43
Mulligan, Casey	R-R	6-2	190	10-5-87	0	1	2.57	6	0	0	4	7	4	3	2	1	2	6	.160	.200	.133	7.71	2.57
Nieto, Arquimedes	R-R	6-0	175	4-28-89	0	2	10.00	2	2	0	0	9	14	11	10	2	6	6	.359	.500	.211	6.00	6.00
Rada, Jose	R-R	6-1	180	4-13-88	1	4	6.75	32	0	0	1	40	53	31	30	9	15	38	.319	.310	.324	8.55	3.38
Rauschenberger, Cory	R-R	6-1	185	7-31-84	1	0	1.69	3	0	0	0	5	3	1	1	1	3	3	.167	.286	.091	5.06	5.06
Reid, Chase	L-R	6-3	215	5-17-88	0	1	3.91	18	0	0	0	23	19	12	10	1	13	17	.229	.281	.196	6.65	5.09

Pitching

Pitching	B-T	HT	WT	DOB	W	L	ERA	G	GS	CG	SV	IP	H	R	ER	HR	BB	SO	AVG	vLH	vRH	K/9	BB/9
Rondon, Jorge	R-R	6-1	175	9-16-88	1	8	9.16	37	0	0	7	37	43	45	38	4	33	30	.295	.380	.250	7.23	7.96
Samuel, Francisco	R-R	6-2	185	12-20-86	0	1	10.38	11	0	0	0	9	11	13	10	0	10	9	.314	.250	.348	9.35	10.38
Sanchez, Eduardo	R-R	5-11	170	2-16-89	0	1	4.15	3	0	0	0	4	3	3	2	0	2	3	.200	.250	.143	6.23	4.15
Schneider, Scott	R-R	6-0	175	6-7-88	7	10	5.98	35	20	0	0	117	133	96	78	15	48	88	.284	.268	.294	6.75	3.68
Simpson, Jesse	R-R	6-0	180	1-29-87	1	0	5.56	18	0	0	1	23	25	14	14	5	7	17	.278	.276	.279	6.75	2.78
Swagerty, Jordan	B-R	6-2	175	7-14-89	0	0	2.89	9	0	0	3	9	8	5	3	1	5	7	.222	.167	.228	6.75	4.82
Thomas, Kevin	R-R	6-3	215	7-8-86	1	7	6.44	33	16	0	0	94	109	73	67	12	49	71	.289	.275	.299	6.82	4.71
Zawacki, Brett	R-R	6-1	190	5-2-89	3	2	8.00	20	0	0	0	27	35	29	24	7	11	17	.304	.256	.329	5.67	3.67

Fielding

Catcher	PCT	G	PO	A	E	DP	PB
Cutler	.994	44	279	31	2	3	3
Derba	.990	27	175	20	2	6	0
Hill	1.000	6	50	6	0	1	0
Perez	.977	52	395	26	10	5	6
Tartamella	1.000	14	103	11	0	1	2

First Base	PCT	G	PO	A	E	DP
Adams	.993	111	1032	60	8	85
Duncan	.952	11	74	6	4	9
Hill	.995	20	177	14	1	15

Second Base	PCT	G	PO	A	E	DP
Bolivar	1.000	13	18	21	0	8
Curtis	.949	16	25	49	4	5
Duncan	.969	32	53	71	4	19
Garcia	.947	67	108	180	16	35
Punto	.800	3	1	3	1	0

Solano	.984	24	37	85	2	15	

Third Base	PCT	G	PO	A	E	DP
Cox	.912	87	36	172	20	16
Curtis	.978	19	6	38	1	2
Derba	.000	1	0	0	0	0
Duncan	.778	4	0	7	2	0
Solano	1.000	1	0	1	0	0
Vasquez	.950	38	19	76	5	12

Shortstop	PCT	G	PO	A	E	DP
Bolivar	1.000	3	4	9	0	1
Garcia	.913	5	10	11	2	3
Jackson	.969	134	201	395	19	80
Solano	1.000	1	2	2	0	0

Outfield	PCT	G	PO	A	E	DP
Ahmady	.947	18	33	3	2	1

	PCT	G	PO	A	E	DP
Castellanos	.953	89	174	10	9	3
Craig	1.000	2	5	0	0	0
Curtis	.981	31	50	2	1	0
Cutler	1.000	5	4	1	0	0
Duncan	1.000	34	54	5	0	0
Garcia	.964	18	26	1	1	0
Henley	1.000	10	14	0	0	0
Hill	1.000	1	1	0	0	0
Ingram	1.000	25	52	2	0	1
Jones	.952	36	58	2	3	0
Luna	.875	14	21	0	3	0
Pham	.978	37	85	6	2	3
Rapoport	.981	38	103	2	2	0
Robinson	1.000	7	20	1	0	0
Swauger	.966	78	109	5	4	0

PALM BEACH CARDINALS   HIGH CLASS A

FLORIDA STATE LEAGUE

Batting

Batting	B-T	HT	WT	DOB	AVG	vLH	vRH	G	AB	R	H	2B	3B	HR	RBI	BB	HBP	SH	SF	SO	SB	CS	SLG	OBP
Ahmady, Alan	R-R	5-11	200	12-14-87	.253	.243	.259	90	304	48	77	19	2	1	41	62	8	0	5	66	2	2	.339	.388
Bogany, Jarred	R-R	6-3	200	1-4-87	.183	.222	.170	21	71	8	13	1	2	1	5	5	0	0	0	31	1	1	.296	.237
Bolivar, Domnit	R-R	5-11	165	5-12-89	.273	.283	.268	88	304	40	83	16	3	8	41	27	5	0	1	73	7	2	.424	.341
Castillo, Juan	R-R	5-11	160	12-13-89	.163	.300	.121	13	43	5	7	2	0	0	4	4	0	0	0	4	0	0	.209	.234
Cerreto, Phil	R-R	6-1	195	10-4-87	.207	.412	.122	15	58	5	12	5	0	0	6	4	0	0	0	13	0	0	.293	.258
Conley, Kyle	R-R	6-4	210	5-7-87	.249	.256	.246	72	273	32	68	18	4	13	50	26	4	0	2	79	0	3	.487	.321
Cox, Zack	L-R	6-0	215	5-9-89	.335	.227	.375	42	164	22	55	8	0	3	20	11	2	0	2	29	2	2	.439	.380
De La Cruz, Luis	R-R	5-10	165	5-6-89	.276	.239	.306	46	152	19	42	11	0	1	18	10	0	0	0	18	3	0	.368	.321
Elkins, Packy	L-R	5-11	175	11-6-87	.195	.143	.222	14	41	9	8	0	0	0	2	9	0	0	0	11	3	0	.195	.340
Garcia, Greg	L-R	6-0	175	8-8-89	.290	.188	.340	59	210	36	61	11	5	2	16	31	8	0	1	42	4	4	.419	.400
Ingram, D'Marcus	R-R	5-9	170	3-30-88	.272	.333	.259	28	103	16	28	7	0	1	4	14	2	0	0	23	13	1	.369	.370
Lara, Edgar	R-R	6-3	210	3-2-89	.257	.230	.268	84	300	29	77	14	0	10	42	16	4	0	6	74	1	2	.403	.298
Mateo, Luis	R-R	6-0	160	5-23-90	.179	.130	.200	56	184	22	33	5	0	2	12	10	5	0	2	31	7	4	.239	.239
Melker, Adam	L-L	5-11	180	1-31-88	.245	.207	.260	94	314	36	77	16	1	0	32	34	6	0	3	69	10	5	.303	.328
Obregon, Ted	B-R	5-11	175	5-4-90	.236	.225	.241	64	208	22	49	1	3	0	12	11	0	0	0	52	13	4	.269	.274
Perez, Audry	R-R	5-9	180	12-23-88	.291	.263	.299	22	86	7	25	4	0	3	10	2	0	0	0	13	0	0	.442	.307
Ramirez, Ronald	R-R	5-11	165	1-30-86	.211	.313	.178	35	133	9	28	2	0	0	3	5	0	0	0	27	2	2	.226	.239
Rodriguez, Ryde	R-R	6-3	232	2-2-88	.220	.200	.226	13	41	4	9	1	0	0	3	1	0	0	0	6	0	0	.244	.238
Rodriguez, Starlin	B-R	5-10	168	12-13-89	.315	.381	.275	45	165	28	52	9	1	4	20	6	6	0	4	34	3	5	.455	.354
Rosario, Rainel	R-R	6-0	188	3-29-89	.270	.282	.265	122	455	52	123	19	6	9	70	40	5	0	5	112	15	8	.398	.333
Scruggs, Xavier	R-R	6-1	210	9-23-87	.260	.275	.254	117	411	57	107	27	3	21	63	40	13	0	6	125	4	1	.494	.340
Stock, Robert	L-R	6-0	175	11-21-89	.262	.250	.265	42	149	16	39	8	1	1	9	18	0	0	1	17	0	1	.349	.339
Tartamella, Travis	R-R	5-11	200	12-17-87	.203	.333	.163	20	64	6	13	3	0	1	8	7	0	0	1	22	0	0	.297	.278
Vasquez, Niko	R-R	5-11	175	2-26-89	.226	.250	.212	86	287	40	65	14	0	7	35	31	5	0	5	70	3	2	.348	.308

Pitching

Pitching	B-T	HT	WT	DOB	W	L	ERA	G	GS	CG	SV	IP	H	R	ER	HR	BB	SO	AVG	vLH	vRH	K/9	BB/9
Augenstein, Bryan	R-R	6-6	230	7-11-86	0	2	10.38	3	2	0	0	4	6	5	5	2	0	6	.316	.556	.100	12.46	0.00
Boyer, Blaine	R-R	6-3	245	7-11-81	0	1	5.06	3	3	0	0	11	6	6	6	1	3	11	.158	.158	.158	9.28	2.53
Bradford, Jared	R-R	6-1	177	4-3-86	0	0	5.40	1	0	0	0	2	1	1	1	0	3	2	.167	.000	.333	10.80	16.20
Butler, Keith	R-R	6-0	180	1-30-89	1	0	1.25	34	0	0	12	36	19	6	5	1	18	52	.151	.183	.121	13.00	4.50
Calhoun, Daniel	L-L	6-3	220	9-5-86	4	3	3.28	36	0	0	1	58	60	23	21	3	15	39	.276	.171	.327	6.09	2.34
Castillo, Richard	R-R	5-11	165	10-11-89	5	4	3.62	13	10	0	0	60	62	25	24	3	22	47	.276	.313	.239	7.09	3.32
Cleto, Maikel	R-R	6-3	235	5-1-89	1	1	2.48	5	5	0	0	29	20	10	8	2	10	33	.190	.178	.200	10.24	3.10
Corrigan, Chris	R-R	6-2	155	12-24-87	1	1	3.48	32	0	0	0	41	49	18	16	1	21	29	.301	.286	.314	6.31	4.57
Fornataro, Eric	R-R	6-1	195	1-2-88	7	13	3.67	24	24	1	0	145	150	68	59	7	50	116	.265	.240	.291	7.22	3.11
Freeman, Sam	R-L	5-11	170	6-24-87	0	0	4.00	7	0	0	0	9	8	5	4	0	4	7	.258	.273	.250	7.00	4.00
Gast, John	L-L	6-1	195	2-16-89	5	4	3.95	13	12	1	0	82	85	40	36	7	28	59	.272	.240	.286	6.48	3.07
Greenwood, Nick	R-L	6-1	180	9-28-87	0	0	9.00	2	0	0	0	3	3	3	3	1	0	3	.250	.200	.286	9.00	0.00
Hooker, Deryk	R-R	6-4	185	6-21-89	0	0	0.00	1	1	0	0	4	3	0	0	0	1	5	.200	.222	.167	11.25	0.00
Kelly, Joe	R-R	6-1	165	6-9-88	5	2	2.60	12	11	0	0	73	56	26	21	1	34	62	.215	.277	.169	7.68	4.21
Lyman, Jeff	R-R	6-3	225	1-14-87	1	0	2.45	7	0	0	0	11	7	4	3	0	10	5	.189	.200	.182	4.09	8.18
Lyons, Tyler	B-L	6-2	195	2-21-88	9	4	4.50	33	12	1	1	94	93	51	47	8	29	79	.255	.268	.249	7.56	2.78
Mahay, Ron	L-L	6-2	190	6-28-71	0	0	0.00	2	0	0	0	2	1	0	0	0	4	.222	.500	.000	18.00	0.00

Pitching

Pitching	B-T	HT	WT	DOB	W	L	ERA	G	GS	CG	SV	IP	H	R	ER	HR	BB	SO	AVG	vLH	vRH	K/9	BB/9
Maness, Seth	R-R	6-0	180	10-14-88	1	0	4.32	3	0	0	0	8	7	4	4	0	2	8	.219	.286	.167	8.64	2.16
Martinez, Carlos	R-R	6-0	165	9-21-91	3	3	5.28	10	10	0	0	46	49	31	27	2	30	48	.269	.307	.243	9.39	5.87
Miller, Shelby	R-R	6-3	195	10-10-90	2	3	2.89	9	9	0	0	53	40	20	17	2	20	81	.204	.238	.165	13.75	3.40
Nieto, Arquimedes	R-R	6-0	175	4-28-89	2	5	4.96	12	7	0	0	49	48	28	27	3	21	37	.253	.306	.210	6.80	3.86
Rada, Jose	R-R	6-1	180	4-13-88	2	0	3.18	2	0	0	0	6	4	2	2	0	0	5	.190	.125	.231	7.94	0.00
Reid, Chase	L-R	6-3	215	5-17-88	2	0	2.28	19	0	0	2	28	21	7	7	1	10	31	.212	.179	.233	10.08	3.25
Rondon, Jorge	R-R	6-1	175	9-16-88	1	5	4.05	21	0	0	6	27	29	13	12	1	13	27	.302	.400	.216	9.11	4.39
Samuel, Francisco	R-R	6-2	185	12-20-86	0	2	18.69	5	0	0	0	4	7	9	9	0	6	6	.350	.444	.273	12.46	12.46
Siegrist, Kevin	L-L	6-5	190	7-20-89	0	3	3.42	11	11	0	0	53	44	23	20	3	30	45	.232	.245	.227	7.69	5.13
Simpson, Jesse	R-R	6-0	180	1-29-87	6	1	1.54	37	0	0	2	47	40	10	8	1	18	40	.233	.200	.252	7.71	3.47
Smith, Justin	R-R	6-0	190	3-23-88	4	8	5.72	29	14	0	0	91	106	67	58	9	42	82	.294	.343	.251	8.08	4.14
Swagerty, Jordan	R-R	6-2	175	7-14-89	2	2	1.82	22	7	0	5	54	42	13	11	1	16	52	.214	.284	.138	8.61	2.65
Terry, Aaron	R-R	5-11	185	12-25-88	3	3	4.33	25	0	0	2	35	35	17	17	3	19	17	.269	.226	.309	4.33	4.84
Wright, Justin	L-L	5-9	175	8-18-89	0	0	0.57	14	0	0	1	16	7	1	1	1	9	16	.140	.125	.154	9.19	5.17
Zawacki, Brett	R-R	6-1	190	5-2-89	0	0	3.55	9	0	0	2	13	12	5	5	0	7	10	.245	.290	.167	7.11	4.97

Fielding

Catcher	PCT	G	PO	A	E	DP	PB
Castillo	.988	12	74	5	1	0	3
De La Cruz	.974	46	330	41	10	4	7
Perez	.985	22	180	20	3	1	5
Stock	1.000	42	324	31	0	4	0
Tartamella	.993	20	138	13	1	0	2

First Base	PCT	G	PO	A	E	DP
Bolivar	1.000	6	25	3	0	3
Cerreto	1.000	13	123	10	0	10
Lara	1.000	16	111	9	0	11
Scruggs	.987	108	928	73	13	84

Second Base	PCT	G	PO	A	E	DP
Bolivar	.963	19	34	44	3	5
Elkins	1.000	6	10	18	0	3

	PCT	G	PO	A	E	DP
Garcia	.986	38	49	95	2	23
Mateo	.991	54	87	145	2	31
Obregon	1.000	1	1	0	0	0
Rodriguez	.950	28	40	74	6	15

Third Base	PCT	G	PO	A	E	DP
Ahmady	1.000	5	6	6	0	0
Bolivar	.905	9	5	14	2	1
Cox	.942	35	14	51	4	2
Elkins	1.000	7	3	15	0	2
Rosario	1.000	1	0	2	0	0
Vasquez	.975	83	49	150	5	14

Shortstop	PCT	G	PO	A	E	DP
Bolivar	.945	44	57	133	11	28
Garcia	.939	8	12	19	2	5

	PCT	G	PO	A	E	DP
Obregon	.934	55	76	136	15	24
Ramirez	.947	34	52	108	9	22

Outfield	PCT	G	PO	A	E	DP
Ahmady	.981	72	95	6	2	3
Bogany	1.000	20	34	2	0	0
Bolivar	.750	5	3	0	1	0
Conley	.975	70	114	5	3	3
Elkins	1.000	1	3	0	0	0
Ingram	1.000	26	65	0	0	0
Lara	1.000	14	19	0	0	0
Melker	.986	94	206	6	3	0
Obregon	1.000	3	2	0	0	0
Rodriguez	.947	11	17	1	1	0
Rosario	.986	114	198	9	3	3
Vasquez	.000	1	0	0	0	0

QUAD CITIES RIVER BANDITS

LOW CLASS A

MIDWEST LEAGUE

Batting	B-T	HT	WT	DOB	AVG	vLH	vRH	G	AB	R	H	2B	3B	HR	RBI	BB	HBP	SH	SF	SO	SB	CS	SLG	OBP
Bergman, Joey	L-R	5-10	190	2-7-88	.288	.233	.307	35	118	24	34	6	1	0	18	16	0	0	1	16	2	2	.356	.370
Castillo, Juan	R-R	5-11	160	12-13-89	.350	.400	.343	13	40	4	14	5	0	0	5	4	1	0	0	5	0	0	.475	.422
Castillo, Yunier	B-R	6-0	160	5-15-89	.194	.105	.214	31	103	11	20	2	0	0	7	8	2	0	1	26	3	2	.252	.263
Conley, Kyle	R-R	6-4	210	5-7-87	.221	.263	.204	20	68	8	15	3	1	3	7	7	0	0	0	23	0	0	.426	.293
Edmondson, Chris	L-R	6-0	200	4-8-88	.260	.228	.270	99	327	51	85	22	6	10	54	39	8	0	6	73	5	3	.456	.347
Elkins, Packy	L-R	5-11	175	11-6-87	.240	.196	.251	80	246	29	59	10	2	1	22	50	4	0	2	55	3	3	.309	.374
Garcia, Greg	L-R	6-0	175	8-8-89	.273	.216	.292	46	150	20	41	10	1	0	10	17	4	0	1	24	4	2	.353	.360
Gil, Ronny	B-R	5-10	150	3-15-89	.260	.333	.225	86	327	63	85	14	3	1	34	27	4	0	6	83	18	2	.330	.319
Hill, Virgil	R-R	5-11	186	9-9-89	.183	.233	.167	37	120	18	22	5	1	2	15	7	1	0	0	51	8	1	.292	.234
Klein, Geoff	B-R	6-3	200	3-27-88	.268	.281	.264	53	205	24	55	17	0	4	33	19	2	0	2	57	1	0	.410	.333
Lara, Edgar	R-R	6-3	210	3-2-89	.188	.143	.200	11	32	4	6	2	0	2	6	5	0	0	1	13	0	0	.438	.289
Longmire, Nick	R-R	6-3	180	1-5-89	.242	.287	.225	97	368	53	89	22	0	8	42	29	4	0	4	83	10	2	.367	.301
Mateo, Luis	R-R	6-0	160	5-23-90	.364	.429	.250	3	11	3	4	0	0	0	2	1	0	0	0	2	0	0	.364	.417
O'Neill, Mike	L-L	5-9	170	2-12-88	.338	.267	.354	25	80	15	27	8	0	0	10	13	0	0	0	13	1	0	.438	.430
Parejo, Freddy	R-R	6-0	165	7-5-90	.160	.222	.140	24	75	11	12	0	0	0	4	10	1	0	0	31	2	2	.320	.267
Rodriguez, Jonathan	R-R	6-2	205	8-21-89	.251	.327	.225	118	394	67	99	27	0	20	70	77	14	0	3	109	4	5	.472	.389
Rodriguez, Starlin	B-R	5-10	168	12-13-89	.263	.306	.248	41	137	18	36	7	3	1	16	11	5	0	2	37	5	2	.380	.335
Ruiz, Romulo	R-R	6-0	170	11-30-89	.119	.222	.091	13	42	4	5	2	0	0	2	6	0	0	1	8	1	0	.167	.224
Sanchez, Victor	R-R	6-1	175	12-30-88	.242	.265	.233	68	240	28	58	16	1	2	28	15	11	0	2	39	4	1	.342	.313
Stanley, Cody	L-R	5-10	190	12-21-88	.264	.308	.246	101	379	54	100	24	2	11	66	27	4	0	3	92	4	2	.435	.317
Stock, Robert	L-R	6-0	175	11-21-89	.176	.050	.258	16	51	4	9	2	0	1	6	5	0	0	2	6	1	0	.275	.241
Swinson, Michael	L-R	6-2	185	9-24-89	.248	.195	.264	93	331	46	82	17	2	2	26	58	1	0	3	59	9	8	.329	.359
Taveras, Oscar	L-L	6-2	180	6-19-92	.386	.360	.396	78	308	52	119	27	5	8	62	32	3	0	4	52	1	4	.584	.444
Teran, Kleininger	R-R	6-1	168	7-23-89	.000	.000	.000	3	5	1	0	0	0	0	0	3	0	0	0	1	0	0	.000	.375
Walsh, Colin	B-R	6-1	202	9-26-89	.239	.243	.238	69	230	36	55	18	1	4	29	43	1	0	1	43	6	2	.378	.360
Wong, Kolten	L-R	5-9	190	10-10-90	.335	.283	.351	47	194	39	65	15	2	5	25	21	3	0	4	24	9	5	.510	.401

Pitching	B-T	HT	WT	DOB	W	L	ERA	G	GS	CG	SV	IP	H	R	ER	HR	BB	SO	AVG	vLH	vRH	K/9	BB/9
Benes, Drew	R-R	6-2	190	11-4-88	1	2	5.40	14	2	0	1	28	35	23	17	1	11	18	.304	.370	.261	5.72	3.49
Blair, Seth	R-R	6-2	185	3-3-89	6	3	5.29	21	21	0	0	82	79	54	48	9	62	70	.259	.305	.226	7.71	6.83
Butler, Keith	R-R	6-0	180	1-30-89	0	1	1.17	12	0	0	5	15	7	2	2	0	5	16	.135	.158	.121	9.39	2.93
Copeland, Ryan	R-L	5-11	180	6-10-88	4	4	4.94	19	11	0	1	82	82	48	45	9	15	82	.258	.270	.252	9.00	1.65
Corpas, Hector	R-R	6-3	170	1-5-90	2	2	7.26	30	0	0	1	40	48	34	32	5	17	31	.302	.339	.278	7.03	3.86
Corrigan, Chris	R-R	6-2	155	12-24-87	0	0	3.27	5	0	0	2	11	8	4	4	1	2	13	.200	.125	.250	10.64	1.64
De Jesus, Angel	R-R	6-6	188	2-3-89	2	2	6.47	42	0	0	4	64	85	50	46	5	30	47	.328	.383	.285	6.61	4.22
Edwards, Justin	L-L	6-2	190	12-3-87	3	2	2.94	20	0	0	1	34	30	14	11	3	17	22*	.242	.167	.280	7.22	4.54
Ferrara, Anthony	R-L	6-1	175	9-2-89	13	7	3.03	23	22	0	0	128	103	48	43	7	53	93	.227	.234	.224	6.56	3.74

Pitching

	B-T	HT	WT	DOB	W	L	ERA	G	GS	CG	SV	IP	H	R	ER	HR	BB	SO	AVG	vLH	vRH	K/9	BB/9
Hernandez, Hector	B-L	6-1	198	2-20-91	1	0	0.00	1	0	0	0	3	3	1	0	0	0	4	.231	.250	.222	12.00	0.00
Johnson, Cale	R-R	6-2	200	8-26-87	1	4	4.33	30	0	0	0	52	58	27	25	5	22	39	.289	.316	.270	6.75	3.81
Kiekhefer, Dean	L-L	6-0	175	6-7-89	4	1	1.26	34	0	0	8	57	35	8	8	1	12	46	.179	.141	.197	7.26	1.89
Lucas, Aiden	R-R	6-2	225	4-21-88	2	4	2.75	33	0	0	11	39	28	16	12	3	18	41	.211	.265	.179	9.38	4.12
Maness, Seth	R-R	6-0	180	10-14-88	1	0	1.80	2	0	0	0	5	4	1	1	0	0	3	.222	.000	.400	5.40	0.00
Martinez, Carlos	R-R	6-0	165	9-21-91	3	2	2.33	8	8	0	0	39	27	10	10	1	14	50	.196	.109	.270	11.64	3.26
Moss, Andy	R-R	6-1	210	10-8-86	2	0	5.79	6	0	0	0	14	12	9	9	2	4	12	.231	.208	.250	7.71	2.57
Nazario, Iden	L-L	6-0	190	3-28-89	1	0	3.90	19	0	0	1	30	19	15	13	1	18	37	.179	.088	.222	11.10	5.40
Rosenthal, Trevor	R-R	6-2	190	5-29-90	7	7	4.11	22	22	1	0	120	111	62	55	7	39	133	.247	.226	.263	9.95	2.92
Russell, Zach	R-R	6-2	185	7-27-89	7	10	4.21	23	23	0	0	113	105	68	53	11	61	98	.245	.237	.253	7.78	4.84
Siegrist, Kevin	L-L	6-5	190	7-20-89	8	1	1.15	9	8	0	0	55	38	12	7	1	15	34	.194	.293	.152	5.60	2.47
Swagerty, Jordan	B-R	6-2	175	7-14-89	3	1	1.50	5	5	0	0	30	18	5	5	2	2	30	.178	.209	.155	9.00	0.60
Tallet, Brian	L-L	6-6	220	9-21-77	0	0	0.00	1	1	0	0	2	0	0	0	0	0	0	.000		.000	22.50	0.00
Whiting, Boone	R-R	6-1	175	8-20-89	5	2	2.41	30	14	0	4	120	82	36	32	8	24	122	.191	.149	.228	9.18	1.81
Wright, Justin	L-L	5-9	175	8-18-89	5	1	1.26	17	0	0	4	36	20	8	5	1	9	54	.155	.178	.143	13.63	2.27

Fielding

Catcher	PCT	G	PO	A	E	DP	PB
Castillo	.983	13	97	18	2	0	2
Klein	.992	31	237	16	2	1	1
Stanley	.986	80	615	68	10	2	9
Stock	.987	16	135	16	2	3	0
Teran	1.000	2	15	1	0	0	0

First Base	PCT	G	PO	A	E	DP
Klein	.986	18	137	7	2	14
Lara	1.000	1	5	0	0	1
Rodriguez	.990	68	573	30	6	45
Ruiz	.989	10	91	3	1	9
Sanchez	.998	47	389	17	1	39

Second Base	PCT	G	PO	A	E	DP
Bergman	1.000	17	37	45	0	13
Elkins	.986	22	31	42	1	14
Garcia	1.000	29	38	70	0	17
Rodriguez	.971	31	52	84	4	10
Walsh	.923	2	7	5	1	2
Wong	.964	46	82	133	8	26

Third Base	PCT	G	PO	A	E	DP
Bergman	.750	4	0	3	1	1
Elkins	.942	49	31	66	6	9
Gil	1.000	2	0	2	0	0
Mateo	1.000	3	0	9	0	0
Rodriguez	.826	34	15	56	15	6
Sanchez	.922	21	12	47	5	4
Walsh	.918	36	22	67	8	6

Shortstop	PCT	G	PO	A	E	DP
Castillo	.924	31	47	75	10	21
Elkins	1.000	11	13	26	0	5
Garcia	.967	18	25	34	2	8
Gil	.925	84	112	232	28	50

	PCT	G	PO	A	E	DP
Walsh	.857	3	1	5	1	2

Outfield	PCT	G	PO	A	E	DP
Conley	1.000	9	8	0	0	0
Edmondson	.969	81	119	4	4	0
Elkins	.000	1	0	0	0	0
Gil	.000	1	0	0	0	0
Hill	.970	36	62	3	2	0
Lara	.846	4	11	0	2	0
Longmire	.983	93	173	3	3	2
O'Neill	1.000	14	14	0	0	0
Parejo	1.000	18	32	2	0	0
Rodriguez	.000	1	0	0	0	0
Swinson	.979	86	129	9	3	1
Taveras	.986	70	133	6	2	4
Walsh	.956	25	40	3	2	1

BATAVIA MUCKDOGS

SHORT-SEASON

NEW YORK-PENN LEAGUE

Batting

	B-T	HT	WT	DOB	AVG	vLH	vRH	G	AB	R	H	2B	3B	HR	RBI	BB	HBP	SH	SF	SO	SB	CS	SLG	OBP
Albitz, Vance	R-R	5-8	160	1-31-88	.283	.167	.324	12	46	9	13	5	0	0	2	4	1	0	0	2	0	0	.391	.353
Bergman, Joey	L-R	5-10	190	2-7-88	.309	.130	.345	34	136	20	42	8	0	2	14	16	2	0	1	28	5	1	.412	.387
Castillo, Juan	R-R	5-11	160	12-13-89	.313	.258	.326	44	166	25	52	11	0	2	17	10	1	0	1	30	3	0	.416	.354
Castillo, Yunier	B-R	6-0	160	5-15-89	.176	—	.176	12	34	5	6	2	0	0	4	3	0	0	0	7	1	0	.235	.243
Cerreto, Phil	R-R	6-1	195	10-4-87	.200	.000	.273	10	30	1	6	1	0	0	3	1	1	0	1	3	0	0	.233	.242
Encarnacion, Victor	R-R	6-2	165	3-8-90	.059	.111	.000	7	17	1	1	1	0	0	0	0	0	0	0	5	0	0	.118	.059
Hill, Virgil	R-R	5-11	186	9-9-89	.245	.152	.274	54	192	21	47	9	6	6	26	9	2	0	3	68	6	3	.448	.282
Ingram, D'Marcus	R-R	5-9	170	3-30-88	.333	.000	.333	1	3	1	1	0	1	0	0	0	0	0	0	1	0	1	1.000	.333
Martini, Nicholas	L-L	5-11	193	6-27-90	.167	.185	.163	57	174	19	29	5	3	0	19	28	3	0	1	34	8	0	.230	.291
Medina, David	L-L	6-3	162	1-1-89	.290	.217	.314	69	248	43	72	14	1	8	31	36	2	0	2	77	2	2	.452	.382
Moscatel, Kevin	R-R	6-1	175	5-16-91	.225	.258	.211	30	102	10	23	6	0	1	8	8	3	0	0	24	1	1	.314	.301
O'Neill, Mike	L-L	5-9	170	2-12-88	.290	.300	.288	25	93	18	27	9	0	1	8	22	2	0	1	10	3	1	.419	.432
Patton, Jeremy	R-R	5-11	195	8-12-88	.292	.250	.302	63	226	32	66	20	2	4	40	30	0	0	1	28	0	2	.451	.374
Rasmus, Jordan	L-R	5-10	175	3-29-90	.230	.300	.222	32	100	11	23	1	1	0	9	8	1	0	2	20	5	3	.260	.288
Reyes, Roberto	L-L	6-0	185	5-10-89	.237	.225	.240	54	194	24	46	10	1	3	24	21	2	0	1	53	9	4	.345	.317
Ruiz, Romulo	R-R	6-0	170	11-30-89	.265	.226	.277	62	230	35	61	20	0	7	38	23	2	0	4	41	7	3	.443	.332
Stienstra, Daniel	R-R	6-2	200	3-1-89	.258	.316	.232	33	120	16	31	4	1	0	9	9	1	0	0	11	3	1	.308	.315
Valera, Cesar	R-R	6-1	180	3-8-92	.213	.167	.226	51	169	20	36	4	1	1	17	17	5	0	1	46	10	3	.266	.302
Williams Jr., Reggie	B-R	6-4	190	9-15-89	.306	.364	.280	14	36	2	11	1	1	1	8	2	0	0	1	12	0	2	.472	.333
Wittels, Garrett	R-R	6-2	205	5-11-90	.262	.325	.242	42	168	23	44	8	1	0	13	12	0	0	2	30	4	2	.321	.308

Pitching

	B-T	HT	WT	DOB	W	L	ERA	G	GS	CG	SV	IP	H	R	ER	HR	BB	SO	AVG	vLH	vRH	K/9	BB/9
Almarante, Jose	R-R	6-1	172	12-19-88	4	2	4.72	15	13	0	0	69	75	38	36	7	10	33	.275	.297	.248	4.33	1.31
Avendano, Javier	R-R	6-3	180	9-6-90	1	2	3.14	9	1	0	2	14	11	5	5	1	8	19	.216	.227	.207	11.93	5.02
Baker, Corey	R-R	6-1	170	11-23-89	5	3	2.89	19	4	0	1	53	54	21	17	1	7	32	.263	.200	.318	5.43	1.19
Benes, Drew	R-R	6-2	190	11-4-88	1	1	3.15	6	2	0	0	20	23	13	7	0	5	19	.284	.355	.240	8.55	2.25
Bileckyj, Adam	L-L	6-3	205	10-17-88	1	3	5.29	20	0	0	0	34	37	29	20	3	18	36	.274	.295	.264	9.53	4.76
Binder, Eric	R-R	6-2	210	9-15-86	3	1	8.74	14	0	0	0	11	16	11	11	2	14	13	.314	.500	.243	10.32	11.12
Bittle, Scott	R-R	6-2	190	8-27-86	0	0	10.13	3	0	0	0	3	5	3	3	0	3	5	.385	.200	.500	16.88	10.13
Cole, Ethan	L-R	6-0	180	10-27-89	1	1	5.91	8	0	0	0	11	15	8	7	0	1	9	.319	.381	.269	7.59	0.84
Cornelius, Jonathan	L-L	6-1	190	5-31-88	1	4	4.02	14	10	0	0	47	36	21	21	2	19	50	.213	.265	.192	9.57	3.64
Daugherty, Pat	L-L	6-5	215	8-30-88	3	5	7.11	14	10	0	0	44	54	40	35	2	31	45	.303	.364	.284	9.14	6.29
De La Cruz, Manuel	L-L	6-2	225	5-8-90	0	0	6.00	5	0	0	0	6	8	5	4	1	0	4	.320	.500	.263	6.00	0.00
Edwards, Justin	L-L	6-2	190	12-3-87	0	0	0.00	1	1	0	0	2	0	0	0	0	2	4	.250	.000	.250	18.00	9.00
Gaviglio, Sam	R-R	6-2	195	5-22-90	0	0	0.00	2	2	0	0	4	2	0	0	0	0	4	.143	.286	.000	9.00	0.00

Pitching	B-T	HT	WT	DOB	W	L	ERA	G	GS	CG	SV	IP	H	R	ER	HR	BB	SO	AVG	vLH	vRH	K/9	BB/9
Hernandez, Hector	B-L	6-1	198	2-20-91	3	2	2.72	12	11	0	0	53	46	21	16	5	18	48	.220	.236	.212	8.15	3.06
Jacob, Kevin	R-R	6-6	225	3-26-89	1	1	4.58	16	0	0	0	18	10	11	9	1	20	18	.161	.200	.135	9.17	10.19
Maness, Seth	R-R	6-0	180	10-14-88	0	1	0.91	10	7	0	0	40	27	11	4	0	3	31	.185	.197	.176	7.03	0.68
Martinez, Ricky	R-R	6-1	195	4-20-88	2	4	3.73	22	0	0	0	31	34	16	13	3	11	18	.281	.333	.239	5.17	3.16
McInnis, Todd	R-R	6-1	140	3-26-88	3	2	1.90	13	11	0	0	62	50	15	13	1	8	36	.218	.255	.191	5.25	1.17
Miller, Travis	R-R	6-1	185	3-15-90	3	1	3.26	28	0	0	1	30	28	15	11	1	18	21	.241	.217	.257	6.23	5.34
Miranda, Danny	L-L	6-0	190	8-25-90	2	2	2.64	27	0	0	15	31	21	10	9	0	7	27	.194	.216	.183	7.92	2.05
Nazario, Iden	L-L	6-0	190	3-28-89	0	1	2.70	2	0	0	0	3	1	1	1	0	3	2	.091	.000	.167	5.40	8.10
Sherriff, Ryan	L-L	6-1	185	5-25-90	1	1	2.70	3	3	0	0	17	14	5	5	0	2	7	.230	.136	.282	3.78	1.08
Watson, Sean	L-L	6-10	220	8-22-87	1	1	3.96	19	0	0	0	36	37	17	16	1	9	20	.266	.250	.273	4.95	2.23

Fielding

Catcher	PCT	G	PO	A	E	DP	PB
Castillo	.982	38	232	36	5	5	9
Moscatel	.990	25	187	9	2	0	4
Rasmus	.990	16	92	12	1	0	7

First Base	PCT	G	PO	A	E	DP
Cerreto	.920	2	22	1	2	1
Medina	.974	29	247	20	7	21
Patton	1.000	1	9	0	0	0
Ruiz	.995	36	339	24	2	29
Stienstra	1.000	10	71	7	0	5

Second Base	PCT	G	PO	A	E	DP
Bergman	.942	13	14	35	3	2
Castillo	.893	6	9	16	3	5
Patton	.971	30	38	95	4	16
Stienstra	.983	12	18	39	1	7
Wittels	.949	17	27	47	4	9

Third Base	PCT	G	PO	A	E	DP
Bergman	.887	19	14	41	7	7
Patton	.913	8	5	16	2	2
Ruiz	.902	23	18	28	5	2
Stienstra	.920	11	11	12	2	2
Wittels	.833	15	7	23	6	1

Shortstop	PCT	G	PO	A	E	DP
Albitz	.986	12	21	48	1	11
Castillo	.923	5	7	17	2	1
Valera	.917	51	92	139	21	24
Wittels	.949	8	16	21	2	5

Outfield	PCT	G	PO	A	E	DP
Cerreto	1.000	7	5	0	0	0
Encarnacion	.900	7	9	0	1	0
Hill	.971	53	100	2	3	1
Ingram	1.000	1	1	0	0	0
Martini	1.000	56	96	3	0	0
Medina	.955	38	62	1	3	0
O'Neill	.950	13	16	3	1	0
Patton	.000	1	0	0	0	0
Reyes	.990	54	98	5	1	0
Williams Jr.	1.000	9	15	1	0	0
Wittels	1.000	3	2	0	0	0

JOHNSON CITY CARDINALS — ROOKIE

APPALACHIAN LEAGUE

Batting	B-T	HT	WT	DOB	AVG	vLH	vRH	G	AB	R	H	2B	3B	HR	RBI	BB	HBP	SH	SF	SO	SB	CS	SLG	OBP
Apelian, Gary	R-R	6-4	206	9-22-90	.298	.306	.295	55	225	35	67	20	1	8	45	13	4	0	3	46	3	0	.502	.343
Bergin, David	R-R	6-2	235	8-25-89	.284	.300	.277	19	67	11	19	4	0	1	10	3	2	0	2	21	0	0	.388	.324
Byrd, Kolby	L-R	6-1	215	3-23-90	.233	.222	.236	37	150	11	35	8	1	1	15	5	0	0	3	36	0	0	.320	.253
Castillo, Ronard	R-R	6-5	200	6-16-92	.245	.382	.202	47	143	25	35	7	4	2	14	9	3	0	0	45	4	2	.392	.303
De La Cruz, Roberto	R-R	6-2	180	11-10-91	.264	.212	.280	59	227	39	60	15	0	16	47	7	5	0	2	57	0	1	.542	.299
Garcia, Anthony	R-R	6-0	180	1-4-92	.308	.360	.288	51	182	38	56	14	4	6	31	21	11	0	2	36	4	1	.527	.407
Garcia, Hector	R-R	6-1	185	5-16-90	.262	.143	.298	17	61	10	16	5	0	2	8	2	1	0	1	12	0	0	.443	.292
Keener, Jonathan	R-R	6-0	195	12-10-89	.250	.222	.257	27	92	10	23	2	0	4	12	4	1	0	0	19	0	1	.402	.289
Martin, Trevor	R-R	6-0	190	8-3-91	.333	.000	.500	1	3	1	1	0	0	0	0	0	0	0	0	2	0	0	.333	.500
Montero, Jesus	R-R	5-11	185	6-21-91	.276	.240	.288	29	98	12	27	7	0	0	11	9	1	0	1	32	1	0	.347	.339
Pritchard, Neal	R-R	6-0	0	2-21-89	.249	.136	.286	54	177	31	44	9	0	4	33	22	6	0	3	34	1	0	.367	.346
Rahmatulla, Tyler	R-R	5-10	190	2-26-90	.314	.328	.309	58	220	49	69	27	3	6	39	26	4	0	4	38	5	3	.545	.390
Ramos, Steve	R-R	6-0	160	7-4-90	.274	.350	.250	60	248	45	68	12	3	2	25	8	2	0	3	59	19	5	.371	.299
Tilson, Charlie	L-L	5-11	175	12-2-92	.467	.500	.462	4	15	2	7	2	0	0	4	1	0	0	0	1	0	0	.600	.500
Valera, Breyvic	B-R	5-11	160	8-1-92	.397	.563	.351	19	73	16	29	4	1	0	8	5	0	0	1	9	7	5	.479	.430
Washington, David	L-L	6-5	200	11-20-90	.248	.234	.252	55	202	33	50	13	2	9	27	23	2	0	1	64	4	1	.470	.329
Williams, Matt	R-R	5-10	170	8-29-89	.293	.327	.282	59	229	47	67	19	1	6	25	27	6	0	0	45	20	2	.463	.382

Pitching	B-T	HT	WT	DOB	W	L	ERA	G	GS	CG	SV	IP	H	R	ER	HR	BB	SO	AVG	vLH	vRH	K/9	BB/9
Bautista, Juan	R-R	5-11	195	6-16-93	0	0	6.00	2	1	0	0	6	6	4	4	2	0	7	.286	.375	.231	10.50	0.00
Billbrough, Logan	R-R	6-0	200	8-4-89	3	0	1.72	23	0	0	5	31	27	7	6	0	6	38	.231	.282	.205	10.91	1.72
Binder, Eric	R-R	6-6	210	9-15-86	0	0	0.00	3	0	0	1	3	0	0	0	0	1	3	.000	.000	.000	10.13	3.38
Canache, Roberto	R-R	6-5	180	5-12-90	3	1	2.40	21	0	0	1	30	29	8	8	2	6	32	.248	.154	.295	9.60	1.80
Constantino, Chris	R-R	6-3	235	10-8-91	0	0	0.00	3	0	0	0	6	3	0	0	0	1	7	.143	.167	.133	10.50	1.50
Creath, Brandon	R-R	6-3	200	2-16-89	1	0	0.00	1	0	0	0	2	0	0	0	0	0	3	.000	.000	.000	13.50	0.00
De La Cruz, Manuel	L-L	6-2	225	5-8-90	0	0	0.00	9	0	0	1	8	3	4	0	0	1	11	.100	.091	.111	12.38	1.13
Freeman, Ben	L-L	6-2	150	2-6-92	4	3	5.11	11	11	1	0	49	53	34	28	3	23	47	.279	.306	.270	8.57	4.20
Gillung, Nicholas	R-L	6-1	185	2-25-89	1	0	1.73	12	2	0	0	26	20	5	5	0	9	25	.211	.200	.215	8.65	3.12
Hald, Kyle	L-L	5-11	195	5-27-89	7	0	1.84	11	7	0	1	54	34	14	11	5	12	63	.178	.151	.188	10.57	2.01
Hiraldo, Eduardo	R-R	6-3	180	8-21-89	2	3	3.71	11	11	0	0	61	60	33	25	10	16	50	.261	.248	.271	7.42	2.37
Jenkins, Tyrell	R-R	6-4	180	7-20-92	4	2	3.86	11	11	0	0	56	63	33	24	3	13	55	.296	.291	.299	8.84	2.09
Lucas, Josh	R-R	6-6	185	11-5-90	4	1	4.00	8	8	0	0	45	57	22	20	6	9	25	.308	.304	.310	5.00	1.80
Melling, Tyler	R-L	6-2	170	9-4-88	0	0	5.40	1	1	0	0	5	6	3	3	1	0	3	.316	.143	.417	5.40	0.00
Mills, Tyler	R-R	6-3	205	1-10-90	2	1	6.84	20	0	0	2	26	30	21	20	6	19	18	.297	.333	.277	6.15	6.49
Nuernberg, Dyllon	R-R	6-1	220	5-28-91	2	2	5.23	21	0	0	2	33	29	23	19	2	15	33	.232	.211	.241	9.09	4.13
Pasen, Jose	R-R	6-1	180	5-19-90	4	4	4.45	11	11	0	0	61	58	39	30	6	17	51	.252	.280	.231	7.57	2.52
Paulino, Willy	R-R	6-2	190	6-21-90	0	0	0.00	1	0	0	1	2	0	0	0	0	1	4	.000	.000	.000	18.00	4.50
Rein, Matt	B-L	5-11	170	5-29-88	2	1	3.60	15	0	0	0	20	23	12	8	0	10	26	.284	.360	.250	11.70	4.50
Santana, Michael	R-R	6-0	155	7-1-90	1	1	1.45	21	0	0	1	31	23	6	5	1	9	27	.202	.190	.208	7.84	2.61
Sherriff, Ryan	L-L	6-1	185	5-25-90	2	2	4.54	9	5	0	0	34	38	18	17	4	8	24	.297	.375	.271	6.42	2.14
Wyatt, Heath	R-R	6-2	190	8-27-88	3	1	3.24	23	0	0	8	25	22	11	9	1	7	30	.237	.267	.222	10.80	2.52

Fielding

Catcher	PCT	G	PO	A	E	DP	PB
Byrd	.988	20	149	16	2	0	5
Keener	1.000	23	176	34	0	0	3
Montero	.964	28	232	32	10	4	6

First Base	PCT	G	PO	A	E	DP
Bergin	.987	8	77	1	1	9
De La Cruz	.750	1	3	0	1	2
Garcia	1.000	9	74	5	0	3
Washington	.992	54	464	30	4	42

Second Base	PCT	G	PO	A	E	DP
Martin	.750	1	2	1	1	1

	PCT	G	PO	A	E	DP
Pritchard	.963	16	35	44	3	12
Rahmatulla	.970	48	76	121	6	29
Valera	.974	10	15	22	1	3

Third Base	PCT	G	PO	A	E	DP
De La Cruz	.814	22	14	34	11	8
Garcia	.952	9	4	16	1	1
Pritchard	.973	40	25	82	3	9
Rahmatulla	1.000	7	7	9	0	2
Valera	.000	1	0	0	0	0

Shortstop	PCT	G	PO	A	E	DP
Rahmatulla	.900	6	3	15	2	1

	PCT	G	PO	A	E	DP
Valera	.897	8	8	18	3	2
Williams	.936	58	82	182	18	34

Outfield	PCT	G	PO	A	E	DP
Apelian	.975	54	107	8	3	1
Bergin	.667	3	2	0	1	0
Castillo	.887	44	54	1	7	1
Garcia	.944	47	66	1	4	0
Ramos	.993	60	131	8	1	2
Tilson	.800	4	6	2	2	0
Valera	1.000	3	4	1	0	0

GCL CARDINALS   ROOKIE

GULF COAST LEAGUE

Batting	B-T	HT	WT	DOB	AVG	vLH	vRH	G	AB	R	H	2B	3B	HR	RBI	BB	HBP	SH	SF	SO	SB	CS	SLG	OBP
Argenal, Jem	L-L	5-11	180	9-19-91	.260	.233	.267	45	150	24	39	6	3	3	18	6	3	0	4	29	1	4	.400	.294
Bryant, Anthony	L-R	6-3	215	1-13-92	.208	.227	.202	36	106	17	22	2	2	1	13	15	3	0	1	40	11	3	.292	.320
Cerreto, Phil	R-R	6-1	195	10-4-87	.125	.167	.115	9	32	4	4	2	0	0	4	5	1	0	2	7	2	0	.188	.250
Conley, Kyle	R-R	6-4	210	5-7-87	.154	.000	.200	5	13	0	2	2	0	0	2	4	0	0	1	5	0	0	.308	.333
Deol, Dutch	R-R	6-3	200	10-20-92	.089	.167	.080	21	56	5	5	1	0	0	1	8	1	0	1	21	0	0	.107	.212
Dodd, Corderious	R-R	6-2	230	2-21-92	.226	.400	.186	18	53	4	12	2	0	1	3	2	2	0	0	18	0	0	.321	.281
Ehrlich, Adam	L-L		200	12-13-92	.237	.286	.222	19	59	3	14	3	0	1	6	7	2	0	1	16	1	0	.339	.333
Encarnacion, Victor	R-R	6-2	165	3-8-90	.217	.263	.203	32	83	16	18	2	1	3	12	9	0	0	1	26	2	1	.373	.290
Garcia, Hector	R-R	6-1	185	5-16-90	.321	.400	.309	21	78	11	25	3	0	1	13	5	0	0	1	12	0	0	.397	.357
Jeffries, Lance	R-R	5-9	185	3-28-93	.256	.250	.258	44	125	20	32	8	2	1	19	15	6	0	0	48	12	5	.376	.363
Knox, Michael	R-R	6-4	230	4-18-89	.211	.111	.229	37	123	16	26	7	0	5	18	21	3	0	2	46	0	1	.390	.336
Mateo, Leandro	B-R	5-11	170	3-17-90	.220	.158	.236	29	91	16	20	4	1	0	11	12	6	0	1	18	8	3	.286	.345
McElroy Jr., C.J.	R-R	5-10	180	5-29-93	.228	.360	.167	23	79	10	18	2	1	0	7	7	2	0	1	15	8	2	.278	.303
Peoples, Kenny	R-R	6-1	180	8-16-93	.239	.263	.232	28	88	8	21	1	0	0	5	9	1	0	1	24	4	4	.250	.313
Perez, Luis	R-R	5-10	160	7-24-91	.296	.400	.267	32	115	19	34	10	1	3	20	9	4	0	1	15	3	0	.478	.364
Robinson, Shane	R-R	5-9	160	10-30-84	.136	.000	.143	6	22	4	3	2	1	0	0	1	0	0	1	0	0	0	.318	.174
Tilson, Charlie	L-L	5-11	175	12-2-92	.167	.000	.200	4	12	2	2	0	0	0	1	2	0	0	0	3	1	0	.167	.286
Tuivailala, Sam	R-R	6-3	195	10-19-92	.253	.261	.252	49	174	19	40	9	0	1	15	12	7	0	1	39	2	2	.329	.331
Valera, Breyvic	B-R	5-11	160	8-1-92	.255	.421	.220	28	110	23	28	5	2	1	13	10	3	0	2	17	7	1	.364	.328
Vargas, Ildemaro	R-R	6-0	170	7-16-91	.289	.333	.277	43	152	21	44	11	1	1	18	23	5	0	4	17	4	0	.395	.391
Velazco, Gerwuins	R-R	6-1	190	10-7-91	.245	.053	.291	30	98	14	24	4	0	1	13	18	1	0	0	17	0	0	.316	.368
Williams Jr., Reggie	B-R	6-4	190	9-15-89	.300	.250	.333	11	10	3	3	1	0	0	0	0	0	0	0	3	1	2	.400	.417

Pitching	B-T	HT	WT	DOB	W	L	ERA	G	GS	CG	SV	IP	H	R	ER	HR	BB	SO	AVG	vLH	vRH	K/9	BB/9
Aguilar, Cesar	R-R	6-3	250	5-15-92	3	1	2.05	16	0	0	0	22	14	8	5	1	17	24	.171	.179	.167	9.82	6.95
Bittle, Scott	R-R	6-2	190	8-27-86	0	1	6.75	3	0	0	0	3	0	2	2	0	5	1	.000	.000	.000	3.38	16.88
Brand, Cole	R-R	6-2	225	5-19-92	0	1	3.81	21	0	0	1	28	23	13	12	1	3	23	.215	.209	.219	7.31	0.95
Creath, Brandon	R-R	6-3	200	2-16-89	3	2	2.22	21	0	0	1	24	23	8	6	0	11	32	.256	.286	.242	11.84	4.07
De Leon, Victor	R-R	6-2	190	4-19-92	0	6	4.47	10	9	0	0	50	56	32	25	2	24	30	.290	.286	.293	5.36	4.29
Hooker, Deryk	R-R	6-4	185	6-21-89	0	1	3.00	2	2	0	0	3	5	2	1	0	0	4	.357	.500	.167	12.00	0.00
Lopez, Stalyn	L-L	5-9	160	12-28-91	1	3	3.40	12	9	0	0	48	48	23	18	2	24	31	.264	.243	.269	5.85	4.53
Lyman, Jeff	R-R	6-3	225	1-14-87	1	0	10.38	3	0	0	0	4	8	6	5	1	3	3	.400	.455	.333	6.23	6.23
Martinez, Bryan	R-R	6-3	172	3-1-91	1	0	6.75	5	0	0	0	5	5	4	4	0	4	3	.227	.250	.214	5.06	6.75
Melling, Tyler	R-L	6-2	170	9-4-88	5	0	3.86	15	0	0	0	30	21	14	13	3	7	28	.191	.222	.185	8.31	2.08
Mendoza, Richard	B-R	6-1	170	2-25-92	1	0	15.58	11	0	0	0	9	7	18	15	1	19	8	.200	.211	.188	8.31	19.73
Montanez, Fermin	R-R	6-4	200	1-1-91	1	1	5.00	13	0	0	0	18	22	10	10	0	5	12	.306	.364	.256	6.00	2.50
Nieto, Arquimedes	R-R	6-0	175	4-28-89	0	0	0.00	1	0	0	0	2	1	0	0	0	2	2	.143	.000	.200	9.00	9.00
Paulino, Willy	R-R	6-2	190	6-21-90	1	0	2.30	23	0	0	12	31	22	9	8	1	9	35	.193	.139	.218	10.05	2.59
Reid, Chase	L-R	6-3	215	5-17-88	1	1	4.50	3	1	0	0	4	4	3	2	1	1	3	.308	.500	.143	6.75	2.25
Samuel, Francisco	R-R	6-2	185	12-20-86	0	0	0.00	1	1	0	0	1	0	0	0	0	0	2	.000	.000	.000	18.00	0.00
Tapia, Angel	R-R	5-11	180	5-21-90	3	0	2.10	18	0	0	0	26	20	8	6	2	6	22	.211	.370	.147	7.71	2.10
Toribio, Arturo	R-R	5-11	180	3-1-92	2	0	1.69	3	0	0	0	16	16	9	3	1	3	16	.239	.231	.244	9.00	1.69
Ulacio, Ramon	R-R	6-1	190	3-17-91	4	3	2.93	12	12	0	0	58	50	31	19	2	20	38	.224	.265	.200	5.86	3.09
Villanueva, Dail	L-L	6-3	180	1-23-90	1	2	3.64	11	10	0	0	47	40	22	19	3	19	43	.229	.313	.210	8.23	3.64
Watson, Bradley	R-R	6-4	185	8-8-89	5	1	2.22	11	8	0	0	49	51	16	12	0	5	37	.264	.232	.282	6.84	0.92
Wright, Justin	L-L	5-9	175	8-18-89	0	0	0.00	1	0	0	0	1	0	0	0	0	0	0	.000	.000	.000	0.00	0.00

Fielding

Catcher	PCT	G	PO	A	E	DP	PB
Ehrlich	.985	17	111	18	2	1	8
Perez	.967	18	132	13	5	2	5
Velazco	.988	23	143	25	2	1	10

First Base	PCT	G	PO	A	E	DP
Argenal	.975	26	185	10	5	12
Cerreto	1.000	2	20	4	0	1
Garcia	1.000	10	82	6	0	4
Knox	.984	22	174	7	3	15

	PCT	G	PO	A	E	DP
Tuivailala	1.000	1	1	0	0	0
Velazco	1.000	2	12	1	0	1

Second Base	PCT	G	PO	A	E	DP
Mateo	.933	17	31	39	5	5
Valera	.976	27	55	69	3	14
Vargas	.970	13	34	30	2	7

Third Base	PCT	G	PO	A	E	DP
Garcia	1.000	8	8	16	0	1
Mateo	.667	4	1	7	4	0

	PCT	G	PO	A	E	DP
Tuivailala	.881	43	41	85	17	4
Vargas	1.000	3	2	3	0	0

Shortstop	PCT	G	PO	A	E	DP
Mateo	.882	4	5	10	2	3
Peoples	.917	25	34	66	9	9
Valera	.000	1	0	0	0	0
Vargas	.941	28	50	78	8	7

Outfield	PCT	G	PO	A	E	DP
Argenal	1.000	15	27	2	0	1

Bryant	.955	32	40	2	2	0
Conley	1.000	5	4	0	0	0
Deol	1.000	16	12	1	0	0
Dodd	.929	14	13	0	1	0
Encarnacion	.981	27	48	4	1	1
Jeffries	.939	44	89	3	6	1
Mateo	.000	1	0	0	0	0
McElroy Jr.	1.000	21	46	1	0	0
Perez	1.000	2	8	0	0	0
Robinson	1.000	6	9	0	0	0
Tilson	1.000	3	2	1	0	0
Williams Jr.	1.000	7	1	0	0	0

DSL CARDINALS   ROOKIE

DOMINICAN SUMMER LEAGUE

Batting	B-T	HT	WT	DOB	AVG	vLH	vRH	G	AB	R	H	2B	3B	HR	RBI	BB	HBP	SH	SF	SO	SB	CS	SLG	OBP
Acevedo, Jhohan	R-R	6-1	173	3-28-93	.255	.346	.236	52	153	19	39	3	1	0	14	20	2	0	1	34	6	3	.288	.347
Agustin, Jose	R-R	6-3	160	4-2-93	.220	.100	.250	35	100	14	22	7	0	2	8	26	10	0	0	26	2	4	.350	.426
Araujo, George	L-L	6-2	170	11-26-93	.136	.125	.138	35	103	7	14	3	0	1	10	10	3	0	1	38	0	1	.194	.231
Baez, Fernando	R-R	6-1	195	1-2-92	.221	.238	.218	50	140	17	31	3	5	5	21	19	2	0	2	22	1	2	.421	.319
Barbuena, Daniel	R-R	6-0	160	3-23-93	.259	.258	.259	55	174	22	45	7	1	2	20	29	3	0	0	44	2	1	.345	.374
Capellan, Amaury	R-R	5-11	190	9-30-92	.305	.269	.313	47	154	26	47	10	1	5	36	27	2	0	2	30	0	3	.481	.411
Celestino, Eduardo	L-R	6-2	175	9-8-92	.267	.259	.270	31	90	12	24	6	2	0	5	5	1	0	0	20	3	2	.378	.313
Cruz, Luis	R-R	6-2	180	5-26-93	.186	.263	.172	36	118	12	22	2	0	0	6	11	0	0	0	23	1	2	.203	.256
Diaz, Domingo	R-R	6-2	165	3-8-92	.216	.095	.235	52	153	28	33	8	2	1	16	26	4	0	0	42	3	0	.314	.344
Garcia, Ronnierd	R-R	6-1	185	3-8-90	.262	.143	.294	42	130	18	34	6	1	3	20	8	7	0	2	29	0	2	.392	.333
Gomez, Jose	R-R	5-11	183	1-30-92	.175	.231	.164	32	80	5	14	2	0	0	8	18	0	0	1	25	0	0	.200	.323
Martinez, Jose	R-R	6-0	175	11-3-92	.152	.100	.174	15	33	4	5	0	0	0	4	7	1	0	0	5	0	2	.152	.317
Medina, Rafael	R-R	6-2	170	10-24-91	.252	.231	.256	49	147	27	37	6	1	3	18	22	2	0	0	27	1	0	.367	.357
Mejia, Alejandro	R-R	6-4	195	3-10-93	.172	.077	.200	20	58	4	10	2	1	0	5	7	1	0	2	20	0	0	.241	.265
Pena, Jose	R-R	6-2	190	5-26-92	.137	.095	.148	38	102	12	14	6	0	0	9	22	7	0	0	50	2	2	.196	.328
Pina, Leobaldo	R-R	6-2	160	6-29-94	.268	.286	.264	51	194	29	52	5	1	0	12	19	5	0	2	32	6	1	.304	.345
Reyes, Robelys	B-R	5-9	150	7-25-90	.378	.370	.381	62	222	43	84	11	5	6	26	27	4	0	1	26	22	9	.554	.453
Torres, Carlos	R-R	6-3	160	10-1-92	.228	.091	.261	29	57	6	13	3	0	1	6	7	1	0	0	9	1	0	.333	.323

Pitching	B-T	HT	WT	DOB	W	L	ERA	G	GS	CG	SV	IP	H	R	ER	HR	BB	SO	AVG	vLH	vRH	K/9	BB/9
Almeida, Alberth	R-R	6-0	190	11-30-91	0	0	34.71	3	0	0	0	2	5	10	9	1	5	1	.417	.667	.333	3.86	19.29
Bautista, Juan	R-R	5-11	195	6-16-93	3	5	3.36	13	11	1	0	56	44	29	21	4	28	47	.215	.158	.228	7.51	4.47
Brito, Ismael	L-L	5-11	170	3-23-93	2	1	2.63	13	0	0	0	24	16	10	7	0	15	21	.186	.500	.163	7.88	5.63
Ceballo, Addelin	R-R	6-0	190	6-29-91	0	3	4.74	15	1	0	2	25	33	18	13	3	15	14	.314	.304	.317	5.11	5.47
De Aguas, John	L-L	5-10	160	12-4-91	1	2	2.81	9	0	0	0	16	12	5	5	0	13	16	.226	.500	.216	9.00	7.31
De La Cruz, Anthony	L-L	6-0	170	3-14-93	0	1	12.18	13	1	0	1	17	28	23	23	2	20	18	.378	.400	.377	9.53	10.59
De La Cruz, Jean	R-R	6-1	190	5-8-92	0	1	18.00	3	0	0	0	3	3	6	6	0	7	1	.273	.500	.222	3.00	21.00
De Los Santos, Hansel	R-R	6-3	160	8-7-91	3	5	2.78	12	12	0	0	65	55	27	20	2	15	57	.229	.159	.257	7.93	2.09
Escudero, Jhonatan	R-R	6-1	165	7-7-93	2	5	4.95	12	9	1	0	44	44	30	24	2	33	33	.267	.387	.239	6.80	6.80
Flores, Fidencio	R-R	6-0	160	9-10-91	5	2	2.22	14	0	0	2	24	21	15	6	1	7	25	.228	.176	.240	9.25	2.59
Garcia, Silfredo	R-R	6-2	170	7-19-91	1	4	2.43	12	11	1	0	63	47	23	17	0	14	45	.208	.291	.181	6.43	2.00
Gerdel, Anderson	R-R	6-4	204	7-19-91	3	2	1.21	15	2	0	1	45	38	10	6	1	4	36	.224	.353	.191	7.25	0.81
Gonzalez, Fernando	R-R	6-4	175	4-22-94	0	3	5.14	8	5	0	0	28	31	20	16	2	9	14	.284	.421	.256	4.50	2.89
Paredes, Norge	R-R	6-3	171	2-12-91	0	1	2.65	6	4	0	0	17	21	8	5	0	8	9	.300	.238	.327	4.76	4.24
Perdomo, Luis	R-R	6-2	159	5-9-93	1	3	5.68	6	5	0	0	19	28	18	12	1	8	16	.364	.333	.369	7.58	3.79
Planchart, Douglas	R-R	6-2	184	12-17-91	1	1	3.32	13	1	1	3	22	22	13	8	0	15	11	.265	.292	.254	4.57	6.23
Polanco, Jhonny	R-R	6-3	191	4-28-92	3	2	4.33	8	6	0	0	35	31	19	17	1	20	30	.246	.300	.229	7.64	5.09
Rodriguez, Delvi	L-L	6-2	170	9-14-90	0	0	2.35	4	0	0	0	8	7	9	2	0	9	2	.219	.333	.207	2.35	10.57
Salazar, Hector	R-R	6-2	165	6-29-94	0	1	3.77	12	3	0	0	29	20	18	12	2	21	22	.194	.118	.209	6.91	6.59
Villegas, Kender	R-R	6-2	170	6-8-93	2	2	1.13	15	0	0	1	32	29	8	4	0	9	33	.238	.350	.216	9.28	2.53

Fielding

Catcher	PCT	G	PO	A	E	DP	PB
Baez	.968	36	186	25	7	1	13
Cruz	.983	21	105	10	2	1	10
Gomez	.965	31	177	18	7	2	10
Medina	1.000	3	2	3	0	1	
Pina	.958	5	13	10	1	5	
Reyes	.971	48	103	99	6		23

First Base	PCT	G	PO	A	E	DP
Baez	.967	14	84	3	3	10
Diaz	.982	23	155	11	3	16
Medina	.971	30	194	7	6	18
Mejia	.987	18	143	4	2	9

Second Base	PCT	G	PO	A	E	DP
Barbuena	.944	22	48	36	5	13

Third Base	PCT	G	PO	A	E	DP
Agustin	.923	30	29	55	7	9
Garcia	.915	30	24	62	8	8
Medina	.885	15	11	35	6	1

Shortstop	PCT	G	PO	A	E	DP
Agustin	1.000	1	1	0	0	0
Barbuena	.837	27	19	58	15	9
Pina	.928	41	52	115	13	16
Reyes	.886	6	10	21	4	6

Outfield	PCT	G	PO	A	E	DP
Acevedo	.980	52	94	5	2	1
Araujo	.911	33	40	1	4	0
Capellan	.968	47	85	7	3	3
Celestino	.923	22	22	2	2	1
Diaz	.964	24	27	0	1	0
Martinez	1.000	11	16	1	0	0
Pena	.889	29	34	6	5	3
Torres	1.000	19	20	3	0	1

ST. LOUIS CARDINALS

San Diego Padres

SEASON IN A SENTENCE: The offseason trade of hometown hero Adrian Gonzalez to the Red Sox hamstrung an already anemic offense, causing the Padres to go from 90 wins in the previous year to 90 losses in 2011.

HIGH POINT: Lost in the shuffle of a disappointing season was the emergence of center fielder Cameron Maybin. The 24-year old, acquired in an offseason trade with the Marlins, finally fulfilled the promise that made him the 10th overall pick in the 2010 draft. Maybin played spectacular defense in the spacious Petco outfield while stealing 40 bases and producing with the bat. Maybin was particularly impressive on the road, where he hit .294/.349/.457.

LOW POINT: Not helped by their home park, the Padres' offense ranked as one of the worst in baseball. San Diego finished in the bottom three in several offensive categories including home runs, average, on-base percentage and slugging. The Padres also ranked near the bottom in various advanced metrics that account for park and league.

NOTABLE ROOKIES: Lefthander Cory Luebke established himself in the rotation, surpassing most expectations by posting a 3.29 ERA while striking out nearly 10 batters per nine innings. Anthony Rizzo is San Diego's first baseman of the future, but when he faltered in his first major league experience, Jesus Guzman took over and broke out in a big way. The minor league veteran became the Padres' best hitter with a .312/.369/.478 line in 76 games.

KEY TRANSACTIONS: In addition to trading for Maybin before the season, the big deal that sent Gonzalez to the Red Sox netted several premium prospects, highlighted by Rizzo. Free-agent acquisition Aaron Harang, a San Diego State alum, returned home and returned to form, throwing 170 innings with a solid 3.64 ERA. After Heath Bell dominated trade deadline rumors, another reliever, Mike Adams, was the one who got traded to the Rangers, bringing back pitching prospects Robbie Erlin and Joe Wieland.

DOWN ON THE FARM: Rizzo was spectacular in Triple-A before struggling in a major league stint. High Class A Lake Elsinore Storm and Double-A San Antonio won their league titles with prospect-laden rosters, and the Missions had one of the best records in the minor leagues, winning 94 games in spite of high roster turnover.

OPENING DAY PAYROLL: $45,869,140 (27th)

PLAYERS OF THE YEAR

MAJOR LEAGUE	MINOR LEAGUE
Cameron Maybin of	**Anthony Rizzo** 1b
.264/.323/.393	(Triple-A)
24 2B, 40 SB	.331/.404/.652
2nd in NL in SB	26 HR, 101 RBIs

ORGANIZATION LEADERS

BATTING *Minimum 250 PA

MAJORS

* AVG	Jesus Guzman	.312
* OPS	Jesus Guzman	.847
HR	Ryan Ludwick	11
RBI	Ryan Ludwick	64

MINORS

* AVG	Jedd Gyorko, Lake Elsinore/San Antonio	.333
* OBP	James Darnell, San Antonio/Tucson	.406
* SLG	Anthony Rizzo, Tucson	.652
R	Jedd Gyorko, Lake Elsinore/San Antonio	119
H	Jedd Gyorko, Lake Elsinore/San Antonio	192
TB	Jedd Gyorko, Lake Elsinore/San Antonio	318
2B	Jedd Gyorko, Lake Elsinore/San Antonio	47
3B	Reymond Fuentes, Lake Elsinore	9
	Rymer Liriano, Lake Elsinore/Fort Wayne	9
HR	Anthony Rizzo, Tucson	26
RBI	Jedd Gyorko, Lake Elsinore/San Antonio	114
BB	Jaff Decker, San Antonio	103
SO	Jaff Decker, San Antonio	145
SB	Rymer Liriano, Lake Elsinore/Fort Wayne	66

PITCHING #Minimum 75 IP

MAJORS

W	Aaron Harang	14
# ERA	Cory Luebke	3.29
SO	Mat Latos	185
SV	Heath Bell	43

MINORS

W	Matt Buschmann, San Antonio/Tucson	12
	Keyvius Sampson, Fort Wayne	12
L	Will Inman, Tucson	11
	Adys Portillo, Fort Wayne	11
# ERA	Mark Hardy, Fort Wayne	2.78
G	Brad Brach, San Antonio/Tucson	67
	Colt Hynes, Tucson/San Antonio	67
GS	Jeremy Hefner, Tucson	28
	Jerry Sullivan, Lake Elsinore	28
SV	Brad Brach, San Antonio/Tucson	34
IP	Jeremy Hefner, Tucson	157.1
BB	Jon Leicester, Tucson	64
SO	Keyvius Sampson, Fort Wayne	143
# AVG	Keyvius Sampson, Fort Wayne	.192

General Manager: Jed Hoyer. **Farm Director:** Randy Smith. **Scouting Director:** Jaron Madison.

Class	Team	League	W	L	PCT	Finish	Manager(s)
Majors	San Diego Padres	National	71	91	.438	t-14th (16)	Bud Black
Triple-A	Tucson Padres	Pacific Coast	65	79	.451	t-13th (16)	Terry Kennedy
Double-A	San Antonio Missions	Texas	94	46	.671	1st (8)	Doug Dascenzo
High A	Lake Elsinore Storm	California	69	71	.493	t-5th (10)	Carlos Lezcano/Phil Plantier
Low A	Fort Wayne Tincaps	Midwest	69	70	.496	9th (16)	Shawn Wooten
Short-season	Eugene Emeralds	Northwest	46	30	.605	1st (8)	Pat Murphy
Rookie	AZL Padres	Arizona	23	33	.411	10th (13)	Jim Gabella
Overall 2011 Minor League Record			366	329	.527	8th (30)	

ORGANIZATION STATISTICS

SAN DIEGO PADRES
NATIONAL LEAGUE

Batting	B-T	HT	WT	DOB	AVG	vLH	vRH	G	AB	R	H	2B	3B	HR	RBI	BB	HBP	SH	SF	SO	SB	CS	SLG	OBP
Bartlett, Jason	R-R	6-0	190	10-30-79	.245	.279	.234	139	554	61	136	22	3	2	40	48	5	0	6	98	23	10	.307	.308
Blanks, Kyle	R-R	6-6	270	9-11-86	.229	.185	.250	55	170	21	39	7	1	7	26	16	2	0	2	51	2	0	.406	.300
Cabrera, Everth	B-R	5-10	175	11-17-86	.125	.500	.000	2	8	1	1	0	0	0	1	0	0	0	0	3	2	0	.125	.222
Cantu, Jorge	R-R	6-3	205	1-30-82	.194	.204	.189	57	144	8	28	4	0	3	16	7	1	0	3	28	0	0	.285	.232
Cunningham, Aaron	R-R	5-11	205	4-24-86	.178	.205	.152	52	90	12	16	6	1	3	9	9	1	0	1	17	1	0	.367	.257
Darnell, James	R-R	6-2	195	1-19-87	.222	.143	.292	18	45	2	10	2	0	1	7	5	0	0	1	7	1	0	.333	.294
Denorfia, Chris	R-R	6-0	195	7-15-80	.277	.328	.245	111	307	38	85	13	2	5	19	28	1	0	2	49	11	6	.381	.337
Forsythe, Logan	R-R	6-1	205	1-14-87	.213	.217	.212	62	150	12	32	9	1	0	12	12	3	0	2	33	3	1	.287	.281
Gonzalez, Alberto	R-R	5-10	195	4-18-83	.215	.257	.198	102	247	18	53	10	2	1	32	13	2	0	4	37	1	2	.283	.256
Guzman, Jesus	R-R	6-1	215	6-14-84	.312	.333	.299	76	247	33	77	22	2	5	44	22	1	0	1	43	9	2	.478	.369
Hawpe, Brad	L-L	6-3	210	6-22-79	.231	.190	.236	62	195	19	45	10	0	4	19	19	1	0	1	68	0	0	.344	.301
Headley, Chase	B-R	6-2	200	5-9-84	.289	.352	.264	113	381	43	110	28	1	4	44	52	2	0	3	92	13	2	.399	.374
Hermida, Jeremy	L-R	6-2	220	1-30-84	.225	.250	.222	20	40	3	9	2	1	1	6	7	1	0	0	19	0	0	.400	.354
2-team total (10 Cincinnati)					.190	—	—	30	58	5	11	2	1	2	9	7	1	0	0	26	0	0	.362	.288
Hudson, Orlando	B-R	6-0	190	12-12-77	.246	.224	.256	119	398	54	98	15	3	7	43	49	2	0	4	84	19	3	.352	.329
Hundley, Nick	R-R	6-1	205	9-8-83	.288	.286	.289	82	281	34	81	16	5	9	29	22	4	0	1	74	1	1	.477	.347
Hunter, Cedric	L-L	6-0	185	3-10-88	.250	.200	.250	6	4	1	1	0	0	0	1	0	0	0	0	0	1	0	.250	.400
Johnson, Rob	R-R	6-1	215	7-22-82	.190	.229	.165	67	179	9	34	6	1	3	16	14	3	0	1	58	3	0	.285	.259
Ludwick, Ryan	R-L	6-3	215	7-13-78	.238	.264	.230	101	378	42	90	18	0	11	64	32	4	0	5	87	1	1	.373	.301
2-team total (38 Pittsburgh)					.237	—	—	139	490	56	116	23	0	13	75	51	4	0	6	124	1	1	.363	.310
Martinez, Luis	R-R	6-0	210	4-3-85	.203	.214	.200	22	59	7	12	1	1	1	10	8	1	0	0	14	1	0	.305	.309
Maybin, Cameron	R-R	6-3	210	4-4-87	.264	.296	.251	137	516	82	136	24	8	9	40	44	2	0	2	125	40	8	.393	.323
Parrino, Andy	R-R	6-0	180	10-31-85	.182	.143	.189	24	44	3	8	1	0	0	4	9	1	0	1	17	1	0	.205	.327
Patterson, Eric	L-R	6-0	170	4-8-83	.180	.250	.176	47	89	8	16	2	1	2	8	12	0	0	2	22	8	2	.292	.272
Phillips, Kyle	L-R	6-1	225	4-3-84	.171	.200	.169	36	76	9	13	3	0	2	10	8	1	0	0	19	0	0	.289	.259
Rizzo, Anthony	L-L	6-3	220	8-8-89	.141	.172	.131	49	128	9	18	8	1	1	9	21	4	0	0	46	2	1	.242	.281
Tekotte, Blake	L-R	5-11	175	5-24-87	.176	.000	.200	19	34	1	6	1	1	0	1	4	0	0	0	21	2	1	.265	.263
Venable, Will	L-L	6-2	205	10-29-82	.246	.174	.256	121	370	49	91	14	7	9	44	31	5	0	4	92	26	3	.395	.310

Pitching	B-T	HT	WT	DOB	W	L	ERA	G	GS	CG	SV	IP	H	R	ER	HR	BB	SO	AVG	vLH	vRH	K/9	BB/9
Adams, Mike	R-R	6-5	195	7-29-78	3	1	1.13	48	0	0	1	48	26	7	6	2	9	49	.155	.194	.107	9.19	1.69
Bass, Anthony	R-R	6-2	190	11-1-87	2	0	1.68	27	3	0	0	48	41	9	9	3	21	24	.236	.243	.230	4.47	3.91
Bell, Heath	R-R	6-3	260	9-29-77	3	4	2.44	64	0	0	43	63	51	20	17	4	21	51	.223	.283	.164	7.32	3.02
Brach, Brad	R-R	6-6	210	4-12-86	0	2	5.14	9	0	0	0	7	9	5	4	0	7	11	.300	.333	.286	14.14	9.00
Carpenter, Drew	R-R	6-3	240	5-18-85	0	0	8.44	6	0	0	0	5	6	5	5	1	3	6	.300	.300	.300	10.13	5.06
2-team total (6 Philadelphia)					0	0	7.98	12	0	0	0	15	19	13	13	3	7	16	—	—	—	9.82	4.30
Deduno, Samuel	R-R	6-3	190	7-2-83	0	0	3.00	2	0	0	0	3	5	1	1	0	3	4	.357	.333	.375	12.00	9.00
Frieri, Ernesto	R-R	6-2	200	7-19-85	1	2	2.71	59	0	0	0	63	51	21	19	3	34	76	.221	.258	.196	10.86	4.86
Fulchino, Jeff	R-R	6-5	285	11-26-79	0	0	16.20	3	0	0	0	2	3	3	3	0	4	2	.375	.250	.500	10.80	21.60
2-team total (36 Houston)					1	4	5.71	39	0	0	0	35	37	22	22	5	22	33	—	—	—	8.57	5.71
Gregerson, Luke	L-R	6-3	200	5-14-84	3	3	2.75	61	0	0	0	56	57	23	17	2	19	34	.266	.329	.225	5.50	3.07
Hamren, Erik	R-R	6-1	195	8-21-86	1	0	4.38	14	0	0	0	12	10	7	6	2	9	10	.244	.077	.321	7.30	6.57
Harang, Aaron	R-R	6-7	260	5-9-78	14	7	3.64	28	28	0	0	171	175	73	69	20	58	124	.269	.277	.261	6.54	3.06
Latos, Mat	R-R	6-6	225	12-9-87	9	14	3.47	31	31	0	0	194	168	82	75	16	62	185	.233	.258	.204	8.57	2.87
LeBlanc, Wade	L-L	6-3	215	8-7-84	5	6	4.63	14	14	0	0	80	84	42	41	7	28	51	.276	.408	.236	5.76	3.16
Luebke, Cory	R-L	6-4	205	3-4-85	6	10	3.29	46	17	0	0	140	105	54	51	12	44	154	.209	.157	.229	9.92	2.84
Moseley, Dustin	R-R	6-4	215	12-26-81	3	10	3.30	20	20	0	0	120	117	59	44	10	36	64	.255	.262	.249	4.80	2.70
Neshek, Pat	B-R	6-3	210	9-4-80	1	1	4.01	25	0	0	0	25	19	12	11	4	22	20	.216	.209	.222	7.30	8.03
Qualls, Chad	R-R	6-5	220	8-17-78	6	8	3.51	77	0	0	0	74	73	30	29	7	20	43	.263	.320	.218	5.21	2.42
Richard, Clayton	L-L	6-5	245	9-12-83	5	9	3.88	18	18	0	0	100	104	52	43	8	38	53	.272	.261	.276	4.79	3.43
Scribner, Evan	R-R	6-3	190	7-19-85	0	0	7.07	10	0	0	0	14	18	11	11	1	4	10	.300	.379	.226	6.43	2.57
Spence, Josh	L-L	6-1	170	1-22-88	0	2	2.73	40	0	0	0	30	14	9	9	2	19	31	.140	.158	.116	9.40	5.76
Stauffer, Tim	R-R	6-1	225	6-2-82	9	12	3.73	31	31	0	0	186	180	81	77	20	53	128	.258	.276	.239	6.20	2.57
Thatcher, Joe	L-L	6-2	230	10-4-81	0	0	4.50	18	0	0	0	10	8	5	5	1	7	9	.216	.158	.278	8.10	6.30

Fielding

Catcher	PCT	G	PO	A	E	DP	PB
Hundley	.989	76	501	60	6	8	4
Johnson	.995	63	362	65	2	3	5
Martinez	1.000	19	122	7	0	1	0
Phillips	.981	24	140	12	3	1	1

First Base	PCT	G	PO	A	E	DP
Blanks	1.000	13	67	6	0	6
Cantu	.990	26	198	8	2	10
Gonzalez	1.000	4	17	1	0	3
Guzman	.990	53	380	35	4	28
Hawpe	.990	44	368	32	4	46
Rizzo	.994	45	316	26	2	28

Second Base	PCT	G	PO	A	E	DP
Cantu	.000	1	0	0	0	0
Forsythe	.952	23	40	40	4	12
Gonzalez	.983	41	53	61	2	14

	PCT	G	PO	A	E	DP
Hudson	.993	114	238	308	4	69
Parrino	1.000	3	6	9	0	2
Patterson	.951	10	20	19	2	8

Third Base	PCT	G	PO	A	E	DP
Cantu	.950	10	5	14	1	1
Darnell	.909	12	7	13	2	2
Forsythe	.985	26	19	47	1	5
Gonzalez	.970	21	6	26	1	2
Headley	.960	107	95	166	11	16
Parrino	1.000	11	6	16	0	2

Shortstop	PCT	G	PO	A	E	DP
Bartlett	.971	138	203	391	18	83
Cabrera	1.000	2	4	5	0	0
Forsythe	.000	1	0	0	0	0
Gonzalez	.990	30	43	61	1	10
Parrino	1.000	4	1	10	0	2

Outfield	PCT	G	PO	A	E	DP
Blanks	.985	37	62	3	1	2
Cunningham	1.000	26	35	1	0	0
Darnell	1.000	3	3	0	0	0
Denorfia	.982	95	162	6	3	2
Guzman	1.000	7	13	0	0	0
Hawpe	1.000	7	11	0	0	0
Hermida	1.000	13	24	1	0	0
Hunter	.000	2	0	0	0	0
Ludwick	.994	96	158	9	1	2
Maybin	.986	136	342	2	5	1
Parrino	1.000	5	5	0	0	0
Patterson	1.000	16	34	0	0	0
Tekotte	1.000	11	10	0	0	0
Venable	.989	109	176	3	2	2

TUCSON PADRES
PACIFIC COAST LEAGUE

TRIPLE-A

Batting	B-T	HT	WT	DOB	AVG	vLH	vRH	G	AB	R	H	2B	3B	HR	RBI	BB	HBP	SH	SF	SO	SB	CS	SLG	OBP
Blanks, Kyle	R-R	6-6	270	9-11-86	.351	.344	.353	35	134	36	47	12	2	11	35	16	1	0	1	37	0	1	.716	.421
Cabrera, Everth	B-R	5-10	175	11-17-86	.297	.268	.305	58	246	52	73	12	4	2	15	29	0	0	1	40	29	8	.402	.370
Cintron, Alex	B-R	6-2	210	12-17-78	.350	.412	.326	17	60	9	21	4	1	1	6	5	0	0	1	9	0	0	.500	.394
Clark, Matt	L-R	6-5	215	12-10-86	.292	.235	.308	129	462	71	135	24	1	23	83	58	1	0	13	116	0	2	.498	.363
Contreras, Anthony	L-R	5-11	185	9-26-83	.223	.217	.225	36	112	12	25	4	1	1	11	9	0	0	1	17	1	1	.304	.279
Cunningham, Aaron	R-R	5-11	205	4-24-86	.329	.395	.311	87	340	65	112	34	4	9	63	38	3	0	3	54	4	4	.532	.398
Daal, Rodney	R-R	5-11	190	3-23-94	.000	.000	.000	1	1	0	0	0	0	0	0	0	0	0	0	1	0	0	.000	.000
Darnell, James	R-T	6-2	195	1-19-87	.261	.419	.187	35	134	20	35	4	0	6	17	16	2	0	2	30	0	0	.425	.344
Denorfia, Chris	R-R	6-0	195	7-15-80	.118	.333	.071	7	17	0	2	1	0	0	0	3	0	0	0	4	0	0	.176	.250
Durango, Luis	B-R	5-9	165	4-23-86	.243	.218	.254	61	177	36	43	3	3	0	15	19	4	0	1	31	10	5	.294	.328
2-team total (47 Oklahoma City)					.257	—	—	108	331	69	85	5	4	0	24	41	4	0	2	54	28	14	.296	.344
Feliz, Pedro	R-R	6-1	210	4-27-75	.217	.333	.176	25	92	9	20	5	0	3	12	0	0	0	0	13	0	1	.370	.217
Forsythe, Logan	R-R	6-1	205	1-14-87	.326	.244	.350	46	178	41	58	12	0	8	34	33	6	0	1	50	8	4	.528	.445
Gale, Rocky	R-R	6-0	180	2-22-88	.250	.000	.250	4	12	1	3	0	1	0	2	0	0	0	0	1	0	0	.417	.250
Guzman, Jesus	R-R	6-1	215	6-14-84	.332	.475	.284	63	244	40	81	22	1	8	57	34	5	0	1	42	4	4	.529	.423
Hoffpauir, Jarrett	R-R	5-9	190	6-18-83	.281	.295	.275	91	306	49	86	26	2	5	34	35	5	0	8	36	2	3	.428	.356
Hudson, Orlando	B-R	6-0	190	12-12-77	.750	1.000	.500	2	4	4	3	2	0	1	3	0	0	0	0	1	0	0	1.250	.857
Hudson, Robbie	R-R	6-0	170	8-31-83	.224	.429	.143	18	49	2	11	3	1	0	7	1	0	0	0	6	0	0	.327	.240
Hundley, Nick	R-R	6-1	205	9-8-83	.273	.600	.000	4	11	3	3	2	0	1	5	2	0	0	0	2	0	0	.727	.385
Hunter, Cedric	L-L	6-1	225	3-10-88	.255	.262	.253	81	282	44	72	17	3	2	33	28	1	0	3	24	9	4	.358	.322
Kielty, Bobby	B-R	6-1	225	8-5-76	.289	.303	.282	62	190	23	55	15	0	7	28	20	1	0	2	43	0	0	.479	.357
Macias, Drew	L-L	6-3	175	3-7-83	.241	.211	.256	19	58	6	14	3	1	1	6	7	2	0	1	10	0	0	.379	.338
Martinez, Alberth	R-R	6-1	170	1-23-91	.118	.000	.200	4	17	2	2	0	0	0	0	0	0	0	0	7	0	0	.118	.118
Martinez, Luis	R-R	6-0	210	4-3-85	.323	.289	.333	58	198	24	64	17	1	1	28	17	2	0	2	46	2	0	.434	.379
Maybin, Cameron	R-R	6-3	210	4-4-87	.200	.000	.333	3	10	1	2	1	0	0	1	1	0	0	0	2	1	0	.300	.273
McKenna, Pat	R-R	5-10	170	6-24-87	.250	.316	.216	25	56	10	14	2	1	1	5	7	0	0	2	25	1	0	.375	.323
Parrino, Andy	B-R	6-0	180	10-31-85	.327	.308	.333	48	153	26	50	13	1	3	24	16	5	0	4	25	2	1	.484	.399
Patterson, Eric	L-R	6-0	170	4-8-83	.253	.286	.236	51	190	31	48	12	4	3	14	9	1	0	2	29	3	3	.405	.287
Payne, Danny	L-L	5-10	185	9-8-85	.286	.000	.333	3	7	1	2	1	0	0	2	0	0	0	0	2	0	0	.429	.286
Phillips, Kyle	L-R	6-1	225	4-3-84	.179	.211	.171	35	95	9	17	2	0	2	9	8	0	0	1	10	0	0	.263	.240
Pozo, Jhonaldo	R-R	6-3	183	3-28-89	—	.000	.000	1	0	0	0	0	0	0	0	0	0	0	0	0	0	0	—	—
Quiroz, Guillermo	R-R	6-1	215	11-29-81	.240	.213	.256	76	250	33	60	18	2	5	44	20	2	0	5	67	0	1	.388	.296
Rizzo, Anthony	L-L	6-3	220	8-8-89	.331	.299	.342	93	356	64	118	34	1	26	101	43	6	0	8	89	7	6	.652	.404
Rodriguez, Eddy	R-R	6-0	205	12-1-85	.158	.500	.118	6	19	3	3	0	0	1	3	2	0	0	0	5	0	0	.316	.238
Solis, Ali	R-R	5-10	225	9-29-87	.211	.273	.185	11	38	3	8	2	0	0	3	1	0	0	0	14	0	0	.263	.231
Stokes, Mykal	R-R	6-4	170	6-2-90	.385	.500	.200	5	13	1	5	0	1	0	1	0	0	0	0	3	1	0	.538	.429
Stubblefield, Tyler	R-R	5-10	185	11-19-87	.000	.000	.000	2	6	0	0	0	0	0	0	0	0	0	0	0	0	0	.000	.000
Tolleson, Steve	R-R	5-11	190	11-1-83	.276	.202	.310	77	312	48	86	21	2	4	36	29	3	0	3	56	16	3	.394	.340
2-team total (46 Sacramento)					.275	—	—	123	487	77	134	27	2	9	55	60	5	0	4	93	24	5	.394	.358
Venable, Will	L-L	6-2	205	10-29-82	.276	.176	.317	14	58	14	16	3	2	3	11	5	0	0	1	13	3	0	.552	.328

Pitching	B-T	HT	WT	DOB	W	L	ERA	G	GS	CG	SV	IP	H	R	ER	HR	BB	SO	AVG	vLH	vRH	K/9	BB/9
Bass, Anthony	R-R	6-2	190	11-1-87	1	0	1.80	1	1	0	0	5	6	1	1	0	0	2	.300	.333	.273	5.40	0.00
Brach, Brad	R-R	6-6	210	4-12-86	1	3	3.90	25	0	0	11	28	28	13	12	1	7	30	.264	.300	.232	9.76	2.28
Burke, Greg	R-R	6-4	215	9-21-82	2	2	5.70	64	0	0	1	79	100	57	50	8	40	76	.313	.328	.303	8.66	4.56
Buschmann, Matt	R-R	6-3	210	2-13-84	6	5	7.31	20	15	1	0	89	129	75	72	11	33	60	.351	.394	.315	6.09	3.35
Castro, Simon	R-R	6-5	210	4-9-88	2	2	10.17	6	6	0	0	26	37	30	29	5	18	21	.333	.278	.386	7.36	6.31
Deduno, Samuel	R-R	6-3	190	7-2-83	4	6	3.93	40	12	0	0	105	101	58	46	2	58	85	.253	.216	.279	7.26	4.96
Flores, Randy	L-L	6-0	190	7-31-75	1	2	2.89	19	0	0	0	19	17	9	6	1	6	19	.243	.200	.300	9.16	2.89
2-team total (10 Nashville)					2	3	3.03	29	0	0	2	30	30	16	10	3	10	30	—	—		9.10	3.03
Frieri, Ernesto	R-R	6-2	200	7-19-85	1	0	2.70	4	0	0	0	3	3	1	1	0	2	5	.231	.600	.000	13.50	5.40
Geer, Josh	R-R	6-3	195	6-2-83	1	0	8.00	2	2	0	0	9	17	8	8	1	2	7	.395	.364	.429	7.00	2.00

Pitching

Pitching	B-T	HT	WT	DOB	W	L	ERA	G	GS	CG	SV	IP	H	R	ER	HR	BB	SO	AVG	vLH	vRH	K/9	BB/9
Gregerson, Luke	L-R	6-3	200	5-14-84	0	0	20.25	2	0	0	0	1	3	3	3	0	2	2	.429	.500	.400	13.50	13.50
Hamren, Erik	R-R	6-1	195	8-21-86	0	0	3.00	2	0	0	1	3	3	1	1	1	3	2	.273	.200	.333	6.00	9.00
Hefner, Jeremy	R-R	6-4	215	3-11-86	9	7	4.98	28	28	0	0	157	178	101	87	21	61	120	.283	.292	.275	6.86	3.49
Hernandez, Pedro	L-L	5-10	200	4-12-89	2	1	6.00	4	4	0	0	18	28	17	12	3	6	7	.364	.250	.385	3.50	3.00
Herr, Zach	L-L	5-9	185	12-1-86	0	0	27.00	1	0	0	0	1	4	3	3	0	2	2	.571	.500	.600	18.00	18.00
Hynes, Colt	L-L	5-11	200	6-28-85	2	1	5.47	22	0	0	0	26	35	16	16	1	9	12	.340	.375	.309	4.10	3.08
Inman, Will	R-R	6-0	215	2-6-87	5	11	6.15	42	17	0	0	117	139	91	80	16	57	120	.294	.296	.294	9.23	4.38
Italiano, Craig	R-R	6-4	215	7-22-86	0	0	20.25	4	0	0	0	4	8	9	9	1	5	6	.400	.375	.417	13.50	11.25
LeBlanc, Wade	L-L	6-3	215	8-7-84	9	1	4.30	17	17	0	0	107	108	54	51	8	28	92	.263	.250	.269	7.76	2.36
Leicester, Jon	R-R	6-3	220	2-7-79	5	9	6.50	27	25	0	0	136	169	105	98	21	64	66	.312	.300	.321	4.38	4.25
Munter, Scott	R-R	6-6	260	3-7-80	3	3	7.04	37	0	0	0	46	55	40	36	3	31	42	.302	.307	.299	8.22	6.07
2-team total (10 Fresno)					4	3	5.92	47	1	0	0	62	70	48	41	5	42	62	—	—	—	8.95	6.06
Musgrave, Rob	L-L	6-1	210	9-26-85	3	2	5.44	9	9	0	0	45	46	31	27	3	21	31	.269	.293	.262	6.25	4.23
Neshek, Pat	B-R	6-3	210	9-4-80	1	2	4.10	24	0	0	3	26	29	12	12	5	10	13	.293	.289	.296	4.44	3.42
Oramas, Juan	L-L	5-10	215	5-11-90	0	1	14.73	1	1	0	0	4	7	7	6	3	1	4	.389	.500	.375	9.82	2.45
Osuna, Stiven	R-R	6-3	170	5-5-87	0	0	9.58	4	0	0	0	10	10	11	11	2	11	7	.263	.417	.192	6.10	9.58
Perdomo, Luis	R-R	6-0	170	4-27-84	0	8	5.40	65	0	0	10	72	86	53	43	6	46	51	.300	.308	.292	6.40	5.78
Poreda, Aaron	L-L	6-6	240	10-1-86	4	3	5.43	41	1	0	0	70	65	47	42	3	63	79	.251	.304	.228	10.21	8.14
Ray, Jason	R-R	5-11	195	7-14-84	0	1	8.53	6	0	0	0	6	9	6	6	1	3	7	.333	.143	.400	9.95	4.26
Scribner, Evan	R-R	6-3	190	7-19-85	2	3	4.71	28	0	0	10	29	25	15	15	2	12	27	.255	.245	.264	8.48	3.77
Thatcher, Joe	L-L	6-2	230	10-4-81	0	0	1.23	8	0	0	0	7	3	1	1	0	3	10	.125	.077	.182	12.27	3.68
Van Benschoten, John	R-R	6-4	215	4-14-80	1	4	7.52	5	5	0	0	26	37	23	22	3	9	14	.336	.390	.275	4.78	3.08
Watt, Michael	L-L	6-1	185	2-24-89	0	1	3.60	1	1	0	0	5	6	2	2	1	0	3	.316	.429	.250	5.40	0.00

Fielding

Catcher

Catcher	PCT	G	PO	A	E	DP	PB
Gale	1.000	4	24	3	0	0	0
Hundley	1.000	3	18	1	0	0	0
Martinez	.986	54	337	27	5	1	2
Phillips	.981	23	141	16	3	2	4
Quiroz	.992	65	439	34	4	3	10
Rodriguez	.952	5	35	5	2	0	0
Solis	.984	9	55	6	1	1	0

First Base

First Base	PCT	G	PO	A	E	DP
Blanks	.987	21	142	11	2	18
Clark	.997	33	267	25	1	29
Guzman	.982	6	49	6	1	6
Phillips	.889	1	7	1	1	0
Quiroz	.947	4	18	0	1	3
Rizzo	.985	88	728	77	12	85

Second Base

Second Base	PCT	G	PO	A	E	DP
Contreras	.974	26	53	61	3	19
Forsythe	.958	27	52	63	5	14
Guzman	1.000	1	0	1	0	0
Hoffpauir	.967	59	122	170	10	53
Hudson	1.000	2	3	2	0	1
Hudson	.986	13	30	43	1	11
McKenna	1.000	5	4	12	0	1
Parrino	.986	16	20	48	1	11

Third Base

	PCT	G	PO	A	E	DP
Patterson	1.000	5	5	14	0	1
Tolleson	1.000	8	22	26	0	7
Third Base	**PCT**	**G**	**PO**	**A**	**E**	**DP**
Contreras	.000	1	0	0	0	0
Cunningham	.000	1	0	0	0	0
Darnell	.955	20	10	32	2	5
Feliz	.984	24	16	47	1	7
Forsythe	.918	17	10	35	4	5
Guzman	.896	46	32	80	13	8
Hoffpauir	.963	12	9	17	1	2
Phillips	1.000	2	3	3	0	0
Stubblefield	.875	2	3	4	1	1
Tolleson	.929	30	21	57	6	5

Shortstop

Shortstop	PCT	G	PO	A	E	DP
Cabrera	.949	55	84	175	14	41
Cintron	.867	13	10	29	6	7
Clark	.000	1	0	0	0	0
Contreras	.955	5	9	12	1	3
Forsythe	.929	4	4	9	1	0
Hoffpauir	.969	9	12	19	1	5
Hudson	.857	1	4	2	1	2
McKenna	.950	13	12	45	3	11
Parrino	.973	27	30	79	3	16
Tolleson	.965	28	36	75	4	21

Outfield

Outfield	PCT	G	PO	A	E	DP
Blanks	1.000	15	18	1	0	0
Buschmann	1.000	1	1	0	0	0
Clark	.991	74	112	1	1	0
Cunningham	.989	82	170	4	2	0
Darnell	1.000	19	24	0	0	0
Denorfia	.875	6	6	1	1	0
Durango	.980	51	95	2	2	1
Guzman	1.000	7	10	1	0	0
Hoffpauir	1.000	6	9	0	0	0
Hunter	.953	73	180	3	9	1
Kielty	.986	34	68	0	1	0
Macias	1.000	19	43	2	0	0
Martinez	1.000	4	9	0	0	0
Martinez	1.000	1	1	0	0	0
Maybin	1.000	2	4	0	0	0
Parrino	1.000	2	4	1	0	1
Patterson	.989	44	85	5	1	2
Payne	1.000	2	3	0	0	0
Pozo	.000	1	0	0	0	0
Quiroz	1.000	1	1	0	0	0
Stokes	1.000	4	8	0	0	0
Tolleson	1.000	13	13	0	0	0
Venable	.929	14	25	1	2	0

SAN ANTONIO MISSIONS

DOUBLE-A

TEXAS LEAGUE

Batting	B-T	HT	WT	DOB	AVG	vLH	vRH	G	AB	R	H	2B	3B	HR	RBI	BB	HBP	SH	SF	SO	SB	CS	SLG	OBP
Altman, Bryan	R-R	6-1	170	8-12-87	.193	.229	.170	41	88	10	17	2	0	0	8	8	2	0	1	12	3	0	.216	.273
Anna, Dean	L-R	5-11	180	11-24-86	.253	.300	.236	70	198	45	50	18	1	2	23	41	3	0	2	19	3	0	.384	.385
Belnome, Vince	L-R	5-11	205	3-11-88	.333	.267	.365	75	267	56	89	19	1	17	62	47	1	0	2	59	0	5	.603	.432
Blanks, Kyle	R-R	6-6	270	9-11-86	.282	.371	.235	44	177	33	50	16	3	4	27	17	4	0	3	41	3	0	.475	.353
Brayton, Ross	R-R	6-3	195	5-16-88	.000	.000	.000	1	4	0	0	0	0	0	0	0	0	0	0	0	0	0	.000	.000
Carroll, Sawyer	L-R	6-4	215	5-9-86	.267	.242	.277	129	460	68	123	24	6	18	71	61	0	0	1	97	11	2	.463	.352
Contreras, Anthony	L-R	5-11	185	9-26-83	.241	.157	.272	77	261	32	63	16	0	4	32	18	0	0	4	57	2	1	.349	.286
Darnell, James	R-R	6-2	195	1-19-87	.333	.392	.304	76	288	62	96	25	1	17	62	52	2	0	4	48	2	1	.604	.434
Decker, Cody	R-R	5-11	220	1-17-87	.237	.362	.176	49	177	32	42	10	1	13	38	11	2	0	0	59	0	1	.525	.289
Decker, Jaff	L-L	5-10	190	2-23-90	.236	.243	.233	133	496	90	117	29	2	19	92	103	8	0	5	145	15	5	.417	.373
Gale, Rocky	R-R	6-0	180	2-22-88	.043	.000	.048	7	23	1	1	1	0	0	1	0	0	0	0	6	0	0	.087	.043
Garcia, Oscar	L-R	6-1	185	12-5-88	.333	.000	.333	2	3	1	1	0	0	0	1	1	0	0	0	0	0	0	.333	.500
Gyorko, Jedd	R-R	5-10	195	9-23-88	.288	.424	.243	59	236	41	68	12	0	7	40	26	1	0	2	50	1	0	.428	.358
Hagerty, Jason	B-R	6-3	220	9-13-87	.231	.267	.220	36	130	15	30	6	1	1	18	14	3	0	1	40	0	1	.315	.318
Hundley, Nick	R-R	6-1	205	9-8-83	.174	.200	.167	7	23	1	4	0	0	0	1	6	0	0	0	10	0	0	.174	.345
Kielty, Bobby	B-R	6-1	225	8-5-76	.417	.429	.400	5	12	1	5	3	0	1	5	1	0	0	0	3	0	0	.917	.462
McKenna, Pat	R-R	5-10	190	4-28-87	.294	.500	.111	6	17	1	5	1	0	0	2	1	0	0	0	6	0	0	.353	.333
Parrino, Andy	B-R	6-0	180	10-31-85	.303	.353	.280	40	152	28	46	7	1	9	32	22	1	0	3	40	3	1	.539	.388
Payne, Danny	L-L	5-10	185	9-8-85	.188	.000	.200	7	16	0	3	2	0	0	0	1	0	0	0	10	0	0	.313	.235

SAN DIEGO PADRES

Batting	B-T	HT	WT	DOB	AVG	vLH	vRH	G	AB	R	H	2B	3B	HR	RBI	BB	HBP	SH	SF	SO	SB	CS	SLG	OBP
Phillips, Kyle	L-R	6-1	225	4-3-84	.316	.346	.300	19	76	10	24	4	0	2	15	4	0	0	2	1	0	0	.447	.341
Pozo, Jhonaldo	R-R	6-3	183	3-28-89	.333	.333	.000	1	3	0	1	0	0	0	0	0	0	0	0	2	0	0	.333	.333
Robertson, Dan	R-R	5-8	175	9-30-85	.283	.299	.276	124	438	97	124	23	5	5	44	55	7	0	3	51	20	6	.393	.370
Rodriguez, Eddy	R-R	6-0	205	12-1-85	.209	.273	.178	18	67	7	14	3	0	1	6	4	1	0	0	18	0	0	.299	.264
Solis, Ali	R-R	5-10	225	9-29-87	.263	.288	.251	73	255	30	67	14	1	6	26	12	5	0	1	65	0	0	.396	.308
Sosa, Carlos	L-R	6-1	195	5-19-83	.312	.280	.324	28	93	12	29	5	0	2	13	9	1	0	1	22	2	0	.430	.375
Tekotte, Blake	L-R	5-11	175	5-24-87	.285	.280	.287	106	414	77	118	27	2	19	67	67	8	0	2	108	36	12	.498	.393
Weems, Beamer	R-R	5-10	175	7-28-87	.246	.224	.257	77	272	38	67	17	1	9	46	28	7	0	1	68	0	2	.415	.331
Zazueta, Amadeo	B-R	5-10	160	1-31-86	.283	.118	.361	15	53	4	15	1	1	1	5	0	0	0	1	9	1	0	.396	.278

Pitching	B-T	HT	WT	DOB	W	L	ERA	G	GS	CG	SV	IP	H	R	ER	HR	BB	SO	AVG	vLH	vRH	K/9	BB/9
Bass, Anthony	R-R	6-2	190	11-1-87	6	4	3.75	13	13	0	0	70	62	31	29	6	21	62	.242	.306	.196	8.01	2.71
Brach, Brad	R-R	6-6	210	4-12-86	2	2	2.25	42	0	0	23	44	32	11	11	3	5	64	.198	.221	.181	13.09	1.02
Breit, Aaron	R-R	6-4	205	4-19-86	4	3	6.51	24	8	0	0	57	80	44	41	5	34	48	.340	.400	.303	7.62	5.40
Buschmann, Matt	R-R	6-3	210	2-13-84	6	1	3.94	12	7	0	0	46	42	22	20	5	19	32	.247	.238	.256	6.31	3.74
Castro, Simon	R-R	6-5	210	4-9-88	5	6	4.33	16	16	0	0	89	95	48	43	9	16	73	.271	.303	.249	7.35	1.61
Erlin, Robbie	L-L	6-0	175	10-8-90	1	0	1.38	6	6	0	0	26	26	4	4	2	4	31	.265	.208	.284	10.73	1.38
2-team total (11 Frisco)					6	2	3.50	17	16	0	0	93	99	38	36	11	11	92	—	—	—	8.94	1.07
Hamren, Erik	R-R	6-1	195	8-21-86	3	0	0.92	33	0	0	0	49	34	7	5	0	12	48	.202	.162	.230	8.82	2.20
Hernandez, Pedro	L-L	5-10	200	4-12-89	3	2	3.48	9	8	0	0	41	39	17	16	4	10	43	.245	.273	.231	9.36	2.18
Hynes, Colt	L-L	5-11	200	6-28-85	0	6	3.72	45	0	0	1	58	64	29	24	1	20	41	.286	.260	.298	6.36	3.10
Italiano, Craig	R-R	6-4	215	7-22-86	6	1	5.00	55	0	0	0	67	78	40	37	6	28	48	.305	.301	.307	6.48	3.78
Kelly, Casey	R-R	6-3	195	10-4-89	11	6	3.98	27	27	0	0	142	153	74	63	8	46	105	.278	.284	.273	6.64	2.91
Kunz, Eddie	R-R	6-6	260	4-8-86	2	1	4.30	52	0	0	0	73	72	42	35	4	34	27	.266	.288	.248	3.31	4.17
Lara, Alexis	R-R	6-0	150	3-23-87	2	0	2.84	11	0	0	0	13	13	5	4	3	8	15	.265	.333	.214	10.66	5.68
Marona, Chase	R-R	6-5	220	8-18-88	1	0	0.00	2	0	0	0	2	1	0	0	0	3	4	.143	.000	.143	18.00	13.50
Mikolas, Miles	R-R	6-5	220	8-23-88	1	0	1.67	28	0	0	9	32	29	6	6	0	6	27	.240	.275	.214	7.52	1.67
Musgrave, Rob	L-L	6-1	210	9-26-85	7	2	3.30	23	12	0	0	79	77	31	29	3	25	65	.258	.236	.268	7.41	2.85
Oramas, Juan	L-L	5-10	215	5-11-90	10	5	3.10	19	18	0	0	105	99	39	36	10	28	102	.249	.254	.247	8.77	2.41
Ray, Jason	R-R	5-11	195	7-14-84	0	0	3.00	2	0	0	0	3	4	2	1	0	1	5	.333	.444	.000	15.00	3.00
Reyes, Jorge	B-R	6-3	195	12-7-87	10	3	3.12	33	20	0	0	113	111	42	39	6	30	98	.261	.243	.275	7.83	2.40
Spence, Josh	L-L	6-1	170	1-22-88	3	1	1.71	35	0	0	0	47	29	9	9	4	11	42	.180	.130	.206	7.99	2.09
Vincent, Nick	R-R	6-0	185	7-12-86	8	2	2.27	66	0	0	3	79	54	20	20	6	20	89	.196	.234	.162	10.10	2.27
Wieland, Joe	R-R	6-3	175	1-21-90	3	1	2.77	5	5	0	0	26	23	10	8	0	6	18	.240	.236	.244	6.23	2.08
2-team total (7 Frisco)					7	1	1.80	12	12	1	0	70	58	19	14	2	17	54	—	—	—	6.94	2.19

Fielding

Catcher	PCT	G	PO	A	E	DP	PB
Brayton	1.000	1	4	1	0	1	0
Gale	.980	7	45	3	1	0	0
Hagerty	1.000	27	181	21	0	2	2
Hundley	.973	5	35	1	1	0	1
Phillips	1.000	19	145	12	0	2	2
Pozo	1.000	1	5	1	0	0	0
Rodriguez	.985	17	118	15	2	1	0
Solis	.981	72	552	57	12	3	8

First Base	PCT	G	PO	A	E	DP
Anna	.950	2	18	1	1	1
Belnome	.989	20	164	11	2	17
Blanks	.994	33	282	24	2	26
Carroll	.988	33	309	19	4	28
Darnell	.960	4	22	2	1	4
Decker	.991	24	219	14	2	24
Hagerty	1.000	9	65	5	0	12
Sosa	.990	22	189	9	2	15

Second Base	PCT	G	PO	A	E	DP
Altman	1.000	11	13	33	0	6
Anna	.965	31	58	81	5	15
Belnome	.980	52	92	149	5	29
Contreras	.977	48	72	144	5	30
McKenna	1.000	5	9	13	0	7
Zazueta	1.000	1	2	4	0	2

Third Base	PCT	G	PO	A	E	DP
Altman	1.000	6	2	11	0	3
Anna	.850	8	4	13	3	1
Belnome	.857	3	2	4	1	2
Contreras	1.000	2	1	3	0	0
Darnell	.932	70	27	96	9	9
Gyorko	.970	56	40	119	5	11

Shortstop	PCT	G	PO	A	E	DP
Altman	1.000	1	1	0	0	0
Anna	.970	11	19	45	2	8
Contreras	.971	8	14	20	1	3
McKenna	1.000	2	1	6	0	2
Parrino	.972	38	66	106	5	24
Weems	.971	77	98	206	9	50
Zazueta	.980	12	13	37	1	7

Outfield	PCT	G	PO	A	E	DP
Anna	1.000	8	13	0	0	0
Blanks	1.000	2	4	0	0	0
Carroll	.993	86	136	8	1	0
Contreras	1.000	1	2	0	0	0
Darnell	1.000	4	12	0	0	0
Decker	.983	126	218	11	4	1
Garcia	1.000	1	1	0	0	0
Kielty	1.000	1	1	0	0	0
Parrino	.000	1	0	0	0	0
Payne	1.000	3	9	0	0	0
Robertson	.977	107	198	17	5	2
Tekotte	.979	102	228	6	5	1

LAKE ELSINORE STORM   HIGH CLASS A

CALIFORNIA LEAGUE

Batting	B-T	HT	WT	DOB	AVG	vLH	vRH	G	AB	R	H	2B	3B	HR	RBI	BB	HBP	SH	SF	SO	SB	CS	SLG	OBP
Anna, Dean	L-R	5-11	180	11-24-86	.311	.321	.308	44	148	25	46	10	2	3	18	19	5	0	3	22	2	0	.466	.400
Baxter, Mike	L-R	6-0	190	12-7-84	.278	.357	.227	11	36	5	10	1	0	0	2	9	0	0	1	8	0	1	.306	.413
Blackwood, Jake	R-R	6-0	195	9-14-85	.251	.231	.257	60	227	31	57	10	1	8	33	18	1	0	2	43	3	1	.410	.306
Brayton, Ross	R-R	6-3	195	5-16-88	.500	1.000	.444	4	10	2	5	0	0	0	1	2	0	0	0	3	0	0	.500	.583
Denorfia, Chris	R-R	6-0	195	7-15-80	.667	.000	.667	2	6	1	4	1	0	0	0	0	0	0	0	1	0	0	.833	.667
Freiman, Nate	R-R	6-7	225	12-31-86	.288	.347	.272	138	548	81	158	35	4	22	111	50	11	0	9	93	6	1	.487	.354
Fuentes, Reymond	L-L	6-0	160	2-12-91	.275	.298	.268	124	510	84	140	15	9	5	45	44	9	0	1	117	41	14	.369	.342
Gale, Rocky	R-R	6-0	180	2-22-88	.141	.217	.104	27	71	7	10	1	0	0	7	2	0	1	0	12	0	1	.155	.235
Galvez, Jonathan	R-R	6-2	175	1-18-91	.291	.339	.275	128	488	84	142	36	5	13	86	41	10	0	5	123	37	9	.465	.355
Garcia, Oscar	L-R	6-1	185	12-5-88	.224	.600	.182	18	49	9	11	1	0	1	6	2	0	0	2	7	1	0	.306	.245
Gyorko, Jedd	R-R	5-10	195	9-23-88	.365	.372	.362	81	340	78	124	35	2	18	74	38	2	0	2	64	11	3	.638	.429
Hagerty, Mike	B-R	6-3	220	9-13-87	.311	.269	.326	68	257	53	80	25	2	8	47	26	7	0	3	62	3	2	.518	.386
Hudson, Orlando	B-R	6-0	190	12-12-77	.571	.000	.571	4	7	6	4	0	0	1	3	6	0	0	0	2	0	1	1.000	.769
Killian, Dan	L-R	6-4	195	1-14-89	.143	.000	.143	6	14	1	2	1	0	0	4	0	0	0	0	1	0	0	.214	.333

SAN DIEGO PADRES

SAN DIEGO PADRES

Batting

Batting	B-T	HT	WT	DOB	AVG	vLH	vRH	G	AB	R	H	2B	3B	HR	RBI	BB	HBP	SH	SF	SO	SB	CS	SLG	OBP
Liriano, Rymer	R-R	6-0	211	6-20-91	.127	.133	.125	15	55	8	7	1	1	0	6	6	0	0	0	13	1	1	.182	.213
Medica, Tommy	R-R	6-1	190	4-9-88	.302	.310	.300	42	139	21	42	10	0	6	17	25	10	0	1	32	0	1	.504	.440
Meeley, Dan	L-L	6-0	190	7-1-89	.268	.231	.278	55	190	25	51	10	1	4	29	12	1	0	2	43	0	0	.395	.312
Noel, Rico	R-R	5-9	175	1-11-89	.210	.241	.197	32	100	19	21	2	2	0	6	13	2	0	0	19	12	1	.270	.313
Olabisi, Wande	R-R	6-0	212	3-18-88	.225	.277	.205	94	293	47	66	8	4	5	31	33	12	0	1	75	25	5	.331	.327
Patterson, Eric	L-R	6-0	170	4-8-83	.000	.000	.000	2	4	0	0	0	0	0	0	2	0	0	0	1	1	0	.000	.333
Payne, Danny	L-L	5-10	185	9-8-85	.245	.309	.230	88	277	49	68	19	5	8	50	62	2	0	4	90	10	5	.437	.383
Pozo, Jhonaldo	R-R	6-3	183	3-28-89	.167	.333	.143	18	48	3	8	2	0	0	2	1	0	0	1	17	0	0	.208	.180
Rincon, Edinson	R-R	6-1	185	8-11-90	.329	.416	.299	74	298	54	98	24	1	8	50	32	4	0	6	59	1	1	.497	.394
Rodriguez, Eddy	R-R	6-0	205	12-1-85	.272	.174	.289	46	158	23	43	10	0	8	21	12	2	0	1	41	0	0	.487	.329
Stokes, Mykal	R-R	6-4	170	6-2-90	.214	.250	.200	12	28	2	6	0	0	0	1	0	0	0	10	2	0	.214	.241
Tremblay, Chris	R-R	5-10	185	11-13-86	.255	.200	.271	53	153	17	39	1	0	0	18	16	0	0	3	33	3	2	.261	.320
Valdez, Jeudy	R-R	5-10	185	5-5-89	.295	.382	.267	122	516	93	152	37	7	15	92	31	5	0	3	108	34	11	.481	.339

Pitching

Pitching	B-T	HT	WT	DOB	W	L	ERA	G	GS	CG	SV	IP	H	R	ER	HR	BB	SO	AVG	vLH	vRH	K/9	BB/9
Beard, Hayden	R-R	6-1	175	1-22-85	4	3	6.17	41	0	0	0	58	81	47	40	6	21	61	.327	.327	.326	9.41	3.24
Breit, Aaron	R-R	6-4	205	4-19-86	2	1	7.01	20	1	0	1	26	39	21	20	1	9	28	.345	.308	.356	9.82	3.16
DePaula, Jose	L-L	6-1	170	3-4-90	10	5	5.22	26	23	0	0	112	129	81	65	4	37	87	.282	.225	.298	6.99	2.97
Fetter, Chris	R-R	6-8	230	12-23-85	1	6	5.80	13	11	0	0	50	70	41	32	7	9	43	.329	.279	.376	7.79	1.63
Hamren, Erik	R-R	6-1	195	8-21-86	2	0	1.08	15	0	0	1	17	12	2	2	0	2	21	.211	.192	.226	11.34	1.08
Harang, Aaron	R-R	6-7	260	5-9-78	0	1	6.75	1	1	0	0	4	5	3	3	0	1	7	.313	.375	.250	15.75	2.25
Hernandez, Pedro	L-L	5-10	200	4-18-89	5	0	2.70	15	6	0	0	57	52	19	17	3	6	44	.239	.288	.220	6.99	0.95
Herr, Zach	L-L	5-9	185	12-1-86	5	3	3.10	52	0	0	3	73	66	31	25	3	27	77	.241	.188	.263	9.54	3.34
Ibarra, Jeff	L-L	6-6	180	8-18-87	3	2	3.93	22	0	0	0	37	31	16	16	1	9	29	.240	.296	.225	7.12	2.21
Lollis, Matt	R-R	6-9	250	9-11-90	4	8	5.35	31	19	0	1	119	135	86	71	12	45	114	.285	.259	.303	8.60	3.39
Marona, Chase	R-R	6-1	205	8-18-88	0	0	0.00	2	0	0	0	2	0	0	0	0	1	3	.000	.000	.000	11.57	7.71
McBryde, Jeremy	R-R	6-2	225	5-1-87	2	4	4.32	63	0	0	9	94	99	55	45	10	29	96	.266	.346	.224	9.22	2.79
Mikolas, Miles	R-R	6-5	220	8-23-88	3	0	1.13	34	0	0	12	40	31	5	5	1	9	42	.214	.148	.262	9.53	2.04
Osuna, Stiven	R-R	6-3	170	5-5-87	0	0	9.18	8	0	0	0	17	27	18	17	5	8	12	.355	.263	.447	6.48	4.32
Pease, Dustin	B-L	5-11	170	10-4-85	0	7	3.18	55	0	0	1	74	69	35	26	7	23	66	.249	.148	.291	8.06	2.81
Ray, Jason	R-R	5-11	195	7-14-84	7	4	2.52	41	0	0	11	54	42	20	15	2	19	64	.222	.262	.202	10.73	3.19
Schmidt, Nick	L-L	6-5	245	10-10-85	3	5	3.84	12	12	0	0	63	62	35	27	7	23	58	.262	.372	.237	8.24	3.27
Schrader, Adam	R-R	6-3	210	3-10-87	0	1	9.00	5	0	0	0	8	14	8	8	0	7	2	.400	.455	.375	2.25	7.88
Sullivan, Jerry	R-R	6-4	220	1-18-88	9	7	5.95	28	28	0	0	135	184	111	89	17	32	74	.323	.330	.318	4.95	2.14
Thatcher, Joe	L-L	6-2	230	10-4-81	0	0	0.00	1	0	0	0	1	0	0	0	0	0	2	.000	.000		18.00	0.00
Watt, Michael	L-L	6-1	185	2-24-89	6	9	5.36	26	26	0	0	124	146	87	74	11	45	119	.289	.322	.275	8.61	3.26
Werner, Andrew	L-L	6-2	215	2-25-87	5	2	3.03	13	13	0	0	68	72	26	23	1	13	55	.266	.169	.296	7.24	1.71
Wilkes, Chris	R-R	6-4	235	9-26-89	1	0	4.91	4	0	0	0	7	9	7	4	2	5	4	.300	.467	.133	4.91	6.14

Fielding

Catcher	PCT	G	PO	A	E	DP	PB
Brayton	1.000	3	17	2	0	0	
Gale	.994	27	160	18	1	0	1
Hagerty	.971	63	458	41	15	6	4
Killian	.973	5	30	6	1	0	1
Pozo	.992	16	115	11	1	1	3
Rodriguez	.989	46	343	30	4	0	1

First Base	PCT	G	PO	A	E	DP
Anna	1.000	2	11	0	0	3
Baxter	1.000	2	17	2	0	1
Blackwood	1.000	1	8	0	0	1
Freiman	.987	135	1127	102	16	85
Hagerty	1.000	1	3	0	0	0
Rodriguez	1.000	1	4	1	0	0
Tremblay	.947	3	18	0	1	1

Second Base	PCT	G	PO	A	E	DP
Anna	.980	20	31	66	2	13
Blackwood	1.000	2	5	6	0	3
Galvez	.960	114	211	287	21	53
Hudson	1.000	4	9	5	0	1
Patterson	1.000	1	2	0	0	0
Tremblay	.974	12	11	26	1	5

Third Base	PCT	G	PO	A	E	DP
Blackwood	.913	49	26	100	12	11
Gyorko	.941	44	29	98	8	5
Rincon	.835	39	25	66	18	6
Tremblay	.939	13	7	24	2	1

Shortstop	PCT	G	PO	A	E	DP
Anna	.931	7	10	17	2	2
Galvez	.919	11	14	20	3	7
Tremblay	.972	8	18	17	1	4
Valdez	.941	121	156	337	31	47

Outfield	PCT	G	PO	A	E	DP
Anna	.906	15	24	5	3	0
Baxter	1.000	6	8	0	0	0
Blackwood	1.000	6	11	0	0	0
Denorfia	1.000	2	4	0	0	0
Fuentes	.974	122	258	6	7	0
Garcia	1.000	15	27	0	0	0
Liriano	.971	15	30	4	1	1
Meeley	.947	45	86	3	5	0
Noel	.954	31	59	3	3	0
Olabisi	.977	88	125	2	3	1
Patterson	.000	1	0	0	0	0
Payne	.969	83	152	5	5	1
Stokes	1.000	8	11	1	0	0
Tremblay	.968	18	29	1	1	0

FORT WAYNE TINCAPS   LOW CLASS A

MIDWEST LEAGUE

Batting	B-T	HT	WT	DOB	AVG	vLH	vRH	G	AB	R	H	2B	3B	HR	RBI	BB	HBP	SH	SF	SO	SB	CS	SLG	OBP
Adamson, Corey	L-R	6-2	185	2-23-92	.167	.000	.167	6	18	0	3	1	0	0	1	0	0	0	0	7	0	0	.222	.167
Altman, Bryan	R-R	6-1	170	8-12-87	.143	.000	.167	3	7	1	1	0	0	0	1	0	0	0	1	3	0	0	.143	.125
Bisson, Chris	L-R	5-11	185	8-14-89	.261	.259	.261	123	418	61	109	11	5	2	43	53	2	0	3	106	21	10	.325	.345
Blackwood, Jake	R-R	6-0	195	9-14-85	.284	.265	.291	71	271	29	77	26	2	9	43	17	2	0	1	51	6	2	.494	.330
Cunningham, Wes	L-R	6-2	200	10-4-87	.268	.179	.295	107	362	43	97	20	3	5	50	42	2	0	3	71	9	7	.381	.345
Domoromo, Luis	L-L	6-1	185	2-4-92	.283	.264	.289	112	435	66	123	20	3	9	68	36	4	0	11	83	7	7	.405	.335
Dore, Jose	L-R	6-1	170	2-9-92	.199	.188	.204	50	161	18	32	8	1	5	14	19	3	0	0	53	0	1	.354	.295
Gale, Rocky	R-R	6-0	180	2-22-88	.267	.296	.254	26	90	9	24	3	0	1	13	6	1	0	3	23	0	1	.333	.310
Gallic, Michael	R-R	6-2	210	4-8-89	.304	.348	.286	25	79	7	24	2	0	0	6	4	1	0	1	17	2	0	.329	.341
Garcia, Oscar	L-R	6-1	185	12-5-88	.234	.043	.276	38	128	19	30	7	0	0	12	19	1	0	2	26	1	2	.289	.333
Guinn, Brian	B-R	5-11	165	4-4-89	.245	.221	.253	123	417	49	102	11	6	1	34	36	3	0	4	104	34	10	.307	.307
Killian, Dan	L-R	6-4	195	1-14-89	.130	.000	.167	14	46	3	6	2	0	1	2	3	1	0	0	24	2	1	.239	.200

Batting	B-T	HT	WT	DOB	AVG	vLH	vRH	G	AB	R	H	2B	3B	HR	RBI	BB	HBP	SH	SF	SO	SB	CS	SLG	OBP
Liriano, Rymer	R-R	6-0	211	6-20-91	.319	.308	.322	116	455	81	145	30	8	12	62	47	6	0	9	95	65	20	.499	.383
Martinez, Alberth	R-R	6-1	170	1-23-91	.000	.000	.000	4	13	0	0	0	0	0	0	0	1	1	0	6	0	1	.000	.133
McKenna, Pat	5-10	170	6-24-87	.071	.250	.000	6	14	2	1	0	0	0	0	3	1	0	0	6	0	0	.071	.278
Medica, Tommy	R-R	6-1	190	4-9-88	.268	.420	.185	44	142	22	38	19	0	3	21	17	5	0	0	33	0	1	.465	.366
Noel, Rico	R-R	5-9	175	1-11-89	.253	.282	.243	94	375	70	95	20	3	3	40	37	16	0	1	75	50	4	.347	.345
Olabisi, Wande	R-R	6-0	212	3-18-88	.211	.429	.083	6	19	1	4	0	0	0	2	2	0	0	0	7	0	0	.211	.286
Powers, Connor	R-R	6-2	220	12-21-87	.338	.344	.336	76	275	48	93	29	1	8	45	42	1	0	4	64	0	0	.538	.422
Pozo, Jhonaldo	R-R	6-3	183	3-28-89	.235	1.000	.188	6	17	1	4	0	0	0	2	5	0	0	0	7	0	0	.235	.409
Quiles, Emmanuel	R-R	5-11	186	10-26-84	.211	.275	.192	87	298	27	63	9	1	3	27	11	1	0	1	64	1	2	.279	.241
Spangenberg, Cory	L-R	6-0	185	3-16-91	.286	.263	.295	47	189	35	54	7	1	2	24	14	3	0	0	42	15	4	.365	.345
Stokes, Mykal	R-R	6-4	170	6-2-90	.125	.000	.133	5	16	1	2	1	0	0	1	1	0	0	0	6	0	0	.188	.176
Stubblefield, Tyler	R-R	5-10	185	11-19-87	.223	.156	.241	42	148	17	33	10	1	0	18	16	5	0	4	45	2	0	.304	.312
Tate, Donavan	R-R	6-3	200	9-27-90	.316	.100	.556	6	19	3	6	2	0	0	2	4	0	0	0	3	2	2	.421	.435
Tremblay, Chris	R-R	5-10	185	11-13-86	.146	.147	.145	25	89	7	13	1	0	0	8	8	0	0	0	31	0	0	.157	.216
Tyrell, Cole	R-R	6-0	185	2-8-88	.193	.238	.179	27	88	16	17	5	1	3	10	12	4	0	0	23	0	1	.375	.317
Williams, Everett	L-R	5-10	200	10-1-90	.300	.400	.200	6	20	5	6	0	0	0	1	2	1	0	0	3	3	0	.300	.391

Pitching	B-T	HT	WT	DOB	W	L	ERA	G	GS	CG	SV	IP	H	R	ER	HR	BB	SO	AVG	vLH	vRH	K/9	BB/9
Branham, Matt	R-R	6-5	220	9-28-87	4	3	4.98	11	10	0	0	47	54	31	26	6	12	49	.287	.248	.337	9.38	2.30
Cates, Zach	R-R	6-3	200	12-17-89	4	10	4.73	25	25	0	0	118	107	75	62	4	53	111	.244	.251	.236	8.47	4.04
Dominick, Adam	R-R	6-5	235	3-30-86	5	6	3.59	59	0	0	10	73	68	37	29	5	13	83	.240	.234	.245	10.28	1.61
Eisenbach, Robert	L-L	6-0	180	4-5-88	0	0	3.68	9	0	0	0	7	9	3	3	0	4	5	.321	.333	.300	6.14	4.91
Franklin, Chris	R-R	6-1	200	11-10-87	2	2	2.97	63	0	0	7	73	67	34	24	5	26	48	.245	.238	.250	5.94	3.22
Haney, Christopher	R-R	5-11	185	2-13-89	0	0	9.00	3	0	0	0	3	8	3	3	0	1	0	.571	.667	.500	0.00	3.00
Hardy, Mark	L-L	6-4	195	5-3-88	11	10	2.78	27	19	1	0	129	117	47	40	9	32	96	.241	.255	.235	6.68	2.23
Ibarra, Jeff	L-L	6-6	180	8-18-87	3	3	3.23	25	0	0	0	31	15	11	11	1	11	36	.144	.136	.156	10.57	3.23
Jackson, Matt	R-R	6-4	190	12-18-87	5	1	1.95	17	8	0	1	65	49	18	14	1	12	68	.205	.198	.211	9.46	1.67
Marona, Chase	R-R	6-1	205	8-18-88	0	0	12.91	14	0	0	0	15	26	26	22	0	18	14	.371	.361	.382	8.22	10.57
Mull, Noah	L-L	5-10	170	11-19-86	1	3	3.77	28	2	0	0	45	52	23	19	6	19	37	.277	.292	.267	7.35	3.77
O'Grady, Dennis	R-R	5-10	200	5-17-89	4	2	4.53	10	10	0	0	52	55	30	26	2	22	43	.267	.303	.227	7.49	3.83
Osuna, Stiven	R-R	6-3	170	5-5-87	2	1	4.13	21	0	0	0	28	26	17	13	4	13	18	.245	.233	.261	5.72	4.13
Portillo, Adys	R-R	6-2	185	12-21-91	3	11	7.11	23	20	0	0	82	89	66	65	10	55	97	.278	.336	.232	10.60	6.01
Privett, Todd	L-L	6-0	185	4-22-86	3	2	4.90	9	9	0	0	45	53	33	21	3	10	42	.301	.186	.365	8.40	2.00
Quackenbush, Kevin	R-R	6-3	207	11-28-88	1	1	0.84	18	0	0	9	21	12	2	2	0	6	38	.158	.200	.130	16.03	2.53
Sampson, Keyvius	R-R	6-0	185	1-6-91	12	3	2.90	24	24	0	0	118	81	42	38	8	49	143	.192	.191	.193	10.91	3.74
Sanchez, Deiber	R-R	5-10	170	3-24-89	3	1	4.33	52	0	0	0	81	71	42	39	9	50	54	.239	.172	.290	6.00	5.56
Werner, Andrew	L-L	6-2	215	2-25-87	2	6	3.44	12	12	0	0	68	70	30	26	4	13	52	.266	.238	.279	6.88	1.72
Wilkes, Chris	R-R	6-4	235	9-26-89	0	0	8.31	3	0	0	0	4	7	5	4	0	2	1	.389	.500	.333	2.08	4.15
Worrell, Josh	R-R	6-5	215	11-17-86	0	0	0.00	3	0	0	0	2	3	0	0	0	1	2	.333	.250	.400	7.71	3.86

Fielding

Catcher	PCT	G	PO	A	E	DP	PB
Gale	.988	26	221	20	3	4	1
Killian	.950	9	50	7	3	2	1
Medica	1.000	4	33	0	0	0	0
Pozo	1.000	6	43	3	0	0	0
Quiles	.989	87	670	78	8	5	5
Tyrell	.983	16	102	11	2	0	9

First Base	PCT	G	PO	A	E	DP
Cunningham	.977	40	275	21	7	26
Medica	.996	26	210	13	1	19
Powers	.985	61	486	37	8	36
Stubblefield	1.000	5	33	5	0	3
Tremblay	.973	5	32	4	1	4
Tyrell	.989	10	85	8	1	7

Second Base	PCT	G	PO	A	E	DP
Altman	.846	2	4	7	2	2
Bisson	.968	82	131	204	11	44
McKenna	1.000	3	8	6	0	2

Spangenberg	.955	46	51	141	9	21
Stubblefield	1.000	3	4	11	0	1
Tremblay	.971	8	16	18	1	2

Third Base	PCT	G	PO	A	E	DP
Altman	.000	1	0	0	0	0
Bisson	.895	35	21	47	8	8
Blackwood	.920	64	31	119	13	10
McKenna	1.000	2	0	4	0	0
Powers	.976	15	14	27	1	6
Stubblefield	.943	23	20	30	3	2
Tremblay	.800	5	5	3	2	0
Tyrell	.600	2	2	1	2	0

Shortstop	PCT	G	PO	A	E	DP
Bisson	.931	8	10	17	2	3
Guinn	.941	120	177	286	29	59
McKenna	1.000	1	2	2	0	1
Stubblefield	.962	7	8	17	1	2
Tremblay	.944	7	3	14	1	1

Outfield	PCT	G	PO	A	E	DP
Adamson	.900	6	9	0	1	0
Bisson	.000	1	0	0	1	0
Cunningham	.000	1	0	0	0	0
Domoromo	.970	99	151	10	5	2
Dore	.965	39	80	3	3	1
Gallic	.967	22	29	0	1	0
Garcia	.984	33	62	1	1	0
Killian	1.000	1	5	0	0	0
Liriano	.944	105	181	6	11	3
Martinez	1.000	4	4	0	0	0
Noel	.992	92	253	9	2	2
Olabisi	.857	6	6	0	1	0
Stokes	1.000	5	13	0	0	0
Stubblefield	1.000	2	5	0	0	0
Tate	.923	6	11	1	1	0
Tremblay	1.000	2	2	0	0	0
Williams	1.000	5	7	0	0	0

EUGENE EMERALDS

SHORT-SEASON

NORTHWEST LEAGUE

Batting	B-T	HT	WT	DOB	AVG	vLH	vRH	G	AB	R	H	2B	3B	HR	RBI	BB	HBP	SH	SF	SO	SB	CS	SLG	OBP
Colantonio, Matthew	L-R	6-0	195	5-17-89	.264	.226	.274	53	148	16	39	7	1	0	22	30	3	0	1	18	5	0	.324	.396
Dore, Jose	L-R	6-1	170	2-9-92	.226	.250	.220	48	164	15	37	9	0	4	21	13	2	0	1	58	3	2	.354	.289
Gaedele, Kyle	R-R	6-3	220	11-1-89	.203	.250	.191	63	197	34	40	6	1	3	29	36	3	0	1	67	9	0	.289	.333
Gallic, Michael	R-R	6-2	210	4-25-89	.290	.190	.341	23	62	11	18	3	0	0	2	4	1	0	1	13	5	3	.339	.338
Garce, Daniel	R-R	6-1	166	6-6-89	.185	.438	.123	26	81	5	15	2	0	1	5	3	2	0	0	27	0	0	.247	.233
Hedges, Austin	R-R	6-1	190	8-18-92	.100	.167	.000	4	10	1	1	1	0	0	0	2	0	0	0	3	0	0	.200	.250
Ingram, Rashad	R-R	6-0	175	5-27-89	.200	.000	.286	9	20	2	4	0	0	0	1	2	1	0	0	5	1	1	.200	.304
Jones, Duanel	R-R	6-3	195	5-11-93	.206	.300	.167	18	68	7	14	5	0	0	5	0	0	0	25	3	0	.279	.260
Killian, Dan	L-R	6-4	195	1-14-89	.175	.333	.147	15	40	8	7	1	0	1	3	1	0	0	15	0	1	.275	.250
Kometani, Zach	R-R	6-0	200	11-26-89	.250	.264	.245	56	192	20	48	13	0	4	39	16	4	0	1	51	4	0	.380	.319

Batting	B-T	HT	WT	DOB	AVG	vLH	vRH	G	AB	R	H	2B	3B	HR	RBI	BB	HBP	SH	SF	SO	SB	CS	SLG	OBP
Martinez, Alberth	R-R	6-1	170	1-23-91	.182	.071	.233	12	44	3	8	2	1	0	3	2	1	0	0	8	4	0	.273	.234
McElroy, Casey	L-R	5-8	180	12-28-89	.301	.143	.365	19	73	11	22	6	0	2	11	10	0	0	1	13	0	2	.466	.381
Miller, Justin	R-R	5-9	190	12-14-88	.308	.308	.308	35	130	24	40	12	0	0	14	21	2	0	1	31	7	3	.400	.409
Minyeti, Jorge	B-R	5-10	180	11-7-90	.209	.250	.200	40	86	11	18	0	1	0	8	10	1	0	0	23	4	2	.233	.299
Moore, Clint	R-R	5-11	195	6-22-89	.222	.231	.220	20	54	15	12	8	0	1	11	5	4	0	2	21	0	0	.426	.323
Orr, Lee	R-R	6-3	205	10-23-88	.219	.105	.244	62	210	45	46	13	2	8	35	38	11	0	2	88	18	2	.414	.364
Peterson, Jace	L-R	6-0	200	5-9-90	.243	.175	.263	73	276	48	67	9	5	2	27	50	2	0	3	53	39	10	.333	.360
Pozo, Jhonaldo	R-R	6-3	183	3-28-89	.167	.000	.167	3	6	0	1	1	0	0	0	0	0	0	0	2	0	0	.333	.167
Rodriguez, Jeremy	R-R	5-8	185	8-30-89	.211	.136	.235	38	90	11	19	1	0	0	13	29	5	0	4	20	0	1	.222	.414
Spangenberg, Cory	L-R	6-0	185	3-16-91	.384	.353	.391	25	86	20	33	10	0	1	20	31	2	0	2	15	10	4	.535	.545
Stokes, Mykal	R-R	6-4	170	6-2-90	.240	.152	.265	37	146	23	35	5	1	1	16	7	4	0	1	37	12	2	.308	.291
Tate, Donavan	R-R	6-3	200	9-27-90	.283	.375	.262	33	127	24	36	8	4	0	20	25	2	0	1	32	17	5	.409	.406
Tyrell, Cole	R-R	6-0	185	2-8-88	.000	.000	.000	5	13	2	0	0	0	0	0	0	0	0	0	8	0	0	.000	.188
Whitmore, Travis	L-R	6-1	190	7-5-88	.297	.333	.290	62	209	27	62	15	5	1	32	24	2	0	1	56	3	5	.431	.373

Pitching	B-T	HT	WT	DOB	W	L	ERA	G	GS	CG	SV	IP	H	R	ER	HR	BB	SO	AVG	vLH	vRH	K/9	BB/9
Andriese, Matt	R-R	6-3	210	8-28-89	5	1	1.51	12	8	0	0	42	29	8	7	0	10	42	.197	.209	.188	9.07	2.16
Barbato, Johnny	R-R	6-2	185	7-11-92	1	4	4.89	15	13	0	0	57	52	39	31	4	31	50	.248	.288	.223	7.89	4.89
Berroa, Simon	R-R	6-4	165	10-28-87	2	0	4.12	32	1	0	0	39	45	20	18	3	19	33	.288	.250	.308	7.55	4.35
Bingham, Paul	R-R	6-3	205	3-7-88	0	0	15.63	6	0	0	0	6	12	12	11	3	5	5	.400	.364	.421	7.11	7.11
Branham, Matt	R-R	6-5	220	9-28-87	0	0	0.00	2	0	0	0	2	1	0	0	0	1	4	.143	.333	.000	18.00	4.50
Brule, Kyle	R-R	6-2	185	6-9-89	4	0	5.47	19	0	0	1	25	32	17	15	1	8	25	.323	.371	.297	9.12	2.92
Campos, Leonel	R-R	6-3	185	7-17-87	0	0	18.00	1	1	0	0	2	5	4	4	1	0	4	.455	.500	.429	18.00	0.00
Cropper, Daniel	R-R	6-4	200	1-13-88	1	0	1.86	7	0	0	0	10	8	2	2	0	4	11	.250	.200	.273	10.24	3.72
De La Cruz, Luis	R-R	6-6	195	6-15-89	1	2	4.28	36	0	0	1	48	40	25	23	3	20	43	.222	.169	.248	8.01	3.72
Gigliotti, Jeremy	L-L	6-1	190	1-16-88	4	3	3.82	23	0	0	2	33	24	15	14	3	16	44	.203	.186	.213	12.00	4.36
Gonzalez, Greg	R-R	5-10	180	9-19-88	4	1	3.99	16	0	0	0	29	18	13	13	5	12	33	.176	.161	.183	10.13	3.68
Haney, Christopher	R-R	5-11	185	2-13-89	1	1	6.97	9	0	0	1	10	8	8	8	0	6	14	.211	.150	.278	12.19	5.23
Hebner, Cody	R-R	5-11	175	11-21-90	2	2	3.35	11	7	0	0	38	28	16	14	0	15	39	.207	.208	.207	9.32	3.58
Herrera, Juan	R-R	6-0	175	8-21-91	2	4	4.50	14	14	0	0	56	51	34	28	4	40	37	.244	.208	.274	5.95	6.43
Jones, James	R-R	6-3	210	12-16-88	0	0	0.00	3	0	0	0	3	6	0	0	0	1	5	.375	.000	.375	13.50	2.70
Mejia, Ruben	R-R	6-1	175	2-23-92	0	0	4.50	1	1	0	0	4	3	2	2	0	2	1	.214	.000	.214	2.25	4.50
Needy, James	R-R	6-6	205	3-30-91	1	4	4.60	12	11	0	0	43	51	28	22	3	16	26	.288	.344	.259	5.44	3.35
Pope, Mark	R-R	6-2	203	8-29-89	3	1	3.41	10	0	0	0	29	26	12	11	4	11	24	.239	.167	.266	7.45	3.41
Quackenbush, Kevin	R-R	6-3	207	11-28-88	1	0	0.44	17	0	0	9	21	13	1	1	0	6	33	.188	.269	.140	14.37	2.61
Rea, Colin	R-R	6-5	225	7-1-90	3	4	2.21	15	15	0	0	53	47	18	13	2	21	43	.236	.279	.214	7.30	3.57
Scott, Will	R-R	6-2	191	9-2-90	2	2	3.17	19	5	0	2	54	45	23	19	0	12	43	.223	.174	.248	7.17	2.00
Slack, Warren	R-R	5-11	175	7-15-89	0	0	16.88	5	0	0	0	5	12	10	10	0	5	1	.480	.667	.455	1.69	8.44
Stites, Matthew	R-R	5-11	170	5-28-90	4	0	1.93	24	0	0	5	33	14	7	7	1	8	36	.125	.089	.149	9.92	2.20
Wilkes, Chris	R-R	6-4	235	9-26-89	5	1	3.28	27	0	0	5	36	29	15	13	3	18	46	.218	.222	.216	11.61	4.54

Fielding

Catcher	PCT	G	PO	A	E	DP	PB
Colantonio	.992	46	319	41	3	5	4
Hedges	1.000	4	19	3	0	0	0
Kometani	1.000	3	10	0	0	0	0
Pozo	1.000	3	15	3	0	0	0
Rodriguez	.990	35	267	29	3	3	5
Tyrell	1.000	1	5	0	0	0	0

First Base	PCT	G	PO	A	E	DP
Garce	.994	21	162	4	1	11
Killian	.962	6	23	2	1	3
Kometani	.987	51	364	27	5	29
Orr	1.000	2	10	0	0	0
Tyrell	1.000	3	20	1	0	1
Whitmore	.980	6	48	0	1	5

Second Base	PCT	G	PO	A	E	DP
Ingram	.929	9	10	16	2	2
McElroy	.986	16	28	41	1	10
Miller	.924	19	22	39	5	4
Minyeti	1.000	5	7	7	0	2
Spangenberg	.963	24	40	63	4	9
Whitmore	1.000	11	12	22	0	7

Third Base	PCT	G	PO	A	E	DP
Garce	1.000	1	0	1	0	0
Jones	.898	18	15	38	6	5
McElroy	1.000	1	0	3	0	0
Minyeti	.881	29	15	37	7	3
Moore	.875	14	8	13	3	1
Tyrell	.000	1	0	0	0	0
Whitmore	.935	31	25	47	5	4

Shortstop	PCT	G	PO	A	E	DP
McElroy	.923	3	3	9	1	2
Minyeti	1.000	7	5	7	0	2
Moore	.500	1	0	1	1	0
Peterson	.944	71	122	180	18	34

Outfield	PCT	G	PO	A	E	DP
Dore	.933	25	41	1	3	0
Gaedele	.980	54	96	4	2	0
Gallic	1.000	12	20	0	0	0
Martinez	1.000	12	25	1	0	0
Miller	.957	15	20	2	1	0
Orr	.983	60	117	0	2	0
Stokes	.984	34	58	2	1	1
Tate	.982	26	54	1	1	0

AZL PADRES   ROOKIE

ARIZONA LEAGUE

Batting	B-T	HT	WT	DOB	AVG	vLH	vRH	G	AB	R	H	2B	3B	HR	RBI	BB	HBP	SH	SF	SO	SB	CS	SLG	OBP
Adamson, Corey	L-R	6-2	185	2-23-92	.245	.234	.248	48	192	23	47	7	3	1	18	22	0	0	2	48	9	8	.328	.319
Alcantara, Yoan	R-R	6-1	175	11-20-92	.348	.378	.339	50	210	50	73	13	8	7	46	4	3	0	1	25	8	2	.586	.367
Blanco, Felipe	R-R	6-1	175	12-9-93	.176	.267	.151	38	136	13	24	0	2	1	16	8	3	0	1	42	6	3	.228	.236
Brayton, Ross	R-R	6-3	195	5-10-88	.200	.000	.200	1	5	1	1	0	0	0	0	0	0	0	0	3	0	0	.200	.200
Cabrera, Felix	R-R	6-0	170	7-14-89	.289	.250	.298	40	128	19	37	5	2	1	19	11	1	0	2	26	10	3	.383	.345
Daal, Rodney	R-R	5-11	190	3-23-94	.243	.200	.260	24	70	8	17	4	0	0	6	14	2	0	0	21	2	1	.300	.384
Decker, Cody	R-R	5-11	220	1-17-87	.344	.571	.280	10	32	4	11	2	0	2	7	6	0	0	1	9	1	0	.594	.436
Filpo, Fabel	R-R	6-1	180	9-28-92	.385	.500	.333	9	26	5	10	1	0	0	8	3	0	0	0	1	1	2	.538	.448
Gabella, Cody	R-R	6-1	175	12-5-91	.169	.143	.178	21	59	5	10	1	0	0	7	8	1	0	0	23	1	0	.186	.279
Garce, Daniel	R-R	6-1	166	6-6-89	.194	.222	.182	16	62	3	12	2	0	0	4	3	0	0	0	24	0	0	.226	.231
Gomez, Jairo	R-R	6-0	170	1-16-92	.278	.350	.260	26	97	14	27	9	0	1	11	5	1	0	0	17	2	3	.402	.320
Hedges, Austin	R-R	6-1	190	8-18-92	.313	.500	.200	5	16	3	5	0	0	1	4	5	1	0	0	1	0	0	.500	.500

Batting	B-T	HT	WT	DOB	AVG	vLH	vRH	G	AB	R	H	2B	3B	HR	RBI	BB	HBP	SH	SF	SO	SB	CS	SLG	OBP
Ingram, Rashad	R-R	6-0	175	5-27-89	.260	.474	.190	25	77	14	20	2	2	0	9	12	2	0	1	20	4	0	.338	.370
Jones, Duanel	R-R	6-3	195	5-11-93	.267	.310	.256	37	150	38	40	7	2	8	23	16	3	0	0	43	1	1	.500	.349
Karmas, Paul	R-R	6-3	220	5-18-89	.276	.357	.255	37	134	20	37	11	0	2	17	18	1	0	2	17	0	0	.403	.361
Killian, Dan	L-R	6-4	195	1-14-89	.375	.500	.357	9	32	6	12	2	1	1	5	6	2	0	0	4	0	0	.594	.500
Kral, Robert	L-R	5-9	190	3-28-89	.275	.000	.314	14	40	9	11	1	1	1	7	13	1	0	0	10	0	1	.425	.463
Lopez, Yair	R-R	6-3	150	9-9-91	.288	.262	.295	45	191	34	55	11	4	6	21	5	3	0	0	58	14	3	.482	.317
Martinez, Alberth	R-R	6-1	170	1-23-91	.354	.389	.346	44	189	31	67	12	6	7	24	10	3	0	1	27	14	3	.593	.394
McElroy, Casey	L-R	5-8	180	12-28-89	.263	.000	.294	5	19	0	5	2	0	0	3	1	0	0	0	9	0	1	.368	.300
McKenna, Pat	R-R	5-10	170	6-24-87	.000	.000	.000	1	2	0	0	0	0	0	0	0	0	0	0	0	0	1	.000	.000
Medica, Tommy	R-R	6-1	190	4-9-88	.391	.167	.471	6	23	8	9	2	0	1	6	4	0	0	1	3	0	0	.609	.464
Miller, Justin	R-R	5-9	190	12-14-88	.407	.417	.405	17	54	8	22	2	2	1	6	6	2	0	1	9	2	1	.574	.476
Quintana, Gabriel	R-R	6-2	190	9-7-92	.267	.200	.300	8	30	3	8	1	0	1	3	3	0	0	0	6	0	1	.400	.333
Rincon, Edinson	R-R	6-1	185	8-11-90	.300	.000	.375	3	10	0	3	0	0	0	1	1	0	0	0	1	0	0	.300	.364

Pitching	B-T	HT	WT	DOB	W	L	ERA	G	GS	CG	SV	IP	H	R	ER	HR	BB	SO	AVG	vLH	vRH	K/9	BB/9
Beard, Hayden	R-R	6-1	175	1-22-85	0	0	0.00	2	0	0	0	3	3	1	0	0	1	4	.231	.000	.333	12.00	3.00
Brule, Kyle	R-R	6-2	185	6-9-89	2	1	2.03	10	0	0	2	13	6	6	3	2	2	12	.120	.053	.161	8.10	1.35
Castillo, Jeury	R-R	6-5	210	1-20-89	0	0	2.25	3	0	0	0	4	3	1	1	0	2	5	.231	.000	.273	11.25	4.50
Claveria, Marlon	R-R	6-3	210	8-30-90	1	4	7.15	12	8	0	0	34	54	45	27	1	22	18	.344	.373	.327	4.76	5.82
Corpas, Jean	R-R	6-2	170	3-9-91	3	1	3.79	21	2	0	0	38	41	21	16	2	11	37	.261	.327	.229	8.76	2.61
Cropper, Daniel	R-R	6-4	200	1-13-88	3	1	2.08	17	0	0	0	30	29	14	7	0	4	34	.236	.273	.215	10.09	1.19
De La Cruz, Vladimir	R-R	6-3	174	9-3-90	0	0	9.82	4	0	0	0	4	7	9	4	0	3	4	.368	.250	.400	9.82	7.36
Eisenbach, Robert	L-L	6-0	180	4-5-88	2	2	3.05	14	4	0	1	38	32	18	13	1	10	32	.227	.171	.245	7.51	2.35
Guerrero, Tayron	R-R	6-7	189	1-9-91	0	4	9.62	16	4	0	0	34	45	42	36	0	41	24	.331	.295	.360	6.42	10.96
Hancock, Justin	R-R	6-4	185	10-28-90	0	3	7.09	11	8	0	0	33	46	30	26	0	21	30	.329	.275	.350	8.18	5.73
Jones, James	R-R	6-3	210	12-16-88	2	1	2.97	27	0	0	8	30	29	14	10	0	4	32	.240	.189	.262	9.49	1.19
Mejia, Ruben	R-R	6-1	175	2-23-92	0	1	4.66	2	2	0	0	10	8	5	5	2	3	7	.211	.313	.136	6.52	2.79
Needy, James	R-R	6-6	205	3-30-91	2	0	2.70	2	2	0	0	10	11	6	3	0	2	7	.282	.286	.281	6.30	1.80
Norwood, Tyler	R-R	6-3	215	2-3-91	0	3	8.51	22	0	0	0	31	37	42	29	2	35	25	.289	.250	.324	7.34	10.27
O'Grady, Dennis	R-R	5-10	200	5-17-89	0	0	6.43	2	1	0	0	7	10	5	5	1	0	4	.323	.250	.368	5.14	0.00
Osuna, Stiven	R-R	6-3	190	5-5-87	0	0	2.25	2	0	0	0	4	4	1	1	1	0	4	.267	.250	.273	9.00	0.00
Paz, Uber	R-R	6-4	194	5-4-91	4	3	5.16	14	12	0	0	59	79	46	34	5	13	50	.317	.329	.311	7.58	1.97
Pearson, Atlee	R-R	6-0	190	9-9-89	0	0	4.91	3	0	0	0	4	4	2	2	0	0	3	.308	.167	.429	7.36	0.00
Pope, Mark	R-R	6-2	203	8-29-89	0	0	9.00	1	0	0	0	4	4	2	2	0	0	3	.444	.667	.333	13.50	0.00
Reyes, Eugenio	R-R	6-3	215	7-13-90	—	—	—	1	0	0	0	0	0	0	0	0	0	0	—	—	—	—	—
Reyes, Genison	R-R	6-5	190	9-19-91	2	6	10.34	18	5	0	0	43	76	58	49	3	19	44	.394	.411	.387	9.28	4.01
Ross, Joseph	R-R	6-3	185	5-21-93	0	0	0.00	1	0	0	0	1	2	0	0	0	0	0	.400	.000	.000	0.00	0.00
Sarria, Daniel	R-R	6-1	190	1-31-88	0	2	8.10	6	5	0	0	17	21	18	15	1	8	9	.309	.286	.325	4.86	4.32
Schmidt, Nick	L-L	6-5	245	10-10-85	1	1	4.50	2	2	0	0	8	8	4	4	0	3	9	.267	.667	.167	10.13	3.38
Slack, Warren	R-R	5-11	175	7-15-89	0	0	1.33	12	1	0	0	20	18	3	3	0	7	25	.234	.258	.217	11.07	3.10
Smith, Burch	R-R	6-4	195	4-12-90	0	0	4.50	2	0	0	1	2	3	2	1	0	1	4	.300	.000	.375	18.00	4.50
Stites, Matthew	R-R	5-11	170	5-28-90	0	0	0.00	2	0	0	0	2	0	0	0	0	0	3	.000	.000	.000	13.50	0.00
Wisler, Matthew	R-R	6-3	175	9-12-92	0	0	—	1	0	0	0	0	2	4	4	0	0	0	1.000	1.000	1.000	—	—
Worrell, Josh	R-R	6-5	215	11-17-86	1	0	15.68	8	0	0	1	10	25	18	18	3	3	8	.463	.357	.500	6.97	2.61

Fielding

Catcher	PCT	G	PO	A	E	DP	PB
Brayton	1.000	1	3	0	0	0	0
Daal	.964	23	164	23	7	1	12
Gomez	.963	23	162	19	7	1	14
Hedges	.882	2	13	2	2	0	0
Kral	.945	12	96	7	6	0	4
Gabella	.971	17	33	33	2	7	
Gomez	1.000	1	2	1	0	0	
Ingram	.833	7	6	14	4	1	
McElroy	1.000	4	10	16	0	5	
McKenna	1.000	1	3	4	0	1	
Miller	.963	9	23	29	2	9	

Shortstop	PCT	G	PO	A	E	DP
Blanco	.842	38	46	103	28	23
Cabrera	.667	2	2	0	1	0
Gabella	.500	3	0	2	2	0
Ingram	.904	15	14	33	5	5
Miller	.882	3	9	6	2	0

First Base	PCT	G	PO	A	E	DP
Brayton	1.000	1	2	1	0	0
Decker	.983	7	58	1	1	2
Garce	.990	12	92	3	1	10
Karmas	.979	31	264	18	6	24
Killian	1.000	6	54	3	0	5

Third Base	PCT	G	PO	A	E	DP
Cabrera	.857	13	11	25	6	2
Daal	1.000	1	0	1	0	0
Gomez	1.000	1	1	0	0	0
Jones	.850	37	23	73	17	8
Quintana	.880	8	5	17	3	1
Rincon	.750	1	1	2	1	0

Outfield	PCT	G	PO	A	E	DP
Adamson	.966	43	55	2	2	0
Alcantara	.901	45	74	8	9	0
Filpo	1.000	8	3	0	0	0
Gomez	.000	1	0	0	0	0
Lopez	.978	37	85	6	2	2
Martinez	.979	41	92	3	2	0
Miller	.000	1	0	0	0	0

Second Base	PCT	G	PO	A	E	DP
Cabrera	.929	23	39	52	7	10

DSL PADRES

ROOKIE

DOMINICAN SUMMER LEAGUE

Batting	B-T	HT	WT	DOB	AVG	vLH	vRH	G	AB	R	H	2B	3B	HR	RBI	BB	HBP	SH	SF	SO	SB	CS	SLG	OBP
Barahona, Luis	B-R	5-11	170	11-27-93	.286	.231	.310	40	84	17	24	6	0	0	17	15	1	0	1	15	9	1	.357	.396
Brito, Malquiel	L-R	6-1	187	8-24-93	.217	.225	.214	48	152	23	33	5	2	0	9	26	5	0	1	37	3	8	.276	.348
Brugeura, Reynaldo	B-R	5-10	170	11-5-91	.213	.222	.211	37	89	23	19	2	0	1	7	20	3	0	0	21	10	9	.270	.375
Castillo, Fabian	R-R	6-1	175	9-26-93	.141	.190	.120	21	71	4	10	1	0	0	7	0	2	0	1	21	2	0	.155	.162
Charles, Henry	L-L	6-1	174	1-3-94	.303	.262	.317	51	165	32	50	8	5	3	20	31	2	0	1	28	6	7	.467	.417
Del Castillo, Miguel	R-R	5-10	170	10-14-91	.223	.280	.208	47	121	15	27	9	0	0	15	14	2	0	5	18	1	1	.298	.303
Diaz, Yorky	R-R	6-2	185	6-18-93	.082	.143	.068	34	73	8	6	0	1	0	8	12	0	0	0	30	3	1	.110	.212
Filpo, Fabel	B-R	6-1	180	9-28-92	.281	.429	.240	26	96	6	27	4	2	1	5	6	2	0	1	20	2	0	.396	.333

SAN DIEGO PADRES

Batting	B-T	HT	WT	DOB	AVG	vLH	vRH	G	AB	R	H	2B	3B	HR	RBI	BB	HBP	SH	SF	SO	SB	CS	SLG	OBP
Gomez, Jairo	R-R	6-0	170	1-16-92	.263	.400	.214	6	19	1	5	2	0	0	2	4	0	0	0	5	1	0	.368	.391
Guzman, Jorge	R-R	6-1	170	7-15-89	.137	.077	.163	41	131	15	18	3	0	0	4	23	3	0	1	36	4	2	.160	.278
Jimenez, Miguel	L-L	6-2	185	10-17-93	.235	.175	.252	59	183	12	43	11	0	0	28	27	2	0	1	62	3	7	.295	.338
Lendor, Moises	B-R	6-1	170	6-25-93	.191	.250	.173	25	68	7	13	1	0	0	2	8	2	0	0	28	4	4	.206	.295
Martinez, Cristhofer	B-R	6-1	175	11-23-92	.221	.190	.230	57	190	29	42	7	6	1	16	31	2	0	1	38	6	2	.337	.335
Moreno, Edwin	L-L	6-1	190	10-07-93	.244	.256	.241	49	176	28	43	5	2	7	27	14	1	0	2	28	4	3	.415	.301
Quintana, Gabriel	R-R	6-2	190	9-7-92	.284	.321	.272	60	211	35	60	16	0	7	34	18	9	0	2	55	3	3	.460	.363
Tejada, Luis	R-R	6-3	175	10-12-92	.276	.346	.255	67	217	48	60	12	2	8	42	35	7	0	2	60	16	6	.461	.391
Valenzuela, Ricardo	R-R	6-0	189	8-4-90	.250	.059	.309	31	72	10	18	6	0	0	6	11	2	0	0	6	1	2	.333	.365

Pitching	B-T	HT	WT	DOB	W	L	ERA	G	GS	CG	SV	IP	H	R	ER	HR	BB	SO	AVG	vLH	vRH	K/9	BB/9
Andujar, Rudi	R-R	6-2	190	5-14-91	1	1	9.11	23	0	0	1	28	16	28	28	0	38	20	.180	.139	.208	6.51	12.36
Brasoban, Yimmi	R-R	6-1	185	6-22-94	3	3	5.65	12	10	0	0	43	42	35	27	1	28	25	.259	.283	.245	5.23	5.86
Cabrera, Erik	R-R	6-1	180	8-15-90	2	5	5.34	12	5	1	0	30	26	24	18	1	19	15	.243	.294	.219	4.45	5.64
Claveria, Marlon	R-R	6-3	210	8-30-90	1	3	9.20	5	4	0	0	15	15	16	15	0	9	10	.273	.294	.263	6.14	5.52
Constanza, Alexander	L-L	6-3	190	7-27-94	0	0	2.25	3	0	0	0	4	3	1	1	0	3	4	.214	.000	.273	9.00	6.75
Cornelio, Andres	R-R	6-1	166	9-12-90	0	3	27.00	14	2	0	0	8	2	31	23	0	36	4	.077	.000	.133	4.70	42.26
Corpas, Jean	R-R	6-2	170	3-9-91	0	1	3.55	3	2	0	0	13	14	6	5	0	5	9	.280	.389	.219	6.39	3.55
Corpas, Juan	R-R	6-0	180	10-28-92	2	1	3.34	14	4	0	1	35	34	16	13	0	13	22	.260	.204	.293	5.66	3.34
De La Cruz, Vladimir	R-R	6-3	174	9-23-90	4	3	4.60	20	0	0	3	29	19	16	15	0	25	37	.190	.185	.192	11.35	7.67
Garces, Frank	L-L	5-11	155	1-17-90	4	3	2.51	15	10	1	1	72	53	28	20	3	20	115	.202	.211	.200	14.44	2.51
Liriano, Elvin	L-L	6-3	190	10-17-92	3	3	3.58	13	8	0	0	50	36	29	20	1	31	35	.196	.227	.191	6.26	5.54
Marcano, Ivan	R-R	6-3	218	6-1-91	1	1	8.33	18	0	0	0	27	20	28	25	1	42	24	.196	.212	.188	8.00	14.00
Mejia, Ruben	R-R	6-1	175	2-23-92	1	1	1.40	5	4	0	0	19	16	7	3	0	10	20	.213	.167	.244	9.31	4.66
Mora, Abel	L-L	6-5	175	12-3-91	0	6	4.14	11	10	0	0	54	41	30	25	5	22	52	.211	.154	.215	8.61	3.64
Oviedo, Jonathan	R-R	6-3	200	5-25-87	2	1	11.00	9	0	0	0	9	11	16	11	0	8	7	.314	.125	.370	7.00	8.00
Paz, Uber	R-R	6-4	194	5-4-91	0	4	5.66	4	4	0	0	21	20	15	13	0	6	17	.256	.286	.240	7.40	2.61
Pena, Arturo	R-R	6-4	200	5-13-94	0	1	5.79	18	0	0	0	28	31	23	18	2	15	20	.279	.300	.268	6.43	4.82
Pimentel, Carlos	B-R	6-2	175	10-24-91	0	0	1.69	7	4	0	0	16	18	12	3	0	9	15	.273	.071	.327	8.44	5.06
Ramirez, Roberto	R-R	6-2	190	6-6-90	1	0	2.45	10	1	0	1	22	17	6	6	2	11	15	.215	.143	.255	6.14	4.50
Rodriguez, Edwin	R-R	6-3	180	9-22-93	0	0	21.00	14	0	0	0	6	10	21	14	1	28	3	.370	.286	.400	4.50	42.00
Rodriguez, Pedro	R-R	6-0	170	4-12-91	1	0	9.00	4	0	0	0	6	2	6	6	1	6	2	.111	.000	.167	3.00	9.00

Fielding

Catcher	PCT	G	PO	A	E	DP	PB
Castillo	.989	15	81	11	1	0	5
Del Castillo	.978	44	278	36	7	1	9
Gomez	.981	5	43	8	1	0	3
Valenzuela	.981	19	93	10	2	0	11
Brugeura	.962	14	23	27	2	5	
Filpo	.000	1	0	0	0	0	
Lendor	.909	3	3	7	1	3	
Martinez	.955	51	106	106	10	21	

First Base	PCT	G	PO	A	E	DP
Filpo	.933	2	13	1	1	0
Jimenez	.988	59	465	28	6	31
Quintana	.750	1	3	0	1	2
Tejada	1.000	7	34	1	0	3
Valenzuela	1.000	6	34	1	0	1

Second Base	PCT	G	PO	A	E	DP
Brito	.880	7	9	13	3	1

Third Base	PCT	G	PO	A	E	DP
Brugeura	.875	9	6	22	4	0
Lendor	1.000	1	0	1	0	0
Martinez	.750	1	1	2	1	1
Quintana	.876	58	50	119	24	6
Valenzuela	.929	5	5	8	1	2

Shortstop	PCT	G	PO	A	E	DP
Brugeura	.938	9	10	20	2	2
Guzman	.947	41	56	105	9	15
Lendor	.829	20	23	40	13	4
Martinez	.889	4	9	7	2	1
Quintana	1.000	1	1	0	0	0

Outfield	PCT	G	PO	A	E	DP
Barahona	.951	35	38	1	2	0
Charles	.920	49	79	1	7	0
Diaz	.923	29	24	0	2	0
Filpo	.875	14	20	1	3	0
Moreno	.911	45	44	7	5	0
Tejada	.963	56	92	12	4	1

San Francisco Giants

SEASON IN A SENTENCE: An offense that ranked in the bottom of the National League in several categories overshadowed one of baseball's best pitching staffs as the Giants fell short of the playoffs in defending their World Series title.

HIGH POINT: The trade deadline brought outfielder Carlos Beltran from the Mets to provide the middle of the order thump the Giants had been lacking. At the time of the trade, Beltran was hitting .289/.391/.513 with 15 home runs and the Giants held a two-game lead over the Arizona Diamondbacks in the NL West and were in the midst of taking a series against the Phillies. Optimism reigned as Beltran was viewed as the piece that would put them over the top.

LOW POINT: Buster Posey, the team's cleanup hitter and catcher, had his second season end suddenly in a violent home plate collision on May 26. He sustained a broken leg and torn ankle ligaments, and for an offense that wasn't potent to begin with, the injury created a gap that proved too much to overcome. Outside of Posey, Giants catchers combined to hit .204/.276/.311.

NOTABLE ROOKIES: Brandon Belt was the club's Opening Day first baseman, but he got off to a slow start and shuttled between Triple-A Fresno and the big league club much of the season. He chipped in nine home runs in only 209 at-bats despite struggling with hitting for average and strikeouts. Lefthander Erik Surkamp gave up one run in six innings of work in his major league debut against the Astros, then provided five more solid September starts.

KEY TRANSACTIONS: After signing a minor league deal before the season, righthander Ryan Vogelsong was an unlikely choice to be the Giants' best pitcher, but arguably he was. After spending time in Japan and three other organizations, the 1998 Giants draftee led the NL with six shutouts and placed fourth with a 2.71 ERA. As noted above, the big in-season deal was getting Beltran from the Mets top pitching prospect Zack Wheeler just days before the trade deadline.

DOWN ON THE FARM: Outfielder Gary Brown dominated the high Class A California League as he led the circuit in batting (.336) and triples (13) while finishing second in runs (115) and steals (53). With their first-round selection in the draft, the Giants selected lefthanded-hitting shortstop Joe Panik out of St. John's, and he became the MVP of the short-season Northwest League.

OPENING DAY PAYROLL: $118,198,333 (8th)

PLAYERS OF THE YEAR

MAJOR LEAGUE	MINOR LEAGUE
Pablo Sandoval 3b	**Gary Brown** of
.315/.357/.552	(High Class A)
26 2B/23 HR	.336/.407/.519
NL All-Star	BA Minors All-Star

ORGANIZATION LEADERS

BATTING		*Minimum 250 PA
MAJORS		
* AVG	Pablo Sandoval	.315
* OPS	Pablo Sandoval	.909
HR	Pablo Sandoval	23
RBI	Pablo Sandoval	70
MINORS		
* AVG	Gary Brown, San Jose	.336
* OBP	Gary Brown, San Jose	.407
* SLG	Brad Eldred, Fresno	.536
R	Gary Brown, San Jose	115
H	Gary Brown, San Jose	188
TB	Gary Brown, San Jose	290
2B	Ryan Cavan, San Jose	38
3B	Gary Brown, San Jose	13
HR	Brett Pill, Fresno	25
RBI	Brett Pill, Fresno	107
BB	Jarrett Parker, San Jose	74
SO	Chris Dominguez, San Jose/Richmond	151
SB	Tyler Graham, Fresno	60

PITCHING		#Minimum 75 IP
MAJORS		
W	Three tied at	13
# ERA	Ryan Vogelsong	2.71
SO	Tim Lincecum	220
SV	Brian Wilson	36
MINORS		
W	Craig Westcott, San Jose	13
L	Shane Loux, Fresno	12
	Daryl Maday, Fresno/Richmond	12
# ERA	Eric Surkamp, Richmond/San Jose	1.94
G	Stephen Harrold, Augusta/San Jose	57
GS	Matt Yourkin, Fresno	29
SV	Heath Hembree, San Jose/Richmond	38
IP	Shane Loux, Fresno	179.1
BB	Ryan Verdugo, Richmond	63
SO	Eric Surkamp, Richmond/San Jose	170
# AVG	Eric Surkamp, Richmond/San Jose	.212

General Manager: Brian Sabean. **Farm Director:** Fred Stanley. **Scouting Director:** John Barr.

Class	Team	League	W	L	PCT	Finish	Manager(s)
Majors	San Francisco Giants	National	86	76	.531	6th (16)	Bruce Bochy
Triple-A	Fresno Grizzlies	Pacific Coast	65	79	.451	t-13th (16)	Steve Decker
Double-A	Richmond Flying Squirrels	Eastern	76	66	.535	3rd (12)	Dave Machemer
High A	San Jose Giants	California	90	50	.643	1st (10)	Andy Skeels
Low A	Augusta GreenJackets	South Atlantic	70	68	.507	7th (14)	Lipso Nava
Short-season	Salem-Keizer Volcanoes	Northwest	34	42	.447	7th (8)	Tom Trebelhorn
Rookie	AZL Giants	Arizona	41	15	.732	1st (13)	Mike Goff
Overall 2011 Minor League Record			376	320	.540	2nd (30)	

ORGANIZATION STATISTICS

SAN FRANCISCO GIANTS

NATIONAL LEAGUE

Batting	B-T	HT	WT	DOB	AVG	vLH	vRH	G	AB	R	H	2B	3B	HR	RBI	BB	HBP	SH	SF	SO	SB	CS	SLG	OBP
Belt, Brandon	L-L	6-5	220	4-20-88	.225	.348	.184	63	187	21	42	6	1	9	18	20	2	0	0	57	3	2	.412	.306
Beltran, Carlos	B-R	6-1	215	4-24-77	.323	.385	.296	44	167	17	54	9	4	7	18	11	1	0	0	27	1	2	.551	.369
2-team total (98 New York)				.300	—	—	142	520	78	156	39	6	22	84	71	3	0	4	88	4	2	.525	.385
Burrell, Pat	R-R	6-4	235	10-10-76	.230	.219	.235	92	183	17	42	9	1	7	21	33	2	0	1	67	0	0	.404	.352
Burriss, Emmanuel	B-R	6-0	205	1-17-85	.204	.143	.220	59	137	14	28	1	0	0	4	6	3	0	0	17	11	3	.212	.253
Cabrera, Orlando	R-R	5-10	195	11-2-74	.222	.179	.241	39	126	4	28	3	0	1	13	4	0	0	3	17	2	2	.270	.241
Christian, Justin	R-R	6-1	190	4-3-80	.255	.370	.100	18	47	6	12	5	0	0	4	2	0	0	0	8	3	2	.362	.286
Crawford, Brandon	L-R	6-2	215	1-21-87	.204	.133	.217	66	196	22	40	5	2	3	21	23	0	0	0	31	1	3	.296	.288
DeRosa, Mark	R-R	6-0	220	2-26-75	.279	.263	.292	47	86	9	24	2	0	0	12	8	2	0	1	18	1	1	.302	.351
Fontenot, Mike	L-R	5-8	165	6-9-80	.227	.255	.220	85	220	22	50	15	3	4	21	25	1	0	4	48	5	1	.377	.304
Ford, Darren	R-R	5-9	190	10-1-85	.286	1.000	.167	26	14	7	4	0	0	0	0	1	1	0	0	5	7	5	.286	.375
Gillaspie, Conor	L-R	6-1	195	7-18-87	.263	.333	.250	15	19	2	5	0	0	1	2	2	0	0	0	1	0	0	.421	.333
Hall, Bill	R-R	6-0	210	12-28-79	.158	.071	.208	16	38	6	6	2	0	0	1	3	0	0	0	8	2	1	.211	.220
2-team total (46 Houston)				.211	—	—	62	185	24	39	9	2	4	14	11	2	0	1	63	3	2	.314	.261
Huff, Aubrey	L-R	6-4	225	12-20-76	.246	.270	.237	150	521	45	128	27	1	12	59	47	2	0	9	90	5	3	.370	.306
Keppinger, Jeff	R-R	6-0	185	4-21-80	.255	.200	.273	56	216	17	55	11	0	2	15	8	2	0	2	17	0	0	.333	.285
2-team total (43 Houston)				.277	—	—	99	379	39	105	20	0	6	35	12	2	0	4	24	0	1	.377	.300
Pill, Brett	R-R	6-4	210	9-9-84	.300	.250	.364	15	50	7	15	3	2	2	9	2	0	0	1	8	0	1	.560	.321
Posey, Buster	R-R	6-1	220	3-27-87	.284	.205	.314	45	162	17	46	5	0	4	21	18	4	0	1	30	3	0	.389	.368
Rohlinger, Ryan	R-R	6-0	195	10-7-83	.000	.357	.000	1	1	0	0	0	0	0	0	0	0	0	0	1	0	0	.000	.000
Ross, Cody	R-L	5-10	195	12-23-80	.240	.234	.241	121	405	54	97	25	0	14	52	49	4	0	3	96	5	2	.405	.325
Rowand, Aaron	R-R	6-0	210	8-29-77	.233	.286	.208	108	331	34	77	22	2	4	21	10	9	0	1	84	2	3	.347	.274
Sanchez, Freddy	R-R	6-0	200	12-21-77	.289	.222	.308	60	239	21	69	15	1	3	24	13	3	0	1	35	0	1	.397	.332
Sanchez, Hector	R-R	5-11	235	11-17-89	.258	.091	.350	13	31	0	8	2	0	0	1	3	0	0	0	6	0	0	.323	.324
Sandoval, Pablo	B-R	5-11	240	8-11-86	.315	.281	.324	117	426	55	134	26	3	23	70	32	0	0	7	63	2	4	.552	.357
Schierholtz, Nate	L-R	6-1	205	2-15-84	.278	.234	.288	115	335	42	93	22	1	9	41	21	4	0	2	61	7	4	.430	.326
Stewart, Chris	R-R	6-4	215	2-19-82	.204	.295	.169	67	162	20	33	8	0	3	10	16	2	0	0	18	0	0	.309	.283
Tejada, Miguel	R-R	5-9	220	5-25-74	.239	.247	.236	91	322	28	77	16	0	4	26	12	3	0	4	35	4	4	.326	.270
Torres, Andres	B-R	5-9	200	1-26-78	.221	.170	.229	112	348	50	77	24	1	4	19	42	4	0	0	95	19	6	.330	.312
Whiteside, Eli	R-R	6-2	220	10-22-79	.197	.250	.186	82	213	14	42	8	2	4	17	18	2	0	2	59	2	1	.310	.264

Pitching	B-T	HT	WT	DOB	W	L	ERA	G	GS	CG	SV	IP	H	R	ER	HR	BB	SO	AVG	vLH	vRH	K/9	BB/9
Affeldt, Jeremy	L-L	6-4	230	6-6-79	3	2	2.63	67	0	0	3	62	47	22	18	5	24	54	.207	.144	.248	7.88	3.50
Bumgarner, Madison	R-L	6-5	225	8-1-89	13	13	3.21	33	33	0	0	205	202	82	73	12	46	191	.260	.243	.264	8.40	2.02
Cain, Matt	R-R	6-3	230	10-1-84	12	11	2.88	33	33	1	0	222	177	82	71	9	63	179	.217	.185	.250	7.27	2.56
Casilla, Santiago	R-R	6-0	220	7-25-80	2	2	1.74	49	0	0	6	52	33	11	10	1	25	45	.183	.234	.155	7.84	4.35
Edlefsen, Steve	R-R	6-2	195	6-27-85	0	0	9.53	13	0	0	0	11	17	12	12	2	10	6	.347	.533	.265	4.76	7.94
Joaquin, Waldis	R-R	6-0	240	12-25-86	1	0	4.26	5	0	0	0	6	6	3	3	0	3	3	.261	.250	.263	4.26	4.26
Lincecum, Tim	L-R	5-11	165	6-15-84	13	14	2.74	33	33	1	0	217	176	74	66	15	86	220	.222	.217	.226	9.12	3.57
Lopez, Javier	L-L	6-4	220	7-11-77	5	2	2.72	70	0	0	1	53	42	16	16	2	20	40	.221	.163	.276	6.79	4.42
Mota, Guillermo	R-R	6-6	240	7-25-73	2	2	3.81	52	0	0	1	80	71	34	34	10	30	77	.240	.234	.243	8.63	3.36
Ramirez, Ramon	R-R	5-11	200	8-31-81	3	3	2.62	66	0	0	4	69	54	24	20	3	26	66	.216	.250	.203	8.65	3.41
Romo, Sergio	R-R	5-10	185	3-4-83	3	1	1.50	65	0	0	1	48	29	8	8	2	5	70	.173	.229	.150	13.13	0.94
Runzler, Dan	L-L	6-4	235	3-30-85	1	2	6.26	31	1	0	0	27	29	21	19	0	16	25	.282	.244	.310	8.23	5.27
Sanchez, Jonathan	L-L	6-0	200	11-19-82	4	7	4.26	19	19	0	0	101	80	54	48	9	66	102	.220	.188	.231	9.06	5.86
Surkamp, Eric	L-L	6-4	190	7-16-87	2	2	5.74	6	6	0	0	27	32	18	17	1	17	13	.311	.429	.302	4.39	5.74
Vogelsong, Ryan	R-R	6-4	215	7-22-77	13	7	2.71	30	28	1	0	180	164	62	54	15	61	139	.244	.258	.233	6.96	3.06
Wilson, Brian	R-R	6-2	205	3-16-82	6	4	3.11	57	0	0	36	55	50	20	19	2	31	54	.240	.223	.257	8.84	5.07
Zito, Barry	L-L	6-2	205	5-13-78	3	4	5.87	13	9	0	0	54	51	35	35	10	24	32	.256	.294	.248	5.37	4.02

Fielding

Catcher	PCT	G	PO	A	E	DP	PB
Posey	.994	41	333	24	2	4	3
Sanchez	1.000	11	51	3	0	1	2
Stewart	.986	63	430	48	7	4	2
Whiteside	.991	81	495	41	5	4	7

First Base	PCT	G	PO	A	E	DP
Belt	.995	31	201	12	1	8
Burriss	1.000	2	10	0	0	1

SAN FRANSISCO GIANTS

DeRosa	1.000	10	33	3	0	3
Huff	.995	120	990	72	5	86
Pill	1.000	14	105	10	0	5
Posey	1.000	2	16	2	0	2
Sandoval	1.000	6	54	6	0	3
Stewart	1.000	3	5	0	0	0

Second Base	PCT	G	PO	A	E	DP
Burriss	.979	39	62	77	3	24
Cabrera	1.000	2	1	3	0	1
DeRosa	1.000	2	1	1	0	0
Fontenot	.963	23	32	47	3	7
Hall	.931	10	17	10	2	2
Keppinger	.991	55	109	114	2	17
Sanchez	.988	58	105	136	3	30

Tejada	1.000	4	5	13	0	2

Third Base	PCT	G	PO	A	E	DP
Burriss	.857	2	3	3	1	0
Cabrera	.000	1	0	0	0	0
DeRosa	.941	16	10	22	2	2
Fontenot	1.000	8	0	6	0	1
Gillaspie	1.000	4	2	1	0	0
Sandoval	.966	106	71	214	10	16
Tejada	.985	44	29	99	2	12

Shortstop	PCT	G	PO	A	E	DP
Burriss	.944	9	5	12	1	3
Cabrera	.966	36	52	91	5	19
Crawford	.972	65	74	167	7	29
Fontenot	.968	37	38	84	4	18

Tejada	.951	42	44	110	8	12

Outfield	PCT	G	PO	A	E	DP
Belt	.945	32	50	2	3	0
Beltran	1.000	43	80	6	0	1
Burrell	.932	54	53	2	4	1
Burriss	1.000	2	2	0	0	0
Christian	1.000	17	27	1	0	0
Ford	1.000	15	11	0	0	0
Hall	1.000	1	2	0	0	0
Huff	1.000	16	22	1	0	0
Ross	.995	115	183	8	1	1
Rowand	.994	84	157	3	1	0
Schierholtz	.982	103	157	9	3	4
Torres	.986	109	204	6	3	2

FRESNO GRIZZLIES

PACIFIC COAST LEAGUE

TRIPLE-A

Batting	B-T	HT	WT	DOB	AVG	vLH	vRH	G	AB	R	H	2B	3B	HR	RBI	BB	HBP	SH	SF	SO	SB	CS	SLG	OBP
Belt, Brandon	L-L	6-5	220	4-20-88	.309	.267	.325	49	165	32	51	12	0	8	32	42	2	0	3	47	4	4	.527	.448
Bond, Brock	B-R	5-11	185	9-11-85	.246	.176	.275	19	57	6	14	1	2	0	3	7	1	0	0	8	1	2	.333	.338
Burrell, Pat	R-R	6-4	235	10-10-76	.000	.000	.000	2	5	0	0	0	0	0	0	0	0	0	0	2	0	0	.000	.000
Burriss, Emmanuel	B-R	6-0	205	1-17-85	.297	.356	.267	45	175	31	52	8	1	2	10	22	4	0	1	19	24	5	.389	.386
Christian, Justin	R-R	6-1	190	4-3-80	.338	.380	.319	64	237	57	80	20	3	10	41	35	4	0	2	31	36	3	.574	.428
Crawford, Brandon	L-R	6-2	215	1-21-87	.234	.174	.250	29	107	13	25	5	1	1	9	9	0	0	0	20	5	2	.327	.291
Cuevas, Jose	R-R	6-2	190	4-5-88	.133	.200	.100	4	15	1	2	0	0	0	1	1	0	0	0	5	0	0	.133	.188
DeRosa, Mark	R-R	6-0	220	2-26-75	.310	.417	.267	11	42	6	13	1	0	0	3	0	0	0	0	8	0	0	.333	.310
Eldred, Brad	R-R	6-6	270	7-12-80	.278	.258	.288	111	371	61	103	23	2	23	57	34	8	0	0	94	9	4	.536	.351
Evans, Terry	R-R	6-4	210	1-19-82	.232	.235	.230	39	95	9	22	7	0	1	11	9	2	0	0	26	8	0	.337	.311
Fontenot, Mike	L-R	5-8	165	6-9-80	.219	.105	.385	10	32	5	7	0	0	1	3	5	0	0	0	4	0	0	.313	.324
Ford, Darren	R-R	5-9	190	10-1-85	.211	.226	.200	18	71	10	15	2	0	2	7	4	1	0	0	23	10	0	.324	.263
Gillaspie, Conor	L-R	6-1	195	7-18-87	.297	.254	.315	124	428	63	127	22	6	11	61	66	1	0	4	79	9	9	.453	.389
Gonzalez, Edgar	R-R	6-0	180	6-14-78	.315	.354	.297	137	505	69	159	30	0	14	82	51	3	0	5	73	14	6	.457	.378
Graham, Tyler	R-R	6-0	180	1-25-84	.273	.308	.256	127	414	82	113	18	3	1	31	31	11	0	4	80	60	12	.338	.337
Hall, Bill	R-R	6-0	210	12-28-79	.274	.433	.217	31	113	17	31	9	0	7	20	9	1	0	2	36	0	0	.540	.328
Honeycutt, Ryan	L-R	6-0	195	9-6-88	.500	.000	.600	2	6	2	3	0	0	0	0	0	0	0	0	0	0	0	.500	.500
Ishikawa, Travis	L-L	6-3	225	9-24-83	.251	.288	.236	56	175	21	44	14	0	3	18	29	4	0	1	54	3	1	.383	.368
La Torre, Tyler	L-R	6-0	219	4-22-83	.262	.250	.264	52	107	13	28	7	0	4	22	10	2	0	2	23	1	0	.439	.331
Liles, Nick	R-R	6-0	165	7-23-87	.417	.500	.333	3	12	0	5	1	0	0	1	1	0	0	0	3	1	0	.500	.462
Lormand, Ryan	R-R	6-0	165	10-30-85	.161	.200	.125	26	31	2	5	0	0	0	3	1	0	0	0	12	3	1	.161	.188
Mergenthaler, Michael	L-L	6-4	210	1-6-89	.000	.000	.000	1	1	0	0	0	0	0	0	0	0	0	0	0	0	0	.000	.000
Neal, Thomas	R-R	6-2	225	8-17-87	.295	.338	.273	60	220	35	65	13	3	2	25	13	6	0	0	50	7	6	.409	.351
Noonan, Nick	L-R	6-0	175	5-4-89	.297	.200	.333	13	37	6	11	0	0	1	4	4	0	0	0	2	1	0	.378	.366
Pill, Brett	R-R	6-4	210	9-9-84	.312	.340	.300	133	536	82	167	36	3	25	107	25	4	0	9	54	6	6	.530	.341
Ramirez, Max	R-R	5-11	175	10-11-84	.318	.321	.316	48	148	24	47	11	1	10	29	14	3	0	0	34	0	0	.608	.388
3-team total (11 Iowa, 24 Oklahoma City)					.278	—	—	83	266	38	74	15	1	13	48	21	4	0	5	58	0	0	.489	.334
Rohlinger, Ryan	R-R	6-0	195	10-7-83	.174	.196	.160	33	121	22	21	4	0	5	16	19	2	0	1	14	2	1	.331	.294
2-team total (70 Colorado Springs)					.247	—	—	103	364	71	90	19	5	10	51	56	5	0	3	57	2	3	.409	.353
Ross, Cody	R-L	5-10	195	12-23-80	.500	.500	.500	2	6	1	3	1	0	0	2	2	0	0	0	1	0	0	.667	.625
Sanchez, Hector	B-R	5-11	235	11-17-89	.261	.326	.236	46	153	15	40	9	0	1	26	13	0	0	2	22	0	1	.340	.315
Sandoval, Pablo	B-R	5-11	240	8-11-86	.278	.500	.167	5	18	4	5	0	0	2	7	2	0	0	2	0	0	0	.611	.318
Simmons, James	R-R	6-3	190	9-3-85	.228	.333	.133	27	57	6	13	0	0	3	6	3	1	0	0	25	0	0	.386	.279
Stewart, Chris	R-R	6-4	215	2-19-82	.221	.148	.250	33	95	9	21	5	0	0	10	11	2	0	1	16	3	1	.274	.312
Torres, Andres	B-R	5-9	200	1-26-78	.273	.364	.250	13	55	10	15	2	2	4	11	6	1	0	0	13	1	0	.600	.355
Villegas, Ydwin	B-R	5-10	180	9-1-94	.143	.100	.182	17	21	0	3	0	0	0	1	2	0	0	0	5	0	0	.143	.217
Williams, Jackson	R-R	5-11	205	5-14-86	.184	.182	.185	56	125	13	23	3	0	1	13	11	2	0	2	36	0	2	.232	.288
Yarrow, Stephen	L-R	6-3	155	11-30-88	.333	.500	.250	2	6	1	2	0	0	0	2	0	1	0	0	3	0	0	.333	.429

Pitching	B-T	HT	WT	DOB	W	L	ERA	G	GS	CG	SV	IP	H	R	ER	HR	BB	SO	AVG	vLH	vRH	K/9	BB/9
Banks, Josh	R-R	6-3	215	7-18-82	5	6	7.27	19	12	0	0	78	113	70	63	12	22	50	.338	.344	.333	5.77	2.54
Casilla, Santiago	R-R	6-0	220	7-25-80	0	0	1.80	4	0	0	0	5	3	1	1	1	1	4	.188	.200	.182	7.20	1.80
Daigle, Casey	R-R	6-6	220	4-4-81	2	0	5.97	36	0	0	2	38	45	26	25	3	17	39	.290	.254	.315	9.32	4.06
Dowdy, Justin	L-L	6-1	175	8-13-83	2	6	5.44	36	1	0	1	45	36	29	27	4	32	39	.224	.234	.216	7.86	6.45
Edlefsen, Steve	B-R	6-2	195	6-27-85	2	4	5.66	32	0	0	1	41	50	28	26	2	19	29	.313	.362	.275	6.31	4.14
Espineli, Geno	L-L	6-4	195	9-8-82	3	5	5.80	31	4	0	0	54	71	42	35	7	28	29	.317	.366	.289	4.80	4.64
2-team total (3 Colorado Springs)					3	5	6.83	34	4	0	0	57	82	51	43	9	30	34	—	—	—	5.40	4.76
Hinshaw, Alex	L-L	6-2	175	10-31-82	0	0	9.00	13	0	0	0	10	15	10	10	0	11	11	.366	.250	.476	9.90	9.90
Joaquin, Waldis	R-R	6-0	240	12-25-86	2	2	3.44	35	0	0	1	50	53	26	19	5	23	27	.279	.263	.291	4.89	4.17
King, Aaron	L-L	6-4	205	4-27-89	0	1	7.71	3	0	0	0	5	4	5	4	2	7	3	.222	.250	.214	5.79	13.50
Kown, Andrew	L-R	6-7	210	10-7-82	10	9	4.48	25	25	0	0	137	142	75	68	15	52	103	.272	.275	.269	6.78	3.42
Kroon, Marc	R-R	6-2	190	4-2-73	2	5	5.11	49	0	0	20	49	48	30	28	8	33	52	.255	.258	.253	9.49	6.02
Lofgren, Chuck	L-L	6-4	190	1-29-86	0	1	15.00	1	1	0	0	3	5	5	5	0	6	0	.417	.333	.444	0.00	18.00
Loux, Shane	R-R	6-2	225	8-31-79	8	12	4.67	28	28	1	0	179	202	101	93	19	41	84	.289	.299	.279	4.22	2.06
Machi, Jean	R-R	6-0	250	2-1-82	1	1	9.00	3	0	0	0	4	5	4	4	0	0	6	.294	.125	.444	13.50	0.00

SAN FRANSISCO GIANTS

Pitching

Pitching	B-T	HT	WT	DOB	W	L	ERA	G	GS	CG	SV	IP	H	R	ER	HR	BB	SO	AVG	vLH	vRH	K/9	BB/9
Maday, Daryl	R-R	6-2	225	8-12-85	0	2	7.07	3	3	0	0	14	25	15	11	3	7	7	.379	.520	.293	4.50	4.50
Mathis, Doug	R-R	6-3	220	6-7-83	0	4	3.60	13	13	0	0	65	65	33	26	5	31	54	.259	.319	.207	7.48	4.29
2-team total (4 Sacramento)					0	5	4.27	17	17	0	0	86	92	49	41	6	40	64	—	—	—	6.67	4.17
Matos, Osiris	R-R	6-1	200	8-6-84	0	0	1.93	6	0	0	0	9	8	2	2	0	3	5	.242	.167	.286	4.82	2.89
Mixon, David	R-R	6-3	190	9-10-84	0	0	8.53	7	0	0	1	13	18	13	12	0	7	7	.340	.333	.343	4.97	4.97
Munter, Scott	R-R	6-6	260	3-7-80	1	0	2.76	10	1	0	0	16	15	8	5	2	11	20	.231	.154	.282	11.02	6.06
2-team total (37 Tucson)						4	35.92	47	1	0	0	62	70	48	41	5	42	62	—	—	—	8.95	6.06
Otero, Danny	R-R	6-0	205	2-19-85	2	3	3.25	33	0	0	12	36	38	15	13	4	7	36	.264	.436	.157	9.00	1.75
Ray, Ronnie	R-R	6-3	215	5-11-84	4	2	4.85	35	1	0	1	52	44	35	28	5	28	33	.222	.265	.200	5.71	4.85
Rodriguez, Wilmin	L-L	6-2	220	5-13-85	0	0	9.00	7	0	0	0	7	10	7	7	0	6	5	.345	.333	.357	6.43	7.71
Romero, Felix	R-R	6-1	215	6-18-80	0	4	6.34	33	7	0	1	61	84	50	43	8	31	55	.327	.314	.336	8.11	4.57
Runzler, Dan	L-L	6-4	235	3-30-85	2	3	3.98	17	10	0	0	52	47	32	23	2	32	59	.237	.270	.222	10.21	5.54
Sanchez, Jonathan	L-L	6-0	200	11-19-82	1	0	3.27	2	2	0	0	11	10	4	4	1	5	13	.256	.455	.179	10.64	4.09
Sosa, Henry	R-R	6-1	205	7-28-85	3	1	10.41	17	0	0	0	23	39	30	27	3	17	21	.371	.366	.375	8.10	6.56
2-team total (1 Oklahoma City)					3	1	8.01	18	1	0	0	30	44	30	27	3	20	24	—	—	—	7.12	5.93
Stevenson, Jason	L-L	6-1	175	8-8-81	1	0	5.56	2	2	0	0	11	13	7	7	4	5	9	.295	.333	.276	7.15	3.97
Vessella, Tom	R-L	6-6	205	10-12-85	0	0	0.00	1	0	0	0	1	0	0	0	0	0	0	.000	.000	.000	0.00	0.00
Vogelsong, Ryan	R-R	6-4	215	7-22-77	2	0	1.59	2	2	0	0	11	8	3	2	1	5	17	.195	.286	.148	13.50	3.97
Yourkin, Matt	R-L	6-3	240	7-4-81	10	8	4.69	29	29	0	0	167	187	94	87	24	56	145	.284	.284	.284	7.81	3.02
Zito, Barry	L-L	6-2	205	5-13-78	2	0	2.55	3	3	1	0	18	10	5	5	1	5	17	.167	.094	.250	8.66	2.55

Fielding

Catcher	PCT	G	PO	A	E	DP	PB
La Torre	.992	25	116	4	1	1	1
Ramirez	.972	25	159	12	5	1	1
Sanchez	.994	42	288	27	2	6	5
Stewart	.996	31	212	20	1	2	7
Williams	.985	51	232	29	4	2	5

First Base	PCT	G	PO	A	E	DP
Belt	.971	12	94	5	3	7
DeRosa	.875	1	7	0	1	0
Eldred	.978	36	252	11	6	23
Gillaspie	1.000	9	73	6	0	8
Gonzalez	1.000	1	9	0	1	0
Ishikawa	.994	24	156	15	1	14
La Torre	1.000	6	19	0	0	3
Pill	.992	83	558	49	5	56
Ramirez	.952	7	19	1	1	1
Sandoval	1.000	1	8	2	0	0
Stewart	1.000	1	1	0	0	0

Second Base	PCT	G	PO	A	E	DP
Bond	.962	15	15	36	2	2
Burriss	.968	26	51	71	4	21
DeRosa	.950	4	5	14	1	2
Downing	1.000	3	3	9	0	0
Fontenot	1.000	9	11	15	0	6

	PCT	G	PO	A	E	DP
Gonzalez	.967	49	42	74	4	14
Hall	.949	15	36	38	4	14
Pill	.977	57	90	125	5	32
Rohlinger	.667	2	1	1	1	1

Third Base	PCT	G	PO	A	E	DP
Cuevas	1.000	2	1	3	0	0
DeRosa	.917	6	2	9	1	3
Eldred	.000	1	0	0	0	0
Gillaspie	.965	111	88	215	11	22
Gonzalez	.905	23	10	28	4	2
Hall	.893	7	6	19	3	4
Pill	.000	1	0	0	1	0
Rohlinger	.833	5	2	8	2	1
Sandoval	1.000	4	7	1	0	1
Yarrow	1.000	2	3	3	0	0

Shortstop	PCT	G	PO	A	E	DP
Burriss	.974	10	13	24	1	4
Crawford	.956	29	43	88	6	16
Cuevas	1.000	2	5	8	0	0
Fontenot	1.000	1	3	1	0	1
Gonzalez	.973	58	75	143	6	27
Hall	1.000	3	8	7	0	2
Lormand	.914	19	6	26	3	5
Noonan	.975	13	16	23	1	5

	PCT	G	PO	A	E	DP
Rohlinger	.959	26	47	69	5	20
Villegas	.938	15	13	17	2	4

Outfield	PCT	G	PO	A	E	DP
Belt	.960	37	68	4	3	1
Burrell	.500	2	1	0	1	0
Burriss	.917	9	11	0	1	0
Christian	.972	63	134	5	4	0
Eldred	.931	47	60	7	5	1
Evans	1.000	34	60	3	0	1
Ford	.979	18	44	2	1	0
Gillaspie	1.000	2	3	0	0	0
Gonzalez	.927	30	50	1	4	0
Graham	.982	119	272	7	5	1
Hall	1.000	6	9	0	0	0
Honeycutt	1.000	2	1	0	0	0
Ishikawa	.918	34	56	0	5	0
Liles	1.000	3	5	0	0	0
Lormand	.000	1	0	0	0	0
Mergenthaler	.000	1	0	0	0	0
Neal	.982	56	102	7	2	0
Pill	1.000	2	1	0	0	0
Ross	1.000	2	0	1	0	0
Simmons	.947	22	35	1	2	0
Torres	1.000	11	33	1	0	0

RICHMOND FLYING SQUIRRELS

DOUBLE-A

EASTERN LEAGUE

Batting	B-T	HT	WT	DOB	AVG	vLH	vRH	G	AB	R	H	2B	3B	HR	RBI	BB	HBP	SH	SF	SO	SB	CS	SLG	OBP
Biery, Drew	R-R	6-2	215	5-14-86	.219	.143	.240	10	32	1	7	1	0	0	4	1	0	0	1	10	0	0	.250	.235
Christian, Justin	R-R	6-1	190	4-3-80	.256	.318	.237	73	273	46	70	12	2	4	32	23	7	0	2	31	18	2	.359	.328
Culberson, Charlie	R-R	6-1	200	4-10-89	.259	.336	.236	137	553	69	143	34	2	10	56	22	6	0	2	129	14	4	.382	.293
Dominguez, Chris	R-R	6-3	215	11-22-86	.244	.148	.269	78	295	35	72	22	2	7	45	9	4	0	5	78	1	5	.403	.272
Fairley, Wendell	L-R	6-2	195	3-17-88	.265	.300	.261	34	98	11	26	3	2	0	7	8	0	0	0	27	2	2	.337	.321
Flores, Jose	B-R	5-11	175	8-17-87	.201	.271	.169	55	189	20	38	1	3	3	19	14	2	0	0	30	5	1	.286	.263
Ford, Darren	R-R	5-9	190	10-1-85	.279	.348	.254	23	86	11	24	3	0	2	9	0	0	0	0	24	6	3	.314	.347
Hodges, Wes	R-R	6-2	205	9-14-84	.279	.288	.277	74	265	30	74	15	1	8	34	14	1	0	2	67	0	1	.434	.316
Kieschnick, Roger	L-R	6-3	215	1-21-87	.255	.218	.266	126	459	71	117	22	5	16	65	34	3	0	5	121	13	7	.429	.307
Koshansky, Joe	L-L	6-4	230	5-26-82	.198	.200	.198	34	126	11	25	8	0	3	12	17	1	0	0	43	2	0	.333	.299
Lollis, Ryan	L-L	6-2	185	12-16-86	.222	.000	.222	3	9	1	2	0	0	0	1	0	0	0	0	1	0	0	.222	.222
Lormand, Ryan	R-R	6-0	165	10-30-85	.190	.176	.194	29	84	9	16	5	0	0	10	11	0	0	0	17	2	2	.250	.284
Lowenstein, Aaron	R-R	6-1	195	6-9-85	.204	.273	.183	36	93	5	19	1	0	0	5	6	0	0	1	28	0	1	.215	.250
McBryde, Mike	R-R	6-1	215	2-25-86	.255	.207	.274	30	102	14	26	4	1	1	12	6	3	0	1	29	4	0	.343	.313
Monell, Johnny	L-R	5-11	205	3-27-86	.249	.255	.247	119	386	46	96	24	1	10	49	48	3	0	3	93	0	3	.394	.334
Noonan, Nick	L-R	6-0	175	5-4-89	.212	.227	.206	71	260	28	55	11	0	3	25	33	2	0	2	60	2	2	.288	.303
Peguero, Francisco	R-R	5-11	195	6-1-88	.309	.281	.316	71	285	34	88	12	6	5	37	5	1	0	5	45	8	1	.446	.318
Perez, Juan	R-R	5-11	185	11-13-86	.256	.211	.272	131	457	58	117	25	10	4	40	28	4	0	3	95	22	6	.381	.303
Schoop, Sharlon	R-R	6-2	190	4-15-87	.218	.091	.265	80	206	25	45	8	0	4	21	20	1	0	2	39	3	2	.316	.288
Stromsmoe, Skyler	B-R	5-10	175	3-30-84	.277	.327	.260	83	195	30	54	6	1	2	20	28	2	0	5	39	3	6	.349	.365
Weeks, Joel	L-R	5-9	185	12-16-86	.179	.286	.156	19	39	2	7	1	0	0	2	3	0	0	1	9	0	1	.205	.233
Williams, Jackson	R-R	5-11	205	5-14-86	.208	.308	.175	18	53	8	11	2	0	3	9	5	1	0	0	9	0	0	.415	.288
Zambrano, Eliezer	B-R	5-11	175	9-16-86	.217	.222	.214	8	23	4	5	2	0	0	3	1	0	0	1	5	0	0	.304	.240

Pitching

Pitching	B-T	HT	WT	DOB	W	L	ERA	G	GS	CG	SV	IP	H	R	ER	HR	BB	SO	AVG	vLH	vRH	K/9	BB/9
Bowlin, Drew	R-R	6-1	190	12-28-86	0	0	2.84	3	0	0	0	6	4	2	2	1	4	4	.174	.333	.000	5.68	5.68
Correa, Hector	R-R	6-3	165	3-18-88	4	1	3.20	23	0	0	1	39	33	14	14	3	12	32	.236	.211	.261	7.32	2.75
Dowdy, Justin	L-L	6-1	175	8-13-83	4	0	0.82	12	0	0	1	22	9	3	2	1	10	21	.129	.148	.116	8.59	4.09
Fitzgerald, Justin	R-R	6-5	225	3-3-86	9	9	3.51	27	27	0	0	146	147	65	57	7	55	111	.267	.259	.273	6.83	3.38
Fleet, Austin	R-R	6-1	175	4-17-87	0	0	2.77	4	0	0	1	13	11	4	4	0	2	6	.239	.190	.280	4.15	1.38
Hembree, Heath	R-R	6-4	210	1-13-89	1	1	2.83	28	0	0	17	29	20	11	9	1	13	34	.194	.217	.175	10.67	4.08
Hinshaw, Alex	L-L	6-2	175	10-31-82	2	0	3.60	32	0	0	1	35	24	15	14	1	28	47	.190	.297	.146	12.09	7.20
Lively, Mitch	R-R	6-5	230	9-7-85	0	4	3.68	18	0	0	1	22	23	12	9	0	9	19	.258	.273	.250	7.77	3.68
Lofgren, Chuck	L-L	6-3	190	1-29-86	3	2	4.02	9	9	0	0	47	43	23	21	5	25	36	.238	.233	.240	6.89	4.79
Maday, Daryl	R-R	6-2	225	8-12-85	4	10	4.47	25	19	0	1	117	124	61	58	14	39	92	.276	.298	.259	7.10	3.01
Matos, Osiris	R-R	6-1	200	8-6-84	3	4	2.84	22	0	0	0	38	33	14	12	2	6	27	.232	.196	.256	6.39	1.42
Mixon, David	R-R	6-3	190	9-10-84	0	0	3.60	3	2	0	0	10	9	6	4	3	2	4	.231	.231	.231	3.60	1.80
Otero, Danny	R-R	6-2	205	2-19-85	2	1	1.42	23	0	0	1	38	34	8	6	0	4	40	.238	.212	.260	9.47	0.95
Quinowski, David	L-L	5-10	170	4-23-86	4	3	3.64	40	1	0	0	54	49	27	22	4	19	39	.234	.184	.263	6.46	3.15
Quirarte, Edwin	R-R	6-2	185	12-20-86	1	2	5.44	35	0	0	0	46	61	36	28	3	20	38	.324	.288	.352	7.38	3.88
Ray, Ronnie	R-R	6-3	215	5-11-84	2	1	0.95	15	0	0	0	28	20	5	3	1	5	29	.202	.250	.169	9.21	1.59
Rodriguez, Wilmin	L-L	6-2	220	5-13-85	4	3	3.77	33	3	0	0	57	64	31	24	4	23	38	.290	.280	.295	5.97	3.61
Schumer, Justin	R-R	6-0	180	8-2-88	1	0	1.29	5	2	0	0	14	11	3	2	0	10	4	.224	.138	.350	2.57	6.43
Sosa, Henry	R-R	6-1	205	7-28-85	5	2	2.68	8	6	0	0	40	41	13	12	1	8	36	.263	.351	.212	8.03	1.79
Stevenson, Jason	L-L	6-1	175	8-8-81	1	0	1.29	1	1	1	0	7	8	1	1	0	2	7	.320	.333	.316	9.00	2.57
Stoffel, Jason	R-R	6-2	225	9-15-88	1	2	3.98	32	0	0	13	32	34	16	14	1	16	31	.276	.352	.217	8.81	4.55
Surkamp, Eric	L-L	6-4	190	7-16-87	10	4	2.02	23	22	1	0	142	110	37	32	5	44	165	.213	.250	.197	10.43	2.78
Tanner, Clayton	L-R	6-2	205	12-5-87	6	10	4.29	22	22	1	0	120	120	71	57	13	35	90	.257	.254	.258	6.77	2.63
Verdugo, Ryan	L-L	6-0	195	4-10-87	8	6	4.35	25	25	0	0	130	115	68	63	14	63	133	.241	.231	.246	9.18	4.35
Vessella, Tom	R-L	6-6	205	10-12-85	1	1	5.54	4	3	0	0	13	10	8	8	1	9	12	.222	.200	.240	8.31	6.23

Fielding

Catcher	PCT	G	PO	A	E	DP	PB
Biery	.000	1	0	0	0	0	
Lowenstein	.985	34	228	28	4	2	3
Monell	.988	93	678	65	9	4	20
Williams	1.000	18	119	8	0	0	0
Zambrano	1.000	8	53	1	0	0	2

First Base	PCT	G	PO	A	E	DP
Biery	1.000	8	61	4	0	3
Flores	1.000	4	37	2	0	4
Hodges	.982	73	522	28	10	49
Koshansky	.994	34	301	26	2	30
Lormand	1.000	11	65	6	0	9
Monell	1.000	1	8	0	0	0
Schoop	.971	20	128	8	4	13
Stromsmoe	1.000	4	14	3	0	1

Second Base	PCT	G	PO	A	E	DP
Culberson	.978	136	240	342	13	74
Flores	1.000	1	3	2	0	2
Lormand	1.000	1	2	2	0	1
Schoop	1.000	3	4	5	0	0
Stromsmoe	.900	3	4	5	1	0

Third Base	PCT	G	PO	A	E	DP
Dominguez	.932	78	45	134	13	16
Flores	.957	44	15	74	4	1
Lormand	.931	9	4	23	2	4
Schoop	.926	11	7	18	2	4
Stromsmoe	1.000	2	1	2	0	0
Weeks	1.000	4	3	6	0	3

Shortstop	PCT	G	PO	A	E	DP
Lormand	1.000	3	2	10	0	0

	PCT	G	PO	A	E	DP
Noonan	.970	71	91	198	9	39
Schoop	.953	34	30	72	5	14
Stromsmoe	.969	33	45	82	4	16
Weeks	.941	9	10	22	2	4

Outfield	PCT	G	PO	A	E	DP
Christian	1.000	58	121	4	0	0
Fairley	.979	22	42	4	1	0
Ford	1.000	20	60	0	0	0
Kieschnick	.989	104	176	7	2	1
Lollis	1.000	1	9	0	0	0
Lormand	1.000	4	1	0	0	0
McBryde	.986	29	63	6	1	2
Peguero	.975	55	115	1	3	1
Perez	.976	125	361	9	9	4
Stromsmoe	1.000	20	24	0	0	0

SAN JOSE GIANTS   HIGH CLASS A

CALIFORNIA LEAGUE

Batting	B-T	HT	WT	DOB	AVG	vLH	vRH	G	AB	R	H	2B	3B	HR	RBI	BB	HBP	SH	SF	SO	SB	CS	SLG	OBP
Adrianza, Ehire	B-R	6-0	170	8-21-89	.300	.355	.280	56	230	34	69	24	3	3	27	23	6	0	2	46	5	1	.470	.375
Anders, Luke	L-L	6-6	225	10-2-86	.246	.243	.247	106	378	62	93	24	2	13	50	41	4	0	0	91	1	1	.423	.326
Belt, Brandon	L-L	6-5	220	4-20-88	.462	.333	.571	4	13	3	6	1	0	0	4	5	0	0	0	1	1	0	.538	.611
Brown, Gary	R-R	6-1	190	9-28-88	.336	.459	.306	131	559	115	188	34	13	14	80	46	23	0	4	77	53	19	.519	.407
Burg, Alex	R-R	6-0	190	8-9-87	.298	.302	.296	72	262	49	78	24	0	14	45	28	3	0	2	80	2	3	.550	.369
Burrell, Pat	R-R	6-4	235	10-10-76	.375	.333	.400	2	8	0	3	0	0	0	2	0	0	0	0	1	0	0	.375	.375
Cavan, Ryan	B-R	5-10	180	6-28-87	.270	.245	.276	130	508	86	137	38	5	12	90	64	6	0	10	92	10	4	.435	.352
Ciriaco, Juan	R-R	6-0	160	8-15-83	.274	.344	.250	43	124	23	34	9	3	0	20	12	0	0	2	19	5	0	.395	.333
Crawford, Brandon	L-R	6-2	215	1-21-87	.322	.500	.302	14	59	14	19	5	1	3	15	9	0	0	0	13	0	0	.593	.412
DeRosa, Mark	R-R	6-0	220	2-26-75	.400	.000	.400	2	5	2	2	1	0	0	1	0	0	0	0	1	0	0	.600	.500
Dominguez, Chris	R-R	6-3	215	11-22-86	.291	.265	.297	63	258	40	75	10	1	11	40	18	1	0	2	73	8	2	.465	.337
Fairley, Wendell	L-R	6-2	195	3-17-88	.245	.359	.219	60	208	28	51	7	1	2	21	20	7	0	2	39	3	1	.317	.329
Flores, Jose	B-R	5-11	175	8-17-87	.233	.194	.243	52	180	23	42	9	0	2	21	25	1	0	2	35	0	0	.317	.327
Haney, Bobby	L-R	6-1	185	8-16-88	.244	.333	.237	14	41	4	10	2	0	0	3	6	0	0	0	11	0	0	.293	.340
Joseph, Tommy	R-R	6-1	220	7-16-91	.270	.258	.274	127	514	80	139	33	2	22	95	29	9	0	7	102	1	0	.471	.317
Jurica, Carter	R-R	5-11	185	9-23-88	.250	.139	.278	55	180	36	45	12	0	4	23	25	5	0	1	44	5	2	.383	.355
La Torre, Tyler	L-R	6-0	219	4-22-83	.263	.500	.200	6	19	4	5	2	0	0	3	3	1	0	0	3	0	0	.368	.391
Liles, Nick	R-R	6-0	165	7-23-87	.281	.225	.300	78	288	30	81	16	2	2	37	17	1	0	6	38	6	0	.372	.317
Lollis, Ryan	L-L	6-2	185	12-16-86	.255	.100	.293	14	51	12	13	2	0	0	5	4	2	0	0	9	0	0	.294	.333
Navarro, Jesus	R-R	6-0	180	1-3-88	.000	.000	.000	3	6	0	0	0	0	0	0	0	0	0	0	4	0	0	.000	.000
Noonan, Nick	L-R	6-0	175	5-4-89	.246	.152	.303	28	122	14	30	6	1	1	16	12	0	0	1	18	1	2	.336	.311
Parker, Jarrett	L-L	6-4	210	1-1-89	.253	.237	.257	127	486	81	123	25	3	13	61	74	8	0	1	144	20	5	.397	.360
Peguero, Francisco	R-R	5-11	195	6-1-88	.324	1.000	.313	16	68	12	22	2	0	2	9	7	0	0	0	8	4	0	.441	.387
Sanchez, Hector	B-R	5-11	235	11-17-89	.302	.420	.265	52	212	31	64	14	1	11	58	11	2	0	3	49	0	1	.533	.338
Sandoval, Pablo	B-R	5-11	240	8-11-86	.000	.000	.000	1	3	1	0	0	0	0	0	0	0	0	0	0	0	0	.000	.000
Simmons, James	R-R	6-3	190	9-3-85	.270	.143	.306	49	159	30	43	6	2	10	27	13	1	0	0	60	4	0	.522	.329

Pitching	B-T	HT	WT	DOB	W	L	ERA	G	GS	CG	SV	IP	H	R	ER	HR	BB	SO	AVG	vLH	vRH	K/9	BB/9
Casilla, Jose	R-R	6-1	210	5-21-89	0	4	9.49	11	0	0	1	12	17	13	13	1	6	4	.354	.400	.321	2.92	4.38
Casilla, Santiago	R-R	6-0	220	7-25-80	0	0	0.00	2	2	0	0	3	3	0	0	0	2	1	.273	.600	.000	3.00	6.00
Correa, Hector	R-R	6-3	165	3-18-88	3	1	1.93	20	0	0	2	42	20	11	9	4	12	37	.141	.217	.104	7.93	2.57
Dunning, Jake	R-R	6-4	188	8-12-88	6	3	4.74	41	7	0	10	76	86	42	40	7	24	71	.294	.341	.272	8.41	2.84
Dunnington, Jake	L-R	6-2	160	2-2-91	2	1	2.82	16	0	0	1	22	13	8	7	1	10	31	.167	.172	.163	12.49	4.03
Gloor, Chris	L-L	6-6	255	3-7-87	1	0	0.00	1	0	0	0	2	1	0	0	0	1	5	.143	1.000	.000	19.29	3.86
Harrold, Stephen	R-R	6-1	200	3-12-89	1	0	5.48	19	0	0	0	23	24	14	14	3	13	24	.261	.243	.273	9.39	5.09
Hembree, Heath	R-R	6-4	210	1-13-89	0	0	0.73	26	0	0	21	25	16	2	2	1	12	44	.182	.167	.190	16.05	4.38
Heston, Chris	R-R	6-4	185	4-10-88	12	4	3.16	24	24	1	0	151	144	64	53	10	40	131	.259	.267	.255	7.81	2.38
King, Aaron	L-L	6-4	205	4-27-89	0	0	4.76	2	0	0	0	6	3	3	3	2	5	4	.176	.000	.214	6.35	7.94
Lively, Mitch	R-R	6-5	230	9-7-85	3	3	1.46	38	0	0	8	49	33	13	8	3	18	52	.190	.250	.167	9.49	3.28
Lofgren, Chuck	L-L	6-3	190	1-29-86	2	0	3.68	18	2	0	1	29	21	12	12	3	15	24	.198	.316	.172	7.36	4.60
Main, Michael	R-R	6-1	170	12-14-88	2	4	6.84	22	8	0	0	53	62	45	40	11	36	46	.295	.300	.293	7.86	6.15
Marte, Kelvin	R-R	6-0	180	11-24-87	12	6	3.47	25	25	0	0	148	158	67	57	11	47	84	.280	.315	.272	5.12	2.86
Matos, Osiris	R-R	6-1	200	8-6-84	0	0	2.25	4	0	0	1	4	5	1	1	0	1	4	.313	.250	.333	9.00	2.25
Mixon, David	R-R	6-3	190	9-10-84	5	1	2.59	10	7	0	1	49	45	16	14	2	6	42	.245	.278	.231	7.77	1.11
Proszek, A.J.	R-R	6-5	260	4-17-87	0	1	6.75	7	0	0	0	9	7	7	7	0	5	9	.206	.385	.095	8.68	4.82
Quirarte, Edwin	R-R	6-2	185	12-20-86	2	1	2.13	12	0	0	1	13	15	5	3	2	1	14	.273	.261	.281	9.95	0.71
Reichard, Andy	R-R	6-4	235	12-4-84	9	4	3.38	28	15	0	0	112	115	49	42	12	25	61	.269	.259	.275	4.90	2.01
Ronick, Ari	L-L	6-4	205	3-25-86	3	1	3.56	45	0	0	1	61	51	28	24	4	36	54	.228	.155	.253	8.01	5.34
Sanchez, Jonathan	L-L	6-0	200	11-19-82	0	0	20.25	1	1	0	0	3	6	6	6	1	2	3	.429	.750	.300	10.13	6.75
Surkamp, Eric	L-L	6-4	220	7-16-87	1	0	0.00	1	1	0	0	6	4	0	0	0	1	5	.190	.333	.167	7.50	1.50
Valdez, Jose	R-R	6-7	250	8-1-88	1	0	6.98	35	0	0	0	39	47	31	30	4	34	44	.307	.318	.303	10.24	7.91
Vessella, Tom	R-L	6-6	205	10-12-85	3	4	4.57	18	5	0	0	45	55	27	23	2	26	30	.284	.294	.319	5.96	5.16
Westcott, Craig	L-R	6-4	225	3-1-86	13	4	3.42	25	24	0	0	155	155	67	59	11	33	87	.262	.289	.245	5.04	1.91
Wheeler, Zack	R-R	6-4	185	5-30-90	7	5	3.99	16	16	0	0	88	74	44	39	7	47	98	.224	.292	.189	10.02	4.81
Wilson, Chris	R-R	6-2	205	11-27-86	0	1	2.35	10	0	0	0	15	13	5	4	1	6	15	.224	.375	.167	8.80	3.52
Zito, Barry	L-L	6-2	205	5-13-78	2	1	2.53	3	3	0	0	21	15	7	6	2	5	19	.205	.167	.213	8.02	2.11

Fielding

Catcher	PCT	G	PO	A	E	DP	PB
Burg	.988	24	139	30	2	2	5
Joseph	.992	91	686	74	6	4	13
Navarro	1.000	3	13	1	0	0	0
Sanchez	.983	31	198	34	4	3	6

First Base	PCT	G	PO	A	E	DP
Anders	.987	103	867	53	12	90
Belt	1.000	4	36	2	0	5
Burg	.983	12	112	4	2	16
Ciriaco	.950	3	18	1	1	2
Joseph	.983	16	162	12	3	16
La Torre	1.000	6	47	3	0	6
Liles	1.000	2	11	2	0	2
Sanchez	1.000	1	5	0	0	2

Second Base	PCT	G	PO	A	E	DP
Burg	1.000	3	4	7	0	3
Cavan	.993	125	295	377	5	100

Ciriaco	1.000	2	2	1	0	0
DeRosa	1.000	1	1	0	0	0
Flores	.921	9	17	18	3	7
Jurica	1.000	2	3	6	0	1
Noonan	1.000	3	6	7	0	2

Third Base	PCT	G	PO	A	E	DP
Burg	.875	16	14	28	6	4
Ciriaco	.875	9	3	11	2	0
DeRosa	1.000	1	0	2	0	0
Dominguez	.924	60	31	126	13	13
Flores	.948	30	18	55	4	8
Liles	1.000	5	3	8	0	1
Noonan	.900	24	10	53	7	7
Sandoval	.000	1	0	0	1	0

Shortstop	PCT	G	PO	A	E	DP
Adrianza	.959	53	76	155	10	32
Cavan	1.000	1	2	2	0	1

Ciriaco	.938	11	10	35	3	8
Crawford	1.000	12	21	46	0	10
Haney	.973	14	18	53	2	12
Jurica	.940	48	76	145	14	33
Liles	.929	3	3	10	1	0
Noonan	1.000	1	3	5	0	1

Outfield	PCT	G	PO	A	E	DP
Brown	.989	120	254	16	3	3
Burg	1.000	2	2	0	0	0
Ciriaco	.960	14	22	2	1	0
Fairley	.978	55	88	1	2	0
Jurica	.000	1	0	0	0	0
Liles	1.000	47	77	2	0	0
Lollis	.958	14	22	1	1	0
Parker	.959	120	226	10	10	2
Peguero	.963	11	23	3	1	0
Simmons	.956	45	86	1	4	0

AUGUSTA GREENJACKETS

LOW CLASS A

SOUTH ATLANTIC LEAGUE

Batting	B-T	HT	WT	DOB	AVG	vLH	vRH	G	AB	R	H	2B	3B	HR	RBI	BB	HBP	SH	SF	SO	SB	CS	SLG	OBP
Adrianza, Ehire	B-R	6-0	170	8-21-89	.231	.243	.226	38	143	18	33	10	1	3	17	18	0	0	1	32	3	2	.378	.315
Arnold, Jeff	R-R	6-2	205	1-13-88	.213	.145	.240	80	268	30	57	16	0	6	23	25	6	0	1	80	2	0	.340	.293
Biery, Drew	R-R	6-2	215	5-14-86	.280	.214	.295	19	75	9	21	3	0	4	13	8	1	0	1	16	0	1	.480	.353
Burkhart, Dan	L-R	5-11	215	3-6-89	.217	.273	.200	13	46	5	10	2	0	0	1	3	0	0	0	17	0	1	.261	.265
Campbell, Raynor	R-R	5-10	175	7-15-87	.226	.256	.212	70	243	31	55	12	1	7	29	28	4	0	3	71	12	5	.370	.313
Duvall, Adam	R-R	6-1	205	9-4-88	.285	.313	.275	116	431	69	123	30	4	22	87	59	14	0	5	98	4	4	.527	.385
Haney, Bobby	L-R	6-1	165	8-16-88	.236	.239	.235	66	237	33	56	11	0	2	23	28	1	0	2	63	1	5	.308	.317
Harris, Devin	R-R	6-3	225	4-23-88	.231	.181	.248	108	399	47	92	26	1	15	58	44	4	0	4	136	6	1	.414	.310
Lofton, Chris	L-R	6-1	175	5-20-90	.237	.190	.252	119	418	59	99	16	2	1	31	49	5	0	2	98	22	14	.292	.323
Lollis, Ryan	L-L	6-2	185	12-16-86	.314	.372	.294	80	296	45	93	22	2	2	37	39	1	0	2	47	10	5	.422	.393
Mazzola, Josh	R-R	6-2	195	4-10-86	.259	.306	.241	104	386	52	100	22	2	13	50	42	8	0	3	90	8	3	.427	.342
Mergenthaler, Michael	L-L	6-4	210	1-6-89	.000	.000	.000	1	4	0	0	0	0	0	0	0	0	0	0	3	0	0	.000	.000
Navarro, Jesus	R-R	6-0	180	1-3-88	.083	.000	.125	4	12	1	1	1	0	0	1	2	0	0	0	4	0	0	.167	.214
Rodriguez, Rafael	R-R	6-5	198	7-13-92	.236	.182	.257	96	364	39	86	15	2	1	30	24	2	0	4	69	1	6	.297	.284
Scoma, Ryan	R-L	6-2	180	9-12-87	.254	.183	.277	119	461	45	117	26	2	6	59	38	2	0	5	80	5	1	.358	.310
Tomlinson, Kelby	R-R	6-2	180	6-16-90	.333	.375		2	9	2	3	0	0	0	1	1	0	0	0	2	0	0	.333	.400
Villegas, Ydwin	B-R	5-10	180	11-5-91	.200	.202		38	134	10	27	5	0	0	9	5	1	0	1	34	2	1	.239	.212
Weeks, Joel	L-R	5-9	185	11-30-84	.295	.220	.319	54	176	27	52	8	1	1	25	26	0	0	3	38	0	1	.369	.380
Willoughby, Carlos	B-R	5-10	170	11-12-88	.240	.219	.248	126	483	80	116	18	6	1	40	63	12	0	2	86	33	10	.308	.341
Windster, Sundrendy	R-R	6-3	185	2-23-89	.108	.083	.120	12	37	4	4	1	0	1	3	5	0	0	1	16	0	0	.216	.209
Zambrano, Eliezer	R-R	5-11	175	9-16-86	.259	.111	.333	18	54	6	14	3	0	1	5	7	0	0	0	5	0	0	.370	.344

Pitching

Pitching	B-T	HT	WT	DOB	W	L	ERA	G	GS	CG	SV	IP	H	R	ER	HR	BB	SO	AVG	vLH	vRH	K/9	BB/9
Bean, Ryan	R-R	6-4	225	3-9-90	0	0	5.40	3	0	0	0	3	4	2	2	1	2	4	.286	.250	.300	10.80	5.40
Berger, Andrew	R-R	6-3	210	11-24-87	1	0	7.20	4	0	0	0	5	6	6	4	0	3	2	.286	.000	.333	3.60	5.40
Bochy, Brett	R-R	6-2	192	8-27-87	1	0	1.38	35	0	0	10	39	22	6	6	1	8	53	.161	.200	.129	12.23	1.85
Bowlin, Drew	R-R	6-1	190	12-28-86	2	0	3.66	45	0	0	3	52	42	22	21	1	26	33	.235	.297	.200	5.75	4.53
Bradley, Ryan	B-L	6-1	180	7-15-88	4	2	4.31	28	10	0	0	79	90	43	38	7	32	48	.300	.310	.301	5.45	3.63
Concepcion, Edward	R-R	6-3	190	10-3-88	1	1	3.61	43	0	0	0	52	53	28	21	4	36	62	.256	.235	.266	10.66	6.19
Dunnington, Jake	L-R	6-2	160	2-2-91	3	3	3.77	32	0	0	1	43	29	23	18	1	32	53	.193	.216	.182	11.09	6.70
Escobar, Edwin	L-L	6-1	185	4-22-92	1	3	18.00	4	2	0	0	6	15	15	12	0	5	5	.455	.250	.483	7.50	7.50
Fleet, Austin	R-R	6-1	175	4-17-87	8	5	4.32	25	8	0	0	67	72	40	32	5	24	48	.280	.302	.262	6.48	3.24
Graham, Matt	R-R	6-4	225	1-5-90	0	0	5.32	12	0	0	0	22	21	14	13	1	18	10	.244	.214	.259	4.09	7.36
Harrold, Stephen	R-R	6-1	200	3-12-89	4	1	1.54	38	0	0	16	41	29	9	7	4	17	39	.200	.214	.191	8.56	3.73
Kickham, Mike	R-R	6-4	205	12-12-88	5	10	4.11	21	21	0	0	112	112	58	51	9	37	103	.261	.228	.273	8.30	2.98
Rodriguez, Mario	L-L	6-2	190	8-21-88	8	5	4.28	41	9	0	0	90	114	51	43	5	22	50	.317	.304	.321	4.98	2.19
Rogers, Taylor	R-R	6-4	200	6-5-87	12	10	2.91	27	27	1	0	155	136	63	50	3	38	86	.241	.257	.232	5.00	2.21
Rosin, Seth	R-R	6-5	235	11-2-88	2	3	3.34	39	10	0	2	89	81	44	33	3	30	93	.247	.257	.242	9.40	3.03
Sanford, Shawn	R-R	6-0	200	8-28-88	10	10	2.55	30	25	0	0	170	143	60	48	10	30	107	.226	.242	.213	5.68	1.59
Santiago, Gaspar	L-L	6-0	200	9-23-89	3	7	4.47	38	14	0	1	95	84	54	47	8	53	88	.240	.317	.216	8.37	5.04
Schumer, Justin	R-R	6-0	180	8-2-88	5	5	5.24	21	12	0	0	81	96	58	47	3	30	49	.294	.323	.275	5.47	3.35
Valdez, Jose	R-R	6-7	250	8-1-88	0	0	0.00	12	0	0	2	14	5	1	0	0	2	21	.109	.071	.077	13.83	1.32
Vessella, Tom	R-L	6-6	205	10-12-85	0	1	8.78	11	0	0	0	13	17	14	13	0	10	8	.327	.286	.342	5.40	6.75

Fielding

Catcher	PCT	G	PO	A	E	DP	PB
Arnold	.995	78	563	56	3	7	9
Biery	1.000	1	5	1	0	0	0
Burkhart	.959	13	64	6	3	3	3
Navarro	1.000	4	23	0	0	0	6
Weeks	.981	32	185	22	4	1	5
Zambrano	1.000	18	149	6	0	1	1

First Base	PCT	G	PO	A	E	DP
Biery	.964	3	27	0	1	1
Mazzola	.992	59	558	30	5	65
Scoma	.988	74	689	32	9	64
Weeks	.968	3	28	2	1	2
Windster	.950	4	36	2	2	5

Second Base	PCT	G	PO	A	E	DP
Campbell	.974	7	17	20	1	6
Haney	1.000	5	12	8	0	3
Villegas	1.000	6	7	16	0	5
Weeks	1.000	2	1	1	0	0
Willoughby	.982	123	237	429	12	100

Third Base	PCT	G	PO	A	E	DP
Campbell	.913	17	10	32	4	0
Duvall	.908	95	62	205	27	21
Haney	1.000	3	1	5	0	0
Mazzola	.899	20	15	47	7	6
Weeks	1.000	6	5	13	0	2

Shortstop	PCT	G	PO	A	E	DP
Adrianza	.959	38	46	140	8	31

	PCT	G	PO	A	E	DP
Campbell	.954	12	18	44	3	10
Haney	.954	59	85	185	13	46
Tomlinson	1.000	2	5	6	0	3
Villegas	.952	29	43	114	8	25
Weeks	1.000	1	1	4	0	1

Outfield	PCT	G	PO	A	E	DP
Campbell	1.000	26	48	2	0	0
Harris	.967	89	143	3	5	1
Lofton	.984	118	236	7	4	0
Lollis	.992	71	117	6	1	1
Mazzola	1.000	1	1	0	0	0
Mergenthaler	1.000	1	1	0	0	0
Rodriguez	.966	94	162	7	6	0
Scoma	1.000	21	34	4	0	2

SALEM-KEIZER VOLCANOES　　　　SHORT-SEASON

NORTHWEST LEAGUE

Batting	B-T	HT	WT	DOB	AVG	vLH	vRH	G	AB	R	H	2B	3B	HR	RBI	BB	HBP	SH	SF	SO	SB	CS	SLG	OBP
Brock, Danny	R-R	6-1	210	12-28-87	.184	.176	.188	55	98	17	18	0	2	1	8	17	2	0	1	23	2	2	.255	.314
Buechele, Garrett	R-R	6-0	200	10-23-89	.235	.297	.221	54	200	22	47	8	0	5	27	14	2	0	3	39	1	0	.350	.288
Burkhart, Dan	L-R	5-11	215	3-6-89	.285	.421	.264	40	144	20	41	10	0	4	21	9	1	0	1	43	1	0	.438	.329
Cutspec, Brice	L-R	6-4	250	12-7-87	.240	.250	.239	28	96	18	23	5	0	6	20	6	1	0	2	23	0	0	.479	.286
Eshleman, John	R-R	6-0	185	4-8-89	.221	.162	.241	44	149	19	33	7	0	0	15	8	1	0	1	32	7	0	.268	.264
Galindo, Jesus	B-R	5-11	175	8-23-90	.276	.366	.258	62	239	49	66	9	3	2	20	25	5	0	3	46	47	8	.364	.353
Honeycutt, Ryan	L-R	6-0	195	9-6-88	.172	.000	.183	28	64	5	11	3	0	1	2	2	0	0	0	16	0	0	.266	.197
Izturis, Julio	B-R	5-11	165	8-29-89	.209	.188	.216	22	67	10	14	0	1	0	2	5	3	0	1	14	6	2	.239	.289
Jones, Chuckie	R-R	6-3	235	7-28-92	.218	.300	.191	41	124	19	27	6	0	2	9	15	5	0	2	48	4	2	.315	.322
Krill, Brett	R-R	6-4	195	1-24-89	.304	.377	.279	52	207	38	63	16	2	6	43	14	2	0	3	44	4	4	.488	.350
Murray, Mike	L-R	5-11	205	4-24-88	.326	.370	.316	63	242	29	79	14	0	6	48	28	1	0	3	37	2	0	.459	.394
Ochoa, Leo	L-R	6-0	180	10-20-89	.265	.222	.269	29	102	13	27	4	0	5	9	10	0	0	0	26	1	1	.451	.330
Panik, Joe	L-R	6-1	193	10-30-90	.341	.309	.349	69	270	49	92	10	3	6	54	28	2	0	4	25	13	5	.467	.401
Payne, Shawn	R-R	6-1	190	7-13-89	.306	.206	.333	57	160	37	49	8	3	0	19	29	6	0	0	32	21	6	.394	.431
Staley, Joe	B-R	6-1	235	5-8-89	.280	.250	.292	43	157	27	44	9	0	8	30	21	5	0	0	38	4	0	.490	.383
Thomas, Ben	L-L	6-1	240	6-3-89	.302	.300	.302	27	96	7	29	6	1	1	17	6	1	0	3	22	2	0	.417	.340

Pitching	B-T	HT	WT	DOB	W	L	ERA	G	GS	CG	SV	IP	H	R	ER	HR	BB	SO	AVG	vLH	vRH	K/9	BB/9
Allen, Brandon	R-R	6-6	190	8-15-91	2	8	6.04	13	13	0	0	57	68	43	38	1	22	25	.292	.263	.307	3.97	3.49
Bilodeau, Keith	R-R	6-4	195	9-17-89	0	0	0.00	3	0	0	0	6	4	0	0	0	2	8	.190	.125	.231	12.00	3.00
Bucardo, Wilber	R-R	6-2	175	11-20-87	0	2	3.86	16	0	0	0	21	26	11	9	0	10	21	.310	.286	.327	9.00	4.29
Davis, Paul	R-R	6-2	210	1-29-90	1	0	1.64	2	2	0	0	11	6	2	2	1	3	9	.176	.250	.071	7.36	2.45
Flick, Brennan	R-R	6-1	190	9-12-89	2	3	5.57	24	0	0	0	32	39	20	20	2	16	30	.291	.370	.250	8.35	4.45
Flores, Kendry	R-R	6-2	175	11-24-91	4	3	5.06	12	11	0	0	48	59	35	27	5	14	47	.304	.371	.266	8.81	2.63
Gloor, Chris	L-L	6-6	255	3-7-87	1	0	2.45	12	0	0	1	22	22	10	6	2	7	26	.256	.200	.286	10.64	2.86
Graham, Matt	R-R	6-4	225	5-1-90	2	2	8.35	21	0	0	0	37	47	35	34	2	22	31	.303	.319	.296	7.61	5.40
Hall, Cody	R-R	6-4	220	1-6-88	3	1	2.63	23	0	0	4	27	21	8	8	1	14	42	.210	.250	.188	13.83	6.26
King, Aaron	L-L	6-4	205	4-27-89	0	1	6.84	15	0	0	1	25	19	19	19	1	24	29	.216	.250	.200	10.44	8.64
Lamb, Cameron	R-R	6-4	195	5-29-89	4	6	5.09	15	15	0	0	74	88	54	42	3	15	58	.290	.283	.295	7.02	1.82
Maloney, Brian	L-L	6-0	176	10-4-88	0	1	18.00	4	0	0	0	5	7	11	10	0	11	7	.350	.600	.267	12.60	19.80
Martinez, Rafael	R-R	6-3	185	7-9-88	2	1	7.53	13	0	0	0	29	32	24	24	7	16	23	.283	.226	.305	7.22	5.02
McCormick, Phil	L-L	6-1	184	9-7-88	1	1	1.19	23	0	0	6	30	19	5	4	1	11	29	.178	.189	.171	8.60	3.26

Pitching	B-T	HT	WT	DOB	W	L	ERA	G	GS	CG	SV	IP	H	R	ER	HR	BB	SO	AVG	vLH	vRH	K/9	BB/9
Mendoza, Lorenzo	R-R	5-10	190	8-6-91	5	5	4.19	14	14	0	0	73	77	37	34	5	16	68	.266	.253	.271	8.38	1.97
Montero, Raymundo	R-R	6-2	185	9-20-89	0	1	9.82	5	0	0	0	7	11	12	8	1	12	14	.324	.308	.333	17.18	14.73
Roibal, Reinier	R-R	6-2	215	1-19-89	1	4	3.74	14	14	0	0	67	82	38	28	3	17	58	.300	.366	.255	7.75	2.27
Shackleford, Stephen	R-R	6-1	185	5-5-89	2	2	5.21	20	3	0	0	47	50	27	27	3	19	41	.272	.368	.204	7.91	3.66
Snodgrass, Jack	L-L	6-6	216	12-10-87	4	1	3.59	19	4	0	0	48	49	24	19	1	14	44	.259	.250	.263	8.31	2.64

Fielding

Catcher	PCT	G	PO	A	E	DP	PB
Burkhart	.988	35	287	31	4	3	2
Murray	1.000	1	7	0	0	0	0
Staley	.980	42	321	17	7	4	5

First Base	PCT	G	PO	A	E	DP
Brock	.993	47	256	15	2	20
Cutspec	.982	27	204	15	4	17
Thomas	.980	26	182	13	4	23

Second Base	PCT	G	PO	A	E	DP
Buechele	1.000	2	1	4	0	0
Downing	.962	41	61	114	7	26

Eshleman	.937	20	30	44	5	12
Izturis	.922	18	34	37	6	9
Payne	.500	1	0	1	1	0

Third Base	PCT	G	PO	A	E	DP
Brock	1.000	8	5	4	0	0
Buechele	.961	52	28	95	5	6
Downing	.786	4	3	8	3	1
Eshleman	.909	17	11	29	4	0
Izturis	.000	1	0	0	0	0

Shortstop	PCT	G	PO	A	E	DP
Eshleman	.962	11	4	21	1	3

Izturis	1.000	2	5	6	0	1
Panik	.964	69	102	215	12	49

Outfield	PCT	G	PO	A	E	DP
Downing	1.000	3	6	0	0	0
Galindo	.973	59	138	5	4	0
Honeycutt	.912	26	28	3	3	3
Jones	.933	37	56	0	4	1
Krill	.956	49	82	4	4	0
Ochoa	1.000	27	38	0	0	0
Payne	.987	53	74	3	1	1

AZL GIANTS

ROOKIE

ARIZONA LEAGUE

Batting	B-T	HT	WT	DOB	AVG	vLH	vRH	G	AB	R	H	2B	3B	HR	RBI	BB	HBP	SH	SF	SO	SB	CS	SLG	OBP
Barnett, Eldred	R-R	6-1	190	5-2-89	.248	.269	.241	28	109	20	27	5	2	2	16	8	4	0	5	30	3	3	.385	.310
Benusa, Gus	L-L	6-1	190	1-30-91	.297	.154	.328	24	74	15	22	2	2	1	7	5	0	0	1	18	3	0	.419	.338
Blair, Elliott	R-R	6-1	181	2-3-88	.333	.290	.349	37	114	28	38	8	4	1	20	9	9	0	1	29	6	0	.500	.421
Buechele, Garrett	R-R	6-0	200	10-23-89	.308	.200	.324	9	39	6	12	2	0	2	5	1	0	0	0	7	0	1	.513	.325
Cornier, Gabriel	B-R	6-0	190	6-10-92	.130	.000	.176	12	23	3	3	0	0	1	3	4	0	0	0	12	0	0	.261	.259
Cuevas, Jose	R-R	6-2	190	4-5-88	.337	.235	.383	46	166	44	56	15	4	9	46	22	3	0	10	20	9	2	.639	.403
de la Cruz, Jose	R-R	6-3	190	4-28-91	.262	.235	.273	17	61	8	16	3	1	1	7	2	1	0	0	9	2	3	.393	.297
Delgado, Jean	R-R	5-11	150	2-5-93	.225	.368	.173	27	71	16	16	3	0	1	15	16	5	0	4	18	1	3	.310	.385
Diaz, Christian	L-L	6-1	170	7-15-93	.231	.000	.273	10	13	2	3	1	0	0	0	2	1	0	0	5	0	0	.308	.375
Duran, Rey	R-R	6-0	200	7-31-89	.091	.000	.125	4	11	1	1	0	0	0	0	0	0	0	0	7	0	0	.091	.091
Ford, Darren	R-R	5-9	190	10-1-85	.375	.400	.368	8	24	9	9	0	1	2	6	6	1	0	1	4	2	1	.708	.500
Fuentes, Leonardo	R-R	6-4	215	11-29-92	.257	.191	.280	46	179	28	46	13	1	5	31	10	4	0	3	55	1	1	.425	.306
Hill, Kentrell	R-R	6-0	180	10-27-90	.256	.263	.254	31	86	13	22	5	2	0	12	6	2	0	1	24	2	2	.360	.316
Honeycutt, Ryan	R-R	6-0	195	9-6-88	.500	1.000	.333	1	4	0	2	0	0	0	0	0	0	0	0	0	0	0	.500	.500
Jurica, Carter	R-R	5-11	185	9-23-88	.224	.400	.179	14	49	6	11	2	0	1	9	4	3	0	1	8	4	1	.327	.316
Mergenthaler, Michael	L-L	6-4	210	1-6-89	.388	.364	.400	31	103	22	40	9	0	4	20	16	3	0	2	19	5	2	.592	.476
Munoz, Luis	R-R	6-0	165	10-10-91	—	.000	.000	1	0	0	0	0	0	0	0	0	0	0	0	0	0	0	—	—
Nicholson, Brian	L-L	6-2	225	10-31-89	.274	.214	.292	32	117	21	32	5	2	2	20	7	4	0	0	38	2	1	.402	.336
Ochoa, Leo	L-R	6-0	180	10-20-89	.300	.000	.300	3	10	2	3	0	0	0	2	1	0	0	0	4	0	1	.300	.364
Paulino, Cristian	R-R	5-10	168	9-4-91	.277	.292	.273	34	112	36	31	7	4	1	16	16	3	0	1	17	10	1	.438	.379
Schroder, Myles	R-R	5-11	180	8-1-87	.282	.200	.313	30	110	22	31	9	3	1	12	6	0	0	4	21	6	2	.445	.308
Sim, Eric	R-R	6-2	215	1-3-89	.352	.378	.340	43	145	30	51	12	2	6	37	17	9	0	5	35	5	1	.586	.438
Thomas, Ben	L-L	6-1	240	6-3-89	.346	.231	.396	32	130	23	45	9	1	6	29	8	1	0	3	19	1	1	.569	.380
Tomlinson, Kelby	R-R	6-2	180	6-16-90	.357	.295	.385	37	140	32	50	10	5	2	26	14	1	0	1	22	11	2	.543	.417
Villegas, Kevin	B-R	5-10	180	9-1-90	.180	.111	.195	14	50	8	9	2	0	1	5	3	0	0	0	7	1	2	.280	.226
Yarrow, Stephen	L-R	6-3	215	11-30-88	.286	.167	.327	18	70	13	20	3	0	1	11	12	3	0	0	10	1	0	.371	.412

Pitching	B-T	HT	WT	DOB	W	L	ERA	G	GS	CG	SV	IP	H	R	ER	HR	BB	SO	AVG	vLH	vRH	K/9	BB/9
Angeles, Luis	R-R	6-0	165	12-15-89	2	1	7.43	16	3	0	1	23	31	22	19	4	7	19	.320	.313	.323	7.43	2.74
Arnold, Demondre	R-R	6-3	208	3-18-92	1	0	1.69	16	0	0	1	27	16	6	5	0	8	32	.182	.185	.180	10.80	2.70
Bean, Ryan	R-R	6-4	225	3-9-90	2	1	4.15	13	3	0	0	22	27	14	10	1	15	28	.297	.278	.309	11.63	6.23
Berger, Andrew	R-R	6-3	210	11-24-87	1	0	12.00	16	0	0	0	15	20	21	20	0	9	15	.313	.400	.273	9.00	5.40
Bilodeau, Keith	R-R	6-4	195	9-17-89	1	0	0.00	5	0	0	0	8	6	0	0	0	2	7	.231	.500	.182	7.88	2.25
Blackburn, Clayton	L-R	6-3	220	1-6-93	3	1	1.08	12	6	0	0	33	16	6	4	2	3	30	.140	.200	.124	8.10	0.81
Crick, Kyle	L-R	6-4	220	11-30-92	1	0	6.43	7	0	0	0	7	9	8	5	0	8	8	.321	.308	.333	10.29	10.29
Davis, Paul	R-R	6-2	210	1-29-90	0	0	3.44	12	9	0	0	37	32	16	14	1	11	27	.230	.237	.225	6.63	2.70
Edlefsen, Steve	B-R	6-2	195	6-27-85	0	0	2.70	4	0	0	0	3	4	4	1	0	4	6	.250	.429	.111	16.20	10.80
Escobar, Edwin	L-L	6-1	185	4-22-92	2	4	5.09	15	12	0	0	46	51	30	26	2	17	42	.293	.243	.307	8.22	3.33
Feliz, Keurin	R-L	6-0	180	8-17-90	2	2	5.14	20	0	0	7	21	23	14	12	0	12	19	.288	.250	.304	8.14	5.14
Ferrer, Miguel	R-R	6-3	168	8-7-90	6	1	1.53	16	0	0	2	29	14	6	5	1	7	36	.139	.133	.143	11.05	2.15
Fleet, Austin	R-R	6-1	175	4-17-87	1	0	0.00	3	0	0	1	4	3	0	0	1	3	.286	.143	.250	6.75	2.25
Gloor, Chris	L-L	6-6	255	3-7-87	1	1	8.44	5	0	0	0	5	6	5	5	1	3	5	.286	.000	.375	8.44	5.06
Gregorio, Joan	R-R	6-7	180	1-12-92	3	0	2.32	12	12	0	0	50	43	14	13	1	16	43	.235	.333	.187	7.69	2.86
Hernandez, Ariel	R-R	6-3	180	3-2-92	1	0	8.40	17	0	0	1	15	19	22	14	0	14	15	.284	.250	.308	9.00	8.40
Law, Derek	R-R	6-3	218	9-14-90	0	0	2.50	15	0	0	4	18	14	5	5	0	2	19	.232	.111	.310	9.50	1.00
Maloney, Brian	L-L	6-0	176	10-4-88	1	0	3.55	9	1	0	1	13	10	6	5	0	5	21	.217	.333	.189	14.92	3.55
Marlowe, Christopher	R-R	6-0	175	10-26-89	1	0	0.00	3	0	0	0	3	3	0	0	0	1	5	.231	.250	.222	15.00	3.00
Matos, Osiris	R-R	6-1	200	8-6-84	0	0	4.50	2	0	0	0	2	4	1	1	0	1	4	.444	.600	.250	4.50	0.00
Montero, Raymundo	R-R	6-2	185	9-20-89	0	1	6.35	7	1	0	0	11	10	10	8	0	8	6	.233	.444	.176	4.76	6.35
Neff, Steven	L-L	6-2	195	2-24-89	0	0	29.25	7	0	0	1	4	16	13	13	1	1	6	.552	.545	.556	13.50	2.25

Pitching	B-T	HT	WT	DOB	W	L	ERA	G	GS	CG	SV	IP	H	R	ER	HR	BB	SO	AVG	vLH	vRH	K/9	BB/9
Paniagua, Armando	R-R	5-11	155	1-11-90	3	0	7.50	11	0	0	0	12	13	10	10	0	5	13	.271	.308	.257	9.75	3.75
Proszek, A.J.	R-R	6-5	260	4-17-87	1	0	2.05	12	0	0	0	22	16	5	5	1	3	21	.200	.296	.151	8.59	1.23
Romo, Sergio	R-R	5-10	185	3-4-83	0	0	0.00	1	1	0	0	1	1	0	0	0	0	3	.250	.333	.000	27.00	0.00
Sandbrink, Danny	R-R	6-2	195	6-23-89	1	0	2.53	15	0	0	1	21	27	10	6	3	3	21	.314	.368	.271	8.86	1.27
Shadle, Jake	R-R	6-2	175	4-25-90	1	0	6.00	3	0	0	0	3	5	2	2	0	0	7	.357	.571	.143	21.00	0.00
Vazquez, Kyle	R-R	6-3	175	6-29-88	2	2	7.36	13	8	0	0	29	37	29	24	2	17	21	.306	.313	.301	6.44	5.22

Fielding

Catcher	PCT	G	PO	A	E	DP	PB
Cornier	.980	10	44	6	1	0	7
Schroder	.988	18	138	27	2	2	4
Sim	.978	38	306	49	8	4	4

First Base	PCT	G	PO	A	E	DP
Blair	1.000	2	2	0	0	1
Cuevas	1.000	1	0	0	0	0
Duran	.958	3	23	0	1	3
Jones	1.000	1	2	9	0	1
Nicholson	.986	24	191	13	3	14
Schroder	1.000	1	2	0	0	0
Thomas	.988	26	240	17	3	12
Yarrow	.986	7	62	8	1	4

Second Base	PCT	G	PO	A	E	DP
Blair	1.000	4	6	10	0	1

Cuevas	1.000	2	2	7	0	1
Delgado	.929	21	28	63	7	10
Paulino	.948	31	58	88	8	13
Tomlinson	1.000	2	6	5	0	1
Villegas	.800	1	2	2	1	0

Third Base	PCT	G	PO	A	E	DP
Buechele	.941	9	7	9	1	1
Cuevas	.890	38	20	69	11	4
Paulino	.000	1	0	0	0	0
Schroder	1.000	1	1	1	0	0
Tomlinson	.857	5	0	6	1	0
Yarrow	.880	8	4	18	3	3

Shortstop	PCT	G	PO	A	E	DP
Cuevas	1.000	3	2	7	0	1
Delgado	.867	6	4	9	2	0

Jurica	.930	14	17	36	4	6
Tomlinson	.924	32	42	80	10	17
Villegas	.979	13	13	33	1	2

Outfield	PCT	G	PO	A	E	DP
Barnett	.955	26	62	2	3	0
Benusa	.967	21	28	1	1	0
Blair	1.000	23	35	2	0	1
de la Cruz	1.000	10	5	0	0	0
Diaz	.857	7	5	1	1	0
Ford	1.000	8	14	0	0	0
Fuentes	.887	40	51	4	7	0
Hill	1.000	30	29	1	0	0
Mergenthaler	.976	30	39	1	1	0
Munoz	.000	1	0	0	0	0
Ochoa	1.000	3	2	0	0	0

DSL GIANTS

ROOKIE

DOMINICAN SUMMER LEAGUE

Batting	B-T	HT	WT	DOB	AVG	vLH	vRH	G	AB	R	H	2B	3B	HR	RBI	BB	HBP	SH	SF	SO	SB	CS	SLG	OBP
Almeida, Alexis	R-R	6-3	215	2-16-93	.248	.310	.229	39	125	6	31	5	0	0	17	2	2	0	2	29	1	2	.288	.267
Astacio, Royel	B-R	6-2	197	9-27-93	.218	.233	.213	50	170	22	37	9	0	2	21	40	2	0	1	49	5	2	.306	.371
Cartagena, Carlos	R-R	6-2	190	12-22-93	.147	.171	.139	43	143	23	21	4	1	2	12	16	13	0	0	46	4	4	.231	.291
Feliz, Victor	R-R	6-0	185	11-23-90	.286	.242	.304	37	112	15	32	4	2	0	13	17	6	0	0	25	7	2	.357	.407
Gonzalez, Nelder	R-R	5-10	175	8-15-93	.214	.273	.176	14	28	4	6	0	0	0	3	7	1	0	0	11	1	0	.214	.389
Hernandez, Emmanuel	R-R	6-1	185	11-2-93	.229	.231	.229	15	48	3	11	3	0	0	5	7	0	0	0	11	1	1	.292	.327
Lopez, Eduardo	L-L	6-0	185	2-23-91	.153	.125	.163	17	59	7	9	0	0	0	7	1	0	0	0	15	0	0	.153	.167
Lopez, Jorge	R-R	6-2	180	9-9-91	.172	.000	.250	13	29	8	5	2	0	1	3	4	1	0	1	11	5	0	.345	.286
Matamoros, Franklin	R-R	6-1	190	6-14-93	.145	.214	.104	24	76	8	11	1	0	0	1	6	2	0	0	18	1	1	.158	.226
Mercedes, Hector	R-R	6-3	188	10-5-91	.199	.213	.193	53	166	23	33	6	2	3	22	14	5	0	0	50	4	3	.313	.281
Mesa, Herody	R-R	5-11	185	4-10-91	.241	.133	.282	22	54	13	13	2	2	1	6	11	1	0	0	24	2	0	.407	.379
Moreno, Rando	R-R	6-1	164	6-6-92	.222	.208	.226	34	117	23	26	3	1	0	6	20	4	0	0	18	6	7	.265	.355
Mujica, Shurendell	R-R	6-1	158	3-22-91	.221	.170	.239	58	195	42	43	5	5	1	21	39	5	0	2	46	24	13	.313	.361
Ortiz, Randy	R-R	5-11	170	6-15-93	.292	.233	.312	57	168	31	49	6	3	0	19	23	6	0	0	49	19	9	.363	.396
Parra, Nicoll	L-L	5-9	160	7-28-94	.067	.273	.000	20	45	6	3	1	0	0	5	10	2	0	1	13	2	3	.089	.259
Pena, Julio	R-R	6-0	185	12-13-92	.207	.179	.216	43	150	20	31	6	0	4	23	17	1	0	2	59	1	2	.327	.288
Pujadas, Fernando	R-R	6-1	179	1-2-92	.256	.240	.262	28	90	8	23	4	0	3	17	6	2	0	0	17	0	0	.400	.316
Robles, Alberto	R-R	5-11	155	9-14-90	.344	.340	.346	55	183	39	63	8	1	0	36	32	7	0	0	19	14	6	.399	.459
Rodriguez, Richard	R-R	6-1	170	10-3-92	.121	.100	.132	34	58	12	7	0	0	0	2	10	1	0	0	13	6	3	.121	.261
Sotelo, Ronny	R-R	5-10	180	11-13-93	.000	.000	.000	3	8	2	0	0	0	0	0	2	1	0	0	4	0	0	.000	.273
Vasquez, Luis	L-R	5-10	170	3-20-91	.262	.333	.239	45	145	19	38	6	0	0	22	20	1	0	3	26	0	4	.303	.349

Pitching	B-T	HT	WT	DOB	W	L	ERA	G	GS	CG	SV	IP	H	R	ER	HR	BB	SO	AVG	vLH	vRH	K/9	BB/9
Barrios, Marvin	R-R	6-3	145	9-23-92	0	0	0.00	2	2	0	0	8	5	1	0	0	3	5	.179	.333	.160	5.87	3.52
De Jesus, Enmanuel	L-L	6-0	175	1-6-94	4	2	1.74	10	8	0	0	47	33	10	9	1	20	59	.202	.143	.208	11.38	3.86
Diaz, Carlos	L-L	6-2	176	11-18-93	2	2	3.31	10	6	1	0	35	30	16	13	0	14	21	.226	.364	.213	5.35	3.57
Diaz, Noel	R-R	6-1	180	9-23-93	1	3	5.91	14	1	0	1	32	35	27	21	4	13	19	.273	.294	.266	5.34	3.66
Fernandez, Ebert	L-L	6-3	192	10-28-90	5	3	4.17	16	2	0	0	50	46	28	23	2	23	36	.243	.286	.238	6.52	4.17
Flores, Alejandro	R-R	6-0	185	9-25-93	2	1	5.33	7	7	0	0	27	36	20	16	1	15	17	.316	.263	.342	5.67	5.00
Freite, Renzo	R-R	6-1	170	1-3-93	1	2	1.93	13	3	0	0	42	44	30	9	1	19	32	.260	.225	.271	6.86	4.07
Garcia, Alexis	R-R	6-4	170	1-17-92	1	0	0.00	1	1	0	0	2	1	0	0	0	1	3	.167	.000	.200	16.20	5.40
Garcia, Bertoni	R-R	5-11	173	7-8-91	1	1	4.10	10	1	0	0	26	26	16	12	2	12	23	.253	.333	.244	7.86	4.10
Martinez, Yeini	R-R	6-3	186	11-29-90	3	6	3.00	16	12	1	0	72	70	36	24	4	24	59	.256	.219	.268	7.38	3.00
Mejia, Adalberto	L-L	6-3	195	6-20-93	5	2	1.42	13	13	0	0	76	58	18	12	0	8	71	.209	.174	.213	8.41	0.95
Minier, Gregorio	R-R	6-0	170	2-20-92	0	1	7.78	10	0	0	0	20	24	23	17	2	21	14	.304	.240	.333	6.41	9.61
Moronta, Reyes	R-R	6-0	175	1-3-93	1	1	2.13	14	0	0	5	42	30	11	10	3	13	36	.195	.189	.197	7.65	2.76
Noel, Franklin	L-L	6-1	175	12-20-88	2	5	3.51	26	0	0	16	33	31	15	13	0	14	37	.248	.462	.223	9.99	3.78
Nova, Juan	R-R	6-3	190	10-7-91	0	0	8.44	2	2	0	0	5	6	5	5	1	3	3	.286	1.000	.250	5.06	5.06
Reyes, Jose	R-R	6-1	184	1-3-91	4	3	2.59	11	10	0	0	56	50	20	16	3	20	42	.246	.298	.226	6.79	3.23
Sierra, Juan	R-R	6-4	185	3-2-91	3	0	6.46	8	0	0	0	15	15	11	0	10	14	.267	.143	.304	8.22	5.87

Fielding

Catcher	PCT	G	PO	A	E	DP	PB
Matamoros	.875	3	14	0	2	0	0
Pujadas	.978	28	190	30	5	1	3
Sotelo	.882	3	9	6	2	0	1

First Base	PCT	G	PO	A	E	DP
Almeida	.975	39	292	19	8	15
Astacio	.959	10	67	4	3	9

Vasquez	.987	42	270	32	4	1	12
Feliz	.969	20	153		3	5	11
Matamoros	.981	14	102		3	2	6
Robles	.000	1	0		0	0	0

Second Base	PCT	G	PO	A	E	DP
Gonzalez	.973	11	20	16	1	1
Mesa	1.000	2	1	3	0	0
Moreno	1.000	1	1	1	0	0
Mujica	.989	23	40	50	1	9
Robles	.978	31	64	68	3	14
Rodriguez	.902	22	31	24	6	9

Third Base	PCT	G	PO	A	E	DP
Astacio	.859	30	15	64	13	4

	PCT	G	PO	A	E	DP
Gonzalez	1.000	1	0	2	0	0
Hernandez	.880	9	7	15	3	1
Matamoros	.875	8	10	18	4	2
Mujica	.333	1	0	1	2	0
Robles	.909	36	30	80	11	9

Shortstop	PCT	G	PO	A	E	DP
Moreno	.944	33	47	89	8	9
Mujica	.943	35	62	104	10	14
Rodriguez	.955	5	11	10	1	2

Outfield	PCT	G	PO	A	E	DP
Cartagena	.946	40	51	2	3	0
Lopez	1.000	12	17	1	0	0
Lopez	.833	10	8	2	2	0
Mercedes	.960	51	66	6	3	3
Ortiz	.950	55	94	2	5	0
Parra	.800	16	16	0	4	0
Pena	.895	36	47	4	6	0

SAN FRANSISCO GIANTS

Seattle Mariners

SEASON IN A SENTENCE: For the sixth time over the last eight years, the Mariners finished in the cellar of the American League West.

HIGH POINT: On July 30, the Mariners beat the Rays 3-2 behind two of their top rookies and hopes for the future. Righthander Michael Pineda allowed two runs on one hit with four walks and 10 strikeouts over six innings, and Dustin Ackley went 2-for-3 with a double and a home run.

LOW POINT: Just a few days earlier the M's had lost to the Yankees, their 17th loss in a row. The team's franchise icon, Ichiro Suzuki, went 0-for-4 in the game, and 2011 marked the first time since coming to the United States that the 37-year-old failed to hit .300, didn't collect 200 hits, wasn't named to the All-Star Game and did not win a Gold Glove. Another down season resulted in the team drawing fewer than 2 million fans for the first time in a full season since 1992.

NOTABLE ROOKIES: In addition to Pineda and Ackley, the Mariners looked at a huge contingent of rookies in 2011. Kyle Seager became the regular third baseman after Chone Figgins' continued decline. Outfielders Trayvon Robinson and Casper Wells both flashed promise after coming in trades at the deadline, and righthander Tom Wilhelmsen made his big league debut after a six-year layoff from baseball and showed he could be a contributor to the back of the bullpen. Righthanders Blake Beavan and Josh Lueke also made their debuts after coming to Seattle in last year's Cliff Lee trade.

KEY TRANSACTIONS: The Mariners were one of the most active teams at the July trade deadline, sending righthanders Doug Fister and David Pauley to the Tigers for minor league third baseman Francisco Martinez, lefthander Charlie Furbush, Wells and righthander Chance Ruffin. The next day, they were part of a three-team deal that sent lefthander Erik Bedard and righthander Josh Fields to Boston for minor league outfielder Chih-Hsien Chiang from the Red Sox and Robinson from the Dodgers.

DOWN ON THE FARM: After the graduations of Ackley and Pineda, pitching is the strength of the system. Righthander Taijuan Walker emerged as one of the best young pitching prospects in the game, and lefthander James Paxton went 6-3, 2.37 with 131 strikeouts and 43 walks over 95 innings between low Class A and Double-A. The Mariners also drafted lefthander Danny Hultzen second overall in the 2011 draft out of Virginia.

OPENING DAY PAYROLL: $86,524,600 (16th)

General Manager: Jack Zduriencik. **Farm Director:** Pedro Grifol. **Scouting Director:** Tom McNamara.

Class	Team	League	W	L	PCT	Finish	Manager(s)
Majors	Seattle Mariners	American	67	95	.414	13th (14)	Eric Wedge
Triple-A	Tacoma Rainiers	Pacific Coast	70	74	.486	t-8th (16)	Daren Brown
Double-A	Jackson Generals	Southern	68	72	.486	6th (10)	Jim Pankovits
High A	High Desert Mavericks	California	59	81	.421	9th (10)	Jose Moreno
Low A	Clinton Lumber Kings	Midwest	63	76	.453	13th (16)	Jesus Azuaje/Eddie Menchaca
Short-season	Everett Aquasox	Northwest	37	39	.487	4th (8)	Scott Steinmann
Rookie	Pulaski Mariners	Appalachian	32	36	.471	6th (10)	Rob Mummau
Rookie	AZL Mariners	Arizona	25	31	.446	9th (13)	Jesus Azuaje
Overall 2011 Minor League Record			354	409	.464	28th (30)	

ORGANIZATION STATISTICS

SEATTLE MARINERS

AMERICAN LEAGUE

Batting	B-T	HT	WT	DOB	AVG	vLH	vRH	G	AB	R	H	2B	3B	HR	RBI	BB	HBP	SH	SF	SO	SB	CS	SLG	OBP
Ackley, Dustin	L-R	6-1	185	2-26-88	.273	.224	.290	90	333	39	91	16	7	6	36	40	0	0	3	79	6	0	.417	.348
Bard, Josh	B-R	6-3	225	3-30-78	.210	.125	.231	26	81	5	17	4	0	2	11	5	0	0	0	20	0	0	.333	.256
Bradley, Milton	B-R	6-0	215	4-15-78	.218	.255	.180	28	101	12	22	6	1	2	13	13	1	0	0	31	4	0	.356	.313
Carp, Mike	L-R	6-2	210	6-30-86	.276	.306	.266	79	290	27	80	17	1	12	46	19	3	0	1	81	0	2	.466	.326
Cust, Jack	L-R	6-1	245	1-7-79	.213	.246	.200	67	225	19	48	15	1	3	23	44	1	0	0	87	0	0	.329	.344
Figgins, Chone	B-R	5-8	180	1-22-78	.188	.152	.204	81	288	24	54	11	1	1	15	21	0	0	2	42	11	6	.243	.241
Gimenez, Chris	R-R	6-2	220	12-27-82	.203	.313	.163	24	59	6	12	1	0	1	6	10	0	0	1	13	0	1	.271	.314
Gutierrez, Franklin	R-R	6-2	190	2-21-83	.224	.224	.224	92	322	26	72	13	0	1	19	16	1	0	2	56	13	2	.273	.261
Halman, Greg	R-R	6-4	200	8-26-87	.230	.258	.214	35	87	7	20	2	1	2	6	2	1	0	0	32	5	1	.345	.256
Kennedy, Adam	L-R	6-1	195	1-10-76	.234	.191	.244	114	380	36	89	23	1	7	38	22	1	0	2	67	8	2	.355	.277
Langerhans, Ryan	L-L	6-3	220	2-20-80	.173	.286	.097	19	52	6	9	0	0	3	6	11	0	0	0	22	0	1	.346	.317
Liddi, Alex	R-R	6-4	230	8-14-88	.225	.429	.115	15	40	7	9	3	0	3	6	3	1	0	0	17	1	0	.525	.295
Moore, Adam	R-R	6-3	220	5-8-84	.167	.200	.000	2	6	0	1	1	0	0	0	0	0	0	0	2	0	0	.333	.167
Olivo, Miguel	R-R	6-0	225	7-15-78	.224	.236	.220	130	477	54	107	19	1	19	62	20	1	0	8	140	6	5	.388	.253
Peguero, Carlos	L-L	6-5	245	2-22-87	.196	.286	.191	46	143	14	28	3	2	6	19	8	3	0	1	54	0	1	.371	.252
Pena, Wily Mo	R-R	6-3	260	1-23-82	.209	.313	.176	22	67	8	14	3	0	2	8	5	2	0	0	20	0	0	.343	.284
Robinson, Trayvon	B-R	5-10	200	9-1-87	.210	.158	.229	44	143	12	30	12	0	2	14	8	0	0	1	61	1	0	.336	.250
Rodriguez, Luis	B-R	5-9	190	6-27-80	.197	.172	.205	44	117	10	23	10	0	2	14	16	2	0	2	21	1	2	.333	.299
Ryan, Brendan	R-R	6-2	195	3-26-82	.248	.255	.245	123	436	51	108	19	3	3	39	34	10	0	5	87	13	3	.326	.313
Saunders, Michael	L-R	6-4	225	11-19-86	.149	.143	.152	58	161	16	24	5	0	2	8	12	0	0	1	56	6	2	.217	.207
Seager, Kyle	L-R	6-0	195	11-3-87	.258	.229	.265	53	182	22	47	13	0	3	13	13	2	0	2	36	3	1	.379	.312
Smoak, Justin	B-L	6-4	230	12-5-86	.234	.252	.227	123	427	38	100	24	0	15	55	55	3	0	4	105	0	0	.396	.323
Suzuki, Ichiro	L-R	5-11	170	10-22-73	.272	.281	.268	161	677	80	184	22	3	5	47	39	0	0	4	69	40	7	.335	.310
Wells, Casper	R-R	6-2	210	11-23-84	.216	.190	.222	31	102	14	22	1	0	7	15	9	5	0	0	42	2	2	.431	.310
2-team total (64 Detroit)					.237	—	—	95	215	30	51	11	0	11	27	18	7	0	0	71	3	2	.442	.317
Wilson, Jack	R-R	6-0	190	12-29-77	.249	.237	.258	62	173	22	43	8	0	0	11	9	0	0	2	27	5	2	.295	.283
Wilson, Mike	R-R	6-2	245	6-29-83	.148	.105	.250	8	27	0	4	1	0	0	3	1	0	0	0	7	0	0	.185	.179

Pitching	B-T	HT	WT	DOB	W	L	ERA	G	GS	CG	SV	IP	H	R	ER	HR	BB	SO	AVG	vLH	vRH	K/9	BB/9
Beavan, Blake	R-R	6-7	240	1-17-89	5	6	4.27	15	15	0	0	97	106	46	46	13	15	42	.278	.314	.236	3.90	1.39
Bedard, Erik	L-L	6-1	200	3-5-79	4	7	3.45	16	16	0	0	91	77	41	35	11	30	87	.226	.239	.221	8.57	2.96
2-team total (8 Boston)					5	9	3.62	24	24	0	0	129	118	63	52	14	48	125	—	—	—	8.70	3.34
Cortes, Dan	R-R	6-6	235	3-4-87	0	2	5.91	10	0	0	0	11	13	7	7	1	6	3	.302	.200	.391	2.53	5.06
Delabar, Steve	R-R	6-5	220	7-17-83	1	1	2.57	6	0	0	0	7	5	2	2	1	4	7	.217	.125	.267	9.00	5.14
Fister, Doug	L-R	6-8	210	2-4-84	3	12	3.33	21	21	3	0	146	139	57	54	7	32	89	.252	.261	.242	5.49	1.97
2-team total (11 Detroit)					11	13	2.83	32	31	3	0	216	193	76	68	11	37	146	—	—	—	6.07	1.54
Furbush, Charlie	L-L	6-5	215	4-11-86	3	7	6.62	11	10	0	0	53	61	41	39	11	16	41	.289	.326	.279	6.96	2.72
2-team total (17 Detroit)					4	10	5.48	28	12	0	0	85	97	59	52	16	30	67	—	—	—	7.07	3.16
Gray, Jeff	R-R	6-3	195	11-19-81	0	1	4.89	24	0	0	0	35	39	19	19	3	17	16	.283	.297	.270	4.11	4.37
2-team total (6 Chicago)					0	1	4.28	30	0	0	1	48	52	23	23	4	21	23	—	—	—	4.28	3.91
Hernandez, Felix	R-R	6-3	225	4-8-86	14	14	3.47	33	33	5	0	234	218	99	90	19	67	222	.248	.252	.243	8.55	2.58
Jimenez, Cesar	L-L	5-11	210	11-12-84	1	0	5.40	8	0	0	0	7	6	4	4	0	3	7	.222	.214	.231	9.45	4.05
Kelley, Shawn	R-R	6-2	220	4-26-84	0	0	0.00	10	0	0	0	13	7	0	0	0	3	10	.159	.278	.077	7.11	2.13
Laffey, Aaron	L-L	6-0	200	4-15-85	1	1	4.01	36	0	0	0	43	54	20	19	7	16	24	.305	.250	.343	5.06	3.38
2-team total (11 New York)					3	2	3.88	47	0	0	0	53	67	24	23	7	21	30	—	—	—	5.06	3.54
League, Brandon	R-R	6-2	205	3-16-83	1	5	2.79	65	0	0	37	61	56	19	19	3	10	45	.239	.254	.224	6.60	1.47
Lueke, Josh	R-R	6-5	220	12-5-84	1	1	6.06	25	0	0	0	33	34	22	22	2	13	29	.270	.220	.313	7.99	3.58
Pauley, David	R-R	6-2	215	6-17-83	5	4	2.15	39	0	0	0	54	38	13	13	2	16	34	.200	.143	.253	5.63	2.65
2-team total (14 Detroit)					5	6	3.16	53	0	0	0	74	64	27	26	6	22	44	—	—	—	5.35	2.68
Pineda, Michael	R-R	6-7	260	1-18-89	9	10	3.74	28	28	0	0	171	133	76	71	18	55	173	.211	.237	.184	9.11	2.89
Ray, Chris	R-R	6-3	210	1-12-82	3	2	4.68	29	0	0	0	33	33	18	17	2	12	22	.270	.308	.243	6.06	3.31
Ruffin, Chance	R-R	6-0	185	9-8-88	1	0	3.86	13	0	0	0	14	13	6	6	2	9	15	.245	.261	.233	9.64	5.79

Pitching

Pitching	B-T	HT	WT	DOB	W	L	ERA	G	GS	CG	SV	IP	H	R	ER	HR	BB	SO	AVG	vLH	vRH	K/9	BB/9
2-team total (2 Detroit)					1	0	4.08	15	0	0	0	18	18	8	8	4	9	18	—	—	—	9.17	4.58
Vargas, Jason	L-L	6-0	210	2-2-83	10	13	4.25	32	32	4	0	201	205	105	95	22	59	131	.260	.278	.255	5.87	2.64
Vasquez, Anthony	L-L	6-0	175	9-19-86	1	6	8.90	7	7	0	0	29	46	35	29	13	10	13	.351	.480	.321	3.99	3.07
Wilhelmsen, Tom	R-R	6-6	230	12-16-83	2	0	3.31	25	0	0	0	33	25	13	12	2	13	30	.210	.200	.220	8.27	3.58
Wright, Jamey	R-R	6-6	230	12-24-74	2	3	3.16	60	0	0	1	68	61	26	24	6	30	48	.246	.226	.266	6.32	3.95

Fielding

Catcher	PCT	G	PO	A	E	DP	PB
Bard	.988	25	156	12	2	2	0
Gimenez	1.000	20	111	9	0	2	0
Moore	1.000	2	11	1	0	0	0
Olivo	.988	127	835	71	11	7	11

First Base	PCT	G	PO	A	E	DP
Ackley	1.000	1	8	0	0	0
Carp	.993	34	253	14	2	27
Gimenez	1.000	2	15	1	0	5
Kennedy	.992	36	217	24	2	21
Rodriguez	1.000	1	3	0	0	0
Smoak	.993	108	884	59	7	87

Second Base	PCT	G	PO	A	E	DP
Ackley	.984	86	144	225	6	49
Kennedy	.993	34	47	100	1	20

	PCT	G	PO	A	E	DP
Rodriguez	.952	7	11	9	1	3
Seager	1.000	3	2	7	0	0
Wilson	.990	45	79	111	2	28

Third Base	PCT	G	PO	A	E	DP
Figgins	.941	80	40	134	11	11
Kennedy	.965	27	18	37	2	3
Liddi	.971	14	9	25	1	2
Rodriguez	1.000	11	7	10	0	3
Seager	.967	42	31	85	4	2
Wilson	1.000	1	2	2	0	1

Shortstop	PCT	G	PO	A	E	DP
Rodriguez	.968	23	35	57	3	15
Ryan	.974	123	186	371	15	79
Seager	.944	10	14	20	2	6
Wilson	.986	13	28	44	1	7

Outfield	PCT	G	PO	A	E	DP
Bradley	.964	26	53	0	2	0
Carp	.927	28	49	2	4	0
Figgins	1.000	2	2	0	0	0
Gimenez	.000	3	0	0	0	0
Gutierrez	1.000	92	237	7	0	3
Halman	1.000	35	59	0	0	0
Langerhans	1.000	17	33	0	0	0
Peguero	.988	43	82	3	1	2
Robinson	.933	41	80	3	6	0
Saunders	1.000	56	139	1	0	0
Suzuki	.985	151	263	7	4	5
Wells	.983	24	55	4	1	2
Wilson	1.000	7	10	1	0	0

TACOMA RAINIERS   TRIPLE-A
PACIFIC COAST LEAGUE

Batting

Batting	B-T	HT	WT	DOB	AVG	vLH	vRH	G	AB	R	H	2B	3B	HR	RBI	BB	HBP	SH	SF	SO	SB	CS	SLG	OBP
Ackley, Dustin	L-R	6-1	185	2-26-88	.303	.299	.304	66	271	57	82	17	3	9	35	55	1	0	1	38	7	3	.487	.421
Agudelo, Jorge	R-R	6-0	175	5-30-89	.250	.250	.250	2	8	1	2	0	0	0	0	0	0	0	0	1	0	0	.250	.250
Bard, Josh	B-R	6-3	225	3-30-78	.301	.283	.307	58	226	28	68	18	0	2	41	21	0	0	1	39	0	0	.407	.359
Bonilla, Leury	R-R	6-3	170	2-8-85	.205	.143	.220	24	73	7	15	0	0	0	5	2	0	0	0	14	2	0	.205	.227
Carp, Mike	L-R	6-2	210	6-30-86	.343	.324	.350	66	251	55	86	14	0	21	64	28	3	0	3	50	6	2	.649	.411
Coleman, Trevor	B-R	6-1	205	1-19-88	.167	.000	.167	3	6	0	1	0	0	0	1	0	1	0	0	2	0	0	.167	.286
Extrano, Jetsy	B-R	6-2	200	8-13-88	.333	.000	.333	1	3	0	1	0	0	0	0	1	0	0	0	0	0	0	.333	.500
Gimenez, Chris	R-R	6-2	220	12-27-82	.265	.333	.261	13	49	8	13	1	0	1	4	7	0	0	0	13	0	1	.347	.357
Gutierrez, Franklin	R-R	6-2	190	2-21-83	.275	.308	.259	11	40	7	11	2	2	0	6	6	0	0	1	7	0	0	.425	.362
Halman, Greg	R-R	6-4	200	8-26-87	.299	.167	.333	40	177	35	53	14	1	3	15	13	3	0	0	53	11	1	.441	.358
Haveman, Brandon	L-R	5-9	165	6-21-86	.200	.154	.227	16	35	3	7	1	0	1	4	2	1	0	1	13	0	0	.314	.256
Henriquez, Ralph	B-R	6-1	190	4-7-87	.256	.200	.272	13	43	14	34	7	0	1	16	5	0	0	4	17	0	0	.331	.275
Jimenez, Luis	L-L	6-3	275	5-7-82	.285	.221	.306	74	284	51	81	12	1	12	57	39	1	0	3	55	2	1	.461	.370
Kazmar, Sean	R-R	5-9	180	8-5-84	.253	.219	.263	127	462	50	117	29	3	3	45	36	6	0	7	68	7	6	.348	.311
Langerhans, Ryan	L-L	6-3	220	2-20-80	.313	.195	.341	57	214	46	67	10	0	16	37	37	2	0	2	63	3	6	.584	.416
2-team total (38 Reno)					.311	—	—	95	344	69	107	20	2	22	60	76	3	0	3	94	11	7	.573	.437
Liddi, Alex	R-R	6-4	230	8-14-88	.259	.219	.271	138	559	121	145	32	3	30	104	61	5	0	10	170	5	1	.488	.332
Limonta, Johan	L-L	6-0	205	8-4-83	.319	.321	.319	108	407	58	130	20	1	14	84	44	0	0	5	75	3	3	.477	.382
Lopez, Danny	R-R	5-11	180	1-21-88	.000	.000	.000	1	4	0	0	0	0	0	0	0	0	0	0	1	0	0	.000	.000
Mangini, Matt	L-R	6-4	230	12-21-85	.336	.189	.380	58	232	34	78	9	1	2	41	24	1	0	1	45	3	1	.409	.399
Peguero, Carlos	L-L	6-5	245	2-22-87	.317	.279	.331	57	240	44	76	15	2	13	47	15	3	0	0	82	8	0	.558	.364
Pena, Wily Mo	R-R	6-3	260	1-23-82	.333	.417	.308	13	51	11	17	4	0	4	14	9	1	0	0	13	0	0	.647	.443
2-team total (63 Reno)					.358	—	—	76	288	63	103	21	3	25	77	34	9	0	1	61	5	2	.712	.440
Robinson, Trayvon	B-R	5-10	200	9-1-87	.111	.000	.143	3	9	1	1	0	0	0	3	0	0	0	4	1	0	.111	.333
2-team total (100 Albuquerque)					.289	—	—	103	377	71	109	9	6	26	71	48	3	0	0	126	9	6	.552	.374
Rodriguez, Luis	B-R	5-9	190	6-27-80	.200	.200	.308	7	31	3	9	1	0	1	3	2	0	0	4	0	1	.419	.333
Saunders, Michael	L-R	6-4	225	11-19-86	.288	.283	.290	64	236	51	68	11	3	7	38	50	2	0	1	71	10	3	.449	.415
Seager, Kyle	L-R	6-0	195	11-3-87	.387	.208	.439	24	106	24	41	8	2	3	17	11	0	0	0	12	3	1	.585	.444
Smoak, Justin	B-L	6-4	230	12-5-86	.000	.000	.000	4	11	1	0	0	0	0	0	3	1	0	0	1	0	0	.000	.267
Triunfel, Carlos	R-R	5-11	175	2-27-90	.279	.304	.273	27	111	3	31	6	1	0	10	2	2	0	1	17	1	0	.351	.302
Tuiasosopo, Matt	R-R	6-2	230	5-10-86	.226	.241	.220	116	439	73	99	20	6	14	77	75	5	0	6	132	11	2	.394	.341
Wilson, Mike	R-R	6-2	245	6-29-83	.331	.365	.322	87	335	73	111	27	0	16	49	45	6	0	2	86	5	2	.555	.418
Yepez, Jose	R-R	6-0	205	6-19-81	.307	.275	.319	48	153	30	47	6	2	3	26	24	4	0	0	22	1	0	.431	.414

Pitching

Pitching	B-T	HT	WT	DOB	W	L	ERA	G	GS	CG	SV	IP	H	R	ER	HR	BB	SO	AVG	vLH	vRH	K/9	BB/9
Aardsma, David	R-R	6-3	210	12-27-81	0	1	15.75	5	0	0	0	4	8	7	7	1	4	5	.444	.500	.417	11.25	9.00
Bautista, Denny	R-R	6-5	190	8-23-80	1	2	4.21	24	0	0	2	36	27	19	17	3	22	49	.208	.182	.227	12.14	5.45
Beavan, Blake	R-R	6-7	240	1-17-89	5	3	4.45	16	16	0	0	93	118	52	46	10	20	64	.305	.330	.281	6.19	1.94
Castro, Fabio	L-L	5-7	185	1-20-85	5	4	3.63	24	12	0	1	79	74	40	32	9	34	64	.244	.255	.239	7.26	3.86
Cortes, Dan	R-R	6-5	235	3-4-87	1	2	5.08	32	0	0	3	39	43	25	22	3	29	46	.289	.277	.298	10.62	6.69
Delabar, Steve	R-R	6-5	220	7-17-83	1	1	0.69	10	0	0	0	13	11	1	1	0	6	18	.224	.059	.313	12.46	4.15
Delcarmen, Manny	R-R	6-2	205	2-16-82	2	2	5.14	18	0	0	0	28	31	17	16	2	12	24	.292	.239	.333	7.39	3.86
2-team total (8 Round Rock)					3	2	5.59	26	0	0	0	39	52	25	24	4	15	33	—	—	—	7.68	3.49
Fields, Josh	R-R	6-0	185	8-19-85	0	0	6.23	9	0	0	0	13	11	10	9	2	13	13	.229	.200	.250	9.00	9.00
French, Luke	L-L	6-4	220	9-13-85	9	9	6.27	26	26	0	0	146	196	115	102	30	61	81	.322	.313	.327	4.98	3.75
Grube, Jarrett	R-R	6-4	220	11-5-81	4	4	4.95	14	7	0	1	60	54	35	33	10	18	51	.226	.195	.245	7.65	2.70
Haeger, Charlie	R-R	6-1	210	9-19-83	2	2	7.74	9	9	0	0	48	53	44	41	5	42	35	.291	.239	.324	6.61	7.93

Pitching

Pitching	B-T	HT	WT	DOB	W	L	ERA	G	GS	CG	SV	IP	H	R	ER	HR	BB	SO	AVG	vLH	vRH	K/9	BB/9
Jimenez, Cesar	L-L	5-11	210	11-12-84	5	4	4.06	43	0	0	1	71	71	33	32	3	35	81	.259	.283	.246	10.27	4.44
Kelley, Shawn	R-R	6-2	220	4-26-84	1	0	1.84	12	0	0	0	15	11	3	3	3	6	15	.208	.188	.216	9.20	3.68
Lueke, Josh	R-R	6-5	220	12-5-84	2	4	2.76	30	0	0	11	42	34	17	13	1	12	35	.217	.213	.219	7.44	2.55
Miller, Justin	R-R	6-2	215	8-27-77	0	0	1.04	6	0	0	0	9	6	1	1	0	5	7	.194	.143	.235	7.27	5.19
3-team total (3 Albuquerque, 11 Round Rock)					1	3	5.73	20	0	0	3	22	18	14	14	3	22	19	—	—	—	7.77	9.00
Paredes, Edward	L-L	6-0	180	9-30-86	2	1	11.37	11	0	0	0	13	21	17	16	3	13	12	.389	.385	.390	8.53	9.24
Patterson, Scott	R-R	6-7	235	6-20-79	3	3	3.99	36	0	0	9	47	47	21	21	4	6	53	.255	.310	.221	10.08	1.14
Ramirez, Erasmo	R-R	5-11	180	5-2-90	3	2	5.10	7	7	0	0	42	51	27	24	4	13	35	.304	.278	.326	7.44	2.76
Ring, Royce	L-L	6-0	220	12-21-80	2	1	6.08	27	0	0	2	24	25	17	16	3	11	33	.266	.218	.333	12.55	4.18
Robertson, Nate	R-L	6-2	225	9-3-77	6	7	7.14	18	18	1	0	93	135	87	74	14	38	55	.339	.315	.348	5.30	3.66
Robles, Mauricio	L-L	5-10	210	3-5-89	1	2	8.74	4	4	0	0	11	7	11	11	3	14	8	.189	.182	.192	6.35	11.12
Roe, Chaz	R-R	6-5	190	10-9-86	0	7	6.59	33	10	0	2	100	133	85	73	16	38	83	.319	.348	.296	7.49	3.43
Seddon, Chris	L-L	6-3	220	10-13-83	9	7	6.27	28	25	0	0	149	180	108	104	20	69	119	.300	.313	.295	7.17	4.16
Smith, Chris	R-R	6-0	190	4-9-81	1	1	6.75	13	0	0	2	19	30	14	14	3	12	22	.366	.294	.417	10.61	5.79
Snow, Forrest	R-R	6-6	195	12-30-88	1	2	5.35	9	2	0	0	35	34	21	21	4	10	36	.256	.189	.300	9.17	2.55
Vasquez, Anthony	L-L	6-0	175	9-19-86	4	3	3.21	8	8	0	0	53	51	22	19	6	18	32	.255	.269	.250	5.40	3.04

Fielding

Catcher	PCT	G	PO	A	E	DP	PB
Bard	.989	56	424	23	5	2	4
Coleman	1.000	3	17	2	0	0	2
Gimenez	1.000	10	70	5	0	0	1
Henriquez	.996	37	252	17	1	6	3
Yepez	.986	47	337	17	5	1	7

First Base	PCT	G	PO	A	E	DP
Carp	1.000	3	25	4	0	1
Gimenez	.909	2	10	0	1	1
Jimenez	1.000	3	18	5	0	2
Langerhans	.985	12	63	2	1	9
Liddi	1.000	2	7	1	0	1
Limonta	.996	26	223	9	1	19
Mangini	.979	35	267	17	6	31
Smoak	1.000	3	20	2	0	1
Tuiasosopo	.989	64	430	36	5	55
Yepez	1.000	1	6	2	0	1

Second Base	PCT	G	PO	A	E	DP
Ackley	.979	66	116	165	6	45

	PCT	G	PO	A	E	DP	PB
Agudelo	.875	2	3	4	1	1	
Bonilla	1.000	3	7	4	0	0	
Kazmar	.976	42	90	113	5	32	
Rodriguez	1.000	2	7	5	0	2	
Seager	1.000	10	16	27	0	9	
Triunfel	1.000	1	2	3	0	2	
Tuiasosopo	.975	22	34	43	2	12	

Third Base	PCT	G	PO	A	E	DP
Bonilla	.000	1	0	0	0	0
Extrano	.000	1	0	0	1	0
Gimenez	1.000	1	0	1	0	0
Liddi	.943	115	101	199	18	23
Mangini	.931	15	10	17	2	2
Seager	.963	11	7	19	1	5
Tuiasosopo	.786	6	6	5	3	0

Shortstop	PCT	G	PO	A	E	DP
Bonilla	1.000	5	9	5	0	0
Kazmar	.938	84	148	200	23	53
Liddi	.948	24	29	63	5	12

	PCT	G	PO	A	E	DP
Rodriguez	.913	5	8	13	2	6
Seager	1.000	4	8	8	0	2
Triunfel	.984	26	47	78	2	19

Outfield	PCT	G	PO	A	E	DP
Bonilla	1.000	14	31	4	0	0
Carp	.959	44	89	4	4	0
Gutierrez	1.000	5	14	0	0	0
Halman	.967	40	86	1	3	0
Haveman	1.000	13	25	0	0	0
Langerhans	.991	47	113	3	1	1
Limonta	.962	53	95	7	4	0
Peguero	.933	55	91	6	7	2
Pena	1.000	1	6	0	0	0
Robinson	1.000	3	8	1	0	0
Saunders	.978	64	177	4	4	0
Tuiasosopo	.983	29	58	1	1	0
Wilson	.979	79	175	8	4	0

JACKSON GENERALS

SOUTHERN LEAGUE

DOUBLE-A

Batting

Batting	B-T	HT	WT	DOB	AVG	vLH	vRH	G	AB	R	H	2B	3B	HR	RBI	BB	HBP	SH	SF	SO	SB	CS	SLG	OBP
Acevedo, Michael	R-R	6-0	185	12-5-90	.143	.000	.200	3	7	0	1	0	0	0	0	0	0	0	0	0	0	0	.143	.143
Agudelo, Jorge	R-R	6-0	175	5-30-89	.600	.000	.600	2	5	2	3	0	0	0	0	0	0	0	1	1	0	.600	.600
Bantz, Brandon	R-R	6-1	211	1-7-87	.216	.208	.220	83	236	27	51	9	0	1	20	32	5	0	1	55	0	1	.267	.321
Bonilla, Leury	R-R	6-3	170	2-8-85	.247	.318	.216	21	73	16	18	0	3	0	5	10	0	0	1	15	2	4	.329	.333
Catricala, Vinnie	R-R	6-2	210	10-31-88	.347	.347	.348	62	239	45	83	29	3	11	45	24	9	0	4	47	9	1	.632	.420
Chavez, Johermyn	R-R	6-3	220	1-26-89	.216	.196	.226	126	439	47	95	16	4	13	50	49	14	0	4	124	6	9	.360	.312
Chiang, Chih-Hsien	L-R	6-2	170	2-21-88	.208	.250	.179	32	130	11	27	7	0	0	10	6	3	0	2	30	1	2	.262	.255
Dunigan, Joe	L-L	6-1	238	3-29-86	.215	.264	.193	49	172	23	37	11	1	7	30	26	0	0	1	81	4	2	.413	.317
Franklin, Nick	B-R	6-1	170	3-2-91	.325	.226	.385	21	83	13	27	3	2	2	6	6	0	0	0	18	5	3	.482	.371
Haveman, Brandon	L-R	5-9	165	6-21-86	.265	.234	.274	67	211	30	56	6	4	2	21	15	1	0	0	42	7	7	.408	.317
Henriquez, Ralph	B-R	6-1	190	4-7-87	.196	.167	.204	42	138	12	27	6	1	1	18	12	0	0	3	29	0	0	.275	.255
Jimenez, Luis	R-R	6-3	275	5-7-82	.317	.333	.314	30	101	17	32	3	1	4	18	18	0	0	1	17	2	0	.485	.417
Limonta, Johan	L-L	6-0	205	8-4-83	.063	.200	.000	4	16	3	1	0	0	1	2	2	0	0	0	6	0	0	.250	.167
Lo, Kuo Hui	R-R	6-2	188	9-26-85	.252	.255	.250	49	151	26	38	9	3	4	24	19	0	0	0	32	6	1	.430	.335
Martinez, Francisco	R-R	6-1	180	9-1-90	.310	.327	.300	33	129	20	40	7	3	3	23	4	0	0	2	24	3	2	.481	.320
Martinez-Esteve, Eddy	R-R	6-2	215	7-14-83	.269	.174	.345	15	52	8	14	4	1	0	5	8	1	0	0	14	0	0	.385	.377
McOwen, Jamie	L-R	6-0	200	9-26-85	.261	.152	.298	72	257	41	67	12	0	4	26	19	1	0	3	50	9	3	.354	.311
Noriega, Gabriel	R-R	6-2	170	9-13-90	.237	.226	.242	25	93	8	22	4	0	0	7	3	1	0	0	20	1	0	.280	.268
Poythress, Rich	R-R	6-4	235	8-11-87	.267	.293	.255	122	450	50	120	24	1	12	64	50	7	0	3	82	2	3	.416	.347
Savastano, Scott	R-R	6-4	190	6-12-86	.283	.298	.274	104	368	54	104	28	1	10	49	45	3	0	4	62	3	2	.446	.362
Seager, Kyle	L-R	6-0	195	11-3-87	.312	.284	.326	66	266	33	83	25	1	4	37	26	5	0	2	38	8	5	.459	.381
Shaffer, Jake	L-L	6-1	190	8-16-87	.287	.281	.290	120	442	57	127	22	7	11	47	30	2	0	4	83	8	8	.443	.333
Sucre, Jesus	R-R	6-0	200	4-30-88	.214	.083	.267	32	84	4	18	3	0	1	9	5	0	0	0	7	0	1	.286	.258
2-team total (40 Mississippi)					.217	—	—	72	221	17	48	8	0	1	19	11	1	0	1	19	0	2	.267	.256
Tenbrink, Nate	L-R	6-2	202	12-21-86	.218	.163	.232	64	211	30	46	9	6	6	25	34	5	0	2	60	11	3	.403	.337
Triunfel, Carlos	R-R	5-11	175	2-27-90	.281	.250	.294	105	395	45	111	22	2	6	35	25	10	0	0	71	5	7	.392	.340

Pitching

Pitching	B-T	HT	WT	DOB	W	L	ERA	G	GS	CG	SV	IP	H	R	ER	HR	BB	SO	AVG	vLH	vRH	K/9	BB/9
Carraway, Andrew	R-R	6-2	190	9-4-86	9	5	3.66	28	21	1	0	138	123	62	56	9	25	106	.237	.227	.244	6.93	1.63
Cooper, Daniel	R-R	6-3	205	11-6-86	1	1	4.24	9	0	0	1	17	12	8	8	0	7	11	.200	.182	.211	5.82	3.71
Corrales, Joshua	R-R	6-2	205	5-25-90	0	0	0.00	1	0	0	0	1	0	0	0	0	0	0	.000	.000	.000	0.00	0.00

Pitching	B-T	HT	WT	DOB	W	L	ERA	G	GS	CG	SV	IP	H	R	ER	HR	BB	SO	AVG	vLH	vRH	K/9	BB/9
Delabar, Steve	R-R	6-5	220	7-17-83	1	3	2.05	23	0	0	12	31	23	10	7	0	26	30	.209	.217	.203	8.80	7.63
Fields, Josh	R-R	6-0	185	8-19-85	1	2	2.77	20	0	0	3	26	17	11	8	0	19	26	.185	.184	.185	9.00	6.58
Gillheeney, Jimmy	L-L	6-1	200	11-8-87	1	3	5.49	7	0	0	0	39	35	24	24	6	19	22	.241	.154	.261	5.03	4.35
Grube, Jarrett	R-R	6-4	220	11-5-81	5	2	3.11	14	14	0	0	84	79	35	29	4	20	69	.251	.286	.217	7.39	2.14
Hensley, Steven	R-R	6-3	180	12-27-86	4	8	4.61	19	18	0	0	96	112	57	49	10	38	65	.296	.227	.344	6.11	3.57
Hernandez, Moises	R-R	6-1	168	3-18-84	4	2	6.25	40	3	0	0	72	94	53	50	10	29	44	.316	.383	.279	5.50	3.63
Kasparek, Kenn	R-R	6-8	200	9-23-85	5	5	4.50	12	12	0	0	62	69	39	31	6	26	40	.279	.271	.286	5.81	3.77
Kelley, Shawn	R-R	6-2	220	4-26-84	0	1	0.00	3	2	0	0	3	4	3	0	0	0	3	.333	.333	.333	9.00	0.00
LaFromboise, Bobby	L-L	6-4	190	6-25-86	3	4	3.10	49	0	0	0	61	62	23	21	6	24	53	.268	.243	.280	7.82	3.54
Medina, Yoervis	R-R	6-3	250	7-27-88	0	1	4.68	4	4	0	0	25	23	13	13	5	9	17	.250	.278	.232	6.12	3.24
Moran, Brian	L-L	6-3	185	9-30-88	5	3	4.60	45	0	0	0	61	60	31	31	9	22	63	.256	.348	.218	9.35	3.26
Paredes, Edward	L-L	6-0	180	9-30-86	1	3	5.24	32	0	0	1	45	50	28	26	5	24	41	.286	.226	.311	8.26	4.84
Patterson, Scott	R-R	6-7	235	6-20-79	1	1	2.53	16	0	0	10	21	18	6	6	1	1	24	.231	.297	.171	10.13	0.42
Paxton, James	L-L	6-4	220	11-6-88	3	0	1.85	7	7	0	0	39	28	10	8	2	13	51	.201	.190	.203	11.77	3.00
Penney, Stephen	R-R	6-7	240	8-14-86	5	2	4.25	38	0	0	2	49	49	28	23	1	24	33	.258	.236	.267	6.10	4.44
Pryor, Stephen	R-R	6-6	225	7-23-89	2	1	1.19	17	0	0	6	23	9	4	3	0	7	27	.123	.179	.089	10.72	2.78
Ramirez, Erasmo	R-R	5-11	180	5-2-90	7	6	4.73	19	19	0	0	110	127	74	58	10	19	81	.285	.300	.272	6.61	1.55
Richard, Steve	R-R	6-3	240	3-7-85	0	1	3.68	6	0	0	0	7	9	4	3	1	3	6	.300	.333	.286	7.36	3.68
Robles, Mauricio	L-L	5-10	210	3-5-89	0	1	4.15	2	2	0	0	9	7	4	4	1	8	6	.219	.286	.200	6.23	8.31
Sena, Jandy	L-R	6-6	245	8-10-89	0	0	0.00	2	0	0	1	6	3	0	0	0	1	4	.136	.250	.071	5.68	1.42
Stanton, Taylor	R-R	6-2	230	1-15-88	1	4	4.35	22	3	0	2	52	56	29	25	3	16	31	.286	.337	.248	5.40	2.79
Vasquez, Anthony	L-L	6-0	175	9-19-86	5	7	3.77	16	16	1	0	100	125	50	42	6	19	59	.316	.215	.348	5.29	1.70
Wilhelmsen, Tom	R-R	6-6	230	12-16-83	4	5	5.49	14	12	0	0	61	66	45	37	8	26	40	.282	.232	.328	5.93	3.86

Fielding

Catcher	PCT	G	PO	A	E	DP	PB
Bantz	.986	83	526	57	8	2	9
Bonilla	.917	3	11	0	1	0	1
Henriquez	.997	39	270	20	1	3	3
Sucre	.979	32	166	22	4	2	1

First Base	PCT	G	PO	A	E	DP
Catricala	1.000	8	68	4	0	7
Jimenez	.971	4	32	1	1	2
Martinez-Esteve	.937	6	53	6	4	8
Poythress	.994	117	940	77	6	95
Savastano	.979	8	41	6	1	8
Tenbrink	1.000	1	12	1	0	2

Second Base	PCT	G	PO	A	E	DP
Acevedo	1.000	3	3	7	0	1
Agudelo	1.000	1	2	1	0	1
Bonilla	.961	10	21	28	2	5

	PCT	G	PO	A	E	DP
Franklin	.943	7	15	18	2	3
Haveman	1.000	1	1	0	0	0
Noriega	1.000	9	21	29	0	8
Savastano	.970	57	98	130	7	25
Seager	.973	54	102	149	7	43
Triunfel	.944	5	9	8	1	3

Third Base	PCT	G	PO	A	E	DP
Bonilla	.893	9	10	15	3	2
Catricala	.897	24	15	55	8	5
Martinez	.919	32	23	68	8	6
Savastano	.967	27	18	41	2	5
Seager	1.000	3	3	6	0	1
Tenbrink	.898	53	36	87	14	7

Shortstop	PCT	G	PO	A	E	DP
Bonilla	.500	1	1	2	3	0
Franklin	.950	14	31	45	4	14

	PCT	G	PO	A	E	DP
Noriega	.977	16	33	51	2	9
Seager	.974	10	16	21	1	6
Triunfel	.943	100	172	293	28	76

Outfield	PCT	G	PO	A	E	DP
Catricala	1.000	26	43	2	0	0
Chavez	.975	122	253	18	7	6
Chiang	.984	28	57	3	1	0
Dunigan	1.000	14	18	0	0	0
Haveman	.981	60	149	5	3	1
Lo	.968	47	90	1	3	0
McOwen	.993	63	146	2	1	0
Shaffer	.976	75	117	7	3	1
Tenbrink	1.000	8	13	3	0	1

HIGH DESERT MAVERICKS

HIGH CLASS A

CALIFORNIA LEAGUE

Batting	B-T	HT	WT	DOB	AVG	vLH	vRH	G	AB	R	H	2B	3B	HR	RBI	BB	HBP	SH	SF	SO	SB	CS	SLG	OBP
Almonte, Denny	B-R	6-2	187	9-24-88	.268	.302	.257	128	504	75	135	28	6	24	97	22	2	0	5	161	18	12	.490	.298
Baron, Steve	R-R	6-0	200	12-7-90	.188	.333	.100	5	16	3	3	1	0	0	1	1	0	0	1	6	0	0	.250	.222
Batista, Yidid	R-R	6-0	150	10-13-89	.000	.000	.000	1	3	0	0	0	0	0	0	0	0	0	0	2	0	0	.000	.000
Bonilla, Leury	R-R	6-3	170	2-8-85	.326	.421	.286	32	129	26	42	5	1	6	21	4	1	0	0	27	2	3	.519	.351
Browning, Matt	R-R	6-0	210	1-7-88	.250	.240	.255	20	76	9	19	2	1	0	6	1	0	1	0	17	1	3	.303	.288
Carroll, Dan	R-R	6-1	175	1-6-89	.299	.301	.298	131	482	117	144	20	6	18	57	88	14	0	4	157	62	14	.477	.418
Catricala, Vinnie	R-R	6-2	210	10-31-88	.351	.400	.336	71	282	56	99	19	1	14	61	33	4	0	4	45	8	3	.574	.421
Cerione, Matt	L-L	6-2	192	1-4-87	.248	.289	.235	48	157	21	39	9	1	3	19	19	7	0	0	40	7	3	.376	.355
Coleman, Trevor	B-R	6-1	205	1-19-88	.265	.186	.288	93	306	40	81	17	1	6	50	58	1	0	4	62	3	2	.386	.379
Dunigan, Joe	L-L	6-1	238	3-29-86	.236	.290	.213	33	106	16	25	3	0	10	19	12	0	0	0	59	0	1	.547	.314
Franklin, Nick	B-R	6-1	170	3-2-91	.275	.247	.286	64	258	50	71	10	5	5	20	31	2	0	1	56	13	1	.411	.356
Giobbi, Andrew	R-R	6-2	194	10-25-86	.195	.208	.189	25	77	8	15	6	0	1	10	5	1	0	1	22	0	0	.312	.250
Hansen, Shaver	B-R	6-0	185	12-19-87	.289	.291	.289	54	197	37	57	10	6	2	28	20	2	0	2	59	2	4	.431	.357
Henriquez, Ralph	B-R	6-1	190	4-7-87	.250	.000	.500	1	4	0	1	1	0	0	0	0	0	0	0	2	0	0	.500	.250
Jones, James	L-L	6-4	193	9-24-88	.247	.262	.242	83	296	42	73	16	4	5	29	42	4	0	1	92	16	3	.378	.347
Lo, Kuo Hui	R-R	6-2	188	9-26-85	.261	.400	.244	11	46	3	12	3	1	1	5	1	0	0	0	17	1	0	.435	.277
Marcoe, Billy	R-R	5-10	195	6-5-87	.167	.118	.189	18	54	3	9	0	0	0	1	1	3	0	0	7	0	0	.167	.224
Marder, Jack	R-R	5-11	185	2-21-90	.324	.250	.362	18	71	11	23	6	0	2	12	2	5	0	1	12	3	1	.493	.380
Martinez, Mario	R-R	6-3	200	11-13-89	.278	.304	.270	109	432	64	120	22	3	11	56	19	6	0	7	137	2	1	.419	.313
McOwen, Jamie	L-R	6-0	200	9-26-85	.291	.341	.265	33	127	16	37	7	1	6	27	7	3	0	7	28	2	1	.504	.326
Morales, Alfredo	R-R	6-2	190	11-6-92	.125	.000	.143	2	8	4	1	0	0	0	2	2	1	0	0	1	0	0	.125	.364
Morris, Tim	L-L	6-3	220	12-11-87	.280	.364	.214	6	25	2	7	0	0	0	1	1	0	0	0	4	0	0	.280	.308
Noriega, Gabriel	R-R	6-2	170	9-13-90	.266	.269	.266	105	383	45	102	16	6	3	50	18	5	0	1	108	4	11	.363	.307
Phillips, Anthony	R-R	5-9	160	4-11-90	.229	.222	.231	14	35	7	8	1	2	1	3	10	0	0	0	12	3	0	.457	.400
Proscia, Steve	R-R	6-2	210	6-26-90	.303	.400	.256	44	185	28	56	11	1	12	42	4	1	0	1	33	3	3	.568	.319
Raben, Dennis	L-L	6-3	200	7-31-87	.330	.316	.335	76	309	61	102	23	3	18	75	28	4	0	5	76	2	1	.599	.387
Salome, Angel	R-R	5-7	200	6-8-86	.474	1.000	.412	5	19	5	9	1	1	3	5	2	0	0	0	3	0	0	1.105	.524

Batting	B-T	HT	WT	DOB	AVG	vLH	vRH	G	AB	R	H	2B	3B	HR	RBI	BB	HBP	SH	SF	SO	SB	CS	SLG	OBP
Sams, Kalian	R-R	6-2	248	8-25-86	.200	.111	.216	20	60	11	12	3	1	6	10	3	0	0	0	26	1	1	.583	.238
Schlander, Jake	R-R	6-2	195	8-4-88	.272	.243	.281	47	158	30	43	12	0	0	17	27	3	0	2	42	4	0	.348	.384
van Heydoorn, Rudy	R-R	6-3	180	4-17-89	.241	.118	.297	19	54	6	13	6	0	1	10	4	0	0	0	21	0	0	.407	.293
Velasquez, Roberto	B-R	5-11	160	2-14-90	.238	.333	.222	8	21	2	5	1	0	0	0	1	1	0	0	6	0	0	.286	.304

Pitching	B-T	HT	WT	DOB	W	L	ERA	G	GS	CG	SV	IP	H	R	ER	HR	BB	SO	AVG	vLH	vRH	K/9	BB/9
Boyce, Tim	R-R	6-2	193	2-6-87	1	0	8.83	10	0	0	0	17	30	17	17	7	3	14	.385	.286	.440	7.27	1.56
Buursma, Jason	R-R	6-3	200	9-9-85	0	0	5.14	12	0	0	0	21	24	17	12	5	7	7	.286	.276	.291	3.00	3.00
Cooper, Daniel	R-R	6-3	205	11-6-86	5	2	5.25	33	0	0	2	58	71	40	34	8	19	38	.301	.413	.244	5.86	2.93
Czyz, Nick	L-L	6-2	215	4-10-87	1	6	8.54	10	10	0	0	45	69	47	43	7	15	28	.348	.271	.373	5.56	2.98
Delabar, Steve	R-R	6-5	220	7-17-83	1	1	4.38	7	0	0	3	12	12	6	6	0	8	20	.245	.250	.241	14.59	5.84
Diaz, Ogui	R-R	6-2	170	12-1-85	2	0	6.75	22	0	0	0	35	45	27	26	8	17	25	.324	.373	.288	6.49	4.41
Fernandez, Anthony	L-L	6-4	180	6-8-90	1	1	7.39	7	7	0	0	28	48	27	23	4	13	26	.384	.333	.396	8.36	4.18
Gillheeney, Jimmy	L-L	6-1	200	11-8-87	6	5	5.35	20	20	0	0	108	119	73	64	21	28	109	.277	.296	.272	9.11	2.34
Hesketh, John	L-L	6-0	175	6-3-86	3	2	6.55	13	4	0	0	33	43	25	24	6	9	34	.314	.357	.295	9.27	2.45
Housey, John	L-R	6-3	178	6-4-88	1	0	8.44	6	0	0	0	11	16	11	10	3	7	7	.340	.250	.387	5.91	5.91
2-team total (1 R. Cucamonga)					1	0	10.03	7	0	0	0	12	19	14	13	4	9	7	—	—	—	5.40	6.94
Hudson, Austin	R-R	6-4	175	1-6-88	4	5	5.35	40	1	0	5	72	95	57	43	3	25	51	.322	.302	.333	6.35	3.11
Hume, Donnie	R-L	6-0	185	8-29-85	0	1	6.75	2	2	0	0	8	8	6	6	1	5	6	.250	.375	.208	5.63	6.75
Jimenez, Jose	L-L	6-0	180	3-23-87	3	2	6.44	45	0	0	4	64	84	51	46	11	26	51	.315	.247	.344	7.13	3.64
Kahn, Stephen	L-R	6-3	220	12-14-83	0	2	5.76	24	1	0	2	45	48	36	29	4	19	32	.273	.250	.284	6.35	3.77
Kasparek, Kenn	R-R	6-8	200	9-23-85	0	1	4.63	2	2	0	0	12	12	7	6	2	1	11	.267	.182	.294	8.49	0.77
Kesler, Willy	R-R	6-0	225	8-11-87	5	3	3.12	28	0	0	11	40	52	20	14	3	13	32	.319	.341	.311	7.14	2.90
Kirkland, Chris	R-R	6-4	220	10-6-85	0	0	9.92	10	0	0	1	16	29	22	18	2	11	13	.387	.345	.413	7.16	6.06
Markovitz, Jason	L-L	6-3	195	8-27-88	3	2	6.20	30	0	0	0	45	67	35	31	7	16	28	.364	.352	.369	5.60	3.20
Maurer, Brandon	R-R	6-5	200	7-3-90	2	4	6.38	9	7	0	0	42	47	32	30	8	11	37	.275	.291	.267	7.87	2.34
Medina, Yoervis	R-R	6-3	250	7-27-88	1	13	6.50	20	19	1	0	101	139	90	73	19	38	73	.333	.333	.332	6.50	3.39
Miller, Trevor	R-R	6-3	190	6-13-91	0	2	21.60	2	2	0	0	7	17	18	16	4	5	4	.515	.636	.455	5.40	6.75
Pryor, Stephen	R-R	6-6	225	7-23-89	1	0	7.67	22	0	0	4	27	28	24	23	2	26	34	.264	.206	.292	11.33	8.67
Reed, Nate	R-R	6-3	180	12-1-87	2	2	5.91	7	7	0	0	35	43	30	23	6	12	30	.297	.378	.260	7.71	3.09
Robles, Mauricio	L-L	5-10	210	3-5-89	0	2	12.41	4	4	0	0	12	19	18	17	2	11	9	.373	.250	.395	6.57	8.03
Sena, Jandy	L-R	6-6	245	8-10-89	3	4	6.22	10	10	0	0	55	77	44	38	5	20	28	.330	.418	.275	4.58	3.27
Snow, Forrest	R-R	6-6	195	12-30-88	2	3	8.10	6	6	0	0	33	49	30	30	7	13	20	.350	.313	.370	5.40	3.51
Sorce, Chris	R-R	6-0	190	10-28-87	8	12	5.07	27	27	1	0	165	206	109	93	17	43	105	.308	.286	.320	5.73	2.35
Stanton, Taylor	R-R	6-2	230	1-15-88	4	5	5.65	11	11	1	0	65	84	43	41	7	13	45	.316	.278	.344	6.20	1.79
Zablan, Keli'i	R-R	5-10	190	10-4-86	0	1	11.02	12	0	0	0	16	26	22	20	4	11	15	.347	.423	.306	8.27	6.06

Fielding

Catcher	PCT	G	PO	A	E	DP	PB
Baron	1.000	5	25	0	0	0	0
Coleman	.988	89	601	65	8	6	16
Giobbi	.983	24	168	10	3	1	4
Henriquez	1.000	1	3	2	0	0	0
Marcoe	.981	16	91	11	2	4	1
Marder	1.000	9	59	5	0	0	2
Salome	1.000	2	6	0	0	0	0
van Heydoorn	1.000	9	4	0	0	1	0

First Base	PCT	G	PO	A	E	DP
Browning	.974	4	35	2	1	6
Catricala	.991	26	204	19	2	26
Dunigan	.984	8	59	2	1	7
Jones	.982	9	51	5	1	10
Martinez	.988	21	154	5	2	13
Morris	1.000	3	32	1	0	4
Proscia	.992	13	119	7	1	8
Raben	.987	51	437	24	6	37
van Heydoorn	.983	12	117	1	2	12

Second Base	PCT	G	PO	A	E	DP
Bonilla	.971	6	16	17	1	7

Catcher							
Browning	.939	9	9	22	2	3	
Franklin	.960	12	16	32	2	7	
Hansen	.978	37	73	108	4	27	
Marder	.889	5	6	10	2	1	
Martinez	1.000	1	1	0	0	2	
Noriega	.940	41	70	101	11	22	
Phillips	1.000	9	24	20	0	11	
Schlander	1.000	24	36	58	0	17	
Velasquez	.960	5	9	15	1	4	

Third Base	PCT	G	PO	A	E	DP
Bonilla	1.000	1	0	4	0	1
Catricala	.936	30	19	69	6	6
Hansen	1.000	2	0	6	0	0
Martinez	.886	70	58	129	24	16
Phillips	.000	1	0	0	0	0
Proscia	.901	28	28	63	10	12
Schlander	.933	10	7	21	2	2
van Heydoorn	1.000	1	1	3	0	0

Shortstop	PCT	G	PO	A	E	DP
Bonilla	.882	19	40	57	13	10
Franklin	.932	47	87	132	16	32

Hansen	.965	12	21	34	2	8	
Noriega	.966	66	104	237	12	48	
Phillips	1.000	2	2	4	0	0	
Schlander	1.000	2	0	2	0	0	

Outfield	PCT	G	PO	A	E	DP
Almonte	.987	128	290	11	4	3
Bonilla	1.000	3	2	0	0	0
Carroll	.981	126	236	16	5	4
Catricala	.909	6	10	0	1	0
Cerione	.929	36	59	6	5	1
Dunigan	1.000	6	15	1	0	0
Jones	.985	72	122	10	2	2
Lo	.957	9	22	0	1	0
Martinez	1.000	5	10	1	0	0
McOwen	.957	33	63	3	3	1
Morales	1.000	1	2	0	0	0
Raben	.000	1	0	0	0	0
Sams	.955	14	18	3	1	0

CLINTON LUMBERKINGS

LOW CLASS A

MIDWEST LEAGUE

Batting	B-T	HT	WT	DOB	AVG	vLH	vRH	G	AB	R	H	2B	3B	HR	RBI	BB	HBP	SH	SF	SO	SB	CS	SLG	OBP
Agudelo, Jorge	R-R	6-0	175	5-30-89	.195	.111	.219	12	41	4	8	1	0	0	2	5	2	0	1	11	2	0	.220	.306
Anston, Robbie	L-L	5-11	190	4-13-88	.243	.227	.248	56	181	25	44	11	2	0	16	31	3	0	0	34	11	8	.326	.363
Baron, Steve	R-R	6-0	200	12-7-90	.197	.250	.176	57	198	17	39	13	0	4	20	17	2	0	1	49	6	3	.323	.266
Blash, Jabari	R-R	6-4	195	7-4-89	.218	.227	.213	42	124	13	27	5	1	3	13	38	0	0	0	43	5	2	.347	.401
Browning, Matt	R-R	6-0	210	1-7-88	.229	.273	.206	55	192	21	44	9	0	2	19	16	6	0	1	29	4	3	.307	.307
Cerione, Matt	L-L	6-2	192	1-4-88	.200	.242	.167	20	75	6	15	1	0	0	5	7	2	0	1	28	3	1	.213	.282
Extrano, Jetsy	R-R	6-2	200	8-13-88	.176	.059	.216	21	68	8	12	2	2	1	7	4	0	0	19	2	0	.309	.291
Hansen, Shaver	B-R	6-0	185	12-19-87	.220	.261	.195	31	123	14	27	3	1	1	12	7	0	0	2	26	4	2	.285	.258
Hicks, John	R-R	6-2	190	8-31-89	.309	.348	.302	38	139	21	43	9	2	2	26	5	1	0	3	17	2	3	.446	.331
Littlewood, Marcus	B-R	6-2	180	3-18-92	.158	.121	.177	27	95	7	15	0	1	1	6	10	0	0	1	23	0	1	.211	.236

Batting	B-T	HT	WT	DOB	AVG	vLH	vRH	G	AB	R	H	2B	3B	HR	RBI	BB	HBP	SH	SF	SO	SB	CS	SLG	OBP
Marcoe, Billy	R-R	5-10	195	6-5-87	.000	.000	.000	1	3	0	0	0	0	0	0	0	0	0	0	2	0	0	.000	.000
McGee, Michael	R-R	6-0	185	3-7-89	.283	.268	.287	60	237	44	67	16	3	4	29	23	3	0	2	40	5	2	.426	.351
Miller, Brad	L-R	6-2	185	10-18-89	.415	.167	.488	14	53	9	22	4	1	0	7	4	1	0	1	9	1	0	.528	.458
Morban, Julio	L-L	6-1	190	2-13-92	.256	.200	.274	80	301	44	77	12	7	4	28	26	1	0	2	99	10	5	.382	.315
Morla, Ramon	R-R	6-1	175	11-20-89	.170	.176	.167	28	106	7	18	3	3	0	7	4	0	0	2	28	5	2	.255	.196
Morris, Tim	L-L	6-3	220	12-11-87	.252	.188	.274	96	337	44	85	12	4	5	42	34	7	0	3	87	21	6	.356	.331
Phillips, Anthony	R-R	5-9	160	4-11-90	.199	.208	.197	100	316	36	63	9	0	4	25	28	8	0	2	77	23	11	.266	.280
Ramirez, Carlos	B-R	5-11	145	12-2-88	.231	.218	.236	81	260	32	60	6	0	5	25	39	4	0	3	50	9	2	.312	.337
Rivers, Kevin	L-R	6-2	210	8-24-88	.249	.222	.256	87	281	40	70	12	1	10	40	34	3	0	4	82	7	2	.406	.332
Romero, Stefen	R-R	6-3	225	10-17-88	.280	.293	.275	116	429	62	120	22	4	16	65	32	11	0	5	69	16	9	.462	.342
Sams, Kalian	R-R	6-2	248	8-25-86	.237	.241	.235	93	321	47	76	13	3	18	56	29	2	0	4	102	25	4	.464	.301
Schlander, Jake	R-R	6-2	195	8-4-88	.130	.105	.143	17	54	3	7	2	0	1	7	7	0	0	0	16	0	0	.222	.230
Tanabe, Carlton	R-R	6-0	190	10-28-91	.219	.190	.231	48	146	13	32	8	1	0	14	7	4	0	1	46	1	1	.288	.272
Wiswall, Mickey	L-R	6-1	200	11-25-88	.240	.227	.245	130	509	49	122	19	1	10	57	25	6	0	4	104	4	4	.340	.281

Pitching	B-T	HT	WT	DOB	W	L	ERA	G	GS	CG	SV	IP	H	R	ER	HR	BB	SO	AVG	vLH	vRH	K/9	BB/9
Arias, Jonathan	R-R	6-3	190	2-8-88	5	3	3.27	39	0	0	9	63	50	25	23	3	38	101	.215	.238	.195	14.35	5.40
Bischoff, Matt	R-R	6-0	190	5-21-87	4	3	3.38	20	0	0	2	37	38	18	14	2	10	46	.262	.189	.304	11.09	2.41
Blandford, Tyler	R-R	6-3	165	1-25-88	1	1	9.70	18	0	0	0	21	32	24	23	2	19	22	.348	.390	.314	9.28	8.02
Burgoon, Tyler	R-R	5-10	160	4-25-89	5	2	2.30	42	0	0	14	63	55	22	16	1	15	66	.236	.231	.240	9.48	2.15
Butler, Tony	L-L	6-7	220	11-18-87	3	4	3.26	12	12	0	0	69	65	29	25	3	30	67	.256	.167	.295	8.74	3.91
Capps, Carter	R-R	6-5	220	8-7-90	1	1	6.00	4	4	0	0	18	19	12	12	1	10	21	.284	.300	.270	10.50	5.00
Elias, Roenis	L-L	6-2	178	8-1-88	4	2	5.45	7	7	0	0	36	41	24	22	7	18	33	.289	.306	.283	8.17	4.46
Fernandez, Anthony	L-L	6-4	180	6-8-90	7	4	2.80	21	19	0	0	125	109	49	39	6	42	107	.238	.206	.254	7.68	3.02
Hesketh, John	L-L	6-0	175	6-3-86	0	1	3.00	8	0	0	1	12	9	8	4	0	12	6	.225	.133	.280	4.50	9.00
Kesler, Willy	R-R	6-0	225	8-11-87	1	0	1.45	8	0	0	1	19	15	4	3	1	0	16	.217	.154	.256	7.71	0.00
Kiel, Ryan	L-L	6-4	230	6-26-87	0	2	3.54	15	1	0	1	28	32	16	11	2	14	29	.283	.257	.295	9.32	4.50
Kim, Seon Gi	R-R	6-2	185	9-1-91	0	2	4.74	4	4	0	0	19	25	13	10	0	5	13	.333	.406	.279	6.16	2.37
Kohlscheen, Stephen	R-R	6-6	200	9-20-88	5	3	4.44	22	7	0	0	73	77	39	36	9	33	71	.267	.243	.282	8.75	4.07
Markovitz, Jason	L-L	6-3	195	8-27-88	1	0	0.00	5	0	0	0	8	5	2	0	0	3	9	.161	.125	.174	9.72	3.24
Martinez, Fray	R-R	6-3	170	5-20-89	0	1	7.00	3	1	0	0	9	14	7	7	2	5	7	.359	.500	.323	7.00	5.00
Maurer, Brandon	R-R	6-5	200	7-3-90	1	3	3.41	7	6	0	0	37	28	16	14	2	14	44	.211	.236	.192	10.70	3.41
Mieses, George	R-R	6-2	180	5-3-91	4	11	4.87	21	21	0	0	115	132	74	62	8	36	56	.295	.279	.310	4.40	2.83
Nava, Jessie	R-R	6-3	165	9-18-87	2	4	3.28	25	1	0	4	49	49	20	18	0	25	50	.266	.314	.224	9.12	4.56
Paxton, James	L-L	6-4	220	11-6-88	3	3	2.73	10	10	0	0	56	45	21	17	1	30	80	.225	.232	.221	12.86	4.82
Reed, Nate	R-R	6-3	180	12-1-87	3	3	3.64	18	4	0	0	47	49	28	19	2	17	42	.268	.288	.255	8.04	3.26
Seco, Edlando	L-L	6-2	178	7-23-88	1	0	5.59	21	6	0	0	48	53	33	30	5	28	43	.288	.294	.286	8.01	5.21
Sena, Jandy	L-R	6-6	245	8-10-89	4	5	4.56	14	5	0	0	47	50	32	24	6	17	19	.279	.254	.293	3.61	3.23
Snow, Forrest	R-R	6-6	195	12-30-88	2	7	3.62	13	13	1	0	75	62	34	30	4	19	71	.223	.184	.250	8.56	2.29
Taylor, John	R-R	5-10	175	3-27-89	0	2	3.78	10	0	0	1	17	12	8	7	1	8	12	.203	.292	.143	6.48	4.32
Versnik, Ben	R-R	6-3	240	12-5-88	0	0	4.50	8	0	0	1	14	9	7	7	2	6	5	.176	.143	.200	3.21	3.86
Walker, Taijuan	R-R	6-4	195	8-13-92	6	5	2.89	18	18	1	0	97	69	33	31	4	39	113	.202	.220	.187	10.52	3.63
Zablan, Keli'i	R-R	5-10	190	10-4-86	0	1	3.92	15	0	0	2	21	22	14	9	1	10	17	.272	.222	.311	7.40	4.35

Fielding

Catcher	PCT	G	PO	A	E	DP	PB
Baron	.987	57	457	63	7	7	7
Extrano	1.000	1	9	0	0	0	0
Hicks	.997	38	307	33	1	3	6
Marcoe	1.000	1	12	1	0	0	0
Tanabe	.990	48	357	54	4	1	7

First Base	PCT	G	PO	A	E	DP
Browning	.976	10	77	6	2	6
Morris	.986	73	596	46	9	47
Wiswall	.993	61	525	50	4	32

Second Base	PCT	G	PO	A	E	DP
Agudelo	.958	12	16	30	2	8
Extrano	.923	3	6	6	1	0
Hansen	.965	30	55	82	5	14
Phillips	1.000	12	20	28	0	4

	PCT	G	PO	A	E	DP
Ramirez	.977	41	58	113	4	18
Romero	.965	49	90	130	8	19

Third Base	PCT	G	PO	A	E	DP
Agudelo	.000	1	0	0	1	0
Browning	.924	37	23	50	6	4
Extrano	.933	14	10	18	2	1
Morla	.950	28	30	65	5	4
Phillips	1.000	8	6	12	0	2
Ramirez	.901	30	18	46	7	1
Rivers	.000	1	0	0	0	0
Romero	.875	23	11	38	7	3
Schlander	.846	6	3	8	2	0
Wiswall	.667	1	1	1	1	0

Shortstop	PCT	G	PO	A	E	DP
Extrano	.900	4	10	8	2	3

	PCT	G	PO	A	E	DP
Littlewood	.954	23	31	52	4	9
Miller	.905	14	15	23	4	3
Phillips	.963	82	132	233	14	48
Ramirez	.912	11	16	15	3	4
Schlander	.921	11	13	22	3	2

Outfield	PCT	G	PO	A	E	DP
Anston	.962	43	72	4	3	2
Blash	.936	40	68	5	5	2
Cerione	.973	17	34	2	1	0
McGee	.992	60	114	3	1	1
Morban	.975	77	114	3	3	0
Rivers	.948	65	86	5	5	1
Romero	1.000	17	23	2	0	0
Sams	.955	87	164	7	8	1
Wiswall	.971	25	28	6	1	0

EVERETT AQUASOX

NORTHWEST LEAGUE

SHORT-SEASON

Batting	B-T	HT	WT	DOB	AVG	vLH	vRH	G	AB	R	H	2B	3B	HR	RBI	BB	HBP	SH	SF	SO	SB	CS	SLG	OBP
Agudelo, Jorge	R-R	6-0	175	5-30-89	.211	.184	.219	51	166	32	35	7	0	7	22	11	6	0	1	43	9	3	.380	.283
Blash, Jabari	R-R	6-4	195	7-4-89	.292	.333	.282	57	195	26	57	16	3	11	43	28	5	0	1	65	10	3	.574	.393
Brady, Patrick	R-R	5-10	175	2-5-88	.284	.250	.291	28	95	18	27	4	2	1	13	14	2	0	2	8	3	3	.400	.381
Burgess, Jarrett	R-R	6-2	180	8-10-90	.220	.194	.227	57	177	22	39	11	2	5	24	21	0	0	2	68	9	3	.390	.300
DeJesus, Jharmidy	R-R	6-3	185	8-30-89	.299	.256	.310	58	201	31	60	8	1	4	33	18	8	0	3	42	3	0	.408	.374
Dowd, Michael	R-R	5-8	205	4-10-90	.228	.237	.226	45	162	15	37	4	0	2	16	7	3	0	1	21	1	0	.290	.272
Extrano, Jetsy	B-R	6-2	200	8-13-88	.192	.222	.182	22	73	11	14	3	2	1	8	7	3	0	1	14	2	2	.329	.286
Gonzalez, Larry	R-R	5-11	170	2-1-88	.246	.333	.225	36	126	11	31	7	1	1	15	10	0	0	0	21	1	0	.341	.301

SEATTLE MARINERS

Batting	B-T	HT	WT	DOB	AVG	vLH	vRH	G	AB	R	H	2B	3B	HR	RBI	BB	HBP	SH	SF	SO	SB	CS	SLG	OBP
Littlewood, Marcus	B-R	6-2	180	3-18-92	.206	.114	.228	62	233	45	48	13	1	8	30	45	1	0	0	81	3	3	.373	.337
Lopez, Danny	R-R	5-11	180	1-21-88	.247	.069	.287	44	158	14	39	6	0	2	17	10	1	0	3	26	1	2	.323	.291
Melendres, Nathan	R-R	5-10	187	4-4-90	.285	.240	.293	46	165	31	47	5	6	1	19	9	5	0	0	27	11	5	.406	.341
Morla, Ramon	R-R	6-1	175	11-20-89	.263	.342	.241	48	179	24	47	5	2	4	21	18	2	0	3	44	10	5	.380	.332
Paquette, Ethan	R-R	6-3	220	3-12-88	.238	.081	.292	46	143	14	34	6	1	0	11	18	7	0	0	30	0	0	.294	.351
Rodriguez, Luis	B-R	5-9	190	6-27-80	.333	.500	.286	3	9	2	3	1	0	0	2	2	0	0	0	1	0	1	.444	.455
van Heydoorn, Rudy	R-R	6-3	180	4-17-89	.161	.000	.192	8	31	5	5	4	0	0	1	0	0	0	0	6	0	0	.290	.161
Wood, James	L-L	6-2	200	12-19-87	.260	.265	.259	61	223	33	58	16	1	9	34	23	1	0	2	77	3	1	.462	.329
Yepez, Mario	B-R	6-2	160	6-15-88	.332	.224	.363	66	262	37	87	17	2	0	20	14	1	0	0	33	5	2	.412	.368

Pitching	B-T	HT	WT	DOB	W	L	ERA	G	GS	CG	SV	IP	H	R	ER	HR	BB	SO	AVG	vLH	vRH	K/9	BB/9
Bischoff, Matt	R-R	6-0	190	5-21-87	2	0	0.00	9	0	0	5	15	5	1	0	0	3	23	.104	.100	.107	13.80	1.80
Butler, Tony	L-L	6-7	220	11-18-87	0	2	2.57	3	3	0	0	14	10	8	4	1	7	18	.196	.308	.158	11.57	4.50
Buursma, Jason	R-R	6-3	200	9-9-85	0	1	7.16	8	0	0	1	16	29	14	13	0	5	8	.387	.321	.426	4.41	2.76
Campos, Vicente	R-R	6-4	195	7-27-92	5	5	2.32	14	14	0	0	81	66	34	21	4	13	85	.214	.237	.195	9.41	1.44
Colvin, David	R-R	6-3	215	1-7-89	0	0	6.75	5	0	0	0	7	10	11	5	1	5	5	.313	.273	.333	6.75	6.75
Corrales, Joshua	R-R	6-2	205	5-25-90	0	0	0.00	2	0	0	0	4	2	0	0	0	0	3	.154	.167	.143	7.36	0.00
de Haas, Jeroen	R-R	6-5	175	1-1-91	0	0	7.59	15	0	0	1	21	28	20	18	1	9	20	.322	.250	.364	8.44	3.80
Diaz, Nolan	R-R	6-1	175	3-28-91	2	3	6.59	16	0	0	0	27	33	22	20	3	20	29	.295	.256	.315	9.55	6.59
DiRocco, Joseph	R-R	6-1	200	9-19-88	1	3	5.13	16	4	0	1	40	37	24	23	6	14	21	.243	.234	.248	4.69	3.12
Griffin, Tim	B-R	6-1	200	3-1-88	3	1	2.09	22	0	0	7	39	31	10	9	3	9	41	.217	.222	.213	9.54	2.09
Hobson, Cameron	L-L	6-0	190	4-10-89	4	2	2.89	12	5	0	0	44	41	16	14	4	8	51	.244	.151	.287	10.51	1.65
Hunter, Kyle	L-L	6-3	205	6-18-89	2	0	1.82	10	0	0	2	25	28	6	5	0	6	31	.277	.222	.297	11.31	2.19
Kittredge, Andrew	R-R	6-1	200	3-17-90	0	0	4.50	1	0	0	0	2	3	1	1	0	1	2	.375	.000	.375	9.00	4.50
Kohlscheen, Stephen	R-R	6-6	200	9-20-88	2	0	3.03	9	7	0	0	36	29	12	12	1	11	31	.220	.242	.197	7.82	2.78
Krakowiak, Max	R-R	6-3	205	6-23-89	1	1	5.50	11	0	0	0	18	23	15	11	2	8	12	.329	.370	.302	6.00	4.00
Landazuri, Steve	R-R	6-0	175	1-6-92	5	4	4.35	14	14	0	0	72	73	39	35	5	29	72	.264	.278	.255	8.96	3.61
Leigh, Bryan	L-R	6-0	200	2-11-88	1	2	4.78	15	0	0	0	26	23	17	14	7	15	24	.232	.267	.217	8.20	5.13
Pries, Jordan	B-R	6-1	195	1-27-90	4	3	3.71	12	6	0	0	51	46	27	21	4	13	46	.241	.206	.260	8.12	2.29
Shipers, Jordan	R-L	5-10	160	6-27-91	1	5	4.71	10	0	0	0	50	50	35	26	4	26	47	.272	.286	.268	8.52	4.71
Versnik, Ben	R-R	6-3	240	12-5-88	0	0	1.42	5	0	0	2	6	5	2	1	0	1	5	.208	.000	.313	7.11	1.42
Weiss, Cody	R-R	5-10	195	8-14-90	0	1	7.07	12	0	0	0	14	21	11	11	3	10	11	.350	.269	.412	7.07	6.43
Whitmore, Ben	L-L	6-4	215	4-17-88	4	6	5.40	13	13	0	0	67	84	44	40	11	13	40	.307	.262	.321	5.40	1.76

Fielding

Catcher	PCT	G	PO	A	E	DP	PB
Dowd	.992	43	333	45	3	3	6
Gonzalez	.994	36	277	42	2	5	3
van Heydoorn	1.000	1	1	0	0	0	0

First Base	PCT	G	PO	A	E	DP
DeJesus	.964	37	282	12	11	25
Extrano	1.000	2	2	0	0	0
Paquette	.992	39	347	36	3	26
van Heydoorn	.984	7	58	4	1	2

Second Base	PCT	G	PO	A	E	DP
Agudelo	.938	47	74	107	12	21
Brady	.963	7	9	17	1	4

	PCT	G	PO	A	E	DP
Extrano	1.000	5	16	15	0	4
Littlewood	.949	12	15	22	2	4
Lopez	1.000	11	12	25	0	3

Third Base	PCT	G	PO	A	E	DP
DeJesus	.936	15	9	35	3	2
Extrano	.875	2	2	5	1	0
Lopez	.927	18	7	31	3	1
Morla	.888	43	38	104	18	8
Paquette	.667	1	0	4	2	0

Shortstop	PCT	G	PO	A	E	DP
Brady	.900	5	8	19	3	2
Extrano	.967	8	8	21	1	3

	PCT	G	PO	A	E	DP
Littlewood	.926	50	62	126	15	25
Lopez	.971	17	24	44	2	8
Rodriguez	.900	2	3	6	1	1

Outfield	PCT	G	PO	A	E	DP
Blash	.933	49	68	2	5	0
Brady	1.000	20	23	1	0	0
Burgess	.971	55	92	7	3	2
Extrano	1.000	4	5	0	0	0
Melendres	.965	43	82	0	3	0
Wood	1.000	10	11	0	0	0
Yepez	.958	64	110	4	5	1

PULASKI MARINERS   ROOKIE
APPALACHIAN LEAGUE

Batting	B-T	HT	WT	DOB	AVG	vLH	vRH	G	AB	R	H	2B	3B	HR	RBI	BB	HBP	SH	SF	SO	SB	CS	SLG	OBP
Acevedo, Michael	R-R	6-0	185	12-5-90	.300	.379	.272	63	227	42	68	12	0	4	42	22	4	0	2	33	1	3	.405	.369
Austin, Jamal	R-R	5-9	180	8-26-90	.335	.333	.335	55	206	35	69	6	2	0	13	22	3	0	1	21	20	8	.383	.405
Brady, Patrick	R-R	5-10	175	2-5-88	.281	.214	.300	21	64	14	18	4	3	0	5	8	1	0	0	9	3	1	.438	.370
Brito, Bryan	R-R	6-2	170	2-24-89	.227	.200	.234	57	203	22	46	7	3	0	14	5	0	0	0	63	3	4	.291	.245
Christian, Frankie	L-L	5-11	192	6-6-91	.176	.143	.182	23	51	7	9	2	0	0	3	7	0	0	0	19	0	0	.216	.276
Hazlett, Dillon	R-R	6-1	190	1-22-89	.243	.261	.237	52	177	19	43	7	1	1	16	23	1	0	1	45	15	5	.311	.332
Hernandez, Jose	R-R	6-1	165	1-12-88	.202	.143	.221	29	89	9	18	1	0	3	10	5	1	0	0	20	0	0	.315	.253
Jimenez, Hassiel	R-R	6-0	185	5-8-91	.174	.176	.172	18	46	4	8	1	0	1	6	2	0	0	0	15	0	1	.261	.296
Lara, Jordy	R-R	6-3	180	5-21-91	.257	.375	.222	51	175	29	45	12	1	8	23	12	2	0	1	51	1	0	.474	.311
Marlette, Tyler	R-R	5-11	195	1-23-93	.156	.133	.167	12	45	4	7	2	0	0	2	0	0	0	0	13	0	0	.200	.162
Morales, Alfredo	R-R	6-2	190	11-6-92	.266	.333	.240	39	143	17	38	7	0	2	19	18	3	0	3	46	0	0	.357	.353
Nunez, Efrain	B-R	6-3	190	2-17-91	.291	.226	.308	44	148	23	43	6	4	6	23	13	5	0	0	47	3	2	.507	.367
Paolini, Daniel	R-R	6-0	190	10-11-89	.284	.362	.256	61	218	32	62	17	5	4	26	27	7	0	2	53	5	2	.463	.378
Pimentel, Guillermo	L-L	6-1	180	10-5-92	.265	.177	.295	65	245	33	65	10	0	11	46	15	2	0	4	73	4	1	.441	.308
Straus, Kenneth	R-R	6-2	190	5-8-91	.150	.139	.155	32	107	7	16	1	0	4	7	3	2	0	0	31	1	0	.271	.188
Villasuso, David	R-R	5-10	195	12-31-89	.240	.190	.253	32	104	11	25	5	1	3	14	5	5	0	1	30	0	1	.394	.304

Pitching	B-T	HT	WT	DOB	W	L	ERA	G	GS	CG	SV	IP	H	R	ER	HR	BB	SO	AVG	vLH	vRH	K/9	BB/9
Colvin, David	R-R	6-3	215	1-7-89	2	1	0.81	11	1	0	0	22	22	5	2	0	8	24	.250	.462	.161	9.67	3.22
Cornwell, Ben	R-R	6-3	220	11-2-88	1	2	3.25	13	2	0	0	28	24	15	10	1	11	27	.233	.286	.197	8.78	3.58
Corrales, Joshua	R-R	6-2	205	5-25-90	2	0	0.96	7	0	0	1	9	4	1	1	1	4	12	.129	.154	.111	11.57	3.86
Dobbs, Jeremy	L-L	6-3	185	10-12-89	0	1	6.16	16	0	0	1	31	41	28	21	1	17	32	.311	.380	.268	9.39	4.99

SEATTLE MARINERS

Pitching

Pitching	B-T	HT	WT	DOB	W	L	ERA	G	GS	CG	SV	IP	H	R	ER	HR	BB	SO	AVG	vLH	vRH	K/9	BB/9
Elias, Roenis	L-L	6-2	178	8-1-88	1	0	0.82	3	1	0	0	11	11	4	1	0	3	8	.262	.300	.250	6.55	2.45
Guaipe, Mayckol	R-R	6-3	175	8-11-90	5	6	3.66	14	14	0	0	64	66	37	26	2	20	49	.262	.298	.232	6.89	2.81
Hidalgo, Ambioris	R-R	6-2	196	2-4-91	1	3	4.98	11	11	0	0	43	52	29	24	3	22	40	.301	.254	.327	8.31	4.57
Hunter, Kyle	L-L	6-3	205	6-18-89	1	2	1.61	10	1	0	0	22	23	6	4	1	3	31	.277	.286	.274	12.49	1.21
Kim, Seon Gi	R-R	6-2	185	9-1-91	1	2	5.76	12	2	0	2	30	33	24	19	2	20	29	.287	.320	.262	8.80	6.07
Raga, Angel	R-R	6-1	168	7-25-89	2	3	4.09	17	6	0	7	44	40	21	20	4	8	47	.255	.239	.267	9.61	1.64
Reeder, Bo	R-R	6-0	195	8-21-90	1	1	4.56	16	0	0	0	26	28	19	13	2	12	22	.277	.250	.295	7.71	4.21
Rodriguez, Leonardo	R-R	6-2	185	4-15-88	0	1	5.68	8	0	0	0	13	11	8	8	2	11	11	.239	.350	.154	7.82	7.82
Sabala, Reynaldo	R-R	6-3	187	8-16-90	1	2	3.07	19	0	0	4	41	30	15	14	4	17	48	.203	.215	.193	10.54	3.73
Shankin, Brett	R-R	6-0	200	10-30-89	0	3	6.67	16	0	0	0	28	25	29	21	1	18	20	.223	.255	.206	6.35	5.72
Shore, Bobby	R-R	6-1	170	1-27-89	0	1	3.06	11	0	0	0	18	20	10	6	1	7	21	.278	.294	.263	10.70	3.57
Taylor, John	R-R	5-10	175	3-27-89	3	0	0.00	6	0	0	2	7	4	0	0	0	1	10	.154	.143	.158	12.86	1.29
Taylor, Luke	R-R	6-6	200	7-14-92	3	2	8.87	13	12	0	0	45	59	45	44	8	29	28	.319	.276	.357	5.64	5.84
Unsworth, Dylan	R-R	6-1	170	9-23-92	6	5	5.16	12	12	0	0	61	73	37	35	7	10	46	.294	.288	.299	6.79	1.48
Valdivia, Jose	R-R	6-4	195	3-19-92	2	1	4.42	9	6	0	0	39	35	22	19	5	15	38	.243	.167	.281	8.84	3.49

Fielding

Catcher	PCT	G	PO	A	E	DP	PB
Hernandez	.978	26	201	17	5	2	11
Jimenez	.985	18	123	9	2	2	6
Marlette	.969	5	26	5	1	0	2
Villasuso	1.000	27	187	15	0	1	5

First Base	PCT	G	PO	A	E	DP
Acevedo	.895	3	16	1	2	1
Brady	1.000	10	78	6	0	7
Hazlett	.974	10	71	4	2	9
Lara	.981	46	381	29	8	35
Straus	1.000	4	34	1	0	1

Second Base	PCT	G	PO	A	E	DP
Acevedo	.950	3	5	14	1	4

Brady	1.000	1	0	2	0	0
Hazlett	.906	6	10	19	3	4
Paolini	.961	59	99	149	10	35

Third Base	PCT	G	PO	A	E	DP
Acevedo	.912	52	20	83	10	4
Brady	1.000	6	2	10	0	3
Hazlett	.913	7	5	16	2	0
Lara	.000	1	0	0	0	0
Straus	.625	4	1	4	3	0

Shortstop	PCT	G	PO	A	E	DP
Acevedo	.909	6	6	14	2	5
Brady	1.000	1	0	1	0	0
Brito	.923	57	81	169	21	32

Hazlett	.939	8	10	21	2	4

Outfield	PCT	G	PO	A	E	DP
Austin	.979	52	93	2	2	0
Brady	.833	2	5	0	1	0
Christian	1.000	9	16	0	0	0
Hazlett	.939	19	29	2	2	0
Morales	.958	36	64	5	3	2
Nunez	.952	26	40	0	2	0
Pimentel	.933	64	95	3	7	0
Straus	.714	10	5	0	2	0
Villasuso	1.000	1	1	0	0	0

AZL MARINERS

ROOKIE

ARIZONA LEAGUE

Batting

Batting	B-T	HT	WT	DOB	AVG	vLH	vRH	G	AB	R	H	2B	3B	HR	RBI	BB	HBP	SH	SF	SO	SB	CS	SLG	OBP
Andreas, Chris	L-R	6-3	215	5-31-88	.336	.292	.348	31	116	18	39	9	0	0	12	10	2	0	0	29	3	5	.414	.398
Batista, Yidid	R-R	6-0	150	10-13-89	.306	.226	.327	42	144	26	44	2	1	1	18	19	6	0	1	18	13	7	.354	.406
Burin, Felipe	R-R	5-10	170	2-10-92	.319	.275	.333	41	163	13	52	12	0	0	22	19	1	0	1	39	3	3	.393	.391
Carmichael, Christian	R-R	5-11	190	4-25-92	.182	.200	.167	5	11	0	2	1	1	0	0	1	0	0	0	3	0	1	.455	.250
Castillo, Phillips	R-R	6-2	190	2-2-94	.300	.324	.294	48	170	36	51	18	5	1	27	15	5	0	4	61	8	5	.482	.366
Cochrane, Stephen	B-R	6-0	180	7-12-88	.143	.000	.150	8	21	2	3	1	0	0	3	2	1	0	0	7	1	1	.190	.250
Franklin, Nick	B-R	6-1	170	3-2-91	.091	.000	.100	3	11	1	1	0	0	0	0	0	0	0	0	6	0	0	.091	.091
Guarnaccia, Luke	B-R	5-11	210	7-11-92	.200	.333	.158	15	45	2	9	0	0	0	7	0	0	0	0	8	2	1	.200	.375
Higgs, Travis	R-R	6-2	210	9-6-88	.300	.438	.259	35	70	13	21	10	0	1	10	6	2	0	0	13	1	0	.486	.372
Jimenez, Charles	R-R	6-3	225	5-19-93	.156	.400	.111	14	32	4	5	0	0	0	2	7	1	0	0	14	3	1	.156	.325
Jimenez, Hassiel	R-R	6-0	205	5-8-91	.250	.000	.273	4	12	3	3	0	0	0	2	4	0	0	2	0	0	0	.250	.357
Lampe, Reginald	R-R	6-3	185	3-1-90	.233	.235	.232	22	73	9	17	5	1	1	12	2	1	0	0	20	1	0	.370	.263
Lawson, Reggie	R-R	6-4	235	8-14-91	.226	.250	.220	42	159	16	36	4	3	1	21	5	4	0	1	43	5	4	.308	.266
Marcoe, Billy	R-R	5-10	195	6-5-87	.300	.000	.333	10	20	4	6	2	0	0	2	3	2	0	0	1	0	2	.400	.440
Martinez, Jose	R-R	6-1	180	7-22-92	.237	.146	.288	53	187	26	48	9	2	1	22	7	5	0	2	59	4	3	.342	.299
McGee, Michael	R-R	6-0	185	3-7-89	.556	.000	.556	2	9	3	5	0	3	0	4	0	0	0	1	1	0	0	21.222	.500
Morales, Alfredo	R-R	6-2	190	11-6-92	.405	.533	.373	19	74	13	30	7	1	2	12	8	0	0	2	19	8	2	.608	.452
Morla, Ramon	R-R	5-11	175	11-20-89	.250	.500	.200	3	12	1	3	1	0	0	1	0	0	0	0	2	1	1	.333	.250
Peguero, Martin	R-R	6-1	185	11-3-93	.279	.382	.252	43	165	23	46	12	1	1	25	6	2	0	2	22	17	5	.382	.309
Ramirez, Ivan	R-R	6-1	190	7-25-92	.167	.000	.250	3	6	0	1	0	0	0	1	1	0	0	0	3	0	0	.167	.286
Rangel, Rigoberto	B-R	6-1	167	6-21-90	.221	.185	.233	35	113	11	25	5	0	1	11	15	3	0	0	29	5	3	.292	.328
Salome, Angel	R-R	5-7	200	6-8-86	.354	.273	.395	17	65	14	23	9	0	0	9	3	0	0	1	14	1	0	.492	.377
Susini, Norberto	B-R	5-10	210	1-24-89	.261	.500	.238	17	23	7	6	0	0	0	1	10	0	0	0	9	1	0	.261	.541
Velasquez, Roberto	R-R	5-11	160	2-14-90	.246	.200	.257	36	130	15	32	4	0	0	10	8	2	0	0	18	6	3	.277	.300
Zamarripa, James	L-L	5-10	190	9-17-93	.266	.207	.282	35	139	22	37	5	2	0	13	13	1	0	2	38	6	3	.331	.329

Pitching

Pitching	B-T	HT	WT	DOB	W	L	ERA	G	GS	CG	SV	IP	H	R	ER	HR	BB	SO	AVG	vLH	vRH	K/9	BB/9
Catapano, Maxx	R-R	6-4	215	10-28-88	2	2	5.65	20	0	0	2	29	34	19	18	3	11	29	.288	.279	.297	9.10	3.45
Chen, Min-Sih	R-R	6-3	205	12-6-89	5	4	6.08	12	11	0	0	53	62	44	36	4	25	39	.290	.257	.306	6.58	4.22
Cornwell, Ben	R-R	6-3	220	11-2-88	0	0	1.80	4	0	0	1	5	6	2	1	0	0	2	.316	.385	.167	3.60	0.00
Corrales, Joshua	R-R	6-2	205	5-25-90	0	1	0.00	11	0	0	6	13	3	1	0	0	6	10	.071	.083	.067	6.92	4.15
DeJesus, Yunior	R-R	6-2	180	9-22-88	6	3	3.24	16	0	0	3	25	26	13	9	1	5	17	.265	.226	.284	6.12	1.80
Elias, Roenis	L-L	6-2	178	8-1-88	0	0	0.00	1	0	0	0	1	1	0	0	0	0	0	.333	.500	.000	0.00	0.00
Hensley, Steven	R-R	6-3	180	12-27-86	0	0	5.40	1	1	0	0	5	5	3	3	1	2	3	.278	.313	.000	5.40	3.60
Holman, David	R-R	6-3	185	5-31-90	2	1	5.04	16	1	0	0	30	36	29	17	4	7	19	.281	.289	.277	5.64	2.08
Huijer, Lars	R-R	6-4	183	9-22-93	0	1	5.40	3	0	0	0	15	19	9	9	2	2	9	.317	.100	.360	5.40	1.20
Kaalekahi, Charles	R-R	6-2	175	5-13-92	3	4	5.24	12	7	0	0	55	69	42	32	5	17	44	.315	.371	.293	7.20	2.78
Kasparek, Kenn	R-R	6-8	200	9-23-85	0	0	5.00	3	0	0	0	9	14	6	5	0	2	8	.350	.333	.368	8.00	2.00
Kiel, Ryan	L-L	6-4	230	6-26-87	0	0	0.00	2	1	0	0	2	0	0	0	0	0	0	.000	.000	.000	0.00	0.00

Pitching

Pitching	B-T	HT	WT	DOB	W	L	ERA	G	GS	CG	SV	IP	H	R	ER	HR	BB	SO	AVG	vLH	vRH	K/9	BB/9
Kim, Seon Gi	R-R	6-2	185	9-1-91	1	0	0.00	3	0	0	0	9	3	0	0	0	4	7	.097	.111	.091	7.00	4.00
Medina, Yoervis	R-R	6-3	250	7-27-88	0	0	7.20	1	1	0	0	5	7	4	4	1	1	9	.333	.333		16.20	1.80
Miller, Trevor	R-R	6-3	190	6-13-91	2	2	3.99	11	7	0	0	50	60	26	22	2	12	36	.305	.383	.270	6.52	2.17
Ogando, Jochi	R-R	6-5	210	5-27-93	1	4	5.84	8	5	0	0	25	23	19	16	1	25	15	.240	.242	.238	5.47	9.12
Plotz, Brandon	R-R	6-3	200	5-22-91	0	0	4.96	10	0	0	0	16	15	12	9	1	11	19	.227	.222	.229	10.47	6.06
Reyna, Marcos	R-R	6-2	185	11-4-89	2	3	4.18	17	0	0	0	32	32	25	15	2	16	31	.244	.200	.257	8.63	4.45
Ronnenbergh, Scott	L-L	6-2	170	1-11-92	1	0	5.90	16	1	0	0	29	42	24	19	2	13	23	.339	.333	.340	7.14	4.03
Saquilon, Gabe	R-R	6-0	180	6-7-93	0	2	5.32	9	3	0	0	22	27	13	13	0	10	19	.307	.257	.340	7.77	4.09
Sunderland, Alex	R-R	6-3	200	8-9-89	0	2	4.91	17	0	0	3	22	23	15	12	4	7	27	.256	.152	.316	11.05	2.86
Valenza, Nick	R-L	5-10	180	3-31-93	0	2	7.90	11	4	0	0	27	29	27	24	2	28	20	.284	.429	.261	6.59	9.22
Versnik, Ben	R-R	6-3	240	12-5-88	0	0	0.00	4	4	0	0	4	3	0	0	0	2	3	.200	.000	.300	6.75	4.50
White, Richard	R-R	5-11	170	2-1-93	0	0	4.09	5	2	0	0	11	10	5	5	1	7	13	.256	.308	.231	10.64	5.73
Zaragoza, Ernesto	R-R	6-1	175	9-26-92	0	0	11.12	2	2	0	0	6	7	10	7	1	6	8	.292	.000	.333	12.71	9.53

Fielding

Catcher	PCT	G	PO	A	E	DP	PB
Carmichael	.920	5	19	4	2	0	0
Cochrane	.966	6	25	3	1	1	4
Guarnaccia	.964	11	38	15	2	1	3
Higgs	.981	34	141	18	3	1	5
Jimenez	1.000	2	5	1	0	0	0
Jimenez	1.000	4	27	3	0	0	0
Marcoe	.979	10	44	3	1	0	2
Ramirez	1.000	3	17	1	0	0	0
Salome	.966	5	25	3	1	1	2
Susini	.935	16	49	9	4	0	2
Lampe	.988	8	78	2	1		6
Martinez	.969	22	173	13	6		15

First Base	PCT	G	PO	A	E	DP
Andreas	.988	29	236	19	3	21
Cochrane	1.000	1	2	0	0	0

Second Base	PCT	G	PO	A	E	DP
Batista	.971	15	33	34	2	10
Burin	.954	33	68	76	7	14
Velasquez	.920	9	20	26	4	7

Third Base	PCT	G	PO	A	E	DP
Batista	.825	15	7	26	7	0
Lampe	.875	4	3	4	1	0
Martinez	.939	32	23	69	6	12
Morla	1.000	3	3	7	0	0
Velasquez	1.000	11	9	12	0	3

Shortstop	PCT	G	PO	A	E	DP
Franklin	.867	3	2	11	2	1
Martinez	.667	2	2	0	1	0
Peguero	.894	40	54	114	20	21
Velasquez	.961	17	15	58	3	9

Outfield	PCT	G	PO	A	E	DP
Batista	1.000	7	14	0	0	0
Castillo	.959	44	68	2	3	1
Jimenez	1.000	9	12	0	0	0
Lampe	1.000	8	11	0	0	0
Lawson	.938	29	58	3	4	1
McGee	1.000	2	4	0	0	0
Morales	.977	19	41	1	1	0
Rangel	.946	30	51	2	3	0
Salome	.000	1	0	0	0	0
Zamarripa	.960	35	92	4	4	3

DSL MARINERS   ROOKIE

DOMINICAN SUMMER LEAGUE

Batting	B-T	HT	WT	DOB	AVG	vLH	vRH	G	AB	R	H	2B	3B	HR	RBI	BB	HBP	SH	SF	SO	SB	CS	SLG	OBP
Alcantara, Ismael	R-R	6-0	185	12-15-93	.148	.083	.163	24	61	6	9	2	0	2	6	11	0	0	0	24	1	1	.279	.278
Batista, David	R-R	5-11	170	8-10-93																				
Berro, Noe	L-R	6-3	180	8-21-93	.214	.158	.224	46	126	16	27	4	2	4	17	14	6	0	0	40	5	3	.373	.322
Brea, Ivan	R-R	6-2	190	7-5-88	.222	.143	.241	13	36	3	8	1	0	0	0	0	0	0	0	12	0	0	.250	.222
Capriata, Alexander	R-R	5-11	190	8-3-92	.253	.250	.253	41	99	13	25	7	0	1	15	9	5	0	2	10	3	3	.354	.339
DeJesus, Jharmidy	R-R	6-3	185	8-30-89	.000	.000	.000	1	4	0	0	0	0	0	0	0	0	0	0	1	0	0	.000	.000
Guerrero, Gabriel	R-R	6-3	190	12-11-93	.236	.243	.234	57	191	24	45	9	0	1	14	14	0	0	0	29	4	3	.298	.288
Marcelino, Westlonder	R-R	6-4	200	3-2-91	.253	.444	.200	30	83	11	21	3	1	2	9	11	0	0	0	11	4	0	.386	.340
Marte, Ketel	B-R	6-1	160	10-12-93	.259	.163	.282	62	220	44	57	5	3	2	22	26	2	0	1	35	16	6	.336	.341
Martinez, Wilton	R-R	6-4	195	12-11-93	.170	.273	.140	49	147	14	25	6	1	1	13	14	5	0	2	29	2	2	.245	.262
Matias, Luis	R-R	6-2	180	8-27-90	.238	.154	.260	43	126	18	30	1	0	2	12	12	3	0	1	25	3	2	.294	.317
Mina, Diego	R-R	5-11	181	10-13-92	.206	.120	.256	35	68	16	14	5	0	0	6	9	3	0	0	21	1	3	.279	.325
Morales, Estarlyn	R-R	6-3	180	10-28-92	.230	.172	.243	54	165	19	38	6	2	1	10	21	3	0	0	20	4	4	.309	.328
Perez, Randy	R-R	6-3	180	2-23-89	.257	.292	.247	50	105	33	27	4	1	7	27	10	0	0		16	22	7	.343	.451
Sanchez, Miguel	R-R	6-2	180	9-27-91	.221	.333	.197	32	86	8	19	6	0	2	11	17	0	0	2	17	3	1	.360	.343
Soto, George	R-R	6-2	190	11-19-89	.232	.200	.238	59	181	24	42	10	2	4	32	32	2	0	5	41	6	9	.376	.345
Wel, Axel	L-L	6-3	180	4-10-91	.267	.267	.268	56	187	28	50	13	1	6	26	21	3	0	1	30	3	2	.444	.349
Zorrilla, Janelfry	R-R	6-2	180	9-2-90	.321	.302	.326	66	224	50	72	21	2	12	61	24	10	0	4	37	13	5	.594	.405

Pitching	B-T	HT	WT	DOB	W	L	ERA	G	GS	CG	SV	IP	H	R	ER	HR	BB	SO	AVG	vLH	vRH	K/9	BB/9
Aquino, Gregorio	R-R	6-5	175	3-5-90	3	4	5.82	14	8	0	0	51	50	43	33	6	34	35	.253	.327	.228	6.18	6.00
Brazoban, Domingo	R-R	6-3	190	8-8-89	9	2	2.96	17	3	1	1	55	51	21	18	3	12	37	.254	.304	.239	6.09	1.98
Cleto, Ramire	R-R	6-0	190	4-4-93	2	2	6.49	13	3	0	0	26	35	23	19	1	15	15	.327	.440	.293	5.13	5.13
Cortoreal, Leonel	L-L	6-5	175	9-6-92	0	1	4.26	5	3	0	0	13	10	6	6	0	8	11	.217	.000	.244	7.82	5.68
De La Cruz, Noel	R-R	6-3	180	12-17-91	3	1	3.79	14	2	0	1	36	31	18	15	2	17	28	.237	.265	.227	7.07	4.29
DeJesus, Yunior	R-R	6-2	180	9-22-88	3	1	0.49	10	0	0	3	18	10	5	1	0	3	16	.152	.278	.104	9.82	1.47
Dominguez, Ronald	R-R	6-2	180	1-13-94	2	1	1.33	10	0	0	4	27	24	5	4	1	7	18	.245	.150	.269	6.00	2.33
Garcia, Oliver	R-R	6-1	188	12-7-90	3	0	2.66	14	0	0	4	24	17	12	7	1	23	25	.210	.333	.175	9.51	8.75
Garcia, Rigoberto	R-R	6-2	202	9-23-93	0	5	4.01	9	9	0	0	25	21	19	11	1	14	18	.216	.360	.167	6.57	5.11
Gonzalez, Yeuri	R-R	6-2	170	12-22-92	2	0	3.26	9	0	0	2	19	21	8	7	0	5	12	.292	.412	.255	5.59	2.33
Julio, Ivan	R-R	6-3	175	8-19-91	5	2	2.80	13	12	1	0	64	64	26	20	3	17	36	.263	.356	.242	5.04	2.38
Marte, Wander	L-L	6-2	180	6-30-92	2	0	0.94	9	8	0	0	38	18	4	4	1	15	49	.136	.308	.118	11.50	3.52
Munoz, Leoncio	L-L	6-4	170	8-18-90	3	0	3.67	13	2	0	0	27	15	11	11	2	5	16	.257	.167	.269	10.00	5.00
Nunez, Junior	R-R	6-3	210	3-1-92	1	1	4.32	13	5	0	0	33	39	20	16	1	19	23	.295	.333	.283	6.21	5.13
Rosario, Enrique	R-R	6-1	180	6-23-91	2	2	1.44	16	0	0	2	31	16	11	5	2	12	27	.147	.107	.160	7.76	3.45
Tamarez, Albert	R-R	6-1	185	11-30-93	0	0	15.88	6	0	0	0	6	6	11	10	0	11	3	.261	.250	.267	4.76	17.47
Torres, Jose	R-R	6-4	165	9-1-93	5	1	2.15	14	13	2	0	75	57	23	18	2	26	42	.214	.311	.185	5.02	3.11

SEATTLE MARINERS

Fielding

Catcher	PCT	G	PO	A	E	DP	PB
Brea	.932	13	66	3	5	1	4
Capriata	.968	41	223	45	9	2	10
Sanchez	.962	27	158	19	7	0	12

First Base	PCT	G	PO	A	E	DP
Alcantara	1.000	1	11	0	0	1
DeJesus	1.000	1	6	1	0	0
DeJesus	1.000	1	9	1	0	1
Marcelino	1.000	24	181	8	0	9
Matias	1.000	11	46	1	0	6
Sanchez	1.000	2	9	0	0	1
Wel	.985	41	314	16	5	26

	PCT	G	PO	A	E	DP
Zorrilla	1.000	1	1	0	0	0

Second Base	PCT	G	PO	A	E	DP
Berro	.934	30	53	46	7	7
Marte	1.000	4	8	11	0	4
Matias	.971	14	12	22	1	4
Mina	.975	23	45	33	2	10
Soto	.978	14	20	25	1	8

Third Base	PCT	G	PO	A	E	DP
Alcantara	.970	16	7	25	1	0
Marcelino	1.000	1	1	3	0	0
Matias	.944	17	9	25	2	0
Mina	1.000	2	2	3	0	0

	PCT	G	PO	A	E	DP
Soto	.927	43	34	81	9	5

Shortstop	PCT	G	PO	A	E	DP
Berro	.879	16	18	33	7	6
Marte	.958	58	87	165	11	26
Matias	.962	6	8	17	1	2

Outfield	PCT	G	PO	A	E	DP
Guerrero	.976	48	79	4	2	1
Martinez	.937	40	55	4	4	1
Morales	.971	45	61	5	2	0
Perez	.905	27	32	6	4	1
Zorrilla	.964	64	152	8	6	0

VSL MARINERS   *ROOKIE*

VENEZUELAN SUMMER LEAGUE

Batting	B-T	HT	WT	DOB	AVG	vLH	vRH	G	AB	R	H	2B	3B	HR	RBI	BB	HBP	SH	SF	SO	SB	CS	SLG	OBP
Brito, Miguel	R-R	6-3	228	9-11-92	.286	.750	.208	8	28	2	8	2	0	0	4	3	0	0	0	5	1	1	.357	.355
Burin, Felipe	B-R	5-10	170	2-10-92	.381	.256	.427	41	160	29	61	18	2	1	38	23	3	0	3	19	1	3	.538	.460
Calderon, Yordi	R-R	6-2	185	2-15-94	.271	.296	.264	68	247	30	67	16	0	7	39	32	8	0	0	62	14	8	.421	.373
Coronel, Ramon	R-R	5-11	155	2-2-92	.352	.378	.345	61	210	36	74	14	1	0	27	14	5	0	0	31	6	3	.429	.406
Diaz, Franklin	B-R	6-1	170	7-20-90	.211	.222	.207	46	128	19	27	5	0	2	16	25	3	0	0	22	4	1	.297	.353
Fernandez, Rafael	B-L	5-10	180	4-21-94	.250	.273	.244	44	100	24	25	3	0	0	8	21	3	0	0	9	9	4	.280	.395
Gonzalez, Ricardo	R-R	6-0	206	3-25-92	.165	.077	.182	29	79	11	13	3	0	1	6	12	1	0	0	20	3	0	.241	.283
Hart, Kenny	R-R	6-3	180	3-21-90	.265	.167	.295	59	181	38	48	15	1	5	24	34	16	0	3	35	13	2	.442	.419
Kalbakgi, Jose	R-R	6-1	200	9-16-92	.182	.185	.180	33	88	6	16	3	0	2	7	8	0	0	0	23	1	0	.284	.250
Lampe, Reginald	R-R	6-3	185	3-19-94	.300	.276	.306	40	140	28	42	8	1	6	31	24	4	0	0	12	16	3	.500	.417
Michel, Rashynol	B-R	6-2	175	11-30-92	.213	.225	.210	59	197	32	42	3	2	0	18	14	5	0	0	38	15	5	.249	.282
Nieto, Arturo	R-R	6-2	195	12-9-92	.231	.250	.227	31	91	7	21	5	0	0	11	6	4	0	0	11	2	1	.286	.307
Okuda, Pedro	L-R	5-10	160	4-20-90	.275	.207	.292	51	149	28	41	6	0	0	17	37	3	0	3	17	7	8	.315	.422
Palma, Alexy	R-R	6-3	195	12-24-92	.263	.355	.243	55	179	27	47	10	1	4	24	28	0	0	1	32	9	8	.397	.361
Quevedo, Johan	B-R	6-1	212	11-6-93	.205	.333	.171	19	44	8	9	0	0	4	7	0	0	0	8	0	0	.205	.314
Ugueto, Jesus	B-R	6-0	170	5-30-91	.262	.208	.276	62	229	38	60	15	2	2	25	36	1	0	1	46	6	2	.371	.363
Wawoe, Gianfranco	B-R	5-11	170	7-25-94	.179	.000	.226	36	78	13	14	2	0	0	8	17	5	0	0	14	3	2	.205	.360

Pitching	B-T	HT	WT	DOB	W	L	ERA	G	GS	CG	SV	IP	H	R	ER	HR	BB	SO	AVG	vLH	vRH	K/9	BB/9
Bishop, Aljeurreau	R-R	6-5	182	9-15-91	0	0	15.75	5	0	0	0	4	6	7	7	0	4	3	.333	.200	.385	6.75	9.00
Carrera, Rafael	R-R	6-0	190	10-29-92	4	0	3.35	16	0	0	3	38	31	20	14	1	18	26	.228	.125	.271	6.21	4.30
Flores, Jose	R-R	6-2	190	12-31-92	5	2	2.61	13	11	0	0	69	51	22	20	2	23	35	.212	.243	.198	4.57	3.00
Gomez, Erick	L-L	6-1	165	1-16-93	3	2	7.79	10	0	0	0	17	26	17	15	1	11	13	.333	.375	.323	6.75	5.71
Gonzalez, Isliexel	R-R	6-3	185	5-10-91	6	3	2.51	14	14	0	0	82	88	35	23	3	18	56	.281	.318	.267	6.12	1.97
Mata, Daniel	R-R	6-2	180	7-3-93	3	4	4.60	14	12	0	0	61	68	35	31	6	19	40	.292	.347	.267	5.93	2.82
Mendoza, Jose	R-R	6-2	193	9-29-92	1	4	6.48	13	0	0	0	25	30	21	18	2	15	12	.309	.367	.284	4.32	5.40
Miliani, Eduardo	R-R	5-11	178	7-8-93	3	3	2.81	13	0	0	1	26	20	16	8	2	13	8	.213	.333	.178	2.81	4.56
Morales, Osmel	R-R	6-3	196	10-30-92	0	0	0.00	2	2	0	0	3	4	1	0	0	1	3	.333	.333	.333	10.13	3.38
Osorio, Neritzon	R-R	6-1	180	12-29-93	4	0	2.72	13	2	0	2	36	27	14	11	0	22	27	.206	.250	.192	6.69	5.45
Pereira, Cruz	L-L	5-10	175	12-18-90	1	4	3.18	17	0	0	2	40	34	20	14	0	24	29	.230	.231	.230	6.58	5.45
Pereira, Ricardo	B-R	6-3	150	4-18-91	1	5	3.86	14	10	1	1	75	82	42	32	1	24	32	.288	.287	.288	3.86	2.89
Pina, Luis	L-L	6-2	178	12-6-93	1	2	3.69	13	12	0	0	54	54	29	22	1	22	28	.270	.298	.261	4.70	3.69
Pirela, Jesus	R-R	6-3	190	9-17-91	0	1	39.00	4	1	0	0	3	9	16	13	0	8	3	.474	.333	.538	9.00	24.00
Quintanilla, Kevin	R-R	6-0	174	5-21-92	0	1	2.00	6	0	0	0	18	18	8	4	1	6	8	.281	.333	.255	4.00	3.00
Vieira, Thyago	R-R	6-2	210	1-7-93	2	0	4.00	12	2	0	0	18	20	11	8	0	22	8	.294	.300	.292	4.00	11.00
Ynfantes, Maykel	R-R	6-0	190	12-6-90	4	3	2.59	20	0	0	8	49	54	21	14	0	9	30	.278	.324	.254	5.55	1.66

Fielding

Catcher	PCT	G	PO	A	E	DP	PB
Diaz	.966	27	112	29	5	2	7
Gonzalez	.973	22	88	19	3	2	5
Nieto	.994	25	127	28	1	2	6
Quevedo	.948	13	40	15	3	0	3

First Base	PCT	G	PO	A	E	DP
Brito	1.000	3	21	3	0	0
Coronel	1.000	1	9	0	0	0
Diaz	1.000	18	151	12	0	12
Gonzalez	1.000	4	35	5	0	3
Kalbakgi	.983	31	223	15	4	14
Lampe	.996	26	234	12	1	16
Nieto	1.000	2	19	2	0	1

	PCT	G	PO	A	E	DP
Okuda	.500	1	1	0	1	0

Second Base	PCT	G	PO	A	E	DP
Burin	.972	36	103	106	6	21
Coronel	.972	14	34	35	2	5
Fernandez	.968	8	16	14	1	2
Okuda	.975	21	51	66	3	12

Third Base	PCT	G	PO	A	E	DP
Brito	1.000	1	0	2	0	0
Calderon	.833	49	38	102	28	5
Coronel	.884	30	22	54	10	3
Fernandez	.000	1	0	0	0	0

Shortstop	PCT	G	PO	A	E	DP
Coronel	.941	21	27	69	6	8
Fernandez	.933	36	52	100	11	21
Okuda	.963	7	14	12	1	0
Wawoe	.926	31	39	86	10	12

Outfield	PCT	G	PO	A	E	DP
Coronel	.000	1	0	0	0	0
Diaz	.000	1	0	0	0	0
Hart	.973	55	64	7	2	2
Lampe	.947	13	17	1	1	0
Michel	.990	55	89	7	1	2
Palma	.950	53	88	8	5	0
Ugueto	.942	54	89	9	6	2

Tampa Bay Rays

SEASON IN A SENTENCE: Despite losing Carl Crawford, Carlos Pena and most of their bullpen, including Rafael Soriano, to free agency, the Rays and their tiny payroll came back to beat out the Red Sox for the American League wild card in one of the most unlikely September races ever.

HIGH POINT: Down to his final out of the season and trailing 7-6 to the Yankees, manager Joe Maddon sent Dan Johnson to the plate. Johnson, who was batting .108/.178/.157, stepped up and cranked a game-tying home run, sending the game to extra innings. Not to be outdone, Evan Longoria blasted a walkoff home run three innings later. The Rays surged into the playoffs when the Orioles staged a late-inning comeback of their own, taking out the Red Sox just minutes before the Rays won. The game capped one of baseball's most memorable nights and capped off a run when the Rays made up a deficit that was as large as nine games on Aug. 27.

LOW POINT: The Rays were unable to carry the momentum from the regular season into the playoffs, falling to the eventual AL champion Rangers in four games in the Division Series.

NOTABLE ROOKIES: Jeremy Hellickson pitched to contact and made use of his superb defense to post a 2.95 ERA and win Baseball America Rookie of the Year honors. Athletic outfielder Desmond Jennings took over for Crawford and provided speed in the outfield and on the bases, while blasting 10 home runs in just 287 plate appearances from the leadoff spot.

KEY TRANSACTIONS: The Rays found three key contributors on the cheap before the season: Casey Kotchman, Johnny Damon and Kyle Farnsworth. Kotchman led the team with a .333 average and played solid defense, Damon hit 16 home runs and stole 19 bases, and Farnsworth had 25 saves.

DOWN ON THE FARM: Matt Moore, the game's best pitching prospect, provided a big boost at the end of the season, with a five-inning 11-strikeout performance against the Yankees. He followed it up with the Rays' only Division Series win, going seven shutout innings in Game One against the Rangers. Shortstop Hak Ju Lee hit .318/.389/.443 with 28 stolen bases in high Class A in his first season since coming over from the Cubs. Thanks to their free-agent losses, the Rays had 12 picks in the first two rounds of the draft. Their first two selections were prep righthander Taylor Guerreri and athletic Louisiana State outfielder Mikie Mahtook.

OPENING DAY PAYROLL: $41,053,571 (29th)

PLAYERS OF THE YEAR

MAJOR LEAGUE	MINOR LEAGUE
Evan Longoria	**Matt Moore**
3b	lhp
.244/.355/.495	(Double-A/Triple-A)
26 2B, 31 HR	12-3, 1.92
Led AL 3B in putouts	210 SO/155 IP

ORGANIZATION LEADERS

BATTING		*Minimum 250 PA
MAJORS		
* AVG	Casey Kotchman	.306
* OPS	Evan Longoria	.850
HR	Evan Longoria	31
RBI	Evan Longoria	99
MINORS		
* AVG	Russ Canzler, Durham	.314
* OBP	Tyler Bortnick, Charlotte	.428
* SLG	Russ Canzler, Durham	.53
R	Hak-Ju Lee, Charlotte/Montgomery	98
H	Stephen Vogt, Montgomery/Durham	152
TB	Stephen Vogt, Montgomery/Durham	252
2B	Russ Canzler, Durham	40
3B	Hak-Ju Lee, Charlotte/Montgomery	15
HR	Derek Dietrich, Bowling Green	22
RBI	Stephen Vogt, Montgomery/Durham	105
BB	Robby Price, Bowling Green	86
SO	Russ Canzler, Durham	129
SB	Tyler Bortnick, Charlotte	43
PITCHING		#Minimum 75 IP
MAJORS		
W	James Shields	16
# ERA	James Shields	2.82
SO	James Shields	225
SV	Kyle Farnsworth	25
MINORS		
W	George Jensen, Bowling Green	13
L	Shane Dyer, Montgomery	11
	Braulio Lara, Bowling Green	11
# ERA	Matt Moore, Montgomery/Durham	1.92
G	Dane De La Rosa, Durham	52
GS	Alexander Colome, Charlotte/Montgomery	28
	Shane Dyer, Montgomery	28
SV	Zachary Quate, Montgomery	20
	Chris Rearick, Bowling Green	20
IP	Alexander Colome, Charlotte/Montgomery	157.2
BB	Christopher Archer, Montgomery/Durham	86
SO	Matt Moore, Montgomery/Durham	210
# AVG	Matt Moore, Montgomery/Durham	.184

General Manager: Andrew Friedman. **Farm Director:** Mitch Lukevics. **Scouting Director:** R.J. Harrison.

Class	Team	League	W	L	PCT	Finish	Manager(s)
Majors	Tampa Bay Rays	American	91	71	.562	4th (14)	Joe Maddon
Triple-A	Durham Bulls	International	80	62	.563	3rd (14)	Charlie Montoyo
Double-A	Montgomery Biscuits	Southern	65	74	.468	7th (10)	Billy Gardner
High A	Charlotte Stone Crabs	Florida State	64	75	.460	9th (12)	Jim Morrison
Low A	Bowling Green Hot Rods	Midwest	77	63	.550	5th (16)	Brady Williams
Short-season	Hudson Valley Renegades	New York-Penn	37	39	.487	9th (14)	Jared Sandberg
Rookie	Princeton Rays	Appalachian	30	38	.441	7th (10)	Mike Johns
Rookie	GCL Rays	Gulf Coast	24	36	.400	13th (15)	Joe Alvarez
Overall 2011 Minor League Record			377	387	.493	19th (30)	

ORGANIZATION STATISTICS

TAMPA BAY RAYS
AMERICAN LEAGUE

Batting	B-T	HT	WT	DOB	AVG	vLH	vRH	G	AB	R	H	2B	3B	HR	RBI	BB	HBP	SH	SF	SO	SB	CS	SLG	OBP
Brignac, Reid	L-R	6-3	195	1-16-86	.193	.150	.201	92	249	18	48	4	0	1	15	10	1	0	0	63	3	1	.221	.227
Canzler, Russ	R-R	6-2	220	4-11-86	.333	.500	.000	3	3	0	1	0	0	0	1	1	0	0	1	1	0	0	.333	.400
Chirinos, Robinson	R-R	6-1	195	6-5-84	.218	.333	.212	20	55	4	12	2	0	1	7	5	0	0	1	13	0	0	.309	.283
Damon, Johnny	L-L	6-2	205	11-5-73	.261	.277	.255	150	582	79	152	29	7	16	73	51	7	0	5	92	19	6	.418	.326
Fuld, Sam	L-L	5-10	180	11-20-81	.240	.192	.255	105	308	41	74	18	5	3	27	32	1	0	1	49	20	8	.360	.313
Guyer, Brandon	R-R	6-1	210	1-28-86	.195	.207	.167	15	41	7	8	1	0	2	3	1	0	0	0	9	0	0	.366	.214
Jaso, John	L-R	6-2	205	9-19-83	.224	.161	.233	89	246	26	55	15	1	5	27	25	1	0	0	36	1	2	.354	.298
Jennings, Desmond	R-R	6-2	200	10-30-86	.259	.256	.260	63	247	44	64	9	4	10	25	31	6	0	0	59	20	6	.449	.356
Johnson, Dan	L-R	6-2	210	8-10-79	.119	.200	.074	31	84	7	10	1	0	2	4	6	1	0	0	20	0	0	.202	.187
Johnson, Elliot	B-R	6-0	190	3-9-84	.194	.213	.176	70	160	20	31	7	2	4	17	14	0	0	1	53	6	7	.338	.257
Joyce, Matt	L-R	6-2	205	8-3-84	.277	.217	.292	141	462	69	128	32	2	19	75	49	4	0	7	106	13	1	.478	.347
Kotchman, Casey	L-L	6-3	220	2-22-83	.306	.289	.313	146	500	44	153	24	2	10	48	48	12	0	3	66	2	2	.422	.378
Lobaton, Jose	B-R	6-0	195	10-21-84	.118	.150	.071	15	34	2	4	1	0	0	4	1	0	0	0	8	0	0	.147	.231
Longoria, Evan	R-R	6-2	210	10-7-85	.244	.258	.240	133	483	78	118	26	1	31	99	80	6	0	5	93	3	2	.495	.355
Lopez, Felipe	B-R	6-0	205	5-12-80	.216	.244	.196	32	97	8	21	4	0	2	8	4	0	0	0	28	1	1	.320	.248
Ramirez, Manny	R-R	6-0	225	5-30-72	.059	.000	.071	5	17	0	1	0	0	0	1	0	0	0	0	4	0	0	.059	.059
Rodriguez, Sean	R-R	6-0	200	4-26-85	.223	.273	.192	131	373	45	83	20	3	8	36	38	18	0	2	87	11	7	.357	.323
Ruggiano, Justin	R-R	6-2	205	4-12-82	.248	.217	.271	46	105	11	26	4	0	4	13	4	0	0	1	26	1	1	.400	.273
Shoppach, Kelly	R-R	6-0	220	4-29-80	.176	.241	.115	87	221	23	39	3	0	11	22	19	9	0	1	79	0	0	.339	.268
Upton, B.J.	R-R	6-3	185	8-21-84	.243	.238	.245	153	560	82	136	27	4	23	81	71	4	0	3	161	36	12	.429	.331
Zobrist, Ben	B-R	6-3	200	5-26-81	.269	.303	.253	156	588	99	158	46	6	20	91	77	2	0	5	128	19	6	.469	.353

Pitching	B-T	HT	WT	DOB	W	L	ERA	G	GS	CG	SV	IP	H	R	ER	HR	BB	SO	AVG	vLH	vRH	K/9	BB/9
Buente, Jay	R-R	6-2	185	9-28-83	0	0	9.00	1	0	0	0	2	2	2	2	0	2	1	.250	.000	.667	4.50	9.00
Cobb, Alex	R-R	6-2	195	10-7-87	3	2	3.42	9	9	0	0	53	49	21	20	3	21	37	.244	.259	.224	6.32	3.59
Cruz, Juan	R-R	6-2	165	10-15-78	5	0	3.88	56	0	0	0	49	36	21	21	5	28	46	.211	.171	.238	8.51	5.18
Davis, Wade	R-R	6-5	220	9-7-85	11	10	4.45	29	29	1	0	184	190	96	91	23	63	105	.267	.289	.246	5.14	3.08
De La Rosa, Dane	R-R	6-7	245	2-1-83	0	0	9.82	7	0	0	0	7	10	8	8	1	3	8	.323	.385	.278	9.82	3.68
Delaney, Rob	L-R	6-3	220	9-8-84	0	0	10.80	4	0	0	0	5	4	6	6	0	7	3	.235	.400	.000	5.40	12.60
Ekstrom, Mike	R-R	6-0	190	8-30-83	0	0	0.00	1	0	0	0	1	1	0	0	0	0	1	.250	.000	.500	9.00	0.00
Farnsworth, Kyle	R-R	6-4	230	4-14-76	5	1	2.18	63	0	0	25	58	45	15	14	5	12	51	.211	.194	.225	7.96	1.87
Gomes, Brandon	R-R	5-11	175	7-15-84	2	1	2.92	40	0	0	0	37	34	15	12	3	16	32	.246	.291	.217	7.78	3.89
Hellickson, Jeremy	R-R	6-1	185	4-8-87	13	10	2.95	29	29	2	0	189	146	64	62	21	72	117	.210	.230	.188	5.57	3.43
Howell, J.P.	L-L	6-0	195	4-25-83	2	3	6.16	46	0	0	1	31	30	24	21	5	18	26	.259	.222	.302	7.63	5.28
McGee, Jake	L-L	6-3	230	8-6-86	5	2	4.50	37	0	0	0	28	30	14	14	5	12	27	.270	.164	.400	8.68	3.86
Moore, Matt	L-L	6-2	205	6-18-89	1	0	2.89	3	1	0	0	9	3	3	3	1	3	15	.243	.222	.250	14.46	2.89
Niemann, Jeff	R-R	6-9	260	2-28-83	11	7	4.06	23	23	1	0	135	131	65	61	18	37	105	.250	.253	.247	6.98	2.46
Peralta, Joel	R-R	5-11	195	3-23-76	3	4	2.93	71	0	0	6	68	44	23	22	7	18	61	.188	.155	.218	8.11	2.39
Price, David	L-L	6-6	225	8-26-85	12	13	3.49	34	34	0	0	224	192	93	87	22	63	218	.230	.171	.250	8.75	2.53
Ramos, Cesar	L-L	6-2	205	6-22-84	0	1	3.92	59	0	0	0	44	36	22	19	4	25	31	.224	.221	.227	6.39	5.15
Russell, Adam	R-R	6-8	255	4-14-83	1	2	3.03	36	0	0	0	33	31	13	11	2	20	13	.254	.135	.306	3.58	5.51
Shields, James	R-R	6-4	220	12-20-81	16	12	2.82	33	33	11	0	249	195	83	78	26	65	225	.217	.219	.215	8.12	2.35
Sonnanstine, Andy	L-R	6-3	190	3-18-83	0	2	5.55	15	4	0	0	36	40	22	22	10	12	12	.292	.299	.286	3.03	3.03
Torres, Alex	L-L	5-10	175	12-8-87	0	1	3.38	4	0	0	0	8	8	4	3	0	7	9	.258	.200	.313	10.13	7.88

Fielding

Catcher	PCT	G	PO	A	E	DP	PB
Chirinos	1.000	19	115	8	0	1	0
Jaso	.992	82	479	26	4	4	4
Lobaton	.989	14	90	3	1	0	0
Shoppach	.994	86	485	37	3	7	1

First Base	PCT	G	PO	A	E	DP
Chirinos	1.000	1	2	1	0	1

	PCT	G	PO	A	E	DP
Damon	1.000	1	2	0	0	0
Johnson	.994	21	151	13	1	10
Johnson	1.000	2	1	0	0	1
Kotchman	.998	146	1119	80	2	109
Lopez	.977	6	39	3	1	2
Rodriguez	1.000	5	24	1	0	1

Second Base	PCT	G	PO	A	E	DP
Johnson	.944	9	6	11	1	0
Rodriguez	.989	48	66	112	2	25
Zobrist	.989	131	213	316	6	68

Third Base	PCT	G	PO	A	E	DP
Johnson	1.000	3	0	2	0	0
Longoria	.962	130	124	229	14	35

	PCT	G	PO	A	E	DP
Lopez	.953	23	14	27	2	1
Rodriguez	1.000	30	15	45	0	6
Shortstop	**PCT**	**G**	**PO**	**A**	**E**	**DP**
Brignac	.979	91	104	217	7	44
Johnson	.993	52	48	100	1	15
Rodriguez	.947	60	55	105	9	22

Outfield	**PCT**	**G**	**PO**	**A**	**E**	**DP**
Damon	1.000	16	19	0	0	0
Fuld	.985	87	190	5	3	0
Guyer	1.000	14	20	0	0	0
Jennings	.992	60	118	3	1	0
Johnson	.000	2	0	0	0	0

	PCT	G	PO	A	E	DP
Joyce	.988	136	231	8	3	3
Rodriguez	1.000	2	1	0	0	0
Ruggiano	1.000	36	64	1	0	0
Upton	.992	151	382	6	3	3
Zobrist	1.000	38	65	1	0	0

DURHAM BULLS

TRIPLE-A

INTERNATIONAL LEAGUE

Batting	B-T	HT	WT	DOB	AVG	vLH	vRH	G	AB	R	H	2B	3B	HR	RBI	BB	HBP	SH	SF	SO	SB	CS	SLG	OBP
Albernaz, Craig	R-R	5-8	195	10-30-82	.167	.000	.211	8	24	1	4	2	0	0	1	1	0	0	0	8	0	0	.250	.200
Anderson, Leslie	L-L	6-1	205	3-30-82	.277	.276	.277	121	462	46	128	24	0	13	65	21	6	0	5	60	2	3	.413	.314
Ashley, Nevin	R-R	6-1	215	8-14-84	.218	.267	.197	32	101	9	22	1	1	2	15	5	3	0	1	29	0	1	.307	.273
Beckham, Tim	R-R	6-0	190	1-27-90	.255	.345	.221	24	106	12	27	3	2	5	13	3	1	0	0	29	2	1	.462	.282
Brignac, Reid	L-R	6-3	195	1-16-86	.231	.214	.240	11	39	7	9	2	1	1	4	7	0	0	0	6	0	1	.410	.348
Canzler, Russ	R-R	6-2	220	4-11-86	.314	.321	.312	131	474	78	149	40	4	18	83	67	4	0	4	129	5	2	.530	.401
Carson, Matt	R-R	6-2	200	7-1-81	.250	.235	.254	22	84	15	21	7	0	5	10	9	2	0	0	25	0	0	.512	.337
Carter, Chris	L-L	6-0	230	9-16-82	.270	.266	.272	54	215	25	58	14	0	10	46	12	2	0	4	28	1	0	.460	.309
2-team total (23 Gwinnett)					.286	—	—	77	283	35	81	15	0	14	63	19	2	0	4	37	1	0	.488	.331
Chirinos, Robinson	R-R	6-1	195	6-5-84	.259	.312	.239	78	282	24	73	13	1	6	24	29	7	0	0	69	1	1	.376	.343
Furmaniak, J.J.	R-R	6-0	190	7-31-79	.215	.224	.211	116	377	41	81	23	0	4	32	26	2	0	3	89	2	2	.308	.267
Guyer, Brandon	R-R	6-1	210	1-28-86	.312	.346	.299	107	388	78	121	29	5	14	61	35	12	0	2	79	16	6	.521	.384
Jaso, John	L-R	6-2	205	9-19-83	.300	.417	.125	6	20	2	6	2	0	0	4	2	0	0	0	3	0	0	.400	.364
Jennings, Desmond	R-R	6-2	200	10-30-86	.275	.284	.272	89	338	68	93	19	3	12	39	45	9	0	1	78	17	1	.456	.374
Johnson, Dan	L-R	6-2	210	8-10-79	.273	.216	.294	93	333	52	91	23	0	13	52	58	2	0	2	65	0	1	.459	.382
Johnson, Elliot	R-R	6-0	190	3-9-84	.222	.000	.250	2	9	1	2	0	0	0	0	0	0	0	0	3	0	0	.222	.222
Kotchman, Casey	L-L	6-3	220	2-22-83	.250	.000	.250	1	4	0	1	0	0	0	0	1	0	0	0	0	0	0	.250	.400
Lobaton, Jose	B-R	6-0	195	10-21-84	.293	.322	.280	54	184	24	54	10	1	8	31	37	0	0	5	50	0	0	.489	.410
Lopez, Felipe	B-R	6-0	205	5-12-80	.305	.297	.310	48	190	25	58	11	0	7	37	14	2	0	1	41	1	0	.474	.357
Luna, Omar	R-R	5-11	165	12-13-86	.203	.120	.238	56	172	15	35	4	0	6	3	13	1	0	1	22	1	1	.227	.229
Matulia, John	L-L	6-0	175	8-19-86	.238	.317	.200	36	126	16	30	5	2	5	16	6	1	0	0	30	0	0	.429	.278
Mayora, Daniel	R-R	5-11	175	7-27-85	.262	.315	.241	51	187	26	49	9	1	2	11	12	3	0	0	30	3	0	.353	.317
Olmedo, Ray	R-R	5-11	165	5-31-81	.260	.267	.258	124	457	60	119	22	3	0	27	27	2	0	2	82	5	4	.322	.303
Ruggiano, Justin	R-R	6-2	205	4-12-82	.304	.302	.304	43	168	29	51	13	1	7	34	20	0	0	0	42	12	2	.518	.378
Shelby III, John	R-R	5-10	185	8-6-85	.000	.000	.000	1	3	0	0	0	0	0	0	0	0	0	0	1	0	0	.000	.000
Vogt, Stephen	L-R	6-0	215	11-1-84	.290	.242	.308	31	124	15	36	14	1	4	20	8	0	0	3	29	0	0	.516	.305

Pitching	B-T	HT	WT	DOB	W	L	ERA	G	GS	CG	SV	IP	H	R	ER	HR	BB	SO	AVG	vLH	vRH	K/9	BB/9
Archer, Chris	R-R	6-3	185	9-26-88	1	0	0.69	2	2	0	0	13	11	1	1	0	6	12	.224	.207	.250	8.31	4.15
Baker, Brian	R-R	6-5	190	1-10-83	7	9	6.62	25	20	0	0	105	116	82	77	17	41	76	.282	.315	.250	6.54	3.53
Bateman, Joe	R-R	6-1	185	5-6-80	1	3	4.71	15	0	0	0	21	20	11	11	2	8	18	.253	.324	.190	7.71	3.43
Bootcheck, Chris	R-R	6-5	210	10-24-78	3	2	3.57	16	7	0	1	58	46	27	23	9	19	48	.218	.200	.238	7.45	2.95
Buente, Jay	R-R	6-2	185	9-28-83	1	3	5.70	24	4	1	1	43	48	31	27	4	17	43	.286	.288	.284	9.07	3.59
Cobb, Alex	R-R	6-2	195	10-7-87	5	1	1.87	12	12	0	0	67	61	19	14	4	16	70	.251	.295	.217	9.36	2.14
Cormier, Lance	R-R	6-1	200	8-19-80	4	3	5.51	20	4	0	0	47	62	34	29	8	18	25	.318	.309	.327	4.75	3.42
De La Rosa, Dane	R-R	6-7	245	2-1-83	6	5	3.20	52	0	0	6	70	63	26	25	8	26	83	.244	.248	.242	10.62	3.33
De Los Santos, Richard	R-R	6-1	170	6-1-84	0	1	6.00	2	2	0	0	6	7	4	4	0	4	4	.280	.300	.267	6.00	6.00
Delaney, Rob	L-R	6-3	220	9-8-84	4	2	1.86	51	0	0	13	68	51	15	14	3	17	57	.213	.226	.201	7.58	2.26
Ekstrom, Mike	R-R	6-0	190	8-30-83	6	4	4.35	46	1	0	5	68	75	37	33	5	29	65	.280	.353	.224	8.56	3.82
Fleming, Marquis	R-R	6-1	181	9-11-86	0	0	0.00	2	0	0	0	2	4	3	0	0	1	1	.364	.500	.200	3.86	3.86
Gomes, Brandon	R-R	5-11	175	7-15-84	0	1	1.07	20	0	0	7	25	17	4	3	1	7	40	.187	.205	.173	14.21	2.49
Gonzalez, Edgar	R-R	6-2	210	2-23-83	3	3	4.56	11	11	0	0	53	62	32	27	4	17	34	.288	.299	.281	5.74	2.87
Hall, Jeremy	R-R	6-3	200	9-16-83	0	2	8.47	5	4	0	0	17	17	19	16	4	13	12	.250	.148	.317	6.35	6.88
Hayhurst, Dirk	L-R	6-3	200	3-24-81	4	4	4.12	11	11	0	0	59	54	29	27	7	21	43	.241	.221	.258	6.56	3.20
Howell, J.P.	L-L	6-0	195	4-25-83	0	0	0.00	4	0	0	0	4	5	4	0	0	1	5	.333	.286	.375	12.27	2.45
McGee, Jake	L-L	6-3	230	8-6-86	4	2	2.70	24	0	0	9	33	30	10	10	4	8	38	.236	.243	.236	10.26	2.16
Moore, Matt	L-L	6-2	205	6-18-89	4	0	1.37	9	9	0	0	53	33	8	8	3	18	79	.179	.211	.165	13.50	3.08
Niemann, Jeff	R-R	6-9	260	2-28-83	1	1	3.86	2	2	0	0	9	10	4	4	0	3	8	.270	.400	.118	7.71	2.89
Paduch, Jim	R-R	6-2	190	11-2-82	1	0	3.86	1	1	0	0	7	8	3	3	0	1	3	.286	.222	.400	3.86	1.29
Phillips, Paul	R-R	6-1	211	11-26-84	1	1	12.71	6	0	0	0	11	20	16	16	5	2	11	.364	.381	.353	8.74	1.59
Ramos, Cesar	L-L	6-2	205	6-22-84	2	0	4.50	4	0	0	0	4	5	2	2	1	2	1	.313	.429	.222	2.25	4.50
Reid, Ryan	L-R	5-11	215	4-24-85	1	1	4.55	26	5	0	0	55	58	31	28	5	18	51	.271	.225	.313	8.30	2.93
Russell, Adam	R-R	6-8	255	4-14-83	0	1	4.24	15	0	0	1	17	14	8	8	2	12	14	.226	.250	.206	7.41	6.35
Sonnanstine, Andy	L-R	6-3	190	3-18-83	3	6	4.82	10	9	0	0	56	64	37	30	4	15	35	.283	.240	.333	5.63	2.41
Swindle, R.J.	L-L	6-3	190	7-7-83	2	0	4.15	39	0	0	1	35	26	16	16	7	17	36	.205	.182	.222	9.35	4.41
Torra, Matt	R-R	6-3	225	6-29-84	5	1	3.67	11	11	0	0	61	58	25	25	6	12	25	.246	.183	.306	4.55	1.76
Torres, Alex	L-L	5-10	175	12-8-87	9	7	3.08	27	27	1	0	146	134	61	50	7	83	156	.249	.278	.237	9.59	5.10
Wade, Cory	R-R	6-2	190	5-28-83	2	1	1.23	21	0	0	0	37	34	5	5	4	6	34	.248	.214	.272	8.35	1.47
2-team total (1 Scranton/W-B)					3	1	1.17	22	0	0	0	38	36	5	5	4	6	35	—	—		8.22	1.41

Fielding

Catcher	PCT	G	PO	A	E	DP	PB
Albernaz	.976	8	39	2	1	0	1
Ashley	.988	31	232	17	3	1	0
Chirinos	.993	63	494	36	4	5	4
Jaso	1.000	4	27	0	0	0	0
Lobaton	.991	38	307	28	3	1	3
Vogt	1.000	6	45	2	0	1	0

TAMPA BAY RAYS

First Base	PCT	G	PO	A	E	DP
Anderson	.990	63	455	40	5	39
Canzler	.974	17	139	13	4	14
Johnson	.992	59	478	44	4	67
Kotchman	1.000	1	8	0	0	1
Lopez	1.000	1	6	0	0	1
Vogt	1.000	5	29	6	0	4

Second Base	PCT	G	PO	A	E	DP
Furmaniak	.985	52	78	120	3	29
Lopez	.971	25	37	64	3	13
Luna	.980	47	79	113	4	31
Mayora	.929	4	4	9	1	3
Olmedo	.974	29	40	72	3	16

Third Base	PCT	G	PO	A	E	DP
Canzler	.877	40	25	68	13	6
Furmaniak	.972	43	31	75	3	4
Johnson	1.000	15	5	15	0	2
Lopez	.969	12	11	20	1	1
Luna	1.000	1	0	1	0	0
Mayora	.901	40	17	65	9	10

Shortstop	PCT	G	PO	A	E	DP
Beckham	.979	24	38	55	2	16
Brignac	.978	11	17	28	1	6
Furmaniak	.922	15	21	38	5	8
Johnson	1.000	1	1	1	0	1
Luna	1.000	1	2	1	0	0
Olmedo	.965	95	155	234	14	71

Outfield	PCT	G	PO	A	E	DP
Anderson	.985	42	61	4	1	2
Canzler	.984	68	122	1	2	1
Carson	1.000	22	43	4	0	2
Carter	1.000	26	39	0	0	0
Furmaniak	1.000	11	14	0	0	0
Guyer	.992	107	228	17	2	4
Jennings	1.000	83	193	4	0	2
Luna	1.000	3	3	0	0	0
Matulia	.987	36	73	1	1	0
Ruggiano	.950	41	76	0	4	0
Shelby III	1.000	1	3	0	0	0
Vogt	.950	10	17	2	1	0

MONTGOMERY BISCUITS

SOUTHERN LEAGUE

DOUBLE-A

Batting	B-T	HT	WT	DOB	AVG	vLH	vRH	G	AB	R	H	2B	3B	HR	RBI	BB	HBP	SH	SF	SO	SB	CS	SLG	OBP
Albernaz, Craig	R-R	5-8	195	10-30-82	.220	.217	.221	30	91	13	20	4	0	0	7	13	4	0	2	19	0	0	.264	.336
Ashley, Nevin	R-R	6-1	215	8-14-84	.280	.256	.289	80	279	35	78	15	2	6	33	36	14	0	2	66	2	3	.412	.387
Beckham, Tim	R-R	6-0	190	1-27-90	.275	.357	.244	107	418	82	115	25	2	7	57	39	3	0	3	91	15	4	.395	.339
Cipriano, Cody	R-R	6-0	200	1-7-85	.186	.250	.148	14	43	3	8	2	0	1	2	1	0	0	0	17	1	0	.302	.205
Figueroa, Cole	L-R	5-10	180	6-30-87	.283	.330	.269	114	410	71	116	20	6	5	51	55	8	0	4	41	9	5	.398	.375
Fronk, Reid	L-R	6-1	200	7-21-86	.203	.145	.230	57	177	17	36	10	1	3	19	27	3	0	1	48	2	2	.322	.317
Jefferies, Jake	L-R	6-2	200	10-30-87	.263	.250	.267	6	19	3	5	0	0	0	3	1	0	0	0	3	0	0	.263	.300
Kang, K.D.	L-L	6-2	180	2-6-88	.263	.244	.270	99	316	54	83	14	4	11	39	53	11	0	3	85	6	3	.437	.384
Lee, Hak-Ju	L-R	6-2	170	11-4-90	.190	.212	.179	24	100	16	19	1	4	1	7	11	1	0	2	22	5	2	.310	.272
Longoria, Evan	R-R	6-2	210	11-16-85	.267	.375	.143	4	15	5	4	0	0	3	3	1	1	0	0	2	0	0	.867	.353
Matulia, John	L-L	6-0	175	8-19-86	.236	.226	.239	55	195	26	46	7	2	7	42	19	3	0	5	48	3	2	.400	.306
Mayora, Daniel	R-R	5-11	175	7-27-85	.305	.325	.296	73	272	51	83	19	4	7	42	31	7	0	2	54	5	3	.482	.388
Nommensen, Brett	L-L	5-11	190	10-6-86	.267	.167	.333	4	15	1	4	0	0	0	1	0	0	0	0	5	0	0	.267	.267
O'Malley, Shawn	R-R	5-11	160	12-28-87	.276	.264	.282	79	308	55	85	5	1	23	42	4	0	1	58	24	13	.344	.369
Sexton, Greg	R-R	6-2	205	2-8-85	.222	.278	.200	54	194	21	43	4	1	4	19	16	3	0	1	0	0	.314	.290
Shelby III, John	R-R	5-10	185	8-6-85	.248	.281	.233	117	415	62	103	20	5	16	52	20	4	0	4	99	7	4	.436	.287
Sweeney, Matt	L-R	6-3	215	4-4-88	.154	.149	.155	82	266	25	41	11	1	7	29	35	4	0	0	92	1	0	.282	.262
Velasquez, Isaias	R-R	5-11	155	5-7-88	.255	.288	.243	63	204	29	52	11	8	2	24	22	2	3	0	32	5	4	.417	.332
Vogt, Stephen	L-R	6-0	215	11-1-84	.301	.274	.311	97	386	52	116	21	6	13	85	30	1	0	10	51	4	2	.487	.344
Wendt, David	R-R	6-5	205	1-2-87	.211	.125	.233	14	38	1	8	5	0	0	5	4	1	0	0	8	0	0	.342	.302
Wrigley, Henry	R-R	6-3	180	8-9-86	.274	.220	.295	118	468	60	128	34	2	17	84	23	2	0	2	73	3	2	.464	.309

Pitching	B-T	HT	WT	DOB	W	L	ERA	G	GS	CG	SV	IP	H	R	ER	HR	BB	SO	AVG	vLH	vRH	K/9	BB/9
Archer, Chris	R-R	6-3	185	9-26-88	8	7	4.42	25	25	0	0	134	136	76	66	11	80	118	.266	.283	.249	7.91	5.36
Barnese, Nick	R-R	6-2	170	1-11-89	6	8	3.76	24	24	0	0	117	109	64	49	8	57	91	.244	.246	.243	6.98	4.37
Bush, Matt	R-R	5-9	180	2-8-86	5	3	4.83	36	0	0	5	50	48	28	27	5	24	77	.251	.244	.257	13.77	4.29
Colome, Alexander	R-R	6-2	184	12-31-88	3	4	4.15	9	9	1	0	52	41	25	24	5	28	31	.219	.143	.273	5.37	4.85
Cruz, Joe	R-R	6-4	190	7-20-88	3	5	8.43	11	11	0	0	47	75	44	44	8	20	42	.369	.412	.327	8.04	3.83
De Los Santos, Frank	L-L	6-0	165	11-17-87	3	6	3.55	33	5	0	3	79	81	43	31	3	23	48	.276	.228	.297	5.49	2.63
Dyer, Shane	R-R	6-3	185	3-9-88	7	11	4.47	28	28	0	0	157	191	85	78	11	45	66	.308	.318	.300	3.78	2.58
Espinosa, Sergio	L-L	5-10	175	1-2-86	1	0	4.81	22	0	0	0	49	55	29	26	9	15	32	.281	.229	.310	5.92	2.77
Fleming, Marquis	R-R	6-1	181	9-11-86	5	4	3.59	41	0	0	4	80	57	33	32	5	42	104	.204	.215	.193	11.65	4.71
Hall, Jeremy	R-R	6-3	200	9-16-83	1	2	5.40	5	1	0	0	15	14	12	9	4	4	13	.237	.172	.300	7.80	2.40
Lobstein, Kyle	L-L	6-2	200	8-12-89	1	1	7.36	2	2	0	0	11	14	9	9	4	6	10	.318	.000	.368	9.00	4.91
Moore, Matt	L-L	6-2	205	6-18-89	8	3	3.20	18	18	1	0	102	68	31	25	8	28	131	.187	.304	.147	11.52	2.46
Newmann, David	R-L	6-2	200	6-24-85	0	0	9.64	3	0	0	0	5	6	5	5	0	6	4	.316	.375	.273	7.71	11.57
Paduch, Jim	R-R	6-2	190	11-2-82	4	6	5.32	17	15	0	0	91	103	62	54	13	37	76	.281	.230	.322	7.49	3.65
Phillips, Paul	R-R	6-1	211	1-26-84	2	4	4.55	35	1	0	1	57	64	32	29	8	16	46	.281	.347	.233	7.22	2.98
Quate, Zach	R-R	6-1	200	9-12-87	4	6	4.68	49	0	0	20	58	65	31	30	5	20	39	.289	.292	.286	6.09	3.12
Reid, Ryan	L-R	5-11	215	4-24-85	2	0	6.75	9	0	0	1	16	27	12	12	4	4	12	.386	.464	.333	6.75	2.25
Schenk, Neil	L-L	6-3	220	6-17-86	1	2	3.76	46	0	0	2	67	55	42	28	5	43	49	.221	.212	.227	6.58	5.78
Thall, Chad	L-L	6-4	220	8-2-85	1	2	5.74	7	0	0	1	16	16	12	10	1	14	11	.271	.304	.250	6.32	8.04

Fielding

Catcher	PCT	G	PO	A	E	DP	PB
Albernaz	.986	29	195	22	3	1	1
Ashley	.990	54	443	42	5	0	3
Jefferies	.923	3	10	2	1	0	0
Vogt	.997	44	308	37	1	4	2
Wendt	1.000	14	58	9	0	1	2

First Base	PCT	G	PO	A	E	DP
Sexton	1.000	6	55	6	0	6
Sweeney	.987	40	296	17	4	29
Vogt	1.000	8	45	1	0	6
Wrigley	.988	92	730	33	9	56

Second Base	PCT	G	PO	A	E	DP
Albernaz	1.000	1	2	0	0	0
Cipriano	1.000	6	9	16	0	3
Figueroa	.987	58	86	138	3	25
Fronk	.000	1	0	0	0	0
Mayora	1.000	2	0	4	0	1
O'Malley	.966	76	126	191	11	32
Sexton	1.000	1	1	0	0	0

Third Base	PCT	G	PO	A	E	DP
Cipriano	.800	5	0	4	1	0
Figueroa	.963	36	25	52	3	5
Longoria	1.000	4	2	7	0	2

	PCT	G	PO	A	E	DP
Mayora	.944	62	50	119	10	13
Sexton	.956	34	31	55	4	3
Wrigley	.786	7	2	9	3	0

Shortstop	PCT	G	PO	A	E	DP
Beckham	.956	106	177	254	20	59
Figueroa	.980	12	17	31	1	4
Lee	.980	24	31	65	2	7
O'Malley	1.000	1	0	1	0	0

Outfield	PCT	G	PO	A	E	DP
Fronk	.992	55	114	5	1	2
Kang	.976	91	159	3	4	0

Matulia	.932	51	89	7	7	1	Shelby III	.978	115	249	12	6	2	Vogt	1.000	40	55 4 0 1
Nommensen	1.000	4	8	0	0	0	Velasquez	.988	58	158	9	2	2	Wrigley	.957	13	20 2 1 0

CHARLOTTE STONE CRABS

HIGH CLASS A

FLORIDA STATE LEAGUE

Batting	B-T	HT	WT	DOB	AVG	vLH	vRH	G	AB	R	H	2B	3B	HR	RBI	BB	HBP	SH	SF	SO	SB	CS	SLG	OBP
Acosta, Mayobanex	R-R	6-1	205	11-20-87	.203	.225	.191	60	202	18	41	13	0	3	24	23	1	0	2	44	1	1	.312	.285
Biell, Dustin	L-R	6-0	175	3-19-89	.201	.194	.204	83	268	31	54	8	3	1	21	24	5	0	0	100	7	7	.265	.279
Bortnick, Tyler	R-R	5-11	185	7-3-87	.306	.301	.308	132	474	96	145	34	7	4	70	79	25	0	4	67	43	4	.432	.428
Cohen, Gabe	R-R	6-2	205	11-7-87	.154	.000	.182	4	13	1	2	1	0	0	1	0	0	0	0	2	0	0	.231	.154
Fronk, Reid	L-R	6-1	200	7-21-86	.193	.152	.213	44	140	9	27	7	0	0	13	23	2	0	3	50	2	2	.243	.310
Hall, Matt	R-R	6-2	180	3-10-87	.237	.218	.248	94	312	39	74	17	1	4	35	30	6	0	4	73	11	4	.337	.313
Jefferies, Jake	L-R	6-2	200	10-30-87	.235	.139	.256	59	204	18	48	12	1	2	29	12	2	0	3	24	1	1	.333	.281
Lee, Hak-Ju	L-R	6-2	170	11-4-90	.318	.339	.308	97	400	82	127	16	11	4	23	42	5	0	0	72	28	14	.443	.389
Lobaton, Jose	B-R	6-0	195	10-21-84	.444	.444	.444	6	18	0	8	4	0	0	2	2	0	0	0	5	0	0	.667	.500
Luna, Omar	R-R	5-11	165	12-13-86	.272	.328	.235	48	169	19	46	10	1	0	12	7	4	0	0	24	6	3	.343	.317
Montero, Lucas	B-R	5-11	180	10-18-84	.077	.100	.069	12	39	4	3	0	1	0	0	1	1	0	0	9	2	0	.128	.122
Morrison, Ty	L-R	6-2	170	7-22-90	.264	.277	.258	67	265	36	70	8	2	0	18	11	5	0	0	67	19	7	.309	.306
Murrill, Chris	L-L	6-2	190	6-5-88	.279	.300	.270	45	165	19	46	5	0	0	9	10	2	0	1	44	10	3	.309	.326
Nommensen, Brett	L-L	5-11	190	10-6-86	.292	.266	.303	87	305	51	89	17	4	4	45	44	18	0	7	52	20	5	.413	.404
Scelfo, Anthony	L-R	5-10	195	9-19-86	.253	.213	.268	112	399	39	101	17	3	3	44	37	3	0	2	92	15	4	.333	.320
Sexton, Greg	R-R	6-2	205	2-8-85	.313	.338	.305	72	281	48	88	22	2	3	59	29	5	0	4	38	1	1	.438	.382
Sheridan, Mike	L-L	6-2	205	8-8-87	.243	.225	.251	127	497	52	121	38	3	3	72	19	6	0	12	72	5	3	.350	.273
Thomas, Mark	R-R	6-1	180	5-5-88	.237	.252	.230	116	422	45	100	25	1	13	64	36	5	0	8	94	6	3	.393	.299
Torres, Alejandro	R-R	6-1	178	9-30-88	.185	.231	.143	11	27	2	5	1	0	0	3	2	0	0	1	11	0	0	.222	.233
Torrez, Riccio	R-R	6-0	205	10-14-89	.194	.111	.227	8	31	2	6	1	0	1	6	1	0	0	0	2	0	0	.323	.242
Wendt, David	R-R	6-5	205	1-2-87	.176	.250	.111	5	17	0	3	1	0	0	1	0	0	0	0	7	0	0	.235	.176

Pitching	B-T	HT	WT	DOB	W	L	ERA	G	GS	CG	SV	IP	H	R	ER	HR	BB	SO	AVG	vLH	vRH	K/9	BB/9
Andujar, Chris	R-R	6-2	180	8-24-87	0	1	5.04	5	5	0	0	25	31	17	14	0	13	13	.310	.325	.300	4.68	4.68
Colome, Alexander	R-R	6-2	184	12-31-88	9	5	3.66	19	19	1	0	106	78	45	43	8	44	92	.214	.214	.214	7.84	3.75
Cruz, Joe	R-R	6-4	190	7-20-88	1	0	5.14	3	3	0	0	14	12	8	8	1	6	6	.240	.231	.250	3.86	3.86
Cruz, Juan	R-R	6-2	165	10-15-78	0	0	0.00	1	1	0	0	1	2	0	0	0	0	2	.400	.333	.500	18.00	0.00
De Los Santos, Frank	L-L	6-0	165	11-17-87	0	1	19.13	3	1	0	0	8	25	17	17	3	2	8	.543	.667	.525	9.00	2.25
Espinosa, Sergio	L-L	5-10	175	1-2-86	2	0	1.95	14	0	0	1	37	27	8	8	1	7	33	.208	.238	.193	8.03	1.70
Fuentes, Felix	R-R	6-0	205	5-17-87	0	0	9.00	1	0	0	0	1	2	1	1	0	2	0	.500	1.000	.000	0.00	18.00
Hill, Hunter	R-R	5-11	185	11-30-88	0	0	7.50	4	0	0	0	6	6	5	5	1	3	5	.250	.250	.250	7.50	4.50
Howell, J.P.	L-L	6-0	195	4-25-83	0	1	2.70	3	3	0	0	3	3	1	1	0	1	4	.231	.000	.300	10.80	2.70
Jannis, Mickey	R-R	6-0	190	12-16-87	0	0	7.20	2	0	0	0	5	10	4	4	0	0	3	.435	.500	.250	5.40	0.00
Jarman, Michael	L-L	6-1	195	6-6-85	7	4	3.33	40	0	0	4	84	82	33	31	5	35	66	.259	.177	.286	7.10	3.76
Kelly, Merrill	R-R	6-2	170	10-14-88	8	7	3.28	25	23	0	0	129	117	52	47	6	51	70	.246	.251	.242	4.88	3.56
Koronis, Alex	R-R	6-2	187	1-4-88	7	8	5.04	27	23	0	0	127	134	85	71	10	49	111	.271	.259	.280	7.89	3.48
Leary, Drew	L-R	6-4	225	12-9-87	0	4	8.20	9	5	0	1	26	39	27	24	4	8	25	.345	.393	.298	8.54	2.73
Liberatore, Adam	L-L	6-3	239	7-5-87	6	5	3.09	38	1	0	1	90	88	34	31	3	31	70	.266	.221	.282	6.97	3.09
Lobstein, Kyle	L-L	6-3	200	8-12-89	9	9	3.71	22	21	1	0	121	120	54	50	11	30	85	.257	.227	.266	6.30	2.23
Mavares, Deivis	R-R	5-11	156	9-19-86	1	6	3.79	37	0	0	2	62	53	38	26	4	40	42	.231	.289	.194	6.13	5.84
Minks, Shane	R-R	6-3	205	4-25-88	0	2	6.14	9	0	0	0	15	14	11	10	1	14	8	.259	.294	.243	4.91	8.59
Niemann, Jeff	R-R	6-9	260	2-28-83	0	0	0.00	1	1	0	0	4	1	0	0	0	2	2	.083	.000	.143	4.50	0.00
Riefenhauser, C.J.	L-L	6-0	180	1-30-90	1	3	4.14	8	7	0	0	37	35	21	17	3	11	24	.252	.147	.286	5.84	2.68
Satow, Josh	L-L	5-10	155	12-18-85	4	5	2.26	45	0	0	13	56	45	15	14	5	14	55	.218	.250	.208	8.89	2.26
Shuman, Scott	R-R	6-3	205	3-28-88	0	4	4.70	42	0	0	2	52	28	30	27	3	59	86	.156	.125	.179	14.98	10.28
Stabelfeld, Matt	L-L	5-10	185	8-21-86	1	2	3.99	29	1	0	1	50	46	26	22	1	31	39	.254	.173	.287	7.07	5.62
Suarez, Albert	R-R	6-2	185	10-8-89	1	1	2.76	4	3	0	0	16	13	6	5	1	3	7	.210	.107	.294	3.86	1.65
Thompson, Jake	R-R	6-3	225	8-8-89	5	7	2.90	22	22	0	0	115	114	47	37	4	37	56	.267	.296	.246	4.40	2.90
Yates, Kirby	R-R	5-10	170	3-25-87	2	0	1.62	16	0	0	2	33	14	6	6	0	22	45	.128	.156	.109	12.15	5.94

Fielding

Catcher	PCT	G	PO	A	E	DP	PB
Acosta	.996	32	199	26	1	2	1
Jefferies	.993	21	123	17	1	0	1
Lobaton	1.000	2	4	0	0	0	0
Thomas	.983	88	609	81	12	8	5
Torres	.955	6	18	3	1	1	0
Wendt	1.000	1	3	0	0	0	0

First Base	PCT	G	PO	A	E	DP
Acosta	1.000	4	35	2	0	10
Jefferies	1.000	1	4	1	0	0
Sexton	1.000	9	76	9	0	7
Sheridan	.995	125	1118	58	6	103
Torres	1.000	1	5	0	0	0

Second Base	PCT	G	PO	A	E	DP
Bortnick	.969	130	244	355	19	96
Hall	.963	6	13	13	1	3
Luna	1.000	2	4	7	0	1
Scelfo	1.000	2	5	2	0	0

Third Base	PCT	G	PO	A	E	DP
Hall	.932	35	33	76	8	10
Luna	.925	32	28	71	8	4
Scelfo	.692	5	1	8	4	1
Sexton	.928	62	44	148	15	19
Torrez	.955	8	3	18	1	0

Shortstop	PCT	G	PO	A	E	DP
Hall	.977	45	68	105	4	24

Lee	.964	94	141	287	16	55
Luna	1.000	1	0	5	0	0

Outfield	PCT	G	PO	A	E	DP
Biell	.984	81	174	7	3	2
Cohen	.750	3	3	0	1	0
Fronk	.978	41	82	6	2	2
Hall	1.000	9	10	0	0	0
Luna	1.000	12	18	0	0	0
Montero	1.000	11	20	0	0	0
Morrison	.980	60	141	5	3	1
Murrill	.987	42	70	4	1	0
Nommensen	.983	85	166	6	3	1
Scelfo	.953	88	154	8	8	0

BOWLING GREEN HOT RODS

LOW CLASS A

MIDWEST LEAGUE

Batting	B-T	HT	WT	DOB	AVG	vLH	vRH	G	AB	R	H	2B	3B	HR	RBI	BB	HBP	SH	SF	SO	SB	CS	SLG	OBP
Acosta, Mayobanex	R-R	6-1	205	11-20-87	.221	.350	.175	23	77	16	17	3	1	3	11	10	4	0	0	20	1	1	.403	.341
Bailey, Luke	R-R	6-0	198	3-11-91	.223	.125	.263	74	247	26	55	17	1	7	35	18	7	0	0	89	5	1	.385	.294
Castillo, Keith	B-R	6-4	215	7-10-87	.330	.227	.360	29	97	19	32	8	0	5	22	10	3	0	0	25	0	1	.567	.409
Cedeno, Julio	R-R	6-2	185	8-25-89	.246	.263	.239	66	264	30	65	13	1	8	31	10	2	0	1	67	4	1	.394	.278
Dietrich, Derek	L-R	6-1	200	7-18-89	.277	.266	.281	127	480	73	133	34	4	22	81	38	15	0	5	128	5	7	.502	.346
Estrada, Robi	B-R	5-10	170	10-8-88	.255	.299	.231	83	220	35	56	8	3	3	25	31	0	0	4	39	14	3	.359	.341
Glaesmann, Todd	R-R	6-4	220	10-24-90	.229	.379	.171	63	210	28	48	8	2	4	21	14	3	0	0	85	6	0	.343	.286
Guevara, Hector	R-R	5-11	170	10-7-91	.248	.338	.211	69	234	24	58	16	2	3	29	14	1	0	2	37	2	4	.372	.291
Holloway, Kyle	R-R	6-0	204	6-13-88	.240	.238	.241	22	75	7	18	4	0	1	6	8	1	0	0	23	0	0	.333	.321
Kiermaier, Kevin	L-R	6-1	200	4-22-90	.241	.171	.266	120	402	54	97	11	8	4	39	37	8	0	3	99	27	10	.338	.316
Motter, Taylor	R-R	6-1	190	9-18-89	.182	.000	.200	3	11	1	2	0	0	1	3	1	0	0	0	4	1	0	.455	.250
Price, Robby	L-R	5-10	188	4-20-88	.283	.262	.291	127	427	85	121	25	5	6	44	86	20	0	0	63	16	7	.407	.426
Rogers, Cody	L-R	6-2	175	9-13-88	.244	.180	.268	122	475	89	116	18	11	12	51	43	12	0	3	111	28	7	.404	.321
Schwaner, Nick	L-R	6-1	215	2-27-88	.229	.179	.248	117	420	43	96	20	5	8	44	23	3	0	3	85	8	4	.357	.272
Tinoco, Steve	R-R	6-0	200	4-11-88	.277	.276	.277	105	372	47	103	15	0	1	49	38	13	0	4	53	3	3	.325	.361
Torres, Alejandro	R-R	6-1	178	9-30-88	.174	.154	.183	37	121	12	21	6	0	1	11	6	1	0	1	30	0	0	.248	.217
Wunderlich, Phil	R-R	6-0	225	11-4-88	.263	.244	.269	132	502	56	132	34	0	17	86	34	17	0	8	83	0	3	.432	.326

Pitching	B-T	HT	WT	DOB	W	L	ERA	G	GS	CG	SV	IP	H	R	ER	HR	BB	SO	AVG	vLH	vRH	K/9	BB/9
Bencomo, Omar	R-R	6-1	168	2-10-89	4	5	3.97	38	0	0	0	79	87	38	35	11	13	52	.281	.224	.324	5.90	1.47
Garcia, Nate	R-R	6-1	190	5-9-88	2	4	3.52	37	0	0	4	64	62	28	25	4	19	64	.256	.245	.265	9.00	2.67
Hiscock, Stephen	R-R	6-2	153	1-23-88	1	2	5.32	40	0	0	1	66	80	46	39	9	29	61	.296	.231	.340	8.32	3.95
Hubbard, Austin	R-R	6-2	206	6-14-88	5	3	2.51	46	0	0	10	68	62	25	19	2	35	68	.237	.278	.208	9.00	4.63
Jensen, George	R-R	6-4	215	4-12-90	13	4	4.28	26	26	0	0	122	137	64	58	16	42	88	.289	.332	.255	6.49	3.10
Lara, Braulio	L-L	6-1	180	12-20-88	5	11	4.94	25	25	0	0	120	117	74	66	10	55	111	.259	.212	.283	8.30	4.11
Linsky, Lenny	R-R	6-2	220	3-4-90	0	0	0.00	4	0	0	0	5	3	0	0	1	3	.188	.250	.125	5.79	1.93
Mateo, Victor	R-R	6-5	180	7-27-89	12	6	3.98	26	20	1	1	124	134	65	55	14	37	102	.278	.320	.241	7.38	2.68
McEachern, Jason	R-R	6-2	160	10-12-90	1	2	7.20	4	4	0	0	20	28	16	16	2	5	14	.341	.353	.333	6.30	2.25
Patterson, Jimmy	R-L	6-0	190	2-9-89	7	4	2.95	39	2	0	1	85	76	31	28	8	25	93	.235	.164	.279	9.81	2.64
Rearick, Chris	L-L	6-3	190	12-5-87	7	2	1.66	50	0	0	20	81	49	18	15	3	16	89	.173	.130	.194	9.85	1.77
Riefenhauser, C.J.	L-L	6-0	180	1-30-90	6	5	2.31	18	18	1	0	101	77	32	26	7	25	99	.212	.120	.261	8.79	2.22
Rodriguez, Wilking	R-R	6-1	160	3-2-90	0	3	4.66	9	9	0	0	37	38	21	19	3	14	34	.266	.280	.250	8.35	3.44
Romero, Enny	L-L	6-3	165	1-24-91	5	5	4.26	26	26	0	0	114	104	67	54	9	68	140	.245	.237	.248	11.05	5.37
Stabelfeld, Matt	L-L	5-10	185	8-21-86	1	1	3.98	11	0	0	0	22	22	9	9	0	11	29	.275	.304	.263	12.84	4.87
Suero, Eliazer	R-R	6-4	170	6-7-89	8	6	4.43	27	10	0	2	108	122	65	53	12	36	72	.288	.322	.261	6.02	3.01

Fielding

Catcher	PCT	G	PO	A	E	DP	PB
Acosta	1.000	22	156	28	0	1	1
Bailey	.987	69	514	76	8	9	9
Castillo	.994	20	143	14	1	0	0
Holloway	.992	14	105	12	1	0	2
Torres	.990	24	178	25	2	3	1

First Base	PCT	G	PO	A	E	DP
Schwaner	1.000	1	1	0	0	0
Tinoco	1.000	23	150	9	0	8
Torres	1.000	2	12	0	0	0
Wunderlich	.993	120	952	64	7	82

Second Base	PCT	G	PO	A	E	DP
Estrada	.981	43	66	85	3	20
Guevara	.977	64	98	153	6	23
Price	.975	37	61	97	4	19

Third Base	PCT	G	PO	A	E	DP
Cedeno	.905	47	27	78	11	6
Estrada	.727	7	6	16	6	0
Motter	1.000	2	0	5	0	0
Price	.941	76	52	138	12	9
Tinoco	.926	11	12	13	2	1

Shortstop	PCT	G	PO	A	E	DP
Dietrich	.952	122	190	306	25	65
Estrada	.947	22	36	54	5	8

Outfield	PCT	G	PO	A	E	DP
Estrada	1.000	2	3	0	0	0
Glaesmann	.989	52	85	3	1	0
Kiermaier	.974	115	279	20	8	6
Price	.000	1	0	0	0	0
Rogers	.957	104	219		5	10	1
Schwaner	1.000	96	140	9	0	0
Tinoco	.984	62	113	7	2	3

HUDSON VALLEY RENEGADES

SHORT-SEASON

NEW YORK-PENN LEAGUE

Batting	B-T	HT	WT	DOB	AVG	vLH	vRH	G	AB	R	H	2B	3B	HR	RBI	BB	HBP	SH	SF	SO	SB	CS	SLG	OBP
Biagini, Tanner	R-R	6-2	200	8-6-88	.215	.185	.223	35	121	12	26	8	0	0	5	4	1	0	1	29	1	1	.281	.244
Bryles, Brian	R-R	6-1	170	11-4-89	.211	.233	.205	62	199	15	42	13	3	0	20	16	2	0	1	62	15	4	.307	.275
Carter, Kes	L-L	6-2	205	3-3-90	.231	.000	.273	3	13	2	3	0	0	0	1	2	0	0	0	1	0	0	.231	.333
Church, Raymond	R-R	5-11	180	11-3-88	.247	.179	.266	55	182	20	45	14	1	0	16	16	3	0	2	39	4	2	.335	.315
Guillen, Cesar	R-R	6-1	175	3-15-89	.239	.171	.259	53	180	18	43	8	0	2	10	20	0	0	1	36	4	3	.317	.313
Holloway, Kyle	R-R	6-0	204	6-13-88	.187	.105	.219	39	134	15	25	7	0	4	22	12	4	0	1	44	0	0	.328	.272
Koscso, Jonathan	R-R	5-11	175	10-28-88	.333	.167	.394	17	45	8	15	2	0	0	3	7	1	0	0	5	2	1	.378	.434
Luis, Diogenes	B-R	5-10	169	5-7-87	.143	.308	.083	15	49	6	7	0	1	0	3	6	0	0	0	18	3	2	.184	.236
Lyerly, Craige	R-R	5-11	175	8-24-88	.285	.295	.281	50	172	23	49	2	1	3	19	15	3	0	2	34	17	3	.360	.349
Malm, Jeff	L-L	6-3	225	10-31-90	.257	.232	.267	73	249	36	64	15	0	12	47	38	13	0	1	65	3	2	.462	.382
Olivares, Gerardo	R-R	6-0	187	8-14-88	.298	.407	.246	24	84	11	25	6	2	2	18	8	0	0	1	20	0	0	.488	.355
Querecuto, Juniel	B-R	5-9	155	9-19-92	.241	.290	.226	70	274	36	66	11	3	0	24	20	1	0	3	45	8	3	.303	.292
Reginatto, Leonardo	R-R	6-2	180	4-10-90	.198	.115	.226	63	207	20	41	5	0	2	17	12	4	0	1	47	11	3	.251	.254
Rice, Matt	R-R	6-3	195	5-8-89	.286	.333	.270	54	192	25	55	7	0	3	21	22	6	0	1	39	5	2	.370	.376
Segovia, Alejandro	R-R	6-0	185	4-27-90	.276	.375	.260	18	58	7	16	2	0	2	9	6	2	0	0	10	0	0	.414	.364
Winder, Chris	R-R	5-10	157	9-28-89	.225	.254	.217	72	271	45	61	8	5	3	21	25	5	0	1	80	16	5	.325	.301

Pitching

Pitching	B-T	HT	WT	DOB	W	L	ERA	G	GS	CG	SV	IP	H	R	ER	HR	BB	SO	AVG	vLH	vRH	K/9	BB/9
Bass, Andy	R-R	6-4	220	3-25-89	0	4	9.25	17	0	0	0	24	31	28	25	4	32	15	.323	.325	.321	5.55	11.84
Bellatti, Andrew	R-R	6-1	170	8-5-91	3	5	2.63	15	13	0	0	72	66	26	21	1	23	63	.250	.240	.259	7.88	2.88
Belter, Brooks	R-R	6-2	205	4-17-88	3	2	3.58	15	1	0	1	33	26	20	13	0	18	29	.215	.220	.211	7.99	4.96
Carpenter, Ryan	L-L	6-5	235	8-22-90	2	1	0.76	8	4	0	0	24	9	2	2	0	4	26	.113	.118	.111	9.89	1.52
Colon, Roque	R-R	5-10	155	4-23-88	0	2	12.60	4	0	0	0	10	20	15	14	1	5	5	.435	.417	.441	4.50	4.50
Cononie, Charlie	R-R	6-7	210	2-25-89	1	1	2.43	16	0	0	6	30	17	11	8	0	12	27	.177	.258	.138	8.19	3.64
Dickmann, Robert	L-L	5-11	200	12-25-86	3	3	1.65	17	5	0	1	49	42	26	9	4	13	45	.221	.139	.240	8.27	2.39
Floethe, Jake	R-R	6-3	205	5-29-89	1	1	1.71	7	5	0	0	21	21	5	4	0	7	15	.266	.265	.267	6.43	3.00
Geith, T.J.	L-L	6-4	170	6-27-89	0	1	1.80	2	0	0	0	5	4	1	1	0	0	4	.250	.200	.273	7.20	0.00
Gomez, Roberto E	R-R	6-5	178	8-3-89	1	0	0.00	2	1	0	0	7	2	0	0	0	3	4	.087	.071	.111	5.14	3.86
Jannis, Mickey	R-R	6-0	190	12-16-87	4	3	2.92	18	2	0	2	52	48	24	17	2	16	42	.250	.239	.260	7.22	2.75
Laufer, Dave	R-R	6-2	210	9-22-88	1	2	5.40	17	0	0	0	25	28	20	15	3	11	15	.286	.323	.269	5.40	3.96
Leary, Drew	L-R	6-4	225	12-9-87	0	0	3.75	3	1	0	2	12	10	5	5	1	2	6	.233	.143	.276	4.50	1.50
Linsky, Lenny	R-R	6-2	220	3-4-90	3	0	1.46	12	0	0	3	25	19	11	4	2	6	27	.207	.235	.190	9.85	2.19
Markel, Parker	R-R	6-4	220	9-15-90	3	4	3.14	13	13	0	0	57	42	26	20	3	23	44	.207	.191	.215	6.91	3.61
McEachern, Jason	R-R	6-2	160	10-12-90	3	0	2.38	7	1	0	0	34	21	12	9	1	9	35	.175	.241	.121	9.26	2.38
Partridge, Jacob	L-L	6-3	200	12-21-90	3	6	3.89	15	15	0	0	74	81	45	32	6	23	57	.283	.239	.292	6.93	2.80
Rodriguez, Wilking	R-R	6-1	160	3-2-90	1	1	6.48	2	2	0	0	8	10	6	6	0	2	9	.303	.333	.278	9.72	2.16
Shull, Trevor	R-R	6-4	180	8-7-90	0	2	4.67	6	6	0	0	27	21	14	14	0	16	14	.231	.324	.175	4.67	5.33
Thomas, Stayton	R-R	5-11	180	4-7-89	3	0	2.05	14	1	0	2	26	26	6	6	1	10	18	.257	.357	.186	6.15	3.42
Woodall, Justin	L-L	6-2	210	11-6-87	2	1	2.25	19	0	0	4	24	18	9	6	1	14	27	.214	.250	.203	10.13	5.25

Fielding

Catcher	PCT	G	PO	A	E	DP	PB
Holloway	.985	24	175	23	3	2	1
Olivares	.987	10	65	11	1	2	1
Rice	.991	33	209	17	2	1	7
Segovia	1.000	10	80	8	0	0	0

First Base	PCT	G	PO	A	E	DP
Biagini	.957	8	63	4	3	10
Malm	.993	70	550	37	4	68
Reginatto	1.000	1	0	1	0	0

Second Base	PCT	G	PO	A	E	DP
Church	.958	55	99	153	11	43

	PCT	G	PO	A	E	DP
Koscso	.959	12	24	23	2	9
Luis	.938	10	17	28	3	11

Third Base	PCT	G	PO	A	E	DP
Biagini	.867	22	16	36	8	2
Koscso	1.000	4	1	9	0	0
Luis	1.000	1	1	1	0	0
Reginatto	.951	55	29	106	7	20

Shortstop	PCT	G	PO	A	E	DP
Luis	1.000	2	2	5	0	1
Querecuto	.912	68	110	161	26	44
Reginatto	.897	7	15	20	4	5

Outfield	PCT	G	PO	A	E	DP
Bryles	.966	62	110	4	4	0
Carter	1.000	1	3	0	0	0
Guillen	.953	46	80	2	4	1
Koscso	1.000	1	1	0	0	0
Luis	.875	2	7	0	1	0
Lyerly	.978	50	83	4	2	1
Winder	.994	72	147	13	1	1

PRINCETON RAYS

ROOKIE

APPALACHIAN LEAGUE

Batting	B-T	HT	WT	DOB	AVG	vLH	vRH	G	AB	R	H	2B	3B	HR	RBI	BB	HBP	SH	SF	SO	SB	CS	SLG	OBP
Brett, Ryan	R-R	5-9	180	10-9-91	.300	.234	.316	61	240	42	72	22	5	3	24	26	2	0	2	24	21	3	.471	.370
Caminero, Leandro	R-R	6-1	185	10-24-89	.330	.310	.336	48	188	25	62	9	6	3	22	5	0	0	0	38	6	7	.489	.347
DePew, Jake	R-R	6-1	220	3-1-92	.214	.125	.230	46	159	14	34	5	0	1	22	20	0	0	5	27	6	4	.264	.293
Dixon, Deshun	R-L	6-0	190	9-20-91	.211	.267	.195	56	199	22	42	8	4	5	20	14	0	0	0	49	5	3	.367	.263
Gonzalez, Felix	B-R	5-10	165	4-4-90	.289	.000	.338	32	90	9	26	3	1	0	6	4	0	0	0	18	3	1	.344	.319
Hager, Jake	R-R	6-1	170	3-4-93	.269	.186	.293	47	193	29	52	11	1	4	17	9	1	0	0	26	5	7	.399	.305
Koscso, Jonathan	R-R	5-11	175	10-28-88	.269	.167	.300	13	26	6	7	0	0	1	3	4	4	0	0	3	1	1	.385	.441
Motter, Taylor	R-R	6-1	190	9-18-89	.323	.391	.311	46	158	37	51	13	0	4	23	33	1	0	3	26	22	2	.481	.436
O'Conner, Justin	R-R	6-0	190	3-31-92	.157	.111	.169	48	178	18	28	8	0	9	29	17	1	0	1	78	4	1	.354	.234
Rodriguez, Junior	R-R	6-3	220	1-24-88	.280	.417	.237	33	100	16	28	7	0	6	14	15	1	0	2	28	0	0	.530	.373
Sale, Josh	L-R	6-0	215	7-5-91	.210	.257	.201	60	214	24	45	11	3	4	35	32	0	0	1	41	4	3	.346	.289
Seitzer, Cameron	L-R	6-5	220	1-11-90	.285	.333	.277	64	221	30	63	14	0	11	42	43	3	0	1	46	6	3	.498	.407
Terry, Ryan	R-R	6-0	185	6-8-89	.226	.267	.212	36	115	20	26	5	1	1	13	6	5	0	0	33	4	0	.313	.294
Vettleson, Drew	L-R	6-1	185	7-19-91	.282	.211	.296	61	234	33	66	13	4	7	40	27	2	0	3	53	20	6	.462	.357

Pitching	B-T	HT	WT	DOB	W	L	ERA	G	GS	CG	SV	IP	H	R	ER	HR	BB	SO	AVG	vLH	vRH	K/9	BB/9
Ames, Jeff	R-R	6-2	225	1-31-91	4	2	7.12	11	5	0	1	30	40	25	24	4	7	39	.317	.333	.308	11.57	2.08
Crawford, Shay	L-L	6-2	190	12-12-87	2	2	5.29	10	0	0	1	17	15	12	10	0	5	23	.227	.280	.195	12.18	2.65
Henderson, Brandon	L-L	6-3	175	4-19-92	4	2	4.30	13	7	0	2	59	65	36	28	7	15	44	.278	.229	.299	6.75	2.30
Irvine, Luke	R-R	6-1	200	12-1-88	0	3	5.33	16	0	0	1	27	31	18	16	1	18	32	.287	.256	.308	10.67	6.00
James, Kevin	L-L	6-4	190	10-1-90	1	2	7.91	11	0	0	0	19	20	19	17	0	27	14	.282	.095	.360	6.52	12.57
Kendall, Ian	R-R	6-0	205	11-11-91	1	4	4.31	14	12	0	1	54	44	30	26	7	30	33	.224	.192	.246	5.47	4.97
Kubiak, Dave	R-R	6-7	245	8-3-89	2	1	3.26	12	0	0	3	19	21	9	7	3	3	27	.273	.346	.235	12.57	1.40
Lopez, Reinaldo	R-R	6-2	221	4-27-91	2	4	3.66	14	6	0	1	52	59	32	21	3	15	28	.291	.282	.296	4.88	2.61
Molina, Jose	L-L	5-11	160	6-26-91	1	1	2.55	13	1	0	1	42	32	17	12	5	20	44	.209	.200	.214	9.35	4.25
Proctor, Marcus	R-R	6-3	170	8-21-91	1	6	4.32	14	0	0	3	42	32	23	20	6	11	39	.211	.241	.191	8.42	2.38
Quinonez, Eduar	R-R	6-3	182	8-9-89	1	5	6.61	12	10	0	0	48	47	39	35	8	24	26	.266	.253	.275	4.53	4.91
Rivero, Felipe	L-L	6-0	151	7-5-91	3	3	4.62	14	12	0	0	60	64	36	31	7	13	57	.264	.234	.272	8.50	1.94
Silvestre, Pedro	R-R	6-2	185	10-23-89	4	0	4.01	15	0	0	0	34	35	23	15	7	14	29	.265	.216	.296	7.75	3.74
Smith, Garret	R-R	6-1	202	10-17-88	0	0	0.82	10	0	0	4	11	8	1	1	0	5	5	.211	.200	.214	4.09	4.09
Spann, Matt	L-L	6-7	185	2-17-91	4	1	3.13	14	10	0	0	63	58	26	22	5	18	61	.239	.210	.249	8.67	2.56
Swilley, Matt	R-R	6-2	175	12-19-90	0	2	3.57	11	3	0	0	23	17	11	9	1	18	24	.202	.146	.253	9.53	7.15

Fielding

Catcher	PCT	G	PO	A	E	DP	PB
DePew	.989	33	246	35	3	3	2
O'Conner	.971	36	262	36	9	4	8
Rodriguez	1.000	4	9	0	0	0	1

First Base	PCT	G	PO	A	E	DP
Rodriguez	.988	11	74	5	1	12
Seitzer	.984	61	510	43	9	33

Second Base	PCT	G	PO	A	E	DP
Brett	.931	59	84	160	18	26
Gonzalez	1.000	5	6	8	0	0

	PCT	G	PO	A	E	DP	
Koscso	.960	7	6	18	1	5	
Terry	.889	3	2	6	1	1	

Third Base	PCT	G	PO	A	E	DP
Gonzalez	.917	17	11	22	3	1
Koscso	.909	3	6	4	1	2
Motter	.877	25	22	42	9	4
Rodriguez	1.000	2	1	4	0	0
Terry	.900	31	24	48	8	6

Shortstop	PCT	G	PO	A	E	DP
Gonzalez	.967	8	14	15	1	5

	PCT	G	PO	A	E	DP
Hager	.962	46	78	123	8	24
Motter	.940	18	29	49	5	7

Outfield	PCT	G	PO	A	E	DP
Caminero	.924	38	80	5	7	1
Dixon	.974	55	105	6	3	2
Gonzalez	1.000	3	3	0	0	0
Koscso	.000	1	0	0	0	0
Sale	.979	56	89	3	2	0
Vettleson	.974	56	107	6	3	4

GCL RAYS   ROOKIE

GULF COAST LEAGUE

Batting	B-T	HT	WT	DOB	AVG	vLH	vRH	G	AB	R	H	2B	3B	HR	RBI	BB	HBP	SH	SF	SO	SB	CS	SLG	OBP
Alexander, John	L-L	6-5	200	4-25-93	.314	.261	.357	12	51	4	16	4	1	2	11	0	1	0	1	12	0	0	.549	.321
Antunez, Ismel	L-R	5-7	166	6-17-91	.235	.318	.193	46	132	19	31	10	0	0	10	12	3	0	1	41	7	7	.311	.311
Bourdon, Mike	R-R	6-3	215	10-12-88	.236	.182	.273	23	55	6	13	2	0	0	3	3	6	0	0	11	1	1	.273	.344
Choate, Brandon	R-R	6-0	205	5-7-89	.275	.389	.212	24	51	4	14	5	0	1	3	7	3	0	0	12	0	0	.431	.393
Dorville, Edward	B-R	6-1	185	11-5-88	.194	.159	.211	44	139	16	27	3	3	3	14	9	2	0	0	57	16	3	.324	.253
Eierman, Johnny	R-R	6-1	195	8-23-92	.254	.308	.212	16	59	7	15	3	2	1	5	5	2	0	1	17	1	1	.424	.328
George, Darryl	R-R	6-1	213	3-14-93	.243	.136	.288	24	74	11	18	3	0	0	7	10	4	0	1	9	4	2	.284	.360
Glaesmann, Todd	R-R	6-4	220	10-24-90	.216	.125	.241	11	37	7	8	1	0	0	5	2	0	0	0	10	6	1	.243	.341
Goetzman, Granden	R-R	6-4	200	11-14-92	.173	.250	.128	25	75	8	13	3	0	0	8	6	1	0	0	17	6	1	.213	.262
Harris, James	R-R	6-1	180	8-7-93	.165	.150	.173	45	158	17	26	6	0	0	8	13	7	0	1	39	13	4	.203	.257
Johnson, Matt	R-R	6-1	195	9-18-88	.221	.212	.225	32	104	21	23	1	0	2	10	17	1	0	2	23	13	1	.288	.331
Martin, Brandon	R-R	5-11	185	8-24-92	.255	.467	.156	19	47	10	12	1	0	1	3	7	3	0	0	12	5	3	.340	.386
Morillo, Julian	R-R	5-11	167	12-10-91	.194	.186	.198	41	124	13	24	4	3	0	12	17	1	0	1	30	3	3	.274	.294
Narvaez, Omar	B-R	5-10	172	2-10-92	.221	.143	.255	47	140	11	31	4	0	0	15	16	1	0	1	16	1	1	.250	.304
Perez, Cesar	R-R	6-2	190	3-8-93	.147	.152	.144	44	150	8	22	0	0	0	12	11	1	0	2	40	1	0	.147	.207
Quinonez, Jonathan	R-R	6-1	187	11-27-90	.293	.319	.276	40	123	18	36	2	2	1	18	12	3	0	2	22	11	2	.366	.364
Rodriguez, Hector	R-R	6-2	210	11-5-89	.194	.243	.167	32	103	10	20	3	0	1	13	9	1	0	3	21	1	1	.252	.259
Segovia, Alejandro	R-R	6-0	185	4-27-90	.071	.000	.100	5	14	2	1	1	0	0	0	1	0	0	0	3	0	0	.143	.133
Soriano, Ariel	R-R	5-11	160	11-9-90	.220	.266	.197	53	191	24	42	11	2	3	22	14	4	0	1	26	10	5	.346	.286
Tomkins, Ian	R-R	6-3	205	2-27-89	.444	.600	.250	4	9	1	4	0	0	0	1	0	0	0	0	0	0	0	.444	.444
Torrez, Riccio	R-R	6-0	205	10-14-89	.231	.211	.242	13	52	4	12	1	0	2	3	1	1	0	0	12	1	1	.365	.259
Velasquez, Isaias	R-R	5-11	155	5-7-88	.222	.500	.143	2	9	1	2	1	0	0	0	0	0	0	0	1	0	0	.333	.222

Pitching	B-T	HT	WT	DOB	W	L	ERA	G	GS	CG	SV	IP	H	R	ER	HR	BB	SO	AVG	vLH	vRH	K/9	BB/9
Bream, Dan	R-R	6-6	185	8-16-88	0	2	3.91	14	0	0	1	23	27	17	10	2	11	21	.290	.227	.347	8.22	4.30
Butler, Zach	R-R	6-3	200	7-28-89	2	1	1.69	16	0	0	0	27	19	6	5	1	14	17	.209	.173	.256	5.74	4.73
Crawford, Shay	L-L	6-2	190	12-12-87	1	0	0.00	6	0	0	0	12	5	1	0	0	1	21	.128	.133	.125	16.20	0.77
Cruz, Joe	R-R	6-4	190	7-20-88	2	0	0.00	4	1	1	0	14	6	0	0	0	2	16	.133	.125	.143	10.54	1.32
Duarte, Hugo	R-R	6-1	169	1-7-90	3	5	3.33	12	6	1	0	54	46	22	20	3	17	39	.237	.221	.256	6.50	2.83
Echarry, Eli	R-R	6-1	150	7-1-92	0	5	7.05	12	6	0	0	45	56	39	35	4	19	38	.306	.275	.337	7.66	3.83
Faria, Jacob	R-R	6-3	175	7-30-93	0	1	2.87	6	2	0	0	16	15	6	5	1	1	14	.250	.188	.321	8.04	0.57
Fuentes, Felix	R-R	6-2	205	5-17-87	0	0	1.08	4	2	0	0	8	5	1	1	0	3	10	.172	.231	.125	10.80	3.24
Geith, T.J.	L-L	6-4	170	6-27-89	4	1	2.13	16	0	0	4	25	21	11	6	1	7	30	.216	.280	.194	10.66	2.49
Gil, Isaac	R-R	6-5	230	10-8-91	1	1	5.14	12	0	0	0	14	7	12	8	1	15	10	.140	.143	.138	6.43	9.64
Gomez, Roberto E	R-R	6-5	178	8-3-89	3	4	2.48	11	8	0	0	54	41	22	15	3	9	42	.203	.239	.161	6.96	1.49
Guerrero, Joan	L-L	6-2	170	1-22-91	1	5	6.68	12	2	0	0	31	47	30	23	0	11	20	.348	.200	.374	5.81	3.19
Havlicek, Stepan	R-L	6-1	160	2-25-93	0	1	4.80	11	0	0	0	15	19	8	8	2	7	8	.328	.000	.365	4.80	4.20
Kubiak, Dave	R-R	6-7	245	8-3-89	0	1	3.00	3	0	0	0	6	5	3	2	1	1	9	.217	.267	.125	13.50	1.50
Orta, Ricky	R-R	6-2	195	11-6-84	0	0	1.13	4	0	0	0	8	7	2	1	0	0	10	.250	.313	.167	11.25	0.00
Shull, Trevor	R-R	6-4	180	8-7-90	1	0	2.51	5	5	0	0	14	10	4	4	0	4	6	.196	.167	.222	3.77	2.51
Smith, Shawn	R-L	6-3	180	9-9-90	1	1	2.25	14	0	0	1	32	23	9	8	2	10	21	.204	.192	.207	5.91	2.81
Snell, Blake	L-L	6-4	180	12-4-92	1	3	3.08	14	8	0	0	26	30	9	9	0	11	26	.291	.261	.300	8.89	3.76
Suarez, Albert	R-R	6-2	185	10-8-89	0	0	1.38	4	0	0	0	13	10	3	2	0	5	10	.213	.208	.217	6.92	3.46
Suero, Bruedlin	L-L	6-4	170	2-28-90	3	4	2.63	11	8	0	0	55	48	24	16	5	8	36	.226	.240	.222	5.93	1.32
Thomas, Stayton	R-R	5-11	180	4-7-89	0	0	0.00	4	0	0	1	6	1	0	0	0	0	2	.059	.167	.000	3.18	0.00
Turner, Ryan	R-R	6-5	195	8-28-88	1	1	6.35	13	0	0	0	17	33	14	12	2	8	17	.423	.528	.333	9.00	4.24
Yates, Kirby	R-R	5-10	170	3-25-87	0	1	2.70	4	0	0	0	7	6	3	2	0	2	3	.231	.188	.300	4.05	2.70

Fielding

Catcher	PCT	G	PO	A	E	DP	PB
Bourdon	1.000	18	109	10	0	0	1
Choate	.986	22	121	21	2	2	7
Harris	1.000	1	5	3	0	0	6
Narvaez	.995	29	172	29	1	1	5
Segovia	1.000	2	2	0	0	0	0
Tomkins	1.000	4	15	1	0	0	0

First Base	PCT	G	PO	A	E	DP
Alexander	.977	10	77	8	2	9

	PCT	G	PO	A	E	DP
Bourdon	.000	1	0	0	0	0
George	.979	15	128	10	3	11
Narvaez	1.000	15	111	10	0	10
Quinonez	.875	1	7	0	1	0
Rodriguez	.991	25	206	10	2	17

Second Base	PCT	G	PO	A	E	DP
Morillo	.973	27	40	67	3	13
Quinonez	1.000	6	6	11	0	2
Soriano	.937	29	70	78	10	19

Third Base	PCT	G	PO	A	E	DP
George	.950	6	8	11	1	2
Morillo	.889	4	2	14	2	2
Perez	.891	42	34	88	15	5
Quinonez	.000	2	0	0	0	0
Soriano	.667	2	1	3	2	0
Torrez	1.000	9	4	18	0	2

Shortstop	PCT	G	PO	A	E	DP
Eierman	.940	11	12	35	3	4

Martin	.957	11	15	29	2	5
Morillo	.939	9	15	16	2	5
Quinonez	.923	17	21	51	6	12
Soriano	.905	17	20	47	7	4

Outfield	PCT	G	PO	A	E	DP
Antunez	1.000	45	66	5	0	0
Bourdon	1.000	1	1	0	0	0
Dorville	.987	43	72	4	1	1
Glaesmann	1.000	5	8	1	0	0
Harris	.959	39	69	2	3	0

Johnson	.985	31	62	3	1	0
Narvaez	1.000	1	1	0	0	0
Quinonez	.933	12	13	1	1	0
Rodriguez	.933	6	13	1	1	0
Soriano	1.000	7	8	0	0	0
Velasquez	1.000	2	5	0	0	0

DSL RAYS   ROOKIE

DOMINICAN SUMMER LEAGUE

Batting	B-T	HT	WT	DOB	AVG	vLH	vRH	G	AB	R	H	2B	3B	HR	RBI	BB	HBP	SH	SF	SO	SB	CS	SLG	OBP
Adolfo, Roberto	R-R	6-1	175	3-31-91	.226	.325	.195	49	168	19	38	6	0	0	23	15	3	0	4	34	6	3	.262	.295
Aguero, Ismael	R-R	6-0	185	6-19-93	.323	.333	.321	40	127	16	41	16	2	2	21	10	4	0	0	21	1	1	.528	.390
Araiza, Jesus	R-R	5-11	185	6-19-93	.256	.385	.219	50	176	29	45	11	0	6	27	28	6	0	3	40	2	0	.420	.371
Araujo, Yoel	R-R	6-0	190	12-3-92	.221	.209	.224	57	190	30	42	11	2	5	23	32	5	0	0	76	6	2	.379	.348
Calderon, Jorge	R-R	5-11	170	2-8-93	.163	.182	.158	48	123	15	20	6	1	0	10	16	3	0	0	50	3	3	.228	.275
De Castro, Raynill	R-R	6-3	175	12-11-89	.208	.167	.220	24	77	12	16	6	0	2	13	13	1	0	0	20	1	1	.364	.330
Infante, Jhancarlos	R-R	6-0	180	10-12-89	.313	.222	.333	21	48	10	15	2	0	0	2	3	3	0	0	6	1	0	.354	.389
Maldonado, Darwin	R-R	6-0	160	7-10-89	.254	.167	.289	18	63	11	16	2	0	0	6	7	1	0	1	17	3	2	.286	.333
Marte, Luis	R-R	6-3	180	2-23-91	.203	.149	.217	65	222	28	45	4	2	2	24	22	10	0	7	80	7	4	.266	.295
Medina, Julio	R-R	5-10	188	12-26-90	.224	.143	.244	36	107	22	24	8	0	1	12	15	5	0	1	16	3	2	.327	.344
Natera, Jiminson	R-R	6-0	180	4-10-92	.273	.226	.287	37	139	18	38	5	3	0	10	16	3	0	2	37	7	0	.353	.331
Paulino, Enmanuel	R-R	6-1	175	11-28-93	.247	.333	.224	53	182	30	45	11	0	0	14	21	2	0	1	60	3	4	.308	.330
Rojas, Jose	R-R	6-0	175	3-11-93	.188	.429	.146	19	48	8	9	1	0	0	1	7	0	0	0	7	1	1	.208	.291
Rosa, Adderly	B-R	6-0	167	7-4-91	.269	.132	.299	64	212	34	57	12	3	2	28	45	2	0	3	40	16	9	.382	.397
Rosario, Francisco	R-R	6-1	175	1-26-91	.265	.273	.263	28	68	8	18	4	0	0	1	9	1	0	1	8	0	0	.324	.354
Simon, Alexander	B-R	6-2	182	9-28-92	.265	.302	.253	60	223	26	59	10	4	0	27	28	1	0	2	49	14	7	.345	.346
Tapia, Juan	B-R	6-0	156	3-1-92	.238	.091	.290	12	42	1	10	2	0	0	2	1	0	0	0	18	2	2	.286	.256

Pitching	B-T	HT	WT	DOB	W	L	ERA	G	GS	CG	SV	IP	H	R	ER	HR	BB	SO	AVG	vLH	vRH	K/9	BB/9
Almonte, Yomelbin	R-R	6-0	202	2-2-93	0	3	4.41	8	5	0	0	16	10	9	8	1	9	6	.179	.000	.222	3.31	4.96
Alonzo, Jose	R-R	6-4	191	2-24-93	2	7	4.11	13	11	0	0	50	49	35	23	1	24	41	.246	.294	.236	7.33	4.29
Arguila, Nelson	R-R	6-0	180	9-4-88	0	0	0.00	2	0	0	1	3	1	0	0	0	3	4	.111	.000	.143	13.50	10.13
Armenta, Oscar	R-L	5-11	170	10-15-93	4	2	3.12	12	6	0	0	52	41	20	18	4	11	51	.220	.214	.221	8.83	1.90
Cano, Joselito	L-L	6-5	190	9-16-92	2	0	1.85	16	1	0	0	34	23	10	7	0	22	36	.193	.222	.191	9.53	5.82
Cedeno, Carlos	R-R	6-2	180	7-19-90	2	5	4.54	14	9	1	0	40	41	26	20	1	21	24	.270	.243	.278	5.45	4.76
De La Cruz, Dionicio	L-L	6-1	170	4-1-92	3	1	2.57	18	0	0	1	28	23	16	8	1	27	24	.219	.200	.220	7.71	8.68
De La Cruz, Geisel	L-L	6-0	139	4-11-93	1	3	2.02	13	12	0	0	58	45	23	13	1	16	59	.216	.235	.215	9.16	2.48
Franco, Jose	R-R	6-2	180	9-11-90	0	0	4.61	8	0	0	1	14	13	9	7	2	6	6	.255	.125	.279	3.95	3.95
Garcia, Carlos	R-R	6-2	218	12-1-90	5	1	2.18	15	0	0	0	33	26	11	8	0	28	25	.220	.200	.223	6.82	7.64
Gomez, Eduardo	R-R	6-0	165	12-31-89	0	0	8.44	5	0	0	0	5	5	7	5	0	6	3	.238	.167	.267	5.06	10.13
Gomez, Roberto E	R-R	6-5	178	8-3-89	2	1	4.26	3	2	0	0	13	16	6	6	1	4	12	.330	.333	.319	8.53	2.84
Guerrero, Joan	L-L	6-2	170	1-22-92	1	0	1.42	3	3	0	0	13	7	5	2	0	8	8	.159	.333	.146	5.68	5.68
Guerrero, Luis	R-R	6-0	170	8-20-90	1	2	4.58	10	0	0	2	18	14	9	9	1	10	15	.230	.353	.182	7.64	5.09
Hernandez, Wilmer	R-R	6-3	175	8-29-91	1	2	2.50	11	10	0	0	36	34	15	10	3	5	16	.248	.120	.277	4.00	1.25
Mercedes, Luis	L-L	5-11	170	3-29-91	0	0	6.75	6	0	0	2	8	8	6	6	2	4	6	.267	.000	.286	6.75	4.50
Nina, Carlos	R-R	6-3	185	3-29-93	0	1	45.00	4	0	0	0	2	3	11	10	0	12	1	.375	.000	.375	4.50	54.00
Polanco, Jose	R-R	6-5	171	1-29-91	1	0	12.27	5	0	0	0	7	10	11	10	0	14	2	.333	.500	.321	2.45	17.18
Ramirez, Emanuel	R-R	6-4	215	11-20-89	0	0	0.68	5	0	0	0	13	13	2	1	0	2	11	.260	.167	.289	7.43	1.35
Rodriguez, Jorge	R-R	5-11	187	12-15-91	2	2	1.00	19	0	0	7	36	24	12	4	2	8	35	.178	.250	.165	8.75	2.00
Rodriguez, Junior	R-R	6-0	189	2-8-89	0	0	3.60	2	1	0	0	5	3	2	2	1	2	4	.167	.000	.214	7.20	3.60
Soriano, Dauris	L-L	6-1	156	12-16-89	0	0	14.21	3	0	0	0	6	10	10	10	2	5	2	.357	.000	.357	2.84	7.11
Suero, Bruedlin	L-L	6-4	170	2-28-90	0	2	3.21	3	2	0	1	14	16	7	5	0	2	8	.296	.167	.313	5.14	1.29
Taveras, Ricardo	R-R	6-2	210	10-17-87	3	0	4.00	13	0	0	3	27	14	14	12	1	22	28	.154	.091	.174	9.33	7.33
Torres, Jose	R-R	6-2	180	4-18-91	5	1	1.29	10	8	0	0	49	31	17	7	1	15	25	.174	.200	.167	4.62	2.77

Fielding

Catcher	PCT	G	PO	A	E	DP	PB
Araiza	.978	47	287	68	8	1	10
Infante	.973	12	63	9	2	0	2
Rojas	.974	12	61	14	2	0	4
Rosario	.931	4	24	3	2	0	1

First Base	PCT	G	PO	A	E	DP
Aguero	.984	33	239	12	4	21
Araujo	1.000	1	7	0	0	1
De Castro	.972	17	134	4	4	12
Medina	.982	8	52	4	1	6
Rosario	.994	24	166	4	1	9

Second Base	PCT	G	PO	A	E	DP
Adolfo	.935	8	15	14	2	4

Medina	.968	7	19	11	1	2
Paulino	.909	3	8	12	2	4
Rosa	.982	55	134	132	5	27
Tapia	.857	1	5	1	1	1

Third Base	PCT	G	PO	A	E	DP
Adolfo	.808	12	3	18	5	1
Aguero	1.000	1	1	6	0	1
Medina	.881	13	12	25	5	2
Simon	.890	48	44	102	18	9

Shortstop	PCT	G	PO	A	E	DP
Adolfo	.933	5	4	10	1	0
Paulino	.903	50	64	141	22	22
Rosa	.906	8	13	16	3	2

Tapia	.900	11	14	31	5	5

Outfield	PCT	G	PO	A	E	DP
Adolfo	.897	15	24	2	3	0
Aguero	1.000	1	3	0	0	0
Alonzo	1.000	1	2	0	0	0
Araujo	.961	47	70	3	3	0
Calderon	.949	43	70	4	4	0
Maldonado	.973	17	36	0	1	0
Marte	.963	63	99	6	4	1
Natera	1.000	34	65	1	0	0
Rosa	1.000	2	0	1	0	0

TAMPA BAY RAYS

VENEZUELAN SUMMER LEAGUE

Batting	B-T	HT	WT	DOB	AVG	vLH	vRH	G	AB	R	H	2B	3B	HR	RBI	BB	HBP	SH	SF	SO	SB	CS	SLG	OBP
Alcala, Franklin	L-L	6-2	200	3-9-91	.192	.258	.172	38	130	13	25	5	1	0	9	7	1	0	0	42	3	2	.246	.239
Aldazoro, Gianfranco	R-R	6-1	205	4-5-94	.149	.182	.143	24	67	3	10	2	0	0	5	5	1	0	1	20	0	0	.179	.216
Antunez, Ismel	L-R	5-7	166	6-17-91	.248	.192	.263	33	125	30	31	1	0	3	10	25	2	0	1	27	22	3	.328	.379
Bellorin, Jose	R-R	6-0	160	12-14-90	.302	.463	.262	60	205	30	62	11	1	3	29	27	3	0	1	25	9	3	.410	.390
Correa, Leopoldo	L-R	6-0	186	12-3-91	.322	.370	.310	64	230	35	74	17	0	8	54	31	5	0	0	31	0	1	.500	.414
Dominguez, Wilmer	R-R	5-10	182	6-19-90	.324	.373	.307	54	188	26	61	9	1	6	32	12	1	0	2	21	4	3	.479	.365
Duran, Douglas	B-R	5-10	150	11-17-92	.276	.238	.290	64	239	45	66	12	4	4	27	39	1	0	2	41	10	10	.410	.377
Epifano, Erick	R-R	6-1	160	3-31-90	.293	.300	.291	50	164	24	48	6	0	0	12	22	1	0	0	24	6	3	.329	.380
Hernandez, Oscar	R-R	6-0	196	7-9-93	.402	.397	.403	69	239	56	96	14	1	21	66	37	15	0	3	44	3	5	.732	.503
Maldonado, Darwin	R-R	6-0	160	7-10-89	.176	.357	.108	12	51	7	9	1	0	0	3	4	0	0	1	16	3	2	.196	.232
Paez, Jose	B-R	6-0	165	8-11-93	.167	.188	.156	12	48	9	8	3	0	1	4	7	1	0	0	14	6	1	.292	.286
Paz, Franklin	R-R	6-1	166	5-7-91	.275	.340	.257	59	229	36	63	11	3	9	34	20	6	0	0	48	11	3	.467	.349
Quinonez, Jonathan	R-L	6-1	187	11-27-90	.326	.300	.333	13	46	9	15	4	0	1	4	3	3	0	0	2	1	0	.478	.404
Reyes, Keiverson	R-R	5-9	152	2-7-91	.227	.200	.235	51	154	28	35	5	1	3	21	14	11	0	1	23	3	9	.331	.333
Silva, Wester	R-L	6-0	170	1-10-92	.203	.158	.217	28	79	10	16	0	0	0	5	8	1	0	0	14	1	0	.203	.284
Suarez, Norly	R-R	5-11	156	9-17-93	.235	.000	.333	9	17	2	4	0	0	0	0	0	0	0	0	6	0	0	.235	.235
Vasquez, Erick	R-R	6-1	186	9-27-93	.222	.279	.206	57	198	26	44	10	0	7	23	14	11	0	0	86	9	5	.379	.309

Pitching	B-T	HT	WT	DOB	W	L	ERA	G	GS	CG	SV	IP	H	R	ER	HR	BB	SO	AVG	vLH	vRH	K/9	BB/9
Alvarez, Freddy	R-R	6-1	170	9-10-93	3	1	2.47	15	6	0	1	47	35	19	13	2	19	41	.200	.273	.176	7.80	3.61
Bier, Deimer	R-R	6-2	174	1-6-91	1	0	1.35	3	0	0	1	7	5	1	1	0	3	7	.227	.429	.133	9.45	4.05
Cabrera, Luis	R-R	6-2	185	8-14-90	4	1	2.84	14	12	0	0	57	48	26	18	3	25	43	.230	.246	.222	6.79	3.95
Cazorla, Kevin	R-R	6-2	190	10-14-93	0	0	7.16	14	0	0	0	28	40	30	22	7	21	13	.328	.364	.315	4.23	6.83
Centeno, Henry	R-R	6-2	174	8-24-94	4	3	3.24	14	3	0	0	42	30	18	15	4	19	24	.201	.235	.184	5.18	4.10
Fernandez, Mario	R-R	6-0	206	9-7-93	0	4	4.14	11	8	0	0	37	32	26	17	2	13	20	.227	.243	.221	4.86	3.16
Garcia, Hugo	R-R	6-2	172	7-26-92	0	0	8.10	6	0	0	0	7	12	12	6	2	7	9	.414	.400	.421	12.15	9.45
Gonzalez, Andres	R-R	6-3	205	2-20-94	0	3	1.93	13	12	0	0	56	51	17	12	1	6	34	.244	.242	.245	5.46	0.96
Gonzalez, Joynerd	R-R	6-1	150	7-22-92	4	3	2.29	17	0	0	2	35	31	14	9	0	19	19	.252	.333	.218	4.84	4.84
Guzman, Luis	R-R	6-3	222	7-21-91	4	2	4.85	13	5	0	0	39	39	35	21	2	26	22	.262	.341	.229	5.08	6.00
Hurtado, Jhefferson	R-R	6-0	181	12-19-91	1	2	3.79	9	6	0	0	19	16	12	8	0	17	5	.242	.118	.286	2.37	8.05
Marval, Johan	R-R	6-1	195	11-24-93	4	1	4.06	16	0	0	0	38	43	20	17	3	14	24	.295	.333	.276	5.73	3.35
Medina, Eduardo	R-R	6-0	170	2-24-92	4	4	2.70	23	0	0	7	40	36	17	12	1	19	35	.247	.283	.230	7.88	4.28
Orasmo, Carlos	L-L	5-9	154	12-13-91	4	1	4.93	13	0	0	1	35	47	28	19	4	7	20	.322	.185	.353	5.19	1.82
Rivero, Brohiglyn	R-R	6-3	185	5-3-93	1	2	7.52	11	7	0	0	20	18	29	17	1	21	7	.254	.263	.250	3.10	9.30
Rosal, Gregory	R-R	6-1	207	9-24-92	1	4	2.73	18	0	0	3	26	25	14	8	0	12	16	.253	.100	.319	5.47	4.10
Sabala, Wilmer	R-R	6-2	184	12-22-91	2	1	4.18	13	3	0	0	28	31	14	13	1	12	17	.290	.229	.319	5.46	3.86
Salazar, Danmar	L-L	6-1	172	7-23-92	1	0	3.45	13	0	0	0	31	35	13	12	2	14	12	.299	.333	.293	3.45	4.02
Sanchez, Yerwin	R-R	6-1	258	5-5-93	0	1	5.12	13	9	0	0	32	19	19	18	2	29	13	.184	.194	.181	3.69	8.24

Fielding

Catcher	PCT	G	PO	A	E	DP	PB
Aldazoro	.954	16	68	15	4	2	4
Dominguez	.991	21	87	23	1	3	1
Hernandez	.973	42	235	57	8	5	12
Reyes	1.000	1	3	0	0	0	0

First Base	PCT	G	PO	A	E	DP
Alcala	.985	35	307	18	5	33
Aldazoro	1.000	1	10	0	0	2
Bellorin	.992	15	115	6	1	13
Dominguez	.987	24	217	11	3	18
Quinonez	1.000	5	54	3	0	5

Second Base	PCT	G	PO	A	E	DP
Bellorin	1.000	2	10	5	0	3

	PCT	G	PO	A	E	DP
Epifano	.970	44	99	130	7	33
Quinonez	1.000	3	7	9	0	2
Reyes	.957	23	52	58	5	17
Suarez	.909	5	2	8	1	0

Third Base	PCT	G	PO	A	E	DP
Bellorin	.943	22	17	49	4	5
Correa	.897	50	42	98	16	9
Epifano	.944	7	5	12	1	2
Quinonez	1.000	2	0	1	0	0

Shortstop	PCT	G	PO	A	E	DP
Duran	.920	61	91	196	25	39
Reyes	.867	13	12	40	8	7
Suarez	.500	4	1	4	5	1

Outfield	PCT	G	PO	A	E	DP
Antunez	.973	32	69	4	2	0
Bellorin	1.000	28	32	6	0	2
Maldonado	.909	12	19	1	2	1
Paez	1.000	12	22	0	0	0
Paz	.930	45	90	3	7	2
Quinonez	.917	4	10	1	1	0
Reyes	1.000	14	25	1	0	0
Silva	1.000	27	43	1	0	0
Vasquez	.921	56	87	6	8	3

Texas Rangers

SEASON IN A SENTENCE: Sporting baseball's most productive and dynamic lineup, the Rangers cruised through the regular season with 95 victories and powered their way to a second straight American League pennant before losing an epic World Series to the Cardinals.

HIGH POINT: The Rangers were riding high after a 15-5 thrashing of the Tigers in Game Six of the AL Championship Series, their 17th win in 21 games. Texas exploded for a nine-run third inning and kept Detroit at bay to win the pennant, sending 51,508 fans at the Ballpark in Arlington into a frenzy.

LOW POINT: After twice being one strike away from winning the first World Series in franchise history in Game Six, the Rangers' season came to a close in a 6-2 Game Seven loss to the Cardinals, as Texas dropped two in a row for the first time in 47 games and became the first team to lose back-to-back Fall Classics since the 1991-92 Braves.

NOTABLE ROOKIES: With an established core, the Rangers didn't see much production from rookies in 2011. Outfielder Craig Gentry played a utility role, batting .271/.347/.346 in 183 at-bats, and Japanese reliever Yoshinori Tateyama made 39 appearances out of the bullpen and went 2-0, 4.50.

KEY TRANSACTIONS: Texas made one of the offseason's most overlooked free agent signings, inking third baseman Adrian Beltre to a six-year deal after losing out on Cliff Lee. Beltre played Gold Glove defense at the hot corner and fit well into the middle of the Rangers' lineup. Texas bolstered its bullpen at the trade deadline by acquiring relievers Mike Adams from the Padres for pitching prospects Robbie Erlin and Joe Wieland, and Koji Uehara from the Orioles for Tommy Hunter and Chris Davis. Farm director Scott Servais left to become an assistant GM with the Angels.

DOWN ON THE FARM: Despite a consistently top-ranked system in the past few years, the Rangers haven't had many homegrown talents contribute at the big league level. That will start to change as top prospects Leonys Martin, Martin Perez, Neil Ramirez and Tanner Scheppers could all contribute in 2012. Shortstop Jurickson Profar ranks as one of the game's top prospects and was the youngest player in the Futures Game. Profar was a product of the Rangers' aggressive international scouting efforts, which spent nearly $30 million in 2011 alone.

OPENING DAY PAYROLL: $92,299,264 (13th)

PLAYERS OF THE YEAR

MAJOR LEAGUE	MINOR LEAGUE
Adrian Beltre	**Jurickson Profar**
3b	ss
.296/.331/.561	(Low Class A)
32 HR, 105 RBIs	.286/.390/.493
Won 3rd Gold Glove	BA All-Star SS

ORGANIZATION LEADERS

BATTING		*Minimum 250 PA
MAJORS		
* AVG	Michael Young	.338
* OPS	Mike Napoli	1.045
HR	Adrian Beltre	32
	Ian Kinsler	32
RBI	Michael Young	106
MINORS		
* AVG	Joey Butler, Frisco/Round Rock	.313
* OBP	Andrew Clark, Hickory/Myrtle Beach	.43
* SLG	Brad Nelson, Round Rock	.501
R	Esteban German, Round Rock	94
H	Esteban German, Round Rock	153
	Renny Osuna, Frisco	153
TB	Michael Bianucci, Frisco	251
2B	Jurickson Profar, Hickory	37
3B	Ryan Strausborger, Myrtle Beach	9
	Jeremy Williams, AZL	9
HR	Michael Bianucci, Frisco	30
RBI	Chad Tracy, Round Rock	109
BB	Andrew Clark, Hickory/Myrtle Beach	83
SO	Jonathan Greene, Frisco	161
SB	Esteban German, Round Rock	44
PITCHING		#Minimum 75 IP
MAJORS		
W	Derek Holland	16
	C.J. Wilson	16
# ERA	C.J. Wilson	2.94
SO	C.J. Wilson	206
SV	Neftali Feliz	32
MINORS		
W	Zach Jackson, Round Rock	13
L	Wilfredo Boscan, Frisco/Myrtle Beach	15
# ERA	Joseph Wieland, Myrtle Beach/Frisco	1.80
G	Justin Miller, Frisco	48
GS	Three tied at	26
SV	Ryan Rodebaugh, Hickory/Myrtle Beach	16
IP	Robert Ross, Myrtle Beach/Frisco	161.1
BB	Carlos Pimentel, Frisco	80
	Matt Thompson, Hickory	80
SO	Miguel De Los Santos, Frisco/AZL/Myrtle Beach	142
# AVG	Robert Erlin, Myrtle Beach/Frisco	.219

General Manager: Jon Daniels. **Farm Director:** Scott Servais. **Scouting Director:** Kip Fagg.

Class	Team	League	W	L	PCT	Finish	Manager(s)
Majors	Texas Rangers	American	96	66	.593	2nd (14)	Ron Washington
Triple-A	Round Rock Express	Pacific Coast	87	57	.604	2nd (16)	Bobby Jones/Spike Owen
Double-A	Frisco RoughRiders	Texas	79	61	.564	2nd (8)	Steve Buechele
High A	Myrtle Beach Pelicans	Carolina	72	67	.518	3rd (8)	Jason Wood
Low A	Hickory Crawdads	South Atlantic	79	58	.577	1st (14)	Bill Richardson
Short-season	Spokane Indians	Northwest	35	41	.461	6th (8)	Tim Hulett
Rookie	AZL Rangers	Arizona	38	18	.679	2nd (13)	Hector Ortiz
Overall 2011 Minor League Record			390	302	.564	1st (30)	

ORGANIZATION STATISTICS

TEXAS RANGERS

AMERICAN LEAGUE

Batting	B-T	HT	WT	DOB	AVG	vLH	vRH	G	AB	R	H	2B	3B	HR	RBI	BB	HBP	SH	SF	SO	SB	CS	SLG	OBP
Andrus, Elvis	R-R	6-0	200	8-26-88	.279	.282	.279	150	587	96	164	27	3	5	60	56	5	0	1	74	37	12	.361	.347
Beltre, Adrian	R-R	5-11	220	4-7-79	.296	.315	.290	124	487	82	144	33	0	32	105	25	5	0	8	53	1	1	.561	.331
Blanco, Andres	B-R	5-10	180	4-11-84	.224	.190	.236	36	76	9	17	3	0	2	3	4	0	0	0	14	0	1	.342	.263
Borbon, Julio	L-L	6-0	195	2-20-86	.270	.300	.254	32	89	10	24	1	3	0	11	3	2	0	1	9	6	2	.348	.305
Chavez, Endy	L-L	6-0	170	2-7-78	.301	.357	.290	83	256	37	77	11	3	5	27	10	0	0	3	30	10	5	.426	.323
Cruz, Nelson	R-R	6-2	240	7-1-80	.263	.340	.243	124	475	64	125	28	1	29	87	33	2	0	3	116	9	5	.509	.312
Davis, Chris	L-R	6-3	230	3-17-86	.250	.294	.237	28	76	9	19	3	0	3	6	5	0	0	0	24	0	0	.408	.296
2-team total (31 Baltimore)					.266	—	—	59	199	25	53	12	0	5	19	11	0	0	0	63	1	0	.402	.305
Gentry, Craig	R-R	6-2	190	11-29-83	.271	.265	.277	64	133	26	36	5	1	1	13	10	6	0	1	27	18	0	.346	.347
German, Esteban	R-R	5-9	195	1-26-78	.455	.500	.429	11	11	6	5	1	0	1	4	1	0	0	1	1	0	.818	.462
Hamilton, Josh	L-L	6-4	240	5-21-81	.298	.260	.314	121	487	80	145	31	5	25	94	39	2	0	10	93	8	1	.536	.346
Kinsler, Ian	R-R	6-0	200	6-22-82	.255	.263	.252	155	620	121	158	34	4	32	77	89	8	0	2	71	30	4	.477	.355
Martin, Leonys	L-R	6-1	180	3-6-88	.375	.000	.375	8	8	2	3	1	0	0	0	0	0	0	0	1	0	0	.500	.375
Moreland, Mitch	L-L	6-2	230	9-6-85	.259	.234	.266	134	464	60	120	22	1	16	51	39	4	0	3	92	2	2	.414	.320
Murphy, David	L-L	6-4	205	10-18-81	.275	.215	.296	120	404	46	111	14	2	11	46	33	0	0	2	61	11	6	.401	.328
Napoli, Mike	R-R	6-0	215	10-31-81	.320	.319	.320	113	369	72	118	25	0	30	75	58	3	0	2	85	4	2	.631	.414
Quintanilla, Omar	L-R	5-9	190	10-24-81	.045	.000	.091	11	22	3	1	0	1	0	2	0	0	0	0	9	0	0	.136	.045
Teagarden, Taylor	R-R	6-1	200	12-21-83	.235	.000	.286	14	34	3	8	2	0	2	2	0	0	0	13	0	0	.294	.278
Torrealba, Yorvit	R-R	5-11	200	7-19-78	.273	.256	.280	113	396	40	108	27	1	7	37	20	0	0	2	65	0	2	.399	.306
Treanor, Matt	R-R	6-0	205	3-3-76	.000	.000	.000	7	10	0	0	0	0	0	1	1	0	0	1	4	0	0	.000	.083
2-team total (65 Kansas City)					.214	—	—	72	196	24	42	6	0	3	22	34	4	0	3	53	2	2	.291	.338
Young, Michael	R-R	6-1	200	10-19-76	.338	.361	.330	159	631	88	213	41	6	11	106	47	2	0	9	78	6	2	.474	.380

Pitching	B-T	HT	WT	DOB	W	L	ERA	G	GS	CG	SV	IP	H	R	ER	HR	BB	SO	AVG	vLH	vRH	K/9	BB/9
Adams, Mike	R-R	6-5	195	7-29-78	2	3	2.10	27	0	0	1	26	18	6	6	3	5	25	.196	.182	.216	8.77	1.75
Bush, Dave	R-R	6-2	205	11-9-79	0	1	5.79	17	3	0	0	37	47	27	24	6	9	23	.309	.293	.329	5.54	2.17
Eppley, Cody	R-R	6-5	205	10-8-85	1	1	8.00	10	0	0	0	9	11	8	8	3	5	6	.306	.385	.261	6.00	5.00
Feldman, Scott	L-R	6-6	230	2-7-83	2	1	3.94	11	2	0	0	32	25	14	14	3	10	22	.216	.155	.276	6.19	2.81
Feliz, Neftali	R-R	6-3	215	5-2-88	2	3	2.74	64	0	0	32	62	42	22	19	4	30	54	.194	.189	.200	7.80	4.33
Gonzalez, Mike	R-L	6-2	215	5-23-78	0	0	5.14	7	0	0	0	7	5	4	4	0	3	5	.208	.231	.182	6.43	3.86
2-team total (49 Baltimore)					2	2	4.39	56	0	0	1	53	51	30	26	7	21	51	—	—	—	8.61	3.54
Hamburger, Mark	R-R	6-4	195	2-5-87	1	0	4.50	5	0	0	0	8	5	4	4	0	3	6	.179	.167	.188	6.75	3.38
Harrison, Matt	L-L	6-4	240	9-16-85	14	9	3.39	31	30	0	0	186	180	79	70	13	57	126	.257	.275	.249	6.11	2.76
Holland, Derek	B-L	6-2	195	10-9-86	16	5	3.95	32	32	4	0	198	201	97	87	22	67	162	.262	.235	.272	7.36	3.05
Hunter, Tommy	R-R	6-3	280	7-3-86	1	1	2.93	8	0	0	0	15	12	6	5	1	5	10	.218	.409	.091	5.87	2.93
2-team total (12 Baltimore)					4	4	4.68	20	11	0	0	85	100	50	44	12	15	45	—	—	—	4.78	1.59
Kirkman, Michael	L-L	6-4	195	9-18-86	1	1	6.59	15	0	0	0	27	26	22	20	5	12	21	.250	.214	.274	6.91	3.95
Lewis, Colby	R-R	6-4	225	8-2-79	14	10	4.40	32	32	2	0	200	187	103	98	35	56	169	.244	.274	.204	7.59	2.52
Lowe, Mark	L-R	6-3	210	6-7-83	2	3	3.80	52	0	0	1	45	46	26	19	6	19	42	.263	.256	.268	8.40	3.80
O'Day, Darren	R-R	6-4	220	10-22-82	0	1	5.40	16	0	0	0	17	17	10	10	7	5	18	.262	.233	.286	9.72	2.70
Ogando, Alexi	R-R	6-4	195	10-5-83	13	8	3.51	31	29	1	0	169	149	73	66	16	43	126	.234	.255	.202	6.71	2.29
Oliver, Darren	R-L	6-2	200	10-6-70	5	5	2.29	61	0	0	2	51	47	17	13	3	11	44	.236	.227	.243	7.76	1.94
Rhodes, Arthur	L-L	6-2	200	10-24-69	3	3	4.81	32	0	0	1	24	28	13	13	6	8	15	.289	.216	.333	5.55	2.96
Strop, Pedro	R-R	6-0	175	6-13-85	0	1	3.72	11	0	0	0	10	7	4	4	0	7	9	.206	.267	.158	8.38	6.52
2-team total (12 Baltimore)					2	1	2.05	23	0	0	0	22	15	5	5	0	10	21	—	—	—	8.59	4.09
Tateyama, Yoshinori	R-R	5-10	165	12-26-75	2	0	4.50	39	0	0	1	44	37	23	22	8	11	43	.220	.260	.189	8.80	2.25
Tobin, Mason	R-R	6-3	210	7-8-87	0	0	6.75	4	0	0	0	5	5	5	4	1	5	0	.278	.429	.182	0.00	8.44
Tomko, Brett	R-R	6-4	220	4-7-73	0	1	4.58	8	0	0	0	18	15	9	9	4	10	14	.246	.333	.176	7.13	5.09
Tucker, Ryan	R-R	6-1	200	12-6-86	0	0	7.20	5	0	0	0	5	6	5	4	1	4	4	.286	.300	.273	7.20	7.20
Uehara, Koji	R-R	6-1	190	4-3-75	1	2	4.00	22	0	0	0	18	13	8	8	5	1	23	.191	.111	.244	11.50	0.50
2-team total (43 Baltimore)					2	3	2.35	65	0	0	0	65	38	17	17	11	9	85	—	—	—	11.77	1.25
Valdez, Merkin	R-R	6-5	230	11-10-81	0	0	6.23	5	0	0	0	4	7	3	3	2	1	6	.350	.462	.143	12.46	2.08
Wilson, C.J.	L-L	6-1	210	11-18-80	16	7	2.94	34	34	3	0	223	191	89	73	16	74	206	.232	.251	.227	8.30	2.98

TEXAS RANGERS

Fielding

Catcher	PCT	G	PO	A	E	DP	PB
Napoli	.996	61	431	25	2	4	1
Teagarden	1.000	14	63	5	0	0	1
Torrealba	.988	98	685	38	9	4	7
Treanor	1.000	7	30	2	0	0	0

First Base	PCT	G	PO	A	E	DP
Davis	1.000	15	87	1	0	11
Moreland	.995	99	731	54	4	88
Napoli	.996	35	223	19	1	21
Young	.989	36	267	13	3	34

Second Base	PCT	G	PO	A	E	DP
Blanco	1.000	5	6	9	0	1
German	1.000	2	0	3	0	1

	PCT	G	PO	A	E	DP
Kinsler	.984	144	268	398	11	103
Quintanilla	1.000	5	5	6	0	2
Young	1.000	14	28	29	0	11

Third Base	PCT	G	PO	A	E	DP
Beltre	.965	112	93	208	11	24
Blanco	.800	6	2	2	1	0
Davis	.875	9	4	17	3	2
German	1.000	4	0	3	0	0
Quintanilla	1.000	3	1	3	0	0
Young	.950	40	30	66	5	9

Shortstop	PCT	G	PO	A	E	DP
Andrus	.963	147	245	407	25	102
Blanco	.958	23	21	47	3	12

	PCT	G	PO	A	E	DP
Quintanilla	1.000	3	7	12	0	2
Young	1.000	1	1	2	0	1

Outfield	PCT	G	PO	A	E	DP
Blanco	1.000	1	0	1	0	0
Borbon	.986	32	70	1	1	0
Chavez	.993	75	133	3	1	0
Cruz	.977	115	244	6	6	1
Gentry	.982	60	109	0	2	0
Hamilton	.979	112	224	5	5	1
Martin	1.000	8	7	0	0	0
Moreland	.982	34	55	0	1	0
Murphy	.980	109	191	5	4	2

ROUND ROCK EXPRESS

TRIPLE-A

PACIFIC COAST LEAGUE

Batting	B-T	HT	WT	DOB	AVG	vLH	vRH	G	AB	R	H	2B	3B	HR	RBI	BB	HBP	SH	SF	SO	SB	CS	SLG	OBP
Barden, Brian	R-R	5-11	200	4-2-81	.357	.311	.377	53	207	38	74	18	1	7	38	17	2	0	5	33	1	1	.556	.403
Beltre, Adrian	R-R	5-11	220	4-7-79	.250	.333	.200	2	8	1	2	0	0	0	0	0	0	0	0	3	0	0	.250	.250
Blanco, Andres	B-R	5-10	180	4-11-84	.227	.286	.200	6	22	3	5	3	0	0	5	3	0	0	0	3	0	0	.364	.320
Borbon, Julio	L-L	6-0	195	2-20-86	.298	.302	.295	32	131	27	39	10	4	0	14	14	3	0	1	22	16	4	.435	.376
Butler, Joey	R-R	6-2	210	3-12-86	.322	.330	.318	113	426	73	137	27	5	12	57	43	4	0	1	138	13	4	.493	.388
Cash, Kevin	R-R	6-0	200	12-6-77	.244	.176	.267	85	291	36	71	15	2	6	45	44	4	0	1	63	0	1	.371	.350
Chavez, Endy	L-L	6-0	170	2-7-78	.305	.250	.323	30	128	16	39	8	2	2	11	6	1	0	0	6	6	0	.445	.353
Cruz, Luis	R-R	6-1	210	2-10-84	.273	.325	.253	67	275	34	75	15	1	9	34	10	1	0	0	40	2	1	.433	.301
Cruz, Nelson	R-R	6-2	240	7-1-80	.455	.667	.375	3	11	3	5	0	0	3	4	2	0	0	1	0	0	1	.538	
Davis, Chris	L-R	6-3	230	3-17-86	.368	.369	.367	48	193	39	71	14	1	24	66	11	3	0	3	58	1	0	.824	.405
Deeds, Doug	L-L	6-2	195	6-2-81	.249	.135	.274	55	205	24	51	13	3	7	32	15	2	0	2	40	1	0	.444	.304
Diaz, Robinzon	R-R	5-11	215	9-19-83	.303	.367	.269	38	142	21	43	3	0	4	14	5	0	0	1	8	0	1	.408	.324
Gentry, Craig	R-R	6-2	190	11-29-83	.245	.241	.247	30	110	21	27	5	1	1	10	11	2	0	0	17	5	1	.336	.325
German, Esteban	R-R	5-9	195	1-26-78	.301	.329	.290	123	508	94	153	29	3	7	56	72	1	0	2	58	44	9	.411	.388
Green, Nick	R-R	5-11	185	9-10-78	.293	.222	.315	36	147	26	43	15	0	2	17	10	4	0	1	29	1	1	.435	.352
Hamilton, Josh	L-L	6-4	240	5-21-81	.182	.250	.143	3	11	2	2	1	0	1	3	2	0	0	0	4	0	0	.545	.308
Kata, Matt	R-R	6-1	185	3-14-78	.293	.272	.302	106	392	60	115	30	2	13	71	24	0	0	11	63	1	1	.480	.353
Majewski, Val	L-L	6-2	220	6-19-81	.333	.206	.376	35	135	25	45	7	3	5	33	18	1	0	1	25	5	1	.541	.413
Martin, Leonys	L-R	6-1	180	3-6-88	.263	.321	.235	40	175	27	46	7	1	0	17	11	3	0	1	24	9	2	.314	.316
Napoli, Mike	R-R	6-0	215	10-31-81	.267	.200	.300	4	15	3	4	1	0	0	2	2	0	0	1	4	0	0	.933	.333
Nelson, Brad	L-R	6-2	260	12-23-82	.281	.298	.275	121	463	83	130	28	1	24	83	60	2	0	8	101	3	1	.501	.360
Quintanilla, Omar	L-R	5-9	190	10-24-81	.298	.333	.282	51	208	46	62	9	4	5	25	23	1	0	1	33	3	1	.452	.369
Rodriguez, Guilder	B-R	6-1	160	3-24-85	.270	.250	.276	41	137	20	37	2	0	0	13	21	0	0	1	14	3	0	.285	.365
Ruiz, Jose	R-R	6-3	235	3-24-85	.246	.400	.204	19	69	7	17	5	0	3	12	6	1	0	1	10	0	0	.449	.312
Teagarden, Taylor	R-R	6-1	200	12-21-83	.285	.283	.286	42	151	30	43	4	3	12	22	21	1	0	0	52	0	0	.589	.376
Tracy, Chad	R-R	6-3	210	7-4-85	.259	.215	.277	134	526	80	136	32	2	26	109	55	13	0	8	104	4	0	.475	.339

Pitching	B-T	HT	WT	DOB	W	L	ERA	G	GS	CG	SV	IP	H	R	ER	HR	BB	SO	AVG	vLH	vRH	K/9	BB/9
Aguero, Ramon	R-R	6-4	205	12-21-84	1	0	0.00	2	0	0	0	2	0	0	0	0	2	1	.000	.000	.000	4.50	9.00
Arguello, Doug	L-L	6-3	215	11-21-84	0	0	9.00	2	0	0	0	3	3	3	3	0	3	3	.231	.500	.182	9.00	9.00
2-team total (31 Oklahoma City)					5	7	3.89	33	7	0	0	72	55	32	31	4	49	64	—	—	—	8.04	6.15
Brazoban, Yhency	R-R	6-1	250	11-6-80	3	0	3.42	15	0	0	1	26	23	12	10	5	11	31	.230	.192	.271	10.59	3.76
2-team total (8 Reno)					4	1	3.22	23	0	0	2	36	31	15	13	6	14	42	—	—	—	10.40	3.47
Delcarmen, Manny	R-R	6-2	205	2-16-82	1	0	6.75	8	0	0	0	11	21	8	8	2	3	10	.429	.400	.441	8.44	2.53
2-team total (18 Tacoma)					3	2	5.59	26	0	0	0	39	52	25	24	4	15	33	—	—	—	7.68	3.49
Eppley, Cody	R-R	6-5	205	10-8-85	4	2	3.90	43	0	0	10	55	51	27	24	3	34	55	.238	.277	.214	8.95	5.53
Feldman, Scott	L-R	6-6	230	2-7-83	2	1	4.43	8	8	0	0	41	48	24	20	5	9	24	.298	.272	.325	5.31	1.99
Hamburger, Mark	R-R	6-4	195	2-5-87	7	4	3.88	31	4	0	0	63	54	27	27	5	20	48	.233	.275	.200	6.89	2.87
Hankins, Derek	R-R	6-4	195	7-1-83	7	6	5.89	24	14	0	0	92	109	68	60	20	34	60	.295	.320	.271	5.89	3.34
Hunter, Tommy	R-R	6-3	280	7-3-86	2	2	5.06	8	5	0	1	27	37	17	15	2	3	16	.322	.333	.309	5.40	1.01
Hurley, Eric	R-R	6-4	195	9-17-85	8	3	5.55	16	16	0	0	84	108	54	52	10	36	46	.317	.295	.333	4.91	3.84
Jackson, Zach	L-L	6-5	220	5-13-83	13	5	5.51	28	23	1	0	152	185	98	93	21	56	78	.304	.302	.305	4.62	3.32
Jones, Beau	L-L	6-1	195	8-25-86	0	1	3.63	39	0	0	1	62	59	28	25	8	26	54	.258	.236	.271	7.84	3.77
Kirkman, Michael	L-L	6-4	195	9-18-86	3	3	5.05	27	7	0	1	73	87	45	41	6	37	84	.295	.231	.337	10.36	4.56
Lowe, Mark	L-R	6-3	210	6-7-83	1	0	2.89	6	0	0	0	9	7	3	3	0	4	13	.200	.294	.111	12.54	3.86
McClung, Seth	L-R	6-6	280	2-7-81	2	3	5.19	19	11	0	0	78	93	50	45	6	34	49	.296	.307	.286	5.65	3.92
Miller, Justin	R-R	6-2	215	8-27-77	1	2	8.49	11	0	0	2	10	11	11	11	2	13	16	.233	.286	.182	7.71	10.03
3-team total (3 Albuquerque, 6 Tacoma)					1	3	5.73	20	0	0	3	22	18	14	14	3	22	19	—	—	—	7.77	9.00
Mobley, Chris	R-R	5-11	170	8-16-83	2	0	3.48	9	0	0	0	21	14	9	8	2	10	15	.194	.229	.162	6.53	4.35
O'Day, Darren	R-R	6-4	220	10-22-82	1	0	2.21	17	1	0	1	20	16	6	5	2	4	26	.211	.280	.176	11.51	1.77
Perez, Martin	L-L	6-0	178	4-4-91	4	4	6.43	10	10	0	0	49	72	38	35	4	20	37	.343	.317	.354	6.80	3.67
Phillips, Zach	L-L	6-1	200	9-21-86	1	3	4.43	33	0	0	3	45	50	26	22	3	21	38	.282	.304	.265	7.66	4.23
Ramirez, Neil	R-R	6-3	185	5-25-89	4	3	3.63	18	18	0	0	74	63	34	30	6	35	86	.229	.248	.208	10.41	4.24
Scheppers, Tanner	R-R	6-4	200	1-17-87	2	0	4.35	11	1	0	2	21	23	10	10	0	12	20	.295	.192	.346	8.71	5.23
Strop, Pedro	R-R	6-0	175	6-13-85	4	4	3.59	39	0	0	11	48	53	21	19	2	24	55	.283	.368	.225	10.38	4.53

Pitching

Pitching	B-T	HT	WT	DOB	W	L	ERA	G	GS	CG	SV	IP	H	R	ER	HR	BB	SO	AVG	vLH	vRH	K/9	BB/9
Tateyama, Yoshinori	R-R	5-10	165	12-26-75	1	0	2.14	14	0	0	1	21	17	5	5	1	4	26	.215	.250	.186	11.14	1.71
Tomko, Brett	R-R	6-4	220	4-7-73	9	6	6.15	21	18	0	0	108	130	81	74	21	42	82	.295	.290	.299	6.81	3.49
Tucker, Ryan	R-R	6-1	200	12-6-86	3	5	5.40	29	8	0	2	68	79	45	41	5	31	64	.288	.280	.295	8.43	4.08
Valdez, Merkin	R-R	6-5	230	11-10-81	1	0	2.35	12	0	0	4	15	14	4	4	1	5	14	.230	.176	.250	8.22	2.93
2-team total (38 Albuquerque)					5	2	3.29	50	0	0	8	66	61	27	24	2	29	57	—	—	—	7.81	3.97
Wood, Tim	R-R	6-0	180	11-16-82	0	0	9.64	4	0	0	1	5	9	5	5	1	3	2	.450	.286	.538	3.86	5.79

Fielding

Catcher	PCT	G	PO	A	E	DP	PB
Cash	.989	81	580	56	7	5	4
Diaz	.967	23	162	13	6	1	4
Napoli	1.000	2	8	0	0	0	0
Teagarden	.987	41	285	27	4	4	2

First Base	PCT	G	PO	A	E	DP
Barden	1.000	1	6	0	0	0
Cash	1.000	3	12	2	0	2
Napoli	1.000	1	8	1	0	0
Nelson	.996	55	451	40	2	61
Ruiz	1.000	19	172	7	0	18
Tracy	.986	68	615	26	9	58

Second Base	PCT	G	PO	A	E	DP
Cruz	.964	19	45	63	4	17
German	.977	43	90	125	5	33
Green	1.000	2	5	4	0	1
Kata	.978	66	144	207	8	41
Rodriguez	1.000	16	41	67	0	15

Third Base	PCT	G	PO	A	E	DP
Barden	.958	49	17	97	5	7
Beltre	1.000	2	1	7	0	1
Blanco	1.000	1	0	2	0	0
Cash	.600	2	1	2	2	0
Cruz	.944	7	4	13	1	2
Davis	.875	26	10	53	9	7
Diaz	.667	2	2	0	1	0
German	.924	57	36	97	11	9
Green	1.000	2	2	1	0	0
Kata	1.000	2	0	3	0	0
Rodriguez	1.000	1	0	1	0	0

Shortstop	PCT	G	PO	A	E	DP
Blanco	.933	5	6	8	1	0
Cruz	.976	34	56	109	4	23
German	.750	1	2	1	1	0
Green	.957	33	39	93	6	19
Kata	.882	4	5	10	2	2

Quintanilla	.991	51	81	140	2	41
Rodriguez	.976	21	33	50	2	17

Outfield	PCT	G	PO	A	E	DP
Borbon	1.000	31	86	2	0	0
Butler	.968	113	209	6	7	1
Chavez	.984	29	60	2	1	0
Cruz	1.000	9	15	2	0	1
Cruz	1.000	3	6	0	0	0
Davis	.885	14	23	0	3	0
Deeds	1.000	47	79	4	0	2
Gentry	.987	30	72	3	1	2
German	1.000	22	43	0	0	0
Kata	.985	31	66	1	1	1
Majewski	.984	32	63	0	1	0
Martin	.972	39	101	2	3	0
Nelson	.958	32	44	2	2	0
Rodriguez	1.000	3	3	0	0	0
Tracy	1.000	3	1	0	0	0

FRISCO ROUGHRIDERS   DOUBLE-A

TEXAS LEAGUE

Batting	B-T	HT	WT	DOB	AVG	vLH	vRH	G	AB	R	H	2B	3B	HR	RBI	BB	HBP	SH	SF	SO	SB	CS	SLG	OBP
Adair, Travis	L-R	5-10	180	12-23-87	.238	.125	.265	33	126	20	30	4	1	2	13	8	0	0	0	19	1	1	.333	.284
Beltre, Engel	L-L	6-2	180	11-1-89	.231	.183	.254	118	437	64	101	15	6	1	28	28	5	0	1	103	16	6	.300	.285
Bianucci, Mike	R-R	6-1	225	6-26-86	.243	.262	.236	133	535	80	130	29	1	30	89	35	12	0	4	136	5	1	.469	.302
Bolden, Jared	L-L	6-2	205	3-17-87	.239	.095	.304	21	67	10	16	1	0	1	10	9	0	0	2	19	1	0	.299	.321
Borbon, Julio	L-L	6-0	195	2-20-86	.000	.000	.000	1	4	0	0	0	0	0	0	0	0	0	0	1	0	0	.000	.000
Butler, Joey	R-R	6-2	210	3-12-86	.227	.000	.303	13	44	11	10	1	0	2	4	7	4	0	0	16	2	1	.386	.382
Cruz, Nelson	R-R	6-2	240	7-1-80	.182	.200	.167	3	11	1	2	1	0	0	1	1	0	0	0	0	0	0	.273	.250
Diaz, Robinzon	R-R	5-11	215	9-19-83	.357	.308	.372	17	56	11	20	1	0	3	8	4	2	0	0	4	0	0	.536	.419
Felix, Jose	R-R	5-10	200	6-28-88	.228	.167	.260	72	263	29	60	12	0	2	28	10	3	0	2	27	1	0	.297	.263
Garcia, Edwin	B-R	6-0	150	3-1-91	.250	.000	.500	1	4	0	1	0	0	0	0	0	0	0	0	1	0	0	.250	.250
Greene, Jonathan	R-R	6-0	200	9-16-85	.292	.301	.287	130	487	73	142	29	0	18	75	30	19	0	4	161	5	2	.462	.354
Hamilton, Josh	L-L	6-4	240	5-21-81	.286	.000	.500	2	7	3	2	0	0	1	3	1	0	0	0	1	0	0	.714	.375
Hilligoss, Mitch	L-R	6-1	195	6-17-85	.264	.255	.268	52	193	20	51	10	2	3	22	12	1	0	1	27	0	0	.383	.309
Leeds, Matt	B-L	6-0	200	12-22-89	.333	.250	.400	3	9	0	3	1	0	0	2	2	0	0	0	1	0	0	.444	.455
Martin, Leonys	L-R	6-1	180	3-6-88	.348	.318	.368	29	112	24	39	9	2	4	24	15	3	0	1	8	10	8	.571	.435
Mendonca, Tommy	L-R	6-1	200	4-12-88	.278	.247	.292	125	504	75	140	27	3	25	87	35	11	0	5	160	0	1	.492	.335
Morrison, Erik	R-R	6-0	190	10-23-85	.000	.000	.000	1	2	0	0	0	0	0	0	0	0	0	0	0	0	0	.000	.000
Osuna, Renny	R-R	6-0	172	4-24-85	.294	.302	.291	123	520	72	153	23	2	10	64	39	1	0	6	63	20	9	.404	.341
Paisano, David	R-R	6-1	165	11-26-87	.227	.179	.244	31	110	15	25	3	0	0	5	5	2	0	1	30	2	1	.255	.271
Rodriguez, Guilder	B-R	6-1	160	7-24-83	.275	.296	.263	80	284	39	78	7	0	0	37	30	1	0	3	40	14	4	.320	.343
Ruiz, Jose	L-R	6-3	235	3-24-85	.275	.269	.277	106	397	47	109	27	2	12	54	40	4	0	4	67	4	2	.443	.344
Sarmiento, Elio	R-R	5-11	200	6-20-86	.279	.271	.283	59	208	33	58	11	4	5	27	16	2	0	2	42	3	1	.442	.333
Stoneburner, Davis	R-R	6-0	175	1-14-85	.269	.279	.265	116	438	64	118	26	5	9	47	38	12	0	4	90	18	5	.413	.341
Swift, Jimmy	R-R	6-2	190	12-21-87	.167	.250	.125	4	12	2	2	0	0	0	1	2	0	0	1	4	0	0	.167	.267

Pitching	B-T	HT	WT	DOB	W	L	ERA	G	GS	CG	SV	IP	H	R	ER	HR	BB	SO	AVG	vLH	vRH	K/9	BB/9
Aguero, Ramon	R-R	6-4	205	12-21-84	2	2	8.18	19	0	0	0	22	23	20	20	5	21	17	.295	.357	.260	6.95	8.59
Bleier, Richard	L-L	6-3	195	4-16-87	7	8	5.60	32	13	0	0	101	142	73	63	5	16	55	.330	.280	.357	4.88	1.42
Boscan, Wilfredo	R-R	6-2	187	10-26-89	1	3	6.95	5	5	0	0	22	30	20	17	5	8	15	.323	.321	.323	6.14	3.27
Brigham, Jake	R-R	6-3	210	2-10-88	6	6	4.49	35	14	0	0	114	107	67	57	13	55	114	.244	.287	.213	8.97	4.33
Castillo, Fabio	R-R	6-1	235	2-19-89	3	6	6.36	42	0	0	9	52	58	40	37	6	23	37	.282	.268	.290	6.36	3.96
De Los Santos, Miguel	L-L	6-1	170	7-10-88	1	3	8.04	6	6	0	0	28	27	25	25	4	17	38	.265	.296	.253	12.21	5.46
Erlin, Robbie	L-L	6-0	175	10-8-90	5	2	4.32	11	10	0	0	67	73	34	32	9	7	61	.282	.292	.278	8.24	0.95
2-team total (6 San Antonio)					6	2	3.50	17	16	0	0	93	99	38	36	11	11	92	—	—	—	8.94	1.07
Feldman, Scott	L-R	6-6	230	2-7-83	1	0	3.00	2	2	0	0	9	5	3	3	0	2	8	.156	.188	.125	8.00	2.00
Feliz, Neftali	R-R	6-3	215	5-2-88	0	0	0.00	1	1	0	0	1	1	0	0	0	0	3	.250	.500	.000	27.00	0.00
Flores, Adalberto	R-R	6-7	225	11-4-86	5	4	3.32	41	2	0	1	81	72	32	30	5	38	80	.236	.227	.243	8.85	4.20
Hamburger, Mark	R-R	6-4	195	2-5-87	1	0	1.83	11	0	0	4	20	11	4	4	3	5	22	.162	.174	.156	10.07	2.29
Hankins, Derek	R-R	6-4	195	7-1-83	1	2	4.82	5	4	0	0	19	22	15	10	2	7	10	.293	.359	.222	4.82	3.38
Hendricks, Kyle	R-R	6-2	165	12-7-89	0	0	3.00	1	1	0	0	3	4	1	1	0	2	2	.308	.400	.250	6.00	6.00
Hunter, Tommy	R-R	6-3	280	7-3-86	0	0	4.50	1	0	0	0	4	3	2	2	1	1	5	.231	.429	.000	11.25	2.25
Jones, Beau	L-L	6-1	195	8-25-86	0	0	0.00	4	0	0	0	6	4	0	0	0	3	5	.174	.200	.167	7.11	4.26

Pitching	B-T	HT	WT	DOB	W	L	ERA	G	GS	CG	SV	IP	H	R	ER	HR	BB	SO	AVG	vLH	vRH	K/9	BB/9
Miller, Justin	R-R	6-3	190	6-13-87	9	1	1.81	48	0	0	13	70	46	14	14	2	24	77	.185	.187	.185	9.95	3.10
Mobley, Chris	R-R	5-11	170	8-16-83	0	0	8.53	5	1	0	1	6	11	8	6	1	5	5	.355	.091	.500	7.11	7.11
O'Day, Darren	R-R	6-4	220	10-22-82	0	0	9.00	1	1	0	0	1	1	1	1	1	0	1	.250	.000	.333	9.00	0.00
Perconte, Mike	R-R	6-4	170	3-18-86	3	0	5.40	19	0	0	0	28	27	17	17	2	15	28	.257	.172	.289	8.89	4.76
2-team total (5 Corpus Christi)					3	0	7.71	24	0	0	0	33	42	28	28	6	17	33	—	—	—	9.09	4.68
Perez, Martin	L-L	6-0	178	4-4-91	4	2	3.16	17	16	1	0	88	80	35	31	6	36	83	.245	.194	.260	8.46	3.67
Pimentel, Carlos	R-R	6-3	180	12-1-89	7	9	4.74	28	26	0	0	142	128	78	75	15	80	110	.246	.273	.221	6.96	5.06
Ramirez, Neil	R-R	6-3	185	5-25-89	1	0	1.89	6	6	0	0	19	13	4	4	1	8	24	.194	.250	.143	11.37	3.79
Ross, Robbie	L-L	5-11	185	6-24-89	1	1	2.61	6	6	0	0	38	33	13	11	5	5	36	.231	.143	.267	8.53	1.18
Scheppers, Tanner	R-R	6-4	200	1-17-87	2	1	3.13	17	0	0	0	23	18	10	8	1	9	24	.212	.189	.229	9.39	3.52
Snyder, Ben	L-L	6-2	225	7-20-85	11	5	3.87	40	14	0	1	119	123	56	51	15	30	67	.273	.202	.301	5.08	2.28
Tufts, Tyler	R-R	6-3	195	12-5-86	4	1	3.23	39	1	0	7	56	68	21	20	2	7	46	.302	.321	.291	7.44	1.13
Webb, Brandon	R-R	6-3	230	5-9-79	0	2	9.75	4	4	0	0	12	21	13	13	1	6	4	.404	.448	.348	6.00	4.50
Wieland, Joe	R-R	6-3	175	1-21-90	4	0	1.23	7	7	1	0	44	35	9	6	2	11	36	.217	.215	.221	7.36	2.25
2-team total (5 San Antonio)					7	1	1.80	12	12	1	0	70	58	19	14	2	17	54	—	—	—	6.94	2.19
Yan, Johan	R-R	6-3	185	9-27-88	0	0	0.34	19	0	0	2	27	18	4	1	0	9	18	.191	.222	.163	6.08	3.04
Young, Corey	L-L	6-2	185	12-30-86	0	3	4.67	35	0	0	0	44	45	28	23	0	17	34	.259	.258	.259	6.90	3.45

Fielding

Catcher	PCT	G	PO	A	E	DP	PB
Diaz	.992	15	120	12	1	1	0
Felix	.990	70	543	73	6	5	2
Sarmiento	.981	57	411	43	9	8	5

First Base	PCT	G	PO	A	E	DP
Bolden	1.000	21	175	5	0	11
Greene	.992	16	124	8	1	15
Hilligoss	.900	1	8	1	1	2
Leeds	1.000	1	6	1	0	0
Ruiz	.988	101	832	62	11	87

Second Base	PCT	G	PO	A	E	DP
Garcia	1.000	1	0	1	0	0
Hilligoss	1.000	3	3	4	0	0

	PCT	G	PO	A	E	DP
Morrison	1.000	1	1	3	0	1
Osuna	.972	43	94	111	6	26
Stoneburner	.964	96	185	241	16	58

Third Base	PCT	G	PO	A	E	DP
Greene	1.000	1	2	1	0	0
Hilligoss	.870	6	9	11	3	1
Mendonca	.941	123	84	221	19	21
Osuna	1.000	9	7	25	0	3
Swift	1.000	2	3	3	0	0

Shortstop	PCT	G	PO	A	E	DP
Osuna	.969	66	126	188	10	38
Rodriguez	.980	75	140	199	7	44
Stoneburner	1.000	1	1	2	0	0

	PCT	G	PO	A	E	DP
Swift	1.000	1	2	2	0	1

Outfield	PCT	G	PO	A	E	DP
Adair	.978	30	44	1	1	0
Beltre	.984	118	295	10	5	7
Bianucci	.988	54	78	6	1	1
Butler	1.000	13	27	0	0	1
Cruz	1.000	1	2	0	0	0
Greene	.991	107	217	15	2	1
Hilligoss	.970	31	63	2	2	0
Martin	.986	29	66	4	1	2
Paisano	1.000	31	60	5	0	0
Rodriguez	1.000	7	16	1	0	0
Snyder	1.000	1	1	0	0	0
Stoneburner	1.000	3	5	0	0	0

MYRTLE BEACH PELICANS

HIGH CLASS A

CAROLINA LEAGUE

Batting	B-T	HT	WT	DOB	AVG	vLH	vRH	G	AB	R	H	2B	3B	HR	RBI	BB	HBP	SH	SF	SO	SB	CS	SLG	OBP
Adair, Travis	L-R	5-10	180	12-23-87	.305	.343	.282	71	279	38	85	14	2	4	33	24	2	0	1	44	1	2	.412	.363
Bolden, Jared	L-L	6-2	205	3-17-87	.271	.245	.290	94	347	48	94	21	6	6	47	21	1	0	1	89	4	5	.418	.314
Clark, Andrew	L-L	6-2	220	8-12-87	.297	.261	.317	20	64	11	19	4	0	2	12	21	1	0	1	11	0	0	.453	.471
DiFazio, Vin	R-R	6-0	215	5-15-86	.232	.267	.210	67	228	29	53	16	1	8	31	43	12	0	1	73	1	0	.417	.380
Garcia, Leury	B-R	5-7	153	3-18-91	.256	.238	.266	109	442	65	113	19	5	3	38	28	4	0	0	100	30	12	.342	.306
Hill, Santiago	R-R	5-10	154	2-11-91	.263	.252	.270	115	422	54	111	18	1	4	41	18	10	0	7	49	3	3	.339	.304
Hilligoss, Mitch	L-R	6-1	195	6-17-85	.253	.189	.293	59	237	29	60	14	0	2	24	15	1	0	1	40	5	1	.338	.299
Hoying, Jared	L-R	6-3	190	5-18-89	.236	.206	.254	116	420	50	99	27	4	5	45	45	9	0	2	98	10	9	.355	.321
James, Andres	B-R	5-9	155	11-25-87	.196	.243	.161	82	270	27	53	7	1	0	15	5	3	0	1	46	6	4	.230	.219
McGuiness, Chris	L-L	6-1	210	4-11-88	.214	.218	.213	53	196	19	42	10	0	2	26	30	1	0	1	51	1	0	.296	.320
Nicholas, Brett	L-R	6-2	210	7-18-88	.111	.000	.333	3	9	0	1	1	0	0	2	0	0	0	0	3	0	0	.222	.273
Olt, Mike	R-R	6-2	210	8-27-88	.267	.297	.248	69	240	39	64	15	0	14	42	48	1	0	3	70	0	1	.504	.387
Paisano, David	R-R	6-1	165	11-26-87	.241	.208	.266	65	245	21	59	13	4	1	22	8	3	0	2	37	1	3	.339	.271
Prince, Jared	R-R	6-3	220	5-25-86	.282	.310	.263	131	482	67	136	30	1	8	72	47	30	0	7	47	2	3	.398	.376
Roof, Jonathan	R-R	6-1	165	1-23-89	.186	.286	.091	12	43	5	8	2	0	0	1	3	0	0	0	9	0	0	.233	.239
Strausborger, Ryan	R-R	6-0	180	3-4-88	.270	.339	.228	126	488	71	132	29	9	8	57	45	15	0	5	91	31	12	.416	.347
Swift, Jimmy	R-R	6-2	190	12-21-87	.167	.231	.143	12	48	5	8	1	0	1	2	2	1	0	0	14	0	0	.250	.216
Zaneski, Zach	R-R	6-2	215	6-27-86	.281	.347	.243	73	274	24	77	17	0	6	42	22	5	0	1	56	0	0	.409	.344

Pitching	B-T	HT	WT	DOB	W	L	ERA	G	GS	CG	SV	IP	H	R	ER	HR	BB	SO	AVG	vLH	vRH	K/9	BB/9
Bell, Chad	R-L	6-3	200	2-28-89	3	2	2.98	32	9	1	1	82	76	30	27	2	23	69	.246	.263	.240	7.60	2.53
Boscan, Wilfredo	R-R	6-2	187	10-26-89	4	12	4.69	22	20	0	0	119	144	74	62	11	30	72	.300	.269	.319	5.45	2.27
De Los Santos, Miguel	L-L	6-1	170	7-10-88	6	3	3.82	13	12	0	0	64	46	32	27	2	28	97	.195	.093	.218	13.71	3.96
Devore, Kyle	R-R	6-4	225	12-23-90	0	0	0.00	1	0	0	0	3	2	0	0	0	0	0	.500	.000	.600	0.00	0.00
Doyle, Andrew	R-R	6-3	220	11-12-87	1	0	4.35	5	0	0	0	10	12	6	5	0	6	13	.293	.267	.308	11.32	5.23
Erlin, Robbie	L-L	6-0	175	10-8-90	3	2	2.14	9	9	0	0	55	25	15	13	7	5	62	.132	.208	.106	10.21	0.82
Gomez, Kennil	R-R	6-3	170	4-8-88	2	7	3.81	35	11	0	1	102	98	54	43	7	41	80	.253	.321	.218	7.08	3.63
Grimm, Justin	R-R	6-3	175	8-16-88	3	2	3.39	16	16	0	0	90	84	40	34	2	30	73	.247	.291	.226	7.27	2.99
Hurley, Trevor	R-R	6-3	215	7-28-87	2	4	2.70	38	0	0	4	57	43	24	17	8	28	69	.205	.263	.183	10.96	4.45
Kelly, Ryan	R-R	6-2	180	10-30-87	3	6	3.95	40	5	0	9	82	74	44	36	6	23	64	.242	.240	.243	7.02	2.52
Kiker, Kasey	L-L	5-10	185	11-19-87	3	4	7.05	30	1	0	0	45	45	39	35	3	52	54	.260	.298	.246	10.88	10.48
Killian, Colby	R-R	6-0	192	6-5-88	0	1	3.65	9	0	0	0	12	15	6	5	1	6	7	.319	.294	.333	5.11	4.38
Loux, Barret	R-R	6-5	215	4-6-89	8	5	3.80	21	21	0	0	109	106	50	46	6	34	127	.252	.241	.257	10.49	2.81
Ortiz, Joseph	L-L	5-7	175	8-13-90	5	5	2.15	40	0	0	5	67	54	16	16	4	14	55	.216	.200	.222	7.39	1.88
Osborne, Zach	R-R	6-5	205	5-9-88	5	2	3.36	34	1	0	3	56	51	24	21	2	13	48	.242	.211	.257	7.67	2.08
Ramirez, Neil	R-R	6-3	185	5-25-89	0	0	0.00	1	1	0	0	5	1	0	0	0	1	6	.063	.000	.077	17.36	1.93

Pitching

Pitching	B-T	HT	WT	DOB	W	L	ERA	G	GS	CG	SV	IP	H	R	ER	HR	BB	SO	AVG	vLH	vRH	K/9	BB/9
Reyes, Jimmy	L-L	5-10	195	3-7-89	0	1	4.15	7	0	0	2	9	9	4	4	1	0	7	.257	.444	.192	7.27	0.00
Rodebaugh, Ryan	L-R	6-0	165	3-30-89	1	1	5.21	16	0	0	2	19	20	11	11	3	9	22	.278	.143	.333	10.42	4.26
Ross, Robbie	L-L	5-11	185	6-24-89	9	4	2.26	21	20	1	0	123	102	37	31	1	28	98	.227	.177	.241	7.15	2.04
Tufts, Tyler	R-R	6-3	195	12-5-86	1	0	1.35	6	0	0	3	7	4	1	1	1	1	9	.174	.375	.067	12.15	1.35
Wieland, Joe	R-R	6-3	175	1-21-90	6	3	2.10	14	13	1	0	86	78	23	20	7	4	96	.240	.256	.230	10.09	0.42
Yan, Johan	R-R	6-3	185	9-27-88	5	3	1.52	26	0	0	10	41	33	11	7	2	13	48	.214	.260	.192	10.45	2.83

Fielding

Catcher	PCT	G	PO	A	E	DP	PB
DiFazio	.995	65	574	56	3	4	4
Nicholas	1.000	3	18	5	0	0	0
Zaneski	.983	73	586	43	11	3	14

First Base	PCT	G	PO	A	E	DP
Bolden	1.000	57	423	32	0	35
Clark	.970	17	155	7	5	10
DiFazio	1.000	1	12	0	0	1
Hilligoss	1.000	22	172	13	0	11
McGuiness	.995	49	404	31	2	32

Second Base	PCT	G	PO	A	E	DP
Adair	.981	14	25	26	1	5

	PCT	G	PO	A	E	DP
Hill	.968	78	160	171	11	42
James	.965	43	80	87	6	21
Roof	1.000	9	17	17	0	7

Third Base	PCT	G	PO	A	E	DP
Hill	.916	37	27	60	8	5
Hilligoss	.923	30	18	66	7	6
James	.000	1	0	0	0	0
Olt	.954	66	43	145	9	13
Roof	.800	2	3	5	2	0
Swift	.895	7	7	10	2	1

Shortstop	PCT	G	PO	A	E	DP
Garcia	.920	106	121	304	37	52

	PCT	G	PO	A	E	DP
James	.937	34	46	88	9	11
Swift	.833	2	1	4	1	0

Outfield	PCT	G	PO	A	E	DP
Adair	.952	32	35	5	2	1
Bolden	1.000	15	26	0	0	0
Hoying	.984	99	182	4	3	1
Paisano	.988	41	79	1	1	0
Prince	.985	118	194	5	3	2
Strausborger	.981	116	242	11	5	1
Swift	1.000	1	2	0	0	0

HICKORY CRAWDADS

LOW CLASS A

SOUTH ATLANTIC LEAGUE

Batting

Batting	B-T	HT	WT	DOB	AVG	vLH	vRH	G	AB	R	H	2B	3B	HR	RBI	BB	HBP	SH	SF	SO	SB	CS	SLG	OBP
Castillo, Yefry	R-R	5-11	175	4-22-90	.296	.278	.302	23	71	8	21	3	2	0	10	1	0	0	2	11	2	2	.394	.297
Clark, Andrew	L-L	6-2	220	8-12-87	.313	.355	.294	103	355	59	111	24	0	12	60	62	8	0	4	62	7	4	.482	.422
Deglan, Kellin	L-R	6-2	195	5-3-92	.227	.218	.230	89	291	39	66	15	1	6	39	34	8	0	4	91	2	0	.347	.320
Garcia, Edwin	B-R	6-0	150	3-1-91	.500	.667	.333	2	6	2	3	1	0	0	1	1	0	0	0	0	0	0	.667	.571
Gomez, Jhonny	R-R	5-11	190	12-21-89	.258	.267	.254	93	295	41	76	9	0	2	31	40	8	0	3	53	3	7	.308	.358
Herrera, David	L-R	5-11	165	12-29-91	.306	.321	.299	119	464	72	142	26	3	3	56	24	8	0	2	78	34	11	.394	.349
Lane, Braxton	R-R	5-10	190	12-30-90	.186	.150	.205	25	59	16	11	2	0	0	1	15	2	0	0	16	6	1	.220	.368
Martinez, Teodoro	R-R	5-11	155	3-16-92	.276	.224	.295	63	214	27	59	10	2	3	25	17	3	0	3	32	20	12	.383	.333
Murphy, Clark	L-L	6-2	190	12-18-89	.133	.111	.143	9	30	1	4	0	0	0	4	0	0	0	0	1	0	0	.133	.235
Profar, Jurickson	B-R	5-11	165	2-20-93	.286	.270	.294	115	430	86	123	37	8	12	65	65	11	0	4	63	23	9	.493	.390
Richmond, Josh	R-R	6-3	205	6-14-89	.247	.262	.241	126	462	73	114	32	5	11	50	40	10	0	4	114	9	4	.409	.318
Roof, Jonathan	R-R	6-1	165	1-23-89	.275	.276	.275	79	236	28	65	15	0	2	38	12	1	0	4	43	15	5	.364	.308
Selen, Alejandro	R-R	5-10	175	3-20-89	.294	.333	.279	62	214	36	63	14	1	11	38	18	4	0	1	64	1	1	.523	.359
Skole, Jake	L-R	6-1	190	1-17-92	.264	.276	.259	124	424	76	112	14	6	9	62	65	6	0	5	138	21	14	.389	.366
Telis, Tomas	B-R	5-8	175	6-18-91	.297	.230	.322	115	461	67	137	28	0	11	69	18	6	0	4	35	12	6	.430	.329
Torres, Kevin	L-R	6-3	195	2-24-90	.500	.000	.500	2	8	2	4	1	0	0	0	0	0	0	0	2	0	0	.625	.500
Villanueva, Christian	R-R	5-11	160	6-19-91	.278	.239	.295	126	467	78	130	30	3	17	84	37	12	0	13	86	32	6	.465	.338

Pitching

Pitching	B-T	HT	WT	DOB	W	L	ERA	G	GS	CG	SV	IP	H	R	ER	HR	BB	SO	AVG	vLH	vRH	K/9	BB/9
Buckel, Cody	R-R	6-1	170	6-18-92	8	3	2.61	23	17	0	0	97	83	34	28	7	27	120	.229	.267	.207	11.17	2.51
Doyle, Andrew	R-R	6-3	220	11-12-87	1	2	3.75	15	0	0	0	24	15	13	10	3	20	24	.183	.222	.152	9.00	7.50
Grimm, Justin	R-R	6-3	175	8-16-88	2	1	3.40	9	9	0	0	50	45	23	19	5	18	54	.247	.225	.265	9.66	3.22
Henry, Ben	R-R	6-4	190	4-9-89	6	3	2.38	24	5	0	1	64	44	22	17	5	31	67	.197	.260	.146	9.37	4.34
Jackson, Luke	R-R	6-2	185	8-24-91	5	6	5.64	19	19	0	0	75	83	57	47	9	48	78	.276	.295	.263	9.36	5.76
Johnson, Kevin	L-L	6-5	215	12-3-87	1	1	3.52	16	1	0	0	23	20	12	9	1	30	22	.238	.320	.203	8.61	11.74
Killian, Colby	R-R	6-0	192	6-5-88	6	4	3.88	33	0	0	1	56	57	29	24	1	29	53	.271	.244	.288	8.57	4.69
Lamb, Will	L-L	6-6	180	9-9-90	2	0	0.48	4	4	0	0	19	10	2	1	0	8	20	.156	.294	.106	9.64	3.86
Marban, Jorge	R-R	6-1	215	12-5-88	1	1	4.61	35	0	0	3	55	45	35	28	2	30	65	.223	.197	.237	10.70	4.94
McBride, Nick	R-R	6-4	180	5-13-91	1	1	6.94	11	2	0	0	23	33	21	18	2	10	14	.340	.321	.348	5.40	3.86
Melo, Carlos	R-R	6-3	180	2-27-91	2	4	8.59	7	6	0	0	22	16	23	21	2	28	27	.205	.370	.118	11.05	11.45
Mendez, Roman	R-R	6-2	180	7-25-90	9	1	3.31	26	20	0	1	117	117	44	43	7	45	130	.259	.280	.246	10.00	3.46
Mendoza, Francisco	R-R	6-0	175	12-7-87	0	0	2.78	19	0	0	9	23	17	7	7	1	5	33	.210	.200	.216	13.10	1.99
Monegro, Jose	R-R	6-3	200	9-19-89	2	0	5.19	9	0	0	1	17	15	10	10	3	3	19	.227	.160	.268	9.87	1.56
Nam, Yoon-Hee	L-L	6-2	190	8-4-87	0	0	0.00	1	0	0	0	2	1	0	0	0	3	3	.143	1.000	.000	13.50	0.00
Osborne, Zach	R-R	6-5	205	5-9-88	1	0	1.26	8	0	0	1	14	9	2	2	0	2	18	.176	.200	.167	11.30	1.26
Perez-Lobo, Andres	R-R	5-11	184	3-3-92	0	2	8.22	6	0	0	0	8	7	8	7	2	10	7	.233	.083	.333	8.22	11.74
Reyes, Jimmy	L-L	5-10	195	3-7-89	6	1	1.88	26	0	0	2	43	44	10	9	2	7	44	.277	.231	.292	9.21	1.47
Rodebaugh, Ryan	L-R	6-0	165	3-30-89	1	2	0.41	28	0	0	14	44	26	4	2	1	12	54	.169	.190	.156	11.13	2.47
Rojas, Randol	R-R	6-0	160	9-28-90	5	1	3.52	9	5	0	0	38	40	18	15	2	11	23	.280	.275	.282	5.40	2.58
Rowen, Ben	R-R	6-4	190	11-15-88	5	4	1.98	33	0	0	2	59	55	26	13	1	18	43	.246	.282	.223	6.56	2.75
Tepesch, Nick	R-R	6-4	200	10-12-88	7	5	4.03	29	23	2	0	138	147	70	62	14	33	118	.279	.267	.287	7.68	2.15
Thompson, Matt	R-R	6-3	210	2-10-90	3	5	5.91	23	18	0	1	88	80	63	58	4	80	96	.243	.259	.232	9.78	8.15
Tullis, Braden	R-R	6-2	200	1-23-90	0	0	12.86	4	0	0	0	7	18	12	10	1	6	2	.545	.857	.462	2.57	7.71
Van Meter, Joe	R-R	6-2	195	10-18-88	5	6	4.15	39	8	0	5	82	79	41	38	10	35	65	.255	.217	.279	7.11	3.83

Fielding

Catcher	PCT	G	PO	A	E	DP	PB
Castillo	.987	10	63	14	1	1	4
Deglan	.982	74	643	71	13	4	13

	PCT	G	PO	A	E	DP	PB
Telis	.986	55	442	61	7	4	10
Torres	1.000	1	6	0	0	0	0

First Base	PCT	G	PO	A	E	DP
Clark	.990	78	647	34	7	70
Gomez	.991	55	424	23	4	36

	PCT	G	PO	A	E	DP
Murphy	1.000	5	46	0	0	2
Selen	.967	4	26	3	1	1

Second Base	PCT	G	PO	A	E	DP
Castillo	1.000	2	5	4	0	1
Herrera	.969	113	199	299	16	72
Roof	1.000	14	20	33	0	8
Selen	.980	14	23	26	1	3

Third Base	PCT	G	PO	A	E	DP
Castillo	1.000	1	1	2	0	1

	PCT	G	PO	A	E	DP
Roof	.737	8	4	10	5	0
Selen	.895	8	5	12	2	1
Villanueva	.942	122	75	251	20	37

Shortstop	PCT	G	PO	A	E	DP
Garcia	1.000	2	2	4	0	1
Herrera	.941	5	6	10	1	3
Profar	.955	114	176	295	22	62
Roof	.895	18	17	34	6	4
Villanueva	1.000	2	2	7	0	0

Outfield	PCT	G	PO	A	E	DP
Castillo	1.000	5	5	0	0	0
Gomez	.979	34	44	3	1	0
Lane	.971	22	33	0	1	0
Martinez	.991	61	103	3	1	0
Richmond	.967	118	186	16	7	3
Roof	.963	37	47	5	2	1
Selen	.977	29	40	3	1	1
Skole	.983	118	228	4	4	2

SPOKANE INDIANS — SHORT-SEASON
NORTHWEST LEAGUE

Batting	B-T	HT	WT	DOB	AVG	vLH	vRH	G	AB	R	H	2B	3B	HR	RBI	BB	HBP	SH	SF	SO	SB	CS	SLG	OBP
Adams, Trever	R-R	6-0	200	9-30-88	.270	.341	.255	66	252	37	68	20	5	1	36	21	4	0	1	75	5	0	.401	.335
Alberto, Hanser	R-R	5-11	175	10-17-92	.267	.146	.301	53	187	21	50	8	1	0	16	9	3	0	2	15	7	1	.321	.308
Alfaro, Jorge	R-R	6-2	185	6-11-93	.300	.343	.288	45	160	18	48	9	1	6	23	4	7	0	0	54	1	0	.481	.345
Castillo, Yefry	R-R	5-11	175	4-22-90	.347	.407	.330	32	118	15	41	8	3	2	19	10	2	0	0	15	3	3	.517	.408
Cone, Zach	R-R	6-2	205	12-14-89	.201	.333	.168	62	224	37	45	15	2	4	29	16	9	0	3	57	11	2	.339	.278
Garcia, Edwin	B-R	6-0	150	3-1-91	.276	.282	.274	47	185	20	51	5	1	2	24	10	0	0	1	28	2	1	.346	.311
Lane, Braxton	B-R	5-10	190	12-30-90	.229	.278	.200	16	48	8	11	2	1	0	4	4	0	0	0	23	4	1	.313	.288
Nicholas, Brett	L-R	6-2	210	7-18-88	.277	.341	.262	63	224	35	62	21	0	6	45	38	5	0	5	45	1	0	.451	.386
Odor, Rougned	L-R	5-11	170	2-3-94	.262	.273	.258	58	233	33	61	9	3	2	29	13	9	0	2	37	10	4	.352	.323
Onaka, Hirotoshi	R-R	5-10	175	7-11-88	.239	.267	.236	46	155	32	37	2	5	1	8	40	4	0	1	46	9	6	.335	.405
Pimentel, Guillermo	R-R	6-1	190	11-12-89	.277	.275	.278	63	220	30	61	3	1	1	15	27	7	0	1	58	7	6	.314	.373
Robinson, Drew	L-R	6-1	185	4-20-92	.163	.100	.179	45	147	18	24	6	0	3	25	22	0	0	4	46	3	1	.265	.266
Rua, Ryan	R-R	6-2	180	3-11-90	.192	.222	.176	7	26	2	5	0	0	1	3	1	1	0	0	6	0	0	.308	.250
Sierra Jr., Ruben	L-L	6-2	172	3-10-91	.256	.125	.286	50	172	25	44	13	0	4	28	10	1	0	0	56	8	4	.401	.301
Swift, Jimmy	R-R	6-2	190	12-21-87	.235	.200	.250	5	17	2	4	1	0	0	2	1	0	0	1	3	0	0	.294	.263
Urbanus, Nick	B-R	6-1	175	3-29-92	.000	.000	.000	1	3	0	0	0	0	0	0	0	1	0	0	2	0	0	.000	.250
Vickerson, Nick	R-R	5-11	205	7-8-89	.201	.194	.203	45	154	24	31	9	3	1	11	26	6	0	0	51	2	2	.318	.339
Vitale, Carson	R-R	6-1	195	8-25-88	.170	.231	.150	16	53	8	9	2	0	0	6	11	0	0	1	17	0	1	.208	.308

Pitching	B-T	HT	WT	DOB	W	L	ERA	G	GS	CG	SV	IP	H	R	ER	HR	BB	SO	AVG	vLH	vRH	K/9	BB/9
Alvarez, Richard	R-R	6-2	180	8-14-92	0	2	7.79	13	4	0	0	35	47	34	30	4	15	36	.324	.250	.376	9.35	3.89
Claudio, Alexander	L-L	6-3	160	1-31-92	1	0	0.00	1	0	0	0	3	2	0	0	0	1	2	.200	.000	.222	6.00	3.00
Eickhoff, Jerad	R-R	6-4	200	7-2-90	1	1	2.51	10	0	0	2	14	8	4	4	1	3	18	.163	.286	.114	11.30	1.88
Grullon, Juan	L-L	6-0	185	3-4-90	5	1	3.11	20	0	0	0	38	32	15	13	3	21	37	.225	.289	.202	8.84	5.02
Hanna, Chris	R-L	6-1	180	3-7-92	4	2	2.58	17	6	0	1	59	48	21	17	2	14	56	.227	.283	.209	8.49	2.12
Hendricks, Kyle	R-R	6-2	165	12-7-89	2	2	1.93	20	0	0	3	33	20	7	7	0	4	36	.169	.123	.192	9.92	1.10
Klein, Phil	R-R	6-7	240	4-30-89	1	2	4.58	9	0	0	0	18	18	13	9	1	15	24	.261	.192	.302	12.23	7.64
Kukuruda, John	R-R	6-4	180	6-9-92	0	3	8.15	5	5	0	0	18	23	21	16	4	10	11	.307	.281	.326	5.60	5.09
Lamb, Will	L-L	6-6	180	9-9-90	1	1	3.89	12	7	0	0	37	35	17	16	3	23	42	.248	.308	.225	10.22	5.59
Martinez, Nicholas	L-R	6-1	175	8-5-90	1	2	2.54	9	7	0	0	39	37	18	11	0	16	37	.252	.290	.224	8.54	3.69
Matthews, Kevin	R-L	5-11	180	11-29-92	0	3	2.70	5	5	0	0	17	14	7	5	0	13	18	.222	.333	.211	9.72	7.02
Mavare, Jose	R-R	6-0	175	2-19-90	0	0	1.98	8	0	0	0	14	10	5	3	0	7	20	.204	.267	.176	13.17	4.61
McBride, Nick	R-R	6-4	180	5-13-91	2	2	3.73	9	0	0	0	51	53	22	21	3	8	30	.269	.296	.254	5.33	1.42
Melo, Carlos	R-R	6-3	180	2-27-91	1	1	8.27	13	1	0	0	21	14	19	19	2	29	31	.194	.276	.140	13.50	12.63
Mendoza, Francisco	R-R	6-0	175	12-7-87	2	1	6.00	8	0	0	1	15	17	10	10	2	7	17	.298	.385	.273	10.20	4.20
Monegro, Jose	R-R	6-3	200	9-19-89	3	0	3.28	12	0	0	2	25	23	10	9	3	12	32	.240	.270	.220	11.68	4.38
Payano, Victor	L-L	6-5	185	10-17-92	2	5	5.44	15	9	0	0	48	53	37	29	7	27	43	.286	.361	.268	8.06	5.06
Perez, David	R-R	6-5	200	12-20-92	1	4	8.60	13	9	0	0	30	25	29	29	2	29	43	.223	.318	.162	12.76	8.60
Perez, Santo	R-R	6-5	200	11-22-88	6	4	4.15	15	14	0	0	69	73	44	32	10	21	48	.269	.286	.260	6.23	2.73
Perez-Lobo, Andres	R-R	5-11	184	3-3-92	1	2	8.20	12	0	0	0	19	22	19	17	2	14	14	.282	.323	.255	6.75	6.75
Robinson, Samuel	L-L	6-2	175	10-26-89	0	1	6.75	5	0	0	0	9	12	8	7	2	1	8	.316	.250	.333	7.71	0.96
Sossamon, Chance	R-R	6-2	185	10-19-89	0	0	0.00	2	0	0	0	2	1	0	0	0	1	2	.143	.167	.000	9.00	4.50
Stanford, Tim	R-R	6-0	191	5-7-89	0	0	6.75	4	0	0	0	9	14	7	7	1	4	8	.359	.333	.370	7.71	3.86
Williams, Greg	L-L	6-4	205	12-30-89	0	0	0.00	1	0	0	0	1	1	0	0	0	0	3	.200	.000	.200	6.75	20.25

Fielding

Catcher	PCT	G	PO	A	E	DP	PB
Alfaro	.971	36	298	42	10	2	12
Castillo	.983	19	154	17	3	2	9
Nicholas	1.000	12	96	11	0	3	0
Vitale	.992	13	116	3	1	1	2

First Base	PCT	G	PO	A	E	DP
Adams	.994	40	289	25	2	35
Castillo	.983	7	55	3	1	3
Garcia	1.000	2	9	0	0	0
Nicholas	.992	30	226	21	2	18

Second Base	PCT	G	PO	A	E	DP
Garcia	.985	14	24	40	1	10

	PCT	G	PO	A	E	DP
Odor	.966	54	119	133	9	27
Urbanus	1.000	1	1	3	0	0
Vickerson	.949	10	15	22	2	6

Third Base	PCT	G	PO	A	E	DP
Garcia	.875	7	2	19	3	1
Robinson	.910	45	40	82	12	13
Rua	1.000	5	6	7	0	0
Swift	.909	4	3	7	1	0
Vickerson	.865	16	7	25	5	0

Shortstop	PCT	G	PO	A	E	DP
Alberto	.902	51	66	118	20	22
Garcia	.920	26	50	65	10	19

	PCT	G	PO	A	E	DP
Rua	.800	2	1	3	1	0
Swift	1.000	1	0	2	0	0

Outfield	PCT	G	PO	A	E	DP
Adams	1.000	8	18	0	0	0
Cone	.983	59	113	5	2	2
Lane	.900	14	16	2	2	0
Onaka	1.000	37	66	1	0	0
Pimentel	.964	59	97	10	4	3
Sierra Jr.	.971	47	63	5	2	1
Vickerson	1.000	13	11	1	0	0

TEXAS RANGERS

AZL RANGERS
ARIZONA LEAGUE

ROOKIE

Batting	B-T	HT	WT	DOB	AVG	vLH	vRH	G	AB	R	H	2B	3B	HR	RBI	BB	HBP	SH	SF	SO	SB	CS	SLG	OBP
Akins, Jordan	R-R	6-3	192	4-19-92	.283	.263	.289	48	180	37	51	12	4	2	31	6	2	0	1	42	13	2	.428	.312
Edmonds, Guy	R-R	6-2	180	3-16-93	.304	.313	.303	32	115	22	35	12	1	4	23	8	0	0	1	28	0	1	.530	.347
Grayson, Christopher	L-L	6-2	195	9-15-89	.288	.441	.252	48	177	34	51	8	5	2	30	9	1	0	2	32	17	5	.424	.323
Harlin, Rashad	R-R	6-0	185	2-7-93	.133	.167	.125	24	60	9	8	1	0	0	4	9	2	0	1	26	5	0	.150	.264
Henry, Desmond	R-R	5-10	150	7-7-93	.140	.083	.156	23	57	8	8	0	0	0	3	9	1	0	0	26	3	2	.140	.269
Johnson, Saquan	R-R	6-2	175	2-26-93	.389	.500	.357	6	18	6	7	1	1	1	3	0	1	0	0	5	1	0	.722	.421
Leeds, Matt	B-L	6-0	200	12-22-89	.272	.222	.286	44	169	39	46	10	4	5	30	28	6	0	2	56	1	1	.467	.390
Maloney, Joseph	R-R	6-2	190	7-27-90	.208	.400	.158	9	24	3	5	0	0	0	4	2	2	0	1	4	0	0	.208	.310
Marte, Luis	R-R	6-1	170	12-15-93	.240	.250	.238	7	25	2	6	1	1	0	4	0	0	0	0	3	1	0	.360	.240
Martin, Leonys	L-R	6-1	180	3-6-88	.267	.333	.250	4	15	2	4	0	2	0	1	1	0	0	0	6	0	1	.533	.313
McGuiness, Chris	L-L	6-1	210	4-11-88	.200	.000	.250	2	5	3	1	0	0	1	2	1	1	0	0	1	0	0	.800	.429
Mendez, Luis	B-R	5-9	155	1-1-93	.254	.310	.235	39	114	23	29	2	1	2	12	18	6	0	2	18	12	2	.342	.379
Murphy, Clark	L-L	6-2	190	12-18-89	.242	.000	.286	10	33	4	8	1	0	2	5	7	0	0	0	11	1	0	.455	.375
Olt, Mike	R-R	6-2	210	8-27-88	.214	.000	.273	4	14	2	3	0	0	1	4	1	0	0	0	5	0	0	.429	.267
Oropeza, Carlos	B-R	6-0	180	7-7-92	.247	.158	.278	27	73	10	18	3	0	0	12	19	5	0	1	19	0	0	.288	.429
Radcliffe, Kendall	L-R	6-2	185	10-17-92	.125	.200	.116	23	48	4	6	4	0	0	5	7	0	0	0	24	0	0	.208	.236
Robinson, Drew	L-R	6-1	185	4-20-92	.500	.000	.692	6	18	9	9	2	0	1	5	6	1	0	0	4	4	1	.778	.640
Rua, Ryan	R-R	6-2	180	3-11-90	.321	.222	.341	45	162	41	52	12	5	3	34	20	1	0	2	34	10	0	.512	.395
Sardinas, Luis	B-R	6-1	150	5-16-93	.308	.300	.310	14	52	11	16	2	1	0	7	4	2	0	2	10	2	1	.385	.367
Swift, Jimmy	R-R	6-2	190	12-21-87	.416	.412	.417	27	89	22	37	7	3	3	23	13	3	0	1	11	3	2	.663	.500
Torres, Kevin	L-R	6-3	195	2-24-90	.345	.317	.352	51	200	40	69	11	4	4	30	26	6	0	1	35	4	1	.500	.433
Urbanus, Nick	B-R	6-1	175	3-29-92	.283	.244	.294	50	205	35	58	5	5	0	30	21	1	0	2	36	12	5	.356	.349
Williams, Jeremy	R-R	6-2	220	4-1-87	.357	.344	.360	42	143	39	51	9	9	5	34	14	4	0	1	25	11	3	.650	.426

Pitching	B-T	HT	WT	DOB	W	L	ERA	G	GS	CG	SV	IP	H	R	ER	HR	BB	SO	AVG	vLH	vRH	K/9	BB/9
Beltre, Omar	R-R	6-3	230	8-24-81	0	0	0.00	2	2	0	0	2	2	0	0	0	2	4	.286	.000	.286	18.00	9.00
Blackwell, Shawn	R-R	6-5	195	11-15-90	5	0	3.58	14	3	0	0	50	44	24	20	2	16	49	.228	.159	.248	8.76	2.86
Castro, Kyle	R-R	6-4	190	8-18-93	2	2	5.68	8	2	0	0	13	17	11	8	0	5	6	.321	.421	.265	4.26	3.55
Claudio, Alexander	L-L	6-3	160	1-31-92	4	0	2.13	15	0	0	1	25	20	8	6	1	9	29	.222	.267	.213	10.30	3.20
De Los Santos, Abel	R-R	6-2	180	11-21-92	7	1	3.67	14	12	0	0	61	55	29	25	5	8	61	.244	.309	.224	8.95	1.17
De Los Santos, Miguel	L-L	6-1	170	7-10-88	0	0	3.00	1	1	0	0	3	4	1	1	0	1	7	.308	.500	.273	21.00	3.00
Dennis, Taylor	R-R	6-1	175	3-31-89	2	1	7.08	14	1	0	1	20	30	17	16	1	11	29	.349	.310	.368	12.84	4.87
Devore, Kyle	R-R	6-4	225	12-23-90	0	0	3.29	12	0	0	0	14	16	5	5	0	2	16	.281	.353	.250	10.54	1.32
Eickhoff, Jerad	R-R	6-4	200	7-2-90	0	1	1.93	4	0	0	1	5	1	1	1	0	1	4	.067	.111	.000	7.71	1.93
Faulkner, Andrew	R-L	6-3	180	9-12-92	0	2	2.16	12	7	0	0	25	17	9	6	1	4	27	.187	.083	.203	9.72	1.44
Haase, Anthony	R-R	6-3	190	3-1-90	0	1	8.31	4	0	0	2	4	3	4	4	0	5	4	.200	.500	.154	8.31	10.38
Johnson, Kevin	L-L	6-5	215	12-3-87	1	0	4.22	8	0	0	2	21	25	11	10	0	11	27	.305	.200	.328	11.39	4.64
Klein, Phil	R-R	6-7	240	4-30-89	0	0	0.00	3	0	0	0	3	2	0	0	0	1	7	.182	.167	.200	23.63	3.38
Martinez, Nicholas	L-R	6-1	175	8-5-90	2	1	1.83	6	4	0	0	20	21	6	4	0	2	19	.266	.414	.180	8.69	0.92
Matthews, Kevin	R-L	5-11	180	11-29-92	1	0	1.50	7	3	0	0	12	10	4	2	1	5	12	.222	.333	.194	9.00	3.75
Mavare, Jose	R-R	6-0	175	2-19-90	0	1	1.93	9	2	0	0	23	14	5	5	0	4	8	.173	.244	.100	13.11	3.09
McKinnon, Steve	R-R	6-4	220	4-17-92	1	0	8.84	12	1	0	0	18	25	19	18	2	9	10	.321	.235	.344	4.91	4.42
Nam, Yoon-Hee	L-L	6-2	190	8-4-87	0	0	13.50	1	0	0	0	1	1	2	2	0	1	2	.200	.500	.000	13.50	6.75
Parra, Luis	L-L	6-2	160	11-21-91	3	4	5.32	15	7	0	1	44	47	28	26	3	23	45	.276	.258	.281	9.20	4.70
Perez-Lobo, Andres	R-R	5-11	184	3-3-92	1	0	8.10	4	0	0	0	7	7	7	6	1	4	5	.250	.222	.263	6.75	5.40
Rijo, Ezequiel	R-R	6-4	190	9-12-90	3	0	5.31	14	6	0	1	41	54	28	24	3	13	36	.327	.341	.322	7.97	2.88
Robinson, Samuel	L-L	6-2	175	10-26-89	1	0	6.23	7	0	0	0	9	8	6	6	1	2	5	.242	.250	.241	5.19	2.08
Stanford, Tim	R-R	6-0	191	5-7-89	0	0	6.35	5	0	0	1	6	7	4	4	0	6	4	.269	.300	.250	9.53	6.35
Strong, Paul	L-L	6-2	195	8-18-90	1	1	3.34	16	4	0	1	32	33	13	12	3	12	25	.277	.105	.310	6.96	3.34
Williams, Greg	L-L	6-4	205	12-30-89	4	1	3.42	13	0	0	1	24	24	10	9	0	6	20	.267	.176	.288	7.61	2.28
Wiser, Kenneth	R-R	6-7	235	11-27-88	0	1	5.00	8	0	0	0	9	10	5	5	0	6	7	.278	.286	.276	7.00	6.00

Fielding

Catcher	PCT	G	PO	A	E	DP	PB
Edmonds	.988	29	220	32	3	4	3
Maloney	.955	4	17	4	1	1	1
Oropeza	.985	16	114	16	2	1	3
Torres	.986	17	126	20	2	1	2

First Base	PCT	G	PO	A	E	DP
Leeds	.988	27	228	18	3	23
McGuiness	1.000	2	13	0	0	1
Murphy	.947	4	34	2	2	6
Oropeza	1.000	6	34	5	0	2
Torres	.990	21	182	19	2	8

Second Base	PCT	G	PO	A	E	DP
Mendez	.980	21	41	56	2	10
Swift	.961	20	35	38	3	13
Urbanus	.967	22	31	56	3	13

Third Base	PCT	G	PO	A	E	DP
Leeds	.714	4	2	3	2	0
Olt	.833	4	2	8	2	1
Oropeza	.667	1	2	4	3	0
Robinson	.941	6	2	14	1	0
Rua	.936	43	29	88	8	7
Swift	.923	9	1	11	1	2

Shortstop	PCT	G	PO	A	E	DP
Marte	1.000	7	6	14	0	2
Mendez	.949	19	18	38	3	8
Rua	1.000	2	3	3	0	0

	PCT	G	PO	A	E	DP
Sardinas	.925	14	15	34	4	7
Urbanus	.941	27	35	60	6	12

Outfield	PCT	G	PO	A	E	DP
Akins	.976	48	80	3	2	1
De Los Santos	.000	1	0	0	0	0
Grayson	.972	46	66	4	2	0
Harlin	.857	23	23	1	4	1
Henry	1.000	20	31	1	0	0
Johnson	1.000	6	5	0	0	0
Martin	.500	4	1	0	1	0
Radcliffe	.952	21	17	3	1	0
Williams	1.000	34	46	3	0	0

DOMINICAN SUMMER LEAGUE

Batting	B-T	HT	WT	DOB	AVG	vLH	vRH	G	AB	R	H	2B	3B	HR	RBI	BB	HBP	SH	SF	SO	SB	CS	SLG	OBP
Abreu, Esdras	R-R	6-3	185	3-21-92	.236	.240	.235	35	106	19	25	5	2	3	18	9	4	0	1	29	2	2	.406	.317
Campos, Belarmino	B-R	5-10	165	6-19-93	.300	.529	.226	22	70	10	21	2	2	0	11	8	4	0	1	6	1	2	.386	.398
Castillo, Elio	R-R	6-1	160	3-1-94	.228	.400	.171	37	101	14	23	3	1	0	10	16	3	0	3	14	4	2	.277	.341
Cedeno, Diego	L-L	5-11	160	5-19-92	.338	.394	.320	56	130	28	44	4	0	0	17	24	2	0	2	20	6	3	.369	.443
Cedeno, Luis	R-R	6-1	165	2-7-92	.221	.182	.234	29	86	11	19	5	0	0	9	7	3	0	3	8	1	0	.279	.293
Feliz, Aneudy	R-R	6-0	180	1-18-93	.200	.267	.183	31	75	8	15	2	1	0	7	7	2	0	0	27	2	0	.253	.286
Garia, Christopher	B-R	6-0	165	12-16-92	.315	.370	.297	61	219	49	69	7	3	0	18	36	4	0	2	45	31	10	.374	.418
Gonzalez, Alex	R-R	5-11	165	7-7-91	.297	.349	.276	52	148	32	44	9	0	0	21	23	6	0	0	34	8	6	.358	.412
Gonzalez, Jose	B-R	6-1	175	3-16-94	.264	.250	.268	39	129	26	34	3	5	0	20	21	3	0	1	35	8	5	.364	.377
Jesus, Anderson	R-R	6-2	168	2-19-94	.260	.302	.246	48	169	23	44	11	3	0	20	6	4	0	2	44	3	1	.361	.298
Lantigua, Smerling	R-R	6-2	180	2-3-94	.260	.245	.265	54	200	21	52	7	3	1	23	17	4	0	1	56	4	4	.340	.329
Larrazabal, Gabriel	L-L	6-0	160	4-13-93	.200	.286	.154	9	20	3	4	0	0	0	2	1	0	0	0	6	1	1	.200	.304
Marte, Luis	R-R	6-1	170	12-15-93	.290	.250	.301	60	231	29	67	16	1	2	42	6	2	0	4	38	17	10	.394	.309
Mendez, Luis	B-R	5-9	155	1-1-93	.250	.500	.200	5	12	4	3	0	0	0	3	5	0	0	0	2	1	0	.250	.471
Obispo, Christefer	R-R	6-3	180	6-21-92	.217	.200	.220	39	120	15	26	7	2	0	18	9	3	0	3	41	6	2	.308	.281
Pirela, Oswaldo	R-R	5-10	165	10-13-91	.254	.217	.271	25	71	12	18	1	0	0	6	8	3	0	1	6	1	1	.268	.349
Santos, Jose	B-R	6-0	170	11-12-93	.000	.000	.000	2	2	0	0	0	0	0	1	0	0	0	0	2	0	0	.000	.333
Triunfel, Alberto	R-R	5-11	160	2-1-94	.257	.154	.279	43	148	28	38	8	1	0	20	11	7	0	2	21	8	2	.324	.333
Urias, Ramon	R-R	5-10	150	6-3-94	.213	.242	.202	49	122	14	26	5	0	1	13	15	9	0	2	20	2	1	.279	.338
Vivili, Fernando	R-R	6-3	210	1-9-94	.189	.154	.198	43	132	16	25	9	1	0	16	16	4	0	0	51	3	0	.273	.296

Pitching	B-T	HT	WT	DOB	W	L	ERA	G	GS	CG	SV	IP	H	R	ER	HR	BB	SO	AVG	vLH	vRH	K/9	BB/9
Beltre, Dario	R-R	6-3	170	11-19-92	0	2	3.38	14	8	0	0	35	27	24	13	0	21	29	.201	.200	.202	7.53	5.45
De Jesus, Jorge	R-R	6-0	205	1-17-92	1	0	12.46	10	0	0	0	13	15	19	18	1	4	10	.283	.250	.297	6.92	2.77
De La Torre, Luis	L-L	6-1	170	1-12-93	0	0	1.62	10	0	0	1	17	13	3	3	0	10	10	.217	.200	.218	5.40	5.40
Fandino, Jesus	R-R	6-2	165	1-27-94	2	2	2.37	15	1	0	0	30	19	12	8	0	14	14	.181	.241	.158	4.15	4.15
Gil, Leonel	L-L	6-0	160	2-5-91	1	3	4.50	17	0	0	0	32	34	19	16	1	19	27	.264	.364	.254	7.59	5.34
Gomez, Jose	R-R	6-1	155	10-4-93	3	2	3.15	18	6	0	1	40	41	22	14	2	11	35	.261	.279	.254	7.88	2.48
Grullon, Geuris	L-L	6-5	185	12-20-89	2	0	3.72	12	0	0	2	10	7	4	4	0	10	12	.194	.000	.206	11.17	9.31
Leclerc, Angelo	R-R	6-0	170	10-9-91	4	1	0.59	20	3	0	4	46	26	8	3	0	19	51	.159	.167	.155	10.05	3.74
Leclerc, Jose	R-R	6-0	165	12-19-93	3	1	2.36	20	1	0	1	34	25	14	9	1	18	27	.203	.289	.165	7.08	4.72
Lopez, Frank	L-L	6-1	175	2-18-94	1	0	2.03	8	7	0	0	31	20	8	7	2	13	29	.180	.400	.158	8.42	3.77
Montero, Dennys	R-R	6-0	170	11-20-89	4	4	2.00	17	0	0	4	27	16	9	6	2	11	15	.167	.107	.191	5.00	3.67
Morel, Luis	R-R	6-2	188	9-14-93	1	0	10.80	4	0	0	0	5	10	8	6	0	2	1	.417	.571	.353	1.80	3.60
Moreno, Luis	R-R	6-0	170	6-18-92	2	1	4.71	18	3	0	1	36	42	20	19	5	10	15	.302	.300	.303	3.72	2.48
Nunez, Nerfy	L-L	6-3	210	8-12-92	2	3	3.10	14	9	0	0	41	43	29	14	0	27	22	.285	.154	.297	4.87	5.98
Pena, Richelson	R-R	6-1	170	9-29-93	3	3	4.00	14	12	1	0	54	57	29	24	2	15	32	.277	.228	.295	5.33	2.50
Rodriguez, Ricardo	R-R	6-2	220	8-31-92	4	1	4.05	11	0	0	1	20	20	13	9	0	6	21	.266	.421	.217	9.45	2.70
Tirado, Pedro	L-L	6-2	180	12-18-90	5	3	4.14	15	10	0	1	59	60	28	27	5	11	38	.268	.235	.271	5.83	1.69
Valdespina, Jose	R-R	6-6	220	3-22-92	2	3	2.82	15	10	0	1	51	40	19	16	1	22	40	.217	.250	.206	7.06	3.88
Vasquez, Kelvin	R-R	6-4	180	4-6-93	0	1	3.24	9	1	0	0	17	20	9	6	0	7	10	.299	.227	.333	5.40	3.78

Fielding

Catcher	PCT	G	PO	A	E	DP	PB
Cedeno	.961	26	127	21	6	0	4
Pirela	.972	23	119	19	4	1	2
Vivili	.990	30	177	23	2	0	7

First Base	PCT	G	PO	A	E	DP
Castillo	.994	20	157	8	1	7
Feliz	1.000	17	106	2	0	6
Gonzalez	1.000	12	88	4	0	9
Larrazabal	1.000	1	1	0	0	1
Obispo	.990	37	295	15	3	34
Urias	.000	1	0	0	0	0

Second Base	PCT	G	PO	A	E	DP
Campos	.833	5	7	8	3	1
Gonzalez	.986	19	25	48	1	7

Marte	.949	12	24	32	3	5
Mendez	1.000	2	5	9	0	3
Triunfel	.988	21	40	45	1	8
Urias	.977	27	35	50	2	10

Third Base	PCT	G	PO	A	E	DP
Campos	.929	9	6	20	2	1
Castillo	.941	11	7	25	2	2
Feliz	1.000	2	0	1	0	1
Gonzalez	1.000	2	1	1	0	0
Lantigua	.846	45	38	99	25	14
Urias	1.000	9	14	12	0	2

Shortstop	PCT	G	PO	A	E	DP
Campos	.789	4	5	10	4	1
Castillo	1.000	3	4	5	0	2

Gonzalez	1.000	1	2	4	0	0
Marte	.945	47	78	129	12	19
Triunfel	.969	21	25	68	3	9
Urias	1.000	1	1	0	0	0

Outfield	PCT	G	PO	A	E	DP
Abreu	.971	26	32	1	1	0
Cedeno	.966	51	80	6	3	0
Garia	.993	60	131	2	1	1
Gonzalez	1.000	16	14	0	0	0
Gonzalez	.984	38	58	3	1	0
Jesus	.938	41	60	0	4	0
Larrazabal	.900	6	8	1	1	0
Urias	1.000	3	1	0	0	0

TEXAS RANGERS

Toronto Blue Jays

SEASON IN A SENTENCE: The Jays had a new outlook under general manager Alex Anthopoulos and first-year manager John Farrell, but the same old results, finishing fourth in the American League East for the fourth consecutive season with an 81-81 record.

HIGH POINT: Jose Bautista showed that he was no one-hit wonder, building on a monstrous 2010 campaign by batting .302/.447/.608 with 43 home runs and 103 RBIs. Ricky Romero emerged as an ace and went 15-11, 2.92 in 32 starts with 178 strikeouts.

LOW POINT: The Jays are depending on young players like Kyle Drabek moving them up in the standings. He made the major league rotation out of spring training and got off to a good start, standing at 2-0, 3.30 after a win over the Rangers at the end of April, but after his ERA ballooned to 5.70 in a loss the the Red Sox on June 12, he found himself back in Triple-A. He went 5-4, 7.44 there, with 45 strikeouts and 41 walks in 75 innings while allowing 111 hits, before returning to the big leagues for a few relief appearances in September.

NOTABLE ROOKIES: While Drabek had his ups and downs, the Jays think they found their young hitting cornerstone in third baseman Brett Lawrie, a Canadian who hit .293/.373/.580 with 21 extra-base hits in 150 at-bats after getting called up. He hit nine home runs, including an extra-inning, walkoff shot against Boston on Sept. 5. Catcher J.P. Arencibia hit just .219, but showed off his power with 23 home runs. Eric Thames was called upon when Travis Snider continued to struggle and held his own by hitting .262/.313/.456.

KEY TRANSACTIONS: Anthopoulos was able to dump Vernon Wells' contract on the Angels in exchange for Mike Napoli, but flipped the catcher to the Rangers for reliever Frank Francisco. He got a potential star from the Cardinals in outfielder Colby Rasmus, who wore out his welcome in St. Louis. He helped the Cardinals shore up their bullpen for their playoff run, but didn't give up any key pieces from an improving farm system.

DOWN ON THE FARM: Double-A New Hampshire went 77-65 during the regular season and went on to win the Eastern League title. Short-season Vancouver won the Northwest League title in its first season as a Jays affiliate, and Toronto's minor league teams had a .537 winning percentage overall, fourth-best in baseball.

OPENING DAY PAYROLL: $62,567,800 (23rd)

PLAYERS OF THE YEAR

KEVIN LITTLEFIELD

MAJOR LEAGUE	MINOR LEAGUE
Jose Bautista	**Travis d'Arnaud**
of	c
.302/.447/.608	(Double-A)
43 HR, 103 RBIs	.311/.371/.542
1.056 OPS, 1st in AL	33 2B, 21 HR

ORGANIZATION LEADERS

BATTING		*Minimum 250 PA
MAJORS		
* AVG	Jose Bautista	.302
* OPS	Jose Bautista	1.055
HR	Jose Bautista	43
RBI	Jose Bautista	103
MINORS		
* AVG	David Cooper, Las Vegas	.364
* OBP	David Cooper, Las Vegas	.439
* SLG	Travis d'Arnaud, New Hampshire	.542
R	Darin Mastroianni, New Hampshire/Las Vegas	92
H	David Cooper, Las Vegas	170
TB	Adam Loewen, Las Vegas	264
2B	David Cooper, Las Vegas	51
3B	Darin Mastroianni, New Hampshire/Las Vegas	9
HR	Brad Glenn, Dunedin	26
RBI	David Cooper, Las Vegas	96
BB	David Cooper, Las Vegas	67
	Marcus Knecht, Lansing	67
SO	Anthony Gose, New Hampshire	154
SB	Anthony Gose, New Hampshire	70
PITCHING		#Minimum 75 IP
MAJORS		
W	Ricky Romero	15
# ERA	Ricky Romero	2.92
SO	Brandon Morrow	203
SV	Frank Francisco	17
MINORS		
W	Drew Hutchison, Lansing/Dunedin/N.H.	14
	Casey Lawrence, Lansing/Dunedin	14
L	Chad Jenkins, Dunedin/New Hampshire	12
# ERA	Nestor Molina, Dunedin/New Hampshire	2.21
G	Wes Etheridge, Dunedin/New Hampshire	54
GS	Drew Hutchison, Lansing/Dunedin/N.H.	27
	Chad Jenkins, Dunedin/New Hampshire	27
SV	Wes Etheridge, Dunedin/New Hampshire	33
IP	Chad Jenkins, Dunedin/New Hampshire	167.2
BB	Joel Carreno, New Hampshire	68
SO	Drew Hutchison, Lansing/Dunedin/N.H.	171
# AVG	Joel Carreno, New Hampshire	.208

2011 PERFORMANCE

General Manager: Alex Anthopoulos. **Farm Director:** Charlie Wilson. **Scouting Director:** Andrew Tinnish.

Class	Team	League	W	L	PCT	Finish	Manager(s)
Majors	Toronto Blue Jays	American	81	81	.500	7th (14)	John Farrell
Triple-A	Las Vegas 51s	Pacific Coast	71	73	.493	t-6th (16)	Marty Brown
Double-A	New Hampshire Fisher Cats	Eastern	77	65	.542	2nd (12)	Sal Fasano
High A	Dunedin Blue Jays	Florida State	79	61	.564	1st (12)	Clayton McCullough
Low A	Lansing Lugnuts	Midwest	77	60	.562	3rd (16)	Mike Redmond
Short-season	Vancouver Canadians	Northwest	39	37	.513	3rd (8)	John Schneider
Rookie	Bluefield Blue Jays	Appalachian	40	28	.588	3rd (10)	Dennis Holmberg
Rookie	GCL Blue Jays	Gulf Coast	27	32	.458	t-9th (15)	Omar Malave
Overall 2011 Minor League Record			410	354	.537	4th (30)	

ORGANIZATION STATISTICS

TORONTO BLUE JAYS
AMERICAN LEAGUE

Batting	B-T	HT	WT	DOB	AVG	vLH	vRH	G	AB	R	H	2B	3B	HR	RBI	BB	HBP	SH	SF	SO	SB	CS	SLG	OBP
Arencibia, J.P.	R-R	6-1	210	1-5-86	.219	.259	.206	129	443	47	97	20	4	23	78	36	4	0	3	133	1	1	.438	.282
Bautista, Jose	R-R	6-0	195	10-19-80	.302	.336	.292	149	513	105	155	24	2	43	103	132	6	0	4	111	9	5	.608	.447
Cooper, David	L-L	6-0	200	2-12-87	.211	.286	.193	27	71	9	15	7	0	2	12	7	1	0	2	14	0	0	.394	.284
Davis, Rajai	R-R	5-10	195	10-19-80	.238	.288	.221	95	320	44	76	21	6	1	29	15	1	0	1	63	34	11	.350	.273
Encarnacion, Edwin	R-R	6-2	235	1-7-83	.272	.276	.271	134	481	70	131	36	0	17	55	43	3	0	3	77	8	2	.453	.334
Escobar, Yunel	R-R	6-2	205	11-2-82	.290	.330	.279	133	513	77	149	24	3	11	48	61	6	0	5	70	3	3	.413	.369
Hill, Aaron	R-R	5-11	200	3-21-82	.225	.226	.224	104	396	38	89	15	1	6	45	23	4	0	6	53	16	3	.313	.270
Johnson, Kelly	L-R	6-1	195	2-22-82	.270	.366	.216	33	115	16	31	4	2	3	9	16	1	0	0	31	3	3	.417	.364
Lawrie, Brett	R-R	6-0	215	1-18-90	.293	.295	.292	43	150	26	44	8	4	9	25	16	3	0	0	31	7	1	.580	.373
Lind, Adam	L-L	6-1	220	7-17-83	.251	.243	.253	125	499	56	125	16	0	26	87	32	3	0	8	107	1	1	.439	.295
Loewen, Adam	L-L	6-6	235	4-9-84	.188	.000	.222	14	32	4	6	1	0	1	4	3	2	0	0	13	0	0	.313	.297
Mastroianni, Darin	R-R	5-11	190	8-26-85	.000	.167	.000	1	2	0	0	0	0	0	0	0	0	0	0	1	0	0	.000	.000
McCoy, Mike	R-R	5-9	180	4-2-81	.198	.190	.201	80	197	26	39	8	0	2	10	25	1	0	0	41	12	2	.269	.291
McDonald, John	R-R	5-9	180	9-24-74	.250	.250	.250	65	168	19	42	8	1	2	20	8	1	0	2	18	2	4	.345	.285
Molina, Jose	R-R	6-2	250	6-3-75	.281	.276	.283	55	171	19	48	12	1	3	15	15	1	0	0	44	2	1	.415	.342
Nix, Jayson	R-R	6-0	195	8-26-82	.169	.273	.149	46	136	15	23	5	1	4	16	12	2	0	1	42	4	1	.309	.245
Patterson, Corey	L-R	5-10	180	8-13-79	.252	.301	.238	89	317	44	80	16	3	6	33	15	1	0	2	65	13	8	.379	.287
Rasmus, Colby	L-L	6-2	200	8-11-86	.173	.146	.188	35	133	14	23	10	0	3	13	5	0	0	1	39	0	0	.316	.201
Rivera, Juan	R-R	6-2	230	7-3-78	.243	.327	.219	70	247	22	60	11	0	6	28	22	2	0	4	41	3	2	.360	.305
Snider, Travis	L-L	6-0	235	2-2-88	.225	.116	.257	49	187	23	42	14	0	3	30	11	1	0	2	56	9	3	.348	.269
Teahen, Mark	L-R	6-3	230	9-6-81	.190	.200	.185	27	42	3	8	1	0	1	3	4	0	0	0	17	0	0	.286	.261
2-team total (51 Chicago)					.200	—	—	78	160	14	32	4	0	4	14	16	0	0	4	45	0	1	.300	.273
Thames, Eric	L-R	6-1	205	11-10-86	.262	.209	.279	95	362	58	95	24	5	12	37	23	5	0	3	88	2	1	.456	.313
Wise, Dewayne	L-L	5-11	195	2-24-78	.125	.125	.125	20	32	4	4	0	1	2	2	0	0	0	0	15	2	0	.375	.125
Woodward, Chris	R-R	6-0	190	6-27-76	.000	.000	.000	11	10	3	0	0	0	0	0	0	0	0	0	4	0	0	.000	.000

Pitching	B-T	HT	WT	DOB	W	L	ERA	G	GS	CG	SV	IP	H	R	ER	HR	BB	SO	AVG	vLH	vRH	K/9	BB/9
Alvarez, Henderson	R-R	6-1	195	4-18-90	1	3	3.53	10	10	0	0	64	64	26	25	8	8	40	.262	.252	.274	5.65	1.13
Beck, Chad	R-R	6-4	245	1-17-85	0	0	0.00	3	0	0	0	2	1	0	0	0	3	1	.125	.500	.000	11.57	0.00
Camp, Shawn	R-R	6-0	205	11-18-75	6	3	4.21	67	0	0	1	66	79	36	31	3	22	32	.303	.347	.263	4.34	2.98
Carreno, Joel	R-R	6-0	190	3-7-87	1	0	1.15	11	0	0	0	16	11	2	2	1	4	14	.200	.250	.161	8.04	2.30
Cecil, Brett	R-L	6-1	235	7-2-86	4	11	4.73	20	20	2	0	124	122	68	65	22	42	87	.256	.186	.282	6.33	3.06
Dotel, Octavio	R-R	6-0	220	11-25-73	2	1	3.68	36	0	0	1	29	20	13	12	5	12	30	.187	.237	.159	9.20	3.68
Drabek, Kyle	R-R	6-1	220	12-8-87	4	5	6.06	18	14	0	0	79	87	54	53	10	55	51	.289	.304	.269	5.83	6.29
Farquhar, Danny	R-R	5-11	180	2-17-87	0	0	13.50	3	0	0	0	2	4	4	3	0	2	1	.500	.667	.400	4.50	9.00
Francisco, Frank	R-R	6-2	250	9-11-79	1	4	3.55	54	0	0	17	51	49	21	20	7	18	50	.253	.246	.292	8.82	3.20
Frasor, Jason	R-R	5-9	180	8-9-77	2	1	2.98	44	0	0	0	42	38	15	14	4	15	37	.244	.260	.228	7.87	3.19
2-team total (20 Chicago)					3	3	3.60	64	0	0	0	60	58	25	24	7	26	57	—	—	—	8.55	3.90
Janssen, Casey	R-R	6-3	225	9-17-81	6	0	2.26	55	0	0	2	56	47	14	14	2	14	53	.228	.220	.234	8.57	2.26
Ledezma, Wil	L-L	6-4	225	1-21-81	0	0	15.00	1	0	0	0	6	11	10	10	1	7	6	.393	.500	.286	9.00	10.50
Lewis, Rommie	L-L	6-5	230	9-2-82	0	0	9.00	6	0	0	0	5	12	8	5	1	2	5	.444	.500	.412	9.00	3.60
Litsch, Jesse	R-R	6-1	225	3-9-85	6	3	4.44	28	8	0	1	75	69	40	37	10	28	66	.245	.279	.203	7.92	3.36
McGowan, Dustin	R-R	6-3	235	3-24-82	0	2	6.43	5	4	0	0	21	20	15	15	4	13	20	.247	.326	.158	8.57	5.57
Miller, Trever	R-L	6-3	200	5-29-73	0	0	4.91	6	0	0	0	6	6	2	2	1	2	2	.375	.667	.000	4.91	4.91
2-team total (3 Boston)					0	0	3.18	9	0	0	0	6	6	2	2	1	2	3	—	—	—	4.76	3.18
Mills, Brad	L-L	6-0	185	3-5-85	1	2	9.82	5	4	0	0	18	23	20	20	4	12	18	.299	.345	.271	8.84	5.89
Morrow, Brandon	R-R	6-3	195	7-26-84	11	11	4.72	30	30	0	0	179	162	103	94	21	69	203	.237	.220	.260	10.19	3.46
Perez, Luis	L-L	6-0	160	1-20-85	3	3	5.12	37	4	0	0	65	74	40	37	9	27	54	.287	.260	.305	7.48	3.74
Purcey, David	L-L	6-4	240	4-22-82	0	0	11.57	5	0	0	0	2	3	3	3	0	4	3	.300	.750	.000	11.57	15.43
3-team total (19 Detroit, 9 Oakland)					1	2	5.61	33	0	0	0	34	33	21	21	2	27	22	—	—	—	5.88	7.22
Rauch, Jon	R-R	6-10	290	9-27-78	5	4	4.85	53	0	0	11	52	56	28	28	11	14	36	.269	.267	.272	6.23	2.42
Reyes, Jo-Jo	L-L	6-2	230	11-20-84	5	8	5.40	20	20	1	0	110	140	78	66	14	35	64	.306	.317	.302	5.24	2.86

Pitching

Pitching	B-T	HT	WT	DOB	W	L	ERA	G	GS	CG	SV	IP	H	R	ER	HR	BB	SO	AVG	vLH	vRH	K/9	BB/9
2-team total (9 Baltimore)					7	11	5.57	29	25	1	0	141	176	99	87	21	48	87	—	—	—	5.57	3.07
Richmond, Scott	R-R	6-5	220	8-30-79	0	0	0.00	1	0	0	0	0	0	0	0	0	0	0	.000	.400	.000	0.00	0.00
Romero, Ricky	R-L	6-0	215	11-6-84	15	11	2.92	32	32	4	0	225	176	85	73	26	80	178	.216	.269	.195	7.12	3.20
Rzepczynski, Marc	L-L	6-1	205	8-29-85	2	3	2.97	43	0	0	0	39	28	16	13	2	15	33	.201	.159	.243	7.55	3.43
Stewart, Zach	R-R	6-2	205	9-28-86	0	1	4.86	3	3	0	0	17	26	9	9	2	5	10	.382	.438	.333	5.40	2.70
2-team total (10 Chicago)					2	6	5.88	13	11	1	0	67	90	44	44	11	18	45	—	—	—	6.01	2.41
Tallet, Brian	L-L	6-6	220	9-21-77	0	1	54.00	1	0	0	0	2	2	2	2	0	2	1	.667	.000	.667	27.00	54.00
Villanueva, Carlos	R-R	6-2	230	11-28-83	6	4	4.04	33	13	0	0	107	103	49	48	11	32	68	.251	.259	.241	5.72	2.69
Walters, P.J.	R-R	6-4	200	3-12-85	0	0	0.00	1	0	0	0	1	0	0	0	0	1	1	.000	.000	.000	9.00	9.00

Fielding

Catcher	PCT	G	PO	A	E	DP	PB
Arencibia	.993	122	822	72	6	4	12
Molina	.997	48	342	24	1	3	8

First Base	PCT	G	PO	A	E	DP
Cooper	.964	15	99	7	4	9
Encarnacion	.980	25	192	9	4	16
Lind	.996	109	952	64	4	88
Rivera	.995	21	178	15	1	20
Teahen	1.000	7	7	1	0	0

Second Base	PCT	G	PO	A	E	DP
Hill	.985	104	193	280	7	71
Johnson	.972	33	53	86	4	21
McCoy	.980	10	16	32	1	4
McDonald	.988	21	24	57	1	13
Nix	1.000	4	4	6	0	1

	PCT	G	PO	A	E	DP
Woodward	1.000	2	0	5	0	1

Third Base	PCT	G	PO	A	E	DP
Bautista	.975	25	17	62	2	1
Encarnacion	.892	36	23	43	8	2
Lawrie	.963	43	38	120	6	10
McCoy	1.000	16	6	10	0	0
McDonald	.983	26	18	39	1	8
Nix	.975	41	32	83	3	8
Teahen	1.000	4	3	10	0	1
Woodward	1.000	1	1	1	0	0

Shortstop	PCT	G	PO	A	E	DP
Escobar	.974	132	182	343	14	73
McCoy	.966	26	38	76	4	14
McDonald	.986	20	21	47	1	14
Woodward	.000	1	0	0	0	0

Outfield	PCT	G	PO	A	E	DP
Bautista	.976	116	233	13	6	5
Davis	.990	91	197	2	2	0
Loewen	.864	8	19	0	3	0
Mastroianni	1.000	1	2	0	0	0
McCoy	1.000	20	40	2	0	0
Nix	.000	1	0	0	0	0
Patterson	1.000	84	162	3	0	0
Rasmus	.963	35	79	0	3	1
Rivera	1.000	27	37	2	0	0
Snider	.969	48	91	4	3	1
Teahen	1.000	6	4	0	0	0
Thames	.987	79	146	2	2	1
Wise	.920	16	22	1	2	0

LAS VEGAS 51S

TRIPLE-A

PACIFIC COAST LEAGUE

Batting	B-T	HT	WT	DOB	AVG	vLH	vRH	G	AB	R	H	2B	3B	HR	RBI	BB	HBP	SH	SF	SO	SB	CS	SLG	OBP
Budde, Ryan	R-R	5-11	210	8-15-79	.234	.183	.253	67	218	34	51	8	1	7	30	30	3	0	3	73	1	2	.376	.331
Cooper, David	L-L	6-0	200	2-12-87	.364	.392	.354	120	467	77	170	51	1	9	96	67	2	0	9	43	1	3	.535	.439
Diaz, Jonathan	R-R	5-9	165	4-10-85	.297	.526	.200	19	64	9	19	3	0	1	10	15	0	0	1	15	2	1	.391	.425
Dominguez, Oliver	B-R	5-9	156	4-23-89	.200	.000	.250	2	5	1	1	1	0	0	1	0	0	0	0	1	0	0	.400	.200
Gomes, Yan	R-R	6-2	215	7-19-87	.214	.000	.333	4	14	1	3	1	0	0	1	0	0	0	0	4	0	0	.286	.267
Hechavarria, Adeiny	R-R	5-11	180	4-15-89	.389	.389	.389	25	108	16	42	6	2	2	11	8	0	0	0	21	1	2	.537	.431
Howard, Kevin	L-R	6-2	190	6-25-81	.291	.308	.287	35	127	20	37	2	0	5	18	9	0	0	0	19	3	3	.425	.338
Hurtado, Luis	R-R	5-11	175	11-4-88	.000	.000	.000	3	6	1	0	0	0	0	0	0	0	0	0	1	0	0	.000	.000
Jeroloman, Brian	L-R	6-0	200	5-10-85	.240	.226	.244	79	271	30	65	9	0	2	26	38	2	0	2	72	3	3	.295	.335
Lane, Jason	R-L	6-2	225	12-22-76	.291	.326	.266	60	213	38	62	16	1	6	34	24	0	0	3	36	1	2	.460	.358
Lawrie, Brett	R-R	6-0	215	1-18-90	.353	.329	.362	69	292	64	103	24	6	18	61	26	6	1	1	53	13	2	.661	.415
Loewen, Adam	L-L	6-6	235	4-9-84	.306	.303	.307	134	520	83	159	46	4	17	85	61	0	0	3	136	11	7	.508	.377
Mastroianni, Darin	R-R	5-11	190	8-26-85	.276	.278	.275	79	319	63	88	18	6	2	23	40	1	0	0	54	20	7	.389	.358
Mayorson, Manny	R-R	5-9	195	3-10-83	.313	.351	.298	97	335	57	105	16	1	3	54	31	2	0	4	25	16	8	.394	.371
McCoy, Mike	R-R	5-9	180	4-2-81	.311	.378	.282	38	148	33	46	6	0	2	20	33	1	0	0	23	14	5	.392	.440
Nanita, Ricardo	L-L	6-0	205	6-12-81	.363	.471	.340	51	193	38	70	13	0	8	33	18	1	0	2	22	6	4	.554	.416
Nix, Jayson	R-R	5-11	195	8-26-82	.270	.206	.287	41	163	30	44	12	2	8	29	14	4	0	1	38	3	0	.515	.341
Perales, Daniel	L-L	6-0	195	3-18-85	.305	.341	.294	51	177	25	54	12	2	1	29	9	1	0	7	27	2	0	.412	.330
Podsednik, Scott	L-L	6-0	185	3-18-76	.254	.118	.310	14	59	12	15	2	2	0	6	10	1	0	1	9	3	0	.356	.366
Romero, Niuman	B-R	6-1	190	1-24-85	.160	.286	.111	8	25	1	4	0	0	0	2	0	0	0	0	9	2	0	.160	.222
Shealy, Ryan	R-R	6-5	240	8-29-79	.272	.240	.282	62	224	38	61	13	0	11	56	31	5	0	0	62	0	1	.478	.373
Snider, Travis	L-L	6-0	235	2-2-88	.327	.286	.345	61	248	47	81	22	2	4	42	25	3	0	1	44	12	1	.480	.394
Stansberry, Craig	R-R	6-0	195	3-03-82	.303	.357	.288	18	66	9	20	3	0	2	14	7	0	0	2	16	3	1	.439	.360
Thames, Eric	L-R	6-1	205	11-10-86	.352	.245	.389	53	210	38	74	25	4	7	45	23	5	0	3	41	5	2	.610	.423
Vazquez, Ramon	L-R	5-11	195	8-21-76	.288	.182	.328	20	80	9	23	1	1	1	14	10	0	0	0	8	1	0	.363	.367
3-team total (40 Memphis, 10 New Orleans)					.267	—	—	70	240	33	64	8	1	1	32	31	0	0	0	39	2	1	.321	.351
Wise, Dewayne	L-L	5-11	195	2-24-78	.338	.366	.326	31	133	28	45	10	3	4	19	6	4	0	1	21	8	3	.549	.382
2-team total (2 New Orleans)					.338	—	—	33	142	28	48	11	3	4	19	6	4	0	1	25	8	3	.542	.379
Woodward, Chris	R-R	6-0	190	6-27-76	.296	.300	.295	108	422	67	125	32	2	13	65	39	1	0	6	70	4	2	.474	.353

Pitching	B-T	HT	WT	DOB	W	L	ERA	G	GS	CG	SV	IP	H	R	ER	HR	BB	SO	AVG	vLH	vRH	K/9	BB/9
Abreu, Winston	R-R	6-2	170	4-5-77	8	5	3.66	53	0	0	0	66	56	31	27	12	34	72	.227	.235	.221	9.77	4.61
Beck, Chad	R-R	6-4	245	1-17-85	2	4	6.70	8	8	0	0	42	61	36	31	7	26	23	.341	.341	.341	4.97	5.62
Boone, Randy	R-R	6-0	200	8-6-84	1	0	1.00	2	2	0	0	9	6	3	1	0	1	7	.182	.308	.100	7.00	1.00
Cecil, Brett	R-L	6-1	235	7-2-86	8	2	5.26	12	12	2	0	79	89	51	46	15	24	63	.283	.275	.288	7.21	2.75
Collazo, Willie	L-L	5-8	180	11-7-79	1	2	4.98	14	6	0	0	47	52	28	26	5	14	26	.289	.278	.296	4.98	2.68
Cordero, Chad	R-R	6-0	220	3-18-82	0	2	8.66	9	2	0	0	18	23	17	17	5	9	7	.329	.310	.341	3.57	4.58
Davies, Kyle	R-R	6-1	210	9-9-83	0	0	3.38	6	0	0	0	8	3	3	3	1	3	8	.111	.118	.100	9.00	3.38
2-team total (2 Omaha)					1	1	1.80	8	1	0	0	20	11	6	4	1	3	22	—	—	—	9.90	1.35
Drabek, Kyle	R-R	6-1	220	12-8-87	5	4	7.44	15	15	1	0	75	111	70	62	12	41	45	.355	.365	.345	5.40	4.92
Everts, Clint	B-R	6-2	195	8-10-84	0	0	6.00	9	0	0	0	15	21	11	10	3	8	12	.344	.367	.323	7.20	4.80
Farquhar, Danny	R-R	5-11	180	2-17-87	4	5	4.70	50	0	0	14	52	63	32	27	4	18	43	.300	.337	.276	7.49	3.14

Pitching	B-T	HT	WT	DOB	W	L	ERA	G	GS	CG	SV	IP	H	R	ER	HR	BB	SO	AVG	vLH	vRH	K/9	BB/9
2-team total (4 Sacramento)					4	5	4.07	54	0	0	15	60	70	33	27	4	21	52	—	—	—	7.84	3.17
Gaudin, Chad	R-R	5-10	190	3-24-83	2	3	6.14	6	6	0	0	29	37	21	20	2	9	13	.319	.333	.304	3.99	2.76
Gonzalez, Rey	R-R	5-9	215	11-1-85	2	3	11.69	5	5	0	0	22	45	29	29	3	13	9	.441	.469	.415	3.63	5.24
Henn, Sean	R-L	6-3	235	4-23-81	3	2	2.79	43	0	0	3	61	55	21	19	3	29	61	.240	.218	.252	8.95	4.26
Hinckley, Mike	R-L	6-3	195	10-5-82	0	0	5.68	5	0	0	0	6	7	5	4	0	3	4	.292	.500	.222	5.68	4.26
Janssen, Casey	R-R	6-3	225	9-17-81	0	0	0.00	1	0	0	0	2	1	0	0	0	0	3	.143	.500	.000	13.50	0.00
Johnson, David	R-R	6-5	205	8-25-82	0	0	9.00	7	0	0	0	9	14	9	9	1	3	7	.359	.364	.353	7.00	3.00
Korecky, Bobby	R-R	5-11	185	9-16-79	1	0	0.68	9	0	0	1	13	4	1	1	0	6	11	.095	.063	.115	7.43	4.05
LaMura, B.J.	R-R	6-1	200	1-1-81	0	0	67.50	2	0	0	0	2	11	15	15	3	5	1	.688	.500	1.000	4.50	22.50
Ledezma, Wil	L-L	6-4	225	1-21-81	1	1	4.50	36	0	0	3	48	49	32	24	6	19	64	.249	.206	.271	12.00	3.56
Lewis, Rommie	L-L	6-5	230	9-2-82	3	3	6.60	42	0	0	4	59	71	47	43	10	29	50	.296	.180	.364	7.67	4.45
Litsch, Jesse	R-R	6-1	225	3-9-85	1	2	8.16	6	6	0	0	29	41	26	26	5	11	27	.333	.356	.313	8.48	3.45
MacDonald, Mike	R-R	6-1	215	10-29-81	6	6	6.59	28	17	1	0	115	168	89	84	8	33	52	.350	.377	.328	4.08	2.59
Mills, Brad	L-L	6-0	185	3-5-85	11	9	4.00	24	24	1	0	157	161	73	70	20	39	136	.267	.260	.270	7.78	2.23
Perez, Luis	L-L	6-0	160	1-20-85	2	2	4.60	8	0	0	0	45	37	23	23	5	23	43	.230	.244	.213	8.60	4.60
Pino, Yohan	R-R	6-2	190	12-26-83	0	0	10.80	1	0	0	0	2	2	2	2	0	2	0	.286	.500	.200	0.00	10.80
Ray, Robert	R-R	6-4	195	1-21-84	1	3	7.22	6	6	0	0	34	41	30	27	9	7	30	.289	.327	.269	8.02	1.87
Richmond, Scott	R-R	6-5	220	8-30-79	6	9	7.33	26	20	0	0	113	149	98	92	24	56	87	.321	.310	.332	6.93	4.46
Roenicke, Josh	R-R	6-3	200	8-4-82	1	3	6.04	16	0	0	0	22	25	21	15	3	15	20	.281	.293	.271	8.06	6.04
2-team total (23 Colorado Springs)					1	4	4.58	39	0	0	0	53	55	35	27	6	22	42	—	—	—	7.13	3.74
Uvieto, Ronald	R-R	6-1	160	10-7-86	1	0	4.74	24	0	0	0	38	36	23	20	5	15	43	.245	.231	.256	10.18	3.55
Walters, P.J.	R-R	6-4	200	3-12-85	1	3	8.38	7	7	0	0	29	44	29	27	4	16	26	.349	.319	.386	8.07	4.97
2-team total (17 Memphis)					8	7	5.17	24	24	1	0	132	149	80	76	13	58	113	—	—	—	7.69	3.94

Fielding

Catcher	PCT	G	PO	A	E	DP	PB
Budde	.985	64	437	38	7	6	5
Gomes	.971	4	33	1	1	0	0
Hurtado	1.000	2	6	1	0	0	1
Jeroloman	.985	78	548	26	9	2	4

First Base	PCT	G	PO	A	E	DP
Budde	1.000	1	10	2	0	1
Cooper	.994	106	874	66	6	104
Lane	1.000	4	37	2	0	5
Loewen	.994	19	173	4	1	22
Shealy	1.000	16	126	5	0	13

Second Base	PCT	G	PO	A	E	DP
Budde	.875	2	2	5	1	1
Diaz	1.000	6	14	11	0	6
Dominguez	1.000	2	4	4	0	0
Howard	1.000	2	5	5	0	1
Mayorson	.982	82	153	230	7	72

	PCT	G	PO	A	E	DP
McCoy	1.000	3	6	8	0	1
Nix	.968	5	8	22	1	6
Romero	1.000	6	13	16	0	5
Stansberry	.976	8	18	23	1	9
Vazquez	1.000	1	13	20	0	4
Woodward	.974	27	54	58	3	26

Third Base	PCT	G	PO	A	E	DP
Howard	.917	26	22	66	8	8
Lawrie	.921	68	47	140	16	14
Nix	.983	19	15	44	1	6
Stansberry	.885	9	4	19	3	3
Woodward	.924	24	11	50	5	3

Shortstop	PCT	G	PO	A	E	DP
Diaz	.973	13	24	49	2	12
Hechavarria	.959	25	34	60	4	19
Mayorson	.951	9	13	26	2	10
McCoy	.954	25	39	86	6	28

	PCT	G	PO	A	E	DP
Nix	1.000	8	6	21	0	5
Romero	1.000	1	1	2	0	0
Stansberry	1.000	1	0	2	0	1
Vazquez	.929	13	18	34	4	6
Woodward	.952	52	74	144	11	30

Outfield	PCT	G	PO	A	E	DP
Lane	1.000	34	46	0	0	0
Loewen	.959	111	220	11	10	3
Mastroianni	.990	75	188	6	2	2
McCoy	.962	10	23	2	1	0
Nanita	1.000	35	59	1	0	0
Nix	1.000	6	11	1	0	0
Perales	.973	42	68	4	2	0
Podsednik	1.000	13	36	1	0	0
Snider	.945	46	83	3	5	0
Thames	.967	52	85	4	3	0
Wise	1.000	21	51	4	0	1

NEW HAMPSHIRE FISHER CATS   DOUBLE-A

EASTERN LEAGUE

Batting	B-T	HT	WT	DOB	AVG	vLH	vRH	G	AB	R	H	2B	3B	HR	RBI	BB	HBP	SH	SF	SO	SB	CS	SLG	OBP
Bowen, Joe	B-R	6-1	190	9-25-87	.000	.000	.000	4	4	1	0	0	0	0	0	1	0	0	0	1	0	0	.000	.200
Calderone, Adam	L-R	6-2	200	3-17-84	.171	.167	.172	10	35	1	6	2	1	1	8	3	0	0	1	7	1	0	.371	.231
2-team total (28 Erie)					.202	—	—	38	129	5	26	7	2	2	19	8	0	0	1	26	5	0	.333	.246
Crabbe, Callix	B-R	5-7	185	2-14-83	.259	.204	.275	69	220	32	57	9	1	7	31	30	1	0	2	29	9	8	.405	.348
d'Arnaud, Travis	R-R	6-2	195	2-10-89	.311	.336	.302	114	424	72	132	33	1	21	78	33	8	0	1	100	4	2	.542	.371
Davis, Rajai	R-R	5-10	195	10-19-80	.300	.400	.200	4	10	1	3	1	0	0	2	2	0	0	0	2	0	2	.400	.500
Diaz, Jonathan	R-R	5-9	165	4-10-85	.252	.230	.261	70	218	29	55	11	0	1	19	28	9	0	1	48	7	5	.317	.359
Dominguez, Oliver	B-R	5-9	156	4-23-89	.000	.000	.000	2	4	0	0	0	0	0	0	0	0	0	0	1	0	0	.000	.000
Gomes, Yan	R-R	6-2	215	7-19-87	.250	.236	.257	79	276	34	69	18	1	13	51	25	4	0	4	75	0	0	.464	.317
Gose, Anthony	L-L	6-1	190	8-10-90	.253	.252	.254	137	509	87	129	20	7	16	59	62	13	0	1	154	70	15	.415	.349
Hechavarria, Adeiny	R-R	5-11	180	4-15-89	.235	.305	.207	111	464	58	109	22	6	6	46	25	3	0	6	78	19	13	.347	.275
Howard, Kevin	L-R	6-2	190	6-25-81	.253	.294	.242	21	79	7	20	3	0	1	13	10	0	0	2	15	0	1	.329	.330
Jackson, Justin	R-R	6-1	186	12-11-88	.212	.050	.262	28	85	11	18	6	1	1	6	8	0	0	0	26	2	0	.341	.280
Mastroianni, Darin	R-R	5-11	190	8-26-85	.254	.333	.228	44	169	29	43	8	1	3	12	22	2	0	3	24	14	3	.355	.342
McDade, Mike	B-R	6-1	260	5-8-89	.281	.252	.292	125	484	71	136	37	0	16	74	28	8	0	4	104	0	1	.457	.328
Murphy, Jack	B-R	6-4	235	4-6-88	.167	.000	.250	3	6	1	1	0	0	0	2	0	0	0	0	2	0	0	.167	.375
Nanita, Ricardo	L-L	6-0	205	6-12-81	.299	.306	.296	58	201	25	60	11	1	3	23	11	3	0	2	24	9	0	.408	.341
Perales, Daniel	L-L	6-0	185	6-18-86	.207	.167	.225	31	116	15	24	5	0	4	18	8	4	0	2	16	5	2	.353	.277
Sierra, Moises	R-R	6-0	225	9-24-88	.277	.295	.270	133	495	81	137	19	3	18	67	39	12	0	4	93	16	14	.436	.342
Sobolewski, Mark	R-R	6-1	220	12-24-86	.273	.283	.268	112	400	49	109	20	0	8	49	30	2	0	3	96	0	0	.383	.324
Stansberry, Craig	R-R	6-0	190	10-31-82	.209	.190	.216	62	153	27	32	9	1	3	16	24	4	0	3	47	7	4	.340	.326
Tolisano, John	B-R	5-11	190	10-7-88	.221	.190	.235	111	339	46	75	22	1	14	53	47	2	0	3	101	7	4	.416	.317

Pitching	B-T	HT	WT	DOB	W	L	ERA	G	GS	CG	SV	IP	H	R	ER	HR	BB	SO	AVG	vLH	vRH	K/9	BB/9
Alvarez, Henderson	R-R	6-1	195	4-18-90	8	4	2.86	15	14	1	0	88	81	31	28	7	17	66	.245	.252	.238	6.75	1.74
Beck, Chad	R-R	6-4	245	1-17-85	7	4	3.69	22	14	0	0	95	92	41	39	7	28	70	.258	.307	.222	6.63	2.65

Pitching

Pitching	B-T	HT	WT	DOB	W	L	ERA	G	GS	CG	SV	IP	H	R	ER	HR	BB	SO	AVG	vLH	vRH	K/9	BB/9
Carreno, Joel	R-R	6-0	190	3-7-87	7	9	3.41	24	23	0	0	135	100	56	51	12	68	152	.208	.234	.188	10.16	4.54
Collazo, Willie	L-L	5-8	180	11-7-79	2	0	2.95	5	3	0	0	18	15	6	6	2	1	11	.224	.200	.238	5.40	0.49
Crawford, Evan	R-L	6-1	175	9-2-86	3	5	3.35	45	0	0	2	51	50	23	19	3	21	62	.260	.323	.231	10.94	3.71
Daly, Matt	R-R	5-9	180	8-14-86	4	0	6.25	29	0	0	0	36	39	26	25	2	28	29	.275	.200	.322	7.25	7.00
Etheridge, Wes	R-R	6-1	185	8-12-84	0	0	3.94	8	0	0	1	16	14	8	7	2	3	7	.237	.222	.250	3.94	1.69
Everts, Clint	B-R	6-2	195	8-10-84	0	1	2.59	40	0	0	5	49	32	18	14	2	20	56	.186	.176	.194	10.36	3.70
Farina, Alan	R-R	5-11	190	8-9-86	2	1	1.56	17	0	0	6	17	15	3	3	2	7	16	.224	.313	.143	8.31	3.63
Gailey, Frank	L-L	5-9	190	11-18-85	1	4	5.70	19	0	0	0	30	32	20	19	4	11	23	.286	.293	.282	6.90	3.30
Garcia, Dumas	R-R	6-2	165	7-7-83	0	0	3.00	2	0	0	0	3	2	2	1	0	1	2	.200	.500	.000	6.00	3.00
Gonzalez, Rey	R-R	5-9	215	11-1-85	8	3	3.36	28	11	0	0	99	113	47	37	2	27	52	.292	.288	.295	4.73	2.45
Hinckley, Mike	R-L	6-3	195	10-5-82	1	0	5.68	18	0	0	0	13	11	9	8	1	7	8	.224	.150	.276	5.68	4.97
Hutchison, Drew	L-R	6-2	165	8-22-90	3	0	1.20	3	3	0	0	15	10	2	2	0	2	21	.192	.179	.208	12.60	1.20
Janssen, Casey	R-R	6-3	225	9-17-81	0	0	0.00	5	0	0	5	5	1	0	0	0	1	7	.063	.000	.091	12.60	1.80
Jenkins, Chad	R-R	6-4	235	12-22-87	5	7	4.13	16	16	1	0	100	93	48	46	8	27	74	.247	.255	.242	6.64	2.42
Korecky, Bobby	R-R	5-11	185	9-16-79	3	3	2.50	35	0	0	12	40	28	11	11	3	10	40	.194	.219	.175	9.08	2.27
LaMura, B.J.	R-R	6-1	200	1-1-81	6	5	4.19	32	11	0	0	88	75	44	41	5	44	76	.231	.188	.262	7.77	4.50
Litsch, Jesse	R-R	6-1	225	3-9-85	0	0	1.04	2	2	0	0	9	6	1	1	0	0	9	.194	.118	.286	9.35	0.00
McGowan, Dustin	R-R	6-3	235	3-24-82	0	2	2.75	5	5	0	0	20	18	7	6	2	7	18	.247	.182	.300	8.24	3.20
McGuire, Deck	R-R	6-6	220	6-23-89	2	1	4.35	4	3	1	0	21	20	10	10	4	7	22	.253	.200	.286	9.58	3.05
Molina, Nestor	R-R	6-1	179	1-9-89	2	0	0.41	5	5	0	0	22	12	2	1	0	2	33	.156	.116	.206	13.50	0.82
Perkins, Vince	L-R	6-5	240	9-27-81	0	0	10.13	3	0	0	0	3	5	3	3	1	5	0	.417	.571	.200	0.00	16.88
Pino, Yohan	R-R	6-2	190	12-26-83	4	8	4.14	36	10	1	0	96	90	47	44	15	14	104	.245	.230	.257	9.78	1.32
2-team total (2 Akron)					4	8	4.08	38	10	1	0	97	92	47	44	15	14	106	—	—	—	9.84	1.30
Ray, Robert	R-R	6-4	195	1-21-84	1	2	6.27	6	6	0	0	33	32	26	23	4	17	29	.256	.333	.203	7.91	4.64
Stewart, Zach	R-R	6-2	205	9-28-86	5	5	4.20	16	16	1	0	94	106	49	44	6	27	74	.286	.284	.287	7.06	2.58
Uviedo, Ronald	R-R	6-1	160	10-7-86	3	1	4.29	26	0	0	1	36	37	17	17	3	13	39	.266	.242	.288	9.84	3.28

Fielding

Catcher	PCT	G	PO	A	E	DP	PB
Bowen	1.000	3	7	1	0	0	0
d'Arnaud	.993	98	775	57	6	7	13
Gomes	.986	43	317	39	5	2	4
Murphy	1.000	3	15	3	0	0	0

First Base	PCT	G	PO	A	E	DP
Gomes	.994	20	152	9	1	21
Howard	1.000	1	11	1	0	0
McDade	.993	115	909	57	7	79
Stansberry	.986	14	67	5	1	4

Second Base	PCT	G	PO	A	E	DP
Crabbe	.991	52	83	137	2	30
Diaz	.994	37	66	110	1	29
Dominguez	.000	1	0	0	0	0

	PCT	G	PO	A	E	DP
Howard	1.000	5	12	12	0	3
Jackson	1.000	2	2	5	0	2
Stansberry	.981	14	23	30	1	7
Tolisano	.969	35	60	95	5	19

Third Base	PCT	G	PO	A	E	DP
Crabbe	.778	3	2	5	2	0
Diaz	1.000	5	2	6	0	0
Dominguez	.500	1	1	0	1	0
Howard	.955	11	8	13	1	2
Sobolewski	.953	102	61	180	12	11
Stansberry	.970	26	26	39	2	7
Tolisano	.000	1	0	0	0	0

Shortstop	PCT	G	PO	A	E	DP
Diaz	.974	29	40	72	3	16

	PCT	G	PO	A	E	DP
Hechavarria	.974	111	138	279	11	68
Howard	.857	2	1	5	1	1
Jackson	1.000	2	4	1	0	1

Outfield	PCT	G	PO	A	E	DP
Calderone	1.000	8	19	0	0	0
Davis	1.000	4	7	0	0	0
Gose	.991	137	300	14	3	3
Jackson	.974	21	34	4	1	1
Mastroianni	.981	44	98	3	2	0
Nanita	1.000	11	24	1	0	0
Perales	1.000	29	54	6	0	1
Sierra	.983	132	224	11	4	2
Tolisano	.965	53	80	3	3	1

DUNEDIN BLUE JAYS

HIGH CLASS A

FLORIDA STATE LEAGUE

Batting	B-T	HT	WT	DOB	AVG	vLH	vRH	G	AB	R	H	2B	3B	HR	RBI	BB	HBP	SH	SF	SO	SB	CS	SLG	OBP
Ahrens, Kevin	B-R	6-1	195	4-26-89	.242	.250	.239	121	429	59	104	24	0	13	54	56	6	0	6	99	0	2	.389	.334
Bailli, Kenen	L-L	6-0	190	1-25-85	.294	.000	.294	7	17	5	5	1	0	1	3	1	0	0	0	4	0	0	.529	.333
Bowen, Joe	B-R	6-1	190	9-25-87	.135	.000	.184	17	52	5	7	0	0	0	3	9	0	0	0	20	0	0	.135	.262
Contreras, Ivan	B-R	5-9	155	1-3-87	.225	.277	.201	91	298	37	67	13	3	2	30	24	1	0	4	65	26	10	.309	.281
Davis, Rajai	R-R	5-10	195	10-19-80	.400	.000	.400	2	5	1	2	0	0	1	1	0	0	0	0	1	0	0	1.000	.400
Diaz, Jonathan	R-R	5-9	165	4-10-85	.400	.400	.400	3	10	3	4	1	0	0	1	3	0	0	0	3	0	0	.500	.538
Glenn, Brad	R-R	6-2	220	4-2-87	.263	.284	.256	111	418	59	110	25	1	26	80	30	6	0	4	123	0	0	.514	.319
Goins, Ryan	L-R	5-10	170	2-13-88	.286	.266	.293	101	353	50	101	24	5	3	52	32	0	0	3	67	2	2	.408	.343
Hawkins, Chris	L-R	6-2	195	8-17-91	.000	.000	.000	2	4	0	0	0	0	0	0	0	0	0	0	2	0	0	.000	.000
Hill, Aaron	R-R	5-11	200	3-21-82	.167	.000	.167	2	6	2	1	0	0	0	1	1	1	0	0	1	0	0	.167	.375
Hopkins, Chris	R-R	5-11	175	9-10-87	.222	.200	.232	58	135	20	30	10	0	0	13	23	3	0	0	32	11	1	.296	.348
Hurtado, Luis	R-R	5-11	175	11-4-88	1.000	.000	1.000	2	2	0	2	0	0	0	0	0	0	0	0	0	0	0	1.000	1.000
Jackson, Justin	R-R	6-1	186	12-11-88	.259	.319	.243	92	316	67	82	16	2	4	24	38	2	0	1	89	8	5	.361	.342
Jimenez, A.J.	R-R	5-11	200	5-1-90	.303	.320	.297	102	379	49	115	29	1	4	52	28	3	0	4	60	11	2	.417	.353
Lawrie, Brett	R-R	6-0	215	1-18-90	.125	.000	.167	4	8	0	1	0	0	0	1	0	0	0	0	1	0	0	.125	.364
Lind, Adam	L-L	6-1	220	7-17-83	.600	.250	.833	3	10	2	6	3	0	0	4	2	0	0	0	1	2	0	.900	.667
Mahler, Tim	R-R	6-3	190	9-21-87	.000	.000	.000	1	1	0	0	0	0	0	1	0	0	0	0	0	0	0	.000	.000
McDonald, John	R-R	5-9	180	9-24-74	.250	.000	.250	1	4	0	1	0	0	0	0	0	0	0	0	0	0	0	.250	.250
McElroy, Brad	L-R	5-11	195	4-24-86	.295	.253	.306	106	356	63	105	24	3	3	42	39	10	0	1	58	31	6	.404	.379
Nix, Jayson	R-R	5-11	200	8-26-82	.083	.111	.000	5	12	0	1	0	0	0	2	1	0	0	0	3	0	0	.083	.154
Nolan, Kevin	R-R	6-2	200	12-13-87	.281	.271	.285	72	242	32	68	20	0	4	20	36	1	0	4	47	2	3	.413	.375
Ochinko, Sean	R-R	5-11	205	10-21-87	.261	.252	.265	121	459	65	120	35	1	16	79	37	7	0	3	77	1	2	.447	.324
Patterson, Corey	L-R	5-10	180	8-13-79	.333	.000	.357	4	15	1	5	0	0	0	1	0	0	0	0	4	3	0	.333	.375
Podsednik, Scott	L-L	6-0	185	3-18-76	.250	.000	.250	3	12	1	3	1	0	0	1	2	0	0	0	2	0	0	.333	.357
Schimpf, Ryan	L-R	5-9	181	3-11-88	.240	.156	.265	57	196	30	47	9	2	10	36	22	7	0	3	52	2	0	.459	.333
Talley, Jon	L-R	6-3	220	2-18-89	.241	.212	.251	102	378	58	91	21	1	20	63	37	3	0	4	99	0	1	.460	.310

Batting	B-T	HT	WT	DOB	AVG	vLH	vRH	G	AB	R	H	2B	3B	HR	RBI	BB	HBP	SH	SF	SO	SB	CS	SLG	OBP
Van Kirk, Brian	R-R	5-11	210	8-10-85	.292	.325	.278	103	359	54	105	21	1	17	66	50	2	0	2	89	1	0	.499	.380
Wilson, Kenny	R-R	5-10	185	1-30-90	.201	.302	.165	48	164	21	33	8	2	0	10	16	6	0	0	52	17	4	.274	.296
Wise, Dewayne	L-L	5-11	195	2-24-78	.273	.000	.273	3	11	4	3	2	0	1	2	2	0	0	2	2	0	0	.727	.385

Pitching	B-T	HT	WT	DOB	W	L	ERA	G	GS	CG	SV	IP	H	R	ER	HR	BB	SO	AVG	vLH	vRH	K/9	BB/9
Alvarez, Henderson	R-R	6-1	195	4-18-90	0	1	6.48	2	2	0	0	8	11	9	6	0	1	4	.306	.316	.294	4.32	1.08
Antolin, Dustin	R-R	6-2	195	8-9-89	1	0	0.00	1	0	0	0	2	0	0	0	0	1	3	.000	.000	.000	16.20	5.40
Beck, Casey	R-R	6-1	215	3-28-87	0	0	3.00	9	0	0	0	9	10	6	3	1	4	5	.278	.333	.200	5.00	4.00
Beck, Chad	R-R	6-4	245	1-17-85	0	0	1.69	1	1	0	0	5	4	1	1	1	1	7	.222	.308	.000	11.81	1.69
Bongiovanni, Vince	R-R	6-5	215	1-11-83	2	0	5.95	4	0	0	0	20	22	13	13	4	7	15	.272	.340	.176	6.86	3.20
Collazo, Willie	L-L	5-8	180	11-7-79	0	0	6.00	1	1	0	0	3	5	2	2	1	0	4	.385	.500	.364	12.00	0.00
Daly, Matt	R-R	5-9	180	8-14-86	0	1	8.59	11	0	0	4	15	18	14	14	4	9	13	.321	.409	.265	7.98	5.52
Etheridge, Wes	R-R	6-1	185	8-12-84	1	1	1.89	46	0	0	32	48	40	11	10	1	7	38	.222	.212	.232	7.17	1.32
Francisco, Frank	R-R	6-2	250	9-11-79	0	1	10.80	5	0	0	0	5	6	7	6	2	4	6	.300	.250	.375	10.80	7.20
Gailey, Frank	L-L	5-9	190	11-18-85	4	2	1.84	26	0	0	2	44	26	9	9	1	10	38	.168	.131	.191	7.77	2.05
Garcia, Dumas	R-R	6-2	165	7-7-83	2	3	3.09	32	0	0	0	44	42	16	15	1	20	43	.256	.197	.296	8.86	4.12
Gracey, Scott	R-R	6-2	190	10-15-86	1	3	3.86	32	3	0	1	51	50	27	22	5	15	41	.255	.250	.259	7.19	2.63
Griffith, Shawn	R-R	5-10	180	5-24-87	0	0	0.00	3	0	0	0	5	3	0	0	0	2	3	.167	.167	.167	5.06	3.38
Hutchison, Drew	L-R	6-2	165	8-22-90	5	3	2.74	11	10	0	0	62	42	20	19	3	14	66	.194	.220	.161	9.53	2.02
Jenkins, Chad	R-R	6-4	235	12-22-87	4	5	3.07	11	11	0	0	67	71	33	23	3	14	44	.267	.264	.270	5.88	1.87
Lawrence, Casey	R-R	6-2	170	10-28-87	3	1	2.84	4	4	1	0	25	26	8	8	3	2	14	.268	.259	.279	4.97	0.71
Liebel, Andrew	R-R	6-0	195	3-22-86	2	3	5.50	8	8	0	0	38	54	25	23	6	12	19	.342	.370	.318	4.54	2.87
Loup, Aaron	L-L	5-11	180	12-19-87	4	3	4.66	48	0	0	5	66	67	38	34	6	27	56	.269	.218	.304	7.68	3.70
Malone, Chris	R-R	6-4	215	6-28-83	1	0	6.75	9	0	0	0	8	6	6	6	1	10	7	.231	.200	.273	7.88	11.25
McGowan, Dustin	R-R	6-3	235	3-24-82	0	2	2.87	7	7	0	0	16	13	5	5	0	7	17	.228	.185	.267	9.77	4.02
McGuire, Deck	R-R	6-6	220	6-23-89	7	4	2.75	19	18	0	0	105	89	38	32	9	38	102	.228	.229	.226	8.77	3.27
Molina, Nestor	R-R	6-1	179	1-9-89	10	3	2.58	21	18	0	0	108	102	37	31	8	14	115	.248	.235	.260	9.55	1.16
Morrow, Brandon	R-R	6-3	195	7-26-84	0	2	7.71	3	3	0	0	9	13	9	8	0	6	11	.310	.320	.294	10.61	5.79
Mozingo, Harold	R-R	6-1	192	3-29-85	2	0	2.82	17	0	0	0	22	20	8	7	2	6	22	.238	.262	.214	8.87	2.42
Phillabaum, Justin	R-R	6-2	180	4-18-86	1	0	9.58	8	0	0	0	10	20	13	11	1	6	8	.400	.500	.308	6.97	5.23
Shopshire, Ryan	R-R	6-5	200	11-8-85	1	2	8.56	16	4	0	0	27	40	26	26	5	26	18	.333	.362	.306	5.93	8.56
Tallet, Brian	L-L	6-6	220	9-21-77	1	0	2.25	4	0	0	0	4	4	1	1	1	0	5	.250	.143	.333	11.25	0.00
Tepera, Ryan	R-R	6-1	180	11-3-87	11	6	4.43	27	23	0	0	146	156	75	72	13	38	93	.276	.311	.246	5.72	2.34
Turnbull, Steve	R-R	6-3	215	11-25-86	1	4	5.28	26	0	0	0	31	36	23	18	2	6	25	.288	.333	.250	7.34	1.76
Villanueva, Carlos	R-R	6-2	230	11-28-83	0	0	0.00	1	1	0	0	1	1	0	0	0	0	2	.200	.000	.500	0.00	0.00
Wojciechowski, Asher	R-R	6-4	235	12-21-88	11	9	4.70	25	22	0	0	130	156	79	68	15	31	96	.292	.302	.282	6.63	2.14
Wright, Matt	L-L	5-10	170	5-7-87	4	2	3.27	50	0	0	1	77	70	30	28	4	18	88	.237	.268	.219	10.29	2.10

Fielding

Catcher	PCT	G	PO	A	E	DP	PB
Bowen	1.000	16	101	10	0	2	0
Hurtado	1.000	1	1	0	0	0	0
Jimenez	.992	98	697	76	6	5	6
Mahler	1.000	1	1	0	0	0	0
Ochinko	.996	31	219	15	1	1	1
Talley	1.000	1	2	0	0	0	0

First Base	PCT	G	PO	A	E	DP
Lind	1.000	1	7	0	0	0
Nolan	.995	23	181	15	1	15
Ochinko	.989	17	170	8	2	18
Talley	.994	102	923	63	6	75

Second Base	PCT	G	PO	A	E	DP
Contreras	.947	87	80	261	19	39
Hill	.833	2	1	4	1	0

	PCT	G	PO	A	E	DP
Jackson	.979	18	35	57	2	12
Nolan	1.000	1	0	1	0	0
Schimpf	.957	37	49	108	7	28

Third Base	PCT	G	PO	A	E	DP
Ahrens	.931	107	49	166	16	13
Contreras	1.000	2	1	4	0	1
Lawrie	1.000	4	1	10	0	1
Nix	1.000	2	0	7	0	0
Nolan	.667	3	1	1	1	0
Ochinko	.943	28	7	43	3	4

Shortstop	PCT	G	PO	A	E	DP
Contreras	1.000	1	1	1	0	1
Diaz	1.000	3	1	8	0	2
Goins	.967	100	175	288	16	65
Jackson	.933	15	23	47	5	8

	PCT	G	PO	A	E	DP
McDonald	1.000	1	0	3	0	1
Nolan	.962	27	32	68	4	14

Outfield	PCT	G	PO	A	E	DP
Bailli	1.000	5	5	0	0	0
Davis	.000	1	0	0	0	0
Glenn	.982	90	164	1	3	0
Hawkins	1.000	2	2	1	0	0
Hopkins	.990	50	93	2	1	1
Jackson	.966	62	109	5	4	0
McElroy	.995	104	177	9	1	1
Nolan	1.000	21	27	1	0	0
Patterson	1.000	3	2	0	0	0
Podsednik	1.000	2	11	0	0	0
Van Kirk	.966	72	112	3	4	0
Wilson	1.000	46	97	2	0	0
Wise	1.000	3	5	0	0	0

TORONTO BLUE JAYS

LANSING LUGNUTS

LOW CLASS A

MIDWEST LEAGUE

Batting	B-T	HT	WT	DOB	AVG	vLH	vRH	G	AB	R	H	2B	3B	HR	RBI	BB	HBP	SH	SF	SO	SB	CS	SLG	OBP
Boike, Eli	L-L	6-0	205	12-26-87	.222	.150	.250	20	72	11	16	4	2	0	10	13	1	0	1	24	2	1	.333	.345
Bowen, Joe	B-R	6-1	190	9-25-87	.333	.000	.333	4	12	3	4	1	0	0	4	2	0	0	0	4	0	0	.417	.429
Brisker, Markus	R-R	6-3	210	8-21-90	.233	.228	.235	97	348	72	81	18	4	5	33	44	9	0	1	112	24	8	.351	.351
Crouse, Michael	R-R	6-4	215	11-22-90	.261	.245	.267	101	364	73	95	26	5	14	55	44	9	0	4	113	38	8	.475	.352
Dominguez, Oliver	B-R	5-9	156	4-23-89	.217	.211	.220	97	322	56	70	11	6	4	39	55	2	0	2	76	15	6	.326	.333
Durham, Lance	L-R	5-11	210	2-28-89	.182	.207	.177	50	159	20	29	11	0	4	29	22	0	0	2	54	2	0	.327	.279
Fuenmayor, Balbino	R-R	6-3	235	11-26-89	.287	.467	.203	29	94	10	27	5	1	0	11	8	1	0	1	19	0	1	.362	.346
Hobson, K.C.	L-L	6-2	205	8-22-90	.250	.218	.262	128	480	65	120	24	2	4	53	61	3	0	3	73	1	0	.333	.336
Hurtado, Luis	R-R	5-11	175	11-4-88	.313	.000	.385	4	16	0	5	0	0	0	4	0	0	0	0	3	0	0	.313	.313
Jones, Jonathan	R-R	5-11	185	3-2-89	.298	.421	.244	35	124	20	37	4	1	1	15	15	3	0	1	23	10	5	.371	.385
Knecht, Marcus	R-R	6-1	200	6-21-90	.273	.269	.275	121	439	77	120	34	3	16	86	67	12	0	10	124	4	3	.474	.377
Marisnick, Jake	R-R	6-4	200	3-30-91	.320	.315	.322	118	462	68	148	27	6	14	77	43	14	0	4	91	37	8	.496	.392
Mooney, Peter	L-R	5-6	155	8-19-90	.360	.167	.421	7	25	3	9	2	2	0	1	5	0	0	0	5	0	1	.600	.467
Murphy, Jack	B-R	6-4	235	4-6-88	.222	.125	.254	50	162	14	36	11	0	3	24	21	1	0	1	43	0	2	.346	.314

Batting	B-T	HT	WT	DOB	AVG	vLH	vRH	G	AB	R	H	2B	3B	HR	RBI	BB	HBP	SH	SF	SO	SB	CS	SLG	OBP
Namba, Bryson	R-R	6-2	210	1-31-91	.191	.247	.171	89	283	35	54	12	2	6	35	35	6	0	4	107	1	0	.311	.290
Nolan, Kevin	R-R	6-2	200	12-13-87	.319	.433	.262	24	91	20	29	6	0	3	19	12	1	0	2	15	2	1	.484	.396
Nuzzo, Matt	R-R	6-0	205	3-18-87	.267	.236	.280	68	258	33	69	15	1	4	32	29	2	0	4	67	4	0	.380	.341
Pena, Gary	R-R	5-11	178	3-10-92	.214	.213	.215	77	280	28	60	11	1	5	24	8	1	0	4	81	2	2	.314	.235
Perez, Carlos	R-R	6-0	193	10-27-90	.256	.218	.273	95	383	58	98	17	6	3	41	37	2	0	6	74	6	2	.355	.320
Pierre, Gustavo	R-R	6-2	183	12-28-91	.187	.196	.184	56	187	25	35	4	2	2	18	13	1	0	0	52	6	3	.262	.244

Pitching	B-T	HT	WT	DOB	W	L	ERA	G	GS	CG	SV	IP	H	R	ER	HR	BB	SO	AVG	vLH	vRH	K/9	BB/9
Anderson, John	L-L	6-2	200	11-9-88	1	1	3.52	5	5	0	0	15	13	8	6	0	6	14	.217	.174	.243	8.22	3.52
Antolin, Dustin	R-R	6-2	195	8-9-89	3	2	4.26	23	0	0	0	32	31	19	15	1	16	35	.263	.245	.277	9.95	4.55
Barnes, Dan	L-R	6-1	195	10-21-89	5	1	2.32	44	2	0	13	66	44	20	17	3	20	99	.184	.153	.215	13.50	2.73
Berl, Brandon	R-R	6-0	185	4-9-88	3	5	2.28	30	0	0	3	51	53	22	13	3	9	42	.256	.319	.204	7.36	1.58
Brown, Eric	L-R	6-1	185	2-23-89	0	0	2.25	2	0	0	0	4	4	1	1	0	2	4	.308	.750	.111	9.00	4.50
Diaz, Misual	R-R	6-2	180	12-20-89	1	3	5.63	12	7	0	0	38	41	33	24	5	24	33	.266	.267	.266	7.75	5.63
Escalante, Alesone	B-R	6-4	180	8-29-88	0	0	6.14	8	0	0	0	15	23	10	10	1	6	14	.383	.500	.294	8.59	3.68
Fields, Matt	R-R	6-3	190	7-10-86	0	0	0.00	1	0	0	0	2	1	1	0	0	1	0	.125	.000	.250	0.00	4.50
Gracey, Scott	R-R	6-2	190	10-15-86	4	1	1.44	15	0	0	0	25	13	4	4	1	5	27	.148	.154	.143	9.72	1.80
Griffith, Shawn	R-R	5-10	180	5-24-87	5	0	4.82	24	1	0	0	37	30	22	20	2	30	41	.221	.194	.239	9.88	7.23
Hutchison, Drew	L-R	6-2	165	8-22-90	6	2	2.63	14	14	0	0	72	68	29	21	1	19	84	.245	.212	.282	10.50	2.38
Jensen, Tucker	R-R	6-2	205	8-3-89	0	0	5.40	1	1	0	0	5	4	3	3	1	0	1	.222	.000	.250	5.40	1.80
Lawrence, Casey	R-R	6-2	170	10-28-87	11	8	3.08	22	21	2	0	126	123	57	43	9	22	97	.252	.264	.238	6.95	1.58
Liebel, Andrew	R-R	6-0	195	3-22-86	2	0	2.38	2	2	0	0	11	7	4	3	0	3	10	.171	.000	.241	7.94	2.38
Litsch, Jesse	R-R	6-1	225	3-9-85	0	0	9.00	1	1	0	0	2	3	3	2	0	1	3	.300	.167	.500	13.50	4.50
Longpre, Bryan	R-R	6-2	195	7-13-87	0	0	18.00	2	0	0	0	2	5	4	4	2	0	2	.500	.250	.667	9.00	0.00
Marze, Dayton	R-R	6-2	185	1-1-89	6	5	4.10	44	0	0	7	86	86	41	39	6	31	71	.263	.276	.261	7.46	3.26
Nicolino, Justin	L-L	6-3	160	11-22-91	1	1	3.12	3	3	0	0	9	11	3	3	0	2	9	.297	.167	.421	9.35	2.08
Nolin, Sean	L-L	6-5	235	12-26-89	4	4	3.49	25	21	0	1	108	102	56	42	9	31	113	.253	.218	.273	9.39	2.58
Pepe, Alex	L-L	6-2	190	4-14-87	2	2	6.35	12	0	0	0	17	19	17	12	0	16	20	.275	.375	.222	10.59	8.47
Permison, Drew	R-R	5-10	170	2-24-89	0	0	12.00	4	0	0	0	6	10	8	8	2	4	4	.385	.417	.357	6.00	6.00
Powell, Tyler	R-R	6-4	210	2-16-89	3	5	4.57	20	6	0	0	65	70	34	33	4	19	36	.278	.318	.246	4.98	2.63
Smith, Egan	L-L	6-5	200	3-16-89	7	7	3.84	24	24	1	0	117	141	67	50	10	24	95	.298	.302	.296	7.29	1.84
Strickland, Sam	L-L	6-5	210	6-9-87	3	1	4.98	33	2	0	2	78	116	57	43	5	25	58	.341	.331	.347	6.72	2.90
Syndergaard, Noah	L-R	6-5	200	8-29-92	0	0	3.00	2	2	0	0	9	8	4	3	0	2	9	.235	.292	.100	9.00	2.00
Turnbull, Steve	R-R	6-3	215	11-25-86	0	1	2.13	25	0	0	15	25	18	6	6	0	7	28	.194	.191	.196	9.95	2.49
Walden, Marcus	R-R	5-10	185	9-13-88	6	6	3.24	28	13	0	0	100	90	48	36	1	28	54	.239	.214	.263	4.86	2.52
Webb, Daniel	R-R	6-3	210	8-18-89	4	5	5.59	18	12	0	2	66	80	53	41	7	24	51	.303	.306	.301	6.95	3.27

Fielding

Catcher	PCT	G	PO	A	E	DP	PB
Bowen	.971	4	31	2	1	1	0
Hurtado	1.000	3	7	0	0	0	1
Murphy	.987	42	341	26	5	3	2
Perez	.982	89	689	72	14	4	18

First Base	PCT	G	PO	A	E	DP
Dominguez	1.000	1	3	0	0	1
Durham	.978	6	44	1	1	7
Fuenmayor	1.000	3	31	1	0	4
Hobson	.979	124	1058	96	25	82
Murphy	1.000	1	4	1	0	1
Namba	.947	4	34	2	2	4

Second Base	PCT	G	PO	A	E	DP
Dominguez	.935	52	67	150	15	22

	PCT	G	PO	A	E	DP
Jones	1.000	1	1	0	0	0
Mooney	.962	5	10	15	1	5
Namba	1.000	1	1	2	0	1
Nolan	.985	13	18	48	1	5
Nuzzo	.971	62	116	189	9	30
Pena	.944	11	14	37	3	3

Third Base	PCT	G	PO	A	E	DP
Dominguez	.861	31	16	52	11	1
Fuenmayor	.898	23	16	28	5	4
Namba	.894	83	45	123	20	8
Nolan	1.000	3	0	1	0	0
Nuzzo	.818	5	4	5	2	1

Shortstop	PCT	G	PO	A	E	DP
Dominguez	.971	8	16	18	1	3

	PCT	G	PO	A	E	
Mooney	.923	3	6	6	1	3
Nolan	.955	11	13	29	2	7
Pena	.960	68	102	206	13	55
Pierre	.836	53	78	106	36	18

Outfield	PCT	G	PO	A	E	DP
Boike	1.000	14	24	0	0	0
Brisker	.966	69	106	9	4	2
Crouse	.971	88	152	13	5	1
Dominguez	1.000	5	5	1	0	0
Jones	1.000	23	32	2	0	0
Knecht	.966	111	164	7	6	0
Marisnick	.988	108	237	5	3	1

VANCOUVER CANADIANS

SHORT-SEASON

NORTHWEST LEAGUE

Batting	B-T	HT	WT	DOB	AVG	vLH	vRH	G	AB	R	H	2B	3B	HR	RBI	BB	HBP	SH	SF	SO	SB	CS	SLG	OBP
Aponte, Yeico	L-L	6-2	190	12-17-88	.239	.154	.259	30	71	9	17	4	0	0	4	4	0	0	0	24	4	0	.296	.280
Baligod, Nick	L-R	5-11	190	9-28-87	.248	.241	.250	70	238	28	59	13	1	2	32	38	2	0	2	38	2	1	.336	.354
Berti, Jon	R-R	5-10	175	1-22-90	.291	.231	.305	60	213	37	62	5	5	1	21	22	12	0	1	44	23	5	.376	.387
Boike, Eli	L-L	6-0	205	12-26-87	.370	.000	.400	7	27	3	10	2	0	0	2	4	0	0	0	7	1	1	.444	.452
Burns, Andy	R-R	6-2	190	8-7-90	.179	.154	.190	23	84	10	15	4	0	2	7	6	0	0	0	14	2	1	.298	.233
Fuenmayor, Balbino	R-R	6-3	235	11-26-89	.234	.196	.243	61	231	24	54	13	0	6	29	14	4	0	1	56	1	0	.368	.288
Hurtado, Luis	R-R	5-11	175	11-4-88	.364	.333	.375	3	11	1	4	0	0	0	4	0	0	0	1	0	0	0	.364	.333
Johnson, Matt	R-R	6-3	210	5-26-88	.233	.333	.179	13	43	7	10	4	1	0	6	1	2	0	1	16	0	0	.372	.277
Jones, Jonathan	R-R	5-11	185	8-2-89	.283	.344	.264	64	254	32	72	13	1	1	26	28	3	0	4	43	18	3	.354	.356
Kervin, Bryan	L-R	5-10	185	3-23-85	.198	.167	.207	34	111	7	22	6	0	0	7	5	0	0	1	28	2	3	.252	.231
Maines, Garrett	R-R	5-11	195	2-7-87	.263	.250	.269	26	76	16	20	4	1	4	17	9	1	0	3	28	1	0	.500	.337
McQuail, Steve	R-R	6-2	225	6-10-89	.200	.152	.213	61	220	30	44	8	0	12	36	31	20	4	0	84	1	1	.400	.278
Newman, Matt	L-L	5-10	170	9-20-88	.228	.240	.226	49	149	17	34	9	0	3	17	18	0	0	4	41	3	5	.349	.304
Opitz, Shane	L-R	6-1	180	1-10-92	.259	.354	.236	63	239	25	62	6	0	0	25	19	0	0	2	34	8	2	.285	.312
Patterson, Kevin	L-R	6-4	220	9-28-88	.270	.286	.264	33	115	16	31	6	2	5	21	18	2	0	2	40	1	0	.487	.372
Rankin, Pierce	R-R	6-1	190	4-26-89	.230	.240	.228	38	126	25	29	4	0	3	8	20	5	0	1	35	2	4	.333	.355

Batting	B-T	HT	WT	DOB	AVG	vLH	vRH	G	AB	R	H	2B	3B	HR	RBI	BB	HBP	SH	SF	SO	SB	CS	SLG	OBP
Salas, Roan	R-R	5-11	175	6-9-90	.259	.379	.227	39	139	19	36	10	1	4	14	5	4	0	0	31	1	0	.432	.304
Schaeffer, Chris	R-R	5-10	195	11-19-87	.210	.125	.231	26	81	6	17	3	0	0	8	9	2	0	0	21	0	0	.247	.304
Schwartz, Randy	R-R	6-4	235	1-25-86	.185	.111	.202	47	146	17	27	6	2	5	13	15	2	0	0	49	2	1	.356	.270

Pitching	B-T	HT	WT	DOB	W	L	ERA	G	GS	CG	SV	IP	H	R	ER	HR	BB	SO	AVG	vLH	vRH	K/9	BB/9
Breault, Zack	L-R	6-4	220	12-6-88	2	2	6.32	15	15	0	0	68	82	52	48	5	33	42	.301	.274	.319	5.53	4.35
Brown, Eric	L-R	6-1	185	2-23-89	0	1	3.62	18	0	0	0	27	25	19	11	3	7	30	.238	.300	.200	9.88	2.30
Brua, Phil	L-R	6-2	185	4-3-89	7	1	2.70	27	0	0	5	40	33	17	12	3	4	23	.228	.177	.265	5.18	0.90
Champlin, Kramer	R-R	6-6	200	3-8-90	0	2	4.91	7	3	0	0	15	20	8	8	1	3	11	.339	.379	.300	6.75	1.84
Cole, Taylor	R-R	6-1	180	8-20-89	1	3	5.88	11	8	0	0	34	35	23	22	3	17	25	.276	.339	.221	6.68	4.54
Davis, Shane	R-L	6-0	195	4-19-88	0	0	7.91	18	0	0	0	19	31	26	17	4	17	16	.344	.278	.389	7.45	7.91
Escalante, Alesone	B-R	6-4	180	8-29-88	1	2	1.41	16	0	0	1	32	21	8	5	2	6	24	.179	.196	.167	6.75	1.69
Garrett, Travis	R-R	5-11	205	10-27-89	4	4	4.28	20	0	0	0	34	31	19	16	3	20	32	.263	.262	.263	8.55	5.35
Hernandez, Jesse	R-R	6-1	200	8-23-88	4	4	4.28	15	15	0	0	76	86	42	36	1	25	52	.286	.287	.285	6.19	2.97
Kaye, Brandon	R-R	6-4	200	8-16-88	1	2	3.65	17	0	0	0	25	19	13	10	0	14	14	.211	.217	.205	5.11	5.11
Longpre, Bryan	R-R	6-2	195	7-13-87	4	3	2.85	22	0	0	2	41	39	18	13	2	14	38	.253	.186	.310	8.34	3.07
McFarland, Blake	R-R	6-5	230	2-2-88	6	7	5.32	14	11	0	0	64	68	41	38	3	23	34	.273	.281	.268	4.76	3.22
Nicolino, Justin	L-L	6-3	160	11-22-91	5	1	1.03	12	9	1	0	52	28	9	6	0	11	64	.156	.229	.139	11.01	1.89
Pepe, Alex	L-L	6-2	190	4-14-87	0	0	4.44	23	0	0	1	26	20	13	13	4	25	22	.213	.250	.200	7.52	8.54
Permison, Drew	R-R	5-10	170	2-24-89	1	1	1.69	29	0	0	15	32	23	8	6	0	8	27	.205	.227	.191	7.59	2.25
Purdy, Nick	R-R	6-5	205	10-2-89	0	0	8.62	8	0	0	0	16	23	16	15	5	9	16	.348	.400	.306	9.19	5.17
Rollins, David	L-L	6-1	195	12-21-89	1	0	2.57	3	0	0	0	14	16	4	4	0	1	11	.276	.150	.342	7.07	0.64
Sanchez, Aaron	R-R	6-4	190	7-1-92	0	1	4.63	3	3	0	0	12	8	6	6	0	8	13	.195	.227	.158	10.03	6.17
Syndergaard, Noah	R-R	6-5	200	8-29-92	1	2	2.00	4	4	0	0	18	15	5	4	0	5	22	.221	.188	.231	11.00	2.50
White, Ben	R-R	6-2	185	5-10-89	1	1	7.00	8	5	0	0	27	36	23	21	3	10	10	.319	.340	.302	3.33	3.33

Fielding

Catcher	PCT	G	PO	A	E	DP	PB
Hurtado	.967	3	25	4	1	0	0
Maines	.991	14	95	11	1	1	2
Rankin	.975	36	240	30	7	4	4
Schaeffer	.989	25	158	22	2	2	1

First Base	PCT	G	PO	A	E	DP
Fuenmayor	.988	18	152	7	2	12
Patterson	.980	29	280	13	6	35
Schwartz	.997	36	326	12	1	36

Second Base	PCT	G	PO	A	E	DP
Berti	.974	58	101	203	8	42

	PCT	G	PO	A	E	DP
Kervin	1.000	13	26	37	0	12
Opitz	.970	6	12	20	1	7
Salas	.944	7	10	7	1	3

Third Base	PCT	G	PO	A	E	DP
Burns	.946	16	8	45	3	2
Fuenmayor	.865	32	14	50	10	3
Johnson	.966	11	12	16	1	1
Salas	.846	17	2	31	6	1
Schwartz	.800	5	1	7	2	0

Shortstop	PCT	G	PO	A	E	DP
Burns	.862	7	4	21	4	5

	PCT	G	PO	A	E	DP
Johnson	1.000	1	0	2	0	0
Kervin	.957	19	25	64	4	9
Opitz	.945	54	82	177	15	55

Outfield	PCT	G	PO	A	E	DP
Aponte	1.000	18	24	2	0	0
Baligod	.975	68	116	3	3	0
Boike	.917	5	11	0	1	0
Jones	.974	61	144	8	4	5
McQuail	.970	45	60	5	2	0
Newman	.954	46	61	1	3	0

BLUEFIELD BLUE JAYS   ROOKIE

APPALACHIAN LEAGUE

Batting	B-T	HT	WT	DOB	AVG	vLH	vRH	G	AB	R	H	2B	3B	HR	RBI	BB	HBP	SH	SF	SO	SB	CS	SLG	OBP
Abraham, Matt	R-R	5-8	165	1-27-87	.250	1.000	.000	2	4	2	1	0	0	0	0	4	0	0	0	1	0	0	.250	.625
Arce, Eric	L-R	5-9	205	11-29-91	.263	.600	.143	6	19	1	5	1	0	0	1	2	0	0	0	4	0	0	.316	.333
Arcila, Daniel	L-R	6-1	170	7-4-90	.243	.237	.244	54	210	43	51	10	5	10	37	24	3	0	0	50	3	3	.481	.329
Bartlett, Cody	R-R	6-5	180	7-22-88	.198	.152	.224	27	91	9	18	7	0	1	17	11	0	0	0	22	2	1	.308	.284
Boike, Eli	L-L	6-0	205	12-26-87	.304	.000	.304	9	23	2	7	2	1	0	8	2	1	0	0	8	1	0	.478	.385
Carroll, George	R-R	6-2	210	4-17-88	.000	.000	.000	1	2	0	0	0	0	0	0	0	0	0	0	1	0	0	.000	.000
Charles, Art	L-L	6-6	221	11-10-90	.240	.235	.242	68	250	46	60	18	3	11	61	39	6	0	4	89	1	1	.468	.351
Fermin, Andy	L-R	6-0	180	7-27-89	.261	.200	.280	59	218	41	57	15	0	5	33	35	2	0	6	37	2	1	.399	.360
Garcia, Melvin	R-R	6-0	175	9-17-91	.167	.167	.167	26	78	9	13	2	0	0	5	7	1	0	1	26	2	1	.192	.241
Hawkins, Chris	L-R	6-2	195	8-17-91	.318	.426	.282	68	242	49	77	15	6	5	52	12	1	0	2	46	14	4	.492	.375
Hernandez, Leonardo	R-R	5-10	195	2-22-90	.333	.348	.329	29	93	10	31	4	1	1	12	2	0	0	3	9	0	0	.430	.337
Hernandez, Yudelmis	R-R	6-4	205	5-18-87	.250	.182	.286	9	32	5	8	2	0	1	5	2	2	0	0	12	0	0	.406	.333
Johnson, Matt	R-R	6-3	210	5-26-88	.203	.059	.246	20	74	10	15	2	0	1	7	2	3	0	0	16	3	2	.270	.253
Mahler, Tim	R-R	5-3	170	3-30-87	.400	.500	.000	4	5	0	2	0	0	0	0	0	0	0	0	2	0	0	.400	.400
Melendez, Ronnie	R-R	5-10	170	9-29-89	.300	.500	.167	6	10	0	3	2	0	0	4	0	0	0	0	2	0	0	.500	.300
Mooney, Peter	L-R	5-6	155	8-19-90	.260	.188	.279	21	77	19	20	7	2	1	11	17	0	0	2	13	1	0	.442	.385
Munoz, Aaron	R-R	5-9	185	12-24-88	.231	.211	.239	45	130	12	30	3	0	0	21	11	4	0	2	28	0	0	.254	.306
Pierre, Gustavo	R-R	6-2	183	12-28-91	.252	.203	.269	63	250	44	63	12	3	6	23	26	1	0	1	73	9	5	.396	.324
Pillar, Kevin	R-R	6-0	200	1-4-89	.347	.458	.311	60	236	44	82	17	3	7	37	10	3	0	3	36	8	4	.534	.377
Pompey, Dalton	B-R	6-1	170	12-11-92	.191	.222	.180	18	68	15	13	3	0	1	5	14	3	0	0	23	4	1	.279	.353
Ramirez, Carlos	R-R	6-3	172	4-24-91	.232	.243	.227	40	112	18	26	7	2	2	9	10	1	0	0	39	2	1	.384	.301
Schaeffer, Chris	R-R	5-10	195	11-19-87	.378	.200	.444	10	37	6	14	4	0	1	7	1	0	0	1	5	0	0	.568	.385
Sweeney, Kellen	L-R	6-0	180	9-14-91	.114	.100	.120	9	35	4	4	1	0	0	1	9	0	0	0	17	1	0	.143	.295
Williams, Javan	L-L	6-2	185	10-18-89	.304	.250	.310	26	46	7	14	1	0	0	5	4	0	0	0	10	5	0	.391	.360

Pitching	B-T	HT	WT	DOB	W	L	ERA	G	GS	CG	SV	IP	H	R	ER	HR	BB	SO	AVG	vLH	vRH	K/9	BB/9
Berryhill, Thomas	R-R	5-10	185	12-9-87	0	0	5.63	6	0	0	0	8	13	5	5	0	5	5	.371	.364	.375	5.63	5.63
Diaz, Misual	R-R	6-2	180	12-20-89	1	0	4.35	6	0	0	1	10	6	5	5	2	5	15	.167	.071	.227	13.06	4.35
Duvall, Myles	R-R	6-5	220	4-23-89	2	1	5.40	14	0	0	1	25	33	19	15	3	9	25	.311	.419	.267	9.00	3.24
Elliott, Drew	L-R	6-3	215	8-2-88	0	0	1.59	4	0	0	0	5	3	1	0		2	6	.238	.333	.222	9.53	3.18
Estrada, Deivy	R-R	5-11	178	8-22-92	3	4	6.94	9	9	0	0	36	46	29	28	5	16	27	.311	.373	.278	6.69	3.96

Pitching	B-T	HT	WT	DOB	W	L	ERA	G	GS	CG	SV	IP	H	R	ER	HR	BB	SO	AVG	vLH	vRH	K/9	BB/9
Gabryszwski, Jeremy	R-R	6-4	195	3-16-93	0	0	0.00	1	0	0	0	1	1	0	0	0	0	1	.250	.500	.000	9.00	0.00
Jaye, Myles	B-R	6-3	170	12-28-91	3	3	3.00	13	9	1	1	54	48	22	18	7	18	49	.239	.257	.229	8.17	3.00
Jensen, Tucker	R-R	6-2	205	8-3-89	0	2	11.12	4	4	0	0	11	26	23	14	2	8	13	.441	.524	.395	10.32	6.35
Kadish, Ian	L-R	6-0	200	8-29-88	2	3	2.67	23	0	0	7	30	24	11	9	0	11	35	.209	.147	.235	10.38	3.26
Lucas, Jon	R-R	5-10	205	12-12-87	3	3	3.93	21	0	0	0	37	31	16	16	2	9	24	.231	.146	.269	5.89	2.21
Meyer, Ajay	L-R	6-6	185	7-19-87	4	2	3.02	13	13	0	0	66	62	26	22	3	13	55	.243	.282	.226	7.54	1.78
Musgrove, Joe	R-R	6-5	230	12-4-92	1	0	0.00	1	0	0	0	3	2	0	0	0	1	2	.222	.200	.250	6.00	3.00
Purdy, Nick	R-R	6-5	205	10-2-89	1	0	2.70	2	0	0	0	7	4	2	2	0	6	6	.167	.182	.154	8.10	8.10
Rollins, David	L-L	6-1	195	12-21-89	3	0	1.25	4	4	0	0	22	12	3	3	2	2	18	.158	.063	.183	7.48	0.83
Sanchez, Aaron	R-R	6-4	190	7-1-92	3	2	5.48	11	6	0	1	43	45	27	26	4	18	43	.269	.237	.287	9.07	3.80
Santana, Kenllie	L-L	6-0	192	7-13-89	0	0	15.58	9	0	0	0	9	13	16	15	1	20	12	.333	.364	.321	12.46	20.77
Santana, Milciades	R-R	6-5	214	1-20-89	1	2	9.47	19	0	0	1	26	30	29	27	4	15	28	.294	.237	.328	9.82	5.26
Sikula, Arik	R-R	6-1	195	12-21-88	1	1	2.97	18	0	0	1	30	38	12	10	2	9	35	.309	.313	.307	10.38	2.67
Syndergaard, Noah	L-R	6-5	200	8-29-92	4	0	1.41	7	5	0	0	32	23	5	5	1	11	33	.198	.132	.231	10.41	3.09
Taylor, Mitchell	L-L	6-0	155	5-11-92	4	2	4.23	13	8	0	0	55	50	28	26	5	14	61	.242	.237	.243	9.92	2.28
Vargas, Jose	L-L	6-0	166	7-19-90	0	1	10.22	4	4	0	0	12	16	15	14	3	11	8	.320	.357	.306	5.84	8.03
Williams, Les	R-R	6-2	220	3-2-89	2	2	4.46	17	1	0	0	36	45	24	18	2	12	26	.296	.345	.268	6.44	2.97
Ybarra, Tyler	L-L	6-2	170	12-11-89	2	0	2.15	14	5	0	0	46	34	12	11	2	16	54	.200	.118	.221	10.57	3.13

Fielding

Catcher	PCT	G	PO	A	E	DP	PB
Carroll	1.000	1	2	0	0	0	0
Hernandez	.983	24	163	15	3	1	4
Mahler	1.000	1	1	0	0	0	0
Munoz	.992	45	343	46	3	2	4
Schaeffer	1.000	8	53	9	0	0	1

First Base	PCT	G	PO	A	E	DP
Charles	.987	64	563	24	8	32
Hernandez	.969	3	30	1	1	2
Johnson	1.000	2	12	1	0	2

Second Base	PCT	G	PO	A	E	DP
Abraham	1.000	1	3	0	0	0

	PCT	G	PO	A	E	DP
Arcila	.988	52	91	147	3	21
Bartlett	.930	13	17	23	3	5
Fermin	1.000	3	9	8	0	2
Mooney	1.000	1	1	4	0	0

Third Base	PCT	G	PO	A	E	DP
Arcila	.000	1	0	0	0	0
Fermin	.933	56	38	128	12	7
Johnson	.778	3	1	6	2	0
Sweeney	.966	9	4	24	1	2

Shortstop	PCT	G	PO	A	E	DP
Abraham	1.000	1	1	2	0	0
Bartlett	.867	13	16	36	8	4

	PCT	G	PO	A	E	DP
Johnson	.910	14	22	39	6	8
Mooney	.963	19	24	54	3	7
Pierre	.909	22	23	57	8	6

Outfield	PCT	G	PO	A	E	DP
Boike	1.000	7	4	0	0	0
Garcia	.979	24	45	2	1	0
Hawkins	.979	62	91	2	2	1
Melendez	1.000	4	6	0	0	0
Pillar	.976	56	114	8	3	0
Pompey	.962	17	24	1	1	0
Ramirez	.986	38	69	1	1	0
Williams	1.000	16	16	1	0	0

GCL BLUE JAYS

GULF COAST LEAGUE

ROOKIE

Batting	B-T	HT	WT	DOB	AVG	vLH	vRH	G	AB	R	H	2B	3B	HR	RBI	BB	HBP	SH	SF	SO	SB	CS	SLG	OBP
Abraham, Matt	R-R	5-8	165	1-27-87	.103	.000	.111	14	29	5	3	0	0	0	4	3	3	0	1	7	0	0	.103	.250
Anderson, Jacob	R-R	6-4	190	11-22-92	.405	.444	.393	9	37	9	15	2	0	2	7	4	1	0	0	8	2	0	.622	.476
Arce, Eric	L-R	5-9	205	11-29-91	.268	.226	.279	49	153	34	41	6	3	14	40	38	11	0	4	48	1	1	.621	.437
Atkinson, Justin	R-R	6-1	205	7-24-93	.279	.250	.282	12	43	6	12	3	1	0	6	2	0	0	2	3	0	0	.395	.298
Bailli, Kenen	L-L	6-0	190	1-25-85	.364	.000	.364	4	11	0	4	0	0	0	1	0	0	0	0	2	0	1	.364	.364
Burns, Andy	R-R	6-2	190	8-7-90	.625	.500	.667	5	16	5	10	0	0	1	7	2	1	0	1	0	0	1	.813	.650
Carroll, George	R-R	6-2	210	4-17-88	.098	.077	.107	16	41	3	4	2	0	0	3	3	1	0	0	15	0	0	.146	.178
Conner, Seth	R-R	6-2	205	1-29-92	.276	.158	.309	50	174	29	48	9	2	4	23	30	5	0	1	37	4	2	.420	.395
Frias, Christian	B-R	5-10	170	7-19-89	.143	.083	.174	33	70	6	10	1	0	0	5	15	3	0	1	13	1	2	.157	.315
Garcia, Melvin	R-R	6-0	175	9-17-91	.238	.125	.265	11	42	7	10	1	0	2	7	3	1	0	0	14	0	0	.405	.304
Goins, Ryan	L-R	5-10	170	2-13-88	.000	.000	.000	1	3	0	0	0	0	0	0	0	0	0	0	1	0	0	.000	.000
Gomez, Angel	B-R	6-2	180	1-12-92	.228	.083	.267	36	114	11	26	3	1	0	6	7	2	0	2	24	5	3	.272	.280
Hernandez, Yudelmis	R-R	6-4	205	5-18-87	.152	.111	.162	28	92	13	14	6	0	2	10	15	1	0	0	50	1	0	.283	.278
Javier, Sony	R-R	6-0	195	6-15-91	.203	.250	.182	23	79	6	16	1	0	1	8	3	0	0	0	17	2	0	.253	.232
Loveless, Derrick	L-R	6-1	200	3-7-93	.059	.000	.071	5	17	2	1	0	0	0	1	3	0	0	0	7	0	0	.059	.200
Mahler, Tim	R-R	6-3	190	9-21-87	.167	.000	.500	2	6	0	1	0	0	0	0	0	0	0	0	0	0	0	.167	.167
Melendez, Ronnie	R-R	5-10	170	9-29-89	.265	.000	.273	10	34	6	9	2	0	0	5	3	0	0	0	3	3	0	.324	.324
Mooney, Peter	L-R	5-6	155	8-19-90	.300	.000	.300	3	10	2	3	1	1	0	1	2	0	0	1	2	0	0	.600	.385
Nessy, Santiago	R-R	6-2	230	12-8-92	.306	.308	.306	35	134	12	41	7	0	3	19	8	1	0	1	29	0	2	.425	.347
Newman, Matt	L-L	5-10	170	9-20-88	.167	.000	.167	2	6	1	1	0	0	0	0	0	0	0	0	2	0	0	.167	.167
Patterson, Kevin	L-R	6-4	200	9-28-88	.370	.286	.424	15	54	11	20	5	0	5	11	5	0	0	0	13	2	0	.741	.424
Peters, Chris	R-R	6-0	175	12-29-88	.246	.357	.211	42	118	13	29	5	3	1	17	14	0	0	2	26	3	0	.364	.321
Pompey, Dalton	B-R	6-1	170	12-11-92	.259	.118	.298	42	158	34	41	7	2	4	12	24	1	0	0	35	19	0	.405	.361
Rodriguez, Alexys	R-R	5-10	200	11-23-88	.233	.318	.206	29	90	9	21	3	0	2	11	4	5	0	1	14	0	0	.333	.300
Taylor, Nico	R-R	6-4	215	2-9-90	.319	.368	.306	30	91	17	29	8	0	3	13	15	1	0	0	24	2	2	.505	.421
Thon, Dickie Joe	R-R	6-2	185	11-16-91	.223	.208	.227	45	121	23	27	3	0	3	15	23	5	0	0	44	6	2	.322	.369
Vega-Rosado, Jorge	R-R	5-8	175	12-5-91	.317	.333	.314	51	183	39	58	12	2	4	30	19	2	0	4	40	22	4	.470	.380

Pitching	B-T	HT	WT	DOB	W	L	ERA	G	GS	CG	SV	IP	H	R	ER	HR	BB	SO	AVG	vLH	vRH	K/9	BB/9
Adams, Zak	L-L	6-2	190	3-19-92	0	1	9.00	7	3	0	0	21	19	21	21	3	19	28	.232	.133	.254	12.00	8.14
Broussard, Colby	R-R	6-4	220	5-8-89	1	2	1.85	18	0	0	6	24	12	6	5	1	8	17	.145	.167	.132	6.29	2.96
Cardona, Adonys	R-R	6-1	170	1-16-94	1	3	4.55	10	7	0	0	32	31	17	16	2	12	35	.256	.200	.284	9.95	3.41
Carmona, Julio	R-R	6-1	205	10-10-90	3	2	6.41	23	0	0	2	27	20	21	19	1	22	30	.208	.156	.234	10.13	7.43
Champlin, Kramer	R-R	6-6	200	3-8-90	0	0	20.25	1	0	0	0	1	6	3	3	1	1	0	.600	.750	.500	0.00	6.75
Diaz, Misual	R-R	6-2	180	12-20-89	1	0	3.86	3	1	0	0	7	6	3	3	1	1	9	.231	.333	.176	11.57	1.29
Dragmire, Brady	R-R	6-1	180	2-5-93	0	0	27.00	1	0	0	0	1	2	3	3	1	1	1	.400	.500	.333	9.00	9.00

Pitching	B-T	HT	WT	DOB	W	L	ERA	G	GS	CG	SV	IP	H	R	ER	HR	BB	SO	AVG	vLH	vRH	K/9	BB/9
Estrada, Deivy	R-R	5-11	178	8-22-92	0	1	2.25	3	3	1	0	16	14	4	4	1	3	18	.233	.231	.235	10.13	1.69
Fields, Matt	R-R	6-3	190	7-10-86	0	0	0.00	1	0	0	0	2	0	0	0	0	0	1	.000	.000	.000	4.50	0.00
Gabryszwski, Jeremy	R-R	6-4	195	3-16-93	0	0	0.00	3	1	0	0	4	3	0	0	0	1	5	.188	.000	.300	10.38	2.08
Jensen, Tucker	R-R	6-2	205	8-3-89	2	2	1.77	8	8	0	0	41	31	10	8	1	6	40	.208	.175	.233	8.85	1.33
Kelly, Adaric	R-R	5-10	180	12-1-92	2	2	7.13	15	1	0	0	24	37	22	19	0	14	18	.359	.359	.359	6.75	5.25
Liebel, Andrew	R-R	6-0	195	3-22-86	0	1	2.40	4	4	0	0	15	13	6	4	0	4	15	.232	.263	.216	9.00	2.40
Mella, Leandro	L-L	6-4	190	5-5-90	0	1	8.00	10	0	0	0	9	8	8	8	1	11	6	.250	.125	.292	6.00	11.00
Mendez, Luis	R-R	6-7	250	10-14-89	2	1	6.58	19	0	0	0	26	24	21	19	4	13	21	.247	.231	.259	7.27	4.50
Murphy, Griffin	R-L	6-3	200	1-16-91	2	2	4.39	11	11	0	0	41	48	27	20	6	16	39	.294	.231	.307	8.56	3.51
Musgrove, Joe	R-R	6-5	230	12-4-92	0	1	4.57	8	7	0	0	22	17	12	11	1	4	16	.227	.229	.225	6.65	1.66
Navarette, Jorge	L-L	6-0	200	9-25-89	1	3	5.33	20	0	0	1	27	39	22	16	5	16	28	.348	.324	.359	9.33	5.33
Purdy, Nick	R-R	6-5	205	10-2-89	3	0	2.88	6	3	0	0	25	25	9	8	0	7	38	.255	.182	.292	13.68	2.52
Ramirez, Alex	R-R	6-2	200	2-11-90	2	1	5.29	20	0	0	1	32	31	20	19	3	22	34	.256	.233	.269	9.46	6.12
Roman, Chris	R-R	6-3	200	4-22-89	4	2	6.12	17	0	0	0	25	26	18	17	4	8	23	.268	.323	.242	8.28	2.88
Santana, Kenllie	L-L	6-0	192	7-13-89	0	0	6.75	1	0	0	0	1	0	1	1	0	3	1	.000	.000	.000	6.75	20.25
Slover, Brian	R-R	6-3	230	6-10-88	0	1	10.38	4	0	0	0	4	4	5	5	0	4	3	.267	.500	.182	6.23	8.31
Thompson, Randall	R-R	6-1	210	5-18-89	1	2	2.87	18	6	0	1	47	42	26	15	3	12	44	.228	.212	.237	8.43	2.30
Valdez, Denny	R-R	6-3	188	5-8-90	0	1	10.38	4	0	0	0	4	6	5	5	1	5	3	.375	.400	.364	6.23	10.38
Vargas, Jose	L-L	6-0	166	7-19-90	0	4	9.47	11	4	0	0	19	35	21	20	3	4	9	.380	.067	.442	4.26	1.89
Webb, Daniel	R-R	6-3	210	8-18-89	0	0	0.00	1	0	0	0	1	2	0	0	0	0	0	.333	.000	.500	0.00	0.00

Fielding

Catcher	PCT	G	PO	A	E	DP	PB
Carroll	.000	3	0	0	1	0	0
Nessy	.967	35	266	28	10	0	8
Rodriguez	.983	29	205	20	4	2	6

First Base	PCT	G	PO	A	E	DP
Carroll	.962	8	49	2	2	2
Conner	.993	16	136	4	1	9
Hernandez	.985	25	183	10	3	21
Patterson	.990	12	92	8	1	7

Second Base	PCT	G	PO	A	E	DP
Frias	.971	32	41	58	3	17
Peters	.986	21	32	37	1	8
Vega-Rosado	.975	27	30	48	2	10

Third Base	PCT	G	PO	A	E	DP
Abraham	.929	4	3	10	1	0
Atkinson	.963	11	6	20	1	1
Burns	.857	3	3	3	1	0
Conner	.888	33	8	63	9	3
Peters	.938	11	6	24	2	3

Shortstop	PCT	G	PO	A	E	DP
Abraham	.957	8	7	15	1	6
Burns	1.000	2	3	1	0	0
Frias	1.000	1	0	2	0	0
Goins	1.000	1	1	3	0	1
Mooney	1.000	2	1	4	0	2
Peters	.962	12	11	14	1	3
Thon	.945	31	22	47	4	8
Vega-Rosado	.929	38	43	75	9	14

Outfield	PCT	G	PO	A	E	DP
Anderson	1.000	9	13	0	0	0
Arce	1.000	28	46	0	0	0
Bailli	1.000	2	3	0	0	0
Garcia	1.000	11	30	0	0	0
Gomez	1.000	36	60	4	0	0
Javier	1.000	22	37	0	0	0
Loveless	.800	5	8	0	2	0
Melendez	.929	10	13	0	1	0
Newman	1.000	2	3	0	0	0
Pompey	1.000	42	81	3	0	0
Taylor	.972	24	32	3	1	1

DSL BLUE JAYS — ROOKIE

DOMINICAN SUMMER LEAGUE

Batting	B-T	HT	WT	DOB	AVG	vLH	vRH	G	AB	R	H	2B	3B	HR	RBI	BB	HBP	SH	SF	SO	SB	CS	SLG	OBP
Aguida, Nelson	R-R	6-1	180	4-22-92	.289	.273	.294	17	45	2	13	2	0	0	5	3	1	0	0	7	2	0	.333	.347
Barazarte, Cesar	R-R	6-1	195	4-19-93	.244	.160	.279	50	172	25	42	7	1	0	14	34	10	0	1	40	11	4	.297	.367
Blanco, Alvaro	R-R	5-10	185	4-29-92	.143	.214	.119	40	112	15	16	1	1	1	10	11	2	0	1	26	4	5	.196	.230
Cenas, Gabriel	R-R	6-1	155	10-16-93	.208	.167	.220	19	53	6	11	1	0	0	3	9	5	0	1	11	1	0	.226	.368
Cipriota, Jacinto	R-R	5-11	180	3-23-90	.205	.286	.180	50	146	15	30	3	0	0	14	23	8	0	1	34	4	5	.226	.343
De La Cruz, Maydawin	L-L	6-1	160	7-16-93	.177	.233	.160	47	130	11	23	4	0	2	8	24	6	0	0	54	2	3	.254	.331
Delgado, John	L-R	6-4	255	9-10-90	.213	.250	.200	35	89	8	19	3	0	0	9	12	0	0	1	17	3	2	.247	.304
Feliz, Angel	R-R	6-1	200	8-21-91	.125	.000	.162	22	48	4	6	3	0	2	5	13	0	0	1	19	0	1	.313	.306
Guerrero, Emilio	R-R	6-4	170	8-21-93	.239	.234	.241	53	180	16	43	11	1	0	22	11	4	0	0	47	4	1	.311	.297
Guillen, Ricardo	R-R	5-10	152	10-26-89	.207	.167	.221	40	140	17	29	4	3	0	13	10	1	0	2	38	4	6	.279	.261
Martin, Luis	R-R	6-4	210	2-12-94	.183	.173	.188	54	180	15	33	7	2	1	14	18	2	0	0	92	5	3	.261	.265
Moreno, Franklin	R-R	6-1	180	3-25-93	.121	.125	.120	13	33	3	4	0	0	0	2	7	0	0	0	15	3	0	.121	.275
Nagahashi, Mauricio	R-R	6-1	165	4-10-92	.202	.135	.227	54	193	23	39	3	3	8	30	13	5	0	0	49	15	6	.249	.328
Perez, Tonguard	R-R	5-9	210	1-8-93	.215	.200	.220	44	135	13	29	9	3	3	17	12	5	0	3	43	1	1	.393	.297
Pumarol, Jonathan	R-R	5-9	194	5-4-92	.205	.296	.176	35	112	8	23	6	2	1	9	15	3	0	0	33	4	0	.321	.315
Quintana, Gabriel	R-R	5-9	155	10-17-92	.207	.316	.154	31	58	11	12	2	0	0	6	9	1	0	0	26	1	4	.241	.324
Rojas, Angel	R-R	5-11	160	4-7-93	.199	.188	.202	62	211	27	42	4	2	0	10	24	4	0	1	62	15	5	.237	.292
Santiago, Kervin	R-R	5-11	185	4-5-93	.259	.172	.287	43	116	12	30	4	1	1	11	15	1	0	2	18	3	0	.336	.343

Pitching	B-T	HT	WT	DOB	W	L	ERA	G	GS	CG	SV	IP	H	R	ER	HR	BB	SO	AVG	vLH	vRH	K/9	BB/9
Agostini, Juan	R-R	6-3	183	8-29-92	0	1	6.75	5	5	0	0	12	15	11	9	1	2	5	.283	.133	.342	3.75	1.50
Cabrera, Juan	R-R	6-2	204	9-21-91	0	2	3.19	15	3	0	1	37	34	18	13	2	14	34	.246	.276	.239	8.35	3.44
Calatayud, Edgar	R-R	6-1	185	6-10-92	1	3	5.40	8	0	0	0	18	23	14	11	0	4	12	.295	.357	.281	5.89	1.96
De La Cruz, Aderly	R-R	6-4	180	10-20-92	2	0	3.60	7	0	0	0	15	10	8	6	1	6	10	.196	.188	.200	6.00	3.60
Del Rosario, Yeyfry	R-R	6-2	182	4-27-94	1	8	2.78	14	13	0	0	45	33	24	14	2	10	31	.195	.256	.175	6.15	1.99
Guerrero, Eyerys	R-R	6-3	208	10-14-92	1	2	5.46	15	9	0	1	31	27	21	19	1	10	29	.229	.179	.244	8.33	2.87
Guillen, Luillyn	L-L	5-10	156	9-19-88	0	0	1.13	2	1	0	0	8	6	1	1	0	0	10	.222	.000	.240	11.25	0.00
Labourt, Jairo	L-L	6-4	204	3-7-94	0	4	2.23	12	12	0	0	36	29	18	9	0	14	29	.220	.000	.236	7.18	3.47
Lopez, Manuel	R-R	6-2	182	3-2-91	3	1	1.40	24	0	0	1	58	40	13	9	1	17	46	.195	.119	.226	6.83	2.64
Manaure, Edgar	R-R	6-1	165	5-20-89	0	2	6.92	12	1	0	0	13	12	14	10	0	25	11	.255	.125	.282	7.62	17.31
Marquez, Erick	L-L	5-11	151	2-9-91	1	5	1.22	23	3	0	3	59	33	21	8	0	17	61	.163	.231	.159	9.31	2.59
Romero, Steven	R-R	6-0	190	8-2-90	3	1	2.22	23	0	0	2	57	46	24	14	0	17	46	.224	.294	.201	7.31	2.70
Sanchez, Cesar	R-R	6-2	210	8-29-91	4	7	3.66	16	11	0	0	64	47	39	26	0	25	63	.200	.182	.207	8.86	3.52

TORONTO BLUE JAYS

Pitching	B-T	HT	WT	DOB	W	L	ERA	G	GS	CG	SV	IP	H	R	ER	HR	BB	SO	AVG	vLH	vRH	K/9	BB/9
Tiburcio, Dariel	R-R	6-2	220	8-14-87	1	2	4.34	18	2	0	1	29	31	22	14	0	17	37	.270	.270	.269	11.48	5.28
Vielma, Gilberto	R-R	6-4	220	11-23-93	1	8	4.97	19	4	0	0	38	39	37	21	1	32	22	.267	.333	.254	5.21	7.58
Zerpa, Luis	R-R	6-1	190	9-28-92	2	3	2.74	25	0	0	0	66	58	31	20	3	13	56	.232	.221	.237	7.68	1.78

Fielding

Catcher	PCT	G	PO	A	E	DP	PB
Aguida	.950	17	87	28	6	0	6
Moreno	1.000	4	20	4	0	0	1
Perez	1.000	1	1	0	0	0	0
Pumarol	.948	25	138	25	9	0	5
Santiago	.982	34	236	35	5	0	5

First Base	PCT	G	PO	A	E	DP
Barazarte	.875	1	6	1	1	1
Cipriota	.989	22	178	7	2	15
Delgado	.977	28	202	9	5	8
Feliz	1.000	2	15	1	0	1
Moreno	.960	6	23	1	1	3
Perez	.968	23	201	13	7	11

Second Base	PCT	G	PO	A	E	DP
Blanco	.944	25	54	65	7	11
Cipriota	.852	5	12	11	4	0
Quintana	.926	18	31	32	5	5
Rojas	.983	31	62	52	2	11

Third Base	PCT	G	PO	A	E	DP
Blanco	.700	6	3	4	3	0
Cenas	.913	15	7	35	4	3
Cipriota	.935	18	13	30	3	2
Guerrero	.857	36	21	69	15	4
Perez	.000	1	0	0	0	0

Shortstop	PCT	G	PO	A	E	DP
Blanco	1.000	3	0	4	0	1

	PCT	G	PO	A	E	DP
Guerrero	.867	4	8	5	2	0
Guillen	.894	40	52	108	19	10
Quintana	.750	1	3	0	1	0
Rojas	.912	27	37	87	12	11

Outfield	PCT	G	PO	A	E	DP
Barazarte	.980	48	92	4	2	0
Blanco	.833	6	5	0	1	0
Cipriota	1.000	1	3	0	0	0
De La Cruz	.889	44	52	4	7	0
Feliz	.857	13	17	1	3	0
Martin	.938	54	89	2	6	0
Nagahashi	.968	53	58	2	2	1
Quintana	1.000	1	1	0	0	0
Rojas	1.000	2	4	0	0	0

Washington Nationals

SEASON IN A SENTENCE: The Nationals, a perennial National League East doormat, reached the 80-win plateau for the first time since 2005 and finished in third place, their highest finish since the 2002 Expos landed in second.

HIGH POINT: Phenom Stephen Strasburg had Tommy John surgery in September 2010 after a stirring debut, and he returned to go 1-1, 1.50 with 24 strikeouts and two walks in 24 innings in five September starts in 2011, showing the same dazzling stuff he displayed before his injury. Strasburg helped the Nationals finish strong, as the team went 17-10 in September.

LOW POINT: While 2011 gave Nationals fans reason to feel hopeful for the first time since the franchise moved to Washington, there is still plenty of work to be done—especially on the pitching staff, which produced just one 10-game winner (John Lannan). During a six-game losing streak at the end of July, Washington starters posted a 7.98 ERA.

NOTABLE ROOKIES: Danny Espinosa broke into the big leagues at the end of 2010 and stuck as the everyday starter in 2011, leading all big league rookies with 21 home runs while fielding at a solid .982 clip. Catcher Wilson Ramos, acquired from the Twins in 2010, emerged as another cornerstone up-the-middle piece.

KEY TRANSACTIONS: The Nationals allowed slugger Adam Dunn to depart via free agency and he posted his worst big league season for the White Sox, while 29-year-old Michael Morse took over first base and had a breakout year, leading the team with 31 homers and 95 RBIs. The Nats' big free agent signing was Jayson Werth, who put up a disappointing .232/.330/.389 line. Their more notable spending came in the draft, where more than $15 milion on bonuses helped bring in blue-chip prospects Anthony Rendon, Brian Goodwin, Matt Purke and Alex Meyer.

DOWN ON THE FARM: A year after signing for a $9.99 million major league deal—the largest ever given to a position player in the draft—outfielder Bryce Harper emerged as baseball's best prospect. He posted a .977 OPS in the the low Class A South Atlantic League as an 18-year-old, earning a two-level promotion to Double-A Harrisburg, where he held his own. The organization enjoyed a strong year from top to bottom, with prospects like Brad Peacock, Tommy Milone and Steve Lombardozzi breaking through to the big leagues.

OPENING DAY PAYROLL: $63,856,928 (22nd).

PLAYERS OF THE YEAR

MAJOR LEAGUE	MINOR LEAGUE
Michael Morse 1b/of	**Brad Peacock** rhp
.303/.360/.550	(Double-A/Triple-A)
31 HR, 95 RBIs	15-3, 2.39
4th in NL in SLG	EL Pitcher of Year

ORGANIZATION LEADERS

BATTING		*Minimum 250 PA
MAJORS		
* AVG	Michael Morse	.303
* OPS	Michael Morse	.91
HR	Michael Morse	31
RBI	Michael Morse	95
MINORS		
* AVG	Archie Gilbert, Potomac/Harrisburg	.313
* OBP	David Freitas, Hagerstown	.409
* SLG	Tyler Moore, Harrisburg	.532
R	Steve Lombardozzi, Harrisburg/Syracuse	86
H	Steve Lombardozzi, Harrisburg/Syracuse	172
TB	Tyler Moore, Harrisburg	276
2B	Tyler Moore, Harrisburg	35
3B	Chris Rahl, Harrisburg	10
HR	Tyler Moore, Harrisburg	31
RBI	Tyler Moore, Harrisburg	90
BB	David Freitas, Hagerstown	82
SO	Jason Martinson, Hagerstown	144
SB	Jeff Kobernus, Potomac	53

PITCHING		#Minimum 75 IP
MAJORS		
W	John Lannan	10
# ERA	Tyler Clippard	1.83
SO	Jordan Zimmermann	124
SV	Drew Storen	43
MINORS		
W	Brad Peacock, Harrisburg/Syracuse	15
L	Erik Davis, Harrisburg/Potomac	12
# ERA	Brad Peacock, Harrisburg/Syracuse	2.39
G	Josh Wilkie, Syracuse	52
GS	Paul Demny, Potomac	26
SV	Hector Nelo, Potomac	18
IP	Daniel Rosenbaum, Potomac/Harrisburg	171.1
BB	Erik Davis, Harrisburg/Potomac	57
SO	Brad Peacock, Harrisburg/Syracuse	177
# AVG	Brad Peacock, Harrisburg/Syracuse	.188

General Manager: Mike Rizzo. **Farm Director:** Bob Boone. **Scouting Director:** Kris Kline.

Class	Team	League	W	L	PCT	Finish	Manager(s)
Majors	Washington Nationals	National	80	81	.497	8th (16)	J. Riggleman/J. McLaren/D. Johnson
Triple-A	Syracuse Chiefs	International	66	74	.471	10th (14)	Randy Knorr
Double-A	Harrisburg Senators	Eastern	80	62	.563	1st (12)	Tony Beasley
High A	Potomac Nationals	Carolina	68	71	.489	5th (8)	Matthew LeCroy
Low A	Hagerstown Suns	South Atlantic	75	64	.540	6th (14)	Brian Daubach
Short-season	Auburn Doubledays	New York-Penn	45	30	.600	3rd (14)	Gary Cathcart
Rookie	GCL Nationals	Gulf Coast	20	33	.377	14th (15)	Bobby Williams
Overall 2011 Minor League Record			354	334	.515	10th (30)	

ORGANIZATION STATISTICS

WASHINGTON NATIONALS
NATIONAL LEAGUE

Batting	B-T	HT	WT	DOB	AVG	vLH	vRH	G	AB	R	H	2B	3B	HR	RBI	BB	HBP	SH	SF	SO	SB	CS	SLG	OBP
Ankiel, Rick	L-L	6-2	225	7-19-79	.239	.228	.243	122	380	46	91	20	0	9	37	29	2	0	1	96	10	3	.363	.296
Bernadina, Roger	L-L	6-2	200	6-12-84	.243	.191	.257	91	309	40	75	12	2	7	27	22	4	0	0	63	17	3	.362	.301
Bixler, Brian	R-R	6-1	195	10-22-82	.205	.212	.194	79	83	9	17	1	2	0	2	7	0	0	0	19	4	3	.265	.267
Brown, Corey	L-L	6-1	205	11-26-85	.000	.000	.000	3	3	0	0	0	0	0	0	0	0	0	0	2	0	0	.000	.000
Cora, Alex	L-R	6-0	200	10-18-75	.224	.300	.219	91	156	12	35	6	1	0	6	12	2	0	1	23	2	0	.276	.287
Desmond, Ian	R-R	6-2	210	9-20-85	.253	.216	.264	154	584	65	148	27	5	8	49	35	4	0	5	139	25	10	.358	.298
Espinosa, Danny	B-R	6-0	190	4-25-87	.236	.283	.222	158	573	72	135	29	5	21	66	57	19	0	4	166	17	6	.414	.323
Flores, Jesus	R-R	6-1	230	10-26-84	.209	.200	.212	30	86	5	18	6	0	1	2	5	0	0	0	27	0	0	.314	.253
Gomes, Jonny	R-R	6-1	225	11-22-80	.204	.278	.158	43	93	11	19	4	1	3	12	10	3	0	1	31	2	0	.366	.299
2-team total (77 Cincinnati)					.209	—	—	120	311	41	65	12	1	14	43	48	8	0	5	105	7	3	.389	.325
Hairston Jr., Jerry	R-R	5-10	190	5-29-76	.268	.235	.283	75	213	25	57	11	1	4	24	22	2	0	0	30	2	2	.385	.342
2-team total (45 Milwaukee)					.270	—	—	120	337	43	91	21	1	5	31	33	5	0	0	46	3	2	.383	.344
LaRoche, Adam	L-L	6-3	205	11-6-79	.172	.098	.200	43	151	15	26	4	0	3	15	25	0	0	1	37	1	0	.258	.288
Lombardozzi, Steve	B-R	6-0	170	9-20-88	.194	.000	.200	13	31	3	6	1	0	0	1	1	0	0	0	4	0	0	.226	.219
Marrero, Chris	R-R	6-3	210	7-2-88	.248	.313	.237	31	109	6	27	5	0	0	10	4	1	0	3	27	0	0	.294	.274
Morse, Mike	R-R	6-5	230	3-22-82	.303	.297	.304	146	522	73	158	36	0	31	95	36	13	0	4	126	2	3	.550	.360
Nix, Laynce	L-L	6-1	220	10-30-80	.250	.111	.263	124	324	38	81	15	1	16	44	23	1	0	3	82	2	2	.451	.299
Ramos, Wilson	R-R	6-0	220	8-10-87	.267	.276	.265	113	389	48	104	22	1	15	52	38	2	0	2	76	0	2	.445	.334
Rodriguez, Ivan	R-R	5-9	205	11-30-71	.218	.238	.214	44	124	14	27	7	0	2	19	10	1	0	0	28	0	0	.323	.281
Stairs, Matt	L-R	5-9	200	2-27-68	.154	.333	.145	56	65	4	10	1	0	0	2	9	0	0	0	23	0	0	.169	.257
Werth, Jayson	R-R	6-5	220	5-20-79	.232	.184	.244	150	561	69	130	26	1	20	58	74	10	0	4	160	19	3	.389	.330
Zimmerman, Ryan	R-R	6-3	230	9-28-84	.289	.338	.279	101	395	52	114	21	2	12	49	41	1	0	3	73	3	1	.443	.355

Pitching	B-T	HT	WT	DOB	W	L	ERA	G	GS	CG	SV	IP	H	R	ER	HR	BB	SO	AVG	vLH	vRH	K/9	BB/9
Balester, Collin	R-R	6-5	200	6-6-86	1	4	4.54	23	0	0	0	36	38	21	18	7	14	34	.268	.235	.286	8.58	3.53
Broderick, Brian	R-R	6-6	205	9-1-86	0	1	6.57	11	0	0	0	12	16	9	9	0	3	4	.320	.400	.240	2.92	2.19
Burnett, Sean	L-L	6-1	200	9-17-82	5	5	3.81	69	0	0	4	57	54	24	24	6	21	33	.254	.200	.297	5.24	3.34
Clippard, Tyler	R-R	6-3	200	2-14-85	3	0	1.83	72	0	0	0	88	48	18	18	11	26	104	.162	.169	.156	10.60	2.65
Coffey, Todd	R-R	6-4	240	9-9-80	5	1	3.62	69	0	0	0	60	55	25	24	4	20	46	.244	.338	.193	6.94	3.02
Detwiler, Ross	R-L	6-5	185	3-6-86	4	5	3.00	15	10	0	0	66	63	26	22	7	20	41	.258	.167	.281	5.59	2.73
Gaudin, Chad	R-R	5-10	190	3-24-83	1	1	6.48	10	0	0	0	8	12	10	6	1	8	10	.333	.429	.273	10.80	8.64
Gorzelanny, Tom	L-L	6-2	210	7-12-82	4	6	4.03	30	15	0	0	105	102	50	47	15	33	95	.258	.157	.287	8.14	2.83
Hernandez, Livan	R-R	6-2	245	2-20-75	8	13	4.47	29	29	1	0	175	199	98	87	16	46	99	.291	.297	.286	5.08	2.36
Kimball, Cole	R-R	6-2	225	8-1-85	1	0	1.93	12	0	0	0	14	8	3	3	0	11	11	.174	.211	.148	7.07	7.07
Lannan, John	L-L	6-4	215	9-27-84	10	13	3.70	33	33	0	0	185	194	90	76	15	76	106	.272	.211	.293	5.17	3.70
Marquis, Jason	L-R	6-1	210	8-21-78	8	5	3.95	20	20	1	0	121	132	58	53	8	39	71	.283	.280	.285	5.30	2.91
2-team total (3 Arizona)					8	6	4.43	23	23	1	0	132	154	74	65	11	43	76	—	—	—	5.18	2.93
Mattheus, Ryan	R-R	6-3	215	11-10-83	2	2	2.81	35	0	0	0	32	26	11	10	1	15	12	.228	.170	.279	3.38	4.22
Maya, Yunesky	R-R	5-11	170	8-28-81	1	1	5.23	10	5	0	0	33	40	19	19	3	10	15	.323	.283	.359	4.13	2.76
Milone, Tom	L-L	6-1	205	2-16-87	1	0	3.81	5	5	0	0	26	28	11	11	2	4	15	.283	.300	.281	5.19	1.38
Peacock, Brad	R-R	6-1	175	2-2-88	2	0	0.75	3	2	0	0	12	7	1	1	0	6	4	.167	.148	.200	3.00	4.50
Rodriguez, Henry	R-R	6-0	220	2-25-87	3	3	3.56	59	0	0	2	66	54	30	26	1	45	70	.220	.238	.206	9.59	6.17
Severino, Atahualpa	L-L	5-9	170	11-6-84	1	0	3.86	6	0	0	0	5	5	2	2	1	1	7	.278	.222	.333	13.50	1.93
Slaten, Doug	L-L	6-5	215	2-4-80	0	2	4.41	31	0	0	0	16	26	10	8	3	9	13	.356	.333	.378	7.16	4.96
Stammen, Craig	R-R	6-3	200	3-9-84	1	1	0.87	7	0	0	0	10	3	1	1	0	4	4	.088	.067	.105	10.45	3.48
Storen, Drew	B-R	6-2	180	8-11-87	6	3	2.75	73	0	0	43	75	57	24	23	8	20	74	.204	.198	.209	8.84	2.39
Strasburg, Stephen	R-R	6-4	220	7-20-88	1	1	1.50	5	5	0	0	24	15	5	4	0	2	24	.179	.125	.227	9.00	0.75
Wang, Chien-Ming	R-R	6-3	230	3-31-80	4	3	4.04	11	11	0	0	62	67	35	28	8	13	25	.272	.368	.186	3.61	1.88
Zimmermann, Jordan	R-R	6-2	220	5-23-86	8	11	3.18	26	26	1	0	161	154	62	57	12	31	124	.251	.252	.251	6.92	1.73

Fielding

Catcher	PCT	G	PO	A	E	DP	PB
Flores	.993	22	140	10	1	0	2
Ramos	.993	108	684	55	5	7	3
Rodriguez	.989	37	245	18	3	4	3

First Base	PCT	G	PO	A	E	DP
Bixler	1.000	2	3	0	0	1
Cora	.875	9	14	0	2	2

LaRoche	1.000	43	380	32	0	34
Marrero	.993	31	254	14	2	17
Morse	.992	85	732	55	6	63
Nix	1.000	9	44	4	0	5
Rodriguez	1.000	1	1	0	0	0
Stairs	1.000	4	11	1	0	0

Second Base	PCT	G	PO	A	E	DP
Cora	.900	5	9	0	1	0
Espinosa	.982	158	305	464	14	101
Hairston Jr.	1.000	3	4	2	0	0
Lombardozzi	1.000	3	6	5	0	0

Third Base	PCT	G	PO	A	E	DP
Bixler	.929	14	3	10	1	1
Cora	.978	31	4	41	1	5
Hairston Jr.	.936	44	27	61	6	4
Lombardozzi	.917	3	2	9	1	0
Zimmerman	.957	97	66	200	12	19

Shortstop	PCT	G	PO	A	E	DP
Bixler	1.000	2	1	4	0	0
Cora	1.000	16	22	47	0	10
Desmond	.966	152	226	437	23	85
Hairston Jr.	1.000	1	0	1	0	0

Lombardozzi	1.000	1	1	1	0	0

Outfield	PCT	G	PO	A	E	DP
Ankiel	.996	113	245	9	1	0
Bernadina	.994	84	159	6	1	0
Bixler	1.000	34	31	1	0	0
Gomes	.979	30	46	0	1	0
Hairston Jr.	.957	30	45	0	2	0
Morse	.989	55	89	4	1	1
Nix	.985	85	122	7	2	3
Werth	.978	149	342	11	8	4

SYRACUSE CHIEFS

TRIPLE-A

INTERNATIONAL LEAGUE

Batting	B-T	HT	WT	DOB	AVG	vLH	vRH	G	AB	R	H	2B	3B	HR	RBI	BB	HBP	SH	SF	SO	SB	CS	SLG	OBP
Ankiel, Rick	L-L	6-2	225	7-19-79	.143	.000	.200	2	7	2	1	1	0	0	0	1	0	0	0	2	1	0	.286	.250
Antonelli, Matt	R-R	6-0	205	4-8-85	.297	.301	.295	86	300	44	89	19	3	8	30	47	3	0	4	59	6	6	.460	.393
Aubrey, Michael	L-L	6-0	190	4-15-82	.273	.128	.303	82	227	34	62	12	0	11	35	32	1	0	2	30	0	0	.471	.363
Bernadina, Roger	L-L	6-2	200	6-12-84	.250	.125	.290	46	164	26	41	9	0	6	14	18	4	0	0	47	14	5	.415	.339
Bixler, Brian	R-R	6-1	195	10-22-82	.314	.368	.299	25	86	17	27	5	0	1	6	16	4	0	1	30	4	1	.407	.439
Blanco, Gregor	L-L	5-11	170	12-24-83	.203	.175	.214	51	143	26	29	7	2	3	10	27	2	0	1	35	15	1	.343	.335
Brown, Corey	L-L	6-1	205	11-26-85	.235	.219	.241	124	396	50	93	18	3	14	39	47	7	0	1	134	4	7	.402	.326
Bynum, Seth	R-R	6-0	185	12-19-80	.259	.303	.240	84	297	35	77	13	2	10	39	26	4	0	2	83	7	2	.418	.325
Curran, Chris	L-R	5-9	170	12-21-87	.278	.429	.182	7	18	2	5	0	1	0	2	1	0	0	1	6	0	1	.389	.300
Flores, Jesus	R-R	6-1	230	10-26-84	.234	.211	.243	56	209	17	49	15	0	5	30	5	1	0	3	54	0	0	.378	.252
Fox, Adam	R-R	5-11	200	11-23-81	.241	.269	.230	29	87	12	21	4	2	2	12	5	0	0	0	20	2	1	.402	.283
Frazier, Jeff	R-R	6-3	195	8-10-82	.226	.241	.221	118	371	37	84	21	0	10	46	33	5	0	4	53	1	3	.364	.295
Hulett, Tug	L-R	5-10	185	2-28-83	.280	.268	.284	104	346	44	97	25	2	6	49	43	1	0	4	67	7	6	.416	.358
Lombardozzi, Steve	B-R	6-0	170	9-20-88	.310	.322	.301	69	294	46	91	13	2	4	29	21	1	0	3	40	14	5	.408	.354
Maldonado, Carlos	R-R	6-2	250	1-7-79	.234	.152	.269	38	111	11	26	9	0	1	12	21	1	0	0	32	0	0	.342	.361
Marrero, Chris	R-R	6-3	210	7-2-88	.300	.356	.276	127	483	59	145	30	0	14	69	58	2	0	3	97	3	2	.449	.375
McConnell, Chris	R-R	5-9	170	12-18-85	.175	.146	.185	57	171	14	30	9	1	1	10	13	4	0	0	41	3	3	.257	.250
Nicol, Sean	R-R	5-10	175	9-25-86	.333	.000	.500	2	3	0	1	0	0	0	0	0	0	0	0	0	0	0	.333	.333
Solano, Jhonatan	R-R	6-0	180	8-12-85	.275	.313	.256	78	255	27	70	14	0	5	33	19	1	0	2	36	1	1	.388	.325
Valdez, Alex	B-R	6-1	160	9-2-84	.156	.150	.158	27	77	8	12	2	1	2	6	7	1	0	0	17	2	0	.286	.235
2-team total (5 Pawtucket)					.165	—	—	32	91	10	15	4	1	3	7	10	1	0	0	23	2	0	.330	.255
Valdez, Jesus	R-R	6-2	170	11-2-84	.271	.298	.258	102	388	48	105	19	0	10	62	28	3	0	9	68	3	2	.397	.318
Whiting, Boomer	R-R	5-10	170	11-5-83	.175	.208	.154	22	63	7	11	1	0	0	3	5	2	0	0	15	3	5	.190	.257
Zimmerman, Ryan	R-R	6-3	230	9-28-84	.222	.000	.400	2	9	1	2	0	0	0	1	0	0	0	0	2	0	0	.222	.222

Pitching	B-T	HT	WT	DOB	W	L	ERA	G	GS	CG	SV	IP	H	R	ER	HR	BB	SO	AVG	vLH	vRH	K/9	BB/9
Arnesen, Erik	R-R	6-3	260	3-19-84	0	2	3.57	3	3	0	0	18	22	7	7	2	3	15	.314	.348	.298	7.64	1.53
Balester, Collin	R-R	6-5	200	6-6-86	2	1	4.35	28	0	0	1	39	47	19	19	2	15	46	.299	.349	.266	10.53	3.43
Bronson, Evan	L-L	6-3	195	2-13-87	1	0	6.23	1	0	0	0	4	3	3	3	0	2	3	.188	.125	.250	6.23	4.15
Carr, Adam	R-R	6-2	220	4-1-84	2	2	6.63	17	0	0	0	19	22	14	14	4	12	13	.286	.276	.292	6.16	5.68
Chico, Matt	L-L	5-11	220	6-10-83	0	2	5.06	8	0	0	0	11	16	7	6	0	5	8	.356	.421	.308	6.75	4.22
Detwiler, Ross	R-L	6-5	185	3-6-86	6	6	4.53	16	16	0	0	87	98	48	44	4	32	63	.285	.289	.284	6.49	3.30
Garcia, Christian	R-R	6-5	215	8-24-85	0	0	0.00	1	0	0	0	2	0	0	0	0	1	2	.000	.000	.000	9.00	4.50
Gaudin, Chad	R-R	5-10	190	3-24-83	0	2	4.38	6	2	0	0	12	17	9	6	0	3	14	.333	.500	.207	10.22	2.19
Gorzelanny, Tom	L-L	6-2	210	7-12-82	0	1	9.00	1	1	0	0	4	5	4	4	1	1	3	.313	.000	.333	6.75	2.25
Hyde, Lee	R-L	6-2	205	2-14-85	2	0	5.68	42	0	0	1	38	40	26	24	5	26	38	.278	.214	.318	9.00	6.16
Kimball, Cole	R-R	6-3	225	8-1-85	1	0	0.00	12	0	0	5	14	8	0	0	0	8	14	.163	.227	.111	9.22	5.27
Mandel, Jeff	R-R	6-3	190	4-30-85	4	4	3.81	43	0	0	3	54	67	25	23	5	16	48	.309	.305	.311	7.95	2.65
Martin, J.D.	R-R	6-2	200	1-2-83	3	7	3.93	30	14	0	2	108	105	51	47	17	17	72	.263	.272	.257	6.02	1.42
Martinez, Carlos	R-R	6-4	180	3-30-84	0	0	27.00	1	0	0	0	2	7	5	5	1	2	0	.636	.833	.400	0.00	10.80
Mattheus, Ryan	R-R	6-3	215	11-10-83	0	0	0.00	9	0	0	2	10	3	0	0	0	3	10	.094	.143	.056	9.00	2.70
Maya, Yunesky	R-R	5-11	170	8-28-81	4	9	5.00	22	22	1	0	130	133	73	72	14	28	98	.265	.255	.274	6.80	1.94
Meyers, Brad	R-R	6-6	195	9-13-85	6	5	3.48	17	16	0	0	96	110	39	37	8	15	74	.293	.261	.322	6.96	1.41
Milone, Tom	L-L	6-1	205	2-16-87	12	6	3.22	24	24	0	0	148	137	55	53	9	16	155	.241	.230	.244	9.40	0.97
Mock, Garrett	R-R	6-4	230	4-25-83	0	3	6.28	16	4	0	0	29	24	20	20	2	24	32	.220	.263	.173	10.05	7.53
Peacock, Brad	R-R	6-1	175	2-2-88	5	1	3.19	9	9	0	0	48	36	18	17	5	24	48	.205	.174	.233	9.00	4.50
Pena, Hassan	R-R	6-2	210	3-25-85	0	4	19.29	7	0	0	1	7	18	15	15	0	2	8	.474	.438	.500	10.29	2.57
Rodriguez, Henry	R-R	6-0	220	2-25-87	0	0	1.08	6	0	0	0	8	5	2	1	0	6	9	.185	.400	.059	9.72	6.48
Romero, J.C.	B-L	5-11	205	6-4-76	0	0	1.29	5	0	0	0	7	3	1	1	0	1	5	.130	.000	.188	6.43	1.29
2-team total (11 Scranton/W-B)					1	0	2.33	16	0	0	0	19	14	6	5	0	6	15	—	—	—	6.98	2.79
Severino, Atahualpa	L-L	5-9	170	11-6-84	1	2	4.50	35	0	0	1	32	37	17	16	2	23	38	.280	.244	.299	10.69	6.47
Slaten, Doug	L-L	6-5	215	2-4-80	0	0	0.00	3	0	0	0	3	2	0	0	0	0	5	.250	.000	.500	16.88	0.00
Stammen, Craig	R-R	6-3	200	3-9-84	10	7	4.75	25	24	1	0	142	163	80	75	18	40	127	.287	.305	.273	8.05	2.54
Strasburg, Stephen	R-R	6-4	220	7-20-88	0	1	1.80	1	1	0	0	5	2	1	1	0	0	7	.118	.000	.222	12.60	0.00
Tatusko, Ryan	R-R	6-5	200	3-27-85	3	4	4.54	23	2	0	0	40	52	20	20	1	19	28	.327	.234	.389	6.31	4.31
Wang, Chien-Ming	R-R	6-3	230	3-31-80	0	1	6.75	2	2	0	0	11	15	8	8	2	2	9	.349	.316	.375	7.59	1.69
Wilkie, Josh	R-R	6-2	190	7-22-84	3	5	3.13	52	0	0	16	60	61	25	21	4	21	57	.263	.287	.242	8.50	3.13
Zinicola, Zech	R-R	6-1	220	3-2-85	1	0	1.98	21	0	0	1	27	20	6	6	2	10	29	.196	.190	.200	9.55	3.29

WASHINGTON NATIONALS

Fielding

Catcher	PCT	G	PO	A	E	DP	PB
Flores	.995	46	362	23	2	2	5
Maldonado	.995	28	200	17	1	1	1
Solano	.991	73	510	61	5	3	6

First Base	PCT	G	PO	A	E	DP
Aubrey	1.000	4	26	2	0	2
Frazier	1.000	11	79	3	0	6
Hulett	1.000	2	6	1	0	1
Marrero	.996	125	1104	67	5	102

Second Base	PCT	G	PO	A	E	DP
Antonelli	.965	24	36	74	4	14
Bixler	.962	5	10	15	1	4
Bynum	.977	23	32	52	2	13
Hulett	.981	23	40	61	2	14
Lombardozzi	1.000	59	104	162	0	35
Nicol	1.000	1	2	3	0	1
Solano	.857	2	3	3	1	0
Valdez	.982	13	20	34	1	7

Third Base	PCT	G	PO	A	E	DP
Antonelli	.971	41	19	82	3	4
Bixler	1.000	8	2	4	0	0
Bynum	1.000	5	5	9	0	1
Fox	.966	24	12	45	2	1
Frazier	1.000	1	0	2	0	0
Hulett	.938	60	36	85	8	8
Lombardozzi	1.000	1	2	2	0	0
Valdez	.895	12	4	13	2	1
Zimmerman	1.000	2	0	6	0	0

Shortstop	PCT	G	PO	A	E	DP
Antonelli	.930	19	14	39	4	8
Bixler	1.000	8	12	14	0	2
Bynum	.970	55	70	153	7	29
Hulett	1.000	5	5	7	0	1
Lombardozzi	1.000	10	16	33	0	8
McConnell	.975	55	81	154	6	41

Outfield	PCT	G	PO	A	E	DP
Ankiel	1.000	2	4	1	0	0
Antonelli	1.000	6	8	0	0	0
Aubrey	1.000	13	13	0	0	0
Bernadina	1.000	45	67	5	0	2
Bixler	1.000	9	10	0	0	0
Blanco	.979	45	91	3	2	0
Brown	.986	121	273	9	4	4
Curran	.875	5	7	0	1	0
Fox	.000	1	0	0	0	0
Frazier	.985	88	132	3	2	0
Hulett	.000	2	0	0	0	0
Valdez	.981	96	150	2	3	1
Whiting	1.000	20	28	1	0	0

HARRISBURG SENATORS

DOUBLE-A

EASTERN LEAGUE

Batting	B-T	HT	WT	DOB	AVG	vLH	vRH	G	AB	R	H	2B	3B	HR	RBI	BB	HBP	SH	SF	SO	SB	CS	SLG	OBP
Ankiel, Rick	L-L	6-2	225	7-19-79	.000	.000	.000	1	4	0	0	0	0	0	0	0	0	0	0	4	0	0	.000	.000
Antonelli, Matt	R-R	6-0	205	4-8-85	.333	.333	.333	4	15	3	5	1	0	0	1	0	0	0	0	1	0	0	.400	.333
Coats, Buck	L-R	6-3	200	6-9-82	.261	.600	.167	9	23	0	6	0	0	0	3	2	0	0	0	2	0	0	.261	.370
Davis, Leonard	L-R	5-10	215	12-24-83	.229	.182	.250	36	144	13	33	7	2	2	15	4	2	0	1	34	4	2	.347	.258
Fox, Adam	R-R	5-11	200	11-23-81	.192	.148	.224	50	146	13	28	8	1	4	21	11	1	0	0	31	1	0	.342	.253
Gilbert, Archie	R-R	5-8	184	7-8-83	.313	.318	.311	98	326	51	102	22	0	12	40	27	10	0	1	35	26	4	.491	.382
Hairston Jr., Jerry	R-R	5-10	190	5-29-76	.167	.200	.000	2	6	1	1	0	0	0	0	2	0	0	0	0	0	0	.167	.375
Harper, Bryce	L-R	6-3	225	10-16-92	.256	.167	.309	37	129	14	33	7	1	3	12	15	0	0	2	26	7	2	.395	.329
Ivany, Devin	R-R	6-2	185	7-27-82	.231	.333	.185	51	156	18	36	8	0	3	22	12	2	0	1	36	3	4	.340	.292
Johnson, Josh R.	B-R	5-11	170	1-11-86	.244	.283	.227	128	447	70	109	24	3	8	36	67	6	0	2	91	21	12	.365	.349
King, Stephen	R-R	6-2	195	10-2-87	.191	.171	.200	95	257	18	49	11	1	5	23	28	3	0	1	94	2	0	.300	.277
Komatsu, Erik	L-L	5-10	175	10-1-87	.234	.237	.233	31	128	12	30	5	0	1	8	11	1	0	1	22	8	3	.297	.298
Lombardozzi, Steve	B-R	6-0	170	9-20-88	.309	.265	.325	65	262	40	81	12	7	4	23	18	6	0	1	38	16	3	.454	.366
McConnell, Chris	R-R	5-9	170	12-18-85	.214	.167	.236	64	187	19	40	9	1	2	15	15	0	0	1	39	4	2	.305	.271
Moore, Tyler	R-R	6-2	185	1-30-87	.270	.289	.263	137	519	70	140	35	4	31	90	30	6	0	6	139	2	0	.532	.314
Nicol, Sean	R-R	5-10	175	9-25-86	.000	.000	.000	4	3	0	0	0	0	0	0	0	0	0	0	1	0	0	.000	.250
Norris, Derek	R-R	6-0	210	2-14-89	.210	.225	.204	104	334	75	70	17	1	20	46	77	7	0	2	117	13	4	.446	.367
Pahuta, Tim	L-R	6-4	225	5-3-83	.260	.227	.267	87	246	29	64	11	1	15	43	20	0	0	3	75	1	1	.496	.312
Peacock, Brian	R-R	6-1	185	8-26-84	.286	.000	.333	3	7	1	2	1	0	0	1	0	0	0	0	3	0	0	.429	.286
Perez, Miguel	R-R	6-3	235	9-25-83	.000	.000	.000	3	5	0	0	0	0	0	0	0	0	0	0	3	0	0	.000	.000
Rahl, Chris	R-R	5-10	185	12-5-83	.280	.303	.271	117	429	52	120	24	10	5	53	23	9	0	2	100	25	6	.417	.328
Rhinehart, Bill	L-L	6-0	202	11-22-84	.283	.203	.304	89	276	55	78	17	2	21	59	39	4	0	3	59	1	1	.587	.376
Rodriguez, Ivan	R-R	5-9	205	11-30-71	.222	.000	.286	3	9	2	2	1	0	0	0	1	0	0	0	1	0	0	.333	.300
Tucker, Jonathan	R-R	5-8	180	7-2-83	.224	.218	.226	75	223	29	50	8	3	2	23	19	1	0	1	30	12	2	.314	.287
Valdez, Alex	B-R	6-1	160	9-2-84	.225	.227	.224	29	89	13	20	6	2	3	14	7	0	0	1	20	2	1	.438	.278
2-team total (6 Portland)					.241	—	—	35	108	16	26	7	2	3	15	10	0	0	1	22	3	1	.426	.303
Valdez, Jesus	R-R	6-2	170	11-2-84	.261	.265	.260	31	111	7	29	8	0	3	14	7	0	0	1	10	0	0	.387	.305

Pitching	B-T	HT	WT	DOB	W	L	ERA	G	GS	CG	SV	IP	H	R	ER	HR	BB	SO	AVG	vLH	vRH	K/9	BB/9
Arnesen, Erik	R-R	6-3	260	3-19-84	8	4	2.43	26	16	0	1	126	114	43	34	7	24	122	.241	.267	.219	8.71	1.71
Atilano, Luis	R-R	6-2	220	5-10-85	0	1	13.50	2	2	0	0	6	12	9	9	0	3	3	.429	.438	.417	4.50	4.50
Barthmaier, Jimmy	R-R	6-5	205	1-6-84	5	3	5.05	39	2	0	1	68	74	42	38	7	31	69	.280	.257	.294	9.18	4.12
Bronson, Evan	L-L	6-3	195	2-13-87	0	0	2.25	1	1	0	0	4	5	1	1	0	2	1	.313	.200	.364	2.25	4.50
Chico, Matt	L-L	5-11	220	6-10-83	1	1	10.93	10	0	0	1	14	25	22	17	3	7	16	.379	.304	.419	10.29	4.50
Davis, Erik	R-R	6-4	200	10-8-86	5	7	4.79	19	18	1	0	94	110	60	50	9	41	93	.289	.287	.290	8.90	3.93
Lehman, Pat	R-R	6-3	210	10-18-86	1	2	3.71	29	0	0	6	34	22	14	14	2	4	34	.186	.185	.188	9.00	1.06
Mandel, Jeff	B-R	6-3	190	4-30-85	0	0	2.25	5	0	0	0	8	8	2	2	0	2	5	.235	.385	.143	5.63	2.25
Martin, Rafael	R-R	6-2	195	5-16-84	4	1	1.77	32	0	0	13	36	26	8	7	1	9	44	.203	.204	.203	11.10	2.27
Martinez, Carlos	R-R	6-4	180	3-30-84	3	4	5.34	32	2	0	2	64	75	40	38	7	16	36	.292	.283	.299	5.06	2.25
Martis, Shairon	R-R	6-1	225	3-30-87	8	6	3.05	23	23	1	0	133	123	53	45	9	39	146	.245	.250	.240	9.88	2.64
Mattheus, Ryan	R-R	6-3	215	11-10-83	2	1	2.45	13	0	0	4	15	9	4	4	1	5	18	.173	.231	.115	11.05	3.07
McCoy, Patrick	L-L	6-4	200	8-3-88	1	2	4.78	49	0	0	4	53	53	32	28	7	16	53	.259	.250	.264	9.06	2.73
Meyers, Brad	R-R	6-6	195	11-3-85	3	2	2.48	6	6	0	0	36	35	10	10	2	0	38	.255	.282	.227	9.41	0.00
Mock, Garrett	R-R	6-4	230	4-25-83	0	1	13.50	2	2	0	0	7	12	11	11	3	3	5	.353	.316	.400	6.14	3.68
Peacock, Brad	R-R	6-1	175	2-2-88	10	2	2.01	16	14	1	0	99	62	25	22	4	23	129	.179	.158	.200	11.77	2.10
Pena, Hassan	R-R	6-2	210	3-26-85	2	2	2.73	40	0	0	10	56	42	20	17	5	12	55	.208	.195	.217	8.84	1.93
Perez, Oliver	L-L	6-3	210	8-15-81	3	5	3.09	16	15	0	0	76	78	34	26	10	27	58	.268	.313	.250	6.90	3.21
Roark, Tanner	R-R	6-2	220	10-5-86	9	9	4.69	21	21	0	0	117	125	64	61	10	39	92	.277	.279	.276	7.08	3.00
Rodriguez, Henry	R-R	6-0	220	2-25-87	0	0	0.00	3	1	0	0	4	3	0	0	0	0	7	.200	.222	.167	15.75	0.00
Rosenbaum, Danny	R-L	6-1	210	10-10-87	3	1	2.29	6	6	0	0	39	27	14	10	0	11	27	.190	.194	.189	6.18	2.52
Slaten, Doug	L-L	6-5	215	2-4-80	0	0	0.00	1	1	0	0	2	2	0	0	0	0	2	.250	.000	.333	9.00	0.00

Pitching	B-T	HT	WT	DOB	W	L	ERA	G	GS	CG	SV	IP	H	R	ER	HR	BB	SO	AVG	vLH	vRH	K/9	BB/9
Strasburg, Stephen	R-R	6-4	220	7-20-88	1	0	0.00	1	1	0	0	6	1	0	0	0	0	4	.056	.000	.067	6.00	0.00
Tatusko, Ryan	R-R	6-5	200	3-27-85	2	4	5.94	12	9	0	0	47	60	33	31	2	26	40	.308	.333	.283	7.66	4.98
VanAllen, Cory	L-L	6-3	180	12-24-84	5	4	2.50	47	0	0	0	58	49	19	16	6	22	71	.236	.202	.261	11.08	3.43
Wang, Chien-Ming	R-R	6-3	230	3-31-80	2	0	0.00	2	2	0	0	11	8	0	0	0	3	3	.205	.250	.133	2.45	0.00
Zinicola, Zech	R-R	6-1	220	3-2-85	2	0	2.08	11	0	0	4	13	11	3	3	1	3	15	.234	.167	.304	10.38	2.08

Fielding

Catcher	PCT	G	PO	A	E	DP	PB
Ivany	.992	45	360	20	3	2	3
Norris	.991	95	787	74	8	2	15
Peacock	1.000	2	17	0	0	0	1
Perez	1.000	2	9	0	0	0	0
Rodriguez	1.000	2	12	1	0	0	0

First Base	PCT	G	PO	A	E	DP
Moore	.992	125	925	90	8	97
Pahuta	.980	12	94	5	2	3
Rhinehart	.980	6	44	6	1	3

Second Base	PCT	G	PO	A	E	DP
Antonelli	1.000	1	3	2	0	1
Davis	1.000	2	3	1	0	0
Fox	.978	15	22	22	1	3
Johnson	.974	62	114	149	7	32
Lombardozzi	.993	63	115	156	2	35

	PCT	G	PO	A	E	DP
McConnell	.923	2	5	7	1	2
Nicol	1.000	1	2	4	0	1
Tucker	.000	1	0	0	0	0
Valdez	.957	4	6	16	1	1

Third Base	PCT	G	PO	A	E	DP
Antonelli	1.000	3	3	1	0	0
Davis	.667	1	0	2	1	1
Fox	.979	25	15	31	1	4
King	.920	73	32	95	11	5
Pahuta	.914	57	41	87	12	7
Valdez	.921	12	9	26	3	1

Shortstop	PCT	G	PO	A	E	DP
Hairston Jr.	.889	2	5	3	1	0
Johnson	.984	63	90	149	4	31
King	.947	24	21	51	4	11
Lombardozzi	1.000	3	6	3	0	1

	PCT	G	PO	A	E	DP
McConnell	.951	61	74	140	11	34
Tucker	.895	7	9	8	2	2

Outfield	PCT	G	PO	A	E	DP
Ankiel	.000	1	0	0	0	0
Coats	1.000	4	11	0	0	0
Davis	.976	19	39	1	1	0
Fox	.000	1	0	0	0	0
Gilbert	.959	89	156	8	7	3
Harper	.955	37	57	7	3	0
Johnson	1.000	8	11	1	0	0
Komatsu	1.000	31	63	0	0	0
Rahl	.976	113	196	5	5	1
Rhinehart	.927	54	73	3	6	0
Tucker	.993	67	136	3	1	1
Valdez	1.000	27	36	2	0	0

POTOMAC NATIONALS
CAROLINA LEAGUE

HIGH CLASS A

Batting	B-T	HT	WT	DOB	AVG	vLH	vRH	G	AB	R	H	2B	3B	HR	RBI	BB	HBP	SH	SF	SO	SB	CS	SLG	OBP
Bloxom, Justin	R-B	6-1	205	4-29-88	.259	.287	.242	88	320	36	83	20	3	9	45	36	1	0	5	75	2	3	.425	.331
Cuevas, Justino	R-R	5-10	160	11-30-88	.323	.273	.333	19	65	7	21	4	1	2	12	2	0	0	2	18	1	0	.508	.333
Curran, Chris	L-R	5-9	170	12-21-87	.149	.273	.111	21	47	4	7	1	0	0	1	4	1	0	0	13	2	2	.170	.231
Dykstra, Cutter	R-R	5-11	180	6-29-89	.212	.242	.198	94	306	26	65	11	1	1	27	21	2	0	3	82	12	4	.265	.265
Gilbert, Archie	R-R	5-8	184	7-8-83	.316	.200	.357	5	19	2	6	1	0	0	2	2	1	0	0	3	5	0	.368	.409
Hague, Rick	R-R	6-2	190	9-18-88	.357	.500	.333	4	14	4	5	2	0	1	4	2	0	0	0	1	0	0	.714	.438
Higley, J.R.	R-R	6-3	210	6-21-88	.234	.272	.211	69	209	36	49	13	0	6	23	23	10	0	0	61	5	2	.383	.339
Hood, Destin	R-R	6-1	225	4-3-90	.276	.258	.286	128	463	61	128	29	5	13	83	58	9	0	6	96	21	6	.445	.364
King, Stephen	R-R	6-2	195	10-2-87	.250	.308	.217	21	72	9	18	6	0	2	6	5	5	0	0	21	1	0	.417	.341
Kobernus, Jeff	R-R	6-2	210	6-30-88	.282	.306	.270	124	489	67	138	22	4	7	52	21	2	0	2	87	53	8	.387	.313
Leon, Sandy	B-R	5-11	175	3-13-89	.251	.248	.253	109	370	36	93	21	1	6	43	33	1	0	3	69	1	3	.362	.312
Lozada, Jose	B-R	6-0	180	12-29-85	.256	.287	.241	99	313	50	80	22	5	6	34	33	8	0	2	69	8	4	.415	.340
Mayo, Jeremy	R-R	5-10	194	6-17-88	.167	.000	.222	5	12	1	2	1	0	0	2	0	0	0	0	7	0	1	.250	.286
Nicol, Sean	R-R	5-10	175	9-25-86	.156	.071	.194	14	45	8	7	1	0	0	3	6	0	0	0	11	0	0	.178	.255
Nieto, Adrian	B-R	6-0	200	11-12-89	.200	.200	.000	2	5	1	1	0	0	0	0	1	1	0	0	2	0	0	.200	.333
Peacock, Brian	R-R	6-1	185	8-26-84	.237	.288	.213	60	186	21	44	9	1	2	20	18	1	0	3	59	7	3	.328	.303
Perez, Eury	R-R	6-0	180	5-30-90	.283	.321	.266	119	424	54	120	9	2	1	41	22	3	0	5	63	45	15	.330	.319
Ramirez, J.P.	L-L	5-10	185	9-29-89	.223	.221	.223	85	310	38	69	14	1	7	29	21	2	0	2	57	3	1	.342	.275
Rodriguez, Ivan	R-R	5-9	205	11-30-71	.333	.500	.000	1	3	1	1	0	0	1	0	0	0	0	0	0	0	0	1.333	.333
Soriano, Francisco	B-R	5-11	169	6-16-87	.229	.243	.221	88	284	48	65	15	3	6	37	55	5	0	3	51	16	4	.366	.360
Souza, Steven	R-R	6-3	205	4-24-89	.228	.258	.213	122	390	58	89	17	2	11	56	75	8	0	5	131	25	9	.367	.360
Walters, Zach	B-R	6-2	195	9-5-89	.293	.289	.295	30	116	15	34	7	1	0	11	8	0	0	1	33	7	1	.371	.336
Zimmerman, Ryan	R-R	6-3	230	9-28-84	.400	.000	.444	3	10	4	2	0	0	1	1	0	0	0	1	0	0	0	.600	.455

Pitching	B-T	HT	WT	DOB	W	L	ERA	G	GS	CG	SV	IP	H	R	ER	HR	BB	SO	AVG	vLH	vRH	K/9	BB/9
Bronson, Evan	L-L	6-3	195	2-13-87	5	5	3.64	23	12	0	0	96	103	43	39	9	28	55	.276	.245	.287	5.14	2.62
Caldera, Alex	L-R	6-3	200	10-1-85	0	1	16.71	3	2	0	0	7	16	13	13	5	3	6	.457	.533	.400	7.71	3.86
Clegg, Mitchell	R-L	6-5	225	12-22-86	4	7	5.50	29	11	0	0	88	120	74	54	6	28	38	.329	.355	.318	3.87	2.85
Davis, Erik	R-R	6-4	200	10-8-86	0	5	6.75	6	6	1	0	33	37	26	25	2	16	24	.289	.341	.262	6.48	4.32
Demmin, Ryan	L-L	6-1	210	4-5-88	0	0	10.03	8	0	0	0	12	16	13	13	6	6	9	.327	.333	.323	6.94	4.63
Demny, Paul	R-R	6-2	200	8-3-89	10	10	4.32	26	26	0	0	144	144	79	69	18	54	108	.261	.267	.257	6.77	3.38
Frias, Marcos	R-R	6-2	190	12-19-88	3	3	2.63	43	4	0	2	75	56	23	22	6	28	67	.207	.243	.185	8.00	3.35
Gaudin, Chad	R-R	5-10	190	3-24-83	0	0	0.00	1	1	0	0	6	0	0	0	0	0	0	.000	.000	.000	0.00	0.00
Holder, Trevor	R-R	6-2	185	1-8-87	3	8	5.77	19	14	1	0	87	107	60	56	7	9	51	.304	.297	.310	5.26	0.93
Holland, Neil	R-R	6-0	190	8-14-88	4	0	2.73	20	0	0	1	30	21	9	9	1	9	20	.206	.247	.181	6.07	2.73
Lehman, Pat	R-R	6-3	210	10-18-86	2	0	1.72	13	0	0	7	16	9	4	3	0	2	16	.167	.067	.205	6.32	0.00
Martin, Rafael	R-R	6-2	195	5-16-84	1	0	1.13	6	0	0	0	8	6	2	1	0	2	10	.207	.182	.222	11.25	2.25
Martinez, Carlos	R-R	6-4	180	3-30-84	0	2	13.50	4	0	0	0	3	7	5	5	0	0	0	.500	.600	.444	0.00	0.00
Mock, Garrett	R-R	6-4	230	4-25-83	0	0	0.00	1	1	0	0	6	4	0	0	0	2	6	.200	.200	.200	9.00	3.00
Morrison, Kyle	R-R	6-1	190	12-22-87	0	0	4.91	5	0	0	0	7	11	5	4	1	5	7	.333	.214	.421	8.59	6.14
Nelo, Hector	R-R	6-1	200	11-5-86	1	0	2.40	36	0	0	18	41	32	17	11	0	16	35	.206	.182	.220	7.62	3.48
Olbrychowski, Adam	R-R	6-3	205	9-7-86	5	7	4.16	31	15	0	1	102	99	53	47	6	56	78	.255	.238	.265	6.90	4.96
Rosenbaum, Danny	R-L	6-1	210	10-10-87	6	5	2.59	20	19	2	0	132	113	52	38	4	41	108	.234	.205	.243	7.36	2.80
Selik, Cameron	R-R	6-2	235	8-25-87	4	9	4.52	22	16	3	0	92	91	57	46	6	26	52	.262	.261	.263	5.11	2.55
Smoker, Josh	L-L	6-2	195	11-26-88	5	2	2.31	46	0	0	2	51	32	16	13	4	37	56	.181	.190	.176	9.95	6.57

Pitching	B-T	HT	WT	DOB	W	L	ERA	G	GS	CG	SV	IP	H	R	ER	HR	BB	SO	AVG	vLH	vRH	K/9	BB/9
Solis, Sammy	R-L	6-5	230	8-10-88	6	2	2.72	10	10	0	0	56	61	20	17	5	11	53	.279	.357	.260	8.47	1.76
Strasburg, Stephen	R-R	6-4	220	7-20-88	0	0	0.00	1	1	0	0	3	2	0	0	0	0	5	.167	.125	.250	15.00	0.00
Testa, Joe	L-L	5-10	175	12-18-85	6	2	1.42	39	0	0	2	38	26	13	6	1	24	34	.198	.167	.221	8.05	5.68
Wang, Chien-Ming	R-R	6-3	230	3-31-80	0	0	0.00	1	1	0	0	4	1	0	0	0	2		.091	.250	.000	4.50	4.50
Weaver, Dean	R-R	6-4	207	5-17-88	1	1	9.37	13	0	0	0	16	22	17	17	4	7	7	.319	.391	.283	3.86	3.86
Wort, Rob	R-R	6-2	170	2-7-89	2	2	4.42	34	0	0	3	37	32	21	18	3	27	37	.234	.354	.169	9.08	6.63

Fielding

Catcher	PCT	G	PO	A	E	DP	PB
Leon	.987	104	669	98	10	10	13
Mayo	1.000	5	14	5	0	0	0
Nieto	1.000	2	19	0	0	0	0
Peacock	.995	33	181	19	1	0	4
Rodriguez	1.000	1	4	0	0	0	0

First Base	PCT	G	PO	A	E	DP
Bloxom	.995	22	186	12	1	19
Nicol	1.000	2	4	0	0	1
Peacock	1.000	4	29	0	0	2
Souza	.989	117	942	66	11	91

Second Base	PCT	G	PO	A	E	DP
Dykstra	.976	24	24	56	2	13
Kobernus	.976	105	206	245	11	61
Lozada	1.000	3	5	6	0	2

	PCT	G	PO	A	E	DP
Nicol	1.000	3	7	6	0	2
Soriano	.980	11	25	23	1	4

Third Base	PCT	G	PO	A	E	DP
Bloxom	.817	49	23	84	24	10
Cuevas	.824	11	9	19	6	1
Dykstra	.833	7	2	8	2	1
King	.960	20	29	43	3	6
Lozada	.962	51	38	114	6	6
Nicol	1.000	3	2	5	0	0
Zimmerman	.889	3	0	8	1	0

Shortstop	PCT	G	PO	A	E	DP
Cuevas	.935	8	15	14	2	4
Hague	.882	4	8	7	2	2
Kobernus	.850	4	6	11	3	3
Lozada	.950	45	77	130	11	29

	PCT	G	PO	A	E	DP
Soriano	.942	55	71	155	14	34
Souza	.000	1	0	0	0	0
Walters	.942	27	34	79	7	13

Outfield	PCT	G	PO	A	E	DP
Curran	.927	20	34	4	3	1
Dykstra	1.000	23	29	1	0	0
Gilbert	1.000	5	9	0	0	0
Higley	.993	65	135	4	1	2
Hood	.996	119	245	12	1	2
Nicol	.944	7	16	1	1	0
Peacock	.000	1	0	0	0	0
Perez	.982	118	270	8	5	2
Ramirez	.971	64	98	3	3	0
Soriano	.964	15	24	3	1	1

HAGERSTOWN SUNS
LOW CLASS A
SOUTH ATLANTIC LEAGUE

Batting	B-T	HT	WT	DOB	AVG	vLH	vRH	G	AB	R	H	2B	3B	HR	RBI	BB	HBP	SH	SF	SO	SB	CS	SLG	OBP
Cuevas, Justino	R-R	5-10	160	11-30-88	.243	.292	.220	21	74	10	18	5	1	1	13	4	1	0	3	22	1	0	.378	.280
Curran, Chris	L-R	5-9	170	12-21-87	.257	.348	.231	34	101	15	26	4	1	2	12	9	0	0	2	25	8	3	.376	.313
Freitas, David	R-R	6-2	225	3-18-89	.288	.214	.316	123	427	67	123	30	0	13	73	82	6	0	1	87	2	1	.450	.409
Harper, Bryce	L-R	6-3	225	10-16-92	.318	.325	.315	72	258	49	82	17	1	14	46	44	3	0	0	61	19	5	.554	.423
Kelso, Blake	R-R	5-10	170	3-28-89	.293	.293	.293	127	512	81	150	17	7	2	52	49	4	0	4	53	23	7	.365	.357
Keyes, Kevin	R-R	6-3	225	3-15-89	.263	.200	.286	85	304	49	80	22	1	17	65	32	3	0	3	86	6	0	.510	.336
Leonida, Cole	R-R	6-2	220	12-25-88	.240	.063	.299	39	129	21	31	7	1	2	16	17	3	0	2	45	1	0	.357	.338
Martinson, Jason	R-R	6-2	190	10-15-88	.252	.246	.254	129	433	64	109	22	3	19	64	66	10	0	5	144	26	6	.448	.360
Moldenhauer, Russ	L-R	6-0	200	9-24-87	.174	.182	.171	14	46	3	8	4	0	0	3	2	1	0	1	9	0	1	.261	.220
Moore, Wade	L-R	6-1	215	12-27-87	.206	.130	.228	100	315	43	65	17	3	3	35	52	4	0	1	86	16	8	.308	.325
Newsome, Brett	L-L	6-2	210	8-24-86	.273	.160	.300	79	267	34	73	13	2	6	38	29	3	0	3	78	2	1	.404	.348
Nicol, Sean	R-R	5-10	175	9-25-86	.304	.306	.303	57	181	31	55	12	2	2	26	21	2	0	2	28	6	5	.425	.379
Nieto, Adrian	R-B	6-0	200	11-12-89	.255	.296	.239	27	98	17	25	8	1	3	12	9	0	0	0	31	0	0	.449	.318
Oduber, Randolph	R-L	6-3	190	3-18-89	.301	.309	.297	56	216	31	65	6	1	5	26	15	6	0	1	64	22	2	.407	.361
Rogers, Mills	R-R	6-1	195	6-8-88	.215	.186	.236	77	237	27	51	12	0	0	19	22	4	0	4	65	3	3	.266	.288
Sanchez, Adrian	B-R	6-0	160	8-16-90	.262	.253	.265	131	538	75	141	30	5	3	51	17	10	0	4	71	25	12	.353	.295
Taylor, Michael	R-R	6-2	190	3-26-91	.253	.278	.244	126	442	64	112	26	7	13	68	32	6	0	4	120	23	12	.432	.310
Zimmerman, Ryan	R-R	6-3	230	9-28-84	1.000	.000	1.000	1	2	2	2	1	0	1	0	1	0	0	0	0	0	0	2.500	1.000

Pitching	B-T	HT	WT	DOB	W	L	ERA	G	GS	CG	SV	IP	H	R	ER	HR	BB	SO	AVG	vLH	vRH	K/9	BB/9
Applebee, Paul	L-L	6-3	195	5-17-88	7	2	3.35	31	5	0	2	97	86	43	36	10	12	78	.235	.333	.206	7.26	1.12
Bates, Colin	R-R	6-1	175	3-10-88	0	0	6.75	4	0	0	1	9	10	8	7	0	3	4	.270	.333	.227	3.86	2.89
Brown, Sam	R-R	6-5	215	6-10-87	4	6	5.34	41	0	0	3	59	76	46	35	7	17	48	.308	.392	.268	7.32	2.59
Cole, A.J.	R-R	6-4	180	1-5-92	4	7	4.04	20	18	0	0	89	87	47	40	6	24	108	.251	.325	.190	10.92	2.43
Demmin, Ryan	L-L	6-1	210	4-5-88	5	2	2.80	12	5	0	0	45	33	18	14	4	17	43	.201	.204	.200	8.60	3.40
Eusebio, Wilson	R-R	6-0	170	8-20-88	1	7	5.56	38	0	0	5	68	75	43	42	14	24	61	.282	.305	.269	8.07	3.18
Gaudin, Chad	R-R	5-10	190	3-24-83	0	0	0.00	1	0	0	0	2	2	0	0	0	0	0	.250	.500	.167	0.00	0.00
Grace, Matt	L-L	6-3	190	12-14-88	12	7	5.17	26	25	0	0	132	169	92	76	8	38	85	.314	.333	.309	5.78	2.58
Graham, Ben	R-R	6-4	195	11-23-87	4	4	3.30	37	0	0	8	46	46	21	17	3	14	32	.253	.321	.225	6.22	2.72
Hanks, Tyler	R-R	6-2	186	3-19-90	0	1	11.25	6	0	0	1	8	16	10	10	1	4	3	.432	.385	.458	3.38	4.50
Hansen, Bobby	L-L	6-5	220	12-17-89	5	1	4.10	10	10	0	0	53	54	27	24	3	14	49	.262	.410	.228	8.37	2.39
Holland, Neil	R-R	6-0	190	8-14-88	1	0	1.13	16	0	0	1	24	21	7	3	2	1	22	.228	.273	.203	8.25	0.38
Holt, Gregory	R-R	6-2	205	6-19-89	0	1	6.00	10	0	0	1	21	23	15	14	1	9	18	.277	.270	.283	7.71	3.86
Jenkins, Chad	L-L	6-4	195	3-12-88	1	0	5.00	6	0	0	0	9	7	5	5	0	6	7	.219	.000	.333	7.00	6.00
Jordan, Taylor	R-R	6-3	190	1-17-89	9	4	2.48	18	17	1	0	94	90	38	26	1	23	63	.247	.261	.239	6.01	2.19
Manno, Chris	L-L	6-3	170	11-4-88	1	3	1.04	34	0	0	12	43	20	9	5	1	15	69	.135	.107	.142	14.33	3.12
McCatty, Shane	R-R	6-3	205	5-18-87	2	3	6.63	30	1	0	1	57	71	46	42	5	22	39	.307	.297	.314	6.16	3.47
McKenzie, Chris	R-R	6-3	185	12-6-89	4	7	6.97	13	10	0	0	50	58	44	39	4	29	31	.289	.344	.263	5.54	5.19
Ray, Robbie	L-L	6-2	170	10-1-91	2	3	3.13	20	20	0	0	89	71	36	31	3	38	95	.221	.244	.214	9.61	3.84
Selik, Cameron	R-R	6-2	235	8-25-87	3	0	0.31	5	5	0	0	29	23	1	1	0	3	30	.219	.308	.190	9.31	0.93
Slaten, Doug	L-L	6-5	215	2-4-80	0	0	4.91	4	2	0	0	4	5	2	2	0	0	3	.313	.500	.250	7.36	0.00
Solis, Sammy	R-L	6-5	230	8-10-88	2	1	4.02	7	7	0	0	40	39	18	18	3	12	40	.253	.269	.250	8.93	2.68
Strasburg, Stephen	R-R	6-4	220	7-20-88	0	1	9.95	3	3	0	0	6	9	9	6	1	3	13	.310	.357	.267	18.47	4.26
Swynenberg, Matt	R-R	6-5	185	2-16-89	6	3	3.68	30	10	0	0	103	103	47	42	9	22	74	.265	.275	.257	6.49	1.93
Wang, Chien-Ming	R-R	6-3	230	3-31-80	0	0	6.00	1	1	0	0	3	4	2	2	0	0	3	.286	.600	.111	9.00	0.00
Weaver, Dean	R-R	6-4	207	5-17-88	2	1	5.40	17	0	0	3	27	27	16	16	4	8	28	.262	.150	.333	9.45	2.70

Fielding

Catcher	PCT	G	PO	A	E	DP	PB
Freitas	.996	86	627	71	3	5	6
Leonida	.974	37	265	37	8	0	2
Nieto	.970	18	116	12	4	1	5

First Base	PCT	G	PO	A	E	DP
Freitas	.973	13	104	3	3	6
Moldenhauer	.973	9	68	3	2	5
Newsome	.990	75	629	53	7	53
Nicol	1.000	2	22	1	0	2
Rogers	.984	48	402	28	7	29

Second Base	PCT	G	PO	A	E	DP
Cuevas	.667	1	2	0	1	0

	PCT	G	PO	A	E	DP	PB
Kelso	.975	15	34	44	2	9	
Nicol	.909	3	3	7	1	1	
Sanchez	.966	124	224	348	20	72	

Third Base	PCT	G	PO	A	E	DP
Cuevas	.870	21	17	43	9	5
Kelso	.956	74	50	166	10	15
Nicol	.896	36	25	70	11	8
Rogers	.880	12	2	20	3	2
Zimmerman	1.000	1	0	1	0	0

Shortstop	PCT	G	PO	A	E	DP
Kelso	.947	25	29	60	5	10
Martinson	.936	113	150	335	33	55

	PCT	G	PO	A	E	DP
Nicol	.778	2	3	4	2	1

Outfield	PCT	G	PO	A	E	DP
Curran	1.000	33	73	3	0	1
Harper	.963	68	125	6	5	1
Keyes	.947	62	107	0	6	0
Moore	.980	86	138	6	3	1
Nicol	1.000	12	20	3	0	1
Oduber	.969	43	59	3	2	0
Rogers	.933	15	14	0	1	0
Taylor	.977	119	239	16	6	2

AUBURN DOUBLEDAYS   SHORT-SEASON

NEW YORK-PENN LEAGUE

Batting	B-T	HT	WT	DOB	AVG	vLH	vRH	G	AB	R	H	2B	3B	HR	RBI	BB	HBP	SH	SF	SO	SB	CS	SLG	OBP
Alvarez, Carlos	B-R	5-11	175	11-25-85	.306	.375	.287	32	111	16	34	7	0	1	15	15	1	0	0	24	2	0	.396	.394
Burns, Billy	R-L	5-9	180	8-30-89	.262	.333	.238	32	107	21	28	3	2	1	18	12	7	0	2	22	13	1	.355	.367
Bynum, Seth	R-R	6-0	185	12-19-80	.273	.429	.200	6	22	7	6	2	0	1	4	2	0	0	0	7	2	0	.500	.333
Hughes, Rick	R-R	6-3	225	5-25-90	.125	.121	.128	22	80	9	10	4	0	0	3	8	0	0	0	36	3	0	.175	.205
Jimenez, Hendry	B-R	5-10	160	12-30-89	.290	.216	.317	54	193	32	56	9	6	5	40	23	3	0	3	50	5	3	.477	.369
Mayo, Jeremy	R-R	5-10	194	6-17-88	.244	.167	.274	27	86	20	21	5	0	4	13	13	2	0	0	32	1	0	.442	.356
Miller, Justin	R-R	6-0	180	11-28-88	.299	.338	.283	63	241	40	72	15	7	7	44	11	10	3	67	4	0	.498	.361
Moldenhauer, Russ	L-R	6-0	200	9-24-87	.289	.234	.308	51	190	20	55	16	0	5	30	21	6	0	4	31	1	1	.453	.371
Montilla, Angelberth	R-R	6-1	180	4-11-89	.249	.246	.250	67	261	33	65	12	3	4	29	11	3	0	1	36	11	2	.364	.286
Nieto, Adrian	B-R	6-0	200	11-12-89	.302	.289	.309	30	106	20	32	5	0	4	22	17	1	0	2	34	2	0	.462	.397
Norfork, Khayyan	R-R	5-10	190	1-19-89	.250	.286	.231	15	40	5	10	1	0	0	5	3	1	0	0	17	5	0	.275	.318
Ortega, Bryce	R-R	5-11	170	9-22-88	.314	.365	.296	56	194	43	61	15	0	0	21	29	3	0	1	34	23	2	.392	.410
Pena, Wilfri	R-R	6-0	180	5-2-87	.222	.154	.247	29	99	11	22	3	0	1	10	7	1	0	0	20	1	0	.283	.280
Perez, Miguel	R-R	6-3	235	9-25-83	.429	.000	.600	2	7	0	3	0	0	0	1	0	0	0	0	1	0	0	.429	.429
Perez, Roberto	R-R	6-1	180	4-4-91	.270	.308	.258	30	115	13	31	6	0	1	15	3	0	0	0	24	0	1	.348	.288
Ramirez, Andruth	R-R	5-11	180	3-10-89	.100	.000	.125	3	10	0	1	0	0	0	0	0	0	0	0	7	0	0	.100	.100
Ramsey, Caleb	L-R	6-2	215	10-7-88	.280	.180	.307	64	239	38	67	11	1	1	26	28	3	0	1	51	15	4	.347	.362
Rogers, Mills	R-R	6-1	195	6-28-89	.000	.000	.000	3	9	0	0	0	0	0	1	0	0	0	1	6	0	0	.000	.000
Rowe, Connor	R-R	6-0	175	8-16-88	.192	.163	.204	44	146	24	28	11	0	2	11	20	1	0	3	59	5	1	.308	.288
Skole, Matthew	L-R	6-4	230	7-30-89	.290	.203	.323	72	272	43	79	23	1	5	48	42	1	0	4	52	2	1	.438	.382

Pitching	B-T	HT	WT	DOB	W	L	ERA	G	GS	CG	SV	IP	H	R	ER	HR	BB	SO	AVG	vLH	vRH	K/9	BB/9
Barrett, Aaron	R-R	6-4	175	1-2-88	1	2	4.05	19	0	0	9	27	16	12	12	2	20	32	.172	.184	.159	10.80	6.75
Bates, Colin	R-R	6-1	175	3-10-88	4	2	2.25	13	7	0	2	48	44	14	12	0	11	29	.237	.202	.265	5.44	2.06
Demmin, Ryan	L-L	6-1	210	4-5-88	3	0	4.15	5	5	0	0	26	21	12	12	4	8	19	.216	.130	.243	6.58	2.77
Dupra, Brian	R-R	6-3	200	12-15-88	4	4	3.46	13	9	0	0	55	52	24	21	1	14	38	.250	.302	.213	6.26	2.30
Encarnacion, Pedro	R-R	6-4	175	6-26-91	0	2	9.00	3	3	0	0	11	14	11	11	2	6	4	.311	.348	.273	3.27	4.91
Estevez, Wirkin	R-R	6-1	170	3-15-92	6	3	4.01	14	13	0	0	67	72	36	30	2	22	55	.278	.252	.300	7.35	2.94
Garcia, Christian	R-R	6-5	215	8-24-85	3	1	2.95	10	0	0	1	18	17	6	6	1	2	28	.239	.200	.268	13.75	0.98
Grisz, Ben	R-R	6-1	230	1-26-90	1	0	1.35	11	0	0	4	20	11	3	3	1	6	11	.159	.265	.057	4.95	2.70
Hanks, Tyler	R-R	6-2	186	3-19-90	0	0	0.00	4	0	0	0	7	5	0	0	1	4	8	.208	.143	.235	5.14	1.29
Hawkins, Ben	L-L	6-2	175	11-4-89	2	0	2.35	8	0	0	0	15	11	4	4	0	8	15	.200	.235	.184	8.80	4.70
Henke, Travis	R-R	6-6	241	7-9-88	4	2	5.40	16	0	0	1	28	34	20	17	0	9	21	.298	.295	.300	6.67	2.86
Hill, Taylor	R-R	6-3	233	3-12-89	0	2	3.16	9	5	0	0	31	32	12	11	1	3	27	.264	.320	.225	7.76	0.86
Holt, Gregory	R-R	6-2	205	6-19-89	1	1	0.64	7	0	0	1	14	8	3	1	0	5	7	.170	.150	.185	4.50	3.21
Jenkins, Chad	L-L	6-4	195	3-12-88	3	0	3.48	16	0	0	1	34	21	14	13	0	30	28	.181	.205	.167	7.49	8.02
Karns, Nathan	R-R	6-5	230	11-25-87	3	2	3.44	8	0	0	0	37	27	14	14	1	27	33	.211	.259	.171	8.10	6.63
Kreis, Alex	R-R	6-1	210	5-30-89	1	1	5.97	18	0	0	2	35	35	19	19	1	19	23	.302	.250	.338	7.22	5.97
Lopez, Kelvin	R-R	6-1	150	1-22-90	2	2	3.65	10	1	0	0	25	22	15	10	0	13	19	.232	.282	.196	6.93	4.74
Medina, Silvio	R-R	6-1	190	6-3-90	0	0	3.38	1	0	0	0	3	4	2	1	0	1	3	.364	.429	.250	10.13	3.38
Meyers, Brad	R-R	6-6	195	9-13-85	0	0	2.70	2	2	0	0	7	5	2	2	0	0	4	.200	.111	.250	5.40	0.00
Meza, Christian	L-L	6-0	185	8-3-90	1	1	5.68	11	10	0	0	44	46	34	28	1	17	34	.260	.379	.236	6.90	3.45
Mirowski, Richard	R-R	6-2	190	4-30-89	1	2	2.59	14	0	0	0	24	24	12	7	0	11	20	.261	.308	.226	7.40	4.07
Monar, Blake	L-L	6-2	198	6-16-89	0	0	0.00	2	0	0	0	4	0	0	0	0	2	4	.000	.000	.000	9.00	4.50
Rivera, Manuel	R-R	6-2	170	7-2-87	3	0	2.81	20	0	0	2	26	20	8	8	1	10	15	.227	.222	.231	5.26	3.51
Rodriguez, Manny	R-R	6-3	205	1-12-89	2	3	4.65	14	12	0	0	50	55	31	26	1	18	39	.275	.290	.262	6.97	3.22

Fielding

Catcher	PCT	G	PO	A	E	DP	PB
Mayo	.985	26	178	15	3	1	5
Nieto	.980	21	131	14	3	1	3
Pena	.989	26	159	19	2	0	6
Perez	1.000	2	13	0	0	0	0
Ramirez	1.000	3	18	4	0	0	0

First Base	PCT	G	PO	A	E	DP
Miller	.991	45	406	27	4	45

	PCT	G	PO	A	E	DP
Moldenhauer	.989	28	262	19	3	24
Perez	1.000	2	17	2	0	0
Rogers	1.000	1	5	0	0	0

Second Base	PCT	G	PO	A	E	DP
Alvarez	.978	11	18	26	1	7
Jimenez	.964	43	82	131	8	31
Miller	1.000	4	7	14	0	3
Norfork	.957	15	16	28	2	6

	PCT	G	PO	A	E	DP
Ortega	1.000	1	0	1	0	0
Perez	1.000	11	19	27	0	6

Third Base	PCT	G	PO	A	E	DP
Alvarez	.778	6	2	12	4	2
Miller	1.000	2	1	2	0	0
Perez	.833	1	1	4	1	0
Rogers	1.000	1	2	2	0	1
Skole	.910	65	47	94	14	6

WASHINGTON NATIONALS

Shortstop	PCT	G	PO	A	E	DP
Alvarez	.887	11	18	37	7	11
Bynum	1.000	5	3	13	0	1
Jimenez	.885	9	20	26	6	5
Ortega	.950	53	78	151	12	38

Perez	.818	3	5	4	2	1

Outfield	PCT	G	PO	A	E	DP
Burns	1.000	32	70	1	0	0
Hughes	.923	21	34	2	3	1
Miller	1.000	5	4	1	0	0

Montilla	.969	64	119	7	4	3
Ramsey	.981	62	91	10	2	2
Rogers	1.000	1	3	0	0	0
Rowe	.989	43	85	3	1	0

GCL NATIONALS — ROOKIE
GULF COAST LEAGUE

Batting	B-T	HT	WT	DOB	AVG	vLH	vRH	G	AB	R	H	2B	3B	HR	RBI	BB	HBP	SH	SF	SO	SB	CS	SLG	OBP
Alvarez, Carlos	B-R	5-11	175	11-25-85	.354	.600	.289	14	48	14	17	3	1	0	4	9	3	0	1	6	5	0	.458	.475
Ankiel, Rick	L-L	6-2	225	7-19-79	.500	.000	.500	1	2	0	1	0	0	0	0	1	0	0	0	0	0	0	.500	.667
Cuevas, Justino	R-R	5-10	160	11-30-88	.286	.000	.286	2	7	0	2	0	0	0	0	0	0	0	0	1	0	1	.286	.286
Curran, Chris	L-R	5-9	170	12-21-87	.382	.286	.407	8	34	7	13	0	2	1	4	3	0	0	0	4	2	0	.588	.432
Difo, Wilmer	R-R	6-0	175	4-2-92	.273	.188	.292	25	88	10	24	4	3	0	8	10	0	0	1	8	5	3	.386	.343
Fernandez, Erick	R-R	5-11	190	11-30-88	.245	.150	.268	28	102	12	25	4	0	1	11	5	1	0	1	11	1	0	.314	.284
Hatcher, Rashad	R-R	6-2	190	6-17-90	.250	.333	.222	5	12	1	3	0	1	0	1	1	0	0	0	3	0	1	.417	.308
Hughes, Rick	R-R	6-3	225	5-25-90	.182	.333	.158	9	22	2	4	1	0	0	0	8	1	0	0	11	1	1	.227	.419
Karlen, Trey	R-R	5-11	188	4-23-88	.188	.125	.196	27	64	11	12	1	2	1	9	11	4	0	1	22	5	0	.313	.338
Martinez, Estarlin	R-L	6-1	185	3-8-92	.289	.282	.291	50	187	36	54	8	4	6	28	29	0	0	3	36	11	2	.471	.379
Mayo, Jeremy	R-R	5-10	194	6-17-88	.200	.200	.200	5	15	3	3	0	0	1	4	2	1	0	0	7	0	0	.400	.333
Mesa, Narciso	R-R	5-11	175	11-16-91	.286	.286	.286	40	168	19	48	10	4	1	19	8	1	0	2	29	6	1	.411	.318
Mozingo, Chad	L-L	5-11	190	9-3-88	.262	.273	.260	20	61	10	16	5	0	0	7	5	0	0	1	14	2	0	.344	.313
Oduber, Randolph	R-L	6-3	190	3-18-89	.500	.500	.500	4	2	4	2	0	0	0	0	2	0	0		4	3	0	.667	.571
Peguero, Arialdi	L-R	6-3	195	9-15-92	.207	.174	.214	42	140	13	29	2	0	5	13	14	3	0	2	52	1	0	.329	.289
Perez, Roberto	R-R	6-1	180	4-4-91	.000	.000	.000	2	7	1	0	0	0	0	1	1	0	0	1	3	0	0	.000	.111
Ramirez, Andruth	R-R	5-11	180	3-10-89	.254	.250	.254	22	71	7	18	2	1	0	14	5	1	0	1	4	0	0	.310	.308
Ramos, Wander	R-R	6-3	192	4-26-90	.313	.310	.314	43	147	32	46	12	1	12	37	19	4	0	2	45	7	4	.653	.401
Rodriguez, Johan	R-R	6-0	165	11-8-90	.211	.188	.215	34	109	11	23	2	0	0	10	4	3	0	1	10	8	1	.229	.256
Schill, Wes	R-R	5-9	170	11-22-89	.255	.243	.258	42	157	24	40	5	2	0	16	16	1	0	1	19	10	5	.312	.326
Severino, Pedro	R-R	6-1	180	7-20-93	.183	.240	.167	32	115	16	21	4	1	2	9	10	2	0	0	27	0	0	.287	.260
Soriano, Francisco	B-R	5-11	169	6-16-87	.222	.333	.167	3	9	2	2	0	0	1	1	0	1	0	0	1	1	0	.556	.300
Williams, Deion	R-R	6-3	190	11-11-92	.157	.130	.165	30	102	6	16	0	0	0	7	8	0	0	1	44	3	1	.157	.216

Pitching	B-T	HT	WT	DOB	W	L	ERA	G	GS	CG	SV	IP	H	R	ER	HR	BB	SO	AVG	vLH	vRH	K/9	BB/9
Arnold, Patrick	R-R	6-1	190	10-31-88	1	0	1.23	6	0	0	0	7	7	3	1	0	2	6	.269	.364	.200	7.36	2.45
Baez, Gregori	L-L	6-3	185	5-5-92	1	3	3.72	13	11	0	0	48	48	20	20	1	29	41	.264	.238	.271	7.63	5.40
Chico, Matt	L-L	5-11	220	6-10-83	2	1	2.95	9	2	0	0	21	19	8	7	0	2	14	.238	.190	.254	5.91	0.84
Davis, Cody	R-R	5-9	170	7-21-90	2	0	3.09	7	0	0	0	12	12	5	4	0	4	11	.279	.286	.276	8.49	3.09
Encarnacion, Pedro	R-R	6-4	175	6-26-91	2	2	4.29	9	8	0	0	36	32	25	17	4	16	29	.224	.189	.244	7.32	4.04
Ferrer, Kenneth	R-R	6-2	220	12-13-89	0	1	13.50	7	0	0	0	7	16	12	11	1	1	5	.444	.364	.480	6.14	1.23
Hanks, Tyler	R-R	6-2	186	3-19-90	1	1	0.93	5	0	0	0	10	6	5	1	0	2	12	.171	.286	.095	11.17	1.86
Harper, Bryan	L-L	6-5	205	12-29-89	0	0	0.00	2	0	0	0	2	1	0	0	0	1	2	.167	.000	.167	9.00	4.50
Hawkins, Ben	L-L	6-2	175	11-4-89	0	0	2.00	4	0	0	2	9	4	2	2	1	4	11	.308	.000	.174	11.00	4.00
Heredia, Inocencio	R-R	5-11	172	12-11-91	0	2	6.75	17	0	0	3	21	32	19	16	2	7	24	.333	.359	.316	10.13	2.95
Herrera, Mark	R-R	6-3	230	3-11-90	0	0	3.38	5	0	0	1	5	6	4	2	0	0	3	.273	.300	.250	5.06	0.00
Holder, Trevor	R-R	6-2	185	1-8-87	0	1	6.75	4	0	0	0	7	12	8	5	1	0	4	.364	.333	.400	5.40	0.00
Karns, Nathan	R-R	6-5	230	11-25-87	0	0	0.00	5	0	0	0	19	2	0	0	0	6	26	.035	.000	.054	12.54	2.89
King, Brandon	R-R	6-4	235	11-14-90	1	4	6.06	9	9	0	0	36	30	27	24	2	12	26	.226	.235	.220	6.56	3.03
Lee, Nicholas	L-L	5-11	185	1-13-91	1	0	4.05	10	0	0	0	13	16	10	6	1	15	15	.302	.333	.293	10.13	10.13
Lucas, Bobby	L-L	6-4	220	8-12-87	1	1	1.69	11	0	0	1	21	14	7	4	0	15	29	.187	.063	.220	12.23	6.33
Marcelino, Anthony	R-R	6-3	175	1-21-93	0	2	10.45	3	1	0	0	10	15	17	12	0	5	8	.341	.333	.350	6.97	4.35
McGeary, Jack	L-L	6-3	195	3-19-89	1	2	2.81	5	5	0	0	16	13	6	5	0	7	12	.241	.357	.200	6.75	3.94
McKenzie, Chris	R-R	6-3	185	12-6-89	1	0	5.40	5	2	0	0	13	12	9	8	0	5	16	.226	.176	.250	10.80	3.38
Medina, Silvio	R-R	6-1	190	6-3-90	4	5	4.61	9	5	0	0	33	40	27	24	3	9	36	.292	.333	.263	9.92	2.48
Meza, Christian	L-L	6-0	185	8-3-90	0	0	0.00	2	0	0	1	7	4	0	0	0	1	8	.160	.000	.200	10.29	1.29
Mieses, Adalberto	R-R	6-3	190	1-1-90	1	2	6.75	8	4	0	0	19	20	16	14	4	16	10	.286	.241	.317	4.82	7.71
Mock, Garrett	R-R	6-4	230	4-25-83	1	1	4.91	7	0	0	0	7	11	5	4	0	0	8	.344	.357	.333	9.82	0.00
Monar, Blake	L-L	6-2	198	6-16-89	0	1	4.50	3	0	0	0	6	5	3	3	0	1	2	.217	.333	.200	10.50	1.50
Peters, John	R-R	6-3	225	6-15-89	2	1	7.45	5	0	0	0	10	16	11	8	2	4	2	.372	.308	.400	1.86	3.72
Santana, Andy	R-R	6-2	187	12-5-90	2	2	4.86	10	0	0	0	17	15	12	9	1	8	14	.246	.200	.278	7.56	4.32
Simko, Todd	L-L	6-5	220	12-5-88	1	2	6.75	5	0	0	0	5	9	12	4	0	3	4	.375	.333	.389	6.75	5.06
Slaten, Doug	L-L	6-5	215	2-4-80	0	0	0.00	1	1	0	0	2	0	0	0	0	0	0	1.000	.000	.000	4.50	0.00
Smith, Jason	R-R	6-3	180	8-7-90	0	0	3.07	14	0	0	0	29	34	22	10	1	7	18	.274	.422	.190	5.52	2.15
Williams, Scott	R-R	6-0	210	7-26-88	0	0	3.46	8	0	0	1	13	14	5	5	0	1	12	.275	.269	.280	8.31	0.69

Fielding

Catcher	PCT	G	PO	A	E	DP	PB
Fernandez	.943	8	40	10	3	0	0
Mayo	1.000	3	14	0	0	1	1
Ramirez	.972	19	122	18	4	0	2
Severino	.989	28	210	53	3	1	8

First Base	PCT	G	PO	A	E	DP
Martinez	.992	14	111	12	1	9

Peguero	.988	31	236	15	3	22
Valdez	.978	10	85	4	2	5

Second Base	PCT	G	PO	A	E	DP
Alvarez	1.000	5	8	16	0	3
Difo	.926	4	15	10	2	3
Karlen	.957	13	26	18	2	4
Martinez	.000	1	0	0	0	0

Perez	1.000	1	1	6	0	2
Rodriguez	.958	14	24	22	2	7
Schill	.947	22	38	52	5	10
Valdez	1.000	2	4	1	0	0

Third Base	PCT	G	PO	A	E	DP
Alvarez	.944	9	5	12	1	1
Cuevas	1.000	2	0	5	0	0

							Schill	.871	15	21	40	9	5	Martinez	.924	33	55	6	5	1
Karlen	.862	10	12	13	4	0	Soriano	1.000	2	1	3	0	0	Mesa	.989	38	90	3	1	0
Peguero	.722	9	10	16	10	1	Williams	.872	18	26	42	10	6	Mozingo	1.000	17	33	1	0	0
Perez	1.000	1	0	4	0	0	**Outfield**	**PCT**	**G**	**PO**	**A**	**E**	**DP**	Oduber	.889	4	8	0	1	0
Schill	1.000	4	1	4	0	0	Ankiel	1.000	1	1	0	0	0	Ramos	.955	41	57	6	3	1
Valdez	.738	13	10	21	11	2	Curran	1.000	8	11	0	0	0	Rodriguez	.935	20	28	1	2	0
Williams	.958	9	9	14	1	3	Hatcher	1.000	4	7	1	0	1	Schill	.000	1	0	0	0	0
Shortstop	**PCT**	**G**	**PO**	**A**	**E**	**DP**	Hughes	.909	7	10	0	1	0	Soriano	1.000	1	1	0	0	0
Alvarez	1.000	2	2	3	0	0	Karlen	.000	1	0	0	0	0	Valdez	1.000	1	1	0	0	0
Difo	.927	22	41	73	9	15														

DSL NATIONALS · ROOKIE

DOMINICAN SUMMER LEAGUE

Batting	B-T	HT	WT	DOB	AVG	vLH	vRH	G	AB	R	H	2B	3B	HR	RBI	BB	HBP	SH	SF	SO	SB	CS	SLG	OBP
Chavez, Victor	R-R	6-1	196	12-27-88	.000	.000	.000	1	1	0	0	0	0	0	0	0	0	0	0	0	0	0	.000	.000
De Los Santos, Juan	R-R	5-11	170	1-11-94	.194	.000	.259	14	36	4	7	1	0	0	4	5	1	0	0	15	0	0	.222	.310
Difo, Wilmer	R-R	6-0	175	4-2-92	.297	.357	.282	39	145	31	43	4	5	1	7	27	3	0	0	20	26	8	.414	.417
Eusebio, Diomedes	R-R	6-0	185	9-8-92	.292	.313	.287	59	226	38	66	16	1	6	30	16	2	0	1	36	5	1	.451	.343
Geraldo, Junior	R-R	6-1	185	1-22-93	.254	.222	.268	18	59	8	15	8	0	3	12	8	3	0	1	12	0	2	.542	.366
Gonzalez, Edgar	B-R	5-11	160	3-5-93	.281	.176	.306	29	89	20	25	7	0	0	12	9	2	0	1	9	2	2	.360	.356
Marmolejos-Diaz, Jose	L-L	6-1	185	1-2-93	.223	.237	.219	54	184	22	41	6	3	1	21	23	7	0	1	32	1	1	.304	.330
Mejia, Bryan	B-R	6-1	170	3-2-94	.200	.108	.228	52	160	18	32	6	6	1	23	9	1	0	3	35	4	1	.331	.243
Mercedes, Yermin	R-R	5-11	175	2-14-93	.302	.300	.303	44	149	16	45	12	1	0	25	8	4	0	1	18	2	3	.396	.352
Novas, Randy	R-R	6-3	180	7-31-94	.207	.269	.189	37	116	14	24	4	1	2	10	10	4	0	1	40	3	3	.310	.290
Ortega, Nelalexfred	R-R	5-11	155	8-1-92	.230	.320	.213	53	161	30	37	3	1	0	15	19	3	0	1	25	23	8	.261	.321
Ramirez, Algenis	R-R	6-3	175	4-11-94	.200	.333	.171	17	50	7	10	4	0	1	4	11	2	0	0	15	2	1	.340	.365
Read, Raudy	R-R	6-0	170	10-29-93	.157	.179	.152	42	140	13	22	5	1	4	22	4	4	0	2	20	1	1	.293	.200
Reyes, Aladin	R-R	6-4	180	8-1-90	.220	.308	.196	43	118	16	26	2	1	3	17	10	2	0	3	33	2	2	.331	.286
Rodriguez, Wilman	R-R	6-1	175	6-7-91	.279	.323	.268	51	154	31	43	7	1	2	13	18	11	0	1	24	20	5	.377	.391
Rosario, Dionicio	R-R	6-3	180	2-14-94	.251	.283	.242	60	199	28	50	11	0	1	26	18	7	0	3	48	4	5	.322	.330
Ruiz, Adderling	R-R	6-1	175	5-3-91	.343	.259	.372	34	105	25	36	11	0	1	21	9	5	0	1	20	7	1	.476	.417
Tillero, Jorge	R-R	5-11	160	12-21-93	.260	.250	.262	20	50	2	13	0	0	3	6	0	0	0	9	0	1	.260	.339
Valdez, Bienvenido	R-R	6-2	180	11-25-90	.200	.154	.209	32	80	12	16	2	1	1	9	8	7	0	0	26	2	3	.288	.326

Pitching	B-T	HT	WT	DOB	W	L	ERA	G	GS	CG	SV	IP	H	R	ER	HR	BB	SO	AVG	vLH	vRH	K/9	BB/9
Baez, Gregori	L-L	6-3	185	5-5-92	0	1	1.00	2	2	0	0	9	2	1	1	1	4	7	.069	.000	.074	7.00	4.00
Barrientos, Joel	L-L	6-2	145	8-16-93	2	3	1.78	17	0	0	0	35	26	12	7	1	11	34	.215	.100	.225	8.66	2.80
De La Cruz, Emmanuel	R-R	6-4	180	4-16-92	0	1	6.75	10	0	0	0	12	10	11	9	1	11	6	.227	.118	.296	4.50	8.25
De Los Santos, Jesus	R-R	6-4	190	11-28-92	0	0	11.57	9	0	0	0	9	16	15	12	0	12	9	.372	.200	.464	8.68	11.57
Escolastico, Brian	R-R	6-3	185	12-15-92	0	1	17.72	11	0	0	0	11	22	25	21	1	22	13	.365	.500	.360	10.97	18.56
Guzman, Jesus	L-L	6-3	175	1-2-91	0	4	3.86	15	7	0	1	49	42	24	21	0	24	39	.246	.444	.235	7.16	4.41
Heredia, Inocencio	R-R	5-11	172	12-11-91	2	1	0.87	7	0	0	2	10	10	4	1	0	2	9	.250	.429	.212	7.84	1.74
Hernandez, Jorge	R-R	6-0	170	4-27-90	2	1	5.70	18	0	0	4	24	30	22	15	2	7	16	.300	.393	.264	6.08	2.66
Lellis, Dennis	R-R	6-2	175	10-17-92	0	0	27.00	1	0	0	0	1	5	3	3	1	1	1	.714	1.000	.500	9.00	9.00
Marcelino, Anthony	R-R	6-3	175	1-21-93	1	0	0.57	3	3	0	0	16	10	7	1	0	4	10	.185	.182	.186	5.74	2.30
Martinez, Anderson	R-R	6-3	180	2-22-93	0	2	4.86	6	2	0	1	17	15	14	9	2	8	13	.246	.269	.229	7.02	4.32
Mendez, Gilberto	R-R	6-0	165	11-17-92	7	0	2.06	13	11	0	0	66	63	24	15	1	12	66	.259	.234	.271	9.05	1.64
Moscat, Felix	R-R	6-2	160	12-2-90	3	7	6.16	12	12	0	0	61	78	54	42	4	24	53	.312	.382	.282	7.78	3.52
Navarro, Miguel	R-R	6-2	180	3-4-93	0	2	15.75	10	4	0	0	16	15	33	28	2	29	16	.227	.211	.234	9.00	16.31
Pineyro, Ivan	R-R	6-1	198	9-29-91	4	6	2.20	14	14	1	0	70	63	27	17	2	20	73	.237	.235	.237	9.43	2.58
Santana, Andy	R-R	6-2	187	12-5-90	2	1	1.69	3	3	0	0	16	6	4	3	1	3	20	.118	.235	.059	11.25	1.69
Silvestre, Hector	L-L	6-3	180	12-14-92	3	1	1.96	12	7	0	0	46	32	13	10	1	23	36	.194	.294	.182	7.04	4.50
Suero, Wander	R-R	6-3	175	9-15-91	3	2	5.49	16	2	0	1	39	35	27	24	4	26	41	.230	.256	.220	9.38	5.95
Vasquez, Daury	R-R	6-4	170	11-21-92	1	1	4.41	15	1	0	1	33	33	19	16	0	12	20	.262	.219	.277	5.51	3.31

Fielding

Catcher	PCT	G	PO	A	E	DP	PB		Mejia	.953	36	61	61	6	16		Ortega	.911	14	18	23	4	3
Mercedes	.993	17	127	20	1	0	3		Ortega	.960	39	69	76	6	18		Valdez	.950	6	7	12	1	3
Read	.968	31	206	35	8	0	8		Valdez	1.000	3	1	3	0	1		**Outfield**	**PCT**	**G**	**PO**	**A**	**E**	**DP**
Ruiz	.966	16	96	16	4	2	4		**Third Base**	**PCT**	**G**	**PO**	**A**	**E**	**DP**		De Los Santos	1.000	3	4	1	0	0
Tillero	.976	14	74	8	2	1	2		Eusebio	.896	57	57	124	21	12		Eusebio	1.000	1	1	0	0	0
First Base	**PCT**	**G**	**PO**	**A**	**E**	**DP**			Geraldo	1.000	2	1	2	0	0		Gonzalez	.966	24	26	2	1	0
Marmolejos-Diaz	.982	50	348	28	7	34			Mejia	1.000	2	0	2	0	0		Marmolejos-Diaz	1.000	5	6	0	0	0
Mejia	.941	4	31	1	2	4			Ortega	.000	2	0	0	0	0		Mejia	1.000	5	3	0	0	0
Mercedes	1.000	7	46	1	0	2			Rosario	1.000	1	0	1	0	0		Novas	.931	32	53	1	4	0
Ruiz	.976	6	39	2	1	3			Valdez	.813	10	4	22	6	1		Ramirez	.971	17	31	2	1	0
Valdez	.959	9	67	4	3	6			**Shortstop**	**PCT**	**G**	**PO**	**A**	**E**	**DP**		Reyes	.964	41	52	2	2	1
Second Base	**PCT**	**G**	**PO**	**A**	**E**	**DP**			Difo	.939	39	75	95	11	21		Rodriguez	.940	47	77	2	5	0
De Los Santos	1.000	4	2	4	0	0			Geraldo	.789	17	25	31	15	5		Rosario	.960	59	90	7	4	3
																	Valdez	.000	1	0	0	0	0

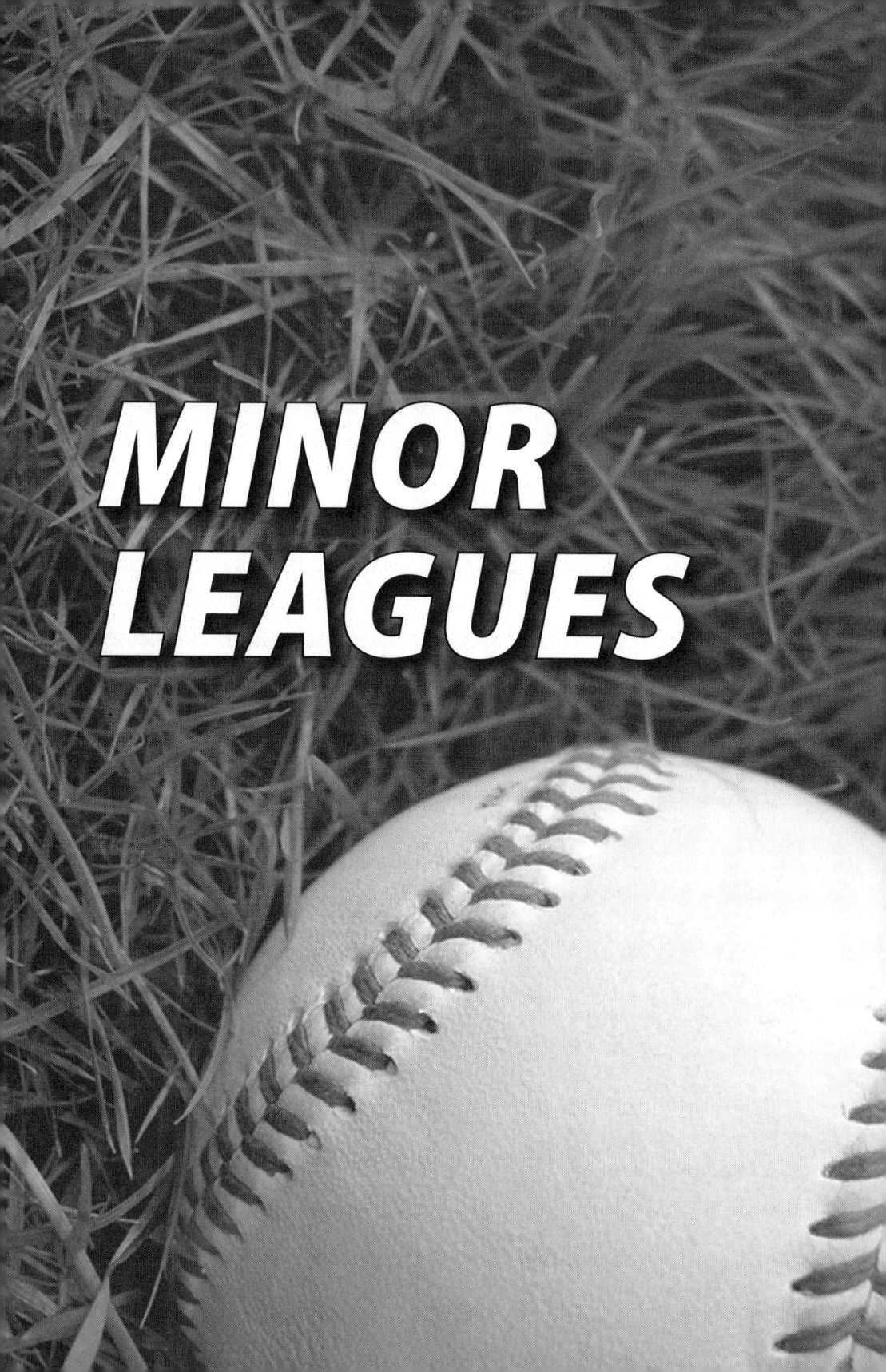

MINOR LEAGUES

Nationals phenom Bryce Harper was the center of attention—both good and bad—in 2011

Minors find success amid challenging year

Minor league baseball proved yet again its ability to thrive in a challenging economic environment, as much of the sport tried to overcome equally difficult weather.

The minors also proved they can crank out fascinating storylines. The top two prospects in baseball were teenagers on Opening Day—one arguably the most hyped draft pick ever, the other rising all the way to the big leagues while winning our Minor League Player of the Year Award. And for the first time in a long time, the sport welcomed only one new ballpark in 2011 and saw many other proposed stadium projects fail, leaving the future of some markets in question.

Let's take a look back at the season in by-the numbers style.

18 years, 5 months, 22 days

Nationals top prospect Bryce Harper's age on Opening Day, when he went 2-for-4 with low Class A Hagerstown against Augusta.

For the second straight season, the Nationals featured the most hyped prospect in minor league baseball. Bryce Harper may not have packed ballparks like Stephen Strasburg did a year ago (the ace helped set three single-game attendance records in 2010), but the right fielder certainly drew more scrutiny.

Harper, the 2010 No. 1 overall pick, earned top prospect honors in the low Class A South Atlantic and Double-A Eastern leagues after hitting a combined .297/.392/.501 with 17 home runs in what should have been his senior year of high school.

"He's figured it out so early in his life, when it takes some a lifetime," Erie manager Cris Cron said of Harper.

However, despite spending half the season in remote Hagerstown, Harper couldn't stay out of the spotlight. His aggressive style of play, plus a $9.9 million contract, drew the ire of opposing teams and fans. Pitchers regularly aimed fastballs at him and fans often lobbed obscenities his way. And when Harper responded—he blew a kiss at an opposing pitcher while circling the bases, went toe-to-toe with a catcher and got tossed for arguing a called strike with an umpire—the media pounced with charges of immaturity and arrogance.

Nationals farm director Doug Harris did Harper no favors in a Sports Illustrated article by comparing the scrutiny Harper was under to what Jackie Robinson faced while integrating baseball. Harris would apologize for his "ill-fated correlation."

83

Home runs hit by Diamondbacks first baseman Paul Goldschmidt in his first three professional sea-

sons, including 30 in 2011 with Double-A Mobile.

That Goldschmidt hit for such power is not surprising. The 6-foot-3, 245-pound first baseman set a school record at Texas State with 36 career homers before the Diamondbacks took him in the eighth round of the 2009 draft. The surprise for many was that he continued to do so as he faced more advanced pitching. He hit eight more homers in 156 at-bats with Arizona, then smacked two more in the postseason—including a grand slam against the Brewers as part of a five-RBI outing.

"That's five RBIs for a kid who was in Double-A this year," manager Kirk Gibson said. "That's pretty impressive."

200 x 2

Rays top pitching prospect Matt Moore surpasses 200 strikeouts for the second straight season.

Moore became the first minor leaguer to tally at least 200 strikeouts in consecutive seasons since Sid Fernandez accomplished the feat in 1982-83. The 22-year-old lefthander recorded a combined 210 strikeouts and 46 walks in 155 innings between Double-A Montgomery and Triple-A Durham. He fell short of topping the minors in strikeouts for a third straight season (high Class A Modesto lefthander Edwar Cabrera had 217), but Moore did go 1-0, 2.89 with 15 strikeouts in three starts with the Rays following a September promotion. He also tossed a gem against the Rangers in Game One in the American League Division Series.

83

Number of domestic minor league teams that saw an increase in attendance in 2011, compared to 63 in 2010.

Overall attendance dipped for a third straight year in 2011, after the minors had set records for five straight seasons. That dip was a mere blip, as attendance fell 0.4 percent to 41,252,053. Minor league officials were quick to note that overall average attendance of 4,029 was up 0.9 percent from 2010, because two fewer Mexican League teams participated this season and 140 more games were lost due to weather.

"We're still operating in a tough economic climate and environment, and for us to be on par with last year in gross attendance and a little higher in average attendance . . . I think we can characterize that as a good year," Minor League Baseball president Pat O'Conner said.

The biggest success story came from one of the smallest markets in Triple-A, as Lehigh Valley (International) topped the minors for a second straight year, averaging 9,249 fans to outpace fellow IL franchises Louisville (8,716) and Columbus

THE ROYAL 9

Nine Royals opened the season in our Top 100 Prospects rankings, the most from a single organization in the 22-year history of the list. Many moved fast—at one point in 2011, the Royals entire infield (plus pitcher) had been promoted through the system—while others took a step backward. Here's a breakdown of The Royal 9 (ranking was their place in the Top 100):

8. Eric Hosmer, 1b, Royals: Arrived in Kansas City on May 6 and batted .293/.334/.465 while showing he's the Royals' everyday first baseman for years to come.

9. Mike Moustakas, 3b, Royals: Hosmer beat him to K.C. and outproduced him, but after an awful start, Moustakas hit .352/.380/.580 in September with 11 of his 24 extra-base hits.

10. Wil Myers, of/c, Royals: Royals moved him to right field before the season. Struggled with injuries and the jump to Double-A but seemed to bounce back in Arizona Fall League.

18. John Lamb, lhp, Royals: Made only eight starts before needing Tommy John surgery. Should return to the mound at some point in 2012.

19. Mike Montgomery, lhp, Royals: Montgomery's plus stuff was undermined by below-average control in his first exposure to Triple-A hitters.

51. Christian Colon, ss, Royals: His prospect status took a significant hit, as he hasn't hit enough to make his otherwise average tools stand out.

68. Danny Duffy, lhp, Royals: Went 4-8, 5.64 after a May promotion to the Royals rotation, and he'll need to show improved command in 2012.

69. Jake Odorizzi, rhp, Royals: Dominated the high Class A Carolina League, but found the going tougher after a midseason promotion to Double-A Northwest Arkansas.

83. Chris Dwyer, lhp, Royals: Showed the same plus stuff, but his inability to locate fastball for strikes often left his curveball on the shelf.

(8,704). Round Rock (Pacific Coast) finished fourth with a 8,587 average, though its 618,261 total was second to Lehigh Valley (628,925).

25

Number of International League games lost due to weather by May 16—more than the Triple-A circuit had in all of 2010.

For many teams and leagues, the 2011 season featured the worst weather in recent memory. Few regions of the country were spared: The season opened with flooding in the Midwest, followed by devastating tornadoes in the Southeast in late April, before another string of tornadoes ripped through the Midwest a few weeks later. Northeast and Midwest teams overcame one of the rainiest springs on record. Hurricane Irene dealt blows to Eastern League franchises Binghamton and Harrisburg, as the Senators concluded their season with the Susquehanna River flowing through their ballpark, which is situated on an island on the river. And nearly every Texas League franchise saw attendance dip as the region endured a record drought.

However, teams persevered and the minor leagues rallied for their patrons—and fellow teams—in need. Huntsville Stars (Southern) general manager Buck Rogers converted the team's ballpark into an emergency shelter, as it was one of the only places in town with power after the tornadoes came through Alabama. Minor League Baseball also raised $60,000 through club donations and its 15 for 15 promotion—in which 46 teams donated 15 percent of online sales over a 15-day stretch—for three different minor league cities.

70

Number of players suspended in 2011 (through Oct. 8) as part of Major League Baseball's drug prevention and treatment program.

Since the Players Association and MLB agreed to expand drug testing before the 2005 season, 515 players have been suspended for drug violations (including 34 major leaguers).

Of the 70 players who tested positive in 2011, 28 were playing in Latin American Rookie leagues. Two active major leaguers tested positive: Brewers righthander Mark Rogers received a 25-game suspension for a stimulant, and Rockies catcher Eliezer Alfonso received a 100-game suspension for a second positive test for a performance-enhancing drug. On Aug. 18, former big leaguer Mike Jacobs became the first player to test positive for use of human growth hormone under MLB's new blood-testing policy for minor leaguers. The 30-year-old first baseman received a 50-game suspension.

42

Career games played by 2009 third overall pick Donavan Tate before he was suspended 50 games in late June (later reduced to 25) following a second positive test for a drug of abuse.

The suspension was just the latest in a series of setbacks for Tate, who received a $6.25 million signing bonus from the Padres. Before he ever took the field, Tate had surgery for a sports hernia and broke his jaw in an ATV accident. A concussion, shoulder injury and virus limited his playing time in 2010. He made his full-season debut with low Class A Fort Wayne in 2011, only to miss three months following an outfield collision with Everett Williams. Then came the suspension.

"Obviously, this is disappointing," Padres GM Jed Hoyer said. "This needs to be a wake-up call."

1956

The year Kinston debuted in the Carolina League. The franchise had been a member continuously

ORGANIZATION STANDINGS

Cumulative domestic farm club records for major league organizations, with winning percentages going back five years. Most organizations have six affiliates.

	2011						
	W	L	PCT	2010	2009	2008	2007
1. Texas	431	332	.565	.522	.495	.556	.489
2. L.A. Dodgers	414	349	.543	.508	.498	.484	.506
3. San Francisco	411	352	.539	.524	.603	.553	.562
4. Philadelphia	437	400	.522	.508	.507	.462	.488
5. St. Louis	428	399	.518	.569	.498	.525	.478
6. Toronto	430	405	.515	.506	.467	.511	.523
7. San Diego	393	370	.515	.485	.501	.517	.465
8. Cleveland	392	369	.515	.504	.501	.506	.535
9. Oakland	392	370	.514	.527	.494	.520	.492
10. Pittsburgh	429	409	.512	.511	.499	.430	.480
11. Washington	387	370	.511	.501	.501	.481	.443
12. Chi. Cubs	421	409	.507	.542	.487	.488	.499
13. L.A. Angels	386	376	.507	.507	.514	.542	.490
14. Cincinnati	420	415	.503	.466	.453	.476	.519
15. Chi. White Sox	386	386	.500	.489	.551	.503	.475
16. N.Y. Mets	450	453	.498	.511	.466	.453	.461
17. Tampa Bay	450	455	.497	.534	.502	.475	.527
18. Colorado	389	397	.495	.480	.513	.499	.496
19. Florida	375	383	.495	.490	.502	.530	.465
20. N.Y. Yankees	412	422	.494	.538	.554	.586	.597
21. Kansas City	408	418	.494	.492	.482	.442	.497
22. Boston	376	392	.490	.491	.505	.518	.501
23. Minnesota	372	387	.490	.434	.535	.532	.534
24. Arizona	409	429	.488	.489	.476	.426	.494
25. Baltimore	374	394	.487	.463	.475	.468	.490
26. Seattle	437	467	.483	.530	.528	.472	.443
27. Atlanta	356	400	.471	.457	.503	.506	.486
28. Detroit	390	445	.467	.485	.492	.448	.531
29. Milwaukee	355	406	.466	.493	.488	.469	.565
30. Houston	337	488	.408	.436	.426	.376	.441

POSTSEASON RESULTS

LEAGUE	CHAMPION	RUNNER-UP
International	Columbus	Lehigh Valley
Pacific Coast	Omaha	Sacramento
Eastern	New Hampshire	Richmond
Southern	Mobile	Tennessee
Texas	San Antonio	Arkansas
California	Lake Elsinore	Stockton
Carolina	Frederick	Kinston
Florida State	Daytona	St. Lucie
Midwest	Quad Cities	Lansing
South Atlantic	Greensboro	Savannah
New York-Penn	Staten Island	Auburn
Northwest	Vancouver	Tri-City
Appalachian	Johnson City	Bluefield
Pioneer	Great Falls	Ogden
Arizona	Dodgers	Giants
Gulf Coast	Yankees	Marlins

since 1978 before playing its final game at Grainger Stadium in the Carolina League championship series against Frederick.

The end of an era has come upon the city of Kinston, N.C. The Kinston Indians—at least in their current form—are no more. A three-way franchise shuffle will send the Southern League's Carolina Mudcats to Pensacola, Fla.; Kinston's Carolina League franchise to Zebulon, N.C., the

Omaha's professional team finally got a home of its own with the debut of Werner Park

former home of the Mudcats; and Kinston to the sidelines.

Kinston's professional baseball history dates back to the early 20th century, and the current franchise had been the high Class A affiliate of the Cleveland Indians since 1987 and under the same ownership since 1994. Cam McRae, the chairman of a nearly 70-member ownership group, cited "fiduciary responsibility" to the investors and a unique set of circumstances among the three cities as the factors that made the timing right to sell.

2020

The year the Professional Baseball Agreement, the contract between Major League Baseball and Minor League Baseball, will now expire.

Off-field peace in professional sports was a rare commodity in 2011, but baseball proved to be the exception. Not only was MLB expected to extend its labor agreement with the players without incident, but it also extended the Professional Baseball Agreement with the minors before the start of the season—and three years before it was set to expire.

The PBA, the agreement that governs the two organizations' relationship, assures major league teams will field at least 160 minor league affiliates. A relationship that was volatile in the 1990s has become the opposite in recent years, so much so that MLB agreed to postpone an agreed-upon increase in the tax rate on tickets that minor league teams pay major league clubs.

25

Consecutive years of new ballparks in minor league baseball, extended in 2011 when the Omaha Storm Chasers moved into Werner Park.

Omaha's professional team finally got a home of its own after sharing Rosenblatt Stadium with the College World Series (and annually spending most of June on the road) when the Storm Chasers' Werner Park debuted this season. The new facility also extended minor league baseball's run of new

ballparks, though the volume of new facilities has decreased. Omaha's was the only ballpark to open in 2011, and only one is scheduled to debut in 2012, in Pensacola. Over the previous 24 seasons, that number had never been fewer than two.

815

Consecutive sellouts by the Midwest League's Dayton Dragons, breaking the record by a professional sports team set by the NBA's Portland Trailblazers (1977-1995).

More than six million fans have passed through the gates at Fifth Third Field since the Dragons debuted in 2000 as the Reds' low Class A affiliate. The stadium offers 7,230 fixed seats, plus three lawn areas that are often packed but don't count toward a sellout. A season-ticket waiting list of about 8,000 would seem to guarantee future success.

"It's sold out no matter what," marveled first-year Dragons manager Delino DeShields, a 13-year major league veteran. "It's like Wrigley Field."

912

Career at-bats by Padres infielder Drew Cumberland before he retired at age 22 due to a rare brain condition.

A supplemental first-round pick of the Padres in 2007, Cumberland delivered on his promise by hitting .316/.380/.430 over four seasons. But Cumberland never got to a fifth season. As a battery of specialists determined over four months during the 2011 season, the severe headaches and wooziness Cumberland had lived with, dating back to high school, were the effects of repeated concussions—from what many athletes would consider inconsequential impacts—as well a condition in which the major nerve of the inner-ear was not sending signals to the brain for balance and vision.

"There were times when I thought I was losing my mind," Cumberland said. "The headaches were

CONTINUED ON PAGE 350

Trout proves scout right

BY J.J. COOPER

If you're a scout, you log your miles and rack up your Marriott points. You sit through the rain delays and sweat in your khakis. You miss your family and worry about your kid's cough from afar. You spend night after night watching baseball because every now and then you see something you've never seen before.

And when you see it, if you're a good scout, you know you've been blessed. Such blessings aren't evenly distributed. If you scout in Florida or Southern California, you've got a pretty good chance of seeing something special on a regular basis.

If you're an area scout in the Northeast, you may see hundreds of games without ever seeing what you've been searching for. In five years as an area scout for the Angels covering the Northeast, Greg Morhardt—known to his friends in the industry simply as Mo— spent a lot of time looking and not much time finding. For five years, he hadn't turned in a position player from his area that he projected to be a major league regular.

And then it happened.

He was at a showcase, just like dozens of other scouts. He looked up and saw a player who intrigued him. It was a 16-year-old middle infielder by the name of Mike Trout. Morhardt checked his scout book for the event and saw Trout was from Millville, N.J.

"How crazy is that?"

When Morhardt was a player himself (the Twins made him the 36th overall pick in the 1984 draft), his roommate for spring training one year and his teammate at Double-A Orlando was Jeff Trout. He remembered Trout as an undersized second baseman who knew how to hit and got every ounce out of his ability. But more than anything, he remembered that Jeff Trout always talked about being from Millville, N.J.

Morhardt was staring at an old teammate's son. And while Jeff Trout may have been short, no one would ever say that about his son. Even at 16, Mike Trout had a physicality that stood out. That was apparent at first glance. Watch a little longer and you'd see something more surprising: he was amazingly fast.

Those tools were apparent to anyone paying attention. Morhardt saw more.

Maybe it was because he knew Trout's father. Maybe it was just the feeling that comes from years of scouting. He felt confident that Mike had his father's intensity and feel for the game just from talking to him. And in Mike's case, the desire and confidence was packaged in a body that gave him a chance to do things most baseball players can only dream of doing. Put it together, and Morhardt was convinced that he was scouting a future star.

"Michael is very strong and fast. You see guys who are fast, you see guys who are strong. It's very unusual when a guy has both elements," Morhardt said. "How many guys have great athletic minds but don't have those qualities? And he had the personality to handle the everyday-ness of baseball."

Morhardt's conviction prompted the Angels to take Trout at the back of the first round in 2009. Just two years later, Trout has already made it to the big leagues after hitting .326/.414/.544 with 11 homers and 33 steals for Double-A Arkansas, and won Baseball America's 2011 Minor League Player of the Year award.

Mike Trout

PLAYER OF THE YEAR

PREVIOUS WINNERS

2001: Josh Beckett, rhp, Brevard County/Portland (Marlins)
2002: Rocco Baldelli, of, Bakersfield/Orlando/Durham (Devil Rays)
2003: Joe Mauer, c, Fort Myers/New Britain (Twins)
2004: Jeff Francis, lhp, Tulsa/Colorado Springs (Rockies)
2005: Delmon Young, of, Montgomery/Durham (Devil Rays)
2006: Alex Gordon, 3b, Wichita (Royals)
2007: Jay Bruce, of, Sarasota/Chattanooga/Louisville (Reds)
2008: Matt Wieters, c, Frederick/Bowie (Orioles)
2009: Jason Heyward, Myrtle Beach/Mississippi (Braves)
2010: Jeremy Hellickson, Montgomery/Durham (Rays)
Full list: BaseballAmerica.com/awards

MINOR LEAGUES

Parnell strikes gold in Richmond

Even the biggest enthusiasts could not have imagined success quite like this when the Eastern League's Connecticut Defenders announced they were moving to the recently vacated Richmond market after the 2009 season. After all, the team would have to play in The Diamond, the longtime home of the Richmond Braves that was in such poor condiition that the team left town after 42 years for a new ballpark in suburban Atlanta. But Richmond vice president Todd Parnell and a dream team of a front office—that includes chief executive Chuck Domino (our 2003 Executive of the Year) and general manager Bill Papierniak—has overcome those conditions and done the unthinkable: turn Richmond into one of the best draws in the minor leagues.

A creative nickname—Flying Squirrels merchandise is a hit in Richmond and the mascot made an appearance at the World Series in St. Louis—and even more creative promotions helped Richmond draw an average of 6,679 fans in 2011, 17th out of 140 minor league

teams).

In many ways, Parnell has been the man behind the magic in Richmond. He has served as the face of the franchise, whether it be during creative on-field stunts (Parnell had his head shaved for charity) or countless speaking engagements around the city. "If you're part of the business community in Richmond, chances are you know Parney," Minor League Baseball president Pat O'Conner said.

CONTINUED FROM PAGE 348

coming from so deep in my brain, it was hard to explain to someone. I would talk to (the Padres') psychiatrist because, honestly, I thought I was going crazy."

102-186

Triple-A Rochester's record over the past two seasons.

The performance of the Twins' Triple-A affiliate over this span was among the worst in Rochester history (which dates back to 1877) and led Minnesota to fire manager Tom Nieto. It's a demonstration that the Twins care deeply about keeping their affiliation in Rochester, even though the player-development contract isn't up for renewal until after the 2012 season. The Twins have been in Rochester since 2003; the city had hosted the Orioles since 1961 before five straight losing seasons led Rochester to cut ties with Baltimore.

4

Number of Blue Jays affiliates that advanced to their league finals, the highest number of any organization. It's also how many Rangers affiliates reached the playoffs (not counting big league club).

Perhaps Toronto's emphasis on scouting and player development under second-year general manager Alex Anthopoulos is starting to pay off. Double-A New Hampshire won the Eastern League, defeating Reading and Richmond while losing only once in each round. Short-season Vancouver rolled to the Northwest League title while losing once each to Eugene and Tri-City. The low Class A Lansing and Rookie-level Bluefield clubs lost the battle of the birds to Cardinals affiliates Quad Cities and Johnson City in the Midwest and Appalachian leagues.

5.68

The average runs per nine innings for Pacific Coast League teams in 2011, the highest average for a full-season league in the past five seasons.

Even as the major leagues have seen batting average (.255) and runs per nine (4.30) dip to their lowest levels in roughly 20 years, the drop did not carry over to the high minors. This year's California League finished at 5.66 runs, trailing only the '07 version of the Cal League (5.67).

While the PCL and Cal League are known for scoreboard-busting run totals, the same can not be said about the Rookie-level Pioneer League. The PL scored 6.02 runs per nine innings, blowing

Sandberg thrives in new role

BY JEFF SCHULER

With every passing season, the gap widens between Ryne Sandberg, Hall of Fame player, and Ryne Sandberg, managerial prospect.

Five years into his quest to return to the big leagues, the 10-time Cubs all-star is being valued as much for his ability as a minor league manager as for his 19-year playing career that earned him a ticket to Cooperstown.

"I think I've noticed that more this year than in the past, and it's gratifying, because that's what I'm pursuing at the moment, what I'm trying to do right now," Sandberg said.

Sandberg won Pacific Coast League manager of the year honors in 2010 when he guided Triple-A Iowa to an 82-62 record. However, this year may have been his best work. Sandberg led the Phillies' Triple-A Lehigh Valley affiliate—a franchise that hadn't spent a day above .500 in its three-year history—to within two wins of the International League championship. The feat earned him Baseball America's 2011 Minor League Manager of the Year award.

MANAGER OF THE YEAR

PREVIOUS 10 WINNERS

2001: Jackie Moore, Round Rock (Astros)
2002: John Russell, Edmonton (Twins)
2003: Dave Brundage, San Antonio (Mariners)
2004: Marty Brown, Buffalo (Indians)
2005: Ken Oberkfell, Norfolk (Mets)
2006: Todd Claus, Portland (Red Sox)
2007: Matt Wallbeck, Erie (Tigers)
2008: Rocket Wheeler, Myrtle Beach (Braves)
2009: Charlie Montoyo, Durham Bulls (Rays)
2010: Mike Sarbaugh, Columbus Clippers (Indians)
Full list: BaseballAmerica.com/awards

"It's a great honor, and it speaks volumes to what we did as a team," said Sandberg, whose team (80-64) spent nearly three months in first place before earning a wild-card berth.

"I think we were expecting a lot from Ryne when we brought him in, but I believe he even exceeded those expectations," Phillies assistant general manager Benny Looper said.

away the PCL and Cal. This year's Arizona League featured the second-highest scoring average (5.90) of the past five seasons, if we consider short-season leagues.

6

Different teams to win the International League's Governors' Cup over the past 10 years, as Columbus became the third team to win consecutive titles during that span before going on to win the Triple-A National Championship for a second straight year.

Columbus won six of seven playoff games while dispatching Durham and Lehigh Valley to win the Governors' Cup. During the regular season, the Clippers led the IL in runs per game (4.97), home runs (152), walks (570), on-base percentage (.347) and OPS (.770). Columbus topped off its season by winning a second consecutive Triple-A National Championship, this time knocking off Pacific Coast League champion Omaha by an 8-3 score.

Both Columbus and Omaha won throughout 2011 despite losing many of their top players to the big leagues. Omaha lost first baseman Eric Hosmer, second baseman Johnny Giavotella, third baseman Mike Moustakas, catcher Salvador Perez and lefthander Danny Duffy to Kansas City. Columbus lost second baseman Jason Kipnis,

Luke Carlin's three RBIs helped Columbus win its second consecutive Triple-A title

third baseman Lonnie Chisenhall, lefthander Nick Hagadone and righthanders Alex White (via the Ubaldo Jimenez trade) and Zach Putnam, who all ranked in the Indians' Top 20.

14

Home runs hit by Blue Jays left fielder Eric Arce, a Rookie-level Gulf Coast League record.

The Blue Jays' 25th-round pick in June, Arce hit .268/.437/.621 with a GCL-leading 38 walks

MINOR LEAGUES

MIKE JANES

TRIPLE-A

Pos	Player, Team (Org)	League	AVG	OBP	SLG	AB	R	H	2B	3B	HR	RBI	BB	SO	SB	CS
C	Devin Mesoraco, Louisville (Reds)	IL	.289	.371	.484	436	60	126	36	2	15	71	52	83	1	1
1B	* Anthony Rizzo, Tucson (Padres)	PCL	.331	.404	.652	356	64	118	34	1	26	101	43	89	7	6
2B	* Jason Kipnis, Columbus (Indians)	IL	.280	.362	.484	343	65	96	16	9	12	55	44	72	12	1
3B	Brett Lawrie, Las Vegas (Blue Jays)	PCL	.353	.415	.661	292	64	103	24	6	18	61	26	53	13	2
SS	Zack Cozart Louisville (Reds)	IL	.310	.357	.467	323	57	100	26	2	7	32	23	51	9	2
CF	Collin Cowgill, Reno (D-backs)	PCL	.354	.430	.554	395	95	140	24	8	13	70	51	63	30	3
OF	Russ Canzler, Durham (Rays)	IL	.314	.401	.530	474	78	149	40	4	18	83	67	129	5	2
OF	# Trayvon Robinson, Alb./Tacoma (LAD/Sea)	PCL	.289	.374	.552	377	71	109	9	6	26	71	48	126	9	6
DH	* Bryan LaHair, Iowa, (Cubs)	PCL	.331	.405	.664	456	91	151	38	0	38	109	60	111	2	0

Pos	Pitcher, Team (Org)	League	W	L	ERA	G	GS	SV	IP	H	HR	BB	SO	G/F	WHIP	AVG
SP	Graham Godfrey, Sacramento (Athletics)	PCL	14	3	2.68	19	18	0	107	92	6	30	89	0.88	1.14	.227
SP	Zach McAllister, Columbus (Indians)	IL	12	3	3.32	25	25	0	155	155	11	31	128	0.84	1.20	.261
SP	Tom Milone, Syracuse (Nationals)	IL	12	6	3.22	24	24	0	148	137	9	16	155	0.77	1.03	.241
SP	Julio Teheran, Gwinnett (Braves)	IL	15	3	2.55	25	24	0	145	123	5	48	122	0.80	1.18	.232
RP	Michael Schwimer, Lehigh Valley (Phillies)	IL	9	1	1.85	47	0	10	68	51	4	22	86	0.75	1.07	.203

Player of the Year: Brett Lawrie, Las Vegas. **Pitcher of the Year:** Julio Teheran, Gwinnett. **Manager of the Year:** Mike Sarbaugh, Columbus.

DOUBLE-A

Pos	Player, Team (Org)	League	AVG	OBP	SLG	AB	R	H	2B	3B	HR	RBI	BB	SO	SB	CS
C	Travis d'Arnaud, New Hampshire (Blue Jays)	EL	.311	.371	.542	424	72	132	33	1	21	78	33	100	4	2
1B	Paul Goldschmidt, Mobile (D-backs)	SL	.306	.435	.626	366	84	112	21	3	30	94	82	92	9	3
2B	* Vince Belnome, San Antonio (Padres)	TL	.333	.432	.603	267	56	89	19	1	17	62	47	59	0	5
3B	James Darnell, San Antonio (Padres)	TL	.333	.434	.604	288	62	96	25	1	17	62	52	48	2	1
SS	Jordy Mercer, Altoona (Pirates)	EL	.268	.329	.487	265	40	71	17	1	13	48	23	35	6	3
CF	Mike Trout, Arkansas (Angels)	TL	.326	.414	.544	353	82	115	18	13	11	38	45	76	33	10
OF	Starling Marte, Altoona (Pirates)	EL	.332	.370	.500	536	91	178	38	8	12	50	22	100	24	12
OF	* Tim Wheeler, Tulsa (Rockies)	TL	.287	.365	.535	561	105	161	28	6	33	86	59	142	21	12
DH	Scott Van Slyke, Chattanooga (Dodgers)	SL	.348	.427	.595	457	81	159	45	4	20	92	65	100	6	1

Pos	Pitcher, Team (Org)	League	W	L	ERA	G	GS	SV	IP	H	HR	BB	SO	G/F	WHIP	AVG
SP	Shelby Miller, Springfield (Cardinals)	TL	9	3	2.70	16	16	0	87	72	2	33	89	0.85	1.21	.229
SP	* Matt Moore, Montgomery (Rays)	SL	8	3	2.20	18	18	0	102	68	8	28	131	0.98	0.94	.187
SP	Brad Peacock, Harrisburg (Nationals)	EL	10	2	2.01	16	14	0	99	62	4	23	129	0.86	0.86	.179
SP	* Eric Surkamp, Richmond (Giants)	EL	10	4	2.02	23	22	0	142	110	5	44	165	0.97	1.08	.213
RP	Luis Marte, Erie (Tigers)	EL	3	0	1.70	23	1	3	53	29	3	18	68	0.96	0.89	.158

Player of the Year: Mike Trout, Arkansas. **Pitcher of the Year:** Matt Moore, Montgomery. **Manager of the Year:** Doug Dascenzo, San Antonio.

HIGH CLASS A

Pos	Player, Team (Org)	League	AVG	OBP	SLG	AB	R	H	2B	3B	HR	RBI	BB	SO	SB	CS
C	Tommy Joseph, San Jose (Giants)	CAL	.270	.317	.471	514	80	139	33	2	22	95	29	102	1	0
1B	* Jonathan Singleton, Clear./Lan. (Phi/Hou)	FSL/CAL	.298	.392	.441	449	68	134	23	1	13	63	70	123	3	3
2B	Jeff Kobernus, Potomac (Nationals)	CAR	.282	.313	.387	489	67	138	22	4	7	52	21	87	53	8
3B	Jedd Gyorko, San Antonio (Padres)	CAL	.365	.429	.638	340	78	124	35	2	18	74	38	64	11	3
SS	* Hak-Ju Lee, Charlotte (Rays)	FSL	.318	.389	.443	400	82	127	16	11	4	23	42	72	28	14
CF	Gary Brown, San Jose (Giants)	CAL	.336	.407	.519	559	115	188	34	13	14	80	46	77	53	19
OF	Kyle Jensen, Jupiter (Marlins)	FSL	.309	.385	.535	391	53	121	20	1	22	66	46	114	0	0
OF	Michael Choice, Stockton (Athletics)	CAL	.285	.376	.542	467	79	133	28	1	30	82	61	134	9	5
DH	Kent Matthes, Modesto (Rockies)	CAL	.334	.378	.642	371	70	124	39	3	23	95	22	80	7	4

Pos	Pitcher, Team (Org)	League	W	L	ERA	G	GS	SV	IP	H	HR	BB	SO	G/F	WHIP	AVG
SP	Chad Bettis, Modesto (Rockies)	CAL	12	5	3.34	27	27	0	170	142	10	45	184	1.14	1.10	.225
SP	Trevor May, Clearwater (Phillies)	FSL	10	8	3.63	27	27	0	151	121	8	67	208	0.70	1.24	.221
SP	Julio Rodriguez, Clearwater (Phillies)	FSL	16	7	2.76	27	27	0	157	102	13	56	168	0.46	1.01	.186
SP	* Robbie Ross, Myrtle Beach (Rangers)	CAR	9	4	2.26	21	20	0	123	102	1	28	98	1.54	1.05	.227
RP	Alejandro Ramos, Jupiter (Marlins)	FSL	1	4	1.78	49	0	25	51	37	2	19	71	0.86	1.11	.200

Player of the Year: Gary Brown, San Jose. **Pitcher of the Year:** Chad Bettis, Modesto. **Manager of the Year:** Aaron Holbert, Kinston.

in 49 games. The 19-year-old is a former Florida State recruit who was drafted out of high school in 2010 by Toronto in the 27th round. He had a lewd battery and lewd molestation charge in April 2010 that was later dropped.

Meanwhile, another Rookie-level home run record nearly fell . . .

41

Combined home runs hit by Rookie-level

LOW CLASS A

Pos	Player, Team (Org)	League	AVG	OBP	SLG	AB	R	H	2B	3B	HR	RBI	BB	SO	SB	CS
C	* Rob Brantly, West Michigan (Tigers)	MWL	.303	.366	.440	284	42	86	16	1	7	44	24	39	2	2
1B	* Andrew Clark, Hickory (Rangers)	SAL	.313	.422	.482	355	59	111	24	0	12	60	62	62	7	4
2B	Ronald Torreyes, Dayton (Reds)	MWL	.356	.398	.457	278	53	99	9	5	3	41	14	19	12	7
3B	Nick Castellanos, West Michigan (Tigers)	MWL	.312	.367	.436	507	65	158	36	3	7	76	45	130	3	2
SS	# Jurickson Profar, Hickory (Rangers)	SAL	.286	.390	.493	430	86	123	37	8	12	65	65	63	23	9
CF	Jake Marisnick, Lansing (Blue Jays)	MWL	.320	.392	.496	462	68	148	27	6	14	77	43	91	37	8
OF	* Bryce Harper, Hagerstown (Nationals)	SAL	.318	.423	.554	258	49	82	17	1	14	46	44	61	19	5
OF	Rymer Liriano, Fort Wayne (Padres)	MWL	.319	.383	.499	455	81	145	30	8	12	62	47	95	65	20
DH	* Oscar Taveras, Quad Cities (Cardinals)	MWL	.386	.444	.584	308	52	119	27	5	8	62	32	52	1	4

Pos	Pitcher, Team (Org)	League	W	L	ERA	G	GS	SV	IP	H	HR	BB	SO	G/F	WHIP	AVG
SP	Greg Billo, Kane County (Royals)	MWL	9	5	1.93	27	18	1	135	113	6	25	119	1.32	1.02	.228
SP	Keyvius Sampson, Fort Wayne (Padres)	MWL	12	3	2.90	24	24	0	118	81	8	49	143	0.72	1.10	.192
SP	Taijuan Walker, Clinton (Mariners)	MWL	6	5	2.89	18	18	0	97	69	4	39	113	1.54	1.12	.202
SP	Daniel Corcino, Dayton (Reds)	MWL	11	7	3.42	26	26	0	139	128	10	34	156	0.91	1.16	.238
RP	* Chris Manno, Hagerstown (Nationals)	SAL	1	3	1.04	34	0	12	43	20	1	15	69	0.72	0.81	.135

Player of the Year: Jurickson Profar, Hickory. **Pitcher of the Year:** Greg Billo, Kane County. **Manager of the Year:** Johnny Rodriguez, Quad Cities.

SHORT-SEASON

Pos	Player, Team (Org)	League	AVG	OBP	SLG	AB	R	H	2B	3B	HR	RBI	BB	SO	SB	CS
C	Jorge Alfaro, Spokane (Rangers)	NWL	.300	.345	.481	160	18	48	9	1	6	23	4	54	1	0
1B	* Dean Green, Connecticut (Tigers)	NYP	.341	.395	.520	246	33	84	19	2	7	44	18	35	1	0
2B	* Cory Spangenberg, Eugene (Padres)	NWL	.384	.545	.535	86	20	33	10	0	1	20	31	15	10	4
3B	* Matt Skole, Auburn (Nationals)	NYP	.290	.382	.438	272	43	79	23	1	5	48	42	52	2	1
SS	* Joe Panik, Salem-Keizer (Giants)	NWL	.341	.401	.467	270	49	92	10	3	6	54	28	25	13	5
CF	* Mason Williams, Staten Island (Yankees)	NYP	.349	.395	.468	269	42	94	11	6	3	31	20	41	28	12
OF	* Pin-Chieh Chen, Boise (Cubs)	NWL	.301	.363	.424	229	34	69	14	4	2	30	25	44	20	6
OF	* Tyler Collins, Connecticut (Tigers)	NYP	.313	.360	.534	163	28	51	10	1	8	31	10	17	6	1
DH	Jabari Blash, Everett (Mariners)	NWL	.292	.393	.574	195	26	57	16	3	11	43	28	65	10	3

Pos	Pitcher, Team (Org)	League	W	L	ERA	G	GS	SV	IP	H	HR	BB	SO	G/F	WHIP	AVG
SP	Jose Campos, Everett (Mariners)	NWL	5	5	2.32	14	14	0	81	66	4	13	85	1.67	0.97	.214
SP	Todd McInnis, Batavia (Cardinals)	NYP	3	2	1.90	13	11	0	62	50	1	8	36	1.64	0.94	.218
SP	* Justin Nicolino, Vancouver (Blue Jays)	NWL	5	1	1.03	12	9	0	52	28	0	11	64	1.44	0.75	.156
SP	Jose Rosario, Boise (Cubs)	NWL	6	3	3.53	15	7	2	64	67	1	18	50	2.83	1.34	.266
RP	Dayan Diaz, Tri-City (Astros)	NYP	7	3	1.98	19	1	2	50	27	0	30	70	1.08	1.14	.158

Player of the Year: Mason Williams, Staten Island. **Pitcher of the Year:** Justin Nicolino, Vancouver. **Manager of the Year:** Tom Slater, Staten Island.

ROOKIE

Pos	Player, Team (Org)	League	AVG	OBP	SLG	AB	R	H	2B	3B	HR	RBI	BB	SO	SB	CS
C	Will Swanner, Casper (Rockies)	PIO	.264	.357	.553	159	33	42	14	1	10	24	20	60	1	2
1B	C.J. Cron, Orem (Angels)	PIO	.308	.371	.629	143	30	44	5	1	13	41	10	34	0	0
2B	* Taylor Lindsey, Orem (Angels)	PIO	.362	.394	.593	290	64	105	28	6	9	46	13	46	10	4
3B	Miguel Sano, Elizabethton (Twins)	APP	.292	.352	.637	267	58	78	18	7	20	59	23	77	5	4
SS	Matt Williams, Johnson City (Cardinals)	APP	.293	.382	.463	229	47	67	19	1	6	25	27	45	20	2
CF	* Eddie Rosario, Elizabethton (Twins)	APP	.337	.397	.670	270	71	91	9	9	21	60	27	60	17	6
OF	* Eric Arce, GCL Blue Jays (Blue Jays)	GCL	.268	.437	.621	153	34	41	6	3	14	40	38	48	1	1
OF	* Joc Pederson, Ogden (Dodgers)	PIO	.353	.429	.568	266	54	94	20	2	11	64	36	54	24	5
DH	Dante Bichette Jr., GCL Yankees	GCL	.342	.446	.505	196	33	67	17	3	3	47	30	41	3	3

Pos	Pitcher, Team (Org)	League	W	L	ERA	G	GS	SV	IP	H	HR	BB	SO	G/F	WHIP	AVG
SP	* Tony Cingrani, Billings (Reds)	PIO	3	2	1.75	13	13	0	51	35	1	6	80	1.30	0.80	.190
SP	J.R. Graham, Danville (Braves)	APP	5	2	1.72	13	8	0	58	52	0	13	52	2.30	1.13	.245
SP	Tyrell Jenkins, Johnson City (Cardinals)	APP	4	2	3.86	11	11	0	56	63	3	15	55	1.83	1.36	.296
SP	* Scott Snodgress, Great Falls (White Sox)	PIO	3	3	3.34	16	12	0	59	61	5	17	68	1.55	1.31	.262
RP	Edwin Carl, Idaho Falls (Royals)	PIO	3	1	1.36	21	0	5	33	17	0	3	71	2.00	0.61	.145

Player of the Year: Eddie Rosario, Elizabethton. **Pitcher of the Year:** Tony Cingrani, Billings. **Manager of the Year:** Dennis Holmberg, Bluefield.

Elizabethton Twins teammates Eddie Rosario and Miguel Sano. Rosario, a center fielder selected in the fourth round of the 2010 draft out of Puerto Rico, batted .337/.397/.670 and mashed a league-high 21 homers in 67 games. Sano, a third baseman signed out of the Dominican Republic, batted .292/.352/.637 with 20 homers in 66 games and was named the Appy's top prospect. However, neither could surpass the league-record 24 home runs set by Mitch Einertson in 2004.

DAVID STONER

TONY FARLOW

Julio Teheran mastered Triple-A hitters in between two brief big league stints

Jurickson Profar was the South Atlantic League's youngest and best player

FIRST TEAM

Pos	Player, Level (Organization)	Age	AVG	OBP	SLG	G	AB	R	H	2B	3B	HR	RBI	BB	SO	SB
C	Ryan Lavarnway, AAA/AA (Red Sox)	24	.290	.376	.563	116	435	75	126	23	0	32	93	57	107	1
1B	Paul Goldschmidt, AA (Diamondbacks)	24	.306	.435	.626	103	366	84	112	21	3	30	94	82	92	9
2B	Jose Altuve, High A/AA (Astros)	21	.389	.426	.591	87	357	59	139	22	10	10	59	26	40	24
3B	Brett Lawrie, High A/AAA (Blue Jays)	21	.347	.414	.647	73	300	64	104	24	6	18	62	26	54	13
SS	# Jurickson Profar, Low A (Rangers)	18	.286	.390	.493	115	430	86	123	37	8	12	65	65	63	23
CF	Mike Trout, AA (Angels)	20	.326	.414	.544	91	353	82	115	18	13	11	38	45	76	33
OF	Gary Brown, High A (Giants)	22	.336	.407	.519	131	559	115	188	34	13	14	80	46	77	53
OF	* Tim Wheeler, AA (Rockies)	23	.287	.365	.535	138	561	105	161	28	6	33	86	59	142	21
DH	* Bryan LaHair, AAA (Cubs)	28	.331	.405	.664	129	456	91	151	38	0	38	109	60	111	2

Pos	Pitcher, Level (Organization)	Age	W	L	ERA	G	GS	SV	IP	H	HR	BB	SO	G/F	AVG	WHIP
SP	Shelby Miller, High A/AA (Cardinals)	20	11	6	2.77	25	25	0	140	112	4	53	170	0.74	.219	1.18
SP	* Matt Moore, AA/AAA (Rays)	22	12	3	1.92	27	27	0	155	101	11	46	210	0.96	.184	0.95
SP	Brad Peacock, AA/AAA (Nationals)	23	15	3	2.39	25	23	0	147	98	9	47	177	0.75	.188	0.99
SP	* Tyler Skaggs, High A/AA (D-backs)	20	9	6	2.96	27	27	0	158	126	10	49	198	1.19	.218	1.11
SP	Julio Teheran, AAA (Braves)	20	15	3	2.55	25	24	0	145	123	5	48	122	0.80	.232	1.18
RP	Addison Reed, Lo A/Hi A/AA/AAA (White Sox)	22	2	1	1.26	43	0	5	78	43	3	14	111	0.69	.157	0.73

SECOND TEAM

Pos	Player, Level (Organization)	Age	AVG	OBP	SLG	G	AB	R	H	2B	3B	HR	RBI	BB	SO	SB
C	Travis d'Arnaud, AA (Blue Jays)	22	.311	.371	.542	114	424	72	132	33	1	21	78	33	100	4
1B	* Anthony Rizzo, AAA (Padres)	22	.331	.404	.652	93	356	64	118	34	1	26	101	43	89	7
2B	* Jason Kipnis, AAA (Indians)	24	.280	.362	.484	92	343	65	96	16	9	12	55	44	72	12
3B	* Taylor Green, AA/AAA (Brewers)	24	.336	.412	.580	123	431	76	145	37	1	22	91	55	75	1
SS	* Hak-Ju Lee, High A/AA (Rays)	20	.292	.365	.416	121	500	98	146	17	15	5	30	53	94	33
CF	Jake Marisnick, Low A (Blue Jays)	20	.320	.392	.496	118	462	68	148	27	6	14	77	43	91	37
OF	* Bryce Harper, Low A/AA (Nationals)	18	.297	.392	.501	109	387	63	115	24	2	17	58	59	87	26
OF	* Oscar Taveras, Low A (Cardinals)	19	.386	.444	.584	78	308	52	119	27	5	8	62	32	52	1
DH	Russ Canzler (Rays)	25	.314	.401	.530	131	474	78	149	40	4	18	83	67	129	5

Pos	Pitcher, Level (Organization)	Age	W	L	ERA	G	GS	SV	IP	H	HR	BB	SO	G/F	AVG	WHIP
SP	Chad Bettis, High A (Rockies)	22	12	5	3.34	27	27	0	170	142	10	45	184	1.14	.225	1.10
SP	* Edwar Cabrera, Low A/High A (Rockies)	23	8	3	3.34	26	26	0	167	155	18	41	217	1.20	.244	1.17
SP	Drew Hutchison, Low A/High A/AA (Jays)	21	14	5	2.53	28	27	0	149	120	4	35	171	1.33	.220	1.04
SP	Trevor May, High A (Phillies)	21	10	8	3.63	27	27	0	151	121	8	67	208	0.70	.221	1.24
SP	* Eric Surkamp, High A/AA (Giants)	24	11	4	1.94	24	23	0	148	114	5	45	170	0.98	.212	1.07
RP	Shawn Tolleson, Low A/High A/AA (Dodgers)	23	7	2	1.17	57	0	25	69	52	3	18	105	1.00	.206	1.01

BayBears roar to the top

BY JACK MAGRUDER

PHOENIX

When the Diamondbacks plotted possible rosters for the 2011 minor league season last winter, they suspected that they might have something special at Double-A Mobile, a likely landing spot for many of their top prospects.

They could not have been more right.

Fortified by a roster that included a stacked pitching staff and arguably the best power-hitting prospect in the minor leagues, Mobile won the Southern League title under first-year manager Turner Ward to become Baseball America's 2011 Minor League Team of the Year. The BayBears won 48 of their final 70 games, beginning with the final two games of the first half, and beat Birmingham and Tennessee to win the league title—their first outright championship since 1998.

"It's a thrill that the group gets that type of notoriety," said Diamondbacks vice president of scouting and player development Jerry Dipoto, who left the team in late October to take over as general manager of the Angels. "We're proud as an organization, and we all took a great deal of pleasure in watching that group come together, the way they played and really the quality of the people involved."

The BayBears finished with an 84-54 record and featured at least a dozen players expected to soon reach the majors. Five have already tasted the big time: first baseman Paul Goldschmidt, lefthander Wade Miley, righthander Jarrod Parker and righthanded relievers Bryan Shaw and Ryan Cook.

Goldschmidt was leading the minor leagues in home runs (30) and RBIs (94) at the time of his callup on Aug. 1, and all he did after that was hit eight more homers in the final two months of the regular season and two more in the NL Division Series against the Brewers. Cy Young Award winners were not immune. He hit two homers off Tim Lincecum, including his first career homer, and another off Cliff Lee. Miley, Parker, Shaw and Cook also were contributors as the parent Diamondbacks won

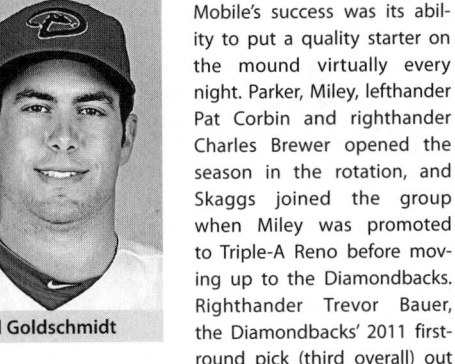

Paul Goldschmidt

TEAM OF THE YEAR

the NL West, with Parker and Shaw making the playoff roster in the bullpen.

The bounty did not stop there. Lefthander Tyler Skaggs, obtained in a package for Dan Haren from the Angels at the 2010 trading deadline, was named the best prospect in the California League and the No. 2 prospect in the Southern League after being promoted at midseason. In between, Skaggs took time out to start for the U.S. team in the Futures Game at Chase Field in Phoenix.

Perhaps the biggest key to Mobile's success was its ability to put a quality starter on the mound virtually every night. Parker, Miley, lefthander Pat Corbin and righthander Charles Brewer opened the season in the rotation, and Skaggs joined the group when Miley was promoted to Triple-A Reno before moving up to the Diamondbacks. Righthander Trevor Bauer, the Diamondbacks' 2011 first-round pick (third overall) out of UCLA, only added to the riches when he joined the team in August.

"When you have the opportunity to run out prospects like that in one rotation at one level, it's pretty extraordinary. When (Brewer) is your fifth starter at Double-A, that's a mother of a rotation," Dipoto said. "I think this is the first time in our time here in Arizona that I can honestly say that the pitching was as significant as the offensive prospects, and that's what made this team pretty special."

PREVIOUS 10 WINNERS

2001: Lake Elsinore/California (Padres)
2002: Akron/Eastern (Indians)
2003: Sacramento/Pacific Coast (Athletics)
2004: Lancaster/California (Diamondbacks)
2005: Jacksonville/Southern (Dodgers)
2006: Tucson/Pacific Coast (Diamondbacks)
2007: San Antonio/Texas (Padres)
2008: Frisco/Texas (Rangers)
2009: Akron/Eastern (Indians)
2010: Northwest Arkansas/Texas (Royals)
Full list: BaseballAmerica.com/awards

MINOR LEAGUES

PHOENIX

Grant Green said he felt a lot more comfortable at the 2011 Futures Game after playing in the 2010 Futures Game. And it showed.

The Athletics second baseman drilled two doubles in two-bats, sparking the game-winning rally with the second. The United States plated three runs in the bottom of the eighth to win its second straight Futures Game, 6-4, at Chase Field. The victory gave the U.S. a 7-6 edge over the World in the event's 13-year history.

Green entered the game in the fifth inning, delivering a pinch-hit RBI double off a 93-mph fastball from Rangers lefthander Martin Perez to put the U.S. ahead 3-0. That lead had disappeared by the time Green led off the eighth against Royals righthander Kelvin Herrera, as the World had scored four runs in the sixth. Herrera delivered one 94-96 mph fastball after another, and Green drilled the seventh off the top of the batting eye in center field.

Rays shortstop Tim Beckham followed with a game-tying double before Herrera rallied to get two outs. Yankees catcher Austin Romine then snapped the tie with a line-drive single to left and scored an insurance run on a double by Rockies third baseman Nolan Arenado.

Sixteen of Green's U.S. teammates from last year's Futures Game already have appeared in the majors. If he couldn't join them there, he said winning MVP honors in Phoenix was the next-best thing.

"I hope this is my last time here," Green said with a chuckle, "but it was a lot of fun. I thought that second double was out of here. After I got to second base, the people in the stands were getting on me and telling me I need to hit the weight room."

The U.S. comeback took the spotlight away from a stunning rally by the World. With two out in the sixth, Dodgers right fielder Alfredo Silverio finally put the World on the board with a two-run homer off a 93 mph fastball from Indians lefthander Drew Pomeranz.

Red Sox left fielder Chih-Hsien Chiang walked and Phillies catcher Sebastian Valle doubled to tie the game and chase Pomeranz. Rangers shortstop Jurickson Profar showed off his pop and speed with a triple off Twins righthander Kyle Gibson, giving the World its first lead.

Indians second baseman Jason Kipnis opened the scoring when he led off the bottom of the first by turning on a 95 mph fastball

FUTURES GAME BOX SCORE

JULY 10 IN PHOENIX
UNITED STATES 6, WORLD 4

WORLD	AB	R	H	BI	U.S.	AB	R	H	BI
Marte, CF	3	0	1	0	Kipnis, 2B	2	1	1	1
Fuentes, PH-CF	2	0	0	0	Green, PH-2B	2	1	2	1
Altuve, 2B	3	0	2	0	Machado, SS	2	0	0	0
Schoop, 2B	1	0	1	0	Beckham, PH-SS	2	1	1	1
Alonso, 1B	2	0	0	0	Harper, LF	4	0	0	0
Viciedo, DH	3	1	1	0	Goldschmidt, 1B	4	0	0	0
Martinez, F, PH-DH	1	0	0	0	Mesoraco, C	1	1	1	0
Liddi, 3B	3	0	0	0	Romine, C	2	1	2	1
Marte, J, 3B	1	0	0	0	Middlebrooks, 3B	2	0	1	0
Silverio, RF	4	1	1	2	Arenado, 3B	2	0	1	1
Chiang, LF	3	1	0	0	Darnell, DH	3	0	0	0
Rosario, W, C	2	0	0	0	Myers, RF	3	0	0	1
Valle, PH-C	2	1	1	1	Brown, G, CF	2	1	1	0
Lee, SS	2	0	0	0	Szczur, CF	1	0	0	0
Profar, PH-SS	2	0	1	1					
Totals	**34**	**4**	**8**	**4**	**Totals**	**32**	**6**	**10**	**6**

WORLD	000 004 000	4 8 0
U.S.	110 010 03X	6 10 0

LOB: World 6, U.S. 4. **2B:** Altuve, Valle, Green 2, Beckham, Arenado. **3B:** Profar. **HR:** Silverio, Kipnis. **GIDP:** Middlebrooks; Myers. **SB:** Brown. **CS:** Schoop.

WORLD	IP	H	R	ER	BB	SO	U.S.	IP	H	R	ER	BB	SO
Teheran	1	1	1	1	0	1	Skaggs	1	1	0	0	1	1
Hendriks	1	2	1	1	0	0	Peacock (H)	1	0	0	0	0	1
Paxton	1	0	0	0	0	0	Miller, S (H)	1	1	0	0	1	1
Martinez	1	0	0	0	0	1	Moore (H)	1	0	0	0	0	1
Perez	1	2	1	1	1	1	Thornburg (H)	1	1	0	0	0	0
Alvarez	1	1	0	0	0	0	Pomeranz (BS)	⅔	3	4	4	1	1
Vizcaino	1	0	0	0	0	1	Gibson	1⅓	2	0	0	0	0
Herrera (L)	⅔	4	3	3	0	1	Cosart (W)	1	0	0	0	0	2
Marinez	⅓	0	0	0	0	1	Turner	⅔	0	0	0	0	0
							Harvey (S)	⅓	0	0	0	0	0
Totals	**8**	**10**	**6**	**6**	**1**	**6**	**Totals**	**9**	**8**	**4**	**4**	**3**	**7**

Umpires: HP: Ben May. **1B:** Will Little. **2B:** Jimmy Volpi. **3B:** Scott Mahoney.

from Braves righthander Julio Teheran, drilling it over the right-field fence. Kipnis, who starred at nearby Arizona State, was serenaded with chants of "ASU! ASU!" as he circled the bases.

"Going into the game, I was just thinking, 'Don't strike out,'" Kipnis said. "To have that kind of at-bat versus that kind of pitcher, I couldn't be happier. It's hard to describe. It's a dream come true."

Rays lefthander Matt Moore and Phillies righthander Jarred Cosart highlighted a dominant U.S. pitching staff. Moore pitched a perfect fourth inning, working from 94-98 mph with his fastball. Cosart earned the victory with a 1-2-3 eighth inning, pitching at 96-97 and registering a strikeout each with his curveball and changeup.

TRIPLE-A: Neither the Pacific Coast League's offense, nor the notorious elevation of Spring Mobile Ballpark in Salt Lake City turned out to be much a problem for the International League's pitching staff. Nine IL pitchers combined for a three-hit shutout, and the IL defeated the PCL 3-0 for its third straight victory in the Triple-A all-star game.

Durham third baseman Russ Canzler provided the only runs of the game in the top of the second inning by depositing a fastball from Las Vegas lefty Brad Mills onto the berm in right-center field for a three-run homer. Canzler played the entire game and earned MVP honors for going 1-for-4 with three RBIs. Canzler signed with the Rays as a minor league free agent in November after spending his first seven pro seasons with the Cubs.

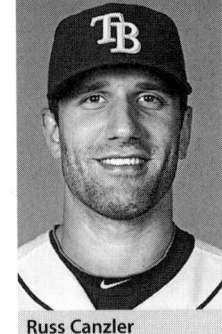

Russ Canzler

IL relievers Shane Lindsay of Charlotte, who touched 99 mph, and Chuck James of Rochester walked the bases loaded in the bottom of the seventh, but the PCL ultimately squandered its best scoring opportunity when James struck out Reno second baseman Tony Abreu for the third out. IL starter Zach McAllister (Columbus) pitched two scoreless innings, striking out two of the final three batters he faced to earn the win.

Canzler's homer notwithstanding, the PCL pitching staff was also effective. After Louisville right fielder Jeremy Hermida and catcher Devin Mesoraco each singled in the third, no IL batters reached base until the seventh.

Omaha righthander Luis Mendoza pitched a scoreless third, after which a succession of PCL relievers completed four perfect innings: Albuquerque lefty Dana Eveland, Fresno righty Andrew Kown, Nashville lefty Sam Narron and Round Rock righty Cody Eppley.

EASTERN LEAGUE: Altoona shortstop Brock Holt hit just his second home run of the season to lift the West to an 8-3 victory at New Hampshire's Merchantsauto.com Stadium. After the East tied the game at two in the sixth, the West responded with RBI hits by Richmond teammates Charlie Culberson and Roger Kieschnick before scoring four runs in the ninth.

SOUTHERN LEAGUE: The North tagged Rays lefthander Matt Moore for four runs on three hits and a walk in two-thirds of an inning and never relinquished its lead in a 6-3 win in Jackson, Tenn. Chattanooga first baseman Scott Van Slyke earned MVP honors after going 2-for-4 with a double and an RBI for the North.

TEXAS LEAGUE: Hometown hero James Darnell smacked a two-homer in the third inning, leading the South to a 3-2 win in San Antonio. San Antonio righthander Casey Kelly got the start and threw a scoreless inning, striking out one, and the rest of the South's pitchers kept the North off the board until the sixth, when Springfield's Matt Adams hit a solo homer.

CALIFORNIA/CAROLINA LEAGUE: Lake Elsinore third baseman Jedd Gyorko had two hits and two RBIs as the Cal League cruised to a 6-1 win at Modesto. The game was scoreless until the bottom of the third, when the first seven Cal League hitters reached base against Frederick's Bobby Bundy. RBI singles by Gyorko and Fresno's Gary Brown got the scoring started, and both came around to score.

FLORIDA STATE LEAGUE: Daytona Beach third baseman Matt Cerda put the North ahead with an RBI double in the fifth, then scored on Cubs teammate Mike Brenly's single as the North won 5-3 at Clearwater. Bradenton first baseman Aaron Baker—who hit a two-run home run in the fourth and walked twice—earned the game's MVP award in a losing effort.

MIDWEST LEAGUE: Burlington second baseman Nino Leyja hit his first home run of the season , a two-run shot in the sixth, and the West added four more in the eighth to knock off the East, 8-3, at Quad Cities.

SOUTH ATLANTIC LEAGUE: Hometown hero Manny Machado, the Orioles' top prospect, went 2-for-4 in his final low Class A action, helping the North to a 6-3 win at Delmarva. Hitting behind Machado was the minors' top prospect, Bryce Harper. The Nationals phenom, nursing a thumb injury, was pulled from the pregame home run derby and went 0-for-2 with an RBI groundout.

(*Full-season teams only)

TEAM

WINS
San Antonio (Texas)	94
San Jose (California)	90
Columbus (International)	88
Sacramento (Pacific Coast)	88
Round Rock (Pacific Coast)	87

LONGEST WINNING STREAK*
Stockton (California)	17
Columbus (International)	13
Daytona (Florida State)	12
San Jose (California)	12
San Jose (California)	12

LOSSES
Rochester (International)	91
Corpus Christi (Texas)	90
Norfolk (International)	87
Carolina (Southern)	86
Lake County (Midwest)	86

LONGEST LOSING STREAK*
Delmarva (South Atlantic)	14
Jupiter (Florida State)	13
Corpus Christi (Texas)	12
West Michigan (Midwest)	12
Potomac (Carolina)	11

BATTING AVERAGE*
Las Vegas (Pacific Coast)	.307
Colo. Springs (Pacific Coast)	.305
Reno (Pacific Coast)	.298
Albuquerque (Pacific Coast)	.292
Round Rock (Pacific Coast)	.289

RUNS
Reno (Pacific Coast)	933
Colorado Springs (Pacific Coast)	932
Tacoma (Pacific Coast)	893
Las Vegas (Pacific Coast)	869
Albuquerque (Pacific Coast)	854

HOME RUNS
Albuquerque (Pacific Coast)	183
Reno (Pacific Coast)	178
Sacramento (Pacific Coast)	178
Round Rock (Pacific Coast)	176
Tacoma (Pacific Coast)	176

STOLEN BASES
Dayton (Midwest)	228
Fort Wayne (Midwest)	220
Potomac (Carolina)	215
Fresno (Pacific Coast)	209
Northwest Arkansas (Texas)	205

EARNED RUN AVERAGE*
Frederick (Carolina)	3.22
Savannah (South Atlantic)	3.26
Myrtle Beach (Carolina)	3.32
Gwinnett (International)	3.33
Dayton (Midwest)	3.39

STRIKEOUTS
Dayton (Midwest)	1292
Gwinnett (International)	1223
Hickory (South Atlantic)	1199
Harrisburg (Eastern)	1187
Bakersfield (California)	1184

INDIVIDUAL BATTING

BATTING AVERAGE*
Jose Altuve (Lancaster/Corpus Christi)	.389
David Cooper (Las Vegas)	.364
Collin Cowgill (Reno)	.354
Vinnie Catricala (High Desert/Jackson)	.349
Juan Lagares (St. Lucie/Binghamton)	.349

RUNS
Robbie Grossman (Bradenton)	127
Alex Liddi (Tacoma)	121
Jedd Gyorko (Lake Elsinore/San Antonio)	119
Matt Long (Inland Empire/Arkansas)	119
Daniel Carroll (High Desert)	117

HITS
Jedd Gyorko (Lake Elsinore/San Antonio)	192
Gary Brown (San Jose)	188
Vinnie Catricala (High Desert/Jackson)	182
Starling Marte (Altoona)	178
Jermaine Mitchell (Midland/Sacramento)	178

TOP HITTING STREAKS
Abraham Almonte (Tampa)	34
Anderson Hernandez (Okla. City)	30
Brian Barden (Round Rock)	28
Josh Rutledge (Modesto)	27
Bryce Brentz (Greenville)	26

MOST HITS (ONE GAME)
Tyler Austin (Staten Island)	6
Omar Quintanilla (Round Rock)	6
D'Vontrey Richardson (Brevard Co.)	6
141 players	5

TOTAL BASES
Jedd Gyorko (Lake Elsinore/San Antonio)	318
Vincent Catricala (High Desert/Jackson)	313
Angelo Songco (Rancho Cucamonga)	310
Bryan LaHair (Iowa)	303
Tim Wheeler (Tulsa)	300

EXTRA-BASE HITS
Angelo Songco (Rancho Cucamonga)	81
Vinnie Catricala (High Desert/Jackson)	77
Bryan LaHair (Iowa)	76
Alfredo Silverio (Chattanooga)	76
Jedd Gyorko (Lake Elsinore/San Antonio)	74
Joe Terdoslavich (Lynchburg)	74

DOUBLES
Joe Terdoslavich (Lynchburg)	52
David Cooper (Las Vegas)	51
Vinnie Catricala (High Desert/Jackson)	48
Angelo Songco (Rancho Cucamonga)	48
Jedd Gyorko (Lake Elsinore/San Antonio)	47

TRIPLES
Jeremy Moore (Salt Lake)	18
Alfredo Silverio (Chattanooga)	18
Cole Gillespie (Reno)	16
Kevin Mattison (Jacksonville)	16
Jermaine Mitchell (Midland/Sacramento)	16

HOME RUNS
Bryan LaHair (Iowa)	38
Ian Gac (Winston-Salem)	33
Tim Wheeler (Tulsa)	33
Matt Adams (Springfield)	32
Corey Dickerson (Asheville)	32
Ryan Lavarnway (Portland/Pawtucket)	32
Jai Miller (Sacramento)	32
Jorge Vazquez (Scranton/WB)	32

RUNS BATTED IN
Nolan Arenado (Modesto)	122
Jedd Gyorko (Lake Elsinore/San Antonio)	114
Angelo Songco (Rancho Cucamonga)	114
Nathan Freiman (Lake Elsinore)	111
Bryan LaHair (Iowa)	109
Nick Stavinoha (Memphis)	109
Chad Tracy (Round Rock)	109

MOST RBIS (ONE GAME)
Corey Dickerson (Asheville)	10
Chad Huffman (Columbus)	10
Chris Wallace (Lexington)	9
Eight tied at	8

WALKS
Robbie Grossman (Bradenton)	104
Jaff Decker (San Antonio)	103
Conner Crumbliss (Stockton)	96
Kody Hinze (Lancaster/Corpus Christi)	94
Jermaine Mitchell (Midland/Sacramento)	93

STRIKEOUTS
Cody Johnson (Trenton/Tampa)	194
Dusty Coleman (Sacramento/Stockton)	185
Jared Mitchell (Winston-Salem)	183
Jai Miller (Sacramento)	179
Keon Broxton (South Bend/Visalia)	172
Trayce Thompson (Kannapolis)	172

STOLEN BASES
Billy Hamilton (Dayton)	103
Anthony Gose (New Hampshire)	70
Rymer Liriano (Lake Elsinore/Fort Wayne)	66
Daniel Carroll (High Desert)	62
Rico Noel (Lake Elsinore/Fort Wayne)	62

CAUGHT STEALING
Rymer Liriano (Lake Elsinore/Fort Wayne)	21
Billy Hamilton (Dayton)	20
Gary Brown (San Jose)	19
Rafael Ortega (Asheville)	19
Lee Haydel (Huntsville)	18
Drew Maggi (West Virginia/Bradenton)	18
Jermaine Mitchell (Midland/Sacramento)	18
Andrelton Simmons (Lynchburg)	18
Jordany Valdespin (Binghamton/Buffalo)	18

ON-BASE PERCENTAGE*
David Cooper (Las Vegas)	.439
Ryan Langerhans (Tacoma/Reno)	.437
Paul Goldschmidt (Mobile)	.435
Adam Eaton (Visalia/Mobile)	.434
Jermaine Mitchell (Midland/Sacramento)	.430

SLUGGING PERCENTAGE*
Bryan LaHair (Iowa)	.664
Anthony Rizzo (Tucson)	.652
Kent Matthes (Modesto)	.642
Corey Dickerson (Asheville)	.629
Cody Ransom (Reno)	.629

ON BASE PLUS SLUGGING*
Bryan LaHair (Iowa)	1.070
Paul Goldschmidt (Mobile)	1.061
Anthony Rizzo (Tucson)	1.056
Cody Ransom (Reno)	1.034
Scott Van Slyke (Chattanooga)	1.022

HIT BY PITCH
Jared Prince (Myrtle Beach)	30
Nate Roberts (Beloit)	29
Tyler Bortnick (Charlotte)	25
Seth Loman (Birmingham)	24
Gary Brown (San Jose)	23
Tony Delmonico (Rancho Cucamonga)	23
Adam Eaton (Visalia/Mobile)	23
Adam Heether (Sacramento/Midland)	23

SACRIFICE BUNTS
Christian Colon (NW Arkansas)	21
Geulin Beltre (Kane County)	16
Angel Franco (Kane County)	16
Tyler Pastornicky (Mississippi/Gwinnett)	16
Anthony Phillips (High Desert/Clinton)	16

SACRIFICE FLIES
Nolan Arenado (Modesto)	14
Matt Clark (Tucson)	13
Christian Villanueva (Hickory)	13
Stephen Vogt (Montgomery/Durham)	13
Michael Sheridan (Charlotte)	12

BATTING AVERAGE*

BY POSITION
Catchers
Ramon Cabrera (Bradenton)	.343
Steve Clevenger (Iowa/Tennessee)	.319
Travis d'Arnaud (New Hampshire)	.311
Yasmani Grandal (Bakersfield/Carolina/Louisville)	.305
A.J. Jimenez (Dunedin)	.303

FIRST BASEMEN
David Cooper (Las Vegas)	.364
Scott Van Slyke (Chattanooga)	.348
Wes Timmons (Midland/Sacramento)	.341
Anthony Rizzo (Tucson)	.331
Bryan LaHair (Iowa)	.331

SECOND BASEMEN
Jose Altuve (Lancaster/Corpus Christi)	.389
Johnny Giavotella (Omaha)	.338
Kyle Seager (Jackson/Tacoma)	.333
Tyler Kuhn (Charlotte/Birmingham)	.333
Josh Satin (Binghamton/Buffalo)	.323

THIRD BASEMEN
Vincent Catricala (High Desert/Jackson)	.349

Taylor Green (Huntsville/Nashville)	.336
Jedd Gyorko (Lake Elsinore/San Antonio)	.333
Elevys Gonzalez (Bradenton)	.322
Cody Ransom (Reno)	.317

SHORTSTOPS

Josh Rutledge (Modesto)	.348
Gil Velazquez (Salt Lake)	.328
Brian Dozier (Fort Myers/New Britain)	.320
Tyler Pastornicky (Mississippi/Gwinnett)	.314
Andrelton Simmons (Lynchburg)	.311

OUTFIELDERS

Collin Cowgill (Reno)	.354
Juan Lagares (St. Lucie/Binghamton)	.349
Denis Phipps (Carolina/Louisville)	.346
Gary Brown (San Jose)	.336
Kent Matthes (Modesto)	.334

DESIGNATED HITTERS

Ricardo Nanita (New Hampshire/Las Vegas)	.330
Clint Robinson (Omaha)	.326
Adrian Cardenas (Sacramento)	.314
Paul McAnulty (Salt Lake)	.311
Donald Lutz (Dayton)	.301

INDIVIDUAL PITCHING

EARNED RUN AVERAGE*

Michael Fiers (Huntsville/Nashville)	1.86
Matt Moore (Montgomery/Durham)	1.92
Greg Billo (Kane County)	1.93
Eric Surkamp (Richmond/San Jose)	1.94
Joseph Wieland (Myrtle Beach/Frisco/San Antonio)	1.97

WORST ERA*

Alan Johnson (Colorado Springs)	7.43
Scott Richmond (Las Vegas)	7.33
Shawn Haviland (Midland)	7.08
Zachary Grimmett (Lancaster)	6.81
Nick Schnaitmann (Modesto/Asheville)	6.64

WINS

Julio Rodriguez (Clearwater)	16
Brad Peacock (Harrisburg/Syracuse)	15
Julio Teheran (Gwinnett)	15
Jared Wesson (Lakeland)	15
Cameron Bayne (Charlotte/Birmingham/Winston-Salem)	15
David Buchanan (Lakewood/Clearwater)	14
Stephen Fife (Portland/Chattanooga)	14
Graham Godfrey (Midland/Sacramento)	14
Drew Hutchison (Lansing/Dunedin/New Hampshire)	14
Casey Lawrence (Lansing/Dunedin)	14
Josh Smith (Dayton)	14

LOSSES

Edgar Olmos (Jupiter)	17
J.R. Bradley (South Bend)	16
Wilfredo Boscan (Frisco/Myrtle Beach)	15
Chad James (Jupiter)	15
Mark Cohoon (Binghamton/Buffalo)	14
Scott Diamond (Rochester)	14
Robert Donovan (Lancaster)	14
Shane Greene (Charleston)	14
Eric Hacker (Rochester)	14
Jay Jackson (Iowa)	14
Yoervis Medina (AZL/High Desert/Jackson)	14

GAMES

Brad Brach (San Antonio/Tucson)	67
Colt Hynes (Tucson/San Antonio)	67
Nick Vincent (San Antonio)	66
Jim Miller (Colorado Springs)	65
Luis Perdomo (Tucson)	65

GAMES STARTED

Matt Yourkin (Fresno)	29
Brian Bass (Lehigh Valley)	28
Josh Bowman (Burlington)	28
Josh Butler (Nashville)	28
Alexander Colome (Charlotte/Montgomery)	28
Shane Dyer (Montgomery)	28
Trevor Feeney (Lakeland/Toledo/Erie)	28
Robert Gilliam (Stockton)	28
Michael Goodnight (Lake County/Kinston)	28
Jeremy Hefner (Tucson)	28
Austin Hyatt (Reading)	28
Austin Kirk (Peoria)	28
Tom Koehler (New Orleans)	28
Shane Loux (Fresno)	28
Kyle McPherson (Bradenton/Altoona)	28

Dan Merklinger (Huntsville)	28
Edgar Olmos (Jupiter)	28
Curtis Partch (Bakersfield/Carolina)	28
Red Patterson (Great Lakes/Rancho Cucamonga)	28
Ariel Pena (Inland Empire/Salt Lake)	28
Amaury Rivas (Nashville)	28
Ross Seaton (Corpus Christi)	28
Tim Sexton (Albuquerque/Great Lakes)	28
Eric Smith (Visalia)	28
Jerry Sullivan (Lake Elsinore)	28
Elih Villanueva (New Orleans)	28

COMPLETE GAMES

Zeke Spruill (Lynchburg/Mississippi)	6
Matt Shoemaker (Salt Lake/Arkansas)	5
Oliver Drake (Norfolk/Frederick/Bowie)	4
Dae-Eun Rhee (Daytona)	4
13 tied at	3

SHUTOUTS

Christian Bergman (Tri-City)	2
Dan Houston (Modesto/Tulsa)	2
Trevor May (Clearwater)	2
D.J. Mitchell (Scranton/WB)	2
Wilson Palacios (Connecticut)	2
Matt Shoemaker (Salt Lake/Arkansas)	2
Joseph Wieland (Myrtle Beach/Frisco/San Antonio)	2

SAVES

Heath Hembree (San Jose/Richmond)	38
Cory Burns (Akron)	35
Preston Guilmet (Kinston)	35
Brad Brach (San Antonio/Tucson)	34
Wes Etheridge (Dunedin/New Hampshire)	33

INNINGS PITCHED

Shane Loux (Fresno)	179.1
Matt Shoemaker (Salt Lake/Arkansas)	177.1
Zeke Spruill (Lynchburg/Mississippi)	174.2
Red Patterson (Great Lakes/Rancho Cucamonga)	173.1
Terry Doyle (Winston-Salem/Birmingham)	173.0

WALKS

Nevin Griffith (Birmingham)	96
Tyler Matzek (Modesto/Asheville)	96
Caleb Brewer (Rome/Lynchburg)	89
Cameron Greathouse (Peoria/Boise/AZL)	87
Christopher Archer (Montgomery/Durham)	86

STRIKEOUTS

Edwar Cabrera (Asheville/Modesto)	217
Matt Moore (Montgomery/Durham)	210
Trevor May (Clearwater)	208
Tyler Skaggs (Visalia/Mobile)	198
Chad Bettis (Modesto)	184

HITS ALLOWED

Manuel Flores (Salt Lake/Inland Empire)	225
Curtis Partch (Bakersfield/Carolina)	216
Ronald Bay (Salt Lake)	207
Tim Sexton (Albuquerque/Great Lakes)	207
Chris Sorce (High Desert)	206

HOME RUNS ALLOWED

Andrew Baldwin (Rochester)	33
Luke French (Tacoma)	30
Thad Weber (Toledo)	28

| James Gillheeney (High Desert/Jackson) | 27 |
| Gaby Hernandez (Charlotte/Reno) | 27 |

STRIKEOUTS PER NINE INNINGS (STARTERS)*

Trevor May (Clearwater)	12.37
Matt Moore (Montgomery/Durham)	12.19
Edwar Cabrera (Asheville/Modesto)	11.69
Tyler Skaggs (Visalia/Mobile)	11.25
Jose Cisnero (Lancaster)	11.09

STRIKEOUTS PER NINE INNINGS (RELIEVERS)*

Christopher Manno (Hagerstown/Bakersfield)	14.92
Jonathan Arias (Clinton)	14.35
Ryan Kussmaul (Winston-Salem)	13.81
Shawn Tolleson (Great Lakes/Rancho/Chattanooga)	13.70
Danny Barnes (Lansing)	13.50
Brad Boxberger (Carolina/Louisville)	13.50

BATTING AVERAGE AGAINST (STARTERS)*

Brad Peacock (Harrisburg/Syracuse)	.183
Matt Moore (Montgomery/Durham)	.184
Julio Rodriguez (Clearwater)	.186
Keyvius Sampson (Fort Wayne)	.192
Tyler Thornburg (Wisconsin/Brevard County)	.195

BATTING AVERAGE AGAINST (RELIEVERS)*

Christopher Manno (Hagerstown/Bakersfield)	.127
Shane Lindsay (Birmingham/Charlotte)	.137
Drew Hayes (Dayton)	.141
Brad Boxberger (Carolina/Louisville)	.152
Addison Reed (Kannapolis/W-S/Birm./Charlotte)	.157

MOST STRIKEOUTS/ONE GAME

Xavier Cedeno (Corpus Christi)	14
Robert Erlin (Frisco)	14
Trevor May (Clearwater)	14
Brad Peacock (Harrisburg)	14
Ariel Pena (Inland Empire)	14
Jon Michael Redding (Rancho Cucamonga)	14
Daniel Renken (Dayton)	14

WILD PITCHES

Matt Thompson (Hickory)	30
Steven Wright (Columbus/Lake County/Kinston/Akron)	27
Caleb Brewer (Rome/Lynchburg)	26
Tyler Cravy (Wisconsin/Helena)	24
Braulio Lara (Bowling Green/Binghamton)	24

BALKS

Frank Del Valle (Daytona/Peoria/AZL)	6
Martin Perez (Round Rock/Frisco)	6
Carlos Perez (Rome)	6
Michael Blazek (Memphis/Springfield)	5
Ryan Feierabend (Lehigh Valley)	5
Wes Mugarian (Billings)	5
Luis Noel (Delmarva)	5
Santo Perez (Spokane)	5
Amaury Rivas (Nashville)	5
Zach Russell (Quad Cities)	5
Manuel Soliman (Beloit)	5
J.C. Sulbaran (Bakersfield)	5

HIT BATTERS

Jheyson Manzueta (Greensboro/Jamestown)	23
Gary Daley (Sacramento/Stockton/Midland)	19
Mitch Atkins (Frederick/Bowie/Norfolk)	16
Tom Ebert (Salem)	16
Joe Gardner (Akron/Tulsa)	16
Alex Koronis (Charlotte)	16
Matt Palmer (Salt Lake)	16
Stolmy Pimentel (Portland/Salem)	16
Josh Ravin (Bakersfield/Carolina)	16
Wes Roemer (Mobile/Reno)	16

INDIVIDUAL FIELDING

MOST ERRORS

Edward Salcedo (Rome)	47
Gustavo Pierre (Lansing/Bluefield)	44
Aderlin Rodriguez (Savannah)	44
Arismendy Alcantara (Peoria)	40
Billy Hamilton (Dayton)	39
Jose Pirela (Trenton)	39
Juan Silverio (Kannapolis/Winston-Salem)	39

JERRY HALE

Michael Fiers

MINOR LEAGUES

MINOR LEAGUES

	INTERNATIONAL LEAGUE	PACIFIC COAST LEAGUE	EASTERN LEAGUE	SOUTHERN LEAGUE	TEXAS LEAGUE	CALIFORNIA LEAGUE	CAROLINA LEAGUE	FLORIDA STATE LEAGUE	MIDWEST LEAGUE	SOUTH ATLANTIC LEAGUE
Best Batting Prospect	Dayan Viciedo, Charlotte	Brett Lawrie, Las Vegas	Will Middlebrooks, Portland	Paul Goldschmidt, Mobile	Mike Trout, Arkansas	Jedd Gyorko, Lake Elsinore	Tyler Townsend, Frederick	Hak-Ju Lee, Charlotte	Jake Marisnick, Lansing	Bryce Harper, Hagerstown
Best Power Prospect	Ryan Lavarnway, Pawtucket	Anthony Rizzo, Tucson	Tyler Moore, Harrisburg	Paul Goldschmidt, Mobile	Tim Wheeler, Tulsa	Michael Choice, Stockton	Bryce Brentz, Salem	Jonathan Singleton, Clearwater	Yazy Arbelo, South Bend	Bryce Harper, Hagerstown
Best Strike-Zone Judgment	Alex Presley, Indianapolis	Dustin Ackley, Tacoma	Alex Hassan, Portland	Paul Goldschmidt, Mobile	Jaff Decker, San Antonio	Kody Hinze, Lancaster	Tyler Holt, Kinston	Robbie Grossman, Bradenton	Nick Shaw, Wisconsin	Ramon Flores, Charleston
Best Baserunner	Ezequiel Carrera, Columbus	Colin Cowgill, Reno	Greg Miclat, Bowie	A.J. Pollock, Mobile	Mike Trout, Arkansas	Gary Brown, San Jose	Jeff Kobernus, Potomac	Tyler Bortnick, Charlotte	Billy Hamilton, Dayton	Felix Sanchez, Greenville
Fastest Baserunner	Jose Constanza, Gwinnett	Dee Gordon, Albuquerque	Anthony Gose, New Hampshire	Kevin Mattison, Jacksonville	Derrick Robinson, Northwest Arkansas	Gary Brown, San Jose	Leury Garcia, Myrtle Beach	Hak-Ju Lee, Charlotte	Billy Hamilton, Dayton	Felix Sanchez, Greenville
Best Pitching Prospect	Julio Teheran, Gwinnett	Jordan Lyles, Oklahoma City	Brad Peacock, Harrisburg	Matt Moore, Montgomery	Garrett Richards, Arkansas	Tyler Skaggs, Visalia	Drew Pomeranz, Kinston	Matt Harvey, St. Lucie	Carlos Martinez, Quad Cities	Jameson Taillon, West Virginia
Best Fastball	Julio Teheran, Gwinnett	Dan Cortes, Tacoma	Henderson Alvarez, New Hampshire	Matt Moore, Montgomery	Shelby Miller, Springfield	Chad Bettis, Modesto	Hector Nelo, Potomac	Carlos Martinez, Palm Beach	Carlos Martinez, Quad Cities	Jameson Taillon, West Virginia
Best Breaking Pitch	Jairo Asencio, Gwinnett	Rex Brothers, Colorado Springs	Eric Surkamp, Richmond	Brad Hand, Jacksonville	Garrett Richards, Arkansas	Tyler Skaggs, Visalia	Arodys Vizcaino, Lynchburg	Jordan Swagerty, Palm Beach	James Paxton, Clinton	Jameson Taillon, West Virginia
Best Changeup	Tom Milone, Syracuse	Brad Mills, Las Vegas	Eric Surkamp, Richmond	Marquis Fleming, Montgomery	Dallas Keuchel, Corpus Christi	Jose Guzman, Stockton	Robbie Erlin, Myrtle Beach	Darin Gorski, St. Lucie	Tyler Thornburg, Wisconsin	Edwar Cabrera, Asheville
Best Control	Tom Milone, Syracyse	Brad Mills, Las Vegas	Brad Peacock, Harrisburg	Pat Corbin, Mobile	Matt Shoemaker, Arkansas	Josh Lansford, Stockton	Joe Wieland, Myrtle Beach	Nestor Molina, Dunedin	David Holmberg, South Bend	Edwar Cabrera, Asheville
Best Reliever	Jairo Asencio, Gwinnett	Jose Ceda, New Orleans	Cory Burns, Akron	Ryan Cook, Birmingham	Brad Brach, San Antonio	Heath Hembree, San Jose	Preston Guilment, Kinston	Wes Etheridge, Dunedin	Steve Turnbull, Lansing	Chris Manno, Hagerstown
Best Defensive Catcher	Devin Mesoraco, Louisville	Anthony Recker, Sacramento	Travis d'Arnaud, Reading	Martin Maldonado, Huntsville	Alberto Rosario, Arkansas	Tommy Joseph, San Jose	Sandy Leon, Potomac	A.J. Jimenez, Dunedin	Micah Gibbs, Peoria	Christian Vazquez, Greenville
Best Defensive First Baseman	Jim Gallagher, Louisville	Efran Navarro, Salt Lake	Chris Parmalee, New Britain	Paul Goldschmidt, Mobile	Ben Paulsen, Tulsa	Anthony Aliotti, Stockton	Tyler Townsend, Frederick	Michael Sheridan, Charlotte	Michael Gonzales, Beloit	Miles Head, Greenville
Best Defensive Second Baseman	Will Rhymes, Toledo	Eric Farris, Nashville	Steve Lombardozzi, Harrisburg	Sergio Miranda, Huntsville	Tyler Ladendorf, Midland	Ryan Cavan, San Jose	Rey Navarro, Wilmington	Cesar Hernandez, Clearwater	Kolten Wong, Quad Cities	Carlos Willoughby, Augusta
Best Defensive Third Baseman	Brandon Laird, Scranton/Wilkes-Barre	Matt Dominguez, New Orleans	Francisco Martinez, Erie	Ryan Wheeler, Mobile	Tommy Mendoca, Frisco	Nolan Arenado, Modesto	Mike Olt, Myrtle Beach	Matt Cerda, Daytona	Giovanny Urshela, Lake County	Christian Villanueva, Hickory
Best Defensive Shortstop	Jose Iglesias, Pawtucket	Everth Cabrera, Tucson	Adeiny Hechavarria, New Hampshire	Taylor Harbin, Mobile	Beamer Weems, San Antonio	Dusty Coleman, Stockton	Andrelton Simmons, Lynchburg	Hak-Ju Lee, Charlotte	Dixon Machado, West Michigan	Jurickson Profar, Hickory
Best Infield Arm	Juan Francisco, Louisville	Everth Cabrera, Tucson	Juan Diaz, Akron	Carlos Triunfel, Jackson	Hector Gomez, Tulsa	Didi Gregorius, Bakersfield	Andrelton Simmons, Lynchburg	Junior Lake, Daytona	Dixon Machado, West Michigan	Jurickson Profar, Hickory
Best Defensive Outfielder	Ezequiel Carrera, Columbus	Colin Cowgill, Reno	Anthony Gose, New Hampshire	A.J. Pollock, Mobile	Mike Trout, Arkansas	Gary Brown, San Jose	Ryan Strausborger, Myrtle Beach	Matt den Dekker, St. Lucie	Matt Szczur, Peoria	Slade Heathcott, Charleston
Best Outfield Arm	Gorkys Hernandez, Indianapolis	Brett Carroll, Nashville	Moises Sierra, New Hampshire	Denis Phipps, Carolina	Jaff Decker, San Antonio	Blake Smith, Rancho Cucamonga	Nick Francis, Wilmington	Aaron Hicks, Fort Myers	Anthony Giansanti, Peoria	Marcell Ozuna, Lakewood
Most Exciting Player	Desmond Jennings, Durham	Collin Cowgill, Reno	Anthony Gose, New Hampshire	Paul Goldschmidt, Mobile	Mike Trout, Arkansas	Gary Brown, San Jose	Andrelton Simmons, Lynchburg	Hak-Ju Lee, Charlotte	Rymer Liriano, Fort Wayne	Bryce Harper, Hagerstown
Best Manager Prospect	Mike Sarbaugh, Columbus	Brett Butler, Reno	Mark Parent, Reading	Andy Barkett, Jacksonville	Steve Buechele, Frisco	Ken Griffey, Bakersfield	Aaron Holbert, Kinston	Dusty Wathan, Clearwater	Mike Redmond, Lansing	Ryan Ellis, Savannah

Awards highlight long-term success

TRIPLE-A: Colorado Springs Sky Sox (Pacific Coast)

Dave Elmore's five minor league teams dot the country and the minor leagues' classifications: from Triple-A Colorado Springs to Rookie-level Idaho Falls. One trait that carries over from team to team is a commitment to his fans and employees.

That has certainly been the case in Colorado Springs, one of the Pacific Coast League's charter members that saw baseball return home when Elmore moved the Honolulu Islanders there in 1988. Elmore assured the team's long-term future in Colorado Springs by paying for the $3.2 million construction of a new ballpark. A naming rights deal led to a $4 million renovation of the ballpark in 2005, which included amenities for players (new clubhouses and underground batting cages) and fans (new concourse, five-tiered picnic area and upgraded luxury suite level).

Colorado Springs is one of the smallest markets in Triple-A, but the Sky Sox have set team attendance records in each of the past three seasons.

DOUBLE-A: Harrisburg Senators (Eastern)

For many years, the Harrisburg Senators' island ballpark had been anything but a destination. With bleacher seating throughout, the franchise had become one of the minors' worst draws. That changed soon after an ownership group headed by Michael Reinsdorf purchased the club in 2007 for a reported $13.25 million and started a facelift that made Metro Bank Park look like new.

Along with an emphasis on marketing and promotions, the team has set attendance records in each of the past three seasons. A new video board now stands in right field, and a 6-by-125-foot LED board runs along the left-field wall. A wrap-around boardwalk concourse is among the ballpark's highlights, taking advantage of its sce-nic setting on the Susquehanna River, as do the 21 luxury suites with glass-enclosed views of the playing field in front and the ballpark in back.

LOW CLASS A: Fort Wayne TinCaps (Midwest)

Like many teams around the minors, Fort Wayne has enjoyed the benefits of a new ballpark and marketing campaign, as the team's name and identity changed with the new TinCaps moniker. But Fort Wayne has hardly relied on those factors as it has become one of the top draws in the Midwest League. The TinCaps have proven to be one of the most creative promotional teams in the minors, and that was rewarded when the club was honored by its peers at the Promo Seminar for its "Opening Night in 3-D" event. The TinCaps turned their 26-by-54 foot videoboard to 3-D and made local headlines as they filled the park despite miserable weather conditions.

SHORT-SEASON: Vancouver Canadians (Northwest)

Vancouver thrived in its first season as a Blue Jays affiliate. Team president Andy Dunn believes that relationship will thrive even more in the future. "Being a Jays affiliate has helped with the fact that we can promote our brands across Canada," Dunn said. "One major league team, one minor league team, all working to bring a World Series Championship to Toronto and Canada. It will really pay off for us in the future when some of the kids who now start in Vancouver will be visible at the major league level in Toronto."

Though the team's affiliation with the Blue Jays is new, Nat Bailey Stadium certainly is not. The 60-year-old facility underwent a lot of changes prior to this season in order to help the club and the atmosphere at the ballpark, Marketing the team to a diverse population has continued to help the success of the Canadians, and saw them sell out 30 of their 38 home games this season.

PREVIOUS WINNERS

TRIPLE-A	DOUBLE-A	CLASS A	SHORT-SEASON
2001: Buffalo (International)	2001: Mobile (Southern)	2001: Delmarva (South Atlantic)	2001: Salem-Keizer (Northwest)
2002: Memphis (Pacific Coast)	2002: Chattanooga (Southern)	2002: Fort Myers (Florida State)	2002: Ogden (Pioneer)
2003: Pawtucket (International)	2003: New Britain (Eastern)	2003: Modesto (California)	2003: Spokane (Northwest)
2004: Sacramento (Pacific Coast)	2004: Round Rock (Texas)	2004: Dayton (Midwest)	2004: Burlington (Appalachian)
2005: Toledo (International)	2005: Tulsa (Texas)	2005: Lakewood (South Atlantic)	2005: Brooklyn (New York-Penn)
2006: Durham (International)	2006: Altoona (Eastern)	2006: Daytona (Florida State)	2006: Aberdeen (New York-Penn)
2007: Albuquerque (Pacific Coast)	2007: Frisco (Texas)	2007: Lake Elsinore (California)	2007: Missoula (Pioneer)
2008: Columbus (International)	2008: Birmingham (Southern)	2008: Greensboro (South Atlantic)	2008: Greeneville (Appalachian)
2009: Iowa (Pacific Coast)	2009: New Hampshire (Eastern)	2009: San Jose (California)	2009: Tri-City (New York-Penn)
2010: Louisville (International)	2010: Corpus Christi (Texas)	2010: Lynchburg (Carolina)	2010: Idaho Falls (Pioneer)

The Columbus Clippers went five years without a league title before winning the Governors' Cup in 2010. They didn't have to wait nearly as long for another, blending veterans and prospects to take home the 2011 crown.

The Clippers posted the best regular season record in the International League, including a 49-23 home record in their third year at Huntington Park. Their success carried over to the postseason, where Columbus swept Durham and dropped just one game to Lehigh Valley in the title round before defeating Omaha for a second straight Triple-A National Championship.

Columbus showed plenty of pop at the plate (.769 team OPS) to go with two of the top International League starting pitching performances. The offense was carried by a strong infield behind the trio of Luis Valbuena, Cord Phelps and Jason Kipnis. Minor league veteran Jared Head slugged 24 home runs to place fourth in the IL. Starting pitchers Jeanmar Gomez topped the IL in ERA (2.55) and Zach McAllister ranked seventh with a 3.32 ERA.

Durham overcame a constantly changing roster to win the Southern Division for a second straight season. Even the late-season callups of 2007 No. 1 overall pick Tim Beckham and top pitching prospect Matt Moore were not enough to overcome losing the likes of outfielder Desmond Jennings, lefthander Jake McGee, righthander Alex Cobb and outfielder Brandon Guyer to the big league club. One mainstay in Durham was league MVP Russ Canzler, who hit .314/.401/.530 with 18 home runs. Lefthander Alex Torres was led the IL with 156 strikeouts.

The league's youngest pitcher was also its most dominant, as Gwinnett Braves righthander Julio Teheran tied for first with a 2.55 ERA while

TOP 20 PROSPECTS

1. Matt Moore, lhp, Durham Bulls (Rays)
2. Julio Teheran, rhp, Gwinnett Braves
3. Devin Mesoraco, c, Louisville Bats (Reds)
4. Desmond Jennings, of, Durham Bulls (Rays)
5. Jesus Montero, c, Scranton/Wilkes-Barre Yankees
6. Domonic Brown, of, Lehigh Valley Ironpigs (Phillies)
7. Jason Kipnis, 2b, Columbus Clippers (Indians)
8. Mike Minor, lhp, Gwinnett Braves
9. Brad Peacock, rhp, Syracuse Chiefs (Nationals)
10. Lonnie Chisenhall, 3b, Columbus Clippers (Indians)
11. Zack Cozart, ss, Louisville Bats (Reds)
12. Dayan Viciedo, of/1b, Charlotte Knights (White Sox)
13. Yonder Alonso, 1b/of, Louisville Bats (Reds)
14. Ryan Lavarnway, c, Pawtucket Red Sox
15. Vance Worley, rhp, Lehigh Valley Ironpigs (Phillies)
16. Josh Reddick, of, Pawtucket Red Sox
17. Brandon Guyer, of, Durham Bulls (Rays)
18. Alex Presley, of, Indianapolis Indians (Pirates)
19. Alex Cobb, rhp, Durham Bulls (Rays)
20. Todd Frazier, of/3b/1b, Louisville Bats (Reds)

topping the circuit in wins (15) and capturing the league's MVP and rookie of the year awards. Louisville catcher Devin Mesoraco was the best position prospect in the league and was one of three catchers to make the IL Top 20 Prospects list, joining Scranton/Wilkes-Barre phenom Jesus Montero and Pawtucket's Ryan Lavarnway.

Scranton made news after the season when it announced that it will play its home games in 2012 on the road while the team's ballpark in Pennsylvania goes through a $40 million renovation. The Yankees will play at the homes of five IL franchises (Buffalo, Lehigh Valley, Pawtucket, Rochester and Syracuse) in addition to Batavia, N.Y., which is home to a New York-Penn League franchise.

The Braves were host to an embarrassment of pitching riches for the duration of the year including lefthander Mike Minor and the late-season additions of righthanders Randall Delgado and Arodys Vizcaino.

OVERALL STANDINGS

	W	L	PCT	GB	Manager(s)	Attendance	Average	Last Pennant
Columbus Clippers (Indians)	88	56	.611	—	Mike Sarbaugh	591,884	8,704	2010
Pawtucket Red Sox (Red Sox)	81	61	.570	6	Arnie Beyeler	578,930	8,270	1984
Durham Bulls (Rays)	80	62	.563	7	Charlie Montoyo	462,682	6,517	2009
Lehigh Valley IronPigs (Phillies)	80	64	.556	8	Ryne Sandberg	628,925	9,249	1995
Gwinnett Braves (Braves)	78	65	.545	9 ½	Dave Brundage	351,565	5,095	2007
Indianapolis Indians (Pirates)	76	68	.528	12	Dean Treanor/Jeff Branson	580,082	8,170	2000
Scranton/WB Yankees (Yankees)	73	69	.514	14	Dave Miley	298,098	4,586	2008
Louisville Bats (Reds)	73	71	.507	15	Rick Sweet	601,372	8,716	2001
Charlotte Knights (White Sox)	69	74	.483	18 ½	Joe McEwing	279,107	4,105	1999
Syracuse Chiefs (Nationals)	66	74	.471	20	Randy Knorr	374,680	5,854	1976
Toledo Mud Hens (Tigers)	67	77	.465	21	Phil Nevin	549,438	7,963	2006
Buffalo Bisons (Mets)	61	82	.427	26 ½	Tim Teufel	521,530	7,784	2004
Norfolk Tides (Orioles)	56	87	.392	31 ½	Gary Allenson	397,889	5,684	1985
Rochester Red Wings (Twins)	53	91	.368	35	Tom Nieto	448,024	6,493	1997

Semifinals: Columbus defeated Durham 3-0 and Lehigh Valley defeated Pawtucket 3-1 in best-of-five series. **Finals:** Columbus defeated Lehigh Valley 3-1 in a best-of-five series.

CLUB BATTING

	AVG	G	AB	R	H	2B	3B	HR	RBI	BB	SO	SB	OBP	SLG
Durham	.271	142	4867	669	1318	287	26	136	631	444	1020	75	.337	.424
Louisville	.266	144	4936	654	1315	288	26	146	619	431	1085	68	.331	.424
Columbus	.264	144	4791	716	1266	250	26	152	661	570	1006	82	.347	.422
Scranton/WB	.264	142	4773	612	1262	233	32	124	578	392	1147	92	.326	.405
Indianapolis	.263	144	4872	622	1282	277	45	91	581	408	981	133	.327	.394
Toledo	.262	144	4821	586	1261	248	22	108	555	451	1099	139	.327	.389
Charlotte	.261	143	4713	614	1231	276	24	136	584	460	1188	108	.331	.417
Gwinnett	.260	143	4765	613	1238	214	20	123	573	419	1056	116	.322	.391
Rochester	.257	144	4786	587	1230	252	30	103	537	465	983	71	.328	.387
Syracuse	.257	140	4626	581	1190	248	20	113	544	481	1011	90	.331	.393
Lehigh Valley	.256	144	4726	601	1209	250	28	117	560	422	1102	120	.324	.395
Buffalo	.255	143	4730	570	1205	234	18	101	532	462	1005	52	.325	.376
Pawtucket	.253	142	4719	657	1194	260	21	132	623	544	1036	104	.335	.401
Norfolk	.251	143	4932	601	1238	216	22	119	565	464	1138	94	.319	.376

CLUB PITCHING

	ERA	G	CG	SHO	SV	IP	H	R	ER	HR	BB	SO	AVG
Gwinnett	3.33	143	2	11	41	1264	1160	541	468	106	505	1223	.244
Pawtucket	3.57	142	1	6	42	1251	1113	546	496	123	459	1118	.239
Lehigh Valley	3.68	144	3	12	47	1248	1253	563	510	110	401	1126	.262
Scranton/WB	3.80	142	8	13	39	1230	1195	551	519	122	483	997	.257
Durham	3.87	142	2	9	44	1259	1226	620	541	129	461	1135	.256
Columbus	3.94	144	6	9	45	1253	1270	622	548	118	417	1142	.263
Louisville	4.01	144	1	4	40	1280	1318	641	570	110	431	995	.266
Indianapolis	4.08	144	1	7	42	1278	1227	629	579	101	500	989	.254
Syracuse	4.17	140	2	9	33	1216	1279	598	563	108	379	1079	.271
Charlotte	4.25	143	2	8	36	1236	1196	634	583	120	517	1121	.254
Toledo	4.27	144	3	4	37	1263	1277	655	599	147	480	1064	.263
Norfolk	4.34	143	3	7	27	1277	1319	686	616	129	512	846	.270
Buffalo	4.36	143	1	3	36	1237	1259	669	599	133	467	1013	.265
Rochester	4.76	144	5	7	20	1235	1347	728	654	145	401	1009	.276

CLUB FIELDING

	PCT	PO	A	E	DP		PCT	PO	A	E	DP
Scranton/WB	.987	3691	1324	67	138	Rochester	.980	3706	1419	107	121
Charlotte	.984	3708	1332	84	112	Columbus	.979	3759	1358	109	116
Pawtucket	.984	3753	1336	84	151	Lehigh Valley	.979	3745	1484	110	148
Syracuse	.984	3648	1429	82	118	Toledo	.979	3788	1395	110	138
Durham	.980	3777	1340	107	139	Norfolk	.978	3811	1430	119	144
Indianapolis	.980	3833	1456	108	107	Buffalo	.977	3710	1377	122	117
Louisville	.980	3840	1495	109	127	Gwinnett	.975	3791	1257	129	112

INDIVIDUAL BATTING LEADERS (Minimum 2.7 PA/Team Game)

	AVG	G	AB	R	H	2B	3B	HR	RBI	BB	SO	SB
De Aza, Alejandro, Charlotte	.322	99	385	64	124	29	5	9	37	32	72	22
Hermida, Jeremy, Louisville	.319	105	395	67	126	28	1	17	55	46	97	3
Bates, Aaron, Rochester	.316	106	358	57	113	23	0	7	37	53	90	1
Canzler, Russ, Durham	.314	131	474	78	149	40	4	18	83	67	129	5
Guyer, Brandon, Durham	.312	107	388	78	121	29	5	14	61	35	79	16
Hague, Matt, Indianapolis	.309	141	534	70	165	37	3	12	75	47	68	4
Bowker, John, Indianapolis	.306	106	421	56	129	27	1	15	76	27	73	2
Rhymes, Will, Toledo	.306	104	405	57	124	17	4	3	24	46	46	13
Perez, Timo, Toledo	.304	122	473	43	144	32	0	6	50	29	41	16
Gomez, Mauro, Gwinnett	.304	135	506	76	154	34	2	24	90	38	131	6

INDIVIDUAL PITCHING LEADERS (Minimum 0.8 IP/Team Game)

	W	L	ERA	G	GS	CG	SV	IP	H	R	ER	BB	SO
Gomez, Jeanmar, Columbus	10	7	2.55	21	21	2	0	138	123	54	39	49	107
Teheran, Julio, Gwinnett	15	3	2.55	25	24	0	0	145	123	46	41	48	122
Redmond, Todd, Gwinnett	10	8	2.92	28	27	2	0	170	152	58	55	47	142
Torres, Alexander, Durham	9	7	3.08	27	27	1	0	146	134	61	50	83	156
Below, Duane, Toledo	9	4	3.13	18	18	0	0	115	99	42	40	37	83
Mitchell, D.J., Scranton/WB	13	9	3.18	28	24	3	0	161	155	60	57	63	112
Milone, Tom, Syracuse	12	6	3.22	24	24	0	0	148	137	55	53	16	155
McAllister, Zach, Columbus	12	3	3.32	25	25	3	0	155	155	61	57	31	128
Pena, Tony, Pawtucket	9	6	3.56	33	14	0	3	116	127	51	46	36	65
Weiland, Kyle, Pawtucket	8	10	3.58	24	24	0	0	128	108	54	51	55	126

ALL-STAR TEAM

C: Devin Mesoraco, Louisville. 1B: Matt Hague, Indianapolis. 2B: Jason Kipnis, Columbus. 3B: Russ Canzler, Durham. SS: Zack Cozart, Louisville. OF: Stefan Gartrell, Gwinnett; Alex Presley, Pirates; Dayan Viciedo, Charlotte. DH: Jorge Vazquez, Scranton/W-B. UTIL: Luis Valbuena, Columbus. SP: Julio Teheran, Gwinnett. RP: Tim Wood, Indianapolis.
Most Valuable Player: Russ Canzler, Durham. **Most Valuable Pitcher:** Julio Teheran, Gwinnett. **Rookie of the Year:** Julio Teheran, Gwinnett. **Manager of the Year:** Mike Sarbaugh, Columbus.

DEPARTMENT LEADERS

BATTING

OBP	Bates, Aaron, Rochester	.408
SLG	Canzler, Russ, Durham	.530
OPS	Canzler, Russ, Durham	.930
R	Thompson, Rich, Lehigh Valley	81
H	Hague, Matt, Indianapolis	165
TB	Gomez, Mauro, Gwinnett	264
XBH	Canzler, Russ, Durham	62
2B	Canzler, Russ, Durham	40
3B	Hernandez, Gorkys, Indianapolis	9
	Kipnis, Jason, Columbus	9
HR	Vazquez, Jorge, Scranton/WB	32
RBI	Gartrell, Stefan, Charlotte, Gwinnett	94
SAC	Escobar, Eduardo, Charlotte	15
	Furmaniak, J.J., Durham	15
BB	Anderson, Lars, Pawtucket	80
HBP	Frandsen, Kevin, Lehigh Valley	16
	Thompson, Rich, Lehigh Valley	16
SO	Strieby, Ryan, Toledo	171
SB	Thompson, Rich, Lehigh Valley	48
CS	De Aza, Alejandro, Charlotte	11
AB/SO	Feliciano, Jesus, Buffalo	12.22

PITCHING

G	Thomas, Justin, Indianapolis	63
GS	Bass, Brian, Lehigh Valley	28
GF	Judy, Josh, Columbus	45
SV	Asencio, Jairo, Gwinnett	26
W	Teheran, Julio, Gwinnett	15
L	Diamond, Scott, Rochester	14
	Hacker, Eric, Rochester	14
IP	Redmond, Todd, Gwinnett	169.7
H	Carroll, Scott, Louisville	186
R	Hacker, Eric, Rochester	103
ER	Weber, Thad, Toledo	95
HB	Gallagher, Sean, Indianapolis	15
BB	Torres, Alexander, Durham	83
SO	Torres, Alexander, Durham	156
SO/9	Torres, Alexander, Durham	9.59
SO/9 (RP)	Schwimer, Michael, Lehigh Valley	11.38
BB/9	Milone, Tom, Syracuse	0.97
WP	Brackman, Andrew, Scranton/WB	19
BK	Feierabend, Ryan, Lehigh Valley	5
HR	Baldwin, Andrew, Rochester	33
AVG	Fox, Matt, Pawtucket	.230

FIELDING

C	FPCT	Montero, Jesus, Scranton/WB	.997
	PO	Kratz, Erik, Lehigh Valley	807
	A	Kratz, Erik, Lehigh Valley	69
	E	Mesoraco, Devin, Louisville	10
	DP	Castillo, Wilkin, Gwinnett	9
		Kratz, Erik, Lehigh Valley	9
	PB	Exposito, Luis, Pawtucket	11
1B	FPCT	Gallagher, Jim, Charlotte	.997
	PO	Marrero, Chris, Syracuse	1104
	A	Hague, Matt, Indianapolis	86
	E	Hague, Matt, Indianapolis	15
	DP	Anderson, Lars, Pawtucket	123
2B	FPCT	Barfield, Josh, Lehigh Valley	.984
	PO	Barfield, Josh, Lehigh Valley	189
	A	Barfield, Josh, Lehigh Valley	302
	E	Valaika, Chris, Louisville	12
	DP	Barfield, Josh, Lehigh Valley	77
3B	FPCT	Laird, Brandon, Scranton/WB	.968
	PO	Bell, Josh, Norfolk	76
	A	Bell, Josh, Norfolk	181
	E	Lambin, Chase, Rochester	21
	DP	Laird, Brandon, Scranton/WB	23
SS	FPCT	Iglesias, Jose, Pawtucket	.973
	PO	Olmedo, Ray, Durham	155
	A	Iglesias, Jose, Pawtucket	284
	E	Iorg, Cale, Toledo	19
	DP	Olmedo, Ray, Durham	71
OF	FPCT	Danks, Jordan, Charlotte	.997
	PO	Danks, Jordan, Charlotte	319
	A	Golson, Greg, Scranton/WB	17
		Guyer, Brandon, Durham	17
	E	Head, Jerad, Columbus	6
	DP	Hernandez, Gorkys, Indianapolis	5

MINOR LEAGUES

Pacific Coast League champions of the past have often been built around high-scoring lineups that take advantage of the hitter-friendly ballparks around the league.

But the newly minted Omaha Storm Chasers bucked that trend and rode the league's best pitching performance to the PCL title. Led by righthander Luis Mendoza, the postseason MVP, the Storm Chasers swept Sacramento in the league finals before falling to defending champion Columbus in the Triple-A National Championship.

The 27-year old Mendoza led the league in ERA (2.15), WHIP (1.25) and opponent average (.241) en route to being named the PCL pitcher of the year. The team's most heralded pitcher, lefthander Mike Montgomery, scuffled in a full season with Omaha, finishing 5-11, 5.32.

The Royals opened the season with the best farm system in baseball and sent a talented group through Omaha. First baseman Eric Hosmer earned an early promotion to Kansas City after hitting .439/.525/.582 in just 98 at-bats. He was later joined by third baseman Mike Moustakas, who hit 10 home runs in 223 at-bats before also moving up to Kansas City. Lefthander Danny Duffy and second baseman Johnny Giavotella also passed through Omaha on their way to the majors.

Sacramento captured a fifth consecutive Southern Division crown. Their pitching staff placed second out of 16 teams in ERA, WHIP and home runs allowed.

Iowa finished the year near the bottom of the standings but featured the league MVP, Bryan LeHair. The 28-year-old first baseman, a 39th-round draft pick in 2002, mashed an Iowa record and league-leading 38 home runs. He also topped the circuit in RBIs (109), extra-base hits (76) and

TOP 20 PROSPECTS

1. Brett Lawrie, 3b, Las Vegas 51s (Blue Jays)
2. Dustin Ackley, 2b, Tacoma Rainiers (Mariners)
3. Mike Moustakas, 3b, Omaha Storm Chasers (Royals)
4. Brandon Belt, 1b/of, Fresno Grizzlies (Giants)
5. Anthony Rizzo, 1b, Tucson Padres
6. Dee Gordon, ss, Albuquerque Isotopes (Dodgers)
7. Mike Montgomery, lhp, Omaha Storm Chasers (Royals)
8. Brett Jackson, of, Iowa Cubs
9. Jordan Lyles, rhp, Oklahoma City Redhawks (Astros)
10. Rex Brothers, lhp, Colorado Springs Sky Sox (Rockies)
11. Jemile Weeks, 2b, Sacramento River Cats (Athletics)
12. Martin Perez, lhp, Round Rock Express (Rangers)
13. Leonys Martin, of, Round Rock Express (Rangers)
14. Matt Dominguez, 3b, New Orleans Zephyrs (Marlins)
15. Eric Thames, of, Las Vegas 51s (Blue Jays)
16. Johnny Giavotella, 2b, Omaha Storm Chasers (Royals)
17. Charlie Blackmon, of, Colorado Springs Sky Sox (Rockies)
18. Logan Schafer, of, Nashville Sounds (Brewers)
19. Alex Liddi, 3b, Tacoma Rainiers (Mariners)
20. Collin Cowgill, of, Reno Aces (Diamondbacks)

total bases (303), while placing second in OPS (1.070).

Reno outfielder Collin Cowgill took home the league's rookie of the year award. In 98 games before earning a major league promotion from the Diamondbacks, Cowgill hit .354/.430/.554 with 13 home runs and 30 stolen bases. Las Vegas third baseman Brett Lawrie didn't qualify for the batting title but hit .353 with 18 home runs. The 21-year-old, acquired by the Blue Jays from the Brewers in an offseason trade for Shaun Marcum, hit .293/.373/.580 in Toronto after getting called up.

The Tucson Padres made their debut in the league, though how long the team stays in town is uncertain. Padres owner Jeff Moorad bought the team and moved it there from Portland, but it was supposed to be a temporary move as he waited for a new ballpark in the San Diego suburb of Escondido. Financing for the project fell through, however, leaving the club's future unclear.

OVERALL STANDINGS

Team (Organization)	W	L	PCT	GB	Manager(s)	Attendance	Average	Last Pennant
Sacramento River Cats (Athletics)	88	56	.611	—	Darren Bush	600,306	8,455	2008
Round Rock Express (Rangers)	87	57	.604	1	Bobby Jones/Spike Owen	618,261	8,587	Never
Omaha Storm Chasers (Royals)	79	63	.556	8	Mike Jirschele	410,326	5,947	2011
Memphis Redbirds (Cardinals)	77	66	.538	10½	Chris Maloney	493,528	7,050	2009
Reno Aces (Diamondbacks)	77	67	.535	11	Brett Butler	432,314	6,089	2006
Las Vegas 51s (Blue Jays)	71	73	.493	17	Marty Brown	314,032	4,486	1988
Nashville Sounds (Brewers)	71	73	.493	17	Don Money	335,143	4,857	2005
Albuquerque Isotopes (Dodgers)	70	74	.486	18	Lorenzo Bundy	578,328	8,145	1994
Tacoma Rainiers (Mariners)	70	74	.486	18	Daren Brown	378,518	5,331	2010
New Orleans Zephyrs (Marlins)	69	74	.483	18½	Greg Norton	372,017	5,315	2001
Okla. City Redhawks (Astros)	68	75	.476	19½	Tony DeFrancesco	378,877	5,262	1965
Iowa Cubs (Cubs)	66	77	.462	21½	Bill Dancy	500,675	7,256	Never
Fresno Grizzlies (Giants)	65	79	.451	23	Steve Decker	494,051	6,958	Never
Tucson Padres (Padres)	65	79	.451	23	Terry Kennedy	242,136	3,410	2006
Colorado Springs Sky Sox (Rockies)	64	80	.444	24	Stu Cole	339,009	4,843	1995
Salt Lake Bees (Angels)	62	82	.431	26	Keith Johnson	437,769	6,438	1979

Semifinals: Omaha defeated Round Rock 3-1 and Sacramento defeated Reno 3-2 in best-of-five series. **Finals:** Omaha defeated Sacramento 3-0 in a best-of-five series.

CLUB BATTING

	AVG	G	AB	R	H	2B	3B	HR	RBI	BB	SO	SB	OBP	SLG
Las Vegas	.307	144	5107	869	1567	352	40	133	822	577	943	135	.378	.470
Colorado Springs	.305	144	5131	932	1564	334	56	166	862	484	955	87	.366	.489
Reno	.298	144	4993	933	1487	302	67	178	869	643	987	143	.381	.492
Albuquerque	.292	144	4961	854	1451	251	39	183	805	571	1081	85	.370	.469
Omaha	.289	142	4859	768	1406	265	50	122	710	476	826	152	.356	.440
Round Rock	.289	144	5086	839	1472	301	39	176	806	514	953	118	.358	.468
Salt Lake	.289	144	4975	755	1436	284	51	120	712	465	1014	140	.352	.439
Tacoma	.289	144	5153	893	1491	284	31	176	840	620	1169	89	.368	.459
Iowa	.284	143	4872	750	1383	292	40	141	703	439	1047	71	.345	.447
Sacramento	.283	144	5052	842	1431	292	27	178	790	630	1064	140	.367	.457
Nashville	.282	144	4912	746	1383	283	23	153	703	510	941	63	.354	.442
Tucson	.282	144	5047	810	1424	334	40	139	759	522	1025	105	.351	.447
Fresno	.277	144	4924	735	1362	264	27	143	682	509	975	209	.350	.428
New Orleans	.273	143	4840	704	1322	281	17	136	659	454	899	95	.343	.423
Memphis	.270	143	4877	722	1318	252	27	129	677	588	1043	84	.354	.412
Oklahoma City	.260	143	4771	619	1242	237	38	88	566	540	1016	143	.341	.381

CLUB PITCHING

	ERA	G	CG	SHO	SV	IP	H	R	ER	HR	BB	SO	AVG
Memphis	4.10	143	2	4	37	1276	1279	645	581	135	493	1002	.264
Sacramento	4.21	144	0	5	38	1290	1285	687	603	129	502	1118	.259
Omaha	4.26	142	3	9	41	1252	1274	666	593	138	490	991	.264
Nashville	4.27	144	2	6	32	1264	1307	677	599	125	570	1003	.268
Oklahoma City	4.63	143	0	4	42	1259	1402	717	647	135	506	984	.285
New Orleans	4.76	143	4	13	43	1247	1324	747	660	136	543	974	.276
Round Rock	4.87	144	1	4	41	1285	1435	759	695	143	536	1048	.283
Fresno	5.03	144	2	4	40	1270	1419	808	710	141	550	981	.284
Tacoma	5.39	144	1	1	34	1283	1459	848	768	162	561	1075	.287
Iowa	5.52	143	1	3	35	1238	1421	817	759	154	526	1021	.291
Salt Lake	5.62	144	6	4	33	1265	1496	866	790	167	501	919	.301
Reno	5.64	144	3	4	29	1258	1467	846	789	164	538	886	.293
Tucson	5.72	144	1	3	36	1284	1509	908	816	135	621	1025	.295
Albuquerque	5.73	144	5	5	27	1256	1456	892	800	169	568	932	.293
Las Vegas	5.76	144	5	8	25	1262	1504	883	807	175	515	1010	.298
Colorado Springs	6.41	144	0	1	30	1260	1711	1005	897	153	522	969	.329

CLUB FIELDING

	PCT	PO	A	E	DP		PCT	PO	A	E	DP
Salt Lake	.983	3795	1650	92	179	Nashville	.977	3792	1525	126	132
Reno	.982	3775	1515	99	140	Las Vegas	.976	3785	1508	132	161
Iowa	.981	3713	1410	97	113	Oklahoma City	.976	3776	1536	133	166
Memphis	.978	3827	1524	118	177	Albuquerque	.975	3769	1557	137	151
New Orleans	.978	3741	1440	119	142	Fresno	.973	3809	1448	144	130
Round Rock	.978	3856	1503	121	152	Omaha	.973	3757	1493	146	136
Sacramento	.978	3869	1298	118	119	Tacoma	.973	3850	1274	143	134
Colorado Springs	.977	3779	1587	124	144	Tucson	.973	3853	1513	149	157

INDIVIDUAL BATTING LEADERS (Minimum 2.7 PA/Team Game)

	AVG	G	AB	R	H	2B	3B	HR	RBI	BB	SO	SB
Cooper, David, Las Vegas	.364	120	467	77	170	51	1	9	96	67	43	1
Cowgill, Collin, Reno	.354	98	395	95	140	24	8	13	70	51	63	30
Giavotella, Johnny, Omaha	.338	110	453	67	153	34	2	9	72	40	57	9
Green, Taylor, Nashville	.336	120	420	74	141	36	1	22	88	55	72	1
Rizzo, Anthony, Tucson	.331	93	356	64	118	34	1	26	101	43	89	7
LaHair, Bryan, Iowa	.331	129	456	91	151	38	0	38	109	60	111	2
Velazquez, Gil, Salt Lake	.328	123	427	78	140	25	5	8	58	49	60	17
Robinson, Clint, Omaha	.326	134	503	86	164	35	0	23	100	58	88	2
Butler, Joey, Round Rock	.322	113	426	73	137	27	5	12	57	43	138	13
Limonta, Johan, Tacoma	.319	108	407	58	130	20	1	14	84	44	75	3

INDIVIDUAL PITCHING LEADERS (Minimum 0.8 IP/Team Game)

	W	L	ERA	G	GS	CG	SV	IP	H	R	ER	BB	SO
Mendoza, Luis, Omaha	12	5	2.18	33	18	1	2	144	126	52	35	54	81
Van Hekken, Andy, Okla. City	9	6	3.40	35	19	0	1	130	152	56	49	47	111
Sampson, Chris, New Orleans	9	2	3.71	20	19	1	0	116	139	50	48	19	62
De La Cruz, Frankie, Nashville	7	6	3.88	25	23	0	0	137	130	67	59	63	126
Dickson, Brandon, Memphis	8	9	3.95	26	25	1	0	157	169	75	69	32	124
Mills, Brad, Las Vegas	11	9	4.00	24	24	1	0	157	161	73	70	39	136
Mazzaro, Vin, Omaha	7	2	4.29	22	22	0	0	124	140	63	59	60	107
Eveland, Dana, Albuquerque	12	8	4.38	25	25	2	0	154	151	83	75	61	107
Kown, Andrew, Fresno	10	9	4.48	25	25	0	0	137	142	75	68	52	103
Banwart, Travis, Sacramento	9	9	4.63	27	25	0	0	150	145	87	77	46	120

ALL-STAR TEAM

C: Anthony Recker, Sacramento. **1B:** Bryan LaHair, Iowa. **2B:** Johnny Giavotella, Omaha. **3B:** Taylor Green, Nashville. **SS:** Cody Ransom, Reno. **OF:** Joey Butler, Round Rock; Collin Cowgill, Reno; Jai Miller, Sacramento. **DH:** Clint Robinson, Omaha. **RHP:** Luis Mendoza, Omaha. **LHP:** Dana Eveland, Albuquerque. **RP:** Victor Marte, Memphis. **Most Valuable Player:** Bryan LaHair, Iowa. **Pitcher of the Year:** Luis Mendoza, Omaha. **Rookie of the Year:** Collin Cowgill, Reno. **Manager of the Year:** Bobby Jones, Round Rock.

DEPARTMENT LEADERS

BATTING

OBP	Cooper, David, Las Vegas	.439
SLG	LaHair, Bryan, Iowa	.664
OPS	LaHair, Bryan, Iowa	1.070
R	Liddi, Alex, Tacoma	121
H	Cooper, David, Las Vegas	170
TB	LaHair, Bryan, Iowa	303
XBH	LaHair, Bryan, Iowa	76
2B	Cooper, David, Las Vegas	51
3B	Moore, Jeremy, Salt Lake	18
HR	LaHair, Bryan, Iowa	38
RBI	Three tied at	109
SAC	Maysonet, Edwin, Nashville	15
BB	Carpenter, Matt, Memphis	84
HBP	Thurston, Joe, New Orleans	17
SO	Miller, Jai, Sacramento	179
SB	Graham, Tyler, Fresno	60
CS	Durango, Luis, Tucson, Oklahoma City	14
AB/SO	Hallberg, Mark, Reno	17.09

PITCHING

G	Miller, Jim, Colorado Springs	65
	Perdomo, Luis, Tucson	65
GS	Yourkin, Matt, Fresno	29
GF	Miller, Jim, Colorado Springs	51
SV	Marte, Victor, Memphis	31
W	Godfrey, Graham, Sacramento	14
L	Jackson, Jay, Iowa	14
IP	Loux, Shane, Fresno	179.3
H	Bay, Ronald, Salt Lake	207
R	Johnson, Alan, Colorado Springs	118
ER	Johnson, Alan, Colorado Springs	109
HB	Palmer, Matt, Salt Lake	16
BB	Rivas, Amaury, Nashville	81
SO	Yourkin, Matt, Fresno	145
SO/9	Inman, Will, Tucson	9.23
SO/9 (RP)	Cabrera, Fernando, Sacramento	10.43
BB/9	Sampson, Chris, New Orleans	1.47
WP	Palmer, Matt, Salt Lake	18
BK	Rivas, Amaury, Nashville	5
HR	French, Luke, Tacoma	30
AVG	Mendoza, Luis, Omaha	.238

FIELDING

C	FPCT	Pacheco, Jordan, Colorado Springs	.991
	PO	Davis, Brad, New Orleans	674
	A	Davis, Brad, New Orleans	59
	E	Donaldson, Josh, Sacramento	14
	DP	Donaldson, Josh, Sacramento	9
	PB	Quiroz, Guillermo, Tucson	10
1B	FPCT	Navarro, Efren, Salt Lake	.998
	PO	Navarro, Efren, Salt Lake	1285
	A	Jacobs, Mike, Colorado Springs	81
	E	Rizzo, Anthony, Tucson	12
	DP	Navarro, Efren, Salt Lake	140
2B	FPCT	Farris, Eric, Nashville	.983
	PO	Thurston, Joe, New Orleans	222
	A	Farris, Eric, Nashville	306
	E	Thurston, Joe, New Orleans	15
	DP	Giavotella, Johnny, Omaha	78
3B	FPCT	Baisley, Jeff, Salt Lake	.973
	PO	Liddi, Alex, Tacoma	101
	A	Baisley, Jeff, Salt Lake	270
	E	Liddi, Alex, Tacoma	18
	DP	Baisley, Jeff, Salt Lake	36
SS	FPCT	Manzella, Tommy, Okla./Reno	.972
	PO	Rohlinger, Ryan, Fresno/Colo. Springs	180
	A	Manzella, Tommy, Okla./Reno	314
	E	Kazmar, Sean, Tacoma	23
		Maysonet, Edwin, Nashville	23
	DP	Manzella, Tommy, Okla./Reno	89
OF	FPCT	Hoffmann, Jamie, Albuquerque	1.000
	PO	Chambers, Adron, Memphis	290
	A	Carroll, Brett, Nashville	17
	E	Loewen, Adam, Las Vegas	10
	DP	Cain, Lorenzo, Omaha	5

MINOR LEAGUES

The New Hampshire Fisher Cats brought home the Eastern League championship in 2011, relying heavily on two of the top prospects in the league: catcher Travis d'Arnaud and outfielder Anthony Gose.

D'Arnaud, the league MVP, came to the Blue Jays from the Phillies after the 2009 season in the Roy Halladay trade. He sustained a concussion in April but bounced back to rank fifth in the league in average (.311) and slugging percentage (.542), and tied for fourth in home runs (21). Scouts also applauded his defensive skills and improvement behind the plate.

Gose, who also came over from the Phillies, helped drive the Fisher Cats with a career-high 16 home runs. When righthanders Henderson Alvarez and Joel Carreno got promoted to Toronto, New Hampshire replaced them with two more quality arms in Drew Hutchison and Deck McGuire.

The Fisher Cats knocked off Richmond in four games after rolling through the regular season with a combination of power (134 homers tied for third in the league) and pitching (fourth-best 3.70 team ERA).

Richmond made a deep run in its second year at The Diamond after moving from Norwich, Conn., and got a big season from lefthander Eric Surkamp, who went 10-4, 2.02 with 165 strikeouts in 142 innings. The Flying Squirrels have been a hit in Richmond, and ranked second in the league in attendance, but their future remains uncertain as plans for a new ballpark have stalled and ownership has made noise about having to move.

Harrisburg had two notable prospects. Bryce Harper took the league by storm after the No. 1 overall pick in the 2010 draft hit .318/.423/.544 in the low Class A South Atlantic League. Harper endured his first significant slump as a pro with Harrisburg, which included a 1-for-25 stretch, but recovered to bat .256 and smacked the league's most talked-about homer: a walkoff, 450-foot shot to straightaway center field on Aug. 12.

Harrisburg righthander Brad Peacock was the league's pitcher of the year after going 10-2, 2.01 with 129 strikeouts in 99 innings. He led the league in strikeouts when he was promoted to Triple-A in mid-July, and he eventually reached the big leagues.

Altoona center fielder Starling Marte proved even better than advertised, as he tracked down balls with ease in center field and led the league in batting at .332. The 22-year-old edged New Britain left fielder Yangervis Solarte (.329). Harrisburg first baseman Tyler Moore hit a league-high 31 homers for the Senators.

Akron's Cory Burns was the top closer in the league. The 6-foot-1 righthander with a fastball in the low 90s and a quality changeup had a league-best 35 saves, posting a 2.11 ERA and holding opposing batters to a .220 average. Burns has 88 saves in three minor league seasons after getting 42 combined last year for low Class A Lake County and high Class A Kinston.

TOP 20 PROSPECTS

1. Bryce Harper, of, Harrisburg Senators (Nationals)
2. Travis D'Arnaud, c, New Hampshire Fisher Cats (Blue Jays)
3. Anthony Gose, of, New Hampshire Fisher Cats (Blue Jays)
4. Brad Peacock, rhp, Harrisburg Senators (Nationals)
5. Jacob Turner, rhp, Erie Seawolves (Tigers)
6. Manny Banuelos, lhp, Trenton Thunder (Yankees)
7. Starling Marte, of, Altoona Curve (Pirates)
8. Will Middlebrooks, 3b, Portland Seadogs (Red Sox)
9. Dellin Betances, rhp, Trenton Thunder (Yankees)
10. Henderson Alvarez, rhp, New Hamp. Fisher Cats (Blue Jays)
11. Eric Surkamp, lhp, Richmond Flying Squirrels (Giants)
12. Derek Norris, c, Harrisburg Senators (Nationals)
13. Jeurys Familia, rhp, Binghamton Mets
14. Francisco Peguero, of, Richmond Flying Squirrels (Giants)
15. Ryan Lavarnway, c, Portland Sea Dogs (Red Sox)
16. Francisco Martinez, 3b, Erie Seawolves (Tigers)
17. Austin Romine, c, Trenton Thunder (Yankees)
18. Chih-Hsien Chiang, of, Portland Sea Dogs (Red Sox)
19. Adeiny Hechavarria, ss, New Hamp. Fisher Cats (Blue Jays)
20. Kyle McPherson, rhp, Altoona Curve (Pirates)

OVERALL STANDINGS

Team (Organization)	W	L	PCT	GB	Manager	Attendance	Average	Last Pennant
Harrisburg Senators (Nationals)	80	62	.563	—	Tony Beasley	291,248	4,221	1999
New Hampshire Fisher Cats (Blue Jays)	77	65	.542	3	Sal Fasano	373,482	5,574	2011
Richmond Flying Squirrels (Giants)	76	66	.535	4	Dave Machemer	447,520	6,679	2002
Bowie Baysox (Orioles)	75	66	.532	4½	Gary Kendall	255,832	3,655	Never
Reading Phillies (Phillies)	74	68	.521	6	Mark Parent	456,957	6,720	2001
Akron Aeros (Indians)	73	69	.514	7	Chris Tremie	266,265	3,916	2009
New Britain Rock Cats (Twins)	72	70	.507	8	Jeff Smith	363,759	5,867	2001
Trenton Thunder (Yankees)	68	73	.482	11½	Tony Franklin	379,501	5,664	2008
Erie SeaWolves (Tigers)	67	75	.472	13	Chris Cron	224,443	3,350	Never
Binghamton Mets (Mets)	65	76	.461	14½	Wally Backman	209,044	3,167	1994
Altoona Curve (Pirates)	64	77	.454	15½	P.J. Forbes	285,906	4,205	2010
Portland Sea Dogs (Red Sox)	59	83	.415	21	Kevin Boles	369,424	5,514	2006

Semifinals: New Hampshire defeated Reading 3-1 and Richmond defeated Harrisburg 3-0 in best-of-five series. **Finals:** New Hampshire defeated Richmond 3-1 in a best-of-five series.

CLUB BATTING

	AVG	G	AB	R	H	2B	3B	HR	RBI	BB	SO	SB	OBP	SLG
Reading	.273	142	4767	668	1302	253	16	136	620	406	945	117	.336	.419
New Britain	.269	142	4703	662	1265	282	37	94	598	470	935	75	.340	.405
Portland	.267	142	4733	684	1265	298	23	129	639	459	1052	117	.339	.422
Erie	.266	142	4756	655	1264	259	41	70	579	449	977	119	.334	.382
Binghamton	.262	141	4646	646	1217	251	34	134	609	455	1168	100	.334	.417
New Hampshire	.259	142	4691	676	1215	256	27	134	623	438	1043	170	.330	.411
Altoona	.258	141	4673	574	1204	231	39	85	525	407	1052	86	.324	.378
Bowie	.256	141	4630	597	1186	237	29	92	545	457	1143	161	.328	.379
Trenton	.253	141	4722	616	1193	240	49	88	565	464	1195	115	.325	.380
Akron	.252	142	4690	620	1182	234	33	89	571	522	977	107	.330	.373
Harrisburg	.249	142	4590	607	1143	242	39	143	564	436	1073	150	.321	.412
Richmond	.247	142	4682	574	1155	225	36	83	519	348	1068	105	.302	.363

CLUB PITCHING

	ERA	G	CG	SHO	SV	IP	H	R	ER	HR	BB	SO	AVG
Richmond	3.46	142	3	9	37	1251	1160	557	481	85	467	1096	.247
Harrisburg	3.61	142	3	12	46	1226	1172	563	492	96	365	1187	.251
Bowie	3.65	141	5	6	48	1229	1145	577	498	101	406	1014	.247
New Hampshire	3.70	142	5	14	27	1230	1129	557	506	97	415	1100	.245
Akron	3.73	142	3	11	44	1231	1176	589	510	84	471	1132	.255
Altoona	3.95	141	1	11	35	1239	1225	607	543	105	364	886	.259
Reading	3.96	142	3	5	36	1243	1198	615	547	121	429	1133	.254
Trenton	4.04	141	1	2	40	1227	1287	667	550	105	472	1001	.270
Erie	4.37	142	3	8	27	1234	1216	667	599	127	478	1056	.261
Binghamton	4.47	141	1	7	38	1209	1272	693	600	114	484	997	.268
Portland	4.78	142	2	7	21	1206	1294	732	641	136	469	1076	.276
New Britain	4.93	142	3	8	38	1217	1317	755	667	106	491	950	.278

CLUB FIELDING

	PCT	PO	A	E	DP		PCT	PO	A	E	DP
New Hampshire	.983	3690	1356	89	120	Reading	.977	3729	1320	117	102
Akron	.982	3693	1512	95	141	Altoona	.976	3716	1546	129	115
Erie	.978	3703	1444	115	138	Bowie	.974	3687	1479	140	129
Richmond	.978	3573	1371	115	116	Portland	.973	3618	1301	135	110
Harrisburg	.977	3677	1340	120	111	Trenton	.970	3680	1401	158	125
New Britain	.977	3652	1405	118	137	Binghamton	.969	3628	1330	160	102

INDIVIDUAL BATTING LEADERS (Minimum 2.7 PA/Team Game)

	AVG	G	AB	R	H	2B	3B	HR	RBI	BB	SO	SB
Marte, Starling, Altoona	.332	129	536	91	178	38	8	12	50	22	100	24
Solarte, Yangervis, New Britain	.329	121	459	64	151	36	3	7	49	24	38	5
Spidale, Michael, Reading	.326	133	494	65	161	16	3	5	35	28	51	20
Satin, Josh, Binghamton	.325	94	338	60	110	35	2	11	60	57	91	2
d'Arnaud, Travis, New Hampshire	.311	114	424	72	132	33	1	21	78	33	100	4
Henry, Justin, Erie	.309	113	376	52	116	24	6	0	46	62	52	21
Hoes, LJ, Bowie	.305	95	344	47	105	17	1	6	54	43	56	16
Middlebrooks, Will, Portland	.302	96	371	54	112	25	1	18	80	21	95	6
Valdespin, Jordany, Binghamton	.297	107	404	62	120	24	3	15	51	21	68	33
Rizzotti, Matt, Reading	.295	139	499	73	147	34	1	24	84	79	125	4

INDIVIDUAL PITCHING LEADERS (Minimum 0.8 IP/Team Game)

	W	L	ERA	G	GS	CG	SV	IP	H	R	ER	BB	SO
Surkamp, Eric, Richmond	10	4	2.02	23	22	1	0	142	110	37	32	44	165
Arnesen, Erik, Harrisburg	8	4	2.43	26	16	0	1	126	114	43	34	24	122
Martis, Shairon, Harrisburg	8	6	3.05	23	23	1	0	133	123	53	45	39	146
Bascom, Timothy, Bowie	9	4	3.11	29	17	0	1	130	113	52	45	34	110
Carreno, Joel, New Hampshire	7	9	3.41	24	23	0	0	135	100	56	51	68	152
Fitzgerald, Justin, Richmond	9	9	3.51	27	27	0	0	146	147	65	57	55	111
Voss, Jay, Erie	9	7	3.67	19	19	1	0	115	96	50	47	37	101
Colla, Mike, Altoona	5	11	3.70	29	23	0	0	134	117	58	55	39	109
Hirschfeld, Steve, New Britain	8	8	3.73	30	21	0	1	128	117	54	53	43	90
Adams, Austin, Akron	11	10	3.77	26	26	0	0	136	147	68	57	63	131

ALL-STAR TEAM

C: Travis d'Arnaud, New Hampshire. **1B:** Tyler Moore, Harrisburg. **2B:** Yangervis Solarte. **3B:** Will Middlebrooks, Portland. **SS:** Adeiny Hechavarria, New Hampshire. **OF:** Chih-Hsien Chiang, Portland; Anthony Gose, New Hampshire; Starling Marte. **UTIL:** Josh Satin, Binghamton. **DH:** Matt Rizzotti, Reading. **RHSP:** Brad Peacock, Harrisburg. **LHSP:** Eric Surkamp, Richmond. **RP:** Cory Burns, Akron. **Most Valuable Player:** Travis d'Arnaud, New Hampshire. **Pitcher of the Year:** Brad Peacock, Harrisburg. **Rookie of the Year:** Starling Marte, Altoona. **Manager of the Year:** Sal Fasano, Reading.

DEPARTMENT LEADERS

BATTING

OBP	Satin, Josh, Binghamton	.423
SLG	Chiang, Chih-Hsien, Portland	.648
OPS	Satin, Josh, Binghamton	.962
R	Johnson, Jamie, Erie	93
H	Marte, Starling, Altoona	178
TB	Moore, Tyler, Harrisburg	276
XBH	Moore, Tyler, Harrisburg	70
2B	Joseph, Corban, Trenton	38
	Marte, Starling, Altoona	38
3B	Perez, Juan, Richmond	10
	Rahl, Chris, Harrisburg	10
HR	Moore, Tyler, Harrisburg	31
RBI	Moore, Tyler, Harrisburg	90
SAC	Johnson, Josh, Harrisburg	15
BB	Johnson, Jamie, Erie	84
HBP	Sanchez, Tony, Altoona	14
SO	Avery, Xavier, Bowie	156
SB	Gose, Anthony, New Hampshire	70
CS	Gose, Anthony, New Hampshire	15
AB/SO	Solarte, Yangervis, New Britain	12.08

PITCHING

G	Robertson, Eric, New Britain	55
GS	Hyatt, Austin, Reading	28
GF	Burns, Cory, Akron	52
SV	Burns, Cory, Akron	35
W	Hyatt, Austin, Reading	12
L	Ramirez, J.C., Reading	12
IP	Packer, Matt, Akron	169.3
H	Lanigan, Bobby, New Britain	184
R	Lanigan, Bobby, New Britain	93
ER	Huntzinger, Brock, Portland	85
HB	Moore, Brandon, Binghamton	14
BB	Crosby, Casey, Erie	77
SO	Hyatt, Austin, Reading	171
SO/9	Surkamp, Eric, Richmond	10.43
SO/9 (RP)	Diekman, Jake, Reading	11.49
BB/9	Pribanic, Aaron, Altoona	1.65
WP	Holt, Bradley, Binghamton	18
BK	Ramirez, J.C., Reading	4
HR	Huntzinger, Brock, Portland	23
AVG	Carreno, Joel, New Hampshire	.208

FIELDING

C	FPCT	Joseph, Caleb, Bowie	.997
	PO	Gosewisch, Tuffy, Reading	851
	A	Holaday, Bryan, Erie	78
	E	Sanchez, Tony, Altoona	18
	DP	Holaday, Bryan, Erie	9
		Joseph, Caleb, Bowie	9
	PB	Monell, Johnny, Richmond	20
1B	FPCT	Bishop, Rawley, Erie	.997
	PO	Bishop, Rawley, Erie	1100
	A	Moore, Tyler, Harrisburg	90
		Parmelee, Chris, New Britain	90
	E	Dykstra, Allan, Binghamton	12
	DP	Bishop, Rawley, Erie	113
2B	FPCT	Holt, Brock, Altoona	.980
	PO	Joseph, Corban, Trenton	243
	A	Joseph, Corban, Trenton	344
	E	Tejeda, Oscar, Portland	24
	DP	Joseph, Corban, Trenton	78
3B	FPCT	Bellows, Kyle, Akron	.962
	PO	Rivero, Carlos, Reading	84
	A	Bellows, Kyle, Akron	259
	E	Martinez, Francisco, Erie	27
	DP	Bellows, Kyle, Akron	26
SS	FPCT	Hechavarria, Adeiny, N. Hampshire	974
	PO	Florimon Jr., Pedro, Bowie	219
	A	Diaz, Juan, Akron	391
	E	Pirela, Jose, Trenton	37
	DP	Diaz, Juan, Akron	83
		Florimon Jr., Pedro, Bowie	83
OF	FPCT	Hassan, Alex, Portland	.995
	PO	Perez, Juan, Richmond	361
	A	Marte, Starling, Altoona	18
	E	Bigley, Evan, New Britain	11
		Maldonado, Brahiam, Binghamton	11
	DP	Benson, Joe, New Britain	5

MINOR LEAGUES

Mobile and Tennessee put together the best seasons in the Southern League with 84 and 83 regular season victories, so it was fitting that the two teams played for the league championship, with Mobile claiming the title in four games.

Mobile righthander Trevor Bauer, the third overall pick in June out of UCLA, wasted no time dominating in pro ball, as he struck out seven in five innings and won the deciding game.

The regular season standout for Mobile was first baseman Paul Goldschmidt, who was the league's MVP after hitting .306 with a league-leading 30 home runs and 94 RBIs. He was in the major leagues by August and flashed his power, with eight homers in 48 regular season games for the Diamondbacks and a grand slam in the National League Division Series against the Brewers. Outfielder A.J. Pollock hit .307 for Mobile with eight homers and 73 RBIs.

The BayBears featured arguably the best rotation in the minors. Righthander Jarrod Parker posted a 2.84 ERA in the second half as he worked his way back from Tommy John surgery. Lefthander Patrick Corbin lmited lefthanded batters to a .218 average, and lefthander Tyler Skaggs arrived in July after dominating the high Class A California League and ranked fourth in the minors with 198 strikeouts. Bauer made three impressive starts with Mobile (striking out 23 in 15 innings) before yielding 10 runs over two innings in his regular season finale. Mike DeMark had 15 saves before being promoted to Triple-A.

Pitching prospects stood out across the league, none more than Montgomery lefthander Matt Moore. He established himself as the top pitching prospect in the minors while with the Biscuits, solidified the notion in Triple-A and put an exclamation point on it by striking out 11 Yankees in five shutout innings in his first big league start.

Pitchers grabbed 13 of the spots on the league's Top 20 Prospects list, and that number would have been higher had Bauer, Chattanooga's Rubby de la

Rosa, Jackson's James Paxton and Birmingham's Addison Reed logged enough work to qualify.

Chattanooga outfielder Scott Van Slyke, the son of former major leaguer Andy, led the league in batting at .348, to go with 20 homers and 92 RBIs.

After the season, league president Don Mincher stepped down after 12 years on the job. Mincher, 73, is a former big leaguer who led a group of investors that bought the Huntsville Stars in 1994 to keep the team in town.

TOP 20 PROSPECTS

1. Matt Moore, lhp, Montgomery Biscuits (Rays)
2. Tyler Skaggs, lhp, Mobile Baybears (Diamondbacks)
3. Paul Goldschmidt, 1b, Mobile Baybears (Diamondbacks)
4. Brett Jackson, of, Tennessee Smokies (Cubs)
5. Jarrod Parker, rhp, Mobile Baybears (Diamondbacks)
6. Arodys Vizcaino, rhp, Mississippi Braves
7. Randall Delgado, rhp, Mississippi Braves
8. Wily Peralta, rhp, Huntsville Stars (Brewers)
9. Yasmani Grandal, c, Carolina Mudcats (Reds)
10. Allen Webster, rhp, Chattanooga Lookouts (Dodgers)
11. Chris Archer, rhp, Montgomery Biscuits (Rays)
12. Alfredo Silverio, of, Chattanooga Lookouts (Dodgers)
13. Nathan Eovaldi, rhp, Chattanooga Lookouts (Dodgers)
14. A.J. Pollock, of, Mobile Baybears (Diamondbacks)
15. Vinnie Catricala, of/3b, Jackson Generals (Mariners)
16. Patrick Corbin, lhp, Mobile Baybears (Diamondbacks)
17. Tyler Pastornicky, ss, Mississippi Braves
18. Chris Withrow, rhp, Chattanooga Lookouts (Dodgers)
19. Brett Oberholtzer, lhp, Mississippi Braves
20. Shawn Tolleson, rhp, Chattanooga Lookouts (Dodgers)

STANDINGS: SPLIT SEASON

FIRST HALF

NORTH	W	L	PCT	GB
Tennessee	43	27	.614	—
Jackson	38	32	.543	5
Huntsville	37	33	.529	6
Chattanooga	35	35	.500	8
Carolina	23	47	.329	20

SOUTH	W	L	PCT	GB
Birmingham	40	30	.571	—
Mobile	38	32	.543	2
Jacksonville	37	33	.529	3
Montgomery	34	36	.486	6
Mississippi	25	45	.357	15

SECOND HALF

NORTH	W	L	PCT	GB
Chattanooga	42	27	.609	—
Tennessee	40	30	.571	2.5
Carolina	30	39	.435	12
Jackson	30	40	.429	12.5
Huntsville	27	40	.403	14

SOUTH	W	L	PCT	GB
Mobile	46	22	.676	—
Mississippi	36	34	.514	11
Jacksonville	33	37	.471	14
Montgomery	31	38	.449	15.5
Birmingham	31	39	.443	16

PLAYOFFS—Semifinals: Tennessee defeated Chattanooga 3-0 and Mobile defeated Birmingham 3-2 in best-of-five series.
Finals: Mobile defeated Tennessee 3-1.

OVERALL STANDINGS

Team (Organization)	W	L	PCT	GB	Manager	Attendance	Average	Last Pennant
Mobile BayBears (Diamondbacks)	84	54	.609	—	Turner Ward	210,956	3,057	2011
Tennessee Smokies (Cubs)	83	57	.593	2	Brian Harper	265,341	3,960	2004
Chattanooga Lookouts (Dodgers)	77	62	.554	7½	Carlos Subero	224,974	3,409	1988
Birmingham Barons (White Sox)	71	69	.507	14	Bobby Magallanes	261,623	3,847	2002
Jacksonville Suns (Marlins)	70	70	.500	15	Andy Barkett	309,310	4,419	2010
Jackson Generals (Mariners)	68	72	.486	17	Jim Pankovits	106,689	1,641	2000
Montgomery Biscuits (Rays)	65	74	.468	19½	Billy Gardner	256,403	3,771	2007
Huntsville Stars (Brewers)	64	73	.467	19½	Mike Guerrero	93,340	1,582	2001
Mississippi Braves (Braves)	61	79	.436	24	Rocket Wheeler	191,653	2,738	2008
Carolina Mudcats (Reds)	53	86	.381	31½	David Bell	255,216	3,699	2003

CLUB BATTING

	AVG	G	AB	R	H	2B	3B	HR	RBI	BB	SO	SB	OBP	SLG
Tennessee	.274	140	4674	694	1280	293	27	131	654	444	889	95	.340	.432
Chattanooga	.273	139	4675	705	1277	320	53	125	642	523	1075	121	.350	.444
Mobile	.272	138	4640	705	1263	243	28	106	645	548	981	112	.353	.405
Carolina	.263	139	4638	664	1222	266	26	115	613	447	1016	126	.334	.406
Jackson	.263	140	4748	622	1248	263	48	104	576	468	1008	93	.335	.404
Birmingham	.260	140	4715	601	1226	257	47	79	552	469	1082	119	.335	.385
Mississippi	.260	140	4675	620	1216	227	24	80	556	451	946	77	.333	.370
Huntsville	.258	137	4507	566	1165	236	29	61	517	447	950	74	.331	.364
Montgomery	.258	139	4629	682	1193	231	53	111	627	479	937	92	.334	.402
Jacksonville	.253	140	4708	634	1190	242	40	103	581	569	1047	101	.341	.387

CLUB PITCHING

	ERA	G	CG	SHO	SV	IP	H	R	ER	HR	BB	SO	AVG
Chattanooga	3.66	139	3	2	46	1228	1196	609	499	86	471	1103	.256
Birmingham	3.77	140	2	11	39	1247	1146	614	522	64	555	1024	.247
Tennessee	3.83	140	1	4	42	1224	1253	616	521	92	489	945	.268
Mobile	3.87	138	4	10	48	1224	1196	601	526	98	422	1055	.259
Mississippi	4.04	140	5	8	29	1221	1216	664	548	89	500	1036	.259
Jackson	4.05	140	2	7	38	1239	1263	652	557	103	427	952	.266
Huntsville	4.08	137	2	7	37	1173	1160	618	532	121	481	983	.260
Jacksonville	4.23	140	1	7	38	1253	1316	679	589	120	476	887	.274
Montgomery	4.39	139	2	6	37	1206	1230	678	588	117	516	1001	.266
Carolina	5.17	139	3	4	24	1193	1304	762	685	125	508	945	.281

CLUB FIELDING

	PCT	PO	A	E	DP		PCT	PO	A	E	DP
Mobile	.981	3672	1436	98	133	Jacksonville	.973	3760	1506	147	133
Huntsville	.977	3520	1343	112	101	Jackson	.972	3717	1430	150	142
Birmingham	.976	3740	1561	128	150	Mississippi	.971	3662	1299	146	96
Carolina	.975	3579	1356	124	108	Tennessee	.971	3673	1505	156	125
Montgomery	.975	3617	1323	126	113	Chattanooga	.968	3683	1384	166	128

INDIVIDUAL BATTING LEADERS (Minimum 2.7 PA/Team Game)

	AVG	G	AB	R	H	2B	3B	HR	RBI	BB	SO	SB
Van Slyke, Scott, Chattanooga	.348	130	457	81	159	45	4	20	92	65	100	6
Kuhn, Tyler, Birmingham	.341	107	414	61	141	28	10	1	55	39	64	16
Ridling, Rebel, Tennessee	.309	125	433	79	134	29	0	20	80	43	89	5
Pollock, A.J., Mobile	.307	133	550	103	169	41	5	8	73	44	86	36
Goldschmidt, Paul, Mobile	.306	103	366	84	112	21	3	30	94	82	92	9
Silverio, Alfredo, Chattanooga	.306	132	533	90	163	42	18	16	85	30	91	11
Negrych, Jim, Jacksonville	.304	121	398	60	121	22	1	5	46	45	52	11
Romero, Alex, Jacksonville	.303	104	353	53	107	25	1	5	37	7	50	33
Vogt, Stephen, Montgomery	.301	97	386	52	116	21	6	13	85	30	51	4
Pastornicky, Tyler, Mississippi	.299	90	355	50	106	13	5	6	36	24	34	20

INDIVIDUAL PITCHING LEADERS (Minimum 0.8 IP/Team Game)

	W	L	ERA	G	GS	CG	SV	IP	H	R	ER	BB	SO
Peralta, Wily, Huntsville	9	7	3.46	21	21	1	0	120	106	57	46	48	117
Carraway, Andrew, Jackson	9	5	3.66	28	21	1	0	138	123	62	56	25	106
Oberholtzer, Brett, Mississippi	9	9	3.74	21	21	1	0	128	119	65	53	42	93
Barnese, Nick, Montgomery	6	8	3.76	24	24	0	0	117	109	64	49	57	91
Parker, Jarrod, Mobile	11	8	3.79	26	26	0	0	131	112	61	55	55	112
Delgado, Randall, Mississippi	5	5	3.84	21	21	2	0	117	116	58	50	46	110
Scarpetta, Cody, Huntsville	8	5	3.85	23	23	0	0	117	100	61	50	61	98
Savage, Will, Chattanooga	12	6	3.95	25	23	1	1	141	150	69	62	27	87
Antonini, Michael, Chattanooga	10	9	4.01	27	27	0	0	148	164	85	66	42	131
Leesman, Charles, Birmingham	10	7	4.03	27	27	0	0	152	150	79	68	83	113

ALL-STAR TEAM

C: Stephen Vogt, Montgomery. **1B:** Paul Goldschmidt, Mobile. **2B:** Tyler Kuhn, Birmingham. **3B:** Ryan Wheeler, Mobile. **SS:** Tyler Pastornicky, Mississippi. **OF:** Dennis Phipps, Carolina; A.J. Pollock, Mobile; Alfredo Silverio, Chattanooga; Scott Van Slyke, Chattanooga. **UTIL:** Tyler Kuhn. **DH:** Ernesto Mejia, Mississippi. **Hustler:** Kevin Mattison, Jacksonville. **RHSP:** Nathan Eovaldi, Chattanooga. **LHSP:** Matt Moore, Montgomery. **RP:** Rafael Dolis, Tennessee.
Most Valuable Player: Paul Goldschmidt, Mobile. **Most Outstanding Pitcher:** Matt Moore, Montgomery. **Manager of the Year:** Turner Ward, Mobile.

DEPARTMENT LEADERS

BATTING

OBP	Goldschmidt, Paul, Mobile	.435
SLG	Goldschmidt, Paul, Mobile	.626
OPS	Goldschmidt, Paul, Mobile	1.061
R	Pollock, A.J., Mobile	103
H	Pollock, A.J., Mobile	169
TB	Silverio, Alfredo, Chattanooga	289
XBH	Silverio, Alfredo, Chattanooga	76
2B	Van Slyke, Scott, Chattanooga	45
3B	Silverio, Alfredo, Chattanooga	18
HR	Goldschmidt, Paul, Mobile	30
	Soto, Neftali, Carolina	30
RBI	Mejia, Ernesto, Mississippi	99
SAC	Bantz, Brandon, Jackson	15
BB	Goldschmidt, Paul, Mobile	82
HBP	Loman, Seth, Birmingham	24
SO	Mejia, Ernesto, Mississippi	156
SB	Berry, Quintin, Carolina	40
CS	Haydel, Lee, Huntsville	18
AB/SO	Cabrera, Willie, Mississippi	11.97

PITCHING

G	Joseph, Donnie, Carolina	57
GS	Dyer, Shane, Montgomery	28
	Merklinger, Dan, Huntsville	28
GF	Quate, Zachary, Montgomery	45
SV	Rosario, Sandy, Jacksonville	23
W	Savage, Will, Chattanooga	12
L	Avery, James, Carolina	12
	Bowman, Michael, Huntsville	12
IP	Corbin, Patrick, Mobile	160.3
H	Dyer, Shane, Montgomery	191
	Edwards, Justin, Birmingham	191
R	Edwards, Justin, Birmingham	103
ER	Edwards, Justin, Birmingham	83
HB	Roemer, Wes, Mobile	15
BB	Griffith, Nevin, Birmingham	96
SO	Corbin, Patrick, Mobile	142
SO/9	Withrow, Chris, Chattanooga	9.09
SO/9 (RP)	Fleming, Marquis, Montgomery	11.65
BB/9	Carraway, Andrew, Jackson	1.63
WP	Archer, Christopher, Montgomery	18
BK	Four tied at	3
HR	Antonini, Michael, Chattanooga	19
	Bowman, Michael, Huntsville	19
AVG	Scarpetta, Cody, Huntsville	.234

FIELDING

C	FPCT	Easley, Ed, Mobile	.998
	PO	Phegley, Josh, Birmingham	620
	A	Maldonado, Martin, Huntsville	63
	E	Kennelly, Mathew, Mississippi	12
	DP	Clevenger, Steve, Tennessee	7
	PB	Phegley, Josh, Birmingham	16
1B	FPCT	Goldschmidt, Paul, Mobile	.996
	PO	Mejia, Ernesto, Mississippi	956
	A	Halton, Sean, Huntsville	87
	E	Mejia, Ernesto, Mississippi	11
	DP	Poythress, Rich, Jackson	95
2B	FPCT	Elmore, Jacob, Mobile	.981
	PO	Elmore, Jacob, Mobile	214
	A	Elmore, Jacob, Mobile	315
	E	Curry, Ryan, Jacksonville	15
	DP	Elmore, Jacob, Mobile	75
3B	FPCT	Linares, Donell, Mississippi	.932
	PO	Wheeler, Ryan, Mobile	65
	A	Wheeler, Ryan, Mobile	184
	E	Vitters, Josh, Tennessee	21
	DP	Linares, Donell, Mississippi	14
SS	FPCT	Harbin, Taylor, Mobile	.969
	PO	Beckham, Tim, Montgomery	177
	A	Gutierrez, Chris, Jacksonville	339
	E	Gutierrez, Chris, Jacksonville	28
		Triunfel, Carlos, Jackson	28
	DP	Harbin, Taylor, Mobile	80
OF	FPCT	Pollock, A.J., Mobile	.996
	PO	Mattison, Kevin, Jacksonville	374
	A	Silverio, Alfredo, Chattanooga	19
	E	Mattison, Kevin, Jacksonville	10
	DP	Chavez, Johermyn, Jackson	6

MINOR LEAGUES

San Antonio dominated the Double-A Texas League from start to finish in 2011, posting 94 regular-season wins and going 6-1 in the playoffs to take the league title.

The Missions also had a wealth of talent, with standouts like righthander Casey Kelly (who won seven of eight starts in a midseason stretch) and third baseman James Darnell (43 of his 96 hits were for extra bases) to start the season. Jedd Gyorko replaced Darnell at third base after the all-star break, and pitchers Robbie Erlin and Joe Wieland moved from Frisco to San Antonio when the Rangers traded for Padres reliever Mike Adams.

Still, the player who commanded the most attention was Arkansas outfielder Mike Trout, Baseball America's Minor League Player of the Year. He was the catalyst in the Travelers' playoff drive, though he was in the big leagues by the time the postseason rolled around, and finished the season ranked first in batting average and on-base percentage, and placed third in slugging.

Another dynamic player, Frisco outfielder Leonys Martin made a big impact during his short stint in the league. Martin, who the Rangers signed out of Cuba in May, dominated TL pitching in just 29 games for the Roughriders. The 23-year-old hit .348/.435/.571 before moving on to Triple-A and ultimately the big leagues.

Righthanders Jarred Cosart and Paul Clemens, two more trade acquisitions who joined Corpus Christi after the parent Astros dealt away Hunter Pence and Michael Bourn, also made a strong impression during late-season stints. Besides a rough seven-run outing against Midland, Cosart yielded just three runs in 33 innings.

Springfield first baseman Matt Adams was the league MVP. The former Slippery Rock star hit an even .300 with 32 homers and 101 RBIs. Tulsa outfielder Tim Wheeler, who hit just 12 home runs last season during his full-season debut in the hitter-friendly California League, topped the TL with 33 homers in 2011.

Matt Shoemaker of Arkansas won the league ERA title, going 12-5, 2.48 to finish one spot

ahead of Reyes. Cardinals top prospect Shelby Miller mowed down 170 batters in 86 innings after earning a midseason promotion from high Class A Palm Beach. The 20-year-old righthander's season hit a bump in the road when an alcohol-related incident led to a one-week suspension in August.

For the third straight year, San Antonio reliever Brad Brach emerged as his league's top closer. The righthander led the SL with 23 saves after topping the California League in 2010 with 41 and the Midwest League in 2009 with 33. He passed through Triple-A Tucson before making his big league debut with the Padres.

TOP 20 PROSPECTS

1. Mike Trout, of, Arkansas Travelers (Angels)
2. Shelby Miller, rhp, Springfield Cardinals
3. Garrett Richards, rhp, Arkansas Travelers (Angels)
4. Martin Perez, lhp Frisco Roughriders (Rangers)
5. Jake Odorizzi, rhp, NW Arkansas Naturals (Royals)
6. Wilin Rosario, c, Tulsa Drillers (Rockies)
7. Casey Kelly, rhp, San Antonio Missions (Padres)
8. Robbie Erlin, lhp, Frisco (Rangers)/San Antonio (Padres)
9. Jedd Gyorko, 3b, San Antonio Missions (Padres)
10. James Darnell, 3b, San Antonio Missions (Padres)
11. Grant Green, ss, Midland Rockhounds (Athletics)
12. Tim Wheeler, of, Tulsa Drillers (Rockies)
13. Wil Myers, of, NW Arkansas Naturals (Royals)
14. Zack Cox, 3b, Springfield Cardinals
15. Chris Dwyer, lhp NW Arkansas Naturals (Royals)
16. Kelvin Herrera, rhp, NW Arkansas Naturals (Royals)
17. Salvador Perez, c, NW Arkansas Naturals (Royals)
18. Joe Wieland, rhp, Frisco (Rangers)/San Antonio (Padres)
19. Matt Adams, 1b, Springfield Cardinals
20. J.D. Martinez, of, Corpus Christi Hooks (Astros)x

STANDINGS: SPLIT-SEASON

FIRST HALF

NORTH			
Arkansas	36	31	.537 —
NW Arkansas	35	32	.522 1
Tulsa	33	37	.471 4.5
Springfield	32	38	.457 5.5

SOUTH			
San Antonio	49	21	.700 —
Frisco	40	30	.571 9
Midland	27	43	.386 22
Corpus Christi	25	45	.357 24

SECOND HALF

NORTH			
NW Arkansas	38	32	.543 —
Tulsa	35	35	.500 3.
Arkansas	32	38	.457 6
Springfield	30	40	.429 8

SOUTH			
San Antonio	45	25	.643 —
Frisco	39	31	.557 6
Midland	36	34	.514 9
Corpus Christi	25	45	.357 20

Playoffs—Semifinals: Arkansas defeated Northwest Arkansas 3-1 and San Antonio defeated Frisco 3-1 in best-of-five series.
Finals: San Antonio defeated Arkansas 3-0 in best-of-five series.

OVERALL STANDINGS

Team (Organization)	W	L	PCT	GB	Manager(s)	Attendance	Average	Last Pennant
San Antonio Missions (Padres)	94	46	.671	—	Doug Dascenzo	294,176	4,203	2007
Frisco Roughriders (Rangers)	79	61	.564	15	Steve Buechele	509,331	7,276	2004
NW Arkansas Naturals (Royals)	73	64	.533	19 ½	Brian Poldberg	310,613	4,779	2010
Arkansas Travelers (Angels)	68	69	.496	24 ½	B. Mosiello/T. Takayoshi/B. Mitchell	300,594	4,625	2008
Tulsa Drillers (Rockies)	68	72	.486	26	Duane Espy	366,291	5,387	1998
Midland Rockhounds (Athletics)	63	77	.450	31	Steve Scarsone	308,810	4,541	2009
Springfield Cardinals (Cardinals)	62	78	.443	32	Ron Warner	337,166	5,109	1994
Corpus Christi Hooks (Astros)	50	90	.357	44	Tom Lawless	395,128	5,645	2006

MINOR LEAGUES

CLUB BATTING

	AVG	G	AB	R	H	2B	3B	HR	RBI	BB	SO	SB	OBP	SLG
Springfield	.278	140	4841	740	1347	246	26	166	696	429	961	53	.343	.443
Midland	.269	140	4800	675	1289	245	33	92	612	539	1012	91	.349	.391
San Antonio	.269	140	4812	801	1293	291	27	159	751	613	1081	102	.355	.440
Northwest Arkansas	.268	137	4529	688	1212	206	30	108	618	490	858	205	.345	.398
Frisco	.267	140	4832	693	1291	239	30	128	629	367	1021	102	.327	.409
Corpus Christi	.258	140	4776	605	1234	222	27	114	560	408	1022	119	.320	.388
Tulsa	.258	140	4750	666	1225	227	29	164	600	421	1106	109	.326	.421
Arkansas	.256	137	4501	611	1152	218	38	100	551	454	962	156	.330	.388

CLUB PITCHING

	ERA	G	CG	SHO	SV	IP	H	R	ER	HR	BB	SO	AVG
San Antonio	3.43	140	0	12	36	1261	1217	533	480	85	387	1087	.257
Arkansas	3.60	137	13	14	26	1198	1128	567	479	117	423	912	.249
Frisco	4.13	140	2	6	38	1267	1249	647	582	113	467	1069	.259
Tulsa	4.39	140	4	11	35	1239	1265	694	604	140	438	951	.267
Northwest Arkansas	4.57	137	4	8	42	1200	1181	688	609	140	486	998	.259
Midland	4.92	140	0	4	33	1234	1379	780	675	125	480	989	.285
Corpus Christi	5.01	140	1	5	23	1233	1295	761	687	150	506	1034	.270
Springfield	5.11	140	1	3	29	1227	1329	809	697	161	534	983	.277

CLUB FIELDING

	PCT	PO	A	E	DP		PCT	PO	A	E	DP
San Antonio	.980	3783	1492	108	138	NW Arkansas	.975	3599	1415	126	145
Arkansas	.978	3595	1352	110	109	Tulsa	.974	3716	1537	142	150
Frisco	.977	3801	1398	122	133	Midland	.972	3702	1513	148	136
Corpus Christi	.976	3700	1396	127	118	Springfield	.972	3682	1503	152	126

INDIVIDUAL BATTING LEADERS (Minimum 2.7 PA/Team Game)

	AVG	G	AB	R	H	2B	3B	HR	RBI	BB	SO	SB
Mitchell, Jermaine, Midland	.355	74	304	67	108	15	13	10	50	54	65	14
Trout, Mike, Arkansas	.326	91	353	82	115	18	13	11	38	45	76	33
Castellanos, Alex, Springfield	.319	93	354	72	113	21	4	19	62	24	94	10
Wikoff, Brandon, Corpus Christi	.308	103	331	40	102	6	0	3	26	47	33	5
Van Ostrand, James, Corpus Christi	.306	104	346	41	106	22	2	11	48	43	52	3
Adams, Matt, Springfield	.300	115	463	80	139	23	2	32	101	40	90	0
Swauger, Chris, Springfield	.296	114	362	52	107	13	2	12	56	24	67	3
Osuna, Renny, Frisco	.294	123	520	72	153	23	2	10	64	39	63	20
Cox, Zack, Springfield	.293	93	352	54	103	19	0	10	48	29	69	0
Greene, Jonathan, Frisco	.292	130	487	73	142	29	0	18	75	30	161	5

INDIVIDUAL PITCHING LEADERS (Minimum 0.8 IP/Team Game)

	W	L	ERA	G	GS	CG	SV	IP	H	R	ER	BB	SO
Shoemaker, Matt, Arkansas	12	5	2.48	23	23	5	0	156	132	47	43	35	129
Reyes, Jorge, San Antonio	10	3	3.12	33	20	0	0	113	111	42	39	30	98
Richards, Garrett, Arkansas	12	2	3.15	22	21	3	0	143	123	50	50	41	103
Keuchel, Dallas, Corpus Christi	9	7	3.17	20	20	1	0	128	116	49	45	27	76
Smith, Will, NW Arkansas	13	9	3.85	27	27	2	0	161	171	78	69	45	108
Snyder, Ben, Frisco	11	5	3.87	40	14	0	1	119	123	56	51	30	67
Scahill, Rob, Tulsa	12	11	3.92	27	26	1	0	161	164	81	70	60	104
Kelly, Casey, San Antonio	11	6	3.98	27	27	0	0	142	153	74	63	46	105
Abreu, Erick, Corpus Christi	6	8	4.29	33	18	0	0	124	124	64	59	27	111
Arenas, Orangel, Arkansas	9	10	4.48	25	25	0	0	149	176	86	74	39	67

ALL-STAR TEAM

C: Wilin Rosario, Tulsa; Salvador Perez, Northwest Arkansas. **1B:** Matt Adams, Springfield. **2B:** Tommy Field, Tulsa. **SS:** Ryan Jackson, Springfield. **3B:** James Darnell, San Antonio. **OF:** J.D. Martinez, Corpus Christi; Mike Trout, Arkansas; Jermaine Mitchell, Midland. **DH:** Tommy Mendonca, Frisco. **UTIL:** Grant Green, Midland. **P:** Brad Brach, San Antonio; Joe Wieland, San Antonio; Shelby Miller, Springfield; Garrett Richards, Arkansas; Matt Shoemaker, Arkansas; Dallas Keuchel, Corpus Christi.
Player of the Year: Matt Adams, Springfield. **Pitcher of the Year:** Matt Shoemaker, Arkansas.
Manager of the Year: Doug Dascenzo, San Antonio.

DEPARTMENT LEADERS

BATTING

OBP	Mitchell, Jermaine, Midland		.453
SLG	Adams, Matt, Springfield		.566
OPS	Trout, Mike, Arkansas		.958
R	Wheeler, Tim, Tulsa		105
H	Wheeler, Tim, Tulsa		161
TB	Wheeler, Tim, Tulsa		300
XBH	Wheeler, Tim, Tulsa		67
2B	Jimenez, Luis, Arkansas		40
3B	Mitchell, Jermaine, Midland		13
	Trout, Mike, Arkansas		13
HR	Wheeler, Tim, Tulsa		33
RBI	Adams, Matt, Springfield		101
SAC	Colon, Christian, NW Arkansas		21
BB	Decker, Jaff, San Antonio		103
HBP	Heether, Adam, Midland		22
SO	Greene, Jonathan, Frisco		161
SB	Robinson, Derrick, NW Arkansas		55
CS	Robinson, Derrick, NW Arkansas		15
AB/SO	Wikoff, Brandon, Corpus Christi		10.03

PITCHING

G	Vincent, Nick, San Antonio		66
GS	Seaton, Ross, Corpus Christi		28
GF	Brach, Brad, San Antonio		40
SV	Brach, Brad, San Antonio		23
W	Smith, Will, NW Arkansas		13
L	Three tied at		12
IP	Smith, Will, NW Arkansas		161.3
H	Haviland, Shawn, Midland		205
R	Haviland, Shawn, Midland		133
ER	Haviland, Shawn, Midland		113
HB	McKiernan, Eddie, Arkansas		15
BB	Pimentel, Carlos, Frisco		80
SO	Shoemaker, Matt, Arkansas		129
SO/9	Brigham, Jacob, Frisco		8.97
SO/9 (RP)	Leon, Arcenio, Corpus Christi		10.16
BB/9	Riordan, Cory, Tulsa		1.58
WP	Thomas, Kevin, Springfield		18
BK	Blazek, Michael, Springfield		5
HR	Blazek, Michael, Springfield		25
AVG	Shoemaker, Matt, Arkansas		.228

FIELDING

C	FPCT	Felix, Jose, Frisco	.990
	PO	Rosario, Wilin, Tulsa	652
	A	Rosario, Wilin, Tulsa	82
	E	Solis, Ali, San Antonio	12
	DP	Three tied at	8
	PB	Rosario, Wilin, Tulsa	13
1B	FPCT	Spina, Michael, Midland	.994
	PO	Paulsen, Ben, Tulsa	1251
	A	Spina, Michael, Midland	77
	E	Paulsen, Ben, Tulsa	11
		Ruiz, Jose, Frisco	11
	DP	Paulsen, Ben, Tulsa	123
2B	FPCT	Field, Tommy, Tulsa	.983
	PO	Stoneburner, Davis, Frisco	185
	A	Field, Tommy, Tulsa	278
	E	Garcia, Jose, Springfield	16
		Stoneburner, Davis, Frisco	16
	DP	Field, Tommy, Tulsa	71
3B	FPCT	Mendonca, Tommy, Frisco	.941
	PO	Jimenez, Luis, Arkansas	98
	A	Parker, Stephen, Midland	224
	E	Cox, Zack, Springfield	20
		Parker, Stephen, Midland	20
	DP	Mendonca, Tommy, Frisco	21
		Parker, Stephen, Midland	21
SS	FPCT	Perez, Darwin, Arkansas	.981
	PO	Jackson, Ryan, Springfield	201
	A	Jackson, Ryan, Springfield	395
	E	Villar, Jonathan, Corpus Christi	23
	DP	Jackson, Ryan, Springfield	80
OF	FPCT	Castillo, Angel, Arkansas	.995
	PO	Wheeler, Tim, Tulsa	302
	A	Barfield, Jeremy, Midland	20
	E	Castellanos, Alex, Springfield	9
	DP	Beltre, Engel, Frisco	7

MINOR LEAGUES

Although the major league team struggled to a bottom-five finish, the success of the Padres' high Class A affiliate was a bright spot in part of the organization's development and rebuilding plan.

Lake Elsinore snuck in the playoffs with a wild-card berth and went on to defeat Inland Empire, Rancho Cucamonga, and Stockton to win the Storm's first title since 2001.

Storm third baseman Jed Gyroko demolished pitching in the first half by leading the league in all three triple-crown categories with a .365 average, 18 home runs and 74 RBIs in just 81 games before earning a promotion.

Third baseman Edinson Rincon filled in nicely for Gyroko in the second half, hitting .328/.393/490. Strong contributors to the championship club also included speedy outfielder Reymond Fuentes, toolsy infielder Jonathan Galvez, and first baseman Nathan Frieman. Frieman hit two home runs in the decisive game of the championship series in the midst of a series clinching 10-3 victory.

Ports center fielder Michael Choice, the 10th overall pick in 2010 out of Texas-Arlington, made an impressive full-season debut by leading the league with 30 home runs.

San Jose's stellar first half was overshadowed by a playoff run that fell short, but 2011 marked the seventh consecutive year the Giants took home the first half trophy. The Giants boasted two of the most impressive talents in outfielder Gary Brown and righthander Zack Wheeler. Brown, a speedy centerfielder, terrorized Cal League opponents in the field, on the basepaths, and with the stick by leading the league in hits (188) while showing surprising pop (he ranked fifth with 61 extra-base hits). The Giants traded Wheeler to the Mets in July for Carlos Beltran after he registered 98 strikeouts in just 88 innings pitched.

Jose Altuve's climb to the big leagues began when the Lancaster second baseman opened the season hitting a minor league best .407 in 213 at-bats with JetHawks. Modesto outfielder Kent

Matthes became the first player in team history to be named the California League MVP. Despite playing his last game on Aug. 3 due to a hand injury, Matthes ranked in the top five in home runs, RBIs, and doubles. Modesto ighthander Chad Bettis, was the league pitcher of the year after placing first in strikeouts and second in ERA. Veteran Nuts manager Jerry Weinstein was named Padres bullpen coach after the season.

TOP 20 PROSPECTS

1. Tyler Skaggs, lhp, Visalia Rawhide (Diamondbacks)
2. Jedd Gyorko, 3b, Lake Elsinore Storm (Padres)
3. Gary Brown, of, San Jose Giants
4. Zack Wheeler, rhp, San Jose Giants
5. Jonathan Singleton, 1b, Lancaster Jethawks (Astros)
6. Nolan Arenado, 3b, Modesto Nuts (Rockies)
7. Michael Choice, of, Stockton Ports (Athletics)
8. Allen Webster, rhp, Rancho Cucamonga Quakes (Dodgers)
9. Chad Bettis, rhp, Modesto Nuts (Rockies)
10. Yasmani Grandal, c, Bakersfield Blaze (Reds)
11. Tommy Joseph, c, San Jose Giants
12. Nick Franklin, ss/2b, High Desert (Mariners)
13. Jean Segura, ss, Inland Empire (Angels)
14. Reymond Fuentes, of, Lake Elsinore (Padres)
15. Jose Altuve, 2b, Lancaster (Astros)
16. Matt Davidson, 1b/3b, Visalia (Diamondbacks)
17. Chris Dominguez, 3b, San Jose (Giants)
18. Johnny Hellweg, rhp, Inland Empire (Angels)
19. Chris Owings, ss, Visalia (Diamondbacks)
20. Kent Matthes, of, Modesto (Rockies)

STANDINGS: SPLIT SEASON

FIRST HALF

NORTH	W	L	PCT	GB
San Jose	51	19	.729	—
Stockton	38	32	.543	13
Bakersfield	35	35	.500	16
Modesto	33	37	.471	18
Visalia	31	39	.443	20

SOUTH	W	L	PCT	GB
Rancho Cuca.	38	32	.543	—
High Desert	32	38	.457	6
Inland Empire	32	38	.457	6
Lake Elsinore	32	38	.457	6
Lancaster	28	42	.400	10

SECOND HALF

NORTH	W	L	PCT	GB
Modesto	41	29	.586	—
San Jose	39	31	.557	2
Stockton	37	33	.529	4
Visalia	32	38	.457	9
Bakersfield	31	39	.443	10

SOUTH	W	L	PCT	GB
Rancho Cuca.	42	28	.600	—
Inland Empire	37	33	.529	5
Lake Elsinore	37	33	.529	5
High Desert	27	43	.386	15
Lancaster	27	43	.386	15

PLAYOFFS—Division Series: Lake Elsinore defeated Inland Empire 2-1 and Stockton defeated Modesto 2-1 in best-of-three series. **Semifinals:** Lake Elsinore defeated Rancho Cucamonga 3-1 and Stockton defeated San Jose 3-1 in best-of-five series. **Finals:** Lake Elsinore defeated Stockton 3-1 in a best-of-five series.

OVERALL STANDINGS

Team (Organization)	W	L	PCT	GB	Manager(s)	Attendance	Average	Last Pennant
San Jose Giants (Giants)	90	50	.643	—	Andy Skeels	222,547	3,225	2010
Rancho Cucamonga Quakes (Dodgers)	80	60	.571	10	Juan Bustabad	155,903	2,227	1994
Stockton Ports (Athletics)	75	65	.536	15	Webster Garrison	198,705	2,839	2008
Modesto Nuts (Rockies)	74	66	.529	16	Jerry Weinstein	180,785	2,659	2004
Inland Empire 66ers (Angels)	69	71	.493	21	Tom Gamboa	185,411	2,649	2006
Lake Elsinore Storm (Padres)	69	71	.493	21	Carlos Lezcano/Phil Plantier	225,769	3,272	2011
Bakersfield Blaze (Reds)	66	74	.471	24	Ken Griffey	40,056	572	1989
Visalia Rawhide (Diamondbacks)	63	77	.450	27	Jason Hardtke	118,065	1,736	1978
High Desert Mavericks (Mariners)	59	81	.421	31	Jose Moreno	119,028	1,725	1997
Lancaster JetHawks (Astros)	55	85	.393	35	Tom Spencer	147,129	2,132	Never

CLUB BATTING

	AVG	G	AB	R	H	2B	3B	HR	RBI	BB	SO	SB	OBP	SLG
Rancho Cucamonga	.287	140	4888	848	1404	279	40	153	781	524	993	107	.362	.455
Bakersfield	.282	140	4844	747	1365	263	29	115	681	425	933	195	.345	.419
Lake Elsinore	.280	140	4970	828	1394	295	46	133	760	512	1097	196	.354	.439
Lancaster	.280	140	4854	749	1359	249	34	121	685	510	1075	135	.352	.420
High Desert	.279	140	4880	798	1363	259	51	158	734	469	1344	157	.348	.450
San Jose	.278	140	4941	814	1372	306	40	139	752	493	1059	129	.350	.440
Inland Empire	.277	140	4844	746	1344	297	48	105	684	500	1027	122	.350	.424
Modesto	.272	140	4827	801	1314	282	45	118	726	463	1103	129	.343	.423
Visalia	.271	140	4837	747	1312	275	32	127	683	451	1161	104	.341	.420
Stockton	.261	140	4853	739	1268	230	35	143	678	566	1266	109	.344	.411

CLUB PITCHING

	ERA	G	CG	SHO	SV	IP	H	R	ER	HR	BB	SO	AVG
San Jose	3.70	140	1	14	48	1262	1212	590	519	106	471	1043	.255
Stockton	4.29	140	0	4	44	1263	1271	701	602	136	356	1134	.261
Rancho Cucamonga	4.55	140	1	1	40	1250	1299	728	632	116	576	1180	.268
Modesto	4.58	140	1	5	30	1249	1261	714	635	111	475	1154	.263
Lake Elsinore	4.60	140	0	5	31	1254	1397	774	641	101	395	1118	.280
Bakersfield	4.94	140	2	4	26	1234	1303	797	678	146	561	1184	.271
Inland Empire	4.98	140	1	6	34	1248	1359	796	691	114	534	1160	.275
Visalia	5.15	140	0	2	22	1223	1359	802	699	122	603	1183	.283
Lancaster	5.96	140	3	4	26	1225	1427	929	811	177	496	971	.292
High Desert	6.24	140	3	6	34	1231	1607	986	854	183	446	931	.317

CLUB FIELDING

	PCT	PO	A	E	DP			PCT	PO	A	E	DP
Modesto	.975	3746	1383	134	113		Inland Empire	.969	3744	1483	165	116
San Jose	.975	3787	1560	139	152		Bakersfield	.968	3702	1382	168	112
Lancaster	.973	3676	1477	144	131		Visalia	.968	3668	1408	166	137
Rancho Cuca.	.973	3749	1384	140	127		High Desert	.967	3693	1497	175	150
Stockton	.970	3788	1431	159	121		Lake Elsinore	.964	3763	1493	194	100

INDIVIDUAL BATTING LEADERS (Minimum 2.7 PA/Team Game)

	AVG	G	AB	R	H	2B	3B	HR	RBI	BB	SO	SB
Gyorko, Jedd, Lake Elsinore	.365	81	340	78	124	35	2	18	74	38	64	11
Rutledge, Josh, Modesto	.348	113	460	91	160	33	9	9	71	41	91	16
Brown, Gary, San Jose	.336	131	559	115	188	34	13	14	80	46	77	53
Matthes, Kent, Modesto	.334	93	371	70	124	39	3	23	95	22	80	7
Buss, Nick, Rancho Cuca.	.328	115	479	86	157	30	8	14	55	27	63	28
Calhoun, Kole, Inland Empire	.324	133	512	94	166	36	6	22	99	73	96	20
Songco, Angelo, Rancho Cuca.	.313	131	534	110	167	48	4	29	114	42	121	4
Long, Matt, Inland Empire	.301	121	481	104	145	29	11	16	73	56	86	26
Wates, Austin, Lancaster	.300	132	526	85	158	23	9	6	75	47	86	26
Nick, David, Visalia	.300	132	564	99	169	35	5	13	68	30	80	5

INDIVIDUAL PITCHING LEADERS (Minimum 0.8 IP/Team Game)

	W	L	ERA	G	GS	CG	SV	IP	H	R	ER	BB	SO
Heston, Chris, San Jose	12	4	3.16	24	24	1	0	151	144	64	53	40	131
Bettis, Chad, Modesto	12	5	3.34	27	27	0	0	170	142	72	63	45	184
Reichard, Andy, San Jose	9	4	3.38	28	15	0	0	112	115	49	42	25	61
Westcott, Craig, San Jose	13	4	3.42	25	24	0	0	155	155	67	59	33	87
Marte, Kelvin, San Jose	12	6	3.47	25	25	0	0	148	158	67	57	47	84
Redding, Jon Michael, Rancho Cuca.	11	7	3.66	25	24	0	0	138	132	64	56	52	130
Straily, Daniel, Stockton	11	9	3.87	28	26	0	0	161	160	78	69	40	154
Buchanan, Jake, Lancaster	5	10	3.91	25	25	1	0	159	157	92	69	35	102
Smith, Murphy, Stockton	6	9	3.94	26	24	0	1	137	151	80	60	33	100
Magill, Matt, Rancho Cuca.	11	5	4.33	26	21	0	0	139	156	78	67	52	126

ALL-STAR TEAM

C: Tommy Joseph, San Jose. **1B:** Nathan Freiman, Lake Elsinore. **2B:** David Nick, Visalia. **3B:** Nolan Arenado, Modesto. **SS:** Josh Rutledge, Modesto. **OF:** Gary Brown, San Jose; Kent Matthes, Modesto; Michael Choice, Stockton. **DH:** Angelo Songco, Rancho Cucamonga. **UT:** Kole Calhoun, Inland Empire. **SP:** Chad Bettis, Modesto; Craig Westcott, San Jose; Jon Michael Redding, Rancho Cucamonga; Tyler Skaggs, Visalia.
Most Valuable Player: Kent Matthes, Modesto. **Most Valuable Pitcher:** Chad Bettis, Modesto. **Manager of the Year:** Juan Bustabad, Rancho Cucamonga.

DEPARTMENT LEADERS

BATTING

OBP	Hinze, Kody, Lancaster	.458
SLG	Matthes, Kent, Modesto	.642
OPS	Gyorko, Jedd, Lake Elsinore	1.068
R	Carroll, Daniel, High Desert	117
H	Brown, Gary, San Jose	188
TB	Songco, Angelo, Rancho Cuca.	310
XBH	Songco, Angelo, Rancho Cuca.	81
2B	Songco, Angelo, Rancho Cuca.	48
3B	Brown, Gary, San Jose	13
HR	Choice, Michael, Stockton	30
RBI	Arenado, Nolan, Modesto	122
SAC	Buss, Nick, Rancho Cuca.	15
BB	Crumbliss, Conner, Stockton	96
HBP	Brown, Gary, San Jose	23
	Delmonico, Tony, Rancho Cuca.	23
SO	Coleman, Dusty, Stockton	171
SB	Carroll, Daniel, High Desert	62
CS	Brown, Gary, San Jose	19
AB/SO	Perez, Rossmel, Visalia	10.58

PITCHING

G	McBryde, Jeremy, Lake Elsinore	63
GS	Three tied at	28
GF	Clark, Kirk, Lancaster	43
SV	Hembree, Heath, San Jose	21
W	Flores, Manuel, Inland Empire	13
	Westcott, Craig, San Jose	13
L	Donovan, Robert, Lancaster	14
IP	Bettis, Chad, Modesto	169.7
H	Flores, Manuel, Inland Empire	217
R	Smith, Eric, Visalia	128
ER	Smith, Eric, Visalia	106
HB	Hellweg, John, Inland Empire	15
	Ravin, Josh, Bakersfield	15
BB	Smith, Eric, Visalia	85
SO	Bettis, Chad, Modesto	184
SO/9	Cisnero, Jose, Lancaster	11.09
SO/9 (RP)	Gomez, Leuris, Modesto	11.1
BB/9	Westcott, Craig, San Jose	1.91
WP	Smith, Eric, Visalia	22
BK	Sulbaran, J.C., Bakersfield	5
HR	Gilliam, Robert, Stockton	24
AVG	Bettis, Chad, Modesto	.225

FIELDING

C	FPCT	Joseph, Tommy, San Jose	.992
	PO	Perez, Rossmel, Visalia	823
	A	Perez, Rossmel, Visalia	112
	E	Perez, Rossmel, Visalia	17
	DP	Garcia, Rene, Lancaster	10
	PB	Perez, Rossmel, Visalia	22
1B	FPCT	Aliotti, Anthony, Stockton	.991
	PO	Freiman, Nathan, Lake Elsinore	1127
	A	Freiman, Nathan, Lake Elsinore	102
	E	Freiman, Nathan, Lake Elsinore	16
	DP	Aliotti, Anthony, Stockton	90
	DP	Anders, Luke, San Jose	90
2B	FPCT	Cavan, Ryan, San Jose	.993
	PO	Cavan, Ryan, San Jose	295
	A	Cavan, Ryan, San Jose	377
	E	Galvez, Jesus, Lake Elsinore	21
	DP	Cavan, Ryan, San Jose	100
3B	FPCT	Meyer, Jonathan, Lancaster	.953
	PO	Meyer, Jonathan, Lancaster	88
	A	Meyer, Jonathan, Lancaster	240
	E	Martinez, Mario, High Desert	24
	DP	Meyer, Jonathan, Lancaster	29
SS	FPCT	Lemmerman, Jake, Rancho Cuca.	.946
	PO	Coleman, Dusty, Stockton	176
	A	Owings, Chris, Visalia	354
	E	Owings, Chris, Visalia	32
	DP	Owings, Chris, Visalia	83
OF	FPCT	Brown, Gary, San Jose	.989
	PO	Cleary Jr., Delta, Modesto	291
	A	LaMarre, Ryan, Bakersfield	19
	E	Parker, Jarrett, San Jose	10
	DP	Long, Matt, Inland Empire	7

MINOR LEAGUES

The success of the Keys' season was built around strong pitching and up-the-middle defense. Frederick dominated from start to finish, as it captured both the regular season title and the Mills Cup, given to the Carolina League postseason champion.

The Keys were spurred by the league's top overall prospect, shortstop Manny Machado, who displayed the talent that made him the No. 3 overall pick in the 2010 draft. The Florida native was named the Carolina League's playoff MVP by batting .344 with a league-leading nine RBIs and eight runs. Machado added a home run in the decisive game of the final series, giving Frederick an 11-3 victory over Kinston.

Joining Machado as his double-play partner was Jonathan Schoop, who heated up during the playoffs with a .314 average while chipping in a home run and two steals. Schoop and Machado joined Frederick midseason following a promotion from low Class A Delmarva.

Frederick's pitching staff led the league in ERA, WHIP, and hits allowed. Bobby Bundy, older brother of 2011 Orioles first-round pick Dylan Bundy, was the staff ace as he placed near the top of the league in ERA, WHIP, and strikeouts.

Kinston lefthander Drew Pomeranz was the talk of the league for his dominating performance in the first half of the regular season. Drafted fifth overall in 2010, Pomeranz used his dominating fastball to strike out 95 batters in only 77 innings pitched while posting a 1.87 ERA. Pomeranz was traded to the Rockies in July and ended his first full professional season in the big leagues.

Myrtle Beach placed a remarkable seven players on the league's top 20 list. Lefthander Robbie Ross paired his lofty prospect ranking with a strong performance as he was named the league's pitcher of the year.

Although Lynchburg finished with the circuit's worst record, they possessed arguably the league's most exciting position player in shortstop Andrelton Simmons. The athletic Simmons began to convert his raw physical tools into baseball skills by leading the league in hitting with a .311 average. Additionally, Simmons wowed observers with his well-above-average arm strength.

The season marked the end of an era in Kinston, as the Indians' long run in the league came to an end. Indians owner Cam McRae sold the team to Double-A Carolina owner Steve Bryant, and the team will relocate to the Mudcats' home in Zebulon, N.C., in 2012. McRae has vowed to return affiliated baseball to Kinston, but had made little progress when the season came to a close.

Winston-Salem minor league veteran Ian Gac showed his maturity by posting league leading totals in home runs, OPS, and RBI on his way to the Carolina League MVP.

TOP 20 PROSPECTS

1. Manny Machado, ss, Frederick (Orioles)
2. Drew Pomeranz, lhp, Kinston Indians
3. Mike Olt, 3b, Myrtle Beach (Rangers)
4. Andrelton Simmons, ss, Lynchburg (Braves)
5. Robbie Erlin, lhp, Myrtle Beach (Rangers)
6. Jonathan Schoop, 2b/ss, Frederick (Orioles)
7. Jake Odorizzi, rhp, Wilmington (Royals)
8. Bryce Brentz, of, Salem Red Sox
9. Joe Wieland, rhp, Myrtle Beach (Rangers)
10. Christian Bethancourt, c, Lynchburg (Braves)
11. Zeke Spruill, rhp, Lynchburg (Braves)
12. Destin Hood, of, Potomac (Nationals)
13. Sammy Solis, lhp, Potomac (Nationals)
14. Anthony Ranaudo, rhp, Salem (Red Sox)
15. Bobby Bundy, rhp, Frederick (Orioles)
16. Leury Garcia, ss, Myrtle Beach (Rangers)
17. Robbie Ross, lhp, Myrtle Beach (Rangers)
18. Justin Grimm, rhp, Myrtle Beach (Rangers)
19. Miguel de los Santos, lhp, Myrtle Beach (Rangers)
20. Tyler Saladino, ss, Winston-Salem (White Sox)

STANDINGS: SPLIT SEASON

FIRST HALF

NORTH	W	L	PCT	GB
Frederick	41	28	.594	—
Wilmington	36	33	.522	5
Lynchburg	30	40	.429	11½
Potomac	29	40	.420	12

SOUTH	W	L	PCT	GB
Myrtle Beach	40	29	.580	—
Kinston	38	31	.551	2
W-S	32	38	.457	8½
Salem	31	38	.449	9

SECOND HALF

NORTH	W	L	PCT	GB
Frederick	39	31	.557	—
Potomac	39	31	.557	—
Lynchburg	30	38	.441	8
Wilmington	30	39	.435	8½

SOUTH	W	L	PCT	GB
Kinston	38	31	.551	—
W-S	37	33	.529	1½
Salem	33	37	.471	5½
Myrtle Beach	32	38	.457	6½

PLAYOFFS—Semifinals: Frederick defeated Potomac 3-2 and Kinston defeated Myrtle Beach 3-1 in best-of-five series. **Finals:** Frederick defeated Kinston 3-1 in best-of-five series.

OVERALL STANDINGS

Team (Organization)	W	L	PCT	GB	Manager(s)	Attendance	Average	Last Pennant
Frederick (Orioles)	80	59	.576	—	Orlando Gomez	296,296	4,422	2011
Kinston (Indians)	76	62	.551	3½	Aaron Holbert	112,181	1,781	2006
Myrtle Beach (Rangers)	72	67	.518	8	Jason Wood	213,200	3,280	2000
Winston-Salem (White Sox)	69	71	.493	11½	Julio Vinas	312,416	4,663	2003
Potomac (Nationals)	68	71	.489	12	Matthew LeCroy	171,096	2,950	2010
Wilmington (Royals)	66	72	.478	13½	Brian Rupp	288,738	4,512	1999
Salem (Red Sox)	64	75	.460	16	Bruce Crabbe	226,337	3,429	2001
Lynchburg (Braves)	60	78	.435	19½	Rick Albert/Luis Salazar	169,367	2,455	2009

MINOR LEAGUES

CLUB BATTING

	AVG	G	AB	R	H	2B	3B	HR	RBI	BB	SO	SB	OBP	SLG
Lynchburg	.262	138	4578	579	1198	280	38	90	528	335	924	110	.320	.398
Myrtle Beach	.256	139	4737	602	1214	258	34	74	550	427	929	95	.328	.372
Salem	.254	139	4538	620	1152	264	30	93	548	449	1017	136	.328	.387
Winston-Salem	.253	140	4609	644	1164	241	41	133	601	455	1119	67	.322	.409
Potomac	.252	139	4472	583	1129	227	30	81	531	449	1010	215	.326	.371
Wilmington	.246	138	4422	528	1086	247	36	77	474	402	1017	126	.313	.370
Frederick	.245	139	4466	569	1093	236	22	101	511	427	982	152	.318	.375
Kinston	.234	138	4461	527	1043	210	28	78	473	489	1094	127	.318	.346

CLUB PITCHING

	ERA	G	CG	SHO	SV	IP	H	R	ER	HR	BB	SO	AVG
Frederick	3.22	139	4	12	47	1212	1052	488	433	92	382	1001	.235
Myrtle Beach	3.32	139	3	12	40	1240	1124	545	458	76	389	1179	.240
Kinston	3.68	138	2	13	46	1207	1108	564	494	101	419	1110	.245
Wilmington	3.86	138	3	10	34	1182	1184	592	507	80	378	1016	.262
Lynchburg	3.89	138	6	7	32	1191	1121	601	514	99	477	998	.251
Winston-Salem	3.96	140	2	12	37	1211	1189	614	533	91	476	989	.257
Potomac	4.00	139	7	8	36	1188	1175	627	528	96	438	879	.260
Salem	4.16	139	1	6	37	1188	1126	621	549	92	474	920	.253

CLUB FIELDING

	PCT	PO	A	E	DP		PCT	PO	A	E	DP
Frederick	.977	3636	1425	119	114	Lynchburg	.973	3572	1447	140	122
Kinston	.977	3620	1366	119	108	Potomac	.972	3563	1410	144	127
Salem	.976	3565	1619	130	120	Wilmington	.970	3545	1360	153	123
Myrtle Beach	.974	3721	1372	138	101	Winston-Salem	.970	3632	1474	157	123

INDIVIDUAL BATTING LEADERS (Minimum 2.7 PA/Team Game)

	AVG	G	AB	R	H	2B	3B	HR	RBI	BB	SO	SB
Simmons, Andrelton, Lynchburg	.311	131	517	69	161	35	6	1	52	29	43	26
Testa, Carlo, Wilmington	.290	100	366	48	106	27	4	7	43	36	109	18
Terdoslavich, Joe, Lynchburg	.286	131	483	72	138	52	2	20	82	41	107	9
Wiley, Keenan, Lynchburg	.285	102	358	59	102	11	5	1	24	22	66	19
Perez, Eury, Potomac	.283	119	424	54	120	9	2	1	41	22	63	45
Kobernus, Jeff, Potomac	.282	124	489	67	138	22	4	7	52	21	87	53
Prince, Jared, Myrtle Beach	.282	131	482	67	136	30	1	8	72	47	47	2
Vitek, Kolbrin, Salem	.281	123	473	78	133	22	6	3	43	45	102	12
Gac, Ian, Winston-Salem	.279	140	516	91	144	31	1	33	96	58	144	0
Wilkins, Andy, Winston-Salem	.278	134	493	72	137	33	0	23	89	56	91	2

INDIVIDUAL PITCHING LEADERS (Minimum 0.8 IP/Team Game)

	W	L	ERA	G	GS	CG	SV	IP	H	R	ER	BB	SO
Ross, Robert, Myrtle Beach	9	4	2.26	21	20	1	0	123	102	37	31	28	98
Rosenbaum, Daniel, Potomac	6	5	2.59	20	19	2	0	132	113	52	38	41	108
Bundy, Robert, Frederick	11	5	2.75	20	20	1	0	121	102	43	37	31	100
Hernandez, Chris, Salem	10	7	3.18	25	25	1	0	127	112	53	45	51	80
Spruill, Zeke, Lynchburg	7	9	3.19	20	20	5	0	130	108	56	46	23	92
Tanaka, Ryohei, Frederick	9	5	3.33	23	18	0	1	114	118	47	42	18	84
Masters, Chris, Lynchburg	9	5	3.34	28	23	0	0	148	128	59	55	65	122
Rienzo, Andre, Winston-Salem	6	5	3.41	25	22	1	0	116	108	50	44	66	118
Pimentel, Elisaul, Wilmington	6	7	3.59	26	22	1	1	133	129	60	53	31	105
Brach, Brett, Kinston	6	9	3.60	21	19	1	0	115	97	48	46	37	72

ALL-STAR TEAM

C: Sandy Leon, Potomac. **1B:** Joey Terdoslavich, Lynchburg. **2B:** Jeff Kobernus, Potomac. **3B:** Mike Olt, Myrtle Beach. **SS:** Andrelton Simmons, Lynchburg. **OF:** Destin Hood, Potomac; Ryan Strausborger, Myrtle Beach; Bryce Brentz, Salem. **DH:** Ian Gac, Winston-Salem. **UT INF:** Andy Wilkins, Winston-Salem. **UT OF:** Jared Prince, Myrtle Beach. **SP:** Robbie Ross, Myrtle Beach. **RP:** Preston Guilmet, Kinston. **Most Valuable Player:** Ian Gac, Winston-Salem. **Pitcher of the Year:** Robbie Ross, Myrtle Beach. **Manager of the Year:** Aaron Holbert, Kinston.

DEPARTMENT LEADERS

BATTING

OBP	Prince, Jared, Myrtle Beach	.376
SLG	Gac, Ian, Winston-Salem	.535
OPS	Gac, Ian, Winston-Salem	.893
R	Gac, Ian, Winston-Salem	91
H	Simmons, Andrelton, Lynchburg	161
TB	Gac, Ian, Winston-Salem	276
XBH	Terdoslavich, Joe, Lynchburg	74
2B	Terdoslavich, Joe, Lynchburg	52
3B	Saladino, Tyler, Winston-Salem	9
	Strausborger, Ryan, Myrtle Beach	9
HR	Gac, Ian, Winston-Salem	33
RBI	Gac, Ian, Winston-Salem	96
SAC	Lozada, Jose, Potomac	12
	Simmons, Andrelton, Lynchburg	12
BB	Holt, Tyler, Kinston	78
HBP	Prince, Jared, Myrtle Beach	30
SO	Mitchell, Jared, Winston-Salem	183
SB	Kobernus, Jeff, Potomac	53
CS	Simmons, Andrelton, Lynchburg	18
AB/SO	Simmons, Andrelton, Lynchburg	12.02

PITCHING

G	Guilmet, Preston, Kinston	52
GS	Four tied at	26
GF	Guilmet, Preston, Kinston	48
SV	Guilmet, Preston, Kinston	35
W	Bayne, Cameron, Winston-Salem	12
L	Britton, Drake, Salem	13
IP	Masters, Chris, Lynchburg	148.3
H	Serafin, Joseph, Winston-Salem	166
R	Sample, Tyler, Wilmington	95
ER	Serafin, Joseph, Winston-Salem	81
HB	Ebert, Tom, Salem	16
BB	House, T.J., Kinston	66
	Rienzo, Andre, Winston-Salem	66
SO	Marks, Justin, Wilmington	140
SO/9	Rienzo, Andre, Winston-Salem	9.16
SO/9 (RP)	Kussmaul, Ryan, Winston-Salem	13.81
BB/9	Tanaka, Ryohei, Frederick	1.43
WP	Loux, Barret, Myrtle Beach	17
BK	Lafferty, Brendan, Wilmington	3
HR	Demny, Paul, Potomac	18
AVG	Ross, Robert, Myrtle Beach	.227

FIELDING

C	FPCT	Butler, Dan, Salem	.995
	PO	Perez, Roberto, Kinston	767
	A	Ward, Brian, Frederick	100
	E	Blanke, Michael, Winston-Salem	12
	DP	Perez, Roberto, Kinston	12
	PB	Zaneski, Zach, Myrtle Beach	14
1B	FPCT	Wilkins, Andy, Winston-Salem	.992
	PO	Souza, Steven, Potomac	942
	A	Terdoslavich, Joe, Lynchburg	72
	E	Burnette, Chase, Kinston	11
		Souza, Steven, Potomac	11
	DP	Souza, Steven, Potomac	91
2B	FPCT	Kobernus, Jeff, Potomac	.976
	PO	Wagner, Daniel, Winston-Salem	239
	A	Wagner, Daniel, Winston-Salem	303
	E	Wagner, Daniel, Winston-Salem	18
	DP	Wagner, Daniel, Winston-Salem	71
3B	FPCT	Mollenhauer, Dale, Frederick	.950
	PO	Mollenhauer, Dale, Frederick	83
	A	Mollenhauer, Dale, Frederick	261
	E	Vitek, Kolbrin, Salem	28
	DP	Mollenhauer, Dale, Frederick	21
SS	FPCT	Gibson, Derrik, Salem	.966
	PO	Simmons, Andrelton, Lynchburg	218
	A	Simmons, Andrelton, Lynchburg	417
	E	Garcia, Leury, Myrtle Beach	37
	DP	Simmons, Andrelton, Lynchburg	89
OF	FPCT	Hood, Destin, Potomac	.996
	PO	Perez, Eury, Potomac	270
	A	Ware, L.V., Lynchburg	16
	E	Brentz, Bryce, Salem	9
	DP	Three tied at	3

MINOR LEAGUES

A six-game win streak to open the regular season became a harbinger of things to come for Daytona. Despite placing only one player in the league Top 20 Prospects list (outfielder Matt Szczur, No. 8), the Cubs rode the momentum of the initial streak to the league's best first-half record and eventually to the Florida State League championship.

The Cubs, which also enjoyed a 12-game and two separate eight-game win streaks during the regular season, went streaking again in the postseason. After dropping the first-round opening game against Dunedin, Daytona won five straight—including a three-game sweep of St. Lucie in the finals. Strong starting pitching set the tone during the playoffs, as Cubs' starters pitched to a 1.50 ERA in the playoffs in over 35 innings of work.

St. Lucie lefthander Darin Gorski earned FSL pitcher of the year honors after leading the league in wins, ERA, WHIP and placed third in strikeouts. The Mets' postseason fortunes might have been different if righthander Matt Harvey had not been promoted to Double-A midseason. During his tenure in the FSL, Harvey dazzled observers by showing a dominant fastball and striking out 92 hitters in 76 innings while posting a 2.37 ERA.

Before bowing out to Daytona in the first round of the playoffs, Dunedin showed off a wealth of young talent. Catcher A.J. Jimenez coupled a plus arm behind the plate with a breakout offensive performance at it, and pitchers Nestor Molina, Deck McGuire, Drew Hutchison, Chad Jenkins, and Asher Wojciechowski showed promise.

Although Clearwater was unable to earn a playoff berth, the Threshers stockpiled several future major leaguers. The Threshers' rotation—which included Jarred Cosart, Brody Colvin, Trevor May, John Pettibone, and Julio Rodriguez—led the league in team ERA, hits allowed, WHIP, and strikeouts. First baseman Jonathan Singleton displayed a great feel for hitting while Jiwan James showed off his toolsy skill set at the plate, in the field, and on the bases. Singleton and Cosart were traded midseason to the Astros for outfielder Hunter Pence.

Bradenton outfielder Robbie Grossman competed for the top spot in runs, hits, steals, OBP, and OPS. Top prospect Shelby Miller overwhelmed hitters, striking out 81 in 53 innings, before moving on to Double-A Springfield.

TOP 20 PROSPECTS

1. Shelby Miller, rhp, Palm Beach Cardinals
2. Matt Harvey, rhp, St. Lucie Mets
3. Hak-Ju Lee, ss, Charlotte Stone Crabs (Rays)
4. Trevor May, rhp, Clearwater Threshers (Phillies)
5. Alex Colome, rhp, Charlotte Stone Crabs (Rays)
6. Carlos Martinez, rhp, Palm Beach Cardinals
7. Jonathan Singleton, 1b/of, Clearwater Threshers (Phillies)
8. Matt Szczur, of, Daytona Cubs
9. Jarred Cosart, rhp, Clearwater Threshers (Phillies)
10. A.J. Jimenez, c, Dunedin Blue Jays
11. Zack Cox, 3b, Palm Beach Cardinals
12. Sebastian Valle c, Clearwater Threshers (Phillies)
13. Drew Hutchison, rhp, Dunedin Blue Jays
14. Tyler Thornburg, rhp, Brevard County Manatees (Brewers)
15. Oswaldo Arcia, of, Fort Myers Miracle (Twins)
16. Drew Smyly, lhp, Lakeland Flying Tigers (Tigers)
17. Deck McGuire, rhp, Dunedin Blue Jays
18. Aaron Hicks, of, Fort Myers Miracle (Twins)
19. Brody Colvin, rhp, Clearwater Threshers (Phillies)
20. Wilmer Flores, ss, St. Lucie Mets

STANDINGS: SPLIT SEASON

FIRST HALF

North	W	L	PCT	GB
Daytona	47	23	.671	—
Clearwater	39	30	.565	7½
Dunedin	39	31	.557	8
Tampa	37	32	.536	9½
Lakeland	36	34	.514	11
Brevard Co.	27	43	.386	20

South	W	L	PCT	GB
St. Lucie	38	32	.543	—
Fort Myers	34	36	.486	4
Jupiter	32	38	.457	6
Charlotte	30	39	.435	7½
Bradenton	30	40	.429	8
Palm Beach	29	40	.420	8½

SECOND HALF

North	W	L	PCT	GB
Dunedin	40	30	.571	—
Tampa	37	32	.536	2½
Clearwater	36	33	.522	3½
Brevard Co.	35	33	.515	4
Daytona	29	38	.433	9.5
Lakeland	28	40	.412	11

South	W	L	PCT	GB
Bradenton	44	23	.657	—
Palm Beach	39	30	.565	6
Charlotte	34	36	.486	11½
St. Lucie	34	36	.486	11½
Fort Myers	29	40	.420	16
Jupiter	28	42	.400	17½

PLAYOFFS: Semifinals: Daytona defeated Dunedin 2-1 and St. Lucie defeated Bradenton 2-1 in best-of-five series. **Finals:** Daytona defeated St. Lucie 3-0 in best-of-five series.

OVERALL STANDINGS

Team (Organization)	W	L	PCT	GB	Manager	Attendance	Average	Last Pennant
Dunedin Blue Jays (Blue Jays)	79	61	.564	—	Clayton McCullough	43,148	654	Never
Daytona Cubs (Cubs)	76	61	.555	1½	Buddy Bailey	154,557	2,342	2011
Clearwater Threshers (Phillies)	75	63	.543	3	Dusty Wathan	177,117	2,567	2007
Bradenton Marauders (Pirates)	74	63	.540	3½	Carlos Garcia	103,978	1,507	1963
Tampa Yankees (Yankees)	74	64	.536	4	Luis Sojo	117,162	1,775	2010
St. Lucie Mets (Mets)	72	68	.514	7	Pedro Lopez	105,379	1,647	2006
Palm Beach Cardinals (Cardinals)	68	70	.493	10	Luis Aguayo	68,620	1,089	2005
Lakeland (Flying Tigers)	64	74	.464	14	Dave Huppert	62,324	959	1992
Charlotte Stone Crabs (Rays)	64	75	.460	14½	Jim Morrison	166,375	2,483	1990
Fort Myers Miracle (Twins)	63	76	.453	15½	Jake Mauer	122,328	1,911	1985
Brevard County Manatees (Brewers)	62	76	.449	16	Jeff Isom	93,903	1,491	2001
Jupiter Hammerheads (Marlins)	60	80	.429	19	Ron Hassey	82,071	1,207	1991

CLUB BATTING

	AVG	G	AB	R	H	2B	3B	HR	RBI	BB	SO	SB	OBP	SLG
Bradenton	.278	137	4483	699	1247	265	42	99	639	516	952	125	.357	.422
St. Lucie	.268	140	4605	625	1232	218	40	91	562	379	913	111	.330	.392
Tampa	.268	139	4669	649	1249	253	45	92	609	430	1061	92	.335	.400
Brevard County	.267	138	4525	625	1209	209	37	108	565	362	967	157	.330	.401
Daytona	.267	137	4609	629	1232	231	36	101	574	380	941	103	.328	.399
Clearwater	.264	139	4643	559	1224	223	30	94	522	355	999	90	.322	.385
Dunedin	.262	140	4651	689	1219	287	22	125	641	490	1053	117	.338	.414
Charlotte	.259	139	4648	611	1204	257	40	45	551	432	949	177	.331	.361
Lakeland	.258	138	4577	587	1180	219	32	84	538	434	997	57	.329	.375
Palm Beach	.255	138	4520	568	1151	221	31	88	526	424	1041	93	.326	.376
Jupiter	.249	140	4589	505	1141	205	26	72	459	419	950	105	.317	.352
Fort Myers	.248	139	4507	549	1118	234	29	56	490	469	954	61	.323	.350

CLUB PITCHING

	ERA	G	CG	SHO	SV	IP	H	R	ER	HR	BB	SO	AVG
Clearwater	3.52	139	3	12	43	1214	1099	529	475	83	405	1117	.244
Jupiter	3.65	140	2	14	34	1221	1232	600	495	81	469	1010	.264
Palm Beach	3.65	138	3	8	34	1192	1121	542	484	64	490	1064	.250
Bradenton	3.78	137	3	9	29	1175	1147	606	493	83	345	855	.254
Daytona	3.79	137	4	6	38	1191	1186	616	501	95	423	1063	.260
St. Lucie	3.82	140	7	14	35	1181	1222	606	502	82	383	989	.268
Charlotte	3.83	139	2	13	27	1225	1140	593	521	76	514	958	.250
Dunedin	3.87	140	1	7	45	1212	1223	590	521	103	356	1026	.261
Lakeland	3.91	138	5	8	32	1190	1213	606	517	95	381	915	.266
Tampa	3.98	139	0	9	39	1210	1253	605	535	92	382	970	.269
Fort Myers	4.56	139	4	8	39	1189	1327	702	603	102	464	883	.283
Brevard County	4.70	138	3	10	38	1175	1243	700	614	99	478	927	.272

CLUB FIELDING

	PCT	PO	A	E	DP		PCT	PO	A	E	DP
Clearwater	.980	3643	1295	100	117	Tampa	.974	3630	1476	138	135
Lakeland	.978	3569	1438	113	117	St. Lucie	.973	3544	1364	134	135
Dunedin	.977	3637	1473	118	119	Brevard County	.971	3525	1356	147	129
Palm Beach	.977	3576	1387	119	117	Bradenton	.970	3525	1432	154	115
Charlotte	.975	3675	1486	134	134	Daytona	.970	3573	1330	150	111
Fort Myers	.975	3568	1362	126	106	Jupiter	.969	3663	1423	161	126

INDIVIDUAL BATTING LEADERS *(Minimum 2.7 PA/Team Game)*

	AVG	G	AB	R	H	2B	3B	HR	RBI	BB	SO	SB
Cabrera, Ramon, Bradenton	.343	92	327	46	112	25	4	3	53	38	29	5
Gonzalez, Elevys, Bradenton	.322	126	454	63	146	36	6	6	83	39	93	7
Lee, Hak-Ju, Charlotte	.318	97	400	82	127	16	11	4	23	42	72	28
Santos, Adalberto, Bradenton	.314	105	353	59	111	22	7	7	49	42	55	27
Jensen, Kyle, Jupiter	.309	109	391	53	121	20	1	22	66	46	114	0
Ruf, Darin, Clearwater	.308	133	484	72	149	43	1	17	82	56	95	0
Crawford, Evan, Daytona	.307	115	446	69	137	24	6	2	50	26	98	32
Bortnick, Tyler, Charlotte	.306	132	474	96	145	34	7	4	70	79	67	43
Jimenez, A.J., Dunedin	.303	102	379	49	115	29	1	4	52	28	60	11
Gennett, Scooter, Brevard County	.300	134	556	74	167	20	6	9	51	27	69	11

INDIVIDUAL PITCHING LEADERS *(Minimum 0.8 IP/Team Game)*

	W	L	ERA	G	GS	CG	SV	IP	H	R	ER	BB	SO
Gorski, Darin, St. Lucie	11	3	2.08	27	21	3	1	139	109	40	32	29	140
Rodriguez, Julio, Clearwater	16	7	2.76	27	27	0	0	157	102	49	48	56	168
Lorin, Brett, Bradenton	7	6	2.84	25	17	1	1	117	103	50	37	19	99
Thompson, Jacob, Charlotte	5	7	2.90	22	22	0	0	115	114	47	37	37	56
Pettibone, Jonathan, Clearwater	10	11	2.96	27	27	0	0	161	149	62	53	34	115
Kelly, Merrill, Charlotte	8	7	3.28	25	25	0	0	129	117	52	47	51	70
Baker, Nathan, Bradenton	10	8	3.34	25	25	0	0	148	151	80	55	51	105
May, Trevor, Clearwater	10	8	3.63	27	27	3	0	151	121	65	61	67	208
Rasmussen, Rob, Jupiter	12	10	3.64	28	27	1	0	148	140	75	60	71	118
Fornataro, Eric, Palm Beach	7	13	3.67	24	24	1	0	145	150	68	59	50	116

DEPARTMENT LEADERS

BATTING

OBP	Bortnick, Tyler, Charlotte	.428
SLG	Jensen, Kyle, Jupiter	.535
OPS	Jensen, Kyle, Jupiter	.919
R	Grossman, Robbie, Bradenton	127
H	Gennett, Scooter, Brevard County	167
TB	Ruf, Darin, Clearwater	245
XBH	Ruf, Darin, Clearwater	61
2B	Ruf, Darin, Clearwater	43
3B	Watkins, Logan, Daytona	12
HR	Glenn, Brad, Dunedin	26
RBI	Plagman, Tony, Lakeland	97
SAC	Hanzawa, Troy, Clearwater	14
	Ibarra, Walter, Tampa	14
BB	Grossman, Robbie, Bradenton	104
HBP	Bortnick, Tyler, Charlotte	25
SO	Gaynor, Wade, Lakeland	137
SB	Bortnick, Tyler, Charlotte	43
CS	James, Jiwan, Clearwater	16
AB/SO	Cabrera, Ramon, Bradenton	11.28

PITCHING

G	Batista, Frank, Daytona	51
GS	Olmos, Edgar, Jupiter	28
GF	Batista, Frank, Daytona	48
	Ramos, Alejandro, Jupiter	48
SV	Etheridge, Wes, Dunedin	32
W	Rodriguez, Julio, Clearwater	16
L	Olmos, Edgar, Jupiter	17
IP	Pettibone, Jonathan, Clearwater	161
H	Moviel, Scott, St. Lucie	177
R	Olmos, Edgar, Jupiter	110
ER	Olmos, Edgar, Jupiter	94
HB	Koronis, Alex, Charlotte	16
BB	Olmos, Edgar, Jupiter	81
SO	May, Trevor, Clearwater	208
SO/9	May, Trevor, Clearwater	12.37
SO/9 (RP)	Wright, Matt, Dunedin	10.29
BB/9	Lorin, Brett, Bradenton	1.46
WP	Allen, Kyle, St. Lucie	17
BK	Three tied at	3
HR	Feeney, Trevor, Lakeland	18
AVG	Rodriguez, Julio, Clearwater	.186

FIELDING

C	FPCT	Valle, Sebastian, Clearwater	.998
	PO	Valle, Sebastian, Clearwater	737
	A	Thomas, Mark, Charlotte	81
	E	Rodriguez, Julio, Lakeland	14
	DP	Thomas, Mark, Charlotte	8
	PB	Cabrera, Ramon, Bradenton	14
1B	FPCT	Welch, Stefan, St. Lucie	.998
	PO	Sheridan, Michael, Charlotte	1118
	A	Baker, Aaron, Bradenton	78
	E	Morris, Hunter, Brevard County	19
	DP	Welch, Stefan, St. Lucie	107
2B	FPCT	Hernandez, Cesar, Clearwater	.975
	PO	Gennett, Scooter, Brevard County	251
	A	Gennett, Scooter, Brevard County	395
	E	Cunningham, Jarek, Bradenton	22
		Gennett, Scooter, Brevard County	22
	DP	Bortnick, Tyler, Charlotte	96
3B	FPCT	Gaynor, Wade, Lakeland	.953
	PO	Gaynor, Wade, Lakeland	104
	A	Gaynor, Wade, Lakeland	257
	E	Marte, Jefry, St. Lucie	28
	DP	Gaynor, Wade, Lakeland	25
SS	FPCT	Hanzawa, Troy, Clearwater	.970
	PO	Flores, Wilmer, St. Lucie	195
	A	Flores, Wilmer, St. Lucie	370
	E	Dominguez, Jeff, Jupiter	30
	DP	Flores, Wilmer, St. Lucie	79
OF	FPCT	McElroy, Brad, Dunedin	.995
	PO	Hicks, Aaron, Fort Myers	331
	A	Hicks, Aaron, Fort Myers	18
	E	Puello, Cesar, St. Lucie	10
	DP	Hicks, Aaron, Fort Myers	10

MINOR LEAGUES

Prospects in low Class A do not often receive an 80 grade on the 20-80 scouting scale, but Dayton shortstop Billy Hamilton's speed might merit such a mark.

The 2009 second-round pick stole a Reds' record 103 bases and became the first minor leaguer to steal 100 since Chris Morris swiped 111 in 2001. Hamilton overcame a sluggish first half to hit .318/.382/.387 in the second half.

Dayton finished the regular season with the league's best overall record behind a strong pitching staff which placed first in team ERA, shutouts, strikeouts and WHIP. Righthander Daniel Corcino ranked among the Midwest League leaders in strikeouts (156) and WHIP (1.16). In the end, however, Dayton fell to Lansing in the playoffs.

In one of the most difficult hitting environments in the minors, Lansing outfielder Jake Marisnick showed off a power-speed combination, stealing 37 bases and hitting 14 home runs.

Quad Cities swept Lansing in the championship series. Throughout the season, the River Bandits were home to hitting machine Oscar Tavares, who led the circuit in batting with a .368 average. Reinforcements came in the form of second baseman Kolten Wong, who signed quickly after being selected in the first round of this year's draft and hit .335/.401/.510 in 47 games.

Fort Wayne outfielder Rhymer Liriano found his second stint in the Midwest League more hospitable as he was named MVP. After a 2010 demotion, he placed third in in hitting with a .319 average with 12 homers and 65 stolen bases.

Clinton righthander Taijuan Walker nosed out Hamilton as the top prospect. Carlos Martinez drew comparisons to Pedro Martinez (no relation) and would have challenged Walker for the top spot had he not been promoted after just eight starts.

TOP 20 PROSPECTS

1. Taijuan Walker, rhp Clinton Lumberkings (Mariners)
2. Billy Hamilton, ss, Dayton Dragons (Reds)
3. Jake Marisnick, of, Lansing Lugnuts (Blue Jays)
4. Nick Castellanos, 3b, West Michigan Whitecaps (Tigers)
5. Rymer Liriano, of, Fort Wayne Tincaps (Padres)
6. Oscar Taveras, of, Quad Cities River Bandits (Cardinals)
7. Zach Lee, rhp Great Lakes Loons (Dodgers)
8. James Paxton, lhp Clinton Lumberkings (Mariners)
9. Matt Szczur, of, Peoria Chiefs (Cubs)
10. Keyvious Sampson, rhp Fort Wayne Tincaps (Padres)
11. Cheslor Cuthbert, 3b, Kane County Cougars (Royals)
12. Kolten Wong, 2b, Quad Cities River Bandits (Cardinals)
13. Cory Spangenberg 2b, Fort Wayne Tincaps (Padres)
14. Drew Hutchison, rhp Lansing Lugnuts (Blue Jays)
15. Enny Romero, lhp Bowling Green Hot Rods (Rays)
16. Daniel Corcino, rhp Dayton Dragons (Reds)
17. Garrett Gould, rhp Great Lakes Loons (Dodgers)
18. Tyler Thornburg, rhp Wisconsin Timber Rattlers (Brewers)
19. Derek Dietrich, ss, Bowling Green Hot Rods (Rays)
20. David Holmberg, lhp, South Bend Silverhawks (Dbacks)

STANDINGS: SPLIT SEASON

FIRST HALF

EASTERN	W	L	PCT	GB
Bowling Green	41	29	.586	—
Lansing	38	29	.567	1½
Great Lakes	39	30	.565	1½
Dayton	35	35	.500	6
South Bend	34	35	.493	6½
West Michigan	32	37	.464	8½
Fort Wayne	30	39	.435	10½
Lake County	28	41	.406	12½

WESTERN	W	L	PCT	GB
Burlington	45	25	.643	—
Quad Cities	40	29	.580	4½
Beloit	38	32	.543	7
Wisconsin	38	32	.543	7
Peoria	33	37	.471	12
Cedar Rapids	32	38	.457	13
Kane County	28	41	.406	16½
Clinton	24	46	.343	21

SECOND HALF

EASTERN	W	L	PCT	GB
Dayton	48	22	.686	—
Fort Wayne	39	31	.557	9
Lansing	39	31	.557	9
West Michigan	38	32	.543	10
Bowling Green	34	36	.514	12
Great Lakes	33	37	.471	15
South Bend	33	37	.471	15
Lake County	25	45	.357	23

WESTERN	W	L	PCT	GB
Quad Cities	41	27	.603	—
Clinton	39	30	.565	2½
Kane County	37	33	.529	5
Beloit	31	37	.456	10
Burlington	31	37	.456	10
Cedar Rapids	29	40	.420	12½
Wisconsin	29	40	.420	12½
Peoria	27	42	.391	14½

PLAYOFFS—Division Series: Lansing defeated Dayton 2-1, Fort Wayne defeated Bowling Green 2-0, Quad Cities defeated Clinton 2-0 and Kane County defeated Burlington 2-1 in best-of-three series. **Semifinals:** Lansing defeated Fort Wayne 2-0 and Quad Cities defeated Kane County 2-0 in best-of-three series. **Finals:** Quad Cities defeated Lansing 3-0 in best-of-five series.

OVERALL STANDINGS

Team (Organization)	W	L	PCT	GB	Manager(s)	Attendance	Average	Last Pennant
Dayton Dragons (Reds)	83	57	.593	—	Delino DeShields	571,886	8,288	Never
Quad Cities River Bandits (Cardinals)	81	56	.591	½	Johnny Rodriguez	223,025	3,485	2011
Lansing Lugnuts (Blue Jays)	77	60	.562	4½	Mike Redmond	345,089	5,392	2003
Burlington Bees (Royals)	76	62	.551	6	Aaron Nieckula	54,284	835	2008
Bowling Green Hot Rods (Rays)	77	63	.550	6	Brady Williams	237,070	3,538	Never
Great Lakes Loons (Dodgers)	72	67	.518	10½	John Shoemaker	264,249	3,830	2000
West Michigan Whitecaps (Tigers)	70	69	.504	12½	Ernie Young	372,555	5,561	2007
Beloit Snappers (Twins)	69	69	.500	13	Nelson Prada	66,982	1,030	1995
Fort Wayne TinCaps (Padres)	69	70	.496	13½	Shawn Wooten	376,022	5,612	2009
South Bend Silver Hawks (Diamondbacks)	67	72	.482	15½	Mark Haley	112,795	1,762	2005
Wisconsin Timber Rattlers (Brewers)	67	72	.482	15½	Matt Erickson	240,998	3,766	1984
Kane County Cougars (Athletics)	65	74	.468	17½	Vance Wilson	410,262	6,123	2001
Clinton LumberKings (Mariners)	63	76	.453	19½	Jesus Azuaje/Eddie Menchaca	115,253	1,746	1991
Cedar Rapids Kernels (Angels)	61	78	.439	21½	Brent Del Chiaro	169,000	2,449	1994
Peoria Chiefs (Cubs)	60	79	.432	22½	Casey Kopitzke	187,915	2,763	2002
Lake County Captains (Indians)	53	86	.381	29 1/2	Ted Kubiak	235,897	3,574	2010

CLUB BATTING

	AVG	G	AB	R	H	2B	3B	HR	RBI	BB	SO	SB	OBP	SLG
Dayton	.264	140	4636	696	1224	215	45	93	627	430	1144	228	.332	.390
Peoria	.262	139	4710	569	1232	233	27	63	520	355	928	79	.319	.363
Fort Wayne	.261	139	4609	641	1202	244	36	67	550	457	1078	220	.333	.373
Quad Cities	.261	137	4582	687	1196	281	33	89	605	550	1025	101	.346	.395
West Michigan	.255	139	4619	550	1176	207	19	77	497	391	1044	82	.318	.358
Bowling Green	.252	140	4634	645	1170	240	43	106	588	421	1041	120	.327	.391
Wisconsin	.252	139	4565	608	1149	204	43	76	537	473	1107	165	.327	.365
Beloit	.251	138	4463	659	1121	249	29	97	597	461	1087	105	.331	.385
Lansing	.250	137	4561	691	1142	243	44	88	610	545	1160	154	.336	.381
Lake County	.246	139	4659	573	1148	247	35	92	496	432	1111	92	.315	.374
Burlington	.245	138	4514	611	1104	231	31	84	533	484	1094	146	.324	.365
Kane County	.242	139	4642	539	1123	210	35	79	465	435	1097	106	.311	.353
South Bend	.241	139	4467	558	1078	234	36	73	489	432	1033	131	.316	.359
Great Lakes	.240	139	4572	552	1096	220	38	102	489	435	1009	87	.314	.371
Clinton	.238	139	4589	566	1093	192	37	91	523	435	1090	166	.311	.356
Cedar Rapids	.237	139	4567	548	1083	195	35	76	491	398	1077	120	.308	.345

CLUB PITCHING

	ERA	G	CG	SHO	SV	IP	H	R	ER	HR	BB	SO	AVG
Dayton	3.39	140	2	14	36	1210	1087	543	455	84	461	1292	.239
Burlington	3.45	138	0	12	34	1209	1104	569	463	82	400	1028	.241
Great Lakes	3.62	139	2	5	48	1218	1129	586	490	69	464	1097	.244
Quad Cities	3.63	137	1	9	43	1198	1037	555	483	83	450	1105	.234
South Bend	3.68	139	2	8	34	1192	1127	580	488	86	378	970	.249
West Michigan	3.68	139	4	8	43	1214	1140	574	497	73	442	1054	.251
Beloit	3.73	138	3	5	29	1199	1159	604	497	92	421	1076	.252
Clinton	3.78	139	2	6	36	1225	1166	613	514	75	506	1166	.253
Lansing	3.78	137	3	8	44	1190	1214	636	500	72	378	1056	.263
Bowling Green	3.81	140	2	12	39	1215	1198	599	515	110	431	1119	.259
Kane County	3.81	139	0	9	32	1237	1233	623	524	75	373	1075	.259
Cedar Rapids	3.89	139	4	5	37	1212	1192	637	524	71	481	962	.259
Peoria	3.92	139	1	6	27	1221	1154	649	532	110	454	953	.251
Fort Wayne	3.99	139	1	11	29	1214	1147	638	539	86	462	1117	.248
Wisconsin	4.01	139	7	7	37	1198	1122	619	534	81	497	1044	.248
Lake County	4.08	139	2	3	28	1216	1128	668	551	104	536	1011	.246

CLUB FIELDING

	PCT	PO	A	E	DP		PCT	PO	A	E	DP
Bowling Green	.975	3646	1370	129	104	Wisconsin	.969	3594	1478	162	116
West Michigan	.973	3642	1417	142	124	Cedar Rapids	.968	3637	1525	170	128
Kane County	.971	3710	1467	157	108	Clinton	.968	3674	1470	168	98
Beloit	.970	3596	1381	154	108	Fort Wayne	.968	3643	1326	165	107
Dayton	.970	3629	1293	152	106	Lake County	.967	3649	1523	176	138
South Bend	.970	3576	1586	158	133	Peoria	.966	3663	1427	180	137
Great Lakes	.969	3565	1387	159	95	Burlington	.964	3627	1403	186	110
Quad Cities	.969	3594	1394	161	123	Lansing	.961	3569	1464	205	111

INDIVIDUAL BATTING LEADERS (Minimum 2.7 PA/Team Game)

	AVG	G	AB	R	H	2B	3B	HR	RBI	BB	SO	SB
Taveras, Oscar, Quad Cities	.386	78	308	52	119	27	5	8	62	32	52	1
Whitaker, Josh, Burlington	.326	113	396	67	129	34	3	17	68	44	107	10
Marisnick, Jake, Lansing	.320	118	462	68	148	27	6	14	77	43	91	37
Liriano, Rymer, Fort Wayne	.319	116	455	81	145	30	8	12	62	47	95	65
Castellanos, Nick, West Michigan	.312	135	507	65	158	36	3	7	76	45	130	3
Jones, Richard, Peoria	.309	123	472	62	146	36	0	24	98	32	125	0
Walters, Zach, South Bend	.302	97	361	69	109	27	6	9	56	42	96	12
Lutz, Donald, Dayton	.301	123	465	85	140	23	3	20	75	34	125	5
Silva, Rubi, Peoria	.300	93	390	59	117	16	7	3	37	13	73	6
Hawn, Cody, Wisconsin	.294	101	377	56	111	24	0	6	50	51	85	3

INDIVIDUAL PITCHING LEADERS (Minimum 0.8 IP/Team Game)

	W	L	ERA	G	GS	CG	SV	IP	H	R	ER	BB	SO
Billo, Greg, Kane County	9	5	1.93	27	18	0	1	135	113	39	29	25	119
Gould, Garrett, Great Lakes	11	6	2.40	27	24	0	0	124	102	47	33	37	104
Whiting, Boone, Quad Cities	5	2	2.41	30	14	0	4	120	82	36	32	24	122
Hassebrock, Blake, Burlington	7	8	2.64	26	26	0	0	140	133	64	41	46	110
Hardy, Mark, Fort Wayne	11	10	2.78	27	19	1	0	129	117	47	40	32	96
Fernandez, Anthony, Clinton	7	4	2.80	21	19	0	0	125	109	49	39	42	107
Sampson, Keyvius, Fort Wayne	12	3	2.90	24	24	0	0	118	81	42	38	49	143
Salcedo, Adrian, Beloit	6	6	2.93	29	20	1	0	135	131	56	44	27	92
Jokisch, Eric, Peoria	9	3	2.96	25	11	0	1	119	106	41	39	32	103
Smith, Josh, Dayton	14	7	2.97	26	26	0	0	142	122	57	47	33	166

ALL-STAR TEAM

C: Rob Brantly, West Michigan. **1B:** Jesus Aguilar, Lake County. **2B:** Hernan Perez, West Michigan.
3B: Nick Castellanos, West Michigan. **SS:** Billy Hamilton, Dayton. **OF:** Michael Crouse, Lansing; Jake Marisnick, Lansing; Rymer Liriano, Fort Wayne. **DH:** Josh Whitaker, Burlington. **RHSP:** Greg Billo, Kane County. **LHSP:** C.J. Riefenhauser, Bowling Green. **RHRP:** Drew Hayes, Dayton. **LHRP:** Chris Rearick, Bowling Green.
Most Valuable Player: Rymer Liriano, Fort Wayne. **Manager of the Year:** Mike Redmond, Lansing.

DEPARTMENT LEADERS

BATTING

OBP	Price, Robby, Bowling Green	.426
SLG	Fletcher, Brian, Kane County	.560
OPS	Whitaker, Josh, Burlington	.957
R	Hamilton, Billy, Dayton	99
H	Castellanos, Nick, West Michigan	158
TB	Jones, Richard, Peoria	254
XBH	Arbelo, Yazy, South Bend	62
2B	Vidal, David, Dayton	37
3B	Landry, Leon, Great Lakes	11
	Rogers, Cody, Bowling Green	11
HR	Arbelo, Yazy, South Bend	31
RBI	Jones, Richard, Peoria	98
SAC	Beltre, Geulin, Kane County	16
	Franco, Angel, Kane County	16
BB	Price, Robby, Bowling Green	86
HBP	Roberts, Nate, Beloit	29
SO	Arbelo, Yazy, South Bend	161
SB	Hamilton, Billy, Dayton	103
CS	Hamilton, Billy, Dayton	20
	Liriano, Rymer, Fort Wayne	20
AB/SO	Gomez, Raywilly, South Bend	10

PITCHING

G	Franklin, Chris, Fort Wayne	63
GS	Bowman, Josh, Burlington	28
	Kirk, Austin, Peoria	28
GF	Hayes, Drew, Dayton	43
	Rearick, Chris, Bowling Green	43
SV	Hayes, Drew, Dayton	22
W	Smith, Josh, Dayton	14
L	Bradley, J.R., South Bend	16
IP	Bowman, Josh, Burlington	154.7
H	Bradley, J.R., South Bend	169
R	Bradley, J.R., South Bend	100
ER	Bradley, J.R., South Bend	79
HB	Lotzkar, Kyle, Dayton	15
	Miller, Matthew, Wisconsin	15
BB	Robles, Tanner, Dayton	69
SO	Smith, Josh, Dayton	166
SO/9	Renken, Daniel, Dayton	11.2
SO/9 (RP)	Arias, Jonathan, Clinton	14.35
BB/9	Lawrence, Casey, Lansing	1.58
WP	Lara, Braulio, Bowling Green	22
BK	Russell, Zach, Quad Cities	5
	Soliman, Manuel, Beloit	5
HR	Cooper, Jordan, Lake County	19
AVG	Whiting, Boone, Quad Cities	.191

FIELDING

C	FPCT	Barnhart, Tucker, Dayton	.998
	PO	Barnhart, Tucker, Dayton	805
	A	Barnhart, Tucker, Dayton	118
	E	Pericht, Michael, Great Lakes	15
	DP	Bailey, Lucas, Bowling Green	9
	PB	Monsalve, Alex, Lake County	20
1B	FPCT	Robbins, James, West Michigan	.994
	PO	Robbins, James, West Michigan	1189
	A	Hobson, K.C., Lansing	96
	E	Hobson, K.C., Lansing	25
	DP	Robbins, James, West Michigan	104
2B	FPCT	Grider, Casio, Great Lakes	.966
	PO	Grider, Casio, Great Lakes	173
	A	Grider, Casio, Great Lakes	286
	E	Hatton, Wes, Cedar Rapids	22
	DP	Grider, Casio, Great Lakes	55
		Perez, Hernan, West Michigan	55
3B	FPCT	Vidal, David, Dayton	.965
	PO	Vidal, David, Dayton	105
	A	Urshela, Giovanny, Lake County	214
	E	Helm, Matt, South Bend	32
	DP	Urshela, Giovanny, Lake County	27
SS	FPCT	Machado, Dixon, West Michigan	.963
	PO	Hamilton, Billy, Dayton	218
	A	Machado, Dixon, West Michigan	371
	E	Hamilton, Billy, Dayton	39
	DP	Machado, Dixon, West Michigan	75
OF	FPCT	Schwaner, Nicholas, Bwl. Green	1.000
	PO	Kiermaier, Kevin, Bwl. Green	279
	A	Giansanti, Anthony, Peoria	24
	E	Moncrief, Carlos, Lake County	12
	DP	Giansanti, Anthony, Peoria	6
		Kiermaier, Kevin, Bowling Green	6

MINOR LEAGUES

The top three picks of the 2010 draft and one of the top international signings of the '09 class spent time in the South Atlantic League this season.

Hagerstown outfielder Bryce Harper and Delmarva shortstop Manny Machado, performed well enough to earn midseason promotions. Although held back in extended spring training to begin the year and under strict pitch counts upon arrival, West Virginia righthander Jameson Taillon showed off the big velocity and premium offspeed stuff that made him the No. 2 pick.

Harper, the game's top prospect entering the season, lived up to the hype in Hagerstown as the 18-year-old smacked 14 home runs in his professional debut before moving up to Double-A at midseason. However, Hickory Crawdads' shortstop Jurickson Profar stole the show. The 18-year-old Profar earned MVP honors as he placed in the top 10 in runs, doubles, triples, on-base percentage and slugging to go with stellar range at shortstop.

Hickory won a first-half title and finished with the league's best overall record behind a strong offense that ranked near the top in runs, stolen bases, and on-base percentage. Third baseman Christian Villanueva was Profar's running mate in the Hickory lineup and also joined him as part of the postseason all-star team.

Hickory fell to eventual champion Greensboro in the first round of the playoffs. Grasshoppers outfielder Christian Yelich hit a two-run walk-off home run in the bottom of the 15th inning to give Greensboro a come-from-behind 5-4 victory in the opening game of the series. Led by Yelich, another 2010 first-round pick, and Marcell Ozuna, a toolsy but unrefined talent, Greensboro never looked back on the way to knocking off the Savannah in the championship.

Lakewood lefthander Jesse Biddle, a 2010 first-round pick, improved throughout the season and

posted a 1.91 ERA in the second half. Kannapolis outfielder Trayce Thompson showed off his prodigious power by smashing 24 homers while former Auburn football commit Brandon Jacobs (Greenville) had a .881 OPS with 30 stolen bases.

TOP 20 PROSPECTS

1. Bryce Harper, of, Hagerstown Suns (Nationals)
2. Manny Machado, ss, Delmarva Shorebirds (Orioles)
3. Jurickson Profar, ss, Hickory Crawdads (Rangers)
4. Jameson Taillon, rhp, West Virginia Power (Pirates)
5. Christian Yelich, of, Greensboro Grasshoppers (Marlins)
6. Jesse Biddle, lhp, Lakewood Blueclaws (Phillies)
7. Marcell Ozuna, of, Greensboro Grasshoppers (Marlins)
8. Brandon Jacobs, of, Greenville Drive (Red Sox)
9. Jonathan Schoop, ss/3b, Delmarva Shorebirds (Orioles)
10. Xander Bogaerts, ss, Greenville Drive (Red Sox)
11. A.J. Cole, rhp, Hagerstown Suns (Nationals)
12. Kyle Parker, of, Asheville Tourists (Rockies)
13. J.T. Realmuto, c, Greensboro Grasshoppers (Marlins)
14. Gary Sanchez, c, Charleston Riverdogs (Yankees)
15. Trayce Thompson, of, Kannapolis Intimidators (White Sox)
16. Bryce Brentz, of, Greenville Drive (Red Sox)
17. Tyler Matzek, lhp, Asheville Tourists (Rockies)
18. Domingo Santana, of, Lakewood (Phi.)/Lexington (Astros)
19. Cody Buckel, rhp, Hickory Crawdads (Rangers)
20. Miles Head, 1b, Greenville Drive (Red Sox)

STANDINGS: SPLIT SEASON

FIRST HALF

NORTH	W	L	PCT	GB
Hickory	40	28	.588	—
Greensboro	40	30	.571	1
Hagerstown	40	30	.571	1
Kannapolis	37	31	.544	3
West Virginia	35	33	.515	5
Delmarva	35	35	.500	6
Lakewood	33	35	.485	7

SOUTH	W	L	PCT	GB
Savannah	39	30	.565	—
Greenville	38	32	.543	1½
Lexington	35	35	.500	4½
Asheville	31	38	.449	8
Augusta	31	39	.443	8½
Charleston	26	44	.371	13½
Rome Braves	25	45	.357	14½

SECOND HALF

NORTH	W	L	PCT	GB
Greensboro	39	30	.565	—
Hickory	39	30	.565	—
Kannapolis	39	31	.557	½
Hagerstown	35	34	.507	4
Lakewood	35	34	.507	4
West Virginia	34	36	.486	5½
Delmarva	20	50	.286	19½

SOUTH	W	L	PCT	GB
Augusta	39	29	.574	—
Greenville	40	30	.571	—
Savannah	40	30	.571	—
Asheville	38	32	.543	2
Rome	35	35	.500	5
Charleston	29	41	.414	11
Lexington	24	44	.353	15

PLAYOFFS—Semifinals: Greensboro defeated Hickory 2-0 and Savannah defeated Augusta 2-1 in best-of-three series. **Finals:** Greensboro defeated Savannah 3-2 in a best-of-five series.

OVERALL STANDINGS

Team (Organization)	W	L	PCT	GB	Manager(s)	Attendance	Average	Last Pennant
Hickory Crawdads (Rangers)	79	58	.577	—	Bill Richardson	131,131	2,049	2004
Greensboro Grasshoppers (Marlins)	79	60	.568	1	Andy Haines	388,218	5,546	2011
Savannah Sand Gnats (Mets)	79	60	.568	1	Ryan Ellis	135,415	1,963	1996
Greenville Drive (Red Sox)	78	62	.557	2½	Billy McMillon	327,558	4,747	1998
Kannapolis Intimidators (White Sox)	76	62	.551	3½	Tommy Thompson	138,487	2,067	2005
Hagerstown Suns (Nationals)	75	64	.540	5	Brian Daubach	123,593	1,931	Never
Augusta GreenJackets (Giants)	70	68	.507	9½	Lipso Nava	200,115	2,943	2008
West Virginia Power (Pirates)	69	69	.500	10½	Gary Robinson	165,996	2,554	1990
Asheville Tourists (Rockies)	69	70	.496	11	Joe Mikulik	157,199	2,346	1984
Lakewood BlueClaws (Phillies)	68	69	.496	11	Chris Truby	382,070	6,263	2010
Rome Braves (Braves)	60	80	.429	20½	Matt Walbeck/Rick Albert	186,345	2,781	2003
Lexington Legends (Astros)	59	79	.428	20½	Rodney Linares	312,349	4,880	2001
Charleston Riverdogs (Yankees)	55	85	.393	25½	Aaron Ledesma	265,465	3,962	Never
Delmarva Shorebirds (Orioles)	55	85	.393	25½	Ryan Minor	211,993	3,072	2001

MINOR LEAGUES

CLUB BATTING

	AVG	G	AB	R	H	2B	3B	HR	RBI	BB	SO	SB	OBP	SLG
Hickory	.277	137	4487	711	1241	261	31	99	629	453	898	187	.351	.415
Asheville	.276	139	4789	799	1322	304	38	163	741	479	1220	137	.352	.458
Greensboro	.269	139	4684	708	1259	262	24	142	656	396	1065	164	.331	.426
Hagerstown	.265	139	4583	683	1216	253	37	105	620	504	1072	183	.344	.405
Greenville	.263	140	4808	752	1266	264	41	125	671	438	1255	199	.334	.413
Kannapolis	.263	138	4634	697	1217	277	37	89	642	423	1109	75	.333	.396
Rome	.261	140	4806	653	1256	256	43	101	582	364	917	106	.320	.396
Charleston	.259	140	4746	612	1231	268	30	89	541	445	1104	95	.330	.385
West Virginia	.256	138	4590	627	1173	245	47	63	547	490	923	151	.332	.371
Lexington	.255	138	4607	645	1177	248	21	109	564	429	1034	102	.327	.389
Savannah	.250	139	4612	572	1153	229	45	68	501	453	981	113	.324	.363
Lakewood	.249	137	4579	560	1141	245	33	78	503	353	1091	168	.313	.368
Augusta	.248	138	4676	612	1159	247	24	86	536	510	1085	109	.327	.366
Delmarva	.242	140	4669	582	1130	217	20	60	508	500	1051	108	.323	.336

CLUB PITCHING

	ERA	G	CG	SHO	SV	IP	H	R	ER	HR	BB	SO	AVG
Savannah	3.26	139	3	13	50	1225	1070	521	444	76	428	1058	.236
Lakewood	3.52	137	2	8	33	1203	1091	564	470	74	470	1094	.243
Kannapolis	3.67	138	3	7	33	1205	1154	598	492	81	399	1025	.251
Augusta	3.70	138	1	7	35	1227	1171	611	505	66	455	962	.254
Hickory	3.77	137	2	8	41	1189	1106	586	498	85	546	1199	.248
Greenville	3.97	140	1	9	32	1236	1230	635	545	107	364	1131	.258
West Virginia	3.98	138	0	13	35	1227	1199	605	542	124	337	1012	.257
Hagerstown	4.10	139	1	12	38	1208	1225	649	551	90	358	1047	.262
Charleston	4.27	140	0	8	32	1216	1190	705	577	110	518	1171	.255
Greensboro	4.29	139	1	11	37	1212	1216	659	578	113	437	1039	.261
Rome	4.49	140	0	4	40	1236	1280	760	617	82	517	1053	.265
Lexington	4.63	138	0	5	34	1189	1295	731	612	136	385	1001	.276
Delmarva	4.74	140	0	5	38	1232	1318	760	648	106	516	988	.275
Asheville	5.28	139	1	2	34	1220	1396	829	716	127	507	1025	.290

CLUB FIELDING

	PCT	PO	A	E	DP		PCT	PO	A	E	DP
Greensboro	.975	3636	1359	130	126	Lakewood	.968	3610	1345	165	120
Hickory	.973	3566	1396	139	124	Savannah	.968	3675	1376	167	123
Augusta	.972	3681	1611	150	155	Delmarva	.967	3695	1616	184	123
West Virginia	.971	3680	1457	153	126	Kannapolis	.967	3616	1462	173	118
Asheville	.970	3661	1551	163	151	Lexington	.967	3566	1389	169	121
Greenville	.970	3708	1403	159	107	Rome	.965	3709	1474	188	115
Hagerstown	.968	3625	1492	168	112	Charleston	.962	3647	1334	198	116

INDIVIDUAL BATTING LEADERS (Minimum 2.7 PA/Team Game)

	AVG	G	AB	R	H	2B	3B	HR	RBI	BB	SO	SB
Gattis, Evan, Rome	.322	88	338	58	109	24	2	22	71	25	53	2
Shoemaker, Brady, Kannapolis	.319	99	373	68	119	28	2	11	65	43	78	7
Clark, Andrew, Hickory	.313	103	355	59	111	24	0	12	60	62	62	7
Yelich, Christian, Greensboro	.312	122	461	73	144	32	1	15	77	55	102	32
Herrera, Odubel, Hickory	.306	119	464	72	142	26	3	3	56	24	78	34
Garcia, Chris, Rome	.305	97	348	51	106	24	0	16	67	59	70	1
Jacobs, Brandon, Greenville	.303	115	442	75	134	32	3	17	80	43	123	30
Telis, Tomas, Hickory	.297	115	461	67	137	28	0	11	69	18	35	12
Perio, Noah, Greensboro	.295	119	488	76	144	30	3	6	52	19	64	15
Ortega, Rafael, Asheville	.294	113	479	77	141	26	8	9	66	28	90	32

INDIVIDUAL PITCHING LEADERS (Minimum 0.8 IP/Team Game)

	W	L	ERA	G	GS	CG	SV	IP	H	R	ER	BB	SO
Whitenton, Taylor, Savannah	5	5	2.49	26	22	1	1	112	77	39	31	48	119
Sanford, Shawn, Augusta	10	10	2.55	30	25	0	0	170	143	60	48	30	107
Rogers, Taylor, Augusta	12	10	2.91	27	27	1	0	155	136	63	50	38	86
Biddle, Jesse, Lakewood	7	8	2.98	25	24	0	0	133	104	51	44	66	124
Mendez, Roman, Hickory	9	1	3.31	26	20	0	1	117	117	44	43	45	130
Northcraft, Aaron, Rome	7	8	3.34	23	19	0	0	113	108	53	42	41	88
Buchanan, David, Lakewood	11	5	3.38	20	20	1	0	125	116	60	47	32	86
Claypool, Garett, Lakewood	5	7	3.47	27	23	0	0	137	111	60	53	46	151
Couch, Keith, Greenville	7	5	3.54	28	18	0	3	137	145	66	54	19	123
Cuan, Angel, Savannah	10	3	3.56	32	14	0	1	124	125	56	49	16	99

ALL-STAR TEAM

C: Evan Gattis, Rome. **1B:** Dan Black, Kannapolis. **2B:** Odubel Herrera, Hickory. **3B:** Adam Duvall, Augusta. **SS:** Jurickson Profar, Hickory. **OF:** Brandon Jacobs, Greenville; Kyle Parker, Asheville; Christian Yelich, Greensboro. **DH:** Jim Murphy, Lakewood. **UT INF:** Christian Villanueva, Hickory. **UT OF:** Brady Shoemaker, Kannapolis. **RHP:** Shawn Sanford, Augusta. **LHP:** Jesse Biddle, Lakewood.
Most Valuable Player: Jurickson Profar, Hickory. **Most Outstanding Pitcher:** Shawn Sanford, Augusta. **Manager of the Year:** Ryan Ellis, Savannah. **Coach of the Year:** Glenn Abbott, Savannah.

DEPARTMENT LEADERS

BATTING

OBP	Clark, Andrew, Hickory	.422
SLG	Dickerson, Corey, Asheville	.629
OPS	Dickerson, Corey, Asheville	.986
R	Thompson, Trayce, Kannapolis	95
H	Kelso, Blake, Hagerstown	150
TB	Black, Dan, Kannapolis	253
XBH	Black, Dan, Kannapolis	65
2B	Black, Dan, Kannapolis	41
3B	Vasquez, Andy, West Virginia	13
HR	Dickerson, Corey, Asheville	32
RBI	Black, Dan, Kannapolis	98
SAC	Duran, Edgar, Lakewood	13
BB	Freitas, David, Hagerstown	82
HBP	Santana, Domingo, Lex./Lakewood	17
SO	Thompson, Trayce, Kannapolis	172
SB	Sanchez, Felix, Greenville	55
CS	Ortega, Rafael, Asheville	19
AB/SO	Telis, Tomas, Hickory	13.17

PITCHING

G	Perez, Juan, Asheville	55
GS	Five tied at	27
GF	Perez, Juan, Asheville	45
SV	Walters, David, Delmarva	30
W	Grace, Matthew, Hagerstown	12
	Rogers, Taylor, Augusta	12
L	Greene, Shane, Charleston	14
IP	Arroyo, Spencer, Kannapolis	170.3
H	Quevedo, Carlos, Lexington	193
R	Brewer, Caleb, Rome	95
ER	Morey, Robert, Greensboro	80
	Von Rosenberg, Zack, West Virginia	80
HB	Manzueta, Jheyson, Greensboro	19
BB	Thompson, Matt, Hickory	80
SO	Claypool, Garett, Lakewood	151
SO/9	Mendez, Roman, Hickory	10
SO/9 (RP)	Rodriguez, Juan, Greenville	13.42
BB/9	Quevedo, Carlos, Lexington	1.13
WP	Thompson, Matt, Hickory	30
BK	Perez, Carlos, Rome	6
HR	Quevedo, Carlos, Lexington	22
AVG	Whitenton, Taylor, Savannah	.193

FIELDING

C	FPCT	Freitas, David, Hagerstown	.996
	PO	Vazquez, Christian, Greenville	788
	A	Vazquez, Christian, Greenville	108
	E	Cordero, Albert, Savannah	17
	DP	Realmuto, Jacob, Greensboro	9
	DP	Rupp, Cameron, Lakewood	9
	PB	Sanchez, Gary, Charleston	26
1B	FPCT	Black, Dan, Kannapolis	.995
	PO	Murphy, Jim, Lakewood	1067
	A	Black, Dan, Kannapolis	111
	E	Burnett, Tyler, Lexington	12
	DP	Murphy, Jim, Lakewood	100
2B	FPCT	Willoughby, Carlos, Augusta	.982
	PO	Willoughby, Carlos, Augusta	237
	A	Willoughby, Carlos, Augusta	429
	E	Perio, Noah, Greensboro	24
	DP	Willoughby, Carlos, Augusta	100
3B	FPCT	Villanueva, Christian, Hickory	.942
	PO	Rodriguez, Aderlin, Savannah	91
	A	Avila, Eric, West Virginia	269
	E	Rodriguez, Aderlin, Savannah	44
	DP	Villanueva, Christian, Hickory	37
SS	FPCT	Adames, Cristhian, Asheville	.966
	PO	Profar, Jurickson, Hickory	176
	A	Adames, Cristhian, Asheville	351
	E	Martinson, Jason, Hagerstown	33
	DP	Adames, Cristhian, Asheville	79
OF	FPCT	Galloway, Isaac, Greensboro	.996
	PO	Thompson, Trayce, Kannapolis	307
	A	Ortega, Rafael, Asheville	18
	E	Fernandez, Rafael, Savannah	16
	DP	Grovatt, Dan, West Virginia	6

MINOR LEAGUES

The Staten Island Yankees have been the New York-Penn League's most successful franchise for more than a decade. They added to their legacy of dominance in 2011, sweeping Auburn in two games to earn their second NY-P title in three years, and their sixth in the last 12 years.

Staten Island was by far the most prospect-laden team in the league, placing five players on the league's Top 20 prospects list, led by No. 1 prospect Mason Williams. The 20-year-old Williams tied for the league lead in triples (six) while ranking second in hitting (.349) and flashing brilliant defense in center field. Fellow 2010 high school draftees Cito Culver (No. 6), Tyler Austin (No. 8) and Angelo Gumbs (No. 14) joined Williams on the league's prospects list.

The Yankees surrounded their young core of high school talent with solid 2011 college draftees, such as slugger Zach Wilson and lefthander Matt Tracy, who struck out four over six shutout innings to earn the win in the decisive game of the championship series. Tracy tossed 12 scoreless innings over two postseason starts. Wilson, a 21st-round pick out of Arizona State in June, hit a solo home run to lift the Yankees to a 2-1 win in that final contest.

Staten Island's lone defeat of the postseason came against Brooklyn, 12-5, in Game Two of the opening-round series. The Yankees yielded just three runs in their remaining four games, including two shutouts against the Cyclones. Four Yankees pitchers (Tracy, William Oliver, Branden Pinder and Philip Wetherell) didn't give up a run over a combined 28 innings.

McNamara Division champion Staten Island edged wild card Brooklyn and Pinckney Division champ Auburn for the NY-P's best overall record during the regular season, and Vermont trumped

TOP 20 PROSPECTS

1. Mason Williams, of, Staten Island Yankees
2. Garin Cecchini, 3b, Lowell Spinners (Red Sox)
3. Parker Markel, rhp, Hudson Valley Renegades (Rays)
4. Maikel Franco, 3b, Williamsport Crosscutters (Phillies)
5. Jose Urena, rhp, Jamestown Jammers (Marlins)
6. Cito Culver, ss, Staten Island Yankees
7. Tony Wolters, ss, Mahoning Valley Scrappers (Indians)
8. Tyler Austin, 3b, Staten Island Yankees
9. Nick Kingham, rhp, State College Spikes (Pirates)
10. Parker Bridwell, rhp, Aberdeen Ironbirds (Orioles)
11. Alex Dickerson, 1b, State College Spikes (Pirates)
12. Aaron Westlake, 1b, Connecticut Tigers
13. Matt Skole, 3b, Auburn Doubledays (Nationals)
14. Angelo Gumbs, 2b, Staten Island Yankees
15. Glynn Davis, of, Aberdeen Ironbirds (Orioles)
16. Bobby Crocker, of, Vermont Lake Monsters (Athletics)
17. Jake Lowery, c/1b, Mahoning Valley Scrappers (Indians)
18. Danny Muno, ss, Brooklyn Cyclones (Mets)
19. Branden Pinder, rhp, Staten Island Yankees
20. Aaron Altherr, of, Williamsport Crosscutters (Phillies)

Connecticut via tie-breaker for the Stedler Division title, rounding out the playoff field. Two of those playoff teams had new affiliations in 2011, as the Nationals moved from Vermont to Auburn after the Blue Jays ended their long-time affiliation with the Doubledays. The Athletics replaced the Nationals in Vermont.

Vermont beat Auburn in the opening game of their playoff matchup, but the Doubledays bounced back to win the next two games and reach the championship series.

As negotiations with most premium 2011 draftees dragged late into the summer, the New York-Penn League lacked its usual college star power. Instead, most of the circuit's top prospects were 2010 high school draftees or international players.

Frontline arms were scarce in the league, as just five pitchers ranked among its Top 20 prospects. Beyond Williams, an easy choice as the league's top prospect, it was hard to find a slam-dunk blue-chipper in this NY-P class.

OVERALL STANDINGS

Team (Organization)	W	L	PCT	GB	Manager	Attendance	Average	Last Pennant
Staten Island Yankees (Yankees)	45	28	.616	—	Tom Slater	192,568	5,664	2011
Brooklyn Cyclones (Mets)	45	29	.608	½	Rich Donnelly	245,087	7,002	2001
Auburn Doubledays (Nationals)	45	30	.600	1	Gary Cathcart	48,429	1,424	2007
Williamsport Crosscutters (Phillies)	43	33	.566	3½	Mickey Morandini	68,124	1,841	2003
Mahoning Valley Scrappers (Indians)	41	34	.547	5	David Wallace	111,048	3,001	2004
Connecticut Tigers (Tigers)	39	35	.527	6½	Andrew Graham	62,317	1,780	1998
Vermont Lake Monsters (Athletics)	39	35	.527	6½	Rick Magnante	88,711	2,464	1996
Batavia Mucdogs (Cardinals)	37	38	.493	9	Dann Bilardello	37,029	1,058	2008
Hudson Valley Renegades (Rays)	37	39	.487	9½	Jared Sandberg	149,243	4,523	1999
Jamestown Jammers (Marlins)	35	40	.467	11	Dave Berg	42,086	1,137	1991
Tri-City ValleyCats (Astros)	33	42	.440	13	Stubby Clapp	156,297	4,342	2010
State College Spikes (Pirates)	31	44	.413	15	Kimera Bartee	139,007	3,757	1994
Lowell Spinners (Red Sox)	29	45	.392	16½	Carlos Febles	167,222	4,645	Never
Aberdeen Ironbirds (Orioles)	24	51	.320	22	Leo Gomez	242,723	6,560	1983

PLAYOFFS: Semifinals—Staten Island defeated Brooklyn 2-1 and Auburn defeated Vermont 2-1 in best-of-three series. **Finals:** Staten Island defeated Auburn 2-0 in best-of-three series.

CLUB BATTING

	AVG	G	AB	R	H	2B	3B	HR	RBI	BB	SO	SB	OBP	SLG
Auburn	.269	75	2528	395	681	150	18	42	359	268	610	95	.347	.393
Staten Island	.265	73	2452	350	651	141	20	35	304	233	547	84	.337	.382
Brooklyn	.261	74	2439	348	637	129	18	42	311	280	563	38	.345	.380
Batavia	.256	75	2484	336	637	139	19	36	290	259	530	67	.331	.371
Connecticut	.253	74	2432	323	615	120	17	46	286	236	481	66	.328	.373
Vermont	.251	74	2417	344	607	104	12	36	291	266	618	117	.334	.349
Mahoning Valley	.247	75	2527	372	625	137	20	23	325	297	502	97	.340	.345
Tri-City	.247	75	2429	345	601	118	16	32	282	272	513	92	.335	.349
Jamestown	.246	75	2543	333	625	103	18	28	276	231	503	62	.316	.333
Lowell	.246	74	2485	320	612	117	18	55	290	244	627	86	.320	.374
Williamsport	.246	76	2508	305	616	115	19	20	276	237	486	82	.316	.331
Hudson Valley	.240	76	2430	299	583	108	16	33	256	229	574	89	.315	.338
Aberdeen	.237	75	2442	254	579	99	10	20	222	242	505	75	.316	.310
State College	.231	75	2451	278	567	117	24	24	236	242	516	90	.314	.328

CLUB PITCHING

	ERA	G	CG	SHO	SV	IP	H	R	ER	HR	BB	SO	AVG
Williamsport	2.98	76	1	4	23	664	609	277	220	28	234	533	.242
Connecticut	3.05	74	8	9	19	646	579	285	219	32	216	500	.236
Brooklyn	3.06	74	0	7	25	641	608	261	218	30	192	582	.251
Hudson Valley	3.25	76	0	8	21	640	563	312	231	30	249	527	.239
Staten Island	3.50	73	0	4	22	642	597	307	250	36	292	644	.247
Mahoning Valley	3.59	75	0	5	16	665	613	320	265	38	252	574	.245
Auburn	3.71	75	0	5	23	650	596	308	268	19	263	512	.243
Vermont	3.71	74	2	4	19	633	601	319	261	39	259	542	.251
Batavia	3.74	75	0	1	19	648	619	336	269	32	222	507	.248
Tri-City	3.78	75	1	5	16	641	643	343	269	36	250	614	.259
State College	4.32	75	0	2	16	660	696	381	317	31	243	426	.268
Jamestown	4.45	75	0	3	16	655	653	364	324	36	263	531	.259
Lowell	4.50	74	0	2	7	639	584	386	319	42	326	546	.241
Aberdeen	4.80	75	0	4	12	647	675	403	345	43	275	537	.265

CLUB FIELDING

	PCT	PO	A	E	DP		PCT	PO	A	E	DP
Brooklyn	.972	1924	719	75	63	Connecticut	.964	1939	739	101	48
Auburn	.970	1949	795	86	74	Hudson Valley	.964	1921	765	101	85
Jamestown	.970	1965	813	85	85	Lowell	.964	1916	691	97	58
Aberdeen	.969	1941	794	87	74	Mahoning Valley	.964	1994	839	105	77
Staten Island	.969	1927	766	85	68	State College	.964	1981	773	103	64
Vermont	.968	1898	759	88	56	Tri-City	.964	1923	773	101	49
Batavia	.964	1943	796	101	64	Williamsport	.964	1993	844	107	67

INDIVIDUAL BATTING LEADERS (Minimum 2.7 PA/Team Game)

	AVG	G	AB	R	H	2B	3B	HR	RBI	BB	SO	SB
Muno, Daniel, Brooklyn	.355	59	220	45	78	23	3	2	24	43	39	9
Williams, Mason, Staten Island	.349	68	269	42	94	11	6	3	31	20	41	28
Green, Dean, Connecticut	.341	65	246	33	84	19	2	7	44	18	35	1
Ortega, Bryce, Auburn	.314	56	194	43	61	15	0	0	21	29	34	23
Myles, Bryson, Mahoning Valley	.302	50	192	36	58	10	3	1	15	24	32	20
Smith, Jordan, Mahoning Valley	.300	65	243	36	73	20	1	0	47	35	30	3
Lucas, Richard, Brooklyn	.300	69	250	46	75	19	3	6	41	31	66	2
Taijeron, Travis, Brooklyn	.299	56	194	24	58	13	5	9	44	22	64	0
Miller, Justin, Auburn	.299	63	241	40	72	17	5	7	47	14	67	4
Duffy, Matthew, Tri-City	.298	63	235	36	70	20	1	2	37	15	41	2

INDIVIDUAL PITCHING LEADERS (Minimum 0.8 IP/Team Game)

	W	L	ERA	G	GS	CG	SV	IP	H	R	ER	BB	SO
Smith, Brennan, Connecticut	4	3	1.53	14	14	2	0	94	76	21	16	19	66
McInnis, Todd, Batavia	3	2	1.90	13	11	0	0	62	50	15	13	8	36
Kingham, Nicholas, State College	6	2	2.15	15	15	0	0	71	63	18	17	15	47
Frankoff, Seth, Vermont	6	3	2.34	14	14	2	0	73	54	25	19	27	63
Jimenez, Danny, Mahoning Valley	4	3	2.39	17	12	0	0	72	66	30	19	24	50
Diaz, Luis, Lowell	4	4	2.53	14	14	0	0	75	57	25	21	15	41
Bellatti, Andrew, Hudson Valley	3	5	2.63	15	13	0	0	72	66	26	21	23	62
Hallock, Kyle, Tri-City	3	4	2.63	13	13	0	0	62	58	29	18	17	61
Martinez, Lino, Williamsport	6	2	2.79	13	13	0	0	68	64	25	21	23	46
Sanz, Luis Angel, Connecticut	6	4	2.81	14	14	3	0	83	67	36	26	23	76

DEPARTMENT LEADERS

BATTING

OBP	Muno, Daniel, Brooklyn	.466
SLG	Taijeron, Travis, Brooklyn	.557
OPS	Muno, Daniel, Brooklyn	.980
R	Wolters, Tony, Mahoning Valley	50
H	Williams, Mason, Staten Island	94
TB	Green, Dean, Connecticut	128
XBH	Lowery, Jake, Mahoning Valley	30
2B	Three tied at	23
3B	Lewis, Taylor, State College	7
HR	Malm, Jeff, Hudson Valley	12
RBI	Skole, Matthew, Auburn	48
SAC	Jamieson, Sean, Vermont	10
BB	Lowery, Jake, Mahoning Valley	54
HBP	Three tied at	13
SO	Schwindenhammer, Seth, Lowell	106
SB	Hudson, Kyrell, Williamsport	28
	Williams, Mason, Staten Island	28
CS	Williams, Mason, Staten Island	12
AB/SO	Leonora, Dudley, Aberdeen	10.91

PITCHING

G	Miller, Travis, Batavia	28
	Tejeda, Enosil, Mahoning Valley	28
GS	Seven tied at	15
GF	Miranda, Danny, Batavia	25
SV	Miranda, Danny, Batavia	15
W	Hodges, Josh, Jamestown	8
L	Cervenka, Hunter, Lowell	8
IP	Smith, Brennan, Connecticut	94
H	Nixon, Rob, Mahoning Valley	99
R	Nixon, Rob, Mahoning Valley	50
ER	Nixon, Rob, Mahoning Valley	43
HB	Benedict, Matt, State College	11
BB	Cervenka, Hunter, Lowell	40
SO	Sanz, Luis Angel, Connecticut	76
SO/9	Perez, Juri, Tri-City	8.96
SO/9 (RP)	Tejeda, Enosil, Mahoning Valley	15.09
BB/9	Neil, Matthew, Jamestown	0.68
WP	Kapteyn, Braden, Lowell	18
BK	Tejeda, Enosil, Mahoning Valley	4
HR	Velette, Raynel, Lowell	9
AVG	Frankoff, Seth, Vermont	.208

FIELDING

C	FPCT	Sawyer, Wynston, Aberdeen	.994
	PO	Lavisky, Alex, Mahoning Valley	348
	A	Lavisky, Alex, Mahoning Valley	46
	E	Gonzalez, Samuel, State College	8
	DP	Lavisky, Alex, Mahoning Valley	6
		McCoy, Nick, Staten Island	6
	PB	Sawyer, Wynston, Aberdeen	15
1B	FPCT	Malm, Jeff, Hudson Valley	.993
	PO	Nunez, Reymond, Staten Island	570
	A	Stassi, Brock, Williamsport	45
	E	Johnson, Zachary, Tri-City	12
	DP	Malm, Jeff, Hudson Valley	68
2B	FPCT	Hankins, Todd, Mahoning Valley	.976
	PO	Leonora, Dudley, Aberdeen	126
	A	Leonora, Dudley, Aberdeen	224
	E	Asche, Cody, Williamsport	15
	DP	Leonora, Dudley, Aberdeen	52
3B	FPCT	Reginatto, Leonardo, H Valley	.951
	PO	Skole, Matthew, Auburn	47
	A	Duffy, Matthew, Tri-City	117
	E	Narron, Connor, Aberdeen	19
	DP	Reginatto, Leonardo, H. Valley	20
SS	FPCT	Jamieson, Sean, Vermont	.970
	PO	Culver, Cito, Staten Island	125
	A	Givens, Mychal, Aberdeen	214
	E	Querecuto, Juniel, H. Valley	26
	DP	Givens, Mychal, Aberdeen	54
OF	FPCT	Three tied at	1.000
	PO	Wright, Chad, Connecticut	190
	A	Muren, Andrew, Tri-City	14
	E	Siliga, Aaron, Mahoning Valley	9
	DP	Davis, Glynn, Aberdeen	4
		Lewis, Taylor, State College	4

MINOR LEAGUES

Vancouver rolled to the Northwest League championship despite seeing the league's top prospect move on to low Class A by the time the postseason got underway.

Leftthander Justin Nicolino, a second-round pick in the 2010 draft, went 5-1, 1.03 with 64 strikeouts and 11 walks in 52 innings. He would have won the league's ERA title had he made enough starts. His election to the postseason all-star team showed that his abbreviated performance did not go without notice.

Beyond Nicolino, the success of the team was primarily a cumulative effort, as the only position player to make the postseason all-star team was second baseman Jonathon Berti, who hit .291/.387/.376. Consecutive 2-1 series wins (best of three) over regular season champion Eugene and Tri-City clinched the league championship for the Canadians.

Eugene featured three of the top six prospects in the league—and six of the top 20. Led by second baseman Cory Spangenburg and shortstop Jace Peterson, the Emeralds manufactured runs by pacing the league in walks and stolen bases on their way to the second-highest run-scoring offense in the league.

Much like Nicolino, Spangenberg's time in the Northwest League was abbreviated due to a midseason promotion to the Midwest League. However, Spangenberg made his presence felt as the 2011 first-rounder showed his polish by hitting .384/.545/.535 in 25 games. Peterson, Spangenberg's double-play partner, stole 39 bases and showed the premium athleticism which many observers believe will allow the McNeese State product to stick at shortstop as he moves up the ladder.

Fellow 2011 first-rounder Joe Panik shined during his professional debut for Salem-Keizer. The St. John's product signed quickly and was named the league's MVP, hitting .341/.401/.467 and led the MWL in average, placed fourth in slugging, and third in OPS (.868).

Everett righthander Jose Campos, a 19 year-old out of Venezuela, posted league bests in ERA

(2.32) and WHIP (0.97) while striking out more than a batter per inning and earned Northwest League pitcher of the year honors.

Boise first baseman Paul Hoilman, a 19th-round pick of the Cubs out of East Tennessee State, ran away with the home run title by slugging 17—no Northwest League player has hit more since Jason Hart smacked 20 for Southern Oregon in 1998. Salem-Keizer 21-year-old outfielder Jesus Galindo stole a league-best 47 bases—the most in the NWL since Yakima's Marland Williams swiped 51 in 2002.

TOP 20 PROSPECTS

1. Justin Nicolino, lhp, Vancouver (Blue Jays)
2. Cory Spangenberg, 2b, Eugene (Padres)
3. Jose Campos, rhp, Everett (Mariners)
4. Joe Panik, ss, Salem-Keizer (Giants)
5. Jace Peterson, ss, Eugene (Padres)
6. Matt Andriese, rhp, Eugene (Padres)
7. Rougned Odor, 2b, Spokane (Rangers)
8. Jorge Alfaro, c, Spokane (Rangers)
9. Jesus Galindo, of, Salem-Keizer (Giants)
10. Reggie Golden, of, Boise (Cubs)
11. Jabari Blash, of, Everett (Mariners)
12. Ben Wells, rhp, Boise (Cubs)
13. Matt West, rhp, Spokane (Rangers)
14. Pin-Chieh Chen, of, Boise (Cubs)
15. Kevin Quackenbush, rhp, Eugene (Padres)
16. Donavan Tate, of, Eugene (Padres)
17. Zeke DeVoss, 2b, Boise (Cubs)
18. Will Lamb, lhp, Spokane (Rangers)
19. John Barbato, rhp, Eugene (Padres)
20. Kyle Hendricks, rhp, Spokane (Rangers)

STANDINGS: SPLIT SEASON

FIRST HALF

EAST	W	L	PCT	GB
Tri—City	22	16	.579	—
Spokane	20	18	.526	2
Boise	17	21	.447	5
Yakima	13	25	.342	9

WEST	W	L	PCT	GB
Eugene	24	14	.632	—
Vancouver	24	14	.632	—
Everett	16	22	.421	8
Salem-Keizer	16	22	.421	8

SECOND HALF

EAST	W	L	PCT	GB
Tri—City	22	16	.579	—
Yakima	20	18	.526	2
Boise	19	19	.500	3
Spokane	15	23	.395	7

WEST	W	L	PCT	GB
Eugene	22	16	.579	—
Everett	21	17	.553	1
Salem-Keizer	18	20	.474	4
Vancouver	15	23	.395	7

PLAYOFFS—Semifinals: Tri-City defeated Boise 2-0 and Vancouver defeated Eugene 2-1 in best-of-three series. **Finals:** Vancouver defeated Tri-City 2-1 in best-of-three series.

OVERALL STANDINGS

Team (Organization)	W	L	PCT	GB	Manager	Attendance	Average	Last Pennant
Eugene Emeralds (Padres)	46	30	.605	—	Pat Murphy	114,690	3,018	1980
Tri-City Dust Devils (Rockies)	44	32	.579	2	Fred Ocasio	85,953	2,262	Never
Vancouver Canadians (Blue Jays)	39	37	.513	7	John Schneider	162,162	4,267	2011
Everett AquaSox (Mariners)	37	39	.487	9	Scott Steinmann	96,345	2,535	2010
Boise Hawks (Cubs)	36	40	.474	10	Mark Johnson	98,860	2,602	2004
Spokane Indians (Rangers)	35	41	.461	11	Tim Hulett	183,458	4,828	2008
Salem-Keizer Volcanoes (Giants)	34	42	.447	12	Tom Trebelhorn	105,973	2,789	2009
Yakima Bears (Diamondbacks)	33	43	.434	13	Audo Vicente	66,545	1,751	2000

CLUB BATTING

	AVG	G	AB	R	H	2B	3B	HR	RBI	BB	SO	SB	OBP	SLG
Salem-Keizer	.277	76	2601	405	721	125	17	54	363	253	544	126	.348	.401
Boise	.259	76	2530	369	655	123	19	49	333	292	567	79	.341	.381
Everett	.257	76	2598	371	668	133	24	56	329	255	607	71	.332	.391
Yakima	.255	76	2643	315	674	120	25	31	272	218	545	66	.318	.355
Spokane	.253	76	2578	365	652	133	26	34	323	263	634	73	.333	.364
Tri-City	.251	76	2540	363	637	130	27	39	326	246	596	73	.324	.369
Eugene	.246	76	2532	382	622	137	21	29	336	370	689	144	.351	.351
Vancouver	.243	76	2574	329	625	120	14	48	292	255	633	72	.319	.356

CLUB PITCHING

	ERA	G	CG	SHO	SV	IP	H	R	ER	HR	BB	SO	AVG
Tri-City	3.03	76	2	10	26	674	597	284	227	33	223	543	.236
Yakima	3.75	76	0	3	17	690	682	365	287	25	275	611	.260
Eugene	3.79	76	0	4	26	680	599	329	286	40	289	644	.236
Everett	4.04	76	0	5	19	675	677	369	303	60	226	625	.259
Boise	4.15	76	0	0	22	665	669	376	307	42	303	590	.262
Vancouver	4.15	76	1	4	24	673	661	372	310	43	260	527	.258
Spokane	4.45	76	0	4	18	666	643	389	329	58	306	665	.253
Salem-Keizer	4.85	76	0	5	12	666	726	415	359	39	270	610	.275

CLUB FIELDING

	PCT	PO	A	E	DP		PCT	PO	A	E	DP
Tri-City	.972	2022	847	83	65	Vancouver	.966	2018	897	102	88
Eugene	.970	2040	737	87	58	Yakima	.965	2049	909	109	87
Salem-Keizer	.969	1999	777	89	67	Everett	.962	2025	827	112	61
Boise	.966	1996	915	103	80	Spokane	.962	1998	759	108	66

INDIVIDUAL BATTING LEADERS (Minimum 2.7 PA/Team Game)

	AVG	G	AB	R	H	2B	3B	HR	RBI	BB	SO	SB
Panik, Joe, Salem-Keizer	.341	69	270	49	92	10	3	6	54	28	25	13
Yepez, Mario, Everett	.332	66	262	37	87	17	2	0	20	14	33	5
Murray, Mike, Salem-Keizer	.326	63	242	29	79	14	0	6	48	28	37	2
Comerota, Jimmy, Yakima	.322	59	227	31	73	11	3	1	34	26	23	13
Lopez, Rafael, Boise	.316	54	196	34	62	8	0	6	37	21	27	1
Downing, Kaohi, Salem-Keizer	.312	52	186	26	58	10	2	1	19	16	36	11
Krill, Brett, Salem-Keizer	.304	52	207	38	63	16	2	6	43	14	44	4
Chen, Pin-Chieh, Boise	.301	60	229	34	69	14	4	2	30	25	44	20
De Jesus, Jharmidy, Everett	.299	58	201	31	60	8	1	4	33	18	42	3
Whitmore, Travis, Eugene	.297	62	209	27	62	15	5	1	32	24	56	3

INDIVIDUAL PITCHING LEADERS (Minimum 0.8 IP/Team Game)

	W	L	ERA	G	GS	CG	SV	IP	H	R	ER	BB	SO
Campos, Jose, Everett	5	5	2.32	14	14	0	0	81	66	34	21	13	85
Gagnon, Tyler, Tri-City	4	3	2.57	14	14	0	0	74	55	23	21	26	64
Bergman, Christian, Tri-City	7	5	2.59	15	15	2	0	97	83	31	28	11	68
Pedrotty, John, Yakima	2	4	3.04	15	13	0	0	68	61	29	23	29	70
Capaul, Alex, Yakima	2	3	3.07	15	11	0	0	73	77	36	25	10	39
Wang, Yao-Lin, Boise	4	4	3.22	14	14	0	0	67	64	25	24	20	77
Alsup, Ben, Tri-City	3	3	3.23	13	11	0	0	61	56	24	22	22	50
Kudryk, Adam, Yakima	5	4	3.40	15	15	0	0	87	95	44	33	34	69
Rosario, Jose, Boise	6	3	3.53	15	7	0	2	64	67	36	25	18	50
Roibal, Reinier, Salem-Keizer	1	4	3.74	14	14	0	0	67	82	38	28	17	58

ALL-STAR TEAM

C: Rafael Lopez, Boise. **1B:** Paul Hoilman, Boise. **2B:** Jon Berti, Vancouver. **3B:** Jimmy Comerota, Yakima; Travis Whitmore, Eugene. **SS:** Joe Panik, Salem-Keizer. **OF:** Brett Krill, Salem-Keizer; Jesus Galindo, Salem-Keizer; Jabari Blash, Everett. **DH:** Mike Murray, Salem-Keizer. **RHSP:** Christian Bergman, Tri-City; Jose Campos, Everett. **LHSP:** Justin Nicolino, Vancouver. **RHRP:** Drew Permison, Vancouver. **LHRP:** Kenneth Roberts, Tri-City.
Most Valuable Player: Joe Panik, Salem-Keizer. **Manager of the Year:** Freddie Ocasio, Tri-City.

DEPARTMENT LEADERS

BATTING

OBP	Payne, Shawn, Salem-Keizer	.431
SLG	Blash, Jabari, Everett	.574
OPS	Blash, Jabari, Everett	.967
R	Galindo, Jesus, Salem-Keizer	49
	Panik, Joe, Salem-Keizer	49
H	Panik, Joe, Salem-Keizer	92
TB	Hoilman, Paul, Boise	126
	Panik, Joe, Salem-Keizer	126
XBH	Blash, Jabari, Everett	30
	Hoilman, Paul, Boise	30
2B	Nicholas, Brett, Spokane	21
3B	Smalling, Timothy, Tri-City	7
HR	Hoilman, Paul, Boise	17
RBI	Panik, Joe, Salem-Keizer	54
SAC	Yepez, Mario, Everett	9
BB	Peterson, Jace, Eugene	50
HBP	Berti, Jonathon, Vancouver	12
SO	Hoilman, Paul, Boise	105
SB	Galindo, Jesus, Salem-Keizer	47
CS	Peterson, Jace, Eugene	10
AB/SO	Pulfer, Daniel, Yakima	11

PITCHING

G	De La Cruz, Luis, Eugene	36
GS	Seven tied at	15
GF	Permison, Drew, Vancouver	24
SV	Permison, Drew, Vancouver	15
W	Three tied at	7
L	Allen, Brandon, Salem-Keizer	8
IP	Bergman, Christian, Tri-City	97.3
H	Kudryk, Adam, Yakima	95
R	Lamb, Cameron, Salem-Keizer	54
ER	Breault, Zack, Vancouver	48
HB	Gutierrez, Teo, Yakima	11
BB	Herrera, Juan, Eugene	40
SO	Campos, Jose, Everett	85
SO/9 (RP)	Wang, Yao-Lin, Boise	10.34
SO/9 (RP)	Gigliotti, Jeremy, Eugene Emeralds	12
BB/9	Bergman, Christian, Tri-City	1.02
WP	Reagan, Miles, Yakima	15
BK	Perez, Santo, Spokane	5
HR	Whitmore, Bennett, Everett	11
AVG	Gagnon, Tyler, Tri-City	.205

FIELDING

C	FPCT	Cabezas, Yaniel, Boise	.995
	PO	Casteel, Ryan, Tri-City	396
	A	Dowd, Michael, Everett	45
	E	Alfaro, Jorge, Spokane	10
	DP	Colantonio, Matthew, Eugene	5
		Gonzalez, Larry, Everett	5
	PB	Alfaro, Jorge, Spokane	12
1B	FPCT	Hoilman, Paul, Boise	.991
	PO	Hoilman, Paul, Boise	498
	A	Hoilman, Paul, Boise	39
	E	De Jesus, Jharmidy, Everett	11
	DP	Comerota, Jimmy, Yakima	48
		Hoilman, Paul, Boise	48
2B	FPCT	Berti, Jonathon, Vancouver	.974
	PO	Odor, Rougned, Spokane	119
	A	Berti, Jonathon, Vancouver	203
	E	DeVoss, Zeke, Eugene	13
	DP	Berti, Jonathon, Vancouver	42
3B	FPCT	Buechele, Garrett, Salem-Keizer	.961
	PO	Robinson, Drew, Spokane	40
	A	Langfels, Jayson, Tri-City	130
	E	Contreras, Willson, Boise	19
	DP	Langfels, Jayson, Tri-City	14
SS	FPCT	Panik, Joe, Salem-Keizer	.964
	PO	Peterson, Jace, Eugene	122
	A	Panik, Joe, Salem-Keizer	215
	E	Alberto, Hanser, Spokane	20
	DP	Opitz, Shane, Vancouver	55
OF	FPCT	Chen, Pin-Chieh, Boise	1.000
	PO	Jones, Jonathan, Vancouver	144
	A	Pimentel, Guillermo, Spokane	10
	E	Golden, Reggie, Boise	6
	DP	Jones, Jonathan, Vancouver	5

MINOR LEAGUES

Johnson City rolled to an Appalachian League-best 45 wins and repeated as league champion by using much the same formula they had in 2010. The Cardinals averaged more than six runs per game to lead all clubs, and they put up 20 runs over three games in their first-round series win against Danville.

In the finals, Johnson City swept two games from Bluefield by more modest scores of 4-3 and 4-1 as pitching ruled the day. Lefty Nick Gillung and righthander Logan Billbrough combined to one hit the Blue Jays in the finale.

Several league prospects had high pedigrees in 2011. A dozen players selected in the first two rounds of the 2010 and '11 drafts qualified for the prospect list and 10 cracked the Top 20, led by '10 supplemental pick Tyrell Jenkins, a righthander for Johnson City. The 19-year-old ranked among the league leaders in ERA (3.86) and strikeout rate (8.8 per nine innings).

Elizabethton third baseman/shortstop Miguel Sano ranked as the No. 1 prospect after dueling teammate Eddie Rosario for the league home run title. Veteran Elizabethton manager Ray Smith says Sano's offensive potential compares favorably with former Appy League standouts Josh Hamilton and Joe Mauer. Sano crushed a league-leading 45 extra-base hits, including 20 homers, in 66 games.

The Twins' Rosario won co-player of the year honors for leading the league in homers (21), triples (nine), runs (71), and slugging (.670) while finishing second in hits (91), extra-base hits (39) and RBIs (60).

Appy League observers also liked the offensive upside of the circuit's No. 2 prospect, Danville third baseman Brandon Drury, a 13th-round pick in 2010 who shared player-of-the-year honors. Drury led the league with 92 hits and hit safely in 25 of his final 26 games, barely losing the batting title to Bluefield's Kevin Pillar, .3475 to .3472.

TOP 20 PROSPECTS

1. Miguel Sano, 3b/ss, Elizabethton Twins
2. Brandon Drury, 3b, Danville Braves
3. Tyrell Jenkins, rhp, Johnson City Cardinals
4. Noah Syndergaard, rhp, Bluefield Blue Jays
5. Eddie Rosario, of, Elizabethton Twins
6. Drew Vettleson, of, Princeton Rays
7. Jake Hager, ss, Princeton Rays
8. J.R. Graham, rhp, Danville Braves
9. Felipe Rivero, lhp, Princeton Rays
10. Ryan Brett, 2b, Princeton Rays
11. Chris Hawkins, of, Bluefield Blue Jays
12. Aaron Sanchez, rhp, Bluefield Blue Jays
13. Josh Sale, of, Princeton Rays
14. Guillermo Pimentel, of, Pulaski Mariners
15. Justin O'Conner, c, Princeton Rays
16. Jeff Ames, rhp, Princeton Rays
17. Madison Boer, rhp, Elizabethton Twins
18. Nick Ahmed, ss, Danville Braves
19. Jordan Scott, of, Greeneville Astros
20. Kevan Smith, c, Bristol White Sox

Princeton may have gone just 30-38, but the Rays monopolized the Top 20 list with seven selections, the majority of them arriving courtesy of recent drafts. Six of the Rays' top 18 picks over the past two years made their way to the Appy League this season, including the organization's top three selections from 2010, as well as third-rounder Ryan Brett, a sparkplug of a second baseman who ranked third in the league with 21 steals and 22 doubles. Right fielder Drew Vettleson, a supplemental pick, impressed league managers while left fielder Josh Sale and catcher Justin O'Conner, first-rounders both, hit just .210 and .157.

The Orioles severed their 53-year affiliation with Bluefield following the 2010 season, but the city found a worthy successor when the Blue Jays moved in and stocked the club with promising talent from the 2010 draft. Noah Syndegaard and Aaron Sanchez, a pair of supplemental-round righties, as well as third-round left fielder Chris Hawkins helped guide the young Jays to the playoffs, where they defeated Elizabethton in the first round but lost to Johnson City in the finals.

STANDINGS

EASTERN DIVISION	W	L	PCT	GB	Manager(s)	Attendance	Average	Last Penn.
Bluefield (Blue Jays)	40	28	.588	—	Dennis Holmberg	26,395	800	2001
*Danville (Braves)	39	29	.574	1	Randy Ingle	28,523	864	2009
Pulaski (Mariners)	32	36	.471	8	Rob Mummau	30,236	889	Never
Princeton (Rays)	30	38	.441	10	Michael Johns	27,685	814	1994
Burlington (Royals)	24	44	.353	16	Nelson Liriano	28,427	836	1993
WESTERN DIVISION	W	L	PCT	GB	Manager(s)	Attendance	Average	Last Penn.
Johnson City (Cardinals)	45	23	.662	—	Mike Shildt	25,961	764	2011
*Elizabethton (Twins)	42	26	.618	3	Ray Smith	28,900	850	2008
Kingsport (Mets)	39	29	.574	6	Frank Fultz	31,988	941	1995
Greeneville (Astros)	25	43	.368	20	Omar Lopez	45,015	1,364	2004
Bristol (White Sox)	24	44	.353	21	Pete Rose Jr.	22,433	701	2002

*Wild-card winner

PLAYOFFS—Semifinals: Johnson City defeated Danville 2-1 and Bluefield defeated Elizabethton 2-1 in best-of-three series. **Finals:** Johnson City defeated Bluefield 2-0 in best-of-three series.

CLUB BATTING

	AVG	G	AB	R	H	2B	3B	HR	RBI	BB	SO	SB	OBP	SLG
Johnson City	.279	68	2412	415	673	167	21	67	354	186	556	68	.339	.449
Elizabethton	.274	68	2384	405	653	128	26	71	343	226	653	51	.343	.439
Kingsport	.269	68	2364	385	637	132	18	49	320	222	529	58	.338	.403
Danville	.266	68	2415	372	643	158	21	44	329	238	528	74	.343	.404
Bluefield	.262	68	2342	399	614	135	26	54	362	252	567	58	.339	.411
Princeton	.260	68	2315	325	602	129	25	59	290	246	490	107	.334	.414
Pulaski	.258	68	2248	308	580	100	20	47	270	191	569	56	.325	.383
Greeneville	.252	68	2293	326	577	119	17	36	293	228	566	69	.330	.365
Burlington	.245	68	2252	300	552	112	18	58	274	234	579	108	.327	.388
Bristol	.243	68	2328	326	565	141	19	43	288	229	615	23	.322	.375

CLUB PITCHING

	ERA	G	CG	SHO	SV	IP	H	R	ER	HR	BB	SO	AVG
Danville	3.15	68	1	2	15	618	559	286	216	25	239	623	.240
Johnson City	3.58	68	1	3	23	614	587	299	244	52	183	583	.252
Elizabethton	3.96	68	0	7	20	609	604	331	268	66	197	616	.258
Kingsport	4.10	68	1	5	20	599	580	339	273	52	233	531	.251
Bluefield	4.23	68	1	2	13	606	608	332	285	50	231	585	.259
Princeton	4.36	68	0	1	18	600	588	357	291	64	245	523	.255
Pulaski	4.46	68	0	2	17	581	601	355	288	45	236	543	.266
Burlington	5.00	68	1	2	13	587	651	422	326	56	219	552	.274
Greeneville	5.12	68	0	2	13	596	650	419	339	53	236	550	.272
Bristol	5.47	68	0	1	9	596	668	421	362	65	233	546	.282

CLUB FIELDING

	PCT	PO	A	E	DP		PCT	PO	A	E	DP
Bluefield	.971	1818	713	76	41	Bristol	.961	1787	728	101	63
Danville	.968	1853	743	85	69	Princeton	.959	1801	718	107	56
Johnson City	.966	1842	756	92	64	Pulaski	.958	1743	670	105	58
Elizabethton	.965	1828	705	91	61	Greeneville	.950	1788	722	131	63
Kingsport	.962	1798	701	98	63	Burlington	.949	1762	622	129	43

INDIVIDUAL BATTING LEADERS (Minimum 2.7 PA/Team Game)

	AVG	G	AB	R	H	2B	3B	HR	RBI	BB	SO	SB
Pillar, Kevin, Bluefield	.347	60	236	44	82	17	3	7	37	10	36	8
Drury, Brandon, Danville	.347	63	265	40	92	23	0	8	54	6	35	3
Scott, Jordan, Greeneville	.337	60	246	41	83	12	3	1	31	19	47	9
Rosario, Eddie, Elizabethton	.337	67	270	71	91	9	9	21	60	27	60	17
Davidson, Chase, Greeneville	.335	43	161	33	54	13	2	11	44	24	51	8
Austin, Jamal, Pulaski	.335	55	206	35	69	6	2	0	13	22	21	20
Caminero, Joel, Princeton	.330	48	188	25	62	9	6	3	22	5	38	6
Williams, JaDamion, Elizabethton	.324	50	185	30	60	12	1	4	24	25	58	10
Motter, Taylor, Princeton	.323	46	158	37	51	13	0	4	23	33	26	22
Vargas, Kennys, Elizabethton	.322	44	174	27	56	11	0	6	33	15	50	0

INDIVIDUAL PITCHING LEADERS (Minimum 0.8 IP/Team Game)

	W	L	ERA	G	GS	CG	SV	IP	H	R	ER	BB	SO
Graham, J.R., Danville	5	2	1.72	13	8	0	0	58	52	15	11	13	52
Christensen, Derek, Elizabethton	5	2	2.84	19	6	0	0	57	43	22	18	26	61
Jaye, Myles, Bluefield	3	3	3.00	13	9	1	1	54	48	22	18	18	49
Meyer, Ajay, Bluefield	4	2	3.02	13	13	0	0	66	62	26	22	13	55
Spann, Matthew, Princeton	4	1	3.13	14	10	0	0	63	58	26	22	18	61
Shibuya, Tim, Elizabethton	8	2	3.30	13	13	0	0	74	70	32	27	11	70
Guaipe, Mayckol, Pulaski	5	6	3.66	14	14	0	0	64	66	37	26	20	49
Hiraldo, Eduardo, Johnson City	2	3	3.71	11	11	0	0	61	60	33	25	16	50
Jenkins, Tyrell, Johnson City	4	2	3.86	11	11	0	0	56	63	33	24	13	55
Ridings, Matt, Burlington	3	4	3.92	14	14	0	0	67	65	36	29	11	60

ALL-STAR TEAM

C: Cam Maron, Kingsport. **1B:** Chase Davidson, Greeneville. **2B:** Tyler Rahmatulla, Johnson City. **3B:** Brandon Drury, Danville. **SS:** Taylor Motter, Princeton. **UTIL INF:** Miguel Sano, Elizabethton. **OF:** Jamal Austin, Pulaski; Kevin Pillar, Bluefield; Eddie Rosario, Elizabethton. **UTIL OF:** Chris Hawkins, Bluefield. **DH:** Art Charles, Bluefield. **RHP:** Tim Shibuya, Elizabethton. **LHP:** Kyle Hald, Johnson City. **RP:** Madison Boer, Elizabethton.
Most Valuable Players: Brandon Drury, Danville/Eddie Rosario, Elizabethton. **Pitcher of the Year:** Tim Shibuya, Elizabethton. **Manager of the Year:** Dennis Holmberg, Bluefield.

DEPARTMENT LEADERS

BATTING

OBP	Motter, Taylor, Princeton	.436
SLG	Rosario, Eddie, Elizabethton	.670
OPS	Davidson, Chase, Greeneville	1.071
R	Rosario, Eddie, Elizabethton	71
H	Drury, Brandon, Danville	92
TB	Rosario, Eddie, Elizabethton	181
XBH	Sano, Miguel, Elizabethton	45
2B	Rahmatulla, Tyler, Johnson City	27
3B	Rosario, Eddie, Elizabethton	9
HR	Rosario, Eddie, Elizabethton	21
RBI	Charles, Art, Bluefield	61
SAC	Trapp, Justin, Burlington	8
BB	Seitzer, Cameron, Princeton	43
HBP	Beckwith, William, Danville	12
SO	Charles, Art, Bluefield	89
SB	Trapp, Justin, Burlington	31
CS	Magee, Joshua, Greeneville	9
AB/SO	Brett, Ryan, Princeton	10

PITCHING

G	Zuloaga, Scott, Greeneville	24
GS	Four tied at	14
GF	Kadish, Ian, Bluefield	20
SV	West, Jared, Kingsport	10
W	Shibuya, Tim, Elizabethton	8
L	Duque, Jean, Bristol	9
IP	Shibuya, Tim, Elizabethton	73.7
H	Icard, Ethan, Bristol	84
R	Icard, Ethan, Bristol	61
ER	Icard, Ethan, Bristol	59
HB	Quintero, Rodney, Greeneville	13
BB	Morris, Akeel, Kingsport	38
SO	Shibuya, Tim, Elizabethton	70
SO/9	Taylor, Mitchell, Bluefield	9.92
SO/9 (RP)	Cornely, John, Danville	13.64
BB/9	Shibuya, Tim, Elizabethton	1.34
WP	Culver, Malcom, Burlington	14
BK	Five tied at	3
HR	Five tied at	10
AVG	Christensen, Derek, Elizabethton	.207

FIELDING

C	FPCT	Munoz, Aaron, Bluefield	.992
	PO	Munoz, Aaron, Bluefield	343
	A	Alvarez, Luis, Greeneville	53
	E	Montero, Jesus, Johnson City	10
	DP	Alvarez, Luis, Greeneville	5
	DP	Parker, Matt, Elizabethton	5
	PB	Alvarez, Luis, Greeneville	12
1B	FPCT	Washington, David, Johnson City	.992
	PO	Charles, Art, Bluefield	563
	A	Seitzer, Cameron, Princeton	43
	E	Seitzer, Cameron, Princeton	9
	DP	Washington, David, Johnson City	42
2B	FPCT	Lockwood, Nick, Elizabethton	.991
	PO	Paolini, Daniel, Pulaski	99
	A	Brett, Ryan, Princeton	160
	E	Brett, Ryan, Princeton	18
	E	Magee, Joshua, Greeneville	18
	DP	Paolini, Daniel, Pulaski	35
3B	FPCT	Fermin, Andy, Bluefield	.933
	PO	Fermin, Andy, Bluefield	38
	A	Fermin, Andy, Bluefield	128
	E	Rivera, Darwin, Greeneville	30
	DP	Rivera, Darwin, Greeneville	12
SS	FPCT	Ahmed, Nick, Danville	.971
	PO	Ahmed, Nick, Danville	88
	A	Williams, Matthew, Johnson City	182
	E	Antonio, Michael, Burlington	25
	DP	Ahmed, Nick, Danville	40
OF	FPCT	Pron, Gregory, Kingsport	1.000
	PO	Ramos, Steven, Johnson City	131
	A	Four tied at	8
	E	Four tied at	7
	DP	Vettleson, Drew, Princeton	4

MINOR LEAGUES

G reat Falls rode the Pioneer League's best second-half record at 25-13 into the post-season behind the circuit's toughest pitching staff. The club's 4.45 ERA paced the PL, led by pitcher of the year Blair Walters, an 11th-round lefthander this year from Hawaii. He went 9-0, 4.03 before winning both of his playoff starts.

Voyagers catcher Kevan Smith, a seventh-rounder from Pittsburgh, served as Great Falls' biggest offensive catalyst in the postseason. He caught every game and hit .478 with two homers, three doubles and eight RBIs in Great Falls' five-game march to the league title. He wasn't alone. Great Falls hit .306 as a team.

Smith struck the deciding blow in Game One of the best-of-three championship series against Ogden, hitting a three-run homer in the fourth and a tie-breaking RBI single in the seventh as Great Falls won 9-7. In Game Two, Walters held Ogden to one run in six innings, while Smith had three more hits in the deciding 7-1 win.

The Angels sent their top two picks from this year's draft to the PL—first-rounder C.J. Cron and third-rounder Nick Maronde, both collegians—as well as two of their top four prep picks from the 2010 draft: first-rounder Kaleb Cowart and supplemental pick Taylor Lindsey. All four players performed well and cracked the top 10.

While Cron was the top 2011 draft pick to play in the league, supplemental first-rounder Trevor Story was the league's top prospect because he's a potential five-tool shortstop who performed well against older competition. He batted .268/.364/.436 with six homers for Casper.

Because the organization does not field an Arizona League team, the Rockies sent two premium high school picks to the PL, though neither corner outfielder fared as well as Story. Second-rounder Carl Thomore hit just .192 in 43 games, while fourth-rounder Dillon Thomas hit .328 but managed just three extra-base hits in 15 games.

Drafted 47th overall by the White Sox this year—two picks after the Rockies took Story—cen- ter fielder Keenyn Walker touched down in Great Falls for two weeks and batted .333/.431/.483 with top-of-the-line speed before moving on to low Class A Kannapolis at the end of July.

The league's best story was probably Idaho Falls righty reliever Edwin Carl. Undrafted after his senior year at New Mexico in 2010, Carl returned this year for a second season in the PL and led all relievers in opponent average (.145) and both strikeouts (19.4) and baserunners (5.7) per nine innings. He struck out 58 percent of the 122 batters he faced.

TOP 20 PROSPECTS

1. Trevor Story, ss/3b, Casper (Rockies)
2. Taylor Lindsey, 2b, Orem (Angels)
3. Joc Pederson, of, Ogden (Dodgers)
4. C.J. Cron, 1b, Orem (Angels)
5. Rosell Herrera, ss/3b, Casper (Rockies)
6. Kaleb Cowart, 3b, Orem (Angels)
7. Nick Maronde, lhp, Orem (Angels)
8. Tony Cingrani, lhp, Billings (Reds)
9. Will Swanner, c, Casper (Rockies)
10. Ryan Wright, 2b, Billings (Reds)
11. James Baldwin III, of, Ogden (Dodgers)
12. Sean Buckley, 3b, Billings (Reds)
13. Nick Mutz, rhp, Orem (Angels)
14. Scott Snodgress, lhp, Great Falls (White Sox)
15. David Goforth, rhp, Helena Brewers
16. Yadiel Rivera, ss, Helena Brewers
17. Kevan Smith, c, Great Falls (White Sox)
18. Danny Winkler, rhp, Casper (Rockies)
19. Kyle Waldrop, of, Billings (Reds)
20. Danny Mateo, 2b/3b, Idaho Falls (Royals)

STANDINGS: SPLIT SEASON

FIRST HALF

NORTH	W	L	PCT	GB
Missoula	25	13	.658	—
Billings	20	18	.526	5
Helena	18	20	.474	7
Great Falls	17	21	.447	8

SOUTH	W	L	PCT	GB
Ogden	22	16	.579	—
Orem	22	16	.579	—
Idaho Falls	17	21	.447	5
Casper	11	27	.289	11

SECOND HALF

NORTH	W	L	PCT	GB
Great Falls	25	13	.658	—
Billings	24	14	.632	1
Missoula	16	22	.421	9
Helena	12	26	.316	13

SOUTH	W	L	PCT	GB
Orem	24	14	.632	—
Ogden	19	19	.500	5
Casper	16	22	.421	8
Idaho Falls	16	22	.421	8

PLAYOFFS—Semifinals: Great Falls defeated Missoula 2-1 and Ogden defeated Orem 2-1 in best-of-three series. **Finals:** Great Falls defeated Ogden 2-0 in best-of-three series.

OVERALL STANDINGS

NORTHERN DIVISION	W	L	PCT	GB	Manager(s)	Attendance	Average	Last Penn.
Billings Mustangs (Reds)	44	32	.579	—	Pat Kelly	109,881	2,970	2001
Great Falls Voyagers (White Sox)	42	34	.553	2	Ryan Newman	59,884	1,618	2011
Missoula Osprey (Diamondbacks)	41	35	.539	3	Hector de la Cruz	86,313	2,271	2006
Helena (Brewers)	30	46	.395	14	Joe Ayrault	37,484	986	2010
SOUTHERN DIVISION	**W**	**L**	**PCT**	**GB**	**Manager(s)**	**Attendance**	**Average**	**Last Penn**
Orem Owlz (Angels)	46	30	.605	—	Tom Kotchman	104,007	2,737	2009
Ogden Raptors (Dodgers)	41	35	.539	5	Damon Berryhill	130,817	3,443	Never
Idaho Falls Chukars (Royals)	33	43	.434	13	Brian Buchanan	94,518	2,487	2000
Casper Ghosts (Rockies)	27	49	.355	19	Tony Diaz	47,982	1,297	Never

CLUB BATTING

	AVG	G	AB	R	H	2B	3B	HR	RBI	BB	SO	SB	OBP	SLG
Orem	.302	76	2729	502	825	151	33	77	466	270	610	54	.372	.466
Idaho Falls	.287	76	2679	428	768	151	28	63	369	227	622	68	.349	.434
Ogden	.286	76	2689	516	769	163	30	94	459	244	720	121	.359	.474
Billings	.284	76	2691	464	765	154	37	97	422	232	675	78	.353	.477
Missoula	.275	76	2668	437	733	147	35	94	384	242	738	85	.340	.462
Great Falls	.273	76	2545	439	695	154	25	52	383	272	641	89	.355	.415
Casper	.259	76	2587	419	671	129	35	79	366	250	719	85	.333	.428
Helena	.257	76	2630	379	676	135	20	56	335	244	715	74	.328	.387

CLUB PITCHING

	ERA	G	CG	SHO	SV	IP	H	R	ER	HR	BB	SO	AVG
Great Falls	4.45	76	0	2	10	662	734	399	327	62	227	692	.280
Helena	4.56	76	0	1	18	681	702	426	345	77	220	701	.267
Billings	4.58	76	0	4	18	677	722	411	344	62	272	675	.273
Missoula	5.05	76	0	3	19	677	673	429	380	84	277	738	.258
Ogden	5.13	76	0	3	13	669	738	463	381	86	290	699	.276
Orem	5.33	76	0	0	23	671	733	452	397	88	238	657	.280
Idaho Falls	5.52	76	0	1	16	665	766	487	408	71	244	719	.286
Casper	5.91	76	1	1	15	658	834	517	432	82	213	559	.304

CLUB FIELDING

	PCT	PO	A	E	DP		PCT	PO	A	E	DP
Orem	.972	2012	798	80	76	Idaho Falls	.963	1996	835	109	75
Missoula	.971	2030	857	87	66	Billings	.960	2030	809	117	62
Great Falls	.966	1985	803	99	66	Casper	.960	1974	850	118	69
Helena	.965	2044	795	103	72	Ogden	.956	2007	810	129	52

INDIVIDUAL BATTING LEADERS (Minimum 2.7 PA/Team Game)

	AVG	G	AB	R	H	2B	3B	HR	RBI	BB	SO	SB
Yakubik, Jerod, Orem	.372	60	215	48	80	17	3	1	34	16	30	2
Lindsey, Taylor, Orem	.362	63	290	64	105	28	6	9	46	13	46	10
Hall, Frazier, Orem	.355	62	228	44	81	19	2	9	46	13	46	1
Pederson, Joc, Ogden	.353	68	266	54	94	20	2	11	64	36	54	24
Mateo, Daniel, Idaho Falls	.348	56	224	33	78	9	4	4	40	17	43	1
Dickson, O'Koyea, Ogden	.333	48	189	33	63	10	1	13	38	19	44	1
Kandilas, David, Casper	.327	61	248	51	81	17	10	6	35	26	44	15
Davis, Runey, Idaho Falls	.326	58	193	42	63	18	3	9	42	28	72	7
Jones, Ryan, Orem	.319	67	257	51	82	18	7	12	61	26	48	3
Espy, Richard, Idaho Falls	.318	62	233	43	74	17	1	7	39	20	59	2

INDIVIDUAL PITCHING LEADERS (Minimum 0.8 IP/Team Game)

	W	L	ERA	G	GS	CG	SV	IP	H	R	ER	BB	SO
Brooks, Aaron, Idaho Falls	6	2	3.84	15	13	0	0	80	89	42	34	8	73
Martin, Brennon, Idaho Falls	4	6	4.02	15	15	0	0	87	102	50	39	9	75
Walters, Blair, Great Falls	9	0	4.03	14	13	0	0	74	72	36	33	17	72
Martinez, Brandon, Ogden	6	3	4.07	15	15	0	0	73	66	40	33	44	58
Shackelford, Kevin, Helena	3	5	4.15	15	8	0	0	65	74	34	30	10	31
Hernandez, Raymond, Missoula	8	3	4.35	14	10	0	0	70	67	38	34	18	71
Peacock, Brian, Idaho Falls	5	5	4.48	15	14	0	1	74	73	45	37	21	89
Moye, Andrew, Helena	7	3	4.48	15	15	0	0	78	87	45	39	19	76
Sanchez, Raydel, Ogden	4	5	4.66	15	15	0	0	75	89	54	39	16	77
Gehle, Pete, Great Falls	5	7	4.67	14	14	0	0	69	71	39	36	11	65

ALL-STAR TEAM

C: Will Swanner, Casper. **1B:** Jon Griffin, Missoula. **2B:** Taylor Lindsey, Orem. **3B:** Sean Buckley, Billings. **SS:** Yadiel Rivera, Helena. **OF:** Ryan Jones, Orem; David Kandilas, Casper; Joc Pederson, Ogden. **DH:** Frazier Hall, Orem. **P:** Aaron Brooks, Idaho Falls; Edwin Carl, Idaho Falls; Raymond Hernandez, Missoula; Taylor Siemens, Missoula; Blair Walters, Great Falls.
Most Valuable Player: Taylor Lindsey, Orem. **Pitcher of the Year:** Blair Walters, Great Falls.
Manager of the Year: Hector de la Cruz, Missoula.

DEPARTMENT LEADERS

BATTING

OBP	Yakubik, Jerod, Orem	.433
SLG	Dickson, O'Koyea, Ogden	.603
OPS	Davis, Runey, Idaho Falls	1.012
R	Lindsey, Taylor, Orem	64
H	Lindsey, Taylor, Orem	105
TB	Lindsey, Taylor, Orem	172
XBH	Lindsey, Taylor, Orem	43
2B	Lindsey, Taylor, Orem	28
3B	Kandilas, David, Casper	10
HR	Griffin, Jonathan, Missoula	18
RBI	Pederson, Joc, Ogden	64
SAC	Martinez, Drew, Orem	8
BB	Riggins, Harold, Casper	46
HBP	Herbek, David, Great Falls	14
SO	Schebler, Scott, Ogden	97
SB	Millender, Qualon, Great Falls	28
CS	Millender, Qualon, Great Falls	11
AB/SO	Yakubik, Jerod, Orem	7.17

PITCHING

G	Pinckard, Brooks, Billings	28
GS	Six tied at	15
GF	Carl, Edwin, Idaho Falls	20
	Pinckard, Brooks, Billings	20
SV	Johnson, D.J., Missoula	10
	Pinckard, Brooks, Billings	10
W	Walters, Blair, Great Falls	9
L	Parker, Geoff, Casper	9
IP	Martin, Brennon, Idaho Falls	87.3
H	Martin, Brennon, Idaho Falls	102
R	Rowland, Robby, Missoula	65
ER	Rowland, Robby, Missoula	61
HB	Six tied at	9
BB	Guillon, Ismael, Billings	46
SO	Peacock, Brian, Idaho Falls	89
SO/9	Gomez, Gustavo, Ogden	11.95
SO/9 (RP)	Carl, Edwin, Idaho Falls	19.36
BB/9	Brooks, Aaron, Idaho Falls	0.9
WP	Cravy, Tyler, Helena	17
BK	Mugarian, Wes, Billings	5
HR	Moye, Andrew, Helena	15
	Rowland, Robby, Missoula	15
AVG	Martinez, Brandon, Ogden	.237

FIELDING

C	FPCT	Aguila, Roidany, Missoula	.996
	PO	Aguila, Roidany, Missoula	452
	A	Baker, Abel, Orem	65
	E	Escobar, Edul, Idaho Falls	13
	DP	Three tied at	5
	PB	Escobar, Edul, Idaho Falls	13
1B	FPCT	Hall, Frazier, Orem	.994
	PO	Riggins, Harold, Casper	563
	A	Riggins, Harold, Casper	61
	E	Riggins, Harold, Casper	11
	DP	Riggins, Harold, Casper	49
2B	FPCT	Lindsey, Taylor, Orem	.976
	PO	De Pinto, Joe, Great Falls	131
	A	De Pinto, Joe, Great Falls	168
		Lindsey, Taylor, Orem	168
	E	De Pinto, Joe, Great Falls	13
	DP	Lindsey, Taylor, Orem	44
3B	FPCT	Court, Ryan, Missoula	.934
	PO	Cowart, Kaleb, Orem	48
	A	Court, Ryan, Missoula	128
		Cowart, Kaleb, Orem	128
	E	Hunt, Jeffrey, Ogden	19
	DP	Cowart, Kaleb, Orem	17
SS	FPCT	Hairgrove, Trevor, Orem	.976
	PO	Herbek, David, Great Falls	100
	A	Rivera, Yadiel, Helena	233
	E	Rivera, Yadiel, Helena	23
	DP	Rivera, Yadiel, Helena	47
OF	FPCT	Bianco, Justin, Missoula	.989
	PO	Walla, Max, Helena	139
	A	Walla, Max, Helena	11
	E	Waldrop, Kyle, Billings	6
		Walla, Max, Helena	6
	DP	Walla, Max, Helena	5

MINOR LEAGUES

The Dodgers joined the Arizona League in 2009 and needed just three years to capture their first championship, as they defeated the perennial contending Giants 4-2 in a one-game final.

Juan Noriega, who started the 2011 season in his native Mexico, earned the win in the finale by pitching four scoreless innings in relief of starter Jose Dominguez. The winners scored all of their runs in the fifth inning, led by shortstop Delvis Morales' two-run single.

The Dodgers qualified for the championship game by beating the Rangers, 3-2, in a one-game semifinal, while the Giants reached the finals by topping the Reds, 9-3.

The league added a 13th team in 2011 with the Diamondbacks moving into their parent organization's new Salt River Fields training facility on the edge of Scottsdale. The 2011 season also marked a return to a split schedule, with night games being played in the first half of the year followed by day games from late July until the end of August. The shift to 11 a.m. games coincided with the arrival of record August heat in the Phoenix area, which resulted in quite a few extremely uncomfortable games during the season's last month.

Padres outfielder Yoan Alcantara was named the league's top prospect after a season in which the Dominican Republic native batted .348/.367/.586, with seven home runs and a league-leading 46 RBIs (tying with two other players). Alcantara, 18, was one of three Padres' position players to rank among the league's best prospects.

A majority of the top 20 prospects were Latin American players, with most high draft picks waiting until the Aug. 15 signing deadline to start their professional careers. Four first-round picks made their pro debuts in the AZL, with Rangers southpaw Kevin Matthews coming closest to

TOP 20 PROSPECTS

1. Yoan Alcantara, of, Padres
2. Phillips Castillo, of, Mariners
3. Elvis Araujo, lhp, Indians
4. Clayton Blackburn, rhp, Giants
5. Luigi Rodriguez, of, Indians
6. Marco Hernandez, ss/2b, Cubs
7. Duanel Jones, 3b, Padres
8. Humberto Arteaga, ss, Royals
9. Gioskar Amaya, inf, Cubs
10. Jorge Martinez, ss, Indians
11. Alberth Martinez, of, Padres
12. Jordan Akins, of, Rangers
13. Alex Santana, 3b, Dodgers
14. Jake Sisco, rhp, Indians
15. Gabriel Rosa, 3b, Reds
16. Felix Sterling, rhp, Indians
17. Luis Sardinas, ss, Rangers
18. Joan Gregorio, rhp, Giants
19. D'andre Toney, of, Royals
20. Martin Peguero, ss, Mariners

inclusion on the prospect list. Matthews fell a few innings short of qualifying when he was promoted to short-season Spokane in early August.

Other first-round picks in the AZL, each of whom made only token appearances, were right-handers Sonny Gray (Athletics) and Joe Ross (Padres) and shortstop Javier Baez (Cubs).

The Indians dominated this year's prospect list by placing five players among the top 20. Lefthander Elvis Araujo, who led all pitchers with nine wins, was ranked third among prospects in his first season back after two years rehabilitating his arm after Tommy John surgery, while 18-year-old outfielder Luigi Rodriguez placed fifth.

Jose Cuevas (Giants) was named MVP and also led the league with nine home runs. The 23-year-old third baseman played in his second AZL season. Cuevas and Joe Winker (Dodgers) tied Alcantara for the RBIs lead. Former major league second baseman Jody Reed was named manager of the year for leading the Dodgers to the crown in his first year in the Arizona League.

OVERALL STANDINGS

Team (Organization)	W	L	PCT	GB	Manager	Last Pennant
Giants	41	15	.732	—	Mike Goff	2008
Rangers	38	18	.679	3	Hector Ortiz	Never
Dodgers	34	22	.607	7	Jody Reed	2011
Reds	31	25	.554	10	Jose Nieves	Never
Indians	30	26	.536	11	Anthony Medrano	Never
Angels	28	28	.500	13	Tyrone Boykin	Never
Cubs	28	28	.500	13	Juan Cabreja	2002
Athletics	27	29	.482	14	Marcus Jensen	2001
Mariners	25	31	.446	16	Jesus Azuaje	2009
Padres	23	33	.411	18	Jim Gabella	2006
Royals	22	34	.393	19	Darryl Kennedy	2003
D-backs	20	36	.357	21	Andy Green	Never
Brewers	17	39	.304	24	Tony Diggs	2010

PLAYOFFS—Semifinals: Giants defeated Reds and Dodgers defeated Rangers in one-game playoffs. **Finals:** Dodgers defeated Giants in a one-game playoff.

CLUB BATTING

	AVG	G	AB	R	H	2B	3B	HR	RBI	BB	SO	SB	OBP	SLG
Cubs	.305	56	2018	350	616	117	47	18	302	164	399	95	.362	.437
Giants	.296	56	2027	412	600	125	34	51	358	198	444	75	.368	.467
Rangers	.289	56	1997	405	578	103	46	36	336	229	461	100	.372	.441
Padres	.284	56	1984	319	563	97	33	43	272	184	447	76	.351	.431
Mariners	.277	56	1952	284	541	116	20	12	242	167	478	90	.345	.376
Indians	.275	56	1945	295	535	105	33	35	253	190	444	78	.342	.417
Royals	.274	56	2016	344	553	108	28	26	294	196	439	89	.350	.394
Athletics	.266	56	1915	289	509	109	22	32	253	175	481	37	.338	.396
Dodgers	.266	56	1948	341	519	111	27	30	283	216	483	61	.348	.397
Reds	.264	56	1928	334	509	100	40	30	273	218	453	113	.350	.404
Angels	.263	56	1911	321	502	96	46	22	280	244	475	86	.360	.396
Diamondbacks	.251	56	1901	284	477	82	24	22	229	221	479	65	.337	.354
Brewers	.247	56	1879	256	464	77	30	22	213	204	548	81	.332	.355

CLUB PITCHING

	ERA	G	CG	SHO	SV	IP	H	R	ER	HR	BB	SO	AVG
Indians	3.70	56	0	6	14	493	453	267	203	24	209	472	.246
Dodgers	3.87	56	0	3	10	502	476	257	216	36	204	505	.251
Cubs	4.08	56	0	1	9	498	551	310	226	35	197	460	.280
Rangers	4.22	56	0	1	12	499	511	266	234	24	175	499	.265
Giants	4.34	56	0	2	20	511	514	300	246	21	196	496	.261
Angels	4.54	56	0	1	16	496	511	294	250	27	163	445	.266
Reds	4.79	56	0	1	11	498	557	328	265	23	194	499	.281
Brewers	4.80	56	0	1	6	491	555	338	262	28	191	454	.280
Mariners	4.91	56	0	2	15	500	556	348	273	37	219	410	.280
Athletics	4.93	56	0	2	14	493	520	342	270	32	229	492	.269
Diamondbacks	5.22	56	0	2	4	490	559	346	284	27	209	405	.286
Padres	5.79	56	0	1	13	491	607	417	316	24	217	437	.298
Royals	6.11	56	0	1	13	502	596	421	341	41	223	457	.295

CLUB FIELDING

	PCT	PO	A	E	DP		PCT	PO	A	E	DP
Rangers	.968	1496	637	70	50	Athletics	.953	1478	594	103	43
Angels	.964	1488	625	78	53	Mariners	.953	1501	607	105	50
Diamondbacks	.960	1469	615	87	50	Indians	.952	1480	582	103	41
Giants	.960	1532	645	90	41	Royals	.951	1506	603	108	46
Dodgers	.959	1506	614	90	44	Brewers	.941	1473	613	131	45
Reds	.959	1494	612	90	50	Padres	.935	1473	569	142	45
Cubs	.954	1494	585	100	48						

INDIVIDUAL BATTING LEADERS (Minimum 2.7 PA/Team Game)

	AVG	G	AB	R	H	2B	3B	HR	RBI	BB	SO	SB
DelGuidice, Nick, Royals	.408	34	125	32	51	16	2	4	24	10	10	2
Rojas, Kelvin, Athletics	.379	48	169	38	64	11	4	3	35	16	42	3
Amaya, Gioskar, Cubs	.377	52	204	37	77	11	8	0	36	13	39	13
Winker, Joseph, Dodgers	.374	43	163	35	61	17	6	4	46	20	37	4
Tomlinson, Kelby, Giants	.357	37	140	32	50	10	5	2	26	14	22	11
Williams, Jeremy, Rangers	.357	42	143	39	51	9	9	5	34	14	25	11
Martinez, Alberth, Padres	.354	44	189	31	67	12	6	7	24	10	27	14
Sim, Eric, Giants	.352	43	145	30	51	12	2	6	37	17	35	5
Alcantara, Yoan, Padres	.348	50	210	50	73	13	8	7	46	4	25	8
Perez, Juan, Reds	.346	33	133	28	46	4	5	2	21	16	18	12

INDIVIDUAL PITCHING LEADERS (Minimum 0.8 IP/Team Game)

	W	L	ERA	G	GS	CG	SV	IP	H	R	ER	BB	SO
Gregorio, Joan, Giants	3	0	2.32	12	12	0	0	50	43	14	13	16	43
Schaub, Michael, Brewers	2	4	2.60	13	4	0	1	45	39	23	13	20	35
Araujo, Elvis, Indians	9	1	2.86	13	11	0	0	63	54	28	20	18	58
McNelis, Brandon, Angels	2	3	3.25	14	9	0	0	53	47	26	19	21	49
Smith, Brian, Cubs	3	4	3.30	14	12	0	0	46	46	22	17	23	41
DeJesus, Luis, Indians	3	2	3.33	13	9	0	0	46	41	20	17	11	45
Bender, Joel, Reds	4	3	3.40	12	8	0	0	53	63	30	20	17	45
Blackwell, Shawn, Rangers	5	0	3.58	14	3	0	0	50	44	23	20	16	49
Gerdeman, Ross, Diamondbacks	4	2	3.64	14	7	0	0	59	57	25	24	13	32
De Los Santos, Abel, Rangers	7	1	3.67	14	12	0	0	61	55	29	25	8	61

ALL-STAR TEAM

C: Kevin Torres, Rangers. **1B:** Ben Thomas, Giants. **2B:** Juan Perez, Reds. **3B:** Jose Cuevas, Giants. **SS:** Gioskar Amaya, Cubs. **OF:** Kelvin Rojas, Athletics; Yoan Alcantara, Padres; Joseph Winker, Dodgers. **DH:** Kevin Torres, Rangers. **SP:** Yoan Gregorio, Giants; Elvis Araujo, Indians. **RP:** Andrew Stueve, Royals; Manuel Ruiz, Brewers.
Most Valuable Player: Jose Cuevas, Giants. **Manager of the Year:** Jody Reed, Dodgers.

DEPARTMENT LEADERS

BATTING

OBP	Winker, Joseph, Dodgers	.442
SLG	Williams, Jeremy, Rangers	.650
OPS	Williams, Jeremy, Rangers	1.076
R	Alcantara, Yoan, Padres	50
H	Amaya, Gioskar, Cubs	77
TB	Alcantara, Yoan, Padres	123
XBH	Alcantara, Yoan, Padres	28
	Cuevas, Jose, Giants	28
2B	Bandy, Jett, Angels	18
	Castillo, Phillips, Mariners	18
3B	Clarke, Chevy, Angels	10
HR	Cuevas, Jose, Giants	9
RBI	Three tied at	46
SAC	Morales, Delvis, Dodgers	8
BB	Moesquit, Kevin, Angels	33
HBP	Bandy, Jett, Angels	18
SO	Mateo, Wagner, Diamondbacks	88
SB	Cuckovich, Nicholas, Royals	24
CS	Toney, D'Andre, Royals	11
AB/SO	Donahue, Pat, Diamondbacks	11.92

PITCHING

G	Jones, James, Padres	27
GS	Meza, Luis, Dodgers	14
GF	Jones, James, Padres	22
SV	Chacin, Alejandro, Reds	11
W	Araujo, Elvis, Indians	9
L	Batista, Lay, Angels	6
	Reyes, Genison, Padres	6
IP	Batista, Lay, Angels	64.7
	Meza, Luis, Dodgers	64.7
H	Avila, Andres, Athletics	83
R	Reyes, Genison, Padres	58
ER	Reyes, Genison, Padres	49
HB	Perry, Blake, Diamondbacks	10
BB	Guerrero, Tayron, Padres	41
SO	Avila, Andres, Athletics	71
SO/9	Avila, Andres, Athletics	10.25
SO/9(RP)	Chacin, Alejandro, Reds	13.91
BB/9	French, Justice, Reds	0.92
WP	Norwood, Tyler, Padres	21
BK	Mavare, Jose, Rangers	3
HR	Three tied at	8
AVG	Araujo, Elvis, Indians	.228

FIELDING

C	FPCT	Edmonds, Guy, Rangers	.988
	PO	Sim, Eric, Giants	306
	A	Sim, Eric, Giants	49
	E	Gomez, Wagner, Reds	12
	DP	Five tied at	4
	PB	Gomez, Wagner, Reds	19
1B	FPCT	Sanchez, Carlos, Reds	.995
	PO	Gaylord, Brian, Royals	446
	A	Marte, Miguel, Athletics	33
	E	Arias, Hitaniel, Brewers	14
	DP	Gaylord, Brian, Royals	34
2B	FPCT	Moesquit, Kevin, Angels	.975
	PO	Ramirez, Jose, Indians	102
	A	Ramirez, Jose, Indians	131
	E	Garcia, Carlos, Royals	16
	DP	Moesquit, Kevin, Angels	32
3B	FPCT	Rua, Ryan, Rangers	.936
	PO	Martinez, Andres, Brewers	32
	A	Rua, Ryan, Rangers	88
	E	Ramirez, Robert, Reds	19
	DP	Martinez, Jose, Mariners	12
SS	FPCT	Arteaga, Humberto, Royals	.932
	PO	Arteaga, Humberto, Royals	68
	A	Arteaga, Humberto, Royals	137
	E	Blanco, Felipe, Padres	28
	DP	Blanco, Felipe, Padres	23
		Hernandez, Marco, Cubs	23
OF	FPCT	Winker, Joseph, Dodgers	1.000
	PO	Brito, Socrates, Diamondbacks	118
		Shines, Devin, Dodgers	118
	A	Three tied at	8
	E	Alcantara, Yoan, Padres	9
	DP	Puello, Ronny, Brewers	3
		Zamarripa, James, Mariners	3

MINOR LEAGUES

While many of the top picks from the 2011 draft played sparingly, Dante Bichette Jr. signed quickly with the Yankees, won the Gulf Coast League MVP and led his team to the league title.

Bichette, who hit .342/.446/.505 in 52 games, homered in the decisive Game Three of the championship series against the Marlins to help the Yankees to a 3-1 victory. During the regular season, Bichette, whose father Dante was a four-time all-star in the 1990s, led the league in hits (67), doubles (17) and RBIs (47).

The Yankees had the GCL's most potent offense, leading the league in runs, average, on-base percentage, slugging, hits and stolen bases. The organization has developed one of the strongest contingents of Latin American prospects in baseball, and the Yankees' young Dominican talent helped carry their offense. Center fielder Ravel Santana was the league's No. 2 prospect and shortstop/second baseman Claudio Custodio was No. 9, while middle infielder Jose Rosario and catcher Isaias Tejeda were both among the league's top performers in 2011.

Marlins center fielder Jesus Solorzano played solid defense and hit .299/.355/.454, while the pitching staff was led by righthanders Jose Rodriguez (2.04 ERA in 53 innings) and Austin Brice (2.96 ERA in 49 innings).

With so many 2011 draft picks holding out to sign until the Aug. 15 deadline, the league's prospects leaned heavily international, particularly from Latin America. After Bichette, the league's next 11 best prospects were all signed out of Latin America, as were 15 of the top 20 prospects. Other than Bichette, fellow sandwich picks Blake Snell (Rays) and Joe Musgrove (Blue Jays) were the only 2011 draftees to make the cut.

TOP 20 PROSPECTS

1. Dante Bichette Jr., 3b, Yankees
2. Ravel Santana, of, Yankees
3. Luis Heredia, rhp, Pirates
4. Brenny Paulino, rhp, Tigers
5. Jose Osuna, 1b/of, Pirates
6. Raul Alcantara, rhp, Red Sox
7. Jose Vinicio, ss, Red Sox
8. Adonys Cardona, rhp, Blue Jays
9. Claudio Custodio, ss, Yankees
10. Danry Vasquez, of, Tigers
11. Jesus Solorzano, of, Marlins
12. Roderick Bernadina, of, Orioles
13. Blake Snell, lhp, Rays
14. Alen Hanson, ss/2b, Pirates
15. Joe Musgrove, rhp, Blue Jays
16. Ethan Stewart, lhp, Phillies
17. Victor Deleon, rhp, Cardinals
18. Eduardo Rodriguez, lhp, Orioles
19. Austin Brice, rhp, Marlins
20. Rafael Montero, rhp, Mets

Though Eric Arce didn't make the GCL Top 20, the Blue Jays' left fielder had an outstanding debut. A 25th-round pick in 2011 who didn't play baseball in the spring, Arce set a GCL record with 14 home runs. The 5-foot-9, 205-pound Arce hit .268/.437/.621 overall, leading the circuit in walks (38), ranking second in slugging, RBIs and extra-base hits and third in on-base percentage.

While he was in the GCL, Red Sox righthander Raul Alcantara was the league's most effective pitcher. Alcantara earned a late-season promotion to short-season Lowell, leaving the GCL after posting a league-low 0.75 ERA in 48 innings, walking just six and allowing just 23 hits.

Tigers righthander Brenny Paulino, an 18-year-old who signed for $100,000 out of the Dominican Republic in 2009, ranked as the GCL's No. 4 prospect with a 2.73 ERA and a 45-18 K-BB mark in 46 innings. Paulino earned praise around the league for his projectable 6-foot-4 frame and his fastball that he ran up to 97 mph.

OVERALL STANDINGS

Team (Organization)	W	L	PCT	GB	Manager	Last Pennant
Marlins	38	16	.704	—	Jorge Hernandez	Never
Orioles	38	22	.633	3	Ramon Sambo	Never
Yankees	37	23	.617	4	Carlos Mendoza	2011
Pirates	34	26	.567	7	Tom Prince	Never
Cardinals	31	24	.564	7½	Steve Turco	Never
Twins	31	29	.517	10	Ramon Borrego	Never
Tigers	29	31	.483	12	Basilio Cabrera	Never
Mets	27	29	.482	12	Luis Rojas	Never
Blue Jays	27	32	.458	13½	Omar Malave	Never
Phillies	27	32	.458	13½	Rolando de Armas	2010
Red Sox	27	33	.450	14	George Lombard	2006
Braves	24	34	.414	16	Jonathan Schuerholz	2003
Rays	24	36	.400	17	Joe Alvarez	Never
Nationals	20	33	.377	17½	Bobby Williams	2009
Astros	20	34	.370	18	Ed Romero	Never

Semifinals: Marlins defeated Pirates and Yankees defeated Orioles in one-game playoffs. **Finals:** Yankees defeated Marlins 2-1 in a best-of-three series.

CLUB BATTING

	AVG	G	AB	R	H	2B	3B	HR	RBI	BB	SO	SB	OBP	SLG
Yankees	.298	60	2094	388	625	150	28	48	345	220	484	116	.378	.466
Marlins	.272	54	1797	291	488	86	18	15	239	197	330	64	.354	.364
Pirates	.261	60	2023	364	527	98	35	26	304	234	414	108	.349	.382
Blue Jays	.256	59	1926	303	494	87	15	51	262	245	478	73	.350	.397
Nationals	.253	53	1811	255	459	69	25	32	219	178	384	75	.327	.372
Phillies	.253	59	1934	252	490	101	19	30	222	173	403	56	.324	.372
Tigers	.247	60	2014	261	497	93	10	42	230	151	416	58	.310	.365
Red Sox	.244	60	1989	220	486	79	23	32	193	171	528	55	.317	.355
Cardinals	.240	55	1813	259	436	87	15	23	215	201	437	67	.329	.343
Braves	.238	58	1906	264	454	81	13	28	219	174	468	105	.315	.338
Orioles	.238	60	1956	260	465	102	25	20	221	184	390	45	.315	.346
Astros	.231	54	1735	215	400	68	19	13	187	160	468	61	.308	.314
Twins	.230	60	1908	215	439	82	15	11	185	198	379	43	.311	.306
Mets	.229	56	1854	227	424	85	11	12	195	204	421	26	.316	.306
Rays	.216	60	1897	222	410	69	13	17	179	177	484	100	.297	.293

CLUB PITCHING

	ERA	G	CG	SHO	SV	IP	H	R	ER	HR	BB	SO	AVG
Orioles	2.07	60	0	6	14	534	398	163	123	15	183	504	.209
Twins	2.89	60	0	6	15	517	449	211	166	14	171	446	.236
Marlins	2.90	54	0	9	17	472	381	190	152	17	194	455	.219
Cardinals	3.32	55	0	3	14	482	437	238	178	21	188	397	.238
Rays	3.32	60	2	5	7	521	487	246	192	28	166	426	.247
Tigers	3.35	60	2	8	14	527	499	265	196	27	175	451	.252
Mets	3.67	56	0	2	16	491	449	235	200	13	175	370	.244
Red Sox	3.81	60	0	2	16	532	466	297	225	23	210	362	.237
Astros	4.19	54	0	1	11	462	474	280	215	20	198	404	.263
Yankees	4.31	60	0	2	17	524	506	324	251	33	230	504	.248
Braves	4.33	58	0	2	11	499	503	284	240	39	139	401	.261
Nationals	4.35	53	0	1	9	464	466	304	224	24	185	414	.259
Pirates	4.69	60	0	2	16	534	550	326	278	47	204	374	.266
Blue Jays	4.85	59	1	2	11	499	501	311	269	43	217	482	.260
Phillies	4.85	59	0	2	17	504	528	322	272	36	232	451	.271

CLUB FIELDING

	PCT	PO	A	E	DP		PCT	PO	A	E	DP
Mets	.969	1473	613	66	49	Cardinals	.960	1446	575	85	37
Orioles	.969	1601	715	73	61	Pirates	.960	1602	613	92	54
Phillies	.969	1513	584	68	27	Marlins	.958	1417	574	88	36
Blue Jays	.968	1498	566	69	46	Twins	.958	1552	682	98	68
Tigers	.967	1581	604	75	52	Red Sox	.955	1595	700	107	47
Braves	.966	1496	637	76	41	Yankees	.949	1571	548	114	42
Rays	.963	1563	678	86	49	Nationals	.946	1391	560	111	40
Astros	.961	1387	530	78	39						

INDIVIDUAL BATTING LEADERS (Minimum 2.7 PA/Team Game)

	AVG	G	AB	R	H	2B	3B	HR	RBI	BB	SO	SB
Eckerle, Brandon, Tigers	.355	45	166	34	59	5	0	0	12	28	16	18
Bichette, Jr., Dante, Yankees	.342	52	196	33	67	17	3	4	47	30	41	3
Osuna, Jose, Pirates	.331	48	178	28	59	14	3	4	32	18	21	3
Rosario, Jose, Yankees	.331	43	172	38	57	6	5	6	28	6	28	11
Valenzuela, Carlos, Phillies	.331	43	160	20	53	9	1	2	18	11	31	2
Tejeda, Isaias, Yankees	.331	39	148	34	49	11	3	6	27	11	20	5
Custodio, Claudio, Yankees	.325	39	157	46	51	9	1	1	19	22	40	26
Vega-Rosado, Jorge, Blue Jays	.317	51	183	39	58	12	2	4	30	19	40	22
Aguasvivas, Juaner, Tigers	.315	48	178	26	56	9	3	10	37	12	47	3
Ramos, Wander, Nationals	.313	43	147	32	46	12	1	12	37	19	45	7

INDIVIDUAL PITCHING LEADERS (Minimum 0.8 IP/Team Game)

	W	L	ERA	G	GS	CG	SV	IP	H	R	ER	BB	SO
Alcantara, Raul, Red Sox	1	1	0.75	9	9	0	0	48	23	5	4	6	36
Morton, Taylor, Yankees	3	2	1.98	12	6	0	0	50	49	19	11	8	35
Rodriguez, Jose, Marlins	4	3	2.04	11	8	0	0	53	35	13	12	15	41
Watson, Bradley, Cardinals	5	1	2.22	11	8	0	0	49	51	16	12	5	37
Gomez, Roberto, Rays	3	4	2.48	11	8	0	0	54	41	22	15	9	42
Suero, Bruedlin, Rays	3	4	2.63	11	8	0	0	55	48	24	16	8	36
Gomez, Sergio, Red Sox	1	3	2.68	12	11	0	0	50	38	18	15	16	37
Gil, Jean Carlos, Braves	2	3	2.91	13	10	0	0	65	65	28	21	12	63
Ulacio, Ramon, Cardinals	4	3	2.93	12	12	0	0	58	50	31	19	20	38
Brice, Austin, Marlins	6	0	2.96	11	9	0	0	49	32	20	16	33	55

ALL-STAR TEAM

C: Isaias Tejeda, Yankees. **1B:** Juaner Aguasvivas, Tigers. **2B:** Jorge Vega-Rosada, Blue Jays. **3B:** Dante Bichette, Yankees. **SS:** Jose Rosario, Yankees. **OF:** Brandon Eckerle, Tigers; Wander Ramos, Nationals; Jesus Solorzano, Marlins. **DH:** Eric Arce, Blue Jays. **SP:** Raul Alcantara, Red Sox. **RP:** Willy Paulino, Cardinals.

Most Valuable Player: Dante Bichette, Yankees. **Most Outstanding Pitcher:** Raul Alcantara, Red Sox. **Manager of the Year:** Carlos Mendoza, Yankees.

DEPARTMENT LEADERS

BATTING

OBP	Eckerle, Brandon, Tigers	.460
SLG	Ramos, Wander, Nationals	.653
OPS	Arce, Eric, Blue Jays	1.058
R	Custodio, Claudio, Yankees	46
H	Bichette, Jr., Dante, Yankees	67
TB	Aguasvivas, Juaner, Tigers	101
XBH	Ramos, Wander, Nationals	25
2B	Bichette, Jr., Dante, Yankees	17
3B	Hanson, Alen, Pirates	7
HR	Arce, Eric, Blue Jays	14
RBI	Bichette, Jr., Dante, Yankees	47
SAC	Hernandez, Yeison, Marlins	11
BB	Arce, Eric, Blue Jays	38
HBP	Reynolds, Javaris, Astros	12
	Schwind, Jonathan, Pirates	12
SO	Perkins, Kendrick, Red Sox	62
SB	Custodio, Claudio, Yankees	26
CS	Vinicio, Jose, Red Sox	10
AB/SO	Villalobos, Alejandro, Phillies	33

PITCHING

G	Robertson, Montreal, Tigers	24
GS	Three tied at	12
GF	Robertson, Montreal, Tigers	21
SV	Paulino, Willy, Cardinals	12
W	Pevny, Logan, Pirates	7
L	Five tied at	6
IP	De La Rosa, Edgar, Tigers	67.7
H	Briceno, Endrys, Tigers	72
	Warner, Josh, Phillies	72
R	Warner, Josh, Phillies	48
ER	Warner, Josh, Phillies	42
HB	Briceno, Endrys, Tigers	14
BB	Brice, Austin, Marlins	33
SO	Gil, Jean Carlos, Braves	63
SO/9	Brice, Austin, Marlins	10.17
SO/9 (RP)	Checo, Mariel, Yankees	13.67
BB/9	Ynoa, Gabriel, Mets	0.75
WP	Mendoza, Richard, Cardinals	20
BK	Villasmil, Edioglis, Mets	4
HR	Castillo, Eduardo, Braves	9
AVG	Alcantara, Raul, Red Sox	.147

FIELDING

C	FPCT	Caldwell, Tony, Marlins	.993
	PO	Tejeda, Isaias, Yankees	295
	A	Severino, Pedro, Nationals	53
	E	Tejeda, Isaias, Yankees	12
	DP	Snitker, Troy, Braves	4
	PB	Gonzalez, Alfredo, Astros	15
1B	FPCT	Alcantara, Aris, Braves	.998
	PO	Aguasvivas, Juaner, Tigers	399
	A	Alcantara, Aris, Braves	45
	E	Munoz, Felix, Marlins	8
	DP	Hendricks, Joshua, Twins	39
2B	FPCT	Pena, Jerome, Orioles	.978
	PO	Pena, Jerome, Orioles	91
	A	Pena, Jerome, Orioles	130
	E	Tavarez, Aneury, Red Sox	12
	DP	Pena, Jerome, Orioles	33
3B	FPCT	Bichette, Jr., Dante, Yankees	.945
	PO	Tuivailala, Samuel, Cardinals	41
	A	Mosby, Michael, Orioles	113
	E	Tuivailala, Samuel, Cardinals	17
	DP	Mosby, Michael, Orioles	12
SS	FPCT	Hernandez, Yeison, Marlins	.939
	PO	Vinicio, Jose, Red Sox	107
	A	Vinicio, Jose, Red Sox	161
	E	Vinicio, Jose, Red Sox	29
	DP	Vinicio, Jose, Red Sox	25
OF	FPCT	Four tied at	1.000
	PO	Smith, Patrick, Tigers	128
	A	Three tied at	8
	E	Jeffries, Lance, Cardinals	6
	DP	Polanco, Gregory, Pirates	4

MINOR LEAGUES

DOMINICAN SUMMER LEAGUE

From start to finish, the Angels were the best team in the Dominican Summer League. After posting the league's best record, the Angels were perfect in the postseason, sweeping the Mariners in the semifinals before winning the championship with a three-game sweep of the Orioles.

Shortstop/second baseman Pedro Toribio led the Angels' offense with his combination of power and speed, hitting .316/.356/.540 to rank among the league leaders in slugging and stolen bases (32). Righthander Jean Carlos Santiago was the team's top pitcher, ranking fourth in the league in ERA (1.38) and third in strikeouts (82).

Cubs third baseman Jeimer Candelario hit .337/.443/.478 in 72 games, while Athletics center fielder Vicmal de la Cruz finished batting .318/.438/.453 in 58 games. Mets righthander Luis Mateo had a stellar 80-5 K-BB mark and a 2.00 ERA in 63 innings

STANDINGS

SANTO DOMINGO NORTH

	W	L	PCT	GB
Mariners	45	24	.652	—
Brewers	44	27	.620	2
Cardinals	27	44	.380	19
Athletics	24	46	.343	21 ½

BOCA CHICA BASEBALL CITY

	W	L	PCT	GB
Orioles	46	24	.657	—
Twins	42	26	.618	3
Rockies	43	28	.606	3 ½
White Sox	35	32	.522	9 ½
Reds	32	36	.471	13
Padres	27	41	.397	18

SAN PEDRO DE MACORIS

	W	L	PCT	GB
Angels	52	17	.754	—
Braves	34	35	.493	18
Tigers	25	41	.379	25 ½
Blue Jays	20	49	.290	32

INDIVIDUAL BATTING LEADERS
(Minimus 2.7 Plate Appearances Per League Game)

PLAYER, TEAM	AVG	G	AB	R	H	2B	3B	HR	RBI	BB	SO	SB
Reyes, Robelys, Cardinals	.378	62	222	43	84	11	5	6	26	27	26	22
Goris, Diego, Pirates	.350	68	266	53	93	20	4	5	46	15	28	15
Gonzalez, Diego, Phillies	.345	47	174	21	60	6	0	0	14	11	20	23
Robles, Alberto, Giants	.344	55	183	39	63	8	1	0	36	32	19	14
Candelario, Jeimer, Cubs	.337	72	249	50	84	16	2	5	53	50	42	4
Vasquez, Jesus, Marlins	.324	66	222	48	72	20	1	11	53	41	58	21
Fortunato, Raul, Pirates	.324	66	244	53	79	10	5	7	32	30	49	34
Zorrilla, Janelfry, Mariners	.321	66	224	50	72	21	2	12	61	24	37	13
De La Cruz, Maikis, Mets	.321	73	265	40	85	19	1	0	31	27	39	33
De La Cruz, Vicmal, A's	.318	58	192	29	61	13	5	1	28	37	27	10

INDIVIDUAL PITCHING LEADERS
Minimum 0.8 Innings Per League Game

PITCHER, TEAM	W	L	ERA	G	GS	CG	SV	IP	H	R	BB	SO
Caramo, Yender, Royals	10	3	1.20	13	12	1	0	68	51	11	8	38
Marquez, Ericdavis, Blue Jays	1	5	1.22	23	3	0	3	59	33	21	17	61
Aquino, Jayson, Rockies	8	2	1.30	14	14	3	0	90	55	21	22	80
Santiago, Jean Carlos, Angels	4	1	1.38	12	12	1	0	65	37	16	12	82
Lopez, Manuel, Blue Jays	3	1	1.40	24	0	0	1	58	40	13	17	44
Mejia, Adalberto, Giants	5	2	1.42	13	13	0	0	76	58	18	8	71
Hurtado, Daniel, Angels	7	3	1.45	14	14	3	0	74	53	23	20	65
Perez, Gabriel, Angels	10	1	1.47	14	14	1	0	74	41	15	28	76
Mateo, Jackson, Dodgers	5	1	1.62	15	15	0	0	72	49	19	18	52
Cleto, Jeffry, Indians	3	4	1.65	14	13	0	0	651	54	26	22	37

BOCA CHICA NORTH

	W	L	PCT	GB
Royals	46	24	.657	—
Dodgers	40	29	.580	5 ½
Pirates	41	30	.577	5 ½
Red Sox	38	33	.535	8 ½
Rays	35	35	.500	11
Indians	31	36	.463	13 ½
Astros	27	40	.403	17 ½
Yankees2	28	42	.400	18
Mets2	28	44	.389	19

BOCA CHICA SOUTH

	W	L	PCT	GB
Cubs2	47	25	.653	—
Rangers	41	30	.577	5 ½
Phillies	38	33	.535	8 ½
Giants	35	32	.522	9 ½
Mets1	34	36	.486	12
Nationals	33	36	.478	12 ½
Yankees1	32	38	.457	14
Marlins	24	43	.358	20 ½

VENEZUELAN SUMMER LEAGUE

The Pirates finished with the best regular season record and were one win away from a title, but the Rays rallied with a 4-3 win and then a 7-2 victory in the decisive Game Three to capture the title.

The Rays led the league in runs scored in large part because of the contributions of catcher Oscar Hernandez, who dominated nearly every major offensive category. Hernandez finished first in the VSL in average, on-base percentage, slugging, hits, runs, extra-base hits, home runs and RBIs. His 21 home runs were more than twice the total of Rays outfielder Franklin Paz, who finished second with nine. Third baseman Dilson Herrera was a key offensive contributor for the Pirates, hitting .308/.413/.472 in 65 games as a 17-year-old.

Reds righthander Oswaldo Mieres returned to the VSL for his second season and led the league with a 2.33 ERA. It was the Phillies who allowed the fewest runs in the league, with righthander Yovan Silva and Moises Rivas ranking fifth and sixth in the league in ERA, respectively.

STANDINGS

	W	L	PCT	GB
Pirates	40	32	.556	—
Rays	38	33	.535	1 ½
Mariners	38	34	.528	2

	W	L	PCT	GB
Reds	38	34	.528	2
Phillies	32	38	.457	7
Tigers	28	43	.394	11 ½

INDIVIDUAL BATTING LEADERS
(Minimus 2.7 Plate Appearances Per League Game)

PLAYER, TEAM	AVG	G	AB	R	H	2B	3B	HR	RBI	BB	SO	SB
Hernandez, Oscar, Rays	.402	69	239	56	96	14	1	21	66	37	44	3
Montilla, Ulises, Pirates	.364	70	253	39	92	21	3	3	47	33	17	11
Astudillo, Willians, Phillies	.361	52	194	31	70	8	3	1	25	15	2	11
Munoz, Edgard, Pirates	.360	52	164	42	59	8	1	1	17	23	14	20
Coronel, Ramon, Mariners	.352	61	210	36	74	14	1	0	27	14	31	6
Mendez, Miguel, Reds	.341	62	208	45	71	16	5	2	35	13	12	12
Dominguez, Wilmer, Rays	.324	54	188	26	61	9	1	6	32	12	21	4
Ustariz, Jesus, Tigers	.324	50	176	25	57	12	1	3	22	14	21	3
Correa, Leopoldo, Rays	.322	64	230	35	74	17	0	8	54	31	31	0
Roman, Jose, Pirates	.317	68	243	39	77	17	0	5	46	34	33	6

INDIVIDUAL PITCHING LEADERS
Minimum 0.8 Innings Per League Game

PITCHER, TEAM	W	L	ERA	G	GS	CG	SV	IP	H	R	BB	SO
Mieres, Oswaldo, Reds	7	4	2.33	14	14	0	0	73	54	23	19	52
Gonzalez, Isliexel, Mariners	6	3	2.51	14	14	0	0	82.1	88	35	18	56
Flores, Jose, Mariners	5	2	2.61	13	11	0	0	69	51	22	20	35
Romero, Franderlin, Reds	3	2	3.02	13	13	1	0	66	69	31	9	34
Silva, Yovan, Phillies	3	4	3.11	12	11	0	0	64	45	25	34	42
Rivas, Moises, Phillies	4	2	3.22	14	11	0	0	73	51	30	34	57
Alvarado, Carlos, Tigers	3	5	3.57	18	13	0	0	68	69	35	22	63
Rojas, Keivi, Phillies	2	4	3.75	13	13	0	0	62	75	34	26	44
Gonzalez, Luis, Reds	4	3	3.84	13	13	0	0	61	65	30	13	23
Pereira, Ricardo, Mariners	1	5	3.86	14	10	1	1	75	82	42	24	32

BY BILL MITCHELL

The Salt River Rafters capped their debut season in the Arizona Fall League by the Surprise Saguaros 9-3 in front of a Scottsdale Stadium crowd of 3,079.

David Nick (Diamondbacks) smacked a seventh-inning, bases-loaded triple to break open the game and Salt River starter Charles Brewer (Diamondbacks) earned the win with four strong innings in which the only runs he yielded came from a third inning two-run homer by Christian Bethancourt (Braves).

The Rafters, managed by Stu Cole (Rockies), took an early lead in the top of the second inning on a sacrifice fly from Jake Goebbert (Astros) and a run-scoring single off the bat of Dixon Machado (Tigers), an advantage that the visitors never relinquished. A solo home run by Nolan Arenado (Rockies) in the third inning added to the Rafters' early lead.

Alex Sanabia (Marlins) took the loss for Surprise, which set a league record with a .722 winning percentage during the AFL season.

"My swing felt good and I didn't want to miss a pitch if it was out over the plate," Nick said about his big hit. "It was a 3-1 pitch and a fastball away. I didn't try to do too much with it. I just put a good swing on it and luckily it found a gap. We were able to score three runs and cash it in."

The Rafters, playing its first year in the new Salt River Fields facility in Scottsdale, earned the championship game berth by finishing in first place in the East Division with a 22-16 record. Their roster included prospects from the Astros, Diamondbacks, Dodgers, Rockies and Tigers farm systems.

Slimmed-Down MVP

Arenado was getting the message loud and clear—he needed to get in better shape if he wanted to stay at the hot corner.

The speculation that the Rockies prospect eventually might need to shift Arenado to first base was part of many scouting reports on him prior to the 2011 season. The 20-year-old Southern California native was even hearing from his parent organization that he had the glove to play the position but that he had to improve his lateral movement.

So Arenado went to work last offseason. He hired a nutritionist and dropped 20 pounds. He also worked hard on his defense during the regular season, taking grounders every day to work on his footwork and lateral movement.

"I took it to heart," Arenado said about the recommendations on improving his defense. "I want to play third base in the big leagues and I know I can, it's just a matter of staying in shape and doing the right things to stay over there."

Arenado's extra effort is paying off. AFL observers now consider him a potential above-AVG defender at third, and his play earned him the Joe Black Award as the AFL's MVP. He batted .388/.424/.636, leading the league in hits (47) and doubles (12).

Salt River manager Cole works in the Rockies system and said his reports indicated Arenado was an above-AVG defender in the high Class A California League this season. He was still impressed by Arenado in Arizona. "One of the best defensive third basemen I've seen in a long time," Cole said.

Arenado is more than just a guy who prevents runs with his glove—he also has a penchant for driving in runs. He drove in a Cal League-high 122 runs and had 33 in 29 AFL games.

"Some guys have that knack for driving in runs and he has that," Cole said. "He's not going to give up any at-bats when he's got a guy out there that he can score."

Arenado takes pride in that part of his game. "I'm not going to say I'm clutch," said Arenado, who played in both the Futures Game in July and the Rising Stars Game in November. "But I believe that when it's the moment to drive people in, I bear down and do what I have to do."

One of the other raps on Arenado in the past was his lack of walks. He improved in that area in 2011, drawing 47 walks while striking out only 53 times. He had an 8-14 walk-strikeout ratio in 121 AFL at-bats.

"Not striking out much is a positive," he said, "but it can also be a negative because I'm swinging at pitches that I can get out on that I probably should be laying off, which can lead to walks."

TOP 10 PROSPECTS

1. Bryce Harper, of, Scorpions (Nationals)
2. Mike Trout, of, Scorpions (Angels)
3. Danny Hultzen, lhp, Javelinas (Mariners)
4. Gerrit Cole, rhp, Solar Sox (Pirates)
5. Wil Myers, of, Saguaros (Royals)
6. Nolan Arenado, 3b, Rafters (Rockies)
7. Mike Olt, 3b, Saguaros (Rangers)
8. Michael Choice, of, Desert Dogs (Athletics)
9. Christian Bethancourt, c, Saguaros (Braves)
10. Jedd Gyorko, 3b, Javelinas (Padres)

MINOR LEAGUES

STANDINGS

EAST	W	L	PCT	GB	WEST	W	L	PCT	GB
Salt River Rafters	22	16	.579	—	Surprise Saguaros	26	10	.722	—
Mesa Solar Sox	17	20	.459	4½	Peoria Javelinas	16	19	.457	9½
Scottsdale Scorpions	14	22	.389	7	Phoenix Desert Dogs	14	22	.389	12

INDIVIDUAL BATTING LEADERS
(MINIMUM 2 PLATE APPEARANCES/LEAGUE GAMES)

PLAYER, TEAM	AVG	G	AB	R	H	RBI
Gyorko, Jedd, Peoria	.437	18	71	17	31	22
Gennett, Scooter, Peoria	.411	22	90	20	37	14
Arenado, Nolan, Salt River	.388	29	121	22	47	33
Grossman, Robbie, Mesa	.375	26	104	20	39	22
Garcia, Leury, Surprise	.361	20	83	18	30	12
Myers, Wil, Surprise	.360	23	86	24	31	18
Vitters, Josh, Mesa	.360	24	100	14	36	17
Olt, Mike, Surprise	.349	27	106	27	37	43
Mattison, Kevin, Surprise	.349	25	109	29	38	23
Eaton, Adam, Surprise	.344	30	122	31	42	16

INDIVIDUAL PITCHING LEADERS
(MINIMUM .4 INNINGS PITCHED/LEAGUE GAMES)

PITCHER, TEAM	W	L	ERA	IP	H	BB	SO
Snow, Forrest, Peoria	1	1	1.10	16	10	3	16
Hultzen, Danny, Peoria	1	0	1.40	19	16	5	18
Whitley, Chase, Phoenix	0	1	1.62	17	12	5	13
Harrold, Stephen, Scottsdale	3	0	1.76	15	10	5	15
Doyle, Terry, Mesa	4	0	1.98	27	12	5	22
Joseph, Donnie, Phoenix	1	1	2.16	17	19	6	17
Liberatore, Adam, Surprise	2	0	2.93	15	15	4	15
Johnson, Steve, Mesa	0	0	2.96	24	24	6	16
Fleet, Austin, Scottsdale	2	1	3.00	18	19	3	17
DeVries, Cole, Mesa	2	1	3.12	26	21	3	19

MESA SOLAR SOX

Player	AVG	AB	R	H	2B	3B	HR	RBI	BB	SO	SB
Avery, Xavier	.288	111	21	32	4	5	0	15	16	25	9
Blanke, Mike	.206	34	4	7	3	0	2	4	2	6	0
Cunningham, Jarek	.222	90	12	20	4	1	3	16	10	14	0
Dozier, Brian	.296	108	27	32	8	0	3	22	11	20	4
Grossman, Robbie	.375	104	20	39	5	0	7	22	20	18	6
Herrmann, Chris	.380	50	11	19	6	0	2	9	7	6	3
Hicks, Aaron	.294	102	25	30	8	5	3	21	18	21	5
Holt, Brock	.240	25	4	6	0	0	3	7	3	3	1
Lake, Junior	.296	115	19	34	8	3	5	21	8	32	18
Lemahieu, D.J.	.302	126	22	38	5	0	2	21	11	18	14
Mahoney, Joe	.325	83	7	27	6	0	4	22	4	14	0
Saladino, Tyler	.286	77	14	22	1	2	0	13	7	17	3
Sarmiento, Elio	.250	4	0	1	0	0	0	0	0	0	0
Short, Brandon	.274	117	23	32	7	1	4	15	12	38	4
Vitters, Josh	.360	100	14	36	6	0	4	17	4	10	4
Ward, Brian	.273	44	10	12	2	0	0	2	8	6	0

Player	W	L	ERA	G	GS	SV	IP	H	BB	SO	AVG
Baker, Nate	1	1	8.80	12	0	0	5	24	12	16	.304
Beliveau, Jeff	0	1	5.40	4	0	0	5	4	1	7	.200
Carpenter, Chris	1	1	3.29	11	0	0	14	15	2	18	.263
Cashner, Andrew	1	0	12.46	9	0	2	9	14	3	7	.326
Cole, Gerrit	2	0	3.00	5	5	0	15	10	4	16	.167
Colla, Mike	0	0	4.20	11	0	2	15	10	10	10	.156
DeVries, Cole	2	1	3.12	8	8	0	26	21	3	19	.212
Doyle, Terry	4	0	1.98	8	8	0	27	12	5	22	.125
Gleason, Sean	1	1	16.62	12	0	0	13	35	5	7	.473
Griffith, Nevin	0	2	9.64	13	0	0	14	20	11	7	.270
Hatley, Marcus	1	3	9.88	12	0	0	14	27	3	6	.386
Inman, Jeff	1	1	7.36	8	0	0	7	6	1	3	.194
Irwin, Phillip	0	0	7.71	1	0	0	2	3	0	0	.273
Jacobson, Brett	1	2	6.94	11	0	0	12	12	8	12	.211
Johnson, Steve	0	0	2.96	8	8	0	24	24	6	16	.255
Kloess, Brandon	0	2	3.65	13	0	2	12	6	4	17	.120
Lambert, Casey	0	1	4.86	12	0	0	17	15	5	7	.231
McCurry, Cole	1	0	5.51	12	0	0	16	21	8	16	.269
McNutt, Trey	0	2	5.00	7	7	0	18	22	7	8	.268
Petricka, Jake	0	1	5.51	13	0	0	16	16	10	18	.205
Pugh, Bruce	0	1	12.21	12	0	0	14	26	15	13	.313
Watts, Dakota	0	1	5.65	11	0	2	14	15	10	9	.227

PEORIA JAVELINAS

Player	AVG	AB	R	H	2B	3B	HR	RBI	BB	SO	SB
Adams, Matt	.250	80	15	20	6	0	4	19	3	28	1
Centeno, Juan	.234	47	4	11	3	0	0	5	6	6	0
Chiang, Chih-Hsien	.263	76	9	20	3	1	1	6	9	15	1
Davis, Kentrail	.325	77	16	25	4	4	1	12	13	24	4
Decker, Jaff	.289	90	17	26	5	1	2	14	17	20	1
Franklin, Nick	.258	89	15	23	4	1	2	14	11	26	1
Gennett, Scooter	.411	90	20	37	7	0	2	14	10	15	2
Gyorko, Jedd	.437	71	17	31	4	0	5	22	10	15	1
Hagerty, Jason	.250	56	6	14	3	0	0	8	3	14	1
Jackson, Ryan	.342	76	13	26	7	1	1	11	13	17	0
Lagares, Juan	.303	66	8	20	4	1	2	18	4	10	4
Marte, Jefry	.333	78	20	26	4	0	4	18	12	12	1
Moore, Adam	.259	54	9	14	3	0	0	8	6	15	0
Schafer, Logan	.302	96	15	29	4	2	2	16	8	9	5
Taveras, Oscar	.307	75	7	23	5	0	1	5	0	12	0
Tovar, Wilfredo	.281	96	17	27	11	1	1	9	4	9	0
Wheeler, Zelous	.276	58	15	16	5	1	0	8	7	14	1

Player	W	L	ERA	G	GS	SV	IP	H	BB	SO	AVG
Bass, Anthony	1	0	4.98	6	5	0	22	25	5	23	.272
Bradley, Jed	1	0	6.48	5	2	0	8	9	4	8	.231
Butler, Keith	1	1	6.75	12	0	0	11	10	11	5	.204
Carson, Robert	0	0	4.15	10	0	0	17	21	1	11	.263
Hensley, Steven	1	1	11.30	11	0	0	14	23	16	15	.277
Hultzen, Danny	1	0	1.40	6	6	0	19	16	5	18	.211
Ibarra, Jeff	0	0	6.00	11	0	0	9	13	6	7	.310
Kintzler, Brandon	0	0	7.36	4	0	0	4	6	1	5	.333
Kopp, David	0	2	10.13	11	0	2	11	19	8	5	.339
Lyons, Tyler	3	2	4.85	7	7	0	30	28	7	28	.237
Manzanillo, Santo	0	1	6.75	3	0	1	3	3	2	1	.214
McHugh, Collin	2	3	6.91	8	7	0	27	42	11	24	.321
Meadows, Sean	0	0	6.57	10	0	0	12	14	7	5	.233
Medlen, Casey	1	2	5.84	8	0	0	12	12	4	12	.231
Mikolas, Miles	0	0	7.15	11	0	3	11	16	4	10	.296
Moran, Brian	1	0	1.32	11	0	1	14	10	4	11	.185
Scarpetta, Cody	0	3	19.64	5	4	0	7	14	13	7	.292
Schmidt, Nick	1	0	5.40	8	4	0	23	25	12	26	.225
Snow, Forrest	1	1	1.10	10	1	1	16	10	3	16	.159
Thornburg, Tyler	1	0	3.38	3	0	0	5	3	4	3	.130
Turgeon, Erik	0	1	3.77	11	0	0	14	14	4	6	.230
Whitenton, Taylor	1	2	4.76	10	0	0	17	17	9	17	.233
Wright, Justin	0	0	11.42	10	0	0	9	12	14	6	.245

PHOENIX DESERT DOGS

Player	AVG	AB	R	H	2B	3B	HR	RBI	BB	SO	SB
Aguilar, Jesus	.339	59	15	20	7	0	3	9	13	14	0
Ahrens, Kevin	.269	93	12	25	8	0	1	13	9	24	1
Choice, Michael	.318	66	16	21	5	0	6	18	9	12	0
Coleman, Dusty	.167	54	4	9	2	1	3	8	2	21	0
Fedroff, Tim	.364	11	4	4	2	0	0	2	2	1	1
Gomes, Yan	.302	63	11	19	4	0	1	8	8	16	0
Gose, Anthony	.250	120	18	30	5	4	3	19	13	41	7
Grandal, Yasmani	.333	12	1	4	2	0	0	3	1	4	0
Green, Grant	.290	107	22	31	9	2	5	19	8	26	1
Greene, Brodie	.288	80	14	23	3	0	4	15	10	12	2
Hechavarria, Adeiny	.250	72	10	18	3	4	1	8	6	17	1
Huffman, Chad	.214	70	6	15	6	0	1	11	10	13	0
Joseph, Corban	.227	97	14	22	8	0	2	11	9	17	1
Moncrief, Carlos	.174	23	4	4	1	0	0	0	5	8	0
Mustelier, Ronnier	.344	64	8	22	3	1	2	6	1	7	3
Ortiz, Ryan	.310	42	8	13	2	0	2	12	13	12	1
Perez, Roberto	.226	53	13	12	1	0	4	11	13	10	0
Puckett, Cody	.147	68	9	10	2	1	3	9	15	29	0
Segedin, Rob	.250	108	21	27	6	1	3	12	17	25	0

Player	W	L	ERA	G	GS	SV	IP	H	BB	SO	AVG
Beck, Chad	0	0	0.00	5	0	0	8	2	1	5	.074
Boxberger, Brad	0	0	5.40	11	0	3	13	13	6	22	.228
Burawa, Daniel	1	4	7.53	12	0	0	24	30	11	10	.267
Burns, Cory	2	1	4.50	12	0	1	14	18	3	12	.286
Capra, Anthony	0	1	21.21	11	0	0	9	15	17	9	.234
Carignan, Andrew	0	2	6.52	12	0	0	12	13	7	16	.236
Chapman, Aroldis	0	0	3.38	2	0	0	3	1	2	2	.111
Christiani, Nick	0	1	5.52	12	0	0	15	15	7	10	.224
Claiborne, Preston	0	2	3.00	12	0	0	12	11	7	8	.204

MINOR LEAGUES

Player	W	L	ERA	G	GS	SV	IP	H	BB	SO	AVG
Crawford, Evan	0	1	3.18	11	0	1	17	13	3	16	.194
Etheridge, Wes	0	0	5.40	6	0	0	8	8	5	3	.211
Guilmet, Preston	0	0	6.43	10	0	0	14	18	8	12	.281
Joseph, Donnie	1	1	2.16	12	0	0	17	19	6	17	.264
Loup, Aaron	1	0	4.86	12	0	0	17	17	2	16	.236
McFarland, T.J.	3	0	3.18	8	7	0	28	30	13	22	.240
Phelps, David	2	2	4.41	8	8	0	33	36	9	28	.255
Ross, Tyson	1	3	5.94	7	7	0	17	24	5	13	.304
Smith, Murphy	1	2	12.46	8	8	0	26	51	10	16	.375
Sturdevant, Tyler	0	0	3.00	10	0	0	12	11	4	13	.200
Webb, Travis	2	1	5.03	7	7	0	20	24	9	24	.270
Whitley, Chase	0	1	1.62	12	0	0	17	12	5	13	.179

SALT RIVER RAFTERS

Player	AVG	AB	R	H	2B	3B	HR	RBI	BB	SO	SB
Arenado, Nolan	.388	121	22	47	12	0	6	33	8	14	0
Austin, Jay	.311	45	6	14	4	1	0	7	6	9	4
Brantly, Rob	.388	49	5	19	5	0	0	7	1	2	0
Castellanos, Alex	.379	29	13	11	2	1	3	7	5	5	4
Castro, Jason	.289	38	6	11	1	0	0	4	8	9	0
Cavazos-Galvez, Brian	.278	54	11	15	2	0	2	10	2	10	2
Eaton, Adam	.344	122	31	42	8	1	2	16	14	29	8
Erickson, Gorman	.213	61	8	13	4	1	1	8	6	13	0
Goebbert, Jake	.247	85	16	21	6	1	2	10	7	19	2
Hinze, Kody	.268	82	14	22	4	0	4	18	12	21	0
Lemmerman, Jake	.156	64	7	10	3	0	0	3	11	12	1
Machado, Dixon	.118	68	7	8	0	2	0	4	5	19	0
Nick, David	.298	84	13	25	4	1	1	9	5	12	2
Paulsen, Ben	.267	90	12	24	8	1	0	13	7	19	0
Pena, Roberto	.250	4	0	1	0	0	0	0	0	0	0
Perez, Hernan	.302	63	10	19	6	0	0	9	2	9	2
Russell, Kyle	.256	39	7	10	0	1	2	3	5	18	0
Wheeler, Ryan	.292	106	12	31	9	0	0	13	7	24	0
Wheeler, Tim	.256	121	18	31	11	1	3	25	17	26	5

Player	W	L	ERA	G	GS	SV	IP	H	BB	SO	AVG
Ames, Steven	0	0	4.15	12	0	0	17	20	5	8	.274
Brewer, Charles	1	1	5.46	8	8	0	28	39	7	22	.312
Crosby, Casey	2	0	1.32	11	0	1	14	12	10	13	.197
Fife, Stephen	1	6	8.06	8	8	0	26	41	14	18	.315
Frazier, Parker	1	1	6.10	13	1	0	21	28	8	15	.289
Gardner, Joe	2	2	5.29	7	7	0	17	17	10	18	.218
Hicks, Chris	0	0	40.50	2	0	0	1	6	1	1	.545
Hoffman, Matt	0	0	0.00	2	0	0	3	1	0	1	.091
Keuchel, Dallas	3	2	5.08	7	6	0	28	36	1	22	.293
Munson, Kevin	1	1	1.32	13	0	3	14	9	3	16	.167
Oliver, Andy	0	1	5.82	8	8	0	17	19	16	15	.229
Scahill, Rob	2	0	7.36	11	0	1	11	17	3	14	.327
Smith, Eric	2	0	5.12	13	0	0	19	20	13	18	.220
St. Clair, Cole	0	0	4.64	15	0	0	21	27	10	15	.267
Stoffel, Jason	0	1	6.87	14	0	0	18	19	21	21	.204
Stohr, Tyler	1	0	4.63	13	0	0	12	8	9	7	.160
Waite, Rob	1	0	9.28	9	0	0	11	22	4	11	.379
Wall, Josh	2	0	2.16	8	0	4	8	10	2	10	.256
Weathers, Casey	1	1	8.18	14	0	0	11	15	13	13	.234
Woodall, Bryan	0	0	4.11	14	0	0	15	19	5	15	.275
Zeid, Josh	2	0	5.00	15	0	0	18	21	9	21	.253

SCOTTSDALE SCORPIONS

Player	AVG	AB	R	H	2B	3B	HR	RBI	BB	SO	SB
Brown, Gary	.220	50	6	11	2	1	0	4	1	10	2
Butler, Daniel	.313	48	7	15	1	0	1	8	13	7	0
Conger, Hank	.217	46	3	10	1	1	0	8	5	8	1
Crawford, Brandon	.287	87	12	25	2	2	2	12	5	21	1
Dent, Ryan	.191	47	1	9	2	1	0	5	8	12	1
Gillies, Tyson	.178	90	15	16	2	0	1	7	14	24	4
Harper, Bryce	.333	93	17	31	6	2	6	26	11	22	4
Hassan, Alex	.253	83	14	21	4	0	2	7	15	16	2
Linares, J.C.	.111	18	2	2	0	0	1	1	0	1	0
Middlebrooks, Will	.250	56	9	14	3	0	4	11	4	19	1
Norris, Derek	.276	76	13	21	2	0	2	11	12	14	4
Overbeck, Cody	.321	81	16	26	6	1	1	7	14	22	1
Panik, Joe	.323	93	6	30	6	1	2	13	9	10	0

Player	AVG	AB	R	H	2B	3B	HR	RBI	BB	SO	SB
Ruf, Darin	.239	67	12	16	1	0	3	14	10	13	0
Segura, Jean	.310	87	17	27	6	2	0	8	5	14	5
Trout, Mike	.245	106	12	26	5	0	1	5	5	33	3
Walters, Zach	.205	83	5	17	5	0	1	10	4	21	0

Player	W	L	ERA	G	GS	SV	IP	H	BB	SO	AVG
Bradley, Ryan	0	1	23.63	4	0	0	3	9	0	2	.529
Carpenter, David	0	0	6.75	9	0	1	9	13	5	10	.277
Clay, Caleb	1	0	1.26	11	0	0	14	12	5	10	.214
Cloyd, Tyler	1	4	4.35	8	8	0	31	37	7	27	.274
Diekman, Jake	0	0	0.79	11	0	2	11	3	6	14	.065
Fleet, Austin	2	1	3.00	11	2	0	18	19	3	17	.260
Fleming, Marquis	0	0	9.00	1	0	0	2	5	0	3	.500
Harrold, Stephen	3	0	1.76	12	0	1	15	10	5	15	.172
Huntzinger, Brock	2	1	5.40	8	6	0	27	35	3	22	.299
Jennings, Daniel	0	0	0.00	1	0	0	2	2	0	1	.333
Kehrt, Jeremy	2	1	9.88	10	3	0	14	27	5	9	.386
Latimer, Will	0	0	9.19	11	0	0	16	22	6	11	.310
Lehman, Pat	0	4	9.82	12	0	0	15	26	3	17	.356
Maday, Daryl	1	2	4.91	3	3	0	11	8	5	11	.170
Martin, Rafael	0	1	1.50	10	0	0	12	8	6	9	.174
Purke, Matt	0	0	13.50	7	1	0	7	12	3	5	.316
Rosenberg, B.J.	0	1	5.14	6	0	0	7	8	3	6	.258
Rosin, Seth	0	0	2.13	9	0	0	13	9	4	9	.180
Scholl, Chris	0	3	9.90	6	6	0	20	27	8	15	.287
Shreve, Colby	0	0	5.59	9	0	0	10	13	7	8	.277
Solis, Sammy	1	1	4.50	7	7	0	26	29	16	25	.242
Taylor, Drew	0	1	8.76	11	0	0	12	19	6	10	.317
Tillman, Daniel	1	1	5.23	9	0	1	10	13	3	10	.295

SURPRISE SAGUAROS

Player	AVG	AB	R	H	2B	3B	HR	RBI	BB	SO	SB
Beckham, Tim	.244	90	18	22	6	2	4	15	15	25	3
Bethancourt, Christian	.306	72	14	22	3	0	5	13	2	17	3
Bortnick, Tyler	.267	45	8	12	3	0	1	3	5	8	2
Colon, Christian	.299	77	12	23	4	0	2	10	5	10	1
Cunningham, Todd	.234	64	11	15	4	1	0	11	5	13	3
Dominguez, Matt	.226	84	11	19	2	0	4	19	8	19	0
Garcia, Leury	.361	83	18	30	6	2	3	12	3	14	7
Gran, Paul	.293	41	7	12	2	1	2	7	5	13	1
Mahtook, Mikie	.338	68	15	23	3	1	3	14	7	16	5
Martin, Leonys	.290	31	6	9	2	1	1	7	4	5	4
Mattison, Kevin	.349	109	29	38	2	5	6	23	15	30	9
Myers, Wil	.360	86	24	31	5	5	4	18	20	18	1
Olt, Mike	.349	106	27	37	5	0	13	43	15	36	0
Sarmiento, Elio	.216	37	3	8	0	0	1	5	0	13	0
Seratelli, Anthony	.317	63	9	20	1	0	2	6	14	14	3
Skipworth, Kyle	.302	53	11	16	2	0	2	8	10	22	0
Strausborger, Ryan	.329	73	12	24	5	1	2	10	2	15	2
Terdoslavich, Joey	.321	84	22	27	6	2	3	14	13	27	1

Player	W	L	ERA	G	GS	SV	IP	H	BB	SO	AVG
Adcock, Nathan	2	2	4.44	6	6	0	24	27	4	23	.265
Bullock, Billy	1	0	14.81	9	0	1	10	19	11	13	.317
Cordier, Erik	0	0	3.38	2	0	0	3	2	3	2	.154
De Los Santos, Miguel	5	0	3.26	9	6	0	30	19	15	40	.153
Dyer, Shane	2	1	4.38	6	6	0	25	28	9	10	.255
Fleming, Marquis	1	0	4.15	7	0	0	13	12	11	10	.194
Gilmartin, Sean	2	1	4.34	8	7	0	29	27	8	26	.229
Hoover, J.J.	2	1	8.03	11	0	1	12	15	3	9	.273
Jeffress, Jeremy	0	1	4.91	11	0	0	11	16	8	15	.286
Jennings, Daniel	0	0	4.50	8	0	0	12	13	5	10	.245
Kelly, Ryan	0	2	8.36	10	2	0	14	14	11	11	.212
Lafferty, Brendan	0	0	7.16	11	0	0	16	18	8	17	.237
Liberatore, Adam	2	0	2.93	10	0	0	15	15	4	15	.246
Miller, Justin	2	0	0.00	2	0	0	2	2	0	2	.200
Moore, Navery	1	0	3.86	5	0	0	7	5	5	4	.172
Paukovits, Bryan	1	1	5.91	10	0	0	11	12	7	9	.231
Ramirez, Neil	0	0	1.29	2	2	0	7	4	1	5	.154
Ramos, A.J.	1	0	5.40	12	0	3	12	7	7	18	.143
Reed, Evan	0	0	2.57	12	0	1	14	12	5	16	.211
Sanabia, Alex	2	1	5.65	7	7	0	29	32	11	23	.252
Yan, Johan	2	0	3.55	11	0	2	13	10	2	8	.189
Yates, Kirby	0	0	6.97	9	0	1	10	11	7	17	.224

INDEPENDENT LEAGUES

Reality, recession hit indy ball hard as landscape shrinks

BY J.J. COOPER

After the great consolidation, independent baseball faced significant obstacles in 2011.

The Great Recession of recent years has made times tougher for all minor league teams, but in independent baseball it has led to significant problems. Where there were once eight leagues, there were five in 2011, and eight fewer teams than started play just one year earlier.

And even with all that consolidation, several teams barely made it to the finish line of the season.

No league had more issues than the North American League. An amalgamation of the remaining teams from the Golden, United and Northern leagues, the new circuit had planned to be a massive league with four former Northern League teams in the Chicago area, four former United League teams in Texas and four former Golden League teams on the West Coast and in Hawaii.

But three of the four Chicago area teams dropped out before the season, leaving Lake County, a team without a permanent stadium, more than 1,000 miles from its closest competitor. At the same time, the four Texas teams decided they would play only each other to cut travel costs.

The Lake County Fielders spent their first month of the season on the road. By the time they played their first home game, players were complaining about not getting their paychecks. Manager Tim Johnson quit, and his replacement Pete LaCock had to use pitchers as position players after much of the team refused to take the field. The Fielders then traded away or released almost the entire roster of a team that was at the time in first place.

The team's radio announcer quit on the air that same week, giving the team another set of unwanted national headlines. Fans stopped coming to the park, and by the end of the season the team had first announced it was quitting the league. It then recanted, but did not finish its assigned schedule, instead playing a series of unofficial games against a hastily assembled group of local players.

With all the financial struggles, the league's plans for a neutral site for its playoffs were scrapped. Instead, the league finished the season a week early, and the Northern and Southern Divisions playered

Lincoln manager Marty Scott left after the season to become Marlins farm director

a series of playoff games. When the Edmonton Capitals won the Northern Division and the right to host the championship series, many of the players of the Southern Division champion Rio Grande Valley WhiteWings did not have the passports necessary for the trip to Canada. So the Texas clubs cobbled together an all-star team of sorts, where the prime requirement was possession of a passport. Edmonton beat the reconstituted WhiteWings 4-1 in the best-of-seven series.

The Can-Am League had troubles of its own, as the Newark Bears drew a series of negative headlines through the season.

While there were financial struggles, independent baseball as a whole seemed remarkably resilient. The five leagues drew an announced 6.79 million fans, with the Atlantic League averaging more than 4,000 fans a game and the American Association averaging more than 3,000. But the stratification of the leagues was also apparent. The top drawing team in the Can-Am League ranked 18th overall, while the top drawing North American League team barely cracked the top 25.

Colabello stars wherever he plays

Growing up as the son of a professional baseball player, Chris Colabello was always around the ballpark. And whether he was watching a big league game, or watching his father pitch for Rimini in the Italian League, he always noticed the hitters.

"I think when I was a little kid, I always noticed what made the best hitters in the world. So .300 was such an important number for me," Colabello said.

Colabello took notes. While his father was a lefthanded pitcher, Colabello wasn't made for the mound. He's a big (6-foot-4, 225 pound) righthanded hitter. And rather than pitching, he always wanted to be considered one of the best hitters around.

If you go by that magic .300 number, Colabello is reaching his goal. In seven years playing the Can-Am League—all of them with the Worcester Tornadoes—Colabello has topped .300 seven times. He is the Can-Am League's all-time leader in hits, doubles and RBIs.

But he has never had a season like the one he had in 2011. The Worcester first baseman hit .348 (second-best in the Can-Am League) with 20 home runs (second-best in the league) and 79 RBIs (second-best in the league). He was also second in the league in hits (127) and led the league in doubles (32) and slugging percentage (.600).

For all of those accomplishments with the bat, Colabello was Baseball America's choice for 2011 Independent League Player of the Year.

When Colabello was playing first base at Assumption College, a Division II school in Worcester, he thought there was a good chance he'd get his shot at playing affiliated ball. The summer before his junior year, he had a strong showing in the New England Collegiate Baseball League, a wood-bat summer league. He made the NECBL all-star team along with future big leaguer Kevin Slowey, who played at Winthrop.

But the 2004 draft came and went without Colabello's name being called. A year later, Colabello again went undrafted. The only team that called was the Worcester Tornadoes, a franchise making its Can-Am League debut. Colabello hit .320 that year as the Tornadoes won the league title.

That next spring, Colabello got what, up to now, has been his only shot at affiliated ball. He made the 60-man tryout roster for the Italian team in the World Baseball Classic. While he didn't make the cut for the active roster, the Tigers noticed him at the workouts and brought him to spring training.

There Colabello found what many other indy players have seen before and since: When you come in with no pedigree, it's tough to make a roster out of spring training.

In the six years since, Colabello has kept putting up numbers in the Can-Am League with a consistency that is remarkable. He doesn't strike out much, he draws walks and he hits for some power.

But he's also a righthanded-hitting first baseman, which is about the toughest position for an independent league player to make the jump to affiliated ball. Colabello has played a little third base in recent years and he's looking to play some outfield next year to add to his versatility.

For now, Colabello keeps plugging away in Worcester. He's grateful for the opportunity the Tornadoes have given him. But he hopes that at some point, he'll get another chance at affiliated ball.

"I don't want Worcester to be the last uniform I put on," Colabello said.

PREVIOUS WINNERS

1996: Darryl Motley, of, Fargo-Moorhead (Northern)
1997: Mike Meggers, of, Winnipeg/Duluth (Northern)
1998: Morgan Burkhart, 1b, Richmond (Frontier)
1999: Carmine Cappucio, of, New Jersey (Northeast)
2000: Anthony Lewis, 1b, Duluth-Superior (Northern)
2001: Mike Warner, of, Somerset (Atlantic)
2002: Bobby Madritsch, lhp, Winnipeg (Northern)
2003: Jason Shelley, rhp, Rockford (Frontier)

2004: Victor Rodriguez, ss, Somerset (Atlantic)
2005: Eddie Lantigua, 3b, Quebec (Can-Am)
2006: Ian Church, of, Kalamazoo (Frontier)
2007: Darryl Brinkley, of, Calgary (Northern)
2008: Patrick Breen, of, Orange County (Golden)
2009: Greg Porter, of, Wichita (American Association)
2010: Beau Torbert, of, Sioux Falls (American Association)

AMERICAN ASSOCIATION

Wherever Ricky Van Asselberg goes, championships soon follow.

In his first year as the Grand Prairie Airhogs manager, Van Asselberg took an AirHogs club that finished nine games under .500 in 2010 and made it the class of the league. Grand Prairie compiled the best record in the league in the regular season, then rallied to win three consecutive elimination games in the American Association championship series to top St. Paul for the title.

Van Asselberg led the Shreveport-Bossier Captains to the American Association crown in 2010, and he won a pair of United League titles before that, giving him four titles in six years as a manager.

STANDINGS

NORTHERN DIVISION	W	L	PCT	GB
Winnipeg	60	40	.600	—
*St. Paul	56	44	.560	4
Fargo-Moorhead	44	56	.440	16
Sioux Falls	42	57	.425	17.5
CENTRAL DIVISION	**W**	**L**	**PCT**	**GB**
Wichita	55	45	.550	—
Gary SouthShore	54	46	.540	1
Lincoln	51	48	.515	3.5
Sioux City	51	49	.510	4
Kansas City	48	52	.480	7
SOUTHERN DIVISION	**W**	**L**	**PCT**	**GB**
Grand Prairie	64	36	.640	—
Fort Worth	48	52	.480	16
Shreveport-Bossier	45	55	.450	19
Amarillo	44	56	.440	20
El Paso	37	63	.370	27

*Wild card

PLAYOFFS: Semifinals—St. Paul defeated Winnipeg 3-2 and Grand Prairie defeated Wichita 3-1 in best-of-five series. **Finals**—Grand Prairie defeated St. Paul 3-2 in best-of-five series.

ATTENDANCE: Winnipeg 275,521, Kansas City 261,115, St Paul 240,206, Fargo-Moorhead 175,918, El Paso 172,742, Wichita 159,239, Gary SouthShore 157,676, Lincoln 157,647, Amarillo 138,865, Grand Prairie 117,861, Fort Worth 108,020, Sioux Falls 76549, Sioux City 64,000, Shreveport-Bossier 56,910.

MANAGERS: Amarillo—John Harris. **El Paso**—Jorge Alvarez. **Fargo-Moorhead**—Doug Simunic. **Gary**—Greg Tagert. **Grand Prairie**—Ricky Van Asselberg. **Fort Worth**—Stan Hough. **Kansas City**—Tim Doherty. **Lincoln**—Marty Scott. **Shreveport-Bossier**—Vince Moore. **Sioux City**—Stan Cliburn. **Sioux Falls**—Steve Shirley. **St. Paul**—George Tsamis. **Wichita**—Kevin Hooper. **Winnipeg**—Rick Forney.

ALL-STAR TEAM

C—Kelley Gulledge, Fort Worth. **1B**—Trent Lockwood, Fort Worth. **2B**—Brad Boyer, Gary SouthShore. **3B**—Juan Richardson, Wichita. **SS**—Josh Horn, Wichita. **OF**—Stephen Douglas, El Paso/Grand Prairie; Ryan Patterson, Fort Worth/Wichita/St. Paul; Ray Sadler, Kansas City. **DH**—Lee Cruz, Amarillo. **SP**—Ben Moore, Sioux Falls. **RP**—Jon Hunton, Grand Prairie. **Player of the Year:** Lee Cruz, Amarillo. **Manager of the Year:** Rick Forney, Winnipeg.

AMARILLO SOX

PLAYER	AVG	AB	R	H	2B	3B	HR	RBI	SB
Alberts, T	.332	382	59	127	30	6	8	72	2
Banda, J	.274	95	13	26	3	1	5	18	1
Butler, K	.281	249	31	70	9	4	2	30	0
Chavez, A	.286	77	18	22	4	0	2	7	3
Cruz, L	.344	418	75	144	38	3	18	94	3
De La Garza, A	.246	366	67	90	20	6	1	42	8
Farnsworth, N	.205	39	2	8	4	0	0	2	0
Fenwick, R	.294	68	7	20	4	0	0	5	3

PLAYER	AVG	AB	R	H	2B	3B	HR	RBI	SB
Johnson, B	.257	148	20	38	10	1	5	22	1
Kain, H	.268	56	9	15	3	0	0	7	4
Lentini, F	.324	312	81	101	30	7	4	56	21
Nash, C	.268	153	25	41	14	1	4	23	0
Pope, V	.299	328	69	98	20	5	10	61	8
Santana, J	.000	5	0	0	0	0	0	0	0
Sauceda, J	.172	29	2	5	1	0	0	2	0
Tucker, M	.270	200	42	54	10	9	1	32	2

PLAYER	W	L	ERA	G	SV	IP	H	BB	SO
Allen, C	1	5	8.83	11	0	54	88	28	23
Altman, K	0	0	27.00	2	0	1	5	2	1
Bass, C	5	5	8.22	32	3	66	97	25	23
Chambliss, A	1	6	6.06	38	0	68	93	29	42
Elliott, M	8	5	5.31	19	0	119	135	48	79
Evans, C	0	1	2.57	7	4	7	5	5	9
Garcia, J	9	5	4.66	21	0	129	162	33	118
Godfrey, K	0	0	11.25	4	0	4	5	6	6
Henry, L	1	0	5.02	9	0	14	12	5	18
Keeler, S	0	1	6.75	7	0	15	17	11	9
Lawler, T	5	5	6.18	18	0	103	113	37	63
Mayes, L	0	1	13.24	16	0	17	31	17	3
Mitchell, R	5	8	4.63	22	0	142	166	34	105
Montalbano, P	0	1	3.27	9	0	11	6	6	4
Oliver, B	0	1	11.25	8	0	12	21	8	9
Overholt, P	1	3	7.45	25	2	29	33	15	20
Pearson, T	0	3	24.55	4	0	4	10	4	4
Perinar, G	0	2	10.66	15	4	13	17	15	15
Pope, V	0	0	0.00	2	0	3	2	2	5
Povich, C	8	3	5.72	41	3	50	65	41	47
Wortham, J	0	1	15.43	13	0	7	12	7	2

EL PASO DIABLOS

PLAYER	AVG	AB	R	H	2B	3B	HR	RBI	SB
Avila, G	.300	90	14	27	3	0	6	22	0
Ballez, B	.152	33	8	5	1	0	0	2	3
Brito, J	.358	204	50	73	22	0	5	36	2
Deleo, A	.231	147	12	34	12	0	3	20	0
Douglas, S	.372	298	57	111	27	3	1	55	17
Drew, K	.255	341	45	87	15	3	2	42	11
Espinosa, A	.326	175	28	57	17	0	7	41	2
Gabriel, C	.349	269	48	94	14	0	3	38	5
Garcia, J	.287	209	40	60	9	3	2	23	14
Gonzalez, M	.335	239	47	80	8	9	0	28	21
Gray, A	.264	106	15	28	4	0	5	23	0
Joynt, B	.295	129	21	38	9	3	1	18	5
Machado, A	.294	401	74	118	19	6	2	41	13
Marquez, U	.347	95	15	33	6	0	0	14	1
Mejia, M	.306	157	22	48	8	4	5	22	4
Nichols, K	.325	212	42	69	19	0	10	53	1
Parra, M	.243	202	24	49	7	2	2	26	4
Ponce, A	.293	41	8	12	0	2	0	6	2
Smith, K	.195	41	6	8	3	1	0	4	0
Teilon, N	.302	182	29	55	17	0	5	34	5

PLAYER	W	L	ERA	G	SV	IP	H	BB	SO
Allen, C	2	2	7.64	10	1	35	53	10	22
Almonte, R	0	1	8.10	7	0	13	20	10	12
Ballez, B	0	0	0.00	2	0	2	2	0	2
Blanco, J	0	1	12.60	2	0	5	9	12	9
Caballero, A	1	1	13.50	5	0	9	11	10	4
Cremers, K	2	2	4.91	20	4	26	31	9	19
Crespo, J	0	0	5.50	11	0	18	21	14	13
Cruz, R	5	8	6.40	20	0	108	132	55	83
Deleo, A	0	0	32.40	2	0	2	3	4	1
Dorado, R	1	1	1.00	12	5	18	11	10	12
Ellis, S	0	3	14.24	5	0	18	42	11	21
Grady, J	0	1	7.04	7	0	8	14	6	2
Hodsdon, S	5	6	4.61	19	1	96	130	28	61
Infante, L	0	1	7.36	4	0	4	3	9	3
Jung, J	1	5	7.34	9	0	42	65	15	10
Kaminsky, A	3	1	6.40	7	1	32	37	13	35
Martinez, R	0	0	108.00	1	0	0	1	3	1
McCarter, J	0	0	5.84	7	0	12	12	6	8
Medina, J	0	2	9.96	16	0	28	45	20	23

PLAYER	W	L	ERA	G	SV	IP	H	BB	SO
Montano, L	2	5	8.41	10	0	41	61	25	26
Montes, A	0	2	4.79	15	0	21	30	3	9
Parra, M	0	0	0.00	1	0	1	0	0	1
Pearson, T	0	1	10.80	3	0	5	6	6	4
Plefka, J	1	1	3.89	29	1	37	42	26	29
Rivas, S	0	0	11.49	12	0	16	28	7	13
Rodriguez, J	0	1	9.95	8	0	19	35	6	13
Rowe, A	3	6	8.16	29	0	61	93	27	27
Sanchez, J	0	0	7.04	5	0	8	11	10	5
Silva, R	3	1	5.72	25	6	28	31	11	21
Starling, W	4	2	5.23	8	0	52	55	27	32
Stephens , A	0	1	12.98	10	0	17	28	7	15
Stone, M	0	0	18.69	5	0	4	9	4	5
Tucker, C	0	2	9.00	3	0	12	15	11	6
Tussey, G	0	0	15.00	5	0	9	21	7	3
Vander Weg, S	2	2	9.52	24	1	41	54	34	36
Whigham , D	2	4	5.71	6	0	35	48	8	25

FARGO-MOORHEAD REDHAWKS

PLAYER	AVG	AB	R	H	2B	3B	HR	RBI	SB
Blunt, D	.154	13	1	2	0	0	1	1	0
Britton, P	.283	159	18	45	12	0	4	28	0
Coles, M	.276	312	43	86	19	1	1	36	17
Cota, C	.287	376	55	108	32	0	13	51	4
Cox, J	.150	40	3	6	1	0	0	0	0
Fasano, J	.292	192	27	56	11	0	4	21	0
Hoorelbeke, J	.295	363	49	107	26	0	15	75	0
Jackson, N	.287	383	52	110	23	1	6	65	28
James, J	.263	190	30	50	16	0	4	27	2
Jennings, T	.273	121	14	33	5	0	0	9	2
Krause, J	.250	52	9	13	2	0	0	3	4
Nichols, K	.222	194	15	43	9	0	6	23	1
Retherford, C	.339	224	34	76	24	0	4	37	1
Ruggiano, B	.209	148	17	31	9	0	1	15	8
Wagle, J	.196	51	9	10	3	2	0	0	0
Wyatt, S	.245	94	15	23	4	0	1	5	5
Zimmerman, K	.211	147	23	31	3	0	2	10	5

PLAYER	W	L	ERA	G	SV	IP	H	BB	SO
Bailey, G	0	1	13.50	2	1	1	4	0	0
Blewett, D	2	5	7.69	11	0	46	59	24	38
Caldera, A	7	3	3.07	18	2	73	60	40	66
Deminsky, D	0	0	16.20	2	0	2	4	1	1
Di Napoli, N	1	0	6.75	12	0	11	14	7	9
Fogelson, S	2	4	5.92	8	0	38	39	27	24
Frawley, J	1	3	7.55	6	0	31	40	13	20
Fuqua, K	1	2	1.60	21	3	34	31	19	28
Harris, J	3	4	3.49	28	1	49	38	21	41
Hartley, J	0	0	4.09	6	0	11	12	4	7
Hoorelbeke, C	2	2	6.03	27	4	31	44	17	16
Jackel, W	1	1	5.54	21	0	26	34	12	19
James, J	0	0	99.99	1	0	0	2	1	0
Kaminsky, A	1	1	6.86	13	0	39	48	23	31
Laber, J	10	7	3.55	23	0	139	142	62	100
Light, K	1	1	7.20	8	0	25	23	24	18
Longfellow, T	2	2	4.00	4	0	18	21	10	20
Mossey, M	1	0	6.08	8	0	13	16	4	7
Odle, O	2	7	5.83	12	0	71	88	16	37
Rhoades, C	0	0	8.82	14	0	16	27	8	7
Siegfried, C	1	1	3.46	9	0	13	12	2	9
Smith, D	1	1	3.93	18	7	18	12	12	26
Smith, J	0	2	5.26	14	0	39	47	18	23
Tollefson, A	1	3	3.19	41	3	37	32	27	39
Ward, Z	4	6	5.06	15	0	89	93	55	55

FORT WORTH CATS

PLAYER	AVG	AB	R	H	2B	3B	HR	RBI	SB
Allen, J	.323	371	62	120	23	2	15	80	1
Ballez, B	.286	105	18	30	3	2	1	16	1
Davis, A	.268	168	41	45	4	1	2	27	14
Fryer, B	.283	279	47	79	7	4	4	31	21
Garcia, I	.000	2	0	0	0	0	0	0	0
Gulledge, K	.339	372	74	126	28	0	14	73	0
Kinzler, D	.221	195	28	43	8	0	0	18	2
Lockwood, T	.338	367	77	124	37	3	20	90	4
Metcalf, T	.275	204	23	56	10	0	4	20	4
Monger, C	.243	37	6	9	1	1	1	4	0

PLAYER	AVG	AB	R	H	2B	3B	HR	RBI	SB
Moore, J	.198	81	8	16	3	0	1	4	2
Morales, C	.283	368	61	104	27	1	2	48	16
Patterson, R	.355	152	31	54	8	0	8	33	0
Rodriguez, M	.341	405	71	138	29	4	4	70	14
Sauceda, J	.227	141	22	32	9	0	4	17	8
Surina, M	.162	37	3	6	0	0	0	0	0
Thomas, C	.360	50	6	18	3	0	0	13	1

PLAYER	W	L	ERA	G	SV	IP	H	BB	SO
Bacsik, M	2	4	4.01	10	0	49	52	14	31
Bailey, G	2	2	3.71	39	1	63	70	18	39
Bartleski, P	5	4	4.50	15	1	78	79	37	42
Blacksher, D	3	6	4.55	12	0	65	69	22	54
Bozeman, T	0	0	8.59	6	0	7	6	5	4
Brandhorst, J	2	0	6.75	16	0	31	30	23	33
Calhoun, W	2	2	6.85	7	0	22	27	15	10
Cunningham, A	2	2	11.44	5	0	20	38	16	10
DeBarr, N	4	6	4.18	40	9	65	70	34	59
Denton, G	0	0	1.59	6	0	17	15	9	15
Haines, T	0	1	4.66	20	0	37	37	24	30
Holguin, C	0	2	17.55	5	0	7	14	8	1
Kennedy, J	0	0	0.00	4	0	4	2	4	1
Kirsten, J	2	1	4.80	3	0	15	20	12	14
Lee, G	0	1	14.54	3	0	9	16	6	1
Mackey, W	8	5	4.41	21	0	120	119	43	53
Manuel, R	0	0	0.54	13	1	17	9	4	19
Moore, J	0	0	0.00	1	0	1	2	1	0
Pollok, D	3	5	4.95	11	0	73	74	12	57
Romero, R	0	0	36.00	3	0	2	4	6	3
Sartor, M	2	2	2.95	12	2	18	10	11	19
Schmidt, J	2	1	6.75	6	0	28	42	2	8
Seaman, T	1	5	7.47	16	0	69	95	43	29
Vander Weg, S	4	1	5.90	16	0	29	36	21	24
White, C	4	2	4.05	15	1	33	31	19	25

GARY SOUTHSHORE RAILCATS

PLAYER	AVG	AB	R	H	2B	3B	HR	RBI	SB
Beachum, J	.161	62	3	10	0	0	0	5	2
Bowden, J	.111	9	1	1	0	0	0	1	0
Boyer, B	.348	353	66	123	21	8	10	68	11
Bryan, N	.000	1	0	0	0	0	0	0	0
Carrara, C	.295	336	59	99	12	1	2	34	17
Guerrero, C	.294	401	52	118	23	3	12	82	5
Haines, K	.309	243	36	75	15	0	1	24	4
Johnson, T	.247	271	39	67	15	3	4	39	7
Klein, A	.299	351	75	105	25	3	1	45	17
Kolb, B	.280	168	26	47	12	0	2	18	5
Maddox, C	.321	137	21	44	8	2	2	21	1
Massaro, M	.344	413	66	142	28	16	1	66	12
Ott, L	.200	10	0	2	0	0	0	3	0
Rohde, M	.290	365	55	106	32	2	6	63	10
Scott, L	.195	118	17	23	3	2	2	11	6
Valadez, M	.193	264	28	51	11	0	0	15	2
Washington, R	.345	29	6	10	2	0	0	8	0

PLAYER	W	L	ERA	G	SV	IP	H	BB	SO
Baker, J	3	1	2.57	42	1	49	42	18	68
Chavez, C	3	0	3.05	16	1	21	16	8	15
Engle, Z	1	2	7.50	16	0	18	26	8	16
Frawley, J	3	5	6.05	16	0	86	118	22	41
Gordon, D	2	2	4.24	6	0	34	30	19	27
Grening, B	5	2	3.70	39	0	58	60	15	48
Hauer, J	2	1	3.65	43	0	49	43	20	24
Krout, W	5	2	1.85	49	1	73	65	8	49
Lare, T	1	2	6.23	3	0	17	29	8	10
Little, C	0	3	4.91	14	0	18	19	7	15
Martinez, J	0	0	0.00	5	0	3	3	2	1
Martinez, R	0	1	63.00	1	0	1	6	1	1
Minix, T	1	2	3.86	30	8	33	33	8	27
Nathanson, D	0	1	5.23	9	6	10	9	3	10
Nelson, T	0	0	15.75	6	0	4	9	5	3
Nicholson, N	4	8	7.37	25	0	101	153	39	47
Quijano, A	4	3	4.61	13	0	70	77	23	40
Reynoso, R	3	4	5.36	8	0	42	56	17	17
Rivas, C	5	1	3.38	13	0	61	67	26	33
Shaw, S	11	6	5.49	23	0	134	151	62	80
Shipman, A	0	0	0.00	5	1	6	4	0	5
Short, B	0	0	10.80	1	0	2	1	0	1

GRAND PRAIRIE AIRHOGS

PLAYER	AVG	AB	R	H	2B	3B	HR	RBI	SB
Alonso, J	.308	364	58	112	25	0	13	68	0
Chavez, Z	.262	149	20	39	5	2	0	21	0
Clement, S	.220	50	3	11	5	0	0	4	0
Douglas, S	.392	125	30	49	11	1	2	21	7
Duran, G	.317	41	9	13	3	0	2	9	3
Espinosa, D	.324	386	85	125	21	11	6	60	20
Figueroa, D	.270	319	64	86	10	1	1	30	31
Frichter, B	.152	33	2	5	1	0	1	2	0
Gomes, J	.311	106	10	33	3	0	2	24	1
Henley, T	.251	227	28	57	15	5	2	42	5
Jordan, D	.333	3	0	1	0	0	0	0	0
Martinez, G	.303	290	45	88	16	5	0	25	11
McMurray, B	.265	215	37	57	16	2	4	32	8
Nicolas, C	.353	309	53	109	29	0	8	73	3
Porter, G	.341	270	48	92	25	0	8	63	2
Sauceda, J	.000	4	0	0	0	0	0	0	0
Taylor, J	.266	192	33	51	8	1	4	25	3
Thomas, D	.273	362	76	99	26	9	11	57	29
Thompson, K	.158	19	5	3	1	0	0	0	2

PLAYER	W	L	ERA	G	SV	IP	H	BB	SO
Abbl, F	0	0	2.08	1	0	4	3	5	0
Brown, T	1	0	3.43	3	0	21	20	2	7
Brownell, J	11	5	3.56	20	0	139	137	51	112
Cameron, D	0	2	1.30	28	0	28	17	7	22
Cross, R	0	0	6.75	3	0	3	4	2	1
Cunningham, J	0	1	10.50	11	0	12	22	3	9
Drucker, S	0	1	2.08	2	0	13	14	0	6
Fulton, J	2	2	2.53	37	0	53	50	16	41
Godfrey, K	0	0	6.75	4	0	4	9	3	6
Gunderson, K	0	1	7.71	7	1	9	9	6	8
Hunton, J	7	2	1.77	49	25	51	38	20	47
James, C	0	0	4.50	2	0	2	2	1	2
Janke, L	6	3	5.40	11	0	62	80	29	51
Jennings, J	10	2	3.59	19	0	118	110	37	92
Jung, J	2	1	7.36	5	0	26	27	11	8
Montgomery, T	0	1	9.64	2	0	9	13	7	9
Moody, J	1	1	3.48	17	0	21	21	10	18
Nathanson, D	1	3	7.91	7	0	39	64	10	17
Railsback, C	1	0	2.31	7	0	12	10	9	7
Rainwater, J	14	6	4.41	20	0	135	162	27	91
Salmon, R	0	0	5.87	4	0	8	7	2	4
Sartor, M	1	1	9.95	8	0	6	9	5	6
Schultz, A	4	3	4.13	37	1	72	80	24	54
Smith, G	3	1	2.54	6	0	39	39	7	31
Taylor, J	0	0	0.00	1	0	1	1	1	2

KANSAS CITY T-BONES

PLAYER	AVG	AB	R	H	2B	3B	HR	RBI	SB
Barrows, P	.280	50	6	14	4	1	0	7	1
Bowden, J	.227	181	23	41	9	0	2	22	2
Caceres, G	.248	157	19	39	6	0	0	18	2
Duran, J	.265	34	6	9	2	0	1	8	1
Eggleston, A	.324	312	51	101	23	2	6	49	15
Espinosa, A	.239	46	7	11	1	0	2	4	0
Farnsworth, N	.273	77	8	21	2	1	1	9	1
Fasano, J	.276	185	33	51	14	0	7	28	0
Garcia, F	.303	66	16	20	3	1	0	8	6
Hulett, J	.217	157	23	34	8	0	6	26	7
Jaspe, J	.296	71	7	21	4	0	1	8	0
Joynt, B	.216	116	14	25	8	2	3	13	2
Kaaihue, K	.286	234	48	67	9	0	22	55	8
Nieblas, L	.235	17	0	4	2	0	0	2	0
Price, R	.000	1	3	0	0	0	0	0	0
Redman, P	.282	71	9	20	2	0	3	9	2
Simon, K	.332	394	86	131	30	16	6	40	25
Snyder, J	.213	61	11	13	2	1	2	6	0
Suarez, G	.111	9	3	1	1	0	0	2	0
Washington, R	.310	361	59	112	20	3	12	75	14
White, D	.178	90	8	16	3	0	3	11	1

PLAYER	W	L	ERA	G	SV	IP	H	BB	SO
Anderson, D	7	8	5.24	21	0	125	159	43	78
Baker, D	0	0	13.50	3	0	2	5	4	2

Cook, A	0	0	7.50	4	0	6	11	3	5
Dahman, K	2	3	4.63	39	9	58	65	30	56
Dewald, M	0	0	3.98	18	0	20	22	8	14
Graham, D	3	1	2.81	24	0	32	17	15	21
Grening, B	1	2	1.98	4	0	14	13	6	3
Hook, R	0	0	2.46	8	0	7	6	2	2
Johnson, K	6	3	3.23	16	0	111	98	51	64
Jones, R	0	0	7.71	7	0	7	9	3	3
Kassavavoid, J	0	0	4.50	2	0	2	3	0	2
Lare, T	3	2	4.53	17	0	46	45	13	33
Large, T	5	7	6.47	22	0	106	124	53	62
Light, K	0	0	36.00	2	0	1	3	2	0
Little, C	1	0	0.00	2	0	2	3	1	3
Lohden, C	1	0	23.14	3	0	2	8	3	1
Mitchell, M	2	5	7.67	12	0	54	68	38	21
Mojica, J	0	0	0.00	1	0	1	0	0	1
Morrison, W	0	0	0.00	5	0	6	2	4	4
Reynoso, R	2	2	7.12	8	0	30	35	20	18
Rocco, M	0	4	8.63	7	0	24	42	8	17
Santos, R	8	6	5.23	21	0	134	173	42	87
Shipman, A	3	4	5.17	32	11	31	39	18	32
Stewart, S	4	5	5.84	36	1	62	81	20	47

LINCOLN SALTDOGS

PLAYER	AVG	AB	R	H	2B	3B	HR	RBI	SB
Albitz, V	.314	223	43	70	8	2	1	22	8
Alcombrack, R	.216	97	11	21	3	1	3	11	1
Alvarez, R	.340	150	24	51	6	1	3	27	3
Dickey , G	.290	359	66	104	19	4	6	49	20
Gailen, B	.406	278	54	113	24	6	8	46	14
Hawke , P	.300	353	74	106	20	1	21	77	3
Howell, J	.269	130	24	35	11	0	5	19	0
Jones , B	.232	298	34	69	15	1	6	39	0
Jova, M	.229	144	12	33	6	0	2	16	0
Nelson, J	.315	73	5	23	6	0	2	16	0
Ramos, J	.268	306	61	82	12	1	4	40	16
Rios, K	.156	122	9	19	2	0	4	9	0
Smith, C	.335	310	46	104	14	4	9	48	6
Smith, N	.200	5	0	1	1	0	0	0	0
Steinhauer, K	.260	100	17	26	7	0	2	8	2
Trettel, P	.237	207	20	49	12	2	7	33	2
Weaver, T	.333	3	0	1	0	0	0	0	0

PLAYER	W	L	ERA	G	SV	IP	H	BB	SO
Bongiovanni, V	1	3	4.66	5	0	29	26	17	19
Brewer, J	1	1	11.17	5	0	10	21	5	6
Brown, T	8	6	3.81	18	0	113	136	21	47
Garcia, J	1	2	5.17	3	0	16	21	3	9
Gonzalez, J	6	1	1.83	10	0	54	46	17	47
Gulin, L	1	7	5.94	9	0	50	74	19	25
Harker, B	0	0	5.14	4	0	7	6	6	8
Hawke , P	0	0	4.70	7	0	8	8	4	4
James, J	9	6	5.28	21	0	116	138	41	50
Junker, S	0	1	10.00	6	0	9	15	5	5
Koss, P	1	4	7.42	32	0	47	70	21	43
Luis, S	1	1	0.83	21	0	22	12	9	30
Maestri, A	8	6	5.72	21	0	118	119	60	62
Medina, J	1	0	2.46	2	0	11	12	4	6
Muyco, J	1	1	6.75	3	0	4	7	4	1
Palica, T	2	1	2.98	11	0	45	36	15	44
Potter, S	0	0	8.03	14	0	25	37	13	10
Schreiber, N	6	1	6.35	37	0	57	79	36	35
Sherrill, G	2	1	3.52	30	0	38	27	21	34
Smith, B	0	0	9.00	1	0	2	2	3	4
Stern, J	2	4	6.08	22	1	50	61	20	31
Zocchi, P	0	2	1.95	36	21	37	38	14	41

SHREVEPORT-BOSSIER CAPTAINS

PLAYER	AVG	AB	R	H	2B	3B	HR	RBI	SB
Cowart, A	.276	217	35	60	10	4	3	25	2
Diffie, M	.081	37	3	3	2	0	0	2	0
Frichter, B	.234	184	20	43	10	0	3	28	5
Gabriel, C	.424	99	22	42	10	1	1	15	2
Gathright, J	.190	79	17	15	2	0	0	3	8
Hulett, J	.237	38	4	9	2	0	0	6	0
Johnson, J	.311	119	27	37	3	3	0	9	12
Karr Jr., P	.245	310	43	76	19	0	12	55	9

INDEPENDENT LEAGUES

PLAYER	AVG	AB	R	H	2B	3B	HR	RBI	SB
Kuhn, A	.190	21	3	4	1	0	0	3	0
Marquez, U	.282	248	41	70	12	1	9	35	14
Perry, R	.272	342	70	93	21	4	4	45	30
Peterson, B	.295	325	52	96	15	6	5	58	14
Provencher, M	.295	383	66	113	22	4	9	52	26
Rodriguez, A	.323	400	66	129	30	2	16	74	7
Sabatella, B	.350	337	55	118	16	4	4	66	16
Thomas, S	.333	39	4	13	1	0	0	4	1
Urtuzuastegui, J	.229	214	27	49	7	1	2	25	9

PLAYER	W	L	ERA	G	SV	IP	H	BB	SO
Bono, R	1	4	9.72	5	0	25	37	15	16
Carrasco, H	0	1	4.60	13	3	16	14	8	15
Cowart, A	0	1	4.15	13	0	13	17	8	6
Cunningham, A	2	7	6.68	12	0	61	94	24	25
DiPietro, R	9	5	4.71	19	0	115	136	37	93
Flores, P	0	0	4.91	1	0	4	3	6	6
Forrest, T	0	0	4.50	1	0	2	2	3	1
Griffin, D	3	1	3.04	27	14	27	19	15	31
Haynes, M	1	3	5.83	47	5	63	74	33	59
Henry, L	3	0	7.39	27	0	39	47	30	34
Hulett, J	0	0	162.00	1	0	0	4	2	0
Kaminsky, A	3	1	2.40	5	0	30	33	7	22
Kent, S	0	3	18.47	3	0	6	13	3	3
Kirsten, J	1	5	9.06	9	0	48	82	14	34
Maj, J	3	3	6.29	49	3	59	80	10	43
McCarter, J	3	1	5.16	31	0	37	46	20	24
McHenry, D	1	1	15.43	3	0	9	19	6	3
Railsback, C	0	1	8.74	6	0	11	18	13	11
Rodriguez, O	5	7	6.46	21	0	114	151	71	91
Salazar, R	4	4	4.61	12	0	70	99	28	52
Shivers, B	0	0	7.71	3	0	5	7	3	2
Strawn, J	3	4	3.95	9	0	57	75	22	22
Urtuzuastegui, J	0	0	0.00	2	0	3	3	2	2
Velazquez, J	1	0	2.57	20	0	28	22	10	16
Young, J	1	3	6.16	15	0	19	24	14	11

SIOUX CITY EXPLORERS

PLAYER	AVG	AB	R	H	2B	3B	HR	RBI	SB
Backman, W	.294	398	55	117	17	2	7	62	6
Bisnette, C	.143	7	1	1	0	0	0	3	0
Bistagne, B	.300	130	22	39	8	1	2	13	6
Bohn, T	.284	349	59	99	20	1	8	49	13
Brito, J	.245	151	20	37	6	0	2	16	0
Flowers, B	.329	173	29	57	11	0	4	38	0
Goodro, T	.245	233	37	57	15	0	5	29	0
Jones, D	.264	413	64	109	24	2	3	59	11
Murphy, M	.301	153	26	46	8	0	1	17	3
Priddy, R	.291	368	58	107	23	4	7	55	6
Sakamoto, K	.347	329	63	114	24	2	8	65	4
Schermerhorn, D	.272	397	66	108	19	3	2	45	20
Schermerhorn, J	.250	8	0	2	0	0	0	0	0
Serrano, R	.320	359	49	115	28	2	12	67	1
Wendte, J	.217	23	4	5	2	0	0	2	2

PLAYER	W	L	ERA	G	SV	IP	H	BB	SO
Carreras, L	0	0	9.00	2	0	3	6	2	3
Delacruz, E	6	7	3.47	48	9	75	66	36	72
Fruto, E	2	3	2.67	21	12	27	19	18	36
Gibbs, M	5	4	6.21	18	0	38	49	21	17
Howard, C	0	1	4.00	14	1	18	19	14	14
Jarvis, J	3	5	5.59	12	0	66	90	28	44
King, T	2	1	5.07	9	0	40	50	10	36
Leonard, J	0	0	11.88	5	0	8	12	8	6
Marotz, T	6	5	4.98	21	0	125	161	39	74
Plefka, J	1	2	5.19	7	0	9	12	6	7
Rossignol, M	0	1	13.50	1	0	3	5	3	3
Salazar, R	3	2	4.31	8	0	54	69	12	35
Schumacher, N	10	5	3.03	23	0	149	137	54	123
Snowdon, A	2	4	5.89	32	4	55	56	24	65
Trahan, D	5	2	2.67	16	0	84	63	42	78
Wilde, B	3	1	5.28	25	0	46	47	30	26
Wright, K	3	6	5.53	15	0	86	124	22	47

SIOUX FALLS PHEASANTS

PLAYER	AVG	AB	R	H	2B	3B	HR	RBI	SB
Abercrombie, R	.304	385	61	117	27	2	17	66	33
Anthonsen, J	.243	387	51	94	8	1	0	21	6

PLAYER	AVG	AB	R	H	2B	3B	HR	RBI	SB
Carby, K	.210	314	30	66	12	2	1	26	11
Contreras, H	.271	255	31	69	13	0	6	41	0
Jobes, H	.249	177	20	44	5	0	6	22	5
Lawhorn, T	.245	302	43	74	19	1	5	32	0
Leandro, F	.280	350	47	98	24	4	6	58	4
Lind, R	.148	27	3	4	1	0	0	0	0
Milner, G	.329	371	71	122	26	3	5	47	14
Powell, M	.194	31	0	6	3	0	0	2	0
Richards, W	.207	87	5	18	0	0	1	5	0
Shorey, M	.283	392	54	111	26	1	11	64	1
Sing, B	.303	346	71	105	28	0	24	70	4

PLAYER	W	L	ERA	G	SV	IP	H	BB	SO
Cotter, J	1	2	3.89	38	13	39	45	16	35
Cowart, A	5	8	6.24	19	0	102	140	28	48
Engles, T	0	0	3.00	1	0	6	6	3	2
Fleckenstein, R	2	1	3.73	42	0	51	58	14	27
Fowler, B	5	6	4.82	12	0	65	85	17	20
Grant, R	0	3	6.21	40	0	42	44	21	45
Litzinger, M	0	1	3.86	8	0	12	16	7	5
McDaniel, D	3	3	3.21	38	0	53	47	32	50
Moore, B	13	4	2.92	22	0	145	124	49	144
Pluta, A	0	1	14.73	3	0	4	7	3	0
Rapoza, B	5	10	5.45	24	0	101	131	35	30
Rosen, B	0	0	15.00	8	0	9	24	6	8
Ruwe, K	4	5	4.62	16	0	99	118	20	29
Salberg, C	3	8	5.70	26	0	96	123	57	67
Stone, B	1	3	8.89	5	0	27	44	11	18
Walls, S	0	2	4.23	28	0	28	28	10	25

ST. PAUL SAINTS

PLAYER	AVG	AB	R	H	2B	3B	HR	RBI	SB
Bernal, H	.189	37	5	7	3	0	1	4	0
Blunt, D	.150	20	2	3	1	0	0	0	0
Bourquin, R	.300	333	59	100	26	1	12	51	6
Cooper, J	.284	377	53	107	21	2	9	68	0
Costa, S	.333	171	25	57	12	1	1	23	3
Eggleston, A	.197	66	8	13	2	1	0	4	2
Garabedian, A	.233	120	12	28	4	0	2	17	0
Hammes, N	.000	8	0	0	0	0	0	0	0
Howell, J	.184	76	10	14	4	0	2	11	0
Krause, B	.111	9	1	1	0	0	1	1	0
Krause, J	.215	93	15	20	5	0	0	6	3
Mays, S	.175	137	14	24	3	0	0	8	0
Mercado, A	.299	338	49	101	20	1	9	39	0
Nunez, A	.368	87	14	32	9	0	3	17	0
Patterson, R	.354	48	11	17	5	0	1	13	4
Sheldon, J	.304	326	51	99	22	2	12	76	0
Snyder, J	.232	241	40	56	12	0	2	20	2
Thompson, K	.286	28	6	8	2	0	1	2	1
Tripp, B	.314	239	36	75	21	2	9	48	7
Van Every, J	.265	298	55	79	16	1	19	50	1

PLAYER	W	L	ERA	G	SV	IP	H	BB	SO
Brandt, D	7	4	5.34	20	0	111	140	48	76
Carr, K	1	2	5.02	27	0	57	63	41	55
Coe, R	3	1	4.93	18	0	38	43	11	19
Cordero, C	0	1	13.50	7	0	6	12	2	5
DePaula, J	1	1	3.86	4	0	12	13	6	10
Edwards, K	1	0	4.15	8	0	17	18	7	9
English, J	0	1	1.76	11	1	15	12	8	19
Foster, K	6	2	1.73	48	6	73	59	18	72
Long, M	6	10	5.62	20	0	122	151	49	62
Manuel, R	3	2	4.73	32	13	32	41	8	37
Mathison, T	1	0	7.50	2	0	12	15	6	6
Mays, S	0	0	6.00	3	0	3	3	1	2
Quijano, A	2	2	9.15	4	0	20	37	15	12
Rolon, A	10	4	4.41	26	0	112	116	51	76
Schmidt, J	7	4	5.02	16	0	86	107	35	61
Severtson, B	0	0	3.00	2	0	3	5	2	2
Thielbar, C	3	3	2.54	43	0	50	41	15	62
Walker, E	3	6	4.53	25	0	91	92	47	77
Walker, T	1	0	1.50	12	5	12	9	2	13
Zaleski, K	1	1	1.88	3	0	14	16	9	14

WICHITA WINGNUTS

PLAYER	AVG	AB	R	H	2B	3B	HR	RBI	SB
Barrows, P	.292	96	18	28	4	2	3	13	4

	AVG	AB	R	H	2B	3B	HR	RBI	SB
Bellorin, E	.256	324	37	83	21	1	5	58	2
Bustamante, G	.179	28	3	5	0	0	0	2	1
Button, E	.333	45	10	15	2	1	1	8	3
Clevlen, B	.310	184	32	57	15	1	10	32	1
Conroy, M	.302	384	66	116	23	10	1	48	16
Delgado, J	.329	368	67	121	29	1	8	70	7
Duran, J	.349	186	27	65	9	3	2	21	11
Einertson, M	.382	55	9	21	6	0	2	13	0
Fitzgerald, T	.265	136	17	36	4	0	0	10	2
Patterson, R	.299	234	53	70	19	2	11	44	12
Powell, M	.174	23	3	4	0	0	0	2	0
Richardson, J	.360	389	81	140	28	5	12	86	3
Rivera, C	.374	91	22	34	6	0	3	16	0
Robbins, T	.000	13	3	0	0	0	0	3	0
Stevens, J	.111	18	2	2	0	0	0	1	0
Workman, J	.325	375	66	122	29	1	10	68	6

PLAYER	W	L	ERA	G	SV	IP	H	BB	SO
Batista, K	1	3	3.16	35	0	37	37	13	31
Blacksher, D	5	3	3.97	10	0	68	64	23	41
Bradford, J	0	2	12.86	3	0	7	18	2	5
Cotter, M	0	0	5.19	7	0	9	10	5	5
Dew, J	3	1	1.13	34	20	40	27	19	62
Ellis, J	0	3	6.55	6	0	34	42	19	18
Fitzgerald, T	0	0	10.80	1	0	2	3	1	0
Garcia, G	0	3	13.50	6	0	5	9	4	4
Gilliland, E	0	0	2.53	25	0	21	23	12	25
Grybash, D	0	0	0.00	1	0	1	0	2	0
Guerra, J	9	3	3.57	20	0	129	109	72	103
Hinson, R	11	5	5.35	20	0	132	135	42	84
Hoch, L	0	0	9.28	16	0	11	15	10	9
Howard , C	2	2	8.31	10	0	9	11	7	7
Lare, T	0	2	10.26	7	0	17	33	8	13
Lee, G	0	0	6.30	9	0	10	10	4	6
Macfarland, S	0	2	27.00	2	0	4	13	5	2
Mathes, B	0	0	4.50	31	1	46	45	24	32
Miller, D	0	1	10.32	7	1	11	18	11	5
Murray, J	3	4	6.90	8	0	46	70	22	23
Nevarez, M	0	1	2.76	18	1	16	8	6	19
Sherman, C	3	3	6.45	10	0	52	57	36	45
Simon, J	4	5	2.93	47	0	55	63	21	48
Singleton, N	11	2	3.57	19	0	98	95	43	87
Tabata, M	3	0	4.67	26	0	35	28	18	32

WINNIPEG GOLDEYES

PLAYER	AVG	AB	R	H	2B	3B	HR	RBI	SB
Alen, L	.322	366	45	118	30	1	5	57	4
Bass, K	.258	314	52	81	11	2	15	53	4
Carpenter, R	.320	125	23	40	11	2	1	17	5
Ferrante, V	.275	131	18	36	7	0	3	10	0
Joynt, B	.265	83	18	22	5	2	3	14	1
Justice, J	.200	20	1	4	0	0	0	1	0
Kaiser, K	.293	423	80	124	22	6	11	60	37
Kendall, P	.324	417	83	135	16	4	2	54	22
Lentini, F	.244	86	17	21	8	0	2	8	3
Long, W	.264	363	56	96	24	0	10	81	9
Myrow, B	.319	364	62	116	21	2	11	70	6
Ott, L	.325	314	56	102	15	2	5	38	12
Pino, W	.238	21	2	5	0	0	0	0	1
Ramon, A	1.000	1	0	1	0	0	0	0	0
Rick, A	.140	107	12	15	1	0	5	13	0
Weber, J	.326	267	49	87	30	3	10	65	3
Wyatt, J	.261	88	9	23	5	1	1	5	1

PLAYER	W	L	ERA	G	SV	IP	H	BB	SO
Baldwin, Z	5	1	4.50	28	0	46	54	16	38
Benefield, C	2	3	4.43	38	2	45	49	13	28
Carpenter, R	0	1	99.99	1	0	0	1	0	0
Carrillo, E	0	0	4.85	3	0	13	14	9	3
Cook, A	1	1	1.01	28	1	27	16	9	18
Ferrante, V	0	0	0.00	1	0	1	0	0	0
Fowler, B	0	1	4.22	6	0	21	20	7	6
Glant, D	1	3	6.21	6	0	29	37	12	21
Hartsock, A	2	1	2.50	45	4	50	44	21	33
Hess, I	8	4	4.15	20	0	104	97	39	88
Jackel, W	0	0	5.24	21	0	22	25	8	12
Kaiser, K	1	0	0.00	1	0	1	1	0	0
Light, K	0	3	6.35	17	0	17	25	10	16

	W	L	ERA	G	SV	IP	H	BB	SO
Plefka, J	1	1	8.31	5	0	4	5	8	6
Salamida, C	11	4	3.82	21	0	115	113	37	109
Thomas, I	6	3	2.20	37	1	57	42	22	72
Uyechi, C	0	0	9.00	4	0	5	6	4	8
Vermilyea, J	3	3	1.81	45	17	55	41	18	41
Villarreal, L	7	4	4.35	17	0	91	104	28	61
Walker, A	10	4	3.37	21	0	142	149	24	73
Williams, M	2	3	7.62	14	0	39	55	20	23
Wright, E	0	0	8.18	7	0	11	19	9	8

ATLANTIC LEAGUE

If this was Vince Harrison's final pro season, he made sure it was one he'll never forget.

The Atlantic League all-star third baseman hit .529 during the playoffs to earn playoff MVP honors. He was the key cog in York's second consecutive Atlantic League title, making the Revolution only the second Atlantic League team to win back-to-back crowns.

Harrison's family, including younger brother Josh, who made his big league debut with the Pirates in 2011, surprised him by coming to the deciding game. After it was over, the 31-year-old Harrison said he is likely to retire and pursue a career in coaching.

Long Island had the league's best regular season record, and the Ducks placed a league-high five players on the all-star team, but in the championship series, they couldn't match the Revolution.

FIRST HALF

FREEDOM DIVISION	W	L	PCT	GB
Lancaster	37	26	.587	—
York	36	27	.571	1
Somerset	26	37	.413	11
Road Warriors	22	41	.349	15
LIBERTY DIVISION	**W**	**L**	**PCT**	**GB**
Long Island	40	23	.635	—
Southern Maryland	36	27	.571	4
Bridgeport	32	31	.508	8
Camden	23	40	.365	17

SECOND HALF

FREEDOM DIVISION	W	L	PCT	GB
York	37	24	.607	—
Lancaster	32	30	.516	5.5
Somerset	23	37	.383	13.5
Road Warriors	16	45	.262	21
LIBERTY DIVISION	**W**	**L**	**PCT**	**GB**
Long Island	38	24	.613	—
Bridgeport	36	28	.563	3
Camden	34	27	.557	3.5
Southern Maryland	29	30	.492	7.5

PLAYOFFS: Semifinals—York defeated Lancaster 3-2 and Long Island defeated Southern Maryland 3-1 in best-of-five series. **Finals**—York defeated Long Island 3-1 in best-of-five series.

ATTENDANCE: Long Island 382,027, Somerset 372,082, Lancaster 323,091, York 261,590, Camden 244,228, Southern Maryland 214,135, Bridgeport 151,168.

MANAGERS: Bridgeport—Willie Upshaw. **Camden**—Von Hayes. **Lancaster**—Butch Hobson. **Long Island**—Kevin Baez. **Somerset**—Sparky Lyle. **Southern Maryland**—Patrick Osborn. **York**—Andy Etchebarren.

ALL-STAR TEAM
C—J.R. House, Long Island. **1B**—Tommy Everidge, Lancaster. **2B**—Ramon Castro, York. **3B**—Vince Harrison, York. **SS**—Javier Colina, Long Island. **Utility**—Lloyd Turner, Camden. **OF**—Kraig Binick, Long Island; Matt Esquivel, Long Island; Steve Moss, Bridgeport; James Shanks, York. **DH**—Wes Bankston, Bridgeport/Chris Nowak, York. **RHP**—Mike Loree, Long Island. **LHP**—Carlos Vasquez, Camden. **RP**—Jay Marshall, Camden. **Closer**—Jim Ed Warden, So Maryland.
Player of the Year: Tommy Everidge, Lancaster. **Pitcher of the Year:** Mike Loree, Long Island. **Manager of the Year:** Andy Etchebarren, York.

BRIDGEPORT BLUEFISH

PLAYER	AVG	AB	R	H	2B	3B	HR	RBI	SB
Bankston, W	.298	450	60	134	39	0	25	95	4
Berroa, A	.263	228	33	60	15	0	6	33	3
Borchard, J	.229	96	8	22	5	0	3	14	1
Chaves, B	.190	42	7	8	0	1	2	7	1
Chavez, A	.254	315	37	80	11	1	2	29	6
Greenberg, A	.259	379	82	98	8	12	10	44	27
Lopez, L	.276	456	59	126	21	0	10	67	0
Mercedes, V	.333	66	8	22	1	0	1	10	1
Molina, F	.171	35	2	6	0	0	0	2	2
Moras, M	.308	130	19	40	6	1	3	13	1
Moss, S	.295	441	82	130	27	4	19	70	20
Munson, E	.143	56	9	8	2	0	0	4	0
Perez, A	.313	339	57	106	23	2	15	54	8
Peterson, B	.272	235	41	64	18	2	11	31	1
Putnam, D	.270	381	57	103	23	2	10	34	4
Redman, P	.286	133	27	38	12	0	8	21	3
Richar, D	.067	15	1	1	0	0	0	1	0
Roberson, C	.213	160	17	34	8	0	6	23	8
Rodriguez, L	.244	307	39	75	15	2	10	43	2

PLAYER	W	L	ERA	G	SV	IP	H	BB	SO
Alfonseca, A	3	6	4.56	50	2	49	55	14	27
Carrasco, H	1	1	8.44	5	0	5	5	5	5
Cunnane, W	4	2	2.82	28	0	38	33	19	21
Diaz, R	10	1	4.12	13	0	83	79	26	55
Furnish, B	2	1	2.70	15	0	37	29	14	32
Gonzalez, L	0	2	4.91	2	0	11	12	4	9
Kensing, L	0	0	1.59	9	0	11	7	4	16
Manon, J	0	5	4.50	23	0	40	36	18	42
Mejia, M	1	3	7.88	13	0	32	47	19	17
Oseguera, P	11	5	4.53	20	0	113	116	47	102
Padilla, J	2	3	5.65	8	0	29	41	7	22
Pike, M	8	8	4.32	25	0	150	180	44	77
Ramos, L	0	0	24.30	4	0	3	5	7	2
Rincon, J	2	1	2.98	42	23	45	43	19	51
Rivera, C	4	0	4.12	49	1	68	78	20	42
Rodriguez, J	3	3	6.46	13	0	46	52	14	26
Ryan, P	6	5	6.07	19	0	102	122	63	94
Saladin, M	0	0	3.27	10	8	11	11	6	6
Silva, R	0	0	0.00	1	0	2	1	1	2
Smith, M	3	8	7.05	36	0	74	103	44	48
Starling, W	4	2	3.21	12	1	67	68	27	48
Yan, J	2	3	6.88	11	0	51	82	12	34
Zaleski, K	2	0	4.15	22	0	26	22	9	17

CAMDEN RIVERSHARKS

PLAYER	AVG	AB	R	H	2B	3B	HR	RBI	SB
Burgamy, B	.259	398	73	103	15	2	18	68	9
Colina, A	.111	9	1	1	0	0	0	2	0
Colina, A	.276	192	29	53	11	0	14	49	0
Dorta, M	.097	31	1	3	1	0	0	2	0
Eigsti, J	.356	45	11	16	5	0	3	12	1
Feliz, P	.298	275	38	82	15	1	11	45	1
Francia, J	.286	384	39	110	13	2	0	32	30
Hall, N	.285	438	66	125	20	6	15	64	3
Hall, T	.255	318	18	81	8	0	2	32	0
Harris, S	.167	12	4	2	0	0	1	3	0
Hill, J	.200	50	6	10	4	0	1	1	0
Jenkins, A	.240	25	1	6	0	0	0	4	0
Lamb, M	.320	169	30	54	12	0	7	32	3
Macias, D	.267	236	37	63	13	3	8	31	6
Otanez, W	.308	91	11	28	8	0	2	6	0
Pacheco, J	.261	230	37	60	6	2	7	27	8
Padron, R	.335	158	23	53	11	0	7	30	0
Richar, D	.282	341	54	96	20	2	11	45	4
Turner, L	.296	433	71	128	23	3	3	40	15
Yan, R	.281	359	48	101	10	3	2	24	26

PLAYER	W	L	ERA	G	SV	IP	H	BB	SO
Baez, F	6	5	5.58	18	0	79	86	33	44
Bale, J	1	2	2.35	52	4	61	57	17	50
Bazardo, Y	1	0	7.50	4	0	6	8	4	3
Camacho, E	7	7	5.12	31	0	104	145	34	59
Cline, Z	1	0	1.35	3	0	13	9	5	5
DAlessandro, J	1	0	6.57	12	0	12	12	9	9

De la Rosa, W	3	2	2.41	7	0	37	29	17	28
Dittler, J	1	5	8.70	7	0	30	44	23	14
Gearhart, K	0	0	0.00	1	0	1	0	0	1
Hammes, Z	0	2	4.56	39	0	49	47	42	31
Hernandez, F	1	0	2.08	13	1	13	8	4	9
Hernandez, S	1	0	1.80	5	0	10	5	6	13
Hunt, J	0	0	27.00	2	0	1	1	3	1
Jarrett, S	1	2	4.15	11	0	26	25	6	9
Johnson, J	0	6	10.92	8	0	30	57	18	15
Koplove, M	3	2	3.19	47	0	48	48	19	46
Marshall, J	1	1	1.73	59	9	52	36	20	25
Mason, C	1	2	5.93	5	0	27	32	13	10
Mathes, J	5	7	5.62	16	0	90	115	17	38
McGuire, M	1	0	0.00	2	0	4	1	0	5
McKeller, R	0	2	4.86	25	0	33	40	17	34
Rivera, M	2	2	3.12	39	1	52	46	32	46
Rohrbaugh, R	1	3	8.68	6	0	28	41	7	17
Rollins, C	0	0	0.00	1	0	1	0	0	0
Sanchez, H	3	1	4.50	6	0	28	20	15	15
Stokes, B	2	3	3.47	31	11	36	31	13	23
Towers, J	5	6	6.15	13	0	72	100	13	39
Vasquez, C	10	6	3.47	30	0	132	150	56	86

LANCASTER BARNSTORMERS

PLAYER	AVG	AB	R	H	2B	3B	HR	RBI	SB
Calderone, A	.299	174	25	52	9	4	6	26	5
Chavez, O	.175	114	11	20	3	0	2	12	2
Colina, A	.220	132	8	29	6	0	1	10	1
Copeland, B	.331	139	26	46	3	3	4	19	8
Douglas, S	.412	17	3	7	1	0	1	3	0
Everidge, T	.319	501	94	160	41	0	28	94	1
Flores, A	.311	119	14	37	3	0	1	11	0
Frostad, E	.280	50	7	14	3	1	2	11	0
Godwin, A	.256	43	9	11	5	0	0	2	1
Herr, A	.287	366	52	105	20	1	12	57	3
Holt, J	.291	247	34	72	7	3	5	35	9
Howard, K	.381	118	20	45	7	0	4	17	2
Jones, B	.268	194	20	52	6	0	4	22	2
King, B	.261	23	3	6	0	0	0	1	0
Lydon, W	.302	172	51	52	9	3	6	25	16
Mejia, G	.286	455	75	130	14	10	4	43	40
Metcalf, T	.261	142	17	37	8	0	6	22	2
Seguignol, F	.287	341	53	98	18	0	20	71	1
Suarez, I	.250	220	23	55	8	1	1	24	3
Tamayo, Y	.208	53	8	11	1	0	2	10	0
Tiffee, J	.293	198	36	58	16	1	13	46	0
Townsend, T	.000	0	0	0	0	0	0	0	0
Tupman, M	.268	179	20	48	8	0	4	17	1
Watson, M	.287	272	51	78	16	0	15	45	0
Wiley, S	.231	26	2	6	2	0	0	0	0

PLAYER	W	L	ERA	G	SV	IP	H	BB	SO
Bayliss, J	2	3	3.54	39	18	41	31	20	30
Beam, T	3	3	4.78	52	1	49	51	30	40
Bennett, J	4	0	0.82	21	3	33	22	13	24
Braun, R	0	0	6.00	3	0	3	1	1	2
Carrillo, C	4	11	7.16	18	0	88	117	42	64
Colina, A	0	0	40.50	1	0	1	1	2	0
Cullen, R	1	1	3.18	6	0	6	9	2	7
Durbin, J	8	4	5.06	18	0	107	132	45	81
Englebrook, E	0	0	6.05	25	0	22	21	11	18
Halama, J	6	6	5.33	15	0	105	143	23	57
Hammond, S	0	0	0.00	2	0	11	4	8	12
Hamulack, T	1	0	0.00	11	7	11	5	0	14
Herr, A	0	0	36.00	1	0	1	2	2	2
Holt, J	0	0	0.00	1	0	1	0	0	0
Huber, J	3	0	4.63	24	0	23	21	14	18
Koronka, J	0	0	0.00	2	0	1	0	4	0
McNab, T	3	4	3.89	54	0	72	84	17	32
Novoa, Y	5	5	5.34	33	0	83	99	24	76
Parker, Z	0	0	9.75	10	0	12	14	23	7
Peeples, R	7	5	5.16	30	0	98	138	27	53
Regas, K	0	0	4.26	29	1	19	17	12	14
Segal, J	5	2	4.46	56	0	77	95	25	31
Tabor, L	1	0	1.74	7	0	10	9	5	3
Walrond, L	1	0	1.39	9	0	13	10	2	15
Williams, J	6	0	2.91	8	0	53	43	12	40

	W	L	ERA	G	SV	IP	H	BB	SO
Wright, M	7	10	3.98	21	0	129	122	38	97
Zink, C	2	2	7.80	8	0	30	31	29	24

LONG ISLAND DUCKS

PLAYER	AVG	AB	R	H	2B	3B	HR	RBI	SB
Binick, K	.343	373	72	128	19	4	4	47	42
Colina, J	.309	431	79	133	21	5	25	90	3
Esquivel, M	.328	332	65	109	22	1	15	69	7
Ford, L	.318	258	57	82	21	2	10	45	2
House, J	.305	420	73	128	22	0	19	81	1
Jones, K	.292	438	82	128	25	11	8	54	28
Kourie, J	.118	17	3	2	2	0	0	1	0
Lyons, D	.283	244	44	69	15	4	2	40	12
Monzon, E	.359	78	17	28	5	0	3	10	5
Navarrete, R	.242	492	86	119	20	0	27	79	0
Padgett, M	.282	418	61	118	24	1	11	67	5
Pennino, J	.143	84	10	12	1	0	1	8	3
Petersen, J	.063	16	1	1	0	0	0	0	0
Rodriguez, J	.313	304	74	95	16	2	18	81	2
Thon, F	.284	345	41	98	18	0	7	47	0

PLAYER	W	L	ERA	G	SV	IP	H	BB	SO
Banks, J	1	1	4.24	3	0	17	17	4	10
Buzachero, B	7	2	3.26	52	22	58	58	11	39
De Los Santos, V	3	4	5.23	21	2	43	52	19	33
Diapoules, M	7	4	5.08	28	0	85	83	33	60
Diaz, J	5	8	6.91	22	0	111	135	67	78
DiNardo, L	2	1	5.09	3	0	18	18	3	17
Flinn, C	0	0	1.59	4	0	6	6	3	6
Ford, L	0	0	18.00	1	0	1	2	0	0
Gregory, S	0	0	8.38	7	0	10	17	5	6
Hill, J	8	2	2.91	48	1	68	64	12	48
Hunton, J	1	0	2.70	3	1	3	3	1	4
Loree, M	14	5	1.98	24	0	123	103	28	131
Lugo, R	5	4	6.48	20	0	83	111	44	48
McCoy, C	3	1	4.42	25	0	59	66	20	26
Monti, J	1	1	3.00	20	0	30	32	8	33
Parisi, M	6	4	3.50	13	0	80	86	29	76
Phillips, H	1	3	4.91	10	0	48	57	26	37
Sanchez, D	0	0	5.00	9	1	9	9	8	9
Walker, T	0	0	4.50	2	0	2	3	0	1
Wassermann, E	4	1	2.57	51	11	63	54	12	66
Williams, D	1	3	4.91	22	0	51	68	21	35
Youman, S	7	1	0.66	13	0	54	39	9	46
Zimmermann, B	2	2	4.41	31	1	67	60	26	54

ROAD WARRIORS

PLAYER	AVG	AB	R	H	2B	3B	HR	RBI	SB
Caballero, J	.188	16	2	3	1	0	0	0	0
Cabral, M	.280	389	49	109	20	3	0	31	4
Cruz, A	.211	251	26	53	17	1	9	29	1
Dorta, M	.353	150	15	53	6	0	2	20	8
Gonzalez, D	.289	343	48	99	22	0	4	37	6
Gutierrez, V	.289	225	24	65	7	1	1	27	4
Guzman, J	.179	39	3	7	2	0	0	2	0
Henry, S	.328	186	33	61	16	2	3	20	4
Jiannetti, J	.215	65	3	14	3	0	1	4	1
Johnson, J	.229	358	36	82	18	1	9	46	1
Jordan, D	.247	146	20	36	6	0	5	19	0
Kelly, K	.176	85	6	15	3	0	3	7	1
Mitchell, T	.316	19	4	6	1	0	0	3	4
Mooney, M	.252	266	37	67	22	2	7	32	6
Nieblas, L	.239	255	19	61	13	0	3	24	0
Ortiz, A	.220	255	31	56	9	4	0	11	19
Pacheco, J	.285	186	23	53	9	0	6	27	9
Pena, A	.146	41	2	6	0	0	0	1	1
Sena, E	.056	36	4	2	0	0	0	1	1
Sosa, C	.330	279	45	92	10	0	17	55	6
Suarez, G	.216	241	22	52	9	0	0	13	1
Thomas, S	.143	35	2	5	0	0	0	1	0
Zazueta, A	.301	319	41	96	16	3	6	33	2

PLAYER	W	L	ERA	G	SV	IP	H	BB	SO
Thomas, A	2	5	1.73	56	17	57	45	12	49
Ramos, E	1	1	2.21	29	3	41	28	10	24
Coffey, D	0	1	3.48	3	0	10	11	8	6
Lugo, J	0	1	3.52	6	0	8	10	4	8
Giron, R	1	0	3.60	18	0	25	27	8	23

	W	L	ERA	G	SV	IP	H	BB	SO
Little, C	0	2	3.72	4	0	19	18	9	12
Rivera, S	2	4	4.29	28	0	42	52	18	29
McCullough, B	4	3	4.42	36	0	57	57	24	39
Martinez, M	6	12	4.79	24	0	128	142	61	66
Javier, O	0	6	5.65	11	0	43	42	25	38
Mannix, K	1	2	5.76	7	0	30	40	11	15
Asleton, K	1	3	5.80	42	2	59	62	28	54
Massetti, L	9	12	5.82	25	0	138	169	26	64
Villa, K	5	10	6.08	25	0	98	118	43	85
Norderum, J	3	7	6.61	36	1	80	103	43	60
Frias, J	3	3	6.69	14	0	38	47	25	16
Kelly, C	0	2	8.06	16	1	22	29	12	10
Mason, J	0	7	8.72	21	0	64	100	41	42
Cruz, A	0	0	9.00	1	0	1	2	2	1
Morales, J	0	0	9.00	2	0	2	3	5	0
Palacio, J	0	0	10.57	7	0	15	25	5	7
Morales, R	0	2	11.15	6	0	15	22	11	3
Thompson, S	0	0	13.50	6	0	5	8	5	1
Astacio, E	2	2	14.40	2	0	5	6	11	1
Cepeda, B	0	1	15.43	5	0	9	13	13	2

SOMERSET PATRIOTS

PLAYER	AVG	AB	R	H	2B	3B	HR	RBI	SB
Ayala, E	.256	207	31	53	8	1	2	19	4
Burke, J	.229	157	13	36	5	0	3	16	7
Carter, Y	.247	150	16	37	9	0	6	19	1
Chaves, B	.077	13	3	1	0	0	0	1	0
Cortez, F	.290	431	53	125	17	3	4	42	18
DeGeorge, D	.256	160	20	41	8	0	1	6	2
Hagen, M	.236	331	41	78	22	1	11	46	7
Hernandez, M	.272	272	37	74	19	0	9	45	0
Holden, J	.272	331	45	90	21	2	1	32	31
Hopf, J	.164	67	6	11	5	0	0	4	0
Hopper, N	.253	265	35	67	8	1	1	31	7
Huber, J	.259	336	48	87	14	1	8	42	5
Lydon, W	.202	178	32	36	3	3	5	11	14
Nettles, J	.266	432	56	115	24	1	15	72	2
Pachot, J	.222	189	14	42	8	0	0	15	0
Pressley, J	.297	404	63	120	32	0	16	75	1
Shubsda, J	.000	3	0	0	0	0	0	0	0
Suarez, I	.136	66	7	9	1	0	0	5	2

PLAYER	W	L	ERA	G	SV	IP	H	BB	SO
Anderson, J	2	2	3.72	23	0	29	31	5	24
Bush, P	0	2	13.50	5	0	5	9	3	3
Cahill, C	2	2	5.46	45	0	59	69	25	24
Cate, T	0	2	6.55	3	0	11	12	5	7
Cromer, J	2	3	3.38	10	0	37	37	14	19
Dobies, A	2	3	2.81	28	5	32	30	3	31
Gordon, D	7	4	2.63	11	0	68	53	23	58
Grezlovski, B	2	3	3.78	45	1	52	66	15	40
Hagen, M	0	0	0.00	1	0	1	1	0	3
Honel, K	0	1	6.23	4	0	17	14	17	10
Houston, R	0	2	2.10	26	11	26	20	13	28
Kennard, J	4	3	2.91	52	2	56	49	21	48
Magrane, J	3	3	4.19	9	0	54	52	24	35
Massingham, E	0	0	8.10	5	0	3	10	3	2
McCall, B	5	8	4.43	18	0	100	103	31	42
McCullough, B	0	0	3.38	10	0	13	17	8	7
Minix, T	0	1	3.86	11	0	14	12	2	12
Oxspring, C	5	9	4.17	18	0	106	114	30	104
Pulsipher, B	3	6	4.00	18	0	92	125	22	55
Reese, K	3	3	5.84	30	0	86	105	23	36
Sommer, L	4	5	4.02	36	1	69	77	13	44
Sweeney, B	1	0	2.57	1	0	7	4	0	8
Ungs, N	4	7	5.45	20	0	101	112	31	51
Villone, R	0	4	12.00	18	0	15	22	15	14
Williamson, S	0	1	14.46	11	2	9	14	16	2

SOUTHERN MARYLAND BLUE CRABS

PLAYER	AVG	AB	R	H	2B	3B	HR	RBI	SB
Barton, B	.304	329	48	100	19	2	12	42	17
Benjamin, C	.270	348	60	94	19	4	13	58	5
Cusick, M	.000	4	0	0	0	0	0	0	0
Espinosa, D	.276	29	4	8	2	1	0	6	2
Garcia, T	.305	259	48	79	18	1	18	57	4
Giannotti, R	.276	98	11	27	5	0	2	11	0

INDEPENDENT LEAGUES

PLAYER	AVG	AB	R	H	2B	3B	HR	RBI	SB
Godwin, A	.326	298	53	97	9	2	2	24	37
Harrison, B	.285	393	63	112	26	2	11	68	4
Herrera, J	.239	117	13	28	8	0	1	18	0
Hopf, J	.186	86	10	16	5	1	1	3	1
Hunt, B	.281	96	18	27	4	0	2	15	5
Jiannetti, J	.232	56	4	13	0	0	1	4	1
Kirkland, K	.245	143	20	35	8	3	6	20	1
Lopez, C	.258	361	45	93	18	2	9	42	9
Mulhern, R	.348	112	22	39	9	3	10	34	0
Owens, J	.236	347	47	82	18	0	13	48	10
Pinckney, B	.293	372	49	109	19	0	4	30	3
Pineiro, L	.222	9	2	2	0	0	0	3	0
Riddick, A	.083	12	2	1	0	0	1	2	0
Rodriguez, J	.261	69	11	18	1	1	0	3	2
Sanchez, Y	.403	231	41	93	17	2	7	40	3
Suarez, I	.275	40	3	11	3	0	0	5	0
Townsend, T	.256	305	35	78	18	1	10	38	1

PLAYER	W	L	ERA	G	SV	IP	H	BB	SO
Dumesnil, B	2	1	3.21	35	0	48	28	22	54
Gannon, J	3	3	4.72	24	1	61	67	30	29
Giannotti, R	0	0	99.99	1	0	0	2	2	0
Green, N	11	6	3.96	26	0	150	158	34	81
Hayes, C	1	2	4.07	5	0	24	24	3	15
Manning, C	2	3	4.04	44	0	49	48	32	62
Moore, B	1	0	3.38	3	0	16	10	7	19
Morlan, E	1	1	1.96	38	0	37	33	8	29
Palazzolo, S	9	5	3.07	53	0	62	49	25	57
Pinckney, B	0	0	0.00	1	0	1	0	0	0
Ramsey, K	2	3	6.35	6	0	28	37	10	22
Rodriguez, E	8	4	4.14	29	1	100	114	34	84
Schlact, M	6	4	4.61	21	0	107	108	25	38
Slocum, B	4	4	4.08	15	0	82	83	25	51
Trahan, D	1	0	2.84	2	0	13	6	5	10
Vasquez, V	8	6	4.25	23	0	140	140	31	80
Waddell, J	4	10	5.31	37	1	95	98	37	88
Warden, J	2	5	2.76	50	28	49	40	14	43

YORK REVOLUTION

PLAYER	AVG	AB	R	H	2B	3B	HR	RBI	SB
Botts, J	.370	54	13	20	4	0	4	13	1
Castro, R	.323	288	50	93	22	1	14	62	1
Eymann, E	.283	279	29	79	15	1	3	43	1
Grimes, S	.268	436	97	117	15	3	15	42	21
Guzman, C	.233	30	2	7	0	0	0	3	0
Harrison, V	.327	431	58	141	23	0	10	61	13
Herrera, J	.283	332	45	94	10	0	9	59	0
Majewski, V	.317	281	63	89	10	4	11	48	10
Martinez, J	.194	31	4	6	2	0	0	1	0
Martinez, O	.273	253	18	69	10	0	1	29	1
Nelson, B	.283	113	18	32	4	0	3	19	1
Nowak, C	.330	297	67	98	19	0	25	66	7
Ori, M	.242	124	14	30	7	0	1	21	0
Paniagua, S	.251	195	17	49	9	0	6	21	0
Pope, V	.206	34	5	7	2	0	0	2	0
Rodriguez, L	.231	238	25	55	9	1	1	23	1
Shanks, J	.314	392	61	123	25	6	12	61	15
Townsend, T	.209	43	4	9	2	0	1	4	0
Walker, C	.287	380	70	109	12	4	4	35	24

PLAYER	W	L	ERA	G	SV	IP	H	BB	SO
Barcelo, J	5	0	3.96	6	0	36	38	6	24
Cline, Z	0	2	7.62	6	0	13	18	8	7
Cody, C	9	5	4.39	18	0	105	113	19	78
Cruz, R	0	2	23.14	4	0	5	13	4	2
DeMark, M	0	0	2.61	13	1	10	8	4	17
DeSalvo, M	6	3	3.89	23	1	106	104	33	108
Edwards, J	1	1	3.27	3	0	11	12	6	8
Garceau, A	4	9	5.45	32	0	119	132	45	102
Garcia, D	2	3	4.70	13	0	31	37	12	34
Geary, G	3	2	3.57	23	0	23	25	5	21
Gomez, R	2	0	2.13	21	2	25	21	12	30
Gonzalez, J	2	1	4.30	4	0	23	22	4	25
Guzman, C	0	0	99.99	1	0	0	1	0	0
Lewis, J	2	0	6.75	7	0	7	11	2	3
Majewski, V	0	0	13.50	1	0	1	1	1	0
Mannix, K	0	1	5.00	4	0	9	11	3	4
Morales, R	2	2	3.81	70	0	59		26	56

PLAYER	W	L	ERA	G	SV	IP	H	BB	SO
Nix, M	0	1	4.08	50	18	46	53	13	50
Pacella, J	0	1	12.27	5	0	4	7	4	1
Polanco, C	0	0	8.10	3	0	3	7	2	2
Regas, K	0	0	0.00	4	0	4	1	1	4
Rice, S	1	0	2.46	15	1	15	9	4	15
Richardson, J	4	0	3.33	19	0	24	15	9	25
Rodriguez, R	3	3	3.61	49	10	52	42	23	51
Sanchez, J	3	2	6.67	6	0	28	46	15	19
Schumacher, N	2	1	4.15	4	0	26	25	5	23
Spradlin, J	0	2	5.10	31	0	48	54	27	44
Stidfole, S	5	4	3.79	60	1	55	58	19	56
Tabor, L	1	1	11.17	7	0	10	19	5	5
Thurman, C	13	3	3.33	25	0	141	135	52	111
VanBenschoten, J	3	2	2.91	8	0	43	46	14	34
Zaleski, K	0	0	27.00	1	0	1	3	0	0

CAN-AM LEAGUE

In the Can-Am League, there are Quebec Capitales and then there is everyone else.

Quebec captured its third consecutive league title and its fourth in six years by beating New Jersey in the league championship series. Quebec has now won more than half of the league's titles since the Can-Am League was reborn in 2005.

The convincing title series win was just the final act of a team that dominated the league all year. Quebec had the best record in the league in the first half and the second half of the season, though New Jersey was clearly the second-best team.

Quebec manager Pat Scalabrini now has two titles in two years leading the club. The previous manager, Michel Laplante, now is the team's president. Pitching led Quebec to the title in the playoffs, as starters Bryan Rembisz, John Mariotti and Karl Gelinas combined to go 5-1, 1.67 in six playoff starts.

FIRST HALF	W	L	PCT	GB
Quebec	35	11	.761	—
New Jersey	27	20	.574	8.5
Brockton	26	20	.565	9
Pittsfield	25	21	.543	10
Newark	23	24	.489	12.5
Worcester	21	26	.447	14.5
Rockland	19	27	.413	16
New York	10	37	.213	25.5

SECOND HALF	W	L	PCT	GB
Quebec	29	15	.659	—
New Jersey	30	16	.652	—
Pittsfield	28	18	.609	2
Worcester	27	18	.600	2.5
Brockton	25	22	.532	5.5
Rockland	21	25	.457	9
Newark	18	28	.391	12
New York	5	41	.109	25

PLAYOFFS: Semifinals—New Jersey defeated Pittsfield 3-0 and Quebec defeated Brockton 3-0 in best-of-five series. **Finals**—Quebec defeated New Jersey 3-1 in best-of-five series.

ATTENDANCE: Quebec 149,330, Rockland 123,518, Brockton 94,112, New Jersey 84,865, Worcester 83,745, Newark 51,854, Pittsfield 37,154.

MANAGERS: Brockton—Bill Buckner. **Newark**—Tim Raines. **New Jersey**—Joe Calfapietra. **New York**—Skip Nathanson. **Quebec**—Pat Scalabrini. **Pittsfield**—Jamie Keefe. **Rockland**—Dave LaPoint. **Worcester**—Ed Riley.

ALL-STAR TEAM
C—Myron Leslie, New Jersey. **1B**—Chris Colabello, Worcester. **2B**—Danny Bomback, Pittsfield. **3B**—Mark Minicozzi, Worcester. **SS**—Dominic Ramos, Brockton. **OF**—Keith Brachold, Brockton; Danny Santiesteban, Newark; Chris Valencia, Brockton. **DH**—Nick Salotti, Worcester.
LHP—Isaac Pavlik, New Jersey. **RHP**—Bryan Rembisz, Quebec. **RP**—Adrian Martin, Rockland.

Player of the Year: Chris Colabello, Worcester. **Manager of the Year:** Jamie Keefe, Pittsfield.

BROCKTON ROX

PLAYER	AVG	AB	R	H	2B	3B	HR	RBI	SB
Barbero, Dan	.300	120	21	36	7	1	5	24	2
Brachold, Keith	.334	356	69	119	22	4	18	80	14
Cuadrado, P	.319	47	7	15	3	0	1	9	0
Falu, Melvin	.283	350	54	99	20	2	9	49	7
Grossman, Chris	.259	332	50	86	16	0	7	38	11
Hernandez, T	.266	192	26	51	9	0	6	35	1
Hunt, J	.194	31	4	6	3	1	0	3	0
Jimenez, J	.271	140	29	38	7	0	5	25	5
Monger, Cameron	.091	11	3	1	0	0	0	0	0
Nathans, T	.311	45	9	14	2	1	0	8	2
Ramos, Dominic	.284	306	52	87	23	2	4	34	17
Rosenbeck, J	.100	20	2	2	1	0	0	0	0
Royster, R	.264	174	25	46	11	2	13	38	0
Sumner, A	.179	39	3	7	0	0	0	4	0
Torres, M	.340	321	47	109	25	3	3	49	8
Valencia, Chris	.342	386	76	132	30	8	5	53	41
Vranau, S	.100	20	2	2	0	0	0	1	0
Wiley, S	.270	37	3	10	2	0	1	5	0
Williams, Shawn	.316	231	40	73	16	0	2	29	9

PLAYER	W	L	ERA	G	SV	IP	H	BB	SO
Birosak, D	7	2	3.30	15	0	85	81	28	63
Bono, R	3	1	5.29	12	0	51	61	19	31
Cruceta, F	0	0	0.00	2	1	2	0	0	3
Flores, F	7	9	4.90	19	0	112	123	30	71
Hale, J	0	3	3.07	41	15	41	33	16	37
Hertzler, B	0	3	2.94	30	0	34	35	10	13
Hughes, T	1	2	5.51	16	6	16	21	8	18
Jackson, R	1	0	3.29	17	0	14	12	10	11
Kelly, J	1	1	2.15	6	0	29	27	10	29
Kennedy, J	3	3	3.70	30	2	41	43	7	29
Loye, J	3	2	3.80	15	0	45	51	18	21
Lynch, C	0	3	5.87	13	0	15	15	6	8
Petrowski, M	0	0	7.04	3	0	8	11	7	5
Richard, S	0	0	1.50	7	0	6	5	1	6
Rosen, M	3	3	3.99	34	0	56	47	31	46
Sampson, J	10	5	3.92	19	0	115	92	55	73
Schmidt, D	2	0	6.55	10	0	11	18	5	5
Smith, M	8	5	3.99	15	0	95	86	33	53
VanLeur, J	0	0	4.80	18	0	15	17	5	11
Woods, Z	2	0	0.72	9	0	25	13	8	23

NEW JERSEY JACKALS

PLAYER	AVG	AB	R	H	2B	3B	HR	RBI	SB
Anderson, C	.244	123	19	30	3	0	8	21	1
Davis, L	.317	208	46	66	18	2	9	36	3
DeJesus, M	.289	353	53	102	17	2	2	35	6
Giarraputo, N	.308	328	52	101	27	3	6	44	3
Jimenez, D	.303	99	19	30	8	0	2	23	5
Jones, M	.266	282	40	75	15	2	7	49	1
Leslie, M	.328	311	59	102	27	1	9	51	14
Madera, S	.289	38	4	11	0	1	1	9	0
Newton, J	.258	124	20	32	7	2	4	12	3
Reyes, A	.306	248	34	76	12	3	2	29	12
Richard, M	.273	11	1	3	1	0	0	1	0
Sabatella, B	.442	52	12	23	4	1	1	16	8
Sanchez, K	.261	307	45	80	22	1	14	59	0
Santomauro, N	.239	109	17	26	6	0	2	14	3
Slayden, J	.252	139	24	35	8	0	7	20	2
Smith, S	.273	139	34	38	3	1	3	16	37
White, C	.230	243	36	56	5	4	4	24	23

PLAYER	W	L	ERA	G	SV	IP	H	BB	SO
Anderson, C	0	0	0.00	1	0	2	3	0	2
Bartleski, P	1	1	10.57	7	0	15	21	9	14
Betteridge, D	0	0	0.00	1	0	1	0	0	1
Clyne, S	0	0	18.00	2	0	1	2	1	1
Ellis, J	0	0	2.89	6	0	9	10	4	11
Ellis, S	5	3	4.13	18	0	72	79	30	61
Fox, S	0	2	2.28	41	4	51	38	15	63
Gagg, B	2	0	3.03	16	0	36	33	11	23
Gogal, J	1	4	3.32	37	15	41	38	11	55
Gunderson, K	1	0	0.00	7	2	8	1	0	5

Hunt, J	0	0	5.87	8	1	8	10	11	8
Kibler, J	3	6	6.03	12	0	66	79	25	47
Kulik, R	2	3	8.91	7	0	33	50	16	26
Leverton, J	8	4	2.38	13	0	87	71	22	64
Locke, J	7	1	3.65	41	1	49	57	13	44
Mendez, J	0	1	16.20	1	0	3	7	1	2
Moore, M	5	1	6.26	10	0	42	43	25	36
Pavlik, I	13	3	2.73	19	0	132	130	25	112
Petrowski, M	0	2	9.30	13	0	20	30	12	15
Pontius, M	0	1	3.77	10	0	14	16	7	12
Railsback, C	0	0	5.79	12	0	19	16	10	15
Vasami, C	2	2	7.27	6	0	26	37	12	18
Wideman, A	7	2	2.52	10	0	61	56	16	28

NEW YORK FEDERALS

PLAYER	AVG	AB	R	H	2B	3B	HR	RBI	SB
Adamkiewicz, F	.087	23	3	2	0	0	0	0	0
Barbaro, A	.250	16	1	4	0	0	0	1	1
Barbero, D	.533	15	4	8	2	0	0	2	0
Bardeguez, A	.299	107	7	32	9	0	2	10	0
Castellano, M	.210	62	4	13	1	0	0	5	0
Coury, D	.227	119	12	27	4	0	5	13	0
DeLeon, S	.238	214	14	51	3	0	0	12	1
Detwiler, S	.238	151	14	36	7	0	2	8	0
Dubben, S	.259	58	5	15	1	0	0	4	0
Dyer, R	.148	135	10	20	8	1	0	8	0
Fabry, J	.258	267	22	69	9	2	3	28	1
Gerhart, K	.120	50	3	6	1	0	0	3	1
Gorang, B	.158	19	1	3	0	0	0	0	0
Jackson, B	.291	223	22	65	13	1	4	26	2
Lantigua, E	.244	234	31	57	9	0	12	32	3
Ledesma, A	.263	19	1	5	2	0	0	0	0
Levy, M	.172	64	4	11	0	0	0	2	1
Maloney, T	.224	299	28	67	15	1	4	25	10
Matos, W	.255	55	7	14	4	0	1	7	1
Nastani, C	.133	15	0	2	0	0	0	0	0
Nathans, T	.278	36	3	10	1	1	0	3	2
Obal, K	.161	93	10	15	2	0	0	0	1
Pinto, S	.188	165	12	31	6	1	1	4	9
Pippin, T	.263	38	6	10	1	0	3	9	0
Pyles, D	.241	112	15	27	6	0	4	13	1
Reyes, J	.135	52	2	7	0	0	0	6	0
Rosenbeck, J	.190	184	17	35	1	1	1	10	0
Schult, J	.364	11	0	4	1	0	0	2	0
Sumner, A	.231	104	11	24	5	0	0	8	1

PLAYER	W	L	ERA	G	SV	IP	H	BB	SO
Ahern, D	0	1	10.80	8	0	12	26	0	4
Anderson, M	1	0	16.50	7	0	6	15	4	4
Aquino, J	0	0	4.50	4	1	4	4	1	4
Asnicar, B	0	0	6.23	2	0	4	5	3	3
Bakowski, A	0	1	4.86	10	0	17	19	5	10
Bierlein, J	0	0	9.37	20	1	16	29	8	11
Briend, S	0	0	1.42	6	2	6	6	3	8
Byron, G	0	1	13.50	5	0	6	14	1	3
Davis, B	0	0	13.50	1	0	1	3	2	0
DeLeon, N	0	0	8.64	7	0	8	13	7	2
Detwiler, S	0	0	18.00	1	0	1	5	0	0
Dyer, R	0	0	6.75	4	0	4	8	0	2
Echeverria, M	0	2	9.64	9	0	14	21	14	12
Fabry, J	0	0	9.00	1	0	1	0	4	0
Foltz, J	1	0	5.16	23	2	23	30	3	23
Gerard, K	0	0	27.00	1	0	0	1	0	0
Gibson, D	0	0	0.00	2	0	1	2	4	1
Granitto, G	0	1	23.63	2	0	5	14	4	4
Guinard, S	0	2	9.00	4	0	5	7	9	4
Hassett, W	2	4	3.74	8	0	43	35	27	27
Hildreth, B	0	1	9.39	2	0	8	21	2	1
Jachno, S	0	0	9.00	1	0	1	3	1	1
Kalb, A	0	1	13.50	2	0	1	2	0	0
Kelly, M	0	0	9.00	1	0	1	3	1	0
Kukucka, J	3	8	8.61	20	0	76	106	50	39
Larson, P	0	0	22.50	2	0	2	3	2	2
Loye, J	0	4	5.02	6	0	29	35	9	21
Lysenko, D	0	1	23.82	8	0	6	19	6	2
Marcotte, T	0	3	16.76	3	0	10	22	5	4
Masklee, J	1	1	3.97	12	0	11	14	6	13

	0	0	10.39	6	0	9	17	5	3
McNamara, J	0	0	10.39	6	0	9	17	5	3
Merslich, S	0	1	27.00	2	0	3	5	6	2
Moore, B	0	4	7.54	4	0	23	39	11	17
Mullen, M	0	0	6.89	29	1	31	35	18	25
Overby, J	0	0	19.29	2	0	2	9	0	2
Pardo, L	0	10	5.83	15	0	76	98	32	48
Peabody, T	0	0	27.00	2	0	3	9	2	2
Penalo, B	1	0	0.00	1	0	1	1	0	0
Petrowski, M	1	2	1.84	7	0	29	23	9	23
Pippin, T	0	0	3.00	2	0	3	4	2	2
Putnam, K	1	9	6.06	13	0	55	61	33	31
Raymond, J	0	1	54.00	1	0	1	5	4	1
Renault, N	0	1	5.40	1	0	2	1	1	0
Rijo, F	0	1	9.00	1	0	4	5	1	0
Schult, J	1	6	5.40	10	0	50	60	30	36
Shaffer, N	0	1	9.82	2	0	11	16	7	9
Shepard, J	2	3	4.34	18	3	19	18	6	20
Streaman, M	1	5	6.80	10	0	49	59	28	32
Watson, A	0	0	18.69	8	0	4	10	4	6
Wells, A	0	2	12.15	2	0	7	14	6	4
Woods, Z	0	1	3.18	4	0	6	3	1	7
Worthington, K	0	0	3.09	10	2	12	10	8	12

NEWARK BEARS

PLAYER	AVG	AB	R	H	2B	3B	HR	RBI	SB
Alvino, B	.305	246	35	75	12	1	2	26	3
Benzel, T	.174	46	5	8	4	0	0	5	0
Biserta, P	.200	75	10	15	5	0	2	12	0
Davis, K	.262	65	9	17	3	0	0	6	1
Dombrowski, B	.154	13	2	2	0	0	0	0	0
Fontaine, C	.235	102	20	24	4	1	1	15	4
Gossage, T	.191	94	16	18	5	0	3	11	1
Jackson, B	.255	51	8	13	2	1	0	3	0
LaMotta, K	.200	75	13	15	2	0	2	9	3
Martinez, J	.318	173	37	55	14	2	8	26	8
Matera, P	.292	202	32	59	15	0	2	32	7
McGee, E	.276	152	26	42	6	0	10	23	1
Nichols, B	.414	29	4	12	2	0	1	5	0
Raines Jr., T	.294	286	55	84	13	3	9	48	20
Reynolds, B	.232	263	41	61	11	3	13	36	11
Santiesteban, D	.326	362	61	118	26	8	13	74	13
Stewart, C	.281	57	12	16	4	0	4	10	2
Swenson, A	.333	3	0	1	0	0	0	0	0
Toth, J	.222	54	6	12	2	1	1	8	0
Walsh, R	.292	216	33	63	11	0	5	34	3
Ward, D	.312	218	40	68	16	1	12	51	5
Watson, B	.323	371	63	120	8	1	6	41	22
Young, B	.375	8	0	3	0	0	1	0	0

PLAYER	W	L	ERA	G	SV	IP	H	BB	SO
Eden, E	4	2	5.80	13	0	45	66	20	21
Estrada, J	3	6	7.02	13	0	68	92	33	48
Fitton, M	0	1	3.43	29	0	45	40	19	31
Gabel, A	0	0	18.47	3	0	6	13	5	2
Gaynor, C	5	4	4.70	13	0	75	87	16	34
Gonzalez, V	0	4	7.64	13	1	33	35	32	24
Hose, T	0	3	3.00	28	0	42	32	14	45
Jachno, K	0	0	54.00	2	0	0	0	4	0
Jennings, D	0	1	27.00	2	0	1	0	4	1
Kalb, A	1	2	5.55	5	0	24	25	12	17
Lane, G	1	0	5.11	9	0	25	39	10	12
Lobban, R	1	0	4.91	2	0	11	10	4	6
Marcotte, T	0	1	11.57	2	0	7	11	5	2
Mehlich, M	1	4	3.29	38	13	38	36	22	29
Morrison, K	3	4	6.02	28	1	55	59	34	67
Nivar, R	0	0	6.75	1	0	4	6	1	2
Parker, B	0	3	3.33	5	0	27	32	6	22
Pluta, A	2	2	3.63	24	1	40	37	27	39
Pluta, A	2	2	4.50	10	0	18	19	2	11
Pontius, M	0	0	0.00	1	0	1	0	2	0
Rivera, P	0	2	11.85	5	0	14	23	12	8
Rollins, C	3	2	3.72	25	0	39	30	23	30
Smith, A	10	3	3.39	19	0	112	103	52	56
Snyder, K	0	0	3.86	6	0	5	7	2	6
Vasami, C	3	3	9.17	8	0	36	58	26	33
Wild, J	2	5	5.40	5	0	30	27	10	18
Yawger, A	0	0	10.80	2	0	3	7	1	0

PITTSFIELD COLONIALS

PLAYER	AVG	AB	R	H	2B	3B	HR	RBI	SB
Beauregard, Keith	.182	33	6	6	0	0	2	6	0
Bomback, D	.355	341	62	121	32	4	5	47	26
Cabreja, R	.185	92	5	17	4	1	0	5	0
Davis, Q	.264	242	39	64	9	0	1	23	19
Edmondson, Jerod	.315	365	76	115	28	3	17	61	23
Fatse, P	.279	251	43	70	12	4	5	41	17
Knazek, S	.252	246	28	62	9	2	6	45	6
Lomack, Jermel	.253	95	16	24	2	0	0	6	10
Molina, Angel	.308	341	56	105	21	2	5	78	12
Mottram, B	.313	320	74	100	22	10	12	62	26
Nandin, Matt	.241	166	29	40	10	0	1	15	12
Pagliarulo, Charlie	.120	25	0	3	0	0	0	1	0
Torres, Chris	.289	187	24	54	10	1	4	30	0
Welch, J	.302	252	55	76	14	2	15	45	7

PLAYER	W	L	ERA	G	SV	IP	H	BB	SO
Cevette, Daniel	0	0	7.36	2	0	7.1	10	10	10
Flores, Miguel	4	9	4.06	18	0	115.1	111	44	110
Garner, Brandon	0	0	7.71	7	0	7	6	8	6
Ibanez, Yosandy	1	1	7.02	12	0	16.2	20	6	16
Katzman, Eric	0	1	14.85	3	0	6.2	7	12	7
King, MacKenzie	2	3	7.42	15	1	47.1	61	20	33
Lluberes, Rafael	1	0	4.86	14	3	16.2	11	10	13
Lyons, Matt	1	1	4.82	11	4	9.1	10	5	13
Moran, P	11	3	3.56	16	0	106.1	119	25	79
Paronto, Chad	9	7	3.8	17	0	118.1	132	25	79
Qualben, David	7	7	3.91	18	0	119.2	137	35	70
Rubio, Chris	1	1	2.86	18	3	28.1	19	7	20
Stronach, Tim	4	2	3.38	9	0	37.1	36	17	35
Torres, C	0	0	8.10	6	0	6.2	10	1	2
Wink, T	5	2	2.56	22	1	59.2	50	28	48
Zenko, M	6	2	1.61	34	7	50.1	40	16	53

QUEBEC CAPITALES

PLAYER	AVG	AB	R	H	2B	3B	HR	RBI	SB
Barbero, D	.264	53	10	14	3	0	0	10	0
Blazynski, M	.360	25	5	9	2	0	0	3	0
Boucher, S	.326	304	54	99	12	1	6	55	21
Colafemina, J	.271	133	22	36	4	1	1	16	11
DAoust, P	.244	254	40	62	22	1	5	33	5
Delaney, M	.248	141	24	35	3	0	4	15	1
Gorang, B	.241	83	10	20	3	0	0	9	2
Helps, J	.269	216	38	58	2	2	0	23	6
Henry, S	.257	307	54	79	16	1	8	39	20
Laforest, P	.268	220	34	59	13	0	6	44	2
Leveret, R	.292	295	58	86	10	0	12	55	2
Naccarata, I	.393	61	10	24	5	0	1	10	2
Thompson, M	.289	149	19	43	11	0	1	21	0
Tomlinson, G	.242	359	57	87	24	1	2	53	25
Vallieres, M	.193	57	6	11	2	1	1	10	0
Wagner, R	.256	313	53	80	16	3	13	59	5

PLAYER	W	L	ERA	G	SV	IP	H	BB	SO
Bobo, D	3	1	3.06	36	1	35	27	15	30
DiPietro, R	2	0	0.00	2	0	14	7	1	9
Duda, J	6	0	1.53	31	1	53	44	15	48
Duguay, G	5	1	2.61	27	0	48	38	8	35
Gelinas, K	8	6	3.49	16	0	106	107	19	87
Mariotti, J	11	1	2.74	18	0	108	103	20	70
Oliveros, R	3	3	4.86	32	0	33	31	5	23
Poirier, M	1	0	13.50	3	0	3	4	2	1
Rembisz, B	9	1	2.56	17	0	106	94	31	52
Ricard, J	0	0	3.09	3	0	12	14	2	7
Rusch, M	6	4	2.99	15	0	102	88	15	84
Sausville, D	6	5	6.19	21	1	96	116	38	65
St-Gelais, A	0	0	0.00	1	0	2	0	2	2
Stanton, T	3	1	3.57	32	15	35	27	9	36
Sullivan, A	1	3	4.26	23	2	25	22	12	24

ROCKLAND BOULDERS

PLAYER	AVG	AB	R	H	2B	3B	HR	RBI	SB
Benitez, D	.132	38	2	5	2	0	0	3	3
Buttler, V	.271	118	22	32	7	2	3	20	6
Candelier, J	.091	22	2	2	0	0	0	3	0
Clement, S	.275	131	12	36	5	0	1	19	0

PLAYER	AVG	AB	R	H	2B	3B	HR	RBI	SB
Duesler, C	.105	19	1	2	1	0	0	0	0
Fitzpatrick, J	.214	28	2	6	2	0	1	6	1
Flynn, E	.167	60	6	10	3	0	0	9	3
Giles, T	.272	136	19	37	8	0	5	27	1
Hage, J	.162	74	9	12	5	0	2	11	0
Hill, M	.267	15	3	4	2	0	0	2	0
Hunt, B	.237	59	7	14	0	1	0	1	4
Hutchins, N	.295	224	36	66	16	1	7	37	1
Jennings, T	.266	79	6	21	3	1	0	11	2
Johnson, G	.176	17	1	3	0	0	1	2	0
Kraft, C	.281	160	22	45	6	2	3	26	4
Lomack, J	.226	124	22	28	2	1	1	6	16
Mollica, R	.301	312	42	94	19	1	10	52	1
Richard, M	.291	151	27	44	5	0	0	8	12
Rodriguez, R	.267	187	23	50	10	0	4	27	10
Santana, C	.281	256	37	72	9	2	1	31	1
Slayden, J	.303	178	24	54	7	1	5	28	0
Smith, D	.195	41	6	8	1	0	0	2	1
Smith, S	.274	164	35	45	10	3	4	28	12
Stokes, R	.268	183	40	49	8	1	3	18	23
Weems, C	.208	106	11	22	3	0	1	7	0
Wesson, B	.282	124	16	35	6	0	5	13	1

PLAYER	W	L	ERA	G	SV	IP	H	BB	SO
Blevins, B	6	8	3.99	19	0	131	125	28	82
Carroll, B	1	0	5.27	37	0	43	57	19	31
Coffey, D	1	0	8.53	4	0	6	8	11	6
Fry, J	0	1	6.25	22	0	40	49	29	47
Gardner, M	1	4	6.27	19	0	19	23	12	18
Hassett, W	4	3	5.19	10	0	50	57	27	33
Hodges, C	3	7	6.36	25	1	81	103	21	49
Hutchins, N	0	0	9.00	1	0	1	2	1	0
Knippschild, R	2	5	6.40	9	0	51	71	17	28
Lincoln, R	1	5	7.10	8	0	46	57	14	30
Martin, A	5	2	2.06	39	22	44	45	4	39
Muller, J	4	6	6.87	18	0	75	96	45	62
Ottman, J	0	0	17.36	3	0	5	11	2	2
Shepard, J	1	1	6.86	22	0	21	26	11	19
Velasquez, J	8	6	4.20	19	0	124	122	45	109
Weems, C	0	0	27.00	2	0	1	2	2	0
Wilson, K	1	3	5.79	14	0	14	18	14	12
Worthington, K	2	1	8.61	21	0	23	24	10	29

WORCESTER TORNADOES

PLAYER	AVG	AB	R	H	2B	3B	HR	RBI	SB
Blanchard, B	.221	86	10	19	4	0	2	11	1
Colabello, Chris	.348	365	75	127	32	0	20	79	1
Crespi, R	.267	273	42	73	10	2	3	27	4
Fabry, J	.130	23	0	3	0	0	0	0	0
Fernandez, A	.230	61	5	14	5	0	1	6	0
Fontaine, C	.216	37	6	8	3	0	1	8	2
Kelliher, B	.261	92	12	24	4	0	1	11	0
Minicozzi, M	.328	323	60	106	18	0	15	77	1
Monger, Cameron	.336	214	40	72	6	5	4	34	14
Nunez, A	.271	314	67	85	19	0	5	34	4
Nunez, A	.308	318	61	98	18	3	2	45	22
O'Neil, C	.095	21	0	2	0	0	0	0	0
Patane, T	.222	198	17	44	5	0	2	20	2
Salotti, N	.298	326	61	97	19	0	23	74	1
Sosnoskie, A	.259	81	9	21	2	1	3	4	0
Trezza, A	.289	315	57	91	20	4	16	57	5

PLAYER	W	L	ERA	G	SV	IP	H	BB	SO
Allen, C	0	2	30.38	2	0	3	11	2	2
Asadoorian, R	1	4	5.16	31	11	30	28	16	32
Ayala, A	1	6	2.93	41	5	40	39	20	42
Bicondoa, R	7	1	3.01	14	0	90	97	20	82
Cooper, K	5	5	5.35	22	0	76	91	33	74
Gedman, M	2	1	5.71	27	0	35	43	19	28
Gilblair, S	6	7	4.37	19	0	111	113	29	98
Goldbranson, S	0	0	0.00	2	0	2	1	1	1
Gregory, S	0	2	3.97	32	0	34	38	17	26
Keeler, S	1	0	4.77	7	0	17	20	7	18
Lobban, R	3	2	4.19	10	0	43	56	19	44
McDonald, M	1	1	4.99	23	0	43	62	16	31
Mullen, M	1	0	3.86	4	0	5	5	1	3
Pacella, J	1	1	9.00	5	0	7	7	2	7
Pardo, L	0	1	6.00	2	0	9	17	3	10

PLAYER	W	L	ERA	G	SV	IP	H	BB	SO
Patane, T	0	0	0.00	1	0	1	1	0	0
Serino, N	3	5	2.46	35	2	62	49	24	73
Smith, M	1	1	7.52	6	0	26	34	16	18
Sosnoskie, A	0	0	12.00	2	0	3	3	1	3
Walfield, R	1	0	3.48	9	0	10	9	6	2
Zuercher, Z	14	5	3.70	20	0	126	112	29	110

FRONTIER LEAGUE

Over the last couple of seasons, the Frontier League has become bigger by adding new markets, and older by tweaking its eligibility rules.

Along the way, it has also become more talented, as scouts and other observers agree that the league has narrowed much of the gap that used to separate it from the older rosters of other independent leagues.

No one had more of that talent in 2011 than the River City Rascals. Steve Brook's club dominated the regular season, led by league MVP Stephen Holdren and pitcher of the year Josh Lowey.

But in the playoffs, the Rascals were upended by Joliet in the championship series. The Jackhammers beat Lowey in Game Two, then got great relief work in the final two games as the Jackhammers bullpen allowed one earned run in nine innings. Reliever Brian Smith picked up back-to-back wins, while all-star reliever Ryan Quigley finished out the clincher by getting Holdren to ground out to end the game.

STANDINGS

EASTERN DIVISION	W	L	PCT	GB
Joliet	56	40	.583	—
*Lake Erie	51	44	.537	4.5
Traverse City	51	45	.531	5
Windy City	48	48	.500	8
Washington	42	53	.442	13.5
Rockford	37	59	.385	19

WESTERN DIVISION	W	L	PCT	GB
River City	68	27	.716	—
*Southern Illinois	58	38	.604	10.5
Normal	46	50	.479	22.5
Gateway	39	56	.411	29
Evansville	39	57	.406	29.5
Florence	39	57	.406	29.5

*Wild card

PLAYOFFS: Semifinals—Joliet defeated Lake Erie 3-0 and River City defeated Southern Illinois 3-1 in best-of-five series. **Finals:** Joliet defeated River City 3-1 in best-of-five series.

ATTENDANCE: Southern Illinois 181,576, Traverse City 169,739, Gateway 166,072, Lake Erie 128,628, Normal 114,917, Joliet 108,610, Washington 104,635, Evansville 97,937, Rockford 97,678, Windy City 86,727, Florence 83,436, River City 71,958.

MANAGERS: Evansville—Andy McCauley. **Florence**—Fran Riordan. **Gateway**—Phil Warren. **Joliet**—Bart Zeller. **Lake Erie**—John Massarelli. **Normal**—Hal Lanier. **River City**—Steve Brook. **Rockford**—Richard Austin. **Southern Illinois**—Mike Pinto. **Traverse City**—Gregg Langbehn. **Washington**—Darin Everson. **Windy City**—Mike Kashirsky.

ALL-STAR TEAM

C—Landon Hernandez, Gateway. **1B**—Logan Parker, River City. **2B**—Will Block, Southern Illinois. **3B**—Chris Curley, Florence. **SS**—Andrew Davis, Lake Erie. **OF**—Stephen Holdren, River City; J.T. Hall, Traverse City; Alvaro Ramirez, Normal. **DH**—Charlie Lisk, Gateway. **SP**—Josh Lowey, River City. **RP**—Ryan Quigley, Joliet. **Most Valuable Player:** Stephen Holdren, River City. **Pitcher of the Year:** Josh Lowey, River City. **Manager of the Year**—Bart Zeller, Joliet.

EVANSVILLE OTTERS

PLAYER	AVG	AB	R	H	2B	3B	HR	RBI	SB
Alexander, G	.277	325	42	90	21	2	8	53	13
Britton, P	.262	168	19	44	11	0	2	15	10
Burns, G	.260	73	11	19	4	1	2	12	4

PLAYER	AVG	AB	R	H	2B	3B	HR	RBI	SB
Caseres, S	.226	208	16	47	16	0	5	40	0
Chamberlain, B	.258	97	10	25	3	0	6	6	0
Durant, M	.282	103	22	29	6	0	6	17	0
Ebert, N	.167	42	2	7	1	0	0	4	0
Foltz, A	.262	206	29	54	6	0	1	11	12
Fontenot, G	.257	218	28	56	8	1	0	20	13
Frazier, T	.250	212	38	53	13	1	3	25	0
Hernandez, J	.348	132	26	46	10	2	5	22	2
Jordan, J	.215	65	5	14	3	0	1	6	0
Kam, S	.000	4	0	0	0	0	0	0	0
Killian, B	.299	77	10	23	4	0	0	9	1
Killian, D	.314	51	5	16	5	0	1	5	0
Mintken, K	.236	89	12	21	4	1	1	11	5
Rahier, B	.200	10	3	2	0	0	0	2	0
Salem, C	.245	49	5	12	0	0	5	13	0
Scarduzio, V	.221	77	10	17	4	0	2	8	0
Sequeira, P	.228	101	12	23	1	1	1	7	0
Spiers, J	.323	300	46	97	11	3	5	40	50
Still, R	.239	234	50	56	4	0	4	21	14
Waltenbury, J	.245	53	7	13	5	0	0	7	0
Walton, J	.298	265	36	79	11	2	10	41	10

PLAYER	W	L	ERA	G	SV	IP	H	BB	SO
Anton, M	0	4	7.23	5	0	23.2	28	17	28
Bagley, J	0	0	0.00	1	0	2	0	1	0
Barry, K	4	7	5.11	21	0	104	117	44	71
Britton, P	0	0	0.00	1	0	1	1	0	0
Cephas, J	4	3	3.46	33	0	41.2	39	28	43
Crider, B	4	3	4.46	55	0	36.1	33	21	37
Eastham, K	0	4	7.18	7	0	31.1	37	18	20
Erwin, D	0	1	4.50	12	0	12	13	5	6
Francis, D	0	3	7.33	10	0	23.1	28	19	15
Jordan, J	1	0	6.31	14	0	25.2	30	13	18
Kelley, S	6	6	5.64	21	0	99	86	76	104
Kitchens, W	0	2	6.75	6	0	14.2	20	14	17
LaMar, T	0	0	6.35	5	0	5.2	10	3	1
Marcacci, D	6	3	4.48	20	0	92.1	108	26	55
Massingham, E	2	3	1.38	38	22	45.2	30	16	47
McKeown, S	0	0	10.80	1	0	1.2	2	1	3
Morris, R	0	1	11.57	1	0	4.2	5	7	4
Odom, J	1	1	5.56	16	0	11.1	10	10	15
Purcell, R	0	1	6.00	16	0	15	18	9	12
Ritchie, B	0	1	10.80	5	0	5	10	2	6
Satriano, J	3	2	7.34	17	1	34.1	34	18	24
Thorne, J	2	7	5.82	12	0	65	90	18	41
Trent, M	1	2	7.94	9	0	39.2	45	25	33
Trudell, C	0	0	3.60	8	0	10	6	9	18
Willinsky, M	1	0	0.71	12	3	12.2	8	4	15
Wisniewski, A	2	1	4.24	31	0	34	39	8	35
Zielinski, M	2	2	3.30	7	0	43.2	42	13	28

FLORENCE FREEDOM

PLAYER	AVG	AB	R	H	2B	3B	HR	RBI	SB
Arrojo, J	.239	247	43	59	12	1	1	20	13
Baker, J	.241	133	23	32	7	3	5	24	0
Campbell, M	.077	13	1	1	0	0	0	0	0
Cisneros, J	.256	129	13	33	5	0	1	17	0
Curley, C	.292	383	60	112	25	0	14	66	20
Dombrowski, B	.000	7	0	0	0	0	0	0	0
Dunbar, J	.225	111	10	25	3	0	2	15	0
Frierson, J	.219	114	9	25	5	0	4	12	5
Haas, K	.257	214	28	55	11	1	3	18	3
Holloway, K	.236	148	22	35	5	0	3	19	3
Holmes, W	.270	100	7	27	5	0	1	18	0
Malloy, J	.272	180	23	49	9	3	3	23	8
Martinez, F	.143	21	2	3	0	0	0	2	3
Miles, C	.308	302	54	93	12	9	2	30	40
Rundle, D	.188	298	44	56	9	3	9	42	12
Samuelson, M	.252	107	22	27	2	0	4	11	0
Sheppard, J	.000	3	0	0	0	0	0	0	0
Shults, S	.200	250	30	50	10	0	13	46	3
Smith, J	.203	79	9	16	3	0	2	6	4
Valdes, J	.240	341	52	82	22	0	7	43	10

PLAYER	W	L	ERA	G	SV	IP	H	BB	SO
Asselin, K	0	1	6.94	4	0	11.2	19	5	8
Bello, A	3	8	4.24	17	0	99.2	116	44	50
Bridgewater, A	2	1	5.68	16	1	12.2	14	10	7

PLAYER	W	L	ERA	G	SV	IP	H	BB	SO
Cann, A	0	2	6.10	9	0	10.1	8	11	7
Carr, M	0	0	16.88	3	0	5.1	9	6	1
Chilcoat, A	0	0	15.00	3	0	3	3	2	1
Clark, A	10	5	3.73	20	0	125.1	119	33	101
Engle, Z	2	2	5.40	24	1	33.1	34	8	29
Frost, J	0	5	5.57	14	0	42	44	18	19
Hanley, M	0	0	2.57	23	0	35	27	19	29
Holmes, T	4	8	4.47	21	0	92.2	101	20	38
Ingoglia, C	4	4	4.33	11	0	62.1	70	14	44
Junker, S	0	1	9.00	1	0	5	9	1	1
Lewis, A	4	7	3.21	19	0	89.2	75	31	76
MacFarland, S	3	0	4.50	8	0	12	6	18	13
Martin, C	2	3	5.04	25	10	25	20	13	21
Mathes, B	1	2	2.54	20	5	28.1	23	12	27
Painter, A	0	1	6.08	8	0	13.1	16	10	8
Robinson, C	2	3	5.45	34	0	34.2	31	19	35
Tarallo, J	0	0	3.00	14	0	15	17	4	8
Tullis, J	1	1	4.13	24	0	32.2	27	23	22
Vancil, P	1	3	6.91	11	0	41.2	62	20	35
Walden, C	0	0	11.25	1	0	4	7	2	1

GATEWAY GRIZZLIES

PLAYER	AVG	AB	R	H	2B	3B	HR	RBI	SB
Agreste, J	.291	378	50	110	24	3	11	70	6
Aldaz, J	.170	88	11	15	5	0	2	13	0
Barnes, J	.103	29	2	3	0	0	0	0	3
Bloom, E	1.000	1	0	1	0	0	0	1	0
Button, E	.304	23	4	7	1	0	2	6	1
Cresswell, J	.200	85	12	17	2	0	1	10	1
Farnsworth, N	.135	52	5	7	0	0	2	6	0
Fitzgerald, D	.301	123	25	37	5	3	2	11	4
Gerst, K	.228	149	25	34	7	2	10	25	6
Harris, B	.211	171	27	36	5	0	3	18	1
Hart, J	.212	85	12	18	3	0	3	10	4
Heil, T	.225	191	33	43	7	0	1	13	9
Hernandez, L	.250	308	54	77	19	1	18	46	0
Jennings, D	.247	81	23	20	4	0	0	9	4
Khoury, R	.320	103	25	33	6	0	5	16	1
Lisk, C	.295	363	65	107	23	4	24	94	5
Parker, L	.355	245	52	87	22	3	11	61	9
Patton, J	.255	102	9	26	3	1	1	11	1
Peters, B	.231	242	36	56	11	0	4	37	2
Phillips, D	.239	71	7	17	3	0	0	7	0
Reed, T	.180	50	4	9	0	0	0	2	0
Rigby, C	.354	99	10	35	7	0	0	9	1
Salters, C	.257	70	13	18	5	0	2	7	4
Sedon, C	.217	143	17	31	6	1	2	11	7

PLAYER	W	L	ERA	G	SV	IP	H	BB	SO
Attard, J	1	1	7.30	9	0	12.1	15	8	7
Barber, B	4	3	4.92	10	0	60.1	56	26	44
Barrett, R	4	4	3.60	32	0	40	35	16	39
Boling, J	1	1	4.40	20	0	28.2	37	18	23
Brackman, M	7	5	2.15	15	0	100.1	92	23	78
Buehler, B	0	0	45.00	2	0	1	5	4	1
Cabral, R	1	1	6.97	7	0	10.1	16	7	9
Caceres Jr., A	2	2	6.15	7	0	33.2	37	26	16
Carillo, E	1	2	4.55	5	0	27.2	25	10	20
Combs, T	0	0	8.44	3	0	5.1	8	6	4
Cudney, J	1	1	2.67	18	0	27	24	12	32
Dail, B	1	3	5.93	5	0	27.1	31	16	18
Davis, J	0	0	10.13	3	0	13.1	20	9	8
Davisson, C	2	3	3.46	16	0	52	49	21	24
Donze, J	0	1	6.10	6	0	20.2	20	19	10
Enourato, C	0	4	3.77	39	11	45.1	40	23	45
Garza, A	2	3	11.41	9	0	23.2	33	12	13
Heil, T	0	0	2.25	5	0	8	6	6	7
Juarez, J	4	4	5.22	11	0	50	52	23	25
Nading, C	0	0	21.94	7	0	5.1	10	10	5
Phillips, B	0	0	11.57	4	0	7	13	5	7
Shafer, B	2	0	0.61	2	0	14.2	10	4	17
Shafer, J	0	0	8.74	11	1	11.1	11	10	11
Shaffer, N	0	1	7.20	7	0	20	24	10	17
Shutt, J	0	0	0.00	1	0	0.2	0	0	0
Stone, B	2	9	6.99	14	0	83.2	112	32	58
Toler, S	0	3	7.04	8	0	23	32	13	20
Tremlin, P	0	0	4.08	10	1	17.2	18	4	11

	2	1	2.81	39	1	41.2	20	48	54
Walters, N	2	1	2.81	39	1	41.2	20	48	54
Whitlock, J	2	3	6.75	6	0	28	32	18	33

JOLIET SLAMMERS

PLAYER	AVG	AB	R	H	2B	3B	HR	RBI	SB
Adeyemi, T	.209	43	6	9	0	1	0	3	0
Chenworth, R	.244	78	11	19	6	0	2	15	0
Creal, T	.286	7	2	2	0	0	0	1	2
Estand, S	.260	288	41	75	15	1	1	28	0
Ferrell, B	.157	70	10	11	0	0	1	5	1
Flores, J	.289	308	67	89	16	6	12	38	35
Fox, D	.278	216	22	60	8	1	7	45	4
Gutierrez, Y	.220	41	8	9	1	0	2	5	1
Hewett, B	.261	161	19	42	3	0	0	18	4
Kasarjian, K	.263	99	10	26	7	0	0	7	4
Leeper, B	.292	236	40	69	11	5	6	30	12
Lis, E	.302	344	51	104	17	1	20	77	0
Lopez, P	.043	23	0	1	0	0	0	0	0
Manz, T	.298	114	12	34	9	1	1	15	3
Maunus, K	.259	316	62	82	17	0	15	56	3
Netzel, B	.277	354	47	98	15	2	3	40	7
Ochoa, N	.205	44	5	9	2	0	2	7	0
Pellot, H	.319	226	41	72	16	1	4	29	10
Peters, B	.217	60	6	13	2	0	0	5	3
Rubin, L	.180	61	6	11	1	1	0	4	1
Shepherd, D	.231	39	4	9	2	0	2	8	0
Wagle, J	.161	56	9	9	1	1	1	5	1
Walters, B	.250	12	1	3	1	0	0	3	0

PLAYER	W	L	ERA	G	SV	IP	H	BB	SO
Crimmel, K	7	5	5.33	21	0	79.1	91	33	68
Deain, A	0	0	7.20	5	0	5	5	0	2
Dott, A	1	0	0.00	11	1	11.1	4	5	16
Fowler, B	4	3	3.08	9	1	52.2	43	23	30
Garner, B	0	0	45.00	1	0	1	2	1	1
Jarvis, J	1	2	5.40	6	0	35	39	16	26
Kriech, K	0	1	3.72	8	0	9.2	14	4	7
Leeper, B	0	0	0.00	1	0	1	1	1	0
Lukanen, C	4	2	3.91	44	1	48.1	40	28	48
Manz, T	0	0	4.50	1	0	2	3	0	1
Mendoza, T	6	2	4.00	12	0	65.1	68	20	44
Miller, R	2	3	4.53	10	0	51.2	46	32	36
Moss, A	5	6	4.86	16	0	87	74	50	59
Pack, C	0	0	4.61	22	0	27.1	27	17	22
Petrick, B	4	7	5.06	28	0	89	103	31	64
Quigley, R	1	3	2.32	43	28	42.2	31	25	72
Renshaw, J	13	4	3.09	19	0	128	105	40	90
Smith, B	1	1	1.24	40	2	43.2	28	4	31
Tietze, J	7	1	4.61	32	1	56.2	59	32	31

LAKE ERIE CRUSHERS

PLAYER	AVG	AB	R	H	2B	3B	HR	RBI	SB
Baumet, T	.333	12	2	4	1	0	0	1	0
Boe, K	.217	83	9	18	6	0	1	8	4
Collins, J	.273	172	17	47	10	0	2	25	1
Davis, A	.339	363	48	123	39	3	12	87	1
Erie, B	.337	89	11	30	5	0	0	15	2
Fontaine, C	.188	16	5	3	1	0	0	1	0
Gliebe, A	.176	51	6	9	3	0	0	6	0
Houin, S	.286	112	18	32	6	3	2	16	2
Kulbacki, K	.269	334	41	90	16	2	6	37	1
Kuzdale, R	.265	102	17	27	5	1	0	5	6
Luick, C	.214	168	20	36	4	2	1	22	3
Mahin, N	.269	182	20	49	9	1	0	18	0
Martinez, F	.182	11	1	2	0	0	0	0	1
Messer, Z	.184	196	25	36	3	1	0	9	5
Milons, J	.251	183	43	46	9	1	1	15	10
Norris, P	.256	324	45	83	10	7	1	35	19
Rivera, J	.252	210	30	53	7	4	3	20	5
Shaffer, K	.220	164	19	36	6	0	5	22	1
Sharpley, E	.221	95	15	21	2	1	1	9	2
Taylor, J	.275	164	19	45	8	1	6	42	17

PLAYER	W	L	ERA	G	SV	IP	H	BB	SO
Allen, C	4	2	1.42	30	2	44.1	38	11	37
Berger, A	0	0	4.66	7	0	9.2	7	6	9
Campbell, T	3	1	2.75	11	0	55.2	30	24	37
Cinadr, J	0	1	12.27	7	0	7.1	12	7	6

	W	L	ERA	G	SV	IP	H	BB	SO
Cuevas, J	1	2	7.17	5	0	21.1	26	5	13
Curry, N	0	0	67.50	1	0	0.2	7	1	0
Daniels, P	5	2	2.31	28	0	46.2	44	14	30
Davis, A	0	0	0.00	1	0	1	0	0	1
Fagan, P	7	11	4.30	22	0	127.2	117	41	89
Flores, R	2	3	2.24	45	21	56.1	30	23	77
Gonzalez-Diaz, E	4	1	3.11	6	0	37.2	31	8	28
Hendrix, G	0	2	4.66	10	0	19.1	20	10	18
Mountain, B	0	0	8.59	5	0	7.1	14	4	7
Risser, T	3	5	3.32	35	6	76	77	20	51
Roberts, J	10	6	3.97	23	0	143	141	35	95
Schellenberg, K	3	2	1.92	39	3	51.2	40	9	27
Sturgill, R	6	1	3.33	16	0	54	52	17	30
Weeks, A	3	3	5.26	13	0	63.1	81	15	31
Wendizki, K	0	1	9.00	1	0	4	4	3	2
Wendziki, R	0	1	6.32	10	0	15.2	16	4	10

NORMAL CORNBELTERS

PLAYER	AVG	AB	R	H	2B	3B	HR	RBI	SB
Agustin, B	.215	93	13	20	6	0	0	7	2
Alexander, S	.257	381	58	98	25	0	22	72	1
Barbaro, A	.250	92	13	23	4	1	4	11	0
Brown, C	.129	31	4	4	1	0	0	2	0
Cox, D	.225	338	50	76	8	1	11	60	3
DeMarco, G	.143	7	4	1	0	0	0	1	0
Dunbar, J	.209	187	22	39	12	0	3	17	0
Keeble, T	.271	229	34	62	13	1	0	27	7
Mansilla, M	.059	17	1	1	0	0	0	1	1
Martinez, F	.305	374	80	114	25	4	14	65	12
McNeely, T	.243	70	13	17	1	0	2	8	1
Miller, A	.196	102	9	20	3	0	1	10	0
Mobbs, M	.288	257	36	74	17	1	7	35	11
Moro, L	.225	138	20	31	4	0	4	18	1
Newton, B	.302	139	23	42	7	1	3	17	8
Ramirez, A	.328	378	65	124	24	7	2	43	23
Sakaguchi, K	.000	9	0	0	0	0	0	0	0
Samuelson, M	.287	87	10	25	1	0	1	12	0
Shah, A	.331	359	50	119	26	1	11	63	0
White, A	.186	43	7	8	1	0	0	1	0

PLAYER	W	L	ERA	G	SV	IP	H	BB	SO
Berger, J	3	2	7.17	8	0	42.2	62	13	33
Brewer, J	0	3	5.03	15	1	19.2	24	9	16
Click, M	0	0	0.00	1	0	0.1	0	0	0
Click, M	1	1	3.79	19	0	40.1	38	12	37
Dunbar, J	0	0	0.00	1	0	0.1	0	0	0
Furrow, D	1	2	3.31	20	2	35.1	40	18	27
Lavigne, T	7	9	3.17	21	0	133.2	120	70	115
Lester, B	4	5	5.31	14	0	76.1	80	51	36
Liedka, J	2	3	3.83	30	2	42.1	41	21	32
Mee, A	2	2	5.30	12	0	18.2	18	3	20
Morrison, W	0	0	6.23	5	0	8.2	7	10	7
Mossey, M	1	5	4.86	11	0	66.2	82	22	45
Ohlmann, L	2	2	5.28	21	2	30.2	30	18	41
Parinar, G	0	0	16.20	2	0	1.2	1	5	0
Paxton, B	1	3	3.28	18	0	24.2	27	12	10
Pritchett, B	9	5	3.57	19	0	123.2	110	45	109
Schuler, M	1	2	1.74	36	12	46.2	42	16	37
Sheldon, R	12	5	2.82	21	0	140.2	115	39	134
Smith, J	0	1	13.50	2	0	1.1	3	2	1

RIVER CITY RASCALS

PLAYER	AVG	AB	R	H	2B	3B	HR	RBI	SB
Banda, J	.176	17	3	3	0	0	1	2	0
Brodin, J	.300	343	71	103	25	0	14	66	19
Burk, B	.272	342	55	93	16	1	17	58	6
Carr, J	.250	32	4	8	0	0	1	5	0
DeBiasse, N	.000	3	0	0	0	0	0	0	0
Farnsworth, N	.140	50	4	7	2	0	0	5	0
Harris, B	.200	65	11	13	1	0	0	5	1
Holdren, S	.332	346	75	115	17	1	21	84	17
Johnson, B	.159	63	12	10	4	0	2	5	7
Long, K	.167	18	1	3	0	0	0	1	0
Maddox, C	.282	355	49	100	17	5	13	56	5
McClendon, C	.332	208	39	69	23	2	4	34	7
Parker, L	.282	103	19	29	5	0	5	25	3
Patton, J	.343	236	33	81	14	1	8	43	13

INDEPENDENT LEAGUES

PLAYER	AVG	AB	R	H	2B	3B	HR	RBI	SB
Sanders, D	.264	330	53	87	12	0	5	41	4
Sawyer, D	.253	281	45	71	17	0	5	36	22
Serna, M	.304	23	6	7	0	1	0	2	2
Weinberg, A	.182	11	2	2	0	0	0	0	0
West, J	.275	.218	45	60	11	2	11	43	11
Williams, E	.289	128	35	37	6	1	0	11	14
Wilson, L	.205	44	6	9	1	0	0	3	0

PLAYER	W	L	ERA	G	SV	IP	H	BB	SO
Arnerich, K	0	1	4.74	6	1	19	20	6	12
Barrett, R	0	0	5.06	7	0	10.2	11	4	11
Burk, B	0	0	0.00	1	0	1	1	1	2
Carillo, E	2	2	7.84	5	0	20.2	29	9	13
Coladonato, M	0	0	9.00	4	0	3	1	6	3
Cunniff, B	4	0	1.54	44	9	46.2	34	24	53
Dewald, M	1	0	5.40	7	0	3.1	4	1	3
Kitchens, W	1	1	5.79	9	0	23.1	18	19	33
Lisi, D	8	2	3.69	17	0	85.1	79	24	57
Lowey, J	11	2	2.44	20	0	129.1	123	46	114
Marsala, T	0	1	16.20	2	0	1.2	2	1	2
Miller, R	3	3	7.02	6	0	16.2	17	8	13
Miramontes, D	9	2	2.21	44	17	53	32	25	68
Moore, K	1	0	9.00	16	0	13	24	7	15
Moran, G	2	0	1.57	3	0	23	15	5	23
Pankau, J	1	0	9.15	13	0	20.2	36	6	20
Rivers, K	5	1	1.72	34	6	36.2	22	20	33
Robertson, Z	9	4	4.50	26	1	88	72	42	77
Rossman, M	0	0	8.38	4	0	9.2	15	2	7
Sterner, Z	10	3	3.04	19	0	124.1	99	44	73
Toler, S	0	2	5.91	11	0	21.1	32	8	16
Umberger, D	3	3	4.52	36	0	61.2	72	19	84
Vancil, P	1	0	4.50	4	0	24	24	8	24
Zink, R	0	0	5.79	1	0	4.2	8	1	4

ROCKFORD RIVERHAWKS

PLAYER	AVG	AB	R	H	2B	3B	HR	RBI	SB
Button, E	.224	107	13	24	4	2	4	11	3
Carrington, J	.059	17	0	1	0	0	0	4	0
Cooper, D	.247	324	54	80	9	3	3	34	42
Curry, C	.198	101	11	20	1	0	0	11	10
DeMarco, G	.289	45	6	13	2	0	0	2	0
Dominguez, C	.239	188	14	45	10	0	1	22	1
Eigsti, J	.340	335	53	114	22	2	12	74	14
Greener, M	.296	338	47	100	24	3	5	43	0
Hamilton, J	.207	174	22	36	12	0	4	22	0
Hur, M	.369	65	11	24	4	0	3	11	1
James, J	.316	98	13	31	5	0	4	17	0
Long, B	.105	19	1	2	0	0	0	1	1
Lopez, C	.077	13	1	1	0	0	0	0	0
Malay, R	.231	91	13	21	5	1	0	6	3
Millan Jr., E	.200	25	5	5	0	0	2	4	1
Parache, L	.282	323	41	91	16	1	8	47	12
Parejo, F	.256	383	63	98	13	2	2	27	24
Perozo, E	.167	6	1	1	0	1	0	0	0
Richter, J	.252	115	18	29	6	3	4	17	1
Satterwhite, C	.204	142	23	29	8	0	6	18	3
Smith, K	.248	117	13	29	5	0	3	13	0
Van Horn, G	.243	144	27	35	5	2	0	14	0

PLAYER	W	L	ERA	G	SV	IP	H	BB	SO
Allen, B	0	0	6.00	14	0	15	24	8	12
Brown, L	0	1	14.21	7	0	6.1	12	11	5
Cadoret, S	0	0	6.30	16	0	10	9	12	4
Durand, B	4	4	1.77	35	16	40.2	27	13	45
Faulkner, S	0	0	9.00	1	0	1	0	3	1
Fonseca, G	2	7	4.91	12	0	66	76	34	41
Frerichs, C	1	1	4.07	24	1	24.1	20	19	13
Garner, B	0	1	5.40	12	1	8.1	3	13	9
Gaudi, N	1	2	6.32	4	0	15.2	16	2	12
Gibbs, M	1	5	11.05	7	0	29.1	51	13	19
Gradney, J	1	2	5.04	20	0	55.1	52	16	35
Hyde, T	1	3	4.91	22	0	22	23	15	8
Kriech, K	0	0	5.16	21	0	22.2	32	9	11
Marsala, T	1	1	3.71	4	0	17	20	5	16
McGee, T	1	1	3.18	8	0	17	16	9	17
Minium, S	0	2	5.63	7	1	8	5	6	8
Nyman, C	2	5	4.50	10	0	50	56	19	25
Osteen, A	0	0	11.12	6	0	5.2	9	6	3

PLAYER	W	L	ERA	G	SV	IP	H	BB	SO
Parker, B	0	4	5.96	4	0	22.2	24	14	12
Patterson, K	2	3	4.81	24	0	43	32	31	38
Reid, S	1	0	7.56	7	0	8.1	15	1	7
Rucinski, D	0	1	31.50	1	0	2	9	1	0
Scarpetta, B	7	6	5.24	25	0	113.1	135	48	54
Scumaci, J	4	4	5.72	15	0	67.2	83	36	43
Smith, R	0	0	2.46	3	0	3.2	4	3	3
Szymanski, A	5	4	4.09	16	0	92.1	81	41	86
Zoltak, M	3	2	6.94	12	0	58.1	69	22	33

SOUTHERN ILLINOIS MINERS

PLAYER	AVG	AB	R	H	2B	3B	HR	RBI	SB
Armenio, A	.182	11	2	2	0	0	0	1	0
Banks, E	.285	137	16	39	10	0	7	23	0
Blanchard, B	.276	199	36	55	6	1	0	16	7
Block, W	.295	295	55	87	24	9	17	57	14
Bullock, T	.197	61	6	12	6	1	0	3	1
Church, E	.100	10	1	1	0	0	0	1	0
Coughlin, S	.242	260	33	63	13	0	11	49	4
Fields, M	.272	224	34	61	11	4	17	45	5
Gregory, K	.325	194	28	63	15	0	1	18	4
Gronkowski, G	.302	106	19	32	7	1	3	21	1
Hall, N	.228	307	37	70	11	3	11	38	2
Harrell, S	.345	194	38	67	10	4	3	21	16
Lester, C	.286	112	18	32	10	1	5	18	3
Manz, T	.222	36	6	8	0	0	1	5	0
Meade, R	.224	58	7	13	3	0	1	6	1
Milons, J	.246	171	22	42	4	2	1	15	13
Randall, J	.260	73	9	19	2	3	0	8	3
Sakaguchi, K	.228	123	14	28	8	0	0	17	1
Suttle, E	.261	329	48	86	15	2	4	41	22
Walton, K	.200	30	3	6	0	0	0	1	0
Wiley, S	.209	110	14	23	5	0	5	11	0
Womack, J	.220	100	19	22	4	3	1	13	8

PLAYER	W	L	ERA	G	SV	IP	H	BB	SO
Augustine, J	3	2	5.40	6	0	28.1	36	11	24
Campbell, I	2	0	3.00	2	0	12	14	1	7
Campbell, T	1	2	2.12	10	0	29.2	29	12	24
Cowsert, C	3	0	0.55	11	2	16.1	9	5	22
Dail, B	0	2	7.79	5	0	17.1	21	14	9
Dill, C	4	1	2.16	25	10	25	21	11	29
Draxton, E	2	3	4.84	41	11	44.2	44	23	51
Harden, D	7	5	2.91	19	0	120.2	109	17	67
Joy, S	6	4	3.92	18	0	105.2	95	26	56
Macy, T	0	0	5.40	2	0	1.2	4	1	2
Malkowski, B	8	3	4.07	16	0	86.1	87	24	38
Manz, T	1	0	0.00	1	0	3	1	2	0
Marshall, J	0	0	20.25	1	0	2.2	5	4	2
Martin, C	0	1	5.40	9	0	8.1	10	1	6
McGraw, R	0	1	2.40	10	0	15	9	14	16
Meade, R	0	0	6.75	3	0	2.2	4	1	1
Quigley, R	6	1	1.68	36	0	48.1	37	19	59
Robichaux, J	0	0	3.00	1	0	3	1	1	1
Shaw, G	1	1	3.51	19	0	33.1	31	5	30
Shivers, B	4	2	3.27	32	4	44	34	14	30
Tarallo, J	0	0	4.91	2	0	3.2	4	4	2
Teague, V	1	2	7.22	8	0	33.2	35	28	10
Tew, D	2	2	5.63	20	1	54.1	66	14	33
Zink, R	7	6	5.33	19	0	109.2	113	32	59

TRAVERSE CITY BEACH BUMS

PLAYER	AVG	AB	R	H	2B	3B	HR	RBI	SB
Baker, J	.154	13	2	2	0	0	1	4	0
Bernal, H	.227	220	30	50	10	5	3	20	3
Brown, M	.299	335	52	100	13	1	2	40	16
Burch, C	.260	308	46	80	13	0	17	55	4
Burns, G	.244	135	21	33	7	3	4	16	11
Codiroli, J	.217	83	15	18	4	1	3	9	3
Flagg, J	.247	223	34	55	12	2	13	31	3
Gebbers, H	.147	34	3	5	1	0	0	4	1
Guerrero, J	.218	110	9	24	8	1	0	15	2
Gusrang, S	.167	6	0	1	0	0	0	0	0
Hall, J	.281	384	59	108	16	4	23	75	21
Kay, C	.169	65	9	11	4	0	1	5	0
Pace, Z	.250	292	53	73	10	3	1	22	12
Parham, J	.257	167	14	43	5	0	1	10	0

PLAYER	AVG	AB	R	H	2B	3B	HR	RBI	SB
Pearl, B	.174	46	6	8	2	0	0	5	3
Peterson, N	.220	41	6	9	3	1	0	6	0
Sharpley, E	.231	78	13	18	2	0	2	7	2
Shults, S	.214	56	9	12	2	0	4	9	0
Vargas, J	.261	368	52	96	28	5	14	63	1
Zebroski, T	.281	210	25	59	15	0	3	25	1

PLAYER	W	L	ERA	G	SV	IP	H	BB	SO
Anderson, J	0	1	5.01	7	0	23.1	27	6	8
Banes, B	10	4	3.07	22	0	117.1	112	40	60
Cinadr, J	2	1	2.81	20	0	32	29	9	26
Codiroli, J	0	0	0.00	1	0	1	1	0	0
Deminsky, D	6	3	3.84	13	0	82	72	23	49
Dunn, S	9	3	2.58	33	1	83.2	75	27	60
Erwin, D	0	0	9.64	4	0	4.2	7	5	2
Gariano, R	2	2	8.59	4	0	14.2	25	5	7
Johnson, D	1	0	1.54	14	0	23.1	17	12	18
Kitchens, W	1	1	5.82	4	0	17	16	14	6
Mazur, J	1	2	8.68	4	0	18.2	25	10	10
Miller, M	1	0	3.08	13	1	26.1	23	8	16
Morrow, B	1	0	6.35	6	0	11.1	11	5	5
Mueller, S	3	3	1.31	44	21	55	41	14	53
Nathanson, D	3	2	4.23	9	0	61.2	68	8	36
Paulun, A	2	2	6.11	6	0	28	30	16	12
Pugliese, D	1	1	3.32	19	0	38	28	29	34
Raraigh, R	0	3	5.57	6	0	21	22	16	13
Reid, S	1	2	2.42	30	1	52	44	19	38
Rodewald, B	0	0	4.32	6	0	16.2	15	9	6
Shaffer, N	5	4	6.75	11	0	42.2	48	18	25
Shelton, S	1	3	6.31	9	0	25.2	24	22	14
Smith, C	0	0	18.90	2	0	3.1	7	3	2
Smith, M	1	6	9.00	7	0	28	33	17	16
Taylor, C	0	0	13.50	1	0	0.2	3	1	1
Thomas, E	0	2	8.03	4	0	12.1	15	10	3

WASHINGTON WILD THINGS

PLAYER	AVG	AB	R	H	2B	3B	HR	RBI	SB
Allaire, S	.222	9	2	2	1	0	0	0	0
Banda, J	.127	63	6	8	1	0	0	1	2
Banks, E	.207	145	15	30	8	0	2	13	1
Battle, T	.221	145	16	32	3	3	1	17	9
Bistagne, B	.000	13	0	0	0	0	0	0	0
Cisneros, J	.167	36	2	6	1	0	1	4	0
Ditthardt, R	.241	187	15	45	12	1	5	23	0
Feiner, K	.211	323	38	68	13	5	2	26	22
Fogle, B	.241	29	2	7	0	0	0	0	0
Harris, E	.227	163	26	37	7	0	8	30	0
Lawson, S	.280	336	52	94	17	1	9	37	16
Morrow, R	.034	29	2	1	0	0	0	1	0
Ochoa, B	.190	247	30	47	11	0	6	27	0
Ontiveros, E	.222	90	10	20	0	0	0	4	0
Perren, B	.245	94	11	23	8	1	0	6	2
Rivera, L	.266	297	32	79	14	0	8	53	21
Rossi, D	.300	40	4	12	1	0	0	6	0
Sidick, C	.287	349	55	100	15	7	9	41	21
Stanton, Z	.148	54	6	8	1	1	0	4	5
Stephens, E	.217	198	22	43	7	1	7	31	4
Thennis, D	.304	286	43	87	23	0	8	33	7

PLAYER	W	L	ERA	G	SV	IP	H	BB	SO
Allaire, S	0	1	5.40	2	0	1.2	5	0	2
Barnes, C	5	5	2.34	13	0	84.2	75	19	51
Barnes, M	0	2	6.35	6	0	17	17	10	19
Bilardello, D	1	2	4.67	27	0	34.2	40	22	26
Cotter, M	0	0	6.35	6	0	5.2	11	9	2
Dupuis, T	0	0	17.18	2	0	3.2	7	4	2
Edwards, J	5	3	2.16	14	0	91.2	64	35	72
Grife, S	3	1	2.36	21	2	26.2	16	16	38
Gusky, R	0	1	3.32	22	1	38	25	22	36
Hall, J	10	7	3.22	20	0	145.1	131	22	104
Hammons, K	4	2	2.62	25	1	34.1	26	23	43
Lee, G	4	6	4.18	16	0	94.2	121	21	44
Mattaliano, M	0	1	5.40	7	0	5	8	2	0
Montoya, J	4	7	3.77	20	0	117	113	51	83
Nuno, V	2	3	2.83	6	0	41.1	35	12	34
Ramsey, J	0	1	15.00	2	0	3	10	2	1
Rossi, D	0	0	5.79	4	0	4.2	3	4	2
Santana, J	0	3	12.00	3	0	9	16	4	2

PLAYER	W	L	ERA	G	SV	IP	H	BB	SO
Smith, C	1	2	4.50	6	0	24	17	12	21
Tarallo, J	0	0	99.99	1	0	0	2	1	0
Thomas, R	0	1	12.27	4	0	3.2	4	6	4
Williams, A	0	0	0.00	3	1	7.2	3	3	8
Williams, M	1	1	7.54	14	0	14.1	15	16	24
Wulf, T	2	4	2.46	33	0	33	27	19	32

WINDY CITY THUNDERBOLTS

PLAYER	AVG	AB	R	H	2B	3B	HR	RBI	SB
Aakhus, Z	.311	318	53	99	20	0	4	64	14
Anderson, B	.287	390	77	112	17	5	1	25	53
Basham, R	.224	165	22	37	9	0	1	19	5
Chavez, N	.244	45	3	11	1	0	0	5	1
Cregar, C	.270	185	23	50	12	0	6	33	0
Del Real, P	.111	18	2	2	0	0	0	2	0
Fitzgerald, D	.190	21	0	4	2	0	0	3	0
Huggins, M	.000	0	0	0	0	0	0	0	0
James, J	.264	72	14	19	4	0	2	8	1
Keeble, T	.275	40	6	11	2	0	0	7	1
Kuroczko, N	.245	237	45	58	9	0	1	24	8
Luquette, Q	.232	95	17	22	2	1	0	4	5
Mahin, N	.170	53	4	9	1	0	0	4	0
Nowlin, B	.280	25	4	7	0	0	1	6	0
Pempek, L	.282	78	17	22	4	1	1	9	1
Porch, C	.233	227	21	53	9	1	1	30	5
Regan, G	.204	54	5	11	4	1	0	7	0
Rubin, L	.264	129	12	34	8	0	2	19	0
Sferra, L	.150	40	1	6	2	0	0	8	2
Shepherd, D	.311	280	38	87	13	4	8	55	5
Swinford, D	.000	8	2	0	0	0	0	0	0
Torres, M	.322	348	62	112	14	2	2	45	35
Wade, C	.253	300	36	76	18	2	2	28	8
Womack, J	.158	38	5	6	0	0	0	3	2

PLAYER	W	L	ERA	G	SV	IP	H	BB	SO
Alsup, W	1	2	4.24	38	8	34	31	22	61
Blanks, B	0	1	4.32	9	5	8.1	5	1	13
Costello, M	4	6	4.39	33	1	65.2	73	22	47
Cotton, B	6	10	4.85	21	0	115	136	37	92
Curry, N	0	0	3.86	1	0	2.1	1	0	3
Durand, B	0	0	5.25	10	3	12	13	2	13
Fonseca, G	1	4	4.03	8	0	44.2	35	18	37
Frymier, K	2	0	5.51	32	0	34.1	38	14	23
Gately, T	0	0	10.80	4	0	6.2	11	4	4
Gaudi, N	0	0	4.67	8	0	17.1	19	8	19
Heston, A	0	0	8.53	4	0	6.1	10	5	7
Jackson, T	0	0	12.46	3	0	4.1	6	6	3
Jernstad, M	8	11	3.71	24	1	140.2	131	50	116
Johnson, G	6	1	2.58	51	1	59.1	61	16	35
Jordat, N	1	0	3.97	8	0	11.1	10	4	16
Lane, G	0	0	23.14	3	0	2.1	8	3	0
Mincone, J	1	2	4.61	6	0	13.2	12	9	8
Oster, J	0	1	12.00	4	0	3	5	2	2
Porch, C	0	0	10.80	2	0	1.2	4	1	1
Privett, T	5	3	2.81	10	0	67.1	55	17	58
Roy, P	0	0	10.29	8	0	7	7	9	11
Scudero, M	1	1	3.86	18	0	30.1	31	9	16
Thieroff, A	0	0	14.73	6	1	3.2	3	3	5
Williams, D	11	6	4.05	25	0	144.1	150	73	157
Zegarac, S	1	0	3.00	6	0	6	8	1	7

INDEPENDENT LEAGUES

NORTH AMERICAN LEAGUE

Few of the memories of the 2011 North American League season come from on the field, but it was fitting that the team's best regular season squad ended up taking home the title.

The Edmonton Capitals edged the Calgary Vipers by two games for first place in the Northern Division during the regular season, topped the Vipers in the playoffs, then easily handled the Rio Grande Valley WhiteWings in the championship series to win the league's first title.

You could argue the original Lake County

Fielders lineup might have been the league's best. They led the league with a 24-13 record when the majority of the roster was either traded or released after players complained that they weren't being paid. From that point the Fielders were 3-23, including a 14-game losing streak to end their season that featured a forfeit for not fielding suitable baseballs. They canceled their final 17 games for financial reasons.

The league's future for 2012 was very much up in the air. In addition to Lake County and Maui's troubles, Calgary and Chico shut down their operations at the end of the season.

NORTHERN DIVISION	W	L	PCT	GB
Edmonton	56	32	.636	—
Calgary	53	33	.616	2
Chico	41	47	.466	15
Lake County	27	36	.429	16.5
Maui	29	40	.420	17.5
SOUTHERN DIVISION	W	L	PCT	GB
San Angelo	52	36	0.591	—
Rio Grande Valley	51	37	.580	1
Edinburg	37	52	.416	15.5
McAllen	37	52	.416	15.5
Yuma	35	53	.398	17

PLAYOFFS: Semifinals—Edmonton defeated Calgary 4-2 and Rio Grande Valley defeated San Angelo 4-0 in best-of-seven series. **Finals**—Edmonton defeated Rio Grande Valley 4-1 in best-of-seven series.

ATTENDANCE: San Angelo 112,228; Edinburg 107,786; Edmonton 102,253; Chico 67,282; Rio Grande Valley 65,916; Calgary 62,308; Yuma 48,700; Maui 31,606; Lake County 26,480; McAllen 18,404.

MANAGERS: Calgary—Morgan Burkhart. **Chico**—Mike Marshall. **Edinburg**—Steve Maddock. **Edmonton**—Orv Franchuk. **Lake County**—Tim Johnson/Pete LaCock/Chris Thompson/Chris Arango. **Maui**—Garry Templeton. **McAllen**— Matt Stark. **Rio Grande Valley**—Eddie Dennis. **San Angelo**—Doc Edwards. **Yuma**—Jose Canseco.

ALL-STAR TEAM: C—Lou Santalongo, Edmonton. **1B**—CJ Ziegler, Lake County/Calgary. **2B**—Wilver Perez, Calgary. **3B**—Landon Camp, San Angelo. **SS**—Enrique Cruz, Edmonton. **OF**—David Peralta, Rio Grande Valley; Todd Linden, Edmonton; Ronnie Gaines, San Angelo; Jake Rife, Chico. **Utility**—Jimmy Rohan Jr., Calgary. **DH**—Daryl Jones, San Angelo.
SP—Chandler Barnard, San Angelo; Jason Stevenson, Chico; Eric Blackwell, Rio Grande Valley; Logan Williamson, San Angelo; Aaron Guerra, Edinburg. **RP**— Edgar Martinez, Rio Grande Valley; Julio Castro, Edinburg; Tom Boleska, Edmonton; JJ Leaper, Yuma; Clayton Uyechi, Maui.
Player of the Year: Todd Linden, Edmonton. **Pitcher of the Year:** Chandler Barnard, San Angelo.

CALGARY VIPERS

PLAYER	AVG	AB	R	H	2B	3B	HR	RBI	SB
Burke, B	.302	192	52	58	9	1	2	28	10
Dunsmore, A	.308	104	21	32	10	1	1	15	3
Ehrnsberger, C	.397	141	33	56	13	0	2	36	0
Fruson, L	.000	2	0	0	0	0	0	0	0
Garcia, L	.329	73	11	24	7	0	2	17	3
Giacomini, J	.277	130	20	36	4	0	1	17	2
Jenkins, A	.295	44	7	13	5	0	0	7	1
Kaplan, J	.368	340	84	125	29	11	7	49	25
Kavanaugh, M	.114	35	5	4	0	0	1	4	1
Miller, D	.337	276	67	93	20	1	12	61	2
Perez, W	.379	338	94	128	26	8	11	86	30
Perren, D	.211	19	3	4	0	0	0	0	0
Price, K	.213	61	8	13	4	0	1	9	0
Quintana, A	.256	39	4	10	1	1	0	5	0
Rios, B	.212	33	2	7	0	0	0	2	1
Rohan, J	.379	301	51	114	24	4	1	58	1
Tellam, J	.277	206	33	57	11	0	7	50	1
Templeton, L	.289	194	46	56	10	2	5	42	4
Ziegler, C	.329	143	39	47	13	0	10	40	0

PLAYER	W	L	ERA	G	SV	IP	H	BB	SO
Ayala, M	3	2	7.76	7	0	29	39	18	31
Bodishbaugh, C	0	1	2.86	32	2	35	48	8	47
Burns, M	7	2	3.35	24	0	38	34	2	38
Cate, T	0	0	13.50	1	0	4	11	1	4
Galva, C	0	3	4.21	28	18	26	27	8	36
Gober, D	7	3	4.68	16	0	85	98	42	47
Hammons, M	0	1	5.40	7	0	7	8	1	7
Hetherington, S	1	2	4.99	12	0	22	27	4	17
Holleran, G	5	7	6.41	17	0	91	119	52	53
Mabee, H	1	0	3.78	13	1	17	22	11	13
Michael, M	8	2	4.17	15	0	82	83	35	69
Morari, D	2	0	1.98	36	0	36	25	11	33
Naegele, R	2	0	5.70	23	0	36	48	14	22
Valdez, E	6	3	7.23	14	0	56	81	13	43
Watson, S	2	1	4.57	36	1	41	56	6	34
Whalen, S	7	5	5.13	14	0	74	93	24	43
Whetsel, J	1	1	6.85	21	1	22	31	22	22

CHICO OUTLAWS

PLAYER	AVG	AB	R	H	2B	3B	HR	RBI	SB
Buschini, A	.288	306	47	88	15	3	9	52	18
Fowler, B	.186	70	8	13	4	0	1	7	0
Gonzalez, D	.310	226	38	70	11	0	0	27	3
Hale, D	.296	71	13	21	6	3	0	10	1
Hibbert, M	.373	67	14	25	2	1	0	4	2
Hill, B	.308	234	64	72	15	3	2	38	6
Lubanski, C	.259	212	34	55	13	1	4	29	2
McFall, B	.247	271	48	67	14	0	13	48	0
Munoz, E	.313	16	5	5	1	1	1	2	1
Pecci, J	.332	316	53	105	21	3	0	37	7
Quintana, A	.297	256	42	76	9	1	5	48	0
Rife, J	.343	309	68	106	23	6	13	71	24
Sigala, O	.258	62	9	16	7	0	0	10	4
Steinhauer, K	.367	169	30	62	11	0	5	33	11
Terry, P	.271	107	12	29	5	0	0	16	2
Wright, W	.267	116	13	31	8	0	1	16	3

PLAYER	W	L	ERA	G	SV	IP	H	BB	SO
Aguilar, O	0	0	4.80	15	3	15	13	14	15
Banks, D	6	7	6.96	18	0	84	115	38	75
Bravo, J	5	5	6.34	16	0	88	114	32	44
Constantine, J	0	1	21.60	2	0	2	4	2	1
Foltz, A	0	1	8.68	8	0	19	30	9	10
Giles, J	1	1	5.06	14	0	16	18	15	14
Gonzalez, D	0	0	7.20	4	0	5	5	4	1
James, C	0	0	0.00	2	0	3	2	4	6
Kane, T	4	3	7.03	25	1	56	86	21	39
Kramer, M	1	0	2.29	6	0	20	24	4	13
Mackintosh, J	1	4	7.44	17	0	52	78	8	34
Muyco, J	2	0	2.70	16	7	20	22	1	21
Paduch, J	1	0	2.57	1	0	7	4	1	7
Riddle, R	1	2	7.13	18	3	18	23	11	20
Roberts, D	2	8	6.87	19	0	75	98	26	61
Roenicke, J	3	3	6.34	32	3	44	62	37	43
Screnar, R	0	1	8.31	1	0	4	6	2	3
Slovak, D	2	0	2.76	33	2	29	22	2	22
Spralin, J	0	0	99.99	1	0	0	1	2	0
Stevenson, J	8	0	1.68	9	1	64	57	14	76
Whigham, D	0	3	12.27	5	0	15	31	11	8
White, E	1	4	5.40	8	0	42	59	15	29
Wilson, K	2	4	5.32	8	0	46	50	22	21
Wright, W	0	0	9.00	1	0	3	5	0	2
Yoshida, E	0	0	9.00	1	0	2	2	5	0

EDINBURG ROADRUNNERS

PLAYER	AVG	AB	R	H	2B	3B	HR	RBI	SB
Aranda, N	.133	15	2	2	0	0	0	1	0
Beatty, C	.326	288	53	94	21	4	13	54	13
DeJesus, A	.353	85	17	30	8	1	0	10	6
Dixon, D	.220	82	6	18	3	0	0	8	0
Dotel, W	.280	211	36	59	15	4	6	28	18
Fernandez, J	.268	71	12	19	1	0	0	7	8
Flores, O	.247	299	50	74	14	0	7	41	8
Gordon, A	.216	74	18	16	6	0	1	4	5
Harris, R	.275	305	65	84	16	0	10	42	21
Hill, J	.225	71	11	16	4	0	2	6	7

INDEPENDENT LEAGUES

PLAYER	AVG	AB	R	H	2B	3B	HR	RBI	SB
Lewis, M	.140	50	9	7	1	0	0	1	5
Marshall, D	.230	61	8	14	2	0	0	9	0
Matlock, R	.280	286	41	80	12	2	1	45	17
McMorris, C	.182	33	6	6	0	1	0	2	5
Memmert, G	.275	295	36	81	19	1	5	44	0
Sanders, B	.200	50	6	10	2	0	0	3	1
Smith, S	.305	357	45	109	14	2	2	46	42
Stroud, C	.154	26	2	4	1	1	0	0	0
Thomas, J	.250	52	7	13	1	1	1	5	1
Wilkerson, B	.210	252	33	53	8	3	3	36	6
Wright, S	.170	47	5	8	0	0	0	8	6

PLAYER	W	L	ERA	G	SV	IP	H	BB	SO
Castro, J	3	1	2.05	26	11	48	35	8	58
Chutchian, M	0	0	7.04	11	0	15	26	8	7
Cortez, R	0	1	5.06	6	0	5	5	3	8
Cross, R	0	0	7.04	11	0	15	17	7	11
Cunningham, E	1	0	8.68	7	0	9	10	3	8
Dowl, A	0	0	9.95	10	0	19	27	15	13
Falcon, R	4	0	0.55	5	0	33	19	4	30
Giulietti, J	0	6	6.00	15	0	51	61	24	44
Gordon, A	0	0	0.00	1	0	1	1	0	0
Goudeau, C	2	6	7.82	18	0	61	89	40	56
Guerra, J	7	7	3.60	19	0	85	106	14	62
Haines, T	0	2	4.12	8	0	39	41	15	41
Harris, R	1	3	7.94	4	0	23	33	8	18
Holbrook, S	0	0	1.59	4	0	6	9	0	9
Marshall, D	0	0	0.00	1	0	2	0	0	3
Miller, G	0	0	13.14	7	0	12	20	11	5
Oyervidez, J	3	1	2.73	5	0	36	29	12	35
Parry, B	2	4	5.36	23	0	50	60	17	37
Quintero, J	6	8	6.41	17	0	79	96	29	53
Schurz, M	1	2	4.66	31	3	39	38	23	45
Trevino, T	4	7	5.62	14	0	83	106	21	64
Wingo, S	3	4	4.75	11	0	66	76	22	48

EDMONTON CAPITALS

PLAYER	AVG	AB	R	H	2B	3B	HR	RBI	SB
Brown, S	.317	183	50	58	5	4	11	39	15
Chavez, A	.288	73	14	21	4	0	1	6	6
Closser, J	.333	96	29	32	3	2	2	23	4
Collaro, T	.269	279	42	75	23	1	14	60	2
Cruz, E	.361	335	72	121	28	4	14	66	9
Duncan, C	.324	241	42	78	16	0	9	56	0
Linden, T	.355	296	85	105	22	5	14	79	23
McGraw, J	.244	90	27	22	2	1	0	2	8
Metheny, B	.325	289	66	94	30	0	10	76	21
Nowlin, C	.147	34	3	5	0	1	0	3	0
Rogelstad, M	.332	316	75	105	23	4	2	46	3
Rundgren, R	.297	111	16	33	6	1	1	18	2
Santangelo, L	.346	185	37	64	11	3	10	45	1
Tountas, P	.169	59	7	10	5	0	1	12	0
Valdez, N	.290	138	24	40	10	2	1	19	2

PLAYER	W	L	ERA	G	SV	IP	H	BB	SO
Arreola, A	0	2	8.02	6	0	21	31	15	8
Arreola, D	6	6	6.75	17	0	95	121	29	75
Blackwell, C	3	0	4.07	35	0	55	63	16	57
Boleska, T	3	3	2.11	33	11	47	34	11	56
Buck, D	5	0	2.08	6	0	35	36	13	14
Davidson, D	1	1	6.12	34	2	32	38	20	36
Fortunato, B	2	1	4.18	23	6	24	24	18	27
Francisco, A	3	3	6.40	9	0	45	61	14	40
Green, S	0	1	18.00	1	0	1	4	1	0
Hrynio, M	1	3	8.53	20	0	44	76	31	35
Lopez, A	3	0	4.15	6	0	26	39	12	12
Mace, J	0	0	6.75	5	0	7	9	1	4
Metheny, B	0	0	9.00	1	0	1	3	1	1
Pote, J	7	5	5.16	17	0	96	116	42	100
Shortell, R	11	4	5.29	19	0	95	117	22	60
Smith, J	2	0	2.25	2	0	12	12	5	10
Vasquez, J	1	3	3.07	31	2	59	40	34	74
Villafuerte, B	4	2	4.79	25	1	26	36	15	32
Whetsel, J	0	0	9.39	7	0	8	10	6	11

LAKE COUNTY FIELDERS

PLAYER	AVG	G	AB	R	H	2B	3B	HR	RBI	SB
Agustin, B	.296	17	54	5	16	4	0	1	4	1

PLAYER	AVG	G	AB	R	H	2B	3B	HR	RBI	SB
Brooks, P	.233	38	150	11	35	5	0	1	10	1
Brown, C	.220	21	59	6	13	1	0	3	7	0
Coleman, D	.286	21	49	9	14	0	0	0	5	1
Dempsey, J	.205	23	73	9	15	1	0	0	6	0
Dziomba, J	.286	23	84	9	24	6	2	0	3	2
Garcia, L	.276	25	87	16	24	5	0	4	20	8
Getsee, Z	.182	19	33	2	6	3	0	0	2	0
Hunt, J	.500	2	6	1	3	0	0	0	2	0
Jova, M	.333	11	42	6	14	2	0	1	7	0
Judah, S	.255	19	51	4	13	3	1	0	6	0
Lopez, T	.237	20	59	4	14	1	1	0	7	0
Luquette, Q	.267	38	116	17	31	7	0	0	13	2
Mansilla, M	.270	36	137	14	37	9	2	2	18	5
Moro, C	.292	16	48	7	14	5	1	0	6	0
Newton, B	.341	31	138	27	47	9	7	2	17	10
Nunez, A	.356	36	146	39	52	11	1	9	28	1
Payne, B	.245	40	94	9	23	0	1	0	5	6
Perren, J	.364	11	44	5	16	2	0	0	3	0
Redding, M	.197	23	66	11	13	2	0	1	13	0
Rick, A	.267	23	75	11	20	2	0	3	9	0
Rundgren, R	.289	36	159	25	46	7	2	0	20	0
Samuelson, M	.304	17	56	10	17	4	0	3	10	0
Weaver, T	.200	5	15	0	3	1	0	0	1	1
White, A	.111	5	9	1	1	0	0	0	0	0
Ziegler, C	.340	38	141	27	48	7	0	14	39	0

PLAYER	W	L	ERA	G	SV	IP	H	BB	SO
Blewett, D	5	1	3.89	7	0	44	50	13	28
Bongiovanni, V	4	0	3.49	8	0	49	46	19	45
Brewer, J	1	1	2.08	4	0	22	17	10	11
Brooks, P	0	1	13.50	1	0	2	4	2	4
Carr, R	1	3	7.83	20	0	33	33	23	28
Cline, Z	2	3	4.94	9	0	51	67	13	33
Daly, B	0	1	13.50	5	0	3	4	4	1
Gaudi, N	2	0	4.18	11	0	28	25	20	29
Gomez, J	0	1	10.80	11	0	12	19	13	14
Gonzalez, J	1	0	2.49	5	0	22	15	2	17
Grife, S	0	0	1.57	16	1	23	15	14	33
Gunderson, R	0	4	12.54	4	0	9	15	15	9
Hildebrand, J	0	3	14.25	5	0	12	30	8	7
Judah, S	0	0	9.00	2	0	4	7	0	3
Junker, S	0	1	3.68	4	0	7	9	3	3
Kennedy, N	0	2	5.23	9	1	10	15	2	13
Kohli, N	0	0	9.00	6	0	10	18	6	13
Kramer, M	1	0	6.75	1	0	4	4	1	1
Lane, G	4	0	3.60	15	0	25	22	11	9
Lee, T	1	2	7.00	9	0	18	24	10	16
Lueck, M	0	2	9.15	8	0	21	40	10	12
Luquette, Q	0	0	0.00	1	0	1	0	1	0
Medina, J	0	3	3.60	5	0	30	29	12	17
Moore, M	2	2	3.48	7	0	31	28	18	16
Moro, C	0	0	0.00	1	0	1	0	1	2
Newton, B	0	0	0.00	1	0	3	4	1	5
Paxton, B	1	1	3.86	18	1	19	10	8	12
Rundgren, R	0	0	36.00	1	0	1	4	1	1
Severtson, B	0	0	2.70	7	0	13	20	4	5
Thompson, J	2	4	3.74	19	12	22	15	15	22
Ziegler, C	0	0	9.00	1	0	1	2	0	1

McALLEN THUNDER

PLAYER	AVG	G	AB	R	H	2B	3B	HR	RBI	SB
Batista, W	.330	74	294	57	97	21	2	11	65	16
Breda, G	.188	15	48	5	9	0	0	0	2	1
Coury, G	.235	20	51	8	12	3	0	0	3	0
Davis, O	.143	2	7	0	1	0	0	0	0	0
Dixon, D	.304	37	138	12	42	5	1	1	16	0
Eiland, R	.325	77	295	66	96	18	1	11	37	14
Ferrante, V	.217	11	46	5	10	2	0	2	8	2
Gallardo, C	.213	25	80	13	17	6	0	0	8	1
Garza, G	.500	2	2	0	1	0	0	0	0	0
Goss, M	.343	69	236	29	81	15	1	3	36	5
Gray, A	.324	46	182	50	59	11	0	11	33	1
Harris, R	.258	19	62	9	16	5	0	1	8	0
Hernandez, A	.222	6	18	2	4	1	0	1	1	0
Hetherington, L	.289	47	166	27	48	11	2	4	21	7
Johnson, C	.264	17	53	6	14	4	0	1	9	5
Kuhn, A	.162	18	37	2	6	0	0	0	4	0

PLAYER	AVG	G	AB	R	H	2B	3B	HR	RBI	SB
Lewis, M	.353	4	17	4	6	0	0	0	1	0
Lilley, J	.241	17	58	12	14	2	0	3	9	2
Mandelblatt, Z	.298	75	235	63	70	10	0	14	46	22
Marshall, D	.223	34	94	12	21	2	0	1	12	5
Matos, A	.260	74	223	33	58	14	1	4	30	16
McMorris, C	.213	19	47	7	10	1	0	0	3	6
Nichols, B	.290	27	107	16	31	9	1	4	17	4
Perez, Y	.224	30	116	15	26	6	1	0	11	7
Perodin, R	.200	12	40	8	8	4	0	0	4	0
Redding, M	.083	19	36	1	3	0	0	0	2	0
Sanders, B	.244	32	86	10	21	3	0	2	15	1
Tamayo, Y	.340	73	303	56	103	20	0	7	50	4

PLAYER	W	L	ERA	G	SV	IP	H	BB	SO
Bright, Q	1	1	5.53	23	1	41	54	14	29
Davenport, C	1	1	13.50	2	0	7	16	5	4
De La Cruz, M	0	1	11.77	3	0	13	26	9	11
Ford, R	4	2	6.51	15	0	55	70	31	39
Garza, A	4	4	5.10	15	0	55	70	22	48
Granitz, G	1	1	4.38	12	1	12	13	5	14
Houck, K	5	9	5.79	15	0	93	127	39	85
James, F	4	2	5.37	20	0	62	76	25	45
Jordan, J	4	7	6.21	24	4	67	84	14	75
Lewis, A	2	0	5.73	4	0	22	25	4	21
Lugo, J	0	1	13.50	1	0	5	7	3	4
Martin, K	2	3	6.12	7	0	32	31	30	36
Matamoros, L	1	1	4.12	27	6	39	42	10	30
Mesa, W	0	1	10.93	3	0	14	18	14	18
Mora, A	1	5	6.92	9	0	52	62	16	41
Oatman, J	1	3	7.77	9	0	24	35	10	27
Papa, D	0	0	12.79	3	0	6	12	2	0
Rossetti, Z	1	0	4.15	4	0	4	3	0	4
Roth, R	1	1	3.48	15	1	21	20	5	42
Smith, B	2	1	4.91	17	0	29	33	11	28
Veronee, B	0	1	13.50	5	0	6	15	5	4
Wilyman, S	0	2	5.61	8	0	26	30	9	32
Zink, J	2	5	7.23	9	0	47	64	12	29

MAUI NA IKAIKA KOA

PLAYER	AVG	AB	R	H	2B	3B	HR	RBI	SB
Bargewell, R	.252	107	12	27	3	1	0	15	1
Boggs, S	.250	72	7	18	1	1	0	6	1
DelReal, P	.267	45	12	12	2	1	0	5	1
Einertson, M	.314	258	46	81	13	4	8	49	2
Fitzgerald, N	.232	56	7	13	0	1	1	10	2
Garcia, S	.212	33	4	7	1	0	0	2	0
Jacobs, J	.241	54	9	13	2	1	2	11	4
Johnson, T	.000	9	1	0	0	0	0	1	0
Kahoohalahala, K	.250	4	2	1	0	0	0	0	0
Kavanaugh, M	.255	94	10	24	9	0	1	18	3
Mochizuki, G	.230	226	35	52	10	3	0	20	13
Muhlsteff, K	.000	17	0	0	0	0	0	1	1
Murray - Thornton, J	.273	205	30	56	13	3	2	26	0
Nishimura, P	.171	41	8	7	0	1	0	4	0
Okano, M	.146	41	5	6	0	0	1	4	4
Pearson, S	.289	253	37	73	14	5	2	40	9
Rose, P	.313	217	36	68	11	1	1	17	10
Ruggiano, B	.333	21	5	7	2	0	1	5	1
Sanchez, J	.354	158	35	56	14	1	1	22	0
Sherrill, J	.330	176	37	58	7	4	9	33	9
Tedesco, S	.244	41	4	10	1	0	0	1	1
White, D	.211	71	5	15	2	1	0	10	1

PLAYER	W	L	ERA	G	SV	IP	H	BB	SO
Altman, K	1	1	8.10	7	0	33	42	22	15
Broughton, M	3	5	5.25	9	0	48	47	32	29
Delucia, D	1	5	7.44	12	0	62	90	32	33
Dinelli, D	1	2	2.49	32	3	51	29	34	64
Hales, C	2	3	6.46	8	0	39	51	27	35
Herrera, B	1	3	3.89	24	0	35	38	30	23
Holley Jr, J	0	5	6.35	18	0	34	37	28	26
Honel, K	0	4	5.28	5	0	29	28	19	21
Jones, R	4	2	6.55	27	2	33	33	26	25
Koons, M	1	2	5.36	18	2	40	52	24	25
Martinez, R	2	0	2.53	12	1	21	17	9	22
Page, R	4	2	7.31	12	0	64	94	23	57
Renault, N	1	3	3.97	7	1	23	24	10	17
Smith, J	0	1	4.50	1	0	6	8	1	5

	W	L	ERA	G	SV	IP	H	BB	SO
Tiffany Jr, C	2	0	2.49	11	0	22	17	16	15
Uyechi, C	4	1	1.65	27	3	33	23	15	29
Yeo, J	1	1	10.50	9	0	12	15	17	10
Yoshida, E	1	0	1.80	1	0	5	4	3	1

RIO GRANDE VALLEY WHITEWINGS

PLAYER	AVG	AB	R	H	2B	3B	HR	RBI	SB
Avila, G	.373	102	22	38	4	0	11	35	2
Batista, W	.275	51	7	14	1	0	0	3	6
Decker, B	.275	207	40	57	6	0	2	25	11
DeJesus, A	.340	244	49	83	16	4	2	24	18
Delgado, L	.188	69	12	13	3	1	2	9	0
Dimitt, W	.214	98	21	21	2	1	3	12	2
Dotel, W	.368	114	31	42	7	1	4	14	20
Fernandez, J	.261	111	18	29	2	0	0	13	3
Gonzalez, E	.325	123	21	40	3	0	2	18	1
Hernandez, A	.262	107	13	28	5	0	5	16	0
Hernandez, F	.194	31	2	6	1	0	0	5	0
Johnson, C	.209	86	18	18	4	2	4	15	1
Oliveras, A	.254	67	13	17	4	1	2	6	0
Ortiz, G	.260	219	29	57	8	0	4	34	9
Peralta, D	.392	339	76	133	30	5	17	81	7
Pino, W	.371	286	52	106	20	2	13	62	13
Rotola, T	.222	18	2	4	0	0	0	1	0
Santana, F	.351	188	51	66	9	3	7	32	16
Trejo, E	.323	285	53	92	14	3	13	47	5
Ventura, L	.323	337	75	109	23	2	20	78	8

PLAYER	W	L	ERA	G	SV	IP	H	BB	SO
Blackwell, E	8	3	3.01	17	0	93	83	34	100
Cassidy, M	3	2	4.35	26	0	60	68	21	42
Cedeno, J	3	1	6.49	17	1	43	57	10	65
Chirinos, L	4	2	3.95	18	0	82	75	34	93
Concepcion, A	8	4	4.76	15	0	87	92	25	89
Cortez, R	0	1	10.39	3	0	4	10	4	4
Cross, D	2	1	5.52	5	0	29	37	10	34
Davenport, C	5	5	5.35	14	0	71	91	29	48
Dennis Jr., E	3	2	8.68	22	0	57	75	40	47
Dotel, W	0	0	0.00	2	0	2	2	0	3
Dowl, A	1	1	5.06	4	0	11	9	5	8
Gonzalez, E	0	0	1.29	2	0	7	5	4	3
Hernandez, E	1	0	7.71	15	0	23	33	15	27
Martinez, E	2	3	2.48	31	20	33	26	6	60
Mesa, W	0	1	20.25	7	0	5	15	6	5
Moody, J	1	0	5.68	2	0	6	7	5	4
Nation, B	0	1	6.75	2	0	5	7	0	5
Orosco, J	0	0	14.29	4	0	6	13	2	3
Peralta, D	0	0	0.00	1	0	1	0	0	1
Perez, W	1	1	1.50	6	1	18	12	6	21
Rondon, D	3	3	5.28	23	1	44	62	20	42
Sanchez, R	0	0	19.80	3	0	5	5	13	9
Santana, J	4	5	5.52	20	0	31	31	16	37
Vasquez, S	0	0	16.20	2	0	2	4	2	2
Ventura, L	0	0	0.00	1	0	1	0	0	1
Wells, A	2	1	6.69	8	0	35	47	17	40

SAN ANGELO COLTS

PLAYER	AVG	G	AB	R	H	2B	3B	HR	RBI	SB
Ballez, B	.333	3	9	1	3	0	0	1	3	0
Beatty, C	.333	13	51	9	17	2	1	4	16	1
Browne, E	.133	5	15	4	2	0	0	0	0	0
Calfee, C	.304	86	339	57	103	21	0	12	64	0
Calloway, T	.206	22	63	9	13	4	0	0	4	1
Camp, L	.319	63	248	57	79	16	1	24	61	2
Carter, T	.307	57	218	30	67	9	1	6	31	1
Crosland, J	.224	29	107	23	24	5	1	7	21	1
Edwards, J	.227	23	75	14	17	3	0	5	15	0
Ferrante, V	.292	25	96	21	28	5	0	4	15	0
Gaines, R	.358	75	313	92	112	25	1	24	79	19
Glad, G	.185	7	27	7	5	1	0	1	1	0
Hernandez, D	.271	67	251	45	68	11	0	6	27	2
Jones, D	.345	85	351	81	121	22	0	28	90	11
Lasprilla, A	.385	3	13	2	5	0	0	0	1	0
Nichols, B	.328	13	58	10	19	2	0	5	10	2
Page, D	.259	45	135	24	35	4	1	4	14	1
Ramos, M	.319	80	285	85	91	14	3	9	51	4
Redding, M	.136	7	22	2	3	2	0	0	3	0

PLAYER	AVG	AB	R	H	2B	3B	HR	RBI	SB
Riddick, A	.250	17	56	17	14	4	0	3	9	1
Riportella, B	.302	14	43	6	13	1	0	1	6	0
Stroud, C	.273	4	11	1	3	0	0	0	0	0
West, J	.152	9	33	5	5	1	0	3	5	1

PLAYER	W	L	ERA	G	SV	IP	H	BB	SO
Barnard, C	12	2	3.25	18	0	114	103	25	98
Boggio, K	0	1	6.31	15	0	26	32	15	25
Caballero, A	0	3	8.53	3	0	13	16	10	5
Casillas, A	3	0	5.51	7	0	34	36	11	33
Cruceta, F	2	1	1.39	11	3	13	8	1	21
Cruerta, F	0	0	0.00	1	0	1	1	0	3
Ferrante, V	0	0	10.80	3	0	3	3	1	4
Giles, J	1	2	4.61	11	0	14	15	6	11
Goodline, W	0	0	13.50	2	0	4	8	1	1
Goudeau, C	0	0	11.46	7	0	11	20	5	6
Hacker, M	0	0	0.00	1	0	1	1	0	1
Henschel, B	7	8	5.03	18	0	113	150	19	64
Huizinga, J	0	0	0.00	2	0	1	1	0	1
Keeler, S	1	0	9.58	2	0	10	18	6	3
Kramer, A	4	3	6.85	20	0	71	93	28	40
Kramer, S	3	5	7.92	24	13	25	24	16	38
MacFarland, S	1	3	8.64	6	0	17	28	14	23
Parker, D	0	0	9.25	18	0	24	37	10	23
Patton, C	2	0	4.34	18	0	19	20	6	19
Ramos, M	0	0	0.00	2	0	2	1	0	1
Riddle, R	0	1	2.89	2	0	9	13	1	6
Rodgers, C	0	1	6.35	3	0	6	7	1	3
Romero, G	4	1	5.12	22	0	58	72	12	32
Vacek, C	1	2	3.07	34	1	44	40	9	51
Wells, A	0	1	11.88	3	0	8	19	3	8
Williamson, L	11	2	4.99	18	0	114	126	36	104

YUMA SCORPIONS

PLAYER	AVG	AB	R	H	2B	3B	HR	RBI	SB
Alfonso, J	.215	144	12	31	7	1	1	16	3
Avila, G	.439	66	12	29	9	0	3	12	1
Aybar, W	.302	43	6	13	1	1	0	3	0
Brooks, P	.292	106	16	31	6	0	1	12	2
Camacho, J	.357	115	16	41	13	0	4	27	1
Canseco, J	.256	199	30	51	10	0	8	46	3
Canseco, O	.258	31	3	8	3	0	0	7	0
Cooper, B	.231	13	1	3	1	0	0	0	0
Diaz, J	.231	65	13	15	2	0	0	5	5
Falls, C	.286	7	2	2	0	0	0	0	0
Gathright, J	.347	222	47	77	9	3	0	21	20
Jaspe, J	.327	168	28	55	10	0	3	26	0

PLAYER	AVG	AB	R	H	2B	3B	HR	RBI	SB
Larson, Z	.282	220	29	62	7	1	4	23	2
Leon, C	.285	214	40	61	8	2	0	33	16
McDonald, J	.329	286	44	94	17	3	6	53	17
Muse, J	.310	319	52	99	32	2	7	52	11
Naegele, N	.308	13	2	4	2	0	0	1	0
Ortiz, G	.333	39	7	13	3	1	0	5	6
Patton, J	.100	10	0	1	0	0	0	0	0
Phillips, T	.269	78	17	21	9	0	0	1	0
Ponce, A	.305	279	48	85	19	4	8	46	10
Rios, B	.333	6	0	2	0	0	0	0	0
Riportella, B	.365	115	20	42	10	3	0	16	5
Stokes, R	.182	11	3	2	0	0	0	0	0
Teilon, N	.215	79	11	17	2	0	0	9	2
Ugueto, L	.267	30	5	8	3	1	0	1	0
Villaescusa, F	.333	3	2	1	0	0	0	0	0

PLAYER	W	L	ERA	G	SV	IP	H	BB	SO
Alexander, S	0	0	0.00	1	0	2	1	1	1
Britton, C	3	2	8.16	10	0	43	70	11	37
Canseco, J	1	3	10.44	11	0	25	41	15	10
Carr, R	0	2	12.66	4	0	11	19	12	2
Cross, J	2	4	9.58	10	0	41	69	17	32
De La Cruz, M	0	1	22.50	3	0	2	6	2	0
De La Vara, G	6	8	6.43	17	0	91	129	54	82
Diaz, J	0	0	9.00	1	0	1	3	1	0
Dorado, R	0	2	9.15	16	0	21	30	14	18
Freeborn, G	0	0	7.50	2	0	6	11	2	4
Garcia, J	4	1	3.93	10	0	53	54	24	38
Gracesqui, F	0	0	3.86	7	1	7	6	9	10
Hoyt, J	2	0	4.34	19	1	37	34	24	50
Huizinga, J	5	5	5.76	18	0	95	119	35	64
Jachno, E	0	0	2.70	2	0	3	3	2	1
Larson, J	0	0	0.00	1	0	1	1	0	0
Leaper, J	0	2	1.39	17	3	26	17	12	31
Lopresti, J	0	0	7.20	4	0	5	6	3	3
McDonald, J	0	0	9.00	1	0	1	1	2	1
Muse, J	0	0	0.00	1	0	1	0	1	3
Nestor, S	0	0	33.75	2	0	1	4	4	2
Romo, A	5	6	4.55	18	0	85	87	33	86
Santana, J	0	1	5.63	8	2	8	14	4	8
Scott, R	1	0	0.00	7	0	11	6	4	19
Sergent, J	0	0	9.53	2	0	6	12	2	1
Smith, B	0	2	9.58	11	0	21	28	16	10
Stolp, E	4	5	6.38	23	0	48	64	32	32
Thompson, C	1	2	7.02	15	6	17	20	16	14
Wiley, J	1	6	4.40	33	1	47	54	29	48

INDEPENDENT LEAGUES

INTERNATIONAL

October Surprise: Dutch, Canada win gold

Netherlands players pose with the World Cup trophy after beating Cuba 2-1 in the finals

EZIO RATTI-IBAF

The only way Tom Stuifbergen could describe the reception he and his teammates from the Netherlands received when they got home was to reference soccer.

"We just arrived in Holland," he e-mailed, a day after helping the Dutch national team win the 2011 World Cup, "and the airport was loaded with press and fans. It was crazy. We kind of felt like the Dutch soccer team, who obviously gets the most attention in Holland. At first the media didn't really care about us beating (the) U.S.A. and Puerto Rico. But when we qualified for the Final apparently the whole country was going nuts. And that showed at the arrival in Holland, which was amazing! That was probably one of the coolest things that I've witnessed with the Dutch baseball team.

"I also hope because of this media attention that more kids are going to play baseball instead of soccer; that way we could become a bigger country in baseball overall."

The World Cup is not the biggest baseball stage in the world, and few fans in North America took note of the event that took place during the first two weeks of October in Panama. But thanks to Stuifbergen (Twins) and other pitchers such as 36-year-old veteran Rob Cordemans, the Netherlands won its first major international tournament, beating Cuba 2-1 in the final and becoming the first European nation to win the World Cup.

Cuba earned silver for the third straight World Cup after winning nine consecutive events from 1984-2005. The United States won the '07 and '09 Cups, but the '11 USA Baseball club had to rally from a 4-4 start, winning its last three games to earn a spot in the medal round. Its bronze-medal game with Canada was rained out, and the teams were named co-bronze medallists, though only Canada's players got actual bronze medals.

Canada then took home a fine consolation prize two weeks later, winning the Pan American Games gold medal for the country's first championship in a major international baseball tournament. Canada beat the U.S. in a taut championship game in Guadalajara, Mexico, winning 2-1 to claim the eight-team event of North American and Caribbean clubs. The field included seven World Cup teams—including Cuba, the Dominican Republic, Panama, Puerto Rico and Venezuela—plus host Mexico.

Those tournament victories show the increased parity of international baseball in the professional era, which began in 1998. In just the past six years, seven different nations have claimed international or continental tournaments, from Canada and the Dutch this year to Cuba (2005 World Cup), Japan (two World Baseball Classics), South Korea ('08 Olympics), the Dominican Republic ('10 Pan Am qualifier) and the U.S. ('07 and '09 World Cups).

"I wanted so bad for those guy to win a gold medal," Team USA manager Ernie Young said of his team, which finished with a 10-6 overall record. "We just came up one run short. I'm proud of them. They came a long way. We didn't play well in Panama at first, but we got better and carried it over to the Pan Ams. We lost two games here—both by one run. They were great ballgames."

The Dutch had never finished higher than fourth in World Cup history previously. They can thank pitchers such as Stuifbergen, who finished his 2011 season with Triple-A Rochester in the Twins system, and Cordemans, who played at

Indian River (Fla.) JC in 1997 and has had a long career at the front of his nation's national team rotation. They can also thank Robert Eenhoorn, the former Yankees and Angels shortstop who is now the technical director of the Netherlands baseball federation. Essentially, he's the team's general manager, and he put together a program and a team that has blended players both from the Netherlands' European mainland and its Caribbean island protectorates into a cohesive unit.

"We have young guys and veterans and I think the whole combination of the team made us good," said Stuifbergen, who went 6-9, 4.29 in 122 innings overall, with all but one outing coming with high Class A Fort Myers. "We had a good team chemistry and lots of talent. Also one of the reasons that we won the World Cup is because of the winning flow. We won all the four practice games and we kept that mood into the tournament."

Dutch coach Brian Farley successfully piloted a team with two consistent offensive threats—veteran outfielder Bryan Engelhardt, who plays in Holland's domestic league; and first baseman Curt Smith, formerly of Vermont and the Cardinals farm system and most recently with independent Lincoln of the American Association—to 11 victories in 12 games. Engelhardt hit .425 with 10 RBIs to pace the offense, while Smith hit .375 with three homers and a tournament-best 13 RBIs.

Prospects DiDi Gregorius (Reds) and brothers Sharlon (Giants) and Jonathan Schoop (Orioles) gave the Dutch an athletic infield defensively, backing the pitching staff led by Stuifbergen, Cordemans, Juan Carlos Sulbaran (Reds) and ex-big leaguer Shairon Martis (Nationals). A powerful Cuban lineup that hit .328 overall in 12 tournament games had just 10 hits in 58 at-bats in two losses to the Dutch. Stuifbergen shut out Puerto Rico and South Korea and got a save against Taiwan as part of his 17 scoreless innings. Cordemans won all three of his starts, beating Japan, host Panama and then the Cubans, pitching into the eighth inning in the gold-medal game.

"His nickname is Cordeboss," Stuifbergen said. "He is the most experienced one on the team and I can't believe he never played (professionally) in the USA. His changeup is probably the nastiest one I've ever seen."

Competitive Events

The tournament's highest-profile players, outside of the Cubans who aren't allowed to play professionally, were non-40-man roster prospects such as Germany's Max Kepler (Twins), Team USA's Brett Jackson (Cubs) and Canada outfielder Tim Smith (Royals), or veterans of foreign leagues, such

USA PAN AM/WORLD CUP TEAM

FINAL RECORD: 10-6

Silver Medal, Pan American Games, Guadalajara, Mexico
3rd Place (tie), World Cup, Panama

BATTERS, POS., 2011 ORG	AVG	AB	R	H	HR	RBI	SB
James McCann, c, Tigers	1.000	1	1	1	0	0	0
Joe Thurston, 2b, Marlins	.424	59	9	25	0	12	3
Brett Jackson, of, Cubs	.400	35	8	14	1	4	2
Brett Carroll, of, Red Sox	.348	46	11	16	2	11	2
Jordy Mercer, ss, Pirates	.319	47	14	15	2	12	1
Matt Clark, 1b/dh, Padres	.294	51	14	15	3	10	0
A.J. Pollock, of, D-backs	.273	55	13	15	2	6	2
Tom Mendonca, 3b, Rangers	.271	59	12	16	4	17	0
Jim Gallagher, of, White Sox	.250	8	2	2	1	6	0
Tuffy Gosewisch, c, Phillies	.227	44	4	10	1	9	0
Travis d'Arnaud, c, Blue Jays	.188	16	1	3	0	2	0
Drew Garcia, 2b/ss, White Sox	.182	22	4	4	0	1	1
Chad Tracy, 1b, Rangers	.132	38	3	5	0	4	0

PITCHERS, POS., 2011 ORG	W-L	ERA	G	SV	IP	H	BB	SO
Drew Smyly, lhp, Tigers	2-0	0.00	3	0	17	10	1	17
Justin Cassel, rhp, White Sox	1-0	0.00	5	0	6	4	3	5
Andy Van Hekken, lhp, Astros	3-1	0.96	4	0	28	21	4	14
Scott Patterson, rhp, Mariners	0-0	1.29	8	3	7	3	0	7
Jeff Beliveau, lhp, Cubs	1-0	1.42	5	0	6	4	1	9
Chuckie Fick, rhp, Cardinals	1-0	2.08	5	0	9	7	0	1
Pete Andrelcyk, rhp, Marlins	0-0	4.15	7	1	9	6	6	8
Todd Redmond, rhp, Braves	0-1	5.23	4	0	21	24	5	13
Randy Williams, lhp, Red Sox	0-1	6.00	5	1	6	9	3	5
Matt Shoemaker, rhp, Angels	1-1	7.00	3	0	9	9	5	8
Jeff Marquez, rhp, White Sox	1-2	8.56	3	0	14	21	1	8
Royce Ring, lhp, Red Sox	0-0	9.00	3	0	1	2	0	2

as Panama slugger Fernando Seguignol.

Team USA had a solid roster with prospects such as outfielders Brett Jackson (Cubs) and A.J. Pollock (Diamondbacks) and lefthander Drew Smyly (Tigers), but catcher Travis d'Arnaud (Blue Jays) was forced out by a thumb injury that required surgery and left the team with only one catcher, Tuffy Gosewisch (Phillies). The Netherlands (7-5 loss), Canada (6-1) and Cuba (8-7) thumped American starters Matt Shoemaker (Angels), Todd Redmond (Braves) and Jeffrey Marquez (Yankees), the last loss leaving Team USA at 4-4.

But Team USA held Australia and South Korea to a run apiece, and the Americans needed to beat Venezuela to earn a medal-round spot. The Americans rallied for six runs in the seventh and final frame. Shortstop Jordy Mercer (Pirates) capped the rally with a tie-breaking three-run homer, and veteran minor leaguer Scott Patterson (Mariners) got the save for what proved to be a medal-clinching victory.

Canada went 8-3 to earn its share of the bronze, led by Smith and Albers (Twins), who worked 15 scoreless innings in a dual role as a spot-starter and reliever. The Canadian team resembled the Dutch club in being a roster of professionals that came together on the field quickly and responded well again in Mexico for its Pan Am title.

There, it rode the left arm of Andrew Albers (Twins) and the bat of Jimmy Van Ostrand (Astros), beating the U.S. 2-1 in the gold-medal game. Albers struck out eight and walked none in 6 2/3 innings to earn the victory, while Van Ostrand had a two-run double in the sixth inning off fellow Astros farmhand Andy Van Hekken. Scott Richmond (Blue Jays) got the final seven outs for the save. Van Ostrand went 9-for-19 in the Pan Ams and had four RBIs to set the offense.

Cuba took the bronze, beating Mexico 6-0 after losing 12-10 in the semifinal to the United States. It was the first time Cuba didn't win Pan Am gold since 1967 and continued the country's recent international slide. It has won only one major international event—the 2010 Intercontinental Cup, in which the U.S. did not participate—since 2005. That coincides with the 2003 defection of Jose Contreras and the aging of former national team aces Pedro Luis Lazo and Norge Vera. Cuba has not developed a next wave of arms to replace them or defectors from Livan and Orlando Hernandez in the late 1990s to Aroldis Chapman, who pitched in the 2009 World Baseball Classic.

WBC, IBAF Future

The 2011 baseball World Cup turned out to be the last one. The International Baseball Federation ceded the title of "world champion" to the winner of the World Baseball Classic, Major League Baseball's international event. The only obstacle now appears to be financial resolutions with Nippon Professional Baseball in Japan—the two-time Classic champion—on how to split the pot.

The WBC expands to 28 teams for its next installment, with 16 countries—including Canada and Taiwan—vying in four four-team pods in the fall of 2012, with the four hosts yet to be determined at press time. The four winners will join the top 12 finishers from the 2009 WBC in the 16-team field in the spring of 2013.

"A lot of effort by a lot of dedicated people at IBAF and around the world have gotten us to this point," said Paul Archey, MLB's senior vice president for international business operations. "It will be a less-cluttered landscape, which I think will be a positive. Clearly, the WBC has quickly become the premier international baseball event. It is the one spot in which the best players in the world, regardless of their professional or amateur status, can play for their country at the highest level."

IBAF president Riccardo Fraccari said his organization's top-level tournament will build off the WBC. Its next major tournament with professionals will be called the Premier 12 and is tentatively scheduled for 2015. Meanwhile, IBAF will con-

WORLD CUP

Oct. 1-15, various sites in Panama

OVERALL STANDINGS

COUNTRY	W	L	PCT	COUNTRY	W	L	PCT
Netherlands	10	1	.909	Dominican Republic	3	4	.429
Cuba	9	1	.900	Italy	3	4	.429
Canada	8	3	.727	Puerto Rico	3	4	.429
United States	7	4	.636	Japan	2	5	.286
Australia	6	5	.545	Taiwan	2	5	.286
South Korea	6	5	.545	Nicaragua	1	6	.143
Panama	6	5	.545	Germany	0	7	.000
Venezuela	5	6	.455	Greece	0	7	.000

Gold Medal Game: Netherlands 2, Cuba 1. **Bronze Medal Game:** Rained out, Canada given medals, USA awarded third-place tie with Canada

MVP: Curt Smith, 1b, Netherlands

INDIVIDUAL BATTING (MINIMUM 20 AB)

BATTERS, COUNTRY	AVG	AB	R	H	2B	3B	HR	RBI	SB
Rusney Castillo, Cuba	.512	41	11	21	4	2	2	6	0
Dwight Britton, Nicaragua	.478	23	4	11	2	0	0	3	2
Jose Abreu, Cuba	.475	40	10	19	3	0	3	8	1
Tom Brice, Australia	.467	30	5	14	1	0	1	6	0
Conception Rodriguez, Panama	.457	35	9	16	3	0	1	9	1
Dionys Cesar, D.R.	.450	20	2	9	3	0	0	7	0
Fernando Seguignol, Panama	.447	38	10	17	3	0	3	13	1
Joe Thurston, USA	.439	41	4	18	6	0	0	10	3
Yonathan Sivira, Venezuela	.419	31	2	13	2	0	0	5	2
Bryan Engelhardt, Netherlands	.417	36	7	15	3	1	2	9	1
Victor Mendez, D.R.	.417	24	8	10	1	0	2	8	1
Brett Jackson, USA	.412	34	8	14	3	0	1	4	2
Emerson Frostad, Canada	.409	22	3	9	1	0	0	5	1
Frederick Cepeda, Cuba	.400	40	12	16	5	3	1	9	0
Alexis Gomez, D.R.	.393	28	8	11	2	0	0	6	0

INDIVIDUAL PITCHING

(Minimum 8 IP)

PITCHERS, COUNTRY	W-L	ERA	G	SV	IP	H	BB	SO
Tom Stuifbergen, Netherlands	2-0	0.00	3	1	17	12	2	8
Andrew Albers, Canada	2-0	0.00	4	0	15	7	3	9
Mario Alvarez, D.R.	1-0	0.00	2	0	11	4	2	6
Drew Smyly, USA	1-0	0.00	2	0	11	6	0	13
Willy Lebron, D.R.	1-1	0.00	2	0	11	6	7	9
Julio Rodriguez, P.R.	1-0	0.00	2	0	9	3	4	15
Dustin Molleken, Canada	0-0	0.00	5	0	8	5	4	4
Hyoun Taek Oh, Korea	2-1	0.44	4	0	21	15	1	34
Andy Van Hekken, USA	2-0	0.64	2	0	14	9	1	5

tinue to press its case for Olympic reinstatement.

"For the Netherlands to win the World Cup is very important, to show baseball is truly a global sport that is growing in Europe," Fraccari said in a phone interview from Rome. "I think we can show to the International Olympic Committee that baseball is not only an American sport.

"Baseball is globalizing. The best athletes are no longer just American. Japan has won the last two Classics. Almost 50 percent of players in MLB (organizations) are not American. With Alex Liddi, Italy has its first major leaguer. And now you have the Netherlands winning the World Cup."

If baseball ever makes it back to the Olympics—the current target date would be 2020—October of 2011 will be the catalyst, for showing how global and competitive international baseball can be.

Quintana Roo rides pitching to championship

Quintana Roo completed a four-game sweep of the Mexico City Diablos to win its 10th Mexican League championship since 1955, getting excellent relief work from former big league righthander Jorge Campillo in the 13-9 clinching victory.

Campillo tossed four shutout innings, allowing one hit, in the high-scoring finale. He entered a game that was tied at 5, and the Tigers put up five runs in the seventh to seize control. Veteran second baseman Carlos Gastelum, a former Angels farmhand, hit two homers, one in the seventh, and had five RBIs on the game. Former Blue Jays and Rockies farmhand Sandy Nin, who had a league-high 24 saves during the regular season, got his seventh postseason save despite allowing four hits and three runs (one earned) in the ninth as the Red Devils didn't go down without a fight.

Quintana Roo posted a 12-4 playoff mark behind its pitching staff, which had a 2.96 ERA, by far the league's best mark. Staff ace Pablo Ortego, 35, set the pace in the regular season (10-3, 3.29) and was better in the postseason, pitching a team-high 32 innings and going 3-1, 1.13 in five starts. Nin worked in 13 of the team's 17 postseason games.

The Tigers finished 13th in the league in batting (.277) and 12th in runs (542) but relied on their pitching, ranking second in team ERA at 4.37. The team's top hitters included 35-year-old outfielder Doug Clark, 36-year-old 5-foot-8 DH Carlos Sievers (who led the club in walks) and catcher Iker Franco, whose 23 homers and 74 RBIs were both team bests.

Veracruz outfielder Jorge Guzman, 27, led the league with 39 home runs in just 103 games after hitting just 22 the previous year. Cuban ex-pat and former Braves farmhand Barbaro Canizares had a huge season as well, batting .396 to lead the league. Canizares and Guzman kept Mexico's Luis Terrero from winning the triple crown (old-fashioned and modern), as he finished second in batting, home runs and on-base percentage (.485 to Canizares' .499) while leading the league in RBIs and slugging (.770).

As is the case in other international leagues, many veteran minor leaguers extend their careers in Mexico. Familiar names such as Marshall McDougall (the 1999 College World Series Most Outstanding Player), Fernando Valenzuela Jr., ex-Mariners lefthander Bobby Livingston and Kevin Barker dot Mexican League rosters, as do ex-big leaguers from Mexico such as Francisco Cordova, Benji Gil and Elmer Dessens.

STANDINGS & LEADERS

NORTH	W	L	PCT	GB
Diablos Rojos del Mexico	63	40	.612	—
Broncos de Reynosa	57	47	.548	6½
Sultanes de Monterrey	54	49	.524	9
Pericos de Puebla	53	53	.500	11½
Vaqueros de la Laguna	48	58	.453	16½
Acereros del Norte	47	59	.443	17½
Saraperos de Saltillo	44	60	.423	19½

SOUTH	W	L	PCT	GB
Tigres de Quintana Roo	62	43	.590	—
Piratas de Campeche	55	45	.550	4½
Rojos del Aguila de Veracruz	54	49	.524	7
Guerreros de Oaxaca	51	51	.500	9½
Olmecas de Tabasco	50	55	.476	12
Petroleros de Minatitlan	47	57	.452	14½
Leones de Yucatan	43	62	.410	19

PLAYOFFS—Division Series: Mexico defeated Puebla 4-2, Monterrey defeated Reynosa 4-2, Quintana Roo defeated Oaxaca 4-2 and Veracruz defeated Campeche 4-3 in best-of-seven series. **Semifinals:** Mexico defeated Monterrey 4-3 and Quintana Roo defeated Veracruz 4-2 in best-of-seven series. **Finals:** Quintana Roo defeated Mexico 4-0 in a best-of-seven series.

ATTENDANCE—Monterrey, 430,420; Saltillo, 429,343; Puebla, 363,011; Mexico, 330,626; Monclova, 307,571; Laguna, 249,548; Yucatan, 202,326; Veracruz, 194,831; Oaxaca, 174,856; Reynosa, 156,714; Quintana Roo, 151,698; Tabasco, 131,749; Minatitlan, 101,318; Campeche, 98,997

INDIVIDUAL BATTING LEADERS

PLAYER, TEAM	AVG	AB	R	H	2B	3B	HR	RBI	BB	SO	SB
Canizares, Barbaro, Oax	.396	308	77	122	15	2	20	76	61	41	1
Terrero, Luis, Mex	.390	382	109	149	27	2	38	110	61	85	30
Amador, Japhet, Mex	.376	351	70	132	22	2	25	84	39	56	1
Valenzuela, Mario, Mex	.374	254	62	95	15	1	21	58	35	52	1
Orantes, Ramon, Tab	.364	352	45	128	13	0	8	58	20	43	0
Valenzuela Jr., F., Yuc	.359	348	40	125	24	1	8	61	29	47	0
Barker, Kevin, Oax	.358	316	59	113	34	2	12	79	56	63	2
Quintero, Edgar, Mont	.357	333	74	119	19	3	32	78	57	101	5
Castillo, Jose, Mex	.357	294	56	105	20	2	10	60	20	23	12
Cervantes, Refugio, Sal	.357	384	76	137	22	0	25	73	39	55	0

INDIVIDUAL PITCHING LEADERS

PLAYER, TEAM	W	L	ERA	G	GS	SV	IP	H	HR	BB	SO
Tovar, Marco, Rey	12	4	3.11	21	21	0	127	122	8	36	80
Meza, Andres, Pue	11	5	3.14	20	20	1	132	133	12	31	75
Ortega, Pablo, QR	10	3	3.29	19	19	2	109	105	4	41	53
Ruiz, Miguel, Cam	5	6	3.36	31	13	0	102	82	7	36	75
Campos, Francisco, Cam	12	5	3.42	23	22	0	137	131	10	38	113
Silva, Walter, Mon	10	4	3.51	19	19	0	108	99	7	50	53
Rivera, Oscar, Yuc	6	10	3.52	22	22	4	133	133	14	37	78
Barcelo, Lorenzo, Pue	10	7	3.54	21	21	3	142	148	17	20	80
Ramirez, Roberto, Mex	10	3	3.59	21	21	1	108	119	12	36	86
Ramirez, Jose, QR	7	4	3.60	19	19	0	105	121	10	27	48
Vargas, Joel, Ver	11	7	3.60	21	21	0	120	137	9	26	75

INTERNATIONAL

Tsunami recovery hampers season

BY WAYNE GRACZYK

The Pacific League's Fukuoka SoftBank Hawks defeated the Central League Chunichi Dragons four games to three to win the 2011 Japan Series. Both clubs finished the regular season in first place in their respective leagues and won the right to play in the Japan Series after winning the final stage of Climax Series playoffs.

In a Japan Series that saw the first six games won by the visiting team, Chunichi took Games One, Two and Six at Fukuoka Yahoo Dome, while SoftBank swept Games Three, Four and Five at the Dragons' Nagoya Dome home. The Hawks finally won at home in Game Seven to secure their first Japan Series title since 2003.

The 2011 Japan pro baseball season will be remembered as a pitcher's year, because scoring was down considerably, as were batting averages, home runs and almost all other offensive categories. The decline in hitting statistics may be attributed to two main factors: a new official ball used league-wide that favored pitchers, and slightly darkened stadium lighting necessitated by electric power-saving measures.

In the wake of the devastating earthquake and tsunami that struck northern Japan on March 11, and worries about the damaged Fukushima nuclear power plant, Opening Day was pushed back from March 25 to April 12. The Japan Series was not completed until Nov. 20.

Eighty foreign-born players were in Japan in 2011, and righthander D.J. Houlton had perhaps the best showing, as he posted a 19-6, 2.19 record. He's the third foreign pitcher since 1950 to win more than 18 games in a season; the others (Gene Bacque and Joe Stanka) both happened in 1964. Houlton, playing his fourth year in Japan, tied Rakuten Eagles ace Masahiro Tanaka (19-5) for the most victories in both leagues.

Wladimir Balentien, playing his first season in Japan, led the Central League in home runs with 31, while Matt Murton, in his second season, hit .311 to rank second in the Central batting race.

Several foreign righthanders found success in Japan in 2011. The list includes Nippon Ham starters Bobby Keppel (14-6) and Brian Wolfe (12-11), Hiroshima's Bryan Bullington (13-11) and Hanshin's Randy Messenger (12-7). SoftBank reliever Brian Falkenborg saved 19 games in a closer role and accumulated 20 holds as the Fukuoka set-up man, while Dennis Sarfate racked up 35 saves for Hiroshima.

Japan's leagues faced off in three all-star games played in 2011, with the Pacific League winning two and the Central one. The PL leads the all-star series 77-71 with nine ties.

The Yokohama BayStars franchise was in the process of being sold by owner Tokyo Broadcasting to an IT company called DeNA. Final approval of the transfer was expected Dec. 1, and the team in 2012 would be called the Yokohama DeNA BayStars.

Among Japanese players looking to go to the major leagues in 2012 were righthander Yu Darvish of Nippon Ham and outfielder Norichika Aoki of Yakult via the posting system, and lefty Tsuyoshi Wada of SoftBank and righty Hisashi Iwakuma of Rakuten as free agents.

Opening Day 2012 was set for March 30, following a scheduled two-game American League series between the Seattle Mariners and Oakland Athletics at Tokyo Dome March 28-29.

CENTRAL LEAGUE

STANDINGS	W	L	T	PCT	GB
Chunichi Dragons	75	59	10	.560	—
Tokyo Yakult Swallows	70	59	15	.543	2½
Yomiuri Giants	71	62	11	.534	3½
Hanshin Tigers	68	70	6	.493	9
Hiroshima Carp	60	76	8	.441	16
Yokohama BayStars	47	86	11	.353	27½

CLIMAX SERIES PLAYOFFS—Stage 1: Tokyo Yakult defeated Yomiuri 2-1 in best-of-three series. Final Stage: Chunichi defeated Tokyo Yakult 4-2 in best-of-seven series.

INDIVIDUAL BATTING LEADERS
(MINIMUM 446 PLATE APPEARANCES)

	AVG.	AB	R	H	2B	3B	HR	RBI	SB
Chono, Hisayoshi, Giants	.316	519	58	164	20	4	17	69	19
Murton, Matt, Tigers	.311	579	66	180	24	1	13	60	6
Miyamoto, Shinya, Swallows	.302	474	30	143	17	1	2	35	2
Toritani, Takashi, Tigers	.300	500	71	150	28	7	5	51	16
Hirano, Keiichi, Tigers	.295	542	62	160	13	5	1	29	6
Kurihara, Kenta, Carp	.293	536	56	157	29	0	17	87	0
Aoki, Norichika, Swallows	.292	583	73	170	18	5	4	44	8
Brazell, Craig, Tigers	.282	422	33	119	21	0	16	69	0
Ramirez, Alex, Giants	.279	477	39	133	12	1	23	73	2
Higashide, Akihiro, Carp	.278	543	60	151	17	3	0	27	8
Hatakeyama, Kazuhiro, Swallows	.269	494	66	133	24	1	23	85	1
Arai, Takahiro, Tigers	.269	550	68	148	25	3	17	93	5
Kawabata, Shingo, Swallows	.268	399	48	107	20	3	4	46	0
Watanabe, Naoto, BayStars	.266	403	33	107	16	2	1	24	7
Araki, Masahiro, Dragons	.263	543	58	143	20	2	2	24	18
Sakamoto, Hayato, Giants	.262	568	69	149	27	2	16	59	8
Ishikawa, Takehiro, BayStars	.260	466	49	121	11	1	0	22	12
Murata, Shuichi, BayStars	.253	530	65	134	28	1	20	70	0
Tanaka, Hiroyasu, Swallows	.252	511	57	129	13	2	1	40	2
Aikawa, Ryoji, Swallows	.244	409	24	100	14	1	1	33	0
Maru, Yoshihiro, Carp	.241	435	48	105	16	4	9	50	9
Morino, Masahiko, Dragons	.232	508	46	118	19	0	10	45	0
Wada, Kazuhiro, Dragons	.232	444	49	103	24	4	12	54	6
Balentien, Wladimir, Dragons	.228	486	63	111	22	1	31	76	3

REMAINING NORTH AMERICAN AND LATIN PLAYERS

	AVG.	AB	R	H	2B	3B	HR	RBI	SB
Barden, Brian, Carp	.281	210	18	59	10	0	3	20	0
Harper, Brett, BayStars	.278	320	23	89	17	0	9	39	0
Sledge, Terrmel, BayStars	.260	339	45	88	15	0	20	57	0
Blanco, Tony, Dragons	.248	278	39	69	13	1	16	48	0
Whitesell, Josh, Swallows	.247	299	29	74	18	0	12	33	0
Tracy, Chad, Carp	.235	149	10	35	12	0	1	19	0
Fields, Josh, Giants	.202	109	9	22	4	1	2	9	0
Ryal, Rusty, Giants	.198	96	6	19	4	0	0	4	0
Guzman, Joel, Dragons	.181	238	15	43	7	0	7	15	0
Guiel, Aaron, Swallows	.138	29	3	4	2	0	1	4	0
Carrasco, Felix, Dragons	.000	4	0	0	0	0	0	0	0

INDIVIDUAL PITCHING LEADERS
(MINIMUM 144 INNINGS)

	W	L	ERA	G	SV	IP	H	BB	SO
Yoshimi, Kazuki, Dragons	18	3	1.65	26	0	191	143	23	120
Utsumi, Tetsuya, Giants	18	5	1.70	28	0	186	153	47	144
Sawamura, Hirokazu, Giants	11	11	2.03	29	0	200	149	45	174
Tateyama, Shohei, Swallows	11	5	2.04	26	0	181	146	29	130
Iwata, Minoru, Tigers	9	13	2.29	25	0	169	121	45	133
Bullington, Bryan, Carp	13	11	2.42	30	0	204	183	43	136
Maeda, Kenta, Carp	10	12	2.46	31	0	216	178	43	192
Nomi, Atsushi, Tigers	12	9	2.52	29	0	200	151	55	186
Nelson, Maximo, Dragons	10	14	2.54	31	0	209	171	49	149
Chen, Wei Yin, Dragons	8	10	2.68	25	0	164	138	31	94
Ishikawa, Masanori, Swallows	10	9	2.73	27	0	178	168	42	127
Messenger, Randy, Tigers	12	7	2.88	25	0	150	129	45	122
Standridge, Jason, Tigers	9	7	2.92	25	0	151	136	44	116
Takasaki, Kentaro, BayStars	5	15	3.45	29	0	177	182	36	127
Tono, Shun, Giants	8	11	3.47	31	2	161	141	55	115

REMAINING U.S. AND LATIN PLAYERS

	W	L	ERA	G	SV	IP	H	BB	SO
Schultz, Mike, Carp	0	0	1.06	19	0	17	22	11	7
Mann, Brandon, BayStars	1	1	1.16	12	0	23	19	8	17
Sarfate, Dennis, Carp	3	1	1.34	57	35	61	40	16	82
Soto, Enyelbert, Dragons	5	1	1.73	20	0	78	65	19	59
Gonzalez, Dicky, Giants	3	3	1.80	13	0	75	58	15	63
Albaladejo, Jonathan, Giants	2	2	2.45	46	2	51	43	19	44
Barnette, Tony, Swallows	1	1	2.68	48	2	47	43	13	54
Alvarado, Giancarlo, Carp	3	7	2.72	18	0	99	82	34	88
Romero, Levi, Giants	1	3	3.29	41	11	41	35	19	36
Soriano, Dioni, Carp	1	3	3.65	8	0	25	15	10	12
Greisinger, Seth, Giants	1	5	4.15	9	0	48	52	18	33
Leach, Brent, BayStars	1	7	5.95	8	0	39	47	21	36
Torres, Carlos, Giants	1	2	6.26	6	0	27	31	11	19
Hamilton, Clayton, BayStars	1	4	7.18	10	0	36	48	11	17
Gonzalez, Luis, BayStars	1	1	12.86	2	0	7	16	1	4
Fernandes, Rafael, Swallows	0	0	54.00	1	0	⅓	1	2	0

PACIFIC LEAGUE

STANDINGS

	W	L	T	PCT	GB
Fukuoka SoftBank Hawks	88	46	10	.657	—
Hokkaido Nippon Ham Fighters	72	65	7	.526	17½
Saitama Seibu Lions	68	67	9	.504	20½
Orix Buffaloes	69	68	7	.504	20½
Tohoku Rakuten Golden Eagles	66	71	7	.482	23½
Chiba Lotte Marines	54	79	11	.406	33½

CLIMAX SERIES PLAYOFFS—Stage 1: Saitama Seibu defeated Hokkaido Nippon Ham 2-0 in best-of-three series. Final Stage: Fukuoka SoftBank defeated Saitama Siebu 4-0 in best-of-seven series.

INDIVIDUAL BATTING LEADERS
(MINIMUM 446 PLATE APPEARANCES)

	AVG.	AB	R	H	2B	3B	HR	RBI	SB
Uchikawa, Seiichi, Hawks	.338	429	48	145	21	3	12	74	4
Itoi, Yoshio, Fighters	.319	489	72	156	30	0	11	54	31
Goto, Mitsutaka, Buffaloes	.312	526	54	164	19	4	8	55	14
Kuriyama, Takumi, Lions	.307	557	87	171	30	2	3	60	6
Honda, Yuichi, Hawks	.305	524	84	159	19	7	0	43	60
Nakajima, Hiroyuki, Lions	.297	566	82	168	27	1	16	100	21
Sakaguchi, Tomotaka, Buffaloes	.297	590	84	175	20	7	3	45	5
Hasegawa, Yuya, Hawks	.293	392	51	115	23	1	4	34	13

Hijirisawa, Ryo, Eagles	.288	496	57	143	19	1	2	42	52
Matsuda, Nobuhiro, Hawks	.282	525	77	148	31	7	25	83	27
Takasu, Yosuke, Eagles	.277	429	28	119	10	1	1	30	5
Yo, Daikan, Fighters	.274	537	66	147	23	4	6	36	19
Nakamura, Takeya, Lions	.269	525	97	141	30	0	48	116	4
Imae, Toshiaki, Marines	.269	499	53	134	30	1	8	51	2
Asamura, Hideto, Lions	.268	437	48	117	17	3	9	45	7
Baldiris, Aarom, Buffaloes	.267	479	49	128	16	1	18	66	2
Kawasaki, Munenori, Hawks	.267	603	71	161	19	7	1	37	31
Okada, Yoshifumi, Marines	.267	577	68	154	7	4	0	35	41
Iguchi, Tadahito, Marines	.265	509	52	135	23	3	9	73	1
Inaba, Atsunori, Fighters	.262	473	49	124	22	3	12	54	4
Ishimine, Shota, Marines	.261	422	52	110	16	6	2	21	32
Matsui, Kazuo, Eagles	.260	538	51	140	34	2	9	48	15
Okada, Takahiro, Buffaloes	.260	492	61	128	26	0	16	85	4
Fernandez, Jose, Lions	.259	529	49	137	21	0	17	81	3
Obiki, Keiji, Buffaloes	.244	405	36	99	15	2	1	34	3
Nakata, Sho, Fighters	.237	527	49	125	32	2	18	91	4
Koyano, Eiichi, Fighters	.237	473	43	112	21	1	5	47	1

REMAINING U.S. AND LATIN PLAYERS

	AVG.	AB	R	H	2B	3B	HR	RBI	SB
Mulhern, Ryan, Lions	.281	57	2	16	1	0	1	8	0
Castillo, Jose, Marines	.269	331	31	89	13	1	5	34	0
Garcia, Luis, Eagles	.261	287	27	75	11	0	8	34	1
Scales, Bobby, Fighters	.261	287	34	75	11	0	9	30	2
Cabrera, Alex, Hawks	.225	311	25	70	13	0	10	35	0
Hoffpauir, Micah, Fighters	.222	329	29	73	14	0	12	36	0
Ortiz, Jose, Hawks	.215	186	11	40	9	0	7	15	0
Ruiz, Randy, Eagles	.195	128	11	25	5	0	6	17	0
Hessman, Mike, Buffaloes	.192	130	9	25	6	0	6	14	0
Brown, Dee, Lions	.155	58	3	9	2	0	0	5	0
Caraballo, Francisco, Buffaloes	.091	11	1	1	0	0	0	0	0

INDIVIDUAL PITCHING LEADERS
(MINIMUM 144 INNINGS)

	W	L	ERA	G	SV	IP	H	BB	SO
Tanaka, Masahiro, Eagles	19	5	1.27	27	0	226	171	27	241
Darvish, Yu, Fighters	18	6	1.44	28	0	232	156	36	276
Wada, Tsuyoshi, Hawks	16	5	1.51	26	0	185	145	40	168
Sugiuchi, Toshiya, Hawks	8	7	1.94	23	0	171	122	49	177
Houlton, D.J., Hawks	19	6	2.19	26	0	172	132	36	121
Karakawa, Yuuki, Marines	12	6	2.41	24	0	168	146	35	122
Kaneko, Chihiro, Buffaloes	10	4	2.43	20	0	155	126	38	123
Takeda, Masaru, Fighters	11	12	2.46	25	0	165	143	18	87
Settsu, Tadashi, Hawks	14	8	2.79	26	0	178	148	31	150
Hoashi, Kazuyuki, Lions	9	6	2.83	26	0	169	172	34	102
Shiomi, Takahiro, Eagles	9	9	2.85	24	0	155	144	34	113
Wakui, Hideaki, Lions	9	12	2.93	26	0	178	184	41	108
Nakayama, Shinya, Buffaloes	8	9	2.94	28	1	156	128	69	119
Terahara, Hayato, Buffaloes	12	10	3.06	25	0	170	162	43	112
Keppel, Bobby, Fighters	14	6	3.22	26	0	162	162	56	66
Naruse, Yoshihisa, Marines	10	12	3.27	26	0	190	189	18	151
Wolfe, Brian, Fighters	12	11	3.60	26	0	150	161	36	90

REMAINING U.S. AND LATIN PLAYERS

	W	L	ERA	G	SV	IP	H	BB	SO
Brazoban, Yhency, Hawks	0	0	0.56	15	1	16	8	5	12
Falkenborg, Brian, Hawks	1	2	1.42	53	19	51	27	16	79
Lerew, Anthony, Hawks	0	0	1.80	4	0	5	6	1	1
Rasner, Darrell, Eagles	3	4	2.04	34	17	53	52	16	46
Rosa, Carlos, Marines	3	4	2.08	62	1	74	62	19	48
Figaro, Alfredo, Buffaloes	8	6	3.42	24	0	123	126	36	90
Penn, Hayden, Marines	2	2	3.46	4	0	26	26	6	15
Jimenez, Kelvin, Eagles	1	7	3.69	13	0	63	74	29	27
Murphy, Bill, Marines	2	5	3.98	10	0	52	56	20	33
Graman, Alex, Lions	2	1	4.26	29	1	25	27	12	13
MacLane, Evan, Buffaloes	3	3	4.50	7	0	30	34	10	22
Speier, Ryan, Eagles	1	4	4.60	30	8	29	29	7	27
Sikorski, Brian, Lions	0	1	4.91	4	0	4	4	2	3
Sanchez, Romulo, Eagles	0	2	4.96	15	0	16	21	7	19
Obispo, Wirfin, Fighters	0	0	54.00	2	0	1	4	3	0

INTERNATIONAL

Lions Win KBO

The Samsung Lions held the defending champion SK Wyverns to seven runs en route to winning the Korean Baseball Organization's championship series in just five games.

The Lions won their first title in five years with pitching and got a shutout in the clincher, winning 1-0 behind a solo homer by Kang Bong-kyu off Wyverns starter Brian Gordon, formerly of the Rangers and Yankees, and seven scoreless innings from Cha Woo-chan.

Reliever Oh Seung-hwan clinched the game by getting the last four outs and earned MVP honors by picking up saves in all four Lions victories. Oh had 47 saves during the regular season without a blown save and went 1-0, 0.63 overall. The Wyverns similarly relied on relievers heavily, with no pitcher surpassing 121 innings.

Samsung, whose 79-50-4 record was the league's best in the regular season, also had the league's most impressive slugger in Choi Hyung-woo, who hit .340 to rank second to Lee Dae-ho in batting. Choi also led the league in home runs (30) and RBIs (118).

STANDINGS & LEADERS

TEAM	W	L	T	PCT	GB
Samsung Lions	79	50	4	.612	—
Lotte Giants	72	56	5	.563	6.5
SK Wyverns	71	59	3	.546	8.5
Kia Tigers	70	63	0	.526	11
Doosan Bears	61	70	2	.466	19
LG Twins	59	72	2	.450	21
Hanwha Eagles	59	72	2	.450	21
Nexen Heroes	51	80	2	.389	29

INDIVIDUAL BATTING LEADERS
BATTING (MIN. 2.0 AB/TEAM GAME)

PLAYER, TEAM	AVG	AB	R	H	2B	3B	HR	RBI	BB	SO
Lee Dae-ho, Lotte	.357	493	76	176	26	1	27	113	63	63
Choi Hyung-woo, Sam	.340	480	80	163	37	3	30	118	76	88
Lee Byung-gyu, LG	.338	485	64	164	24	0	16	75	28	47
Lee Yong-gyu, Kia	.333	421	84	140	16	2	3	33	63	33
Song Ah-seop, Lotte	.326	442	79	144	25	5	15	83	43	80
Ahn Chi-hong, Kia	.315	378	54	119	21	4	5	46	33	55
Choi Jeong, SK	.310	403	64	125	25	1	20	75	46	72
Hong Seong-heon, Lotte	.306	474	70	145	24	2	6	67	53	80
Lee Jong-wook, Doosan	.303	436	64	132	11	5	5	44	49	51
Park Yong-taek, LG	.302	414	57	125	21	1	15	65	26	71

INDIVIDUAL PITCHING LEADERS
(MIN. 120 IP)

PLAYER, TEAM	W	L	ERA	G	SV	IP	H	HR	BB	SO
Oh Seung-hwan, Sam	1	0	0.63	54	47*	57	27	2	11	76
Yoon Suk-min, Kia	17	5	2.45	27	0	172	137	10	44	178
Dustin Nippert, Doosan	15	6	2.55	29	0	187	150	8	64	150
Kim Sun-woo, Doosan	16	7	3.13	28	0	176	188	12	35	89
Jang Won-jun, Lotte	15	6	3.14	29	0	181	195	7	62	129
Yoon Sung-hwan, Sam	14	5	3.54	24	0	137	151	8	30	83
Ben Jukich, LG	10	8	3.60	32	0	188	174	9	53	150
Cha Woo-chan, Sam	10	6	3.69	24	0	149	156	22	62	114
Radhames Liz, LG	11	13	3.88	30	0	165	149	11	84	122
Ryan Sadowski, Lotte	11	8	3.91	25	0	140	130	15	52	79

Lions Overcome Monkeys

The Lamigo Monkeys had the league's best record in the regular season in their first year after moving from Kaohsiung to Taoyuan County, and changing their name from the La New Bears. The Monkeys had the league's MVP in catcher Lin Hong-yu, but they couldn't overcome the Uni-President Lions, who beat them four games to one in the best-of-seven Taiwan Series.

It was quite a turnaround for the Lions, who finished last in the four-team league in 2010 but stormed out of the gates to win the first-half title. In the championship series, three of the Lions' wins came by one run. They won the clincher 10-6 with a 16-hit attack against former big leaguer Ken Ray, the Lamigo starter who led the league in ERA during the season. Chang Tai-shan hit a first-inning grand slam that set the tone for the victory.

After the season, a team of Major League Baseball players came to Taiwan for a five-game exhibition series, winning all five against a team of Taiwan players that included big leaguer Chien-Ming Wang (Nationals), minor leaguers such as Chun-Hsiu Chen (Indians), Che-Hsuan Lin (Red Sox) and Pin-Chieh Chen (Cubs).

STANDINGS & LEADERS

TEAM	W	L	T	PCT	GB
#Lamigo Monkeys	66	52	2	.559	—
*Uni-President Lions	65	52	3	.556	0.5
Brother Elephants	60	60	0	.500	7
Sinon Bulls	45	72	3	.385	20.5

*First-half champion #Second-half champion

INDIVIDUAL BATTING LEADERS
BATTING (MIN. 2.0 AB/TEAM GAME)

PLAYER, TEAM	AVG	AB	R	H	2B	3B	HR	RBI
Chang Cheng-wei, Elephants	.351	484	96	170	22	10	0	44
Lin Zhi-sheng, Monkeys	.336	375	72	126	27	1	18	72
Kao Kuo-ching, Lions	.333	472	74	157	29	4	22	84
Chen Guan-ren, Elephants	.333	375	52	125	25	2	3	74
Zhang Jian-ming, Bulls	.323	439	62	142	23	4	1	55
Lin Hung-yu, Monkeys	.321	439	78	141	28	2	22	106
Zheng Da-hong, Bulls	.319	433	64	138	26	2	5	71
Lin Yi-quan, Bulls	.318	368	56	117	29	0	8	55
Zhong Chen-gyou, Monkeys	.318	444	64	141	29	3	15	73
Su Jien-rong, Bulls	.312	324	48	101	11	0	4	43

INDIVIDUAL PITCHING LEADERS
(MIN. 120 IP)

PLAYER, TEAM	W	L	ERA	G	SV	IP	WHIP
Ken Ray, Monkeys	13	10	2.85	29	1	183	1.11
Tyler Lumsden, Elephants	10	11	3.21	21	0	143	1.29
Orlando Roman, Brothers	16	6	3.36	33	0	204	1.21
Dan Reichert, Lions	12	10	3.66	26	0	160	1.38
Steve Hammond, Monkeys	9	9	4.14	21	0	126	1.44
Chen Huan-yang, Bulls	5	7	4.32	57	0	123	1.41
Lin Qi-wei, Bulls	3	12	4.35	38	2	126	1.56

INTERNATIONAL

Italy: San Marino's Big Year

BY HARVEY SAHKER

In a year that saw Alex Liddi become the first player born and raised in Italy to make the major leagues, a team from outside Italy claimed the country's domestic competition. San Marino—a 24-square-mile independent republic in the country's northeast, near Rimini—won the Italian Baseball League pennant and defeated Nettuno four games to three in the Italy Series after losing the first two games at home. It was San Marino's third Italy Series appearance in four years and its second IBL title.

Italian-Canadian Anthony Granato was chosen as the Italy Series MVP. Leading off and playing short-

BILL NICHOLS

Josh Phelps

stop for San Marino, the 30-year old former minor and independent leaguer batted .379 in the series and led all batters with three homers and nine runs batted in. Former Blue Jays farmhand Jairo Ramos feasted on Nettuno pitching in the series. The 40-year old Venezuelan DH hit .625 and scored 10 runs. Cuban Laidel Chapelli, 39, also caused problems for Nettuno. A career .284 hitter in his native country's Serie Nacional, Chapelli hit .379 and scored seven runs. San Marino hit .331 as a team in the series.

Nettuno starting pitcher Carlos Richetti and manager Ruggero Bagialemani were both ejected during Game Five and suspended for the remainder of the series. Nettuno shortstop Olmo Rosario was also banned from Games Six and Seven as punishment for failing a random drug test that had been administered a few weeks earlier. His suspension was later extended to six months. The 31-year old Dominican was the Can-Am League's Player of the Year in 2007.

The Italy Series was less than memorable for Nettuno hurler Kris Wilson, who was 0-1, 12.27, in three appearances. The former big leaguer pitched a total of 4⅓ innings in two starts. It was a disappointing way to end the campaign for Wilson, who threw a no-hitter and logged 17 strikeouts in a 7-0 win against Godo on April 22.

Wilson, Chapelli, Ramos and Granato all played in the inaugural IBL All-Star Game, which was played at Nettuno's Steno Borghese Stadium. Some 6,000 fans saw Granato go 4-for-6 and score three runs to lead Italy to a 12-4 victory over the All-Stars.

Less than two weeks after it knocked off Nettuno, San Marino was crowned as continental champs when it captured the European Cup in the Czech city of Brno. San Marino defeated the Holland Series champion Amsterdam Pirates and last year's Italy Series winners Parma in the competition's Final Four. It was San Marino's second European Cup title, following victory in 2006.

STANDINGS & LEADERS

TEAM	W	L	GB
San Marino	31	11	—
*Bologna	29	13	2.0
*Parma	28	14	3.0
*Nettuno	25	17	6.0
Rimini	24	18	7.0
Grosseto	18	24	13.0
Godo	10	32	21.0
Novara	3	39	28.0

*Advanced to playoffs

INDIVIDUAL BATTING LEADERS

PLAYER, TEAM	AVG	AB	R	H	2B	3B	HR	RBI
Rodney Medina, Par	.377	151	30	57	10	3	5	28
Edgar Clemente, Bol	.372	121	24	45	9	1	5	34
Luis Perez, Gross	.371	89	16	33	4	2	1	18
Mario Chiarini, Rim	.360	114	29	41	9	0	6	33
Francis Chaves, Rim	.351	148	43	52	9	3	2	20
Lorenzo Avagnina, SM	.348	141	28	49	10	0	5	26
Wuillians Vasquez, SM	.344	160	37	55	11	0	8	26
Josh Phelps, Rim	.338	139	32	47	7	1	4	28
Bryant Nelson, Rim	.336	146	25	49	9	0	4	38
Juan Camilo, Nett	.333	93	19	31	6	1	4	20

INDIVIDUAL PITCHING LEADERS

PLAYER, TEAM	W	L	ERA	G	SV	IP	H	BB	SO
Darwin Cubillan, SM	6	0	0.41	12	2	44	16	13	59
Marco Grifantini, Par	7	1	1.27	14	2	71	38	45	62
Enorbel Marquez, Rim	8	2	1.46	12	0	68	47	22	49
Kris Wilson, Nett	6	3	1.68	13	0	91	64	13	76
Jesus Matos, Bol	8	3	1.88	14	0	86	81	15	62
Justin Cicatello, Bol	2	2	1.96	18	4	37	26	15	31
Mihai Burlea, Par	9	3	2.00	13	0	77	78	30	63
Fabio Betto, Bol	9	0	2.12	13	0	81	67	13	25
Sandy Patrone, Rim	5	3	2.24	14	0	76	61	15	48
Jose Cruz, Nett	3	1	2.27	13	1	48	40	20	29

INTERNATIONAL

Netherlands: Cordemans Does It All

The autumn of 2011 will always be a special one for righthander Rob Cordemans. Five weeks after winning the Holland Series with the Amsterdam Pirates, Cordemans led the Netherlands to a 2-1 victory over Cuba in the final of the Baseball World Cup in Panama. It was the first true world championship for a European nation, as the other came in 1938 when a team of Canadians playing for the United Kingdom won a series against the United States in what is now recognized as the first World Cup.

Former Twins farmhand Wesley Connor was the Holland Series MVP. The 26-year old outfielder hit .455 in the series with a homer and five RBIs. Connor won Game One of the series in

Rob Coredemans

the 14th inning by stealing home on a missed squeeze bunt. It was the longest game in Holland Series history. The Pirates defeated the Hoofddorp Pioniers four games to one to claim their second Dutch championship in four years.

Cordemans (9-1, 0.31) was virtually untouchable for the Pirates during the regular season, holding opponents to a .135 average while allowing just 40 hits in 88 innings. In June, Cordemans became the fourth DML pitcher to reach 1,500 strikeouts and the second to notch 140 wins.

In July, DML batting champ Dirk van't Klooster of Kinheim became the second DML player to reach 1,000 hits en route to a .400 season.

Utrecht-based UVV returned to the DML for the first time since 1988, featuring 50-year-old Cuban slugger Fausto Alvarez, who hit .336, eighth in the league. UVV finished the season with the best won-loss record of any newly promoted DML team in many years.

Neptunus led the league in hitting (.296) and ERA (2.31) during the regular season but stumbled

in the new round-robin semifinals, losing its last two games to the Pirates and failing to make it to the Holland Series for only the fourth time in the last 14 years.

STANDINGS & LEADERS

TEAM	W	L	T	GB
*Neptunus	31	11	0	—
*Pirates	30	11	1	0.5
*Kinheim	30	12	0	1
*Hoofddorp	25	16	1	5.5
UVV	17	25	0	14
Sparta/Feyenoord	16	26	0	15
HCAW	13	29	0	18
ADO	5	37	0	26

*Advanced to playoffs

INDIVIDUAL BATTING LEADERS

PLAYER, TEAM	AVG	AB	R	H	2B	3B	HR	RBI	SB
Dirk van't Klooster, Kin	.400	180	30	72	10	4	0	27	6
Vince Rooi, Ams	.381	139	35	53	15	2	4	37	3
Dirimo Chavez, HCAW	.363	157	28	57	12	0	2	27	0
Dwayne Kemp, Nep	.363	171	47	62	14	5	2	28	22
Basil de Jong, Ams	.354	164	28	58	16	0	1	28	3
Bryan Engelhardt, Kin	.350	123	29	43	11	0	10	38	6
Gyenuar Lopez, ADO	.347	121	13	42	8	3	0	11	8
Fausto Alvarez, UVV	.336	113	17	38	3	0	4	22	0
Jason Halman, Kin	.333	165	28	55	20	0	1	32	2
Sidney de Jong, Ams	.329	140	44	46	7	1	7	36	3

PITCHING

PLAYER, TEAM	W	L	ERA	G	SV	IP	H	BB	SO
Rob Cordemans, Ams	9	1	0.31	13	0	88	40	10	127
Craig Anderson, Nep	5	1	1.09	16	1	58	40	13	34
D. Markwell, Nep	10	1	1.71	13	0	79	56	26	50
Eddie Aucoin, Hoof	11	1	1.98	14	0	100	77	12	84
Patrick Beljaards, Kin	7	2	2.06	26	1	39	40	12	32
David Bergman, Kin	8	3	2.11	14	0	94	74	19	101
Kevin Heijstek, Nep	7	2	2.38	12	0	76	60	17	57
Orlando Yntema, UVV	7	7	2.38	15	0	102	96	31	82
Derek Tarapacki, UVV	4	3	2.70	24	7	47	39	15	62
Shane Gnade, Hoof	2	4	2.83	19	0	41	45	15	14

AROUND EUROPE

■ Technika Brno won the Czech Extraleague, winning a best-of-five series three games to one against AVG Draci Brno. AVG had won the last 16 Extraleague championships.

■ In France, the Rouen Huskies came back from an 0-2 deficit in the best-of-five finals and beat the Montpelier Barracudas to defend their league championship, extending their run of titles to seven years. Rouen won the final three games 4-2, 4-1 and 4-3, all at home.

■ Regensberg's Buchbinder Legioinaere won the German Bundesliga championship, winning the fifth and deciding game of the series against Untouchables Paderborn 5-1 in front of 2,630 fans in Regensburg. It's the third title in four years for Legionaere.

MORRIS FOSTOFF

INTERNATIONAL

Pinar del Rio claims No. 50

The best regular-season team doesn't always win in the postseason. That's true across baseball and was true for the second straight year in Cuba, where Pinar del Rio celebrated the 50th Serie Nacional with a league championship.

The Vegueros (Tobacco Pickers) tied for the fifth-best record in the 90-game regular season, going 50-39-1 under famed manager Alfonso Urquiola, who played for and has managed Cuba's national team in the past. Named the league manager of the year, he piloted a Pinar team that lacks the island's bigger stars or many national team regulars to the finals against Ciego de Avila, which made its first-ever trip to the finals but earned its second top-three finish in the last three seasons.

Pinar topped Ciego in six games to win its first championship in 12 season. The Vegueros featured slugging third baseman Donald Duarte, their lone league all-star, as well as postseason MVP Yosvani Torres, a righthander who went 10-5, 4.01 in the regular season before winning four times in the postseason. Two of those victories came against Ciego and ace Vladimir Garcia, including the Game six clincher.

Signs of Cuba's baseball decline, however, remain abundant. The nation's national team didn't win any of the tournaments it entered in 2011—losing to Taiwan at the World Port tournament in the Netherlands in June, then falling to the Netherlands in the finals of the World Cup in Panama, held in October. Less than two weeks later, Cuba's streak of Pan American Games gold medals ended with a 12-10 loss to the United States in the semifinals in Mexico. Cuba had won every Pan Ams baseball tournament since 1971.

Another sign is the outlandish numbers being put up by Cuban hitters. While scouts rave about

Alfredo Despaigne

IBAF

the talent of players such as Alexei Bell, Alfredo Despaigne, and 2010-11 MVP Jose Dariel Abreu, the first baseman for Cienfuegos, their outlandish numbers point to a wide disparity in the quality of play in the game, similar to the U.S. majors in the pre-World World II era.

Abreu hit .453/.597/.986 with a record-tying 33 home runs over 212 at-bats. He drew 58 walks, which helped him fall short of winning the traditional triple crown—he had 93 RBIs, while Yoennis Cespedes—who left the island following the season, seeking to play in the major leagues—had 99.

STANDINGS & LEADERS

EAST	W	L	PCT	GB
Ciego de Avila	55	35	.611	—
Granma	53	37	.589	2
Guantanamo	51	39	.567	4
Villa Clara	50	39	.556	4.5
Santiago de Cuba	45	45	.500	10
Las Tunas	43	47	.478	12
Camaguey	41	49	.456	14
Holguin	29	60	.326	25.5

WEST	W	L	PCT	GB
Cienfuegos	59	31	.656	—
Pinar del Rio	50	39	.562	8.5
Sancti Spiritus	49	41	.544	10
La Havana	49	41	.544	10
Industriales	44	46	.489	15
Matanzas	38	52	.422	21
Isla de la Juventud	34	55	.378	24.5
Metropolitanos	28	62	.311	31

INDIVIDUAL BATTING LEADERS

PLAYER, TEAM	AVG	AB	R	H	2B	3B	HR	RBI	BB	SO
Jose Dariel Abreu, Cien	.453	212	79	96	14	0	33	93	58	32
Michel Enriquez, Juven	.401	304	67	122	29	0	13	52	62	15
Frederich Cepeda, SS	.397	305	84	121	25	3	28	81	77	36
Yordanis Samon, Gran	.385	327	65	126	20	3	21	76	52	38
Urmaris Guerra, Gran	.379	322	83	122	26	3	16	72	43	36
Yosvani Alarcon, LT	.368	280	43	103	17	4	13	47	25	39
Serguei Perez, Ind	.366	336	52	123	16	1	12	80	26	16
Dariel Alvarez, Cam	.363	344	65	125	22	2	20	81	18	20
Yoandri Urgelles, Ind	.359	340	81	122	26	2	9	67	48	33
Jorge Luis Barcelan, Met	.357	314	47	112	32	0	11	70	15	34
Donal Duarte, PdR	.356	303	79	108	20	3	21	62	49	21
Alfredo Despaigne, Gran	.356	261	56	93	7	0	27	74	33	42
4 tied with	.350									

INDIVIDUAL PITCHING LEADERS

PLAYER, TEAM	W	L	ERA	G	SV	IP	H	HR	BB	SO
Freddy Alvarez, VC	8	4	1.89	17	1	109	96	7	37	73
Ismel Jimenez, SS	13	5	2.53	19	0	139	125	13	24	84
Noelvis Entenza, Cien	11	4	2.54	20	0	131	90	9	75	97
Norberto Gonzalez, Cien	13	2	2.76	21	0	131	139	13	33	73
Yadier Pedroso, Habana	7	4	3.03	13	0	92	77	6	30	73
Norge Vera, Santiago	8	3	3.05	12	1	86	87	9	13	59
Luis Manuel Suarez, Juven	6	5	3.10	17	0	110	110	8	36	64
Misael Silverio, VC	9	7	3.12	18	0	101	86	5	47	94
Miguel Gonzalez, Habana	8	5	3.19	16	0	113	111	9	29	74
Pedro Echemendia, Ciego	5	2	3.19	25	6	85	79	6	28	31

Obregon claims title for Mexico's first since 2005

The final day of the Caribbean Series in Mayaguez, Puerto Rico, began with a chance all four teams could have ended the round-robin format tied, sending the tournament into a playoff.

Instead, Mexico defeated Venezuela and got help from the Dominican Republic to finish alone atop the standings and win the country's first title since 2005.

The Obregon Yaquis went 4-2 in the tournament, finishing a game ahead of the Dominican Republic's Toros del Este and Puerto Rico's Caguas. Venezuela's Caribes finished in last at 2-4.

First baseman Jorge Vazquez led Mexico to a 3-2 victory in its final game, going 2-for-4 with a home run. Righthander Luis Ayala closed the game with a perfect final 12/3 innings to earn his second save of the series. The Yankees later rewarded Ayala for his five shutout innings in the tournament with a minor league contract and spring training invitation. Vazquez, a Yankees farmhand, led Mexico offensively through the series. He hit .310/.310/.552 with a tournament-high six RBIs. Vazquez and former big leaguer Karim Garcia each hit two home runs in the tournament. The only other player to hit two home runs in the series was Venezuelan first baseman Luis Antonio Jimenez.

Padres shortstop Everth Cabrera hit just .238/.304/.238 in the series, but did score a run in Mexico's last-day victory.

This year's tournament was dedicated to Roberto Alomar, who was elected to the Hall of Fame in January and was also inducted into the Caribbean Series Hall of Fame with fellow Puerto Ricans Carlos Baerga and Candy Maldonado.

Mexico got off to a good start in the tournament, defeating the Dominican Republic 4-3 in 15 innings in the opening game.

After losing to Puerto Rico on the tournament's second day, Mexico won back-to-back games to regain control of the series. Attempting a comeback for the island's first Caribbean Series title since 2000, Puerto Rico defeated Mexico 7-6 on the fifth day of the tournament, pulling into a first-place tie with Mexico to set up the tournament's final day.

In the first game of the final day, Mexico's vic-

Dee Gordon won Winter Player of the Year

LARRY GOREN

tory eliminated Venezuela and the Dominican Republic, which meant Puerto Rico would need a win to force a one-game playoff. But the Dominican Republic closed the Caribbean Series with a 3-0 win, setting off Mexico's celebration.

This year was the second time in four years Obregon represented Mexico in the Caribbean Series. Its last appearance came in 2008, but it finished 2-4.

Dodgers farmhand Dee Gordon, son of ex-big league pitcher Tom Gordon, earned BA's Winter Player of the Year award after hitting .361/.396/.493 with Gigantes de Carolina in the Puerto Rican League, which returned after a one-year hiatus.

—Teddy Cahill

DOMINICAN LEAGUE

TEAM	W	L	PCT	GB
Estrellas de Oriente	27	22	.551	—
Leones del Escogido	27	22	.551	—
Toros del Este	27	22	.551	—
Gigantes del Cibao	25	24	.510	2
Aguilas Cibaenas	24	25	.490	3
Tigres del Licey	17	32	.347	10

ROUND ROBIN	W	L	PCT	GB
Toros del Este	12	6	.667	—
Estrellas de Oriente	10	9	.526	2.5
Gigantes del Cibao	9	10	.474	3.5
Leones del Escogido	6	12	.333	6

LIDOM Championship: Toros defeated Estrellas 5-0

INDIVIDUAL BATTING LEADERS
(MIN. 3.1 PA/LEAGUE GAMES)

PLAYER, TEAM	AVG	AB	R	H	2B	3B	HR	RBI	SB
Hector Luna, Aguilas	.349	172	34	60	17	0	4	28	6
Juan Francisco, Gigantes	.322	152	29	49	12	0	8	30	0
Andy Dirks, Toros	.315	165	27	52	7	7	5	26	10
Alexi Casilla, Gigantes	.303	155	38	47	5	2	2	18	7

INTERNATIONAL

	AVG	AB	R	H	2B	3B	HR	RBI	SB
Michael Martinez,, Estrellas	.301	173	19	52	6	2	1	18	5
Alex Valdez, Estrellas	.299	157	22	47	17	1	2	20	1
Jeff Frazier, Estrellas	.299	137	18	41	12	0	7	21	4
Felix Pie, Estrellas	.290	124	18	36	5	3	2	14	1
Erick Almonte, Gigantes	.285	158	25	45	7	0	3	22	0
Elian Herrera, Aguilas	.280	143	19	40	3	3	2	17	6

INDIVIDUAL PITCHING LEADERS
PITCHING (MIN. 0.8 IP/LEAGUE GAMES)

PLAYER, TEAM	W	L	ERA	G	SV	IP	H	BB	SO
Yunesky Maya, Leones	4	2	1.32	8	0	41	27	9	42
Radhames Liz, Estrellas	4	3	1.59	11	0	57	37	20	47
Aneury Rodriguez, Toros	4	2	2.06	9	0	44	34	11	37
Fabio Castro, Gigantes	4	2	2.65	10	0	51	38	21	61
Raul Valdez, Toros	5	3	2.95	10	0	55	53	13	49
Ryan Ketchner, Estrellas	2	3	3.18	10	0	45	43	16	22
Nerio Rodriguez, Leones	2	4	3.28	10	0	49	43	13	56
Ramon Ortiz, Tigres	1	4	3.97	9	0	45	55	10	35
John Halama, Aguilas	4	4	4.39	12	0	55	60	13	28
Lorenzo Barcelo, Aguilas	2	6	5.30	10	0	53	56	8	37

MEXICAN PACIFIC LEAGUE

TEAM	W	L	PCT	GB
Culiacan	39	29	.574	—
Los Mochis	38	30	.559	1
Hermosillo	38	30	.559	1
Obregon	38	30	.559	1
*Guasave	36	32	.529	3
Mazatlan	33	35	.485	6
Mexicali	31	37	.456	8
Navojoa	19	49	.279	20

*first-half champion

FINALS: Obregon defeated Guasave, 4-3.

INDIVIDUAL BATTING LEADERS
(MIN. 3.1 PA/LEAGUE GAMES)

PLAYER, TEAM	AVG	AB	R	H	2B	3B	HR	RBI	SB
Sandy Madera, LM	.362	221	41	80	8	1	14	48	0
Justin Christian, LM	.356	253	60	90	22	0	10	32	24
Geronimo Gil, Herm	.338	234	30	79	8	0	3	36	1
Erubiel Durazo, Herm	.329	213	49	70	5	0	12	34	0
Ramon Orantes, LM	.323	220	38	71	18	0	14	42	1
Barbaro Canizares, Obr	.310	197	32	63	6	0	12	46	0
Yurendell de Caster, Gua	.319	238	46	76	12	0	14	44	0
Heber Gomez, Maz	.318	233	30	74	13	0	5	32	2
Tike redman, Nav	.316	196	45	62	12	0	4	19	4
Rolando Acosta, Nav	.315	203	33	64	7	0	11	31	3

INDIVIDUAL PITCHING LEADERS
(MIN. 0.8 IP/LEAGUE GAMES)

PLAYER, TEAM	W	L	ERA	G	SV	IP	H	BB	SO
Luis Mendoza, Obr	6	3	2.11	14	0	68	57	17	45
Marco Quevedo, Obr	6	1	2.63	14	0	79	79	15	35
Matt Buschmann, Cul	7	2	2.70	13	0	83	56	28	61
Alfonso Sanchez, Maz	7	5	2.73	14	0	79	73	19	41
Andres Meza, Cul	7	3	2.74	13	0	76	64	21	41
Walter Silva, Maz	4	7	2.87	15	0	91	87	29	58
Francisco Campos, Cul	7	5	3.82	13	0	73	59	20	48
Dan Serafini, LM	5	2	3.84	14	0	89	90	36	62
Rolando Valdez, Obr	6	4	3.86	13	0	72	65	23	84
Alberto Castillo, LM	9	2	3.94	13	0	78	65	35	57

VENEZUELAN LEAGUE

TEAM	W	L	PCT	GB
Aguilas del Zulia	35	28	.556	—
Leones del Caracas	35	28	.556	—
Caribes de Anzoategui	34	29	.540	1
Tigres de Aragua	33	30	.524	2
Bravos de Margarita	31	30	.508	3
Cardenales de Lara	28	35	.444	7
Navegantes del Magallanes	28	35	.444	7
Tiburones de La Guaira	26	35	.426	8

ROUND ROBIN	W	L	PCT	GB
Caribes del Anzoategui	11	5	.688	—
Tigres de Aragua	11	6	.647	0.5
Leones del Caracas	10	7	.588	1.5
Bravos de Margarita	5	11	.313	6
Aguilas del Zulia	4	12	.250	7

LVBP Championship: Caribes defeated Tigres 4-3

INDIVIDUAL BATTING LEADERS
(MIN. 2.7 PA/LEAGUE GAMES)

PLAYER, TEAM	AVG	AB	R	H	2B	3B	HR	RBI	SB
Josh Kroeger, Car	.369	149	32	55	13	4	8	36	7
Cesar Suarez, Ori	.338	213	27	72	17	1	4	26	5
Alex Romero, Ara	.325	200	35	65	14	2	4	36	7
Marwin Gonzalez, Car	.324	210	41	68	12	1	2	38	3
Wilson Ramos, Ara	.322	180	34	58	17	0	9	36	1
Hernan Iribarren, Ara	.318	154	31	49	4	4	2	11	8
Luis A. Jimenez, Mar	.312	186	36	58	8	0	12	40	4
Jesus Guzman, Car	.306	252	33	77	11	1	6	52	5
Alexi Amarista, Ori	.295	217	41	64	14	4	9	34	6
Gerardo Parra, Zul	.287	150	20	43	5	1	2	17	5

INDIVIDUAL PITCHING LEADERS
PITCHING (MIN. 0.8 IP/LEAGUE GAMES)

PLAYER, TEAM	W	L	ERA	G	SV	IP	H	BB	SO
Andrew Baldwin, Ori	5	2	2.08	13	0	74	55	20	47
Jan Granado, Zul	6	2	2.21	15	0	53	53	17	19'
Ryan Vogelson, LG	6	2	2.25	11	0	60	39	30	53
Yusmeiro Petit, Mar	5	3	2.39	10	0	60	52	13	45
Ronald Uviedo, Car	4	2	2.39	17	0	64	61	10	32
Yorman Bazardo, Ara	7	2	2.63	12	0	72	57	17	28
Josh Schmidt, Zul	5	3	2.79	14	0	71	52	33	69
Seth Etheron, Ara	4	4	2.81	13	0	67	53	14	53
Jesus Silva, Mar	3	3	2.89	13	0	65	59	17	36
Dwayne Pollok, Zul	3	3	3.83	13	0	56	54	17	36

PUERTO RICAN LEAGUE

TEAM	W	L	PCT	GB
Caguas	31	16	.660	—
Ponce	29	19	.604	2.5
Carolina	27	21	.563	4.5
San Juan	20	28	.417	11.5
Mayaguez	12	35	.255	19

FINALS: Caguas defeated Ponce, 4-3.

INDIVIDUAL BATTING LEADERS
(MIN. 2.7 PA/LEAGUE GAMES)

PLAYER	AVG	AB	R	H	2B	3B	HR	RBI	BB	SO	SB
Luis Figueroa, Cag	.361	155	25	56	10	3	2	18	11	11	1
Dee Gordon, Car	.341	144	26	52	4	6	1	13	5	15	8
Sergio Miranda, SJ	.353	156	18	55	6	3	0	18	14	11	5
Felix Perez, Pon	.344	128	18	44	8	4	1	11	3	17	2
Wilberto Ortiz, Car	.329	143	24	47	13	1	1	16	10	18	2
Pedro Valdes, Car	.316	136	16	43	9	0	4	27	24	12	0
Irving Falu, May	.302	159	26	48	4	4	0	5	19	15	8
Javier Valentin, Cag	.283	127	14	36	4	1	3	15	17	14	0
Jorge Jimenez, Pon	.283	152	11	43	10	0	0	19	13	14	0
Jeff Dominguez, Car	.281	135	17	38	5	2	4	15	7	28	2

INDIVIDUAL PITCHING LEADERS
PITCHING (MIN. 0.8 IP/LEAGUE GAMES)

PITCHER	W	L	ERA	G	SV	IP	H	BB	SO
Kyler Newby, Pon	4	2	1.55	10	0	46	40	16	45
Graham Godfrey, SJ	3	3	1.93	11	0	56	56	13	31
Juan Padilla, Pon	3	4	1.94	13	0	51	42	10	16
Julio Rodriguez, Car	3	1	2.00	11	0	45	36	16	29
Xavier Cedeno, Car	1	2	2.32	12	0	43	32	13	31
Erik Arnesen, Cag	3	2	2.35	7	0	38	40	6	15
Mario Santiago, Car	6	2	2.66	10	0	51	47	14	50
Sho Iwasaki, Cag	8	1	3.19	10	0	54	57	9	40
Willie Collazo, Car	2	2	3.70	7	0	41	33	11	23
Steve Hirschfeld, May	1	4	3.72	11	0	48	53	13	38

COLLEGE

CHRIS PROCTOR

South Carolina got to dogpile again after winning its second straight national championship

Gamecocks take back-to-back titles

BY AARON FITT

For two years, South Carolina coach Ray Tanner has insisted his team is not "imposing" or "great" or "formidable" or—as he put it in his final College World Series press conference of 2011—"awesome."

It's time to revise that position.

Maybe the Gamecocks don't score runs by the truckload or blast towering home runs. Maybe they win a lot of close games in the late innings, and do it in improbable fashion. But when it comes to the business of winning, nobody is more imposing or great or formidable than South Carolina—which won its second consecutive national championship with a dominating 5-2 victory against Florida, sweeping the best-of-three CWS Finals.

"I'd say we're pretty awesome, yeah," said South Carolina senior second baseman Scott Wingo, the College World Series Most Outstanding Player. "Our talent might not be a bunch of first-rounders, but I think I'd play with these guys more than any other team. We don't give you one yard . . . and we're tough to beat."

So tough, in fact, that the Gamecocks haven't been beaten in their last 16 NCAA tournament games, the longest postseason winning streak ever. They have not lost in the postseason since their first game at the 2010 CWS. They ran through the loser's bracket en route to a thrilling national title then, and extended their CWS winning streak to a record 11 games with an unbeaten run to the 2011 title.

It was the same route Oregon State took to consecutive national titles in 2006-07—a run through the loser's bracket followed by a 5-0 showing the next year in Omaha. Those '07 Beavers showed that a confident, fundamentally sound team can prevail against teams with more talent. South Carolina slammed that message home in 2011, when it opened TD Ameritrade Park Omaha the same way it closed Rosenblatt Stadium—with a championship.

"At the beginning of the year, I said, 'We finished up the old one; let's try to open the new one up,' " Wingo said. "Coach thought we might not get it, but I'm the type of guy that, I had a feeling we were going to do it. And I kept thinking of the Oregon State team the whole year. I had a feeling we would get back and win this thing, and we did."

COACHING CAROUSEL

SCHOOL	NEW COACH (PREVIOUS JOB)	FORMER COACH (REASON FOR DEPARTURE)
Akron	Rick Rembielak (Georgia Tech volunteer assistant)	Pat Bangston (resigned)
Alabama State	Mervyl Melendez (Bethune-Cookman head coach)	Larry Watkins (resigned)
Bethune-Cookman	Jason Beverlin (Tennessee assistant)	Mervyl Melendez (Alabama State head coach)
UC Davis	Matt Vaughn (UC Davis associate head coach)	Rex Peters (UCLA assistant)
UC Santa Barbara	Andrew Checketts (Oregon assistant)	Bob Brontsema (reassigned)
Cal State Fullerton	Rick Vanderhook (UCLA associate head coach)	Dave Serrano (Tennessee head coach)
Fairfield	Bill Currier (Fairfield associate head coach)	John Slosar (retired)
Florida A&M	Willie Brown (Maclay, Fla., HS head coach)	Brett Richardson (served as interim head coach)
Fordham	Kevin Leighton (Manhattan head coach)	Nick Restaino (resigned)
Hartford	Justin Blood (Connecticut assistant)	Jeff Calcaterra (fired)
Manhattan	Jim Duffy (Seton Hall assistant)	Kevin Leighton (Fordham head coach)
Md.-Baltimore County	Bob Mumma (UMBC assistant)	John Jancuska (resigned)
Nebraska	Darin Erstad (Nebraska volunteer assistant)	Mike Anderson (fired)
New York Tech	*Butch Caufield (New York Tech assistant)	Bob Hirschfield (retired)
North Carolina A&T	Joel Sanchez (Daytona State, Fla, JC assistant)	Keith Shumate (resigned)
North Carolina Central	Jim Koerner (Buffalo assistant)	Henry White (resigned)
Old Dominion	Chris Finwood (Western Kentucky head coach)	Nate Goulet (served as interim head coach)
Sam Houston State	David Pierce (Rice assistant)	Mark Johnson (retired)
Santa Clara	Dan O'Brien (UC San Diego head coach)	Mark O'Brien (resigned)
South Alabama	Mark Calvi (South Alabama associate head coach)	Steve Kittrell (retired)
South Dakota State	Dave Schrage (Notre Dame head coach)	Ritchie Price (Kansas assistant)
Temple	Ryan Wheeler (Richmond assistant)	Rob Valli (resigned)
Tennessee	Dave Serrano (Cal State Fullerton head coach)	Todd Raleigh (fired)
Western Kentucky	Matt Myers (WKU associate head coach)	Chris Finwood (Old Dominion head coach)

*Interim

Wingo was a driving force behind this title run. He delivered a walk-off hit in South Carolina's CWS opener against Texas A&M, then provided a game-tying RBI single in the eighth inning of the finals opener. His sensational defense bailed out the Gamecocks over and over again—most notably in the first finals game against Florida, when he made two great plays to extract South Carolina from a bases-loaded, no-out jam in the ninth.

He came up huge again in the championship clincher, driving in South Carolina's first run with a sacrifice fly in the third inning against Karsten Whitson, helping key a three-run rally that put the Gamecocks in command. He added an RBI single over a drawn-in infield in the eighth to give the Gamecocks a three-run cushion.

Lefthander Michael Roth added to his own South Carolina legend, starting the CWS clincher on three days' rest for the second consecutive year. In 2010, it was just his second start of the season, and he earned a no-decision with five innings of one-run ball. This time he was a first-team All-American making his third start of this CWS—and he earned the win, holding the Gators to two runs on five hits and two walks while striking out six.

The Gamecocks had enough key parts in place to garner a No. 7 preseason ranking, but they had to replace two weekend rotation stalwarts in Blake

Cooper and Sam Dyson. They entered the spring without any pitchers who had proven themselves in starting roles over a full season.

"The thing coming into the season was the pitching staff—was it going to be good enough, was the starting rotation going to be good enough?" Roth said. "I think some of us had something to prove. And thus far I think we've done a good job."

Roth lowered his career CWS ERA to 1.17 in 38⅓ innings—second-lowest all-time among pitchers with at least 30 career innings. Only Ohio State's Steve Arlin (0.96 in 1965-66) has a lower ERA. In five years or 50, Roth's name will be mentioned in the same breath as Arlin's. "It's like the saying goes, 'History happens here,' " Roth said. "We're in the history books now."

Matt Price's name is right there with Roth's. South Carolina's fearless closer appeared in all five of his team's CWS games, going 2-0, 0.00 with two saves in nine innings of work. He worked 1⅓ perfect innings in the clincher, after working an inning in the first game the day before and 5⅔ taxing innings two days earlier against Virginia. The performance against the Cavaliers was an epic high-wire act. Virginia loaded the bases three times after the ninth inning—once with no outs—but failed to score a run, as Price willed his way through a season-high 95-pitch outing. The two teams combined to go 3-for-25 with runners in scoring position and 0-for-21 with two outs in that white-knuckle affair.

The finals opener against Florida was similarly stressful. Despite freshman righthander Forest Koumas' strong outing, the Gamecocks trailed 1-0 through seven innings, as Florida ace Hudson Randall was in control. South Carolina tied the game in the eighth, then escaped a bases-loaded, no-outs jam in the ninth on back-to-back web gems by Wingo and catcher Robert Beary.

Eventually, sophomore first baseman Christian Walker scored the winning run for South Carolina in the 11th. Just as the Gamecocks scored the winning run against Virginia on back-to-back errors, they scored the winning run against Florida on back-to-back errors—on the same play. After Walker hit a one-out single up the middle, he headed to second on a hit-and-run play, but Adam Matthews swung through the pitch. Catcher Mike Zunino's throw to second sailed into center field, so Walker bolted for third. And center fielder Bryson Smith's throw to third bounced in the dirt and out of play, allowing Walker to waltz home. Walker finished the game 2-for-5 with a double, a single and the game-winning run.

An hour before game time, Walker wasn't even in the lineup because of a broken hamate bone in his left wrist, diagnosed that morning. South Carolina flew in two doctors from the school's orthopedics and sports medicine center, and they treated Walker—with massages, ice and a brace—after he stretched with the team before the game.

Price recorded the final three outs to save the 11-inning thriller. The next day, Price picked up a four-out save, getting pinch-hitter Ben McMahan to fly out to center field for the final out—setting off a dogpile around Price at the pitcher's mound.

"It's been phenomenal, the success that those guys have enjoyed," Tanner said of Roth and Price. "It's just like they've been almost unblemished. Ask me to bring up some days where they didn't do very well, I'd have to think long and hard, because it seems like every time the chips have been down, they've been able to perform."

Price led another tour de force postseason performance by the South Carolina bullpen, which went 6-0, 0.53 with five saves in 34 innings in the NCAA tournament—without allowing an extra-base hit. Set-up man John Taylor, like Price, was a critical figure, appearing in all 12 postseason games and 50 games in all, one shy of the NCAA record. In a CWS dominated by pitching, South Carolina's staff was the most dominant, posting a 0.88 ERA in five games, the fourth-lowest team

ERA in CWS history and the lowest since 1972.

"We've really played some great baseball while we were here, and it's hard for me to understand it all right now," Tanner said. "I'll have to let it sink in a little bit . . .

"Our players, they've made it happen between the lines. They made plays. They made pitches. They got big hits. They always felt they had a chance to win. They believed."

And belief is a powerful thing.

COLLEGE WORLD SERIES

STANDINGS

BRACKET ONE	W	L
Florida	3	0
Vanderbilt	2	2
North Carolina	1	2
Texas	0	2

BRACKET TWO	W	L
South Carolina	3	0
Virginia	2	2
California	1	2
Texas A&M	0	2

CWS FINALS (BEST OF THREE)

June 27: South Carolina 2, Florida 1 (11)
June 28: South Carolina 5, Florida 2

ALL-TOURNAMENT TEAM

C: Robert Beary, South Carolina. **1B:** Christian Walker, South Carolina. **2B:** *Scott Wingo, South Carolina. **3B:** Cody Dent, Florida. **SS:** Peter Mooney, South Carolina. **OF:** Tony Kemp, Vanderbilt; Connor Harrell, Vanderbilt; Bryson Smith, Florida. **DH:** Brady Thomas, South Carolina. **P:** Matt Price, South Carolina; Michael Roth, South Carolina.
*Named Most Outstanding Player.

BATTING
(Minimum 10 PA)

PLAYER	AVG	AB	R	H	2B	3B	HR	RBI	SB
Ben Bunting, UNC	.462	13	2	6	1	1	0	1	0
Keith Werman, UVa.	.455	11	3	5	0	0	0	2	0
Connor Harrell, VU	.417	12	3	5	0	0	2	6	0
Tony Kemp, VU	.400	15	2	6	0	2	0	2	1
John Barr, UVa.	.400	15	0	6	0	0	0	2	1
Jacob Stallings, UNC	.400	10	0	4	2	0	0	2	0
Kenny Swab, UVa.	.385	13	1	5	0	0	0	0	0
Conrad Gregor, VU	.385	13	4	5	1	0	0	2	0
Bryson Smith, UF	.368	19	2	7	1	0	0	2	0
Brady Thomas, SC	.364	22	0	8	2	0	0	4	0

PITCHING
(Minimum 6 IP)

PITCHER	W-L	ERA	G	SV	IP	H	BB	SO
Danny Hultzen, UVa.	0-0	0.00	2	0	9	4	3	14
Matt Price, SC	2-0	0.00	5	2	9	8	5	8
Kent Emanuel, UNC	1-0	0.00	1	0	9	4	1	5
John Taylor, SC	2-0	0.00	5	0	8	5	4	1
Michael Roth, SC	1-0	1.23	3	0	22	13	9	17
Hudson Randall, UF	1-0	1.26	2	0	14	8	1	11
Taylor Hill, VU	1-0	1.29	1	0	7	4	4	4
Tyler Wilson, UVa.	2-0	1.80	2	0	10	8	0	7
Karsten Whitson, UF	0-1	1.93	2	0	9	8	3	9
Ross Stripling, TAMU	0-0	2.25	1	0	8	7	1	6

COLLEGE WORLD SERIES CHAMPIONS

Undefeated

YEAR	CHAMPION	COACH	RECORD	RUNNER-UP	MOST OUTSTANDING PLAYER
1947	California*	Clint Evans	31-10	Yale	None selected
1948	Southern California	Sam Barry	40-12	Yale	None selected
1949	Texas*	Bibb Falk	23-7	Wake Forest	Charles Teague, 2b, Wake Forest
1950	Texas	Bibb Falk	27-6	Washington State	Ray VanCleef, of, Rutgers
1951	Oklahoma*	Jack Baer	19-9	Tennessee	Sid Hatfield, 1b-p, Tennessee
1952	Holy Cross	Jack Barry	21-3	Missouri	Jim O'Neill, p, Holy Cross
1953	Michigan	Ray Fisher	21-9	Texas	J.L. Smith, p, Texas
1954	Missouri	Hi Simmons	22-4	Rollins	Tom Yewcic, c, Michigan State
1955	Wake Forest	Taylor Sanford	29-7	Western Michigan	Tom Borland, p, Oklahoma State
1956	Minnesota	Dick Siebert	33-9	Arizona	Jerry Thomas, p, Minnesota
1957	California*	George Wolfman	35-10	Penn State	Cal Emery, 1b-p, Penn State
1958	Southern California	Rod Dedeaux	35-7	Missouri	Bill Thom, p, Southern California
1959	Oklahoma State	Toby Greene	27-5	Arizona	Jim Dobson, 3b, Oklahoma State
1960	Minnesota	Dick Siebert	34-7	Southern California	John Erickson, 2b, Minnesota
1961	Southern California*	Rod Dedeaux	43-9	Oklahoma State	Littleton Fowler, p, Oklahoma State
1962	Michigan	Don Lund	31-13	Santa Clara	Bob Garibaldi, p, Santa Clara
1963	Southern California	Rod Dedeaux	37-16	Arizona	Bud Hollowell, c, Southern California
1964	Minnesota	Dick Siebert	31-12	Missouri	Joe Ferris, p, Maine
1965	Arizona State	Bobby Winkles	54-8	Ohio State	Sal Bando, 3b, Arizona State
1966	Ohio State	Marty Karow	27-6	Oklahoma State	Steve Arlin, p, Ohio State
1967	Arizona State	Bobby Winkles	53-12	Houston	Ron Davini, c, Arizona State
1968	Southern California*	Rod Dedeaux	45-14	Southern Illinois	Bill Seinsoth, 1b, Southern California
1969	Arizona State	Bobby Winkles	56-11	Tulsa	John Dolinsek, of, Arizona State
1970	Southern California	Rod Dedeaux	51-13	Florida State	Gene Ammann, p, Florida State
1971	Southern California	Rod Dedeaux	53-13	Southern Illinois	Jerry Tabb, 1b, Tulsa
1972	Southern California	Rod Dedeaux	50-13	Arizona State	Russ McQueen, p, Southern California
1973	Southern California*	Rod Dedeaux	51-11	Arizona State	Dave Winfield, of-p, Minnesota
1974	Southern California	Rod Dedeaux	50-20	Miami	George Milke, p, Southern California
1975	Texas	Cliff Gustafson	56-6	South Carolina	Mickey Reichenbach, 1b, Texas
1976	Arizona	Jerry Kindall	56-17	Eastern Michigan	Steve Powers, dh-p, Arizona
1977	Arizona State	Jim Brock	57-12	South Carolina	Bob Horner, 3b, Arizona State
1978	Southern California*	Rod Dedeaux	54-9	Arizona State	Rod Boxberger, p, Southern California
1979	Cal State Fullerton	Augie Garrido	60-14	Arkansas	Tony Hudson, p, Cal State Fullerton
1980	Arizona	Jerry Kindall	45-21	Hawaii	Terry Francona, of, Arizona
1981	Arizona State	Jim Brock	55-13	Oklahoma State	Stan Holmes, of, Arizona State
1982	Miami	Ron Fraser	57-18	Wichita State	Dan Smith, p, Miami
1983	Texas	Cliff Gustafson	66-14	Alabama	Calvin Schiraldi, p, Texas
1984	Cal State Fullerton	Augie Garrido	66-20	Texas	John Fishel, of, Cal State Fullerton
1985	Miami*	Ron Fraser	64-16	Texas	Greg Ellena, dh, Miami
1986	Arizona	Jerry Kindall	49-19	Florida State	Mike Senne, of, Arizona
1987	Stanford	Mark Marquess	53-17	Oklahoma State	Paul Carey, of, Stanford
1988	Stanford	Mark Marquess	46-23	Arizona State	Lee Plemel, p, Stanford
1989	Wichita State	Gene Stephenson	68-16	Texas	Greg Brummett, p, Wichita State
1990	Georgia	Steve Webber	52-19	Oklahoma State	Mike Rebhan, p, Georgia
1991	Louisiana State*	Skip Bertman	55-18	Wichita State	Gary Hymel, c, Louisiana State
1992	Pepperdine*	Andy Lopez	48-11	Cal State Fullerton	Phil Nevin, 3b, Cal State Fullerton
1993	Louisiana State	Skip Bertman	53-17	Wichita State	Todd Walker, 2b, Louisiana State
1994	Oklahoma*	Larry Cochell	50-17	Georgia Tech	Chip Glass, of, Oklahoma
1995	Cal State Fullerton*	Augie Garrido	57-9	Southern California	Mark Kotsay, of-p, Cal State Fullerton
1996	Louisiana State*	Skip Bertman	52-15	Miami	Pat Burrell, 3b, Miami
1997	Louisiana State*	Skip Bertman	57-13	Alabama	Brandon Larson, ss, Louisiana State
1998	Southern California	Mike Gillespie	49-17	Arizona State	Wes Rachels, 2b, Southern California
1999	Miami*	Jim Morris	50-13	Florida State	Marshall McDougall, 2b, Florida State
2000	Louisiana State*	Skip Bertman	52-17	Stanford	Trey Hodges, rhp, Louisiana State
2001	Miami*	Jim Morris	53-12	Stanford	Charlton Jimerson, of, Miami
2002	Texas*	Augie Garrido	57-15	South Carolina	Huston Street, rhp, Texas
2003	Rice	Wayne Graham	58-12	Stanford	John Hudgins, rhp, Stanford
2004	Cal State Fullerton	George Horton	47-22	Texas	Jason Windsor, rhp, Cal State Fullerton
2005	Texas*	Augie Garrido	56-16	Florida	David Maroul, 3b, Texas
2006	Oregon State	Pat Casey	50-16	North Carolina	Jonah Nickerson, rhp, Oregon State
2007	Oregon State*	Pat Casey	49-18	North Carolina	Jorge Reyes, rhp, Oregon State
2008	Fresno State	Mike Batesole	47-31	Georgia	Tommy Mendonca, 3b, Fresno State
2009	Louisiana State	Paul Mainieri	56-17	Texas	Jared Mitchell, of, Louisiana State
2010	South Carolina	Ray Tanner	54-16	UCLA	Jackie Bradley Jr., of, South Carolina
2011	South Carolina*	Ray Tanner	55-14	Florida	Scott Wingo, 2b, South Carolina

New World Of BBCOR

The advent of new bat standards before the 2011 season dramatically changed the complexion of college baseball.

The new BBCOR bats—which stands for Batted Ball Coefficient of Restitution, a new, more stringent test of bat liveliness—were far less potent than their BESR predecessors, and offense was down across the board in 2011. The average Division I team batting average dropped from .305 in 2010 to .282 in 2011, the lowest average since 1976—just the third year of the metal bat era. Scoring dropped from 6.98 runs per game to 5.58 runs per game, the first time scoring dipped below six runs per game since 1977. Home runs dropped from 0.94 per game to 0.52 per game, the lowest since 1975. So winning teams—like College World Series participant Virginia—found other ways to produce offense.

"We're a team that's not going to try to sell out for the home run," Virginia coach Brian O'Connor said. "We'll try to execute, try to be good consistent hitters, put the ball in play. If you look across the country, there's not many people hitting many home runs. The last two years, we had the kind of hitters that you could stand up there and let them swing away. We broke our home run record two years in a row here. This team's a little bit different, and the game's a little bit different as a whole in all of college baseball."

Texas, like Virginia, set a school record for home runs in a season in 2010 (81). But in 2011, it was back to Augie Ball—bunting constantly, manufacturing runs. The Longhorns hit just 17 homers with the BBCOR bats.

"It really goes back to old-school baseball, because of the bat," Longhorns coach Augie Garrido said after his team went homerless in an early-season series win against Stanford. "You see the home runs (totals). How many balls were hit off the fence? How many balls were hit to the fence? How many balls one-bounced to the fence? None. We didn't even hit them out in batting practice. So, one thing, we don't use as many balls—saving money. Well, it's a recession."

The average staff ERA fell from 5.95 to 4.67 in 2011, the lowest since 1980. And with balls coming off bats at lower speeds, the composite Division I fielding percentage climbed from .962 to a record .964. The lesson: It's more important than ever to throw strikes and play sound defense.

"Particularly this year, if you walk people and make an error, you create a four- or five-run inning, it's going to be near impossible to catch up

RPI RANKINGS

The Ratings Percentage Index is an important tool used by the NCAA in selecting at-large teams for the 64-team Division I regional tournament. The NCAA now releases its RPI rankings during the season. These were the top 100 finishers for 2011. A team's rank in the final Baseball America Top 25 is indicated in parentheses, and College World Series teams are in **bold**.

1. North Carolina (5)	51-16		51. Kansas State	36-25
2. Florida (2)	53-19		52. St. John's	36-22
3. Virginia (3)	56-12		53. Cal State Bakersfield	33-22
4. Vanderbilt (4)	54-12		54. Oregon	33-26
5. South Carolina (1)	55-14		55. Florida Atlantic	32-25
6. Florida State (8)	46-19		56. Mercer	39-20
7. Arizona State (9)	43-18		57. Seton Hall	34-25
8. Clemson (21)	43-20		58. Belmont	38-26
9. Texas A&M (7)	47-22		59. Southeastern La.	35-22
10. Georgia Tech (20)	42-21		60. Illinois State	36-18
11. Texas (6)	49-19		61. Washington State	26-28
12. Rice (15)	42-21		62. College of Charleston	39-22
13. Stanford (13)	35-22		63. Houston	27-32
14. Arkansas (24)	40-22		64. Missouri State	33-23
15. CS Fullerton (14)	41-17		65. Long Beach State	29-27
16. Georgia	33-32		66. Wake Forest	25-31
17. Miami (23)	38-23		67. Samford	37-23
18. Mississippi State (17)	38-25		68. Hawaii	34-25
19. Arizona	39-21		69. Nebraska	30-25
20. Stetson	43-20		70. Rhode Island	31-22
21. Texas Christian (19)	43-19		71. Wichita State	39-26
22. Central Florida	39-23		72. Oral Roberts	39-22
23. Fresno State	40-16		73. Charlotte	43-16
24. Southern Mississippi	39-19		74. Alabama-Birmingham	29-28
25. Oregon State (10)	41-19		75. Gonzaga	32-19
26. California (11)	38-23		76. Missouri	27-32
27. UC Irvine (16)	43-18		77. Tulane	31-26
28. Louisiana State	36-20		78. Sam Houston State	35-24
29. East Carolina (25)	41-21		79. Virginia Tech	30-25
30. Oklahoma	41-19		80. Georgia Southern	36-26
31. Baylor	31-28		81. La.-Lafayette	31-27
32. Connecticut (12)	45-20		82. Michigan State	36-21
33. Alabama	35-28		83. Stony Brook	42-12
34. UCLA (22)	35-24		84. Liberty	35-24
35. Creighton	45-16		85. Texas A&M-CC	37-24
36. North Carolina State	35-27		86. Sacred Heart	34-23
37. Kent State	45-17		87. UNLV	33-25
38. Florida International	40-20		88. Western Kentucky	33-24
39. East Tenn. State	36-21		89. Southern California	25-31
40. Texas State	41-23		90. San Francisco	32-25
41. Dallas Baptist (18)	42-20		91. VMI	27-24
42. Ole Miss	30-25		92. Gardner-Webb	34-23
43. Auburn	29-29		93. Stephen F. Austin	37-23
44. Coastal Carolina	42-20		94. UNC Greensboro	34-20
45. Oklahoma State	35-25		95. Kennesaw State	32-25
46. Jacksonville	37-24		96. South Florida	25-29
47. Elon	36-21		97. Louisville	32-29
48. James Madison	42-19		98. Loyola Marymount	30-25
49. Troy	43-19		99. South Alabama	30-28
50. Texas Tech	33-25		100. UNC Wilmington	31-28

if the other team's throwing strikes," Kansas State coach Brad Hill said.

And outfield speed really matters now.

"Balls that have been hit pretty hard in the gaps, the outfielders have a chance to run them down," said now-retired Sam Houston State coach Mark Johnson. "The old aluminum didn't expose the outfielders as much."

FIRST TEAM

POS.	NAME	YEAR	AVG	OBP	SLG	AB	R	H	HR	RBI	BB	SO	SB
C	Mike Zunino, Florida	So.	.371	.442	.674	264	75	98	19	67	32	52	7
1B	C.J. Cron, Utah	Jr.	.434	.517	.803	198	51	86	15	59	31	21	1
2B	Kolten Wong, Hawaii	Jr.	.378	.492	.560	209	48	79	7	53	42	20	23
3B	Colin Moran, North Carolina	Fr.	.335	.442	.540	248	46	83	9	71	47	33	2
SS	Brad Miller, Clemson	Jr.	.395	.498	.559	195	53	77	5	50	40	34	21
OF	Jason Krizan, Dallas Baptist	Jr.	.413	.498	.700	247	63	102	10	81	42	23	13
OF	Mikie Mahtook, Louisiana State	Jr.	.383	.496	.709	196	61	75	14	56	41	32	29
OF	Victor Roache, Georgia Southern	So.	.326	.438	.778	230	58	75	30	84	37	42	3
DH	Jake Lowery, James Madison	Jr.	.359	.442	.797	251	80	90	24	91	38	47	9
UT	Danny Hultzen, Virginia	Jr.	.309	.396	.441	136	18	42	1	35	18	12	6

	NAME	YEAR	W	L	ERA	G	CG	SV	IP	H	BB	SO	AVG
SP	Trevor Bauer, UCLA	Jr.	13	2	1.25	16	10	0	137	73	36	203	.154
SP	Sean Gilmartin, Florida State	Jr.	12	2	2.09	18	1	0	120	92	21	130	.209
SP	Taylor Jungmann, Texas	Jr.	13	3	1.60	19	5	0	141	81	36	126	.165
SP	Michael Roth, South Carolina	Jr.	14	3	1.06	20	1	0	145	104	41	112	.208
RP	Cody Martin, Gonzaga	Sr.	2	1	0.86	25	0	12	52	30	19	63	.167
UT	Danny Hultzen, Virginia	Jr.	12	3	1.37	18	0	0	118	76	23	165	.184

SECOND TEAM

POS.	NAME	YEAR	AVG	OBP	SLG	AB	R	H	HR	RBI	BB	SO	SB
C	Nick Rickles, Stetson	Jr.	.347	.408	.600	245	47	85	12	62	25	10	0
1B	Aaron Westlake, Vanderbilt	Jr.	.344	.463	.640	250	59	86	18	56	47	54	2
2B	Tommy La Stella, Coastal Carolina	Jr.	.398	.476	.680	231	59	92	14	70	32	18	7
3B	Jason Esposito, Vanderbilt	Jr.	.340	.403	.530	268	55	91	9	59	17	45	15
SS	Joe Panik, St. John's	Jr.	.398	.509	.642	226	60	90	10	57	44	24	21
OF	Trever Adams, Creighton	Sr.	.387	.465	.665	230	46	89	14	57	28	41	15
OF	Bryson Myles, Stephen F. Austin	Jr.	.411	.484	.581	241	69	99	8	36	23	36	53
OF	George Springer, Connecticut	Jr.	.343	.450	.608	245	61	84	12	77	36	40	31
DH	Adam Brett Walker, Jacksonville	So.	.411	.486	.685	241	65	99	13	75	34	63	14
UT	Nick Ramirez, Cal State Fullerton	Jr.	.291	.391	.507	213	40	62	9	49	32	42	4

	NAME	YEAR	W	L	ERA	G	CG	SV	IP	H	BB	SO	AVG
SP	Matt Barnes, Connecticut	Jr.	11	5	1.93	17	3	0	121	79	33	117	.187
SP	Grayson Garvin, Vanderbilt	Jr.	13	2	2.48	18	0	0	113	98	25	11	.232
SP	Sam Gaviglio, Oregon State	Jr.	12	3	2.54	17	4	0	121	91	33	116	.210
SP	Sonny Gray, Vanderbilt	Jr.	12	4	2.43	19	3	0	126	97	51	132	.213
RP	Corey Knebel, Texas	Fr.	3	2	1.13	38	0	19	56	28	12	61	.151
UT	Nick Ramirez, Cal State Fullerton	Jr.	1	1	2.13	22	0	16	25	15	10	33	.167

THIRD TEAM

POS.	NAME	YEAR	AVG	OBP	SLG	AB	R	H	HR	RBI	BB	SO	SB
C	Tyler Ogle, Oklahoma	Jr.	.343	.464	.552	201	53	69	9	45	34	34	10
1B	Christian Walker, South Carolina	So.	.358	.438	.554	271	64	97	10	62	36	30	4
2B	Dan Paolini, Siena	Sr.	.346	.440	.664	211	48	73	19	67	32	36	13
3B	Matt Leeds, College of Charleston	Jr.	.345	.447	.672	232	66	80	18	80	39	61	8
SS	Chad Zurcher, Memphis	Jr.	.443	.547	.557	203	47	90	0	34	33	14	12
OF	Daniel Aldrich, Coll. of Charleston	Fr.	.347	.399	.739	222	43	77	22	73	18	59	1
OF	James Ramsey, Florida State	Jr.	.364	.442	.580	250	58	91	10	67	31	52	11
OF	Dusty Robinson, Fresno State	Jr.	.310	.364	.662	210	44	65	16	55	16	55	10
DH	Joey DeMichele, Arizona State	So.	.368	.412	.663	193	37	71	9	51	14	27	6
UT	Bo Reeder, East Tennessee State	Jr.	.316	.361	.566	244	59	77	15	60	14	61	3

	NAME	YEAR	W	L	ERA	G	CG	SV	IP	H	BB	SO	AVG
SP	Greg Gonzalez, Fresno State	Sr.	11	1	1.79	16	2	0	105	76	28	124	.199
SP	Mark Pope, Georgia Tech	Jr.	11	4	1.74	16	5	0	114	91	24	88	.218
SP	Matt Summers, UC Irvine	Jr.	11	4	2.15	18	2	0	117	81	33	100	.195
SP	Michael Wacha, Texas A&M	So.	9	4	2.29	19	2	0	130	117	30	123	.243
RP	Matt Price, South Carolina	Jr.	7	3	1.83	36	0	20	59	44	20	75	.213
UT	Bo Reeder, East Tennessee State	Jr.	0	1	1.95	24	0	18	28	16	12	32	.165

"You can still hit some doubles, but the ball that you hit into the gap that used to get through now gets cut off sometimes, and the ball that goes over an outfielder's head doesn't happen nearly as much," Florida State coach Mike Martin said.

"When the ball goes in the air, many times in the past I've said, 'Uh-oh'. Now the ball goes in the air, I go, 'OK, who's the next hitter?' "

The trend continued in Omaha, where the new bats and the pitcher-friendly dimensions and wind conditions at TD Ameritrade Park led to the least offensive College World Series in decades. The 2.66 combined ERA by the eight Omaha teams was the lowest since 1973, the final year of the wood-bat era, when the eight teams posted a 2.51 ERA. The nine home runs and .239 batting average were the lowest since the 1974 Series, when teams hit eight homers and batted .227.

"There may not be the home runs, but I think offensively it's been exciting—the grinding out of at-bats, the hit-and-runs, the drags, the pushes, defending the bunt, the walk is now a huge part of the offense," Florida coach Kevin O'Sullivan said before the Finals. "So maybe home runs are down. But as far as the offensive excitement, I think it's as good as it's ever been."

The reduction in offense—and new rules that regulate the time between pitches and innings—caused the pace of play to pick up considerably. Overall, an average D-I game took two hours, 48 minutes in 2011—19 minutes faster than the 2010 average. An average CWS game was completed in three hours, 10 minutes—14 minutes faster than 2010 games in Omaha.

Coaches, players and fans can get behind a faster-paced game. So it took coaches some time to adjust to the new style of play, but they eventually made their peace with the new bats, by and large. American Baseball Coaches Association executive director Dave Keilitz said in Omaha that he conducted a survey of all NCAA coaches (73 percent responded). Just 16 percent of Division I coaches responded that they didn't like the new bats, while 42 percent said they liked the bats, and 41 percent said they are acceptable, Keilitz said.

"I'm enjoying it a lot—I like it," SHSU's Johnson said. "The bunting game's become a little bit more important. That game within the game got lost with the (old) bat sometimes, and you didn't get to see some of the other things that are going on. Now we're moving runners more, hitting behind runners becomes a little more important—the things that champions do."

AROUND THE NATION

■ Minutes after Florida watched South Carolina celebrate its second straight national championship from the first-base dugout at TD Ameritrade Park, Gators coach **Kevin O'Sullivan** exchanged postgame handshakes with South Carolina's players and coaches, then turned to accept handshakes from a couple of reporters. "We'll be back," he said. "We'll be back."

Indeed, the foundation is rock-solid for the Gators, who entered 2011 atop the national rankings and are strong favorites to be preseason No. 1 in 2012 as well. Florida followed its historically strong 2009 recruiting class with another banner haul in 2010, leaving the Gators' roster stacked with experienced stars such as **Mike Zunino**, **Hudson Randall**, **Brian Johnson**, **Austin Maddox** and **Nolan Fontana** heading into 2012.

The bright future provided solace for the Gators, though in the immediate aftermath of a national runner-up finish, it was small consolation. Florida has gone from winning a regional to reaching the College World Series to making the CWS Finals in the last three years under O'Sullivan, but the progression of the program provided little comfort.

"It's nice to make steps," O'Sullivan said. "But to be honest with you, the idea is to win this thing. And I think there's a lot of disappointed players in that locker room right now. Our goal year in, year out is going to be to win a national championship. I think we have the pieces in place—facilities, etc.—to be one of those teams year in, year out. And we're going to be back here. We just—we want to finish this thing off."

■ California shocked the college baseball world by announcing in September 2010 that it would cut its 108-year-old baseball program in response to budget woes. Supporters fought for months to save the program, and the school's chancellor finally agreed to reinstate Cal baseball in April, after donors pledged about $9 million. Cal's players bonded together in the face of adversity, spending most of the season in the Top 25 and rebounding from a late-season swoon to win the Houston Regional in thrilling fashion, storming back from a three-run ninth-inning deficit to beat Baylor in the championship game. They hosted their first super regional (on the campus of Santa Clara) against fellow upstart Dallas Baptist, sweeping the best-of-three series to reach Omaha for the first time since 1992.

"We were cut as a program when we were just in informal workouts in September. We hadn't even had our first full team practice," Cal coach **David Esquer** said after his team had clinched its storybook run to the CWS. "To watch our kids go out and play baseball that Saturday like nothing had happened, like that's what they were meant to do—then behind the scenes to have to deal with all the pressures of trying to figure out their lives. So to be here today, I could not be prouder of a bunch of kids who had to go through what we did and come out the other side. They'll never forget this the rest of their lives."

■ Florida International shortstop **Garrett Wittels** ended the 2010 season riding a 56-game hitting streak, just two games off Division I record owned by former Oklahoma State star **Robin Ventura**. He had to wait eight months to resume his pursuit of Ventura, only to go 0-for-4 on Opening Day against Southeastern Louisiana, snapping his streak.

■ Virginia junior righthander **Will Roberts** threw the first perfect game in school history in a 2-0 midweek win against George Washington in March. He needed just 98 pitches to record the first Division I perfect game since Auburn's **Eric Brandon** did it in 2002. Since 1957, there have been just seven other nine-inning perfect games, and just 18 other perfect games of any length. Roberts' gem was also the second perfect game in Atlantic Coast Conference history (Maryland's **Dick Reitz** threw the last one in 1959 against Johns Hopkins). Roberts struck out 10 and recorded 14 groundball outs.

REGIONALS

JUNE 3-6

64 teams, 16 four-team, double-elimination tournaments. Winners advance to super regionals.

CHARLOTTESVILLE, VA.
Host: Virginia (No. 1 national seed).
Participants: No. 1 Virginia (49-9), No. 2 East Carolina (39-19), No. 3 St. John's (35-20), No. 4 Navy (33-23-1).
Champion: Virginia (3-0).
Runner-up: East Carolina (2-2)
Outstanding player: Danny Hultzen, lhp/1b, Virginia.

LOS ANGELES
Host: UCLA.
Participants: No. 1 UCLA (33-23), No. 2 Fresno State (40-14), No. 3 UC Irvine (39-16), No. 4 San Francisco (31-23).
Champion: UC Irvine (3-0).
Runner-up: UCLA (2-2).
Outstanding player: Ronnie Shaeffer, c, UC Irvine.

FORT WORTH, TEXAS
Host: Texas Christian
Participants: No. 1 Texas Christian (42-17), No. 2 Oklahoma (41-17), No. 3 Dallas Baptist (39-17), No. 4 Oral Roberts (36-20).
Champion: Dallas Baptist (3-1).
Runner-up: Oral Roberts (3-2).
Outstanding player: Landon Anderson, of, Dallas Baptist.

HOUSTON
Host: Rice (No. 8 national seed).
Participants: No. 1 Rice (41-19), No. 2 Baylor (29-26), No. 3 California (31-20), No. 4 Alcorn State (27-28).
Champion: California (4-1).
Runner-up: Baylor (2-2).
Outstanding player: Devon Rodriguez, 1b, California.

TALLAHASSEE, FLA.
Host: Florida State (No. 5 national seed).
Participants: No. 1 Florida State (42-17), No. 2 Central Florida (38-21), No. 3 Alabama (33-26), No. 4 Bethune-Cookman (36-23).
Champion: Florida State (3-0).
Runner-up: Alabama (2-2).
Outstanding player: James Ramsey, of, Florida State.

COLLEGE STATION, TEXAS
Host: Texas A&M.
Participants: No. 1 Texas A&M (42-18), No. 2 Arizona (36-19), No. 3 Seton Hall (33-23), No. 4 Wright State (36-17).
Champion: Texas A&M (3-1).
Runner-up: Arizona (3-2).
Outstanding player: Tyler Naquin, of, Texas A&M.

CLEMSON, S.C.
Host: Clemson.
Participants: No. 1 Clemson (41-18), No. 2 Connecticut (41-17-1), No. 3 Coastal Carolina (41-18), No. 4 Sacred Heart (34-21).
Champion: Connecticut (4-1).
Runner-up: Clemson (2-2).
Outstanding player: Greg Nappo, lhp, Connecticut.

COLUMBIA, S.C.
Host: South Carolina (No. 4 national seed).
Participants: No. 1 South Carolina (45-14), No. 2 Stetson (41-18), No. 3 North Carolina State (34-25), No. 4 Georgia Southern (36-24).
Champion: South Carolina (3-0).
Runner-up: Stetson (2-2).
Outstanding player: Robert Beary, c, South Carolina.

GAINESVILLE, FLA.
Host: Florida (No. 2 national seed).
Participants: No. 1 Florida (45-16), No. 2 Miami (36-21), No. 3 Jacksonville (36-22), No. 4 Manhattan (34-17).
Champion: Florida (3-0).
Runner-up: Miami (2-2).
Outstanding player: Preston Tucker, of, Florida.

ATLANTA
Host: Georgia Tech.
Participants: No. 1 Georgia Tech (40-19), No. 2 Southern Mississippi (39-17), No. 3 Mississippi State (34-23), No. 4 Austin Peay State (33-22).
Champion: Mississippi State (3-0).
Runner-up: Georgia Tech (2-2).
Outstanding player: C.T. Bradford, of, Mississippi State.

TEMPE, ARIZ.
Host: Arizona State.
Participants: No. 1 Arizona State (39-16), No. 2 Arkansas (38-20), No. 3 Charlotte (42-14), No. 4 New Mexico (20-39).
Champion: Arizona State (3-0).
Runner-up: Arkansas (2-2).
Outstanding player: Joey DeMichele, dh, Arizona State.

AUSTIN, TEXAS
Host: Texas (No. 7 national seed).
Participants: No. 1 Texas (43-15), No. 2 Texas State (40-21), No. 3 Kent State (43-15), No. 4 Princeton (23-22).
Champion: Texas (4-1).
Runner-up: Kent State (2-2).
Outstanding player: Tant Shepherd, 1b, Texas.

NASHVILLE, TENN.
Host: Vanderbilt (No. 6 national seed).
Participants: No. 1 Vanderbilt (47-10), No. 2 Oklahoma State (35-23), No. 3 Troy (42-17), No. 4 Belmont (36-24).
Champion: Vanderbilt (3-0).
Runner-up: Belmont (2-2).
Outstanding player: Jason Esposito, 3b, Vanderbilt.

CORVALLIS, ORE.
Host: Oregon State.
Participants: No. 1 Oregon State (38-17), No. 2 Creighton (44-14), No. 3 Georgia (31-30), No. 4 Arkansas-Little Rock (24-32).
Champion: Oregon State (3-0).
Runner-up: Georgia (2-2).
Outstanding player: Sam Gaviglio, rhp, Oregon State.

FULLERTON, CALIF.
Host: Cal State Fullerton.
Participants: No. 1 Cal State Fullerton (40-15), No. 2 Stanford (32-20), No. 3 Kansas State (36-23), No. 4 Illinois (28-25).
Champion: Stanford (3-0).
Runner-up: Illinois (2-2).
Outstanding player: Jordan Pries, rhp, Stanford.

CHAPEL HILL, N.C.
Host: North Carolina (No. 3 national seed).
Participants: No. 1 North Carolina (45-14), No. 2 Florida International (40-18-1), No. 3 James Madison (40-17), No. 4 Maine (32-22).
Champion: North Carolina (3-0).
Runner-up: James Madison (2-2).
Outstanding player: Patrick Johnson, rhp, North Carolina.

SUPER REGIONALS

JUNE 10-13

16 teams, best-of-three series. Winners advance to College World Series.

UC IRVINE AT VIRGINIA
Site: Charlottesville, Va.
Virginia wins 2-1, advances to CWS.

DALLAS BAPTIST AT CALIFORNIA
Site: Santa Clara, Calif.
California wins 2-0, advances to CWS.

TEXAS A&M AT FLORIDA STATE
Site: Tallahassee, Fla.
Texas A&M wins 2-1, advances to CWS.

CONNECTICUT AT SOUTH CAROLINA
Site: Columbia, S.C.
South Carolina wins 2-0, advances to CWS.

MISSISSIPPI STATE AT FLORIDA
Site: Gainesville, Fla.
Florida wins 2-1, advances to CWS.

ARIZONA STATE AT TEXAS
Site: Austin, Texas.
Texas wins 2-1, advances to CWS.

OREGON STATE AT VANDERBILT
Site: Nashville, Tenn.
Vanderbilt wins 2-0, advances to CWS.

STANFORD AT NORTH CAROLINA
Site: Chapel Hill, N.C.
North Carolina wins 2-0, advances to CWS.

UCLA's Bauer cruises to top

PLAYER OF THE YEAR

After a while, you run out of new ways to describe greatness.

UCLA righthander Trevor Bauer dominated college hitters throughout his career.

"That's kind of how it feels—the ho-hum part. It's like, 'Eh,' " Bauer said then, after a four-hit shutout of Arizona, striking out 13.

If you were expecting a different reaction after what turned out to be his final career start in the Los Angeles Regional, after Bauer struck out 14 Fresno State hitters and allowed just a run on six hits in UCLA's 3-1 win, you were disappointed. Bauer did it every week—really. It was his ninth consecutive complete game, and his 14th double-digit strikeout game in 16 starts. It improved him to 13-2, 1.25 on the season—tying him for the national lead in wins and moving him up to third in the national ERA race—and cemented him as Baseball America's 2011 College Player of the Year.

Trevor Bauer

"The one thing Trevor is is very consistent," UCLA coach John Savage said. "He's the same guy in a lot of different situations—on the road, at home, in big games. I thought he was himself (against Fresno). That's what makes him so good. It was just Trevor being Trevor."

Trevor being Trevor meant Trevor blowing hitters away with a fastball that peaked repeatedly at 96 mph and sat at 93-95 for all nine innings. It meant a hammer curveball, a putaway slider, a deceptive changeup, a "reverse slider" that runs away from lefties and even a couple of splitters.

"I had all six pitches going today—it was good," Bauer said. "My reverse was really good today. I've kind of struggled with my feel for it lately, and I haven't thrown it too much, but I worked on it a lot this week. It was really good—it was a good weapon to lefties, and I threw it really effectively. My changeup was really good, got a couple weak contacts on it, and a couple of swing-and-misses. My fastball was OK—velocity was decent, location could have been a little bit better but was workable, my curveball was workable. My slider was, 'Eh.' "

There's that word again—"Eh." Savage marvels at Bauer's ability to dig deep in tough spots, and the way he rises to the occasion against the best competition. "Right when you think the guy is going to crack or not pitch as well, he goes out and out-does himself," Savage said. "He's as consistent as any guy I've ever been around, and he's as competitive a guy as I've ever been around. The guy's just a hell of a pitcher, and I think that's how you describe him. The guy just keeps coming at you and gets better as the game goes on."

Bauer is famously cerebral, and it should be no surprise that he has a deep appreciation for the history of the game. His remarkable season has put him in rare company, and he knows it—and values it.

"There are certain achievements that are good, and they're a little surreal to me," Bauer said. "To get mentioned up there with the likes of Mark Prior and Tim Lincecum and Stephen Strasburg, with some of those stats, it's pretty cool."

PREVIOUS WINNERS

1981: Mike Sodders, 3b, Arizona State	**1991:** David McCarthy, 1b, Stanford	**2001:** Mark Prior, rhp, Southern California
1982: Jeff Ledbetter, of/lhp, Florida State	**1992:** Phil Nevin, 3b, Cal State Fullerton	**2002:** Khalil Greene, ss, Clemson
1983: Dave Magadan, 1b, Alabama	**1993:** Brooks Kieschnick, dh/rhp, Texas	**2003:** Rickie Weeks, 2b, Southern
1984: Oddibe McDowell, of, Arizona State	**1994:** Jason Varitek, c, Georgia Tech	**2004:** Jered Weaver, rhp, Long Beach State
1985: Pete Incaviglia, of, Oklahoma State	**1995:** Todd Helton, 1b/lhp, Tennessee	**2005:** Alex Gordon, 3b, Nebraska
1986: Casey Close, of, Michigan	**1996:** Kris Benson, rhp, Clemson	**2006:** Andrew Miller, lhp, North Carolina
1987: Robin Ventura, 3b, Oklahoma State	**1997:** J.D. Drew, of, Florida State	**2007:** David Price, lhp, Vanderbilt
1988: John Olerud, 1b/lhp, Washington St.	**1998:** Jeff Austin, rhp, Stanford	**2008:** Buster Posey, c/rhp, Florida State
1989: Ben McDonald, rhp, Louisiana State	**1999:** Jason Jennings, rhp, Baylor	**2009:** Stephen Strasburg, rhp, San Diego State
1990: Mike Kelly, of, Arizona State	**2000:** Mark Teixeira, 3b, Georgia Tech	**2010:** Anthony Rendon, 3b, Rice

O'Sullivan builds winner in Florida

COACH OF THE YEAR

BY AARON FITT

Shortly after South Carolina won its first national championship in 2010, Gamecocks coach Ray Tanner received a note from Florida athletics director Jeremy Foley.

"I wrote him back," Tanner recalled, "and I said, 'Your team is outstanding, your coach is the best, and you will win a national championship sooner than later.'"

Little did Tanner know that his Gamecocks would beat the Gators in the College World Series Finals a year later. Tanner, who won Baseball America's Coach of the Year award in 2010, submitted another masterful coaching performance in 2011—but so did Florida coach Kevin O'Sullivan.

In four years at the helm, O'Sullivan has transformed the Gators into an elite college baseball powerhouse. After missing regionals in 2006 and '07, Florida exceeded expectations to make a regional in O'Sullivan's first season in 2008. The next year, the Gators won a regional. The year after that, they made it to Omaha. And in 2011, they ably shouldered the weight of a preseason No. 1 ranking, ending the regular season atop the rankings and advancing all the way to the CWS Finals. For constructing a model program with a rock-solid foundation, O'Sullivan is Baseball America's 2011 Coach of the Year.

Coaches who crossed paths with O'Sullivan over the years knew he was destined for great things. Tanner said he knew even when O'Sullivan was an assis-

Kevin O'Sullivan

tant coach at rival Clemson that he would make a great head coach.

"There was never any doubt in my mind," Tanner said. "This guy's the best. He has been for a long time, and now he's a young head coach. He just does it the right way."

O'Sullivan carved out a reputation as a rising star in the coaching world for his work as Clemson's pitching coach, but also for his relentlessness on the recruiting trail.

"It all starts with recruiting and getting players, and Sully is one of the best at that," said Florida sophomore catcher Mike Zunino. "He gets all the right guys in. And then from there on out it's up to the players to bond, work hard and try to get here."

Florida's ability to recruit an incredibly deep pitching staff has made it easier for the coaches to protect their arms, which in turn attracts more elite arms. The most notable arm, of course, belonged to righthander Karsten Whitson, who opted to attend Florida rather than sign with the Padres as the No. 9 overall pick last year.

"You know, Jeremy Foley made it loud and clear when he hired me: This isn't a two- or three-year deal. This isn't about 2011," O'Sullivan said. "This is about making Florida like a South Carolina, like a Florida State, like a Miami—year in, year out, you have a chance to play for a national championship. Never once did he say, 'You have to win a national championship.' It was all about consistency and being one of the elite programs in the country."

Mission accomplished.

PREVIOUS WINNERS

1981: Ron Fraser, Miami	**1991:** Jim Hendry, Creighton	**2001:** Dave Van Horn, Nebraska
1982: Gene Stephenson, Wichita State	**1992:** Andy Lopez, Pepperdine	**2002:** Augie Garrido, Texas
1983: Barry Shollenberger, Alabama	**1993:** Gene Stephenson, Wichita State	**2003:** George Horton, Cal State Fullerton
1984: Augie Garrido, Cal State Fullerton	**1994:** Jim Morris, Miami	**2004:** David Perno, Georgia
1985: Ron Polk, Mississippi State	**1995:** Pat Murphy, Arizona State	**2005:** Rick Jones, Tulane
1986: Skip Bertman, LSU/Dave Snow, LMU	**1996:** Skip Bertman, Louisiana State	**2006:** Pat Casey, Oregon State
1987: Mark Marquess, Stanford	**1997:** Jim Wells, Alabama	**2007:** Dave Serrano, UC Irvine
1988: Jim Brock, Arizona State	**1998:** Pat Murphy, Arizona State	**2008:** Mike Fox, North Carolina
1989: Dave Snow, Long Beach State	**1999:** Wayne Graham, Rice	**2009:** Paul Mainieri, Louisiana State
1990: Steve Webber, Georgia	**2000:** Ray Tanner, South Carolina	**2010:** Ray Tanner, South Carolina

Unsung Moran makes his mark

Like Dustin Ackley before him, Colin Moran was under the radar and undrafted out of high school. Like Ackley, Moran is a gifted lefthanded hitter who went to North Carolina and earned a starting job immediately as a corner infielder. And like Ackley, Moran became Baseball America's Freshman of the Year.

That's not to say Ackley and Moran are really similar players. They are built much differently—Ackley is a lithe, rather slight, quick-twitch athlete, while Moran is bigger, slower and stronger at 6-foot-3, 180 pounds. But, boy, can Moran hit—just like his UNC predecessor, who won Freshman of the Year honors in 2007 and is now playing in the big leagues with the Mariners. Moran earned first-team All-America honors by hitting .339/.444/.547 with nine homers and 71 RBIs in 245 at-bats.

Colin Moran

FRESHMAN OF THE YEAR

"I wouldn't put him quite in Dustin Ackley's category yet, because that's the best player I've ever coached," North Carolina coach Mike Fox said. "He's a little bit slow-twitch from his waist down, his feet and his biceps—it's a little contrast. But he does have that ability from what I call elbows to fingers, at the last minute. He's nice and loose, he gets in that good power position with his hands, and he lets the bat go, and he swings hard. He swings hard every time in batting practice. But not too hard—he just doesn't take any swings off."

That mental approach, in fact, is the first thing Moran cites when dissecting his offensive success.

"I don't like to take an at-bat off," he said. "Baseball's so mental, I try to lock in on every at-bat. I know that doesn't happen sometimes, but I try to take every pitch like it's my last, try to grind it out, I guess."

PREVIOUS WINNERS

1982: Cory Snyder, 3b, Brigham Young
1983: Rafael Palmeiro, of, Mississippi State
1984: Greg Swindell, lhp, Texas
1985: Jack McDowell, rhp, Stanford
1986: Robin Ventura, 3b, Oklahoma State
1987: Paul Carey, of, Stanford
1988: Kirk Dressendorfer, rhp, Texas
1989: Alex Fernandez, rhp, Miami
1990: Jeffrey Hammonds, of, Stanford
1991: Brooks Kieschnick, rhp-dh, Texas
1992: Todd Walker, 2b, Louisiana State
1993: Brett Laxton, rhp, Louisiana State
1994: R.A. Dickey, rhp, Tennessee
1995: Kyle Peterson, rhp, Stanford
1996: Pat Burrell, 3b, Miami
1997: Brian Roberts, ss, North Carolina
1998: Xavier Nady, 2b, California
1999: James Jurries, 2b, Tulane
2000: Kevin Howard, 3b, Miami
2001: Michael Aubrey, of/lhp, Texas
2002: Stephen Drew, ss, Florida State
2003: Ryan Braun, ss, Miami
2004: Wade LeBlanc, lhp, Alabama
2005: Joe Savery, lhp, Rice
2006: Pedro Alvarez, 3b, Vanderbilt
2007: Dustin Ackley, 1b, North Carolina
2008: Chris Hernandez, lhp, Miami
2009: Anthony Rendon, 3b, Rice
2010: Matt Purke, lhp, Texas Christian

FRESHMAN ALL-AMERICA TEAMS

FIRST TEAM

		AVG	OBP	SLG	AB	R	H	HR	RBI	SB
C	Zane Evans, Georgia Tech	.270	.327	.398	226	34	61	5	46	2
1B	Brian Ragira, Stanford	.329	.370	.465	213	31	70	4	46	2
2B	Jordan Hankins, Austin Peay	.351	.436	.505	188	29	66	4	31	7
3B	Colin Moran, North Carolina	.335	.443	.551	236	46	79	9	69	2
SS	Luke Tendler, N.C. A&T	.380	.404	.606	213	33	81	6	53	7
OF	Daniel Aldrich, Charleston	.347	.399	.739	222	43	77	22	73	1
OF	Tony Kemp, Vanderbilt	.325	.430	.401	237	56	77	0	32	16
OF	Michael Lorenzen, CS Fullerton	.342	.427	.479	146	33	50	2	31	19
DH	Kris Bryant, San Diego	.365	.482	.599	197	57	72	9	36	18
UT	Marco Gonzales, Gonzaga	.291	.403	.382	110	20	32	0	14	1

		W	L	ERA	G	SV	IP	H	BB	SO	AVG
SP	Kent Emanuel, North Carolina	8	1	2.55	19	0	95	92	22	84	.254
SP	Austin Kubitza, Rice	6	5	2.34	15	0	100	95	24	102	.251
SP	Adam Plutko, UCLA	7	4	2.01	16	0	108	73	24	92	.193
SP	Karsten Whitson, Florida	8	0	2.45	17	0	88	76	25	83	.235
RP	Corey Knebel, Texas	3	2	1.15	37	19	55	27	12	60	.148
UT	Marco Gonzales, Gonzaga	11	2	2.57	15	0	105	83	21	90	.221

SECOND TEAM

C—Jared Bales, Southern Mississippi (.281-2-20); **1B**—Dominic Ficociello, Arkansas (.335-4-50); **2B**—JaCoby Jones, Louisiana State (.338-4-32); **3B**—Erich Weiss, Texas (.358-4-44); **SS**—Logan Kirkland, South Alabama (.339-1-27); **OF**—Krey Bratsen, Texas A&M (.331-0-36), Phillip Ervin, Samford (.371-4-41), Kyle Wren, Georgia Tech (.340-1-32); **DH**—Brad Zebedis, Presbyterian (.425-13-57); **UT**—Josh Desze, Ohio State (.332-4-42). **SP**—Tyler Barnette, Charlotte (9-3, 2.29, 90 IP/56 SO), Kurt McCune, Louisiana State (7-3, 3.31, 90 IP/68 SO), Andrew Mitchell, Texas Christian (6-1, 2.84, 76 IP/73 SO), Bryan Radziewski, Miami (9-2, 3.35, 91 IP/92 SO); **RP**—Kyle Porter, California (5-0, 1.59, 2 SV, 51 IP/53 SO). **UT**—Josh Desze, Ohio State (4-2, 5.53, 28 IP/32 SO).

BATTING

Minimum 120 plate appearances, 3.0 plate appearances per team game

BATTING AVERAGE

RANK NAME, TEAM	YEAR	G	AB	H	AVG
1. Chad Zurcher, Memphis	Jr.	55	203	90	.443
2. Effrey Valdez, New York Tech	Sr.	51	183	80	.437
3. C.J. Cron, Utah	Jr.	49	198	86	.434
4. Bo Cuthbertson, Southern Utah	Jr.	51	192	83	.432
5. Tyler Jones, Long Island	Jr.	51	167	71	.425
6. Ross Heffley, Western Carolina	Jr.	53	229	96	.419
7. Scott Davis, Delaware State	Jr.	50	177	74	.418
8. Taylor Davis, Morehead State	Jr.	47	174	72	.414
9. Frazier Hall, Southern	Sr.	48	179	74	.413
10. Jason Krizan, Dallas Baptist	Sr.	62	247	102	.413
11. Bryson Myles, Stephen F. Austin	Jr.	60	241	99	.411
12. Chris O'Brien, Wichita State	Jr.	65	244	100	.410
13. Adam Brett Walker, Jacksonville	So.	61	242	99	.409
14. Jake Hibberd, Wright State	Jr.	55	236	96	.407
15. Cody Fick, Evansville	Sr.	53	212	86	.406
16. Matt Gedman, Massachusetts	Sr.	45	189	76	.402
17. Chris Benson, Utah Valley	Sr.	56	250	100	.400
18. Tommy La Stella, Coastal Carolina	Jr.	61	231	92	.398
19. Joe Panik, St. John's	Jr.	58	226	90	.398
20. Zac Fisher, New Mexico State	So.	52	171	68	.398
21. Kevan Smith, Pittsburgh	Sr.	54	209	83	.397
22. Parker Hipp, New Mexico State	So.	49	169	67	.396
23. Thomas Pope, UNC Wilmington	Jr.	59	202	80	.396
24. Trenton Moses, Southeast Mo. State	Sr.	54	177	70	.395
25. Brad Miller, Clemson	Jr.	56	195	77	.395
26. Ronnie Freeman, Kennesaw State	So.	57	217	85	.392
27. Matt Holland, Texas A&M-CC	Sr.	61	238	93	.391
28. Eric Phillips, Georgia Southern	Jr.	62	251	98	.390
29. Tanner Waite, New Mexico State	Fr.	57	175	68	.389
30. Trever Adams, Creighton	Sr.	61	230	89	.387
31. A.J. Miller, Lafayette	Sr.	48	161	62	.385
32. Tom Murphy, Buffalo	So.	52	190	73	.384
33. Greg Kumpel, Saint Joseph's	So.	48	177	68	.384
34. Brandon Elliott, Murray State	So.	45	159	61	.384
35. Mikie Mahtook, Louisiana State	Jr.	56	196	75	.383
36. Danny Poma, Hofstra	Jr.	47	178	68	.382
37. Ryan Terry, Monmouth	Sr.	52	220	84	.382
38. Will Faulkner, IPFW	Sr.	51	189	72	.381
Tyler Naquin, Texas A&M	So.	68	273	104	.381
40. Andrew Deeds, Morehead State	Jr.	49	184	70	.380
41. Luke Tendler, N.C. A&T	Fr.	55	213	81	.380
42. Brandon Eckerle, Michigan State	Sr.	57	253	96	.379
43. Tobi Adeyemi, Florida A&M	Sr.	57	222	84	.378
44. Kolten Wong, Hawaii	Jr.	57	209	79	.378
45. C.J. Gillman, Dayton	Jr.	59	241	91	.378
46. Mike McCarthy, Texas-Pan American	Jr.	53	191	72	.377
47. Ricky Pacione, Marist	Sr.	52	202	76	.376
48. Jeff Holm, Michigan State	Sr.	57	226	85	.376
49. Ben Packard, Northern Colorado	So.	48	179	67	.374
50. Steve Antolik, High Point	Sr.	56	222	83	.374
Joel Blake, South Dakota State	Sr.	54	222	83	.374
52. Zach Tanner, Wright State	Jr.	52	214	80	.374
53. Brant Jones, Longwood	Sr.	45	182	68	.374
54. Pablo Bermudez, Florida International	Jr.	58	233	87	.373
55. John Rasberry, Norfolk State	Sr.	49	180	67	.372
56. James Brooks, Utah	Jr.	49	223	83	.372
57. Jj Edwards, Sacred Heart	Sr.	57	215	80	.372
58. Zack Leonard, Eastern Michigan	Sr.	59	234	87	.372
Casey McElroy, Auburn	Jr.	58	234	87	.372
60. Seth Granger, McNeese State	Jr.	55	226	84	.372
61. Richie Goodenow, Lipscomb	Sr.	55	210	78	.371
Thomas McCarthy, Kentucky	Jr.	55	210	78	.371
63. Mike Zunino, Florida	So.	72	264	98	.371
64. Phillip Ervin, Samford	Fr.	58	213	79	.371
65. Mitchell Kauweloa, Southern Utah	Jr.	50	189	70	.370
66. Tyler Hannah, Troy	Jr.	62	235	87	.370
67. Dan Gulbransen, Jacksonville	So.	61	227	84	.370
68. Torsten Boss, Michigan State	So.	57	219	81	.370
69. Dustin Torchio, Pacific	So.	53	195	72	.369
70. Jeremy Maas, Penn	Sr.	36	141	52	.369
71. Matt Serna, Illinois-Chicago	Sr.	53	198	73	.369
Josh Wright, Old Dominion	Jr.	53	198	73	.369
73. Ben Klafczynski, Kent State	Sr.	62	247	91	.368
Brig Tison, George Mason	Jr.	54	247	91	.368
75. Eldred Barnett, Grambling State	Jr.	48	182	67	.368
76. Trent Cook, UNLV	Jr.	58	231	85	.368
77. Joey DeMichele, Arizona State	So.	52	193	71	.368
78. Chris Burke, Iona	Jr.	51	185	68	.368
79. Alex Dickerson, Indiana	Jr.	54	215	79	.367
80. Jarryd Reid, Florida A&M	Jr.	43	147	54	.367
81. Tyler Hall, Central Michigan	Jr.	58	229	84	.367
82. Matt Hillsinger, Radford	Jr.	56	221	81	.367
83. Kendall Logan, Jackson State	Jr.	50	183	67	.366
84. Dan Schafferman, George Mason	Jr.	42	164	60	.366
85. Kris Bryant, San Diego	Fr.	53	197	72	.365
86. Byron McKoy, Temple	Sr.	53	230	84	.365
87. Zach Maxfield, Fla. Gulf Coast	Sr.	55	222	81	.365
Trey Rallis, Yale	Sr.	41	148	54	.365
89. Brandon Hairston, Norfolk State	Sr.	52	181	66	.365
90. Stephen Piscotty, Stanford	So.	57	225	82	.364
91. Nick Baligod, Oral Roberts	Sr.	61	247	90	.364
92. James Ramsey, Florida State	Jr.	65	250	91	.364
93. Preston Aldridge, Saint Peter's	Jr.	49	176	64	.364
Grant Buckner, West Virginia	Sr.	55	209	76	.364
Eric Helmrich, Marist	Jr.	43	132	48	.364
96. Jarrod Parks, Mississippi State	Sr.	62	212	77	.363
97. Pete Rajkovich, Centenary	Fr.	40	124	45	.363
98. Michael Adamson, Southeast Mo. State	Sr.	56	226	82	.363
99. Pat Dameron, Delaware	Sr.	52	204	74	.363
100. Corey LeVier, San Diego	Jr.	50	182	66	.363

ON-BASE PERCENTAGE

RANK NAME, TEAM	OBP
1. Chad Zurcher, Memphis	.547
2. Tyler Jones, Long Island	.545
3. Effrey Valdez, New York Tech	.525
4. Frazier Hall, Southern	.524
5. Anthony Rendon, Rice	.520
6. C.J. Cron, Utah	.517
7. Scott Davis, Delaware State	.516
8. Tyler Robbins, Dallas Baptist	.510
9. Taylor Davis, Morehead State	.510
10. Joe Panik, St. John's	.509
11. Tanner Waite, New Mexico State	.509
12. Jarrod Parks, Mississippi State	.508
13. Parker Hipp, New Mexico State	.507
14. Trenton Moses, Southeast Mo. State	.502
15. Jason Krizan, Dallas Baptist	.498
16. Brad Miller, Clemson	.498
17. Jamie Wallschlaeger, St. Bonaventure	.496
18. Mikie Mahtook, Louisiana State	.496
19. Bo Cuthbertson, Southern Utah	.496
20. Chris O'Brien, Wichita State	.495
21. Jimmy Brenneman, Campbell	.493
22. Kolten Wong, Hawaii	.492
23. Dan Gulbransen, Jacksonville	.491
24. Zeke DeVoss, Miami	.491
25. Taylor Roy, Southern	.490
26. Ryan Still, Houston	.488
27. Pablo Bermudez, Florida International	.488
28. Thomas Pope, UNC Wilmington	.488
29. Ronnie Freeman, Kennesaw State	.487
30. Adam Brett Walker, Jacksonville	.486
31. A.J. Miller, Lafayette	.485
32. Tyler McNeely, Illinois State	.485
33. Peter Copa, Massachusetts	.484
34. Bryson Myles, Stephen F. Austin	.484
35. Ross Heffley, Western Carolina	.483
36. Erich Weiss, Texas	.483
37. Kris Bryant, San Diego	.482
38. Scott Woodward, Coastal Carolina	.480
39. Brandon Hairston, Norfolk State	.480
40. Johnny Bladel, James Madison	.478
41. Tyler Hannah, Troy	.477
42. Michael Chiaravalloti, Iona	.477
43. Tommy La Stella, Coastal Carolina	.476

44. Dan Schafferman, George Mason	.475	
45. Xavier Macklin, N.C. A&T	.474	
46. Billy Burns, Mercer	.473	
47. Zach Price, Army	.472	
48. James Taylor, Norfolk State	.472	
49. Rob Kral, Col. of Charleston	.471	
50. Ricky Pacione, Marist	.471	

SLUGGING PERCENTAGE

RANK NAME, TEAM	SLG
1. C.J. Cron, Utah	.803
2. Jake Lowery, James Madison	.797
3. Xavier Macklin, N.C. A&T	.781
4. Victor Roache, Georgia Southern	.778
5. Daniel Aldrich, Col. of Charleston	.739
6. Taylor Davis, Morehead State	.736
7. Paul Hoilman, East Tenn. State	.724
8. Effrey Valdez, New York Tech	.721
9. Mikie Mahtook, Louisiana State	.709
10. A.J. Miller, Lafayette	.708
11. Andrew Rash, Virginia Tech	.707
12. Jason Krizan, Dallas Baptist	.700
13. Bo Cuthbertson, Southern Utah	.688
14. Frazier Hall, Southern	.687
15. Adam Brett Walker, Jacksonville	.682
Josh Wright, Old Dominion	.682
17. Tommy La Stella, Coastal Carolina	.680
18. Kendall Logan, Jackson State	.678
19. Kevan Smith, Pittsburgh	.675
20. Mike Zunino, Florida	.674
21. David Herbek, James Madison	.672
22. Matt Leeds, Col. of Charleston	.672
23. Trenton Moses, Southeast Mo. State	.672
24. Doug Shribman, Bucknell	.670
25. Trever Adams, Creighton	.665
26. David Chester, Pittsburgh	.665
27. Dan Paolini, Siena	.664
28. Joey DeMichele, Arizona State	.663
29. Dusty Robinson, Fresno State	.662
30. Jonathan Griffin, Central Florida	.661
31. Ross Heffley, Western Carolina	.659
32. Will Skinner, Middle Tenn. State	.655
33. Dario Pizzano, Columbia	.654
34. Casey Kalenkosky, Texas State	.653
35. Peter Copa, Massachusetts	.649
36. Jarod Berggren, Northern Colorado	.646
37. Chris O'Brien, Wichita State	.643
38. Joe Panik, St. John's	.642
39. Cody Fick, Evansville	.642
40. Aaron Westlake, Vanderbilt	.640
41. Cody Asche, Nebraska	.639
42. Sean Jamieson, Canisius	.635
43. Bryan Chaikowsky, Md.-Eastern Shore	.634
44. Cameron Edman, Gonzaga	.632
45. Zac Fisher, New Mexico State	.632
46. Zach Johnson, Oklahoma State	.631
47. Ben Thomas, Xavier	.631
48. Andrew Deeds, Morehead State	.630
49. Joe Winker, Mercer	.630
50. Tom Murphy, Buffalo	.626

HOME RUNS

RANK NAME, TEAM	HR
1. Victor Roache, Georgia Southern	30
2. Jake Lowery, James Madison	24
3. Daniel Aldrich, Col. of Charleston	22
Paul Hoilman, East Tenn. State	22
Xavier Macklin, N.C. A&T	22
6. Casey Kalenkosky, Texas State	21
7. Jonathan Griffin, Central Florida	19
Dan Paolini, Siena	19
Mike Zunino, Florida	19
10. Matt Leeds, Col. of Charleston	18
Andrew Rash, Virginia Tech	18
Aaron Westlake, Vanderbilt	18

13. David Chester, Pittsburgh	16
Brandon Miller, Samford	16
Dusty Robinson, Fresno State	16
Doug Shribman, Bucknell	16
Will Skinner, Middle Tenn. State	16
18. Andy Chriscaden, Kennesaw State	15
C.J. Cron, Utah	15
Zack Helgeson, George Mason	15
David Herbek, James Madison	15
Brendon Kelliher, George Washington	15
Mike Martinez, Florida International	15
Dylan Pratt, East Tenn. State	15
Bo Reeder, East Tenn. State	15
Jacob Tanis, Mercer	15
Ben Thomas, Xavier	15
Preston Tucker, Florida	15
29. Trever Adams, Creighton	14
D.J. Hicks, Central Florida	14
Tommy La Stella, Coastal Carolina	14
Mikie Mahtook, Louisiana State	14
Peter O'Brien, Bethune-Cookman	14
Travis Shaw, Kent State	14
Derek Trent, East Tenn. State	14
Steve Ulaky, Delaware	14
37. Taylor Davis, Morehead State	13
Tim Egerton, Belmont	13
Ryan Fleming, Georgia State	13
John Hogan, Austin Peay State	13
Sean Jamieson, Canisius	13
Zach Johnson, Oklahoma State	13
Joey Rapp, Louisiana-Monroe	13
Rony Rodriguez, Miami	13
Richie Shaffer, Clemson	13
Effrey Valdez, New York Tech	13
Adam Brett Walker, Jacksonville	13
Joe Winker, Mercer	13
Nate Woods, Belmont	13
Zach Wright, East Carolina	13

RUNS BATTED IN

RANK NAME, TEAM	RBI
1. Jake Lowery, James Madison	91
2. Victor Roache, Georgia Southern	84
3. Jason Krizan, Dallas Baptist	81
4. Matt Leeds, Col. of Charleston	80
5. George Springer, Connecticut	77
6. David Herbek, James Madison	76
7. Jacob Tanis, Mercer	75
8. Andy Chriscaden, Kennesaw State	74
Preston Tucker, Florida	74
Adam Brett Walker, Jacksonville	74
11. Daniel Aldrich, Col. of Charleston	73
12. Cody Fick, Evansville	71
Colin Moran, North Carolina	71
14. Tommy La Stella, Coastal Carolina	70
Chris O'Brien, Wichita State	70
16. Casey Kalenkosky, Texas State	69
Peter O'Brien, Bethune-Cookman	69
18. Frazier Hall, Southern	67
Xavier Macklin, N.C. A&T	67
Dan Paolini, Siena	67
James Ramsey, Florida State	67
Justin Riddell, Cincinnati	67
Mike Zunino, Florida	67
24. Adam Bryant, Troy	66
D.J. Hicks, Central Florida	66
Kyle Kubitza, Texas State	66
27. Ross Heffley, Western Carolina	65
28. Chris Baker, Old Dominion	63
Garrett Buechele, Oklahoma	63
Ben Carhart, Stetson	63
John Hogan, Austin Peay State	63
Zach Johnson, Oklahoma State	63
33. Nick Rickles, Stetson	62
Christian Walker, South Carolina	62

Nate Woods, Belmont	62
36. Saxon Butler, Samford	61
Jeff Holm, Michigan State	61
38. Jeremy Baltz, St. John's	60
Jarod Berggren, Northern Colorado	60
Jayce Boyd, Florida State	60
David Chester, Pittsburgh	60
Goose Kallunki, Utah Valley	60
Mike Martinez, Florida International	60
Bo Reeder, East Tenn. State	60
Hunter Ridge, UNC Wilmington	60
46. Ryan Aguayo, New Mexico State	59
Torsten Boss, Michigan State	59
Daniel Bowman, Coastal Carolina	59
Johnny Coy, Wichita State	59
C.J. Cron, Utah	59
Chris Elder, Oral Roberts	59
Jason Esposito, Vanderbilt	59
John Hicks, Virginia	59
Jason King, Kansas State	59
Steven Proscia, Virginia	59
Matt Rice, Western Kentucky	59

DOUBLES

RANK NAME, TEAM	2B
1. Jason Krizan, Dallas Baptist	39
2. D.J. Peterson, New Mexico	32
3. Cody Asche, Nebraska	27
William Carmona, Stony Brook	27
Ryan Fuller, Connecticut	27
Tyler Hannah, Troy	27
Chadd Krist, California	27
8. James Brooks, Utah	26
Adam Bryant, Troy	26
Saxon Butler, Samford	26
C.J. Cron, Utah	26
Devon Travis, Florida State	26
13. Austin Heaps, Utah Valley	25
Chris O'Brien, Wichita State	25
Dusty Quattlebaum, Gardner-Webb	25
16. Joey DeBernardis, Penn State	24
Eduardo Gonzalez, Alcorn State	24
18. James Beck, Iona	23
Chris Benson, Utah Valley	23
Cameron Edman, Gonzaga	23
Jacob Esch, Georgia Tech	23
Brandon Loy, Texas	23
L.J. Mazzilli, Connecticut	23
Tyler Naquin, Texas A&M	23
Steve Nikorak, Temple	23
Lee Orr, McNeese State	23
Jeremy Schaffer, Tulane	23
George Springer, Connecticut	23
Alex Staehely, Creighton	23
Preston Tucker, Florida	23
Adam Brett Walker, Jacksonville	23
Mike Zunino, Florida	23
33. Pat Dameron, Delaware	22
Zac Elgie, Troy	22
Jason Esposito, Vanderbilt	22
C.J. Gillman, Dayton	22
Paul Hoilman, East Tenn. State	22
Scott Hornstra, Miss. Valley State	22
Matt Koch, Loyola Marymount	22
Zack Kometani, San Diego	22
Jake Lowery, James Madison	22
Phil Pohl, Clemson	22
Jared Reaves, Alabama	22
44. Chris Baker, Old Dominion	21
Nick Baligod, Oral Roberts	21
Alex Bast, Air Force	21
Ken Battiston, Eastern Mich.	21
Phillip Chapman, Memphis	21
Garrett Customs, Air Force	21
Sam Eberle, Jacksonville State	21

Cody Fick, Evansville	21
Matt Fleishman, Villanova	21
Rudy Flores, Florida International	21
Jake Hibberd, Wright State	21
John Hicks, Virginia	21
Zach Johnson, Oklahoma State	21
Paul Karmas, St. John's	21
Mason Katz, Louisiana State	21
Stephen Marino, Stony Brook	21
Pratt Maynard, North Carolina State	21
Mark Onorati, Manhattan	21
Adrian Perez, Temple	21
Daniel Pigott, Florida	21
Christian Walker, South Carolina	21
Jantzen Witte, Texas Christian	21
Chris Wychock, Towson	21

TRIPLES

RANK NAME, TEAM	3B
1. Tyler Hall, Central Mich.	11
2. Bryan Chaikowsky, Md.-Eastern Shore	9
Trevor Willis, Iowa	9
4. Kendall Logan, Jackson State	8
Jake Lowery, James Madison	8
Jace Peterson, McNeese State	8
Dane Phillips, Oklahoma State	8
Jarryd Reid, Florida A&M	8
Joe Sclafani, Dartmouth	8
10. Landon Anderson, Dallas Baptist	7
Isaac Ballou, Marshall	7
Jarod Berggren, Northern Colorado	7
Nathan Carter, Air Force	7
Shaun Cooper, Utah	7
Bo Cuthbertson, Southern Utah	7
Joey DeMichele, Arizona State	7
Andrew Deeds, Morehead State	7
Pete Diresta, Albany	7
Aaron Dobbs, Kennesaw State	7
Mac Doyle, Wofford	7
Jonathan Houston, Central Arkansas	7
Tony Kemp, Vanderbilt	7
Kyle Kubitza, Texas State	7
David Lyon, Kent State	7
Tyler Naquin, Texas A&M	7
Robby Ort, Indiana State	7
Billy Stitz, South Dakota State	7
Adrian Turner, Grambling State	7
Erich Weiss, Texas	7
Kyle Wren, Georgia Tech	7
31. Jared Baehl, Evansville	6
Ken Battiston, Eastern Mich.	6
Brandon Beans, Navy	6
Jon Berti, Bowling Green State	6
James Brooks, Utah	6
Thomas Brown, Grambling State	6
Kameron Brunty, Southern Miss.	6
Dylan Craig, Belmont	6
Angel Ibanez, Texas-Pan American	6
Alex Jones, Northern Illinois	6
Matt Juengel, Texas A&M	6
Jason King, Kansas State	6
Mike Lang, Rutgers	6
Michael Lowe, Miss. Valley State	6
Chris Marconcini, Duke	6
John McCambridge, Xavier	6
Ryan McIntyre, Cal State Bakersfield	6
Tristan Moore, Wright State	6
Shawn Payne, Georgia Southern	6
Robert Refsnyder, Arizona	6
Tim Smalling, Virginia Tech	6
Jake Williams, South Carolina	6

STOLEN BASES

RANK NAME, TEAM	SB	CS
1. Bryson Myles, Stephen F. Austin	53	15

2. Ryan Brenner, Miami (Ohio)	39	9
Dexter Kelley, Savannah State	39	6
4. Brandon Hollins, Alcorn State	38	8
5. Brooks Pinckard, Baylor	36	3
6. Shawn Payne, Georgia Southern	33	3
7. Zeke DeVoss, Miami	32	10
R.J. Talamantes, Centenary	32	5
9. Krey Bratsen, Texas A&M	31	9
Chad Hinshaw, Illinois State	31	6
George Springer, Connecticut	31	7
Cory Tilton, Charlotte	31	4
Scott Woodward, Coastal Carolina	31	4
14. Steven Brooks, Wake Forest	30	3
Travis Jankowski, Stony Brook	30	4
Jace Peterson, McNeese State	30	10
17. Aaron Barbosa, Northeastern	29	5
Michael Blanchard, Austin Peay	29	5
Billy Burns, Mercer	29	3
Anthony Flenoy, Texas Southern	29	6
John Lynch, Norfolk State	29	9
Mikie Mahtook, Louisiana State	29	9
Khayyan Norfork, Tennessee	29	4
Michael O'Neill, Michigan	29	8
Jeff Simpson, Stetson	29	4
26. Rob Elliott, Bradley	28	6
Tyler Grimes, Wichita State	28	4
Matt Hillsinger, Radford	28	4
John McCambridge, Xavier	28	6
Jamodrick McGruder, Texas Tech	28	6
Ryan Mooney, Sam Houston State	28	3
32. Patrick Biondi, Michigan	27	5
Zack MacPhee, Arizona State	27	7
Ian Parmley, Liberty	27	10
Eric Stamets, Evansville	27	10
Joe Torres, Iona	27	5
Jamison Wells, Northern Illinois	27	7
38. Jamal Austin, Ala.-Birmingham	26	6
Johnny Bladel, James Madison	26	8
Jimmy Brenneman, Campbell	26	4
Derek Hamblen, Belmont	26	4
Matt Johns, Western Carolina	26	0
Eric Phillips, Georgia Southern	26	5
Nick Vickerson, Mississippi State	26	3
45. Willie Argo, Illinois	25	10
Marty Gantt, Col. of Charleston	25	5
Brock Hebert, Southeastern La.	25	5
Jerry Hildreth, Miss. Valley State	25	12
Bryce Ortega, Arizona	25	4
Taylor Ratliff, Jacksonville	25	4
Rand Ravnaas, Georgetown	25	4
Kevin Tokarski, Illinois State	25	9
Justin Wilson, Charlotte	25	7

RUNS

RANK NAME, TEAM	R
1. Jake Lowery, James Madison	80
2. Tyler Robbins, Dallas Baptist	78
3. Mike Zunino, Florida	75
4. Landon Anderson, Dallas Baptist	72
Billy Burns, Mercer	72
6. Derek Hamblen, Belmont	70
Shawn Payne, Georgia Southern	70
8. Johnny Bladel, James Madison	69
Bryson Myles, Stephen F. Austin	69
10. Tyler Naquin, Texas A&M	68
11. Nick Baligod, Oral Roberts	67
Tyler Grimes, Wichita State	67
Jace Peterson, McNeese State	67
14. Matt Leeds, Col. of Charleston	66
15. Adam Brett Walker, Jacksonville	65
16. Michael Adamson, SE Missouri State	64
Jonathan Murphy, Jacksonville	64
Christian Walker, South Carolina	64
19. Pablo Bermudez, Florida International	63
Adam Bryant, Troy	63

Marty Gantt, Col. of Charleston	63
Dan Gulbransen, Jacksonville	63
Jason Krizan, Dallas Baptist	63
Kendall Logan, Jackson State	63
Chris Taylor, Virginia	63
26. Chris Benson, Utah Valley	62
Tyler Hannah, Troy	62
John Hinson, Clemson	62
Ryan Jones, Michigan State	62
Rob Kral, Col. of Charleston	62
Eric Phillips, Georgia Southern	62
Richie Shaffer, Clemson	62
Tyler Sibley, Texas State	62
34. Anthony Gomez, Vanderbilt	61
Dexter Kelley, Savannah State	61
Mikie Mahtook, Louisiana State	61
George Springer, Connecticut	61
Jacob Tanis, Mercer	61
39. Taylor Dugas, Alabama	60
Sean Jamieson, Canisius	60
Joe Panik, St. John's	60
Wesley Starkes, New Mexico State	60
Mike Yastrzemski, Vanderbilt	60
44. Zeke DeVoss, Miami	59
Casey Kalenkosky, Texas State	59
Kyle Kubitza, Texas State	59
Tommy La Stella, Coastal Carolina	59
Bo Reeder, East Tenn. State	59
Ronnie Richardson, Central Florida	59
Kevan Smith, Pittsburgh	59
Aaron Westlake, Vanderbilt	59

HITS

RANK NAME, TEAM	H
1. Tyler Naquin, Texas A&M	104
2. Jason Krizan, Dallas Baptist	102
3. Chris Benson, Utah Valley	100
Chris O'Brien, Wichita State	100
5. Bryson Myles, Stephen F. Austin	99
Adam Brett Walker, Jacksonville	99
7. Eric Phillips, Georgia Southern	98
Mike Zunino, Florida	98
9. Christian Walker, South Carolina	97
10. Brandon Eckerle, Michigan State	96
Anthony Gomez, Vanderbilt	96
Ross Heffley, Western Carolina	96
Jake Hibberd, Wright State	96
14. Matt Holland, Texas A&M-CC	93
L.J. Mazzilli, Connecticut	93
Mike Nemeth, Connecticut	93
17. John Hicks, Virginia	92
Tommy La Stella, Coastal Carolina	92
Brandon Loy, Texas	92
20. Adam Bryant, Troy	91
Jason Esposito, Vanderbilt	91
C.J. Gillman, Dayton	91
Ben Klafczynski, Kent State	91
James Ramsey, Florida State	91
Brig Tison, George Mason	91
26. Nick Baligod, Oral Roberts	90
Jake Lowery, James Madison	90
Joe Panik, St. John's	90
Kyle Wren, Georgia Tech	90
Chad Zurcher, Memphis	90
31. Trever Adams, Creighton	89
Landon Anderson, Dallas Baptist	89
Krey Bratsen, Texas A&M	89
Taylor White, South Alabama	89
35. Sam Eberle, Jacksonville State	88
Steven Proscia, Virginia	88
Tony Renda, California	88
Preston Tucker, Florida	88
Garrett Wittels, Florida International	88
40. Jared Andreoli, Western Kentucky	87

Pablo Bermudez, Florida International	87
Tyler Hannah, Troy	87
Zack Leonard, Eastern Mich.	87
Casey McElroy, Auburn	87
Tyler Sibley, Texas State	87
Chris Taylor, Virginia	87
47. Matt Campbell, UNC Wilmington	86
C.J. Cron, Utah	86
Cody Fick, Evansville	86
Riley Good, Texas-San Antonio	86
Jonathan Griffin, Central Florida	86
Brian Hernandez, UC Irvine	86
Levi Hyams, Georgia	86
Joey Rickard, Arizona	86
Aaron Westlake, Vanderbilt	86

TOTAL BASES

RANK NAME, TEAM	TB
1. Jake Lowery, James Madison	200
2. Victor Roache, Georgia Southern	179
3. Mike Zunino, Florida	178
4. Jason Krizan, Dallas Baptist	173
5. Jonathan Griffin, Central Florida	166
6. Adam Brett Walker, Jacksonville	165
7. Daniel Aldrich, Col. of Charleston	164
8. Casey Kalenkosky, Texas State	160
Aaron Westlake, Vanderbilt	160
10. C.J. Cron, Utah	159
11. Tommy La Stella, Coastal Carolina	157
Chris O'Brien, Wichita State	157
13. Matt Leeds, Col. of Charleston	156
Preston Tucker, Florida	156
15. Paul Hoilman, East Tenn. State	155
16. Adam Bryant, Troy	154
David Herbek, James Madison	154
18. Trever Adams, Creighton	153
19. Ross Heffley, Western Carolina	151
20. Christian Walker, South Carolina	150
21. Matt Holland, Texas A&M-CC	149
George Springer, Connecticut	149
23. Chris Benson, Utah Valley	148
24. Tyler Naquin, Texas A&M	147
Nick Rickles, Stetson	147
26. Ben Klafczynski, Kent State	146
27. Joe Panik, St. John's	145
James Ramsey, Florida State	145
Jacob Tanis, Mercer	145
30. Jake Hibberd, Wright State	144
Will Skinner, Middle Tenn. State	144
32. Xavier Macklin, N.C. A&T	143
33. Jason Esposito, Vanderbilt	142
Zach Johnson, Oklahoma State	142
35. Kevan Smith, Pittsburgh	141
36. Bryson Myles, Stephen F. Austin	140
Dan Paolini, Siena	140
Ben Thomas, Xavier	140
Steve Ulaky, Delaware	140
Ryan Wright, Louisville	140
41. Tyler Hannah, Troy	139
John Hicks, Virginia	139
Mikie Mahtook, Louisiana State	139
Dusty Robinson, Fresno State	139
45. Sean Deegan, Penn State	138
Bo Reeder, East Tenn. State	138
47. Landon Anderson, Dallas Baptist	137
Andy Chriscaden, Kennesaw State	137
Steve Nikorak, Temple	137
50. Nick Baligod, Oral Roberts	136
Taylor Dugas, Alabama	136
Cody Fick, Evansville	136
Derek Hamblen, Belmont	136
Brendon Kelliher, George Washington	136
Jason King, Kansas State	136

WALKS

RANK NAME, TEAM	BB
1. Anthony Rendon, Rice	80
2. Rob Kral, Col. of Charleston	61
3. Sherman Johnson, Florida State	59
4. Zeke DeVoss, Miami	57
Tyler Grimes, Wichita State	57
Tyler Robbins, Dallas Baptist	57
7. Marty Gantt, Col. of Charleston	55
8. Kyle Kubitza, Texas State	54
9. Rob Lind, Georgia State	53
Erich Weiss, Texas	53
11. Pat Blair, Wake Forest	52
Nolan Fontana, Florida	52
13. Pablo Bermudez, Florida International	51
Steven Brooks, Wake Forest	51
15. Dan Gulbransen, Jacksonville	50
Jeff Simpson, Stetson	50
17. Ryan Aguayo, New Mexico State	49
Zack MacPhee, Arizona State	49
Levi Michael, North Carolina	49
20. Jordan Castaldo, Arkansas State	48
21. Colin Moran, North Carolina	47
Aaron Westlake, Vanderbilt	47
23. Keith Hernandez, Delaware State	46
Mike McGee, Florida State	46
Taylor Motter, Coastal Carolina	46
Danny Muno, Fresno State	46
27. Mike Nemeth, Connecticut	45
Kevin Tokarski, Illinois State	45
Devon Travis, Florida State	45
30. Mikel Alvarez, Fla. Gulf Coast	44
Shane Basen, Charlotte	44
Aaron Buchanan, Lamar	44
Chas Crane, Winthrop	44
Trey Hernandez, Texas A&M-CC	44
Peter Mooney, South Carolina	44
Joe Panik, St. John's	44
Jarrod Parks, Mississippi State	44
Richie Shaffer, Clemson	44
Matt Skole, Georgia Tech	44
Jacob Stallings, North Carolina	44
Tanner Waite, New Mexico State	44
Scott Wingo, South Carolina	44
43. Chaz Frank, North Carolina	43
Paul Hoilman, East Tenn. State	43
Jace Peterson, McNeese State	43
John Schultz, Pittsburgh	43
Jomel Torres, San Diego State	43
Mike Yastrzemski, Vanderbilt	43
49. Jeremy Baltz, St. John's	42
Johnny Bladel, James Madison	42
Spiker Helms, Missouri State	42
Jabari Henry, Florida International	42
Jason Krizan, Dallas Baptist	42
Sean Madigan, UC Irvine	42
Jeremy Patton, Florida International	42
Wesley Starkes, New Mexico State	42
Ryan Still, Houston	42
Alex Swenson, Jacksonville	42
Kolten Wong, Hawaii	42

TOUGHEST TO STRIKE OUT

RANK NAME, TEAM	AB/SO
1. Marquis Riley, N.C. A&T	51.8
2. Mark Onorati, Manhattan	40.2
3. Chris Dudics, Toledo	33.6
4. Jordan Fox, UC Irvine	31
5. Danny Stienstra, San Jose State	26.8
6. Tyler Koelling, Southern Miss.	25.8
7. Nick Rickles, Stetson	24.5
8. Dillon Checkal, San Diego	24.4
9. Corey LeVier, San Diego	22.8
10. Tanner Mathis, Ole Miss	22.6
11. Craig Manuel, Rice	21.9

12. Alex Swim, Elon	21.5
13. Kevin Plawecki, Purdue	21.1
14. Anthony Gomez, Vanderbilt	20.4
15. Hunter Phillips, Sacred Heart	20.3
16. Casey McMurray, Illinois	20
17. Angel Ibanez, Texas-Pan American	18.4
18. Ryan Jones, Michigan State	18.2
19. Alex Azor, Navy	18
Maxx Tissenbaum, Stony Brook	18
Derek Vigoa, Penn	18
22. T.J. Rivera, Troy	17.9
23. Jeff Cammans, Rhode Island	17.7
24. A.J. Rusbarsky, Seton Hall	17.6
25. Bret Atwood, Texas State	17

HIT BY PITCH

RANK NAME, TEAM	HBP
1. Jimmy Brenneman, Campbell	31
Tyler Robbins, Dallas Baptist	31
3. Chris Cook, George Mason	26
4. Jamodrick McGruder, Texas Tech	25
5. Jeremy Gum, West Virginia	23
6. John Koszulinski, Western Illinois	22
Mark Onorati, Manhattan	22
Kevin Quaranto, Siena	22
Scott Woodward, Coastal Carolina	22
10. Landon Appling, Houston	21
Cody Cotter, Saint Louis	21
12. Jett Bandy, Arizona	20
Jonathan Koscso, South Florida	20
Jarrod Parks, Mississippi State	20
15. Cole Frenzel, Arizona	19
Tyler Grimes, Wichita State	19
Ivan Hartle, Western Kentucky	19
Cameron Perkins, Purdue	19
Ronnie Richardson, Central Florida	19
20. Marlon Calbi, Villanova	18
Trevor Edwards, UNC Greensboro	18
Taylor Featherston, Texas Christian	18
Braden Kapteyn, Kentucky	18
Paul Nice, Va. Commonwealth	18
Bryan Peters, Nebraska	18
Kevin Plawecki, Purdue	18
George Springer, Connecticut	18
Ivory Thomas, Cal State Fullerton	18

SACRIFICE BUNTS

RANK NAME, TEAM	SH
1. Keith Werman, Virginia	27
2. Bret Fanning, Northern Colorado	22
Nick Judkins, Creighton	22
Justin Roland, Charlotte	22
Zach Thoma, Western Mich.	22
6. Brandon Bednar, Fla. Gulf Coast	21
Brock Bennett, Alabama	21
8. Ben Morgan, Georgia Southern	20
9. Krey Bratsen, Texas A&M	19
Drew Geissinger, High Point	19
Hayes Orton, Coastal Carolina	19
Mark Paytono, Texas	19
13. Bobby Martin, UNC Greensboro	18
Justin McDavid, West Virginia	18
Bryan Peters, Nebraska	18
16. Junior Carlin, South Florida	17
Denver Chavez, Cal Poly	17
18. Jordan Bourque, La.-Lafayette	16
Austin Cowen, Western Illinois	16
Greg Fontenot, La.-Lafayette	16
Jonathan Johnson, Loyola Marymount	16
Zach McCool, Iowa	16
Brad Moss, Samford	16
Marcus Semien, California	16

SACRIFICE FLIES

RANK NAME, TEAM	SF
1. Jason King, Kansas State	12

2. Tom Coulombe, Rhode Island	10
David Herbek, James Madison	10
Logan Kirkland, South Alabama	10
5. Jett Bandy, Arizona	9
Tyler Bream, Liberty	9
Nolan Fontana, Florida	9
Byron McKoy, Temple	9
9. Ryan Behmanesh, Dallas Baptist	8

Johnny Bladel, James Madison	8
Torsten Boss, Michigan State	8
Ben Carhart, Stetson	8
Bobby Glover, Dayton	8
Victor Gomez, Marshall	8
Mason Heyne, Rider	8
John Hicks, Virginia	8
Shane Hoelscher, Rice	8

Wilmy Marrero, Southern	8
Mike Mergenthaler, Richmond	8
Stephen Notaro, Western Carolina	8
Sam Sivilotti, Milwaukee	8
George Springer, Connecticut	8
Billy Urban, St. Bonaventure	8
Zach Wilson, Arizona State	8

PITCHING

Minimum 50 IP, 1 IP per team game

EARNED RUN AVERAGE

RANK NAME, TEAM	YEAR	G	IP	R	ER	ERA
1. Cody Martin, Gonzaga	Sr.	25	52	7	5	0.86
2. Michael Roth, South Carolina	Jr.	21	145	36	17	1.06
3. John Taylor, South Carolina	Sr.	50	71	12	9	1.14
4. Trevor Bauer, UCLA	Jr.	16	137	22	19	1.25
5. Danny Hultzen, Virginia	Jr.	18	118	26	18	1.37
6. Kyle Winkler, Texas Christian	Jr.	14	91	18	14	1.39
7. Tanner Peters, UNLV	Jr.	15	120	30	20	1.50
8. Caleb Reed, Mississippi State	Jr.	29	64	14	11	1.55
9. Brad Mincey, East Carolina	Sr.	31	69	20	12	1.57
10. D.J. Baxendale, Arkansas	So.	19	85	19	15	1.58
11. Taylor Jungmann, Texas	Jr.	19	141	32	25	1.60
12. Mike McCarthy, Cal State Bakersfield	Sr.	17	128	40	23	1.62
13. Evan Marshall, Kansas State	Jr.	30	61	20	11	1.62
14. John Stilson, Texas A&M	Jr.	15	91	22	17	1.68
15. Noe Ramirez, Cal State Fullerton	Jr.	14	91	21	17	1.69
16. Jeremy Gendlek, Utah Valley	Jr.	14	90	23	17	1.71
17. Seth Maness, East Carolina	Sr.	15	105	31	20	1.71
18. Drew Bowen, Oral Roberts	Jr.	13	68	16	13	1.73
19. Mark Pope, Georgia Tech	Jr.	16	114	28	22	1.74
20. Michael Rocha, Oklahoma	Sr.	16	113	33	22	1.75
21. Sam Stafford, Texas	Jr.	19	81	20	16	1.77
22. Will Roberts, Virginia	Jr.	18	106	27	21	1.79
23. Greg Gonzalez, Fresno State	Sr.	16	105	33	21	1.79
24. Max Perlman, Harvard	Sr.	10	60	26	12	1.80
25. Andrew Smith, Charlotte	Jr.	16	109	27	22	1.81
26. Nick Tropeano, Stony Brook	Jr.	14	93	23	19	1.84
27. Sean McKeown, Marist	Sr.	15	63	17	13	1.87
28. Jon Prosinski, Seton Hall	So.	15	94	33	20	1.91
29. Justin Frane, Valparaiso	Sr.	13	61	29	13	1.93
30. Kyle Hallock, Kent State	Sr.	17	106	38	23	1.95
31. Mike Hamann, Toledo	So.	9	60	13	13	1.96
32. Joe DiRocco, Seton Hall	Sr.	17	119	30	26	1.97
33. Carson Smith, Texas State	Jr.	17	113	40	25	1.99
34. Adam Plutko, UCLA	Fr.	16	108	28	24	2.01
35. Matt Barnes, Connecticut	Jr.	17	121	33	27	2.01
36. Andrew Chafin, Kent State	Jr.	14	89	24	20	2.02
37. Brandon McNitt, Stony Brook	Fr.	16	80	20	18	2.03
38. Matt Rein, Coastal Carolina	Sr.	18	74	22	17	2.07
39. Burny Mitchem, Dayton	Jr.	21	104	38	24	2.07
40. Jonas Dufek, Creighton	Sr.	18	113	28	26	2.08
41. Keegan Linza, Liberty	Sr.	15	108	37	25	2.08
42. Sean Gilmartin, Florida State	Jr.	18	120	41	28	2.09
43. Matt Whitehouse, UC Irvine	So.	23	72	21	17	2.12
44. Matt Summers, UC Irvine	Jr.	18	117	35	28	2.15
45. Anthony Meo, Coastal Carolina	Jr.	16	108	31	26	2.16
46. Hudson Randall, Florida	So.	19	124	40	30	2.17
47. Brent McNeil, Eastern Illinois	Sr.	21	54	15	13	2.18
48. David Starn, Kent State	Jr.	17	107	31	26	2.18
49. Mac Thoreson, Miami (Ohio)	So.	16	101	32	25	2.22
50. Brook Hart, Yale	Sr.	11	65	26	16	2.23
51. David Haselden, Clemson	Jr.	25	77	30	19	2.23
52. Tyler Wilson, Virginia	Sr.	19	104	29	26	2.24
53. Josh Biggs, Evansville	So.	15	56	21	14	2.25
54. Kevin Brandt, East Carolina	Jr.	19	92	33	23	2.26
55. Derek Self, Louisville	Jr.	21	76	21	19	2.26
56. Madison Boer, Oregon	Jr.	18	99	27	25	2.27
57. Tyler Pill, Cal State Fullerton	Jr.	17	99	46	25	2.28
58. Charlie McCready, Charleston Southern	Jr.	27	59	20	15	2.29
59. Michael Wacha, Texas A&M	So.	19	130	45	33	2.29
60. Ross Stripling, Texas A&M	Jr.	24	126	42	32	2.29
61. Eddie Orozco, UC Riverside	Jr.	12	71	22	18	2.29
62. Tyler Barnette, Charlotte	Fr.	16	90	34	23	2.29
63. Tyler Johnson, Stony Brook	Jr.	13	78	27	20	2.30
64. Dillon Overton, Oklahoma	Fr.	23	74	30	19	2.30
65. Seth Webster, Nicholls State	Sr.	16	109	35	28	2.31
66. Justin Amlung, Louisville	So.	15	105	31	27	2.31
67. Kent Emanuel, North Carolina	Fr.	20	104	30	27	2.33
68. Tyler Anderson, Oregon	Jr.	15	108	33	28	2.34
69. Austin Kubitza, Rice	Fr.	15	100	38	26	2.34
70. Mike Thomas, Rider	Sr.	14	96	30	25	2.34
71. Jordan John, Oklahoma	Fr.	20	61	23	16	2.35
72. Cody Forsythe, Southern Illinois	So.	15	103	37	27	2.35
73. Anthony Kupbens, UC Davis	Jr.	15	103	31	27	2.36
74. Cody Fick, Evansville	Sr.	11	80	28	21	2.36
75. Tanner Perkins, Western Kentucky	So.	15	99	38	26	2.36
76. Shaun Coughlin, Maine	Fr.	20	57	17	15	2.37
77. Tyler Ray, Troy	Jr.	16	117	35	31	2.39
78. Andy Moye, Georgia Southern	Sr.	15	79	30	21	2.39
79. Matt Murray, Georgia Southern	Jr.	26	68	23	18	2.39
80. Karsten Whitson, Florida	Fr.	19	97	29	26	2.40
81. Kurt Heyer, Arizona	So.	20	138	41	37	2.41
82. Chris Pike, Fordham	Fr.	16	93	31	25	2.41
83. Matthew Neil, Brigham Young	Sr.	20	86	31	24	2.42
84. Sonny Gray, Vanderbilt	Jr.	19	126	38	34	2.43
85. Colin O'Connell, Cal State Fullerton	Jr.	17	77	34	21	2.45
86. Charles Basford, Samford	Jr.	16	88	30	24	2.45
87. Hoby Milner, Texas	So.	32	84	26	23	2.46
88. Casey Hauptman, Nebraska	Sr.	28	62	22	17	2.46
89. Kyle Hendricks, Dartmouth	Jr.	9	62	18	17	2.47
90. Patrick Johnson, North Carolina	Sr.	18	113	33	31	2.47
91. Grayson Garvin, Vanderbilt	Jr.	18	113	36	31	2.48
92. Scott Garner, Bethune-Cookman	Fr.	14	83	32	23	2.48
93. Alex Gillingham, Loyola Marymount	Jr.	14	112	35	31	2.49
94. Brian Muransky, Xavier	Sr.	19	72	29	20	2.50
95. Jonathan Smart, Alabama	Sr.	31	86	28	24	2.50
96. Jordan Nicholson, La.-Lafayette	Jr.	12	72	29	20	2.51
97. Rick Anton, Utah	Sr.	15	100	35	28	2.52
98. Brooks Fiala, Miami (Ohio)	So.	17	82	31	23	2.53
99. Sam Gaviglio, Oregon State	Jr.	17	121	48	34	2.54
100. Mike Frongello, Davidson	Sr.	39	67	30	19	2.54

WINS

RANK NAME, TEAM	W	L
1. Ross Stripling, Texas A&M	14	2
Michael Roth, South Carolina	14	3
3. Trevor Bauer, UCLA	13	2
Grayson Garvin, Vanderbilt	13	2
Patrick Johnson, North Carolina	13	2
Taylor Jungmann, Texas	13	3
7. Tyler Ray, Troy	12	0
Jonas Dufek, Creighton	12	1
Nick Tropeano, Stony Brook	12	1
Sean Gilmartin, Florida State	12	2
Sam Gaviglio, Oregon State	12	3
Danny Hultzen, Virginia	12	3
Sonny Gray, Vanderbilt	12	4
14. Greg Gonzalez, Fresno State	11	1
Marco Gonzales, Gonzaga	11	2
Will Roberts, Virginia	11	2
Buck Farmer, Georgia Tech	11	3
Keegan Linza, Liberty	11	3
Hudson Randall, Florida	11	3
Kyle Simon, Arizona	11	3
Mark Pope, Georgia Tech	11	4
Matt Summers, UC Irvine	11	4
Matt Barnes, Connecticut	11	5
24. Tyler Wilson, Virginia	10	0
Paul Davis, Florida Atlantic	10	1
Sean Tierney, James Madison	10	1
Justin Amlung, Louisville	10	2
D.J. Baxendale, Arkansas	10	2
Kurt Wunderlich, Michigan State	10	2
Keith Bilodeau, Maine	10	3

Ty Blach, Creighton	10	3
Seth Maness, East Carolina	10	3
Anthony Meo, Coastal Carolina	10	3
Greg Nappo, Connecticut	10	3
Michael Rocha, Oklahoma	10	3
John Soldinger, Manhattan	10	3
Geoffrey Thomas, Southern Miss.	10	3
Kyle Hallock, Kent State	10	4
Andrew Smith, Charlotte	10	4
Burch Smith, Oklahoma	10	4
Tyler Watkins, Southeastern La.	10	4
Brandon Williamson, Dal. Baptist	10	4
Ryan Beck, New Mexico State	10	5
Charlie Lowell, Wichita State	10	5
Michael Palazzone, Georgia	10	5
Todd Simko, Texas A&M-CC	10	6

SAVES

RANK NAME, TEAM	SV
1. Matt Price, South Carolina	20
2. Corey Knebel, Texas	19
3. Bo Reeder, East Tenn. State	18
Tyler Maloof, Georgia	18
Kyle McMillen, Kent State	18
Branden Kline, Virginia	18
7. Abram Williams, Radford	17
James Allen, Kansas State	17
9. Nick Ramirez, Cal State Fullerton	16
10. Daniel Miranda, Miami	15
Tyler Smith, Rider	15
Adam Wisniewski, Old Dominion	15
Todd Hornsby, Jacksonville State	15
Jon Ivie, Belmont	15
Andrew Jones, Samford	15
Chris Haney, Dallas Baptist	15
Daniel Bennett, Florida State	15
18. Lenny Linsky, Hawaii	14
Nick Pepitone, Tulane	14
20. Evan Zerff, Long Island	13
Dan Kickham, Missouri State	13
Kevin Vance, Connecticut	13
Pat Christensen, La Salle	13
Tony Zych, Louisville	13
Kurt Spomer, Creighton	13
26. Kyle Glancy, Northern Illinois	12
Charlie Robertson, Fresno State	12
Cody Martin, Gonzaga	12
Tyler Wagner, Utah	12
Taylor Miller, Appalachian State	12
Brian Hernandez, UC Irvine	12
Jordan LeGros, McNeese State	12
Tony Bryant, Oregon State	12
Kevin Quackenbush, South Florida	12
Caleb Reed, Mississippi State	12
Nick Wittgren, Purdue	12
Caleb Dudley, Louisiana Tech	12
Tony Cingrani, Rice	12
39. Matt Zahel, Toledo	11
Scott Matyas, Minnesota	11
Navery Moore, Vanderbilt	11
Jonathan Smart, Alabama	11
Chris Anderson, Jacksonville	11
44. Eric Heckaman, Western Mich.	10
Ryan Hawthorne, Loyola Marymount	10
Zack Jones, San Jose State	10
Mark Montgomery, Longwood	10
Travis Parker, Saint Louis	10
Paris Shewey, Washington State	10
Jason West, Stephen F. Austin	10
Dylan Cole, Furman	10
Blake Drake, Indiana State	10
Hugh Adams, Florida Atlantic	10
Chris Dennis, Portland	10
Trever Vermeulen, South Dakota State	10
J.B. Johnson, Kennesaw State	10

Michael Morin, North Carolina	10

STRIKEOUTS

RANK NAME, TEAM	SO
1. Trevor Bauer, UCLA	203
2. Danny Hultzen, Virginia	165
3. Cory Mazzoni, North Carolina State	137
4. Kurt Heyer, Arizona	134
5. Sonny Gray, Vanderbilt	132
6. Sean Gilmartin, Florida State	130
7. Carson Smith, Texas State	129
8. Jonas Dufek, Creighton	128
9. Taylor Jungmann, Texas	126
10. Patrick Johnson, North Carolina	125
11. Greg Gonzalez, Fresno State	124
Charlie Lowell, Wichita State	124
Tyler Wilson, Virginia	124
14. Michael Wacha, Texas A&M	123
15. Gerrit Cole, UCLA	119
Nick Tropeano, Stony Brook	119
17. Matt Barnes, Connecticut	117
David Starn, Kent State	117
19. Sam Gaviglio, Oregon State	116
Mike McCarthy, Cal State Bakersfield	116
21. Anthony Meo, Coastal Carolina	115
22. Tyler Anderson, Oregon	114
23. Ross Stripling, Texas A&M	113
24. Michael Roth, South Carolina	112
25. Corey Maines, Illinois State	110
Alex Meyer, Kentucky	110
Tyler Pill, Cal State Fullerton	110
28. Chris Beck, Georgia Southern	109
29. Kyle Hald, Old Dominion	108
30. Ryan Carpenter, Gonzaga	107
31. Jed Bradley, Georgia Tech	106
Buck Farmer, Georgia Tech	106
Kyle Hansen, St. John's	106
34. Logan Billbrough, William & Mary	105
Andrew Chafin, Kent State	105
Cameron Hobson, Dayton	105
Phil Klein, Youngstown State	105
Tanner Peters, UNLV	105
39. Cole Green, Texas	104
40. Mark Leiter, NJIT	103
Noe Ramirez, Cal State Fullerton	103
42. Erik Johnson, California	102
Austin Kubitza, Rice	102
44. Grayson Garvin, Vanderbilt	101
45. Ty Blach, Creighton	100
Alex Gonzalez, Oral Roberts	100
Matt Summers, UC Irvine	100
48. Kyle Winkler, Texas Christian	99
49. Justin Meza, Texas A&M-CC	98
50. James Crockett, Southern Utah	97
Marc Zecchino, Virginia Tech	97

STRIKEOUTS PER NINE INNINGS

RANK NAME, TEAM	SO/9
1. Trevor Bauer, UCLA	13.37
2. Marcus Stroman, Duke	12.60
3. Danny Hultzen, Virginia	12.58
4. Bobby Lucas, George Washington	11.92
5. Nick Tropeano, Stony Brook	11.52
6. Jose De Leon, Southern	11.51
7. Lex Rutledge, Samford	11.29
8. Jacob Barnes, Fla. Gulf Coast	11.13
9. Matthew Reckling, Rice	11.03
10. James Crockett, Southern Utah	10.95
11. Kyle McMyne, Villanova	10.89
12. Cody Martin, Gonzaga	10.84
13. Charlie Lowell, Wichita State	10.80
14. Paul Cusick, Penn	10.79
15. Nate Koneski, Holy Cross	10.76
16. Cory Mazzoni, North Carolina State	10.75
17. Tyler Wilson, Virginia	10.70

18. Andrew Chafin, Kent State	10.62
19. Richie Goodenow, Lipscomb	10.61
20. Greg Gonzalez, Fresno State	10.60
21. Corey Maines, Illinois State	10.57
22. Jordan Egan, Norfolk State	10.46
23. Robbie Collier, North Florida	10.41
24. Justin Meza, Texas A&M-CC	10.34
25. Terrance Washington, Jackson State	10.29

FEWEST HITS PER NINE INNINGS

RANK NAME, TEAM	H/9
1. Corey Knebel, Texas	4.52
2. Trevor Bauer, UCLA	4.81
3. Cody Martin, Gonzaga	5.16
4. Taylor Jungmann, Texas	5.17
5. Vinny Lally, Yale	5.35
6. Noe Ramirez, Cal State Fullerton	5.56
7. John Taylor, South Carolina	5.68
8. Brian Muransky, Xavier	5.75
9. Danny Hultzen, Virginia	5.80
10. Erik Johnson, California	5.83
11. Matt Barnes, Connecticut	5.88
12. Andrew Chafin, Kent State	5.97
13. Sam Stafford, Texas	5.98
14. Zack Weiss, UCLA	6.00
15. Sean McKeown, Marist	6.03
16. Nick Tropeano, Stony Brook	6.10
17. Adam Plutko, UCLA	6.10
18. Matt Purke, Texas Christian	6.15
19. Andrew Mitchell, Texas Christian	6.16
20. E.J. Encinosa, Miami	6.17
21. Jonas Dufek, Creighton	6.23
22. Matt Summers, UC Irvine	6.23
23. Abel Flores, Texas Southern	6.24
24. Tyler Anderson, Oregon	6.27
25. Steven Ewing, Miami	6.30

FEWEST WALKS PER NINE INNINGS

RANK NAME, TEAM	BB/9
1. Casey Hauptman, Nebraska	0.43
2. Austin Drewyer, UMBC	0.62
3. Ethan Mildren, Pittsburgh	0.76
4. Kyle Simon, Arizona	0.77
5. Michael Palazzone, Georgia	0.82
6. Brady Rodgers, Arizona State	0.82
7. Ken Graveline, Rhode Island	0.91
8. Colin O'Connell, Cal State Fullerton	0.93
9. Hudson Randall, Florida	0.94
10. Cody Forsythe, Southern Illinois	0.96
11. Tyler Watkins, Southeastern La.	0.97
12. Tommy Hoenshell, CS Bakersfield	1.02
13. Michael Schum, Wright State	1.02
14. Randy Fontanez, South Florida	1.03
15. Tyler Deetjen, Valparaiso	1.05
16. Matthew Neil, Brigham Young	1.05
17. Steven Hill, Penn State	1.06
18. Garrett Baker, Liberty	1.09
19. Dustin Crenshaw, South Alabama	1.14
20. Kyle Kraus, Portland	1.14
21. Matteo D'Angelo, Winthrop	1.16
22. Will Roberts, Virginia	1.19
23. Mike Hauschild, Dayton	1.20
24. Mike Hamann, Toledo	1.21
25. Todd Miller, Notre Dame	1.22

BATTING

SCORING

RANK TEAM	G	R	R/G
1. James Madison	61	541	8.9
2. New Mexico State	58	495	8.5
3. Dallas Baptist	62	509	8.2
4. Southern	48	382	8.0
5. Mercer	59	455	7.7
6. Jacksonville	61	453	7.4
7. Temple	53	389	7.3
8. Col. of Charleston	61	446	7.3

9.	Grambling State	49	358	7.3
10.	Florida State	65	474	7.3
11.	Stony Brook	54	389	7.2
12.	Purdue	57	407	7.1
13.	Savannah State	52	371	7.1
14.	Florida International	61	435	7.1
15.	Clemson	63	449	7.1
16.	Dartmouth	42	297	7.1
17.	Vanderbilt	66	459	7.0
18.	Louisiana State	56	388	6.9
19.	Virginia	68	471	6.9
20.	Oklahoma	60	415	6.9
21.	Southeast Mo. State	56	387	6.9
22.	Central Florida	62	428	6.9
23.	South Dakota State	57	393	6.9
24.	Utah Valley	56	386	6.9
25.	Troy	62	427	6.9

BATTING AVERAGE

RANK	TEAM	AVG
1.	New Mexico State	.337
2.	Wright State	.323
3.	Arizona	.320
4.	James Madison	.319
5.	Temple	.319
6.	Clemson	.318
7.	Michigan State	.318
8.	Stony Brook	.316
9.	Florida International	.316
10.	Southeast Mo. State	.316

HOME RUNS

RANK	TEAM	HR
1.	East Tenn. State	86
2.	Col. of Charleston	81
3.	Mercer	80
	James Madison	80
5.	Florida	69
6.	Belmont	64
	Florida International	64
8.	Florida State	61
9.	Dallas Baptist	60
	Virginia Tech	60

DOUBLES

RANK	TEAM	2B
1.	Florida State	152
2.	Troy	149
3.	Virginia	148
4.	Stony Brook	146
5.	Florida	143
6.	Texas Christian	141
7.	Florida International	140
8.	Dallas Baptist	139
	Central Florida	139
10.	South Carolina	136

TRIPLES

RANK	TEAM	3B
1.	Grambling State	36
2.	Texas A&M	30
3.	Arkansas-Pine Bluff	29
4.	Virginia Tech	28
	Arizona State	28
6.	Dartmouth	27
	Northern Colorado	27
	James Madison	27
9.	Arizona	26
	Texas	26
	North Carolina	26

SLUGGING PERCENTAGE

RANK	TEAM	SLG
1.	James Madison	.517

2.	East Tenn. State	.498
3.	Mercer	.492
4.	Col. of Charleston	.486
5.	Virginia Tech	.485
6.	Florida International	.478
7.	New Mexico State	.474
8.	Southeast Mo. State	.474
9.	Dallas Baptist	.473
10.	Texas Christian	.464

STOLEN BASES

RANK	TEAM	SB	CS
1.	Savannah State	159	34
2.	James Madison	155	47
3.	Alcorn State	134	35
4.	Connecticut	127	43
5.	Kansas State	123	28
6.	Arkansas	122	27
7.	Dayton	121	47
8.	Liberty	119	32
9.	Rhode Island	117	30
10.	Miss. Valley State	116	40

WALKS

RANK	TEAM	BB
1.	Florida State	381
2.	North Carolina	358
3.	New Mexico State	333
4.	Dallas Baptist	310
5.	Rice	305
6.	Clemson	304
7.	Col. of Charleston	297
8.	Wichita State	296
9.	Georgia State	294
10.	James Madison	289

PITCHING

EARNED RUN AVERAGE

RANK	TEAM	ERA
1.	Virginia	2.24
2.	Texas	2.35
3.	UCLA	2.44
4.	Vanderbilt	2.44
5.	South Carolina	2.45
6.	Kent State	2.66
7.	East Carolina	2.67
8.	Seton Hall	2.68
9.	Georgia Tech	2.76
10.	Charlotte	2.81
11.	Cal State Bakersfield	2.87
12.	Cal State Fullerton	2.88
13.	California	2.90
14.	Texas A&M	2.90
15.	Fresno State	2.91
16.	Florida	2.93
17.	UC Irvine	2.95
18.	Coastal Carolina	2.97
19.	Oregon	2.99
20.	Oklahoma	3.00
21.	Louisville	3.06
22.	Samford	3.11
23.	Connecticut	3.16
24.	Rice	3.18
25.	Gonzaga	3.19

STRIKEOUTS PER NINE INNINGS

RANK	TEAM	SO/9
1.	Virginia	9.8
2.	UCLA	9.8
3.	North Carolina	9.0
4.	Vanderbilt	8.8
5.	Rice	8.6
6.	Georgia Tech	8.6

7.	Cal State Fullerton	8.4
8.	Miami	8.3
9.	Texas	8.3
10.	Oregon	8.2

FEWEST HITS PER NINE INNINGS

RANK	TEAM	H/9
1.	Texas	6.38
2.	UCLA	6.61
3.	Virginia	6.84
4.	Vanderbilt	7.19
5.	South Carolina	7.42
6.	Charlotte	7.43
7.	Miami	7.52
8.	Connecticut	7.58
9.	Kent State	7.71
10.	Oregon	7.74

FEWEST WALKS PER NINE INNINGS

RANK	TEAM	BB/9
1.	Florida	1.82
2.	Dayton	2.18
3.	Dartmouth	2.24
4.	Virginia	2.28
5.	Cal State Fullerton	2.33
6.	Miami (Ohio)	2.35
7.	Cal State Bakersfield	2.45
8.	Arizona State	2.47
9.	Liberty	2.50
10.	Texas A&M	2.51

FIELDING

FIELDING PERCENTAGE

RANK	TEAM	PCT
1.	San Francisco	.985
2.	Stony Brook	.985
3.	Texas	.982
4.	Creighton	.980
5.	North Carolina	.979
6.	UC Irvine	.979
7.	Virginia	.978
8.	Kent State	.978
9.	Central Florida	.978
10.	Evansville	.977
11.	Fairfield	.977
12.	Boston College	.977
13.	Memphis	.977
14.	Arizona	.976
15.	Western Kentucky	.976
16.	UCLA	.976
17.	Oregon	.976
18.	UC Riverside	.976
19.	Troy	.976
20.	Indiana State	.976
21.	Nebraska	.975
22.	UNC Greensboro	.975
23.	Texas A&M	.975
24.	Michigan State	.975
25.	Alabama-Birmingham	.975

DOUBLE PLAYS PER NINE INNINGS

RANK	TEAM	DP/G
1.	Southern Mississippi	1.40
2.	Penn State	1.30
3.	Cleveland State	1.29
4.	Pepperdine	1.25
5.	Illinois-Chicago	1.24
6.	Oklahoma State	1.22
7.	Central Connecticut State	1.19
8.	Northwestern	1.18
9.	Middle Tennessee State	1.16
10.	South Carolina	1.16

Batters: 10 or more at-bats. **Pitchers:** 5 or more innings.

1. SOUTH CAROLINA

Coach: Ray Tanner. **Record:** 55-14.

PLAYER, POS., YEAR	AVG	AB	R	H	2B	3B	HR	RBI	SB
Christian Walker, 1b, So.	.358	271	64	97	21	1	10	62	4
Scott Wingo, 2b, Sr.	.338	240	47	81	8	1	4	31	7
Brady Thomas, dh, Sr.	.316	231	32	73	10	3	4	43	1
Evan Marzilli, of, So.	.291	220	39	64	14	2	3	31	6
Robert Beary, c, Sr.	.289	211	31	61	14	1	3	35	4
Adrian Morales, 3b, Sr.	.281	249	44	70	16	0	3	40	7
Peter Mooney, ss, Jr.	.280	254	45	71	15	1	4	37	3
Jake Williams, of, Jr.	.268	209	29	56	10	6	2	38	1
Jackie Bradley Jr., of, Jr.	.247	162	32	40	10	1	6	27	2
Greg Brodzinski, c, Fr.	.333	12	3	4	0	0	0	2	0
Adam Matthews, of, Jr.	.264	110	26	29	4	2	2	14	4
Steven Neff, dh, Jr.	.254	71	11	18	7	0	5	7	0
Michael Roth, dh, Jr.	.200	15	3	3	1	0	0	4	0
DeSean Anderson, of, Fr.	.191	47	10	9	4	0	0	5	1

PLAYER, POS., YEAR	W	L	ERA	G	SV	IP	H	BB	SO
Michael Roth, lhp, Jr.	14	3	1.06	21	0	145	108	41	112
John Taylor, rhp, Sr.	8	1	1.14	50	0	71	45	28	63
Forrest Koumas, rhp, Fr.	6	1	2.96	19	0	73	59	29	63
Colby Holmes, rhp, So.	7	3	3.69	18	0	85	76	21	77
Patrick Sullivan, rhp, So.	2	0	1.35	10	1	20	14	9	21
Jose Mata, rhp, Sr.	3	0	1.76	23	1	20	30	13	16
Matt Price, rhp, So.	7	3	1.83	36	20	59	44	20	75
Steven Neff, lhp, Jr.	3	1	2.45	12	0	37	29	10	29
Tyler Webb, lhp, So.	3	1	3.00	22	0	36	34	17	28
Bryan Harper, lhp, Jr.	1	0	5.40	22	1	18	17	17	18
Adam Westmoreland, lhp, So.	1	1	5.77	11	0	34	41	18	26
Logan Munson, lhp, Jr.	0	0	7.71	11	0	7	12	2	5

South Carolina lefthander Michael Roth will return for his senior season

CHRIS PROCTOR

2. FLORIDA

Coach: Kevin Sullivan. **Record:** 53-19.

PLAYER, POS., YEAR	AVG	AB	R	H	2B	3B	HR	RBI	SB
Mike Zunino, c, So.	.371	264	75	98	23	0	19	67	7
Daniel Pigott, of, Jr.	.331	257	44	85	21	1	5	40	15
Josh Adams, 2b, Jr.	.323	260	34	84	11	1	6	43	1
Preston Tucker, of, Jr.	.308	286	55	88	23	0	15	74	5
Brian Johnson, 1b, So.	.307	192	26	59	11	2	5	29	2
Nolan Fontana, ss, So.	.289	256	57	74	12	5	5	49	6
Austin Maddox, 3b, So.	.280	239	30	67	3	0	6	35	1
Vickash Ramjit, 1b, So.	.382	76	17	29	5	0	1	7	2
Bryson Smith, of, Sr.	.328	174	40	57	14	0	2	22	6
Tyler Palmer, 3b, Fr.	.286	14	3	4	1	0	0	2	0
Kamm Washington, of, So.	.284	67	15	19	2	1	1	8	3
Tyler Thompson, of, So.	.264	110	15	29	6	1	1	17	3
Zack Powers, 3b, Fr.	.250	64	8	16	4	1	0	7	0
Jeff Moyer, 3b, Jr.	.246	61	8	15	4	0	2	11	0
Ben McMahan, c, Jr.	.236	55	10	13	2	0	1	3	3
Cody Dent, 3b, So.	.207	82	11	17	1	1	0	7	1

PLAYER, POS., YEAR	W	L	ERA	G	SV	IP	H	BB	SO
Steven Rodriguez, lhp, So.	4	2	1.91	32	2	38	31	12	44
Nick Maronde, lhp, Jr.	0	1	2.09	36	3	43	27	9	55
Greg Larson, rhp, Jr.	1	1	2.09	33	0	39	37	7	30
Hudson Randall, rhp, So.	11	3	2.17	19	0	124	104	13	73
Karsten Whitson, rhp, Fr.	8	1	2.40	19	0	97	84	28	92
Brian Johnson, lhp, So.	8	3	3.62	16	0	80	78	15	72
Alex Panteliodis, lhp, Jr.	6	2	3.71	18	0	63	61	9	47
Tommy Toledo, rhp, Jr.	6	3	3.99	29	1	38	39	10	32
Anthony Desclafani, rhp, Jr.	5	3	4.33	28	3	44	48	6	39
Keenan Kish, rhp, Fr.	0	0	0.63	12	0	14	11	7	12
Austin Maddox, rhp, So.	3	0	0.67	21	5	27	20	3	21
Justin Poovey, rhp, Jr.	0	0	3.52	5	0	8	6	2	3
Matt Campbell, rhp, Sr.	1	0	5.28	15	1	15	19	5	13
Daniel Gibson, lhp, Fr.	1	0	13.06	14	0	10	23	3	10

3. VIRGINIA

Coach: Brian O'Connor. **Record:** 56-12.

PLAYER, POS., YEAR	AVG	AB	R	H	2B	3B	HR	RBI	SB
David Coleman, of, Sr.	.362	185	37	67	12	0	2	40	8
John Hicks, c, Jr.	.332	277	52	92	21	1	8	59	5
Steven Proscia, 3b, Jr.	.320	275	52	88	19	1	8	59	11
Kenny Swab, of, Sr.	.318	198	44	63	17	2	1	29	11
Chris Taylor, ss, So.	.305	285	63	87	18	2	2	49	15
John Barr, of, Jr.	.290	248	46	72	14	2	0	35	9
Keith Werman, 2b, Jr.	.223	197	39	44	5	0	0	31	5
Colin Harrington, dh, So.	.353	51	10	18	3	1	0	7	5
Jared King, 1b, Jr.	.321	165	39	53	12	2	2	29	5
Danny Hultzen, dh, Jr.	.309	136	18	42	11	2	1	35	6
Ryan Levine, c, So.	.304	69	15	21	3	1	0	13	0
Reed Gragnani, of, So.	.272	136	26	37	5	2	0	31	1
Tyler Biddix, of, So.	.261	23	3	6	4	0	0	5	0
Stephen Bruno, ss, So.	.240	25	4	6	2	0	0	2	0
Mitchell Shifflet, of, Fr.	.237	38	16	9	2	0	0	7	9
Shane Halley, ph, Jr.	.077	13	1	1	0	0	1	1	0

PLAYER, POS., YEAR	W	L	ERA	G	SV	IP	H	BB	SO
Danny Hultzen, lhp, Jr.	12	3	1.37	18	0	118	76	23	165
Will Roberts, rhp, Jr.	11	2	1.79	18	0	106	80	14	93
Tyler Wilson, rhp, Jr.	10	0	2.24	19	0	104	75	22	124
Cody Winiarski, rhp, Sr.	6	4	2.92	19	1	77	60	23	58
Artie Lewicki, rhp, Fr.	0	1	0.96	9	0	9	1	6	10
Branden Kline, rhp, So.	4	1	1.88	32	18	43	30	22	56
Kyle Crockett, lhp, So.	3	0	1.97	27	0	32	27	9	32
Corey Hunt, rhp, Sr.	1	0	2.81	11	0	16	13	3	13
Whit Mayberry, rhp, So.	5	0	3.00	17	1	33	35	7	32
Justin Thompson, rhp, Jr.	3	1	3.46	22	0	39	39	13	41
Scott Silverstein, lhp, Fr.	1	0	3.77	14	0	14	17	5	11
Shane Halley, rhp, Jr.	0	0	5.40	8	1	12	6	7	18

4. VANDERBILT

Coach: Tim Corbin. **Record:** 54-12.

PLAYER, POS., YEAR	AVG	AB	R	H	2B	3B	HR	RBI	SB
Conrad Gregor, dh, Fr.	.353	170	33	60	11	0	3	32	2
Aaron Westlake, 1b, Jr.	.344	250	59	86	18	1	18	56	2
Jason Esposito, 3b, Jr.	.340	268	55	91	22	1	9	59	15
Anthony Gomez, ss, So.	.336	286	61	96	12	2	0	48	7
Riley Reynolds, 2b, Jr.	.331	166	26	55	7	0	0	18	4
Tony Kemp, of, Fr.	.329	252	58	83	8	7	0	34	17
Curt Casali, c, Sr.	.303	238	40	72	20	0	7	53	1
Mike Yastrzemski, of, So.	.296	230	60	68	8	1	3	42	23
Connor Harrell, of, So.	.289	197	35	57	12	1	9	36	7
Sam Lind, 2b, So.	.255	47	7	12	4	0	1	14	0
Joe Loftus, of, Jr.	.222	45	5	10	2	0	0	7	0
Bryan Johns, 2b, Sr.	.211	57	7	12	4	1	1	5	1
Jack Lupo, of, So.	.192	26	7	5	2	0	0	2	1
Drew Fann, c, Jr.	.158	19	0	3	0	0	0	3	0

PLAYER, POS., YEAR	W	L	ERA	G	SV	IP	H	BB	SO
Navery Moore, rhp, Jr.	4	2	1.21	28	11	30	18	12	25
Sam Selman, lhp, So.	0	0	1.42	7	0	6	5	3	6
T. J. Pecoraro, rhp, Fr.	7	0	1.59	17	0	40	26	13	41
Kevin Ziomek, lhp, Fr.	3	0	1.59	27	1	45	33	16	47
Mark Lamm, rhp, Sr.	5	0	2.00	26	1	27	26	3	21
Sonny Gray, rhp, Jr.	12	4	2.43	19	0	126	97	51	132
Grayson Garvin, lhp, Jr.	13	2	2.48	18	0	113	98	25	101
Jack Armstrong, rhp, Jr.	0	1	2.65	13	0	17	6	18	17
Taylor Hill, rhp, Sr.	6	1	2.73	17	0	99	89	26	92
Will Clinard, rhp, So.	2	2	2.75	35	3	39	36	10	48
Corey Williams, lhp, So.	2	0	4.46	29	2	38	30	14	37

5. NORTH CAROLINA

Coach: Mike Fox. **Record:** 51-16.

PLAYER, POS., YEAR	AVG	AB	R	H	2B	3B	HR	RBI	SB
Colin Moran, 3b, Fr.	.335	248	46	83	20	2	9	71	2
Tommy Coyle, 2b, So.	.311	270	57	84	16	3	2	36	18
Jacob Stallings, c, Jr.	.292	233	52	68	18	1	4	43	4
Levi Michael, ss, Jr.	.289	242	53	70	14	3	5	48	15
Jesse Wierzbicki, 1b, Sr.	.287	230	50	66	13	3	7	40	7
Ben Bunting, of, Sr.	.287	279	54	80	6	4	1	40	17
Chaz Frank, of, So.	.278	230	45	64	8	4	0	35	10
Seth Baldwin, of, Jr.	.245	151	25	37	8	2	5	27	3
Greg Holt, dh, Sr.	.397	68	15	27	7	0	3	23	1
Jeff Bouton, of, Fr.	.256	39	13	10	0	1	1	5	3
Brian Holberton, dh, Fr.	.250	88	12	22	6	1	1	15	0
Matt Roberts, c, Fr.	.205	39	7	8	3	0	0	2	0
Tom Zengel, dh, Fr.	.204	113	17	23	4	2	1	23	3
Parks Jordan, of, Fr.	.179	28	5	5	1	0	0	3	0

PLAYER, POS., YEAR	W	L	ERA	G	SV	IP	H	BB	SO
Kent Emanuel, lhp, Fr.	9	1	2.33	20	0	104	96	23	89
Patrick Johnson, rhp, Sr.	13	2	2.47	18	0	113	85	32	125
Chris Munnelly, rhp, So.	6	5	4.09	21	1	70	71	31	57
Tate Parrish, rhp, Fr.	0	0	2.20	32	0	16	9	10	15
Cody Stiles, rhp, So.	4	0	2.43	12	0	37	29	13	29
Jimmy Messer, rhp, So.	0	0	2.70	12	0	10	10	4	11
Andrew Smith, rhp, Fr.	3	1	2.77	24	0	26	27	11	27
Shane Taylor, rhp, Fr.	2	3	3.00	27	0	36	45	12	38
R.C. Orlan, lhp, So.	2	0	3.79	32	0	19	18	11	24
Greg Holt, rhp, Sr.	7	2	4.15	33	2	61	57	32	68
Bryant Gaines, rhp, Sr.	0	0	4.50	10	0	18	14	5	20
Michael Morin, rhp, So.	4	2	4.64	32	10	64	63	18	66
Cody Penny, rhp, So.	1	0	5.62	22	5	16	17	9	18

6. TEXAS

Coach: Augie Garrido. **Record:** 49-19.

PLAYER, POS., YEAR	AVG	AB	R	H	2B	3B	HR	RBI	SB
Erich Weiss, 3b, Fr.	.348	224	46	78	12	7	4	45	11
Brandon Loy, ss, Jr.	.342	269	50	92	23	3	1	30	19
Tant Shepherd, 1b, Sr.	.303	254	54	77	20	5	5	41	9
Paul Montalbano, of, Sr.	.270	196	35	53	9	2	0	28	4
Mark Payton, of, Fr.	.263	240	37	63	11	2	0	25	6
Jonathan Walsh, of, So.	.254	189	26	48	16	2	2	27	6

PLAYER, POS., YEAR	AVG	AB	R	H	2B	3B	HR	RBI	SB
Jordan Etier, 2b, Jr.	.237	215	28	51	12	3	2	27	6
Cohl Walla, of, So.	.229	144	19	33	7	1	0	18	3
Jacob Felts, c, Fr.	.215	186	22	40	3	0	1	20	5
Lucas Kephart, c, Jr.	.216	74	9	16	6	0	0	16	0
Tim Maitland, of, Jr.	.206	34	9	7	0	0	0	3	4
Kevin Lusson, dh, Jr.	.198	121	9	24	4	0	2	25	2
Christian Summers, 3b, Fr.	.182	11	1	2	0	1	0	2	1
Alex Silver, 3b, Fr.	.172	29	2	5	0	0	0	1	0

PLAYER, POS., YEAR	W	L	ERA	G	SV	IP	H	BB	SO
Taylor Jungmann, rhp, Jr.	13	3	1.60	19	0	141	81	36	126
Sam Stafford, lhp, Jr.	6	2	1.77	19	0	81	54	42	91
Hoby Milner, lhp, So.	7	4	2.45	32	1	84	60	33	62
Cole Green, rhp, Sr.	8	4	3.14	20	0	106	89	20	104
Corey Knebel, rhp, Fr.	3	2	1.13	38	19	56	28	12	61
Nathan Thornhill, rhp, Fr.	3	0	1.89	22	0	38	30	6	38
Kendal Carrillo, rhp, Sr.	6	1	2.33	35	1	39	27	11	31
Josh Urban, rhp, So.	0	0	2.65	13	0	17	12	10	23
Andrew McKirahan, lhp, Jr.	3	0	3.57	24	0	23	22	6	14
Keifer Nuncio, rhp, So.	0	2	4.00	8	1	9	8	6	4
Kirby Bellow, lhp, Fr.	0	1	5.73	13	0	11	14	9	7
Stayton Thomas, rhp, Sr.	0	0	6.55	12	1	11	8	5	5

7. TEXAS A&M

Coach: Rob Childress. **Record:** 47-22.

PLAYER, POS., YEAR	AVG	AB	R	H	2B	3B	HR	RBI	SB
Tyler Naquin, of, So.	.381	273	68	104	23	7	2	44	6
Krey Bratsen, of, Fr.	.332	268	45	89	5	3	0	36	31
Matt Juengel, 3b, Jr.	.308	253	46	78	13	6	7	50	15
Jacob House, 1b, Jr.	.301	272	46	82	16	2	3	52	5
Kenny Jackson, ss, Sr.	.278	234	36	65	9	0	2	28	5
Kevin Gonzalez, c, Sr.	.252	210	28	53	10	1	5	28	0
Gregg Alcazar, c, Sr.	.299	67	6	20	4	0	0	12	1
Charlie Curl, 2b, Fr.	.276	116	18	32	4	0	1	18	4
Brandon Wood, of, So.	.264	159	23	42	7	5	1	29	6
Andrew Collazo, 2b, Sr.	.256	129	28	33	2	1	1	14	18
Adam Smith, 3b, Sr.	.238	168	26	40	10	2	7	27	7
Scott Arthur, ss, Jr.	.233	30	14	7	1	0	0	2	8
Jace Statum, of, Fr.	.218	101	13	22	4	2	0	9	3
Troy Stein, c, Fr.	.192	26	4	5	0	0	1	5	1

PLAYER, POS., YEAR	W	L	ERA	G	SV	IP	H	BB	SO
John Stilson, rhp, Jr.	5	2	1.68	15	1	91	75	29	92
Michael Wacha, rhp, So.	9	4	2.29	19	0	130	117	30	123
Ross Stripling, rhp, Jr.	14	2	2.29	24	4	126	91	18	113
Nick Fleece, rhp, Sr.	7	1	1.41	36	3	45	44	10	32
Joaquin Hinojosa, rhp, Sr.	2	2	3.28	31	8	36	36	11	31
Estevan Uriegas, lhp, Jr.	1	0	3.60	19	0	20	18	8	16
Kyle Martin, rhp, Sr.	2	3	3.67	33	1	42	38	13	38
Dylan Mendoza, lhp, So.	3	2	4.01	15	0	34	40	8	17
Brandon Parrent, lhp, So.	2	4	4.21	24	0	47	47	17	29
Ross Hales, lhp, So.	1	1	5.00	3	0	9	7	5	6
Derrick Hadley, rhp, Fr.	0	1	5.40	15	0	37	40	16	18
Steve Martin, rhp, Sr.	1	0	7.15	11	0	11	10	7	5

8. FLORIDA STATE

Coach: Mike Martin. **Record:** 46-19.

PLAYER, POS., YEAR	AVG	AB	R	H	2B	3B	HR	RBI	SB
James Ramsey, of, Jr.	.364	250	58	91	18	3	10	67	11
Jayce Boyd, 1b, So.	.343	245	44	84	17	4	8	60	10
Devon Travis, 2b, So.	.329	231	58	76	26	0	6	33	5
Rafael Lopez, c, Sr.	.325	212	43	69	19	0	7	37	9
Mike McGee, of, Sr.	.321	234	57	75	16	0	10	58	7
Justin Gonzalez, ss, So.	.264	231	50	61	13	1	8	40	8
Sherman Johnson, 3b, Jr.	.256	238	51	61	18	0	1	40	10
Stuart Tapley, of, Sr.	.232	164	28	38	4	0	7	29	1
Sean O'Brien, dh, Fr.	.355	31	2	11	2	0	1	9	0
Taiwan Easterling, of, Jr.	.296	115	28	34	5	0	1	19	6
Parker Brunelle, c, Jr.	.232	112	20	26	7	1	1	13	1
Sean Gilmartin, dh, Jr.	.182	22	3	4	0	0	0	2	0
Seth Miller, of, So.	.178	101	15	18	4	0	1	12	8
Robby Stahl, of, Sr.	.167	18	7	3	1	0	0	2	0
Eric Arce, of, Fr.	.100	10	3	1	0	0	0	1	0

PLAYER, POS., YEAR	W	L	ERA	G	SV	IP	H	BB	SO
Sean Gilmartin, lhp, Jr.	12	2	2.09	18	0	120	92	21	130
Tye Buckley, rhp, Sr.	0	0	1.32	17	0	13	5	6	13
Tyler Everett, rhp, Sr.	1	1	2.29	14	0	20	20	6	10
Daniel Bennett, rhp, Sr.	3	1	2.29	39	15	55	46	23	52
Robert Benincasa, rhp, So.	2	2	3.58	20	0	33	30	12	24
Adam Simmons, rhp, Jr.	1	0	3.75	10	0	12	10	10	6
Gary Merians, rhp, Jr.	6	2	4.03	13	0	38	42	13	26
Brian Busch, lhp, Jr.	6	2	4.29	26	1	63	66	29	44
Hunter Scantling, rhp, Jr.	3	3	4.45	17	0	59	52	21	48
Mack Waugh, rhp, Jr.	2	1	4.58	21	2	39	45	16	31
Mike McGee, rhp, Sr.	4	3	4.68	18	5	42	32	33	40
Robby Scott, lhp, Sr.	0	0	4.82	16	0	9	3	9	9
Scott Sitz, rhp, So.	4	2	5.92	18	1	52	58	24	33
Jack Posey, rhp, Jr.	0	0	6.35	8	0	6	11	3	6
David Trexler, rhp, So.	2	0	7.80	10	0	15	19	6	17

9. ARIZONA STATE

Coach: Tim Esmay. **Record:** 43-18.

PLAYER, POS., YEAR	AVG	AB	R	H	2B	3B	HR	RBI	SB
Joey Demichele, dh, So.	.368	193	37	71	16	7	9	51	6
Xorge Carrillo, c, Sr.	.330	106	23	35	13	0	1	24	2
Johnny Ruettiger, of, Sr.	.327	245	53	80	8	4	0	37	23
Austin Barnes, c, Jr.	.320	153	27	49	14	1	1	15	3
Deven Marrero, ss, Jr.	.315	219	33	69	14	3	2	20	10
Riccio Torrez, 3b, Jr.	.307	228	37	70	17	4	4	54	15
Andy Workman, of, Jr.	.292	96	18	28	5	1	3	18	2
Andrew Aplin, of, So.	.284	141	23	40	9	3	1	19	3
Matt Newman, of, Jr.	.280	207	33	58	12	2	6	27	2
Zack MacPhee, 2b, Jr.	.279	222	49	62	11	2	1	25	26
Zach Wilson, 1b, Jr.	.258	236	33	61	13	1	7	44	6
Michael Benjamin, ss, Fr.	.182	22	7	4	1	0	1	3	0
Abe Ruiz, 1b, Jr.	.176	17	2	3	1	0	1	4	0
Brandon Magee, of, Jr.	.154	13	2	2	1	0	0	0	0

PLAYER, POS., YEAR	W	L	ERA	G	SV	IP	H	BB	SO
Trevor Williams, rhp, Fr.	1	0	2.50	32	1	40	28	6	35
Alex Blackford, rhp, So.	4	1	2.66	24	1	61	52	23	55
Brady Rodgers, rhp, So.	9	4	2.75	15	0	98	88	9	87
Kramer Champlin, rhp, Jr.	9	4	2.85	17	0	117	105	37	95
Kyle Ottoson, lhp, Jr.	3	1	3.38	15	0	53	47	22	48
Jake Barrett, rhp, So.	7	4	4.14	14	0	76	75	21	72
Mitchell Lambson, lhp, Jr.	7	4	4.31	31	9	56	59	12	67
Josh McAlister, rhp, Fr.	0	0	1.80	3	0	5	6	1	4
Mark Lambson, rhp, Fr.	2	0	1.90	10	0	23	18	3	13
Joseph Lopez, rhp, Jr.	1	0	3.00	14	1	18	12	11	14

10. OREGON STATE

Coach: Pat Casey. **Record:** 41-19.

PLAYER, POS., YEAR	AVG	AB	R	H	2B	3B	HR	RBI	SB
Jake Rodriguez, 2b, Fr.	.320	75	9	24	5	1	1	7	3
Luke Acosta, of, Jr.	.306	36	5	11	4	0	0	8	0
Kavin Keyes, 2b, Fr.	.302	182	28	55	10	0	1	30	3
Carter Bell, 3b, Jr.	.299	174	24	52	12	1	2	23	4
Andrew Susac, c, So.	.298	141	31	42	9	4	5	32	0
Jared Norris, 1b, Sr.	.282	149	19	42	10	1	2	24	3
Ryan Dunn, ss, Jr.	.280	168	30	47	8	1	4	26	1
Danny Hayes, dh, So.	.279	140	30	39	10	0	4	32	2
Brian Stamps, of, Jr.	.271	155	29	42	11	2	2	23	7
Parker Berberet, 1b, Jr.	.259	166	25	43	12	2	5	39	2
Michael Miller, of, So.	.252	107	22	27	3	0	1	6	2
Jordan Poyer, of, Fr.	.250	12	1	3	1	0	0	0	1
Ryan Barnes, of, So.	.248	165	26	41	9	2	1	25	8
Tyler Smith, ss, So.	.221	113	18	25	4	0	0	11	4
Garrett Nash, of, So.	.208	106	27	22	5	0	3	14	8
Max Gordon, of, So.	.130	46	11	6	1	0	0	2	3
Dylan Jones, if, Fr.	.105	19	1	2	0	0	0	5	0

PLAYER, POS., YEAR	W	L	ERA	G	SV	IP	H	BB	SO
Tony Bryant, rhp, So.	3	2	1.52	28	12	47	39	11	40
Matt Boyd, lhp, So.	0	0	1.57	30	4	46	42	11	35
Cole Baylis, rhp, Fr.	1	0	2.25	14	0	12	11	7	12
Sam Gaviglio, rhp, Jr.	12	3	2.54	17	0	121	91	33	116
James Nygren, rhp, Sr.	8	3	3.44	17	0	73	71	15	56

PLAYER, POS., YEAR	W	L	ERA	G	SV	IP	H	BB	SO
Scott Schultz, rhp, Fr.	4	1	3.61	21	1	53	46	14	28
Josh Osich, lhp, Jr.	6	4	3.64	16	0	77	62	34	79
Ben Wetzler, lhp, Fr.	6	3	4.66	17	1	68	74	18	50
Adam Duke, rhp, Fr.	1	0	4.76	6	0	6	3	5	3
Cam Booser, lhp, Fr.	0	1	6.97	6	0	10	13	7	6
Ryan Gorton, rhp, Jr.	0	0	9.00	8	0	9	16	5	9
Dan Child, rhp, Fr.	0	1	9.00	4	0	5	7	2	2

11. CALIFORNIA

Coach: David Esquer. **Record:** 38-23.

PLAYER, POS., YEAR	AVG	AB	R	H	2B	3B	HR	RBI	SB
Tony Renda, 2b, Jr.	.332	265	38	88	14	2	3	44	9
Austin Booker, of, Sr.	.313	214	31	67	9	2	1	24	9
Dwight Tanaka, of, Sr.	.308	13	5	4	1	0	0	1	0
Vince Bruno, of, So.	.299	164	27	49	11	0	0	13	5
Chadd Krist, c, Jr.	.297	226	37	70	27	1	2	43	1
Louie Lechich, of, Fr.	.286	56	11	16	1	0	1	5	0
Michael Theofanopoulos, of, Fr.	.286	21	4	6	1	0	1	4	0
Devon Rodriguez, 1b, So.	.279	233	29	65	13	1	5	35	3
Chad Bunting, of, Jr.	.276	127	21	35	4	1	7	25	2
Darrel Matthews, of, So.	.275	149	27	41	5	4	0	18	3
Marcus Semien, ss, Jr.	.275	229	41	63	11	3	5	35	9
Derek Campbell, ss, Fr.	.263	57	7	15	4	0	0	7	2
Mitch Delfino, 3b, So.	.260	192	32	50	13	1	4	21	1
Andrew Knapp, c, Fr.	.212	66	7	14	3	0	1	15	0
Danny Oh, of, Jr.	.209	86	12	18	1	0	1	10	4
Paul Toboni, dh, So.	.200	10	1	2	0	0	0	1	0

PLAYER, POS., YEAR	W	L	ERA	G	SV	IP	H	BB	SO
Joey Donofrio, rhp, Jr.	0	0	0.71	10	0	13	8	3	15
Matt Flemer, rhp, Jr.	4	2	1.83	30	6	39	32	8	41
Kyle Porter, lhp, Jr.	6	0	1.89	25	2	57	49	15	57
Erik Johnson, rhp, Jr.	7	4	2.83	18	0	105	68	59	102
Justin Jones, lhp, So.	9	6	2.93	20	1	120	113	31	81
Logan Scott, rhp, So.	1	2	3.09	24	1	47	42	10	30
Kevin Miller, rhp, So.	6	4	3.12	23	1	84	79	13	91
Dixon Anderson, rhp, Jr.	4	4	3.86	14	0	70	70	22	44
Louie Lechich, lhp, Fr.	1	1	4.58	7	0	20	18	14	14

12. CONNECTICUT

Coach: Jim Penders. **Record:** 45-20.

PLAYER, POS., YEAR	AVG	AB	R	H	2B	3B	HR	RBI	SB
Mike Nemeth, 1b, Sr.	.359	259	49	93	15	1	3	51	3
George Springer, of, Jr.	.343	245	61	84	23	3	12	77	31
L.J. Mazzilli, 2b, So.	.338	275	48	93	23	5	3	32	11
Nick Ahmed, ss, Jr.	.326	190	52	62	11	2	2	35	23
John Andreoli, of, Jr.	.317	262	41	83	6	1	0	31	22
Ryan Fuller, 3b, Jr.	.316	244	40	77	27	4	6	58	11
Tim Martin, dh, Jr.	.298	141	22	42	6	0	4	29	2
Doug Elliot, c, Sr.	.296	247	29	73	11	0	2	33	0
Billy Ferriter, of, So.	.284	197	45	56	1	3	0	24	16
Mike Friel, of, Jr.	.264	72	9	19	2	0	0	8	1
John Sulzicki, c, Jr.	.250	16	5	4	0	0	1	2	1
Tom Verdi, ss, Fr.	.230	100	13	23	5	0	1	7	3
Ryan Moore, of, So.	.200	20	6	4	0	0	0	1	3
Anthony Aceto, of, Fr.	.167	30	1	5	0	0	0	0	0
Kevin Vance, 3b, Jr.	.103	39	3	4	2	0	0	2	0

PLAYER, POS., YEAR	W	L	ERA	G	SV	IP	H	BB	SO
Matt Barnes, rhp, Jr.	11	5	1.93	17	0	121	79	33	117
Bob Van Woert, rhp, Sr.	4	1	2.01	7	0	40	36	18	28
Kevin Vance, rhp, Jr.	1	0	2.12	27	13	30	14	7	31
Dan Feehan, rhp, So.	2	2	2.19	27	1	37	27	19	24
David Fischer, rhp, Jr.	2	1	2.20	24	2	49	38	24	43
Greg Nappo, lhp, Sr.	10	3	2.63	17	0	96	79	41	57
Anthony Marzi, lhp, Fr.	2	0	2.79	7	0	10	6	5	6
Brian Ward, lhp, Fr.	6	1	3.28	14	0	60	50	27	53
Will Jolin, rhp, So.	2	2	3.76	24	0	38	29	15	35
Elliot Glynn, lhp, Sr.	2	4	4.13	11	0	53	49	26	30
Pat Butler, rhp, So.	3	1	5.33	7	0	27	37	13	6
Ryan Moore, rhp, So.	0	0	5.65	12	0	14	22	13	15
Michael Zaccardo, rhp, So.	0	0	9.45	7	0	7	12	2	6
Stephen Catalina, rhp, So.	0	0	12.60	9	1	10	18	4	8

13. STANFORD

Coach: Mark Marquess. **Record:** 35-22.

PLAYER, POS., YEAR	AVG	AB	R	H	2B	3B	HR	RBI	SB
Stephen Piscotty, 3b, So.	.364	225	35	82	13	1	3	40	2
Brian Ragira, 1b, Fr.	.329	213	31	70	7	5	4	46	2
Tyler Gaffney, of, So.	.327	199	42	65	10	5	3	35	7
Austin Wilson, of, Fr.	.311	196	25	61	7	0	5	30	1
Lonnie Kauppila, 2b, Fr.	.298	205	24	61	10	1	1	25	1
Kenny Diekroeger, ss, So.	.293	225	31	66	8	1	2	31	2
Jake Stewart, of, So.	.287	174	32	50	15	1	0	19	8
Brett Michael Doran, dh, Fr.	.286	14	2	4	2	0	0	1	0
Brian Guymon, of, Fr.	.283	53	8	15	2	0	0	1	0
Dave Giuliani, of, Sr.	.277	65	9	18	3	0	0	2	0
Danny Diekroeger, dh, Fr.	.258	31	1	8	0	0	0	8	0
Zach Jones, c, Sr.	.255	212	43	54	15	2	4	28	6
Eric Smith, 2b, So.	.250	24	0	6	2	0	0	2	0
Ben Clowe, c, Sr.	.245	143	22	35	10	1	4	14	3

PLAYER, POS., YEAR	W	L	ERA	G	SV	IP	H	BB	SO
Sahil Bloom, rhp, So.	1	0	0.90	5	0	10	6	2	8
Chris Reed, lhp, Jr.	6	2	2.56	29	9	53	39	17	52
Brian Busick, rhp, Jr.	2	0	2.79	9	0	19	22	4	20
Mark Appel, rhp, So.	6	7	3.02	17	0	110	114	29	86
A.J. Vanegas, rhp, Fr.	1	0	3.35	23	0	40	37	21	30
Danny Sandbrink, rhp, So.	4	1	3.39	13	1	61	53	15	45
Jordan Pries, rhp, Jr.	6	6	3.41	17	0	98	97	32	76
Dean McArdle, rhp, So.	7	4	4.21	16	0	58	56	23	30
A.J. Talt, rhp, Jr.	0	0	4.61	8	0	14	13	4	8
Scott Snodgress, lhp, Jr.	2	2	4.94	26	2	31	28	28	38
Elliott Byers, rhp, Jr.	0	0	8.22	6	0	8	10	6	7

14. CAL STATE FULLERTON

Coach: Dave Serrano. **Record:** 41-17.

PLAYER, POS., YEAR	AVG	AB	R	H	2B	3B	HR	RBI	SB
Michael Lorenzen, of, Fr.	.342	146	33	50	8	3	2	31	19
Carlos Lopez, of, So.	.342	158	17	54	8	4	2	34	8
Richy Pedroza, ss, So.	.331	163	37	54	9	2	0	22	9
Tyler Pill, of, Jr.	.323	155	25	50	11	2	1	30	3
Anthony Trajano, 3b, Jr.	.313	147	29	46	4	1	0	23	5
Jared Deacon, c, Fr.	.298	131	22	39	1	3	0	12	1
Ivory Thomas, of, So.	.294	160	46	47	6	2	1	17	20
Nick Ramirez, 1b, Jr.	.291	213	40	62	17	1	9	49	4
Greg Velazquez, 2b, Fr.	.344	64	12	22	5	0	1	12	5
Casey Watkins, of, So.	.286	28	4	8	1	0	0	3	2
Keegan Dale, ss, Fr.	.264	53	4	14	1	0	0	6	2
Joe Terry, 3b, Jr.	.257	74	10	19	3	3	0	9	5
Austin Kingsolver, of, So.	.241	79	13	19	1	1	0	6	9
Chad Wallach, 1b, Fr.	.222	27	2	6	0	0	0	3	0
Blake Barber, 3b, Jr.	.186	59	4	11	2	1	1	10	3
Anthony Hutting, of, So.	.169	71	8	12	2	1	0	8	1
Zach Tanida, c, Sr.	.167	30	2	5	0	0	0	3	1
Matt Orloff, 2b, So.	.160	50	6	8	1	0	0	1	0
Walker Moore, 1b, Sr.	.128	47	5	6	2	0	0	4	1
Nick O'Loughlin, c, Jr.	.000	11	0	0	0	0	0	0	0

PLAYER, POS., YEAR	W	L	ERA	G	SV	IP	H	BB	SO
Raymond Hernandez, rhp, Sr.	3	0	1.37	18	1	26	28	6	18
Noe Ramirez, rhp, Jr.	8	4	1.69	14	0	91	56	20	103
Nick Ramirez, lhp, Jr.	1	1	2.13	22	16	25	15	10	33
Tyler Pill, rhp, Jr.	7	1	2.28	17	0	99	77	22	110
Colin O'Connell, rhp, Jr.	7	3	2.44	17	0	77	68	8	55
Jake Floethe, rhp, Jr.	6	3	3.82	19	2	64	57	26	49
David Hurlbut, lhp, Jr.	2	1	4.08	10	0	18	19	9	20
Dylan Floro, rhp, So.	4	2	4.23	25	1	55	74	13	39
Chris Devenski, rhp, Jr.	2	0	4.98	15	2	22	29	8	26
Christi Coronado, rhp, Fr.	1	1	5.06	10	0	21	17	6	15
Ryan Ackland, rhp, Sr.	0	1	5.40	8	0	10	12	3	4

15. RICE

Coach: Wayne Graham. **Record:** 42-21.

PLAYER, POS., YEAR	AVG	AB	R	H	2B	3B	HR	RBI	SB
Anthony Rendon, 3b, Jr.	.327	214	58	70	20	2	6	37	13
Michael Ratterree, 2b, So.	.327	260	46	85	20	1	6	53	6
Craig Manuel, c, Jr.	.309	175	24	54	6	0	1	35	1
J.T. Chargois, 1b, So.	.299	261	52	78	9	3	2	31	2
Shane Hoelscher, 3b, Fr.	.281	210	30	59	13	0	3	37	4
Keenan Cook, of, Fr.	.276	203	28	56	6	1	1	23	6
Ryan Lewis, of, So.	.269	171	32	46	7	3	1	28	4
Michael Fuda, of, Jr.	.255	161	25	41	7	0	0	18	1
Derek Hamilton, ss, Fr.	.248	226	31	56	7	0	0	30	3
Chase McDowell, of, So.	.313	16	2	5	0	0	1	5	0
Jeremy Rathjen, of, Jr.	.295	61	7	18	5	0	1	18	2
Geoff Perrott, c, So.	.286	42	14	12	3	0	1	8	0
Michael Aquino, of, Fr.	.279	43	8	12	0	0	0	4	1
Daniel Gonzales-Luna, of, Jr.	.182	55	12	10	1	0	0	8	0

PLAYER, POS., YEAR	W	L	ERA	G	SV	IP	H	BB	SO
Austin Kubitza, rhp, Fr.	6	5	2.34	15	0	100	95	24	102
Abe Gonzales, lhp, Sr.	8	2	2.91	25	1	74	70	20	43
Matthew Reckling, rhp, Jr.	4	1	3.10	17	0	78	63	48	96
Tony Cingrani, lhp, Sr.	4	2	1.74	34	12	57	47	10	66
Tyler Duffey, rhp, So.	8	2	2.52	30	2	61	54	18	76
John Simms, rhp, Fr.	3	2	3.32	23	1	62	81	18	63
Holt McNair, lhp, So.	0	1	3.48	12	0	10	7	6	7
Tyler Spurlin, rhp, So.	2	0	3.52	12	0	15	16	8	11
Taylor Wall, lhp, Jr.	1	0	3.60	14	0	35	36	15	16
Jeremy Fant, rhp, So.	2	1	3.71	21	0	27	26	14	29
Chase McDowell, rhp, So.	2	1	5.14	7	1	28	36	5	19
Andrew Benak, rhp, So.	1	2	8.18	6	0	11	17	2	5
J.T. Chargois, rhp, So.	0	2	13.50	7	2	7	8	9	7

16. UC IRVINE

Coach: Mike Gillespie. **Record:** 43-18.

PLAYER, POS., YEAR	AVG	AB	R	H	2B	3B	HR	RBI	SB
Brian Hernandez, 3b, Jr.	.341	252	47	86	12	1	0	32	2
Drew Hillman, of, Sr.	.333	240	45	80	14	2	6	51	7
Jordan Fox, 3b, Jr.	.323	186	35	60	5	2	0	25	9
D.J. Crumlich, ss, Jr.	.300	233	51	70	15	2	1	27	4
Jordan Leyland, dh, Jr.	.289	211	30	61	13	2	4	44	1
Tommy Reyes, 2b, Jr.	.289	173	32	50	11	0	0	29	3
Sean Madigan, of, Sr.	.287	216	38	62	8	3	1	35	9
Christian Ramirez, of, Jr.	.282	163	26	46	10	5	0	32	6
Scott Gottschling, of, So.	.282	39	10	11	2	0	0	2	2
Ronnie Shaeffer, c, Jr.	.264	208	27	55	6	0	1	31	2
Jonathan Hurst, c, Sr.	.212	66	8	14	3	0	1	10	0
Dillon Moyer, 2b, Fr.	.143	28	6	4	0	1	0	1	2

PLAYER, POS., YEAR	W	L	ERA	G	SV	IP	H	BB	SO
Phillip Ferragamo, rhp, Fr.	2	0	2.03	19	0	27	23	7	24
Matt Whitehouse, lhp, So.	4	0	2.12	23	0	72	54	15	63
Matt Summers, rhp, Jr.	11	4	2.15	18	0	117	81	33	100
Andy Lines, lhp, So.	5	2	2.57	22	0	28	22	18	27
Jimmy Litchfield, lhp, Fr.	2	1	2.89	34	3	44	43	7	34
Brian Hernandez, rhp, Jr.	3	2	3.29	27	12	27	28	10	23
Nick Hoover, rhp, Jr.	2	4	3.44	22	0	34	27	9	24
Crosby Slaught, rhp, Jr.	7	2	3.80	15	0	69	69	20	47
Andrew Thurman, rhp, Fr.	4	3	3.82	23	1	75	82	21	64
Kyle Hooper, rhp, So.	3	0	4.06	17	1	44	49	17	31

17. MISSISSIPPI STATE

Coach: John Cohen. **Record:** 38-25.

PLAYER, POS., YEAR	AVG	AB	R	H	2B	3B	HR	RBI	SB
Jarrod Parks, 3b, Sr.	.363	212	54	77	13	3	3	36	4
Nick Vickerson, 2b, Sr.	.319	204	57	65	17	3	9	37	26
C.T. Bradford, of, Fr.	.303	244	37	74	12	2	0	34	11
Jaron Shepherd, of, Sr.	.289	166	31	48	9	0	4	29	12
Cody Freeman, dh, Sr.	.282	213	32	60	11	0	2	28	3
Brent Brownlee, of, Jr.	.279	140	18	39	4	3	1	24	5
Daryl Norris, 1b, Sr.	.277	94	19	26	5	1	0	20	1
Adam Frazier, ss, Fr.	.274	95	10	26	0	0	0	14	4
Jonathan Ogden, ss, Sr.	.259	205	37	53	10	2	8	36	6
Ryan Collins, 1b, So.	.252	202	32	51	7	1	11	33	10
Wes Thigpen, c, Jr.	.237	152	15	36	5	0	1	26	2
Trey Johnson, of, Sr.	.232	69	11	16	6	0	0	9	1
Sam Frost, 2b, So.	.184	38	11	7	1	0	0	3	4
Taylor Stark, of, Fr.	.182	33	9	6	1	1	1	5	0
Demarcus Henderson, ss, Fr.	.167	12	3	2	0	0	0	2	0

PLAYER, POS., YEAR	AVG	AB	R	H	2B	3B	HR	RBI	SB
Hunter Renfroe, c, Fr.	.154	26	4	4	1	0	0	2	0

PLAYER, POS., YEAR	W	L	ERA	G	SV	IP	H	BB	SO
Caleb Reed, rhp, Jr.	1	2	1.55	29	12	64	51	23	66
Taylor Stark, rhp, Fr.	3	0	2.95	15	2	18	5	9	18
Daryl Norris, rhp, Fr.	2	0	3.20	14	1	25	20	12	19
Kendall Graveman, rhp, So.	5	0	3.65	14	0	57	55	9	38
Nick Routt, lhp, Jr.	3	3	3.86	13	0	56	64	21	49
Devin Jones, rhp, Jr.	2	5	4.37	19	0	60	59	26	49
Luis Pollorena, lhp, So.	7	5	4.45	22	0	59	61	21	34
Evan Mitchell, lhp, Fr.	6	2	4.62	15	0	49	50	24	49
Tim Statz, lhp, Jr.	0	1	4.64	14	0	21	25	15	15
Chris Stratton, rhp, So.	5	7	5.21	17	0	76	83	27	76
Chad Girodo, lhp, So.	3	0	5.76	17	0	30	37	11	29
Victor Diaz, rhp, Fr.	0	0	8.10	9	0	10	14	8	10
Andrew Busby, rhp, So.	1	0	10.38	13	0	13	23	11	11
C.C. Watson, lhp, So.	0	0	4.91	4	0	4	4	3	6
Hunter Renfroe, rhp, Fr.	0	0	9.64	6	0	5	8	4	2
C.T. Bradford, lhp, Fr.	0	0	9.72	7	1	8	13	3	10

18. DALLAS BAPTIST

Coach: Dan Heefner. **Record:** 42-20.

PLAYER, POS., YEAR	AVG	AB	R	H	2B	3B	HR	RBI	SB
Jason Krizan, of, Sr.	.413	247	63	102	39	1	10	81	13
Landon Anderson, of, Jr.	.356	250	72	89	13	7	7	58	21
Ryan Behmanesh, 1b, Jr.	.318	242	57	77	18	3	4	51	3
Tyler Robbins, 2b, Sr.	.316	206	78	65	17	1	10	40	4
Joel Hutter, ss, Jr.	.303	231	47	70	15	1	9	50	3
Kenny Hatcher, 3b, Jr.	.287	223	38	64	15	0	2	48	1
Duncan McAlpine, c, So.	.270	174	35	47	4	0	9	38	3
Austin Elkins, of, So.	.245	196	46	48	5	3	4	37	13
Josh Wilson, of, Sr.	.242	149	34	36	7	1	0	25	1
Chris Haney, c, Jr.	.357	28	5	10	1	0	0	5	0
Michael Miller, c, Fr.	.273	11	2	3	2	0	0	1	0
K.J. Alexander, c, Fr.	.253	91	24	23	1	0	4	23	0
Logan Brumley, dh, So.	.250	16	5	4	1	0	1	7	0
Patrick Hicks, of, Fr.	.200	15	2	3	1	0	0	1	0
Tyler Ervine, 1b, Fr.	.077	13	0	1	0	0	0	1	0

PLAYER, POS., YEAR	W	L	ERA	G	SV	IP	H	BB	SO
Jared Stafford, rhp, Sr.	8	5	3.27	16	0	105	93	35	63
Brandon Williamson, rhp, Sr.	10	4	4.24	21	0	123	139	41	71
Chris Haney, rhp, Jr.	4	2	2.17	32	15	37	33	13	44
Will Lane, rhp, So.	3	1	4.58	13	0	37	36	29	25
Aaron Gilbreath, lhp, So.	1	1	4.60	9	0	31	34	11	8
Taylor Massey, lhp, Jr.	0	0	4.85	10	1	13	7	16	17
Michael Smith, rhp, Jr.	1	2	4.86	24	0	50	65	26	46
Ryan Behmanesh, rhp, Jr.	0	0	5.00	9	0	9	9	3	7
Jordan Staples, rhp, Jr.	6	2	5.27	15	0	55	55	29	26
Stuart Pudenz, rhp, So.	4	1	6.50	20	0	36	37	20	38
Duncan McAlpine, rhp, So.	1	2	8.79	10	0	14	24	14	13
Patrick Hicks, lhp, Fr.	1	0	9.35	9	0	9	13	5	4
Jake Johansen, rhp, So.	3	0	12.15	11	0	13	16	16	12

19. TEXAS CHRISTIAN

Coach: Jim Schlossnagle. **Record:** 43-19.

PLAYER, POS., YEAR	AVG	AB	R	H	2B	3B	HR	RBI	SB
Taylor Featherston, ss, Jr.	.335	245	53	82	13	4	3	42	6
Josh Elander, c, So.	.333	171	38	57	11	2	5	38	9
Jantzen Witte, 3b, So.	.331	254	51	84	21	1	4	45	7
Jason Coats, of, Jr.	.325	249	52	81	16	4	8	56	8
Brance Rivera, of, Jr.	.324	244	48	79	19	3	7	36	14
Zac Jordan, of, Jr.	.303	132	18	40	13	1	4	24	4
Aaron Schultz, of, Jr.	.302	162	23	49	8	2	4	26	8
Joe Weik, 1b, Sr.	.301	186	39	56	10	0	8	39	2
Jerome Pena, 2b, Sr.	.263	217	38	57	15	3	1	31	9
Brett Johnson, 1b, Fr.	.286	63	12	18	1	1	2	12	0
Kyle Von Tungeln, of, So.	.267	86	24	23	6	2	0	11	8
Jimmie Pharr, c, Sr.	.239	113	17	27	8	1	4	13	3
Davy Wright, 2b, So.	.125	16	3	2	0	0	0	1	0

PLAYER, POS., YEAR	W	L	ERA	G	SV	IP	H	BB	SO
Kyle Winkler, rhp, Jr.	8	2	1.39	14	0	91	65	14	99
Andrew Mitchell, rhp, Jr.	6	1	2.84	22	2	76	52	31	73
Steven Maxwell, rhp, Sr.	5	1	3.13	11	0	63	56	18	53

PLAYER, POS., YEAR	W	L	ERA	G	SV	IP	H	BB	SO
Trent Appleby, rhp, Sr.	4	3	3.49	25	1	67	67	20	35
Erik Miller, rhp, So.	7	7	4.63	26	5	80	88	18	58
Matt Purke, lhp, So.	5	1	1.71	11	0	53	36	20	61
Stefan Crichton, rhp, Fr.	6	3	1.98	26	5	50	38	10	42
Nick Frey, rhp, Fr.	1	0	3.45	10	0	29	32	4	18
Kyle Starratt, rhp, Jr.	1	1	4.85	13	0	30	33	5	18
Tyler Duffie, rhp, Jr.	0	0	5.79	8	1	9	7	15	8
Teddy Nowell, lhp, Jr.	0	0	8.31	12	1	9	10	7	10

20. GEORGIA TECH

Coach: Danny Hall. **Record:** 42-21.

PLAYER, POS., YEAR	AVG	AB	R	H	2B	3B	HR	RBI	SB
Matt Skole, 3b, Jr.	.348	233	56	81	16	0	10	58	1
Jake Davies, 1b, Jr.	.347	222	39	77	13	1	5	35	0
Kyle Wren, of, Jr.	.340	265	57	90	11	7	1	32	16
Jacob Esch, ss, Jr.	.319	263	55	84	23	2	6	41	9
Sam Dove, of, So.	.310	171	30	53	6	1	0	18	6
Brandon Thomas, of, So.	.307	205	29	63	12	2	3	29	19
Daniel Palka, of, Fr.	.297	232	41	69	18	3	12	52	3
Mott Hyde, 2b, Fr.	.275	229	39	63	13	1	4	47	6
Zane Evans, c, Fr.	.270	226	34	61	14	0	5	46	2
Chase Butler, 3b, Fr.	.233	30	5	7	2	0	0	6	1
DeAndre Smelter, of, Fr.	.222	45	11	10	1	0	0	7	2
Evan Martin, of, Jr.	.200	35	4	7	0	0	2	4	1
Connor Winn, ss, Jr.	.200	10	4	2	0	0	0	0	1
Alex Cruz, 2b, Fr.	.188	16	0	3	0	0	0	1	0
Paul Kronenfeld, of, Fr.	.143	28	1	4	1	0	0	1	0

PLAYER, POS., YEAR	W	L	ERA	G	SV	IP	H	BB	SO
DeAndre Smelter, rhp, Fr.	2	1	0.52	14	0	17	16	11	8
Clay Dalton, rhp, So.	0	0	0.79	14	0	11	5	7	9
Mark Pope, rhp, Jr.	11	4	1.74	16	0	114	91	24	88
Jacob Esch, rhp, Jr.	0	0	1.80	6	1	5	4	2	6
Kevin Jacob, rhp, Sr.	0	1	2.25	17	0	16	8	14	23
Conner Kendrick, lhp, Fr.	0	0	2.57	12	0	7	4	7	4
Luke Bard, rhp, So.	2	2	2.72	25	8	50	41	19	46
Dusty Isaacs, rhp, Fr.	1	1	2.72	25	0	36	29	13	40
Buck Farmer, rhp, Fr.	11	3	2.82	16	0	108	95	31	106
Taylor Wood, lhp, Sr.	0	2	3.29	17	0	14	15	16	14
Devin Stanton, lhp, Fr.	1	0	3.38	18	0	8	5	3	8
Jed Bradley, lhp, Jr.	7	3	3.49	16	0	98	89	31	106
Matt Grimes, rhp, Fr.	7	4	4.15	15	0	74	69	27	77
Brad Markey, rhp, Fr.	0	0	5.06	6	0	5	9	1	4

21. CLEMSON

Coach: Jack Leggett. **Record:** 43-20.

PLAYER, POS., YEAR	AVG	AB	R	H	2B	3B	HR	RBI	SB
Brad Miller, ss, Jr.	.395	195	53	77	11	3	5	50	21
Will Lamb, of, Jr.	.348	227	46	79	11	4	3	39	13
Phil Pohl, dh, Jr.	.333	228	43	76	22	0	4	33	5
John Hinson, 3b, Jr.	.331	245	62	81	12	3	9	41	23
Jeff Schaus, of, Sr.	.323	229	43	74	20	2	0	43	10
Richie Shaffer, 1b, Sr.	.315	222	62	70	15	2	13	55	8
Chris Epps, of, Sr.	.292	195	44	57	6	2	10	42	11
Jason Stolz, 2b, Jr.	.285	193	30	55	10	0	1	27	8
Spencer Kieboom, c, So.	.282	170	22	48	10	0	1	31	0
Mike Dunster, 2b, Fr.	.500	12	6	6	1	0	0	2	0
Dominic Attanasio, of, Fr.	.367	60	11	22	2	1	1	11	3
Jon McGibbon, of, Fr.	.339	62	8	21	4	0	1	14	1
Jay Cox, of, Jr.	.182	11	0	2	1	0	0	2	0
Addison Johnson, of, Sr.	.176	34	3	6	1	0	0	1	2
Steve Wilkerson, 2b, Fr.	.173	52	13	9	0	0	0	5	1

PLAYER, POS., YEAR	W	L	ERA	G	SV	IP	H	BB	SO
David Haselden, rhp, Jr.	6	1	2.23	25	3	77	65	14	49
Justin Sarratt, rhp, Sr.	7	2	2.57	18	0	80	72	14	65
Jonathan Meyer, rhp, Jr.	5	2	3.31	23	1	68	55	19	63
Dominic Leone, rhp, Jr.	6	2	3.70	15	0	65	53	30	72
Kevin Pohle, rhp, Fr.	5	2	1.93	17	0	33	37	10	17
Scott Firth, rhp, So.	5	1	3.06	16	0	50	42	27	38
Matt Campbell, rhp, Fr.	1	0	3.09	16	2	23	12	15	25
Alex Frederick, rhp, Sr.	0	3	3.34	27	3	35	28	13	29
Kevin Brady, rhp, So.	2	0	3.86	10	0	23	19	1	33
Scott Weismann, rhp, Jr.	3	5	4.89	24	7	57	62	17	51

PLAYER, POS., YEAR	W	L	ERA	G	SV	IP	H	BB	SO
Will Lamb, lhp, Jr.	1	1	5.11	10	0	25	24	11	29
Joseph Moorefield, lhp, So.	2	1	5.28	24	0	15	19	5	9

22. UCLA
Coach: John Savage. Record: 35-24.

PLAYER, POS., YEAR	AVG	AB	R	H	2B	3B	HR	RBI	SB
Dean Espy, 1b, Jr.	.320	231	32	74	15	0	3	40	7
Cody Keefer, of, So.	.303	201	29	61	13	1	1	18	7
Beau Amaral, of, So.	.299	221	37	66	16	3	2	29	8
Cody Regis, 3b, So.	.284	194	20	55	10	2	6	45	4
Jeff Gelalich, of, So.	.268	183	35	49	13	4	2	13	10
Chris Giovinazzo, of, Sr.	.250	192	28	48	12	4	2	18	15
Pat Valaika, ss, Fr.	.238	160	21	38	10	0	1	20	2
Trevor Brown, 2b, So.	.217	106	10	23	3	0	0	8	1
Steve Rodriguez, c, Jr.	.196	148	9	29	5	0	0	17	1
Brenton Allen, of, Fr.	.300	10	2	3	0	0	0	0	0
Tyler Heineman, c, So.	.261	46	8	12	2	0	0	7	0
Tyler Rahmatulla, 2b, Jr.	.250	68	12	17	3	0	0	6	5
Kevin Williams, 2b, Fr.	.210	62	6	13	1	0	0	6	0
Adrian Williams, ss, Jr.	.206	34	4	7	0	0	0	1	2
Marc Navarro, of, Jr.	.200	45	6	9	3	0	0	7	2
Brian Carroll, of, Fr.	.167	18	2	3	0	0	0	2	1
Pat Gallagher, 1b, Fr.	.083	12	0	1	1	0	0	1	0

PLAYER, POS., YEAR	W	L	ERA	G	SV	IP	H	BB	SO
Trevor Bauer, rhp, Jr.	13	2	1.25	16	0	137	73	36	203
Adam Plutko, rhp, Fr.	7	4	2.01	16	0	108	73	24	92
Mitchell Beacom, lhp, Jr.	0	2	2.20	25	0	33	27	9	38
Zack Weiss, rhp, Fr.	5	3	2.86	22	0	66	44	22	53
Nick Vander Tuig, rhp, Jr.	3	4	2.90	28	9	31	29	8	31
Gerrit Cole, rhp, Jr.	6	8	3.31	16	0	114	103	24	119
Brandon Lodge, rhp, Jr.	0	0	1.59	11	0	11	16	3	5
Scott Griggs, rhp, So.	1	1	5.60	9	0	18	13	21	21
Ryan Deeter, rhp, Fr.	0	0	7.11	5	0	6	8	3	7

23. MIAMI
Coach: Jim Morris. Record: 38-23.

PLAYER, POS., YEAR	AVG	AB	R	H	2B	3B	HR	RBI	SB
Zeke DeVoss, 2b, Jr.	.340	215	59	73	13	3	2	27	32
Nathan Melendres, of, Jr.	.326	190	38	62	14	2	2	25	24
Rony Rodriguez, of, Jr.	.308	198	43	61	16	1	13	44	5
Harold Martinez, 3b/1b, Jr.	.301	209	31	63	8	1	3	38	7
Brad Fieger, 3b, Fr.	.280	225	28	63	14	0	2	29	1
Dale Carey, of, Fr.	.271	155	30	42	8	0	1	24	5
Stephen Perez, ss, So.	.263	175	25	46	12	3	0	31	14
Michael Broad, 2b, So.	.248	125	20	31	8	2	3	21	1
Chris Pelaez, of, So.	.235	81	7	19	3	0	0	8	1
Chantz Mack, of, So.	.232	138	21	32	6	0	3	16	4
Cade Kreuter, dh, So.	.228	57	7	13	4	0	1	9	1
David Villasuso, c, Jr.	.217	69	8	15	5	0	1	8	0
Shane Rowland, c, Fr.	.175	120	14	21	3	0	1	13	3
Corey Janson, c, Fr.	.167	18	1	3	0	0	1	2	0

PLAYER, POS., YEAR	W	L	ERA	G	SV	IP	H	BB	SO
Steven Ewing, lhp, So.	8	2	2.66	13	0	74	52	23	77
Eric Whaley, rhp, So.	7	5	2.70	16	0	93	81	22	82
Bryan Radziewski, lhp, Fr.	9	2	3.35	16	0	91	87	37	92
E.J. Encinosa, rhp, So.	5	6	3.45	16	0	86	59	33	70
Sam Robinson, lhp, Jr.	1	1	1.79	37	6	40	16	18	37
Travis Miller, rhp, Jr.	2	2	2.53	17	0	21	10	5	28
Daniel Miranda, lhp, Jr.	3	1	2.67	28	15	30	27	4	37
Sam Abrams, rhp, Fr.	0	0	3.72	7	0	10	9	4	5
Michael Rudman, rhp, Sr.	0	0	4.05	7	0	7	11	6	8
Adam Sargent, rhp, Fr.	2	2	4.40	29	0	31	25	15	25
A.J. Salcines, lhp, Fr.	1	0	5.27	18	0	27	33	13	27
Javi Salas, rhp, Fr.	0	2	5.59	21	0	29	31	8	13

24. ARKANSAS
Coach: Dave Van Horn. Record: 40-22.

PLAYER, POS., YEAR	AVG	AB	R	H	2B	3B	HR	RBI	SB
Dominic Ficociello, 1b, Fr.	.335	224	29	75	15	1	4	50	5
James McCann, c, Jr.	.306	209	35	64	14	1	6	38	11
Jarrod McKinney, of, Jr.	.301	166	24	50	10	3	2	20	8
Bo Bigham, 2b, Jr.	.291	237	41	69	7	3	2	20	17
Kyle Robinson, of, Sr.	.286	213	38	61	9	4	10	49	9
Collin Kuhn, of, Sr.	.282	206	44	58	13	2	7	41	22
Matt Reynolds, 3b, So.	.243	202	36	49	11	1	3	22	16
Tim Carver, ss, Jr.	.232	177	30	41	4	0	1	13	24
Kyle Atkins, of, So.	.286	21	10	6	0	0	0	1	3
Franco Broyles, of,	.242	33	1	8	0	0	0	6	0
Sam Bates, of, Jr.	.237	59	3	14	6	0	0	7	1
Matt Vinson, of, So.	.221	77	9	17	5	1	2	8	2
Jacob Morris, of, Fr.	.194	67	14	13	4	0	0	5	2
Jake Wise, c, Fr.	.163	43	3	7	0	0	1	5	0
Jacob Rice, of, Fr.	.152	46	4	7	1	0	0	3	2
Eric Fisher, 1b, Fr.	.143	35	3	5	1	0	0	5	0

PLAYER, POS., YEAR	W	L	ERA	G	SV	IP	H	BB	SO
D.J. Baxendale, rhp, So.	10	2	1.58	19	3	85	69	21	77
Cade Lynch, lhp, So.	4	4	3.11	20	1	64	55	27	63
Brandon Moore, rhp, Fr.	4	1	3.45	17	0	70	73	20	38
Randall Fant, lhp, So.	3	5	3.89	20	0	69	67	15	35
Ryne Stanek, rhp, Fr.	4	2	3.94	15	1	64	50	26	41
Colby Suggs, rhp, Fr.	2	1	0.90	12	0	20	8	17	22
Barrett Astin, rhp, Fr.	5	2	2.72	27	3	60	57	20	57
Trent Daniel, lhp, So.	2	0	2.91	26	4	43	28	22	48
Nolan Sanburn, rhp, Fr.	2	4	3.62	24	8	33	28	15	35
Geoffrey Davenport, lhp, Jr.	3	1	4.95	6	0	20	18	7	22
Zack Hall, lhp, So.	0	0	5.19	7	0	9	9	8	3
Jeff Harvill, lhp, Fr.	1	0	6.35	6	0	6	8	4	6

25. EAST CAROLINA
Coach: Billy Goodwin. Record: 41-21.

PLAYER, POS., YEAR	AVG	AB	R	H	2B	3B	HR	RBI	SB
Corey Thompson, 3b, Jr.	.328	229	36	75	11	0	6	47	3
Trent Whitehead, of, Sr.	.325	246	45	80	20	1	4	29	17
Chase McDonald, 1b, Fr.	.314	188	26	59	11	0	4	31	2
Jack Reinheimer, ss, Fr.	.311	212	33	66	4	0	0	23	3
Philip Clark, of, So.	.310	174	30	54	4	0	3	28	13
Ben Fultz, of, Fr.	.303	178	25	54	9	4	4	26	2
John Wooten, 1b, So.	.298	245	36	73	16	2	1	28	5
Chris Gosik, of, So.	.283	92	7	26	3	0	1	12	2
Zach Wright, c, Jr.	.272	228	47	62	15	1	13	39	6
Mike Ussery, 2b, Jr.	.264	121	17	32	3	0	0	18	1
Tim Younger, 2b, Jr.	.250	80	13	20	5	0	0	10	0
Austin Homan, of, Sr.	.236	55	8	13	1	0	1	9	0
Drew Reynolds, 2b, Fr.	.200	50	4	10	0	0	0	1	0
Jonathan Holt, of, Fr.	.294	34	5	10	1	0	0	8	1
Jacob Davis, of, So.	.200	10	1	2	0	0	0	1	0

PLAYER, POS., YEAR	W	L	ERA	G	SV	IP	H	BB	SO
Jake Harris, lhp, So.	0	1	1.15	14	2	16	7	6	21
Brad Mincey, rhp, Sr.	6	4	1.57	31	3	69	61	18	55
Seth Maness, rhp, Sr.	10	3	1.71	15	0	105	84	17	80
Austin Chrismon, rhp, Fr.	1	0	1.93	10	0	18	14	8	11
Kevin Brandt, lhp, Jr.	7	3	2.26	19	0	92	78	27	63
Seth Simmons, rhp, Sr.	6	2	2.78	29	6	36	32	23	50
Mike Wright, rhp, Jr.	6	4	2.79	16	0	100	81	30	75
Joseph Hughes, rhp, So.	0	0	4.09	18	0	22	22	11	21
Zach Woods, rhp, So.	2	3	4.28	14	0	40	44	14	38
Shawn Armstrong, rhp, So.	3	1	4.63	19	0	45	47	22	50
Tanner Merritt, rhp, Fr.	0	0	5.62	6	0	8	9	1	5
Mike Anderson, rhp, Sr.	0	0	6.23	9	0	9	12	7	8

CONFERENCE STANDINGS & LEADERS

NCAA regional teams in bold. Conference category leaders in bold.
*Team won conference's automatic regional bid. #Category leader who did not qualify for batting or pitching title.

AMERICA EAST CONFERENCE

	Conference		Overall	
	W	L	W	L
Stony Brook	22	2	42	12
*Maine	18	6	33	24
Binghamton	13	10	21	28
Albany	11	11	21	31
Hartford	3	20	6	43
Maryland-Baltimore County	2	20	10	37

ALL-CONFERENCE TEAM: C—Pat Cantwell, Jr., Stony Brook. **1B**—Dave Ciocchi, Jr., Binghamton. **2B**—Maxx Tissenbaum, So., Stony Brook. **SS**—Chad Marshall, Sr., Stony Brook. **3B**—Stephen Marino, Sr., Stony Brook. **OF**—Peter Bregartner, Sr., Binghamton; Travis Jankowski, So., Stony Brook; Joey Martin, Sr., Maine. **DH**—William Carmona, So., Stony Brook. **SP**—Mike Augliera, Jr., Binghamton; Keith Bilodeau, Jr., Maine; Tyler Johnson, Jr., Stony Brook; Nick Tropeano, Jr., Stony Brook. **RP**—Zach Juliano, Sr., Binghamton.

Player of the Year: William Carmona, Stony Brook. **Pitcher of the Year:** Nick Tropeano, Stony Brook. **Rookie of the Year:** Brand McNitt, Stony Brook. **Coach of the Year:** Matt Senk, Stony Brook.

INDIVIDUAL BATTING LEADERS
(Minimum 2.5 at-bats per team game)

	AVG	AB	R	H	2B	3B	HR	RBI	SB
Carmona, William, Stony Brook	**.357**	**224**	48	**80**	**27**	3	6	41	4
Jankowski, Travis, Stony Brook	.355	186	39	66	7	3	2	38	**30**
Bregartner, Peter, Binghamton	.348	178	38	62	19	2	4	37	11
Tissenbaum, Maxx, Stony Brook	.343	198	**55**	68	20	3	5	43	0
Ciocchi, Dave, Binghamton	.343	178	35	61	15	3	4	31	12
Marino, Stephen, Stony Brook	.333	210	41	70	21	1	5	42	0
Ream, D.J., UMBC	.331	124	18	41	11	0	1	19	0
Leisenheimer, Justin, Maine	.327	150	33	49	9	2	**8**	25	2
Martin, Joey, Maine	.325	197	33	64	8	3	4	**44**	17
Taylor, Corey, Binghamton	.318	176	37	56	7	3	4	26	11
Fransoso, Michael, Maine	.317	164	41	52	15	2	5	32	17
Himmelstein, Max, UMBC	.315	168	24	53	12	0	2	31	0
Conlon, Rich, UMBC	.314	140	24	44	10	0	0	8	1
Marshall, Chad, Stony Brook	.314	220	40	69	12	0	2	33	6
Nivins, Tanner, Stony Brook	.313	179	38	56	14	4	2	35	8
Cantwell, Pat, Stony Brook	.308	208	46	64	14	2	0	23	11
Gaige, Nolan, Albany	.307	202	48	62	8	2	4	28	11
Lewis, Taylor, Maine	.288	205	44	59	8	**5**	3	27	20
Calbick, Alex, Maine	.286	189	29	54	8	1	5	30	1
Kean, Kevin, UMBC	.283	120	17	34	6	2	1	9	8
Nethaway, Josh, Albany	.280	175	21	49	13	0	3	36	2
Patzalek, Tyler, Maine	.278	198	21	55	9	0	1	28	0
Howell, John, Binghamton	.277	148	14	41	10	0	0	14	0
Walker, Matt, Hartford	.277	141	18	39	12	0	4	26	1
Lukach, Ryan, Hartford	.276	127	19	35	7	2	1	16	6
McCabe, Rob, UMBC	.270	141	23	38	7	1	0	10	6
Crean, Kyle, Albany	.268	179	29	48	10	2	4	25	1
Lukaszewski, C.J., Binghamton	.265	155	24	41	5	0	2	9	1
Wilmot, Rodger, Hartford	.264	129	14	34	11	4	0	17	3
Mason, Joshua, Stony Brook	.256	160	29	41	9	2	3	28	2

INDIVIDUAL PITCHING LEADERS
(Minimum 1 IP per team game)

	W	L	ERA	G	SV	IP	H	BB	SO
#Carmona, William, Stony Brook	1	0	1.76	11	**4**	15	12	7	9
Tropeano, Nick, Stony Brook	**12**	1	**1.84**	14	0	**93**	63	24	**119**
Mcnitt, Brandon, Stony Brook	7	3	2.03	16	3	79	64	18	42
Johnson, Tyler, Stony Brook	9	3	2.30	13	0	78	63	17	62
Bilodeau, Keith, Maine	10	2	2.87	14	0	84	75	34	77
Augliera, Mike, Binghamton	6	5	3.01	14	0	92	84	14	71
Peraskslis, Stephen, Maine	6	4	3.63	16	0	67	57	36	54
Gibbs, Jeffrey, Maine	7	5	3.69	13	0	68	53	43	61
Graham, Kasceim, Albany	4	2	3.88	13	1	72	63	32	50
#Juliano, Zach, Binghamton	2	3	3.90	19	**4**	28	31	17	32
Lynch, Jay, Binghamton	5	5	4.42	13	0	79	90	20	52
Kraham, Zach, Albany	5	6	4.48	14	0	82	86	29	65

Bazdanes, A.J., Maine	1	4	4.66	14	0	67	62	36	62
Kubiak, Dave, Albany	6	7	4.72	14	0	82	91	25	73
Drewyer, Austin, UMBC	3	8	5.24	14	0	87	118	6	29
Giulietti, James, Binghamton	5	6	5.53	14	0	83	112	19	62
Diblasi, Luke, UMBC	2	3	5.76	18	0	50	59	14	34
Mannuccia, Anthony, Hartford	2	7	6.49	12	0	51	70	18	36
Swetnam, Sean, UMBC	1	6	7.69	15	0	57	82	23	23
Mitchell, Mike, UMBC	2	10	7.81	14	0	66	115	18	22

ATLANTIC COAST CONFERENCE

	Conference		Overall	
ATLANTIC	W	L	W	L
Florida State	19	11	46	19
Clemson	17	13	43	20
North Carolina State	15	15	35	27
Wake Forest	15	15	25	31
Boston College	7	22	17	33
Maryland	5	25	21	35

COASTAL	W	L	W	L
*Virginia	22	8	56	12
Georgia Tech	22	8	42	21
North Carolina	20	10	51	16
Miami	19	10	38	23
Virginia Tech	11	19	30	25
Duke	7	23	26	30

ALL-CONFERENCE TEAM: C—John Hicks, Jr., Virginia; Pratt Maynard, Jr., North Carolina State. **1B**—Richie Shaffer, So., Clemson. **2B**—Devon Travis, So., Florida State. **3B**—Colin Moran, Fr., North Carolina; Steven Proscia, Jr., Virginia. **SS**—David Coleman, Sr., Virginia; James Ramsey, Jr., Florida State; Andrew Rash, So., Virginia Tech; Kyle Wren, Fr., Georgia Tech. **DH/UT**—Mike McGee, Sr., Florida State. **SP**—Sean Gilmartin, Jr., Florida State; Danny Hultzen, Jr., Virginia; Mark Pope, Jr., Georgia Tech. **RP**—Branden Kline, So., Virginia.

Player of the Year: Brad Miller, Clemson. **Pitcher of the Year:** Danny Hultzen, Virginia. **Freshman of the Year:** Colin Moran, North Carolina. **Coach of the Year:** Brian O'Connor, Virginia.

INDIVIDUAL BATTING LEADERS
(Minimum 2.5 at-bats per team game)

	AVG	AB	R	H	2B	3B	HR	RBI	SB
Miller, Brad, Clemson	**.395**	195	53	77	11	3	5	50	21
Ramsey, James, Florida State	.364	250	58	91	18	3	10	67	11
Coleman, David, Virginia	.362	185	37	67	12	0	2	40	8
Lamb, Will, Clemson	.348	227	46	79	11	4	3	39	13
Skole, Matt, Georgia Tech	.348	233	56	81	16	0	10	58	1
Davies, Jake, Georgia Tech	.347	222	39	77	13	1	5	35	0
Kremer, Jeff, Duke	.347	199	37	69	14	1	1	19	3
Boyd, Jayce, Florida State	.343	245	44	84	17	4	8	60	10
DeVoss, Zeke, Miami	.340	215	59	73	13	3	2	27	**32**
Wren, Kyle, Georgia Tech	.340	265	57	90	11	**7**	1	32	16
Moran, Colin, North Carolina	.335	248	46	83	20	2	9	**71**	2
Rash, Andrew, Virginia Tech	.335	191	49	64	17	0	**18**	53	4
Pohl, Phil, Clemson	.333	228	43	76	22	0	4	33	5
Hicks, John, Virginia	.332	277	52	**92**	21	1	8	59	5
Hinson, John, Clemson	.331	245	62	81	12	3	9	41	23
Travis, Devon, Florida State	.329	231	58	76	**26**	0	6	33	5
Melendres, Nathan, Miami	.326	190	38	62	14	2	2	25	24
Lopez, Rafael, Florida State	.325	212	43	69	19	0	7	37	9
Maynard, Pratt, N.C. State	.323	251	46	81	21	1	5	41	1
Schaus, Jeff, Clemson	.323	229	43	74	20	2	0	43	10
King, Jared, Virginia	.321	165	39	53	12	2	2	29	5
McGee, Mike, Florida State	.321	234	57	75	16	0	10	58	7
Procia, Steven, Virginia	.320	275	52	88	19	1	8	59	11
Esch, Jacob, Georgia Tech	.319	263	55	84	23	2	6	41	9
Balisteri, Tony, Virginia Tech	.318	214	45	68	12	2	5	26	13
Swab, Kenny, Virginia	.318	198	44	63	17	2	1	29	11
Shaffer, Richie, Clemson	.315	222	62	70	15	2	13	55	8
Riggins, Harold, N.C. State	.314	207	33	65	11	2	4	35	2
Smalling, Tim, Virginia Tech	.314	220	39	69	14	6	9	42	5
Coyle, Tommy, North Carolina	.311	270	57	84	16	3	2	36	18

Dove, Sam, Georgia Tech	.310	171	30	53	6	1	0	18	6
#Taylor, Chris, Virginia	.305	285	**63**	87	18	2	2	49	15

INDIVIDUAL PITCHING LEADERS
(Minimum 1 IP per team game)

	W	L	ERA	G	SV	IP	H	BB	SO
Hultzen, Danny, Virginia	12	3	**1.37**	16	0	118	76	23	**165**
Pope, Mark, Georgia Tech	11	4	1.74	16	0	113	91	24	88
Roberts, Will, Virginia	11	2	1.79	18	0	105	80	14	93
#Kline, Branden, Virginia	4	1	1.88	32	**18**	43	30	22	56
Gilmartin, Sean, Florida State	12	2	2.09	18	0	**120**	92	21	130
Wilson, Tyler, Virginia	10	0	2.24	19	0	104	75	22	124
Emanuel, Kent, North Carolina	9	1	2.33	20	0	104	96	23	89
Johnson, Patrick, North Carolina	**13**	2	2.47	18	0	113	85	32	125
Sarratt, Justin, Clemson	7	2	2.57	18	0	80	72	14	65
Ewing, Steven, Maryland	8	2	2.66	13	0	74	52	23	77
Whaley, Eric, Maryland	7	5	2.70	16	0	93	81	22	82
Farmer, Buck, Georgia Tech	11	3	2.82	16	0	108	95	31	106
Winiarski, Cody, Virginia	6	4	2.92	19	1	77	60	23	58
Holmes, Brian, Wake Forest	3	4	3.00	15	0	69	58	28	66
Cooney, Tim, Wake Forest	7	3	3.01	14	0	98	104	18	91
Parsons, Joe, Virginia Tech	7	3	3.21	15	1	75	76	29	54
Mazzoni, Cory, N.C. State	6	6	3.30	16	0	114	91	29	137
Meyer, Jonathan, Clemson	5	2	3.31	23	1	68	55	19	63
Radziewski, Bryan, Maryland	9	2	3.35	16	0	91	87	37	92
Encinosa, E.J., Maryland	5	6	3.45	16	0	86	59	33	70
Bradley, Jed, Georgia Tech	7	3	3.49	16	0	98	89	31	106
O'Grady, Dennis, Duke	6	3	3.65	15	0	86	91	38	75
Leone, Dominic, Clemson	6	2	3.70	15	0	65	53	30	72
Munnelly, Chris, North Carolina	6	5	4.09	21	1	70	71	31	57
Grimes, Matt, Georgia Tech	7	4	4.15	15	0	73	69	27	77
Chamra, Rob, N.C. State	8	3	4.35	17	0	68	66	32	39
Mantiply, Joe, Virginia Tech	5	8	4.36	14	0	84	97	32	66
Huber, Robert, Duke	4	1	4.37	16	0	56	69	21	40
Ogburn, Ethan, N.C. State	6	4	4.52	20	0	62	65	21	47
Zecchino, Marc, Virginia Tech	6	5	4.66	14	0	85	83	32	97
Carroll, David, Maryland	5	5	4.70	14	0	74	83	37	40
Potter, Eric, Maryland	3	7	4.80	18	0	65	48	48	68

ATLANTIC SUN CONFERENCE

	Conference		Overall	
	W	L	W	L
Stetson	23	7	43	20
Jacksonville	19	11	37	24
Kennesaw State	18	11	32	25
Mercer	17	12	39	20
East Tennessee State	16	12	36	21
*Belmont	17	13	38	26
Florida Gulf Coast	16	14	27	28
North Florida	13	17	27	27
South Carolina-Upstate	10	18	19	36
Lipscomb	10	20	19	36
Campbell	3	27	17	37

ALL-CONFERENCE TEAM: C—Nick Rickles, Jr., Stetson. **1B**—Adam Brett Walker, So., Jacksonville. **2B**—Robert Crews, Jr., Stetson. **SS**—Mark Jones, Jr., Stetson. **3B**—Jacob Tanis, Jr., Mercer. **OF**—Dylan Craig, Jr., Belmont; Aaron Dobbs, Jr., Kennesaw State; Blake Green, Sr., South Carolina-Upstate; Dan Gulbransen, So., Jacksonville. **DH**—Nate Woods, Sr., Belmont. **SP**—Matt Hamann, Jr., Belmont; Brandon Love, Jr., Mercer; Kurt Schluter, So., Stetson. **RP**—Bo Reeder, Jr., East Tennessee State. **Player of the Year:** Adam Brett Walker, Jacksonville. **Pitcher of the Year:** Kurt Schluter, Stetson. **Freshman of the Year:** Alex Bacon, North Florida. **Coach of the Year:** Pete Dunn, Stetson.

INDIVIDUAL BATTING LEADERS
(Minimum 2 at-bats per team game)

	AVG	AB	R	H	2B	3B	HR	RBI	SB
Walker, Adam Brett, Jack.	**.409**	242	65	**99**	**23**	2	13	74	14
Green, Blake, S.C.-Upstate	.399	238	50	95	11	2	0	24	1
Freeman, Ronnie, Kennesaw	.392	217	49	85	20	0	10	51	1
Goodenow, Richie, Lipscomb	.371	210	33	78	11	0	5	33	5
Bumgardner, Gaither, USC-U	.371	159	30	59	6	2	1	28	3
Gulbransen, Dan, Jacksonville	.370	227	63	84	18	2	6	52	12
Maxfield, Zach, Fla. Gulf Coast	.365	222	45	81	20	0	10	55	1

Winker, Joe, Mercer	.359	192	41	69	11	1	13	50	2
Holskey, Josh, Campbell	.359	195	35	70	14	0	6	42	2
Karmeris, Andrew, North Florida	.357	207	43	74	16	1	11	43	7
Burns, Billy, Mercer	.357	224	**72**	80	12	2	6	33	**29**
Williams, M.L., Lipscomb	.354	237	48	84	17	3	3	28	24
Sujo, Javi, Fla. Gulf Coast	.354	192	23	68	10	0	2	31	0
Bacon, Alex, North Florida	.352	199	46	70	18	1	9	42	3
Trent, Derek, ETSU	.351	208	45	73	12	1	14	56	1
Tanis, Jacob, Mercer	.350	237	61	83	17	0	15	**75**	6
Rickles, Nick, Stetson	.347	245	47	85	20	3	12	62	0
Woods, Nate, Belmont	.338	228	48	77	19	0	13	62	8
Carroll, Thomas, Mercer	.336	235	58	79	17	4	10	56	7
Lowe, Ellis, Campbell	.335	230	48	77	16	1	4	42	15
Jones, Mark, Stetson	.333	237	47	79	12	4	5	37	17
Crews, Robert, Stetson	.332	250	53	83	12	0	4	38	10
Workman, Derrick, Mercer	.332	232	39	77	12	1	9	47	11
Ratliff, Taylor, Jacksonville	.330	206	58	68	9	1	1	24	25
Dahl, Kyle, North Florida	.326	132	22	43	12	0	6	31	0
#Hoilman, Paul, ETSU	.313	214	57	67	22	0	**22**	50	2
#Liput, Austin, S.C.-Upstate	.307	228	40	70	11	**8**	4	36	5

INDIVIDUAL PITCHING LEADERS
(Minimum 1 IP per team game)

	W	L	ERA	G	SV	IP	H	BB	SO
#Reeder, Bo, ETSU	0	1	1.95	24	**18**	28	16	12	32
Haman, Matt, Belmont	**9**	2	**2.81**	23	1	86	76	28	51
#Boyd, Jake, Stetson	**9**	1	2.93	38	0	61	47	17	62
Love, Brandon, Mercer	8	1	3.26	16	0	80	81	23	66
French, Justice, Mercer	6	2	3.26	15	0	80	93	19	59
Sinclair, Connor, Lipscomb	2	7	3.27	15	0	88	90	24	**86**
Brookshire, Chase, Belmont	6	4	3.33	15	0	**103**	103	24	72
Blough, Bryan, Kennesaw State	4	4	3.61	14	0	84	94	20	84
Bushey, Derek, ETSU	6	5	3.69	17	0	85	80	26	66
Tomshaw, Matthew, Jacksonville	8	4	3.69	17	0	102	115	20	76
Fanchier, Garrett, Belmont	4	3	3.75	32	0	69	76	41	40
Donahue, Tucker, Stetson	3	3	3.76	28	1	79	76	43	63
Moore, Tyler, North Florida	4	3	3.92	16	0	59	50	28	53
Carr, Josh, Kennesaw State	5	6	3.94	14	0	82	82	31	66
Eagerton, Steve, Jacksonville	9	0	4.09	14	0	83	105	19	42
Mollica, Tony, Jacksonville	3	4	4.24	15	0	63	45	61	48
Forjet, Jason, Fla. Gulf Coast	3	5	4.28	18	2	67	93	15	50
Wagoner, Jack, Fla. Gulf Coast	5	3	4.34	18	0	58	62	21	53
Dorsey, Will, Stetson	7	6	4.52	21	0	83	108	24	64
Barnes, Jacob, Fla. Gulf Coast	1	4	4.58	20	4	55	55	25	68
Collier, Robbie, North Florida	4	5	4.89	14	0	70	72	31	81
Medlen, Casey, North Florida	5	2	5.05	18	1	62	72	20	70

ATLANTIC 10 CONFERENCE

	Conference		Overall	
	W	L	W	L
*Charlotte	17	7	43	16
Rhode Island	16	8	31	22
Dayton	15	9	32	27
Xavier	14	10	30	27
Richmond	13	11	29	27
La Salle	13	11	28	26
St. Bonaventure	13	11	23	23
Fordham	12	11	31	23
St. Joseph's	11	13	21	31
Saint Louis	10	14	29	26
George Washington	9	15	19	36
Massachusetts	8	15	17	29
Temple	4	20	24	29

ALL-CONFERENCE TEAM: C—Ross Steedley, Jr., Charlotte. **1B**—Ben Thomas, Sr., Xavier. **2B**—Seth Willoughby, So., Xavier. **3B**—Matt Gedman, Sr., Massachusetts. **SS**—Brian Blasick, Jr., Dayton. **OF**—Greg Annarummo, Jr., Rhode Island; Brandon Kelliher, Sr., George Washington; John McCambridge, Sr., Xavier. **DH**—Billy Barber, Sr., Richmond. **SP**—Burney Mitchem, Jr., Dayton; Andrew Smith, Jr., Charlotte. **RP**—Pat Christensen, So., La Salle. **Player of the Year:** Ben Thomas, Xavier. **Pitcher of the Year:** Andrew Smith, Charlotte. **Rookie of the Year:** Tyler Barnette, Charlotte. **Coach of the Year:** Jim Foster, Rhode Island.

INDIVIDUAL BATTING LEADERS
(Minimum 2.5 at-bats per team game)

	AVG	AB	R	H	2B	3B	HR	RBI	SB
Gedman, Matt, Massachusetts	.402	189	43	76	11	3	5	32	4
Kumpel, Greg, St. Joseph's	.384	177	31	68	14	1	3	32	1
Gillman, C.J., Dayton	.378	241	48	91	22	0	5	41	22
Blasik, Brian, Dayton	.369	195	44	72	11	5	6	37	23
McKoy, Byron, Temple	.365	230	50	84	18	3	3	39	18
Nikorak, Steve, Temple	.359	220	56	79	23	1	11	58	6
Kelliher, Brendon, GW	.358	218	40	78	13	0	15	41	11
McCambridge, John, Xavier	.354	237	56	84	14	6	4	34	28
Copa, Peter, Massachusetts	.351	151	42	53	10	1	11	42	14
Cammans, Jeff, Rhode Island	.349	195	47	68	9	1	2	30	22
Thomas, Ben, Xavier	.347	222	42	77	16	1	15	58	5
Roy, Jeff, Rhode Island	.345	145	35	50	6	5	1	15	9
Steedley, Ross, Charlotte	.342	158	22	54	9	1	2	31	0
Perez, Adrian, Temple	.342	243	45	83	21	1	4	50	3
Annarummo, Greg, Rhode Island	.341	173	34	59	10	5	2	34	6
Wilson, Justin, Charlotte	.341	229	48	78	8	5	2	38	25
Steinbach, Brad, St. Bon.	.331	181	37	60	4	1	2	22	20
Urban, Billy, St. Bonaventure	.327	168	31	55	13	1	3	41	0
Bruening, Brian, Xavier	.327	214	37	70	10	0	0	28	7
Willoughby, Seth, Xavier	.326	181	27	59	10	0	5	36	2
Radwan, Jason, St. Bon.	.324	182	35	59	10	0	5	33	3
Bauer, Phil, Xavier	.324	207	40	67	9	2	3	32	10
Ingraham, Austin, St. Bon.	.323	130	18	42	10	1	2	16	5
#Tilton, Cory, Charlotte	.284	224	46	63	12	4	2	45	31

INDIVIDUAL PITCHING LEADERS
(Minimum 1 inning pitched per team game)

	W	L	ERA	G	SV	IP	H	BB	SO
#Christensen, Pat, La Salle	3	2	1.17	28	13	38	29	5	39
Smith, Andrew, Charlotte	10	4	1.81	16	0	109	83	26	92
Mitchem, Burny, Dayton	8	2	2.07	21	3	104	93	23	88
Barnette, Tyler, Charlotte	9	2	2.19	16	0	90	72	24	56
Pike, Chris, Fordham	8	1	2.41	16	3	93	78	33	70
Muransky, Brian, Xavier	3	4	2.50	19	0	72	46	25	72
Crane, Jordan, St. Bonaventure	4	2	2.76	14	1	62	56	22	32
Fuqua, Kevin, La Salle	6	4	2.92	15	0	104	108	25	75
Alemann, Alex, Saint Louis	5	6	3.05	14	0	88	103	21	46
Peterson, Stephen, Rhode Island	6	4	3.06	14	0	85	75	22	69
Yermal, Joe, Charlotte	6	3	3.06	12	0	61	52	14	42
Bury, Tim, Dayton	4	2	3.23	21	1	83	89	25	57
Roberts, Corey, Charlotte	7	3	3.23	13	1	78	56	27	71
Mullen, Kyle, St. Joseph's	6	5	3.45	14	0	88	87	27	68
Gray, Eddie, St. Bonaventure	6	2	3.47	12	0	80	90	37	57
Pendergast, Brian, Fordham	2	8	3.51	14	0	88	90	27	52
Cafagna, Anthony, Richmond	7	3	3.57	16	1	75	85	22	36
Hauschild, Michael, Dayton	9	7	3.59	18	1	97	106	13	85
Van Wyk, Eric, La Salle	3	4	3.64	14	0	89	90	16	51
Williams, Bret, Richmond	7	3	3.67	15	0	95	89	35	58
Richard, Jon, Xavier	5	5	3.67	15	0	95	111	25	56
Nittoli, Vinny, Xavier	7	1	3.75	13	0	69	54	28	48
Johnson, Cael, St. Bonaventure	4	4	3.75	13	0	50	54	34	36
Graveline, Ken, Rhode Island	7	4	3.83	15	0	89	100	9	67
#Hobson, Cameron, Dayton	5	6	4.23	16	0	104	116	18	105

BIG EAST CONFERENCE

	Conference		Overall	
	W	L	W	L
Connecticut	22	5	45	20
St. John's	18	8	36	22
Pittsburgh	16	11	33	23
*Seton Hall	14	13	34	25
Cincinnati	14	13	30	27
Louisville	14	13	32	29
West Virginia	14	13	28	27
Notre Dame	13	13	23	29
South Florida	13	14	25	29
Rutgers	11	16	20	30
Villanova	7	20	20	32
Georgetown	5	22	23	33

ALL-CONFERENCE TEAM: C—Kevan Smith, Sr., Pittsburgh. **1B**—David Chester, Sr., Pittsburgh. **2B**—Ryan Wright, Jr., Louisville. **3B**—Jonathan Koscso, Sr., South Florida. **SS**—Joe Panik, Jr., St. John's. **OF**—Jeremy Baltz, So., St. John's; Rand Ravnaas, Jr., Georgetown; George Springer, Jr., Connecticut. **DH**—Jeremy Gum, Sr., West Virginia. **P**—Justin Amlung, So., Louisville; Matt Barnes, Jr., Connecticut; Joe DiRocco, Sr., Seton Hall; Kyle Hansen, So., St. John's.

Player of the Year: George Springer, Connecticut. **Pitcher of the Year:** Matt Barnes, Connecticut. **Rookie of the Year:** Trey Mancini, Notre Dame. **Coach of the Year:** Jim Penders, Connecticut.

INDIVIDUAL BATTING LEADERS
(Minimum 2.5 at-bats per team game)

	AVG	AB	R	H	2B	3B	HR	RBI	SB
Panik, Joe, St. John's	.398	226	60	90	19	3	10	57	21
Smith, Kevan, Pittsburgh	.397	209	59	83	17	4	11	56	10
Buckner, Grant, West Virginia	.364	209	48	76	14	1	8	46	3
Nemeth, Mike, Connecticut	.359	259	49	93	15	1	3	51	3
Ravnaas, Rand, Georgetown	.352	213	37	75	18	4	5	37	26
Riddell, Justin, Cincinnati	.346	211	30	73	17	1	9	67	7
Wright, Ryan, Louisville	.346	234	49	81	15	4	12	52	6
Chester, David, Pittsburgh	.345	200	48	69	12	2	16	60	4
Lang, Michael, Rutgers	.344	192	39	66	10	6	2	13	7
Springer, George, Connecticut	.343	245	61	84	23	3	12	77	31
Koscso, Jonathan, South Florida	.340	212	39	72	10	0	0	15	4
Gum, Jeremy, West Virginia	.339	177	33	60	16	1	4	38	3
DiBartolomeo, Dan, West Va.	.338	148	39	50	5	1	6	28	6
Mazzilli, L.J., Connecticut	.338	275	48	93	23	5	3	32	11
Whitmore, Travis, Pittsburgh	.336	211	29	71	12	4	4	41	12
Wilson, Brady, West Virginia	.330	215	45	71	8	1	2	27	12
Ahmed, Nick, Connecticut	.326	190	52	62	11	2	2	35	23
Glass, Justin, Cincinnati	.326	227	39	74	14	1	4	45	9
Kline, Braden, Cincinnati	.326	181	23	59	12	2	5	31	1
Fleishman, Matt, Villanova	.325	203	27	66	21	4	5	42	6
Calbi, Marlon, Villanova	.325	191	32	62	11	0	0	12	6
Mancini, Trey, Notre Dame	.323	189	33	61	15	3	9	34	4
Andreoli, John, Connecticut	.317	262	41	83	6	1	0	31	22
Fuller, Ryan, Connecticut	.316	244	40	77	27	4	6	58	11
Fernandez, Erick, Georgetown	.315	184	30	58	16	1	4	35	2
Baltz, Jeremy, St. John's	.311	209	42	65	12	3	6	60	7
Karmas, Paul, St. John's	.310	216	48	67	21	1	5	40	5
Martin, Tim, Connecticut	.298	141	22	42	6	0	4	29	2

INDIVIDUAL PITCHING LEADERS
(Minimum 1 IP per team game)

	W	L	ERA	G	SV	IP	H	BB	SO
Prosinski, Jon, Seton Hall	7	4	1.91	15	0	94	79	30	56
Barnes, Matt, Connecticut	11	5	1.93	17	0	121	79	33	117
Dirocco, Joe, Seton Hall	8	2	1.97	17	0	118	91	40	82
#Vance, Kevin, Connecticut	1	0	2.12	27	13	30	14	7	31
Self, Derek, Louisville	3	3	2.26	21	1	75	65	13	34
Amlung, Justin, Louisville	10	2	2.31	15	0	105	78	27	80
Nappo, Greg, Louisville	10	3	2.63	17	0	95	79	41	57
Iannazzo, Matt, Pittsburgh	8	3	2.73	14	0	102	92	22	62
Johnson, Cole, Notre Dame	5	7	2.76	15	0	101	78	31	87
Caravella, Alex, Pittsburgh	4	3	2.81	25	5	57	49	18	55
Fontanez, Randy, South Florida	5	6	2.92	14	0	95	86	11	74
#Zych, Tony, Louisville	0	2	3.00	28	13	30	29	14	30
Hansen, Kyle, St. John's	8	7	3.09	17	1	107	87	41	106
Dupra, Brian, Notre Dame	3	7	3.10	15	0	104	116	29	93
Jensen, Dan, Cincinnati	4	5	3.11	15	0	89	87	30	79
Gebler, Tyler, Rutgers	5	5	3.22	14	0	103	111	19	5
Koch, Matt, Louisville	5	5	3.48	16	0	67	73	21	46
Gilbert, Brian, Seton Hall	2	4	3.80	17	1	64	68	25	29
Hagan, Sean, St. John's	7	2	4.05	20	0	66	74	18	56
Berry, Andy, West Virginia	8	4	4.09	15	0	103	114	30	48
Miller, Todd, Notre Dame	4	3	4.09	14	0	81	94	11	41
Reed, Matt, South Florida	5	4	4.11	15	0	65	64	28	21

BIG SOUTH CONFERENCE

	Conference		Overall	
	W	L	W	L
*Coastal Carolina	20	7	42	20
Liberty	18	9	35	24
Charleston Southern	15	12	29	30
Winthrop	15	12	27	30
Gardner-Webb	14	13	34	23
Radford	14	13	31	25
Virginia Military Institute	14	13	27	24
Presbyterian	9	18	24	32
High Point	9	18	24	32
UNC Asheville	7	20	15	37

ALL-CONFERENCE TEAM: C—Alex Haitsuka, Sr., VMI. **1B**—Matt Mack, Jr., Radford. **2B**—Tommy La Stella, Jr., Coastal Carolina. **3B**—Scott Woodward, Sr., Coastal Carolina. **SS**—Sam Roberts, Sr., VMI. **DH**—Brad Zebedis, Fr., Presbyterian. **OF**—Steve Antolik, Sr., High Point; Matt Hillsinger, Jr., Radford; Matt Still, Sr., Charleston Southern. **SP**—Keegan Linza, Sr., Liberty; Anthony Meo, Jr., Coastal Carolina; Matt Rein, Sr., Coastal Carolina. **RP**—Charlie McCready, Jr., Charleston Southern; Abram Williams, Jr., Radford.

Player of the Year: Tommy La Stella, Coastal Carolina. **Pitcher of the Year:** Matt Rein, Coastal Carolina. **Freshman of the Year:** Brad Zebedis, Presbyterian. **Coach of the Year:** Stuart Lake, Charleston Southern.

INDIVIDUAL BATTING LEADERS
(Minimum 2.5 at-bats per team game)

	AVG	AB	R	H	2B	3B	HR	RBI	SB
Zebedis, Brad, Presbyterian	.425	212	47	90	23	0	13	57	1
La Stella, Tommy, Coastal	.398	231	**59**	**92**	15	4	**14**	**70**	7
Antolik, Steve, High Point	.374	222	47	83	20	0	6	44	2
Hillsinger, Matt, Radford	.367	221	49	81	14	4	6	30	28
Still, Matt, Charleston So.	.358	176	36	63	20	2	3	37	1
Sullivan, Graham, VMI	.358	204	42	73	16	0	5	40	8
Mack, Matt, Radford	.358	204	44	73	16	5	1	31	10
Quattlebaum, Walt, Charl. So.	.355	211	32	75	11	1	3	31	5
Watts, Jake, Gardner-Webb	.354	237	47	84	15	2	3	53	6
Bream, Doug, Liberty	.349	209	32	73	14	3	2	41	9
Roberts, Sam, VMI	.347	202	46	70	14	2	5	37	13
Micklon, Tony, Presbyterian	.343	207	46	71	17	0	12	51	3
Woodward, Scott, Coastal	.342	193	57	66	17	1	4	37	**31**
Sustar, Jaren, Charleston So.	.342	237	39	81	14	0	1	41	10
Rohan, Eddie, Winthrop	.342	199	33	68	11	2	5	38	8
Lurie, Jordan, UNC Asheville	.339	221	34	75	11	1	1	23	13
Williams, Matt, Liberty	.336	226	41	76	17	2	9	38	16
Piccirilli, George, VMI	.332	196	36	65	13	1	4	34	4
Chinners, Nick, Charleston So.	.330	179	28	59	4	0	5	36	6
Miller, Aaron, Gardner-Webb	.326	218	55	71	6	3	1	30	17
Williams, Andrew, Presbyterian	.325	**243**	39	79	13	**5**	1	24	9
Haitsuka, Alex, VMI	.323	192	33	62	16	0	6	37	2
McFarland, Adam, G-W	.321	193	32	62	15	1	5	48	4
Walters, Cam, Winthrop	.321	184	28	59	5	0	0	21	11
Quattlebaum, Dusty, G-W	.320	219	37	70	**25**	0	6	49	0
Gajdosz, Grant, UNC Asheville	.318	170	26	54	15	0	2	27	1
Guerra, Alex, Radford	.317	205	35	65	13	0	4	40	15
Robertston, Michael, Liberty	.316	215	39	68	12	2	2	36	18
Gliebe, Adam, Winthrop	.316	212	32	67	4	3	3	38	11
Hite, Mack, Presbyterian	.316	212	38	67	6	0	0	15	6
Parmley, Ian, Liberty	.314	210	48	66	8	4	0	19	27
Harris, John, Gardner-Webb	.314	175	31	55	13	0	0	33	4

INDIVIDUAL PITCHING LEADERS
(Minimum 1 IP per team game)

	W	L	ERA	G	SV	IP	H	BB	SO
Rein, Matt, Coastal	9	2	**2.07**	18	1	74	56	15	44
Linza, Keegan, Liberty	**11**	3	2.08	15	0	108	104	22	67
Meo, Anthony, Coastal	10	3	2.16	16	0	**108**	91	31	**115**
McCready, Charlie, Charleston So.	6	2	2.29	27	5	59	53	19	40
Conway, Josh, Coastal	8	2	2.69	20	3	77	70	23	70
Baker, Garrett, Liberty	6	5	2.73	25	3	66	58	8	46
Evans, Steven, Liberty	7	3	2.87	16	0	100	75	29	83
Allen, Cody, High Point	4	6	3.12	13	0	84	77	29	89
#Williams, Abram, Radford	0	2	3.48	24	**17**	31	41	12	28
Niggli, John, Liberty	4	4	3.69	15	0	85	85	16	43
Cowgill, Coby, VMI	4	3	3.73	13	0	72	61	31	59
Mizenko, Tyler, Winthrop	5	3	3.79	15	0	90	88	19	65
Bolling, Bobby, Radford	6	6	3.80	15	0	85	87	18	73
Brase, Stew, Charleston So.	6	7	3.86	14	0	89	98	42	39
Peterson, Mark, Radford	4	4	4.00	15	0	90	96	30	59
Caldwell, Mike, High Point	5	3	4.09	13	0	66	79	13	28
Butler, Eddie, Radford	9	2	4.15	15	0	95	90	27	72
Brown, Jeremy, VMI	5	3	4.33	14	0	69	69	15	52
Pace, Jordan, Presbyterian	2	8	4.44	13	0	81	103	16	36
D'Angelo, Matteo, Winthrop	4	8	4.54	17	0	77	97	10	34
Pagan, Emilio, Gardner-Webb	4	4	4.54	17	1	69	61	36	44

BIG TEN CONFERENCE

	Conference		Overall	
	W	L	W	L
Michigan State	15	9	36	21
*Illinois	15	9	30	27
Purdue	14	10	37	20
Minnesota	13	11	25	24
Ohio State	13	11	26	27
Penn State	12	12	32	22
Indiana	11	13	30	25
Northwestern	10	13	20	29
Iowa	9	15	20	32
Michigan	7	16	17	37

ALL-CONFERENCE TEAM: C—Kevin Plawecki, So., Purdue. **1B**—Jeff Holm, Sr., Michigan State. **2B**—Ryan Jones, So., Michigan State. **SS**—A.J. Pettersen, Jr., Minnesota. **3B**—Torsten Boss, So., Michigan State. **OF**—Sean Deegan, Jr., Penn State; Brandon Eckerle, Sr., Michigan State; Barrett Serrato, So., Purdue. **DH**—Alex Dickerson, Jr., Indiana. **SP**—Tony Bucciferro, Jr., Michigan State; Joey DeNato, Fr., Indiana; Kurt Wunderlich, Sr., Michigan State. **RP**—Scott Matyas, Sr., Minnesota.

Player of the Year: Jeff Holm, Michigan State. **Pitcher of the Year:** Kurt Wunderlich, Michigan State. **Freshman of the Year:** Josh Dezse, Ohio State. **Coach of the Year:** Jake Boss, Michigan State.

INDIVIDUAL BATTING LEADERS
(Minimum 2.5 at-bats per team game)

	AVG	AB	R	H	2B	3B	HR	RBI	SB
Eckerle, Brandon, Mich. State	.379	253	53	**96**	10	0	0	19	22
Holm, Jeff, Michigan State	.376	226	51	85	15	3	9	**61**	20
Boss, Torsten, Michigan State	.370	219	44	81	17	5	7	59	7
Dickerson, Alex, Indiana	.367	215	33	79	10	0	9	49	2
DeMuth, Dustin, Indiana	.360	236	43	85	12	2	0	23	8
Lashmet, Chris, Northwestern	.353	190	36	67	16	1	3	29	5
Charles, Eric, Purdue	.351	225	49	79	17	4	3	39	11
Perkins, Cameron, Purdue	.349	232	42	81	15	4	8	53	13
Snieder, Paul, Northwestern	.347	176	33	61	13	0	6	42	1
Pettersen, A.J., Minnesota	.344	209	33	72	10	2	1	12	8
Jones, Ryan, Michigan State	.344	218	**62**	75	18	1	1	29	12
Plawecki, Kevin, Purdue	.341	211	46	72	14	0	2	39	3
Hook, Jared, Michigan State	.341	173	19	59	7	1	4	30	1
Johnson, Micah, Indiana	.335	209	43	70	12	4	3	34	19
Deegan, Sean, Penn State	.333	222	54	74	18	**5**	**12**	40	14
Cappetta, Pete, Illinois	.333	162	34	54	11	1	2	17	15
Dezse, Josh, Ohio State	.332	193	30	64	11	2	4	43	0
McQuillan, Ryan, Iowa	.330	200	30	66	11	0	2	31	7
DeBernardis, Joey, Penn State	.329	207	36	68	**24**	1	0	33	2
Spillner, Tyler, Purdue	.328	229	47	75	17	1	4	33	11
Cypret, Ryan, Ohio State	.323	201	37	65	10	1	3	34	5
Steranka, Jordan, Penn State	.323	217	46	70	14	5	8	57	6
Parr, Justin, Illinois	.317	208	25	66	11	4	0	32	3
Serrato, Barrett, Purdue	.313	211	50	66	12	2	2	42	6
Hendrickson, Davis, Illinois	.311	193	27	60	5	3	2	27	9
Hohl, Brandon, Illinois	.311	193	26	60	13	2	5	39	0
O'Neill, Michael, Michigan	.307	218	30	67	8	2	2	29	**30**
Gominsky, Justin, Minnesota	.307	189	30	58	8	3	0	18	8
Blaser, Tyson, Iowa	.306	180	26	55	18	1	1	21	9
Stevens, Trevor, Northwestern	.305	177	40	54	5	4	0	18	10

INDIVIDUAL PITCHING LEADERS
(Minimum 1 IP per team game)

	W	L	ERA	G	SV	IP	H	BB	SO
Hill, Steven, Penn State	6	5	2.57	15	0	102	110	12	58
DeNato, Joey, Indiana	7	3	2.80	15	0	64	61	31	53
Sinnery, Brandon, Michigan	2	5	2.91	15	0	68	59	26	46
Fangman, Tim, Iowa	2	1	2.94	25	3	52	17	11	32
Rucinski, Drew, Ohio State	5	3	2.95	13	0	82	81	18	53
Hippen, Jarred, Iowa	4	6	3.14	14	0	95	97	20	61
Isaksson, Phil, Minnesota	4	5	3.16	14	0	77	76	28	50
Wunderlich, Kurt, Mich. State	10	2	3.19	15	0	102	102	29	65
#Wittgren, Nick, Purdue	2	3	3.18	29	12	51	47	10	55
Walter, John, Penn State	6	4	3.19	15	0	85	72	53	59
Oakes, T.J., Minnesota	5	5	3.26	14	0	86	93	21	52
Farrell, Luke, Northwestern	6	3	3.33	13	0	81	81	31	65
Bucciferro, Tony, Michigan State	8	3	3.38	15	0	101	99	16	66
Haase, Joe, Purdue	6	4	3.39	17	0	82	99	22	55
Martin, Chad, Indiana	2	5	3.41	17	2	71	67	19	34
Monar, Blake, Indiana	6	3	3.52	14	0	79	84	34	61
Morgan, Matt, Purdue	6	2	4.00	13	0	72	68	30	65
Anderson, John, Illinois	8	6	4.13	17	0	98	95	25	55
Dermody, Matt, Iowa	4	6	4.15	14	0	84	87	26	75
Jahns, Michael, Northwestern	2	5	4.30	16	0	58	57	27	49
Lubinsky, Austin, Minnesota	5	6	4.36	14	0	74	75	24	53

BIG 12 CONFERENCE

	Conference		Overall	
	W	L	W	L
Texas	19	8	49	19
*Texas A&M	19	8	47	22
Oklahoma	14	11	41	19
Oklahoma State	14	12	35	25
Baylor	13	14	31	28
Kansas State	12	14	36	25
Texas Tech	12	15	33	25
Missouri	11	15	27	32
Nebraska	9	17	30	25
Kansas	9	18	26	30

ALL-CONFERENCE TEAM: C—Tyler Ogle, Jr., Oklahoma. **IF**—Cody Asche, Jr., Nebraska; Garrett Buechele, Jr., Oklahoma; Brandon Loy, Jr., Texas; Max Muncy, So., Baylor; Erich Weiss, Fr., Texas. **OF**—Barrett Barnes, So., Texas Tech; Krey Bratsen, Fr., Texas A&M; Tyler Naquin, So., Texas A&M. **DH**—Dane Phillips, So., Oklahoma State. **UT**—David Paiz, Fr., Texas Tech; Brooks Pinckard, Jr., Baylor. **SP**—Taylor Jungmann, Jr., Texas; Michael Rocha, Sr., Oklahoma; Ross Stripling, Jr., Texas A&M. **RP**—James Allen, Jr., Kansas State; Corey Knebel, Fr., Texas.
Player of the Year: Tyler Naquin, Texas A&M. **Pitcher of the Year:** Taylor Jungmann, Texas. **Newcomer of the Year:** Zach Johnson, Oklahoma State. **Freshman of the Year:** Erich Weiss, Texas. **Coaches of the Year:** Augie Garrido, Texas/Rob Childress, Texas A&M.

INDIVIDUAL BATTING LEADERS
(Minimum 2.5 at-bats per team game)

	AVG	AB	R	H	2B	3B	HR	RBI	SB
Naquin, Tyler, Texas A&M	.381	273	68	104	23	7	2	44	6
Seitzer, Cameron, Oklahoma	.358	212	37	76	17	2	4	41	1
Johnson, Zach, Oklahoma State	.356	225	51	80	21	1	13	63	0
Weiss, Erich, Texas	.348	224	46	78	12	7	4	45	11
Ogle, Tyler, Oklahoma	.343	201	53	69	15	0	9	45	10
Loy, Brandon, Texas	.342	269	50	92	23	3	1	30	19
Phillips, Dane, Oklahoma State	.339	245	44	83	16	8	4	32	2
Bratsen, Krey, Texas A&M	.332	268	45	89	5	3	0	36	31
Asche, Cody, Nebraska	.327	208	46	68	27	1	12	56	2
King, Jason, Kansas State	.326	230	46	75	19	6	10	59	16
Martini, Nick, Kansas State	.326	221	48	72	15	4	1	44	24
Muncy, Max, Baylor	.322	227	40	73	10	3	9	44	6
Redman, Reid, Texas Tech	.320	200	37	64	12	2	0	34	6
Buechele, Garrett, Oklahoma	.317	243	33	77	9	1	8	63	0
Schmidt, Jonah, Missouri	.317	218	34	69	17	1	6	38	11
Mistich, Evan, Oklahoma	.316	155	35	49	6	2	2	16	3
Juengel, Matt, Texas A&M	.308	253	46	78	13	6	7	50	15
King, Jared, Kansas State	.307	176	34	54	12	2	8	40	13
Tomlinson, Kelby, Texas Tech	.307	218	42	67	7	2	1	43	21

	AVG	AB	R	H	2B	3B	HR	RBI	SB
House, Jacob, Texas A&M	.301	272	46	82	16	2	3	52	5
Kalkowski, Kash, Nebraska	.299	194	30	58	12	3	5	42	11
Miller, Jake, Baylor	.299	187	21	56	10	1	3	27	3
Popescu, Nick, Texas Tech	.299	174	27	52	10	1	1	32	10
Elgie, Zac, Kansas	.297	202	26	60	22	1	7	37	4
Pinckard, Brooks, Baylor	.295	176	35	52	7	5	2	16	36
Champagne, Brannon, Missouri	.294	218	30	64	6	0	0	27	13
McGruder, Jamodrick, Texas Tech	.293	174	38	51	3	4	2	29	28
Ginther, Mark, Oklahoma State	.292	236	40	69	17	3	10	33	0
Duren, Davis, Oklahoma	.291	230	39	67	10	0	3	25	6
Christensen, Chad, Nebraska	.292	209	24	61	6	1	1	16	5

INDIVIDUAL PITCHING LEADERS
(Minimum 1 IP per team game)

	W	L	ERA	G	SV	IP	H	BB	SO
#Knebel, Corey, Texas	3	2	1.13	38	19	56	28	12	61
Jungmann, Taylor, Texas	13	3	1.60	19	0	141	81	36	126
Marshall, Evan, Kansas State	5	5	1.62	30	1	61	47	11	16
Stilson, John, Texas A&M	5	2	1.68	15	1	91	75	29	92
Rocha, Michael, Oklahoma	10	3	1.75	16	0	113	89	17	82
Stafford, Sam, Texas	6	2	1.77	19	0	81	54	42	91
Wacha, Michael, Texas A&M	9	4	2.29	19	0	130	117	30	123
Stripling, Ross, Texas A&M	14	2	2.29	24	4	126	91	18	113
Overton, Dillon, Oklahoma	8	4	2.30	23	0	74	72	32	59
John, Jordan, Oklahoma	4	2	2.35	20	0	61	55	18	54
Milner, Hoby, Texas	7	4	2.45	32	1	84	60	33	62
Hauptman, Casey, Nebraska	6	3	2.45	28	8	62	62	3	57
Verrett, Logan, Baylor	7	6	2.93	17	0	101	95	31	96
Neely, John, Texas Tech	9	1	2.97	30	7	61	59	21	56
Green, Cole, Texas	8	4	3.14	20	0	106	89	20	104
Turley, Josh, Baylor	4	5	3.39	17	0	96	103	19	63
Strong, Mike, Oklahoma State	5	1	3.61	15	0	72	64	25	70
Jon Keller, Nebraska	3	6	3.62	15	0	65	69	37	54
Propst, Brad, Oklahoma State	7	6	3.66	16	0	103	95	20	69
Stites, Matt, Missouri	3	6	3.72	15	0	92	90	41	77
Smith, Burch, Oklahoma	10	4	3.90	16	0	88	85	32	90

BIG WEST CONFERENCE

	Conference		Overall	
	W	L	W	L
*Cal State Fullerton	19	5	41	17
UC Irvine	16	8	43	18
Cal Poly	15	9	27	26
Long Beach State	12	12	29	27
UC Riverside	11	13	29	23
UC Santa Barbara	10	14	26	26
UC Davis	10	14	18	36
Pacific	9	15	17	37
Cal State Northridge	6	18	23	33

ALL-CONFERENCE TEAM: C—Ronnie Shaeffer, Jr., UC Irvine. **1B**—Nick Ramirez, Jr., Cal State Fullerton. **2B**—Sean Williams, Sr., UC Santa Barbara. **3B**—Brian Hernandez, Sr., UC Irvine. **SS**—Trevor Hairgrove, Sr., UC Riverside. **OF**—Bobby Crocker, Jr., Cal Poly; Mark Haddow, Sr., UC Santa Barbara; Drew Hillman, Sr., UC Irvine. **DH**—David Popkins, Jr., UC Davis. **UT**—Brian Hernandez, Sr., UC Irvine; Dustin Torchio, So., Pacific. **SP**—Mason Radeke, Jr., Cal Poly; Noe Ramirez, Jr., Cal State Fullerton; Matt Summers, Jr., UC Irvine. **RP**—Bryce Uhrig, Sr., UC Santa Barbara. **CP**—Nick Ramirez, Jr., Cal State Fullerton.
Player of the Year: Nick Ramirez, Cal State Fullerton. **Pitcher of the Year:** Matt Summers, UC Irvine. **Defensive Player of the Year:** Brian Hernandez, UC Irvine. **Freshman Player of the Year:** Michael Lorenzen, Cal State Fullerton. **Freshman Pitcher of the Year:** Dylan Stuart, UC Riverside. **Coach of the Year:** Dave Serrano, Cal State Fullerton.

INDIVIDUAL BATTING LEADERS
(Minimum 2.5 at-bats per team game)

	AVG	AB	R	H	2B	3B	HR	RBI	SB
Torchio, Dustin, Pacific	.369	195	35	72	11	1	1	17	5
Haddow, Mark, UCSB	.356	191	40	68	10	4	6	41	16
Martin, Brian, Pacific	.351	208	29	73	6	0	4	31	2
Williams, Sean, UCSB	.343	201	35	69	11	4	3	25	1
Lorenzen, Michael, CS Fullerton	.342	146	33	50	8	3	2	31	19
Lopez, Carlos, CS Fullerton	.342	158	17	54	8	4	2	34	8
Hernandez, Brian, UC Irvine	.341	252	47	86	12	1	0	33	2

Carvutto, Matthew, Pacific	.341	223	36	76	19	1	1	35	8
Crocker, Bobby, Cal Poly	.339	189	37	64	13	1	5	20	9
Hairgrove, Trevor, UC Riverside	.336	214	36	72	16	0	3	32	5
Hillman, Drew, UC Irvine	.333	240	45	80	14	2	6	51	7
Pedroza, Richy, CS Fullerton	.331	163	37	54	9	2	0	22	9
Fox, Jordan, UC Irvine	.323	186	35	60	5	2	0	25	9
Pill, Tyler, CS Fullerton	.323	155	25	50	11	2	1	30	3
Popkins, David, UC Davis	.321	196	22	63	9	3	4	23	1
Bowen, Marty, CS Northridge	.320	172	16	55	5	0	1	23	0
Goetz, Ryan, UC Riverside	.318	220	42	70	15	1	2	27	4
Trajano, Anthony, CS Fullerton	.313	147	29	46	4	1	0	23	5
Andriese, David, UC Riverside	.307	179	22	55	6	4	4	30	1
Muren, Drew, CS Northridge	.306	193	39	59	17	1	3	32	9
Miller, Mike, Cal Poly	.306	144	18	44	9	1	0	23	6
Carpenter, Ridge, CS Northridge	.304	207	37	63	10	4	4	21	16
Crumlich, D.J., UC Irvine	.300	233	51	70	15	2	1	27	4
Thomas, Ivory, CS Fullerton	.294	160	46	47	6	2	1	17	20
Shults, Justin, UC Riverside	.293	191	42	56	11	1	4	26	0
Ramirez, Nick, CS Fullerton	.291	213	40	62	17	1	9	49	4
Thompson, J.J., Cal Poly	.291	179	20	52	12	0	1	15	5
Marjama, Mike, Long Beach	.290	217	21	63	8	4	1	27	8
Riley, Allen, Pacific	.290	214	19	62	14	3	4	38	2
Leyland, Jordan, UC Irvine	.289	211	30	61	13	2	4	44	1
Reyes, Tommy, UC Irvine	.289	173	32	50	11	0	0	29	3
#Ramirez, Christian, UC Irvine	.282	163	26	46	10	5	0	32	6

INDIVIDUAL PITCHING LEADERS
(Minimum 1 IP per team game)

	W	L	ERA	G	SV	IP	H	BB	SO
Ramirez, Noe, CS Fullerton	8	4	1.69	14	0	91	56	20	103
Whitehouse, Matt, UC Irvine	4	0	2.12	23	0	72	54	15	63
#Ramirez, Nick, CS Fullerton	1	1	2.13	22	16	25	15	10	33
Summers, Matt, UC Irvine	11	4	2.15	18	0	117	81	33	100
Pill, Tyler, CS Fullerton	7	1	2.28	17	0	99	77	22	110
Orozco, Eddie, UC Riverside	5	2	2.29	12	0	71	61	30	60
Kupbens, Anthony, UC Davis	5	8	2.36	15	0	103	93	25	69
O'Connell, Colin, CS Fullerton	7	3	2.44	17	0	77	68	8	55
Andriese, Matt, UC Riverside	4	5	2.63	14	0	96	92	25	74
Gagnon, Andrew, Long Beach	4	10	2.81	15	0	99	79	38	84
Radeke, Mason, Cal Poly	8	4	3.07	15	0	100	91	31	95
Stuart, Shawn, Long Beach	4	4	3.16	18	2	74	71	31	70
Davis, Greg, UCSB	6	5	3.30	18	4	87	87	27	40
Fischback, Steven, Cal Poly	7	3	3.33	14	0	92	87	20	77
Frank, Trevor, UC Riverside	2	3	3.35	13	1	83	84	14	55
Roberts, Vincent, CS Northridge	3	6	3.44	16	1	81	67	32	55
Wagman, Joey, Cal Poly	4	3	3.62	17	1	65	54	17	52
Meaux, Jesse, UCSB	3	5	3.70	10	0	66	72	14	34
Loredo, Nick, UCSB	4	3	3.81	22	4	57	65	14	41
Floethe, Jake, CS Fullerton	6	3	3.82	19	2	64	57	26	49
Thurman, Andrew, UC Irvine	4	3	3.82	23	1	75	82	21	64

COLONIAL ATHLETIC ASSOCIATION

	Conference		Overall	
	W	L	W	L
*James Madison	21	9	42	19
Old Dominion	19	11	30	26
UNC Wilmington	18	12	31	28
Georgia State	17	13	37	21
Delaware	16	14	27	26
William & Mary	16	14	26	29
Towson	15	15	26	28
Virginia Commonwealth	12	18	22	32
Northeastern	12	18	18	33
Hofstra	12	18	15	32
George Mason	7	23	21	32

ALL-CONFERENCE TEAM: C—Jake Lowery, Jr., James Madison. **1B**—Steve Ulaky, Sr., Delaware. **2B**—Rob Lind, Sr., Georgia State. **3B**—Brandon Williams, Jr., Georgia State. **SS**—Josh Wright, Jr., Old Dominion. **OF**—Pat Dameron, Sr., Delaware; Mark Micowski, Sr., Georgia State; Danny Poma, Jr., Hofstra. **UT**—Taylor Perkins, Jr., Virginia Commonwealth. **DH**—Thomas Pope, Jr., UNC Wilmington. **SP**—Logan Billbrough, Sr., William & Mary; Kyle Hald, Sr., Old Dominion. **RP**—Adam Wisniewski, Sr., Old Dominion.

Player of the Year: Jake Lowery, James Madison. **Pitchers of the Year:** Logan Billbrough, William & Mary/Kyle Hald, Old Dominion. **Defensive Player of the Year:** Nick Natoli, Towson. **Rookie of the Year:** Aaron Barbosa, Northeastern. **Coach of the Year:** Nate Goulet, Old Dominion.

INDIVIDUAL BATTING LEADERS
(Minimum 125 at-bats)

	AVG	AB	R	H	2B	3B	HR	RBI	SB
Pope, Thomas, UNCW	.396	202	48	80	13	2	5	46	19
Poma, Danny, Hofstra	.382	178	38	68	16	2	2	28	20
Wright, Joshua, ODU	.369	198	53	73	16	5	12	44	18
Tison, Brig, GMU	.368	247	44	91	16	3	0	42	8
Schafferman, Dan, Delaware	.366	164	34	60	11	1	5	40	8
Dameron, Pat, Delaware	.363	204	46	74	22	0	5	45	5
Herbek, David, James Madison	.362	229	56	83	20	3	15	76	13
Bladel, Johnny, James Madison	.360	211	69	76	12	5	4	41	26
Foltz, Alex, James Madison	.359	195	44	70	12	1	7	44	16
Lowery, Jake, James Madison	.359	251	80	90	22	8	24	91	9
Hammer, Jared, Hofstra	.358	134	17	48	8	0	1	25	2
Ridge, Hunter, UNCW	.354	237	53	84	17	0	9	60	6
Lenherr, John, VCU	.353	215	44	76	11	5	2	22	21
Micowski, Mark, Ga. State	.351	239	51	84	20	4	5	48	12
Williams, Brandon, Ga. State	.342	222	43	76	13	0	1	36	12
Tenaglia, Matt, James Madison	.341	232	47	79	11	1	9	54	13
Cook, Christopher, GMU	.340	191	46	65	13	0	4	29	6
Ulaky, Steve, Delaware	.339	230	44	78	18	1	14	54	3
Campbell, Matt, UNCW	.337	255	48	86	15	3	6	26	10
Barbosa, Aaron, Northeastern	.335	209	31	70	8	3	1	13	29
Lind, Rob, Georgia State	.327	199	52	65	11	1	10	37	14
Harclerode, Austin, Towson	.327	208	41	68	9	2	5	42	7
Cheatham, Michael, VCU	.324	185	32	60	9	4	1	34	4
Cullen, Bill, VCU	.324	210	40	68	12	4	1	33	15
Shields, Drew, Georgia State	.321	140	35	45	4	1	0	20	5
Cujas, Joey, VCU	.321	209	32	67	9	1	2	41	4
Perkins, Taylor, VCU	.320	197	36	63	15	1	4	38	8
Osteen, Derrick, William & Mary	.318	201	35	64	12	0	0	26	7
Bower, Tadd, William & Mary	.315	197	30	62	6	0	5	40	9
Miller, Matt, Northeastern	.314	188	28	59	14	1	1	24	6

INDIVIDUAL PITCHING LEADERS
(Minimum 50 IP)

	W	L	ERA	G	SV	IP	H	BB	SO
Billbrough, Logan, W&M	7	2	2.58	14	0	98	81	32	105
Koehler, Brett, W&M	4	3	2.73	27	8	59	45	19	58
Crispell, Corey, Delaware	6	3	2.86	17	0	57	46	17	46
Campbell, Will, Georgia State	9	3	2.86	15	0	94	80	19	54
Ali, Dean, ODU	0	3	2.86	27	0	57	58	20	46
#Wisniewski, Adam, ODU	0	0	2.89	29	15	28	32	10	35
Acker, Chris, Towson	4	1	3.04	15	0	50	48	17	34
Tomchick, Ben, ODU	8	4	3.15	15	0	91	92	26	81
Haynes, Kyle, VCU	6	7	3.36	14	0	80	83	23	57
Cononie, Charlie, Towson	8	3	3.39	14	0	85	68	42	94
Tierney, Sean, James Madison	10	1	3.43	18	0	63	62	25	47
Leenhouts, Andrew, Northeastern	3	8	3.67	13	0	83	80	38	66
Hald, Kyle, ODU	8	3	3.67	14	0	96	82	46	108
Malone, Justin, UNCW	7	1	3.81	14	0	85	94	15	52
Bradley, Travis, UNCW	2	5	3.96	17	0	50	61	13	20
Cropper, Daniel, UNCW	8	3	3.97	14	0	91	92	19	80
Williams, Les, Northeastern	5	6	3.98	13	0	95	101	18	77
Young, Eric, Delaware	5	2	4.00	13	0	72	74	20	40
Brown, D.J., James Madison	9	1	4.00	23	4	97	90	30	92
McCarthy, Phil, ODU	9	4	4.05	14	0	96	110	27	61
Wainman, Matt, W&M	5	3	4.06	22	0	58	62	19	62

CONFERENCE USA

	Conference		Overall	
	W	L	W	L
Southern Mississippi	16	8	39	19
*Rice	16	8	42	21
East Carolina	14	10	41	21
Central Florida	12	12	39	23
Memphis	12	12	30	27
Houston	12	12	27	32
Tulane	10	14	31	26

Alabama-Birmingham	9	15	29 28
Marshall	7	17	20 31

ALL-CONFERENCE TEAM: C—Jeremy Schaffer, Jr., Tulane. **IF**—Jonathan Griffin, Jr., Central Florida; Michael Ratterree, So., Rice; B.A. Vollmuth, Jr., Southern Mississippi; Chad Zurcher, Jr., Memphis. **OF**—Jamal Austin, Jr., Alabama-Birmingham; Marc Bourgeois, Sr., Southern Mississippi; Tyler Koelling, Sr., Southern Mississippi. **DH**—Anthony Rendon, Jr., Rice. **P**—Austin Kubitza, Fr., Rice; Seth Maness, Sr., East Carolina; Todd McInnis, Sr., Southern Mississippi; Geoffrey Thomas, Jr., Southern Mississippi. **RP**—Nick Pepitone, Sr., Tulane.
Player of the Year: Chad Zurcher, Memphis. **Pitcher of the Year:** Todd McInnis, Southern Mississippi. **Rookie of the Year:** Austin Kubitza, Rice. **Newcomer of the Year:** Dillon Napoleon, Alabama-Birmingham. **Coach of the Year:** Scott Berry, Southern Mississippi.

INDIVIDUAL BATTING LEADERS
(Minimum 150 at-bats)

	AVG	AB	R	H	2B	3B	HR	RBI	SB
Zurcher, Chad, Memphis	.443	203	47	90	19	2	0	34	12
Koelling, Tyler, Southern Miss	.362	232	43	84	18	1	4	46	5
Bourgeois, Marc, Southern Miss	.358	201	46	72	10	2	7	38	1
Austin, Jamal, UAB	.351	225	38	79	8	2	0	28	26
Hicks, D.J., UCF	.351	251	42	80	11	0	14	66	1
Griffin, Jonathan, UCF	.343	210	53	86	19	2	19	58	1
Schaffer, Jeremy, Tulane	.338	287	45	71	23	2	6	37	0
Socorro, Kenny, Marshall	.337	200	32	63	5	0	1	27	5
Doleac, Adam, Southern Miss	.335	289	33	67	14	3	2	39	3
Still, Ryan, Houston	.333	175	45	63	3	3	0	21	12
Graham, Robby, Memphis	.331	239	23	58	10	0	4	34	3
Martinez, Drew, Memphis	.331	229	56	79	14	0	0	24	20
Gomez, Victor, Marshall	.330	214	31	65	11	1	6	39	1
Thompson, Corey, East Carolina	.328	260	36	75	11	0	6	47	3
Rendon, Anthony, Rice	.327	246	58	70	20	2	6	37	13
Ratterree, Michael, Rice	.327	261	46	85	20	1	6	53	6
Whitehead, Trent, East Carolina	.325	209	45	80	20	1	4	29	17
Taylor, Beau, UCF	.325	175	51	75	11	2	5	47	0
Chapman, Phillip, Memphis	.321	244	36	67	21	2	5	42	6
Stafford, Rhett, Marshall	.320	223	30	56	8	2	10	41	7
Jensen, Chase, Houston	.320	188	42	78	12	3	3	45	5
Ramsey, Caleb, Houston	.318	237	38	71	17	4	0	46	5
McDonald, Chase, East Carolina	.314	212	26	59	11	0	4	31	2
Richardson, Ronnie, UCF	.312	174	59	74	12	4	2	34	15
Reinheimer, Jack, East Carolina	.311	213	33	66	4	0	0	23	3
Clark, Philip, East Carolina	.310	223	30	54	4	0	3	28	13
Crawford, Nick, UAB	.310	204	40	66	6	1	0	21	18
Shreve, Travis, UCF	.309	275	51	69	15	0	0	20	22
Ramos, Victor, Marshall	.309	189	42	63	16	4	1	25	16
Manuel, Craig, Rice	.309	178	24	54	6	0	1	35	1
#Ballou, Isaac, Marshall	.283	187	40	53	4	7	1	29	18

INDIVIDUAL PITCHING LEADERS
(Minimum 1 IP per team game)

Player, team	W	L	ERA	G	SV	IP	H	BB	SO
Mincey, Brad, East Carolina	6	4	1.57	31	3	69	61	18	55
Maness, Seth, East Carolina	10	3	1.71	15	0	105	84	17	80
#Cingrani, Tony, Rice	4	2	1.74	34	12	57	47	10	66
Brandt, Kevin, East Carolina	7	3	2.26	19	0	92	78	27	63
Kubitza, Austin, Rice	6	5	2.34	15	0	100	95	24	102
McInnis, Todd, Southern Miss	8	3	2.65	15	0	99	94	32	87
Wright, Mike, East Carolina	6	4	2.79	16	0	100	81	30	75
Napoleon, Dillon, UAB	5	3	2.87	13	0	85	70	26	56
Gonzales, Abe, Rice	8	2	2.91	25	1	74	70	20	43
Pepitone, Nick, Tulane	3	3	3.02	27	14	45	45	22	27
Woolley, Ryan, UAB	7	6	3.06	17	0	106	87	29	75
Thomas, Geoffrey, So. Miss	10	3	3.09	14	0	84	75	34	54
Reckling, Matthew, Rice	4	1	3.10	17	0	78	63	38	96
Byo, Alex, Tulane	3	2	3.32	12	0	60	56	20	39
Thompson, Jonathan, So. Miss	7	1	3.49	14	0	70	75	25	43
Lewis, Jordan, Houston	5	3	3.75	16	0	82	63	28	55
Flynn, Conrad, Tulane	3	7	4.32	15	0	90	56	20	66
Langfield, Dan, Memphis	3	3	4.32	15	0	85	75	49	94
Adkins, Brian, UCF	6	5	4.40	16	0	88	88	22	45
Zizinia, Drew, Tulane	3	1	4.57	20	0	65	92	37	59
Holland, Ryan, Memphis	5	3	4.61	17	0	96	77	54	78

Wiley, Mo, Houston	4	4	4.63	15 0 70 100 23 31

GREAT WEST CONFERENCE

	Conference		Overall	
	W	L	W	L
Utah Valley	22	2	34	21
Northern Colorado	19	7	24	32
Houston Baptist	16	12	22	40
New York Tech	13	12	19	31
New Jersey Tech	12	16	20	35
Texas-Pan American	10	19	21	31
North Dakota	7	17	12	35
Chicago State	4	19	9	41

ALL-CONFERENCE TEAM: C—Mike McCarthy, Jr., Texas-Pan American. **1B**—Effrey Valdez, Sr., New York Tech. **2B**—T.J. Berge, Sr., Northern Colorado. **3B**—Vincent Mejia, Jr., Texas-Pan American. **SS**—Kai Hatch, Jr., Utah Valley. **DH**—Robbie Buller, Jr., Houston Baptist. **OF**—Chris Benson, Sr., Utah Valley; Jarod Berggren, Jr., Northern Colorado; Josh Ray, Sr., North Dakota. **UT**—D.J. Roche, So., New Jersey Tech. **P**—Trip Davis, So., New Jersey Tech; Jeremy Gendlek, Sr., Utah Valley; Blake Krahenbuhl, Jr., Utah Valley. **RP**—Ryan Dillabough, So., New York Tech.
Player of the Year: Effrey Valdez, New York Tech. **Pitcher of the Year:** Jeremy Gendlek, Utah Valley. **Newcomer of the Year:** Jeremy Gendlek, Utah Valley. **Coach of the Year:** Eric Madsen, Utah Valley.

INDIVIDUAL BATTING LEADERS
(Minimum 125 at-bats)

	AVG	AB	R	H	2B	3B	HR	RBI	SB
Valdez, Effrey, NY Tech	.437	183	39	80	13	0	13	39	4
Benson, Chris, Utah Valley	.400	250	62	100	23	5	5	53	10
Sadler, Andy, North Dakota	.385	182	40	70	10	2	0	22	4
Packard, Ben, Northern Colo.	.374	179	27	67	17	4	4	43	1
McCarthy, Mike, UTPA	.372	183	27	68	11	2	1	43	0
Carpen, Michael, Chicago State	.360	197	35	71	8	1	1	18	8
Berggren, Jarod, Northern Colo.	.360	189	50	68	19	7	7	60	2
Ray, Josh, North Dakota	.354	192	32	68	9	7	3	31	5
Bernal, Roger, UTPA	.353	190	37	67	9	1	2	25	7
Mejia, Vincent, UTPA	.352	182	44	64	16	0	4	38	0
Ibanez, Angel, UTPA	.347	213	42	74	11	6	3	36	13
Arnst, Kolby, Houston Baptist	.343	230	42	79	15	4	2	36	5
Kwak, Kris, North Dakota	.339	168	30	57	17	2	5	25	3
Heaps, Austin, Utah Valley	.339	221	50	75	25	0	3	38	1
Smith, Jerry, New York Tech	.335	179	32	60	5	0	2	27	8
Hilker, Adam, Northern Colo.	.335	221	41	74	14	3	2	34	11
Hatch, Kai, Utah Valley	.335	206	35	69	8	4	2	33	11
Rodriguez, Ali, New York Tech	.331	181	36	60	7	1	3	25	18
Berge, T.J., Northern Colo.	.330	203	47	67	17	3	1	31	6
Burgess, Billy, Utah Valley	.320	200	33	64	10	1	4	36	9
McWhorter, Cole, Utah Valley	.320	147	36	47	6	1	4	23	10
Tomczyk, Matt, NJ Tech	.318	214	40	68	12	1	4	27	8
Magner, Jake, North Dakota	.313	166	27	52	13	1	7	38	0
Kallunki, Goose, Utah Valley	.311	222	33	69	14	0	4	60	1
Lewis, Weston, Chicago State	.310	145	25	45	6	1	1	19	7
Cafiero, Rob, New York Tech	.310	129	28	40	7	3	5	32	4
Hetzler, Collin, Houston Baptist	.309	236	41	73	7	1	0	28	4
Carpen, Jonathan, Chi. State	.307	189	33	58	2	2	2	30	3
Coy, Casey, Northern Colo.	.306	186	41	57	10	1	2	29	2
Valenzuela, Marcus, N. Colo.	.302	126	23	38	11	0	2	27	4
#Buller, Robbie, Houston Baptist	.298	228	57	68	16	0	16	55	1

INDIVIDUAL PITCHING LEADERS
(Minimum 50 IP)

	W	L	ERA	G	SV	IP	H	BB	SO
Gendlek, Jeremy, Utah Valley	7	3	1.71	14	0	90	82	25	36
#Swenson, Josh, Utah Valley	1	2	2.38	19	6	34	31	22	26
Krahenbuhl, Blake, Utah Valley	7	2	2.65	15	0	85	68	30	60
Davis, Tripp, New Jersey Tech	6	6	3.69	15	0	107	110	27	87
Dillabough, Ryan, New York Tech	4	4	3.95	19	5	57	78	15	37
Baker, Cory, North Dakota	1	5	4.19	15	4	62	69	35	50
Leiter, Mark, New Jersey Tech	5	3	4.76	15	0	91	90	53	103
Dickerson, Kyle, Houston Baptist	5	2	5.00	16	0	63	72	35	41
Flores, Luis, UTPA	2	5	5.04	10	0	50	61	25	27
Nikonchik, Stephen, HB	5	4	5.14	24	2	68	96	24	41
Perez, Marcos, New York Tech	5	4	5.24	13	0	67	79	28	48

	W	L	ERA	G	SV	IP	H	BB	SO
Willman, Joe, Northern Colorado	7	5	5.24	13	0	81	98	29	58
Duggan, John, New York Tech	3	5	5.25	13	0	62	63	50	33
Olson, Preston, Utah Valley	3	0	5.26	16	0	53	67	32	44
Storey, Jamie, Houston Baptist	2	8	5.28	15	0	77	90	20	48
Roche, D.J., New Jersey Tech	2	5	5.94	11	0	53	63	34	49
Hernandez, Chase, HB	4	5	6.07	13	1	73	100	27	41
Spies, David, North Dakota	3	3	6.17	11	1	58	95	18	20
Schafer, Dalton, Houston Baptist	3	10	6.20	17	0	90	131	24	42
Borst, Derek, Chicago State	0	9	6.25	18	0	68	99	32	16
Hall, Brendan, Northern Colo.	1	1	6.41	**27**	0	39	41	16	37
Delgado, Jonathan, UTPA	2	5	6.54	12	0	54	80	15	36

	W	L	ERA	G	SV	IP	H	BB	SO
Pierce, Chad, Milwaukee	6	4	3.21	15	0	**101**	87	29	82
Semmelhack, Eric, Milwaukee	3	4	3.44	14	0	86	75	28	63
Klein, Phil, YSU	5	5	3.61	15	0	92	83	34	**105**
Deetjen, Tyler, Valparaiso	3	5	3.71	9	0	61	59	10	32
Bates, Coty, Cleveland State	1	7	3.95	14	0	66	61	30	45
Silvestri, Dom, Butler	6	5	4.07	14	1	86	101	30	56
McCormick, Damon, Valparaiso	2	5	4.22	9	0	64	51	17	56
Gulbransen, Jon, Valparaiso	3	5	4.53	10	0	56	61	18	54
Woytek, Michael, Wright State	7	4	4.64	15	0	85	109	26	39
Henn, Casey, Wright State	7	4	4.83	16	0	86	102	21	59
Begel, Joey, UIC	4	3	4.98	14	0	81	115	26	25
Schneider, Mike, Milwaukee	4	2	5.03	13	0	54	44	30	47
Sambula, Anthony, CSU	3	8	5.05	15	0	87	90	45	60
Weinberg, Charlie, UIC	6	5	5.17	18	1	54	59	30	32
McCulloh, Kevin, YSU	4	9	5.29	22	1	63	81	30	49
Wagoner, Jared, Butler	5	6	5.47	14	0	77	95	25	60
Heaslip, Matt, UIC	5	5	5.78	18	0	86	114	35	40
Hernandez, Mike, Butler	5	6	5.81	15	0	79	115	17	60
#Cooper, Brandon, CSU	3	3	6.18	**32**	0	55	71	25	29

HORIZON LEAGUE

	Conference		Overall	
	W	L	W	L
*Wright State	16	7	36	17
Illinois-Chicago	16	7	28	26
Wisconsin-Milwaukee	15	10	28	28
Valparaiso	14	10	25	32
Butler	11	14	23	28
Youngstown State	7	16	14	41
Cleveland State	5	20	12	43

ALL-CONFERENCE TEAM: C—Corey Davis, Jr., Wright State. **1B**—Jake Hibberd, Jr., Wright State. **2B**—Cole Kraft, Sr., Wisconsin-Milwaukee. **3B**—Zach Tanner, Jr., Wright State. **SS**—Justin Kopale, So., Wright State. **OF**—Doug Dekoning, Sr., Wisconsin-Milwaukee; Alex Johnson, Jr., Cleveland State; Tristan Moore, Jr., Wright State. **DH**—Will Hagel, Jr., Valparaiso. **UT**—Andy Leonard, Sr., Illinois-Chicago. **P**—Chad Pierce, Sr., Milwaukee; Michael Schum, Jr., Wright State.
Player of the Year: Jake Hibbard, Wright State. **Pitcher of the Year:** Chad Pierce, Wisconsin–Milwaukee. **Relief Pitcher of the Year:** Michael Schum, Wright State. **Newcomer of the Year:** Corey Davis, Wright State. **Coach of the Year:** Rob Cooper, Wright State.

INDIVIDUAL BATTING LEADERS
(Minimum 125 at-bats)

	AVG	AB	R	H	2B	3B	HR	RBI	SB
Hibberd, Jake, Wright State	.407	236	42	**96**	**21**	0	9	56	5
Tanner, Zach, Wright State	.374	214	45	80	15	4	5	34	7
Serna, Matt, UIC	.369	198	36	73	12	1	0	32	8
Dekoning, Doug, Milwaukee	.362	221	47	80	17	2	8	47	16
Kraft, Cole, Milwaukee	.354	237	39	84	17	1	3	39	13
Moore, Tristan, Wright State	.352	210	49	74	17	**6**	5	46	8
Fillipitch, Grant, Butler	.340	200	46	68	17	0	3	33	0
Letzter, Michael, Butler	.331	178	33	59	12	1	6	36	2
Gaedele, Kyle, Valparaiso	.324	139	31	45	11	2	3	26	10
Ganek, Jason, UIC	.321	184	35	59	14	0	8	39	0
Kopale, Justin, Wright State	.321	162	21	52	11	0	3	28	2
Capasso, Jonathan, Milwaukee	.313	192	27	60	5	0	3	27	11
Davis, Corey, Wright State	.312	189	38	59	15	2	8	40	4
Picchiotti, Sam, Wright State	.308	198	37	61	13	1	2	28	5
Hoenecke, Paul, Milwaukee	.304	184	24	56	13	1	5	31	5
Hoscheit, Mike, Butler	.302	139	24	42	11	1	1	27	5
Leonard, Andy, UIC	.301	193	40	58	6	3	1	32	9
Ashe, Ryan, Wright State	.301	176	22	53	12	1	1	29	4
Duncan, Luke, Butler	.300	213	27	64	8	1	3	26	5
Banks, Jeremy, YSU	.300	150	30	45	2	1	0	15	2
Marsh, Dan, Wright State	.298	208	**52**	62	8	0	0	26	9
Schroth, Neil, YS	.297	182	23	54	9	4	0	16	5
Scoby, Steven, Valparaiso	.287	136	25	39	7	1	0	13	5
Iacobucci, Joe, YSU	.284	204	30	58	5	1	1	23	7
Eckhardt, Andrew, Butler	.280	168	34	47	3	3	1	13	10
Sambula, Anthony, CSU	.276	174	13	48	3	1	0	16	5
Johnson, Alex, CSU	.274	208	23	57	16	1	3	28	18
Addison, Nick, UIC	.272	184	31	50	9	0	4	28	6
Leon, David, YSU	.268	168	21	45	6	1	3	11	4
Taylor, Tell, Milwaukee	.267	135	15	36	1	0	1	18	4
#Calhoun, Kyle, CSU	.254	201	26	51	8	0	1	19	**20**

INDIVIDUAL PITCHING LEADERS
(Minimum 50 IP)

	W	L	ERA	G	SV	IP	H	BB	SO
#Schum, Michael, Wright State	9	2	1.37	29	**9**	53	42	6	41
Salemi, Matt, UIC	4	5	3.00	14	0	72	59	30	21

IVY LEAGUE

	Conference		Overall	
GEHRIG	W	L	W	L
*Princeton	15	5	23	24
Pennsylvania	10	10	19	21
Columbia	9	11	19	25
Cornell	7	13	10	30
ROLFE	W	L	W	L
Dartmouth	14	6	30	12
Yale	11	9	23	19
Brown	9	11	13	29
Harvard	5	15	9	36

ALL-CONFERENCE TEAM: C— Will Davis, Jr., Pennsylvania; Sam Mulroy, Jr., Princeton. **1B**—Trey Rallis, Sr., Yale. **2B**—Jeff Reynolds, Jr., Harvard. **3B**—Dan Williams, Sr., Pennsylvania. **SS**—Joe Sclafani, Jr., Dartmouth. **OF**—Jason Banos, Sr., Columbia; Dario Pizzano, So., Columbia; Greg Zebrack, So., Pennsylvania. **DH**—Spencer Branigan, So., Pennsylvania. **UT**—Mickey Brodsky, Sr., Cornell. **SP**—Paul Cusick, Sr., Pennsylvania; Kyle Hendricks, Jr., Dartmouth; Vinny Lally, Sr., Yale; Max Perlman, Sr., Harvard; Cole Sulser, Jr., Dartmouth. **RP**—Ryan Smith, Sr., Dartmouth. **Hitter of the Year:** Trey Rallis, Yale. **Pitcher of the Year:** Paul Cusick, Pennsylvania. **Rookie of the Year:** Mike Ford, Princeton.

INDIVIDUAL BATTING LEADERS
(Minimum 2.5 at-bats per team game)

	AVG	AB	R	H	2B	3B	HR	RBI	SB
Maas, Jeremy, Penn	.369	141	28	52	9	0	5	23	9
Rallis, Trey, Yale	.365	148	25	54	12	0	4	30	1
Coble, Ennis, Dartmouth	.361	147	29	53	14	3	1	**40**	9
Pizzano, Dario, Columbia	.359	156	34	56	15	2	**9**	36	0
Cox, Nick, Columbia	.353	139	34	49	12	1	2	16	18
Sclafani, Joe, Dartmouth	.349	172	46	**60**	12	8	4	34	3
Zebrack, Greg, Penn	.336	146	35	49	11	3	7	27	4
Bean, Sam, Dartmouth	.335	164	35	55	12	1	1	26	9
Megee, Andy, Yale	.329	167	28	55	11	0	2	28	4
O'Dowd, Chris, Dartmouth	.328	161	**49**	53	8	4	7	23	12
Yanzick, Marshall, Cornell	.323	134	19	44	2	0	0	11	9
Banos, Jason, Columbia	.320	130	24	42	9	0	6	30	3
Mulroy, Sam, Princeton	.315	178	31	57	11	3	7	39	3
Brenner, Ryan, Yale	.311	111	20	35	10	1	1	18	13
Brodsky, Mickey, Cornell	.306	151	17	47	8	1	3	29	4
Bowman, Matt, Princeton	.306	**193**	39	59	8	2	0	20	4
Vigoa, Derek, Penn	.304	144	22	44	5	0	1	24	6
Davis, Will, Penn	.301	138	31	42	**16**	1	6	27	2
Colantonio, Matt, Brown	.301	136	31	41	12	1	1	13	1
Reynolds, Jeff, Harvard	.300	163	17	49	11	1	2	19	4
Ford, Mike, Princeton	.300	170	30	51	9	1	3	31	1
Hunter, Jacob, Yale	.299	120	17	36	9	0	0	25	1
Engelhardt, Brando, Penn	.299	157	21	47	5	3	0	25	2
Flink, Alex, Princeton	.296	134	16	40	6	1	0	10	8
Branigan, Spencer, Penn	.292	125	26	37	8	0	7	23	0
Billigen, Brian, Cornell	.291	120	32	35	5	4	8	24	1
Mishu, John, Princeton	.288	165	29	48	9	5	0	29	11

	AVG	AB	R	H	2B	3B	HR	RBI	SB
Williams, Dan, Penn	.287	153	29	44	9	1	2	28	6
Sheridan, John, Brown	.287	136	18	39	5	0	0	9	23
Peters, Brenton, Cornell	.285	105	13	30	7	2	1	14	3

INDIVIDUAL PITCHING LEADERS
(Minimum 1 IP per team game)

	W	L	ERA	G	SV	IP	H	BB	SO
Perlman, Max, Harvard	2	5	1.80	10	0	60	46	17	55
Giel, Tim, Columbia	1	2	2.05	16	5	26	29	9	26
Hart, Brook, Yale	4	5	2.23	11	0	65	64	13	47
Hendricks, Kyle, Dartmouth	5	3	2.47	9	0	62	53	11	70
Lally, Vinny, Yale	5	1	2.54	13	0	67	40	43	70
Sulser, Cole, Dartmouth	4	1	2.59	8	0	49	39	4	49
Cusick, Paul, Penn	5	3	2.70	11	0	67	56	31	80
Mayo, Heath, Brown	3	1	3.06	12	0	53	54	20	22
Hermans, Zak, Princeton	5	2	3.18	11	0	71	67	21	55
#O'Hare, Christopher, Yale	5	1	3.25	8	0	36	39	9	31
#Thomson, Cody, Penn	5	5	3.35	17	2	38	43	8	22
Olson, Stefan Columbia	2	2	3.63	9	1	45	34	22	34
Schmeltzer, Jadd, Cornell	3	4	3.63	9	0	52	51	20	38
Kimball, Matthew, Brown	3	4	3.74	8	0	53	59	9	42
Hunter, Kyle, Dartmouth	5	3	3.77	9	0	62	66	16	43
Ford, Mike, Princeton	5	4	4.08	11	0	71	75	17	38
Bracey, Dan, Columbia	4	5	4.10	9	0	53	56	10	33
Voiro, Vince, Penn	4	5	4.28	11	0	61	73	24	57
Wood, Taylor, Cornell	3	6	4.30	10	0	61	68	18	44
Whitaker, Geoff, Columbia	3	5	4.55	9	0	55	65	10	41
Lower, Pat, Columbia	1	5	4.62	9	0	49	52	31	37
Eadington, Eric, Harvard	0	7	4.99	10	0	52	56	21	54
Bowman, Matt, Princeton	2	7	5.05	10	0	52	73	8	45
Ludwig, Pat, Yale	4	3	5.10	8	0	48	55	17	49
Pappel, Corey, Cornell	0	9	5.69	10	0	55	58	29	35
#Palms, David, Princeton	3	3	5.73	22	2	33	34	21	23
McNulty, Chris, Penn	1	4	7.36	12	0	51	80	22	26

METRO ATLANTIC ATHLETIC CONFERENCE

	Conference		Overall	
	W	L	W	L
*Manhattan	20	2	34	19
Rider	16	7	33	18
Siena	14	10	28	30
Canisius	12	10	26	32
Marist	13	11	35	17
Fairfield	13	11	22	25
Iona	7	17	17	34
St. Peter's	5	18	16	34
Niagara	5	19	8	40

ALL-CONFERENCE TEAM: C—Bryce Nugent, Jr., Marist. 1B—Brian Burton, Sr., Canisius. 2B—Dan Paolini, Jr., Siena. 3B—Chris Burke, Jr., Iona. SS—Sean Jamieson, Sr., Canisius. OF—Brandon Cotton, Jr., Rider; Mike McCann, Sr., Manhattan; Mark Onorati, Sr., Manhattan. DH—James Beck, Jr., Iona; Eric Helmrich, So., Marist. UT—Ricky Pacione, Jr., Marist. P—John Soldinger, So., Manhattan; Mike Thomas, Sr., Rider. Players of the Year: Sean Jamieson, Canisius/Dan Paolini, Siena. Pitcher of the Year: John Soldinger, Manhattan. Relief Pitcher of the Year: Tyler Smith, Rider. Rookie of the Year: Nick Crescenzo, Rider. Coach of the Year: Kevin Leighton, Manhattan.

INDIVIDUAL BATTING LEADERS
(Minimum 125 at-bats)

	AVG	AB	R	H	2B	3B	HR	RBI	SB
Burke, Chris, Iona	.368	185	43	68	13	0	11	44	22
Helmrich, Eric, Marist	.364	132	22	48	9	1	3	32	0
Aldridge, Preston, St. Peter's	.364	176	24	64	9	2	1	29	9
McCann, Mike, Manhattan	.355	186	33	66	12	2	6	38	7
Crescenzo, Nick, Rider	.355	155	25	55	6	0	0	31	7
Jamieson, Sean, Canisius	.350	197	60	69	13	2	13	51	22
Paolini, Dan, Siena	.346	211	48	73	10	0	19	67	13
Pettit, Drew, Canisius	.345	203	32	70	12	1	6	40	3
Nathans, Tucker, Fairfield	.344	180	39	62	16	3	5	35	13
Beck, James, Iona	.339	186	29	63	23	2	7	42	2
Chiaravalloti, Michael, Iona	.333	135	21	45	10	1	4	25	2

	AVG	AB	R	H	2B	3B	HR	RBI	SB
Ortega, Ramon, Manhattan	.331	160	21	53	11	0	2	25	1
Cotton, Brandon, Rider	.331	178	43	59	16	2	4	29	9
Onorati, Mark, Manhattan	.328	201	58	66	21	2	6	26	15
Salem, Chad, Manhattan	.328	198	37	65	19	1	9	50	5
Wagner, Adam, Niagara	.327	171	22	56	9	1	0	11	6
Sheffield, Austin, Manhattan	.309	175	27	54	9	0	3	29	0
Burton, Brian, Canisius	.308	195	36	60	16	1	5	47	2
Stupienski, Russ, St. Peter's	.307	150	21	46	6	1	1	13	4
Nugent, Bryce, Marist	.300	190	36	57	11	0	5	34	0
Grimes, Chris, St. Peter's	.297	158	19	47	9	0	2	27	2
Furbeck, Ryan, Fairfield	.296	159	27	47	7	0	2	15	6
Albee, A.J., Rider	.295	190	33	56	9	0	2	29	12
Stykemain, Cam, Niagara	.293	181	30	53	10	1	1	16	12
Citro, Vincent, Siena	.293	191	38	56	3	1	0	24	6
Gallic, Michael, Marist	.292	192	43	56	14	3	6	43	12
Kriss, Matt, Iona	.287	167	20	48	7	0	1	22	3
Torres, Joe, Iona	.287	195	45	56	10	1	0	8	27
Schwind, Jon, Marist	.287	202	47	58	15	1	5	32	4
Heyne, Mason, Rider	.287	188	24	54	15	1	3	37	1
#Hink, Eric, Niagara	.263	179	22	47	6	4	0	25	2
#Rooney, John, Siena	.258	229	41	59	9	1	0	15	7

INDIVIDUAL PITCHING LEADERS
(Minimum 50 IP)

	W	L	ERA	G	SV	IP	H	BB	SO
McKeown, Sean, Marist	6	1	1.87	15	1	63	42	13	38
Thomas, Mike, Rider	9	3	2.34	14	0	96	83	37	92
#Smith, Tyler, Rider	3	3	2.58	29	15	38	26	7	41
Shulick, Brett, Fairfield	4	3	2.75	12	0	69	62	23	41
Gallagher, Chad, Marist	9	3	2.87	14	0	97	88	17	56
Wiley, Justin, Iona	6	5	2.97	14	0	88	85	21	67
Davis, Shane, Canisius	5	6	3.23	15	0	98	91	19	59
Brantley, Justin, Siena	6	6	3.29	15	0	88	80	43	51
Hartman, Zach, Siena	6	4	3.29	16	0	104	102	34	69
Soldinger, John, Manhattan	10	1	3.57	16	1	106	97	40	66
Luksis, Eric, Manhattan	7	4	3.68	15	0	86	80	40	69
Gussaroff, Scott, Fairfield	5	6	3.72	13	0	87	74	37	89
Calogero, Joe, Rider	2	3	3.82	11	0	68	82	14	33
Giordano, Mike, Manhattan	8	2	3.86	15	0	91	79	25	78
Sumple, Kyle, Siena	4	6	3.98	15	0	86	102	43	69
Eppley, Nate, Rider	6	7	4.27	14	0	86	81	30	50
Bordonaro, Mark, Fairfield	2	3	4.42	21	5	59	54	23	38
Warwick, Scott, Fairfield	5	5	4.43	12	0	69	64	34	58
Martin, Billy, Canisius	4	3	4.81	15	2	73	76	23	32
Macaluso, Dom, St. Peter's	4	9	4.92	15	0	82	102	28	48
Cortright, Garret, Canisius	4	4	5.05	15	1	62	63	25	29

MID-AMERICAN CONFERENCE

	Conference		Overall	
EAST	W	L	W	L
*Kent State	21	5	45	17
Miami (Ohio)	18	9	35	25
Bowling Green State	11	14	20	31
Ohio	11	16	27	27
Akron	7	20	16	37
Buffalo	3	21	14	37
WEST	W	L	W	L
Central Michigan	17	9	31	27
Eastern Michigan	16	11	37	22
Northern Illinois	16	11	30	27
Toledo	15	12	26	29
Western Michigan	12	14	26	31
Ball State	11	15	15	35

ALL-CONFERENCE TEAM: C—Tom Murphy, So., Buffalo. 1B—Kyle Weldon, Sr., Miami (Ohio). 2B—Zack Leonard, Sr., Eastern Michigan. 3B—Travis Shaw, Jr., Kent State. SS—Alex Jones, Jr., Northern Illinois. OF—Ken Battison, Sr., Eastern Michigan; Ben Klafczynski, Sr., Kent State; Drew Turocy, Jr., Akron. DH—Jeff Zimmerman, Fr., Northern Illinois. UT—Jon Berti, Sr., Bowling Green State. SP—Andrew Chafin, So., Kent State; Kyle Hallock, Sr., Kent State; David Starn, Jr., Kent State; Mac Thoreson, So., Miami (Ohio). RP—Jeff Zimmerman, Fr., Northern Illinois.
Player of the Year: Tom Murphy, Buffalo. Pitcher of the Year: Kyle

Hallock, Kent State. **Freshman of the Year:** Jeff Zimmerman, Northern Illinois. **Coach of the Year:** Scott Stricklin, Kent State.

INDIVIDUAL BATTING LEADERS
(Minimum 125 at-bats)

	AVG	AB	R	H	2B	3B	HR	RBI	SB
Murphy, Tom, Buffalo	.384	190	34	73	16	0	10	44	7
Leonard, Zack, Eastern Mich.	.372	234	53	87	18	0	2	37	5
Klafczynski, Ben, Kent State	.368	247	56	91	19	3	10	57	4
Hall, Tyler, Central Mich.	.367	229	46	84	13	11	3	34	16
Berti, Jon, Bowling Green	.356	180	34	64	8	6	2	26	18
Jones, Alex, Northern Ill.	.352	233	43	82	15	6	3	47	8
Turocy, Drew, Akron	.347	199	35	69	12	5	7	29	10
Ohrman, Brent, Eastern Mich.	.339	248	51	84	18	1	2	37	20
Newton, Ethan, Ohio	.330	224	44	74	10	1	1	17	20
Hammer, Ben, Toledo	.330	194	26	64	10	1	1	27	10
Battiston, Ken, Eastern Mich.	.329	237	51	78	21	6	6	44	10
Arnold, William, Central Mich.	.326	193	28	63	8	2	3	38	5
Zimmerman, Jeff, Northern Ill.	.326	215	34	70	13	0	11	47	0
Elliott, Cody, Ball State	.325	197	34	64	12	5	3	38	14
Wells, Jamison, Northern Ill.	.321	240	56	77	16	2	2	26	27
Baldock, Alex, Buffalo	.320	194	40	62	18	1	4	24	1
Magsig, Ben, Eastern Mich.	.316	206	41	65	12	0	4	33	4
Lyon, David, Kent State	.315	238	36	75	12	7	9	53	1
Widau, Mitch, Ball State	.313	166	29	52	6	1	1	26	6
Barnes, Bryan, Ohio	.313	192	34	60	7	3	4	25	5
Longo, Lee, Eastern Mich.	.312	138	22	43	10	0	4	25	0
McMillin, Ryan, Western Mich.	.312	186	33	58	12	3	7	40	7
Edgington, Jon, Miami (Ohio)	.311	206	40	64	9	0	2	25	17
Dean, Jordan, Central Mich.	.310	226	29	70	12	0	2	29	17
Shaw, Travis, Kent State	.307	244	48	75	14	2	14	51	0
Redeker, Bryce, Miami (Ohio)	.307	231	36	71	20	2	7	50	10
Dudics, Chris, Toledo	.306	235	34	72	8	2	2	18	13
Duncan, Clay, Bowling Green	.305	174	28	53	8	0	2	30	3
Russell, Daniel, Eastern Mich.	.305	223	34	68	11	4	2	38	9
White, Troy, Northern Ill.	.304	217	46	66	11	4	3	45	12
#Rider, Jimmy, Kent State	.281	267	41	75	16	3	1	46	5
#Brenner, Ryan, Miami (Ohio)	.254	185	35	47	7	2	0	17	39

INDIVIDUAL PITCHING LEADERS
(Minimum 50 IP)

	W	L	ERA	G	SV	IP	H	BB	SO
#Bassitt, Chris, Akron	2	5	1.42	28	7	38	24	15	48
#McMillen, Kyle, Kent State	1	2	1.80	28	18	30	18	12	31
Hallock, Kyle, Kent State	10	4	1.95	17	0	106	101	26	88
Hamann, Mike, Toledo	2	3	1.96	9	0	60	47	8	51
Chafin, Andrew, Kent State	8	1	2.02	14	0	89	59	23	105
Starn, David, Kent State	9	3	2.18	17	0	107	91	24	117
Thoreson, Mac, Miami (Ohio)	6	4	2.22	16	0	101	89	20	71
Fiala, Brooks, Miami (Ohio)	7	4	2.53	17	0	82	77	12	56
Mace, Ryan, Kent State	5	3	2.67	14	0	64	64	16	49
Howard, Trent, Central Mich.	4	4	2.78	14	0	87	76	22	96
Webber, Casey, Western Mich.	4	7	2.86	15	0	88	82	37	77
Brown, Andrew, Akron	4	7	2.97	15	0	103	87	27	70
Stroud, Brian, Western Mich.	8	4	3.20	15	0	101	103	25	74
Cooper, Zach, Central Mich.	6	3	3.26	15	0	91	86	39	88
Wendzicki, Rob, Eastern Mich.	6	6	3.38	16	0	107	110	22	76
Bowling, Cal, Ball State	5	5	3.41	14	0	90	85	31	48
Coombs, Morgan, Ball State	4	4	3.46	12	0	55	56	18	43
Melling, Tyler, Miami (Ohio)	8	2	3.51	15	0	90	85	14	72
Gerdeman, Ross, Bowling Green	2	1	3.57	22	1	58	63	20	42
Barry, Tom, Northern Illinois	5	5	3.79	14	0	74	79	39	51

MID-EASTERN ATHLETIC CONFERENCE

	Conference		Overall	
	W	L	W	L
*Bethune-Cookman	18	10	36	25
Delaware State	11	7	26	29
North Carolina A&T	10	8	21	34
Norfolk State	9	9	24	29
Maryland-Eastern Shore	7	11	9	41
Florida A&M	6	12	17	40
Coppin State	2	16	5	39

ALL-CONFERENCE TEAM: C—Peter O'Brien, Jr., Bethune-Cookman. **1B**—Ryan Haas, So., Delaware State. **2B**—Scott Davis, Jr., Delaware State. **3B**—Ryan Montgomery, So., Norfolk State. **SS**—Luke Tendler, Fr., North Carolina A&T. **OF**—Xavier Macklin, Jr., North Carolina A&T; John Rasberry, Sr., Norfolk State; Jarryd Reid, Jr., Florida A&M. **DH**—Bryan Chalkovsky, Sr., Maryland-Eastern Shore. **SP**— Scott Garner, Fr., Bethune-Cookman; Patrick Goelz, So., Bethune-Cookman. **RP**—Jordan Dailey, So., Bethune-Cookman.
Player of the Year: Scott Davis, Delaware State. **Pitcher of the Year:** Scott Garner, Bethune-Cookman. **Rookie of the Year:** Scott Garner, Bethune-Cookman. **Coach of the Year:** Mervyl Melendez, Bethune-Cookman.

INDIVIDUAL BATTING LEADERS
(Minimum 2 at-bats per team game)

	AVG	AB	R	H	2B	3B	HR	RBI	SB
Davis, Scott, Delaware State	.418	177	48	74	17	1	1	32	9
Tendler, Luke, N.C. A&T	.380	213	33	81	20	5	6	53	7
Adeyemi, Tobi, Florida A&M	.378	222	46	84	13	5	4	29	8
Rasberry, John, Norfolk State	.372	180	38	67	7	2	4	39	11
Reid, Jarryd, Florida A&M	.367	147	37	54	6	8	4	34	16
Hairston, Brandon, NSU	.365	181	37	66	11	3	5	43	12
Montgomery, Ryan, NSU	.362	152	21	55	10	3	0	25	3
Chaikowsky, Bryan, UMES	.360	164	36	59	9	9	6	35	6
Johnson, Tre-von, UMES	.359	195	38	70	11	3	0	22	15
Haas, Ryan, Del. State	.356	202	32	72	9	1	5	50	2
Macklin, Xavier, N.C. A&T	.355	183	57	65	6	3	22	67	9
Riley, Marquis, N.C. A&T	.353	207	54	73	12	3	6	38	14
Taylor, James, Norfolk State	.338	154	43	52	4	0	1	24	12
Johnson, Brashad, B-CU	.337	202	36	68	11	2	1	31	6
Freeman, Kelvin, N.C. A&T	.335	194	37	65	17	1	7	40	3
McKoy, Andre, N.C. A&T	.327	220	47	72	9	2	2	25	15
Franklin, Cory, Florida A&M	.326	190	34	62	14	0	6	40	5
Richards, Derek, Coppin State	.325	154	21	50	10	0	0	20	2
Lynch, John, Norfolk State	.319	216	49	69	10	1	1	40	29
Wright, Matt, B-CU	.316	152	42	48	18	5	6	33	7
Drummond, Troy, Del. State	.306	160	39	49	3	4	0	17	16
Sanchez, Alejandro, B-CU	.305	223	46	68	6	2	4	27	8
O'Brien, Peter, B-CU	.304	230	41	70	14	1	14	69	3
Nales, Mark, N.C. A&T	.304	171	24	52	10	3	0	23	3
Terrell, Jimmie, Florida A&M	.301	136	22	41	11	1	0	22	5
Johnson, Nick, B-CU	.297	185	30	55	12	2	6	36	0
Hernandez, Keith, Del. State	.293	191	50	56	8	1	1	37	6
Cecil, Cameron, Del. State	.290	169	26	49	9	1	4	28	4
Copeland, Carvell, N.C. A&T	.290	183	35	53	4	2	0	10	18
Durrence, Ryan, B-CU	.285	221	54	63	19	1	10	48	3

INDIVIDUAL PITCHING LEADERS
(Minimum 1 IP per team game)

	W	L	ERA	G	SV	IP	H	BB	SO
#Dailey, Jordan, B-CU	1	1	1.99	29	8	54	50	14	49
Garner, Scott, B-CU	9	2	2.48	14	0	83	71	20	50
Goelz, Patrick, B-CU	8	3	3.09	14	0	67	60	32	75
Vanassche, Ryan, NSU	7	6	3.47	18	0	80	85	32	56
Shook, Ryan, Norfolk State	4	3	3.75	15	1	72	76	29	79
Oelker, Nick, N.C. A&T	8	3	4.36	17	0	85	98	40	71
Matt Witte, UMES	3	7	4.50	13	0	74	95	28	54
Jordan Elliot, Delaware State	6	5	4.58	18	0	94	103	29	70
Jordan Egan, NSU	3	3	4.78	16	2	70	68	33	81
Justin Bhatti, NSU	3	6	4.92	15	0	57	64	32	59
Esterlin Paulino, N.C. A&T	6	6	5.00	15	0	99	123	15	90
Elliot Gardner, Delaware State	5	7	5.19	17	0	69	74	33	65
Matt McClain, Delaware State	4	8	5.46	17	0	87	107	22	59
Heath Blackburn, Florida A&M	1	10	6.80	15	0	94	135	38	52
Craig Erskine, N.C. A&T	2	7	7.00	17	1	63	74	47	23
Zach Spahn, Coppin State	2	6	7.62	14	0	67	100	43	49
Brent Moore, N.C. A&T	3	7	7.62	13	0	70	103	24	36
Barwick, Thomas, Florida A&M	3	5	7.69	13	0	60	83	36	26
Foreman, Jacob, UMES	3	9	8.37	14	0	76	106	40	50

MISSOURI VALLEY CONFERENCE

	Conference		Overall	
	W	L	W	L
*Creighton	15	6	45	16
Wichita State	14	7	39	26
Illinois State	13	8	36	18
Missouri State	11	9	33	23
Southern Illinois	11	10	23	34
Indiana State	8	13	29	28
Evansville	7	13	28	25
Bradley	4	17	22	32

ALL-CONFERENCE TEAM: C—Chris O'Brien, Jr., Wichita State. **1B**—Johnny Coy, So., Wichita State. **2B**—Kevin Medrano, Jr., Missouri State. **SS**—Jimmy Swift, Sr., Creighton. **3B**—Ryan Court, Sr., Illinois State. **OF**—Trever Adams, Sr., Creighton; Tyler McNeeley, Sr., Illinois State; Robby Ort, So., Indiana State. **DH**—Preston Springer, Sr., Wichita State. **UT**—Cody Fick, Sr., Evansvlle. **SP**—Jonas Dufek, Sr., Creighton; Cody Forsythe, So., Southern Illinois; Charlie Lowell, Jr., Wichita State. **RP**—Dan Kickham, Jr., Missouri State; Kenny Long, Jr., Illinois State.
Player of the Year: Chris O'Brien, Wichita State. **Pitcher of the Year:** Charlie Lowell, Wichita State. **Newcomer of the Year:** Dan Kickham, Missouri State. **Freshman of the Year:** Nick Petree, Missouri State. **Coach of the Year:** Ed Servais, Creighton.

INDIVIDUAL BATTING LEADERS
(Minimum 2.5 at-bats per team game)

	AVG	AB	R	H	2B	3B	HR	RBI	SB
O'Brien, Chris, Wichita State	.410	244	56	100	25	1	10	70	1
Fick, Cody, Evansville	.406	212	39	86	21	1	9	71	6
Adams, Trever, Creighton	.387	230	46	89	14	4	14	57	15
McNeeley, Tyler, Illinois State	.344	180	50	62	12	0	12	48	6
Chaffin, Brock, Missouri State	.344	160	31	55	13	1	6	37	4
Tauchman, Mike, Bradley	.343	172	26	59	7	2	0	32	16
Lucas, Jeremy, Indiana State	.333	177	30	59	10	2	3	28	0
Medrano, Kevin, Missouri State	.325	206	34	67	4	4	0	34	13
Conway, Aaron, Missouri State	.325	231	52	75	16	5	3	32	19
Court, Ryan, Illinois State	.323	295	47	63	15	4	6	35	7
Ort, Robby, Indiana State	.320	222	56	71	9	7	10	53	7
Kraemer, Koby, Indiana State	.318	236	44	75	14	4	4	39	9
Leblebijian, Jason, Bradley	.315	203	28	64	14	2	0	19	12
Wallace, Greg, Evansville	.314	207	45	65	16	5	7	36	9
Copeland, Trentt, Evansville	.308	182	34	56	17	1	1	22	10
Wampler, Tyler, Indiana State	.306	183	26	56	3	0	0	17	5
Sivertsen, Jordan, Southern Ill.	.302	202	40	61	17	2	9	48	1
Baehl, Jared, Evansville	.300	203	25	61	15	6	1	30	7
Grimes, Tyler, Wichita State	.300	243	67	73	10	2	5	32	28
Murphy, Chris, Southern Ill.	.300	237	34	71	13	2	1	28	5
Stamets, Eric, Evansville	.292	212	51	62	13	0	2	21	27
Colon, Josh, Illinois State	.291	141	23	41	12	1	0	15	2
Montgomery, Austin, Southern Ill.	.291	172	23	50	10	1	2	18	1
Helms, Spiker, Missouri State	.290	210	34	61	6	0	1	30	9
Springer, Preston, Wichita State	.289	266	42	77	17	0	10	56	4
Seifert, Brent, Missouri State	.289	232	35	67	16	1	9	43	5
McComack, Travis, Mo. State	.288	191	31	55	7	1	0	19	1
Voit, Luke, Missouri State	.286	203	30	58	13	0	6	35	6
Kimball, Brad, Bradley	.286	147	22	41	9	1	4	30	0
Staehely, Alex, Creighton	.285	228	37	65	23	3	3	36	8
#Hinshaw, Chad, Illinois State	.244	197	46	48	10	3	0	22	31

INDIVIDUAL PITCHING LEADERS
(Minimum 1 IP per team game)

	W	L	ERA	G	SV	IP	H	BB	SO
Dufek, Jonas, Creighton	12	1	2.08	18	0	113	78	29	128
#Spomer, Kurt, Creighton	3	4	2.22	35	13	49	35	13	37
Biggs, Josh, Evansville	5	2	2.25	15	0	56	51	17	34
Forsythe, Cody, Southern Illinois	8	5	2.35	15	0	103	105	11	69
Fick, Cody, Evansville	7	4	2.36	11	0	80	65	35	59
Blach, Ty, Creighton	10	3	2.65	19	0	102	94	29	100
Lowell, Charlie, Wichita State	10	5	2.79	17	0	103	84	39	124
Petree, Nick, Missouri State	9	2	2.81	16	2	96	86	27	81
Maines, Corey, Illinois State	9	4	2.88	15	0	94	80	34	110
Winkelman, Mark, Creighton	1	1	2.95	35	1	43	34	18	28
Bircher, Joe, Bradley	6	6	3.00	15	0	105	86	33	71

Smith, Josh, Wichita State	7	4	3.00	15	0	78	73	25	56
McGraw, Reese, Creighton	6	1	3.00	35	5	42	33	19	34
Barber, Blake, Missouri State	8	4	3.09	15	0	93	100	17	67
Bever, Andrew, Southern Illinois	5	6	3.28	16	0	80	75	30	47
Hochstedler, Reggie, Ind. State	4	1	3.38	16	1	59	58	11	53
Rea, Colin, Indiana State	8	4	3.68	30	1	95	69	48	76
Hellhake, Greg, Creighton	4	4	3.91	18	0	71	55	30	35
Savas, Dan, Illinois State	3	4	3.92	16	0	67	62	32	68
Learnard, J.D., Illinois State	8	2	4.04	14	0	78	88	32	41
Doerr, Tory, Bradley	2	4	4.14	17	0	63	71	16	31
Van Skike, Jason, Indiana State	4	5	4.25	16	0	83	90	48	57
Gordon, Grant, Missouri State	3	6	4.26	15	0	70	82	41	50
#Kickham, Dan, Missouri State	2	3	1.84	25	13	29	20	16	24

MOUNTAIN WEST CONFERENCE

	Conference		Overall	
	W	L	W	L
Texas Christian	20	3	43	19
Utah	16	7	29	21
Brigham Young	11	12	31	27
San Diego State	11	13	22	36
Nevada-Las Vegas	10	13	33	25
*New Mexico	10	14	20	41
Air Force	4	20	19	36

ALL-CONFERENCE TEAM: C—Garrett Custons, So., Air Force. **1B**—C.J. Cron, Jr., Utah. **2B**—Jerome Pena, Sr., Texas Christian; Michael Beltran, Sr., Utah. **3B**—Jantzen Witte, So., Texas Christian. **SS**—Taylor Featherston, Jr., Texas Christian. **OF**—Jaycob Brugman, Fr., Brigham Young; Jason Coats, Jr., Texas Christian; Shaun Cooper, Jr., Utah. DH/ **UT**—Brandon Bayardi, So., Nevada-Las Vegas. **P**—Rick Anton, Sr., Utah; Tanner Peters, Jr., Nevada-Las Vegas; Kyle Winkler, Jr., Texas Christian. **RP**—Tyler Wagner, So., Utah.
Player of the Year: C.J. Cron, Utah. **Pitcher of the Year:** Tanner Peters, Nevada-Las Vegas. **Freshman of the Year:** Jacob Brugman, Brigham Young. **Coach of the Year:** Jim Schlossnagle, Texas Christian.

INDIVIDUAL BATTING LEADERS
(Minimum 125 at-bats)

	AVG	AB	R	H	2B	3B	HR	RBI	SB
Cron, C. J., Utah	.434	198	51	86	26	1	15	59	1
Brooks, James, Utah	.372	223	55	83	26	6	3	32	11
Cook, Trent, UNLV	.368	231	51	85	14	1	2	44	5
Dysinger, Scott, UNLV	.345	148	25	51	4	1	0	19	4
Featherston, Taylor, TCU	.335	245	53	82	13	4	3	42	6
Elander, Josh, TCU	.333	171	38	57	11	2	5	38	9
Cooper, Shaun, Utah	.332	202	42	67	14	7	8	43	2
Witte, Jantzen, TCU	.331	254	51	84	21	1	4	45	7
Custons, Garrett, Air Force	.330	209	42	69	21	3	6	23	13
Roundy, Rance, UNLV	.330	182	35	60	15	0	8	37	5
Bayardi, Brandon, UNLV	.325	163	31	53	13	0	10	51	9
Coats, Jason, TCU	.325	249	52	81	16	4	8	56	8
Rivera, Brance, TCU	.324	244	48	79	19	3	7	36	14
Bernal, Ryan, BYU	.323	198	38	64	16	4	6	32	4
Bast, Alex, Air Force	.318	211	37	67	21	3	3	30	5
Nielsen, Trey, Utah	.318	173	25	55	17	0	9	41	3
Brugman, Jaycob, BYU	.317	205	37	65	19	5	9	49	13
Peterson, D.J., New Mexico	.317	246	39	78	32	3	6	48	0
Grant, Quay, New Mexico	.316	177	23	56	8	0	0	26	4
Kirk, Trevor, UNLV	.314	207	56	65	5	2	1	28	12
Smith, Cody, San Diego State	.311	193	27	60	11	4	2	30	15
Scott, Ryan, UNLV	.306	157	15	48	7	0	2	20	0
Jordan, Zac, TCU	.303	132	18	40	13	1	4	24	4
Schultz, Aaron, TCU	.302	162	23	49	8	2	4	26	8
Campbell, Luke, New Mexico	.301	143	26	43	4	1	5	24	1
Zier, Tim, San Diego State	.301	219	30	66	6	0	0	20	7
Weik, Joe, TCU	.301	186	39	56	10	0	8	39	2
Garver, Mitchell, New Mexico	.300	230	38	69	13	2	2	27	2
Thomas, Cash, UNLV	.299	157	22	47	6	1	0	21	5
Hall, Austin, BYU	.296	199	40	59	16	5	2	28	19

INDIVIDUAL PITCHING LEADERS
(Minimum 50 IP)

	W	L	ERA	G	SV	IP	H	BB	SO
Winkler, Kyle, TCU	8	2	1.39	14	0	91	65	14	99
Peters, Tanner, UNLV	9	4	1.50	15	0	120	92	24	105
Purke, Matt, TCU	5	1	1.71	11	0	53	36	20	61
Crichton, Stefan, TCU	6	3	1.98	26	5	50	38	10	42
#Wagner, Tyler, Utah	4	3	2.04	25	12	35	27	17	33
Neil, Matthew, BYU	6	4	2.42	20	3	86	77	10	73
Anton, Rick, Utah	9	1	2.52	15	0	100	100	25	85
Mitchell, Andrew, TCU	6	1	2.84	22	2	76	52	31	73
Cole, Taylor, BYU	5	5	2.99	16	0	93	83	37	67
Maxwell, Steven, TCU	5	1	3.13	11	0	63	56	18	53
Swanson, Cole, San Diego State	4	2	3.23	15	0	78	64	32	61
Appleby, Trent, TCU	4	3	3.49	25	1	67	67	20	35
Black, Corey, San Diego State	4	5	3.56	19	0	73	67	42	78
Carley, Sean, Air Force	3	5	3.94	12	0	82	89	24	62
Poulson, Desmond, BYU	6	0	4.15	15	1	56	50	21	49
Jaramillo, Rudy, New Mexico	4	8	4.25	16	0	104	108	20	69
Pond, Joe, Utah	4	4	4.36	16	0	74	69	43	65
Miller, Erik, TCU	7	7	4.63	26	5	80	88	18	58
Mares, Bobby, New Mexico	4	4	4.84	18	1	67	66	30	57
Robinson, Joe, UNLV	5	7	4.88	15	0	90	97	31	35
Capper, Chris, BYU	3	6	4.91	16	0	84	95	27	75
#Colangelo, Stephen, Air Force	1	2	5.52	30	7	31	35	14	33

NORTHEAST CONFERENCE

	Conference		Overall	
	W	L	W	L
Monmouth	25	7	36	19
*Sacred Heart	23	9	34	23
Long Island	19	11	28	23
Bryant	19	12	30	23
Central Connecticut State	17	14	26	25
Wagner	12	20	18	33
Quinnipiac	11	21	15	32
Fairleigh Dickinson	9	23	12	38
Mount St. Mary's	7	25	15	35

ALL-CONFERENCE TEAM: C—Tyler Jones, Jr., Long Island. **1B**—Rob Griffith, Jr., Sacred Heart. **2B**—Ryan Terry, Sr., Monmouth. **3B**—Mitch Wells, Jr., Central Connecticut State. **SS**—David Soltis, Jr., Bryant. **OF**—J.J. Edwards, Sr., Sacred Heart; Jake Matuszak, Jr., Central Connecticut State; Steve Tedesco, Sr., Sacred Heart. **DH**—Nick Pulsonetti, Sr., Monmouth. **UT**—Andrew Caron, Sr., Mount St. Mary's. **SP**—Chris Franzese, Sr., Long Island; Nick Meyers, Sr., Monmouth. **RP**—Andrew McGee, Fr., Monmouth.
Player of the Year: Ryan Terry, Monmouth. **Pitcher of the Year:** Nick Meyers, Monmouth. **Rookie of the Year:** Nick Leningen, Sacred Heart. **Coach of the Year:** Don Maines, Long Island.

INDIVIDUAL BATTING LEADERS
(Minimum 125 at-bats)

	AVG	AB	R	H	2B	3B	HR	RBI	SB
Jones, Tyler, Long Island	.425	167	40	71	7	4	1	36	6
Terry, Ryan, Monmouth	.382	220	53	84	19	2	7	43	13
Edwards, J.J., Sacred Heart	.372	215	41	80	5	1	0	30	6
Wells, Mitch, CCSU	.360	203	34	73	12	2	2	43	4
Soltis, David, Bryant	.348	178	34	62	16	1	1	33	8
Kresky, Ryan, FDU	.344	189	41	65	10	3	5	21	7
Tedesco, Steve, Sacred Heart	.337	202	39	68	13	0	1	27	16
Nisson, Kyle, Quinnipiac	.336	152	17	51	4	0	0	21	2
Griffith, Rob, Sacred Heart	.335	209	41	70	12	4	4	44	5
Schifano, M.J., Sacred Heart	.332	205	36	68	11	2	2	28	12
Boyd, Seth, Wagner	.330	179	27	59	16	1	0	25	11
Higgins, Tommy, Wagner	.329	170	21	56	13	0	1	24	10
Matuszak, Jake, CCSU	.328	186	36	61	4	4	0	18	4
Leonello, Pete, Long Island	.328	180	46	59	12	4	0	21	19
Phillips, Hunter, Sacred Heart	.325	203	39	66	10	2	0	35	5
Pulsonetti, Nick, Monmouth	.324	176	40	57	11	1	8	39	5
Flynn, Tommy, MSM	.324	176	35	57	17	2	5	17	13
Amanti, Mickey, Quinnipiac	.324	185	33	60	11	0	0	16	9
Eyler, Shane, MSM	.321	165	21	53	7	0	3	24	3
Caron, Andrew, MSM	.318	157	28	50	12	1	3	31	4

Sciamarelli, Sam, Long Island	.311	167	38	52	11	3	1	25	8
Delacruz, Dylan, CCSU	.308	169	27	52	4	1	1	25	2
Farina, Ben, Quinnipiac	.305	187	26	57	4	1	1	17	13
Helman, Zach, MSM	.303	152	18	46	8	1	3	25	3
Dillon, Brian, FDU	.301	183	31	55	9	2	7	23	3
Murphy, John, Sacred Heart	.300	210	35	63	7	4	3	43	11
Rosenkranz, Jamie, Monmouth	.299	187	30	56	11	2	1	23	8
McDonnell, Kevin, Wagner	.299	167	33	50	11	1	4	31	14
Epps, Pat, CCSU	.298	181	37	54	14	0	4	30	2
Martin, Ed, Monmouth	.298	191	39	57	6	0	2	19	4
#Brown, Kevin, Bryant	.294	201	30	59	16	4	5	28	11

INDIVIDUAL PITCHING LEADERS
(Minimum 50 IP)

	W	L	ERA	G	SV	IP	H	BB	SO
Ryan, John Michael, Bryant	6	3	2.57	15	0	67	67	24	46
Savatsky, Todd, CCSU	7	4	2.57	14	0	70	66	19	36
Nuemann, Nick, CCSU	5	3	2.61	12	0	72	75	16	53
Glynne, Harry, CCSU	3	3	2.65	12	1	58	51	10	29
Meyers, Nick, Monmouth	9	1	2.85	13	0	88	81	18	68
Brittenham, Max, MSM	4	6	2.86	14	0	88	93	23	54
Lisanti, Salvatore, Bryant	5	3	3.12	13	1	61	57	21	37
Lamaccia, Derek, Quinnipiac	4	5	3.41	11	0	63	68	28	47
Krasnowiecki, Dave, CCSU	5	4	3.42	12	0	74	75	39	59
McCormick, Matt, Long Island	6	2	3.52	17	0	72	85	21	43
Smith, Dan, Monmouth	5	3	3.69	13	0	76	89	18	47
O'Neil, Brian, Bryant	4	3	3.98	14	0	61	51	23	27
Kelich, Peter, Bryant	6	3	4.04	13	1	71	75	19	58
Light, Pat, Monmouth	4	5	4.04	14	0	76	83	17	61
Franzese, Chris, Long Island	7	4	4.06	19	0	84	98	22	57
Schifano, M.J., Sacred Heart	3	3	4.11	13	3	50	45	10	30
Lucas, Jon, Wagner	4	6	4.15	12	0	69	77	21	53
McDonnell, John, Monmouth	5	1	4.33	11	0	52	53	23	20
Topa, Justin, Long Island	6	7	4.46	14	0	67	68	21	53
Leiningen, Nick, Sacred Heart	7	4	4.46	15	1	83	81	27	39
#Scribner, Troy, Sacred Heart	9	3	4.55	15	0	95	115	23	36
#Zerff, Evan, Long Island	3	3	5.53	24	13	28	35	17	27
#Kisling, Zach, FDU	3	0	6.82	27	0	30	41	15	9

OHIO VALLEY CONFERENCE

	Conference		Overall	
Team	W	L	W	L
*Austin Peay State	17	6	34	24
Southeast Missouri State	14	8	34	22
Jacksonville State	14	9	36	23
Tennessee Tech	12	12	25	29
Eastern Kentucky	11	13	21	36
Tennessee-Martin	10	13	20	36
Eastern Illinois	9	12	18	33
Murray State	9	13	19	32
Morehead State	6	16	10	39

ALL-CONFERENCE TEAM: C—Taylor Davis, Jr., Morehead State. **1B**—John Hogan, So., Austin Peay State. **2B**—Blake Seguin, Sr., Jacksonville State. **SS**—Reed Harper, So., Austin Peay State. **3B**—Trenton Moses, Jr., Southeast Missouri State. **OF**—Michael Adamson, Sr., Southeast Missouri; Zach Borenstein, Jr., Eastern Illinois; Jacob Daniel, Jr., Eastern Kentucky. **DH**—Phil Sorensen, Jr., Tennessee-Martin. **UT**—Chad Oberacker, Sr., Tennessee Tech. **SP**—Jeremy Dobbs, Jr., Austin Peay State; Stephen Hefler, Sr., Eastern Kentucky. **RP**—Todd Hornsby, Jr., Jacksonville State.
Player of the Year: Trenton Moses, Southeast Missouri State. **Pitcher of the Year:** Jeremy Dobbs, Austin Peay State. **Rookie of the Year:** Bryan Soloman, Eastern Kentucky. **Coach of the Year:** Gary McClure, Austin Peay State.

INDIVIDUAL BATTING LEADERS
(Minimum 2.5 at-bats per team game)

	AVG	AB	R	H	2B	3B	HR	RBI	SB
Davis, Taylor, Morehead State	.414	174	46	72	17	0	13	48	2
Moses, Trenton, SE Mo.	.395	177	44	70	14	1	11	53	4
Elliott, Brandon, Murray State	.384	159	40	61	11	2	1	22	4
Deeds, Andrew, Morehead State	.380	184	44	70	17	7	5	49	7
Adamson, Michael, SE Mo.	.363	226	64	82	11	0	7	38	16
Rodriguez, Richie, Eastern Ky.	.357	230	44	82	14	5	2	26	19

Eberle, Sam, JSU	.356	247	50	**88**	**21**	1	8	54	9
Underwood, Eik, JSU	.354	212	34	75	10	1	0	28	3
Hankins, Jordan, Austin Peay	.351	188	29	66	15	1	4	31	7
Borenstein, Zach, Eastern Ill.	.349	195	38	68	13	3	7	29	9
Bluestein, Kyle, JSU	.346	159	38	55	13	4	7	38	3
Waldrip, Ben, JSU	.344	192	33	66	7	1	10	46	0
Sorensen, Phil, Tenn.-Martin	.340	147	18	50	15	1	4	33	0
Ritzheimer, Paul, Murray State	.336	152	27	51	2	0	1	27	4
Noonan, Zach, Murray State	.335	182	37	61	19	1	4	39	2
Blanchard, Coty, JSU	.335	233	43	78	16	1	2	32	8
Blanchard, Michael, Austin Peay	.333	189	47	63	13	5	1	27	**29**
Daniel, Jacob, Eastern Ky.	.330	200	31	66	7	3	9	44	5
Harper, Reed, Austin Peay	.329	222	38	73	17	2	4	43	11
Rhodes, Jacob, Murray State	.328	180	24	59	9	0	3	31	0
Donaldson, Casanova, Tenn. Tech	.327	214	42	70	10	3	5	36	10
Oberacker, Chad, Tenn. Tech	.325	200	39	65	10	2	10	48	14
Rupp, Tim, Southeast Mo.	.325	151	26	49	7	0	4	27	4
Ferguson, Shawn, Eastern Ill.	.324	136	10	44	9	0	2	22	1
Sharrock, Jake, JSU	.322	205	40	66	11	1	5	33	4
Jones, Casey, SE Mo.	.320	200	33	64	19	1	5	44	0
Seguin, Blake, JSU	.316	212	41	67	6	3	1	17	11
Terry, Cody, Tenn.-Martin	.316	228	39	72	15	3	1	35	9
Mcmanus, T.J., Eastern Ill.	.316	152	24	48	12	0	3	27	0
Bachman, Greg, Austin Peay	.312	205	47	64	18	0	7	45	4
#Hogan, John, Austin Peay	.310	232	42	72	12	1	**13**	**63**	1

INDIVIDUAL PITCHING LEADERS
(Minimum 1 IP per team game)

	W	L	ERA	G	SV	IP	H	BB	SO
#Hornsby, Todd, JSU	5	4	2.16	30	**15**	58	49	24	49
McNeil, Brent, Eastern Ill.	3	2	**2.18**	21	1	54	48	12	35
Beistline, Jordan, JSU	6	1	3.48	13	0	62	62	12	30
Snodgrass, Jack, Austin Peay	4	6	3.50	15	0	80	98	27	67
Labruyere, Brad, SE Mo.	**9**	2	3.55	14	0	76	83	20	46
Dobbs, Jeremy, Austin Peay	**9**	3	3.59	18	0	90	89	52	**87**
Hefler, Stephen, Eastern Ky.	7	5	3.77	15	0	88	86	34	54
Elias, Aaron, JSU	7	3	3.78	15	0	88	101	16	71
Park, Cullen, Tenn. Tech	3	3	4.27	14	4	59	54	25	67
Hebert, Mike, Austin Peay	2	1	4.39	**34**	2	41	51	13	31
Dicus, Jon, SE Mo.	6	4	4.50	16	0	80	106	22	38
Underwood, Jordan, SE Mo.	5	1	4.68	15	0	83	83	49	56
Fyffe, Matt, Eastern Ky.	0	5	4.70	18	2	67	82	23	62
Toney, Zach, Austin Peay	6	3	4.72	19	2	76	91	46	72
Donze, Jake, Murray State	6	5	5.49	14	0	80	90	35	52
Hoekstra, Mike, Eastern Ill.	5	6	5.53	14	0	85	114	15	50
Tobik, Dan, Tenn.-Martin	3	7	5.64	19	1	**91**	121	36	67
Shepherd, Matthew, Tenn. Tech	3	7	5.67	17	0	75	88	31	64
Archer, Tristan, Tenn. Tech	7	4	5.94	16	1	89	114	22	67
Boshers, Alex, Tenn.-Martin	4	4	6.00	24	2	80	103	24	28
Kelley, Danny, Tenn.-Martin	1	7	6.04	21	0	78	115	22	30
Bushur, Luke, Eastern Ill.	4	5	6.14	15	0	57	71	22	49

PACIFIC-10 CONFERENCE

	Conference		Overall	
	W	L	W	L
*UCLA	18	9	34	21
Arizona State	17	10	39	16
Oregon State	17	10	38	17
Arizona	15	12	36	19
Stanford	14	12	32	20
California	13	13	31	20
Southern California	13	14	25	31
Oregon	11	16	33	26
Washington State	10	17	26	28
Washington	6	21	17	37

ALL-CONFERENCE TEAM: C—Austin Barnes, Jr., Arizona State; Chadd Krist, Jr., California. **1B**—Taylor Ard, So., Washington State; Cole Frenzel, So., Arizona; Ricky Oropesa, Jr., Southern California. **2B**—Danny Pulfer, Jr., Oregon; Tony Renda, So., California. **SS**—Deven Marrero, So., Arizona State; Alex Mejia, So., Arizona. **3B**—Stephen Piscotty, So., Stanford; Riccio Torrez, Jr., Arizona State. **DH**—Joey DeMichele, So., Arizona State; Kavin Keyes, Fr., Oregon State. **OF**—Beau Amaral, So., UCLA; Robert Refsnyder, So., Arizona; Joey Rickard, So., Arizona; Johnny Ruettiger, Jr.,

Arizona State. **RHP**—Trevor Bauer, Jr., UCLA; Tony Bryant, So., Oregon State; Sam Gaviglio, Jr., Oregon State; Kurt Heyer, So., Arizona; Erik Johnson, Jr., California; Adam Plutko, Fr., UCLA; Kyle Simon, Jr., Arizona. **LHP**—Tyler Anderson, Jr., Oregon.
Player of the Year: Tony Renda, California. **Pitcher of the Year:** Trevor Bauer, UCLA. **Defensive Player of the Year:** Deven Marrero, Arizona State. **Freshman of the Year:** Brian Ragira, Stanford. **Coach of the Year:** Pat Casey, Oregon State.

INDIVIDUAL BATTING LEADERS
(Minimum 2.5 at-bats per team game)

	AVG	AB	R	H	2B	3B	HR	RBI	SB
DeMichele, Joey, Arizona State	**.368**	193	37	71	16	**7**	9	51	6
Piscotty, Stephen, Stanford	.364	225	35	82	13	1	3	39	2
Ortega, Bryce, Arizona	.353	221	**57**	78	8	3	1	28	25
Pulfer, Danny, Oregon	.351	225	38	79	16	2	2	20	8
Rickard, Joey, Arizona	.347	248	49	86	11	1	4	37	16
Frenzel, Cole, Arizona	.346	228	48	79	16	1	3	48	9
Ard, Taylor, Washington State	.337	196	40	66	17	0	**10**	**55**	3
Mejia, Alex, Arizona	.335	230	40	77	12	4	0	42	7
Renda, Tony, California	.332	265	38	**88**	14	2	3	44	9
Carrillo, Xorge, Arizona State	.330	106	23	35	13	0	1	24	2
Ragira, Brian, Stanford	.329	213	31	70	7	5	4	46	2
Gaffney, Tyler, Stanford	.327	199	42	65	10	5	3	35	7
Ruettiger, Johnny, Arizona State	.327	245	53	80	8	4	0	37	23
Oropesa, Rick, USC	.322	208	35	67	10	1	7	44	4
Espy, Dean, UCLA	.320	231	32	74	15	0	3	40	7
Barnes, Austin, Arizona State	.320	153	27	49	14	1	1	15	3
Healy, Ryon, Oregon	.320	122	20	39	10	1	4	20	2
Refsnyder, Robert, Arizona	.320	241	51	77	13	6	6	55	9
Sherrod, Alex, USC	.318	173	28	55	11	0	6	34	1
Meggs, Joe, Washington	.317	164	20	52	12	0	1	17	2
Marrero, Deven, Arizona State	.315	219	33	69	14	3	2	20	10
Mejias-Brean, Seth, Arizona	.313	195	30	61	7	3	0	25	7
Lamb, Jacob, Washington	.311	212	20	66	13	2	3	26	2
Wilson, Austin, Stanford	.311	196	25	61	7	0	5	30	1
Roundtree, Kevin, USC	.309	207	38	64	11	3	1	11	2
Garcia, Brandon, USC	.309	136	11	42	6	0	2	22	2
Booker, Austin, California	.308	214	31	66	9	2	1	24	9
Slaybaugh, Collin, WSU	.308	104	25	32	3	3	0	13	9
Torrez, Riccio, Arizona State	.307	228	37	70	17	4	4	54	15
Keefer, Cody, UCLA	.303	201	29	61	13	1	1	18	7
#Krist, Chadd, California	.297	236	37	70	**27**	1	2	43	1
#MacPhee, Zack, Arizona State	.279	222	49	62	11	2	1	25	**27**

INDIVIDUAL PITCHING LEADERS
(Minimum 1 IP per team game)

	W	L	ERA	G	SV	IP	H	BB	SO
Bauer, Trevor, UCLA	**13**	2	**1.25**	16	0	137	73	36	**203**
#Bryant, Tony, Oregon State	3	2	1.52	28	**12**	47	39	11	40
Porter, Kyle, California	6	0	1.89	25	2	57	49	15	57
Plutko, Adam, UCLA	7	4	2.01	16	0	108	73	24	92
Boer, Madison, Oregon	3	6	2.27	18	3	99	81	35	74
Anderson, Tyler, Oregon	8	3	2.34	15	0	108	75	35	114
Heyer, Kurt, Arizona	8	5	2.41	20	0	**138**	122	27	134
Gaviglio, Sam, Oregon State	12	3	2.54	17	0	121	91	33	116
Reed, Chris, Stanford	6	2	2.56	29	9	53	39	17	52
Blackford, Alex, Arizona State	4	1	2.66	24	1	61	52	23	55
Simon, Kyle, Arizona	11	3	2.72	19	0	129	114	11	86
Rodgers, Brady, Arizona State	9	4	2.75	15	0	98	88	9	87
Johnson, Erik, California	7	4	2.83	18	0	105	68	59	102
Champlin, Kramer, Arizona State	9	4	2.85	17	0	117	105	37	95
Weiss, Zack, UCLA	5	3	2.86	22	0	66	44	22	53
Keudell, Alex, Oregon	7	3	2.89	17	0	90	86	24	71
Jones, Justin, California	9	6	3.01	20	1	120	114	31	81
Appel, Mark, Stanford	6	7	3.02	17	0	110	114	29	86
Miller, Kevin, California	6	4	3.12	23	1	84	79	13	91
Wade, Konner, Arizona	3	0	3.21	17	0	62	56	19	28
Jones, Christian, Oregon	7	2	3.24	16	0	78	69	34	73
#Chaffee, Matt, Arizona	6	3	4.85	**36**	7	43	39	21	59

PATRIOT LEAGUE

	Conference		Overall	
	W	L	W	L
*Navy	12	8	33	25
Army	11	9	22	26
Lafayette	10	10	18	30
Bucknell	10	10	25	28
Holy Cross	9	11	24	23
Lehigh	8	12	24	21

ALL-CONFERENCE TEAM: C—A.J. Miller, Sr., Lafayette. **1B**—Doug Shribman, Sr., Bucknell. **2B**—Zach Price, Jr., Army. **3B**—Steve May, Sr., Army. **SS**—Clint Moore, Sr., Army. **OF**—Nick Ciardiello, Sr., Holy Cross; Drew Constable, Sr., Bucknell; Rob Froio, Sr., Lafayette; Ben Koenigsfeld, Sr., Army. **DH**—Dave Milanes, So., Navy. **SP**—Ryan Ebner, Jr., Bucknell; John Pedrotty, Jr., Holy Cross. **RP**—Wes Olson, Sr., Navy.
Hitter of the Year: A.J. Miller, Lafayette. **Pitcher of the Year:** Ryan Ebner, Bucknell. **Rookie of the Year:** Taylor Cato, Navy. **Coach of the Year:** Paul Kostacopoulos, Navy.

INDIVIDUAL BATTING LEADERS
(Minimum 2.5 at-bats per team game)

	AVG	AB	R	H	2B	3B	HR	RBI	SB
Miller, A.J., Lafayette	.385	161	35	62	14	1	12	52	1
Goldman, Billy, Lehigh	.358	134	30	48	10	2	3	24	10
Mihalik, Kevin, Lehigh	.355	155	32	55	10	0	4	27	9
Ciardiello, Nick, Holy Cross	.345	168	31	58	14	1	8	43	1
Price, Zach, Army	.331	169	39	56	9	1	0	15	13
Runyan, Gerry, Bucknell	.330	179	29	59	11	2	3	31	2
Azor, Alex, Navy	.329	234	49	77	15	1	0	33	6
Laurendeau, Jack, Holy Cross	.329	155	40	51	7	3	0	27	14
Dupell, Greg, Navy	.327	211	49	69	14	4	7	35	4
Henshaw, Joey, Army	.325	160	27	52	13	0	5	31	3
#Shribman, Doug, Bucknell	.325	194	41	63	13	3	16	49	0
#McGaheran, Brendan, Lehigh	.317	180	38	57	13	0	3	30	19
#Oxford, Eric, Holy Cross	.310	184	19	57	16	0	4	41	5
#Beans, Brandon, Navy	.256	168	31	43	11	6	0	21	11

INDIVIDUAL PITCHING LEADERS
(Minimum 1 IP per team game)

	W	L	ERA	G	SV	IP	H	BB	SO
Olson, Wes, Navy	7	1	2.51	18	2	57	51	15	43
#Colella, John, Holy Cross	3	2	3.00	24	9	42	31	16	40
Ebner, Ryan, Bucknell	6	1	3.53	11	0	66	54	33	54
Lee, Logan, Army	4	9	3.99	13	0	79	75	27	55
Long, Sam, Navy	5	5	4.24	15	0	81	92	32	52
Pedrotty, John, Holy Cross	7	2	4.62	11	0	60	64	26	56
Rowley, Chris, Army	5	4	4.68	12	0	73	86	19	54
Nelson, Ben, Navy	6	6	4.91	16	0	92	101	20	80
Perro, Ethan, Lafayette	3	4	5.37	14	0	55	63	27	39
Gentile, John, Lafayette	2	7	5.50	11	1	56	77	21	33
Seeley, Dylan, Bucknell	2	7	6.24	13	0	66	101	19	35
Koneski, Nate, Holy Cross	2	6	6.66	10	0	53	70	21	63

SOUTHEASTERN CONFERENCE

EAST	Conference		Overall	
	W	L	W	L
South Carolina	22	8	55	14
Vanderbilt	22	8	54	12
*Florida	22	8	53	19
Georgia	16	14	33	32
Kentucky	8	22	25	30
Tennessee	7	23	25	29

WEST	W	L	W	L
Arkansas	15	15	40	22
Mississippi State	14	16	38	25
Alabama	14	16	35	28
Auburn	14	16	29	29
Louisiana State	13	17	36	20
Mississippi	13	17	30	25

ALL-CONFERENCE TEAM: C—Mike Zunino, So., Florida. **1B**—Aaron Westlake, Jr., Vanderbilt. **2B**—Scott Wingo, Sr., South Carolina. **3B**—Thomas McCarthy, Jr., Kentucky. **SS**—Casey McElroy, Jr., Auburn.

OF—Tony Kemp, Fr., Vanderbilt; Mikie Mahtook, Jr., Louisiana State; Preston Tucker, Jr., Florida. **DH**—Brian Johnson, So., Florida. **P**—Grayson Garvin, Jr., Vanderbilt; Michael Roth, Jr., South Carolina. **RP**—Matt Price, So., South Carolina.
Player of the Year: Mike Zunino, Florida. **Pitcher of the Year:** Grayson Garvin, Vanderbilt. **Freshman of the Year:** Tony Kemp, Vanderbilt. **Coach of the Year:** Ray Tanner, South Carolina.

INDIVIDUAL BATTING LEADERS
(Minimum 3 plate appearances per team game)

	AVG	AB	R	H	2B	3B	HR	RBI	SB
Mahtook, Mikie, LSU	.383	196	61	75	12	5	14	56	29
McElroy, Casey, Auburn	.372	234	46	87	18	0	9	53	1
McCarthy, Thomas, Kentucky	.371	210	32	78	19	2	7	39	8
Zunino, Mike, Florida	.371	264	75	98	23	0	19	67	7
Parks, Jarrod, Mississippi State	.363	212	54	77	13	3	3	36	4
Rhymes, Raph, LSU	.360	214	43	77	18	0	3	42	8
Wright, Chad, Kentucky	.359	217	42	78	16	3	6	40	16
Walker, Christian	.358	271	64	97	21	1	10	62	4
Gregor, Conrad, Vanderbilt	.353	170	33	60	11	0	3	32	2
Yarbrough, Alex, Mississippi	.350	214	49	75	14	3	7	38	4
Dugas, Taylor, Alabama	.349	241	60	84	20	4	8	33	8
Westlake, Aaron, Vanderbilt	.344	250	59	86	18	1	18	56	2
Reaves, Jared, Alabama	.340	241	51	82	22	2	4	47	4
Esposito, Jason, Vanderbilt	.340	268	55	91	22	1	9	59	15
Jones, JaCoby, LSU	.338	195	36	66	11	1	4	32	12
Bennett, Brock, Alabama	.338	225	39	76	7	0	0	22	9
Wingo, Scott, South Carolina	.338	240	47	81	8	1	4	31	7
Katz, Mason, LSU	.337	190	40	64	21	2	4	53	6
Mathis, Tanner, Mississippi	.336	226	37	76	9	0	0	27	7
Gomez, Anthony, Vanderbilt	.336	286	61	96	12	2	0	48	7
Ficociello, Dominic, Arkansas	.335	224	29	75	15	1	4	50	5
Hyams, Levi, Georgia	.332	259	49	86	17	2	5	38	8
Norfork, Khayyan, Tennessee	.332	205	36	68	15	2	4	37	29
Caldwell, Tony, Auburn	.332	190	37	63	13	1	7	44	5
Pigott, Daniel, Florida	.331	257	44	85	21	1	5	40	15
Osborne, Zach, Tennessee	.330	176	27	58	9	1	1	19	5
Kemp, Tony, Vanderbilt	.329	252	58	83	8	7	0	34	17
Adams, Josh, Florida	.323	260	34	84	11	1	6	43	1
Black, Taylor, Kentucky	.319	229	43	73	16	2	4	38	12
Vickerson, Nick. Miss. State	.319	204	57	65	17	3	9	37	26
#Tucker, Preston, Florida	.308	286	55	88	23	0	15	74	5

INDIVIDUAL PITCHING LEADERS
(Minimum 1 IP per team game)

	W	L	ERA	APP	SV	IP	H	BB	SO
Roth, Michael, South Carolina	14	3	1.06	21	0	145	108	41	112
Taylor, John, South Carolina	8	1	1.14	50	0	71	45	28	63
Reed, Caleb, Mississippi State	1	2	1.55	29	12	64	51	23	66
Baxendale, DJ, Arkansas	10	2	1.58	19	3	85	69	21	77
#Price, Matt, South Carolina	7	3	1.83	36	20	59	44	20	75
Randall, Hudson, Florida	11	3	2.17	19	0	124	104	13	73
Whitson, Karsten, Florida	8	1	2.40	19	0	97	84	28	92
Gray, Sonny, Vanderbilt	12	4	2.43	19	0	126	97	51	132
Garvin, Grayson, Vanderbilt	13	2	2.48	18	0	113	98	25	101
Smart, Jonathan, Alabama	5	3	2.50	31	11	86	88	15	43
Hill, Taylor, Vanderbilt	6	1	2.73	17	0	99	89	26	92
Meyer, Alex, Kentucky	7	5	2.94	14	0	101	78	46	110
Koumas, Forrest, South Carolina	6	1	2.96	19	0	73	59	29	63
Lynch, Cade, Arkansas	4	4	3.11	20	1	64	55	27	63
Kilcrease, Nathan, Alabama	3	4	3.12	16	0	101	100	28	88
Palazzone, Michael, Georgia	10	5	3.14	18	0	120	121	11	78
McCune, Kurt, LSU	7	3	3.31	14	0	90	73	25	68
Crouse, Matt, Mississippi	7	4	3.41	14	0	90	88	19	62
Moore, Brandon, Arkansas	4	1	3.45	17	0	70	73	20	38
Gausman, Kevin, LSU	5	6	3.51	14	0	90	70	23	86

SOUTHERN CONFERENCE

	Conference		Overall	
	W	L	W	L
Elon	23	7	36	21
UNC Greensboro	22	8	34	20
College of Charleston	18	12	39	22
Samford	18	12	37	23

*Georgia Southern	18	12	36	26
Appalachian State	15	15	33	27
Furman	13	16	24	33
Western Carolina	12	18	23	31
Wofford	9	21	22	33
Davidson	8	21	18	30
The Citadel	8	22	20	36

ALL-CONFERENCE TEAM: C—Trevor Edwards, So., UNC Greensboro. **1B**—Saxon Butler, Jr., Samford. **2B**—Ross Hefley, Jr., Western Carolina. **3B**—Matt Leeds, Jr., College of Charleston. **SS**—Eric Phillips, Jr., Georgia Southern. **OF**—Daniel Aldrich, Fr., College of Charleston; Nick Orvin, Jr., The Citadel; Victor Roache, So., Georgia Southern. **DH**—Stephen Notaro, Sr., Western Carolina. **SP**—Josh Renfro, Sr., College of Charleston; Warren Slack, Sr., UNC Greensboro. **RP**—Matt Murray, Jr., Georgia Southern. **Hitter of the Year:** Victor Roache, Georgia Southern. **Pitcher of the Year:** Matt Murray, Georgia Southern. **Freshman of the Year:** Daniel Aldrich, College of Charleston. **Coach of the Year:** Mike Gaski, UNC Greensboro.

INDIVIDUAL BATTING LEADERS
(Minimum 2.5 at-bats per team game)

	AVG	AB	R	H	2B	3B	HR	RBI	SB
Heffley, Ross, W. Carolina	.419	229	52	96	18	2	11	65	3
Phillips, Eric, Ga. Southern	.390	251	62	98	13	3	4	39	26
Ervin, Phillip, Samford	.371	213	44	79	15	2	4	41	7
Gadaire, Drew, Davidson	.362	174	25	63	15	3	5	36	7
Butler, Saxon, Samford	.355	228	49	81	26	0	9	61	2
Zupcic, Tyler, ASU	.350	220	47	77	14	0	3	29	15
Thompkins, Aaron, Furman	.348	204	38	71	14	2	1	26	6
Aldrich, Daniel, Charleston	.347	222	43	77	17	2	22	73	1
Leeds, Matt, Charleston	.345	232	66	80	18	2	18	80	8
Johnson, Michael, Samford	.342	240	56	82	10	3	2	22	11
Notaro, Stephen, W. Carolina	.335	188	34	63	10	0	6	42	1
Diamaduros, K., Wofford	.332	217	27	72	8	5	0	36	9
Gantt, Marty, Charleston	.329	237	63	78	15	3	7	44	25
Ladd, William, The Citadel	.327	205	40	67	7	1	1	32	18
Roache, Victor, Ga. Southern	.326	230	58	75	10	2	30	84	3
Cochrane, Steve, Ga. Southern	.327	224	38	73	19	1	6	56	4
Owens, Will, Furman	.321	224	42	72	7	0	1	27	13
Orvin, Nick, The Citadel	.320	231	47	74	14	1	9	32	19
Kral, Rob, Col. of Charleston	.319	213	62	68	17	1	11	48	6
Edwards, Trevor, UNCG	.318	179	36	57	18	2	8	51	0
Johns, Matt, W Carolina	.318	223	55	71	16	2	6	44	26
DeKerlegand, Drew, The Citadel	.317	208	32	66	11	4	2	24	0
Myers, Jack, ASU	.317	224	30	71	10	0	0	26	19
Crespo, Hector, ASU	.316	190	42	60	8	3	1	25	18
Payne, Shawn, Ga. Southern	.314	242	70	76	16	6	6	39	33
Rakar, Cole, Charleston	.307	238	55	73	13	0	4	28	16
Foster, James, Wofford	.306	222	31	68	10	1	0	22	22
Gomez, Sebastian, Elon	.305	167	30	51	6	1	2	28	14
Gehringer, Drew, UNCG	.303	188	40	57	9	3	3	31	15
Mackert, Justin, The Citadel	.303	218	40	66	14	1	2	33	17
Doyle, Mac, Wofford	.300	213	47	64	13	7	10	46	10
Burrus, Michael, Ga. Southern	.300	273	51	82	11	5	3	46	9

INDIVIDUAL PITCHING LEADERS
(Minimum 1 IP per team game)

	W	L	ERA	G	SV	IP	H	BB	SO
Moye, Andy, Ga. Southern	7	2	2.39	15	0	79	64	40	63
Murray, Matt, Ga. Southern	4	3	2.39	26	9	68	50	21	72
Basford, Charles, Samford	7	4	2.45	16	1	88	76	26	66
Frongello, Mike, Davidson	4	3	2.54	39	5	67	69	20	27
Clark, Dylan, Elon	3	3	2.78	18	1	68	67	27	43
Arrowood, Ryan, ASU	8	3	2.96	19	0	94	93	31	83
Powell, Christian, Charleston	8	1	3.09	16	0	82	69	29	63
Collins, Cash, Wofford	8	4	3.15	18	0	97	98	32	59
Beck, Chris, Ga. Southern	9	5	3.23	20	0	103	79	39	109
Putkonen, Kyle, Samford	7	2	3.25	13	0	80	91	18	65
Girdwood, Thomas, Elon	4	5	3.39	16	2	63	59	33	45
Hyatt, Colby, UNCG	8	3	3.43	18	1	94	98	14	29
Renfro, Josh, Charleston	9	3	3.66	15	0	96	95	21	77
Rutledge, Lex, Samford	5	6	3.71	17	0	63	51	45	79
Lamb, Chris, Davidson	1	7	3.75	14	0	82	82	19	85
Browne, Brandon, UNCG	2	2	3.78	16	0	67	55	42	45

Lyne, Bobby, Furman	4	4	3.84	13	0	80	80	32	53
Talley, Matt, The Citadel	3	7	3.95	13	0	82	101	29	72
Miller, Jarett, UNCG	4	2	4.01	28	3	61	50	38	66
Benedict, Matt, W. Carolina	2	4	4.01	14	0	85	96	34	70
#Jones, Andrew, Samford	1	3	1.49	31	15	36	25	6	35
#Adams, Josh, Ga. Southern	9	6	4.79	21	0	71	76	35	39

SOUTHLAND CONFERENCE

	Conference		Overall	
	W	L	W	L
*Texas State	23	9	40	23
Stephen F. Austin State	20	13	37	23
Texas A&M-Corpus Christi	19	14	37	24
Southeastern Louisiana	18	14	35	22
Sam Houston State	17	16	35	24
Texas-San Antonio	16	17	27	32
Texas-Arlington	15	17	27	28
Lamar	15	18	29	27
Nicholls State	15	18	28	29
McNeese State	14	19	26	29
Central Arkansas	13	20	24	29
Northwestern State	11	21	22	32

ALL-CONFERENCE TEAM: C—Jarid Scarafiotti, Jr., Stephen F. Austin State. **1B**—Casey Kalenkosky, Jr., Texas State. **2B**—Tyler Sibley, Jr., Texas State. **3B**—Kyle Kubitza, Jr., Texas State. **SS**—Jace Peterson, Jr., McNeese State. **OF**—Matt Holland, Jr., Texas A&M-Corpus Christi; Bryson Myles, Jr., Stephen F. Austin State; Lee Orr, Jr., McNeese State. **DH**—Chris Andreas, Sr., Sam Houston State. **P**—Matt Shelton, Sr., Sam Houston State; Carson Smith, Jr., Texas State; Seth Webster, Jr., Nicholls State. **Player of the Year:** Bryson Myles, Stephen F. Austin State. **Pitcher of the Year:** Carson Smith, Texas State. **Relief Pitcher of the Year:** Jordan LeGros, McNeese State. **Freshman of the Year:** Jonathan Davis, Central Arkansas. **Newcomer of the Year:** Bryson Myles, Stephen F. Austin State. **Coach of the Year:** Ty Harrington, Texas State.

INDIVIDUAL BATTING LEADERS
(Minimum 125 at-bats)

	AVG	AB	R	H	2B	3B	HR	RBI	SB
Myles, Bryson, SFA	.411	241	69	99	11	3	8	36	53
Holland, Matt, Texas A&M-CC	.391	238	44	93	20	3	10	53	7
Granger, Seth, McNeese State	.372	226	37	84	15	3	3	55	1
Nephew, Brian, UT-Arlington	.358	229	29	82	17	0	2	31	1
Davis, Jonathan, Central Ark.	.350	157	43	55	6	3	5	30	21
Scarafiotti, Jarid, SFA	.350	203	30	71	8	1	5	45	2
Jaramillo, Chase, Nicholls State	.349	235	41	82	7	3	3	35	15
Pace, Jonathan, SE La.	.343	216	49	74	13	1	1	39	3
Hutson, Ryan, UTSA	.342	152	30	52	11	1	10	35	4
Bear, Colin, Northwestern State	.340	206	28	70	19	1	5	41	1
Hebert, Brock, SE La.	.340	200	46	68	11	2	2	31	26
Sibley, Tyler, Texas State	.340	256	62	87	12	3	6	37	20
Good, Riley, UTSA	.337	255	42	86	15	3	2	32	16
Weber, Renny, McNeese State	.335	170	26	57	10	0	0	33	0
Peterson, Jace, McNeese State	.335	224	67	75	9	8	2	34	30
Boudreaux, Justin, SE La.	.333	222	54	74	13	3	8	48	15
Andreas, Chris, SHSU	.332	223	39	74	18	2	12	54	5
Abt, Jeff, Lamar	.329	155	31	51	9	4	2	38	13
Perales, Jacob, Texas A&M-CC	.329	213	43	70	13	4	5	44	6
Mooney, Ryan, SHSU	.328	247	49	81	16	1	1	24	28
Marek, Jeramie, Texas A&M-CC	.328	195	34	64	6	0	0	25	14
Kalenkosky, Casey, Texas State	.327	245	59	80	17	0	21	69	6
Orr, Lee, McNeese State	.322	239	58	77	23	3	6	54	18
Hernandez, Trey, Texas A&M-CC	.322	208	51	67	14	2	11	49	2
Walker, Ryan, UT-Arlington	.322	236	43	76	13	0	0	37	11
Smith, Garrett, SFA	.319	226	46	72	11	4	0	40	8
McVaney, Jeff, Texas State	.319	238	53	76	11	1	10	47	12
Hargis, Cass, Southeastern La.	.315	222	42	70	11	3	0	27	9
Dozier, Hunter, SFA	.315	197	38	62	13	1	5	34	5
Dickson, Zack, Central Ark.	.313	160	36	51	1	1	1	20	4

INDIVIDUAL PITCHING LEADERS
(Minimum 50 IP)

	W	L	ERA	G	SV	IP	H	BB	SO
Smith, Carson, Texas State	9	3	1.99	17	0	113	90	48	129
#Legros, Jordan, McNeese State	3	2	2.27	27	12	31	21	11	38

Webster, Seth, Nicholls State	7	3	2.30	16	0	109	109	20	69
Shreve, Patrick, Nicholls State	4	2	2.56	11	0	60	56	10	32
Shelton, Matt, SHSU	7	3	2.87	16	0	94	81	37	89
Selsor, Casey, UTSA	5	5	2.90	15	0	99	99	38	79
West, Jared, Stephen F. Austin	7	3	3.08	15	0	79	85	38	58
Tromblee, Stephen, Lamar	3	3	3.10	21	1	52	51	14	38
Smith, Caleb, Sam Houston State	4	3	3.18	17	0	62	45	26	54
#Pittman, Fielding, Texas State	2	2	3.19	31	0	37	43	9	21
Taylor, Zack, Stephen F. Austin	5	2	3.20	16	0	82	73	34	63
Kimbrel, Brandon, SHSU	7	4	3.26	15	0	102	100	27	74
Watkins, Tyler, Southeastern La.	10	4	3.26	16	0	102	112	11	50
Ford, Blake, Lamar	6	4	3.42	16	1	103	112	31	78
Campbell, Ian, Texas A&M-CC	8	4	3.47	19	0	106	114	36	88
Steinmetz, Andy, Central Ark.	1	4	3.54	24	1	53	55	23	42
Bear, Colin, Northwestern State	3	4	3.54	14	0	76	73	31	66
Oberto, Michael, Texas-Arlington	2	0	3.58	20	0	50	54	24	27
Day, Lance, Texas-Arlington	4	7	3.62	15	0	97	104	28	64
Pitts, Mitchell, Texas State	6	3	3.66	19	0	106	111	34	72
Efferson, Brandon, SE La.	8	5	3.72	15	0	97	87	40	86
Northcott, Dustin, NW State	2	6	3.73	26	4	51	53	17	38

SOUTHWESTERN ATHLETIC CONFERENCE

	Conference		Overall	
EAST	W	L	W	L
*Alcorn State	19	4	27	30
Mississippi Valley State	14	9	18	36
Jackson State	14	10	27	26
Alabama State	6	18	14	29
Alabama A&M	6	18	10	37
WEST	W	L	W	L
Southern	16	8	26	18
Grambling State	14	10	23	26
Prairie View A&M	13	11	25	21
Texas Southern	10	14	24	28
Arkansas-Pine Bluff	7	17	11	34

ALL-CONFERENCE TEAM: C—Evan Richard, Jr., Prairie View A&M. **1B**—Frazier Hall, Sr., Southern. **2B**—Ray Hernandez, Jr., Texas Southern. **3B**—Scott Hornstra, Jr., Mississippi Valley State. **SS**—Jerry Hildreth, Sr., Mississippi Valley State. **OF**—Eldred Barnett, Jr., Grambling State; Charles Epperson, So., Jackson State; Wilmy Marerro, Jr., Southern. **DH**—Kilby Perdomo, Sr., Alcorn State. **SP**—Dakota Laufenberg, Sr., Texas Southern. **RP**—Cody Hall, Sr., Southern.
Player of the Year: Frazier Hall, Southern. **Pitcher of the Year:** Dakota Laufenberg, Texas Southern. **Freshman of the Year**: Desmond Russell, Jackson State. **Coach of the Year:** Eldred Barnett, Grambling State.

INDIVIDUAL BATTING LEADERS
(Minimum 100 at-bats)

	AVG	AB	R	H	2B	3B	HR	RBI	SB
Hall, Frazier, Southern	.416	178	51	74	16	3	9	67	8
Barnett, Eldred, Grambling	.368	182	46	67	13	5	6	52	15
Logan, Kendall, Jackson State	.366	183	63	67	5	8	12	44	19
Marrero, Wilmy, Southern	.357	185	34	66	14	2	9	50	3
Hornstra, Scott, MVSU	.348	181	36	63	22	3	7	52	11
Perdomo, Kilby, Alcorn State	.346	191	48	66	18	1	10	49	8
Gonzalez, Eduardo, Alcorn State	.344	218	43	75	24	1	4	48	6
Angel, Giovanni, Prairie View	.343	172	31	59	9	2	1	29	1
Roy, Taylor, Southern	.336	143	49	48	8	3	1	28	8
Mims, Jordan, Alabama State	.333	135	29	45	5	2	2	24	4
Logan, Cameron, TSU	.333	144	26	48	8	3	9	30	2
Perez, Rafael, Prairie View	.331	136	25	45	9	3	1	33	8
Rowry, Bryan, Southern	.331	151	29	50	4	3	0	25	2
Pitts, Andrew, Alabama State	.330	115	23	38	5	3	3	24	4
Wolfe, Chris, Grambling	.326	178	54	58	6	2	1	30	21
Flenoy, Anthony, TSU	.324	182	38	59	6	2	0	22	29
Hines, Colby, Prairie View	.321	156	32	50	5	3	0	10	5
Ellis, Demari, Southern	.318	176	37	56	11	1	1	29	7
Austin, Trey, Ark.-Pine Bluff	.317	164	29	52	10	3	0	19	6
Pace, Matthew, Ark.-Pine Bluff	.315	149	32	47	18	1	3	30	0
Richard, Evan, Prairie View	.313	115	20	36	8	1	2	23	2
Lamis, Ozzie, Southern	.313	144	38	45	1	5	0	24	9

Rivera, Frankie, TSU	.313	182	24	57	12	2	0	24	3
Russell, Desmond, Jackson State	.310	197	37	61	13	4	5	49	10
Prater, Sean, Ark.-PB	.308	130	24	40	6	1	0	14	3
McDonley, Barry, Ark.-PB	.307	166	34	51	16	3	3	28	0
Cook, Justin, Texas Southern	.304	158	35	48	15	1	1	23	0
Duarte, Kency, Alabama A&M	.302	162	16	49	7	2	2	17	3
Solis, Frank, Jackson State	.372	137	27	51	1	5	0	36	10
#Hollins, Brandon, Alcorn State	.282	177	39	50	1	2	0	20	38

INDIVIDUAL PITCHING LEADERS
(Minimum 50 IP)

	W	L	ERA	G	SV	IP	H	BB	SO
Laufenberg, Dakota, TSU	4	4	3.54	19	4	81	77	28	83
Flores, Abel, Texas Southern	5	2	3.57	18	2	71	49	42	40
Bautista, Richard, Grambling	7	2	3.58	13	0	98	125	29	57
Hall, Cody, Southern	4	2	3.71	15	2	61	55	18	62
Nelson, Cortney, JSU	4	4	4.04	14	1	62	68	21	37
Washington, Terrance, JSU	5	5	4.09	16	0	77	68	46	88
Dominguez, Devin, Ala. State	3	4	4.15	12	0	65	68	25	49
#Wahl, Kyle, Southern	0	3	4.22	17	5	44	50	16	34
Drains, Quintavious, Jackson State	7	3	4.24	17	1	100	102	33	95
Mitchell, Derrick, Prairie View	7	3	4.25	13	0	72	72	30	74
#Smith, Bryan, Texas Southern	2	5	4.30	17	5	44	50	16	34
Russell, Desmond, Jackson State	4	6	4.52	16	3	82	82	32	79
Vicars, Cole, Alcorn State	5	3	4.57	14	0	65	68	22	43
#Parker, Cody, MVSU	0	1	4.72	34	1	27	37	13	25
Easter, Steve, Alcorn State	8	6	4.82	18	1	112	122	24	77
Barnes, Steven, MVSU	5	9	4.84	20	2	89	86	54	84
Listi, Michael, Prairie View	5	4	4.94	13	0	75	76	22	65
Williams, Troy, Alcorn State	7	6	5.01	16	0	97	127	37	43
Hefflinger, Ricky, MVSU	5	0	5.16	17	0	59	59	24	27
Newby, Michael, Ark.-Pine Bluff	4	4	5.29	13	0	66	74	13	38
Lora, Manny, Alabama A&M	2	6	5.31	13	1	61	63	36	50
Young, Curtis, Alabama State	2	4	5.36	15	1	50	55	25	46
Mitchell, Matt, Grambling	5	4	5.45	12	0	78	93	28	47

SUMMIT LEAGUE

	Conference		Overall	
	W	L	W	L
*Oral Roberts	21	7	39	22
South Dakota State	20	8	37	20
North Dakota State	15	12	22	32
Western Illinois	13	15	21	38
IPFW	12	16	17	34
Southern Utah	11	17	23	31
Oakland	10	18	19	31
Centenary	9	18	12	31

ALL-CONFERENCE TEAM: 1B—Joel Blake, Sr., South Dakota State. **2B**—Tommy Jablonski, Sr., Oakland. **3B**—R.J. Talamantes, Fr., Centenary. **SS**—Bo Cuthbertson, Jr., Southern Utah. **OF**—Nick Baligod, Sr., Oral Roberts; Chris Elder, Sr., Oral Roberts; Beau Hanowski, Jr., South Dakota State. **C**—Ryan Waldhart, Sr., Oakland. **DH**—Brandon King, Jr., Oral Roberts. **UT**—Mitchell Kauweloa, Jr., Southern Utah. **SP**—James Crockett, Sr., Southern Utah; Alex Gonxalez, Fr., Oral Roberts; Blake Treinen, Sr., South Dakota State. **RP**—Trever Vermeulen, Sr., South Dakota State.
Player of the Year: Bo Cuthbertson, Southern Utah. **Pitcher of the Year:** Alex Gonzalez, Oral Roberts. **Freshman of the Year**: Alex Gonzalez, Oral Roberts. **Coach of the Year:** Rob Walton, Oral Roberts.

INDIVIDUAL BATTING LEADERS
(Minimum 2.5 plate appearances per team game)

	AVG	AB	R	H	2B	3B	HR	RBI	SB
Cutherbertson, Bo, So. Utah	.432	192	51	83	20	7	5	47	15
Faulkner, Will, IPFW	.381	189	28	72	9	0	1	29	11
Blake, Joel, SDSU	.374	222	48	83	16	0	1	45	0
Kauweloa, Mitchell, So. Utah	.370	189	30	70	12	0	5	47	7
Baligod, Nick, Oral Roberts	.364	247	67	90	21	2	7	41	15
Rajkovich, Pete, Centenary	.363	124	21	45	7	0	0	18	5
Wick, Aaron, Oakland	.357	168	24	60	7	0	0	30	7
Gillean, Mark, Centenary	.355	121	18	43	4	2	0	12	8
Talamantes, R.J., Centenary	.350	160	38	56	7	0	0	22	32
Hanowski, Beau, SDSU	.349	212	49	74	8	1	1	26	5
Turbak, Blake, NDSU	.349	152	20	53	4	0	0	19	0

COLLEGE

BaseballAmerica.com

Baseball America 2012 Almanac • **473**

	AVG	AB	R	H	2B	3B	HR	RBI	SB
Jablonski, Tommy, Oakland	.344	154	25	53	15	0	0	16	6
Schiller, Cam, Oral Roberts	.342	228	48	78	17	1	7	56	3
Shaw, Taylor, So. Utah	.338	151	34	51	7	3	4	35	13
Phelen, Andrew, SDSU	.333	177	42	59	11	3	2	27	6
Colwell, Tim, NDSU	.333	168	26	56	8	1	0	22	10
Carson, Mike, Oakland	.329	173	31	57	12	0	6	27	2
Elder, Chris, Oral Roberts	.326	233	54	76	19	0	12	59	5
Cain, Eric, SDSU	.322	214	40	69	11	3	2	46	2
Ryan, Tim, Oakland	.319	188	41	60	10	0	0	20	16
King, Brandon, Oral Roberts	.319	229	46	73	13	1	10	56	2
Rhodes, Zach, SDSU	.318	170	29	54	13	1	6	42	5
Igara, Matt, Western Illinois	.317	240	45	76	19	1	4	36	10
Thomas, Nate, IPFW	.317	139	15	44	3	1	0	15	1
Stitz, Billy, SDSU	.316	244	46	77	14	7	0	32	4
Satszinger, Wes, NDSU	.308	159	23	49	11	2	2	35	1
Jarrad, D.J., Oakland	.304	191	37	58	8	3	2	33	14
Waldhart, Ryan, Oakland	.303	142	27	43	8	0	2	27	9
Cowen, Austin, Western III.	.302	212	33	64	13	1	1	37	1
#Sawyer, Jesse, SDSU	.266	207	35	55	9	0	12	42	4

INDIVIDUAL PITCHING LEADERS
(Minimum 1 IP per team game)

	W	L	ERA	G	SV	IP	H	BB	SO
Bowen, Drew, Oral Roberts	6	2	1.73	13	0	68	48	28	53
#Vermeulen, Trever, SDSU	2	5	2.98	28	10	51	36	20	56
Treinen, Blake, SDSU	7	3	3.00	13	0	84	81	25	84
Gonzalez, Alex, Oral Roberts	8	7	3.49	19	0	106	96	43	100
Tognetti, Colby, NDSU	4	6	3.57	13	0	81	85	19	32
Sterling, Zach, Western III.	5	4	3.93	15	1	66	62	45	60
Russell, Dan, Western III.	6	7	4.21	16	0	103	103	38	80
Wachholder, Ryan, Western III.	3	8	4.34	17	1	77	87	38	46
Oberle, Alex, SDSU	4	5	4.61	18	0	84	105	24	27
Opitz, Nick, IPFW	4	8	4.71	12	0	86	102	17	44
Luxton, Russell, Oakland	4	4	4.72	11	1	55	79	20	30
Bougher, Stephen, SDSU	6	4	4.89	13	0	81	101	21	43
Emery, Kolton, SDSU	7	1	5.09	16	1	76	93	14	32
Chung, Chris, Southern Utah	6	6	5.21	14	1	66	84	18	41
Wick, Aaron, Oakland	4	7	5.23	12	0	76	101	26	39
August, Ryan, IPFW	3	4	5.25	12	0	58	70	32	28
Lugo, Seth, Centenary	3	7	5.57	16	2	73	82	39	70
Ransbottom, Matt, IPFW	4	3	5.61	25	0	59	81	25	26
Crockett, James, Southern Utah	5	6	5.65	15	1	80	76	51	97
Anderson, Luke, NDSU	2	3	5.69	14	0	62	58	35	46
Walker, Samuel, IPFW	5	5	5.90	13	0	76	84	40	59
Parrott, Nic, Centenary	2	2	6.11	14	0	46	58	21	12
Leichtman, Mark, Oakland	2	5	6.14	11	0	59	78	32	27
Dalzell, Derek, Centenary	2	8	6.71	16	2	51	71	22	24

SUN BELT CONFERENCE

	Conference		Overall	
	W	L	W	L
Troy	21	9	43	19
Florida International	20	9	40	20
Louisiana-Lafayette	18	12	31	27
Western Kentucky	17	13	33	24
Florida Atlantic	17	13	32	25
South Alabama	15	15	30	28
Arkansas State	13	16	27	31
*Arkansas-Little Rock	10	20	24	34
Middle Tennessee State	9	21	18	37
Louisiana-Monroe	9	21	24	30

ALL-CONFERENCE TEAM: C—Matt Rice, Sr., Western Ky.. **1B**—Joey Rapp, Sr., Louisiana-Monroe. **2B**—Raymond Church, Sr., Florida Atlantic. **3B**—Tyler Hannah, Jr., Troy; Jeremy Patton, Jr., Florida International. **SS**—Adam Bryant, Sr., Troy. **OF**—Todd Baumgartner, Sr., Arkansas State; Pablo Bermudez, Sr., Florida International; Kes Carter, Western Ky.. **DH**—Nick Rountree, Sr., Arkansas-Little Rock. **SP**—Paul Davis, Sr., Florida Atlantic; Tyler Ray, Jr., Troy. **RP**—Hugh Adams, Sr., Florida Atlantic. **UT**—Tyson Workman, Jr., Troy.
Players of the Year: Pablo Bermudez, Florida International/Adam Bryant, Troy. **Pitcher of the Year:** Tyler Ray, Troy. **Freshman of the Year:** Justin Hageman, Western Kentucky. **Coach of the Year:** Bobby Pierce, Troy.

INDIVIDUAL BATTING LEADERS
(Minimum 2.5 at-bats per team game)

	AVG	AB	R	H	2B	3B	HR	RBI	SB
Bermudez, Pablo, FIU	.373	233	63	87	16	2	5	37	17
Hannah, Tyler, Troy	.370	235	62	87	27	2	7	53	6
Rice, Matt, Western Ky.	.360	236	45	85	14	2	9	59	1
Hudak, Alex, Fla. Atlantic	.360	203	41	73	16	1	3	35	4
Patton, Jeremy, FIU	.359	237	54	85	15	0	7	53	6
Andreoli, Jared, Western Ky.	.352	247	49	87	9	5	3	38	17
Petello, Mike, La.-Lafayette	.351	205	38	72	10	4	9	42	13
Church, Raymond, Fla. Atlantic	.351	228	51	80	15	0	6	32	13
Parma, Myles, UALR	.350	160	25	56	8	0	3	21	4
Guidry, Justin, MTSU	.349	232	39	81	13	2	4	32	7
Wittels, Garrett, FIU	.345	255	49	88	16	0	4	40	11
Carter, Kes, Western Ky.	.344	215	46	74	17	3	7	40	8
Tanner, Brent, South Ala.	.342	228	44	78	15	0	10	55	7
Delguidice, Nick, Fla. Atlantic	.341	220	34	75	20	0	5	50	3
Skinner, Will, MTSU	.341	220	45	75	17	2	16	51	6
Baumgartner, Todd, Ark. State	.340	244	56	83	18	0	9	48	9
Kirkland, Logan, South Ala.	.339	224	43	76	10	2	1	27	3
Aulds, Les, La.-Monroe	.339	192	41	65	4	1	2	22	24
Houston, Jason, UALR	.338	222	42	75	12	2	6	28	8
Bryant, Adam, Troy	.337	270	63	91	26	2	11	66	8
Barroso, Yoandy, FIU	.335	185	42	62	18	4	2	31	8
White, Taylor, South Ala.	.333	267	49	89	12	1	3	19	20
Earley, Nolan, South Ala.	.330	221	41	73	20	1	2	40	2
Fontenot, Greg, La.-Lafayette	.330	212	41	70	13	1	1	31	12
Behar, Jose, FIU	.330	185	30	61	13	1	5	31	2
Hook, Brad, South Ala.	.328	189	44	62	13	1	7	41	4
Rapp, Joey, La.-Monroe	.318	198	46	63	15	0	13	46	3
McRae, Todd, Troy	.316	187	33	59	9	1	1	38	2
Garcia, Greg, UALR	.315	168	32	53	6	0	4	25	8
DeBlieux, Jeff, South Ala.	.314	159	27	50	7	2	0	25	9
Emery, Ryan, Ark. State	.314	210	36	66	9	0	3	40	1
#Marvel, Lance, La.-Lafayette	.304	158	20	48	5	5	1	23	9

INDIVIDUAL PITCHING LEADERS
(Minimum 1 IP per team game)

	W	L	ERA	G	SV	IP	H	BB	SO
Perkins, Tanner, Western Ky.	7	4	2.36	15	0	99	89	22	75
Ray, Tyler, Troy	12	0	2.39	16	0	117	103	16	69
Nicholson, Jordan, La.-Lafayette	5	2	2.51	12	0	72	65	18	42
Davis, Paul, Fla. Atlantic	10	1	2.87	16	0	100	96	34	73
Fondon, R.J., FIU	6	6	3.05	16	0	97	95	27	55
Hageman, Justin, Western Ky.	8	5	3.22	18	0	101	99	30	85
Lee, Jacob, Ark. State	5	4	3.25	15	1	91	95	32	69
Satriano, Joey, La.-Lafayette	4	5	3.29	24	2	68	58	32	54
Haig, Phil, FIU	9	4	3.44	16	0	99	96	32	72
Ferguson, Andy, Ark. State	7	4	3.57	14	0	88	73	28	80
Harris, Garrett, South Ala.	8	3	3.61	15	0	115	120	32	95
Hubbell, Taylor, La.-Lafayette	5	7	3.61	16	0	95	95	22	59
Wetherell, Phil, Western Ky.	1	3	4.10	30	5	59	67	19	44
DeSimone, Daniel, FIU	5	2	4.24	13	0	70	81	19	48
Paris, Carlton, South Ala.	3	5	4.44	16	0	81	88	32	45
Meiers, Jake, Fla. Atlantic	4	5	4.45	17	1	59	67	14	26
Geith, T.J., La.-Lafayette	6	5	4.59	14	0	82	92	27	55
Granier, Drew, La.-Monroe	4	5	4.60	14	0	86	76	39	86
Briley, Luke, La.-Monroe	4	2	4.61	18	1	57	72	8	26
Crenshaw, Dustin, South Ala.	7	3	4.63	16	0	103	135	13	58
Edelen, Brian, Western Ky.	7	2	4.74	23	1	74	71	28	60
#Hugh, Adam, Fla. Atlantic	0	1	3.44	28	10	37	31	7	28

WEST COAST CONFERENCE

	Conference		Overall	
	W	L	W	L
*San Francisco	16	5	32	25
Gonzaga	15	6	32	29
Loyola Marymount	11	10	30	25
Portland	11	10	23	31
San Diego	11	10	22	31
St. Mary's	9	12	27	28
Pepperdine	7	14	22	34
Santa Clara	4	17	17	34

ALL-CONFERENCE TEAM: C—Cameron Edman, Sr., Gonzaga; Travis Higgs, Sr., San Francisco; Matt Koch, Jr., Loyola Marymount; Zack Kometani, Jr., San Diego. **1B**—Nik Balog, Jr., San Francisco; Marco Gonzales, Fr., Gonzaga; Corey LeVier, Jr., San Diego. **2B**—Joe Sever, So., Pepperdine. **3B**—Kris Bryant, Fr., San Diego; Patrick Wisdom, So., St. Mary's; Stephen Yarrow, Sr., San Francisco. **UT**—Bryan Haar, Jr., San Diego. **OF**—Connor Bernatz, Sr., San Francisco; Tyler Chism, Sr., Gonzaga; Turner Gill, Fr., Portland; Brian Humphries, Jr., Pepperdine; Pete Lavin, Sr., San Francisco. **P**—Martin Agosta, So., St. Mary's; Kyle Barraclough, Jr., St. Mary's; Ryan Carpenter, Jr., Gonzaga; Aaron Gates, Jr., Pepperdine; Alex Gillingham, Jr., Loyola Marymount; Cory Hall, Sr., Santa Clara; Kyle Kraus, Jr., Portland; Cody Martin, Sr., Gonzaga; Kyle Zimmer, So., San Francisco.

Players of the Year: Kris Bryant, San Diego/Marco Gonzales, Gonzaga.
Freshmen of the Year: Kris Bryant, San Diego/Marco Gonzales, Gonzaga. **Pitcher of the Year:** Ryan Carpenter, Gonzaga. **Defensive Player of the Year:** Stephen Yarrow, San Francisco. **Coach of the Year:** Nino Giarratano, San Francisco.

INDIVIDUAL BATTING LEADERS
(Minimum 3 plate appearances per team game)

	AVG	AB	R	H	2B	3B	HR	RBI	SB
Bryant, Kris, San Diego	**.365**	197	57	72	17	1	**9**	36	18
LeVier, Corey, San Diego	.363	182	23	66	10	0	1	34	1
Kometani, Zack, San Diego	.355	**217**	27	77	22	1	4	**54**	7
Wisdom, Patrick, St. Mary's	.351	208	33	73	16	1	8	46	5
Lowenstein, Matt, LMU	.349	186	32	65	9	1	0	21	9
Lavin, Pete, San Francisco	.347	236	42	**82**	20	**4**	2	27	16
Edman, Cameron, Gonzaga	.346	182	35	63	**23**	1	**9**	36	2
Moon, Billy, Gonzaga	.337	193	31	65	14	1	3	41	2
Gill, Turner, Portland	.332	184	26	61	18	0	3	33	0
Haar, Bryan, San Diego	.330	188	27	62	13	1	2	29	14
Checkal, Dillon, San Diego	.316	171	33	54	4	2	0	20	4
Lane, Eric, Gonzaga	.314	210	39	66	7	0	1	19	3
Chism, Tyler, Gonzaga	.313	201	33	63	10	1	5	27	7
Koch, Matt, LMU	.313	211	30	66	22	1	4	39	2
Terry, Patrick, Santa Clara	.312	186	18	58	10	0	3	30	4
Scott, Kramer, Portland	.299	157	26	47	9	2	1	19	6
Armijo, Kevin, Portland	.294	187	26	55	15	3	3	26	2
Bernatz, Connor, San Francisco	.292	212	33	62	11	2	2	24	7
Kalfus, Brenden, St. Mary's	.292	209	24	61	17	2	3	25	5
Herbst, Lucas, Santa Clara	.289	190	25	55	9	0	1	28	6
Higgs, Travis, San Francisco	.289	180	27	52	19	2	4	27	2
Humphries, Brian, Pepperdine	.288	208	28	60	8	2	3	28	11
Bolinger, Royce, Gonzaga	.283	191	28	54	11	1	3	25	4
DeMello, Toby, St. Mary's	.282	170	18	48	10	0	0	19	1
DeMerritt, Kyle, Santa Clara	.280	186	29	52	8	0	0	27	2
Roe, Shon, LMU	.279	190	23	53	5	3	0	26	10
Sever, Joe, Pepperdine	.279	208	30	58	13	0	6	32	5
Balog, Nik, San Francisco	.274	215	23	59	13	0	4	34	1
Muno, Kevin, San Diego	.274	215	35	59	11	3	1	9	**22**
Johnson, Jonathan, LMU	.274	197	32	54	8	3	0	24	7
Diedrich, Trent, Pepperdine	.272	151	16	41	7	0	3	18	0
#Mardesich, Matt, Portland	.263	205	35	54	16	2	**9**	37	3

INDIVIDUAL PITCHING LEADERS
(Minimum 1 IP per team game)

	W	L	ERA	G	SV	IP	H	BB	SO
Martin, Cody, Gonzaga	2	1	**0.86**	25	**12**	52	30	19	63
Gillingham, Alex, LMU	8	4	2.04	10	0	112	104	24	78
Gonzales, Marco, Gonzaga	**11**	2	2.57	15	0	105	83	21	90
Carpenter, Ryan, Gonzaga	8	2	2.62	14	0	96	72	33	**107**
Agosta, Martin, St. Mary's	7	6	2.81	15	0	90	81	19	76
Griffin, Aaron, LMU	7	3	2.99	19	1	72	73	18	41
Gates, Aaron, Pepperdine	4	5	3.15	14	0	94	67	59	57
Hall, Cory, Santa Clara	4	7	3.26	15	0	105	110	24	80
Drummond, Calvin, San Diego	3	4	3.29	14	0	77	73	37	55
Gaham, J.R., Santa Clara	3	5	3.34	23	3	62	53	6	45
Anderson, Mark, St. Mary's	8	6	3.50	15	0	108	90	26	80
Johnson, Chris, Portland	3	5	3.56	14	0	83	80	22	58
Barraclough, Kyle, St. Mary's	6	5	3.60	15	0	105	90	36	78
Sewald, Paul, San Diego	2	4	3.63	22	2	67	67	16	49
Paez, Paul, San Diego	7	4	3.64	28	1	72	68	25	58
Zimmer, Kyle, San Francisco	6	5	3.73	20	1	92	93	24	89
Wheeler, Jason, LMU	6	4	3.84	14	0	103	105	24	71
Jensen, Chris, San Diego	3	7	3.95	18	2	82	80	36	73
Olson, Tyler, Gonzaga	6	5	3.97	14	0	79	89	29	63
Hiserman, Matt, San Francisco	6	4	4.01	18	1	94	93	18	63
Lujan, Matt, San Francisco	5	3	4.08	13	0	79	76	35	63
Kraus, Kyle, Portland	6	5	4.12	14	0	103	111	13	59
Moscot, Jon, Pepperdine	2	2	4.27	12	1	72	69	27	48
Jones, Owen, Portland	5	6	4.60	15	0	90	101	17	64
Maurer, Matt, Pepperdine	3	6	4.63	18	1	68	84	30	59
Najera, Alex, Pepperdine	1	4	4.79	17	0	62	69	41	24
Mendoza, Chris, Santa Clara	3	6	5.62	20	1	58	86	23	18
Simon, Brock, Santa Clara	3	8	6.28	19	0	76	101	26	25

WESTERN ATHLETIC CONFERENCE

	Conference		Overall	
	W	L	W	L
*Fresno State	17	7	40	16
Hawaii	17	7	34	25
Louisiana Tech	12	12	34	27
Nevada	12	12	24	31
San Jose State	11	13	35	26
New Mexico State	9	15	34	24
Sacramento State	6	18	19	39

ALL-CONFERENCE TEAM: C—Austin Wynns, So., Fresno State. **1B**—Jordan Ribera, Sr., Fresno State; Brock Stassi, Sr., Nevada; Danny Stienstra, Sr., San Jose State. **2B**—Kolten Wong, Jr., Hawaii. **3B**—Danny Muno, Sr., Fresno State. **SS**—Garrett Weber, Sr., Fresno State. **OF**—Aaron Judge, Fr., Fresno State; Dusty Robinson, Jr., Fresno State; Kyle Roliard, Jr., Louisiana Tech; Tanner Waite, Jr., New Mexico State. **DH**—Zack Swasey, Jr., Hawaii. **SP**—Greg Gonzalez, Sr., Fresno State; Mike Jefferson, Jr., Louisiana Tech; Roberto Padilla, Jr., San Jose State. **RP**—Scott Coffman, Jr., New Mexico State.
Player of the Year: Dusty Robinson, Fresno State. **Pitcher of the Year:** Greg Gonzalez, Fresno State. **Freshman of the Year:** Aaron Judge, Fresno State. **Coach of the Year:** Mike Trapasso, Hawaii.

INDIVIDUAL BATTING LEADERS
(Minimum 2.5 at-bats per team game)

	AVG	AB	R	H	2B	3B	HR	RBI	SB
Fisher, Zach, NMSU	**.398**	171	35	68	16	0	8	56	0
Hipp, Parker, NMSU	.396	169	45	67	10	1	6	58	7
Waite, Tanner, NMSU	.389	175	49	68	12	1	1	43	4
Wong, Kolten, Hawaii	.378	209	48	79	11	3	7	53	**23**
Stassi, Brock, Nevada	.360	203	29	73	19	3	2	34	5
Judge, Aaron, Fresno State	.358	187	38	67	12	1	2	30	11
Forney, Tyler, NMSU	.356	146	36	52	6	1	1	27	6
Karraker, Bryan, NMSU	.350	160	55	56	13	1	4	33	4
Stienstra, Danny, San Jose State	.349	**241**	42	**84**	15	0	3	54	8
Muno, Danny, Fresno State	.348	204	47	71	14	1	3	52	14
Aguayo, Ryan, NMSU	.332	193	48	64	19	1	5	**59**	1
Roliard, Kyle, Louisiana Tech	.330	230	44	76	14	1	1	26	7
Starkes, Wesley, NMSU	.329	207	**60**	68	10	2	3	44	13
Voight, Zachary, NMSU	.327	196	55	64	9	3	2	38	1
Hertler, Craig, San Jose State	.326	190	39	62	10	4	1	23	17
Wynns, Austin, Fresno State	.326	175	41	57	9	0	2	21	0
Swasey, Zack, Hawaii	.320	225	27	72	12	2	1	44	11
Jones, Zack, San Jose State	.316	155	29	49	7	3	3	26	4
Robinson, Dusty, Fresno State	.310	210	44	65	**20**	3	**16**	55	10
Van Doornum, Jeff, Hawaii	.309	217	34	67	17	2	3	38	13
Threlkeld, Mark, Louisiana Tech	.309	230	45	71	19	1	9	45	8
Valdez, Jacob, San Jose State	.307	192	37	59	10	2	1	24	9
Hedges, Austin, Louisiana Tech	.304	158	25	48	4	0	0	13	2
Melino, Nick, Nevada	.303	201	43	61	19	0	4	27	6
Almadova, Breland, Hawaii	.298	191	54	57	16	2	1	22	16
Ford, Joey, Louisiana Tech	.296	223	26	66	15	0	1	24	1
Bennett, Collin, Hawaii	.292	161	22	47	10	0	0	20	1
Wise, Kenny, Fresno State	.289	159	28	46	12	3	7	26	4
Miller, Blake, Sacramento State	.289	187	21	54	9	1	7	30	6
Escobar, Carlos, Nevada	.289	142	22	41	8	0	4	25	0
Montplaisir, Sean, Hawaii	.289	194	30	56	12	**5**	1	25	5

INDIVIDUAL PITCHING LEADERS
(Minimum 1 IP per team game)

	W	L	ERA	G	SV	IP	H	BB	SO
#Linsky, Lenny, Hawaii	1	1	1.30	27	14	34	25	9	34
Gonzalez, Greg, Fresno State	11	1	1.79	16	0	105	76	28	124
Poytress, Josh, Fresno State	7	3	2.85	18	0	79	89	17	56
Padilla, Roberto, San Jose State	9	6	3.19	16	0	99	83	46	81
Guzman, Esteban, San Jose State	5	4	3.33	18	0	76	78	22	74
Jefferson, Mike, Louisiana Tech	6	4	3.56	18	0	86	79	46	70
Sisto, Matt, Hawaii	5	5	3.67	15	0	83	81	28	55
Harlan, Tom, Fresno State	5	3	3.84	19	1	63	77	16	45
Sandoval, Brandon, Sac. State	4	3	3.90	15	2	62	72	31	36
Marks, Troy, Nevada	2	6	4.21	17	1	73	64	28	52
McFarland, Blake, San Jose State	8	2	4.21	15	0	83	95	31	61
Maas, Karl, Sac. State	4	5	4.30	14	0	82	77	31	36
Arakawa, Jarrett, Hawaii	5	4	4.50	16	0	80	89	29	65
Gallagher, Zach, Hawaii	5	3	4.52	17	0	66	77	13	40
Stefan, Jeb, Louisiana Tech	7	4	4.52	14	0	66	63	37	51
Hennessey, Andy, San Jose State	3	4	4.73	16	0	72	78	35	59
Jameson, Tom, Nevada	6	6	4.84	15	0	84	103	35	41
Cole, Jeremy, Nevada	4	5	4.90	15	0	64	80	21	26
Petersen, Trevor, Louisiana Tech	6	4	5.08	18	1	83	90	49	45
Mendonca, Tanner, Sac. State	2	6	5.73	14	1	66	75	31	33
Beck, Ryan, NMSU	10	5	5.96	16	0	91	121	39	73
Reid, Dan, NMSU	7	4	7.01	15	0	77	107	30	48
Mack, Tyler, NMSU	6	5	9.68	15	0	61	75	55	52

INDEPENDENTS

	Overall	
	W	L
Dallas Baptist	42	20
Longwood	28	18
Cal State Bakersfield	33	22
Savannah State	29	23
Le Moyne	23	20
Southern Illinois-Edwardsville	28	24
Seattle	21	30
North Carolina Central	7	39
New Orleans	4	50

INDIVIDUAL BATTING LEADERS
(Minimum 125 at-bats)

	AVG	AB	R	H	2B	3B	HR	RBI	SB
Krizan, Jason, DBU	.413	247	63	102	39	1	10	81	13
Jones, Brant, Longwood	.374	182	43	68	12	5	6	29	11
Anderson, Landon, DBU	.356	250	72	89	13	7	7	58	21
Sanay, Oscar, CSUB	.355	220	36	78	12	1	0	34	2
Dickason, Matt, Longwood	.349	166	28	58	8	1	1	22	4
Schaaf, Don, LeMoyne	.348	141	22	49	9	0	3	30	8
Hawkins, Zach, SIU-E	.345	197	29	68	12	1	3	44	2
Barkley, Emory, SSU	.338	130	20	44	11	0	0	22	2
McCrary, Joseph, SSU	.337	190	41	64	8	6	4	37	21
Kelley, Dexter, SSU	.335	182	60	61	16	2	1	28	39
Lacy, Justin, Longwood	.331	181	29	60	15	0	5	29	3
Rodriguez, Jeremy, CSUB	.328	198	40	65	11	0	3	30	0
Vazquez, James, SIU-E	.325	200	51	65	9	3	2	27	6
Oleszczuk, Trent, Seattle	.322	180	39	58	7	0	1	21	8
Behmanesh, Ryan, DBU	.318	242	57	77	18	3	4	51	3

Sollars, Dustin, Longwood	.317	167	32	53	8	0	3	24	10
Robbins, Tyler, DBU	.316	206	78	65	17	1	10	40	4
Caldwell, Devin, SIU-E	.314	191	41	60	16	2	6	53	5
Greatting, Joel, SIU-E	.312	173	26	54	8	0	5	28	3
Legg, DC, CSUB	.312	199	25	62	13	1	3	42	0
Botsford, Brett, Le Moyne	.311	196	41	61	13	0	0	19	20
Drayton, Dylan, NCCU	.309	188	26	58	9	1	1	17	5
McIntyre, Ryan, CSUB	.309	217	47	67	11	6	2	25	14
Newman, Robby, Longwood	.308	133	28	41	11	0	4	25	3
Becherer, Travis, SIU-E	.307	192	39	59	5	1	0	21	19
Hutter, Joel, DBU	.303	231	47	70	15	1	9	50	3
Matecki, Mitch, SIU-E	.302	169	33	51	7	5	1	30	11
Williamson, Carter, NCCU	.298	151	14	45	7	0	1	22	2
Mahoney, Ryan, Le Moyne	.292	192	39	56	7	2	6	31	9
Oglesby, Matthew, SSU	.292	178	33	52	6	2	2	29	8
Letourneau, Andrew, CSUB	.288	226	41	65	2	0	0	26	13
Pegues, Edward, NCCU	.288	132	17	38	3	0	0	14	5
Hatcher, Kenny, DBU	.287	223	38	64	15	0	2	48	1
Medina, Martin, CSUB	.287	209	38	60	11	1	9	53	0
Wheeless, Cameron, UNO	.287	143	18	41	7	1	2	11	2
Kincaid, Doug, Seattle	.274	186	33	51	13	2	8	33	11
Marrow, Troy, NCCU	.272	158	24	43	11	0	0	16	3
Plummer, Ross, NCCU	.271	144	25	39	6	1	2	15	2
Burkett, Scott, Longwood	.270	174	24	47	9	0	3	34	2
McAlpine, Duncan, DBU	.270	174	35	47	4	0	9	38	3

INDIVIDUAL PITCHING LEADERS
(Minimum 50 IP)

	W	L	ERA	G	SV	IP	H	BB	SO
McCarthy, Mike, CSUB	8	6	1.62	17	0	127	99	28	116
#Haney, Chris, DBU	4	2	2.17	32	15	37	33	13	42
Patton, Spencer, SIU-E	9	3	2.55	15	0	88	70	29	109
Felax, Travis, SIU-E	5	2	2.62	13	0	68	63	19	37
Tardiff, Jeff, Le Moyne	3	2	2.81	10	0	57	59	16	41
Hoenshell, Tommy, CSUB	7	7	2.89	16	0	106	117	12	62
Briere, Chris, Longwood	7	3	3.27	11	0	71	74	20	42
Stafford, Jared, DBU	8	5	3.27	16	0	104	93	35	63
Howe, Seafth, Seattle	4	4	3.42	14	0	73	67	19	33
Kohout, Ed, Le Moyne	1	6	3.49	17	5	59	55	18	56
Montoya, Jonathan, CSUB	8	5	3.67	16	0	115	104	48	86
Malin, Josh, SIU-E	5	4	3.91	15	0	89	95	19	51
Ramsey, Cory, Longwood	6	3	3.95	10	0	54	51	21	37
Williamson, Brandon, DBU	10	4	4.24	21	0	123	139	41	71
Kuzma, Mark, Le Moyne	3	6	4.53	10	0	59	66	30	36
Allegretti, Michael, SSU	7	2	4.63	13	0	56	61	20	47
McGowin, Kyle, SSU	5	4	4.79	16	0	77	80	48	76
Smith, Michael, DBU	1	2	4.86	24	0	50	65	26	46
Kizer, Brandon, Seattle	6	5	4.91	13	0	77	68	21	49
Nelson, Cory, Le Moyne	2	6	4.95	13	0	63	63	29	53
Whieldon, Max, Seattle	0	6	4.98	16	0	59	73	12	23
Daniels, Ryan, SIU-E	1	4	5.12	16	0	51	58	21	32
Zielinski, Derek, Le Moyne	3	4	5.20	10	0	55	69	23	48
Staples, Jordan, DBU	6	2	5.27	15	0	54	55	29	26
Herlihy, Kevin, SSU	5	5	5.38	14	0	80	103	20	55
Evasick, Arlo, Seattle	4	4	5.63	16	0	54	60	24	29
Robinson, Drew, NCCU	2	7	5.90	12	0	61	79	35	23
Frye, Glenn, NCCU	2	8	6.64	15	1	64	88	41	67
Fulmer, Sam, NCCU	1	4	6.87	13	0	55	70	40	38

NCAA DIVISION II

West Florida right-hander Daniel Vargas-Vila capped a dominant senior season in championship fashion.

Vargas-Vila gave up two runs in eight innings and won his second game in the NCAA Division II World Series as West Florida rolled past Winona State 12-2 in the championship game at the USA Baseball National Training Complex in Cary, N.C.

Vargas-Vila pitched eight shutout innings in the Argonauts' Series opener to get West Florida off on an undefeated run through the series with a 13-0 victory over Southern Connecticut. West Florida (52-9) also defeated Sonoma State (Calif.) 5-4 and host Mount Olive (N.C.) 5-3 en route to its first Division II championship.

Vargas-Vila was the undisputed ace for the Argonauts, compiling the best season in school history. He finished 16-1 with a 1.86 ERA and pitched a school-record 121 innings.

In the title game, West Florida scored four runs in the first inning to take charge against Winona State (Minn.), getting consecutive RBI hits from Josh Huggins, Leo Lamarche and Zach Taylor. The Argonauts added three in the fourth and built an 11-0 lead with two seventh-inning runs.

"When you get four runs in the first inning, you go out there and just pitch to contact – throw strikes, not try to strike everyone out," Vargas-Vila said. "Our hitters did what they've done all year, just try to put the ball in play and let the ball do the work. Our defense was amazing again today. It's just a great job all around."

Argonauts third baseman Huggins led West Florida offensively in the series, hitting .533 (8-for-15) with nine RBIs. Huggins and outfielders Larry Taye and Greg Pron were named to the All-Tournament team along with Vargas-Vila, who was co-most outstanding player for the Series along with Winona State outfielder-pitcher Tony Mueller. Taye and Huggins had three hits each in the title game for West Florida.

Despite getting up early in the final, Taye said, the Argonauts stayed focused until the end. "Jumping out to a big lead like that was huge," Taye said. "We were excited throughout the whole game, but still trying to stay focused, stay in the moment, not lose ourselves. It's just a great feeling."

Pron led the team in the triple crown categories, batting .423 with 10 home runs (tied for team honors) and 69 RBIs.

DIVISION II WORLD SERIES

Site: Cary, N.C.
Participants: Winona State, Minn. (39-17). Central Missouri (49-8), Millersville, Pa. (43-10), Mount Olive, N.C. (45-8), Sonoma State, Calif. (36-20), Grand Valley State, Mich. (52-3), West Florida (48-9), Southern Connecticut State (43-7-1).
Champion: West Florida.
Runner-up: Winona State.
Co-Outstanding players: Daniel Vargas-Vila, rhp, West Florida; Tony Mueller, of-rhp, Winona State.
PRELIMINARIES
Winona State 4, Central Missouri 3
Mount Olive 3, Millersville 1
Sonoma State 7, Grand Valley State 6 (11 innings)
West Florida 13, Southern Connecticut State 0
Winona State 9, Mount Olive 3
Millersville 1, Central Missouri 0 (Central Missouri eliminated)
Mount Olive 5, Millersville 2 (Millersville eliminated)
West Florida 5, Sonoma State 4
Southern Connecticut State 8, Grand Valley State 6 (Grand Valley State eliminated)
Southern Connecticut State 6, Sonoma State 4 (Sonoma State eliminated)
Winona State 7, Southern Connecticut State 5 (Southern Connecticut eliminated)
West Florida 5, Mount Olive 3 (Mount Olive eliminated)

NCAA DIVISION III

Marietta (Ohio) College bounced back from its lone bump in a near-perfect season to defeat Chapman (Calif.) University 18-5 for the Division III crown.

Heading into the title game, the Pioneers had a 46-3 record and were in the midst of a 22-game winning streak that saw them bully their way through the Mideast Regional, outscoring opponents 38-9 in four games, and the World Series, outscoring opponents 33-7 in four games.

Needing to win one of two in the championship, the 'Etta Express lost the first game 15-4, despite having senior Brian Gasser—the ABCA/Rawlings co-national player of the year and D3baseball.com's national pitcher of the year—on the mound. Marietta jumped out on top in the winner-take-all finale, though, with a run-scoring double by sophomore center fielder Aaron Hopper giving it the lead.

Then John Snyder made a run-saving catch in the bottom of the first, and Snyder, Hopper and first-team all-American Tim Saunders powered Marietta its fifth overall national championship, tops among D-III schools. The three Pioneers went 8-for-19 in game two with nine runs scored and seven RBIs sparking a seven-run third en route to the drubbing.

Marietta's pitching staff dominated for much of the season, posting an impressive 1.74 team ERA. The Express were lead by Gasser (14-1, 1.06, 86 strikeouts in 93 IP), and junior Austin Blaski (12-

2, 1.62, 86 strikeouts in 95 IP), who was named the tournament's most outstanding player after his six innings of two-hit work in the clinching win.

DIVISION III WORLD SERIES

Site: Appleton, Wis.
Participants: Chapman, Calif. (33-11), Kean, N.J. (42-9), Salisbury, Md. (33-12), Marietta, Ohio (42-3), Wisconsin-Whitewater (36-11), Buena Vista, Iowa (32-16), Western New England, Mass. (42-9), Keystone, Pa. (36-10).
Champion: Marietta.
Runner-up: Chapman.
Outstanding player: Austin Blaski, rhp, Marietta.
PRELIMINARIES
Chapman 9, Kean 4
Marietta 8, Salisbury 0
Buena Vista 5, Wisconsin-Whitewater 4
Keystone 2, Western New England 1
Salisbury 10, Kean 3 (Kean eliminated)
Wisconsin-Whitewater 8, Western New England (Western New England eliminated)
Marietta 9, Chapman 4
Buena Vista 8, Keystone 5
Chapman 4, Wisconsin-Whitewater 2 (Wisconsin-Whitewater eliminated)
Keystone 7, Salisbury 2 (Salisbury eliminated)
Marietta 5, Buena Vista 1
Chapman 3, Buena Vista 2 (Buena Vista eliminated)
Marietta 11, Keystone 2 (Keystone eliminated)

NAIA

Ninth-seeded Concodia (Calif.) rebounded from a loss in its second game at the NAIA World Series to roll to the national championship at Lewiston, Idaho.

The Eagles (43-19) peaked late in the season, winning 25 of their final 28 games to become the first team from the Golden State Athletic Conference to claim an NAIA title.

The Eagles defeated Lubbock Christian (Texas) 9-3 in the championship game.

"It's a great group of guys," Concordia coach Mike Grahovac said. "They did everything right while were were [at the Series], and they did everything right throughout the year—even when things were going wrong [on the field]. It really showed for us."

Series MVP Matt Ivanoff, an Eagles outfielder, went 10-for-24 (.417) in six Series games with eight RBIs. Ivanoff was 2-for-5 with an RBI in the title game.

Blake Harrison went the distance in the championship game, giving up six hits and two earned runs with no walks and three strkeouts to wrap up an 8-1 season.

NAIA WORLD SERIES

Site: Lewiston, Idaho.
Participants: Embry-Riddle, Fla. (50-9), Oklahoma City (46-10), Oklahoma Baptist (45-12), LSU Shreveport (45-13), Lee, Tenn. (47-12), Lubbock Christian, Texas (46-12), Lewis-Clark State, Idaho (37-15), Faulkner, Ala. (48-13), Concoria, Calif. (38-18), Tennessee Wesleyan

(40-19).
Champion: Concordia.
Runner-up: Lubbock Christian.
Outstanding player: Matt Ivanoff, of, Concordia.

JUNIOR COLLEGES

NJCAA DIVISION I

Navarro (Texas) College displayed a flair for the dramatic as it came away from Grand Junction, Colo., with its first national title.

Bulldogs catcher J.T. Files, the Series MVP, shook off a bunt sign and hit a two-run, walk-off home run in the 10th inning to lift Navarro (45-17) to a 6-4 victory over Central Arizona in the championship game.

With a runner on first base in the bottom of the 10th, Files was given the sign to bunt. When he saw the Central Arizona first and third basemen charge toward home in case of a bunt, he swung away and sent the all over the fence to touch off a Bulldogs celebration.

Navarro went 5-1 in the Series, losing to 11-8 to Central Arizona in its fourth game. The Bulldogs bounced back with a 9-5 win over Iowa Western to advance to the championship game.

Third baseman David Harris hit .526 (10-for-19) in the Series for Navarro with four homers and 12 RBIs. Outfielder Garrett Autrey batted .500 (7-for-14) with two homers and nine RBIs. Files hit .364 (8-for-22).

NJCAA DIVISION I

Site: Grand Junction, Colo.
Participants: Potomac State, W.Va. (35-10), Jefferson, Mo. (43-20), South Georgia (33-31), Central Arizona (52-13), Southern Union State, Ala. (41-18), Navarro, Texas (42-17), Chipola, Fla. (39-20), Grayson County, Texas (42-15), Seward County, Kan. (44-18), Iowa Western (40-18).
Champion: Navarro
Runner-up: Central Arizona.
Outstanding player: J.T. Files, c, Navarro.

NJCAA DIVISION II

Western Oklahoma State rode its potent offense, which used an eye-popping .402 team batting average to produce a 51-16 season, to its first NJCAA Division II national championship.

Roberto Duran Jr. went 4-for-5 and drove in six runs to lead the Pioneers to an 11-1 victory over Jones County, Ala., in the title game. Western went 5-1 in the tournament, scoring 60 runs (an average of 10 per game) en route to the title.

Sophomore outfielder Jhiomar Veras, the national player of the year, hit .471 with 23 home runs and 84 RBIs to lead the Pioneers for the season. Michael Cruz hit .464 with 16 homers and 90 RBIs, while Duran hit .399 average with 11 homers.

NJCAA DIVISION II WORLD SERIES

Site: Enid, Okla.
Participants: Gateway, Ariz. (40-21); Des Moines, Iowa (46-16); Madison, Wis. (42-14); Heartland, Ill. (53-9); Kellogg, Mich. (30-25); Jones County, Miss. (42-15); Western Oklahoma State (46-15); Southeastern, N.C. (35-19); Connecticut-Avery Point (39-9); Cecil, Md. (39-13-1).
Champion: Western Oklahoma State.
Runner-up: Jones County.
Outstanding Player: Roberto Duran Jr., ss, Western Oklahoma State.

NJCAA DIVISION III

Eastfield, Texas, rallied after losing its opener and beat defending champion Gloucester County (N.J.) twice en route to winning its third D-III national championship, all since 2001. Eastfield became just the second team to lose its first game and still win the national title. Freshman third baseman Nathan Hancock led the tournament with 17 hits, 12 RBIs and 10 runs to earn MVP honors.

NJCAA DIVISION III WORLD SERIES

Site: Tyler, Texas.
Participants: Erie, N.Y. (28-16); Joliet, Ill. (39-21); Eastfield, Texas (34-19); Westmoreland County, Pa. (21-17-1); Rochester, Minn. (31-17); Suffolk County, N.Y. (32-11); Gloucester County, N.J. (28-16); Manchester, Conn. (24-22).
Champion: Eastfield.
Runner-up: Gloucester.
Outstanding Player: Nathan Hancock, 3b, Eastfield.

CALIFORNIA CC ATHLETIC ASSOCIATION

In a state title series matching the top two seeds from Northern California, San Joaquin Delta, based in Stockton, defeated defending state champion Ohlone twice to win its first state juco championship since 1959.

In the clincher at Bakersfield JC, lefthander Jeff McKenzie earned his first victory since his American Legion days in 2009. McKenzie was a .237 hitter as the Mustangs' regular center fielder and had pitched five innings in four games over the last two seasons prior to the state championship game. Named the tournament MVP, McKenzie went the distance, striking out seven. He allowed an unearned run and seven hits while walking three, and he picked four runners off at first base.
Site: Bakersfield, Calif.
Participants: Glendale (28-14); Ohlone (26-17); San Joaquin Delta (31-11); Santa Ana (30-12).
Champion: San Joaquin Delta.
Runner Up: Ohlone.

NORTHWEST ATHLETIC ASSOCIATION OF CCS

Bellevue (Wash.) won its third championship in the last five seasons and its fifth overall, beating defending champion Lower Columbia (Wash.) on its home field 5-3 in the tournament title game.
Site: Longview, Wash.
Participants: Bellevue, Wash. (33-13, 21-3); Columbia Basin, Wash. (32-14, 22-6); Everett, Wash. (34-9, 20-4); Lane, Ore. (24-18, 19-11); Lower Columbia, Wash. (32-10, 18-6); Mount Hood, Ore. (26-11, 22-8); Pierce, Wash. (31-7, 20-4); Yakima Valley, Wash. (32-10, 22-6).
Champion: Bellevue.
Runner-Up: Lower Columbia.
Outstanding Player: Tyler Bumgartner, of, Bellevue.

It was an unusual summer for USA Baseball's Collegiate National Team, but largely a successful one.

Team USA's summer tour was short and sweet, featuring no trials, no international travel and no major tournaments. The highlight of the summer schedule was the 38th series against a team of Japanese collegiate all-stars, which is now a bi-annual event. Team USA won the five-game series 3-1-1, capping an 11-2-1 summer campaign that ended at TD Ameritrade Park Omaha.

"It was a great success to win the Japan series," said Eric Campbell, USA Baseball's general manager of national teams. "Tim (Jamieson) and his staff were willing to do it with no trials, and they got the team ready to play. The ultimate goal is to win the Japan series, and we did that . . . I'm just really proud of this team. They did a great job—we had a great staff, great team. We were just so different this year; it was a short tour, but I think these guys all will have great memories from this summer."

It wasn't easy for Missouri's Jamieson, who served as Team USA's head coach this summer, and his staff to get the team ready to face Japan in a short period of time. With no trials, the team convened on June 22 for a day of practice in Keene, N.H., and its tour through the New England Collegiate League was set to begin the next day. At that point, 10 of the 19 players who had been given official roster spots were still at the College World Series. Several key players, like Team USA veterans Nolan Fontana and Brian Johnson of Florida, played deep into the CWS, so more than a dozen alternates logged playing time at various points of the short schedule.

Some alternates, like Oral Roberts' undrafted senior Chris Elder (.300/.397/.380 in 14 games), made the most of their opportunities and became fixtures on the team. Elder was signed as a free agent by the Royals at the end of the summer, and another undrafted senior—San Francisco third baseman Stephen Yarrow (.286/.400/.524 in six games)—signed as a free agent with the Giants.

"We had so many alternate-type guys in the camp, we wanted to throw a bone to those guys a little bit," Campbell said. "We had a lot of guys decline (invitations), but we ended up with some great stories at the end. To have Stephen Yarrow come in and help us, and not get offered a final slot, but he knew his ultimate goal was playing pro baseball—that was one of the great stories of our summer. Chris Elder ended up making our club, got some great at-bats and signed with the Royals at the end of our tour. So there were some great stories."

And it proved to be a very resilient team. USA had to come from behind in all three of its victories against Japan, highlighted by the series opener,

COLLEGIATE NATIONAL TEAM STATS

Year indicates 2010-11 class standing

PLAYER, POS.	YEAR	SCHOOL	AVG	OBP	SLG	G	AB	R	H	2B	3B	HR	RBI	BB	SO	SB
Ronnie Freeman, c	So.	Kennesaw State	.500	.583	.500	6	10	4	5	0	0	0	0	1	2	0
Brian Johnson, 1b/dh	So.	Florida	.417	.533	1.167	4	12	4	5	0	0	3	5	3	2	0
Josh Elander, c	So.	Texas Christian	.327	.421	.510	14	49	7	16	5	2	0	7	6	9	2
Deven Marrero, ss	So.	Arizona State	.322	.385	.441	14	59	9	19	5	1	0	14	6	13	6
Tyler Naquin, rf	So.	Texas A&M	.321	.373	.547	12	53	11	17	4	1	2	10	5	13	5
Michael Lorenzen, cf	Fr.	CS Fullerton	.317	.440	.512	14	41	11	13	3	1	1	10	6	10	5
Chris Elder, of	Sr.	Oral Roberts	.300	.397	.380	14	50	9	15	4	0	0	5	5	6	5
Stephen Yarrow, 1b	Sr.	San Francisco	.386	.400	.524	6	21	3	6	3	1	0	3	4	5	1
Dominic Ficociello, 1b	Fr.	Arkansas	.283	.346	.370	13	46	7	13	4	0	0	9	5	10	5
David Lyon, c	Jr.	Kent State	.263	.364	.368	10	19	3	5	2	0	0	1	3	7	1
Matt Reynolds, 3b	So.	Arkansas	.227	.292	.227	6	22	3	5	0	0	0	2	2	5	3
Erich Weiss, 3b	Fr.	Texas	.161	.308	.226	12	31	5	5	2	0	0	5	4	11	0
L.J. Mazzilli, 2b	So.	Connecticut	.143	.250	.190	6	21	3	3	1	0	0	2	1	5	2
Nolan Fontana, 2b	So.	Florida	.125	.348	.125	5	16	4	2	0	0	0	0	2	5	2

PITCHER, POS.	YEAR	SCHOOL	W	L	ERA	G	GS	SV	IP	H	R	ER	BB	SO	AVG
Eric Anderson, rhp	So.	Missouri	2	0	0.00	2	2	0	12	8	0	0	2	7	.195
Marcus Stroman, rhp	So.	Duke	0	0	0.00	7	0	4	8	0	0	0	1	17	.000
Branden Kline, rhp	So.	Virginia	0	0	0.00	3	0	0	4	2	0	0	1	3	.154
Michael Wacha, rhp	So.	Texas A&M	1	0	0.79	2	2	0	11	7	5	1	3	12	.167
Ryne Stanek, rhp	Fr.	Arkansas	1	0	1.00	2	1	0	9	13	1	1	1	12	.361
Andrew Mitchell, rhp	Fr.	Texas Christian	2	0	1.08	7	0	0	8	5	1	1	8	13	.167
Hoby Milner, lhp	So.	Texas	1	0	1.35	6	0	0	7	5	1	1	2	5	.238
Matt Boyd, lhp	So.	Oregon State	1	0	1.42	5	0	0	6	8	4	1	1	8	.276
Cory Knebel, rhp	Fr.	Texas	0	0	1.80	5	0	0	5	6	1	1	1	5	.333
Brady Rogers, rhp	So.	Arizona State	2	0	2.08	3	3	0	17	9	5	4	3	8	.158
Kevin Gausman, rhp	Fr.	Louisiana State	0	0	2.08	2	2	0	9	5	2	2	3	9	.161
D.J. Baxendale, rhp	So.	Arkansas	0	1	3.38	3	3	0	13	12	11	5	4	12	.245
Mark Appel, rhp	So.	Stanford	0	0	5.00	5	1	1	9	7	6	5	2	11	.194

when the Americans overcame a 6-2 deficit with five runs in the seventh inning. Dominic Ficociello (Arkansas) tied that game with a two-run single, then scored the winning run on a single by Elder and an error. Closer Marcus Stroman (Duke), the de facto MVP of the Japan series, extracted USA from an eighth-inning jam en route to the save. He worked 4 1/3 scoreless innings over three appearances against Japan, finishing the summer with a 0.00 ERA, 17 strikeouts and one walk in eight innings.

As usual, pitching was Team USA's strength. It posted a 1.73 team ERA and a 127-33 strikeout-walk mark in 125 innings. Arizona State's Brady Rodgers (2-0, 2.08), Texas A&M's Michael Wacha (1-0, 0.79), Louisiana State's Kevin Gausman (0-0, 2.08) and Missouri's Eric Anderson (2-0, 0.00) came up big in starting roles, though Anderson did not make the final roster for the Japan series. Branden Kline (Virginia), Andrew Mitchell (Texas Christian), Hoby Milner (Texas), Corey Knebel (Texas), Mark Appel (Stanford), Matt Boyd (Oregon State) and Johnson joined Stroman in a stellar, overpowering bullpen.

The lineup took some time to gel, but wound up holding its own. Texas A&M's Tyler Naquin (.321 with two homers and 10 RBIs) and Cal State Fullerton's Michael Lorenzen (.317, one homer, 10 RBIs) helped anchor the lineup and brought incredible arm strength to the outfield. Arizona State's Devn Marrero (.322, 14 RBIs) came up with a number of big hits, and Texas Christian's Josh Elander (.327/.421/.510) emerged as a physical presence in the lineup while also handling the bulk of the catching. Elander has caught sparingly over two years at TCU, but Horned Frogs coach Jim Schlossnagle assured Team USA that he could handle the catching duties—and it became imperative for him to do so after Florida catcher Mike Zunino backed out of playing for the national team.

Harwich Wins Cape Title

The Harwich Mariners swept the Falmouth Commodores in the Cape Cod League championship series to capture their second league title in four years.

The Mariners won the decisive game, 7-5, via gutsy relief efforts and timely hitting. With the score tied at five apiece in the seventh inning, starting pitcher and No. 3 hitter Jake Davies, a rising senior at Georgia Tech, doubled in two runs to put Harwich ahead for good. Davies had three hits in the game and hit .370 during the postseason.

On the mound, Davies allowed four runs (one

earned) in two innings before handing the game over to Mississippi State's Caleb Reed. Reed, Grant Gordon (Missouri State), Blake Hauser (Virginia Commonwealth), and Chris Overman (N.C. State) stifled the Commodore bats, yielding one run the rest of the game. Gordon earned the win while Overman recorded his third save of the postseason. A rising junior, Overman did not allow a run in 34 innings this summer.

The middle of the Mariners lineup provided the bulk of their offense, combining to knock in five runs on nine hits. In addition to Davies, series and team MVP Mike Garza (Georgetown) had three hits, Austin Wilson (Stanford) added two, and John Wooten (East Carolina) hit a home run and drove in three.

Harwich dropped the first game of the playoffs to Brewster, but rattled off six straight wins to finish on top. In Game One of the title series, Garza had a pair of base hits and Hauser worked three innings and struck out five in relief.

SUMMER LEAGUE ROUNDUP

■ After cruising through the first six games of the National Baseball Congress World Series without a defeat, the Santa Barbara Foresters claimed their third championship in five years by knocking off the Kenai Peninsula Oilers, 1-0, in an unusual pitchers duel in Wichita, Kan.

Wichita State righthander Mitch Mormann allowed just four hits over seven innings for the championship victory, and Spencer Messmore (Cal State Bakersfield) earned the save with two spotless innings of relief.

"We won big in this tournament and we won small, like tonight, 1-0," Santa Barbara coach Bill Pintard told the Wichita Eagle following the victory. "We finished undefeated. It's really sweet."

Alaska League champion Kenai entered the final with one defeat in the double-elimnation event and would have needed to beat Santa Barbara twice to win the title. With a taxed pitching staff that faced the possibility of playing four games in three days, Kenai coach Dennis Machado decided to use his entire staff against the Foresters. Kenai used eight pitchers in the defeat, none tossing more than one inning.

"Our approach to today's game was kind of out of necessity," Machado told the Wichita Eagle. "We didn't have a starter to go in any of these games today, so we have a lot of guys in the bullpen who are very capable.

"What we decided to do was run one guy out for three outs at a time. Their whole focus was three outs. They did a great job holding the Foresters down to four hits."

The Haysville Heat and St. Joseph's Mustangs, champions of the Jayhawk and MINK League, respectively, also made appearances in the NBC World Series. Haysville went 5-2 and advanced to the final six. The Mustangs finished the tournament with a 2-2 record.

COLLEGE SUMMER LEAGUES

For players who played for multiple teams:
1: Stats with first team 2: Stats with second team
3: Stats with third team T: combined stats

CAPE COD LEAGUE

EAST	W	L	T	PCT	PTS
Orleans	24	17	3	.545	51
Harwich	24	19	1	.545	49
Brewster	20	20	4	.455	44
Yarmouth-Dennis	19	21	4	.432	42
Chatham	15	28	1	.341	31

WEST	W	L	T	PCT	PTS
Hyannis	29	15	0	.659	58
Wareham	23	21	0	.523	46
Bourne	22	20	2	.500	46
Falmouth	19	25	0	.432	38
Cotuit	14	30	0	.318	28

PLAYOFFS: Semifinals: Harwich defeated Yarmouth-Dennis 2-0 and Falmouth defeated Wareham 2-0 in best-of-three series. **Finals:** Harwich defeated Falmouth 2-0 in best-of-three series.

TOP 30 PROSPECTS: 1. Deven Marrero, ss, Cotuit (Jr., Arizona State). 2. Chris Beck, rhp, Cotuit (Jr., Georgia Southern). 3. Ryne Stanek, rhp, Bourne (So., Arkansas). 4. Brian Johnson, 1b/lhp, Yarmouth-Dennis (Jr., Florida). 5. John Sims, rhp, Falmouth (So., Rice). 6. Victor Roache, of, Cotuit (Jr., Georgia Southern). 7. Colin Moran, 3b, Bourne (So., North Carolina). 8. Kyle Zimmer, rhp, Cotuit (Jr., San Francisco). 9. Ryan Eades, rhp, Bourne (So., Louisiana State). 10. Travis Janikowski, of, Bourne (Jr., Stony Brook). 11. Richie Schaffer, 1b/3b, Chatham (Jr., Clemson). 12. Stephen Piscotty, 3b/1b/of, Yarmouth-Dennis (Jr., Stanford). 13. Brandon Thomas, of, Wareham (Jr., Georgia Tech). 14. Jason Monda, of, Brewster (So., Washington State). 15. Konner Wade, rhp, Wareham (So., Arizona). 16. J.T. Chargois, rhp, Brewster (Jr., Rice). 17. Andrew Heaney, lhp, Falmouth (Jr., Oklahoma State). 18. Bobby Wahl, rhp, Cotuit (So., Mississippi). 19. Josh Conway, rhp, Bourne (Jr., Coastal Carolina). 20. Buck Farmer, rhp, Chatham (Jr., Georgia Tech). 21. Carter Capps, rhp, Harwich (SIGNED: Mariners). 22. Kyle Hansen, rhp, Yarmouth-Dennis (Jr., St. John's). 23. Jack Armstrong, rhp, Yarmouth-Dennis (SIGNED: Astros). 24. Adam Brett Walker, of/1b, Hyannis (Jr., Jacksonville). 25. Austin Wilson, of, Harwich (So., Stanford). 26. James Ramsey, of, Yarmouth-Dennis (Sr., Florida State). 27. Jeremy Baltz, of, Falmouth (Jr., St. John's). 28. Dylan Floro, rhp, Hyannis (Jr., Cal State Fullerton). 29. Dane Phillips, c/1b/of, Chatham (Jr., Arkansas). 30. Andrew Toles, of, Brewster (So., Tennessee)

INDIVIDUAL BATTING LEADERS
(MINIMUM 2.7 PLATE APPEARANCES PER TEAM GAME)

	AVG	G	AB	R	H	HR	RBI
Phillips, Dane, Chatham	.349	41	129	23	45	4	34
Piscotty, Stephen, Yarmouth-Dennis	.349	29	106	20	37	3	21
Duffy, Matt, Orleans	.346	39	133	16	46	1	16
Vick, Logan, Cotuit	.337	37	101	13	34	0	9
Monda, Jason, Brewster	.333	32	123	13	41	1	16
Janikowski, Travis, Bourne	.329	44	173	31	57	0	22
Palka, Daniel, Wareham	.327	35	110	11	36	1	13
Baltz, Jeremy, Falmouth	.321	42	140	21	45	2	23
Roache, Victor, Cotuit	.316	42	136	29	43	6	28
Coyle, Tommy, Bourne	.315	29	108	12	34	1	16

INDIVIDUAL PITCHING LEADERS
(MINIMUM 0.8 INNINGS PITCHED PER TEAM GAME)

	W	L	ERA	IP	H	BB	SO
Firth, Scott, Hyannis	3	0	1.15	39	28	23	30
Bircher, Joe, Falmouth	2	2	1.44	44	35	9	48
Amlung, Justin, Wareham	3	1	1.76	41	22	13	29
Bucciferro, Tony, Brewster	1	4	1.90	47	34	8	37
Johnson, Tyler, Orleans	4	1	2.04	40	33	11	17
Beck, Chris, Cotuit	2	3	2.12	51	48	13	41
Hagan, Sean, Falmouth	1	3	2.27	36	25	9	14
DeNato, Joey, Yarmouth-Dennis	4	0	2.38	42	36	18	25
Aizenstadt, Andrew, Falmouth	2	1	2.46	37	34	11	26
Bard, Luke, Brewster	2	2	2.61	41	34	21	32

BOURNE

	AVG	AB	R	H	2B	3B	HR	RBI	SB
Barrett, Jake	.500	2	1	1	1	0	0	0	0
Martinez, Drew	.359	145	26	52	2	0	1	18	22
Oh, Danny	.299	97	17	29	7	1	0	16	3
Featherston, Taylor	.267	30	2	8	2	0	0	3	1
Ard, Taylor	.263	118	13	31	9	0	1	14	6
Walla, Cohl	.259	85	9	22	5	0	0	7	6

	AVG	AB	R	H	2B	3B	HR	RBI	SB
Norfork, Khayyan	.258	31	7	8	2	0	0	2	6
Dowd, Mike	.244	41	2	10	1	0	0	2	6
1 Andreoli, John	.240	25	4	6	3	0	0	2	5
T Andreoli, John	.243	70	10	17	5	0	0	6	11
Melendres, Nathan	.225	71	7	16	3	1	1	5	13
Berti, Jon	.225	102	15	23	5	0	0	9	13
Jones, Derek	.211	90	9	19	5	1	0	12	3
Burns, Andy	.211	152	19	32	6	1	1	18	25
Singer, Kirk	.206	107	12	22	2	1	1	7	3

	W	L	ERA	G	SV	IP	H	BB	SO
Bladel, Johnny	0	0	0.00	3	0	3	1	0	3
Eades, Ryan	3	0	0.84	7	0	32	19	7	23
Orlan, R.C.	0	0	1.50	11	0	18	8	9	21
Conway, Josh	2	0	1.88	6	0	29	24	10	28
Farrell, John	1	1	2.30	12	0	16	13	6	22
Connolly, Ryan	3	2	2.70	18	0	30	26	5	29
Alvarez, R.J.	0	2	2.70	16	7	17	10	7	22
Smith, Slade	1	4	2.86	16	0	35	37	7	21
Ward, Brian	2	1	3.18	4	0	17	14	8	13
Brandt, Kevin	1	1	3.24	7	0	33	38	4	30
Pickering, Chris	1	3	3.32	8	0	38	45	7	23
Melotakis, Mason	1	1	3.38	14	0	19	18	2	22
Stanek, Ryne	2	1	4.50	3	0	16	15	4	16
Norris, Logan	1	2	4.50	3	0	10	10	4	5
Green, Chad	0	1	6.85	11	0	22	43	9	10

BREWSTER

	AVG	AB	R	H	2B	3B	HR	RBI	SB
Soule, Billy	.500	4	0	2	0	0	0	0	0
Monda, Jason	.333	123	13	41	4	4	1	16	13
Toles, Andrew	.302	149	16	45	4	3	0	9	14
Altobelli, J.J.	.295	105	14	31	3	1	0	8	3
Jones, Ryan	.283	138	16	39	6	0	0	11	7
Hayes, Danny	.262	42	6	11	2	0	0	1	1
Nivins, Tanner	.259	147	23	38	10	1	5	20	5
Steckenrider, Drew	.250	4	0	1	0	0	0	0	0
Tam Sing, Trace	.242	66	9	16	3	0	1	5	5
Ard, Taylor	.231	121	14	28	5	1	4	16	1
Mayfield, Jack	.225	71	9	16	4	0	1	4	1
Anselment, Chase	.219	96	11	21	4	0	1	8	0
Tkowski, Steve	.205	44	7	9	1	0	1	5	1
Rodriguez, Devon	.182	88	2	16	2	0	0	7	2
Chargois, J.T.	.091	22	0	2	0	0	0	3	0
Bard, Luke	.000	0	1	0	0	0	0	0	0
Langfield, Dan	.000	1	0	0	0	0	0	0	0
Snell, Jeff	.000	0	0	0	0	0	0	0	0

	W	L	ERA	G	SV	IP	H	BB	SO
Chargois, J.T.	0	0	0.43	17	7	21	16	4	20
Biagini, Joe	0	1	1.37	16	0	20	17	6	20
Bucciferro, Tony	1	4	1.90	8	0	47	34	8	37
Voth, Austin	0	0	1.98	14	0	27	18	14	30
Love, Brandon	4	1	2.20	10	0	33	21	13	29
Steckenrider, Drew	2	0	2.35	15	2	15	10	13	23
Bard, Luke	2	2	2.61	7	0	41	34	21	32
Griggs, Scott	1	3	3.03	9	0	33	20	29	28
Snell, Jeff	3	1	3.26	17	0	19	16	2	13
Langfield, Dan	1	2	3.86	6	0	28	22	10	26
Lowery, Patrick	3	2	4.05	15	0	40	38	22	29
Garner, Max	2	2	4.07	7	1	24	30	5	17
Soule, Billy	0	1	4.50	14	0	16	15	14	11
Locante, Will	0	0	18.00	2	0	1	0	1	1

CHATHAM

	AVG	AB	R	H	2B	3B	HR	RBI	SB
Jones, Zack	.400	5	1	2	0	0	0	0	0
Phillips, Dane	.349	129	23	45	7	2	4	34	0
Reilly, Sean	.274	62	4	17	1	0	2	3	0
Sever, Joe	.270	174	16	47	10	0	2	19	4
Shaffer, Richie	.263	137	21	36	11	2	6	22	2
Matthews, Darrell	.250	76	9	19	2	1	0	6	2
Amaral, Beau	.242	95	11	23	3	0	1	5	5
Perez, Stephen	.233	120	12	28	5	0	1	7	10
Bryant, Kris	.223	130	16	29	6	2	3	16	0
Calbick, Alex	.205	122	12	25	2	0	1	11	0

	AVG	AB	R	H	2B	3B	HR	RBI	SB
Blair, Patrick	.184	49	3	9	1	1	0	2	1
Roberts, Matthew	.167	42	5	7	2	0	1	2	0
Gianis, John	.160	50	4	8	1	0	1	4	1
Marzilli, Evan	.159	69	12	11	1	0	0	1	2
Watkins, J.T.	.106	47	6	5	0	0	1	2	0

	W	L	ERA	G	SV	IP	H	BB	SO
Koch, Matthew	1	0	1.19	17	5	23	15	3	22
Bilodeau, Keith	1	1	1.48	5	0	30	25	11	34
Healy, Tucker	0	1	2.08	14	0	17	8	7	27
Penny, Cody	0	0	2.13	10	0	13	12	5	15
Leone, Dominic	2	3	3.15	8	0	40	32	22	40
Cooney, Tim	2	5	3.54	9	0	48	47	8	46
Light, Pat	0	5	3.77	12	0	31	33	10	24
Jones, Zack	1	1	5.23	11	5	10	12	6	15
Gallagher, Chad	3	3	5.27	12	0	27	40	6	13
Farmer, Buck	2	1	5.57	4	0	21	27	4	17
Kime, Dace	1	4	5.91	11	0	43	43	15	34
Munnelly, Chris	1	2	6.75	6	0	24	24	8	16
Jaffe, Eric	1	0	7.94	7	0	6	6	10	6
Gibbs, Jeffrey	0	1	8.44	7	0	11	13	11	8
Marino, Harry	0	1	8.68	12	0	9	15	6	9
Davis, Trae	0	0	9.18	12	0	17	17	16	8

COTUIT

	AVG	AB	R	H	2B	3B	HR	RBI	SB
Vick, Logan	.337	101	13	34	4	5	0	9	6
Marrero, Deven	.326	46	6	15	2	1	0	5	3
Roache, Victor	.316	136	29	43	12	0	6	28	2
Sabol, Stefan	.299	77	11	23	5	0	1	7	0
Mager, Kevin	.284	74	7	21	5	0	0	6	3
Wren, Kyle	.282	131	17	37	4	0	0	8	18
Leyland, Jordan	.275	40	3	11	3	0	0	5	0
Yarbrough, Alex	.268	138	19	37	11	1	3	21	0
Yastrzemski, Michael	.253	75	7	19	4	0	1	12	4
Bratsen, Krey	.250	60	7	15	0	0	0	2	6
Healy, Ryon	.244	82	4	20	2	0	1	8	3
Boss, Torsten	.237	76	5	18	2	2	0	12	2
Johnson, Micah	.212	85	6	18	3	0	0	9	5
Roundtree, Kevin	.211	95	9	20	4	1	0	3	1
Biondi, Patrick	.172	87	10	15	0	0	0	4	12

	W	L	ERA	G	SV	IP	H	BB	SO
Vick, Logan	1	0	0.00	2	0	3	2	1	3
Stiles, Cody	0	0	0.00	4	0	10	5	5	9
Wahl, Bobby	1	1	1.23	6	6	22	15	11	38
Beck, Chris	2	3	2.12	9	0	51	48	13	41
Graveman, Kendall	1	0	2.36	13	0	27	26	15	18
Keudell, Alex	2	2	3.03	10	1	39	36	10	30
Zimmer, Kyle	2	5	3.38	10	1	48	41	14	37
Clevinger, Michael	0	1	3.98	14	1	20	23	8	25
Ziomek, Kevin	2	3	4.36	6	0	21	27	12	16
Fondon, R.J.	2	3	4.40	8	0	47	50	15	33
Kish, Keenan	0	0	4.50	6	0	10	13	5	6
McVay, Mason	1	1	6.43	17	1	21	27	16	11
Fleck, Kaleb	0	1	10.61	5	0	9	14	5	6
Healy, Ryon	0	0	18.00	1	0	1	1	2	2

FALMOUTH

	AVG	AB	R	H	2B	3B	HR	RBI	SB
Baltz, Jeremy	.321	140	21	45	13	0	2	23	1
Ferriter, Billy	.272	114	17	31	2	1	0	7	6
Rodriguez, Jake	.267	131	16	35	7	0	0	10	1
Redman, Reid	.267	30	2	8	1	0	0	0	1
White, Max	.250	108	18	27	4	2	4	22	0
Garcia, Eric	.246	118	16	29	4	0	1	17	10
Barnes, Barrett	.233	120	18	28	8	1	2	12	4
Kieboom, Spencer	.221	113	7	25	3	0	0	9	2
VonTungeln, Kyle	.213	94	11	20	4	0	0	9	4
King, Jared	.202	104	8	21	3	0	1	10	1
Rowland, Shane	.196	51	5	10	2	2	0	2	1
Santigate, R.J.	.125	16	1	2	0	0	0	0	0
Smelter, DeAndre	.000	3	0	0	0	0	0	0	0

	W	L	ERA	G	SV	IP	H	BB	SO
Moore, Ryan	1	0	0.00	1	0	2	0	2	2
Simms, John	0	0	0.00	13	8	19	5	6	29
Koneski, Nate	0	0	1.03	13	0	26	24	6	24
Thornhill, Nathan	2	0	1.11	7	0	24	14	4	18
Easley, Josh	1	1	1.26	11	3	14	11	1	16

	W	L	ERA	G	SV	IP	H	BB	SO
Bircher, Joe	2	2	1.44	8	0	44	35	9	48
Smelter, DeAndre	0	1	2.13	10	0	13	12	5	12
Hagan, Sean	1	3	2.27	7	0	36	25	9	14
Aizenstadt, Andrew	2	1	2.46	8	0	37	34	11	26
Duffey, Tyler	3	3	3.33	10	0	27	26	8	20
Heaney, Andrew	4	4	3.38	8	0	45	39	14	46
Emanuel, Kent	0	4	4.18	5	0	24	30	5	13
Gardeck, Ian	0	1	5.87	9	0	8	4	13	12
Sandefur, Taylor	3	2	6.11	16	0	18	20	10	13
Battipaglia, Jerry	0	2	6.75	7	0	12	17	2	16
Smith, Andrew	0	2	8.00	7	0	9	13	6	9

HARWICH

	AVG	AB	R	H	2B	3B	HR	RBI	SB
Burns, Billy	.329	73	12	24	3	0	0	6	4
Sweeney, Darnell	.282	103	14	29	6	1	0	12	15
Garza, Mike	.254	142	18	36	11	0	1	15	6
Swim, Alex	.253	91	11	23	0	0	0	4	2
Voit, Luke	.250	92	12	23	6	0	3	14	5
Werman, Keith	.250	52	10	13	0	0	0	3	1
Wooten, John	.245	110	15	27	6	2	1	16	3
Henry, Jabari	.241	137	18	33	10	2	4	17	6
Davies, Jake	.241	112	11	27	4	1	1	13	0
Jones, Jacoby	.234	47	6	11	1	1	0	5	5
Nola, Austin	.217	138	17	30	5	1	0	15	8
Wilson, Austin	.204	93	11	19	6	0	1	13	1
Rash, Andrew	.196	51	2	10	2	0	1	6	1
Richardson, Ronnie	.192	120	18	23	3	0	2	11	17

	W	L	ERA	G	SV	IP	H	BB	SO
Enns, Dietrich	3	1	0.65	15	4	28	9	8	18
Wittgren, Nick	3	0	0.95	17	9	19	15	7	29
Firth, Scott	3	0	1.15	8	0	39	28	23	30
Gibson, Ryan	3	0	1.27	11	0	21	13	14	26
Browder, Kolt	0	0	2.25	11	0	12	6	5	15
Floro, Dylan	4	1	2.48	7	1	29	24	13	27
Moscot, Jon	2	3	2.91	8	1	43	40	8	46
Dermody, Matt	1	1	3.00	7	0	24	23	10	21
Masek, Trey	2	1	3.32	4	0	19	20	7	16
McArdle, Dean	2	1	3.41	7	0	32	28	8	18
Kraus, Kyle	3	1	3.60	10	0	20	24	1	13
Ruth, Eric	1	0	3.71	12	0	17	18	5	8
Flemer, Matthew	0	2	3.86	7	0	9	8	6	5
Roberts, Corey	1	1	3.96	7	0	25	23	6	22
Cooper, Zach	0	1	4.40	7	0	14	17	5	13

HYANNIS

	AVG	AB	R	H	2B	3B	HR	RBI	SB
Rickard, Joey	.311	148	23	46	6	3	0	17	14
Gulbransen, Dan	.303	122	15	37	7	1	1	6	7
Elkins, Austin	.284	88	10	25	6	0	2	16	3
Frost, John	.282	78	9	22	3	0	0	6	1
Stamets, Eric	.277	159	21	44	2	0	0	12	11
McGruder, Jamodrick	.263	19	4	5	0	0	0	1	5
Plawecki, Kevin	.262	130	13	34	5	0	1	15	6
Towey, Cal	.260	77	8	20	2	1	0	8	7
Vincej, Zach	.247	81	11	20	3	0	0	6	5
Pedroza, Richie	.240	50	4	12	1	0	0	1	2
Krist, Chadd	.237	76	5	18	4	1	0	11	2
Walker, Adam	.216	134	15	29	4	0	4	17	8
DeMichele, Joey	.210	105	16	22	5	1	2	14	4
Gonzalez, Justin	.179	67	13	12	2	2	2	6	3

	W	L	ERA	G	SV	IP	H	BB	SO
Enns, Dietrich	3	1	0.65	15	4	28	9	8	18
Wittgren, Nick	3	0	0.95	17	9	19	15	7	29
Firth, Scott	3	0	1.15	8	0	39	28	23	30
Gibson, Ryan	3	0	1.27	11	0	21	13	14	26
Browder, Kolt	0	0	2.25	11	0	12	6	5	15
Floro, Dylan	4	1	2.48	7	1	29	24	13	27
Moscot, Jon	2	3	2.91	8	1	43	40	8	46
Dermody, Matt	1	1	3.00	7	0	24	23	10	21
Masek, Trey	2	1	3.32	4	0	19	20	7	16
McArdle, Dean	2	1	3.41	7	0	32	28	8	18
Kraus, Kyle	3	1	3.60	10	0	20	24	1	13
Ruth, Eric	1	0	3.71	12	0	17	18	5	8
Flemer, Matthew	0	2	3.86	7	0	9	8	6	5
Roberts, Corey	1	1	3.96	7	0	25	23	6	22
Cooper, Zach	0	1	4.40	7	0	14	17	5	13

COLLEGE

ORLEANS

	AVG	AB	R	H	2B	3B	HR	RBI	SB
Duffy, Matt	.346	133	16	46	8	0	1	16	7
Gragnani, Reed	.311	74	13	23	6	1	1	10	8
Gomez, Anthony	.292	89	13	26	1	0	2	10	6
Waldrip, Ben	.276	134	11	37	4	0	6	23	1
Aplin, Andrew	.263	95	19	25	7	1	3	16	7
Shaeffer, Ronnie	.250	64	8	16	2	0	1	4	0
Tissenbaum, Maxx	.229	96	16	22	3	0	3	17	2
Koch, Matt	.222	45	10	10	2	0	1	4	1
Stewart, Jake	.210	81	12	17	4	2	1	8	4
Senay, Tarran	.205	73	14	15	3	0	3	8	0
Boyd, Jayce	.204	108	17	22	7	0	2	16	1
Flores, Rudy	.176	68	3	12	3	0	1	4	1
Lowenstein, Matt	.143	63	12	9	0	0	0	2	2

	W	L	ERA	G	SV	IP	H	BB	SO
Gott, Trevor	0	0	1.29	18	12	21	14	4	26
Boyd, Matt	0	0	1.71	8	0	21	16	8	15
Johnson, Tyler	4	1	2.04	10	0	40	33	11	17
Brebbia, John	2	2	2.43	9	0	30	23	9	26
Heyer, Kurt	2	0	2.70	10	1	27	26	8	23
Long, Kenny	2	2	3.33	19	0	24	21	8	30
Hauschild, Mike	3	1	3.62	11	1	37	33	7	31
Gebler, Tyler	1	1	3.64	12	1	30	41	3	19
Wheeler, Jason	3	5	4.38	8	0	37	43	15	25
Ottoson, Kyle	1	0	5.87	5	0	8	8	3	7
Butler, Patrick	0	0	7.98	9	0	15	23	8	7
Flemer, Matthew	0	2	3.86	7	0	9	8	6	5
Roberts, Corey	1	1	3.96	7	0	25	23	6	22
Cooper, Zach	0	1	4.40	7	0	14	17	5	13

WAREHAM

	AVG	AB	R	H	2B	3B	HR	RBI	SB
Palka, Daniel	.327	110	11	36	6	0	1	13	0
Refsnyder, Robert	.308	133	17	41	9	4	0	11	13
Muncy, Max	.282	156	17	44	6	0	1	23	6
Thomas, Brandon	.273	132	18	36	9	3	0	3	12
Field, Johnny	.261	119	20	31	7	1	2	18	6
2 Andreoli, John	.255	110	15	28	2	0	0	7	9
Mazzilli, L.J.	.223	112	13	25	6	0	0	7	5
Reynolds, Jeff	.222	90	6	20	5	0	0	9	0
Bradford, C.T.	.200	65	6	13	1	2	0	8	2
Carmona, William	.196	97	11	19	2	0	2	13	6
Dennis, Derek	.194	36	4	7	0	0	0	5	2
Ross, Tyler	.168	95	6	16	1	0	0	10	0
Hyde, Mott	.151	93	7	14	3	1	0	2	7
Fischer, Michael	.133	15	3	2	0	0	0	1	0

	W	L	ERA	G	SV	IP	H	BB	SO
Wade, Konner	1	1	1.33	17	12	20	13	6	23
Amlung, Justin	3	1	1.76	7	0	41	22	13	29
Boyd, Jake	0	0	2.25	1	0	4	4	1	5
Astin, Barrett	2	1	2.63	8	0	27	24	8	15
Perakslis, Stephen	0	1	2.70	10	1	17	9	6	17
Turley, Joshua	4	2	2.78	7	0	36	27	8	27
Feehan, Daniel	1	1	2.78	22	4	23	22	11	18
Flynn, Joseph	0	0	3.09	12	0	12	11	5	4
Brosnahan, Bobby	3	3	3.94	8	0	30	26	12	24
Suter, Brent	2	3	3.96	10	0	39	36	11	30
Newman, Dillon	2	1	4.33	15	0	27	31	6	26
Farrell, Luke	4	4	4.46	8	0	36	35	25	33
Fischer, David	0	0	4.50	9	0	16	13	8	18
Grimes, Matthew	0	2	5.63	7	0	32	40	13	20
Bradford, C.T.	0	0	6.75	3	0	4	2	2	8
Flett, Andy	1	1	6.75	10	0	11	9	9	11
Palka, Daniel	0		18.00	1	0	1	3	2	1

YARMOUTH-DENNIS

	AVG	AB	R	H	2B	3B	HR	RBI	SB
Piscotty, Stephen	.349	106	20	37	8	0	3	21	1
Reynolds, Matt	.322	87	7	28	7	0	2	20	5
Ramsey, James	.313	112	29	35	5	3	6	17	7
Zunino, Michael	.303	33	5	10	2	0	0	3	0
Keefer, Cody	.282	110	16	31	4	1	1	13	6
Johnson, Brian	.280	50	6	14	2	0	2	14	0
Katz, Mason	.272	136	24	37	9	1	3	18	5
Taylor, Chris	.270	89	12	24	8	1	0	11	5
Melchionda, Anthony	.259	81	7	21	3	0	0	5	1
Lamb, Jacob	.253	87	11	22	5	0	0	10	1
Hanover, Tyler	.245	94	12	23	4	1	0	11	3
Harrell, Connor	.244	45	5	11	2	1	0	2	4
ONeill, Michael	.219	64	3	14	3	0	0	6	4
Wessinger, Matt	.218	124	14	27	6	0	0	5	11
Chung, Derrick	.167	54	9	9	2	0	0	5	2
Pickar, Bennett	.158	38	1	6	1	0	0	1	3

	W	L	ERA	G	SV	IP	H	BB	SO
Reckling, Matt	0	2	0.87	9	0	10	3	11	16
Piscotty, Stephen	0	1	1.93	5	0	5	4	3	5
DeNato, Joey	4	0	2.04	11	0	40	32	18	24
Appel, Mark	0	1	2.25	2	0	12	7	1	15
Lomangino, James	2	0	2.39	7	0	26	24	6	12
Gonzalez, Alex	2	4	3.08	7	0	38	39	17	25
Hansen, Kyle	0	0	3.52	13	4	23	19	10	28
Thurman, Andrew	3	2	3.82	10	0	33	36	12	22
Carasiti, Matt	0	0	3.92	16	3	21	16	13	20
Vanegas, A.J.	0	1	4.13	8	0	24	22	15	20
Johnson, Brian	2	0	4.30	3	0	15	14	4	19
Gibson, Daniel	1	1	4.42	8	1	18	21	7	23
Armstrong, Jack	1	1	4.60	5	0	16	15	5	14
Rogers, Joe	0	2	5.19	8	0	17	23	7	20
Weiss, Zack	1	1	5.23	8	0	31	35	14	15
Benincasa, Robert	1	3	5.65	11	0	14	21	9	12

ALASKA LEAGUE

	W	L	PCT	GB
Kenai Peninsula Oilers	24	12	.667	—
Mat-Su Miners	21	15	.583	3
Anchorage Glacier Pilots	17	19	.472	7
Anchorage Bucs	16	20	.444	8
Alaska Fire	12	24	.333	12

TOP 10 PROSPECTS: 1. Aaron Judge, of, Anchorage Glacier Pilots (So., Fresno State). 2. Patrick Wisdom, 3b, Kenai Peninsula (Jr., St. Mary's). 3. Kyle Finnegan, rhp, Anchorage Bucs (So., Texas State). 4. Jordan Mills, lhp, Kenai Peninsula (So., St. Mary's). 5. Jon Maciel, rhp, Kenai Peninsula (So., Long Beach State). 6. Tanner Rust, of/if, Kenai Peninsula (So., New Mexico State). 7. Ben Griset, lhp, Kenai Peninsula (So., St. Mary's). 8. Conner Kendrick, lhp, Anchorage Bucs (So., Georgia Tech). 9. Cameron McVey, rhp, Kenai Peninsula (SIGNED: Giants). 10. Mike Miller, ss, Kenai Peninsula (Sr., Cal Poly).

INDIVIDUAL BATTING LEADERS
(MINIMUM 3 PLATE APPEARANCES PER TEAM GAME)

	AVG	PA	R	H	2B	3B	HR	RBI	SB
Miller, Mike, Oilers	.364	150	25	44	8	3	1	19	9
Harjung, Matthew, Bucs	.327	122	8	34	2	0	0	8	1
Hohl, Brady, Pilots	.316	143	17	37	5	0	1	14	14
Channing, Troy, Oilers	.306	152	14	38	9	0	4	19	2
Branca, Stephen, Miners	.299	145	14	38	7	2	1	21	4
Zier, Tim, Miners	.295	115	10	31	1	0	0	14	4
Valdez, Jake, Bucs	.292	139	17	31	2	1	0	15	8
Mallory, Chris, Oilers	.290	161	20	40	8	1	1	18	2
Judge, Aaron, Pilots	.289	121	19	28	8	2	0	11	6

INDIVIDUAL PITCHING LEADERS
(MINIMUM 0.9 INNINGS PITCHED PER TEAM GAME)

	W	L	ERA	G	SV	IP	ER	BB	SO
Anderson, Mark, Miners	4	1	1.03	8	0	35	4	11	14
Mills, Jordan, Oilers	5	1	1.24	7	0	36	5	21	29
Maciel, John, Oilers	2	1	1.40	6	0	39	6	9	16
Belleque, Christian, Pilots	2	1	1.62	7	0	33	6	7	24
Gibson, David, Miners	4	1	2.03	8	0	40	9	16	32
Linehan, Tyler, Pilots	2	1	2.06	8	0	44	10	27	39
Salles, J.D., Miners	3	2	2.41	12	0	34	9	6	26
Gillies, Charlie, Fire	4	1	2.44	8	0	55	15	26	50
Asakura, Gabriel, Oilers	1	1	2.70	7	0	33	10	15	26
Work, Andrew, Fire	0	5	3.18	8	0	45	16	18	26

ATLANTIC COLLEGIATE LEAGUE

WOLFF

	W	L	PCT	GB
Jersey Pilots	24	10	.706	—
Lehigh Valley Catz	21	17	.553	5
Quakertown Blazers	18	20	.474	8
North Jersey Eagles	12	25	.324	13½

KAISER	W	L	PCT	GB
Staten Island Tide	21	14	.600	—
New York Atlantics	18	19	.486	4
Long Island Collegians	13	22	.371	8
HAMPTON	**W**	**L**	**PCT**	**GB**
Westhampton Aviators	21	19	.525	—
Southampton Breakers	21	19	.525	—
Sag Harbor Whalers	20	20	.500	1
North Fork Ospreys	20	20	.500	1
Riverhead Tomcats	18	22	.450	3

PLAYOFFS: Staten Island defeated Westhampton in a one-game championship.

TOP 10 PROSPECTS: 1. Brandon Kuter, rhp, Westhampton (Jr., George Mason). 2. Charlie Curl, 2b/ss/of, Sag Harbor (So., Texas A&M). 3. Kevin McCarthy, rhp, Sag Harbor (So., Marist). 4. Jordan Patterson, 1b/lhp, Westhampton (So., South Alabama). 5. Lou Trivino, rhp, Quakertown (So., Slippery Rock, Pa.). 6. Matt Carroll, 1b, North Fork (So., San Jose State). 7. Kevin Heller, of, Westhampton (Sr., Amherst, Mass.). 8. Stuart Turner, c, Southampton (So., LSU-Eunice JC). 9. Mike Ahmed, if/rhp, Westhampton (So., Holy Cross). 10. Matt Soren, rhp, New York (Jr., Delaware).

INDIVIDUAL BATTING LEADERS
(MINIMUM 74 PLATE APPEARANCES)

	AVG	AB	R	H	2B	3B	HR	RBI	SB
Maruri, Alex, New York	.410	83	22	34	11	1	0	14	1
Knabe, Henry, Jersey	.364	99	20	36	8	1	2	21	7
Colon, Alexi, Jersey	.357	84	16	30	7	1	4	21	7
Brockett, Ryan, North Fork	.356	118	19	42	7	1	0	14	13
Kelly, Martin, North Jersey	.354	99	21	35	5	1	1	12	9
Schwindel, Frank, Riverhead	.349	109	18	38	6	0	6	36	0
Kanzler, Jason, Staten Island	.333	129	30	43	6	4	5	24	17
Glozzy, Scott, Jersey	.333	63	15	21	1	0	2	13	1
Selden, Chris, Staten Island	.328	128	23	42	5	0	1	21	12
Romano, Eric, Riverhead	.327	98	19	32	5	0	1	11	3

INDIVIDUAL PITCHING LEADERS
(MINIMUM 35 INNINGS)

	W	L	ERA	G	SV	IP	H	BB	SO
Phelan, Chris, Southhampton	4	0	0.68	5	0	40	37	4	26
McCarthy, Kevin, Sag Harbor	3	2	1.38	7	0	46	29	12	34
Nichols, Christopher, Lehigh Valley	4	3	1.50	10	0	54	42	11	27
Corsi, Rob, Jersey	5	2	1.54	9	0	47	37	16	56
Black, Taylor, Westhampton	4	2	1.70	7	0	42	27	12	40
Angelucci, Ray, Westhampton	2	1	1.74	6	0	41	28	11	27
Melchiorre, Steven, Jersey	5	1	2.00	7	0	36	22	10	38
Lubreski, Ryan, Lehigh Valley	2	3	2.14	9	0	42	37	17	37
Trivino, Lou, Quakertown	4	2	2.20	10	0	45	35	29	50
Casey, Ryan, North Jersey	2	3	2.40	17	1	49	51	14	28

CAL RIPKEN COLLEGIATE LEAGUE

	W	L	PCT	GB
Bethesda Big Train	33	9	.786	—
Youse's Orioles	24	16	.600	8
Southern Maryland Nationals	24	16	.600	8
Baltimore Redbirds	23	19	.548	10
Vienna River Dogs	18	23	.439	14½
Rockville Express	17	24	.415	15½
Alexandria Aces	16	25	.390	16½
Herndon Braves	16	26	.381	17
Silver Spring-Takoma T-Bolts	13	26	.333	18½

PLAYOFFS: Bethesda defeated Baltimore in the championship of a four-team, double-elimination tournament.

TOP 10 PROSPECTS: 1. K.J. Hockaday, 3b/of, Youse's Orioles (Fr., Maryland). 2. Ryan Farrar, lhp, Youse's Orioles (Jr., Virginia Commonwealth). 3. Austin Urban, rhp, Youse's Orioles, (SIGNED: Cubs). 4. Hunter Renfroe, c/rhp, Bethesda, (So., Mississippi State). 5. Sander Beck, rhp, Youse's Orioles (Sr., Maryland). 6. Tucker Donahue, rhp, Bethesda (Sr., Stetson). 7. Ben Lively, rhp, Youse's Orioles (So., Central Florida). 8. Matt Bowman, rhp, Bethesda (Jr., Princeton). 9. Sean Godfrey, of, Southern Maryland (So., Ball State). 10. Adam Barry, 3b, Bethesda (Sr., Cal State Northridge).

INDIVIDUAL BATTING LEADERS
(MINIMUM 2.7 PLATE APPEARANCES PER TEAM GAME)

	AVG	AB	R	H	2B	3B	HR	RBI	SB
Berry, Adam, Bethesda	.414	162	38	67	14	3	1	43	3
Ibanez, Angel, Rockville	.391	156	22	61	9	1	0	19	21
Eggleston, Brian, Herndon	.379	124	16	47	7	1	1	11	2
Gerstenslager, Bill, T-Bolts	.374	139	26	52	8	1	5	27	1

Morley, Jacob, Vienna	.368	136	18	50	6	1	5	19	3
Godfrey, Sean, S. Maryland	.357	143	28	51	9	3	1	18	20
McInturff, Cole, Vienna	.357	129	18	46	4	0	2	11	9
Smucker, Jordon, Herndon	.355	169	25	60	4	3	1	20	4
Jensen, Cory, Baltimore	.339	124	27	42	11	0	1	14	15
Ayers, Chris, Youse's	.328	116	17	38	8	0	0	20	1

INDIVIDUAL PITCHING LEADERS
(MINIMUM 0.8 INNINGS PITCHED PER TEAM GAME)

	W	L	ERA	G	SV	IP	H	BB	SO
Bowman, Matt, Bethesda	5	2	0.82	9	0	55	31	6	46
Secrest, Kelly, Bethesda	4	2	0.97	7	0	37	29	8	25
Rhodes, Jarius, Rockville	0	2	1.32	6	0	34	24	11	31
Hibberd, Houston, Rockville	4	2	2.08	9	0	61	48	11	32
Beck, Sander, Youse's	3	1	2.25	6	0	32	23	14	41
Markey, Bradley, Youse's	5	2	2.36	8	0	50	46	11	35
Kuhl, Chad, Youse's	5	2	2.63	8	0	51	43	11	39
Mitchell, Mike, Vienna	4	2	2.70	8	0	47	51	7	24
Poretz, Austin, S. Maryland	5	1	2.85	12	1	54	50	18	43
Love, Cameron, Bethesda	4	0	2.92	7	0	37	38	12	31

CALIFORNIA COLLEGIATE LEAGUE

	W	L	PCT	GB
San Luis Obispo Blues	24	12	.667	—
Santa Barbara Foresters	24	12	.667	—
Orange County Pioneers	20	16	.556	4
Team Vegas Baseball Club	20	16	.556	4
Conejo Oaks	17	19	.472	7
Glendale Angelenos	11	25	.306	13
Academy Barons	10	26	.278	14

TOP 10 PROSPECTS: 1. Austin Kubitza, rhp, Santa Barbara (So., Rice). 2. Greg Bird, 1b/c, Team Vegas (SIGNED: Yankees). 3. Aaron Brown, of, Glendale (Fr., Pepperdine). 4. Stephen Johnson, rhp, Santa Barbara (Jr., St. Edward's, Texas). 5. Michael Ratterree, 2b, Santa Barbara (Jr., Rice). 6. Ricky Jacquez, rhp, Team Vegas (Fr., Texas). 7. Mitch Mormann, rhp, Santa Barbara (Sr., Wichita State). 8. Travis Radke, lhp, Conejo (Fr., Portland). 9. Nick Grim, rhp, San Luis Obispo (Jr., Cal Poly). 10. Austin Dicharry, rhp, Santa Barbara (Sr., Texas).

INDIVIDUAL BATTING LEADERS
(MINIMUM 2.5 PLATE AT-BATS PER TEAM GAME)

	AVG	AB	R	H	2B	3B	HR	RBI	SB
McVaney, Jeff, Santa Barbara	.412	136	38	56	12	6	2	21	15
Bernard, Wyton, OC	.375	120	29	45	5	1	2	19	23
Zebrack, Greg, Orange County	.336	137	28	46	14	5	5	31	8
Legg, Derek, Santa Barbara	.336	152	19	51	5	3	3	31	9
Frazier, Adam, SLO	.333	102	22	34	6	0	0	12	4
McNeil, Jeff, Santa Barbara	.331	118	27	39	2	5	0	9	20
Wharton, James, SB	.328	128	35	42	13	1	7	34	6
Sharrar, Jo Jo, SLO	.325	123	28	40	13	0	1	24	0
Boggan, Nick, Conejo	.324	148	32	48	10	1	1	20	1
Aguayo, J.C., Conejo	.319	160	34	51	16	1	2	32	0

INDIVIDUAL PITCHING LEADERS
(MINIMUM 0.8 INNINGS PITCHED PER TEAM GAME)

	W	L	ERA	SV	IP	H	BB	SO
Sidhu, Harmen, SLO	5	0	0.26	1	34	16	10	42
Moskovits, Danny, OC	3	1	1.08	0	25	13	14	30
McCarthy, Ian, Santa Barbara	4	0	1.38	0	33	12	15	37
Smith, Patrick, Academy	2	3	1.73	0	42	30	7	42
Aguayo, J.C., Conejo	7	1	1.78	0	56	33	19	84
McGreevy, T.J., Santa Barbara	4	1	1.86	2	29	14	3	28
DiMartino, Kyle, Team Vegas	2	1	1.93	6	33	15	8	32
Morehouse, Codey, Santa Barbara	3	0	2.04	1	35	28	11	33
Barry, Tom, SLO	5	3	2.28	1	51	39	24	53
Huber, Travis, SLO	4	0	2.47	0	47	29	14	56

COASTAL PLAIN LEAGUE

NORTH	W	L	PCT	GB
Edenton Steamers	44	11	.800	—
Peninsula Pilots	27	29	.482	17½
Outer Banks Daredevils	26	28	.481	17½
Wilson Tobs	25	31	.446	19½
Petersburg Generals	13	43	.232	31½
SOUTH	**W**	**L**	**PCT**	**GB**
Fayetteville SwampDogs	34	22	.607	—
Wilmington Sharks	29	27	.518	5
Morehead City Marlins	27	29	.482	7

Florence RedWolves	27	29	.482	7
Columbia Blowfish	19	37	.339	15
WEST	**W**	**L**	**PCT**	**GB**
Thomasville HiToms	31	25	.554	—
Asheboro Copperheads	30	25	.545	0½
Forest City Owls	30	25	.545	0½
Gastonia Grizzlies	29	26	.527	1½
Martinsville Mustangs	25	29	.463	5

PLAYOFFS: Gastonia defeated Edenton 2-1 in a best-of-three championship series of an eight-team tournament.

TOP 10 PROSPECTS: 1. Jake Cave, 1b/lhp, Peninsula (SIGNED: Yankees). 2. Shawn Armstrong, rhp, Morehead City (SIGNED: Indians). 3. Ryan Mathews, of, Wilson (Sr., N.C. State). 4. Zack Smith, 1b/of, Columbia (So., Erskine, S.C.). 5. Chase McDonald, 1b, Morehead City (So., East Carolina). 6. Daniel Aldrich, of, Wilmington (So., College of Charleston). 7. Joe Wendle, 2b, Edenton (Sr., West Chester, Pa.). 8. Joe Sclafani, ss, Morehead City (Sr., Dartmouth). 9. Adam Engel, of, Florence (So., Louisville). 10. Deshorn Lake, rhp, Peninsula (Fr., East Carolina).

INDIVIDUAL BATTING LEADERS
(MINIMUM 149 PLATE APPEARANCES)

	AVG	AB	R	H	2B	3B	HR	RBI	SB
McDonald, Chase, M. City	.403	181	36	73	8	0	13	51	0
Wendle, Joe, Edenton	.377	215	46	81	12	2	4	39	5
Sclafani, Joe, M. City	.375	160	40	60	10	3	5	32	1
Grabe, Eric, Fayetteville	.355	155	33	55	9	1	2	23	15
Smith, Zack, Columbia	.354	223	35	79	15	0	11	46	7
Slaybaugh, Collin, M-ville	.349	146	29	51	3	2	1	24	15
Sciacca, Tyler, Outer Banks	.346	185	36	64	16	4	1	37	9
Harvey, Ian, Martinsville	.341	135	24	46	12	0	3	20	11
Carman, Chad, Outer Banks	.333	153	25	51	6	0	5	28	4
Hebert, Brock, Thomasville	.330	209	42	69	13	0	5	22	34

INDIVIDUAL PITCHING LEADERS
(MINIMUM 44 INNINGS)

	W	L	ERA	G	SV	IP	H	BB	SO
Campbell, Matthew, Florence	1	0	1.19	8	0	45	23	17	41
Rivera, Stephen, Asheboro	2	1	1.64	12	0	49	46	7	26
Batts, Mat, Wilmington	3	3	1.89	9	0	62	53	15	54
Jankowski, Jordan, Thomasville	3	1	2.13	11	1	51	35	26	66
Brown, Andrew, Forest City	3	2	2.27	10	0	63	58	19	56
Lomascolo, Nick, Forest City	5	2	2.4	8	0	56	43	26	43
Holmes, Brian, Thomasville	5	1	2.4	10	0	60	33	31	54
Macaluso, Dom, Fayetteville	3	6	2.43	11	0	63	62	20	31
Brooks, Derek, Fayetteville	7	1	2.48	13	1	62	55	14	42
Sinclair, Connor, Outer Banks	5	3	2.52	10	0	64	55	20	67

FLORIDA COLLEGIATE SUMMER LEAGUE

	W	L	T	PCT	GB
Leesburg Lightning	29	12	0	.707	—
Winter Park Diamond Dawgs	22	14	1	.595	4½
DeLand Suns	23	17	0	.575	5½
Sanford River Rats	16	22	1	.410	11½
Orlando Freedom	14	26	0	.350	14½
Winter Haven Loggerheads	13	26	0	.333	15

PLAYOFFS: Sanford defeated Winter Park in five-team playoff.

TOP 10 PROSPECTS: 1. Garrett Nuss, rhp, Orlando (Fr., Central Florida). 2. Ted Blackman, of, Winter Park (Jr., Coastal Carolina). 3. Omar Cotto, of, Winter Park (So., Southern California). 4. Ethan Bader, rhp, Leesburg (So., Armstrong Atlantic, Ga., State). 5. Todd Hankins, 2b, Winter Park (SIGNED: Indians). 6. Anthony Caronia, ss, Orlando (Jr., Tampa). 7. Peter Miller, rhp, Winter Haven (So., Florida State). 8. James Ramsay, of, Sanford (So., South Florida). 9. Mike Heller, rhp, Winter Haven (So., Miami-Dade JC). 10. Kevin Gude, rhp, Winter Park (So., Polk State, Fla., JC).

INDIVIDUAL BATTING LEADERS
(MINIMUM 2.7 PLATE APPEARANCES PER TEAM GAME)

	AVG	AB	R	H	2B	3B	HR	RBI	SB
Blackman, Ted, Winter Park	.425	106	38	45	10	0	3	19	28
Sicking, Thomas, Leesburg	.396	111	23	44	4	1	0	21	10
Tillotson, Jacob, Leesburg	.371	170	42	63	9	1	2	24	5
Zimmerman, B.J., WP	.355	110	20	39	5	0	3	30	3
Coronia, Anthony, Orlando	.353	133	22	47	5	0	0	16	21
Lehane, Kevin, Orlando	.350	117	24	41	10	0	3	18	4
Cruz, Alex, Winter Park	.337	98	20	33	4	1	1	18	3
Chubb, Austin, Winter Park	.333	99	19	33	5	0	0	13	2
Lindheim, Kevin, DeLand	.330	88	14	29	4	2	1	17	2
Mendez, Alex, Sanford	.326	132	28	43	9	1	1	12	10

INDIVIDUAL PITCHING LEADERS
(MINIMUM 0.8 INNINGS PITCHED PER TEAM GAME)

	W	L	ERA	G	SV	IP	H	BB	SO
DuRapau, Montana, DeLand	2	1	1.09	8	0	33	20	12	29
Acevedo, Jairo, DeLand	3	2	1.35	12	0	33	22	7	15
Brown, Ben, Winter Park	4	1	1.35	8	0	40	26	3	32
Jackson, Austin, DeLand	3	2	2.13	9	1	38	33	10	21
Modomo, Chad, Winter Park	4	2	2.25	8	0	44	37	11	21
Nuss, Garrett, Orlando	3	1	2.80	7	0	35	25	18	43
Hathcock, Dylan, Leesburg	2	2	2.81	9	0	48	44	18	43
Ortega, Dylan, Leesburg	4	2	2.98	9	0	48	47	9	28
Kovacs, Nic, Leesburg	5	1	3.38	11	0	56	67	3	45
Rood, Chad, DeLand	3	2	3.74	8	0	34	43	11	21

FUTURES COLLEGE BASEBALL LEAGUE

	W	L	PCT	GB
Nashua Silver Knights	27	16	.628	—
Torrington Titans	27	17	.614	0½
Martha's Vineyard Sharks	23	21	.523	4½
Seacoast Mavericks	10	33	.233	17

PLAYOFFS: Nashua defeated Torrington in the championship of a four-team, double-elimination tournament.

TOP 5 PROSPECTS: 1. Eric Perrault, lhp, Nashua (Jr., Keene, N.H., State). 2. Robbie Zinsmeister, ss/2b/of, Martha's Vineyard (Jr., Indiana, Pa.). 3. Jeramy Matos, of, Martha's Vineyard (Jr., Central Florida). 4. Donald Hissa, rhp, Seacoast (So., Notre Dame). 5. Dylan Maki, rhp, Nashua (Jr., Northeastern).

INDIVIDUAL BATTING LEADERS
(MINIMUM 2.7 PLATE APPEARANCES PER TEAM GAME)

	AVG	AB	R	H	2B	3B	HR	RBI	SB
Gillis, Logan, Nashua	.376	165	42	62	11	0	2	21	13
Matos, Jeremy, MV	.346	156	20	54	7	1	13	34	0
Jacobs, Matt, Nashua	.342	161	37	55	10	2	2	31	14
Zinsmeister, Robbie, MV	.326	172	41	56	10	3	9	26	25
Jensen, Eric, MV	.313	150	21	47	4	1	0	20	8
Katsiroubas, James, Nashua	.312	138	26	43	11	2	7	39	4
Corona, Anthony, MV	.309	152	20	47	6	0	3	19	3
Sanborn, Mark, Nashua	.306	160	32	49	6	0	6	35	3
Simms, Josh, Torrington	.300	110	21	33	4	3	1	11	3
Boix, Anthony, MV	.293	140	23	41	5	2	2	16	5

INDIVIDUAL PITCHING LEADERS
(MINIMUM 0.8 INNINGS PITCHED PER TEAM GAME)

	W	L	ERA	G	SV	IP	H	BB	SO
McCullough, Gavin, Torrington	6	0	1.24	8	0	51	45	19	43
Fishem, Geoff, Nashua	6	0	1.53	8	0	59	50	10	31
Perrault, Eric, Nashua	5	0	1.57	9	0	46	32	20	48
Erickson, Tyler, Torrington	4	3	1.79	10	1	55	40	6	42
Kasper, Kody, MV	3	4	2.47	9	0	51	51	20	28
Hissa, Donald, Seacoast	0	5	2.82	8	0	45	41	26	60
McMahon, Conner, Torrington	4	2	3.00	8	0	54	35	15	33
Swinford, Jay, MV	5	3	3.04	9	0	50	32	32	39
Terill, Travis, Nashua	2	1	3.11	10	0	38	41	13	16
Torres, Dennis, Seacoast	1	3	3.15	7	0	40	40	20	39

GREAT LAKES LEAGUE

NORTH	**W**	**L**	**PCT**	**GB**
Lima Locos	29	14	.674	—
Licking County Settlers	22	21	.512	7
Lake Erie Monarchs	20	22	.476	8½
Stark County Terriers	19	23	.452	9½
Grand Lake Mariners	11	29	.275	16½
SOUTH	**W**	**L**	**PCT**	**GB**
Southern Ohio Copperheads	29	13	.69	—
Hamilton Joes	24	18	.571	5
Xenia Scouts	23	19	.548	6
Cincinnati Steam	22	20	.524	7
Lexington Hustlers	10	30	.25	18

PLAYOFFS: Lima defeated Southern Ohio in the championship of a six-team, double-elimination tournament.

TOP 10 PROSPECTS: 1. Dusty Isaacs, rhp, Hamilton (So., Georgia Tech). 2. David Garner, rhp, Southern Ohio (So., Michigan State). 3. J.T. Riddle, 2b/rhp, Lexington (So., Kentucky). 4. Marcus Davis, of/1b, Hamilton (So., Hillsborough, Fla., CC). 5. Marcus Davis, of/1b, Hamilton (So., Walters State, Tenn., CC). 6. Zach Isler, rhp, Cincinnati (Jr., Cincinnati). 7. Greg Greve, rhp, Stark County (So., Ohio State). 8. Seth Streich, rhp, Southern

Ohio (Jr., Ohio). 9. Jake Proctor, of, Cincinnati (Jr., Cincinnati). 10. Chuck Ghysels, rhp, Hamilton (Sr., Maryland).

INDIVIDUAL BATTING LEADERS
(MINIMUM 2.7 PLATE APPEARANCES PER TEAM GAME)

	AVG	AB	R	H	2B	3B	HR	RBI	SB
Grogg, Taylor, Southern Ohio	.379	103	27	39	4	0	0	8	17
Lapikas, Mark, Stark County	.375	120	29	45	11	1	6	31	6
Palensky, Caleb, Xenia	.374	123	32	46	12	1	1	25	2
Meadows, Wes, Licking Co.	.366	134	22	49	10	1	5	26	2
Bower, Kevin, Cincinnati	.361	119	19	43	8	1	6	29	2
Riddle, J.T., Lexington	.343	108	19	37	10	2	3	17	2
Proctor, Jake, Cincinnati	.342	114	28	39	8	2	1	18	14
Elwell, Mark, Cincinnati	.340	106	21	36	7	0	0	10	7
Hirschberg, Pat, Lake Erie	.336	143	18	48	5	2	1	19	4
Chriscaden, Andy, Lima	.333	153	28	51	14	1	5	25	0

INDIVIDUAL PITCHING LEADERS
(MINIMUM 0.8 INNINGS PITCHED PER TEAM GAME)

	W	L	ERA	G	SV	IP	H	BB	SO
Radon, Alex, Lake Erie	4	1	0.81	10	0	45	33	13	33
Alexander, Tyler, Hamilton	3	1	1.71	7	0	42	26	24	45
Bagshaw, Blake, Cincinnati	4	0	1.90	6	0	38	32	7	24
Vaske, Tyler, Licking County	5	2	1.97	8	0	46	41	13	37
Ghysels, Chuck, Hamilton	4	3	1.98	9	0	50	21	32	62
Scott, Tyler, Lake Erie	3	3	2.15	8	0	38	32	12	27
Porter, Grant, Licking County	2	2	2.29	7	0	39	41	16	23
Isaacs, Dusty, Hamilton	5	1	2.24	9	0	44	31	22	50
Scott, James, Xenia	3	1	2.46	9	1	37	26	16	29
Walter, Johnny, Lake Erie	3	3	2.54	8	0	39	37	13	29

HAWAII COLLEGIATE LEAGUE

	W	L	PCT	GB
Oahu Paddlers	22	13	.629	—
Waikiki Surfers	20	15	.571	2
Waimea Waves	18	17	.513	4
Kamuela Paniolos	17	18	.486	5
Kauai Menehunes	14	21	.400	8
Hawaii Aliis	14	21	.400	8

PLAYOFFS: Kamuela defeated Waikiki in a six-team, double-elimination tournament.

TOP 10 PROSPECTS: 1. Trey Teakell, rhp, Kauai (R-Fr., Texas Christian). 2. Kai'iana Eldredge, 2b/c, Oahu (So., Kansas). 3. Jonathan Hochstatter, lhp, Waimea (Fr., Stanford). 4. Jacob Wakamatsu, ss/2b, Waimea (Fr., Arizona State). 5. Jimmy Filter, ss, Oahu (Sr., Northeastern). 6. Luke Esquerra, of, Waimea (Jr., Cal Baptist). 7. James Yacabonis, rhp, Waikiki (So., St. Joseph's). 8. James Stanfield, c, Kamuela (Sr., Kansas). 9. Robert Kahana, rhp, Oahu (Fr., Kansas). 10. Ben McQuown, of, Waikiki (Jr., Campbell).

INDIVIDUAL BATTING LEADERS
(MINIMUM 3.1 PLATE APPEARANCES PER TEAM GAME)

	AVG	AB	R	H	2B	3B	HR	RBI	SB
Marnati, Matthew, Hawaii	.350	120	16	42	6	2	0	16	6
Filter, Jimmy, Oahu	.327	113	18	37	14	2	2	16	8
Eldredge, Kai'iana, Oahu	.327	113	28	37	6	1	0	6	14
Flax, Jeffery, Hawaii	.321	137	22	44	6	1	0	14	8
Howard, Tom, Waimea	.319	119	18	38	5	0	0	8	5
Reiling, Michael, Kamuela	.311	122	22	38	4	3	0	16	3
Castoldi, Pete, Oahu	.311	106	15	33	4	2	1	14	3
Greve, Brad, Hawaii	.306	121	29	37	3	1	0	11	15
Esquerra, Luke, Waimea	.306	108	22	33	8	3	0	24	12
Brandt, Forrest, Oahu	.298	121	18	36	8	0	0	19	11

INDIVIDUAL PITCHING LEADERS
(MINIMUM 0.8 INNINGS PITCHED PER TEAM GAME)

	W	L	ERA	G	SV	IP	H	BB	SO
Pasquale, Nicholas, Waimea	2	2	0.84	7	2	32	25	7	26
Teakell, Trey, Kauai	3	2	0.91	8	0	59	39	11	46
Johnson, Matthew, Hawaii	4	1	1.66	11	1	54	38	10	46
Rafferty, Chad, Waimea	2	2	1.78	8	0	30	33	13	22
Quinney, Drew, Waikiki.	1	4	1.93	16	2	33	20	17	22
Ferguson, Kevin, Kamuela	3	1	2.18	7	0	33	23	13	31
Kenolio, Bryson, Kamuela	3	2	2.20	11	0	45	39	18	22
Haynal, Austin, Kamuela	3	2	2.20	9	0	45	32	18	35
Rooke-Ley, Travis, Oahu	3	3	2.44	8	0	48	35	17	24
Aldrete, Blake, Waikiki	1	1	2.45	15	0	51	53	21	44

JAYHAWK LEAGUE

	W	L	PCT	GB
Haysville Heat	22	12	.647	—
Hays Larks	20	14	.588	2
Derby Twins	19	15	.559	3
Liberal BeeJays	18	15	.545	3½
Dodge City A's	11	22	.333	10½
El Dorado Broncos	11	23	.324	11

TOP 10 PROSPECTS: 1. Josh Smith, lhp, Liberal (Sr., Wichita State). 2. Aaron Cornell, of, Hays (So., Oklahoma State). 3. Cale Elam, rhp, Liberal (So., Wichita State). 4. Cass Ingvardsen, rhp, Dodge City (Jr., Stephen F. Austin State). 5. Zeb Sneed, rhp, Haysville (Jr., Northwest Nazarene, Idaho). 6. Jared Moore, lhp, Liberal (So., Kansas State). 7. Ryan Gebhart, of, El Dorado (Sr., Florida Gulf Coast). 8. Robbie Ingram, lhp, Liberal (So., Mesa, Ariz., CC). 9. John Nasshan, rhp, El Dorado (Jr., Bradley). 10. Jon Ryan, of, Hays (So., Illinois-Chicago).

INDIVIDUAL BATTING LEADERS
(MINIMUM 80 PLATE APPEARANCES)

	AVG	AB	H	2B	3B	HR	RBI
Gebhart, Ryan, El Dorado	.382	89	34	5	1	4	12
Hagel, Will, Dodge City	.364	132	48	12	0	2	30
Wilson, Sean, Hays	.364	132	48	2	0	1	15
Burnham, Kyle, Derby	.356	118	42	6	1	2	11
Gougler, Cody, Hays	.346	130	45	8	0	1	20
Cornell, Aaron, Hays	.336	119	40	12	1	7	26
Rea, Robbie, El Dorado	.327	98	32	4	0	0	17
Parr, Jordan, Derby	.327	113	37	6	0	5	24
Walterhous, Ryan, Derby	.319	113	36	1	0	5	21
Kivett, Ross, Liberal	.314	104	33	3	1	1	13

INDIVIDUAL PITCHING LEADERS
(MINIMUM 20 INNINGS)

	W	L	ERA	IP	H	SO
Spitsnogle, Dexter, Haysville	4	0	0.00	30	20	16
Schmit, Matt, Hays	0	0	1.23	22	23	11
Elam, Cale, Liberal	0	1	1.25	23	15	16
Burchett, Michael, Hays	0	1	1.48	24	19	17
Ziegler, Justin, Hays	4	0	1.60	39	21	32
Collazo, Anthony, Haysville	4	0	1.74	31	21	47
Ingvardsen, Case, Dodge City	4	1	1.80	30	23	28
Shreve, Patrick, Liberal	3	2	1.99	42	39	34
Moore, Jared, Liberal	0	3	2.21	38	25	27
Blades, Spencer, Derby	1	2	2.54	28	28	12

MINK LEAGUE

NORTH

	W	L	PCT	GB
St. Joseph Mustangs	34	10	.773	—
Clarinda A's	22	20	.524	11
Chillicothe Mudcats	21	22	.488	12½
Omaha Diamond Spirit	19	24	.442	14½

SOUTH

	W	L	PCT	GB
Sedalia Bombers	24	18	.571	—
Nevada Griffons	25	19	.568	—
Ozark Generals	14	28	.333	10
Joplin Outlaws	12	30	.286	12

PLAYOFFS: St. Joseph defeated Nevada 2-0 in best-of-three championship series.

TOP 10 PROSPECTS: 1. Nick Petree, rhp, Sedalia (So., Missouri State). 2. Mark Robinette, rhp, St. Joseph (Jr., Oklahoma State). 3. Brent Seifert, 3b, St. Joseph (Sr., Missouri State). 4. Matt Skipper, 1b, Sedalia (Jr., Embry-Riddle, Fla.). 5. Ryan Esquerra, of, Chillicothe (So., California Baptist). 6. Aaron Baker, rhp, Sedalia (Jr., Central Missouri). 7. Will Landsheft, rhp, Sedalia (So., Drury, Mo.). 8. Kraig Kelley, c, Chillicothe (So., Central Arkansas). 9. Jeff Roy, of, St. Joseph (So., Rhode Island). 10. Peter Barrows, of, Nevada (SIGNED: Wichita Wingnuts).

INDIVIDUAL BATTING LEADERS
(MINIMUM 2.7 PLATE APPEARANCES PER TEAM GAME)

	AVG	AB	R	H	2B	3B	HR	RBI	SB
Barrows, Peter, Nevada	.404	141	39	57	12	1	8	44	5
Skipper, Matt, Sedalia	.402	127	32	51	13	1	5	35	0
Scornaienchi, Ryan, Clarinda	.367	109	23	40	8	0	0	15	7
Wilson, Brad, Nevada	.358	95	31	34	5	3	0	11	5
Ford, Cory, Chillcothe	.357	168	34	60	7	4	1	12	8
Johnston, Bryce, Omaha	.355	124	19	44	4	1	2	14	8
Pritchard, Mike, Sedalia	.353	133	27	47	9	1	0	19	23
Seifert, Brent, St. Joseph	.353	167	43	59	23	3	2	35	10
Drake, Patrick, Joplin	.349	109	14	38	9	1	2	11	5

Krist, A.J., Nevada	.333	111	23	37	7	0	2	22	6

INDIVIDUAL PITCHING LEADERS
(MINIMUM 0.8 INNINGS PITCHED PER TEAM GAME)

	W	L	ERA	G	SV	IP	H	BB	SO
Kuligowski, Steve, Nevada	5	3	1.46	10	0	58	44	17	46
Baker, Aaron, Sedalia	3	1	1.62	8	0	52	50	9	39
Malin, Josh, Nevada	7	2	1.65	10	0	72	68	8	70
Maddox, Adam, St. Joseph	4	1	1.69	7	0	41	29	17	25
Huett, Jayson, St. Joseph	4	0	1.82	6	0	42	31	10	28
Stewart, Glenn, Ozark	3	2	1.85	8	0	42	31	11	14
Smith, Curtis, Omaha	2	3	1.91	8	0	40	39	8	33
Alva, Austin, Clarinda	3	2	1.92	9	0	47	52	16	49
Landssheft, Will, Sedalia	4	1	2.00	8	0	42	31	25	46
Rand, Jon, Chillcothe	1	3	2.01	17	1	52	44	28	32

NEW ENGLAND COLLEGIATE LEAGUE

EASTERN

	W	L	PCT	GB
Newport Gulls	29	13	.690	—
North Shore Navigators	22	20	.524	7
Sanford Mainers	20	22	.476	9
Laconia Muskrats	18	24	.429	11
New Bedford Blue Sox	16	26	.381	13
Old Orchard Beach Raging Tide	9	33	.214	20

WESTERN

	W	L	PCT	GB
Keene Swamp Bats	28	14	.667	—
Holyoke Blue Sox	28	14	.667	—
Vermont Mountaineers	26	16	.619	2
Danbury Westerners	25	17	.595	3
Mystic Schooners	18	24	.429	10
North Adams SteepleCats	13	29	.310	15

PLAYOFFS: Keene defeated Laconia 2-0 in best-of-three series.
TOP 10 PROSPECTS: 1. Tom Murphy, c, Holyoke (Jr., Buffalo). 2. Ronnie Freeman, c, Holyoke (Jr., Kennesaw State). 3. Conrad Gregor, of, Newport (So., Vanderbilt). 4. Jeff Thompson, rhp, Keene (So., Louisville). 5. Chris Costantino, rhp, Laconia (SIGNED: Cardinals). 6. Trey Mancini, 1b, Holyoke (So., Notre Dame). 7. Chris Jenkins, rhp, Holyoke (Jr., Stanford). 8. Tyler Mizenko, rhp, Sanford (SIGNED: Giants). 9. Dario Pizzano, of, North Shore (Jr., Columbia). 10. Tyler Horan, of, Danbury (So., Virginia Tech).

INDIVIDUAL BATTING LEADERS
(MINIMUM 2.7 PLATE APPEARANCES PER TEAM GAME)

	AVG	AB	R	H	2B	3B	HR	RBI	SB
Garner, Andrew, Danbury	.384	112	28	43	9	1	5	27	7
Bereszniewicz, Billy, Old Orchard	.378	127	19	48	2	0	0	4	11
Freeman, Ronnie, Holyoke	.373	150	32	56	12	0	5	25	0
Pizzano, Dario, North Shore	.365	148	29	54	12	2	4	27	0
Ravnass, Rand, Newport	.342	111	23	38	6	5	4	33	9
Horan, Tyler, Danbury	.341	129	26	44	7	0	11	35	7
Johnson, Kyle, Newport	.331	139	26	46	8	0	2	12	13
Krietemeier, Tanner, Danbury	.329	149	30	49	12	1	2	21	8
Kiene, Tim, Newport	.325	126	16	41	4	0	9	30	0
Brown, Kevin, Keene	.325	160	33	52	6	3	8	29	6

INDIVIDUAL PITCHING LEADERS
(MINIMUM 0.8 INNINGS PITCHED PER TEAM GAME)

	W	L	ERA	G	SV	IP	H	BB	SO
Lee, Jacob, Newport	4	0	0.66	7	0	41	30	10	39
Sinnery, Brandon, Newport	3	1	1.00	10	1	45	35	6	34
Mount, Ben, Holyoke	5	1	1.36	8	0	46	34	12	45
Shepard, Fred, Vermont	3	0	1.42	7	0	38	27	16	33
Lawrence, Tommy, Sanford	1	2	1.48	9	0	43	25	10	28
Norris, Alex, Mystic	5	0	1.90	8	0	38	32	14	21
Thompson, Jeff, Keene	2	2	1.90	8	0	38	27	15	53
Williams, Taylor, Keene	6	1	2.18	11	1	41	27	16	41
Terhune, Greg, New Bedford	2	1	2.29	11	0	39	37	12	18
Costantino, Chris, Laconia	3	3	2.30	8	0	47	28	18	60

NEW YORK COLLEGIATE LEAGUE

WEST

	W	L	PCT	GB
Webster Brewers	30	14	.682	—
Niagara Power	24	20	.545	6
Geneva Red Wings	24	20	.545	6
Hornell Dodgers	22	22	.500	8
Allegany County Nitros	20	24	.455	10
Alfred Thunder	14	30	.318	16

EAST

	W	L	PCT	GB
Utica Brewers	32	12	.727	—
Oneonta Outlaws	29	15	.659	3
Rome Thunderbolts	27	17	.614	5
Syracuse Jr. Chiefs	16	28	.364	16
Syracuse Salt Cats	14	30	.318	18
Sherill Silversmiths	12	32	.273	20

PLAYOFFS: Webster defeated Oneonta 2-0 in a best of three series.
TOP 10 PROSPECTS: 1. Mike Johnson, lhp, Utica (SIGNED: Angels). 2. Chris Bostick, 2b/ss, Webster (SIGNED: Athletics). 3. Scott Weathersby, rhp, Oneonta (Fr., Mississippi). 4. Artie Lewicki, rhp, Oneonta (So., Virginia). 5. Matt Chavez, if/rhp, Oneonta (Sr., San Francisco). 6. Brady Wager, rhp, Oneonta (Jr., Grand Canyon, Ariz., CC). 7. Carlos Asuaje, 2b, Oneonta (So., Nova Southeastern, Fla.). 8. Daniel Mims, of, Utica (Jr., Southeastern, Fla.). 9. Dan Fiorito, 3b, Syracuse Salt Cats (Jr., Manhattanville, N.Y.). 10. Scott Krutel, 3b, Utica (Sr., Missouri Baptist).

INDIVIDUAL BATTING LEADERS
(MINIMUM 2.0 PLATE APPEARANCES PER TEAM GAME)

	AVG	AB	R	H	2B	3B	HR	RBI	SB
Costantino, Branden, Sherill	.417	151	37	63	9	2	3	22	63
Bostick, Chris, Webster	.413	138	38	57	6	6	5	32	18
Stimpson, Leon, Geneva	.378	135	30	51	6	0	14	14	23
Howell, John, Oneonta	.375	128	31	48	4	0	1	30	10
Asuaje, Carlos, Oneonta	.369	149	35	55	8	4	3	26	19
Scahill, Dan, Rome	.368	144	25	53	11	1	1	18	5
Bostick, Ben, Webster	.362	177	36	64	12	7	0	21	19
Matuszak, Jacob, Hornell	.360	175	41	63	10	4	0	16	18
Collins, Brendan, Niagara	.353	156	33	55	7	2	0	15	18
Compton, Chase, Oneonta	.351	134	24	47	8	2	0	24	5

INDIVIDUAL PITCHING LEADERS
(MINIMUM 0.8 INNINGS PITCHED PER TEAM GAME)

	W	L	ERA	G	SV	IP	H	BB	SO
Petit, Jacob, Utica	7	1	0.71	9	0	51	30	17	50
Frosch, Kenny, Rome	2	1	1.12	20	1	48	36	16	46
Krauss, Brent, Utica	4	2	1.30	7	0	42	18	29	36
Storey, Julius, Allegany	3	2	1.40	10	0	51	54	12	23
Knox, Chandler, Hornell	3	2	1.48	10	0	61	56	16	34
Mann, Tyler, Rome	5	0	1.64	9	0	44	33	15	31
Greenfield, Joe, Webster	4	2	1.80	14	0	60	37	19	37
Croteau, Jeff, Geneva	5	1	1.96	8	0	41	38	9	15
Galligan, Bryan, Oneonta	4	1	1.97	8	0	46	35	26	32
Weathersby, Scott, Oneonta	4	2	2.01	11	1	49	39	9	56

NORTHWOODS LEAGUE

NORTH

	W	L	PCT	GB
Alexandria Beetles	28	11	.718	—
Willmar Stingers	22	16	.579	5½
Mankato MoonDogs	19	18	.514	8
Thunder Bay Border Cats	18	17	.514	8
St. Cloud River Bats	20	19	.513	8
Rochester Honkers	16	22	.421	11½
Brainerd Lakes Area Lunkers	15	24	.385	13
Duluth Huskies	13	24	.351	14

SOUTH

	W	L	PCT	GB
Battle Creek Bombers	23	13	.639	—
Green Bay Bullfrogs	22	14	.611	1
La Crosse Loggers	22	14	.611	1
Waterloo Bucks	17	18	.486	5½
Madison Mallards	16	18	.471	6
Eau Claire Express	16	21	.432	7½
Wisconsin Rapids Rafters	16	21	.432	7½
Wisconsin Woodchucks	12	25	.324	11½

PLAYOFFS: Battle Creek defeated Mankato 2-0 in best-of-three championship series.
TOP 20 PROSPECTS: 1. Nolan Sanburn, rhp, Battle Creek (So., Arkansas). 2. Andrew Knapp, c, La Crosse (So., California). 3. Mitch Haniger, of, Green Bay (Jr., Cal Poly). 4. Carlos Escobar, c, Wisconsin (Jr., Nevada). 5. Sam Selman, lhp, Mankato (Jr., Vanderbilt). 6. Dan Child, rhp, La Crosse (So., Oregon State). 7. Anthony Bazzani, rhp, Alexandria (Jr., Eastern Kentucky). 8. Cameron Perkins, 3b, Waterloo (Jr., Purdue). 9. Phillip Ervin, of, Green Bay (So., Samford). 10. Matt Milroy, rhp, Madison (Jr., Illinois). 11. Jonathon Crawford, rhp, Madison (So., Florida). 12. Ty Forney, ss, Eau Claire (Sr., New Mexico State). 13. Louie Lechich, of, La Crosse (So., California). 14. Sean Dwyer, of, Willmar (So., Florida Gulf Coast). 15. Shaun Cooper, of, Mankato (Sr., Utah). 16. Chase Stevens, rhp, Waterloo (Jr., Oklahoma State). 17. Tom Windle, lhp, Madison (So., Minnesota).

18. Jordan Haseltine, lhp, La Crosse (So., San Francisco). 19. Trevor Teykl, rhp, La Crosse (R-Fr., Texas). 20. Carlos Lopez, 1b, St. Cloud (Jr., Cal State Fullerton).

	AVG	AB	R	H	2B	3B	HR	RBI	SB
Brantley, Justin, Albany	4	2	3.94	8	0	48	51	17	43
Carter, Jordan, Elmira	4	4	3.95	9	0	57	65	14	34

PROSPECT LEAGUE

EAST	W	L	PCT	GB
West Virginia Miners	29	27	.518	—
Lorain County Ironmen	27	27	.500	1
Slippery Rock Sliders	26	29	.473	2½
Chillicothe Paints	26	30	.464	3
Richmond River Rats	26	30	.464	3
Butler Blue Sox	25	29	.463	3
WEST	W	L	PCT	GB
Quincy Gems	38	18	0.679	—
Terre Haute Rex	34	22	0.607	4
Nashville Outlaws	29	24	0.547	7½
Hannibal Cavemen	29	26	0.527	8½
Danville Dans	25	29	0.463	12
Springfield Sliders	25	30	0.455	12½
DeKalb County Liners	23	32	0.418	14½
Dubois County Bombers	22	31	0.415	14½

PLAYOFFS: Quincy defeated West Virginia in the championship of an eight-team playoff.

TOP 10 PROSPECTS: 1. Stephen Bruno, ss, Terre Haute (Jr., Virginia). 2. Sean Manaea, lhp, DuBois County (So., Indiana State). 3. Chris Serritella, 1b, Quincy (Sr., Southern Illinois). 4. Shae Simmons, rhp, Nashville (Jr., Southeast Missouri State). 5. Evan Mitchell, rhp, Danville (So., Mississippi State). 6. Nick Rumbelow, rhp, Danville (So., Louisiana State). 7. Clayton Schulz, lhp, Chillicothe (SIGNED—Royals). 8. Trenton Moses, 3b, Dekalb County (Sr., Southeast Missouri State). 9. Koby Kraemer, 2b, Terre Haute (Jr., Indiana State). 10. Nolan Earley, of, Richmond (Jr., South Alabama).

INDIVIDUAL BATTING LEADERS
(MINIMUM 2.7 PLATE APPEARANCES PER TEAM GAME)

INDIVIDUAL BATTING LEADERS
(MINIMUM 2.7 PLATE APPEARANCES PER TEAM GAME)

	AVG	AB	R	H	2B	3B	HR	RBI	SB
Knapp, Andrew, La Crosse	.400	155	30	62	8	0	5	33	1
Mahoney, Cullen, TB	.347	213	33	74	7	5	4	29	10
Escobar, Carlos, Wisconsin	.345	197	38	68	16	0	7	33	4
Perkins, Cameron, Waterloo	.344	247	49	85	19	1	10	46	13
Forney, Ty, Eau Claire	.338	213	35	72	12	0	5	30	13
Stover, Pat, Willmar	.337	169	23	57	10	1	3	25	1
Cooper, Shaun, Mankato	.335	242	55	81	14	4	20	61	15
Susdorf, Danny, Wisconsin	.335	182	31	61	11	0	2	28	16
Rowan, Mitch, Willmar	.333	225	41	75	19	0	0	21	22
Brault, Steven, Brainerd	.330	215	25	71	10	1	2	31	8

INDIVIDUAL PITCHING LEADERS
(MINIMUM 0.8 INNINGS PITCHED PER TEAM GAME)

	W	L	ERA	G	SV	IP	H	BB	SO
Schwartz, Blake, Mankato	6	1	1.71	11	0	63	51	15	75
Novak, Joey, Duluth	4	4	1.82	13	0	74	55	18	54
Wisecarver, Mike, Waterloo	6	0	1.91	9	0	57	46	19	44
Hunter, Andy, Green Bay	5	2	1.97	17	0	59	42	11	68
Shellhorn, Rusty, Madison	5	2	2.30	14	0	63	46	40	71
Giel, Tim, Green Bay	7	3	2.33	12	0	70	62	22	44
Vocca, Tony, Eau Claire	2	3	2.33	11	0	58	47	27	63
Tessar, Brando, La Crosse	6	1	2.46	11	0	77	67	17	51
Winter, Kyle, Brainerd	4	5	2.57	11	0	70	72	25	65
Willman, Joe, Brainerd	4	1	2.64	11	0	61	54	18	54

PERFECT GAME COLLEGIATE LEAGUE

EAST	W	L	PCT	GB
Glen Falls Golden Eagles	31	17	.646	—
Amsterdam Mohawks	30	17	.638	0½
Mohawk Valley	18	29	.383	12½
Albany Dutchmen	18	29	.383	12½
WEST	W	L	PCT	GB
Cooperstown Hawkeyes	25	20	.556	—
Newark Pilots	26	22	.542	0½
Elmira Pioneers	22	25	.468	4
Watertown Wizards	18	29	.383	8

PLAYOFFS: Newark defeated Amsterdam 21 in best-of-three series.

TOP 10 PROSPECTS: 1. Josh Anderson, 3b, Glen Falls (So., Yavapai, Ariz., JC). 2. Luke Maile, c/1b, Amsterdam (Jr., Kentucky). 3. Erick Gaylord, of, Watertown (Sr., Campbell). 4. Tyler Kane, rhp, Mohawk Valley (So., Washington). 5. Kyle Ruchim, rhp/2b, Glen Falls (So., Northwestern). 6. Ricky Claudio, of/rhp, Glen Falls (Jr., St. Thomas, Fla.). 7. Carson Beauchaine, rhp, Newark (Jr., Saginaw Valley, Mich., State). 8. Jude Vidrine, of, Amsterdam (So., Lamar). 9. Mark Leiter Jr., rhp, Amsterdam (Jr., New Jersey Tech). 10. Willie Gabay, rhp, Mohawk Valley (So., Herkimer County, N.Y., CC).

INDIVIDUAL BATTING LEADERS
(MINIMUM 140 PLATE APPEARANCES)

	AVG	AB	R	H	2B	3B	HR	RBI
Aanderud, Bryan, Cooperstown	.379	132	13	50	6	1	2	26
Normoyle, Ryan, Elmira	.379	177	35	67	9	0	1	34
Anderson, Josh, Glen Falls	.368	136	23	50	13	1	9	38
Gaylord, Erick, Watertown	.360	161	37	58	8	2	10	42
Vidrine, Jude, Amsterdam	.348	158	34	55	7	3	8	29
Bolling, Michael, Newark	.343	166	35	57	13	2	1	19
Shank, Zach, Amsterdam	.341	170	38	58	10	2	2	17
Ruchim, Kyle, Glen Falls	.333	165	37	55	16	1	6	27
Maldonado, Alex, Watertown	.329	164	30	54	10	1	0	12
Deeds, Andrew, Albany	.326	178	31	45	6	3	1	25

INDIVIDUAL PITCHING LEADERS
(MINIMUM 1.0 INNINGS PITCHED PER TEAM GAME)

	W	L	ERA	G	SV	IP	H	BB	SO
Ruscitti, Dominick, Newark	6	1	1.82	9	0	59	42	15	49
Mazzio, Derek, Glen Falls	2	1	1.99	10	0	54	56	13	58
Beauchaine, Carson, Newark	2	1	2.00	9	0	54	29	15	60
Leiter, Mark, Amsterdam	4	3	2.67	10	0	43	19	16	74
Whitehead, Scott, Watertown	4	2	2.78	11	0	65	65	27	27
Houseal, Brett, Amsterdam	5	1	3.06	10	0	47	51	7	41
Blankenship, Collin, Coop.	2	3	3.74	9	1	53	44	15	37
Kono, Chris, Cooperstown	3	1	3.91	8	0	48	48	17	27

INDIVIDUAL BATTING LEADERS
(MINIMUM 2.7 PLATE APPEARANCES PER TEAM GAME)

	AVG	AB	R	H	2B	3B	HR	RBI	SB
Moses, Trenton, DeKalb	.388	196	36	76	20	1	6	38	1
Anderson, Steve, Chillicothe	.380	192	35	73	22	1	3	28	9
Massey, Craig, Nashville	.367	158	34	58	10	0	3	20	8
Serritella, Chris, Quincy	.359	170	35	61	13	1	15	62	0
Coffman, Cody, Springfield	.355	183	41	65	19	2	3	43	0
Joyce, Doug, Nashville	.355	214	32	76	19	1	6	52	3
Miller, Zach, Danville	.351	174	33	61	11	2	1	25	5
Guidry, Justin, Nashville	.350	217	38	76	12	1	1	27	7
Roberts, Blake, West Virginia	.350	177	37	62	17	5	2	33	11
Houck, Shayne, Butler	.347	199	33	69	19	1	10	44	4

INDIVIDUAL PITCHING LEADERS
(MINIMUM 0.8 INNINGS PITCHED PER TEAM GAME)

	W	L	ERA	G	SV	IP	H	BB	SO
Janway, Josh, Quincy	3	3	1.36	16	5	46	46	8	27
Beach, Adam, Lorain County	6	1	1.47	12	0	61	39	26	65
Schulz, Clayton, Chillicothe	5	2	1.63	9	0	55	43	12	49
Duffy, Brad, Butler	4	2	1.68	8	0	54	42	15	52
Diaz, Julian, Butler	1	2	1.80	21	5	45	35	18	38
Lengel, Matt, Butler	3	3	1.94	8	0	46	44	19	33
Webber, Casey, Chillicothe	2	2	2.20	12	0	57	47	15	61
Rodriguez, Tomas, Dubois Co.	4	2	2.25	10	0	52	55	21	36
Kendzora, T.J., Quincy	8	0	2.58	11	0	70	64	14	43
Heefner, Daniel, Terre Haute	5	0	2.40	16	0	71	68	22	33

TEXAS COLLEGIATE LEAGUE

FINAL STANDINGS	W	L	PCT	GB
East Texas PumpJacks	41	21	.661	—
Coppell Copperheads	37	27	.578	5
Acadiana Cane Cutters	29	29	.500	10
Brazos Valley Bombers	31	33	.484	11½
Victoria Generals	28	31	.475	11½
Alexandria Aces	16	41	.281	22½

PLAYOFFS: Coppell defeated Brazos Valley 2-0 in best-of-three championship series.

TOP 10 PROSPECTS: 1. Tyler Collins, of, Coppell (SIGNED: Tigers). 2. Taylor Dugas, of, Acadiana (Sr., Alabama). 3. Hunter Dozier, 3b, East Texas (So., Stephen F. Austin). 4. Josh Burris, of, Acadiana (SIGNED: Twins). 5. Alec Mills, rhp, Brazos Valley (Jr., Tennessee-Martin). 6. Jason Jester, rhp, East Texas (Jr., Texas A&M). 7. Jaden Dillon, rhp, East Texas (Sr., Texas A&M-Kingsville). 8. Adam Smith, ss/rhp, Brazos Valley (SIGNED: Yankees). 9. Kirby Pellant, ss/2b, East Texas (Jr., Ohio State). 10. Damian Rivera, lhp, Brazos Valley (So., Saint Louis).

COLLEGE

INDIVIDUAL BATTING LEADERS
(MINIMUM 2.7 PLATE APPEARANCES FOR TEAM GAME)

	AVG	AB	R	H	2B	3B	HR	RBI	SB
Porras, Trey, Brazos Valley	.344	209	36	72	4	1	0	21	4
Dugas, Taylor, Acadiana	.329	155	36	51	8	0	0	24	30
Kruse, Chase, Victoria	.325	237	44	77	13	3	0	26	7
Granger, Seth, East Texas	.314	207	48	65	9	5	3	38	13
Girouard, Tyler, East Texas	.308	146	22	46	6	1	1	26	9
Dozier, Hunter, East Texas	.300	180	27	54	10	1	1	34	10
Pellant, Kirby, East Texas	.286	203	44	58	2	0	0	18	33
Hilger, Tid, Alexandria	.286	154	20	44	8	0	1	19	0
Marlow, Ty, East Texas	.283	191	27	54	8	1	3	20	12
Migi, Tyler, Coppell	.282	177	35	50	9	2	2	34	17

INDIVIDUAL PITCHING LEADERS
(MINIMUM 0.8 IP PER TEAM GAME)

	W	L	ERA	G	SV	IP	H	BB	SO
Mils, Alec, Brazos Valley	4	3	1.98	11	1	59	50	7	55
Rivera, Damian, Brazos Valley	7	0	2.01	14	1	58	49	25	33
O'Neal, Carlton, Coppell	6	2	2.23	14	1	69	54	24	51
Ashby, Doug, Coppell	4	1	2.44	15	0	63	66	17	42
Suit, Ben, Alexandria	5	4	2.46	14	1	48	42	18	33
Adams, Andrew, Acadiana	3	1	2.47	12	0	47	29	30	65
Dillon, Jaden, East Texas	7	1	2.48	11	0	62	58	16	42
Munson, Matt, East Texas	5	2	2.61	12	0	69	58	17	38
Manuel, Kaleb, Acadiana	4	2	2.72	8	0	50	43	15	34
Goebel, Ross, Victoria	5	2	2.76	9	0	59	48	25	31

VALLEY LEAGUE

NORTH	W	L	PCT	GB
Winchester Royals	31	18	.633	—
Front Royal Cardinals	20	27	.426	10
Haymarket Senators	19	26	.422	10
Strasburg Express	15	29	.341	13½
CENTRAL	W	L	PCT	GB
Harrisonburg Turks	34	14	.708	—
New Market Rebels	23	24	.489	10½
Woodstuck River Bandits	20	24	.455	12
Luray Wranglers	19	25	.432	13
SOUTH	W	L	PCT	GB
Waynesboro Generals	26	20	.565	—
Covington Lumberjacks	27	25	.519	3
Rockbridge Rapids	26	25	.510	3½
Staunton Braves	22	25	.468	4½

PLAYOFFS: Covington defeated Rockbridge 2-1 in a best of three series.
TOP 10 PROSPECTS: 1. Mac Williamson, of, Harrisonburg (Jr., Wake Forest). 2. Matt Snyder, 1b, Winchester (Sr., Mississippi). 3. Chris Devenski, rhp, Woodstock (SIGNED: White Sox). 4. Dale Carey, of, Luray (So., Miami). 5. Jay Gonzalez, of, Harrisonburg (So., Auburn). 6. Brady Wilson, of, Winchester (Jr., West Virginia). 7. Brad Zebedis, 1b, Strasburg (So., Presbyterian). 8. Jake Boyd, rhp, Luray (Sr., Stetson). 9. Tanner Leighton, of, Woodstock (Jr., The Master's, Calif.). 10. Dodson McPherson, of/1b, Harrisonburg (Sr., Wingate, N.C.).

INDIVIDUAL BATTING LEADERS
(MINIMUM 2.5 PLATE APPEARANCES PER TEAM GAME)

	AVG	AB	R	H	2B	3B	HR	RBI	SB
Zebedis Brad, Strasburg	.420	174	39	73	19	2	5	36	0
Williamson, Mac, Haymarket	.381	126	31	48	11	0	10	38	5
Lopez, Brett, Woodstock	.365	170	28	62	9	1	1	24	6
Walton, Jordan, Waynesboro	.364	165	31	60	9	3	1	32	1
Vigoa, Derek, Woodstock	.357	129	32	46	6	0	0	19	11
Dineen, Ryan, Covington	.350	180	41	63	5	2	3	30	13
Briones, Gibby, Winchester	.348	155	31	54	9	1	0	17	15
Owens, Arthur, Staunton	.346	130	17	45	5	0	1	22	8
Gonzalez, Jay, Harrisonburg	.344	157	45	54	5	1	0	24	32
Dove, Sam, Harrisonburg	.343	143	26	49	14	0	0	30	8

INDIVIDUAL PITCHING LEADERS
(MINIMUM 1.0 INNINGS PITCHED PER TEAM GAME)

	W	L	ERA	G	SV	IP	H	BB	SO
Luchterhand, Aaron, Harris.	4	1	1.60	12	0	73	42	18	48
Spezial, Niko, Harrisonburg	3	1	1.91	9	0	57	61	33	37
Welsh, Greg, Winchester	7	1	2.04	17	0	53	47	19	30
Voiro, Vince, Woodstock	4	2	2.04	9	0	57	46	22	60
Overcash, Ryan, Rockbridge	4	4	2.48	8	0	58	52	8	43
Bouthilette, Sean, Winchester	4	2	2.56	10	0	53	63	9	55
Kelich Peter, Haymarket	5	3	2.57	11	1	67	65	19	51
Rassi, Lincoln, Winchester	3	1	2.89	20	6	53	40	26	71
Tighe, Sean, Covington	2	2	3.04	8	0	56	47	10	47
Cole, Garrett, Covington	5	2	3.05	10	0	65	62	14	41

WEST COAST LEAGUE

EAST	W	L	PCT	GB
Wenatchee AppleSox	39	15	.722	—
Walla Walla Sweets	26	28	.481	13
Bellingham Bells	21	32	.396	17½
Kelowna Falcons	19	34	.358	19½
WEST				
Corvallis Knights	37	17	.685	—
Bend Elks	29	25	.537	8
Cowlitz Black Bears	28	26	.519	9
Kitsap BlueJackets	24	30	.444	13
Klamath Falls Gems	19	35	.352	18

PLAYOFFS: Corvallis defeated Walla Walla 2-0 in a best of three series.
TOP 10 PROSPECTS: 1. Jace Fry, lhp, Corvallis (Fr., Oregon State). 2. Mitchell Walding, ss, Cowlitz (SIGNED: Phillies). 3. Adrian Sampson, rhp, Bellingham (So., Bellevue, Wash., JC). 4. Ben Wetzler, lhp, Corvallis (So., Oregon State). 5. Spencer O'Neil, of, Cowlitz (Fr., Oregon). 6. Breland Almadova, of, Wenatchee (Jr., Hawaii). 7. Adam Nelubowich, 3b/1b, Wenatchee (So., Washington State). 8. Billy Flamion, of, Cowlitz (Fr., Oregon). 9. Jimmie Sherfy, rhp, Corvallis (So., Oregon). 10. Chase Johnson, rhp, Corvallis (So., Cal Poly).

INDIVIDUAL BATTING LEADERS
(MINIMUM 2.7 PLATE APPEARANCES PER TEAM GAME)

	AVG	AB	R	H	2B	3B	HR	RBI	SB
Cawley Lamb, Payden, Wen.	.350	183	34	64	12	1	0	24	7
Stanford, Alex, Walla Walla	.340	194	25	66	12	0	2	11	15
Barnes, Ryan, Wenatchee	.336	125	20	42	4	0	0	18	11
Almadova, Breland, Wen.	.328	180	32	59	12	3	2	32	17
Davis, Cory, Corvallis	.317	145	18	46	4	0	1	17	3
Folkinga, Bo, Kelowna	.310	155	21	48	8	0	0	10	6
Sanguinetti, Rich, KF	.309	207	28	64	6	2	0	18	15
Walter, Bo, Bend	.304	138	20	42	6	0	0	17	1
Nelubowich, Adam, Wen.	.304	204	35	62	10	2	8	36	6
Saiko, Graham, KF	.301	173	23	52	14	1	0	16	2

INDIVIDUAL PITCHING LEADERS
(MINIMUM 0.8 INNINGS PER TEAM GAME)

	W	L	ERA	G	SV	IP	H	BB	SO
Richardson, Ryan, Walla Walla	3	3	1.53	11	0	53	37	7	35
Pulido, Andrew, Bellingham	2	1	1.57	8	0	52	39	5	35
Watson, Brett, Walla Walla	3	2	1.62	10	0	50	34	26	26
Ochoa, Richie, Bellingham	2	3	1.65	12	1	49	38	13	43
Sampson, Adrian, Bellingham	4	4	1.71	9	0	63	42	20	71
Ostapeck, Stephen, Bend	5	3	1.81	15	2	50	43	11	28
Chavez, Daniel, Bend	6	3	1.84	10	0	68	51	11	35
Phillips, Alex, Wenatchee	5	1	1.89	12	0	62	41	6	59
Jones, Owen, Wenatchee	7	1	2.00	15	0	77	53	20	78
Thompson, Cole, Kitsap	2	3	2.12	12	0	47	38	17	20

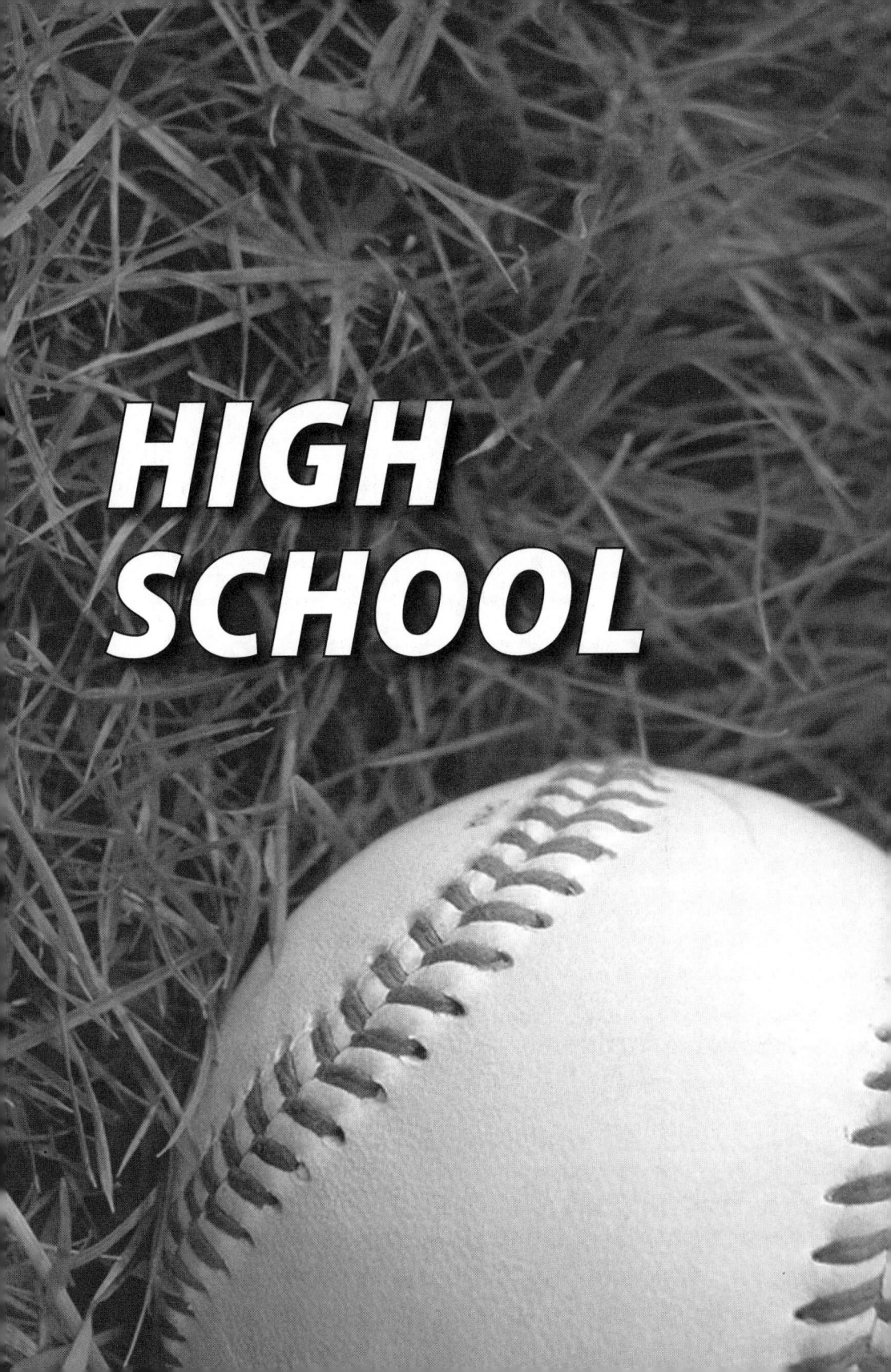

HIGH
SCHOOL

The Mavericks beat Tampa's Jesuit High in the 4-A championship for the second straight year

Archbishop McCarthy makes case for No. 1

BY NATHAN RODE

Ranking the top high school teams in the country is an inexact science, but a key factor to look for is big wins—beating a team's ace, winning a tournament or state title or defeating another national-caliber program. Archbishop McCarthy High in Southwest Ranches, Fla., pulled off a few of those tasks in dramatic fashion, beating nationally-ranked Jesuit High of Tampa in the 4-A state championship game. On the mound for Jesuit was the Tigers' ace and a top pitching prospect for the 2012 draft, righthander Lance McCullers Jr.

Already coming off a 2010 state title with several returning players, the Mavericks rolled to 29-3 record in 2011 and polished their resume with the win over Jesuit to finish the season atop the Baseball America/National High School Baseball Coaches Association Top 25, making them the High School Team of the Year.

"It was an incredible journey," head coach Rich Bielski said. "That's something we preached to the kids all year long: Enjoy the journey. We knew we were going to have a very strong team coming back. We knew last year that this year was going to be a very powerful year as well. The experience we had last year helped us this year."

Turning Point

The Mavericks had a sound pitching staff with a team ERA of 2.08 and crushed opponents on offense, outscoring them by double digits in 15 games. Two of the three losses were by a total of four runs, but a 5-0 loss to Miami's Columbus High on March 14 was the most shocking. Lefthander Luis Collazo, a junior, hurled a no-hitter against the Mavericks. They were expecting to face the Explorers' ace, lefthander Andrew Suarez, a ninth-round pick of the Blue Jays and Miami signee. When they learned he wasn't starting, Bielski says his team got overconfident and Collazo took advantage. That only fueled the fire, however, as the Mavericks bounced back, winning the next nine games.

"That was a changing point in our season, no doubt about it," Bielski said. "The next few games, we scored like 15 runs a game. It angered the players that it was even possible with our lineup and as many good hitters as we had. It was unconscionable. It was a slap in the face, a wakeup call that we couldn't just walk out there because we were Archbishop McCarthy and won the state championship the year before (that) we're going to win games. We had to stay focused, no matter who was pitching."

Rank	School	Record	Season conclusion
1	Archbishop McCarthy HS, Southwest Ranches, Fla.	29-3	Florida 4-A Champion
2	Spanish Fork (Utah) HS	29-3	Utah 4-A Champion
3	Broken Arrow (Okla.) HS	37-2	Oklahoma 6-A Champion
4	Marist School, Atlanta	33-4	Georgia 4-A Champion
5	Buchanan HS, Clovis, Calif.	30-2	CIF Central Section D-I Champion
6	Bishop Gorman HS, Las Vegas	35-4	Nevada 4-A Champion
7	Bishop Amat HS, La Puente, Calif.	29-4	CIF Southern Section D-IV Champion
8	Maize (Kan.) HS	25-0	Kansas 6-A Champion
9	West Boca HS, Boca Raton, Fla.	28-4	Florida 5-A Champion
10	Mountain Pointe HS, Phoenix	28-5	Arizona 5-A-I Champion
11	Owasso (Okla.) HS	37-2	Oklahoma 6-A Runner-Up
12	North HS, Riverside, Calif.	27-7	CIF Southern Section D-I Champion
13	Bishop Verot HS, Fort Myers, Fla.	28-4	Florida 3-A Champion
14	Saguaro HS, Scottsdale, Ariz.	34-4	Arizona 4-A-I Champion
15	Edison HS, Huntington Beach, Calif.	25-4	CIF Southern Section D-I Quarterfinalist
16	Brazoswood HS, Clute, Texas	30-8	Texas 5-A Champion
17	Alonso HS, Tampa	23-5	Florida 6-A Champion
18	Parkview HS, Lilburn, Ga.	29-10	Georgia 5-A Champion
19	JSerra Catholic HS, San Juan Capistrano, Calif.	24-5	CIF Southern Section D-I Runner-Up
20	Columbus (Ga.) HS	30-9	Georgia 3-A Champion
21	Rider HS, Wichita Falls, Texas	38-7	Texas 4-A Champion
22	Jesuit HS, Tampa	26-6	Florida 4-A Runner-Up
23	Gloucester Catholic HS, Gloucester City, N.J.	31-2	New Jersey Non-Public B Champion
24	Petal (Miss.) HS	24-12	Mississippi 6-A Champion
25	Bingham HS, South Jordan, Utah	24-3	Utah 5-A Champion
26	Mater Dei HS, Santa Ana, Calif.	24-6	CIF Southern Section D-I Quarterfinalist
27	Rancho Bernardo HS, San Diego	27-3	CIF San Diego Section D-I Champion
28	Jesuit HS, New Orleans	29-5	Louisiana 5-A Champion
29	Great Bridge HS, Chesapeake, Va.	23-4	Virginia 3-A Champion
30	North Florida Christian School, Tallahassee	27-4	Florida 2-A Champion
31	Carroll HS, Corpus Christi	36-7	Texas 5-A Semifinalist
32	Howell HS, St. Charles, Mo.	32-3	Missouri 4-A Champion
33	Farragut HS, Knoxville	37-8	Tennessee 3-A Champion
34	Washington HS, New York	22-0	PSAL A Champion
35	Westview HS, Portland	27-5	Oregon 6-A Champion
36	Calallen HS, Corpus Christi	39-6	Texas 4-A Runner-Up
37	South County HS, Lorton, Va.	28-1	Virginia 3-A Runner-Up
38	La Cueva HS, Albuquerque	24-5	New Mexico 5-A Champion
39	Brenham (Texas) HS	36-8	Texas 4-A Semifinalist
40	Palo Alto (Calif.) HS	28-9	CIF Central Coast Section D-I Champion
41	Shawnee Heights HS, Tecumseh, Kan.	25-0	Kansas 5-A Champion
42	Regis Jesuit HS, Aurora, Colo.	20-7	Colorado 5-A Champion
43	Archbishop Spalding HS, Severn, Md.	26-5	Maryland MIAA A Champion
44	Spalding HS, Griffin, Ga.	32-5	Georgia 3-A Runner-Up
45	Palm Desert (Calif.) HS	28-5	CIF Southern Section D-IV Runner-Up
46	Don Bosco Prep, Ramsey, N.J.	24-1	New Jersey Non-Public A Quarterfinalist
47	Clements HS, Fort Bend, Texas	34-5	Texas 5-A Region Semifinalist
48	Lakota East HS, Liberty Township, Ohio	25-7	Ohio D-I Champion
49	Orangewood Christian HS, Maitland, Fla.	33-2	Florida 2-A Runner-Up
50	Central Hardin HS, Cecilia, Ky.	36-4	Kentucky Champion

The Mavericks would lose just one more game in their last 20 on their way to the championship. They were led by senior infielders Alexander Fernandez and Jose Brizuela and junior lefthander Andre Martinez. Fernandez and Brizuela were both drafted in the 46th round by the Tigers and Reds, respectively. Fernandez, the son of former major leaguer Alex Fernandez, was a two-way threat, hitting .470 with four home runs and 13 stolen bases. On the mound, he went 10-0, 2.39 in 56 innings with 51 strikeouts and 24 walks. Brizuela hit .477 with seven home runs and got some relief work in, earning five saves in 18 innings over 12 appearances. He struck out 37 and walked eight while

stepping in as a team leader. Martinez went 12-2, 1.50 with 96 strikeouts in 54 innings.

The 2010 squad was led by Nick Castellanos, a supplemental first-round pick by the Tigers and recipient of a $3.45 million bonus. His graduation would be a big loss for any team, but Brizuela says they are best friends and he received some very useful advice in the offseason.

"When he came back in November we trained together," Brizuela said. "I told him it would be different without him. He told me this, 'Keep your composure. You know you can do it. Keep the guys intact. Don't let them get too riled up. And just have fun.' Honestly, I learned a lot from him. I had to fill big shoes. I tried my best to be as good as him and follow his footsteps. Not only as a leader, but as a player and a brother to my teammates. He's a great friend and he's taught me a lot."

Previously a self-titled jokester, Brizuela switched things up this spring and showed maturity. He told his teammates all season that he would lead them to The Port—referring to the state championship being played in Port St. Lucie at the Mets' spring training complex.

"I knew it was going to be a great season," Brizuela added. "I knew I had to step up as a leader. I was always confident in my team no matter if we were losing. I knew we were always in the game and be there to come back and win. It was an honor to play with those guys. They're special guys. They're like my brothers."

On Bielski's coaching staff is Alex Fernandez, owner of a major league no-hitter and a World Series champion with the 1997 Marlins. Coach Alex, as Bielski calls him, was in charge of putting the schedule together for the season. He put together a challenging one in 2010, but increased the difficulty for 2011. A flashy record was the last thing on the coaches' minds. They wanted a schedule that would prepare them for playoffs. It worked out in two ways. The Mavericks finished with a stellar record that prepared them for the playoffs and strengthened their resume for a national championship.

"This is the kind of schedule (where) we're not going to have a pretty record," Bielski said. "You can't. It's tough. Every week you're facing somebody tough. Coach Alex and I have been on the same page. It's never been about our record. It's been about being prepared come playoff time."

Special Experience

Fernandez has had the unique opportunity to experience a championship as a professional player and now a coach. To add to it, his son was a key factor in the team's success and the deciding one in the championship against Jesuit and McCullers.

In the third inning with McCullers sitting in the mid-90s and two runners on base, the young Fernandez sat on a fastball and smoked it to left field for a three-run home run. He also started the game, pitching three innings and allowing one run on four hits. Even a walk-off in a World Series couldn't outrank that experience for the elder Fernandez.

"That is like a storybook ending," he said. "He had a great high school season. He came into his own. To be able to be on the mound and pitch in that game and hit the three-run homer was pretty impressive. I'm especially happy for him. You go

through a lot growing up as the son of a major league baseball player and there's a lot of added pressure, which is really not fair. To come this way and put an exclamation point on his high school career was really impressive."

Bielski described the moment as dreamlike, saying everything went into slow motion and fell silent for him. He snapped back to reality as the ball cleared the wall.

"I felt like that was the shot heard around the world," Bielski said. "That home run would become legendary as far as the history of our program and with the school. I'm sure he's going to get congratulated on that home run for the rest of his life. That's a lifetime memory."

Archbishop McCarthy had experience on its side, also defeating Jesuit in the 2010 finals with lefthander Daniel Gibson going for the Tigers and McCullers in relief. The only difference is the Mavericks are now on top of the nation.

"It was on our focus from day one to try and repeat," Bielski said. "We thought we had a good opportunity to repeat. That was our focus all year. It was always out there, always ahead of us. We felt that if we could get hot and play good baseball at the right time that we would have a shot. We knew it would be a daunting task, going back-to-back because you're not sneaking up on anybody, you have a big target on your back and you're seeing everybody's ace. But that would only make us better throughout the season."

Geographical Oddity

On the high school side, there was a noticeable shift in the draft landscape for 2011. Georgia had a historic year in 2010, producing five first-round picks and 12 picks in the first four rounds, but talent in the Peach State was below-par in 2011. Southern California and Texas also lacked their usual impact talent. This led to the theme of having to look elsewhere for talent.

"There are so many high school guys in small towns this year," an American League crosschecker told Baseball America in May. "Typically you can spend 10 days in Atlanta and see a bunch of guys within a little bit of a radius, but not this year—you're all over Oklahoma, Wyoming, just out-of-the-way places."

Fourteen of the first 33 picks were high school players and they represented 10 different states. Among those were righthanders Dylan Bundy (fourth overall) and Archie Bradley (seventh overall), who hail from Oklahoma; outfielder Bubba Starling (fifth overall), from Kansas; outfielder Brandon Nimmo (13th overall), the highest-drafted player ever from Wyoming; righthander Tyler

Beede (21st overall) from Massachusetts; catcher Blake Swihart (26th overall) from New Mexico; and shortstop Jake Hager (32nd overall), the latest impact talent from Nevada.

While California and Texas had down years, the state of Florida held strong in producing draft picks. Fourteen players from Florida were popped before the conclusion of the second round, with 10 of them being from the high school ranks. Shortstops Franciso Lindor and Javier Baez went back-to-back at the eighth and ninth picks, but also offered an interesting dynamic. Neither attended traditional baseball powers. Baez was at Arlington Country Day School in Jacksonville, an instituion that isn't recognized by the Florida High School Athletic Association, while Lindor's Montverde Academy failed to qualify for the postseason.

Shifting Spring

High school baseball may be witnessing another shift with the increasing emphasis put on travel teams and showcases. A few players have decided to quit their high school team to join a club league in Southern California that plays during the spring. Righthander Cody Poteet of Christian High in El Cajon, Calif., and infielder Tanner Rahier of Palm Desert (Calif.) High are two of the highest profile players to make the decision.

If there is support in the scouting and coaching community for these decsions, it's hard to find.

"It's absolutely the wrong message you're sending younger kids that it's OK to not pitch for their high school team," a scout told BA's Kirk Kenney in August. "From a scout's perspective, we want to see them compete. And this is not competition. At showcases we can't get a good feel for the kid if he's going to come out here for one inning and throw as hard as he can. It does no good for us scouts to see a guy in a showcase but not see him be in a competitive situation. It's 100 percent the wrong path to take. They need to show us they're competitors."

Poteet, a UCLA signee, may find opposition elsewhere.

"I don't like it," UCLA head coach John Savage told the Los Angeles Times. "I think it sends a poor message. It's about your team and developing on and off the field with your teammates."

More Gold

With a 9-0 victory over Cuba in the 2011 IBAF World 'AA'/16U Youth Championships, Team USA claimed its sixth straight gold medal in international competition. Righthander Keegan Thompson (Cullman, Ala., HS) continued a dominating tournament performance by throwing

a complete-game shutout against Cuba, striking out 12 while allowing just four hits and one walk. He went 2-0, 1.29 with 18 strikeouts in 14 innings at the tournament in Lagos de Moreno, Mexico.

"Keegan Thompson is legit," head coach Ernie Padron said. "He didn't let up. He was pounding the strike zone. He had three innings with single-digit pitch counts. He had command, mound presence and he went 4-for-5 at the plate—his out was a one-hop shot at the second baseman."

Thompson has an athletic frame a 6-foot-2, 175 pounds and works with a low-90s fastball, curveball, slider and changeup. Padron said his command and demeanor stood out against Cuba.

"He could throw wherever he wanted to throw, everything," Padron said. "The composure he exhibited for a 16-year-old was mind boggling."

Infielder Zach Collins (American Heritage HS, Plantation, Fla.) was named MVP after hitting .536/.618/.964 with 16 RBIs in 28 at-bats. Outfielder Austin Meadows (Grayson HS, Loganville, Ga.) set a 16U record with 26 RBIs and was named to the all-tournament team.

A member of the 2013 class, Meadows is arguably the best draft prospect on the 16U team. He has a physical frame at 6-foot-3, 200 pounds, and showed an ability to hit for average and power, and run for Team USA.

"We started him as the leadoff guy," Padron said. "I thought he would bring a lot to the team there. Then he got seven RBIs in the first game and we dropped him to third. We did a good job in front of him. He's got three tools that anybody would want. He's a quiet leader. He just goes out and does what he has to do."

The 16U program did see its 45-game winning streak end in an 8-6, 10-inning, second-round loss to Japan. Its last loss had come against Cuba in the gold medal game of the 2005 World Youth Championships. That team featured future big league first baseman Freddie Freeman and right-hander Blake Beavan.

"The win streak was something nice," 16U team director Jeff Singer said. "Had we won against Japan and not Cuba, it wouldn't have meant anything. We were fortunate with a remarkable and crazy win the night before against Venezuela. The goal from the start was August 28 (the date of the gold medal game)."

Lagos de Moreno is at an elevation of over 6,000 feet so there was no shortage of offense for Team USA, who went 4-0 in the first round and outscored opponents 70-21. All four games were shortened under the mercy rule. In the second round, Team USA didn't run into trouble until facing Venezuela. The 16Us were down 5-0 after the second inning, but got

AMATEUR/YOUTH CHAMPIONS 2011

TEAM USA
18U

Event	Site	Champion	Runner-up
Tournament of Stars	Cary, N.C.	Babe Ruth	AABC

16U

Event	Site	Champion	Runner-up
USA Junior Olympics—East	Palm Beach County, Fla.	So. Fla. Elite Black	Team Elite White
USA Junior Olympics—West	Phoenix	Colton Nighthawks	Placentia Mustangs

14U

Event	Site	Champion	Runner-up
USA Junior Olympics—East	Fort Myers, Fla.	The Gravel	Lamorinda National
USA Junior Olympics—West	Phoenix	ABD Bulldogs Navy	Bomberz Baseball 13U

ALL-AMERICAN AMATEUR BASEBALL ASSOCIATION (AAABA) HEADQUARTERS: Zanesville, Ohio

Event	Site	Champion	Runner-up
World Series (21-and-Under)	Johnstown, Pa.	Baltimore	New Orleans

AMATEUR ATHLETIC UNION (AAU) HEADQUARTERS: Lake Buena Vista, Fla.

Event	Site	Champion	Runner-up
10-and-Under Diamond (60-foot)	Orlando, Fla.	Team Miami	Team MVP
10-and-Under Gold (60-foot)	Orlando, Fla.	Boca Storm	Tampa Legends
11-and-Under Diamond (70-foot)	Orlando, Fla.	Central Fla. Gators	All-American Pride
11-and-Under Gold (70-foot)	Orlando, Fla.	Tampa Titans	Team Rawlings
12-and-Under Diamond (70-foot)	Orlando, Fla.	MBA Pride Elite	Mozido Fury Elite
12-and-Under Gold (70-foot)	Orlando, Fla.	Capital Diamondrats	SW Spartans
13-and-Under Diamond (90-foot)	Orlando, Fla.	Lamorinda Monarchs	Naples Naturals
13-and-Under Gold (90-foot)	Orlando, Fla.	Orlando Assault	Boston Jr. Rams
14-and-Under Diamond (90-foot)	Viera, Fla.	Richmond Braves	Florida Stars
14-and-Under Gold (90-foot)	Viera, Fla.	BCC Hurricanes	Beyel Brothers Bulldogs
Underclassmen Diamond	Fort Myers, Fla.	East Cobb Titans	Connecticut Blue Jays
Underclassmen Gold	Acadiana, La.	Westchester County Nats	South Florida Stingers
Upperclassmen Diamond	Acadiana, La.	Tallahassee Baseball	Brazos Valley Renegades

AMERICAN AMATEUR BASEBALL CONGRESS (AABC) HEADQUARTERS: Farmington, N.M.

Event	Site	Champion	Runner-up
Gil Hodges	Brooklyn, N.Y.	Cincy Flames	Connecticut Combat
Pee Wee Reese (12 & U)	Toa Baja, Puerto Rico	San Diego Stars	Dallas Tigers
Sandy Koufax (13 & U)	Battle Creek, Mich.	B.C./Kalamazoo Broncos	Sayo Grays
Sandy Koufax (14 & U)	Surprise, Ariz.	Puerto Rico Vaqueros	New York Youth Service
Ken Griffey, Jr. (15 & U)	Owasso, Okla.	Dallas Tigers	
Mickey Mantle (16 & U)	McKinney, Texas	DBAT Mustangs Sharp	So Cal Bombers
Don Mattingly (17 & U)	Tempe, Ariz.	ABD Bulldogs	EJ Sports Warriors
Connie Mack (18 & U)	Farmington, N.M.	Midland Redskins	Arizona Firebirds
Stan Musial (open)	Huntsville, Texas	Canton Stallions	Houston N.W. Wildcats

BABE RUTH BASEBALL HEADQUARTERS: Trenton, N.J.

Event	Site	Champion	Runner-up
Cal Ripken (10 & U)	Winchester, Va.	Southeastern Lexington, Ky.	Winchester, Va.
Cal Ripken 12-year old (60 ft)	Visalia, Calif.	Visalia, Calif.	Southeastern Lexington, Ky.
Cal Ripken 13-year old (70 ft)	Aberdeen, Md.	Southeastern Lexington, Ky.	Japan
13-year old	Clifton Park, N.Y.	Tri-Valley, Calif.	Clifton Park, N.Y.
14-year old	Glen Allen, Va.	Tualatin Hills, Calif.	Glen Allen, Va.
13-15 year old	Jamestwon, N.Y.	Tri-Valley, Calif.	Tri-Township, Pa.
16-18 year-old	Ephrata, Wash.	Mobile, Ala.	Portland, Ore.

AMERICAN LEGION BASEBALL HEADQUARTERS: Indianapolis

Event	Site	Champion	Runner-up
World Series (19 & U)	Shelby, N.C.	Eden Prairie, Minn.	Tupelo, Miss.

locked into a back-and-forth battle. Venezuela was up 13-9 in the bottom of the eighth, when Team USA put up a five-spot. Venezuela responded with two in the ninth, before the U.S. tied it at 15. Venezuela plated two runs in the 10th, but Team USA again came back and won on a sacrifice fly from outfielder Willie Abreu (Mater Academy, Hialeah, Fla.).

USA Baseball's 18U Team defeated Canada in Cartagena, Colombia, to finish 9-0 and win the COPABE Pan Am Championship, giving USA Baseball the amateur trifecta for 2011. The 14U team won its Pan Am tournament while the 16U squad captured the IBAF World Championship.

The clincher was a 12-2, mercy-rule shortened game. Team USA sent 12 batters to the plate and scored seven runs in the bottom of the first. The big blow came off the bat of shortstop Addison Russell, who hit a grand slam.

CONTINENTAL AMATEUR BASEBALL ASSOCIATION (CABA) HEADQUARTERS: Westerville, Ohio

Event	Site	Champion	Runner-up
8-and-Under	Sylvania, Ohio	Michigan Blue Jays	Brecksville Bees
9-and-Under	Woodstock, Ill.	Cincy Flames	Illinois Mavericks
10-and-Under	Westfield, Ind	Indiana Prospects	Illinois Mavericks
11-and-Under	McHenry/Johnsburg, Ind.	Top Tier	Tinley Park Bulldogs
12-and-Under	Sylvania, Ohio	Upper Deck Stars	Ohio Diamond Hawks
13-and-Under	Westfield, Ind.	East Cobb Astros	Dulin Dodgers
14-and-Under (60x90)	Lebanon, Tenn.	Gravel Baseball	NorCal Baseball
15-and-Under (Aluminum)	Northern Illinois	Schaumberg Seminoles	East Cobb Astros
15-and-Under (Wood)	Charleston, S.C.	SC Shockwave No. 2	Arena Starz No. 1
16-and-Under	Marietta, Ga.	East Cobb Astros	
17-and-Under/HS (Aluminum)	Euclid, Ohio	Bergen Beach	T3 Pelicans
17-and-Under/HS (Wood)	Charleston, S.C.	Hm. Plate Chili Dogs No. 1	Diamond Devils Black No. 2
18-and-Under (Aluminum)	Charleston, S.C.	Diamond Devils Black No. 1	Team New York Scout No. 2
18-and-Under (Wood)	Youngstown, Ohio	Oakland Bulldogs	Astro Falcons

LITTLE LEAGUE BASEBALL HEADQUARTERS: Williamsport, Pa.

Event	Site	Champion	Runner-up
Little League (11-12)	Williamsport, Pa.	Ocean View, Calif.	Japan
Junior League (13-14)	Taylor, Mich.	Palma Ceia, Fla.	Taiwan
Senior League (15-16)	Bangor, Maine	Hilo, Hawaii	Rose Capital East, Texas
Big League (17-18)	Easley, S.C.	S.C. District 7	San Juan, P.R. District 1

NATIONAL AMATEUR BASEBALL FEDERATION (NABF) HEADQUARTERS: Bowie, Md.

Event	Site	Champion	Runner-up
Sophomore (14 & U)	Lynchburg, Va.	Frederick Hustlers	Long Island Storm
Junior (16 & U)	Northville, Mich.	Ohio Glaciers	Bloomington/Normal Gold
High School (17 & U)	Knoxville	Maryland Monarchs	Allen Baseball
Senior (18 & U)	Youngstown, Ohio	Toronto Mets	Houston Raiders

PERFECT GAME/BCS FINALS HEADQUARTERS: Cedar Rapids, Iowa

Event	Site	Champion	Runner-up
14-and-Under	Fort Myers, Fla.	East Cobb Titans	Boca Thunder Baseball
15-and-Under	Fort Myers, Fla.	East Cobb Astros	Orlando Scorpions 2014
16-and-Under	Fort Myers, Fla.	So. Fla. Prospects	Midland Braves
17-and-Under	Fort Myers, Fla.	Texas Sun Devils	Orlando Scorpions Purple
18-and-Under	Fort Myers, Fla.	East Cobb Braves/Bullets Baseball	

PERFECT GAME/WORLD WOOD BAT ASSOCIATION SUMMER CHAMPIONSHIPS
HEADQUARTERS: Cedar Rapids, Iowa

Event	Site	Champion	Runner-up
14-and-Under	Marietta, Ga.	East Cobb Astros	Kentucky Baseball Club
15-and-Under	Marietta, Ga.	East Cobb Astros	Dulin Dodgers
16-and-Under	Marietta, Ga.	So. Fla. Elite Black	Orlando Scorpions Purple
17-and-Under	Marietta, Ga.	East Cobb Braves	Florida Travel Baseball
18-and-Under	Marietta, Ga.	San Diego Show	East Cobb Yankees

PONY BASEBALL HEADQUARTERS: Washington, Pa.

Event	Site	Champion	Runner-up
Mustang (9-10)	Burleson, Texas	Santa Clarita, Calif.	Caguas (Villa Nueva), P.R.
Bronco (11-12)	Chesterfield, Va.	North Tampa, Fla.	Torrance, Calif.
Pony (13)	Fullerton, Calif.	West Covina, Calif.	Fullerton, Calif.
Pony (13-14)	Washington, Pa.	Laredo, Texas	Taiwan
Colt (15-16)	Lafayette, Ind.	Los Gatos, Calif.	Levittown, P.R.
Palomino (17-18)	Compton, Calif.	CM Stars	Lynnhaven Baseball

REVIVING BASEBALL IN INNER CITIES (RBI) HEADQUARTERS: New York

Event	Site	Champion	Runner-up
Junior (13-15)	Minneapolis	Dominican Republic	Los Angeles
Senior (16-18)	Minneapolis	Venice, Calif.	Harrisburg, Pa.

U.S. SPECIALTY SPORTS ASSOCIATION (USSSA) HEADQUARTERS: Petersburg, Va.

Event	Site	Champion	Runner-up
10-and-Under/Majors Elite	Orlando	Oakley Sting Rays	Georgia Yard Dogs Black
11-and-Under/Majors Elite	Orlando	Team Florida	Banditos Black
12-and-Under/Majors Elite	Orlando	Bandits Baseball	Team Florida
13-and-Under/Majors Elite	Orlando	VooDoo Baseball	East Cobb Astros
14-and-Under/Majors Elite	Orlando	Louisiana Tigers	Beaver Valley Red

Bundy Rolls The Competition

When Dylan Bundy takes the mound, people stop to watch. The physical righthander from Oklahoma's Owasso High used an elite arsenal to dominate the competition this season, striking out 158 batters in 71 innings while allowing just five walks and two earned runs. He won all 11 of his starts and also earned a save.

His performance and draft status made him the overwhelming selection for Baseball America's 2011 High School Player of the Year. After being selected by the Orioles with the fourth overall pick, Bundy signed just the eighth major league contract for a high school pick in draft history. He received a $4 million bonus as part of a pact guaranteeing him $6.25 million overall.

We let Bundy, his head coach, Larry Turner, as well as his catcher, Drew Stiner and rotation partner Phillip Wilson tell the story of his remarkable season.

TURNER: "He's the most incredible player that I've ever coached as far as his work ethic. It is unmatched. It made us a better team, better program by rubbing off on other players. In one game in particular, we're playing in a tournament in Bartlesville and he pitches against an out of state team at 7:30 at night. It runs late and we don't get back until about 11 to Owasso. We're playing the next morning at 9 a.m. so we have to leave at 7 to get up there to get ready. He's in the weight room at 5:30 in the morning, running on the treadmill, getting his workout in before we have to go play. He has that kind of commitment and knows what it takes to be successful. He has been a true pleasure to coach. He never thought he was bigger than the program. He was just a team guy."

STINER: "We've played together since we were about 7 years old. Whenever he takes the mound I feel real comfortable. He's right there every time. He's very consistent. He's made me better too. He was a big part of our success at Owasso. He led us. I've hit off of him since we've been little. He's a lot easier to catch than hit."

WILSON: "It was nice to have him pitch in front of you because you knew you were always going to win that game when he pitched. That game was set, so all you had to do was concentrate on your game and that

gave you a little more time to prepare.

"It's just complete domination. When he takes the mound every time, you know he's going to do his best and put everything he has in it for the team. He's prepared enough for that start and the next one."

BUNDY: "Me, my dad and brother, we've prepared our whole lives for this whole year, everything. It's finally coming to reality that I was picked by the Orioles, the same team my brother is on. It's pretty amazing I get the opportunity to be on the same team as my brother.

"We had a very successful season as a team. We came up short last year in the ninth. This year we came up short losing to Broken Arrow. I consider both years I was here a success even though we didn't win. I really didn't think of the draft that much. I was concentrating on being the best teammate I could and doing the most I could to help our team win and having fun while I was doing it.

"I didn't really think of the draft that much beforehand. I didn't know who was going to pick me. The first thing that popped in my head when they said my name was my brother Bobby and I might get the opportunity to play with him. I wouldn't say I cried, but I got a little teary eyed."

Dylan Bundy

Dante Bichette Jr.

PHIL SEARS

FIRST TEAM

Pos.	Name	School	Yr.	AVG	AB	R	H	2B	3B	HR	RBI	SB	DRAFTED
C	Tomas Nido	Orangewood Christian HS, Maitland, Fla.	Jr.	.577	104	44	60	8	1	17	64	2	Not Eligible
IF	Javier Baez	Arlington Country Day School, Jacksonville, Fla.	Sr.	.771	83	46	64	20	6	22	52	28	Cubs (1)
IF	Dante Bichette Jr.	Orangewood Christian HS, Orlando	Sr.	.640	86	58	55	15	2	10	40	15	Yankees (1s)
IF	Trevor Mitsui	Shorewood (Wash.) HS	Sr.	.712	52	39	37	7	1	13	26	6	Rays (12)
IF	David Thompson	Westminster Christian School, Miami	Jr.	.525	99	45	52	9	2	17	45	9	Not Eligible
OF	Josh Bell	Dallas Jesuit HS	Sr.	.575	87	54	50	8	0	13	52	17	Pirates (2)
OF	Austin Cousino	Dublin Coffman (Ohio) HS	Sr.	.529	87	42	29	17	2	10	31	25	Undrafted
OF	Larry Greene	Berrien County HS, Nashville, Ga.	Sr.	.562	89	58	50	11	1	19	52	13	Phillies (1s)
DH	Kevin Cron	Mountain Pointe HS, Phoenix	Sr.	.560	109	32	61	11	0	27	65	0	Mariners (3)
UT	Jake Thompson	Rockwall-Heath HS, Rockwall, Texas	Jr.	.504	131	45	66	17	1	15	58	3	Not Eligible

Pos.	Name	School	Yr.	W	L	ERA	G	SV	IP	H	BB	K	DRAFTED
RHP	Hudson Boyd	Bishop Verot HS, Fort Myers, Fla.	Sr.	13	0	0.44	15	0	80	37	26	131	Twins (1s)
RHP	Archie Bradley	Broken Arrow (Okla.) HS	Sr.	12	1	0.29	14	1	71	33	11	137	D-Backs (1)
RHP	Dylan Bundy	Owasso (Okla.) HS	Sr.	11	0	0.20	12	1	71	20	5	158	Orioles (1)
RHP	Dillon Maples	Pinecrest HS, Southern Pines, N.C.	Sr.	9	0	0.53	11	2	67	18	25	139	Cubs (14)
RHP	Kyle Smith	Santaluces HS, West Palm Beach, Fla.	Sr.	9	1	0.40	13	0	69	46	13	116	Royals (4)
UT	Jake Thompson	Rockwall-Heath HS, Rockwall, Texas	Jr.	12	3	1.90	16	2	88	67	33	131	Not Eligible

SECOND TEAM

Pos.	Name	School	Yr.	AVG	AB	R	H	2B	3B	HR	RBI	SB	DRAFTED
C	Brett Austin	Providence HS, Charlotte	Sr.	.537	82	47	44	10	0	12	38	14	Padres (1s)
IF	Gavin Cecchini	Barbe HS, Lake Charles, La.	Jr.	.532	111	44	59	13	3	11	45	32	Not Eligible
IF	Jake Hager	Sierra Vista HS, Las Vegas	Sr.	.547	128	75	70	22	3	11	57	28	Rays (1)
IF	Andres Sanchez	Flanagan HS, Pembroke Pines, Fla.	Jr.	.500	72	33	36	5	3	17	51	5	Not Eligible
IF	Dan Vogelbach	Bishop Verot HS, Fort Myers, Fla.	Sr.	.467	92	42	43	6	4	19	54	5	Cubs (2)
OF	Ryan O'Hearn	Wakeland HS, Frisco, Texas	Sr.	.505	97	38	49	13	0	15	55	2	Undrafted
OF	Fernelys Sanchez	Washington HS, New York	Jr.	.425	101	44	43	10	8	5	24	41	Not Eligible
OF	Dwight Smith Jr.	McIntosh HS, Peachtree City, Ga.	Sr.	.577	52	31	30	6	1	4	17	5	Blue Jays (1s)
DH	Joey Gallo	Bishop Gorman HS, Las Vegas	Jr.	.471	121	64	57	5	4	25	78	9	Not Eligible
UT	Keegan Thompson	Cullman (Ala.) HS	So.	.433	150	59	65	15	3	17	66	3	Not Eligible

Pos.	Name	School	Yr.	W	L	ERA	G	SV	IP	H	BB	K	DRAFTED
RHP	Tyler Beede	Lawrence Academy, Groton, Mass.	Sr.	8	0	0.69	9	0	51	13	8	102	Blue Jays (1)
RHP	Jose Fernandez	Alonso HS, Tampa	Sr.	13	1	1.35	16	0	93	51	21	134	Marlins (1)
RHP	Michael Fulmer	Deer Creek HS, Edmond, Okla.	Sr.	10	2	0.72	15	3	68	22	24	127	Mets (1s)
LHP	Henry Owens	Edison HS, Huntington Beach, Calif.	Sr.	12	1	1.15	17	3	92	45	30	140	Red Sox (1s)
RHP	Robert Stephenson	Alhambra HS, Martinez, Calif.	Sr.	8	2	1.19	14	0	76	33	23	142	Reds (1)
UT	Keegan Thompson	Cullman (Ala.) HS	So.	9	2	1.70	15	0	83	52	16	123	Not Eligible

DRAFT

Depth of power arms gives 2011 draft class its identity

BY CONOR GLASSEY

K ris Kline had it easy.

The 2009 and 2010 drafts were defined by one player, and the Nationals' scouting director held the first pick both times. In 2009, righthander Stephen Strasburg captured the country's attention as one of the most dominating college pitchers ever. The year after that it was all about Las Vegas phenom Bryce Harper, who graduated high school two years early to become draft-eligible.

In 2011, after a 57-105 campaign the year prior, the Pirates held the first pick, but the class didn't have a no-brainer option like 2009 and 2010.

The top three players coming into the season all had some hiccups. Rice third baseman Anthony Rendon was mostly used as a DH while nursing a shoulder injury. UCLA righthander Gerrit Cole was inconsistent and didn't dominate lineups like his stuff would indicate, while Texas Christian lefthander Matt Purke was sidelined with shoulder soreness.

The 2011 draft marked the fourth time the Pirates held the No. 1 pick, and in the end, they chose Cole. In 1986 the franchise selected shortstop Jeff King out of Arkansas. In 1996 Clemson righthander Kris Benson was the top choice, and Pittsburgh famously chose Ball State righthander

UCLA's Gerrit Cole (right) and Trevor Bauer were picked first and third overall in 2011

JESSE SOLL

DRAFT

FIRST-ROUND BONUS PROGRESSION

Teams spent an average of $2,653,375 on first-round picks in 2011, breaking the record of $2,458,714 established three years earlier. The 2011 average represented an increase of 19.5 percent from 2010, the biggest one-year increase since 1997-98.

After the first draft in 1965, first-round bonuses rose by an average of just 0.6 percent annually for the rest of the 1960s and 5.2 percent per year in 1970s. Bonus inflation started to pick up in the 1980s, averaging 10.2 percent annually, and soared to 26.9 percent per year in the 1990s. Since MLB instituted an informal slotting system in 2000, first-round bonuses have risen by an average of 3.8 percent.

Below are the annual averages for first-round bonuses since the draft started in 1965 (averages include the value of college scholarship and incentive bonus plans from 1965-82, and cash bonuses only from 1983 on):

YEAR	AVERAGE	CHANGE						
1965	$42,516	—	1980	$74,025	+8.7%	1996*	$944,404	+2.9%
1966	$44,430	+4.5%	1981	$78,573	+6.1%	1997	$1,325,536	+40.4%
1967	$42,898	-3.4%	1982	$82,615	+5.1%	1998	$1,637,667	+23.1%
1968	$43,850	+2.2%	1983	$87,236	+5.6%	1999	$1,809,767	+10.5%
1969	$43,504	-0.8%	1984	$105,391	+20.8%	2000	$1,872,586	+3.5%
1970	$45,230	+3.9%	1985	$118,115	+12.1%	2001	$2,154,280	+15.0%
1971	$45,197	-0.1%	1986	$116,300	-1.6%	2002	$2,106,793	-2.2%
1972	$44,952	-0.5%	1987	$128,480	+10.5%	2003	$1,765,667	-16.2%
1973	$48,832	+8.6%	1988	$142,540	+10.9%	2004	$1,958,448	+10.9%
1974	$53,333	+9.2%	1989	$176,008	+23.5%	2005	$2,018,000	+3.0%
1975	$49,333	-7.5%	1990	$252,577	+43.5%	2006	$1,933,333	-4.2%
1976	$49,631	+0.6%	1991	$365,396	+44.7%	2007	$2,098,083	+8.5%
1977	$48,813	-1.6%	1992	$481,893	+31.9%	2008	$2,458,714	+17.2%
1978	$67,892	+39.1%	1993	$613,037	+27.2%	2009	$2,434,800	-1.0%
1979	$68,094	+0.2%	1994	$790,357	+28.9%	2010	$2,220,966	-8.8%
			1995	$918,019	+16.1%	2011	$2,653,375	+19.5%

*Doesn't include four loophole free agents.

Bryan Bullington in 2002 over B.J. Upton.

Bucs scouting director Greg Smith had selected within the top four picks the past three years and used those choices to grab third baseman Pedro Alvarez (second overall in 2008), Tony Sanchez (fourth, 2009) and Jameson Taillon (second, 2010). For Smith, 2011 was the second time he's had first dibs on any player—his first year as scouting director in Detroit was 1997, when the team drafted Rice righthander Matt Anderson.

Smith has scouted literally thousands of players since that pick and felt the extra experience made him much more prepared this time around.

"I don't know if many first-year scouting directors are prepared to have the No. 1 pick, just for all the things that go into the process," Smith said in May. "Yeah, you can go out and scout players and you can travel, but when you take all the dynamics that go into a No. 1 selection, I think we as an organization in Pittsburgh and myself, individually, are much more prepared and much more equipped to make the selection now."

Despite the uncertainty at the top, this year's class did offer good depth. It may even wind up as a better class than 2005—a year that featured Justin Upton, Ryan Zimmerman, Ryan Braun, Troy Tulowitzki, Andrew McCutchen, Jay Bruce and Colby Rasmus, to name a few.

"I've been doing it a while and I would say not even in the 2000s, or maybe even before that, was the last time I saw this kind of depth," a National League scouting director said. "It's been a long time."

While 2005 obviously featured a lot of high-upside position players, this class was very strong on the mound. There was a surprising amount of velocity and it was an above-average year for high school players. As usual (and unlike '05), there weren't a lot of impact bats at the college level and things thinned out quickly at up-the-middle positions teams covet, like catcher and shortstop.

"It's a really good draft," an American League scouting director said during the spring. "In this year's draft, there might be some fourth- and fifth-round picks that maybe in an average year could be late first-round, early second-round picks."

It's a bit surprising that it was such a strong collection of talent because none of the typical hotbed states—California, Texas, Florida and Georgia—was home to a banner crop this year. Instead, many premium players were from non-traditional states.

"There are so many high school guys in small towns this year," an American League crosschecker said. "Typically you can spend 10 days in Atlanta

DRAFT EXPENDITURES BY CLUB

Teams didn't just break the industry record for draft spending for the fourth straight year, they shattered it. They spent a combined $228 million on bonuses, up from $195.8 million in 2011. Including guaranteed salaries included in major league contracts for Danny Hultzen (Mariners), Trevor Bauer (Diamondbacks), Dylan Bundy (Orioles), Anthony Rendon (Nationals) and Matt Purke (Nationals), clubs paid a total of $236.1 million. The Pirates ($17,005,700) set a new record for bonus spending by a single team, with the Nationals, Royals, Cubs and Diamondbacks also surpassing the previous mark of $11,927,200 set by Washington in 2010. Ten different clubs topped $10 million, compared to eight in the first 46 years of the draft.

TEAM	2011	2010	2009
Pirates	$17,005,700	$11,900,400	$8,918,900
Nationals	$15,002,100	$11,927,200	$11,511,500
Royals	$14,066,000	$6,697,000	$6,657,000
Cubs	$11,994,550	$4,727,100	$4,044,200
Diamondbacks	$11,930,000	$4,399,300	$9,328,200
Rays	$11,482,900	$7,150,800	$4,004,500
Mariners	$11,330,500	$4,942,500	$10,945,600
Padres	$11,020,600	$4,262,000	$9,139,000
Blue Jays	$10,996,500	$11,594,400	$4,895,200
Red Sox	$10,978,700	$10,664,400	$7,095,400
Orioles	$8,432,100	$9,159,900	$8,730,200
Indians	$8,225,000	$9,381,500	$4,943,000
Brewers	$7,509,300	$2,432,200	$6,759,500
Mets	$6,782,500	$4,721,200	$3,134,300
Reds	$6,378,900	$5,739,300	$5,855,400
Yankees	$6,324,500	$6,652,500	$7,564,500
Giants	$6,266,000	$4,102,900	$6,289,000
Twins	$5,902,300	$3,511,300	$4,694,100
Astros	$5,545,800	$7,275,530	$4,212,800
Phillies	$4,689,800	$3,927,900	$3,229,500
Cardinals	$4,554,000	$6,692,200	$5,388,500
Rangers	$4,193,000	$8,487,800	$4,684,200
Marlins	$4,135,000	$4,380,500	$4,142,800
Rockies	$3,967,900	$4,785,700	$7,924,300
Braves	$3,735,700	$3,925,100	$4,400,500
Dodgers	$3,509,300	$7,992,900	$4,037,100
Angels	$3,318,100	$8,095,300	$6,792,900
Athletics	$3,067,300	$5,022,400	$6,439,400
Tigers	$2,878,700	$7,301,400	$9,395,100
White Sox	$2,786,300	$3,930,200	$4,178,600
Total	**$228,009,050**	**$195,782,830**	**$189,335,200**
Average	**$7,600,302**	**$6,526,094**	**$6,311,173**

and see a bunch of guys within a little bit of a radius, but not this year—you're all over Oklahoma, Wyoming, just out-of-the-way places."

The 2011 first round featured players from 21 states. There was outfielder Bubba Starling in Kansas, a Nebraska football signee who became the highest-drafted high schooler the Sunflower State has produced when the Royals selected him fifth overall. Oklahoma had prep righthanders Dylan Bundy (Orioles, fourth overall) and Archie Bradley (Diamondbacks, seventh overall). Connecticut featured a pair of first-rounders in outfielder George Springer (Astros, 11th overall) and righthander Matt Barnes (Red Sox, 19th overall), and high school catcher Blake Swihart (Red Sox, 26th overall) hails from New Mexico.

The state of Oregon produced one first-rounder

(Jacoby Ellsbury) over the past 16 years, but got another this year with Ducks lefthander Tyler Anderson, who went to the Rockies as the 20th overall pick. The first round also featured first baseman C.J. Cron from Utah (Angels, 17th overall), second baseman Kolten Wong from Hawaii (Cardinals, 22nd overall) and high school outfielder Brandon Nimmo from Wyoming (Mets, 13th overall).

Shuffled At The Top

The drama started early in the first round of the 2011 draft.

The Pirates took away a bit of the anticipation the night before draft day, when multiple sources confirmed they would select UCLA righthander Gerrit Cole first overall. Cole became the first Bruin ever taken with the No. 1 pick.

The real drama started with the Mariners and the second overall pick. Seattle had long been tied to a position player, most notably linked to Rendon, Starling and Florida prep shortstop Francisco Lindor.

Instead, the Mariners surprised the industry and selected Virginia lefthander Danny Hultzen. Hultzen's reaction on MLB Network's draft broadcast was a mix of shock and speechlessness. "I did not (expect to picked No. 2)," he said. "This is completely unexpected."

Mariners scouting director Tom McNamara told reporters, "I believe in taking the best player or the best pitcher (available), and Dan was the best guy

at pick No. 2, no doubt."

Hultzen's selection set off a chain reaction, as the top six prospects on Baseball America's Top 200 still went in the first six picks, just not to the teams rumored to be most interested before the draft.

The Diamondbacks took Cole's UCLA teammate, righthander Trevor Bauer, at No. 3 overall. And when the Orioles selected Oklahoma prep righthander Dylan Bundy at No. 4, that was the first time that the first four picks in any draft had been spent on pitchers.

"I thought it was unique with all the velocity," said Rays scouting director R.J. Harrison, who evaluated the class with an eye on Tampa Bay's record haul of 10 picks in the first 60. "I saw a lot of it this spring . . . Pointing to one thing that was unique, it was power, radar-gun type of velocity."

The Rays greatly benefited from the free agent compensation system. After losing Carl Crawford, Rafael Soriano, Grant Balfour, Brad Hawpe, Joaquin Benoit, Randy Choate and Chad Qualls to free agency, the Rays inherited 10 extra picks in the first and supplemental first round. Combined with their own first-round pick, the Rays had 11 of the first 75 selections.

"Tampa's having the best draft in 2011," a third National League scouting director said. "You can book it right now. Just get it right on 40 percent of the (extra) picks and that'll do it."

Two players expected to go higher—South Carolina prep righthander Taylor Guerrieri and Louisiana State outfielder Mikie Mahtook—fell to Tampa's first two picks at Nos. 24 and 31, and the club found three high school position players and two lefthanders among its next eight selections.

"The most agonizing part of the whole night was waiting to see who we were going to get at 24, and after that, it all fell into place for us because we prepared so well," Harrison said. "We grinded it out pretty good all week, kind of eliminated guys and moved guys, and then the day before the draft—it was the first time we had done it—we had two mock drafts. The guys tried to create a chaotic situation in one of them, and the other was a little more straightforward.

"(They) simulated some tougher situations for us, so once the draft came around, things just kind of fell into place real well."

A Sort Of Homecoming

The pitcher run left the Royals picking between Rendon and Starling. They took the hometown hero, Starling, and had to buy him out of a football commitment to Nebraska.

"We got the player we wanted, we got the most electric athlete and player in the draft, and it just happened to be in our backyard as well," Royals scouting director Lonnie Goldberg said in a conference call after the draft. "Obviously, his athleticism and probably his competitiveness and his desire to be a Royal as well, so it fit all of our needs. He's got raw power, he's got speed, he's got a plus arm. You name it, pick one. He's got a lot of them."

That left Rendon at No. 6 overall, where the Nationals snapped him up. For the third straight season, Washington wound up taking the No. 1 player on BA's Top 200, as Rendon joined Strasburg and Harper in Washington's fold.

UCLA Duo Ties Record

Cole had some time to prepare his reaction to becoming the first overall pick in the 2011 draft. Word filtered out early on the night before the draft that the Pirates would take Cole with the top choice, and the club called him about a half-

Kansas prep outfielder Bubba Starling became the state's highest-drafted prep

hour before the start of the draft to notify him officially.

There was a little more suspense for Bauer, the College Player of the Year. But Cole was ready when commissioner Bud Selig announced that the Diamondbacks had taken Bauer with the third overall selection.

"I gave him a call right after he got picked," Cole said. "We were both ecstatic—just kind of (exchanged) congratulations back and forth, really. I had a little more time to think about the conversation than he did, and that kind of jumped on him pretty quick. So there wasn't really a lot of substance because I think we're both pretty much

FIRST-ROUND TRENDS

Year	College	HS	Hitters	Pitchers	Average Bonus	Change
2000	12	18	13	17	$1,872,586	+3.5%
2001	18	12	10	*20	$2,154,280	+15.0%
2002	14	16	14	16	$2,106,793	-2.2%
2003	18	12	*20	10	$1,765,667	*-16.2%
2004	17	13	11	19	$1,958,448	+10.9%
2005	19	10	17	13	$2,018,000	+3.0%
2006	16	13	12	18	$1,933,333	-4.2%
2007	13	17	13	17	$2,098,083	+8.5%
2008	*21	9	11	19	$2,458,714	+17.2%
2009	15	16	16	16	$2,434,800	-1.0%
2010	15	17	18	14	$2,220,966	-8.8%
2011	19	14	14	19	*$2,653,375	+19.5%

*Draft record.

DRAFT RECORDS BY ROUND

ROUND	PLAYER, POS, TEAM	YEAR	BONUS
1st	Gerrit Cole, rhp, Pirates	2011	$8,000,000
Supp. 1st	Nick Castellanos, 3b, Tigers	2010	$3,450,000
2nd	Josh Bell, of, Pirates	2011	$5,000,000
3rd	Matt Purke, lhp, Nationals	2011	$2,750,000
4th	A.J. Cole, rhp, Nationals	2010	$2,000,000
5th	Ryan Westmoreland, of, Red Sox	2008	$2,000,000
6th	Jack McGeary, lhp, Nationals	2007	$1,800,000
7th	Brett Hunter, rhp, Athletics	2008	$1,100,000
8th	Colton Cain, lhp, Pirates	2009	$1,125,000
9th	Clay Holmes, rhp, Pirates	2011	$1,200,000
10th	Luis Cota, rhp, Royals*	2003	$1,050,000
11th	Chris Huseby, rhp, Cubs	2006	$1,300,000
12th	Mike Rozier, lhp, Red Sox	2004	$1,575,000
13th	Jimmy Barthmaier, rhp, Astros	2003	$750,000
14th	Dillon Maples, rhp, Cubs	2011	$2,500,000
15th	J.P. Ramirez, of, Nationals	2008	$1,000,000
Post-15th	Sean Henn, lhp, Yankees*	2000	$1,701,000

*Signed following year as draft-and-follow.

THE BONUS RECORD

Rick Monday, the No. 1 overall pick in baseball's first draft in 1965, signed with the Athletics for $100,000—a figure that no draftee bettered for a decade. The record has been broken several times since, with Gerrit Cole setting a new standard last August when the Pirates signed 2011's No. 1 overall pick for $8 million. The list below represents only cash bonuses and doesn't include guaranteed money from major league deals, college scholarship plans or incentives. It also considers only players who signed with the clubs that drafted them and doesn't include draft picks who signed after being granted free agency, such as Bill Bordley ($200,000 from the Giants after the Reds selected him in the January 1979 draft) and Matt White ($10.2 million from the Devil Rays after the Giants chose him in the 1996 draft).

YEAR	PLAYER, POS., CLUB (ROUND)	BONUS
1965	Rick Monday, of, Athletics (1)	$100,000
1975	Danny Goodwin, c, Angels (1)	$125,000
1978	Kirk Gibson, of, Tigers (1)	$150,000
	*Bob Horner, 3b, Braves (1)	$162,000
1979	Todd Demeter, 1b, Yankees (2)	$208,000
1988	Andy Benes, rhp, Padres (1)	$235,000
1989	Tyler Houston, c, Braves (1)	$241,500
	*Ben McDonald, rhp, Orioles (1)	$350,000
	*John Olerud, 1b, Blue Jays (3)	$575,000
1991	Mike Kelly, of, Braves (1)	$575,000
	Brien Taylor, lhp, Yankees (1)	$1,550,000
1994	Paul Wilson, rhp, Mets (1)	$1,550,000
	Josh Booty, 3b, Marlins (1)	$1,600,000
1996	Kris Benson, rhp, Pirates (1)	$2,000,000
1997	Rick Ankiel, lhp, Cardinals (2)	$2,500,000
	Matt Anderson, rhp, Tigers (1)	$2,505,000
1998	*J.D. Drew, of, Cardinals (1)	$3,000,000
	*Pat Burrell, 3b, Phillies (1)	$3,150,000
	Mark Mulder, lhp, Athletics (1)	$3,200,000
	Corey Patterson, of, Cubs (1)	$3,700,000
1999	Josh Hamilton, of, Devil Rays (1)	$3,960,000
2000	Joe Borchard, of, White Sox (1)	$5,300,000
2005	Justin Upton, ss, Diamondbacks (1)	$6,100,000
2008	Tim Beckham, ss, Rays (1)	$6,150,000
	Buster Posey, c, Giants (1)	$6,200,000
2009	Donavan Tate, cf, Padres (1)	$6,250,000
	*Stephen Strasburg, rhp, Nationals (1)	$7,500,000
2011	Gerrit Cole, rhp, Pirates (1)	$8,000,000

*Part of major league contract.

speechless."

"I think he probably had my number ready and hit 'call,' " Bauer said, "because the call came in a couple seconds after the pick was announced."

The two Bruins matured together in three years at UCLA, and so did their relationship—which was once a bit rocky. They drove each other and made each other better, and they became the first pair of college teammates to be drafted among the top three picks since Arizona State's Bob Horner and Hubie Brooks in 1978.

"I think it really speaks to the talent pool in Southern California, and also being on a staff with him," Bauer said. "When you have that competition on the same staff as you, it pushes you to get better. It's been a motivating factor for me to go out and compete and try to out-pitch him. I think it pushes everyone on the staff to try to get better."

UCLA coach John Savage said he thinks the competition between Bauer and Cole helped both pitchers "a ton."

"They're two of the most competitive guys I've ever been around," Savage said. "Gerrit pitched on Friday, Trevor pitched on Saturday for most of their careers at UCLA. There were a lot of competitions going back and forth—strikeouts, performances, number of hits—and I think they fed off each other. Sometimes it doesn't work, but I think in this case it did for both of them. Coming out of college being the first and third picks, I don't think a lot of people could argue that both of them performed and fed off it in a positive way."

Cole and Bauer both heaped praise on Savage and his staff for helping them develop, and so did Pirates scouting director Greg Smith.

"Obviously (Savage has) done a good job devel-

oping young men, quality student-athletes," Smith said. "It's just a credit to what the UCLA Bruins are doing out there."

"It's really a credit to coach Savage and his recruiting, and his knowledge about pitching," Bauer said. "Without him, I don't think either of us would have been drafted that high. He's taught me and Gerrit a whole lot in our time at UCLA—we've spent three years with him. We've picked up countless amounts of knowledge: the changeup, how important it is to command the fastball to both sides of the plate, when to throw the breaking ball in the dirt, stuff like that . . . I feel like we've done a good job taking a program that was building momentum and carrying that on."

Bauer signed on July 25 and started his professional career with high Class A Visalia before getting a promotion at the end of the season to

DRAFT

The Nationals got BA's highest-ranked player with Rice's Anthony Rendon

ANDREW WOOLLEY

Double-A Mobile. Over his first seven pro games, Bauer went 1-2, 5.96 with 43 strikeouts and 12 walks over 26 innings. Cole signed at the deadline and made his debut in the Arizona Fall League.

Surprise Picks

Two of the oddest picks in the draft came in the ninth round, when the Mariners took shortstop Cavan Cohoes and the Angels selected righthander Nick Mutz.

Cohoes, whose father is in the Army, attended an American high school on the Patch Barracks in Germany, so he was the rare European prospect who is also draft-eligible.

A 6-foot-2, 185-pound shortstop, Cohoes is raw even by European standards but gets attention for his projectable body and excellent athleticism. He was one of the best athletes in Europe and a plus runner with an above-average arm. His hands need work but he has the speed to play center field if he can't stick at shortstop.

Scouts' biggest question with Cohoes is his bat. He has a quick stroke, but he has trouble maintaining his swing and is raw at the plate. He has hit well against his high school competition but he hasn't had to face Europe's best prospects. He was committed to Ohio State, but chose to sign for $650,000 instead.

Mutz, meanwhile, left NAIA Dakota State

(S.D.) in 2010 and did not pitch last spring. The Angels received a tip on him, however, and brought him into a predraft workout. Mutz threw a 20-25-pitch bullpen session, and that's all the Halos needed to see to pop the 6-foot-1, 190-pounder. Mutz showed an easy 94-95 mph fastball with life down in the zone and good angle for his size. Mutz also showed flashes of an above-average cutter. The Angels followed his progress in the Cape Cod League and signed him for $100,000.

TOP 100 PICKS

The Rays had 12 of the first 100 picks, led by South Carolina prep righthander Taylor Guerrieri

TEAM, PLAYER, POS., SCHOOL	BONUS
1. Pirates. Gerrit Cole, rhp, UCLA	$8,000,000
2. Mariners. Danny Hultzen, lhp, Virginia	$6,350,000
3. Diamondbacks. Trevor Bauer, rhp, UCLA	$3,400,000
4. Orioles. Dylan Bundy, rhp, HS—Owasso, Okla.	$4,000,000
5. Royals. Bubba Starling, of, HS—Gardner, Kan.	$7,500,000
6. Nationals. Anthony Rendon, 3b, Rice	$6,000,000
7. D-Backs. Archie Bradley, rhp, HS—Broken Arrow, Okla.	$5,000,000
8. Indians. Francisco Lindor, ss, HS—Montverde, Fla.	$2,900,000
9. Cubs. Javier Baez, ss, HS—Jacksonville, Fla.	$2,625,000
10. Padres. Cory Spangenberg, 2b, Indian River (Fla.) JC	$1,863,000
11. Astros. George Springer, of, Connecticut	$2,525,000
12. Brewers. Taylor Jungmann, rhp, Texas	$2,525,000
13. Mets. Brandon Nimmo, of, HS—Cheyenne, Wyo.	$2,100,000
14. Marlins. Jose Fernandez, rhp, HS—Tampa	$2,000,000
15. Brewers. Jed Bradley, lhp, Georgia Tech	$2,000,000
16. Dodgers. Chris Reed, lhp, Stanford	$1,589,000
17. Angels. C.J. Cron Jr., 1b, Utah	$1,467,000
18. Athletics. Sonny Gray, rhp, Vanderbilt	$1,540,000
19. Red Sox. Matt Barnes, rhp, Connecticut	$1,500,000
20. Rockies. Tyler Anderson, lhp, Oregon	$1,400,000
21. Blue Jays. Tyler Beede, rhp, HS—Groton, Mass.	Did not sign
22. Cardinals. Kolten Wong, 2b, Hawaii	$1,300,000
23. Nationals. Alex Meyer, rhp, Kentucky	$2,000,000
24. Rays. Taylor Guerrieri, rhp, HS—Columbia, S.C.	$1,600,000
25. Padres. Joe Ross, rhp, HS—Oakland	$2,750,000
26. Red Sox. Blake Swihart, c, HS—Rio Rancho, N.M.	$2,500,000
27. Reds. Robert Stephenson, rhp, HS—Martinez, Calif.	$2,000,000
28. Braves. Sean Gilmartin, lhp, Florida State	$1,134,000
29. Giants. Joe Panik, ss, St. John's	$1,116,000
30. Twins. Levi Michael, ss, North Carolina	$1,175,000
31. Rays. Mikie Mahtook, of, Louisiana State	$1,150,000
32. Rays. Jake Hager, ss, HS—Las Vegas	$963,000
33. Rangers. Kevin Matthews, lhp, HS—Richmond Hill, Ga.	$936,000
34. Nationals. Brian Goodwin, of, Miami Dade JC	$3,000,000
35. Blue Jays. Jacob Anderson, of, HS—Chino, Calif.	$990,000
36. Red Sox. Henry Owens, lhp, HS—Huntington Beach, Calif.	$1,550,000
37. Rangers. Zach Cone, of, Georgia	$873,000
38. Rays. Brandon Martin, ss, HS—Corona, Calif.	$860,000
39. Phillies. Larry Greene, of, HS—Nashville, Ga.	$1,000,000
40. Red Sox. Jackie Bradley, of, South Carolina	$1,100,000
41. Rays. Tyler Goeddel, 3b, HS—Mountain View, Calif.	$1,500,000
42. Rays. Jeff Ames, rhp, Lower Columbia (Wash.) JC	$650,000
43. Diamondbacks. Andrew Chafin, lhp, Kent State	$875,000
44. Mets. Michael Fulmer, rhp, HS—Edmond, Okla.	$937,500
45. Rockies. Trevor Story, ss, HS—Irving, Texas	$915,000
46. Blue Jays. Joe Musgrove, rhp, HS—El Cajon, Calif.	$500,000
47. White Sox. Keenyn Walker, of, Central Arizona JC	$795,000
48. Padres. Mike Kelly, rhp, HS—West Boca Raton, Fla.	$718,000
49. Giants. Kyle Crick, rhp, HS—Sherman, Texas	$900,000
50. Twins. Travis Harrison, 3b, HS—Tustin, Calif.	$1,050,000

TEAM, PLAYER, POS., SCHOOL	BONUS
51. Yankees. Dante Bichette Jr., of, HS—Orlando Fla.	$750,000
52. Rays. Blake Snell, lhp, HS—Shoreline, Wash.	$684,000
53. Blue Jays. Dwight Smith Jr., of, HS—McIntosh, Ga.	$800,000
54. Padres. Brett Austin, c, HS—Charlotte N.C.	Did not sign
55. Twins. Hudson Boyd, rhp, HS—Fort Myers, Fla.	$1,000,000
56. Rays. Kes Carter, of, Western Kentucky	$625,000
57. Blue Jays. Kevin Comer, rhp, HS—Tabernacle, N.J.	$1,650,000
58. Padres. Jace Peterson, ss, McNeese State	$624,600
59. Rays. Grayson Garvin, lhp, Vanderbilt	$370,000
60. Rays. James Harris, of, HS—Oakland	$490,000
61. Pirates. Josh Bell, of, HS—Dallas	$5,000,000
62. Mariners. Brad Miller, ss, Clemson	$750,000
63. Diamondbacks. Anthony Meo, rhp, Coastal Carolina	$625,000
64. Orioles. Jason Esposito, 3b, Vanderbilt	$600,000
65. Royals. Cam Gallagher, c, HS—Lancaster, Pa.	$750,000
66. Phillies. Roman Quinn, ss, HS—Port St. Joe, Fla.	$775,000
67. Indians. Dillon Howard, rhp, HS—Searcy, Ark.	$1,850,000
68. Cubs. Dan Vogelbach, 1b, HS—Fort Myers, Fla.	$1,600,000
69. Astros. Adrian Houser, rhp, HS—Locust Grove, Okla.	$530,100
70. Brewers. Jorge Lopez, rhp, HS—Cayey, P.R.	$690,000
71. Mets. Cory Mazzoni, rhp, North Carolina State	$437,500
72. Marlins. Adam Conley, lhp, Washington State	$625,000
73. Dodgers. Alex Santana, 3b, HS—Cape Coral, Fla.	$499,500
74. Blue Jays. Daniel Norris, lhp, HS—Johnson City, Tenn.	$2,000,000
75. Rays. Granden Goetzman, of, HS—Palmetto, Fla.	$490,000
76. Tigers. James McCann, c, Arkansas	$577,900
77. Rockies. Carl Thomore, of, HS—East Brunswick, N.J.	$480,000
78. Blue Jays. Jeremy Gabryszwski, rhp, HS—Crosby, Texas	$575,000
79. Cardinals. Charlie Tilson, of, HS—Winnetka, Ill.	$1,275,000
80. White Sox. Erik Johnson, rhp, California	$450,000
81. Red Sox. Williams Jerez, of, HS—Brooklyn	$443,700
82. Padres. Austin Hedges, c, HS—San Juan Capistrano, Calif.	$3,000,000
83. Rangers. Will Lamb, lhp, Clemson	$430,200
84. Reds. Gabriel Rosa, of, HS—Rio Grande, P.R.	$500,000
85. Braves. Nick Ahmed, ss, Connecticut	$417,600
86. Giants. Andrew Susac, c, Oregon State	$1,100,000
87. Twins. Madison Boer, rhp, Oregon	$405,000
88. Yankees. Sam Stafford, lhp, Texas	Did not sign
89. Rays. Lenny Linsky, rhp, Hawaii	$392,400
90. Phillies. Harold Martinez, 3b, Miami	$387,000
91. Pirates. Alex Dickerson, 1b, Indiana	$380,700
92. Mariners Kevin Cron, 1b, HS—Phoenix	Did not sign
93. Diamondbacks. Justin Bianco, of, HS—Canonsburg, Pa.	$369,000
94. Orioles. Mike Wright, rhp, East Carolina	$363,300
95. Royals. Bryan Brickhouse, rhp, HS—The Woodlands, Texas	$1,500,000
96. Nationals. Matt Purke, lhp, Texas Christian	$2,750,000
97. Indians. Jake Sisco, rhp, Merced (Calif.) JC	$325,000
98. Cubs. Zeke DeVoss, of, Miami	$500,000
99. Astros. Jack Armstrong Jr., rhp, Vanderbilt	$750,000
100. Brewers. Drew Gagnon, rhp, Long Beach State	$340,000

ARIZONA DIAMONDBACKS (3)

1. **Trevor Bauer, rhp, UCLA**
1. **Archie Bradley, rhp, Broken Arrow (Okla.) HS** (Supplemental pick—seventh—for failure to sign 2010 first-round pick Barret Loux)
1. **Andrew Chafin, lhp, Kent State** (Supplemental pick—43rd—for loss of Type B free agent Adam LaRoche)
2. **Anthony Meo, rhp, Coastal Carolina**
3. **Justin Bianco, of, Peters Township HS, Canonsburg, Pa.**
4. **Evan Marshall, rhp, Kansas State**
5. **Michael Perez, c, Colegio Vocacional, San Juan, P.R.**
6. Matt Price, rhp, South Carolina
7. Ben Roberts, of, Sentinel HS, Missoula, Mont.
8. **Jesse Darrah, rhp, Fresno Pacific**
9. **John Leonard, ss, Connellsville (Pa.) Area HS**
10. **Kyle Winkler, rhp, Texas Christian**
11. **Will Locante, lhp, Cumberland (Tenn.)**
12. **Josh Parr, ss, Illinois**
13. **John Pedrotty, lhp, Holy Cross**
14. **Cody Geyer, rhp, Walters State (Tenn.) CC**
15. **Steve Rodriguez, c, UCLA**
16. **Michael Blake, lhp, Hawaii**
17. Adam Choplick, lhp, Ryan HS, Denton, Texas
18. **Taylor Siemens, lhp, California Baptist**
19. **Danny Pulfer, 2b, Oregon**
20. Tommy Williams, ss, Palm Beach Gardens (Fla.) HS
21. **John Griffin, 1b, Central Florida**
22. **Garrett Weber, ss, Fresno State**
23. **Ryan Court, 3b, Illinois State**
24. Matt Ogden, rhp, Smoky Hill HS, Aurora, Colo.
25. Brett Williams, of, North Carolina State
26. **Austin Platt, rhp, Bradenton, Fla. (No school)**
27. Wyatt Strahan, rhp, Villa Park (Calif.) HS
28. **Matt Sample, rhp, Rogers State (Okla.)**
29. **Carter Bell, 3b, Oregon State**
30. **Dexter Price, rhp, South Carolina-Beaufort**
31. **Matt Jensen, 2b, Cal Poly**
32. Alex Vetter, rhp, Feather River (Calif.) JC
33. Anthony Banda, lhp, Sinton (Texas) HS
34. **Zach Jones, c, Stanford**
35. **Ross Gerdeman, rhp, Bowling Green State**
36. **Brian Henry, c, Keystone (Pa.)**
37. **Elroy Urbina, lhp, Incarnate Word (Texas)**
38. **Kerry Jenkins, of, San Jose State**
39. **Chris Ellison, of, Oklahoma**
40. **Seth Simmons, rhp, East Carolina**
41. Michael Cederoth, rhp, Steele Canyon HS, Spring Valley, Calif.
42. **Tyler Bream, 3b, Liberty**
43. **Alex Capaul, rhp, Hawaii**
44. **Derek Luciano, 3b, Central Florida**
45. Jake Lane, of, Coral Shores HS, Tavernier, Fla.
46. **Joe Loftus, of, Vanderbilt**
47. Tucker Ward, rhp, UMS-Wright Prep, Mobile, Ala.
48. **Raymond Hernandez, rhp, Cal State Fullerton**
49. **Jake Williams, 1b, South Mountain (Ariz.) CC**
50. David Masters, ss, Timberland HS, Wentzville, Mo.

ATLANTA BRAVES (25)

1. **Sean Gilmartin, lhp, Florida State**
2. **Nick Ahmed, ss, Connecticut**
3. **Kyle Kubitza, 3b, Texas State**
4. **J.R. Graham, rhp, Santa Clara**
5. **Nick DeSantiago, c, Blinn (Texas) JC**
6. **Mark Lamm, rhp, Vanderbilt**
7. **Cody Martin, rhp, Gonzaga**
8. **Tommy La Stella, 2b, Coastal Carolina**
9. **Chase Larsson, of, Cameron (Okla.)**
10. **Logan Robbins, ss, Western Kentucky**
11. **Seth Moranda, ss, Buchanan HS, Clovis, Calif.**
12. **Matt Chaffee, lhp, Arizona**
13. **Tony Mueller, of, Winona State (Minn.)**
14. **Navery Moore, rhp, Vanderbilt**

15. **John Cornely, rhp, Wofford**
16. **Adam Holland, rhp, St. Joseph's**
17. **Gus Schlosser, rhp, Florida Southern**
18. **Greg Ross, rhp, Frostburg State (Md.)**
19. **Troy Snitker, c, North Georgia College & State**
20. Carlos Rodriguez, lhp, Iolani HS, Honolulu
21. **Jarrett Miller, rhp, UNC Greensboro**
22. **Clint Wright, rhp, Columbia State (Tenn.) CC**
23. **Sam Munson, of, Tennessee Weslyan**
24. **Brian Stamps, of, Oregon State**
25. **Will Skinner, of, Middle Tennessee State**
26. **Kirk Walker, ss, Oklahoma City**
27. **Charlie Robertson, rhp, Fresno State**
28. **Matt Talley, lhp, The Citadel**
29. **Chad Comer, c, Texas-Arlington**
30. Jon Youngblood, of, Lafayette HS, Lexington, Ky.
31. **Jackson Laumann, 1b, Boone County HS, Florence, Ky.**
32. Matt Kimbrel, rhp, Shelton State (Ala.) CC
33. **Nick Popescu, 3b, Texas Tech**
34. **Chris Bullard, of, Western Kentucky**
35. **Mike Hashem, lhp, Fisher (Mass.)**
36. **Gardner Adams, rhp, Asbury (Ky.)**
37. **Ryne Harper, rhp, Austin Peay State**
38. Nate Williams, rhp, Valley Center (Kan.) HS
39. Daniel Arellano, of, Centennial HS, Corona, Calif.
40. Jacoby Almaraz, 3b, San Jacinto (Texas) JC
41. Keelin Rasch, c, Harrisburg (Ill.) HS
42. **Cody Livesay, of, Anna-Jonesboro HS, Jonesboro, Ill.**
43. Jake Lueneberg, 1b, Kishwaukee (Ill.) JC
44. Sutton Whiting, 2b, Ballard HS, Louisville
45. Sako Chapjian, 3b, Glendale (Calif.) JC
46. John Means, lhp, Gardner-Edgerton HS, Gardner, Kan.
47. Dane Gronewald, lhp, Jefferson (Mo.) CC
48. Erwin Real, 3b, Boulder Creek HS, Anthem, Ariz.
49. Cody Cox, rhp, Thomas Nelson (Va.) CC
50. Kevin McKague, rhp, Army

BALTIMORE ORIOLES (4)

1. **Dylan Bundy, rhp, Owasso (Okla.) HS**
2. **Jason Esposito, 3b, Vanderbilt**
3. **Mike Wright, rhp, East Carolina**
4. **Kyle Simon, rhp, Arizona**
5. **Matt Taylor, lhp, Middle Georgia JC**
6. **Nicky Delmonico, 3b, Farragut HS, Knoxville**
7. **Trent Howard, lhp, Central Michigan**
8. **John Ruettiger, of, Arizona State**
9. **Devin Jones, rhp, Mississippi State**
10. **Tyler Wilson, rhp, Virginia**
11. **Adam Davis, c, Illinois**
12. Jason Coats, of, Texas Christian
13. Derek Jones, of, Washington State
14. K.J. Hockaday, 3b, Carroll School, Bel Air, Md.
15. **Eric Wooten, lhp, Central Arizona JC**
16. **Mark Blackmar, rhp, Temple (Texas) JC**
17. Nick Carmichael, rhp, Palomar (Calif.) JC
18. Brad Roney, 3b, Wetumpka (Ala.) HS
19. **Dustin Ward, lhp, Central Arkansas**
20. Marc Wik, of, Chabot (Calif.) JC
21. **Jose Rivera, rhp, Hill (Texas) JC**
22. Mike Miedzianowski, ss, Martin County HS, Stuart, Fla.
23. Adam Matthews, of, South Carolina
24. **Jalen Simmons, of, Camden County HS, Kingsland, Ga.**
25. Mike Finnigan, lhp, San Bernardino Valley (Calif.) JC
26. **Zach Davies, rhp, Mesquite HS, Gilbert, Ariz.**
27. Chris Oliver, rhp, Shiloh Christian HS, Springdale, Ark.
28. Nate Raubinger, 1b, Arroyo Grande (Calif.) HS
29. **Cameron Edman, c, Gonzaga**
30. Mike Reynolds, ss, Paradise Valley (Ariz.) CC
31. John Costa, rhp, Summit Christian HS, West Palm Beach, Fla.
32. Ryan Meyer, rhp, Oviedo (Fla.) HS
33. Sander Beck, rhp, Maryland
34. **Zach Fowler, lhp, Texas Tech**

35. Lindsey Caughel, rhp, Stetson
36. Jeffrey Zona, rhp, Hanover HS, Mechanicsville, Va.
37. Nick Skala, c, Concordia (Ill.)
38. **Jerome Pena, 2b, Texas Christian**
39. Pat Cantwell, c, Stony Brook
40. **Bennett Parry, lhp, Poway, Calif. (No school)**
41. Chris Mariscal, ss, Clovis North HS, Fresno
42. **Jason McCracken, rhp, Pierce (Calif.) JC**
43. David Reynolds, rhp, Edmonds (Wash.) CC
44. Patrick Merkling, lhp, Chattanooga State (Tenn.) JC
45. Andrew Millner, rhp, Feather River (Calif.) JC
46. Mark Reyes, lhp, Jessieville (Ark.) HS
47. Devon Conley, of, New Mexico JC
48. Tyler Hunter, of, Lowndes HS, Valdosta, Ga.
49. Ronnie Shaban, rhp, Virginia Tech
50. Brendan Butler, of, Carroll School, Bel Air, Md.

BOSTON RED SOX (21)

1. **Matt Barnes, rhp, Connecticut** (Pick from Tigers as compensation for Type A free agent Victor Martinez)
1. (Pick to Rays as compensation for Type A free agent Carl Crawford)
1. **Blake Swihart, c, Cleveland HS, Rio Rancho, N.M.** (Pick from Rangers as compensation for Type A free agent Adrian Beltre)
1. **Henry Owens, lhp, Edison HS, Huntington Beach, Calif.** (Supplemental pick—36th—for loss of Martinez)
1. **Jackie Bradley, of, South Carolina** (Supplemental pick—40th—for loss of Beltre)
2. **Williams Jerez, of, Grand Street HS, Brooklyn**
3. **Jordan Weems, c, Columbus (Ga.) HS**
4. **Noe Ramirez, rhp, Cal State Fullerton**
5. **Mookie Betts, ss, Overton HS, Brentwood, Tenn.**
6. **Miguel Pena, lhp, San Jacinto (Texas) JC**
7. **Cody Kukuk, lhp, Free State HS, Lawrence, Kan.**
8. Senquez Golson, of, Pascagoula (Miss.) HS
9. **Travis Shaw, 3b, Kent State**
10. **Cody Koback, of, Wisconsin-Stevens Point**
11. **Kevin Brahney, lhp, Chico State (Calif.)**
12. Deshorn Lake, rhp, Menchville HS, Newport News, Va.
13. **Matty Ott, rhp, Louisiana State**
14. **Mike McCarthy, rhp, Cal State Bakersfield**
15. **Braden Kapteyn, 1b, Kentucky**
16. Daniel Gossett, rhp, Byrnes HS, Duncan, S.C.
17. Blake Forslund, rhp, Liberty
18. **Andrew Jones, rhp, Samford**
19. Sikes Orvis, 1b, Freedom HS, Orlando
20. **Zach Good, lhp, Grayson County (Texas) CC**
21. Austin Davidson, 2b, Oxnard (Calif.) HS
22. **Joe Holtmeyer, rhp, Nebraska-Omaha**
23. Jarrett Brown, lhp, Salem HS, Conyers, Ga.
24. **Drew Turocy, of, Akron**
25. Taylor Ard, 1b, Washington State
26. Cody Dill, rhp, Los Osos HS, Rancho Cucamonga, Calif.
27. Alex Massey, rhp, Catholic HS, Baton Rouge
28. **Brenden Shepherd, rhp, Stonehill (Mass.)**
29. **Matt Spalding, rhp, St. Xavier HS, Louisville**
30. **Nick Moore, 3b, Brookwood HS, Snellville, Ga.**
31. Tyler Wells, of, Lexington (Ky.) Catholic HS
32. Julius Gaines, ss, Luella HS, Locust Grove, Ga.
33. **David Chester, 1b, Pittsburgh**
34. Sean Dartnell, lhp, Vauxhall (Alb.) HS
35. **Carlos Coste, c, Academia Bautista HS, San Juan, P.R.**
36. Jace Herrera, rhp, Wekiva HS, Apopka, Fla.
37. Robert Youngdahl, of, Hill-Murray HS, Maplewood, Minn.
38. Tyler Poole, rhp, Hickory (N.C.) HS
39. **Corey Vogt, rhp, Keene State (N.H.)**
40. Jordan Gross, lhp, Don Bosco Prep, Ramsey, N.J.
41. **Matt Marquis, of, Maryland**
42. Derek O'Dell, 3b, Canyon (Texas) HS
43. Brandon Downes, of, South Plainfield (N.J.) HS
44. Matt Martin, c, Pendleton School, Bradenton, Fla.
45. **Matt Gedman, 2b, Massachusetts**
46. Mac Williamson, of, Wake Forest
47. Sam Wolff, rhp, JC of Southern Nevada
48. David Sosebee, rhp, White County HS, Cleveland, Ga.
49. **Jadd Schmeltzer, rhp, Cornell**

50. John Gorman, rhp, Catholic Memorial HS, West Roxbury, Mass.

CHICAGO CUBS (8)

1. **Javier Baez, ss, Arlington Country Day HS, Jacksonville, Fla.**
2. **Dan Vogelbach, 1b, Bishop Verot HS, Fort Myers, Fla.**
3. **Zeke DeVoss, of, Miami**
4. **Tony Zych, rhp, Louisville**
5. **Tayler Scott, rhp, Notre Dame Prep, Scottsdale, Ariz.**
6. **Neftali Rosario, c, PR Baseball Academy, Gurabo, P.R.**
7. **Trevor Gretzky, 1b, Oaks Christian HS, Westlake Village, Calif.**
8. Taylor Dugas, of, Alabama
9. **Garrett Schlecht, of, Waterloo (Ill.) HS**
10. **Daniel Lockhart, ss, Hebron Christian Academy, Dacula, Ga.**
11. **Shawon Dunston Jr., of, Valley Christian HS, San Jose**
12. Jacob Lindgren, lhp, St. Stanislaus HS, Bay St. Louis, Miss.
13. **Trey Martin, of, Brookwood HS, Snellville, Ga.**
14. **Dillon Maples, rhp, Pinecrest HS, Southern Pines, N.C.**
15. **Justin Marra, c, Power/St. Joseph HS, Toronto**
16. **Rafael Lopez, c, Florida State**
17. **John Andreoli, of, Connecticut**
18. **James Pugliese, rhp, Mercer County (N.J.) CC**
19. **Paul Hoilman, 1b, East Tennessee State**
20. **Ben Klafczynski, of, Kent State**
21. **Andrew McKirahan, lhp, Texas**
22. Ethan Elias, rhp, Grand Trunk HS, Evansburg, Alb.
23. **Bradley Zimmer, of, La Jolla (Calif.) HS**
24. George Asmus, rhp, Ohlone (Calif.) JC
25. **Rock Shoulders, 1b, State JC of Florida**
26. **Michael Jensen, rhp, Hartnell (Calif.) JC**
27. **Taiwan Easterling, of, Florida State**
28. Chris Garrison, rhp, Western Nevada CC
29. Drew Weeks, 3b, Clay HS, Green Cove Springs, Fla.
30. **Arturo Maltos-Garcia, rhp, Lamar (Colo.) CC**
31. Ronnie Richardson, of, Central Florida
32. **Pete Levitt, rhp, Mount Olive (N.C.)**
33. **Sheldon McDonald, lhp, British Columbia**
34. Bobby Kelley, of, Calhoun (Ala.) CC
35. **Ian Dickson, rhp, Lafayette (Pa.)**
36. **Travis Garcia, 3b, Martin Methodist (Tenn.)**
37. Steven Maxwell, rhp, Texas Christian
38. Casey Lucchese, rhp, College of Charleston
39. Ricky Jacquez, rhp, Franklin HS, El Paso
40. **P.J. Francescon, rhp, Trevecca Nazarene (Tenn.)**
41. **Austin Urban, rhp, Des Moines Area CC**
42. **Brad Zapenas, ss, Boston College**
43. Jay Calhoun, rhp, Second Baptist HS, Houston
44. **Kenny Socorro, ss, Marshall**
45. Tanner Kichler, rhp, Sherwood (Ore.) HS
46. **Scott Weismann, rhp, Clemson**
47. David Ernst, rhp, South HS, Fargo, N.D.
48. Sam Howard, lhp, Cartersville (Ga.) HS
49. Antonio Gonzales, lhp, Damien HS, La Verne, Calif.
50. Cody Edwards, rhp, Bellevue (Wash.) CC

CHICAGO WHITE SOX (20)

1. (Pick to Nationals as compensation for Type A free agent Adam Dunn)
1. **Keenyn Walker, of, Central Arizona JC** (Supplemental pick—47th—for loss of Type B free agent J.J. Putz)
2. **Erik Johnson, rhp, California**
3. **Jeff Soptic, rhp, Johnson County (Kan.) CC**
4. **Kyle McMillen, rhp, Kent State**
5. **Scott Snodgress, lhp, Stanford**
6. **Marcus Semien, ss, California**
7. **Kevan Smith, c, Pittsburgh**
8. Ian Gardeck, rhp, Angelina (Texas) JC
9. **Matt Lane, lhp, Northwest Florida State JC**
10. Ben O'Shea, lhp, Santa Fe (Fla.) CC
11. **Blair Walters, lhp, Hawaii**
12. **Andrew Virgili, rhp, Lynn (Fla.)**
13. Chadd Krist, c, California
14. Mark Ginther, 3b, Oklahoma State
15. **David Herbek, ss, James Madison**
16. **Chris Bassitt, rhp, Akron**
17. **Collin Kuhn, of, Arkansas**
18. **Bryan Blough, rhp, Kennesaw State**

19. **Kevin Vance, rhp, Connecticut**
20. **Martin Medina, c, Cal State Bakersfield**
21. **Joe DePinto, 2b, Southern California**
22. **Blake Drake, rhp, Indiana State**
23. **Mike Marjama, c, Long Beach State**
24. **Mark Haddow, of, UC Santa Barbara**
25. **Chris Devenski, rhp, Cal State Fullerton**
26. **Grant Buckner, 3b, West Virginia**
27. **Jake Cose, rhp, San Joaquin Delta (Calif.) JC**
28. **Kyle Robinson, 1b, Arkansas**
29. Dustin Hayes, of, Langley, B.C. (No school)
30. **Brandon Parrent, lhp, Texas A&M**
31. **Michael Johnson, ss, Samford**
32. **Brent Tanner, c, South Alabama**
33. **Bryce Mosier, c, Valhalla HS, El Cajon, Calif.**
34. Dakota Freese, rhp, Washington HS, Cedar Rapids, Iowa
35. **Joseph Dvorsky, rhp, Texas State**
36. **Cody Winiarski, rhp, Virginia**
37. **Todd Kibby, lhp, St. Petersburg (Fla.) JC**
38. **Keegan Linza, rhp, Liberty**
39. Javier Reynoso, lhp, Brooks-DeBartolo Collegiate HS, Tampa
40. Jake Reed, rhp, Helix Charter HS, La Mesa, Calif.
41. Chandler Shepherd, rhp, Lawrence County HS, Louisa, Ky.
42. Aaron Pangilinan, rhp, Escalon (Calif.) HS
43. Joel Effertz, rhp, Madison (Wis.) JC
44. Joe Pistorese, lhp, Flathead HS, Kalispell, Mont.
45. **Cory Farris, of, Cumberland (Tenn.)**
46. Mike Mancuso, rhp, Brecksville-Broadview Heights (Ohio) HS
47. Robert Liera, c, Hialeah (Fla.) HS
48. Dontrell Rush, of, Harlan Community HS, Chicago
49. Zach Regier, of, Gilbert (Ariz.) HS
50. Jack Graham, 2b, Seneca Valley HS, Harmony, Pa.

CINCINNATI REDS (24)

1. **Robert Stephenson, rhp, Alhambra HS, Martinez, Calif.**
2. **Gabriel Rosa, of, Colegio Hector Urdaneta, Rio Grande, P.R.**
3. **Tony Cingrani, lhp, Rice**
4. **Kyle McMyne, rhp, Villanova**
5. **Ryan Wright, 2b, Louisville**
6. **Sean Buckley, 3b, St. Petersburg (Fla.) JC**
7. **James Allen, rhp, Kansas State**
8. **Jon Matthews, rhp, St. Petersburg (Fla.) JC**
9. **Cole Green, rhp, Texas**
10. **Brooks Pinckard, rhp, Baylor**
11. **Vaughn Covington, rhp, Killarney SS, Vancouver, B.C.**
12. Joe Serrano, ss, Salpointe HS, Tucson, Ariz.
13. **Nick Fleece, rhp, Texas A&M**
14. **Leo Kemp, rhp, St. Joseph's**
15. Will Dorton, rhp, Lugoff-Elgin HS, Lugoff, S.C.
16. Conor Costello, of, Santa Fe HS, Edmond, Okla.
17. Morgan Phillips, ss, Douglas Academy, New York
18. **Jimmy Moran, rhp, South Florida**
19. **Chris Joyce, lhp, Santa Barbara (Calif.) CC**
20. **Dan Jensen, rhp, Cincinnati**
21. **Carlos Gonzalez, rhp, Cal State Northridge**
22. **Amir Garrett, lhp, Henderson (Nev.) International School**
23. **Sal Romano, rhp, Southington (Conn.) HS**
24. **Nick O'Shea, 1b, Minnesota**
25. **Justice French, rhp, Mercer**
26. **Juan Perez, 2b, JC of the Canyons (Calif.)**
27. **Taylor Wrenn, 2b, Tampa**
28. **Vordanys Perez, of, Calabasas, Calif. (No school)**
29. Dariel Delgado, rhp, Miami (No school)
30. **Joe Terry, 3b, Cal State Fullerton**
31. **Erik Miller, rhp, Texas Christian**
32. **Mike Dennhardt, rhp, Boston College**
33. **Steve Selsky, of, Arizona**
34. **Bryson Smith, of, Florida**
35. Sammy Kimmell, 2b, Indian River (Fla.) JC
36. **Randy Yard, rhp, Hawaii**
37. Michael Suiter, of, Punahou HS, Honolulu
38. Daniel Bowman, of, Coastal Carolina
39. Justin Amlung, rhp, Louisville
40. Sam Travis, 3b, Providence Catholic HS, New Lenox, Ill.
41. Carson Baranik, rhp, Parkway HS, Bossier City, La.

42. Jacob Stallings, c, North Carolina
43. **Ty Washington, 2b, Plano (Texas) East HS**
44. Shon Carson, of, Lake City (S.C.) HS
45. Travis Radke, lhp, Oaks Christian HS, Westlake Village, Calif.
46. Jose Brizuela, 3b, Archbishop McCarthy HS, Southwest Ranches, Fla.
47. Kirby Pellant, 2b, Chandler-Gilbert (Ariz.) CC
48. Jon Webb, lhp, South Carolina
49. **Eric Alessio, rhp, Marist**
50. Austin Robichaux, rhp, Notre Dame HS, Crowley, La.

CLEVELAND INDIANS (7)

1. **Francisco Lindor, ss, Montverde (Fla.) Academy**
2. **Dillon Howard, rhp, Searcy (Ark.) HS**
3. **Jake Sisco, rhp, Merced (Calif.) JC**
4. **Jake Lowery, c, James Madison**
5. **Will Roberts, rhp, Virginia**
6. **Bryson Myles, of, Stephen F. Austin State**
7. **Eric Haase, c, Divine Child HS, Dearborn, Mich.**
8. Stephen Tarpley, lhp, Gilbert (Ariz.) HS
9. **Jordan Smith, 3b, St. Cloud State (Minn.)**
10. **Jeff Johnson, rhp, Cal Poly**
11. **Luis DeJesus, rhp, Angelina (Texas) JC**
12. **Grant Sides, rhp, Samford**
13. **Zack MacPhee, 2b, Arizona State**
14. **Cody Anderson, rhp, Feather River (Calif.) JC**
15. **Todd Hankins, 2b, Seminole State (Fla.) JC**
16. **Ryan Merritt, lhp, McLennan (Texas) CC**
17. Kevin Brady, rhp, Clemson
18. **Shawn Armstrong, rhp, East Carolina**
19. **Shawn Morimando, lhp, Ocean Lakes HS, Virginia Beach**
20. Dillon Peters, lhp, Cathedral HS, Indianapolis
21. **Cody Elliott, of, Ball State**
22. Matthew Reckling, rhp, Rice
23. **Cody Allen, rhp, High Point**
24. Taylor Sparks, 3b, St. John Bosco HS, Bellflower, Calif.
25. Kevin Kramer, ss, Turlock (Calif.) HS
26. Austin Diemer, of, Rocklin (Calif.) HS
27. **Evan Frazar, ss, Galveston (Texas) JC**
28. Tyler Nurdin, lhp, Temple (Texas) JC
29. Jared Ruxer, rhp, Lawrence Central HS, Indianapolis
30. John Polonius, ss, Genesee (N.Y.) CC
31. Michael Roth, lhp, South Carolina
32. Cole Pitts, rhp, Colquitt County HS, Moultrie, Ga.
33. **Jack Wagoner, rhp, Florida Gulf Coast**
34. Tyler Maloof, rhp, Georgia
35. **Mason Radeke, rhp, Cal Poly**
36. **Abel Guerrero, lhp, Galveston (Texas) JC**
37. Taylor Starr, rhp, Oregon State
38. **Yhoxian Medina, ss, Southeastern (Iowa) CC**
39. **John Barr, of, Virginia**
40. Matt Eureste, ss, St. Pius X HS, Houston
41. **Brian Ruiz, of, Lincoln West HS, Cleveland**
42. **K.C. Serna, ss, Oregon**
43. **Geoff Davenport, lhp, Arkansas**
44. Adam Griffin, rhp, Forsyth Country Day HS, Lewisville, N.C.
45. Will Jamison, of, Evangelical Christian HS, Cordova, Tenn.
46. **Robert Nixon, rhp, Adelphi (N.Y.)**
47. Corey Embree, of, Moberly (Mo.) HS
48. Blaine O'Brien, rhp, Keystone (Pa.)
49. Brian Hanson, rhp, St. Cloud State (Minn.)
50. Tyler Baker, c, Shawnee Heights HS, Tecumseh, Kan.

COLORADO ROCKIES (17)

1. **Tyler Anderson, lhp, Oregon**
1. **Trevor Story, ss, Irving (Texas) HS** (Supplemental pick—45th—for loss of Type B free agent Octavio Dotel)
2. **Carl Thomore, of, East Brunswick (N.J.) HS**
3. Peter O'Brien, c, Bethune-Cookman
4. **Dillon Thomas, of, Westbury Christian HS, Houston**
5. **Taylor Featherston, ss, Texas Christian**
6. **Chris Jensen, rhp, San Diego**
7. **Harold Riggins, 1b, North Carolina State**
8. **Roberto Padilla, lhp, San Jose State**
9. Ross Stripling, rhp, Texas A&M
10. **Ben Hughes, rhp, St. Olaf (Minn.)**

11. **Alex Gillingham, rhp, Loyola Marymount**
12. David Schuknecht, c, Palm Desert (Calif.) HS
13. **Kyle Roliard, lhp, Louisiana Tech**
14. **Brian Humphries, of, Pepperdine**
15. **Tim Smalling, ss, Virginia Tech**
16. Preston Tucker, 1b, Florida
17. **Will Rankin, rhp, Southern Polytechnic State (Ga.)**
18. **Ben Alsup, rhp, Louisiana State**
19. **Jesse Meaux, rhp, UC Santa Barbara**
20. **Danny Winkler, rhp, Central Florida**
21. **Jordan Ribera, 1b, Fresno State**
22. **Logan Mahon, lhp, Southeast Missouri State**
23. **Brook Hart, lhp, Yale**
24. Connor McKay, of, Regis Jesuit HS, Aurora, Colo.
25. **Patrick Johnson, rhp, North Carolina**
26. **Mike Wolford, rhp, UC Riverside**
27. **Matt Argyropoulos, 3b, Washington State**
28. Joshua Correa, of, Caguas Military Academy, Caguas, P.R.
29. Matt Dermody, lhp, Iowa
30. John Curtiss, rhp, Carroll HS, Southlake, Texas
31. **Sam Mende, ss, South Florida**
32. **Jarod Berggren, of, Northern Colorado**
33. **Jaron Shepherd, of, Mississippi State**
34. **Chris Dennis, rhp, Portland**
35. **Richard Pirkle, c, Georgia College & State**
36. Tyler Servais, c, Douglas County HS, Castle Rock, Colo.
37. Brandon Bonilla, lhp, Pendleton School, Bradenton, Fla.
38. Boo Vazquez, of, Cardinal Mooney HS, Youngstown, Ohio
39. Chase Williams, rhp, Broken Arrow (Okla.) HS
40. Drew Stankiewicz, 2b, Gilbert (Ariz.) HS
41. Taylor Martin, rhp, Lexington (Ky.) Catholic HS
42. Jordan Johnson, rhp, Franklin HS, Elk Grove, Calif.
43. Garrett Brown, of, Erwin HS, Asheville, N.C.
44. Robert Kahana, rhp, Campbell HS, Ewa Beach, Hawaii
45. Will Price, of, Greenbrier HS, Evans, Ga.
46. Nathaniel Causey, c, Gilbert (Ariz.) HS
47. Casey Scott, 2b, Notre Dame Prep, Scottsdale, Ariz.
48. Clay Bauer, rhp, JC of San Mateo (Calif.)
49. Tyler Bernard, ss, Palomar (Calif.) JC
50. Heath Holder, of, Loganville (Ga.) HS

DETROIT TIGERS (16)

1. (Pick to Red Sox as compensation for Type A free agent Victor Martinez)
2. **James McCann, c, Arkansas**
3. **Aaron Westlake, 1b, Vanderbilt**
4. **Jason King, 3b, Kansas State**
5. **Brandon Loy, ss, Texas**
6. **Tyler Collins, of, Howard (Texas) JC**
7. **Brian Flynn, lhp, Wichita State**
8. **Jason Krizan, of, Dallas Baptist**
9. **Chad Wright, of, Kentucky**
10. **Curt Casali, c, Vanderbilt**
11. **Dean Green, 1b, Barry (Fla.)**
12. **Jeff Holm, of, Michigan State**
13. **Ryan Woolley, rhp, Alabama-Birmingham**
14. **Pat Smith, of, Middle Georgia JC**
15. **Tyler Gibson, of, Stratford Academy, Macon, Ga.**
16. **Ismael Salgado, of, International Baseball Academy, Cieba, P.R.**
17. **Chad Smith, rhp, Southern California**
18. **Brett Harrison, 3b, Green Valley HS, Henderson, Nev.**
19. **Daniel Bennett, rhp, Florida State**
20. **Tyler Barrett, lhp, Lewis-Clark State (Idaho)**
21. Scott Squier, lhp, Greenway HS, Phoenix
22. **Tommy Collier, rhp, San Jacinto (Texas) JC**
23. Trent Daniel, lhp, Arkansas
24. **Matt Crouse, lhp, Mississippi**
25. Mitch Mormann, rhp, Wichita State
26. **Colin Kaline, 2b, Florida Southern**
27. **Scott Matyas, rhp, Minnesota**
28. **Guido Knudson, rhp, UC San Diego**
29. **Montreal Robertson, rhp, Coahoma (Miss.) CC**
30. Greg Milhorn, rhp, Arkansas HS, Texarkana, Ark.
31. **Brian Stroud, rhp, Western Michigan**
32. **Brandon Eckerle, of, Michigan State**
33. **Dan Kickham, rhp, Missouri State**

34. **Zach Maggard, c, Florida Southern**
35. **Eric Heckaman, rhp, Western Michigan**
36. **Jake Sabol, rhp, Central Michigan**
37. **Nick Avila, rhp, Nova Southeastern (Fla.)**
38. Blaise Salter, c, St. Mary's Prep, Orchard Lake Village, Mich.
39. Cole Brocker, rhp, Sacramento CC
40. Ryan Krill, 1b, Portage (Mich.) Central HS
41. Jimmy Pickens, of, Brother Rice HS, Bloomfield Hills, Mich.
42. Tim Chadd, c, Bishop Carroll HS, Wichita, Kan.
43. Greg Fettes, c, Lamphere HS, Madison Heights, Mich.
44. **Chretien Matz, of, Arkansas-Pine Bluff**
45. Andrew Allen, 1b, Cal State Los Angeles
46. Alex Fernandez Jr., of, Archbishop McCarthy HS, SW Ranches, Fla.
47. Ryan MacPhail, c, Dutch Fork HS, Irmo, S.C.
48. Lavaris McCullough, of, Palatka (Fla.) HS
49. Brett Impemba, of, Dakota HS, Macomb, Mich.
50. Brandon Webber, of, Bishop Carroll HS, Wichita, Kan.

FLORIDA MARLINS (12)

1. **Jose Fernandez, rhp, Alonso HS, Tampa**
2. **Adam Conley, lhp, Washington State**
3. Connor Barron, ss, Sumrall (Miss.) HS
4. Tyler Palmer, 2b, Wayne County HS, Jesup, Ga.
5. **Mason Hope, rhp, Broken Arrow (Okla.) HS**
6. **Charlie Lowell, lhp, Wichita State**
7. **Ryan Rieger, 1b, JC of the Sequoias (Calif.)**
8. **Dejal Oliver, rhp, Seminole State (Fla.) JC**
9. **Austin Barnes, c, Arizona State**
10. **Scott Lyman, rhp, UC Davis**
11. **Jacob Esch, rhp, Georgia Tech**
12. **Ryan McIntyre, of, Cal State Bakersfield**
13. **Josh Adams, ss, Florida**
14. Nick Grim, rhp, Monterey Peninsula (Calif.) JC
15. **Jhiomar Veras, of, Western Oklahoma State JC**
16. Adrian Sampson, rhp, Bellevue (Wash.) CC
17. Derek Varnadore, rhp, Auburn
18. **Greg Nappo, lhp, Connecticut**
19. **Connor Burke, 2b, La Serna HS, Whittier, Calif.**
20. Devon Reed, ss, Milford (Del.) HS
21. **Chase Wier, rhp, Stephen F. Austin State**
22. **Collin Cargill, rhp, Southern Mississippi**
23. **Tyler Higgins, rhp, Lansing (Mich.) CC**
24. **Tony Caldwell, c, Auburn**
25. **Sean Donatello, rhp, Connecticut-Avery Point JC**
26. **Ryan Goetz, 3b, UC Riverside**
27. **Frankie Reed, lhp, Cal Poly**
28. **Brad Mincey, rhp, East Carolina**
29. **Matthew Neil, rhp, Brigham Young**
30. **Jose Behar, c, Florida International**
31. **Kenny Jackson, 3b, Texas A&M**
32. **Sharif Othman, c, California Baptist**
33. **James Nygren, rhp, Oregon State**
34. **John Schultz, of, Pittsburgh**
35. **Johnny Omahen, rhp, Cal State San Marcos**
36. Damek Tomscha, 3b, Iowa Western CC
37. Jacob Ehret, rhp, San Dimas (Calif.) HS
38. Joe Ceja, rhp, Marquette HS, Ottawa, Ill.
39. Travis Huber, rhp, JC of Southern Idaho
40. Trent Gilbert, ss, Torrance (Calif.) HS
41. Matt Anderson, rhp, Chaffey (Calif.) JC
42. Jerad Grundy, lhp, Heartland (Ill.) CC
43. Drew Leenhouts, lhp, Northeastern
44. Zack LaNeve, ss, Pine-Richland HS, Gibsonia, Pa.
45. Tim Zufall, of, Lamar (Colo.) CC
46. Zach Cooper, rhp, Central Michigan
47. Joel Thys, c, Ohlone (Calif.) JC
48. Chris Nunez, 2b, Goddard HS, Roswell, N.M.
49. Connor Little, rhp, Hawaii
50. Cory Caruso, lhp, Cal State San Bernardino

HOUSTON ASTROS (9)

1. **George Springer, of, Connecticut**
2. **Adrian Houser, rhp, Locust Grove (Okla.) HS**
3. **Jack Armstrong, rhp, Vanderbilt**
4. **Chris Lee, lhp, Santa Fe (Fla.) CC**

5. Nick Tropeano, rhp, Stony Brook
6. Brandon Meredith, of, San Diego State
7. Javaris Reynolds, of, King HS, Tampa
8. Brandon Culbreth, rhp, Forsyth Country Day HS, Lewisville, N.C.
9. Jonas Dufek, rhp, Creighton
10. Kyle Hallock, lhp, Kent State
11. Justin Gominsky, of, Minnesota
12. Miles Hamblin, c, Mississippi
13. John Hinson, 2b, Clemson
14. Gandy Stubblefield, rhp, Lufkin (Texas) HS
15. Zach Johnson, 1b, Oklahoma State
16. Scott Zuloaga, lhp, Scottsdale (Ariz.) CC
17. Tyson Perez, rhp, Fresno CC
18. Kevin Miller, rhp, California
19. Mitchell Lambson, lhp, Arizona State
20. Matt Duffy, 3b, Tennessee
21. Jimmy Howick, ss, Jacksonville
22. Drew Muren, of, Cal State Northridge
23. Ruben Sosa, 2b, Oklahoma City
24. Jesse Wierzbicki, 1b, North Carolina
25. Billy Flamion, of, Central Catholic HS, Modesto, Calif.
26. Jared Fisher, rhp, Newport HS, Bellevue, Wash.
27. Alex Todd, ss, Sonoma State (Calif.)
28. Jordan John, lhp, Oklahoma
29. Wallace Gonzalez, of, Bishop Amat HS, La Puente, Calif.
30. Jordan Steranka, 3b, Penn State
31. Jarrod McKinney, of, Arkansas
32. Zach Dando, rhp, Central Arizona JC
33. Dominique Taylor, of, Salt Lake CC
34. Dustin Kellogg, rhp, Caney Creek HS, Conroe, Texas
35. Chris Morales, rhp, Clear Creek HS, League City, Texas
36. Kevin Gonzalez, c, Texas A&M
37. Steven Martin, rhp, Texas A&M
38. Brad Propst, rhp, Oklahoma State
39. David Haerle, rhp, JC of the Canyons (Calif.)
40. Buddy Lamothe, rhp, San Jacinto (Texas) JC
41. Chase Davidson, 1b, Georgia
42. Hoke Granger, of, Northside Methodist Academy, Dothan, Ala.
43. David Grimes, of, Upton Lakes Christian HS, Clinton Corners, N.Y.
44. Blake Ford, rhp, Lamar
45. Chris Epps, of, Clemson
46. Justin Shults, 1b, UC Riverside
47. Zack Hardoin, lhp, Missouri
48. A.J. Murray, c, Westfield (N.J.) HS
49. David Peterson, rhp, College of Charleston
50. Colton Davis, of, Lake Wales (Fla.) HS

KANSAS CITY ROYALS (5)

1. Bubba Starling, of, Gardner-Edgerton HS, Gardner, Kan.
2. Cam Gallagher, c, Manheim Township HS, Lancaster, Pa.
3. Bryan Brickhouse, rhp, The Woodlands (Texas) HS
4. Kyle Smith, rhp, Santaluces HS, Lantana, Fla.
5. Patrick Leonard, of, St. Thomas HS, Houston
6. Cesar Ogando, lhp, Caribbean (P.R.) JC
7. Kellen Moen, rhp, Oregon
8. Evan Beal, rhp, South County HS, Lorton, Va.
9. Aaron Brooks, rhp, Cal State San Bernardino
10. Matt Murray, rhp, Georgia Southern
11. Jerrell Allen, of, Milford (Del.) HS
12. Adam Schemenauer, lhp, Park Hill South HS, Riverside, Mo.
13. Stephen Lumpkins, lhp, American (D.C.)
14. D'Andre Toney, of, Gulf Coast (Fla.) CC
15. Dean Espy, 1b, UCLA
16. Jack Lopez, ss, Deltona (Fla.) HS
17. Nic Cuckovich, rhp, Riverside (Calif.) CC
18. Andy Ferguson, rhp, Arkansas State
19. Matt Flemer, rhp, California
20. Terrance Gore, of, Gulf Coast (Fla.) CC
21. Kenny Swab, c, Virginia
22. Dave Middendorf, lhp, Northern Kentucky
23. Lance Harper, c, Scottsdale (Ariz.) CC
24. Spencer Patton, rhp, Southern Illinois-Edwardsville
25. Matt Threlkeld, 3b, Louisiana Tech
26. Joseph Moorefield, lhp, Clemson
27. Lee Clubb, of, Iowa Park (Texas) HS

28. Jordan Ramsey, rhp, North Davidson HS, Lexington, N.C.
29. Jake Junis, rhp, Rock Falls (Ill.) HS
30. Mark Binford, rhp, Mercersburg (Pa.) Academy
31. Chris Serritella, 1b, Southern Illinois
32. Nick Piscotty, rhp, Amador Valley HS, Pleasanton, Calif.
33. Abel Gonzales, lhp, Rice
34. Ali Williams, rhp, Charleston Southern
35. Gabriel Gray, of, Hazlehurst (Miss.) HS
36. Christian Witt, rhp, Truman State (Mo.)
37. Matt Wessinger, ss, St. John's
38. Andrew Durden, rhp, Nova Southeastern (Fla.)
39. Garrett Mattlage, ss, West HS, Stinnett, Texas
40. Ben Waldrip, 1b, Jacksonville State (Ala.)
41. Travis Lane, c, Central Arizona JC
42. Joey Hawkins, 2b, Sinclair SS, Whitby, Ont.
43. Tyler Chism, of, Gonzaga
44. Andrew Vasquez, rhp, Los Osos HS, Rancho Cucamonga, Calif.
45. Julio Morales, rhp, Bethune-Cookman
46. Adrian Bringas, 3b, Chico State (Calif.)
47. Patrick Corbett, rhp, Tabb HS, Yorktown, Va.
48. Matt Beaty, c, Dresden (Tenn.) HS
49. Adrian Morales, 3b, South Carolina
50. Kash Kalkowski, 3b, Nebraska

LOS ANGELES ANGELS (14)

1. C.J. Cron Jr., 1b, Utah
2. (Pick to Blue Jays as compensation for Type A free agent Scott Downs)
3. Nick Maronde, lhp, Florida
4. Mike Clevinger, rhp, Seminole State (Fla.) JC
5. Andrew Ray, of, Northeast Texas CC
6. Austin Wood, rhp, Southern California
7. Abel Baker, c, Grayson County (Texas) CC
8. Logan Odom, rhp, Southern California
9. Nick Mutz, rhp, Cotati, Calif. (No school)
10. Drew Martinez, of, Memphis
11. Garrett Baker, lhp, Liberty
12. Joe Krehbiel, 3b, Seminole (Fla.) HS
13. Jackson Whitley, 1b, North Augusta (S.C.) HS
14. Wayne Taylor, c, Memorial HS, Houston
15. Domonic Jose, of, Boca Raton (Fla.) HS
16. Frazier Hall, 1b, Southern
17. Hunter Lockwood, c, Bell HS, Hurst, Texas
18. Trevor Hairgrove, ss, UC Riverside
19. Ryan Crowley, lhp, Northwest Florida State JC
20. Junior Carlin, lhp, South Florida
21. Shane Riedie, rhp, Tampa
22. Brennan Gowens, of, Fresno State
23. Zach Borenstein, of, Eastern Illinois
24. Jarrod Parks, 3b, Mississippi State
25. Josh Alvarado, rhp, Phoenix (No school)
26. John Gianis, of, North Carolina State
27. Brian Hernandez, 3b, UC Irvine
28. Daniel Vargas-Vila, rhp, West Florida
29. Greg Larson, rhp, Florida
30. Mike Papi, of, Tunkhannock (Pa.) Area HS
31. Jett Bandy, c, Arizona
32. John Leonard, rhp, Boston College
33. Erik Forgione, ss, West HS, Chehalis, Wash.
34. Andy Workman, of, Arizona State
35. Stephen Tromblee, lhp, Lamar
36. Brandon Brewer, ss, West Florida
37. Brandon Efferson, rhp, Southeastern Louisiana
38. Frank DeJiulio, rhp, Tampa
39. Chris Giovinazzo, of, UCLA
40. Joe Church, rhp, Marshall
41. Brandon McNelis, rhp, Northeastern
42. Jason Nappi, 3b, Harding (Ark.)
43. Kyle Mahoney, c, High Point
44. Landis Ware, 2b, Baylor
45. Matt Scioscia, c, Notre Dame
46. Michael Johnson, lhp, Hillsborough (Fla.) CC
47. Brandon Lodge, rhp, UCLA
48. Ricky Pacione, c, Marist
49. Matt Vedo, rhp, UC Santa Barbara
50. Trent Garrison, c, Fresno State

LOS ANGELES DODGERS (13)

1. Chris Reed, lhp, Stanford
2. Alex Santana, 3b, Mariner HS, Cape Coral, Fla.
3. Pratt Maynard, c, North Carolina State
4. Ryan O'Sullivan, rhp, Oklahoma City
5. Scott McGough, rhp, Oregon
6. Scott Barlow, rhp, Golden Valley HS, Santa Clarita, Calif.
7. Scott Woodward, of, Coastal Carolina
8. Rick Anton, lhp, Utah
9. Tyler Ogle, c, Oklahoma
10. Jamaal Moore, lhp, Westchester HS, Los Angeles
11. Scott Wingo, ss, South Carolina
12. O'Koyea Dickson, 1b, Sonoma State (Calif.)
13. David Palladino, rhp, Emerson (N.J.) HS
14. Justin Boudreaux, ss, Southeastern Louisiana
15. Craig Stem, rhp, Trevecca Nazarene (Tenn.)
16. Jeff Schaus, of, Clemson
17. Jesus Valdez, 3b, Oxnard (Calif.) JC
18. Chris O'Brien, c, Wichita State
19. Garrett Bush, rhp, Seminole State (Fla.) JC
20. Vince Spilker, rhp, Johnson County (Kan.) CC
21. Zak Qualls, lhp, Rancho HS, Las Vegas
22. Kyle Conwell, of, Bellevue (Wash.) CC
23. Garrett Bolt, rhp, Western Illinois
24. Matt Shelton, rhp, Sam Houston State
25. Travis Burnside, of, Spartanburg Methodist (S.C.) JC
26. Freddie Cabrera, rhp, Central Methodist (Mo.)
27. Taylor Garrison, rhp, Fresno State
28. Joey Winker, of, Mercer
29. Joe Robinson, rhp, Nevada-Las Vegas
30. Adam McConnell, ss, Richmond
31. Mickey McConnell, ss, St. Mary's
32. Hunter Jennings, of, Delgado (La.) CC
33. Malcolm Holland, 2b, Hamilton HS, Chandler, Ariz.
34. Rob Chamra, rhp, North Carolina State
35. Mike Thomas, lhp, Rider
36. Kevin Taylor, 2b, Western Nevada CC
37. Reid Redman, 3b, Texas Tech
38. Devin Shines, of, Oklahoma State
39. Jordan Kipper, rhp, Mountain Pointe HS, Phoenix
40. Stefan Jarrin, 2b, San Gabriel, Calif. (No school)
41. Casey Thomas, 2b, Desert Vista HS, Phoenix
42. Max Povse, rhp, Green Hope HS, Cary, N.C.
43. Alex Hermeling, rhp, Glenbrook North HS, Northbrook, Ill.
44. Austin Slater, ss, Bolles School, Jacksonville, Fla.
45. James Lynch, of, Salisbury (Conn.) HS
46. Victor Munoz, c, Claremont (Calif.) HS
47. Gregg Downing, lhp, Franklin Pierce (N.H.)
48. Kevin Thompson, ss, Eastern New Mexico
49. J.J. Ethel, c, Louisville
50. Chris Ellis, rhp, Spain Park HS, Birmingham

MILWAUKEE BREWERS (10)

1. Taylor Jungmann, rhp, Texas
1. Jed Bradley, lhp, Georgia Tech (Supplemental pick—15th—for failure to sign 2010 first-round pick Dylan Covey)
2. Jorge Lopez, rhp, Academia de Milagrosa, Cayey, P.R.
3. Drew Gagnon, rhp, Long Beach State
4. Nick Ramirez, 1b, Cal State Fullerton
5. Michael Reed, of, Leander (Texas) HS
6. Danny Keller, rhp, Newbury Park HS, Thousand Oaks, Calif.
7. David Goforth, rhp, Mississippi
8. Dustin Houle, c, Brookswood SS, Langley, B.C.
9. Malcolm Dowell, of, La Grange (Ga.) HS
10. Mike Strong, lhp, Oklahoma State
11. Tommy Toledo, rhp, Florida
12. Andrew Cain, of, UNC Wilmington
13. Mallex Smith, of, Rickards HS, Tallahassee, Fla.
14. Jacob Barnes, rhp, Florida Gulf Coast
15. Andy Moye, rhp, Georgia Southern
16. Carlos Rodon, lhp, Holly Springs (N.C.) HS
17. Mario Amaral, c, Reagan HS, Hialeah, Fla.
18. Chris McFarland, ss, Lufkin (Texas) HS
19. Renaldo Jenkins, ss, Whitewater HS, Fayetteville, Ga.

20. Brandon Williamson, rhp, Dallas Baptist
21. Mike Nemeth, 1b, Connecticut
22. Dennis Jones, of, Davis HS, Montgomery, Ala.
23. Ben McMahan, c, Florida
24. Michael Palazzone, rhp, Georgia
25. Parker Berberet, c, Oregon State
26. Josh Smith, lhp, Wichita State
27. Chad Thompson, rhp, Orange Coast (Calif.) CC
28. BreShon Kimbrell, c, Mesquite (Texas) HS
29. David Lucroy, rhp, Umatila (Fla.) HS
30. Trent Boras, 3b, JSerra HS, San Juan Capistrano, Calif.
31. Sean Albury, rhp, Nova Southeastern (Fla.)
32. Alfredo Rodriguez, ss, Maryland
33. Steven Okert, lhp, Grayson County (Texas) CC
34. Adam Weisenburger, c, Miami (Ohio)
35. Doug Elliot, c, Connecticut
36. Mitch Conner, rhp, Elon
37. Casey Medlen, rhp, North Florida
38. Chad Pierce, rhp, Wisconsin-Milwaukee
39. Elliot Glynn, lhp, Connecticut
40. Keaton Aldridge, c, Glenwood School, Smiths Station, Ala.
41. Jalen Harris, 3b, Lambrick Park SS, Victoria, B.C.
42. Caleb Whalen, ss, Union HS, Camas, Wash.
43. Clint Wilson, rhp, Navarro (Texas) JC
44. Steve Adam, of, Ecole Secondaire L'Essor, Tecumseh, Ont.
45. Adrian Williams, ss, UCLA
46. Ahmad Christian, ss, Trinity Christian Academy, Deltona, Fla.
47. Jecid Tarazona, of, North Broward Prep, Coconut Creek, Fla.
48. Mike Francisco, lhp, Villanova
49. Gant Elmore, 2b, Yale
50. Matt Franco, of, St. Thomas Aquinas HS, Ft. Lauderdale, Fla.

MINNESOTA TWINS (27)

1. Levi Michael, ss, North Carolina
1. Travis Harrison, 3b, Tustin (Calif.) HS (Supplemental pick—50th—for loss of Type B free agent Orlando Hudson)
1. Hudson Boyd, rhp, Bishop Verot HS, Ft. Myers, Fla. (Supplemental pick—55th—for loss of Type B free agent Jesse Crain)
2. Madison Boer, rhp, Oregon
3. Corey Williams, lhp, Vanderbilt
4. Matt Summers, rhp, UC Irvine
5. Tyler Grimes, ss, Wichita State
6. Dereck Rodriguez, of, Pace (Fla.) HS
7. Steve Gruver, lhp, Tennessee
8. Jason Wheeler, lhp, Loyola Marymount
9. Adam Bryant, ss, Troy
10. Brett Lee, lhp, St. Petersburg (Fla.) JC
11. Tyler Jones, rhp, Louisiana State
12. Matt Koch, c, Loyola Marymount
13. Steven Evans, lhp, Liberty
14. Adam McCreery, lhp, Bonita HS, La Verne, Calif.
15. Josue Montanez, lhp, Miami Dade JC
16. Austin Malinowski, lhp, Centennial HS, Circle Pines, Minn.
17. Josh Burris, rhp, Louisiana State-Eunice JC
18. Corey Kimes, lhp, Illinois
19. Tyler Koelling, of, Southern Mississippi
20. Brian Anderson, ss, Deer Creek HS, Edmond, Okla.
21. Michael Howard, lhp, Prescott (Ariz.) HS
22. James Ramsey, of, Florida State
23. Tim Shibuya, rhp, UC San Diego
24. Nick Burdi, rhp, Downers Grove (Ill.) South HS
25. A.J. Pettersen, ss, Minnesota
26. Trent Higginbotham, rhp, Clay-Chalkville HS, Trussville, Ala.
27. Chris Mazza, rhp, Menlo (Calif.)
28. David Hurlbut, lhp, Cal State Fullerton
29. Derek Thompson, lhp, Teutopolis (Ill.) HS
30. Will Clinard, rhp, Vanderbilt
31. Garrett Jewell, rhp, Southern New Hampshire
32. Dylan Chavez, lhp, American River (Calif.) JC
33. Stephen Wickens, ss, Florida Gulf Coast
34. Ryan Tella, of, Ohlone (Calif.) JC
35. Phillip Chapman, c, Memphis
36. Austin Barrois, of, Belle Chasse (La.) HS
37. Drew Leachman, of, Birmingham-Southern
38. Alex Keudell, rhp, Oregon

39. Rocky McCord, rhp, Spanish Fort (Ala.) HS
40. Kyle Barraclough, rhp, St. Mary's
41. T.J. Oakes, rhp, Minnesota
42. Matthew Tomshaw, lhp, Jacksonville
43. Bobby O'Neill, rhp, Biola (Calif.)
44. Cole Johnson, rhp, Notre Dame
45. Julio Torres, 2b, Puerto Rico Baseball Academy, Gurabo, P.R.
46. Jared Dettmann, lhp, Somerset (Wis.) HS
47. John Hochstatter, lhp, San Ramon Valley HS, Danville, Calif.
48. Garret Peterson, rhp, DuBois (Pa.) Area HS
49. Drake Roberts, 2b, Brenham (Texas) HS
50. Bryan Burgher, rhp, Emerald Ridge HS, Puyallup, Wash.

NEW YORK METS (11)

1. Brandon Nimmo, of, East HS, Cheyenne, Wyo.
1. Michael Fulmer, rhp, Deer Creek HS, Edmond, Okla.
   (Supplemental pick—44th—for loss of Type B free agent Pedro Feliciano)
2. Cory Mazzoni, rhp, North Carolina State
3. Logan Verrett, rhp, Baylor
4. Tyler Pill, rhp, Cal State Fullerton
5. Jack Leathersich, lhp, Massachusetts-Lowell
6. Joe Tuschak, of, Northern HS, Dillsburg, Pa.
7. Cole Frenzel, 1b, Arizona
8. Danny Muno, ss, Fresno State
9. Alex Panteliodis, lhp, Florida
10. Matthew Budgell, rhp, Woodbridge HS, Irvine, Calif.
11. Christian Montgomery, rhp, Lawrence Central HS, Indianapolis
12. Kenny Matthews, lhp, Diamond Bar (Calif.) HS
13. Robert Gsellman, rhp, Westchester HS, Los Angeles
14. Xorge Carrillo, c, Arizona State
15. Phillip Evans, ss, La Costa Canyon HS, Carlsbad, Calif.
16. Brad Marquez, of, Odessa (Texas) HS
17. Jonathan Clark, of, Lee (Tenn.)
18. Travis Taijeron, of, Cal Poly Pomona
19. Dustin Lawley, of, West Florida
20. Mason Robbins, of, George County HS, Lucedale, Miss.
21. John Gant, rhp, Wiregrass Ranch HS, Wesley Chapel, Fla.
22. Casey Turgeon, ss, Dunedin (Fla.) HS
23. Jeff Diehl, c, Cranston (R.I.) West HS
24. Tant Shepherd, 1b, Texas
25. A.J. Reed, lhp, Terre Haute (Ind.) South HS
26. Casey Hauptman, rhp, Nebraska
27. Randy Fontanez, rhp, South Florida
28. Jharel Cotton, rhp, Miami Dade JC
29. Josh Ake, ss, Hunterdon Central HS, Flemington, N.J.
30. Jake Hansen, lhp, Walshe HS, Fort Macleod, Alb.
31. Chad Zurcher, ss, Memphis
32. Carlos Leyva, ss, Cal State Dominguez Hills
33. Tyson Seng, rhp, Oklahoma
34. Seth Lugo, rhp, Centenary
35. Chase Bradford, rhp, Central Florida
36. Ryan Hutson, 1b, Texas-San Antonio
37. Craig Missigman, rhp, Olympic HS, Charlotte
38. Dustin Emmons, rhp, UC Riverside
39. Charley Thurber, of, Tennessee
40. Alexis Mercado, c, Otay Ranch HS, Chula Vista, Calif.
41. Mark Picca, lhp, Texas-Arlington
42. Greg Pron, of, West Florida
43. Jacob Decker, ss, Piedmont (Okla.) HS
44. Clint Sharp, rhp, Howard (Texas) JC
45. Andrew Marra, rhp, St. Thomas of Villanova SS, LaSalle, Ont.
46. Rich Ruff, rhp, Quincy (Ill.)
47. Cole Limbaugh, rhp, Childersburg (Ala.) HS
48. Malcolm Clapsaddle, rhp, Santa Fe (Fla.) CC
49. Sean Buckle, lhp, Wilson HS, Long Beach
50. Eddie Rohan, c, Winthrop

NEW YORK YANKEES (28)

1. (Pick to Rays as compensation for Type A free agent Rafael Soriano)
1. Dante Bichette Jr., of, Orangewood Christian HS, Orlando
   (Supplemental pick—51st—for loss of Type B free agent Javier Vazquez)
2. Sam Stafford, lhp, Texas
3. Jordan Cote, rhp, Winnisquam HS, Northfield, N.H.

4. Matt Duran, 3b, New Rochelle (N.Y.) HS
5. Greg Bird, c, Grandview HS, Aurora, Colo.
6. Jake Cave, of, Kecoughtan HS, Hampton, Va.
7. Austin Jones, 1b, Edmonds-Woodway HS, Edmonds, Wash.
8. Phil Wetherell, rhp, Western Kentucky
9. Zach Arneson, rhp, Lewis-Clark State (Idaho)
10. Jon Gray, rhp, Eastern Oklahoma State JC
11. Mark Montgomery, rhp, Longwood
12. Cody Grice, of, Grand Valley State (Mich.)
13. Justin James, of, Sacramento CC
14. Rookie Davis, rhp, Dixon HS, Holly Ridge, N.C.
15. Tyler Molinaro, of, Pitt (N.C.) CC
16. Branden Pinder, rhp, Long Beach State
17. Mathew Troupe, rhp, Chaminade Prep HS, Chatsworth, Calif.
18. Hayden Sharp, rhp, Morris (Okla.) HS
19. Ben Paullus, rhp, Memphis
20. Daniel Camarena, lhp, Cathedral Catholic HS, San Diego
21. Zach Wilson, 1b, Arizona State
22. Nick Goody, rhp, State JC of Florida
23. Corey Maines, rhp, Illinois State
24. Matt Tracy, lhp, Mississippi
25. Adam Smith, rhp, Texas A&M
26. Jordan Foley, rhp, The Colony (Texas) HS
27. Chaz Hebert, lhp, Breaux Bridge (La.) HS
28. Josean Lazaro, rhp, North Broward Prep, Coconut Creek, Fla.
29. Scott Hoffman, rhp, Desert Ridge HS, Mesa, Ariz.
30. John Brebbia, rhp, Elon
31. Aaron Bummer, lhp, Sunrise Mountain HS, Peoria, Ariz.
32. Garrett Nuss, rhp, Mount Dora HS, Sorrento, Fla.
33. Spencer O'Neil, of, Southridge HS, Kennewick, Wash.
34. Skylar Janisse, rhp, St. Thomas of Villanova SS, LaSalle, Ont.
35. Chris McCue, rhp, Ardrey Kell HS, Charlotte
36. Ryan Thompson, rhp, Franklin Pierce (N.H.)
37. Ryan Harris, rhp, Jupiter (Fla.) Community HS
38. Joey Maher, rhp, Bedford (N.H) HS
39. Taylor Guilbeau, lhp, Zachary (La.) HS
40. Tyler Hanover, ss, Louisiana State
41. Jeremy Rathjen, of, Rice
42. Kevin Cornelius, ss, Weatherford (Texas) HS
43. Tyler Farrell, rhp, Galesburg (Ill.) HS
44. Adam Ravenelle, rhp, Lincoln-Sudbury HS, Sudbury, Mass.
45. Cass Ingvardsen, rhp, Weatherford (Texas) JC
46. Conner Mach, 3b, Missouri
47. Ethan Springston, of, Seton Catholic HS, Chandler, Ariz.
48. Wes Benjamin, lhp, St. Charles (Ill.) East HS
49. Tyler Mapes, rhp, Navarro (Texas) JC
50. Cody Stewart, of, Great Oak HS, Temecula, Calif.

OAKLAND ATHLETICS (15)

1. Sonny Gray, rhp, Vanderbilt
2. (Pick to Rays as compensation for Type A free agent Grant Balfour)
3. B.A. Vollmuth, 3b, Southern Mississippi
4. Bobby Crocker, of, Cal Poly
5. Beau Taylor, c, Central Florida
6. Dayton Alexander, of, Feather River (Calif.) JC
7. Blake Treinen, rhp, South Dakota State
8. Colin O'Connell, rhp, Cal State Fullerton
9. Jace Fry, lhp, Southridge HS, Beaverton, Ore.
10. Dusty Robinson, of, Fresno State
11. Chris Lamb, lhp, Davidson
12. Xavier Macklin, of, North Carolina A&T
13. Jacob Tanis, 3b, Mercer
14. Nick Rickles, c, Stetson
15. T.J. Walz, rhp, Kansas
16. Tanner Peters, rhp, Nevada-Las Vegas
17. Sean Jamieson, ss, Canisius
18. Brent Powers, lhp, Sam Houston State
19. Eric Potter, lhp, Maryland
20. Kurt Wunderlich, rhp, Michigan State
21. Brandon Magee, of, Arizona State
22. Rhett Stafford, of, Marshall
23. Cecil Tanner, rhp, Georgia
24. Max Kuhn, ss, Zionsville (Ind.) Community HS
25. Chad Oberacker, of, Tennessee Tech
26. Sam Roberts, rhp, Virginia Military Institute

27. Derek Self, rhp, Louisville
28. Thomas Girdwood, rhp, Elon
29. **Nate Eppley, rhp, Rider**
30. **Nathan Kilcrease, rhp, Alabama**
31. Sasha Kuebel, lhp, St. Louis University HS
32. **Drew Granier, rhp, Louisiana-Monroe**
33. **Austin Booker, 2b, California**
34. Alfredo Unzue, lhp, Calabasas, Calif. (No school)
35. **Max Perlman, rhp, Harvard**
36. Brenden Farney, ss, Vacaville (Calif.) HS
37. Eric Wood, 3b, Oshawa, Ontario (No school)
38. Alex Blandino, ss, St. Francis HS, Mountain View, Calif.
39. **Shane Boras, 2b, Southern California**
40. Nic Coffman, 3b, Wilson HS, Portland, Ore.
41. Brett Bittiger, ss, Pius X HS, Bangor, Pa.
42. Brett Geren, c, San Ramon Valley HS, Danville, Calif.
43. Adam Frank, lhp, Field HS, Gilbert, Ariz.
44. **Chris Bostick, ss, Aquinas Institute, Rochester, N.Y.**
45. C.J. Jacobe, of, Vacaville (Calif.) HS
46. Nate Esposito, c, Granite Bay (Calif.) HS
47. Jeriel Waller, of, Grossmont (Calif.) JC
48. Travis Feeney, of, Pinole Valley HS, Pinole, Calif.
49. Charles Sheffield, of, Pendleton School, Bradenton, Fla.
50. Travis Pitcher, rhp, Cypress (Calif.) JC

PHILADELPHIA PHILLIES (30)

1. (Pick to Rangers as compensation for Type A free agent Cliff Lee)
1. **Larry Greene, of, Berrien County HS, Nashville, Ga.** (Supplemental pick—39th—for loss of Type A free agent Jayson Werth)
2. **Roman Quinn, ss, Port St. Joe (Fla.) HS** (Pick from Nationals as compensation for Werth)
2. **Harold Martinez, 3b, Miami**
3. **Adam Morgan, lhp, Alabama**
4. **Cody Asche, 3b, Nebraska**
5. **Mitch Walding, ss, St. Mary's HS, Stockton, Calif.**
6. **Zach Wright, c, East Carolina**
7. **Kenny Giles, rhp, Yavapai (Ariz.) JC**
8. **Austin Wright, lhp, Mississippi**
9. **Logan Moore, c, Northeastern (Col.) JC**
10. Jake Overbey, ss, University School, Jackson, Tenn.
11. **Tyler Greene, ss, West Boca Raton (Fla.) HS**
12. **Yacksel Rios, rhp, Cuevas HS, Gurabo, P.R.**
13. **Colton Murray, rhp, Kansas**
14. **Trey Ford, 3b, South Mountain (Ariz.) CC**
15. Ryan Garvey, of, Palm Desert (Calif.) HS
16. **Taylor Black, ss, Kentucky**
17. **Jesen Dygestile-Therrien, rhp, Ahuntsic (Que.) JC**
18. **Drew Hillman, 3b, UC Irvine**
19. **John Hill, c, Concordia (Calif.)**
20. **Pete Lavin, of, San Francisco**
21. Riley Moore, c, San Marcos (Calif.) HS
22. **Matt Holland, of, Texas A&M-Corpus Christi**
23. **Cody Fick, rhp, Evansville**
24. **Matt Campbell, rhp, Florida**
25. **Ryan Duke, rhp, Oklahoma**
26. Michael Rocha, rhp, Oklahoma
27. **Braden Shull, lhp, Mount Pleasant (Iowa) HS**
28. **Ian Durham, rhp, California Lutheran**
29. **Paul Cusick, rhp, Pennsylvania**
30. **Mike Marshall, 1b, Lubbock Christian (Texas)**
31. Kyle Olson, c, Jackson HS, Mill Creek, Wash.
32. **Greg Herbst, rhp, St. Mary's (Texas)**
33. **Brock Stassi, of, Nevada**
34. Brandon Pletsch, ss, Rancho HS, Las Vegas
35. Kyle Freeland, lhp, Jefferson HS, Denver
36. Brendon Hayden, rhp, Wilmot (Wis.) Union HS
37. Mike Nastold, rhp, Louisville
38. Brett Maggard, lhp, Hernando HS, Brooksville, Fla.
39. Tim Ponto, rhp, Roberts HS, Pottstown, Pa.
40. Brendan Hendriks, 1b, Vauxhall (Alb.) HS
41. Austin Dicharry, rhp, Texas
42. **Andre Kinder, lhp, Peru State (Neb.)**
43. Austin Knight, c, Sumrall (Miss.) HS
44. Nevin Wilson, lhp, Chaparral HS, Scottsdale, Ariz.
45. A.J. Ladwig, rhp, Millard West HS, Omaha

46. Scott Tomassetti, c, Sierra Vista HS, Las Vegas
47. Andrew Amaro, 2b, Penn Charter HS, Philadelphia
48. Kewby Meyer, 1b, Kamehameha HS, Honolulu
49. **Johnny Knight, of, Sebring (Fla.) HS**
50. Koyla Stephenson, rhp, Ocean City (N.J.) HS

PITTSBURGH PIRATES (1)

1. **Gerrit Cole, rhp, UCLA**
2. **Josh Bell, of, Dallas Jesuit HS**
3. **Alex Dickerson, 1b, Indiana**
4. **Colten Brewer, rhp, Canton (Texas) HS**
5. **Tyler Glasnow, rhp, Hart HS, Santa Clarita, Calif.**
6. **Dan Gamache, 3b, Auburn**
7. **Jake Burnette, rhp, Buford (Ga.) HS**
8. **Jason Creasy, rhp, Clayton (N.C.) HS**
9. **Clay Holmes, rhp, Slocomb (Ala.) HS**
10. **Taylor Lewis, of, Maine**
11. Jo-El Bennett, of, Houston Academy, Dothan, Ala.
12. **Candon Myles, of, South Grand Prairie (Texas) HS**
13. Brandon Platts, rhp, Mason City (Iowa) HS
14. Jordan Dunatov, of, Horizon HS, Scottsdale, Ariz.
15. Kody Watts, rhp, Skyview HS, Vancouver, Wash.
16. Eric Skoglund, lhp, Sarasota (Fla.) HS
17. Aaron Brown, of, Chatsworth (Calif.) HS
18. **Josh Poytress, lhp, Fresno State**
19. Tayler Nunez, rhp, Salmen HS, Slidell, La.
20. Trea Turner, ss, Park Vista HS, Lake Worth, Fla.
21. **Alex Fuselier, of, Louisiana-Lafayette**
22. **Mike Jefferson, lhp, Louisiana Tech**
23. **Jordan Cooper, rhp, Kentucky**
24. **Brian Sharp, ss, California Baptist**
25. Josh Martin, rhp, Samford
26. Nick Flair, ss, Belle Chasse (La.) HS
27. **Ryan Hornback, c, San Jacinto (Texas) JC**
28. Brandon Zajac, lhp, Walker Valley HS, Cleveland, Tenn.
29. **Kirk Singer, ss, Long Beach State**
30. **Matt Benedict, rhp, Western Carolina**
31. **Derek Trent, c, East Tennesse State**
32. **David Jagoditsh, rhp, Pima (Ariz.) CC**
33. **Chris Lashmet, 3b, Northwestern**
34. Hommy Rosado, 1b, Louisiana State-Eunice JC
35. Reid Matthews, 2b, Dobyns-Bennett HS, Kingsport, Tenn.
36. Isaac Ballou, of, Marshall
37. **Rodarrick Jones, of, Southern**
38. D.J. Crumlich, ss, UC Irvine
39. Rand Ravnaas, of, Georgetown
40. Raph Rhymes, 2b, Louisiana State
41. **Jon Schwind, c, Marist**
42. Nick Hibbing, rhp, Lakes Community HS, Antioch, Ill.
43. Willie Argo, of, Illinois
44. Bobby LeCount, 3b, Edmonds (Wash.) CC
45. Robbie Ingram, lhp, Yavapai (Ariz.) JC
46. Jeff Schalk, of, Wheaton (Ill.) North HS
47. Jordan DeLuca, of, Tussey Mountain HS, Saxton, Pa.
48. Zach Thompson, rhp, Grace Prep Academy, Arlington, Texas
49. Austin White, 3b, Arkansas HS, Texarkana, Ark.
50. Zechariah Lemond, rhp, Waltrip HS, Houston

ST. LOUIS CARDINALS (19)

1. **Kolten Wong, 2b, Hawaii**
2. **Charlie Tilson, of, New Trier HS, Winnetka, Ill.**
3. **C.J. McElroy Jr., of, Clear Creek HS, League City, Texas**
4. **Kenny Peoples, ss, Westchester HS, Los Angeles**
5. **Sam Gaviglio, rhp, Oregon State**
6. **Adam Ehrlich, c, Campbell Hall HS, North Hollywood, Calif.**
7. **Nick Martini, of, Kansas State**
8. **Daniel Miranda, lhp, Miami**
9. **Tyler Mills, rhp, Michigan**
10. **Lance Jeffries, of, McCluer HS, St. Louis**
11. **Seth Maness, rhp, East Carolina**
12. **Danny Stienstra, 1b, San Jose State**
13. **Kolby Byrd, c, Copiah-Lincoln (Miss.) CC**
14. Kevin Medrano, 2b, Missouri State
15. **Matt Williams, ss, Liberty**
16. **Travis Miller, rhp, Miami**

17. **Dutch Deol, of, Aliso Niguel HS, Aliso Viejo, Calif.**
18. **Kyle Hald, lhp, Old Dominion**
19. **Nick Gillung, lhp, Mercyhurst (Pa.)**
20. Aramis Garcia, c, Pembroke Pines (Fla.) Charter HS
21. Chris Kirsch, lhp, Lackawanna (Pa.) JC
22. **Justin Kamplain, lhp, Walker HS, Jasper, Ala.**
23. Kyle Deese, rhp, Western Carolina
24. **Jonathan Cornelius, lhp, Florida Tech**
25. **Todd McInnis, rhp, Southern Mississippi**
26. Brett Graves, rhp, Howell HS, St. Charles, Mo.
27. **Gary Apelian, of, Santa Ana (Calif.) JC**
28. **Ryan Sherriff, lhp, Glendale (Calif.) JC**
29. Chris Matulis, lhp, Central Florida
30. **David Bergin, rhp, Tennessee Wesleyan**
31. **Kevin Jacob, rhp, Georgia Tech**
32. **Jonathan Keener, c, Cal State Dominguez Hills**
33. **Heath Wyatt, rhp, Southeastern Oklahoma State**
34. **Tyler Rahmatulla, 2b, UCLA**
35. Drew Madrigal, rhp, California Baptist
36. **Jordan Rasmus, c, Liberty**
37. **Brad Watson, rhp, Wartburg (Iowa)**
38. **Jeremy Patton, 3b, Florida International**
39. **Tyler Melling, lhp, Miami (Ohio)**
40. Kyle Arnsberg, c, McLennan (Texas) CC
41. **Mike Knox, 1b, Mt. Olive (N.C.)**
42. Cody Poarch, rhp, Walters State (Tenn.) CC
43. **Chris Costantino, rhp, Walters State (Tenn.) CC**
44. **Brandon Creath, rhp, Embry-Riddle (Fla.)**
45. Cooper Moseley, 2b, Central Alabama CC
46. Chadwick Kaalekahi, c, Campbell HS, Ewa Beach, Hawaii
47. David Schmidt, rhp, Christian Brothers HS, St. Louis
48. Brock Asher, of, Aiea (Hawaii) HS
49. **Corey Baker, rhp, Pittsburgh**
50. Tyler Sibley, 2b, Texas State

SAN DIEGO PADRES (22)

1. **Cory Spangenberg, 2b, Indian River (Fla.) JC** (Supplemental pick–10th–for failure to sign 2010 first-round pick Karsten Whitson)
1. **Joe Ross, rhp, Bishop O'Dowd HS, Oakland**
1. **Michael Kelly, rhp, West Boca Raton (Fla.) HS** (Supplemental pick–48th–for loss of Type B free agent Jon Garland)
1. **Brett Austin, c, Providence HS, Charlotte** (Supplemental pick–54th–for loss of Type B free agent Yorvit Torrealba)
1. **Jace Peterson, ss, McNeese State** (Supplemental pick–58th–for loss of Type B free agent Kevin Correia)
2. **Austin Hedges, c, JSerra HS, San Juan Capistrano, Calif.**
3. **Matt Andriese, rhp, UC Riverside**
4. **Cody Hebner, rhp, Green River (Wash.) CC**
5. **Mark Pope, rhp, Georgia Tech**
6. **Kyle Gaedele, of, Valparaiso**
7. **Matt Wisler, rhp, Bryan (Ohio) HS**
8. **Kevin Quackenbush, rhp, South Florida**
9. **Justin Hancock, rhp, Lincoln Trail (Ill.) CC**
10. **Rob Kral, c, College of Charleston**
11. **Casey McElroy, ss, Auburn**
12. **Colin Rea, rhp, Indiana State**
13. **Lee Orr, of, McNeese State**
14. **Burch Smith, rhp, Oklahoma**
15. **Greg Gonzalez, rhp, Fresno State**
16. **Jeremy Rodriguez, c, Cal State Bakersfield**
17. **Matt Stites, rhp, Missouri**
18. **Mike Gallic, of, Marist**
19. **Jeremy Gigliotti, lhp, East Stroudsburg (Pa.)**
20. **Chris Haney, rhp, Dallas Baptist**
21. **Zach Kometani, 1b, San Diego**
22. **Matt Colantonio, c, Brown**
23. **R.L. Eisenbach, lhp, Faulkner (Ala.)**
24. Erick Fedde, rhp, Las Vegas HS
25. **Paul Karmas, 1b, St. John's**
26. Roberto Suppa, rhp, St. Thomas Aquinas SS, West London, Ont.
27. Arby Fields, of, Cypress (Calif.) JC
28. **Rashaad Ingram, 2b, St. Augustine's (N.C.)**
29. Vimeal Machin, c, Puerto Rico Baseball Academy, Gurabo, P.R.
30. **Justin Miller, of, Southeastern Oklahoma**
31. **Clint Moore, ss, Army**

32. **Kyle Brule, rhp, Oklahoma Baptist**
33. **James Jones, rhp, Louisiana-Monroe**
34. **Dennis O'Grady, rhp, Duke**
35. **Travis Whitmore, 2b, Pittsburgh**
36. Andrew Rash, of, Virginia Tech
37. Cody Semler, ss, Allen (Texas) HS
38. Pat Connaughton, rhp, St. John's Prep, Danvers, Mass.
39. Josh Pond, rhp, Cal State San Bernardino
40. Taylor Murphy, 3b, Torrey Pines HS, San Diego
41. Dante Flores, 2b, St. John Bosco HS, Bellflower, Calif.
42. Garrett Boulware, c, Hanna HS, Anderson, S.C.
43. **Cody Gabella, ss, Southeastern (Iowa) CC**
44. Spenser Linney, lhp, Head-Royce School, Oakland
45. Will Gross, of, Tupelo (Miss.) HS
46. Eddie Solomon, 2b, Beaumont (Calif.) HS
47. Vince Voiro, rhp, Pennsylvania
48. Kent Rollins, ss, South Gwinnett HS, Snellville, Ga.
49. Ryan Hutchison, of, Western Kentucky

SAN FRANCISCO GIANTS (26)

1. **Joe Panik, ss, St. John's**
1. **Kyle Crick, rhp, Sherman (Texas) HS** (Supplemental pick–49th–for loss of Type B free agent Juan Uribe)
2. **Andrew Susac, c, Oregon State**
3. **Ricky Oropesa, 1b, Southern California**
4. **Bryce Bandilla, lhp, Arizona**
5. **Chris Marlowe, rhp, Oklahoma State**
6. **Josh Osich, lhp, Oregon State**
7. **Ray Black, rhp, Pittsburgh**
8. **Jean Delgado, ss, Caguas (P.R.) Military Academy**
9. **Derek Law, rhp, Miami Dade JC**
10. **Kentrell Hill, of, Arkansas Baptist JC**
11. **Christian Diaz, of, PR Baseball Academy, Gurabo, P.R.**
12. **Kelby Tomlinson, ss, Texas Tech**
13. Adam Paulencu, rhp, Vancouver Island (B.C.)
14. **Garrett Buechele, 3b, Oklahoma**
15. Tyler Leslie, rhp, Silverado HS, Victorville, Calif.
16. **Clayton Blackburn, rhp, Santa Fe HS, Edmond, Okla.**
17. **Paul Davis, rhp, Florida Atlantic**
18. **Cristian Otero, ss, PR Baseball Academy, Gurabo, P.R.**
19. **Cody Hall, rhp, Southern**
20. **Mitchell Beacom, lhp, UCLA**
21. Andrew Triggs, rhp, Southern California
22. **Cameron McVey, rhp, Biola (Calif.)**
23. **Jonathan Jones, 3b, Vanier (Que.) JC**
24. **Keith Bilodeau, rhp, Maine**
25. **DeMondre Arnold, rhp, Middle Georgia JC**
26. **Joe Biagini, rhp, UC Davis**
27. **Jack Snodgrass, lhp, Austin Peay State**
28. **Tyler Mizenko, rhp, Winthrop**
29. **Eldred Barnett, of, Grambling State**
30. Dave Fischer, rhp, Connecticut
31. **Phil McCormick, lhp, Missouri**
32. **Mike Mergenthaler, of, Richmond**
33. Brock Bennett, c, Alabama
34. **Ben Thomas, 1b, Xavier**
35. **Shawn Payne, of, Georgia Southern**
36. Austin Lubinsky, rhp, Minnesota
37. Michael Williams, c, Kentucky
38. **Bryan Nicholson, 1b, Concordia (Calif.)**
39. Ryan Holland, lhp, Memphis
40. Alan Garcia, rhp, Eastern Arizona JC
41. **Steven Neff, lhp, South Carolina**
42. **Danny Sandbrink, rhp, Stanford**
43. **Drew Stiner, c, Owasso (Okla.) HS**
44. **Travious Relaford, ss, Hinds (Miss.) CC**
45. **Brian Maloney, lhp, Franklin Pierce (N.H.)**
46. **Elliott Blair, of, Oklahoma**
47. Marc Frazier, 3b, Newnan (Ga.) HS
48. **Jake Smith, rhp, Campbell**
49. Benny Sosnick, 2b, Jewish Community HS of the Bay, San Francisco
50. Waldyvan Estrada, of, International Baseball Academy, Cieba, P.R.

SEATTLE MARINERS (2)

1. **Danny Hultzen, lhp, Virginia**

2. Brad Miller, ss, Clemson
3. Kevin Cron, 1b, Mountain Pointe HS, Phoenix
3. Carter Capps, rhp, Mount Olive (N.C.) (Supplemental pick—121st—for failure to sign 2010 third-round pick Ryne Stanek)
4. John Hicks, c, Virginia
5. Tyler Marlette, c, Hagerty HS, Oviedo, Fla.
6. James Zamarripa, of, Rancho Cucamonga (Calif.) HS
7. Steve Proscia, 3b, Virginia
8. Carson Smith, rhp, Texas State
9. Cavan Cohoes, ss, Patch HS, Stuttgart, Germany
10. Dan Paolini, 2b, Siena
11. Cameron Hobson, lhp, Dayton
12. Mike Dowd, c, Franklin Pierce (N.H.)
13. Jamal Austin, of, Alabama-Birmingham
14. Cody Weiss, rhp, La Salle
15. Mike McGee, of, Florida State
16. Jack Marder, c, Oregon
17. Nathan Melendres, of, Miami
18. Nick Valenza, lhp, Horizon HS, Scottsdale, Ariz.
19. Luke Guarnaccia, c, Palm Beach (Fla.) CC
20. Dillon Hazlett, 2b, Emporia State (Kan.)
21. Joe DiRocco, rhp, Seton Hall
22. John Taylor, rhp, South Carolina
23. Richard White, rhp, St. Croix Educational HS, St. Thomas, V.I.
24. Tanner Chleborad, rhp, Stevens HS, Rapid City, S.D.
25. Gabe Saquilon, rhp, Horizon Christian HS, San Diego
26. Kenny Straus, 3b, Georgia Perimeter JC
27. David Colvin, rhp, Pomona Pitzer (Calif.)
28. Brett Shankin, rhp, Wayne State
29. Keone Kela, rhp, Chief Sealth HS, Seattle
30. Jordan Pries, rhp, Stanford
31. Kyle Hunter, lhp, Kansas State
32. Ryan Hawthorne, lhp, Loyola Marymount
33. Jeremy Dobbs, lhp, Austin Peay State
34. Taylor Brennan, 2b, Edmonds (Wash.) CC
35. Cory Scammell, c, St. Francis Xavier HS, Edmonton
36. Bo Reeder, rhp, East Tennessee State
37. Jeremy Null, rhp, Bunker Hill HS, Claremont, N.C.
38. Alex Sunderland, rhp, Claremont McKenna (Calif.)
39. Chris Andreas, of, Sam Houston State
40. Trevor Miller, rhp, San Joaquin Delta (Calif.) JC
41. Bobby Shore, rhp, Oklahoma
42. David Villasuso, c, Miami
43. Marcos Reyna, rhp, Bakersfield (Calif.) JC
44. Josh Corrales, rhp, Cal State Dominguez Hills
45. Charles Jimenez, of, Milton (Fla.) HS
46. Maxx Catapano, rhp, Lee (Tenn.)
47. Brandon Plotz, rhp, Chabot (Calif.) JC
48. Max Krakowiak, rhp, Fordham
49. Andrew Grifol, 1b, Santa Fe (Fla.) CC
50. Esteban Tresgallo, 1b, Colegio Marista de Guaynabo (P.R.)

TAMPA BAY RAYS (29)

1. Taylor Guerrieri, rhp, Spring Valley HS, Columbia, S.C. (Pick from Red Sox as compensation for Type A free agent Carl Crawford)
1. Mikie Mahtook, of, Louisiana State (Pick from Yankees as compensation for Type A free agent Rafael Soriano)
1. Jake Hager, ss, Sierra Vista HS, Las Vegas
1. Brandon Martin, ss, Santiago HS, Corona, Calif. (Supplemental pick—38th—for loss of Soriano)
1. Tyler Goeddel, 3b, St. Francis HS, Mountain View, Calif. (Supplemental pick—41st—for loss of Crawford)
1. Jeff Ames, rhp, Lower Columbia (Wash.) JC (Supplemental pick—42nd—for loss of Type A free agent Grant Balfour)
1. Blake Snell, lhp, Shorewood HS, Shoreline, Wash. (Supplemental pick—52nd—for loss of Type B free agent Brad Hawpe)
1. Kes Carter, of, Western Kentucky (Supplemental pick—56th—for loss of Type B free agent Joaquin Benoit)
1. Grayson Garvin, lhp, Vanderbilt (Supplemental pick—59th—for loss of Type B free agent Randy Choate)
1. James Harris, of, Oakland Technical HS (Supplemental pick—60th—for loss of Type B free agent Chad Qualls)
2. Granden Goetzman, of, Palmetto (Fla.) HS (Pick from Athletics as compensation for Balfour)
2. Lenny Linsky, rhp, Hawaii

---

3. Johnny Eierman, of, Warsaw (Mo.) HS
4. Riccio Torrez, 3b, Arizona State
5. J.D. Davis, 3b, Elk Grove (Calif.) HS
6. Jake Floethe, rhp, Cal State Fullerton
7. Ryan Carpenter, lhp, Gonzaga
8. John Alexander, 1b, Glendora (Calif.) HS
9. Matt Rice, c, Western Kentucky
10. Jacob Faria, rhp, Gahr HS, Cerritos, Calif.
11. Cameron Seitzer, 1b, Oklahoma
12. Trevor Mitsui, 1b, Shorewood HS, Shoreline, Wash.
13. Tanner English, of, St. James HS, Murrells Inlet, S.C.
14. Matt Young, of, Compton (Calif.) CC
15. Tyler Parmenter, ss, Cibola HS, Yuma, Ariz.
16. Brett McAfee, ss, Pine Tree HS, Longview, Texas
17. Taylor Motter, ss, Coastal Carolina
18. Andy Bass, rhp, Davidson
19. Matt Ramsey, rhp, Tennessee
20. Garrett Smith, ss, Boston College
21. Ryan Terry, 3b, Monmouth
22. Brad Hendrix, rhp, Auburn
23. Matt Johnson, of, Arkansas Tech
24. Charlie Cononie, rhp, Towson
25. Brooks Belter, rhp, Occidental (Calif.)
26. Raymond Church, 2b, Florida Atlantic
27. Luke Irvine, rhp, Northwestern State
28. Blake Grant-Parks, c, Yuba City (Calif.) HS
29. Jonathan Koscso, 2b, South Florida
30. Chris Burgess, rhp, Black Hawk (Ill.) JC
31. Isaac Gil, rhp, Advanced Software Analysis (N.Y.) JC
32. Ryan Turner, rhp, Tarleton State (Texas)
33. Dan Bream, rhp, Southern Arkansas
34. Zach Butler, rhp, McNeese State
35. John Magliozzi, rhp, Dexter HS, Brookline, Mass.
36. Dave Kubiak, rhp, Albany
37. Tanner Poppe, rhp, Kansas
38. Brandon Choate, c, Southern Arkansas
39. T.J. Geith, lhp, Scottsdale (Ariz.) CC
40. Joe Perricone, rhp, Hersey HS, Arlington Heights, Ill.
41. Shay Crawford, lhp, Lee (Tenn.)
42. Mike Bourdon, c, Tampa
43. Stayton Thomas, rhp, Texas
44. Jordan Leyland, 1b, UC Irvine
45. Kevin Lusson, c, Texas
46. Max Rossiter, c, Central Arizona JC
47. Derek Vaughn, rhp, Texas Wesleyan
48. Brandon Liebrandt, lhp, Marist School, Atlanta
49. Alan Baldwin, c, Kailua (Hawaii) HS
50. Ian Tomkins, c, Abilene Christian (Texas)

TEXAS RANGERS (23)

1. (Pick to Red Sox as compensation for Type A free agent Adrian Beltre)
1. Kevin Matthews, lhp, Richmond Hill (Ga.) HS (Pick from Phillies as compensation for Type A free agent Cliff Lee)
1. Zach Cone, of, Georgia (Supplemental pick—37th—for loss of Lee)
2. Will Lamb, lhp, Clemson
3. Kyle Castro, rhp, Pleasant Grove HS, Elk Grove, Calif.
4. Desmond Henry, of, Centennial HS, Compton, Calif.
5. Brandon Woodruff, rhp, Wheeler (Miss.) HS
6. Derek Fisher, of, Cedar Crest HS, Lebanon, Pa.
7. Max Pentecost, c, Winder-Barrow HS, Winder, Ga.
8. Kyle Hendricks, rhp, Dartmouth
9. Rashard Harlin, of, Helix Charter HS, La Mesa, Calif.
10. Joe Maloney, c, Limestone (S.C.)
11. Connor Sadzeck, rhp, Howard (Texas) JC
12. Greg Williams, lhp, Marshall
13. Chris Grayson, of, Lee (Tenn.)
14. Andrew Faulkner, lhp, South Aiken (S.C.) HS
15. Jerad Eickhoff, rhp, Olney Central (Ill.) JC
16. Trever Adams, of, Creighton
17. Ryan Rua, ss, Lake Erie (Ohio)
18. Nick Martinez, rhp, Fordham
19. Nathan Harsh, lhp, Brunswick (Ga.) HS
20. Nick Vickerson, ss, Mississippi State
21. Chance Sossamon, rhp, Wichita State
22. T.J. Costen, ss, First Colonial HS, Virginia Beach

23. Mike Mason, lhp, Marshall
24. Zach Fish, c, Gull Lake HS, Richland, Mich.
25. Jordan Remer, lhp, San Francisco
26. Ryan Bores, rhp, Cuyahoga (Ohio) CC
27. **Kyle DeVore, rhp, Sacramento CC**
28. **Saquan Johnson, of, East Bladen HS, Elizabethtown, N.C.**
29. Nick Sawyer, rhp, Howard (Texas) JC
30. **Phil Klein, rhp, Youngstown State**
31. **Matt Leeds, 3b, College of Charleston**
32. **Sam Robinson, lhp, Miami**
33. Jonathan Taylor, of, Georgia
34. **Taylor Dennis, rhp, Southern Indiana**
35. Cy Sneed, rhp, Twin Falls (Idaho) HS
36. **Jeremy Williams, of, Mobile (Ala.)**
37. Bryce Greager, ss, Fountain Hills (Ariz.) HS
38. Tucker Donahue, rhp, Stetson
39. Trumon Jefferson, of, Decatur (Ga.) HS
40. Josh Peterson, rhp, Unaka HS, Elizabethton, Tenn.
41. Tyler Scott, of, Marin Catholic HS, Kentfield, Calif.
42. Joey Pankake, ss, Easley (S.C.) HS
43. Kaleb Merck, rhp, Texas Christian
44. Philip Pfeifer, lhp, Farragut HS, Knoxville
45. Brandon Finnegan, lhp, Southwest HS, Fort Worth
46. Tyler Powell, rhp, Myers Park HS, Charlotte
47. Kevin Moriarty, rhp, Shorewood HS, Shoreline, Wash.
48. **Carl Edwards, rhp, Mid-Carolina HS, Prosperity, S.C.**
49. Mick Van Vossen, rhp, Forest Hills Central HS, Grand Rapids, Mich.
50. **K.C. Wiser, rhp, Linfield (Ore.)**

TORONTO BLUE JAYS (18)

1. Tyler Beede, rhp, Lawrence Academy, Groton, Mass.
1. **Jacob Anderson, of, Chino (Calif.) HS** (Supplemental pick—35th—for loss of Type A free agent Scott Downs)
1. **Joe Musgrove, rhp, Grossmont HS, El Cajon, Calif.** (Supplemental pick—46th—for loss of Type B free agent John Buck)
1. **Dwight Smith Jr., of, McIntosh (Ga.) HS** (Supplemental pick—53rd—for loss of Type B free agent Kevin Gregg)
1. **Kevin Comer, rhp, Seneca HS, Tabernacle, N.J.** (Supplemental pick—57th—for loss of Type B free agent Miguel Olivo)
2. **Daniel Norris, lhp, Science Hill HS, Johnson City, Tenn.** (Pick from Angels as compensation for Downs)
2. **Jeremy Gabryszwski, rhp, Crosby (Texas) HS**
3. **John Stilson, rhp, Texas A&M**
4. **Tom Robson, rhp, Delta SS, Ladner, B.C.**
5. Andrew Chin, lhp, Buckingham Browne & Nichols HS, Cambridge, Mass.
6. **Anthony DeSclafani, rhp, Florida**
7. **Christian Lopes, ss, Edison HS, Huntington Beach, Calif.**
8. **Mark Biggs, rhp, Warren East HS, Bowling Green, Ky.**
9. Andrew Suarez, lhp, Columbus HS, Miami
10. Aaron Garza, rhp, Ball HS, Galveston, Texas
11. **Andy Burns, ss, Arizona**
12. John Norwood, of, Seton Hall Prep, Orange, N.J.
13. **Matt Dean, 3b, The Colony (Texas) HS**
14. Cole Wiper, rhp, Newport HS, Bellevue, Wash.
15. Cody Glenn, lhp, Westbury Christian HS, Houston
16. Richard Prigatano, 1b, St. Francis HS, Mountain View, Calif.
17. **Brady Dragmire, rhp, Bradshaw Christian School, Sacramento**
18. **Jon Berti, 2b, Bowling Green State**
19. Luke Weaver, rhp, DeLand (Fla.) HS
20. Joel Seddon, rhp, St. Clair (Mich.) HS
21. **Peter Mooney, ss, South Carolina**
22. Aaron Nola, rhp, Catholic HS, Baton Rouge
23. K'Shawn Smith, ss, Indian River (Fla.) JC
24. **David Rollins, lhp, San Jacinto (Texas) JC**
25. Eric Arce, 1b, Tampa (No school)
26. **Justin Atkinson, ss, North Surrey (B.C.) SS**
27. **Derrick Loveless, of, Solon (Iowa) HS**
28. Jorge Vega-Rosado, ss, Miami Dade JC
29. **Taylor Cole, rhp, Brigham Young**
30. **Kevin Patterson, 1b, Auburn**
31. Austin Nola, ss, Louisiana State
32. **Kevin Pillar, of, Cal State Dominguez Hills**
33. **Kramer Champlin, rhp, Arizona State**
34. **Luis Munoz, c, Northwestern State**
35. Jerrick Suiter, rhp, Valparaiso (Ind.) HS

36. **Arik Sikula, rhp, Marshall**
37. **Les Williams, rhp, Northeastern**
38. **Nico Taylor, of, Northwood (Texas)**
39. Chris Cox, rhp, Canisus
40. **Nick Baligod, of, Oral Roberts**
41. **Cody Bartlett, ss, Washington State**
42. **Shane Davis, lhp, Canisius**
43. Jake Eliopoulos, lhp, Newmarket, Ont. (No school)
44. **Colby Broussard, rhp, Faulkner (Ala.)**
45. Johnny Coy, 3b, Wichita State
46. **Shane Farrell, rhp, Marshall**
47. Austin Davis, 3b, Central Columbia HS, Bloomsburg, Pa.
48. Jake Wakamatsu, of, Keller (Texas) HS
49. Charlie LaMar, lhp, Clearwater (Fla.) Central Catholic HS
50. **Eric Brown, rhp, British Columbia**

WASHINGTON NATIONALS (6)

1. **Anthony Rendon, 3b, Rice**
1. **Alex Meyer, rhp, Kentucky** (Pick from White Sox as compensation for Type A free agent Adam Dunn)
1. **Brian Goodwin, of, Miami Dade JC** (Supplemental pick—34th—for loss of Dunn)
2. (Pick to Phillies as compensation for Type A free agent Jayson Werth)
3. **Matt Purke, lhp, Texas Christian**
4. **Kylin Turnbull, lhp, Santa Barbara (Calif.) CC**
5. **Matt Skole, 3b, Georgia Tech**
6. **Taylor Hill, rhp, Vanderbilt**
7. **Brian Dupra, rhp, Notre Dame**
8. **Greg Holt, rhp, North Carolina**
9. **Dixon Anderson, rhp, California**
10. **Manny Rodriguez, rhp, Barry (Fla.)**
11. **Caleb Ramsey, of, Houston**
12. **Blake Monar, lhp, Indiana**
13. Casey Kalenkosky, 1b, Texas State
14. Cody Stubbs, of, Walters State (Tenn.) CC
15. Zach Houchins, ss, Louisburg (N.C.) JC
16. **Deion Williams, ss, Redan HS, Stone Mountain, Ga.**
17. Esteban Guzman, rhp, San Jose State
18. **Nick Lee, lhp, Weatherford (Texas) JC**
19. Hawtin Buchanan, rhp, Biloxi (Miss.) HS
20. Josh Laxer, rhp, Madison (Miss.) Central HS
21. **Todd Simko, lhp, Texas A&M**
22. **Travis Henke, rhp, Arkansas-Little Rock**
23. **Khayyan Norfork, 2b, Tennessee**
24. Kyle Ottoson, lhp, Arizona State
25. **Erick Fernandez, c, Georgetown**
26. **Shawn Pleffner, of, Tampa**
27. **Bobby Lucas, rhp, George Washington**
28. **Ken Ferrer, rhp, Elon**
29. Sean Cotten, c, Tusculum (Tenn.)
30. **Bryan Harper, lhp, South Carolina**
31. Josh Tobias, ss, Southeast Guilford HS, Greensboro, N.C.
32. **Billy Burns, of, Mercer**
33. **Trey Karlen, 2b, Tennessee-Martin**
34. Calvin Drummond, rhp, San Diego
35. **Alex Kreis, rhp, Jamestown (N.D.)**
36. **Ben Hawkins, lhp, West Florida**
37. Derrick Bleeker, rhp, Howard (Texas) JC
38. **Brett Mooneyham, lhp, Stanford**
39. Peter Verdin, of, Georgia
40. Cory Collum, of, Cartersville (Ga.) HS
41. **Bryce Ortega, 3b, Arizona**
42. David Kerian, ss, Bishop Heelan HS, Sioux City, Iowa
43. Mitch Morales, ss, Wellington (Fla.) HS
44. Matt Snyder, 3b, Mississippi
45. **Richie Mirowski, rhp, Oklahoma Baptist**
46. Tyler Thompson, of, Florida
47. Tim Montgomery, lhp, Rockmart (Ga.) HS
48. Mike Bisenius, of, Wayne State (Mich.)
49. Hunter Cole, of, Dorman HS, Roebuck, S.C.
50. Tony Nix, of, UC Riverside

DRAFT

APPENDIX

■ **Billy Baldwin**, an outfielder who played two seasons in the major leagues, died June 29 in Hudson, Ohio. He was 60.

Baldwin came up through the Tigers organization and played 30 games for Detroit in 1975, hitting .221. He was traded to the Mets that offseason and played in nine games for New York in 1976.

■ **Hal Bamberger**, an outfielder who played briefly in the major leagues, died Nov. 14, 2010, in Reading, Pa. He was 86.

Bamberger appeared in seven games for the New York Giants in September 1948, going 1-for-12.

■ **Reno Bertoia**, a third baseman who played 10 seasons in the majors, died April 15 in Windsor, Ontario. He was 76.

Bertoia played a part-time role for Detroit from 1954-58. He was traded to the Washington Senators before the 1959 season and saw his most extensive action there in 1960, batting .265 in 511 at-bats as Washington's primary third baseman.

■ **George Binks**, an outfielder who played five seasons in the majors, died Nov. 13, 2010, in Woodbury, Tenn. He was 96.

Binks was a regular in the Senators' lineup in 1945, hitting .278 over 550 at-bats. He continued on in a part-time role for the Senators in 1946, followed by stints with the Philadelphia Athletics and St. Louis Browns in 1947-48.

■ **Eddie Bockman**, a third baseman who played in four major league seasons, died Sept. 29 in Millbrae, Calif. He was 91.

Bockman made his debut with the Yankees in September 1946 and went on to play part-time roles with the Indians and Pirates from 1947-49.

■ **Edward "Red" Borom**, a second baseman who played two seasons in the majors, died Jan. 7 in Dallas. He was 95.

Borom got to the majors in 1944, appearing in seven games for the Tigers. Borom served in a utility role for the World Series-winning 1945 Tigers, appearing in 55 games and batting .269.

■ **Steve Boros**, a third baseman who played seven seasons in the major leagues, died Dec. 29, 2010, in Deland, Fla. He was 74.

Boros was a regular in Detroit from 1961-62. Boros went on to play for Cubs and Reds over his final three seasons from 1963-65. He later spent parts of three seasons managing in the big leagues with the Athletics (1983-84) and Padres (1986).

■ **Don Buddin**, a shortstop who played six seasons in the big leagues, died June 30 in Greenville, S.C. He was 77.

Buddin was the Red Sox's everyday shortstop for five seasons from 1956-61, along with missing the 1957 season due to military service.

■ **Joe Caffie**, an outfielder who played two seasons for the Indians, died Aug. 1 in Warren, Ohio. He was 80.

■ **Scott Cary**, a lefthander who pitched for the Washington Senators for one year, died Feb. 28 in Coldwater, Mich. He was 87.

■ **Phil Cavarretta**, a first baseman who played 22 seasons in the majors and was the 1945 National League MVP, died Dec. 18, 2010, in Lilburn, Ga. He was 94.

Cavarretta was just 18 years old when he made his major league debut in September 1934, yet he was in the big leagues to stay. Cavarretta made his first of three all-star games in 1944, when he batted .321 and led the National League in hits with 197. Cavarretta peaked in 1945, when he won the NL batting title with a .355 average and the NL MVP award. From 1946-51, Cavarretta batted .295 collectively, including two seasons in which he hit over .300.

■ **Gino Cimoli**, an outfielder who played 10 seasons in the majors and was an all-star in 1957, died Feb. 12 in Roseville, Calif. He was 81.

Cimoli made the 1957 National League All-Star team in his first full season in the majors with the Dodgers, batting .293 with 10 homers. Following the Dodgers' first season in Los Angeles in 1958, Cimoli was traded to the Cardinals where he would play for one year before being traded to the Pirates in 1959. Cimoli was part of Pittsburgh's 1960 World Series championship team, primarily serving as a reserve outfielder.

Cimoli was kept on the move over the next few seasons, beginning with a trade to the Milwaukee Braves in June 1961 and a selection in the Rule 5 draft by the Kansas City Athletics after the season. Cimoli's last two notable seasons followed in 1962 when he led the league with 15 triples and in 1963 where he placed in the top 5 in both triples and outfield assists.

■ **Wes Covington**, an outfielder who played 11 seasons in the major leagues, died July 4 in Edmonton. He was 79.

Covington was a semi-regular in the Milwaukee Braves' outfield in the late 1950s. In five seasons with the Braves, he never played more than 103 games but hit over 20 homers twice, helping the Braves reach the World Series in 1957 and '58. Covington spent most of the second half of his career with the Phillies, playing there from 1961-65.

■ **George Crowe**, a first baseman who played in the major leagues for nine seasons, died Jan. 18

in Rancho Cordova, Calif. He was 89.

Crowe debuted with the Boston Braves in 1952, splitting time at first base and batting .258 in 217 at-bats. Crowe moved with the Braves to Milwaukee in 1953 and continued serving in a part-time role. Crowe was sent back to the minors in 1954 but retuned to Milwaukee again as a part-timer in 1955.

Crowe was traded to the Reds before the 1956 season and became the Reds' primary first baseman in 1957. The '57 season was Crowe's most productive big league campaign, as he hit 31 homers while batting .271. Crowe was traded to the Cardinals after '58 season and played three years in St. Louis, again in a part-time capacity.

■ **Walt Dropo**, a first baseman who was the 1950 American League rookie of the year, died Dec. 17, 2010, in Peabody, Mass. He was 87.

Dropo is best remembered for his 1950 rookie season with the Red Sox, when he belted 34 home runs, ranking second in the AL, while batting .322. He also led the league in RBIs with 144 and beat out Whitey Ford for the league's rookie of the year award.

Unfortunately, Dropo was never able to replicate that success in subsequent years. He managed to hit 29 homers in 1952, a season during which he was traded from the Red Sox to the Tigers, but that was the only other season in which he surpassed the 20-homer plateau.

■ **Ryne Duren**, a righthander who pitched 10 seasons in the majors and was a three-time all-star, died Jan. 6 in Lake Wales, Fla. He was 81.

Duren blossomed after the Yankees brought him up as a reliever in 1958. Duren posted a 2.02 ERA while striking out 87 batters in 76 innings, earning him a spot on the American League all-star team. He also issued 43 walks, and he would become well known for his blend of wildness and a blazing fastball. Duren earned his second trip to the All-Star Game in 1959, putting up a 1.88 ERA in 77 innings with 96 strikeouts.

Duren made one more all-star trip in 1961, a season during which he was traded from the Yankees to the Angels. Duren pitched four more seasons and while he was still effective, he never quite recaptured the success he'd found in New York. He posted a combined 3.91 ERA over stops with the Angels, Phillies, Reds and Washington Senators from 1962-65.

■ **George Estock**, a righthander who pitched one season for the Boston Braves, died Nov. 7, 2010, in Sebastian, Fla. He was 86.

Estock pitched in 37 games for the 1951 Braves, making one start, and went 0-1, 4.33 in 60 innings.

■ **Bob Feller**, a Hall of Fame pitcher who was arguably the greatest Indians player of all time, died Dec. 15, 2010, in Cleveland. He was 92.

Feller led the league with 240 strikeouts (and 208 walks) as a 19-year-old in 1939, the first of four straight seasons as the strikeout king before he left the game to enlist in the Navy two days after Japan bombed Pearl Harbor on Dec. 7, 1941. Feller racked up three consecutive seasons with at least 24 victories and 296 innings pitched before missing nearly four seasons in the prime of his career.

Feller picked up where he left off before the war in 1946. He went 26-15, 2.18 for a sixth-place club, recorded 36 complete games and 10 shutouts, and struck out 348 batters in 371 innings. Feller injured his back slipping off a wet mound early in 1947, later admitting that his fastball "was never the same after that."

Feller went on to pitch nine more seasons and completed his career with 266 wins, a 3.25 ERA and 2,581 strikeouts. Feller became the first president of the first players association in 1956 after his retirement. He was voted into the Hall of Fame in his first year of eligibility in 1962.

■ **Mike Flanagan**, a lefthander who pitched 18 seasons in the majors and won the 1979 American League Cy Young Award, died Aug. 24 in Monkton, Md., of an apparent suicide. He was 59.

Flanagan was a mainstay in the Orioles rotation for a decade. He won 15 games with a 3.64 ERA in his first full season in the majors in 1977 and made his only trip to the All-Star Game in 1978, when he went 19-15, 4.03 with 17 complete games. He had his best year in 1979, capturing the AL Cy Young Award with a 23-9, 3.08 season in which he led the league in wins and finished third in strikeouts with 190.

Flanagan battled injuries and his numbers began dropping off in 1985, though he did have a brief rejuvenation with the Blue Jays after a late-season trade there in 1987. After his playing career, Flanagan continued working for the Orioles in various capacities. He served as big league pitching coach in 1995 and '98 and was the club's general manager from 2003-2007. In other years, Flanagan worked as color commentator on Orioles TV broadcasts.

■ **Joe Frazier**, an outfielder who played in four big league seasons, died Feb. 16 in Broken Arrow, Okla. He was 88.

Frazier was a baseball lifer as he enjoyed decades of time in the game as a player and then a manager.

He spent most of his playing career as a reserve for the Indians, Cardinals, Reds and Orioles, ending in 1956. However, Frazier's time in the sport was far from over, as he began a long managing career that lasted until 1982. Frazier was most notable for managing the Mets big league club in 1976 and part of 1977, compiling a 101-106 record, before being replaced by player-manager Joe Torre.

■ **Woodie Fryman**, a lefthander who pitched 18 seasons in the major leagues with six teams, died Feb. 4 in Lexington, Ky. He was 70.

Fryman broke out with the Phillies in 1968. Although he went just 12-14 pitching for a non-contending Phillies squad in 1968, he had a 2.78 ERA in 214 innings, earning his first trip to the All-Star Game. Fryman didn't replicate that success over the next two seasons but he rebounded to go 10-7, 3.38 in 149 innings in 1971.

The Tigers picked Fryman up on waivers in August 1972, and he went 10-3, 2.06 down the stretch to help Detroit win the American League East. Fryman pitched two more seasons in Detroit before being traded to the Montreal Expos in December 1974. Fryman made his second All-Star Game appearance in 1976 at age 36, going 13-13, 3.37 for the Expos.

■ **Greg Goossen**, a first baseman who played six seasons in the majors, died Feb. 26 in Sherman Oaks, Calif. He was 65.

Goossen saw limited action with the Mets from 1965-68. He had his best year in 1969, appearing in 52 big league games for the Seattle Pilots and batting .309 with 10 homers.

■ **Ted Gray**, a lefthander who was an all-star in 1950 and played nine seasons in the majors, died June 15 in Delray Beach, Fla. He was 86.

Gray became a regular in the Tigers' rotation in 1949. Gray won at least 10 games four times, and went 10-7, 4.40 in his all-star season of 1950.

■ **Hideki Irabu**, a righthander who had a long career in Japan and played in six seasons in the majors, died July 27 in Rancho Palos Verdes, Calif., after an apparent suicide. He was 42.

Irabu pitched his first full season in the Japanese Pacific League at age 19 in 1988. Irabu went on to win back-to-back Pacific League ERA titles in 1995 (2.53) and '96 (2.40). He had three mostly tumultuous seasons for the Yankees, though he did win 13 games with a 4.06 ERA for the 1998 Yankees and 11 for the '99 Yankees. Irabu was traded to the Montreal Expos after the '99 season. He spent two injury-plagued years in Montreal in 2000 and 2001, making just 14 starts. The Rangers gave Irabu a chance to be their closer in

2002 and he had 16 saves but with a 5.74 ERA in 47 innings. Irabu returned to Japan in 2003.

■ **Eddie Joost**, a shortstop who played 17 seasons in the majors and was a two-time all-star, died April 12 in Fair Oaks, Calif. He was 94.

Joost came up with the Reds in 1936 and started getting regular playing time in 1941. Joost was best known for his tenure with the Philadelphia Athletics from 1947-54, when he made all-star appearances in 1949 and '52.

■ **Harmon Killebrew**, a Hall of Fame slugger who played in 22 major league seasons, died May 17 in Scottsdale, Ariz. He was 74.

Killebrew was baseball's most prolific home run hitter of the 1960s, hitting 393 during the decade. Killebrew didn't become the Washington Senators' regular third baseman in 1959, and he made a splash immediately, hitting 42 home runs to tie for the American League lead.

After the Senators moved to Minnesota before the 1961 season, Killebrew began a streak of four straight 40-homer seasons, capped off by his hitting 49 with 111 RBIs in 1964. Killebrew hit over 40 home runs in a season three times after turning 30, and he captured the American League MVP award in 1969 at age 33, when he hit 49 homers, matching his career high. He made 11 all-star teams, including nine straight from 1963-71. He hit 573 career home runs, which ranked him fifth on the all-time list at the time of his retirement. Killebrew was inducted into the Hall of Fame in 1984, and his number 3 was retired by the Twins.

■ **Clyde King**, a righthander who pitched six seasons in the majors, died Nov. 2, 2010, in Goldsboro, N.C. He was 86.

King was just 20 years old when he made his major league debut with the Brooklyn Dodgers in June 1944. He posted a 3.09 ERA in 44 innings as a rookie and was a mainstay of the Dodgers' bullpen in 1945. King was sent back to the minors in 1946. He made it back to Brooklyn in 1951, going 14-7, 4.17 in 121 innings. He was traded to the Reds after the 1952 season and pitched his final big league year there in 1953.

King stayed around the game after his playing career. He had three stints as a big league manager with the Giants, Braves and Yankees, going 464-229 in parts of five seasons. He was the Yankees' general manager from 1985-86.

■ **Gene Kirby**, who worked in baseball as an executive and broadcaster for many years, died April 27 in St. Petersburg, Fla. He was 95.

Kirby spent more than 20 years working with Dizzy Dean at ABC and CBS. He later worked for

APPENDIX

several big league teams in various capacities. He was a traveling secretary for the Montreal Expos and director of broadcasting for the Expos, Phillies and Red Sox. He also wrote stories which appeared in Baseball America and The Sporting News.

■ **Ed Kirkpatrick**, an outfielder who had a 16-year major league career, died Nov. 15, 2010, in Laguna Niguel, Calif. He was 66.

Kirkpatrick spent his first full year in the majors in 1966, at age 21, when he was a regular in the Angels' outfield and hit .192 with nine homers in 312 at-bats. Kirkpatrick played two more seasons with the Angels before being traded to the Royals in December 1968.

Kirkpatrick played five seasons in Kansas City, where he was utilized at catcher and first base in addition to the outfield. He hit 32 home runs over his first two seasons in a Royals uniform, easily the best two year stretch of his big league career. His best season overall might have been in 1972, when he hit a career-best .275 with nine homers.

■ **Mike Krsnich**, an outfielder who played in parts of two big league seasons, died April 30 in Mesquite, Nev. He was 79.

Krsnich appeared in 15 big league games with the Milwaukee Braves during the 1960 and '62 seasons, batting .190 with four RBIs.

■ **Bill Lajoie**, who was general manager of the Tigers for seven seasons, died Dec. 28, 2010, in Sarasota, Fla. He was 76.

Lajoie played 10 seasons in the minors before joining the Tigers as a scout in 1968. He worked his way up to become assistant GM in 1979 and was named general manager in 1984. Under Lajoie's watch, the Tigers won the 1984 World Series and captured another division title in 1987.

■ **Buddy Lewis**, a third baseman and outfielder who played 11 seasons for the Washington Senators and was a two-time all-star, died Feb. 18 in Gastonia, N.C. He was 94.

Lewis earned a spot in the Senators' everyday lineup in 1936, batting .291 with 67 RBIs as the club's third baseman. Lewis hit over .300 three times in the next five seasons, and made the All-Star Game in 1938, a season in which he hit .296 with a career-best 12 homers.

Lewis moved to right field in 1940, but his career was interrupted when he was drafted in the U.S. Army in 1941. Lewis played two more seasons, making the All-Star Game again in 1947, before a hip injury prompted him to retire. He sat out the 1948 season but was lured back for one more go-around with Washington in 1949.

■ **Danny Litwhiler**, an outfielder who played 11 seasons in the major leagues, died Sept. 23 in Clearwater, Fla. He was 95.

Litwhiler was a regular in the Phillies' outfield early in his career. He hit .305 with 18 homers in 1941, his first full season, and made the All-Star Game in 1942. However, he was traded to the Cardinals in June 1943, and spent the rest of his career mostly as a part-time player.

■ **Marty Marion**, a shortstop who as an eight-time all-star in the 1940s, died March 15 in Ladue, Mo. He was 93.

Marion broke into the majors as a 22-year-old with the Cardinals in 1940, taking over as the team's everyday shortstop, a role he would fill for the next decade. Marion had his best offensive season in 1942, when he hit .276 with 54 RBIs and a league-leading 38 doubles. The Cardinals went to the World Series four times in five years from 1942-46 with Marion as their shortstop, winning three times. Along the way, he captured the 1944 NL MVP award, a year in which he hit .267 with 63 RBIs, and made the NL all-star team every year from 1943-50.

■ **Dan McDevitt**, a lefthander who pitched six seasons in the major leagues, died Nov. 20, 2010, in Covington, Ga. He was 78.

McDevitt was called up to the Dodgers for the first time in June 1957, during their final season in Brooklyn, and made 22 appearances, including 17 starts, going 7-4, 3.25. McDevitt pitched the next three seasons for the relocated Los Angeles Dodgers, winning 10 games in 1959. He was sold to the Yankees after the 1960 season and pitched two more seasons in the majors with the Yankees, Twins and Kansas City Athletics.

■ **Gil McDougald**, a second baseman who was the 1951 American League rookie of the year and a five time all-star, died Nov. 28, 2010, in Wall Township, N.J. He was 82.

McDougald was a fixture with the dominant Yankees squads of the 1950s. Although McDougald played more games at second base than any other during his career, he was versatile and saw regular action at third base and shortstop over the years. McDougald made his first all-star team in 1952, when he hit .263 with 78 RBIs, and he would make the all-star team in four consecutive seasons from 1956-59.

■ **Charlie Metro**, an outfielder who played three seasons in the major leagues, died March 10 in Beckingham, Va. He was 91.

Metro made his big league debut in 1943, appearing in 44 games for the Tigers mostly as a pinch-runner and defensive replacement Metro was a regular in the A's outfield for parts of the 1945 season, but he hit just .210 and was sent back to the minors in 1946. He later had stints as manager of the Cubs in 1962 and Royals in 1970.

■ **Jim Northrup**, an outfielder who played 12 seasons in the majors, died June 8 in Grand Blanc, Mich. He was 71.

Northrup was a regular in the Tigers' outfield from 1966-74. Although he was never an all-star, Northrup was a capable hitter by the standards of his era, belting over 20 homers three times and hitting 153 homers in his career.

■ **Karl Olson**, an outfielder who played six seasons in the major leagues, died Dec. 25, 2010, in Reno, Nev. He was 80.

Olson was a part-time outfielder with the Red Sox, Washington Senators and Tigers, playing in the majors in 1951 and then 1953-57.

■ **Bo Osborne**, a first baseman who played six big league seasons and had a long scouting career, died April 15 in Woodstock, Ga. He was 75.

Osborne was a reserve infielder for the Tigers from 1957-62 and Washington Senators in 1963. He went on to spend 19 years as a scout with the Giants, working in various roles including regional cross-checker and major league scout.

■ **Jose Pagan**, a shortstop who played in 15 major league seasons, died June 7 in Sebring, Fla. He was 76.

Pagan came up with the Giants in 1959 and was their everyday shortstop from 1961-64. The Giants traded him to the Pirates in 1965, and he served in a utility role for Pittsburgh through 1972.

■ **Ron Piche**, a righthander who pitched in the major leagues for six seasons, died Feb. 3 in Montreal. He was 75.

Piche broke into the major leagues in 1960 and pitched in parts of four seasons for the Milwaukee Braves, working mostly out of the bullpen. After his playing career ended in 1972, Piche worked for the Montreal Expos in a number of capacities, ranging from public relations to being a minor league pitching instructor.

■ **Duane Pillette**, a righthander who pitched eight seasons in the majors, died May 6 in San Jose. He was 88.

Pillette spent most of his career with the St. Louis Browns/Baltimore Orioles organization. A reliever early in his big league career, Pillette became primarily a starter in 1951 and won 10 games twice, in 1952 and '54.

■ **Mel Queen**, an outfielder and righthander pitcher who spent nine seasons in the majors, died May 11 in Morro Bay, Calif. He was 69.

Queen came up to the majors as an outfielder with the Reds in 1964, but he converted to pitching during the 1966 season. Queen joined the Reds rotation in 1967 and immediately went 14-8, 2.76 in his first full season on the mound. However, Queen battled injuries over the next two seasons and moved to the bullpen with the California Angels in 1970.

■ **Bob Rush**, a righthander who pitched 13 seasons in the majors, died March 19 in Mesa, Ariz. He was 85.

Rush was a two-time all-star with the Cubs, pitching for them from 1948-57. Rush made his first all-star team in 1950 and returned in 1952, when he had his best season, winning a career-high 17 games with a 2.70 ERA. For his career, Rush won 127 games and had a 3.65 ERA.

■ **Fred Sanford**, a righthander who pitched in the big leagues for seven seasons, died March 15 in Salt Lake City. He was 91.

Sanford pitched his first four seasons with the St. Louis Browns, highlighted by his posting a 3.71 ERA in 187 innings there in 1947. He was traded to the Yankees before the 1949 season and was a member of their 1949 and '50 World Series winning teams.

■ **Ron Santo**, a third baseman who was a nine-time all-star for the Cubs, died Dec. 2, 2010, in Scottsdale, Ariz. He was 70.

Santo took over as the Cubs regular third baseman in 1960 and held the job for the next 13 years, becoming one of the most popular players in the team's history. In a difficult era for offense, Santo was one of the National League's shining stars. He hit 23 home runs in 1961, his first full season in the majors, and in 1963 he hit 25 homers, beginning a run of seven consecutive seasons in which he finishing among the NL's top 10 home run hitters. He hit 30 homers four times, peaking at 33 in 1965. He also won five consecutive Gold Gloves at third base from 1964-68.

■ **Dave Sisler**, a righthander who pitched in the major leagues for seven seasons, died Jan. 9 in St. Louis. He was 79.

A son of Hall of Famer George Sisler, Dave began the 1956 season in the majors with the Red Sox. Sisler worked as both a starter and reliever during his first big league season, going 9-8, 4.62 in 142 innings. Sisler spent most of the next two years in Boston's rotation, winning 15 games over the 1957 and 1958 seasons. Sisler was traded to the Tigers in May 1959 and converted back to the bullpen, pitching for the Tigers, Washington Senators and Reds trhough 1962.

■ **Paul Splittorff**, a righthander who pitched 15 seasons for the Royals, died May 25 in Blue Springs, Mo. He was 64.

Splittorff made his big league debut in 1970 and became a full-time member of the Royals' rotation in 1971, a position he maintained through 1983. Splittorff won 20 games for the Royals in 1973 and posted three more seasons of at least 15 wins. He was the Royals' all-time wins leader with 166 and had a 3.81 career ERA.

■ **R.C. Stevens**, a first baseman who played in parts of four big league seasons, died Nov. 30, 2010, in Davenport, Iowa. He was 76.

Stevens saw action with the Pirates and Washington Senators from 1958-61, batting .210 in 162 big league at-bats.

■ **Chuck Tanner**, an outfielder who played eight seasons in the majors and had a long managerial career, died Feb. 11 in New Castle, Pa. He was 82.

Tanner is best known for his managerial prowess as he navigated four major league teams from 1970-1988, particularly his time with the Pirates. During his nine seasons in Pittsburgh (1977-1985), Tanner took his team to a World Series championship in 1979 and had winning records six times.

■ **Tom Underwood**, a lefthander who pitched 11 seasons in the majors, died Nov. 22, 2010, in West Palm Beach, Fla. He was 56.

Underwood pitched for six teams in an 11-year career from 1974-84. He worked as a starter and reliver at various times, with his best season coming in 1980, when he went 13-9, 3.66 for the Yankees.

■ **Jay Van Noy**, an outfielder who played briefly in the majors as part of an 11-year pro career, died Nov. 6, 2010, in Logan, Utah. He was 82.

Van Noy reached the majors in his second season in pro ball, appearing in six games, including one start, with the Cardinals in June 1951.

■ **Jose Vidal**, an outfielder who played four seasons in the major leagues, died Jan. 7 in La Romana, Dominican Republic. He was 70.

Vidal's pro career spanned from 1958-75, but his time in the majors was confined to the 1966-69 seasons. Vidal played less than 20 games in three of his four major league seasons, his most extensive action coming in 1968 when he got into 37 games for the Indians and hit .167 with two homers in 54 at-bats.

■ **Bill Weiss**, one of the most significant statisticians in baseball history, died on Aug. 16 in San Mateo, Calif. He was 86.

In 1948, Weiss was hired to be the Class D Longhorn League's statistician. Before he was done, Weiss was the statistician for most leagues West of the Mississippi River. He was one of the original members of the Society of American Baseball Research (SABR). He also served on the National Association's Scoring Rules Committee and compiled biographical information and career stats for leagues and organizations for decades.

■ **Bill Werle**, a lefthander who pitched six seasons in the major leagues, died Nov. 27, 2010, in San Mateo, Calif. He was 89.

Werle was a starter for the Pirates for two seasons, winning 12 games as a rookie in 1949. Pittsburgh moved him to relief in 1951, and he also pitched for the Cardinals and Red Sox over his last three seasons.

■ **Dick Williams**, a Hall of Fame manager and former major league player, died July 7 in Las Vegas. He was 82.

As a player, Williams broke into the major leagues with the Brooklyn Dodgers in 1951 and played in 13 seasons for five teams. Primarily a left fielder and third baseman, Williams hit .260 over his big league career, which lasted until 1964. He was hired to manage Boston's big league club in 1967, despite being just 37 years old at the time. The Red Sox had finished in ninth place in the American League in 1966, but Williams' "Impossible Dream" squad won the pennant and pushed the Cardinals to seven games in the 1967 World Series.

He landed with the star-studded Athletics in 1971. Williams' A's won back-to-back World Series titles in 1972 and '73. In all, he won 3,023 games in 21 seasons with two World Series titles and four pennants. He is one of only two managers, along with Bill McKechnie, to take three different teams to the World Series. Williams was elected to the Hall of Fame as a manager in 2008.

■ **Gus Zernial**, an outfielder who played 11 seasons in the major leagues and was an all-star in 1953, died Jan. 20 in Fresno. He was 87.

Zernial was one of the most productive power hitters of the early 1950s. Playing mostly for non-competitive Philadelphia A's squad, he finished in the top five in the A.L. in home runs five times, highlighted by his 1953 season when he belted 42 homers, finishing second to Cleveland's Al Rosen, and made his only All-Star Game appearance. Zernial finished second again, this time to Mickey Mantle, in 1955 with 30 homers. He ended his career in 1959 with 237 homers and a .265 lifetime average.

APPENDIX

Get in the game at the grassroots level!

APPENDIX